No. CCXXVI.
1st April, 1895.

Published Quarterly.
Price 10s. 6d.

THE
NEW ARMY LIST,
MILITIA LIST,
AND
YEOMANRY CAVALRY LIST;

EXHIBITING THE
RANK, STANDING, AND A SUMMARY OF THE WAR SERVICES
OF EVERY REGIMENTAL OFFICER IN THE ARMY
SERVING ON FULL PAY,
INCLUDING
THE ROYAL MARINES,
THE
INDIAN STAFF CORPS AND LOCAL INDIAN FORCES;
DISTINGUISHING THOSE
WHO HAVE RECEIVED MEDALS AND OTHER DISTINCTIONS,
AND
WHO HAVE BEEN WOUNDED, AND IN WHAT ACTIONS;
WITH THE PERIOD OF SERVICE BOTH ON FULL AND HALF PAY.
GIVING ALSO
THE DATES OF EVERY OFFICER'S COMMISSIONS,
AND
DISTINGUISHING THOSE OBTAINED BY PURCHASE.
WITH AN INDEX.

BY THE LATE
LIEUTENANT GENERAL H. G. HART.
EDITED BY HIS SON.

LONDON:
JOHN MURRAY, ALBEMARLE STREET.
1895

Foreign Orders.

The Foreign Orders mentioned in the War Services belong to the following Countries, and the Dates are those of the Institution of the respective Orders :—

Affghanistan—Dooranée Empire (3 Classes) 1839.
Austria—Maria Theresa (3 Classes) 18 June 1757.
    Leopold (3 Classes) 14 July 1806.
Bavaria—Maximilian Joseph (3 Classes) 1 Jan. 1806.
Belgium—Leopold (3 Classes) 11 July 1832.
France—Military Merit (3 Classes) March 1759.
    Legion of Honor (5 Classes) 13 May 1802.
Greece—Saviour (5 Classes) 1 June 1833.
Hanover—Guelphs (3 Classes) 18 June 1815.
Naples—St. Januarius (1 Class) July 1738.
    St. Ferdinand and Merit (3 Classes) 1 April 1800.
    St. George and Reunion (3 Classes) 1 Jan. 1819.
Netherlands—Wilhelm (4 Classes) 30 April 1815.
Persia—Lion and Sun (3 Classes) 1801.
Portugal—Tower and Sword (3 Classes) 17 April 1748.
    St. Bento d'Avis (2 Classes) 1789.
    Conception (3 Classes) 6 Feb. 1818.
Prussia—Black Eagle—18 Jan. 1701.
    Military Merit—1740.
    Red Eagle (3 Classes) 12 June 1792.

Russia—St. Andrew—30 Nov. 1698.
    St. Alexander Nowski—1722.
    St. Ann (2 Classes) 3 Feb. 1735.
    St. George (4 Classes) 26 Nov. 1769.
    St. Wladimir (5 Classes) 4 Oct. 1782. [1572.
Sardinia—St. Maurice and St. Lazarus (2 Classes) 3 Nov.
    Military Order of Savoy.
Saxony—St. Henry (3 Classes) 7 Oct. 1736.
    Ernestine (4 Classes) 25 Dec. 1833.
Spain—Charles the Third (3 Classes) 19 Sept. 1771.
    San Fernando (5 Classes) 31 Aug. 1811.
    St. Hermenigilde (2 Classes) 10 July 1815.
    St. Isabella the Catholic (3 Classes) 1815.
Sweden—Sword (3 Classes) 17 April 1748.
Turkey—Crescent (2 Classes) 6 July 1804.
    Medjidie (5 Classes).
    Osmanieh (4 Classes).
Tuscany—St. Joseph (3 Classes) 1807.
Wirtemburg—Military Merit (3 Classes) 1758.

NOTICE.

Communications concerning the contents of "Hart's Army List" should be addressed ONLY to
    The EDITOR of HART'S ARMY LIST,
        50, Albemarle Street,
            LONDON, W.

War Services should be sent so as to reach the Editor not later than the end of the second month of the Quarter preceding that in which publication is desired.

For the following matter, not given in this volume, see "Hart's Annual Army List," price 21s., namely:—

General and Field Officers on the Active List, with full particulars; the Reserve of Officers; Retired General and Field Officers; Officers on the Unemployed Supernumerary List; Officers on Retired or Half Pay; General and Field Officers Retired by Sale, Commutation, with a Gratuity, or by Surrender of Half Pay; Field Officers Retired from the Militia and Yeomanry Cavalry—IN ALL CASES WITH THEIR WAR SERVICES.

EXPLANATIONS.

K.G. Knight of the Order of the Garter.
K.T. Knight of the Order of the Thistle.
K.P. Knight of the Order of St. Patrick.
G.C.B. Knight *Grand Cross* of the Order of the Bath.
K.C.B. Knight *Commander* of the Order of the Bath.
C.B. *Companion* of the Order of the Bath.
G.C.S.I. Knight *Grand Commander* of the Order of the Star of India.
K.C.S.I. Knight *Commander* of the Star of India.
C.S.I. *Companion* of the Star of India.
G.C.M.G. Knight *Grand Cross* of the Order of St. Michael and St. George.
K.C.M.G. Knight *Commander* of ditto ditto.
C.M.G. *Companion* of ditto ditto.

G.C.I.E. *Grand Commander* of the Indian Empire.
K.C.I.E. *Knight Commander* ditto ditto.
C.I.E. *Companion* ditto ditto.
D.S.O. *Companion* of the Order of Distinguished Service.
G.C.H. Knight *Grand Cross* of the Royal Hanoverian Guelphic Order.
K.C.H. Knight *Commander* of ditto ditto.
K.H. Knight of ditto ditto.
K.C. Knight of the Crescent.

V.C. Victoria Cross.
[R] Reward for Distinguished or Meritorious Services.
The Figures prefixed to the Names denote the Battalions to which the Officers are *actually attached*.
c. before the name denotes that the Officer has received a certificate from the Senior Department of the Royal Military College.
The Letters p.s.c. are placed *before* the Names of Officers who have passed the Staff College.
The Letter r. is placed *after* the names of Officers of the Royal Marines employed on the *Recruiting Service*.
The * before the Name or Date of Commission denotes Temporary Rank only.
The Letter p before the Date indicates that the Commission was *purchased*.
v.d. signifies Volunteer Officers' Decoration.

In the Medical Departments,—

BA.......... signifies Bachelor of Arts.
BCh.&BS. ,, Bachelor of Surgery.
BSc. ...... ,, Bachelor of Science.
DPH. ..... ,, Diploma in Public Health.
FRCS. ... ,, Fellow of the Royal College of Surgeons of England.
FRCS.Ed. ,, Ditto of Edinburgh.
FRCSI..... ,, Ditto of Ireland.
LAH.Dub. ,, Licentiate of Apothecaries' Hall, Dublin.
LCh.&M.Dub.,, Licentiate of Surgery and Medicine, Dublin.
LFPS.Glas. ,, Licentiate of the Faculty of Physicians and Surgeons, Glasgow.
LRCP.... ,, Licentiate of the Royal College of Physicians of London.
LRCP.Ed. ,, Ditto of Edinburgh.
LRCPI. ,, Licentiate of the Royal College of Physicians in Ireland.
LRCS.Ed. ,, Licentiate of the Royal College of Surgeons of Edinburgh.

LRCSI.... signifies Licentiate of the Royal College of Surgeons of Ireland.
LSA. ...... ,, Licentiate of the Society of Apothecaries in London.
MA. ...... ,, Master of Arts.
MB. ...... ,, Bachelor of Medicine.
MCh. ,, Master of Surgery.
MD. ...... ,, Doctor of Medicine.
MRCP.... ,, Member of the Royal College of Physicians of London.
MRCP.Ed. ,, Ditto of Edinburgh.
MRCPI. ,, Member of the Royal College of Physicians in Ireland.
MRCS.... ,, Member of the Royal College of Surgeons of England.
A.G.M....... ,, Alexander Gold Medal (triennial).
P.G.M...,... ,, Parkes ditto ditto.
H.P.N....... ,, Herbert Prize at Netley.
M.P.N....... ,, Montefiore Prize and Medal at Netley.
M.M.N. ... ,, Martin Gold Medal at Netley.
P.M.N....... ,, Parkes Bronze Medal at Netley.

In the Militia and Yeomanry Cavalry,—

(H) signifies qualified for appointment as Instructor of Musketry.
(I) signifies qualified for appointment as Instructor of Artillery.
(S) obtained Certificate as Instructor in Army Signalling.
[T] obtained Special Mention in Examination in Tactics laid down for Captains in the Army before 1 Jan. 90.
(P) passed full course in Submarine Mining.
p. Certificate of Proficiency, or otherwise qualified as Proficient for higher rank.

(p.) Subaltern's Certificate of Proficiency.
p. Certificate of Proficiency, or otherwise qualified as Proficient.
p.s. passed School of Instruction.
p.s. passed School of Instruction for higher rank.
(p.s.) School Certificate for Yeomanry Subalterns.
[t] passed the examination in Tactics laid down for Captains in the Army.
(T) obtained Special Mention at examination in Tactics laid down for Lieutenants in the Army before 1 Jan. 90.
(t) passed the examination in Tactics laid down for Lieutenants in the Army.

The words subscribed to the titles of Regiments, as "Peninsula," "Waterloo," &c., denote the Honorary Distinctions permitted to be borne by such Regiments on their colours and appointments, in commemoration of their Services.

TABLE OF CONTENTS
IN ORDER OF ARRANGEMENT.

	PAGE
The Queen	1
Private Secretary to the Queen	1
Aides de Camp to the Queen	1
War Office	2
Staff of the Army	2
Field Marshals	4
General Officers, Active List	4
Colonels, ditto	16
Lieutenant Colonels, ditto	40
Majors, ditto	47
Staff at Home	97
Staff Abroad	100
Regimental District Staff	109

MILITARY ESTABLISHMENTS:—

Educational Establishments.

	PAGE
Royal Military College, Sandhurst	113
Royal Military Academy, Woolwich	113
Staff College	113
School of Gunnery	114
Artillery College	114
School of Military Engineering, Chatham	114
School of Musketry, Hythe	114
School of Signalling	114
Medical School, Netley	114
Royal Military School of Music, Kneller Hall	114
Duke of York's Royal Military School, Chelsea	115
Royal Hibernian Military School	115
Army Schools	115

Ordnance Factories.

	PAGE
Arsenal, Woolwich	115
Small Arms Factory, Enfield	115
Do. Birmingham	115
Gunpowder Factory, Waltham Abbey	115
Army Clothing Department	115
Committees and Inspection Staff	115

Miscellaneous Establishments.

	PAGE
Cavalry Depot	116
Remount Establishment	117
Royal Hospitals — Chelsea, Kilmainham	117
Pay Office	117
Judge Adv. General's Office	117
Prisons	117
Officers who have received Certificates at the Senior Department, Royal Military College	119
Officers who have passed the Staff College	119
Gentlemen at Arms	130
Yeomen of the Guard	132
Cavalry	133
Artillery	164
Engineers	204
Infantry	229
Army Service Corps	366
Ordnance Store Department	369
Army Pay Department	371
Army Medical Staff	377
Army Veterinary Department	395
Army Chaplains' Department	396
Marines	397
Indian Army	403
Index	537
Honourable Artillery Company of London	579
Militia	579
Yeomanry Cavalry	607
Appointments, Promotions, Retirements, &c., since last publication	635

TABLE OF CONTENTS, IN ALPHABETICAL ORDER.

N.B.—By means of this Table, Regiments can be found in this book by their new titles.

	PAGE
Academy, Royal Military	113
Active List	3
Aden Troop	524
African Commissariat	368
Aides de Camp to the Queen	1
Albany's (Duke of) Seaforth Highldrs. (Ross-shire Buffs)	318
Aldershot District Staff	98
Antigua & Leeward Islands Staff	107
Appointments, Promotions, &c., since last publication	635
Argyll and Suther. Highlanders	337
Armourers, Corps of	362
Army Pay Department	371
——— Schools	115
——— Service Corps	366
Arsenal, Woolwich	115
Artillery College	114
——— District Officers	185
——— Malta	186
——— Militia	579
——— Royal	164
——— by Batteries	184
——— Royal Marine	397
Australia, Staff in	104
Bahamas, Staff in	107
Ballooning, School of	114
Barbadoes, Staff in	106
Bedfordshire Regiment	255
Belfast, Staff at	100
Bengal Cavalry	443
——— General List	404
——— Eccles. Department	460
——— Infantry	444
——— General List	404
——— Medical Department	453
——— Mountain Batteries	444
——— Sappers and Miners	444
——— Staff in	101
——— Veterinary Department	460
Berkshire Regiment	293
Bermuda, Staff in	107
Bheel Corps	449b
Bhopaul Battalion	449b
Birmingham Small Arms Factory	115
Black Watch	286
Bombay Artillery (Native)	524
——— Cavalry	523
——— General List	404a
——— Eccles. Department	532
——— Infantry	525
——— General List	404a
——— Medical Department	529
——— Sappers and Miners	525
——— Staff in	103
——— Veterinary Department	531
Border Regiment	258
Buffs, The (East Kent Regt.)	237
Cambridge's (Duke of) Own Middlesex Regiment)	301
Caicos Islands, Staff in	107
Cameron Highlanders	325
Cameronians	270
Canada, Staff in	106
Canadians (Royal), Prince of Wales' Leinster Regiment	346
Canterbury, Cavalry Depot at	117
Carriage Factory, Woolwich	115
Cavalry Depot, Canterbury	117
——— Regiments of	133
Central India Horse	449a
Ceylon, Staff in	104
Chaplains (Honorary) to the Queen	1
Chaplains' Department	396
Chatham, Staff at	98
Chelsea, Royal Hospital	117
——— Royal Military School	115
Cheshire Regiment	264
Chester, Staff at	97
China, &c., Staff in	104
City of London Regiment	243
Clothing Department	115
Coast Battalion	223
Colchester, Staff at	97
College, Royal Military	113
——— Staff	113
Colonels on the Active List	16
Committees and Inspection Staff	115
Connaught Rangers	334
Cork, Staff at	100
Cornwall's (Duke of) Light Inf.	276
Curragh, Staff at the	100
Cyprus, Staff in	101
Deaths since last publication	644
Deolee Irregular Force	449a
Depot, Cavalry, at Canterbury	117
——— and Training School, Aldershot	387
Derbyshire Regiment	289
Devonport, Staff at	97
Devonshire Regiment	249
District Officers (Artillery)	185
Dorsetshire Regiment	283
Dover, Staff at	98
Dragoon Guards	136
Dragoons, Hussars, & Lancers	143-163
Dublin Fusiliers	348
——— Staff in	100
Durham Light Infantry	314
Eastern District Staff	97
Ecclesiastical Department, Bengal	460
——— Bombay	532
——— Madras	506
Edinburgh's (Duke of) Wiltshire Regiment	308
Edinburgh, Staff at	99
Educational Establishments	113
Egypt, Staff of the Force in	105
Enfield Small Arms Factory	115
Engineers, Militia	584
——— Royal	204
Equerries to the Queen	1
Erinpoorah Irregular Force	449a
Essex Regiment	288
Falkland Islands, Staff in	107
Field Marshals	4
Fiji Islands, Staff in	105
Foreign Orders	Back of Title page
General Officers on the Active List	4
Gentlemen at Arms	130
Gibraltar, Staff at	100
Gloucestershire Regiment	272
Gold Coast Colony, Staff in	106
Good Hope (Cape of), Staff in	105
Goorkha Regiments	445-6, 449
Gordon Highlanders	321
Gradation List of General and Field Officers	4
Guards	229
Guernsey and Alderney Staff	99
Guiana, British, Staff in	107
Guides, Corps of	446a
Gun Factory	115
Gunnery, School of	114
Gunpowder Factory, Waltham Abbey	115
Hampshire Regiment	281
Head Quarters Staff	2
Hibernian Military School	115
Highland Light Infantry	317
Home District Staff	98
Honduras, Staff in	107
Hong Kong, &c., Staff in	104
Hong Kong Regiment	362
Honourable Artillery Company of London	579
Horse Guards—Staff of the Army	2
——— District Staff	98
——— Blue	135
Hospital, Chelsea	117
——— Kilmainham	117
Hussars, Lancers, & Dragoons	143-163
Hyderabad Contingent	449b
Hythe School of Musketry	114
Index	537
Indian Army	403
——— Local Forces	403
——— Staff Corps	405
India, Staff in	101
Infantry, Regiments of	229
Inniskilling Fusiliers	271
Inspection Staff	115
Ireland, Staff in	99
Irish Fusiliers	333
——— Regiment	258
——— Rifles	329
Jamaica, Staff in	107
Jersey District Staff	99
Judge Advocate General's Office	117
Kent (East) Regiment	237
——— (West) Regiment	294
Kilmainham, Royal Hospital	117

Table of Contents.

	PAGE
King's (Shropshire Light Inf.)..	297
—— Liverpool Regiment	244
—— Own Lancaster Regiment	238
—— Own Scottish Borderers	269
—— Own Yorkshire Light Inf.	295
—— Royal Rifle Corps	304
Kneller Hall, School of Music	114
Laboratory, Royal	115
Labuan, Staff in	104
Lagos, Staff in	106
Lancashire (East) Regiment	274
—— Fusiliers	261
—— (Loyal North) Regt.	291
—— (South) Regiment	284
Lancaster Regiment	238
Lancers, Dragoons, and Hussars	143-163
Leeward Islands, Staff in	107
Leicestershire Regiment	256
Leinster Regiment	346
Lieutenant Colonels	40
Life Guards	133
Lincolnshire Regiment	246
Liverpool Regiment	244
Local Indian Forces	403
London, Hon. Art. Company of	579
Lothian Regiment	234
Louise's (Princess) Sutherland and Argyll Highlanders	337
Loyal North Lancashire Regt.	291
Madras Cavalry	495
—— General List	404a
—— Eccles. Department	506
—— Infantry	497
—— General List	404a
—— Medical Department	504
—— Sappers and Miners	496
—— Staff in	102
—— Veterinary Department	506
Major Generals	5
Majors	49
Malta Artillery	186
—— Militia	607
—— Staff at	100
Malwah Bheel Corps	449b
Manchester Regiment	309
Marines	397
Mauritius, Staff in	106
Medical Department, Bengal	453
—— Bombay	529
—— Madras	504
—— School, Netley	114
—— Staff	377
Meywar Bheel Corps	449b
Mhairwarra Battalion	449b
Middlesex Regiment	301
Military Engineering, School of	114
—— Establishments	113
—— Mounted Police	362
—— Prisons	117
Militia Artillery	579
—— Channel Islands	607
—— Engineers	584
—— Infantry	585
—— Royal Malta	607
Miscellaneous Establishments	117
Munster Fusiliers	347
Music, School of, Kneller Hall	114
Musketry, School of (Hythe)	114
Natal, Staff in	105
Naval Ordnance Department	402
Netley Medical School	114
Newfoundland, Staff in	106
New Guinea, Staff in	105
New South Wales, Staff in	104

	PAGE
New Zealand, Staff in	105
Norfolk Regiment	245
North British District Staff	99
North Eastern District Staff	97
Northamptonshire Regiment	292
Northumberland Fusiliers	240
Ordnance Factories	115
—— Store Department	369
Oxfordshire Light Infantry	287
Pay Department	371
Pay Office	117
Physicians (Honorary) to the Queen	1
Poona Horse	523
Portsmouth, Staff at	97
Prince Albert's (Somersetshire Light Infantry)	252
Prince Consort's Own Rifle Brig.	356
Prisons	117
Promotions, &c., since last publication	635
Provisional Battalion	362
Punjab Cavalry	446
—— Frontier Force	446
—— Infantry	448
Purchase Commission	117
Queen, The	1
Queen's Own Cameron Highldrs.	325
—— (West Kent) Regt.	294
—— Royal West Surrey Regt.	236
Queensland, Staff in	105
Rangoon Eccles. Establishment	507
Regimental District Staff	109
Remount Establishment	117
Retirements, &c., since last publication	642
Rifle Brigade	356
Rifle Depot	111
Ross-shire Buffs	318
Royal Fusiliers	243
—— Highlanders (Black Watch)	286
—— Military Acad. Woolwich	113
—— College, Sandhurst	113
—— Officers who have Certificates from the Senior Department	119
Royal Military School, Chelsea	115
—— Scots (Lothian Regt.)	234
St. Helena, Staff in	106
Sandhurst, R. Military College	113
—— Staff College	113
School of Gunnery	114
—— Military Engineering	114
—— Music, Kneller Hall	114
—— Musketry at Hythe	114
—— Signalling	114
School, Royal Hibernian Military	115
Schools, Army	115
Scottish Borderers, King's Own	269
—— Rifles	270
Scots Fusiliers	262
Seaforth Highlanders	318
Senior Department, R. M. College, Officers who have received Certificates from	119
Seychelles Islands, Staff in	106
Sherwood Foresters (Derbyshire Regiment)	289
Shropshire Light Infantry	297
Signalling, School of	114
Sikh Infantry	447
Small Arms Factory, Enfield	115
—— Birmingham	115
Somersetshire Light Infantry	252
South Australia, Staff in	104
South Eastern District Staff	98

	PAGE
South Wales Borderers	267
Southern District Staff	97
Staff Abroad	100
—— at Home	97
—— College	113
—— Officers passed	119
—— Corps	410
—— of the Army	2
—— Regimental District	109
Staffordshire (North) Regiment	310
—— (South) Regiment	282
Straits Settlements, Staff in	104
Suffolk Regiment	250
Surgeons (Hon.) to the Queen	1
Surrey (East) Regiment	275
—— (West) Regiment	236
Sussex Regiment	279
Sutherland Highlanders	337
Tasmania, Staff in	105
Thames District Staff	98
Tobago, Staff in	107
Tower of London	111
Trinidad, Staff in	107
Turks and Caicos Islands, Staff in	107
Unattached List	362
Veterinary Department	395
—— Bengal	460
—— Bombay	532
—— Madras	506
Victoria, Staff in	104
Victoria's (Princess) Irish Fus.	333
Wales' (Prince of) Leinster Regiment (Royal Canadians)	346
—— N. Staff. Regt.	310
—— Own (West Yorkshire Regiment)	253
—— Volunteers (S. Lancashire Regiment)	284
—— (Princess Charlotte of) Berkshire Regiment	293
—— (Princess of) Own (Yorkshire Regiment)	259
Waltham Abbey, Gunpowder Factory at	115
War Office	2
Warwickshire Regiment	242
Wellington's (Duke of) West Riding Regiment	277
Welsh Fusiliers	265
—— Regiment	285
West Africa Settlements, Staff in	106
—— India Regiment	360
—— Indies, Staff in	107
—— Riding Regiment	277
Western Australia, Staff in	104
—— District Staff	97
Wiltshire Regiment	308
Windward Islands, Staff in	107
Woolwich Arsenal	115
—— Royal Military Academy	113
—— District Staff	98
Worcestershire Regiment	273
Yeomanry Brigades	614
—— Cavalry	607
Yeomen of the Guard	132
York and Lancaster Regiment	311
York, Staff at	97
York's (Duke of) Royal Military School, Chelsea	115
Yorkshire Light Infantry	295
—— Regiment	259
—— (East) Regiment	254
—— (West) Regiment	253
Zululand, Staff in	105

Changes in the Titles of Regiments of Infantry.

N.B.—By means of this Table, Regiments can be found in this book by their old numbers.

REGT.	NEW TITLE.	PAGE
1st	Royal Scots (Lothian Regiment)	234
2nd	Queen's (Royal West Surrey Regiment)	236
3rd	Buffs (East Kent Regiment)	237
4th	King's Own (Royal Lancaster Regiment)	238
5th	Northumberland Fusiliers	240
6th	Royal Warwickshire Regiment	242
7th	Royal Fusiliers (City of London Regiment)	243
8th	King's (Liverpool Regiment)	244
9th	Norfolk Regiment	245
10th	Lincolnshire Regiment	246
11th	Devonshire Regiment	249
12th	Suffolk Regiment	250
13th	Prince Albert's (Somersetshire Light Infantry)	252
14th	Prince of Wales' Own (W. Yorkshire Regt.)	253
15th	East Yorkshire Regiment	254
16th	Bedfordshire Regiment	255
17th	Leicestershire Regiment	256
18th	Royal Irish Regiment	258
19th	Princess of Wales' Own (Yorkshire Regt.)	259
20th	Lancashire Fusiliers	261
21st	Royal Scots Fusiliers	262
22nd	Cheshire Regiment	264
23rd	Royal Welsh Fusiliers	265
24th	South Wales Borderers	267
25th	King's Own Borderers	269
26th	1st Batt. The Cameronians (Scottish Rifles)	270
27th	1st Batt. Royal Inniskilling Fusiliers	271
28th	1st Batt. Gloucestershire Regiment	272
29th	1st Batt. Worcestershire Regiment	273
30th	1st Batt. East Lancashire Regiment	274
31st	1st Batt. East Surrey Regiment	275

Table of Contents.

REGT.	NEW TITLE.	PAGE
32nd	... 1st Batt. Duke of Cornwall's Light Infantry	276
33rd	... 1st Batt. Duke of Wellington's (West Riding Regiment)	277
34th	... 1st Batt. The Border Regiment	278
35th	... 1st Batt. Royal Sussex Regiment	279
36th	... 2nd Batt. Worcestershire Regiment	273
37th	... 1st Batt. Hampshire Regiment	281
38th	... 1st Batt. South Staffordshire Regiment	282
39th	... 1st Batt. Dorsetshire Regiment	283
40th	... 1st Batt. Prince of Wales' Volunteers (South Lancashire Regiment)	284
41st	... 1st Batt. Welsh Regiment	285
42nd	... 1st Batt. The Black Watch (Royal Highlanders)	286
43rd	... 1st Batt. Oxfordshire Light Infantry	287
44th	... 1st Batt. Essex Regiment	288
45th	... 1st Batt. Sherwood Foresters (Derbyshire Regiment)	289
46th	... 2nd Batt. Duke of Cornwall's Light Infantry	276
47th	... 1st Batt. The Loyal North Lancashire Regt.	291
48th	... 1st Batt. Northamptonshire Regiment	292
49th	... 1st Batt. Princess Charlotte of Wales' (Royal Berkshire Regiment)	293
50th	... 1st Batt. Queen's Own (R. West Kent Regt.)	294
51st	... 1st Batt. King's Own Yorkshire Light Infantry	295
52nd	... 2nd Batt. Oxfordshire Light Infantry	287
53rd	... 1st Batt. King's (Shropshire Light Infantry)	297
54th	... 2nd Batt. Dorsetshire Regiment	283
55th	... 2nd Batt. The Border Regiment	278
56th	... 2nd Batt. Essex Regiment	288
57th	... 1st Batt. Duke of Cambridge's Own (Middlesex Regiment)	301
58th	... 2nd Batt. Northamptonshire Regiment	292
59th	... 2nd Batt. East Lancashire Regiment	274
60th	... King's Royal Rifle Corps	304
61st	... 2nd Batt. Gloucestershire Regiment	272
62nd	... 1st Batt. Duke of Edinburgh's (Wiltshire Regiment)	308
63rd	... 1st Batt. Manchester Regiment	309
64th	... 1st Batt. Prince of Wales' (North Staffordshire Regiment)	310
65th	... 1st Batt. York and Lancaster Regiment	311
66th	... 2nd Batt. Princess Charlotte of Wales' (Royal Berkshire Regiment)	293
67th	... 2nd Batt. Hampshire Regiment	281
68th	... 1st Batt. Durham Light Infantry	314
69th	... 2nd Batt. Welsh Regiment	285
70th	... 2nd Batt. East Surrey Regiment	275
71st	... 1st Batt. Highland Light Infantry	317
72nd	... 1st Batt. Seaforth Highlanders (Ross-shire Buffs, The Duke of Albany's)	318
73rd	... 2nd Batt. The Black Watch (Royal Highlanders)	286
74th	... 2nd Batt. Highland Light Infantry	317
75th	... 1st Batt. Gordon Highlanders	321
76th	... 2nd Batt. Duke of Wellington's (West Riding Regiment)	277
77th	... 2nd Batt. Duke of Cambridge's Own (Middlesex Regiment)	301
78th	... 2nd Batt. Seaforth Highlanders (Ross-shire Buffs, The Duke of Albany's)	318
79th	... 1st Batt. Queen's Own Cameron Highlanders	325
80th	... 2nd Batt. South Staffordshire Regiment	282
81st	... 2nd Batt. Loyal North Lancashire Regt.	291
82nd	... 2nd Batt. Prince of Wales' Volunteers (South Lancashire Regiment)	284
83rd	... 1st Batt. Royal Irish Rifles	329
84th	... 2nd Batt. York and Lancaster Regiment	311
85th	... 2nd Batt. King's (Shropshire Light Inf.)	297
86th	... 2nd Batt. Royal Irish Rifles	329
87th	... 1st Batt. Princess Victoria's (R. Irish Fus.)	333
88th	... 1st Batt. Connaught Rangers	334
89th	... 2nd Batt. Princess Victoria's (R. Irish Fus.)	333
90th	... 2nd Batt. Cameronians (Scottish Rifles)	270
91st	... 1st Batt. Princess Louise's (Argyll and Sutherland Highlanders)	337
92nd	... 2nd Batt. Gordon Highlanders	321
93rd	... 2nd Batt. Princess Louise's (Argyll and Sutherland Highlanders)	337
94th	... 2nd Batt. Connaught Rangers	334
95th	... 2nd Batt. Sherwood Foresters (Derbyshire Regiment)	289
96th	... 2nd Batt. Manchester Regiment	309
97th	... 2nd Batt. The Queen's Own (Royal West Kent Regiment)	294
98th	... 2nd Batt. Prince of Wales' (North Staffordshire Regiment	310
99th	... 2nd Batt. Duke of Edinburgh's (Wiltshire Regiment)	308
100th	... 1st Batt. The Prince of Wales' Leinster Regiment (Royal Canadians)	346
101st	... 1st Batt. Royal Munster Fusiliers	347
102nd	... 1st Batt. Royal Dublin Fusiliers	348
103rd	... 2nd Batt. Royal Dublin Fusiliers	348
104th	... 2nd Batt. Royal Munster Fusiliers	347
105th	... 2nd Batt. The King's Own Yorkshire Light Infantry	295
106th	... 2nd Batt. Durham Light Infantry	314
107th	... 2nd Batt. Royal Sussex Regiment	279
108th	... 2nd Batt. Royal Inniskilling Fusiliers	271
109th	... 2nd Batt. The Prince of Wales' Leinster Regiment (Royal Canadians)	346

Changes in the Titles of Regiments of Militia.

ARTILLERY.

		PAGE
Antrim	... to be Antrim Art. (Southern Div. R. Art.)	579
Argyll & Bute	... Argyll & Bute Art. "	582
Cardigan	... Cardigan Art. (West. Div. R. Art.)	583
Carmarthen	... Carmarthen Art. "	583
Clare	... Clare Art. (Southern Div. R. Art.)	582
Cornwall and Devon Miners	} Cornwall and Devon Miners Art. (Western Div. R. Art.)	582
Cork City, West Cork	} Cork Artillery (South. Div. R. Art.)	58
Devon	... Devon Art. (Western Div. R. Art.)	582
Donegal	... Donegal Art. (South. Div. R. Art.)	580
Dublin City	... Dublin City Art. "	580
Durham	... Durham Art. (Western Div. R. Art.)	583
Edinburgh	... Edinburgh Art. (South. Div. R. Art.)	580
Fife	... Fife Artillery "	580
Forfar & Kincardine	} Forfar and Kincardine Artillery (Southern Div. R. Art.)	581
Glamorgan	... Glamorgan Art. (West. Div. R. Art.)	583
Haddington	... Haddington Art. (South. Div. R. Art.)	580
Hampshire	to be Hampshire Art. (South. Div. R. Art.)	581
Kent	... Kent Art. (Eastern Div. R. Art.)	579
Lancashire	... Lancashire Art (South. Div. R. Art.)	581
Limerick City	... Limerick City Art. "	581
Londonderry	... Londonderry Art. "	582
Mid-Ulster	... Mid-Ulster Art. "	581
Norfolk	... Norfolk Art. (Eastern Div. R. Art.)	579
Northumberland	{ Northumberland Artillery (Western Div. R. Art.)	583
Pembroke	... Pembroke Art. "	583
Sligo	... Sligo Art. (Southern Div. R. Art.)	582
Suffolk	... Suffolk Art. (Eastern Div. R. Art.)	579
Sussex	... Sussex Artillery "	579
1st or South Tipperary	} Tipperary Art. (South. Div. R. Art.)	581
Waterford	... Waterford Artillery "	582
Wicklow	... Wicklow Artillery "	582
Wight (Isle of)	Isle of Wight Art. "	581
York	... Yorkshire Art. (West. Div. R. Art.)	583

INFANTRY.—ENGLAND AND WALES.

	PAGE
Bedford Militia to be 3 Bn. Bedfordshire Regiment	589
Berks ... 3 Bn. Princess Charlotte of Wales' (Berkshire Regiment)	598
Bucks ... 3 Bn. Oxfordshire Light Infantry	596
Cambridge ... 4 Bn. Suffolk Regiment	588
Carnarvon ... 4 Bn. Royal Welsh Fusiliers	591
1 Cheshire ... 3 Bn. Cheshire Regiment	591
2 Cheshire ... 4 Bn. Cheshire Regiment	591
Cornwall Rang. 3 Bn. Duke of Cornwall's Lt. Inf.	594
Cumberland ... 3 Bn. Border Regiment	595
Denbigh and Merioneth ... 3 Bn. Royal Welsh Fusiliers	591
1 Derby ... 5 Bn. The Sherwood Foresters (Derbyshire Regiment)	598
2 Derby ... 3 Bn. Ditto	597
1 Devon ... 4 Bn. Devonshire Regiment	588
2 Devon ... 3 Bn. Devonshire Regiment	588
Dorset ... 3 Bn. Dorsetshire Regiment	596

Table of Contents.

vii

County	Regiment	Page
1 Durham	3 Bn. Durham Light Infantry	601
2 Durham	4 Bn. Durham Light Infantry	602
Essex Rifles	3 Bn. Essex Regiment	597
West Essex	4 Bn. Essex Regiment	597
Flint	6 Bn. King's Royal Rifles	600
Glamorgan	3 Bn. Welsh Regiment	596
South Glo'ster	3 Bn. Gloucestershire Regiment	593
North Glo'ster	4 Bn. Gloucestershire Regiment	593
Hampshire	3 Bn. Hampshire Regiment	595
Hereford	4 Bn. Shropshire Regiment	599
Hertford	4 Bn. Bedfordshire Regiment	589
Huntingdon	5 Bn. King's Royal Rifles	600
East Kent	3 Bn. The Buffs (E. Kent Regt.)	585
West Kent	3 & 4 Bns. The Queen's Own Royal (West Kent Regiment)	598
1 Lancashire	3 & 4 Bns. The King's Own Royal (Lancaster Regiment)	585
2 Lancashire	& 4 Bns. The King's (Liverpool Regiment)	587
3 Lancashire	3 & 4 Bns. Loyal N. Lancashire Regt.	598
4 Lancashire	3 Bn. Prince of Wales' Volunteers (South Lancashire Regiment)	596
5 Lancashire	3 Bn. East Lancashire Regiment	594
6 Lancashire	3 & 4 Bns. Manchester Regiment	601
7 Lancashire	3 Bn. Lancashire Fusiliers	591
Leicestershire	3 Bn. Leicestershire Regiment	589
North Lincoln	3 Bn. Lincolnshire Regiment	587
South Lincoln	4 Bn. Lincolnshire Regiment	587
London	4 Bn. Royal Fusiliers (City of London Regiment)	586
East Middlesex	4 Bn. The Duke of Cambridge's Own (Middlesex Regiment)	599
2 Middlesex	7 Bn. King's Royal Rifles	600
3 Middlesex	3 Bn. Royal Fusiliers (City of London Regiment)	586
4 Middlesex	5 Bn. Royal Fusiliers (City of London Regiment)	586
5 Middlesex	3 Bn. The Duke of Cambridge's Own (Middlesex Regiment)	599
Montgomery	4 Bn. South Wales Borderers	592
1 Norfolk	3 Bn. Norfolk Regiment	587
2 Norfolk	4 Bn. Norfolk Regiment	587
Northampton & Rutland	3 & 4 Bns. Northamptonshire Regt.	598
Northumberl'nd	3 Bn. Northumberland Fusiliers	585
Nottingham	4 Bn. The Sherwood Foresters (Derbyshire Regiment)	597
Oxfordshire	4 Bn. Oxfordshire Light Infantry	597
Shropshire	3 Bn. Shropshire Light Infantry	599
1 Somerset	3 Bn. Prince Albert's (Somersetshire Light Infantry)	588
2 Somerset	4 Bn. Ditto	588
South Wales Borderers	3 Bn. South Wales Borderers	592
1 Stafford	3 & 4 Bns. South Staffordshire Regt.	595
2 Stafford	3 Bn. The Prince of Wales' (North Staffordshire Regiment)	601
3 Stafford	4 Bn. Ditto	601
West Suffolk	3 Bn. Suffolk Regiment	588
1 Surrey	3 Bn. East Surrey Regiment	594
2 Surrey	3 Bn. The Queen's Royal (West Surrey Regiment)	585
3 Surrey	4 Bn. East Surrey Regiment	594
Sussex	3 & 4 Bns. Royal Sussex Regiment	595
1 TowerHamlets	7 Bn. Rifle Brigade (Prince Consort's Own)	607
2 TowerHamlets	5 Bn. Ditto	606
1 Warwick	3 Bn. Royal Warwickshire Regiment	586
2 Warwick	4 Bn. Royal Warwickshire Regiment	586
Westmoreland	4 Bn. Border Regiment	595
Wiltshire	3 Bn. Duke of Edinburgh's (Wiltshire Regiment)	600
Worcester	3 & 4 Bns. Worcestershire Regiment	593
East York	3 Bn. East Yorkshire Regiment	589
North York	4 Bn. Princess of Wales' Own (Yorkshire Regiment)	550
1 West York	3 Bn. The King's Own Yorkshire Light Infantry	599
2 West York	3 Bn. Prince of Wales' Own (West Yorkshire Regiment)	589
3 West York	3 Bn. York and Lancaster Regiment	601
4 West York	4 Bn. Prince of Wales' Own (West Yorkshire Regiment)	589
5 West York	3 Bn. Princess of Wales' Own (Yorkshire Regiment)	590
6 West York	3 & 4 Bns. The Duke of Wellington's (West Riding Regiment)	594

SCOTLAND.

County	Regiment	Page
Aberdeenshire	3 Bn. Gordon Highlanders	602
Ayr and Wigtown	3 Bn. Royal Scots Fusiliers	591
Edinburgh	3 Bn. Royal Scots (Lothian Regt.)	585
Highland Borderers	3 Bn. Princess Louise's (Argyll and Sutherland Highlanders)	604
Highland Lt. Inf.	2 Bn. The Queen's Own (Cameron Highlanders)	602
Highland Rifles	3 Bn. Seaforth Highlanders	602
1 Lanark	3 Bn. Highland Light Infantry	602
2 Lanark	3 & 4 Bns. Cameronians (Scottish Rifles)	592
Perth	3 Bn. The Black Watch (Royal Highlanders)	596
Renfrew	4 Bn. Princess Louise's (Argyll and Sutherland Highlanders)	605
Scottish Borderers	3 Bn. King's Own Scottish Borderers	592

IRELAND.

County	Regiment	Page
Antrim	4 Bn. Royal Irish Rifles	603
Armagh	3 Bn. Princess Victoria's (R. Irish Fus.)	603
Carlow	8 Bn. King's Royal Rifles	600
Cavan	4 Bn. Princess Victoria's (R. Irish Fus.)	604
North Cork	9 Bn. King's Royal Rifles	600
South Cork	3 Bn. Royal Munster Fusiliers	605
Donegal	5 Bn. Royal Inniskilling Fusiliers	593
North Down	3 Bn. Royal Irish Rifles	603
South Down	5 Bn. Royal Irish Rifles	603
Dublin County	5 Bn. Royal Dublin Fusiliers	606
Dublin City	4 Bn. Royal Dublin Fusiliers	606
Fermanagh	3 Bn. Royal Inniskilling Fusiliers	592
Galway	4 Bn. Connaught Rangers	604
Kerry	4 Bn. Royal Munster Fusiliers	605
Kildare	3 Bn. Royal Dublin Fusiliers	606
Kilkenny	5 Bn. Royal Irish Regiment	590
King's County	3 Bn. Prince of Wales' Leinster Regiment (Royal Canadians)	605
Leitrim	8 Bn. Rifle Brigade (Prince Consort's Own)	607
Royal Limerick County	5 Bn. Royal Munster Fusiliers	601
Longford Rifles	6 Bn. Rifle Brigade (Prince Consort's Own)	606
Louth	6 Bn. Royal Irish Rifles	603
South Mayo & North Mayo	3 Bn. Connaught Rangers	604
Meath	5 Bn. Prince of Wales' Leinster Regiment (Royal Canadians)	605
Monaghan	5 Bn. Princess Victoria's (R. Irish Fus.)	604
Queen's County	4 Bn. Prince of Wales' Leinster Regiment (Royal Canadians)	605
Roscommon	3 Bn. Connaught Rangers	604
North Tipperary	4 Bn. Royal Irish Regiment	590
Tyrone Fus.	4 Bn. Royal Inniskilling Fusiliers	593
Westmeath	9 Bn. Rifle Brigade (Prince Consort's Own)	607
Wexford	3 Bn. Royal Irish Regiment	590

HER MAJESTY QUEEN VICTORIA.

Private Secretary to the Queen .... General *Sir* Henry Frederick Ponsonby, *GCB.*

Aides de Camp to the Queen.

Personal Aides de Camp
- Field Marshal *His Royal Highness the Prince of* Wales, *KG. KT. KP. GCB. GCSI. GCMG. GCIE*
- General *His Royal Highness the Duke of* Connaught, *KG. KT. KP. GCSI. GCMG. GCIE. KCB.*
- Field Marshal *His Royal Highness the Duke of* Cambridge, *KG. KT. KP. GCB. GCSI. GCMG. GCIE. Commander in Chief.*

- Colonel W. A. *Marquis of* Exeter, 3rd and 4th Batts. Northamptonshire Regt. (Northampton Militia).
- — William Bell, *CB.* Royal Guernsey Militia.
- — Rt. Hon. Frederick Arthur, *Earl of* Derby, *GCB.* late Lt. and Captain Grenadier Guards; 3rd Batt. Lancaster Regiment (*Supernumerary*).
- — *Sir* James Godfray, *Knt.* Royal Jersey Militia.
- — Francis, *Earl of* Wemyss, 7 Middlesex Rifle Volunteers (*Supernumerary*).
- — *Sir* James Gardiner Baird, *Bart.* 1 Midlothian Artillery Volunteers.
- — Hugh Lupus, *Duke of* Westminster, *KG.* Cheshire Yeomanry Cavalry, and 13 Middlesex Rifle Volunteers (*Supernumerary*).
- — Rt. Hon. W. J. *Visct.* Oxenbridge, 3 Bn. Lincoln Regiment (North Lincoln Militia).
- — Henry Hallam Parr, *CB. CMG.* h.p. Somerset Light Infantry.
- — *VC p.s.c.* Mark Sever Bell, *CB.* (from R. Engineers).
- — Robert Macgregor Stewart, *CB.* (from R. Artillery).
- — *Lord* Claud John Hamilton, 5 Batt. Inniskilling Fusiliers.
- — Rt. Hon. W. H. J. C. *Earl of* Limerick, *KP.* 5 Battalion Munster Fusiliers (*Supernumerary*).
- — Rt. Hon. C. A. *Earl of* Home, Lanark Yeomanry Cavalry (*Supernumerary*).
- — Rt. Hon. W. H. *Earl of* Mount Edgecumbe, 2 Volunteer Battalion Devonshire Regt. (*Supernumerary*).
- — *Sir* Horatio Herbert Kitchener, *KCMG. CB.* Royal Engineers.
- — William Jones Thomas, 3 Bn. S.Wales Borderers.
- — Rt. Hon. R. E. St. L. *Earl of* Cork and Orrery, *KP.* North Somerset Yeomanry.

- Colonel *Hon.* Reg. A. J. Talbot, *CB.* (from h.p. 1 Life Guards.)
- — John Palmer Brabazon, *CB.* 4 Hussars.
- — John Ramsay Slade, *CB.* h.p. Royal Artillery.
- — *VC* Arthur George Hammond, *CB. DSO.* Indian Staff Corps.
- — Reginald Garnett, *CB.* h.p. Seaforth Highlanders.
- — John Henry Barnard, *CB. CMG.* Regtl District.
- — J. H. Rivett-Carnac, *CIE.* 4 Administrative Battalion North West Provinces Volunteers.
- — James Charles Cavendish, 2 Volunteer Battalion Derby Regiment.
- — Right Hon. C. *Lord* Suffield, *KCB.* late Norfolk Artillery (E. Div. R. Art.).
- — Right Hon. Henry, *Earl* Percy, 3 Bn. Northumberland Fusiliers.
- — *p.s.c.* Edward Thomas Henry Hutton, *CB.* (from h.p. King's Royal Rifles).
- — Alfred Gaselee, *CB.* Indian Staff Corps.
- — William Campbell, Royal Marine Artillery.
- — *Sir* Reginald H. A. Ogilvy, *Bart.*, Forfar and Kincardine Artillery (S. Div. R. Artillery).
- — Montague Protheroe, *CB. CSI.* Indian Staff Corps.
- — George, *Earl of* Haddington, Lothians and Berwick Yeomanry.
- — Henry *Lord* Belper, Nottingham Yeomanry Cavalry.
- — Arch. C. *Lord* Blythswood, 3 Vol. Bn. Highland Lt. Inf.
- — Bryan G. D. Cooke, 2 Vol. Bn. Welsh Fusiliers.
- — Gordon L. C. Money, *DSO.* Cameron Highlanders.
- — John Jopp, Indian Staff Corps.
- — Francis Howard, Rifle Brigade.
- — *Sir* Casimir S. Gzowski, *KCMG.* Staff Officer to Engineer Force in Canada (*Honorary*).

Equerries to the Queen.

- General Henry Lynedoch Gardiner, *CB.* R. Artillery.
- Colonel *Hon.* Henry Wm. John Byng, late Coldstream Guards, *Hon. Colonel* 7 Bn. *King's Royal Rifles.*
- *VC* Major General *Sir* John Carstairs M'Neill, *KCB. KCMG.*
- Major Arthur John Bigge, *CB. CMG.* Royal Artillery.
- Major *Hon.* H. C. Legge, Coldstream Guards.
- Lieut. F. E. G. Ponsonby, Grenadier Guards.
- General Rt. *Hon. Sir* Henry Frederick Ponsonby, *GCB.* (*extra*).

- General Rt. *Hon.* Alex. N. *Visct.* Bridport, *KCB.* (*extra*).
- Lt. Colonel Stanier Waller, Royal Engineers (*extra*).
- Lt. Colonel *Sir* F. I. Edwards, *KCB.* R. Eng. (*extra*).
- *p.s.c.* Captain *Count* Gleichen, Grenadier Guards (*extra*).
- Major General Charles Taylor Du Plat, *CB.* r.f.p. R. Art. (*extra*).
- General Aug. C. L. *Duke of* Grafton, *KG. CB.* (*honorary*).

Honorary Physicians to the Queen.

- Director General *Sir* Thomas Galbraith Logan, *MD. KCB.* half pay.
- Surgeon General Samuel Currie, *MD. CB.* half pay.
- Surgeon General Charles Alexander Gordon, *MD. CB.* half pay.
- Surgeon General John Irvine, *MD.* retired pay.
- Surgeon General Alexander Smith, *CB. MD.* retired pay.
- Surgeon Major General William Arthur Thomson, *MB.* retired pay.
- Inspector General *Sir* William Mackenzie, *MD. KCB. CSI.* late Madras Estab.

- Surgeon General *Sir* Joseph Fayrer, *MD. KCSI.* late Bengal Estab.
- Deputy Surgeon General Thomas Edmondstone Charles, *MD.* late Bengal Estab.
- Surgeon General William Robert Cornish, *CIE.* late Madras Estab.
- Surgeon General *Sir* William James Moore, *KCIE.* late Bombay Estab.
- Surgeon Major General John Pinkerton, *MD.* late Bombay Estab.

Honorary Surgeons to the Queen.

- Deputy Surgeon General John Ashton Bostock, *CB.* half pay.
- Surgeon General *Sir* Thomas Longmore, *Knt. CB.* half pay.
- Surgeon General *Sir* John Harrie Ker Innes, *KCB.* half pay.
- Director General *Sir* Thomas Crawford, *MD. KCB.* retired pay.
- *VC* Surgeon General *Sir* James Mouat, *KCB.* half pay.
- Surgeon Major General *Sir* W. A. Mackinnon, *KCB.* Director General Army Medical Department.

- Surgeon Major Alexander Grant, late Indian Army.
- Inspector General John Henry Orr, *CB. MD.* late Madras Estab.
- Surgeon General *Sir* William Guyer Hunter, *MD. KCMG.* late Bombay Estab.
- Deputy Surgeon General Samuel Bowen Partridge, *CIE.* late Bengal Estab.
- Surgeon General James Macnabb Cuningham, *MD. CSI.* late Bengal Estab.
- Deputy Surgeon General Henry Vandyke Carter, *MD.* late Bombay Estab.

Honorary Chaplains to the Queen.

Rev. J. C. Edghill, *DD. Chaplain General.* | Rev. R. H. Bullock, *DCL. Chaplain 1st Class,* ret. pay.

HER MAJESTY'S SECRETARY OF STATE FOR WAR	Right Hon. H. CAMPBELL-BANNERMAN, MP.
Private Secretary	Hon. R. C. F. Leigh.
Assistant Private Secretaries	Captain J. Sinclair, MP. (unpaid).
	A. C. Strange.
HER MAJESTY'S PARLIAMENTARY UNDER-SECRETARY OF STATE FOR WAR	R. Lord Monkswell.
Private Secretary	R. H. Brade.
HER MAJESTY'S PERMANENT UNDER SECRETARY OF STATE FOR WAR	Sir Ralph W. Thompson, KCB.
Private Secretary	F. G. Sills.
Assistant Under Secretary of State	Sir Arthur Lawrence Haliburton, KCB.

Finance Department.

Financial Secretary	W. Woodall, MP.
Private Secretary	H. J. Gibson.
Accountant General	R. H. Knox, CB.
Deputy Accountant General	H. T. De la Bère, CB.
Assistant Accountants General	T. Cave-Browne-Cave.
	A. Major.
	F. T. Marzials.
Director of Contracts	George Lawson, CB.
Assistant Director of Contracts	W. J. Stacey.
Director of Clothing	G. D. A. Fleetwood Wilson, CB.
Assistant Director of Clothing	H. D. De la Bère.
Director General of Ordnance Factories	W. Anderson, M.Inst.C.E. DCL.

STAFF OF THE ARMY.

COMMANDER IN CHIEF.

Field Marshal *His Royal Highness* GEORGE W. F. C. DUKE OF CAMBRIDGE, KG. KT. KP. GCB. GCSI. GCMG. GCIE. Aide de Camp to the Queen, Colonel of the Grenadier Guards, &c.

Private Secretary	Colonel A. C. F. FitzGeorge, h.p. 11 Hussars, 14 July 86.
Aides de Camp	Colonel Lord A. C. Gordon-Lennox (from h.p. Grenadier Guards).
	Colonel G. W. A. FitzGeorge, h.p. 20 Hussars.
	Major A. Davidson, King's Royal Rifles.
	Colonel H. R. Visct. Downe, CIE. (from 10 Hussars);
	p.s.c. Colonel Sir J. C. Ardagh, KCIE. CB. h.p. Royal Engineers, (extra).
Military Secretary	General Sir Reginald Gipps, KCB. 23 Mar. 92.
Assistant Military Secretaries	Colonel R. B. Lane (from h.p. Rifle Brigade), 2 July 92.
	General J. J. H. Gordon, CB. Indian Staff Corps, 8 Oct. 90 (for Indian affairs).

ADJUTANT GENERAL'S DEPARTMENT.

Adjutant General (with rank of General)	VC Lieut.General Rt. Hon. Sir R. H. Buller, GCB. KCMG. 1 Oct. 90.
Deputy Adjutant General (with rank of Major General)	p.s.c. Colonel J. Duncan (from h.p. Dublin Fusiliers), 29 Sept. 93.
Assistant Adjutant Generals	Colonel H. Kingscote (from h.p. Oxford Light Infantry), 28 Dec. 93.
	p.s.c. Colonel Hon. N. G. Lyttelton (from h.p. Rifle Brigade), 5 Dec. 94.
	Colonel H. H. Parr, CB. CMG. (from h.p. Somerset Light Infantry), 25 Jan. 95.
Deputy Assistant Adjutant Generals	p.s.c. Major G. F. Browne, DSO. Northamptonshire Regt. 19 Jan. 91.
	p.s.c. Major F. R. C. Carleton, Durham Light Infantry, 22 Aug. 94.
Staff Captain	p.s.c. Captain G. F. Ellison, West Surrey Regiment, 1 Sept. 94.
Director of Military Intelligence	p.s.c. Lieut.General E. F. Chapman, CB. R. (Bengal) Art. 1 Apr. 91.
Assistant Adjutant General (Ditto)	p.s.c. Colonel W. Everett, CMG. (from h.p. W. Riding Regt.), 7 June 93.
Deputy Assistant Adjutant Generals (Ditto)	p.s.c. Lt.Colonel J. K. Trotter (from h.p. Royal Artillery), 1 Sept. 92.
	p.s.c. Captain C. à Court, Rifle Brigade, 1 Feb. 93.
	p.s.c. Major H. J. Foster, Royal Engineers, 24 May 93.
	p.s.c. Captain E. Agar, Royal Engineers, 1 Feb. 94.
	p.s.c. Captain W. E. Fairholme, Royal Artillery, 15 July 94.
Staff Captains (Ditto)	p.s.c. Major Hon. M. G. Talbot, Royal Engineers, 15 Nov. 92.
	p.s.c. Major J. S. S. Barker, Royal Artillery, 1 Feb. 93.
	p.s.c. Major H. P. Northcott, Leinster Regiment, 24 May 93.
	p.s.c. Captain H. D. Laffan, Royal Engineers, 1 Feb. 94.
	p.s.c. Captain W. A. Macbean, Royal Artillery, 15 July 94.
	Hon. H. D. Napier, Indian Staff Corps, 1 Jan. 95.
Inspector General of Auxiliary Forces and Recruiting	Major General Sir F. W. Grenfell, GCMG. KCB. 1 Aug. 94.
Assistant Adjutant General for Recruiting	Colonel G. Cox (from h.p. Irish Fusiliers), 1 Aug. 94.
Deputy Assistant Adjutant General ditto	Bt.Major C. Crutchley, Scots Guards, 25 Mar. 89.

Staff of the Army.

ROYAL ARTILLERY.

Deputy Adjutant General (with rank of Major General)	Colonel F. T. Lloyd, *CB.*, 21 Feb. 94.
Assistant Adjutant General	Colonel A. E. Turner, *CB.* 2 Apr. 94.
Deputy Assistant Adjutant General	p.s.c. Major F. G. Stone, 1 Sept. 94.

ROYAL ENGINEERS.

Deputy Adjutant General (with rank of Major General)	Colonel J. M. H. Maitland, *CB.* 21 Apr. 91.
Assistant Adjutant General	Colonel D. A. Scott, *DSO.* 8 June 94.

QUARTER MASTER GENERAL'S DEPARTMENT.

Quarter Master General	p.s.c. ℣℃ Lt. General *Sir* Henry Evelyn Wood, *GCB. GCMG.* 9 Oct. 93.
Assistant Quarter Master Generals	p.s.c. Colonel C. J. Burnett (from h.p. Irish Rifles), 29 Sept. 93. Colonel J. T. Skinner, *CB. DSO.* Army Service Corps, 4 Dec. 93.
Deputy Assistant Quarter Master Generals	p.s.c. Bt.Major H. M. Lawson, Royal Engineers, 29 Sept. 93. Lt.Colonel H. N. Bunbury, Army Service Corps, 4 Dec. 91. Lt.Colonel J. A. Boyd, Army Service Corps, 1 Jan. 95.
Director General of Military Education	Major General *Sir* C. W. Wilson, *KCB. KCMG.* Royal Eng. 22 Jan. 95.
Assistant Director of Military Education (ranking as Assistant Adjutant General)	p.s.c. Colonel A. M. Delavoye (from h.p. Essex Regt.), 2 July 91.
Director of Army Schools	p.s.c. Colonel D. F. Jones (from h.p. Royal Artillery), 18 June 92.

Inspector General of Cavalry in Great Britain and Ireland	Major General G. Luck, *CB.* 1 Apr. 95.
Aide de Camp	Captain D. Haig, 7 Hussars, 28 Apr. 94.
Assistant Adjutant General	Colonel H. S. Gough (from 8 Hussars), 8 July 93.

Inspector General of Fortifications, and of Royal Engineers (with rank of Lt.General)	p.s.c. Major General R. Grant, *CB.* 18 Apr. 91.
Aide de Camp	Captain W. C. Hussey, Royal Engineers, 20 Apr. 91.
Deputy Inspectors General of Fortifications	Colonel H. Locock, *CB.* (from Royal Engineers), 1 Nov. 87. Colonel W. Salmond, *CB.* (from Royal Engineers), 18 May 91. Colonel H. F. Turner (from Royal Engineers), 6 Nov. 94.
Assistant Inspectors General of Fortifications	p.s.c. Lt.Colonel C. M. Watson, *CMG.* Royal Engineers, 14 May 91. Lt.Colonel J. Matheson, Royal Engineers, 1 Jan. 92. Lt.Colonel G. Hildebrand, Royal Engineers, 1 July 94. Lt.Colonel R. M. Hyslop, Royal Engineers, 4 July 94. Lt.Colonel G. Barker, Royal Engineers, 1 Sept. 94. p.s.c. Lt.Colonel H. H. Settle, *DSO.* Royal Engineers.
Artillery Adviser to the Inspector General of Fortifications	p.s.c. Lt.Colonel J. R. J. Jocelyn (from h.p. R. Artillery), 1 Apr. 94.
Inspector of Submarine Defences	Major R. M. Ruck, Royal Engineers, 1 July 91.
Assistant Inspector of do.	Major C. Penrose, Royal Engineers, 1 July 91.
Director of Artillery	Lt.General *Sir* R. J. Hay, *KCB.* Royal Artillery, 31 Oct. 91.
Assistant Director of Artillery	p.s.c. Colonel N. L. Walford (from h.p. R. Artillery), 10 Jan. 93.
Assistants to the Director of Artillery	Captain E. Tinker, Royal Artillery, 1 Oct. 93. Deputy Com. Gen. of Ordnance J. Steevens, 1 Dec. 93.
Staff Paymaster	J. E. Kitson, 21 Aug. 93.

Inspector General of Remounts	Major General E. A. Gore, 1 Jan. 94.

Director General of Army Medical Department	*Sir* William Alexander Mackinnon, *KCB. FRCS.Ed.* 7 May 89.
Professional Assistant	Surgeon Major General J. Jameson, *MD.* 1 Apr. 93.
Director General Veterinary Department	Veterinary Colonel J. Drummond Lambert, *CB.* 28 June 90.
Chaplain General	Rev. J. C. Edghill, *DD.* 8 Feb. 85, *Chaplain Tower of London.*

ACTIVE LIST.

FIELD MARSHALS.

	CORNET, 2nd LIEUT. or ENSIGN.	LIEUT.	CAPTAIN.	MAJOR.	LIEUT. COLONEL.	COLONEL.	MAJOR GENERAL.	LIEUT. GENERAL.	GENERAL.	FIELD MARSHAL.
His Royal Highness George William Frederick Charles, Duke of Cambridge,¹ KG. KT. KP. GCB. GCSI. GCMG. GCIE. Colonel of the Royal Artillery and Royal Engineers, 10 May 61; Colonel of the Grenadier Guards, 15 Dec. 61; Colonel in Chief of the King's Royal Rifles, 3 March 69; Colonel in Chief of the 17th Lancers, 21 June 76; Commanding in Chief, 15 July 56; Commander in Chief, 25 Nov. 87	14 Dec. 37	15 Oct. 39	9 Nov. 46	14 July 5	12 Dec. 54	3 Nov. 37	7 May 45	19 June 54	9 Nov. 62	9 Nov. 62
His Royal Highness Albert Edward, Prince of Wales and Duke of Cornwall, KG. KT. KP. GCB. GCSI. GCMG. GCIE. to Hussars, and Colonel of the 1st and 2nd Life Guards and the Royal Horse Guards	21 June 39	15 Dec. 40	16 May 46	7 June 49	2 Aug. 50	9 Nov. 58				29 May 75
Sir John Lintorn Arabin Simmons,³ GCB. GCMG. Royal Engineers	12 Oct. 40	3 Jan. 44	1 June 54	19 Jan. 58	20 July 58					
Sir Frederick Paul Haines,⁴ GCB. GCSI. CIE. Scots Fusiliers								27 Aug. 72	1 Oct. 77	21 May 90
Sir Donald Martin Stewart, Bart.⁵ GCB. GCSI. CIE.							25 Nov. 64	23 May 73	1 Oct. 77	21 May 90
Garnet Joseph, Viscount Wolseley,⁶ KP. GCB. GCMG. Commanding the Forces in Ireland, 1 Oct. 90 [R]	12 Mar. 52	16 May 52	26 Jan. 55	24 Mar. 58	26 Apr. 59	24 Dec. 68	6 Mar. 68	1 Oct. 77	1 July 78	26 May 94
					5 June 65	6 Mar. 68	25 Mar. 78	18 Nov. 82	26 May 94

GENERALS.

	CORNET, 2nd LIEUT. or ENSIGN.	LIEUT.	CAPTAIN.	MAJOR.	LIEUT. COLONEL.	COLONEL.	MAJOR GENERAL.	LIEUT. GENERAL.	GENERAL.
H.R.H. Prince Frederic Christian Charles Augustus of Schleswig-Holstein, KG							3 July 66	14 Aug. 74	1 Oct. 77
John Michel le Courcy Meade,¹ Royal Marines	20 Feb. 49	27 Dec. 52	1 Aug. 60	23 Apr. 73	25 Dec. 77	3 Dec. 8:	7 Nov. 85	22 June 87	8 Sept. 89
Francis William Thomas,¹ Royal Marines	28 June 49	15 Aug. 53	26 Apr. 61	17 May 74	1 Apr. 78	1 Apr. 82	1 Feb. 86	23 Mar. 87	20 Nov. 89
Sir Peter Stark Lumsden,¹ GCB. CSI. Indian Staff Corps	10 Dec. 47	23 May 54	18 Feb. 61	19 Feb. 74	1 Aug. 66	16 Mar. 70	1 July 81	8 Jan. 87	17 Aug. 90
F.C. Frederick Sleigh, Lord Roberts of Kandahar and Waterford,¹ GCB. GCSI. GCIE. Royal Artillery	12 Dec. 51	31 May 57	12 Nov. 65	15 Aug. 68	30 Jan. 75	1 Dec. 75	31 Dec. 78	26 July 83	28 Nov. 90
Sir John Ross,²⁵ GCB. [R]	14 Apr. 40	29 Dec. 48	29 Sept. 54	6 June 56	20 July 58	23 May 66	1 Apr. 65	1 Mar. 86	1 Apr. 91
Sir Edward Gascoigne Bulwer,²⁹ KCB. [R]	21 Aug. 49	13 Dec. 50	21 Aug. 58	26 Jan. 58	26 Apr. 59	23 May 66	1 Oct. 77	1 Jan. 87	1 Apr. 91
Sir George Tomkyns Chesney,¹ KCB. CSI. CIE. M.P. Royal Engineers	8 Oct. 48	1 Aug. 54	27 Aug. 58	28 Apr. 60	15 Jan. 64	16 Feb. 67	15 Jan. 72	16 Mar. 87	1 Apr. 92
Sir Robert Biddulph,¹ GCMG. CB. Royal Artillery	22 June 53	30 May 54	1 Apr. 60	1 Feb. 61	15 Jan. 64	28 Mar. 68	1 July 69	1 Oct. 87	1 Apr. 92
H.R.H. Hon. William Henry Adelbert Feilding,¹³ Insp. Gen. of Recruiting 31 July 91 [R]	13 Feb. 52	26 July 53	15 Feb. 54				4 Mar. 80	1 Oct. 87	1 Nov. 92
H.R.H. the Duke of Connaught,¹ KG. KT. KP. GCSI. GCMG. GCIE. KCB. Rifle Brigade, Personal Aide de Camp to the Queen, and Commanding at Aldershot, 9 Oct. 93		19 June 68	1 May 71	7 Aug. 75	27 Sept. 76	29 May 80	22 Feb. 89	1 Apr. 93
John Hart Dunne,⁴⁴ Lieutenant of the Tower of London 5 Feb. 94 [R]	21 Sept. 52	27 Jan. 54	27 July 55	3 Mar. 63	25 Nov. 65	25 Nov. 70	1 July 81	27 July 89	7 June 93
Thomas Casey Lyons,⁴⁷ CB. Governor and Commander in Chief of Bermuda, 2 July 92 [R]	31 Oct. 48	2 Nov. 49	27 July 55	20 Apr. 59	25 Dec. 65	25 Dec. 70	1 July 81	30 Nov. 89	21 June 93
F.C. Sir Wilbraham Oates Lennox,¹ KCB. Royal Engineers	27 June 52	7 Feb. 54	25 Nov. 57	24 Mar. 58	26 Apr. 59	26 Apr. 64	13 Aug. 81	12 Feb. 88	28 June 93
Francis Charles John Stanley Gough,¹ KCB. Bengal Cavalry	27 Dec. 52	14 Mar. 54	8 Oct. 63	1 Oct. 77	5 Apr. 80	1 Apr. 84	22 Nov. 86	21 May 88	6 Aug. 93
John James Hood Gordon,¹ CB. Indian Staff Corps	20 Mar. 48	1 Sept. 49	29 June 57	20 July 58	24 Jan. 67	27 Nov. 75	2 July 85	3 June 89	1 Apr. 94
F.C. Sir Hugh Henry Gough,¹ KCB. Indian Staff Corps	22 Aug. 49	9 Jan. 54	2 Dec. 59	30 Nov. 60	23 Mar. 59	28 Feb. 77	20 Dec. 86	5 Jan. 91	1 Apr. 94
F.C. Sir Reginald Gipps,⁴⁸ KCB. Military Secretary, 23 Mar. 92 [R]	4 Sept. 53	9 Aug. 55	5 Jan. 61	30 Mar. 69	1 Oct. 77	1 Feb. 78	1 Feb. 87	13 June 91	16 May 94
F.C. Hugh Rowlands,⁵⁰ CB. Commanding Scottish District 5 Jan. 94 [R]	25 Sept. 49	21 Apr. 51	25 Aug. 54	2 Nov. 55	28 Nov. 65	28 Mar. 71	1 July 81	1 Jan. 90	16 Oct. 94

LIEUTENANT GENERALS.

	CORNET, 2nd LIEUT. or ENSIGN.	LIEUT.	CAPTAIN.	MAJOR.	LIEUT. COLONEL.	COLONEL.	MAJOR GENERAL.	LIEUT. GENERAL.
Sir Henry Brackenbury,¹ KCB. Royal Artillery	6 Aug. 56	7 Apr. 56	8 Aug. 66	1 Apr. 74	23 Oct. 75	15 June 85	1 Apr. 88
Sir Robert John Hay,¹ KCB. Royal Artillery	27 Dec. 54	17 May 56	17 Mar. 54	15 Feb. 61	28 May 70	16 Dec. 86	1 Apr. 89
Geoffrey Mairis,¹ Royal Marines	28 Aug. 54	24 Feb. 56	27 Aug. 64	4 Nov. 76	13 Apr. 79	4 June 82	20 May 86	8 Sept. 89
Howard Sutton Jones,¹ CB. Royal Marines	29 Mar. 54	31 May 55	5 Nov. 64	1 Oct. 63	7 July 79	7 July 82	18 Nov. 82	18 July 86	20 Nov. 89
Frederick Gaspar Le Grand,¹ Royal Marines	20 Mar. 54	1 May 55	5 Nov. 64	1 Oct. 64	1 July 80	4 July 83	15 Apr. 87	20 Nov. 89
p.s.c. F.C. Sir Henry Evelyn Wood,⁵² GCB. GCMG. Quarter Master General, 9 Oct. 93 [R]	7 Sept. 56	1 Feb. 56	16 Feb. 60	10 Aug. 62	19 Jan. 73	1 Apr. 78	15 Apr. 87	20 Nov. 89
Sir Arthur James Lyon-Fremantle, 56 KCMG. CB. Governor and Commander in Chief at Malta 5 Jan. 94 [R]	10 Dec. 52	29 Apr. 53	6 Nov. 54		20 Apr. 60	6 Sept. 71	1 Apr. 82	1 Apr. 90

Lieutenant Generals and Major Generals.

	2nd LIEUT. OR ENSIGN.	LIEUT.	CAPTAIN.	MAJOR.	LIEUT. COLONEL.	COLONEL.	MAJOR GENERAL.	LIEUT. GENERAL.
LIEUTENANT GENERALS.								
Sir George Richards Greaves, GCB, KCMG. [R]	30 Nov. 49	16 Jan. 52	11 Oct. 59	1 Mar. 64	1 Mar. 65	1 Sept. 72	11 Oct. 82	1 Oct. 90
Sir William John Williams,¹ KCB. Royal Artillery	2 May 47	30 June 48	24 Aug. 54	2 Nov. 55	24 Oct. 65	1 Jan. 76	1 Jan. 86	1 Nov. 90
Harry M'Leod, Royal Artillery	11 June 52	28 Feb. 54	29 Feb. 56	5 July 72	28 Sept. 76	1 July 81	1 Apr. 87	1 Apr. 91
Sir Charles Knight Pearson,² KCMG. CB. [R]	3 Nov. 52	15 June 55	15 Feb. 56	2 May 56	4 Mar. 64	4 Aug. 67	4 Apr. 85	22 Jan. 91
John Davis,⁶⁴ CB. Commanding at Portsmouth 9 Nov. 93 [R]	13 Feb. 54	20 June 54	4 Aug. 59	24 Aug. 66	15 Feb. 68	15 Sept. 72	15 Feb. 83	1 Apr. 91
F.C. Rt. Hon. Sir Redvers Henry Buller,⁶⁵ GCB. KCMG. Adjutant General, with rank of General, 1 Oct. 90 [R]	13 May 58	9 Dec. 58	28 May 58	1 Apr. 74	1 Apr. 74	1 Feb. 78	17 May 84	1 Apr. 91
Hon. Charles Wemyss Thesiger,¹ 5 Lancers [R]	5 Aug. 53	30 Dec. 53	2 July 58	3 July 58	8 Oct. 61	2 Dec. 73	1 Apr. 87	1 Apr. 91
Æneas Perkins,¹ CB. Royal Engineers	1 Dec. 54	17 Aug. 56	12 Mar. 62	30 June 65	4 June 76	4 June 79	10 Mar. 87	1 May 91
p.s.c. William Howley Goodenough,¹ CB. Royal Artillery; Commanding the Forces in South Africa, 8 Dec. 94...	1 Dec. 40	1 Apr. 51	21 Feb. 56	26 July 58	5 Mar. 68	5 July 77	1 Apr. 86	19 May 91
Alexander George Montgomery Moore, 18 Hussars; Commanding the Forces in Canada 1 June 93 [R]	18 Dec. 56	6 July 57	9 May 60	14 Sept. 67	23 Dec. 68	23 July 73	30 Oct. 86	10 Mar. 92
Somerset Molyneux Wiseman-Clarke,⁷⁹ CB. [R]	23 Nov. 49	5 Mar 52	5 Dec. 54	14 Jan. 63	29 May 68	2 July 75	1 Sept. 84	1 Apr. 92
Sir Edward Henry Clive⁸²	18 Aug. 54	8 Dec. 55	11 July 62	8 Mar. 64	8 Mar. 64	28 June 76	22 Dec. 85	1 Apr. 92
Nathaniel Stevenson, Lieutenant Governor of Guernsey 16 Mar. 94...	25 Aug. 58	7 Nov. 62	11 Feb. 66	7 Feb. 70	28 Feb. 71	28 June 76	11 Mar. 86	1 Apr. 92
His Royal Highness Ernest Augustus William Adolphus George Frederick, Duke of Cumberland, KG...		8 June 55	17 Apr. 58	2 Sept. 64	15 Apr. 68	27 May 76	19 Mar. 85	1 Apr. 92
D.C. Charles Augustus Goodfellow,¹ Royal Engineers	14 June 50	15 July 52	15 July 53	15 Apr. 57	12 July 68	12 June 76	1 Apr. 89	1 June 92
Henry James Buchanan,⁸³ CB. [R]	23 Nov. 49	30 May 52	1 Apr. 56	9 Apr. 61	1 Jan. 72	19 Mar. 76	19 Mar. 86	11 Nov. 92
Sir William Stirling,¹ KCB. Royal Artillery, Governor and Commandant, Royal Military Academy, 15 Apr. 90	22 June 53	30 May 54	1 Apr. 60	31 Dec. 78	22 Nov. 75	1 Oct. 77	1 Oct. 87	25 Nov. 92
p.s.c. Edward Francis Chapman,¹ CB. Royal Artillery	27 Oct. 54	27 Oct. 54	4 Feb. 62	1 Jan. 63	31 Oct. 71	24 Sept. 89	24 Sept. 89	13 Dec. 92
William Godfrey Dunham Massy,¹ CB. 4 Dragoon Guards [R]	27 July 54	27 Aug. 56	9 Feb. 66	9 Feb. 66	2 Nov. 78	22 May 77	28 Aug. 86	15 Feb. 93
Arthur Lyttelton Lyttelton-Annesley⁹² [R]	16 Apr. 52	23 Mar. 55	11 Nov. 57	31 Jan. 61	12 Dec. 74	12 May 77	13 Nov. 86	1 Apr. 93
James Keith Fraser,⁸⁵ CMG.		31 July 55	26 July 62	1 Oct. 64	17 May 74	14 July 79	20 Feb. 88	1 Apr. 93
p.s.c. Sir Richard Harrison,¹ KCB. CMG. Royal Engineers	19 Dec. 51	28 Aug. 57	31 Mar. 62	5 Aug. 70	4 June 72	4 June 77	22 Dec. 86	4 May 93
Henry Fanshawe Davies⁹⁴	16 Sept. 53	6 June 54	30 Mar. 55	18 Aug. 65	1 Mar. 85	22 Dec. 77	18 Nov. 86	2 June 93
Henry Richard Legge Newdigate,⁹⁶ CB. [R]	18 Jan. 54	4 Jan. 56	4 Jan. 66	8 Feb. 82	11 July 77	11 July 77	1 Apr. 90	6 June 93
Adam George Forbes Hogg,⁷ CB. Indian Staff Corps	5 Dec. 54	31 Mar. 55	15 Mar. 56	15 Aug. 82	8 Jan. 85	6 Apr. 76	8 Feb. 88	21 June 93
Godfrey Clerk,⁹⁶ CB. [R]	28 Apr. 54	3 June 54	30 Nov. 65	1 Oct. 77	30 Mar. 59	6 Apr. 76	1 Apr. 87	2 June 93
Henry Brasnell Tuson,¹ CB. Royal Marine Artillery	20 Oct. 55	3 June 55	30 Nov. 59	1 Oct. 77	18 Nov. 82	18 Nov. 82	21 May 88	29 Aug. 93
p.s.c. Cuthbert Collingwood Suther, Royal Marine Artillery	20 Oct. 55	4 May 59	3 Aug. 60	5 July 79	5 July 79	26 Oct. 87	9 Mar. 90	15 Feb. 94
Robert Nicholl Dawson-Scott	14 Aug. 54	20 Aug. 54	1 Feb. 60	9 June 77	1 Apr. 79	6 Apr. 80	1 Sept. 91	1 Apr. 94
Sir William Stephen Alexander Lockhart,¹ KCB. CSI. Bengal Infantry; Commanding Punjab Frontier Force	4 Oct. 58	19 June 59	16 Dec. 62	17 Sept. 70	6 Apr. 77	6 Apr. 83	1 Mar. 87	1 Apr. 94
Henry Clement Wilkinson,¹⁰⁰ CB. [R]	15 Feb. 56	5 Aug. 59	22 Sept. 63	17 Apr. 63	13 July 70	6 Apr. 82	1 Mar. 87	26 May 94
Horace Searle Anderson,¹ CB. Indian Staff Corps	21 Jan. 53	16 Mar. 55	22 Nov. 59	2 Jan. 70	14 Dec. 71	22 Dec. 77	1 Apr. 90	20 Sept. 94
Cecil D'Urban La Touche, ¹ Indian Staff Corps	4 Aug. 53	28 Nov. 54	11 Jan. 62	14 Dec. 71	27 Jan. 71	22 Dec. 77	1 Apr. 90	20 Sept. 94
Philip Henry Farrell Harris, ¹ CB. Indian Staff Corps	20 Jan. 51	5 Oct. 55	20 Nov. 56	20 Oct. 70	20 Dec. 70	18 Nov. 87	1 July 81	1 Nov. 94
Henry Rowband, ¹ Bengal Infantry	19 Dec. 50	22 Oct. 57	16 Dec. 57	1 Oct. 75	30 Aug. 76	29 Sept. 77	5 Apr. 93	1 Nov. 94
Julian Hamilton Hall,¹⁴² Commanding North Western District 1 Apr. 90	21 Jan. 53	16 Mar. 54	13 Feb. 54	0 Jan. 54	6 Apr. 72	1 Oct. 81	14 May 87	2 Nov. 94
p.s.c. George Digby Barker,¹⁴ CB. Commanding at Hong Kong 18 Apr. 90 [R]	4 Aug. 53	28 Nov. 54	12 Apr. 61	14 Dec. 71	12 Dec. 71	22 Dec. 77	30 Apr. 87	8 Jan. 95
Sir Richard Campbell Stewart,¹ KCB. Madras Cavalry, Commanding Secunderabad District	20 Jan. 51	20 Jan. 55	17 Nov. 57	16 Apr. 73	23 Jan. 71	22 Dec. 77	15 Apr. 93	13 Mar. 95
Seafield Falkland Murray Treasure Grant,¹ Indian Staff Corps	19 Dec. 50	22 Oct. 51	15 Oct. 55	15 July 72	15 Jan. 76	15 Jan. 81	1 Apr. 90	1 Mar. 95
Edwin Markham,¹ Royal Artillery		22 Oct. 57	17 Nov. 57		1 Apr. 76	1 Apr. 76	30 Apr. 90	27 Mar. 95
MAJOR GENERALS.								
Samuel James Graham,¹ CB. Royal Marines	20 Mar. 54	1 Mar. 55	5 Nov. 64	1 Oct. 77	1 Oct. 77	6 Aug. 80	22 June 87	
George Hay Moncrieff,¹¹⁷ Commanding Dublin District 1 May 91	6 June 54	4 Aug. 54	15 Jan. 56		19 Aug. 62	26 Mar. 81	31 Dec. 87	
f.C. Sir Geo. Stewart White,¹⁴⁶ GCIE. KCB. Commander in Chief, East Indies, with temporary rank of Lt. General and local rank of General, 8 Apr. 93 [R]	4 Nov. 53	29 Jan. 55	10 July 63	24 Dec. 73		2 Mar. 81	2 Mar. 85	
Sir Frederick William Edward Forestier Walker,¹¹⁶ KCB. CMG. Com. the Troops in Egypt to Dec. 90 [R]			5 Sept. 62	1 Oct. 65		1 Feb. 73	15 Oct. 81	
Charles Mansfield Clarke,¹ KCB. Commander in Chief, Madras, with rank of Lieutenant General, 18 Oct. 93...	1 Mar. 56	18 Nov. 56	25 Sept. 58	26 July 76		7 Apr. 78	12 Aug. 88	
Ardley Henry Falwasser Barnes, Royal Marines	20 Mar. 54	22 June 55	20 June 65			7 Nov. 78	29 Aug. 88	
Cecil James East,¹²⁶ CB. Governor and Comdt. of the Royal Military College, Sandhurst, 19 Dec. 93 [R]	18 Jan. 54	5 June 55	17 Nov. 63	1 Sept. 77		24 Nov. 79	7 Nov. 75	
Lord William Frederick Ernest Seymour,¹²⁵ Commanding South-Eastern District 24 Feb. 91	13 Apr. 54	18 Jan. 55	13 May 59	1 Oct. 77		23 Oct. 67	29 Jan. 80	
p.s.c. Francis Francis Munro,¹ Royal Artillery	19 Apr. 54	22 June 65	29 Sept. 65	1 Oct. 77		6 Feb. 75	6 Feb. 80	
Gustavus Lennox Forster,¹ Royal Artillery		1 Oct. 55	22 June 65	12 July 65		6 Feb. 75	6 Feb. 80	
Bowes Lennox Forster,¹ Royal Artillery		1 Oct. 55	22 June 65	24 July 65		1 Apr. 74	18 Apr. 80	
Sir Baker Creed Russell,¹ KCB. KCMG. 13 Hussars; Commanding North Western District 1 Apr. 95 [R]	2 Nov. 55	1 Aug. 56	18 Feb. 59	24 Dec. 65		1 Apr. 74	30 Apr. 80	

Major Generals.

MAJOR GENERALS.	CORNET, 2ND LIEUT. OR ENSIGN.	LIEUT.	CAPTAIN.	MAJOR.	LIEUT. COLONEL.	COLONEL.	MAJOR GENERAL.
John Plumptre Carr Glyn,[152] *Commanding at Colchester* 20 Jan. 92	25 Aug. 54	2 Dec. 54	12 Mar. 58	5 July 72	1 Apr. 74	1 Apr. 75	17 Apr. 8...
p.s.c. Richard Blundell-Hollinshead-Blundell, *Commanding a District, Bombay Army*, 29 Mar. 91	7 Mar. 56	19 Feb. 58	4 Mar. 59	23 Feb. 65	4 Nov. 74	4 Nov. 8...	23 July 8...
Sir Francis Wallace Grenfel,[153] GCMG, KCB, *Inspector General of Auxiliary Forces and Recruiting* 1 Aug. 94	5 Aug. 59	18 July 93	28 Oct. 71	1 Oct. 78	29 Nov. 79	18 Nov. 8...	1 Aug. 8...
Arthur Huntly Hill Walsh,[1] Royal Marines	19 Apr. 58	22 June 55	10 Nov. 65	15 Dec. 77	19 Apr. 82	1 Feb. 8...	8 Sept. 8...
John Cairncross,[1] Royal Marines	18 Aug. 58	5 July 55	21 Nov. 65	4 Apr. 77	1 Feb. 82	1 Feb. 8...	20 Nov. 8...
Lord Ralph Drury Kerr,[152] CB, *Commanding Curragh District* 13 May 91	24 Nov. 57	12 Jan. 55	8 Aug. 61	8 Sept. 65	14 June 76	31 May 81	1 Jan. 9...
Sir James Browne,[1] KCSI, CB, *Commanding a District, Bengal*, 15 Oct. 90	11 Dec. 57	15 June 58	23 Aug. 61	26 Mar. 73	31 May 76	14 June 81	30 Nov. 8...
p.s.c. Sir William Kidston Elles,[145] KCB, *Commanding a District, Bengal*, 15 Oct. 90	6 June 54	27 July 55	18 June 58	7 May 70	5 Sept. 77	22 June 82	1 Jan. 9...
Paul Sanford Lord Methuen,[150] CB, CMG, *Commanding Home District* 2 Apr. 92	...	2 Feb. 65	13 June 67	...	15 July 79	11 May 83	1 Apr. 9...
Edward Christian Griffin,[1] Royal Artillery	9 Dec. 54	8 Jan. 58	15 July 64	Aug. 72	1 May 79	1 May 83	5 June 9...
Edward Osborne Howett, CMG, Royal Engineers	14 Aug. 58	20 Oct. 54	1 Feb. 60	5 July 72	21 Oct. 77	1 Oct. 81	14 June 9...
William Henry Ralston,[153] CB	18 Dec. 57	23 July 58	5 Apr. 64	15 Dec. 72	17 Mar. 76	1 July 81	23 July 9...
John Fryer,[1] CB, *Commanding Cork District* 1 Oct. 93	9 Mar. 60	30 Mar. 60	1 Apr. 64	15 Dec. 72	5 Apr. 79	5 Apr. 81	11 June 9...
p.s.c. Oliver Henry Atkins Nicolls,[155]	22 Dec. 53	20 June 54	5 Apr. 64	1 Apr. 67	1 July 77	1 July 81	23 July 9...
George Joseph Smart,[1] Royal Artillery	21 Feb. 55	20 Apr. 55	15 Dec. 63	31 Oct. 68	29 Aug. 77	29 Aug. 81	27 Aug. 9...
Charles Edward Nairne,[1] CB, Royal Artillery	18 June 54	19 July 55	3 May 58	14 June 70	20 Apr. 77	1 July 81	1 Oct. 9...
William Clive Justice,[139] CMG, *Commanding the Troops in Ceylon* 5 Mar. 93	7 Dec. 55	24 Apr. 56	24 Mar. 65	2 Nov. 67	1 May 80	1 May 84	6 Nov. 9...
John Arthur Tillard,[1] CB, Royal Artillery	7 Dec. 55	27 Apr. 58	8 Mar. 65	1 Apr. 69	1 Oct. 77	1 Oct. 81	28 Nov. 9...
Archibald Hammond Utterson,[141] CB	25 Aug. 54	2 Mar. 55	15 May 65	28 Apr. 71	2 Mar. 81	2 Mar. 81	28 Jan. 9...
p.s.c. Thomas Erskine Arthur Hall	2 Oct. 55	3 Sept. 53	1 June 64	28 June 71	1 July 78	1 July 82	5 May 9...
p.s.c. Robert Grant,[1] CB, Royal Engineers; *Inspector General of Fortifications, with rank of Lt.-General,* 18 Apr. 91	2 Oct. 55	1 Feb. 56	25 May 65	5 July 72	1 July 78	1 July 82	19 May 9...
p.s.c. Sir George Benjamin Wolseley,[1,68] KCB,	28 Feb. 55	24 Aug. 58	22 May 65	1 Oct. 72	19 July 78	19 July 82	19 May 9...
Edward Francis Beville,[1] CB, Indian Staff Corps	4 Sept. 55	4 Jan. 58	6 May 65	5 July 72	11 Nov. 78	11 Nov. 82	24 Dec. 9...
Sir Edward Arthur Gore,[171] *Inspector General, Remount Establishment,* 1 Jan. 94	18 Sept. 57	24 Aug. 85	1 Apr. 59	...	1 Nov. 78	2 Mar. 85	1 Apr. 9...
Sir William Francis Butler,[172] KCB, *Commanding a Brigade at Aldershot* 11 Nov. 93 [R]	25 Aug. 58	...	4 Sept. 67	2 Feb. 74	11 July 78	1 Oct. 82	15 June 9...
Sir John Withers McQueen,[1] KCB, Indian Staff Corps	17 Sept. 57	17 Nov. 63	4 Apr. 64	29 May 69	1 Oct. 77	1 Oct. 81	2 July 9...
William Henry Mackesy,[1] Indian Staff Corps	4 Apr. 54	4 June 55	13 Apr. 57	4 Apr. 74	18 Apr. 80	18 Nov. 82	12 Nov. 9...
Andrew Smythe Montague Browne[173]	18 Aug. 54	4 Dec. 54	4 Apr. 66	4 Apr. 74	22 Apr. 81	3 Feb. 82	10 Dec. 9...
p.s.c. Wilsone Black,[174] CB, *Commanding at Hong Kong* 28 Feb. 95 [R]	11 Nov. 53	16 Mar. 55	24 Dec. 58	30 June 69	1 July 77	1 July 82	10 Dec. 9...
Sir Charles Warren, GCMG, KCB, Royal Engineers	9 Feb. 55	9 Feb. 55	4 Jan. 70	1 Apr. 72	21 July 77	1 July 82	23 Feb. 9...
Thomas Mauburg Bailie	23 Dec. 57	4 Dec. 54	24 Oct. 69	10 June 71	1 Oct. 78	1 Oct. 82	1 Apr. 9...
H.C. George Nicolas Channer,[1] CB, Indian Staff Corps	29 July 59	2 June 65	3 June 68	1 June 71	1 Oct. 78	1 Nov. 82	1 July 9...
George Luck,[176] CB, *Inspector General of Cavalry* 1 Apr. 95	4 Sept. 59	4 May 61	4 Sept. 71	22 Apr. 76	22 Apr. 82	22 Apr. 82	27 Apr. 9...
Thomas Rennie Stevenson,[177] CB	16 Apr. 58	25 Dec. 59	9 Nov. 67	10 Oct. 77	28 May 79	28 May 83	11 May 9...
p.s.c. John Moorsom,[178] *Commanding Belfast District* 28 Feb. 95	4 Jan. 61	16 Jan. 61	30 Mar. 66	14 Dec. 77	1 Oct. 77	1 Dec. 81	22 June 9...
p.s.c. Henry Alexander Little,[1] CB, Indian Staff Corps	16 July 54	8 Nov. 54	4 Dec. 57	4 Oct. 72	22 June 79	22 June 83	2 June 9...
Sir Arthur Power Palmer,[1] KCB, Indian Staff Corps	16 Mar. 58	8 Mar. 55	4 Oct. 68	31 Mar. 75	4 Apr. 81	13 May 83	7 June 9...
Hon. Henry Parnell,[179] CB	11 Aug. 57	23 Dec. 54	8 Feb. 61	20 Feb. 69	22 Nov. 77	22 Nov. 83	22 June 9...
His Highness Francis P.C. L.A. the Duke of Teck,[180] GCB	23 May 59	9 Nov. 55	25 Sept. 62	20 Feb. 77	1 Oct. 77	1 Oct. 81	22 June 9...
Reginald Thomas Thynne,[181] CB, *Commanding North Eastern District* 1 Oct. 94	...	...	...	...	...	...	1 July 9...
Malcolm John Robert MacGregor[182]	20 June 57	5 Aug. 57	6 Nov. 63	5 July 71	15 Mar. 73	1 Oct. 82	8 July 9...
Arthur French,[1] CB, Royal Marine Artillery	4 Feb. 58	8 Dec. 58	10 Sept. 67	10 Oct. 77	18 Nov. 82	18 Nov. 82	11 Aug. 9...
Charles Smith Maclean, CB, CIE, Indian Staff Corps	14 Dec. 53	23 Nov. 56	14 Dec. 65	14 Dec. 72	14 Dec. 72	1 Oct. 81	10 Sept. 9...
Charles Tucker,[183] CB, *Brigadier General on the Staff, South Africa,* 13 Sept. 93	20 Sept. 58	1 July 61	1 May 68	16 May 76	1 Apr. 79	1 July 83	12 Sept. 9...
Henry Archibald McNair, Bengal Infantry	...	...	...	...	1 Apr. 77	13 July 83	13 Sept. 9...
Charles Samuel Steward,[1] Madras Cavalry	4 Oct. 54	30 Sept. 55	21 Apr. 61	11 May 71	24 May 77	1 July 81	1 Oct. 9...

Major Generals.

MAJOR GENERALS.	CORNET, ONDLIEUT. FRENSIGN.	LIEUT.	CAPTAIN.	MAJOR.	LIEUT. COLONEL.	COLONEL.	MAJOR GENERAL.
Sir Robert Cunliffe Low,[1] KCB, Bengal Cavalry, *Commanding Oude District*	26 Aug. 54	29 Sept. 55	1 Jan. 62	5 Feb. 72	8 Feb. 78	8 Feb. 82	5 Oct. 93
Thomas Phillips	26 Sept. 56	24 Sept. 58	24 May 69	11 July 74	31 Dec. 79	31 Dec. 81	6 Oct. 93
Edmund Faunce,[1] CB, Indian Staff Corps	20 Dec. 54	10 Feb. 57	20 Dec. 66	20 Dec. 74	20 Dec. 80	20 Dec. 84	12 Nov. 93
Robert Byng Patrick Price Campbell,[1] CB, Indian Staff Corps	4 Sept. 55	4 Sept. 57	4 Sept. 67	4 Sept. 75	22 Nov. 79	22 Nov. 83	19 Nov. 93
Hamilton Chapman,[1] CB, Indian Staff Corps	15 July 5	2 Nov. 56	15 July 68	15 July 76	22 Nov. 79	22 Nov. 83	9 Dec. 93
William Galbraith,[186] CB, *Adjutant General in India* 15 Oct. 90	1 June 55	30 Nov. 55	25 Apr. 65	1 Oct. 77	26 Feb. 76	14 May 82	1 Jan. 94
David Makgill Crichton Maitland	31 May 59	16 June 61	8 May 67		29 Nov. 77	29 Nov. 83	20 Jan. 94
Alexander George Ross,[1] CB, Indian Staff Corps	4 Nov. 57	12 Dec. 59	4 Nov. 69	4 Oct. 77	29 Nov. 77	29 Nov. 83	7 Feb. 94
John Fletcher Owen[186]		22 Oct. 58	1 Oct. 69	1 Oct. 75	12 Mar. 77	3 Oct. 83	13 Feb. 94
Robert Hastie Inglis,[1] Bengal Infantry	28 June 58	22 Oct. 58	19 Oct. 68	31 Oct. 75	12 Mar. 77	8 Oct. 83	15 Feb. 94
p.s.c. Harcourt Mortimer Bengough,[187] CB, *Commanding the Troops in Jamaica* 25 Oct. 93	22 Mar. 55	3 Oct. 55	30 Dec. 64	1 Oct. 75	17 Apr. 77	29 Nov. 83	7 Mar. 94
Sir Charles William Wilson,[1] KCB, KCMG, Royal Engineers, *Director General of Military Education*, 22 Jan. 95		24 Sept. 55	20 June 64	23 May 73	19 Apr. 79	19 Apr. 83	15 Mar. 94
Henry Hardinge Denne Stracey[188]		30 Sept. 55	15 June 60		2 Feb. 71	2 Feb. 81	19 Mar. 94
Francis James Caldecott,[1] CB, Royal Artillery		8 June 60	15 May 72	1 Apr. 80	2 Mar. 81	2 Mar. 83	1 Apr. 94
James May,[1] CB, Bengal Infantry	20 Feb. 59	20 Feb. 59	1 Feb. 66	9 Feb. 79	2 Feb. 81	4 Feb. 84	1 Apr. 94
George Robertson Hennessy,[1] CB, Indian Staff Corps	4 Feb. 54	11 Dec. 57	4 Feb. 66	4 Feb. 74	4 Feb. 80	1 Mar. 83	10 May 94
Arthur Harness,[1] CB, Royal Artillery		23 June 57	25 Nov. 63	25 June 77	21 Nov. 78	21 July 80	21 July 84	24 May 94
John Mawby Clossy Galloway,[1] Madras Cavalry	20 Oct. 56	23 Jan. 57	17 Nov. 63	18 Apr. 74	21 July 80	21 July 84	24 May 94
Sir Frederick Carrington,[189] KCMG	1 Sept. 57	10 Mar. 58	31 May 64	13 Aug. 76	15 Dec. 80	15 Dec. 84	26 May 94
Julius Middleton Boyd,[1] Indian Staff Corps	16 July 58	30 Sept. 59	13 July 67	31 May 76	22 Nov. 78	22 Nov. 79	26 Jan. 85	8 June 94
John Edmund Waller,[1] Bengal Infantry	4 July 59	20 Feb. 61	16 Dec. 68	4 July 79	2 Feb. 81	2 Feb. 85	9 June 94
Edward Alexander Wood,[190] CB, *Commanding at Shorncliffe*, 1 Jan. 95	20 Feb. 54	23 Nov. 56	20 Feb. 66	4 Apr. 76	2 Feb. 81	2 Feb. 85	8 Aug. 94
Edmund Leach,[191] CB, *Brigadier General on the Staff, Barbadoes*, 8 Aug. 94	3 Dec. 54	1 Oct. 56	29 June 69	22 Nov. 79	2 Nov. 79	2 Mar. 85	8 Aug. 94
Dawsonne Melancthon Strong,[1] CB, Bengal Infantry	10 Dec. 56	13 July 62	1 Mar. 69	1 Mar. 79	2 Feb. 81	2 Mar. 85	20 Aug. 94
John Richard Breeks Atkinson,[1] Bengal Infantry	7 June 61	30 July 62	29 June 69	6 Sept. 74	6 Sept. 80	6 Sept. 85	8 Sept. 94
William Paget La Touche,[1] Indian Staff Corps	6 Sept. 54	23 Nov. 56	6 Sept. 66	6 Sept. 74	22 Nov. 80	22 Nov. 84	8 Sept. 94
Swinton John Browne,[1] CB, Indian Staff Corps	20 Jan. 55	23 Nov. 56	20 Jan. 61	29 Nov. 74	22 Nov. 78	22 Nov. 82	16 Oct. 94
p.s.c. George Hatchell[192]	22 Oct. 58	31 Mar. 58	24 Jan. 65	29 Nov. 77	Jan. 81	15 Dec. 85	1 Nov. 94
William Jacob,[1] Indian Staff Corps	9 Dec. 55	31 Mar. 58	31 Oct. 68	9 Dec. 79	9 Dec. 79	9 Nov. 76	1 Nov. 94
Malcolm Hassells Nicholson,[1] CB, Bombay Infantry	27 Nov. 57	23 Mar. 60	7 May 70	1 Apr. 81	17 Apr. 79	5 July 82	17 Nov. 94
p.s.c. Charles Walker Robinson,[193] CB, *Lt. Governor of Chelsea Hospital*	12 Dec. 56	27 Apr. 58	24 Mar. 65	17 Apr. 81	17 Apr. 81	17 Apr. 85	1 Dec. 94
Arthur Frank Hamilton,[1] Royal Engineers	6 July 55	7 Aug. 58	4 Jan. 71	4 Mar. 78	4 July 81	July 85	2 Dec. 94
Alexander Walker,[1] CSI, Royal Engineers	18 Dec. 55	7 Feb. 60	29 Oct. 65	17 Apr. 78	17 Nov. 81	Nov. 82	2 Dec. 94
p.s.c. Edward Lutwyche England,[194] CB, Lt.Col. Com. West Counties Brig. Inf. Vol. 4 June 91	18 Dec. 56	29 Oct. 69	23 Mar. 65	4 Feb. 78	29 Nov. 78	29 Nov. 82	1 Jan. 95
p.s.c. Albert Lancelot Walker[195]		21 Sept. 66	23 June 65	1 Apr. 78	2 Apr. 78	11 May 84	1 Jan. 95
Hon. William Shotto Douglas Horne[122]		27 June 66	5 Mar. 65	20 Mar. 68	28 May 76	72 May 85	3 Feb. 95
William Edward Montgomery[196]	5 Mar. 58	3 June 59	16 Jan. 68	13 June 76	13 Sept. 76	2 Mar. 85	4 Dec. 95
p.s.c. Cornelius Francis Clery,[195] CB	13 June 56	14 Sept. 57	13 Dec. 64	15 Feb. 65	13 Sept. 85	2 Mar. 85	24 Dec. 95
Frederick Lance,[1] CB, Indian Staff Corps		18 Oct. 56	8 Feb. 65	6 Oct. 78	73 Dec. 85	2 Mar. 85	8 Jan. 95
George Edward Langham Somerset Sanford,[1] CB, CSI, Royal Engineers	4 Feb. 60	1 Jan. 60	29 Oct. 69	4 Mar. 80	2 Mar. 85	2 Mar. 85	1 Jan. 95
Wm. Walters Biscoe, Bengal Cavalry	4 Mar. 60	20 Apr. 62	20 Jan. 68	4 Mar. 80	2 Mar. 81	2 Mar. 85	13 Feb. 95
Revell Eardley-Wilmot, Bengal Infantry	26 June 56	30 Apr. 58	26 June 68	June 76	2 Mar. 81	2 Mar. 85	3 Mar. 95
Joseph Barnard Smith, Indian Staff Corps							

War Services of the Field Marshals.

[1] The Duke of Cambridge commanded the 1st Division of the Eastern Army throughout the campaign of 1854, including the battles of the Alma, Balaklava, and Inkerman (horse shot), and siege of Sebastopol (mentioned in despatches, received the thanks of the House of Commons, Medal with four Clasps, and Turkish Medal).

[2] Sir Lintorn Simmons was employed for three years in the disputed territory on the N.E. frontier of the United States in constructing works for its defence and in making military explorations. Happening to be in Turkey in 1853 he was specially employed by Lord Stratford de Redcliffe on several important services; joined Omar Pasha in March 1854; escorted the new Governor into Silistria after the former one had been killed, and was present during part of the siege of that fortress; laid out and threw up the lines of Slobodzie and Georgevo on the Danube, having entire charge of the operation with 20,000 men of all arms under his command, a Russian Army of 70,000 men being within seven miles: was present during the occupation of Wallachia and had frequent charge of reconnaissances upon the enemy's rear. Went to the Crimea in Dec. 1854 to concert with the allied Commanders in Chief as to the movements of the Turkish Army: was present at the battle of Eupatoria, laid out and threw up the entrenched camp round that place; afterwards was before Sebastopol from April 1855 until after its fall, and then went to Mingrelia and was present at the forced passage of the Ingur, where he commanded the Division which crossed the river and turned the enemy's position, capturing his works and guns: Omar Pasha in his despatch attributed the success of the day chiefly to Lt.Colonel Simmons. He served as Her Majesty's Commissioner to the Ottoman Army throughout the war and was employed in all the negotiations having reference to the movements of Omar Pasha's Army. Has received the Crimean Medal with Clasp, the Turkish Gold Medal for the Danubian campaign, the Order of Medjidie 3rd Class, and a Sword of Honor from the Turkish Government; also the 4th Class of the Legion of Honor. Was Her Majesty's Commissioner for laying out the Turco-Russian boundary in Asia, and granted the 2n l Class of the Medjidie by the Sultan, but was refused permission to accept it.

[4] Sir Frederick Paul Haines' services:—On the formation of the Army of the Sutlej in 1845 he was appointed to officiate as Military Secretary to the Commander in Chief in India, Sir Hugh Gough, and in that capacity he was present at the battles of Moodkee and Ferozeshah (Medal and one Clasp); in the latter engagement he was severely wounded by grape-shot at the attack on the enemy's works, his horse being killed under him at the same moment. At the recommendation of Lord Gough he was promoted to a Company in the 10th Foot, without purchase. As Military Secretary to his Lordship he served the Punjaub campaign of 1848-49, and was present at the affair of outposts at Ramnuggur, 22 Nov. 1848, and subsequent operations resulting in the passage of the Chenab, and the battles of Chillianwallah and Goojerat (Brevet of Major, Medal with two Clasps). Served with the 21st Fusiliers the Eastern campaign of 1854-55, including the battles of Alma, Balaclava, and Inkerman, and siege of Sebastopol (Brevet of Lt.Colonel, Medal with four Clasps, 5th Class of the Medjidie, and Turkish Medal). During the Afghan war he directed the military operations as Commander in Chief from September 1879 to September 1880 (received the thanks of both Houses of Parliament).

[5] Sir Donald Stewart served against the hill tribes on the Peshawur frontier in 1854-55 (mentioned in despatches), and against the Akba Kheyl and Bussee Kheyl Tribes in 1855 (mentioned in despatches, Medal with Clasp). Commanded the Volunteers serving in the Allyghur district in May and June 1857, and all communication with the Upper Provinces having been cut off he volunteered to carry despatches from the Government of the North-West Provinces to the Officer commanding at Delhi; on arriving in camp was appointed Deputy Assistant Adjutant General of the Field Force and served throughout the siege of Delhi (mentioned in despatches, and Brevet of Major); afterwards served as Assistant Adjutant General of the Army at the siege and capture of Lucknow, and throughout the operations in Rohilcund (mentioned in despatches, Brevet of Lt.Colonel, Medal with two Clasps). Commanded the Bengal Brigade with the expedition to Abyssinia in 1867-68 (mentioned in despatches, Medal, and CB.). Commanded the forces in Southern Afghanistan from December 1878 till April 1880, including the occupation of Candahar. Commanded the Candahar Field Force in the actions at Ahmed Kheyl and Urzoo near Ghuznee. Was in Chief Command of the forces in Southern and Eastern Afghanistan from May 1880 until the evacuation of Cabul in August 1880. Received the thanks of the Government of India and of both Houses of Parliament (KCB., GCB., Baronet, and Medal with Clasp).

[6] Lord Wolseley served with the 80th Regiment in the Burmese war of 1852-53 (Medal for Pegu), was with the expedition under Sir John Cheape against the robber chief Myattoon, and was severely wounded when leading the storming party against the chief's stronghold on the 19th March (mentioned in despatches). Landed in the Crimea with the 90th Light Infantry on 5th Dec. 1854, and was employed in the trenches as Acting Engineer until Sebastopol was taken; was engaged in the assault and defence of the Quarries on 7th June, and on duty in the Trenches at the attack of the 18th June; severely wounded in a sortie 30th August, when in charge of the advanced sap—several times mentioned in despatches (Brevet of Major, Medal with Clasp, Knight of the Legion of Honor. 5th Class of the Medjidic, and Turkish Medal). Served in the Indian campaigns of 1857-59, and was present at the relief of Lucknow, defence of the Alumbagh by Outram, with the several engagements there, siege and capture of Lucknow, subsequently as D.A.Q.M. General to Grant's division and with it at the affair of Baree, action at Nawabgunger and all the others fought by that force (repeatedly mentioned in despatches, Brevet of Lt.Colonel, Medal with Clasp). Served in the war of 1860 in China upon the Quarter Master General's Staff, and was present at the assault of the Taku Forts, and in all the engagements throughout the campaign (promoted Major unattached, Medal with two Clasps). Commanded the Expedition sent in 1870 from Canada to the Red River Territory for the suppression of the Rebel Government established at Fort Garry against the Queen's authority, and was created a Knight of St. Michael and St. George and Companion of the Bath for his services upon that occasion. Was Governor and Commander of the Forces on the Gold Coast during the Ashanti War of 1873-74 (received the thanks of both Houses of Parliament, promoted to be Major General for distinguished service in the field, GCMG. KCB. and Medal with Clasp). At a meeting of the Common Council of the Corporation of London it was unanimously resolved as follows:—" That the honorary freedom of this City, with a sword of the value of 100 guineas, be presented to Major-General Sir Garnet Joseph Wolseley, KCB., GCMG., in recognition of his gallant services in the British Army, and especially in reference to the distinguished ability and gallantry displayed by him in his command of the expedition to the Gold Coast, by which he obtained results conducive to peace, commerce, and civilisation on the continent of Africa. And this Court desires also to record its admiration of the patient endurance of hardship exhibited, and the valuable co-operation and assistance rendered to Sir Garnet Wolseley, by the gallant officers and men of both services and of all arms engaged in the expedition." Was sent to South Africa in June 1879 as Governor and High Commissioner of Natal and lands adjacent, with local rank of General. Completed the subjugation of the Zulus and brought the Zulu war to a conclusion. Afterwards overpowered Sekukuni's hostile nation and destroyed their stronghold; and finally subdued the disaffected Boers and completed the annexation of the Transvaal (GCB., Medal with Clasp). Was Commander in Chief of the British Expeditionary Army throughout the Egyptian war of 1882, in which campaign that Army in the space of 25 days effected disembarkation at Ismailia, traversed the desert, and seized the capital of Egypt together with its citadel and the rebel chief, having in that period fought and defeated the enemy five times—finally at Tel-el-Kebir where the enemy's strongly entrenched position was taken at the point of the bayonet after an arduous night march, all his guns captured, and his army overwhelmed (received the thanks of both Houses of Parliament, raised to the Peerage, promoted General for distinguished service in the field, Medal with Clasp, 1st Class of the Osmanieh, and Khedive's Star). Commanded the forces in the Soudan campaign in 1884-85 (received the thanks of both Houses of Parliament, was raised to a Viscount in the peerage, and received two Clasps).

War Services of the General Officers.   9

[1] For the War Services of General Officers being Colonels of Regiments, &c., see the Corps to which they respectively belong.

[25] Sir John Ross served with the Rifle Brigade in the Eastern campaign, including the battles of Alma and Inkerman, and siege of Sebastopol, until February 1855 (Medal with three Clasps, Brevet of Major, 5th Class of the Medjidie, and Turkish Medal). Served also in the Indian campaign of 1857-58, including the action of Cawnpore, siege and capture of Lucknow. Commanded the Camel Corps at the capture of Calpee and during the subsequent campaign in Central India (mentioned in despatches, Brevet of Lt.Colonel, CB., Medal with two Clasps). Served with the Rifle Brigade in the North West Frontier of India campaigns of 1863-64 (Medal with Clasp). Commanded the Bengal troops during the operations in the Malay Peninsula in 1875-76 mentioned in General Orders of the Government of India. Medal with Clasp. Commanded the Indian Expeditionary Force which was sent to the Mediterranean in 1878. Served in the Afghan war of 1878-80; commanded the 2nd Division Cabul Field Force which defeated the enemy at Shekabad (received the thanks of the Governor General in Council and of the Commander in Chief in India); accompanied Sir Frederick Roberts in the march to Candahar in command of the Infantry Division and as 2nd in command, and was present at the battle of Candahar (mentioned in despatches, received the thanks of both Houses of Parliament, KCB., Medal with Clasp, and Bronze Decoration).

[29] Sir Edward Bulwer served the Eastern campaign of 1854 with the 23rd Fusiliers, including the battle of Alma and siege of Sebastopol (Medal with two Clasps, and Turkish Medal). Served in the Indian mutiny of 1857-59, including the siege and capture of Lucknow, and operations across the Goomtee under Outram. Commanded a Column of troops with the Left Wing of the 23rd Fusiliers in the Bueswarra district of Oude, including the capture of the Fort of Solimpore, and two other successful engagements at Julrowlee and Poorwah, commanded Left Wing of the 23rd at the defeat of Benee Madho by Lord Clyde at Buxarghat (Brevet of Lt.Colonel, CB., Medal with two Clasps, and mentioned in despatches).

[43] General Hon. W. H. A. Feilding accompanied the French Head Quarters as Military Attaché during the Franco-German war of 1870-71 (Chevalier of the Legion of Honour).

[46] General J. H. Dunne served with the 21st Fusiliers in the Eastern campaign of 1854, including the battles of Alma, Balaklava, and Inkerman, siege of Sebastopol, and attack on the Redan on the 18th June (Medal with four Clasps, 5th Class of the Medjidie, and Turkish Medal). Served with the 99th Regiment in the campaign of 1860 in the north of China, including the action of Sinho, taking of Tangku, assault and capture of the inner North Taku Fort, actions of the Chang-kin-wan and Paliatchow, and surrender of Pekin (Medal with two Clasps).

[47] General T. C. Lyons served in the 20th Regiment in the Indian campaign of 1857-58, and commanded the selected marksmen of the Regiment in the actions of Chanda, Umeerpore, Sultanpore, and Fort of Dhowraha, whence he assisted in bringing away two guns under a heavy fire; was present at the siege and capture of Lucknow, the subsequent operations in Oude and affair of Mohan, and commanded four Companies at Morar Mow and Beerah, Fort of Simree, and action of Buxar Ghat; served as Brigade Major to the 2nd Brigade Oude Force, and was present at the capture of Fort Oohmrea (three times mentioned in despatches, Medal with Clasp, and Brevet of Major).

[48] Sir Reginald Gipps served the Eastern campaign of 1854, including the battles of Alma (bayonet wound of hand), Balaklava, and Inkerman (severely wounded, shot through neck), siege of Sebastopol and sortie on the 26th Oct. (Medal with four Clasps, Brevet of Major, Knight of the Legion of Honor, 5th Class of the Medjidie, and Turkish Medal).

[50] General H. Rowlands served the Eastern campaign of 1854-55 with the 41st Regiment, including the battles of Alma and Inkerman (severely wounded), siege and fall of Sebastopol, sortie of 26th October, attack of the Quarries on 7th June and twice on the Rifle-pits, attacks of the Redan on the 18th June and 8th September—wounded (Medal with three Clasps, Victoria Cross, Brevet of Major, Knight of the Legion of Honor, 5th Class of the Medjidie, and Turkish Medal): received the VC "for rescuing Colonel Haly, of the 47th Regiment, from Russian soldiers, Colonel Haly having been wounded and surrounded by them, and for gallant exertions in holding the ground occupied by his advanced piquet against the enemy, at the commencement of the battle of Inkerman, 5th November 1854." Served in the Kafir war in 1877-79 on special service at Luneberg, and commanded the troops in the engagement at Tolako Mountain (mentioned in despatches, Medal with Clasp).

[52] Sir Henry Evelyn Wood entered the Navy in April 1852, and served in the Naval Brigade as Aide de Camp to Captain Peel from 1st Oct. 1854 to 18 June 1855, when he was severely wounded carrying up scaling-ladders to the Redan: mentioned in Lord Raglan's despatches (Medal with two Clasps, Knight of the Legion of Honor, 5th Class of the Medjidie, and Turkish Medal). Served in the Indian campaign of 1858 as Brigade Major in Somerset's Brigade, and was present at Rajghur, Sindwaho (mentioned in General Michel's despatch), Kharee, and Barede —mentioned in despatches (Medal). Employed in 1859-60, while commanding 1st Regiment Beatson's Horse, in hunting down rebels in the Serongo Jungles; thanked by the Government of India for an attack made on a band in December 1859, and gazetted to the Victoria Cross "for having on the 19th October 1858, during action at Sindwaho, when in command of a Troop of the 3rd Light Cavalry, attacked with much gallantry, almost single-handed, a body of rebels who had made a stand, whom he routed. Also for having subsequently, near Sindhora, gallantly advanced with a duffadar and sowar of Beatson's Horse, and rescued from a band of robbers a Potail, Chemmum Singh, whom they had captured and carried off to the Jungles, where they intended to hang him." Raised the 2nd Regiment Central India Horse. Accompanied Sir Garnet Wolseley to the Gold Coast in September 1873 on special service, and served throughout the Ashanti war of 1873-74. Organized the natives forming "Wood's Regiment." Commanded the attacking force at the action of Essaman (received the expression of Her Majesty's approbation). Commanded the troops at the head of the road following the enemy from Mensu to the river Prah prior to the arrival of the European troops, including the reconnaissance in force of the 27th November. Commanded the Right Column at the battle of Amoaful (slightly wounded); and commanded the Head Quarters of his regiment at the battle of Ordahsu and capture of Coomassie (several times mentioned in despatches, Brevet of Colonel, CB., Medal with Clasp). Served throughout the Gaika war of 1878 in command of a column (several times mentioned in despatches). Served throughout the Zulu war of 1879 in command of No. 4 Column. As Political Agent raised a contingent of 1,000 friendly Zulus, known as "Wood's Irregulars." Two days after the British reverse at Isanhlwana he surprised and defeated a force of several thousands of the enemy and then maintained an advanced position in the enemy's country for which he was specially commended by the High Commissioner. Nominated KCB. Defeated the Zulus in the action of Kambula on the 29th March. Appointed Brigadier General in April. Led the advance on Ulundi with a flying column, and was present in the engagement there on the 4th July (mentioned in despatches, Medal with Clasp). Served in the Boer war of 1881 with the rank of Major General, and on the death of Sir George Colley, as Governor of Natal and Commander-in-Chief of the British forces (GCMG.). Served in the Egyptian war of 1882 in command of the 4th Brigade in the operations near Alexandria, including the surrender of Kafr Dowar and Damietta (mentioned in despatches, received the thanks of both Houses of Parliament, Medal, 2nd Class of the Medjidie, and Khedive's Star). Served during the Nile Expedition in 1884-85 in command of the Line of Communications (mentioned in despatches, 1st Class of the Medjidie, Clasp).

[56] Sir Arthur Lyon Fremantle commanded at the defence of Suakin from July 1884 till February 1885, and in the Soudan campaign in 1885 he commanded the Brigade of Guards, including the engagement at Hasheen and the destruction of Temai (mentioned in despatches, CB., 2nd Class of the Medjidie, Medal with Clasp, and Khedive's Star).

[60] Sir George Greaves served at Peshawur during the Indian mutiny in 1857-58. Served as Deputy Assistant Adjutant General in the Eusofzye Expedition of 1858 under Sir Sydney Cotton (mentioned in despatches, Medal with Clasp). Served in the war in New Zealand as D.A. Quarter Master General from January 1862 to January 1866. Surveyed the Waikato River under circumstances of great difficulty and danger, and piloted up it the gunboats *Avon* and *Pioneer*. Was present at nearly the whole of the engagements, and was repeatedly mentioned in despatches—mentioned as being "always conspicuous for energy and daring" (Brevets of Major and Lt.Colonel, and Medal). Served as Chief of the Staff of the Ashanti Expedition of 1873-74, and was present at the battle of Amoaful, battle of Ordahsu and capture of Coomassie, including the minor engagements on the road. Mentioned in despatches by Sir Garnet Wolseley in the following terms:—"Colonel Greaves assumed the duties of Chief of the Staff on the 17th December. His great knowledge of the army, his experience as a Staff Officer, the zeal and ability he brings to bear upon his work mark him out as eminently qualified for the post he occupied. He has

rendered the most valuable assistance" (Medal with Clasp, and CB.). Served in the Soudan campaign in 1885 as Chief of the Staff to Sir Gerald Graham (mentioned in despatches, KCB., and Medal with Clasp).

[63] Sir Charles Knight Pearson served as Adjutant of the 31st Regiment in the Crimea from 3rd Sept. 1855, including the siege and fall of Sebastopol and attack of the 8th Sept. (Medal with Clasp, and Turkish Medal). Served in the Zulu war of 1879 in command of No. 1 Column, a force of all arms, which invaded Zululand by the passage of the Lower Tugela. On the 22nd January he defeated in the action of Inyezane a Zulu force which in superior numbers had taken up position to overwhelm him at a formidable pass called Majia's Hill. He then advanced and formed the fortified post of Ekowe and held it while invested by the enemy for two months, after which the place was relieved by Lord Chelmsford (KCMG., Medal with Clasp).

[64] Lieut.General John Davis served with the 35th Regiment in the Shahabad district during the Indian Mutiny campaign in 1858-59 (Medal). Served in the Soudan expedition under Sir Gerald Graham in 1884 in command of the 2nd Infantry Brigade, and was present in the engagements at El Teb and Temai (several times mentioned in despatches, CB., Medal with Clasp, and Khedive's Star). Served in the Soudan campaign in 1885 (Clasp).

[68] Sir Redvers Henry Buller served with the 2nd Battalion 60th Rifles throughout the campaign of 1860 in China (Medal with two Clasps). Served with the 1st Battalion on the Red River expedition of 1870. Accompanied Sir Garnet Wolseley to the Gold Coast in September 1873, and served as D. A. Adjutant and Quarter Master General and Head of the Intelligence Department throughout the Ashanti war of 1873-74, including the action of Essaman, battle of Amoaful, advanced guard engagement at Jarbinbah, battle of Ordahsu (slightly wounded) and capture of Coomassie (several times mentioned in despatches, Brevet of Major, CB., Medal with Clasp). Served in the Kafir war of 1878-79, and commanded the Frontier Light Horse in the engagement at Taba ka Udoda and in the operations at Molyneux Path and against Manyanyoba's stronghold (several times mentioned in despatches). Served throughout the Zulu war of 1879, and commanded the cavalry in the engagements at Zlobane Mountain and Kambula; conducted the reconnaissance before Ulundi, and was present in the engagement at Ulundi (several times mentioned in despatches, thanked in General Orders, Brevet of Lt.Colonel, Aide de Camp to the Queen, Victoria Cross, CMG., Medal with Clasp) : received the VC "for his gallant conduct at the retreat at Inhlobana, on the 28th March 1879, in having assisted, whilst hotly pursued by Zulus, in rescuing Captain C. D'Arcy, of the Frontier Light Horse, who was retiring on foot, and carrying him on his horse until he overtook the rear guard. Also for having on the same date, and under the same circumstances, conveyed Lieutenant C. Everitt, of the Frontier Light Horse, whose horse had been killed under him, to a place of safety. Later on, Colonel Buller, in the same manner, saved a trooper of the Frontier Light Horse, whose horse was completely exhausted, and who otherwise would have been killed by the Zulus, who were within eighty yards of him." Served in the Boer war of 1881 as Chief of the Staff to Sir Evelyn Wood with the local rank of Major General. Served in the Egyptian war of 1882 in charge of the Intelligence Department, and was present in the action at Kassasin (9th September), and at the battle of Tel-el-Kebir (mentioned in despatches, KCMG., Medal with Clasp, 3rd Class of the Osmanieh, and Khedive's Star). Served in the Soudan Expedition under Sir Gerald Graham in 1884 in command of the 1st Infantry Brigade and as second in command of the expedition, and was present in the engagements at El Teb and Temai (twice mentioned in despatches, promoted Major General for distinguished service in the field, two Clasps). Served in the Soudan campaign in 1884-85 as Chief of the Staff to Lord Wolseley; when Sir Herbert Stewart was wounded and Colonel Burnaby had been killed, he took command of the Desert Column and withdrew it from Gubat to Gakdul in face of the enemy, defeating them at Abu Klea Wells on the 16th and 17th February (mentioned in despatches, KCB., and Clasp).

[79] Lieut. General Wiseman-Clarke served with the 93rd Highlanders the Eastern campaign of 1854-55, including the battles of Alma and Balaklava, siege and fall of Sebastopol, capture of Kertch and Yenikale (Medal with three Clasps, and Turkish Medal). Also the Indian campaign of 1857-59, including relief of Lucknow by Lord Clyde, battle of Cawnpore on 6th Dec., pursuit of the enemy and capture of their guns at Seraighat, action at Kallee Nuddie; taking of Futtehghur, expedition to Mhow under Brigadier Hope, siege and capture of Lucknow (mentioned in Sir E. Lugard's despatches), and subsequent affairs ending in the capture of Bareilly (Medal with two Clasps).

[82] Lieut.General Clive served in the Eastern campaign in 1855-56 after the fall of Sebastopol.

[83] Lieut.General H. J. Buchanan served the Eastern campaign of 1854-55 as Adjutant of the 47th Regiment, including the battles of Alma and Inkerman, sortie of 26th Oct., siege and fall of Sebastopol—appointed Town Major (Medal with three Clasps, Sardinian and Turkish Medals, 5th Class of the Medjidie). Commanded a Column of the Field Force under Brigadier General Ross against the Afreedees on the North West Frontier in 1877-78 (mentioned in despatches, CB., Medal with Clasp).

[92] Lieut.General A. L. Lyttelton-Annesley served with the 11th Hussars in the Crimea from 29th July 1855, including the siege and fall of Sebastopol (Medal and Clasp, and Turkish Medal).

[93] Lieut.General J. K. Fraser served as Orderly Officer to Sir Edmund Lyons on the Expedition to Kinbourn in 1855, and was present at its bombardment and surrender (Medal). Has received a Gold Medal from the President of the French Republic in recognition of his devoted services to the wounded on the field of battle in the Franco-German campaign of 1870-71.

[94] Lieut.General H. F. Davies served in the Royal Navy in the Burmese war (Medal). Also in the Baltic in the Russian war (Medal). Served in the Zulu war of 1879 as Commandant at Conference Hill and afterwards as Commandant of Fort Newdigate (mentioned in despatches, Medal with Clasp).

[96] Lieut.General H. R. L. Newdigate landed in the Crimea with the 2nd Battalion Rifle Brigade, and was present at the battle of Alma (Medal with Clasp, and Turkish Medal). Served also during the Indian campaign of 1857-58, including the action of Cawnpore, and capture of Lucknow; and with Ross' Camel Corps at the capture of Calpee and operations in Central India (Brevet of Major, Medal with two Clasps). Served in the Afghan war in 1878-79 with the Peshawur Valley Field Force in command of the 4th Battalion of the Rifle Brigade, commanded the Lower Koorum Brigade from April to Aug. 1880 (CB., and Medal).

[98] Lieut.General Godfrey Clerk served with the Rifle Brigade in the Indian mutiny, and was present at the Alumbagh and relief of Lucknow (Brevet of Major, Medal with Clasp). Served in the campaign on the North-West Frontier of India in 1864, and was present in the engagement at Shubkudder (Medal with Clasp).

[100] Lieut. General H. C. Wilkinson served with the 95th Regiment in the Indian campaign of 1858, and was present at the siege and capture of Awah, siege assault and capture of Kotah, battle of Kotakeserai, general action resulting in the capture of Gwalior, assault and capture of Rowa, siege and capture of Pouree, battle of Beejapore, and affair of Koondry (Medal with Clasp). Served in the Afghan war in 1880 in command of the Cavalry Brigade in Southern Afghanistan, and took part in the march to Candahar with the force under Major General Phayre (mentioned in despatches, Medal with Clasp). Served in the Egyptian war of 1882 in command of the Cavalry Brigade of the Indian Contingent, and was present at the battle of Tel-el-Kebir (twice mentioned in despatches, CB., Medal with Clasp, 2nd Class of the Medjidic, and Khedive's Star).

[102] Lieut.General J. H. Hall served at the siege of Sebastopol from 20th Nov. 1854 to 16th Jan. 1855 (Medal with Clasp, and Turkish Medal).

[104] Lieut. General G. D. Barker served with the 78th Highlanders in the Persian war in 1857, including the night attack and battle of Kooshab, bombardment of Mohumrah, and expedition to Ahwaz (Medal with Clasp). Served in Bengal with Havelock's Column from its first taking the field in 1857, including the actions of Futtehpore, Aoung, Pandoo Nuddee, Cawnpore, Onao, Buseerutgunge (first and second), Boorbeakeechowkee, and the several actions leading to and ending in the relief of the Residency of Lucknow and subsequent defence, including several sorties wounded); with Outram's Force at Alumbagh, including the repulse of the numerous attacks, and in the operations ending in the final capture of Lucknow, where he officiated as D.A.Q.M. General, 1st Division, and was mentioned in despatches; the Rohilcund campaign in 1858, and capture of Bareilly (mentioned in despatches, Medal with two Clasps, Brevet of Major, and a year's service for Lucknow).

[106] Sir George White served with the 27th Regiment on the North-West Frontier during the Indian mutiny in 1857-59 (Medal). Served with the 92nd Highlanders in the Afghan war in 1879-80, and was present in the engagement at Charasiab on the 6th October 1879, and in the various operations around Cabul in December 1879, including the investment of Sherpore; was also present in the engagement at Charasiab on the 25th April 1880; accompanied Sir Frederick Roberts in the march to Candahar, and was present at the reconnoissance of 31st August and at the battle of Candahar (frequently mentioned in despatches, Brevet of Lt.Colonel, CB., Victoria Cross, Medal with three Clasps, and Bronze Decoration): was awarded the VC "for conspicuous bravery during

War Services of the General Officers.

the engagement at Charasiab on the 6th October 1879, when, finding that the artillery and rifle fire failed to dislodge the enemy from a fortified hill which it was necessary to capture, Major White led an attack upon it in person. Advancing with two companies of his regiment, and climbing from one steep ledge to another, he came upon a body of the enemy, strongly posted, and outnumbering his force by about 8 to 1. His men being much exhausted, and immediate action being necessary, Major White took a rifle, and, *going on by himself*, shot the leader of the enemy. This act so intimidated the rest that they fled round the side of the hill, and the position was won. Again, on the 1st September 1880, at the battle of Candahar, Major White, in leading the final charge, under a heavy fire from the enemy, who held a strong position and were supported by two guns, rode straight up to within a few yards of them, and, seeing the guns, dashed forward and secured one, immediately after which the enemy retired." Served with the Nile Expedition in 1884-85, during the latter part of the time as Assistant Adjutant and Quarter Master General (Medal with Clasp, and Khedive's Star). Served with the Burmese Expedition in 1885-89 in command of the 2nd Infantry Brigade and commanded at Mandalay during the insurrection; commanded the Upper Burmah Field Force after the capture of Mandalay (received the thanks of the Government and of the Commander in Chief in India, promoted Major General for distinguished service in the field, frequently mentioned in despatches, KCB., and Medal with Clasp). Commanded the Zhob Field Force in 1890 (received the thanks of the Government and Commander in Chief in India).

[117] Major General G. H. Moncrieff served in the Crimea from 2nd May 1855, including the siege and fall of Sebastopol (Medal with Clasp, and Turkish Medal).

[118] Sir Frederick Forestier Walker served as Assistant Military Secretary to Lieut. General Sir Arthur Cunynghame during the Kafir war of 1878 (mentioned in despatches, CB.). Was employed on special service throughout the Zulu war of 1879, first as Principal Staff Officer to No 1 Column, being present at the action of Inyezane, and during the occupation of Ekowe, and subsequently on the Line of Communications, and in command of Fort Pearson and the Lower Tugela District (mentioned in despatches, Medal with Clasp). Served with the Bechuanaland Expedition under Sir Charles Warren in 1884-85 as Assistant Adjutant and Quarter Master General (CMG.).

[121] Lieut. General Manefield Clarke served in the 57th Regiment with the Column under Colonel Warre on the Taptee river in co-operation with the Central India Field Force in 1858. Served also in the New Zealand war of 1861, and was present at the operations before Te Arei. Also during the war in 1863-66, present as Adjutant of the 57th at the action of Katikara (mentioned in despatches), and as D.A.Q.M.General from June 1863 to March 1866 in the Province of Taranaki, including the action near Poutoko, capture of the Maori positions at Ahuahu, Kaitake, Mataitawa, and Te Arei, operations at Warea and Te Puru, and various minor affairs (repeatedly mentioned in despatches, Medal). Served in the Zulu campaign of 1879; commanded the 57th Regiment in the engagement at Gingindhlovu (mentioned in despatches) and relief of Ekowe; afterwards commanded the 2nd Brigade 1st Division, and subsequently was appointed to the command of "Clarke's Column"—a force of all arms—formed by Sir Garnet Wolseley for the following objects: the second advance to Ulundi, the capture of King Cetywayo, the subjugation of the Zulu tribes near the Middle Drift of the River Tugela, and the pacification of Zululand; these objects were successfully accomplished—thanked in General Orders (mentioned in despatches as having "performed the duties of his responsible command in the most highly efficient manner," Brevet of Colonel, CB., Medal with Clasp). On the conclusion of the war was appointed Commandant General of the Colonial Forces in South Africa.

[126] Major General C. J. East served with the 82nd Regiment in the Crimea from the 2nd September 1855, and was present at the siege and fall of Sebastopol (Medal with Clasp, and Turkish Medal). Also in the Indian campaign in 1857, and was severely wounded at Cawnpore on the 26th November (Medal). When belonging to the 41st Regt. served as Assistant Quarter Master General with the Chittagong column of the Lushai Expeditionary Force in 1871-72 (mentioned in despatches, received the thanks of the Governor-General in Council, Medal with Clasp, and Brevet of Major). Served in the latter part of the Zulu war of 1879 as Deputy Adjutant and Quarter Master General, and was present in the engagement at Ulundi (mentioned in despatches, Brevet of Colonel, Medal with Clasp). Served with the Burmese Expedition in 1886-89 in command of the 1st Brigade after the capture of Mandalay (mentioned in despatches, CB., and two Clasps).

[128] Lord William Seymour served as a Midshipman with the Baltic Fleet in 1854 (Medal). Served with the 2nd Battalion Coldstream Guards in the Egyptian war 1882, and was present in the engagement at Tel-el-Mahuta, and at the battle of Tel-el-Kebir (Medal with Clasp, 3rd Class of the Osmanieh, and Khedive s Star).

[132] Major General J. P. C. Glyn served with the Rifle Brigade in the Crimea from the 17th June 1855, including the siege and fall of Sebastopol (Medal with Clasp, and Turkish Medal). Embarked for the Gold Coast with the 2nd Battalion Rifle Brigade, and served throughout the second phase of the Ashanti war in 1874, including the battle of Amoaful, battle of Ordahsu, and capture of Coomassie (Brevet of Lt.Colonel, Medal with Clasp).

[134] Sir Francis Grenfell served as Aide de Camp to Sir Arthur Cunynghame in the operation of 1877-8 in the Transkei; also as Staff Officer to Colonel Glyn, commanding a field force in the Transkie, and was present in the engagement with the Galekas and Gaikas at Quintana Mountain on the 7th Feb. 1878 (mentioned in despatches, Brevet of Major). Served in the Kafir war of 1878 as Deputy Assistant Adjutant and Quarter Master General at Head Quarters. Served in the Zulu war of 1879 as Deputy Assistant Adjutant General at Head Quarters, and was present in the engagement at Ulundi (mentioned in despatches, Brevet of Lt.Colonel, Medal with Clasp). Served under Sir Evelyn Wood in the Boer war of 1881 as Assistant Quarter Master General. Served in the Egyptian war of 1882 as Assistant Adjutant and Quarter Master General on the Head Quarters Staff, and was present at the engagements of Tel-el-Mahuta and Kassassin (9th Sept.), and in the battle of Tel-el-Kebir (mentioned in despatches, Aide de Camp to the Queen, Medal with Clasp, 3rd Class of the Medjidie, and Khedive's Star). Served with the Nile Expedition in 1884-85 on the Lines of Communication (mentioned in despatches, CB., and Clasp). Served with the Egyptian Frontier Field Force in 1885-86, and was present in the engagement at Giniss in command of a Division (mentioned in despatches, KCB., and promoted to 1st Class of the Medjidie and 3rd Class of the Osmanieh). Commanded the troops during the operations near Suakin in December 1888 including the engagement at Gemaizah (mentioned in despatches, Clasp). Also commanded the Nile Field Force in 1889 at the engagement at Toski (mentioned in despatches, promoted Major General for distinguished service in the field, and Clasp).

[137] Lord Frankfort de Montmorency served with the 33rd Regiment in the Crimea in 1855, including the siege and fall of Sebastopol and attack of the Redan on the 8th Sept. (Medal with Clasp, Sardinian and Turkish Medals). Commanded a Detachment of the 33rd against the rebels, and after the death of the senior Officer commanded the Dohud Field Force in suppressing the insurgent Bheels in the Rewa Kanta, Guzerat. Served with a Wing of the Regiment at the siege and occupation of Dwarka, Okamundel. Served in the Abyssinian campaign of 1867-68 (Medal). Commanded the Frontier Field Force during the operations in the Soudan in 1886-87 (Khedive's Star). Commanded the British Column of the Frontier Field Force during the operations on the Nile in 1889 (mentioned in despatches).

[142] Lord R. D. Kerr served in the Afghan war in 1878-79, and was present at the engagement at Futtehabad in command of the 10th Hussars (mentioned in despatches, CB., and Medal).

[148] Sir William Elles served with the 38th Regiment in the Crimea in 1854-55, including the siege and fall of Sebastopol, the attack and occupation of the Cemetery on the 18th June (mentioned in despatches, Medal with Clasp, Knight of the Legion of Honor, and Turkish Medal). Served in the Indian Mutiny campaign from Nov. 1857, including the battle of Cawnpore and defeat of the Gwalior Contingent on 6th Dec. 1857, capture of Meeangunge, siege and capture of Lucknow, affairs of Barree and Nuggur (Medal with Clasp). Served in the Hazara campaign of 1868 and accompanied the expedition to the Black Mountain under Major General Wilde as Deputy Assistant Adjutant General (mentioned in despatches, Medal with Clasp). Served with the Burmese Expedition in 1886-87 (mentioned in despatches, CB., and Clasp). Served with the Hazara Expedition in 1891 in command of the Force (received the thanks of the Government of India and of the Commander in Chief in India, mentioned in despatches, KCB,, and Clasp).

[150] Lord Methuen served in the second phase of the Ashanti war from the 17th Dec. 1874, and was present at the battle of Amoaful (Medal with Clasp). Served in the Egyptian war of 1882 as Assistant Adjutant and Quarter Master General and Commandant at Head Quarters, and was present at the engagements of Tel-el-Mahuta and Kassasin (9th Sept.), and in the battle of Tel-el-Kebir (mentioned in despatches, CB., Medal with Clasp, 3rd Class of the Osmanieh, and Khedive's Star). Served with the Bechuanaland Expedition under Sir Charles Warren in 1884-85 in command of Methuen's Horse (mentioned in despatches, CMG.).

War Services of the General Officers.

[153] Major General W. H. Ralston served with the 70th Regiment in the New Zealand war of 1863-65, and was present at Katikara and Rangiawhia, and commanded the Expedition landed at White Cliffs (received the thanks of the Major General Commanding, Medal). Served with the 70th Regiment in the Afghan war in 1878-79 (mentioned in despatches, Medal). Served in the Soudan campaign in 1885 (mentioned in despatches, CB., and Medal with Clasp).

[154] Major General John Fryer commanded the Carabiniers throughout the Afghan war of 1879-80. On the 13th January 1880, in command of a force of Royal Horse Artillery and Cavalry, he repulsed with heavy loss a large body of Mohmunds at Ali Boghan. Commanded the Cavalry in the expeditions under Lt.General Bright to the Lughman Valley and against the Wuzeeree Khugianis. On the 5th July 1880, he commanded a force of Carabiniers and 4th Bengal Cavalry at the attack and destruction of the Ghilzai villages of Nargozi, Arab Kheyl, and Jokan. (CB., Medal).

[155] Major General O. H. A. Nicolls served in the Crimean campaign of 1854 till October of that year. Served also the campaign of 1855 from September, including the siege and fall of Sebastopol (Medal with Clasp, and Turkish Medal). Was in command of the Royal Artillery throughout the operations in Perak in 1875-77 under Major General the Hon. Sir F. Colborne, including the advance on and capture of Kinta in December 1875 (Brevet of Lt.Colonel, Medal with Clasp).

[157] Major General C. B. Knowles served with the 77th Regiment in the Crimea from the 11th July 1855, including the siege and fall of Sebastopol, and was wounded at the assault of the Redan on the 8th September (Medal with Clasp, and Turkish Medal). Commanded the 67th Regiment throughout the Afghan war of 1878-80, and was present in the engagements at Charasiab on 6th October 1879 (mentioned in despatches) and in the operations around Cabul in December 1879, including the engagement at the Asmai Heights on 14th December—mentioned in despatches (CB., Medal with two Clasps).

[159] Major General W. C. Justice served with the 75th Regiment during the Indian campaign of 1857, and was present at the siege of Delhi from 23rd June (in command of the Light Company from 13th Sept.), storm and capture of the city (Medal with Clasp).

[161] Major General A. H. Utterson served with the 17th Regiment in the Crimea from the 11th July 1855 including the siege and fall of Sebastopol, and assault of the Redan on the 8th September; was also at the bombardment and surrender of Kinbourn (Medal with Clasp, and Turkish Medal). Served with the 17th Regiment in the Afghan war in 1878-79, and was present at the capture of Ali Musjid and in the expeditions into the Bazar Valley, including the engagement at Deh Sarak (mentioned in despatches, Medal with Clasp).

[164] Major General J. N. Crealock served with the 95th Regiment in the Indian mutiny campaign in 1858, including the siege and capture of Kotah, battle of Kota ke Serai (wounded), and general action resulting in the capture of Gwalior, siege and capture of Pourie, and surprise of the rebel camp of Kunrye (Medal with Clasp, and twice mentioned in despatches). Served throughout the Kafir war of 1878 and the Zulu war of 1879 as Assistant Military Secretary to Lt.General Lord Chelmsford commanding the forces, and was present at the action at Gingindhlovu (slightly wounded) and relief of Ekowe, and in the engagement at Ulundi (several times mentioned in despatches, Brevet of Lt.Colonel, CB., Medal with Clasp). Served with the 2nd Battalion Derbyshire Regiment in the Egyptian war of 1882, and commanded the troops in Alexandria from the 25th August to the 14th September (Medal, and Khedive's Star).

[166] Major General E. Hopton served with the 88th Regiment in the Crimea from 17th June 1855, including the siege and fall of Sebastopol, and attacks of the Redan on the 18th June and 8th September—severely wounded (Medal with Clasp, and Turkish Medal). Served also in suppression of the Indian mutiny in 1857-58, including the siege of Lucknow in March 1858, and siege of Calpee (Medal with Clasp for Central India). Served with the 88th Regiment throughout the Kafir war of 1877-78 (mentioned in despatches, Brevet of Lt.Colonel), and throughout the Zulu war of 1879, during the first portion of the latter as Director of Transport (Medal with Clasp).

[167] Sir H. J. Alderson served throughout the Eastern campaign of 1854-55, including the battles of Alma and Inkerman, siege and fall of Sebastopol, in the Trenches with the siege train, and bombardments of 17th October, 9th April, and 6th and 17th June (Medal with three Clasps, Knight of the Legion of Honor, and Turkish Medal).

[168] Sir G. B, Wolseley served with the 84th Regiment during the latter part of the Indian mutiny, and was engaged in all the minor affairs in the Shahabad district under Sir John Douglas (Medal). Served in the Afghan war in 1878-79 as Assistant Adjutant General with the Candahar Field Force (Brevet of Lt.Colonel, Medal). Served in the Egyptian war of 1882 as Assistant Adjutant General with the Head Quarters of the Army, and was present at the battle of Tel-el-Kebir (mentioned in despatches, Aide de Camp to the Queen, Medal with Clasp, 3rd Class of the Medjidie, and Khedive's Star); also served with the Nile Expedition in 1884-85 as Assistant Adjutant General at Head Quarters, and afterwards commanded at Abu Gus (mentioned in despatches, CB., and Clasp). Served with the Burmese Expedition in 1887 and 1889-91 in command of a Brigade (mentioned in despatches, KCB., and Medal with Clasp). Commanded the troops during the operations in the Wuntho Territory in 1891 (received the thanks of the Government of India).

[171] Major General Gore commanded the Inniskilling Dragoons in the Boer war in 1881.

[172] Sir William Butler served in the 69th Regiment with the Field Force which repelled an incursion of Fenians into Canada in May 1870. Served throughout the Ashanti war from the 23rd October 1873, and was employed as Special Commissioner to the Western Akims (mentioned in despatches, substantive rank of Major, CB., Medal with Clasp). Served in the Egyptian war of 1882 as Assistant Adjutant and Quarter Master General on the Head Quarters Staff, and was present at the engagements of El Magfar, Tel-el-Mahuta, and Kassasin (9th September), and in the battle of Tel-el-Kebir (mentioned in despatches, Aide de Camp to the Queen, Medal with Clasp, 3rd Class of the Medjidie, and Khedive's Star). Served with the Nile Expedition in 1884-85 as Assistant Adjutant and Quarter Master General, and was present at the action at Kirbekan (twice mentioned in despatches, two Clasps). Served with the Egyptian Frontier Field Force in 1885-86 in command of a Brigade and was present in the engagement at Giniss (mentioned in despatches, KCB.).

[173] Major General A. S. M. Browne served with the Scots Greys in the Crimea from 30th July to 1st Sept. and from Oct. to Dec. 1855, including the battle of the Tchernaya, and siege of Sebastopol (Medal with Clasp, and Turkish Medal).

[174] Major General Wilsone Black served with the 42nd Highlanders in the Crimea from 14th June 1855, including the siege and fall of Sebastopol (Medal with Clasp, and Turkish Medal). Served in the Kafir war in 1878, including the engagement at Taba-ka-Udoda. Served also in the Zulu war of 1879, and commanded the party which recovered the lost colours of the 24th Foot (mentioned in despatches, CB., Medal with Clasp).

[176] Major General G. Luck was present at the operations against the Jowaki Afreedees in January 1878 (Medal with Clasp). Served with the Candahar Column in the Afghan war of 1878-80, including the advance to Khelat-i-Ghilzai; commanded a squadron of the 15th Hussars and a troop of the 1st Punjaub Cavalry in engagements with the Afghan cavalry at Takht-i-Pul on the 4th January 1879 (slightly wounded, mentioned in despatches, Medal). Served with the Thull-Chotiali Field Force under Brigadier General Biddulph, and accompanied Major General Phayre, in command of his regiment, in the march to the relief of Candahar in August 1880 (mentioned in despatches, Medal). Served in the Boer war of 1881 in command of the 15th Hussars.

[177] Major General T. R. Stevenson served in the Egyptian war of 1882 in command of the 1st Battalion Royal Irish Fusiliers, and was present at the battle of Tel-el-Kebir (mentioned in despatches, CB., Medal with Clasp, and Khedive's Star).

[178] Major General C. J. Moorsom served with the 30th Regiment in the Crimea from the 1st to the 28th September 1855, including the siege and fall of Sebastopol and assault of the Redan on the 8th September—severely wounded in the left arm (Medal with Clasp, and Turkish Medal).

[179] Major General Hon. H. Parnell served with the 3rd Buffs in the Crimea subsequent to the fall of Sebastopol. Commanded the 2nd Battalion 3rd Buffs throughout the Zulu war of 1879, and was present at the engagement of Inyezane and during the occupation of Ekowe (mentioned in despatches, CB., Medal with Clasp).

[180] The Duke of Teck served in the Egyptian war of 1882, and was present in the engagement at Tel-el-Mahuta and at the battle of Tel-el-Kebir (appointed Colonel in the Army, Medal with Clasp, and Khedive's Star).

[181] Major General R. T. Thynne served in the Zulu war of 1879, and was present in the engagement at Ulundi (Medal with Clasp). Served with the 2nd Battalion Grenadier Guards in the Egyptian war of 1882 (Medal, 4th Class of the Osmanieh, and Khedive's Star). Served in the Soudan campaign in 1885, after the engagement at Hasheen, in command of the 3rd Battalion of the Grenadier Guards (mentioned in despatches, CB., and Clasp).

War Services of the General Officers.

¹⁸² Major General M. J. R. MacGregor served with the 18th Royal Irish in the Afghan war in 1880 (Medal).

¹⁸³ Major General C. Tucker served with the 80th Regiment with the left attack during the Bhootan Expedition of 1865 (Medal with Clasp). Served in the Perak operations in 1876, part of the time as Brigade Major; commanded the left attack in the operations against Sekukuni in 1878; commanded the 80th Regiment in the Column under Colonel Rowlands on the Swazi border in the Zulu war of 1879, and subsequently the troops at Luneberg; also commanded the regiment in Wood's Column during the march through Zululand and in the engagement at Ulundi (CB., Medal with Clasp).

¹⁸⁵ Major General W. Galbraith served in the Afghan war of 1878-80, first as Assistant Adjutant General in the Koorum Division, being present at the capture of the Peiwar Kotal (mentioned in despatches), in the operations in the Hariab and Khost Valleys, in the engagement at Charasiab on the 6th October 1879 (mentioned in despatches), and in the subsequent occupation of Cabul; afterwards served with the 85th Regiment in the Koorum Division including the Zaimusht Expedition (Brevet of Lt.Colonel, Medal with two Clasps). Served with the Hazara Expedition in 1888 in command of a Brigade (CB., and Medal with Clasp).

¹⁸⁶ Major General J. F. Owen served with Wood's Column in the Zulu war of 1879 in command of a Mounted Gatling Battery, and was present in the engagement at Ulundi (mentioned in despatches, Brevet of Lt.Colonel, Medal with Clasp).

¹⁸⁷ Major General H. M. Bengough commanded a Battalion of the Natal Native Contingent during the Zulu war of 1879, and was present in the engagement at Ulundi (mentioned in despatches, Brevet of Lt.Colonel, Medal with Clasp). Served with the Burmese Expedition in 1885-86 as Assistant Adjutant and Quarter Master General (mentioned in despatches, CB., and Medal with Clasp).

¹⁸⁸ Major General H. H. D. Stracey served in the expedition to the Soudan in 1885 with the 2nd Battalion of the Scots Guards, and was present in the engagements at Hasheen and Temai (mentioned in despatches, Medal with Clasp, and Khedive's Star).

¹⁸⁹ Sir Frederick Carrington organised and commanded Mounted Infantry in the expedition to the Diamond Fields in 1875, and Carrington's Horse (mounted infantry) at the annexation of the Transvaal in 1877. Served in the Kafir war in the Transkei in 1877, and raised and commanded the "Frontier Light Horse," and was present in the engagement at Quintana (mentioned in despatches) and subsequent operations in the Transkei and Perie Bush. Served in the operations against Sekukuni in 1878-79 as Commandant of the Transvaal Volunteer Force, and commanded the advance guard and left attack at the capture of the stronghold (mentioned in despatches, Brevets of Major and Lt.Colonel, CMG., and Medal with Clasp). Commanded the Cape Mounted Rifles at the siege of Mafeteng by the Basutos, and commanded the Colonial Forces in Basutoland during the operations against the Basutos from November 1880 to March 1881—severely wounded (mentioned in Colonial despatches). Served with the Bechuanaland Expedition under Sir Charles Warren in 1884-85 in command of the 2nd Mounted Rifles (mentioned in despatches). Served in the operations in Zululand in 1888 as Commandant of Native Levies.

¹⁹⁰ Major General E. A. Wood commanded the 10th Hussars in the Afghan war of 1878-79, and was present at the attack and capture of Ali Musjid (mentioned in despatches, Brevet of Lt.Colonel, Medal with Clasp). Served in the Soudan Expedition under Sir Gerald Graham in 1884 in command of the 10th Hussars, and was present in the engagements at El Teb and Temai (mentioned in despatches, CB., Medal with Clasp, and Khedive's Star).

¹⁹¹ Major General E. Leach served in the 50th Regiment in the Crimea, subsequent to the fall of Sebastopol, from the 19th September 1855 until the evacuation on 12th July 1856. Served also in the New Zealand war of 1863-66 as Orderly Officer to Colonel Waddy when commanding a Field Force in the Waikato in 1864; present at Waiari; appointed Aide de Camp to Brigadier General Waddy 7th Jan. 1865; and present at the attack and repulse of the enemy at Nukumaru (mentioned in despatches); appointed Deputy Assistant Adjutant General 26th Jan. 1865, and present at the repulse of the enemy at Kakaramea (mentioned), and served throughout the campaign Wanganui district under Sir D. Cameron. Accompanied Major General Chute as D.A. Adjutant General during his campaign on the West Coast in 1865-66, and present at the assault and capture of Okatuku, Putahi, Otapawa, Ketemari, and Waikoko Pah (mentioned in despatches, Brevet of Major, and Medal). Served with the 1st Battalion West Kent Regiment throughout the Egyptian war of 1882, and was present at the action at Kassasin on the 9th of September (Medal, 4th Class of the Osmanieh, and Khedive's Star). Served in the Nile Expedition in 1884-85 in command of the 1st Battalion of the West Kent Regiment (mentioned in despatches, CB., and Clasp).

¹⁹² Major General G. Hatchell served in the Afghan war in 1878-79, and took part in the second expedition into the Bazar Valley under Lieut. General Maude (mentioned in despatches, Brevet of Lt.Colonel, Medal).

¹⁹³ Major General C. W. Robinson served with the 2nd Battalion Rifle Brigade in the Indian Mutiny (Medal). Served throughout the second phase of the Ashanti war, from 12th December 1873, as Brigade Major to the European Brigade, including the battle of Amoaful, battle of Ordahsu and capture of Coomassie (mentioned in despatches, Brevet of Major, Medal with Clasp). Served in the Zulu war of 1879, and was present in the engagement at Ulundi (mentioned in despatches, Brevet of Lt.Colonel, Medal with Clasp).

¹⁹⁴ Major General E. L. England served in the Indian Mutiny campaign in 1858, and was present at the actions at Amorah on the 17th and 25th April (Medal). Served in the operations against Sekukuni in the Transvaal in 1878, including the storming of Tolyana's Stadt; also throughout the Zulu war of 1879, taking part in the engagements at Zungin Nek and Kambula Hill, and, in command of the 1st Battalion, in the action at Ulundi (mentioned in despatches, Brevet of Lt.Colonel, Medal with Clasp).

¹⁹⁵ Major General C. F. Clery served in the Zulu war of 1879, and was present in the engagements at Isandhlwana and Ulundi (mentioned in despatches, Brevet of Lt.Colonel, Medal with Clasp). Served in the Egyptian war of 1882 as Brigade Major at Alexandria (Medal, and Khedive's Star). Served in the Soudan Expedition under Sir Gerald Graham in 1884 as Assistant Adjutant General, and was present in the engagements at El Teb and Temai (twice mentioned in despatches, Brevet of Colonel, CB., and two Clasps); also served with the Nile Expedition in 1884-85 (Clasp).

¹⁹⁶ Major General A. L. Walker served with the 99th Regiment throughout the campaign of 1860 in China, including the actions of Chankinwan and Paliatchow and surrender of Pekin (Medal with Clasp). Served throughout the Zulu war of 1879. Was present in the action of Gingindhlovu; afterwards served as Assistant Adjutant General of the 1st Division (Medal with Clasp).

¹⁹⁷ Major General Hon. W. S. D. Home served with the 2nd Battalion Grenadier Guards in the Egyptian war of 1882, and was present at the battle of Tel-el-Kebir (Medal with Clasp, 4th Class of the Osmanieh, and Khedive's Star). Served in the Soudan campaign in 1885 in command of the 3rd Battalion of the Grenadier Guards until after the engagement at Hasheen (Clasp).

¹⁹⁸ Major General W. E. Montgomery served in the Zulu war in 1879 as Deputy Assistant Adjutant and Quarter Master General 2nd Division from the 6th May to the 27th July, and was present in the engagement at Ulundi (mentioned in despatches, Medal with Clasp).

Colonels.

	CORNET, 2nd LIEUT. or ENSIGN.	LIEUT.	CAPTAIN.	MAJOR.	LIEUT. COLONEL.	COLONEL.	WHEN PLACED ON HALF PAY.
p.s.c. John Duncan[1] (from h.p. Dublin Fus.), D.A.G. War Office, 29 Sept. 93	20 Dec. 56	10 Sept. 57	22 Jan. 68	24 Feb. 77	7 June 79	7 June 83	
Thos. Maynard Hazlerigg, Lt.Col. R. Art.; A.A.Gen., Woolwich, 12 Feb. 91		23 Dec. 57	28 Sept. 71	10 Apr. 78	22 Nov. 79	22 Nov. 83	
Chas. John Moysey, CMG. Lt.Col. h.p. R. Engineers		1 Oct. 57	2 Sept. 67	1 Oct. 77	29 Nov. 79	29 Nov. 83	1 Aug. 94
Jas. M. H. Maitland, CB. Col. (from R. Engineers)		20 Apr. 55	1 Apr. 62	5 July 72	20 Dec. 79	20 Dec. 88	
John Cecil Russell,[2] Lt.Col.h.p. 12 Lanc. Equerry to H.R.H. the Prince of Wales	18 Sept. 60	16 Aug. 64	28 May 70	1 Apr. 74	29 Nov. 79	7 Feb. 84	29 Apr. 92
p.s.c. Wm. Liston Dalrymple,[10] CB. Lt. Col. (from h.p. Connaught Rangers), Brig. Gen. Com. a District, Beng. Army	17 July 63	9 July 68	28 Oct. 71	1 Apr. 74	29 Nov. 79	18 Feb. 84	
Henry Augustus Bushman,[21] CB. Lt. Col. (from h.p. 9 Lancers); A.A. General, Netley, 25 July 92	9 Nov. 58	30 June 63	9 Mar. 72	27 June 79	21 Apr. 80	21 Apr. 84	
Kennett Gregg Henderson,[32] CB. Lt. Col. (from h.p. King's Royal Rifles) Comdg. the Garrison at Alexandria, with rank of Major General, 2 Nov. 93	23 Apr. 55	6 May 56	30 June 63	27 Mar. 74	5 June 80	5 June 84	
Charles M. Stockwell,[43] CB. Lt. Col. h.p. Regimental District **[R]**	17 Nov. 54	22 June 55	12 Apr. 64	15 Aug. 77	2 Sept. 80	2 Sept. 84	29 Dec. 90
p.s.c. George Upton Prior,[54] Colonel (from h.p. Royal Scots), Assistant Adj. General, Gibraltar, 19 Feb. 91	4 July 60	19 Aug. 62	23 Aug. 64	1 Oct. 77	22 Nov. 79	1 Oct. 84	
Henry Trotter, Lt.Col. h.p. Grenadier Guards, H.M. Consul at Galatz; Comdg. West London Brig. Vol.Inf.		4 Oct. 62	16 Oct. 66		31 Oct. 71	4 Nov. 84	17 July 94
Martin P. Blake, h.p. Regimental Dist.	23 Mar. 60	17 May 61	1 Feb. 68	31 Oct. 71	1 Oct. 73	7 Nov. 84	21 June 94
Wm. J. Gascoigne, Lt.Col. Scots Guards		31 Mar. 63	6 Feb. 66		25 June 75	1 Dec. 84	
James Browne,[65] Lt.Col. h.p. Regimental District	30 July 59	28 Dec. 60	2 Oct. 66	18 Dec. 79	27 Dec. 80	27 Dec. 84	16 Feb. 91
p.s.c. Chas. John Burnett,[76] CB. Lt.Col. (from h.p. Irish Rifles); A.Q.M.Gen. War Office, 29 Sept. 93	2 July 61	8 Jan. 64	1 Dec. 69	1 Apr. 74	2 Mar. 81	2 Mar. 85	
Hugh Pearce Pearson,[87] CB. Lt.Col. (from h.p. Regimental District), Commanding a Dist. Madras Army 1 Apr. 94	28 Feb. 56	25 Aug. 57	15 Oct. 61	6 Feb. 75	2 Mar. 81	2 Mar. 85	
Ross Thompson, Lt.Col. Royal Engineers	11 June 58	27 Aug. 58	6 Dec. 68	20 Nov. 75	2 Mar. 81	2 Mar. 85	
Geo. C. Bird, CB. Lt. Col. Indian Staff C.	20 Sept. 56	17 Oct. 57	20 Sept. 68	20 Sept. 76	2 Mar. 81	2 Mar. 85	
Robert C. R. Clifford, CB. Lt.Col. Indian Staff Corps	13 Dec. 56	6 June 57	13 Dec. 68	13 Dec. 76	2 Mar. 81	2 Mar. 85	
Henry M. Pratt, CB. Lt.Col. Indian Staff Corps	13 Dec. 56	30 Apr. 58	13 Dec. 68	13 Dec. 76	2 Mar. 81	2 Mar. 85	
James C. Stewart, CB. Lt. Col. Indian Staff Corps	4 Sept. 57	17 June 58	4 Sept. 69	4 Sept. 77	2 Mar. 81	2 Mar. 85	
Charles R. Pennington, CB. Lt. Col. Indian Staff Corps	4 Oct. 57	18 May 58	4 Oct. 69	4 Oct. 77	2 Mar. 81	2 Mar. 85	
Wm. J. Frampton,[98] Lt.Col. h.p. Regimental District	12 Dec. 56	18 Sept. 59	29 Sept. 65	20 Oct. 77	2 Mar. 81	2 Mar. 85	
Horace M. Evans, CB. Lt.Col. Indian Staff Corps	20 June 58	22 Jan. 59	11 Jan. 67	20 June 78	2 Mar. 81	2 Mar. 85	12 June 93
Frs. Wm. Collis, CB. Lt.Col. Indian Staff Corps	10 Dec. 58	29 Mar. 59	10 Dec. 70	10 Dec. 78	2 Mar. 81	2 Mar. 85	
John Munro Sym, CB. Lt.Col. Indian Staff Corps	11 Dec. 58	15 July 59	11 Dec. 70	11 Dec. 78	2 Mar. 81	2 Mar. 85	
Arth. G. Handcock, CB. Lt.Col. Indian Staff Corps	11 Dec. 58	20 Aug. 59	11 Dec. 70	11 Dec. 78	2 Mar. 81	2 Mar. 85	
Edward S. Reynolds, Lt.Col. Indian S. C.	27 Oct. 59	1 Jan. 62	27 Oct. 71	27 Oct. 79	2 Mar. 81	2 Mar. 85	
Alex. Angus Airlie Kinloch,[103] CB. Lt.Col. h.p. King's Royal Rifles; Brig. Gen. Com. a District, Bengal, 15 Oct. 90	22 Nov. 55	24 Sept. 58	8 May 70	22 Nov. 79	2 Mar. 81	2 Mar. 85	15 Oct. 90
Boyce Albert Combe,[114] CB. Lt.Col. (from h.p. 19 Hus.), Com. Cav. Brig. at Aldershot, with rank of Major Gen. 1 Jan. 95	27 Aug. 60	6 May 65	12 Feb. 73	22 Nov. 79	2 Mar. 81	2 Mar. 85	
Alex. R. Badcock, CB. Lt.Col. Indian S.C.	1 Oct. 61	1 Oct. 62	1 Oct. 73	22 Nov. 79	2 Mar. 81	2 Mar. 85	
Montagu G. Gerard, CB. Lt.Col. Indian S.C.		19 Apr. 64	19 Apr. 76	22 Nov. 79	2 Mar. 81	2 Mar. 85	
Robert G. Woodthorpe, CB. Major, R. Eng.		22 June 65	22 May 78	22 Nov. 79	2 Mar. 81	2 Mar. 85	
W Edward Pemberton Leach, CB. Lt.Col. Royal Engineers		17 Apr. 66	31 Dec. 78	22 Nov. 79	2 Mar. 81	2 Mar. 85	
Robt. Fras. C. A. Tytler, Lt.Col. Bengal Infantry	2 Oct. 60	1 Jan. 62	27 Nov. 69	21 Sept. 80	2 Mar. 81	2 Mar. 85	
Edw. Stedman, CB. Lt.Col. Indian Staff Corps		19 Dec. 60	19 Dec. 72	19 Dec. 80	2 Mar. 81	2 Mar. 85	
Fras. E. Hastings, CB. Lt.Col. Ben. Inf.	10 Dec. 59	2 Oct. 61	22 June 69	10 Dec. 79	2 Mar. 81	7 Mar. 85	
p.s.c. M. W. E. Gosset,[127] CB. Col. (from h.p. Dorsetshire Regiment), Com. a District, Madras Army, 1 Dec. 91	8 July 56	31 Aug. 58	17 Apr. 67	11 Nov. 78	29 Nov. 79	18 Mar. 85	
Chas. R. Matthews, Lt.Col. Indian S. C.	20 Mar. 55	30 Apr. 58	20 Mar. 67	20 Mar. 75	20 Mar. 81	20 Mar. 85	
David Milne Home,[128] Col. Comdg. Regimental District, Exeter	6 May 62	29 Dec. 65	2 Dec. 68		6 Apr. 81	6 Apr. 85	
William Osborne Barnard,[130] Col. (from h.p. Regimental District) Commanding at the Mauritius, 1 Feb. 95	15 Apr. 56	21 May 58	18 Nov. 59	5 July 72	18 May 81	18 May 85	
Hugh M'Calmont,[131] CB. Lt.Col. h.p. 4 Dragoon Guards	23 June 65	27 July 66	29 May 69	30 Nov. 78	24 July 80	15 June 85	7 Mar. 92
Stuart James Nicholson,[132] Lt.Col. h.p. Royal Artillery		31 July 55	3 Oct. 63	5 July 72	1 July 81	15 June 85	3 Mar. 92
p.s.c. Sir J. Chas. Ardagh, KCIE. Col. (from R. Engineers); Aide de Camp to H.R.H. the Duke of Cambridge		1 Apr. 59	3 Aug. 72	30 Nov. 78	18 Nov. 82	15 June 85	
p.s.c. Thos. Fraser, CB. CMG. Lt.Col. h.p. Royal Engineers		25 June 62	19 Aug. 74	30 Nov. 78	18 Nov. 82	15 June 85	3 May 94

Colonels. 17

	CORNET, 2nd LIEUT. or ENSIGN.	LIEUT.	CAPTAIN.	MAJOR.	LIEUT. COLONEL.	COLONEL.	WHEN PLACED ON HALF PAY.
James Alleyne, CB. Col. (from R. Art.), Brig. Gen. on the Staff Com. Royal Artillery, Aldershot, 15 Dec. 93	......	25 June 62	14 Apr. 75	29 Nov. 79	18 Nov. 82	15 June 85	
p.s.c. John Fred. Maurice, CB. Lt.Col. Royal Artillery	......	18 Dec. 61	10 Mar. 75	21 Apr. 80	18 Nov. 82	15 June 85	
p.s.c. Coleridge Grove,[134] CB. Major, h.p. East Yorkshire Regiment	17 Mar. 63	15 June 66	30 Aug. 71	1 July 81	18 Nov. 82	15 June 85	17 Nov. 94
Leopold Victor Swaine,[135] CB. CMG. Col. (from h.p. Rifle Brigade); Military Attaché at Berlin 2 Jan. 92	24 July 59	16 Aug. 64	21 Sept. 72	1 July 81	18 Nov. 82	15 June 85	
John Barton Sterling, Lt.Col. h.p. Coldstream Guards	5 Nov. 61	31 Dec. 61	20 July 66	......	5 July 73	1 July 85	5 Feb. 95
John Booth Richardson,[145] Lt.Col. h.p. R. Art. Colonel on the Staff, Devonport, 17 Sept. 88	......	20 Apr. 55	17 Dec. 62	5 July 72	1 July 81	1 July 85	9 Mar. 85
Turner Van Straubenzee,[146] CB. Lt.Col. (from h.p. R. Art.), Brig. Gen. Com. a District, Madras Army, 28 Feb. 91	......	20 Apr. 55	12 Feb. 63	5 July 72	1 July 81	1 July 85	
Herbert Locock, CB. (from h.p. R. Eng.)	......	7 Apr. 56	7 Jan. 65	25 Aug. 73	1 July 81	1 July 85	
Samuel Parr Lynes, h.p. Royal Artillery	......	1 Oct. 55	10 May 65	11 Mar. 74	1 July 81	1 July 85	7 May 94
p.s.c. Francis Shirley Russell,[151] CMG. Lt.Col. h.p. 1 Dragoons; Comdg. Aberdeen Brigade Inf. Volunteers 13 Feb. 92	6 Feb. 63	23 Aug. 64	13 June 68	1 Apr. 74	1 July 81	1 July 85	27 Oct. 91
Charles Trench, Lt.Col. (from h.p. Royal Art.), Director Artillery Coll. 19 July 90	......	19 Dec. 55	20 Sept. 65	1 Apr. 74	1 July 81	1 July 85	
Julius Dyson Dyson-Laurie,[152] Lt.Col. h.p. Regimental District	16 Feb. 55	13 July 55	11 June 61	1 Aug. 74	1 July 81	1 July 85	11 Oct. 92
Eustace Lovelace Hercy, Lt.Col. h.p. Regimental District	5 Feb. 58	11 Feb. 59	14 Mar. 65	23 Oct. 75	1 July 81	1 July 85	22 Oct. 92
Robert William May Wetherell, Lt.Col. h.p. Regimental District	15 Apr. 58	23 Mar. 60	2 Nov. 66	22 June 76	1 July 81	1 July 85	1 Sept. 92
p.s.c. Hastings D'Oyly Farrington,[159] Lt. Col. h.p. Regimental District	8 July 56	10 July 58	29 July 62	24 June 76	1 July 81	1 July 85	17 Oct. 92
William Byam,[160] CB. Lt.Col. h.p. Regimental District	25 Jan. 59	8 Sept. 63	25 Apr. 68	9 Dec. 76	1 July 81	1 July 85	1 Apr. 92
p.s.c. Geo. Salis-Schwabe,[162] Lt.Col. h.p. Regimental District	23 Sept. 63	9 June 65	29 May 67	17 Mar. 77	1 July 81	1 July 85	18 Jan. 95
Charles Edward King, Lt.Col. h.p. Regimental District	24 Sept. 58	9 Dec. 62	18 July 65	21 Apr. 77	1 July 81	1 July 85	1 Apr. 92
Frederick Charles Ruxton, Lt.Col. h.p. Regimental District	3 June 59	3 Dec. 61	20 Feb. 63	6 July 77	1 July 81	1 July 85	19 Dec. 92
Henry Edward Davidson, Lt.Col. h.p. Regimental District	29 June 58	3 July 60	7 Apr. 63	29 Sept. 77	1 July 81	1 July 85	5 Jan. 93
p.s.c. Thomas Kelly-Kenny,[164] CB. Lt.Col. (from h.p. West Surrey Regt.), A. A. General, Aldershot. 28 Dec. 93	22 Feb. 58	12 Oct. 60	20 July 66	29 Sept. 77	1 July 81	1 July 85	
Charles Edw. Foster,[169] Lt.Col. h.p. Regimental District	31 Dec. 58	23 Nov. 60	29 Mar. 64	1 Oct. 77	1 July 81	1 July 85	21 Apr. 94
Frederick George Berkeley, Lt.Col. h.p. Regimental District	13 July 58	14 Feb. 60	21 June 64	1 Oct. 77	1 July 81	1 July 85	21 July 93
Clifton de Neufville Gw Stockwell, Lt.Col. (from h.p. Lincolnshire Regt.), Comdt. Hibernian Mil. School 31 May 89	26 Apr. 58	16 Apr. 61	11 Oct. 64	1 Oct. 77	1 July 81	1 July 85	
Ernest Adolphus Carey, Lt.Col. h.p. Regimental District; Comdg. Welsh Border Brigade Vol. Infantry 29 Nov. 93	13 Apr. 58	7 Oct. 59	3 Jan. 65	1 Oct. 77	1 July 81	1 July 85	27 Sept. 93
Frederick John Faue, Lt.Col. h.p. Regimental District	18 Dec. 57	13 Dec. 59	8 Sept. 65	1 Oct. 77	1 July 81	1 July 85	20 June 94
Frederick Taylor Hobson,[171] Lt.Col. h.p. Regimental District	30 Oct. 57	30 Sept. 59	29 June 66	10 Mar. 78	1 July 81	1 July 85	17 Oct. 92
John Robert Collins,[173] Col. Comdg. Regimental District, Bury St. Edmunds	31 May 59	22 Feb. 61	17 Apr. 67	23 June 78	1 July 81	1 July 85	
George Clayton Swiney,[175] Lt.Col. h.p. Regimental District	20 Oct. 57	18 May 58	15 May 66	31 Dec. 78	1 July 81	1 July 85	7 Mar. 93
John Fletcher Caldwell,[176] Lt.Col. h.p. Regimental District	28 May 58	15 Nov. 61	30 Oct. 66	5 Feb. 79	1 July 81	1 July 85	12 July 92
Oswald Robert Middleton,[178] Lt.Col. h.p. Regimental District	19 June 57	15 Oct. 58	15 June 66	27 Apr. 79	1 July 81	1 July 85	2 Jan. 93
Henry Langtry,[179] Col. Comdg. Regimental District, Leicester	16 Aug. 61	24 Jan. 65	3 Apr. 69	29 Apr. 79	1 July 81	1 July 85	
Henry Richard Abadie,[182] CB. Lt.Col. Commandant Cavalry Depot 19 Apr. 94	6 Aug. 58	18 Dec. 60	14 Feb. 72	22 Nov. 79	1 July 81	1 July 85	
Robert Fowler Butler,[183] Lt.Col. h.p. Regimental District	10 Feb. 58	11 Feb. 62	18 Dec. 67	21 June 80	1 July 81	1 July 85	3 Nov. 93
William Hanning Lee, Lt.Col. h.p. 2 Dragoon Guards	21 Nov. 65	21 Oct. 67	5 Nov. 70	1 Dec. 80	1 July 81	1 July 85	25 July 92
Charles Falkiner Morton, h.p. 14 Hussars	18 Feb. 62	21 July 63	12 June 69	10 Apr. 81	1 July 81	1 July 85	19 Oct. 92
Charles Swinhoe, Lt.Col. Indian S. C.	27 July 55	8 Sept. 59	27 July 67	27 July 75	27 July 81	27 July 35	
Henry Jardine Hallowes,[185] Lt.Col. (from Regimental District), Colonel on the Staff, Jamaica, with rank of Major General 19 Dec. 94	11 May 55	11 Sept. 57	18 Feb. 62	29 May 75	15 Aug. 81	15 Aug. 85	
Robert Spencer Liddell,[187] Lt.Col. h.p. Regimental District	28 Mar. 58	22 July 59	2 May 68	1 July 81	13 Sept. 81	13 Sept. 85	3 June 94
Constantine Maguire, Col. Comdg. Regimental District, Warley	25 Jan. 59	3 July 60	1 Sept. 69	16 Sept. 76	16 Sept. 81	16 Sept. 85	
Herbert Charles Borrett,[190] Lt.Col. h.p. Regimental District	29 Oct. 58	7 Dec. 62	22 Oct. 70	23 June 80	7 Oct. 81	7 Oct. 85	10 Mar. 95
p.s.c. John Boughey, Lt.Col. h.p. Wiltshire Regt	8 July 62	7 Nov. 65	3 Feb. 69	1 July 81	28 Oct. 81	28 Oct. 85	17 Apr. 94
Henry Colebrook Lewes, Lt.Col. (from h.p. R. Art.) Insp. Gen. of Art. in India, with rank of Major General 28 Mar. 92	......	19 Dec. 55	1 Nov. 65	31 Oct. 74	31 Oct. 81	31 Oct. 85	

Colonels.

	CORNET, 2nd LIEUT. or ENSIGN.	LIEUT.	CAPTAIN.	MAJOR.	LIEUT. COLONEL.	COLONEL.	WHEN PLACED ON HALF PAY.
George T. Pretyman, *Lt.Col.* h.p. R. Art.	......	21 Mar. 63	1 Oct. 77	22 Nov. 79	2 Mar. 81	6 Nov. 85	22 Nov. 94
Hon. Walter John Stewart, *Lt.Col.* h.p. 12 Lancers....................	14 Oct. 68	9 Oct. 69	3 Oct. 74	1 July 81	30 Nov. 81	30 Nov. 85	19 Apr. 94
William Henry Thompson,[196] *Col. Comdg.* Regimental District, *Taunton*	10 May 64	20 Feb. 67	12 Feb. 73	1 July 81	9 Dec. 81	9 Dec. 85	
Fred. C. Keyser,[197] *CB.Lt.Col.* h.p. R. Fus.	28 May 58	4 Mar. 62	18 Apr. 68	27 Aug 80	12 Dec. 81	12 Dec. 85	1 Jan. 94
Henry Edw. Colvile, *CB. CMG. Major,* Grenadier Guards..................	......	1 Oct. 70	15 Mar. 72		1 Nov. 82	2 Jan. 86	
Edward Draper Elliott, *Lt.Col.* Royal Art.	11 Dec. 57	27 Apr. 58	29 May 66	16 Jan. 75	16 Jan. 82	16 Jan. 86	
Francis William Ward, *CB, Lt.Col.* R. Art.	11 Dec. 57	21 May 58	5 Oct. 66	16 Jan. 75	16 Jan. 82	16 Jan. 86	
Fred. Charles St. John.*Lt.Col.* Indian S.C.	20 Jan. 56	17 Aug. 59	20 Jan. 68	20 Jan. 76	20 Jan. 82	20 Jan. 86	
Sebastian White Rawlins, *Lt.Col.* h.p. Regimental District	5 Feb. 58	10 May 61	21 Feb. 65	1 Oct. 77	25 Jan. 82	25 Jan. 86	22 May 93
Frederick Augustus Le Mesurier, *CB. Lt.Col.* h.p. Royal Engineers	......	1 Oct. 57	11 July 67	1 Oct. 77	18 Feb. 82	18 Feb. 86	6 Nov. 94
William Vesey Brownlow,[201] *CB. Lt.Col.* h.p. Regimental District	29 Apr. 59	12 May 61	18 May 70	29 Nov. 79	18 Feb. 82	18 Feb. 86	30 Aug. 94
Edmund Smith Brook,*Lt.Col.*Connaught Rangers	7 Aug. 66	25 Jan. 71	3 Dec. 78	1 July 81	18 Feb. 82	18 Feb. 86	
Geo. Paton,[203] *CMG. Lt.Col.* (from h.p. Regimental District), *Commandant School of Musketry* 17 July 94	23 Aug. 59	5 Sept. 62	30 Oct. 69	19 May 80	25 Feb. 82	25 Feb. 86	
Evelyn E. T. Lord Falmouth, *CB. Lt.Col.* Coldstream Guards	......	22 July 66	5 Mar. 70		16 Feb. 78	27 Feb. 86	
C Reg. Wm. Sartorius, *CMG. Col.* Bengal Infantry	20 Jan. 58	18 May 58	1 Nov. 68	1 Apr. 74	12 Sept. 78	27 Feb. 86	
Arthur G. H. Church,[207] *Lt.Col.* h p. Regimental District	5 Nov. 61	9 Jan. 63	25 Dec. 67	1 July 81	18 Mar. 82	18 Mar. 86	12 July 93
Fred. Benjamin Price White,*Lt.Col.*h.p. 1 West India Regt..........	18 Dec. 63	4 Apr. 65	26 Feb. 67	24 Mar. 77	24 Mar. 82	24 Mar. 86	4 Oct. 93
Barrington B. D. Campbell, *Lt.Col.* Scots Guards	......	10 May 64	18 Dec. 66		17 May 76	1 Apr. 86	
William S. Curzon, *Lt.Col.* h.p. R. Art.	......	7 Apr. 56	7 Sept. 66	1 Apr. 75	1 Apr. 82	1 Apr. 86	8 May 94
Thomas Arthur Cooke,[201] *Lt.Col.* (from h.p. 17 Lancers), *Commanding Sind District, Bombay Army*, 9 Jan. 94	16 May 62	9 July 65	20 July 70	1 July 81	1 Apr. 82	1 Apr. 86	
Alex. Tulloch Rolland, *Lt.Col.* Indian S.C.	4 Apr. 56	26 Jan. 57	4 Apr. 68	4 Apr. 76	4 Apr. 82	4 Apr. 86	
Gerald de Courcy Morton,[210] *CB. Col.* (from h.p. Munster Fus.) *Commanding a District, Bengal Army*, 24 Apr. 91 ...	9 Jan. 63	13 July 67	27 Mar. 77	22 Nov. 79	2 Mar. 81	6 Apr. 86	
John E. Whitting,[211] *Col. Comdg.* Regimental District, *Winchester*	4 Sept. 57	5 Oct. 58	22 Sept. 65	19 Oct. 77	21 Apr. 82	21 Apr. 86	
p.s.c.Wm. F. Gatacre,[212] *DSO.Col.* (from h.p. Middlesex Regt.); *Commanding a District, Bombay Army*, 30 Jan. 94	18 Feb. 62	23 Dec. 64	7 Dec. 70	23 Mar. 81	29 Apr. 82	29 Apr. 86	
Wm. J. Holt,[214] *CB.Col.*h.p. Regimental District	24 July 57	15 Feb. 59	2 Sept. 68	23 Jan. 78	6 May 82	6 May 86	25 Mar. 95
Montague Protheroe, *CB. CSI. Lt.Col.* Indian Staff Corps	4 Jan. 58	9 Mar. 60	4 Jan. 70	4 Jan. 78	4 Jan. 84	17 May 86	
Russell Upcher,[215] *DSO. Col. Com.* Regimental District, *Newcastle*	21 Nov. 62	29 Oct. 66	31 Oct. 71	11 Nov. 78	9 June 82	9 June 86	
Edward Eyre-Williams, *Col. Com.* Regimental District, *Warrington*	6 Jan. 60	27 Sept. 61	6 Mar. 67	27 May 80	10 June 82	10 June 86	
Theophilus Higginson, *CB. Lt.Col.* Indian Staff Corps	26 June 56	24 July 58	26 June 68	26 June 76	26 June 82	26 June 86	
p.s.c. Alex. B. Tulloch,[216] *CB, CMG. Col.* (from h.p. Welsh Regt.), *Hon. Major General* 3 Nov. 94	23 May 55	30 July 57	29 Mar. 64	1 Oct. 77	11 July 82	11 July 86	
Joseph Philips, *CB. Col. Com.* R. Marines	24 Dec. 56	12 July 59	19 June 72	29 Nov. 79	21 June 85	11 July 86	
George Swinley, *CB. Lt.Col.* Royal Art.	......	6 Nov. 60	16 Jan. 75	22 Nov. 79	2 Mar. 81	21 July 86	
Hon. Reginald A. J. Talbot,[219] *Lt.Col.* (from h.p. 1 Life Gds.), *Military Attaché in Paris*, 10 July 89, *and Aide de Camp to the Queen*	13 May 59	28 July 63	8 May 67	14 July 80	21 July 82	21 July 86	
John F. F. Cologan, *Lt.Col.* Indian S. C.	20 Sept. 57	15 Aug. 58	20 Sept. 69	20 Sept. 77	2 Mar. 81	22 July 86	
George Baker,[221] *CB. Lt.Col. Comdg.* Regimental District, *Bury*............	18 Dec. 57	30 Nov. 60	29 May 67	21 July 80	29 Aug. 82	29 Aug. 86	
Fred. Lorn Campbell, *Major*, Scots Gds.	......	12 Aug. 68	24 Apr. 27		1 Oct. 81	11 Sept. 86	
Hy. Phipson Peacock, *Col.* Bengal Cav.	20 Sept. 56	9 Jan. 57	6 May 65	23 July 76	1 July 82	20 Sept. 86	
Maurice Tweedie, *Lt.Col.* Indian S. C.	20 Sept. 56	17 May 59	20 Sept. 68	20 Sept. 76	20 Sept. 82	20 Sept. 86	
W. Nesbitt Wroughton, *Lt.Col.* Indian Staff Corps	23 Sept. 56	28 Apr. 58	23 Sept. 68	23 Sept. 76	23 Sept. 82	23 Sept. 86	
Richard Kerr Bayly,[226] *CB. Lt.Col.* h.p. Black Watch.........	16 Mar. 55	2 Oct. 58	5 July 65	1 Apr. 74	29 Sept. 82	29 Sept. 86	30 Aug. 94
John Jopp, *CB. Lt.Col.* Indian Staff Corps	20 Oct. 56	4 Aug. 60	20 Oct. 68	20 Oct. 76	20 Oct. 82	20 Oct. 86	
Wm. Walpole Murdoch, *Col.* (from h.p.) Royal Artillery)	......	21 June 56	6 July 67	28 Oct. 75	28 Oct. 82	28 Oct. 86	
Laurence J. Oliphant, *Lt.Col.* Gren. Gds.	......	17 Oct. 66	29 Dec. 69		9 Dec. 76	1 Nov. 86	
Chas. Alf. Moore, *Col.* Bombay Cavalry	4 Nov. 56	1 Jan. 58	6 May 63	10 Apr. 74	14 July 80	4 Nov. 86	
Robt. M. Jennings, *Col.* Bengal Cav.	20 May 59	20 May 60	15 Jan. 68	1 Oct. 77	18 Nov. 82	18 Nov. 86	
Wm. Salmond, *Lt.Col.* h.p.R. Eng.	......	1 Oct. 57	10 Nov. 68	21 Oct. 77	18 Nov. 82	18 Nov. 86	10 Feb. 90
p.s.c. Richard H. O'Grady Haly,[230] *DSO Col.* (from h.p. Suffolk Regt.); *Assist. Adjutant General, Belfast*, 25 Sept. 91	6 Nov. 58	11 Feb. 62	31 Aug. 66	20 Nov. 79	18 Nov. 82	18 Nov. 86	
Binton Blood, *CB. Lt.Col.* h.p. R. Eng.	......	19 Dec. 60	25 Aug. 73	29 Nov. 79	18 Nov. 82	18 Nov. 86	10 July 93
p.s.c. Geoffry Barton,[229] *CB. Col.* (from h.p. Royal Fusiliers), *Assistant Adjutant General, Chatham*, 16 Feb. 95	3 Oct. 62	14 Feb. 65	1 Apr. 74	29 Nov. 79	18 Nov. 82	18 Nov. 86	
p.s.c. Arthur FitzRoy Hart, *CB. Lt.Col.* East Surrey Regt. (31 Foot)	23 Dec. 64	29 May 67	13 June 74	29 Nov. 79	18 Nov. 82	18 Nov. 86	
Ronald Bertram Lane,[231] *Major* (from h.p. Rifle Brig.), *Assist. Military Secretary* 2 July 92	1 Feb. 67	4 Oct. 71	5 Oct. 78	29 Nov. 79	18 Nov. 82	18 Nov. 86	

Colonels.

Name	Cornet, 2nd Lieut. or Ensign.	Lieut.	Captain.	Major.	Lieut. Colonel.	Colonel.	When Placed on Half Pay.
Frederick A. Ogle,[232] CB. Col. Com. Royal Marine Artillery	29 July 56	20 Apr. 60	30 July 68	5 Apr. 80	18 Nov. 82	18 Nov. 86	
Alliston C. Toker, CB. Lt.Col. Ind. S. C.	4 May 60	1 Jan. 62	4 May 72	4 May 80	18 Nov. 82	18 Nov. 86	
Arthur George Yeatman-Biggs, CB. Lt.Col. (from h.p. Royal Artillery)		18 Dec. 60	4 Feb. 74	24 July 80	18 Nov. 82	18 Nov. 86	
Geo. Cox,[233] Lt.Col. (from h.p. Irish Fus.) A. A. General for Recruiting, War Office, 1 Aug. 94	4 Jan. 61	12 July 64	22 June 67	8 Nov. 80	18 Nov. 82	18 Nov. 86	
John E. Boyes,[234] Col. Comdg. Regimental District, Aberdeen	29 Oct. 61	18 Jan. 67	14 Oct. 68	18 Dec. 80	18 Nov. 82	18 Nov. 86	
p.s.c. ŸC Euston Henry Sartorius,[235] Major, h.p. East Lanc. Regt.	8 July 62	18 July 65	30 Sept. 74	2 Mar. 81	18 Nov. 82	18 Nov. 86	21 Aug. 94
Charles Needham,[237] Lt.Col. h.p. 1 Life Guards	17 Nov. 63	11 Jan. 67	5 May 70	1 July 81	18 Nov. 82	18 Nov. 86	21 July 92
p.s.c. Kenelm Digby Murray,[238] DSO. Lt. Col. h.p. Irish Fusiliers	4 Sept. 60	26 Feb. 64	30 June 69	1 July 81	18 Nov. 82	18 Nov. 86	6 Jan. 94
Richard Leigh,[239] Lt.Col. h.p. Highland Light Infantry (74 Foot)	30 Dec. 60	13 Mar. 66	12 Feb. 73	1 July 81	18 Nov. 82	18 Nov. 86	3 Apr. 93
Sir Arthur Wm. Mackworth, Bart. Lt.Col. (from h.p. Royal Engineers)		1 July 61	11 Dec. 73	1 July 81	18 Nov. 82	18 Nov. 86	
George Wm. Nesbitt Rogers,[240] Col. Comdg. Regimental District, Birr	17 Jan. 65	1 Feb. 68	14 June 76	1 July 81	18 Nov. 82	18 Nov. 86	
p.s.c. Edward J. Lugard, Lt.Col. Lancaster Regiment (4 F.)	16 Jan. 63	11 Jan. 67	28 Oct. 76	1 July 81	18 Nov. 82	19 Nov. 86	
p.s.c. ŸC Reginald Clare Hart, Col. (from Royal Engineers); Director of Military Education, India, 20 July 89		13 Jan. 69	1 July 81	18 Jan. 82	18 Nov. 82	18 Nov. 85	
Hon. Neville G. Lyttelton,[241] Lt.Col. (from h.p. Rifle Brigade); A. A. Gen. War Office 5 Dec. 94	17 Jan. 65	14 July 69	13 Oct. 77	22 Feb. 82	18 Nov. 82	18 Nov. 86	
p.s.c. Henry J. T. Hildyard,[242] Lt.Col. (from h.p. Highland Lt. Inf.), Commandant Staff College 12 Aug. 93	9 Mar. 67	16 Sept. 68	28 Oct. 76	6 May 82	18 Nov. 82	18 Nov. 86	
Hy. Hallam Parr,[246] CB. CMG. Lt.Col. (from h.p. Somerset Lt. Infantry); Aide de Camp to the Queen and Assist. Adj. Gen. War Office 25 Jan. 95	8 Sept. 65	30 Oct. 69	23 Jan. 78	18 Nov. 82	21 May 84	24 Nov. 86	
Henry S. Jarrett, CIE. Indian S. C.	13 Dec. 56	11 July 57	13 Dec. 68	13 Dec. 76	13 Dec. 82	13 Dec. 86	
Leopold J. H. Grey, CSI. Lt.Col. Indian S.C.	13 Dec. 56	15 Sept. 57	13 Dec. 68	13 Dec. 76	13 Dec. 82	13 Dec. 86	
George A. Jacob, Lt.Col. Indian S. C.	13 Dec. 56	20 May 58	13 Dec. 68	13 Dec. 76	13 Dec. 82	13 Dec. 86	
Thos. O. Underwood, Lt. Col. Indian S.C.	13 Dec. 56	1 Oct. 59	13 Dec. 68	13 Dec. 76	13 Dec. 82	13 Dec. 86	
Charles A. Porteous, Lt.Col. Indian S. C.	13 Dec. 56	27 June 61	13 Dec. 68	13 Dec. 76	13 Dec. 82	13 Dec. 86	
Hy. B. Sanderson, CIE. Lt.Col. Indian S. C.	20 Dec. 56	8 June 57	20 Dec. 68	20 Dec. 76	20 Dec. 82	20 Dec. 86	
George Atkins, Lt.Col. Indian S. C.	20 Dec. 56	30 Apr. 58	20 Dec. 68	20 Dec. 76	20 Dec. 82	20 Dec. 86	
Chas. J. O. Chambers, Lt.Col. Indian S.C.	20 Dec. 56	29 Sept. 59	20 Dec. 68	20 Dec. 76	20 Dec. 82	20 Dec. 86	
William H. Wilson, Lt.Col. Indian S. C.	20 Dec. 56	2 May 61	20 Dec. 68	20 Dec. 76	20 Dec. 82	20 Dec. 86	
Malcolm Furlong, Lt.Col. Indian S. C.	4 Jan. 57	14 Feb. 59	4 Jan. 67	4 Jan. 77	4 Jan. 83	4 Jan. 87	
Robert Morris, Col. Bengal Cavalry	4 Aug. 57	18 May 58	8 Aug. 65	16 Dec. 76	8 Jan. 83	8 Jan. 87	
p.s.c. Hugh T. Jones-Vaughan,[249] CB. Lt.Col. (from h.p. East Yorkshire Regt.), Commanding the Troops, Straits Settlements, 13 Apr. 94	20 Nov. 57	14 Aug. 59	16 Oct. 67	8 May 80	2 Mar. 81	10 Jan. 87	
George Aug. Strover, Lt.Col. Indian S.C.	20 Jan. 57	7 Jan. 59	20 Jan. 69	20 Jan. 77	20 Jan. 83	20 Jan. 87	
William Vertue, Lt.Col. Indian S. C.	20 Jan. 57	6 Mar. 60	20 Jan. 69	20 Jan. 77	20 Jan. 83	20 Jan. 87	
Hon. Albert B. de Montmorency, Lt.Col. Royal Artillery	12 June 58	27 Aug. 58	13 July 68	4 Feb. 76	4 Feb. 83	4 Feb. 87	
Philip D. Henderson, CSI. Col. Madras Cavalry	20 Feb. 57	13 Sept. 59	28 Apr. 64	8 July 74	5 Oct. 80	20 Feb. 87	
Charles Henry Ewart, Lt.Col. Indian S.C.	20 Feb. 57	30 Apr. 58	20 Feb. 69	20 Feb. 77	20 Feb. 83	20 Feb. 87	
Jas. Hen. Prendergast, Lt.Col. Indian S.C.	3 Mar. 57	21 Sept. 59	3 Mar. 69	3 Mar. 77	3 Mar. 83	3 Mar. 87	
Chas. Peter Newport, Lt.Col. Indian S.C.	4 Mar. 57	28 Nov. 58	4 Mar. 69	4 Mar. 77	4 Mar. 83	4 Mar. 87	
Charles J. O. Fitzgerald, CB. Lt.Col. Indian Staff Corps	4 Mar. 57	27 Nov. 59	4 Mar. 69	4 Mar. 77	4 Mar. 83	4 Mar. 87	
George Henry Oakes, Lt.Col. Indian S.C.	4 Mar. 57	2 Sept. 60	4 Mar. 69	4 Mar. 77	4 Mar. 83	4 Mar. 87	
Lord Algernon Chas. Gordon-Lennox,[253] Major (from h.p. Grenadier Guards), Aide de Camp to H.R.H. the Duke of Cambridge	11 Jun. 67	29 May 67	23 Mar. 70		1 Oct. 77	8 Mar. 87	
p.s.c. ŸC Mark Sever Bell, CB. Lt.Col. h.p. Royal Engineers		25 June 62	19 Aug. 74	25 June 82	29 Oct. 84	16 Mar. 87	10 May 94
Henry F. H. Sewell, Lt.Col. Indian S. C.	20 Mar. 57	4 July 58	20 Mar. 69	20 Mar. 77	20 Mar. 83	20 Mar. 87	
Robert W. Hesketh, Lt.Col. Indian S. C.	20 Mar. 57	2 Feb. 60	20 Mar. 69	20 Mar. 77	20 Mar. 83	20 Mar. 87	
Hon. Herbert F. Eaton, Lt.Col. h.p. Grenadier Guards		29 May 67	9 Apr. 70		2 Mar. 78	29 Mar. 87	23 July 94
Jas. Geo. Cockburn,[256] Lt.Col. h.p. Warwickshire Regt.	15 Apr. 56	26 Feb. 58	3 May 64	1 Oct. 77	3 Apr. 83	3 Apr. 87	16 Feb. 95
Charles Tennant Wallace,[257] Col. Comdg. Regimental District, Perth	13 Aug. 58	19 Aug. 62	27 Nov. 67	1 July 81	3 Apr. 83	3 Apr. 87	
Fras. Hen. Vanderzee, Lt.Col. Indian S.C.	7 Apr. 57	18 Feb. 60	7 Apr. 69	7 Apr. 77	7 Apr. 83	7 Apr. 87	
Jas. H. Gordon, CB. DSO. Lt.Col. Indian S.C.	20 Apr. 57	24 June 59	20 Apr. 69	20 Apr. 77	20 Apr. 83	20 Apr. 87	
William R. Truman, Lt.Col. (from h.p.) Regimental District), Assist. Insp. Remount Establishment, 1 Apr. 93	8 Aug. 62	8 Dec. 65	24 July 72	1 July 81	21 Apr. 83	21 Apr. 87	
Chas. S. Perry,[258] Col. h.p. Regimental District, Norwich	29 May 57	2 Oct. 58	8 May 66	31 Dec. 78	1 May 83	1 May 87	26 Mar. 95
Wm. Alex. Lawrence, Lt.Col. Indian S. C.	4 Feb. 61	20 Dec. 64	4 Feb. 73	4 Feb. 81	4 Feb. 83	4 Feb. 87	
Bruce Brine, Lt.Col. h.p. R. Engineers		15 May 57	6 July 67	6 June 77	22 May 83	22 May 87	1 Apr. 94
Geo. H. F. Codrington, Lt.Col. Indian S.C.	13 June 57	19 Jan. 58	13 June 69	13 June 77	13 June 83	13 June 87	
Hon. C. A. Szczepauski, Lt.Col. Indian S.C.	13 June 57	18 May 58	13 June 69	13 June 77	13 June 83	13 June 87	
Thomas Aug. Scott, Lt.Col. Indian S. C.	13 June 57	18 May 58	13 June 69	13 June 77	13 June 83	13 June 87	
Joshua W. Swifte, Lt.Col. Indian Staff C.	13 June 57	2 Dec. 58	13 June 69	13 June 77	13 June 83	13 June 87	
Robt. Vaughan Malden, Lt.Col. Ind. S. C.	13 June 57	16 Jan. 59	13 June 69	13 June 77	13 June 83	13 June 87	

Colonels.

	CORNET, 2nd LIEUT. or ENSIGN.	LIEUT.	CAPTAIN.	MAJOR.	LIEUT. COLONEL.	COLONEL.	WHEN PLACED ON HALF PAY.
John Gatacre, *CB. Lt.Col.* Indian S. C. ...	13 June 57	9 Mar. 59	13 June 69	13 June 77	13 June 83	13 June 87	
Fras. S. FitzPatrick, *Lt.Col.* Indian S. C.	13 June 57	15 Aug. 60	13 June 69	13 June 77	13 June 83	13 June 87	
Robert MacGregor Stewart, *CB. Lt.Col.* (from R. Art.), *Commandant, School of Gunnery*, 9 Mar. 94		18 Dec. 60	4 Feb. 74	22 Nov. 79	15 June 85	18 June 87	
Geo. Terry Luder Carwithen,²⁵⁹ *Col. Comdg. Regtl. Dist., Berwick-on-Tweed*	27 Nov. 57	13 Jan. 60	16 Aug. 64	1 Oct. 77	27 June 83	27 June 87	
Geo. Conrad Sartorius, *CB.Lt.Col.* Ind.S.C.		1 Oct. 57	1 Oct. 66	1 Oct. 77	1 Oct. 83	1 July 87	
Edmund H. Eyre, *CB. Lt.Col.* Indian S.C.	4 Mar. 58	1 Jan. 62	4 Mar. 70	4 Mar. 78	4 Mar. 84	1 July 87	
Henry S. Elton, *Lt.Col.* Indian Staff C.	20 Oct. 58	14 Feb. 61	20 Oct. 70	20 Oct. 78	20 Oct. 84	1 July 87	
Elliott A. Bruce, *Lt.Col.* Indian Staff C.	6 Jan. 59	4 Aug. 61	6 Jan. 71	6 Jan. 79	6 Jan. 85	1 July 87	
Wm. P. Symons,²⁶⁰ *CB.Lt.Col.* (from h.p. South Wales Borderers), *A.A.Gen. for Musketry, Bengal,* 8 Apr. 93	6 Mar. 63	30 Oct. 66	16 Feb. 78	1 July 81	17 May 86	1 July 87	
Hugh R. Hope, *Col.* Madras Cavalry ...	4 Nov. 60	1 Jan. 62	15 Dec. 70	4 Nov. 80	4 Nov. 86	1 July 87	
Frederick Kilgour, *Lt.Col.* Indian S. C.	11 July 57	25 May 60	11 July 69	11 July 77	11 July 83	11 July 87	
John Roberts Hogg, *Lt.Col.* h.p. R. Engrs.		1 Oct. 57	8 Jan. 68	1 Oct. 77	14 July 83	14 July 87	14 June 94
Sir Wm. S. Seton, *Bart.Lt.Col.* Indian S.C.	20 July 57	2 June 60	20 July 69	20 July 77	20 July 83	20 July 87	
Lord Arth. C. Wellesley, *Lt.Col.* Gren. Gds.		13 June 68	15 Feb. 71		5 Apr. 79	1 Aug. 87	
Herbert Charles Chermside,²⁶³ *CB. CMG. Major* (from R. Engineers) ...		23 July 70	23 July 82	27 Sept. 82	15 June 85	3 Aug. 87	
George Scott Hills, *Lt.Col.* Indian S. C.	4 Aug. 57	18 May 58	4 Aug. 69	4 Aug. 77	4 Aug. 83	4 Aug. 87	
Henry G. Waterfield, *Lt.Col.* Indian S. C.	4 Aug. 57	18 May 58	4 Aug. 69	4 Aug. 77	4 Aug. 83	4 Aug. 87	
Coryndon T.P. Luxmoore, *Lt.Col.* Indian Staff Corps	4 Aug. 57	11 June 59	4 Aug. 69	4 Aug. 77	4 Aug. 83	4 Aug. 87	
Henry William Blair, *Lt.Col.* Indian S. C.	4 Aug. 57	18 Nov. 59	4 Aug. 69	4 Aug. 77	4 Aug. 83	4 Aug. 87	
William Frederick Cavaye,²⁶³ *Lt.Col.* (from h.p. Sussex Regiment); *A.A. General, Portsmouth,* 8 Nov. 90	25 Apr. 65	9 Mar. 67	13 Dec. 74	1 July 81	15 Aug. 83	15 Aug. 87	
Samuel B. Miles, *Lt.Col.* Indian S. C. ...	20 Aug. 57	2 Jan. 61	20 Aug. 69	20 Aug. 77	20 Aug. 83	20 Aug. 87	
Hon. Henry W. L. Corry,²⁶⁴ *Lt.Col.* h.p. Coldstream Guards		20 July 66	2 Sept. 68		29 Sept. 77	29 Aug. 87	10 Nov. 93
George Manners Onslow, *Lt.Col.* h.p. 20 Hussars; *Assist. Commandant Cavalry Depot,* 19 Apr. 92	20 May 61	13 Nov. 66	30 Apr. 73	1 July 81	4 Feb. 83	16 Sept. 87	2 July 84
George Wm. Adolphus FitzGeorge,²⁶⁵ *Major,* h.p. 20 Hussars; *Aide de Camp to H.R.H. the Duke of Cambridge*	15 Jan. 61	18 Dec. 63	9 Apr. 70	1 July 81	5 Oct. 82	20 Sept. 87	20 June 83
Richmond I. Crawford, *Lt.Col.* Indian Staff Corps	4 Oct. 57	25 Oct. 59	4 Oct. 69	4 Oct. 77	4 Oct. 83	4 Oct. 87	
Charles Albert Dodd, *Lt.Col.* Indian Staff Corps	4 Oct. 57	18 Feb. 61	4 Oct. 69	4 Oct. 77	4 Oct. 83	4 Oct. 87	
Sir Henry R. Thuillier, *KCIE. Lt.Col.* Royal Engineers	12 June 57	27 Aug. 58	10 Nov. 69	7 Oct. 76	7 Oct. 83	7 Oct. 87	
Alex. Thomas Fraser, *Lt.Col.* R. Eng.	11 June 58	27 Aug. 58	10 Nov. 69	7 Oct. 76	7 Oct. 83	7 Oct. 87	
Willoughby T. Brereton, *Lt.Col.* Indian Staff Corps	10 Oct. 57	17 Feb. 60	10 Oct. 69	10 Oct. 77	10 Oct. 83	10 Oct. 87	
Geo. Elphinstone Erskine, *Col.* Bom. Cav.	4 Nov. 57	4 Apr. 60	4 Nov. 69	4 Nov. 77	4 Nov. 83	4 Nov. 87	
Norman M. T. Horsford, *Lt.Col.* Indian Staff Corps	20 Nov. 57	26 May 58	20 Nov. 69	20 Nov. 77	20 Nov. 83	20 Nov. 87	
Henry Wm. H. Cox, *Lt.Col.* Indian S. C.	20 Nov. 57	31 Oct. 59	20 Nov. 69	20 Nov. 77	20 Nov. 83	20 Nov. 87	
Nowell Fitz U. Way, *CB. Col. Com. R. Mar*	23 Nov. 55	7 May 59	8 June 68	6 Aug. 80	23 Nov. 83	23 Nov. 87	
William Stenhouse, *Col.* Madras Infantry	11 Dec. 58	1 Jan. 62	10 Dec. 70	12 Oct. 75	26 Nov. 75	26 Nov. 87	
James Philips, *Lt.Col.* Indian Staff Corps	27 Nov. 57	2 July 61	27 Nov. 69	27 Nov. 77	27 Nov. 83	27 Nov. 87	
Theodore Wm. Hogg, *Lt.Col.* Indian S. C.	4 Dec. 57	18 May 58	4 Dec. 69	4 Dec. 77	4 Dec. 83	4 Dec. 87	
John Pennycuick, *Lt.Col.* R. Engineers....		10 Dec. 58	13 Oct. 70	8 Dec. 76	8 Dec. 83	8 Dec. 87	
Thomas R. Tabuteau, *Lt.Col.* Indian S. C.	11 Dec. 57	1 Jan. 62	11 Dec. 69	11 Dec. 77	11 Dec. 83	11 Dec. 87	
Wm. Henry Wilkins, *Lt.Col.* Indian S. C.	12 Dec. 57	27 Aug. 58	12 Dec. 69	12 Dec. 77	12 Dec. 83	12 Dec. 87	
John Grierson, *Lt.Col.* Indian Staff Corps	12 Dec. 57	27 Aug. 58	12 Dec. 69	12 Dec. 77	12 Dec. 83	12 Dec. 87	
Elphinstone Shaw, *Lt.Col.* Indian S. C.	12 Dec. 57	11 July 59	12 Dec. 69	12 Dec. 77	12 Dec. 83	12 Dec. 87	
George Chrystie, *Lt.Col.* Indian Staff C.	12 Dec. 57	1 Feb. 60	12 Dec. 69	12 Dec. 77	12 Dec. 83	12 Dec. 87	
Horace R. Spearman, *Lt.Col.* Indian S. C.	18 Dec. 57	25 Apr. 60	18 Dec. 69	18 Dec. 77	18 Dec. 83	18 Dec. 87	
Jas. D. Macpherson, *Lt.Col.* Indian S. C.	19 Dec. 57	11 Aug. 59	19 Dec. 69	19 Dec. 77	19 Dec. 83	19 Dec. 87	
Arthur Peel,²⁶⁶ *Col.* (from h.p. 7 Hus.), *A.A. General, Colchester,* 18 May 91	8 June 61	19 Nov. 63	21 Aug. 69	1 July 81	19 Dec. 83	19 Dec. 87	
Herbert Bruce Jacob, *Lt.Col.* Indian S. C	20 Dec. 57	13 Dec. 59	20 Dec. 69	20 Dec. 77	20 Dec. 83	20 Dec. 87	
Henry Fludyer, *Lt.Col.* Scots Guards ...		29 May 66	21 Aug. 69		19 Dec. 77	21 Dec. 87	
Wm. Eliott Lockhart, *Lt.Col.* R. Artillery	12 June 58	27 Aug. 58	1 Sept. 69	29 Jan. 77	1 Jan. 84	1 Jan. 88	
George Bean Macdonell, *Lt.Col.* R. Art.	12 June 58	27 Aug. 58	12 Sept. 69	29 Jan. 77	1 Jan. 84	1 Jan. 88	
Geo. Thos. Halliday, *Col.* Bengal Cavalry	20 Dec. 58	29 May. 59	4 Apr. 68	1 Oct. 77	1 Jan. 84	1 Jan. 88	
Neville F. Parker, *Lt.Col.* Bengal Inf.	9 Apr. 58	25 July 60	1 Nov. 68	22 Dec. 77	1 Jan. 84	1 Jan. 88	
Thomas Jas. Cotton, *Lt.Col.* Indian S. C.	4 Jan. 58	9 Sept. 59	4 Jan. 70	4 Jan. 78	4 Jan. 84	4 Jan. 88	
Charles J. S. Cahill, *Lt.Col.* Indian S.C.	20 Jan. 58	21 Feb. 59	20 Jan. 70	20 Jan. 78	20 Jan. 84	20 Jan. 88	
Horace Ricardo, *Lt.Col.* Grenadier Guards		17 Apr. 69	17 May 71		24 May 79	29 Jan. 88	
Cecil Beadon, *Col.* Madras Cavalry	4 Feb. 58	4 Feb. 58	22 June 62	29 Aug. 73	1 Jan. 80	4 Feb. 88	
Robert Atkins, *Lt.Col.* Indian Staff Corps	4 Feb. 58	7 June 58	4 Feb. 70	4 Feb. 78	4 Feb. 84	4 Feb. 88	
Jas. Richard Marett, *Lt.Col.* Indian S. C.	4 Feb. 58	25 Dec. 58	4 Feb. 70	4 Feb. 78	4 Feb. 84	4 Feb. 88	
Chas. Jas. T. Whitlock, *Lt.Col.* Indian S. C.	20 Jan. 58	9 Mar. 60	20 Feb. 70	20 Feb. 78	20 Feb. 84	20 Feb. 88	
John Biddulph, *Lt.Col.* Indian Staff Corps	20 Feb. 58	18 May 58	20 Jan. 70	8 Dec. 77	24 Feb. 84	24 Feb. 88	
Henry Marsh Sept. Magrath, *Lt.Col.* Indian Staff Corps	4 Mar. 58	1 Feb. 59	4 Mar. 70	4 Mar. 78	4 Mar. 84	4 Mar. 88	
Edwin Glass Fenn, *Col. Comdg. Regimental District, Halifax*	16 Sept. 59	11 Feb. 62	17 Mar. 69	1 July 81	15 Mar. 84	15 Mar. 88	
Robert W. W. Follett,²⁶⁸ *Lt.Col.* b.p. Coldstream Guards		21 July 66	17 Feb. 69		29 Sept. 77	26 Mar. 88	29 Sept. 94
p.s.c. Henry Manvers Mecrsom, *Lt.Col.* h.p. R. Artillery		1 Oct. 57	7 Sept. 71	20 Feb. 78	19 Feb. 86	30 Mar. 88	19 Feb. 91
Wm. Reeves Bunbury, *Lt.Col.* Indian S.C.	31 Mar. 58	17 Mar. 63	31 Mar. 70	31 Mar. 78	31 Mar. 84	31 Mar. 88	
Jas. W. A. Michell, *Lt.Col.* Indian S. C.	4 Apr. 58	25 Jan. 61	4 Apr. 70	4 Apr. 78	4 Apr. 84	4 Apr. 88	
Sir Horatio H. Kitchener, *KCMG. CB. Major,* Royal Engineers		4 Jan. 71	4 Jan. 83	8 Oct. 84	15 June 85	11 Apr. 88	
Willoughby W. Hooper, *Col.* Madras Cav.	20 Apr. 58	21 Dec. 59	20 Apr. 70	20 Apr. 78	4 Apr. 84	20 Apr. 88	
Charles J. O'N. Ferguson, *Lt.Col.* h.p. Royal Engineers		1 Oct. 57	4 Mar. 68	1 Oct. 77	10 May 84	10 May 88	24 Jan. 91

Colonels.

	2nd LIEUT. or ENSIGN.	LIEUT.	CAPTAIN.	MAJOR.	LIEUT. COLONEL.	COLONEL.	WHEN PLACED ON HALF PAY.
Edmund Antrobus, *Lt. Col.* Gren. Gds......		18 Feb. 69	17 May 71	......	24 May 79	11 May 88	
Thos. J. C. A. Studdy, *Lt.Col.* R. Art......	12 Dec. 57	27 Aug. 58	2 Jan. 68	27 Nov. 78	11 May 84	11 May 88	
Fras. T. Lloyd, *CB. Lt.Col.* (from R. Art.)	......	1 Oct. 57	28 May 70	24 Nov. 77	21 May 84	21 May 88	
Edmund Hunt Holley, *Lt.Col.* h.p. R. Art.	......	19 June 60	23 Nov. 72	13 Mar. 81	21 May 84	21 May 88	1 Oct. 92
Geo. H. T. Colwell, *CB. Col. Com.* R. Mar...	11 Aug. 58	20 Apr. 60	14 Nov. 72	1 July 81	21 May 84	21 May 88	
Alexander Ferrier Kidston,[275] *Col.Comdg.* Regimental District, *Lancaster*..........	9 Nov. 58	2 Dec. 62	12 Feb. 73	1 July 81	21 May 84	21 May 88	
Reginald Wm. Dalgety, *CB. Lt.Col.* York and Lancaster Regt. (65 Foot)	8 June 67	8 Aug. 68	12 July 74	1 July 81	21 May 84	21 May 88	
Hugh Sutlej Gough,[273] *CMG. Lt.Col.* (from 18 Hussars), *A. A. General for Cavalry* 8 July 93	2 May 68	28 Oct. 71	23 June 75	13 Sept.81	21 May 84	21 May 88	
Elliott Wood, *CB. Major* (from R. Eng)	......	15 Jan. 64	30 Sept. 77	18 Nov. 82	21 May 84	21 May 88	
Killingworth R. Todd, *Lt.Col.* R. Eng. ...	......	24 June 63	6 June 77	24 June 84	21 May 84	21 May 88	
William Freeman Kelly,[216] *CB. Major,* (from h.p. Sussex Regt.), *D. A. A. General, Ireland,* 30 Oct. 94	7 Mar. 67	28 Oct. 71	24 Jan. 80	5 Mar. 84	21 May 84	21 May 88	
Andrew Gilbert Wauchope, *CB. CMG. Lt.Col.* Black Watch (42 Foot)	21 Nov. 65	23 June 67	14 Sept. 78	14 Mar. 84	21 May 84	21 May 88	
Mildmay W. Willson, *CB. Maj.*ScotsGds.	......	3 Aug. 66	3 Sept. 70	......	1 Dec. 78	1 June 88	
Wm. Livesay,[277] *Col. Comdg.* Regimental District, *Oxford*	26 Oct. 55	3 Apr. 57	30 Apr. 64	19 June 76	19 June 83	1 June 88	
Wm. F. Vetch, *Lt.Col.* (from h.p. Dublin Fus.) *Assist. Adj. Gen. York,* 22 Sept. 92	8 Mar. 64	1 July 69	22 May 75	18 June 81	7 June 84	7 June 88	
Frank H. B. Marsh, *Lt.Col.* Bengal Inf...	20 May 59	19 Sept.60	1 Nov. 68	2 May 78	10 June 84	10 June 88	
Kenneth J. L. Mackenzie, *CIE. Lt.Col.* Indian Staff Corps	11 June 58	27 Aug. 58	11 June 70	11 June 78	11 June 84	11 June 88	
James Wm. Macdougall, *Lt. Col.* Ind. S.C.	11 June 58	27 Aug. 58	11 June 70	11 June 78	11 June 84	11 June 88	
John Lannoy Tweedie,[278] *DSO. Col. Comdg.* Regimental District, *Dorchester*	3 July 60	4 Nov. 64	2 Jan. 69	9 Sept. 79	11 June 84	11 June 88	
Geo. Herbert Trevor, *CSI. Lt.Col.* Ind. S.C.	12 June 58	27 Aug. 58	12 June 70	12 June 78	12 June 84	12 June 88	
Mathew Morton Bowie, *Lt. Col.* Indian S.C.	12 June 58	27 Aug. 58	12 June 70	12 June 78	12 June 84	12 June 88	
Montagu M. Carpendale, *Lt.Col.* Indian S.C.	12 June 58	2 June 59	12 June 70	12 June 78	12 June 84	12 June 88	
Henry Chas. Morse, *Lt.Col.* Indian S. C...	12 June 58	1 Oct. 58	12 June 70	12 June 78	12 June 84	12 June 88	
David T. Hatchell, *Lt.Col.* Indian S. C. ...	12 June 58	19 July 60	12 June 70	12 June 78	12 June 84	12 June 88	
Alex. Sinclair Grove, *DSO. Lt. Col.* Indian Staff Corps	12 June 58	1 Oct. 61	12 June 70	12 June 78	12 June 84	12 June 88	
Chas. A. Cuningham, *Lt.Col.* Indian S.C.	20 June 58	26 July 61	20 June 70	20 June 78	20 June 84	20 June 88	
Richard M. Clifford, *Lt. Col.* Indian S. C.	25 June 58	22 Oct. 58	25 June 70	25 June 78	25 June 84	25 June 88	
Henry de S. Isaacson, *Lt.Col.* h.p. R.Art....		23 June 57	10 Nov. 68	1 July 77	1 July 84	1 July 88	17 Aug. 90
Henry H. H. Hallett, *Lt. Col.* Indian S. C.	4 July 58	2 Jan. 60	4 July 70	4 July 78	4 July 84	4 July 88	
Harvey Woodhouse, *Col.* Bengal Inf.....	11 Dec. 58	1 Feb. 60	1 Nov. 68	1 June 75	16 July 76	16 July 88	
Wm. Henry Hoskins, *Lt. Col.* Indian S. C.	20 July 58	31 July 60	20 July 70	20 July 78	20 July 84	20 July 88	
Vincent W. Tregear, *CB. Lt.Col.* Ben. Inf.	11 June 59	7 Nov. 60	1 Nov. 68	23 July 78	4 Aug. 84	4 Aug. 88	
Wilfred Tolson,[281] *Col.Comdg.*Regimental District, *Chichester*	6 Jan. 60	20 Feb. 63	25 Oct. 75	1 July 81	6 Aug. 84	6 Aug. 88	
George Young, *Lt. Col.* Indian Staff C. ...	20 Aug. 58	22 Apr. 60	20 Aug. 70	20 Aug. 78	20 Aug. 84	20 Aug. 88	
Michael A. Rowlandson, *Lt. Col.* Ind. S.C.	20 Aug. 58	17 June 60	20 Aug. 70	20 Aug. 78	20 Aug. 84	20 Aug. 88	
Chas. M. Stockley,[282] *CB. Col. Comdg.* Regimental District, *Omagh*	4 Jan. 62	10 Sept.64	22 July 71	2 Mar. 81	20 Aug. 84	20 Aug. 88	
Fred. G. Jackson, *Col. Comdg.* Regimental District, *Ayr*	30 Mar. 58	6 May 59	22 Sept.65	11 Oct. 77	25 Aug 84	25 Aug. 88	
Geo. Arthur Lee,[283] *Col. Comdg.* Regimental District, *Bedford*	16 May 62	26 Jan. 66	25 Mar. 71	1 July 81	27 Aug. 84	27 Aug. 88	
James Ord Goldie, *Lt.Col.* Indian S. C. ...	4 Sept.58	1 Jan. 60	4 Sept. 70	4 Sept.78	4 Sept. 84	4 Sept. 88	
Dudley North,[284] *Col.* (from h.p. North Lancashire Regt.), *A. A. General,* *Canada,* 25 Feb. 92	10 Sept.58	15 Oct. 61	5 June 66	1 Apr. 74	10 Sept 84	10 Sept. 88	
Robert Hamilton Vetch, *CB. Lt.Col.* (from R. Eng.), *Deputy Inspector General of Fortifications, War Office,* 1 July 89 ...	......	23 Dec. 57	30 July 69	16 Feb. 78	14 Sept. 84	14 Sept. 88	
Charles Robert Rowley,[285] *Major,* h.p. Grenadier Guards	......	19 May 69	9 Sept.71	......	7 June 79	17 Sept.88	10 Aug. 92
Adolphus Vallings, *Lt.Col.* Indian S.C.	20 Sept.58	24 May 59	20 Sept.70	20 Sept. 78	20 Sept. 84	20 Sept. 88	
p.s.c. Henry Fane Grant,[286] *CB. Lt. Col.* h.p. 7 Dragoon Guards, *Inspector General of Cavalry in India,* 1 Apr. 93	23 Dec. 68	8 Dec. 69	10 Jan. 79	1 July 81	24 Sept.84	24 Sept.88	31 Mar. 91
Patrick FitzGerald Gallwey, *Lt.Col.* h.p. Royal Artillery, *Inspector General of Ordnance, Bengal,* 1 Feb. 90	......	1 Oct. 57	15 Nov. 69	1 Oct. 77	1 Oct. 84	1 Oct. 88	17 Aug. 85
Charles Henry Fairfax Ellis, *Lt.Col.* (from h.p. R. Artillery), *Member of Ordnance Committee* 10 Jan. 93	......	1 Oct. 57	24 Nov. 69	1 Oct. 77	1 Oct. 84	1 Oct. 88	
Jas. G. Duff Walker, *Col.* Madras Cav. ...	4 Oct. 58	12 Apr. 59	4 Oct. 70	4 Oct. 78	4 Oct. 84	4 Oct. 88	
p.s.c. Reginald Laurence H. Curteis, *Lt.Col.* (from h.p. Bedfordshire Regt.), *Assist. Adj. Gen. Bombay,* 1 July 90 ...	5 Jan. 60	22 Mar. 64	14 Sept.67	10 Oct. 79	10 Oct. 84	10 Oct. 88	
John Chadwick Doveton, *Lt.Col.* Ind. S.C.	20 Oct. 58	1 Oct. 61	20 Oct. 70	20 Oct. 78	20 Oct. 84	20 Oct. 88	
Reginald Pole-Carew, *CB. Lt.Col.* Coldstream Guards	......	12 May 69	14 Aug. 72	......	4 July 83	25 Oct. 88	
Geo. Crawford Hogg, *Col.* Bombay Cav...	27 Oct. 58	16 Oct. 60	27 Oct. 70	27 Oct. 78	27 Oct. 84	27 Oct. 88	
Algernon Currie, *Col.* Bombay Cavalry...	27 Oct. 58	25 Dec. 60	27 Oct. 70	27 Oct. 78	27 Oct. 84	27 Oct. 88	
Edward Nicolls Peters, *Lt.Col.*h.p.R.Eng.	......	23 Dec. 57	20 Oct. 69	17 Apr. 78	3 Nov. 84	3 Nov. 88	3 Nov. 89
Wm. Jackson Parker, *Lt.Col.* Indian S. C.	4 Nov. 58	26 Aug. 60	4 Nov. 70	4 Nov. 78	4 Nov. 84	4 Nov. 88	
Francis James Mortimer, *Lt.Col.* R. Art.	......	11 Dec. 58	29 July 70	1 Dec. 78	4 Nov. 84	4 Nov. 88	
James L. N. Willis, *Lt.Col.* Indian S. C.	13 Nov. 58	11 June 61	13 Nov. 70	3 Nov. 78	13 Nov. 84	13 Nov. 88	
Fendall Currie, *Col.* Bengal Cavalry	20 Nov. 58	29 May 59	11 Sept. 70	20 Nov. 78	20 Nov. 84	20 Nov. 88	
Jas. Wm. S. Butler, *Lt.Col.* Indian S.C.	20 Nov. 58	26 Apr. 61	20 Nov. 70	20 Nov. 78	20 Nov. 84	20 Nov. 88	
Alfred Henry Cormick Lynch, *Col.Comdg.* Regimental District, *Hamilton*	8 May 62	4 Dec. 66	21 Aug. 69	1 July 81	22 Nov. 84	22 Nov. 88	
Herbert S. Marshall, *Lt.Col.* Bengal Inf.	16 June 59	2 Dec. 60	10 Nov. 68	14 Sept.78	25 Nov. 84	25 Nov. 88	
Alf. Geo. Hutchins, *Lt.Col.* Madras Inf.	20 Feb. 59	20 Feb. 60	10 Apr. 70	20 Feb. 79	18 Feb. 85	28 Nov. 88	
Lopton Scott Stewart, *Lt. Col.* Indian S.C.	4 Dec. 58	1 Oct. 61	4 Dec. 70	4 Dec. 78	4 Dec. 84	4 Dec. 88	

C 2

Colonels.

	CORNET, 2nd LIEUT. or ENSIGN.	LIEUT.	CAPTAIN.	MAJOR.	LIEUT. COLONEL.	COLONEL.	WHEN PLACED ON HALF PAY.
Saml. S. Jacob, *CIE. Lt.Col.* Indian S. C.	......	10 Dec. 58	10 Dec. 70	10 Dec. 78	10 Dec. 84	10 Dec. 88	
Fras. Ward Major, *Lt.Col.* Indian S. C....	......	10 Dec. 58	10 Dec. 70	10 Dec. 78	10 Dec. 84	10 Dec. 88	
Jonathan Wm. Elmes, *Col.* Army Service Corps (*Hon. Col.* 9 Aug. 86)	Regtl. and Depart-	Depart- mental	mental Service	Service 29$^{11}/_{12}$ yrs.	29$^{11}/_{12}$	11 Dec. 88	
Fred. FitzC.Goddard, *Col.* Army Service Corps (*Hon. Col.* 15 Sept. 88)	Depart-	mental	Service	21$^{9}/_{12}$	years.	11 Dec. 88	
Chas. Willis Godfrey, *Lt.Col.* Indian S. C.	......	11 Dec. 58	11 Dec. 70	11 Dec. 78	11 Dec. 84	11 Dec. 88	
Clayton Turner Lane, *Lt.Col.* Indian S.C.	11 Dec. 58	29 Mar. 59	11 Dec. 70	11 Dec. 78	11 Dec. 84	11 Dec. 88	
Wm. Saurin Brooke, *Lt.Col.* Indian S.C.	11 Dec. 58	12 June 59	11 Dec. 70	11 Dec. 78	11 Dec. 84	11 Dec. 88	
Edm. S. Ludlow, *CIE. Lt.Col.* Indian S.C.	11 Dec. 58	1 Sept. 60	11 Dec. 70	11 Dec. 78	11 Dec. 84	11 Dec. 88	
Henry L. Nutt, *Lt.Col.* Indian Staff C.	11 Dec. 58	30 July 62	11 Dec. 70	11 Dec. 78	11 Dec. 84	11 Dec. 88	
Hon. HenengeLegge,[287] *Lt.Col.*h.p.9 Lan...	......	11 Sept.63	11 Dec. 66	29 Apr. 80	15 Dec. 84	15 Dec. 88	15 Dec. 90
Thos. G. Crawley,[288] (from h.p L'pool Regt.); *A.A. Gen. Bengal*, 28 July 90 *p.s.c.*	5 July 60	9 Jan. 63	14 Aug. 67	21 Dec. 80	17 Dec. 84	17 Dec. 88	
Chas. Lacon Harvey,[289] (from h.p. Wiltshire Regt.); *A. A. Gen. Bengal*, 7 Jan. 90	5 Mar. 58	10 July 60	23 Oct. 67	9 Nov. 79	24 Dec. 84	24 Dec. 88	
Sir Chas. Holled Smith,[290] *KCMG. CB. Col.* (from h.p. King's R. Rifles); *Comdt. Victorian Local Forces, with local rank of Major General*.	1 Dec. 65	3 Feb. 69	19 Dec. 77	18 Nov. 82	15 June 85	28 Dec. 88	
Alex. James Donnelly Hawes, *DSO. Lt.Col.* Indian Staff Corps	6 Jan. 59	9 Nov. 60	6 Jan. 71	6 Jan. 79	6 Jan. 85	6 Jan. 89	
Robert M. B. Thomas, *Lt.Col.* Indian S.C.	6 Jan. 59	9 Nov. 60	6 Jan. 71	6 Jan. 79	6 Jan. 85	6 Jan. 89	
Sir Benjamin Parnell Bromhead, *Bart. CB. Lt.Col.* Indian Staff Corps	18 Jan. 59	7 Mar. 63	18 Jan. 71	18 Jan. 79	18 Jan. 85	18 Jan. 89	
John Dawson,[291] *Col.Comdg.*Regimental District, *Belfast*	21 Sept.60	13 Feb. 63	1 Aug. 68	1 July 81	30 Jan. 85	30 Jan. 89	
Charles James Bromhead,[292] *CB. Col. Comdg.* Regimental District, *Brecon*...	30 Aug. 59	20 Feb. 63	19 Oct. 72	1 Apr. 74	31 Jan. 85	31 Jan. 89	
Anthony Hepburn Murray, *Lt.Col.* R. Art	12 Dec. 57	27 Aug. 58	14 Dec. 68	31 Dec. 78	1 Feb. 85	1 Feb. 89	
John D. Pinkstone French,[293] *Lt.Col.* h.p. 19 Hussars	......	28 Feb. 74	16 Oct. 80	3 Apr. 83	7 Feb. 85	7 Feb. 89	7 Feb. 93
Wm. Hy. Mackinnon, *Major* (from h.p. Gren. Gds.); *A.A.Gen. Home District*, 26 July 93	......	22 June 70	Aug. 72	......	1 Jan. 81	10 Feb. 89	
James Webber Webber,[294] *Col. Comdg.* Regimental District, *Clonmel*	9 Oct. 63	13 Nov. 66	27 Apr. 70	1 July 81	11 Feb. 85	11 Feb. 89	
Arthur Wm. Roberts, *Lt.Col.* Bengal Cav.	20 Feb. 59	12 July 59	25 Oct. 66	28 Mar. 77	16 July 83	20 Feb. 89	
John Hibbert, *Lt.Col.* Bombay Infantry	27 Feb 59	21 Feb. 61	1 Mar. 69	27 Feb. 79	27 Feb. 85	27 Feb. 89	
Thos. Jas. Quin, *Lt.Col.* Bengal Infantry	4 Mar. 59	11 May 60	19 Oct. 68	28 Oct. 7	1 Jan. 84	4 Mar. 89	
Hy. Wm. John Senior, *Lt.Col.* Indian S.C.	4 Mar. 59	9 Nov. 60	4 Mar. 71	4 Mar. 79	4 Mar. 85	4 Mar. 89	
Allan Graeme Raper,[295] *Col.Comdg.* Regimental District, *Lichfield*	18 Feb. 62	21 Mar. 65	23 Nov. 70	6 Mar. 80	6 Mar. 85	6 Mar. 89	
William Crosby Siddons Mair.[296] *Col. Comdg.* Regimental District, *Warwick*	28 Mar. 58	16 Aug. 59	8 Aug. 65	1 Oct. 77	18 Mar. 85	18 Mar. 89	
p.s.c. Henry Harcourt Griffiths,[297] *Col. Comdg.* Regimental District, *Burnley*	6 Jan. 60	18 Sept.63	21 Aug. 67	26 Dec. 80	18 Mar. 85	18 Mar. 89	
Rich. Westmacott, *CB.DSO.Lt.Col.*Ind.S.C	19 Mar. 59	20 Feb. 61	19 Mar. 71	19 Mar. 79	19 Mar. 85	19 Mar. 89	
Elphinstone W. Begbie, *DSO. Lt.Col.* Madras Infantry	4 Apr. 59	25 Apr. 61	8 Mar. 71	4 Apr. 79	4 Apr. 85	4 Apr. 89	
Wm. L. Ranking, *Lt.Col.* Madras Inf. ...	4 Apr. 59	13 Sept.61	4 Apr. 71	4 Apr. 79	4 Apr. 85	4 Apr. 89	
p.s.c. Wm. Francis Moore Hutchinson, *Lt.Col.* h.p. Royal Artillery	......	1 Oct. 57	31 July 69	1 Oct. 77	1 Oct. 84	9 Apr. 89	23 May 90
William A. Salmon, *Lt.Col.* Indian S. C.	12 Apr. 59	14 May 61	12 Apr. 71	12 Apr. 79	12 Apr. 85	12 Apr. 89	
Francis A. Graves-Sawle, *Lt.Col.* Coldstream Guards	20 June 68	25 Nov. 68	7 Oct. 71	......	10 Dec. 81	18 Apr. 89	
Victor Edw. Law, *Lt.Col.* Madras Cavalry	20 Apr. 59	20 Apr. 60	16 July 64	28 Apr. 75	1 July 81	20 Apr. 89	
John B. B. Dickson,[298] *CB. Col. Comdg.* Regimental District, *Reading*	20 Jan. 60	1 Jan. 52	31 Dec. 72	1 July 81	25 Apr. 85	25 Apr. 89	
Henry Fyers Turner, *Lt.Col.* h.p. R. Engineers	......	23 Dec. 57	12 Aug. 71	31 Dec. 78	6 May 85	16 May 89	6 May 90
Edw. Lee Street,[299] *Lt.Col.* (from Regimental District), *Assistant Adjutant General, Edinburgh*, 17 Apr. 94	21 Feb. 60	8 Jan. 64	1 Sept.69	1 July 81	19 May 85	19 May 89	
Frederick Smalley, *Lt.Col.* Madras Inf...	20 May 59	1 Oct. 61	20 May 71	20 May 79	20 May 85	20 May 89	
Howard Kingscote,[300] *Lt.Col.* (from h.p. Oxfordshire Light Infantry), *Assistant Adjutant General, War Office*, 28 Dec.93	4 Mar. 62	6 Apr. 63	2 Sept.68	1 July 81	20 May 85	20 May 89	
Allan Maclean, *Col. Comdg.* Regimental District, *Northampton*	5 Sept.62	29 Mar. 64	8 June 70	1 July 81	20 May 85	20 May 89	
James Waterhouse, *Lt.Col.* Indian S. C...	......	10 June 59	10 June 71	10 June 79	10 June 85	10 June 89	
George E. Hancock, *Lt.Col.* Indian S. C...	......	10 June 59	10 June 71	10 June 79	10 June 85	10 June 89	
James Hay, *Lt.Col.* Indian Staff Corps...	11 June 59	22 Nov. 60	11 June 71	11 June 79	11 June 85	11 June 89	
James L. Fagan, *Lt.Col.* Indian S. C.....	11 June 59	9 July 61	11 June 71	11 June 79	11 June 85	11 June 89	
Thomas Richd Byng, *Lt.Col.* Indian S. C.	11 June 59	1 Jan. 62	11 June 71	11 June 79	11 June 85	11 June 89	
Arthur Singleton Wynne,[301] *CB. Col.* (from h.p. Yorkshire Lt. Inf.), *Deputy Adjutant General, Malta*, 12 Oct. 94...	4 Aug. 63	21 Aug. 67	22 Apr. 71	22 Nov. 79	15 June 85	15 June 89	
GeorgeR. J. Shakespear, *Lt.Col.*Ind.S.C.	7 Sept.60	17 Mar. 65	7 Sept.72	7 Sept.80	15 June 85	15 June 89	
Leyland Hornby,[302] *Col. Comdg.* Regimental District, *Kingston*	22 Sept.63	16 Jan. 66	14 Oct. 71	1 July 81	15 June 85	15 June 89	
Hon. Chas. C. G. Byng,[302]† *Lt.Col.* h.p. 1 Life Guards	8 June 67	30 Sept.68	9 Aug. 73	1 July 81	15 June 85	15 June 89	6 Dec. 93
Alf. Edw. Turner, *CB. Lt.Col.* R. Art.....	......	19 Dec. 60	11 Mar. 74	1 July 81	15 June 85	15 June 89	
Thomas Davison,[303]*Lt.Col.* h.p. 16 Lancers	8 June 67	31 July 69	7 Aug. 75	1 July 81	15 June 85	15 June 89	27 Jan. 92
Marsden Samuel James Sunderland,[304] *DSO. Col. Comdg.* Regtl. Dist., *Stirling*	24 May 61	17 Jan. 65	19 Jan. 76	5 Dec. 81	15 June 85	15 June 89	
Frederick Harvey Maturin, *Major*, East Surrey Regt	22 Sept.65	27 Feb. 69	9 Mar. 78	20 May 82	15 June 85	15 June 89	
Philip Durham Trotter,[305] *Lt.Col.* h.p. Argyll and Sutherland Highlanders	18 Oct. 64	1 Feb. 68	16 Feb. 78	21 Oct. 82	15 June 85	15 June 89	23 July 94
Fred. Meyer Wardrop,[306] *CB. Lt.Col.* h.p. 12 Lancers	30 June69	10 Aug. 70	1 May 78	18 Nov. 82	15 June 85	15 June 89	21 Dec. 92

Colonels.

	CORNET, 2nd LIEUT. or ENSIGN.	LIEUT.	CAPTAIN.	MAJOR.	LIEUT. COLONEL.	COLONEL.	WHEN PLACED ON HALF PAY.
John Compton Hanford, Lt. Col. 19 Hussars	.....	26 Mar. 74	1 July 81	18 Nov. 82	15 June 85	15 June 89	
Douglas Alex. Scott, DSO. Major (from Royal Engineers)	.....	8 Jan. 70	8 Jan. 82	18 Nov. 82	15 June 85	15 June 89	
Charles Coghlan Smyth,[307] CB. Major h.p. Welsh Regt.	5 Nov. 61	23 Aug. 67	14 Dec. 78	8 Dec. 82	15 June 85	15 June 89	10 Aug. 91
William FitzHenry Spaight, Lt. Col. Royal Engineers	.....	24 June 63	6 June 77	24 June 83	15 June 85	15 June 89	
p.s.c. Sir Edwin Henry H. Collen, KCIE. Lt.Col. Indian Staff Corps	.....	1 July 63	1 July 75	1 July 83	15 June 85	15 June 89	
Fras. John Graves,[308] Lt. Col. h.p. 20 Hus.	23 Jan. 69	28 Oct. 71	7 June 79	3 Oct. 83	15 June 85	15 June 89	9 Sept. 91
Morgan Samuel Crofton,[309] DSO. Major (from h.p. South Stafford Regiment), A. A. Gen. South Africa, 13 July 94	2 Sept. 68	7 May 70	31 Jan. 77	31 Oct. 83	15 June 85	15 June 89	
Francis Ventris, Major. Essex Regiment	.....	11 Feb. 75	5 Nov. 81	16 Dec. 83	15 June 85	15 June 89	
Woodburn Hunter, Major, R. Art.	.....	21 Mar. 65	1 Oct. 77	1 Jan. 84	15 June 85	15 June 89	
James Ford Dorward, Lt.Col. Royal Eng.	.....	19 July 64	1 Oct. 77	19 July 84	15 June 85	15 June 89	
Douglas M. Baillie Hamilton, Earl of Dundonald, Lt.Col. 2 Life Guards	6 July 70	28 Oct. 71	10 Apr. 78	12 Jan. 85	15 June 85	15 June 89	
Richard S. R. Fetherstonhaugh, Lt.Col. King's Royal Rifles	25 Sept. 67	28 Oct. 71	7 May 80	18 Apr. 85	15 June 85	15 June 89	
Robt. E. Cox, Lt.Col. Madras Infantry	16 June 59	1 Jan. 62	16 June 71	16 June 79	16 June 85	16 June 89	
John Talbot Coke,[310] Col. (from h.p. King's Own Scottish Borderers), Assist. Adj. Gen. Curragh, 12 Oct. 94	24 June 59	23 Aug. 61	21 Aug. 66	4 Nov. 79	21 June 85	21 June 89	
John Randal Wilmer, Lt.Col. Indian S. C.	.....	22 June 59	22 June 71	22 June 79	22 June 85	22 June 89	
Colin Hubert Garbett, Lt.Col. Indian S. C.	27 June 59	4 Feb. 61	27 June 71	27 June 79	27 June 85	27 June 89	
W. Scott Peat, Lt.Col. Bombay Cavalry	27 June 59	6 Feb. 61	27 June 71	27 June 79	27 June 85	27 June 89	
Robert Athorpe, Col. (from h.p. Royal Engineers)	.....	22 June 58	27 Jan. 72	11 June 79	2 July 85	2 July 89	
James Fellowes, Lt.Col. h.p. Royal Eng.	.....	22 June 58	17 Feb. 72	8 Sept. 79	2 July 85	2 July 89	2 July 90
Edwin M. L. Marriott, Lt.Col. Bengal Inf.	9 July 59	20 Feb. 61	16 Dec. 68	9 July 79	9 July 85	9 July 89	
Fred. George Slade, CB. Major, R. Art.	.....	15 Dec. 71	13 July 81	21 May 84	15 June 85	10 July 89	
Geo. Edw. Reade, Lt.Col. Bengal Infantry	15 July 59	1 Mar. 61	16 Dec. 68	15 July 79	15 July 85	15 July 89	
Hy. Richd. Shelley, Lt.Col. Madras Inf.	20 July 59	1 Jan. 62	16 Dec. 71	20 July 79	20 July 85	20 July 89	
Henry Hodson Hooke,[311] Col. Comdg. Regimental District, Derby	13 Aug. 58	17 Sept. 61	23 Oct. 67	1 July 81	21 July 85	21 July 89	
Henry Coker Adams, Lt.Col.h.p. Oxford Light Infantry	12 June 63	26 Jan. 66	30 Sept. 68	1 July 81	27 July 85	27 July 89	27 July 91
Michael Henry Saward, Lt.Col. (from Royal Artillery)	.....	9 Dec. 59	11 Dec. 72	26 May 80	28 July 85	28 July 89	
Edward Mockler, Lt.Col. Bombay Inf.	2 Aug. 59	1 Jan. 62	14 Oct. 69	2 Aug. 79	2 Aug. 85	2 Aug. 89	
Fred. Day Mander, Lt.Col. Bombay Inf.	2 Aug. 59	1 Jan. 62	14 Oct. 69	2 Aug. 79	2 Aug. 85	2 Aug. 89	
Jas. Rutherford, Lt.Col. Bombay Infantry	4 Aug. 59	1 Jan. 62	14 Oct. 69	4 Aug. 79	4 Aug. 85	4 Aug. 89	
Geo. Edw. Weston, Lt.Col. Madras Inf.	4 Aug. 59	1 Jan. 62	4 Aug. 71	4 Aug. 79	4 Aug. 85	4 Aug. 89	
Jas. M'Cleverty,[312] Col. Comdg. Regimental District, Preston	10 July 68	27 July 70	4 Aug. 75	1 July 81	4 Aug. 85	4 Aug. 89	
John Purefoy E. Jervoise, Lt.Col.h.p. 3 Hus.	16 Nov. 66	3 June 68	21 June 71	1 July 81	5 Aug. 85	5 Aug. 89	14 Apr. 91
George R. Peart, Lt.Col. Indian S. C.	12 Aug. 59	1 Jan. 62	14 Oct. 69	12 Aug. 79	12 Aug. 85	12 Aug. 89	
Cresswell K. C. Rooke,[313] Lt.Col. h.p. Royal Scots	20 Mar. 57	2 Mar. 60	2 Sept. 68	1 July 81	14 Aug. 85	14 Aug. 89	14 Aug. 91
Fras. Walter Cary, Col. Comdg. Regimental District, Shrewsbury	8 Feb. 61	29 May 63	24 July 69	1 July 81	15 Aug. 85	15 Aug. 89	
Thomas Walker, Lt.Col. Royal Artillery	.....	10 June 59	22 Mar. 71	18 June 79	17 Aug. 85	17 Aug. 89	
p.s.c. Ivor John C. Herbert, CB. Major, Grenadier Guards	.....	5 Nov. 70	25 Nov. 74	18 Nov. 82	2 May 83	18 Aug. 89	
David Wm. Inglis, Lt.Col. Bengal Inf.	20 Aug. 59	5 May 61	29 Jan. 69	13 Aug. 79	20 Aug. 85	20 Aug. 89	
Chas. Freuk. Hughes, Lt.Col. Indian S C	7 June 61	31 Jan. 63	7 June 73	2 Mar. 81	7 June 87	23 Aug. 89	
Alex. Clark-Kennedy, Lt.Col. Ind. S C	29 July 62	15 Nov. 64	29 July 74	29 July 82	29 July 88	23 Aug. 89	
John P. Brabazon, CB. Major, 4 Hus.	.....	13 June 74	13 Nov. 79	2 Mar. 81	21 May 84	28 Aug. 89	
Edw. G. Lillingston, Lt.Col. Indian S. C.	30 Aug. 59	17 Nov. 63	30 Aug. 71	30 Aug. 79	30 Aug. 85	30 Aug. 89	
Robert Alexander, Lt.Col. Royal Artillery	.....	9 Dec. 59	1 Aug. 72	24 Jan. 80	1 Sept. 85	1 Sept. 89	
James Ffoord Hilton,[314] Col. Comdg.Regimental District, Carlisle	11 Feb. 62	3 June 64	14 June 72	1 July 81	2 Sept. 85	2 Sept. 89	
Duncan Geo. Pitcher, Lt.Col. Indian S.C	3 Sept. 59	10 June 61	3 Sept. 71	3 Sept. 79	3 Sept. 85	3 Sept. 89	
George John Burgmann, Lt.Col. R. Art.	.....	1 Oct. 57	8 Sept. 71	20 Feb. 78	2 Feb. 85	4 Sept. 89	
Herbert H. P. Cowper, Lt.Col.Bengal Cav.	4 Sept. 59	4 Sept. 60	13 Oct. 70	4 Sept. 79	4 Sept. 85	4 Sept. 89	
Edw. Jas. Gunthorpe, Lt.Col. Indian S. C.	7 Sept. 59	1 Jan. 62	7 Sept. 71	7 Sept. 79	7 Sept. 85	7 Sept. 89	
Geo. John Skinner, DSO. Lt. Col. Ind. S.C	15 Sept. 59	22 Dec. 63	16 Sept. 71	16 Sept. 79	16 Sept. 85	16 Sept. 89	
Frank W. Chatterton, CIE. Lt.Col.Ben.Inf.	20 Sept. 59	6 July 61	29 Jan. 69	20 Sept. 79	20 Sept. 85	20 Sept. 89	
Fras. Wm. Rhodes, DSO.Lt.Col.h.p. 1 Drag.	.....	23 Apr. 75	15 Oct. 84	19 Sept. 85	20 Sept. 85	20 Sept. 89	19 May 91
Edm. Donough C. O'Brien, Lt.Col. h.p. Royal Engineers	.....	1 Oct. 58	3 Aug. 72	13 Sept. 79	22 Sept. 85	22 Sept. 89	22 Sept. 90
John Kinder Spilling, Lt.Col. h.p. 13 Hus.	3 June 68	4 Feb. 71	15 July 78	1 July 81	29 Sept. 85	29 Sept. 89	1 July 92
Ralph Leeke, Major, h.p. Gren. Guards	.....	23 Mar. 70	17 Feb. 72	.....	7 Aug. 80	1 Oct. 89	10 Dec. 90
Richd. T. M. Lang, Lt.Col. Bengal Cav.	12 Oct. 59	9 Dec. 60	6 Apr. 71	12 Oct. 79	12 Oct. 85	12 Oct. 89	
Chas. H. T. Marshall, Lt.Col. Indian S. C.	12 Oct. 59	23 July 61	12 Oct. 71	12 Oct. 79	12 Oct. 85	12 Oct. 89	
Alfred Anderson, Lt.Col. Madras Inf.	20 Oct. 59	1 Jan. 62	20 Oct. 71	20 Oct. 79	20 Oct. 85	20 Oct. 89	
Geo. D'A. Jackson, Lt.Col. Bengal Cav.	20 Nov. 59	1 Jan. 62	20 Nov. 71	20 Nov. 79	20 Nov. 85	20 Nov. 89	
H. St. J. V. Le M. Thomas-Le Marchant, Lt.Col. h.p. Royal Artillery	.....	1 Oct. 57	7 Jan. 71	1 Jan. 78	1 Jan. 85	28 Nov. 89	28 Nov. 90
Arthur W. L. Anderson, Lt.Col. Mad. Inf.	4 Dec. 59	1 Jan. 62	4 Dec. 71	4 Dec. 79	4 Dec. 85	4 Dec. 89	
p.s.c. Ralph Edward Allen, Lt.Col. East Yorkshire Regiment	7 Apr. 65	12 June 69	21 Oct. 76	26 July 82	9 Dec. 85	9 Dec. 89	
Charles Edmond Knox,[315] Lt.Col. h.p. Shropshire Light Infantry	30 June 65	7 Aug. 67	11 June 76	1 July 83	9 Dec. 85	9 Dec. 89	11 Feb. 94
Richard Henry Jelf, Lt.Col. R. Eng.	.....	22 June 65	17 Apr. 78	22 June 85	9 Dec. 85	9 Dec. 89	
John Edw. Campbell, Lt.Col. Indian S. C	10 Dec. 59	28 Oct. 61	10 Dec. 71	10 Dec. 79	10 Dec. 85	10 Dec. 89	
p.s.c. Hon. George Hugh Gough, CB. Lt.Col. 14 Hussars	28 Oct. 71	28 Oct. 71	23 July 79	18 Nov. 82	15 June 85	16 Dec. 89	
Edw. P. Mainwaring, Lt.Col. Ben. Inf.	20 Dec. 59	14 Nov. 61	29 June 69	20 Dec. 79	20 Dec. 85	20 Dec. 89	
Jas. G. R. D. MacNeill, CB.Lt.Col.Mad.Inf.	22 Dec. 59	1 Apr. 62	21 Dec. 71	22 Dec. 79	22 Dec. 85	22 Dec. 89	
William Head Bayly,[316] Col.Comdg.Regimental District, Maidstone	26 Feb. 67	22 June 70	8 Dec. 77	1 July 81	23 Dec. 85	23 Dec. 89	

Colonels.

	CORNET, 2nd LIEUT. OR ENSIGN	LIEUT.	CAPTAIN.	MAJOR.	LIEUT. COLONEL.	COLONEL.	WHEN PLACED ON HALF PAY.
Jos. G. Fagan, *Lt.Col.* Bombay Cavalry	27 Dec. 59	10 June 61	27 Dec. 71	27 Dec. 79	27 Dec. 85	27 Dec. 89	
Thos. Oliver Wingate, *Lt.Col.* Indian S.C.	30 Dec. 59	17 Nov. 63	30 Dec. 71	30 Dec. 79	30 Dec. 85	30 Dec. 89	
Josceline Henenge Wodehouse, *CB*, *CMG. Major,* R. Art.		2 May 72	1 Oct. 81	21 May 84	2 Jan. 86	2 Jan. 90	
Fras. Hy. Thomas, *Lt.Col.* Bengal Inf.	4 Jan. 60	1 Jan. 62	25 Aug. 69	4 Jan. 80	4 Jan. 85	4 Jan. 90	
Evolyn S. Skinner, *Lt.Col.* Indian S.C.	4 Jan. 60	22 May 62	4 Jan. 72	4 Jan. 80	4 Jan. 86	4 Jan. 90	
Wm. F. Prideaux, *CSI. Lt.Col.* Indian S.C.	12 Jan. 60	9 Mar. 62	12 Jan. 72	12 Jan. 72	12 Jan. 86	12 Jan. 90	
James Cook, *Lt.Col.* Indian Staff Corps	8 June 61	30 July 62	8 June 73	22 Nov. 79	27 Jan. 86	27 Jan. 90	
John Ramsay Slade, *CB. Major,* h.p.; Royal Art.; *A. D. C. to the Queen*		18 Dec. 61	16 Jan. 75	2 Mar. 81	8 July 87	29 Jan. 90	8 July 87
Edw. Lee Rose, *Col. and Com.* R. Mar.	14 Apr. 59	22 Dec. 60	24 Mar. 74	1 July 81	1 Feb. 86	1 Feb. 90	
D℅ Arthur Geo. Hammond, *CB. DSO.* *Lt.Col.* Indian Staff Corps	7 June 61	14 May 62	7 June 73	7 June 81	7 June 87	12 Feb. 90	
p.s.c. Wm. Assheton Earnley Wilmot, *Dep. Judge Advocate, London,* 17 Jan. 86	29 Mar. 61	9 Aug. 64	14 June 76	1 July 81	22 Feb. 86	22 Feb. 90	
Charles W. H. Wilson,[317] *Col. Comdg.* Regimental District, *Wrexham*	29 Dec. 57	15 Nov. 51	4 Sept. 67	13 Feb. 81	24 Feb. 86	24 Feb. 90	
Chas. L. Prendergast, *Lt.Col.* Bengal Inf.	4 Mar. 60	1 Jan. 62	29 Oct. 69	4 Mar. 80	4 Mar. 85	4 Mar. 90	
Fred. Wm. Harington,[318] *Col. Comdg.* Regimental District, *York*	28 May 58	3 Oct. 6	8 May 72	1 July 81	7 Mar. 86	7 Mar. 90	
Walter Scott, *Lt.Col.* Indian Staff Corps	12 Mar. 60	27 May 62	12 Mar. 72	12 Mar. 80	12 Mar. 86	12 Mar. 90	
Henry Blackburne Hamilton,[319] *Lt.Col.* h.p. 14 Hussars	21 July 64	15 May 66	24 Mar. 69	1 July 81	17 Mar. 86	17 Mar. 90	1 July 91
Norman R. Stewart, *Major,* Indian S. C.		3 Dec. 71	29 Oct. 79	2 Mar. 81	15 June 85	28 Mar. 90	
Mark M. Gillies,[320] *Col. Comdg.* Regimental District, *Bodmin*	15 June 55	20 Apr. 58	20 Feb. 64	1 Oct. 77	28 Mar. 86	28 Mar. 90	
Hon. Everard C. Digby,[321] *Major,* h.p. Grenadier Guards		24 June 70	19 Oct. 72		1 Apr. 82	31 Mar. 90	2 July 90
Villiers Hatton, *Major,* Grenadier Guards		27 Aug. 70	4 Dec. 72		5 July 82	31 Mar. 90	
Thomas A. St. Quintin,[322] *Col.* (from h.p. 8 Hussars), *Assist. Inspector of Remounts,* 19 Oct. 92	30 Dec. 59	16 Jan. 63	17 Aug. 70	12 Nov. 79	31 Mar. 86	31 Mar. 90	
Jas. Edw. Harris, *Lt.Col.* h.p. Suffolk Regt.	6 Jan. 60	3 Oct. 62	2 Dec. 68	1 July 81	1 Apr. 86	1 Apr. 90	4 July 94
Henry Brooke Wilson,[323] *Col.* (from *Lt.Col.* Northampton Regt.), *Assist. Adj. General, Cork,* 19 Jan. 91	24 Aug. 58	10 June 62	16 Sept. 68	1 July 81	7 Apr. 86	7 Apr. 90	
Reginald Garnett,[324] *CB. Lt.Col.* h.p. Seaforth Highlanders; *Aide de Camp to the Queen*	30 Jan. 63	26 May 65	6 July 74	2 Mar. 81	8 May 89	9 Apr. 90	8 May 93
p.s.c. Francis Cochran,[325] *Col. Comdg.* Regimental District, *Galway*	8 July 62	31 May 64	23 Mar. 66	31 Dec. 78	21 Apr. 86	21 Apr. 90	
Wm. Brooks Butlin, *Col. Comdg.* Regimental District, *Chester*	22 June 60	7 Nov. 62	19 Feb. 70	1 July 81	21 Apr. 86	21 Apr. 90	
Almeric George Spencer,[337] *Lt.Col.* (from h.p. Essex Regiment), *Commanding West India Depot* 27 Sept. 93	29 Jan. 61	28 July 63	12 Nov. 70	1 July 81	21 Apr. 86	21 Apr. 90	
John Henry Barnard,[328] *CB. CMG. Col. Comdg.* Regimental District, *Tralee; Aide de Camp to the Queen*	8 May 66	28 July 69	7 Mar. 77	2 Mar. 81	20 May 89	23 Apr. 90	
Starling Meux Benson, *Lt.Col.* h.p. 17 Lancers	20 Oct. 65	27 Feb. 67	27 July 70	1 July 81	27 Apr. 86	27 Apr. 90	15 Jan. 92
Wm. B. Warner, *Lt.Col.* Madras Cavalry	1 July 61	1 July 62	1 July 73	1 July 81	17 May 86	17 May 90	
George Simpson, *Lt.Col.* Indian S.C.	27 Nov. 61	13 Oct. 64	27 Nov. 73	27 Nov. 81	17 May 86	17 May 90	
Aug. Chas. Fred. FitzGeorge, *Major,* n.p. Hussars; *Equerry in Waiting to H.R.H. the Duke of Cambridge*	23 Dec. 64	14 July 69	24 Nov. 77	1 July 81	18 May 86	18 May 90	14 July 86
p.s.c. Edward S. Creek,[329] *Col.* (from h.p. Welsh Fusiliers), *Assist. Adj. General, Portsmouth,* 21 Aug. 94	25 June 61	9 Sept. 64	3 May 71	1 July 81	26 May 86	26 May 90	
Henry Collingwood,[330] *Col. Comdg.* Regimental District, *Devizes*	26 July 57	18 May 58	16 Sept. 68	1 July 81	31 May 86	31 May 90	
Joseph G. T. Carruthers, *Lt.Col.* Ben. Inf.	8 June 60	1 Jan. 62	27 Nov. 69	25 May 80	25 May 86	8 June 90	
Fred. Alex. Wilson, *Lt.Col.* Indian S. C.		8 June 60	8 June 72	8 June 80	8 June 86	8 June 90	
Vincent Rivaz, *Lt.Col.* Indian Staff C.		8 June 60	8 June 72	8 June 80	8 June 86	8 June 90	
Farquhar Glennie,[332] *Lt.Col.* (from h.p. S. Wales Borderers), *Commandant R.M. School of Music* 20 Sept. 94	31 July 60	26 Feb. 64	26 Mar. 73	1 July 81	9 June 86	9 June 90	
p.s.c. Arch. Glen, *Col. Comdg.* Regimental District, *Lincoln*	4 Feb. 62	19 July 64	22 Mar. 76	1 July 81	18 June 86	18 June 90	
Inigo R. Jones, *Major,* Scots Guards		18 Dec. 66	4 Feb. 71		15 Mar. 79	1 July 90	
p.s.c. Hy. L. Dundas,[334] *Major* h.p., East Yorkshire Regiment; *Assistant Adjutant General, Dublin,* 1 Jan. 92	17 July 63	27 July 66	25 June 73	1 July 81	1 July 86	1 July 90	2 July 89
Thos. Rennie Cowie, *Lt.Col.* Indian S.C.	4 July 60	1 Jan. 62	4 July 72	4 July 80	4 July 86	4 July 90	
William Gordon, *Col. Comdg.* Regimental District, *Fort George*	15 Oct. 61	2 Oct. 63	22 Jan. 67	1 May 80	11 July 86	11 July 90	
C. Pilcher Temple,[336] *DSO. Col. Comdg.* Regimental District, *Worcester*	19 Aug. 62	14 Mar. 65	23 May 74	1 July 81	14 July 86	14 July 90	
Elliot Alex. Money, *Lt.Col.* Indian S.C.	16 July 60	22 Aug. 63	16 July 72	16 July 80	16 July 86	16 July 90	
Herbert M. Ramsay, *Lt.Col.* Bengal Inf.	4 Aug. 60	1 Jan. 62	27 Nov. 69	20 July 80	4 Aug. 86	4 Aug. 90	
Hugh Richard, *Visct.* Downe,[337] *CIE.* (from 10 Hussars); *Aide de Camp to the Duke of Cambridge* 3 Aug. 92	8 Aug. 65	10 Nov. 69	25 June 73	29 Nov. 79	14 July 86	7 Aug. 90	
Edmund Carrington,[338] *Col.* (from h.p. Worcester Regiment), *Dep. Qr. Mr. General, Bombay Army,* 8 Mar. 91	7 Nov. 62	4 Nov. 64	9 Oct. 69	1 July 81	11 Aug. 86	11 Aug. 90	
Wm. G. Cumming, *CIE. Lt.Col.* R. Eng.		8 June 60	3 Aug. 72	30 Dec. 78	12 Aug. 86	12 Aug. 90	
Fredk. Jervis Home, *CSI. Lt.Col.* R. Eng.	11 June 58	27 Aug. 62	14 Dec. 70	31 Dec. 78	12 Aug. 86	12 Aug. 90	
Edw. D'Oyley Twemlow, *Lt.Col.* R. Eng.		9 Dec. 59	14 Jan. 71	31 Dec. 78	12 Aug. 86	12 Aug. 90	
Hy. Hills Goodeve, *Lt.Col.* (from R. Art.)		1 Oct. 58	1 Oct. 71	1 Jan. 79	1 Jan. 86	17 Aug. 90	
James Murray Murray, *Lt.Col.* (from Royal Artillery)		22 June 59	11 Nov. 71	27 June 79	27 June 86	7 Sept. 90	

Colonels.

Name	Cornet, 2nd Lieut. or Ensign.	Lieut.	Captain.	Major.	Lieut. Colonel.	Colonel.	When placed on half pay.
Trevor Bruce Tyler, *Lt.Col.* h.p. R. Artillery	......	22 June 59	23 Dec. 71	23 Aug. 79	7 Sept. 86	7 Sept. 90	30 Sept. 93
George Strahan, *Lt.Col.* Royal Engineers	......	10 Dec. 58	14 Jan. 71	10 May 81	8 Sept. 86	8 Sept. 90	
Francis Capel Manley,[343] *Major*, h.p. Coldstream Guards	......	16 Mar. 70	19 Nov. 73	......	7 Nov. 83	29 Sept. 90	29 July 91
Chas. G. Leggett,[344] *Col. Comdg.* Regimental District, *Naas*	14 Aug. 60	24 Nov. 63	3 May 71	1 July 81	29 Sept. 86	29 Sept. 90	
Chas. F. Lawson, *Col. Comdg.* Regimental District, *Richmond*	18 Jan. 61	1 Mar. 64	17 Feb. 72	1 July 81	29 Sept. 86	29 Sept. 90	
William Hutchinson Mulloy, *Lt.Col.* h.p. Royal Engineers	......	21 Dec. 58	3 Aug. 72	8 Nov. 79	1 Oct. 86	1 Oct. 90	1 Oct. 91
William Randall Slacke, *Lt.Col.* h.p. Royal Engineers	......	21 Dec. 58	3 Aug. 72	9 Nov. 79	1 Oct. 86	1 Oct. 90	1 Oct. 91
Montague J. King - Harman, *Lt.Col.* Indian Staff Corps	......	2 Oct. 60	2 Oct. 72	2 Oct. 80	2 Oct. 86	2 Oct. 90	
Douglas C. De Wend, *Col. Comdg.* Regimental District, *Beverley*	4 July 60	12 July 64	15 Apr. 74	1 July 81	6 Oct. 86	6 Oct. 90	
Arthur H. Luck, *Col. Comdg.* Regimental District, *Pontefract*	19 Aug. 62	18 Apr. 65	9 Nov. 67	1 July 81	13 Oct. 86	13 Oct. 90	
Andrew McC. Bruce, *Lt.Col.* Bengal Inf.	4 Nov. 60	1 Jan. 62	27 Nov. 69	4 Nov. 80	4 Nov. 86	4 Nov. 90	
John Donaldson Cruickshank, *Lt.Col.* Royal Engineers	......	9 Dec. 59	14 Jan. 71	4 July 79	6 Nov. 86	6 Nov. 90	
Allan Chaplin, *Lt. Col.* Madras Infantry	12 Nov. 60	10 Dec. 62	12 Nov. 72	12 Nov. 80	12 Nov. 86	12 Nov. 90	
George Lecky, *Lt.Col.* Indian Staff Corps	12 Nov. 60	30 Dec. 62	12 Nov. 72	12 Nov. 80	12 Nov. 86	12 Nov. 90	
Fred. Wm. Buller, *Lt.Col.* Madras Cav.	4 Dec. 60	1 Jan. 62	15 Aug. 71	4 Dec. 80	4 Dec. 86	4 Dec. 90	
Robert Vansittart Riddell, *Lt.Col.* R.Eng.	......	10 June 59	20 Jan. 71	3 June 81	6 Dec. 86	6 Dec. 90	
William Frederick Kerr,[345] *Col. Comdg.* Regimental District, *Canterbury*	23 Mar. 58	5 Feb. 62	16 May 68	1 July 81	10 Dec. 86	10 Dec. 90	
James Brown M'Dougal, *Col. Comdg.* Regimental District, *Bristol*	3 Aug. 66	29 Jan. 70	15 Feb. 71	1 July 81	11 Dec. 86	11 Dec. 90	
p.s.c. Edwin Wardroper,[346] *Lt.Col.* h.p. Sussex Regiment (107 Foot)	9 Mar. 66	29 July 67	17 Feb. 76	1 July 81	14 Dec. 86	14 Dec. 90	14 Dec. 90
Louis H. E. Tucker, *CIE. Lt.Col.* Ben.Inf.	19 Dec. 60	1 Jan. 62	28 Nov. 69	18 Dec. 80	19 Dec. 86	19 Dec. 90	
Chas. Edw. Shepherd, *Lt.Col.* Indian S.C.	19 Dec. 60	1 Jan. 62	19 Dec. 72	19 Dec. 80	19 Dec. 86	19 Dec. 90	
John Alex. Temple, *Lt.Col.* Indian S. C.	19 Dec. 60	1 Jan. 62	19 Dec. 72	19 Dec. 80	19 Dec. 86	19 Dec. 90	
Alex. John Shaw, *Lt.Col.* Madras Inf.	20 Dec. 60	23 Mar. 63	20 Dec. 72	20 Dec. 80	20 Dec. 86	20 Dec. 90	
Robt. G. E. Dalrymple, *Lt.Col.* Indian S.C.	20 Dec. 60	12 Oct. 69	20 Dec. 72	20 Dec. 80	20 Dec. 86	20 Dec. 90	
Francis Thos. Ebden, *Lt.Col.* Indian S.C.	29 Dec. 60	5 Oct. 62	29 Dec. 72	29 Dec. 80	29 Dec. 86	29 Dec. 90	
Wm. Gustavus Nicholson, *CB. Major* (from h.p. Royal Engineers)	......	21 Mar. 65	16 Mar. 78	2 Mar. 81	1 July 87	1 Jan. 91	
p.c. Lord Wm. L. De la Poer Beresford,[348] *KCIE. Major*, h.p. 9 Lancers	8 June 67	6 July 70	27 Dec. 76	15 Dec. 84	1 July 87	1 Jan. 91	27 Jan. 94
John Thomas Watling, *Lt.Col.* Indian S.C.	26 Nov. 61	26 July 64	26 Nov. 73	26 Nov. 81	26 Nov. 87	20 May 91	
p.s.c. Alex. Marin Delavoye, *Col.* (from h.p. Essex Regt.) ; *Assist. Director of Military Education* 2 July 91	9 Feb. 64	22 Dec. 68	14 Sept. 78	3 Jan. 82	17 Apr. 88	2 July 91	
Thos. Hungerford Holdich, *CB. CIE. Lt.Col.* Royal Engineers	......	17 Dec. 62	4 June 76	2 Mar. 81	16 Feb. 87	1 Sept. 91	
Aug. Henry Turner, *Lt.Col.* Indian S.O	24 May 61	14 July 65	24 May 73	24 May 81	24 May 87	1 Sept. 91	
Celadon C. Brownlow, *Lt.Col.* Ind. S.C.	8 June 61	30 July 62	8 June 73	8 June 81	8 June 87	1 Sept. 91	
p.s.c. Patrick Douglas Jeffreys,[350] *Major* (from h.p. Connaught Rangers), *A. A. Gen. Bengal*, 6 Jan. 94	9 Nov. 66	9 Feb. 70	13 Mar. 78	1 July 81	1 July 87	1 Sept. 91	
John Becher Ormsby, *Col.* (from h.p. R. Art.), *Supdt. R. Gunpowder Factory* 27 July 94	......	19 June 60	23 Nov. 72	19 Feb. 81	8 Apr. 87	30 Sept. 91	
Matthew Townsend Sale, *CMG. Lt.Col.* (from h.p. Royal Engineers)	......	1 July 61	26 Aug. 73	1 July 81	1 July 88	30 Sept. 91	
p.s.c. Sir St. Vincent Alex. Hammick,[351] *Bart. Major* h.p. Oxford Lt. Infantry; *Assist. Adj. Gen. Egypt*, 10 Nov. 91	12 Mar. 61	29 May 63	26 Feb. 70	1 July 81	21 June 87	10 Nov. 91	22 June 91
Ian S. M. Hamilton,[352] *DSO. Col.* (from Gordon Highlanders) *Military Secretary to Sir G. S. White* 8 Apr. 93	......	24 Apr. 73	25 Feb. 82	7 Nov. 85	1 July 87	25 Nov. 91	
p.s.c. Edm. Roche Elles, *CB. Major* (from Royal Artillery)	......	15 Jan. 67	5 Dec. 78	18 Nov. 82	7 Dec. 88	7 Dec. 91	
Geo. Fred. Young, *Lt.Col.* Indian S. C.	30 June 65	30 Mar. 69	30 June 77	30 June 85	7 Dec. 88	7 Dec. 91	
Robert Patch, *Lt. Col.* Indian Staff Corps	12 June 63	27 July 66	12 June 75	12 June 83	7 Dec. 88	7 Dec. 91	
Arthur Broadwood, *Major*, Scots Guards	......	5 May 69	28 Oct. 71	......	20 Mar. 81	2 June 92	
p.s.c. Douglas Forde Jones, *Major* (from h.p. R. Art.), *Director of Army Schools*, 18 June 92	......	17 July 66	18 June 78	18 June 84	17 June 89	18 June 92	
Pelham Jas. Maitland, *Lt.Col.* Indian S.C.	2 May 66	8 Feb. 70	2 May 78	2 May 86	16 Feb. 87	11 Aug. 92	
Edward W. G. Byam, *Col.* 2nd Com. R. Mar.	12 May 59	26 Dec. 61	30 Nov. 75	1 July 81	12 May 87	8 Sept. 92	
Thomas Deane, *Lt.Col.* Indian Staff Corps	4 Mar. 62	24 Aug. 68	4 Mar. 74	4 Mar. 82	4 Mar. 88	21 Sept. 92	
Robt. Hy. F. Rennick, *Lt.Col.* Indian S.C.	......	18 Dec. 61	18 Dec. 73	18 Dec. 81	1 July 87	5 Oct. 92	
George Arthur French, *CMG. Lt.Col.* (from Royal Artillery)	......	19 June 60	11 Dec. 72	1 July 81	1 Oct. 87	2 Nov. 92	
John Ignatius Morris, *Col. 2nd Com.* Royal Marines	12 May 59	15 Jan. 62	6 Dec. 75	1 July 81	12 May 87	20 Nov. 92	
Thomas William Visct. Coke,[354] *Major*, h.p. Scots Guards, *Lt. Colonel Norfolk Art. East Div. R. Artillery*	......	15 Feb. 68	30 Aug. 71	......	1 Dec. 80	29 Nov. 92	21 Feb. 94
Robert Hunter Murray, *Major*, Seaforth Highlanders	18 Dec. 67	28 Oct. 71	8 Apr. 80	2 Mar. 81	18 Nov. 82	10 Dec. 92	
Albert Jas. Hepper, *DSO. Lt.Col.* h.p. R. Eng.	......	22 Dec. 59	21 Sept. 72	1 July 81	1 Oct. 87	20 Dec. 92	1 Oct. 91
p.s.c. Edward Thomas Henry Hutton,[355] *CB. Major*, h.p. King's Royal Rifles, *Aide de Camp to the Queen, & Com. Colonial Forces, N. S. Wales, with local rank of Major General*, 20 Apr. 93	9 Aug. 67	9 Aug. 71	14 July 79	18 Nov. 82	29 May 89	21 Dec. 92	29 May 89
Arthur Gethin Creagh, *Major*, R. Art.	......	12 Feb. 74	14 Apr. 83	15 Apr. 83	1 June 85	1 Jan. 93	
Alfred Gaselee, *CB. Lt.Col.* Indian S. C.	9 Jan. 63	11 Oct. 66	9 Jan. 75	2 Mar. 81	9 Jan. 89	1 Feb. 93	

Colonels.

Name	CORNET, 2ND LIEUT. OR ENSIGN.	LIEUT.	CAPTAIN.	MAJOR.	LIEUT. COLONEL.	COLONEL.	WHEN PLACED ON HALF PAY.
H.R.H. Prince Henry Maurice of Battenberg, K G. Gov. of the Isle of Wight and of Carisbrooke Castle	......	......	......	......	21 June 87	22 Feb. 93	
William Albert Bridge, Col. Comdg. Regimental District, Glencorse	3 June 59	4 June 61	12 Feb. 67	21 May 80	21 June 87	25 Feb. 93	
Edward A. Brind,356 Lt. Col. (from Regimental Dist.), Chief Recruiting Officer, London, 18 Sept. 94	9 Feb. 64	21 Aug. 66	18 Dec. 75	23 June 81	1 July 87	16 Mar. 93	
Wm. Percival Tomkins, CIE. Lt. Col. R. Eng.	......	8 June 60	3 Aug. 72	1 July 81	26 May 88	12 Apr. 93	
Charles Strahan, Lt. Col. R. Engineers	......	8 June 60	20 Aug. 72	2 Mar. 81	1 July 88	12 Apr. 93	
Ralph R. E. Drake-Brockman, Lt. Col. h.p. Royal Engineers	......	19 Dec. 60	25 Aug. 73	1 July 81	1 July 88	22 Apr. 93	1 July 93
p.s.c. William Everett, CMG. Lt. Col. (from h.p. West Riding Regt.), A. A. Gen. for Intelligence, War Office, 7 June 93	28 June 64	11 Jan. 67	9 Sept. 74	1 July 81	11 Jan. 88	7 June 93	
Robert C. Græme,357 Col. Comdg. Regimental District, Ashton	1 Apr. 62	15 May 67	22 Mar. 71	1 July 81	4 July 87	12 July 93	
Francis Harwood Poore, Col. Sec. Com. R. Marine Artillery	14 Apr. 59	13 Sept. 60	1 Mar. 70	1 July 81	14 Apr. 87	6 Aug. 93	
Donald J. S. McLeod, DSO. Lt. Col. Madras Cavalry	20 July 61	20 July 62	20 July 73	20 July 81	20 July 87	12 Aug. 93	
John Farquharson, CB. Lt. Col. (from h.p. Royal Engineers)	......	22 June 59	3 Aug. 72	1 July 81	17 Mar. 87	29 Aug. 93	
Rowland Walkey, Lt. Col. (from R. Art.)	......	19 June 60	23 Nov. 72	19 Feb. 81	8 Apr. 87	29 Aug. 93	
Chas. Edw. Hussey, Col. Comdg. Regimental District, Hounslow	20 Mar. 59	10 June 62	14 Sept. 70	1 July 81	21 June 87	29 Aug. 93	
Henry John Wolsteyn Geble, Lt. Col. h.p. Royal Engineers	......	21 Dec. 59	3 Aug. 72	1 July 81	27 Aug. 87	29 Aug. 93	27 Aug. 92
Wm. Hy. Patten, Lt. Col. (from h.p. R. Eng.)	......	21 Dec. 59	28 Aug. 72	1 July 81	1 Oct. 87	29 Aug. 93	
Robert D. E. Lockhart, Lt. Col. h.p. R. Art.	......	19 June 60	11 Dec. 72	1 July 81	1 Oct. 87	29 Aug. 93	1 Oct. 92
p.s.c. Henry Knollys, Lt. Col. h.p. R. Art.	......	1 Nov. 60	16 Apr. 73	1 July 81	29 Jan. 88	29 Aug. 93	26 Apr. 93
p.s.c. William Toke Dooner,358 Col. Comdg. Regimental District, Armagh	30 Jan. 63	6 Feb. 66	24 Mar. 75	1 July 81	1 Feb. 88	29 Aug. 92	
Fred. Vincent G. Bird, Col. 2nd Com. R. Marines	29 Mar. 60	10 Dec. 63	27 Sept. 77	1 July 81	29 Mar. 88	29 Aug. 93	
William Campbell, Lt. Col. R. Mar. Art.	27 June 64	3 Aug. 67	20 Mar. 77	11 July 82	27 June 92	29 Aug. 93	
Jas. F. Willoughby, Lt. Col. Bombay Inf.	27 Jan. 61	30 Oct. 62	4 Feb. 71	27 Jan. 81	27 Jan. 87	29 Aug. 93	
Edward Molloy, Lt. Col. Indian S. C.	7 June 61	9 June 62	7 June 73	2 Mar. 81	7 June 87	29 Aug. 93	
John E. Sandeman, Lt. Col. Indian S. C.	7 June 61	19 May 62	7 June 73	7 June 81	7 June 87	29 Aug. 93	
Percy W. Smith, Lt. Col. Bengal Infantry	8 June 61	30 July 62	30 Mar. 70	8 June 81	8 June 87	29 Aug. 93	
Chas. Fred. Thomas, Lt. Col. Bengal Inf.	8 June 61	30 July 62	26 May 70	8 June 81	8 June 87	29 Aug. 93	
Henry Strafford Tandy, Lt. Col. Indian S.C.	12 June 61	4 Oct. 63	12 June 73	1 July 81	12 June 87	29 Aug. 93	
Edward Barry Bishop, Lt. Col. Indian S.C.	2 Dec. 62	2 Dec. 65	2 Dec. 74	2 Mar. 81	1 July 87	29 Aug. 93	
Robert Alexander Swetenham, Lt. Col. Indian Staff Corps	26 May 65	23 June 68	26 May 77	26 May 85	1 July 89	29 Aug. 93	
Alfred Lionel M'Nair, Lt. Col. Indian S.C.	27 Aug. 61	26 Oct. 64	27 Aug. 73	27 Aug. 81	27 Aug. 87	29 Aug. 93	
Walter S. Hore, Lt. Col. Bombay Infantry	12 Sept. 61	29 Feb. 64	21 Feb. 71	1 July 81	12 Sept. 87	29 Aug. 93	
Henry Wylie, CSI. Lt. Col. Bengal Inf.	4 Oct. 61	4 Oct. 63	13 Dec. 70	1 July 81	4 Oct. 87	29 Aug. 93	
Wm. H. Meiklejohn, CMG. Lt. Col. Ben. Inf.	4 Dec. 61	11 Dec. 62	24 May 71	1 July 81	4 Dec. 87	29 Aug. 93	
Arthur Melvill Hogg, Lt. Col. Indian S.C.	12 Dec. 61	14 June 64	12 Dec. 73	12 Dec. 81	12 Dec. 87	29 Aug. 93	
Robt. Warburton, CSI. Lt. Col. Indian S.C.	......	18 Dec. 61	18 Dec. 73	2 Mar. 81	18 Dec. 87	29 Aug. 93	
Binfield Wemyss, Lt. Col. Bengal Inf.	20 Jan. 60	24 Mar. 63	18 July 71	1 July 81	20 Jan. 88	29 Aug. 93	
William Glencross, Lt. Col. (from h.p. Lanc. Fus.) Commandant, Discharge Depot, Fort Brockhurst, 1 June 94	16 Apr. 58	5 May 59	30 Jan. 70	1 July 81	21 June 87	29 Sept. 93	
Arthur Hill, Lt. Col. (from h.p. Royal Engineers)	......	18 Dec. 60	25 Aug. 73	1 July 81	4 Apr. 88	29 Sept. 93	
p.s.c. William S. Cooke,359 Lt. Col. (from h.p. Cheshire Regt.), A.A. Gen. Devonport, 29 Dec. 93	3 July 60	8 Jan. 64	5 July 71	1 July 81	21 Apr. 88	29 Sept. 93	
Jasper Burne, Lt. Col. Indian Staff Corps	6 May 62	17 Nov. 66	6 May 74	6 May 82	6 May 88	29 Sept. 93	
Chas Wm. Thomson, Col. (from h.p. R. Art.)	......	1 Nov. 60	9 Aug. 73	1 July 81	12 May 88	29 Sept. 93	
Francis Wm. Nixon, Lt. Col. (from h.p. Royal Engineers)	......	18 Dec. 60	25 Aug. 73	11 Nov. 78	22 May 88	29 Sept. 93	
William Verner Ellis, Lt. Col. Indian S.C.	10 June 62	9 Dec. 64	10 June 74	2 Mar. 81	10 June 88	29 Sept. 93	1 June 94
Herbert Wynne Apperley,361 Lt. Col. h.p. 9 Lancers	22 Sept. 63	27 July 66	9 Sept. 74	2 Mar. 81	1 July 88	29 Sept. 93	
Geo. F. L. Marshall, CIE. Lt. Col. R. Eng.	......	8 June 60	1 Apr. 74	1 July 81	1 July 88	29 Sept. 93	25 Dec. 94
p.s.c. Emilius Clayton, Lt. Col. h.p. R. Art.	......	1 July 61	10 Oct. 74	1 July 81	31 July 88	29 Sept. 93	
George W. Rogers, DSO. Lt. Col. Ind. S.C.	......	1 Sept. 62	1 Sept. 74	22 Nov. 79	1 Sept. 88	29 Sept. 93	1 Apr. 94
Clervaux Morley, Lt. Col. h.p. R. Art.	......	18 Dec. 60	17 Dec. 73	1 July 81	7 Sept. 88	29 Sept. 93	
Henry Paterson, Lt. Col. Indian S. C.	23 Sept. 62	17 May 66	23 Sept. 74	2 Mar. 81	23 Sept. 88	29 Sept. 93	1 Jan. 94
Harry William Rooke, Lt. Col. h.p. R. Art.	......	18 Dec. 60	18 Feb. 74	1 July 81	1 Oct. 88	29 Sept. 93	14 July 94
William M'Clintock, Lt. Col. h.p. R. Art.	......	18 Dec. 60	11 Mar. 74	1 July 81	1 Oct. 88	29 Sept. 93	
Edm. Bainbridge, Lt. Col. (from h.p. R. Art.), Supdt. Royal Laboratory 6 June 92	......	18 Dec. 60	11 Mar. 74	1 July 81	1 Oct. 88	29 Sept. 93	27 Aug. 94
Charles Henry Spragge, Lt. Col. h.p. R. Artillery	......	19 Dec. 60	1 July 74	1 July 81	29 Oct. 88	29 Sept. 93	24 Nov. 92
Ernle Kerr Amyatt Burney, Lt. Col. h.p. 3 Dragoon Guards	28 Oct. 68	30 June 69	31 Oct. 74	24 Nov. 82	24 Nov. 87	29 Sept. 93	
Malcolm Wm. Rogers, Lt. Col. R. Eng.	......	18 Dec. 60	11 Dec. 73	2 Mar. 81	18 Dec. 88	29 Sept. 93	
Richard Arth. Sargeaunt, Lt. Col. R. Eng.	......	18 Dec. 61	11 Dec. 73	18 Dec. 81	18 Dec. 88	29 Sept. 93	
Lestock Francis Boileau, Lt. Col. R. Eng.	......	18 Dec. 61	13 Mar. 74	18 Dec. 81	18 Dec. 88	29 Sept. 93	
Andrew Wilson Baird, Lt. Col. R. Eng.	......	18 Dec. 61	4 Apr. 74	18 Dec. 81	18 Dec. 88	29 Sept. 93	
p.s.c. Henry Hamilton Settle, DSO. Lt. Col. Royal Engineers	......	10 July 67	9 Nov. 79	15 June 85	28 Dec. 88	29 Sept. 93	
p.s.c. Herbt. Scott Gould Miles, Lt. Col. (from h.p. Munster Fusiliers), A.A. Gen., Aldershot, 29 Sept. 93	4 Feb. 69	27 Apr. 70	23 Aug. 76	1 July 81	29 Dec. 88	29 Sept. 93	
p.s.c. Robert Elias,363 Lt. Col. (from h.p. E. Lancashire Regt.)	28 Oct. 64	21 Aug. 67	11 June 75	15 Oct. 81	14 Dec. 86	2 Nov. 93	
Etwall W. Smyth, Lt. Col. Bengal Infantry	7 June 61	30 July 62	10 Mar. 70	7 June 81	7 June 87	28 Dec. 93	
Jas. T. Cummins, DSO. Lt. Col. Indian S.C.	8 June 61	24 July 63	8 June 73	2 Mar. 81	8 June 87	28 Dec. 93	

Colonels. 28

	CORNET, 2nd LIEUT. or ENSIGN.	LIEUT.	CAPTAIN.	MAJOR.	LIEUT. COLONEL.	COLONEL.	WHEN PLACED ON HALF PAY.
John Alfred Sweny, *Col. 2nd Com. R. Marines*	20 Sept. 59	29 Dec. 62	4 May 77	1 July 81	17 Nov. 87	28 Dec. 93	
Neville F.F.Chamberlain,*Major*,Indian Staff Corps		9 Aug. 74	9 Aug. 85	7 Nov. 85	1 July 87	6 Jan. 94	
Samuel Pym, *Lt.Col.* h.p. Royal Artillery		1 Apr. 61	1 July 74	1 July 81	29 Oct. 88	6 Jan. 94	20 Nov. 94
Alex.JohnForsythReid,*Lt.Col.*IndianS.C.	18 Jan. 67	6 May 71	18 Jan. 79	2 Mar. 81	7 Dec. 88	6 Jan. 94	
Wm. Gage Armstrong, *Lt.Col.* R. Marines	2 Jan. 61	5 Nov. 64	2 Dec. 77	2 Jan. 82	2 Jan. 89	6 Jan. 94	
p.s.c. Robt. Aula,*Major*(from h.p.Northumberland Fusiliers), *A. A. Gen. Chester*, 21 Aug. 94	13 Jan. 69	28 Oct. 71	13 Apr. 81	27 Jan. 86	16 Mar. 89	6 Jan. 94	
Alured DeVere Brooke,*Lt.Col.*h.p.R.Eng.		18 Dec. 61	11 Dec. 73	18 Dec. 81	19 Mar. 89	6 Jan. 94	19 Mar. 94
p.s.c. Arthur Wilkinson, *Lt.Col.* h.p. S. Lancashire Regiment	9 May 65	9 Oct. 69	1 Apr. 75	1 July 81	27 Mar. 89	6 Jan. 94	27 Mar. 93
Henry Champernowne,*Lt.Col.*h.p.R.Eng.		18 Dec. 61	10 Feb. 74	18 Dec. 81	4 Apr. 89	6 Jan. 94	4 Apr. 94
Gerard Septimus Burton,366 *Lt.Col.* h.p. Norfolk Regiment	28 Jan. 59	28 Dec. 61	5 July 73	15 Oct. 81	1 May 89	6 Jan. 94	1 May 93
James Fox Brough, *Lt.Col.* h.p. R. Art		19 Dec. 60	11 Mar. 74	1 July 81	7 May 89	6 Jan. 94	7 May 94
Alex. Dingwall Anderson, *Lt.Col.* R.Art.		8 June 60	9 May 74	1 July 81	8 June 89	6 Jan. 94	
Thos. Henry Anstey, *Lt.Col.* h.p. R. Eng.		25 June 62	12 Aug. 75	25 June 81	11 June 89	6 Jan. 94	11 June 94
Barrett L. Tollner, *Major* (from h.p. R. Art.), *Assist.Insp.of Remounts* 23 June 89		18 Dec. 61	16 Jan. 75	25 Nov. 81	23 June 89	6 Jan. 94	
Desmond D.T.O'Callaghan,*Lt.Col.*R.Art.		18 Dec. 61	16 Jan. 75	18 Dec. 81	23 June 89	6 Jan. 94	
Vernor Chater,367 *Lt.Col.* h.p. Argyll and Sutherland Highlanders	12 July 64	29 Jan. 70	12 Feb. 75	1 July 81	27 June 89	6 Jan. 94	27 June 93
Archibald Hunter, *DSO. Major,* Lancaster Regiment		13 June 74	30 Aug. 82	15 June 85	17 Aug. 89	6 Jan. 94	
Henry M. L. Rundle, *DSO. Major*, R. Art.		14 Aug. 76	13 Mar. 85	15 June 85	17 Aug. 89	6 Jan. 94	
Edw. Harry G. Ravenhill,368 *Lt.Col.* h.p. Shropshire Light Infantry	25 Apr. 65	20 July 67	19 Jan. 76	30 Sept. 82	19 Aug. 89	6 Jan. 94	19 Aug. 93
Henry Vere Hunt, *Lt.Col.* Indian S. C.	11 Sept. 63	2 Mar. 68	25 Dec. 77	2 Mar. 81	11 Sept. 89	6 Jan. 94	
John R. Burlton-Bennett,*Lt.Col.* Ind.S.C.	24 Nov. 63	1 Feb. 68	24 Nov. 75	24 Nov. 83	24 Nov. 89	6 Jan. 94	
H. John de B. de Berniere, *Lt.Col.* h.p. Worcester Regiment	24 Nov. 63	2 Nov. 68	1 Apr. 75	1 July 81	9 Oct. 89	6 Jan. 94	9 Oct. 93
Joseph Henry Laye,369 *Lt.Col.* h.p.Scottish Rifles	20 July 67	27 Oct. 71	23 Jan. 78	29 Nov. 79	10 Oct. 89	6 Jan. 94	10 Oct. 93
p.s.c. George Poignand, *Lt.Col.* h.p. Leinster Regiment	18 Sept. 63	1 Feb. 67	1 Apr. 75	15 Oct. 81	2 Dec. 89	6 Jan. 94	2 Dec. 93
p.s.c. Mackenzie Churchill,370 *Major* (from h.p. Northampton Regt.)	1 Feb. 68	6 July 70	15 Sept. 78	16 Dec. 82	16 Dec. 89	6 Jan. 94	
John Lombard Hunt, *Lt.Col.* h.p. 7 Hussars, *Superintendent Reserve Remount Depot, Calcutta,* 19 Dec. 93	19 Aug. 62	22 Nov. 64	22 June 70	1 July 81	19 Dec. 89	6 Jan. 94	19 Dec. 93
Clement de Beauvoir Carey,*Lt.Col.* h.p. Royal Engineers		17 Dec. 62	27 Oct. 76	18 Nov. 82	20 Dec. 89	6 Jan. 94	20 Dec. 94
John George Sparkes,371 *Lt.Col.* h.p. Derbyshire Regiment	26 Feb. 70	28 Oct. 71	12 Feb. 79	28 May 84	1 Jan. 90	6 Jan. 94	1 Jan. 94
p.s.c. Geo. H. More-Molyneux, *Major*, Indian Staff Corps	5 Jan. 70	27 Oct. 71	5 Jan. 82	5 Jan. 90	6 Jan. 90	6 Jan. 94	
p.s.c. Neville Lloyd Walford,376 *Lt.Col.* (from h.p. R. Art.), *assist. Director of Art. at Head Quarters*, 10 Jan. 93		18 July 65	1 Oct. 77	1 Jan. 84	1 Jan. 89	6 Jan. 94	
George Malcolm Fox,378 *Lt.Col.* (from h.p. Black Watch), *Insp. of Gymnasia, Aldershot*, 12 Feb. 90	22 Dec. 63	9 June 65	10 June 71	25 July 83	25 July 88	21 Apr. 94	
p.s.c. Albert Edw. W. Goldsmid, *Col. Comdg. Regimental District, Cardiff*	29 June 66	28 Nov. 68	1 May 78	29 Aug. 83	29 Aug. 88	21 Apr. 94	
Frederick B. J. Jerrard,374 *Lt.Col.* h.p. West Riding Regiment	18 Oct. 64	14 Oct. 67	23 June 75	14 Sept. 81	14 Sept. 88	25 May 94	14 Sept. 88
Wm. Fred. Campbell, *Lt.Col.* R. Marines	2 Jan. 61	13 Nov. 64	25 Dec. 77	2 Jan. 82	2 Jan. 89	25 May 94	
Edmund S. B. Lockyer,*Lt.Col.*h.p.R.Art.		18 Dec. 61	16 Jan. 75	18 Dec. 81	24 June 89	25 May 94	20 Feb. 95
John Corsane Robinson, *Lt.Col.* R. Art.		18 Dec. 61	7 Feb. 75	11 Nov. 78	8 July 89	25 May 94	
Chas. Henry Stoddart, *Lt.Col.* Indian S.C.	11 Sept. 63	3 Apr. 67	11 Sept. 75	11 Sept. 83	11 Sept. 89	25 May 94	
Wm.Hans Rathborne, *Lt.Col.* h.p. R.Eng.		17 Dec. 62	22 Jan. 77	17 Dec. 82	17 Dec. 89	25 May 94	24 Jan. 95
Chas. Henry Scott Kennedy,379 *Lt.Col.* h.p. Wiltshire Regiment	11 Sept. 63	27 Feb. 67	27 June 74	25 Oct. 81	7 Jan. 90	25 May 94	7 Jan. 94
Arthur Fishe, *Lt.Col.* Indian Staff Corps	15 Jan. 64	18 Dec. 68	15 Jan. 76	15 Jan. 84	15 Jan. 90	25 May 94	
John Thos.Carruthers,*Lt.Col.*Indian S.C.	2 Feb. 64	19 Aug. 68	2 Feb. 76	2 Feb. 84	1 Feb. 90	25 May 94	
Charles Harington Scale, *Lt.Col.* R. Mar.	4 Feb. 62	19 Sept. 65	30 Mar. 78	4 Feb. 83	4 Feb. 90	25 May 94	
William Mogg Rolph, *Lt.Col.* h.p. Leicester Regiment	7 Aug. 61	11 Oct. 64	24 Jan. 74	1 July 81	5 Feb. 90	25 May 94	5 Feb. 94
Edward Nesbitt,380 *Lt.Col.* h.p. West Riding Regiment	1 Sept. 65	13 July 67	9 Sept. 74	1 July 81	15 Mar. 90	25 May 94	15 Mar. 94
Robt. Benj. Cotton,381 *Lt.Col.* h.p. Wiltshire Regiment	18 Oct. 64	14 Sept. 70	31 Oct. 77	7 Jan. 82	19 Mar. 90	25 May 94	19 Mar. 94
Geo. Wilmot M. Turnbull, *Lt.Col.* R. Art.		18 Dec. 61	7 Feb. 75	18 Dec. 81	5 Apr. 90	25 May 94	
p.s.c. Henry Studholme Brownrigg,382 *Lt.Col.* h.p. Rifle Brigade, *A. A. Gen. Bengal*, 15 Oct. 93	30 Apr. 61	10 Nov. 65	30 Apr. 73	2 Mar. 81	12 Apr. 90	25 May 94	15 Oct. 93
Henry Donald Browne,383 *Lt.Col.* h.p. King's Royal Rifles; *Commanding Rifle Depot, Winchester*	13 June 63	14 Aug. 66	27 Mar. 74	1 July 81	16 Apr. 90	25 May 94	16 Apr. 94
George Henry Marshall, *Lt.Col.* R. Art.		18 Dec. 61	10 Mar. 75	18 Dec. 81	16 Sept. 89	26 July 94	
Thomas Robert Disney, *Lt.Col.* R. Art.		18 Dec. 61	1 Apr. 75	18 Dec. 81	1 Oct. 89	26 July 94	
p.s.c. Wy. Duppa A. Cutbill,385 *Lt.Col.* h.p. Irish Rifles	22 Dec. 60	21 Nov. 63	1 Apr. 73	19 Nov. 81	28 Dec. 89	26 July 94	4 June 94
V C Wm. John Vousden, *Lt.Col.* Ind. S.C.	8 Jan. 64	4 Oct. 67	8 Jan. 76	2 Jan. 84	8 Jan. 90	25 July 94	
Herbert Paget Knocker, *Lt.Col.* R. Eng.		24 June 63	6 June 77	24 June 83	6 May 90	26 July 94	
Henry Pipon, *Lt.Col.* Royal Artillery		18 Dec. 61	6 Feb. 75	2 Jan. 84	8 May 90	26 July 94	
St. Aubyn Molesworth, *Lt.Col.* R. Art.		18 Dec. 61	10 Mar. 75	18 Dec. 81	20 May 90	26 July 94	
Henry P. Douglas Willan,386 *Lt.Col.*h.p. 1 Dragoon Guards	12 Oct. 67	14 July 69	17 Dec. 77	1 Feb. 82	14 June 90	25 July 94	14 June 94
Granville Vernon, *Lt.Col.* h.p. Bedford Regt.	9 Aug. 64	29 Nov. 66	28 Oct. 71	1 July 81	1 July 90	25 July 94	1 July 94

Colonels.

	CORNET, 2nd LIEUT. or ENSIGN.	LIEUT.	CAPTAIN.	MAJOR.	LIEUT. COLONEL.	COLONEL.	WHEN PLACED ON HALF PAY.
Fred. Wm. Vans Leckie, *Lt. Col.* Ind. S.C.	5 July 64	13 June 68	14 Mar. 74	3 Jan. 85	5 July 90	26 July 94	
Richard Wace, *Lt. Col.* (from R. Art.), *Insp. Gen. of Ordnance, Bengal,* 6 Oct. 93	......	19 Jan. 64	9 Aug. 76	22 Nov. 79	26 July 90	26 July 94	
Harold P. Leach, *DSO. Major*, R. Eng...	......	2 Aug. 71	2 Aug. 83	15 June 85	28 July 90	28 July 94	
p.s.c. Edw. James Courtenay, *Lt. Col.* (from h.p. Sussex Regt.), *A.A. Gen.* Ireland, 28 Oct. 94	30 June 65	16 Mar. 70	2 Feb. 78	24 Oct. 83	6 Aug. 90	6 Aug. 94	
p.s.c. Arch. Graham Wavell,³⁹⁷ *Lt. Col.* (from h.p. Black Watch), *Dep. Assist. Adj. General, Edinburgh,* 13 Sept. 94	28 July 63	5 June 66	1 May 78	21 Mar. 82	20 Aug. 90	20 Aug. 94	
James M'Gregor Whitton,³⁸⁸ *Lt. Col.* h.p. Scots Fusiliers	14 Aug. 60	1 July 63	24 Dec. 70	1 July 81	21 June 87	25 Aug. 94	25 Aug. 94
Ellis Lee, *Lt. Col.* h.p. York and Lancaster Regt.	8 July 62	9 Mar. 66	31 Oct. 71	1 July 81	27 Aug. 90	27 Aug. 94	27 Aug. 94
Charles Talbot Peyton,³⁸⁹ *Lt. Col.* h.p. Durham Light Infantry	8 Jan. 68	28 Oct. 71	31 Oct. 77	1 July 81	27 Aug. 90	27 Aug. 94	27 Aug. 94
James Keith, *DSO. Lt. Col.* R. Artillery	......	18 Dec. 61	1 Apr. 75	18 Dec. 81	1 Sept. 90	1 Sept. 94	
John Leith Ross,³⁹⁰ *Lt. Col.* h.p. King's Own Scottish Borderers	26 July 64	21 Aug. 67	19 Mar. 75	1 July 81	10 Sept. 90	10 Sept. 94	10 Sept. 94
Vincent Robert Biscoe, *Lt. Col.* h.p. N. Lancashire Regiment	21 June 64	9 Nov. 67	8 Dec. 77	1 July 81	10 Sept. 90	10 Sept. 94	10 Sept. 94
Alex. G. M'Kean, *CMG. Lt. Col.* 6 Drag.	28 Oct. 71	28 Oct. 71	12 Nov. 78	23 Jan. 83	18 Oct. 88	17 Sept. 94	
Chas. E. Ilderton,³²² *DSO. Lt. Col.* h.p. West Surrey Regiment	5 Sept. 62	20 May 68	31 Oct. 71	1 July 81	21 June 87	29 Sept. 94	29 Sept. 94
Edw. Primrose T. Goldsmith, *Lt. Col.* h.p. Lancashire Fusiliers	11 Feb. 62	11 July 68	21 July 75	1 July 81	31 July 90	15 Oct. 94	15 Oct. 94
Reginald Chalmer,³⁹³ *Lt. Col.* h.p. King's Royal Rifles	17 Mar. 63	21 Feb. 65	2 Apr. 74	2 Mar. 81	15 Oct. 90	15 Oct. 94	15 Oct. 94
p.s.c. Aug. W. Morris,³⁹⁵ *Lt. Col.* h.p. Northampton Regiment	5 July 64	2 Dec. 69	24 July 78	1 July 81	22 Nov. 90	22 Nov. 94	22 Nov. 94
Chas. R. Macgregor, *DSO. Lt. Col.* Ind. S.C.	14 Mar. 68	28 Oct. 71	14 Mar. 80	2 Mar. 81	2 Aug. 88	3 Dec. 94	
Charles Fred. Wm. Moir, *Lt. Col.* h.p. Leicester Regiment	3 Dec. 61	11 Oct. 64	30 Sept. 77	2 Mar. 81	23 Sept. 90	3 Dec. 94	3 Dec. 94
p.s.c. John C. R. Glasgow,³⁹⁶ *Lt. Col.* h.p. Suffolk Regiment	16 Aug. 64	8 Aug. 68	1 May 78	7 Sept. 82	9 Dec. 90	9 Dec. 94	9 Dec. 94
James A. F. H. Stewart Mackenzie, *Lt. Col.* 9 Lancers	1 May 67	8 June 70	15 July 76	2 Mar. 81	15 Dec. 90	15 Dec. 94	
John Russell Mecham, *Lt. Col.* h.p. Scottish Rifles	19 July 64	23 June 69	4 Mar. 78	14 Jan. 83	15 Dec. 90	15 Dec. 94	15 Dec. 94
Edw. H. Hanning-Lee, *Lt. Col.* 2 LifeGds.	22 Sept. 65	15 Feb. 71	26 July 76	26 Nov. 83	14 Mar. 88	12 Jan. 95	12 Jan. 95
Lorn Robt. H. Dick Campbell, *Lt. Col.* Indian Staff Corps	28 Aug. 63	20 Jan. 68	28 Aug. 75	28 Aug. 83	28 Aug. 89	15 Jan. 95	
C. G. *Earl of* Erroll, *Lt. Col.* h.p. Royal Horse Guards	7 July 69	19 Aug. 71	11 Sept. 75	1 July 81	24 Sept. 87	18 Jan. 95	18 Jan. 95
Gordon Lorn Campbell Money, *DSO. Lt. Col.* Cameron Highlanders	8 Feb. 68	28 Oct. 71	18 Aug. 80	1 Feb. 84	1 Jan. 88	23 Jan. 95	
Francis Howard, *Lt. Col.* Rifle Brigade...	3 Apr. 66	28 May 70	30 Apr. 78	13 Apr. 82	23 Aug. 89	30 Jan. 95	
Wm. Oliver Thompson, *Lt. Col.* Indian S.C.	18 Mar. 63	12 Oct. 66	18 Mar. 75	18 Mar. 83	18 Mar. 89	1 Feb. 95	
Francis Dorling, *Lt. Col.* h.p. Sussex Regt.	2 Jan. 69	15 Feb. 71	13 Mar. 79	1 July 83	2 Feb. 91	2 Feb. 95	2 Feb. 95
John James Hamilton, *Major,* h.p. Liverpool Regiment	6 Aug. 61	30 Dec. 65	8 Nov. 74	1 July 81	30 July 90	4 Feb. 95	4 Feb. 95
Wm. Godfrey Thomas,³⁹⁷ *Lt. Col.* h.p. South Stafford Regiment	26 June 61	14 Sept. 64	14 June 73	1 July 81	17 Jan. 90	11 Feb. 95	11 Feb. 95
John Edw. Hale Prior, *Lt. Col.* South Stafford Regiment (80 Foot)	21 Mar. 68	30 Aug. 71	18 Nov. 77	29 Nov. 79	11 Feb. 91	11 Feb. 95	
Thomas Stanhope Gildea,³⁹⁸ *Lt. Col.* h.p. Gordon Highlanders	22 Dec. 63	27 Nov. 67	7 Mar. 76	1 July 81	14 Feb. 91	14 Feb. 95	14 Feb. 95
Walter Hailes, *Lt. Col.* Indian Staff Corps	16 Oct. 63	10 Feb. 69	16 Oct. 75	16 Oct. 83	1 July 87	23 Feb. 95	

War Services of the Colonels not belonging to Regiments or Corps.

[For the War Services of other Colonels, vide their respective Regiments or Corps.]

[1] Colonel J. Duncan served in the Indian Mutiny campaign of 1857-58, including the action of Soorajpore, defence of the Alumbagh under Colonel M'Intyre, storming of the Secundrabagh and Shah Nujiff and relief of Lucknow by Lord Clyde, occupation of the Alumbagh under Outram, capture of Lucknow, campaign of 1858 in Oude, with passage of the Goomtee, action at Shabpore, and other minor affairs (Medal with two Clasps, and a year's service for Lucknow). Served with the Bechuanaland Expedition in 1884-85 as Assistant Adjutant and Quarter Master General at the Base and Lines of Communication.

[2] Colonel J. C. Russell served throughout the 2nd phase of the Ashanti war in 1874 as Aide de Camp to Sir Archibald Alison, and was present at the battle of Amoaful, the attack and capture of Becquah, the battle of Ordahsu and capture of Coomassie (twice mentioned in despatches, Brevet of Major, Medal with Clasp). Served in the Kafir war of 1878-79 in the operations against Sekukuni under Colonel Rowlands. Served in the Zulu war of 1879 and was present in the engagements of Zlobane Mountain and Kambula (several times mentioned in despatches, Brevet of Lt. Colonel, Medal with Clasp).

[10] Colonel W. L. Dalrymple served in the Ashanti war in 1874, as Special Commissioner to the Wassaws and Denkeras, on the left flank of the Main line of Advance, and subsequently on the Transport Service (mentioned in despatches, Brevet of Major, Medal with Clasp). Served in the latter part of the Kafir war of 1878. Also served in the Zulu war of 1879, first as Staff Officer to Colonel Glyn's Column, and afterwards as Brigade Major to the 1st Brigade, 2nd Division; was present in the engagement at Ulundi (mentioned in despatches, Brevet of Lt. Colonel, Medal with Clasp).

War Services of the Colonels.

²¹ Colonel H. A. Bushman served with the 9th Lancers in the Afghan war in 1879-80, and accompanied Sir Frederick Roberts in the march to Candahar, and was present at the battle of Candahar (mentioned in despatches, Medal with Clasp, and Bronze Decoration).

³⁴ Colonel K. G. Henderson served with the 60th Rifles in the suppression of the mutiny in the Shahabad district of Bengal in 1858 (Medal). Also throughout the campaign of 1860 in China (Medal with two Clasps for Taku Forts and Pekin). Served with the Nile Expedition in 1884-85 as Assistant Adjutant and Quarter Master General; was Commandant at Shellal and at Assouan (mentioned in despatches, Medal with Clasp, and Khedive's Star).

⁴³ Colonel C. M. Stockwell served with the 72nd Highlanders in the Crimea from 16th July to 18th Sept, 1855, including the siege and fall of Sebastopol (Medal with Clasp, and Turkish Medal). Served with the 72nd Highlanders throughout the Afghan war of 1878-80 with the Koorum, Cabul, and Cabul-Candahar Field Forces, including the Khost Expedition; was present in the engagements at Mattoon and Charasiab, and in the operations around Cabul in December 1879 (twice mentioned in despatches); commanded the rear guard of the Division at Zahidabad during the night attack of 4th October 1879; accompanied Sir Frederick Roberts in the march to Candahar, and commanded the Regiment at the battle of Candahar after the death of Colonel Brownlow, and brought it out of action (mentioned in despatches, Medal with Clasp, and Bronze Decoration). Served in the Egyptian war of 1882 in command of the 1st Battalion Seaforth Highlanders, and was present at the battle of Tel-el-Kebir (mentioned in despatches, Medal with Clasp, 3rd Class of the Medjidie, and Khedive's Star). Received a Reward for Distinguished Service, 1882.

⁴⁴ Colonel G. U. Prior served in the Afghan war in 1878-79 as Deputy Assistant Quarter Master General Candahar Field Force, took part in the advance to Khelat-i-Ghilzie and in the operations in the Arghasan Valley and on the Thull Chotiali line, and was present in the engagement at Baghao in command of half of the column (mentioned in despatches, Brevet of Lt.Colonel, Medal).

⁶⁵ Colonel James Browne served with the 94th Regiment in the Zulu war of 1879, and was present in the engagement at Ulundi and in the subsequent operations against Sekukuni, including the storming of the stronghold (Medal with Clasp). Served in the Boer war in 1881, part of the time as Commandant at Newcastle.

⁷⁶ Colonel C. J. Burnett served in the Ashanti war from the 30th November 1873. Did the duties of Adjutant of Russell's Regiment from the Prah till invalided at Quarman, including the attack and capture of Adubiassie; commanded the post of Quarman at the commencement of the enemy's attack upon it on the 31st January (Brevet of Major, Medal with Clasp). Served in the Afghan war in 1879-80 as Assistant Adjutant General 1st Division Candahar Field Force, and was present at the defence of Candahar (mentioned in despatches) including the sortie of Deh Khojah (mentioned in despatches, Brevet of Lt.Colonel, Medal).

⁸⁷ Colonel H. P. Pearson served in the 84th Regiment throughout the operations of the Column under Havelock, including the actions of Futtehpore, Aoung, Pandoo Nuddee, Cawnpore (wounded), Oonao, Buscerut Gunge (first and second), Boorbeake Chowkee, Bithoor, Mungawar, and Alum Bagh, relief of Lucknow, commanded a Company of the 84th Regiment in the sortie of 26th September 1857, and at the storming of the Hirn Khana; served with Outram's force at the Alum Bagh, also at the assault and capture of Lucknow, relief of Azimghur, and pursuit of Koer Singh (Medal and two Clasps, and a year's service). Served in the Afghan war of 1878-80, first as D. A. Q. M. General in command of the Signallers with Sir Samuel Browne's Division, with which he was present at the capture of Ali Musjid; afterwards as Brigade Major to Brigadier General Doran's Brigade, being present at the affairs at Kam Dakka and Besud (Medal with Clasp, Brevet of Lt.Colonel).

⁹⁸ Colonel W. J. Frampton served in the Afghan war of 1878-80 in the Quetta, afterwards the Ghuznee Field Force under Sir Donald Stewart, and was present in the engagements at Ahmed Kheyl and at Urzoo near Ghuznee (Brevet of Lt.Colonel, Medal with Clasp).

¹⁰³ Brigadier General Kinloch served in the Afghan war of 1878-80 as Deputy Assistant Quarter Master General, and was present at the attack and capture of Ali Musjid, with the expeditions into the Bazar Valley under Lieut. General Maude (mentioned in despatches), and in the advance to Cabul under Brigadier General Charles Gough (mentioned in despatches, Brevets of Major and Lt.Colonel, Medal with two Clasps).

¹¹⁴ Major General B. A. Combe served with the 3rd Sind Horse in the Abyssinian campaign, and was present as Orderly Officer to Colonel Fraser at the action of Arogee, and capture of Magdala (Medal). Served throughout the Afghan war of 1878-80, first as Brigade Major of Cavalry 1st Division Peshawur Valley Field Force, including the attack and capture of Ali Musjid and the engagement at Futtehabad; afterwards as Deputy Assistant Quarter Master General, and was present in the engagement at Charasiab on the 6th October 1879, in the operations around Cabul in December 1879 including the investment of Sherpore, and in the engagement at Shekabad; accompanied Sir Frederick Roberts in the march to Candahar, and was present at the battle of Candahar (frequently mentioned in despatches, Brevets of Major and Lt.Colonel, Medal with four Clasps, and Bronze Decoration).

¹²⁷ Colonel M. W. E. Gosset served with the 54th Regiment during the Indian Mutiny,—in Eastern Bengal in 1857 against the Chittagong mutineers, and in Lord Clyde's campaign in Oude in 1858-59 (Medal). Served as Aide de Camp to Lord Chelmsford in the Kafir war of 1878, and was present in all the actions with the Gaikas in the Buffalo Mountains and Perie Bush (mentioned in despatches, and Brevet of Major). Served in the Zulu war of 1879 as Aide de Camp to Lord Chelmsford in the first advance into Zululand in January, and was present in the actions fought by the Centre Column up to the 22nd January. Was afterwards Assistant Quarter Master General to the 2nd Division in the second advance into Zululand, and was present in the engagement at Ulundi (mentioned in despatches, Brevet of Lt.Colonel, Medal with Clasp). Went to South Africa on special service in January 1881, and served under Sir Evelyn Wood in the Boer war as Assistant Adjutant and Quarter Master General. Commanded the Mandalay District, Burmah, during the operations against the Kachins on the North East Frontier in 1891-92 (Medal with Clasp).

¹²⁸ Colonel D. M. Home served with the Royal Horse Guards in the Egyptian war of 1882, and was present in the engagements at El Magfar and Mahsama, and in the action at Kassasin on the 28th August (Medal, 4th Class of the Osmanieh, and Khedive's Star).

¹³⁰ Colonel W. O. Barnard commanded the 2nd Battalion Manchester Regiment throughout the Egyptian war of 1882 (Medal, 3rd Class of the Medjidie, and Khedive's Star).

¹³¹ Colonel H. M'Calmont served in the Red River Expedition in 1870 (brought home the despatches). Accompanied Sir Garnet Wolseley to the Gold Coast in September 1873, as Aide de Camp (Ashanti Medal). Was appointed a military attaché to the British Embassy at Constantinople on the outbreak of the Russo-Turkish war in 1877, and accompanied the Turkish armies in the field throughout the campaign in Armenia (Brevet of Major). Accompanied Sir Garnet Wolseley to South Africa as Aide de Camp in 1879, and was present in the subsequent operations, including those against Sekukuni (mentioned in despatches, Brevet of Lt.Colonel, Medal with Clasp). Served on the Staff of Brigadier General Macgregor in the expedition against the Marris in 1880 (mentioned in despatches). Served in the Egyptian war of 1882 as Brigade Major of the 1st Cavalry Brigade, and was present in the engagement at Mahsama, in the two actions at Kassasin, and at the battle of Tel-el-Kebir and the capture of Cairo (mentioned in despatches, Medal with Clasp, 3rd Class of the Medjidie, and Khedive's Star). Served with the Nile Expedition in 1884-85 as second in command and afterwards in command of the Light Camel Regiment, including the operations of the Desert Column (mentioned in despatches, Brevet of Colonel, CB., and Clasp).

¹³² Colonel S. J. Nicholson served in the Soudan campaign in 1885, and was present in the engagements at Hasheen and the Tofrek zereba and at the destruction of Temai (mentioned in despatches, Brevet of Colonel, Medal with two Clasps, and Khedive's Star).

¹³⁴ Colonel C. Grove served in the Egyptian war of 1882 as Deputy Assistant Adjutant and Quarter Master General on the Head Quarters Staff, and was present at the engagements of Tel-el-Mahuta and Kassasin (9th Sept.), and in the battle of Tel-el-Kebir (mentioned in despatches, Brevet of Lieut-Colonel, Medal with Clasp, 4th Class of the Osmanieh, and Khedive's Star). Served with the Nile Expedition in 1884-85 and in the campaign in the Soudan in 1885 as Assistant Adjutant General for Boat Service; Commandant at Gemal, and Assistant Adjutant General and Acting Military Secretary at Head Quarters (mentioned in despatches, Brevet of Colonel, two Clasps).

¹³⁵ Colonel L. V. Swaine served in the Egyptian war of 1882 as Military Secretary to Sir Garnet Wolseley, and was present at the engagements of El Magfar, Tel-el-Mahuta, and Kassasin (9th Sept.), and in the battle of Tel-el-Kebir (mentioned in despatches, Brevet of Lt.Colonel, CB., Medal with Clasp, 3rd Class of the Medjidie, and

Khedive's Star). Served with the Nile Expedition in 1884-85 as Military Secretary to Lord Wolseley (mentioned in despatches, Brevet of Colonel, Clasp).

[145] Colonel J. B. Richardson was present with three Batteries of Royal Artillery under Colonel M'Crea in the revolution which upset the Emperor Fausti in Hayti in Jan. 1859 ; landed and protected the Europeans at Port au Prince, and carried off the Emperor his family and ministers ; received the thanks of the English and French Governments.

[146] Brigadier General Van Straubenzee served in the Egyptian war of 1882 in command of Royal Artillery Indian Contingent, and was present at the battle of Tel-el-Kebir (mentioned in despatches, CB., Medal with Clasp, 3rd Class of the Medjidie, and Khedive's Star).

[151] Colonel F. S. Russell served in the Ashanti war from the 17th December 1873; was attached to Wood's Regiment, and commanded the post of Accrofoomu on the line of communication (Brevet of Major, Medal with Clasp). Served in the latter part of the Zulu war of 1879 as Deputy Assistant Adjutant General 2nd Division, and was present in the engagement at Ulundi (Medal with Clasp). Also served in the Boer war of 1881.

[152] Colonel J. D. Dyson-Laurie served with the 34th Regiment in the Crimea from the 10th August 1855, including the siege and fall of Sebastopol, and was severely wounded at the assault of the Redan on the 8th September, was also wounded on a former occasion (Medal with Clasp, and Turkish Medal). Served also in the Indian campaigns in 1858-59, including the capture of Meeangunge, siege and capture of Lucknow, relief of Azimghur, defeat of the rebels at Bootwul, and affair at Bhowanie (Medal with Clasp). Served in Afghanistan in 1878-79 superintending communications on the Khyber line (Medal).

[159] Colonel H. D'O. Farrington served in the Indian Mutiny campaign in 1858-59 (Medal).

[160] Colonel W. Byam served with the 65th Regiment in the New Zealand war in 1863-65 (Medal). Served in the expedition to the Soudan under Sir Gerald Graham in 1884 with the 1st Battalion York and Lancaster Regiment, and was present in the engagements at El Teb and Temai (mentioned in despatches, CB., Medal with Clasp, and Khedive's Star).

[162] Colonel G. Salis-Schwabe served in the latter part of the Zulu war of 1879, in command of the Native Carrier Corps (2,000 strong), which he organised (Medal with Clasp).

[164] Colonel T. Kelly-Kenny served the campaign of 1860 in North China as Orderly Officer to Brigadier Jephson including the action of Sinho (mentioned in despatches), taking of Tangku and Taku Forts (Medal with Clasp). Served the campaign of 1867-68 in Abyssinia in command of a Division of the Transport Train (mentioned in despatches for "zeal, energy, and ability," Medal).

[169] Colonel C. E. Foster served in the Zulu war in 1879 (Medal with Clasp).

[171] Colonel F. T. Hobson served in the campaign of 1860 in China (Medal with Clasp for the Taku Forts).

[173] Colonel J. R. Collins served with the 70th Regiment in the New Zealand war of 1863-65 in the provinces of Taranaki and Waikato (Medal). Served with the 70th Regiment in the Afghan war in 1879 (Medal). Served in the expedition to the Soudan in 1885 with the 2nd Battalion of the East Surrey Regiment, and was present in the engagement at Hasheen, at the attack on the convoy on the 26th March, and in the subsequent advance to Temai (mentioned in despatches, Medal with Clasp).

[175] Colonel G. C. Swiney served in the Indian Mutiny campaign in 1857-58 with the 7th Hussars and was present in an engagement near Allahabad in Dec. 1857.

[176] Colonel J. F. Caldwell served in the Kafir war in 1877-78, and was present in the operations against the Gaikas, including the engagement in the Perie Bush (Medal with Clasp).

[178] Colonel O. R. Middleton served in the Zulu war of 1879 as Staff Officer to the Northern Division (Medal with Clasp).

[179] Colonel H. Langtry served with the 3rd Dragoon Guards in the Abyssinian campaign in 1868, and was present at the storming and capture of Magdala (Medal). Served with the 15th Hussars in the Candahar Column in the Afghan war of 1878-80, including the advance to Khelat-i-Ghilzai; commanded a detached squadron of his Regiment at the affair in the Ghlo Pass, 4th January 1879; also served with the Thull-Chotiali Field Force under Brigadier General Biddulph, and accompanied Major General Phayre in his march to Candahar (Medal). Served in the Boer war of 1881 with the 15th Hussars.

[182] Colonel H. R. Abadie served in the Abyssinian campaign with the Transport Train, and was present at the action at Arogee (mentioned in despatches), and capture of Magdala (Medal). Served with the 9th Lancers in the Afghan war in 1879-80, including the engagement at Takht-i-Pul (mentioned in despatches), the advance on and occupation of Candahar, and the affair at Saif-u-deen; accompanied Sir Frederick Roberts in the march to Candahar, and was present at the battle of Candahar (Brevet of Major, Medal with Clasp, and Bronze Decoration).

[183] Colonel R. F. Butler served in the Afghan war in 1879-80 in Southern Afghanistan (Medal).

[185] Brigadier General Hallowes served with Brigadier General Gough's Brigade in the Afghan war of 1879-80, and was present during the march to and subsequent occupation of Cabul, and in the operations at Jugdulluck (mentioned in despatches, Medal with Clasp).

[187] Colonel R. S. Liddell served in the Soudan Expedition in 1884 with the 10th Hussars, and was present in the engagements at El Teb and Temai (mentioned in despatches, Medal with Clasp, 3rd Class of the Medjidie, and Khedive's Star).

[190] Colonel H. C. Borrett served throughout the Abyssinian campaign, and was present at the action of Arogee and capture of Magdala (Medal).

[196] Colonel W. H. Thompson served with the King's Dragoon Guards in the Zulu war of 1879 in the squadron under Major Marter, including the cavalry affair at Erzungayan (Medal with Clasp).

[197] Colonel F. C. Keyser served in the Afghan war in 1879-80, and was present as Orderly Officer to Brigadier General Brooke in the engagement at Kokeran (mentioned in despatches), as Superintendent of Army Signalling in the defence of Candahar (mentioned in despatches), and at the battle of Candahar (Medal with Clasp). Served as Assistant Adjutant and Quarter Master General of Army Signallers in the Egyptian war of 1882, and was present in the engagement at Tel-el-Mahuta, in the action at Kassasin (9th September), and at the battle of Tel-el-Kebir (mentioned in despatches, CB., Medal with Clasp, 3rd Class of the Medjidie, and Khedive's Star).

[201] Colonel W. V. Brownlow served with the King's Dragoon Guards in the Zulu war of 1879, and was Orderly Officer to Colonel Drury Lowe, commanding the cavalry in the engagement at Ulundi (mentioned in despatches). Afterwards commanded a squadron of his Regiment in Baker Russell's Flying Column (Brevet of Major, Medal with Clasp). Served in the Boer war of 1881 in command of the Mounted Squadron of the Natal Field Force, and was present in the action at Lang's Nek (twice wounded and horse shot) and in the engagement at Ingogo River (twice mentioned in despatches, Brevet of Lt.Colonel).

[203] Colonel G. Paton served in the operations in the Malay Peninsula in 1875-76 (Medal with Clasp). Served in the Kafir war in 1877-78, including the operations against the Galekas ; also served in the Zulu war in 1879 (CMG., and Medal with Clasp).

[207] Colonel A. G. H. Church served with the 2nd Battalion Manchester Regiment throughout the Egyptian war of 1882 (Medal, and Khedive's Star).

[209] Colonel T. A. Cooke served with the 17th Lancers throughout the Zulu war of 1879, and was present in the engagements at Zuinguin Mountain and Ulundi (Medal with Clasp).

[210] Colonel G. de C. Morton served as Adjutant of the 1st Battalion 6th Regiment in the Hazara campaign of 1868, including the subsequent operations in the Black Mountain (Medal with Clasp). Served as Brigade Major and as Assistant Adjutant General during the Afghan war of 1878-80, and was present at the attack and capture of the Peiwar Kotal (mentioned in despatches), in the engagement at Charasiab on the 6th October 1879 (mentioned in despatches), and in the operations around Cabul in December 1879 (mentioned in despatches) ; accompanied Sir Frederick Roberts in the march to Candahar, and was present at the battle of Candahar (mentioned in despatches, Brevets of Major and Lt.Colonel, Medal with four Clasps, and Bronze Decoration).

[211] Colonel J. E. Whitting served as an Ensign in the Indian Army, and was attached to the 23rd Fusiliers during the Indian Mutiny from Nov. 1857 to Oct. 1858. Also served as a Lieutenant with the 8th Regiment during the Oude campaign till Feb. 1859 (Medal with Clasp for Lucknow).

[212] Brigadier General Gatacre served with the Hazara Expedition in 1888 as Deputy Adjutant and Quarter Master General (DSO., and Medal with Clasp).

War Services of the Colonels. 34

²¹⁴ Colonel W. J. Holt was thanked in General Orders dated at Poona 12th July 1866 for his "noble efforts" in saving life on the occasion of the wreck of the Pilgrim ship *Diamond*, and his conduct was deemed by the Commander in Chief at Bombay as "deserving of the warmest admiration." Served in the Abyssinian campaign in 1867-68, as Provost Marshal at Zoula, and subsequently in the Transport Train; was attacked by a large force at Belago Pass whilst in charge of Convoy, and his conduct on the occasion met with the entire approval of Lord Napier (mentioned in despatches, Medal, and promoted to Captain unattached). Served with the Burmese Expedition in 1886-88 in command of the 2nd Battalion Royal West Surrey Regiment, including the operations under Sir William Lockhart in the Pyinmana, Yemethen, and Meiktila Districts (mentioned in despatches, CB., and Medal with two Clasps).

²¹⁵ Colonel R. Upcher served in the Kaffir war in 1877-78 in command of the Left Column, and was present in the engagements at Quintana in command of the troops (mentioned in despatches), and at Kei River; also served in the Zulu war in 1879, and commanded the 1st Battalion of the 24th Foot after the engagement at Isandhlwana (Brevet of Major, Medal with Clasp). Served with the Burmese Expedition in 1885-89 (mentioned in despatches, DSO., and Medal with two Clasps).

²¹⁶ Major General Tulloch served in the Eastern campaign with the 1st Royals from December 1855 till June 1850. Was present with the Spanish National troops during the Carlist war in the campaign in the Pyrenees, which resulted in the relief of Bilbao. Served as D. A. Q. M. General to the expeditionary force in the south of China under Sir Charles Straubenzee; and in the 1st Royals the campaign of 1860 in the north of China, including the taking of Sinho and Tangku, occupation of Tientsin, and surrender of Pekin (Medal with two Clasps). Served in the Egyptian war of 1882, and was present at the bombardment of the Alexandria Forts as Military Staff Officer to the Admiral Commanding in Chief (mentioned in despatches, Brevet of Lt.-Colonel); was one of sixteen volunteers who landed from H.M.S. *Invincible* during the action, swam through the surf, and spiked the guns in the Mex Battery when its garrison had retired to the citadel in rear; afterwards served in the Intelligence Department, and was present at the action at Kassasin on the 9th Sept, (as Acting Assistant Adjutant General to Graham's Force) and at the battle of Tel-el-Kebir (mentioned in despatches, CB., Medal with two Clasps, 3rd Class of the Medjidie, and Khedive's Star).

²¹⁹ Colonel the Hon. R. Talbot served in the latter part of the Zulu war of 1879 on the Staff of Colonel Baker Russell's Column (Medal with Clasp). Served with the 1st Life Guards in the Egyptian war of 1882, and was present in the engagements at El Magfar and Marsama, in the two actions at Kassasin, at the battle of Tel-el-Kebir, and at the capture of Cairo (mentioned in despatches, Medal with Clasp, 4th Class of the Osmanieh, and Khedive's Star). Served with the Nile Expedition in 1884-85 in command of the Heavy Camel Regiment, and was present in the engagements at Abu Klea, El Gubat, and Metammeh; also commanded the Column convoying sick and wounded when attacked near Shabacat Wells on the 14th February 1885 (mentioned in despatches, CB., and two Clasps).

²²¹ Colonel George Baker served with the 67th Regiment throughout the campaign of 1860 in China, and carried the regimental Colour at the action of Sinho, taking of Tangku, and with the storming party at the Taku Fort, the ditch of which he crossed and planted the Colour on the cavalier; also present at the surrender of Pekin (Medal with two Clasps). Served with the 67th Regiment throughout the Afghan war of 1878-80, and was present in the engagement at Charasiab on the 6th October 1879, and in the operations around Cabul in December 1879 including the investment of Sherpore (mentioned in despatches, Medal with two Clasps). Served with the Burmese Expedition in 1885-86 in command of the 2nd Battalion of the Hampshire Regiment until after the surrender of Mandalay (mentioned in despatches, CB., Medal with Clasp).

²²³ Colonel R. K. Bayly served in the Crimea from the 13th October 1855 till the 23rd July 1856. Served with the 42nd Highlanders in the campaign of 1857-58 against the mutineers in India including the actions at Cawnpore (6th Dec. 1857), Seraighat, Kudygunge, and Shumsabad, siege and fall of Lucknow and assault of the Martiniere and Banks' Bungalow, attack on the Fort of Rooyah, action of Allygunge, attack and capture of Bareilly and action at Sisseaghat—wounded (Medal with Clasp). Embarked for the Gold Coast with the 42nd Highlanders. Served in the second phase of the Ashanti war in 1874, and was present at the battle of Ordahsu and capture of Coomassie (Brevet of Major, Medal with Clasp). Served with the 1st Battalion Black Watch in the Egyptian war of 1882, and was present at the battle of Tel-el-Kebir (Medal with Clasp, 4th Class of the Osmanieh, and Khedive's Star). Served in the Soudan Expedition in 1884 with the 1st Battalion Black Watch, and was present in the engagement at El Teb (3rd Class of the Medjidie, two Clasps). Served in the Nile Expedition in 1884-85 with the 1st Battalion of the Black Watch, took part with the River Column under Major General Earle, and was present in the engagement at Kirbekan (mentioned in despatches, CB., and two Clasps).

²²⁹ Colonel G. Barton served in the Ashanti war of 1873-74 in the Transport service, and afterwards in Russell's Regiment, including the battle of Amoaful, attack and capture of Becquah, advanced guard engagement of Jarbinbah, skirmishes and ambuscade affairs between Adwabin and the river Ordah (slightly wounded), battle of Ordahsu and capture of Coomassie (mentioned in despatches, promoted Captain, Medal with Clasp). Served throughout the Zulu war of 1879; first, as Staff Officer to No. 2 Column (Durnford's), and, subsequently, in command of the 4th Battalion of Natal Native Contingent, to the end of the war, taking part in the engagement of Gingindhlovu and the operations of Clarke's Column (mentioned in despatches, Brevet of Major, Medal with Clasp). Served in the Egyptian war of 1882 as Deputy Assistant Adjutant General in command of the Military Police, and was present in the action at Kassasin (9th Sept.), and in the battle of Tel-el-Kebir (mentioned in despatches, Brevet of Lieut.Colonel, Medal with Clasp, 4th Class of the Osmanieh, and Khedive's Star); also served in the Soudan campaign in 1885 as Assistant Military Secretary to Sir Gerald Graham (Clasp).

²³⁰ Colonel R. H. O'G. Haly served with the 2nd Battalion York and Lancaster Regiment throughout the Egyptian war of 1882, and was present in the engagements at El Magfar and Tel-el-Mahuta, in the two actions at Kassasin, and at the battle of Tel-el-Kebir (Brevet of Lt.Colonel, Medal with Clasp, and Khedive's Star). Served with the Hazara Expedition in 1888 in command of the 2nd Column under Brigadier General Channer (mentioned in despatches, DSO., and Medal with Clasp).

²³¹ Colonel R. B. Lane served in the Zulu war of 1879 as Aide de Camp to Major General Newdigate, and was present at the engagement at Ulundi (mentioned in despatches, Brevet of Major, Medal with Clasp). Served in the Boer war of 1881 under Sir Evelyn Wood as Deputy Assistant Quarter Master General. Served in the Egyptian war of 1882 as Aide de Camp to H.R.H. Major General the Duke of Connaught, Commanding the 1st Brigade, and was present in the battle of Tel-el-Kebir (mentioned in despatches, Brevet of Lt.Colonel, Medal with Clasp, 4th Class of the Osmanieh, and Khedive's Star).

²³² Colonel F. A. Ogle was landed from H.M.S. *Brisk* in command of a detachment of Royal Marines for the protection of Cape Coast Castle during the mutiny of the Gold Coast Artillery in October 1862, and received a vote of thanks from the Colonial Government. Served in China in H.M.S. *Rodney* from September 1867 to September 1869; commanded the Royal Marine Artillery of the Battalion of Royal Marines from the Squadron at the occupation of Yangchow in Nov. 1868; served with the Battalion at the attack and capture of three walled villages in January 1869 (mentioned in despatches) Served with the Battalion of Royal Marine Artillery throughout the Egyptian war of 1882, and was present in the engagements at El Magfar and Tel-el-Mahuta (slightly wounded), in the actions at Kassasin on the 28th August (mentioned in despatches) and 9th September, and at the battle of Tel-el-Kebir (Brevet of Lt.Colonel, Medal with Clasp, 4th Class of the Osmanieh, and Khedive's Star).

²³³ Colonel G. Cox served in the Egyptian war of 1882 as Deputy Assistant Adjutant General at the Base, Ismailia (Brevet of Lt.Colonel, Medal, and Khedive's Star).

²³⁴ Colonel J. E. Boyes served throughout the Egyptian war of 1882 with the 1st Battalion Gordon Highlanders, and was present in the engagement at Tel-el-Kebir (mentioned in despatches, Brevet of Lt.Colonel, Medal with Clasp, 4th Class of the Osmanieh, and Khedive's Star); also served in the Soudan Expedition in 1884 with the 1st Battalion Gordon Highlanders, and was present in the engagements at El Teb and Temai (two Clasps). Served in the Nile Expedition in 1884-85 with the 1st Battalion of the Gordon Highlanders and with the River Column under Major General Earle (Clasp).

²³⁵ Colonel E. H. Sartorius served with the 59th Regiment in the Afghan war in 1879-80, and was present in the engagement at Shahjui (mentioned in despatches, Brevet of Major, Victoria Cross, and Medal): was awarded the VC "for conspicuous bravery during the action at Shah-jui, on the 24th October 1879, in leading a party of

five or six men of the 59th Regiment against a body of the enemy, of unknown strength, occupying an almost inaccessible position on the top of a precipitous hill. The nature of the ground made any sort of regular formation impossible, and Captain Sartorius had to bear the first brunt of the attack from the whole body of the enemy, who fell upon him and his men as they gained the top of the precipitous pathway; but the gallant and determined bearing of this officer, emulated as it was by his men, led to the most perfect success, and the surviving occupants of the hill top, seven in number, were all killed. In this encounter Captain Sartorius was wounded by sword cuts in both hands, and one of his men was killed." Served in the Egyptian war of 1882 as Deputy Assistant Adjutant and Quarter Master General on the Base and Lines of Communication (mentioned in despatches, Brevet of Lt.Colonel, Medal, 4th Class of the Osmanieh, and Khedive's Star). [See also Civil Decorations for Gallantry, "Hart's Annual Army List," p. 786.]

²³⁷ Colonel C. Needham served with the 1st Life Guards in the Egyptian war of 1882, and was present in the engagements at El Magfar and Mahsama, in the action at Kassasin (28th August), at the battle of Tel-el-Kebir, and at the capture of Cairo (Brevet of Lt.Colonel, Medal with Clasp, and Khedive's Star).

²³⁸ Colonel K. D. Murray served in the Egyptian war of 1882 as Deputy Assistant Adjutant and Quarter Master General 2nd Division, and was present at the battle of Tel-el-Kebir (mentioned in despatches, Brevet of Lt.Colonel, Medal with Clasp, 4th Class of the Osmanieh, and Khedive's Star). Served with the Egyptian Frontier Field Force in 1885-86 as Assistant Adjutant and Quarter Master General, and was present in the engagement at Giniss (mentioned in despatches, DSO.).

²³⁹ Colonel R. Leigh served with the 2nd Battalion Highland Light Infantry in the Egyptian war of 1882, and was present at the battle of Tel-el-Kebir (mentioned in despatches, Brevet of Lt.Colonel, Medal with Clasp, 4th Class of the Osmanieh, and Khedive's Star).

²⁴⁰ Colonel G. W. N. Rogers served in the Egyptian war of 1882, and was present at the action of Kassasin on the 9th September and at the battle of Tel-el-Kebir (mentioned in despatches, Brevet of Lt.Colonel, Medal with Clasp, 4th Class of the Osmanieh, and Khedive's Star). Served with the Hazara Expedition in 1888 with the 2nd Battalion Royal Irish Regiment (mentioned in despatches, Medal with Clasp).

²⁴¹ Colonel the Hon. N. G. Lyttelton served with the 4th Battalion Rifle Brigade in the Jowaki campaign in 1877 (Medal with Clasp.) Served in the Egyptian war of 1882 as Aide de Camp to Sir John Adye, Chief of the Staff, and was present in the engagements of Tel-el-Mahuta, Kassasin (9th Sept.), and in the battle of Tel-el-Kebir (mentioned in despatches), Brevet of Lt.Colonel, Medal with Clasp, 4th Class of the Osmanieh, and Khedive's Star).

²⁴² Colonel H. J. T. Hildyard served in the Egyptian war of 1882 as Deputy Assistant Adjutant and Quarter Master General 1st Division, and was present in the engagements at El Magfar and Tel-el-Mahuta, at the action at Kassasin on the 9th September, and at the battle of Tel-el-Kebir (mentioned in despatches, Brevet of Lt.Colonel, Medal with Clasp, 4th Class of the Osmanieh, and Khedive's Star).

²⁴⁹ Colonel H. T. Jones-Vaughan served in Bengal with the 10th Regiment in suppression of the mutiny in 1857-58; including the actions of Chanda, Ummeerapore and Sultanpore, siege and capture of Lucknow (Medal with Clasp). Served in the Afghan war of 1878-80 as Brigade Major, Peshawur Field Force, and was present at the capture of Ali Musjid; took part in the expedition into the Bazar Valley as Orderly Officer to Brigadier General Tytler, and in the expedition into the Lughman Valley as Brigade Major (mentioned in despatches); was afterwards Brigade Major with the Koorum Field Force, and served with the Zaimusht Expeditionary Force, including the affair at Zawa (mentioned in despatches, Brevet of Lt.Colonel, Medal with Clasp).

²⁴³ Lord Algernon Gordon-Lennox served with the 2nd Battalion Grenadier Guards in the Egyptian war of 1882, and was present at the battle of Tel-el-Kebir (Medal with Clasp, and Khedive's Star).

²⁵⁶ Colonel J. G. Cockburn served as Brigade Major to the 2nd Brigade of the Hazara Field Force of 1868, including the subsequent operations in the Black Mountain (mentioned in despatches, Medal with Clasp). Served in the Looshai campaign of 1871-72 as Aide de Camp to Brigadier General Brownlow (mentioned in despatches, Clasp).

²⁵⁷ Colonel C. T. Wallace served with the 2nd Battalion Highland Light Infantry in the Egyptian war of 1882, and was present at the battle of Tel-el-Kebir (Medal with Clasp, 4th Class of the Osmanieh, and Khedive's Star).

²⁵⁸ Colonel C. S. Perry served with the Burmese Expedition in 1887-89 (Medal with Clasp).

²⁵⁹ Colonel G. T. L. Carwithen served with the 25th King's Own Borderers in the Afghan war in 1878-79 with the Peshawur Valley Field Force, including the Bazar Valley Expedition under Lieut. General Maude (Medal).

²⁶⁰ Colonel W. P. Symons served in the operations against the Galekas in 1877-78, and in the Zulu war in 1879 (Medal with Clasp). Served with the Burmese Expedition in 1885-89 as Deputy Assistant Adjutant and Quarter Master General, and organized and commanded the Mounted Infantry; also as Brigadier General in command of the Chin Field Force (several times mentioned in despatches, Brevets of Lt.Colonel and Colonel, Medal with Clasp).

²⁶³ Colonel W. F. Cavaye served in the Zulu war of 1879 (Medal with Clasp).

²⁶⁴ Colonel Hon. H. W. L. Corry served in the expedition to the Soudan in 1885 with the 1st Battalion of the Coldstream Guards, and was present in the engagement at Hasheen, at that near Tofrek on the 24th March, and at the destruction of Temai (Medal with Clasp, and Khedive's Star).

²⁶⁵ Colonel G. W. A. FitzGeorge went on special service to Egypt in August 1882, served in the campaign on the personal staff of General Sir Garnet Wolseley, and was present at the battle of Tel-el-Kebir, after which he took home the despatches (mentioned in despatches, Brevet of Lieut.Colonel, Medal with Clasp, 4th Class of the Osmanieh, and Khedive's Star).

²⁶⁶ Colonel A. Peel served in the 101st Fusiliers throughout the Indian N.W. Frontier campaign of 1863 and was present at the storming of the Conical Hill, also at the attack and capture of the Crag Piquet and Umboyla (Medal with Clasp).

²⁶⁸ Colonel R. W. W. Follett served with the 2nd Battalion Coldstream Guards in the Egyptian war of 1882, and was present in the engagement at Tel-el-Mahuta, and at the battle of Tel-el-Kebir (Medal with Clasp, and Khedive's Star). Served in the expedition to the Soudan in 1885 with the 1st Battalion of the Coldstream Guards, and was present in the engagement at Hasheen, at that near Tofrek on the 24th March, and at the destruction of Temai (Clasp).

²⁷³ Colonel H. Gough served in the Afghan war in 1878-79 on special duty, and was present at the attack and capture of Ali Musjid (Medal with Clasp). Served in the Soudan Expedition in 1884 with the 10th Hussars, and was present in the engagements at El Teb and Temai (mentioned in despatches, Brevet of Lt.Colonel, Medal with Clasp, and Khedive's Star). Served with the Bechuanaland Expedition in 1884-85 under Sir Charles Warren, when he raised and commanded a Regiment of Mounted Rifles (CMG.).

²⁷⁵ Colonel A. F. Kidston served with the 42nd Highlanders throughout the second phase of the Ashanti war in 1874, and was present at the battle of Amoaful, capture and destruction of the town of Becquah, battle of Ordahsu and capture of Coomassie (mentioned in despatches, Medal with Clasp). Served with the 1st Battalion Black Watch in the Egyptian war of 1882, and was present at the battle of Tel-el-Kebir (Medal with Clasp, 4th Class of the Osmanieh, and Khedive's Star). Served in the Soudan Expedition in 1884 with the 1st Battalion Black Watch, and was present in the engagement at El Teb (Brevet of Lt.Colonel, two Clasps). Served in the Nile Expedition in 1884-85 with the 1st Battalion of the Black Watch, and took part with the River Column under Major General Earle, and was present in the engagement at Kirbekan (two Clasps).

²⁷⁶ Colonel W. F. Kelly served in the Egyptian war of 1882 (Medal and Khedive's Star). Served in the Soudan Expedition under Sir Gerald Graham in 1884 as Brigade Major 1st Brigade, and was present in the engagements at El-Teb (wounded) and Temai (mentioned in despatches, Brevet of Lt.Colonel, 4th Class of the Medjidie, two Clasps). Served in the Soudan campaign in 1885 as Brigade Major, and was present in the engagement at the Tofrek zereba (mentioned in despatches, two Clasps).

²⁷⁷ Colonel William Livesay served in the suppression of the Indian Mutiny from Dec. 1857 to Jan. 1860, including actions at Sahuo and Puttrai (Medal). Also served in the New Zealand war in 1864-65, including expeditions in the province of Taranaki and in command of outposts, destroying many Pahs and fortified villages (Medal).

²⁷⁸ Colonel J. L. Tweedie served in the Boer war of 1881 with the Natal Field Force. Served in the Nile Expedition in 1884-85 with the 1st Battalion of the West Kent Regiment (Medal with Clasp, and Khedive's Star); also served with the Soudan Frontier Field Force in 1885-86, and was present in the engagement at Giniss in command of the Battalion (DSO.).

281 Colonel W. Tolson served in the Egyptian war of 1882 (Medal, and Khedive's Star). Served in the Nile Expedition in 1884-85 with the 1st Battalion of the Royal Sussex Regiment, and took part in the operations of the Desert Column under Sir Herbert Stewart (Clasp).

282 Colonel C. M. Stockley served in the Indian N.W. Frontier war of 1863, and was present at the attack on the Crag Piquet, and severely wounded on the Umbeyla Heights on the 19th November (Medal with Clasp). Served in the Jowaki campaign of 1877-78 as Brigade Major to the 1st Brigade (Clasp). Served throughout the Afghan war of 1878-80, first as Brigade Major 1st Infantry Brigade 1st Division Southern Afghanistan Field Force, and afterwards with the 2nd Battalion 9th Foot in Northern Afghanistan, including the affair at Shekabad under Major General Ross (mentioned in despatches, Brevet of Major, Medal).

283 Colonel G. A. Lee served with the Soudan Frontier Field Force in 1885-86 in command of a Reserve Battalion and was present in the engagement at Giniss (Medal, and Khedive's Star).

28* Colonel D. North served in the Ashanti war in 1874 in the Transport Service, and was dangerously wounded at the defence of Fommanah (mentioned in despatch, Brevet of Major, Medal with Clasp). Served with the Zhob Valley Expedition in 1884 in command of the Half Battalion of the North Lancashire Regiment.

285 Colonel C. R. Rowley served in the Nile Expedition in 1884-85 with the Guards Camel Regiment, and was present at the actions at Abu Klea and El Gubat (Medal with two Clasps, and Khedive's Star).

286 Colonel H. F. Grant while serving with the Egyptian army in 1884 suppressed a mutiny of the Turkish Battalion (Brevet of Lt.Colonel, 3rd Class of the Medjidie). Served with the Nile Expedition in 1884-85, and in the subsequent operations in the Soudan in 1885 in command of a Battalion of Mounted Infantry (mentioned in despatches, CB., Medal with two Clasps, and Khedive's Star).

287 Colonel the Hon. H. Legge served with the 9th Lancers in the Afghan war in 1879-80, and was present in the engagement at Shekabad; accompanied Sir Frederick Roberts in the march to Candahar, and was present at the battle of Candahar (Medal with Clasp, and Bronze Decoration).

288 Colonel T. G. Crawley served in the Burmese Expedition in 1885-87 with the 2nd Battalion of the Liverpool Regiment (Medal with Clasp).

289 Colonel C. L. Harvey was attached by the Government to the service of the British National Society for Aid to the Sick and Wounded in the Franco-German war of 1870-71, and was awarded the Bavarian Order of Merit. Served in the operations against Sekukuni in 1878 as Staff Officer for the Transvaal. Served in the Zulu war of 1879 as Staff Officer of No. 5 Column, and afterwards as Brigade Major 1st Brigade, and Deputy Assistant Quarter Master General in the 1st Division (Brevet of Major, Medal with Clasp). [See also Civil Decorations for Gallantry, "Hart's Annual Army List," p. 786.]

290 Sir C. Holled Smith served with the 3rd Battalion 60th Rifles in the Zulu war from April to September 1879 (Medal with Clasp). Also served in the Boer war of 1881, and was present in the engagements at Lang's Nek and the Ingogo River (mentioned in despatches). Served with the 3rd Battalion King's Royal Rifle Corps in the Egyptian war of 1882, and was present in the reconnaissance in force from Alexandria on 5th August, in the engagement at Tel-el-Mahuta, the action at Kassasin (9th September), and at the battle of Tel-el-Kebir (mentioned in despatches, Brevet of Major, Medal with Clasp, and Khedive's Star). Served in the Nile Expedition in 1884-85 with the Egyptian Army, and was employed on the Lines of Communication; was afterwards Commandant at Semneh (mentioned in despatches, Brevet of Lt.Colonel, Clasp). Served in the operations of the Soudan Frontier Field Force in 1885-86. Commanded a Brigade during the operations near Suakin in December 1888 including the engagement at Gemaizah (mentioned in despatches, Brevet of Colonel, Clasp). Commanded the force during the operations in February 1891 including the capture of Tokar.

291 Colonel J. Dawson served with the 2nd Battalion 8th Foot throughout the Afghan war of 1878-80, and was present in the action of the 28th Nov. 1878 in the Kobrum Valley, and at the attack and capture of the Peiwar Kotal (mentioned in despatches, Medal with Clasp).

292 Colonel C. J. Bromhead accompanied Sir Garnet Wolseley to the Gold Coast in Sept. 1873 on special service, and served throughout the Ashanti war of 1873-74. Was sent as Special Commissioner first to the King of Eastern Assin and then to the King of Abra. Was Staff Officer to Colonel Festing at the action of the 27th October near Dunquah. Commanded the Abras at the repulse of the Ashanti Army at Abrakrampa during the 5th and 6th November 1873. Commanded the reconnaissance in force of the 8th November. Afterwards served with Russell's Regiment at the capture and destruction of Aduhiassie, battle of Amoaful, capture and destruction of Becquah, advanced guard engagement at Jarbinbah, skirmishes and ambuscade affairs between Adwabin and the river Ordah, battle of Ordahsu and capture of Coomassie (mentioned in despatches, Brevet of Major, Medal with Clasp). Served in the Zulu war of 1879 (Medal with Clasp). Served with the Burmese Expedition in 1887-89 (Medal with Clasp).

293 Colonel J. D. P. French served in the Nile Expedition in 1884-85 with the 19th Hussars, and was present in the engagements at Abu Klea and Metammeh (mentioned in despatches, Medal with two Clasps, and Khedive's Star).

294 Colonel J. W. Webber served in the Nile Expedition in 1884-85 with the 1st Battalion of the South Staffordshire Regiment, and was present in the action at Kirbekan, where he commanded the storming party after the death of Colonel Eyre—horse shot—(Medal with two Clasps, and Khedive's Star). [See also Civil Decorations for Gallantry, "Hart's Annual Army List," p. 786.]

295 Colonel A. G. Raper served with the Zhob Valley Expedition in 1884.

296 Colonel W. C. S. Mair served throughout the New Zealand war of 1860-61, including the capture of the Pahs at Kihihi, capture of Matarikoriko, relief and repulse of the night attack on No. 3 Redoubt, action of Huirangi, and skirmish in front of Te Arei. Served during the first part of the Waikato campaign, also as Adjutant of the Flying Column during the war of 1863-66 (Medal).

297 Colonel H. H. Griffiths served with the 59th Regiment in the Afghan war of 1878-80 with the Candahar Column under Sir Donald Stewart, including the advance on and occupation of Khelat-i-Ghilzie; was present in the engagements at Ahmed Kheyl and Urzoo near Ghuznee, and in the subsequent operations in the Logar Valley (Medal with Clasp).

298 Colonel J. B. B. Dickson served in the latter part of the Zulu war of 1879 with the Native Carrier Corps (Medal with Clasp). Served in the Nile Expedition in 1884-85 with the Camel Corps, and was present in the action at Abu Klea—severely wounded (Medal with two Clasps, and Khedive's Star).

299 Colonel E. L. Street served with the 11th Regiment in the Afghan war in 1879-80 (Medal).

300 Colonel E. H. Kingscote served in the Bhootan campaign of 1864-68—wounded (Medal with Clasp).

301 Colonel A. S. Wynne served as Superintendent of Army Signalling in the Jowaki campaign in 1877 (mentioned in despatches, Medal with Clasp). Served in the Afghan war in 1878-79 as Superintendent of Field Telegraphs, and was present at the capture of the Peiwar Kotal in charge of Army Signalling with the Koorum Valley Field Force, and in the engagements in the Mungiar Pass and at Mattoon Khost (mentioned in despatches, Brevet of Major, Medal with Clasp). Served in the Boer war of 1881 with the Natal Field Force as Deputy Assistant Adjutant and Quarter Master General for Signalling. Served with the Nile Expedition in 1884-85 on the Lines of Communication (mentioned in despatches, Brevet of Lt.Colonel, Medal with Clasp, 4th Class of the Medjidie, and Khedive's Star).

302 Colonel L. Hornby served with the 70th Regiment in the New Zealand war of 1864-65 (Medal). Served with the 70th Regiment in the Afghan war in 1878-79 (Medal). Served in the expedition to the Soudan in 1885 with the 2nd Battalion of the East Surrey Regiment, and was present at the engagement at Hasheen, at the attack on the convoy on the 26th March, and in the subsequent advance to Temai (mentioned in despatches, Brevet of Lt.Colonel, Medal with Clasp, and Khedive's Star).

302† Colonel Hon. C. C. G. Byng served in the Nile Expedition in 1884-85 in command of the 1st Life Guards detachment of the Heavy Camel Regiment, and was present in the engagements at Abu Klea, El Gubat, and Metammeh, and at the attack on the convoy on the 14th February 1885 (mentioned in despatches, Brevet of Lt.Colonel, Medal with two Clasps, and Khedive's Star).

403 Colonel T. Davison served in the Nile Expedition in 1884-85 with the Heavy Camel Regiment, and was present at the action of Abu Klea and in the reconnaissance to Metammeh (twice mentioned in despatches, Brevet of Lt.Colonel, Medal with two Clasps, and Khedive's Star).

304 Colonel M. S. J. Sunderland served in the Nile Expedition in 1884-85 with the 1st Battalion of the Royal Sussex

Regiment, and took part in the operations of the Desert Column under Sir Herbert Stewart, including the action at Abu Klea and the engagement at Metammeh, where he commanded a half-battalion (twice mentioned in despatches, Brevet of Lt.Colonel, Medal with two Clasps, and Khedive's Star). Served in the Hazara campaign in 1888 in command of the 2nd Battalion Royal Sussex Regiment (mentioned in despatches, *DSO.*, and Medal with Clasp).

305 Colonel P. D. Trotter served with the Nile Expedition in 1884-85; was commandant of Dal and of Kaibar and was employed on the Lines of Communication (Brevet of Lt.Colonel, Medal with Clasp, Khedive's Star, 3rd Class of the Medjidie " in recognition of his services with the Egyptian Army ").

306 Colonel F. M. Wardrop served in the Egyptian war of 1882 as Aide de Camp to Sir Garnet Wolseley, and was present at the engagements of El Magfar, Tel-el-Mahuta, Kassasin (9th Sept.), and in the battle of Tel-el-Kebir (mentioned in despatches, Brevet of Major, Medal with Clasp, 4th Class of the Medjidie, and Khedive's Star). Served with the Nile Expedition in 1884-85 as Deputy Assistant Adjutant and Quarter Master General with the Desert Column, and was present at the action of Abu Klea, in the reconnaissance to Metammeh, and in the engagement at Abu Klea Wells on the 16th and 17th February (several times mentioned in despatches, Brevet of Lt.Colonel, two Clasps).

307 Colonel C. C. Smyth served in the Transport Department on the Red River Expedition from Canada of 1870. Served with the 51st Light Infantry in the Jowaki campaign in 1877 (Medal with Clasp). Served with the 51st Light Infantry in the Afghan war of 1878-80, and was present at the attack and capture of Ali Musjid, in the first expedition to the Bazar Valley (mentioned in despatches), and in the advance to the relief of Cabul including the affair at Jugdulluck (Medal with Clasp). Served with the Nile Expedition in 1884-85 in command of Kroomen (mentioned in despatches, Brevet of Lt.Colonel, Medal with Clasp, and Khedive's Star); also served in the operations near Suakin in December 1888 including the engagement at Gemaizah (mentioned in despatches, Clasp, and 3rd Class of the Medjidie).

308 Colonel F. J. Graves served in the Soudan campaign in 1885 in command of Mounted troops of the 2nd Brigade, and was present in the engagement at the Tofrok zereba (mentioned in despatches, Brevet of Lt.Colonel, Medal with two Clasps, and Khedive's Star).

309 Colonel M. S. Crofton proceeded on special service to South Africa in June 1879, and was employed as Staff Officer and Deputy Assistant Quarter Master General at Durban from October 1879 till April 1880 (Medal). Served with the Nile Expedition in 1884-85 (mentioned in despatches, Brevet of Lt.Colonel, Medal with Clasp, and Khedive's Star). Also served with the Soudan Frontier Field Force in 1885-86 as Brigade Major on Intelligence Duty, and was present in the engagement at Giniss (mentioned in despatches, *DSO.*).

310 Colonel J. T. Coke served in command of the 2nd Battalion King's Own Scottish Borderers with the Suakin Field Force in December 1888 during the investment of Suakin and was present in the engagement at Gemaizah (mentioned in despatches, 3rd Class of the Medjidie, Medal with Clasp, and Khedive's Star). Also served in the operations on the Soudan frontier in 1889, in command of the 2nd Battalion King's Own Scottish Borderers.

311 Colonel H. H. Hooke served in the Abyssinian campaign in 1868 (Medal).

312 Colonel J. M'Cleverty served with the Sikkim Expedition in 1888 in command of the 2nd Battalion Derbyshire Regiment and was present in the engagement at the Jelapla (mentioned in despatches, Medal with Clasp).

313 Colonel C. K. C. Rooke served the campaign of 1860 in China, including the taking of Sinho and Tangku, occupation of Tientsin, actions of the 18th and 21st Sept., and surrender of Pekin (Medal with two Clasps). Served in the Bechuanaland Expedition under Sir Charles Warren in 1884-85 with the 1st Battalion of the Royal Scots.

314 Colonel Hilton served with the Hazara Expedition in 1888 in command of the Left Half Battalion 2nd Seaforth Highlanders (mentioned in despatches, Medal with Clasp). Also served in the Hazara Expedition in 1891 in command of the 2nd Battalion Seaforth Highlanders (mentioned in despatches, Clasp).

315 Colonel Knox served with the Bechuanaland Expedition in 1884-85 under Sir Charles Warren, when he raised and commanded the 4th Pioneer Regiment (Brevet of Lt.Colonel).

316 Colonel W. H. Bayly served with the 1st Battalion West Kent Regiment throughout the Egyptian war of 1882 (Medal, and Khedive's Star). Served in the Nile Expedition in 1884-85 with the 1st Battalion of the West Kent Regiment (Clasp).

317 Colonel C. W. H. Wilson served with the 6th Regiment throughout the operations against the hill tribes of Sikkim in 1861; also in the Hazara campaign of 1868, including the subsequent operations in the Black Mountain Medal with Clasp).

318 Colonel F. W. Harington served in the New Zealand war of 1863-65, including the actions of Kohewa, Gate Pah and Tauranga (Medal). Served in the Afghan war in 1880, and was present in the affair at Mazeena and with the Kama Expedition (Medal).

319 Colonel Hamilton served with the Carabiniers in the Afghan war in 1880, commanded a detached party of the Regiment (40 Sabres) with Lt.Colonel Hodding's expeditionary column against the Mohmunds in March 1880, and commanded a detached squadron of the Regiment during the expedition into the Lughman Valley under Brigadier General Arbuthnot, and took part in the attack and destruction of the Ghilzai villages of Nargozi, Arab Kheyl, and Jokan (Medal).

320 Colonel Gillies served on the Bhootan Expedition in 1855 (Medal with Clasp).

321 Colonel Hon. E. C. Digby served in the Soudan campaign in 1885 (Medal with Clasp, and Khedive's Star).

322 Colonel T. A. St. Quintin served with the 10th Hussars in the Afghan war in 1878-79, and was present at the attack and capture of Ali Musjid, and in the engagement at Futtehabad as Orderly Officer to Brigadier General C. Gough (mentioned in despatches, Brevet of Major, Medal with Clasp).

323 Colonel H. B. Wilson served with the 71st Highland Light Infantry throughout the campaign of 1863 against the Boneyrs and other hill tribes on the N.W. Frontier of India. Commanded the Sharpshooters from the 11th November to the 1st December, from which latter date till the end of the campaign he acted as Adjutant of the Regiment (Medal with Clasp).

324 Colonel R. Garnett served with the 72nd Highlanders throughout the Afghan war of 1878-80 with the Kocrum, Cabul, and Cabul-Candahar Field Forces; was present at the attack and capture of the Peiwar Kotal and in the engagement at Charasiab and the operations around Cabul in December 1879; accompanied Sir Frederick Roberts in the march to Candabar, and was present at the battle of Candahar (mentioned in despatches, Brevet of Major, Medal with four Clasps, and Bronze Decoration). Served with the 1st Battalion Seaforth Highlanders in the Egyptian war of 1882, and was present in the engagement at Chalouf (mentioned in despatches) and at the battle of Tel-el-Kebir (Medal with Clasp, and Khedive's Star). Served in the Hazara Expedition in 1888 with the 2nd Battalion Seaforth Highlanders (Medal with Clasp).

325 Colonel F. Cochran served in the Burmese Expedition in 1887-89 in command of the 1st Battalion Hampshire Regiment, part of the time in command of Military and Police in the Ruby Mines District (Medal with Clasp).

327 Colonel A. G. Spencer served in the Nile Expedition in 1884-85 with the 2nd Battalion of the Essex Regiment (Medal with Clasp, and Khedive's Star).

328 Colonel J. H. Barnard served in the 19th Regiment in the Hazara campaign of 1868, including the expedition against the tribes on the Black Mountain (Medal with Clasp). Served as a volunteer under Captain Glover, R.N. in the Ashanti war of 1873-74. Led the Advanced Guard at the capture of Abogoo. Commanded for five days a detached force of 650 men which captured Jaashi and Adoomassie. Commanded a detachment of 150 men which drove the enemy out of their camps in the North bank of the Anoom (mentioned in despatches for "great discretion and judgment," and on two occasions for "gallant conduct," *CMG.*, Medal with Clasp. Promoted Captain " in recognition of his services in the Ashanti Expedition of 1874"). Served in the Afghan war in 1879-80 as Aide de Camp to Lieut.General Bright, first with the Peshawur Valley Field Force, and afterwards with the Khyber Line Force (Brevet of Major, Medal). Served in the Soudan Expedition in 1885 under Sir Gerald Graham as Deputy Assistant Adjutant General (Medal with Clasp, and Khedive's Star).

329 Colonel Creek served in the Burmese Expedition in 1886-87 with the 1st Battalion Royal Welsh Fusiliers including the expedition to the relief of Thila (which he commanded) and the expedition to Woonthoo (mentioned in despatches, Medal with Clasp).

330 Colonel Collingwood served with the 97th Regiment in Bengal in suppressing the mutiny in 1857-58, and was present in the actions of Nusrutpore, Chanda, Ummeerpore, and Sultanpore, also at the siege and capture of Lucknow (Medal with Clasp).

332 Colonel F. Glennie served in the Kafir war in 1877-78, and was present in the engagement at Taba ka Udoda (dangerously wounded); also served in the Zulu war in 1879 (Medal with Clasp).

334 Colonel H. L. Dundas served in the Afghan war in 1880 as Brigade Major 2nd Infantry Brigade Candahar Field Force from the 23rd August (Medal). [See also Civil Decorations for Gallantry, "Hart's Annual Army List," p. 786.]

336 Colonel C. P. Temple served with the Egyptian Frontier Field Force in 1885-86, and was present in the engagement at Giniss in command of the 1st Battalion Berkshire Regiment (mentioned in despatches, DSO., Medal, and Khedive's Star).

337 Lord Downe served in the Zulu war of 1879 as Aide de Camp to Major General Marshall, commanding the Cavalry Brigade (Brevet of Major, Medal with Clasp).

338 Colonel F. Carrington served with the Zhob Valley Expedition in 1884.

343 Colonel F. C. Manley served with the 2nd Battalion Coldstream Guards in the Egyptian war of 1882, and was present in the engagement at Tel-el-Mahuta and at the battle of Tel-el-Kebir (Medal with Clasp, and Khedive's Star). Served in the expedition to the Soudan in 1885 with the 1st Battalion of the Coldstream Guards, and was present in the engagement at Hasheen, at that near Tofrek on the 24th March, and at the destruction of Temai (Clasp).

344 Colonel C. G. Leggett served in the Zulu war in 1879 (Medal with Clasp).

345 Colonel Kerr served throughout the operations in the Malay Peninsula in 1875-76 (Medal with Clasp).

346 Colonel E. Wardroper served in the Hazara campaign in 1888 with the 2nd Battalion Royal Sussex Regiment (mentioned in despatches, Medal with Clasp).

348 Lord William Beresford served with the Jowaki Afreedee Expedition in 1877-78 (Medal with Clasp). Served in the Zulu war of 1879, and was present in the engagement at Ulundi (mentioned in despatches, Victoria Cross, and Medal with Clasp): was awarded the VC "for gallant conduct in having at great personal risk, during the retirement of the reconnoitring party across the 'White Unvolosi River' on 3rd July 1879, turned to assist Sergeant Fitzmaurice, 1st Battalion 24th Foot (whose horse had fallen with him), mounted him behind him on his horse, and brought him away in safety under the close fire of the Zulus, who were in great force, and coming on quickly. Lord William Beresford's position was rendered most dangerous from the fact that Sergeant Fitzmaurice twice nearly pulled him from his horse." Served with the 9th Lancers in the Afghan war of 1878-80 and was present at the capture of Ali Musjid (mentioned in despatches, Medal with Clasp). Served with the Burmese Expedition in 1886 as Military Secretary to the Governor General of India (mentioned in despatches, Brevet of Lt.Colonel, and Clasp).

350 Colonel P. D. Jeffreys served with the 88th Regiment throughout the Zulu war of 1879 (Medal with Clasp). Served with the Burmese Expedition in 1886-87 as Brigade Major 3rd Brigade, and commanded the Column which captured his bivouac and killed the Kemendine Prince on the 1st January 1887 (mentioned in despatches, Brevet of Lt.Colonel, Medal with Clasp). Served with the Zhob Field Force under Sir George White in 1890 as Assistant Adjutant General of the Force (mentioned in despatches, Brevet of Colonel).

351 Sir St. Vincent Hammick served in the New Zealand war in 1864-65, and was mentioned in despatches as having "performed his duty as Acting Adjutant with great coolness and courage under a heavy fire" in the action at Te Ranga (Medal).

352 Colonel I. S. M. Hamilton served with the 92nd Highlanders in the Afghan war of 1878-80, and was present in the engagement at Charasiab on 6th October 1879 including the subsequent pursuit of the Afghans (mentioned in despatches) and in the operations around Cabul in December 1879 (mentioned in despatches), Medal with two Clasps). Served in the Boer war of 1881—severely wounded (mentioned in despatches). Served with the Nile Expedition in 1884-85 with the 1st Battalion Gordon Highlanders; was Captain of the Guard to Major General Earle, Commanding the River Column, and was present at the action of Kirbekan (mentioned in despatches, Brevet of Major, Medal with two Clasps, and Khedive's Star). Served with the Burmese Expedition in 1886-87 (mentioned in despatches, Brevet of Lt.Colonel, Medal with Clasp).

354 Lord Coke served with the 1st Battalion Scots Guards in the Egyptian war of 1882, and was present at the battle of Tel-el-Kebir (Medal with Clasp, and Khedive's Star). Served in the expedition to the Soudan in 1885 with the 2nd Battalion of the Scots Guards, and was present in the engagements at Hasheen and Tamai (Clasp).

355 Major General E. T. H. Hutton served with the 3rd Battalion 60th Rifles in the Zulu war of 1879; was present at the action of Gingindhlovu and relief of Ekowe; and afterwards served as Aide de Camp to Major General Crealock, commanding the 1st Division (Medal with Clasp). Served in the Boer war in 1881 with Barrow's Mounted Infantry. Served throughout the Egyptian war of 1882 as Aide de Camp to Major General Sir Archibald Alison, raised and organised the Mounted Infantry Corps, and was present at the reconnaissance in force from Alexandria (5th August), and at the battle of Tel-el-Kebir (mentioned in despatches, Brevet of Major, Medal with Clasp, 4th Class of the Medjidie, and Khedive's Star). Served with the Nile Expedition in 1884-85 as Commandant of Mounted Infantry, and subsequently as Deputy Assistant Adjutant General; raised the 1st and 2nd Battalions of Mounted Infantry (Clasp).

356 Colonel E. A. Brind served with the 88th Regiment throughout the Zulu war of 1879 (Medal with Clasp).

357 Colonel R. C. Græme served with the 51st Light Infantry in the Umbeyla Expedition in 1863. Also served in the Jowaki campaign in 1877 (Medal with Clasp). Served with the 51st Light Infantry in the Afghan war in 1878-79, and was present at the attack and capture of Ali Musjid (Medal with Clasp).

358 Colonel W. T. Dooner accompanied Sir Garnet Wolseley to the Gold Coast in September 1873 on special service; trained the Opobo Company of Russell's Regiment and commanded it throughout the Ashanti war of 1873-74, including the capture and destruction of Adubiassie, the battle of Amoaful, capture and destruction of Becquah, the advanced guard engagement of Jarbinbah, the skirmishes and ambuscade affairs between Adwabin and the river Ordah, battle of Ordahsu and capture of Coomassie. Also surveyed for the Intelligence Department portions of road between Cape Coast and the Prah (mentioned in despatches, Medal with Clasp).

359 Colonel W. S. Cooke served in the Burmese Expedition in 1887-89 with the 2nd Battalion Cheshire Regiment (Medal with Clasp).

361 Colonel H. W. Apperley served with the 9th Lancers in the Afghan war of 1878-80, and took part with the Bazar Valley Expedition, in the engagement at Charasiab in October 1879, and in the operations around Cabul in December 1879 (mentioned in despatches); accompanied Sir Frederick Roberts in the march to Candahar, and was present at the battle of Candahar (mentioned in despatches, Brevet of Major, Medal with three Clasps, and Bronze Decoration).

363 Colonel R. Elias served with the 59th Regiment in the Afghan war of 1878-80, and was present in the engagements at Ahmed Kheyl and Urzoo near Ghuznee (Medal with Clasp).

366 Colonel G. S. Burton served with the 9th Foot in the Afghan war in 1879-80, and took part in the advance to Cabul under Brigadier General Charles Gough as Brigade Major, including the engagements at Jugdulluck and Saidabad, and the relief of Sherpore (Medal with Clasp). Served in the Burmese Expedition in 1887-89 with the 2nd Battalion Norfolk Regiment (Medal with Clasp).

367 Colonel V. Chater served in the latter part of the Zulu war of 1879, part of the time as Provost Marshal and Deputy Assistant Adjutant General to the 1st Division (Medal with Clasp).

368 Colonel E. H. G. Ravenhill served in the Afghan war in 1879-80 with the Koorum Division, including the Zaimusht Expedition (Medal).

369 Colonel J. H. Laye served with the 90th Light Infantry in the Gaika war of 1878, and was present in the various operations in the Waterkloof and Perie Bush, and acted as Staff Officer to Colonel Palmer's Column (mentioned in despatches). Served in Wood's Flying Column throughout the Zulu war of 1879, and was present in the engagements at Zungin Nek, Kambula Hill, and Ulundi (mentioned in despatches, Brevet of Major, Medal with Clasp).

370 Colonel M. Churchill served in the Zulu war of 1879 (Medal with Clasp). Served in the Boer war of 1881 as Deputy Assistant Adjutant General at the defence of Pretoria (mentioned in despatches).

371 Colonel J. G. Sparkes served with the 2nd Battalion Derbyshire Regiment in the Egyptian war of 1882 (Medal, and Khedive's Star).

374 Colonel F. B. J. Jerrard served in the Ashanti war in 1874, in the Transport Service (Medal).

376 Colonel N. L. Walford served in the Egyptian war of 1882 (Medal, and Khedive's Star).

D

War Services of the Colonels.

³⁷⁸ Colonel G. M. Fox served with the 1st Battalion Black Watch in the Egyptian war of 1882, and was present at the battle of Tel-el-Kebir—wounded (Medal with Clasp, and Khedive's Star).

³⁷⁹ Colonel C. H. S. Kennedy served with the 99th Regiment in the Zulu war of 1879, and was present in the action of Inyezane and in the engagement at Gingindhlovu (Medal with Clasp).

³⁸⁰ Colonel E. Nesbitt served with the 33rd Regiment throughout the Abyssinian campaign of 1867-68, and was present at the storming and capture of Magdala (Medal).

³⁸¹ Colonel R. B. Cotton served with the 99th Regiment throughout the Zulu war of 1879 (Medal with Clasp).

³⁸² Colonel H. S. Brownrigg served as Deputy Assistant Quarter Master General to Brigadier General Ross's Column in the Jowaki Expedition in 1877-78 (mentioned in despatches, Medal with Clasp). Served in the Afghan war in 1878-79 as Deputy Assistant Quarter Master General to the 2nd Division Peshawur Valley Field Force, and was present in the expeditions into the Bazaar Valley and in the operations in the Shuliman Valley (mentioned in despatches, Brevet of Major, Medal).

³⁸³ Colonel Donald Browne served in the Boer war in 1881 as Aide de Camp to Major General Buller, Chief of the Staff.

³⁸⁵ Colonel H. D. A. Cutbill served throughout the New Zealand war of 1863-66, took part in the expeditions to the Thames and the Waikato, and was present at the taking of Orakau and in the engagement at Omaranui (Medal).

³⁸⁶ Colonel Douglas Willan served with the King's Dragoon Guards in the Zulu war of 1879 (Medal with Clasp).

³⁸⁷ Colonel A. G. Wavell served in the Zulu war in 1879 (Medal with Clasp).

³⁸⁸ Colonel J. McG. Whitton served in the Boer war of 1881 with the Natal Field Force, and had charge of a Laager during the engagement at Lang's Nek.

³⁸⁹ Colonel C. T. Peyton served with the 10th Regiment in the expedition into the Native State of Sunghie Ujong, Malay Peninsula, in 1874, and was present at the attack and capture of the Kapayan Stockades. Also served during the Perak Expedition of 1875-76 during the operations in the Native States of Sunghie Ujong, Sri Mananti, and Terrachee, and was present at the action of Paroa (mentioned in despatches for gallant conduct, and promoted in recognition of his services from Lieutenant 10th Regt. to Captain 106th Regt., Medal with Clasp). Served with the Soudan Frontier Field Force in 1885-86, and was present in the engagement at Giniss, (Medal, and Khedive's Star).

³⁹⁰ Colonel J. L. Ross served with the 2nd Battalion King's Own Borderers in the Afghan war of 1878-80, first, with the Peshawur Valley Field Force under Lieut.General Maude, and afterwards with the Khyber Line Force under Lieut.General Bright, including the reconnaissance in the Shiliman Valley and the attack and destruction of the villages of Nargozi, Arab Kheyl and Jokan (mentioned in despatches, Medal). Served with the 2nd Battalion King's Own Scottish Borderers with the Suakin Field Force in December 1888 during the investment of Suakin and was present in the engagement at Gemaizah (Medal with Clasp, and Khedive's Star). Also served in the operations on the Soudan Frontier in 1889.

³⁹² Colonel C. T. Ilderton served with the 68th Light Infantry in the New Zealand war in 1864-66, and was present at the attack on the Gate Pah (Medal). Served with the Burmese Expedition in 1886-88 including the operations under Sir William Lockhart in the Pynmana, Yemethen and Meiktila districts (mentioned in despatches, DSO., and Medal with two Clasps).

³⁹³ Colonel R. Chalmer served with the 2nd Battalion 60th Rifles in the Afghan war from February 1879 to November 1880 during the occupation of Candahar, and as Brigade Major to Brigadier General Barter's Brigade, and was present in the engagements at Ahmed Khoyl and Urzoo near Ghuznee (mentioned in despatches), and in the subsequent operations in the Logar Valley; accompanied Sir Frederick Roberts in the march to Candahar as Brigade Major to Brigadier General MacGregor's Brigade, and was present at the battle of Candahar (mentioned in despatches, Brevet of Major, Medal with two Clasps, and Bronze Decoration). Also served as Brigade Major to Brigadier General MacGregor in the Marri Expedition (mentioned in despatches). Served in the Boer war of 1881 with the 2nd Battalion King's Royal Rifles in the Natal Field Force. Served with the Manipore Expedition in 1891 in command of the 4th Battalion King's Royal Rifles (mentioned in despatches, Medal with Clasp).

³⁹⁵ Colonel A. W. Morris served in the Zulu war of 1879, and was present in the engagement at Ulundi (Medal with Clasp). Served in the Boer war of 1881—severely wounded (mentioned in despatches).

³⁹⁶ Colonel J. C. R. Glasgow served with the 1st Battalion 12th Foot in the Afghan war in 1880 (Medal).

³⁹⁷ Colonel W. G. Thomas served in the Afghan war of 1878-79 with the Transport Train in the advance on Candahar under Sir Donald Stewart, and afterwards with the expedition into the Argand Valley under Major General Biddulph (Medal).

³⁹⁸ Colonel T. S. Gildea served with the 72nd Highlanders from the commencement of the Afghan war in 1878 till August 1879 with the Koorum Field Force, and was present at the attack and capture of the Peiwar Kotal (mentioned in despatches, Medal with Clasp).

Lieutenant Colonels. 40

Name	CORNET, 2nd LIEUT. or ENSIGN.	LIEUT.	CAPTAIN.	MAJOR.	LIEUT. COLONEL.	WHEN PLACED ON HALF PAY.
Arthur Henry Paget, *Major*, Scots Guards	......	12 June 69	29 June 72	......	1 Apr. 82	
Wm. Pringle Harrison, *Lt.Col.* Bengal Infantry ...	4 Jan. 61	6 Feb. 62	1 Jan. 70	21 Dec. 80	4 Jan. 87	
Horace R. Le M. Carey, *Lt.Col.* Indian S. C. ...	15 Jan. 61	4 Dec. 66	15 Jan. 73	15 Jan. 81	15 Jan. 87	
Walter Charles Farwell, *Lt.Col.* Bengal Infantry...	20 Jan. 61	17 Mar. 62	1 Jan. 70	31 Dec. 80	20 Jan. 87	
Robert A. Prideaux, *Lt.Col.* Bombay Infantry	27 Mar. 61	1 Dec. 62	4 Feb. 71	27 Mar. 81	27 Mar. 87	
Edw. Evans Grigg, *Lt.Col.* Bengal Infantry	7 June 61	25 July 62	1 Mar. 70	30 May 81	7 June 87	
Chas. Ransford, *Lt.Col.* Bengal Infantry	7 June 61	30 July 62	1 Mar. 70	7 June 81	7 June 87	
Wm. W. Hopton Scott, *Lt.Col.* Bengal Infantry ...	7 June 61	30 July 62	26 Mar. 70	7 June 81	7 June 87	
Freeman H. Jackson, *Lt.Col.* Bombay Infantry ...	7 June 61	5 Feb. 63	4 Feb. 71	7 June 81	7 June 87	
Henry Byam Abbott, *Lt.Col.* Indian Staff Corps ...	8 June 61	30 July 62	7 June 73	7 June 81	7 June 87	
Jas. Agnew M'Neale, *Lt.Col.* Bengal Infantry	8 June 61	30 July 62	9 May 70	8 June 81	8 June 87	
Chas. Michael Browne, *Lt.Col.* Bombay Infantry...	8 June 61	19 Sept. 63	4 Feb. 71	8 June 81	8 June 87	
Alfred Hercules Mayhew, *Lt.Col.* Indian S. C. ...	8 June 61	23 May 65	8 June 73	8 June 81	8 June 87	
Fred. Mercer Hunter, *CB. CSI. Lt.Col.* Indian S. C.	8 June 61	25 July 65	8 June 73	8 June 81	8 June 87	
Frederick Wilson Hemming, *Major*, 5 Dragoon Gds	25 Apr. 68	28 Oct. 71	31 Oct. 78	2 Mar. 81	1 July 87	
Edward Vincent Stace, *CB. Lt.Col.* Indian S. C. ...	......	1 July 61	1 July 73	1 July 81	1 July 87	
William Clark, *Lt.Col.* Oxford Light Inf. (43 F.)......	11 Feb. 62	30 Apr. 64	20 Sept. 71	30 Nov. 81	1 July 87	
William Aitken, *Lt.Col.* Royal Artillery	......	15 Jan. 67	31 Dec. 78	20 Sept. 84	1 July 87	
William Cooke, *Lt.Col.* Indian Staff Corps	7 Nov. 65	7 Nov. 67	7 Nov. 77	7 Nov. 85	1 July 87	
Ralph A. P. Clements, *DSO, Major*, S. Wales Borderers	......	2 Dec. 74	4 Dec. 80	24 Feb. 86	1 July 87	
Stuart Erskine Roiland, *Lt.Col.* Indian Staff Corps	9 Nov. 66	9 Nov. 67	9 Nov. 78	9 Nov. 86	1 July 87	
William Henry Browne, *Lt.Col.* Indian Staff Corps	20 Oct. 61	17 July 66	20 Oct. 73	20 Oct. 81	20 Oct. 87	
Geo. Farquharson Pengelley, *Lt.Col.* R. Mar. Art.	23 Dec. 59	18 May 65	10 Nov. 74	1 July 81	23 Dec. 87	
Malcolm W. Stevens, *Lt.Col.* Bombay Infantry ...	27 Dec. 61	16 July 64	19 Aug. 71	1 July 81	27 Dec. 87	
Arch. C. Bigg-Wither, *Lt.Col.* Bengal Infantry ...	2 Jan. 62	25 Jan. 63	11 July 71	1 July 81	2 Jan. 88	
Hy. John Lawrence, *Lt.Col.* Bengal Infantry	4 Jan. 62	10 Mar. 63	18 July 71	1 July 81	4 Jan. 88	
William Loch, *Lt.Col.* Bengal Infantry	4 Jun. 62	13 Mar. 63	18 July 71	1 July 81	4 Jan. 88	
Allan S. Roberts, *Lt.Col.* Bengal Infantry	20 Feb. 62	24 Mar. 63	18 July 71	1 July 81	20 Feb. 88	
p.s.c. John Spence, *Lt.Col.* (from h.p. Yorkshire Light Inf.), *Assist. Adj. Gen., Dover*, 28 Dec. 93	17 Jan. 63	29 May 67	12 Apr. 79	1 July 81	21 June 88	
Henry Townley Scott Yates, *Lt.Col.* Royal Artillery	......	8 Jan. 68	1 July 79	6 Feb. 85	2 Aug. 88	
Jacob Pieter D. Vanrenen, *Lt.Col.* Indian Staff C. ...	8 Aug. 62	27 Apr. 69	8 Aug. 74	8 Aug. 82	8 Aug. 88	
p.s.c. James Walton Fowell Buxton, *Major* (from h.p. Innis. Fus.), *D.A.A. Gen. Jersey*, 7 May 93	10 July 63	2 Jan. 69	10 Nov. 77	15 Oct. 81	15 Oct. 88	
Harrison Ross Lewin Morgan, *CB. Lt.Col.* R. Art. ...	......	1 Sept. 63	11 Mar. 76	2 Mar. 81	7 Dec. 88	
Francis J. G. Cook, *Lt.Col.* Army Service Corps (*Hon. Lt.Col.* 1 Apr. 85)	Depart-	mental	Service	22²/₁₂ yrs.	11 Dec. 88	
Fred. H. Bridgman, *Lt.Col.* Army Service Corps (*Hon. Lt.Col.* 1 Apr. 85)	Regtl.	and Deptl.	Service	25¹/₁₂ yrs.	11 Dec. 88	
Thomas B. Stewart, *Lt.Col.* Army Service Corps (*Hon. Lt.Col.* 1 May 85)	Depart-	mental	Service	21⁵/₁₂ yrs.	11 Dec. 88	
James A. Clarke, *Lt.Col.* Army Service Corps (*Hon. Lt.Col.* 1 May 85)	Depart-	mental	Service	21⁴/₁₂ yrs.	11 Dec. 88	
George Coates, *Lt.Col.* Army Service Corps (*Hon. Lt.Col.* 17 June 85)	Depart-	mental	Service	21³/₁₂ yrs.	11 Dec. 88	
Edward T. Christie, *Lt.Col.* Army Service Corps (*Hon. Lt.Col.* 1 Aug. 85)	Depart-	mental	Service	22²/₁₂ yrs.	11 Dec. 88	
Robert D. Noake, *Lt.Col.* Army Service Corps (*Hon. Lt.Col.* 2 Sept. 85)	Regtl.	and Deptl.	Service	25⁷/₁₂ yrs.	11 Dec. 88	
Wodehouse D. Richardson, *CB. Lt.Col.* Army Service Corps (*Hon. Lt.Col.* 9 Dec. 85)	Depart-	mental	Service	16⁶/₁₂ yrs.	11 Dec. 88	
Walter A. Dunne, *Lt.Col.* Army Service Corps (*Hon. Lt.Col.* 12 Dec. 85)	Depart-	mental	Service	15⁸/₁₂ yrs.	11 Dec. 88	
Robert A. Chermside, *Lt.Col.* Army Service Corps (*Hon. Lt.Col.* 1 Apr. 86)	Depart-	mental	Service	18⁸/₁₂ yrs.	11 Dec. 88	
Walter T. M'Leod, *Lt.Col.* Army Service Corps (*Hon. Lt.Col.* 17 May 86)	Depart-	mental	Service	17⁸/₁₂ yrs.	11 Dec. 88	
Edwin Fitz-Stubbs, *Lt.Col.* Army Service Corps (*Hon. Lt.Col.* 13 June 86)	Depart-	mental	Service	2₁²/₁₂ yrs.	11 Dec. 88	
Ernest Grattan, *Lt.Col.* Army Service Corps (*Hon. Lt.Col.* 24 June 86)	Depart-	mental	Service	17⁸/₁₂ yrs.	11 Dec. 88	
Thomas P. Shannon, *Lt.Col.* Army Service Corps (*Hon. Lt.Col.* 13 July 86)	Depart-	mental	Service	17⁷/₁₂ yrs.	11 Dec. 88	
Charles J. Bannister, *Lt.Col.* Army Service Corps (*Hon. Lt.Col.* 8 Aug. 87)	Depart-	mental	Service	17⁵/₁₂ yrs.	11 Dec. 88	
Robert A. Nugent, *CB. Lt.Col.* Army Service Corps (*Hon. Lt.Col.* 1 Sept. 87)	Depart-	mental	Service	16⁶/₁₂ yrs.	11 Dec. 88	
Alfred Ely, *Lt.Col.* Army Service Corps (*Hon. Lt.Col.* 10 Sept. 87)	Depart-	mental	Service	16⁶/₁₂ yrs.	11 Dec. 88	
Casimir A. Bourne, *Lt.Col.* Army Service Corps (*Hon. Lt.Col.* 6 Sept. 88)	Depart-	mental	Service	16⁶/₁₂ yrs.	11 Dec. 88	
Lewis A. Clutterbuck, *Lt.Col.* Army Service Corps	Depart-	mental	Service	16⁶/₁₂ yrs.	19 Dec. 88	
William John Irwin, *Major*, 20 Hussars	23 Jan. 69	28 Oct. 71	30 Nov. 79	9 Sept. 85	28 Dec. 88	
Hen. Mackenzie M. Wood, *Lt.Col.* Indian S. C. ...	17 Jan. 63	17 Jan. 66	17 Jan. 75	17 Jan. 83	17 Jan. 89	
John Davidson, *Lt.Col.* Indian Staff Corps	24 Mar. 63	24 Mar. 66	24 Mar. 75	22 Nov. 79	24 Mar. 89	
George Masson Abbott, *Lt.Col.* Indian Staff Corps	31 Mar. 63	4 Oct. 66	31 Mar. 75	2 Mar. 81	31 Mar. 89	
Arthur Wellesley White, *Lt.Col.* Royal Artillery ...	......	23 Dec. 64	14 July 77	1 Jan. 84	1 May 89	
Edward Quin, *Lt.Col.* Indian Staff Corps	12 May 63	8 Nov. 66	12 May 75	12 May 83	12 May 89	
Hon. Charles Dutton,[1] *Major* (from h.p. Shropshire Light Infantry), *Recruiting Staff Officer, Devonport*, 20 Nov. 93	12 Mar. 61	26 July 64	7 Oct. 71	2 Mar. 81	15 May 89	
Alfred A. Baker, *Lt.Col.* Army Service Corps	Depart-	mental	Service	16⁶/₁₂ yrs.	21 May 89	
Marcus E. R. Rainsford, *Lt.Col.* Army S. C.	Depart-	mental	Service	16⁶/₁₂ yrs.	21 May 89	
George V. Hamilton, *Lt.Col.* Army Service Corps	Depart-	mental	Service	15⁸/₁₂ yrs.	21 May 89	
Frank E. Stevens, *Lt.Col.* Army Service Corps ...	Depart-	mental	Service	16⁶/₁₂ yrs.	12 June 89	
George Robert Hodgson, *Lt.Col.* Indian Staff C.	23 June 63	26 Apr. 67	23 June 75	23 June 83	23 June 89	
George F. O. Boughey, *Lt.Col.* Royal Engineers ...	......	25 June 62	15 Feb. 73	25 June 82	25 June 89	
John Hill, *Lt.Col.* Royal Engineers	......	25 June 62	12 Sept. 75	25 June 82	25 June 89	
Hy. Donald Buchanan-Dunlop, *Lt.Col.* h.p. R. Art.	......	17 July 66	7 Aug. 78	23 June 84	27 June 89	27 June 89
p.s.c. Burnett Groive Hall, *Lt.Col.* R. Marine Art.	1 July 61	3 Aug. 67	1 Apr. 76	1 July 82	1 July 89	
Robert Stevenson, *Major* (from h.p. 6 Dragoon Guards), *Recruiting Staff Officer, Leeds*, 4 Apr. 92	1 Mar. 64	18 Dec. 67	30 June 69	5 July 82	5 July 89	
Henry Affleck Graves, *Lt.Col.* Indian Staff Corps ...	......	16 July 63	16 July 75	16 July 83	16 July 89	

D 2

Lieutenant Colonels.

Name	Cornet, 2nd Lieut. or Ensign	Lieut.	Captain	Major	Lieut. Colonel	When placed on Half Pay
Jas. Bird Hutchinson, *Lt.Col.* Indian Staff Corps...	17 July 63	17 July 66	17 July 75	17 July 83	17 July 89	
Allan H. Langdon, *Lt.Col.* Army Service Corps ...	Departmental Service			16⁶/₁₂ yrs.	13 Aug. 89	
Thomas H. H. Garrett, *Major,* h.p. 16 Lancers ...	13 July 70	4 Feb. 71	24 Feb. 76	21 July 82	21 Aug. 89	21 Aug. 89
Harvey Hamilton Harvey-Kelly, *Lt.Col.* Indian S. C.	16 Feb. 64	28 Oct. 66	31 May 71	6 Feb. 85	23 Aug. 89	
Charles H. Bridge, *Lt.Col.* Army Service Corps ...	Departmental Service			16⁶/₁₂ yrs.	25 Aug. 89	
Francis Jas. Kempster, *DSO, Major,* Munster Fus.		10 Mar. 76	18 Nov. 82	4 Sept. 89	5 Sept. 89	
James Graves Kelly, *Lt.Col.* Indian Staff Corps...	11 Sept. 03	30 Aug. 67	11 Sept 75	11 Sept. 83	11 Sept. 89	
Wm. Henry Auchinleck, *Major,* R. Artillery		25 June 62	1 Apr. 75	25 June 82	1 Oct. 89	
William Mallins, *Major,* Royal Artillery		25 June 62	24 Apr. 75	25 June 82	1 Oct. 89	
Henry Blomfield Kingscote, *Major,* R.Artillery......		1 Sept. 62	8 Sept. 75	1 Sept. 82	1 Oct. 89	
John Briscoe Watts, *Lt.Col.* Indian Staff Corps	2 Oct. 63	9 Feb. 67	2 Oct. 75	2 Oct. 83	2 Oct. 89	
Arthur Hill Sandys Montgomery, *Lt.Col.* Provisional Battalion	18 Jan. 61	5 Aug. 65	23 Apr. 73	1 July 81	16 Oct. 89	
Ernest Frederick Cambier, *Major,* Royal Art.......		1 Mar. 63	8 Dec. 75	1 Nov. 82	1 Nov. 89	
William Savage Langley, *Major,* Royal Artillery ...		1 Mar. 63	23 Dec. 75	1 Nov. 82	1 Nov. 89	
Frank Barrow, *Lt.Col.* Indian Staff Corps	6 Nov. 63	18 Sept. 67	6 Nov. 75	6 Nov. 83	6 Nov. 89	
John G. Y. Wilson, *Lt.Col.* Army Service Corps ...	Departmental Service			16⁶/₁₂ yrs.	17 Nov. 89	
Fred. East Apthorp, *Lt.Col.* h.p. Inniskilling Fus....	11 Aug. 63	18 Jan. 67	10 Dec. 75	1 July 81	1 Dec. 89	1 Dec. 93
Geo. Alban Lewes, *Major* (from h.p. Northampton Regt.), *Professor R. M. College,* 1 Sept. 92...	23 Dec. 64	14 Mar. 68	2 Feb. 80	16 Dec. 82	16 Dec. 89	
Thomas Gracey, *Major,* Royal Engineers		17 Dec. 62	1 Oct. 76	17 Dec. 82	17 Dec. 89	
Henry Hardy Cole, *Major,* h.p. Royal Engineers...		17 Dec. 62	6 June 77	17 Dec. 82	17 Dec. 89	11 Dec. 93
p.s.c. James Latimer Crawshay St. Clair,⁸ *Major,* (from h.p. Argyll and Sutherland Highlanders), *D. A. A. Gen. Guernsey,* 15 May 92	23 Sept. 71	28 Oct. 71	1 Oct. 80	31 Jan. 83	31 Jan. 90	
Thos. Mercer Maxwell, *Major,* Derbyshire Regt......	18 Dec. 60	11 Aug. 63	6 Mar. 74	14 Feb. 82	14 Feb. 90	
John Fras. Jas. Miller, *Lt.Col.* Indian Staff Corps.	1 Mar. 64	8 Sept. 68	1 Mar. 76	1 Mar. 84	1 Mar. 90	
Crawford Boyd Cooke, *Lt.Col.* Indian Staff Corps..	8 Mar. 64	3 Apr. 67	8 Mar. 76	8 Mar. 84	8 Mar. 90	
Francis Wm. Jas. Barker, *Lt.Col.* (from R. Art.) *Supdt. Small Arms Factory, Birmingham,* 1 Oct. 92		24 June 63	15 Jan. 76	28 Mar. 83	28 Mar. 90	
Chas. Anglesea Empson, *Lt.Col.* (from R. Art.), *1st Class Ordnance Officer, Bengal,* 12 July 86		27 June 63	15 Jan. 76	28 Mar. 83	28 Mar. 90	
Wm. Fred. de Hubbenet Curtis, *Lt.Col.* R. Art.......		6 July 63	15 Jan. 76	28 Mar. 83	28 Mar. 90	
Walter Treslove Ellis, *Lt.Col.* h.p. Northampton Regt.	21 Nov. 62	6 Mar. 67	1 Dec. 69	1 July 81	1 Apr. 90	1 Apr. 94
p.s.c. Jas. Cecil Dalton, *Major,* h.p. R. Artillery ...		13 Jan. 69	27 Sept.79	1 Apr. 85	1 Apr. 90	1 Sept.92
Hugh de la Motte Hervey, *Lt.Col.* Indian S. C......	5 Apr. 64	3 Apr. 67	5 Apr. 76	5 Apr. 84	5 Apr. 90	
John Muir Hunter, *Lt.Col.* Indian Staff Corps		12 Apr. 64	12 Apr. 76	12 Apr. 84	12 Apr. 90	
Francis Frederick Ditmas, *Lt.Col.* Royal Art		1 Sept. 63	21 Feb. 76	17 Apr. 82	17 Apr. 90	
James George Proudfoot, *Lt.Col.* Indian S.C........	6 Apr. 64	3 May 67	26 Apr. 76	26 Apr. 84	26 Apr. 90	
William Henry Browne, *Lt.Col.* Indian Staff Corps.	3 May 64	4 Sept. 68	3 May 76	3 May 84	3 May 90	
Arthur Augustus Saunders, *Lt.Col.* (from Royal Art.), *Chief Inst. School of Gunnery,* 29 Nov. 93		1 Sept. 63	11 Mar. 76	12 May 83	12 May 90	
Arthur James Pearson, *Lt.Col.* Royal Artillery		11 Sept. 63	29 Apr. 76	12 May 83	12 May 90	
p.s.c. Harry Cooper,¹⁰ *Major* (from h.p. N. Lancashire Regt.), *D. A. A. Gen. Dublin,* 21 Nov. 93...	10 Nov. 65	23 Nov. 70	23 Jan. 78	1 July 81	31 May 90	
Chas. Robert Kerr, *Lt.Col.* h.p. Dublin Fus. (102 F.)	23 Jan. 69	28 Oct. 71	17 Mar. 77	1 July 81	7 June 90	7 June 94
Samuel Job Lea, *Lt.Col.* Army Service Corps	6 Mar. 72	6 Mar. 72	19 Sept.81	15 June 85	15 June 90	
Arthur W. Collard, *Lt.Col.* Army Service Corps (*Hon. Major,* 15 June 85)	Deptl.	Service	16⁶/₁₂ yrs.	11 Dec. 88	15 June 90	
Bernard Heygate, *Lt.Col.* Army Service Corps (*Hon. Major,* 15 June 85)	Deptl.	Service	15⁸/₁₂ yrs.	11 Dec. 88	15 June 90	
James R. Edwards, *Lt.Col.* Army Service Corps (*Hon. Major,* 15 June 85)	Deptl.	Service	15⁸/₁₂ yrs.	11 Dec. 88	15 June 90	
Joseph Whitley, *Lt.Col.* Army Service Corps (*Hon. Major,* 15 June 85)	Deptl.	Service	14⁸/₁₂ yrs.	11 Dec. 88	15 June 90	
Edward W. D. Ward, *Lt.Col.* Army Service Corps (*Hon. Major,* 15 June 85)	Deptl.	Service	14⁸/₁₂ yrs.	11 Dec. 88	15 June 90	
John A. Boyd, *Lt.Col.* Army Service Corps (*Hon. Major,* 15 June 85)	Deptl.	Service	13⁸/₁₂ yrs	11 Dec. 88	15 June 90	
Geo. Westrenen Sawyer, *Lt.Col.* Indian S.C.	28 June 64	20 May 67	28 June 76	28 June 84	28 June 90	
Wm. Sinclair Smith Bisset, *CIE. Major,* R. Eng....		29 June 63	15 June 77	2 Mar. 81	29 June 90	
George Will, *Major,* Royal Artillery		2 Nov. 63	19 June 76	1 July 83	1 July 90	
Henry Pincke Lee, *Lt.Col.* Royal Engineers		24 June 63	6 June 77	24 June 83	2 July 90	
Allen Aug. William Beamish, *Major,* R. Engineers		17 Dec. 62	9 Apr. 77	6 July 83	6 July 90	
Albert de Clancy Rennick, *Lt.Col.* Indian S. C.....	6 July 64	18 July 68	6 July 76	6 July 84	6 July 90	
H. Saml. Spiller Watkin, *CB. Major*(from R. Art.), *Chief Inspector of Position Finding* 26 July 90 ...		1 Mar. 64	8 Sept.76	26 July 83	26 July 90	
Wm. Hy. Dawes Jones, *Lt.Col.* Indian Staff Corps	26 July 64	21 Aug. 67	26 July 76	26 July 84	26 July 90	
George Henry, *Lt.Col.* Royal Engineers		8 Jan. 68	29 July 80	12 Feb. 87	28 July 90	
John Graham Stone, *Major* (from R. Artillery), *Supdt. of Factories, Bengal,* 23 Feb. 83		22 Mar. 64	21 Dec. 76	1 Aug. 83	1 Aug. 90	
Harry Croker Fox, *Major,* Royal Engineers		3 Aug. 63	22 Aug. 77	3 Aug. 83	3 Aug. 90	
Stannus Verner Gordon, *Lt.Col.* Indian Staff Corps	9 Aug. 64	22 Aug. 67	9 Aug. 76	2 Mar. 81	9 Aug. 90	
Henry Torkington, *Lt.Col.* Royal Artillery		3 June 64	14 Feb. 77	1 Sept. 83	1 Sept. 90	
Christopher S. F. Fagan, *Lt.Col.* Royal Marines ...	31 Dec. 62	23 Aug. 66	5 July 78	1 Sept. 83	1 Sept. 90	
Paul Fred. Michael Baddeley, *Lt.Col.* (from Royal Artillery), *Supdt. of Factories, Bengal,* 22 May 88		16 Aug. 64	30 Apr. 77	2 Sept. 83	2 Sept. 90	
William Purvis Wright, *Lt.Col.* Royal Marines	31 Dec. 62	13 Sept. 66	2 Sept. 78	8 Sept. 83	8 Sept. 90	
Lewis Forbes Heath, *Lt.Col.* Indian Staff Corps ...	9 Sept. 64	11 Jan. 67	9 Sept. 76	9 Sept. 84	9 Sept. 90	
Wm. Geo. Craigie Halkett, *Lt.Col.* Indian S. Corps	9 Sept. 64	16 Apr. 68	9 Sept. 76	9 Sept. 84	9 Sept. 90	
Henry Boileau, *Lt.Col.* Indian Staff Corps	9 Sept. 64	12 Jan. 69	9 Sept. 76	9 Sept. 84	9 Sept. 90	
Edw. Alex. Fraser, *Lt.Col.* Indian Staff Corps	13 Sept. 64	29 May 67	13 Sept. 76	13 Sept. 84	13 Sept. 90	
Wm. Reginald Houison Craufurd,¹³ *Major,* h.p. Argyll and Sutherland Highlanders	6 Mar. 69	14 Sept. 70	15 Dec. 82	23 Mar. 79	17 Sept. 90	1 Dec. 94
David Wm. Keith Barr, *Lt.Col.* Indian S. C..........	20 Sept. 64	22 July 68	20 Sept. 76	20 Sept. 84	20 Sept. 90	
Edmund P. B. Smith, *Lt.Col.* Army Service Corps (*Hon. Major,* 10 Oct. 85)	Deptl.	Service	16⁶/₁₂ yrs.	11 Dec. 88	10 Oct. 90	
Norton Charles Martelli, *Lt.Col.* Indian Staff C. ...	11 Oct. 64	1 Oct. 70	11 Oct. 76	11 Oct. 84	11 Oct. 90	
William F. Moore, *Lt.Col.* Army Service Corps (*Hon. Major,* 15 Oct. 85)	Deptl.	Service	15⁸/₁₂ yrs.	11 Dec. 88	15 Oct. 90	
Edward Thomas Browell, *Lt.Col.* R. Artillery		16 Aug. 64	30 Apr. 77	16 Oct. 83	16 Oct. 90	
Sir Fleetwood Isham Edwards, *KCB. Lt.Col.* R. Eng.		30 June 63	5 July 77	30 June 83	22 Oct. 90	
John W. B. Parkin, *Lt.Col.* Army Service Corps (*Hon. Major,* 14 Nov. 85)	Deptl.	Service	15⁸/₁₂ yrs.	11 Dec. 88	14 Nov. 90	

Lieutenant Colonels.

	CORNET, 2nd LIEUT. OF ENSIGN.	LIEUT.	CAPTAIN.	MAJOR.	LIEUT. COLONEL.	WHEN PLACED ON HALF PAY.
Montagu Wynyard,[14] *Major*, h.p. W. Kent Regt. (50 Foot); *Assist. Comdt. R. M. College* 17 Nov. 90	16 Jan. 66	28 Oct. 71	6 Mar. 80	17 Nov. 83	17 Nov. 90	17 Nov. 90
Malcolm Graham, *Lt.Col.* Army Service Corps (*Hon. Major*, 15 June 85)	Deptl.	Service	16 6/12 yrs.	11 Dec. 88	10 Dec. 90	
George Hugh C. Dyce, *Lt.Col.* Indian Staff Corps	30 Dec. 64	7 May 68	30 Dec. 76	30 Dec. 84	30 Dec. 90	
John Minnitt Tabor, *Lt.Col.* Royal Artillery		28 Oct. 64	1 July 77	31 Dec. 83	31 Dec. 90	
Henry George F. Siddons, *Lt.Col.* R. Artillery		11 Nov. 64	1 July 77	31 Dec. 83	31 Dec. 90	
Edward Lake, *Major*, Royal Artillery		11 Nov. 64	1 July 77	31 Dec. 83	31 Dec. 90	
p.s.c. Arthur G. Walker, *Major*, Royal Artillery		21 Mar. 65	1 Oct. 77	11 Jan. 83	1 Jan. 91	
Philip K. Lonsdale Beaver, *Lt.Col.* Royal Artillery		24 Mar. 65	1 Oct. 77	28 June 83	1 Jan. 91	
Augustus Browne, *Lt.Col.* Royal Artillery		9 Dec. 64	1 July 77	1 Jan. 84	1 Jan. 91	
Alfred Foulger Fletcher, *Major*, h.p. R. Artillery		16 Dec. 64	14 July 77	1 Jan. 84	1 Jan. 91	1 Jan. 91
James Carnegie Gillespie, *Major*, R. Artillery		21 Feb. 65	6 Sept. 77	1 Jan. 84	1 Jan. 91	
Norton Powlett, *Lt.Col.* Royal Artillery		24 Mar. 65	1 Oct. 77	1 Jan. 84	1 Jan. 91	
Sydney Drummond Turnbull, *Lt.Col.* Indian S. C.	3 Jan. 65	8 Sept. 68	3 Jan. 77	1 Jan. 84	1 Jan. 91	
Ramsay W. Rainsford-Hannay, *Major*, h.p. Royal Artillery		18 July 65	1 Jan. 78	9 Jan. 84	9 Jan. 91	9 Jan. 91
John George Uppleby, *Major*, Royal Artillery		12 Jan. 65	2 Jan. 78	9 Jan. 84	9 Jan. 91	
Francis Mascall, *Major*, R. Engineers		15 Jan. 64	1 Sept. 77	15 Jan. 84	15 Jan. 91	
Henry Elsdale, *Major*, Royal Engineers		15 Jan. 64	1 Oct. 77	15 Jan. 84	15 Jan. 91	
Frank Vincent Corbett, *Major*, R. Engineers		15 Jan. 64	1 Oct. 77	15 Jan. 84	15 Jan. 91	
John Walter Ottley, *Major*, Royal Engineers		15 Jan. 64	1 Oct. 77	15 Jan. 84	15 Jan. 91	
St. John Fancourt Michell, *Major*, Indian S. C.	1 Dec. 69	28 Oct. 71	1 Dec. 81	1 Dec. 89	17 Jan. 91	
John Fielden Brocklehurst, *Lt.Col.* R. Horse Guards		2 Dec. 74	18 May 81	15 June 85	18 Jan. 91	
Howel Gunter, *Lt.Col.* h.p. Norfolk Regiment; *Comdt. Queensland Defence Force*	8 July 62	23 June 65	7 July 74	10 July 81	29 Jan. 91	20 Aug. 94
Charles Warren Walker, *Lt.Col.* Indian Staff Corps	31 Jan. 65	10 May 71	31 Jan. 77	31 Jan. 85	31 Jan. 91	
p.s.c. John Thomas Bury, *Lt.Col.* Royal Artillery		21 Mar. 65	1 Oct. 77	1 Jan. 84	10 Feb. 91	
Augustus Bury Liardet, *Major*, h.p. R. Marines, *Barrack Master, Portsmouth*, 27 Sept. 91	24 June 63	10 Nov. 66	19 Oct. 78	11 Feb. 84	11 Feb. 91	27 Sept. 91
*Joseph Speranza, *Lt.Col.* Royal Malta Artillery	26 June 58	25 Jan. 61	13 Aug. 77	10 Nov. 85	14 Feb. 91	
Alexander Donald M'Arthur, *Major*, R. Eng.		16 Feb. 64	1 Oct. 77	16 Feb. 84	16 Feb. 91	
Jasper Selwyn Tupper, *Major* (from h.p.W.Surrey Regt.), *Recruiting Staff Officer, Glasgow*, 31 Aug. 93	29 July 62	4 Oct. 64	8 Apr. 74	6 May 82	19 Feb. 91	
Charles Mitchell Smith, *Lt.Col.* Royal Artillery		23 Dec. 64	1 Oct. 77	1 Jan. 84	1 Mar. 91	
Edward J. H. Spratt,[15] *Lt.Col.* h.p. Worcester Regt.	3 Mar. 65	12 Dec. 68	31 Aug. 78	24 July 82	2 Mar. 91	2 Mar. 95
Arthur Montagu Bowles,[16] *Lt.Col.* h.p. N. Stafford Rgt.	28 Oct. 68	27 Oct. 71	29 June 78	22 July 83	6 Mar. 91	6 Mar. 95
Henry Moore,[17] *Major* (from h.p. Lancaster Regt.) *Recruiting Staff Officer, Woolwich*, 4 Apr. 92	15 Jan. 64	27 Mar. 69	1 Apr. 77	1 July 81	7 Mar. 91	
p.s.c. Jas. Edw. Goodwyn,[18] *Lt.Col.* h.p.E.Lanc.Regt.	17 Mar. 63	12 Sept. 65	9 Aug. 73	1 July 81	18 Mar. 91	18 Mar. 95
Arthur Walter Noyes, *Lt.Col.* W. York. Regt. (14 F.)	9 Mar. 64	14 Aug. 67	16 Feb. 78	7 Mar. 82	20 Mar. 91	
David Geo. Johnston, *Lt.Col.* Munster Fus. (101 F.)	9 Feb. 70	28 Oct. 71	31 Oct. 77	1 July 81	26 Mar. 91	
Walter Creagh, *Lt.Col.* 7 Dragoon Guards	4 Oct. 64	28 Oct. 68	1 Apr. 75	1 July 81	31 Mar. 91	
James Frederick Harman, *Lt.Col.* Royal Artillery, *Assistant Director, Artillery College*, 1 Apr. 91		17 July 66	25 May 78	20 Aug. 84	1 Apr. 91	
Compton Norman, *Lt.Col.* Welsh Fusiliers (23 F.)	2 Sept. 62	12 Jan. 66	1 June 74	24 Dec. 81	2 Apr. 91	
Charles Wm. H. Helyar, *Lt.Col.* 3 Hussars	2 Feb. 64	1 Dec. 65	31 Oct. 71	15 Oct. 81	15 Apr. 91	
Alexander Evans Gordon, *Lt.Col.* Indian Staff Corps	18 Apr. 65	2 Apr. 69	18 Apr. 77	18 Apr. 85	18 Apr. 91	
Arthur Bouverie Stopford, *Lt.Col.* R. Artillery		22 Mar. 68	4 Apr. 79	18 Nov. 82	1 May 91	
Walter John Morse, *Lt.Col.* Indian Staff Corps	25 Apr. 65	3 Sept. 68	25 Apr. 77	25 Apr. 85	25 Apr. 91	
Ponsonby Wm. Watts, *Major*, h.p. Irish Regt. (18 F.)	8 July 62	12 Sept. 65	18 Nov. 76	1 July 81	29 Apr. 91	29 Apr. 91
Edward Thompson Dickson, *Lt.Col.* Berkshire Regt.	23 Jan. 69	14 Apr. 71	20 Oct. 78	2 Feb. 84	30 Apr. 91	
Frederick Cooper Turner,[19] *Major*, h.p. Northampton Regt.	8 Aug. 65	26 Feb. 70	30 Nov. 78	21 June 83	6 May 91	
Arth.Wm. Sheringham, *Lt.Col.* Cheshire Regt. (22F.)	29 June 66	3 Oct. 70	19 July 77	20 Dec. 82	19 May 91	
Philip Henry Smith, *Lt.Col.* Devonshire Regt.	16 Jan. 63	10 July 66	7 Mar. 77	18 Jan. 82	19 May 91	
Henry Tomkinson, *Lt.Col.* 1 Dragoons	23 Apr. 61	10 May 64	8 July 68	23 Dec. 84	20 May 91	
William Guise Tucker, *CB. Lt.Col.* Roy. Marine Art.		24 June 68	24 Mar. 79	18 Nov. 82	1 May 91	
Charles Francis Massy, *Lt.Col.* Indian Staff Corps	26 May 65	14 Aug. 67	26 May 77	26 May 85	26 May 91	
Adolphus Brett Crosbie, *Lt.Col.* Royal Marines	28 Dec. 64	4 Apr. 79	7 Dec. 79	28 May 91		
Alexander Walter Ferrier, *Lt.Col.* Royal Artillery		24 June 63	1 Jan. 76	14 Feb. 83	29 May 91	
John Humfrey, *Lt.Col.* Indian Staff Corps	2 June 65	4 Nov. 68	2 June 77	2 June 85	2 June 91	
Frederick Hutchinson Forjett, *Lt.Col.* Indian S. C.	10 June 65	30 Mar. 70	10 June 77	10 June 85	10 June 91	
John Lloyd Dickin, *Major*, h.p. Gloucester Regt.	10 May 64	20 July 67	3 Aug. 70	1 July 81	17 June 91	17 June 91
p.s.c. Fredk. de Lamare Morison, *Lt.Col.* R. Scots	16 Jan. 61	8 Aug. 65	21 June 71	1 July 81	21 June 91	
Herbert St. George Schomberg, *Lt.Col.* R. Marines	24 June 65	13 Feb. 67	13 Apr. 79	11 July 82	24 June 91	
Sydney Tyers, *Major*, h.p. Royal Marines, *Barrack Master, Chatham*, 3 June 92	24 June 63	15 Jan. 67	12 May 79	24 June 84	24 June 91	3 June 92
James E. W. Smyth Caulfeild, *Lt.Col.* W. I. Regt.		14 May 74	2 Feb. 78	1 Jan. 83	29 June 91	
Howard Melliss, *CSI. Lt.Col.* Indian Staff Corps	30 June 65	31 Mar. 69	30 June 77	18 Nov. 82	30 June 91	
James Grant, *Lt.Col.* Indian Staff Corps	30 June 65	4 Aug. 68	30 June 77	30 June 85	30 June 91	
John Olphert Gage, *Lt.Col.* Border Regt. (34 F.)	16 Mar. 60	2 Sept. 62	5 Jan. 70	1 July 81	1 July 91	
Francis Henry A. Disney-Roebuck, *Lt.Col.* Duke of Cornwall's Light Infantry	26 Feb. 64	17 Apr. 67	9 Apr. 70	1 July 81	1 July 91	
George Conner, *Lt.Col.* Gloucester Regt. (28 F.)	2 June 65	3 June 68	25 Mar. 71	1 July 81	1 July 91	
Edmond Charles Browne, *Lt.Col.* Scots Fusiliers	23 Sept. 62	7 July 66	19 Oct. 74	1 July 81	1 July 91	
Henry Blackwood MacCall, *Lt.Col.* King's R. Rifles	16 Feb. 64	19 Feb. 67	1 Apr. 75	1 July 81	1 July 91	
Sir G. Albert de H. Larpent, *Burt. Lt.Col.* Connaught Rangers (88 F.)	21 Nov. 65	15 Sept. 69	24 Nov. 77	1 July 81	1 July 91	
Waldron E. R. Kelly, *Lt.Col.* The Buffs.	16 Aug. 64	16 Oct. 67	1 Apr. 75	14 Sept. 81	1 July 91	
Frederic John Cartin, *Lt.Col.* Gloucester Regt.	15 Jan. 64	16 Oct. 66	9 Jun. 78	19 Nov. 81	1 July 91	
Frank Ryley, *Lt.Col.* North Lancashire Regt.(47 F.)	12 June 67	24 Dec. 70	7 Jan. 80	23 May 82	1 July 91	
Wm. Henry MacGeorge, *Lt.Col.* 6 Dragoon Guards	13 July 70	28 Oct. 71	14 July 77	7 May 82	1 July 91	
Robert Henry Oxley, *Lt.Col.* Gordon Highlanders	9 Mar. 67	15 Dec. 69	28 Oct. 76	13 Feb. 85	1 July 91	
Sidney Beckwith Blyth, *Lt.Col.* Welsh Fusiliers	1 Dec. 65	30 Mar. 67	4 Aug. 79	10 Apr. 85	1 July 91	
Joseph Henry Newill, *Lt.Col.* Indian Staff Corps	4 July 65	7 Nov. 68	4 July 77	4 July 85	4 July 91	
p.s.c. Thomas Prickett, *Lt.Col.* (from h.p. Essex Regt.) *Assist. Adjutant General, Bengal*	2 June 65	2 Jan. 69	24 July 75	5 Nov. 81	6 July 91	
Francis Charles Burton, *Lt.Col.* Indian Staff Corps	11 July 65	20 May 69	11 July 77	2 Mar. 81	11 July 91	
James Aloysius Miley, *Lt.Col.* Indian Staff Corps	18 July 65	20 May 69	18 July 77	18 July 85	18 July 91	
Charles Brenton Wickham, *Lt.Col.* R. Artillery		11 Oct. 64	10 Dec. 81	22 July 91		
Thomas Francis Hobday, *Lt.Col.* Indian Staff Corps	25 July 65	24 July 68	25 July 77	22 Nov. 79	25 July 91	
Edward Hales Wilson, *Lt.Col.* Indian Staff Corps	25 July 65	13 July 69	25 July 77	25 July 85	25 July 91	
Arthur Bucknall Shakespear, *Major*, R. Marine Art.		24 June 68	19 Oct. 79	11 Mar. 88	29 July 91	

Lieutenant Colonels.

Name	Cornet, 2nd Lieut. or Ensign	Lieut.	Captain.	Major.	Lieut. Colonel.	When placed on half pay.
Richard Corbett, *Lt. Col.* Royal Artillery	......	1 Sept. 63	14 Mar. 75	2 Mar. 81	1 Aug. 91	
Samuel H. Winter, *Lt.Col.* Army Service Corps (*Hon. Major*, 1 Aug. 86)	Deptl.	Service	15 8/12 yrs.	11 Dec. 88	1 Aug. 91	
Robert Alexander Gilchrist, *Lt.Col.* Indian S. C.	4 Aug. 65	19 July 69	4 Aug. 77	4 Aug. 85	4 Aug. 91	
Johnson William Savage, *Lt.Col.* Royal Engineers	......	15 Jan. 64	1 Oct. 77	15 Jan. 84	6 Aug. 91	
Donald Robertson, *Lt.Col.* Indian Staff Corps	8 Aug. 65	8 Aug. 67	8 Aug. 77	8 Aug. 85	8 Aug. 91	
William Geo. Currie Johnstone, *Lt.Col.* Indian S. C.	8 Aug. 65	18 May 69	8 Aug. 77	8 Aug. 85	8 Aug. 91	
Alfred G. Hipwell, *Lt.Col.* Army Service Corps (*Hon. Major*, 8 Aug. 86)	Deptl.	Service	15 8/12 yrs.	11 Dec. 88	8 Aug. 91	
p.s.c. Evelyn C. Money, *Lt.Col.* Irish Fusiliers	3 Jan. 65	27 July 66	19 Feb. 70	21 Sept. 82	12 Aug. 91	
Adrien Samuel Woods, *Lt.Col.* Leinster Regt. (109 F.)	2 Dec. 68	28 Oct. 71	2 Feb. 81	18 Nov. 82	12 Aug. 91	
William Lees Greenstreet, *Lt. Col.* Royal Engineers	......	18 Oct. 64	1 Oct. 77	18 Oct. 84	12 Aug. 91	
Hendley Paul Kirkwood, *Lt.Col.* Royal Engineers	......	15 Jan. 64	1 Oct. 77	15 Jan. 84	13 Aug. 91	
Russell Richard Pulford, *Lt.Col.* Royal Engineers	......	17 Mar. 05	17 Mar. 78	24 Mar. 85	13 Aug. 91	
Frederick Coningham, *Lt.Col.* Royal Scots	20 May 64	13 July 67	11 Apr. 75	1 July 81	14 Aug. 91	
Henry Bellingham Le Mottée, *Lt.Col.* E. York Regt.	22 Jan. 64	1 Jan. 67	12 Nov. 73	1 July 81	15 Aug. 91	
Wm. Villeneuve Gregory, *Lt.Col.* Royal Artillery	......	3 Oct. 63	10 May 76	20 June 83	17 Aug. 91	
Jas. Nicholson Sodon Kirkwood, *Lt.Col.* Indian S.C.	1 Sept. 65	11 Jan. 67	1 Sept. 77	1 Sept. 85	1 Sept. 91	
Vaughan Jenkins, *Major*, West Riding Regiment	......	30 Dec. 71	1 Oct. 81	7 May 86	1 Sept. 91	
Charles Comyn Egerton, *DSO. Lt.Col.* Indian S.C.	8 June 67	19 Oct. 69	8 June 79	8 June 87	1 Sept. 91	
William Terence Shone, *DSO. Major*, R. Engineers	......	4 Jan. 71	4 Jan. 83	17 Apr. 89	1 Sept. 91	
Hugh Gough Grant, *Lt. Col.* Seaforth Highlanders	28 July 63	26 Oct. 65	5 Nov. 72	2 Mar. 81	2 Sept. 91	
Edward Albert Olivant, *Lt.Col.* Royal Artillery	......	22 Mar. 64	13 Sept. 76	26 July 83	7 Sept. 91	
Maule Campbell Brackenbury, *Lt.Col.* R. Engineers	......	22 June 65	17 Apr. 78	22 June 85	8 Sept. 91	
Hon. Miles Stapleton, *Lt. Col.* 20 Hussars	......	5 May 69	3 Aug. 72	2 July 84	9 Sept. 91	
Rodney Edward Mundy, *Major*, R. Artillery	......	19 July 64	10 Ap 77	1 Jan. 84	11 Sept. 91	
Patrick Francis Robertson,[20] *Major*, h.p. Gordon Highlanders	14 Mar. 63	29 May 67	29 Jan. 75	29 Oct. 81	16 Sept. 91	16 Sept. 91
William Wood, *Lt.Col.* Essex Regiment (44 F.)	31 Mar. 63	2 Jan. 69	1 Apr. 75	8 Feb. 82	16 Sept. 91	
Sydney Long Jacob, *Lt.Col.* Royal Engineers	......	22 Dec. 63	23 May 78	22 Dec. 85	16 Sept. 91	
Philip L. Macgregor, *Lt.Col.* Royal Artillery	......	15 Jan. 67	31 Dec. 78	20 Sept. 84	20 Sept. 91	
James Edward Porteous, *Lt.Col.* Indian Staff Corps	22 Sept. 65	2 May 68	22 Sept. 77	22 Sept. 85	22 Sept. 91	
Robert Hugh Wallace, *Lt.Col.* Royal Artillery	......	12 Apr. 64	21 Dec. 76	1 Aug. 83	1 Oct. 91	
Richard Francis Williams, *Lt.Col.* Royal Engineers	......	3 May 64	1 Feb. 77	31 Aug. 83	1 Oct. 91	
Sydenham John Lambert, *Lt.Col.* Royal Engineers	......	15 Jan. 64	1 Oct. 77	15 Jan. 84	1 Oct. 91	
John Lawrence Macpherson, *Lt.Col.* R. Engineers	......	1 Mar. 64	1 Oct. 77	1 Mar. 84	1 Oct. 91	
p.s.c. Walter W. M. Smith, *Lt.Col.* Royal Artillery	......	10 July 67	31 Dec. 78	1 Oct. 84	1 Oct. 91	
William Poyntz Blandy, *Lt. Col.* (from R. Artillery)	......	10 July 67	1 Jan. 79	1 Oct. 84	1 Oct. 91	
William George Knox, *CB. Lt.Col.* Royal Artillery	......	10 July 67	23 Jan. 79	21 Apr. 80	2 Oct. 91	
John Ford Baily, *Lt.Col.* (from Royal Artillery)	......	19 July 64	1 Apr. 77	1 Sept. 83	12 Oct. 91	
Godfrey Hildebrand, *Lt.Col.* Royal Engineers	......	18 Oct. 64	5 Dec. 77	18 Oct. 84	18 Oct. 91	
Napoleon Arnott, *Lt.Col.* Royal Engineers	......	22 Dec. 65	11 July 78	22 Dec. 85	19 Oct. 91	
v.s.c. James Keith Trotter, *Major*, h.p. Royal Art.	......	8 Jan. 70	21 Aug. 80	1 Feb. 86	22 Oct. 91	22 Oct. 91
p.s.c. George Clement Wynne, *Lt.Col.* Royal Art.	......	16 Aug. 64	10 Apr. 77	1 Sept. 83	1 Nov. 91	
David S. Skirving, *Lt. Col.* Army Service Corps (*Hon. Major*, 12 Feb. 85)	Deptl.	Service	16 6/12 yrs.	11 Dec. 88	1 Nov. 91	
Gerald G. Challice, *Lt.Col.* Army Service Corps (*Hon. Major*, 9 Aug. 86)	Deptl.	Service	15 8/12 yrs.	11 Dec. 88	1 Nov. 91	
William R. Winter, *Lt.Col.* Army Service Corps (*Hon. Major*, 1 Nov. 88)	Deptl.	Service	15 8/12 yrs.	11 Dec. 88	1 Nov. 91	
Duncan MacNeil Campbell, *Lt.Col.* Royal Eng.	......	22 Dec. 65	14 July 78	22 Dec. 85	6 Nov. 91	
George Morton Stevens, *Lt.Col.* Royal Engineers	......	10 July 67	30 Jan. 79	7 Nov. 84	7 Nov. 91	
Caledon Philip Egerton, *Lt.Col.* Dorset Regiment	3 Mar. 65	22 July 68	18 Jan. 79	18 Nov. 82	19 Nov. 91	
Charles Edward Swaine, *Lt.Col.* 11 Hussars	13 June 68	27 July 70	1 Jan. 80	18 Nov. 82	19 Nov. 91	
Archibald Broadfoot, *CB. Lt.Col.* Royal Engineers	......	23 Dec. 64	30 Aug. 77	2 Mar. 81	21 Nov. 91	
Arthur Edward Ward, *Lt.Col.* Indian Staff Corps	21 Nov. 67	8 Sept. 68	21 Nov. 77	21 Nov. 85	21 Nov. 91	
George Carew Fenwick, *Lt.Col.* Indian Staff Corps	21 Nov. 65	28 July 70	21 Nov. 77	21 Nov. 85	21 Nov. 91	
C. H. Peregrine Christie, *Lt.Col.* Royal Engineers	......	17 Apr. 66	31 Dec. 78	17 Apr. 86	23 Nov. 91	
Robert H. W. Plunkett, *Lt.Col.* Royal Artillery	......	16 Aug. 64	7 May 77	4 Nov. 83	30 Nov. 91	
David Stanley Cuninghame, *Lt.Col.* Indian S. C.	1 Dec. 65	1 Oct. 69	1 Dec. 77	2 Mar. 81	1 Dec. 91	
Lionel Richd. Stopford Sackville, *Lt.Col.* Rifle Brig.	13 June 63	9 Mar. 67	13 May 75	1 July 81	1 Dec. 91	
Wm. James Alexander Birch, *Lt.Col.* Indian S. C.	1 Dec. 65	5 Aug. 69	1 Dec. 77	1 Dec. 85	1 Dec. 91	
Samuel Compton Turner, *Lt. Col.* Royal Engineers	......	17 Apr. 66	31 Dec. 78	17 Apr. 86	6 Dec. 91	
p.s.c. Justinian G. Ponsonby, *Lt.Col.* Berkshire Regt.	23 Sept. 71	28 Oct. 71	8 Apr. 80	1 Feb. 84	7 Dec. 91	
Thomas George Thomson, *Lt.Col.* Indian S. C.	......	8 Dec. 65	18 July 68	8 Dec. 77	8 Dec. 85	8 Dec. 91
Gardiner Frederic Guyon, *Lt.Col.* Royal Fus. (7 F.)	31 Jan. 65	22 July 68	18 Aug. 78	7 Aug. 78	20 Dec. 82	11 Dec. 91
Robert Wm. F. Phillips, *Lt.Col.* E. Surrey Regt.	18 Dec. 66	25 Dec. 67	23 Jan. 78	19 Nov. 81	14 Dec. 91	
Cecil Harley St. Paul, *Lt.Col.* Rifle Brigade	16 Aug. 64	13 Jan. 69	27 Nov. 77	15 Oct. 81	16 Dec. 91	
p.s.c. H. T. Hughes Hallett, *Lt.Col.* Middlesex Regt.	13 Jan. 69	27 Oct. 70	28 Apr. 75	4 Jan. 82	17 Dec. 91	
Andrew Kennedy Macpherson, *Lt.Col.* Indian S. C.	19 Dec. 65	14 Dec. 69	19 Dec. 77	19 Dec. 85	19 Dec. 91	
Wm. Alexander Eden, *Lt.Col.* Royal Artillery	......	28 Oct. 64	1 July 77	29 Dec. 83	21 Dec. 91	
Stanier Waller, *Lt. Col.* Royal Engineers	......	9 Dec. 64	6 Feb. 78	18 Nov. 82	31 Dec. 91	
p.s.c. George Macdonald, *Lt.Col.* Royal Engineers	......	19 July 64	1 Oct. 77	19 July 84	31 Dec. 91	
Henry Rhodes G. Georges, *Lt.Col.* R. Engineers	......	30 Aug. 64	1 Oct. 77	30 Aug. 84	31 Dec. 91	
Frederick Baldwin, *Lt.Col.* Royal Marines	1 Jan. 64	3 Aug. 67	31 May 79	1 Jan. 85	1 Jan. 92	
William Hill, *Lt.Col.* Indian Staff Corps	5 Jan. 66	14 Dec. 69	5 Jan. 78	2 Mar. 81	5 Jan. 92	
John Matheson, *Lt.Col.* Royal Engineers	......	23 Dec. 64	16 Feb. 78	23 Dec. 84	6 Jan. 92	
William Edward Hilliard,[21] *Major*, h.p. York Lt. Inf., *Assist. Adj. Gen.* Bombay 10 Jan. 92	4 Feb. 69	28 Oct. 71	29 Jan. 79	4 July 83	10 Jan. 92	10 Jan. 92
Charles Arthur Cresswell, *Lt.Col.* Indian S. C.	......	12 Jan. 66	12 Jan. 78	12 Jan. 86	12 Jan. 92	
William Campbell Black, *Lt.Col.* Indian S. C.	......	12 Jan. 66	12 Jan. 78	12 Jan. 86	12 Jan. 92	
William Harry Salmon, *Lt.Col.* Indian Staff Corps	12 Jan. 66	31 Mar. 71	12 Jan. 78	12 Jan. 86	12 Jan. 92	
Ernest Augustus Belford, *Lt.Col.* 17 Lancers	27 July 66	24 Apr. 69	12 Aug. 74	7 Jan. 82	15 Jan. 92	
Dennett Thomas Kinder, *Lt.Col.* Devonshire Regt.	9 May 63	14 May 68	31 Oct. 77	18 Nov. 82	18 Jan. 92	
Arthur Clifford Alexander, *Lt.Col.* Royal Engineers	......	23 Dec. 64	6 Feb. 78	23 Dec. 84	18 Jan. 92	
James Melville Babington, *Lt.Col.* 16 Lancers	......	6 Sept. 73	20 Feb. 80	30 July 90	27 Jan. 92	
Benjamin Chamney Graves, *Lt.Col.* Indian S. C.	......	30 Jan. 68	30 Jan. 78	30 Jan. 86	30 Jan. 92	
William Alexander Wetherall, *Lt.Col.* Indian S. C.	30 Jan. 66	8 Dec. 69	30 Jan. 78	30 Jan. 86	30 Jan. 92	
Wm. Fred. Nuthall, *Major* (from h.p. Manchester Regt.), *Assist. Insp. of Warlike Stores* 21 June 94	6 July 67	26 Mar. 71	6 Aug. 69	30 Sept. 84	3 Feb. 92	
Charles Henry Scott, *Lt.Col.* (from h.p. R. Artillery)	......	8 Jan. 68	23 July 79	6 Feb. 85	6 Feb. 92	
Edward Henry Bingham, *Lt.Col.* Indian S. C.	13 Feb. 66	7 Sept. 68	13 Feb. 78	13 Feb. 86	13 Feb. 92	
John Morison Alves, *Lt.Col.* Royal Artillery	......	23 Dec. 64	1 Sept. 77	1 Jan. 84	15 Feb. 92	
Hougham Charles Huntley, *Lt.Col.* Lincoln Regt.	8 Sept. 63	9 May 65	31 Oct. 77	29 Nov. 79	17 Feb. 92	

Lieutenant Colonels. 44

	CORNET, 2nd LIEUT. OR ENSIGN.	LIEUT.	CAPTAIN.	MAJOR.	LIEUT. COLONEL.	WHEN PLACED ON HALF PAY.
James Butler, *Lt. Col.* Indian Staff Corps	20 Feb. 66	9 July 68	20 Feb. 78	20 Feb. 86	20 Feb. 92	
Wilfred Fitz Allan Way, *Lt. Col.* Northumberland Fus.	18 Oct. 64	22 Aug. 68	15 May 78	25 July 83	22 Feb. 92	
Frank Longbourne, *Lt. Col.* Warwickshire Regt.	27 July 66	28 May 70	1 Jan. 79	20 Sept. 84	24 Feb. 92	
Arthur Bosworth, *Lt. Col.* West India Regiment		11 Feb. 75	1 July 81	3 Aug. 87	24 Feb. 92	
Geoffrey Stanley, *Lt. Col.* Army Service Corps (*Hon. Major*, 24 Feb. 87)	Deptl.	Service	14 8/12 yrs.	11 Dec. 88	14 Feb. 92	
Leslie Trevor Bishop, *Lt. Col.* Indian Staff Corps	2 Mar. 65	1 Mar. 69	2 Mar. 78	2 Mar. 81	2 Mar. 92	
Hy. Edw. Railston, *Major* (fromh.p. Scottish Rifles), *Recruiting Staff Officer, Manchester*, 1 Apr. 92	12 Nov. 70	23 Oct. 71	3 May 81	19 Sept. 83	2 Mar. 92	
William Loch, *Lt. Col.* Indian Staff Corps	2 Mar. 66	14 May 68	2 Mar. 78	2 Mar. 86	2 Mar. 92	
Thomas Morris Jenkins, *Lt. Col.* Indian Staff Corps	2 Mar. 66	19 June 69	2 Mar. 78	2 Mar. 86	2 Mar. 92	
Frederic Howard, *Lt. Col.* Royal Artillery		3 Mar. 65	20 Sept. 77	1 Jan. 84	3 Mar. 92	
Edw. Henry Corse-Sc tt, *Lt. Col.* Warwick Regt.	10 Feb. 60	28 Oct. 71	30 Oct. 80	3 Mar. 86	3 Mar. 92	
Charles Steward Gord n, *Lt. Col.* W. York Regt.	27 June 68	28 Oct. 71	24 Jan. 80	20 Mar. 83	7 Mar. 92	
Philip Kavanagh Doyne, *Lt. Col.* 4 Dragoon Guards	14 Mar. 68	16 May 70	9 Feb. 82	3 Aug. 87	7 Mar. 92	
Andrew Henry Macintire, *Lt. Col.* Indian Staff Corps	9 Mar. 66	30 Sept. 68	9 Mar. 78	9 Mar. 86	9 Mar. 92	
Thomas Edward Verner, *Lt. Col.* Lincoln Regt.	25 Jan. 65	23 Mar. 66	21 Apr. 77	1 Aug. 87	11 Mar. 92	
Hon. John Pleydell-Bouverie,[24] *Major*, h.p. 17 Lancers	27 Feb. 67	18 Aug. 69	28 Mar. 77	1 Apr. 82	16 Mar. 92	16 Mhr. 92
James Johnstone, *Lt. Col.* Oxfordshire Light Inf.	20 Feb. 66	30 Sept. 68	14 Feb. 74	15 Aug. 83	16 Mar. 92	
John Arthur Barlow, *Lt. Col.* Manchester Regt.	8 Jan. 68	18 Aug. 69	15 Jan. 79	14 Feb. 83	18 Mar. 92	
p.s.c. Peter Hy. Hammond, *Major* (from h.p. R. Art.)		15 July 68	27 Aug. 79	18 Mar. 85	18 Mar. 92	
Geo. Lloyd Reilly Richardson, *CIE. Lt. Col.* Ind. S.C.	23 Mar. 66	5 Mar. 69	23 Mar. 78	2 Mar. 81	23 Mar. 92	
p.s.c. Robert A. Montgomery, *Lt. Col.* h.p. R. Art.		15 July 68	27 Aug. 79	19 Mar. 85	19 Mar. 92	1 Sept. 94
Hillyard Henry Angus Cameron, *Major*, h.p. Bedford Regiment; *Recruiting Staff Officer, Birmingham*, 12 Nov. 92	16 Aug. 64	14 Aug. 67	19 Mar. 74	1 July 81	29 Mar. 92	29 Mar. 92
Henry Travers Lugard, *Lt. Col.* h.p. Royal Art.		13 Jan. 69	20 Sept. 79	2 Mar. 8:	1 Apr. 92	1 Apr. 92
Owen Williams, *Lt. Col.* Suffolk Regiment	10 Nov. 65	17 Apr. 69	7 Aug. 78	11 Oct. 82	1 Apr. 92	
William Musson Campbell, *Lt. Col.* h.p. Royal Art.		13 Jan. 69	4 Oct. 79	1 Apr. 85	1 Apr. 92	1 Apr. 92
Arthur C. G. Lydiard, *Lt. Col.* Indian Staff Corps	3 Apr. 66	19 Feb. 65	3 Apr. 78	3 Apr. 86	3 Apr. 92	
John Frederick Garwood, *Lt. Col.* Royal Artillery		17 Apr. 66	31 Dec. 78	17 Apr. 86	4 Apr. 92	
George Atherley W. Forrest,[25] *Major* (from h.p. Hampshire Regiment), *Comd. Duke of York's Royal Military School*, 18 Oct. 93	9 Mar. 66	1 Sept. 69	17 Apr. 80	15 Apr. 84	6 Apr. 92	
Charles Russell, *Lt. Col.* h.p. Royal Artillery		13 Jan. 69	15 Nov. 79	10 Apr. 85	10 Apr. 92	10 Apr. 92
Henry Opie Woodhouse, *Lt. Col.* Indian Staff Corps	10 Apr. 66	22 Aug. 68	10 Apr. 78	10 Apr. 86	10 Apr. 92	
Rich. G. T. Cotton,[26] *Major*, h.p. Shropshire Lt. Inf.	30 Aug. 64	14 Sept. 66	2 Mar. 78	3 Apr. 82	13 Apr. 92	13 Apr. 92
p.s.c. Richard Charles Hare, *Lt. Col.* Cheshire Regt.	23 June 63	29 May 67	17 Mar. 75	18 Nov. 82	21 Apr. 92	
p.s.c. Algernon G. A. Durand, *CB. Capt.* Indian S.C.		21 Dec. 72	21 Dec. 84	11 Nov. 89	27 Apr. 92	
Robert B. M'Comb, *Lt. Col.* Army Service Corps (*Hon. Major*, 6 May 87)	Deptl.	Service	14 8/12 yrs.	11 Dec. 88	6 May 92	
Fras. Onslow Barrington Foote, *Lt. Col.* h.p. R. Art.		13 Jan. 69	23 Dec. 79	12 May 85	12 May 92	12 May 92
Edm. Geo. Henry Bingham, *Lt. Col.* (from h.p. R. Art.)		13 Jan. 69	30 Dec. 79	12 May 85	12 May 92	
Edm. Baker Standbridge, *Lt. Col.* (from h.p. R. Art.)		7 July 69	17 Jan. 80	13 May 85	13 May 92	
Edgar Holford Walker, *Lt. Col.* (from h.p. R. Art.)		7 July 69	17 Jun. 80	4 June 77	1 July 81	1 May 92
Frederick Fras. Wilder Taylor, *Lt. Col.* Dublin Fus.	29 July 66	30 June 69	9 June 77	1 July 81	21 May 92	
George Ernest Harley, *Lt. Col.* The Buffs	4 Oct. 64	7 Dec. 67	7 May 75	23 Dec. 81	23 May 92	
Hy. Aitken Cherry, *Lt. Col.* Northumberland Fus.	25 July 65	17 Apr. 66	3 Apr. 83	23 May 92		
Robert Samuel Watson, *Lt. Col.* Royal Artillery		17 July 66	16 Oct. 78	26 Aug. 84	25 May 92	
Annesley John Garrett, *Lt. Col.* Indian Staff Corps	29 May 66	8 Oct. 68	29 May 78	29 May 86	29 May 92	
Edward Chichester Hart, *Lt. Col.* Royal Engineers		22 June 65	10 Apr. 78	22 June 85	3 June 92	
James Ritchie, *Major* (from h.p. R. Art. District Officer), *Staff Officer, Horse Guards, War Office*		1 Apr. 72	7 June 78	26 Apr. 85	8 June 92	8 June 92
Geo. Stanhope Banister, *Lt. Col.* S. Wales Borderers	8 July 68	28 Oct. 71	5 Feb. 79	15 Aug. 85	9 June 92	
Lewis A. Hope, *Lt. Col.* Army Service Corps (*Hon. Major*, 17 June 87)	Deptl.	Service	14 8/12 yrs.	11 Dec. 88	17 June 92	
Ernest Richard Hope Torin, *Lt. Col.* 13 Hussars	15 Feb. 71	28 Oct. 71	14 Dec. 70	29 Sept. 85	1 July 92	
Alfred Cholmeley E. Welby, *Lt. Col.* 2 Dragoons	18 Oct. 67	1 Dec. 70	1 Apr. 76	21 Oct. 85	5 July 92	
p.s.c. Richd. H. L. Brickenden, *Lt. Col.* Black Watch	18 July 65	11 Jan. 67	29 Sept. 77	18 July 86	17 July 92	
Charles Wm. Hy. Sealy, *Lt. Col.* Indian Staff Corps		17 July 66	17 July 78	17 July 86	20 July 92	
Francis Richard Begbie, *Lt. Col.* Indian Staff Corps	20 July 66	7 May 69	20 July 78	20 July 86	20 July 92	
Edward Blaksley, *Lt. Col.* Royal Artillery		16 Dec. 64	9 July 77	24 July 86	20 July 92	
Sir Simon M. Lockhart, *Bart. Lt. Col.* 1 Life Guards	17 May 67	17 Aug. 70	21 July 77	21 July 86	27 July 92	
p.s.c. Hon. Jas. P. Napier,[29] *Major* (from h.p. 10 Hussars); *D. A. A. Gen. for Instruction, York*, 23 Aug. 90		19 Oct. 72	12 Nov. 79	1 Mar. 84	27 July 92	
Walter Neville Lockyer, *Major* (from h.p. R. Art.)		7 July 69	1 Mar. 80	27 July 85	27 July 92	
Wm. G. W. M'Clintock, *Lt. Col.* Yorkshire Regt.	4 Aug. 65	23 Jan. 69	13 Mar. 78	4 Feb. 82	28 July 92	
Metcalfe S. Brownrigg, *Major* (from h.p. Yorkshire Regt.), *Recruiting Staff Officer, London*, 1 Apr. 92	1 Dec. 63	17 Apr. 67	10 Nov. 69	11 Mar. 82	31 July 92	
Manners Charles Wood, *Lt. Col.* 10 Hussars	1 Sept. 69	27 Oct. 71	2 Feb. 78	6 Apr. 82	3 Aug. 92	
Arthur Ashley, *Lt. Col.* Army Service Corps (*Hon. Major*, 3 Aug. 87)	Deptl.	Service	14 8/12 yrs.	11 Dec. 88	3 Aug. 92	
p.s.c. Cherles Edward Beckett, *Lt. Col.* 2 Dr. Guards	17 Apr. 69	22 Apr. 71	23 Jan. 79	18 Nov. 82	17 Aug. 92	
Francis Palmer Washington, *Lt. Col.* R. Engineers		22 June 65	22 May 78	22 June 85	17 Aug. 92	
John Eyles Blundell, *Lt. Col.* Hampshire Regiment	16 Jan. 63	20 Apr. 67	22 Nov. 70	1 July 81	29 Aug. 92	
John James Congdon, *Lt. Col.* Royal Artillery		18 July 65	24 Nov. 77	1 Jan. 84	2 Sept. 92	
Thomas Alfred Beale, *Lt. Col.* N. Stafford Regt.		14 Aug. 73	25 Aug. 80	22 Jan. 85	14 Sept. 92	
Alfred George Yaldwyn, *Lt. Col.* Indian Staff Corps	14 Sept. 66	2 Dec. 69	14 Sept. 78	14 Sept. 86	14 Sept. 92	
Edw. Warren Broderick, *Lt. Col.* W. Surrey Regt.	28 Aug. 63	1 May 66	21 July 75	10 June 82	29 Sept. 92	
p.s.c. Chas. Moore Watson, *CMG. Lt. Col.* R. Engineers		17 Apr. 66	25 Dec. 78	18 Nov. 82	1 Oct. 92	
Henry Holmes Costobadie, *Lt. Col.* Royal Artillery		24 Mar. 65	1 Oct. 77	1 Oct. 77	1 Oct. 92	
John Douglas Douglas, *Lt. Col.* Royal Artillery		18 July 65	1 Oct. 77	1 Jan. 84	1 Oct. 92	
p.s.c. Chas. Fred. Cobbe Beresford, *Lt. Col.* R. Eng.		22 Dec. 65	1 June 78	22 Dec. 85	1 Oct. 92	
William Robert Purchas, *Lt. Col.* Royal Engineers		22 Dec. 65	4 Sept. 78	22 Dec. 85	1 Oct. 92	
Herbert Jekyll, *CMG. Lt. Col.* Royal Engineers		17 Apr. 66	30 Dec. 78	17 Apr. 86	1 Oct. 92	
W. O'Moore Creagh, *Lt. Col.* Indian Staff Corps	2 Oct. 66	16 Feb. 70	2 Oct. 78	22 Nov. 79	2 Oct. 92	
Alexander Thos. Seton A. Rind, *CMG. Lt. Col.* Indian Staff Corps	2 Oct. 66	18 Jan. 70	2 Oct. 78	2 Mar. 81	2 Oct. 92	
p.s.c. Herbert Anthony Sawyer, *Lt. Col.* Indian S.C.	2 Oct. 66	17 Aug. 70	1 July 77	2 Oct. 86	5 Oct. 92	
James Herbert Yule, *Lt. Col.* Devon Regt. (11 F.)	22 Dec. 65	22 Aug. 68	16 Feb. 78	7 July 83	5 Oct. 92	
Cecil Conor, *Lt. Col.* West Riding Regt.	9 Mar. 67	19 Jan. 70	7 Jan. 79	6 Sept. 83	6 Oct. 92	
John Edward Broadbent, *Lt. Col.* Royal Engineers		17 July 66	31 Dec. 78	17 July 86	7 Oct. 92	
p.s.c. Alex. Martin Paterson, *Lt. Col.* Bedford Regt.	10 Oct. 65	9 Oct. 67	30 Oct. 74	1 July 81	10 Oct. 92	

Lieutenant Colonels.

	CORNET, 2nd LIEUT. OF ENSIGN.	LIEUT.	CAPTAIN.	MAJOR.	LIEUT. COLONEL.	WHEN PLACED ON HALF PAY.
Eden Moyle Baker, *Major*, h.p. Royal Artillery		15 Dec. 71	2 July 81	12 Oct. 87	12 Oct. 92	12 Oct. 92
Hon. George James Playfair, *Major*, h.p. R. Art.		8 Jan. 70	19 May 80	15 Oct. 85	15 Oct. 92	15 Oct. 92
Dudley Elphinstone Gouldsbury, *Lt.Col.* Indian S.C.		17 Apr. 69	16 Oct. 78	16 Oct. 86	16 Oct. 92	
William Henry Lyster, *Lt.Col.* Indian Staff Corps	16 Oct. 66	6 July 70	16 Oct. 78	16 Oct. 86	16 Oct. 92	
Francis Crichton Maltby, *Lt.Col.* Indian S. C.	16 Oct. 65	14 Oct. 70	16 Oct. 78	16 Oct. 86	16 Oct. 92	
James Davidson, *Lt.Col.* 8 Hussars		2 Dec. 74	13 Apr. 81	14 Nov. 83	19 Oct. 92	
Rowland Hill Martin, *Lt.Col.* 21 Hussars	14 Jan. 69	28 Oct. 71	16 Dec. 78	2 Feb. 84	26 Oct. 92	
William H. C. Wyllie, *CIE. Lt.Col.* Indian S. C.	30 Oct. 66	5 Oct. 68	30 Oct. 78	30 Oct. 86	30 Oct. 92	
William Gordon, *Lt.Col.* Durham Lt. Infantry	8 Jan. 68	22 Apr. 71	9 Feb. 79	15 Nov. 83	31 Oct. 92	
James Edward Josselyn, *Lt.Col.* Royal Artillery		18 July 65	4 Oct. 77	1 Jan. 84	1 Nov. 92	
John Lovell, *Major*, h.p. 21 Hussars	26 Feb. 64	9 Nov. 66	1 May 78	18 Mar. 82	6 Nov. 92	6 Nov. 92
Robert Brooke Kirchhoffer, *Lt.Col.* Royal Marines	28 Dec. 64	3 Aug. 67	13 Oct. 79	7 Nov. 85	7 Nov. 92	
James Plomer Freeth, *Lt.Col.* Royal Artillery		12 Jan. 66	20 Feb. 78	9 Jan. 84	9 Nov. 92	
Alister William Jamieson, *Lt.Col.* Indian Staff C.	9 Nov. 65	9 Feb. 70	9 Nov. 78	9 Nov. 86	9 Nov. 92	
Henry Alexander Vincent, *Lt.Col.* Indian Staff C.	9 Nov. 65	9 Feb. 70	9 Nov. 78	9 Nov. 86	9 Nov. 92	
Gabriel R. Ruscombe Poole, *Major*, h.p. 12 Lancers	2 Jan. 69	3 Aug. 70	31 Oct. 71	1 July 81	23 Nov. 92	23 Nov. 92
Edw. Crozier Sibbald Moore, *Lt.Col.* R. Engineers.		17 Apr. 66	31 Dec. 78	17 Apr. 86	17 Apr. 92	
Roger Kennedy Parke, *Lt.Col.* 3 Dragoon Guards.	10 Aug. 70	28 Oct. 71	26 May 79	21 Dec. 87	24 Nov. 92	
Townley Ward Dowding, *Lt.Col.* Royal Marines	28 June 65	4 Dec. 67	15 Nov. 79	1 Sept. 80	11 Dec. 92	
Josiah P. Crampton Neville, *Lt.Col.* Indian Staff C.	11 Dec. 66	4 Dec. 63	11 Dec. 78	2 Mar. 81	11 Dec. 92	
William H. Moberly, *Lt.Col.* Hampshire Regiment	7 Aug. 66	30 Mar. 67	3 Jan. 78	8 Sept. 81	11 Dec. 92	
Henry Stanhope Holmes, *Lt.Col.* Welsh Regiment	1 Aug. 68	8 June 70	24 Nov. 77	25 Jan. 82	12 Dec. 92	
Matthew Henry Purcell, *Lt.Col.* Royal Engineers		17 Apr. 66	31 Dec. 78	17 Apr. 86	19 Dec. 92	
Charles Edward Beck, *Lt.Col.* 12 Lancers		3 Aug. 72	12 Nov. 78	30 Nov. 85	21 Dec. 92	
Thomas Herbert Brock, *Lt.Col.* West Kent Regt.		24 July 72	20 Mar. 80	17 Nov. 83	23 Dec. 92	
Stanley Napier Roberts, *Lt.Col.* Liverpool Regt.	17 July 63	11 Jan. 67	25 Feb. 75	1 Feb. 82	28 Dec. 92	
Roger Pine Coffin, *Lt.Col.* Royal Marines	28 Dec. 64	3 Aug. 67	21 June 80	18 Nov. 82	28 Dec. 92	
p.s.c. Henry T. W. Allatt, *Major* (from h.p. Duke of Cornwall's Lt. Inf.), *D.A.A. General for Instruction, Shorncliffe*, 1 Nov. 92	30 Oct. 66	22 Oct. 70	26 July 76	1 Jan. 86	1 Jan. 93	
ⅎ John Rouse Merriott Chard, *Lt.Col.* Royal Eng.		15 July 68	21 Jan. 79	23 Jan. 79	8 Jan. 93	
Chas. Arundel Barker, *Lt.Col.* Irish Fusiliers (89 F.)		23 June 69	23 Apr. 77	14 May 81	9 Jan. 93	
Folliott S. Furneaux Stokes, *Lt.Col.* Irish Rifles	9 Apr. 70	27 Oct. 71	19 Oct. 78	10 Oct. 85	10 Jan. 93	
Sir Charles Henry Leslie, *Bart. Lt.Col.* Indian S.C.	11 Jan. 67	22 Jan. 68	11 Jan. 79	11 Jan. 87	11 Jan. 93	
George Wemyss Anson, *Lt.Col.* Indian Staff Corps	11 Jan. 67	29 June 69	11 Jan. 79	11 Jan. 87	11 Jan. 93	
Frederick Drummond Battye, *Lt.Col.* Indian S. C.	11 Jan. 67	2 Dec. 69	11 Jan. 79	11 Jan. 87	11 Jan. 93	
Bowes Thorpe M. Gomperts, *Lt.Col.* Indian S. C.	11 Jan. 67	18 Mar. 70	11 Jan. 79	11 Jan. 87	11 Jan. 93	
Montague James, *Lt.Col.* Indian Staff Corps	11 Jan. 67	26 Apr. 70	11 Jan. 79	11 Jan. 87	11 Jan. 93	
John James Money-Simons, *Lt.Col.* Indian S. C.	11 Jan. 67	2 Jan. 71	11 Jan. 79	11 Jan. 87	11 Jan. 93	
Adelbert Cecil Talbot, *CIE. Lt.Col.* Indian S. C.		15 Jan. 67	15 Jan. 79	15 Jun. 87	15 Jan. 93	
George Hunter O'Malley, *Lt.Col.* Royal Artillery		18 July 65	7 Nov. 77	1 Jan. 84	19 Jan. 93	
p.s.c. Frederick Lutman-Johnson, *Major* (from h.p. York and Lancaster Regt.), *D.A.A. General for Instruction, Malta*, 24 Dec. 94	16 Oct. 65	7 Nov. 69	19 Apr. 76	1 July 81	22 Jan. 93	
Henry Graham, *Major*, h.p. 16 Lancers	14 July 69	10 June 71	10 Feb. 78	27 Jan. 86	27 Jan. 93	27 Jan. 93
Samuel Gardiner Smyth, *Lt.Col.* Royal Artillery		13 Mar. 78	31 Jan. 78	9 Jan. 84	28 Jan. 93	
Henry Crawford, *Lt.Col.* Inniskilling Fus. (108 F.)	30 Mar. 66	22 Oct. 67	14 Jan. 76	9 May 83	1 Feb. 93	
Thomas Greenaway, *Lt.Col.* Indian Staff Corps	12 Feb. 67	1 Jan. 69	12 Feb. 79	12 Feb. 87	7 Feb. 93	
Bernard Chamier, *DSO. Lt.Col.* Indian Staff Corps	13 Feb. 67	14 Feb. 68	13 Feb. 79	13 Feb. 87	13 Feb. 93	
James L. Aberigh-Mackay, *Lt.Col.* Indian Staff C.	13 Feb. 67	10 Sept. 69	13 Feb. 79	13 Feb. 87	13 Feb. 93	
Edward Brooke Anderson, *Lt.Col.* Indian Staff C.	19 Feb. 67	14 Apr. 70	19 Feb. 79	19 Feb. 87	19 Feb. 93	
Robert Fred. Willoughby,³³ *Major* (from h.p. Scots Fusiliers), *Recruiting Staff Officer, Dublin*, 1 Feb. 94	16 Oct. 63	15 Feb. 68	29 May 77	2 Feb. 85	20 Feb. 93	
Henry Metcalfe Rose, *DSO. Lt.Col.* Indian Staff C.	8 Mar. 67	24 May 69	8 Mar. 79	8 Mar. 87	8 Mar. 93	
Leonard Wm. Christopher, *Lt.Col.* Indian Staff C.	9 Mar. 67	18 Jan. 70	9 Mar. 79	9 Mar. 87	9 Mar. 93	
William G. W. Mackay, *Lt.Col.* Indian Staff Corps	12 July 67	10 May 70	23 Mar. 79	18 Nov. 82	23 Mar. 93	
Charles Linton, *Lt.Col.* S. Lancashire Regt. (40 F.)	21 Nov. 65	24 Sept. 70	1 May 78	25 July 83	27 Mar. 93	
Edw. Archibald Bruce, *Lt.Col.* York Regt. (19 F.)	23 Jan. 69	28 Oct. 71	1 Mar. 79	29 Sept. 82	29 Mar. 93	
John du Terreau Bogle, *Lt.Col.* Royal Engineers		17 July 66	24 Jan. 79	1 July 85	1 Apr. 93	
William Dunne, *Lt.Col.* Army Service Corps (Hon. *Major*, 1 Apr. 88)	Deptl.	Service	13⁸/₁₂ yrs.	11 Dec. 88	1 Apr. 93	
Edmund Spencer E. Childers, *Major*, Royal Eng.		29 Apr. 73	8 Jan. 85	9 Jan. 85	2 Apr. 93	
p.s.c. John H.S.Craigie,*Lt.Col.*Highland Lt.Inf.(74F.)	8 July 68	17 Nov. 69	22 Apr. 78	6 May 82	3 Apr. 93	
Charles Marsh Keighley, *DSO. Lt.Col.* Indian S. C.	3 Apr. 67	7 June 67	3 Apr. 79	3 Apr. 87	3 Apr. 93	
p.s.c. William Aldworth Home Hare, *Lt.Col.* R.Eng.		15 Jan. 67	13 Sept. 79	13 Nov. 86	4 Apr. 93	
William F. D. Cochrane,³⁵ *Major*, h.p. Duke of Cornwall's Light Infantry	31 Aug. 66	14 June 81	18 Feb. 82	5 Apr. 93	5 Apr. 93	
ⅎ Edward S. Browne, *Lt.Col.* South Wales Bordrs.	23 Sept. 71	28 Oct. 71	19 May 80	2 Nov. 85	8 Apr. 93	
Henry Cecil B. Farrant, *Lt.Col.* N. Lanc. Regt.	4 Sept. 67	25 Mar. 71	6 Mar. 80	9 July 84	11 Apr. 93	
John Owen Quirk, *DSO. Lt.Col.* Welsh Regiment	1 Dec. 69	28 Oct. 71	1 Dec. 80	18 Feb. 84	14 Apr. 93	
p.s.c. Arthur Octavius Green, *Lt.Col.* Royal Eng.		15 Jan. 67	13 Sept. 79	21 May 84	19 Apr. 93	
Frederick G. T. Welch, *Lt.Col.* Indian Staff Corps	20 Apr. 67	15 Aug. 69	20 Apr. 79	20 Apr. 87	20 Apr. 93	
p.s.c. Alex. Hy. Fraser, *Lt.Col.* S. Lancashire Regt.	11 Jan. 67	15 Sept. 69	31 Jan. 78	29 Oct. 81	21 Apr. 93	
Stephen J. M. Jopp,³⁴ *Major* (from h.p. Northampton Regt.), *Instructor R.M. College*, 4 Oct. 88		17 May 77	12 Mar. 81	22 Apr. 86	22 Apr. 93	
Maunsell Bowers, *Lt.Col.* 5 Dragoon Guards		13 Apr. 72	21 Aug. 78	21 Apr. 83	25 Apr. 93	
p.s.c. Frederick Wm. Benson,*Lt.Col.* from h.p. 17 Lancers, *Dep. Assist. Adj. Gen. for Inst. Dublin*, 2 Feb. 95	13 Jan. 69	9 Apr. 70	4 Jan. 80	27 Apr. 86	27 Apr. 93	
Chas. Herbert Shepherd, *DSO. Lt.Col.* Norfolk Regt.	2 May 65	15 Feb. 71	1 Sept. 80	10 Jan. 83	1 May 93	
p.s.c.Chas.Fitzgerald Thomson,³⁹*Maj.*h.p. 7 Hussars	27 July 65	22 June 70	14 June 73	15 June 85	5 May 93	5 May 93
Frederick Cyril Morgan, *Lt.Col.* R. Artillery		8 Jan. 68	8 Apr. 79	20 Nov. 84	6 May 93	
p.s.c. John A. Fergusson, *Major* (from h.p. Rifle Brigade), *Professor R.M. College*, 1 Sept. 93	8 Dec. 65	7 May 70	20 Mar. 78	13 Apr. 82	7 May 93	
Chas. J. B. Stewart, *Lt.Col.* Seaforth Highlanders (78 Foot)	9 Aug. 64	9 Mar. 67	28 May 73	25 Mar. 82	8 May 93	
Thomas Harris,⁴⁰ *Major* (from h.p. Middlesex Regiment)	18 Dec. 63	7 Jan. 68	10 Oct. 74	8 Jan. 83	9 May 93	
Lewis Dening, *DSO. Lt.Col.* Indian Staff Corps	11 May 67	20 Apr. 71	11 May 79	11 May 87	11 May 93	
John Richard Povah,⁴¹ *Major*, h.p. Dublin Fusiliers	12 Nov. 70	28 Oct. 71	15 Nov. 79	7 June 84	17 May 93	17 May 93
John Geo. Cockburn Curtis, *Major*, h.p. Oxford Lt. Inf. *A.A. Gen. for Musketry, Bombay*, 24 Feb. 91		30 Dec. 71	12 Mar. 81	19 May 86	19 May 93	19 May 93
James Frederick Lewis, *Lt.Col.* Royal Engineers		15 Jan. 67	13 Sept. 79	11 Dec. 85	22 May 93	

Lieutenant Colonels.

Name	CORNET, 2nd LIEUT. or ENSIGN.	LIEUT.	CAPTAIN.	MAJOR.	LIEUT. COLONEL.	WHEN PLACED ON HALF PAY.
Henry Hall, *Major*, h.p. Derbyshire Regiment	20 Apr. 64	30 Sept. 68	29 Dec. 77	26 May 85	26 May 93	26 May 93
Felician Rola de Wolski, *Lt. Col.* Royal Engineers		10 July 67	13 Sept. 79	17 Dec. 86	26 May 93	
Charles Archibald Mercer, *Lt. Col.* Indian S. C.	8 June 67	18 Jan. 70	8 June 79	8 June 87	8 June 93	
Thomas Holbrow Goldney, *Lt. Col.* Indian S. C.	9 June 67	24 July 69	9 June 79	9 June 87	9 June 93	
John B. Symes-Bullen, *Lt. Col.* 15 Hussars	22 May 66	14 July 69	23 June 75	29 Apr. 84	12 June 93	
Gerald Ward Martin, *Lt. Col.* Indian Staff Corps	22 June 67	24 Mar. 71	22 June 79	22 June 87	22 June 93	
p.s.c. Edward Robert Prevost Woodgate, *Lt. Col.* Lancaster Regiment	7 Apr. 65	7 July 69	2 Mar. 78	29 Nov. 79	25 June 93	
p.s.c. Hy. Humphreys Crookenden, *Lt. Col.* R. Art.		12 Jan. 66	13 Mar. 78	16 Jan. 84	26 June 93	
Ormelie Campbell Hannay, *Lt. Col.* Argyll and Sutherland Highlanders (93 Foot)	5 Oct. 67	28 Oct. 71	17 Nov. 78	1 Jan. 84	27 Jun. 93	
James R. Silver O. Hewitt, *Lt. Col.* Royal Artillery		12 Jan. 66	13 Mar. 78	16 Jan. 84	28 June 93	
Arthur Emerson Chapman, *Major*, Royal Marines	28 June 65	3 Aug. 67	26 Aug. 80	28 June 86	28 June 93	
Robert Martin Barklie, *Lt. Col.* Royal Engineers		10 July 67	13 Sept. 79	31 Dec. 86	1 July 93	
Henry Walter Trench, *Lt. Col.* W. Surrey Regt.	16 Feb. 64	13 July 67	23 Oct. 75	29 Sept. 82	3 July 93	
Francis Grant Maltby, *Lt. Col.* Indian Staff Corps	6 July 67	18 May 69	6 July 79	6 July 87	6 July 93	
Henry Doveton Hutchinson, *Lt. Col.* Indian S. C.	6 July 67	6 Aug. 69	6 July 79	6 July 87	6 July 93	
Edward Groves Paley, *Lt. Col.* 18 Hussars	2 Jan. 69	19 Feb. 70	16 Dec. 74	28 Nov. 83	8 July 93	
Frederick Robertson Ditmas, *Lt. Col.* Indian S. C.		10 July 67	10 July 79	10 July 87	10 July 93	
Alexander William Smart, *Lt. Col.* Royal Engineers		15 July 68	20 Nov. 80	23 July 87	10 July 93	
Courtney Clarke Rawson, *Lt. Col.* Royal Engineers		15 July 68	9 Feb. 81	1 Oct. 87	10 July 93	
Edward H. Fitzherbert, *Major*, h.p. Lancaster Regiment, *Commandant Deolali Depot*, 12 July 93	11 July 65	9 Feb. 70	31 Aug. 78	19 Nov. 81	12 July 93	12 July 93
George Hambley Elliott, *Lt. Col.* Indian Staff Corps	13 July 67	10 July 67	13 July 79	2 Mar. 81	13 July 93	
p.s.c. William George Morris, *CMG. Lt. Col.* R. Eng.		10 July 67	9 Oct. 79	31 Dec. 86	14 July 93	
John Newman Walker, *Lt. Col.* Indian Staff Corps	20 July 67	17 Aug. 70	20 July 79	20 July 87	20 July 93	
Spencer R. Rawlinson, *DSO. Lt. Col.* Indian S. C.	20 July 67	17 Jan. 71	20 July 79	20 July 87	20 July 93	
Arthur John Bigge, *CB. CMG. Lt. Col.* h.p. R. Art.		7 July 69	22 Feb. 80	27 July 85	22 July 93	
William Wylly Lawrence, *Lt. Col.* Irish Regiment	27 June 68	18 Oct. 71	18 Sept. 79	1 Mar. 83	23 July 93	22 July 93
p.s.c. Henry Elliott Chevallier Kitchener,[45] *Major*, (from h.p. Duke of Cornwall's Light Infantry) ; *Dep. Assist. Adj General, Jamaica*, 17 Dec. 93	10 July 66	10 Feb. 69	13 Nov. 75	26 July 85	26 July 93	
Wm. Barrington Browne, *Lt. Col.* Duke of Cornwall's Light Infantry	8 Jan. 68	16 Mar. 70	1 July 76	18 Nov. 82	31 July 93	
Edward Willock Chalmers, *Lt. Col.* Indian S. C.	14 Aug. 67	25 Feb. 71	14 Aug. 79	14 Aug. 87	14 Aug. 93	
James Anson F. Nutt, *Lt. Col.* Royal Artillery		12 Jan. 66	1 Apr. 78	1 Mar. 84	19 Aug. 93	
p.s.c. Francis Wingfield Robinson, *Lt. Col.* Shropshire Light Infantry (85 F.)	10 Oct. 65	7 Aug. 67	22 June 76	15 May 84	19 Aug. 93	
Knighton Arnold, *Lt. Col.* Army Service Corps (*Hon. Major*, 1 Sept. 88)	Deptl.	Service	13⁸/₁₂ yrs.	11 Dec. 88	1 Sept. 93	
Jas. A. Lawrence Montgomery, *Lt. Col.* Indian S.C.	14 Sept. 67	9 Oct. 69	14 Sept. 79	14 Sept. 87	14 Sept. 93	
Arthur Parry Thornton, *Lt. Col.* Indian Staff Corps	14 Sept. 67	8 Sept. 71	14 Sept. 79	14 Sept. 87	14 Sept. 93	
Masters John Godfery, *Lt. Col.* Army Service Corps (*Hon. Major*, 15 Sept. 88)	Deptl.	Service	13⁸/₁₂ yrs.	11 Dec. 88	15 Sept. 93	
Alfred A. Garstin, *Lt. Col.* Middlesex Regt. (57 F.)	23 Sept. 71	28 Oct. 71	12 Aug. 80	14 Apr. 83	18 Sept. 93	
Wm. H. B. Little, *Lt. Col.* E. Lanc. Regt. (59 F.)	27 Nov. 67	27 Oct. 71	17 Apr. 80	12 Mar. 84	23 Sept. 93	
Frederick William Birch, *Lt. Col.* Lancashire Fus.	10 Nov. 65	14 Oct. 68	10 Feb. 77	19 Nov. 81	25 Sept. 93	
George Hobart, *Major*, h.p. R. Marines, *Paymaster*	13 Dec. 65	3 Aug. 67	26 Aug. 80	29 Sept. 86	29 Sept. 93	
Arthur Domville Corbet, *CB. Lt. Col.* Royal Marines	13 Dec. 65	3 Aug. 67	11 Sept. 80	29 Sept. 86	29 Sept. 93	22 Jan. 95
George B. N. Martin, *CB. Lt. Col.* Royal Artillery		17 July 66	25 May 78	18 Nov. 82	30 Sept. 93	
p.s.c. Julian Robt. J. Jocelyn, *Major* (from h.p. R. Art.)		4 Jan. 71	1 Jan. 81	4 Sept. 86	4 Oct. 93	
Henry Philip Dawson, *Major* (from h.p. R. Art.)		4 Jan. 71	1 Feb. 81	22 Sept. 86	4 Oct. 93	
p.s.c. John Adye, *Major*, Royal Artillery		2 Feb. 76	23 Jan. 85	24 Jan. 85	5 Oct. 93	
Arthur James Dunnage, *Lt. Col.* Royal Artillery		30 Jan. 66	23 Apr. 78	18 Mar. 84	6 Oct. 93	
John Francis Egerton, *Lt. Col.* Worcestershire Regt.	21 Aug. 66	9 Feb. 70	15 Nov. 79	27 Aug. 84	9 Oct. 93	
p.s.c. Percy John Hughes, *Lt. Col.* Scottish Rifles	8 July 68	28 Oct. 71	15 Mar. 79	23 May 83	10 Oct. 93	
Hon. Montagu Curzon, *Lt. Col.* Rifle Brigade	10 Nov. 65	19 Jan. 70	2 Mar. 78	9 Apr. 32	15 Oct. 93	
Chas. Geo. Brind, *Lt. Col.* Border Regt. (55 Foot)	12 Jan. 66	5 Jan. 70	7 Feb. 80	20 Oct. 83	20 Oct. 93	
Hy. Murray Ashley Warde,[47] *Lt. Col.* h.p. 19 Hussars		21 Aug. 74	17 Dec. 81	7 Feb. 85	25 Oct. 93	25 Oct. 93
Arthur James Brander, *Lt. Col.* Indian Staff Corps	6 Nov. 67	28 Oct. 71	6 Nov. 79	6 Nov. 87	6 Nov. 93	
Chas. Edw. Yate, *CSI. CMG. Lt. Col.* Indian S. C.	9 Nov. 67	22 Mar. 71	9 Nov. 79	9 Nov. 87	9 Nov. 93	
Edward Rea Milner Crooke, *Major*, R. Marine Art		8 Dec. 66	3 Aug. 67	17 Sept. 77	15 June 85	22 Nov. 93
Albert P. Wodehouse, *Lt. Col.* Inniskilling Fus. (108 F.)	4 Aug. 65	5 May 69	12 Feb. 75	2 Feb. 85	1 Dec. 93	
p.s.c. John Beckwith Leefe, *Major*, R. Marine Art.	21 June 67	3 Aug. 67	17 Sept. 77	1 Dec. 86	1 Dec. 93	
Alexander Wm. Anstruther, *Lt. Col.* R. Artillery		17 July 65	24 Aug. 78	27 June 84	9 Dec. 93	
Nicholas P. O'Gorman,[48] *Major* (from h.p. Lincoln Regt.), *Dep. Assist. Adj. Gen. Hong Kong*, 18 Jan. 95	7 Mar. 65	21 Aug. 69	21 Aug. 78	10 Jan. 85	16 Dec. 93	
Harrie Archbold Reid, *Lt. Col.* 7 Hussars	5 July 64	26 Nov. 68	24 Dec. 70	19 Dec. 83	19 Dec. 93	
Benjamin H. Pollard, *Lt. Col.* Indian Staff Corps	25 Dec. 67	18 Jan. 70	25 Dec. 79	25 Dec. 87	25 Dec. 93	
p.s.c. Richd. M. Greenfield, *Major*, Inniskilling Fus.		13 June 74	14 Sept. 31	10 Aug. 90	29 Dec. 93	
p.s.c. Claude Kennedy, *Major*, h.p. Suffolk Regt.; *Inspector of Signalling, Aldershot*, 1 Jan. 94		31 Aug. 72	7 Sept. 82	26 Apr. 85	30 Dec. 93	30 Dec. 93
George Burges Allen, *Lt. Col.* Royal Artillery		12 Jan. 66	12 Mar. 78	30 July 84	31 Dec. 93	
Alex. L. Scott Burrowes, *Major*, R. Marine Art.		6 Dec. 67	17 May 78	31 Dec. 86	31 Dec. 93	
Sidney Smith, *Lt. Col.* Royal Engineers		13 Jan. 69	1 July 81	18 Nov. 82	1 Jan. 94	
Archibald Edward Duthy, *Lt. Col.* Royal Artillery		17 July 66	7 Aug. 78	20 Aug. 84	1 Jan. 94	
Cameron M. H. Downing, *Lt. Col.* Royal Artillery		17 July 66	7 Aug. 78	25 Aug. 84	1 Jan. 94	
Walter Neil Jervis, *Lt. Col.* Royal Artillery		15 Jan. 67	9 Oct. 78	26 Aug. 84	1 Jan. 94	
John Wm. T. Hume, *Lt. Col.* Derbyshire Regiment	8 July 64	28 Oct. 71	18 Dec. 80	1 Dec. 84	1 Jan. 94	
John H. H. S. D. Hogarth, *Lt. Col.* K. O. Scottish Brdrs.	5 Mar. 67	28 May 70	1 July 78	15 Dec. 85	1 Jan. 94	
Henry Clarke, *Lt. Col.* Royal Engineers		13 Jan. 69	1 July 81	5 Dec. 87	1 Jan. 94	
Charles John Blake, *Lt. Col.* Royal Artillery		15 Jan. 67	29 Oct. 78	27 Aug. 84	3 Jan. 94	
Wm. Whitmore Smith, *Lt. Col.* Royal Artillery		15 Jan. 67	1 Dec. 78	37 Aug. 84	4 Jan. 94	
Robert Hayne, *Lt. Col.* Wiltshire Regt. (62 F.)	25 Sept. 67	26 Feb. 70	11 May 78	19 June 82	7 Jan. 94	
Hon. Keith Turnour, *Lt. Col.* King's Royal Rifles	2 Oct. 66	9 Feb. 70	30 Sept. 79	19 Aug. 85	7 Jan. 94	
Chas. H. Ellison Adamson, *CIE. Lt. Col.* Ind. S. C.		8 Jan. 68	8 Jan. 80	8 Jan. 88	8 Jan. 94	
p.s.c. Richd. K. Ridgeway, *Lt. Col.* Indian S. C.		8 Jan. 68	8 Jan. 80	8 Jan. 88	8 Jan. 94	
Goffery Lawrence Eliot, *Lt. Col.* Indian Staff Corps	8 Jan. 68	22 Feb. 70	8 Jan. 80	8 Jan. 88	8 Jan. 94	
Fred. Babington Peile, *Lt. Col.* Indian Staff Corps	8 Jan. 68		8 Jan. 80	8 Jan. 88	8 Jan. 94	
James Beverley Lynch, *Lt. Col.* Indian Staff Corps	8 Jan. 68	12 Oct. 70	8 Jan. 80	8 Jan. 88	8 Jan. 94	
Robert Gordon, *Lt. Col.* Indian Staff Corps	8 Jan. 68	8 Sept. 71	8 Jan. 80	8 Jan. 88	8 Jan. 94	
Herbert Edw. Penton, *Lt. Col.* Indian Staff Corps	8 Jan. 68	3 Oct. 71	8 Jan. 80	8 Jan. 88	8 Jan. 94	
Francis Jeromy Day, *Lt. Col.* Royal Engineers		8 Jan. 68	13 Dec. 79	8 Jan. 87	12 Jan. 94	
Charles Lawford Dale, *Lt. Col.* West India Regt.		11 Feb. 76	12 Oct. 82	2 Feb. 87	17 Jan. 94	

Lieutenant Colonels.

Name	CORNET, 2nd LIEUT. or ENSIGN.	LIEUT.	CAPTAIN.	MAJOR.	LIEUT. COLONEL.	WHEN PLACED ON HALF PAY.
Edw. Locke Elliot, *DSO. Lt.Col.* Indian Staff Corps	22 Jan. 68	23 Aug. 70	22 Jan. 80	22 Jan. 88	22 Jan. 94	
Clayton Wm. James Hingston, *Lt.Col.* Indian S. C.	22 Jan. 68	28 Oct. 71	22 Jan. 80	22 Jan. 88	22 Jan. 94	
p.s.c. De Courcy Daniell, *Lt.Col.* Royal Artillery		15 Jan. 67	14 Dec. 78	20 Sept. 84	31 Jan. 94	
p.s.c. Lionel G. Fawkes, *Lt.Col.* (from h.p. Royal Artillery), *Instructor R. M. College*, 1 Sept. 93		1 Dec. 70	12 Dec. 80	21 July 86	3 Feb. 94	
p.s.c. Colwyn W. Vulliamy, *Lt.Col.* Leicester Regiment (17 F.)	29 Sept. 65	18 Aug. 69	23 Jan. 79	15 Nov. 84	5 Feb. 94	
Pulteney H. Murray, *Lt.Col.* Shropshire Lt. Inf.	27 Feb. 69	28 Oct. 71	3 Apr. 80	21 June 85	11 Feb. 94	
Fred. S. C. Hare, *Lt.Col.* Army Service Corps	Deptl.	Service	13 8/12 yrs.	14 Feb. 89	14 Feb. 94	
Henry Alexius Abbott, *Lt.Col.* Indian Staff Corps	15 Feb. 68	18 Nov. 70	15 Feb. 80	15 Feb. 88	15 Feb. 94	
Gilbert Gaisford, *Lt.Col.* Indian Staff Corps	22 Feb. 68	23 Mar. 70	22 Feb. 80	22 Feb. 88	22 Feb. 94	
Henry Breffney Ternan, *Lt.Col.* Indian Staff Corps	22 Feb. 68	28 Oct. 71	22 Feb. 80	22 Feb. 88	22 Feb. 94	
George Colquhoun Madden, *CB. DSO. Lt.Col.* West India Regiment		12 May 75	24 Aug. 81	29 Jan. 88	7 Mar. 94	
Louis Faulkner Brown, *Lt.Col.* Royal Engineers		8 Jan. 68	20 Dec. 79	2 Mar. 81	8 Mar. 94	
Fred. Duncan Raikes, *CIE. Lt.Col.* Indian S. C.	14 Mar. 68	3 May 71	14 Mar. 80	14 Mar. 88	14 Mar. 94	
Chas. Wm. Gore, *Lt.Col.* West Riding Regt. (76 F.)	24 Apr. 69	28 Oct. 71	15 Dec. 79	28 June 84	15 Mar. 94	
Henry Garde Rice, *Lt.Col.* Army Service Corps	Deptl.	Service	13 8/12 yrs.	16 Mar. 89	16 Mar. 94	
John C. Cautley, *Lt.Col.* West Kent Regt. (97 F.)	13 Jan. 69	22 June 70	2 Feb. 78	9 Sept. 84	19 Mar. 94	
Wm. Bowles Williams, *Lt.Col.* Wiltshire Regt. (62 F.)	30 Oct. 67	3 Apr 70	13 July 78	28 Oct. 85	19 Mar. 94	
Duncan Alexander Johnston, *Lt.Col.* R. Engineers		8 Jan. 68	24 Dec. 79	18 Jan. 87	19 Mar. 94	
George P. F. Byng, *Lt.Col.* York Lt. Inf. (51 F.)	11 Jan. 67	18 May 69	14 June 76	20 May 82	26 Mar. 94	
Charles Hervey Bagot, *Lt.Col.* Royal Engineers		8 Jan. 68	17 Aug. 80	27 Feb. 87	28 Mar. 94	
Thos. C. O. Powlett, *Lt.Col.* Northampton Regt. (48F.)	16 Oct. 66	14 Mar. 68	28 Oct. 71	10 June 82	1 Apr. 94	
Sir George S. Clarke, *KCMG. Lt.Col.* Royal Eng.		15 July 68	22 Aug. 80	17 Mar. 87	1 Apr. 94	
Herbert N. Bunbury, *Lt.Col.* Army Service Corps		15 Dec. 71	2 July 81	1 Oct. 87	1 Apr. 94	
George Alex. Cockburn, *Lt.Col.* Royal Engineers		15 July 68	19 Sept. 80	16 June 87	4 Apr. 94	
Henry Oliphant Selby, *Lt.Col.* Royal Engineers		13 Jan. 69	1 July 81	17 Dec. 87	5 Apr. 94	
Fras. Geo. A. Wiehe,[50] *Major* (from h.p. Durham Lt. Inf.), *Chief Inst. School of Musk.*, 28 July 94	28 Oct. 71	28 Oct. 71	7 Jan. 80	29 Oct. 84	11 Apr. 94	
Chas. Waring Darwin, *Major*, h.p. Durham Lt. Inf. *Brig. Major Tyne and Tees Brigade Vol. Inf.*		9 Aug. 74	22 July 80	29 Oct. 84	11 Apr. 94	11 Apr. 94
St. George Mervyn Kirke, *Lt.Col.* R. Engineers		15 July 68	22 Sept. 80	1 July 87	3 May 94	
Hon. Arthur Wm. Hill-Trevor, *Major*, 1 Life Gds.		6 Sept. 75	7 July 80	5 Oct. 92	5 May 94	
Alex. Wm. Dury,[52] *Major*, h.p. West Kent Regt.	30 June 65	9 Feb. 70	1 Jan. 78	31 Dec. 84	9 May 94	9 May 94
Mark Hy. Geo. Goldie, *Lt.Col.* Royal Engineers		15 July 68	2 Oct. 80	11 July 87	10 May 94	
Edm. Percival Wilford, *Major*, h.p. Gloucester Regt.	25 July 65	27 June 68	27 Sept. 79	19 July 82	11 May 94	11 May 94
Frederick T. N. Spratt, *Lt.Col.* Royal Engineers		13 Jan. 69	1 July 81	2 July 87	18 May 94	
Wm. Lloyd Brereton, *Lt.Col.* Munster Fusiliers		21 Sept. 74	22 June 81	30 Jan. 85	20 May 94	
Arthur Thomas Preston, *Lt.Col.* Royal Engineers		15 July 68	22 Jan. 81	23 July 87	21 May 94	
Basil Lloyd Anstruther, *Lt.Col.* Manchester Regiment (63 F.)		17 July 73	13 June 79	1 Aug. 83	31 May 94	
William Potter Newall, *Lt.Col.* Indian Staff Corps	3 June 68	7 Dec. 70	3 June 80	3 June 88	3 June 94	
Wm. Fras. Hungerford Grey, *Lt.Col.* Indian S. C.	3 June 68	28 Oct. 71	3 June 80	3 June 88	3 June 94	
Robert John Knox, *Lt.Col.* Irish Rifles (83 F.)	8 Aug. 68	28 Oct. 71	12 Mar. 81	26 Apr. 86	4 June 94	
William Carre Riddell, *Lt.Col.* Dublin Fus. (103 F.)	12 Jan. 67	25 Mar. 68	15 Aug. 77	15 Mar. 82	7 June 94	
Alex. Herbert Mason, *Major*, Royal Engineers		17 Aug. 74	17 Aug. 85	8 June 94	9 June 94	
p.s.c. Richard C. B. Lawrence, *Lt.Col.* 1 Drag. Gds.		1 Feb. 76	1 June 80	18 Nov. 82	14 June 94	
John Miller Elgee Waddy, *Lt.Col.* Somerset Lt. Inf.	11 Jan. 67	24 Nov. 69	10 Apr. 78	8 May 85	14 June 94	
Edwin Law, *Major*, h.p. Gloucestershire Regiment	12 Sept. 65	16 June 71	20 Jan. 79	5 May 86	16 June 94	16 June 94
Arthur R. F. Dorward, *DSO. Lt.Col.* R. Engineers		15 July 68	1 May 81	1 July 87	21 June 94	
George A. L. Rawstorne, *Major*, R. Marine Art.		24 June 68	21 July 79	22 June 87	23 June 94	
James Stoneman, *Lt.Col.* Army Service Corps	Deptl.	Service	13 8/12 yrs.	25 June 89	25 June 94	
Thomas F. Dunscomb Bridge, *Major*, R. Marines	26 June 66	23 Aug. 67	6 May 81	15 June 81	26 June 94	
Harry Barron, *Lt.Col.* Royal Artillery		10 July 67	1 Jan. 80	1 Oct. 84	27 June 94	
Fred. John Harden, *Lt.Col.* Bedfordshire Regt. (16F.)	11 Apr. 68	23 Nov. 70	23 Aug. 76	10 Oct. 84	1 July 94	
Robert Maxwell Hyslop, *Lt.Col.* Royal Engineers		15 July 68	1 May 81	1 Oct. 87	7 July 94	
Charles Arthur Ross Sage, *Lt.Col.* Indian Staff C.	8 July 68	3 Oct. 71	8 July 80	8 July 88	8 July 94	
Charles Grenville Mansel, *Lt.Col.* Indian Staff C.	8 July 68	20 July 71	8 July 80	8 July 88	8 July 94	
Charles Thomas Bingham, *Lt.Col.* Indian Staff C.	8 July 68	31 Aug. 70	8 July 80	8 July 88	8 July 94	
Benjamin Alex. Napier Parrott, *Lt.Col.* Indian S.C.	8 July 68	8 Dec. 70	8 July 80	8 July 88	8 July 94	
Douglas Davidson Pryce, *Lt.Col.* Indian Staff C.	8 July 68	15 July 71	8 July 80	8 July 88	8 July 94	
Francis Forsyth Robert Burgess, *Lt.Col.* Ind. S.C.	8 July 68	27 Oct. 71	8 July 80	8 July 88	8 July 94	
Cathcart Dempster, *Lt.Col.* Indian Staff Corps	9 July 68	28 Feb. 70	9 July 80	9 July 88	9 July 94	
Edward Bruce, *Lt.Col.* Indian Staff Corps	10 July 68	28 Oct. 71	10 July 80	2 Mar. 81	10 July 94	
Thos. Johnson Seppings, *Lt.Col.* York Lt. Inf. (105 F.)	12 July 68	10 June 71	11 Aug. 78	13 June 83	13 July 94	
Thomas Edward Spencer, *Lt.Col.* Indian Staff C.	22 July 68	30 Mar. 70	1 July 77	15 June 85	22 July 94	
Frank Abbott, *Lt.Col.* Indian Staff Corps	22 July 68	28 Oct. 71	22 July 80	22 July 88	22 July 94	
John David Fetherstonhaugh, *Lt.Col.* Argyll and Sutherland Highlanders (93 Foot)	1 Sept. 69	28 Oct. 71	17 May 79	28 May 84	23 July 94	
Geo. Bulstrode Edmund Radcliffe, *Lt.Col.* Ind. S.C.	23 July 68	2 Nov. 70	23 July 80	23 July 88	23 July 94	
p.s.c. William Andrew Yule,[53] *Lt.Col.* (from h.p. Scots Fus.); *D.A.A. General, Bermuda*, 7 Nov. 94	2 Oct. 66	10 Feb. 69	1 Aug. 78	2 Feb. 85	26 July 94	
Henry Craigie Halkett, *Lt.Col.* Indian Staff Corps	2 Aug. 68	11 Apr. 71	2 Aug. 80	2 Aug. 88	2 Aug. 94	
Arthur S. H. Gem, *Lt.Col.* Sussex Regt. (107 F.)	28 Oct. 71	28 Oct. 71	10 Feb. 80	10 Nov. 83	6 Aug. 94	
Horatio Arthur Yorke, *Lt.Col.* Royal Engineers		13 June 69	3 June 81	15 June 85	6 Aug. 94	
Solomon Chas. Fred. Peile, *Major*, Indian S. C.		9 Aug. 74	9 Aug. 85	9 Aug. 94	10 Aug. 94	
John James Scott Chisholme, *Lt.Col.* 5 Lancers		10 June 72	2 Mar. 78	2 Mar. 81	11 Aug. 94	
Fred. Augustus Yorke, *Lt.Col.* Royal Artillery		10 July 67	1 Jan. 79	1 Oct. 84	13 Aug. 94	
Divie K. Robertson, *Lt.Col.* Norfolk Regt. (9 F.)	26 Sept. 69	28 Oct. 71	27 June 81	28 June 84	22 Aug. 94	
p.s.c. Hon. Fred. Wm. Stopford,[54] *Lt.Col.* (from h.p. Gren. Gds.) *D.A.A. Gen. Aldershot*, 22 Aug. 94		28 Oct. 71	7 May 84	15 June 85	22 Aug. 94	
Arthur Howlett, *Lt.Col.* Indian Staff Corps	22 Aug. 68	21 Nov. 70	22 Aug. 80	22 Aug. 88	22 Aug. 94	
p.s.c. Arthur J. O. Pollock, *Lt.Col.* Scots Fusiliers	6 Feb. 66	2 Jan. 69	2 Mar. 78	2 Feb. 85	25 Aug. 94	
Fred. H. Whitby, *Lt.Col.* Durham Lt. Inf. (106 F.)		9 Aug. 73	3 July 79	20 Jan. 84	27 Aug. 94	
C. J. Whitaker, *Lt.Col.* York and Lanc. Regt. (55 F.)	8 July 69	4 Jan. 71	14 Dec. 78	24 Feb. 88	27 Aug. 94	
John Morpott Piercy, *Lt.Col.* Dorset Regt. (39 F.)	24 Dec. 70	28 Oct. 71	6 Apr. 81	25 Sept. 89	28 Aug. 94	
Guthrie H. Jessop, *Lt.Col.* Army Service Corps	Dep. Ser.	13 2/12 yrs.	11 Dec. 88	1 Sept. 89	1 Sept. 94	
Somerset Henry Paul Graves, *Lt.Col.* Indian S. C.	2 Sept. 68	15 Dec. 69	2 Sept. 80	2 Sept. 88	2 Sept. 94	
p.s.c. Charles L. Mortimer, *Lt.Col.* Royal Fusiliers	1 Sept. 69	28 Oct. 71	21 June 80	11 Dec. 85	3 Sept. 94	
Edward Wheeler, *Major*, Royal Marine Artillery		24 June 68	1 Jan. 79	12 Sept. 87	12 Sept. 94	
Henry Hay, *Lt.Col.* Indian Staff Corps	16 Sept. 68	28 Oct. 71	16 Sept. 80	16 Sept. 88	16 Sept. 94	
Arthur Herbert Nourse, *Lt.Col.* West Surrey Regt.	7 Dec. 67	12 July 71	26 Feb. 81	10 Sept. 85	29 Sept. 94	
Archibald Mungo Muir, *Lt.Col.* Indian Staff Corps	30 Sept. 68	28 Oct. 71	30 Sept. 80	30 Sept. 88	30 Sept. 94	

Lieutenant Colonels.

	CORNET, 2nd LIEUT. or ENSIGN.	LIEUT.	CAPTAIN.	MAJOR.	LIEUT. COLONEL.	WHEN PLACED ON HALF PAY.
William Arthur Broome, *Lt.Col.* Indian Staff Corp[s]	30 Sept. 68	28 Oct. 71	30 Sept. 80	30 Sept. 88	30 Sept. 94	
George Barker, *Lt.Col.* Royal Engineers	......	13 Jan. 69	21 June 81	18 Nov. 82	1 Oct. 94	
Cuthbert G. Collingwood, *Lt.Col.* Lancashire Fus.	14 Sept. 67	3 Sept. 70	11 May 78	27 June 82	15 Oct. 94	
Horatio Reg. Mends, *Lt.Col.* King's Royal Rifles...	......	30 Dec. 71	12 Jan. 81	9 Oct. 85	15 Oct. 94	
John Rogers, *Lt.Col.* Army Service Corps	Dep. Ser.	13⁸/₁₂ yrs.	11 Dec. 88	28 Oct. 89	28 Oct. 94	
Sydney Hume Lynn, *Lt.Col.* Army Service Corps	Dep. Ser.	13⁸/₁₂ yrs.	11 Dec. 88	28 Oct. 89	28 Oct. 94	
Horatio Dove, *Lt.Col.* Royal Engineers	......	13 Jan. 69	1 July 81	19 Oct. 87	3 Nov. 94	
Malcolm Alex. Gray, *Lt.Col.* Indian Staff Corps ...	7 Nov. 68	6 May 71	7 Nov. 80	7 Nov. 88	7 Nov. 94	
Arthur Close Borton, *Lt.Col.* Somerset Light Inf...	24 July 69	28 Oct. 71	9 Jan. 79	28 Dec. 86	8 Nov. 94	
Edward Owen Hay, *Lt.Col.* Royal Artillery	......	10 July 67	1 Apr. 79	18 Nov. 82	15 Nov. 94	
Robert J. Chaytor, *Lt.Col.* Northampton Regt. ...	6 Mar. 67	14 Oct. 68	21 Jan. 81	6 Aug. 83	22 Nov. 94	
Francis M. Reid, *Lt.Col.* Highland Lt. Inf.(71 F.)	8 July 68	27 Aug. 70	20 Apr. 78	7 Apr. 86	22 Nov. 94	
Henry Grey Dixon, *Lt.Col.* King's Own Scot.Bord.	23 Dec. 68	2 Aug. 71	12 Feb. 79	17 Feb. 86	3 Dec. 94	
William Gregg, *Lt.Col.* Leicestershire Regiment ..	......	24 July 72	5 Mar. 81	11 Apr. 88	3 Dec. 94	
Algernon S. Griffiths, *Lt.Col.* Royal Artillery......	......	8 Jan. 68	27 June 79	10 Dec. 84	8 Dec. 94	
Algernon St. L. Burrowes, *Major,* Royal Marines	8 Dec. 66	3 Aug. 67	1 July 81	15 June 85	8 Dec. 94	
Lourenço Edye, *Major,* Royal Marines	8 Dec. 65	3 Aug. 67	1 July 81	8 Dec. 87	8 Dec. 94	
Richard T. E. Dowse, *Lt.Col.* Suffolk Regt. (12 F.)	1 Aug. 68	28 May 7:	11 Nov. 79	4 June 84	9 Dec. 94	
Frederick M. Turner, *Lt.Col.* Royal Artillery	......	8 Jan. 68	1 July 79	13 Dec. 84	10 Dec. 94	
p.s.c. James C. Barker, *Lt.Col.* Royal Engineers...	......	13 Jan. 69	1 July 81	17 Dec. 87	10 Dec. 94	
Henry de Courcy Rawlins, *Lt.Col.* Scot.Rifles(26 F.)	......	23 Apr. 74	11 Oct. 79	30 May 83	15 Dec. 94	
James Cameron, *Lt.Col.* Royal Engineers	......	13 Jan. 69	1 July 81	1 Apr. 88	17 Dec. 94	
John Henry Aug. Spyer, *Lt.Col.* Irish Regt. (18 F.)	......	30 Dec. 71	1 Jan. 81	3 Oct. 88	17 Dec. 94	
p.s.c. Wm. Peacocke, *CMG, Lt.Col.* R. Engineers	......	7 July 69	7 July 81	17 Dec. 87	20 Dec. 94	
Richard Theodore Orpen, *Lt.Col.* Royal Engineers	......	7 July 69	7 July 81	1 Apr. 88	1 Jan. 95	
Henry Thomas Curling, *Lt.Col.* Royal Artillery ...	......	15 July 68	16 Aug. 79	6 Feb. 85	4 Jan. 95	
Daniel Alex. Blest, *Lt.Col.* Essex Regiment (56 F.)	7 July 69	27 Oct. 71	9 Oct. 79	5 July 82	8 Jan. 95	
Audley Dallas Neeld, *Major,* 2 Life Guards	15 Feb. 71	28 Oct. 71	13 Apr. 81	24 Sept. 87	12 Jan. 95	
James Ramsay Hobday, *Lt.Col.* Indian Staff Corps	13 Jan. 69	28 Mar. 71	13 Jan. 81	1 July 87	13 Jan. 95	
George Williams Deane, *Lt.Col.* Indian Staff Corps	13 Jan. 69	28 Oct. 71	13 Jan. 81	13 Jan. 89	13 Jan. 95	
Edmund George Barrow, *Major,* Indian Staff Corps	......	30 Dec. 71	30 Dec. 83	16 Feb. 87	16 Jan. 95	
George, Lord Binning, *Major,* R. Horse Guards...	11 Sept. 80	1 Apr. 81	14 May 87	22 Dec. 94	18 Jan. 95	
Geo. Hart Dyke,⁵⁶ *Major,* h.p.Northumberland Fus.	7 Nov. 65	19 Jan. 70	16 Jan. 80	25 July 83	21 Jan. 95	21 Jan. 95
Francis William Snell, *Lt.Col.* Indian Staff Corps...	23 Jan. 69	28 Oct. 71	23 Jan. 81	23 Jan. 89	23 Jan. 95	
George Robert Rollo Savage, *Lt.Col.* R. Engineers	......	7 July 69	7 July 81	1 Apr. 88	24 Jan. 95	
Malby Edward Crofton, *Major,* h.p. Lancaster Regt.	16 June 66	12 Nov. 70	9 July 79	9 Mar. 86	25 Jan. 95	25 Jan. 95
Benjamin Arthur Milne, *Major,* R. Marine Artillery	......	24 June 68	2 Oct. 79	25 Jan. 88	25 Jan. 95	
Henry Kilgour,⁵⁸ *Major,* h.p. Northumberland Fus.	13 Feb. 66	8 June 70	4 May 80	2 Mar. 81	27 Jan. 95	27 Jan. 95
Robert Purdy, *Lt.Col.* Royal Artillery	......	15 July 68	16 Aug. 79	16 Feb. 85	1 Feb. 95	
Charles Haydon W. Cafe, *Lt.Col.* Sussex Rgt. (35 F.)	28 Oct. 71	28 Oct. 71	1 Feb. 80	5 Mar. 84	2 Feb. 95	
Thomas Harding Mackenzie, *Lt.Col.* Indian S.O.	3 Feb. 69	28 Oct. 71	3 Feb. 81	3 Feb. 89	3 Feb. 95	
Fred. A. Le Poer Trench, *Lt.Col.* Army Service Corps (Hon. Capt. 1 May 80)	Dep.Serv.	12¹¹/₁₂ yrs.	11 Dec. 88	3 Feb. 90	3 Feb. 95	
George Robert Stone, *Lt.Col.* Liverpool Rgt. (8 F.)	......	28 Feb. 74	19 May 81	17 Dec. 84	4 Feb. 95	
John Fraser Dingwall Fordyce, *Lt.Col.* Indian S.C.	4 Feb. 69	28 Oct. 71	4 Feb. 81	4 Feb. 89	4 Feb. 95	
Henry St. Patrick Maxwell, *CSI. Lt.Col.* Indian S.C.	6 Feb. 69	27 Apr. 71	6 Feb. 81	6 Feb. 89	6 Feb. 95	
Alfred Jas. Phayre Nuthall, *Lt.Col.* Indian S.C......	10 Feb. 69	28 Oct. 71	10 Feb. 81	10 Feb. 89	10 Feb. 95	
Henry Robert Dacres Thomas, *Lt.Col.* Indian S.C.	10 Feb. 69	28 Oct. 71	10 Feb. 81	10 Feb. 89	10 Feb. 95	
Archibald Borthwick Horsbrugh, *Lt.Col.* South Staffordshire Regt. (38 Foot)........................	......	28 Feb. 74	5 Apr. 81	11 Feb. 85	11 Feb. 95	
Robert V. Day, *Lt.Col.* Army Service Corps (Hon. Capt. 1 May 80)	Dep.Serv.	12¹¹/₁₂ yrs.	11 Dec. 88	13 Feb. 90	13 Feb. 95	
Henry Harding Mathias, *Lt.Col.* Gordon H. (75 F.)	17 Apr. 69	31 May 71	8 Mar. 79	27 Nov. 83	14 Feb. 95	
William James Fowler, *Lt.Col.* Royal Artillery......	......	15 July 68	16 Aug. 79	24 Feb. 85	20 Feb. 95	
Edward Deedes Newnham-Smith, *Lt.Col.*	27 Feb. 69	28 Oct. 71	27 Feb. 81	27 Feb. 89	27 Feb. 95	
Pechell Haslett, *Lt.Col.* Royal Engineers	......	7 July 69	7 July 81	1 Apr. 81	1 Mar. 95	
William Senhouse Clarke, *Lt.Col.* Worcester Regt. (29 F.)	8 Jan. 68	27 Oct. 71	1 Feb. 79	11 Aug. 86	2 Mar. 95	
Henry D. Williams, *Lt.Col.* N. Stafford Regt. (98 F.)	......	9 Aug. 73	6 Mar. 80	17 June 85	6 Mar. 95	
Henry T. Penrhys Evans, *Lt.Col.* E. Lanc. Regt.	27 Aug. 7c	28 Oct. 71	24 May 79	1 June 85	18 Mar. 95	

War Services of the Lieutenant Colonels not belonging to Regiments or Corps.

[For the War Services of other Lieutenant Colonels, vide their respective Regiments or Corps.]

³ Lt.Colonel Hon. C. Dutton served in the Afghan war in 1879-80 as Assistant Quarter Master General 2nd Division Cabul Field Force, and was present in the affair at Shekabad (mentioned in despatches, Brevet of Major, Medal).

⁸ Lt.Colonel J. L. C. St. Clair served with the 91st Highlanders as Adjutant in the Zulu war of 1879, and was present at the action of Gingindhlovu and relief of Ekowe (Medal with Clasp). Served in the Egyptian war of 1882 as Aide de Camp to Major General Harman (Medal, and Khedive's Star).

¹⁰ Lt.Colonel H. Cooper served in the Ashanti war in 1874 in the Transport Service (Medal). Served in the Boer war of 1881 in Barrow's Mounted Infantry. Served with the Burmese Expedition in 1886 as Aide de Camp to the Governor General of India (Medal with Clasp).

¹³ Lt.Colonel Houison Craufurd served with the 91st Highlanders in the Zulu war of 1879, and was present in the action of Gingindhlovu and relief of Ekowe (Medal with Clasp).

¹⁴ Lt.Colonel M. Wynyard served with the 50th Regiment in New Zealand during General Chute's campaign of 1866 (Medal). Served as Adjutant 1st Battalion West Kent Regiment in the Egyptian war of 1882 till invalided from Kassasin (Medal, and Khedive's Star).

¹⁵ Lt.Colonel E. J. H. Spratt served as Sub-Director of transport throughout the Zulu war of 1879, and was present with the 2nd Division in the engagement at Ulundi. Served in the operations against Sekukuni in 1879, and [was present as Orderly Officer to Colonel Russell, commanding the troops, at the storming of the stronghold (mentioned in despatches, Brevet of Major, Medal with Clasp). Served in the Boer war of 1881 as a Deputy Assistant Adjutant and Quarter Master General.

¹⁶ Lt.Colonel A. M. Bowles served with the 2nd Battalion Derbyshire Regiment in the Egyptian war of 1882 (Medal, and Khedive's Star).

¹⁷ Lt.Colonel H. Moore served in the Zulu war in 1879 (Medal with Clasp).

¹⁸ Lt.Colonel J. E. Goodwyn.—See Civil Decorations for Gallantry, "Hart's Annual Army List," p. 786.

¹⁹ Lt Colonel F. C. Turner served as a Midshipman in the Indian Navy from 1858 to 1863, and was present at the assault on the Island of Beyt in October 1859, and served with a Naval Brigade in the Okamandel Field Force in the operations before Dwarka, and at its capture in Nov. 1859. Served also in the China campaign of 1860, and was present at the capture of the Taku Forts (Medal with Clasp). Served with the 4th King's Own throughout the Abyssinian campaign of 1867-68, and was present at the action of Arrogee and capture of Magdala (Medal).

²⁰ Lt.Colonel P. F. Robertson served with the 92nd Highlanders in the Afghan war in 1879-80, and was present, in the engagement at Charasiab on 25th April 1880 (mentioned in despatches); accompanied Sir Frederick Roberts in the march to Candahar, and was present at the reconnaissance on the 31st August and at the battle of Candahar (Medal with Clasp, and Bronze Decoration). Served in the Boer war of 1881.

²¹ Lt.Colonel W. E. Hilliard served with the Expeditionary Field Force under Colonel J. R. Mackenzie in Arabia from the 27th October to the 20th December 1873, including the investment, surrender, occupation, and destruction of the fort at Al-Hota, and subsequent march to Zaidi in pursuit of Ally Bin Mana, the chief of Honshabi. Served in the Burmese Expedition in 1886-87 with the 1st Battalion of the Yorkshire Light Infantry (mentioned in despatches, Medal with Clasp).

²⁴ Lt.Colonel Hon. John Pleydell-Bouverie served with the 17th Lancers in the Zulu war of 1879, and was present in the engagements at Zuinguin Mountain and Ulundi (Medal with Clasp).

²⁵ Lt.Colonel G. A. W. Forrest served with the Burmese Expedition in 1889-90 (dangerously wounded).

²⁶ Lt.Colonel R. G. T. Cotton served in the occupation of Suakin by British troops in 1885-86.

²⁹ Lt.Colonel Hon. J. P. Napier served with the 10th Hussars in the Afghan war in 1878-79 (Medal).

³¹ Lt.Colonel C. Roberts served as Superintendent of Elephant Transport with the Duffla Expedition of 1874. Served with the 72nd Highlanders in the Afghan war from 1st May 1880 with the Cabul and Cabul-Candahar Field Forces; accompanied Sir Frederick Roberts in the march to Candahar, and was present at the battle of Candahar (Medal with Clasp, and Bronze Decoration).

³³ Lt.Colonel R. F. Willoughby served with the 91st Fusiliers in the Zulu war of 1879, and afterwards in the operations against Sekukuni, and was present at the storming of the stronghold (slightly wounded, Medal with Clasp).

³⁵ Lt.Colonel W. F. D. Cochrane served in the Zulu war of 1879, and was present in the engagement at Isanhlwana on 22nd January as Orderly Officer to Colonel Durnford; served afterwards with Wood's Column in command of the Natal Native Horse, taking part in the engagements at Zoblane Mountain, Kambula, and Ulundi (Brevet of Major, Medal with Clasp). Served as Assistant Adjutant General (Principal Staff Officer) to the Cape Colonial Forces during the Basuto war in 1880-81, and was present at the capture of Lerothodi's stronghold and several minor engagements. Served in the Egyptian war of 1882 with the Commissariat and Transport Corps (Medal, and Khedive's Star).

³⁸ Lt.Colonel S. J. M. Jopp was employed in Natal during the Zulu war in 1879 (Medal). Served in the Boer war of 1881, and was present in the engagements at Lang's Nek (mentioned in despatches) and the Ingogo River.

³⁹ Lt.Colonel C. F. Thomson served in the Boer war of 1881. Served in the Soudan campaign in 1885 as Brigade Major of Cavalry (mentioned in despatches, Brevet of Major, Medal with Clasp, and Khedive's Star).

⁴⁰ Lt.Colonel T. Harris served in the Afghan war in 1879-80 as Deputy Assistant Quarter Master General Candahar Field Force, and was present in the engagements at Girishk (wounded) and on the Helmund (mentioned in despatches), in the action at Maiwand (wounded), and in the defence of Candahar (Medal).

⁴¹ Lt.Colonel J. R. Povah served in the Afghan war of 1878-79 as Transport Officer 2nd Brigade 1st Division Candahar Field Force, and was present at the occupation of Candahar and Khelat-i-Ghilzie (Medal).

⁴⁵ Lt.Colonel H. E. C. Kitchener served with the Burmese Expedition in 1891 as Senior Transport Officer with the Wuntho Field Force (mentioned in despatches); also served with the Tammu Column of the Manipore Field Force in 1891 as Senior Transport Officer (mentioned in despatches, Medal with Clasp).

⁴⁷ Lt.Colonel H. M. A. Warde served with the 19th Hussars in the Egyptian war of 1882, and was present in the action at Kassasin on the 9th September (Medal and Khedive's Star).

⁴⁸ Lt.Colonel N. P. O'Gorman served in the Hazara campaign in 1888 as Deputy Assistant Adjutant General in the 1st Brigade under Brigadier General Channer from 3rd October to 9th November (mentioned in despatches, Medal with Clasp).

⁵⁰ Lt.Colonel F. G. A. Wiehe served in the Afghan war in 1879-80 as Brigade Transport Officer with the Khyber Field Force (Medal).

⁵² Lt.Colonel A. W. Dury served with the 4th Regiment in the Abyssinian campaign in 1868 (Medal).

⁵³ Lt.Colonel W. A. Yule served in the Afghan war in 1878-79, and was present at the attack and capture of Ali Musjid (Medal with Clasp).

⁵⁴ Lt.Colonel the Hon. F. W. Stopford served in the Egyptian war of 1882 as Aide de Camp to Sir John Adye, Chief of the Staff, and was present at the engagement of Tel-el-Mahuta, Kassasin (9th Sept.), and in the battle of Tel-el-Kebir (mentioned in despatches, Medal with Clasp, 5th Class of the Medjidie, and Khedive's Star). Served in the Soudan campaign in 1884-85 a Aide de Camp to Major General Lyon Freemantle and afterwards as Brigade Major to the Brigade of Guards, and was present in the engagement at Hasheen (mentioned in despatches, Brevet of Major, Clasp).

⁵⁶ Lt.Colonel G. H. Dyke served in the Afghan war of 1878-80, took part in the two expeditions into the Bazar Valley, and was present in the engagement at Kam Dakka (mentioned in despatches, Medal).

⁵⁷ Lt.Colonel M. E. Crofton served in the Zulu war of 1879 (Medal with Clasp).

⁵⁸ Lt.Colonel H. Kilgour served in the Afghan war in 1878-79, and took part in the two expeditions into the Bazar Valley as Transport Officer including the engagement at Deh Sarakh, and with the Besud and Kama Expeditions (Brevet of Major, Medal).

Majors. 49

	CORNET, 2nd LIEUT. or ENSIGN.	LIEUT.	CAPTAIN.	MAJOR.	WHEN PLACED ON HALF PAY.
Bloomfield Gough, *Major*, 9 Lancers..................................	27 Apr. 70	28 Oct. 71	17 July 78	2 Mar. 81	
Hon. John Scott Napier, *Major*, Gordon Highlanders (92 Foot)	14 Aug. 67	17 May 71	17 Apr. 80	2 Mar. 81	
Charles Whittingham Horsley Douglas, *Major*, Gordon Highlanders (92 F.)	16 Dec. 69	27 Oct. 71	29 July 80	2 Mar. 81	
Thomas Everard Hungerford,[1] *Major*, h.p. Royal Marines, *Barrack Master, Deal*, 21 Jan. 87	26 June 60	5 Feb. 64	1 Oct. 77	1 July 81	21 Jan. 87
Lionel Godolphin Brooke, *Major*, Connaught Rangers (94 F.)	5 May 69	28 Oct. 71	15 Apr. 79	1 July 81	
Henry J. L. Norcock,[1] *Major*, h.p. Royal Marines, *Barrack Master, Plymouth Division, with hon. rank of Lt. Col.* 6 Oct. 83	12 Oct. 60	7 July 64	1 Oct. 77	12 Oct. 81	6 Oct. 85
Alexander Allen, *Major*, h.p. Royal Marine Artillery; *Barrack Master*, 2 July 92	13 Dec. 65	3 Aug. 67	8 May 77	11 July 82	2 July 92
Edward Selby Innes, *Major*, h.p. Royal Marines, *Paymaster, Deal*, 27 Sept. 91	31 Mar. 63	23 Oct. 66	9 Oct. 78	11 July 82	17 June 89
Francis Fred. Fyler Roupell, *Major*, East Surrey Regiment...	5 Oct. 67	24 Sept. 70	7 Aug. 78	1 Aug. 82	
Lionel Edward B. Booth, *Major*, West Riding Regt. (33 F.)...	......	10 Jan. 72	6 Aug. 78	6 Sept. 82	
Sir Claude M. MacDonald, *KCMG, Major*, Highland Light Infantry (74 Foot)	......	16 Mar. 72	12 Feb. 81	18 Nov. 82	
James Maitland Hunt, *Major*, Cameron Highlanders (79 F.)	......	12 Feb. 74	12 Feb. 81	18 Nov. 82	
p.s.c. Edwd. A. W. S. Grove, *Major*, West Kent Regt. (50 F.)	......	12 Nov. 73	13 Apr. 81	18 Nov. 82	
William Johnston Kirkpatrick, *Major*, York and Lancaster Regiment	......	28 Feb. 74	1 July 81	18 Nov. 82	
Charles Aug. Rochfort-Boyd, *Major*, Royal Engineers	......	23 July 70	23 July 82	18 Nov. 82	
p.s.c. Henry Vivian Cowan, *Major*, Royal Artillery............	......	11 Sept. 73	1 Nov. 82	18 Nov. 82	
Robert Albert Hickson, *Major*, The Buffs (3 F.)..................	26 June 67	29 Dec. 69	26 Feb. 76	14 Mar. 83	
Henry John Knight, *Major*, Seaforth Highlanders (72 F.) ...	9 Mar. 67	24 July 69	27 Mar. 78	27 Mar. 83	
George Lycett Engledue May, *Major*, Lancashire Fusiliers ...	13 June 67	19 Aug. 71	22 Nov. 78	4 Apr. 83	
Charles Stafford Stephen Whitehill, *Major*, Yorkshire Light Infantry	1 Aug. 68	6 Nov. 70	21 Apr. 77	21 June 83	
Wm. M'Curthy O'Leary, *Major*, S. Lancashire Regt. (40 F.)...	17 Apr. 69	15 Feb. 71	20 Mar. 78	13 Aug. 83	
Henry Gritton, *Major*, h.p. R. Marines, *Paymaster, Chatham*, 1 Aug. 90	31 Dec. 62	28 June 66	2 July 78	1 Sept. 83	1 Aug. 90
Adolphus James Price, *Major*, West Yorkshire Regiment	11 Dec. 66	21 July 71	4 Mar. 80	5 Sept. 83	
Charles S. B. Parsons, *Major*, Royal Artillery	......	17 Aug. 74	13 Oct. 81	14 Oct. 83	
p.s.c. Theodore Edward Stephenson, *Major*, Essex Regiment	......	21 Sept. 74	1 July 81	27 Nov. 83	
George Humphrys Leathem, *Major*, East Surrey Regiment (31 Foot)	23 Mar. 67	11 Apr. 68	2 Mar. 78	28 Nov. 83	
Henry Whistler Smith-Rewse, *Major*, Royal Engineers.........	......	15 Dec. 71	15 Dec. 83	29 Dec. 83	
Charles Hawtrey B. Norcott, *Major*, Rifle Brigade	14 Aug. 67	28 Oct. 71	1 Apr. 79	1 Jan. 84	
George Seaforth Rodon, *Major*, Royal Scots (1 Foot)	17 Apr. 67	7 Dec. 70	21 July 77	13 Feb. 84	
Arthur Law Woodland, *Major*, Durham Lt. Infantry (68 F.)	1 Feb. 67	12 Oct. 70	29 June 75	23 Mar. 84	
Arthur Charles Jackson, *Major*, The Buffs (3 Foot)	1 Apr. 68	29 June 70	10 Mar. 78	16 Apr. 84	
William Alexander Ramsay, *Major*, 4 Hussars	1 Sept. 69	14 Jan. 71	2 Mar. 79	21 May 84	
Charles Bradford H. Wolseley-Jenkins, *Major*, 19 Hussars ...	......	13 June 74	1 July 81	21 May 84	
Herbert C. Thornton Littledale, *Major*, 4 Dragoon Guards ...	......	21 Sept. 74	8 Mar. 82	21 May 84	
Edward Wm. Herbert, *Major*, King's Royal Rifles	......	2 Dec. 74	19 Aug. 83	21 May 84	
Wm. Augustus Collings, *Major*, Berkshire Regiment (49 F.)	......	16 Mar. 73	4 Oct. 80	28 June 84	
Frederick Alexander Currie, *Major*, Norfolk Regiment (9 F.)	......	3 July 72	28 Nov. 81	28 June 84	
Arthur Ely Heathcote Tottenham, *Major*, Argyll and Sutherland Highlanders (91 Foot)	......	1 Feb. 73	1 July 81	11 July 84	
Walter G. Crole Wyndham, *Major*, 21 Hussars	......	11 Feb. 75	19 May 80	16 July 84	
George Hardon, *Major*, Sussex Regiment (35 Foot)	......	30 Dec. 71	19 Feb. 81	6 Aug. 84	
Fred. Edward Power, *Major*, Northamptonshire Regiment ...	25 Apr. 68	27 Oct. 71	20 Apr. 81	20 Aug. 84	
William Edward Morrison Rough, *Major*, 7 Dragoon Guards	23 Sept. 71	28 Oct. 71	22 Mar. 79	26 Aug. 84	
Charles Parker Ridley, *Major*, Manchester Regiment (96 F.)	......	9 Aug. 73	13 Dec. 70	30 Sept. 84	
p.s.c. Arthur Grey Tidy, *Major*, N. Lancashire Regt............	8 Jan. 68	24 Apr. 69	30 May 77	22 Nov. 84	
John Guyse Sparke, *Major*, Yorkshire Light Infantry (51 F.)	3 Sept. 70	28 Oct. 71	4 Feb. 81	10 Jan. 85	
Frederick Carpenter, *Major*, Connaught Rangers (88 F.) ...	3 Aug. 70	28 Oct. 71	30 Mar. 81	1 Feb. 85	
Peter Blackburn, *Major*, Royal Artillery	......	15 July 68	27 Aug. 79	24 Feb. 85	
p.s.c. John Charles Duke, *Major*, West Riding Regt. (33 F.)...	23 Sept. 71	28 Oct. 71	24 Aug. 81	25 Feb. 85	
Francis John Burridge, *Major*, Royal Artillery..................	......	15 July 68	27 Aug. 79	13 Mar. 85	
Roger Charles Edward North, *Major*, Royal Artillery.........	......	15 July 68	27 Aug. 79	13 Mar. 85	
Arundel James Nixon, *Major*, Royal Artillery	......	15 July 68	13 Sept. 79	19 Mar. 85	
John Leach, *Major*, Royal Artillery	......	13 Jan. 69	25 Sept. 79	1 Apr. 85	
Lionel James Archer Chapman, *Major*, Royal Artillery.........	......	13 Jan. 69	14 Nov. 70	7 Apr. 85	
Charles Richard Townley, *Major*, Suffolk Regt. (12 Foot) ...	14 Jan. 69	28 Oct. 71	10 Apr. 80	9 Apr. 85	
Thomas Mayhew, *Major*, Royal Artillery........................	......	13 Jan. 69	27 Nov. 79	10 Apr. 85	
George Osborne Smith, *Major*, Irish Fusiliers (89 Foot)	13 July 67	12 Dec. 68	6 Mar. 80	11 Apr. 85	
Arthur Davidson, *Major*, King's Royal Rifles (60 F.)	......	10 Sept. 76	23 Apr. 85	23 Apr. 85	
Henry Robert Roberts, *Major*, Lincolnshire Regt. (10 F.)...	19 Feb. 67	15 Feb. 71	17 May 79	15 June 85	
Augustus West Hill, *Major*, Middlesex Regt. (57 F.)	......	1 Jan. 79	27 Sept. 80	8 May 85	
George Dodsworth Stawell, *Major*, Devonshire Regt. (11 F.)	2 May 68	9 Feb. 70	19 May 80	19 May 85	
Evelyn Broomfield Pocklington, *Major*, Oxfordshire Light Infantry (52 F.)	1 May 67	3 Feb. 69	15 Jan. 78	20 May 85	
Charles Maximilian Western, *Major*, Royal Artillery	......	7 July 69	24 Jan. 80	25 May 85	
William Leslie Davidson, *Major*, Royal Artillery..................	......	7 July 69	24 Jan. 80	7 June 85	
Harold Paget, *Major*, 7 Hussars	23 Jan. 69	22 Feb. 71	23 July 79	15 June 85	
Alexander Nelson Rochfort, *Major*, Royal Artillery	......	4 Jan. 71	9 Mar. 81	15 June 85	
Cecil Wyburn Peters, *Major*, 4 Hussars..........................	......	11 Feb. 75	27 Apr. 81	15 June 85	
p.s.c. Henry William Newton Guinness, *Major*, Irish Regt. ...	......	9 Aug. 73	22 May 81	15 June 85	
John Hope Wynne Eyton, *Major*, Shropshire Lt. Inf. (53 F.)	......	14 Feb. 74	1 July 81	15 June 85	
Samuel Job Lea, *Captain*, Army Service Corps..................	6 Mar. 72	6 Mar. 72	19 Sept. 81	15 June 85	
Charles Boyd Wilkieson, *Major*, Royal Engineers	......	23 July 70	23 July 82	15 June 85	
Ferdinando Wallace Bennet, *Major*, Royal Engineers	......	4 Jan. 71	15 June 82	15 June 85	
Charles Berkeley Pigott, *DSO. Major*, 21 Hussars	......	......	......	15 June 85	
William Graydon Carter, *Major*, Essex Regiment (56 F.) ...	19 Feb. 79	9 Feb. 81	31 Jan. 83	15 June 85	
Henry Parry Carden, *Major*, Duke of Cornwall's Lt. Inf.	......	10 Sept. 75	14 Mar. 83	15 June 85	
George Evan Lloyd, *DSO. Major*, South Stafford Regt.........	......	13 June 74	8 May 83	15 June 85	
David Phelips Chapman, *Major*, Cheshire Regt.	......	29 Nov. 76	20 June 83	15 June 85	
Henry Bowles, *Major*, Yorkshire Regiment (19 F.)	......	28 Mar. 74	13 Aug. 83	15 June 85	
Henry Alfred Walsh, *Major*, Somerset Lt. Infantry..................	......	26 Feb. 77	6 Sept. 83	15 June 85	
Eyre Macdonnell Stewart Crabbe, *Major*, Grenadier Gds. ...	......	28 Feb. 74	20 Oct. 83	15 June 85	
Robert George Kekewich, *Major*, Inniskilling Fusiliers	......	2 Dec. 74	30 Nov. 83	15 June 85	

Majors.

	CORNET, 2nd LIEUT. or ENSIGN.	LIEUT.	CAPTAIN.	MAJOR.	WHEN PLACED ON HALF PAY.
Henry Crichton Sclater, *Major*, Royal Artillery	......	28 Jan. 75	21 Dec. 83	15 June 85	
Gilbert Fred. Allan Norton, *Major*, Royal Artillery	......	28 Jan. 75	1 Jan. 84	15 June 85	
David Stanley William, *Earl of* Airlie, *Major*, 10 Hussars	......	13 June 75	18 Feb. 84	15 June 85	
Richard H. F. W. Wilson, *Captain*, 10 Hussars	......	26 July 76	1 Mar. 84	15 June 85	
p.s.c. William B. Capper, *Major*, Shropshire Lt. Inf. (85 F.)	......	12 Feb. 76	15 May 84	15 June 85	
Henry Slane Fleming, *Captain*, Essex Regiment	25 Sept. 78	25 Aug. 80	30 July 84	15 June 85	
Rawdon Edward Dennys Reilly, *Major*, Indian Staff Corps	......	31 Aug. 72	31 Aug. 84	15 June 85	
Arthur Henry Bagnold, *Major*, Royal Engineers	......	12 Sept. 72	12 Sept. 84	15 June 85	
Frederick Hammersley, *Captain*, Lancashire Fus. (20 F.)	......	11 Sept. 76	2 Feb. 85	15 June 85	
Lord Frederick FitzGerald, *Major*, King's Royal Rifles	......	11 Feb. 76	16 Mar. 85	15 June 85	
Hon. Henry Charles Legge, *Major*, Coldstream Guards	......	31 Aug. 73	18 Apr. 85	15 June 85	
William Christian Anderson, *Major*, Royal Artillery	......	25 Jan. 77	12 May 85	15 June 85	
p.s.c. William Randolph Routh, *Major*, Suffolk Regiment	7 July 69	28 Oct. 71	1 Jan. 81	18 June 85	
William Henry M'Laren, *Major*, 1 Dragoons	......	15 Mar. 74	30 Sept. 80	19 June 85	
Thomas French Ross, *Major*, Royal Scots (1 Foot)	8 July 68	27 Oct. 71	24 Nov. 77	21 June 85	
Henry Woolgar Griffith, *Major*, Welsh Fusiliers (23 Foot)	2 Mar. 66	10 June 71	13 Sept. 79	21 June 85	
Robert Henry Sherston Baker, *Major*, Royal Artillery	......	7 July 69	1 Feb. 80	15 June 85	
Edward Cecil Dowse, *Major*, Derbyshire Regt. (45 F.)	......	30 Dec. 71	23 Mar. 81	21 July 85	
Arthur Howard Whitehorne, *Major*, Royal Artillery	......	8 Jan. 70	13 Mar. 80	27 July 85	
Andrew Green Thompson, *Major*, 6 Dragoons	......	30 Dec. 71	1 Mar. 79	29 July 85	
Robert Gordon Webb Hepburne, *Major*, Royal Artillery	......	8 Jan. 70	24 Mar. 80	5 Aug. 85	
Alfred George Watson, *Major*, East Lancashire Regt. (30 F.)	3 Sept. 70	28 Oct. 71	23 June 80	5 Aug. 85	
Frederick Wm. Nicholas M'Cracken, *Captain*, Berkshire Regt.	13 Aug. 78	28 July 80	15 Dec. 84	14 Aug. 85	
Cecil Henry Collette, *Major*, Shropshire Lt. Infantry (53 F.)	8 Jan. 68	28 Oct. 71	30 Sept. 84	19 Aug. 85	
Arthur Reginald Fraser, *Major*, Royal Artillery	......	8 Jan. 70	12 Apr. 80	1 Sept. 85	
p.s.c. John Winston Thomas Spencer, *Major*, Royal Artillery	......	8 Jan. 70	12 May 80	9 Sept. 85	
George Dalrymple Fanshawe, *Major*, Royal Artillery	......	8 Jan. 70	12 May 80	9 Sept. 85	
Thomas Stock, *Major*, Essex Regiment	......	11 Feb. 75	8 Feb. 82	15 Sept. 85	
John H. F. Jacson, *Major*, Gloucestershire Regt. (28 F.)	15 Mar. 67	28 Oct. 71	5 Oct. 80	22 Sept. 85	
Peter Legh Clowes, *Major*, 8 Hussars	......	20 Nov. 75	21 Feb. 83	2 Oct. 85	
Montagu C. B. F. Walker, *Major*, King's Royal Rifles (60 F.)	......	6 Mar. 72	10 Feb. 81	9 Oct. 85	
Rowland Broughton Mainwaring, *Major*, Welsh Fus. (23 F.)	......	30 Dec. 71	13 June 80	10 Oct. 85	
Charles Herbert Payne, *Major*, Gordon Highlanders (75 F.)	......	11 Nov. 78	10 Oct. 85	10 Oct. 85	
Henry Napier Jervois, *Major*, Royal Artillery	......	8 Jan. 70	28 May 80	16 Oct. 85	
William Prinn Neon, *Major*, Devonshire Regt. (11 F.)	11 Feb. 70	28 Oct. 71	8 June 81	26 Oct. 85	
John Henry Spurgin, *Major*, Scots Fusiliers (21 F.)	15 Feb. 68	28 Oct. 71	19 Feb. 79	2 Nov. 85	
Henry G. Mainwaring, *Major*, South Wales Borderers (24 F.)	......	21 Sept. 73	7 July 80	2 Nov. 85	
Geoffrey G. Grimwood, *Major*, King's Royal Rifles (60 F.)	......	24 July 72	1 Oct. 81	4 Nov. 85	
*Paolo Bernard, *Major*, Royal Malta Artillery	17 Sept. 58	25 Jan. 61	5 Sept. 77	19 Nov. 85	
George Robert Moore, *Major*, Royal Artillery	......	8 Jan. 70	25 June 80	26 Nov. 85	
Wilfred Heaton, *Major*, South Wales Borderers (24 F.)	......	28 Feb. 74	4 Sept. 80	28 Nov. 85	
Albert Edward Ommanney, *Major*, The Buffs (3 F.)	30 Oct. 69	27 Oct. 71	1 Nov. 78	30 Nov. 85	
Julius Batt Backhouse, *Major*, The Buffs (3 F.)	......	15 May 72	15 Mar. 80	30 Nov. 85	
Walter Rupert Kenyon-Slaney, *Major*, Rifle Brigade	10 Nov. 69	28 Oct. 71	14 June 80	1 Dec. 85	
Edward George Grogan, *Major*, Black Watch (42 F.)	24 July 69	28 Oct. 71	19 June 79	4 Dec. 85	
Octavius Allcard, *Major*, Norfolk Regiment (9 F.)	29 May 67	28 Oct. 71	15 Feb. 81	12 Dec. 85	
Gordon George Monck-Mason, *Major*, Royal Artillery	......	8 Jan. 70	9 July 80	25 Dec. 85	
Francis John William Eustace, *Major*, Royal Artillery	......	8 Jan. 70	9 July 80	25 Dec. 85	
Samuel Holt Lomax, *Major*, Scottish Rifles	......	13 June 74	21 July 80	1 Jan. 86	
Arthur C. FitzH. Vincent, *Major*, Scottish Rifles (90 F.)	......	11 Feb. 75	26 Feb. 81	1 Jan. 86	
George Ashby Ashby, *Major*, Duke of Cornwall's Lt. Inf.	......	20 Nov. 75	1 Jan. 81	1 Jan. 86	
Henry Charles Harford, *Major*, Wiltshire Regiment (99 F.)	5 Nov. 70	28 Oct. 71	30 Mar. 81	7 Jan. 86	
Henry Vere, *Major*, King's Royal Rifles (60 F.)	......	5 Oct. 72	22 Dec. 81	7 Jan. 86	
p.s.c. Richard Stanley H. Moody, *Major*, The Buffs	......	9 Aug. 73	24 Oct. 80	14 Jan. 86	
James Arthur Strachan, *Major*, Oxford Light Infantry	5 Feb. 71	28 Oct. 71	19 Sept. 79	15 Jan. 86	
Harry Molyneux Carter, *Major*, Wiltshire Regiment (62 F.)	8 Jan. 68	28 Oct. 71	7 Aug. 78	17 Jan. 86	
James Volant Vashon Baker, *Major*, Royal Artillery	......	8 Jan. 70	28 July 80	20 Jan. 86	
Edward Beresford Coke, *Major*, Royal Artillery	......	8 Jan. 70	1 Aug. 80	20 Jan. 86	
Francis Edw. Romulus Pollard-Urquhart, *Major*, R. Artillery	......	8 Jan. 70	10 Aug. 80	26 Jan. 86	
Frederick Arthur Aylmer, *Major*, Royal Artillery	......	8 Jan. 70	1 Sept. 80	7 Feb. 86	
Richard H. Wm. Henry Harris, *Major*, h.p. East Surrey Regt.	10 Apr. 70	28 Oct. 71	21 June 80	17 Feb. 86	8 Feb. 95
Charles James Long, *Major*, Royal Artillery	......	23 July 70	11 Sept. 80	19 Feb. 86	
Richard D. Buckley Rutherford, *Major*, Highland Light Infantry	9 Oct. 69	28 Oct. 71	29 Apr. 79	24 Feb. 86	
Edward James Montagu Stuart Wortley, *CMG. Major*, King's Royal Rifles (60 Foot)	13 Oct. 77	13 Mar. 80	1 Mar. 86	2 Mar. 86	
John Grogan Glancy, *Major*, Leinster Regiment (100 F.)	......	11 Feb. 75	7 Jan. 82	3 Mar. 86	
Richard Hawes MacCurthy, *Major*, Lancaster Regt. (4 F.)	23 Jan. 69	3 May 71	7 Jan. 80	9 Mar. 86	
Robert Gustavus Alexander, *Major*, 3 Hussars	......	26 Mar. 73	19 Sept. 81	9 Mar. 86	
Thomas Cole Porter, *Major*, 6 Dragoon Guards	......	24 Feb. 73	5 Oct. 78	17 Mar. 86	
Henry Somerset Hassard, *Major*, Berkshire Regt. (49 F.)	......	23 Nov. 73	28 July 80	27 Mar. 86	
John Henry Edward Hinde, *Major*, Border Regt. (34 F.)	4 Apr. 67	19 Jan. 70	7 Jan. 80	31 Mar. 86	
Charles Fred. Alexander Turnbull, *Major*, Duke of Cornwall's Light Infantry (32 F.)	9 Mar. 66	22 July 68	26 May 80	5 Apr. 86	
James Spens, *Major*, Shropshire Light Infantry	......	29 May 72	1 July 83	7 Apr. 86	
William Edmund Franklyn, *Major*, Yorkshire Regt. (19 F.)	......	13 June 74	30 Mar. 81	20 Apr. 86	
Cyril Wood, *Major*, Essex Regiment (56 F.)	17 July 72	17 July 74	16 Aug. 82	21 Apr. 86	
Charles Donovan Cave, *Major*, Suffolk Regiment (12 F.)	......	18 June 72	3 Apr. 82	26 Apr. 86	
Mortimer Graham Neeld, *Major*, 17 Lancers	......	12 Nov. 73	7 Jan. 82	27 Apr. 86	
Frederick Seymour Allen, *Major*, E. Yorkshire Regt. (15 F.)	18 Nov. 68	24 Sept. 70	15 Aug. 77	6 May 86	
Walter Illingworth Haynes, *Major*, Sussex Regt. (35 Foot)	18 Apr. 68	6 July 70	23 July 79	26 May 86	
George F. R. Henderson, *Captain*, York and Lancaster Regt.	1 May 78	24 June 79	2 June 86	3 June 86	
Lawrence Worthington Parsons, *Major*, Royal Artillery	......	23 July 70	16 Sept. 80	1 July 86	
Hon. Walter Philip Alexander, *Major*, 2 Dragoons	3 Feb. 69	10 May 71	24 Nov. 77	5 July 86	
Arthur Gregory Scrocold Wade, *Major*, Royal Artillery	......	23 July 70	27 Oct. 80	7 July 86	
Charles Carroll Rich, *Major*, Royal Artillery	......	23 July 70	27 Nov. 80	7 July 86	
Bernhard Drysdale Möller, *Major*, 18 Hussars	......	8 May 73	18 Dec. 80	7 July 86	
George Francis De Bude Davidson, *Major*, BlackWatch (73 F.)	2 Mar. 66	19 Feb. 67	11 Nov. 76	11 July 86	
Thomas Perrott, *Major*, Royal Artillery	......	1 Dec. 70	12 Dec. 80	21 July 86	
John James Swinton, *Major*, Royal Artillery	......	4 Jan. 71	19 Dec. 80	27 July 86	
p.s.c. Rees J. Fras. Banfield, *Major*, Welsh Regiment	23 Sept. 71	28 Oct. 71	8 Mar. 81	1 Aug. 86	
Hammond Astley Tapp, *Major*, Hampshire Regiment (67 F.)	22 Mar. 71	8 Oct. 7	9 Apr. 81	1 Aug. 86	

Majors. 51

Name	CORNET, 2nd LIEUT. or ENSIGN.	LIEUT.	CAPTAIN.	MAJOR.	WHEN PLACED ON HALF PAY.
Benjamin Arthur Satterthwaite, *Major*, North Lancashire Regiment (81 F.)	16 Oct. 67	28 Oct. 71	28 May 80	28 Aug. 86	
William Egginton Briggs, Hampshire Regiment (67 F.)	......	27 Mar. 72	8 June 81	29 Aug. 86	
Francis Hugh Plowden, *Major*, Oxfordshire Light Infantry (52 F.)	......	5 Oct. 72	19 Aug. 81	1 Sept. 86	
Newton Plomer Fowell, *Major*, Royal Artillery	......	4 Jan. 71	19 Jan. 81	4 Sept. 86	
George Richardson Price, *Major*, Royal Artillery	......	4 Jan. 71	19 Jan. 81	7 Sept. 86	
John Stratford Collins, *Major*, West Surrey Regt. (2 F.)	2 Jan. 69	28 Oct. 71	16 Mar. 81	29 Sept. 86	
Herbert William Brackenbury, *Major*, Royal Artillery	......	4 Jan. 71	1 Feb. 81	1 Oct. 86	
Robert Hugh Fraser, *Major*, Northamptonshire Regt. (48 F.)	21 Aug. 69	28 Oct. 71	1 July 81	1 Oct. 86	
Arthur E. R. Curran, *Major*, West Riding Regt.	......	11 Sept. 74	1 Oct. 81	6 Oct. 86	
Alfred John C. Wrench, *Major*, Welsh Fusiliers	......	13 June 75	29 Oct. 81	6 Oct. 86	
Robert Wm. P. Robertson, *Major*, Royal Artillery	......	4 Jan. 71	9 Feb. 81	9 Oct. 86	
Richard George Randall-Bruxner, *Major*, Lancashire Fusiliers (20 F.)	8 June 70	28 Oct. 71	24 Jan. 80	10 Oct. 38	
Henry Vaughan Hunt, *Major*, Royal Artillery	......	4 Jan. 71	26 Feb. 81	12 Oct. 86	
p.s.c. Arthur John Watson, *Major*, Suffolk Regiment (12 F.)	......	9 Aug. 73	14 Apr. 83	21 Oct. 86	
Lewis Edmund Coker, *Major*, Royal Artillery	......	4 Jan. 71	27 Feb. 81	29 Oct. 86	
James Hurley Rosseter, *Major*, Royal Artillery	......	4 Jan. 71	13 Mar. 81	29 Oct. 86	
Willoughby E. G. Forbes, *Major*, Warwick Regiment (6 F.)	10 Nov. 69	28 Oct. 71	1 June 81	29 Nov. 86	
Warren Hastings Frith, *Major*, Royal Artillery	......	4 Jan. 71	15 Mar. 81	30 Nov. 86	
John William Hind, *Major*, The Buffs (3 F.)	......	28 Feb. 74	27 Dec. 81	10 Dec. 86	
Robert Preston Birkett Redick, *Major*, Royal Fusiliers	9 Feb. 70	28 Oct. 71	10 Sept. 80	19 Dec. 86	
Charles David Myers Gall, *Major*, Royal Fusiliers (7 F.)	......	9 Aug. 73	28 Jan. 82	19 Dec. 86	
John Hotham, *Major*, Royal Artillery	......	2 Aug. 71	6 Apr. 81	21 Dec. 86	
Hans Charles Maunsell Woods, *Major*, Royal Artillery	......	2 Aug. 71	6 Apr. 81	21 Dec. 86	
Edward John Fownes, *Major*, Somerset Light Infantry	8 Feb. 70	28 Oct. 71	8 June 79	28 Dec. 86	
Edmond Joseph Gallwey, *Major*, Somerset Light Infantry	6 July 70	28 Oct. 71	26 Feb. 80	28 Dec. 86	
Fitzgerald Wintour, *Captain*, West Kent Regiment (50 F.)	11 Aug. 80	1 July 81	2 Feb. 87	3 Feb. 87	
John A. W. Falls, *Major*, Army Service Corps	......	29 Nov. 76	12 Feb. 81	13 Feb. 87	
p.s.c. Arthur Fredk. Barrow, *CMG. Major*, Indian Staff Corps	18 Aug. 69	28 Oct. 71	18 Aug. 81	16 Feb. 87	
St. George Corbet Gore, *Major*, Royal Engineers	......	8 Jan. 70	8 Jan. 82	16 Feb. 87	
Harry H. Rose Heath, *Major*, Indian Staff Corps	......	24 July 72	24 July 84	16 Feb. 87	
p.s.c. Hon. Milo George Talbot, *Major*, Royal Engineers	......	29 Apr. 73	8 Jan. 85	16 Feb. 87	
Francis H. R. Drummond, *Major*, Indian Staff Corps	......	11 Feb. 75	11 Feb. 86	16 Feb. 87	
Henry Boughey, *Major*, York and Lancaster Regiment	27 Nov. 67	28 Oct. 71	3 Apr. 78	23 Mar. 87	
Beauchamp J. Colclough Doran, *Captain*, Irish Regiment (18 Foot)	14 Jan. 80	1 July 81	22 May 87	23 May 87	
Charles Crutchley, *Captain*, Scots Guards	......	21 Sept. 74	29 June 87	30 June 87	
William Arthur James Frere, *Major*, Scots Fusiliers (21 F.)	15 July 68	28 Oct. 71	27 Dec. 80	1 July 87	
William Bernard Wilson, *Major*, Indian Staff Corps	24 Apr. 69	28 Oct. 71	24 Apr. 81	1 July 87	
Vernon Ansdell Schalch, *Major*, Indian Staff Corps	29 May 69	28 Oct. 71	29 May 81	1 July 87	
Macan William Saunders, *Major*, Royal Artillery	......	15 Dec. 71	13 July 81	1 July 87	
Alfred Astley Pearson, *Major*, Indian Staff Corps	8 Feb. 70	28 Oct. 71	8 Feb. 82	1 July 87	
Charles Pulley, *Major*, Indian Staff Corps	28 Oct. 71	28 Oct. 71	28 Oct. 83	1 July 87	
Stuart Brownlow Beatson, *Captain*, Indian Staff Corps	......	9 Aug. 73	8 Jan. 85	1 July 87	
Herbert F. S. Ramsden, *Captain*, Indian Staff Corps	......	10 Sept. 75	10 Sept. 86	1 July 87	
Arthur F. G. Richardson, *Major*, S. Lancashire Regt. (40 F.)	......	5 Oct. 73	15 Mar. 80	13 July 87	
George Pridham Owen, *Major*, Royal Artillery	......	2 Aug. 71	8 May 81	15 Aug. 87	
Augustus John English, *Major*, 14 Hussars	......	30 Dec. 73	16 Jan. 84	17 Aug. 87	
Frederick Tyssen Mackinlay Beaver, *Major*, Royal Artillery	......	2 Aug. 71	23 May 81	24 Aug. 87	
Charles Leslie Casey, *Major*, Royal Artillery	......	2 Aug. 71	27 May 81	21 Sept. 87	
Douglas Charles Dean-Pitt, *Major*, Royal Artillery	......	2 Aug. 71	27 May 81	21 Sept. 87	
Solomon Watson, *Major*, Royal Artillery	......	2 Aug. 71	11 June 81	21 Sept. 87	
Patrick Charles Eric Newbigging, *Major*, Royal Artillery	......	2 Aug. 71	11 June 81	21 Sept. 87	
Alfred Luther Lane, *Major*, Royal Artillery	......	2 Aug. 71	1 July 81	21 Sept. 87	
Henry Hewitt Pengree, *Major*, Royal Artillery	......	2 Aug. 71	1 July 81	21 Sept. 87	
Robert Ambrose Cecil King, *Major*, Royal Artillery	......	15 Dec. 71	1 July 81	28 Sept. 87	
George Richards Challenor, *Major*, Royal Artillery	......	15 Dec. 71	1 July 81	28 Sept. 87	
Frederick Augustus Bowles, *Major*, Royal Artillery	......	15 Dec. 71	11 July 81	1 Oct. 87	
Ernest Charles Wace, *DSO. Major*, Royal Artillery	......	15 Dec. 71	1 July 81	1 Oct. 87	
Taylor Dalrymple Wilson, *Major*, Scots Fusiliers (21 F.)	2 Jan. 69	28 Oct. 71	4 Feb. 81	19 Oct. 87	
William Sworder Walford, *Major*, Royal Artillery	......	15 Dec. 71	13 July 81	25 Oct. 87	
Walter Ferrier Graham, *Major*, Royal Artillery	......	15 Dec. 71	13 July 81	29 Oct. 87	
Charles Baker Goodrich Dick, *Major*, h.p. Royal Marines Paymaster	8 Dec. 66	3 Aug. 67	1 July 81	8 Dec. 87	1 July 93
Charles Edward Sawyer, *Major*, North Lancashire Regiment (47 F.)	23 Jan. 69	28 Oct. 71	29 Sept. 80	14 Dec. 87	
Edward Hegan, *Major*, 5 Dragoon Guards	......	11 Sept. 76	31 Jan. 82	22 Dec. 87	
p.s.c. Frederick William Romilly, *DSO. Major*, Scots Guards	......	30 Apr. 73	1 Apr. 87	1 Jan. 88	
William Hodgson Suart, *Major*, Royal Artillery	......	15 Dec. 71	13 July 81	19 Jan. 88	
John Reeves, *Major*, Irish Fusiliers (89 F.)	......	21 Jan. 74	25 June 81	25 Jan. 88	
Frederick Crofton Heath, *Captain*, Royal Engineers	......	25 Jan. 77	25 Jan. 88	26 Jan. 88	
Andrew Graham Thomson, *Captain*, Royal Engineers	......	25 Jan. 77	25 Jan. 88	26 Jan. 88	
Arthur M'Leod Mills, *Major*, Indian Staff Corps	1 Feb. 68	9 Feb. 70	1 Feb. 80	1 Feb. 88	
William Henry Young, *Major*, Bedfordshire Regiment	20 June 69	30 Nov. 70	30 Dec. 76	7 Mar. 88	
George William Addison, *Major*, Royal Engineers	......	7 July 69	7 July 81	1 Apr. 88	
Alfred Porcelli, *Major*, Royal Engineers	......	7 July 69	7 July 81	1 Apr. 88	
James White Thurburn, *Major*, Royal Engineers	......	7 July 69	7 July 81	1 Apr. 88	
Frederic Gosset, *Major*, Royal Engineers	......	7 July 69	7 July 81	1 Apr. 88	
p.s.c. Henry Merrick Lawson, *Captain*, Royal Engineers	......	19 June 77	1 Apr. 88	2 Apr. 88	
Chandos Hoskyns, *Major*, Royal Engineers	......	2 Aug. 71	1 July 81	4 Apr. 88	
Charles Duncan Cooper, *Major*, Dublin Fusiliers	8 July 68	28 Oct. 71	1 Nov. 79	18 Apr. 88	
John Deering, *Major*, Cheshire Regiment (22 F.)	8 July 68	28 Oct. 71	Jan. 80	21 Apr. 88	
Seymour Charles Hale Monro, *Captain*, Seaforth Highlanders (72 F.)	......	17 May 77	25 Apr. 80	26 Apr. 88	
George Arthur Mills, *Major*, Dublin Fusiliers (102 F.)	......	12 Nov. 73	26 May 80	21 May 88	
Charles Joseph Cheetham, *Major*, R. Marine Artillery	......	5 Nov. 69	8 June 80	21 May 88	
Edward Robert Hussey, *Major*, Royal Engineers	......	7 July 69	7 July 81	22 May 88	
John Wm. Ainslie Drummond, *Captain*, Scots Guards	......	11 Feb. 77	23 May 88	24 May 88	
p.s.c. John Wm. Godfray, *Major*, King's Own Scottish Bord (25 F.)	24 Sept. 71	28 Oct. 71	22 Dec. 79	22 Dec. 79	
Herbert Eyre Robbins, *Major*, Royal Marines	22 June 67	3 Aug. 67	1 July 81	22 June 88	
Cosmo George Gordon, *Major*, Royal Marines	22 June 67	3 Aug. 67	1 July 81	22 June 88	

Majors.

	CORNET, 2nd LIEUT. or ENSIGN.	LIEUT.	CAPTAIN.	MAJOR.	WHEN PLACED ON HALF PAY.
Francis Henry Hall, *Major*, Royal Artillery		15 Dec. 71	13 July 81	26 June 88	
Thomas Barnes Weston, *Major*, 20 Hussars		23 Apr. 73	1 Jan. 80	1 July 88	
Thomas Currie, *Major*, North Staffordshire Regt. (98 F.)		28 Feb. 74	12 Mar. 81	1 July 88	
Charles Edward Bradley, *Major*, N. Staffordshire Regt.(64 F.)		28 Feb. 74	1 July 81	1 July 88	
Robert Oliver Lloyd, *Major*, Royal Engineers		8 Jan. 70	8 Jan. 82	1 July 88	
Claude Reignier Conder, *Major*, Royal Engineers		8 Jan. 70	8 Jan. 82	1 July 88	
Frederick Henry Munn, *Major*, Irish Fusiliers (87 F.)		11 Sept. 76	30 Mar. 83	1 July 88	
Richard de Villamil, *Major*, Royal Engineers		8 Jan. 70	8 Jan. 82	10 July 88	
Woodforde George du Boulay, *Major*, Royal Engineers		8 Jan. 70	8 Jan. 82	14 July 88	
Joseph Alexander Lambert, *Major*, 2 Dragoon Guards		2 Dec. 74	1 Dec. 80	21 July 88	
Edmund William Creswell, *Major*, Royal Engineers		8 Jan. 70	8 Jan. 82	1 Aug. 88	
Alexander Bulstrode Fenton, *Major*, Indian Staff Corps		12 Nov. 73	8 Jan. 85	2 Aug. 88	
Constantine Rodney Wm. Hervey, *Major*, Royal Artillery		15 Dec. 71	16 July 81	4 Aug. 88	
Edward Montagu Flint, *Major*, Royal Artillery		15 Dec. 71	16 July 81	4 Aug. 88	
Claude Rainier Rogers, *Major*, Irish Fusiliers (89 F.)		24 June 7	28 Aug. 83	12 Aug. 88	
George Digby Filmer Sullivan, *Major*, 15 Hussars	13 June 63	28 Oct. 71	24 June 76	15 Aug. 88	
Walter S. Davies Liardet, *Major*, Leicestershire Regiment		17 July 72	20 Mar. 81	15 Aug. 88	
Peter Fisher Percival Hamilton, *Major*, Royal Artillery		15 Dec. 71	25 July 81	15 Aug. 88	
Henry Clerk, *Major*, 2 Dragoon Guards		9 Aug. 75	11 Oct. 81	15 Aug. 88	
Herbert Percival Willoughby, *Major*, Royal Artillery		6 Jan. 72	17 Aug. 81	1 Oct. 88	
William Drury Shaw, *Major*, Royal Scots (1 F.)	11 Dec. 66	28 Oct. 71	13 Nov. 78	3 Oct. 88	
Francis Seymour Allen, *Major*, Worcestershire Regt.		9 Mar. 72	29 June 81	3 Oct. 88	
Francis Fawkes Johnstone, *Major*, Bedfordshire Regiment.	2 Sept.68	22 Feb. 71	10 Sept.77	10 Oct. 88	
p.s.c. Hy. Beaufoy Mortimer, *Major*, North Stafford Regt.		28 Feb. 74	19 Nov. 81	10 Oct. 88	
William Frederick Curteis, *Major*, Cheshire Regiment (22 F.)		13 Apr. 72	16 Aug. 82	10 Oct. 88	
Ernest Veness Elwes, *Major*, Royal Artillery		6 Jan. 72	17 Aug. 81	13 Oct. 88	
William Powlett Thring, *Major*, Royal Artillery		6 Jan. 72	17 Aug. 81	29 Oct. 88	
Hugh Aboukir Scott, *Major*, Royal Artillery		6 Jan. 72	7 Sept.81	29 Oct. 88	
Alexander John Montgomery, *Major*, Royal Artillery		6 Jan. 72	7 Sept.81	29 Oct. 88	
Eaton Aylmer Travers, *Captain*, Indian Staff Corps		10 Sept.75	10 Sept. 86	2 Nov. 88	
Herbert Mansfield, *Captain*, Indian Staff Corps		20 Nov. 75	20 Nov. 86	2 Nov. 88	
William Moore, South Staffordshire Regiment		28 Feb. 74	4 Oct. 81	18 Nov. 88	
John Edw. Fitzmaurice Hughes Roche, *Major*, 3 Dr. Gds.	13 Aug. 79	11 Feb. 80	25 Sept.84	24 Nov. 88	
John Wm. Hastings Potts, *Major*, Royal Artillery		2 May 72	17 Sept.81	29 Nov. 88	
Albert Henry Cullwell, *Major*, Royal Artillery		2 May 72	18 Sept.81	29 Nov. 88	
FitzGerald Muirson Banister, *Major*, Royal Artillery		2 May 72	1 Oct. 81	5 Dec. 88	
p.s.c. Wm. Thompson Adair, *Major*, Royal Marines		6 Dec. 67	1 July 81	6 Dec. 88	
Edward Ernest Pyne, *Major*, Royal Marines		6 Dec. 67	1 July 81	6 Dec. 88	
Howard Stanley Thompson, *Major*, Royal Marines		6 Dec. 67	1 July 81	6 Dec. 88	
Alfred O. De Blaquiere Nepean, *Major*, Royal Marines		6 Dec. 67	1 July 81	6 Dec. 88	
Henry Napier M'Rae, *Captain*, Indian Staff Corps	25 Mar. 71	28 Oct. 71	25 Mar. 83	7 Dec. 88	
Suene Grant, *Major*, Royal Engineers		2 Aug. 71	2 Aug. 83	7 Dec. 88	
Charles Hogge, *Captain*, Indian Staff Corps	23 Sept.71	28 Oct. 71	23 Sept.83	7 Dec. 88	
Oswald Claude Radford, *Captain*, Indian Staff Corps	26 Sept.71	28 Oct. 71	26 Sept.83	7 Dec. 88	
Philip Thomas Buston, *Major*, Royal Engineers		12 Sept.72	12 Sept.84	7 Dec. 88	
Martin Martin, *Major*, Royal Engineers		7 July 69	11 May 82	16 Dec. 88	
Thomas Ryder Main, *Major*, Royal Engineers		23 July 70	23 July 82	18 Dec. 88	
Charles William Sherrard, *Major*, Royal Engineers		23 July 70	23 July 82	18 Dec. 88	
Henry Waugh Renny-Tailyour, *Major*, Royal Engineers		23 July 70	23 July 82	18 Dec. 88	
William Pitt, *Major*, Royal Engineers		23 July 70	23 July 82	18 Dec. 88	
Charles Wilkinson, *Major*, Royal Engineers		23 July 70	23 July 82	18 Dec. 88	
John M'Donnell, *Major*, Royal Artillery		2 May 72	1 Oct. 81	21 Dec. 88	
John Temple, *Major*, Royal Artillery		2 May 72	6 Oct. 81	21 Dec. 88	
Benjamin D. Alsop Donne, *Major*, Sussex Regiment		10 Sept.75	20 Oct. 83	28 Dec. 88	
James Alfred Coxhead, *Major*, Royal Artillery		2 May 72	24 Oct. 81	1 Jan. 89	
Percy Alexander MacMahon, *Major*, Royal Artillery		12 Sept.72	29 Oct. 81	1 Jan. 89	
p.s.c. Henry Chesshyre Claughton Walker, *Major*, Royal Art.		12 Sept.72	29 Oct. 81	1 Jan. 89	
Reginald Oakes, *Major*, Royal Artillery		12 Sept.72	29 Oct. 81	1 Jan. 89	
Edward Nathaniel Henriques, *Major*, Royal Artillery		12 Sept.72	29 Oct. 81	1 Jan. 89	
p.s.c. James Wolfe Murray, *Major*, Royal Artillery		12 Sept.72	1 Nov. 81	9 Jan. 89	
James Douglas Standen, *Major*, Irish Fusiliers		28 Apr. 77	14 May 84	9 Jan. 89	
Edward Guy Selby-Smyth, *Major*, Irish Rifles	7 May 0	28 Oct. 71	28 Apr. 81	10 Jan. 89	
Horatio Holt Hart, *Major*, Royal Engineers		23 July 70	23 July 82	10 Jan. 89	
Ernest Cassan, *Major*, Royal Artillery		12 Sept. 72	1 Nov. 81	11 Jan. 89	
Owen Vidal Boddy, *Major*, Royal Engineers		23 July 70	23 July 82	12 Jan. 89	
Francis Reginald Wingate, *DSO*, *Captain*, Royal Artillery		27 July 80	14 Jan. 89	15 Jan. 89	
Charles Evans-Gordon, *Major*, Berkshire Regiment		13 June 75	16 Apr. 81	23 Jan. 89	
Hugh Bertram Nathaniel Bewicke, *Major*, Manchester Regt.	28 Oct. 71	28 Oct. 71	2 Feb. 81	25 Jan. 89	
John Burton Forster, *Major*, Irish Regiment		23 Nov. 72	26 Feb. 81	6 Feb. 89	
Henry Newport Chas. Heath, *Captain*, Yorkshire Lt. Infantry		22 Oct. 81	6 Feb. 89	7 Feb. 89	
p.s.c. Richard Fras. Johnson, *Major*, Royal Artillery		12 Sept.72	14 Mar. 81	16 Feb. 89	
Lionel Langley, *Major*, Royal Engineers		23 July 70	23 July 82	9 Mar. 89	
Hon. Arthur Edward Dalzell, *Major*, Oxfordshire Lt. Infantry	20 Feb. 70	28 Oct. 71	11 Mar. 82	11 Mar. 89	
p.s.c. Charles R. Robert M'Grigor, *Captain*, King's R. Rifles	13 Aug. 79	1 July 81	11 Mar. 89	12 Mar. 89	
Rowland Fearnley K. Money, *Major*, Royal Scots	22 Feb. 71	28 Oct. 71	11 Feb. 80	27 Mar. 89	
Gother Fyers Mann, *Major*, Royal Engineers		23 July 70	25 July 82	30 Mar. 89	
James Tayler Johnston, *Major*, Royal Engineers		23 July 70	23 July 82	1 Apr. 89	
Edward Dickinson, *Major*, Royal Engineers		23 July 70	23 July 82	1 Apr. 89	
William Frederick Noel Noel, *Major*, Royal Engineers		23 July 70	23 July 82	1 Apr. 89	
Henry Lethbridge Jessep, *Major*, Royal Engineers		23 July 70	23 July 82	1 Apr. 89	
Francis Burton Grant D'Aguilar, *Major*, Royal Engineers		1 Dec. 70	1 Dec. 82	1 Apr. 89	
Edmund Spencer, *Major*, Highland Light Infantry	28 Oct. 71	28 Oct. 71	30 Apr. 77	3 Apr. 89	
Edward Reginald Courtenay, *Major*, 11 Hussars		9 Aug. 73	1 July 81	10 Apr. 89	
Monier Williams Skinner, *Major*, Royal Engineers		4 Jan. 71	4 Jan. 83	17 Apr. 89	
Walter Hanbury White, *Major*, Royal Engineers		4 Jan. 71	4 Jan. 83	3 May 89	
Henry Campbell Lamb, *Major*, Royal Engineers	5 May 69	28 Oct. 71	5 May 81	5 May 89	
Edward Vernon Peshall Monteith, *Major*, Indian Staff Corps	5 May 69	28 Oct. 71	5 May 81	15 May 89	
James Montague T. Badgley, *Major*, Royal Engineers		4 Jan. 71	4 Jan. 83	17 May 89	
Spenser Jackson, *Major*, North Lancashire Regiment		15 Mar. 72	2 Feb. 81	10 May 89	
Henry William Duperier, *Major*, Royal Engineers		4 Jan. 71	4 Jan. 83	10 May 89	
Jefferson Serroll Wood, *Major*, Border Regiment	28 May 70	27 Oct. 71	23 June 80	5 May 89	
William MacLaughlin, *Major*, Shropshire Light Infantry		23 Apr. 75	13 Apr. 84	5 May 89	

Majors. 53-4

Name	CORNET, 2nd LIEUT. or ENSIGN.	LIEUT.	CAPTAIN.	MAJOR.	WHEN PLACED ON HALF PAY.
Thomas Duncan Richey, *Major*, R. Artillery (District Officer), (*Qr. Master*, 1 April 76)	......	25 Aug. 77	10 June 82	19 May 89	
Gregory Haines, *Major*, Warwickshire Regiment	......	9 Aug. 73	25 Apr. 83	29 May 89	
Alfred Heathcote, *Major*, Royal Engineers	......	4 Jan. 71	4 Jan. 83	11 June 89	
Arthur Gambier Holland, *Major*, 15 Hussars	24 July 69	28 Oct. 71	29 Apr. 79	12 June 89	
Gervas Selwyn Eyre, *Major*, Indian Staff Corps	12 June 69	27 Oct. 71	12 June 81	12 June 89	
Richard Thompson, *Major*, Royal Engineers	......	4 Jan. 71	4 Jan. 83	21 June 89	
Frank Alexander Newington, *Major*, Royal Marines	......	24 June 68	1 July 81	24 June 89	
Richard Denny, *Major*, Royal Marines	......	24 June 68	1 July 81	24 June 89	
John Jerome Quill, *Major*, Royal Marines	......	24 June 68	1 July 81	24 June 89	
Edm. Jas. Thos. Ross of Bladensburg, *Major*, Royal Eng.	......	4 Jan. 71	4 Jan. 83	25 June 89	
Stewart M'Murdo Maycock, *Major*, Royal Engineers	......	4 Jan. 71	4 Jan. 83	25 June 89	
p.s.c. Edmund Balfe, *Major*, Indian Staff Corps	30 June 69	28 Oct. 71	30 June 81	30 June 89	
Edward John Dewing, *Major*, Royal Engineers	......	4 Jan. 71	4 Jan. 83	6 July 89	
William John Orr, *Major*, Indian Staff Corps	7 July 69	19 Apr. 71	7 July 81	7 July 89	
Duncan Alex. Allan Macpherson, *Major*, Indian Staff Corps	7 July 69	28 Oct. 71	7 July 81	7 July 89	
Charles Wemyss Muir, *CIE. Major*, Indian Staff Corps	7 July 69	28 Oct. 71	7 July 81	7 July 89	
George Cadell Dobbs, *Major*, Indian Staff Corps	7 July 69	28 Oct. 71	7 July 81	7 July 89	
Bradshaw Lewis Philip Reilly, *Major*, Indian Staff Corps	7 July 69	28 Oct. 71	7 July 81	7 July 89	
Alexander William Croker Bell, *Major*, Indian Staff Corps	7 July 69	28 Oct. 71	7 July 81	7 July 89	
Thomas Robert Matheson Macpherson, *Major*, Indian S. C.	7 July 69	28 Oct. 71	7 July 81	7 July 89	
Edward Duncan Fred Bignell, *Major*, Indian Staff Corps	7 July 69	28 Oct. 71	7 July 81	7 July 89	
George Brougham Austin, *Major*, Indian Staff Corps	8 July 69	28 Oct. 71	8 July 81	8 July 89	
Vesey John Dawson, *Major*, Coldstream Guards	......	28 Oct. 71	25 Oct. 84	10 July 89	
George Edward Money, *Major*, Indian Staff Corps	14 July 69	28 Oct. 71	14 July 81	14 July 89	
John Clibborn, *Major*, Indian Staff Corps	14 July 69	28 Oct. 71	14 July 81	14 July 89	
p.s.c. John Stewart Scott Barker, *Major*, Royal Artillery	......	12 Sept. 72	22 Nov. 81	17 July 89	
Alexander Sprot, *Major*, 6 Dragoon Guards	......	28 Feb. 74	26 Apr. 82	19 July 89	
Alexander William Cockburn, *Major*, Royal Engineers	......	2 Aug. 71	2 Aug. 83	20 July 89	
Noel Montagu Lake, *Major*, Royal Engineers	......	2 Aug. 71	2 Aug. 83	20 July 89	
Frederic Brice Bunny, *Major*, Royal Artillery	......	12 Sept. 72	29 Nov. 81	31 July 89	
Henry Lake Wells, *Major*, Royal Engineers	......	2 Aug. 71	2 Aug. 83	31 July 89	
Charles Haggard, *Major*, Irish Rifles	......	27 Mar. 72	19 Nov. 81	3 Aug. 89	
Edward Raban, *Major*, Royal Engineers	......	2 Aug. 71	2 Aug. 83	6 Aug. 89	
Alfred Mansel, *DSO. Major*, Royal Artillery	......	12 Sept. 72	30 Nov. 81	13 Aug. 89	
George Glencairn Cunningham, *Captain*, Derbyshire Regt.	......	22 Oct. 81	14 Aug. 89	15 Aug. 89	
John Grenfell Maxwell, *DSO. Captain*, Black Watch	22 Mar. 79	1 July 81	28 Nov. 87	17 Aug. 89	
William Butler Ferris, *Major*, Indian Staff Corps	18 Aug. 69	7 Oct. 71	18 Aug. 81	18 Aug. 89	
Hugh Claude Edward Lucas, *Major*, Indian Staff Corps	21 Aug. 69	7 Oct. 71	21 Aug. 81	21 Aug. 89	
Edward Chamier Kellie, *Major*, Indian Staff Corps	21 Aug. 69	28 Oct. 71	21 Aug. 81	21 Aug. 89	
Atwell Robert Porter, *Major*, Indian Staff Corps	21 Aug. 69	28 Oct. 71	21 Aug. 81	21 Aug. 89	
Henry Charles Savage, *Major*, South Staffordshire Regiment	......	13 June 74	3 Feb. 82	23 Aug. 89	
Edward Arthur Smith,[s] *Major*, h.p. Royal Artillery	......	12 Feb. 74	7 July 83	23 Aug. 89	7 Apr. 94
Charles Henry Westmorland, *Major*, Indian Staff Corps	......	21 Sept. 74	21 Sept. 85	23 Aug. 89	
George Dalrymple More Nisbett, *Major*, Bedfordshire Regt.	8 June 70	28 Oct. 71	9 Mar. 79	28 Aug. 89	
Arthur Houstoun Hewat, *Major*, Royal Artillery	......	12 Sept. 72	30 Nov. 81	1 Sept. 89	
Harry George Weir, *Major*, Royal Artillery	......	12 Sept. 77	21 Dec. 81	2 Sept. 89	
Buchanan Scott, *CIE. Major*, Royal Engineers	......	2 Aug. 71	2 Aug. 83	4 Sept. 89	
John Dacres Cunningham, *Major*, Royal Artillery	......	12 Sept. 72	21 Dec. 81	14 Sept. 89	
George Fred. Farquharson Shirreff, *Major*, Royal Artillery	......	12 Sept. 72	21 Dec. 81	16 Sept. 89	
James Grove White, *Major*, Middlesex Regiment	......	12 Nov. 73	2 Jan. 81	18 Sept. 89	
Henry John Lyster, *Major*, Royal Artillery	......	12 Sept. 72	21 Dec. 81	1 Oct. 89	
Arthur Mordaunt Murray, *Major*, Royal Artillery	......	12 Sept. 72	24 Dec. 81	1 Oct. 89	
Philip Saltmarshe, *Major*, Royal Artillery	......	9 Jan. 73	31 Dec. 81	1 Oct. 89	
Henry Byron Jeffreys, *Major*, Royal Artillery	......	9 Jan. 73	11 Jan. 82	1 Oct. 89	
p.s.c. Walter Blunt Fletcher, *Major*, Royal Artillery	......	9 Jan. 73	18 Jan. 82	1 Oct. 89	
John William Hawkins, *Major*, Royal Artillery	......	9 Jan. 73	21 Jan. 82	1 Oct. 89	
Frederick Milbank Bland, *Major*, Royal Artillery	......	9 Jan. 73	17 May 82	1 Oct. 89	
Edwin Hay Pickwoad, *Major*, Royal Artillery	......	9 Jan. 73	27 May 82	1 Oct. 89	
Edward Ward, *Major*, Royal Artillery	......	9 Jan. 73	1 June 82	1 Oct. 89	
Arthur Pole-Penton, *Major*, Royal Artillery	......	9 Jan. 73	7 June 82	1 Oct. 89	
George Frederick Wilson, *Major*, Royal Engineers	......	2 Aug. 71	2 Aug. 83	1 Oct. 89	
Orbell Henry Oakes, *Major*, Worcestershire Regiment	......	10 Jan. 72	17 Dec. 81	9 Oct. 89	
Thomas Moore, *Major*, Royal Marine Artillery	......	5 Nov. 69	3 July 80	12 Oct. 89	
Robert Williams Andrews, *Major*, Border Regiment	6 July 70	18 Oct. 71	6 Sept. 81	20 Oct. 89	
James Laing Fixott, *Major*, Royal Artillery	......	9 Jan. 73	12 June 82	1 Nov. 89	
John Charles Frederick Gordon, *Major*, Indian Staff Corps	10 Nov. 69	28 Oct. 71	10 Nov. 81	10 Nov. 89	
p.s.c. John F. G. Ross of Bladensburg, *CB. Major*, Coldst. Gds.	......	15 July 68	18 Mar. 85	10 Nov. 89	
FitzRoy Somerset Lanyon Penno, *Major*, Welsh Regiment	......	9 Aug. 73	2 Feb. 81	13 Nov. 89	
Bowes Leslie Eman, *Major*, Royal Artillery	......	9 Jan. 73	24 June 82	13 Nov. 89	
Owen Stuart Smyth, *Major*, Royal Artillery	......	9 Jan. 73	24 June 82	13 Nov. 89	
Charles Henry Vincent Garbett, *Major*, Indian Staff Corps	17 Nov. 69	28 Oct. 71	17 Nov. 81	17 Nov. 89	
Richard Hobart Morrison, *Major*, 18 Hussars	......	13 June 74	31 Oct. 82	19 Nov. 89	
Andrew William Proudfoot, *Major*, Indian Staff Corps	24 Nov. 69	28 Oct. 71	24 Nov. 81	24 Nov. 89	
Thomas M. G. Thackeray, *Major*, Inniskilling Fusiliers	25 Nov. 68	27 Oct. 71	23 Mar. 81	1 Dec. 89	
p.s.c. Alfred Edward Codrington, *Major*, Coldstream Guards	......	1 Feb. 73	18 Apr. 85	4 Dec. 89	
Charles A. de P. Burroughs, *Major*, S. Lancashire Regiment	12 Oct. 70	28 Oct. 71	8 Sept. 81	8 Dec. 89	
Robert Francis Trotter, *Major*, Indian Staff Corps	8 Dec. 69	28 Oct. 71	8 Dec. 81	8 Dec. 89	
Aubrey de Vere Alexander, *Major*, Indian Staff Corps	8 Dec. 69	28 Oct. 71	8 Dec. 81	8 Dec. 89	
Edward Archibald Young, *Major*, Indian Staff Corps	15 Dec. 69	28 Oct. 71	15 Dec. 81	15 Dec. 89	
Charles Aloysius Ryan, *Major*, Royal Artillery	......	9 Jan. 73	8 July 82	15 Dec. 89	
Parkins Hearle, *Major*, Royal Marines	......	10 Dec. 67	1 July 81	16 Dec. 89	
Richard Matthews Ruck, *Major*, Royal Engineers	......	2 Aug. 71	1 Aug. 83	17 Dec. 89	
Simeon Hardy Exham, *Major*, Royal Engineers	......	2 Aug. 71	1 Aug. 83	17 Dec. 89	
Edward Glennie, *Major*, Royal Engineers	......	2 Aug. 71	1 Aug. 83	17 Dec. 89	
Herbert Hugh Muirhead, *Major*, Royal Engineers	......	2 Aug. 71	1 Aug. 83	17 Dec. 89	
William Harold Chippindall, *Major*, Royal Engineers	......	2 Aug. 71	1 Aug. 83	17 Dec. 89	
Alfred Crawford Bruce, *Major*, Royal Engineers	......	2 Aug. 71	1 Aug. 83	20 Dec. 89	
Henry Averell Eagar, *Major*, Irish Rifles	......	2 Dec. 74	18 Jan. 82	28 Dec. 89	
Arthur H. Croker Phillpotts, *Major*, Royal Artillery	......	29 Apr. 73	8 July 82	4 Jan. 90	
p.s.c. Thomas Stanford Baldock, *Major*, Royal Artillery	......	29 Apr. 73	15 July 82	4 Jan. 90	
Archibald J. A. Wright, *Major*, East Lancashire Regiment	22 Oct. 70	28 Oct. 71	10 Nov. 80	8 Jan. 90	
Layard Livingstone Fenton, *Major*, Indian Staff Corps	......	8 Jan. 70	8 Jan. 82	8 Jan. 90	
Henry John Blagrove, *Major*, 13 Hussars	......	11 Feb. 75	16 Mar. 83	8 Jan. 90	

E

Majors.

	CORNET, 2nd LIEUT. or ENSIGN.	LIEUT.	CAPTAIN.	MAJOR.	WHEN PLACED ON HALF PAY.
Arthur Edmund Simpson, *Major*, Manchester Regiment	......	21 Sept. 74	18 June 81	17 Jan.	17 Jan. 90
Edmond William Cotter, *Major*, Royal Engineers	......	2 Aug. 71	2 Aug. 83	18 Jan.	90
Pierce Edward Hughes, *Major*, Border Regiment	12 Nov. 70	28 Oct. 71	1 Dec. 80	19 Jan.	90
Charles Edward Harman, *Major*, Connaught Rangers	......	21 Sept. 75	30 Mar. 81	21 Jan.	90
Edward John Bor, *Major*, Royal Engineers	......	2 Aug. 71	2 Aug. 83	25 Jan.	90
Henry Robert Kelham, *Major*, Highland Light Infantry	......	28 May 73	7 Jan. 82	31 Jan.	90
Henry Edward M'Callum, *CMG. Major*, Royal Engineers	......	15 Dec. 71	15 Dec. 83	1 Feb.	90
John Andrew Mackenzie-Grieve, *Major*, Royal Artillery	......	29 Apr. 73	21 July 82	2 Feb.	90
Francis William Reader, *Major*, Leicester Regiment	......	2 Dec. 74	15 Nov. 81	5 Feb.	90
Willoughby Pitcairn Kennedy, *Major*, Indian Staff Corps	8 Feb. 70	28 Oct. 71	8 Feb. 82	8 Feb.	90
Henry Macan Mason, *Major*, Indian Staff Corps	8 Feb. 70	28 Oct. 71	8 Feb. 82	8 Feb.	90
Francis Stevenson, *Major*, Indian Staff Corps	8 Feb. 70	28 Oct. 71	8 Feb. 82	8 Feb.	90
William Frederick Cleeve, *Major*, Royal Artillery	......	29 Apr. 73	1 Sept. 82	12 Feb.	90
William Bicknell Coney, *Major*, Derbyshire Regiment	......	11 Feb. 75	1 Apr. 82	14 Feb.	90
George Hawkes, *Major*, Indian Staff Corps	19 Feb. 70	28 Oct. 71	19 Feb. 82	19 Feb.	90
Henry Matthew Ridley, *Major*, 7 Hussars	......	27 Mar. 74	19 Dec. 82	21 Feb.	90
John Henry Chenevix Harrison, *Major*, Royal Engineers	......	15 Dec. 71	15 Dec. 83	1 Mar. 90
Ruscombe Field Westmacott, *Major*, Lancashire Fusiliers	9 Oct. 69	28 Oct. 71	23 Mar. 81	12 Mar. 90
John Frederic Inglis, *Major*, Wiltshire Regiment (99 F.)	......	12 Feb. 73	19 May 80	19 Mar. 90
Napoleon Joseph R. Blake, *Major*, Middlesex Regt. (77 F.)	......	12 Nov. 73	14 Mar. 81	19 Mar. 90
Francis Colebrooke Farmer, *Major*, Royal Artillery	......	29 Apr. 73	9 Sept. 82	19 Mar. 90
p.s.c. Francis Wm. Bromfield, *Major*, Cheshire Regiment	......	29 May 72	22 Sept. 83	24 Mar. 90
p.s.c. Charles St. Leger Barter, *Major*, Yorkshire Lt. Infantry	......	10 Sept. 75	15 Mar. 81	26 Mar. 90
James Wyndham Hughes-Hallett, *Major*, Seaforth Highlanders (78 F.)	......	26 June 73	2 Sept. 80	27 Mar. 90
Edward Gunner, *Major*, Royal Artillery	......	29 Apr. 73	9 Sept. 82	28 Mar. 90
Albert Burton, *Major*, Royal Artillery	......	29 Apr. 73	16 Sept. 82	28 Mar. 90
Hubert Burton, *Major*, Royal Artillery	......	29 Apr. 73	16 Sept. 82	29 Mar. 90
John Stirling Napier, *Major*, Argyll and Suth. Highlanders	......	21 Sept. 74	27 Jan. 82	31 Mar. 90
p.s.c. Francis Waldron, *Major*, Royal Artillery	......	29 Apr. 73	1 Oct. 82	1 Apr. 90
Frederick Francis Johnson, *Major*, Army Service Corps	......	28 Feb. 74	17 Nov. 83	1 Apr. 90
Robert Addison Rigg, *Major*, Royal Artillery	......	29 Apr. 73	1 Oct. 82	1 Apr. 90
Charles A. Edes, *Major*, Army Service Corps. (*Hon. Capt.* 1 May 80)	Dep. Serv. 12 11/12 yrs.	11 Dec. 88	2 Apr. 90	
Edward Umfreville Blackett, *Major*, Royal Artillery	......	29 Apr. 73	1 Oct. 82	5 Apr. 90
Hon. Edward Noel, *Major*, Rifle Brigade	......	27 Mar. 72	20 Aug. 80	12 Apr. 90
William Grant de Jersey, *Major*, Royal Artillery	......	29 Apr. 73	1 Oct. 82	17 Apr. 90
James Kellie, *Major*, Royal Engineers	......	15 Dec. 71	15 Dec. 83	19 Apr. 90
Harris England Buchanan, *Major*, Northumberland Fusiliers	8 June 70	28 Oct. 71	9 Mar. 82	23 Apr. 90
Edward John Kenworthey Priestley, *Major*, Royal Artillery	......	29 Apr. 73	1 Oct. 82	25 Apr. 90
Reginald Campbell Hadow, *Major*, Indian Staff Corps	27 Apr. 70	28 Oct. 71	27 Apr. 82	27 Apr. 90
John Wm. Robinson Parker, *Major*, Yorkshire Regt. (19 F.)	......	12 Feb. 76	8 June 81	2 May 90
Pelham George Von Donop, *Major*, Royal Engineers	......	15 Dec. 71	15 Dec. 83	6 May 90
Lawrence Richard Connolly, *Major*, Royal Marine Artillery	......	18 Feb. 71	25 Sept. 80	7 May 90
Harry Shuldham Lye, *Major*, Irish Regiment	......	9 Aug. 73	23 May 81	7 May 90
William Lewis Clinton Baddeley, *Major*, Royal Engineers	......	15 Dec. 71	15 Dec. 83	10 May 90
Charles John Spottiswoode, *Major*, Yorkshire Regt. (19 F.)	......	5 June 76	29 Sept. 82	11 May 90
Ernest Vaughan-Hughes, *Major*, Royal Artillery	......	29 Apr. 73	20 July 82	12 May 90
Charles Frederick Hadden, *Major*, Royal Artillery	......	11 Sept. 73	1 Oct. 82	12 May 90
James Milford Sutherland Brunker, *Major*, Royal Artillery	......	1 Sept. 73	4 Oct. 82	20 May 90
Wm. John Fortescue Morgan, *Major*, Irish Regiment (18 F.)	......	2 Nov. 73	18 June 81	22 May 90
Gerald Grant-Dalton, *Major*, West Yorkshire Regt. (14 F.)	......	8 June 72	18 May 81	23 May 90
John Chivas Shirres, *Major*, Royal Artillery	......	11 Sept. 73	4 Oct. 82	23 May 90
Edw. Coxwell Morris, *Major*, North Lancashire Regt. (81 F.)	......	9 Aug. 73	23 Feb. 81	31 May 90
Ernest Frederic David, *Captain*, Royal Marines	......	1 Sept. 81	31 May 90	1 June 90
p.s.c. Chas. Edw. de la Poer Beresford, *Major*, Wiltshire Regt.	7 July 69	28 Oct. 71	10 Jan. 83	4 June 90
Henry Tempest Hicks, *Major*, Dublin Fusiliers	......	27 Mar. 73	10 Nov. 80	7 June 90
George T. W. Hewat, *Major*, King's Own Scottish Borderers	27 Sept. 71	28 Oct. 71	1 Jan. 81	14 June 90
Cecil Henry Law, *Major*, Dorsetshire Regiment	7 July 69	28 Oct. 71	24 Jan. 83	21 June 90
Morey Quayle Jones, *Major*, Warwickshire Regiment	......	12 Nov. 73	25 Apr. 83	21 June 90
Martyn John Edward Fenwick, *Major*, Dorsetshire Regt.	......	3 Aug. 72	12 Sept. 83	21 June 90
Robert Henry Gunning, *Major*, King's Royal Rifles	......	26 Mar. 73	1 Aug. 83	25 June 90
Thomas Tweed Vaughan, *Major*, Royal Artillery	......	11 Sept. 73	25 Nov. 82	28 June 90
Henry Dacres Olivier, *Major*, Royal Engineers	......	15 Dec. 71	15 Dec. 83	29 June 90
Justice Chapman Tilly, *Major*, Bedfordshire Regiment	14 Dec. 70	28 Oct. 71	30 Apr. 79	1 July 90
Manley Ogden Hopkins, *Major*, Royal Artillery	......	11 Sept. 73	25 Nov. 82	1 July 90
Henry James Seton, *Major*, Irish Rifles	......	2 Dec. 74	26 Apr. 82	2 July 90
John Edward Blackburn, *Major*, Royal Engineers	......	15 Dec. 71	15 Dec. 83	2 July 90
Hon. John Townshend St. Aubyn, *Captain*, Grenadier Gds.	19 Oct. 78	1 July 81	1 July 90	2 July 90
Charles Oldfield Nicholetts, *Major*, Indian Staff Corps	6 July 70	6 June 71	6 July 82	6 July 90
James Hayes Sadler, *Major*, Indian Staff Corps	6 July 70	28 Oct. 71	6 July 82	6 July 90
John Edmund Mein, *Major*, Indian Staff Corps	6 July 70	28 Oct. 71	6 July 82	6 July 90
William Octavius Harris, *Major*, Indian Staff Corps	6 July 70	28 Oct. 71	6 July 82	6 July 90
Ernest Armond Barclay, *Major*, Indian Staff Corps	6 July 70	21 Jan. 74	6 July 82	6 July 90
Harry D'Arch Breton, *Major*, Royal Engineers	......	15 Dec. 71	15 Dec. 83	6 July 90
Charles William Ross Kitching, *Major*, Royal Marines	......	21 July 70	15 July 82	16 July 90
Charles Cecil Hayford Thorold, *Major*, Welsh Fusiliers	......	13 June 74	25 Oct. 82	16 July 90
Malcolm Edw. H. Owen Welch, *Major*, Indian Staff Corps	20 July 70	28 Oct. 71	20 July 82	20 July 90
Maxwell Archibald Close, *Major*, 13 Hussars	......	2 Dec. 74	25 Sept. 80	25 July 90
Frederick Stapleton Gwatkin, *Captain*, Indian Staff Corps	......	27 Mar. 72	27 Mar. 84	28 July 90
Wensly James Hodson Bond, *Captain*, Indian Staff Corps	......	30 Nov. 76	30 Nov. 87	28 July 90
Arthur Harry Clark-Kennedy, *Captain*, Indian Staff Corps	......	11 Nov. 77	11 Nov. 88	28 July 90
Berkeley Crosbie Quill, *Major*, York and Lancaster Regt.	......	21 Aug. 72	24 June 79	30 July 90
William Tylden, *Major*, Royal Artillery	......	11 Sept. 73	27 Dec. 82	30 July 90
Charles James Blomfield, *Major*, Lancashire Fusiliers	......	11 Feb. 75	1 July 81	31 July 90
Stephen Dickson Rainsford, *Major*, Royal Artillery	......	11 Sept. 73	31 Dec. 82	1 Aug. 90
Arthur Henry Wilford Brett, *Major*, Royal Artillery	......	11 Sept. 73	14 Feb. 83	1 Aug. 90
Francis Dale Tagart, *Major*, 18 Hussars	......	2 Dec. 74	1 Oct. 83	1 Aug. 90
Grey Skipwith, *Major*, Royal Marines	......	1 Oct. 73	26 Jan. 84	1 Aug. 90
Henry Spencer Wheatley, *Major*, Indian Staff Corps	3 Aug. 70	28 Oct. 71	3 Aug. 82	3 Aug. 90
Henry Palmer Knight, *Major*, Royal Engineers	......	15 Dec. 71	15 Dec. 83	3 Aug. 90
William Henry Goldney, *Major*, Royal Engineers	......	15 Dec. 71	15 Dec. 83	3 Aug. 90
Albert Evelyn Houghton, *Major*, Royal Marines	......	1 Oct. 73	11 Feb. 84	10 Aug. 90
William Gibbs Straghan, *Major*, Norfolk Regiment	......	6 Mar. 73	21 Mar. 82	20 Aug. 90

Majors. 57

Name	CORNET, 2ND LIEUT. OR ENSIGN.	LIEUT.	CAPTAIN.	MAJOR.	WHEN PLACED ON HALF PAY.
Frederic Percy Lousada, *Major*, York and Lancaster Regt...	......	28 Feb. 74	1 July 81	27 Aug. 90	
John Henry Collier Coode, *Major*, Black Watch	......	10 Sept.75	17 Apr. 82	27 Aug. 90	
Harry Howlett Young, *Major*, Indian Staff Corps	27 Aug. 70	28 Oct. 71	27 Aug. 82	27 Aug. 90	
Foster Lionel Cunliffe, *Major*, Royal Artillery	......	11 Sept.73	14 Feb. 83	27 Aug. 90	
Terence England Rowan, *Major*, Royal Artillery	......	11 Sept.73	16 Feb. 83	1 Sept. 90	
John William Marsdin Newton, *Major*, Royal Artillery..........	......	11 Sept.73	28 Feb. 83	2 Sept. 90	
George Davidson Campbell Gaatrell,*Major*,Indian Staff Corps	3 Sept.70	28 Oct. 71	3 Sept.82	3 Sept. 90	
Edward Evans Kenny, *Major*, Indian Staff Corps	3 Sept.70	28 Oct. 71	3 Sept.82	3 Sept. 90	
George Lindsay Garstin, *Major*, Indian Staff Corps	3 Sept.70	28 Oct. 71	30 May 83	3 Sept. 90	
Colin George Donald, *Major*, Royal Fusiliers..................	......	21 Sept.74	30 May 83	3 Sept. 90	
Edgar Gaussen, *Major*, Army Service Corps (*Hon. Captain* 6 Mar. 80)	Dep.&h.p. 13⁹/₁₂ yrs.	11 Dec. 88	3 Sept. 90		
p.s.c. John Henry Sewell, *Major*, Norfolk Regiment	......	8 May 72	1 Apr. 82	5 Sept. 90	
Henry Leycester Aylmer, *Major*, 16 Lancers..................	25 Sept.69	28 Oct. 71	11 Dec. 80	10 Sept. 90	
Harry Stewart Bruce Hodgkinson, *Major*, N. Staff. Regt. ...	......	12 Nov. 73	3 Apr. 81	10 Sept. 90	
Lewis Horace Phillips, *Major*, Norfolk Regiment	......	2 Dec. 74	19 July 82	19 Sept. 90	
Francis Seymour Leslie, *Major*, Royal Engineers	......	15 Dec. 71	15 Dec. 83	22 Sept. 90	
Arthur William M'Kinstry, *Major*, Leicestershire Regiment ...	......	5 June 75	7 Mar. 83	23 Sept. 90	
Wentworth Grenville Bowyer, *Major*, Royal Engineers	......	15 Dec. 71	15 Dec. 83	24 Sept. 90	
Stewart John Trench, *Major*, West Riding Regiment (76 F.)	......	6 Oct. 75	24 Jan. 83	26 Sept. 90	
William Robert Le Geyt Anderson, *Major*, Indian Staff C ...	1 Oct. 70	28 Oct. 71	1 Oct. 82	1 Oct. 90	
William Hugh Edward Dobie, *Major*, Royal Artillery	......	11 Sept.73	28 Feb. 83	1 Oct. 90	
John William Edward Angelo, *Major*, Indian Staff Corps ...	2 Oct. 70	28 Oct. 71	2 Oct. 82	2 Oct. 90	
Henry Donald Rosseter, *Major*, Durham Light Infantry......	......	11 Feb. 75	2 Feb. 81	8 Oct. 90	
Robert John Romanes, *Major*, King's Own Scottish Borderers (25 F.)	......	29 May 72	26 Apr. 81	8 Oct. 90	
Arthur Abney Sandys, *Major*, 4 Dragoon Guards	......	13 June 74	10 June 82	8 Oct. 90	
Charles Ernest Heath, *Captain*, Army Service Corps	......	9 Aug. 74	1 Oct. 83	9 Oct. 90	
Claude Mason Haggard, *Major*, Royal Artillery	......	11 Sept.73	8 Feb. 83	16 Oct. 90	
Carmichael Light Young, *Major*, Royal Engineers............	......	15 Dec. 71	25 Dec. 83	22 Oct. 90	
Ulick George Campbell de Burgh, *Major*, 7 Dragoon Guards	......	11 Sept.76	1 July 81	31 Oct. 90	
George Franklend Francis, *Major*, Indian Staff Corps.........	5 Nov. 70	28 Oct. 71	5 Nov. 82	5 Nov. 90	
John Willoughby Wray, *Major*, Indian Staff Corps	12 Nov. 70	23 Oct. 71	12 Nov. 82	12 Nov. 90	
Alexander Thomas Weller, *Major*, Indian Staff Corps	12 Nov. 70	28 Oct. 71	12 Nov. 82	12 Nov. 90	
Guillum Scott Baugh, *Major*, Indian Staff Corps..............	12 Nov. 70	28 Oct. 71	12 Nov. 82	12 Nov. 90	
Charles William Henry Evans, *Major*, West Kent Regiment	......	28 Feb. 74	17 Nov. 83	17 Nov. 90	
Standish Henry Harrison, *Major*, Liverpool Regiment.........	......	2 Dec. 74	1 July 81	19 Nov. 90	
Carteret Walter Carey, *Major*, Highland Light Infantry	......	12 Nov. 73	25 Jan. 82	22 Nov. 90	
p.s.c. George Fitzherbert Browne, *DSO. Major*, Northampton Regiment (58 F.)	6 July 70	28 Oct. 71	16 Dec. 82	22 Nov. 90	
Llewellyn Salusbury Mellor, *Major*, Liverpool Regiment	......	15 Jan. 75	1 July 81	26 Nov. 90	
Alexander Masters, *Major*, Indian Staff Corps..................	30 Nov. 70	28 Oct. 71	30 Nov. 82	30 Nov. 90	
Frederick Gordon Alexander, *Major*, Indian Staff Corps ...	7 Dec. 70	28 Oct. 71	7 Dec. 82	7 Dec. 90	
Francis Cecil Ricardo, *Major*, Grenadier Guards...............	......	11 Sept.72	8 June 84	10 Dec. 90	
Arthur Reginald Hennell, *Major*, Hampshire Regiment......	1 Apr. 68	28 Oct. 71	1 July 81	20 Dec. 90	
George Wade Robertson Fulton, *Major*, Royal Artillery......	......	11 Sept.73	28 Mar. 83	31 Dec. 90	
Thomas Henry Jackson Woodrow, *Major*, Royal Artillery...	......	11 Sept.73	1 Apr. 83	31 Dec. 90	
Arthur Henry Browne, *Major*, Royal Artillery	......	11 Sept.73	1 Apr. 83	31 Dec. 90	
Horace John James Kentish, *Major*, Dorsetshire Regiment...	......	10 Sept.75	19 Mar. 84	31 Dec. 90	
David Erskine Dewar, *Major*, Royal Artillery..................	......	11 Feb. 74	3 Apr. 83	1 Jan. 91	
Gerald Talbot Kelaart, *Major*, Royal Artillery.................	......	12 Feb. 74	17 Apr. 83	1 Jan. 91	
Arthur Churchill Bailward, *Major*, Royal Artillery	......	12 Feb. 74	18 Apr. 83	1 Jan. 91	
Frederick Ernest Arundell Hunter, *Major*, Royal Artillery ...	......	12 Feb. 74	12 May 83	1 Jan. 91	
Harry Alexander Dyer Curtis, *Major*, Royal Artillery.........	......	12 Feb. 74	12 May 83	1 Jan. 91	
Alfred Keene, *DSO. Major*, Royal Artillery	......	12 Feb. 74	12 May 83	1 Jan. 91	
Henry O'Brien Owen, *Major*, Royal Artillery	......	12 Feb. 74	23 May 83	1 Jan. 91	
p.s.c. Julian John Leverson, *Major*, Royal Engineers	......	6 Jan. 72	6 Jan. 84	1 Jan. 91	
Henry Percy Poingdestre Leigh, *CIE. Major*, Indian S. C.	......	4 Jan. 72	4 Jan. 83	4 Jan. 91	
Richard Carnac Temple, *CIE. Major*, Indian Staff Corps ...	4 Jan. 71	28 Oct. 71	4 Jan. 83	4 Jan. 91	
Frederick Guy Vivian, *Major*, Indian Staff Corps	4 Jan. 71	28 Oct. 71	4 Jan. 83	4 Jan. 91	
William Arthur Plant, *Major*, Royal Artillery	......	12 Feb. 74	18 June 83	9 Jan. 91	
Thomas Julian Penrhys Evans, *Major*, Royal Marines.........	......	1 July 74	17 May 84	9 Jan. 91	
John Anstruther Smith-Cuninghame, *Major*, 2 Life Guards	......	11 Feb. 76	10 Apr. 83	12 Jan. 91	
David Francis Lewis, *Major*, Cheshire Regiment	......	11 Feb. 75	20 Feb. 84	14 Jan. 91	
Richard Lionel Hippisley, *Major*, Royal Engineers............	......	6 Jan. 72	6 Jan. 84	15 Jan. 91	
Robert Charles Hellard, *Major*, Royal Engineers	......	6 Jan. 72	6 Jan. 84	15 Jan. 91	
John Colin Livington Campbell, *Major*, Royal Engineers ...	......	6 Jan. 72	6 Jan. 84	15 Jan. 91	
George Davidson, *Major*, Royal Engineers	......	6 Jan. 72	6 Jan. 84	15 Jan. 91	
Henry John R. St. G. Richardson, *Major*, Liverpool Regt.....	......	10 Sept.75	1 Feb. 82	16 Jan. 91	
p.s.c. Cosmo Huntly Gordon, *Major*, The Buffs	......	28 Feb. 74	19 Mar. 82	21 Jan. 91	
Robert Maziere Brady, *Major*, Royal Artillery	......	12 Feb. 74	1 July 83	25 Jan. 91	
Archibald Morden Carthew-Yorstoun, *Major*, Black Watch	......	20 Nov. 75	1 Oct. 82	29 Jan. 91	
James Browne, *Major*, Devonshire Regiment	19 May 69	28 Oct. 71	21 July 81	4 Feb. 91	
Douglas Minto Allen, *Major*, West India Regiment	......	22 Sept.75	16 Jan. 85	4 Feb. 91	
Robert Dunn Loudon, *Major*, Royal Artillery..................	......	12 Feb. 74	6 July 83	7 Feb. 91	
Hon. Ulick de Rupe Burke Roche, *Major*, S. Wales Borderers	......	6 Sept.76	18 June 81	10 Feb. 91	
Walter Dubbon Garnett-Botfield, *Major*, Royal Artillery......	......	12 Feb. 74	7 July 83	10 Feb. 91	
Martin Thackeray, *Major*, South Staffordshire Regiment ...	......	21 Sept.74	19 July 82	11 Feb. 91	
John Stacpole, *Major*, Army Service Corps	......	21 Jan. 74	26 Mar. 84	11 Feb. 91	
John de Courcy O'Grady, *Major*, Connaught Rangers	......	28 Sept.78	13 Apr. 81	11 Feb. 91	
Ralph Bromfield Willington Fisher, *Major*, 10 Hussars	......	27 June 74	28 Apr. 82	12 Feb. 91	
*Antonio Gatt, *Major*, Royal Malta Artillery	......	21 Feb. 65	18 Apr. 82	14 Feb. 91	
James Alastair Campbell, *Major*, Seaforth Highlanders	......	29 Nov. 76	22 Apr. 86	14 Feb. 91	
Cuthbert George Knocker, *Major*, Army Service Corps	......	11 Feb. 75	15 Apr. 82	15 Feb. 91	
Ellis Charles Fletcher Holland, *Major*, Royal Artillery	......	12 Feb. 74	7 July 83	16 Feb. 91	
Wastel Jameson Lister, *Major*, Royal Engineers	......	6 Jan. 72	6 Jan. 84	16 Feb. 91	
George Leonard Thomson, *Major*, Sussex Regiment	......	28 May 75	26 July 82	18 Feb. 91	
George Ewbank Briggs, *Major*, Royal Fusiliers	......	13 June 74	16 Feb. 84	18 Feb. 91	
*Alfred Cavarra, *Major*, Royal Malta Artillery	......	2 May 68	15 May 83	22 Feb. 91	
Hon. Algernon Sidney, *Major*, Royal Artillery	......	12 Feb. 74	26 July 83	26 Feb. 91	
Francis Wilford Botelor, *Major*, Royal Artillery	......	12 Feb. 74	1 Aug. 83	1 Mar. 91	
Allan Moss, *Major*, Worcestershire Regiment (20 foot)	......	19 Apr. 76	1 Jan. 84	2 Mar. 91	
VC William Henry Dick-Cunyngham, *Major*, Argyll and Sutherland Highlanders..................................	......	17 Feb. 73	19 Oct. 81	4 Mar. 91	

E 2

Majors.

Name	CORNET, 2nd LIEUT. OF ENSIGN.	LIEUT.	CAPTAIN.	MAJOR.	WHEN PLACED ON HALF PAY.
Henry George Purdon, *Major*, N. Lancashire Regt.		11 Sept. 74	5 Jan. 84	6 Mar. 91	
Arthur Spencer Pratt, *Major*, Royal Artillery		12 Feb. 74	1 Aug. 83	13 Mar. 91	
William Edward Blewitt, *Major*, Royal Artillery		12 Feb. 74	1 Aug. 83	14 Mar. 91	
Digby de la Motte Du Boulay, *Major*, 7 Dragoon Guards		11 Sept. 77	1 Oct. 81	31 Mar. 91	
Charles Arthur Hadfield, *Major*, Army Service Corps		2 Dec. 74	14 Jan. 84	1 Apr. 91	
Hon. Reginald Henry Bertie, *Major*, Welsh Fusiliers		21 Sept. 74	10 May 83	2 Apr. 91	
Charles Evan Maberly, *Major*, Royal Artillery		12 Feb. 74	22 Aug. 83	19 Apr. 91	
John Frederick Irwin, *Major*, East Lancashire Regiment	8 Jan. 68	28 Oct. 71	30 Sept. 81	22 Apr. 91	
Henry Melville Hatchell, *Major*, Irish Regiment		28 Feb. 74	1 July 81	29 Apr. 91	
Frederick John Brown, *Major*, Essex Regiment		10 Sept. 75	16 Aug. 82	29 Apr. 91	
Frederick George Pogson, *Major*, East Yorkshire Regiment	27 Aug. 70	28 Oct. 71	4 Mar. 82	3 May 91	
Algernon Hildebrand, *Major*, Royal Engineers		4 Jan. 71	4 Jan. 83	4 May 91	
Charles Knight Wood, *Major*, Royal Engineers		6 Jan. 72	6 Jan. 84	6 May 91	
Gerald Hope Wildig O'Sullivan, *Major*, Royal Engineers		6 Jan. 72	6 Jan. 84	9 May 91	
W. Charles James William Grant, *Captain*, Indian S. C.		10 May 82	10 May 91	11 May 91	
Francis Campbell Pearson, *Major*, 4 Hussars		2 Dec. 74	9 Sept. 80	13 May 91	
Charles Henry Kelly, *Major*, Provisional Battalion		26 June 72	18 June 81	13 May 91	
p.s.c. George Mackworth Bullock, *Major*, Devonshire Regt.		24 Apr. 72	22 Feb. 82	19 May 91	
Montagu William Battye, *Major*, East Lancashire Regiment		12 Feb. 73	8 Jan. 83	23 May 91	
Charles Victor Bremer Kuper, *Major*, Royal Artillery		12 Feb. 74	31 Aug. 83	29 May 91	
Edward Crichton Hawkshaw, *Major*, Royal Artillery		12 Aug. 74	31 Aug. 83	3 June 91	
Arthur Clifton Hansard, *Major*, Royal Artillery		17 Aug. 74	1 Sept. 83	3 June 91	
Granville de la Motte Faunce, *Major*, Berkshire Regt. (66 F.)		29 Nov. 76	30 Oct. 83	8 June 91	
Augustus Simeon Le Quesne, *Major*, Royal Marine Art.		18 Feb. 71	27 Sept. 80	12 June 91	
Ernest Blunt, *Major*, Royal Engineers		6 Jan. 72	6 Jan. 84	12 June 91	
Thos. Wm. Crawford Leathem, *Major*, Gloucester Regiment	16 Oct. 66	20 Oct. 69	22 June 80	17 June 91	
p.s.c. Fras. Richd. Pennefather Kane, *Major*, E. Surrey Regt.		12 Nov. 73	28 Feb. 81	21 June 91	
Bolden Dundas Porterfield, *Major*, R. Art. (District Officer)		25 Aug. 77	16 Sept. 82	22 June 91	
Somerset E. O'Brien Kevill-Davies, *Major*, Gordon Highlanders (92 F.)		12 Nov. 73	18 June 81	1 July 91	
Daniel de Hoghton, *Major*, North Lancashire Regt. (47 F.)		28 Feb. 74	10 July 81	1 July 91	
Allan Gilmore, *Major*, Gloucestershire Regiment	8 July 68	28 Oct. 71	7 Aug. 81	1 July 91	
Fred. Geo. Vigor, *Major*, Duke of Cornwall's Lt. Inf. (46 F.)		11 Sept. 73	1 Sept. 81	1 July 91	
Robert Frederick Lindsell, *Major*, Gloucester Regt. (28 F.)		21 Sept. 74	19 Nov. 81	1 July 91	
Francis Edward Wallerstein, *Major*, York & Lancaster Regt.		11 Sept. 76	29 May 82	1 July 91	
Attiwell Henry Wood, *Major*, Connaught Rangers		2 Dec. 74	16 Sept. 82	1 July 91	
Arthur Dillon Denis Kelly, *Major*, Border Regiment (34 F.)		12 Nov. 73	13 Aug. 83	1 July 91	
p.s.c. Percy Hy. Noel Lake, *Major*, East Lanc. Regt. (59 F.)		9 Aug. 73	31 Oct. 83	1 July 91	
Frederick Morris, *Major*, Welsh Fusiliers		2 Dec. 74	1 July 84	1 July 91	
Sir Hy. Allen Wm. Johnson, Bart., *Major*, York Lt. Inf. (51 F.)		28 Feb. 74	6 Feb. 82	4 July 91	
Hugh Ingoldsby Massey, *Major*, Essex Regiment (44 F.)		20 Nov. 75	30 Aug. 82	6 July 91	
Hector Archibald MacDonald, DSO. *Major*, Royal Fusiliers	7 Jan. 80	1 July 81	18 Jan. 88	8 July 91	
Gerald Hedley Ovens, *Major*, Border Regiment (55 F.)		21 Sept. 74	20 Oct. 83	9 July 91	
Benjamin Burton, *Major*, Royal Artillery		17 Aug. 74	1 Sept. 83	25 July 91	
Frank Robt. Crofton Carleton, *Maj.* Durham Lt. Inf. (106 F.)		21 Sept. 74	8 June 81	28 July 91	
p.s.c. Douglas Fred. Rawdon Dawson, *Maj.* Coldstream Gds.		21 Jan. 74	19 Sept. 82	29 July 91	
John Richard Howard Allen, *Major*, Royal Artillery		17 Aug. 74	1 Sept. 83	30 July 91	
John Robert Young, *Major*, East Yorkshire Regiment		6 Mar. 72	26 July 82	5 Aug. 91	
Alexander M'Donnell Moore, *Major*, Irish Fusiliers	23 July 79	1 Dec. 80	12 Aug. 85	5 Aug. 91	
Walter Waterfield Ward, *Major*, East Yorkshire Regiment		30 Apr. 73	25 Jan. 84	6 Aug. 91	
p.s.c. John Burn-Murdoch, *Major*, Royal Engineers		2 May 72	2 May 84	6 Aug. 91	
Edward Elliott Carr, *Major*, Scots Fusiliers		9 Aug. 73	14 July 83	10 Aug. 91	
Arnold H.N. Urquhart Champion, *Maj.* Leinster Regt. (100 F.)		30 Dec. 71	23 May 83	12 Aug. 91	
Charles Conyngham Ellis, *Major*, Royal Engineers		2 May 72	2 May 84	12 Aug. 91	
r.s.c. James Birch Sharpe, *Major*, Royal Engineers		2 May 72	2 May 84	13 Aug. 91	
Thomas Digby, *Major*, Royal Engineers		2 May 72	2 May 84	13 Aug. 91	
Alan William Low Rickards, *Major*, Royal Scots		30 Dec. 71	18 June 81	14 Aug. 91	
Cecil Francis Garnett, *Major*, East Yorkshire Regiment		28 Feb. 74	3 May 84	15 Aug. 91	
James Wilfred Stirling, *Major*, Royal Artillery		17 Aug. 74	2 Sept. 83	17 Aug. 91	
William Peel Nash, *Major*, Manchester Regiment		11 Feb. 75	15 Sept. 81	19 Aug. 91	
Oswald James Henry Ball, *Major*, Welsh Regiment		28 Feb. 74	1 Apr. 81	20 Aug. 91	
Trenchard Fred. Thomas Fowle, *Major*, Royal Artillery		17 Aug. 74	5 Sept. 83	20 Aug. 91	
Herbert Martin, *Major*, Leinster Regiment	30 Jan. 78	1 Oct. 78	6 June 83	21 Aug. 91	
John Percy Fell, *Major*, Royal Artillery		17 Aug. 74	8 Sept. 83	22 Aug. 91	
St. John James St. Leger, *Major*, Leinster Regiment (100 F.)	20 Mar. 78	30 Nov. 78	6 June 83	26 Aug. 91	
Percy Wm. Albert Alfred Milton, *Major*, Yorkshire Lt. Inf.	11 May 78	14 Dec. 78	1 Jan. 84	1 Sept. 91	
Claude Frederic Gambier, *Major*, Indian Staff Corps		30 Dec. 71	30 Dec. 83	1 Sept. 91	
Edwin Capel Currie Sandys, *Major*, Indian Staff Corps		2 May 72	2 May 84	1 Sept. 91	
Alfred Robert Martin, *Major*, Indian Staff Corps		2 Dec. 74	2 Dec. 85	1 Sept. 91	
Hugh Frederick Lyons-Montgomery, *Captain*, Indian S.C.		13 June 75	13 June 86	1 Sept. 91	
William du Gard Gray, *Captain*, Indian Staff Corps		10 Sept. 75	10 Sept. 86	1 Sept. 91	
Dudley Richard Apthorp, *Major*, 19 Hussars		20 Nov. 75	26 Apr. 82	2 Sept. 91	
Kenneth Ross MacKenzie, *Maj.* Seaforth Highlandrs. (78 F.)		9 Aug. 73	27 Mar. 83	3 Sept. 91	
Robert Arthur Gwynne Harrison, *Major*, Royal Artillery		17 Aug. 74	26 Sept. 83	7 Sept. 91	
Maurice Charles Barton, *Major*, Royal Engineers		2 May 72	2 May 84	8 Sept. 91	
Philip Farrer, *Major*, Dorsetshire Regiment (39 Foot)		20 Nov. 75	18 July 84	10 Sept. 91	
Ronald Charles Maxwell, *Major*, Royal Engineers		2 May 72	2 May 84	16 Sept. 91	
Walter Andrew Urquhart, *Major*, Royal Artillery		17 Aug. 74	7 Oct. 83	20 Sept. 91	
Henry C. Cotton Gibbings, *Major*, Inniskilling Fus. (108 F.)		11 Feb. 75	10 Aug. 83	21 Sept. 91	
Percy Schletter, *Major*, Liverpool Regiment (8 F.)		13 June 76	7 Mar. 82	22 Sept. 91	
Frederick Charles Maisey, *Major*, Indian Staff Corps	23 Sept. 71	28 Oct. 71	23 Sept. 83	23 Sept. 91	
George Wingate, *Major*, Indian Staff Corps	23 Sept. 71	28 Oct. 71	23 Sept. 83	23 Sept. 91	
p.s.c. John William Hogge, CIE. *Major*, Indian Staff Corps	23 Sept. 71	28 Oct. 72	23 Sept. 83	23 Sept. 91	
Henry Cuthbert Connell D. Simpson, *Major*, R. Artillery		17 Aug. 72	23 Oct. 83	24 Sept. 91	
Thos. Horatio de Montmorency Roche, *Major*, R. Marines		1 July 74	28 May 84	27 Sept. 91	
Henry Davison Love, *Major*, Royal Engineers		12 Sept. 72	12 Sept. 8	30 Sept. 91	
William Edward Ligonier Balfour, *Major*, Royal Artillery		17 Aug. 74	1 Nov. 8	1 Oct. 91	
Hubert George Howard Galton, *Major*, Royal Artillery		17 Aug. 74	4 Nov. 8	1 Oct. 91	
Alexander Burridge Purvis, *Major*, Royal Artillery		17 Aug. 74	7 Nov. 8	1 Oct. 91	
Rowley Wynyard, *Major*, Royal Artillery		17 Aug. 74	14 Nov. 8	1 Oct. 91	
John Warre Sill, *Major*, Royal Engineers		12 Sept. 72	12 Sept. 8	1 Oct. 91	
Kenneth Mackean, *Major*, Royal Engineers		12 Sept. 72	12 Sept. 8	1 Oct. 91	
p.s.c. Edward William Fleming, *Major*, Royal Artillery		28 Jan. 75	14 Nov. 8	2 Oct. 91	

Majors.

Name	CORNET, 2nd LIEUT. or ENSIGN.	LIEUT.	CAPTAIN.	MAJOR.	WHEN PLACED ON HALF PAY.
George Robert Townshend, *Major*, Royal Artillery		28 Jan. 75	16 Nov. 83	4 Oct. 91	
John Rowlandson, *Major*, Lancaster Regiment (4 F.)		10 Jan. 72	22 Sept. 80	7 Oct. 91	
Andrew Bell-Irving, *Major*, Royal Artillery		28 Jan. 75	1 Dec. 83	12 Oct. 91	
Alfred Montanaro, *Major*, Indian Staff Corps		14 Oct. 71	14 Oct. 83	14 Oct. 91	
Willoughby Verner Constable, *Major*, Royal Engineers		12 Sept. 72	12 Sept. 84	19 Oct. 91	
Robt. Wm. Peter Lodwick, *Major*, Gloucester Regt. (28 F.)		9 Aug. 73	18 June 81	21 Oct. 91	
Alwyn de Blaquiere V. Paget, *Major*, Durham Lt.Inf. (106 F.)		11 Feb. 75	24 Aug. 81	21 Oct. 91	
John Wilmot Robyns, *Major*, Royal Marines		1 Oct. 74	23 July 84	21 Oct. 91	
Charles Tom Reay, *Major*, Manchester Regiment (63 F.)		11 Feb. 75	18 Mar. 82	24 Oct. 91	
Malcolm Thomas Lyde, *Major*, Indian Staff Corps		28 Oct. 71	29 Apr. 82	28 Oct. 91	
William Henry Fothergill MacMullen, *Major*, Indian S.C.	28 Oct. 71	28 Oct. 71	28 Oct. 83	28 Oct. 91	
Francis Sheffield Sorell, *Major*, Indian Staff Corps	28 Oct. 71	28 Oct. 71	28 Oct. 83	28 Oct. 91	
Lambart John Browne, *Major*, Indian Staff Corps	28 Oct. 71	28 Oct. 71	28 Oct. 83	28 Oct. 91	
Percy Edward Henderson, *Major*, Indian Staff Corps	28 Oct. 71	28 Oct. 71	28 Oct. 83	28 Oct. 91	
Robert Feild Jameson, *Major*, Indian Staff Corps	28 Oct. 71	28 Oct. 71	28 Oct. 83	28 Oct. 91	
John Haughton, *Major*, Indian Staff Corps	28 Oct. 71	28 Oct. 71	28 Oct. 83	28 Oct. 91	
Arthur George Frederic Browne, DSO. *Major*, Indian S.C.	28 Oct. 71	28 Oct. 71	28 Oct. 83	28 Oct. 91	
Arthur Wapshare, *Major*, Indian Staff Corps	28 Oct. 71	28 Oct. 71	28 Oct. 83	28 Oct. 91	
George Henry B. Coats, *Major*, Indian Staff Corps	28 Oct. 71	28 Oct. 71	28 Oct. 83	28 Oct. 91	
Thomas Davison, *Major*, Cheshire Regiment (22 F.)	27 Apr. 70	27 Oct. 71	20 Feb. 84	28 Oct. 91	
p.s.c. Harry James Craufurd, *Major*, Grenadier Guards		29 Mar. 73	9 July 84	28 Oct. 91	
Thomas Vaughan Wynn Phillips, *Major*, Royal Artillery		28 Jan. 75	22 Dec. 83	29 Oct. 91	
Robert H. Jennings, *Major*, Royal Engineers		12 Sept. 72	12 Sept. 84	6 Nov. 91	
John Murray Simpson, *Major*, h.p. Royal Artillery		17 Aug. 74	12 Sept. 83	7 Nov. 91	20 Jan. 95
Charles Napier Simpson, *Major*, Royal Artillery		28 Jan. 75	29 Dec. 83	7 Nov. 91	
Edward Sinclair May, *Major*, Royal Artillery		28 Jan. 75	31 Dec. 83	7 Nov. 91	
Victor Alexander Farquharson, *Major*, Royal Scots		29 May 72	18 June 81	15 Nov. 91	
p.s.c. George Dudley Carleton, *Major*, Leicester Regt. (17 F.)		11 Sept. 76	25 Mar. 84	15 Nov. 91	
Richard Louis Milne, DSO. *Major*, Leicester Regiment		31 Aug. 73	18 Mar. 85	18 Nov. 91	
Lord Edmund Bernard Talbot, *Major*, 11 Hussars		20 Nov. 73	14 Sept. 81	19 Nov. 91	
p.s.c. Joseph Howard Poett, *Major*, Dorsetshire Regt. (39 F.)		11 Sept. 76	18 July 84	19 Nov. 91	
Reginald Pemberton Leach, *Major*, Royal Artillery		28 Jan. 75	1 Jan. 84	21 Nov. 91	
Algernon Campbell Foley, *Major*, Royal Engineers		2 May 73	2 May 84	23 Nov. 91	
Henry Charles Barton Gray, *Major*, Welsh Regiment		30 Dec. 71	30 Aug. 81	25 Nov. 91	
George T. F. Downman, *Major*, Gordon Highlanders		29 Nov. 76	28 Nov. 83	25 Nov. 91	
George F. C. Mackenzie, *Major*, Suffolk Regiment		12 Feb. 76	14 July 83	30 Nov. 91	
Octavius Rowe, *Major*, Royal Artillery		28 Jan. 75	1 Jan. 84	30 Nov. 91	
p.s.c. Wm. W. Cole Verner, *Major*, Rifle Brigade		12 Nov. 73	13 Apr. 81	2 Dec. 91	
Charles Henry Darling, *Major*, Royal Engineers		12 Sept. 72	12 Sept. 84	6 Dec. 91	
Charles Mackenzie Edwards, *Major*, Berkshire Regiment	22 Jan. 79	14 Nov. 79	28 June 84	7 Dec. 91	
Charles Coningham, *Major*, Worcestershire Regiment		23 Mar. 72	1 Feb. 82	9 Dec. 91	
Charles Gilbert Colvin Money, *Major*, Northumberland Fus.		29 May 72	1 Sept. 82	9 Dec. 91	
Wm. James Holmes Frodsham, *Major*, E. Surrey Regt.		28 Feb. 74	30 Sept. 82	14 Dec. 91	
William John Butterworth Bird, *Major*, Indian Staff Corps		15 Dec. 71	15 Dec. 83	15 Dec. 91	
Frank S. Whittington Raikes, *Major*, Rifle Brigade		28 Feb. 74	29 June 81	16 Dec. 91	
Reginald Evelyn Boothby, *Major*, Royal Artillery		28 Jan. 75	1 Jan. 84	21 Dec. 91	
Richard Woodroofe Graham, *Major*, Middlesex Regiment		21 Jan. 74	1 July 81	23 Dec. 91	
Edward Morris Poynton, *Major*, Somerset Light Infantry		12 Nov. 73	23 May 83	23 Dec. 91	
Chas. Theodore Becker, *Major*, King's Own Scottish Brdrs.		9 Aug. 73	1 July 81	30 Dec. 91	
John Francis Wegg-Prosser, *Major*, Rifle Brigade		9 Aug. 74	15 Aug. 81	30 Dec. 91	
Alex. Wm. Dennistown Campbell, *Major*, Indian S.C.		30 Dec. 71	30 Dec. 83	30 Dec. 91	
Charles Stuart Wheler, *Major*, Indian Staff Corps		30 Dec. 71	30 Dec. 83	30 Dec. 91	
Allan Smith, *Major*, Indian Staff Corps		30 Dec. 71	30 Dec. 83	30 Dec. 91	
William Grenville Mansel, *Major*, Indian Staff Corps		30 Dec. 71	30 Dec. 83	30 Dec. 91	
Maurice Crosby Cooke-Collis, *Major*, Indian Staff Corps		30 Dec. 71	30 Dec. 83	30 Dec. 91	
William Selwood Hewett, *Major*, Indian Staff Corps		30 Dec. 71	30 Dec. 83	30 Dec. 91	
Francis George Lawrence Mainwaring, *Major*, Indian S.C.		30 Dec. 71	30 Dec. 83	30 Dec. 91	
Alexander Bowes Mein, *Major*, Indian Staff Corps		30 Dec. 71	30 Dec. 83	30 Dec. 91	
Mossom Innis Gibbs, *Major*, Indian Staff Corps		30 Dec. 71	30 Dec. 83	30 Dec. 91	
Charles Mordaunt FitzGerald, *Major*, Indian Staff Corps		30 Dec. 71	30 Dec. 83	30 Dec. 91	
Arthur Cautley Bunny, *Major*, Indian Staff Corps		30 Dec. 71	30 Dec. 83	30 Dec. 91	
John Jervois, *Major*, Royal Engineers		12 Sept. 72	12 Sept. 84	31 Dec. 91	
Herbert Edward Rawson, *Major*, Royal Engineers		12 Sept. 72	12 Sept. 84	31 Dec. 91	
William Jacob Mackenzie, *Major*, Royal Engineers		12 Sept. 72	12 Sept. 84	31 Dec. 91	
Henry Speed Andrews-Speed, *Major*, Royal Engineers		12 Sept. 72	12 Sept. 84	31 Dec. 91	
William Henry Darby, *Major*, Royal Artillery		28 Jan. 75	1 Jan. 84	1 Jan. 92	
John George Adamson, *Major*, Yorkshire Light Infantry		6 Sept. 76	8 Dec. 82	10 Jan. 92	
Charles Hamilton Des Vœux, *Major*, Indian Staff Corps		10 Jan. 72	10 Jan. 84	10 Jan. 92	
Samuel Keith Harries, *Major*, Devonshire Regiment		26 June 74	18 Nov. 82	18 Jan. 92	
John Charles Tyler, *Major*, Royal Engineers		12 Sept. 72	12 Sept 84	18 Jan. 92	
David Fitzgerald Downing, *Major*, Royal Artillery		28 Jan. 75	16 Nov. 83	27 Jan. 92	
Walter Fullarton Ludovic Lindsay, *Major*, Royal Artillery		28 Jan. 75	1 Jan. 84	27 Jan. 92	
Stephen Frewen, *Major*, 16 Lancers	24 July 78	9 Jan. 80	5 May 86	27 Jan. 92	
Edward Grant Wilkinson, *Major*, Royal Marines		1 July 74	19 July 84	1 Feb. 92	
Arthur Gorham Howard Hayne, *Major*, Indian Staff Corps		3 Feb. 72	3 Feb. 84	3 Feb. 92	
George Thorpe Onslow, *Major*, Royal Marines		1 Jan. 76	22 Sept. 84	3 Feb. 92	
Richard Bannatine-Allason, *Major*, Royal Artillery		28 Jan. 75	1 Jan. 84	6 Feb. 92	
p.s.c. Henry Cleland Dunlop, *Major*, Royal Artillery		28 Jan. 75	1 Jan. 84	6 Feb. 92	
Capel George Adye, *Major*, West Yorkshire Regiment		20 Nov. 75	6 Nov. 81	10 Feb. 92	
James Owen Hodgson, *Major*, Royal Artillery		28 Jan. 75	1 Jan. 84	15 Feb. 92	
Frank Robert Lowth, *Major*, Lincolnshire Regiment	30 Nov. 70	28 Oct. 71	11 Mar. 81	17 Feb. 92	
Robert John Maude, *Major*, Rifle Brigade		2 Dec. 74	9 Apr. 82	17 Feb. 92	
Robert Fulton, *Major*, Indian Staff Corps		17 Feb. 72	17 Feb. 84	17 Feb. 92	
p.s.c. Edmund Roger Allday Kerrison, *Major*, R. Artillery		28 Jan. 75	1 Jan. 84	19 Feb. 92	
Richard L. A. Pennington, *Major*, Northumberland Fusiliers		11 Sept. 76	9 Sept. 82	22 Feb. 92	
p.s.c. Ernest Walter Yeatherd, *Major*, Lancaster Regiment		13 Nov. 72	7 Oct. 81	24 Feb. 92	
Nevill Francis Augustus Maunsell, *Major*, Warwick Regt.		20 Nov. 72	1 July 81	24 Feb. 92	
Arthur Bor, *Major*, West India Regiment		18 Dec. 75	16 Jan. 85	24 Feb. 92	
Home Johnstone Fergusson, *Major*, Scottish Rifles		12 Nov. 73	1 July 81	2 Mar. 92	
Francis Charles Annesley, *Major*, Royal Fusiliers		27 June 75	24 Mar. 82	2 Mar. 92	
Ralph Henry Fenwick Lombe, *Major*, Norfolk Regiment		11 Sept. 72	21 July 82	2 Mar. 92	
Cecil William Park, *Major*, Devonshire Regiment		5 June 75	9 Jan. 83	2 Mar. 92	
Frederick James Gavin, *Major*, Irish Regiment	1 May 78	9 July 79	21 May 84	2 Mar. 92	
Donald MacDougall, *Major*, 7 Dragoon Guards		6 Sept. 76	1 Jan. 85	2 Mar. 92	

Majors.

	CORNET, 2nd LIEUT. or ENSIGN.	LIEUT.	CAPTAIN.	MAJOR.	WHEN PLACED ON HALF PAY.
William Henry Muir Lowe, *Major*, 7 Dragoon Guards..........	......	22 Oct. 82	9 Mar. 87	2 Mar. 92	
Sir Godfrey Vignoles Thomas, *Bart.*, *Major*, Royal Artillery	......	28 Jan. 75	1 Jan. 84	3 Mar. 92	
Arthur Wm. Frank Jackson, *Major*, Warwick Regiment	......	22 May 76	12 Feb. 84	3 Mar. 92	
Courtney Vor Trower, *Major*, South Wales Borderers.........	......	17 May 77	8 Oct. 81	4 Mar. 92	
p.s.c. Fred. Walter Kitchener, *Major*, West York Regiment	......	11 Sept. 76	11 Nov. 82	7 Mar. 92	
Frank Montague Rundall, *DSO*. *Major*, Indian Staff Corps	......	9 Mar. 72	9 Mar. 84	9 Mar. 92	
Chas. Maximilian Thos. Western, *Major*, Royal Artillery ...	......	28 Jan. 75	1 Jan. 84	16 Mar. 92	
George Hamilton Sim, *Major*, Royal Engineers	......	12 Sept.72	12 Sept.84	16 Mar. 92	
James William Dunlop, *Major*, Royal Artillery	......	28 Jan. 75	1 Jan. 84	18 Mar. 92	
Wm. Bannatyne Graham, *Major*, Manchester Regt. (96 F.)	......	11 Sept.76	9 July 84	18 Mar. 92	
Thomas Hampden Evans Acton, *Major*, Royal Artillery ...	......	28 Jan. 75	1 Jan. 84	19 Mar. 92	
Robert Lewis Haines, *Major*, Royal Artillery	......	28 Jan. 75	1 Jan. 84	23 Mar. 92	
Hamilton James Elverson, *Major*, West Surrey Regt. (2 F.).	1 Sept.69	28 Oct. 71	1 May 81	25 Mar. 92	
George Blakiston Renny, *Major*, Indian Staff Corps	......	27 Mar. 72	27 Mar. 84	27 Mar. 92	
William Henry Riddell, *Major*, Bedfordshire Regt. (16 F.)...	......	30 Dec. 71	19 June 79	29 Mar. 92	
Edward Stokes Evans, *Major*, Munster Fusiliers (101 F.) ...	......	13 June 74	1 July 81	1 Apr. 92	
Percy Stanley Druitt, *Major*, Munster Fusiliers (101 F.)	......	21 Sept.74	4 May 82	1 Apr. 92	
James Charles Oughterson, *Major*, Army Service Corps......	......	12 Nov. 73	11 Nov. 82	1 Apr. 92	
Gilbert H. Fearon Mathison, *Major*, Yorkshire Regt. (19 F.)	......	10 Mar. 77	14 Nov. 83	1 Apr. 92	
Hugh Palliser Hickman, *Major*, Royal Artillery	......	19 Aug. 75	1 Jan. 84	1 Apr. 92	
John Charles Campbell, *Major*, Royal Engineers	......	9 Jan. 73	8 Jan. 85	1 Apr. 92	
Sir Robt. Aug. Wm. Colleton, *Bart.*, *Major*, Welsh Fusiliers	......	2 Dec. 74	20 Mar. 85	2 Apr. 92	
Frederick Thomas Clayton, *Major*, Army Service Corps......	......	29 Nov. 76	4 June 84	3 Apr. 92	
Henry Finnis, *Major*, Royal Engineers	......	9 Jan. 73	8 Jan. 85	4 Apr. 92	
Edward Henry Le Marchant, *Major*, Hampshire Regt.(67 F.)	......	28 Feb. 74	9 Sept.83	9 Apr. 92	
Alfred Heyland Parratt Turner, *Major*, Royal Artillery ...	......	19 Aug. 75	9 Jan. 84	10 Apr. 92	
Mervyn Edward Archdale, *Major*, Gloucester Regt. (28 F.).	......	10 Mar. 76	10 May 83	13 Apr. 92	
Arthur Thomas Swaine, *Major*, Irish Rifles (86 F.)	......	17 May 76	19 July 82	18 Apr. 92	
William Keane Richardson, *Major*, Cheshire Regt. (22 F.)...	......	13 June 77	10 Sept.84	21 Apr. 92	
Bedford Morant Allen, *Major*, Indian Staff Corps	......	24 Apr. 72	24 Apr. 84	24 Apr. 92	
Philip Arnold Buckland, *Major*, Indian Staff Corps	......	24 Apr. 72	24 Apr. 84	24 Apr. 92	
Henry Compton Sowell Goldfrap, *Major*, Lincoln Regt. (10 F.)	......	30 Apr. 73	3 May 81	25 Apr. 92	
Colin John Mackenzie, *Captain*, Seaforth Highlanders	22 Jan. 81	1 July 81	25 Oct. 89	27 Apr. 92	
Robert Henry Twigg, *Captain*, Indian Staff Corps.............	13 Aug. 79	26 Dec. 80	13 Aug. 90	27 Apr. 92	
Ernest Cooke, *Major*, Scottish Rifles (26 F.)....................	......	15 July 76	24 Jan. 83	29 Apr. 92	
Walter Stanbury Churchward, *Major*, Royal Artillery......	......	19 Aug. 75	9 Jan. 84	30 Apr. 92	
James Archibald Ferrier, *DSO*. *Major*, Royal Engineers ...	......	9 Jan. 73	8 Jan. 85	3 May 92	
Edward Cyril Mills, *Major*, West Yorkshire Regt. (14 F.) ...	......	29 Oct. 76	11 Nov. 82	6 May 92	
Wm. Caldwell Faure Field, *Major*, Indian Staff Corps	......	8 May 72	8 May 84	8 May 92	
Charles Withers Ravenshaw, *Major*, Indian Staff Corps......	......	8 May 72	8 May 84	8 May 92	
John R. H. Richards, *Major*, W. Surrey Regt. (2 F.).........	17 Nov. 69	28 Oct. 71	1 July 81	11 May 92	
p.s.c. Horace L. Smith-Dorrien, *DSO*. *Major*, Derbyshire Regiment (95 F.)	......	26 Feb. 76	22 Aug. 82	11 May 92	
Knightley Stalker Dunsterville, *Major*, Royal Artillery	......	19 Aug. 75	9 Jan. 84	12 May 92	
Arthur Tracey, *Major*, Royal Artillery	......	19 Aug. 75	16 Jan. 84	12 May 92	
p.s.c. William Apsley Smith, *Major*, Royal Artillery.........	......	19 Aug. 75	13 Mar. 84	13 May 92	
Henry Octavius Piers, *Major*, Royal Artillery	......	19 Aug. 75	31 May 84	13 May 92	
Edmund Richard Scott, *Major*, Leicester Regiment (17 F.)..	......	5 June 75	26 Mar. 84	18 May 92	
Reginald P. Macdonald, *DSO*. *Major*, Hampshire Regt. (37 F.)	30 Jan. 78	28 Mar. 78	15 Apr. 84	19 May 92	
Arthur Charles Greaves Banning, *Major*, Liverpool Regt. ...	......	10 Sept.76	15 Apr. 82	20 May 92	
Spencer Godfrey Bird, *Major*, Dublin Fusiliers	......	28 Feb. 74	12 Mar. 81	21 May 92	
Francis Smith, *Major*, The Buffs	......	2 Dec. 74	29 Sept.80	23 May 92	
John Warre Malet, *Major*, Northumberland Fusiliers (5 F.).	......	29 Nov. 76	11 Oct. 82	23 May 92	
p.s.c. *Hon.* North de Coigny Dalrymple, *Major*, Scots Guards	......	28 Oct. 71	15 Aug. 83	23 May 92	
George Hastings Bittleston, *Major*, Royal Artillery	......	19 Aug. 75	18 Mar. 84	23 May 92	
William John Hicks, *Major*, Royal Artillery	......	19 Aug. 75	18 Mar. 84	25 May 92	
Cecil Arthur Howard, *Major*, Royal Artillery	......	19 Aug. 75	13 June 84	25 May 92	
John Davidson Fullerton, *Major*, Royal Engineers	......	9 Jan. 73	8 Jan. 85	25 May 92	
Thomas Caldwell Pears, *Major*, Indian Staff Corps	......	29 May 72	29 May 84	29 May 92	
Edmund Augustine Burrows, *Major*, Royal Artillery	......	19 Aug. 75	2 July 84	2 June 92	
Francis Henry Penny, *Major*, Munster Fusiliers	......	2 Dec. 74	26 July 82	3 June 92	
Charles Reginald Hoskyn, *Major*, Royal Engineers............	......	9 Jan. 73	8 Jan. 85	3 June 92	
Henry Cecil Eagles, *Major*, Royal Marines	......	1 July 74	19 Jan. 85	3 June 92	
Henry Martindale Temple, *Major*, Indian Staff Corps	......	8 June 72	8 June 84	8 June 92	
George Champney Palmes, *Major*, South Wales Borderers	......	10 Sept.77	9 June 82	9 June 92	
Robert George Buchanan-Riddell, *Major*, King's R. Rifles...	......	20 Nov. 75	9 Sept.84	10 June 92	
p.s.c. Wallcourt Holy H. Waters, *Major*, Royal Artillery ...	......	19 Aug. 75	30 July 84	22 June 92	
Robert Stephenson S. Baden-Powell, *Major*, 13 Hussars......	......	11 Sept.76	16 May 83	1 July 92	
Edward Barrington Crake, *Major*, Rifle Brigade	......	2 Dec. 74	19 Apr. 82	2 July 92	
Thomas Robert Swinburne, *Major*, Royal Marine Artillery	......	15 July 72	26 Jan. 84	2 July 92	
p.s.c. Francis Seymour Inglefield, *Major*, E. Yorkshire Regt.	......	13 June 74	30 June 84	2 July 92	
Murray Venables Hilton, *Major*, Worcestershire Regiment	30 Jan. 78	31 Aug. 78	20 Nov. 85	6 July 92	
Hugh Wodehouse Pearse, *Major*, East Surrey Regiment ...	......	11 Feb. 75	30 June 83	12 July 92	
Edgar Charles Spilsbury, *Major*, Royal Engineers	......	9 Jan. 73	8 Jan. 85	12 July 92	
Hugh James Archdale, *Major*, Welsh Fusiliers	......	11 Feb. 75	20 Mar. 85	13 July 92	
Harry John Bolton, *Major*, Indian Staff Corps	......	17 July 72	17 July 84	17 July 92	
p.s.c. Albert Farrar Gatliff, *Major*, Royal Marines............	......	27 Jan. 76	23 Mar. 85	18 July 92	
Philip Bell Baldwin, *Major*, Royal Engineers	......	9 Jan. 73	8 Jan. 85	19 July 92	
Arthur Dolben Bulpett, *Major*, Derbyshire Regiment	......	20 Nov. 75	19 Jan. 83	21 July 92	
Charles Dormer Cottrell, *Major*, Royal Artillery...............	......	19 Aug. 75	30 July 84	21 July 92	
Fra. A. O. Claughton, *Major*, King's Own Scottish Borderers	......	28 Feb. 74	31 Oct. 83	27 July 92	
p.s.c. Charles Molyneux Hutton, *Major*, Lancashire Fusiliers	......	9 Aug. 75	15 Nov. 83	27 July 92	
Philip Francis Durham, *Major*, 10 Hussars	......	20 Nov. 75	18 Feb. 84	27 July 92	
Alfred Henry Carter, *Major*, Royal Artillery	......	19 Aug. 75	1 Aug. 84	27 July 92	
Edgar Alan Lambart, *Major*, Royal Artillery	......	19 Aug. 75	14 Aug. 84	27 July 92	
p.s.c. Gerard Charles Kitson, *Major*, King's Royal Rifles ...	......	11 Feb. 75	1 Jan. 85	27 July 92	
George Turner Jones, *Major*, Royal Engineers	......	9 Jan. 73	8 Jan. 85	27 July 92	
Edward John Bentley Buckle, *Major*, Yorkshire Regiment	8 Dec. 77	8 Dec. 77	1 Aug. 84	28 July 92	
p.s.c. John Francis Burn-Murdoch, *Major*, 1 Dragoons	4 Dec. 78	2 Feb. 80	28 Jan. 85	3 Aug. 92	
Alexander Gordon Duff, *Major*, Black Watch	......	28 Apr. 75	4 Dec. 85	3 Aug. 92	
Frederick Edward Verney Taylor, *Major*, Derbyshire Regt.	......	17 May 77	22 July 83	4 Aug. 92	
Herbert Edwards Irwin, *Major*, Warwickshire Regiment ...	......	19 Jan. 76	4 June 84	6 Aug. 92	
William Daniel Conner, *Major*, Royal Engineers	......	9 Jan. 73	8 Jan. 85	6 Aug. 92	

Majors.

	CORNET, 2nd LIEUT. or ENSIGN.	LIEUT.	CAPTAIN.	MAJOR.	WHEN PLACED ON HALF PAY.
Arthur James Ramsay Van Cortlandt, *Major*, 3 Hussars ...	28 Oct. 71	28 Oct. 71	15 Oct. 81	10 Aug. 92	
Richard Martin Crofton, *Major*, Royal Artillery............	......	19 Aug. 75	17 Aug. 84	10 Aug. 92	
Francis Lloyd, *Major*, Grenadier Guards	......	18 Mar. 75	1 Apr. 85	10 Aug. 92	
John Willoughby Astley Marshall, *Major*, Irish Fusiliers ...	......	30 Nov. 77	5 Oct. 87	10 Aug. 92	
Percy John Tonson Lewis, *Captain*, Army Service Corps ...	......	23 Feb. 81	1 Apr. 89	10 Aug. 92	
Edward Roderic Owen, *DSO. Captain*, Lancashire Fusiliers	......	11 Sept. 76	4 Aug. 84	16 Aug. 92	
p.s.c. Hon. Arthur Stewart Hardinge, *Captain*, Scots Fus....	1 May 78	11 Sept.80	25 Aug. 86	16 Aug. 92	
James Selby Robson Scott, *Major*, 3 Hussars	21 Apr. 77	4 Dec. 79	18 July 85	17 Aug. 92	
James Farish Malcolm Fawcett, *Major*, 5 Lancers	1 May 73	30 June 81	9 June 84	19 Aug. 92	
Waldemar Delmar Lindley, *Major*, Royal Engineers	......	9 Jan. 73	8 Jan. 85	27 Aug. 92	
Alfred Clemons Maxwell Gompertz,[12] *Major*, h.p. Hampshire Regiment	30 Jan. 78	6 Sept.78	22 Sept.84	29 Aug. 92	22 Apr. 94
Charles Hubert Blount, *Major*, Royal Artillery	......	19 Aug. 75	20 Aug. 84	2 Sept.92	
p.s.c. Charles Herbert Farquharson, *Major*, 3 Dragoon Gds.	......	27 Jan. 83	12 Feb. 87	5 Sept. 92	
p.s.c. Benjamin Reddie Hawes, *Major*, Munster Fus. (104 F.)	......	20 Nov. 75	1 Apr. 85	6 Sept.92	
Edward Andrée Wylde, *Major*, Royal Marines	......	27 Jan. 76	13 Apr. 85	8 Sept.92	
William Walter Lean, *Major*, Indian Staff Corps	......	11 Sept.72	11 Sept.84	11 Sept.92	
George Alfred Money, *Major*, Indian Staff Corps	......	11 Sept.72	11 Sept.84	11 Sept.92	
Arthur Wildman Prior, *Major*, N. Staffordshire Regiment	......	13 June 75	14 Jan. 84	14 Sept. 92	
Alexander Houghton Abercrombie, *Major*, Scots Fusiliers	......	26 July 76	21 Sept.83	15 Sept. 92	
Gerald Lionel J. Goff, *Major*, Argyll and Sutherland Hldrs...	......	10 Mar. 75	1 July 84	21 Sept.92	
Arthur Edmund Horniblow, *Major*, Royal Marines	......	27 Jan. 76	17 May 85	28 Sept. 92	
Robert Thomas Hanford-Flood, *Major*, West Surrey Regt.	7 Dec. 70	28 Oct. 71	15 Apr. 82	29 Sept. 92	
George Newton Halifax Barlow, *Major*, Royal Artillery	......	19 Aug. 75	25 Aug. 84	1 Oct. 92	
Frederick Baumgardt Elmslie, *Major*, Royal Artillery	......	19 Aug. 73	27 Aug. 84	1 Oct. 92	
p.s.c. Norman Bruce Inglefield, *Major*, Royal Artillery	......	19 Aug. 75	27 Aug. 84	1 Oct. 92	
p.s.c. Henry Stopford Dawkins, *Major*, Royal Artillery	......	19 Aug. 75	1 Sept. 84	1 Oct. 92	
p.s.c. Edward Hugh Bethell, *Major*, Royal Engineers	......	9 Jan. 73	8 Jan. 85	1 Oct. 92	
Frederick William Town Attree, *Major*, Royal Engineers...	......	9 Jan. 73	8 Jan. 85	1 Oct. 92	
Alexander Lechmere Mein, *Major*, Royal Engineers	......	29 Apr. 73	8 Jan. 85	1 Oct. 92	
Philip Francis Tallents, *Major*, Lancashire Fusiliers	......	26 Feb. 75	15 Oct. 81	5 Oct. 92	
George Borlase Stevens, *Captain*, Indian Staff Corps	......	19 Sept. 77	19 Sept. 88	5 Oct. 92	
Percy Temple Rivett-Carnac, *Major*, W. Riding Regt. (76 F.)	......	3 July 73	19 Dec. 83	6 Oct. 92	
p.s.c. Samuel A. Einem Hickson, *DSO. Major*, Royal Eng.	......	29 Apr. 73	8 Jan. 85	7 Oct. 92	
Frederick Williams Becher, *Major*, Bedford Regiment	......	21 Sept.72	10 Oct. 79	10 Oct. 92	
William Augustus Scott, *Major*, Gordon Highlanders........	......	21 Sept.74	1 Dec. 83	10 Oct. 92	
John James Purdon, *Major*, Inniskilling Fusiliers	......	11 Nov. 76	26 July 84	12 Oct. 92	
Henry Capel Lofft Holden, *Major*, Royal Artillery	......	19 Aug. 75	1 Oct. 84	12 Oct. 92	
*Alexander Mattei, *Major*, Royal Malta Artillery...............	......	30 Nov. 70	15 Nov. 84	12 Oct. 92	
Nigel Maxwell, *Major*, Royal Artillery	......	19 Aug. 75	1 Oct. 84	15 Oct. 92	
Sydney Philip Strong, *Major*, Scottish Rifles.................	30 Jan. 78	7 Aug. 78	11 Sept. 83	16 Oct. 92	
David Edward Wood, *Major*, 8 Hussars	......	28 Feb. 75	3 Oct. 83	19 Oct. 92	
Ivar MacIvor, *CIE. Major*, Indian Staff Corps	......	19 Oct. 72	19 Oct. 84	19 Oct. 92	
Walter F. C. Chichele Plowden, *Major*, Indian Staff Corps..	......	19 Oct. 72	19 Oct. 84	19 Oct. 92	
Roderick William MacLeod, *Major*, Indian Staff Corps......	......	19 Oct. 72	19 Oct. 84	19 Oct. 92	
Lawrence Jamieson Torrie, *Major*, Indian Staff Corps	......	19 Oct. 72	19 Oct. 84	19 Oct. 92	
Gerald Charles Penrice Onslow, *Major*, Royal Engineers...	......	29 Apr. 73	8 Jan. 85	21 Oct. 92	
Hon. Henry Arthur Ormsby Gore, *Major*, 11 Hussars......	......	11 Nov. 76	25 July 83	24 Oct. 92	
O'Donnel Colley Grattan, *Major*, Liverpool Regiment	......	10 Mar. 77	20 Sept.82	26 Oct. 92	
John Charles Farrell, *Major*, Sussex Regiment	......	6 Sept. 76	10 Nov. 83	26 Oct. 92	
Herbert Swayne FitzGerald, *Major*, Durham Light Infantry	......	11 Feb. 75	5 July 82	31 Oct. 92	
Raymond Charles Foster, *Major*, Royal Artillery............	......	2 Feb. 76	2 Oct. 84	1 Nov. 92	
Cholmeley E.C.Branfill Harrison, *Major*, W.Kent Regt.(97 F.)	......	11 Sept. 76	4 Sept.84	2 Nov. 92	
Peter Robert Bairnsfather, *Major*, Indian Staff Corps	......	2 Nov. 72	2 Nov. 84	2 Nov. 92	
William Francis Howard Stafford, *Major*, R. Engineers ...	......	29 Apr. 73	8 Jan. 85	5 Nov. 92	
Richard Owen, *Major*, 21 Hussars	......	12 Nov. 73	13 June 83	6 Nov. 92	
Arthur Graves Spratt, *Major*, Devonshire Regiment	......	23 May 75	20 Mar. 82	9 Nov. 92	
p.s.c. Francis Spencer Thornton, *Major*, Rifle Brigade	......	13 June 75	1 June 82	9 Nov. 92	
p.s.c. John Lindesay Keir, *Major*, Royal Artillery	......	2 Feb. 76	2 Oct. 84	9 Nov. 92	
Francis Algernon Curteis, *Major*, Royal Artillery	......	2 Feb. 76	4 Oct. 84	9 Nov. 92	
Goodson Adye, *Major*, Indian Staff Corps	......	13 Nov. 72	13 Nov. 84	13 Nov. 92	
Henry Richard Marrett, *Major*, Indian Staff Corps	......	13 Nov. 72	13 Nov. 84	13 Nov. 92	
Redmond Conyngham S. Macausland, *Major*, Indian S. C.	......	13 Nov. 72	13 Nov. 84	13 Nov. 92	
John Monteith, *Major*, Indian Staff Corps	......	13 Nov. 72	13 Nov. 84	13 Nov. 92	
Edmund Augustus Waller, *Major*, Royal Engineers	......	29 Apr. 73	8 Jan. 85	13 Nov. 92	
Acheson Whitmore St. George, *Major*, W. Yorkshire Regt.	23 Jan. 78	28 June 78	28 Feb. 83	16 Nov. 92	
James Bruce Darling, *Major*, Royal Marines...................	......	27 Jan. 76	17 May 85	18 Nov. 92	
Percy Owen Lang, *Major*, Royal Marines	......	27 Jan. 76	4 June 85	20 Nov. 92	
Thomas Alexander Hill, *Major*, 12 Lancers.....................	......	26 Mar. 75	30 Nov. 81	23 Nov. 92	
Richard Eyre Goold-Adams, *Major*, Highland Light Inf. ...	......	13 June 74	11 Dec. 82	23 Nov. 92	
Henry Montague Pakington Hawkes, *Major*, Indian S. C.	......	23 Nov. 72	23 Nov. 84	23 Nov. 92	
Arthur Herbert Kenney, *CMG. Major*, Royal Engineers ...	......	29 Apr. 73	8 Jan. 85	23 Nov. 92	
William de Bathe Hatton, *Major*, Seaforth Highlanders ...	......	28 Apr. 77	27 Mar. 85	23 Nov. 92	
Arthur Patrick Douglas Lushington, *Major*, 3 Dragoon Gds.	11 Aug. 80	1 July 81	7 May 87	24 Nov. 92	
Acheson F. Acheson Lyle, *Major*, Shropshire Lt.Inf. (85 F.)	......	11 Feb. 75	11 May 84	30 Nov. 92	
Winton Seton, *Major*, Leinster Regiment (100 F.)	......	11 Feb. 75	1 Jan. 83	1 Dec. 92	
Robert Alexander Wahab, *Major*, Royal Engineers	......	29 Apr. 73	8 Jan. 85	1 Dec. 92	
Cuthbert Pilkington Dawson, *Major*, 2 Dragoon Guards ...	10 Apr. 78	13 July 78	12 June 85	9 Dec. 92	
Robert Howden Kellie, *Major*, S. Lancashire Regt. (82 F.)	......	30 Dec. 71	29 Oct. 81	11 Dec. 92	
Aubrey Francis White, *Major*, Welsh Regiment (69 F.)	......	13 June 74	25 Jan. 82	12 Dec. 92	
Francis John Paul Butler, *Major*, h.p. 18 Hussars	......	6 Oct. 77	13 Feb. 84	14 Dec. 92	20 June 94
William Augustus Edm. St. Clair, *Major*, Royal Engineers	......	29 Apr. 73	8 Jan. 85	19 Dec. 92	
Richard Charles Graham Mayne, *Major*, Indian Staff Corps	......	21 Dec. 72	21 Dec. 84	21 Dec. 92	
Arthur Gillespie Churchill, *Major*, 12 Lancers	11 Aug. 80	1 July 81	1 May 86	21 Dec. 92	
Arthur Templeman Morse, *Major*, West Kent Regiment ...	......	28 Apr. 77	9 Sept.84	23 Dec. 92	
William Vieris Dickinson, *Major*, Welsh Regiment	......	12 Feb. 76	1 Jan. 83	28 Dec. 92	
Lawrence Charles Dundas, *DSO. Major*, Liverpool Regt. ...	30 Jan. 78	30 Jan. 80	16 Jan. 84	28 Dec. 92	
Alexander Pringle, *Major*, Indian Staff Corps	......	30 Dec. 72	30 Dec. 84	30 Dec. 92	
Edward James Fandon Wood, *Major*, Indian Staff Corps...	......	1 Jan. 73	1 Jan. 85	1 Jan. 93	
Hubert James M'Laughlin, *Major*, 5 Lancers	11 Aug. 80	1 July 81	30 May 88	1 Jan. 93	
Harold Gore-Browne, *Major*, King's Royal Rifles............	......	11 Feb. 76	19 May 83	4 Jan. 93	
Arden Lowndes Bayley, *Major*, West India Regiment	11 Aug. 80	1 July 81	8 Sept. 86	4 Jan. 93	
Beresford Robert Hamilton, *Major*, Lincoln Regiment	......	12 Nov. 73	18 June 81	8 Jan. 93	
Hastings Read, *Major*, Indian Staff Corps	......	15 Jan. 73	8 Jan. 85	8 Jan. 93	

Majors.

	CORNET 2nd LIEUT. OR ENSIGN.	LIEUT.	CAPTAIN.	MAJOR.	WHEN PLACED ON HALF PAY.
Charles James Robarts, *Major*, Indian Staff Corps	......	12 Feb. 73	8 Jan. 85	8 Jan. 93	
Wm. Arthur D'Oyly O'Mealy, *Major*, Indian Staff Corps ...	......	12 Feb. 73	8 Jan. 85	8 Jan. 93	
Edward Hogarth Molesworth, *Major*, Indian Staff Corps...	......	24 Feb. 73	8 Jan. 85	8 Jan. 93	
Robt. Ramsay Napier Sturt, *Major*, Indian Staff Corps	......	9 Mar. 73	8 Jan. 85	8 Jan. 93	
George Alfred Tower, *Major*, Royal Engineers	......	29 Apr. 73	8 Jan. 85	8 Jan. 93	
Frederick John Tobin, *Major*, Irish Rifles (86 Foot)	......	12 May 77	1 Apr. 83	10 Jan. 93	
Cuthbert Dunn, *Major*, West India Regiment...................	18 May 81	1 July 81	26 Oct. 87	17 Jan. 93	
Egerton Fayler Morgan-Payler, *Major*, Royal Scots	......	12 Nov. 73	14 Aug. 81	18 Jan. 93	
Joseph Oxley English, *Major*, Royal Artillery	......	2 Feb. 76	18 Oct. 84	19 Jan. 93	
p.s.c. Fred. John Arthur Trench, *Major*, Royal Artillery	......	2 Feb. 76	4 Nov. 84	19 Jan. 93	
p.s.c. Herbert C. O. Plumer, *Major*, York and Lancaster Regt.	......	11 Sept. 76	29 May 82	22 Jan. 93	
William Alexander Campbell, *Major*, Warwick Regt..........	......	9 Aug. 73	30 July 84	25 Jan. 93	
Windham Henry Wyndham-Quin, *Major*, 16 Lancers..........	7 Aug. 78	20 Feb. 80	23 June 86	27 Jan. 93	
Charles Alexander Anderson, *Major*, Royal Artillery	......	2 Feb. 76	7 Nov. 84	29 Jan. 93	
p.s.c. Wm. Aldworth, *DSO. Major*, Bedfordshire Regt. (16 F.)	......	13 June 74	30 Mar. 81	1 Feb. 93	
Henry George Daniel, *Major*, Inniskilling Fusiliers (27 F.) ...	5 Sept. 77	21 Mar. 78	4 Oct. 84	1 Feb. 93	
Duncan Campbell Carter, *Major*, Royal Artillery...............	......	2 Feb. 76	7 Nov. 84	1 Feb. 93	
p.s.c. Herbert Eversley Belfield, *Major*, Munster Fusiliers...	......	26 Feb. 76	20 May 85	1 Feb. 93	
Edmund Kendal Grimstone Aylmer, *Major*, 19 Hussars ...	11 Aug. 80	1 July 81	7 Nov. 83	7 Feb. 93	
Maurice George Moore, *Major*, Connaught Rangers	......	13 June 74	1 Nov. 82	8 Feb. 93	
Alexander Wm. Day Maclean, *Major*, Connaught Rangers	30 Jan. 78	20 Aug. 79	15 Aug. 85	8 Feb. 93	
Algernon William Collings, *Major*, Scots Fusiliers (21 F.)...	......	20 Nov. 75	1 Mar. 84	10 Feb. 93	
Thomas Fras. Arch. Kennedy, *Major*, Cameron Highldrs.	......	27 Jan. 75	20 Jan. 86	22 Feb. 93	
Thomas James Atherton, *Major*, 12 Lancers	11 Aug. 80	1 July 81	2 Feb. 87	22 Feb. 93	
Frank James Carandini, *Major*, 5 Lancers	23 Jan. 78	1 July 81	1 Apr. 84	1 Mar. 93	
William Richard Goold-Adams, *Major*, Army Pay Dept. ..	1 May 78	30 Nov. 80	11 June 84	1 Mar. 93	
Walter Adye, *Major*, Irish Rifles............................	30 Jan. 78	19 Oct. 78	14 Nov. 84	2 Mar. 93	
Henry Weston Helyar, *Major*, Warwickshire Regiment ...	30 Jan. 78	17 May 79	20 Sept. 84	3 Mar. 93	
Leonard Barrett, *Major*, Royal Artillery	......	2 Feb. 76	19 Nov. 84	4 Mar. 93	
Wilford Neville LLoyd, *Major*, Royal Artillery	......	2 Feb. 76	19 Nov. 84	16 Mar. 93	
Reginald Hawkins Hall, *Major*, South Lanc. Regt. (40 F.)	......	12 Nov. 73	15 July 83	27 Mar. 93	
Charles George Donaldson, *Major*, Border Regiment	......	15 July 77	15 May 84	28 Mar. 93	
James Ahmuty Fearon, *Major*, Yorkshire Regiment	23 Jan. 78	23 Jan. 78	10 Aug. 84	29 Mar. 93	
George Pensam Bourcicault, *Major*, Army Service Corps	......	10 Sept. 76	15 Apr. 84	1 Apr. 93	
Cecil Vernon Wingfield-Stratford, *Major*, Royal Engineers	......	29 Apr. 73	8 Jan. 85	1 Apr. 93	
William Arthur Ince Anderton, *Major*, Grenadier Guards	......	21 Jan. 75	18 Apr. 85	1 Apr. 93	
Frank Maxwell, *Major*, Highland Light Infantry	......	21 Sept. 74	5 Feb. 83	3 Apr. 93	
Cedric Maxwell, *Major*, Royal Engineers.....................	......	29 Apr. 73	8 Jan. 85	4 Apr. 93	
John Hamilton Verschoyle, *Major*, Duke of Cornwall's Light Infantry (32 F.)	......	13 June 75	29 Dec. 83	5 Apr. 93	
William Pitcairn Campbell, *Major*, King's Royal Rifles ...	......	10 Mar. 76	18 Apr. 85	5 Apr. 93	
William Weallens, *Major*, South Wales Borderers	11 May 78	23 Jan. 79	30 Sept. 82	8 Apr. 93	
John Davidson, *Major*, North Lancashire Regt. (47 F.)......	......	28 Feb. 74	1 Oct. 81	11 Apr. 93	
James Christopher Reynolds, *Major*, Welsh Regiment	......	6 Sept. 76	2 June 83	14 Apr. 93	
Walter Coles, *Major*, Royal Engineers	......	29 Apr. 73	8 Jan. 85	19 Apr. 93	
George Frend, *Major*, Northumberland Fusiliers (5 F.) ...	......	29 Nov. 76	14 July 83	22 Apr. 93	
Henry Cuthbert Denny, *Major*, Northampton Regt. (48 F.)	31 Oct. 77	29 Oct. 79	20 Oct. 83	22 Apr. 93	
Henry Beaufoy Thornhill, *Major*, Indian Staff Corps.........	......	23 Apr. 73	8 Jan. 85	23 Apr. 93	
William James Mackeson, *Major*, 5 Dragoon Guards	......	10 Sept. 77	2 May 83	25 Apr. 93	
Otway Mayne, *Major*, Norfolk Regiment	......	28 Feb. 76	30 Dec. 82	1 May 93	
James Walter Grant, *Major*, Royal Marine Artillery	......	15 July 72	15 July 84	2 May 93	
Lovick Bransby Friend, *Major*, Royal Engineers...............	......	11 Sept. 73	8 Jan. 85	3 May 93	
Hon. Richard Thompson Lawley, *Major*, 7 Hussars	......	11 Feb. 76	21 July 85	5 May 93	
Richard Arthur Milton Henn, *Major*, Royal Artillery	......	19 Aug. 75	1 Oct. 84	6 May 93	
p.s.c. Francis Gleadowe Stone, *Major*, Royal Artillery.........	......	2 Feb. 76	20 Nov. 84	6 May 93	
Arthur Ralph Pemberton, *Major*, Rifle Brigade	......	11 Feb. 76	1 Jan 84	7 May 93	
Edw. Henry Hopton Montresor. *Major*, Indian Staff Corps	......	8 May 73	8 Jan. 85	8 May 93	
Sydney Bellingham Jameson, *Major*, Seaforth Highldrs....	3 Oct. 77	13 Nov. 78	18 Jan. 88	8 May 93	
Wm. Henry Morris Bent, *Major*, South Stafford Regt. (38 F.)	......	28 Feb. 75	3 Mar. 83	10 May 93	
Robert Charles Pentland, *Major*, Dublin Fusiliers	......	21 Aug. 72	6 July 82	17 May 93	
Charles Theo. Evelyn Metcalfe. *Major*, Rifle Brigade.........	......	21 Sept. 74	1 Jan. 84	17 May 93	
Gerald Edward Shute, *Major*, Royal Engineers	......	11 Sept. 73	8 Jan. 85	22 May 93	
Percy Hugh Hamon Massy, *Major*, 6 Dragoon Guards	......	11 Feb. 75	19 July 82	24 May 93	
Charles King Colhoun, *Major*, York & Lancaster Regt.......	......	12 Feb. 77	14 Mar. 84	24 May 93	
Harold Carmichael Wylly, *Major*, Derbyshire Regiment ...	......	11 Sept. 78	1 May 84	26 May 93	
Frederick Rainsford-Hannay, *Major*, Royal Engineers	......	11 Sept. 73	8 Jan. 85	26 May 93	
William Hope Young, *Major*, Indian Staff Corps	......	29 May 73	8 Jan. 85	29 May 93	
Henry Wiley, *Major*, Lincolnshire Regiment	......	28 Feb. 74	11 Mar. 82	31 May 93	
p.s.c. Charles Rudyerd Simpson, *Major*, Lincoln Regiment	......	21 Sept. 74	19 July 82	7 June 93	
George Wentworth Forbes, *Major*, 1 Dragoon Guards	24 Aug. 81	......	4 Dec. 86	7 June 93	
Charles Emilius Curll, *Major*, South Wales Borderers	14 Sept. 78	23 Jan. 79	5 Jan. 84	9 June 93	
Oswald James Daniell, *Major*, West Kent Regiment	11 May 78	8 May 80	17 Dec. 84	12 June 93	
p.s.c. John Moore Gawne, *Major*, Lancaster Regiment	......	13 June 75	28 May 84	26 June 93	
Arthur Cairns Daniell, *Major*, Royal Artillery	......	2 Feb. 76	20 Nov. 84	26 June 93	
John Hasluck Campbell, *Major*, Argyll and Sutherland Highlanders (93 F.)	......	10 Sept. 77	8 Oct. 84	27 June 93	
William Henry Hippisley, *Major*, 2 Dragoons	......	22 May 75	1 June 84	28 June 93	
William Hanna, *Major*, Royal Artillery	......	2 Feb. 76	24 Nov. 84	28 June 93	
p.s.c. Herbert de Haga Haig, *Major*, Royal Engineers	......	11 Sept. 73	8 Jan. 85	1 July 93	
Douglas John Kysh, *Major*, Royal Marines	......	24 Nov. 77	15 June 85	1 July 93	
Edward Owen Fisher Hamilton, *Major*, W. Surrey Regt....	......	9 Aug. 73	19 Dec. 83	3 July 93	
Charles Augustus King Hall, *Major*, Munster Fus. (104 F.)	......	20 Nov. 75	26 Sept. 83	8 July 93	
Charles Edward Duff, *Major*, 8 Hussars	11 May 78	1 July 81	19 Sept. 85	8 July 93	
Cooper Penrose, *Major*, Royal Engineers	......	11 Sept. 73	8 Jan. 85	10 July 93	
John George Day, *Major*, Royal Engineers	......	11 Sept. 73	8 Jan. 85	10 July 93	
Frank Broadwood Matthews, *Major*, Lancaster Regiment	......	15 July 78	18 Apr. 85	12 July 93	
Geoffrey Morehead Porter, *Major*, Royal Engineers	......	11 Sept. 73	8 Jan. 85	14 July 93	
George Dalhousie Churchill Raitt, *Major*, R. Marine Art....	......	15 July 72	15 July 84	15 July 93	
William Charles Nicholls, *Captain*, Royal Marine Artillery	......	15 July 72	15 July 84	15 July 93	
Charles William Knox, *Major*, Hampshire Regiment	11 May 78	15 June 79	14 Feb. 85	19 July 93	
Anthony John Abdy, *Major*, Royal Artillery	......	2 Feb. 76	5 Dec. 84	22 July 93	
Alan George Chichester, *Major*, Irish Regiment	4 Dec. 78	1 Jan. 80	3 Dec. 84	23 July 93	
Frederick Power Lawrence White, *Major*, Indian S. C. ...	......	24 July 73	8 Jan. 85	24 July 93	
Henry Streatfeild, *Major*, Grenadier Guards...................	......	26 Aug. 76	29 Apr. 85	29 July 93	

Majors. 66

	CORNET, 2nd LIEUT. or ENSIGN.	LIEUT.	CAPTAIN.	MAJOR.	WHEN PLACED ON HALF PAY.
Wolstan Francis, *Major*, Duke of Cornwall's Lt. Infantry	......	20 Nov. 75	17 Feb. 86	31 July 93	
Henry Joseph Walker Jerome, *Major*, Royal Engineers ...	......	11 Sept.73	8 Jan. 85	1 Aug. 93	
Charles Grant, *Major*, Argyll and Sutherland Highlanders	......	9 Aug. 73	14 Jan. 84	2 Aug. 93	
Robert Francis Gartside-Tipping, *Major*, Indian S. C.	......	3 Aug. 73	8 Jan. 85	3 Aug. 93	
Horace George Proctor Beauchamp, *Major*, 20 Hussars ...	......	11 Oct. 78	15 Oct. 84	9 Aug. 93	
Valens Congreve Tonnochy, *Major*, Indian Staff Corps......	......	9 Aug. 73	8 Jan. 85	9 Aug. 93	
Malcolm John Meade, *Major*, Indian Staff Corps...............	......	9 Aug. 73	8 Jan. 85	9 Aug. 93	
John de Courcy Dashwood Meade, *Major*, Indian S. C.......	......	9 Aug. 73	8 Jan. 85	9 Aug. 93	
Harry Everard Passy, *Major*, Indian Staff Corps	......	9 Aug. 73	8 Jan. 85	9 Aug. 93	
Edward Steuart Masters, *Major*, Indian Staff Corps	......	9 Aug. 73	8 Jan. 85	9 Aug. 93	
Eustace Edward Melville Lawford, *Major*, Indian S. C. ...	......	9 Aug. 73	8 Jan. 85	9 Aug. 93	
Francis William Egerton, *Major*, Indian Staff Corps.........	......	9 Aug. 73	8 Jan. 85	9 Aug. 93	
Edward Montgomerie Nedham, *Major*, Indian Staff Corps	......	9 Aug. 73	8 Jan. 85	9 Aug. 93	
Arthur Mackworth Monteith, *Major*, Indian Staff Corps ...	......	9 Aug. 73	8 Jan. 85	9 Aug. 93	
George Henry Robinson, *Major*, Indian Staff Corps	......	9 Aug. 73	8 Jan. 85	9 Aug. 93	
Arthur Wilbraham Twining Radcliffe, *Major*, Indian S. C	......	9 Aug. 73	8 Jan. 85	9 Aug. 93	
Charles Mervyn Barlow, *Major*, Royal Artillery	......	2 Feb. 76	11 Dec. 84	19 Aug. 93	
Gilbert Henry Claude Hamilton, *Major*, 14 Hussars	......	1 Sept.75	24 July 85	23 Aug. 93	
Charles Wellesley Parish, *Major*, Royal Marines.............	......	27 Jan. 76	21 June 85	29 Aug. 93	
Elmhirst Rhodes, *DSO. Major*, Berkshire Regt. (49 Foot)...	25 May 78	4 Mar. 80	16 Oct. 84	30 Aug. 93	
Lawrence Litchfield Steele, *Major*, East Yorkshire Regt. ...	......	2 Dec. 74	1 Oct. 84	6 Sept.93	
St. John Corbet Gore, *Major*, 5 Dragoon Guards	22 Jan. 79	1 July 81	25 Feb. 85	6 Sept.93	
Alfred G. G. Elton, *Major*, Connaught Rangers...............	5 Sept.77	20 June 79	30 July 85	6 Sept.93	
Alexander MacWhirter Renny, *Major*, Indian Staff Corps ..	......	11 Sept.73	8 Jan. 85	11 Sept.93	
George Kenneth Scott-Moncrieff, *Major*, Royal Engineers	......	11 Sept.73	8 Jan. 85	11 Sept.93	
Edwin Loftus M'Causland, *Major*, Royal Marines	......	1 Sept. 76	8 Aug. 85	11 Sept. 93	
Herbert Cecil Money, *Major*, Royal Marines	......	1 Sept. 76	28 Aug. 85	11 Sept. 93	
Ernest Vernon Bellers, *Major*, Middlesex Regiment	......	21 Sept.74	23 May 84	18 Sept. 93	
Walter Henry Scott, *Major*, East Lancashire Regiment......	......	20 Nov. 75	12 Mar. 84	23 Sept.93	
Forbes Macbean, *Major*, Gordon Highlanders	......	11 Nov. 76	2 July 84	23 Sept.93	
William Henry Forbes Taylor, *Major*, Royal Artillery	......	2 Feb. 76	13 Dec. 84	23 Sept.93	
John Francis Wm. Charley, *Major*, Inniskilling Fusiliers...	30 Jan. 78	1 Nov. 78	13 Jan. 85	23 Sept.93	
George Edward Capel Cure, *Major*, Lancashire Fusiliers...	......	20 Nov. 75	11 May 83	25 Sept.93	
Robert Eccles, *Major*, Oxford Light Infantry	......	28 Feb. 74	26 Mar. 84	27 Sept.93	
James Willcocks, *DSO. Major*, Leinster Regiment	30 Jan. 78	20 Oct. 79	21 Aug. 84	29 Sept.93	
John Francis Craig, *Major*, Royal Artillery	......	2 Feb. 76	10 Jan. 85	30 Sept. 93	
Lewis M. Murray Hall, *Major*, Indian Staff Corps............	......	1 Oct. 73	8 Jan. 85	1 Oct. 93	
John Blaxell Woon, *Major*, Indian Staff Corps	......	1 Oct. 73	8 Jan. 85	1 Oct. 93	
Robt. Fras. Ladeveze Napier, *Major*, Cam. Highldrs. (79 F.)	......	29 Nov. 76	14 July 83	4 Oct. 93	
Johnston Stoney Talbot, *Major*, Shropshire Lt. Infantry ...	......	6 Oct. 75	27 Aug. 84	4 Oct. 93	
p.s.c. William Lewis White, *Major*, Royal Artillery............	......	2 Feb. 76	3 Feb. 85	4 Oct. 93	
William Heremon O'Neill, *Major*, Royal Artillery	......	2 Feb. 76	3 Feb. 85	4 Oct. 93	
Arbuthnott James Hughes, *Major*, Royal Artillery	......	2 Feb. 76	4 Feb. 85	4 Oct. 93	
p.s.c. Wm. Geo. Balfour Western, *Major*, West Kent Regt....	13 Aug. 79	12 July 80	6 Mar. 85	4 Oct. 93	
Frederick Rennell Thackeray, *Major*, Royal Artillery	......	2 Feb. 76	6 Feb. 85	6 Oct. 93	
Francis Gibson Cotter, *Major*, Royal Marines	......	1 Sept.76	6 Oct. 85	6 Oct. 93	
William Arbuthnot Lenox Conyngham, *Major*, Worcester Regiment (29 F.)	1 May 78	1 Feb. 79	20 Jan. 86	9 Oct. 93	
Edward Douglas Kennedy, *Major*, Scottish Rifles	......	15 July 78	14 Nov. 83	10 Oct. 93	
p.s.c. Finlay Cochrane Beatson, *Major*, Wiltshire Regiment	......	12 Nov. 73	11 Mar. 81	11 Oct. 93	
p.s.c. Arthur Edw. Wm. Colville, *Major*, Rifle Brigade	......	10 Sept.75	1 Aug. 84	11 Oct. 93	
Charles Anthony Lamb, *Major*, Rifle Brigade	......	11 Feb. 76	1 Aug. 84	15 Oct. 93	
Edmund John Hollway, *Major*, Duke of Cornwall's Light Infantry (32 F.)	......	11 Sept.76	2 May 86	18 Oct. 93	
↑℃ Fenton John Aylmer, *Captain*, Royal Engineers	......	27 July 80	2 Oct. 89	18 Oct. 93	
Welby Francis Montresor, *Major*, Indian Staff Corps	......	19 Oct. 73	8 Jan. 85	19 Oct. 93	
Hamilton Macdonald Richards, *Major*, Border Regiment...	22 Jan. 79	27 Feb. 80	21 Jan. 85	20 Oct. 93	
Latham Charles Miller Blacker, *Major*, Royal Artillery......	......	2 Feb. 76	18 Feb. 85	21 Oct. 93	
Hew Dalrymple Fanshawe, *Major*, 19 Hussars..................	......	28 Jan. 82	2 July 84	25 Oct. 93	
James Molesworth Candy, *Major*, Indian Staff Corps.........	......	2 Nov. 73	8 Jan. 85	2 Nov. 93	
Henry Fortescue, *Major*, 17 Lancers	......	15 July 76	6 June 82	6 Nov. 93	
Francis Douglas Lumley, *Major*, Middlesex Regt. (57 F.)...	......	16 Mar. 75	28 June 84	6 Nov. 93	
Francis Robt. Millington Synge, *Major*, S. Lancashire Regt.	......	23 Nov. 73	15 July 83	8 Nov. 93	
p.s.c. Thos. Edw. Compton, *Major*, Northamptonshire Regt.	30 Jan. 78	15 Nov. 79	14 Nov. 83	8 Nov. 93	
Horace Robert Stopford, *Major*, Coldstream Guards.........	......	13 June 74	19 Oct. 85	10 Nov. 93	
William Lambert, *Major*, Indian Staff Corps	......	12 Nov. 73	8 Jan. 85	12 Nov. 93	
Harry Leonard Dawson, *Major*, Indian Staff Corps	......	12 Nov. 73	8 Jan. 85	12 Nov. 93	
William Gordon Yate, *Major*, Indian Staff Corps............	......	12 Nov. 73	8 Jan. 85	12 Nov. 93	
Alexander Wilson, *Major*, Argyll and Sutherland Highlanders (93 Foot)	22 Feb. 79	1 July 31	13 Nov. 84	18 Nov. 93	
Charles Henry Gostling, *Major*, Royal Scots	......	13 June 74	29 Aug. 83	29 Nov. 93	
Henry M'Leod Young, *Major*, Inniskilling Fusiliers	30 Jan. 78	13 Nov. 78	2 Feb. 85	1 Dec. 93	
Thomas Hope Stavert, *Major*, Leinster Regiment	14 Jan. 80	25 Aug. 80	28 June 85	2 Dec. 93	
Ernest Charles Lambert Congdon, *Major*, Royal Marines...	......	1 Sept.76	1 Nov. 85	5 Dec. 93	
Charles Napier Miles, *Major*, 1 Life Guards	......	20 Nov. 75	24 Nov. 82	6 Dec. 93	
Henry Sherwood Smith, *Major*, Manchester Regiment......	......	29 Nov. 76	9 July 84	6 Dec. 93	
Arthur Eardley-Wilmot, *Major*, Royal Artillery	......	2 Feb. 76	9 Feb. 85	9 Dec. 93	
George Herbert Chippindall, *Major*, West Riding Regiment	......	13 June 74	12 Nov. 83	13 Dec. 93	
Frederick John Evelegh, *Major*, Oxfordshire Lt. Infantry	......	13 June 74	23 May 85	13 Dec. 93	
Beamish St. John Barter, *Major*, Lincolnshire Regiment...	......	11 Sept.76	16 Feb. 85	16 Dec. 93	
Henry Townsend Butcher, *Major*, Royal Artillery	......	14 Aug. 76	22 Feb. 85	16 Dec. 93	
George Alfred Penrhys Evans, *Major*, 7 Hussars	......	2 Feb. 75	8 Aug. 80	19 Dec. 93	
Archer Parry Crawley, *Major*, Grenadier Guards	13 Oct. 77	28 Apr. 80	16 Nov. 88	20 Dec. 93	
Thomas Hulkes Bingham Day, *Major*, Lincolnshire Regt.	......	29 Nov. 76	7 Apr. 83	23 Dec. 93	
Edward Robt. John Presgrave, *DSO.Major*, Indian Staff C.	......	11 Feb. 75	11 Feb. 86	29 Dec. 93	
Henry Yelverton Beale, *Captain*, Norfolk Regiment	22 Jan. 81	1 July 81	29 Feb. 88	29 Dec. 93	
Henry D'Urban Keary, *DSO. Captain*, Indian Staff Corps	......	10 Sept.77	10 Sept.88	29 Dec. 93	
Frederick William Scudamore, *Major*, Suffolk Regiment...	......	22 Mar. 76	4 June 84	30 Dec. 93	
Arthur Elias, *Major*, West Surrey Regiment	......	28 Feb. 74	19 Sept.84	30 Dec. 93	
Henry Bowden Gundry, *Major*, Royal Artillery	......	14 Aug. 76	24 Feb. 85	31 Dec. 93	
Anthony Lumb, *Major*, Somerset Light Infantry............	......	12 Feb. 75	1 Apr. 85	31 Dec. 93	
Geo. Nisbet Mayne, *Major*, King's Own Scottish Borderers	......	13 June 74	2 June 84	1 Jan. 94	
Francis Clements Godley, *Major*, Derbyshire Regt. (95 F.)	......	11 Sept.78	4 Oct. 84	1 Jan. 94	
p.s.c. Hugh Montgomerie Sinclair, *Major*, Royal Engineers	......	12 Feb. 74	12 Feb. 85	1 Jan. 94	

Majors.

	CORNET, 2nd LIEUT. OR ENSIGN.	LIEUT.	CAPTAIN.	MAJOR.	WHEN PLACED ON HALF PAY.
Henry Walter Morrieson, *Major*, Royal Artillery		14 Aug. 76	28 Feb. 85	1 Jan. 94	
William Hugh Williams, *Major*, Royal Artillery		14 Aug. 76	1 Mar. 85	1 Jan. 94	
George Gregory Simpson, *Major*, Royal Artillery		14 Aug. 76	12 Mar. 85	1 Jan. 94	
Thomas William Powles, *Major*, Royal Artillery		14 Aug. 76	13 Mar. 85	3 Jan. 94	
William Gore Alban, *Captain*, Indian Staff Corps	13 Aug. 79	9 Nov. 80	13 Aug. 90	3 Jan. 94	
George Duncan Atkinson, *Captain*, Indian Staff Corps	11 Aug. 80	1 July 81	11 Aug. 91	3 Jan. 94	
Henry Martin Sandbach, *Major*, Royal Artillery		14 Aug. 76	13 Mar. 85	4 Jan. 94	
Claud Henry Alexander, *Major*, Wiltshire Regt. (99 F.)		21 Sept. 74	1 July 81	7 Jan. 94	
Edward Ranulph Kenyon, *Major*, Royal Engineers		12 Feb. 74	12 Feb. 85	12 Jan. 94	
p.s.c. Robert Calverley A. B. Bewicke-Copley, *Major*, King's Royal Rifles		2 Feb. 77	9 Oct. 85	15 Jan. 94	
Ralph Egerton, *Major*, West India Regiment	18 June 81	1 July 81	11 Jan. 88	17 Jan. 94	
Herbert Sturges Barlow, *Major*, Seaforth Highlanders	8 Dec. 77	30 Apr. 79	15 Mar. 88	26 Jan. 94	
Henry Earle, *DSO. Major*, Yorkshire Light Infantry		11 Sept. 76	14 Feb. 83	31 Jan. 94	
Richd. Makdougall Brisbane F. Kelly, *Major*, R. Artillery		14 Aug. 76	13 Mar. 85	31 Jan. 94	
Hon. Rupert Leigh, *Major*, 15 Hussars		11 Feb. 76	17 Mar. 86	31 Jan. 94	
Maxwell Robertson Hyslop, *Major*, Leicester Regiment		11 Sept. 76	15 July 84	5 Feb. 94	
Philip Bulman, *Major*, Shropshire Lt. Infantry (85 F.)		11 Sept. 76	4 Feb. 85	11 Feb. 94	
Hew Francis Cadell, *Major*, Indian Staff Corps		12 Feb. 74	12 Feb. 85	12 Feb. 94	
Henry Turner Faithfull, *Major*, Indian Staff Corps		12 Feb. 74	12 Feb. 85	12 Feb. 94	
Samuel Charles Norton Grant, *Major*, Royal Engineers		12 Feb. 74	12 Feb. 85	12 Feb. 94	
Charles M'Guire Bate, *Major*, Royal Engineers		12 Feb. 74	12 Feb. 85	12 Feb. 94	
John Crawford Middlemass, *Major*, Royal Engineers		12 Feb. 74	12 Feb. 85	12 Feb. 94	
Frederick Peel, *Major*, Royal Engineers		12 Feb. 74	12 Feb. 85	12 Feb. 94	
John Gallwey Lutyens, *Major*, Royal Engineers		12 Feb. 74	12 Feb. 85	12 Feb. 94	
Alexander Towers-Clark, *Major*, Middlesex Regiment		22 May 75	1 Jan. 85	21 Feb. 94	
Archibald Spencer Drummond, *Major*, Scots Guards		28 Oct. 71	1 July 85	21 Feb. 94	
Hugo Montgomery-Campbell, *Major*, Royal Artillery		14 Aug. 76	18 Mar. 85	24 Feb. 94	
Edward Hay M. Elliot, *Major*, S. Lancashire Regt. (40 F.)		2 Dec. 74	4 June 84	26 Feb. 94	
Warren Hastings, *Major*, Indian Staff Corps		28 Feb. 74	28 Feb. 85	28 Feb. 94	
Henry Lushington Ramsay, *Major*, Indian Staff Corps		28 Feb. 74	28 Feb. 85	28 Feb. 94	
James Loughnan O'Bryen, *Major*, Indian Staff Corps		28 Feb. 74	28 Feb. 85	23 Feb. 94	
James Philip Sparling, *Major*, Indian Staff Corps		28 Feb. 74	28 Feb. 85	28 Feb. 94	
Henry George Ryland, *Major*, Indian Staff Corps		28 Feb. 74	28 Feb. 85	28 Feb. 94	
Frederick George Preston, *Major*, Indian Staff Corps		28 Feb. 74	28 Feb. 85	28 Feb. 94	
Harold Arthur Deane, *Major*, Indian Staff Corps		28 Feb. 74	28 Feb. 85	28 Feb. 94	
Charles Edward Wylde Macdonald, *Major*, Indian Staff C.		28 Feb. 74	28 Feb. 85	28 Feb. 94	
Edward Spence Hastings, *DSO. Major*, Indian Staff Corps		28 Feb. 74	28 Feb. 85	28 Feb. 94	
John Franklin Worlledge, *Major*, Indian Staff Corps		28 Feb. 74	28 Feb. 85	28 Feb. 94	
Harry Stanley Massy, *Major*, Indian Staff Corps		28 Feb. 74	28 Feb. 85	28 Feb. 94	
p.s.c. Alfred Edwin Jones, *Major*, Indian Staff Corps		28 Feb. 74	28 Feb. 85	28 Feb. 94	
Frederic Edmond Kent, *Major*, Royal Artillery		14 Aug. 76	25 Mar. 85	14 Mar. 94	
Hubert Cornwall Legh, *Major*, King's Royal Rifles		6 Oct. 78	7 Jan. 86	14 Mar. 94	
Henry Wilmot Mitchell, *Major*, 14 Hussars	13 Aug. 79	1 July 81	26 Nov. 86	14 Mar. 94	
James Alex. Skene Thomson, *Major*, West Riding Regiment (76 F.)		24 Mar. 75	24 Jan. 83	15 Mar. 94	
Edward Cleary Hill, *Major*, Wiltshire Regiment (99 F.)		2 Dec. 74	1 July 81	19 Mar. 94	
George William Maunsell, *Major*, West Kent Regiment	11 May 78	17 Aug. 80	2 May 85	19 Mar. 94	
Francis Macdonald Drury, *Major*, Indian Staff Corps		26 Mar. 74	26 Mar. 85	26 Mar. 94	
Charles John Dennys, *Major*, Indian Staff Corps		26 Mar. 74	26 Mar. 85	26 Mar. 94	
Thos. David Kirkpatrick, *Major*, Yorkshire Regt. (19 F.)	8 Dec. 77	1 Jan. 78	15 Aug. 84	28 Mar. 94	
Henry Blosse Lynch, *Major*, Dorsetshire Regiment (54 F.)		11 Feb. 76	22 Nov. 84	28 Mar. 94	
Edward William Dun, *DSO. Major*, Indian Staff Corps		28 Mar. 74	28 Mar. 85	28 Mar. 94	
Archibald James Erskine, *Major*, Army Service Corps		1 Sept. 77	1 Jan. 84	1 Apr. 94	
Wm. Francis Fawcett, *Major*, Northampton Regiment	12 June 78	14 Apr. 80	25 Mar. 84	1 Apr. 94	
Alexander John Lindsay, *Major* (District Officer), R. Art.		24 Nov. 77	10 Jan. 86	1 Apr. 94	
Thomas Pepper Ernest Lowry, *Major*, West India Regt.		12 May 76	31 Mar. 85	1 Apr. 94	
Henry Beresford Bourke, *DSO. Major*, West India Regt.		30 Nov. 78	5 Oct. 87	1 Apr. 94	
Richard Joseph Norris, *DSO. Major*, West India Regt.	19 Feb. 79	1 Dec. 80	29 Jan. 88	1 Apr. 94	
Arthur Russell Loscombe, *Major*, West India Regiment	11 Aug. 80	1 July 81	29 Jan. 88	1 Apr. 94	
Percival Havelock Acheson, *Major*, Army Service Corps	4 Dec. 78	21 June 80	1 Mar. 88	1 Apr. 94	
Maurice Alexander Cameron, *Major*, Royal Engineers		17 Aug. 74	17 Aug. 85	5 Apr. 94	
George Markham Davison, *Major*, Durham Lt. Inf. (106 F.)		13 June 75	14 Mar. 83	11 Apr. 94	
Herbert Ringwood, *Major*, East Surrey Regiment		11 Sept. 76	28 Nov. 83	11 Apr. 94	
George Morley Saunders, *Major*, Durham Lt. Inf. (106 F.)		26 Aug. 76	20 Jan. 84	11 Apr. 94	
Chas. Arch. Townshend Boultbee, *Major*, King's R. Rifles	21 July 77	7 Apr. 80	21 Apr. 86	16 Apr. 94	
Henry Bourchier Fowler, *Major*, West Surrey Regt. (2 F.)		13 June 74	25 Mar. 85	17 Apr. 94	
Archibald Cyril Cubitt, *Major*, Suffolk Regiment		11 Sept. 76	1 Dec. 85	18 Apr. 94	
Fred. W. Bainbridge Landon, *Major*, Army Service Corps	13 Aug. 79	19 May 80	19 Sept. 85	18 Apr. 94	
James Robert Parkinson, *Major*, Hampshire Regiment	2 July 79	11 Oct. 79	26 Aug. 85	22 Apr. 94	
James Robert Johnstone, *Major*, Royal Marines		1 Sept. 70	7 Nov. 83	1 May 94	
George Backhouse Sandham, *Major*, S. Staff. Regt.(80 F.)		17 May 76	2 Oct. 83	2 May 94	
Richard Alexander Scott, *Major*, 2 Dragoon Guards		28 Apr. 76	1 Jan. 85	2 May 94	
Arch. John Joseph Ross, *Major*, Lancaster Regt. (4 F.)	1 May 78	6 Mar. 80	24 Mar. 86	3 May 94	
Alfred Edward Wrottesley, *Major*, Royal Engineers		17 Aug. 74	17 Aug. 85	3 May 94	
Thos. Charles Pleydell Calley, *Major*, 1 Life Guards		11 Sept. 76	21 July 86	5 May 94	
Charles Henry Alexander, *Major*, Royal Artillery		14 Aug. 76	1 Apr. 85	9 May 94	
John James Porteous, *Major*, Royal Artillery		14 Aug. 76	1 Apr. 85	9 May 94	
p.s.c. Laurence Brock-Hollinshead, *Major*, W. Kent Regt.	13 Aug. 79	31 Aug. 85	23 Dec. 85	9 May 94	
Stewart Dalrymple Cleeve, *Major*, Royal Engineers		17 Aug. 74	17 Aug. 85	10 May 94	
Cuthbert Johnson Baines, *Major*, Gloucester Regt.		28 Oct. 77	18 Oct. 84	15 May 94	
Wm. Henry Slingsby O'Neill, *Major*, Dublin Fus. (102 F.)		10 Sept. 75	29 Jan. 84	16 May 94	
George Hay Montgomerie Conran, *Major*, E. Yorkshire Regt. (15 F.)		12 Feb. 76	1 Oct. 84	16 May 94	
Geo. Wm. Hacket Pain, *Major*, Worcestershire Regiment		20 Nov. 75	15 Feb. 86	16 May 94	
Alfred Creagh MacDonnell, *Major*, Royal Engineers		17 Aug. 74	17 Aug. 85	18 May 94	
Ferdinand William Greatrex, *Major*, 1 Dragoons	13 Aug. 79	1 July 81	19 June 85	19 May 94	
Alf. Herrick Butler Clough, *Major*, Munster Fus. (101 F.)		24 Mar. 76	20 May 85	19 May 94	
Frederick Hacket-Thompson, *Major*, Cameron Highlanders (79 F.)	6 Aug. 79	22 May 80	20 Feb. 84	21 May 94	
Ernest Joseph George Boyce, *Major*, Royal Engineers		17 Aug. 74	17 Aug. 85	21 May 94	
John Collinson, *Major*, Northampton Regiment	22 Jan. 79	8 May 80	20 Aug. 84	30 May 94	

Majors.

Name	Cornet, 2nd Lieut. or Ensign.	Lieut.	Captain.	Major.	When placed on half pay.
Charles Robert Brown, *Major*, Manchester Regt. (63 F.)...	......	11 Oct. 78	28 Aug. 85	31 May 94	
John Southwell Brown, *Major*, Irish Rifles (83 F.)............	1 May 78	12 Apr. 79	15 Apr. 85	4 June 94	
William Henry Thackwell, *Major*, Hampshire Regt. (67 F.)	13 Aug. 79	17 Dec. 79	19 Sept. 85	6 June 94	
George Arthur Shadforth, *Major*, Dublin Fusiliers	......	28 Apr. 76	7 June 84	7 June 94	
Juxon Henry Jones, *Major*, Indian Staff Corps	......	10 June 74	10 June 85	10 June 94	
Henry Appleton, *Major*, Royal Engineers.........................	......	17 Aug. 74	17 Aug. 85	11 June 94	
Charles Hay Cox, *Major*, West Yorkshire Regiment........	30 Jan. 78	19 Sept.78	2 Apr. 84	13 June 94	
Charles Herbert, *Major*, Indian Staff Corps	......	13 June 74	13 June 85	13 June 94	
Hudson Henry Ozzard, *Major*, Indian Staff Corps............	......	13 June 74	13 June 85	13 June 94	
George Atkins Collins, *Major*, Indian Staff Corps	......	13 June 74	13 June 85	13 June 94	
William Charles Aslett, *Major*, Indian Staff Corps	......	13 June 74	13 June 85	13 June 94	
Lumley Scobell Peyton, *Major*, Indian Staff Corps	......	13 June 74	13 June 85	13 June 94	
p.s.c. Alfred Wm. Lambart Bayly, *DSO. Major*, Indian S. C.	......	13 June 74	13 June 85	13 June 94	
William Henry Jameson, *Major*, Indian Staff Corps	......	13 June 74	13 June 85	13 June 94	
Arthur Adye, *Major*, Indian Staff Corps...........................	......	13 June 74	13 June 85	13 June 94	
John Arch. Henry Pollock, *Major*, Indian Staff Corps	......	13 June 74	13 June 85	13 June 94	
Chas. Grant Mausell Fasken, *Major*, Indian Staff Corps...	......	13 June 74	13 June 85	13 June 94	
Lionel Grafton Beckham, *Major*, Indian Staff Corps.........	......	13 June 74	13 June 85	13 June 94	
p.s.c. Raymond Burlton Williams, *Major*, Somerset Lt.Inf.	......	13 June 74	1 Apr. 85	14 June 94	
John Edward Benbow, *Major*, 1 Dragoon Guards............	22 Jan. 81	1 July 81	25 Jan. 88	14 June 94	
Stanley Humphery, *Major*, Gloucester Regiment (28 F.)	30 Jan. 78	21 Apr. 80	17 Apr. 85	16 June 94	
George Robert Brown Patten, *Major*, 18 Hussars	......	22 Oct. 81	1 Apr. 86	20 June 94	
John Elford Dickie, *Major*, Royal Engineers	......	17 Aug. 74	17 Aug. 85	22 June 94	
Newton Seymour Allen, *Major*, S.Staffordshire Regt. (80 F.)	......	6 Oct. 76	31 Oct. 83	27 June 94	
Charles Prideaux Triscott, *DSO. Major*, Royal Artillery...	......	14 Aug. 76	15 Apr. 85	27 June 94	
Charles John Lewis Stuart, *Major*, Indian Staff Corps.....	......	27 June 74	27 June 85	27 June 94	
Alfred Robert LLoyd, *Major*, Bedfordshire Regiment	......	2 Dec. 74	1 Sept. 83	1 July 94	
Henry Edward Tyler, *Major*, Royal Engineers	......	17 Aug. 74	17 Aug. 85	7 July 94	
Arthur W. Alsager Pollock, *Major*, Somerset Lt.Infantry	......	20 Nov. 75	8 May 85	10 July 94	
Henry Crosbie, *Major*, Derbyshire Regiment	......	26 June 74	18 Jan. 82	11 July 94	
Edmund Walter St. George Welchman, *Major*, Indian S.C.	......	11 July 74	11 July 85	11 July 94	
Dacre Lennard Barrett, *Major*, Royal Marines	......	1 Sept. 76	11 Dec. 85	11 July 94	
Arthur Cadell Tait Boileau, *Major*. Royal Artillery	......	25 Jan. 77	15 Apr. 85	14 July 94	
Robert Homfray Alexander, *Captain*, R. Marine Artillery	......	17 July 72	21 May 84	15 July 94	
Walter Blake Butler-Creagh, *Major*, Yorkshire Lt. Inf. ...	7 Aug. 78	9 Aug. 80	26 Mar. 84	19 July 94	
Stanley Paterson, *Major*, Argyll and Sutherland Highlanders (91 F.)	9 July 79	1 July 81	1 Feb. 86	23 July 94	
Henry Goulburn, *Major*, Grenadier Guards..................	11 May 78	1 July 81	18 Oct. 89	23 July 94	
George Alfred Keef, *Major*, Scots Fusiliers (21 F.)	......	11 Sept. 76	2 Feb. 85	6 Aug. 94	
p.s.c. James Charles Young, *Major*, Sussex Regiment.....	......	11 Nov. 76	5 Mar. 84	6 Aug. 94	
John William Dent, *Major*, 4 Dragoon Guards	11 May 78	13 Apr. 81	18 Jan. 85	6 Aug. 94	
Herbert Edward Stacy Abbott, *Major*, Royal Engineers	......	17 Aug. 74	17 Aug. 85	6 Aug. 94	
Harry Wetherell Rowden, *Major*, Wiltshire Regiment.....	......	2 Dec. 74	25 Oct. 81	8 Aug. 94	
John Patrick Walter Spankie, *Major*, Indian Staff Corps	......	9 Aug. 74	9 Aug. 85	9 Aug. 94	
Augustus Carter King, *Major*, 5 Lancers	23 Oct. 80	1 July 81	21 Aug. 89	12 Aug. 94	
Charles Frederick Magrath, *Major*, Royal Artillery.........	......	25 Jan. 77	16 Apr. 85	13 Aug. 94	
John Watkins, *Major*, North Staffordshire Regt. (98 F.)...	......	27 June 76	1 July 84	15 Aug. 94	
p.s.c. Beauchamp Duff, *Major*, Indian Staff Corps	......	4 May 74	8 May 80	17 Aug. 94	
James Lorne Govan, *Major*, Norfolk Regiment	30 Jan. 78	25 Aug. 80	26 Mar. 84	20 Aug. 94	
Ernest Maxwell Willshire, *Major*, R. Highlanders (73 F.)	13 Oct. 77	25 May 78	15 May 85	20 Aug. 94	
Henry Lee Pennell, *Major*, 1 Dragoon Guards...............	......	28 Jan. 82	23 Oct. 88	22 Aug. 94	
Hon. Henry Frederick White, *Major*, Grenadier Guards	14 Sept.78	1 July 81	18 Oct. 89	22 Aug. 94	
William Kingsdown Curling, *Major*, Durham Light Inf.	......	24 June 78	1 Sept.84	27 Aug. 94	
Ernest Chamier Broughton, *Major*, York and Lancaster Regiment (65 F.)	......	11 Nov. 78	29 Nov. 85	27 Aug. 94	
Stephen Eaton Lamb, *Major*, Dorsetshire Regt. (39 F.)...	14 Jan. 80	1 Jan. 81	14 Apr. 86	28 Aug. 94	
Wm. Lueg Harvey, *Major*, Duke of Cornwall's Light Infantry (46 F.)	30 Jan. 78	18 June 81	1 July 87	31 Aug. 94	
Graham Claude Herbert, *Major*, Royal Fusiliers	......	11 Feb. 76	24 Sept. 84	3 Sept. 94	
Maurice Wm. Palmer Block, *Major*, Royal Artillery	......	19 Aug. 75	25 Apr. 85	5 Sept. 94	
Malcolm Orme Little, *Major*, 9 Lancers	11 May 78	25 Feb. 80	20 Oct. 86	5 Sept. 94	
James H. E. Reid, *Major*, K. O. Scottish Brdrs. (25 F.) ...	......	11 Feb. 75	21 June 85	10 Sept. 94	
Francis Blayney L. Woodwright, *Major*, 4 Dragoon Gds...	......	2 Aug. 82	8 May 88	12 Sept. 94	
David Alexander Kinloch, *Major*, Grenadier Guards	11 May 78	1 July 81	18 Oct. 89	12 Sept. 94	
p.s.c. Hubert John Foster, *Major*, Royal Engineers.........	......	28 Jan. 75	28 Jan. 86	20 Sept. 94	
Stewart Douglas Gordon, *Major*, Indian Staff Corps	......	21 Sept. 74	21 Sept. 85	21 Sept. 94	
Jenico Edward Preston, *DSO. Major*, Indian Staff Corps	......	21 Sept. 74	21 Sept. 85	21 Sept. 94	
Frederick Hawkins, *Major*, Indian Staff Corps	......	21 Sept. 74	21 Sept. 85	21 Sept. 94	
Henry Philip Picot, *Major*, Indian Staff Corps.................	......	21 Sept. 74	21 Sept. 85	21 Sept. 94	
William Spiller Birdwood, *Major*, Indian Staff Corps	......	21 Sept. 74	21 Sept. 85	21 Sept. 94	
William Simpson Marshall, *Major*, Indian Staff Corps ...	......	21 Sept. 74	21 Sept. 85	21 Sept. 94	
William Conrad Faithfull, *Major*, Indian Staff Corps	......	21 Sept. 74	21 Sept. 85	21 Sept. 94	
Henry C. Page-Henderson, *Major*, 6 Dragoons	......	11 Sept. 78	20 Oct. 83	26 Sept. 94	
Charles Edwyn Jervois, *Major*, Royal Artillery...............	......	25 Jan. 77	6 May 85	29 Sept. 94	
Walter Clare Savile, *Major*, Royal Artillery	......	25 Jan. 77	6 May 85	29 Sept. 94	
William Samuel Burrell, *Major*, West Surrey Regiment...	......	10 Sept.75	10 Sept.85	29 Sept. 94	
p.s.c. Hon. Arthur Henry Henniker-Major, *Major*, Coldstream Guards	......	20 Nov. 75	10 Nov. 85	29 Sept. 94	
p.s.c. Wm. Inglefield Eastman, *Captain*, R. Marine Art. ...	......	1 Oct. 73	8 Jan. 85	1 Oct. 94	
John Blandford Ratteclyffe Butler, *Major*, Indian S. C....	......	1 Oct. 74	1 Oct. 85	1 Oct. 94	
Clarence Henry Hayes, *Major*, Indian Staff Corps	......	1 Oct. 74	1 Oct. 85	1 Oct. 94	
Charles Edward Haynes, *Major*, Royal Engineers	......	28 Jan. 75	28 Jan. 86	1 Oct. 94	
Vesey Mangles Stockley, *Major*, Indian Staff Corps	......	5 Oct. 74	5 Oct. 85	5 Oct. 94	
Horace William Scott, *Major*, Lancashire Fusiliers	......	11 Feb. 76	9 June 84	15 Oct. 94	
Cameron Charles Douglas, *Major*, Scottish Rifles (26 F.)	1 May 78	31 Mar. 80	10 Oct. 85	15 Oct. 94	
p.s.c. Henry Ponting Northcott, *Major*, Leinster Regt.......	......	17 Feb. 77	12 Feb. 85	17 Oct. 94	
p.s.c. Edw. Richd. Coryton Graham, *Major*, Cheshire Regiment (22 F.)	1 May 78	19 June 79	6 Sept.85	24 Oct. 94	
Horace Hutton Barnet, *Major*, Royal Engineers	......	28 Jan. 75	28 Jan. 86	24 Oct. 94	
Harry Finn, *Major*, 21 Hussars.....................................	22 Jan. 81	1 July 81	23 Nov. 87	24 Oct. 94	
Oliver Edwal Ruck, *Major*, Royal Engineers	......	28 Jan. 75	28 Jan. 86	3 Nov. 94	
Archibald Gell Cochran, *Major*, Royal Marines	......	1 Feb. 77	5 Jan. 86	5 Nov. 94	
Frederick Paul English, *Major*, Dublin Fusiliers	22 Jan. 79	12 Jan. 81	1 July 87	6 Nov. 94	

Majors.

Name	CORNET, and LIEUT. or ENSIGN	LIEUT.	CAPTAIN.	MAJOR.	WHEN PLACED ON HALF PAY.
Theodore Gordon Barclay, *Major*, Irish Fusiliers		9 Aug. 73	4 Oct. 84	7 Nov. 94	
Charles Mannoir Sumner, *Major*, South Lancashire Regt.	1 May 78	28 May 79	3 Nov. 85	7 Nov. 94	
Richard Lloyd Payne, *DSO. Major*, Somerset Lt. Inf. (13 F.)		5 Jan. 76	8 May 85	8 Nov. 94	
Reginald Whitworth Porter, *Major*, Oxford Lt. Inf. (43 F.)		6 Sept. 76	11 Jan. 86	9 Nov. 94	
Ribton Gore, *Major*, Sussex Regiment (35 F.)		26 Feb. 74	5 Mar. 84	14 Nov. 94	
p.s.c. John Sherston, *DSO. Major*, Rifle Brigade		12 Feb. 76	20 Aug. 84	14 Nov. 94	
George Cockburn, *Major*, Rifle Brigade		11 Nov. 76	20 Aug. 84	14 Nov. 94	
Albert Dallas Enriquez, *Major*, Indian Staff Corps		14 Nov. 74	14 Nov. 85	14 Nov. 94	
Charles Edward Johnson, *Captain*, Indian Staff Corps	22 Jan. 81	1 July 81	22 Jan. 92	14 Nov. 94	
Jeffery Charles Marston, *Major*, Royal Artillery		25 Jan. 77	6 May 85	15 Nov. 94	
William Arthur Young, *Major*, Scots Fusiliers		3 May 78	2 Nov. 85	21 Nov. 94	
James Mitchell-Innes, *Major*, Highland Lt. Inf. (71 F.)		12 Nov. 73	25 Oct. 84	22 Nov. 94	
Henry Morgan, *Major*, Northamptonshire Regiment	22 Jan. 79	31 May 80	25 Oct. 84	22 Nov. 94	
Ernest Digby Mansel, *Major*, Highland Lt. Inf. (74 F.)		28 Feb. 74	10 Oct. 85	22 Nov. 94	
William John Langford, *Major*, Royal Marines		19 Sept. 77	1 Feb. 86	25 Nov. 94	
Ernest Henry Burney, *Major*, Berkshire Regiment	22 Jan. 79	8 Apr. 80	10 Dec. 84	29 Nov. 94	
Robert Wm. Freebairn Monteith, *Major*, Army Ser. C.	6 Aug. 79	29 Sept. 80	7 Sept. 86	1 Dec. 94	
Charles Edward Wyncoll, *Major*, Army Service Corps	15 Aug. 77	17 May 79	1 Feb. 85	1 Dec. 94	
Alfred Law Sinclair, *DSO. Major*, Indian Staff Corps		2 Dec. 74	2 Dec. 85	2 Dec. 94	
John Lamb, *Major*, Indian Staff Corps		2 Dec. 74	2 Dec. 85	2 Dec. 94	
Edward Hodding Peacock, *Major*, Leicestershire Regt.		26 Feb. 77	31 Oct. 84	3 Dec. 94	
Leonard Gordon, *Major*, King's Own Scottish Borderers		6 Sept. 76	23 Sept. 85	3 Dec. 94	
George Francis Leslie, *Major*, Rifle Brigade	24 Nov. 77	12 Apr. 79	3 Dec. 84	5 Dec. 94	
Arthur Nugent, *Major*, Royal Fusiliers		29 Nov. 76	31 Dec. 84	5 Dec. 94	
Edward Bleiddian Herbert, *Major*, 17 Lancers		29 Nov. 76	27 Apr. 86	5 Dec. 94	
John Forster Manifold, *Major*, Royal Artillery		25 Jan. 77	12 May 85	8 Dec. 94	
Charles Blair Mayne, *Major*, Royal Engineers		28 Jan. 75	28 Jan. 86	8 Dec. 94	
Frank Graham, *Major*, Suffolk Regiment	11 May 78	5 Aug. 80	18 Mar. 85	9 Dec. 94	
Henry Edward Goodwyn, *Major*, Royal Engineers		28 Jan. 75	28 Jan. 86	12 Dec. 94	
Sydney Gordon Grant, *Major*, Scottish Rifles (90 F.)	1 May 78	29 Sept. 80	16 Oct. 85	15 Dec. 94	
Henry Charles Thomas Kelly, *Major*, Royal Marines		19 Sept. 77	4 Feb. 86	15 Dec. 94	
Chas. H. Lethbridge Baskerville, *Major*, Irish Regiment	13 Aug. 79	22 Dec. 80	16 May 85	17 Dec. 94	
Walter Andrew Gale, *Major*, Royal Engineers		28 Jan. 75	28 Jan. 86	17 Dec. 94	
Walter Francis Hawkins, *Major*, Royal Engineers		19 Aug. 75	19 Aug. 86	20 Dec. 94	
Horace Augustus Terry, *Major*, Oxford Light Infantry		29 Nov. 76	19 May 86	22 Dec. 94	
Mortimer John Slater, *Major*, Royal Engineers		19 Aug. 75	19 Aug. 86	22 Dec. 94	
Julian Oswald, *Major*, 16 Lancers	22 Mar. 79	16 Oct. 80	8 Dec. 86	22 Dec. 94	
John de Winton Lardner-Clarke, *Major*, Royal Artillery		14 Aug. 76	12 May 85	25 Dec. 94	
Alfred Herbert Randolph, *Major*, Royal Engineers		19 Aug. 75	19 Aug. 86	1 Jan. 95	
Henry Edward Maxwell, *Major*, Royal Highlanders		11 Sept. 78	15 May 85	3 Jan. 95	
Frederick Houlton Ward, *Major*, R. Artillery		14 Aug. 76	27 July 85	4 Jan. 95	
James R. Leslie Macdonald, *Captain* Royal Engineers		22 Feb. 82	7 June 90	5 Jan. 95	
Henry Hartland Higginson, *Major*, N. Staffordshire Regiment (64 F.)		29 Jan. 76	1 July 84	9 Jan. 95	
Robert Douglas Longe, *Major*, Middlesex Regiment		11 Sept. 76	8 May 85	9 Jan. 95	
William Crawford Middleton, *Major*, 2nd Dragoons	13 Mar. 78	6 May 80	21 Oct. 85	9 Jan. 95	
Dudley G. Richard Ryder, *Major*, King's Royal Rifles	1 May 78	28 Apr. 80	10 June 86	9 Jan. 95	
Charles F. St. Clair Anstruther Thomson, *Major*, 2 Life Guards		13 June 74	12 Jan. 85	12 Jan. 95	
Sir John Christopher Willoughby, *Bart. Major*, Royal Horse Guards	23 Oct. 80	18 May 81	14 May 87	18 Jan. 95	
Hon. Charles Lambton, *Major*, Northumberland Fus.		31 May 77	25 July 83	21 Jan. 95	
John Hulke Plumbe, *Major*, Royal Marines		19 Sept. 77	5 Mar. 86	22 Jan. 95	
Louis Charles Jackson, *Major*, Royal Engineers		19 Aug. 75	19 Aug. 86	24 Jan. 95	
John Lewis Rooke Maclurcan, *Major* Royal Marines		19 Sept. 77	2 Apr. 86	25 Jan. 95	
Joseph Ignatius Bonomi, *Major*, Lancaster Regiment	11 May 78	6 Mar. 80	9 May 86	25 Jan. 95	
Thos. G. Lowry Herbert Armstrong, *Major*, Northumberland Fusiliers	19 Dec. 77	3 Apr. 78	24 Jan. 85	27 Jan. 95	
William Eden Sturges, *Major*, Northumberland Fus.	36 Jan. 78	7 Jun. 80	4 May 85	30 Jan. 95	
Charles H. Eyre Coote, *Major*, 11 Hussars	13 Aug. 79	29 June 81	14 Oct. 85	30 Jan. 95	
Richard Francis M'Crea, *Major*, Royal Artillery		25 Jan. 77	3 Aug. 85	1 Feb. 95	
Edward Wheler, *Major*, Sussex Regiment	22 Jan. 79	23 July 79	29 July 84	2 Feb. 95	
Horatio James Evans, *Major*, Liverpool Regiment	30 Jan. 78	25 Feb. 80	16 Jan. 84	4 Feb. 95	
p.s.c. Herbert Conyers Surtees, *Major*, Coldstream Gds.		11 Sept. 76	7 May 87	5 Feb. 95	
Victor John Fergus Ferguson, *Major*, Royal Horse Gds.		6 Feb. 84	7 Mar. 88	6 Feb. 95	
Henry Wightman Benson, *Major*, East Surrey Regiment		15 July 76	10 Aug. 84	8 Feb. 95	
Charles Herbert Wylly, *Major*, S. Staffordshire Regt.		11 Sept. 78	20 Nov. 83	11 Feb. 95	
William Tomes Fairbrother, *Major*, Indian Staff Corps		11 Feb. 75	11 Feb. 86	11 Feb. 95	
John George Ramsay, *Major*, Indian Staff Corps		11 Feb. 75	11 Feb. 86	11 Feb. 95	
Andrew Pennell Williamson, *Major*, Indian Staff Corps		11 Feb. 75	11 Feb. 86	11 Feb. 95	
Hugh Dillon Massy Minchin, *Major*, Indian Staff Corps		11 Feb. 75	11 Feb. 86	11 Feb. 95	
Frederick Augustus Blyth, *Major*, Indian Staff Corps		11 Feb. 75	11 Feb. 86	11 Feb. 95	
Alfred Lloyd Barrett, *DSO. Major*, Indian Staff Corps		11 Feb. 75	11 Feb. 86	11 Feb. 95	
John William Parker, *Major*, Indian Staff Corps		11 Feb. 75	11 Feb. 86	11 Feb. 95	
Christopher G. F. Fagan, *Major*, Indian Staff Corps		11 Feb. 75	11 Feb. 86	11 Feb. 95	
William St, John Richardson, *Major*, Indian Staff Corps		11 Feb. 75	11 Feb. 86	11 Feb. 95	
Robert Baker Shawe, *Major*, Indian Staff Corps		11 Feb. 75	11 Feb. 86	11 Feb. 95	
Spencer Walpole Follett, *Major*, 9 Lancers		20 Nov. 75	24 Aug. 81	13 Feb. 95	
John Tyrwhitt-Walker, *Major*, Dorsetshire Regiment		28 Feb. 74	6 Jan. 86	13 Feb. 95	
Richard Money Maxwell, *Captain*, Indian Staff Corps	13 Aug. 79	26 Feb. 81	13 Aug. 90	13 Feb. 95	
Harry Wright, *Major*, Gordon Highlanders (92 Foot)		29 Nov. 76	9 Mar. 86	14 Feb. 95	
Herbert Thomas De C. Hobbs, *Major*, West Yorkshire Regiment		11 Feb. 75	17 Jan. 82	20 Feb. 95	
William George Massy, *Major*, Royal Artillery		25 Jan. 77	13 Aug. 85	20 Feb. 95	
Ralph Pudsay Littledale, *Major*, Royal Engineers		19 Aug. 75	19 Aug. 86	1 Mar. 95	
George O'Connor, *Major*, 6 Dragoons		9 Sept. 82	1 June 88	6 Mar. 95	
Arthur George Burn, *Major*, Indian Staff Corps		10 Mar. 75	10 Mar. 86	10 Mar. 95	
George James Francis Talbot, *Major*, Royal Artillery		25 Jan. 77	13 Aug. 85	20 Mar. 95	

War Services of the Majors not belonging to Regiments or Corps.

[For the War Services of other Majors, vide their respective Regiments or Corps.]

¹ Majors Hungerford and Norcock.—For War Services, see Royal Marines.

⁸ Major E. A. Smith served with the Jowaki Afreedee Expedition in 1877-78 (Medal with Clasp). Served in the Afghan war of 1878-80, and was present in the engagements at Mattoon and Lataband (mentioned in despatches), and in the operations round Cabul in December 1879; accompanied Sir Frederick Roberts in the march to Candahar, and was present at the battle of Candahar (mentioned in despatches, Medal with two Clasps, and Bronze Decoration). Served with the Burmese Expedition in 1888-89 (mentioned in despatches, Brevet of Major, and Clasp).

¹² Major Gompertz served with the 67th Regiment in the Afghan war of 1878-80, and was present in the engagement at Charasiab on the 6th October 1879, and in the operations around Cabul in December 1879 including the investment of Sherpore (Medal with two Clasps). Served in the Burmese Expedition in 1887-89 with the 1st Battalion Hampshire Regiment (Medal with Clasp).

STAFF AT HOME.

1. NORTH EASTERN DISTRICT.—Head Quarters, York.

Major General Commanding	Major General R. T. Thynne, *CB*. 1 Oct. 94.
Aide de Camp	Captain the *Hon*. O. V. G. A. Lumley, 11 Hussars, 1 Oct. 94.
Commanding R. Art. (*Colonel on the Staff*)	Colonel H. St. J. V. Le M. Thomas Le Marchant, 23 May 94.
Commanding R. Eng. (*Colonel on the Staff*)	Colonel A. de V. Brooke.
Assistant Adjutant Generals	Colonel W. F. Vetch (from h.p. Dublin Fusiliers), 22 Sept. 92.
	Colonel F. F. Goddard, Army Service Corps, 1 July 89.
Deputy Assistant Adjutant General	*p.s.c.* Major H. M. Sinclair, Royal Engineers, 1 Apr. 92.
Dep. Assist. Adj. Gen. for Instruction	*p.s.c.* Lt. Col. *Hon*. J. P. Napier (from h.p. 10 Hussars), 23 Aug. 90.
District Inspector of Musketry	Major E. E. Carr, Scots Fusiliers, 24 Feb. 93.
Recruiting Staff Officers (Class I.)	Lt. Colonel R. Stevenson (from h.p. 6 Dr. Gds.), 4 Apr. 92. *Leeds*.
Staff Captain, Royal Artillery	*p.s.c.* Captain E. J. Granet, 1 Jan. 92.
Commanding Militia and Volunteer Artillery	Colonel J. C. Robinson. *Scarborough*.
Senior Ordnance Store Officer	Deputy Commissary General of Ordnance
District Paymaster	Chief Paymaster P. D. Costa.
Principal Medical Officer	Surgeon Colonel J. W. Maxham, *MD*.

2. NORTH WESTERN DISTRICT.—Head Quarters, Chester.

Major General Commanding	Lieut. General J. H. *Sir* B. C. Russell, *KCB*. 13 Hussars.
Aide de Camp	*p.s.c.* Captain F. E. Cooper, Royal Artillery, 1 July 90.
Commanding Royal Artillery	Lt. Colonel A. J. Dunnage. *Seaforth*.
Commanding R. Eng. (*Colonel on the Staff*)	Colonel W. R. Slacke, 1 Dec. 91.
Assistant Adjutant General	*p.s.c.* Col. R. Auld (from h.p. Northumberland Fus.), 21 Aug. 94.
Deputy Assistant Adjutant Generals	*p.s.c.* Captain E. A. Altham, Royal Scots, 16 Jan. 93.
	Lt. Colonel S. H. Lynn, Army Service Corps, 30 Jan. 94.
District Inspector of Musketry	Captain H. C. *Visct*. Hardinge, Rifle Brigade, 1 Jan. 93.
Recruiting Staff Officers (Class I.)	Lt. Col. H.E. Railston (from h.p. Scot. Rifles), 1 Apr. 92. *Manchester*.
	Lt. Colonel H. H. A. Cameron (from h.p. Bedfordshire Regiment), 12 Nov. 92. *Birmingham*.
Recruiting Staff Officer (Class II.)	Captain A. C. Seton-Christopher, Seaforth Highlanders, 15 Apr. 92. *Liverpool*.
Staff Captain, Royal Artillery	*p.s.c.* Captain A. R. Stuart, 15 Aug. 92.
Commanding Militia and Volunteer Artillery	Lt. Colonel A. J. Dunnage.
Senior Ordnance Store Officer	Assistant Commissary General of Ordnance R. T. Stainforth.
District Paymaster	Chief Paymaster J. G. Hamilton.
Principal Medical Officer	Surgeon Colonel H. S. Muir, *MD*.

3. EASTERN DISTRICT.—Head Quarters, Colchester.

Major General Commanding	Major General J. P. C. Glyn, 20 Jan. 92.
Aide de Camp	Captain A. E. Jenkins, Rifle Brigade, 1 Oct. 94.
Assistant Adjutant General	Colonel A. Peel (from h.p. 7 Hussars), 18 May 91.
Deputy Assistant Adjutant Generals	*p.s.c.* Captain N. W. Barnardiston, Middlesex Regiment, 1 Dec. 94.
	Lt. Colonel W. T. McLeod, Army Service Corps, 4 Dec. 91.
Dep. Assist. Adj. Gen. for Instruction	*p.s.c.* Lt. Colonel P. H. Hammond (from h.p. R. Art.), 18 Mar. 92.
District Inspector of Musketry	Major A. R. Hennell, Hampshire Regiment, 14 July 93.
Commanding R. Art. (*Colonel on the Staff*)	*p.s.c.* Colonel J. F. Maurice, *CB*. 25 May 94.
Commanding R. Eng. (*Colonel on the Staff*)	Colonel H. J. W. Gehle, 24 Jan. 95.
Staff Captain, Royal Artillery	*p.s.c.* Captain J. F. Cadell, 15 Aug. 94.
Commanding Militia and Volunteer Artillery	Lt. Colonel W. V. Gregory. *Great Yarmouth*.
Senior Ordnance Store Officer	Assistant Commissary General of Ordnance T. P. Battersby.
District Paymaster	Chief Paymaster R. O. Richmond.
Principal Medical Officer	Surgeon Colonel W. A. Catherwood, *MD*.

4. WESTERN DISTRICT.—Head Quarters, Devonport.

Major General Commanding	*p.s.c.* Lt. General *Sir* R. Harrison, *KCB*. *CMG*. R. Eng. 15 Apr. 90.
Aides de Camp	Lieut. G. R. Lascelles, Royal Fusiliers, 1 May 90.
Commanding R. Art. (*Colonel on the Staff*)	Colonel R. Walkey, 1 Dec. 93.
Commanding R. Eng. (*Colonel on the Staff*)	*p.s.c.* V℃ Colonel M. S. Bell, 6 Nov. 94.
Assistant Adjutant General (for Severn Defences and Milford Haven)	Colonel H. H. Goodeve (from R. Art.), 24 May 91. *Pembroke Dock*.
Assistant Adjutant Generals	*p.s.c.* Colonel W. S. Cooke (from h.p. Cheshire Regt.), 29 Dec. 93.
	Colonel J. W. Elmes, Army Service Corps, 1 Apr. 90.
Deputy Assistant Adjutant General	*p.s.c.* Captain L. W. Bodé, Middlesex Regiment, 15 Nov. 92.
Dep. Assist. Adj. Gen. for Instruction	*p.s.c.* Major C. E. de la P. Beresford, Wiltshire Regiment, 1 July 92
District Inspector of Musketry	Major F. Hacket-Thompson, Cameron Highlanders, 2 Aug. 92.
Recruiting Staff Officer (Class I.)	Lt. Colonel *Hon*. C. Dutton (from h.p. Shropshire Light Infantry), 20 Nov. 93. *Newport, Mon*.
Brigade Major, Royal Artillery	*p.s.c.* Captain C. E. Callwell, Royal Artillery, 9 Sept. 93.
Commanding Militia and Volunteer Artillery	Lt. Colonel G. B. Allen. *Cardiff*.
Senior Ordnance Store Officer	Deputy Commissary General of Ordnance H. Taylor.
District Paymaster	Chief Paymaster G. L. C. Whittington.
Principal Medical Officer	Surgeon Colonel F. H. Welch.

5. SOUTHERN DISTRICT.—Head Quarters, Portsmouth.

Lieutenant General Commanding	Lt. General John Davis, *CB*. 9 Nov. 93.
Aides de Camp	Lieut. J. Shawe-Taylor, Cheshire Regiment, 9 Jan. 94.
	Major C. M. Sumner, S. Lancashire Regiment, 3 Feb. 94.
Commanding R. Art. (*Major Gen. on the Staff*)	Major General H. Le G. Geary, *CB*. 28 Apr. 90.
Commanding R. Eng. (*Colonel on the Staff*)	*p.s.c.* Colonel T. Fraser, *CB*. *CMG*. 1 Sept. 94.
Assistant Adjutant Generals	Colonel W. F. Cavaye (from h.p. Sussex Regiment), 8 Nov. 90.
	Colonel H.A. Bushman, *CB*. (from h.p. 9 Lancers), 15 July 92. *Netley*.
	p.s.c. Colonel E. S. Creek (from h.p. Welsh Fusiliers), 21 Aug. 94.
Deputy Assistant Adjutant Generals	*p.s.c.* Captain B. M. Hamilton, E. York Regt. 27 Jan. 94.
	Lt. Colonel W. A. Dunne, Army Service Corps, 31 Dec. 92.
	Captain T. J. O'Dell, Army Service Corps, 1 Apr. 94.
Deputy Assistant Adjutant General & Deputy Assist. Adj. Gen. for Instruction	*p.s.c.* Captain H. D. Drake, Royal Marine Artillery, 16 July 90.
District Inspector of Musketry	Captain J. E. B. Martin, King's Royal Rifles, 15 July 93.
Brigade Major, Royal Artillery	Major Arthur Pole-Penton, 1 Oct. 93.
Commanding Militia and Volunteer Artillery	Lt. Colonel A. W. Ferrier. *Gosport*.
Senior Ordnance Store Officer	Deputy Commissary General of Ordnance
District Paymaster	Chief Paymaster W. Hughes.
Principal Medical Officer	Surgeon Major General J. Davis.
Quarter Master, Invalid Depot	William Henry Hirst,[1] 1 April 85; *Hon*. *Lieut*. *Netley*.
Comm. Discharge Depot, Fort Brockhurst, Gosport	Colonel W. Glencross (from h.p. Lancashire Fusiliers), 2 June 9
Adjutant	Lieut. A. F. H. Cox, Inniskilling Fusiliers, 1 Apr. 92.
Paymaster	Staff Paymaster O. M. Johnston.
Quarter Master	William Neate, 7 May 84; *Hon*. *Captain* 9 May 94.

[1] Lieut. Hirst served in the Egyptian war of 1882 (Medal, and Khedive's Star).

Staff at Home. 98

6. THAMES DISTRICT.—Head Quarters, *Chatham*.

Major General Commanding	Major General B. L. Forster, R. Artillery, 1 May 92.
Aide de Camp	
Commanding R. Art. (*Colonel on the Staff*)	Colonel E. D. Elliott, 2 Aug. 00.
Commanding R. Eng (*Colonel on the Staff*)	Colonel A. Hill, 1 Aug. 94.
Assistant Adjutant General	p.s.c. Colonel G. Barton CB. (from h.p. R. Fusiliers), 16 Feb. 95.
Deputy Assistant Adjutant General	Lt.Colonel A. G. Hipwell, Army Service Corps, 23 Feb. 95.
Staff Captain, Royal Artillery	p.s.c. Captain A. B. N. Churchill, R. Artillery, 27 Nov. 93.
Commanding Militia and Volunteer Artillery	Lt.Colonel A. J. Pearson. *Woolwich*.
Senior Ordnance Store Officer	Assistant Commissary General of Ordnance F. O. Leggott.
District Paymaster	Staff Paymaster C. F. Casey.
Senior Medical Officer	Brigade Surgeon Lt.Colonel J. Williamson, *MB*.

7. SOUTH EASTERN DISTRICT.—Head Quarters, *Dover*.

Major General Commanding	Major General *Lord* W. F. E. Seymour, 24 Feb. 91.
Aide de Camp	
Brigadier General on the Staff	Major General E. A. Wood, CB. 1 Jan. 95. *Shorncliffe*.
Commanding R. Art. (*Colonel on the Staff*)	Colonel J. G. Burgmann, 19 Mar. 94.
Commanding R. Eng. (*Colonel on the Staff*)	Colonel E. D. C. O'Brien, 31 Dec. 91.
Assistant Adjutant General	p.s.c. Colonel J. Spence (from h.p. Yorkshire Lt. Inf.), 28 Dec. 93.
Deputy Assistant Adjutant General	Lt.Colonel B. Heygate, Army Service Corps, 1 Jan. 95.
Brigade Major	p.s.c. Bt.Major *Hon.* A.S. Hardinge, Scots Fus. 11 July 93. *Shorncliffe*.
Brigade Major, Royal Artillery	p.s.c. Capt. J. W. G. Dawkins, 1 July 94. [1 Nov. 92. *Shorncliffe*.
Dep. Assist. Adj. Gen. for Instruction	p.s.c. Lt.Col. H.T.W. Allatt (from h.p. Duke of Cornwall's Lt. Inf.)
District Inspector of Musketry	Major E. H. Le Marchant, Hampshire Regiment, 1 Jan. 93.
Commanding Militia and Volunteer Artillery	Lt.Colonel F. Ditmas.
Senior Ordnance Store Officer	Assistant Commissary General of Ordnance L. F. Graham.
District Paymaster	Chief Paymaster J. J. Tuak.
Principal Medical Officer	Surgeon Colonel T. F. O'Dwyer, *MD*.

8. HOME DISTRICT.—Head Quarters, *Horse Guards*.

Major General Commanding	Major General *Lord* Methuen, CB. CMG. 1 Apr. 92.
Aide de Camp	Captain L. G. Drummond, Scots Guards, 1 Apr. 92.
Assistant Adjutant General	Colonel W. H. Mackinnon (from h.p. Grenadier Guards), 26 July 93.
Deputy Assistant Adjutant Generals	{ Lt.Colonel J. A. Clarke, Army Service Corps, 11 Dec. 88. Captain C. W. King, Army Service Corps, 1 July 94.
Brigade Major	p.s.c. Captain H. G. D. Shute, Coldstream Guards, 1 Jan. 94.
Dep. Assist. Adj. Gen. for Instruction	p.s.c. Major J. H. Poett, Dorsetshire Regiment, 16 Dec. 92.
District Inspector of Musketry	Captain J. D. Hunt, Highland Light Infantry, 1 Aug. 91.
Commanding R. Eng. (*Colonel on the Staff*)	Colonel R. Athorpe, 19 May 91.
Commanding Militia and Volunteer Artillery	Lt.Colonel A. J. Pearson. *Woolwich*.
Senior Ordnance Store Officer	Assistant Commissary General of Ordnance F. E. Mulcahy.
District Paymaster	Chief Paymaster T. P. Senior.
Principal Medical Officer	Surgeon Colonel C. F. Churchill, *MB*.
Chief Recruiting Staff Officer	Colonel E. A. Brind (from Regimental District), 18 Sept. 94.
Recruiting Staff Officers (*Class II.*)	{ Lt.Colonel M. S. Brownrigg (from h.p. Yorkshire Regt.), 1 Apr. 92. *East London*. Captain J. R. P. Gordon, 15 Hussars, 25 March 94. *West London*.
Paymaster for Recruiting Duties	Staff Paymaster W. C. Kennedy.
Medical Officers for Recruiting Duties	{ Deputy Surgeon General W. G. Don, *MD*., retired pay. *½C*. Brigade Surgeon W. Temple, *MD*., retired pay. Brigade Surgeon Lt.Colonel G. W. M'Nalty, *MD*., retired pay.

9. WOOLWICH DISTRICT.

Major General Commanding	Major General G. J. Smart, 4 Feb. 94.
Aide de Camp	Lieut. J. F. N. Birch, Royal Artillery, 1 Apr. 94.
Assistant Adjutant General	Colonel T. M. Hazlerigg (from Royal Artillery), 12 Feb. 91.
Deputy Assistant Adjutant General	Lt.Colonel R. D. Noake, Army Service Corps, 20 Mar. 91.
Col. on the Staff (*Com. Horse and Field Art.*)	Colonel R. D. E. Lockhart, 22 May 94.
Commanding Royal Engineer	Colonel R. T. Orpen.
Commanding Militia and Volunteer Artillery	Lt.Colonel A. J. Pearson.
District Paymaster	Chief Paymaster C. H. Chauncey.
Principal Medical Officer	Surgeon Colonel A. F. Churchill, *MD*.
District Veterinary Officer	Veterinary Lt.Colonel W. A. Russell.
Recruiting Staff Officer (*Class I.*) for Recruiting Duties	Lt.Colonel H. Moore (from h.p. Lancaster Regt.), 4 Apr. 92 *Woolwich*.
Dep. Assist. Adj. Gen. for Supply Reserves	Lt.Col. G. V. Hamilton, A. S. C., 1 Jan. 95. *Woolwich Dockyard*.
Dep. Assist. Adj. Gen. (for Transport Duties)	Lt.Colonel F.E.Stevens, A. S. Corps, 14 Jan. 92. *Woolwich Arsenal*.

10. ALDERSHOT DISTRICT.

Commanding the Division	{ General *H.R.H.* the Duke of Connaught, KG. KT. KP. GCSI. GCMG. GCIE. KCB. Rifle Brigade, 9 Oct. 93.
Aides de Camp	{ Captain C. R. Burn, 1 Dragoons, 9 Oct. 93. Captain G. C. *Lord* Bingham, Rifle Brigade, 9 Oct. 93 (*extra*).
Assistant Adjutant Generals	{ p.s.c. Colonel H. S. G. Miles (from h.p. Munster Fus.), 29 Sept. 93. p.s.c. Colonel T. Kelly-Kenny, CB. (from h.p. West Surrey Regt.), 28 Dec. 93.
Deputy Assistant Adjutant Generals	{ p.s.c. Captain J. E. Lindley, 1 Dragoons, 31 Aug. 93. p.s.c. Lt.Colonel *Hon.* F. W. Stopford (from h.p. Grenadier Guards), 22 Aug. 94. Lt.Colonel E. FitzStubbs, Army Service Corps, 11 Dec. 88.
Deputy Assistant Adjutant General and Deputy Assist. Adj. Gen. for Instruction	p.s.c. Major H. E. Belfield, Munster Fusiliers, 4 May 93.
Dep. Assist. Adj. Gen. for Instruction	Major J. W. Murray, Royal Artillery, 10 Jan. 94.
Inspector of Gymnasia	Colonel G. M. Fox (from h.p. Black Watch), 12 Feb. 90.
Assistant Inspector of Gymnasia	Major F. W. Greatrex, 1 Dragoons, 1 Aug. 92.
Inspector of Signalling	p.s.c. Lt.Colonel C. Kennedy (from h.p. Suffolk Regt.), 1 Jan. 94.
Assistant Inspector of Signalling	Major E. Rhodes, *DSO*. Berkshire Regiment, 1 Jan. 95.
Instructor in Ballooning	Colonel J. L. B. Templer, 7 Bn. King's Royal Rifles, 1 Apr. 87.
District Inspector of Musketry	Major A. D. Bulpett, Derbyshire Regiment, 16 Dec. 94.
Senior Ordnance Store Officer	Assistant Commissary General of Ordnance F. G. Wintle, *DSO*.
District Paymaster	Chief Paymaster W. M. Playfair.
Principal Medical Officer	Surgeon Major General H. F. Paterson, *MD*.
District Veterinary Officer	Veterinary Lt.Colonel G. A. A. Oliver.
Camp Quarter Master	John Thomas Brind, 20 July 91; *Hon. Major*, 20 July 91.
Quarter Master	James Maguiro, 20 Jan. 83; *Hon. Capt.* 20 Jan. 93.
Provost Marshal	{ John Lindas Emerson, Military Mounted Police Corps, 31 Aug. 94½. *Hon. Lieut*.
Professor Army Veterinary School	Veterinary Major S. Longhurst, 1 Dec. 92.
Assistant Professor Army Veterinary School	Veterinary Captain E. R. C. Butler, 1 June 92.

Staff at Home.

Commanding Royal Artillery (*Brigadier General on the Staff, with rank of Major General*)	Brigadier General J. Alleyne, *CB*, 15 Dec. 93.
Brigade Major of Artillery	*p.s.c.* Captain J. M. Grierson, 1 Jan. 95.
Commanding Royal Engineer (*Col. on Staff*)	Colonel Sir A. W. Mackworth, *Bart.*, 1 Apr. 94.

Cavalry Brigade.

Commanding Brigade *with rank of Major General*	Colonel B. A. Combe, *CB.* (from h.p. 19 Hussars), 1 Jan. 95.
Aide de Camp	
Brigade Major	*p.s.c.* Major C. W. Peters, 4 Hussars, 10 Mar. 94.

1st Infantry Brigade.

Commanding Brigade	*p.s.c.* Major General H. M. Bengough, *CB.* 1 Dec. 94.
Aide de Camp	Captain A. I. S. Godfrey, West Riding Regiment, 1 Dec. 94.
Brigade Major	Major C. W. H. Douglas, Gordon Highlanders, 4 May 93.

2nd Infantry Brigade.

Commanding Brigade	Major General Sir W. F. Butler, *KCB.* 11 Nov. 93.
Aide de Camp	*p.s.c.* Captain R. N. Reade, Shropshire Lt. Inf. 17 Nov. 93.
Brigade Major	*p.s.c.* Captain J. S. Cowans, Rifle Brigade, 1 Sept. 94.

3rd Infantry Brigade.

Commanding Brigade	*p.s.c.* Major General C. F. Clery, *CB.* 20 Jan. 95.
Aide de Camp	Captain R. F. Alison, Seaforth Highlanders, 1 Feb. 95.
Brigade Major	*p.s.c.* Captain F. S. Robb, Durham Light Infantry, 19 Nov. 92.

11. NORTH BRITISH DISTRICT.—Head Quarters, *Edinburgh.*

Lieut. General Commanding	℔ General H. Rowlands, *CB.* 5 Jan. 94.
Aides de Camp	{ *p.s.c.* Captain R. N. Gamble, Lincolnshire Regiment, 16 Jan. 94. { Captain D. Baird, Black Watch, 1 Mar. 94.
Assistant Adjutant General	Colonel E. L. Street (from h.p. Regimental District), 17 Apr. 94.
Deputy Assistant Adjutant General	Lt.Colonel R. A. Nugent, *CB*, Army Service Corps, 21 Oct. 94.
Dep. Assist. Adj. Gen. and also for Instruction	*p.s.c.* Colonel A.G. Wavell (from h.p. R. Highlanders), 13 Sept. 94.
District Inspector of Musketry	Major J. F. Inglis, Wiltshire Regiment, 26 Oct. 93.
Recruiting Staff Officer (*Class I.*)	{ Lt.Colonel J. S. Tupper (from h.p. West Surrey Regt.), 31 Aug. 93. { *Glasgow.*
Recruiting Staff Officer (*Class II.*)	Captain P. Sinclair, Qr.Mr. Highland Lt.Inf. 6 Apr. 92. *Edinburgh.*
Commanding Royal Artillery (*Colonel on the Staff*)	Colonel C. W. Thomson, 4 Feb. 95.
Commanding Royal Engineer (*Colonel on the Staff*)	Colonel W. H. Patten (from h.p.), 2 Feb. 94.
Commanding Militia and Volunteer Artillery	{ Lt.Colonel J. M. Alves. *Leith Fort.* { Lt.Colonel G. Will. *Aberdeen.*
Senior Ordnance Store Officer	Assistant Commissary General of Ordnance H. H. St. George.
District Paymaster	Chief Paymaster E. Roberts.
Principal Medical Officer	Surgeon Colonel

12. JERSEY DISTRICT.

Lieut.Governor and Commanding the Troops	Lt. General E. Markham, Royal Artillery, 1 Nov. 92.
Deputy Assistant Adjutant General	{ *p.s.c.* Lt.Colonel J. W. F. Buxton (from h.p. Inniskilling Fusi- { liers), 7 May 93.
Commanding Royal Artillery	Major H. A. Scott.
Commanding Royal Engineer	Lt.Colonel H. Dove.
Senior Ordnance Store Officer	{ Dep. Assistant Commissary General of Ordnance P. de S. Bass, { *Captain Irish Regiment.*
District Paymaster	Staff Paymaster H. M. Caine.
Senior Medical Officer	Brigade Surgeon Lt.Colonel J. F. Supple.

13. GUERNSEY AND ALDERNEY DISTRICT.

Lieut.Governor and Commanding the Troops	Lt.General N. Stevenson, 16 Mar. 94.
Deputy Assistant Adjutant General	{ *p.s.c.* Lt.Colonel J. L. C. St. Clair (from h.p. Argyll and Suther- { land Highlanders), 15 May 92.
Commanding Royal Artillery	Major C. R. W. Hervey.
Commanding Royal Engineer	Lt.Colonel F. J. Day.
Senior Ordnance Store Officer	{ Dep. Assist. Com. Gen. of Ordnance J. H. Hale, *Captain East* { *Lancashire Regiment.*
District Paymaster	Staff Paymaster H. C. Ryder.

IRELAND.

Lieutenant General & General Governor	The Right Hon. R. O. A. Lord Houghton.

Aides de Camp.

Captain A. B. Ridley, Lancaster Regiment, 3 Oct. 92.	Captain H. H. P. Dundas, 15 Hussars, 25 Apr. 93 (*extra*).
Captain C. W. M. Feilden, 2 Dragoons, 3 Oct. 92.	Captain J. W. Burns, 3 Hussars, 15 Jan. 94 (*extra*).
Captain F. Douglas-Pennant, King's Royal Rifles, 3 Oct. 92.	Lieut. E. Crawley, 12 Lancers, 19 Feb. 94 (*extra*).
Lt. St.J. Meyrick, Gordon Highlanders 3 Oct. 92 (*extra*).	Lieut. *Lord* C. C. Bentinck, 9 Lancers, 6 Oct. 94 (*extra*).

Commanding the Forces	Field Marshal G. J. *Visct.* Wolseley, *KP. GCB. GCMG.* 1 Oct. 90.
Assistant Military Secretary	Bt.Colonel E. S. E. Childers, R. Engineers, 1 Oct. 90.
Aides de Camp	{ Captain W. C. Smithson, 13 Hussars, 2 Dec. 91. { Lieut. Hon. R. F. Somerset, Grenadier Guards, 22 Dec. 92.
Deputy Adjutant General	Colonel W. F. Kelly, *CB.* (from h.p. Sussex Regt.), 30 Oct. 94.
Assistant Adjutant General	{ *p.s.c.* Colonel E. J. Courtenay (from h.p. Sussex Regiment), { 28 Oct. 94.
Deputy Assistant Adjutant Generals	{ *p.s.c.* Major R. C. A. B. Bewicke-Copley, King's Royal Rifles, { 25 March 92. { Lt.Colonel E. W. D. Ward, Army Service Corps, 1 Apr. 92.
District Inspector of Musketry	Major R. F. Lindsell, Gloucestershire Regiment, 31 May 93.
Deputy Assist. Adjutant General R. Artillery	Major H. C. Sclater, 18 Oct. 92.
Chief Engineer (*Colonel on the Staff*)	Colonel R. H. Vetch, *CB.* 6 Nov. 92.
Brigade Major, Royal Engineers	*p.s.c.* Major E. H. Bethell, Royal Engineers, 19 Aug. 90.
Deputy Judge Advocate	
Senior Ordnance Store Officer	Deputy Commissary General of Ordnance W. R. Mayo.
Chief Paymaster	Chief Paymaster E. H. Gorges.
Principal Medical Officer	Surgeon Major General J. Colahan, *MD.*
District Veterinary Officer	Veterinary Lt.Colonel C. Phillips.

Staff at Home.

BELFAST DISTRICT.
COMMANDING BELFAST DISTRICT	Major General C. J. Moorsom, 28 Feb. 95.
Aide de Camp	
Assistant Adjutant General	p.s.c. Col.R.H.O'G. Haly, DSO.(from h.p.SuffolkRegt.), 25 Sept. 91.
Deputy Assistant Adjutant General	Captain F. C. A. Gilpin, Army Service Corps, 11 Dec. 94.
Commanding Royal Artillery	Lt.Colonel J. R. S. O. Hewitt. Londonderry.
Commanding Royal Engineer	Lt.Colonel J. Cameron.
Commanding Militia Artillery	Lt.Colonel J. R. S. O. Hewitt.
Senior Ordnance Store Officer	{ Deputy Assist. Commissary General of Ordnance C. K. Greene, Captain East Kent Regiment. Enniskillen.
District Paymaster	Staff Paymaster A. W. H. Gelston.
Principal Medical Officer	Surgeon Colonel M. Cogan.

DUBLIN DISTRICT.
COMMANDING DUBLIN DISTRICT	Major General G. H. Moncrieff, 1 May 91.
Aide de Camp	Lieut. F. J. Heyworth, Scots Guards, 1 May 91.
Assistant Adjutant General	p.s.c. Colonel H. L. Dundas (from h.p. E. York. Regt.), 1 Jan. 92.
Deputy Assistant Adjutant Generals	{ p.s.c. Lt.Col. H. Cooper (from h.p. N. Lancashire Regt.),21 Nov.93. Lt.Col. W. D. Richardson, CB. Army Service Corps, 8 Aug. 94.
Deputy Assist. Adjutant General for Instruction	p.s.c. Lt.Colonel F. W. Benson (from h.p. 17 Lancers), 2 Feb. 95.
Commanding Royal Engineer	Lt.Colonel C. H. Bagot.
Commanding Militia Artillery	Lt.Colonel J. R. S. O. Hewitt. Londonderry.
Senior Ordnance Store Officer	Assistant Commissary General of Ordnance J. L. Wheeler.
District Paymaster	Chief Paymaster E. H. Gorges.
Recruiting Staff Officer (Class I.)	Lt.Colonel R. F. Willoughby (from h.p. Scots Fus.), 1 Feb. 94.
Medical Officer for Recruiting Duties	Surgeon Major M. L. White, retired pay, 3 Oct. 88.

CURRAGH DISTRICT.
COMMANDING CURRAGH BRIGADE	Major General Lord R. D. Kerr, CB. 13 May 91.
Aide de Camp	Lieut. J. C. Aitken, Gordon Highlanders, 27 June 91. [12 Oct. 94.
Assistant Adjutant General	Colonel J. T. Coke (from h.p. King's Own Scottish Borderers),
Deputy Assistant Adjutant General	Lt.Colonel L. A. Hope, Army Service Corps, 1 Oct. 92.
Dep. Assist. Adj. Gen. for Instruction	p.s.c. Major A. E. W. Colville, Rifle Brigade, 27 Aug. 91.
Commanding Royal Artillery (Colonel on Staff)	p.s.c. Colonel W. F. M. Hutchinson, 1 Apr. 91.
Brigade Major, Royal Artillery	p.s.c. Captain P. J. R. Crampton, 23 July 94.
Commanding Royal Engineer	Lt.Colonel J. W. Savage.
Senior Ordnance Store Officer	Quarter Master E. B. D'Arcy, Hon. Captain.
District Paymaster	Staff Paymaster G. Dewar.
Senior Medical Officer	Brigade Surgeon Lt.Colonel J. Barry, MD.
Camp Quarter Master	H. Gibbs, 20 July 91; Hon. Lieut.
Assistant Provost Marshal	C. Burroughs, Mil. Mounted Police Corps, 16 Sept. 94; Hon.Lieut.

CORK DISTRICT.
COMMANDING CORK DISTRICT	Major General John Fryer, CB. 1 Oct. 93.
Aide de Camp	
Commanding Royal Artillery (Colonel on Staff)	Colonel E. H. Holley, 26 Jan. 94.
Commanding Royal Engineer	Colonel W. F. Spaight.
Assistant Adjutant General	Colonel H. B. Wilson (from Northampton Regt.), 19 Jan. 91.
Deputy Assistant Adjutant Generals	{ p.s.c. Bt.Major C. R. R. M'Grigor, King's Royal Rifles, 22 June 91. Lt.Colonel J. G. Y. Wilson, Army Service Corps.
District Inspector of Musketry	Major W. H. Riddell, Bedfordshire Regiment, 27 May 94.
Commanding Militia Artillery	Lt.Colonel J. M. Tabor. Templemore.
Senior Ordnance Store Officer	Assistant Commissary General of Ordnance H. T. Wyon.
District Paymaster	Staff Paymaster W. R. Kaye.
Principal Medical Officer	Surgeon Colonel C. A. Maunsell, MD.

STAFF ABROAD.—EUROPE.

GIBRALTAR.
Governor and Commander in Chief	General Sir R. Biddulph, GCMG. CB. Royal Artillery, 6 Oct. 93.
Assistant Military Secretary	Major E. W. Herbert, King's Royal Rifles, 3 Jan. 95.
Aides de Camp	{ Captain F. M. Beaumont, King's Royal Rifles, 10 Oct. 93. Lieut. H. Biddulph, Royal Artillery, 18 Oct. 93.
Commanding Brigade	Major General E. Hopton, CB. 25 May 93.
Aide de Camp	p.s.c. Captain C. Delmé-Radcliffe, Connaught Rangers, 7 Nov. 93.
Assistant Adjutant General	p.s.c. Colonel G. U. Prior (from h.p. Royal Scots), 19 Feb. 91.
Deputy Assistant Adjutant General	Lt.Colonel L. A. Clutterbuck, Army Service Corps, 2 Feb. 94.
Deputy Assistant Adjutant General and Deputy Assistant Adjutant General for Instruction	p.s.c. Captain W. D. Jones, Wiltshire Regiment, 1 May 91.
Brigade Major	p.s.c. Captain C. B. Vyvyan, East Kent Regiment, 1 Jan. 95.
Commanding R. Art. (Brigadier General on the Staff), with rank of Major General	Colonel J. B. Richardson, 9 Mar. 94.
Brigade Major, Royal Artillery	p.s.c. Major W. B. Fletcher, 5 Mar. 91.
Commanding Royal Engineer (Colonel on the Staff)	Colonel J. Fellowes, 12 Feb. 91.
Senior Ordnance Store Officer	Assistant Commissary General of Ordnance E. E. Markwick.
District Paymaster	Chief Paymaster J. W. Drage.
Principal Medical Officer	Surgeon Major General R. Lower.
Garrison Adjutant and Quarter Master	Richard Frederick Rankin,[1] 15 Aug. 89; Hon. Major.

[1] Major Rankin served in the Ashanti war in 1873-74 and was present in the actions of Amoaful and Quaman Dah, and at the capture of Coomassie (Medal with Clasp).

MALTA.
Governor and Commander in Chief (with rank of General)	Lt.General Sir Arthur J. Lyon Fremantle, KCMG. CB. 5 Jan. 94.
Assistant Military Secretary	p.s.c. Captain J. S. Ewart, Cameron Highlanders, 5 Jan. 94.
Aides de Camp	{ Captain G. G. A. Egerton, Seaforth Highlanders, 2 Feb. 94.
Colonial Aide de Camp	Captain N. Grech-Biancardi, Royal Malta Militia, 13 Jan. 94.
Commanding Brigade	p.s.c. Major General C. B. Knowles, CB. 29 Jan. 92.
Aide de Camp	Lieut. F. J. Bowker, Hampshire Regiment, 10 Feb. 94.
Deputy Adjutant General	Colonel A. S. Wynne, CB. (from h.p. York Light Inf.), 12 Oct. 94.
Deputy Assistant Adjutant Generals	{ p.s.c. Captain E. M. Woodward, Leicester Regiment, 1 Nov. 93. Major C. E. Wyncoll, Army Service Corps, 15 Mar. 92. Lt.Colonel E. Grattan, Army Service Corps, 8 Feb. 95.
Deputy Assistant Adjutant Gen. for Instruction	{ p.s.c. Lt.Col. F. Luttman-Johnson (from h.p. York and Lancaster Regiment), 14 Dec. 94.
Brigade Major	{ p.s.c. Major E. J. Montagu-Stuart-Wortley, CMG. King's Royal Rifles, 18 Aug. 93.
Commanding R. Artillery (with rank of Major Gen.)	Colonel S. J. Nicholson (from Royal Artillery), 4 Nov. 92.
Brigade Major, Royal Artillery	Captain A. Hamilton Gordon, 3 Aug. 94.
Commanding Royal Engineer (Colonel on the Staff)	Colonel E. Wood, CB. 8 June 94.
Senior Ordnance Store Officer	Assistant Commissary General of Ordnance A. W. Bridgman.
District Paymaster	Chief Paymaster J. L. Hewson.
Principal Medical Officer	Surgeon Major General J. Inkson, MD.

F

Staff Abroad.

CYPRUS.

High Commissioner and Commander in Chief	Sir Walter Joseph Sendall, *KCMG*. *Nicosia*.
Aide de Camp	Captain R. B. Feilden, Royal Artillery, 1 May 90.
Brigadier General	
Deputy Assistant Adjutant General	
Commanding Royal Engineer	Major P. Haslett.
Senior Ordnance Store Officer	Deputy Assistant Commissary General of Ordnance F. B. Simpson, *Captain 2 Dragoons*.
District Paymaster	Paymaster E. L. R. Thackwell.
Senior Medical Officer	Surgeon Major W. W. Kenny, *MB*.

ASIA.
INDIA.
[NOTE.—The Staff in India is corrected to the 1st March only.]

Viceroy and Governor General	The Rt. Hon. the Earl of Elgin and Kincardine, *GMSI*. *GMIE*. 27 Jan. 94.
Private Secretary	Henry Babington Smith, Bengal Civil Service, 16 Apr. 94.
Military Secretary	p.s.c. Bt.Lt.Colonel A. G. A. Durand, *CB*, Indian Staff Corps, 27 Jan. 94.
Aides de Camp	Captain R. E. Grimston, Indian Staff Corps, 27 Jan. 94. Lieut. S. H. Pollen, Wiltshire Regiment, 27 Jan. 94. Lieut. F. L. Adam, Scots Guards, 27 Jan. 94. Lieut. R. G. T. Baker Carr, Rifle Brigade, 17 Feb. 94 (*extra*). Lieut. J. M. F. Fuller, Wilts Yeomanry, 21 Feb. 94 (*extra*). Lieut. C. P. A. Hull, Scots Fusiliers, 19 Dec. 94 (*extra*). Lieut. H. Coape-Smith, Indian Staff Corps, 28 Dec. 94 (*extra*).
Surgeon	Brigade Surgeon Lt.Colonel B. Franklin, Bengal Establishment, 27 Jan. 94.
Commander in Chief (with rank of General)	VC Lieut.General *Sir* George Stewart White, *GCIE*. *KCB*. 8 Apr. 93.
Military Secretary	Colonel I. S. M. Hamilton, *DSO*. (from Gordon Highlanders), 8 Apr. 93.
Interpreter	Captain L. Herbert, Indian Staff Corps, 10 May 93.
Aides de Camp	Lieut. C. H. H. Gough, Indian Staff Corps, 8 Apr. 93. Lieut. Q. G. K. Agnew, Scots Fusiliers, 8 Apr. 93. Lieut. C. H. Stuart, Inniskilling Fusiliers, 13 Apr. 94.
Surgeon	Surgeon Major F. H. Treherne, Army Medical Staff, 8 Apr. 93.

ADJUTANT GENERAL'S DEPARTMENT AT HEAD QUARTERS.

Adjutant General	Major General W. Galbraith, *CB*, 15 Oct. 90.
Deputy Adjutant General	Colonel R. M. Jennings, Bengal Cavalry, 20 Nov. 92.

Assistant Adjutant Generals.

p.s.c. Colonel P. D. Jeffreys (from h.p. Connaught Rangers), 6 Jan. 94 .... Simla.
Colonel A. G. Yeatman-Biggs, (from h.p. Royal Artillery), 4 Jan. 94 .... Simla.

Deputy Assistant Adjutant Generals.

p.s.c. Major B. Duff, Indian Staff Corps, 7 Sept. 91 .... Simla.—Waziristan Field Force.
Major W. G. Bowyer, Royal Engineers, 3 Nov. 90 .... Simla (for R. Engineers).—Furl.

QUARTER MASTER GENERAL'S DEPARTMENT AT HEAD QUARTERS.

Quarter Master General (with rank of Major General)	Colonel E. Stedman, Indian Staff Corps, 12 Mar. 92.
Deputy Quarter Master General	p.s.c. Colonel E. R. Elles, *CB*. (from Royal Artillery), 30 Nov. 93.
Assistant Quarter Master General	Colonel G. F. Young, Indian Staff Corps, 4 Nov. 90.
Dep. Assist. Qr.Mr. Gen. (Mobilization)	p.s.c. Captain G. V. Kemball, Royal Artillery, 11 Mar. 91.
Assistant Quarter Master General, Intelligence Branch	p.s.c. Colonel G. H. More-Molyneux, Indian Staff Corps, 30 Nov. 93.
Dep. Assist. Quarter Master Generals, do.	p.s.c. Captain A. J. W. Allen, East Kent Regiment, 31 Aug. 90.—Furlough. Capt. E.F.H. M'Swiney, *DSO*. Indian S.C. 5 June 92.—Waziristan Field Force. Bt.Lt.Colonel A. H. Mason, *DSO*. R. Eng. 7 July 92.—Waziristan Field Force. Captain G. H. H. Couchman, *DSO*. Somerset Lt.Inf. 18 Apr. 93.—Burma. Captain H. Bower, Indian Staff Corps, 18 Apr. 93.—Special duty, China.
Staff Captains, do.	Captain P. Holland, Indian Staff Corps, 29 Apr. 90.—Offg. D. A. Q. M. Gen. Captain F. C. Colomb, Indian Staff Corps, 4 Nov. 91.—Simla. Captain H. R. Davies, Oxford Light Infantry, 16 Oct. 93.—Burma.
Staff Lieutenant, do.	Lieut. W. R. Robertson, 3 Dr. Gds. 5 June 92.—Offg. D. A. Q. M. Gen. Simla.
Inspector General of Artillery for India (with rank of Major General)	Colonel H. C. Lewes (from h.p. Royal Artillery), 28 Mar. 92.
Brigade Major	Captain F. E. Johnson, Royal Artillery, 25 Nov. 93.

Assistant Adjutant General for Artillery in India.

Colonel A. B. Stopford, 15 Nov. 94 .... Simla.

Inspector General of Cavalry in India (with rank of Major General)	p.s.c. Colonel H. F. Grant, *CB*. (from h.p. 7 Dragoon Guards), 1 Apr. 93.
Brigade Major	Captain F. W. P. Angelo, Indian Staff Corps, 15 Oct. 94.

Director of Military Education in India.

p.s.c. VC Colonel R. C. Hart (from Royal Engineers), 20 July 89 .... Simla.

Assistant Adjutant General for Musketry.

Colonel W. P. Symons, *CB*. (from h.p. South Wales Borderers), 8 Apr. 93 ... {Simla.—Con. Reserve Brigade, Waziristan Field Force.

Bengal.
Deputy Assistant Adjutant Generals for Musketry.

Captain C. L. Woollcombe, King's Own Scottish Borderers, 10 May 90 .... 5th Circle, Umballa.
Captain H. H. Dobbie, Indian Staff Corps, 26 Jan. 91 .... 4th Circle, Meerut.
Captain F. Campbell, Indian Staff Corps, 22 Aug. 91 .... 2nd Circle, Allahabad.
Bt.Major B. J. C. Doran, Irish Regiment, 6 Nov. 91 .... 1st Circle, Fort William.
Major H. C. Wylly, Derbyshire Regiment, 8 May 92 .... 3rd Circle, Lucknow.
Captain H. S. Mayhew, Border Regiment, 31 Mar. 94 .... 6th Circle, Meean Meer.
Major W. E. Sturges, Northumberland Fusiliers, 20 Apr. 94 .... 7th Circle, Rawul Pindee.
Captain A. A. E. Campbell, Indian Staff Corps, 13 May 94 .... 8th Circle, Abbottabad.
Inspector of Gymnasia............Major Hon. A. E. Dalzell, Oxford Light Infantry, 15 Apr. 92.

District Recruiting Officers.

Captain E. Vansittart, Indian Staff Corps, 1 Apr. 92 .... Goruckpore.
Captain R. T. Crowther, Indian Staff Corps, 10 Apr. 92 .... Umritsur.
Captain W. J. Newell, Indian Staff Corps, 12 Apr. 92 .... Lucknow.
Captain G. P. Rankcn, Indian Staff Corps, 14 Apr. 92 .... Peshawur.
Captain A. Hamilton, Indian Staff Corps, 16 Apr. 92 .... Rawul Pindee.
Captain K. P. Burno, Indian Staff Corps, 25 Apr. 92 .... Sealkote.
Captain F. G. R. Ostrehan, Indian Staff Corps, 20 June 92 .... Delhi.
Inspector of Army Signalling...Captain T. E. O'Leary, Irish Fusiliers, 1 Sept. 93 Kussowlie.
Assistant do. ....Captain G. W. Rawlins, Indian Staff C. 1 Nov. 94 Kusswlie.

Deputy Assistant Adjutant Generals for Instruction.

Captain J. E. Nixon, Indian Staff Corps, 2 Apr. 88 .... Chuckrata.
p.s.c. Major A. J. Watson, Suffolk Regiment, 20 July 89 .... Dalhousie.
p.s.c. Major A. M. Renny, Indian Staff Corps, 2 Apr. 92 .... Ranikhet.
p.s.c. Major J. Sherston, *DSO*, Rifle Brigade, 7 Mar. 93 .... Kussowlie.

Staff Abroad.

Garrison Quarter Master.
Lieut. E. Witham, 7 Dragoon Guards, 7 Apr. 92 .... Fort William.

FIRST CLASS DISTRICT COMMANDERS.
Commanding Lahore District .... Major General R. H. Visct. Frankfort de Montmorency, 11 Mar. 99.
Aide de Camp .... Captain W. H. Booth, East Kent Regiment, 26 Apr. 93.
Commanding Rawul Pindee District ...... p.s.c. Major General Sir W. K. Elles, KCB, 15 Oct. 90.
Aide de Camp .... Captain A. W. Elles, Yorkshire Light Infantry, 27 Apr. 93.
Commanding Punjab Frontier Force ... { Lt.Genera Sir W. S. A. Lockhart, KCB, CSI. Bengal Inf., 1 Apr. 93.—Commanding Waziristan Field Force.
Aide de Camp ....
Commanding Oude District .... Major General Sir R. C. Low, KCB, Bengal Cavalry, 1 Apr. 92.
Aide de Camp .... Lieut. R. B. Low, Indian Staff Corps, 1 Apr. 92.
Commanding Quetta District .... Major General G. Luck, CB. 8 Apr. 93.
Aide de Camp .... Lieut. Hon. R. H. Marsham, 7 Hussars, 4 Sept. 93.
Commanding Meerut District, with rank } Colonel G. E. L. S. Sanford, CB. CSI. (from h.p. R. Engineers), 22 Sept. 93.
of Major General ....
Aide de Camp .... Captain C. R. A. Bond, Indian Staff Corps, 23 Sept. 93.

SECOND CLASS DISTRICT COMMANDERS.
Brigadier General A. A. A. Kinloch, CB. (from h.p. King's Royal Rifles,) } Peshawur.
15 Oct. 90.
Brigadier General G. de C. Morton, CB. (from h.p. Munster Fusiliers,) } Bundelcund.
24 Apr. 92.
Major General F. Lance, CB. Indian Staff Corps, 6 Apr. 92 .... Presidency.
p/c Major General G. N. Channer, CB. Indian Staff Corps, 22 Apr. 92 ..... Rohilcund.
Major General Sir A. P. Palmer, KCB. Indian Staff Corps, 21 Apr. 93 ...... Allahabad,—Furlough.
p.s.c. Brig.Gen.W.L.Dalrymple, CB.(from h.p. Connaught Rangers), 15 Nov. 93 Nerbudda.
Brigadier General C. R. Pennington, CB. Indian Staff Corps, 1 Dec. 94 .... Assam.

Colonels on the Staff.
Colonel A. G. Handcock, CB. Indian Staff Corps, 23 Feb. 91 .... Delhi.
Colonel H. G. Waterfield, Indian Staff Corps, 6 Apr. 92 .... Ferozepore.
Colonel G. Swinley, CB. Royal Artillery, 22 Apr. 92 .... Sealkote.
Major General W. W. Biscoe, Bengal Cavalry, 4 Jan. 93 .... Mooltan.
Colonel R. C. R. Clifford, CB. Indian Staff Corps, 28 March 94 .... Cawnpore.—Furlough.
Colonel H. M. Evans, CB. Indian Staff Corps, 31 March 94 .... Fyzabad.—Offg.in.Comd.Allahabad.

Second Class Station Commanders.
Colonel J. W. A. Michell, Indian Staff Corps, 31 March 92 .... Dinapore.   [Field Force.
Lt.Colonel W. O. Thompson, Indian Staff Corps, 30 Sept. 93 .... Dera Ismail Khan.—Waziristan
Lt.Colonel G. E. Harley, East Kent Regiment, 28 Jan. 94 .... Jullunder.
Lt.Colonel C. Norman, Welsh Fusiliers, 8 Feb. 94 .... Jhansi.
Lt.Colonel C. C. Egerton, DSO. Indian Staff Corps, 10 Apr. 94 .... Kohat.—Waziristan Field Force.
Lt.Colonel W. W. H. Scott, Indian Staff Corps, 28 Apr. 94 .... Nowshera.   [Force.
Major A. C. Bunny, Indian Staff Corps .... Edwardesabad.—Waziristan Field
Lt.Colonel W. A. Broome, Indian Staff Corps .... Loralai.
                                                                            Saugor.

Assistant Adjutant Generals.
p.s.c. Colonel C. L. Harvey (from h.p. Wiltshire Regiment), 7 Jan. 90 ..... Oude.
Colonel T. G. Crawley (from h.p. Liverpool Regiment), 28 July 90 .... Allahabad.
Colonel G. R. J. Shakespear, Indian Staff Corps, 25 Oct. 90 .... Rawul Pindee.
Bt.Lt.Colonel St. J. F. Michell, Indian Staff Corps, 25 March 91 .... Presidency.   [Field Force.
Bt.Major A. R. Martin, Indian Staff Corps, 1 Feb. 92 .... Punjab Frontier Force.—Waziristan
Colonel R. M. Clifford, Indian Staff Corps, 6 Feb. 93 .... Peshawur.
p.s.c. Colonel H. S. Brownrigg (from h.p. Rifle Brigade), 1 Oct. 93 ...... Meerut.
Major E. A. Young, Indian Staff Corps, 10 Oct. 93 .... Lahore.
Lt.Colonel G. Henry, Royal Engineers, 6 Jan. 94 .... Quetta.
p.s.c. Major H. L. Smith Dorrien, DSO. Derbyshire Regiment, 27 Oct. 94 ... Sirhind.

Deputy Assistant Adjutant Generals.
Captain J. G. Ramsay, Indian Staff Corps, 1 Apr. 90 .... Punjab Frontier Force.—Furlough.
Major L. C. Dundas, DSO. Liverpool Regiment, 30 June 90 .... Presidency.
p.s.c. Captain W. G. Hamilton, East Lancashire Regiment, 28 July 90 ...... Lahore.
Major Hon. U. De R. B. Roche, South Wales Borderers, 25 Oct. 90 .... Peshawur.
Captain K. S. Davison, Indian Staff Corps, 1 Jan. 91 .... Meerut.—Waziristan Field Force.
Captain A. C. Batten, Indian Staff Corps, 31 Jan. 91 .... Bundelcund.
Captain D. W. Hickman, Indian Staff Corps, 20 Jan. 92 .... Sirhind.
Bt.Major C. J. Mackenzie, Seaforth Highlanders, 2 June 92 .... Quetta.—Waziristan Field Force.
Bt.Major W. du G. Gray, Indian Staff Corps, 14 Nov. 92 .... Nerbudda.—Furlough.
Bt.Major E. A. Travers, Indian Staff Corps, 27 Apr. 93 .... Rawul Pindee.
Captain E. T. Paul, Indian Staff Corps, 23 Apr. 94 .... Assam.
p.s.c. Captain W. P. Blood, Irish Fusiliers, 27 June 94 .... Allahabad.
Captain E. D. J. O'Brien, 3 Dragoon Guards, 16 Sept. 94 .... Rohilcund.
p/c Major W. H. Dick-Cunyngham, Argyll and Suth. Highlanders, 30 Oct. 94 . Oude.
p.s.c. Captain W. E. Bunbury, Indian Staff Corps, 26 Dec. 94 .... Nerbudda.

Madras.
Governor .... The Right Hon. Beilby, Lord Wenlock, GCIE. 23 Jan. 91.
Private Secretary .... Charles Falkiner MacCartie, Madras Civil Service, 18 Dec. 91.
Military Secretary .... Major Hon. R. T. Lawley, 7 Hussars, 23 Jan. 91.
                                      { Captain Hon. E. Baring, 10 Hussars, 23 Jan. 91.
Aides de Camp .... { Captain Lord D. J. C. Compton, 9 Lancers, 16 Nov. 92.
                                      { Capt. Hon. G.A.Lascelles, 3 Bn. Yorkshire Regt., 16 May 92 (extra).
                                      { Captain G. H. Arbuthnot, DSO. 24 Jan. 95 (extra).
Surgeon .... Surgeon Major W. B. Browning, Madras Estab., 29 May 92.
Commander in Chief (with rank of Lt. } Major General C. Mansfield Clarke, CB. 28 Oct. 93.
General) ....
Military Secretary .... Major R. G. Kekewich, Inniskilling Fusiliers, 28 Oct. 93.
Aides de Camp .... { Captain Hon. F. R. Bingham, R. Artillery, 28 Oct. 93.—And Offg. Interp.

ADJUTANT GENERAL'S DEPARTMENT AT HEAD QUARTERS.
Adjutant General ......
Deputy Adjutant General ...... Colonel E. W. Bagbie, DSO. Madras Infantry, 29 Oct. 91.—Offg. Adjutant General.
Assistant Adjutant Generals ... { Colonel W. E. Lockhart, Royal Artillery, 31 Oct. 89.

QUARTER MASTER GENERAL'S DEPARTMENT AT HEAD QUARTERS.
Quarter Master General (with rank of } Colonel E. H. Eyre, CB. Indian Staff Corps, 12 Oct. 90.—Furlough.
Brigadier General) ....
Deputy Quarter Master General .... Colonel G. Simpson, Indian Staff Corps, 28 Nov. 93.—Offg. Qr. Mr. Gen.

Staff Abroad.

Assistant Adjutant General for Musketry.
Major R. L. A. Pennington, Northumberland Fusiliers, 27 Oct. 94.... 1st Circle, Bangalore, &c.

Deputy Assistant Adjutant Generals for Musketry.
Captain H. T. King, Indian Staff Corps, 1 Nov. 92 .... 2nd Circle, Secunderabad, &c.
Captain B. A. Johnstone, Indian Staff Corps, 16 May 94 ... 3rd Circle, Burmah.

Deputy Assistant Adjutant General for Instruction.
p.s.c. Captain C. E. Poynder, Indian Staff Corps, 20 Oct. 94. Bangalore.

FIRST CLASS DISTRICT COMMANDERS.
Commanding Secunderabad District .... Lieut.General Sir R. C. Stewart, KCB. Madras Cavalry, 26 Oct. 90.
Aide de Camp ....
Commanding Burmah District .... p.s.c. Major General J. North Crealock, CB, 13 Nov. 93.
Aide de Camp .... Captain L. A. M. Stopford, Derbyshire Regiment, 6 Dec. 93.

SECOND CLASS DISTRICT COMMANDERS.
Major General A. F. Hamilton, Royal Engineers, 6 Nov. 90 .... Rangoon.
Brigadier General T. Van Straubenzee, CB. (from Royal Artillery), 28 Feb. 91 .... } Madras.
p.s.c. Brigadier General M. W. E. Gosset, CB. (from h.p. Dorsetshire Regiment), 1 Dec. 91 .... } Bangalore.
Brigadier General G. C. Bird, Indian Staff Corps, 15 March 94 .... Mandalay.
Brigadier General H. P. Pearson, CB. (from h.p. Regimental District), 1 Apr. 94 .... } Belgaum.
Brigadier General J. G. H. Prendergast, Indian Staff Corps, 11 July 94 Southern District.

Colonels on the Staff.
Colonel F. C. St. John, Indian Staff Corps, 14 July 90 .... Bellary.—Furlough.
Colonel W. B. Warner, Madras Cavalry, 7 Aug. 94 .... Bhamo.—Offg. in Comd. Mandalay.

Assistant Adjutant Generals.
p.s.c. Major J. H. Sewell, Norfolk Regiment, 17 Apr. 91................ Mandalay.
p.s.c. Major F. W. Bromfield, Cheshire Regiment, 7 Sept. 91 .... Madras.
Colonel A. S. Grove, DSO. Indian Staff Corps, 22 Oct. 91 .... Burmah.
p.s.c. Major H. B. Jeffreys, Royal Artillery, 12 Nov. 91 .... Rangoon.
Colonel W. L. Ranking, Madras Infantry, 1 June 93 .... Belgaum.—Sick Furlough.   [Mil. Dept.
Colonel D. J. S. M'Leod, DSO. Madras Cavalry, 12 Aug. 93 .... Secunderabad.—Offg. Sec. to Madras Govt.,,
Major C. W. Park, Devonshire Regiment, 15 Nov. 93 .... Southern.
Bt.Major G. B. Stevens, Indian Staff Corps, 8 May 94.................. Bangalore.

Deputy Assistant Adjutant Generals.
Captain G. J. Shaw, Indian Staff Corps, 17 April 91 .... Madras.—Furlough.
Captain R. F. Clothier, Indian Staff Corps, 1c June 92 .... Chin Hills.—Furlough.
Captain C. B. Little, Somerset Light Infantry, 14 June 92 .... Secunderabad.—Offg. A. A. Gen.
Major H. Finn, 21 Hussars, 25 Jan. 93 .... Bangalore.
Captain C. Stevens, Indian Staff Corps, 19 Oct. 93 .... Belgaum.—Offg. A. A. Gen.
Captain E. M. Reed, Indian Staff Corps, 15 Nov. 93..................... Bangalore.
Captain T. A. H. Davies, DSO. Devonshire Regiment, 7 Feb. 94 ... Burmah.
Captain A. H. B. Cavaye, King's Own Scottish Borderers, 3 Oct. 94.. Rangoon.
Captain T. H. Haughton, Indian Staff Corps, 3 Oct. 94 .... Burmah (additional).

Bombay.

Governor .... Rt. Hon. W. Lord Sandhurst, GCIE.
Private Secretary ....
Military Secretary...................... Major R. Owen, 21 Hussars.
Aides de Camp .... { Captain H. G. Heneage, 12 Lancers.
                                          { Lieut. B. J. T. Levett, Scots Guards.

Surgeon .... Surgeon Major Henry Martin, MB. Army Medical Staff.
Commander in Chief, with rank of Lt.-Gen. Major General Charles Edward Nairne, CB. Royal Artillery, 4 Sept. 93.
Military Secretary .... Captain H. F. Mercer, Royal Artillery, 4 Sept. 93.
Aides de Camp .... { Captain R. St. C. Lecky, Royal Artillery, 4 Sept. 93.
                                          { Captain C. E. Baynes, Indian Staff Corps, 30 Sept. 93.—And Interpreter.

ADJUTANT GENERAL'S DEPARTMENT AT HEAD QUARTERS.
Adjutant General ....
Deputy Adjutant General............... Colonel J. T. Watling, Indian Staff Corps, 10 Dec. 92.—Furlough.
Assistant Adjutant Generals .... { p.s.c. Colonel R. L. H. Curtois (from h.p. Bedfordshire Regt.), 1 July 90.—
                                         Offg. Adjutant General.

QUARTER MASTER GENERAL'S DEPARTMENT AT HEAD QUARTERS.
Quarter Master General (with rank of Brigadier General)............. } Colonel G. C. Hogg, Bombay Cavalry, 3 Mar. 91.
Deputy Quarter Master General .... Colonel E. Carrington (from h.p. Worcester Regiment), 8 Mar. 91.

Assistant Adjutant General for Musketry.
Lt.Colonel J. G. C. Curtis (from h.p. Oxford Light Infantry), 24 Feb. 91 .... 1st Circle, Poona.

Deputy Assistant Adjutant Generals for Musketry.
Captain W. A. M. Wilson, Indian Staff Corps, 29 May 94 .... 2nd Circle, Mhow.
Captain G. A. Carleton, Lancaster Regiment, 8 June 94 .... 3rd Circle, Bombay.—Sick Furl.

FIRST CLASS DISTRICT COMMANDERS.
Commanding Mhow District .... Lieut.General H. S. Anderson, Indian Staff Corps, 16 Mar. 91.
Aide de Camp .... Captain G. W. W. Savile, Middlesex Regiment, 22 Oct. 91.
Commanding Poona District .... p.s.c. Major General R. B. H. Blundell, 29 Mar. 91.
Aide de Camp............................... Captain B. Upperton, Oxford Light Infantry, 2 June 91.

SECOND CLASS DISTRICT COMMANDERS.
Brigadier General J. Jopp, CB. Indian Staff Corps, 14 May 90 .... Aden.
Brigadier General J. Gatacre, CB. Indian Staff Corps, 1 Nov. 91 .... Nagpore.
Brigadier General T. A. Cooke (from h.p. 17 Lancers), 9 Jan. 94....................... Sind.
p.s.c. Brigadier General W. F. Gatacre, DSO (from h.p. Middlesex Regt.), 30 Jan. 94 Bombay.
Major General M. H. Nicolson, CB. Bombay Infantry, 27 June 94 .... Deesa.

Staff Abroad.
Colonel on the Staff.

Colonel G. C. Sartorius, *CB*. Indian Staff Corps, 6 Apr. 94 .... Nusseerabad.

Assistant Adjutant Generals.

Major C. E. Sawyer, North Lancashire Regiment, 19 July 90 .... Mhow.
Lt.Colonel W. E. Hilliard (from h.p. Yorkshire Light Infantry), 10 Jan. 92 .... Bombay.
Colonel A. Currie, Bombay Cavalry, 15 Dec. 93 .... Sind.
Colonel R. Westmacott, *CB. DSO*. Indian Staff Corps, 2 March 94 .... Deesa.
Colonel H. S. Tandy, Indian Staff Corps, 12 May 94 .... Poona.—Offg. Dep. Adj. Gen.

Deputy Assistant Adjutant Generals.

Captain E. A. D'A. Thomas, Worcester Regiment, 10 Feb. 91 .... Nagpore.
Captain C. R. Philipps, Indian Staff Corps, 24 March 91 .... Aden.—Furlough.
Captain J. C. Swann, Indian Staff Corps, 2 Sept. 91 .... Bombay.
Major C. J. Blomfield, Lancashire Fusiliers, 27 Oct. 92 .... Poona.
p.s.c. Captain H. Chance, Royal Artillery, 4 Feb. 94 .... Sind. [Poona.
p.s.c. Major Sir H. A. W. Johnson, *Bart*. Yorkshire Light Infantry, 10 Mar. 04 ... Bombay.—Offg.Assist.Adj.Gen.
Major J. Willcocks, *DSO*. Leinster Regiment, 1 Aug. 94 .... Mhow.

Deputy Assistant Adjutant General for Instruction.

p.s.c. Major F. W. Kitchener, West Yorkshire Regiment, 15 Aug. 91 .... Poona.

Inspector of Gymnasia, Madras and Bombay.

Captain C. F. H. Davidson, Argyll and Sutherland Highlanders, 7 Nov. 94 .... Poona.

Inspector of Army Signalling, Madras and Bombay.

Captain J. R. K. Birch, Cheshire Regiment, 4 July 92 .... Poona.

CEYLON.

Governor and Commander in Chief .... Sir Arthur Elibank Havelock, *GCMG*. Colombo.
Aide de Camp .... Captain A. H. W. Lowndes, Rifle Brigade, 22 Dec. 94.
Brigadier General .... Major General W. C. Justice, *CMG*. 3 Mar. 93.
Aide de Camp .... Lieut. C. W. Justice, York and Lancaster Regiment, 5 Mar. 94.
Deputy Assistant Adjutant Generals .... { p.s.c. Major R. B. Williams, Somerset Lt. Infantry, 15 Dec. 93.
{ Captain F. Horniblow, Army Service Corps, 31 Jan. 95.
Commanding Royal Artillery .... Lt.Colonel C. J. Blake.
Commanding Royal Engineer .... p.s.c. Lt.Colonel C. F. C. Beresford.
Senior Ordnance Store Officer .... Assistant Commissary General of Ordnance A. Sadler.
District Paymaster .... Staff Paymaster H. F. G. Webster.
Senior Medical Officer .... Brigade Surgeon Lt.Colonel J. Maturin.

CHINA AND HONG KONG, AND STRAITS SETTLEMENTS.

Governor and Commander in Chief of Hong Kong... Sir William Robinson, *KCMG*. Victoria.
Aide de Camp .... Lieut. J. T. Sterling, Coldstream Guards, 17 Apr. 92.
Major General .... p.s.c. Major General W. Black, *CB*. 28 Feb. 95.
Aide de Camp ....
Deputy Assistant Adjutant Generals .... { Lt.Colonel N. P. O'Gorman (from h.p. Lincoln Regt.), 18 Jan. 95.
{ Captain A. H. Thomas, Army Service Corps, 14 June 93.
Commanding Royal Artillery (Colonel on the Staff) Colonel G. B. Macdonell, 16 Dec. 90.
Commanding Royal Engineer (Colonel on the Staff) Colonel W. H. Mulloy, 15 Oct. 91.
Senior Ordnance Store Officer .... Assistant Commissary General of Ordnance R. F. N. Clarke.
District Paymaster .... Chief Paymaster W. L. Barr.
Principal Medical Officer .... Surgeon Colonel A. F. Preston, *MB*.

Straits Settlements.
(*Including Prince of Wales' Island, Malacca, Singapore, and Christmas Island.*)

Governor and Commander in Chief .... { Lt.Colonel Sir Charles Bullen Hugh Mitchell, *KCMG*. ret. pay
{ R. Marines. *Singapore.*
Aide de Camp .... Lieut. E. A. Herbert, 6 Dragoons, 5 Jan. 94.
Colonel on the Staff (with rank of Major General) { p.s.c. Colonel H. T. Jones-Vaughan, *CB*. (from h.p. E. Yorkshire
{ Regt.), 13 Apr. 94.
Deputy Assistant Adjutant General .... p.s.c. Major T. E. Compton, Northampton Regiment, 7 Feb. 91.
Garrison Adjutant .... Captain W. L. Warren, Royal Artillery, 20 Apr. 94. *Singapore.*
Commanding Royal Artillery .... Lt.Colonel R. H. W. Plunkett. *Singapore.*
Commanding Royal Engineer ....)(Lt.Colonel J. R. M. Chard. [*Regt.*
Senior Ordnance Store Officer .... Dep.Assist.Com.Gen.of Ordnance H. D. E.Parsons,*Capt.W.Surrey*
District Paymaster .... Staff Paymaster L. R. Dowdall.
Senior Medical Officer .... Brigade Surgeon Lt.Colonel J. H. Hughes, *MD*.

LABUAN AND ITS DEPENDENCIES.

Governor and Commander in Chief .... C. V. Creagh, *CMG*.

AUSTRALIA.
New South Wales.

Governor and Commander in Chief ....
Aides de Camp .... {

Victoria.

Governor and Commander in Chief .... Rt. Hon. T. Lord Brassey, *KCB*. *Melbourne.*
Aides de Camp .... {

South Australia.

Governor and Commander in Chief .... Rt. Hon. A. H. T. Earl of Kintore, *GCMG*. *Adelaide.*
Aide de Camp .... Captain E. Milner, Scots Guards, 18 Mar. 92.

Western Australia.

Governor and Commander in Chief .... Sir William Clewer Francis Robinson, *GCMG*. *Perth*.
Aide de Camp ....

Staff Abroad.

Queensland.
Governor and Commander in Chief .... General Sir H. W. Norman, *GCB. GCMG. CIE. Brisbane.*
Aide de Camp .... Lieut. C. E. M. Pyne, Warwickshire Regiment, 28 Jan. 94.

Tasmania.
Governor and Commander in Chief .... Rt. Hon. J. W. J. Visct. Gormanstown, *KCMG. Hobart Town.*
Aide de Camp ....

NEW ZEALAND.
Governor and Commander in Chief .... Rt. Hon. Earl of Glasgow, *GCMG. Wellington.*
Aides de Camp .... { Major E. H. M. Elliot, South Lancashire Regiment, 12 Jan. 94.
  Lieut. E. F. Clayton, Scots Guards, 9 April 92.
  Captain R. W. P. Clarke-Campbell-Preston, 3 Bn. R. Highlanders, 25 July/94.

FIJI ISLANDS.
Governor and Commander in Chief, and High Commissioner for the Western Pacific .... } Sir John Bates Thurston, *KCMG. Suva.*
Aide de Camp ....

BRITISH NEW GUINEA.
Administrator .... Sir William Macgregor, *MD. KCMG.*

AFRICA.
EGYPT, FORCE IN.
Major General .... Major General Sir F. W. E. F. Walker, *KCB. CMG.* 19 Dec. 90. Cairo
Aides de Camp .... { Captain F. Lee, 4 Hussars, 21 Oct. 93.
  Captain F. St. J. Hughes, S. Wales Borderers, 27 Sept. 93 (extra).
Assistant Adjutant General .... { p.s.c. Colonel Sir St. V. A. Hammick, Bart. (from h.p. Oxford Lt. Infantry), 10 Nov. 91.
Deputy Assistant Adjutant General .... Lt. Colonel M. E. R. Rainsford, Army Service Corps, 9 Feb. 94.
Dep. Assist. Adj. General and do. for Instruction .. p.s.c. Major J. M. Gawne, Lancaster Regiment, 3: Jan. 95.
Staff Captains .... { Captain P. R. Phipps, Dorsetshire Regiment, 1 Jan. 93.
  Captain G. O. Welch, Army Service Corps, 1 Apr. 94.
Commanding Royal Artillery .... Major J. P. Fell.
Commanding Royal Engineer .... p.s.c. Lt. Colonel A. O. Green.
Senior Ordnance Store Officer .... Assistant Commissary General of Ordnance C. E. Vansittart.
District Paymaster .... Chief Paymaster F. Treffry.
Principal Medical Officer .... Surgeon Colonel W. Nash, *MD.*
Senior Veterinary Officer .... Veterinary Major J. Hammond.

Garrison of Alexandria.
Colonel on the Staff (with rank of Major General) .. Colonel K. G. Henderson, *CB.* (from h.p. King's R. Rifles), 2 Nov. 93.
Deputy Assistant Adjutant General .... p.s.c. Capt. A. B. Hamilton, King's Own Scottish Bords. 10 Dec. 93.
Staff Captain (Military Police) .... Captain T. S. Fox-Strangways, Irish Rifles, 1 June 91.
Commanding Royal Engineer .... Lt. Colonel R. M. Barklie.
Senior Ordnance Store Officer .... Quarter Master P. Mullen, Ordnance Store Department.

Governor of the Frontier and Commandant of the Frontier Field Force .... } Colonel A. Hunter, *DSO.* Lancaster Regiment, 2 July 94.

Suakin.
Governor General of the Red Sea Littoral and Commandant at Suakin (with rank of Lt. Col.) ...... } Major G. E. Lloyd, *DSO.* South Staffordshire Regt. 29 July 94.

CAPE OF GOOD HOPE.
Governor and Commander in Chief, and High Commissioner for South Africa .... } Rt. Hon. Sir Hercules George Robert Robinson, *GCMG.*
Military Secretary .... Captain C. T. Dawkins, Shropshire Light Infantry.
Aide de Camp ....
Lieutenant General .... Lt. General W. H. Goodenough, Royal Artillery, 8 Dec. 94.
Assistant Military Secretary and Aide de Camp ... Major A. M. Murray, Royal Artillery.
Aide de Camp .... Lieut. R. J. Vernon, King's Royal Rifles.
Assistant Adjutant General .... Colonel M. S. Crofton, *DSO.* (from h.p. S. Stafford Regt.) 13 July 94.
Deputy Assistant Adjutant Generals .... { p.s.c. Major J. C. Young, Sussex Regiment, 23 Jan. 92.
  Major G. P. Bourcicault, Army Service Corps, 2 April 92.
Commanding Royal Artillery .... Lt. Colonel A. W. White.
Commanding Royal Engineer (Colonel on the Staff) Colonel F. W. Nixon.
Senior Ordnance Store Officer .... Assistant Commissary General of Ordnance C. G. Jeans.
District Paymaster .... Chief Paymaster G. H. Anson.
Principal Medical Officer .... Surgeon Colonel J. B. Hamilton, *MD.*
Senior Veterinary Officer .... Veterinary Major J. C. Berne.

NATAL AND ZULULAND.
Governor and Commander in Chief .... Hon. Sir Walter Fras. Hely-Hutchinson, *KCMG. Pietermaritzburg.*
Aide de Camp .... Lieut. J. A. Bell-Smyth, 1 Dragoon Guards, 2 Sept. 93.
Brigadier General on the Staff .... Major-General C. Tucker, *CB.* 13 Sept. 93.
Deputy Assistant Adjutant General .... p.s.c. Captain C. H. Watts, Derbyshire Regiment, 18 Jan. 92.
Commanding Royal Engineer .... Lt. Colonel H. Elsdale.
Senior Ordnance Store Officer .... Assistant Commissary General of Ordnance G. R. Hobbs.
District Paymaster .... Staff Paymaster W. B. Caulfeild-Stoker.

Staff Abroad.

SAINT HELENA.

Governor and Commander in Chief	William Grey-Wilson, *CMG*. *James Town*.
Senior Ordnance Store Officer and Acting District Paymaster	Deputy Assist. Commissary General of Ordnance E. H. Seymour, *Captain Dublin Fusiliers*.

MAURITIUS.

Governor and Commander in Chief	Sir Hubert Edward Henry Jerningham, *KCMG*. *Port Louis*.
Aide de Camp	
Colonel on the Staff (with rank of Major General)	Colonel W. O. Barnard (from h.p. Regimental District), 1 Feb. 95.
Deputy Assistant Adjutant General	p.s.c. Captain A. T. P. Hudson, Manchester Regiment, 1 Mar. 95.
Commanding Royal Artillery	Major T. Mayhew.
Commanding Royal Engineer	Lt.Colonel F. R. de Wolski.
Senior Ordnance Store Officer	Dep. Assist. Com. Gen. of Ord. W. M. Tracy, *Capt. W. Surrey Regt*.
District Paymaster	Paymaster A. H. Lindop.
Senior Medical Officer	Brigade Surgeon Lt.Colonel J. Fraser, *MD*.

SEYCHELLES ISLANDS.

Administrator	T. R. Griffith, *CMG*.

GOLD COAST COLONY.

Governor and Commander in Chief	William Edward Maxwell, *CMG*. *Accra*.

COLONY OF LAGOS.

Governor and Commander in Chief	Sir Gilbert Thomas Carter, *KCMG*.

WEST AFRICA SETTLEMENTS.

(At Sierra Leone and on the Gambia.)

Governor and Commander in Chief	p.s.c. Colonel Frederick Cardew, *CMG*. ret. pay S. Lancashire Regiment. *Free Town*.
Aide de Camp	
Garrison Adjutant	Captain G. Oates, West India Regt. 9 Apr. 94. *Sierra Leone*.
Commanding Royal Artillery (with rank of Major)	Captain A. F. Montanaro. *Sierra Leone*.
Commanding Royal Engineer (with rank of Captain)	Lieut. C. W. Gwynn, *DSO*. *Sierra Leone*.
Senior Medical Officer	Surgeon Major W. G. Clements.
District Paymaster	Paymaster C. F. H. Beardmore.
GAMBIA.—*Governor and Commander in Chief*	
Administrator	Robert Baxter Llewellyn, *CMG*.

AMERICA.

CANADA.

COMPRISING ALL THE PROVINCES WITHIN AND ADJACENT THERETO.

Governor General of the Dominion of Canada	The Right Hon. the Earl of Aberdeen, 3 June 93. *Ottawa*.
Military Secretary	
Aides de Camp	Captain O. P. W. Kindersley, Coldstream Guards, 7 Sept. 93. Captain B. C. Urquhart, Cameron Highlanders, 7 Sept. 93.
Lieutenant General	A. G. Montgomery Moore, 18 Hussars, 1 June 93. *Halifax*.
Assistant Military Secretary and Aide de Camp	Major W. A. Smith, Royal Artillery, 24 June 93.
Aide de Camp	Capt. Hon. J. G. R. U. Colborne, S. Staffordshire Regt., 1 June 93.
Commanding the Militia of the Dominion (with rank of Major General)	p.s.c. Colonel I. J. C. Herbert, *CB*. Grenadier Guards, 20 Nov. 90.
Aide de Camp	Lieut. E. Streatfeild, Gordon Highlanders, 5 Dec. 90.
Assistant Adjutant General	Colonel Dudley North (from h.p. N. Lancashire Regt.), 25 Feb 92.
Deputy Assistant Adjutant Generals	Lt.Colonel T. P. Shannon, Army Service Corps, 10 Apr. 94. p.s.c. Major F. Waldron, Royal Artillery, 1 Oct. 90.
Commanding Royal Artillery (Colonel on the Staff)	Colonel H. de S. Isaacson, 18 July 93.
Commanding Royal Engineer	V C Colonel E. P. Leach, *CB*.
Senior Ordnance Store Officer	Assistant Commissary General of Ordnance H. G. Fincham.
District Paymaster	Staff Paymaster D. Creagh.
Principal Medical Officer	Surgeon Colonel S. Archer.

NEWFOUNDLAND.

Governor and Commander in Chief	Bt.Lt.Colonel Sir J. T. N. O'Brien, *KCMG*. late 20 Foot.
Aide de Camp	Captain W. S. Melvill, Leicestershire Regiment, 20 June 92.

BARBADOES, &c.

Governor and Commander in Chief	Sir James Shaw Hay, *KCMG*. .... *Bridgetown*.
Aide de Camp	Lieut. F. R. Barton, West India Regiment, 23 May 93.
Brigadier General on the Staff	Major General E. Leach, *CB*. 8 Aug. 94.
Deputy Assistant Adjutant Generals	p.s.c. Bt.Major F. W. N. M'Cracken, Berkshire Regt. 13 Apr. 92. Major C. G. Knocker, Army Service Corps, 7 Nov. 94.
Commanding Royal Artillery	Major D. F. Downing. *St. Lucia*.
Commanding Royal Engineer	Lt.Colonel S. J. Lambert. [*Regiment*.
Senior Ordnance Store Officer	Dep. Assist. Com. Gen. of Ordnance R. H. Gill, *Captain Hampshire*
District Paymaster	Staff Paymaster S. D. Crookenden.
Senior Medical Officer	Brigade Surgeon Lt.Colonel H. J. O'Brien, *MB*.

ANTIGUA AND LEEWARD ISLANDS.

Governor and Commander in Chief	Sir Francis Fleming, KCMG	St. John's.
Aide de Camp		
ANTIGUA.—Island Secretary	F. Evans, Esq. CMG	St. John's.
St. Christopher and Nevis.—Commissioner	J. K. G. T. S. Churchill, Esq.	Basseterre.
Dominica.—Commissioner	G. R. Le Hunte, Esq.	Roseau
Montserrat.—Commissioner	E. Baynes, Esq.	Plymouth.
Virgin Islands.—Commissioner	E. J. Cameron, Esq.	Tortola.

BAHAMAS.

Governor and Commander in Chief	Sir William Frederick Haynes Smith, KCMG.	Nassau.
Aide de Camp		

WINDWARD ISLANDS.

Governor and Commander in Chief	Sir Charles Bruce, KCMG	St. George, Grenada.
St. Vincent.—Administrator	Harry Langhorne Thompson, Esq.	Kingstown.
St. Lucia.—Administering the Government	Surg.Lt.Colonel V.S.Gouldsbury,CMG.MD. retired pay.	Castries.
Garrison Adjutant	Captain W. B. Stansfeld, West India Regiment, 22 Jan. 92.	

BRITISH GUIANA.

Governor and Commander in Chief	Sir Charles Cameron Lees, KCMG	George Town.
Aide de Camp		

HONDURAS.

Governor and Commander in Chief	Sir Cornelius Alfred Moloney, KCMG.	Belize.
Aide de Camp	Major G. C. Bayly, 5 Bn. Rifle Brigade, 2 Sept. 91.	

JAMAICA.

Captain General and Governor in Chief	Sir Henry Arthur Blake, KCMG. ......Kingston.
Aide de Camp	Captain G. H. P. Colley. 3 Bn. Irish Regiment, 30 Jan. 95.
Colonel on the Staff (with rank of Major General)	Colonel H. J. Hallowes (from Regimental District), 19 Dec. 94.
Deputy Assistant Adjutant Generals	{ p.s.c. Lt.Colonel H. E. C. Kitchener (from h.p. Duke of Cornwall's Light Infantry), 17 Dec. 93. Major F. W. B. Landon, Army Service Corps, 12 Nov. 90.
Garrison Adjutant	Lieut. A. E. Burchard, West India Regiment, 1 Oct. 93.
Commanding Royal Artillery	Major G. F. A. Norton.
Commanding Royal Engineer	Lt.Colonel L. F. Brown.
Senior Ordnance Store Officer	Assist. Com. Gen. of Ordnance J. N. Salmon, Capt. R. Artillery.
District Paymaster	Staff Paymaster H. Potter.
Principal Medical Officer	Brigade Surgeon Lt.Colonel R. N. Mally.

TRINIDAD AND TOBAGO.

Governor and Commander in Chief	Sir Frederick Napier Broome, KCMG.	Port of Spain.
Aide de Camp	Lieut. A. O. Cockayne Cust, Somerset Light Infantry, 24 Oct. 94.	
Tobago.—Commissioner	W. Low, Esq.	

TURKS AND CAICOS ISLANDS.

Commissioner	H. Higgins, Esq.	Grand Turk.

BERMUDA.

Governor and Commander in Chief	General T. C. Lyons, CB. 2 July 92. Hamilton.
Assistant Military Secretary and Aide de Camp...	
Aide de Camp	Captain A. J. W. Dowell, Berkshire Regiment, 14 Oct. 94.
Deputy Assistant Adjutant Generals	{ p.s.c. Lt.Colonel W. A. Yule (from h.p. Scots Fusiliers), 7 Nov. 94. Lt.Colonel W. R. Winter, Army Service Corps, 31 May 94.
Commanding Royal Artillery	Lt.Colonel F. C. Morgan.
Commanding Royal Engineer	Lt.Colonel E. C. S. Moore.
Senior Ordnance Store Officer	Assistant Commissary General of Ordnance W. B. Cooke.
District Paymaster	Staff Paymaster G. H. Moore-Lane.
Principal Medical Officer	Brigade Surgeon Lt.Colonel H. Comerford, MD.

FALKLAND ISLANDS.

Governor and Commander in Chief	Sir Roger Tuckfield Goldsworthy, KCMG.	Stanley.

REGIMENTAL DISTRICT STAFF.

No. 1. *Regimental District,* **GLENCORSE.** *Counties,* EDINBURGH, PEEBLES, HADDINGTON, BERWICK, LINLITHGOW.
Lieutenant Colonel.—William A. Bridgo, 25 Feb. 93; *Colonel,* 21 June 87.
Territorial Regiment, Royal Scots (1 F. and Edinburgh Militia).—*Volunteers,* The Queen's Rifle Volunteer Brigade, 4th, 5th, 6th, 7th, *and* 8th Volunteer Battalions Royal Scots.

No. 2. *Regimental District,* **GUILDFORD.** *County, Part of* SURREY.
Lieutenant Colonel.—
Territorial Regiment, West Surrey Regt. (2 F. and 2nd Surrey Militia).—*Volunteers,* 1st, 2nd, 3rd, *and* 4th Volunteer Battalions West Surrey Regiment.

No. 3. *Regimental District,* **CANTERBURY.** *County, Part of* KENT.
Lieutenant Colonel.—William F. Kerr, 17 Oct. 92; *Colonel,* 10 Dec. 90.
Territorial Regiment, East Kent Regiment (3 F. *and* East Kent Militia).—*Volunteers,* 1st and 2nd Volunteer Battalions East Kent Regiment.

No. 4. *Regimental District,* **LANCASTER.** *County, Part of* LANCASHIRE.
Lieutenant Colonel.—Alexander F. Kidston, 2 Jan. 93; *Colonel,* 21 May 88.
Territorial Regiment, Lancaster Regt. (4 F. *and* 1st Lancashire Militia).—*Volunteers,* 1st Volunteer Battalion Lancaster Regiment.

No. 5. *Regimental District,* **NEWCASTLE.** *Counties,* NORTHUMBERLAND, DURHAM.
Lieutenant Colonel.—Russell Upcher, 8 April 94; *Colonel,* 9 June 86.
Territorial Regiment, Northumberland Fusiliers (5 F. *and* Northumberland Militia).—*Volunteers,* 1st, 2nd, *and* 3rd Volunteer Battalions Northumberland Fusiliers.

No. 68. *Territorial Regiment,* Durham Light Infantry (68 F. *and* 106 F. *and* 1st and 2nd Durham Militia).—*Volunteers,* 1st, 2nd, 3rd, 4th, *and* 5th Volunteer Battalions Durham Light Infantry.

No. 6. *Regimental District,* **WARWICK.** *County,* WARWICK.
Lieutenant Colonel.—William C. S. Mair, 17 Oct. 92; *Colonel,* 18 March 89.
Territorial Regiment, Royal Warwickshire Regt. (6 F. *and* 1st and 2nd Warwick Militia).—*Volunteers,* 1st and 2nd Volunteer Battalions Royal Warwickshire Regiment.

No. 7. *Regimental District,* **HOUNSLOW.** *County,* MIDDLESEX, *and* METROPOLITAN.
Lieutenant Colonel.—Charles E. Hussey, 17 Apr. 94; *Colonel,* 29 Aug. 93.
Territorial Regiment, 1, 2, 3, 4 *and* 5 Bns. Royal Fusiliers (7 F. *and* Westminster, London, *and* South Middlesex Militia).—*Volunteers,* 1st, 2nd, *and* 3rd Volunteer Battalions Royal Fusiliers.

No. 57. *Territorial Regiment,* Middlesex Regt. (57 F. *and* 77 F. *and* East Middlesex *and* 5th Middlesex Militia).—*Volunteers,* 3rd Middlesex, 2nd Vol. Bn. Middlesex Regt., 17th Middlesex.

No. 8. *Regimental District,* **WARRINGTON.** *County, Part of* LANCASHIRE.
Lieutenant Colonel.—Edward Eyre-Williams, 10 Oct. 92; *Colonel,* 10 June 86.
Territorial Regiment, Liverpool Regt. (8 F. *and* 2nd Lancashire Militia).—*Volunteers,* 1st, 2nd, 3rd, 4th, 5th, *and* 6th Volunteer Battalions Liverpool Regiment (7th Volunteer Battalion Liverpool Regiment *attached to* 6th).

No. 40. *Territorial Regiment,* South Lancashire Regt. (40 F. *and* 82 F. *and* 4th Lancashire Militia).—*Volunteers,* 1st and 2nd Volunteer Battalions South Lancashire Regiment.

No. 9. *Regimental District,* **NORWICH.** *County,* NORFOLK.
Lieutenant Colonel.—
Territorial Regiment, Norfolk Regt. (9 F. & 1st & 2nd Norfolk Militia).—*Volunteers,* 1st, 2nd, 3rd, & 4th Volunteer Battalions Norfolk Regiment.

No. 10. *Regimental District,* **LINCOLN.** *County,* LINCOLN.
Lieutenant Colonel.—p.s.c. Archibald Glen, 17 Apr. 94; *Colonel,* 18 June 90.
Territorial Regiment, Lincolnshire Regt. (10 F. *and* N. *and* S. Lincoln Militia).—*Volunteers,* 1st and 2nd Volunteer Battalions Lincolnshire Regiment.

No. 11. *Regimental District,* **EXETER.** *County,* DEVONSHIRE.
Lieutenant Colonel.—David Milne Home, 7 May 90; *Colonel,* 6 Apr. 85.
Territorial Regiment, Devonshire Regiment (11 F. *and* 2nd *and* 1st Devon Militia).—*Volunteers,* 1st, 2nd, 3rd, 4th, *and* 5th Volunteer Battalions Devonshire Regiment.

No. 12. *Regimental District,* **BURY ST. EDMUNDS.** *Counties,* SUFFOLK, CAMBRIDGE.
Lieutenant Colonel.—John R. Collins, 12 May 90; *Colonel,* 1 July 85.
Territorial Regiment, Suffolk Regt. (12 F. *and* West Suffolk *and* Cambridge Militia).—*Volunteers,* 1st, 2nd, 3rd, *and* 4th Volunteer Battalions Suffolk Regiment.

No. 13. *Regimental District,* **TAUNTON.** *County,* SOMERSET.
Lieutenant Colonel.—William H. Thompson, 4 June 91; *Colonel,* 9 Dec. 85.
Territorial Regiment, Somersetshire Light Infantry (13 F. & 1 & 2 Somerset Militia).—*Volunteers,* 1st, 2nd, *and* 3rd Volunteer Battalions Somersetshire Light Infantry.

No. 14. *Regimental District,* **YORK.** *County, Part of* WEST RIDING OF YORK.
Lieutenant Colonel.—Fred. W. Harington, 1 Apr. 93; *Colonel,* 7 Mar. 90.
Territorial Regiment, West Yorkshire Regt. (14 F. *and* 2nd *and* 4th West York Militia), 3 Bn. Yorkshire Regt. (attached).—*Volunteers,* 1st, 2nd, *and* 3rd Volunteer Battalions West Yorkshire Regiment.

No. 15. *Regimental District,* **BEVERLEY.** *County,* EAST RIDING OF YORK.
Lieutenant Colonel.—Douglas C. De Wend, 19 Dec. 94; *Colonel,* 6 Oct. 90.
Territorial Regiment, East Yorkshire Regt. (15 F. *and* East York Militia).—*Volunteers,* 1st and 2nd Volunteer Battalions East Yorkshire Regiment.

No. 16. *Regimental District,* **BEDFORD.** *Counties,* HUNTINGDON, BEDFORD, HERTFORD.
Lieutenant Colonel.—George Arthur Lee, 1 Sept. 92; *Colonel,* 27 Aug. 88.
Territorial Regiment, Bedfordshire Regt. (16 F. *and* Bedford *and* Hertford Militia), 5 Bn. King's Royal Rifles (attached).—*Volunteers,* 1st, 2nd, *and* 3rd Volunteer Battalions Bedfordshire Regiment.

No. 17. *Regimental District,* **LEICESTER.** *Counties,* NOTTINGHAM, LEICESTER.
Lieutenant Colonel.—Henry Langtry, 4 March 91 ; *Colonel,* 1 July 85.
Territorial Regiment, Leicestershire Regt. (17 F. *and* Leicestershire Militia).—*Volunteers,* 1st Volunteer Battalion Leicestershire Regiment.

No. 18. *Regimental District,* **CLONMEL.** *Counties,* KILKENNY, TIPPERARY, WEXFORD, WATERFORD.
Lieutenant Colonel.—James W. Webber, 3 Nov. 92 ; *Colonel,* 11 Feb. 89.
Territorial Regiment, Royal Irish Regiment (18 F. *and* Wexford, North Tipperary, *and* Kilkenny Militia).

No. 19. *Regimental District,* **RICHMOND** (Yorkshire). *County,* NORTH RIDING OF YORK.
Lieutenant Colonel.—Charles F. Lawson, 30 Aug. 94 ; *Colonel,* 29 Sept. 90.
Territorial Regiment, Yorkshire Regt. (19 F. *and* 5th W. York and North York Militia).—*Volunteers,* 1st and 2nd Volunteer Battalions Yorkshire Regiment.

No. 20. *Regimental District,* **BURY.** *County, Part of* LANCASHIRE.
Lieutenant Colonel.—George Baker, *CB.* 30 June 91 ; *Colonel,* 29 Aug. 86.
Territorial Regiment, Lancashire Fusiliers (20 F. *and* 7th Lancashire Militia).—*Volunteers,* 1st, 2nd and 3rd Volunteer Battalions Lancashire Fusiliers.

No. 21. *Regimental District,* **AYR.** *Counties,* AYR, WIGTOWN, KIRKCUDBRIGHT.
Lieutenant Colonel.—Frederick G. Jackson, 21 Jan. 91 ; *Colonel,* 25 Aug. 88.
Territorial Regiment, Royal Scots Fusiliers (21 F. *and* Scottish Borderers, *and* Ayr and Wigtown Militia).—*Volunteers,* 1st and 2nd Volunteer Battalions Scots Fusiliers, Galloway.

No. 22. *Regimental District,* **CHESTER.** *County,* CHESHIRE.
Lieutenant Colonel.—William B. Butlin, 30 Aug. 94 ; *Colonel,* 21 April 90.
Territorial Regiment, Cheshire Regt. (22 F. *and* 1st *and* 2nd Cheshire Militia).—*Volunteers,* 1st, 2nd, 3rd, 4th, and 5th Volunteer Battalions Cheshire Regiment.

No. 23. *Regimental District,* **WREXHAM.** *Counties,* ANGLESEA, CARNARVON, DENBIGH, FLINT, MERIONETH.
Lieutenant Colonel.—Charles W. H. Wilson, 3 June 94 ; *Colonel,* 24 Feb. 90.
Territorial Regiment, Royal Welsh Fusiliers (23 F. *and* Denbigh and Flint *and* Merioneth and Carnarvon Militia), 6th Battalion King's Royal Rifles (*attached*).—*Volunteers,* 1st and 2nd Volunteer Battalions Royal Welsh Fusiliers.

No. 24. *Regimental District,* **BRECON.** *Counties,* CARDIGAN, RADNOR, BRECON, MONMOUTH, MONTGOMERY.
Lieutenant Colonel.—Charles J. Bromhead, *CB.* 13 Feb. 92 ; *Colonel,* 31 Jan. 89
Territorial Regiment, South Wales Borderers (24 F. *and* South Wales Borderer *and* Montgomery Militia).—*Volunteers,* 1st, 2nd, 3rd, *and* 4th Volunteer Battalions South Wales Borderers.

No. 25. *Regimental District,* **BERWICK-ON-TWEED.** *Counties,* DUMFRIES, ROXBURGH, SELKIRK.
Lieutenant Colonel.—George T. L. Carwithen, 1 Apr. 90 ; *Colonel,* 27 June 87.
Territorial Regiment, King's Own Scottish Borderers (25 F. *and* Scottish Borderers Militia).—*Volunteers,* 1st Roxburgh and Selkirk, 2nd *and* 3rd Volunteer Battalions King's Own Scottish Borderers.

No. 26. *Regimental District,* **HAMILTON.** *County, Part of* LANARK.
Lieutenant Colonel.—Alfred H. C. Lynch, 17 March 92 ; *Colonel,* 22 Nov. 88.
Territorial Regiment, Scottish Rifles (26 F. *and* 90 F. *and* 2 Lanark Militia).—*Volunteers,* 1st Lanark, 2nd Volunteer Battalion Scottish Rifles, 3rd Lanark, 4th *and* 5th Volunteer Battalions Scottish Rifles.

No. 71. *Territorial Regiment,* Highland Lt. Inf. (71 F. *and* 74 F. *and* 1st Lanark Mil.).—*Volunteers,* 1st, 2nd, *and* 3rd Vol. Bns. Highland Lt. Inf., 9th Lanarkshire, 5th Vol. Bn. Highland Lt. Inf.

No. 27. *Regimental District,* **OMAGH.** *Counties,* LONDONDERRY, DONEGAL, TYRONE, FERMANAGH.
Lieutenant Colonel.—Charles M. Stockley, *CB.* 12 July 92 ; *Colonel,* 20 Aug. 88.
Territorial Regiment, Inniskilling Fus. (27 F. *and* 108 F. *and* Fermanagh, Tyrone *and* Donegal Militia).

No. 28. *Regimental District,* **BRISTOL.** *County,* GLOUCESTER.
Lieutenant Colonel.—James B. M'Dougal, 18 Jan. 95 ; *Colonel,* 11 Dec. 90.
Territorial Regiment, Gloucestershire Regt. (28 F. *and* 61 F. *and* South *and* North Gloucester Militia).—*Volunteers,* 1st *and* 2nd Volunteer Battalions Gloucestershire Regiment.

No. 29. *Regimental District,* **WORCESTER.** *County,* WORCESTERSHIRE.
Lieutenant Colonel.—C. Pilcher Temple, 19 Dec. 92 ; *Colonel,* 14 July 90.
Territorial Regiment, Worcester Regt. (29 F. *and* 36 F. *and* Worcester Militia).—*Volunteers,* 1st *and* 2nd Volunteer Battalions Worcester Regiment.

No. 30. *Regimental District,* **BURNLEY.** *County, Part of* LANCASHIRE.
Lieutenant Colonel.—p.s.c. Henry H. Griffiths, 12 June 93 ; *Colonel,* 18 Mar. 89.
Territorial Regiment, E. Lancashire Regt. (30 F. & 59 F. & 5th Lancashire Militia).—*Volunteers,* 1st and 2nd Volunteer Battalions East Lancashire Regt.

No. 31. *Regimental District,* **KINGSTON.** *County, Part of* SURREY.
Lieutenant Colonel.—Leyland Hornby, 1 Dec. 91 ; *Colonel,* 15 June 89.
Territorial Regiment, East Surrey Regt. (31 F. *and* 70 F. *and* 1st *and* 3rd Surrey Militia).—*Volunteers,* 1st Surrey, 2nd, 3rd, *and* 4th Volunteer Battalions East Surrey Regiment.

No. 32. *Regimental District,* **BODMIN.** *County,* CORNWALL.
Lieutenant Colonel.—Mark M. Gillies, 7 March 93 ; *Colonel,* 28 March 90.
Territorial Regiment, Duke of Cornwall's Light Infantry (32 F. *and* 46 F. *and* Cornwall Rangers Militia).—*Volunteers,* 1st and 2nd Volunteer Battalions Duke of Cornwall's Light Infantry.

No. 33. *Regimental District,* **HALIFAX.** *County, Part of* WEST RIDING OF YORK.
Lieutenant Colonel.—Edwin G. Fenn, 27 Jan. 91 ; *Colonel,* 15 March 88.
Territorial Regiment, Duke of Wellington's West Riding Regt. (33 F. *and* 76 F. *and* 6th West York Militia).—*Volunteers,* 1st, 2nd, *and* 3rd Volunteer Battalions West Riding Regiment.

No. 34. *Regimental District,* **CARLISLE.** *Counties,* CUMBERLAND, WESTMORELAND.
Lieutenant Colonel.—James F. Hilton, 27 Aug. 93 ; *Colonel,* 2 Sept. 89.
Territorial Regiment, The Border Regt. (34 F. *and* 55 F. *and* Cumberland *and* Westmoreland Militia).—*Volunteers,* 1st *and* 2nd Volunteer Battalions Border Regiment.

No. 35. *Regimental District,* **CHICHESTER.** *County,* SUSSEX.
Lieutenant Colonel.—Wilfred Tolson, 3 Nov. 93 ; *Colonel,* 6 Aug. 88.
Territorial Regiment, The Royal Sussex Regiment (35 F. *and* 107 F. *and* Sussex Militia).—*Volunteers,* 1st *and* 2nd Volunteer Battalions Royal Sussex Regiment, 1st Cinque Ports.

Regimental District Staff.

No. 37. *Regimental District,* **WINCHESTER.** *County,* HAMPSHIRE.
Lieutenant Colonel.—John E. Whitting, 12 Apr. 91; *Colonel,* 21 Apr. 86.
Territorial Regiment, Hampshire Regt. (37 F. and 67 F. and Hampshire Militia).—*Volunteers,* 1st, 2nd, 3rd, 4th, and 5th (Isle of Wight "Princess Beatrice's") Volunteer Battalions Hampshire Regiment.

No. 38. *Regimental District,* **LICHFIELD.** *County of* STAFFORD.
Lieutenant Colonel.—Allan G. Raper, 12 Nov. 92; *Colonel,* 6 March 89.
Territorial Regiment, South Staffordshire Regt. (38 F. and 80 F. and 1 Stafford Militia).—*Volunteers,* 1st, 2nd, and 3rd Volunteer Battalions South Staffordshire Regiment.

No. 64. *Territorial Regiment,* North Staffordshire Regt. (64 F. and 98 F. and 2nd and 3rd Stafford Militia).—*Volunteers,* 1st and 2nd Volunteer Battalions North Staffordshire Regiment.

No. 39. *Regimental District,* **DORCHESTER.** *County,* DORSET.
Lieutenant Colonel.—John L. Tweedie, DSO. 1 Apr. 92; *Colonel,* 11 June 88.
Territorial Regiment, Dorsetshire Regt. (39 F. and 54 F. and Dorset Militia).—*Volunteers,* 1st Volunteer Battalion Dorsetshire Regiment.

No. 41. *Regimental District,* **CARDIFF.** *Counties,* PEMBROKE, CARMARTHEN, GLAMORGAN.
Lieutenant Colonel.—Albert E. W. Goldsmid, 21 Apr. 94; *Colonel,* 21 Apr. 94.
Territorial Regiment, Welsh Regt. (41 F. and 69 F. and Glamorgan Militia).—*Volunteers,* 1st, 2nd, and 3rd Volunteer Battalions Welsh Regiment, 3rd Glamorganshire.

No. 42. *Regimental District,* **PERTH.** *Counties,* FORFAR, PERTH, FIFE.
Lieutenant Colonel.—Charles T. Wallace, 23 July 90; *Colonel,* 3 Apr. 87.
Territorial Regiment, Royal Highlanders (42 F. and 73 F. and Perth Militia).—*Volunteers,* 1st, 2nd, 3rd, 4th, 5th, and 6th Volunteer Battalions Royal Highlanders.

No. 43. *Regimental District,* **OXFORD.** *Counties,* OXFORD, BUCKS.
Lieutenant Colonel.—William Livesay, 10 Nov. 92; *Colonel,* 1 June 88.
Territorial Regiment, Oxford Light Infantry (43 F. and 52 F. and Bucks and Oxford Militia).—*Volunteers,* 1st and 2nd Volunteer Battalions Oxford Light Infantry, 1st Buckinghamshire, 4th Volunteer Battalion Oxford Light Infantry.

No. 44. *Regimental District,* **WARLEY.** *County,* ESSEX.
Lieutenant Colonel.—Constantine Maguire, 1 Apr. 90; *Colonel,* 16 Sept. 85.
Territorial Regiment, Essex Regt. (44 F. and 56 F. and Essex Rifles and West Essex Militia).—*Volunteers,* 1st, 2nd, 3rd, and 4th Volunteer Battalions Essex Regiment.

No. 45. *Regimental District,* **DERBY.** *County,* DERBY.
Lieutenant Colonel.—Henry H. Hooke, 28 Aug. 90; *Colonel,* 21 July 89.
Territorial Regiment, Derbyshire Regt. (45 F. and 95 F. and 2nd Derby, Sherwood Foresters, and 1st Derby Militia).—*Volunteers,* 1st and 2nd Volunteer Battalions Derbyshire Regiment, 1st Nottingham, 4th (Notts) Volunteer Battalion Derbyshire Regiment.

No. 47. *Regimental District,* **PRESTON.** *County, Part of* LANCASHIRE.
Lieutenant Colonel.—James M'Cleverty, 21 July 93; *Colonel,* 4 Aug. 83.
Territorial Regiment, North Lancashire Regt. (47 F. & 81 F. & 3 Lancashire Militia).—*Volunteers,* 1st and 2nd Volunteer Battalions North Lancashire Regiment.

No. 48. *Regimental District,* **NORTHAMPTON.** *Counties,* NORTHAMPTON, RUTLAND.
Lieutenant Colonel.—Allan Maclean, 21 Apr. 94; *Colonel,* 20 May 89.
Territorial Regiment, Northampton Regt. (48 F. and 58 F. and Northampton Militia).—*Volunteers,* 1st Volunteer Battalion Northampton Regiment.

No. 49. *Regimental District,* **READING.** *County,* BERKSHIRE.
Lieutenant Colonel.—John B. B. Dickson, 10 March 95; *Colonel,* 25 Apr. 89.
Territorial Regiment, Royal Berkshire Regiment (49 F. and 66 F. and Berks Militia).—*Volunteers,* 1st Volunteer Battalion Royal Berkshire Regiment.

No. 50. *Regimental District,* **MAIDSTONE.** *County, Part of* KENT.
Lieutenant Colonel.—Wm. Head Bayly, 12 July 94; *Colonel,* 23 Dec. 89.
Territorial Regiment, Royal West Kent Regiment (50 F. and 97 F. and West Kent Militia).—*Volunteers,* 1st, 2nd, and 3rd (Woolwich) Volunteer Battalions Royal West Kent Regiment.

No. 51. *Regimental District,* **PONTEFRACT.** *County,* WEST RIDING OF YORKSHIRE.
Lieutenant Colonel.—Arthur H. Luck, 1 Apr. 92; *Colonel,* 13 Oct. 90.
Territorial Regiment, The King's Own Yorkshire Light Infantry (51 F. and 105 F. and 1 W. York Militia).—*Volunteers,* 1st Volunteer Battalion Yorkshire Light Infantry.

No. 65. *Territorial Regiment,* York and Lancaster Regt. (65 F. and 84 F. and 3rd West York Militia).—*Volunteers,* 1st and 2nd Volunteer Battalions York and Lancaster Regiment.

No. 53. *Regimental District,* **SHREWSBURY.** *Counties,* SHROPSHIRE and HEREFORD.
Lieutenant Colonel.—Francis W. Cary, 27 Sept. 93; *Colonel,* 15 Aug. 89.
Territorial Regiment, Shropshire Light Infantry (53 F. and 85 F. and Shropshire and Hereford Militia).—*Volunteers,* 1st and 2nd Volunteer Battalions Shropshire Light Infantry, 1st Herefordshire.

No. 62. *Regimental District,* **DEVIZES.** *County,* WILTSHIRE.
Lieutenant Colonel.—Henry Collingwood, 3 Apr. 93; *Colonel,* 31 May 90.
Territorial Regiment, Wiltshire Regt. (62 F. and 99 F. and Wiltshire Militia).—*Volunteers,* 1 Wiltshire, 2nd Volunteer Battalion Wiltshire Regiment.

No. 63. *Regimental District,* **ASHTON.** *County, Part of* LANCASHIRE.
Lieutenant Colonel.—Robert C. Græme, 12 July 93; *Colonel,* 12 July 93.
Territorial Regiment, Manchester Regt. (63 F. and 96 F. and 6th Lancashire Militia).—*Volunteers,* 1st, 2nd, 3rd, 4th, 5th, and 6th Volunteer Battalions Manchester Regiment.

No. 72. *Regimental District,* **FORT GEORGE.** *Counties,* ORKNEY and SHETLAND, SUTHERLAND, CAITHNESS, ROSS and CROMARTY, INVERNESS, NAIRN and ELGIN.
Lieutenant Colonel.—William Gordon, 6 June 94; *Colonel,* 1 July 90.
Territorial Regiment, Seaforth Highlanders (72 F. and 78 F. and Highland Rifle Militia) —*Volunteers,* 1st Vol. Bn. Seaforth Highlanders, 1st Sutherland, 3rd Vol. Bn. Seaforth Highlanders.

Regimental District Staff.

No. 75. *Regimental District,* **ABERDEEN.** *Counties,* ABERDEEN, BANFF, KINCARDINE.
Lieutenant Colonel.—John E. Boyes, 1 Apr. 92; *Colonel,* 18 Nov. 86.
Territorial Regiment, Gordon Highlanders (75 F. *and* 92 F. *and* Aberdeenshire Militia).—*Volunteers,* 1st, 2nd, 3rd (The Buchan), 4th, 5th (Deeside Highland), *and* 6th Volunteer Battalions Gordon Highlanders.

No. 79. *Regimental District,* **INVERNESS.**
Lieutenant Colonel.—William Gordon, 6 June 94; *Colonel,* 11 July 90.
Territorial Regiment, Cameron Highlanders (79 F. *and* Highland Light Infantry Militia).—*Volunteers,* 1st Volunteer Battalion Cameron Highlanders.

No. 83. *Regimental District,* **BELFAST.** *Counties,* ANTRIM, DOWN.
Lieutenant Colonel.—John Dawson, 22 Oct. 92; *Colonel,* 30 Jan. 89.
Territorial Regiment, Royal Irish Rifles (83 F. *and* 86 F. *and* N. Down, Antrim, S. Down, *and* Louth Militia).

No. 87. *Regimental District,* **ARMAGH.** *Counties,* CAVAN, MONAGHAN, ARMAGH, LOUTH.
Lieutenant Colonel.—*p.s.c.* William Toke Dooner, 19 Apr. 94; *Colonel,* 29 Aug. 93.
Territorial Regiment, Royal Irish Fusiliers (87 F. *and* 89 F. *and* Armagh, Cavan, *and* Monaghan Militia).

No. 88. *Regimental District,* **GALWAY.** *Counties,* LEITRIM, SLIGO, ROSCOMMON, MAYO, GALWAY.
Lieutenant Colonel.—*p.s.c.* Francis Cochran, 21 June 94; *Colonel,* 21 Apr. 90.
Territorial Regiment, Connaught Rangers (88 F. *and* 94 F. *and* South *and* North Mayo, Galway, *and* Roscommon Militia), 8 Bn. Rifle Brigade (*attached*).

No. 91. *Regimental District,* **STIRLING.** *Counties,* KINROSS and CLACKMANNAN, STIRLING, DUMBARTON, ARGYLL, BUTE, RENFREW.
Lieutenant Colonel.—Marsden S. J. Sunderland, 6 Dec. 92; *Colonel,* 15 June 89.
Territorial Regiment, Argyll and Sutherland Highlanders (91 F. *and* 93 F. *and* Highland Borderers *and* Renfrew Militia).—*Volunteers,* 1st, 2nd, 3rd, 4th *and* 5th Volunteer Battalions Argyll & Sutherland Highlanders, 1st Dumbarton, 7th Volunteer Battalion Argyll & Sutherland Highlanders.

No. 100. *Regimental District,* **BIRR.** *Counties,* MEATH, WESTMEATH, LONGFORD, KING'S CO., QUEEN'S CO.
Lieutenant Colonel.—George W. N. Rogers, 17 Feb. 95; *Colonel,* 18 Nov. 86.
Territorial Regiment, Prince of Wales' Leinster Regt. (100 F. *and* 109 F. *and* King's County, Queen's County *and* Meath Militia), 6 *and* 9 Bns. Rifle Brigade (*attached*).

No. 101. *Regimental District,* **TRALEE.** *Counties,* LIMERICK, KERRY, CORK, CLARE.
Lieutenant Colonel.—John H. Barnard, *CB. CMG.* 26 Oct. 94; *Colonel,* 23 Apr. 90.
Territorial Regiment, Royal Munster Fusiliers (101 F. *and* 104 F. *and* South Cork, Kerry, *and* Limerick County Militia), 9 Bn. King's Royal Rifles (*attached*).

No. 102. *Regimental District,* **NAAS.** *Counties,* DUBLIN, WICKLOW, KILDARE, CARLOW.
Lieutenant Colonel.—Charles G. Leggett, 20 June 94; *Colonel,* 29 Sept. 90.
Territorial Regiment, Royal Dublin Fusiliers (102 F. *and* 103 F. *and* Kildare, Dublin City, *and* Dublin County Militia), 8 Bn. King's Royal Rifles (*attached*).

Rifle Depot, **WINCHESTER.**
Lieutenant Colonel.—Henry D. Browne, 25 May 94; *Colonel,* 25 May 94.
Quarter Master.—Thomas Riley, 8 Feb. 88; *Hon. Captain,* 27 Sept. 92.
Line Battalions, 1st to 9th Bns. King's Royal Rifles (60 F. *and* Huntingdon, Flint, 2nd Middlesex, Carlow, *and* North Cork Militia).—*Volunteers,* 1st, 2nd, 4th (14th *attached*), 5th (9th *attached*), 12th (25th *and* 26th *attached*), 13th, 21st, *and* 22nd Middlesex, 1st, 2nd, *and* 3rd London.
Line Battalions, 1st to 9th Bns. Rifle Brigade (Rifle Brigade *and* Queen's Own Tower Hamlets, Longford, King's Own Tower Hamlets, Leitrim *and* Westmeath Militia).—*Volunteers,* 7th, 15th, 16th, 18th, 19th, 20th, *and* 24th Middlesex, 1st Tower Hamlets, 2nd Tower Hamlets.

The following Regiments of Militia and Volunteers are attached to the Brigade of Foot Guards:—
Command of Lt. Colonel Grenadier Guards.—*Militia:* 4th Bn. Royal Fusiliers. *Volunteers:* 15th *and* 24th Middlesex, 1st, 2nd, *and* 3rd London, 1st *and* 2nd Tower Hamlets.
Command of Lt. Colonel Coldstream Guards.—*Militia:* 7th Bn. King's Royal Rifles. *Volunteers:* 1st, 16th, 18th, 19th, 21st, *and* 22nd Middlesex.
Command of Lt. Colonel Scots Guards.—*Militia;* 5th *and* 7th Bns. Rifle Brigade. *Volunteers:* 2nd, 4th (14th *attached*), 5th (9th *attached*), 7th, 12th (25th *and* 26th *attached*), 13th *and* 20th Middlesex.

GUARDS' DEPOT.—*Caterham.*
Officer Commanding.—*Hon.* A. H. Henniker-Major, Coldstream Guards, 1 Jan. 95.
Adjutant.—Lieut. H. C. Ruggles-Brise, Grenadier Guards, 1 Jan. 95.
Quarter Master.—Thomas Widdowes Gunton,[1] 4 Jan. 90; *Hon. Captain,* 7 Jan. 90.

WEST INDIA DEPOT.
Lieutenant Colonel.—Almeric G. Spencer, 27 Sept. 93; *Colonel,* 21 Apr. 90.

[1] Captain Gunton served in the Egyptian war of 1882 with the 2nd Battalion of the Grenadier Guards, and was present in the engagement at Tel-el-Mahuta and at the battle of Tel-el-Kebir (Medal with Clasp, and Khedive's Star).

ALPHABETICAL LIST OF REGIMENTAL DISTRICT STATIONS.

Aberdeen	75	Cardiff	41	Inverness	79	Preston	47
Armagh	87	Carlisle	34	Kingston	31	Reading	49
Ashton	63	Chester	22	Lancaster	4	Richmond (Yorks.)	19
Ayr	21	Chichester	35	Leicester	17	Rifle Depot	page 111
Bedford	16	Clonmel	18	Lichfield	38, 64	Shrewsbury	53
Belfast	83	Derby	45	Lincoln	10	Stirling	91
Berwick-on-Tweed	25	Devizes	62	Maidstone	50	Taunton	13
Beverley	15	Dorchester	39	Naas	102	Tralee	101
Birr	100	Exeter	11	Newcastle	5, 68	Warley	44
Bodmin	32	Fort George	72	Northampton	48	Warrington	40
Brecon	24	Galway	88	Norwich	9	Warwick	6
Bristol	28	Glencorse	1	Omagh	27	Winchester	37
Burnley	30	Guildford	2	Oxford	43	Worcester	29
Bury	20	Halifax	33	Perth	42	Wrexham	23
Bury St. Edmunds	12	Hamilton	26, 71	Pontefract	51, 65	York	14
Canterbury	3	Hounslow	7, 57				

Tower of London.

Constable, General Sir Daniel Lysons, *GCB.* Derbyshire Regiment, 24 Mar. 90.
Lieut. General J. H. Dunne, 5 Jan. 94.
Major, Lieut. General G. B. Milman, *CB.* 29 Aug. 70.

Chaplain, Rev. J. C. Edghill, *D.D.* 1 Apr. 87; *Chaplain General.*
Medical Officer, Surgeon Captain H. P. G. Elkington.

EDUCATIONAL ESTABLISHMENTS.

Royal Military College, Sandhurst.

President.—Field Marshal *H.R.H. the Duke of* Cambridge, *KG. KT. KP. GCB. GCSI. GCMG. GCIE. Commander in Chief.*
Governor and Commandant.—p.s.c. Major General C. J. East, *CB*, 19 Dec. 93.
Assistant Commandant and Secretary.—Lt. Colonel M. Wynyard (from h.p. West Kent Regiment), 1 Jan. 90.
Quarter Master.—Thomas King Bunting, 1 Apr. 84; *Hon. Captain,* 1 Apr. 94.
Riding Master.—Jacob Hodgins, 13 Feb. 84; *Hon. Captain,* 1 July 81; *Hon. Major,* 30 Oct. 89.
Surgeon.—Brig. Surg. A. F. S. Clarke, *MD.* retired pay, 1 Sept. 82.
Assist. Surg.—Surg.Lt.Col. J. N. Stock, ret. pay, 1 Apr. 89.
Chaplain.—Rev. A. J. Townend, *MA.* 15 Sept. 94.
   MILITARY PROFESSORS AND INSTRUCTORS.
Professor of Fortification.—Major W. H. Chippindall, Royal Engineers, 1 Oct. 92.
   Instructors in Fortification.
Captain A. M. C. Cooper-Key, R. Artillery, 23 May 89.
p.s.c. Major A. F. Gatliff, Royal Marines, 16 Aug. 90.
Captain E. G. Wynyard, *DSO,* Welsh Regt. 22 Aug. 90.
p.s.c. Major F. S. Inglefield, E. York Regt. 1 Sept. 92.
Captain W. N. Bolton, Wiltshire Regiment, 1 Sept. 92.
Captain A. F. Mockler-Ferryman, Oxford Lt. Infantry.
Professor of Military Topography.—Lt. Colonel G. A. Lewes (from h.p. Northamptonshire Regt.) 1 Sept. 92.
   Instructors in Military Topography.
Major R. E. Goold-Adams, Highland Lt. Inf. 10 Feb. 88.
Major F. Macbean, Gordon Highlanders, 1 Sept. 88.
Lt. Colonel S. J. M. Jopp (from h.p. Northampton Regt.), 4 Oct. 88.
Captain A. H. C. Kenney-Herbert, Northampton Regt. 16 Apr. 90.
Captain R. Armstrong, Cheshire Regiment, 6 Oct. 90.
Major J. R. Young, East York Regiment, 8 Oct. 91.
p.s.c. Captain C. M. Lester, W. York Regt. 1 Sept. 92.
Captain B. W. S. Van Straubenzee, South Wales Borderers, 1 Sept. 92.
p.s.c. Lt. Colonel L. G. Fawkes (from h.p. R. Artillery), 1 Sept. 93.
Professor of Tactics, Military Administration and Law.
p.s.c. Lt. Colonel J. A. Ferguson (from h.p. Rifle Brigade), 1 Sept. 93.
   Instructors in Tactics, Military Administration and Law.
p.s.c. Captain W. O. Cavenagh, Bedford Regt. 1 Feb. 89.
p.s.c. Captain C. G. Morrison, 5 Dragoon Gds. 1 Jan. 91.
p.s.c. Captain P. Wildman-Lushington, King's Own Scottish Borderers, 13 Feb. 93.
p.s.c. Captain B. R. James, East Surrey Regt. 1 Sept. 93.
Captain W. C. W. Rawlinson, Lincoln Regt. 1 Sept. 94.
p.s.c. Captain W. E. Lascelles, Rifle Brigade, 10 Feb. 95.

Royal Military Academy at Woolwich.

President.—Field Marshal *H.R.H. the Duke of* Cambridge, *KG. KT. KP. GCB. GCSI. GCMG. GCIE. Commander in Chief,* 8 Feb. 70.
Governor.—Lieut. General Sir W. Stirling, *KCB,* Royal Artillery, 15 Apr. 90.
Assistant Commandant and Secretary.—Colonel J. M. Murray (from Royal Artillery), 20 Sept. 91.
   Lieutenants of the Company of Gentlemen Cadets.
Lieut. F. H. Young, Royal Artillery, 28 Dec. 91.
Lieut. A. E. J. Perkins, Royal Artillery, 20 Feb. 92.
Lieut. H. Coningham, Royal Artillery, 17 Oct. 92.
Adjutant & Qr. Master.—Captain A. Handley, Royal Artillery, 26 Feb. 94.
Surgeon.—Surg.Lt.Colonel W. C. Gasteen, *MB.,* ret. pay.
Professor of Mathematics and Mechanics.—H. Hart, *MA.*
   Instructors of Mathematics.
E. F. S. Tylecote, *MA.* 19 March 73.
W. Foord-Kelcey, *BA.* 27 Apr. 86.
E. J. Brook-Smith, *BA. LLM.* 1 Mar. 89.
C. S. Jackson, *BA.* 17 Mar. 91.
Professor of Fortification and Geometrical Drawing.
Major W. D. Conner, Royal Engineers, 25 July 93.
   Instructors of Fortification and Geometrical Drawing.
Captain J. E. Edmonds, Royal Engineers, 1 Mar. 90.
Captain A. Grant, Royal Engineers, 1 April 92.
Captain H. L. C. Stafford, Royal Engineers, 20 Aug. 92.
Captain H. J. W. Brownrigg, Royal Engineers, 15 Aug. 93.
   Professor of Artillery.
Major F. A. Curteis, Royal Artillery, 15 Sept. 93.
   Instructors of Artillery.
Captain A. M. C. Dale, Royal Artillery, 13 Apr. 91.
Captain F. H. Crampton, Royal Artillery, 15 Sept. 93.
Captain S. B. Von Donop, Royal Artillery, 1 March 95.
   Professor of Military Topography.
Major E. S. May, Royal Artillery, 30 July 91.
   Instructors of Military Topography.
Captain W. St. P. Bunbury, R. Artillery, 26 Sept. 90.
p.s.c. Captain A. Crawford, Royal Artillery, 16 Jan. 92.
Captain A. B. Denne, Royal Artillery, 5 Dec. 92.
Major J. W. Sill, Royal Engineers, 26 Sept. 94.
Professor of Tactics, Military Administration, and Military Law.—p.s.c. Lt. Colonel H. D. Buchanan-Dunlop (from Royal Artillery) 24 Sept. 89.

Instructors in Electricity.
Captain W. P. Brett, Royal Engineers, 1 Apr. 94.
Lieut. M. C. Maunsell, Royal Artillery, 1 Apr. 94.
Professor of French.—Mons. Albert Barrère.
Professor of German.—A. Weiss, *Ph.D. MA.*
Professor of Landscape Drawing.—Lt. Colonel D. T. C. Belgrave, ret. pay West Kent Regiment, 13 Nov. 90.
Instructor of Landscape Drawing.—J. B. Jameson.
Professor of Chemistry and Physics.—W. R. E. Hodgkinson, *Ph.D.* 23 March 82.

Staff College, Sandhurst.

Governor and Commandant.—p.s.c. Colonel H. J. T. Hildyard (from h.p. Highland Light Infantry), 12 Aug. 93.
   PROFESSORS.
Military Art and History.—Lt. Colonel G. F. R. Henderson, York and Lancaster Regiment, 17 Dec. 92.
Fortification and Artillery.—p.s.c. Lt. Colonel H. C. C. Walker, Royal Artillery, 1 Sept. 92.
Military Topography.—p.s.c. Lt. Colonel F. C. Beatson, Wilts Regiment, 13 Sept. 92.
Staff Duties, Military Administration and Law.—p.s.c. Lt Colonel C. R. Simpson, 12 Sept. 94.
French.—Mons. M. Deshumbert.
German.—Dr. H. O. Sommer.
Instructor in Military Topography.—Major J. S. Talbot, Shropshire Light Inf. 16 Dec. 92.

   STUDENTS.
   Senior Division.
Captain C. E. Keith-Falconer, Northumberland Fus.
Capt. D. Henderson, Argyll and Suth. Highlanders.
Lieut. E. Peach, Indian Staff Corps.
Captain D. J. M. Fasson, Royal Artillery.
Capt. H. d'E. Vallancey, Argyll and Suth.-Highlanders.
Lieut. W. M. Marter, 1 Dragoon Guards.
Lieut. H. H. H. Dowding, Essex Regiment.
Lieut. G. Sandilands, Royal Scots.
Captain L. H. Ducrôt, Royal Artillery.
Captain G. D. R. Williams, Berkshire Regiment.
Captain A. A. Chichester, Dorsetshire Regiment.
Lieut. C. Coffin, Royal Engineers.
Major W. G. Massy, Royal Artillery.
Captain R. T. Kirkpatrick, Leinster Regiment.
Captain E. R. O. Ludlow, Army Service Corps.
Captain A. S. Dunlop, Royal Artillery.
Captain W. G. Gwatkin, Manchester Regiment.
Major H. J. Evans, Liverpool Regiment.
Captain S. Bird, Royal Fusiliers.
Captain E. T. Taylor, Cheshire Regiment.
Captain F. R. Maunsell, Royal Artillery (*admitted without competition*).
Captain H. O. D. Hickman, Inniskilling Fus. (*do.*).
Captain E. A. H. Alderson, West Kent Regt. (*do.*).
Captain F. A. Fortescue, King's Royal Rifles (*do.*).
Major W. Adye, Irish Rifles (*do.*).
Captain C. M. Ducat, Indian Staff Corps (*do.*).
Lieut. I. Philipps, Indian Staff Corps (*do.*).

   Junior Division.
Captain H. W. G. Graham, *DSO.,* 5 Lancers.
Captain E. M. Perceval, Royal Artillery.
Lieut. W. A. M. Thompson, Royal Artillery.
Lieut. H. L. Tennant, Royal Artillery.
Captain W. Ewbank, Royal Engineers.
Lieut. G. M. Kirkpatrick, Royal Engineers.
Lieut. D. A. Friederichs, Royal Engineers.
Lieut. S. Earle, Coldstream Guards.
Captain N. H. Vertue, East Kent Regiment.
Major B. St. J. Barter, Lincoln Regiment.
Captain C. M. De Gruyther, Suffolk Regiment.
Captain J. S. Knox, East Yorkshire Regiment.
Captain J. R. F. Sladen, East York Regiment.
Captain C. H. S. Walker, Scottish Rifles.
Captain H. S. Sloman, East Surrey Regiment.
Captain F. St. D. Skinner, Sussex Regiment.
Captain W. C. Bridge, South Stafford Regiment.
Captain H. Jennings-Bramly, Royal Highlanders.
Captain A. H. Barthorp, Northampton Regiment.
Captain L. A. H. Hamilton, York Light Infantry.
Captain C. E. Spearman, Munster Fusiliers.
Lieut. J. A. E. MacBean, Dublin Fusiliers.
Captain R. J. Strachey, Rifle Brigade.
Captain E. E. Carter, Army Service Corps.
Captain H. W. L. Holman, Royal Marines.
Lieut. F. de B. Young, Indian Staff Corps.
Lieut. C. H. Clay, Indian Staff Corps.
Lieut. J. K. Tod, Indian Staff Corps.
Captain *Hon.* H. A. Lawrence, 17 Lancers (*admitted without competition*).
Captain H. J. Du Cane, Royal Artillery (*do*).
Lieut. F. S. Maude, Coldstream Guards (*do*).
Captain H. E. Wise, Derbyshire Regiment (*do*).

Educational Establishments.

School of Gunnery.

Commandant & Superintendent.—Colonel R. M. Stewart, *CB*. 9 March 94.

Chief Instructors.
Lt.Col. R. W. R. Hannay (*Woolwich*), 27 Apr. 92.
Colonel G. H. Marshall, 30 Sept. 93.
Lt.Col. A. A. Saunders (*Comdt. Golden Hill*), 4 Jan. 94.
Lt.Colonel J. F. Bally, 22 Dec. 93.
Lt.Col. E. G. H. Bingham (*Comdt.Devonport*), 22 Mar. 94.
Brigade Major.—p.s.c. Major N. B. Inglefield, 1 Jan. 94.

Staff Captains.
Captain H. A. Inglis (*Golden Hill*), 1 Nov. 91.
Captain P. E. Gray (*Devonport*), 1 Apr. 92.

Instructors in Gunnery.
Major A. C. Hansard (*Woolwich*), 1 April 90.
Major A. J. Hughes, 1 April 90.

Lt.Colonel E. H. Walker (*Aldershot*), 1 Oct. 90.
Captain H. W. M. Shewell (*Woolwich*), 1 June 91.
Major A. S. Pratt (*Sheerness*), 1 Nov. 91.
Captain G. D'A. Alexander (*Devonport*), 1 Apr. 92.
Captain E. G. Nicolls, 28 May 92.
Captain J. E. W. Headlam, 1 July 92.
Captain J. T. Johnston (*Woolwich*), 5 July 92.
Major H. T. Butcher, 26 Jan. 93.
Captain H. S. Jeudwine, 22 March 94.
Captain F. M. Lowe (*Golden Hill*), 9 May 94.
Assistant Supdt. of Experiments.—Major F. B. Elmslie 13 March 91.
2nd do.—Captain G. Tyacke, 1 Feb. 93.
3rd do.—Lieut. F. P. Hutchinson, 8 Sept. 94.
Adjutant.—Captain A. J. Mullins, 28 Oct. 92.
Quarter Master.—

Artillery College.

Director.—Colonel C. Trench (from h.p.), 19 July 90.
Assistant Director.—Lt.Colonel R. S. Watson, 3 May 92.
Insts. in Artillery.—Lt.Colonel E. M. Baker, 1 May 86.
Major G. R. Townshend, 1 Apr. 91.
Major P. A. MacMahon, 14 Apr. 91.
Captain Instructor Royal Gun Factories.—Major H. P. Willoughby, 1 Apr. 88.
Captain Instructor Royal Carriage Department.—Major E. V. Elwes, 23 Feb. 89.

Captain Instructor Royal Laboratory.—Captain J. W. Ormiston, 23 Apr. 94.
Professor of Applied Mathematics.—A. G. Greenhill, *MA*.
Lecturer on Metallurgy.—H. Bauerman, *FGS*.
Lecturer on Armour Plates.—Captain C. O. Browne, late of R. Art., 3 Sept. 80. [*Ph.D.*
Lecturer on Chemistry & Physics.—W. R. E. Hodgkinson,
Lecturer on Practical Mechanics.—H. W. Jones.
Veterinary Lecturer.—Veterinary Major G. D. Whitfield, 19 Feb. 85.

School of Military Engineering.
(*For Instructing the Corps in Military Field Works, at Chatham.*)

Commandant.—Major General E. O. Hewett, *CMG*, 1 Apr. 93.
Assistant Commandant.—Colonel K. R. Todd, 5 Oct. 92.
Brigade Major & Secretary.—p.s.c. Bt.Major F. C. Heath, 12 July 94.
Instructor in Construction and Estimating.—Major G. K. Scott-Moncrieff, 1 Nov. 93.
Assistant Instructors do. { Lieut. E. M. Paul, 24 July 93.
{ Capt J. I. Lang, 1 Oct. 94.
Instructor in Surveying.—Major C.W. Sherrard, 21 June 93.
Assistant Instructors in Surveying.—Capt.C. H. Enthoven, 7 Sept. 93 ; Lieut. A. E. G. Watherston, 1 July 94.
Instructor in Fortification.—Major T. R. Main, 13 Aug.91.

Assist. Instructors in Fortification.—Capt. J. R. Young, 1 March 91 ; Lieut. E. M'L. Blair, 9 Mar. 92.
Assistant Instructor for Charge of Workshops.—Captain H. F. Gaynor, 10 June 93.
Instructor in Electricity. — Major A. H. Bagnold, 30 Jan. 91.
Assistant Instructor in Electricity.—Lt. A. H. Dumaresq, 26 Feb. 94.
Assistant Instructor in Chemistry, Photography, &c.—Captain E. H. Hills, 1 Aug. 93.
Instructor in Tactics.—Major G. H. Sim, 28 June 93.
Adjutant.—Captain S. R. Rice, 10 Aug. 92.
Quarter Master.—Major Crichton Walker, 1 Apr. 94.

Schools of Submarine Mining.

Chief Instructors.
Captain G. A. Carr, 16 May 92.—*S.M.E.*, Chatham.
Captain W. S. Vidal, 16 May 92.—*Portsmouth*.
Captain M. A. Boyd, 16 May 92.—*Plymouth*.

Assistant Instructors.
Lieut. E. C. Seaman, 16 May 92.—*S.M.E.*, Chatham.
Captain W. G. Lawrie, 16 May 92.—*Portsmouth*.
Captain H. B. Roberts, 16 May 92.—*S.M.E.*, Chatham.
Captain W. B. Brown, 15 June 92.—*Portsmouth*.

School of Musketry at Hythe.

Commandant.—Colonel G. Paton, *CMG*. (from h.p. Regimental District), 17 July 94.
Deputy Assistant Adjutant General.—Captain T. N. Bagnall, East Yorkshire Regiment, 31 May 93.
Chief Instructor.—Lt.Colonel F. G. A. Wiehe (from h.p. Durham Light Infantry), 28 July 94.
Captain Instructors. { Captain J. G. Mayne, Inniskilling Fusiliers, 1 Aug. 91.
{ Captain G. E. W. Withington, South Lancashire Regiment.
Lieutenant Instructors. { Lieut. H. C. de la M. Hill, The Buffs, 4 Feb. 92.
{ Lieut. H. C. E. Smithett, York and Lancaster Regiment.
Quarter Master and Acting Adjutant.—Frank Bourne,[1] 1 May 93; *Hon. Lieut.*
Surgeon.—Deputy Surgeon General H. J. Rose, retired pay, 17 Aug. 90.

[1] Lieut. Bourne served in the Kafir war in 1877-78 and took part in the operations against the Galekas ; also in the Zulu war in 1879 including the defence of Rorke's Drift (mentioned in despatches, Medal with Clasp, and Medal for Distinguished Conduct in the Field). Served with the Burmese Expedition in 1887-89 (Medal with Clasp).

School of Signalling.

Inspector of Signalling.—p.s.c. Lt.Colonel C. Kennedy (from h.p. Suffolk Regiment), 1 Jan. 94. Aldershot.
Assistant Inspector of Signalling.—Major E. Rhodes, *DSO*. Berkshire Regiment, 1 Jan. 95. Aldershot.

School of Ballooning.
Instructor in Ballooning.—Lt.Colonel J. L. B. Templer, 7 Bn. King's Royal Rifles, 1 Apr. 87. Aldershot.

Army Medical School, Netley.

SENATE.
Sir W. A. Mackinnon, *KCB. FRCS.Edin.*, Director General Army Medical Department, President.
The Professors of the Army Medical School.
The Principal Medical Officer at Netley (*ex officio*).

PROFESSORS.
Clinical and Military Surgery.—Brigade Surgeon Lt.Col. W. F. Stevenson, *MB*, 10 Aug. 92.
Clinical and Military Medicine.—Deputy Surgeon General Henry Cayley, late Bengal Estab., 4 June 89.
Military Hygiene.—Brigade Surgeon Lt.Colonel J. L. Notter, *MD*, 6 Oct. 88.
Pathology.—Almroth Edw.Wright, Esq., *MD*. 1 Sept. 92.

ASSISTANT PROFESSORS.
Clinical and Military Surgery.—Surgeon Captain H. R. Whitehead.
Clinical and Military Medicine. — Brigade Surgeon Lt.Colonel E. J. Fairland.
Military Hygiene.—Surgeon Captain R. H. Firth.
Pathology.—Surgeon Captain D. Semple, *MD*.
Secretary.—Surg. Capt. W. W. Webb, late Bengal Estab.

Royal Military School of Music, Kneller Hall.

Commandant.—Colonel F. Glennie (from h.p. S. Wales Borderers), 20 Sept. 94.
Quarter Master.— Fred. H. Mahony, 15 Aug. 87; *Hon. Captain* 21 May 84.

Director of Music.—Quarter Master Samuel G. Griffiths, 24 Dec. 90; *Hon. Lieut.*
Chaplain (Acting).—Rev. R. Tahourdin, *MA*, 1 Apr. 88.

The Duke of York's Royal Military School.

Commissioners.

Ex Officio.

The Secretary of State for War, *President.*
H.R.H. the Commander in Chief, *Vice President.*
The Bishop of London.
The Bishop of Winchester.
The Paymaster General.
The Under Secretaries of State for War.
The Quarter Master General.
The Adjutant General.
The Governor of Chelsea Hospital.
The Lieutenant Governor of Chelsea Hospital.
The Governor of the Royal Military College.
The Chaplain General.
The Judge Advocate General.
The Director General of Military Education.

Specially Appointed.

Field Marshal H.R.H. The Duke of Cambridge, *KG. KT, KP, GCB, GCSI, GCMG, GCIE*. Gren. Gds., &c.
Colonel H.R.H. The Duke of York, *KG.*, 3 Bn. W. York Regiment.
General Rt. Hon. Sir Edward Lugard, *GCB*. East Surrey Regiment.
General Sir R. C. H. Taylor, *KCB*. Cameron Highlanders.
p.s.c. Major General J. P. Battersby, retired pay.
General Sir A. J. Herbert, *KCB*.
Commandant.—Lt.Colonel G. A. W. Forrest (from h.p. Hampshire Regiment), 18 Oct. 93.
Quarter Master and Adjutant.—E. C. Thomas, 3 Aug. 86; *Hon. Captain.*
Medical Officer.—Brigade Surgeon J. H. C. Whipple, *MD.*, retired pay.
Chaplain.—Rev. G. H. Andrews, *MA.*

MODEL SCHOOL. *Head Master*—T. Carson, *Hon. Captain*, 1 June 88. *Masters*—W. Townley, 25 Apr. 90; A. Gott, 10 Aug. 93; E. C. Whittle, 6 Dec. 93; T. Glynn, 17 Feb. 94.

Royal Hibernian Military School, Dublin.

Commandant.—Colonel C. de N. O. Stockwell (from h.p. Lincoln Regiment), 31 May 89.
Quarter Master and Adjutant. — Benjamin Smyth, *Hon. Captain*, 24 Jan. 95.
Surgeon.—Dep. Surg. Gen. J. H. Whittaker, retired pay, 1 Apr. 85.
Chaplains.—Rev. Robert Foster, *BA.*, Rev. J. M. Hamilton, *MA.*, Rev. M. Donovan.
Head Master—W. Gooding, 23 Jan. 94.; *Hon. Lieut.* Masters—M. Flanagan, 14 June 80; P. Holland, 1 Dec. 92.; J. W. Cunningham, 1 Jan. 93.

Army Schools.

Inspectors of Army Schools, with hon. rank of Captain.
Thomas Carson .... 11 Feb. 90
Thomas W. Smith .... 27 Feb. 94
George Green .... 19 Apr. 94

Inspectors of Army Schools, with hon. rank of Lieut.
John Masterson 12 Apr. 85	John M. Gilmore 1 Apr. 91
Frederic Major... 12 Aug. 85	William H. Jupp 1 Apr. 92
John C. Perkins 1 June 86	Fred. W. Browne 6 May 92
Wm. Gooding ... 1 Apr. 89	Wm. F. Blount 13 July 92
Charles S. Coo ... 3 Jan. 90	Wm. Harding ... 30 Dec. 92
John A. Smears 20 Apr. 90	Wal. W. Clarke 23 Jan. 94
Wm. Irwin, *BA*. 25 June 90	Henry M'Ilroy 28 Feb. 94
Wm. Langford 1 Sept. 90	Samuel Logan... 2 July 94
Robt. Raymer... 18 Feb. 91	Fred.G. Hendley 28 Dec. 94
Henry Jerram... 20 Feb. 91	Thomas Murray 28 Dec. 94

ORDNANCE FACTORIES.

Director General Ordnance Factories .... W. Anderson, *M.Inst.C.E. DCL. FRS.* 1 Aug. 89.
First Military Assistant .... Commander B. H. Chevallier, R.N. 15 Apr. 90.
Second Military Assistant .... Captain H.W.W. Barlow, R. Artillery, 12 June 93.
Civil Assistant .... G. M. Tapp.
Experimental Officer .... Lieut. A. T. Dawson, R.N. 1 Sept. 92.

Royal Arsenal, Woolwich.

Royal Carriage Factory.
Superintendent, Lt.Colonel Sir G. S. Clarke, *KCMG*. Royal Engineers .... 27 July 94

Royal Laboratory.
Superintendent, Colonel E. Bainbridge (from h.p. R. Artillery) .... 6 June 92
In charge of Danger Buildings, Captain H. Waring, Royal Artillery .... 1 July 93
Lieut. H. B. Strange, Royal Artillery .... 1 Apr. 93

Royal Gun Factory.
Superintendent, Captain J. Ingles, R.N. .... 10 July 94

Building Works.
Superintendent, Colonel M.T. Sale, *CMG*.(from h.p. Royal Engineers) .... 1 Apr. 88
First Assistant, Major S. H. Exham, R. Eng.... 6 Mar. 89
Second Assistant, Captain H. Huleatt, Royal Engineers .... 1 Aug. 93
Railway Traffic Manager, Lieut. E. P. C. Girouard, R. Engineers .... 1 July 90

Medical Officers (Royal Arsenal).
Surgeon Lt.Colonel J. M. Beamish, *MD*....... 13 July 92
Surgeon Captain R. J. S. Simpson, *MB*. ...... 19 May 91
Surgeon Captain S. G. Allen .... 24 Dec.

Royal Small Arms Factory at Enfield.
Superintendent, J. Rigby, Esq., *MA.* .... 15 Oct. 87

Royal Small Arms Factory at Birmingham.
Superintendent, Lt.Col. F. W. J. Barker (from Royal Artillery)............................ 1 Oct. 92

Royal Gunpowder Factory at Waltham Abbey
Superintendent, Colonel J. B. Ormsby .... 27 July 94
In charge of Danger Buildings.
Captain F. L. Nathan, Royal Artillery ....
Lieut. A. S. Buckle, Royal Artillery .... 8 Sept. 94

Army Clothing Department.

Director of Clothing, G. D. A. Fleetwood Wilson, *CB.*
Assistant Director, H. D. De la Bère.
Storekeeper, H. L. Kennedy.

Medical Officer, Dep. Surg. Gen. H. R. L. Veale, *MD.* retired pay.
Inspector of Colours, Sir Albert Wm. Woods, *KCMG. CB.* Garter King of Arms.

COMMITTEES AND INSPECTION OF WARLIKE STORES

(Under the Director of Artillery)

Ordnance Committee.

President .... Major General Sir H. J. Alderson, *KCB*. 31 Oct. 91.
Vice-President .... Rear Admiral E. Rice, R.N., 21 Nov. 94.

Members.
Colonel C. H. F. Ellis (from h.p. R. Art.) ... 10 Jan. 93
Captain A. A. C. Parr, R.N. .... 12 May 94
Col. A. J. Hepper, *DSO.* (from h.p. R. Eng) 20 Dec. 92
Colonel D. D. T. O'Callaghan (from R. Art.) ... 6 June 92
Lt.Colonel C. H. Scott (from h.p. R. Art.), Ord.
Consulting Officer for India, *ex-officio*........ 13 Nov. 92
Captain P. M. Scott, R.N. .... 20 Nov. 93
Sir F. J. Bramwell, *Bt, M.Inst.CE. FRS.* ..... 1 Apr. 81
Sir B. Baker, *KCMG. M.Inst.CE. FRS. LLD.*

Lt.Colonel G.H.Marshall,R.Art.(*for Field Art.*)30 Sept.93
Lt.Col. E. H.Walker, R. Art. (*for Rangefinders*) 25 Nov. 90
The Com. R. Eng. Shorncliffe (*ex-officio*)—*for Lydd Experiments*.
Captain E. Druitt, R. Eng. (*for Lydd Experiments*).
Major T. R. Main, R. Eng.(*for Lydd Experiments*).
Dr. A. Dupré, *FRS.* (*for Explosives*).
Director Gen. Ord. Factories (*for Cordite*).
Lt.Colonel J. F. Harman (from R. Art.), 1 May 92 (*special as Inspector of Warlike Stores for the Australasian Colonies*).

Associate Members.
Lt.Colonel R. W. R. Hannay (from R. Art.) *for Siege Artillery*, 22 Mar. 94.

Secretary................... Major W. E. Blewitt, R. Artillery .... 1 Apr. 94.
Assistant Secretary ...... Commander J. Honner, R.N. .... 29 Aug. 92.

Committees and Inspection of Warlike Stores.

Department of Director of Artillery.

Lt.Colonel H. S. S. Watkin, CB. *Chief Inspector of Position Finding* .... 1 Apr. 86
Captain H. H. Rich................................ 1 Apr. 93
Captain W. L. Farmar.............................. 1 Apr. 93
Captain F. A. Randolph .... 3 May 93
Lieut.S.M'A.Walker,Qr.Mr.Crd.StoreDept....22 Dec. 94

INSPECTION STAFF.

SMALL ARMS.
Chief Inspector.—Lt.Colonel W. N. Lockyer (from h.p. Royal Artillery), 21 June 94.
Inspectors.
Captain T. F. Bushe, R. Artillery, 1 Apr. 93.
Lt.Colonel W. F. Nuthall (from h.p. Manchester Regiment), 21 June 94.
2nd Class Assistant Inspectors.
Captain Hon. A. Lambart, R. Artillery, 10 Apr. 94.
Major F. F. Johnstone, Bedford Regiment, 21 June 94.

STEEL.
Inspector.—Lt.Col.W. P.Blandy(from R.Art.),27 Aug. 94.
2nd Class Assistant Inspectors.
Major T. H. E. Acton, R. Artillery, 26 Aug. 94.
Lieut. R. P. Robinson, R. Engineers, 1 Apr. 93.
Lieut. R. J. Macdonald, R. Artillery, 1 Apr. 93.

ROYAL ARSENAL.
Chief Inspector.—Major C. F. Hadden, R. Artillery, 1 Apr. 93.
Inspectors.
Major H. C. L. Holden, R. Artillery, 1 Feb. 88.
Captain A. H. W. Dod, R. Artillery, 1 Apr. 93.
Major A. H. W. Brett, R. Artillery, 1 Apr. 93.
Captain H. R. Adair, R. Artillery, 1 Apr. 93.
Major W. A. Urquhart, R. Artillery, 1 Apr. 93.
1st Class Assistant Inspector.
Captain W. Lambert, R. Artillery, 1 Apr. 93.
2nd Class Assistant Inspectors.
Captain S. G. R. Horton, R. Artillery, 1 Apr. 93.
Lieut. A. J. Saltren-Willett, R. Artillery, 1 Apr. 93.
Captain J. H. Mansell, R. Artillery, 1 Apr. 93.
Captain N. B. Heffernan, R. Artillery, 1 Apr. 93.
Captain F. T. Fisher, R. Artillery, 1 Apr. 93.
Captain W. W. Griffin, R. Artillery, 18 May 93.
Captain F. F. Minchin, R. Artillery, 1 Apr. 93.
Captain W. J. Honner, R. Artillery, 25 May 93.
Major W. S. Churchward, R. Artillery, 19 June 93.
p.s.c. Captain G. D. Baker, R. Artillery, 15 Aug. 93.

ROYAL ENGINEER STORES.
Inspector.—Captain A. M. Stuart, 1 Apr. 94.
Assistant Inspector.— Lieut. W. Mongomery, Coast Battalion, 1 Apr. 94.
MACHINERY.
Superintending Engineer and Constructor of Shipping.—J. A. C. Hay, CE., 1 Apr. 91.
Assistant do.—H. Travis, 13 Apr. 93.
GENERAL STORES.
Superintendent.—p.s.c. Commissary General of Ordnance J. T. Barrington, retired pay, 1 Apr. 88.
Assistant Superintendents.
Quarter Master W. McCanlis, Ordnance Store Department, 1 Apr. 88, Hon. Captain.
F. Tims, 1 Apr. 92, Hon. Captain Ord. Store Dept.
ASSISTANT INSPECTORS AT OUTSTATIONS.
First Class.
Gibraltar.—Captain H. C. W. Eteson, R. Artillery, 18 May 93.
Malta.—Major L. Barrett, R. Artillery, 5 May 93.
Second Class.
Bermuda.—Lieut. F. M. Thrupp, R. Artillery, 6 Apr. 93.
Cape Town.—Captain H. S. le M. Guille, R.Art. 27 Aug.92.
Ceylon.—Captain C. E. Rolt, R. Artillery, 1 Apr. 92.
Cork.— Captain J. R. Foster, R. Artillery, 1 Apr. 91.
Devonport.—Major R. P. Leach, R. Artillery, 15 May 94.
Halifax, N.S.—Major C. H. Alexander, R. Art. 5 Apr. 91.
Hong Kong.—Lieut. C. S. Taylor, R. Art, 29 Mar. 91.
Mauritius.—Lieut. R. Waring, R. Artillery, 4 July 94.
Portsmouth.—Lt.Colonel H. P. Dawson (from h.p. Royal Artillery), 1 Apr. 91.
Jamaica.—Captain H. C. Marshall, R. Art. 9 Dec. 91.
INSPECTORS OF POSITION FINDING.
Woolwich.—Captain T. E. Carte, R. Artillery, 1 July 93.
Malta.—Captain H. T. Hawkins, R. Art. 21 Aug. 94.
Golden Hill.—Capt. E. F. Hoblyn, R. Art. 15 July 88.
Gibraltar.—Captain H. de T. Phillips, R. Art. 10 Oct. 94.
Woolwich (2nd Class).—Lieut. A. H. Thorp, R. Art. 24 July 93.

Valuation and Inspection of Military Equipment (India Committee).
Col. G. A. Crawford, ret. pay R. Art. (*for War Office*). | Captain A. B. Hawes, late Indian Army (*for India Office*).

Joint Naval and Military Committee on Defence.
President ....The Parliamentary Under Secretary of State for War.
Members, Naval and Military.

The Senior Naval Lord of the Admiralty.
The Admiral Superintendent of Naval Reserve.
The Director of Naval Ordnance.
The Director of Naval Intelligence.
The Adjutant General.
The Inspector General of Fortifications and of R. Eng.
The Director of Artillery.
The Director of Military Intelligence.

Joint Secretaries.
Colonel H. F. Turner (from R. Engineers). | Captain G. A. Callaghan, R.N.

Army Sanitary Committee.
President .... HC p.s.c. Lt.General Sir H. E. Wood, GCB. GCMG. 9 Oct. 93.
Members.

Colonel H. Locock (from h.p. R. Engineers), 1 Nov. 87.
Surgeon General Sir J. Fayrer, KCSI. MD. (for India).
Surg. Gen. J. M. Cuningham, CSI. MD. late Bengal Estab. (do.), 10 March 91.
Surgeon Lt.Colonel W. S. Pratt, MB. 1 Apr. 93.
Sir D. Galton, KCB. FRS. late Capt. R. Eng. 1 July 90.
Surg. Gen. J. A. Marston, CB. MD. ret. pay, 1 July 90.
Sir C. A. Cameron, Knt. MD. 9 Sept. 90.
Secretary........................... J. J. Frederick, 1 Dec. 62.

Royal Engineer Committee.
President.................................. Major General E. O. Hewett, CMG. .... 1 Apr. 93.
Ex-officio Members.

Colonel D. A. Scott, DSO. .... 8 June 94
Lt.Colonel G. Barker .... 6 Nov. 94
Major T. R. Main .... 13 Aug. 91
Major C. W. Sherrard .... 21 June 93
Major R. M. Ruck................................... 1 July 92
Major A. H. Bagnold .... 30 Jan. 91
Major G. K. Scott-Moncrieff....................... 1 Nov. 93
Captain G. A. Carr .... 16 May 92

Associate Members.
Major D. C. Courtney, ret. pay (*for India*)... 20 Apr. 87
Major E. Dickinson .... 1 Oct. 92
Major P. G. Von Donop .... 1 July 94
Major R. L. Hippisley .... 30 Jan. 91
Major O. Penrose .... 1 July 91
Captain A. M. Stuart .... 9 Mar. 94
W. Kellner, Ph.D.

Secretary .... Major E. Druitt.
Experimental Officer, Submarine Mining Service ....Captain P. R. Burn-Murdoch, 16 May 92.

Dress and Equipment Committee.
President..............p.s.c. Colonel H. S. G. Miles.
Members.

Lt. Colonel C. H. Bridge, Army Service Corps.
Brigade Surgeon Lt.Colonel W. H. M'Namara, MD.
Assist. Com. Gen. of Ord. F. G. Wintle, DSO.
Lt.Colonel A. C. E. Welby, 2 Dragoons.
Lt.Colonel A. R. F. Dorward, DSO. Royal Engineers.
Major E. M. Flint, Royal Artillery.

Secretary..................... p.s.c. Captain J. E. Lindley, 1 Dragoons.

MISCELLANEOUS ESTABLISHMENTS.

Cavalry Depot at Canterbury.

Commandant.—Colonel H. R. Abadie, CB. (from Regimental District), 19 Apr. 94.
Assistant Commandant and Superintendent of the Riding Department.—Colonel G. M. Onslow (from h.p. 20 Hussars), 19 Apr. 92.
Adjutant.—Captain E. C. Knox, 18 Hussars, 25 Apr. 94.

Paymaster.—Staff Paymaster D. C. O. Spiller.
Riding Master.—Thomas Henry Jones, 25 June 79; Hon. Major, 15 June 87.
Quarter Master.—Jas. Wm. Humphrey,[1] 5 Oct. 93; Hon. Captain, 18 July 93.

[1] Captain Humphrey served in the Afghan war in 1879-80 (Medal). Served in the Boer war of 1881.

Remount Establishment.

Inspector General.—Major General E. A. Gore, 1 Jan. 94. *Head Quarters.*

Assistant Inspectors.
Colonel B. L. Tollner (from h.p. Royal Artillery), 23 June 89. *Woolwich.*
Colonel T. A. St. Quintin (from h.p. 8 Hussars), 19 Oct. 92. *Dublin.*
Colonel W. R. Truman (from Regimental District), 1 Apr. 93. *London.*

Deputy Assistant Adjutant General.
Captain P. F. Dwyer, 3 Hussars, 10 Apr. 91. *Head Quarters.*

Staff Captains.
Major D. E. Wood, 8 Hussars, 1 July 92. *Dublin.*
Captain H. M. Ferrar, R. Art. 26 Sept. 93. *Woolwich.*

Royal Hospital, Chelsea.

Governor.—

Lt. Governor & Secretary.—*p.s.c.* Major General C. W. Robinson, C.B.
Assistant Secretary.—J. Dowling.
Adjutant.—John James Charles Irby,[1] h.p. Unattached, 7 Sept. 55; *Ens.* P 17 Jan. 51; *Lt.* 8 Oct. 54; *Capt.* 16 Jan. 63; *Hon. Major,* 20 Mar. 78.
Chaplain.—Rev. Sydney Clark, MA. h.p. 2 Feb. 78.

Physician and Surgeon.—J. A. M'Munn,[2] MD. h.p. 4 Nov. 68.
Deputy Surgeon.—Thomas Ligertwood,[3] MD. h.p. 13 Jan. 69.
Quarter Master.—Richd. Barry Jupp, ret. pay, Jan. 85; Hon. Captain, 9 Sept. 81.

Captains of Invalids.
J.Vander H.Rees, late 40F.
Major J. W. Daniell, ret. pay.
Major E. W. Humphry, ret. pay.
Colonel A. Green, ret. pay.
Major E. Brutton, ret. pay.
Major A. S. Carter, retired pay.

[1] Major Irby served the Eastern campaign of 1854-55, including the battles of Alma and Inkerman, capture of Balaklava, siege of Sebastopol, repulse of sortie on 26th Oct. 1855, and storming the Quarries on 7th June 1855— severely wounded, left leg amputated (mentioned in despatches, Medal with three Clasps, and Turkish Medal).
[2] Doctor J. A. M'Munn served in the Eastern campaign of 1854-55, including the siege of Sebastopol (Medal with Clasp, and Turkish Medal).
[3] Doctor T. Ligertwood served throughout the Crimean campaign of 1854-55, including the battles of Alma (mentioned in despatches) and Inkerman, siege and fall of Sebastopol (Medal with three Clasps, Knight of the Legion of Honor, and Turkish Medal).

Judge Advocate General's Office.

Judge Advocate General.—Rt. Hon. Sir F. H. Jeune.
Deputy Judge Advocate General.—J. C. O'Dowd, Esq. CB.
Deputy Judge Advocate.—*p.s.c.* Colonel Sir W. A. Eardley Wilmot, Bart. h.p. Northumberland Fusiliers, London. Office, 35, Great George Street, Westminster.

Royal Hospital, Kilmainham.

Master.—The Commander of the Forces in Ireland.
Joint Dep. Masters. { The Deputy Adj. Gen. in Ireland.
{ The Dep. Quarter Master Gen. do.
Captain of Invalids.
Major George Cresswell, retired pay.
Adjutant.—Joshua Fielding,[1] 3 Nov. 91; *Qr. Mr. and Hon. Captain.*
Physician and Surgeon.—William Carte,[2] 13 Aug. 58.
Secretary.—Langrishe F. Banks.
Quarter Master.—
Solicitor.—R. J. Ferguson, Esq.

Army Pay Office.

Paymaster General.—Rt. Hon. C. Seale-Hayne, MP.
Assistant Paymaster General.—C. J. Maude, Esq.

Army Purchase Commission.

Commissioners { J. C. O'Dowd, CB. 30 Sept. 71.
{ *p.s.c.* Colonel Sir W. A. E. Wilmot, Bt. 23 May 91.

Military Prisons.

Inspector General.—Major General Sir E. F. Du Cane, KCB., ret. pay R. Eng.
Inspector.—W. J. Stopford.
Aldershot.—*Chief Warder,*
Med. Off., Brig. Surg. W. F. Ruttledge, ret. pay.
Cork.—*Chief Warder,* J. Martin.
Med. Off., Brigade Surg. U. A. Jenings, MD. ret. pay.
Dublin.—*Chief Warder,* C. Jacups.
Med. Off., Surgeon Major N. Alcock, ret. pay.
Gosport.—*Gov.,* Lt.Colonel H. Waring, ret. pay 2 Foot.
Med. Off., Surgeon E. Chandler, h.p.
Malta.—*Chief Warder,* P. Prior.

Blue.—*Facings* Red.

[1] Captain Fielding served in the Egyptian war of 1882, and was present in the engagements at Tel-el-Mahuta and Mahsama, at the action at Kassasin on the 28th August, at the battle of Tel-el-Kebir, and at the capture of Cairo (Medal with Clasp, and Khedive's Star).
[2] Surgeon Carte served in the Eastern campaign of 1854-55, including the battles of Balaklava and Inkerman, siege of Sebastopol, and sortie of 26th Oct. (Medal with Clasps, and Turkish Medal).

G

List of Officers, now serving in the Army, who passed the Examination and received Certificates at the Senior Department, Royal Military College.

Cameron, General Sir Wm. Gordon, KCB. Lancaster Regiment, May 1853.
Cox, Major General J. W. CB. Bedford Regt. Nov. 1847.
Cranfield, Captain G. D. h.p. Unatt.
D'Oyly, Major General J. W. Nov. 1847.
Ewart, General Sir J. A., KCB. Gordon Highlanders, May 1845.
Gordon, Major General C. E. P. CB. Nov. 1844.
Hutchinson, Gen. W. N. Yorkshire Regt.(33 F.), Nov.1833.
Jarvis, Colonel S. P. CMG. h.p. 82 F. May 1856.
M'Cleverty, General W. A. Northampton Regt. Dec. 1830.
Paterson, Colonel Wm. Unatt. Nov. 1855.
Pencocke, Major General G. J. Dec. 1856.
Stapylton, Major General G. G. C. May 1849.
Stewart, Major A. F. h.p. 36 F. Dec. 1857.

List of Officers, now serving, who have passed the Staff College.

Passed, December 1860.
Feilding, General Hon. W. H. A.
*Grant, Lt.General R., CB. R. Eng.

Passed, December 1861.
Hall, Major General T. E. A.

Passed, December 1862.
East, Major General C. J., CB.
Elles, Major Gen. Sir W. K., KCB.
Black, Major General W., CB.

Passed, December 1864.
Goodenough, Lt.General W. H., CB. R. Artillery.
Clive, Lt.General E. H.
VC Wood, Lt.General Sir H. E., GCB. GCMG.
Knowles, Major General C. B., CB.

Passed, December 1865.
Swther, Lt.General C. C., R. M. Art.
Robinson, Col. C. W., CB. h.p. Rifle Brig.
Knollys, Colonel H., h.p. R. Art.

Passed, December 1866.
Barker, Lt. General G. D., CB.
Hatchell, Major General G.
Farrington, Colonel H. D'O., h.p. Regimental District.
Blundell, Major General R. B. M.

Passed, December 1867.
Griffiths, Col. H. H., Regtl. District.
Pitman, Captain W., h.p. R. M. Art.
Prior, Colonel G. U., h.p. Royal Scots.
Moorsom, Colonel H. M., h.p. R. Art.

Passed, December 1868.
Walker, Major General A. L.
Hollist, Major E. O., R. Art.
Crealock, Major General J. N., CB.

Passed, December 1869.
Boughey, Colonel J., h.p. Wilts Regt.
Cooke, Col. W. S., h.p. Cheshire Regt.
Tulloch, Colonel A. B., CB. CMG. h.p. Welsh Regiment.
Chapman, Lt.General E. F., CB. R. Art.

Passed, December 1870.
Maurice, Colonel J. F., CB., R. Art.
Clery, Major General C. F., CB.
Harvey, Colonel C. L. (from h.p. Wilts Regt.)
VC Sartorius, Colonel E. H., h.p. East Lancashire Regt. (59 F.)
Little, Maj.Gen. H.A., CB. Indian S.C.

, In the foregoing lists the names are placed in the Order of Merit in which the Officers passed the final Examination, as officially notified; but, the Order of Merit in which Officers have passed out of the Staff College having ceased to be disclosed, their names in the following lists are consequently given in the Order of Merit in which they passed into the Staff College.

Passed, December 1871.
Schwabe, Col. G. S., h.p. Regtl. Dist.
Jones-Vaughan, Colonel H. T., CB. h.p. East Yorkshire Regt.
Nicolls, Major General O. H. A., R. Art.
Dundas, Colonel H. L., h.p. East Yorkshire Regt. (15 F.)

Passed, December 1872.
Hart, Colonel A. FitzRoy, CB. East Surrey Regt. (31 F.)
Hemmick, Colonel Sir St. V. A., Bt. h.p. Oxford Light Infantry (43 F.)
England, Major General E. L., CB.
Gosset, Col. M. W.E., CB. h.p. Dorset Regt.
Hall, Lt.Colonel B. G., R. Mar. Art.
Buxton, Lt.Colonel J. W. F., h.p. Inniskilling Fusiliers.
Brickenden, Lt.Colonel R.H.L., Black Watch (42 F.)
Dooner, Colonel W. T., Regimental District.
Collen, Colonel Sir E. H. H., KCIE. Indian Staff Corps (passed into the College with the preceding Class).

Passed, December 1873.
Clayton, Colonel E., h.p. R. Art.
Dalrymple, Colonel W. L., CB. h.p. Connaught Rangers (88 F.)
Walford, Colonel N. L., h.p.R. Art.
Bury, Lt.Colonel J. T., R. Art.
Russell, Col. F. S., CMG. h.p. 1 Drs.
Cooper, Lt.Colonel H. h.p. North Lancashire Regiment.
Duncan, Col.J., h.p. Dublin Fusiliers.
Poignand, Colonel G., h.p. Leinster Regiment.
Burnett, Col. C.J., CB. h.p. Irish Rifles.
*Hutchinson, Colonel W. F. M., h.p. R. Artillery.

Passed, December 1874.
Hare, Lt.Colonel W. A. H., R. Eng.
Ardagh, Colonel Sir J. C., KCIE. CB. (from R. Engineers).
Walker, Lt.Colonel A. G., R. Art.
Creek, Colonel E. S., h.p. Welsh Fus.
Delavoye, Col. A. M. (from Essex Regt.)
Courtenay, Lt.Col. E. J., h.p. Sussex Regiment.
Gatacre, Colonel W. F., DSO, h.p. Middlesex Regt. (77 F.)
Lugard, Colonel E. J., Lancaster Regt.

Passed, December 1875.
Morris, Lt.Col. W. G., CMG. R. Eng.
Yule, Lt.Col. W. A., h.p. Scots Fus.
Kitchener, Lt.Col. H. E. C., h.p. Duke of Cornwall's Lt. Infantry.
Brownrigg, Col. H. S., h.p. Rifle Brig.
Kelly-Kenny, Col. T., CB. h.p. W. Surrey Regt.
Elias, Colonel R. (from h.p. E. Lancashire Regt.)
Curteis, Col. R.L.H., h.p. Bedford Regt.
Glen, Colonel A., Regtl. District.
Wardroper, Col. E., h.p. Sussex Regt.
Eardley-Wilmot, Colonel W. A.
*Harrison, Lt.General Sir R., KCB. CMG.

Passed, December 1876.
Murray, Colonel K.D., DSO. h.p. Irish Fusiliers.
Bengough, Major General H. M., CB.
Money, Lt.Colonel E. C., Irish Fus.
Fraser, Lt.Col. A. H., S. Lanc. Regt.

Passed, December 1877.
Jones, Col. D. F. (from h.p. R. Art.)
Smith, Lt. Col. W. W. M., R. Art.
Barker, Lt.Colonel J. C., R. Eng.
Hildyard, Colonel H. J. T., h.p. Highland Lt. Infantry (71 F.)
Ross of Bladensburg, Major J. F. G., CB. Coldstream Guards.
Woodgate, Lt.Colonel E. R. P., Lancaster Regt. (4 F.)
Goldsmid, Colonel A. E. W. Regimental District.
Morison, Lt.Colonel F. de L., R.Scots.
Hughes-Hallett, Lt.Colonel H. T., Middlesex Regt. (57 F.)
Cochran, Colonel F., Regtl. District.
Auld, Colonel J., h.p. Northumberland Fusiliers.
Vulliamy, Lt.Col. C.W., Leicester Regt.
Hare, Lt.Col. R. C., Cheshire Regt.

Passed, December 1878.
VC Bell, Colonel M. S., CB. h.p. Royal Engineers.
Everett, Colonel W., CMG. h.p. West Riding Regt.
Luttman-Johnson, Lt.Colonel F., h.p. York and Lancaster Regt.
Fergusson, Lt.Col. J. A. (from h.p. Rifle Brigade.)
Miles, Lt.Col. H.S.G., h.p. Munster Fus.
Paterson, Lt.Colonel A. M., Bedford Regiment.
Goodwyn, Lt.Col. J. E., h p E. Lanc. Regiment.

Passed, December 1879.
Grove, Col. C., CB. h.p. E.York Regt.
Leverson, Major J. J., R. Engineers.
M'Donald, Lt.Col. G., R. Engineers.
Elles, Colonel E. R., CB., R. Art.
Jocelyn, Lt.Col. J. R. J., h.p. R. Art.
Pollock, Lt.Col. A. J. O., Scots Fus.
Glasgow, Col. J.C.R., h.p. Suffolk Reg.
Tidy, Major A. G., N. Lanc. Regt.
Ponsonby, Lt.Col. J. G., Berks Regt.
Craigie, Lt.Col. J. H. S., Highland Light Infantry (71 F.)
*Spencer, Major J. W. T., R. Art.

Passed, December 1880.
Beresford, Lt.Col. C. F. C., R. Eng.
Montgomery, Lt.Col. R. A., h.p. R. Art.
Buchanan-Dunlop, Lt.Colonel H. D., Royal Artillery.
Benson, Lt.Col. F.W., h.p. 17 Lancers.
Browne, Major G. F., DSO. Northamptonshire Regt. (48 F.)
Romilly, Major F. W., DSO. Scots Guards.
Bullock, Major G. M., Devon Regt.
Allatt, Lt.Colonel H. T. W., h.p. Duke of Cornwall's Light Infantry.
Thomson, Lt.Col. C.F., h.p. 7 Hussars.
Prickett, Lt.Col. T., h.p. Essex Regt.
Godfray, Major J. W., King's Own Scottish Borderers.
*Fraser, Colonel T., CB. CMG., h.p. Royal Engineers.
VC Hart, Colonel Reginald C. (from Royal Engineers).

* Passed the Final Examination without having gone through the College.

List of Officers, now serving, who have passed the Staff College. 120

*Watson, Lt.Col. C. M., *CMG*. R. Eng.
Crookenden, Lt.Col. H. H., R. Art. *(passed into the College with the preceding Class)*.
Jeffreys, Colonel P. D., h.p. Connaught Rangers (88 F.) *(do)*.
Spence, Lt.Colonel J., h.p. York Lt. Inf. *(do)*.

Passed, December 1881.

Green, Lt.Col. A. O., R. Engineers.
Murray, Major J. W., R. Artillery.
Daniell, Lt.Col. De C., R. Artillery.
Johnson, Major R. F., R. Artillery.
Hughes, Lt.Col. P. J., Scottish Rifles.
Tidy, Major F. J., E. Lancashire Regt.
Routh, Major W. R., Suffolk Regt.
Herbert, Major General I. J. C., *CB*. Grenadier Gds.
Haly, Colonel R. H. O'G., *DSO*. h.p. Suffolk Regt.
Yeatherd, Maj. E.W., Lancaster Regt.
Dawson, Major D. F. R., Coldst. Gds.
Cutbill, Colonel H. D. A., h.p. Irish Rifles.
Peacocke, Lt.Col.W., *CMG.R.E.(passed into College with the preceding Class)*.
Barton, Colonel G., *CB*. h.p. Royal Fusiliers *(do.)*
Hutton, Major General E. T. H., *CB*. *(do.)*.

Passed, December 1882.

Morris, Colonel A.W., h.p. Northamptonshire Regt.
Haig, Major H. de H., R. Engineers.
Leefe, Bt.Lt.Col. J. B., R. Mar. Art.
Trotter, Lt. Col.J.K., h.p.R.Artillery.
Dalton, Lt.Col. J. C., h.p. R. Art.
Mortimer, Major H. B., North Staffordshire Regt. (64 F.)
Allen, Colonel R. E. E. York Regt.
Hutton, Major C. M., Lanc. Fusiliers.
Stephenson, Major T. E., Essex Regt.
Bromfield, Maj. F. W., Cheshire Regt.
Balfe, Major E., Indian Staff Corps.

Passed, December 1883.

Grove, Maj. E.A.W.S., W. Kent Regt.
Gough, Col. *Hon*. G. H., *CB*. 14 Hus.
Beckett, Lt.Colonel C. E., 2 Dr. Gds.
Codrington, Major A. E., Coldst. Gds.
Verner, Major W. W. C., Rifle Brig.
Stone, Major F. G., R. Artillery.
Settle, Colonel H. H., *DSO*. Royal Engineers.
Barrow, Maj. A. F., *CMG*. Indian S.C.
St. Clair, Lt.Colonel J. L. C., h.p. Argyll and Sutherland Highldrs.
Grant, Colonel H. F., *CB*. h.p. 7 Dragoon Guards
*y*C Ridgeway, Lt.Col. R. K., Ind.S.C.
Barter, Major C. St. L., York Lt. Inf.
Mortimer, Lt.Col. C. L., R. Fusiliers.
Wilkinson, Col. A., h.p. S. Lanc. Regt.
Duke, Capt. J. C., W. Riding Regt

Passed, December 1884.

Sawyer, Lt.Col. H. A., Indian S. C.
Lake, Major P. H. N., E. Lanc. Regt.
Wynne, Lt. Colonel G.C., R. Artillery.
Moody, Major R. S. H., The Buffs.
More-Molyneux, Colonel G. H., Indian Staff Corps.
Banfield, Major R. J. F., Welsh Regt.
Sharpe, Capt. E. J., Middlesex Regt.
Hammond, Lt.Col. P. H., h.p.R. Art.
Lawrence, Lt.Col. R. C. B., 1 Dr. Gds.
Watson, Major A. J., Suffolk Regt.
Thornton, Major F. S., Rifle Brigade

Passed, December 1885.

Stopford, Lt.Colonel *Hon*. F. W., h.p. Grenadier Guards.
Grierson, Captain J. M., Royal Art.
Walker, Lt.Col. H. C. C., Royal Art.
Foster, Major H. J., R. Engineers.
Sharpe, Major J. B., Royal Engineers.

Dunlop, Major H. C., Royal Art.
Penton, Capt. H. E., Indian S.C.
Colville, Major A. E. W., Rifle Brig.
Adair, Major W. T., Royal Marines.
Hogge, Major J. W., Indian Staff C.
Inglefield, Major F. S., E. York Regt.
Napier, Lt.Col. *Hon*. J. P., h.p. 10 Hus.
Wavell, Lt.Col.A.G., h.p.BlackWatch.
Cavenagh, Capt. W. O., Bedford Regt.
Durand, Col. A. G. A., *CB*. Indian S.C.
Johnstone, Lt.Col. J., Oxford Lt. Inf.
Robinson, Lt.Col. F. W., Shropshire Lt. Infantry.
Sherston, Major J., *DSO*. Rifle Brig.

Passed, December 1886.

Wyndham, Major W.G.C., 21 Hussars.
Paget, Major H., 7 Hussars.
Allen, Captain A. J. W., The Buffs.
Callwell, Captain C. E., R. Artillery.
Fleming, Major E. W., R. Artillery.
Agar, Captain E., Royal Engineers.
Northcott, Maj. H. P., Leinster Regt.
Smith, Major W. A., R. Artillery.
Fletcher, Major W. B., R. Artillery.
Daniell, Captain J. F., R. Marines.
Poynder, Captain C. E., Indian S. C.
Jones, Major A. E., Indian S. C.
Smythe, Captain H. H., Scots Fus.
Urmston, Captain E. B., Argyll and Sutherland Highlanders.
Farrant, Lt.Colonel H. C. B. (from h.p. N.Lanc. Regt.)
Bethune, Capt. E. C., 6 Dr. Guards.
Simpson, Major C. R., Lincoln Regt.
Mackenzie, Major G. F. C., Suffolk Regt.
Barkworth, Captain H. A. S., Northampton Regiment.
Bodé, Capt. L. W., Middlesex Regt.
Churchill, Colonel M. (from h.p. Northampton Regt.)
Williams, Maj. R. B., Somerset Lt. Inf.
Wogan-Brown, Capt. P. W. N., 3 Hus.
Kitchener, Maj. F. W., W.York Regt.
Eastman, Major W. I., R. M. Art.

Passed, December 1887.

Reade, Captain R. N. R., Shropshire Light Infantry.
Fawkes, Lt.Col. L. G., h.p. R. Art.
Banning, Capt. S. T., Munster Fus.
Waters, Major W. H. H., R. Art.
Waldron, Major F., R. Artillery.
Hamilton, Capt. W. G., E. Lanc. Regt.
Franklyn, Major W. E., York Regt.
Beatson, Lt.Colonel F. C., Wilts Regt.
Caunter, Captain J. E., Welsh Regt.
Plumer, Major H. C. O., York and Lancaster Regiment.
Kitson, Maj. G. C., King's R. Rifles.
Griffith, Capt. E. H., Leicester Regt.
Gatliff, Major A. F., Royal Marines.
Morrison, Captain C. G., 5 Dr. Gds.
Cockburn, Capt. C. J., Warwick Regt.
Lawson, Bt.Major H.M., R.Engineers.
Renny, Captain A. M., Ind. S. C. *(passed into College with preceding Class)*.
Creagh, Colonel A. G., R. Art. *(do.)*.
Collings, Major W. A., Berks Regt. *(do.)*.
Hammersley, Bt.Major F., Lanc. Fus. *(do.)*.
Craufurd, Major H.J., Gren.Gds. *(do.)*.
Beresford, Major C. E. de la P., Wiltshire Regiment *(do.)*.

Passed, December 1888.

Reeves, Major J., Irish Fusiliers.
Barker, Major J. S. S., Royal Art.
Baldock, Major T. S., Royal Art.
Cooper, Captain F. E., Royal Art.
Kemball, Captain G. V., Royal Art.
Burn-Murdoch, Major J., R. Eng.
O'Leary, Captain W. E., Irish Rifles.
à Court, Captain C., Rifle Brigade.
Paris, Captain A., Royal Marine Art.
Carleton, Maj. G. D., Leicester Regt.
Heath, Bt.Major F. C., R. Engineers
Hegan, Major E., 5 Dragoon Guards.
Smith Dorrien, Major H. L., *DSO*. Derbyshire Regt.

Kennedy, Lt.Colonel C. (from h.p. Suffolk Regiment.)
Munro, Captain L., Hampshire Regt.
Guilding, Captain E. S., Essex Regt.
M'Grigor, Bt.Major C. R. R., King's Royal Rifles.
Watts, Captain C. N., Derby Regt.
Barnardiston, Captain N. W., Middlesex Regiment.
Gordon, Major C. H., The Buffs.
Sewell, Major J. H., Norfolk Regt.
Stawell, Major G. D., Devon Regt.
Burney, Captain H. H., Gordon Highlanders.
Bewicke-Copley, Major R. C. A. B., King's Royal Rifles.
Armitage, Captain J. L., Inniskilling Fusiliers.
Adye, Bt.Lt.Colonel J., R. Artillery.
Henniker-Major, Major *Hon*. A. H. Coldstream Guards.

Passed, December 1889.

Bethell, Major E. H., R. Engineers.
Sinclair, Major H. M., R. Engineers.
Benson, Captain G. E., R. Artillery.
M'Cracken, Bt.Major F. W. N., Berkshire Regiment.
Kerrison, Major E. R. A., R. Art.
Duff, Major B., Indian Staff Corps.
Robb, Capt. F. S., Durham Lt. Inf.
Drake, Capt. H. D., R. Marine Art.
Ellison, Capt. G. F., W. Surrey Regt.
Leverson, Captain G. F., R. Eng.
Belfield, Major H. E., Munster Fus.
Jeffreys, Major H. B., R. Artillery.
Hamilton, Captain A. B., King's Own Scottish Borderers.
Shute, Capt. H. G. D., Coldst. Gds.
White, Major J. G., Middlesex Regt.
Guinness, Major H. W. N., Irish Regt.
Altham, Capt. E. A., Royal Scots.
Goldschmidt, Captain E. S. D., Welsh Regiment.
Lester, Captain C. M., W. York Regt.
Littledale, Major H. C. T., 4 Dr. Gds.
Geoghegan, Capt. T. P., Indian S. C.
Dalrymple, Major *Hon*. N. de C., Scots Guards.
Cavendish, Captain A. E. J., Argyll and Sutherland Highlanders.
Wildman-Lushington, Captain P., King's Own Scottish Borderers.
Compton, Major T. E., Northampton Regt.
Jones, Captain W. D., Wilts Regt.
Kane, Major F. R. P., E. Surrey Regt.
Brook-Hollinshead, Major L., West Kent Regt.
du Boulay, Captain N. W. H., R. Art.
Burn-Murdoch, Major J. F., 1 Drs.
Wilson, Bt.Major R. H. F.W., 10 Hus.

Passed, December 1890.

De Brath, Captain E., Indian S.C.
Pemberton, Capt. E. St. C., R. Eng.
Chance, Capt. H., Royal Artillery.
Inglefield, Major N. B., R. Artillery.
Western, Major W.G.B., W.Kent Regt.
Fairholme, Capt. W. E., R. Artillery.
Semini, Captain V., Leicester Regt.
Wigram, Capt. H. H., Scots Guards.
Granet, Capt. E. J., Royal Artillery.
Cole, Capt. A. W. G. L., Welsh Fus.
Poett, Major J. H., Dorset Regt.
Monro, Capt. C. C., W. Surrey Regt.
Denne, Capt. H. W. D., Gordon High.
Ventris, Colonel F., Essex Regt.
Pedley, Lieut. O. H., Conn. Rangers.
Young, Major J. C., Sussex Regt.
Western, Capt. J. S. E., Indian S.C.
Macdonald, Capt. N. D., Wilts Regt.
Greenfield, Bt.Lt.Colonel R. M., Inniskilling Fusiliers.
Lascelles, Captain W. E., Rifle Brig.
Lawrence, Capt. H. D., East Surrey Regiment.
Broadwood, Capt. R.G., 12 Lancers.
Sitwell, Capt. W. H., Northumberland Fusiliers.
Gawne, Major J. M., Lancaster Regt.
Courtenay, Major E. J., 11 Hussars.
Wortley, Major E. J. M. S., *CMG*. King's Royal Rifles.
*y*C Lysons, Capt. H., Scottish Rifles.

* Passed the Final Examination without having gone through the College; these Officers are here placed in order of Army Rank.

G 2

List of Officers, now serving, who have passed the Staff College.

Passed, December 1891.

Talbot, Major Hon. M. G., R. Eng.
Laffan, Captain H. D., R. Engineers.
Davies, Lieut. F. J., Grenadier Gds.
Bunbury, Captain W. E., Indian S.C.
Allen, Major D. M., West India Regt.
Crawford. Captain A., R. Artillery.
Wintour, Bt. Major F., W. Kent Regt.
Walter, Capt. W. F., Lancashire Fus.
Stuart, Captain A. R., R. Artillery.
Hawkins, Major J. W., R. Artillery.
Vyvyan, Captain C. B., E. Kent Regt.
Gleichen, Capt. A.E.W. Count, Gr. Gds.
Woodward. Capt. E. M., Leicstr. Regt.
Blood, Captain W. P., Irish Fusiliers.
Lindley, Captain J. E., 1 Dragoons.
Hudson, Captain A. T. P., Manchester Regiment.
Ewart, Capt. J. S., Cameron Highldrs.
Aston, Captain G. G., R. Mar. Art.
Gamble, Capt. R. N., Lincoln Regt.
Walker, Major M. C. B. F., King's Royal Rifles.
Hamilton, Capt. B. M., E. York Regt.
Cowans, Captain J. S., Rifle Brigade.
Richardson, Capt.A. J., E. York Regt.
Pinney, Captain R. J., R. Fusiliers.
Peters, Major C. W., 4 Hussars.
Hardinge, Major Hon.A. S., Scots Fus.
Johnson, Major Sir H. A. W., Bart., York Light Infantry.
Younghusband, Capt. G. J., Ind.S.C.

Passed, December 1892.

Rycroft, Capt. W. H., 7 Dragoon Gds.
Wathen, Captain E. O., 5 Lancers.
Coknyne Frith, Capt. R.C., 15 Hussars.
Cowan, Major H. V., R. Artillery.
Dawkins, Major H. S., R. Artillery.
Baker, Capt. G. D., Royal Artillery.
Churchill, Capt. A. B. N., Royal Art.
Stanton, Captain H. E., DSO. R. Art.
Macbean, Capt. W. A., Royal Art.
Hickson, Major S. A. E., DSO.R.Eng.
Heath, Capt. G.M., Royal Engineers.
Surtees, Major H., Coldstream Gds.
Smith, Captain G. R. F., Coldstream Guards.
Pilcher, Captain T. D., Northumberland Fusiliers.

Walter, Captain J. M., Devon Regt.
Graham, Maj. E.R.C., Cheshire Regt.
Lomax, Major S. H., Scottish Rifles.
James, Capt.B.R., East Surrey Regt.
Dunne, Captain E. M., Border Regt.
Bonus, Captain W. J., Dorset Regt.
Shekleton, Capt. H. P., S.Lanc.Regt.
Gosset, Captain E. A. G., Derby Regt.
Fitton, Capt. H. G., Berkshire Regt.
Morland, Captain T. L. N., King's Royal Rifle Corps.
Hughes, Captain E. H., York and Lancaster Regiment.
Carleton, Major F.R.C., Durham L.I.
Delmé-Radcliffe, Captain C., Connaught Rangers.
Foster, Lieut. A., Argyll and Sutherland Highlanders.
Hawes, Major B. R., Munster Fus.
Watkis, Capt. H. B. B., Indian S.C.
Selwyn, Captain C. H., Indian S. C.

Passed, December 1893.

Shadwell, Capt. L. J., Suffolk Regt.
Dawkins, Major J. W. G., Royal Art.
Crampton, Capt. P. J. R., Royal Art.
Hamilton-Gordon, Capt. A., R. Art.
Cadell, Capt. J. F., Royal Artillery.
Haldane, Capt J.A.L., Gordon Hldrs
Rose, Capt. J. M., R. Marine Art.
Clauson, Captain J. E., Royal Eng.
Massy, Major P. H. H., 6 Drag. Gds.
White, Capt. Hon. R., Welsh Fus.
Bowes, Capt. W. H., Scots Fusiliers.
White, Capt. R. W. P., Welsh Regt.
Edwards, Lieut. F. M., Indian S. C.
Tweddell, Lieut. F., Indian Staff C.
Wilson, Capt. H. H., Rifle Brigade.
Hamilton, Capt.H.I.W., W.Surrey Rg.
Rawlinson, Captain H. S., Coldstream Guards.
Churchill, Major A. G., 12 Lancers.
Dyas, Capt. J.R., Warwickshire Regt.
Holland, Captain W. T., North Staffordshire Regiment.
Ley, Capt.W.G., N.Staffordshire Regt.
Watson, Capt. W. A., Indian Staff C.
Donne, Capt. H. R. B., Norfolk Regt.
Prichard, Capt. H. C., Northampton R.
Banks, Capt. W. S., Dorsetshire Regt.

Marrable, Capt. A. G., York Lt. Inf.
Montagu, Capt. E., Suffolk Regt.
Gordon, Capt. F., Gordon Highlanders.
Gaisford, Captain R. B., Scots Fus.
Snow, Capt. T. D'O., Somerset Lt.Inf.
Bayly, Major A. W. L., DSO., Indian Staff Corps.

Passed, December 1894.

Kenny, Captain H. T., Indian S. C.
Doran, Captain W. R. B., Irish Regt.
Montgomery, Capt. R. A. K., R. Art.
Loch, Captain H. F., Indian S. C.
Keir, Major J. L., Royal Artillery.
Norie, Captain E. W. M., Middlesex Regiment.
Trench, Major F. J. A., Royal Art.
Shute, Lieut. C. D., Welsh Regiment.
Rowley, Capt. R. A. D., Irish Rifles.
White, Major W. L., Royal Artillery.
Bevington, Lieut. S. N., West Surrey Regiment.
Napier, Capt. G. S. F., Oxford Lt. Inf.
Farquharson, Major C. H., 3 Dr. Gds.
Cuthbertson, Captain N. W., Royal Highlanders.
Dudgeon, Captain F. A., South Lancashire Regiment.
Heard, Capt. E. S., Northumb. Fus.
Nicholson, Lieut. C. L., York Regt.
Gosset, Captain E. F., E. York Regt.
Carleton, Captain L. R., Essex Regt.
Brander, Captain H. R., Indian S. C.
Copland, Captain C. S., Northampton Regiment.
Conway-Gordon, Captain L., Royal Marine Artillery.
Jenner, Capt. W. K. W., 9 Lancers.
Kiggell, Capt. L. E., Warwick Regt.
Fortescue, Capt. Hon.O.G., Rif. Brig.
Warner, Captain R. H. L., Army Service Corps.
Byng, Captain Hon. J. H. G., 10 Hus.
Hume, Capt. C. V., Royal Artillery.
Wood, Captain H. St. L. DSO., East Yorkshire Regiment.
Aldworth, Major W., DSO., Bedford Regiment.
Mitford, Capt. B. R., E. Surrey Regt.
Capper, Major W. B., Shrop. Lt. Inf.

Officers under Section V., Paragraph 74, of the Queen's Regulations Qualified for Staff Employment in consequence of Service on the Staff in the Field, without Passing the Staff College.

MAJOR GENERALS.

Grenfell, Sir F. W., GCMG. KCB.
Butler, Sir W. F., KCB.

COLONELS.

Alleyne, J., CB.
Colvile, H. E., CB., Grenadier Guards.
Morton, G. de C., CB. h.p. Munster Fusiliers.
Lane, R. B.
Yeatman-Biggs, A. G., CB.
Cockburn, J. G.
Stewart, R. McG., CB.
Kitchener, Sir H. H., KCMG. CB., Royal Engineers.
Wood, E., CB.
Kelly, W. F., CB.
Wynne, A. S. CB.
Turner, A. E., CB.
Crofton, M. S., DSO.
Slade, F. G., CB., Royal Artillery.
Brabazon, J. P., CB., 4 Hussars.
Slade, J. R., CB., h.p. Royal Artillery.
Nicholson, W. G., CB.
DC Beresford, Lord W. L. de la P., KCIE. h.p.
Murray, R. H., Seaforth Highlanders.
Rundle, H. M. L., DSO. Royal Artillery.
McKean, A. C., CMG. 6 Dragoons.
Chalmer, R., h.p.
Money, G. L. C., DSO., Cameron Highlanders.

LIEUTENANT COLONELS

Hemming, F. W., 5 Dragoon Guards.
Clark, W., Oxford Light Infantry.
Clements, R. A. P., DSO. South Wales Borderers.
Cates, H. T. S., Royal Artillery.
Sutton, Hon. C.
Pearson, A. J., Royal Artillery.

Jenkins, V., West Riding Regiment.
Grant, H. G., Seaforth Highlanders.
Hilliard, W. E.
Childers, E. S. E., Royal Engineers.
Cochrane, W. F. D.
Quirk, J. O., DSO., Welsh Regiment.
Mason, A. H., DSO., Royal Engineers.
Spratt, F. T. N., Royal Engineers.

MAJORS.

Douglas, C. W. H., Gordon Highlanders.
Smith-Rewse, H. W., Royal Engineers.
Chapman, D. P., Cheshire Regiment.
Kekewich, R. G., Inniskilling Fusiliers.
Sclater, H. C., Royal Artillery.
Airlie, D. S. W., Earl of, 10 Hussars.
p.s.c. Wortley, E. J. M. S., CMG., King's Royal Rifles.
Cave, C. D., Suffolk Regiment.
Crutchley, C., Scots Guards.
Saunders, M. W., Royal Artillery.
Wingate, F. R., DSO., Royal Artillery.
Milne, R. L., DSO., Leicester Regiment.
p.s.c. Hon. N. de C. Dalrymple, Scots Guards.
Owen, E. R., DSO., Lancashire Fusiliers.
p.s.c. Hickson, S. A. E., DSO., Royal Engineers.
FitzGerald, H. S., Durham Light Infantry.
Triscott, C. P., DSO., Royal Artillery.
Douglas, C. C., Scottish Rifles.
Carter, F. C., Berkshire Regiment.

CAPTAINS.

Holme, B. F., East Kent Regiment.
Pink, F. J., DSO., West Surrey Regiment.
Hickman, T. E., DSO., Worcester Regiment.
Ternan, T. P. B., DSO., Manchester Regiment.

Her Majesty's Body Guard of

Honourable Corps of Gentlemen-at-Arms,
The Body Guard of the Sovereign on all Public and State occasions.
(ESTABLISHED IN THE YEAR 1509.)

Captain.................. Edwyn Francis, *Earl of* Chesterfield, 13 March 94.
Lieutenant .... Henry Hugh Oldham,[1] Colonel retired pay Cameron Highlanders, 25 June 91.
Standard Bearer...... Philip Limborch Tillbrook,[2] late Major Unatt., 18 Dec. 86.

GENTLEMEN-AT-ARMS.

Stapleton Charles Cotton	16 Oct. 49	Arthur Allen Owen,[38] Colonel retired pay 88th Connaught Rangers	3 Mar. 85
Fra. C. Wemyss, Colonel *late 3 Bn. West Riding Regt.* (6 *West York Militia*)	15 Nov. 60	Herbert Alex. St. John Mildmay,[39] Lt.Colonel late Rifle Brigade	16 Oct. 85
Stanhope Leonard Douglas Willan,[3] late Captain 2 F.	8 Oct. 63	Charles Clitherow Gore,[40] Colonel retired pay Irish Rifles	27 Jan. 87
Paget John Bourke,[6] late Captain 11 F.........	25 Apr. 64	John Edward Varty Rogers,[42] Lt.Colonel retired pay 102 F.	27 Apr. 87
Henry Jobling Wallack,[7] late Captain 77 F. ...	17 Dec. 64	Charles Wheler Hume,[44] Bt. Major late Rifle Brigade; *Hon. Col. late 4 Bn. W. Kent Regt.*	9 Jan. 88
John Henry Lowndes,[8] late Lt.Colonel 6 F. ...	17 Dec. 64	Christopher Middlemass Davidson,[45] Lt.Col. retired pay Munster Fusiliers	5 May 89
John Walrond Clarke,[9] late Captain 10 Hus. ...	8 Mar. 65	George Kellie M'Callum,[46] Lt.Colonel retired pay Gordon Highlanders	21 May 89
Wm. Cuninghame Cuninghame,[12] late Captain 70 F.	18 Aug. 67	Walter Frederick Kelsey,[47] Colonel retired pay Seaforth Highlanders	1 Jan. 90
John Chas. D. Morrison,[13] late Col. R. Marines	30 Mar. 69	Charles Wyndham Murray,[48] Colonel retired pay Gloucester Regiment; *M.P. for Bath* ...	1 Jan. 91
Jas. Ainslie Stewart,[14] late Colonel R. Marines	4 June 69	Augustus James Hill,[49] Lt.Colonel retired pay Royal Marine Artillery	17 July 91
John Glas Sandeman,[15] late Captain 1 Drs....	18 June 69	Henry Herbert Edwards,[50] Major retired pay Welsh Fusiliers	18 Mar. 92
Cha. Edwyn Wyatt,[17] late Bt.Major 8 Hussars	20 July 69	Henry Arthur Fletcher,[51] Lt.Colonel late Bengal Cavalry	16 May 92
Walter Clopton Wingfield,[19] late Major *Montgomery Yeomanry Cavalry*..................	22 Apr. 70	Walter Henry Holbech,[52] Lt.Colonel retired pay King's Royal Rifles	1 July 93
V. C. John Grant Malcolmson,[20] late Lieut. 3 Bombay Cavalry	25 May 70	Edward Tufnell,[53] Lt.Colonel retired pay Irish Regiment	21 Mar. 94
John Hampden Waller,[21] late Lieut. 28 F.	24 Aug. 70	Edward George Keppel,[57] Lt.Colonel retired pay Manchester Regiment	17 July 94
Wm. Chester Master, C.B.[22] late Colonel 28 F.	31 Oct. 70		
Edward Andrew Nool,[24] late Captain 31 Foot	19 Mar. 75		
Reynold Alleyne Clement,[27] late Capt. 68 Foot, and late *Lt. Colonel 2 Bucks Rifle Volunteers*...	1 Apr. 76		
Charles Cooch,[28] Colonel retired pay	14 Mar. 77		
Edward Brown,[29] Colonel r.f.p. 101 F.........	1 July 77		
Geo. Henry Pocklington,[30] late Lt.Col. 18 F...	1 July 77		
Henry Brackenbury,[31] late Major Depot Batt.	8 Nov. 77		
Jas. Hornby Buller,[33] late Col. Military Train	22 Mar. 81		
Lord Henry Edward Brudenell Somerset,[36] late Lieut. Royal Horse Guards, *Hon. Major Gloucestershire Yeomanry Cavalry*	19 Feb. 84		

Clerk of the Cheque and Adjutant.—Aubone George Fife,[43] Colonel late 6 Dragoon Guards, 4 July 91.
Sub Officer.—Lt.Colonel J. G. Sandeman,[15] late Captain 1 Dragoons, 21 Feb. 74.
Scarlet—Facings Blue Velvet. | *Agents*, Messrs. Cox and Co.

Gentlemen-at-Arms on Half Pay.

Bevil Granville,[54] late Bt.Major 23 Foot	9 Sept. 63	William Mathew Dunbar,[56] Colonel retired pay 24 Foot	16 June 82
Francis Pavy,[55] late Captain 74 Foot	20 July, 69		

[1] Colonel H. H. Oldham served in the China Expeditionary Force of 1860, and was present in the actions of Sinho and Tangku, assault and capture of the North Taku Fort, and surrender of Pekin (Medal with two Clasps). Served in the Cossyah and Jynteah Hill campaign in 1863.

[2] Major P. L. Tillbrook served with the 50th Regiment in the Crimea from the 22nd August 1855, including the siege and fall of Sebastopol (Medal with Clasp, and Turkish Medal).

[5] Captain Willan landed in the Crimea on 30th June 1855 with the 13th Light Infantry, and was present at the battle of the Tchernaya, siege and fall of Sebastopol (Medal with Clasp, and Turkish Medal).

[6] Captain Bourke served with the Cape Mounted Rifles in the Kaffir war of 1850-51 (Medal); and in 1852-53 in the Orange River Territory, where he commanded several successful patrols.

[7] Captain Wallack served with the 9th Regt. throughout the Sutlej campaign of 1845-46 and was present at the battles of Moodkee, Ferozeshah, and Sobraon (Medal and two Clasps).

[8] Lt.Colonel Lowndes served with the 47th Regt. throughout the Eastern campaign of 1854-55, including the battles of Alma and Inkerman, capture of Balaklava, siege and fall of Sebastopol, sortie of 26th Oct., and storming the Quarries on 7th June—severely wounded (Medal with three Clasps, Brevets of Major and Lt.Colonel, Knight of the Legion of Honor, Sardinian and Turkish Medals, and 5th Class of the Medjidie).

[9] Captain Clarke served with the 10th Hussars in the Crimean campaign from 17th April 1855, including the siege and fall of Sebastopol, capture of Tchorgaum, battle of the Tchernaya where he commanded a squadron in support of a troop of Horse Artillery, and an affair with the Cossacks near Kertch (Medal with Clasp, and Turkish Medal).

[12] Captain Cuninghame served with the 79th Highlanders in the Crimean campaign of 1854 up to 26th Nov., and also from Jan. to 9th Feb. 1855, including the battles of Alma and Balaklava, and siege of Sebastopol (Medal with three Clasps, and Turkish Medal).

[13] Colonel Morrison was present when the batteries of Obligado in the River Parana were attacked and carried 20th Nov. 1845. Served on the China expedition of 1857-59, including the blockade of the Canton river, the landing before, storm and capture of the city. Served as Provost Marshal to the expedition, and afterwards as D.A.A. General to the Army in garrison at Canton (Brevet of Major). Served the campaign in the north of China in 1860, including the action of Sinho, taking of Tongoo, storm and capture of the North Takoo fort (mentioned in despatches), and subsequent operations (Medal with three Clasps, and Brevet of Lt.Colonel).

[14] Colonel Stewart served throughout the campaign in Syria in 1840,—at the Camp at D'Jouni as Acting Engineer the storm and capture of Sidon, surrender of Beyrout, bombardment and capture of St. Jean d'Acre (War Medal with Clasp, and Turkish Medal). Served also on the West Coast of Africa from 1841 to 1844; commanded a detachment of Marines at the destruction of several Barracoons in 1842 and liberated 1,200 slaves at Kabenda, Ambriz, Black Point, Loango, Punta da Linha, 25 miles up the river Congo; and a second time at Kabenda, three miles inland, when he was attacked by a much superior force, and after liberating the slaves and destroying the barracoons effected a safe retreat to the beach with three men mortally wounded, closely pressed by a large force of armed Africans (mentioned in despatches). Served with the battalion of Royal Marines sent to Japan from 1864 to 1866, and was present at the bombardment of the batteries at the Straits of Simonosaki, the entrance of the inland sea of Japan, on the 5th and 6th Sept. 1864.

[15] Lt.Colonel Sandeman served with the 1st Royal Dragoons in the Crimean campaign from the 6th Oct. 1854 and was present at the battles of Balaklava, Inkerman, and Tchernaya, siege and fall of Sebastopol (Medal with three Clasps, and Turkish Medal).

[17] Major Wyatt served with the 14th Light Dragoons in the Persian expedition of 1857 (Medal with Clasp). Also in the Central India Field Force under Sir Hugh Rose in 1858 and was present at the siege and capture of Rahutghur, action of Barodia, relief of Saugor, capture of Gurrakota, forcing the Muddunpore Pass, siege and capture of Jhansi (Medal with Clasp).

[19] Major Wingfield served with the 1st Dragoon Guards throughout the campaign of 1860 in China, and was present at the fall of the Taku Forts, and engaged in the action of Sinho, also those of the 18th and 21st September. Commanded the Cavalry force sent to Tungchon with Mr. Wade to demand the giving up of the prisoners on the 20th September, and present at the surrender of Pekin (Medal with two Clasps).

[20] Lieutenant Malcolmson served in the 3rd Bombay Light Cavalry with the Persian Expeditionary Force in 1856-57, including the assault and capture of Reshire, surrender of Bushire, expedition to Borazjoon, and action of Kooshab (Victoria Cross, and Medal with Clasp); was awarded the V.C. under the following circumstances :—"On the occasion of an attack on the enemy on the 8th February 1857, led by Lieutenant Colonel Forbes, C.B., Lieutenant Moore, the Adjutant of the regiment, was, perhaps, the first of all by a horse's length. His horse leaped into the square, and instantly fell dead, crushing down his rider, and breaking his sword as he fell amid the broken ranks of the enemy. Lieutenant Moore speedily extricated himself, and attempted with his broken sword to force his way through the press; but he would assuredly have lost his life had not the gallant young Lieutenant Malcolmson, observing his peril, fought his way to his dismounted comrade through a crowd of enemies to his rescue, and, giving him his stirrup, safely carried him through everything out of the throng. The thoughtfulness for others, cool determination, devoted courage and ready activity shown in extreme danger by this young Officer, Lieutenant Malcolmson, appear to have been most admirable, and to be worthy of the highest honour." Served also with the Central India Field Force, including the siege of Ratghur and fall of Calpee (Medal with Clasp).

[21] Lieut. Waller served in the Oude campaign in 1858, including the capture of the fort of Kaili (Medal).

[22] Colonel Master commanded the 5th Fusiliers at the relief of Lucknow in Nov. 1857, and served with it in Outram's Force at the Alum Bagh in all the operations of the succeeding months, and commanded the Regt. at the capture of Lucknow, as also throughout the Oude campaign of 1858-59, including the action of Dounderkeira and Buxarghat, and capture of the Fort of Oomorea (several times mentioned in despatches, Brevet of Lt. Colonel, C.B., Medal with two Clasps, and a year's service).

[24] Captain Noel served with the 31st Regiment throughout the Sutlej Campaign of 1845-46, and was present at the battles of Moodkee, Ferozeshah, Buddiwal, Aliwal, and Sobraon (Medal and three Clasps).

[27] Lt.Colonel Clement served in the New Zealand war in 1864-66 (Medal).

[28] Colonel Cooch served with the 62nd Regiment in the Crimea from 12th Nov. 1854, including the siege and fall of Sebastopol and the sorties of the 5th 9th and 10th May, defence of the Quarries 7th June, assaults of the Redan on the 18th June (in command of the Wool-bag party of his regiment) and 8th September (mentioned in despatches, Brevet of Major, Medal with Clasp, Knight of the Legion of Honor, 5th Class of the Medjidie, Sardinian and Turkish Medals). Appointed Town Major in Sebastopol immediately after its fall for his services during the siege and final assault.

[29] Colonel E. Brown served throughout the Sutlej campaign of 1845-46, including the battles of Ferozeshah and Sobraon (Medal and Clasp). Burmese war of 1852-53, including the recapture of Pegu on 21st Nov., relief of its garrison on 14th Dec., and operations in the vicinity (Medal with Clasp for Pegu). Suppression of the Indian Mutiny, including the battle of Budleekeserai, siege of Delhi and assault of the Eedgate, wounded in five places, in one dangerously (Brevet of Major, Medal with Clasp). Served in the Indian N.W. Frontier war of 1863, and was present at the attack and capture of the Conical Hill and Umbeyla (Clasp).

[30] Lt.Colonel G. H. Pocklington served with the 18th Royal Irish in the Burmese campaign of 1852-53 (Medal with Clasp for Pegu). Served also in the Crimea from 1st June 1855, including the siege and fall of Sebastopol, and attack of the 18th June (Medal with Clasp, and Turkish Medal).

[31] Major Brackenbury served with the 61st Regiment in the Punjaub campaign of 1848-49, and was present at the battle of Goojerat, and with the Field Force in pursuit of the enemy to the Khyber Pass in February and March 1849 (Medal with Clasp). Present with the expedition to the Euzofzie Country and at the attack and capture of insurgent villages on the 11th and 14th Dec. 1849 (Medal with Clasp). Served with the rank of Captain with the Turkish Contingent and performed duty as an Engineer Officer in the Crimea in 1855-56 (Turkish Medal).

[33] Colonel Buller served with the 57th Regiment in the Eastern campaign of 1854, and was very severely wounded in the trenches before Sebastopol, and again whilst being carried back to the camp (Medal with Clasp and Turkish Medal).

[36] Lord Henry Somerset served with the Royal Horse Guards in the Egyptian war of 1882, and was present in the engagements at El Magfar and Mahsama, in the two actions at Kassasin, and at the battle of Tel-el-Kebir (Medal with Clasp, and Khedive's Star).

[38] Colonel A. A. Owen served in the Kafir war in 1877-78, first as Assistant Adjutant General to Colonial Forces and afterwards as Assistant Adjutant General to the Transkei Field Force, and commanded the attacking column in the action at Newmaka and subsequent engagements in the Chicaba and Kei River Valley (mentioned in despatches, and received the thanks of Colonel Glyn, Commanding Transkei Field Force, for having, with assistance, saved the life of a private soldier, who was very severely wounded, by carrying him to a place of shelter under a very heavy fire); also served in the Zulu war in 1879 in command of a draft battalion at Pinetown (Brevet of Lt.Colonel, Medal with Clasp).

[39] Lt.Colonel H. A. St. John Mildmay served with the Rifle Brigade in the Crimean campaign from the 6th Sept. 1885, including the siege and fall of Sebastopol (Medal with Clasp, and Turkish Medal). Served in the campaign on the North-West Frontier of India in 1864 (Medal).

[40] Colonel C. C. Gore was present with the 83rd Regiment at the siege and capture of Kotah on the 30th March, 1858, affair at Sanganeer, defeat of the Gwalior rebels at Kotaria, surprise of and attack on the rebels at Seckur (Medal with Clasp). Served with the Natal Field Force in the Boer war of 1881.

[42] Lt.Colonel J. E. V. Rogers served the campaign in Oude from June to Dec. 1858, including the occupation of Fyzabad, capture of Sultanpore, passage of the Goomtee, action of Shahpore, capture of the Fort of Kaili, and other minor affairs (Medal).

[43] Colonel A. G. Fife served with the Carabiniers in the Afghan war in 1879-80 with the Khyber Division of the Cabul Field Force, and took part in the expeditions against Asmatulla Khan in the Lughman Valley and against the Wuzeeree Khugianis; was also present at the attack and destruction of the villages of Nargozi, Arab Kheyl, and Jokan, and in the engagement at Nargashai (Medal). Served with the Burmese Expedition in 1886-87 (Medal with Clasp). Granted a step of honorary rank for service in the Field.

[44] Colonel C. W. Hume served with the 3rd Battalion Rifle Brigade during the Indian Mutiny campaign of 1857-58, including the siege and capture of Lucknow, battle of Nawabgungo, and capture of Fort Birwah. Was Staff Officer to a Field Force under Brigadier General Wheeler in the final campaign in Bundlecund in 1859 (Medal with Clasp). Promoted to an unattached Company for service in the Field.

[45] Lt. Colonel C. M. Davidson served in the Abyssinian campaign as Adjutant of the 4th Regiment, and was present at the action of Arogee and capture of Magdala (Medal).

[46] Lt.Colonel G. K. M'Callum served with the 92nd Highlanders in the Afghan war in 1879-80, and was present in the affair at Karatiga, in the engagement at Charasiab on 6th October 1879, and in the various operations around Cabul in December 1879 (mentioned in despatches, Medal with two Clasps). Served in the Boer war in 1881.

[47] Colonel W. F. Kelsey served with the 72nd Highlanders from the commencement of the Afghan war in 1878 till June 1879 with the Koorum Field Force, including the Khost Expedition, and was present in the engagement at Mattoon (Medal). Served with the 1st Battalion Seaforth Highlanders in the Egyptian war of 1882, and was present in the engagement at Chalouf on the 20th August in command of four companies of his Battalion, and at the battle of Tel-el-Kebir (mentioned in despatches, Brevet of Lt.Colonel, Medal with Clasp, 4th Class of the Osmanieh, and Khedive's Star).

[48] Colonel C. W. Murray served in the Zulu war of 1879, first as Aide de Camp to Major General Crealock, commanding the 1st Division, and afterwards as Deputy Assistant Quarter Master General in the Intelligence Branch of the Division; was finally attached in this capacity to Clarke's Column, reconnoitred the country beyond Ulundi as far as the Ngome region, and made a reconnaissance of the route to be traversed by the column from Ulundi to the Middle Drift of the Tugela River (mentioned in despatches, Brevet of Major, Medal with Clasp). Served in the Afghan war in 1880 with the 72nd Highlanders, and was Orderly Officer to Brigadier General Baker in the expedition to the Logar Valley (Medal). Served in the Marri Expedition in 1881 under Brigadier General Tanner. Served in the Egyptian war of 1882 as Deputy Assistant Adjutant and Quartermaster General on the Base and Lines of Communication, and was present at the battle of Tel-el-Kebir (mentioned in despatches, Brevet of

Lt.Colonel, Medal with Clasp, 4th Class of the Osmanieh, and Khedive's Star). Served in the Bechuanaland Expedition under Sir Charles Warren in 1885 as Deputy Assistant Adjutant and Quartermaster General.

49 Lt.Colonel A. J. Hill served in the Ashanti war of 1873-74 (Medal).

50 Major H. H. Edwards served in the Boer war of 1881 in Barrow's Mounted Infantry. Served with the Mounted Infantry in the Egyptian War of 1882, and was present at the action at Kassasin on the 28th August—wounded (mentioned in despatches, Medal, and Khedive's Star).

51 Lt.Colonel Fletcher served in the campaign on the North West Frontier of India in 1863-64, and was present in the engagement with the Mohmunds near Shubkudder (Medal with Clasp). Served in the Egyptian war in 1882 (Medal and Khedive's Star).

52 Lt.Colonel W. H. Holbech served on the Red River Expedition of 1870.. Served in the Egyptian war of 1832 and was present in the engagement at Tel-el-Mahuta, in the action at Kassasin (9th September), and at the battle of Tel-el-Kebir as Brigade Major to the 2nd Infantry Brigade (mentioned in despatches, Brevet of Major, Medal with Clasp, 4th Class of the Medjidie, and Khedive's Star).

53 Lt.Colonel E. Tufnell served in the Nile Expedition in 1884-85 with the 1st Battalion of the Royal Irish Regiment (Medal with Clasp, and Khedive's Star).

54 Major Granville served with the 23rd Fusiliers in the Eastern campaign of 1854 including the battles of Alma and Inkerman, and siege of Sebastopol (Medal with three Clasps, and Turkish Medal). Joined Lord Clyde's Army before Lucknow on 14 Nov. 1857, and was at the relief of the garrisons, also at the defeat of the Gwalior Contingent at Cawnpore on 6th December, and at the fall of Lucknow in Mar. 1858 (Brevet of Major, Medal with two Clasps).

55 Captain Pavy served in the Indian Mutiny campaign in 1858 with the 74th Highlanders, and was present at the storm and capture of Capaul (Medal).

56 Colonel W. M. Dunbar served with the 34th Regiment in the Crimea from the 12th July 1855, including the siege and fall of Sebastopol, and assault of the Redan on the 8th Sept. (Medal with Clasp and Turkish Medal). Also in the Indian campaign in 1857-59, including the actions at Cawnpore on 26th, 27th and 28th Nov. 1857, siege and capture of Lucknow, relief of Azimghur, defeat of the rebels at Bootwul, and affair at Bhowanie (Medal with Clasp). Served with the 2nd Battalion 24th Regiment in the Kafir war of 1878. Commanded the 1st Battalion 24th Regiment in the second advance into Zululand in the war of 1879, and was present in the engagement at Ulundi (Brevet of Lt.Colonel, Medal with Clasp).

57 Lt.Colonel E. G. Keppel served with the 2nd Battalion Highland Light Infantry in the Egyptian war of 1882, and was present at the battle of Tel-el-Kebir (Medal with Clasp, and Khedive's Star).

Yeomen of the Guard.

Her Majesty's Body Guard.
(INSTITUTED BY HENRY VII. IN THE YEAR 1495.)

Captain .... William, *Lord* Kensington, 25 Aug. 92.
Lieutenant .... Lt.Colonel Horatio Page Vance,[1] late of 38 Foot, 9 Dec. 93.
Ensign .... Lt.Colonel Richard George Ellison,[2] late of 49 Foot, *Hon. Col.* 2 *Vol. Bn. Lincoln Regt.* 4 Oct. 92.

EXONS.
Lt.Colonel Charles Doyle Patterson,[3] late of 10 Foot, 13 Feb. 62.
Major Edmund Halbert Elliot,[4] ret. pay Royal Artillery, 7 May 92.
Bt.Major *Hon.* Francis Lionel Lydston Colborne,[5] ret. pay Irish Rifles, 16 Nov. 92.
Colonel Reginald Hennell,[6] *DSO?* late Bombay Infantry, 24 Feb. 94.
Clerk of the Cheque and Adjutant.—

140 Yeomen.
*Agents.—*Messrs. Cox and Co.

1 Lt.Colonel Vance served with the 38th Regiment in the Crimea from January to the 15th April 1855, including the siege of Sebastopol (Medal with Clasp, and Turkish Medal). Also in the Indian campaign from Nov. 1857, and was present at the storm and capture of Meeangunge, siege and capture of Lucknow, affairs of Barree and Nuggur (mentioned in despatches, Brevet of Major, Medal with Clasp).

2 Colonel Ellison served the Eastern campaign of 1854-55 in the 47th Regt., including the battles of Alma and Inkerman, capture of Balaklava, siege of Sebastopol, and sortie on 26th Oct. (Medal with three Clasps, Sardinian and Turkish Medals, and 5th Class of the Medjidie).

3 Lt.Colonel Patterson served with the 10th Regt. in the Sutlej campaign of 1845-46, including the battle of Sobraon (Medal). Also the Punjaub campaign of 1848-49, including the whole of the siege operations before Mooltan, action of Soorjkhoond, carrying the heights before Mooltan, capture of the Dowlut Gate in command of the storming party, surrender of the fortress, and battle of Goojerat (Medal with two Clasps). Commanded three companies of the 10th Regt. in Shahabad with Major Eyre's field force at Dilawur, and capture of Jugdespore, and was mentioned in despatches for his gallantry (Brevet of Major, and Medal).

4 Major E. H. Elliot served in the Zulu war in 1879, and was present in the engagement at Ulundi (Medal with Clasp).

5 Major the Hon. F. L. L. Colborne served in the Afghan War in 1879-80, and took part in the march to Candahar with the force under Major-General Phayre (Medal). Served with the Natal Field Force in the Boer war of 1881. Was employed with the Boats during the Nile Expedition in 1884-85, and was present at the action of Kirbekan (mentioned in despatches, Brevet of Major, Medal with two Clasps, and Khedive's Star). Served with the Soudan Frontier Field Force in a 885-86 as Senior Officer in charge of Water Transport.

6 Colonel R. Hennell served in the Abyssinian war in 1867-68 (Medal). Served in the Afghan war in 1879-80 (Medal). Served with the Burmese Expedition in 1885-87 (mentioned in despatches, DSO., and Medal with Clasp).

1st Life Guards. [Regent's Park.

The Royal Arms. "DETTINGEN" "PENINSULA" "WATERLOO" "EGYPT, 1882" "TEL-EL-KEBIR."

Colonel-in-Chief.—Field Marshal *His Royal Highness* Albert Edward, *Prince of* Wales and *Duke of* Cornwall *KG. KT. KP. GCB. GCSI. GCMG. GCIE.* 29 May 80.

Colonel.—*H.S.H. Prince Wm. Aug. Edward of Saxe-Weimar*,[1] *KP. GCB. Ens.* 1 June 41; *Ens. & Lt.* P8 June 41; *Lt & Capt.* P19 May 46; *Bt. Major*, 20 June 54; *Bt.Lt.Colonel*, 12 Dec. 54; *Capt. & Lt.Colonel*, P18 May 55; *Colonel*, 5 Oct. 55; *Major General*, 6 Mar. 68; *Lieut. General*, 6 July 77; *General*, 14 Nov. 79; *Colonel 1st Life Guards*, 14 Nov. 88.

Years Ser. — Full Pay 27

Lieutenant Colonel.—*Sir* Simon Macdonald Lockhart,[6] *Bart., Cornet & Sub Lt.* P17 May 68; *Lt.* P17 Aug. 70; *Captain*, 21 July 77; *Major*, 21 July 86; *Bt.Lt.Colonel*, 21 July 92; *Lt.Colonel*, 6 Dec. 93.

Years Ser. Full Pay	Half Pay	MAJORS.	2ND LIEUT.	LIEUT.	CAPTAIN.	BREVET MAJOR.	MAJOR.
20	...	Hon. Arthur William Hill-Trevor (*Brevet Lt.Colonel*, 5 May 94)	......	6 Sept. 75	7 July 80	......	5 Oct. 92
20	...	Charles Napier Miles[9]	......	20 Nov. 75	24 Nov. 82	......	6 Dec. 93
19	...	Thomas Charles Pleydell Calley[10]	......	11 Sept. 76	21 July 86	......	5 May 94
		CAPTAINS.					
16	...	Gordon Carter (*Riding Master* 24 Jan. 80)	......	23 Mar. 81	28 Sept. 87		
16	...	George Lindsay Holford, *CIE. Equerry in Waiting to H.R.H. the Prince of Wales*	31 Jan. 80	1 July 81	1 July 88		
9	...	Hon. Ronald Henry Fulke Greville	......	21 July 86	21 July 92		
9	...	John Richard Geers Cotterell	......	8 Sept. 86	10 Aug. 92		
13	...	Hon. Cecil Edward Bingham	......	9 Sept. 82	26 Oct. 92		
13	...	George Francis Milner	......	27 Jan. 83	11 Jan. 93		
7	...	Henry Arthur Clowes	8 Dec. 88	16 July 90	10 May 93		
5	...	Edwin Berkeley Cook, **Adjutant** 1 Apr. 94	9 July 90	4 July 91	5 May 94		
		LIEUTENANTS.					
5	...	Ernest William Clowes	30 July 90	2 Sept. 91			
5	...	Hugh Crauford Fraser[12]	3 Dec. 90	2 Nov. 92			
4	...	James Albert Edward, *Marquis of* Hamilton	12 Aug. 91	2 Nov. 92			
4	...	Harold Maxwell Walker	5 Dec. 91	25 Jan. 93			
3	...	Harold Maxwell Grenfell	17 Aug. 92	9 Aug. 93			
3	...	Bertram D'Avenant Corbet	28 Dec. 92	22 Nov. 93			
3	...	Hon. Charles Henry Wyndham	28 Dec. 92	31 Jan. 94			
2	...	Charles Shuldham Schreiber	23 Sept. 93	13 Feb. 95			
		SECOND LIEUTENANTS.					
2	...	Simon Joseph, *Lord* Lovat	23 Dec. 93				
1	...	Philip Blencowe Cookson	18 Apr. 94				
1	...	Hon. John Sackville Richard Tufton	27 June 94				

6	...	*Riding Master.*—Douglas Hall, 8 May 89; *Hon. Lieut.*	
9	...	*Quarter Master.*—William Wragg, 6 Nov. 86; *Hon. Lieut.*	
		Surgeon Lt.Colonel.—James Stevenson Forrester,[11] 25 Oct. 94; *Surgeon Captain*, 30 Sept. 74; *Surgeon Major*, 25 Oct. 94; *Surgeon Lt.Colonel*, 25 Oct. 94.	
		Surgeon Captain.—Horatio R. O. Cross,[13] 26 Sept. 94; *Surgeon Captain*, 4 Aug. 78.	
19	...	*Veterinary Captain.*—John D. Edwards,[14] 11 Sept. 89; *Vet. Captain* 4 Aug. 76; *1st Class*, 6 Aug. 86.	

Scarlet—*Facings* Blue.—*Agents*, Messrs. Cox and Co.
Returned from France, January 1816.

---

[1] Prince Edward of Saxe-Weimar served the Eastern Campaign of 1854 with the Grenadier Guards, including the battles of Alma, Balaklava, and Inkerman, and siege of Sebastopol (wounded in the leg in the Trenches, 19 Oct., and mentioned in despatches, Aide de Camp to the Queen and Colonel, *CB.*, Medal with four Clasps, Officer of the Legion of Honor, 4th Class of the Medjidie, and Turkish Medal).

[6] Sir Simon Lockhart served with the 1st Life Guards in the Egyptian war of 1882, and was present in the engagements at El Magfar and Mahsama, in the two actions at Kassasin, at the battle of Tel-el-Kebir, and at the capture of Cairo (Medal with Clasp, and Khedive's Star).

[9] Major Miles served with the 1st Life Guards in the Egyptian war of 1882, and was present in the engagements at El Magfar and Mahsama, in the two actions at Kassasin, at the battle of Tel-el-Kebir, and at the capture of Cairo (Medal with Clasp, and Khedive's Star).

[10] Major Calley served with the 1st Life Guards in the Egyptian war of 1882, and was present in the engagements at El Magfar and Mahsama, in the two actions at Kassasin, at the battle of Tel-el-Kebir, and at the capture of Cairo (Medal with Clasp, and Khedive's Star).

[12] Lieut. Fraser.—See Civil Decorations for Gallantry, "Hart's Annual Army List," p. 736.

[13] Surgeon Lt.Colonel Forrester and Surgeon Captain Cross.—For War Services, see Army Medical Staff.

[14] Veterinary Captain Edwards.—For War Services, see Army Veterinary Department.

Hyde Park.] **2nd Life Guards.** 134

The Royal Arms. "DETTINGEN" "PENINSULA" "WATERLOO" "EGYPT, 1882" "TEL-EL-KEBIR."

Colonel-in-Chief.—Field Marshal *His Royal Highness* Albert Edward, *Prince of* Wales and *Duke of* Cornwall, KG. KT. KP. GCB. GCSI. GCMG. GCIE. 29 May 80.

Colonel.—Richard William Penn, *Earl* Howe,¹ CB. *Ens. & Lt.* P14 July 38; *Lt. & Capt.* P5 Apr. 44; *Bt. Major*, 28 May 53; *Capt. & Lt.Colonel*, 20 June 54; *Colonel*, 17 Nov. 57; *Major General*, 6 Mar. 68; *Lt.General*, 1 Oct. 77; *General*, 16 March 80; *Colonel* 17th Foot, 25 June 79; *Colonel* 2nd Life Guards, 5 Jan. 90.

Lieutenant Colonel.—Douglas Mackinnon Baillie Hamilton, *Earl of* Dundonald,⁶ *Cornet*, P6 July 70; *Lt.* 28 Oct. 71; *Capt.* 10 April 78; *Major*, 12 Jan. 85; *Bt.Lt.Colonel*, 15 June 85; *Lt.Colonel*, 12 Jan. 95; *Colonel*, 15 June 89.

Years'Ser. Full Pay	Half Pay	MAJORS.	CORNET, SUB. LIEUT., OR 2ND LIEUT.	LIEUT.	CAPTAIN.	BREVET MAJOR.	MAJOR.
25	...	Audley Dallas Neeld (*Bt.Lt.Colonel*, 12 Jan. 95)	P15 Feb. 71	28 Oct. 71	13 April 81	......	24 Sept. 87
20	...	John Anstruther Smith-Cuninghame¹⁰	......	11 Feb. 76	10 April 83	......	12 Jan. 91
21	...	Charles Fred. St.Clair Anstruther-Thomson	......	13 June 74	12 Jan. 85	......	12 Jan. 95
		CAPTAINS.					
19	...	Hon. William Spencer Bateman-Hanbury¹²	......	29 Nov. 76	21 Jan. 85		
22	...	Houston French,¹³ **Adjutant** 26 Oct. 92	......	12 Nov. 73	24 Sept. 87		
15	...	Mountifort John Courtnay Longfield¹⁶	23 Oct. 30	1 July 81	14 Mar. 88		
13	...	Herbert Scarisbrick Naylor-Leyland	......	2 Aug. 82	12 Jan. 91		
12	...	Michael James Hughes	......	31 Oct. 83	5 July 92		
11	...	Oswald Henry Ames	......	14 May 84	26 Oct. 92		
10	...	Reginald Arthur Haworth Peel	......	6 May 85	19 Nov. 93		
9	...	Thomas, *Earl of* Longford	5 Feb. 87	16 May 88	12 Jan. 95		
		LIEUTENANTS.					
7	..	Algernon-Francis Holford Ferguson	22 Aug. 88	12 Jan. 91			
6	...	Richard Todd Ellison	17 July 89	8 Apr. 91			
5	...	Sydney Thornhill Hankey	28 June 90	13 Apr. 92			
5	...	John Chaytor Brinton	28 Jan. 91	13 Apr. 92			
4	...	Algernon Richard Trotter	10 Feb. 92	5 Apr. 93			
3	...	Hon. William Edwardes	22 June 92	5 Apr. 93			
3	...	Hon. Nevill Windsor Hill-Trevor	28 Dec. 92	19 Nov. 93			
3	...	Francis Simon Low	28 Dec. 92	12 Jan.† 95			
		SECOND LIEUTENANTS.					
2	...	Mervyn Edward George Rhys Wingfield	14 Feb. 94				
1	...	Sir Edward Paulet Stracey, *Bart.*	22 Aug. 94				
1	...	Hon. Osbert Cecil Molyneux	2 Jan. 95				

14	...	*Riding Master.*—Charles Henry Burt, 8 June 81; *Hon. Captain*, 8 June 91.	
9	...	*Quarter Master.*—Thomas George Entwistle, 13 Oct. 86; *Hon. Lieut.*	

Surgeon Major.—Percy Gordon Radstock Young, 13 Oct. 80; *Surgeon*, 3 Feb. 78; *Surgeon Major*, 12 Aug. 90.
Surgeon Captain.—Henry Mitchell,¹⁷ 3 June 91; *Surgeon Captain*, 2 Aug. 84.
Veterinary Captain.—Thomas Flintoff,¹⁸ 10 June 91; *Vet. Capt.* 23 June 75; *1st Class*, 23 June 85.

Scarlet—*Facings* Blue.—*Agents*, Messrs. Cox and Co.

Returned from France, February 1816.

---

¹ Earl Howe served as Aide de Camp to Sir George Cathcart in the Kaffir war in 1852-53 (Medal), for which service he was promoted to the Brevet rank of Major. Served at the siege of Delhi in 1857, as Acting Quarter Master General of the Queen's Troops (Colonel, CB., Medal with Clasp).

⁶ Lord Dundonald served with the Nile Expedition in 1884-85 in command of the 2nd Life Guards detachment of the Camel Corps; carried the despatches to Korti announcing the seizure of the Gakdul wells; commanded the transport and baggage of the Desert Column under Sir Herbert Stewart in the advance to Metammeh; was present at the action of Abu Klea and in the engagement at Gubat; acted as guide to the convoys which left Gubat on the evenings of 23rd January and 1st February, and also to the reinforcements to Abu Klea; carried the despatches from Gubat announcing the fall of Khartoum (mentioned in despatches, Brevet of Lieut.Colonel, Medal with two Clasps, and Khedive's Star).

¹⁰ Major Smith-Cuninghame served with the 2nd Life Guards in the Egyptian war of 1882, and was present in the two actions at Kassasin and at the battle of Tel-el-Kebir (Medal with Clasp, and Khedive's Star).

¹² Captain Hon. W. S. Bateman-Hanbury served with the 2nd Life Guards in the Egyptian war of 1882, and was present in the engagements at El Magfar and Mahsama, in the two actions at Kassasin, and at the battle of Tel-el-Kebir (Medal with Clasp, and Khedive's Star).

¹³ Captain French served with the 2nd Life Guards in the Egyptian war of 1882, and was present in the engagements at El Magfar and Mahsama, in the action at Kassasin (28th August), and at the battle of Tel-el-Kebir (Medal with Clasp, and Khedive's Star).

¹⁶ Captain Longfield served in the Nile Expedition in 1884-85 with the 2nd Life Guards detachment of the Camel Corps (Medal with Clasp, and Khedive's Star).

¹⁷ Surgeon Captain Mitchell.—For War Services, see Army Medical Staff.

¹⁸ Veterinary Captain Flintoff.—For War Services, see Army Veterinary Department.

Royal Horse Guards. [Windsor.

The Royal Arms. "DETTINGEN" "PENINSULA" "WATERLOO" "EGYPT, 1882" "TEL-EL-KEBIR."

Colonel-in-Chief.—Field Marshal *His Royal Highness* Albert Edward, *Prince of* Wales and *Duke of* Cornwall, *KG, KT, KP, GCB, GCSI, GCMG, GCIE.* 29 May 80.

Colonel.—

Years' Ser. Full Pay.	Half Pay.		2ND LIEUT.	LIEUT.	CAPTAIN.	BREV. MAJ.	MAJOR.
21	...	**Lieutenant Colonel.**—John Fielden Brocklehurst,[1] *Lt.* 2 Dec. 74; *Capt.* 18 May 81; *Bt. Major,* 15 June 85; *Major,* 24 Sept. 87; *Bt.Lt.Colonel,* 18 Jan. 91; *Lt.Colonel,* 18 Jan. 95.					
		MAJORS.					
15	...	George, *Lord* Binning,[12] *Bt.Lt.Col.* 18 Jan. 95	11 Sept. 80	11 Apr. 81	14 May 87	......	22 Dec. 94
15	...	Sir John Christopher Willoughby,[13] *Bt. serving under Brit. South Africa Company*	23 Oct. 80	18 May 81	14 May 87	......	18 Jan. 95
12	...	Victor John Fergus Ferguson	......	6 Feb. 84	7 Mar. 88	......	6 Feb. 95
		CAPTAINS.					
11	...	Edward George, *Lord* Skelmersdale	......	21 May 84	21 May 90		
11	...	Henry Thos. Fenwick, *MP. for Houghton le Spring, Durham*	......	11 Mar. 85	15 Apr. 91		
15	...	William Anstruther-Thomson	17 Apr. 80	1 July 81	30 Dec. 93		
10	...	Arthur Vaughan Hanning Vaughan-Lee ...	......	18 July 85	18 Apr. 94		
8	...	Gordon Chesney Wilson	4 May 87	5 Dec. 88	21 Nov. 94		
8	...	Charles Hyde Villiers	23 Nov. 87	1 June 89	22 Dec. 94		
7	...	Wilfred Francis Ricardo	16 May 88	18 Sept. 89	6 Feb. 95		
		LIEUTENANTS.					
6	...	Gerald James FitzGerald	17 July 89	24 Sept. 90			
6	...	*Hon.* George Cecil Beaumont Weld Forester	17 July 89	15 Oct. 90			
6	...	Arthur Jocelyn Charles, *Visct.* Sudley, *Adjutant* 1 Dec. 93	20 Nov. 89	13 Apr. 92			
5	...	William Dixon Mann-Thomson	4 Mar. 91	5 Apr. 93			
3	...	Charles Ernest Rose	23 Apr. 92	5 Apr. 93			
3	...	John George, *Marquis of* Tullibardine	28 Dec. 92	30 Dec. 93			
3	...	*Hon.* Algernon Henry Charles Hanbury-Tracy	28 Dec. 92	18 Apr. 94			
3	...	Edmund Butler Charteris	28 Dec. 92	22 Dec. 94			
2	...	Sir Samuel Edward Scott, *Bart.*	7 Feb. 94	6 Feb. 95			
		SECOND LIEUTENANTS.					
1	...	Henry William, *Visct.* Crichton	5 May 94				
1	...	*Hon.* Reginald Ward	6 Feb. 95				
1	...	*Hon.* Arthur Vesey Meade	13 Feb. 95				
2	...	*Riding Master.*—James Ashley, 20 Dec. 93; *Hon. Lieut.*					
13	...	*Quarter Master.*—Wyndham Drake, 18 Feb. 83; *Hon. Captain,* 18 Feb. 93.					

Surgeon Lt.Colonel.—Heinrich Freidrich Lawaetz Melladew,[16] *MD.* 4 Sept. 80.
Surgeon Captain.—Joseph Fayrer, *MD.* 8 Nov. 94; *Surgeon Captain,* 28 July 86 (*attached*).
Veterinary Major.—James Reilly,[17] 15 Nov. 93.

Blue—*Facings* Scarlet.—*Agents,* Messrs. Cox and Co.

Returned from France, 2 February 1816.

---

[1] Lt.Colonel Brocklehurst served with the Royal Horse Guards in the Egyptian war of 1882, and was present in the engagements at El Magfar and Mahsama, in the two actions at Kassasin, and at the battle of Tel-el-Kebir (Medal with Clasp, and Khedive's Star). Served with the Nile Expedition in 1884-85 in charge of the Remount Depot (mentioned in despatches, Brevet of Major, Clasp).

[12] Lord Binning served with the Royal Horse Guards and in command of the Signallers of the Cavalry Brigade in the Egyptian war of 1882, and was present in the action at Kassasin on the 9th September, at the battle of Tel-el-Kebir and at the capture of Cairo (Medal with Clasp, and Khedive's Star). Served in the Nile Expedition in 1884-85 with the Heavy Camel Corps in the Desert Column, and was present at the actions at Abu Klea and El Gubat, the affair before Metammeh and the attack on the Convoy on 14th February (two Clasps). Served in the Hazara Expedition in 1888 with the River Column, and was present in the engagement at Kotkai (mentioned in despatches, Medal with Clasp).

[13] Sir John Willoughby served with the Royal Horse Guards in the Egyptian war of 1882, and was present in the action at Kassasin on the 9th September and at the battle of Tel-el-Kebir (Medal with Clasp, and Khedive's Star). Served with the Nile Expedition in 1884-85 on Transport duty (mentioned in despatches, Clasp).

[16] Surgeon Lt.Colonel Melladew.—For War Services, see Army Medical Staff.

[17] Veterinary Major Reilly.—For War Services, see Army Veterinary Department.

1st (The King's) Dragoon Guards.

The Royal Cypher within the Garter. "BLENHEIM" "RAMILLIES" "OUDENARDE" "MALPLAQUET" "DETTINGEN" "WATERLOO" "SEVASTOPOL" "TAKU FORTS" "PEKIN" "SOUTH AFRICA, 1879."

Colonel.—James Robert Steadman Sayer,[1] CB. Cornet, [P]23 May 45; Lt. [P]31 March 48; Capt. [P]22 Nov. 50; Major, [P]6 Feb. 57; Lt.Colonel, [P]21 Oct. 59; Colonel, 21 Oct. 64; Major General, 6 Feb. 70; Lieut. General, 13 March 85; Colonel 1st Dragoon Guards, 25 June 86.

Lieutenant Colonel.—p.s.c. Richard Charles Bernard Lawrence,[4] Lt. 12 Feb. 76; Capt. 1 June 80; Bt.Major, 18 Nov. 82; Major, 25 Jan. 88; Lt.Colonel, 14 June 94.

Years' Ser. Full Pay	Half Pay		2ND LIEUT.	LIEUT.	CAPTAIN.	BREV.MAJ.	MAJOR.
		MAJORS.					
14	...	George Wentworth Forbes[8]	24 Aug. 81	1 July 81	4 Dec. 86	......	7 June 93
15	...	John Edward Benhow, Army Pay Dept.	22 Jan. 81	1 July 81	25 Jan. 88	......	14 June 94
14	...	Henry Lee Pennell	......	28 Jan. 82	23 Oct. 88	......	22 Aug. 94
		CAPTAINS.					
13	...	Alfred Hamilton Mackenzie Edwards,[10] Adjutant Behar Light Horse, 16 Oct, 91	......	27 Jan. 83	18 Feb. 89		
12	...	William Henry Birkbeck[11]	......	25 Aug. 83	31 Jan. 90		
12	...	Charles Loftus Bates	......	30 Jan. 84	14 June 90		
14	...	Steuart Bogle Smith	......	28 Jan. 82	17 Feb. 92		
11	...	Harry Plumridge Levita[12]	......	23 Aug. 84	5 Aug. 91		
12	...	William James Smyth Fergusson[13]	......	6 Feb. 84	29 June 90		
10	...	Charles James Briggs, **Adjutant** 13 Nov. 94	......	30 Jan. 86	1 Mar. 93		
9	...	Frederick Courtenay Longuet Hulton, Supdt. of Gymnasia, Dublin, 1 May 94	......	24 Nov. 86	18 Oct. 93		
10	...	Hugh de Crespigny Eastwood	......	19 Aug. 85	14 June 94		
		LIEUTENANTS.					
8	...	Francis Churchill Quicke	4 May 87	1 Apr. 90			
8	...	John Ambard Bell-Smyth, Aide de Camp to the Governor of Natal, 2 Sept. 93	21 Dec. 87	1 Apr. 90			
6	...	Frederic Graham	1 Mar. 90	17 Feb. 92			
9	...	William Maurice Marter, at Staff College	5 Feb. 87	18 Feb. 91			
5	...	Herbert Francis Langton	8 Oct. 90	7 Sept. 92			
5	...	Henry John Williams	4 Mar. 91	1 Mar. 93			
4	...	Francis Hood Fernie	12 Mar. 92	17 Jan. 94			
3	...	Edmund Deacon	5 Oct. 92	5 Sept. 94			
2	...	Charles Hampton Tuthill	22 Nov. 93	20 Feb. 95			
		SECOND LIEUTENANTS.					
1	...	Denham Parker	30 Jan. 95				
1	...	Richard John Arthur Wynne	13 Feb. 95				
1	...	Hugh Fforde Searight	6 Mar. 95				

| 14 | | Riding Master.—George Matthews, 8 Feb. 82; Hon. Captain, 8 Feb. 92. |
| 3 | | Quarter Master.—William Henry Collins, 1 Mar. 93; Hon. Lieut. |

Scarlet—*Facings* Blue.—*Agents*, Messrs. Cox and Co.
Returned from India, 1 Nov. 91.

[1] Lieut.General Sayer served with the 1st Dragoon Guards in the Crimean campaign from 18th Aug. 1855, including the siege and fall of Sebastopol (Medal with Clasp, and Turkish Medal). Commanded the Regiment in China throughout the campaign of 1860, including the action of Sinho, and those of the 18th and 21st September, also the surrender of Pekin (mentioned in despatches, CB., Medal with two Clasps).

[4] Lt.Colonel Lawrence served in the Egyptian war of 1882 (mentioned in despatches, Brevet of Major, Medal, 4th Class of the Medjidie, and Khedive's Star).

[8] Major Forbes served in the Zulu war in 1879, and was present in the cavalry affair at Erzungayan and in the engagement at Ulundi (Medal with Clasp).

[10] Captain Edwards served with the Hazara Expedition in 1888 as Assistant Provost Marshal (Medal with Clasp).

[11] Captain Birkbeck served with the Hazara Expedition in 1888 as Assistant Superintendent of Army Signalling (mentioned in despatches, Medal with Clasp). Served with the Chin-Lushai Expeditionary Force in 1889-90 as Assistant Superintendent of Army Signalling (mentioned in despatches, Clasp).

[12] Captain Levita served in the Soudan Expedition in 1885 with the 19th Hussars (Medal with Clasp, and Khedive's Star).

[13] Captain Fergusson served with the Nile Expedition in 1884-85 with the 2nd Battalion of the Duke of Cornwall's Light Infantry, and took part in the operations of the Advance Column under Major General Earle (Medal with Clasp, and Khedive's Star).

2nd Dragoon Guards (*Queen's Bays*). [Egypt. Depot, Canterbury.

The Royal Cypher within the Garter. "LUCKNOW."

Years' Ser.								
Full Pay	Half Pay							

Colonel.—William Henry Seymour,[1] *CB. Ensign,* P 7 May 47; *Lt.* 10 June 52; *Capt.* 29 Dec. 54; *Major,* 13 May 58; *Lt. Colonel,* 7 July 58; *Colonel,* 7 July 63; *Major General,* 24 Dec. 68; *Lieut. General,* 30 Sept. 82; *General,* 1 Jan. 85; *Colonel* 3rd Dragoon Guards, 2 Nov. 83; *Colonel* 13th Hussars, 5 Jan. 91; *Colonel* 2nd Dragoon Guards, 20 Jan. 94.

26 ... **Lieutenant Colonel.**—p.s.c. Charles Edward Beckett,[4] *Cornet,* P 17 Apr. 69; *Lieut.* P 22 Apr. 71; *Captain,* 23 Jan. 79; *Bt. Major,* 18 Nov. 82; *Major,* 4 Nov. 84; *Lt. Colonel,* 17 Aug. 92.

		MAJORS.	2ND LIEUT.	LIEUT.	CAPTAIN.	BREV. MAJ.	MAJOR.
21	...	Joseph Alexander Lambert	......	2 Dec. 74	1 Dec. 80	......	21 July 88
20	...	Henry Clerk	......	9 Aug. 75	11 Oct. 81	......	15 Aug. 88
17	4/12	Cuthbert Pilkington Dawson	10 Apr. 78	13 July 78	12 June 85	......	9 Dec. 92
19	...	Richard Alexander Scott	......	28 Apr. 76	1 Jan. 85	......	2 May 94

		CAPTAINS.					
17	...	George Berthon Preston	22 Jan. 79	2 July 79	20 Jan. 86		
15	...	George Prescott Douglas[4]	19 Feb. 81	1 July 81	20 July 87		
13	...	James Edward Dewar[11]	......	29 July 82	20 July 87		
13	...	William Kirk (*Depot*)	......	2 Aug. 82	25 July 88		
13	...	Cecil Henry Saunders-Knox-Gore	......	31 Jan. 83	23 May 91		
10	...	Valentine Geo. Whitla,[13] *Adjutant* 1 Nov. 93	......	6 May 85	9 Dec. 92		

		LIEUTENANTS.					
10	...	William Horsley Perse	......	6 May 85			
11	...	Charles Kendal Bushe[12]	......	23 Aug. 84			
10	...	Edward Robertson Gordon	......	25 Nov. 85			
10	...	James O'Hara, *Army Pay Department*	......	30 Jan. 86			
10	...	Herbert William Wilberforce[14]	......	10 Mar. 86			
8	...	William Alexander Crawford Cockburn	8 June 87	1 Apr. 90			
8	...	Edward William Llewhellin Urquhart	14 Sept. 87	24 Feb. 92			
8	...	Harold Platt Sykes	16 Nov. 87	9 Dec. 92			

		SECOND LIEUTENANTS.					
8	...	Robert Douglas Herron (*Depot*)	14 Mar. 88				
8	...	Percy Molesworth Sykes, *Vice Consul at Kerman, Persia*	29 Feb. 88				
7	...	Nevill Maskelyne Smyth[15]	22 Aug. 88				
5	...	Thomas Ward	23 July 90				
4	...	Reginald Limond Benwell	10 Oct. 91				
4	...	William Robert Bindloss	12 Mar. 92				
3	...	Frank Griffiths Davey	15 Mar. 93				
1	...	William Bennet Andrew (*Depot*)	2 June 94				

Paymaster.—Lieut. H. P. Sykes (acting).

16 ... *Riding Master.*—Henry Andrew Hughes, 23 July 79; *Hon. Captain,* 23 July 89.
8 ... *Quarter Master.*—Frank Hamilton Charters, 14 May 87; *Hon. Lieut.*

Scarlet—*Facings* Buff.—*Agents,* Messrs. Cox and Co.
Embarked for India, 22 Nov. 1885.

---

[1] General Seymour served during the Crimean campaign of 1854-55 with the 68th Light Infantry, including the battles of Alma, Balaklava, and Inkerman, and siege of Sebastopol (Medal with four Clasps, and Turkish Medal). Served in the Indian Mutiny campaigns of 1858-59 with the 2nd Dragoon Guards, including the action of Nusseratpore, siege and capture of Lucknow (charger wounded), and subsequent operations, action of Nawabgungo (in command of three squadrons of the Regiment), and re-occupation of Fyzabad. Commanded the Bays throughout the Oude campaign, including the action of Jamo (wounded), assault and capture of Birwah, and Trans-Gogra affairs at Bungaon (Gazetted Brevet Major on 20th July 1858, frequently mentioned in despatches, Medal with Clasp, and *CB.*).

[2] Lt. Colonel Beckett served in the Egyptian war of 1882 in command of Military Mounted Police, and was present in the action at Kassasin on the 9th September and at the battle of Tel-el-Kebir (mentioned in despatches, Brevet of Major, Medal with Clasp, 4th Class of the Medjidie, and Khedive's Star). Served throughout the Nile Expedition in 1884-85 with the Light Camel Regiment, and took part in the operations of the Desert Column including the engagement at Abu Klea Wells on the 16th and 17th February (Clasp).

[4] Captain Douglas served in the Egyptian war of 1882 with the 7th Dragoon Guards as a volunteer, and was present in the engagements at El Magfar and Mahsama, at the two actions at Kassasin, and at the battle of Tel-el-Kebir and capture of Cairo (Medal with Clasp, and Khedive's Star).

[11] Captain Dewar served in the Soudan campaign in 1885 as Orderly Officer to Brigadier General Ewart, Commanding the Cavalry Brigade (Medal with Clasp, and Khedive's Star),

[12] Lieut. Bushe served in the Nile Expedition in 1884-85 with the 1st Battalion of the Gordon Highlanders and with the River Column under Major General Earle (Medal with Clasp, and Khedive's Star).

[13] Captain V. G. Whitla served in the Egyptian war of 1882 as Midshipman on board H.M.S. *Sultan*, and was present at the bombardment of the Alexandrian Forts; afterwards landed with the Naval Brigade (Medal with Clasp, and Khedive's Star).

[14] Lieut. Wilberforce served in the Hazara Expedition in 1891 as Orderly Officer to Major General Elles, Commanding the Force (mentioned in despatches, Medal with Clasp).

[15] Second Lieut. Smyth served with the Zhob Valley Expedition in 1890-91.

Natal.
Depot, Canterbury.] **3rd (*The Prince of Wales'*) Dragoon Guards.** 138

The Prince's Plume. The Rising Sun and Red Dragon. "BLENHEIM" "RAMILLIES" "OUDENARDE" "MALPLAQUET" "TALAVERA" "ALBUHERA" "VITTORIA" "PENINSULA" "ABYSSINIA."

Colonel.—Conyers Tower,[1] *CB. Cornet*, P7 June 44; *Lt.* P6 June 45; *Capt.* P18 Jan. 50; *Major*, P17 May 61; *Lt.Colonel*, P4 Aug. 63; *Colonel*, 4 Aug. 68; *Major General*, 20 Mar. 78; *Lieut.General*, 20 March 83; *Colonel* 3rd Dragoon Guards, 5 Jan. 91.

25 ... Lieutenant Colonel.—Roger Kennedy Parke, *Cornet*. P10 Aug. 70; *Lt.* 28 Oct. 71; *Capt.* 26 May 79; *Major*, 21 Dec. 87; *Lt.Colonel*, 24 Nov. 92.

Years' Ser. Full Pay / Half Pay			2ND LIEUT.	LIEUT.	CAPTAIN.	BREV.MAJ.	MAJOR.
		MAJORS.					
16	...	John Edward Fitzmaurice Hughes Roche	13 Aug. 79	11 Feb. 80	25 Sept. 84	......	24 Nov. 88
13	...	Charles Herbert Farquharson		27 Jan. 83	12 Feb. 87	......	5 Sept. 92
15	...	Arthur Patrick Douglas Lushington	11 Aug. 80	1 July 81	7 May 87	......	24 Nov. 92
		CAPTAINS.					
17	...	Edmund Donough John O'Brien,[4] *D. A. A. Gen., Bengal*, 16 Sept. 94	11 May 78	28 Aug. 79	17 Jan. 87		
12		Herbert Mercer		30 Jan. 84	8 Apr. 90		
13	...	Stephen Walter		7 Mar. 83	22 Jan. 90		
11		Olive Skene Keith, *Ordnance Store Dept.*		14 May 84	4 July 92		
11		Acland Alfred Gordon Anderson		23 Aug. 84	4 July 92		
11		Charles Leonard Cotton		7 Feb. 85	5 Sept. 92		
10		Walter Triggs,[5] *Army Pay Department*		27 Mar. 86	24 Nov. 92		
9	...	Charles Inglis Scott, *Adjutant* 6 July 91		8 Dec. 86	24 May 93		
10		Herbert Arthur Lafone (*Depot*)		17 Feb. 86	7 June 93		
9	...	Andrew Bellew Nolan	5 Feb. 87	31 July 89	5 July 93		
		LIEUTENANTS.					
7	...	William Robt. Robertson, *Staff Lieut., Intelligence Branch, Bengal*, 5 June 92	27 June 88	1 Mar. 91			
7	...	Francis John Ryder (*Depot*)	30 Jan. 89	17 Sept. 91			
6	...	Oswald Buckley Bingham Smith-Bingham	8 June 89	23 Dec. 91			
5	...	James William Ferguson	26 Apr. 90	5 Sept. 92			
4	...	Robert Hume M'Corquodale, *serving with the Royal Niger Company*	5 Dec. 91	24 May 93			
3		William Croughton Peel	16 Dec. 91	7 June 93			
4	...	William Ernest Davis Goff	12 Mar. 92	7 June 93			
3	...	Frederick Agnew Gill	15 Mar. 93	16 May 94			
2	...	Alexander Ian Mitchell	1 Nov. 93	23 Feb. 95			
		SECOND LIEUTENANTS.					
2	...	Percival Naylor Kent	10 Jan. 94				
2	...	Antony Ernest Wentworth Harman	31 Jan. 94				
2	...	Charles Edward Irvine M'Nalty	31 Jan. 94				
1	...	Richard William Longfield	6 Mar. 95				

1 ... Paymaster.—
Riding Master.—William Sykes, 20 Feb. 95; *Hon. Lieut.*
14 ... Quarter Master.—Thomas Brown, 30 Nov. 81; *Hon. Captain*, 30 Nov. 91.
Scarlet—*Facings* Yellow.—*Agents*, Messrs. Holt and Co.
Embarked for India, 10 Oct. 1884.

[1] Lt.General Tower served with the 6th Dragoons the Eastern campaign of 1854, including the battle of Balaklava and siege of Sebastopol (Medal with two Clasps, and Turkish Medal). Commanded the 3rd Dragoon Guards during the Abyssinian campaign in 1868, and was present at the assault and capture of Magdala (mentioned in despatches, *CB.*, and Medal).

[4] Captain O'Brien served in the Afghan war in 1880, and was present with the 1st Punjaub Cavalry in the affair at Fudkao Shana (mentioned in Brigadier General Palliser's despatch). Was attached to the 15th Sikhs as a volunteer in the march from Cabul to Candahar under Sir Frederick Roberts, and was engaged in the reconnaissance on the 31st August and in the battle of Candahar (Medal with Clasp, and Bronze Decoration).

[5] Captain Triggs served in the Afghan war in 1879-80 (Medal).

Record of the Services of the 3rd (The Prince of Wales') Dragoon Guards.

Raised in 1685. Germany, to 1758 (battles of Blenheim, Ramillies, Oudenarde and Malplaquet). England, to 1780. France, to 1794. England, to 1809. The Peninsula, to 1809 (battles of Talavera, Albuhera and Vittoria). England, to 1815. France, to Jan. 1816. England, to June 1816. Ireland, to 1829. England, to 1834. Ireland, to 1837. England, to 1843. Ireland, to 1846. Scotland, to 1848. England, to 1852. Ireland, to March 1857. England, to August 1857. India, to Feb. 1868. Abyssinia, to May 1868 (Abyssinian war). England, to 1875. Ireland, to 1881. Scotland, to 1883. England, to 1884. India, 1884.

4th (*Royal Irish*) Dragoon Guards.

[Rawul Pindee, Bengal. Depot, Shorncliffe.]

The Harp and Crown, and the Star of St. Patrick, with the motto "*Quis separabit?*" "PENINSULA" "BALAKLAVA" "SEVASTOPOL" "EGYPT, 1882" "TEL-EL-KEBIR."

Colonel.—William Godfrey Dunham Massy,[1] *CB. Ensign*, 27 Oct. 54; *Lieut*. 9 Feb. 55; *Capt*. 20 Feb. 57; *Major*, P23 Jan. 63; *Lt.Colonel*, P31 Oct. 71; *Colonel*, 31 Oct. 76; *Major General*, 28 Aug. 86; *Lieut. General*, 21 Jan. 93; *Colonel* 4 Dragoon Guards, 11 Dec. 94.

Lieutenant Colonel.—Philip Kavanagh Doyne, *Cornet*, P14 Mar. 68; *Lieut*. P16 Mar. 70; *Capt*. 9 Feb. 82; *Major*, 3 Aug. 87; *Lt.Colonel*, 7 Mar. 92.

Years' Ser. Full Pay.	Half Pay	MAJORS.	2ND LIEUT.	LIEUT.	CAPTAIN.	BREV.MAJ.	MAJOR.
21	...	Arthur Abney Sandys[2]	......	13 June 74	10 June 82	......	8 Oct. 90
21	...	v.s.c. Herbert Charles Thornton Littledale[10]	......	21 Sept. 74	8 Mar. 82	21 May 84	13 June 94.
17	...	John William Dent........................	11 May 78	13 April 81	18 Jan. 85	......	6 Aug. 94
13	...	Francis Blayney Lucas Woodwright	......	2 Aug. 82	8 May 88	......	12 Sept. 94
		CAPTAINS.					
13	...	Charles Michael Edgeworth Brinkley, *Ordnance Store Department*................	......	29 July 82	7 Mar. 88		
13	...	Gerald Burrell Geach, *Adjutant Pembroke Yeomanry Cavalry* 15 Apr. 91	......	2 Aug. 82	18 June 90		
10	...	Hon. William Wrottesley........................	......	23 May 85	5 Mar. 91		
10	...	Robert Wilton Morley..........................	......	31 Mar. 86	3 Apr. 91		
12	...	Malcolm. M'Neill[13] (*Depot*)................	......	5 Dec. 83	4 May 92		
11	...	John Flint, **Adjutant** 14 Dec. 92	......	2 July 84	16 Oct. 91		
7	...	William Belk	30 Jan. 89	11 June 90	18 Apr. 94		
6	...	David Plenderleath Sellar................	8 June 89	30 Sept. 90	6 Aug. 94		
6	...	Bampfylde Leonard Carew..................	8 June 89	8 Oct. 90	12 Sept. 94		
		LIEUTENANTS.					
6	...	Thomas Frederick Newcome Jones............	17 July 89	8 Oct. 90			
5	...	George Frederick Mappin (*Depot*)	29 Nov. 90	23 Apr. 92			
4	...	Cecil Robert Gaunt	27 June 91	8 Apr. 92			
5	...	Clement Parker Toulson	3 Dec. 90	24 May 92			
5	...	Ernest Frank Holden	28 June 90	13 Nov. 93			
3	...	Edward Rickards	5 Oct. 92	18 Apr. 94			
10	...	Maurice FitzGerald	......	25 Nov. 85			
2	...	Rintoul Archer Milward-Jones	10 Jan. 94	10 Oct. 94			
		SECOND LIEUTENANTS.					
1	...	Arthur Robert Liddell......................	2 June 94				
1	...	Herbert Timbrell M'Clellan	11 July 94				
1	...	Brownlow Henry Hamilton Mathew-Lannowe	8 Aug. 94				
1	...	John Hardress Lloyd	10 Oct. 94				
1	...	Charles Crosbie..............................	10 Oct. 94				
1	...	Jeremy Taylor Marsh	12 Dec. 94				
1	...	Augustus George Aimé Jerrard	12 Dec. 94				
1	...	Charles Mackenzie Grogan	12 Dec. 94				
2	...	Francis Charles Philips	21 Oct. 93				

Paymaster.—Lieut. C. R. Gaunt (*acting*).
8 ... *Riding Master*.—Ernest Pettitt Cant, 25 Jan. 88; *Hon. Lieut*.
4 ... *Quarter Master*.—Joseph Hopkins, 3 Nov. 91; *Hon. Lieut*.

Scarlet—*Facings* Blue.—*Agents*, Messrs. Holt and Co.
Embarked for India, 12 Sept. 94.

[1] Lieut.General Dunham Massy served at the latter part of the siege of Sebastopol, was under fire at the battle of the Tchernaya, and commanded the Grenadiers of the 19th Regt. at the assault of the Redan on the 8th Sept., where with minor injuries he was dangerously wounded by a ball which passed through his left thigh, shattering the bone. Being left on the ground, he fell into the hands of the enemy the ensuing night, who, supposing him to be mortally wounded, did not remove him with their prisoners. Was recommended in a special despatch by the Commander in Chief in the Crimea for his gallantry at the Redan, his fortitude, and the patient endurance with which he bore his most severe suffering during a confinement to his camp stretcher of nearly six months (promoted Captain, Medal with Clasp, Knight of the Legion of Honor, and Turkish Medal). Served in the Afghan war in 1879-80 in command of a Cavalry Brigade, and was present at the battle of Charasiab on the 6th October 1879, the capture of the cantonment of Sherpore, the engagement in the Chardeh Valley, and the operations around Cabul in December 1879 including the investment of Sherpore (twice mentioned in despatches, Medal with two Clasps).

[2] Major Sandys served with the 4th Dragoon Guards in the Egyptian war of 1882, and was present in the engagement at Tel-el-Mahuta, the two actions at Kassasin, the battle of Tel-el-Kebir, and the capture of Cairo (Medal with Clasp, and Khedive's Star).

[10] Major Littledale served in the expedition to the Soudan under Sir Gerald Graham in 1884 with the 1st Battalion York and Lancaster Regiment, and was present in the engagement at El Teb—severely wounded (mentioned in despatches, Brevet of Major, Medal with Clasp, and Khedive's Star).

[13] Captain M'Neill served with the expedition to the Soudan in 1885 with the 5th Lancers and as Orderly Officer to Sir Henry Ewart, Commanding the Cavalry Brigade, and was present in the engagement at Hasheen and at the destruction of Temai (Medal with Clasp, and Khedive's Star).

Record of the Services of the 4th (Royal Irish) Dragoon Guards.

Raised in 1685 as a Regiment of Cuirassiers, "The Sixth Horse." Designated "The Fifth Horse," 1690. To Flanders, 1691. To England, 1697. To Ireland, 1698. Designated "First Irish Horse," or "The Blue Horse," 1746. Designated "Fourth Royal Irish Regiment of Dragoon Guards," 1788. To England, 1793. To Ireland, 1795. To England, 1799. To Ireland, 1802. To England, 1804. To Portugal, 1811 (Peninsular War). To England, 1813. To Ireland, 1814. To England, 1818. To Ireland, 1822. To England, 1826. To Ireland, 1832. To England, 1835. To Ireland, 1841. To England, 1845. To Ireland, 1851. To the Crimea, 1854 (battle of Balaklava and siege of Sebastopol). To England, 1856. To Ireland, 1861. To England, 1867. To Ireland, 1872. To England, 1878. To Egypt, 1882 (campaign of 1882 and battle of Tel-el-Kebir). To England, 1882. Detachment to the Nile, 1884-85. To Ireland, 1886. To England, 1891. To India, 1894.

5th (*Princess Charlotte of Wales'*) Dragoon Guards.

Meerut, Bengal.
Depot, Canterbury.

"*Vestigia nulla retrorsum.*"—"BLENHEIM" "RAMILLIES" "OUDENARDE" "MALPLAQUET" "SALAMANCA" "VITTORIA" "TOULOUSE" "PENINSULA" "BALAKLAVA" "SEVASTOPOL."

Years' Ser. Full Pay.	Half Pay.		CORNET OR 2ND LIEUT.	LIEUT.	CAPTAIN.	BREV. MAJ.	MAJOR.
23	...	**Colonel.**—Hon. Somerset John Gough Calthorpe,[1] *Cornet*, P 23 May 48; *Lieut.* P 23 May 51; *Capt.* P 14 Sept. 55; *Bt.Major*, 2 Nov. 55; *Major*, 22 July 56; *Lt.Colonel*, P 15 Feb. 61; *Colonel*, 15 Feb. 66; *Major General*, 25 July 70; *Lieut.General*, 1 July 81; *Colonel* 5th Lancers, 18 Nov. 87; *Colonel* 5th Dragoon Guards, 24 Jan. 92.					
		Lieutenant Colonel.—Maunsell Bowers, *Lieut.* 13 Apr. 72; *Captain*, 21 Aug. 78; *Major*, 21 Apr. 83; *Lieut.Colonel*, 25 Apr. 93.					
		MAJORS.					
27	...	Fred. Wilson Hemming³ (*Bt.Lt.Colonel*, 1 July 87)	P 25 Apr. 68	28 Oct. 71	31 Oct. 78	2 Mar. 81	19 Dec. 83
19	...	p.s.c. Edward Hegan⁴		11 Sept. 76	31 Jan. 82		22 Dec. 87
18	...	William James Mackeson⁵		10 Sept. 77	2 May 83		25 Apr. 93
17	...	St. John Corbet Gore⁷	22 Jan. 79	1 July 81	25 Feb. 85		6 Sept. 93
		CAPTAINS.					
18	...	James Henry Aspinwall,⁸ *Adjutant* 2 Yeomanry Brigade 1 June 93	2 Mar. 78	22 Mar. 79	26 Aug. 84		
13	...	William Eden Stobart⁹		10 Mar. 83	24 Aug. 87		
16	...	Llewellin Washington Matthews	17 Dec. 79	15 Mar. 81	1 Oct. 87		
18	...	Alfred René Heneage¹⁰ (*Depot*)		11 Sept. 77	23 May 88		
17	...	p.s.c. Colquhoun Grant Morrison, *Instructor, Royal Military College*, 1 Jan. 91	22 Jan. 79	18 June 81	27 Mar. 89		
11	...	Henry Bagwell-Purefoy¹²		23 Aug. 84	27 Mar. 89		
11	...	William Leetham		7 Feb. 85	25 Apr. 93		
10	...	Herbert Hoare, *Adjutant*, 15 Jan. 95		23 May 85	6 Sept. 93		
8	...	Frederick Adolphus Dawson Oliver Eustace	16 Nov. 87	6 Feb. 89	15 Jan. 95		
		LIEUTENANTS.					
7	...	Percy Henry Darbyshire	9 Jan. 89	26 Mar. 90			
6	...	John Charles Wilmot	8 June 89	20 Aug. 90			
5	...	Henry Gerard Hegan Kennard	8 Oct. 90	21 Oct. 91			
5	...	Frederick Thomas Parker	4 Mar. 91	1 July 92			
4	...	Bertram Robert Mitford Glossop	30 May 91	25 Apr. 93			
3	...	James Robert Lindsay Garrard	13 July 92	6 Sept. 93			
3	...	William Quintyne Winwood	15 Mar. 93	24 Jan. 94			
3	...	Charles Hodgkinson	18 June 92	24 Jan. 95			
		SECOND LIEUTENANTS.					
2	...	Hugh Price Travers	28 June 93				
2	...	Roland Langharne Clennell Wilkinson	9 Sept. 93				
2	...	Bertie Gordon Clay	21 Oct. 93				
2	...	Henry Hodge Lamb	25 Oct. 93				
2	...	Philip Guy Reynolds	28 June 93				
2	...	Guy Hartley Watson	23 Dec. 93				
2	...	Hon. Ralph Legge Pomeroy	23 Dec. 93				
2	...	William Peverell Marley	7 Feb. 94				
1	...	Lewis Maxwell Dunbar	12 Dec. 94				

Paymaster.—Lieut. Henry H. Lamb (*acting*).

17 ... *Riding Master.*—Robert Gifford, 3 April 78; *Hon. Captain*, 3 Apr. 88.
10 ... *Quarter Master.*—Charles George Perkins, 13 May 85; *Hon. Lieut.*

Scarlet—*Facings* Green.—*Agents*, Messrs. Cox and Co.
Embarked for India, 7 September 1893.

---

[1] Lt.General Hon. S. J. G. Calthorpe served in the Eastern campaign of 1854-55 as Aide de Camp to Lord Raglan, including the battles of Alma, Balaklava, and Inkerman, affairs of Bulganak and M'Kenzie's Farm, and siege of Sebastopol (Medal with four Clasps, Brevet of Major, Knight of the Legion of Honour, 5th Class of the Medjidie, and Turkish Medal).

[3] Lt.Colonel Hemming served in the Afghan war in 1878-79 as Aide de Camp to Lieut.General Maude, and was present with the two expeditions into the Bazar Valley (Brevet of Major, Medal). Served with the Burmese Expedition in 1885-86, as Deputy Assistant Adjutant and Quarter Master General in charge of the Intelligence Branch (mentioned in despatches, Brevet of Lt.Colonel, Medal with Clasp).

[4] Major Hegan served in the Boer war of 1881 with the Inniskilling Dragoons.

[5] Major Mackeson served in the Nile Expedition in 1884-85 with the Camel Corps (Medal with Clasp, and Khedive's Star).

[7] Major Gore served in the Nile Expedition in 1884-85 with the Camel Corps (Medal with Clasp, and Khedive's Star).

[8] Captain Aspinwall served with the 7th Dragoon Guards in the Egyptian war of 1882, and was present in the engagements of El Magfar and Mahsama, in the action at Kassasin on the 28th August, and at the battle of Tel-el-Kebir and the capture of Cairo (Medal with Clasp, and Khedive's Star).

[9] Captain Stobart served in the Nile Expedition in 1884-85 with the Heavy Camel Regiment (Medal with Clasp, and Khedive's Star).

[10] Captain Heneage served with the 2nd Battalion Highland Light Infantry in the Egyptian war of 1882, and was present at the battle of Tel-el-Kebir—wounded (Medal with Clasp, and Khedive's Star).

[12] Captain Bagwell-Purefoy served with the Bechuanaland Expedition under Sir Charles Warren in 1884-85 with the Inniskilling Dragoons.

6th Dragoon Guards (Carabiniers). [York.

"BLENHEIM" "RAMILLIES" "OUDENARDE" "MALPLAQUET" "SEVASTOPOL" "DELHI"
"AFGHANISTAN, 1879-80."

Years Ser			2ND LIEUT.	LIEUT.	CAPTAIN.	BREV. MAJ.	MAJOR.
Full Pay	Half Pay						

Colonel.—Alexander James Hardy Elliot,[1] *CB.*, Cornet, 18 July 48; Lieut. P 14 June 50; Capt. 22 Dec. 54; Bt. Major, 17 July 55; Major, 29 July 56; Bt. Lt. Colonel, 29 May 63; Colonel, 1 Feb. 71; Major General, 1 July 81; Colonel 6 Dragoon Guards, 3 Jan. 92.

25 | ... | Lieutenant Colonel.—William Henry MacGeorge, Cornet, P 13 July 70; Lieut. 28 Oct. 71; Capt. 13 July 7; Major, 5 July 82; Lt. Colonel, 1 July 91.

MAJORS.

Years		Name	2ND LIEUT.	LIEUT.	CAPTAIN.	BREV. MAJ.	MAJOR.
23	...	Thomas Cole Porter[11]	......	24 Feb. 73	5 Oct. 78	......	17 Mar. 86
22	...	Alexander Sprot[13]	......	28 Feb. 74	26 Apr. 82	......	19 July 89
21	...	p.s.c Percy Hugh Hamon Massy[15]	......	11 Feb. 75	19 July 82	......	24 May 98

CAPTAINS.

Years		Name	2ND LIEUT.	LIEUT.	CAPTAIN.	BREV. MAJ.	MAJOR.
18	...	Henry Mostyn Owen[17]	30 Jan. 78	1 July 81	4 Dec. 86		
20	...	p.s.c. Edward Cecil Bethune[18]		10 Sept. 75	1 Feb. 84		
18	...	Frederick Henry Arthur Des Vœux[6]	16 Feb. 78	1 July 81	1 July 87		
15	2	Francis Sudlow Garratt[7]	1 May 78	1 July 81	3 Oct. 87		
16	...	Montagu Cradock[20]	6 Aug. 79	1 July 81	20 Oct. 87		
13	...	Arthur Cochrane Hamilton	......	10 May 82	13 June 88		
12	...	John Robert Donne	......	25 Aug. 83	11 Jan. 90		
9	...	Thomas Wootton Blakeway, Adjutant, 3 Feb. 95	......	30 June 86	22 June 92		

LIEUTENANTS.

Years		Name				
9	...	Kenneth J. R. Campbell (*Lieut. Lancaster Regiment*, 18 Aug. 86), Vice Consul Niger Coast Protectorate 12 Oct. 91	6 July 87	1 Aug. 88		
9	...	William John Chesshyre Butler	5 Feb. 87	8 May 89		
7	...	Charles Kershaw Elworthy	30 Jan. 89	16 Apr. 90		
7	...	Charles Melville Johnstone	22 Aug. 88	2 Feb. 90		
5	...	Walter Dougall	28 June 90	28 Oct. 91		
5	...	Edward Leopold Reiss	28 June 90	28 Oct. 91		
5	...	Owen Lyall Francis	28 June 90	8 June 92		
3	...	John Leslie Reid	11 May 92	28 Dec. 92		
6	...	Claud Herbert Campbell	9 Nov. 89	28 Dec. 92		

[24] Captain Brittlebank served in the Afghan war in 1879-80, and was present with the expeditions into the Lughman Valley and against the Wuzeeree Khugianis, and at the attack and destruction of several villages (Medal).

SECOND LIEUTENANTS.

Years		Name		
3	...	John ffarthing Hopkinson	16 Nov. 92	
3	...	Lonsdale Richard Douglas Smith	15 Feb. 93	
3	...	Stuart Rodger Kirby	15 Mar. 93	

| 4 | ... | Riding Master.—Benjamin Turner,[23] 29 July 91; Hon. Lieut. |
| 14 | ... | Quarter Master.—Joseph Brittlebank,[24] 13 April 81; Hon. Captain, 13 Apr. 91. |

Blue—*Facings* White.—*Agents*, Messrs. Cox & Co.
Returned from India, 20 November 1888.

---

[1] Major General Elliot served five years in India, the last two on Lord Hardinge's staff, prior to entering the Royal Army, and was present with his regiment, the 8th Bengal Cavalry, at the battle of Punniar (Bronze Star); also in the Sutlej campaign, including the battles of Ferozeshah and Sobraon (Medal). Served in the Crimean campaign from Oct. 1854 to 1st April 1855 as Aide de Camp to General Scarlett, including the battle of Balaklava (severely wounded) and siege of Sebastopol (Medal with two Clasps, Brevet of Major, Commander of the Legion of Honor, and Turkish Medal).

[6] Captain Des Vœux served with the Carabiniers in the Afghan war in 1879-80, and took part in the expeditions into the Lughman Valley and against the Wuzeeree Khugianis; was also present at the attack and destruction of the villages of Nargozi, Arab Kheyl, and Jokan (Medal).

[7] Captain Garratt served with the Carabiniers in the Afghan war in 1879-80 (Medal).

[11] Major Porter served with the Carabiniers in the Afghan war in 1879-80, including the affair at Ali Boghan under Lt. Colonel Fryer, the expeditions into the Lughman Valley and against the Wuzeeree Khugianis and to the Hissarik Valley, and at the attack and destruction of the villages of Nargozi, Arab Kheyl, and Jokan (Medal).

[13] Major Sprot served with the Carabiniers in the Afghan war in 1879-80, including the engagement with the Mohmunds at Dakka (Medal).

[15] Major Massy served with the Carabiniers in the Afghan war of 1879-80, and took part in the expedition against the Wuzeeree Khugianis (Medal).

[17] Captain Owen served with the Carabiniers in the Afghan war in 1879-80, including the engagement with the Mohmunds at Dakka and the expedition against the Wuzeeree Khugianis (Medal).

[18] Captain Bethune served in the Afghan war of 1878-80, and was present in the operations around Cabul in December 1879 (Medal with Clasp). Served with the 92nd Highlanders in the Boer war of 1881.

[20] Captain Cradock served with the Carabiniers in the Afghan war in 1879-80, and took part in the expeditions into the Lughman Valley and against the Wuzeeree Khugianis, and was present at the attack and destruction of the villages of Nargozi, Arab Kheyl, and Jokan (Medal).

[23] Lieut. Turner served in the Afghan war of 1878-80, took part with the Koorum and Khost Expeditions, and was present at the reconnaissance of the Peiwar Kotal and in the engagements at Mattoon and Futtehabad (Medal). Served in the Nile Expedition in 1884-85 with the Light Camel Corps, and was present at the attack on the convoy on the 14th February and in the action at Abu Klea (mentioned in despatches, Medal with Clasp, Khedive's Star, and Medal for Distinguished Conduct in the Field).

Record of the Services of the 6th Dragoon Guards.

Raised in 1685 (Monmouth's Rebellion). To Ireland, 1688 to 1691. England, to March 1692. Flanders, to 1697. England, to 1702. Flanders, to 1713. Ireland, to 1744. England, 1744, and returned to Ireland (date uncertain). In Ireland, 1747 to 1760. Germany, to 1763. Ireland, to 1793. Low Countries, to 1795. England, to 1796. Ireland to 1803. England (4 troops to Buenos Ayres, 1806) and Scotland, to 1813. Ireland, to 1815. England and Scotland, to 1821. Ireland, to 1824. England and Scotland, to 1830. Ireland, to March 1834. England, to 1840. Ireland, to 1842. England and Scotland, to 1846. Ireland, to 1852. England, to 1855. Crimea, to 1856. England, to August 1856. India, to 1861. England, to 1866. Ireland, to May 1872. England, to December 1877. India, to September 1879. Afghanistan to October 1880. India, to October 1888. Home, November 1888.

Shorncliffe.] **7th (*The Princess Royal's*) Dragoon Guards.** 142

"BLENHEIM" "RAMILLIES" "OUDENARDE" "MALPLAQUET" "DETTINGEN" "SOUTH AFRICA, 1846-7"
"EGYPT, 1882" "TEL-EL-KEBIR."

Years' Ser. Full Pay.	Half Pay.						
31	...	Colonel.—Andrew Nugent,¹ Cornet, P17 Dec. 52; Lieut. P24 Nov. 54; Captain, PS Feb. 56; Major, 31 Mar. 66; Lt.Col. P3 Feb. 69; Colonel, 3 Feb. 74; Major General, 19 Feb. 85; Lt. General, 13 Nov. 86; Colonel 7 Dragoon Guards, 30 Apr. 92.						
31	...	Lieutenant Colonel.—Walter Creagh, Cornet, 4 Oct. 64; Lieut.P 28 Oct. 68; Capt.1 Apr. 75; Major, 1 July 81; Lt.Colonel, 31 March 91.						

		MAJORS.	CORNET OR 2ND LIEUT.	LIEUT.	CAPTAIN.	BREV.MAJ.	MAJOR.
24	...	William Edward Morrison Rough³	23 Sept. 71	28 Oct. 71	22 Mar. 79	......	26 Aug. 84
19	...	Ulick George Campbell de Burgh⁴	......	11 Sept. 76	1 July 81	......	31 Oct. 90
15	3	Digby de la Motte du Boulay⁵	......	11 Sept. 77	1 Oct. 81	......	31 Mar. 91
19	...	Donald MacDougall	......	6 Sept. 76	1 Jan. 85	......	2 Mar. 92
14	...	William Henry Muir Lowe⁹	......	22 Oct. 81	9 Mar. 87	......	2 Mar. 92

		CAPTAINS.					
14	...	Charles William Thompson¹⁰ (*Depot*)	......	28 Jan. 82	9 Mar. 87		
13	...	William Edwin Danby	......	2 Aug. 82	19 Dec. 87		
16	...	p.s.c. William Henry Rycroft¹²	13 Aug. 79	1 July 81	11 Apr. 88		
12	...	Richard William Burton-Phillipson	......	5 Dec. 83	31 Oct. 90		
10	...	John Weston Parsons Peters¹³	......	9 May 85	31 Mar. 91		
10	...	Frederick George Bick Smerdon, *Army Pay Department*	......	9 June 85	31 Mar. 91		
10	...	Henry Spencer Follett	......	29 Aug. 85	2 Mar. 92		

		LIEUTENANTS.					
10	...	Robert Cooper	......	29 Aug. 85			
10	...	John Edmund Mackenzie	......	17 June 85			
9	...	Edward Witham, *Garrison Quarter Master, Fort William*, 7 Apr. 92	16 Mar. 87	5 Dec. 88			
7	2⁹/₁₂	Bernard Russel Dietz	......	30 Jan. 86			
8	...	George Langworthy	4 May 87	6 Nov. 89			
8	...	Cecil William Battine	4 May 87	26 Feb. 90			
8	...	Wm. Eliot Peyton, *Adjutant* 20 June 92	18 June 87	1 Apr. 90			
7	...	William Daniel M'Swiney	28 Nov. 88	20 Nov. 90			
8	...	Henry Anderson Lempriere	14 Mar. 88	23 Dec. 91			
5	...	John Edward Frederick Dyer	28 June 90	2 Mar. 92			
4	...	John Sanders Cayzer	10 Oct. 91	9 Nov. 92			

		SECOND LIEUTENANTS.					
4	...	Richard Sparrow	12 Mar. 92				
4	...	Moreton Foley Gage	12 Mar. 92				
3	...	Christopher Goddard Jackson	5 Oct. 92				

Paymaster.—
| 11 | ... | *Riding Master.—*Lawrence Cunningham, 7 May 84; *Hon. Captain*, 7 May 94. |
| 12 | ... | *Quarter Master.—*William Cumberland,¹⁴ 3 Jan. 84; *Hon. Captain*, 3 Jan. 94. |

Scarlet—*Facings* Black.—*Agents*, Messrs. Cox and Co.
Returned from India, 10 Nov. 94.

¹² Captain Rycroft served in the Nile Expedition in 1884-85 attached to the 1st Battalion of the Royal Irish Regiment including the operations of the Desert Column, and afterwards with the Mounted Infantry (Medal with Clasp, and Khedive's Star). Served with the Soudan Frontier Field Force in 1887 in command of the Irregular Troops of the Egyptian Army, and was present in the engagement at Sarras (mentioned in despatches, 4th Class of the Medjidie).
¹³ Captain Peters served with the Chin-Lushai Expeditionary Force in 1888-89 on special service with Brigadier-General Tregear's Column (Medal with Clasp). Served with the Expedition to the Black Mountain in 1891 as Superintendent of Signalling (Clasp).
¹⁴ Captain Cumberland served in the Egyptian war of 1882 with the 7th Dragoon Guards (Medal, and Khedive's Star).

¹ Lt.General Nugent served in the Eastern campaign of 1854-55 with the Scots Greys, including the battles of Balaklava, Inkerman, and Tchernaya, siege and fall of Sebastopol (Medal with three Clasps, and Turkish Medal).
³ Major Rough served with the 7th Dragoon Guards in the Egyptian war of 1882, and was present in the engagements of El Magfar and Mahsama, in the two actions at Kassasin, and at the battle of Tel-el-Kebir and the capture of Cairo (Medal with Clasp, and Khedive's Star).
⁴ Major do Burgh served with the 7th Dragoon Guards in the Egyptian war of 1882, and was present as Adjutant in the engagements of El Magfar and Mahsama, in the two actions at Kassasin, and at the battle of Tel-el-Kebir and the capture of Cairo (Medal with Clasp, and Khedive's Star).
⁵ Major Du Boulay served in the Egyptian war of 1882 in command of the Signallers of the Cavalry Division, and was present in the engagements at El Magfar and Mahsama, in the two actions at Kassasin, and at the battle of Tel-el-Kebir and the capture of Cairo (Medal with Clasp, and Khedive's Star).
⁹ Major Lowe served with the 7th Dragoon Guards in the Egyptian war of 1882, and was present in the engagements of El Magfar and Mahsama, in the action at Kassasin on the 28th August, and at the battle of Tel-el-Kebir and the capture of Cairo (Medal with Clasp, and Khedive's Star). Served with the Burmese Expedition in 1886-87 on special service (Medal with Clasp).
¹⁰ Captain Thompson served with the 7th Dragoon Guards in the Egyptian war of 1882, and was present in the two actions at Kassasin, and at the battle of Tel-el-Kebir and the capture of Cairo (Medal with Clasp, and Khedive's Star).

Record of the Services of the 7th (*Princess Royal's*) Dragoon Guards.

Raised in 1688 as the "10th Horse, or Devonshire's Regiment." To Ireland, 1689. To the Netherlands as "Schomberg's Horse," 1691. To England, 1698. To Holland, 1702 (battles of Blenheim, Ramillies, Oudenarde, and Malplaquet). To Ireland, 1714. Entitled "Ligonier's Horse," 1720. To Germany, 1742 (battle of Dettingen). To England, 1745. Entitled "4th Irish Horse, or The Black Horse," 1746. To Ireland, 1747. To Germany, 1760. To Ireland, 1763. Entitled "7th Dragoon Guards (The Princess Royal's Regiment)," 1788. To England, 1799. To Ireland, 1814. To Scotland, 1820. To England, 1822. To the Cape, 1846 (first Kafir war). To England, 1847. To India, 1857. To England, 1868. To Ireland, 1872. To England, 1878. To Egypt, 1882, actions at Kassasin and battle of Tel-el-Kebir). To India, 1885. To Egypt, 1893. To England, 1894.

H

1st (Royal) Dragoons. [Dublin.

The Crest of England within the Garter. An Eagle. *"Spectemur agendo."*
"Dettingen" "Peninsula" "Waterloo" "Balaklava" "Sevastopol."

Colonel in Chief.—*His Majesty* William II. German Emperor and *King of* Prussia, *KG.* 5 May 94.
Colonel.—Frederick Marshall,[1] *CMG. Cornet,* P18 Sept. 49; *Lieut.* P16 Sept. 51; *Captain,* P4 Feb. 59; *Major and Lt.Colonel,* P6 Mar. 63; *Lt.Colonel,* P8 Mar. 64; *Colonel,* 6 Mar. 68; *Major General,* 20 Oct. 77; *Lt. General,* 5 Sept. 84; *Colonel* 1st Dragoons, 29 Mar. 90.
Lieutenant Colonel.—Henry Tomkinson, *Cornet,* P23 Apr. 61; *Lieut.* P10 May 64; *Capt.* P8 July 68; *Major* 23 Dec. 84; *Lt. Colonel,* 20 May 91.

Years Ser. Full Pay	Halt Pay		2ND LIEUT.	LIEUT.	CAPTAIN.	BREV.MAJ.	MAJOR.
34	1/12						
		MAJORS.					
22	...	William Henry M'Laren		15 Mar. 74	30 Sept. 80	......	19 June 85
17	...	*p.s.c.* John Francis Burn-Murdoch,[4] *Comdt. of Cavalry, Egyptian Army*	4 Dec. 78	2 Feb. 81	18 Jan. 85	......	3 Aug. 92
17	...	Ferdinand Wm. Greatrex, *Assist. Inspector of Gymnasia, Aldershot,* 1 Aug. 92	13 Aug. 79	1 July 81	19 June 85	......	19 May 94
		CAPTAINS.					
17	...	Charles Rosdew Burn,[5] *Aide de Camp to H.R.H. the Duke of Connaught* 9 Oct. 93	1 May 78	1 July 81	2 Feb. 85		
21	...	James Andrew Murphy		9 Aug. 74	13 May 85		
14	...	*p.s.c.* John Edward Lindley, *D.A.A. General, Aldershot,* 31 Aug. 93		22 Oct. 81	18 Nov. 86		
13	...	George Limbrey Lord Basing		2 Aug. 82	1 Oct. 87		
11	...	Ralph Henry Carr-Ellison, *Adjutant* 12 *Yeomanry Brigade* 25 Sept. 94		22 Nov. 84	25 Nov. 91		
11	...	John Middleton Rogers		7 Feb. 85	25 Nov. 91		
10	...	Kenneth Robert Balfour, *Adjutant Portsmouth Yeomanry Brigade* 20 Nov. 93		6 May 85	1 Aug. 92		
10	...	Francis Yorke M'Mahon		23 May 85	2 Aug. 92		
10	...	John Wreford Julian Hardman, *Adjutant* 22 Dec. 94		29 Aug. 85	31 Aug. 93		
8	...	John William Massey Wood	5 Nov. 87	20 May 91	27 June 94		
8	...	*Prince* Victor Albert Jay Duleep Singh	22 Feb. 88	26 Aug. 91	27 June 94		
7	...	*H.S.H. Prince* Francis Joseph Leopold Frederick *of* Teck	30 Jan. 89	26 Aug. 91	25 July 94		
11	...	Hon. Henry William Mansfield		11 Feb. 85	6 Apr. 94		
		LIEUTENANTS.					
4	...	Robert Wyld Trayner	9 Jan. 92	14 Dec. 92			
4	...	Ernest Makins	23 Jan. 92	31 Aug. 93			
3	...	Reginald Arthur Wombwell	24 Aug. 92	23 Sept. 93			
3	...	George Frederick Steele	7 Sept. 92	20 Nov. 93			
2	...	Hon. Arthur Hamilton-Russell	21 Oct. 93	27 June 94			
5	1	Roderick Beauclerk Webb (*2nd Lieut. S. Stafford Regt.* 6 July 89; *Lieut.* 28 Jan. 91)	20 Dec. 93	9 Jan. 95			
2	...	Henry Donald M'Neile	31 Jan. 94	9 Jan. 95			
1	...	Thomas Morton Stanhope Pitt	20 June 94	27 Feb. 95			
		SECOND LIEUTENANTS.					
1	...	Charles Archibald Calvert	12 Dec. 94				
1	...	Hon. Christian Henry Charles Guest	12 Dec. 94				
1	...	Edward York	12 Dec. 94				
12	...	*Riding Master.*—William Robert Banting, 25 July 83; *Hon. Captain,* 25 July 93.					
15	...	*Quarter Master.*—Humphrey Lakin Webb, 8 May 80; *Hon. Captain,* 8 May 90.					

Scarlet—*Facings* Blue.—*Agents,* Messrs. Cox and Co.
Returned from the Crimea, 27 May 1856.

[1] Lt. General Marshall served in the Crimea from 1st to 26th Sept. 1855, as Aide de Camp to Sir James Scarlett (Medal with Clasp for Sebastopol, and Turkish Medal). Served in the Zulu war of 1879 in command of the Cavalry Brigade, and after the dissolution of the Brigade commanded the advanced posts on the Lines of Communication (Medal with Clasp, and *CMG.*).

[4] Major Burn Murdoch served in the Nile Expedition in 1884-85 with the Royal Dragoons Detachment of the Camel Corps; commanded a Transport Company in the first march to Gakdul; was present at the action of Abu Klea, and commanded the detachment in the engagement at El Gubat (Medal with two Clasps, and Khedive's Star).

[5] Captain Burn served with the Hazara Expedition in 1888 as Orderly Officer to Major General M'Queen, Commanding the Hazara Field Force (mentioned in despatches, Medal with Clasp).

2nd Dragoons (Royal Scots Greys). — Aldershot.

The Thistle within the Circle and Motto of St. Andrew. An Eagle. "Second to None."—"BLENHEIM" "RAMILLIES" "OUDENARDE" "MALPLAQUET" "DETTINGEN" "WATERLOO" "BALAKLAVA" "SEVASTOPOL."

Colonel in Chief.—*His Imperial Majesty* Nicholas II. *Emperor of* Russia, 8 Dec. 94.
Colonel.—George Calvert Clarke,[1] *CB. Ensign,* P 30 May 34; *Lt.* P 7 Oct. 36; *Capt.* P 20 Sept. 39; *Bt. Major,* 11 Nov. 51; *Bt.Lt.Colonel,* 12 Dec. 54; *Major,* 26 Feb. 58; *Colonel,* 23 Apr. 60; *Lt.Colonel,* 31 March 66; *Major General,* 6 March 68; *Lieut.General,* 1 Oct. 77; *General,* 1 July 81; *Colonel* 6 Dragoon Guards, 4 Oct. 80; *Colonel* 2 Dragoons, 23 Sept. 91.
Lieutenant Colonel.—Alfred Cholmeley Earle Welby, *Cornet,* P 16 Oct. 67; *Lt.* P 7 Dec. 70; *Capt.* 1 Apr. 76; *Major,* 21 Oct. 85; *Lt.Colonel,* 5 July 92.

Years' Ser. Full Pay.	Half Pay.		CORNET OR 2ND LIEUT.	LIEUT.	CAPTAIN.	BREV. MAJ.	MAJOR.
		MAJORS.					
27	...	Hon. Walter Philip Alexander	P 3 Feb. 69	P 10 May 71	24 Nov. 77	......	5 July 86
20	...	William Henry Hippisley[7]		22 May 75	1 June 84		28 June 93
18	...	William Crawford Middleton[8]	13 Mar. 78	6 May 80	21 Oct. 85	......	9 Jan. 95
		CAPTAINS.					
16	...	Henry Jenner Scobell, *Adjutant Wiltshire Yeomanry Cavalry* 9 Oct. 89	13 Aug. 79	10 Nov. 80	27 Jan. 86		
16	...	Arthur William Mordaunt Richards	6 Aug. 79	22 Dec. 80	3 July 86		
15	...	Francis Henry Toovey Hawley, *Adjutant* 18 Jan. 92	11 Aug. 80	29 June 81	1 Oct. 87		
15	...	Robert Henry Adams, *serving with the Egyptian Army*	19 Feb. 81	1 July 81	9 Oct. 85		
13	...	John Crabbie		10 May 82	9 Oct. 85		
13	...	Cecil William Montague Feilden, *Aide de Camp to the Lord Lt. of Ireland* 3 Oct. 92		2 Aug. 82	14 Feb. 91		
16	...	Francis Blake Simpson, *Ordnance Store Department*	13 Aug. 79	1 July 81	19 Aug. 91		
11	...	Charles James Maxwell		16 Apr. 84	19 Aug. 91		
11	...	Alfred Douglas Miller		7 Feb. 85	28 June 93		
9	...	Charles Bulkeley Bulkeley-Johnson	5 Feb. 87	16 Mar. 89	13 June 94		
		LIEUTENANTS.					
8	...	Eustace Addison Maude	24 Aug. 87	16 Mar. 89			
7	...	William Fellowes Collins	6 Feb. 89	15 Oct. 90			
6	...	John Collinson Harrison	5 June 89	23 May 91			
6	...	Patrick Moir-Byres, *serving with Lagos Constabulary*	23 Oct. 89	19 Aug. 91			
6	...	Edward Ussher	29 Mar. 90	21 Sept. 91			
3	...	Algernon Lawson	28 Dec. 92	25 Apr. 94			
2	...	Thomas Conolly	28 June 93	5 Dec. 94			
2	...	Arthur Campbell Duckworth	23 Dec. 93	5 Dec. 94			
		SECOND LIEUTENANTS.					
1	...	Hon. Robert Hamilton Lindsay	10 Oct. 94				
1	...	Christopher Erle	12 Dec. 94				
1	...	William Donald Paul Watson	12 Dec. 94				
1	...	Alwyn William Jennings Bramly	6 Mar. 95				
5	...	*Riding Master.*—Frederick Fanstone, 9 July 90; *Hon. Lieut.*					
2	...	*Quarter Master.*—Peter Fraser Fleming, 21 Feb. 94; *Hon. Lieut.*					

Scarlet—*Facings* Blue.—*Agents,* Messrs. Cox and Co.
Returned from the Crimea, 4 July 1856.

[1] General Clarke served the Eastern campaign of 1854-55 with the Scots Greys, including the affair of M'Kenzie's Farm, battles of Balaklava (sabre cut on the neck), Inkerman, and Tchernaya, siege and fall of Sebastopol (Medal with three Clasps, Brevet of Lt.Colonel, Knight of the Legion of Honor, 5th Class of the Medjidie, and Turkish Medal).

[7] Major Hippisley served with the King's Dragoon Guards in the Zulu war of 1879 in the squadron under Major Marter, including the cavalry affair at Ezungayan (Medal with Clasp). Accompanied the reinforcements sent to South Africa during the Boer war of 1881, and served as Staff Officer of Pine Town Camp. Served with the Nile Expedition in 1884-85 in command of a detachment of the Scots Greys attached to the Heavy Camel Regiment, and took part in the operations of the Desert Column, including the actions at Abu Klea and Abu Kru and the reconnaissance to Metammeh; was appointed Adjutant to the Heavy Camel Regiment after Lord St. Vincent had been killed in action (Medal with two Clasps, and Khedive's Star).

[8] Major Middleton served in the Nile Expedition in 1884-85 with the Heavy Camel Regiment (Medal, with Clasp, and Khedive's Star).

Record of the Services of the Royal Scots Greys (formerly "The Royal Regiment of Scots Dragoons" and "The Royal North British Dragoons").

Raised in Scotland in 1678, and proceeded to Flanders in 1694. To Scotland, 1698. To Holland, 1702 (battles of Blenheim, Ramillies, Oudenarde and Malplaquet). To England, 1713. To the Continent, 1743. To England, 1748. To Germany, 1758. To England, 1763. Four troops to Holland, 1793 to 1795. The Regiment embarked for Belgium, 1815 (battle of Waterloo). To England, 1816. To the Crimea, 1854 (battle of Balaklava and siege of Sebastopol). To England, 1855. To Ireland, 1856. To Scotland, 1861. To England, 1863. To Ireland, 1865. To Scotland, 1871. To England, 1873. To Ireland, 1878. To Scotland, 1883. To England, 1885. To Ireland, 1888.

3rd (*The King's Own*) Hussars. [Newbridge.

The White Horse within the Garter. "*Nec aspera terrent.*" "DETTINGEN" "SALAMANCA" "VITTORIA" "TOULOUSE" "PENINSULA" "CABOOL, 1842" "MOODKEE" "FEROZESHAH" "SOBRAON" "PUNJAUB" "CHILLIANWALLAH" "GOOJERAT."

Years' Ser.			CORNET OR 2ND LIEUT.	LIEUT.	CAPTAIN.	BREV.MAJ.	MAJOR.
Full Pay	Half Pay	Colonel.—Edward Howard-Vyse, Cornet, P21 Aug. 49; Lieut. P3 Feb. 54; Captain, P17 Feb. 57; Major, P10 June 62 ; Lt. Colonel, P18 Oct. 64 ; Colonel, 18 Oct. 69; Major General, 25 Apr. 80 ; Lt. General, 25 Apr. 85 ; Colonel 3 Hussars, 23 Sept. 91.					
32	...	Lieutenant Colonel.—Charles William Hawker Helyar, Cornet, P2 Feb. 64 ; Lieut. P1 Dec. 65; Capt. P31 Oct. 71; Major, 15 Oct. 81 ; Lt. Colonel, 15 Apr. 91.					
		MAJORS.					
23	...	Robert Gustavus Alexander		26 Mar. 73	19 Sept. 81	......	9 Mar. 86
24	...	Arthur James Ramsay Van Cortlandt	28 Oct. 71	28 Oct. 71	15 Oct. 81	......	10 Aug 92
18	...	James Selby Robson Scott[1]	21 April 77	4 Dec. 79	18 July 85	......	17 Aug. 92
		CAPTAINS.					
19	...	p.s.c. Frank William Nicholas Wogan-Browne		30 Nov. 76	15 Aug. 85		
17	...	St. Clair Oswald	14 Sept. 78	29 June 81	17 Oct. 85		
17	...	Herbert Bethune Patton-Bethune[8]	22 Jan. 79	1 July 81	13 Apr. 87		
17	...	Duncan Vernon Pirie[10]	7 June 79	4 Dec. 82	16 Dec. 85		
10	...	John William Burns, *Aide de Camp to the Lord Lieutenant of Ireland* 15 Jan. 94		25 Nov. 85	13 Feb. 91		
12	...	Philip Fogarty Dwyer,[11] *D.A.A. General, Remount Establishment*, 10 Apr. 91		19 Mar. 84	25 Mar. 91		
10	...	Walter Goring, **Adjutant** 27 Oct. 91		25 Nov. 85	10 Apr. 91		
8	...	William Scott Stewart	16 Nov. 87	8 May 89	16 Nov. 92		
		LIEUTENANTS.					
7	...	Edmund Charles Hamilton	5 Sept. 88	22 Oct. 90			
7	...	Walter Graham Murray	30 Jan. 89	23 May 91			
4	...	Alfred Alexander Kennedy	10 Oct. 91	16 Nov. 92			
4	...	William Maitland Tower	9 Jan. 92	16 Nov. 92			
3	...	Albert Maitland Tabor	17 Dec. 92	6 Dec. 93			
3	...	Mounteney Kortright	25 Jan. 93	21 Feb. 94			
2	...	Alfred James Arnold, *serving under the Royal Niger Company*	23 Aug. 93	25 July 94			
2	...	Henry Charlton Chaworth-Musters	9 Sept. 93	12 Dec. 94			
		SECOND LIEUTENANTS.					
2	...	Eugene Felix Simeon Aron	23 Dec. 93				
1	...	Clement William Onley Unthank	12 Dec. 94				
1	...	Gerald Hugh Charles Madden	29 Dec. 94				
1	...	John Guy Baron Lethbridge	6 Feb. 95				
16	...	*Riding Master.*—Harry Richard James Willis, 13 March 80 ; *Hon. Captain*, 13 March 90.					
4	...	*Quarter Master.*—Frederick Durman, 4 Feb. 92 ; *Hon. Lieut.*					

Blue—*Facings* Scarlet.—*Agents*, Messrs. Cox and Co.
Returned from India, 1879.

[1] Major Scott served with the 19th Hussars in the Egyptian war of 1882, and was present at the action at Kassasin on the 28th August (Medal, and Khedive's Star). Served throughout the Nile Expedition in 1884-85 with the Light Camel Regiment, and took part in the operations of the Desert Column (Clasp).

[8] Captain Patton-Bethune served in the Boer war of 1881 as a volunteer attached to the Inniskilling Dragoons. Served as a volunteer attached to the 4th Dragoon Guards in the Egyptian war of 1882, and was present in the engagement at Mahsama, the two actions at Kassasin, the battle of Tel-el-Kebir and the capture of Cairo (Medal with Clasp, and Khedive's Star).

[10] Captain Pirie served with the 4th Dragoon Guards in the Egyptian war of 1882, and was present in the engagements at El Magfar and Mahsama, and at the two actions at Kassasin (mentioned in despatches, Medal, and Khedive's Star) ; also served with the Soudan Expedition under Sir Gerald Graham in 1884 with the Staff of the Cavalry Brigade, and was present in the engagements at El Teb and Temai (two Clasps). Served with the Nile Expedition in 1884-85 as Boat Officer and subsequently as Staff Officer to the Cavalry with the River Column under Major General Earle, and was present in the action at Kirbekan (mentioned in despatches, two Clasps).

[11] Captain Dwyer served in the Zulu war in 1879 with the 17th Lancers, and was present in the engagement at Ulundi (Medal with Clasp).

Record of the Services of the 3rd (King's Own) Hussars.

Raised in 1685. To Holland, 1694. To England, 1697. To Spain, 1702, and returned same year. To Spain, 1707. To England, 1708. To Germany, 1712. To England, 1745. To France, 1758, and returned same year. To Holland, 1809, and returned same year. To Spain, 1811. To England, 1814. To France, 1815. To England, 1818. To India, 1837. To England, 1852. To India, 1868. To England, 1879.

4th (*The Queen's Own*) Hussars

"DETTINGEN" "TALAVERA" "ALBUHERA" "SALAMANCA" "VITTORIA" "TOULOUSE" "PENINSULA" "AFGHANISTAN" "GHUZNEE" "ALMA" "BALAKLAVA" "INKERMAN" "SEVASTOPOL."

Colonel.—Alexander Low,[1] *CB. Cornet,* P 2 Oct. 35; *Lt.* P 6 July 38; *Capt.* P 14 July 43; *Bt. Major,* 20 June 54; *Major,* 26 Oct. 54; *Bt.Lt.Colonel,* 12 Dec. 54; *Lt. Colonel,* 1 May 57; *Major General,* 6 March 68; *Lieutenant General,* 1 Oct. 77; *General,* 22 May 80; *Colonel* 4th Hussars, 27 Oct. 81.

Lieutenant Colonel.—John Palmer Brabazon, *CB.*[2] *Aide de Camp to the Queen; Lieut.* 13 June 74; *Captain,* 13 Nov. 79; *Brevet Major,* 2 Mar. 81; *Major,* 10 Aug. 89; *Bt.Lt.Colonel,* 21 May 84; *Colonel,* 28 Aug. 89; *Lt. Colonel,* 12 Feb. 91.

Years' Ser. Full Pay	Half Pay		CORNET OR 2ND LIEUT.		LIEUT.		CAPTAIN.		BREV. MAJ.		MAJOR.	
		MAJORS.										
26	...	William Alexander Ramsay	P 1 Sept.	69	P 14 Jan.	71	2 Mar.	79			21 May	84
21	...	Francis Campbell Pearson			2 Dec.	74	9 Sept.	80			13 May	91
21	...	*p.s.c.* Cecil Wyburn Peters,[4] *Brigade Major, Aldershot,* 10 March 94			11 Feb.	75	27 April	81	15 June	85	4 Nov.	91
		CAPTAINS.										
17	...	Edward Asheton Critchley, *Adj. Shropshire Yeomanry Cavalry* 1 May 90	22 Jan.	79	9 Sept.	80	25 July	85				
16	...	Ronald Kincaid-Smith[5]	27 Aug.	79	27 April	81	6 Feb.	87				
14	...	Lewis Edward Starkey[7]	23 Apr.	81	1 July	81	17 Dec.	87				
13	...	Frederick David Baillie			29 July	82	1 July	88				
13	...	Hon. Frederick Rossmore Wauchope Eveleigh-de Moleyns, **Adjutant** 10 May 93			9 Sept.	82	1 May	90				
10	...	Reginald Hoare			30 Jan.	86	10 May	93				
9	...	Francis Lee, *Aide de Camp to Sir F. W. E. F. Walker* 21 Oct. 93			1 Sept.	86	10 Mar.	94				
8	...	Edgar Mortimore Lafone	11 Feb.	88	6 Nov.	89	17 Oct.	94				
8	...	Daniel Pearce Sunderland[8]	17 Aug.	87	6 Feb.	89	6 Feb.	95				
8	...	Joseph William Underwood	29 Feb.	88	18 Dec.	89	13 Feb.	95				
		LIEUTENANTS.										
7	...	Charles Lanfear Graham	29 Dec.	88	3 Sept.	90						
6	...	Arthure Lockwood Trevor-Boothe	23 Oct.	89	13 May	91						
6	...	Alan Ogilvie Francis	23 Oct.	89	4 Nov.	91						
5	...	Reginald Walter Ralph Barnes	31 Dec.	90	10 May	93						
4	...	Charles Henry Brydges Gaine, *serving under the Royal Niger Company*	23 Jan.	92	21 Oct.	93						
3	...	Albert Savory	12 Oct.	92	10 Mar.	94						
		SECOND LIEUTENANTS.										
1	...	Henry George Watkin	10 Oct.	94								
1	...	Henry James Frank Newbould	10 Oct.	94								
1	...	Edmund Ricardo Clutterbuck	10 Oct.	94								
1	...	William Edward Long	12 Dec.	94								
1	...	Winston Leonard Spencer Churchill	20 Feb.	95								
21	...	*Riding Master.*—Hugh Ernest Elliott, 30 Sept. 74; *Honorary Captain,* 30 Sept. 84.										
11	...	*Quarter Master.*—John Rhodes, 26 Oct. 84; *Hon. Captain,* 26 Oct. 94.										

Blue.—*Agents,* Messrs. Cox and Co.
Returned from India, 1878.

[1] General Low served the Eastern campaign of 1854-55, including the battles of Alma, Balaklava, Inkerman, and Tchernaya, siege and fall of Sebastopol, also present with the Light Cavalry Brigade at Eupatoria; at Inkerman he commanded the Regiment (Medal with four Clasps, Brevet of Lt. Colonel, Knight of the Legion of Honor, Sardinian and Turkish Medals, and 4th Class of the Medjidie).

[2] Colonel Brabazon, formerly Lieut. and Captain Grenadier Guards, served as a volunteer in the Ashanti war in 1874 and was attached to the expedition under Captain Butler to Western Akim, and afterwards to the Transport service (Medal with Clasp). Served in the Afghan war of 1878-80, first with the 10th Hussars; afterwards as Officiating Brigade Major and Staff Officer of Cavalry Brigade Koorum Field Force, and was present at the capture of the Peiwar Kotal, in the operations in the Khost Valley, in the engagement at Charasiab on the 6th October 1879, and in the operations around Cabul in December 1879 including the investment of Sherpore; accompanied Sir Frederick Roberts in the march to Candahar as Brigade Major of Cavalry, and was present also in the reconnaissance of the 31st August and at the battle of Candahar (several times mentioned in despatches, Brevet of Major, Medal with four Clasps, and Bronze Decoration). Served in the Soudan Expedition in 1884 with the 10th Hussars, and was present in the engagements at El Teb and Temai (Brevet of Lt. Colonel, Medal with Clasp, and Khedive's Star). Served throughout the Nile Expedition in 1884-85 with the Light Camel Regiment, and took part in the operations of the Desert Column including the engagement at Abu Klea Wells on the 16th and 17th February (Clasp).

[4] Major Peters served throughout the Nile Expedition in 1884-85 with the Light Camel Regiment as Quarter Master, and took part in the operations of the Desert Column including the engagement at Abu Klea Wells on the 16th and 17th February (mentioned in despatches, Brevet of Major, Medal with Clasp, and Khedive's Star).

[5] Captain Kincaid-Smith served throughout the Nile Expedition in 1884-85 with the Light Camel Regiment, took part in the operations of the Desert Column, and was present at the action at Abu Klea (Medal with two Clasps, and Khedive's Star).

[7] Captain Starkey served in the Egyptian war of 1882 attached to the 4th Dragoon Guards, and was present at the battle of Tel-el-Kebir (Medal with Clasp, and Khedive's Star).

[8] Captain Sunderland served with the Burmese Expedition in 1885-87 (Medal with Clasp).

5th (Royal Irish) Lancers.

{Muttra, Bengal.
Depot, Canterbury.

The Harp and Crown. "*Quis Separabit?*"—"BLENHEIM" "RAMILLIES" "OUDENARDE" "MALPLAQUET" "SUAKIN, 1885."

Colonel.—*Hon.* Charles Wemyss Thesiger,[1] *Cornet*, P5 Aug. 53; *Lieut.* P30 Dec. 53; *Capt.* P2 July 58 ‡. *Major*, P3 Dec. 61; *Lt.Colonel*, P2 Dec. 68; *Colonel*, 2 Dec. 73; *MajorGeneral*, 7 Oct. 84; *Lieut.General*, 1 Apr. 91; *Colonel* 5th Lancers, 24 Jan. 92.

Lieutenant Colonel.—John James Scott Chisholme,[6] *Lieut.* 10 Jan. 72; *Captain*, 2 Mar. 78; *Brevet Major*, 2 Mar. 81; *Major*, 15 Dec. 84; *Lt.Colonel*, 12 Aug. 94.

Years Ser. Full / Half Pay			2ND LIEUT.	LIEUT.	CAPTAIN.	BREV.MAJ.	MAJOR.
		MAJORS.					
17	...	James Farish Malcolm Fawcett............	1 May 78	30 June 81	9 June 84	......	19 Aug. 92
15	...	Hubert James M'Laughlin[12]	11 Aug. 80	1 July 81	30 May 88	......	1 Jan. 93
18	...	Frank James Carandini[13].................	23 Jan. 78	1 July 81	1 Apr. 84	......	1 Mar. 93
15	...	Augustus Carter King[16]..................	23 Oct. 80	1 July 81	21 Aug. 89	......	12 Aug. 94
		CAPTAINS.					
12	...	Mordaunt Berners Doyne[17]...............	......	30 Jan. 84	6 Nov. 89		
11	...	Robert John Spurrell,[15] *Adjutant Nagpore Rifle Volunteers* 15 Mar. 92	......	2 July 84	2 July 92		
12	...	Herman Witsius Gore Graham,[18] *DSO. Staff College*	......	5 Mar. 84	2 July 92		
11	...	Henry Vincent Bailey, **Adjutant** 9 May 92	......	14 May 84	2 July 92		
10	7/12	Wilfrid Edward Russell Collis, *Adjutant 4 Yeomanry Brigade* 28 Oct. 94	......	12 Nov. 84	9 Nov. 92		
13	...	p.s.c. Edward Owen Wathen[19]	......	10 May 82	18 Jan. 89		
8	...	Arthur Parker. *(Depot)*	16 Nov. 87	8 May 89	12 Aug. 94		
9	...	William Augustus Adams..................	5 Feb. 87	31 July 89	4 Nov. 93		
8	...	Edwin Bryce Wilson	16 Nov. 87	3 July 89	28 Oct. 94		
		LIEUTENANTS.					
8	...	Montague Percy Rowland Oakes	16 Nov. 87	26 Mar. 90			
7	...	John Barclay Scriven.....................	3 Oct. 88	14 Mar. 90			
7	...	Alexander Vaughan Leipzic Wood	3 Oct. 88	10 Sept. 90			
7	...	Ernest Edward West	10 Nov. 88	29 Apr. 91			
7	...	Harold Hatton Hulse	30 Jan. 89	9 Mar. 92			
6	...	John Alexander M'Lean	8 June 89	22 June 92			
6	...	James Bruce Jardine	12 Mar. 90	2 July 92			
5	...	Reginald Preston Jermy Gwyn............	31 May 90	7 Sept. 92			
5	...	Robert Clayton Browne-Clayton.........	24 Dec. 90	12 Aug. 94			
4	...	Cyril Harry Haworth....................	30 May 91	28 Oct. 94			
		SECOND LIEUTENANTS.					
5	...	Charles Theobald Mathew	11 Mar. 91				
3	...	John Hodgkinson	18 June 92				
3	...	Henry Urmston Bell	21 Sept. 92				
3	...	Gerald FitzGerald	5 Oct. 92				
2	...	Walter Temple Willcox	8 Nov. 93				
1	...	Wm. Maurice Copland DuQuesne Caillard	10 Oct. 94				
1	...	Cyril Arkwright	10 Oct. 94				
1	...	Maxwell Fielding McTaggart............	20 Feb. 95				

Paymaster.—*Lieut.* J. B. Scriven *(acting).*
7 ... **Riding Master.**—Henry Payne, 18 July 88; *Hon. Lieut.*
6 ... **Quarter Master.**—George Waterman, 15 Feb. 88; *Hon. Lieut.*

Blue.—*Facings* Scarlet.—*Agents*, Messrs. Cox and Co.
Embarked for India, 21 November 1888.

[1] Lieut.General the Hon. C. W. Thesiger acted as Orderly Officer to Brigadier Pattle commanding the Cavalry Brigade during the campaign of 1860 in China, and was present at the affairs of the 12th August, 18th and 21st Sept. and capture of Pekin (Medal with two Clasps).

[6] Lt.Colonel Chisholme served with the 9th Lancers in the Afghan war of 1878-80, and was present at the capture of Ali Musjid, in the affair at Siah Sung (severely wounded), and in the operations around Cabul in December 1879—wounded (mentioned in despatches, Brevet of Major, Medal with two Clasps).

[12] Major M'Laughlin served in the Boer war of 1880-81, and took part in the defence of Standerton. Served in the Nile Expedition in 1884-85 with the 19th Hussars (Medal with Clasp, and Khedive's Star).

[13] Major Carandini served in the Afghan war in 1879-80 with the 8th Hussars (Medal).

[15] Captain Spurrell served with the Hazara Expedition in 1891 as Provost Marshal 2nd Brigade (mentioned in despatches, Medal with Clasp).

[16] Major King served in the Burmese Expedition in 1885-87 with the 1st Battalion Royal Welsh Fusiliers and was present in the engagement at Yuatho (where he commanded), at the relief of Thila as Staff Officer, and in the expedition to Woonthoo (mentioned in despatches, Medal with Clasp).

[17] Captain Doyne served with the expedition to the Soudan in 1885, and was present in the engagements at Hasheen and the Tofrek zereba, and at the destruction of Temai (Medal with two Clasps, and Khedive's Star).

[18] Captain Graham served in the operations against the Awunahs, on the West Coast of Africa, in 1889 (mentioned in despatches, *DSO.*).

[19] Captain Wathen served with the Burmese Expedition in 1886-87 (Medal with Clasp).

Manchester.] **6th (*Inniskilling*) Dragoons.** 148

The Castle of Inniskilling with the St. George's Colours, and the word "Inniskilling" underneath.
"DETTINGEN" "WATERLOO" "BALAKLAVA" "SEVASTOPOL."

Years'Ser. Full Pay.	Half Pay.		2ND LIEUT.	LIEUT.	CAPTAIN.	BREV.MAJ.	MAJOR.
		Colonel.—Sir Charles Cameron Shute,[1] KCB., Cornet, P 19 July 34; Lt. P 13 May 39; Capt. P 5 Mar. 47; Major, 1 June 54; Bt.Lt.Colonel, 12 Dec. 54; Lt.Colonel, P 19 Feb. 58; Colonel, 21 Sept. 58; Major General, 6 Mar. 68; Lieut.General, 1 Oct. 77; General, 1 July 81; Colonel 6th Dragoons, 28 March 86.					
24	...	Lieutenant Colonel.—Alexander Chalmers M'Kean,[6] CMG. Cornet, 28 Oct. 71; Lieut. 28 Oct. 71; Captain, 12 Nov. 78; Major, 23 Jan. 83; Bt.Lt.Colonel, 18 Oct. 88; Lt.Colonel, 17 Sept. 90; Colonel, 17 Sept. 94.					
		MAJORS.					
24	...	Andrew Green Thompson[7]	......	30 Dec. 71	1 Mar. 79	......	29 July 85
17	...	Henry Cockcroft Page-Henderson,[13]*Adj.* Worcester Yeomanry Cavalry 8 June 91..	......	11 Sept. 78	20 Oct. 83	......	26 Sept. 94
13	...	George O'Connor	......	9 Sept. 82	1 June 88	......	6 Mar. 95
		CAPTAINS.					
15	...	Charles Travers Breton,[14] *serving under the British South Africa Company*	22 Jan. 81	1 July 81	5 June 85		
14	...	Raleigh Grey, *serving with the Bechuanaland Police Force*	23 April 81	1 July 81	29 July 85		
14	...	Michael Frederic Rimington[16]	......	22 Oct. 81	26 Oct. 87		
13	...	Edmund Henry Hynman Allenby[17]	......	10 May 82	10 Jan. 83		
13	...	John Watkins Yardley[15]	......	10 May 82	17 Oct. 88		
12	...	Guy Lindsey Jennings-Bramly,[15] *Army Pay Department*	......	31 Oct. 83	16 Nov. 88		
11	...	Camborne Haweis Paynter	......	23 Aug. 84	8 May 89		
11	...	Arthur Rowland Mosley[18]	......	12 Nov. 84	23 May 91		
12	...	John Christian Appold Anstice, Adjutant 12 July 93	......	25 Aug. 83	8 Sept. 88		
11	...	James William Gully Philip Jeffcock	......	28 Feb. 85	7 Feb. 94		
		LIEUTENANTS.					
9	...	Edmund Arthur Herbert, *Aide de Camp to Governor of Straits Settlements* 5 Jan. 94	......	10 Nov. 86			
10	...	Edmund Sylvester Jackson	......	29 Aug. 85			
8	...	James Stevenson-Hamilton	14 Mar. 88	20 Feb. 90			
5	...	Frederick Arthur Bashford Fryer	8 Oct. 90	17 Feb. 92			
5	...	Ernest Charles Holland	4 Mar. 91	17 Aug. 92			
4	...	Neil Wolseley Haig	30 May 91	17 Aug. 92			
4	...	Arthur Francis Morse	10 Oct. 91	8 Feb. 93			
4	...	Cuthbert Francis Dixon-Johnson	28 Oct. 91	30 Aug. 93			
3	...	Francis Salisbury Atkinson, *Army Service Corps*	25 Jan. 93	5 Jan. 94			
2	...	Ewing Paterson	9 Sept. 93	1 Jan. 95			
		SECOND LIEUTENANTS.					
1	...	George Kirkpatrick Ansell	18 Apr. 94				
1	...	Chippindall Holmes Higgin	2 June 94				
1	...	Edward Maunsell Bruce	6 Mar. 95				
3	...	Riding Master.—Alfred Charles Shawyer, 28 Dec. 92; *Hon. Lieut.*					
1	...	Quarter Master.—Thomas Humphreys, 15 Aug. 94; *Hon. Lieut.*					

Scarlet—*Facings* Yellow.—*Agents*, Messrs. Cox and Co.
Returned from South Africa, 13 Nov. 1890.

[1] Sir Charles Shute acted as Adjutant with the right wing of the 13th Light Dragoons in the campaign against the Rajah of Kurnool, East Indies, in 1839. Served with the 6th Dragoons the Eastern campaign of 1854-56 as Assistant Adjutant General of the Cavalry Division from 23rd Nov. 1854 to 2nd July 1856, when the division was finally broken up, including the battles of Balaklava (mentioned in Sir James Scarlett's despatch) and Inkerman, siege and fall of Sebastopol, night attack on the Russian outposts on the 19th Feb. 1855, and battle of the Tchernaya (Medal with three Clasps, Brevet of Lt.Colonel, Knight of the Legion of Honor, 5th Class of the Medjidie, Turkish Medal, and CB.).
[6] Colonel M'Kean served with the Inniskilling Dragoons in the Boer war of 1881. Served in the operations in Zululand in 1888 (Brevet of Lt.Colonel).
[7] Major Thompson served with the Inniskilling Dragoons in the Boer war of 1881.
[13] Major Page-Henderson served in the Boer war of 1881 with the Inniskilling Dragoons. Served in the Bechuanaland Expedition under Sir Charles Warren in 1884-85 with the Inniskilling Dragoons.
[14] Captain Breton served in the Boer war of 1881. Served with the Bechuanaland Expedition under Sir Charles Warren in 1884-85 with the Inniskilling Fusiliers. Served in the operations in Zululand in 1888.
[15] Captains Yardley and Jennings-Bramly served with the Bechuanaland Expedition under Sir Charles Warren in 1884-85 with the Inniskilling Dragoons.
[16] Captain Rimington served with the Bechuanaland Expedition under Sir Charles Warren in 1884-85 with the Inniskilling Dragoons. Served in the operations in Zululand in 1888 as Adjutant Inniskilling Dragoons.
[17] Captain Allenby served with the Bechuanaland Expedition under Sir Charles Warren in 1884-85 with the Inniskilling Dragoons. Served in the operations in Zululand in 1888.
[18] Captain Mosley served in the operations in Zululand in 1888.

Record of the Services of the 6th (*Inniskilling*) *Dragoons.*

Raised in 1689 and served in Ireland till 1763. To England, 1763. To the Low Countries, 1793 (battle of Dettingen). To England, 1797. To Scotland, 1808. To Ireland, 1809. To England, 1814. To Belgium and France, 1815 (battle of Waterloo). To England and Scotland, 1816. To Ireland, 1819. To Scotland, 1823. To England, 1824. To Ireland, 1829. To Scotland, 1833. To England, 1834. To Ireland, 1838. To England, 1841. To Scotland, 1842. To England, 1843. To Ireland, 1846. To Scotland, 1851. To England, 1852. To the Crimea, 1854 (battle of Balaklava and siege of Sebastopol). To England, 1856. To India, 1858. To England, 1866. To Ireland, 1871. To Scotland, 1877. To England, 1880. To South Africa 1881 (Boer war of 1881 and Bechuanaland Expedition in 1884-85). To England, 1890.

7th (The Queen's Own) Hussars. [Mhow, Bombay. Depot, Canterbury.

The Royal Cypher within the Garter. "DETTINGEN" "ORTHES" "PENINSULA" "WATERLOO" "LUCKNOW."

Years Ser. Full Pay	Half Pay						
31	...	Colonel.—William Thomas Dickson, *Cornet*, P23 April 47; *Lt.* P25 Feb. 48; *Capt.* P25 April 51; *Major*, P19 May 54; *Bt.Lt.Colonel*, 26 Oct. 58; *Lt.Colonel*, P3 Oct. 62; *Colonel*, 5 Jan. 64; *Major General*, 18 July 69; *Lieut.General*, 1 July 81; *Colonel* 7th Hussars, 19 July 84.						
		Lieutenant Colonel.—Harrie Archbold Reid, *Cornet*, P5 July 64; *Lieut.* 26 Nov. 68; *Captain*, P24 Dec. 70; *Major*, 19 Dec. 83; *Lt.Colonel*, 19 Dec. 93.						

		MAJORS.	CORNET OR 2ND LIEUT.	LIEUT.	CAPTAIN.	BREV.MAJ.	MAJOR.
27	...	p.s.c. Harold Paget[1]	P23 Jan. 69	P22 Feb. 71	23 July 79	15 June 85	5 May 86
22	...	Henry Matthew Ridley[7]	......	27 Mar. 74	19 Dec. 83	......	21 Feb. 90
20	...	Hon. Richard Thompson Lawley,[8] *Mil.Sec.* to *Governor of Madras* 23 Jan. 91	......	11 Feb. 76	21 July 85	......	5 May 93
21	...	George Alfred Penrhys Evans[10]	......	13 June 74	8 Aug. 80	......	19 Dec. 93
		CAPTAINS.					
16	...	Richard Lionel Walter	31 Jan. 80	1 July 81	15 Dec. 86		
12	...	George Albert Lade Carew	......	31 Oct. 83	19 Dec. 89		
12	...	John Sanctuary Nicholson	......	6 Feb. 84	23 Jan. 91		
10	...	Douglas Haig, *Aide de Camp to Lt.General J. K. Fraser*, 28 Apr. 94	......	7 Feb. 85	23 Jan. 91		
11	...	George Lewis Holdsworth	......	23 Aug. 84	6 Feb. 91		
17	...	Charles Hamlyn Agnew[11] (*Depot*)	1 May 78	1 Oct. 80	28 Aug. 86		
11	...	Claude Brittain FitzHenry[12]	......	14 May 84	11 May 91		
10	...	Bernhard Robert Liebert	......	17 Feb. 86	5 May 93		
		LIEUTENANTS.					
9	...	Robert Montagu Poore	......	28 Apr. 86			
9	...	Ronald George Brooke	......	13 Oct. 86			
9	...	Hon. John Graham Hope Horsley Beresford, **Adjutant** 25 July 92	5 Feb. 87	10 Apr. 89			
10	...	James Logan Stewart[13]	......	9 May 85			
8	...	Hon. Reginald Hastings Marsham, *Aide de Camp to Major General G. Luck* 4 Sept. 93	8 Feb. 88	1 Nov. 90			
7	...	Keith Alexander Fraser (*Depot*)	8 Dec. 88	4 July 91			
6	...	Charles Ernest Graham Norton	9 Oct. 89	15 Mar. 93			
6	...	Henry Barkly Dalgety	26 Feb. 90	5 May 93			
5	...	Harold Fielden	28 June 90	26 June 93			
5	...	John Fryer	26 Nov. 90	26 June 93			
5	...	John Vaughan	11 Mar. 91	4 Sept. 93			
4	...	Frederick William Wormald	29 Apr. 91	24 Oct. 94			
		SECOND LIEUTENANTS.					
2	...	Charles Herbert Rankin	21 Oct. 93				
2	...	Alexander Frederic Aimé Imbert-Terry	21 Oct. 93				
2	...	Hon. Charles Beresford Fulke Greville	23 Dec. 93				
2	...	Henry Arthur Johnstone	7 Mar. 94				
2	...	James Henry Edward Holford	7 Mar. 94				
1	...	H.S.H. Prince Alexander Aug. Fred. Wm. Alfred George of Teck	24 Oct. 94				
1	...	Lawrence Rawstorne	12 Dec. 94				

Paymaster.—Captain B. R. Liebert (*acting*).
| 7 | ... | *Riding Master.*—Harry Dibble, 31 Oct. 88 ; *Hon. Lieut.* |
| 19 | ... | *Quarter Master.*—William John Waite,[14] 11 Oct. 76 ; *Hon. Captain*, 11 Oct. 86. |

Blue.—*Agents*, Messrs. Cox and Co.
Embarked for India, 26 *Nov.* 1886.

[1] Major Paget served throughout the Nile Expedition in 1884-85 as Adjutant to the Light Camel Regiment, and took part in the operations of the Desert Column including the engagement at Abu Klea Wells on the 16th and 17th February—wounded (mentioned in despatches, Brevet of Major, Medal with Clasp, and Khedive's Star).

[7] Major Ridley served with the 19th Hussars in the Egyptian war of 1882, and was present in the action at Kassasin (9th September), and at the battle of Tel-el-Kebir (Medal with Clasp, and Khedive's Star).

[8] Major Hon. R. T. Lawley served throughout the Nile Expedition in 1884-85 with the Light Camel Regiment, and took part in the operations of the Desert Column including the engagement at Abu Klea Wells on the 16th and 17th February (Medal with Clasp, and Khedive's Star).

[10] Major Evans served in the Afghan war in 1879 with the 9th Lancers (Medal).

[11] Captain Agnew served in the Burmese Expedition in 1885-87 with the 2nd Battalion Royal Scots Fusiliers (Medal with Clasp).

[12] Captain FitzHenry served with the Nile Expedition in 1884-85, and was present at the action of Kirbekan (Medal with two Clasps, and Khedive's Star). Served with the Soudan Frontier Field Force during the operations on the Upper Nile in 1885-86.

[13] Lieut. Stewart served with the Burmese Expedition in 1887-88 on Transport duty (Medal with Clasp).

[14] Captain Waite served in a squadron of the 7th Hussars with the expedition against the Mohmund Tribes in 1863-64 under Colonel A. Macdonell (Medal with Clasp).

Hounslow.] **8th** (*The King's Royal Irish*) **Hussars.** 150

The Harp and Crown. "*Pristinæ virtutis memores.*"—"LESWARREE" "HINDOOSTAN" "ALMA" "BALAKLAVA" "INKERMAN" "SEVASTOPOL" "CENTRAL INDIA" "AFGHANISTAN, 1879-80."

Years'Ser.							
Full Pay	Half Pay						

Colonel.—VC Sir Charles Craufurd Fraser,[1] KCB., *Cornet*, P3 Dec. 47; *Lieut.* P14 June 50; *Capt.* P21 April 54; *Bt.Major*, 20 July 58; *Major*, P13 May 59; *Lt.Colonel*, P18 Jan. 61; *Colonel*, 18 Jan. 66; *Major General*, 25 July 70; *Lieut.General*, 1 Oct. 86; *Colonel* 8th Hussars, 25 June 86.

21 ... Lieutenant Colonel.—James Davidson,[5] *Lt.* 2 Dec. 74; *Capt.* 13 Apr. 81; *Major*, 14 Nov. 83; *Lt.Colonel*, 19 Oct. 92.

		MAJORS.	2ND LIEUT.	LIEUT.	CAPTAIN.	BREV.MAJ.	MAJOR.
20	...	Peter Legh Clowes[6]		20 Nov. 75	21 Feb. 83	......	2 Oct. 85
21	...	David Edward Wood,[7] *Staff Captain, Remount Establishment,* 1 July 92	......	28 Feb. 75	3 Oct. 83	......	19 Oct. 92
17	...	Charles Edward Duff[4]	11 May 78	1 July 81	19 Sept. 85	......	8 July 93
		CAPTAINS.					
15	...	Charles Nicholas Colthurst Vesey	23 Oct. 80	1 July 81	9 Dec. 85		
14	...	Philip Walter Jules Le Gallais, Adjutant 16 July 93	23 Apr. 81	1 July 81	19 Mar. 88		
13	...	Bryan Thomas Mahon, *serving with the Egyptian Army*	......	27 Jan. 83	19 Apr. 88		
12	...	Philip Langdale	......	25 Aug. 83	19 Oct. 92		
11	...	Harry Newman Morgan Thoyts	......	23 Aug. 84	1 Mar. 93		
10	...	John Acheson Henderson	......	6 May 85	8 July 93		
11	...	Henry Foulkes Deare	......	7 Feb. 85	17 Feb. 94		
9	...	Hervey Greathed	5 Feb. 87	18 Apr. 90	28 July 94		
9	...	Ernest Gordon Bedingfeld	5 Feb. 87	30 July 90	17 Oct. 94		
		LIEUTENANTS.					
8	...	David Murray Anderson	14 Sept. 87	25 Mar. 91			
7	...	Lincoln Sandwith	9 May 88	28 Apr. 91			
5	...	Francis William Mussendon	11 June 90	30 July 91			
4	...	Isaac William Burns-Lindow, *Superintendent of Gymnasia, S.E. Dist.* 22 Dec.94	9 Jan. 92	16 July 93			
4	...	Francis John Charles Howard	9 Jan. 92	16 July 93			
2	...	Louis Ferdinand Ricardo	9 Sept. 93	17 Oct. 94			
1	...	Maximilian de Bathe	4 Apr. 94	17 Oct. 94			
		SECOND LIEUTENANTS.					
1	...	Walter Boyd Chandless Burdon	18 Apr. 94				
1	...	Egerton Augustus Stafford O'Brien	2 June 94				
1	...	Hon. Christopher Edward Howard	29 Dec. 94				
1	...	Alan George Cameron Bruce	6 Mar. 95				

[4] Major Duff served in the Afghan war in 1879-80 with the 8th Hussars (Medal).
[7] Major Wood served with the 8th Hussars in the Afghan war in 1879-80, and took part in the Znimusht Expedition including the engagement at Mazeena (Medal)

8 ... *Riding Master.*—Edward Griffith Tomblings, 3 Aug. 87; *Hon. Lieut.*
5 ... *Quarter Master.*—Louis Cecil Page, 6 Dec. 90; *Hon. Lieut.*

Blue.—*Agents,* Messrs. Cox and Co.
Returned from Bengal, Nov. 1889.

[1] Sir Charles Fraser served as Orderly Officer to Brigadier Campbell at the affair of Munseata near Allahabad, on the 5th Jan. 1858, and subsequently with the 7th Hussars in the Indian Mutiny campaign from Feb. to July 1858, and from Dec. 1858 to March 1859, and was present at the affair of Meengunge, siege and capture of Lucknow, affairs of Barree and Sirsee (horse wounded), action of Nawabgunge (severely wounded whilst leading a squadron against a body of Gazzie fanatics, mentioned in Sir Hope Grant's despatch for "most conspicuous gallantry," Brevet of Major), throughout the Trans-Gogra campaign, including the affair near Churda and pursuit, taking the fort of Meejedia, attack on Bankee with pursuit to the Raptee, advance into Nepaul and affair at Sitkaghat (Victoria Cross, Medal with Clasp): received the VC "for conspicuous and cool gallantry, on the 31st December 1858, in having volunteered, at great personal risk, and under a sharp fire of musketry, to swim to the rescue of Captain Stisted and some men of the 7th Hussars, who were in imminent danger of being drowned in the River Raptee, while in pursuit of the rebels. Major Fraser succeeded in this gallant service, although at the time partially disabled, not having recovered from a severe wound received while leading a Squadron in a charge against some fanatics in the action of Nawabgunge, on the 13th June 1858." Served in the Abyssinian campaign in 1868 as Commandant at Head Quarters, and in charge of the outposts, and was present at the action of Arogee and capture of Magdala (mentioned in despatches "for unceasing vigilance," CB. and Medal). [See also Civil Decorations for Gallantry, "Hart's Annual Army List," p. 786.]

[5] Lt.Colonel Davidson served in the Egyptian war of 1882 with the 13th Bengal Lancers, and was present at the action at Kassasin (9th September) and at the battle of Tel-el-Kebir (Medal with Clasp, and Khedive's Star).

[6] Major Clowes served with the 8th Hussars in the Afghan war in 1879-80 including the engagement at Mazeena (Medal).

9th (The Queen's Royal) Lancers. [Aldershot.

The Royal Cypher within the Garter. "PENINSULA" "PUNNIAR" "SOBRAON" "PUNJAUB" "CHILLIANWALLAH" "GOOJERAT" "DELHI" "LUCKNOW" "CHARASIAH" "KABUL, 1879" "KANDAHAR, 1880" "AFGHANISTAN, 1878-80."

Colonel.—Sir William Drysdale,[1] *KCB. Cornet*, P29 Dec. 35; *Lt.* P31 Aug. 38; *Capt.* P29 Oct. 47; *Bt.Major*, 9 Jan. 58; *Major*, 5 March 58; *Bt.Lt.Colonel*, 20 July 58; *Lt.Colonel*, P24 May 61; *Colonel*, 20 June 64; *Major General*, 2 Jan. 70; *Lieut.General*, 1 July 81; *Colonel 18 Hussars*, 16 March 85; *Colonel 9 Lancers*, 11 June 91.

Lieutenant Colonel.—James Alexander Francis Humberston Stewart Mackenzie,[2] *Cornet*, P1 May 67; *Lieut.* P8 June 70; *Capt.* 15 July 76; *Bt.Major*, 2 Mar. 81; *Major*, 1 July 81; *Lt.Col.* 15 Dec. 90; *Colonel*, 15 Dec. 94.

Years' Ser.		MAJORS.	CORNET OR 2ND LIEUT.	LIEUT.	CAPTAIN.	BREV.MAJ.	MAJOR.
25	...	Bloomfield Gough[10]	P27 Apr. 70	28 Oct. 71	17 July 78	2 Mar. 81	8 Dec. 86
17	...	Malcolm Orme Little[18]	11 May 78	25 Feb. 80	20 Oct. 86		5 Sept. 94
20	...	Spencer Walpole Follett		20 Nov. 75	24 Aug. 81		13 Feb. 95
		CAPTAINS.					
16	...	Charles Bishop	13 Aug. 79	10 Nov. 80	8 Dec. 86		
15	...	Walter Kentish William Jenner	16 Oct. 80	1 July 81	23 May 88		
15	...	Forrester Farnell Colvin, *Adjutant* 1 *Yeomanry Brigade* 17 Sept. 94	23 Oct. 80	1 July 81	10 Aug. 88		
15	...	Frederick William Duff, *Adjutant* 11th *Yeomanry Brigade* 8 Sept. 93	19 Feb. 81	1 July 81	10 Mar. 89		
11	...	*Hon.* Claude Henry Comaraich Willoughby		12 Nov. 84	4 Dec. 89		
8	...	Frederick Thwaites Lund	17 Aug. 87	15 Feb. 88	11 May 92		
10	...	*Lord* Douglas Jas. Cecil Compton, *Aide de Camp to the Gov. of Madras* 16 Nov. 92		2 Sept. 85	5 Sept. 94		
9	...	Herbert Foster Wentworth Stanley	26 Feb. 87	21 Nov. 88	5 Sept. 94		
8	...	Henry Edw. Twisleton-Wykeham-Fiennes	30 Apr. 87	21 Nov. 88	17 Sept. 94		
		LIEUTENANTS.					
8	...	Gilbert Frank Henry	16 Nov. 87	5 June 89			
7	...	George Paget Ellison	22 Aug. 88	4 Jan. 90			
7	...	David Graham Mushiet Campbell	16 Mar. 89	9 Dec. 90			
6	...	*Lord* Charles Cavendish Bentinck, *A.D.C. to the Lord Lieutenant of Ireland* 6 Oct. 94	8 June 89	23 Jan. 91			
6	...	William Henry von Schröder	4 Dec. 89	1 Oct. 91			
4	...	Desmond John Edward Beale-Browne, *Adjutant* 13 March 95	30 May 91	1 Jan. 93			
4	...	Ernest Fitzroy Bell	5 Dec. 91	5 Sept. 94			
3	...	James Stewart Forbes	25 Jan. 93	7 Nov. 94			
		SECOND LIEUTENANTS.					
3	...	Frederick Henry Allhusen	25 Jan. 93				
1	...	Thomas Malcolm Harvey Kincaid-Smith	10 Oct. 94				
1	...	Victor Reginald Brooke	12 Dec. 94				
1	...	*Riding Master.*—George Parker, 27 Feb. 95; *Hon. Lieut.*					
2	...	*Quarter Master.*—David Laing, 23 Dec. 93; *Hon. Lieut.*					

Blue—*Facings* Scarlet.—*Agents*, Messrs. Cox and Co.
Returned from India, 23 Nov. 1885.

[1] Sir William Drysdale served with the 4th Light Dragoons during the campaign in Affghanistan under Lord Keane, and was present at the siege and capture of Ghuznee (Medal). Served with the 9th Lancers in the Gwalior campaign, including the action at Punniar, 29th Dec. 1843 (Bronze Star). The Sutlej campaign in 1845-46, including the battle of Sobraon (Medal and Clasp). The Punjaub campaign of 1848-49, including the passage of the Chenab at Ramnuggur, and battles of Chillianwallah and Goojerat (Medal with two Clasps). The Indian campaign of 1857-59, and present at Delhi during the siege operations, commanding the Regt. from 18th Aug. to the fall of the city—horse shot at the assault; commanded the Regt. with Greathed's Column, in action at Bolundshuhur, horse shot (wounded), and present in the actions of Allyghur and Agra (mentioned in despatch); also present at the relief of Lucknow (Brevet of Lt.-Colonel, CB., Medal with two Clasps).

[2] Colonel Mackenzie served with the 9th Lancers in the Afghan war of 1878-80, and took part with the Bazar Valley Expedition, the expedition to Maidan, the affair at Killa Kazi (when he brought the regiment out of action, and was severely wounded), and in the operations around Cabul in December 1879 (mentioned in despatches); accompanied Sir Frederick Roberts in the march to Candahar, and was present at the battle of Candahar (mentioned in despatches, Brevet of Major, Medal with two Clasps, and Bronze Decoration).

[10] Major Gough served with the 9th Lancers in the Afghan war of 1878-80, and was present at the capture of Ali Musjid, the affair at Killa Kazi, and in the operations around Cabul in December 1879; accompanied Sir Frederick Roberts in the march to Candahar, and took part in the battle of Candahar (several times mentioned in despatches, Brevet of Major, Medal with three Clasps, and Bronze Decoration).

[18] Major Little served with the 9th Lancers in the Afghan war of 1878-80, and took part in the expedition to Maidan and in the operations around Cabul in December 1879; accompanied Sir Frederick Roberts in the march to Candahar, and was present at the battle of Candahar as Orderly Officer to Brigadier General H. Gough (mentioned in despatches, Medal with two Clasps, and Bronze Decoration).

Record of the Services of the 9th (Queen's Royal) Lancers.

Raised in Ireland in 1715. To England, 1803. To Monte Video, 1806. To England, 1807. To Walcheren, July 1809. To England, 1809. To the Peninsula, 1811. To England, 1813. To Ireland, 1814. To England, 1815. To Ireland, 1823. To Scotland, 1826. To England, 1827. To Ireland, 1832. To England, 1835. To Scotland, 1837. To England, 1838. To India, 1842 (battle of Sobraon; Punjab campaign—battles of Chillianwallah and Goojerat; Indian Mutiny—Delhi, Lucknow). To England, 1859. To Ireland, 1864. To England, 1869. To India, 1875 (Afghanistan, 1878-80—battles of Charasiah and Candahar). To England, 1885. To Ireland, 1890.

10th (*The Prince of Wales' Own Royal*) Hussars.

The Prince's Plume. The Rising Sun and Red Dragon. "PENINSULA" "WATERLOO" "SEVASTOPOL"
"ALI MUSJID" "AFGHANISTAN, 1878-79" "EGYPT, 1884."

Years' Ser.							
Full Pay	Half Pay						
26	...	**Colonel.**—*His Royal Highness* Albert Edward, *Prince of* Wales and *Duke of* Cornwall, *KG. KT. XP. GCB. GCSI. GCMG. GCIE. Colonel*, 9 Nov. 58; *General*, 9 Nov. 62; *Field Marshal*, 29 May 75; *Colonel* 10th Hussars, 18 April 63.					
		Lieutenant Colonel.—Manners Charles Wood,[1] *Cornet,* P[1] Sept. 69; *Lieut.* P27 Oct. 71; *Captain,* 2 Feb. 78; *Major,* 6 Apr. 82; *Lt. Colonel,* 3 Aug. 92.					

			2ND LIEUT.	LIEUT.	CAPTAIN.	BREV.MAJ.	MAJOR.
		MAJORS.					
21	...	Ralph Bromfield Willington Fisher[3]	......	27 June 74	28 Apr. 82	......	12 Feb. 91
20	...	Philip Francis Durham[4]	......	20 Nov. 75	18 Feb. 84	......	27 July 92
20	...	David Stanley William, *Earl of* Airlie [5]	......	13 June 75	18 Feb. 84	15 June 85	3 Aug. 92
		CAPTAINS.					
19	...	p.s.c. Richard Henry Fras. Wharton Wilson[6]	......	26 July 76	1 Mar. 84	15 June 85	
18	...	Hon. George Leopold Bryan[11]	8 Dec. 77	1 July 81	13 Sept. 87		
16	...	Harvey Alexander, *Adjutant Suffolk Yeomanry Cavalry* 1 Feb. 90	24 Jan. 80	1 July 81	16 Mar. 89		
15	...	Charles Bateson Harvey,[9] *Adjutant* 17 *Yeomanry Brigade* 24 July 94	22 Jan. 81	1 July 81	21 July 89		
13	...	Arthur Hughes-Onslow[9]	......	10 May 82	4 Jan. 90		
13	...	Hon. Julian Hedworth George Byng[9]	......	27 Jan. 83	4 Jan. 90		
12	...	Charles Toler M'Murragh Kavanagh	......	6 Feb. 84	1 Feb. 90		
11	...	Hon. Everard Baring, *Aide de Camp to the Governor of Madras* 23 Jan. 91	......	23 Aug. 84	1 Feb. 90		
8	...	Cameron Barclay	14 Sept. 87	6 Mar. 89	23 Mar. 92		
8	...	*Lord* William Augustus Cavendish-Bentinck	16 Nov. 87	10 Aug. 89	1 Feb. 93		
		LIEUTENANTS.					
8	...	Bertram Chas. Christopher Spencer Meeking	11 Feb. 88	18 Sept. 89			
7	...	*Lord* Geo. William Montagu-Douglas-Scott	27 Mar. 89	11 June 90			
6	...	Hon. Thomas Walter Brand, **Adjutant** 30 May 94	20 Nov. 89	10 June 91			
6	...	Anthony Ashley Cooper, *Earl of* Shaftesbury	29 Mar. 90	10 June 91			
5	...	Nathaniel William Curzon	4 Mar. 91	14 Sept. 92			
4	...	Hon. John Dawnay	5 Dec. 91	14 June 93			
3	...	Reginald Spencer Chaplin...................	5 Oct. 92	18 Oct. 93			
3	...	John Peniston Milbanke......................	23 Nov. 92	18 Apr. 94			
		SECOND LIEUTENANTS.					
1	...	Robert Gardner	2 June 94				
1	...	Stanley Leonard Barry	2 June 94				
1	...	Hon. Dudley Roger Hugh Anderson-Pelham	10 Oct. 94				
5	...	*Riding Master.*—Albert William Waite, 27 Aug. 90; *Hon. Lieut.*					
13	...	*Quarter Master.*—Arthur Edward Poole,[17] 2 Dec. 82; *Hon. Captain,* 2 Dec. 92.					

[11] Captain Hon. G. L. Bryan served with the 10th Hussars in the Afghan war in 1878-79, and was present at the attack and capture of Ali Musjid and in the engagement at Futtehabad (mentioned in despatches, Medal with Clasp). Served throughout the Nile Expedition in 1884-85 with the Light Camel Regiment, and took part in the operations of the Desert Column including the engagement at Abu Klea Wells on the 16th. and 17th February (Medal with Clasp, and Khedive's Star).

Blue.—*Agents,* Messrs. Cox and Co.
Embarked for India, 10 January 1873. *Returned from Egypt,* 21 April 1884.

---

[1] Lt. Colonel Wood served with the 10th Hussars in the Afghan war in 1878-79, and was present in the engagement at Futtehabad (mentioned in despatches, Medal).

[3] Major Fisher served throughout the Afghan war of 1878-80, and was present at the attack and capture of the Peiwar Kotal, in the engagements at Mattoon and Futtehabad, with the expedition into the Khost Valley, in the operations in the Shutargardan (mentioned in despatches), and in the operations around Cabul in December 1879 (mentioned in despatches); accompanied Sir Frederick Roberts in the march to Candahar, and was present at the battle of Candahar (mentioned in despatches, Medal with three Clasps, and Bronze Decoration). Served as Transport Officer with the Mahsood Wuzeeree Expedition in 1881 under Brigadier General Gordon (mentioned in despatches).

[4] Major Durham served with the 10th Hussars in the Afghan war in 1878-79, and was present in the engagement at Mattoon, in the operations in the Khost Valley, and in the engagement at Futtehabad (Medal). Served in the Soudan Expedition in 1884 with the 10th Hussars, and was present in the engagements at El Teb and Temai (Medal with Clasp, and Khedive's Star).

[5] Lord Airlie served with the 10th Hussars in the Afghan war in 1878-79, and was present at the attack and capture of Ali Musjid, and in the engagement at Futtehabad (Medal with Clasp). Served in the Soudan Expedition in 1884 as Adjutant 10th Hussars, and was present in the engagement at Temai (Medal with Clasp, 4th Class of the Medjidie, and Khedive's Star). Served with the Nile Expedition in 1884-85 as Brigade Major under Sir Herbert Stewart, and was present at the action at Abu Klea (slightly wounded), in the engagement at Abu Klea Wells on the 16th and 17th February, and in the reconnaissance to Metammeh—slightly wounded (twice mentioned in despatches, Brevet of Major, two Clasps).

[6] Major Wilson served in the Ashanti campaign in 1873 as Midshipman on board H.M.S. *Rattlesnake*, and received a slight gunshot wound on the 14th August (Medal). Served with the 10th Hussars in the Afghan war of 1878-80, and was present at the attack and capture of Ali Musjid, in the engagement at Futtehabad, and in the operations around Cabul in December 1879 as Transport Officer Cabul Field Force, including the investment of Sherpore (mentioned in despatches); accompanied Sir Frederick Roberts in the march to Candahar, and was present at the battle of Candahar (mentioned in despatches, Medal with three Clasps, and Bronze Decoration). Served in the Soudan Expedition in 1884 with the 10th Hussars, and was present in the engagements at El Teb and Temai (Medal with Clasp, and Khedive's Star). Served in the Soudan campaign in 1885 attached to the Cavalry Brigade (Brevet of Major, Clasp).

[9] Captains Harvey, Hughes-Onslow, and Hon. J. H. G. Byng served in the Soudan Expedition in 1884 with the 10th Hussars, and were present in the engagements at El Teb and Temai (Medal with Clasp, and Khedive's Star).

[17] Captain Poole served in the Soudan Expedition in 1884 with the 10th Hussars (Medal, and Khedive's Star).

11th (*Prince Albert's Own*) Hussars.

[Sealkote, Bengal. Depot, Canterbury.]

The Crest and Motto of the late Prince Consort. "EGYPT" (with the Sphinx). "SALAMANCA" "PENINSULA" "WATERLOO" "BHURTPORE" "ALMA" "BALAKLAVA" "INKERMAN" "SEVASTOPOL."

Colonel.—William Charles Forrest,[1] *CB, Cornet,* P11 March 36; *Lt.* P5 Jan. 39; *Capt.* P7 Sept. 41; *Major,* P3 Oct. 48; *Bt.Lt.Colonel,* 12 Dec. 54; *Lt.Colonel,* P5 Aug. 59; *Colonel,* 8 March 60; *Major General,* 6 March 68; *Lieut.General,* 1 Oct. 77; *General,* 1 July 81; *Colonel* 11th Hussars, 8 Feb. 86.

Lieutenant Colonel.—Charles Edward Swaine,[4] *Cornet,* P13 June 68; *Lt.* P 27 July 70; *Capt.* 1 Jan. 80; *Bt.Major,* 18 Nov. 82; *Major,* 1 Dec. 83; *Lt.Colonel,* 19 Nov. 91.

Years' Ser. Full Pay / Half Pay: 27 ...

		MAJORS.	2ND LIEUT.	LIEUT.	CAPTAIN.	BREV.MAJ.	MAJOR.
22	...	p.s.c. Edward Reginald Courtenay[5]		9 Aug. 73	1 July 81		10 Apr. 89
20	...	Lord Edmund Bernard Talbot, *MP. for Chichester*		20 Nov. 75	14 Sept. 81		19 Nov. 91
19	...	Hon. Henry Arthur Ormsby Gore		11 Nov. 76	25 July 83		24 Oct. 92
16	...	Charles Henry Eyre Coote, *Adjutant* 7 *Yeomanry Brigade* 1 Feb. 95	13 Aug. 79	29 June 81	14 Oct. 85		30 Jan. 95

CAPTAINS.

			2ND LIEUT.	LIEUT.	CAPTAIN.		
15	...	Thomas Morrall Jones-Tailby, *Adj.* 14 *Yeomanry Brigade* 1 Apr. 93	22 Jan. 81	1 July 81	29 Sept. 86		
15	...	William Wheat Waring,[6] *Adjutant* 1 *Fife-shire Light Horse Volunteers* 16 Dec. 90...	22 Jan. 81	1 July 81	2 Mar. 87		
14	...	Hon.OsbertVictor Geo. Atheling Lumley, *Aide de Camp to Major General R. T. Thynne* 1 Oct. 94		22 Oct. 81	2 Mar. 87		
14	...	Frederick Hope Lehmann		22 Oct. 84	19 Nov. 87		
11	...	Boyce Combe		12 Nov. 84	19 Nov. 91		
10	...	Esme Stuart Erskine Harrison		9 May 85	4 Jan. 92		
10	...	Lewis Owen Williams (*Depot*)		25 Nov. 85	10 Aug. 92		
9	...	Francis Temple Bacon	26 Feb. 87	6 Feb. 88	8 Mar. 93		
9	...	Thomas Anderdon Salt[7]		25 Aug. 86	8 Mar. 93		
8	...	Julian Dallas Tyndale Tyndale-Biscoe	30 Nov. 87	22 July 90	1 Oct. 94		
8	...	William Bailey	29 Feb. 88	22 July 90	30 Jan. 95		

LIEUTENANTS.

			2ND LIEUT.	LIEUT.			
7	...	John Alan Le Norreys Daniell	16 May 88	31 Mar. 91			
6	...	Thomas Tait Pitman, **Adjutant** 8 Jan. 94	9 Oct. 89	6 Apr. 91			
4	...	Frank Ford Fenton	29 Apr. 91	10 Aug. 92			
4	...	Herbert William Mascall Kenrick (*Depot*)	30 May 91	10 Aug. 92			
5	...	William Robert Codrington	31 Dec. 90	24 Oct. 92			
4	...	Martin Jones	12 Mar. 92	28 June 93			
4	...	Ralph Stapleton Ward Jackson	12 Mar. 92	28 June 93			
3	...	James Jardine Richardson	5 Oct. 92	18 July 94			
3	...	Harry Bertram Abadie	5 Oct. 92	20 Sept. 94			
3	...	Samuel Pearson Yates	17 Dec. 92	1 Oct. 94			
3	...	Sidney Vernon Occleston	17 Dec. 92	22 Oct. 94			
3	...	Norman Marshall Johnstone	15 Mar. 93	30 Jan. 95			

SECOND LIEUTENANTS.

			2ND LIEUT.				
3	...	Rowland James Percy Anderson	15 Mar. 93				
2	...	Godfrey Trevelyan Williams	23 Dec. 93				
2	...	Percy Desmond Fitzgerald	23 Dec. 93				
1	...	William Scott-Elliot	12 Dec. 94				
1	...	Cuthbert von Essen Moberly	12 Dec. 94				
1	...	Archibald Fraser Home	20 Feb. 95				
1	...	Ralph Maximilian Yorke	6 Mar. 95				

3 .. *Riding Master.*—Henry Hume Morton, 23 Nov. 92; *Hon. Lieut.*
5 ... *Quarter Master,*—George Page, 4 June 90; *Hon. Lieut.*

Blue.—*Agents*, Messrs. Cox and Co.
Embarked for South Africa, 22 July 1890.

[1] General Forrest served with the 4th Dragoon Guards the Eastern campaign of 1854-55, including the battles of Balaklava and Inkerman, siege of Sebastopol, night attack on Russian outposts 19th Feb. 1855, and battle of Tchernaya; commanded the 4th Royal Irish Dragoons from 18th February to 1st July 1855 (Medal with three Clasps, Brevet of Lt.Colonel, Sardinian and Turkish Medals, and 5th Class of the Medjidie).

[4] Lt.Colonel Swaine served with the 17th Lancers in the Zulu war of 1879, and was present in the engagement at Ulundi (Medal with Clasp). Served in the Boer war of 1881 as Aide de Camp to Major General Drury Lowe, Commanding the Cavalry Brigade. Served in the Egyptian war of 1882 as Aide de Camp to Major General Drury Lowe, Commanding the Cavalry Division, and was present at the engagements of El Magfar and Tel-el-Mahuta, the two actions at Kassassin, the battle of Tel-el-Kebir, and the capture of Cairo (mentioned in despatches, Brevet of Major, Medal with Clasp, 4th Class of the Medjidie, and Khedive's Star). Served in the Nile Expedition in 1884-85 with the Light Camel Regiment, and took part in the operations of the Desert Column (Clasp).

[5] Major Courtenay served throughout the Zulu war of 1879 as Staff Officer of the mounted troops of the Lower Tugela Column, and was present at the engagement of Inyezane, the action of Gingindhlovu, and the relief of Ekowe (mentioned in despatches, Medal with Clasp). Served throughout the Nile Expedition in 1884-85 in command of the troop of 20th Hussars with the Light Camel Regiment, and took part in the operations of the Desert Column, including the attack on the convoy on the 14th February and the engagement at Abu Klea Wells on the 16th and 17th February (Medal with Clasp, and Khedive's Star). Also served with the Egyptian Frontier Field Force in 1885-86 as Adjutant to the 20th Hussars and as Staff Officer to Mounted troops, and was present in the engagement at Giniss.

[6] Captain Waring served as a volunteer with the 4th Dragoon Guards in the Egyptian war of 1882, and was present at the action at Kassassin on 28th August (Medal, and Khedive's Star).

[7] Captain Salt served with the expedition against the Younies, on the West Coast of Africa, in 1887-88 (mentioned in despatches, Medal with Clasp).

Record of the Services of the 11th (*Prince Albert's Own*) Hussars.

Raised in 1715 and proceeded to France in 1758. To Flanders, 1794. To England, 1796. To Holland 1799. A detachment to Egypt, 1802 (received the badge of "Egypt"—with the Sphinx). To the Peninsula, 1811 (battle of Salamanca). To England, 1813. To Belgium and France, 1815 (battle of Waterloo and Army of Occupation in Paris). To England, 1818. To India, 1819 (battle of Bhurtpore). To England, 1838. To Ireland, 1843. To England, 1846. To Ireland, 1852. To the Crimea, 1854 (battles of Alma, Balaklava, and Inkerman, and siege of Sebastopol). To England, 1856. To Ireland, 1861. To England, 1865. To India, 1866. To England, 1877. To Ireland, 1884. To England, 1889. To South Africa, 1890.

Edinburgh.] **12th (*The Prince of Wales' Royal*) Lancers.** 154

The Prince's Plume. The Rising Sun and Red Dragon. "EGYPT" (with the Sphinx) "PENINSULA" "WATERLOO" "SOUTH AFRICA, 1851-2-3" "SEVASTOPOL" "CENTRAL INDIA."

Colonel.—Robert Hale, *Cornet*, P11 June 52; *Lieut.* 14 Sept. 55; *Capt.* 1 Jan. 59; *Major*, P21 Aug. 69;. *Lt. Colonel*, P22 Feb. 71; *Colonel*, 22 Feb. 76; *Major General*, 20 Dec. 85; *Colonel* 12 Lancers, 10 Feb. 94.

Lieutenant Colonel.—Charles Edward Beck, *Lt.* 3 Aug. 72; *Capt.* 12 Nov. 78; *Major*, 30 Nov. 85; *Lt. Colonel*, 21 Dec. 92.

Years' Ser. Full Pay.	Half Pay.		2ND LIEUT.	LIEUT.	CAPTAIN.	BREV. MAJ.	MAJOR.
		MAJORS.					
21	...	Thomas Alexander Hill	......	26 Mar. 75	30 Nov. 81	......	23 Nov. 92
15	...	p.s.c. Arthur Gillespie Churchill	11 Aug. 80	1 July 81	1 May 86	......	21 Dec. 92
15	...	Thomas James Atherton	11 Aug. 80	1 July 81	2 Feb. 87	......	22 Feb. 93
		CAPTAINS.					
15	...	Antonio Stephen Ralli	11 Aug. 80	1 July 81	1 Jan. 88		
15	...	p.s.c. Robert George Broadwood, *serving with the Egyptian Army*	22 Jan. 81	1 July 81	15 Feb. 88		
13	...	William Frederick Honywood Hinde	......	2 Aug. 82	15 Aug. 88		
12	...	John Charles Basil Eastwood, Adjutant 1 May 91	......	25 Aug. 83	10 June 89		
11	...	John Maxwell Gordon	......	14 May 84	17 Sept. 90		
11	...	Francis Egerton-Green	......	5 July 84	4 Sept. 92		
9	...	John Owens Johnson	5 Feb. 87	18 July 88	23 Nov. 92		
8	...	William Buller Chapell Hodge	21 May 87	18 July 88	21 Dec. 92		
7	...	Henry Granville Heneage, *Aide de Camp to the Governor of Bombay*	16 May 88	18 Sept. 89	17 May 93		
		LIEUTENANTS.					
7	...	Eustace Loder	8 Dec. 88	3 Sept. 90			
6	...	Howard Clifton Brown	8 June 89	3 Sept. 90			
6	...	Eustace Crawley, *Aide de Camp to the Lord Lieutenant of Ireland* 19 Feb. 94	7 Aug. 89	7 Jan. 91			
6	...	Frank Wormald	20 Nov. 89	25 Mar. 91			
5	...	Cecil Vivian Sloane Stanley	31 May 90	4 Sept. 92			
5	...	Benjamin Herbert Piercy	3 Dec. 90	23 Nov. 92			
5	...	Miles Halton Tristram	4 Mar. 91	21 Dec. 92			
3	...	Gerald Walton Hobson	5 Oct. 92	9 Aug. 93			
		SECOND LIEUTENANTS.					
3	...	Godfrey Charles de Cardonnel Wright	15 Mar. 93				
2	...	Ralph Charles Donaldson-Hudson	21 Oct. 93				
1	...	Walter Howorth Greenly	20 Feb. 95				
14	...	*Riding Master.*—Frank Shearme, 8 June 81; *Hon. Captain*, 8 June 91.					
3	...	*Quarter Master.*—William Barrows, 10 Aug. 92; *Hon. Lieut.*					

Blue—*Facings* Scarlet.—*Agents*, Messrs. Cox and Co.
Returned from India, 24 November 1887.

Record of the Services of the 12th (*The Prince of Wales' Royal*) Lancers.

Raised in 1715 as the 12th Dragoons. To Ireland, 1718, remaining there 75 years. In 1768 designated "The Prince of Wales's Regiment," and constituted "Light Dragoons." To the Mediterranean, 1793 (capture of Corsica). To Italy, 1794. To England, 1795. To Portugal, 1797. To Egypt, 1801 (investment of Cairo). To England, 1802. To Ireland, 1803. To England, 1805. To Holland, 1809. To England, 1810. To Portugal, 1811; through the Peninsular War and marched through France, embarking at Calais for England, 1814. To Ostend 1815 (at the battles of Quatre Bras and Waterloo, and in the Army of Occupation in France). Converted into "Lancers," 1816. To England, 1818. To Ireland, 1820. To England, 1824. To Portugal, 1827. To England, 1828. To Scotland, 1829. To Ireland, 1830. To England, 1833. To Ireland, 1841. To Scotland and England, 1843. To Ireland, 1848. Returned to England and embarked for South Africa, 1851. To India, 1854. To the Crimea, 1855 (marching through Egypt). To England, 1856. To India, 1857. To England, 1860. To Ireland, 1865. To England, 1870. To India, 1877. To England, 1887.

13th Hussars. [Dundalk.

"*Vivet in Æternum.*" "ALBUHERA" "VITTORIA" "ORTHES" "TOULOUSE" "PENINSULA"
"WATERLOO" "ALMA" "BALAKLAVA" "INKERMAN" "SEVASTOPOL."

Years' Ser. Full Pay.	Half Pay.							
25	...	**Colonel.**—*Sir* Baker Creed Russell,[1] *KCB, KCMG. Commanding at Chester* 1 Apr. 95; Cornet, 2 Nov. 55; Lieut. 1 Aug. 56; Capt. P18 Feb. 59; Bt.Major, 24 Jan. 65; Bt.Lt.Colonel, 1 Apr. 74; Major, 15 July 78; Colonel, 18 Feb. 80; Lt.Colonel, 29 Sept. 80; Major General, 1 Apr. 89; Colonel 13 Hussars, 20 Jan. 94.							
	...	**Lieutenant Colonel.**—Ernest Richard Hope Torin, *Cornet,* P15 Feb. 71; *Lt.* 28 Oct. 71; *Capt.* 14 Dec. 79; *Major,* 29 Sept. 85; *Lt.Colonel,* 1 July 92.							

		MAJORS.		2ND LIEUT.	LIEUT.	CAPTAIN.	BREV.MAJ.	MAJOR.
21	...	Henry John Blagrove[5]		......	11 Feb. 75	16 Mar. 83	......	8 Jan. 90
21	...	Maxwell Archibald Close		......	2 Dec. 74	25 Sept. 80	......	25 July 90
19	...	Robt. Stephenson Smyth Baden-Powell[6]		......	11 Sept. 76	16 May 83	......	1 July 92
		CAPTAINS.						
16	...	Walter Charles Smithson, *Aide de Camp to Lord Wolseley* 2 Dec. 91		7 Jan. 80	1 July 81	29 Sept. 85		
16	...	Frederick James Murphy[8]		23 July 79	25 Feb. 80	18 Aug. 83		
16	...	George John William Noble		14 Jan. 80	1 July 81	27 Oct. 86		
16	...	Coventry Williams		4 Jan. 80	1 July 81	24 Nov. 86		
15	...	Kenneth MacLaren, **Adjutant** 2 Dec. 91		11 Aug. 80	1 July 81	3 Aug. 87		
15	...	Angus Howard Reginald Ogilvy, *Adj. Kent Yeomanry Brigade* 11 June 94		22 Jan. 81	1 July 81	1 July 88		
12	...	Thomas Brocklehurst Phillips		......	5 Dec. 83	1 Jan. 90		
12	...	Edward Woodriff Jaffray		......	12 May 83	1 Aug. 90		
12	...	Ernest William Newsham Pedder		......	25 Aug. 83	8 Oct. 90		
10	...	Edgar Askin Wiggin		......	29 Aug. 85	12 Nov. 90		
		LIEUTENANTS.						
9	...	John Hearle Tremayne		......	19 May 86			
9	...	Richard Arthur Lennox Massy Bolton		......	25 Aug. 86			
8	...	Lionel Richard James Scholefield Battye		7 Mar. 88	11 June 90			
5	...	Francis Hubert Wise		30 July 90	29 Apr. 91			
4	...	John Fletcher Church		2 May 91	23 Nov. 92			
4	...	Henry Phelps Dangar		30 May 91	23 Nov. 92			
4	...	Adolphe Symons		12 Mar. 92	7 June 93			
3	...	Abdy Fellowes Anderson		15 Mar. 93	2 May 94			
		SECOND LIEUTENANTS.						
2	...	Ernest Wriothesley Denny		28 June 93				
2	...	Herbert Eames Spencer		9 Sept. 93				
1	...	Henry Julius Joseph Stern		10 Oct. 94				
1	...	*Riding Master.*—Robert MacWalter, 26 Sept. 94; *Hon. Lieut.*						
14	...	*Quarter Master.*—William Carter, 7 Jan. 82; *Hon. Captain,* 7 Jan. 92.						

Blue—*Facings* Buff.—*Agents,* Messrs. Cox and Co.
Returned from Natal, 3 Nov. 1885.

[1] Sir Baker Creed Russell was at Meerut with the Carabineers at the outbreak of the Sepoy mutiny, and at Kurnaul when Colonel Gerrard was killed; was afterwards present with Seaton's Moveable Column at the battle of Gungaree, where—his three senior officers being killed—he commanded the Squadron of his Regt., and a Detachment of the 9th Lancers; again, on the 17th Dec. 1857, he commanded the Cavalry in the action of Putteali, where over 700 Sepoys were killed,—"To Lieut. Russell," writes Sir Thomas Seaton in his despatch, "who commanded the Cavalry, as well as to his brave companions in arms, my thanks are specially due, for their gallantry in action and vigour in pursuit." He commanded the Cavalry also at Mynpooree, where 250 of the rebels were killed, and was with his Regiment when General Penny was killed and Bareilly taken; present at the relief of Bareilly, relief of Shahjehanpore, capture of the Fort of Remai and pursuit with destruction of the Fort of Mahundee, action of Bunkagaon, operations in Oude and actions of Mohudipore and Russoolpore, attack and capture of Fort Mitoulee, actions of Alligungo and Biswa; also served with the Agra Field Force under Brigadier Showers in Central India in pursuit of Tantia Topee (Medal with Clasp). Accompanied Sir Garnet Wolseley to the Gold Coast in September 1873 on special service. Organized the natives forming "Russell's Regiment," and commanded it throughout the Ashanti war of 1873-74. During the repulse of the Ashanti Army at Abrakrampa on the 5th and 6th November he commanded the defending forces. His regiment with Lord Gifford's Scouts formed the Advanced Guard of the Army from the River Prah to the north side of the Adansi Hills. Commanded the regiment, now forming part of the augmented Advanced Guard under Colonel M'Leod, at the attack and capture of Adubinssie, battle of Amoaful, attack and capture of Becquah, Advanced Guard engagement of Jarbinbah, skirmishes and ambuscade affairs between Adwabin and the River Ordah, battle of Ordahsu and capture of Coomassie (several times mentioned in despatches, Brevet of Lt.Colonel, *CB.,* Medal with Clasp). Accompanied Sir Garnet Wolseley to South Africa in 1879, and commanded the forces in the operations against Sekukuni resulting in the storming of the stronghold and subjugation of the tribe (mentioned in despatches, *KCMG.,* Aide de Camp to the Queen, Medal with Clasp). Served in the Egyptian war of 1882, first as Assistant Adjutant General for Cavalry, and afterwards in command of a brigade of Cavalry, and was present at the engagements of El Magfar and Tel-el-Mahuta, the two actions at Kassasin, the battle of Tel-el-Kebir and the capture of Cairo (mentioned in despatches, *KCB.,* Medal with Clasp, 2nd Class of the Medjidie, and Khedive's Star).

[5] Major Blagrove served in the Egyptian war of 1882 as Orderly Officer to Sir Baker Russell, Commanding 1st Cavalry Brigade, and was present at the action at Kassasin on the 9th September, at the battle of Tel-el-Kebir, and at the capture of Cairo (Medal with Clasp, and Khedive's Star).

[6] Major Baden-Powell served in the operations in Zululand in 1888 as Assistant Military Secretary to the General Officer Commanding and as Intelligence Officer (mentioned in despatches).

[8] Captain Murphy served with the 7th Dragoon Guards in the Egyptian war of 1882, and was present in the engagements of El Magfar and Mahsama, and at the action at Kassasin on the 28th August (Medal, and Khedive's Star).

14th (The King's) Hussars

The Royal Crest within the Garter. The Prussian Eagle. "DOURO" "TALAVERA" "FUENTES D'ONOR" "SALAMANCA" "VITTORIA" "ORTHES" "PENINSULA" "PUNJAUB" "CHILLIANWALLAH" "GOOJERAT" "PERSIA" "CENTRAL INDIA."

Years' Ser. Full Pay	Half Pay		2ND LIEUT.	LIEUT.	CAPTAIN.	BREV. MAJ.	MAJOR.
24	...	**Colonel.**—Charles William Thompson,[1] *Ensign,* P 26 Feb. 36; *Lieut.* P 17 Jan. 40; *Capt.* P 1 Dec. 48; *Major* P 9 Nov. 55; *Lt. Colonel,* 17 Sept. 57; *Colonel,* 17 Sept. 62; *Major General,* 28 June 68; *Lieutenant General,* 5 Oct. 80; *General,* 1 July 81; *Colonel* 14th Hussars, 1 May 82.					
		Lieutenant Colonel.—p.s.c. Hon. George Hugh Gough,[4] *CB. Cornet,* 28 Oct. 71; *Lieut.* 28 Oct. 71; *Captain,* 23 July 79; *Brev. Major,* 18 Nov. 82; *Bt.Lt.Colonel,* 15 June 85; *Major,* 16 Dec. 85; *Colonel,* 16 Dec. 89; *Lt.Colonel,* 1 July 91.					
		MAJORS.					
22	...	Augustus John English[5]	......	30 Dec. 73	16 Jan. 84	......	17 Aug. 87
20	...	Gilbert Henry Claude Hamilton[9]	......	1 Sept. 75	24 July 85	......	23 Aug. 93
16	...	Henry Wilmot Mitchell[10]	13 Aug. 79	1 July 81	26 Nov. 86	......	14 Mar. 94
		CAPTAINS.					
14	...	Arthur Brooks Broadhurst	......	28 Jan. 82	31 Dec. 87		
11	...	Lionel James Richardson, *Adjutant* 13 Yeomanry Brigade 1 June 93	......	14 May 84	24 Mar. 88		
15	...	Robert Mervyn Richardson[12]	19 Feb. 81	1 July 81	25 July 88		
12	...	Edward Douglas Brown	......	7 Nov. 83	8 Aug. 88		
10	...	John Murray	......	27 Jan. 86	1 July 91		
11	...	Edw. James Tickell, *Adjutant* 1 Sept. 92	......	7 Feb. 85	1 June 92		
12	7/12	Ælla Molyneux Berkeley Gage	......	9 Sept. 82	9 Nov. 92		
9	...	Cyril Stacey	5 Feb. 87	8 Aug. 88	21 Dec. 92		
9	...	Denis Menezes Miller	5 Feb. 87	8 Aug. 88	1 June 93		
8	...	Richard Gylby Brooksbank	14 Sept. 87	5 Dec. 88	14 Mar. 94		
		LIEUTENANTS.					
8	...	Henry Bodvel Lewis Hughes	14 Dec. 87	10 April 89			
7	...	William Gardiner Eley	10 Nov. 88	12 Mar. 90			
5	...	Robert Campbell Stephen	2 April 90	1 July 91			
5	...	William Prevost	8 Nov. 90	23 Jan. 92			
5	...	Charles Bosvile Tottenham	29 Oct. 90	23 Nov. 92			
4	...	William Henry	3 Feb. 92	22 Feb. 92			
3	...	William Jeffery Lockett	15 Mar. 93	10 Jan. 94			
3	...	Clement George Montague Adam	13 July 92	27 June 94			
		SECOND LIEUTENANTS.					
2	...	Freeling Ross Lawrence	7 Mar. 94				
1	...	Harry Frederick Hamilton Hardy	10 Oct. 94				
		Paymaster.—					
15	...	**Riding Master.**—Richard Odlum, 9 June 80; *Hon. Captain,* 9 June 90.					
13	...	**Quarter Master.**—Frederick Mugford, 20 Sept. 82; *Hon. Captain,* 20 Sept. 92.					

Blue.—**Agents,** Messrs. Cox and Co.
Returned from India, 24 Nov. 1886.

[1] General Thompson served as a Captain in the British Legion, and was engaged at Hernani, 30th Aug. 1835; at Arlaban, 16th, 17th and 18th Jan.; and the action before San Sebastian, 5th May 1836, when he was severely wounded in the hip and the hand (*KSF.* and Medal). Served the campaign of the Punjaub in the 14th Light Dragoons, was engaged at Ramnuggur (horse wounded) 22nd Nov. 1848, at Chillianwallah 13th Jan., and at Goojerat 21st Feb. 1849 (Medal with two Clasps). Present also at the crossing of the Chenab, Jhelum, and Indus; at the surrender of the Sikh army at Rawul Pindee, the capture of the Bridge of Boats at Attock, and pursuit of the Affghans to Peshawur. Commanded the 7th Dragoon Guards in India continuously from 1857 to 1867.

[4] Colonel the Hon. G. H. Gough served in the Boer war of 1881, first as Aide-de-Camp to Sir Thomas Baker, and afterwards as Aide de Camp to Sir Evelyn Wood. Served in the Egyptian war of 1882 as Aide de Camp to Sir Edward Hamley, Commanding the 2nd Division, and was present at the battle of Tel-el-Kebir—horse killed (mentioned in despatches, Brevet of Major, Medal with Clasp, 4th Class of the Madjidie, and Khedive's Star). Served through the Nile Expedition in 1884-85 in command of Mounted Infantry, and was present at the action at Abu Klea.—severely wounded (mentioned in despatches, Brevet of Lt.Colonel, two Clasps).

[5] Major English served in the Boer war of 1881.

[9] Major Hamilton served in the Afghan war of 1878-80 as Aide de Camp to Sir Samuel Browne, Commanding the 1st Division Peshawur Field Force (mentioned in despatches, Medal). Served in the Boer war in 1881 with the 14th Hussars.

[10] Major Mitchell served in the Boer war of 1881.

[12] Captain Richardson served with the Seaforth Highlanders in the Egyptian war of 1882, and was present in the engagement at Chalouf and at the battle of Tel-el-Kebir (Medal with Clasp, and Khedive's Star). Served through the Nile Expedition in 1884-85 with the 20th Hussars Troop Light Camel Regiment, including the operations of the Desert Column (Clasp). Served with the Egyptian Frontier Field Force in 1885-86, and was present in the engagement at Giniss.

15th (*The King's*) Hussars. [Dublin.

The Crest of England within the Garter. "*Merebimur.*" "EMSDORF" "VILLIERS EN COUCHE" "EGMONT-OP-ZEE" "SAHAGUN" "VITTORIA" "PENINSULA" "WATERLOO" "AFGHANISTAN, 1878-80."

Years' Ser.			Cornet or 2nd Lieut.	Lieut.	Captain.	Brev. Maj.	Major.
Full Pay.	Half Pay.						
29	...	Colonel.—Sir Frederick Wellington John FitzWygram, Bart.,[1] *MP. for Fareham*; Cornet, P28 July 43; Lt. P17 May 44; Capt. P22 Dec. 48; Major, P19 Feb. 58; Lt.Colonel, 26 July 58; Colonel, 26 July 63; Major General, 23 Mar. 69; Lieut.General, 1 Apr. 83; Colonel 3 Hussars, 16 Apr. 84; Colonel 15 Hussars, 19 Apr. 91. Lieutenant Colonel.—John Bullen Symes Bullen,[5] Cornet, P22 May 66; Lt. P14 July 69; Capt. 23 June 75; Major, 9 Apr. 84; Lt.Colonel, 12 June 93.					
		MAJORS.					
27	...	George Digby Filmer Sulivan[6]...............	P13 June 68	28 Oct. 71	24 June 76	......	15 Aug. 88
26	...	Arthur Gambier Holland[7].................	P24 July 69	28 Oct. 71	29 April 79	......	12 June 89
20	...	Hon. Rupert Leigh,[10] *Army Pay Department*.............	......	11 Feb. 76	17 Mar. 86	......	31 Jan. 94
		CAPTAINS.					
17	...	James Redmond Patrick Gordon,[14] *Recruiting Staff Officer, West London, 25 March 94*.............	22 Jan. 79	25 Jan. 81	15 Aug. 88		
17	...	Harry Evelyn Stracey Pocklington,[13] *Adj. 15 Yeomanry Brigade 23 Oct. 93* ...	13 Nov. 78	25 Jan. 81	15 Aug. 88		
16	...	Tyrell Other William Champion de Crespigny[11]..........	2 July 79	1 July 81	24 Aug. 88		
13	...	p.s.c. Reginald Cokayne Cokayne-Frith...	......	10 May 82	24 Aug. 88		
13	...	Basil St. John Mundy[12]	......	2 Aug. 82	10 Aug. 87		
11	...	Frederick Charlton Meyrick	......	17 May 84	2 Mar. 91		
10	...	Henry Herbert Philip Dundas, *A.D.C. to the Lord Lieut. of Ireland 25 April 93*...	......	17 Feb. 86	25 May 92		
7	...	Frederick John Dalgety	9 May 88	31 July 89	25 Mar. 94		
		LIEUTENANTS.					
7	...	Francis Evelyn Campbell Bald	19 Sept. 88	18 Dec. 89			
7	...	Robert Lowndes Aspinall	19 Sept. 88	18 Dec. 89			
7	...	Henry West Hodgson, **Adjutant** 17 Dec. 93	6 Feb. 89	2 Mar. 91			
6	...	William Campbell Anderson	29 Mar. 90	25 May 92			
5	...	Harold Arthur Lewis Tagart	3 Dec. 90	25 May 92			
4	...	Henry Duncombe Bramwell............	29 Apr. 91	11 Oct. 92			
3	...	Lionel Edward Kennard	18 June 92	12 June 93			
2	...	Percival Otway Hambro	18 June 92	24 Jan. 94			
3	...	Frederick William Vincent Greetham	2 Nov. 92	25 Mar. 94			
		SECOND LIEUTENANTS.					
2	...	James Alexander Stewart Balmain	1 Nov. 93				
1	...	Ernest Herbert Campbell Bald.............	2 June 94				
1	...	Frederick Carlisle Pilkington...............	12 Dec. 94				
23	...	*Riding Master.*—David Noble Smith, 8 June 72; *Hon. Captain*, 8 June 82.					
2	...	*Quarter Master.*—Harold Wilberforce Bell, 18 Oct. 93; *Hon. Lieut.*					

Blue.—*Agents*, Messrs. Cox and Co. *Returned from Natal*, 1882.

[1] Sir Frederick FitzWygram served in the Crimea with the 6th Dragoons, was present at the battle of Tchernaya and fall of Sebastopol (Medal with Clasp, and Turkish Medal).

[5] Lt.Colonel Symes-Bullen served with the 15th Hussars in the Boer war of 1881.

[6] Major Sulivan served with the 15th Hussars in the Candahar Column in the Afghan war of 1878-80, including the advance to Khelat-i-Ghilzai; also served with the Thull-Chotiali Field Force under Brigadier General Biddulph, and in the Column under Major General Phayre in Southern Afghanistan (Medal). Served in the Boer war of 1881.

[7] Major Holland served with the 15th Hussars in the Candahar Column in the Afghan war of 1878-80, including the advance to Khelat-i-Ghilzai, and was present in the engagements with the Afghan Cavalry at Takht-i-Pul (mentioned in despatches); also served with the Thull Chotiali Field Force under Brigadier General Biddulph, and accompanied Major General Phayre in his march to Candahar (Medal). Served in the Boer war of 1881. Served throughout the Nile Expedition in 1884-85 with the Light Camel Regiment, and took part in the operations of the Desert Column including the engagement at Abu Klea Wells on the 16th and 17th February (Medal with Clasp, and Khedive's Star).

[10] Major the Hon. R. Leigh served with the 15th Hussars in the Candahar Column in the Afghan war of 1878-80, including the advance to Khelat-i-Ghilzai, and was present in the engagements with the Afghan cavalry at Takht-i-Pul (mentioned in despatches); also served with the Thull-Chotiali Field Force under Brigadier General Biddulph, and accompanied Major General Phayre in his march to Candahar (Medal). Served in the Boer war of 1881. Served with the 19th Hussars in the Egyptian war of 1882, and was present in the action at Kassasin (9th September), and at the battle of Tel-el-Kebir (Medal with Clasp, and Khedive's Star). Served with the Bechuannaland Expedition under Sir Charles Warren in 1884-85 on special service as Assistant Commandant of the Remount Depot.

[11] Captain de Crespigny served with the 15th Hussars in the Afghan war in 1880 (Medal). Served in the Boer war of 1881. Served with the 19th Hussars in the Egyptian war of 1882, and was present in the action at Kassasin (9th September), and at the battle of Tel-el-Kebir (Medal with Clasp, and Khedive's Star).

[12] Captain Mundy served with the expedition to the Soudan in 1885, and was present in the engagement at Hasheen and at the destruction of Temai (Medal with Clasp, and Khedive's Star).

[13] Captain Pocklington served with the 15th Hussars in the Afghan war in 1880 (Medal). Served in the Boer war of 1881.

[14] Captain Gordon served in the Afghan war in 1880 with the 15th Hussars (Medal). Served in the Boer war of 1881 as Adjutant 15th Hussars. Served with the Bechuanaland Expedition in 1884-85 under Sir Charles Warren as Adjutant of Methuen's Horse. Served with the Burmese Expedition in 1887 (mentioned in despatches, Medal with Clasp). Served with the expedition against the Jebus, on the West Coast of Africa, in 1892 (mentioned in despatches, Medal with Clasp).

Lucknow, Bengal.
Depot, Canterbury.   **16th (The Queen's) Lancers.**   158

The Royal Cypher within the Garter. "*Aut Cursu, aut Cominus armis.*" "TALAVERA" "FUENTES D'ONOR" "SALAMANCA" "VITTORIA" "NIVE" "PENINSULA" "WATERLOO" "BHURTPORE" "AFGHANISTAN" "GHUZNEE" "MAHARAJPORE" "ALIWAL" "SOBRAON."

Years'Ser. Full Pay.	Half Pay.		CORNET OR 2ND LIEUT.	LIEUT.	CAPTAIN.	BREV.MAJ.	MAJOR.
		Colonel.—Sir Charles John Foster,[1] *KCB.*, *Member of the Council of the Secretary of State for India*; Cornet, P8 Apr. 36; Lt. 21 Dec. 38; Capt. P1 Dec. 47; Major, P21 Sept. 52; Lt. Colonel, P17 Feb. 57; Colonel, 20 Sept. 61; *Major General*, 6 March 68; *Lieut.General*, 27 May 79; *General*, 13 March 85; *Colonel 16th Lancers*, 28 March 86.					
22	...	**Lieutenant Colonel.**—James Melville Babington,[5] *Lt.* 6 Sept. 73; *Capt.* 20 Feb. 80; *Major*, 30 July 90; *Lt.Colonel*, 27 Jan. 92.					
		MAJORS.					
26	...	Henry Leycester Aylmer[7]	25 Sept. 69	28 Oct. 71	1 Dec. 80	......	10 Sept. 90
17	...	Stephen Frewen, *Adjutant* 9 *Yeomanry Brigade* 1 April 93	24 July 78	9 Jan. 80	5 May 86	......	27 Jan. 92
17	...	Windham Henry Wyndham-Quin,[9] *Adjutant* 3 *Yeomanry Brigade* 9 Oct. 94	7 Aug. 78	20 Feb. 80	23 June 86	......	27 Jan. 93
17	...	Julian Oswald	22 Mar. 79	16 Oct. 80	8 Dec. 86	......	22 Dec. 94
		CAPTAINS.					
15	...	James Alexander Orr-Ewing	11 Sept. 80	15 Mar. 81	21 July 88		
15	...	Lovelace Stamer, *Adjutant* 8 *Yeomanry Brigade* 1 Sept. 94	22 Jan. 81	1 July 81	25 July 88		
15	...	Herbert Crowe Dugdale, *Adjutant* 6 *Yeomanry Brigade* 1 Jan. 95	22 Jan. 81	1 July 81	9 Jan. 89		
12	...	Henry Pownall Kirkpatrick	......	5 Dec. 83	2 Sept. 90		
11	...	Guy Percy Wyndham (*Depot*)	......	23 Aug. 84	10 Sept. 90		
10	...	Edw. de Grey Beaumont, **Adjutant** 8 Aug.94	......	17 June 85	27 Jan. 92		
9	...	Alister Grant Dallas	......	25 Aug. 86	7 Mar. 92		
8	...	Ronald Francis Assheton Sloane-Stanley	14 Sept. 87	8 May 89	27 Jan. 93		
7	...	Henry Hugh Peter Deasy	10 Nov. 88	29 Jan. 90	17 Feb. 94		
7	...	*Hon.* Lewis Arthur Milles	8 Dec. 88	23 July 90	1 Sept. 94		
7	...	Hubert De La Poer Gough	6 Mar. 89	23 July 90	22 Dec. 94		
		LIEUTENANTS.					
6	...	Bernard Elliot Church	18 Sept. 89	13 May 91			
5	...	Maurice Lilburn MacEwen	23 April 90	23 May 91			
5	...	Telford Mackenzie Young	28 June 90	23 May 91			
5	...	Reginald St. Clair Battine..................	23 July 90	23 May 91			
5	...	Edward Bagwell-Purefoy	23 July 90	9 Sept. 91			
5	...	Richard Lucas Mullens (*Depot*)	8 Oct. 90	27 Jan. 92			
5	...	Clive Macdonnell Dixon	8 Oct. 90	27 Jan. 93			
5	...	Robert Leny Macalpine-Leny	8 Oct. 90	17 Feb. 94			
5	...	George Edward Tuson	8 Oct. 90	31 July 94			
5	...	Arthur Irwin Maling, *serving in the Niger Coast Protectorate*	8 Oct. 90	1 Sept. 94			
4	...	Alexander Edward, *Visct.* Fincastle	30 May 91	1 Sept. 94			
4	...	Edmund Francis Macnaghten..............	10 Oct. 91	13 Mar. 95			
		SECOND LIEUTENANTS.					
4	...	Robert Walter Dillon Bellew	12 Mar. 92				
3	...	George Howard Fanshawe Abadie.........	22 Mar. 93				
1	...	Edwin Francis Fitzroy Osborne	2 June 94				
1	...	Cuthbert John Eccles	1 Aug. 94				
1	...	Roland Haig	14 Nov. 94				
1	...	Charles Lionel Kirwan Campbell	13 Feb. 95				
1	...	Algernon Ernest Hesketh	20 Feb. 95				
32	...	*Paymaster.*—William Henry Battanshaw, 23 June 63; *Hon. Major*, 23 June 78.—At Station Pay Office, Captain H. H. P. Deasy (*acting*). [Aldershot.					
3	...	*Riding Master.*—James Laing, 11 May 92; *Hon. Lieut.*					
3	...	*Quarter Master.*—Israel Hart, 23 Nov. 92; *Hon. Lieut.*					

Scarlet—*Facings* Blue.—*Agents*, Messrs. Cox and Co.
Embarked for India, 3 September 1890.

[1] Sir Charles Foster served with the 16th Lancers during the campaign in Affghanistan under Lord Keane, including the siege and capture of Ghuznee (Medal with Clasp). He served also at the battle of Maharajpore, 9th Dec. 1843 (Bronze Star); and in the campaign on the Sutlej in 1846, including the battles of Buddiwal, Aliwal (as Aide de Camp to Brigadier Cureton), and Sobraon (Medal and Clasp).
[5] Lt.Colonel Babington served with the Bechuanaland Expedition under Sir Charles Warren in 1884-85.
[7] Captain Aylmer served in the Ashanti war from the 30th November 1873; commanded the Cape Coast Volunteers of Wood's Regiment, with the advanced guard under Major Furze during the march to the Prah; and afterwards commanded the post of Essiaman on the line of communications (Medal with Clasp).
[9] Major Wyndham Quin served with the Inniskilling Dragoons in the Boer war of 1881.

Record of the Services of the 16th (The Queen's) Lancers.

Raised as the 16th Regiment of Light Dragoons in 1759. Served at the siege of Belle Isle and in Portugal till the end of the Seven Years' War. To America, 1776. Four Troops to Flanders, 1793 (remainder uncertain). To England, 1796. To Ireland, 1802. To England, 1805. To the Peninsula, 1809 (battles of Talavera, Fuentes d'Onor, Salamanca, Vittoria, and Nive). To England, 1814. To Belgium, 1815 (battle of Waterloo). To England, 1815. To Ireland, 1816. To England, 1819. To Ireland, 1821. To England, 1822. To India, 1822 (battle of Bhurtpore, capture of Ghuznee, battles of Maharajpore, Aliwal, and Sobraon). To England, 1845. To Ireland, 1852. To Scotland, 1857. To England, 1859. To India, 1865. To England, 1876. To Ireland, 1882. To England, 1888. To India, 1890.

I

17th (*The Duke of Cambridge's Own*) Lancers. [Leeds.

Death's Head, with the Motto, "*Or Glory.*"—"ALMA" "BALAKLAVA" "INKERMAN" "SEVASTOPOL"
"CENTRAL INDIA" "SOUTH AFRICA, 1879."

Years' Ser. Full Pay / Half Pay				2ND LIEUT.	LIEUT.	CAPTAIN.	BREV. MAJ.	MAJOR.
29	...	Colonel in Chief.—Field Marshal *His Royal Highness* George W. F. C., Duke of Cambridge,[1] KG. KT. KP. GCB. GCSI. GCMG. GCIE. Commander in Chief, 21 June 76.						
		Colonel.—Sir Drury Curzon Drury-Lowe,[2] KCB. Cornet, P28 July 54; Lieut. 7 Nov. 54; Capt. P9 Nov. 56; Major, P10 June 62; Lt.Colonel, P15 June 66; Colonel, 15 June 71; Major General, 9 Dec. 81; Lieut. General, 1 Apr. 90; Colonel 17th Lancers, 24 Jan. 92.						
		Lieutenant Colonel.—Ernest Augustus Belford,[5] Cornet, P27 July 66; Lieut. P24 April 69; Capt. 12 Aug. 74; Major, 7 Jan. 82; Lt.Colonel, 15 Jan. 92.						
		MAJORS.						
22	...	Mortimer Graham Neeld[8]		......	12 Nov. 73	7 Jan. 82	......	27 Apr. 86
19	...	Henry Fortescue[11]		......	15 July 76	6 June 82		6 Nov. 93
19	...	Edward Bleiddian Herbert[13]		......	29 Nov. 76	27 Apr. 86		5 Dec. 94
		CAPTAINS.						
17	...	Hon. Lionel Henry Dudley Fortescue[14], Condt. School of Inst. Aux. Forces, Aldershot, 1 Jan. 95.		......	11 Nov. 78	6 Nov. 86		
17	...	Charles James Anstruther,[15] Adjutant 13 May 94		11 May 78	27 Apr. 81	6 Nov. 86		
17	...	William Gordon Renton		22 Mar. 79	1 July 81	15 Jan. 88		
15	...	Charles Coventry[18]		29 Sept. 80	1 July 81	15 Jan. 88		
14	...	Harry William Ralph Ricardo			28 Jan. 82	7 Apr. 88		
13	...	Hon. Herbert Alexander Lawrence, *Staff College*.		......	10 May 82	25 Feb. 92		
12	...	Charles Algernon Simeon Warner			30 Jan. 84	5 Dec. 94		
10	...	Bertram Percy Portal			29 Aug. 85	1 Jan. 95		
		LIEUTENANTS.						
9	...	Norman Tom Nickalls			10 Nov. 86			
9	...	Herbert Merton Jessel			10 Nov. 86			
9	...	Victor Staunton Sandeman			10 Nov. 86			
8	...	Thomas Gerrard Collins		9 Nov. 87	26 Oct. 92			
7	...	H.S.H. Prince Adolphus C.A.A.E.G.P.L.L. of Teck		11 Apr. 88	11 Jan. 93			
7	...	Henry Cecil Noel		2 May 88	31 Jan. 93			
6	...	William Arthur Tilney		10 Apr. 89	5 Dec. 94			
4	...	Sir Francis Burdett, Bart.		30 May 91	1 Jan. 95			
		SECOND LIEUTENANTS.						
1	...	Houston Michael Shaw Stewart		12 Dec. 94				
1	...	Hon. Algernon William John Clotworthy Skeffington		20 Feb. 95				
1	...	Hugh Wyndham Montgomery		20 Feb. 95				
9	...	Riding Master.—William Pilley, 19 May 86; *Hon. Lieut.*						
3	...	Quarter Master.—Charles Clarke, 21 Dec. 92; *Hon. Lieut.*						

[14] Captain the Hon. L.H.D. Fortescue served with the 17th Lancers in the Zulu war of 1879, and was present in the engagements at Zuingnin Mountain and Ulundi (Medal with Clasp).
[15] Captain Anstruther served with the 17th Lancers in the Zulu war of 1879, and was present in the engagement at Ulundi (Medal with Clasp).

Blue—*Facings* White.—*Agents*, Messrs. Cox and Co.
Returned from India, 3 Nov. 1890; *Squadron from Egypt*, 2 Nov. 91.

---

[1] The Duke of Cambridge commanded the 1st Division of the Eastern Army throughout the campaign of 1854, including the battles of the Alma, Balaklava, and Inkerman (horse shot), and siege of Sebastopol (mentioned in despatches, received the thanks of the House of Commons, Medal with four Clasps, and Turkish Medal).

[2] Sir D. C. Drury-Lowe served with the 17th Lancers in the Crimea from 18th June 1855, including the battle of the Tchernaya, siege and fall of Sebastopol (Medal with Clasp, and Turkish Medal). Also the Indian campaign of 1858-59, including pursuit of rebel force under Tantia Topee, and the action of Zeerapore (Medal with Clasp for Central India). Commanded the 17th Lancers and the Cavalry of the 2nd Division in the Zulu war of 1879, and was present in the engagement at Ulundi—wounded (CB., Medal with Clasp). Served in the Boer war of 1881 under Sir Evelyn Wood in command of the Cavalry Brigade. Served in the Egyptian war of 1882 in command of the Cavalry Division, and was present at the engagements of El Magfar, Mahsama, the two actions at Kassasin, and the battle of Tel-el-Kebir, immediately after which he commenced a forced march with the Cavalry by which he obtained possession of Cairo, the surrender of its citadel, and of the rebel chief Arabi (six times mentioned in despatches, received the thanks of both Houses of Parliament, KCB., Medal with Clasp, 2nd Class of the Osmanieh, and Khedive's Star).

[5] Lt.Colonel Belford served with the 17th Lancers in the Zulu war of 1879, and was present in the engagement at Ulundi (Medal with Clasp).

[8] Major Neeld served with the 17th Lancers in the Zulu war of 1879, and was present as Orderly Officer to Colonel Drury Lowe, commanding the Cavalry Brigade in the engagement at Ulundi (Medal with Clasp).

[11] Major Henry Fortescue served with the 17th Lancers in the Zulu war of 1879 (Medal with Clasp).

[13] Major Herbert served with the 17th Lancers in the Zulu war of 1879, and was present in the engagement at Ulundi (Medal with Clasp).

[18] Captain Coventry served in the Zulu war of 1879, and was present in the engagement at Ulundi (Medal with Clasp).

Record of the Services of the 17th (Duke of Cambridge's Own) Lancers (formerly the 17th Light Dragoons).

Raised in 1759 as the 18th Light Dragoons; disbanded in 1763, and again raised as the 17th Light Dragoons. To Ireland, 1764. To North America, 1776. To England, 1783. To the West Indies, 1765. To England, 1797 (shipwrecked *en route*). To South America, 1806 (capture of Monte Video). To England and thence to India, 1808. To England, and became Lancers, 1823. To Ireland, 1828. To England, 1832. To Ireland, 1838. To Scotland, 1841. To England, 1842. To Ireland, 1846. To England, 1857. To the Crimea, 1854 (battles of Alma, Balaklava, and Inkerman, and siege of Sebastopol). To Ireland, 1856. To East Indies, 1857 (Indian Mutiny—"Central India"). To England, 1865. To Scotland, 1869. To Ireland, 1870. To England, 1876. To South Africa, 1879 (Zulu war, 1879). To India, 1879. To England, 1890, one squadron remaining in Egypt.

18th Hussars — 160

Umballa, Bengal. Depot, Canterbury.

"Pro Rege, pro Lege, pro Patria conamur." "PENINSULA" "WATERLOO."

Colonel.—Alexander George Montgomery Moore, *Commanding the Forces in Canada* 1 June 94; *Cornet*, P13 Dec. 50; *Lt.* P6 July 52; *Capt.* P9 May 56; *Major*, 14 Sept. 67; *Lt. Colonel*, P23 Dec. 68; *Colonel*, 23 Dec. 73; *Major General*, 30 Dec. 84; *Lt. General*, 10 Mar. 92; *Colonel* 18th Hussars, 4 Jan. 92.

Lieutenant Colonel.—Edward Groves Paley, *Cornet*, P2 Jan. 69; *Lt.* P19 Feb. 70; *Capt.* 16 Dec. 74; *Major*, 28 Nov. 83; *Lt. Colonel*, 8 July 93.

Years' Ser. Full Pay.	Half Pay.		2ND LIEUT.	LIEUT.	CAPTAIN.	BRVT. MAJ.	MAJOR.
27	...						
		MAJORS.					
22	...	Bernhard Drysdale Möller	......	8 May 73	18 Dec. 80	......	7 July 86
21	...	Richard Hobart Morrison	......	13 June 74	31 Oct. 82	......	19 Nov. 89
21	...	Francis Daie Tagart (*Depot*)	......	2 Dec. 74	3 Oct. 83	......	1 Aug. 90
14	...	George Robert Brown Patten, *Army Pay Department*	......	22 Oct. 81	1 Apr. 86	......	20 June 94
		CAPTAINS.					
13	...	Eustace Chaloner Knox,[1] *Adjutant Cavalry Depot* 25 Apr. 94	......	30 Aug. 82	14 Apr. 86		
15	...	VC Percival Scrope Marling[6]	11 Aug. 80	1 July 81	22 Dec. 86		
18	...	Ernest Charles Penn Curzon, *Adjutant Leicestershire Yeomanry Cav.* 1 Jan. 90	8 Dec. 77	23 June 80	30 Apr. 87		
13	...	Henry Thornton Laming	......	10 Mar. 83	14 Mar. 88		
13	...	William Maxwell Sherston[7]	......	10 June 82	8 Aug. 88		
11	...	Henry Algernon Fulke Charles Ferdinand Stephan Greville	......	7 Feb. 85	1 Oct. 91		
9	...	William Pollok Morris Pollok	......	25 Aug. 86	12 Feb. 92		
9	...	Montagu Sinclair Wellby	......	25 Aug. 86	25 April 94		
8	...	Horace Scott Davey	14 Sept. 87	16 Mar. 89	20 June 94		
		LIEUTENANTS.					
7	...	Arthur Hayward Barclay (*Depot*)	19 Sept. 88	25 June 90			
7	...	Charles Harold Corbett	10 Nov. 88	25 June 90			
6	...	Chas. Kenyon Burnett, *Adjutant* 7 Nov. 92	11 Sept. 89	23 Jan. 91			
6	...	Harold Cotton Richards	23 Oct. 89	29 July 91			
6	...	Charles Henry Leveson	23 Oct. 89	29 July 91			
6	...	Emil Carl Haag	1 Mar. 90	11 May 92			
5	...	John Haslett Gosselin	8 Oct. 90	14 Dec. 92			
4	...	Robert Cecil Harbottle	10 Oct. 91	12 Feb. 93			
4	...	John Lockhart Wood	12 Mar. 92	29 June 94			
3	...	Edward Arthur Williams	18 June 92	14 Nov. 94			
3	...	Cecil Duncan Field	17 Dec. 92	14 Nov. 94			
		SECOND LIEUTENANTS.					
3	...	James Howard Adolphus Annesley	15 Feb. 93				
2	...	Charles Joseph Thackwell	28 June 93				
2	...	Albert Charles M'Lachlan	23 Dec. 93				
1	...	Ralph Bryan Henry Gibbins	4 July 94				
1	...	Montagu Brotherhood	10 Oct. 94				
1	...	Edmund Heseltine Bayford	10 Oct. 94				
1	...	Herbert Anderson Cape	12 Dec. 94				
		Paymaster.—Lieut. Charles H. Corbett (*acting*).					
1	...	*Riding Master.*—William Edgar Mummery, 30 Jan. 95; *Hon. Lieut.*					
7	...	*Quarter Master.*—Joseph Baker, 18 July 88; *Hon. Lieut.*					

Blue.—*Agents*, Messrs. Cox and Co.   *Embarked for India*, 20 November 1889.

[1] Captain Knox served throughout the Nile Expedition in 1884-85 with the Light Camel Regiment, and took part in the operations of the Desert Column (Medal with Clasp, and Khedive's Star).

[6] Captain Marling served with the 3rd Battalion 60th Rifles in the Boer war in 1881, and was present in the engagements at Lang's Nek and the Ingogo River. Served with the 3rd Battalion King's Royal Rifle Corps in the Egyptian war of 1882, and was present in the engagement at Tel-el-Mahuta, in the action at Kassasin (9th September), and at the battle of Tel-el-Kebir (Medal with Clasp, and Khedive's Star). Served throughout the Soudan Expedition in 1884 with the Mounted Infantry, and was present in the engagements at El Teb and Temai (mentioned in despatches, Victoria Cross, two Clasps): was awarded the VC "for his conspicuous bravery at the battle of Temai, on 13th March, 1884, in risking his life to save that of Private Morley, Royal Sussex Regiment, who, having been shot, was lifted and placed in front of Lieutenant Marling on his horse. He fell off almost immediately, when Lieutenant Marling dismounted, and gave up his horse for the purpose of carrying off Private Morley, the enemy pressing close on to them until they succeeded in carrying him about 80 yards to a place of comparative safety." Served in the Nile Expedition in 1884-85 with the Mounted Infantry, and was present at the actions of Abu Klea and Abu Kru, in the reconnaissance before Metammeh, and in the second action at Abu Klea (two Clasps).

[7] Captain Maxwell Sherston served in the Nile Expedition in 1884-85 with the Mounted Infantry, and was present at the engagements at Abu Klea and Abu Kru and in the reconnaissance to Metammeh (Medal with two Clasps, and Khedive's Star). Served with the Burmese Expedition in 1886-87 as Aide de Camp to Sir Frederick Roberts (mentioned in despatches, Medal with Clasp).

Record of the Services of the 18th Hussars.

Raised in 1759 as the 19th Light Dragoons. Numbered 18th Light Dragoons, 1763. To Jamaica, 1793. To St. Domingo, 1796. To England, 1797. To Holland, 1799. To England, 1799. To Ireland, 1804. To the Peninsula, 1808. To England, 1809. To the Peninsula, 1813. To Belgium, 1815 (battle of Waterloo). To England, 1818. To Ireland, 1819. Disbanded in 1821. Again raised in 1858. To England, 1858. To India, 1864. To England, 1875. To Ireland, 1881. To England, 1887. To India, 1889.

19th (*Princess of Wales's Own*) Hussars.

[Bangalore, Madras. Depot, Canterbury.

The Elephant.—"MYSORE" "ASSAYE" "NIAGARA" "EGYPT, 1882, 1884" "TEL-EL-KEBIR" "NILE, 1884-85" "ABU KLEA."

Yrs. Serv. Full Pay	Yrs. Serv. Half Pay		2ND LIEUT.	LIEUT.	CAPTAIN.	BREV.MAJ.	MAJOR.
22	...	**Colonel.**—Coote Synge Hutchinson,[1] *Cornet*, [P]14 June 50; *Lieut.* [P]1 Aug. 51; *Capt.* [P]30 Nov. 55; *Major*, 7 July 58; *Bt.Lt.Colonel*, 26 Apr. 59; *Colonel*, 19 Nov. 66; *Major General*, 1 Oct. 77; *Lieut.General*, 1 July 81; *Colonel* 19 Hussars, 24 Mar. 89.					
		Lieutenant Colonel.—John Compton Hanford,[6] Lt. 26 Mar. 74; Capt. 1 July 81; Bt.Major, 18 Nov. 82; Major, 20 Sept. 84; Bt.Lt.Colonel, 15 June 85; Colonel, 15 June 89; Lt.Colonel, 7 Feb. 93.					
		MAJORS.					
21	...	Chas. Bradford Harries Wolseley-Jenkins[7]		13 June 74	1 July 81	21 May 84	11 Nov. 84
20	...	Dudley Richard Apthorp[9]		20 Nov. 75	26 Apr. 82		2 Sept. 91
15	...	Edmund Kendal Grimstone Aylmer[10] (*Depot*)	11 Aug. 80	1 July 81	7 Nov. 83		7 Feb. 93
13	...	Hew Dalrymple Fanshawe[13]		28 June 82	2 July 84		25 Oct. 93
		CAPTAINS.					
13	...	Harry Graham Marsh[14]		29 July 82	18 April 85		
13	...	John Charles Arthington Walker[15]		29 July 82	20 Jan. 86		
13	...	Hugh Gerald Stewart Young[16]		2 Aug. 82	6 Feb. 89		
13	...	Harold George De Pledge[18]		2 Aug. 82	11 June 90		
13	...	Pandia John Zigomala[23]		10 Mar. 83	2 Sept. 91		
11	...	Adam Bruck-Boyd-Wilson[24]		12 Nov. 84	8 June 91		
		LIEUTENANTS.					
6	...	Eustace Tickell Hill	10 July 89	6 Aug. 90			
6	...	Alfred Jennings-Bramly, **Adjutant** 1 Jan. 94	9 Oct. 89	6 Aug. 90			
6	...	Philip Walhouse Chetwode (*Depot*)	20 Nov. 89	6 Aug. 90			
4	...	Andrew Jackson Moseley	30 May 91	2 July 92			
4	...	Albert Lawrence Powell	30 May 91	2 July 92			
4	...	George Algernon Egerton	10 Oct. 91	18 Oct. 92			
4	...	Robert Frederick Cox	10 Oct. 91	18 Oct. 93			
4	...	Carlisle Vincent Henderson	10 Oct. 91	18 Oct. 93			
4	...	Montagu George Erskine Woodmass	7 Nov. 91	23 Nov. 93			
4	...	Ernest Snowdon St. Quintin	5 Dec. 91	31 Jan. 94			
4	...	Wellington Robert Paul Stapleton-Cotton	12 Mar. 92	20 Feb. 94			
3	...	Arthur Reginald Armstrong	5 Oct. 92	15 Aug. 94			
		SECOND LIEUTENANTS.					
3	...	Norman Fyfe Uniacke	9 Nov. 92				
3	...	Martin Archer-Shee	15 Mar. 93				
2	...	Archibald John Campbell	23 Dec. 93				
2	...	George Despard Franks	7 Mar. 94				
1	...	Steuart Scott Binny	2 June 94				
1	...	Herbert Alfred Porter	2 June 94				
1	...	James Frederick Ritchie	2 June 94				

[23] Captain Zigomala served in the Nile Expedition in 1884-85 with the 19th Hussars (Medal with Clasp, and Khedive's Star).

Paymaster.—Lieut. A. L. Powell (*acting*).

4 ... **Riding Master.**—William Frank Graham Percy, 4 Nov. 91; *Hon. Lieut.*

11 ... **Quarter Master.**—V℅ William Thomas Marshall,[26] 20 Jan. 85; *Hon. Captain*, 20 Jan. 95.

Blue.—*Agents*, Messrs. Cox and Co.   *Embarked for India*, 1891.

---

[1] Lt.General Hutchinson served with the 2nd Dragoon Guards in the Indian campaign in 1858-59, including the siege and capture of Lucknow and subsequent operations, and commanded a detached Squadron in the action of Barree, and Trans-Gogra affairs at Bungaon and Newabghur (mentioned in despatches, Medal with Clasp, and Brevet of Lt.Colonel).

[6] Colonel Hanford served with the 19th Hussars in the Egyptian war of 1882, and was present in the action at Kassasin (9th September), and at the battle of Tel-el-Kebir (mentioned in despatches, Brevet of Major, Medal with Clasp, 4th Class of the Medjidie, and Khedive's Star). Served in the Soudan Expedition in 1884 with the 19th Hussars, and was present in the engagements at El Teb and Temai (4th Class of the Osmanieh, two Clasps). Served in the Nile Expedition in 1884-85 with the 19th Hussars, and was present in the action at Kirbekan (mentioned in despatches, Brevet of Lt.Colonel, two Clasps).

[7] Major Wolseley-Jenkins served with the 19th Hussars in the Egyptian war of 1882, and was present in the action at Kassasin (9th September), and at the battle of Tel-el-Kebir (Medal with Clasp, and Khedive's Star). Served in the Soudan Expedition in 1884 with the 19th Hussars, and was present in the engagements at El Teb and Temai (mentioned in despatches, Brevet of Major, 4th Class of the Medjidie, two Clasps).

[9] Major Apthorp served with the 19th Hussars in the Egyptian war of 1882, and was present in the action at Kassasin on the 9th September (Medal, and Khedive's Star). Served in the Soudan Expedition in 1884 with the 19th Hussars, and was present in the engagements at El Teb and Temai (two Clasps). Served in the Soudan Expedition in 1885 with the 19th Hussars (Clasp).

[10] Major Aylmer served with the 19th Hussars in the Egyptian war of 1882, and was present in the engagements at El Magfar and Mahsama, and at the battle of Tel-el-Kebir (Medal with Clasp, and Khedive's Star). Served in the Soudan Expedition in 1884 with the 19th Hussars, and was present in the engagements at El Teb and Temai (two Clasps). Served in the Nile Expedition in 1884-85 with the 19th Hussars, and was present in the action at Kirbekan (two Clasps).

[13] Major Fanshawe served with the 19th Hussars in the Egyptian war of 1882, and was present in the action at Kassasin on the 9th September and at the battle of Tel-el-Kebir (Medal with Clasp, and Khedive's Star). Served in the Soudan Expedition in 1884 with the 19th Hussars, and was present in the engagements at El Teb and Temai (mentioned in despatches, two Clasps). Served in the Nile Expedition in 1884-85 with the 19th Hussars, and was present in the engagements at Abu Klea and Metammeh (two Clasps).

[14] Captain Marsh served in the Soudan Expedition in 1884 with the 19th Hussars, and was present in the engagements at El Teb and Temai (Medal with Clasp, and Khedive's Star). Served in the Nile Expedition in 1884-85 with the 19th Hussars (Clasp).

[15] Captain Walker served in the Soudan Expedition in 1884 with the 19th Hussars, and was present in the engagements at El Teb and Tema (Medal with Clasp, and Khedive's Star). Served in the Nile Expedition in 1884-85 with the 19th Hussars (Clasp).

[16] Captain Young served in the Soudan Expedition in 1884 with the 19th Hussars, and was present in the engagement at Temai (Medal with Clasp, and Khedive's Star). Served in the Nile Expedition in 1884-85 with the 19th Hussars, and was present in the engagements at Abu Klea and Metammeh (two Clasps).

[18] Captain De Pledge served in the Soudan Expedition in 1884 with the 19th Hussars, and was present in the engagements at El Teb and Temai (Medal with Clasp, and Khedive's Star). Served in the Nile Expedition in 1884-85 with the 19th Hussars, and was present in the engagements at Abu Klea and Metammeh (two Clasps).

[24] Captain Boyd-Wilson served during the Nile Expedition in 1884-85 with the 1st Battalion Yorkshire Regiment in the Line of Communication up the Nile. Served with the Soudan Frontier Field Force under Sir Frederick Stephenson in 1885-86, and was present in the engagement at Giniss (Medal, and Khedive's Star).

[26] Captain Marshall served in the Egyptian war of 1882 and was present at the battle of Tel-el-Kebir (Medal with Clasp, and Khedive's Star). Also served in the expedition to the Soudan in 1884 and was present in the engagements at El Teb and Temai (mentioned in despatches, Victoria Cross, and two Clasps): was awarded the V℅ "for his conspicuous bravery during the Cavalry charge at El Teb on 29th February last, in bringing Lt.Colonel Barrow, 19th Hussars, out of action. That officer, having been severely wounded and his horse killed, was on the ground surrounded by the enemy, when Quartermaster-Sergeant Marshall, who stayed behind with him, seized his horse and dragged him through the enemy back to the regiment. Had Lt. Colonel Barrow been left behind he must have been killed."

20th Hussars.

"VIMIERA" "PENINSULA" "SUAKIN, 1885."

Colonel.—Sir Roger William Henry Palmer,[1] *Bart., Cornet,* P22 Jan. 53; *Lt.* 4 Sept. 54; *Capt.* P22 July 59; *Major and Lt.Colonel,* P8 Mar. 64; *Colonel,* 8 Mar. 69; *Major General,* 15 Mar. 79; *Lt.General,* 1 July 81; *Colonel* 20 Hussars, 11 June 91.

26 **Lieutenant Colonel.**—Miles *Lord* Beaumont,[4] *Lt.* P5 May 69; *Capt.* 3 Aug. 72; *Major,* 2 July 84; *Lt.Colonel,* 9 Sept. 91.

Yrs Ser.		CORNET OR 2ND LIEUT.	LIEUT.	CAPTAIN.	BREV.MAJ.	MAJOR.
	MAJORS.					
27	William John Irwin[5] (*Bt. Lt.Colonel* 28 Dec. 88)	23 Jan. 69	28 Oct. 71	30 Nov. 79	......	9 Sept. 85
22	Thomas Barnes Weston............................	......	23 April 73	1 Jan. 80	......	1 July 88
17	Horace George Proctor Beauchamp[9]............	......	11 Oct. 78	15 Oct. 84	......	9 Aug. 93
	CAPTAINS.					
14	Henry Graham[8]	23 Apr. 81	1 July 81	14 July 86		
14	William Douglas Whatman[10]............	......	22 Oct. 81	16 Mar. 87		
13	Norton Legge,[11] *serving with the Egyptian Army*	......	2 Aug. 82	23 Dec. 87		
12	Arthur Morgan Bulkeley Jones[17]............	......	31 Oct. 83	11 Dec. 89		
10	Graham Thomas George Edwards............	......	29 Aug. 85	18 Oct. 93		
10	James Whitaker, **Adjutant** 24 July 93 ...	......	25 Nov. 85	6 Apr. 94		
10	Herbert Roberts Manton[20]............	......	30 Jan. 86	10 Oct. 94		
9	Ponsonby May Lynn Carew............	......	4 Dec. 86	13 Feb. 95		
	LIEUTENANTS.					
9	Herbert Wiltshire[21]	......	11 Dec. 86			
7	Arthur Otway Jacob............	19 Dec. 88	14 June 93			
5	Gerald Walter James FitzGerald Stannus	23 June 90	9 Aug. 93			
4	Henry Bremner............	23 Jan. 92	18 Oct. 93			
2	Hugh Leonard Acland-Troyte............	23 Dec. 93	10 Oct. 94			
2	Hubert Balfour Ogilvy Williams............	17 Jan. 94	10 Oct. 94			
	SECOND LIEUTENANTS.					
2	Thomas Elliott Bayley............	31 Jan. 94				
1	William Wyborgh James	13 Oct. 94				
1	Gilbert Mars Reginald Alexander Swiney	12 Dec. 94				
1	Harry Romer Lee	20 Feb. 95				

[11] Captain Legge served in the Soudan campaign in 1885, and was present in the engagement at Hasheen, the attack on the convoy on the 24th March, and at the destruction of Temai (Medal with Clasp, and Khedive's Star). Served with the Egyptian Frontier Field Force in 1885-86, and was present at the investment of Kosheh, the relief of Ambigole, and the engagement at Giniss (mentioned in despatches).

1 *Riding Master.*—John Rolan Crawshaw, 27 Feb. 95; *Hon. Lieut.* to 1 Life Guards.
6 *Quarter Master.*—Frank Talland, 10 May 89; *Hon. Lieut.*

Blue.—*Agents,* Messrs. Cox and Co. *Returned from Egypt,* 19 November 1887.

---

[1] Sir Roger Palmer served in the Eastern campaign of 1854, and up to 26th August 1855 with the 11th Hussars, including the affair of Bulganak, battles of Alma, Balaklava, and Inkerman, and siege of Sebastopol (Medal with four Clasps, and Turkish Medal).

[4] Lord Beaumont served in the Bechuanaland Expedition under Sir Charles Warren in 1884-85 with the Volunteer Mounted troops. Served with the Egyptian Frontier Field Force in 1885-86, and was present in the engagement at Giniss (Medal, and Khedive's Star).

[5] Major Irwin served in the operations near Suakin in December 1888 including the engagement at Gemaizah (mentioned in despatches, Brevet of Lt. Colonel, Medal with Clasp, and Khedive Star); also served in the operations on the Soudan frontier in 1889 including the engagement at Toski (mentioned in despatches, 3rd Class of the Medjidie, and Clasp).

[8] Captain Graham served in the Soudan campaign in 1885, and was present in the engagement at the Tofrek zereba (Medal with two Clasps, and Khedive's Star).

[9] Major Beauchamp served in the Soudan campaign in 1885 (Medal with Clasp, and Khedive's Star). Served with the Soudan Frontier Field Force in 1885-86 and was present in the engagement at Giniss; also served in the operations near Suakin in December 1888 including the engagement at Gemaizah (mentioned in despatches, Clasp).

[10] Captain Whatman served in the Soudan campaign in 1885 (Medal with Clasp, and Khedive's Star). Served with the Egyptian Frontier Field Force in 1885-86, and was present in the engagement at Giniss.

[17] Captain Jones served with the Egyptian Frontier Field Force in 1885-86, and was present in the engagement at Giniss in command of the escort to the General Officer Commanding (Medal, and Khedive's Star).

[20] Captain Manton served in the operations near Suakin in December 1888 including the engagement at Gemaizah (Medal with Clasp, 5th Class of the Medjidie, and Khedive's Star).

[21] Lieut. Wiltshire served in the Egyptian war of 1882, and was present in the engagement at Mahsama, in the two actions at Kassasin, at the battle of Tel-el-Kebir, and the capture of Cairo (Medal with Clasp, and Khedive's Star). Served in the operations in the Soudan in 1889, including the engagement at Toski (Clasp).

Record of the Services of the 20th Hussars.

Raised in 1759 as the 20th Inniskilling Light Dragoons. Ireland till 1763, when it was disbanded. Raised in 1779 as the 20th Light Dragoons. United Kingdom till 1783, when it was disbanded. Raised in 1791 as the 2cth Jamaica Light Dragoons. Jamaica to 1802. England to 1803. To the Mediterranean, 1805. (A wing to San Salvador in 1805, thence to the Cape in 1805, and South America (capture of Monte Video), returning to England, 1807.] Head Quarters at Barcelona, June 1806; a detachment to Maida, 1807; a detachment to Egypt, June 1808 six troops in England and four troops in Sicily, July 1808. Head Quarters to the Peninsula (battle of Vimiera). The whole Regiment to Messina, Sept. 1809. Head Quarters to Palermo. May 1812; Sicily and Malta, 1815; and in September embarked for England. To Ireland, 1817. Disbanded, December 1818. Raised in 1860 as 20th Light Dragoons at Muttra of volunteers from the 2nd European Bengal Light Cavalry on the amalgamation of the British and Indian Forces. Soon afterwards changed to Hussars. India till Oct. 1872. England till Nov. 1879. Ireland till Aug. 1884. Head Quarters and four troops to Suakin, one troop to the Nile, 1885. In Egypt and Soudan till Oct. 1887. Then to England.

21st Hussars.

[Secunderabad, Madras. Depot at Canterbury.]

Years' Ser. Full Pay.	Half Pay.			2ND LIEUT.	LIEUT.	CAPTAIN.	BREV. MAJ.	MAJOR.
27	...	Colonel.—Sir Robert Whit KCB. Cornet, P15 Oct. 47; Lieut. P22 Dec. 48; Capt. P26 March 52; Brevet Major, 12 Dec. 54; Major, 12 July 58; Lt.Colonel, P21 Feb. 60; Colonel, 21 Feb. 65; Major General, 1 March 70; Lieut.General, 8 July 85; General, 11 Nov. 90; Colonel 21 Hussars, 28 March 86. Lieutenant Colonel.—Rowland Hill Martin,[3] Cornet, 14 Jan. 69; Lieut. 28 Oct. 71; Captain, 16 Dec. 78; Major, 2 Feb. 84; Lt.Colonel, 26 Oct. 92.						
		MAJORS.						
21	...	o.s.c. Walter George Crole Wyndham[4] ...		......	11 Feb. 75	19 May 80	......	16 July 84
17	...	Charles Berkeley Pigott,[6] DSO.		19 Feb. 79	9 Feb. 81	31 Jan. 83	15 June 85	26 Oct. 92
22	...	Richard Owen,[7] Military Secretary, Bombay		......	12 Nov. 73	13 June 83	......	6 Nov. 92
15	...	Harry Finn,[9] D.A.A.General, Madras, 25 Jan. 93		23 Mar. 81	1 July 81	23 Nov. 87	......	24 Oct. 94
		CAPTAINS.						
15	...	John Fowle[8]		22 Jan. 81	1 July 81	23 Nov. 87		
15	...	Henry Charles Higgs,[10] Adjutant Devon Yeomanry Brigade 1 June 93		11 Aug. 80	1 July 81	16 July 88		
13	...	William Markham Doyne............		......	27 Jan. 83	9 Sept. 88		
12	...	Frank Henry Eadon		......	30 Jan. 84	6 Nov. 89		
11	...	Thursby Henry Ernest Dauncey[11]		......	20 Sept. 84	26 Oct. 92		
10	...	James George Fair (Depot)............		......	29 Aug. 85	26 Oct. 92		
9	...	David Bowly............		......	25 Aug. 86	25 Jan. 93		
13	...	William Wilfred Cordeaux		......	10 Mar. 83	30 Jan. 95		
		LIEUTENANTS.						
9	...	Paul Aloysius Kenna............		......	25 Aug. 86			
8	...	Sir Edward Hudson Hudson-Kinahan, Bart............		21 May 87	31 July 89			
8	...	Charles James Clerk (Depot)		5 Oct. 87	6 Nov. 89			
8	...	Hon. Raymond Harvey Lodge Joseph de Montmorency, Adjutant 1 July 93		24 Sept. 87	6 Nov. 89			
8	...	Francis Edward Paulet		5 Oct. 87	1 Apr. 90			
8	...	Donald Maclachlan		16 Nov. 87	21 Apr. 90			
7	...	James Stamers Roche[13]		3 Oct. 88	13 Aug. 90			
7	...	Arthur Murray Pirie............		30 Jan. 89	11 Nov. 91			
7	...	Miles John Stapylton		30 Jan. 89	26 Oct. 92			
6	...	Robert Napier Smyth		12 Feb. 90	6 Nov. 92			
5	...	Arthur Henry Mendle Taylor		28 June 90	25 Jan. 93			
		SECOND LIEUTENANTS.						
5	...	Theobald Michael Langton		4 Mar. 91				
3	...	Norman Baskervyle Glegg Strong		18 June 92				
3	...	Arthur Duncan Champion............		21 Sept. 92				
3	...	Ernest Hastings Lewis		17 Dec. 92				
3	...	Edward William Woodward Scott		15 Mar. 93				
2	...	William Walter Maurice Tweedie		28 June 93				
1	...	William Augustus Cumming Fraser		2 June 94				
1	...	Craufuird George Graham Hutchison ...		2 June 94				

[13] Lieut. Roche served throughout the Nile Expedition in 1884-85 with the 20th Hussars Troop of the Light Camel Corps, including the operations of the Desert Column and the engagement at Abu Klea Wells on the 16th and 17th February (Medal with Clasp, and Khedive's Star). Served with the Soudan Frontier Field Force in 1885-86, and was present in the engagement at Giniss.

| 10 | ... | Paymaster.—Lieut. D. Maclachlan (acting). Riding Master.—William Henry King, 10 June 85; Hon. Lieut. |
| 10 | ... | Quarter Master.—George Leslie Graham, 24 June 85; Hon. Lieut. |

Blue.—Agents, Messrs. Cox and Co.   Embarked for India, 23 November 1887.

---

[1] Sir Robert White served in the Eastern campaign of 1854 with the 17th Lancers, including the affair of Bulganak, battles of Alma and Balaklava, and siege of Sebastopol. At Balaklava he led the squadron of direction was severely wounded, and had his horse shot (Medal with three Clasps, Brevet of Major, 5th Class of the Mediidie, and Turkish Medal). Proceeded with his Regiment to India in 1857, and served throughout the campaign in Central India in 1858-59, part of the time in command of a Flying Column, including the action of Barode (Medal).

[3] Lt.Colonel Martin served with the Bechuanaland Expedition under Sir Charles Warren in 1884-85, during the latter part of the time in command of a Regiment of Mounted Rifles.

[4] Major Wyndham served with King's Dragoon Guards in the Zulu war of 1879, and subsequently in Baker Russell's Flying Column (Medal with Clasp). Served throughout the Nile Expedition in 1884-85 with the Light Camel Regiment, and took part in the operations of the Desert Column (Medal with Clasp, and Khedive's Star).

[6] Major Pigott served with the 3rd Battalion 60th Rifles in the Zulu war from April to September 1879 (Medal with Clasp). Also served with the Mounted Infantry in the Boer war in 1881, and was present in the engagements at Lang's Nek and the Ingogo River. Served with the Mounted Infantry in the Egyptian war of 1882, was present in the reconnaissance in force from Alexandria on 5th August, and commanded the Mounted Infantry in the engagements at Tel-el-Mahuta and Mahsama (mentioned in despatches, promoted Captain for distinguished service), and at the action at Kassasin on the 28th August—severely wounded (twice mentioned in despatches, Medal, 5th Class of the Medjidie, and Khedive's Star); also served in the expedition to the Soudan in 1884 with the 19th Hussars, and was present in the engagements at El Teb and Temai (two Clasps). Served with the Nile Expedition in 1884-85 in command of a company of Mounted Infantry, took part in the operations of the Desert Column under Sir Herbert Stewart, and was present at the actions of Abu Klea and Abu Kru, in the reconnaissance to Metammeh, and in the engagement at Abu Klea Wells on the 16th and 17th February; carried the despatches across the Bayuda Desert from El Gubat to Korti (mentioned in despatches, Brevet of Major, two Clasps). Served in the expedition against the Yonne and other tribes on the West Coast of Africa in 1887-88 as second in command (mentioned in despatches, DSO.).

[7] Major Owen served in the Afghan war of 1879-80, first attached to the 9th Lancers, and afterwards as Aide de Camp to Sir Donald Stewart (Medal). Served with the 14th Hussars in the Boer war of 1881 under Sir Evelyn Wood. Served during the Burmese Expedition in 1885-87 as Aide de Camp to Sir Frederick Roberts (Medal with Clasp).

[8] Captain Fowle served in the Nile Expedition in 1884 with the Light Camel Regiment (Medal with Clasp, and Khedive's Star).

[9] Major Finn served in the Afghan war of 1878-80, and was present in the engagements at Killa Kazi and Siah Sung, and in the operations around Cabul in December 1879 including the investment of Sherpore (mentioned in despatches, Medal with Clasp, Medal for distinguished service in the Field).

[10] Captain Higgs served in the Nile Expedition in 1885 with the Light Camel Regiment (Medal with Clasp, and Khedive's Star).

[11] Captain Dauncey served in the Egyptian war of 1882 with the 7th Dragoon Guards, and was present in the engagements at El Magfar and Mahsama, at the two actions at Kassasin, and at the battle of Tel-el-Kebir and the capture of Cairo (Medal with Clasp, and Khedive's Star). [See also Civil Decorations for Gallantry, "Hart's Annual Army List," p. 785.]

Royal Regiment of Artillery.

The Royal Arms and supporters, with a Cannon, and the Motto "*Ubique*," over the Gun, and "*Quo fas et gloria ducunt*," below it.

NOTE.—The letters A, B, C, &c., prefixed to the Names denote Horse Batteries, the Figures Field Batteries.—G.C. Gentleman Cadet Company.—R.R. Riding Establishment.—*p.a.c.* after the Name denotes Passed the Senior Class, Artillery College; E. Eastern Division; S. Southern Division; W. Western Division; RD. Field Artillery; RHA. Royal Horse Artillery; D.S. District Staff; MN. Mountain Artillery.

Colonel.—Field Marshal His Royal Highness George W. F. C. Duke of Cambridge,[1] *KG. KT. KP. GCB. GCSI. GCMG. GCIE. Commander in Chief, 10 May 1861.*

Ent. ist.	COLONELS COMMANDANT.	SECOND LIEUT.	FIRST LIEUT.	CAPTAIN.	BREVET MAJOR.	MAJOR.	BREVET LT.-COL.	LT.-COL.	BREVET COLONEL.	COLONEL.	COLONEL COMM.	MAJOR GENERAL.	LIEUT. GENERAL.	GENERAL.
60	B C Dickson, Sir Collingwood,[2] *GCB*.	18 Dec. 35	29 June 37	1 Apr. 46	22 May 46	......	20 June 54	23 Feb. 56	5 Apr. 66	17 Nov. 75	24 Aug. 66	8 June 76	1 Oct. 77
65	Fitzmayer, Sir James William,[4] *KCB. R. H. A.*	6 Nov. 30	31 Oct. 31	22 Apr. 42	20 June 54	......	2 Nov. 54	29 June 54	1 Apr. 60	26 Nov. 76	29 Dec. 67	15 Apr. 77	1 Oct. 77
56	Askwith, William Harrison[5].	18 Dec. 29	6 Nov. 30	23 Nov. 41	28 Jan. 42	......	20 June 54	20 July 54	26 Oct. 68	15 Apr. 77	1 Jan. 68	20 Apr. 77	27 June 79
57	D'Aguilar, Sir Charles Lawrence,[6] *GCB*.	18 Dec. 29	7 July 30	12 Apr. 42	12 Dec. 54	......	26 Dec. 56	2 Mar. 59	1 Jan. 68	8 Nov. 80	8 Mar. 68	1 Oct. 77	1 Apr. 84
59	Adye, Sir John Miller,[7] *GCB*.	13 Dec. 36	7 July 39	22 July 46	22 Sept. 54	......	26 Dec. 54	29 Apr. 57	19 May 60	4 Nov. 81	28 June 68	27 June 79	20 Nov. 84
58	Gardiner, Henry Lyndoch,[8] *CB. Equerry to the Queen*	14 Dec. 30	16 Mar. 40	9 Nov. 46	20 July 55	......	......	9 Aug. 58	6 July 67	7 Nov. 84	6 July 67	26 Nov. 80	1 Oct. 82
52	Biddulph, Sir Michael Anthony Shrapnel,[9] *KCB. Keeper of the Jewels, Tower of London.*	17 June 43	26 Apr. 44	4 Oct. 50	12 Dec. 54	......	6 June 56	10 Aug. 64	14 Aug. 63	17 June 74	14 July 85	30 Mar. 69	13 Feb. 81	1 Nov. 86
58	Radcliffe, Robert Parker	14 Dec. 37	13 May 40	9 Nov. 46	......	......	26 Oct. 58	26 Dec. 58	6 July 67	22 May 86	17 May 69	1 Sept. 83	
53	Fraser, Hon. Sir David Macdowall,[10] *KCB*.	11 Jan. 40	14 Jan. 41	17 May 50	2 Nov. 55	......	26 Apr. 59	27 June 64	8 Oct. 73	22 May 89	1 May 80	20 Apr. 84	1 July 85
48	*p.a.c.* Yates, Henry Peel,[11] *CB*.	18 Dec. 38	6 Nov. 40	16 July 54	12 Dec. 54	......	26 Apr. 59	24 Dec. 70	24 June 79	24 Apr. 90	1 May 80	20 Nov. 84	1 May 85
54	Williams, Edward Arthur,[12] *CB*.	1 May 42	8 Nov. 42	1 Nov. 48	......	......	24 June 62	24 Jan. 68	24 Apr. 72	24 Sept. 90	1 May 80	1 May 85	
54	Johnson, George Vanderheyden[13]	1 Jan. 42	4 Apr. 43	1 Nov. 48	......	......	24 Jan. 63	24 Jan. 68	24 Apr. 72	8 Mar. 91	17 May 80	10 Dec. 83	1 Apr. 86
53	Pipon, Philip Gosset,[14] *CB*.	18 June 42	8 Aug. 43	6 Sept. 49	12 Dec. 54	......	7 May 61	1 Mar. 63	24 Apr. 72	13 Nov. 80	6 Oct. 92	4 Jan. 86	31 July 90
52	Arbuthnot, Sir Charles George,[15] *GCB*.	17 June 43	1 Feb. 45	4 Apr. 51	......	......	29 Oct. 64	1 Dec. 69	1 Dec. 70	16 Jan. 75	3 Aug. 93	1 July 81	1 July 86	1 Oct. 87
52	Hastings, Francis William[16]	17 June 43	5 Apr. 45	24 July 51	2 Nov. 55	......	25 Nov. 64	1 June 65	......	......	16 Sept. 93	7 July 82	16 July 86	19 May 89
52	Smyth, Sir Henry Augustus,[17] *KCMG.*	20 Dec. 43	5 Apr. 45	21 Aug. 51	12 Feb. 63	......	31 Aug. 65	31 Jan. 70	10 Jan. 75	17 Oct. 94	1 Nov. 82	1 Nov. 86	1 Oct. 87	25 Nov. 92
42	Biddulph, Sir Robert,[18] *GCMG. CB. Governor and Commander in Chief, Gibraltar, 6 Oct. 93 [R] Removed from the Regt. having ranked as General Officers.*	22 June 53	30 May 54	1 Apr. 60	15 Feb. 61	5 July 72	15 Jan. 64	17 May 79	25 Jan. 72	6 Mar. 95	......	28 Mar. 83	1 Oct. 87	
39	Brackenbury, Sir Henry,[19] *KCB. Member of the Governor General's Council, India*	......	7 Apr. 56	8 Aug. 61	1 Apr. 74	10 Feb. 75	25 Oct. 75	5 Dec. 82	25 Oct. 80	......	......	15 June 85	1 Apr. 88	
19	Hay, Sir Robert John,[20] *KCB. Director of Artillery,* *War Office, 31 Oct. 91 [R]*	6 Aug. 46	7 May 47	17 Mar. 54	1 Feb. 61	......	28 May 70	25 May 75	20 Feb. 78	......	......	16 Dec. 85	1 Apr. 89	
48	Williams, Sir William John,[21] *KCB. [R]*	2 May 47	30 June 48	24 Aug. 54	2 Nov. 55	......	24 Oct. 65	17 Jan. 71	7 Jan. 76	10 Sept. 79	......	4 Jan. 86	19 May 90	1 Nov. 90
46	*p.a.c.* Goodenough, William Howley,[22] *CB. [R] Commanding the Troops in South Africa 3 Dec. 94*	19 Dec. 49	24 Apr. 51	23 Feb. 56	20 July 58	5 July 72	25 Mar. 69	13 Jan. 75	5 July 77	7 Sept. 81	......	1 Apr. 86	19 May 91	
42	Stirling, Sir Wm.,[23] *KCB. Gen. K.M. Acad. 13 Apr. 90 [R]*	27 June 53	30 May 54	1 Apr. 60	9 Apr. 61	5 July 72	5 Jan. 72	17 May 79	1 Oct. 77	......	......	1 Oct. 87	25 Nov. 92	
40	Forster, Bowes Lennox,[24] *Com. Thames Dist., May 92 [R]*	1 Oct. 55	22 June 65	17 July 74	6 Feb. 75	19 July 76	1 Oct. 82	6 Feb. 80	......	......	1 Apr. 89			
45	Markham, Edwin,[25] *Lieut. Governor and Officer Commanding Troops, Jersey, 1 Nov. 92*	29 Dec. 50	22 Oct. 52	17 Nov. 57	......	5 July 72	......	15 Jan. 76	15 Jan. 81	7 Dec. 88	......	30 Apr. 90	27 Mar. 95	
42	*p.a.c.* Nicolls, Oliver Henry Atkins	21 Dec. 53	20 June 54	1 Apr. 60	......	5 July 72	19 July 76	23 Jan. 79	1 Nov. 87	1 Nov. 81	......	27 Aug. 90		
42	Smart, George Joseph,[26] *Comdg. at Woolwich, 4 Feb. 94*	18 June 57	12 July 53	5 May 58	......	5 July 72	......	20 Apr. 77	1 Oct. 82	......	......	1 Nov. 90		
41	Geary, Henry Le Guay,[30] *CB. Brigadier General on the Staff, Portsmouth, 10 May 91*	28 Feb. 55	1 Apr. 55	12 May 62	15 Aug. 68	5 July 72	......	7 Sept. 81	1 Oct. 82	......	......	1 May 91		
43	Aiderson, Sir Henry James,[31] *KCB. President of the Ordnance Committee, 31 Oct. 91*	23 June 52	17 Feb. 54	1 Apr. 59	......	5 July 77	......	1 Oct. 77	1 Oct. 83	......	......	9 July 92		
38	Owen, John Fletcher[33]	......	1 Oct. 57	1 Apr. 69	......	29 Nov. 79	......	29 Nov. 83	......	......	7 Feb. 94			
38	Harness, Arthur,[34] *CB*.	......	23 June 57	25 Oct. 68	......	28 June 77	11 July 78	11 May 85	1 Nov. 82	......	......	11 Apr. 94		
	COLONELS on Half Pay.													
	Richardson, John Booth,[37] *Commanding R. R. Art., Gibraltar,* *with rank of Major General, 14 Mar. 94.*	......	20 Apr. 55	17 Dec. 62	1 Apr. 59	5 July 72	1 July 81	29 Oct. 81	1 July 85	......				
	Nicholson, Stuart James,[38] *Commanding R. Art., Malta, with rank of Major General, 4 Nov. 92*	......	31 July 55	3 Oct. 63	1 Apr. 69	5 July 72	1 July 81	11 Jan. 82	15 June 85	......				
	Lynes, Samuel Parr	......	1 Oct. 55	10 May 65	......	11 Mar. 74	1 July 81	1 July 82	1 July 85					
	Lewes, Henry Colebrook,[14] *Insp. Gen. R. Art., India,* *with rank of Major General, 28 Mar. 92*	......	19 Dec. 55	1 Nov. 65	......	31 Oct. 74	31 Oct. 81	1 Oct. 82	31 Oct. 85					

Royal Artillery.

Colonels on Half Pay.

Yrs Ser.		Colonels on Half Pay.	Second Lieut.	First Lieut.	Captain.	Brevet Major.	Major.	Brevet Lt. Col.	Lt. Col.	Lt. Col. R. Art.	Brevet Colonel.	Colonel.
		Pretyman, George Tyndal[15]		21 Mar. 67	1 Oct. 77	22 Nov. 79	1 Jan. 84	2 Mar. 81	6 Oct. 85		6 Nov. 85	
		Curzon, William Southwell		7 Apr. 56	7 Sept. 66		1 Apr. 75	1 Apr. 82	1 Apr. 84		1 Apr. 86	
		Murdoch, William Walpole, Commanding Royal Artillery, Raewul Pindee Circle, 17 Nov. 90		21 June 56	6 July 67		28 Oct. 75	28 Oct. 82	27 Aug. 84		1 Oct. 86	
		Gallwey, Patrick FitzGerald,[40] Inspector General of Ordnance, Bengal, 1 Apr. 90		1 Oct. 57	15 Nov. 69		1 Oct. 77		1 Oct. 84		1 Oct. 88	
	p.s.c.	Hutchinson, Wm. Francis Moore, Colonel on the Staff, Com. R. A. Curragh, 1 Apr. 91		1 Oct. 57	31 July 69		1 July 77	1 July 84	1 May 85		9 Apr. 89	
		Isaacson, Henry de Stuteville, Colonel on the Staff, Halifax, 18 July 93		23 June 57	10 Nov. 68				21 July 85		1 July 88	
		Lloyd, Francis Thomas,[43] CB. Deputy Adjutant General for Royal Artillery, War Office, with rank of Major General, 21 Feb. 94		1 Oct. 57	28 May 70		24 Nov. 77	21 Mar. 84	24 Nov. 84		21 May 88	
		Thomas-Le Marchant, Hy. St. John Vaughan Le Marchant, Col. on Staff York, 23 May 94		1 Oct. 57	1 Jan. 71		1 Feb. 78		1 Jan. 85		28 Nov. 89	
		Moorsom, Henry Manvers[48]		1 Oct. 57	7 Sept. 71		20 Feb. 78		20 Feb. 85		30 Mar. 88	
	p.s.c.	Burgmann, George John, Colonel on the Staff, Commanding R. Art. Dover, 19 Mar. 94		1 Oct. 57	28 Sept. 71		10 Apr. 78		1 Feb. 85		4 Sept. 89	
		Hazlerigg, Thomas Maynard,[50] Assistant Adjutant General, Woolwich, 12 Feb. 91		23 Dec. 57	1 Nov. 71		27 June 79	22 Nov. 79	13 July 86		22 Nov. 83	
		Murray, James Murray[51] Assistant Commandant, Royal Military Academy, 20 Sept. 91		22 June 59	23 Dec. 71		23 Aug. 79		27 June 86		7 Sept. 90	
		Tyler, Trevor Bruce, Colonel on the Staff, Commanding R. Art. Kirkee, 28 Oct. 93		18 Dec. 60	4 Feb. 74	22 Nov. 79	7 Sept. 81	15 June 83	1 Sept. 86		7 Sept. 90	
		Stewart, Robt. MacGregor,[72] CB. A.D.C. to the Queen, and Comdt. School of Gun. 9 Mar. 94		19 June 60	23 Nov. 72		7 Feb. 81		1 Jan. 89		18 June 87	
		Walkey, Rowland, Colonel on the Staff, Commanding R. Artillery, Devonport, 1 Dec. 93		19 June 60	23 Nov. 72		13 Mar. 81	21 May 84	8 Apr. 87		21 May 88	
		Holley, Edmund Hunt,[56] Colonel on the Staff, Commanding R. Art. Cork, 26 Jan. 94		15 Jan. 67	5 Dec. 72		20 Sept. 81	7 Dec. 88	1 Oct. 87		21 May 89	
	p.s.c.	French, George Arthur, CMG. Colonel on the Staff, Commanding R. Art. Bombay, 28 Oct. 93		18 Dec. 60	18 Feb. 74		7 Sept. 81	18 Nov. 82	1 Jan. 88		2 Nov. 92	
		Yeatman-Biggs, Arthur Godolphin,[74] CB. Assist. Adj. General, Bengal Army, 4 Jan. 94		18 Dec. 60	18 Feb. 74		1 Oct. 81		1 Oct. 88		18 Nov. 86	
		Rooke, Harry William		18 Dec. 60	16 Jan. 75		8 July 82		1 Oct. 88		29 Sept. 93	
		M'Clintock, William		18 Dec. 60	17 Dec. 73		8 July 81	15 June 85	8 July 88		29 Jan. 90	
		Morley, Clervaux		19 Dec. 60	1 Mar. 74		7 Sept. 81		7 May 89		29 Sept. 93	
		Slade, John Ramsay,[42] CB. Aide de Camp to the Queen		18 Dec. 60	18 Feb. 74		1 Oct. 81	18 Nov. 82	23 May 90		15 June 89	
		Turner, Alfred Edward,[41] CB. Assist. Adj. General, for R. Art. War Office, 2 Apr. 94		19 Dec. 60	15 Mar. 74						15 June 85	
	p.s.c.	Maurice, John Fred. CB.[89] Colonel on the Staff, Comdg. R.A. East. Dist. 25 May 94		19 Dec. 60	11 Dec. 72	21 Apr. 30	9 Sept. 82					
		Lockhart, Robert Dundas Eliott, Colonel on the Staff, Commanding Horse and Field Art. Woolwich, 22 May 94					13 July 81		1 Oct. 87		29 Aug. 93	
		Pym, Samuel		1 Apr. 61	1 July 74	1 July 81	29 Oct. 81		1 Oct. 87		29 Aug. 93	
	p.s.c.	Clayton, Emilius		1 July 61	1 Oct. 74	1 July 81	29 Oct. 81		29 July 83		6 Jan. 94	
		Thomson, Charles William. Colonel on the Staff, Edinburgh, 4 Feb. 95		1 Nov. 60	9 Aug. 75	1 Oct. 81	30 July 81		31 July 88		29 Sept. 93	
		Lockyer, Edward Stougnuon Braithwaite		18 Dec. 61	16 Jan. 75	18 Dec. 81	24 June 82		24 June 89		25 May 94	

Lieutenant Colonels.

Yrs Ser.				First Lieut.	Captain.	Brevet Major.	Major.	Brevet Lt. Col.	Lt. Col.	Lt. Col. R. Art.	Brevet Colonel.
34	so	O'Callaghan, Desmond Dykes Tynte, Member of Ordnance Committee 8 June 92		18 Dec. 61	16 Jan. 75	18 Dec. 81	23 June 82		23 June 89	1 Feb. 90	6 Jan. 94
34	wn	Robinson, John Corsane[84]		18 Dec. 61	7 Feb. 75	11 Nov. 78	23 July 82		8 July 89	1 Apr. 90	2 May 94
34	fd	Turnbull, George Wilmot Maitland[85]		18 Dec. 61	7 Feb. 75	18 Dec. 81	15 July 82			5 Apr. 90	25 May 94
34	rha	Pipon, Henry,[88] Commanding Royal Horse Artillery, Newbridge		18 Dec. 61	10 Feb. 75	1 Mar. 81	9 Sept. 82			12 May 90	26 July 94
34	rha	Molesworth, St. Aubyn		18 Dec. 61	10 Mar. 75	18 Dec. 81	9 Sept. 82			20 May 90	30 June 90
34	so	Disney, Thomas Robert[90]		18 Dec. 61	18 Feb. 75	18 Dec. 81	1 Oct. 82			1 Sept. 90	1 July 94
34	mn	Keith, James,[103] DSO		18 Dec. 61	1 Apr. 75	18 Dec. 81	1 Oct. 82		1 Oct. 89	25 Jan. 91	26 July 94
33	so	Auchinleck, William Henry		18 Dec. 61	24 Apr. 75	25 June 82	1 Oct. 82		1 Oct. 89		1 June 94
33	fd	Mullins, Henry		25 June 62	8 Sept. 75	1 Sept. 82	1 Oct. 82		1 Oct. 89	6 Feb. 91	1 Sept. 94
33	fd	Kingscote, Henry Blomfield		1 Mar. 63	8 Dec. 75		1 Nov. 82		1 Nov. 89	19 Feb. 91	
33	fd	Laugley, William Savage[91]		1 Mar. 63	23 Jan. 76		14 Feb. 83			30 July 91	
32	so	Ferrier, Alexander Walter		24 June 63	15 Jan. 76		28 Mar. 83		28 Mar. 90	13 July 91	
32	rha	Curtis, Wm. Frederick de Hubbenet,[34] Commanding Militia and Volunteer Artillery, Home Dist.		6 July 63	1 Apr. 76		18 Apr. 83		17 Apr. 90	21 July 91	
32	ra	Dutmas, Francis Frederick		1 Sept. 63	14 Mar. 76	2 Mar. 81	16 Apr. 83	7 Dec. 88		11 Aug. 91	
32	mn	Morgan, Harrison Ross Lewin,[119] CB.		1 Sept. 63	12 Apr. 76	2 Mar. 81	12 May 83		22 May 90	17 Aug. 91	
32	rha	Corbett, Richard[12]		3 Oct. 63	10 May 76		20 June 83				
32	ea	Pearson, Arthur James,[98] Commanding Militia and Volunteer Artillery, Secunderabad									
32	ea	Gregory, Wm. Villeneuve, Commanding Militia and Volunteer Art., Great Yarmouth									

Royal Artillery.

Yrs. Ser.		LIEUTENANT COLONELS.	LIEUT.	CAPTAIN.	BREVET MAJOR.	MAJOR.	BREVET LT.COL.	LT. COL.	LT. COL. R. ART.	BREVET COLONEL.
32	SO	Will, George, *Commanding Militia and Volunteer Artillery, Aberdeen.*	2 Nov. 63	19 June 76	......	1 July 83	......	1 July 90	3 Sept. 91	......
32	RHA	Ollivant, Edward Albert[127]	2 Mar. 64	13 Sept. 76	......	26 July 83	......	......	7 Sept. 91	......
32	RHA	Wallace, Robert Hugh	12 Mar. 64	21 Dec. 76	......	1 Aug. 83	......	......	1 Oct. 91	......
31	WN	Williams, Richard Francis	3 May 64	1 Feb. 77	......	31 Aug. 83	......	......	1 Oct. 91	......
31	SO	Torkingson, Henry	16 Aug. 64	14 Feb. 77	......	1 Sept. 83	......	1 Sept. 90	12 Oct. 91	......
31	SO	*p.s.c.* Wynne, George Clement, *p.a.c.*	16 Aug. 64	10 Apr. 77	......	16 Sept. 83	......	......	29 Oct. 91	......
31	DS	Browell, Edward Thomas[133]	16 Aug. 64	30 Aug. 77	......	16 Oct. 83	......	16 Oct. 90	1 Nov. 91	......
31	SO	Plunkett, Robert Hastings Willoughby,[134] *Commanding Royal Artillery, Straits Settlements*	16 Aug. 64	7 May 77	......	4 Nov. 83	......	......	30 Nov. 91	......
31	FD	Wickham, Charles Brenton	11 Oct. 64	26 June 77	......	10 Dec. 83	......	22 July 91	21 Dec. 91	......
31		Eden, William Alexander	28 Oct. 64	1 July 77	......	22 Dec. 83	......	......	21 Dec. 91	......
31	RHA	Siddons, Henry George Fombelle[140]	11 Nov. 64	1 July 77	......	31 Dec. 83	......	31 Dec. 90	21 Dec. 91	......
31	WN	Smith, Charles Mitchell	23 Dec. 64	14 July 77	......	1 Jan. 84	......	1 Mar. 91	21 Dec. 91	......
31	WN	Browne, Augustus	9 Dec. 64	14 July 77	......	1 Jan. 84	......	1 Jan. 89	1 Jan. 92	......
31	WF	White, Arthur Wellesley, *p.a.c.*	23 Dec. 64	14 July 77	......	1 Jan. 84	......	1 May 89	15 Feb. 92	......
31	SO	Alves, John Morison, *Commanding Militia and Volunteer Artillery, Leith*	3 Mar. 65	20 Sept. 77	......	1 Jan. 84	......	......	3 Mar. 92	......
31	RA	Howard, Frederic	11 Nov. 64	1 Oct. 77	11 Jan. 83	1 Jan. 84	......	1 Jan. 91	1 Apr. 92	......
31	FD	*p.s.c.* Walker, Arthur Greenwood	11 Nov. 64	1 July 77	......	1 Dec. 83	......	31 Dec. 90	8 Apr. 92	......
31	FD	Lake, Edward,[13] *Offg. Assistant Adjutant General for Royal Artillery, Bombay,* 22 Apr. 94	19 July 64	10 Apr. 77	......	1 Jan. 84	......	1 Sept. 91	18 May 92	......
31	SO	Hunter, Woodburn,[150] *p.a.c.*	21 Mar. 65	1 Oct. 77	......	1 Jan. 84	15 June 83	2 Oct. 91	12 May 92	15 June 88
31	FD	*p.s.c.* Bury, John Thomas	21 Mar. 65	1 Oct. 77	......	1 Jan. 84	......	10 Feb. 91	8 June 92	......
31	WN	Powlett, Norton,[165] *Commanding Royal Artillery, Kurrachee*	24 Mar. 65	1 Oct. 77	......	1 Jan. 84	......	21 July 91	21 July 92	......
31	RE	Blaksley, Edward[142]	16 Dec. 64	9 July 77	......	1 Jan. 84	......	21 Nov. 91	21 July 92	......
31	WN	Beaver, Philip Keith Lonsdale[145]	24 Mar. 65	30 Aug. 77	28 June 83	1 Jan. 84	......	2 Sept. 91	2 Sept. 92	......
31	RHA	Broadfoot, Archibald,[146] CB. *Commanding Royal Artillery, Kirkee*	23 Dec. 64	1 July 77	2 Mar. 81	1 Jan. 84	......	1 Jan. 91	1 Oct. 92	......
31	SO	Congdon, John James[157]	11 Nov. 64	24 Nov. 77	......	1 Jan. 84	......	......	1 Oct. 92	......
31	FD	Gillespie, James Carnegie	21 Feb. 65	6 Sept. 77	......	1 Jan. 84	......	9 Jan. 91	1 Oct. 92	......
31	RHA	Costobadie, Henry Holmes	24 Mar. 65	2 Jan. 78	31 Oct. 83	1 Jan. 84	......	1 Oct. 91	1 Nov. 92	......
31	FD	Douglas, John Douglas	18 July 65	4 Oct. 77	......	1 Jan. 84	......	1 Nov. 91	9 Nov. 92	......
31	FD	Josselyn, James Edward	18 July 65	7 Nov. 77	......	1 Jan. 84	......	9 Nov. 91	9 Nov. 92	......
31	FD	Freeth, James Plomer,[161] *p.a.c.*	12 Jan. 66	20 Feb. 78	......	1 Jan. 84	......	29 Jan. 93	29 Jan. 93	......
30	FD	O'Malley, George Hunter	12 Jan. 66	13 Mar. 78	......	31 Dec. 83	......	26 June 93	31 Mar. 93	......
30	FD	Smyth, Samuel Gardiner[170]	28 Oct. 65	13 Mar. 78	......	1 Jan. 84	......	......	28 June 93	......
30	SO	Tabor, John Minnitt,[169] *Commanding Militia Artillery, Cork*	12 Jan. 66	3 Mar. 78	......	1 Mar. 84	......	28 June 93	19 Aug. 93	......
30	SO	Hewitt, James Robert Silver Oliver[164]	12 Jan. 66	1 Apr. 78	......	13 Mar. 84	......	19 Aug. 93	30 Sept. 93	......
30	FD	Nutt, James Anson Francis,[166] *Commanding Royal Artillery, St. Thomas's Mount*	17 July 66	25 May 78	18 Nov. 82	18 Mar. 84	......	19 Apr. 91	30 Sept. 93	......
30	SO	Stopford, Arthur Bouverie,[166] *Assistant Adjutant General, Simla,* 15 Nov. 94	17 July 66	23 Apr. 78	......	27 May 84	......	30 Sept. 93	6 Oct. 93	......
30	FD	Martin, George Blake Napier,[172] CB.	17 July 66	24 Aug. 78	......	27 June 84	......	6 Dec. 93	31 Dec. 93	......
30	SO	Dunnage, Arthur James, *Commanding Royal Artillery, Chester*	12 Jan. 66	24 June 78	......	30 July 84	......	31 Dec. 93	1 Jan. 94	......
30	WN	Anstruther, Alexander William, *p.a.c.*	12 Jan. 66	25 May 78	......	20 Aug. 84	......	1 Apr. 93	1 Jan. 94	......
29	WN	Allen, George Burges, *Commanding Militia and Volunteer Artillery, Cardiff*	17 July 66	1 Mar. 78	......	25 Aug. 84	......	1 Jan. 94	1 Jan. 94	......
29	FD	Harman, James Frederick, *Inspector of Warlike Stores for the Australian Colonies,* 3 May 92	17 July 66	25 May 78	......	25 Aug. 84	......	1 Jan. 94	1 Jan. 94	......
29	MN	Duthy, Archibald Edwards[175]	17 July 66	7 Aug. 78	......	25 Aug. 84	......	25 May 92	1 Jan. 94	......
29	FD	Downing, Cameron Macartney Harwood[176]	17 July 66	1 Oct. 78	......	26 Aug. 84	......	1 May 92	1 Jan. 94	......
29	FD	Watson, Robert Samuel, *p.a.c. Assistant Director Artillery College,* 3 May 92	15 Jan. 67	16 Oct. 78	......	26 Aug. 84	......	3 Jan. 91	3 Jan. 94	......
29	FD	Jervis, Walter Neil	15 Jan. 67	29 Nov. 78	......	27 Aug. 84	......	1 Jan. 94	3 Jan. 94	......
29	SO	Blake, Charles John	15 Jan. 67	1 Oct. 78	......	20 Sept. 84	......	4 Jan. 94	4 Jan. 94	......
29	SO	Smith, William Whitmore[177]	15 Jan. 67	14 Dec. 78	......	20 Sept. 84	......	......	31 Jan. 94	......
29	SO	*p.s.c.* Daniell, De Courcy	15 Jan. 67	31 Dec. 78	......	1 Oct. 84	......	30 Sept. 91	11 May 94	......
29	RA	Macgregor, Philip Leighton	15 Jan. 67	31 Dec. 78	......	20 Sept. 84	......	24 Feb. 94	25 May 94	......
28	FD	*p.s.c.* Smith, Walter William Marriott[167]	10 July 67	31 Dec. 78	......	1 Oct. 84	1 July 87	1 Oct. 91	8 June 94	......

Royal Artillery.

Yrs. Ser	LIEUTENANT COLONELS.	LIEUT.	CAPTAIN.	BREVET MAJOR.	MAJOR.	BREVET LT.COL.	LT.COL.	LT. COL. R. ART.	BREVET COLONEL.
28	RA Barron, Harry	10 July 67	1 Jan. 79		1 Oct. 84		27 June 94	27 June 94	
28	RD Yorke, Frederick Augustus	10 July 67	1 Jan. 79		1 Oct. 84		13 Aug. 94	13 Aug. 94	
28	WN Knox, William George,[182] CB.	10 July 67	23 Jan. 79	21 Apr. 80	2 Oct. 84		27 Oct. 94	27 Oct. 94	
28	RA Stevens, George Morton, Commanding Royal Artillery, Bombay	10 July 67	1 Apr. 79		7 Nov. 84		7 Nov. 94	7 Nov. 94	
28	RD Hay, Edward Owen[187]	10 July 67	1 Apr. 79	13 Nov. 82	15 Nov. 84		15 Nov. 94	15 Nov. 94	
28	WN Morgan, Frederick Cyril	8 Jan. 68	8 Apr. 79		20 Nov. 84		6 May 94	8 Dec. 94	
28	SO Griffiths, Algernon Sydney	8 Jan. 68	27 June 79		8 Dec. 84		8 Dec. 94	8 Dec. 94	
28	RA Turner, Frederick Mansel	8 Jan. 68	1 July 79		13 Dec. 84		10 Dec. 94	25 Dec. 94	
28	RD Yates, Henry Townley Scott[189]	8 Jan. 68	23 July 79		6 Feb. 85	2 Aug. 88	25 Dec. 94	25 Dec. 94	
27	Scott, Charles Henry, Ordnance Consulting Officer for India	15 July 68	16 Aug. 79		6 Feb. 85		4 Jan. 95	4 Jan. 95	
27	RD Curling, Henry Thomas[191]	15 July 68	16 Aug. 79		6 Feb. 85		6 Feb. 95	6 Feb. 95	
27	RD Purdy, Robert[192]	15 July 68	16 Aug. 79		24 Feb. 85		20 Feb. 95	20 Feb. 95	
27	RD Fowler, William James[193]	15 July 68	16 Aug. 79		24 Feb. 85		20 Feb. 95	20 Feb. 95	

LIEUTENANT COLONELS AND COLONELS on Half Pay.

	p.s.c. Knollys, Henry	1 Nov. 60	16 Apr. 73	1 July 81	30 July 81		29 Jan. 88		29 Aug. 9
	p.s.c. Buchanan-Dunlop, Henry Donald, Professor Royal Military Academy	17 July 66	7 Aug. 78	1 July 81	27 June 84		27 June 89		
	Bainbridge, Edmond, Member of the Ordnance Committee	18 Dec. 60	11 Mar. 74	1 July 81	1 Oct. 84		1 Oct. 88		29 Sept. 93
	Spragge, Charles Henry	19 Dec. 60	11 Mar. 74	1 July 81	29 Oct. 84		29 Oct. 88		29 Sept. 93
	Brough, James Fox[196]		14 July 74		7 May 85		7 May 89		6 Jan. 94
	p.s.c. Dalton, James Cecil[195]	13 Jan. 69	17 Sept. 79		1 Apr. 85		1 Apr. 89		
	Fletcher, Alfred Fouiger,[144] Deputy Director General of Ordnance, Bengal, 6 Oct. 93	16 Dec. 64	11 July 76		1 Apr. 85		1 Apr. 89		
	Saunders, Arthur Augustus, Chief Instructor School of Gunnery, 4 Jan. 94	1 Sept. 63	11 Mar. 76		12 May 85		12 May 90		
	Rainsford-Hannay, Ramsay William, Chief Instructor Royal Military Repository, Woolwich	18 July 65	1 Apr. 77		9 Jan. 84		9 Jan. 91		
	Blandy, William Poyntz, Inspector of Warlike Stores, 1 Apr. 91	19 July 67	1 Apr. 77		1 Sept. 85		1 Oct. 91		
	Bally, John Ford,[130] Chief Instructor, School of Gunnery, Shoeburyness, 22 Dec. 93	19 July 67	1 Apr. 77		2 Sept. 85		12 Oct. 91		
	p.s.c. Trotter, James Keith,[230] Deputy Assistant Adjutant Gen., Intelligence Branch, War Office, 1 Sept. 92	8 Jan. 79	1 Aug. 79		18 Mar. 85		22 Oct. 91		
	p.s.c. Hammond, Peter Henry, Deputy Assistant Adjutant General for Instruction, Colchester, 12 Mar. 91	15 Jan. 69	1 Aug. 79		18 Mar. 85		18 Mar. 92		
	p.s.c. Montgomery, Robert Arthur	15 Jan. 69	4 Oct. 79		1 Apr. 85		1 Apr. 92		
	Lugard, Henry Travers[195]	13 Jan. 69	15 Nov. 79		10 Apr. 85		10 Apr. 92		
	Russell, Charles	13 Jan. 69	23 Dec. 79	2 Mar. 81	12 May 85		12 May 92		
	Foote, Francis Onslow George Barrington[198]	13 Jan. 69	30 Dec. 79		12 May 85		12 May 92		
	Bingham, Edmund Baker, Superintendent Gun Carriage Factory, Fuztehghur, 15 Mar. 91	7 July 69	11 Jan. 80		13 May 85		13 May 92		
	Standbridge, Edmund Baker, Superintendent Gun Carriage Factory, 1 Oct. 90	7 July 69	17 Jan. 80		13 May 85		13 May 92		
	Walker, Edgar Holford, Instructor, School of Gunnery, Birmingham, 21 June 94	7 July 69	1 Mar. 80		27 July 85		27 July 92		
	Locker, Walter Nevill,[221] Instructor Artillery College 1 May 86	15 Dec. 71	2 July 80		12 Oct. 85		12 Oct. 92		
	Baker, Eden Moyle,[221] Instructor Artillery College 1 May 86	8 Jan. 70	19 May 80		15 Oct. 85		15 Oct. 92		
	Playfair, Hon. George James	7 July 69	22 Feb. 80		27 July 85		22 July 93		
	Bigge, Arthur John,[238] CB. CMG. Equerry in Ordinary to Her Majesty	18 Dec. 61	10 Mar. 75	18 Dec. 81	16 Sept. 82		16 Sept. 80		26 July 94
	Marshall, George Henry, Chief Instructor, School of Gunnery, 30 Sept. 93								
	p.s.c. Jocelyn, Julian Robert John, p.a.c. Artillery Adviser to the Inspector General of Fortifications at Head Quarters	4 Jan. 71	1 Jan. 81		4 Sept. 86		4 Oct. 93		
	Dawson, Henry Philip, Assistant Inspector of Warlike Stores, Portsmouth, 1 Apr. 91	4 Jan. 71	1 Feb. 81		22 Sept. 86		4 Oct. 93		
	p.s.c. Fawkes, Lionel Grimston, Instructor, Royal Military College, 1 Sept. 93	1 Dec. 70	12 Dec. 80		21 July 86		3 Feb. 94		

MAJORS.

27	30 Blackburn, Peter[194]	15 July 68	27 Aug. 79		24 Feb. 85				
27	WN Burridge, Francis John	15 July 68	27 Aug. 79		13 Mar. 85				
27	WN North, Roger Charles Edward	15 July 68	27 Aug. 79		13 Mar. 85				
27	WN Nixon, Arundel James	13 Jan. 69	13 Dec. 79		19 Mar. 85				
27	M RHA Leach, John[165]	13 Jan. 69	15 Sept. 79		1 Apr. 85				
27	48 Chapman, Lionel James Archer	13 Jan. 69	14 Nov. 79		10 Apr. 85				
27	WN Mayhew, Thomas	13 Jan. 69	27 Jan. 80		25 May 85				
27	WN Western, Charles Maximilian[202]	7 July 69	24 Jan. 80		25 May 85				
26	J RHA Davidson, William Leslie[204]	7 July 69	21 Jan. 80		7 June 85				

Royal Artillery. 167

Yrs. Ser.	MAJORS.	LIEUT.	CAPTAIN.	BREVET MAJOR.	MAJOR.
26	39 Baker, Robert Henry Sherston,[206]	7 July 69	1 Feb. 80		1 July 85
26	61 Whitehorne, Arthur Howard	8 Jan. 70	13 Mar. 80		27 July 85
26	35 Hepburne, Robert Gordon Webb[210]	8 Jan. 70	24 Mar. 80		5 Aug. 85
26	RA Fraser, Arthur Reginald	8 Jan. 70	12 Apr. 80		1 Sept. 85
26	72 p.s.c. Spencer, John Winston Thomas[211]	8 Jan. 70	12 May 80		9 Sept. 85
26	80 Fanshawe, George Dalrymple[165]	8 Jan. 70	12 May 80		9 Sept. 85
26	WN Jervois, Henry Napier[213]	8 Jan. 70	28 May 80		16 Oct. 85
26	FD Moore, George Robert[134] (2-1 *Depot*)	8 Jan. 70	25 June 80		26 Nov. 85
26	WN Monck-Mason, Gordon George[215] (: *Sub-Depot*)	8 Jan. 70	9 July 80		25 Dec. 85
26	D RHA Eustace, Francis John William[217]	8 Jan. 70	9 July 80		25 Dec. 86
26	80 Baker, James Volant Vashon[219]	8 Jan. 70	28 July 80		20 Jan. 86
26	A DEP RHA Coke, Edward Beresford[134]	8 Jan. 70	1 Aug. 80		20 Jan. 86
26	R RHA Pollard-Urquhart, Francis Edward Romulus	8 Jan. 70	10 Aug. 80		26 Jan. 86
26	80 Aylmer, Frederick Arthur (1 *Sub-Depot*)	8 Jan. 70	1 Sept. 80		5 Feb. 86
25	T RHA Long, Charles James[134]	23 July 70	11 Sept. 80		19 Feb. 86
25	67 Parsons, Lawrence Worthington	23 July 70	16 Sept. 80		1 July 86
25	RA Wade, Arthur Gregory Scrocold	23 July 70	27 Oct. 80		7 July 86
25	F RHA Rich, Charles Carroll[224]	23 July 70	27 Nov. 80		7 July 86
25	WN Perrott, Thomas	1 Dec. 70	12 Dec. 80		21 July 86
25	80 Swinton, John James[225] (*Depot*)	4 Jan. 71	19 Dec. 80		27 July 86
25	22 Fowell, Newton Plomer[226]	4 Jan. 71	19 Jan. 81		4 Sept. 86
25	17 Price, George Richardson	4 Jan. 71	19 Jan. 81		7 Sept. 86
25	26 Brackenbury, Herbert William[228]	4 Jan. 71	1 Feb. 81		1 Oct. 86
25	80 Robertson, Robert William Peacock[229]	4 Jan. 71	9 Feb. 81		9 Oct. 86
25	G RHA Hunt, Henry Vaughan[230]	4 Jan. 71	26 Feb. 81		12 Oct. 86
25	DB Coker, Lewis Edmund	4 Jan. 71	27 Feb. 81		29 Oct. 86
25	C RHA Rochfort, Alexander Nelson[232]	4 Jan. 71	9 Mar. 81	15 June 85	29 Oct. 86
25	RA Rosseter, James Hurley	4 Jan. 71	13 Mar. 81		29 Oct. 86
25	60 Frith, Warren Hastings	4 Jan. 71	15 Mar. 81		30 Nov. 86
24	N RHA Hotham, John	2 Aug. 71	6 Apr. 81		21 Dec. 86
24	7 Woods, Hans Charles Maunsell[235]	2 Aug. 71	6 Apr. 81		21 Dec. 86
24	74 Owen, George Pridham	2 Aug. 71	8 May 81		15 Aug. 87
24	FD Beaver, Frederick Tysson Mackinlay (1-2 *Depot*)	2 Aug. 71	23 May 81		24 Aug. 87
24	80 Casey, Charles Leslie	2 Aug. 71	27 May 81		21 Sept. 87
24	WN Dean-Pitt, Douglas Charles (1 *Sub Depot*)	2 Aug. 71	27 May 81		21 Sept. 87
24	79 Watson, Solomon	2 Aug. 71	11 June 81		21 Sept. 87
24	63 Newbigging, Patrick Charles Eric[243]	2 Aug. 71	11 June 81		21 Sept. 87
24	80 Lane, Alfred Luther	2 Aug. 71	1 July 81		21 Sept. 87
24	27 Pengree, Henry Hewitt[245]	2 Aug. 71	1 July 81		21 Sept. 87
24	King, Robert Ambrose Cecil,[246] *Indian Ordnance Department*	15 Dec. 71	1 July 81		28 Sept. 87
24	14 Challenor, George Richards[247]	15 Dec. 71	1 July 81		28 Sept. 87
24	MN Bowles, Frederick Augustus[248]	15 Dec. 71	1 July 81		1 Oct. 87
24	RA Wace, Ernest Charles,[249] *DSO*	15 Dec. 71	1 July 81		1 Oct. 87
24	80 Walford, William Sworder	15 Dec. 71	13 July 81		25 Oct. 87
24	80 Slade, Frederick George,[252] *CB. (Bt.Lt.Colonel, 15 June 85; Brevet Colonel, 10 July 89)*	15 Dec. 71	13 July 81	21 May 84	29 Oct. 87
24	80 Graham, Walter Ferrier	15 Dec. 71	13 July 81		29 Oct. 87
24	40 Saunders, Macan William[253]	15 Dec. 71	13 July 81	1 July 87	1 Nov. 87
24	S RHA Suart, William Hodgson[170]	15 Dec. 71	13 July 81		19 Jan. 88
24	1-1 FD DEP Hall, Francis Henry[225]	15 Dec. 71	13 July 81		26 June 88
24	WN Hervey, Constantine Rodney William	15 Dec. 71	16 July 81		4 Aug. 88
24	P RHA Flint, Edward Montagu	15 Dec. 71	16 July 81		4 Aug. 88
24	37 Hamilton, Peter Fisher Percival[254]	15 Dec. 71	25 July 81		15 Aug. 88
24	Willoughby, Herbert Percival,[255] *Inst. Art. College* 1 Apr. 88	6 Jan. 72	17 Aug. 81		1 Oct. 88
24	Elwes, Ernest Veness,[256] *Instructor Artillery College* 3 Feb. 89	6 Jan. 72	17 Aug. 81		13 Oct. 88
24	66 Thring, William Powlett[257]	6 Jan. 72	17 Aug. 81		29 Oct. 88
24	WN Scott, Hugh Aboukir	6 Jan. 72	7 Sept. 81		29 Oct. 88
23	23 Montgomery, Alexander John	6 Jan. 72	7 Sept. 81		29 Oct. 88
23	K RHA Potts, John William Hastings[134]	2 May 72	17 Sept. 81		29 Nov. 88
23	WN Callwell, Albert Henry[25]	2 May 72	18 Sept. 81		29 Nov. 88
23	I RHA Wodehouse, Josseline Heneage,[259] *CB. CMG. (Bt.Lt.Col. 2 Jan. 86; Colonel 2 Jan. 90).*	2 May 72	1 Oct. 81	21 May 84	30 Nov. 88
23	2 Banister, FitzGerald Muirson[165]	2 May 72	1 Oct. 81		5 Dec. 88
23	E RHA M'Donnell, John[134]	2 May 72	1 Oct. 81		21 Dec. 88
23	5 Temple, John	2 May 72	6 Oct. 81		21 Dec. 88
23	B RHA Coxhead, James Alfred	2 May 72	24 Oct. 81		1 Jan. 89
23	MacMahon, Percy Alex. *p.a.c. Inst. Artillery College* 14 Apr. 91	12 Sept. 72	29 Oct. 81		1 Jan. 89
23	*p.s.c.* Walker, Henry Chesshyre Claughton, *Professor at Staff College, with rank of Lieut.Colonel, 1 Aug. 90*	12 Sept. 72	29 Oct. 81		1 Jan. 89
23	64 Oakes, Reginald	12 Sept. 72	29 Oct. 81		1 Jan. 89
23	8 Henricies, Edward Nathaniel[262]	12 Sept. 72	29 Oct. 81		1 Jan. 89
23	*p.s.c.* Murray, James Wolfe, *Deputy Assistant Adjutant General for Instruction, Aldershot*, 10 Jan. 94	12 Sept. 72	1 Nov. 81		9 Jan. 89
23	15 Cassan, Ernest	12 Sept. 72	1 Nov. 81		11 Jan. 89
23	WN *p.s.c.* Johnson, Richard Francis	12 Sept. 72	14 Nov. 81		16 Feb. 89
23	*p.s.c.* Barker, John Stewart Scott, *Staff Captain, Intelligence Branch, War Office*, 1 Feb. 93	12 Sept. 72	22 Nov. 81		17 July 89
23	WN Bunny, Frederic Brice (*Depot*)	12 Sept. 72	29 Nov. 81		31 July 89
23	WN Mansel, Alfred,[266] *DSO*	12 Sept. 72	30 Nov. 81		13 Aug. 89
23	L RHA Hewat, Arthur Houstoun[267]	22 Sept. 72	32 Nov. 81		1 Sept. 89
23	RA Weir, Harry George[165] (2 *Sub Depot*)	12 Sept. 72	21 Dec. 81		2 Sept. 89
23	MN Cunningham, John Dacres[268]	12 Sept. 72	21 Dec. 81		14 Sept. 89
23	43 Shirreff, George Frederick Farquharson	12 Sept. 72	21 Dec. 81		16 Sept. 89
23	53 Lyster, Henry John[269]	12 Sept. 72	24 Dec. 81		1 Oct. 89
23	RA Murray, Arthur Mordaunt,[270] *Assist. Mil. Sec. Cape of Good Hope*	12 Sept. 72	24 Dec. 81		1 Oct. 89
23	80 Saltmarshe, Philip[165]	9 Jan. 73	31 Dec. 81		1 Oct. 89
23	*p.s.c.* Jeffreys, Henry Byron, *A. A. General, Rangoon,* 12 Nov. 91	9 Jan. 73	11 Jan. 82		1 Oct. 89
23	*p.s.c.* Fletcher, Walter Blunt, *Brigade Major Royal Artillery, Gibraltar,* 6 March 91	9 Jan. 73	18 Jan. 82		1 Oct. 89
23	H RHA *p.s.c.* Hawkins, John William[271]	9 Jan. 73	21 Jan. 82		1 Oct. 89
23	77 Bland, Frederick Milbank[272]	9 Jan. 73	17 May 82		1 Oct. 89
23	4 Pickwoad, Edwin Hay[165]	9 Jan. 73	27 May 82		1 Oct. 89
23	80 Ward, Edward, *p.a.c.*	9 Jan. 73	1 June 82		1 Oct. 89

Royal Artillery.

Yrs. Ser.	MAJORS.	LIEUT.	CAPTAIN.	BT. MAJOR.	MAJOR.
23	Penton, Arth. Pole-,²¹³ *Brigade Maj. R.Art. Portsmouth*, 1 Oct. 93	9 Jan. 73	7 June 82	......	1 Oct. 89
23	Fixott, James Laing, *Indian Ord. Department, Kirkee*, 5 March 86	9 Jan. 73	12 June 82	......	1 Nov. 89
23	wn Eman, Bowes Leslie	9 Jan. 73	24 June 82	......	13 Nov. 89
23	mn Smyth, Owen Stuart,²⁷⁷ *DSO.*	9 Jan. 73	24 June 82	......	13 Nov. 89
23	wn Ryan, Charles Aloysius²⁷⁸	9 Jan. 73	8 July 82	......	15 Dec. 89
22	o rha Phillpotts, Arthur Henry Croker²⁷⁹	29 Apr. 73	8 July 82	......	4 Jan. 90
22	58 p.s.c. Baldock, Thomas Stanford	29 Apr. 73	15 July 82	......	4 Jan. 90
22	69 Mackenzie-Grieve, John Andrew	29 Apr. 73	21 July 82	......	2 Feb. 90
22	mn Cleeve, William Frederick²⁸¹	29 Apr. 73	1 Sept. 82	......	12 Feb. 90
22	54 Farmer, Francis Colebrooke	29 Apr. 73	9 Sept. 82	......	19 Mar. 90
22	mn Gunner, Edward²⁸²	29 Apr. 73	9 Sept. 82	......	28 Mar. 90
22	51 Burton, Albert	29 Apr. 73	16 Sept. 82	......	28 Mar. 90
22	29 Burton, Hubert	29 Apr. 73	16 Sept. 82	......	29 Mar. 90
22	p.s.c. Waldron, Francis, *Dep. Assist. Adj. Gen. Canada*, 1 Oct. 90	29 Apr. 73	1 Oct. 82	......	1 Apr. 90
22	80 Rigg, Robert Addison	29 Apr. 73	1 Oct. 82	......	2 Apr. 90
22	wn Blackett, Edward Umfreville, *Comdt. Dalhousie Depot*, 1 Dec. 93	29 Apr. 73	1 Oct. 82	......	5 Apr. 90
22	41 de Jersey, William Grant	29 Apr. 73	1 Oct. 82	......	17 Apr. 90
22	ra Priestley, Edward John Kenworthey	29 Apr. 73	1 Oct. 82	......	25 Apr. 90
22	18 Vaughan-Hughes, Ernest²⁸⁰	29 Apr. 73	20 July 82	......	12 May 90
22	Hadden, Charles Fred. *Chief Inspector, Royal Arsenal*, 1 Apr. 93	11 Sept. 73	1 Oct. 82	......	12 May 90
22	Q rha Brunker, James Milford Sutherland¹⁷⁰	11 Sept. 73	4 Oct. 82	......	20 May 90
22	mn Shirres, John Chivas²⁸⁵	11 Sept. 73	4 Oct. 82	......	23 May 90
22	a rha p.s.c. Cowan, Henry Vivian¹⁸⁶	11 Sept. 73	1 Nov. 82	18 Nov. 82	19 June 90
22	Vaughan, Thomas Tweed, *Indian Ordnance Department*	11 Sept. 73	25 Nov. 82	......	28 June 90
22	80 Hopkins, Manley Ogden¹⁷⁰	11 Sept. 73	25 Nov. 82	......	1 July 90
22	6 Tylden, William	11 Sept. 73	27 Dec. 82	......	30 July 90
22	ra Rainsford, Stephen Dickson²⁸⁷	11 Sept. 73	31 Dec. 82	......	1 Aug. 90
22	Brett, Arthur H. Wilford, *Inspector of Warlike Stores* 1 Apr. 93	11 Sept. 73	14 Feb. 83	......	1 Aug. 90
22	rha Cunliffe, Foster Lionel¹⁶⁵ (*B. Depot*)	11 Sept. 73	14 Feb. 83	......	27 Aug. 90
22	Rowan, Terence England, *Ordnance Officer, 3rd Class*	11 Sept. 73	16 Feb. 83	......	1 Sept. 90
22	12 Newton, John William Marsdin²⁸⁹	11 Sept. 73	28 Feb. 83	......	2 Sept. 90
22	wn Dobie, William Hugh Edward	11 Sept. 73	28 Feb. 83	......	1 Oct. 90
22	24 Haggard, Claude Mason²⁹⁰	11 Sept. 73	28 Feb. 83	......	16 Oct. 90
22	mn Fulton, George Wade Robertson	11 Sept. 73	28 Mar. 83	......	31 Dec. 90
22	80 Woodrow, Thomas Henry Jackson²²⁵	11 Sept. 73	1 Apr. 83	......	31 Dec. 90
22	80 Browne, Arthur Henry²⁹¹	11 Sept. 73	1 Aug. 83	......	31 Dec. 90
22	42 Dewar, David Erskine²⁹²	11 Feb. 74	3 Apr. 83	......	1 Jan. 91
22	65 p.s.c. Creagh, Arthur Gethin²⁹³ (*Bt. Lt. Colonel*, 15 June 85; *Brevet Colonel*, 1 Jan. 93)	12 Feb. 74	14 Apr. 83	15 Apr. 83	1 Jun. 91
22	80 Kelsart, Gerald Talbot, p.a.c.	12 Feb. 74	17 Apr. 83	......	1 Jan. 91
22	55 Bailward, Arthur Churchill²⁵⁴	12 Feb. 74	17 Apr. 83	......	1 Jan. 91
22	rh Hunter, Frederick Ernest Arundell²⁹⁵	12 Feb. 74	18 Apr. 83	......	1 Jan. 91
22	45 Curtis, Harry Alexander Dyer²⁹⁶	12 Feb. 74	12 May 83	......	1 Jan. 91
22	mn Keene, Alfred,²⁹⁷ *DSO.*	12 Feb. 74	13 May 83	......	1 Jan. 91
22	59 Owen, Henry O'Brien	12 Feb. 74	23 May 83	......	1 Jan. 91
22	47 Plant, William Arthur²⁹⁸	12 Feb. 74	28 June 83	......	9 Jan. 91
22	wn Brady, Robert Maziere	12 Feb. 74	1 July 83	......	25 Jan. 91
22	80 Loudon, Robert Dunn	12 Feb. 74	6 July 83	......	7 Feb. 91
22	86 Garnett-Botfield, Walter Dubbon²⁹⁹	12 Feb. 74	7 July 83	......	10 Feb. 91
22	21 Holland, Ellis Charles Fletcher¹⁶⁵	12 Feb. 74	7 July 83	......	16 Feb. 91
22	31 Sidney, *Hon.* Algernon	12 Feb. 74	26 July 83	......	26 Feb. 91
22	46 Boteler, Francis Wilford, p.a.c.	12 Feb. 74	1 Aug. 83	......	1 Mar. 91
22	Pratt, Arthur Spencer, *Instructor School of Gunnery* 1 Nov. 91	12 Feb. 74	1 Aug. 83	......	13 Mar. 91
22	Blewitt, William Edward, *Secretary to the Ordnance Committee*	12 Feb. 74	1 Aug. 83	......	14 Mar. 91
22	19 Maberly, Charles Evan³⁰¹	12 Feb. 74	22 Aug. 83	......	19 Apr. 91
22	71 Kuper, Charles Victor Bremer	12 Feb. 74	31 Aug. 83	......	29 May 91
21	70 Hawkshaw, Edward Crichton	12 Aug. 74	31 Aug. 83	......	3 June 91
21	Hansard, Arthur Clifton, *Instructor School of Gunnery* 1 Apr. 90	17 Aug. 74	1 Sept. 83	......	3 June 91
21	25 Burton, Benjamin	17 Aug. 74	1 Sept. 83	......	25 July 91
21	80 Allen, John Richard Howard	17 Aug. 74	1 Sept. 83	......	30 July 91
21	38 Stirling, James Wilfred	17 Aug. 74	2 Sept. 83	......	17 Aug. 91
21	Fowle, Trenchard Frederick Thomas,³⁰³ *Com. of Ord., 3rd Class*	17 Aug. 74	5 Sept. 83	......	20 Aug. 91
21	ra Fell, John Percy	17 Aug. 74	8 Sept. 83	......	22 Aug. 91
21	76 Harrison, Robert Arthur Gwynne	17 Aug. 74	26 Sept. 83	......	7 Sept. 91
21	Parsons, Charles Sim Bremridge,³⁰⁴ *serving with Egyptian Army with the rank of Lt. Colonel*	17 Aug. 74	7 Oct. 83	14 Oct. 83	11 Sept. 91
21	Urquhart, Walter Andrew, p.a.c. *Inspector of Warlike Stores, Royal Arsenal*, 1 Apr. 93	17 Aug. 74	7 Oct. 83	......	20 Sept. 91
21	80 Simpson, Henry Cuthbert Connell Dunlop³⁰⁶	17 Aug. 74	23 Oct. 83	......	23 Sept. 91
21	ra Balfour, William Edward Ligonier	17 Aug. 74	1 Nov. 83	......	1 Oct. 91
21	57 Galton, Hubert George Howard³⁰⁷	17 Aug. 74	4 Nov. 83	......	1 Oct. 91
21	ra Purvis, Alexander Burridge	17 Aug. 74	7 Nov. 83	......	1 Oct. 91
21	44 Wynyard, Rowley	17 Aug. 74	14 Nov. 83	......	1 Oct. 91
21	28 p.s.c. Fleming, Edward William³⁰⁸	28 Jan. 75	14 Nov. 83	......	2 Oct. 91
21	Townshend, George Robert, *Instructor Art. College* 1 Apr. 91	28 Jan. 75	16 Nov. 83	......	4 Oct. 91
21	34 Bell-Irving, Andrew³⁰²	28 Jan. 75	1 Dec. 83	......	15 Oct. 91
21	Sclater, Hy. Crichton,³¹⁰ *Dep. Assist. Adj. Gen., Dublin*, 18 Oct. 92	28 Jan. 75	21 Dec. 83	15 June 85	22 Oct. 91
21	80 Phillips, Thomas Vaughan Wynn¹³⁴	28 Jan. 75	22 Dec. 83	......	29 Oct. 91
21	ra Simpson, Charles Napier	28 Jan. 75	29 Dec. 83	......	7 Nov. 91
21	May, Edward Sinclair, *Professor R. Military Academy* 30 July 91	28 Jan. 75	31 Dec. 83	......	7 Nov. 91
21	Leach, Reg. Pemberton, *Assist. Insp. Warlike Stores* 15 May 94	28 Jan. 75	1 Jan. 84	......	21 Nov. 91
21	ra Rowe, Octavius³¹¹	28 Jan. 75	1 Jan. 84	......	30 Nov. 91
21	49 Boothby, Reginald Evelyn²²⁵	28 Jan. 75	1 Jan. 84	......	21 Dec. 91
21	ra Darby, William Henry (*Depot*)	28 Jan. 75	1 Jan. 84	......	1 Jan. 92
21	wn Downing, David Fitzgerald, *Commanding R. Artillery, Barbadoes*	28 Jan. 75	16 Nov. 83	......	27 Jan. 92
21	75 Lindsay, Walter Fullarton Ludovic³¹²†	28 Jan. 75	1 Jan. 84	......	27 Jan. 92
21	68 Bannatine-Allason, Richard³¹³	28 Jan. 75	1 Jan. 84	......	1 Feb. 92
21	9 p.s.c. Dunlop, Henry Cleland	28 Jan. 75	1 Jan. 84	......	6 Feb. 92
21	wn Hodgson, James Owen	28 Jan. 75	1 Jan. 84	......	15 Feb. 92
21	1 p.s.c. Kerrison, Edmund Roger Allday	28 Jan. 75	1 Jan. 84	......	19 Feb. 92
21	11 Thomas, Sir Godfrey Vignoles, *Bart.*³¹⁴	28 Jan. 75	1 Jan. 84	......	3 Mar. 92
21	50 Western, Charles Maximilian Thomas	28 Jan. 75	1 Jan. 84	......	16 Mar. 92
21	3 Dunlop, James William³¹⁵	28 Jan. 75	1 Jan. 84	......	18 Mar. 92
21	wn Norton, Gilbert Fred. Allan,³¹⁶ *Commanding R. Art., Jamaica*	28 Jan. 75	1 Jan. 84	15 June 85	19 Mar. 92

Yrs. ser	MAJORS.	LIEUT.	CAPTAIN.	BT.MAJOR.	MAJOR.
21	Acton, Thomas Hampden Evans, *Assistant Inspector of Warlike Stores* 26 Aug. 94	28 Jan. 75	1 Jan. 84	......	19 Mar. 92
21	wn Haines, Robert Lewis[318]	28 Jan. 75	1 Jan. 84	......	23 Mar. 92
20	wn Hickman, Hugh Palliser	19 Aug. 75	1 Jan. 84	......	1 Apr. 92
20	ea Turner, Alfred Heyland Parrott	19 Aug. 75	9 Jan. 84	......	10 Apr. 92
20	so Churchward, Walter Stanbury[320]	19 Aug. 75	9 Jan. 84	......	30 Apr. 92
20	Dunsterville, Knightley Stalker, *Com. of Ord., 1st Class*	19 Aug. 75	9 Jan. 84	......	12 May 92
20	wn Tracey, Arthur	19 Aug. 75	16 Jan. 84	......	12 May 92
20	so Piers, Henry Octavius[170]	19 Aug. 75	31 May 84	......	13 May 92
20	p.s.c. Smith, Wm. Apsley,[322] *Assist. Mil. Sec. Canada,* 24 June 93	19 Aug. 75	13 Mar. 84	......	13 May 92
20	ea Bittleston, George Hastings[323]	19 Aug. 75	18 Mar. 84	......	23 May 92
20	so Hicks, William John	19 Aug. 75	18 Mar. 84	......	25 May 92
20	ea Howard, Cecil Arthur	19 Aug. 75	13 June 84	......	25 May 92
20	36 Burrows, Edmund Augustine[296]	19 Aug. 75	2 July 84	......	2 June 92
20	p.s.c. Waters, Wallecourt Hely-Hutchinson, *Military Attaché, St. Petersburg, with rank of Lt.Colonel,* 14 Apr. 93	19 Aug. 75	30 July 84	......	22 June 92
20	so Cottrell, Charles Dormer *(Depot)*	19 Aug. 75	30 July 84	......	21 July 92
20	ea Carter, Alfred Henry	19 Aug. 75	1 Aug. 84	......	27 July 92
20	13 Lambart, Edgar Alan[324]	19 Aug. 75	14 Aug. 84	......	27 July 92
20	56 Crofton, Richard Martin	19 Aug. 75	17 Aug. 84	......	10 Aug. 92
20	20 Blount, Charles Hubert	19 Aug. 75	20 Aug. 84	......	2 Sept. 92
20	ea Barlow, George Newton Halifax	19 Aug. 75	25 Aug. 84	......	1 Oct. 92
	Elmslie, Frederick Baumgardt, *Assist. Supt. of Experiments, Shoeburyness,* 13 Mar. 91	19 Aug. 75	27 Aug. 84	......	1 Oct. 92
20	p.s.c. Inglefield, Norman Bruce,[324] *Brigade Major, School of Gunnery,* 1 Jan. 94	19 Aug. 75	27 Aug. 84	......	1 Oct. 92
20	so p.s.c. Dawkins, Henry Stopford	19 Aug. 75	1 Sept. 84	......	1 Oct. 92
20	Holden, Henry Capel Lofft, *Insp. Dept. of Dir. of Art.* 1 Feb. 88	19 Aug. 75	1 Oct. 84	......	12 Oct. 92
20	ea Maxwell, Nigel	19 Aug. 75	1 Oct. 84	......	15 Oct. 92
20	so Foster, Raymond Charles	2 Feb. 76	2 Oct. 84	......	1 Nov. 92
20	16 p.s.c. Keir, John Lindesay	2 Feb. 76	2 Oct. 84	......	9 Nov. 92
20	Curteis, Francis Algernon,[325] *Prof. R. Mil. Acad.* 15 Sept. 93	2 Feb. 76	4 Oct. 84	......	9 Nov. 92
20	so English, Joseph Oxley	2 Feb. 76	18 Oct. 84	......	19 Jan. 93
20	so p.s.c. Trench, Frederick John Arthur[326]	2 Feb. 76	4 Nov. 84	......	19 Jan. 93
20	10 Anderson, Charles Alexander[327]	2 Feb. 76	7 Nov. 84	......	29 Jan. 93
20	78 Carter, Duncan Campbell[328]	2 Feb. 76	7 Nov. 84	......	1 Feb. 93
20	Barrett, Leonard,[329] *Inspector of Warlike Stores, Malta,* 12 Apr 90	2 Feb. 76	19 Nov. 84	......	4 Mar. 93
20	52 LLoyd, Wilford Neville[320]	2 Feb. 76	19 Nov. 84	......	16 Mar. 93
20	so Henn, Richard Arthur Milton	19 Aug. 75	1 Oct. 84	......	6 May 93
20	p.s.c. Stone, Francis Gleadowe,[165] *Deputy Assistant Adjutant General Royal Artillery, War Office,* 1 Sept. 94	2 Feb. 76	20 Nov. 84	......	6 May 93
20	62 Daniell, Arthur Cairns[331]	2 Feb. 76	20 Nov. 84	......	26 June 93
20	ea Hanna, William	2 Feb. 76	24 Nov. 84	......	28 June 93
20	Abdy, Anthony John, *Secretary Royal Artillery Institution*	2 Feb. 76	5 Dec. 84	......	22 July 93
20	73 Barlow, Charles Mervyn	2 Feb. 76	11 Dec. 84	......	19 Aug. 93
20	Taylor, William Hy. Forbes,[333] *Staff Officer and Chief Gunnery Instructor, Artillery Volunteers, Cape Colony,* 1 Apr. 93	2 Feb. 76	13 Dec. 84	......	23 Sept. 93
20	so Craig, John Francis[334]	2 Feb. 76	10 Jan. 85	......	30 Sept. 93
20	ea p.s.c. Adye, John,[335] *(Brevet Lt. Colonel,* 5 Oct. 93)	2 Feb. 76	23 Jan. 85	24 Jan. 85	4 Oct. 93
20	ea p.s.c. White, William Lewis[337]	2 Feb. 76	29 Jan. 85	......	4 Oct. 93
20	33 O'Neill, William Heremon,[338] *Adj. Jubbulpore*	2 Feb. 76	3 Feb. 85	......	4 Oct. 93
20	Hughes, Arbuthnott James, *Inst. School of Gunnery,* 1 Apr. 90	2 Feb. 76	4 Feb. 85	......	4 Oct. 93
20	wn Thackeray, Frederick Rennell[134]	2 Feb. 76	4 Feb. 85	......	6 Oct. 93
20	wn Blacker, Latham Charles Miller[340]	2 Feb. 76	18 Feb. 85	......	21 Oct. 93
20	so Eardley-Wilmot, Arthur[341]	2 Feb. 76	20 Feb. 85	......	9 Dec. 93
19	Butcher, Henry Townsend, *Inst. School of Gunnery* 26 Jan. 93	14 Aug. 76	22 Feb. 85	......	16 Dec. 93
19	ea Gundry, Henry Bowden[312]	14 Aug. 76	24 Feb. 85	......	31 Dec. 93
19	so Morrieson, Henry Walter	14 Aug. 76	28 Feb. 85	......	1 Jan. 94
19	32 Williams, William Hugh, *Commanding Royal Artillery, Egypt*	14 Aug. 76	1 Mar. 85	......	1 Jan. 94
19	so Simpson, George Gregory[170]	14 Aug. 76	12 Mar. 85	......	1 Jan. 94
19	Rundle, Henry Macleod Leslie,[345] *DSO. (Bt. Lt. Colonel,* 17 Aug. 89; *Brevet Colonel* 6 Jan. 94), *with Egyptian Army*	14 Aug. 76	13 Mar. 85	15 June 85	1 Jan. 94
19	so Powles, Thomas William[316]	14 Aug. 76	13 Mar. 85	......	3 Jan. 94
19	2-2 sub dep pd Sandbach, Henry Martin[347]	14 Aug. 76	13 Mar. 85	......	4 Jan. 94
19	ea Kelly, Rd. Macdougall Brisbane F.[348] *Inst. in Gunnery, Hooghly*	14 Aug. 76	13 Mar. 85	......	31 Jan. 94
19	mn Montgomery-Campbell, Hugo,[499] *Aide de Camp to Major General G. J. Smart* 4 Feb. 94	14 Aug. 76	18 Mar. 85	......	24 Feb. 94
19	so Kent, Frederic Edmond[349]	14 Aug. 76	25 Mar. 85	......	14 Mar. 94
19	Alexander, Chas. Hy. *Insp. of Warlike Stores, Halifax, N.S.* 5 Apr. 91	14 Aug. 76	1 Apr. 85	......	9 May 94
19	so Porteous, John James[351]	14 Aug. 76	1 Apr. 85	......	9 May 94
19	mn Triscott, Charles Prideaux,[353] *DSO.*	14 Aug. 76	1 Apr. 85	......	27 June 94
19	so Boileau, Arthur Cadell Tait (2 Sub Depot)	25 Jan. 77	15 Apr. 85	......	14 July 94
19	so Magrath, Charles Frederick	25 Jan. 77	16 Apr. 85	......	13 Aug. 94
20	ea Block, Maurice William Palmer	19 Aug. 75	25 Apr. 85	......	5 Sept. 94
19	ea Jervois, Charles Edwyn[255]	25 Jan. 77	6 May 85	......	29 Sept. 94
19	so Savile, Walter Clare	25 Jan. 77	6 May 85	......	29 Sept. 94
19	wn Marston, Jeffery Charles[134]	25 Jan. 77	6 May 85	......	15 Nov. 94
19	so Manifold, John Forster	25 Jan. 77	12 May 85	......	8 Dec. 94
19	ea Anderson, William Christian[357]	25 Jan. 77	12 May 85	15 June 85	10 Dec. 94
19	ea Lardner-Clarke, John de Winton	25 Jan. 77	12 May 85	......	25 Dec. 94
19	ea Ward, Frederick Houlton	14 Aug. 76	27 July 85	......	4 Jan. 95
19	ea M'Crea, Richard Francis, Adjutant	25 Jan. 77	5 Aug. 85	......	1 Feb. 95
19	Masey, William George, *Staff College*	25 Jan. 77	13 Aug. 85	......	20 Feb. 95
19	Talbot, George James Francis	25 Jan. 77	13 Aug. 85	......	20 Mar. 95

CAPTAINS.

Yrs. ser	CAPTAINS.	LIEUT.	CAPTAIN.		
19	so Minter, John Surtees[170]	14 Aug. 76	10 Apr. 85		
19	Mercer, Harvey Frederic,[358] *Brig. Maj. to Insp. Gen. of Art., India,* 25 Mar. 90	25 Jan. 77	13 Aug. 85		
19	75 Graeme, Frederick James	25 Jan. 77	13 Aug. 85		
19	so Reynolds, Cecil Edward	25 Jan. 77	19 Aug. 85		
19	q rha Jervis-White-Jervis, John Henry[360]	25 Jan. 77	1 Sept. 85		
19	31 Connolly, William Hallett[356]	25 Jan. 77	2 Sept. 85		
19	so Briscoe, Edward William, **Adjutant** 1 Feb. 94	25 Jan. 77	16 Oct. 85		
19	so Slater, Henry Martyn,[362] Adjutant	19 June 77	7 Nov. 85		
19	mn Fegen, Magrath Fogarty[361]	19 June 77	26 Nov. 85		
19	wn Heyman, Cecil Edward Hamilton[295]	19 June 77	25 Dec. 85		

Royal Artillery.

CAPTAINS.	LIEUT.	CAPTAIN.	CAPTAINS.	LIEUT.	CAPTAIN.
51 Blewitt, Charles Turner	19 June 77	27 Dec. 85	Thornton, Sidney Vernon	18 Dec. 78	29 Oct. 86
28 Paterson, Edward Hamilton	19 June 77	1 Jan. 85	WN Dallas, John Henry Langford	18 Dec. 78	1 Nov. 86
WN Inglis, Thomas Drummond, Adjutant 28 Jan. 93	19 June 77	1 Jan. 85	I RHA M'Laughlin, George Hall³⁹¹	18 Dec. 78	28 Nov. 86
MN Robinson, Charles Taylor,³⁶³ Adj. Quetta.	19 June 77	2 Jan. 86	RHA Du Cane, Hubert John,³⁹¹†	18 Dec. 78	20 Dec. 86
Anderson, Edmund Bullar,³⁶⁵			57 Darley, George Roe	18 Dec. 78	21 Dec. 86
Adj. Fife Art. 1 Feb. 92	19 June 77	4 Jan. 86	RA Nelson, Edgar Forbes	18 Dec. 78	21 Dec. 86
WN Hanham, Phelips Brooke	19 June 77	4 Jan. 86	RA Block, Arthur Hugh	18 Dec. 78	21 Dec. 86
G RHA Chapman, Herbert Alex.	19 June 77	11 Jan. 86	RA Oldfield, Henry Elliott	18 Dec. 78	1 Jan. 87
Foster, John Raffray, Assistant Inspector, Cork, 1 Apr. 91	19 June 77	11 Jan. 86	Thomson, Jocelyn Home,³⁵⁴ H.M.'s Inspector of Explosives, Home Office, 12 June 93	18 Dec. 78	2 Jan. 87
60 Beatson, Wm. John Arnold,³⁶⁷	19 June 77	11 Jan. 86	12 Beever, Henry Holt	18 Dec. 78	24 Feb. 87
78 Vans-Agnew, John Fraser	19 June 77	11 Jan. 86	Findlay, Neil Douglas,³⁷⁸ Adjutant 1 March 94	18 Dec. 78	28 Apr. 87
Gordon, Arthur William Bolton,³⁶⁸ Staff Captain	19 June 77	11 Jan. 86	Lambart, Hon. Arthur, Assist. Insp. Warlike Stores 10 Apr. 94	18 Dec. 78	7 May 87
Nelson, Horace Sydney, Instructor in Range Finding	19 Oct. 77	13 Jan. 86	RHA Paget, Wellesley Lynedoch H., Adjutant 15 Jan. 95	18 Dec. 78	11 May 87
p.s.c. Grierson, J. Moncrieff,³⁶⁹ Brigade Major, R. Art., Aldershot, 1 Jan. 95	9 Oct. 77	20 Jan. 86	Johnston, James Thomason, Inst. Sch. of Gun. 5 July 92	6 Apr. 79	25 May 87
Honner, William James,³⁷⁰ Inspection Branch, Director of Artillery's Dept. 25 Apr. 93	9 Oct. 77	20 Jan. 86	Ricardo, Hy. Geo. Adj. 2 Middlesex Vol. Art. 14 Oct. 93	6 Apr. 79	28 May 87
Smith, Stanley George Drew,¹⁷⁰ Supdt. Gun Carriage Factory, Bombay, 15 March 91	9 Oct. 77	20 Jan. 86	Minchin, Fred. Falkiner,³⁹² Assist. Insp. of Warlike Stores, 1 Apr. 93	6 Apr. 79	1 June 87
Townsend, Charles Collingwood, Superintendent Gun Carriage Factory, Madras, 6 Oct. 93	9 Oct. 77	20 Jan. 86	Inglis, Hy. Alves,³⁹³ Staff Capt. School of Gunnery, 1 Nov. 91	6 Apr. 79	6 June 87
Wilson, Chas. Hy. Luttrell Fahie Ordnance Officer, 4th Class	9 Oct. 77	20 Jan. 86	RA Chamberlain, Thomas Hoster Smith, Sydenham Campbell	6 Apr. 79	17 June 87
DSP. 80 Bell, Leonard	9 Oct. 77	20 Jan. 86	Urquhart, Inst. in Gunnery	6 Apr. 79	29 June 87
80 Toms, Francis Bevill Read³⁷²	9 Oct. 77	26 Jan. 86	48 Burrowes, Henry Gray	6 Apr. 79	1 July 87
E RHA Phipps-Hornby, Edmund John³⁷³	9 Oct. 77	1 Feb. 86	N RHA Hobday, Edmund Arthur Ponsonby	6 Apr. 79	1 July 87
34 Leslie, John Henry	9 Oct. 77	1 Feb. 86	80 Wright, George, Adj., Roorkee	6 Apr. 79	15 Aug. 87
Nicolls, Edmund Gustavus, Inst. in Gunnery	9 Oct. 77	5 Feb. 86	Smith, Gilbert Boys³²⁴	6 Apr. 79	29 Aug. 87
Shute, Arthur Blagden	9 Oct. 77	5 Feb. 86	Ogilvie, Norman Stuart,¹⁷⁰ Commissary of Ordnance, 3rd Class	6 Apr. 79	2 Sept. 87
Shewell, H. Williamson Macan, Instructor School of Gunnery 1 June 91	9 Oct. 77	12 Feb. 86	p.s.c. Hume, Charles Vernon³⁹⁵ D RHA Goulburn, Cuthbert Edward Davidson, John Robert Barkly, Ordnance Officer, 3rd Class	6 Apr. 79	21 Sept. 87
Jackson, Montague Bertie Gosset,³⁷⁴ employed with Egyptian Army	9 Oct. 77	16 Feb. 86	Close, Fredk. Macdonald, Adj. Cornwall and Devon Miners Art. (W. Div.) 25 March 91	6 Apr. 79	21 Sept. 87
Molesworth, Hickman Crawford, Adj. Forfar and Kincardine Art. South Div. 1 June 91	9 Oct. 77	19 Feb. 86	O RHA Enthoven, Percy Henry³⁹⁶ Lowe, Francis Manley, Instr. School of Gunnery, 9 May 94	6 Apr. 79	21 Sept. 87
K RHA Vereker, Hon. Jeffrey Edw. Prendergast	9 Oct. 77	23 Feb. 86	80 Lane, C. W. Moore, p.a.c.	31 Jan. 78	21 Sept. 87
			2-1 DEP. FD Forsyde, Richard Lionel p.s.c. Fairholme, Wm. Ernest, D. A. A. General, Intell. Dept. War Office, 15 July 94	6 Apr. 79	21 Sept. 87
RA Jackson, Francis Benjamin¹³⁴	9 Oct. 77	25 Feb. 86	5 Guinness, Eustace	6 Apr. 79	21 Sept. 87
Waller, John Dawson Hutchinson, 2nd Cl. Com. of Ord.	9 Oct. 77	25 Feb. 86	56 Balguy, John Henry	6 Apr. 79	21 Sept. 87
R RHA Fanshawe, Edward Arthur³⁷⁹	31 Jan. 78	17 Mar. 86	Lambert, Walter, p.a.c. Assist. Insp. Warlike Stores, 1 Apr. 93		
p.s.c. Callwell, Charles Edw.³⁸⁰ Brig. Maj. R. Art. Devonport	31 Jan. 78	24 Mar. 86	WN Gardiner, Henry Lawrence³⁹⁷ p.s.c. Chance, Harry,³⁹⁴ D.A.A. Gen., Sind Dist.	30 July 79	28 Sept. 87
Bunbury, William St. Pierre,¹⁷⁰ Instructor R. M. Academy 26 Sept. 90	31 Jan. 78	24 Mar. 86	Nathan, Frederic Lewis, in charge of Danger Buildings, R. Gunpowder Fact. 1 Oct. 92	30 July 79	1 Oct. 87
Birch, Frederic Henry John³⁸¹	31 Jan. 78	24 Mar. 86	p.s.c. Stuart, Alex. Ramsay, Staff Capt. R. Art., Chester, 15 Aug. 92	30 July 79	1 Oct. 87
S RHA Lecky, Fred. Beauchamp³⁸²	31 Jan. 78	24 Mar. 86			
Blane, Charles Forbes	31 Jan. 78	8 May 85			
A RHA Watkins, Charles Bell³⁸⁴	31 Jan. 78	8 May 86	RA Cummings, Wilfrid Heron	30 July 79	1 Oct. 87
Bushe, Thomas Francis, Insp. of Warlike Stores 1 Apr. 93	31 Jan. 78	16 June 86	37 Tawney, Edw. Plowden Archer	30 July 79	1 Oct. 87
Douglas, James Stewart³⁵⁴	31 Jan. 78	18 June 86	Turner, Archer Lloyd Marischal, Com. of Ord. 2nd Cl.	30 July 79	1 Oct. 87
19 M'Leod, Reginald George M'Queen	31 Jan. 78	3 July 86	Rundle, Geo. Richard Tyrell, Staff Capt. Royal Art., Oude, 3 Dec. 90	30 July 79	1 Oct. 87
Mahon, Reg. Hy. Supdt. Foundry & Shell Factory, Cossipore, 15 March 91	31 Jan. 78	7 July 86	80 Goold-Adams, Hy. Edw. Fane	30 July 79	1 Oct. 87
45 Helyar, Arthur Beaumont	31 Jan. 78	7 July 86	Lane, Samuel Willington	30 July 79	1 Oct. 87
76 Hibbert, Archibald Louis	31 Jan. 78	15 July 86	Simmonds, Percy Richard, Hong Kong	30 July 79	1 Oct. 87
Matthews, Alfred, Inspector Range Finding, Gibraltar	31 Jan. 78	21 July 86	MN Fendall, Chas. Pears,³⁹⁸ DSO	30 July 79	2 Oct. 87
80 Powell, Atherton ffolliott³⁸⁵	31 Jan. 78	21 July 86	WN Lewes, John	30 July 79	12 Oct. 87
7 Guise, Howard	31 Jan. 78	21 July 86	WN Harkness, Thomas Robert	30 July 79	25 Oct. 87
p.s.c. Granet, Edward John,³⁸⁶ Staff Capt. R. Art. N. E. Dist., York, 1 Jan. 92	31 Jan. 78	27 July 86	Labalmondiere, Julian Arthur	30 July 79	25 Oct. 87
			66 Langley, John Penrice	30 July 79	25 Oct. 87
J RHA Taylor, Philip Beauchamp	18 Dec. 78	29 July 86	10 Forde, Lionel¹²⁹⁶	30 July 79	29 Oct. 87
p.s.c. Kemball, George Vero,³⁸⁷ D.A.Q.M.G. for Mobilization, India, 11 March 91	18 Dec. 78	7 Sept. 86	Tothill, Fras. Wm. Galbraith, Adj. Jersey Art. Mil. 24 Oct. 92	30 July 79	29 Oct. 87
M RHA Armitage, Edw. Hume³⁸⁸	18 Dec. 78	8 Sept. 86	WN Morris, Maurice Morgan	30 July 79	29 Oct. 87
MN Harvey, John Edward	18 Dec. 78	8 Sept. 86	WN Tyrwhitt, Hon. Rupert	30 July 79	21 Dec. 87
36 Wedderburn, Alex. Scrymgeour³⁸⁹	18 Dec. 78	1 Oct. 86	69 Guinness, Charles Davis	30 July 75	10 Jan. 88
Alexander, G. D'Arragon, Instructor in Gunnery, Devonport, 1 Apr. 92	18 Dec. 78	1 Oct. 86	80 Osborn, George ¹⁷⁰	18 Feb. 80	19 Jan. 88
			p.s.c. Baker, Geo. Duff, Assist. Inspector of Warlike Stores	18 Feb. 80	21 Jan. 88
9 Jellett, John Hewitt	18 Dec. 78	12 Oct. 86	H RHA Johnston, Thomas Kelly Evans	18 Feb. 80	31 Jan. 88
p.s.c. Cooper, Francis Edw.³⁹⁰	18 Dec. 78	12 Oct. 86	Cockburn, William Frederick Taylor, Hy. Clarence Grant,⁴⁰⁰ Adj. Haddington Artillery 6 Jan. 92	18 Feb. 80	1 Feb. 88
B RHA Jackson, Herbert Kendall	18 Dec. 78	29 Oct. 86		18 Feb. 80	1 Feb. 88

Royal Artillery

CAPTAINS.	LIEUT.	CAPTAIN.
Prinsep, Douglas Gordon, Adj. 3 Middlesex Art. Vols. 1 Mar. 91	18 Feb. 80	1 Mar. 88
80 Weigall, George Edward	18 Feb. 80	1 Mar. 88
Von Donop, Stanley Brenton, Inst. R.M. Academy 1 Mar. 95	18 Feb. 80	1 Apr. 88
p.s.c. Hamilton-Gordon, Alex Brig. Major R. Art. Malta	18 Feb. 80	1 Apr. 88
Buckley, E. Duncombe H. Adj. Glamorgan Art. Mil. 2 Dec. 91	18 Feb. 80	1 Apr. 88
Chamier, George Daniel, Adjutant Lancashire Art. (South. Div. R. Art.) 12 Jan. 91	18 Feb. 80	1 Apr. 88
p.s.c. Crampton, Philip J. R., Brig. Maj. R. Art., Curragh	18 Feb. 80	1 Apr. 88
Foster, William Yorke, Staff Captain, Meerut, 23 May 92..	18 Feb. 80	1 Apr. 88
WN Bryant, Gilbert Edward[296]	18 Feb. 80	3 Apr. 88
RHA Stokes, Alfred,[401] Adjutant...	18 Feb. 80	25 Apr. 88
Winter, Frederic John	18 Feb. 80	12 May 88
Tinker, Edward, Assist. Director of Art., War Office, 1 Oct. 93	18 Feb. 80	12 May 88
T RHA Neish, Colin Graham	18 Feb. 80	12 May 88
Elliot, William,[402]	18 Feb. 80	8 June 88
Dale, Alfred Morris Cecil,[402]† Instructor R. M. Academy 13 Apr. 91	18 Feb. 80	13 June 88
35 de Jersey, Colebrooke	18 Feb. 80	26 June 88
Tisdall, Fr. Arthur Lance,[403] Adj. Londonderry Art. 15 Mar. 92	18 Feb. 80	26 June 88
Carden, Louis Peile, Adj. Clare Art. (S. Div.) 2 Jan 94	18 Feb. 80	26 June 88
HA Hunter-Blair, Walter Charles..	18 Feb. 80	15 July 88
Wood, Creighton, Com. of Ordnance, 3rd Class	18 Feb. 80	25 July 88
P RHA p.s.c. Benson, Geo. Elliott[404]	19 May 80	28 July 38
Stuart, Robt. Chas. Ochiltree,[405] Ordnance Officer, 3rd Class...	19 May 80	1 Aug. 88
80 p.s.c. Du Boulay, Noel Wilmot Houssemayne[403]†	19 May 80	4 Aug. 88
Perceval, Edward Maxwell, Staff College	19 May 80	4 Aug. 88
RHA Horne, Henry Sinclair, Adj. Kirkee	19 May 80	17 Aug. 88
C RHA Wing, Frederick Drummond Vincent	19 May 80	12 Sept. 88
Carte, Thomas Elliott, Insp. of Position Finding 1 July 93	19 May 80	13 Sept. 88
Wiseman-Clarke, Chas. Camden, Adj. 1 Durham Vol. Art. ...	19 May 80	13 Oct. 88
Cooper-Key, Aston M'Neil,[406] Inst. R. M. College, 23 May 89	19 May 80	13 Oct. 88
St. John, Geo. Francis Wm.[410] Comdt. No. 1 Mountain Battery Punjab Frontier Force	19 May 80	22 Oct. 88
Crampton, Fiennes Henry,[407] Inst. R.M. Academy 15 Sept. 93	19 May 80	29 Oct. 88
80 Pollock, Evelyn (3 Sub Depot)..	19 May 80	29 Oct. 88
Barlow, Hilaro Wm. Wellesley, 2nd Assist. to Director Gen. Ordnance Factories 12 June 93	19 May 80	2 Nov. 88
James, Wm. Reginald Wullwyn	19 May 80	24 Nov. 88
Briscoe, Alexander Villiers, 1 Sub Depot	19 May 80	29 Nov. 88
WN Butcher, Arthur E, Aveling, Adjutant	19 May 80	29 Nov. 88
Carroll, Arthur Lyons,[407]† Adj. 1 West Riding of York Art. Volunteers 10 Oct. 91	19 May 80	30 Nov. 88
K RHA Vores, Chas. H. Stiverd[409] ...	19 May 80	30 Nov. 88
Hawkins, Henry Theodore,[406] Instructor in Position Finding, Malta	19 May 80	5 Dec. 88
F RHA Blunt, Edwd. Walter, Aide de Camp to H.R.H. the Duke of Connaught	19 May 80	5 Dec. 38
EM Molesworth, Arthur Ludovic...	19 May 80	8 Dec. 88
Brook-Smith, Wilfrid Lionel, Inst. in Gunnery, Aden	19 May 80	21 Dec. 88
Burt, John Marshall, Adj. York Art. W. Div. 15 Jan. 95	19 May 80	31 Dec. 88
Milward, Clement Henry,[411] Adj. Waterford Art. 10 Jan. 93	19 May 80	1 Jan. 89
58 King, Charles Dickson[412]	19 May 80	1 Jan. 89
Walker, Edmond Somerville Forestier, Assist. Supdt. of Factories, Bengal, 1 Sept. 89	19 May 80	1 Jan. 89
DEP. WN Preston, D'Arcy Brownlow	19 May 80	1 Jan. 89
Kerrich, Walter Edmund, Indian Ordnance Department	19 May 80	9 Jan. 89
49 Bethell, Henry Arthur	27 July 80	11 Jan. 89
80 Powell, Fred. Acton Lambart	19 May 80[?]	14 Jan. 89
Martel, Charles Philip	27 July 80	14 Jan. 89
80 Meeres, Charles Stuart	27 July 80	14 Jan. 89
Wingate, Francis Reginald,[413] DSO. (Bt. Maj. 15 Jan. 89) serving with the Egyptian Army	27 July 80	14 Jan. 89

CAPTAINS.	LIEUT.	CAPTAIN.
Wynne, John George Erskine Instructor in Range Finding	27 July 80	14 Jan. 89
English, Cha. Ernest, Prof. R. M. Academy, Kingston, Canada	27 July 80	14 Jan. 89
Watkins, Leonard George,[295] Assist. Inspector Gen. of Ordnance, Bengal, 1 Apr. 90	27 July 80	14 Jan. 89
Fuller, Richard Woodfield	27 July 80	14 Jan. 89
Gartside-Tippinge, Ernest A., Adj. 4 Lancashire Artillery Vols. 1 Feb. 93	27 July 80	15 Feb. 89
Renny, Sidney Mercer,[414] Ordnance Officer 3rd Cl., Bombay	27 July 80	15 Feb. 89
Johnson, Frank Ernest, Brig. Major to Insp. Gen. of Art. in India, 25 Nov. 93	27 July 80	15 Feb. 89
Griffin, William Wandby	27 July 80	16 Feb. 89
80 Duhan, Wm. Waugh Taylor	27 July 80	16 Feb. 89
p.s.c. Churchill, Arthur B. Norton,[296] Staff Captain for R. Art. Chatham, 27 Nov. 93	27 July 80	18 Mar. 89
Bickford, Edward,[414]† Adj. and Inst. in Gunnery, Rangoon	27 July 80	20 Mar. 89
WN Brownlow, Henry Blaikie[416]	27 July 80	26 Mar. 89
p.s.c. Dawkins, John Wyndham George, Brigade Major R. Artillery, Dover, 1 July 94	27 July 80	1 Apr. 89
Hamilton, C. de Courcy,[416]† Staff Captain R. Artillery, Rawul Pindee	27 July 80	1 Apr. 89
Strange, Robert George,[406] Adj. Northumberland Art. (W.Div.) 20 March 91	27 July 80	1 Apr. 89
63 Rhodes, Bernard Maitland	27 July 80	1 Apr. 89
Birch, Alex. Harry Colvin[415]†	27 July 80	1 Apr. 89
Mullins, Arthur John, Adj. School of Gunnery 28 Oct. 92	27 July 80	8 May 89
Morris, Robert,[417] Adj. Cossipore Art. Vols. 20 July 93	27 July 80	14 May 89
EA Baker, Augustus Theodore	19 May 80	1 June 89
74 Bond, Ralph Francis Xavier McGeough	27 July 80	1 June 89
Birch, Henry George,[418] Adj. Tipperary Art. 26 Jan. 90	27 July 80	1 July 89
13 Tremaine, Richard	27 July 80	1 July 89
EA Brooke, Edward Sabine[419]	27 July 80	1 July 89
EA p.s.c. Montgomery, Robert Arundel Kerr	23 Feb. 81	1 July 89
Phillips, Herbert de Touffreville,[419]† Inspector of Position Finding, 10 Oct. 94	23 Feb. 81	1 July 89
p.s.c. Crawford, Archibald,[420] Instructor, R. M. Academy, 16 Jan. 92	23 Feb. 81	6 July 89
80 Burney, Percy de Sausmarez[421]	23 Feb. 81	17 July 89
RHA Scott, Arthur Binny, Adjutant	23 Feb. 81	31 July 89
Wolley-Dod, A.Hurt, p.a.c. Insp. of Warlike Stores 1 Apr. 93...	23 Feb. 81	1 Aug. 89
Heffernan, Nesbitt Breillat, p.s.c. Assistant Inspector of Warlike Stores, 1 Apr. 93	23 Feb. 81	1 Aug. 89
Moore-Lane, William,[420] Adj. 1 Cinque Ports Art. Vols. (E. Div. R. Art.) 1 Apr. 90	23 Feb. 81	14 Aug. 89
Rich, Harold Hampden, Dept. of Director of Art. 1 Apr. 93	23 Feb. 81	24 Aug. 89
79 Smith, John Leslie	23 Feb. 81	24 Aug. 89
24 Longfield, Alfred Purcell,[408]	23 Feb. 81	1 Sept. 89
WN Maunsell, Francis Richard	23 Feb. 81	14 Sept. 89
4 Henshaw, Clinton Grant	23 Feb. 81	14 Sept. 89
Cole, Frederick Temple	23 Feb. 81	1 Oct. 89
80 Lawless, Skerrett E. George	23 Feb. 81	1 Oct. 89
Perry, Hugh Whitchurch, O. S. Department	23 Feb. 81	1 Oct. 89
Percy-Smith, Rennell	23 Feb. 81	1 Oct. 89
EA Carr, Robert Cattley	23 Feb. 81	1 Oct. 89
d.s. Cleeve, Fredk. John Stewart[421]†	23 Feb. 81	1 Oct. 89
59 Coghill, Charles Edward	23 Feb. 81	1 Oct. 89
Stanford, Hy. Bedell, Adj. Isle of Wight Art. S. Div. 3 Nov. 90	23 Feb. 81	1 Oct. 89
MacMahon, John Joseph, Adj. Limerick City Art., S. Div., 15 Jan. 94	23 Feb. 81	1 Oct. 89
6 Addington, Hon. Harold William	23 Feb. 81	9 Oct. 89
38 Campbell, Herbert Montgomery	25 June 81	18 Oct. 89
46 Tyndale-Biscoe, A. Sandeman	26 July 81	1 Nov. 89
14 Capel-Cure, Alfred,[422]	26 July 81	1 Nov. 89
50 Rodwell, Reginald Mandeville	26 July 81	13 Nov. 89
Bryan, Thomas William Guy[428]†	26 July 81	13 Nov. 89
80 Ducrot, Louis Hhy,[424] at S. Coll.	26 July 81	30 Nov. 89
Muspratt-Williams, Charles Augustus, Supdt. Gunpowder Factory, Ishapore	26 July 81	2 Dec. 89
Richardson, Charles William, Adj. and Inst. in Gunnery, Kurrachee, 1 Mar. 94	26 July 81	2 Dec. 89

Royal Artillery

CAPTAINS.	LIEUT.	CAPTAIN.
80 Sankey, Cyril Charles	26 July 81	4 Dec. 89
Scott, Chas. Darracott,⁴²⁵ *Adj. Edin. Art. S.Div.* 25 Nov. 90	26 July 81	20 Dec. 89
EA Drake, Bernard Francis	26 July 81	20 Dec. 89
Walker, Melville, *Assistant Supdt. of Factories, Bengal,* 1 Dec. 89	26 July 81	20 Dec. 89
Handley, Arthur, *Adj. Royal Military Academy* 26 Feb. 94	26 July 81	20 Dec. 89
20 Belfield, Sydney	26 July 81	1 Jan. 90
Jackson, Landon Dealtry²⁵⁶	26 July 81	1 Jan. 90
68 Slee, Percy Henry	26 July 81	1 Jan. 90
MN Stanton, Hy. Ernest,⁴²⁶ D.S.O.	26 July 81	1 Jan. 90
1-2 DEP FD Brendon, Herbert Alg.	26 July 81	4 Jan. 90
WN Anderson, Robert Douglas⁴²⁷	26 July 81	4 Jan. 90
65 Vigne, Robert Austen	26 July 81	15 Jan. 90
Montanaro, Arthur Forbes, *Comdg. R. Art. Sierra Leone, with local rank of Major*	26 July 81	16 Jan. 90
Carleton, Montgomery Launcelot,⁴²⁷† *Adj. Devon Art. (W. Div. R. Art.)* 16 Feb. 95	26 July 81	26 Jan. 90
WN O'Sullyn, *Hon.* Ranulph Edw. Montague	26 July 81	1 Feb. 90
80 Riddulph, George Warren, **Adjutant** 1 Apr. 92	26 July 81	10 Mar. 90
Gurdon, William, *Adj. Suffolk Artillery* 23 Nov. 91	26 July 81	19 Mar. 90
Underwood, Walter John, *Adj. Tynemouth Vol. Art.* 4 Jan. 92	26 July 81	28 Mar. 90
11 Calley, Henry	26 July 81	29 Mar. 90
B DEP RHA Paget, Victor Fred. William Augustus	26 July 81	31 Mar. 90
80 Nowlan, Thomas Bowman	26 July 81	1 Apr. 90
MN Gonne, Charles Melvill	26 July 81	1 Apr. 90
2 SUB DEP 80 Connal, Alex.Campbell	26 July 81	1 Apr. 90
1 SUB DEP 80 Torry, William Gordon⁴²⁸	26 July 81	1 Apr. 90
1-1 DEP FD Hanwell, Joseph⁴¹⁵	26 July 81	1 Apr. 90
p.s.c. Cadell, John Francis, *Staff Capt. Royal Artillery, Colchester,* 15 Aug. 94	22 Feb. 82	1 Apr. 90
30 Askwith, John Browning Harrison	22 Feb. 82	2 Apr. 90
Bicknell, Maldion Byron,⁴²⁹ *Com. of Ordnance, 3rd Class*	22 Feb. 82	2 Apr. 90
EA Dorehill, Phillip Henry Marcus	22 Feb. 82	5 Apr. 90
Johnson, Arthur Graham	22 Feb. 82	12 Apr. 90
72 Burrard, William Dutton	22 Feb. 82	12 Apr. 90
Crowe, John Hy. Verinder, *A.D.C. to Lt. Gov. Punjab,* 26 Apr. 92	22 Feb. 82	17 Apr. 90
EA Fisher, Charles John, **Adjutant** 1 Apr. 92	22 Feb. 82	21 Apr. 90
WN Breakey, Arthur John, **Adjutant** 4 Mar. 93	22 Feb. 82	25 Apr. 90
WN Scott, Archibald Galbraith	22 Feb. 82	26 Apr. 90
Guille, Hy. Stevens le Marchant, *p.a.c. Insp. of Warlike Stores, Cape of Good Hope,* 27 Aug. 92	22 Feb. 82	26 Apr. 90
Hoblyn, Edward Florance, *Inspector of Position Finding, Golden Hill,* 15 July 88	22 Feb. 82	30 Apr. 90
WN 1 SUB DEP Short, Anthony Holbeche⁴³⁰	22 Feb. 82	30 Apr. 90
Braid, Arthur Reade, *Ord. Dept. India*	26 July 81	6 May 90
Ormiston, James Walker,²⁵⁸ *Inst.R.L.Art.Coll.* 23Apr.94	22 Feb. 82	12 May 90
WN Yunge-Bateman, Geo. Marcus	22 Feb. 82	12 May 90
FD M'Leod, William Kelty, *Adjutant*	22 Feb. 82	20 May 90
Balfour, Arthur Mackintosh, *Adjutant Sussex Art. East Div.,* 1 Jan. 94	22 Feb. 82	22 May 90
18 Johnstone, Francis Buchanan	22 Feb. 82	23 May 90
33 Hutchinson, Charles Hammond	22 Feb. 82	1 Aug. 90
26 Browne, Sherwood Dighton⁴³¹	22 Feb. 82	1 Sept. 90
MN Dowell, George Cecil,⁴³² *Acting Adjutant*	22 Feb. 82	31 Dec. 90
Jeudwine, Hugh Sandham, *Instructor in Gunnery,School of Gunnery,* 22 Mar. 94	22 Feb. 82	1 Jan. 91
Duffus, Græme Sym, **Adjutant** 1 Apr. 94	27 June 82	10 Jan. 91
FD Jenkinson, Henry Law Acland, **Adjutant** 13 May 92	25 July 82	25 Jan. 91
27 Harrison, Halford Claude Vaughan	25 July 82	10 Feb. 91
54 Caulfeild, Charles Trevor	25 July 82	10 Feb. 91
71 Coates, John Unett	25 July 82	13 Feb. 91
Lane, Herbert Edw. Bruce,⁴³³ *Adj. Pembroke Art. Militia* 13 March 93	25 July 82	13 Feb. 91
Birch, Downward Perceval Lea, *Adj. 1 Renfrew & Dumbarton Vol. Art.* 15 Aug. 93	25 July 82	26 Feb. 91

CAPTAINS.	LIEUT.	CAPTAIN.
40 FD Hussey, Arthur Herbert	25 July 82	28 Feb. 91
80 White, Hans Stannard	25 July 82	11 Mar. 91
Young, Norman Edward, *with Egyptian Army*	25 July 82	29 May 91
Lecky, Robert St.Clair, *Aide de Camp to Lt.Gen. C.E. Nairne* 4 Sept. 93	25 July 82	3 June 91
Denne, Alured Barkley, *Inst. R. M. Academy* 5 Dec. 92	25 July 82	3 June 91
De Butts, Fred. Robt. McCrea²²⁶	25 July 82	20 June 91
MN Grier, Harry Dixon⁴³³†	25 July 82	20 June 91
Jennings, Herbert Alex. Kaye, *Com. of Ord. 2nd Class*	25 July 82	22 July 91
Adair, Hugh Robert, *Inspector of Warlike Stores* 1 Apr. 93	25 July 82	25 July 91
Stretton, Wm. de Courcy, *Adj. 1 Cheshire Art.Vols.* 1 Feb. 91	25 July 82	25 July 91
EA Stevenson, Robert Crawford	25 July 82	25 July 91
53 Young, Arthur Davidson⁴⁰⁵	25 July 82	30 July 91
Parry, Llewellyn Humffreys	25 July 82	3 Sept. 91
Taylor, Howbray,⁴³⁴ *O.S. Dept.*	25 July 82	23 Sept. 91
16 King, Algernon D'Aguilar	25 July 82	23 Sept. 91
80 Cooper, Edward Shewell,⁴³⁴†	25 July 82	1 Oct. 91
Gay, Arthur William,⁴³⁵ **Adjutant** 17 July 93	1 Oct. 82	1 Oct. 91
80 Baker, Arthur Slade	1 Oct. 82	1 Oct. 91
Babington, David Melville, *Ordnance Officer, 4th Class*	1 Oct. 82	7 Oct. 91
Waring, Hy., *in Charge Danger Buildings, Royal Laboratory,* 1 July 93	1 Oct. 82	7 Oct. 91
Parker, John Lewes⁴³⁶	1 Oct. 82	7 Oct. 91
Radcliffe, Wm.Charles Alfred, *Ordnance Officer, 4th Class*	1 Oct. 82	7 Oct. 91
Foote, Henry Bruce, *Ordnance Officer, 4th Class*	1 Oct. 82	12 Oct. 91
Cookson, William Whicher, *Com. of Ordnance, 3rd Class*	1 Oct. 82	22 Oct. 91
Bell, Charles Thornhill, *Ordnance Officer, 3rd Class*	1 Oct. 82	22 Oct. 91
Horton, Sydney Geo.*Assist. Insp. of Warlike Stores* 1 Apr. 93	1 Oct. 82	22 Oct. 91
67 Gubbins, Russell Dunmore	1 Oct. 82	22 Oct. 91
Fisher, Francis Torriano, *p.a.c. Assist. Inspector of Warlike Stores* 1 Apr. 93	1 Oct. 82	29 Oct. 91
Eteson, Harold Carlton Wetherall, *Assist. Insp. of Warlike Stores* 1 Apr. 93	1 Oct. 82	1 Nov. 91
Giles, Francis Henry Synge⁴²³	1 Oct. 82	29 Oct. 91
WN Noble, Montague Mark⁴²³†	1 Oct. 82	29 Oct. 91
MN Smeaton, Charles Oswald⁴³⁷	1 Oct. 82	29 Oct. 91
EA Currie, Arthur Cecil²⁹⁶	1 Oct. 82	1 Nov. 91
Mills, Wm. Holroyd, *Adj. 1 Cornwall Vol. Art.* 10 Feb. 91	1 Oct. 82	1 Nov. 91
Pollock, Arthur Julius, *Adj. 1 Sussex Art. Vols.* 15 May 91	1 Oct. 82	1 Nov. 91
29 Butler, Henry Hugh,⁴³⁸	1 Oct. 82	1 Nov. 91
Farmar, Wm. Lawrance, *p.a.c. Royal Arsenal, Woolwich*	1 Oct. 82	1 Nov. 91
MN Donaldson, Frederick Leverton⁴³⁹	1 Oct. 82	1 Nov. 91
61 Fox, Robert Fanshawe de Berry, *Geo. John Lewes, Adj. 1 Kent Vol. Art.* 23 Nov. 91	1 Oct. 82	4 Nov. 91
32 Cloeté, Evelyn R. Hy. Josins⁴⁰⁰	1 Oct. 82	4 Nov. 91
Vincent, Henry Osman, *Adj. 1 Gloucester Art.Vols.* 1 Apr. 90	1 Oct. 82	4 Nov. 91
WN Brownlow, Charles William⁴³⁹† *p.s.c. Macbean, Wm. Alleyne, Staff Captain, Intell. Dept., War Office,* 15 July 94	1 Oct. 82	4 Nov. 91
Campbell, Malcolm Sydenham Clarke,²⁵⁸ *Com. of Ordnance 4th Class*	14 Feb. 83	4 Nov. 91
80 Drake, Fras. Richd⁴⁴¹	14 Feb. 83	23 Nov. 91
44 Owen, Charles Cunliffe	14 Feb. 83	23 Nov. 91
WN Robinson, Walter Henry⁴⁴¹†	14 Feb. 83	23 Nov. 91
73 Breeks, Richard William	14 Feb. 83	30 Nov. 91
8 Herbert, George Frederick⁴⁰⁰	14 Feb. 83	2 Dec. 91
Oldfield, Christopher George	14 Feb. 83	1 Jan. 92
Williamson, Oswald Charles⁴⁴³	14 Feb. 83	1 Jan. 92
39 Goff, Alg. Hamilton Stannus	14 Feb. 83	27 Jan. 92
80 Kaye, Ralph Arthur,⁴⁴⁰	14 Feb. 83	27 Jan. 92
Pullen, Arthur Fox,⁴⁴⁴	14 Feb. 83	27 Jan. 92
Dodgson, Heathfield Butler, *Adj. Guernsey Art. Mil.* 17 Oct. 92	14 Feb. 83	27 Jan. 92
80 Buckle, Chris. Reginald	14 Feb. 83	1 Feb. 92
Thorp, John Claude,⁴⁴⁵	14 Feb. 83	1 Feb. 92
80 Benson, Rion Philip	14 Feb. 83	1 Feb. 92
FD Berkley, James, **Adjutant**	14 Feb. 83	1 Feb. 92
EA Stanton, Frederick William Starkey²⁵⁸	14 Feb. 83	1 Feb. 92
WN Molesworth, Herbert Crofton St. George	14 Feb. 83	1 Feb. 92
Cook, Henry Rex,⁴¹⁵ *Adj. Cork Art. (S. Div.)* 27 June 92	14 Feb. 83	1 Feb. 92

Royal Artillery. 173

CAPTAINS.	LIEUT.	CAPTAIN.	CAPTAINS.	LIEUT.	CAPTAIN.
80 Shepherd, Jas. Laurance Fred.	14 Feb. 83	6 Feb. 92	3 Furse, William Thomas	5 July 84	30 May 93
Muter, St. John Arthur Douglas, Ordnance Officer, 4th Class...	14 Feb. 83	15 Feb. 92	WN Fowler, Francis Charles	5 July 84	30 May 93
RA Persse, William Arthur****†	14 Feb. 83	15 Feb. 92	Feilden, Rolt. Basil, Aide de Camp to the High Commr. of Cyprus	5 July 84	26 June 93
77 Mackenzie, Cortlandt Gordon	14 Feb. 83	19 Feb. 92	70 Geddes, George Hessing	5 July 84	26 June 93
Galbraith, Gerald Edward,⁴¹⁵† Inst. in Gunnery, Gibraltar	14 Feb. 83	19 Feb. 92	SUB. DEP. 2 EA Coxhead, Thomas Langhorne,⁴⁵⁴ DSO.	5 July 84	26 June 93
80 Gordon, Lawrence Christian⁴⁴⁶†	14 Feb. 83	3 Mar. 92	Marshall, Hawtrey Chas. Insp. of Warlike Stores, Jamaica, 9 Dec. 01	5 July 84	28 June 93
Logan, David Finlay Hosken,⁴⁴⁷ Adj. 1 Glamorgan Art. Vols.	14 Feb. 83	3 Mar. 92	Kirke, Henry Lushington, Adj. Caithness Vol. Art. 6 Apr. 93	5 July 84	28 June 93
Ferrar, Hy. Minchin, Staff Capt. Remount Estab. 26 Sept. 93	14 Feb. 83	3 Mar. 92	Dunlop, Arch. Sam. at Staff Coll.	5 July 84	28 June 93
EA Lyall, Charles Noel⁴⁴⁶	28 Feb. 83	15 Mar. 92	2-2 DEP FD Kilner, Charles Harold	5 July 84	1 Aug. 93
Randolph, Francis Arthur, p.a.c.⁴⁰⁰	28 Feb. 83	16 Mar. 92	80 Norris, Arthur Gambier	5 July 84	15 Aug. 93
43 Tyler, Charles William	7 Mar. 83	16 Mar. 92	80 Warren, Wm. Lewis, Garrison Adj. Singapore, 20 Apr. 94...	5 July 84	19 Aug. 93
WN Vans-Agnew, Francis	9 Mar. 83	18 Mar. 92	1 Lachlan, Ernest Moncrieff	5 July 84	19 Aug. 93
Pasley, Montagu Wynyard Sabine 4th Class Commissary of Ord.	21 Mar. 83	19 Mar. 92	DEP EA Radcliffe, R. Edm. Lowndes	5 July 84	14 Sept. 93
55 Knox, Arthur Rice	28 Mar. 83	19 Mar. 92	EA Rouse, Hubert	5 July 84	4 Oct. 93
Gray, Phillip Easson, Instructor School of Gunnery 1 Apr. 92	26 June 83	19 Mar. 92	Lloyd, Maurice Brickdale	5 July 84	13 Oct. 93
Headlam, John Emerson Wharton, Instructor School of Gunnery 1 July 92	28 July 83	23 Mar. 92	EA Humphreys, Gardiner	5 July 84	14 Oct. 93
			Playfair, Frederick Lyon, Adj. 1 Edinburgh (City) Vol. Art.	5 July 84	21 Oct. 93
			WN Roberts, Michael Bradley	5 July 84	21 Oct. 93
80 Perceval, Claude John	28 July 83	1 Apr. 92	80 Cuming, Arthur Thomas	5 July 84	23 Oct. 93
25 Johnston, Fredk. Campbell⁴⁴⁸	28 July 83	1 Apr. 92	80 Askwith, Henry Francis	5 July 84	15 Nov. 93
Rolt, Chas. Edw., Insp. of Warlike Stores, Ceylon, 1 Apr. 92	28 July 83	1 Apr. 92	Dickinson, Thomas Malcolm, Adjutant 1 Ayrshire & Galloway Vol. Art. 6 Apr. 93	5 July 84	9 Dec. 93
80 Napier, William John	28 July 83	1 Apr. 92	Parry, James Bacchus, Adj. Mid Ulster Art. S. Div. 20 Feb. 95	5 July 84	9 Dec. 93
RA Chamier, Saunders Jas. Adjutant	28 July 83	1 Apr. 92			
23 Maunsell, Frederick Guy	28 July 83	1 Apr. 92			
41 Smith, Edmund Perceval	28 July 83	13 May 92	Bateman, Bernard M., St. Helena	5 July 84	16 Dec. 93
EA Onslow, William Henry	28 July 83	18 May 92	Merriman, Reginald Gordon,⁴⁴² DSO. Adj. Kent Art. E. Div. 1 Mar. 95	9 Dec. 84	31 Dec. 93
Mansell, John Herbert, Assist. Insp. of Warlike Stores 1 Apr. 93	28 July 83	25 May 92			
Bertie-Clay, Neville Sneyd, Asst. Supdt. of Factories, Bengal, 15 Mar. 91	28 July 83	25 May 92	80 Hardy, William Kyle⁴⁵⁵	9 Dec. 84	1 Jan. 94
			52 White, George Francis	9 Dec. 84	3 Jan. 94
80 M'Meekan, Francis Henry Fromout Reader⁴⁵⁰	28 July 83	25 May 92	Foster, Philip	9 Dec. 84	4 Jan. 94
			EA Cooper, Philip Templer	9 Dec. 84	10 Feb. 94
47 Geddes, John Gordon	28 July 83	27 July 92	WN Wood, Thomas Birchall	9 Dec. 84	14 Mar. 94
15 Walker, Alexander Lamond	28 July 83	10 Aug. 92	FD Norris, Ernest Euward	9 Dec. 84	14 Mar. 94
80 Williams-Wynn, Henry Cunliffe	28 July 83	10 Aug. 92	RA du Plat-Taylor, St. John Louis Hyde	9 Dec. 84	22 Mar. 94
Bingham, Hon. Fras. Rd. Aide de Camp to Commander in Chief Madras, 28 Oct. 93	28 July 83	15 Aug. 92	WN Lambert, Edward Parry	9 Dec. 84	1 Apr. 94
			80 Battiscombe, Charles	9 Dec. 84	1 Apr. 94
Gordon, Lochinvar Alex. Chas. Hony Kong Art.	28 July 83	1 Oct. 92	21 Browne, James Frederick⁴⁵⁶	9 Dec. 84	1 Apr. 94
			WN Cleeve, Egerton Stewart	9 Dec. 84	9 May 94
80 Ritchie, John Robert	28 July 83	17 Oct. 92	80 Raby, Montague Henry Burton	9 Dec. 84	14 July 94
EA Ross, Horatio St. George	28 July 83	17 Oct. 92	Bidgood, Thomas Edward Wingfield, Adjutant Sligo Art. S. Div. 20 Aug. 94	9 Dec. 84	14 July 94
64 Corbyn, Hector	28 July 83	14 Dec. 92			
WN Eyre, Morland Stanhope⁴⁴⁹	28 July 83	10 Jan. 93			
22 Gordon, Lawrence Geo. Frank	1 Aug. 83	10 Jan. 93	80 Watson, Christopher Godfrey⁴⁵⁷	9 Dec. 84	29 Sept. 94
2 Smith, Herbert Guthrie	15 Feb. 84	10 Jan. 93	80 Grover, William Montague	9 Dec. 84	15 Nov. 94
Tyacke, George, 2nd Assistant Supdt. of Experiments, School of Gunnery, 1 Feb. 93	15 Feb. 84	13 Jan. 94	WN Lyon, Charles	9 Dec. 84	10 Dec. 94
			EA Cameron, Ewan Cornwalli	9 Dec. 84	25 Dec. 94
WN Sandilands, Henry George	15 Feb. 84	18 Jan. 93	Campbell, Edm. Arth., Adj. 1 Newcastle-on-Tyne Vol. Art. 10 Feb. 91	9 Dec. 84	1 Jan. 95
EA Robinson, William Arthur⁴⁵¹	15 Feb. 84	19 Jan. 93			
WN Lushington, Stephen, Adj. Cardigan Art. W. Div. 16 Feb. 95	15 Feb. 84	29 Jan. 93	Freeth, Fras. Edw., Adj. 1 East Riding of York Vol. Art. 20 Nov. 91	9 Dec. 84	1 Jan. 95
WN Burnett, John Chaplyn (2 Sub Depot)	15 Feb. 84	1 Feb. 93	EA Hall, Ernest Frederic	9 Dec. 84	1 Jan. 95
WN Cameron, Ewen Donald Charles²³⁸	15 Feb. 84	1 Feb. 93	Harrison, Arthur Estcourt, Adj. Durham Art. W. Div. 5 Jan. 95	9 Dec. 84	4 Jan. 95
Warden, Richard Edward, Adj. 1 North Riding of Yorkshire Art. Vols. 9 Apr. 90	15 Feb. 84	1 Feb. 93	80 Peake, Malcolm	9 Dec. 84	5 Jan. 95
			80 White-Thomson, Hugh Davie	9 Dec. 84	9 Jan. 95
Bremner, Donald, Adj. 2 Northumberland Art. Vols.	15 Feb. 84	1 Feb. 93	WN Forestier - Walker, George Townshend	9 Dec. 84	1 Feb. 95
80 Ford, Charles Hopewell	15 Feb. 84	1 Feb. 93	EA Lamb, George Rothney⁴⁵⁸	29 Apr. 85	20 Feb. 95
62 Schofield, Harry Norton	15 Feb. 84	1 Feb. 93			
Campbell, Henry Montgomery	15 Feb. 84	1 Feb. 93			
Kemmis, Wm. Henry Olphert	15 Feb. 84	1 Feb. 93			
EA Bampfylde, Henry Edward	15 Feb. 84	1 Mar. 93	**LIEUTENANTS.**		**LIEUT.**
80 Casement, Roger	15 Feb. 84	1 Mar. 93	Maunsell, Mannel Charles, Inst. R. M. Academy, Woolwich, 1 Apr. 94		29 Apr. 85
Anderson, James Douglas	15 Feb. 84	3 Mar. 93			
Salmon, James Nelson, O. S. Dept.	15 Feb. 84	4 Mar. 93	Ogg, George Sim,⁴⁵⁹ Ord. Officer, 4th Class		29 Apr. 85
Du Cane, John Philip, Adjutant Norfolk Art. E. Div. 16 Feb. 94	15 Feb. 84	4 Mar. 93	Money, Arthur Wigram⁴⁶⁰		29 Apr. 85
Lawrie, Charles Edward,⁴⁵² serving with Egyptian Army	15 Feb. 84	4 Mar. 93	Macgowan, Robt. Stuart, Adj. 1 Fifeshire Art. Vols. with rank of Capt. 1 Oct. 92		29 Apr. 85
Dennis, Meade James Crosbie, Adj. Wicklow Art. South Div. R. Art. 1 June 94	15 Feb. 84	4 Mar. 93	Saltren-Willett, Archibald John, Assist. Inspector of Warlike Stores 1 Apr. 93		29 Apr. 85
			Young, Francis Henry, Lieut. of a Company of Gentlemen Cadets 28 Dec. 91		29 Apr. 85
17 Graham, Lancelot	15 Feb. 84	16 Mar. 93	E RHA Staveley, William Cathcart		29 Apr. 85
RA Maxwell, James M'Call	15 Feb. 84	1 Apr. 93	WN Marsh, Hopton Eliott		29 Apr. 85
80 Fasson, Disney John Menzies, at Staff College	15 Feb. 84	1 Apr. 93	80 Gooch, John Sherlock		29 Apr. 85
Lyle, George Samuel Bateson	15 Feb. 84	1 Apr. 93	Birch, Jas. Fred. Noel, A.D.C. to Major General G. J. Smart, 1 Apr. 94		29 Apr. 85
Wray, John Cecil, Adj. Hon. Art., Co. of London 1 Dec. 94	15 Feb. 84	6 May 93	D RHA Thompson, Wm. A. Murray, Staff College		29 Apr. 85
80 Bainbridge, Percy Agnew	15 Feb. 84	13 May 93	Dykes, Lionel Erle Ballantine, Inst. in Range Finding, Cork		29 Apr. 85
Pratt, Hy. Arthur, Assist. Inst. in Range Finding 1 Apr. 92	15 Feb. 84	30 May 93	Iles, Henry Wilson,⁴⁶¹ Adj. 1 Devon Art. Vols. with rank of Captain, 11 Feb. 92		29 Apr. 85

K

Royal Artillery

LIEUTENANTS.	LIEUT.
Vanderzee, Henry Frank,462 Ordnance Officer 4th Class	29 Apr. 85
Hudson, Thomas Ros Christopher	29 Apr. 85
G RHA Prescott-Decie, Cyril	29 Apr. 85
K RHA de Rougemont, Cecil Henry	29 Apr. 85
Stansfield, James Rawdon, Adj. 2 Sussex Vol. Art. with rank of Captain.	29 Apr. 85
Biddulph, Hope, Aide de Camp to Sir R. Biddulph 18 Oct. 93	29 Apr. 85
T RHA Cardew, George Ambrose	29 Apr. 85
SUB. DEP. 2 WN TEDLANT, Henry Lancelot, Staff College	29 Apr. 85
MN Marshall, Thomas Edward463	29 Apr. 85
J RHA Heath, Francis William	29 Apr. 85
I RHA Blacker, Stewart Ward William	29 Apr. 85
J RHA Elton, Fred Algernon George Young	29 Apr. 85
M RHA Norwood, William Blakeney	29 Apr. 85
Strange, Harry Bland,464 Insp. of Danger Buildings, R. Laboratory, 1 Apr. 93	30 June 85
Moren, James Alexander, Instructor R. M. College, Kingston, Canada	30 June 85
Hodgins, Charles Richard, Adj. 3 Lancashire Vol. Art. with hon. rank of Captain 26 May 94	30 June 85
9 Duffus, Edward John	30 June 85
Worsley, George Stanley	30 June 85
72 Potts, Frederick	16 Sept. 85
80 Bruce-Kingsmill, Julian Claud de Kenne465	16 Sept. 85
C RHA Milne, George Francis	16 Sept. 85
Harvest, Hector Horatio, in charge of Defences, King George's Sound, West Australia, 30 Mar. 93	16 Sept. 85
N RHA Simonds, Cecil Barrow	16 Sept. 85
-2 DEP. FD Prendergast, Frederick	16 Sept. 85
22-2 DEP. FD Clark, Charles Watson	16 Sept. 85
41 Wilson, Joseph Reginald	16 Sept. 85
B DEP. RHA Winwood, Henry James Hoyte	16 Sept. 85
Hill, Charles Edward,466 Adj. 1 London Vol. Art. with rank of Captain 1 Apr. 94	16 Sept. 85
DEP. WN Tyler, Arthur Malcolm	16 Sept. 85
Reid, John Watt, Adjutant Hants Vol. Art. with rank of Captain, 1 Jan. 94	16 Sept. 85
Langhorne, Harold Stephen	16 Sept. 85
35 Glanville, Arthur George	16 Sept. 85
Perkins, Arthur John Ernest,467 Lieut. of a Company of Gentlemen Cadets, 20 Feb. 92	16 Sept. 85
Davidson, Francis Middleton	16 Sept. 85
Calvert, George, Adj. 7 Lancashire Art. Vols. with rank of Captain, 28 Jan. 92	16 Sept. 85
East, Lionel William Pellew,468 DSO	16 Sept. 85
P RHA Morris, Charles James Ussher	16 Sept. 85
G RHA Powell, Henry Lloyd	16 Sept. 85
Moore, Robt. Thornton, Ord. Officer, 4th Class	16 Sept. 85
Quinton, Francis William Drummond, Adj. 2 Hants Art. Vols. with rank of Capt.	16 Sept. 85
65 Uniacke, Herbert Crofton Campbell	16 Sept. 85
MN Blunt, Charles Jasper	16 Sept. 85
Baldwin, John Grey469	16 Sept. 85
Lyle, Henry Duntze470	16 Sept. 85
Q RHA Ravenhill, Frederick Thornhill	16 Sept. 85
C RHA Lennox, Amyot Maitland Augustus	17 Feb. 86
Ouseley, Ralph Glynn	17 Feb. 86
Jenour, Arthur Stawell, Adj. 4 Durham Art. Vols. with rank of Capt. 28 Mar. 92	17 Feb. 86
60 White, Henry Arthur Pilkington	17 Feb. 86
1-1 DEP. FD England, Edward Parker	17 Feb. 86
78 Olivier, William Henry	17 Feb. 86
Nicholson, William Cyril Alwynne, Adj. 1 Orkney Vol. Art. with rank of Captain	17 Feb. 86
73 Oldnall-Russell, Henry Cairns	17 Feb. 86
28 Carey, George Glas Sandeman	17 Feb. 86
36 Stockdale, Herbert Edward	17 Feb. 86
I RHA Elkington, Robert James Goodall	17 Feb. 86
Tancred, Thomas Agnew, serving with Bechuanaland Border Police	17 Feb. 86
G RHA Butler, Arthur Townley	17 Feb. 86
Woodifield, A. Hudson, Adj. 2 Cinque Ports Art. Vols. with rank of Capt. 2 Jan. 93	17 Feb. 86
2-1 DEP. FD Sharp, Frederick Leonard	17 Feb. 86
K RHA Combe, Kenneth	17 Feb. 86
Wingfield, William Edward	17 Feb. 86
Tancock, Osborne Kendall	17 Feb. 86
Pringle, Geo. Octavius Shaw, Sierra Leone	17 Feb. 86
Alexander, William Patrick	17 Feb. 86
66 Campbell-Johnston, Gordon	17 Feb. 86
Nichol, William Dale,471 Adj. 3 Durham Vol. Art. with rank of Capt. 16 Jan. 63	17 Feb. 86
Crowe, Mordaunt Abingdon Carlisle	17 Feb. 86
H RHA Boulnois, William Arthur	17 Feb. 86
Malleson, Wilfrid, Ord. Officer, India	17 Feb. 86
72 Usborne, Thomas Masters	17 Feb. 86
55 Crockett, Walter Macandrew	17 Feb. 86
40 Palmer, Hugh Robert	17 Feb. 86
Aikenhead, Frank, Adj. 1 Lancashire Art. Vols. with rank of Captain	17 Feb. 86
B RHA Arbuthnot, Dalrymple	17 Feb. 86

LIEUTENANTS.	LIEUT.	
Q RHA Perrott, William Henry Willy	18 Feb. 86	
32 Symonds, George Davey	18 Feb. 86	
55 Stevens, Charles Frederick	18 Feb. 86	
80 Davies, Ernest Wilson (Depot)	18 Feb. 86	
MN Phipps, Charles Edward	18 Feb. 86	
Gorton, Reginald St. George482	18 Feb. 86	
Head, Harry Francis	18 Feb. 86	
Phillips, Thomas Richmond	18 Feb. 86	
Brake, Herbert Edward John	18 Feb. 86	
Chepmell, Claude Herrie, Mauritius	18 Feb. 86	
22 Shortt, Alexander Graham	18 Feb. 86	
Brewster, Robert Ferdinand	18 Feb. 86	
Reid, Harold Arthur	18 Feb. 86	
C RHA FitzMaurice, Robert	18 Feb. 86	
E RHA Cowper-Smith, Arthur Monro de Lasalle	18 Feb. 86	
Knapp, Kempster Kenmure471†	18 Feb. 86	
1-1 DEP. WD Tyler, James Arbuthnot	24 July 86	
T RHA Hickie, Arthur Francis	24 July 86	
80 Armitage, William Stuart	24 July 86	
Hamilton, Percy Douglas, Instructor in Gunnery, Portsmouth	24 July 86	
80 Kelsall, Harry Joseph	24 July 86	
Hare, Robert Hugh	24 July 86	
SUB DEP. EA Adair, Charles Osborn	24 July 86	
O RHA Kennard, Arthur Mulloy	24 July 86	
Forestier-Walker, Claude Edward	24 July 86	
Fawcett, Percy Harrison	24 July 86	
2 MacCarthy, Morgan John	24 July 86	
MN Church, George Ross Marryat	24 July 86	
EA Pitman, Alfred Cyril	24 July 86	
DEP. 80 Macgowan, James Murray	24 July 86	
80 Traherne, George Gilbert472	24 July 86	
D RHA Ellice, Robert Frederick	24 July 86	
H Lovita, Cecil Bingham	24 July 86	
Griffin, Henry Lysaght, Adj. 2 East Riding of York Art. Vols. with rank of Captain, 25 July 92	24 July 86	
Courtenay, Michael Hudson, Act. Adj. Donegal Art. 18 Oct. 94	24 July 86	
Graham-Clarke, Lionel Altham, Adjutant 4 West Riding of York Vol. Art. with rank of Captain, 26 Feb. 94	24 July 86	
Broadrick, Fredk. Benjamin Dumaresq, Adjutant 1 Lincoln Artillery (W. Div. R. Art.), with rank of Captain, 21 Dec. 93	24 July 86	
Smallwood, Frank Graham,484 Com. of Ord. 4th Class	24 July 86	
Seagrim, Dudley Gillum485	24 July 86	
14 Watson, John Capron	24 July 86	
T RHA Ross-Johnson, Cyril Maxwell	24 July 86	
Q RHA Godfrey-Faussett, Percival Godfrey	24 July 86	
P RHA Kirk, John Charters	24 July 86	
80 Matthews, John Williams (2 Sub. Depot)	24 July 86	
S RHA Cameron, Ewan Duncan	24 July 86	
18 Allen, Frederick Edward Halstead	24 July 86	
31 Cadell, Harry Ernest	24 July 86	
2-1 DEP. FD Van Straubenzee, Casimir Cartwright	25 Dec. 86	
	2ND LIEUT.	
D RHA Fordyce-Buchan, Geo. Chas.	16 Feb. 87	16 Feb. 90
Curme, William Charles, Devonport	16 Feb. 87	16 Feb. 90
80 Peacocke, Charles Leslie	16 Feb. 87	16 Feb. 90
B RHA Pack-Beresford, Arthur Wm.	16 Feb. 87	16 Feb. 90
69 M'Kay, Donald	16 Feb. 87	16 Feb. 90
MN Jones, Walter Howel487	16 Feb. 87	16 Feb. 90
1-2 DEP. FD Tapp, Jas. Hanson Wm.	16 Feb. 87	16 Feb. 90
WN Thornton, James Aylmer	16 Feb. 87	16 Feb. 90
L RHA Wellesley, Rd. Colley	16 Feb. 87	16 Feb. 90
Phillipps, Chas. Inst. in Gun., Cork	16 Feb. 87	16 Feb. 90
MN Kenyon, Lionel Richard	16 Feb. 87	16 Feb. 90
46 Lake, Hubert Atwell	16 Feb. 87	16 Feb. 90
60 Woodcock, Henry Stephen	16 Feb. 87	16 Feb. 90
Stewart, James Anthony	16 Feb. 87	16 Feb. 90
68 Smith, Arthur Murray423	16 Feb. 87	16 Feb. 90
MN Boynton, Henry L. Norman	16 Feb. 87	16 Feb. 90
Taylor, Cecil Salusbury, Assist. Inspector of Warlike Stores, Hong Kong, 29 March 91	16 Feb. 87	16 Feb. 90
2-2 DEP. FD Bell, Kenneth Dowie	16 Feb. 87	16 Feb. 90
Comyn, Edward Walter, Adj. 1 Dorset Art. Vols. with rank of Captain, 16 Feb. 93	16 Feb. 87	16 Feb. 90
54 Douglas, Archibald Philip	16 Feb. 87	16 Feb. 90
H RHA Taylor, Herb. Wodehouse	16 Feb. 87	16 Feb. 90
EA Ruthven, Robert Mervyn Bermingham	16 Feb. 87	16 Feb. 90
Molony, Clement A.,488 Ceylon	16 Feb. 87	16 Feb. 90
Barron, Netterville Guy, Adj. 1 Norfolk Vol. Art. with rank of Captain, 1 Dec. 94	16 Feb. 87	16 Feb. 90
Gordon, Wm. Neville, St. Lucia	16 Feb. 87	16 Feb. 90
80 Farrell, Henry John William	16 Feb. 87	16 Feb. 90
N RHA Jones, Tertius	16 Feb. 87	16 Feb. 90
80 Stiffe, Arch. Frns. Everitt	16 Feb. 87	16 Feb. 90
M RHA FitzGerald, George Alfred	16 Feb. 87	16 Feb. 90

Royal Artillery.

LIEUTENANTS.	2ND LIEUT.	LIEUT.
1-1 DEP. FD Thwaites, William	16 Feb. 87	16 Feb. 90
MN Miller, Alan Stewart	16 Feb. 87	16 Feb. 90
Macdonald, Reginald James, 2nd Class Assistant Inspector of Warlike Stores 1 Apr. 93	16 July 87	6 July 90
A RHA Sandys, Wm. Bain Richardson	23 July 87	23 July 90
Bland, William St. Colum	23 July 87	23 July 90
Molesworth, Richard Pigot	23 July 87	23 July 90
Chapman, Lawrence Joseph	23 July 87	23 July 90
Leahy, Henry Gordon, Inst. in Range Finding, Harwich	23 July 87	23 July 90
WN Matthews, William Arthur	23 July 87	23 July 90
O RHA Farrant, Rbt. Kincaid (Depot)	23 July 87	23 July 90
Fraser, Lyons David, Mauritius	23 July 87	23 July 90
58 Head, Charles Octavius	23 July 87	23 July 90
39 Laird, Gordon	23 July 87	23 July 90
EA Desborough, A. Peregrine Hy.	23 July 87	23 July 90
Pottinger, Eldred Charles	23 July 87	23 July 90
80 Rice, George William	23 July 87	23 July 90
71 Skipwith, Philip Armfield	23 July 87	23 July 90
25 Spedding, Edward Wilfrid	23 July 87	23 July 90
A DEP. RHA Williams, Masterman S.	23 July 87	23 July 90
MN Patch, Francis Robert[120]	23 July 87	23 July 90
DEP. A RHA Hooper, Stuart Huntly	23 July 87	23 July 90
37 Kirby, Arthur Durham	23 July 87	23 July 90
U1 Sclater-Booth, Hon. W. Dashwood	23 July 87	23 July 90
MN Lyon, Francis	23 July 87	23 July 90
MN Fisher, John Francis	23 July 87	23 July 90
Franks, George M'Kenzie	23 July 87	23 July 90
80 Ward, Hon. Maxwell R. Crosbie	23 July 87	23 July 90
Savage, A. R. Boscawen, Adj. 2 West Riding of York. Vol. Art. with rank of Capt. 15 Nov. 94	23 July 87	23 July 90
1 SUB DEP. WN Battine, Alex. James	23 July 87	23 July 90
MN Stuart, Ralph Esme	23 July 87	23 July 90
WN Parken, Philip Hugh (Depot)	23 July 87	23 July 90
63 Roberts, Hugh Bradley	23 July 87	23 July 90
Young, Henry Alfred, Ordnance Officer, 4th Class	17 Feb. 88	17 Feb. 91
RA Peile, Alfred James	17 Feb. 88	17 Feb. 91
74 Crozier, Thomas Henry	17 Feb. 88	17 Feb. 91
16 Parsons, E. H. Thornbrough	17 Feb. 88	17 Feb. 91
23 Owen, Frederick Cunliffe	17 Feb. 88	17 Feb. 91
Coley-Bromfield, John Coley, Inst. in Gunnery, Dover	17 Feb. 88	17 Feb. 91
Lee, Arthur Hamilton, Prof. R. M. College, Canada, with local rank of Capt. 17 Aug. 93	17 Feb. 88	17 Feb. 91
Crawford, Alfred Temple	17 Feb. 88	17 Feb. 91
6 Earle, Cecil Arthur	17 Feb. 88	17 Feb. 91
38 Seddon, Edward M'Mahon	17 Feb. 88	17 Feb. 91
Hutchinson, Fred. Pierrepont, 3rd Assist. Supdt. Expts. Sch. of Gunnery, 8 Sept. 94		
9 Stewart, Charles Edward	17 Feb. 88	17 Feb. 91
R RHA Wellesley, Richard A. Colley	17 Feb. 88	17 Feb. 91
80 Scott, Alex. Francis Sinclair, Adj. 1 Lanark Vol. Art. with rank of Capt. 1 March 95	17 Feb. 88	17 Feb. 91
34 Rotton, John Guy	17 Feb. 88	17 Feb. 91
MN Carter, Ernest Pasley	17 Feb. 88	17 Feb. 91
20 Lithgow, Hugh Lancaster	17 Feb. 88	17 Feb. 91
59 Sanders, George Herbert	17 Feb. 88	17 Feb. 91
75 Ward, Montagu Chas. Pearson	17 Feb. 88	17 Feb. 91
80 Jennings, Walton	17 Feb. 88	17 Feb. 91
WN Moore, St. Leger Montgomery	17 Feb. 88	17 Feb. 91
EA Phillips, Ernest Robert	17 Feb. 88	17 Feb. 91
65 Rugge-Price, Charles Frederick	17 Feb. 88	17 Feb. 91
Tulloch, T. G. Inst. in Gun. Malta	17 Feb. 88	17 Feb. 91
58 Alford, Frederick Lewis, Adj. 2 Devon Vol. Art. with rank of Capt. 15 March 95	17 Feb. 88	17 Feb. 91
Arthy, Walter, Adj. 1 Argyll and Bute Vol. Art. with rank of Captain, 1 Sept. 94	17 Feb. 88	17 Feb. 91
Parker, Henry Wm. Manwaring[174]	17 Feb. 88	17 Feb. 91
Harper, Leonard Llewellyn, Garrison Artillery, Queensland	17 Feb. 88	17 Feb. 91
Christie, Herbert Willie Andrew, Adj. 1 Midlothian Vol. Art. with rank of Capt. 26 Jan. 94	17 Feb. 88	17 Feb. 91
R RHA Cartwright, Garnier Norton	17 Feb. 88	17 Feb. 91
9 Molony, Trevor Charles Wheler	17 Feb. 88	17 Feb. 91
B RHA Herbert, Percy Thos. Colthurst	17 Feb. 88	17 Feb. 91
Carey, W. Havilland, Hong Kong	17 Feb. 88	17 Feb. 91
Thrupp, F. Morton, Assist. Insp. of Warlike Stores, Bermuda	17 Feb. 88	17 Feb. 91
80 Langdon, Paul Perram	17 Feb. 88	17 Feb. 91
71 Davidson, Gordon Villiers	17 Feb. 88	17 Feb. 91
61 MacMillan, John St. Clair	17 Feb. 88	17 Feb. 91
Buckle, Archie S., Danger Buildings Officer, Waltham Abbey 8 Sept. 94	17 Feb. 88	17 Feb. 91
54 Anderson, Austin Thomas	17 Feb. 88	17 Feb. 91
B DEP. RHA Russell, Edmund Stuart Eardley Wilmot	17 Feb. 88	17 Feb. 91

LIEUTENANTS.	2ND LIEUT.	LIEUT.
Bray, Arthur Le Mesurier	17 Feb. 88	17 Feb. 91
MN Brett, Herbert George	17 Feb. 88	17 Feb. 91
10 Ballard, Chas. Naesmyth Bruere	17 Feb. 88	17 Feb. 91
13 Saunders, William Power	17 Feb. 88	17 Feb. 91
DEP. EA Pennethorne, Hy. Evelyn	17 Feb. 88	17 Feb. 91
WN Elliot, Harry Macintire	17 Feb. 88	17 Feb. 91
MN M'Hardy, Alexander Anderson	17 Feb. 88	17 Feb. 91
Corrie, Wm. Fr. Taylor, Singapore	17 Feb. 88	17 Feb. 91
75 Geoghegan, Robert	17 Feb. 88	17 Feb. 91
80 Lambarde, Francis Fane	17 Feb. 88	17 Feb. 91
MN Walters, Hubert de Lancey	17 Feb. 88	17 Feb. 91
36 Rettie, William John Kerr	17 Feb. 88	17 Feb. 91
80 Morrison, Maskell M. D.	17 Feb. 88	17 Feb. 91
42 Gotto, Harold Ralph	17 Feb. 88	17 Feb. 91
MN Grepe, Arthur Wellesley	17 Feb. 88	17 Feb. 91
3 Smith, Edward Pelham	17 Feb. 88	17 Feb. 91
29 Reed, Hamilton Lyster	17 Feb. 88	17 Feb. 91
56 Massy, Edward Charles	17 Feb. 88	17 Feb. 91
6 Tyler, Ralph Edward	17 Feb. 88	17 Feb. 91
32 Nicholson, Graham H. Whalley	17 Feb. 88	17 Feb. 91
40 Boger, Richard Wharton	17 Feb. 88	17 Feb. 91
DEP. EA Wailes, William Eteson	17 Feb. 88	17 Feb. 91
80 Kirkpatrick, Alex. Ronald Vane	17 Feb. 88	17 Feb. 91
MN Moultrie, Hugh Crawford	17 Feb. 88	17 Feb. 91
Edlmann, Ernest Elliot	17 Feb. 88	17 Feb. 91
MN Freeland, Anthony Drage	17 Feb. 88	17 Feb. 91
EA Tomkins, Ernest Leith	17 Feb. 88	17 Feb. 91
Home, Robert Elton	17 Feb. 88	17 Feb. 91
57 Barker, Frederic Edward Lloyd	28 June 88	28 June 91
Cayley, A. M. Inst. in Gun. Halifax	28 June 88	28 June 91
Johnston, George Napier, Adj. 1 London Vol. Art. with rank of Captain, 29 Oct. 94	28 June 88	28 June 91
Stewart, Cosmo Gordon	27 July 88	27 July 91
Tighe, Francis Alfred	27 July 88	27 July 91
7 Crockett, Sydney Laurence	27 July 88	27 July 91
Smith, Wm. H. U., Inst. Range Finding, Bermuda	27 July 88	27 July 91
15 Galloway, Frank Lennox	27 July 88	27 July 91
Bellairs, Norman Ed. Breton	27 July 83	27 July 91
Lethbridge, Sydney	27 July 88	27 July 91
Coningham, Henry, Lieut. of a Co. of Gent. Cadets 17 Oct. 92	27 July 88	27 July 91
2 SUB DEP. WN Butcher, Frederick Spurrell	27 July 88	27 July 91
MacMunn, Geo. Fletcher,[192] DSO	27 July 88	27 July 91
80 Morrice, Herbert	27 July 88	27 July 91
73 Coates, Douglas Richardson	27 July 88	27 July 91
WN Johnstone, Hope (2 Sub. Depot)	27 July 88	27 July 91
2-1 DEP. FD Choke, Edward Geo.	27 July 88	27 July 91
L RHA Bellhouse, John	27 July 88	27 July 91
K RHA Nairne, Edward Spencer	27 July 88	27 July 91
41 Strong, William	27 July 88	27 July 91
Waymouth, Ernest Glanville Adj. Det. School of Gunnery	27 July 88	27 July 91
Mackintosh, John Burn	27 July 88	27 July 91
59 Hill, Howard Berkeley	27 July 88	27 July 91
Nixon, Frederick Eckersall	27 July 88	27 July 91
MN M'Culloch, Robert Henry Frederick	27 July 88	27 July 91
Dent, Frank Wilkinson, Adj. 2 Glamorgan Vol. Art. with rank of Captain, 15 Nov. 94	27 July 88	27 July 91
MN Metcalfe, Fenwick Henry	27 July 88	27 July 91
Massie, Roger Henry	27 July 88	27 July 91
Thorp, Arth. Hugh, Inspector of Position Finding, Woolwich, 24 July 93	27 July 88	27 July 91
52 Nicholson, Walter Adams	27 July 88	27 July 91
MN Kendall, John Kaye	27 July 88	27 July 91
58 Pim, Edward Hugh	27 July 88	27 July 91
Benwell, Albert, Jamaica	27 July 88	27 July 91
MN Ellershaw, Arthur	27 July 88	27 July 91
L Hichens, Thomas Sikes	15 Feb. 89	15 Feb. 92
Hardcastle, J. Herschel	15 Feb. 89	15 Feb. 92
M RHA Brock, Henry Jenkins	15 Feb. 89	15 Feb. 92
I RHA Thomson, Alex. Fred. Roberts	15 Feb. 89	15 Feb. 92
J RHA Budyerth, Chas. Edw. Dutton	15 Feb. 89	15 Feb. 92
80 Farmar, William Cecil Russell	15 Feb. 89	15 Feb. 92
Redfern, P. Youngson, Jamaica	15 Feb. 89	15 Feb. 92
26 Oldham, Frank Trevor	15 Feb. 89	15 Feb. 92
59 Gordon, Neil Fraser	15 Feb. 89	15 Feb. 92
Templer, Cyril Frank	15 Feb. 89	15 Feb. 92
8 Goldie, Adrian Hope	15 Feb. 89	15 Feb. 92
80 Williams, Arthur Cecil	15 Feb. 89	15 Feb. 92
WN Hunt, William Holdsworth	15 Feb. 89	15 Feb. 92
EA Bishop, Charles Frederick	15 Feb. 89	15 Feb. 92
S RHA Boggs, Arthur Addison	15 Feb. 89	15 Feb. 92
37 Forbes, Arthur	15 Feb. 89	15 Feb. 92
Woods, George Greville	15 Feb. 89	15 Feb. 92
61 Coates, Reginald Carlyon	15 Feb. 89	15 Feb. 92
WN Noott, Cuthbert Cecil	15 Feb. 89	15 Feb. 92
80 Blanford, William George	15 Feb. 89	15 Feb. 92
MN Poole, Frederick Cuthbert	15 Feb. 89	15 Feb. 92
A RHA Simpson-Baikie, Hugh A. D.	15 Feb. 89	15 Feb. 92
80 Barnes, Henry Marshall	15 Feb. 89	15 Feb. 92

K 2

176 *Royal Artillery.*

Lieutenants.	2nd Lieut.	Lieut.
69 Hardman, Reginald Stanley ...	15 Feb. 89	15 Feb. 92
F RHA Dixon, George Frederic	15 Feb. 89	15 Feb. 92
KA Craig, Robert Annesley	15 Feb. 89	15 Feb. 92
Bruce, John Elliot Lidderdale[494]	15 Feb. 89	15 Feb. 92
BA Pilkington, W. A. Cunningham	15 Feb. 89	15 Feb. 92
MN Craster, Edm. Hen. Bertram[493]	15 Feb. 89	15 Feb. 92
S RHA Hobson, John Alexander ...	15 Feb. 89	15 Feb. 92
so Stockley, Arthur Uniacke	15 Feb. 89	15 Feb. 92
17 Geary, Henry George Fredk. ...	15 Feb. 89	15 Feb. 92
F RHA Vallentin, Henry Edward ...	15 Feb. 89	20 Sept. 92
MN Thomas, Henry Melville	15 Feb. 89	15 Feb. 92
Duff, G. Graham Kayll, *Hong Kong*	15 Feb. 89	15 Feb. 92
64 Sandars, Edward Carew	15 Feb. 89	15 Feb. 92
KA Eaton-Evans, Harry James ...	15 Feb. 89	15 Feb. 92
19 Dawson, Henry Finch	15 Feb. 89	15 Feb. 92
DEP WN Sherer, James Donnelly ..	15 Feb. 89	15 Feb. 92
so Quain, John	15 Feb. 89	15 Feb. 92
15 Le Mottée, Reginald Edward A.	15 Feb. 89	15 Feb. 92
DA Vereker, Charles Granville......	15 Feb. 89	15 Feb. 92
de Brett, Harry Simonds	15 Feb. 89	15 Feb. 92
7 Hay, James	15 Feb. 89	15 Feb. 92
MN Orr, Charles William James ...	15 Feb. 89	15 Feb. 92
48 Nevinson, Tom St. Aubyn Barrett-Lennard	15 Feb. 89	15 Feb. 92
so Baker, Godfrey Hugh Massy...	27 June 89	27 June 92
11 Emery, William Basil	27 July 89	27 July 92
N RHA Gillman, Webb	27 July 89	27 July 92
80 Jacob, Walter Henry Bell	27 July 89	27 July 92
KA Kane, Arthur Hyde	27 July 89	27 July 92
80 Harington, Elliott Copeland (*2 Sub Depot*)	27 July 89	27 July 92
24 Grove, Ernest Williams	27 July 89	27 July 92
EA De Sausmarez, Cecil.........	27 July 89	27 July 92
1 Ayre, Percy Thorney...............	27 July 80	27 July 92
Chartres, Richard Carew *St. Lucia*	27 July 89	27 July 92
70 Campbell, Gordon M'Clelland	27 July 89	27 July 92
44 Marsden, Richard Travers	27 July 89	27 July 92
80 Howorth H. Godfrey (*3 Sub. Depot*)	27 July 89	27 July 92
EA Smith, Archibald George	27 July 89	27 July 92
80 Burton, Harry Charles Hay ...	27 July 89	27 July 92
1 Bowring, Arthur Hautayne ...	27 July 89	27 July 92
EA Fife, Robert Bainbridge	27 July 89	27 July 92
A RHA Bright, Reginald Arthur ...	27 July 89	27 July 92
74 Lewis, Gerald	27 July 89	27 July 92
WN Bushe, Charles Kendal	27 July 89	27 July 92
43 Broome, Guy Saville Frederick	27 July 89	27 July 92
B DEP RHA Aldridge, John Barttelot	27 July 89	27 July 92
so Waddington, Percy Michael ...	27 July 89	27 July 92
E RHA Elwes, Walter Valentine J. C.	27 July 89	27 July 92
24 Hepper, Lionel Lees	27 July 89	27 July 92
RE Peel, Edward John Russell......	27 July 89	27 July 92
R RHA Powell, E. Weyland Martin	27 July 89	27 July 92
56 James, Jno. Edgcumbe	27 July 89	27 July 92
80 Cleghorn, Charles Angus	27 July 89	27 July 92
80 Tulloch, Donald Fiddes...........	27 July 89	27 July 92
WN Kempson, John Wedgwood ...	27 July 89	27 July 92
51 Allen, William Jefferies Benett	27 July 89	27 July 92
60 Alexander, Ernest Wright	27 July 89	27 July 92
WN M'Gildowny, William	27 July 89	27 July 92
O RHA Sykes, Clement Arthur	27 July 89	27 July 92
75 Clerke, Augustus Basil Holt ...	27 July 89	27 July 92
1·2 DEP. FD Metcalfe, Syd. Fortescue	27 July 89	27 July 92
19 de Winton, Richard Stretton...	27 July 89	27 July 92
23 Sheppard, Herbert Cecil.........	13 Nov. 89	13 Nov. 92
28 Alderne, David Davies	13 Nov. 89	13 Nov. 92
78 Cape, George Augustus Stewart	13 Nov. 89	13 Nov. 92
51 Hewetson, Alexander William	13 Nov. 89	13 Nov 92
RE Gillson, Godfrey....................	13 Nov. 89	13 Nov. 92
47 Hext, Lyonel John	14 Feb. 90	14 Feb. 93
55 Kelly, Hen. Edward Theodore	14 Feb. 90	14 Feb. 93
3 SUB DEP. so FitzRoy, P. FitzWm.	14 Feb. 90	14 Feb. 93
76 Wylde, Robert Darell	14 Feb. 90	14 Feb. 93
43 Gray, Charles Lloyd Rashleigh	14 Feb. 90	14 Feb. 93
66 Willis, Edward Henry	14 Feb. 90	14 Feb. 93
KA Owen, Chas. Rich. Blackstone	14 Feb. 90	14 Feb. 93
47 Curtis, Arthur William[493].........	14 Feb. 90	14 Feb. 93
80 Ashworth, Leonard Temple ...	14 Feb. 90	14 Feb. 93
so Watson, John George Maitland	14 Feb. 90	14 Feb. 93
so Scott, Archibald O'Connor......	14 Feb. 90	14 Feb. 93
H RHA Greathed, Robert Napier ...	14 Feb. 90	14 Feb. 93
KA Ziegler, Chas. Hy. (*Sub. Depot*)	14 Feb. 90	14 Feb. 93
80 Hinton, Godfrey B..................	14 Feb. 90	14 Feb. 93
P RHA Probyn, Dighton Gordon ...	14 Feb. 90	14 Feb. 93
WN Townsend, Sam. Chs. Chetwode	14 Feb. 90	14 Feb. 93
WN Wynter, Fras. Arthur, *S.S.O., Roorkee*, 5 May 94..............	14 Feb. 90	14 Feb. 93
DEP. A RHA Stirling, Charles	14 Feb. 90	14 Feb. 93
63 Browell, William Basil	14 Feb. 90	14 Feb. 93
21 Talbot, Geo. Reginald FitzRoy	14 Feb. 90	14 Feb. 93
EA Lewes, Price Kinnear	14 Feb. 90	14 Feb. 93
80 Paine, James Henry	14 Feb. 90	14 Feb. 93
F RHA Harman, Ramsay St. Clair	14 Feb. 90	14 Feb. 93
Waring, Richard, Insp. of Warlike Stores, Mauritius, 4 July 94	14 Feb. 90	14 Feb. 93
62 Phillpotts, Louis Murray	14 Feb. 90	14 Feb 93
57 Best, Philip George	14 Feb. 90	14 Feb. 9[illegible]

Lieutenants.	2nd Lieut.	Lieut.
45 Manley, William George Henry	14 Feb. 90	14 Feb. 93
1·2 DEP. FD Parry, C. F. Pilkington	14 Feb. 90	14 Feb. 93
22 Barlow, John Frederick	14 Feb. 90	14 Feb. 93
27 Bayly, Abingdon Robert	14 Feb. 90	14 Feb. 93
80 Parker, Lionel Lewis..............	14 Feb. 90	14 Feb. 93
WN Drake, Henry Manning	14 Feb. 90	14 Feb. 93
so Cochrane, Norman Denneys ...	14 Feb. 90	14 Feb. 93
76 Mallock, Art. Maude Raymond	14 Feb. 90	14 Feb. 93
MN O'Connor, Wm. Fred. Travers	14 Feb. 90	14 Feb. 93
80 Smith, Lionel Abel................	14 Feb. 90	14 Feb. 93
57 Wilson, Charles Holmes	14 Feb. 90	14 Feb. 93
73 Williams, Arthur Stuart	14 Feb. 90	14 Feb. 93
WN Bullen, Stephen Darley	14 Feb. 90	14 Feb. 93
50 Donovan, Charles Creagh	14 Feb. 90	14 Feb. 93
50 Gosselin, Bertrand	14 Feb. 90	14 Feb. 93
30 Ruck-Keene, Robert Francis...	10 May 90	10 May 93
DEP so Eady, Charles Edward......	10 May 90	10 May 93
80 Osborn, Lestock Latham Hatton	10 May 90	10 May 93
Morris, Robert Cochrane	4 July 90	4 July 93
26 Cruickshank, Hugh Alexander	25 July 90	25 July 93
80 Cotter, Harry John[493]	25 July 90	25 July 93
WN Crichton, Hew	25 July 90	25 July 93
80 Partridge, Richard Grenville...	25 July 90	25 July 93
WN Stevens-Nash, Chas Geo. Edw.	25 July 90	25 July 93
WN Low, Charles Frederick Gemley	25 July 90	25 July 93
so Haynes, Kenneth Edward.........	25 July 90	25 July 93
so Poulter, Douglas Ryley	25 July 90	25 July 93
EA Easton, Frederick Arthur	25 July 90	25 July 93
10 Robinson, Stratford Watson......	25 July 90	25 July 93
80 Delaforce, Edwin Francis	25 July 90	25 July 93
36 Bell, Maurice Douglas	25 July 90	25 July 93
18 De Prée, Hugo Douglas	25 July 90	25 July 93
20 Madocks, Wm. Robarts Napier	25 July 90	25 July 93
12 Le Pelley, Edward Carey	25 July 90	25 July 93
2 Tudor, Henry Hugh................	25 July 90	25 July 93
47 Palmer, Cyril Eustace	25 July 90	25 July 93
so Lowry, Hubert Leslie	25 July 90	25 July 93
6 Kirwan, Bertram Richard.........	25 July 90	25 July 93
WN Lyddon, William George	25 July 90	25 July 93
4 Livingstone Learmonth, Lennox Christian....................	25 July 90	25 July 93
WN Lawrence-Archer, James Henry	25 July 90	25 July 93
WN Walker, Edward William May...	25 July 90	25 July 93
so Whitehead, Edmond L'Estrange	25 July 90	25 July 93
WN Wilkinson, Arthur Clement	25 July 90	25 July 93
54 Boyce, Harry Augustus............	25 July 90	25 July 93
5 Lane, Frederick Cecil	25 July 90	25 July 93
34 Watts, Charles Donald Raynsford	25 July 90	25 July 93
53 Perreau, Arthur Montagu	25 July 90	25 July 93
23 Cottingham, Henry Langrishe...	25 July 90	25 July 93
42 Douglas, Sholto William...........	25 July 90	25 July 93
64 Washington, Cecil Francis Geo.	25 July 90	25 July 93
30 Holloway, William Octavius......	25 July 90	25 July 93
3 White, Geoffrey Herbert Anthony	25 July 90	25 July 93
64 Reade, Piercy Nevill Graham ...	25 July 90	25 July 93
so Hope, William Henry Webley ...	25 July 90	25 July 93
17 Peckard, Henry Norrington......	25 July 90	25 July 93
45 Henning, Philip Walter Beresford	25 July 90	25 July 93
49 Henderson, George James.........	25 July 90	25 July 93
27 Stewart, Davison Bruce...........	25 July 90	25 July 93
5 Biddulph, Michael	25 July 90	25 July 93
80 Ravenhill, Collingwood	25 July 90	25 July 93
14 Birch, Arthur Charles...............	25 July 90	25 July 93
12 Baillie, George	25 July 90	25 July 93
so Lewis, Penton Shakespear.........	25 July 90	25 July 93
2 Green, Gilbert Victor	25 July 90	25 July 93
58 Robertson, Charles Chetwode ...	25 July 90	25 July 93
WN Bowen, Herbert Walter............	25 July 90	25 July 93
32 Farquhar, Hercules Thomas ...	1 Nov. 90	1 Nov. 93
50 Muspratt-Williams, Reg. Lawford	1 Nov. 90	1 Nov. 93
70 Henry, John	1 Nov. 90	1 Nov. 93
WN Moor, Hatherley George	1 Nov. 90	1 Nov. 93
KA Boyd, Alexander Charles	13 Feb. 91	13 Feb. 94
7 Macgowan, George Lionel	13 Feb. 91	13 Feb. 94
KA Oldfield, Arthur Radulphus ...	13 Feb. 91	13 Feb. 94
80 Parker, Robert Hamilton	13 Feb. 91	13 Feb. 94
WN Slator, George Francis	13 Feb. 91	13 Feb. 94
80 Westerman, Joseph Francis ...	13 Feb. 91	13 Feb. 94
WN Jebb, Sydney Gladwyn	13 Feb. 91	13 Feb. 94
51 Short, William Ambrose	13 Feb. 91	13 Feb. 94
BA Bland-Hunt, Ernest S. de Vere	13 Feb. 91	13 Feb. 94
KA Rumbold, William Edwin	13 Feb. 91	31 Feb. 94
4 Ramsden, Henry	13 Feb. 91	13 Feb. 94
80 Appleyard, George Crossley ...	13 Feb. 91	13 Feb. 94
21 Smyth, George Abraham	13 Feb. 91	13 Feb. 94
WN England, Raymond................	13 Feb. 91	13 Feb. 94
79 Montgomery, H. M. de Fellenberg	13 Feb. 91	13 Feb. 94
24 Browne, Samuel Swinton	13 Feb. 91	13 Feb. 94
80 Christie, Lindsay Bruce Stark...	13 Feb. 91	13 Feb. 94
72 Plummer, Edmund Waller	13 Feb. 91	13 Feb. 94
50 Donaldson, John Wm. Edward	13 Feb. 91	13 Feb. 94
43 M'Neile, Donald Hugh	13 Feb. 91	13 Feb. 94
KA Mackenzie, Ar. Mackenzie Nutt	13 Feb. 91	13 Feb. 94
80 Hamilton, Robert Sydney........	13 Feb. 91	13 Feb. 94
77 Pehrers, Clive	13 Feb. 91	13 Feb. 94
67 Kay, William Heape	13 Feb. 91	13 Feb. 94

Royal Artillery.

	LIEUTENANTS.	2nd LIEUT.	LIEUT.	SECOND LIEUTENANTS.	2nd LIEUT.
wn	Mayne, Herbert Blair	13 Feb. 91	13 Feb. 94	Hay, Westwood Norman	24 July 91
so	Manley, Reginald Harwood	13 Feb. 91	13 Feb. 94	mn Fowler, Willoughby Jones	15 Mar. 92
wn	Twiss, Francis Arthur	13 Feb. 91	13 Feb. 94	so Lockhart, Robert Norman	16 Mar. 92
wn	Fergusson, Arthur Charles	13 Feb. 91	13 Feb. 94	ba Corrie, George Gowan Wyatt	18 Mar. 92
	Davidson, Arthur Noel	13 Feb. 91	13 Feb. 94	so Graene, Albert James Rothwell	19 Mar. 92
1	Overton, Harry Rudall	13 Feb. 91	13 Feb. 94	66 Tilney, Norman Eccles	19 Mar. 92
33	Cubitt, Thomas Astley	13 Feb. 91	13 Feb. 94	ba Stülpnagel, Charles William	23 Mar. 92
	Palmer, Cecil Chas., St. Helena	13 Feb. 91	13 Feb. 94	wn Riddell, Robert Buchanan	28 Mar. 92
61	Dalby, John	13 Feb. 91	13 Feb. 94	39 Ellershaw, Wilfrid	1 Apr. 92
56	Hankey, John C. Giffard Alers	13 Feb. 91	13 Feb. 94	wn Hamer, John Connor	1 Apr. 92
16	Stapylton, Granville J. C.	13 Feb. 91	13 Feb. 94	ba Byron, John	1 Apr. 92
80	Driffield, John	13 Feb. 91	13 Feb. 94	ba Wilkinson, Maurice Lean	1 Apr. 92
80	Clark-Kennedy, Alex. William	13 Feb. 91	13 Feb. 94	so Currie, Ivor Bertram Fendall	1 Apr. 92
46	Bruce, Thomas	13 Feb. 91	13 Feb. 94	53 Swann, Clarence John Henry	1 Apr. 92
wn	Warren, Frank	13 Feb. 91	13 Feb. 94	wn Scott, Edward Balfol	1 Apr. 92
68	Hale, Edmund Thomas	13 Feb. 91	13 Feb. 94	21 Garstin, Henry Edward	1 Apr. 92
wn	Halse, Stanley Clarence	13 Feb. 91	13 Feb. 94	35 Oldfield, Leopold Charles Louis	1 Apr. 92
31	Bruce, Chas. Maurice Dundas	16 May 91	16 May 94	wn Westropp, Richard Gibbings	1 Apr. 92
80	Mathew-Lannowe, Geo. Richd. Monckton	16 May 91	16 May 94	wn Nuttall, Charles Montague	1 Apr. 92
				so Porcher, Alec Francis	1 Apr. 92
48	Wheatley, Philip	16 May 91	16 May 94	33 Boyd, Stuart Ogilvy	1 Apr. 92
60	Ramage-Dawson, Wm. Hutchison	16 May 91	16 May 94	ba Massie, John Hamon	1 May 92
53	Wemyss, Robt. Edw. Fitzmayer	16 May 91	16 May 94	22 Luke, Thomas Mawe	4 May 92
ba	Scott, Robert Kellock	16 July 91	16 July 94	34 FitzGibbon, John Augustine	13 May 92
11	Evans, Cuthbert	24 July 91	24 July 94	wn Mackenzie, Frederick William	13 May 92
50	Downes, Leonard Sawbridge	24 July 91	24 July 94	20 Houstoun, Alexander	18 May 92
13	Ward, Harry Dudley Ossulston	24 July 91	24 July 94	ba Kelly, Courtenay Russell	18 May 92
25	Monkhouse, William Percival	24 July 91	24 July 94	so Holbrooke, Philip Lancelot	25 May 92
8	Charlton, Claud Edw. Charles Graham	24 July 91	24 July 94	so Holman, Bertram William	25 May 92
				so de Bury, Henry Robert Visart	4 July 92
80	Young, John Edgar Harington	24 July 91	24 July 94	44 Walshe, Frederick William Henry	22 July 92
35	Carbutt, Edward Goddard	24 July 91	24 July 94	46 Foulkes, Henry Drury	22 July 92
	Capper, Alfred Stewart	24 July 91	24 July 94	5 Wilson, Herbert Stanley	22 July 92
44	Haymes, Robert Leycester	24 July 91	24 July 94	29 Bond, Henry Hendley	22 July 92
80	Merrick, George Charleton	24 July 91	24 July 94	so Collingwood, Clennell William	22 July 92
wn	Trevor, Arthur Prescott	24 July 91	24 July 94	ba Perceval, Philip	22 July 92
78	Foster, Percival Lloyd	24 July 91	24 July 94	so de Berry, Philip Patrick Evolyn	27 July 92
80	Anley, William Bower	24 July 91	24 July 94	ba Rickard, Frank Martyn	27 July 92
1	Ashmore, Edward Bailey	24 July 91	24 July 94	ba Brewin, Bertram Robert	27 July 92
3	Vincent, Berkeley	24 July 91	24 July 94	so Webb, Andrew Henry	10 Aug. 92
sub dep. so	Myers, Alfred Edw Cecil	24 July 91	24 July 94	wn Godfray, Hugh Culpeper Weston	10 Aug. 92
ba	Browning, Hanworth Stephens	24 July 91	24 July 94	63 Courage, Miles Rafe Fergusor	10 Aug. 92
mn	Dennistoun, James George	24 July 91	24 July 94	so Buzzard, Charles Norman	15 Aug. 92
ba	Hunt, Vere de Vere	24 July 91	24 July 94	wn Hanks, John James	23 Aug. 92
80	MacDougall, James Taylor	24 July 91	24 July 94	ba Carey, Walter Louis John	14 Sept.92
ba	Chrystie, John	24 July 91	24 July 94	17 Ollivant, John Spencer	1 Oct. 92
ba	Manley, William Edward	24 July 91	24 July 94	ba O'Kinealy, James	12 Oct. 92
80	Gordon, Alfred Ernest	24 July 91	24 July 94	so Keyworth, Robert Geoffrey	17 Oct. 92
27	Evans, William	24 July 91	24 July 94	wn Wood, Charles Hastings	17 Oct. 92
	Field.			28 Seligman, Herbert Spencer	17 Oct. 92
74	Devenish, Arthur Henry Noel	1 Nov. 91	1 Nov. 94	Hood, Hon. Neville Albert	30 Oct. 92
65	Montgomery, Archibald Armar	4 Nov. 91	4 Nov. 94	39 Macnaghten, Ernest Brandon	9 Nov. 92
37	Hine-Haycock, Vaughan R.	20 Nov. 91	20 Nov. 94	wn M'Vittie, Robert Henry	9 Dec. 92
79	Kincaid-Smith, Kenneth John	23 Nov. 91	23 Nov. 94	so Carter, Gerard Edward	14 Dec. 92
67	Hildyard, Harold Chas Thoroton	24 Nov. 91	24 Nov. 94	so Edgar, John Stewart	20 Dec. 92
30	Gosling, Seymour Frederick	1 Dec. 91	1 Dec. 94	ba Loring, William	21 Dec. 92
76	Atkinson, Ben	2 Dec. 91	2 Dec. 94	79 Lamont, John William Fraser	2 Jan. 93
38	Becke, Archibald Frank	1 Jan. 92	1 Jan. 95	ba Gordon, George Alexander Steuart	2 Jan. 93
16	Jeffcoat, Henry Jameson Powell	27 Jan. 92	27 Jan. 95	80 Ewart, Charles Nicholson	10 Jan. 93
15	Lloyd, Horace Giesler	12 Feb. 92	12 Feb. 95	ba Buchanan, Bertram George	11 Jan. 93
42	Liveing, Charles Hawker	12 Feb. 92	12 Feb. 95	52 Stanley, Hon. George Frederic	10 Jan. 93
69	Davson, Harry Miller	12 Feb. 92	12 Feb. 95	80 Ponsonby, Edward Francis Talbot	16 Jan. 93
8	Tyrrell, Gerald Ernest	12 Feb. 92	12 Feb. 95	80 Stevenson, Edward Hall	18 Jan. 93
70	Maule, Henry Noel St. John	12 Feb. 92	12 Feb. 95	so Howard-Vyse, Cecil	19 Jan. 93
19	Spencer, Harrison	12 Feb. 92	12 Feb. 95	wn Hope, Graham Archibald	29 Jan. 93
49	Wardrop, Alexander Ernest	12 Feb. 92	12 Feb. 95	41 Harpur, Edmund Herbert	1 Feb. 93
31	Bowcroft, Claude Harold	19 Feb. 92	19 Feb. 95	33 Wynter, Hugh Talbot	1 Feb. 93
26	Bridges, George Tom Molesworth	19 Feb. 92	19 Feb. 95	so Waters, Edmond Egerton Nash	1 Feb. 93
62	Johnstone, James Henry Waller	3 Mar. 92	3 Mar. 95	80 Fisher, Charles Alexander	1 Feb. 93
	Garrison.			29 Newman, Edward Harding	1 Feb. 93
ba	Alderson, Samuel Frank	1 Nov. 91	1 Nov. 94	80 Meares, Hugh Poynder	1 Feb. 93
80	Kennedy, Andrew Campbell	4 Nov. 91	4 Nov. 94	ba Davies, Walter Percy Lionel	1 Feb. 93
80	Hammond, Harry Durham	4 Nov. 91	4 Nov. 94	48 Thompson, William George	16 Feb. 93
wn	Moore, Frank B. Hamilton	4 Nov. 91	4 Nov. 94	80 Galwey, Reginald Hugh	24 Feb. 93
ba	Moorhouse, Harry Claude	4 Nov. 91	4 Nov. 94	80 Symon, Walter Conover	1 Mar. 93
wn	Innes, Hector Munro	16 Nov. 91	16 Nov. 94	14 Johnson, Ronald Marr	1 Mar. 93
80	Ollivant, Alfred Henry	23 Nov. 91	23 Nov. 94	ba Clarke, George Vernon	1 Mar. 93
wn	Corbett, Edwy Frank	23 Nov. 91	23 Nov. 94	80 Thorp, Austin	4 Mar. 93
80	Pritchard, Clive Gordon	23 Nov. 91	23 Nov. 94	wn Eden, William Rushbrooke	4 Mar. 93
ba	Molesworth, Herbert Ellicombe	23 Nov. 91	23 Nov. 94	wn Tyrrell, John Frederick	13 Mar. 93
ea	Hall, Henry Constable	23 Nov. 91	23 Nov. 94	so Nutt, Arthur Charles Rothery	16 Mar. 93
80	Marton, Richard Oliver	23 Nov. 91	23 Nov. 94	ba Locke, Brian John Michael	30 Mar. 93
wn	Austin, John Gardiner	26 Nov. 91	26 Nov. 94	so Wilson, Lancelot Machell	1 Apr. 93
wn	Phipps, Charles Foskett	30 Nov. 91	30 Nov. 94	wn Hamilton, Claud Lorn Campbell	1 Apr. 93
ba	Gooding, Lancelot Newton	1 Jan. 92	1 Jan. 95	25 Lascelles, Alfred	1 Apr. 93
80	Wyatt, Francis Ogilvy	1 Jan. 92	1 Jan. 95	wn Doyle, John Francis Innes Hay	1 Apr. 93
wn	Wheeler, Guy Danvers	27 Jan. 92	27 Jan. 95	wn Goodwin, Robert Hamilton	1 Apr. 93
ba	Nicholl, Donald FitzRoy	12 Feb. 92	12 Feb. 95	ba Brierley, Geoffrey Tetlo	1 Apr. 93
ea	Mackenzie, George Birnie	12 Feb. 92	12 Feb. 95	ba Sargeaunt, Herbert Gaussen	1 Apr. 93
80	Froeth, Charles John David	12 Feb. 92	12 Feb. 95	12 Roberts, Charles Percy	1 Apr. 93
ba	Owen, Charles Harold Wells	12 Feb. 92	12 Feb. 95	so Hart, Henry Travers	1 Apr. 93
80	Smithett, Bertie Dalrymple Hamilton	12 Feb. 92	12 Feb. 95	4 Cairnes, James Elliot	1 Apr. 93
				so Broughton, Legh Harley Dolves	6 Apr. 93
ba	McCheane, Montagu Wm. Hiley	15 Feb. 92	15 Feb. 95	so Playfair, Charles Murray	6 Apr. 93
80	Robinson, Henry	15 Feb. 92	15 Feb. 95	so Carey, Harold Eustace	6 Apr. 93
ba	Forman, Douglas Evans	19 Feb. 92	19 Feb. 95	wn Armitage, William Thompson	1 May 93
62	Sturrock, George Colleymore	3 Mar. 92	3 Mar. 95		

Royal Artillery

	SECOND LIEUTENANTS.	2ND LIEUT.		SECOND LIEUTENANTS.	2ND LIEUT.
so	Drake, William Hacche	1 May 93	wn	Coode, Henry Penrose Rushton	31 Dec. 93
so	Nugent, George Roubiliac Hodges	1 May 93	wn	Odevaine, Ferdinand James	1 Jan. 94
wn	Kongh, Thomas Macgregor	6 May 93	wn	Saunders, Edward Aldborough	1 Jan. 94
so	Keogh, John Henry	13 May 93	wn	Dwyer, George Toulmin Cunynghame	1 Jan. 94
wn	Riddell, Edward Vansittart Dick	30 May 93	so	Jacob, Stephen Hector	1 Jan. 94
18	Stanton, Francis Henry Guy	30 May 93	ra	Blanford, Charles Edward	1 Jan. 94
45	Clarke, Henry Calvert Stanley	30 May 93	so	Falcon, Archibald Anthony	3 Jan. 94
ra	Ritchie, Charles MacIver	14 June 93	ra	Thompson, Aubrey Julian	3 Jan. 94
so	Suther, Percival	16 June 93	so	Dalyell, John Arthur	16 Feb. 94
ra	Keane, Sir John, Bart.	17 June 93	ra	Stoddart, George	26 Feb. 94
so	Wilkins, George Hubert Carey	24 June 93	wn	Forman, Arthur Baron	14 Mar. 94
ra	Athy, Hugh Wordsworth	26 June 93	ra	Keddie, Herbert William Graham	14 Mar. 94
38	O'Malley, Charles Loughlin	26 June 93	ra	Stobart, George Herbert	16 Mar. 94
so	Hollinshead, Henry Neville Brock	27 June 93	wn	Ellissen, Gustav Edmund	16 Mar. 94
ra	Taylor, Archibald John Scriven	28 June 93	so	Fair, Arthur Edward Balfour	22 Mar. 94
ra	Kettlewell, Archibald Middleton	28 June 93	so	Birley, Richard Archibald	1 Apr. 94
so	Muir, George Tagore	30 June 93	wn	Crofton, Robert Benjamin	1 Apr. 94
	Edwards, Arthur Clement	1 Aug. 93	so	Brown, Frank Tatton	1 Apr. 94
ra	Ogg, William Mortimer	1 Aug. 93	so	Lewin, Henry Frederick Elliott	1 Apr. 94
wn	Brooke, Edward William Saurin	11 Aug. 93	49	Edwards, William Egerton	1 Apr. 94
ra	Seagram, Tom Ogle	11 Aug. 93	77	Paley, Raymond Edward	1 Apr. 94
ra	Stallard, Stacy Frampton	11 Aug. 93	wn	Walthall, Edw. Chas. Walthall Delves	1 Apr. 94
ra	Chevallier, Francis Edward de Carteret	15 Aug. 93	wn	Moore, William Henry	4 July 94
so	Swettenham, Wm. Alexander Whybault	17 Aug. 93	wn	Trimnell, William Duncan Conybeare	14 July 94
wn	Hawkes, Corlis St. Leger Gillman	19 Aug. 93	wn	Jacob, Arthur Lawrance Baldwin	14 July 94
	Ollivant, Alfred	19 Aug. 93	so	Izat, Alexander Rennie	14 July 94
wn	Cotton, Arthur Stedman	1 Sept. 93	wn	Schofield, Sydney Vaughan	14 July 94
ra	Deane, Dennis	14 Sept. 93		Conolly, Edward Michael	14 July 94
71	Wigram, Clive	4 Oct. 93	so	FitzGerald, Mordaunt John Fortescue	1 Sept. 94
ra	Radcliffe, Percy Pollexfen de Blaquiere	4 Oct. 93	so	Gemmell, William Alexander Stewart	29 Sept. 94
so	Simpson, Arthur Cyril Stanley Ward	11 Oct. 93	so	Grayson, Ambrose Dixon Holdrege	4 Oct. 94
ra	Thatcher, Gerald Gane	14 Oct. 93	so	Cruickshank, Percy Hamilton	15 Nov. 94
so	Musgrave, Arthur David	21 Oct. 93	wn	Curteis, Cyril Samuel Sackville	15 Nov. 94
wn	Phipps, Henry Ramsay	21 Oct. 93		Dickson, Bertram	15 Nov. 94
61	Arbuthnot, Alexander George	21 Oct. 93		Kemble, William Edward	15 Nov. 94
ra	Koebel, Henry Arthur	21 Oct. 93		Blount, George Percy Cosmo	1 Dec. 94
so	Tyler, Francis Cameron	23 Oct. 93		Barnes, Christopher Chevallier	25 Dec. 94
ra	Keyes, Alfred John Hudleston	4 Nov. 93		Finch, George Forbes Carpenter	1 Jan. 95
ra	Montrésor, Louis Basset	4 Nov. 93		Lloyd-Thomas, Thomas Carrington	4 Jan. 95
wn	Hardcastle, Edward Lewis	23 Nov. 93		Wheeler, Edgar Lockyer	5 Jan. 95
77	Hope, Charles Dunbar	9 Dec. 93		Ravenhill, Harold William	9 Jan. 95
wn	Wade, Harry Amyas Leigh Herschel	16 Dec. 93		Grose, James	1 Feb. 95
so	Rolland, Charles Edward Tulloch	16 Dec. 93		Ingham, Charles St. Maur	1 Mar. 95
wn	Castens, William Ernest	21 Dec. 93			

DEPUTY ADJUTANT GENERAL.
Major General F. T. Lloyd, CB. 21 Feb. 94.

ASSISTANT ADJUTANT GENERAL.

DEPUTY ASSISTANT ADJUTANT GENERAL.
p.s.c. Major F. G. Stone, 1 Sept. 94.

	RIDING MASTERS.	RG.MR.AND HON. LT.	HON. CAPTAIN.
FD	Donnelly, Robert (Hon. Major,) 23 Jan. 95	1 Apr. 75	1 Apr. 85
R.H.A.	Draper, Frederick, Umballa	1 Apr. 75	1 Apr. 85
FD	Hensch, Christopher, Aldershot	15 Nov. 79	15 Nov. 89
R.H.A.	Goode, Richard John, Newbridge	15 Nov. 79	15 Nov. 89
R.H.A.	Stevens, John, Kirkee	24 Jan. 80	24 Jan. 90
FD	Wilken, John, Hilsea	19 June 80	19 June 90
R.H.A.	Simpson, Robert, Meerut	31 Dec. 81	31 Dec. 91
RE	Shipman, William, Woolwich	31 Dec. 81	31 Dec. 91
FD	M'Lennan, John, Woolwich	18 Mar. 85	18 Mar. 95
FD	Bevington, John, Colchester	10 June 85	
	Nicholas, John, Supt. Royal Mews, Buckingham Palace	15 Aug. 88	
FD	Trusler, James, Bangalore	24 Nov. 88	
FD	Thorne, James, Newcastle-on-Tyne	15 May 89	
FD	Brogan, Thos. Hy. Trimulgherry	14 Sept. 89	
R.H.A.	Caringhan, John, Aldershot	20 Feb. 92	
RE	M'Combie, Alex. Wm. Woolwich	5 Apr. 93	
FD	Learmont, John (Depot) Woolwich	27 Jan. 94	
FD	Fleming, Frederick, India	3 Feb. 94	
FD	Clarke, Tom	6 Mar. 95	

	QUARTER MASTERS.	QR.MR.AND HON. LT.	
	Ward, Thomas, Ipswich	26 June 72	26 June 82
	Murdoch, Robert Hamilton, Hon. Major 15 June 67, Assist.Supdt. R.A. Records, Woolwich	19 Feb. 73	1 Mar. 79
DEP. FD	M'Kenna, John, Woolwich	10 Mar. 75	10 Mar. 85
p.s.	Seath, Alexander, Woolwich	8 Sept. 75	8 Sept. 85
	Powell, John Jos. Chas. War Office (Hon. Major, 30 Oct. 80)	1 Apr. 78	1 Apr. 84
	Wilbond, Jas. 497 Antrim Art. S. Div. 11 June 81	11 June 81	11 June 91
	Russell, Henry, Norfolk Art. E. Div. 6 Apr. 87	17 Sept. 81	17 Sept. 91
so	Cook, George, 499 Portsmouth	27 May 82	27 May 92
R.H.A.	Paton, William, 500 Aldershot	27 May 80	27 May 2

	QUARTER MASTERS.	QR.MR.AND HON. LT.	HON. CAPTAIN.
FD	Martin, Alexander, 501 Woolwich	1 Apr. 84	1 Apr. 94
	Firth, Samuel, 502 Scarboro'	1 Apr. 84	1 Apr. 94
so	Wishart, Richard James, Malta Div. 26 Oct. 85	6 Aug. 84	6 Aug. 94
	Paulson, John, Donegal Art. S. Div. 26 Oct. 85	11 July 85	
	Robinson, William, 504 Forfar & Kincardine Art. 9 Sept. 85	9 Sept. 85	
	Shakespear, George Joseph, Durham Art. W.Div.14 Apr. 86	14 Apr. 86	
	Jarvis, Wm. Kent Art. E. Div. 24 Nov. 86	24 Nov. 86	
	Edwards, James, Limerick City Art. S. Division, 21 May 87	21 May 87	
RA	Cooper, Thos. Francis, Gibraltar	11 June 87	
	Small, Alex. Wicklow Art. S. Div. 20 July 87	20 July 87	
	Usmar, George Alleyne, Edinburgh Artillery, 23 Nov. 94	26 Sept. 88	
	M'Cafferty, Charles, Cork Art. 8 Mar. 95	4 Dec. 89	
	Anderson, William, Ennis	30 Apr. 90	
	Murray, Edward Jas., Argyll and Bute Art. S. Div.	18 June 90	
so	Perry, Wm. Change, Cork	6 Dec. 90	
	Dickens, John, Londonderry	6 Dec. 90	
RA	Lawrence, William, Sheerness	25 July 91	
	Stevens, Thomas, School of Gunnery, Shoeburyness	25 July 91	
	Seager, William, Northumberland Art. W. Div. 11 Nov. 91	11 Nov. 91	
so	Whitley, William Thos. Gosport	20 Feb. 92	
wn	Coombes, Samuel, Devonport	9 Mar. 92	
R.H.A.	Richardson, Fredk. Woolwich	9 Mar. 92	
	Stephens, William, Cardigan Art. Aberystwith	6 Apr. 92	
	Williams, Thomas, Carmarthen Art. Carmarthen	6 Apr. 92	
	Cox, John, Seaforth	18 May 92	
	Murray, John, Dunbar	15 Oct. 92	
	Dawson, Joseph Temperley, Art. College, Woolwich	13 June 94	
so	Clements, John Samuel, Templemore	22 Dec. 94	

RIDING ESTABLISHMENT.
Superintendent.—Lt.-Colonel J. F. Brough.
Major.—F. E. A. Hunter.
Lieutenants.—E. J. R. Peel and G. Gillson.

Agents, Messrs. Cox and Co.

Royal Artillery (late Bengal Artillery).

179

Yrs. Ser.	COLONELS COMMANDANT.	SECOND LIEUT.	FIRST LIEUT.	BREVET CAPTAIN.	CAPTAIN.	BREVET MAJOR.	MAJOR.	BREVET LT.COL.	LIEUT. COLONEL.	BREVET COLONEL.	COLONEL.	COLONEL COMM.	MAJOR GENERAL.	LIEUT. GENERAL.	GENERAL.
74	Lane, John Theophilus,¹ CB.	9 June 21	1 May 24	9 June 36	22 Aug. 38	23 Dec. 42	10 Feb. 49	30 Apr. 44	30 Oct. 55	20 June 54	18 Feb. 61	7 Oct. 72	8 June 56	6 Mar. 68	6 Oct. 72
72	Abbott, Sir James,² KCB.	6 June 23	28 Sept. 27	6 June 38	4 Aug. 41	7 June 49	6 Mar. 54	28 Nov. 54	4 July 57	28 Nov. 57	18 Feb. 61	27 Feb. 77	19 June 66	27 Feb. 77	1 Oct. 77
72	Carleton, Henry Alexander,³ CB.	11 June 30	12 Sept. 39	11 June 45	6 Feb. 48	5 Dec. 55	20 July 58	14 Oct. 58	......	20 Sept. 65	1 Jan. 83	10 Mar. 68	6 Mar. 68	10 July 79
65	Thuillier, Sir Henry Edward Landor, CSI.	14 Dec. 32	1 Sept. 40	14 Dec. 47	2 Feb. 51	......	......	......	18 Feb. 61	26 Feb. 67	7 June 88	26 Apr. 82	26 Mar. 70	1 Oct. 77	1 July 81
63	de Teissier, Baron Henry Price⁴	11 Dec. 37	17 Aug. 41	11 Dec. 52	3 Mar. 53	......	......	24 Mar. 58	18 Feb. 61	18 Feb. 66	1 Oct. 77	1 Jan. 83	1 Oct. 77	13 Mar. 83
58	Olpherts, Sir William,⁵ KCB.	11 June 39	27 Aug. 41	......	3 Mar. 53	19 Jan. 58	5 July 72	......	1 Aug. 72	26 Feb. 64	4 Aug. 88	4 Aug. 88	28 June 68	1 Oct. 77	31 Mar. 83
56		13 Dec. 45	1 Jan. 52	......	27 Aug. 58					1 Aug. 77	17 July 72	19 June 93	12 May 82	31 Dec. 88
50	Cordiner, James Edward														
	Removed from the Regt. having rank as General Officers.														
44	Ʋᴱ Roberts of Kandahar and Waterford, Frederick Sleigh, Lord,¹¹ GCB. GCSI. GCIE.	12 Dec. 51	31 May 57	......	......	12 Nov. 60	13 Nov. 60	5 July 72	15 Aug. 68	......	......	30 Jan. 75	......	31 Dec. 78	26 July 83	28 Nov. 90
37	p.s.c. Chapman, Edward Francis,⁵⁶ CB., Director of Military Intelligence [R]	12 June 58	27 Aug. 58	......	21 Jan. 72	......	31 Dec. 78	22 Nov. 79	14 Apr. 87	11 May 79	31 Dec. 81	......	20 Sept. 89	13 Dec. 92	
41	Griffin, Edward Christian²⁵	9 Dec. 54	8 Jan. 58	......	15 July 64	......	1 Aug. 72	......	......	11 May 79	11 May 83	......	5 June 90		
40	Nairne, Charles Edward,²⁷ CB., Commander in Chief, Bombay Army, with rank of Lieut. General, 5 Sept. 93	7 Dec. 55	27 Apr. 58	......	24 Mar. 65	......	2 Nov. 72	......	1 May 80	1 May 84	6 Nov. 90				
36	Tillard, John Arthur,²⁸ CB. [R]	12 Dec. 57	27 Aug. 58	......	1 June 67	......	21 Oct. 76	2 Mar. 81	1 Jan. 84	2 Mar. 85	......	......	28 Nov. 90		
37	Cowie, Crombie,³⁸ CB. Inspector General of Ordnance, Bengal, 1 April 90	12 June 58	27 Aug. 58	......	1 Aug. 72	......	16 Jan. 79	2 Mar. 81	21 July 87	2 Mar. 85	......	......	1 Feb. 92		
39	Walker, Alexander,³⁴ CSI. Director Gen. of Ordnance and Magazines, India, 1 Feb. 90	12 Dec. 56	27 Apr. 58	......	24 Mar. 65	......	4 Feb. 74	1 July 81	1 Jan. 84	1 July 85	......	......	1 Dec. 94		

LIEUTENANT COLONELS *Removed from the Regiment, as substantive Colonels in the Army.*
Murray, Anthony Hepburn, *Colonel on the Staff, Commanding Royal Artillery, Oude*, 19 Oct. 92
Biscard, Michael Henry
Swinley, George,¹³ CB. *Colonel on the Staff, Commanding Royal Artillery, Sealkote*, 16 Apr. 92

Yrs. Ser.		SECOND LIEUT.	FIRST LIEUT.	BREVET CAPTAIN.	CAPTAIN.	BREVET MAJOR.	MAJOR.	BREVET LT.COL.	LIEUT. COLONEL.	BREVET COLONEL.
38		12 Dec. 57	27 Aug. 58	......	14 Dec. 68	......	29 May 66	......	16 Jan. 82	1 Jan. 85	1 Feb. 85
36		......	2 Dec. 59	......	11 Dec. 72	......	......	......	10 Jan. 82	1 Jan. 85	28 July 89
35		......	6 Nov. 60	......	16 Jan. 74	22 Nov. 79	......	......	2 Mar. 81	26 Sept. 89	21 July 86

LIEUTENANT COLONELS (*on Indian Supernumerary List*).
Elliott, Edward Draper, *Colonel on the Staff for Royal Artillery, Chatham*
Ward, Francis William,³⁸ CB.
Studdy, Thomas James Charles Aylmer
Anderson, Alexander Dingwall[?]

Yrs. Ser.		SECOND LIEUT.	FIRST LIEUT.	BREVET CAPTAIN.	CAPTAIN.	BREVET MAJOR.	MAJOR.	BREVET LT.COL.	LIEUT. COLONEL.	BREVET COLONEL.
38		11 Dec. 57	27 Apr. 58	......	29 May 66	......	16 Jan. 75	31 Dec. 78	1 Jan. 82	16 Jan. 84	16 Jan. 86
38		11 Dec. 57	21 May 58	......	5 Oct. 66	......	16 Jan. 75	26 May 80	1 Jan. 82	16 Jan. 84	16 Jan. 86
38		12 Dec. 57	27 Aug. 58	......	2 Jan. 68	......	27 Nov. 78	11 July 82	......	11 May 84	11 May 88
35		......	8 June 60	......	9 May 74	1 July 81	11 July 82	2 Mar. 81	8 June 89	6 Jan. 94

Royal Artillery (late Madras Artillery).

Yrs. Ser.	Colonels Commandant.	Second Lieut.	First Lieut.	Brevet Captain.	Captain.	Brevet Major.	Major.	Brevet Lt.Col.	Lieut. Colonel.	Brevet Colonel.	Colonel.	Colonel Comm.	Major General.	Lieut. General.	General.
53	Cadell, Sir Robert,[1] KCB.	11 June 42	13 July 45	11 June 57	27 Aug. 58	23 Aug. 58	......	26 Apr. 58	14 Dec. 68	1 Feb. 67	1 Oct. 77	15 June 85	31 Dec. 78	27 Feb. 82	31 Mar. 83
52	Campbell, Napier George.	8 Dec. 43	2 Aug. 48	......	27 Aug. 58	......	5 July 72	......	1 Sept. 69	1 Sept. 74	1 Oct. 77	6 Oct. 85	31 Dec. 78	31 Mar. 83	31 Dec. 91
50	Pearse, George Godfrey,[6] CB. p. h. a.	14 June 45	2 July 51	......	27 Aug. 58	26 Apr. 59	5 July 72	4 June 70	1 Aug. 72	1 Aug. 77	31 Jan. 87	23 Jan. 87	26 Feb. 80	7 Sept. 85	
49	Playfair, Elliot Minto[7] *Removed from the Regt. having Rank as General Officer (on Active List).*	11 Dec. 46	11 May 54	......	27 Aug. 58	......	......	......	1 Aug. 72	1 Aug. 77	31 Mar. 94	13 Mar. 94	1 Oct. 82	31 Dec. 88	
42	McLeod, Harry,[10] *Her Britannic Majesty's Consular Agent, Pondicherry and Karikal*} 19 Aug. 91 [R]	11 June 53	27 Apr. 58	......	29 Feb. 64	......	5 July 72	......	23 Sept. 76	1 July 81	14 Sept. 84	......	7 Apr. 88	28 Nov. 90	

Lieut.Colonel *Removed from the Regiment, as substantive Colonel in the Army.*
Alexander, Robert,[20] Colonel on the Staff, Commanding R. Artillery, Madras, 7 June 92

Lieutenant Colonels (on Indian Supernumerary List).

Yrs.Ser.		Second Lieut.	First Lieut.	Brevet Captain.	Captain.	Brevet Major.	Major.	First Lieut.	Second Lieut.	Captain.	Brevet Major.	Major.	Brevet Lt.Col.	Lieut. Colonel.	Brevet Colonel.
36	de Montmorency, Hon. Albert Bouchard[16]							9 Dec. 59				24 Jan. 80	1 Aug. 72		1 Sept. 85
37	Lockhart, William Elliott, *Assistant Adjutant General, Royal Artillery, Madras*								12 June 58	27 Aug. 58	19 Jan. 58	4 Feb. 76	13 July 68	4 Feb. 83	31 Mar. 83	4 Feb. 87
37	Macdonell, George Bean,[17] *Commanding Royal Artillery, Hong Kong*								12 June 58	27 Aug. 58	20 July 58	29 Jan. 77	1 Sept. 69		1 Jan. 84	1 Jan. 88
37									12 June 58	27 Aug. 58		29 Jan. 77	12 Sept. 69		1 Jan. 84	1 Jan. 88

Royal Artillery (late Bombay Artillery).

Yrs.Ser.	Colonels Commandant.	Second Lieut.	First Lieut.	Brevet Captain.	Captain.	Brevet Major.	Major.	Brevet Lt.Col.	Lieut. Colonel.	Brevet Colonel.	Colonel.	Colonel Comm.	Major General.	Lieut. General.	Brevet Colonel.
58	Kemball, Sir Arnold Burrowes,[1] KCB.KCSI.	11 Dec. 37	17 Aug. 41	......	28 Feb. 51	19 Jan. 58	......	......	11 Apr. 60	......	1 Sept. 63	30 June 78	6 Mar. 68	1 Oct. 77	26 Feb. 80
55	Aitken, William David[4]	11 June 40	27 June 42	......	25 June 52	......	......	......	18 Feb. 61	......	3 Aug. 65	27 Nov. 35	28 Oct. 68	1 Oct. 77	31 Mar. 87
55	Fuller, Charles Bowdler[5] *Removed from the Regt. having rank as General Officer (on Active List).*	11 June 40	28 June 42	......	18 July 52	......	......	......	18 Feb. 61	......	3 Aug. 65	12 Nov. 92	9 Nov. 68	1 Oct. 77	31 Mar. 83
35	Caldecott, Francis James[20]		8 June 60		15 May 72		1 Apr. 80	2 Mar. 85	17 Aug. 85	2 Mar. 85		19 Mar. 94			

Lieutenant Colonels (on Indian Supernumerary List).

Yrs.Ser.		Second Lieut.	First Lieut.	Captain.	Brevet Major.	Major.
37	Mortimer, Francis James,[21] 1st Class Commissary of Ordnance	11 Dec. 58	29 July 70		31 Dec. 78	4 Nov. 88
36	Walker, Thomas, *Inspector General of Ordnance, Madras*, 15 Mar. 91	10 June 59	22 Mar. 71		18 June 79	17 Aug. 89

Additional column values (Lieut. Colonel, Brevet Colonel) row 1: 4 Nov. 84; row 2: 17 Aug. 85

ROYAL REGIMENT OF ARTILLERY.

Horse Artillery.

STAFF AT HOME.

Lieutenant Colonels.
E. A. Ollivant, Sheffield.
R. H. Wallace, Aldershot.
Col. St. A. Molesworth, Newbridge.
Col. H. Pipon, Woolwich.

Riding Masters.
Capt. R. J. Goode, Newbridge.
Lieut. J. Carnaghan, Aldershot.

Quarter Master.
Capt. W. Paton, Aldershot.

STAFF IN INDIA.

Lieutenant Colonels.
R. Corbett, Meerut.
W. F. de H. Curtis, Secunderabad.
A. Broadfoot, CB, Kirkee.
W. A. Eden, Umballa.
H. H. Costobadie, Bangalore.

Riding Masters.
Captain F. Draper, Umballa.
Capt. J. Stevens, Kirkee.
Capt. R. Simpson, Meerut.

A Battery, Umballa.
Major.—p.s.c H. V. Cowan.
Captain.—C. B. Watkins.
Lieuts.—W. B. R. Sandys.
H. A. D. Simpson-Baikie
R. A. Bright.

B Battery, Rawul Pindee.
Major.—J. A. Coxhead.
Captain.—H. K. Jackson.
Lieuts.—D. Arbuthnot.
A. W. Pack-Beresford.
P. T. C. Herbert.

C Battery, Meerut.
Major.—A. N. Rochfort.
Captain.—F. D. V. Wing.
Lieuts.—G. F. Milne.
R. FitzMaurice.
A. M. A. Lennox.

D Battery, St. John's Wood.
Major.—F. W. J. Eustace.
Captain.—C. E. Goulburn.
Lieuts.—R. F. Ellice.
C. B. Levita.
G. C. Fordyce-Buchan.

E Battery, Woolwich.
Major.—J. McDonnell.
Captain.—E. J. Phipps Hornby.
Lieuts.—A. M. de L. Cowper-Smith.
W. C. Staveley.
W. V. J. C. Elwes.

F Battery, Aldershot.
Major.—C. C. Rich.
Capt.—Hon. J. E. P. Vereker.
Lieuts.—H. E. Vallentin.
G. F. Dixon.
R. St. C. Harman.

G Battery, Woolwich.
Major.—H. V. Hunt.
Captain.—H. A. Chapman.
Lieuts.—C. Prescott-Decie.
H. L. Powell.
A. T. Butler.

H Battery, Umballa.
Major.—p.s.c J. W. Hawkins.
Captain.—T. K. E. Johnston.
Lieuts.—H. W. Taylor.
W. A. Boulnois.
R. N. Creathed.

I Battery, Mhow.
Major.—Colonel J. H. Wodehouse, CB. CMG.
Captain.—G. H. M'Laughlin.
Lieuts.—S. W. W. Blacker.
R. J. G. Elkington.
A. F. R. Thomson.

J Battery, Aldershot.
Major.—W. L. Davidson.
Captain.—P. B. Taylor.
Lieuts.—F. A. G. Y. Elton.
C. E. D. Budworth.
F. W. Heath.

K Battery, Lucknow.
Major.—J. W. H. Potts.
Captain.—C. H. S. Vores.
Lieuts.—C. H. de Rougemont.
K. Combe.
E. S. Nairne.

L Battery, Kirkee.
Major.—A. H. Hewat.
Captain.—H. M. Campbell.
Lieuts.—R. C. Wellesley.
J. Bellhouse.
T. S. Hichens.

M Battery, Bangalore.
Major.—J. Leach.
Captain.—E. H. Armitage.
Lieuts.—W. B. Norwood.
G. A. FitzGerald.
H. J. Brock.

N Battery, Meerut.
Major.—J. Hotham.
Captain.—E. A. P. Hobday.
Lieuts.—C. B. Simonds.
T. Jones.
W. Gillman.

O Battery, Newbridge.
Major.—A. H. C. Phillpotts
Captain.—P. H. Enthoven.
Lieuts.—R. K. Farrant.
A. M. Kennard.
C. A. Sykes.

P Battery, Aldershot.
Major.—E. M. Flint.
Captain.—p.s.c G. E. Benson.
Lieuts.—J. C. Kirk.
C. U. Morris.
D. G. Probyn.

Q Battery, Sealkot.
Major.—J. M. S. Brunker.
Captain.—Sir J. H. Jervis White-Jervis, Bt.
Lieuts.—F. T. Ravenhill.
W. H. W. Perrott.
P. G. Godfrey-Faussett.

R Battery, Newbridge.
Major.—F. E. R. Pollard-Urquhart.
Captain.—E. A. Fanshawe.
Lieuts.—R. A. C. Wellesley.
G. N. Cartwright.
E. W. M. Powell.

S Battery, Trimulgherry.
Major.—W. H. Suart.
Captain.—F. B. Lecky.
Lieuts.—E. D. Cameron.
A. A. Boggs.
J. A. Hobson.

T Battery, Dorchester.
Major.—C. J. Long.
Captain.—C. G. Neish.
Lieuts.—G. A. Cardew.
C. M. Ross-Johnson.
A. F. Hickie.

DEPOT.
Woolwich.
Lt. Colonel.—E. Blaksley.
Adjutant.—Captain W. L. H. Paget.
Riding Master.—Lieut. A. W. McCombie.
Qr. Master.—Lieut. F. Richardson.

A Battery, Woolwich.
Major.—E. B. Coke.
Captain.—C. F. Blane.
Lieuts.—M. S. Williams.
S. H. Hooper.
C. Stirling.

B Battery, Woolwich.
Major.—F. L. Cunliffe.
Capt.—V. F. W. A. Paget.
Lieuts.—J. H. J. H. Winwood.
E. S. E. W. Russell.
J. B. Aldridge.

RIDING ESTABLISHMENT.
Woolwich.
Lt. Colonel.—E. Blaksley.
Riding Masters.—Major R. Donnelly.
Capt. W. Shipman.
Major.—F. E. A. Hunter.
Lieuts.—E. J. R. Peel.
G. Gillson.

Field Artillery.

STAFF AT HOME.

Lieutenant Colonels.
J. C. Gillespie, Weedon.
C. M. H. Downing, Aldershot.
S. G. Smyth, Ipswich.
G. H. O'Malley, Shorncliffe.
F. A. Yorke, Woolwich.
H. T. S. Yates, Newcastle-on-Tyne.
W. Mallins, Limerick.
H. T. Curling, Hilsea.
G. B. N. Martin, CB., Exeter.
p.s.c. W. W. M. Smith, Colchester.
Col. G. W. M. Turnbull, Athlone.
E. O. Hay, Aldershot.

Riding Masters.
Capt. C. Henson, Aldershot.
Capt. J. Wilken, Hilsea.
Lieut. J. Bevington, Colchester.
Lieut. J. Thorne, Newcastle.

STAFF IN INDIA.

J. E. Josselyn, Jhansi.
E. F. Cambier, Neemuch.
E. Lake, Bombay.
C. B. Wickham, Rawul Pindee.
J. D. Douglas, Meean Meer.
J. A. F. Nutt, St. Thomas's Mount.
W. N. Jervis, Lucknow.
W. Aitken, Campbellpore.

Riding Masters.
Lieut. J. Trasler, Bangalore.
Lieut. T. H. Brogan, Secunderabad.
Lieut. F. Fleming, Rawul Pindee.

1 Battery, Woolwich.
Major.—p.s c. E. R. A. Kerrison.
Captain.—E. M. Lachlan.
Lieuts.—H. R. Overton.
E. B. Ashmore.
P. T. Ayre.

2 Battery, Dinapore.
Major.—F. M. Banister.
Captain.—H. G. Smith.
Lieuts.—M. J. MacCarthy.
H. H. Tudor.
G. V. Green.

3 Battery, Aldershot.
Major.—J. W. Dunlop.
Captain.—W. T. Furse.
Lieuts.—E. P. Smith.
G. H. A. White.
B. Vincent.

4 Battery, Shorncliffe.
Major.—E. H. Pickwood.
Captain.—C. G. Henshaw.
Lieuts.—L. C. Livingstone-Learmonth.
H. Ramsden.
J. E. Cairnes.

5 Battery, Bangalore.
Major.—J. Temple.
Captain.—E. Guinness.
Lieuts.—F. C. Lane.
M. Biddulph.
H. S. Wilson.

6 Battery, Saugor.
Major.—W. Tylden.
Captain.—Hon. H. W. Addington.
Lieutenants.—C. A. Earle.
B. R. Kirwan.

7 Battery, Newcastle.
Major.—H. C. M. Woods.
Captain.—H. Guise.
Lieuts.—S. L. Crockett.
J. Hay.
G. L. Macgowan.

8 Battery, Jhansi.
Major.—E. N. Henriques.
Captain.—G. F. Herbert.
Lieuts.—A. H. Goldie.
C. E. C. G. Charlton.
G. E. Tyrrell.

9 Battery, Agra.
Major.—p.s.c. H. C. Dunlop.
Captain.—J. H. Jollett.
Lieuts.—E. J. Duffus.
T. C. W. Molony.
C. E. Stewart.

10 Battery, Rawul Pindee.
Major.—C. A. Anderson.
Captain.—L. Forde.
Lieuts.—C. N. B. Ballard.
S. W. Robinson.
E. F. Delaforce.

Royal Artillery.

11 Battery, Clonmel.
Maj.—Sir G. V. Thomas, Bt.
Captain.—H. Calley.
Lieuts.—Hon. W. D. Sclater-Booth.
W. E. Emery.
C. Evans.

12 Battery, Hilsea.
Major.—J. W. M. Newton.
Captain.—H. H. Beever.
Lieuts.—E. C. Le Pelley.
G. Baillie.
C. P. Roberts.

13 Battery, Aldershot.
Major.—E. A. Lambart.
Captain.—R. Tremaine.
Lieuts.—W. P. Saunders.
J. Byron.
H. D. O. Ward.

14 Battery, Ipswich.
Major.—G. R. Challenor.
Captain.—A. Capel-Cure.
Lieuts.—J. C. Watson.
A. C. Birch.
R. M. Johnson.

15 Battery, Campbelipore.
Major.—E. Cassan.
Captain.—A. L. Walker.
Lieuts.—R. E. A. Le Mottée.
F. L. Galloway.
H. G. Lloyd.

16 Battery, Aldershot.
Major.—J. L. Keir, Staff College.
Captain.—A. D. A. King.
Lieuts.—E. H. T. Parsons.
G. J. C. Stapylton.
H. J. P. Jeffcoat.

17 Battery, Jubbulpore.
Major.—G. R. Price.
Captain.—L. Graham.
Lieuts.—H. G. F. Geary.
H. N. Packard.
J. S. Ollivant.

18 Battery, Exeter.
Maj.—E. Vaughan-Hughes.
Captain.—F. B. Johnstone.
Lieuts.—F. E. H. Allen.
H. D. De Prée.
F. H. G. Stanton.

19 Battery, Christchurch.
Major.—C. E. Maberly.
Captain.—R. G. M. M'Leod.
Lieuts.—R. S. de Winton.
H. F. Dawson.
H. Spencer.

20 Battery, Shorncliffe.
Major.—C. H. Blount.
Captain.—S. Belfield.
Lieuts.—H. L. Lithgow.
W. R. N. Madocks.
A. Houstoun.

21 Battery, Bangalore.
Major.—E. C. F. Holland.
Captain.—J. F. Browne.
Lieuts.—G. R. FitzR.Talbot.
G. A. Smyth.
H. E. Garstin.

22 Battery, Nusseerabad.
Major.—N. P. Fowell.
Captain.—L. G. F. Gordon.
Lieuts.—A. G. Shortt.
J. F. Barlow.
T. M. Luke.

23 Battery, St. Thomas's Mount.
Major.—A. J. Montgomery.
Captain.—F. G. Maunsell.
Lieutenants.—F. C. Owen.
H. L. Cottingham.
H. C. Sheppard.

24 Battery, Meean Meer.
Major.—C. M. Haggard.
Captain.—A. P. Longfield.
Lieuts.—E. W. Grove.
S. S. Browne.
L. H. Hepper.

25 Battery, Limerick.
Major.—B. Burton.
Captain.—F. C. Johnston.
Lieuts.—E. W. Spedding.
W. P. Monkhouse.
A. Lascelles.

26 Battery, Kamptee.
Major.—H.W.Brackenbury.
Captain.—S. D. Browne.
Lieuts.—F. T. Oldham.
H. A. Cruickshank.
G. T. M. Bridges.

27 Battery, Kirkee.
Major.—H. H. Pengree.
Captain.—H. C. V. Harrison.
Lieuts.—D. B. Stewart.
A. R. Bayly.
W. Evans.

28 Battery, Shorncliffe.
Major.—p.s.c.E.W.Fleming.
Captain.—E. H. Paterson.
Lieuts.—G. G. S. Carey.
D. D. Arderne.
H. S. Seligman.

29 Battery, Belgaum.
Major.—H. Burton.
Captain.—H. H. Butler.
Lieuts.—H. L. Reed.
E. H. Newman.
H. H. Bond.

30 Battery, Colchester.
Major.—P. Blackburn.
Captain.—J. B. H. Askwith.
Lieuts.—W. O. Holloway.
R. F. Ruck-Keene.
S. F. Gosling.

31 Battery, Cawnpore.
Major.—Hon. A. Sidney.
Captain.—W. H. Connolly.
Lieuts.—H. E. Cadell.
O. M. D. Bruce.
C. H. Rowcroft.

32 Battery, Egypt.
Major.—W. H. Williams.
Captain.—E. R. H. J. Cloete.
Lieuts.—G.H.W. Nicholeon.
D. Symonds.
H. T. Farquhar.

33 Battery, Trimulgherry.
Major.—W. H. O'Neill.
Captain.—C. H. Hutchinson.
Lieuts.—T. A. Cubitt.
S. O. Boyd.
F. A. Wynter.

'34 Battery, Meerut.
Major.—A. Bell-Irving.
Captain.—J. H. Leslie.
Lieutenants.—J. G. Rotton.
C. D. R. Watts.
J. A. FitzGibbon.

35 Battery, Ahmedabad.
Major.—R. G.W.Hepburne.
Captain.—O. de Jersey.
Lieuts.—A. G. Glanville.
E. G. Carbutt.
L. C. L. Oldfield.

36 Battery, Kirkee.
Major.—E. A. Burrows.
Captain.—A.S. Wedderburn.
Lieuts.—H. E. Stockdale.
M. D. Bell.
W. J. K. Rettie.

37 Battery, Hilsea.
Major.—P. F. P. Hamilton.
Captain.—E. P. A. Tawney.
Lieuts.—A. Forbes.
A. D. Kirby.
V. R. Hine-Haycock.

38 Battery, Aldershot.
Major.—J. W. Stirling.
Captain.—E. W. Blunt.
Lieuts.—E. M'M. Seddon.
A. F. Becke.
C. L. O'Malley.

39 Battery, Fyzabad.
Major.—R. H. S. Baker.
Captain.—A. H. S. Goff.
Lieuts.—G. Laird.
E. B. Macnaghten.
W. Ellershaw.

40 Battery, Ahmednagar.
Major.—M. W. Saunders.
Captain.—A. H. Hussey.
Lieuts.—H. R. Palmer.
R. W. Boger.
W. C. Symon.

41 Battery, Weedon.
Major.—W. G. de Jersey.
Captain.—E. P. Smith.
Lieuts.—J. R. Wilson.
W. Strong.
E. H. Harpur.

42 Battery, Trimulgherry.
Major.—D. E. Dewar.
Captain.—G. M. Yunge-Bateman.
Lieutenants.—H. R. Gotto.
S. W. Douglas.
C. H. Liveing.

43 Battery, Barrackpore.
Major.—G. F. F. Shirreff.
Captain.—C. W. Tyler.
Lieuts.—G. S. F. Broome.
C. L. R. Gray.
D. H. M'Neile.

44 Battery, Neemuch.
Major.—R. Wynyard.
Captain.—C. C. Owen.
Lieuts.—R. T. Marsden.
R. L. Haymes.
F. W. H. Walshe.

45 Battery, Bellary.
Major.—H. A. D. Curtis.
Captain.—A. B. Helyar.
Lieuts.—W. G. H. Manley.
P. W. B. Henning.
H. C. S. Clarke.

46 Battery, Meean Meer.
Major.—F.W. Boteler.
Captain.—A. S. Tyndale-Biscoe.
Lieuts.—H. A. Lake.
T. Bruce.
H. D. Foulkes.

47 Battery, Kurrachee.
Major.—W. A. Plant.
Captain.—J. G. Geddes.
Lieuts.—A. W. Curtis.
E. Palmer.
L. J. Hext.

48 Battery, Bareilly.
Major.—L. J. A. Chapman.
Captain.—H. G. Burrowes.
Lieuts.—T. St. A. B. L. Nevinson.
P. Wheatley.
W. G. Thompson.

49 Battery, St. Thomas's Mount.
Major.—R. E. Boothby.
Captain.—H. A. Bethell.
Lieuts.—J. Henderson.
A. E. Wardrop.
W. E. Edwards.

50 Battery, Jullunder.
Major.—C. M. T. Western.
Captain.—R. M. Rodwell.
Lieuts.—B. Gosselin.
J. W. E. Donaldson.
L. S. Downes.

51 Battery, Meerut.
Major.—A. Burton.
Captain.—C. T. Blewitt.
Lieuts.—W. J. B. Allen.
A. W. Hewetson.
W. A Short.

52 Battery, Colchester.
Major.—W. N. LLoyd.
Captain.—G. F. White.
Lieuts.—W. A. Nicholson.
A. H. Bowring.
Hon. G. F. Stanley.

53 Battery, Kurrachee.
Major.—H. J. Lyster.
Captain.—A. D. Young.
Lieuts.—A. M. Perreau.
R. F. Wemyss.
C. J. H. Swann.

54 Battery, Allahabad.
Major.—F. C. Farmer.
Captain.—C. T. Caulfeild.
Lieutenants.—A. P. Douglas.
A. T. Anderson.
H. A. Boyce.

55 Battery, Deesa.
Major.—A. C. Bailward.
Captain.—A. R. Knox.
Lieuts.—C. F. Stevens.
W. M. Crockett.
H. E. T. Kelly.

56 Battery, Exeter.
Major.—R. M. Crofton.
Captain.—J. H. Balguy.
Lieutenants.—E. C. Massy.
J. C. G. A. Hankey.
J. E. James.

57 Battery, Woolwich.
Major.—H. G. H. Galton.
Captain.—G. R. Darley.
Lieuts.—C. H. Wilson.
P. G. Best.
F. E. L. Barker.

58 Battery, Woolwich.
Major.—p.s.c.T. S. Baldock.
Captain.—C. D. King.
Lieutenants.—C. O. Head.
E. H. Pim.

59 Battery, Nowgong.
Major.—H. O'B. Owen.
Captain.—C. E. Coghill.
Lieuts.—N. F. Gordon.
G. H. Sanders.
H. B. Hill.

60 Battery, Mooltan.
Major.—W. H. Frith.
Captain.—W. J. A. Beatson.
Lieutenants.—H. A. P.White.
E. W. Alexander.
H. S. Woodcock.

61 Battery, Aldershot.
Major.—A. H. Whitehorne.
Captain.—R. F. Fox.
Lieuts.—R. O. Coates.
J. Dalby.
A. G. Arbuthnot.

62 Battery, Ipswich.
Major.—A. C. Daniell.
Capt.—H. N. Schofield.
Lieuts.—J. St. C. Macmillan.
L. M. Phillpotts.
J. H. W. Johnstone.

63 Battery, Newcastle.
Maj.—P. C. E. Newbigging.
Captain.—B. M. Rhodes.
Lieuts.—H. B. Roberts.
W. B. Browell.
M. R. F. Courage.

64 Battery, Sheffield.
Major.—R. Oakes.
Captain.—W. Corbyn.
Lieuts.—E. C. Sandars.
P. N. G. Reade.
C. F. G. Washington.

65 Battery, Neemuch.
Major.—p.s.c. Colonel A. G. Creagh.
Captain.—R. A. Vigne.
Lieuts.—H. C. O. Uniacke.
C. F. Rugge-Price.
A. A. Montgomery.

66 Battery, Glasgow.
Major.—W. P. Thring.
Captain.—P. Langley.
Lieuts.—G. Campbell-Johnston.
E. H. Willis.
N. E. Tilney.

67 Battery, Fermoy.
Major.—L. W. Parsons.
Captain.—R. D. Gubbins.
Lieutenants.—W. H. Kay.
H. C. T. Hildyard.

Royal Artillery.

184b

68 Battery, Peshawur.
Major.—R. Bannatine-Allason.
Captain.—P. H. Slee.
Lieuts.—C. C. Robertson.
E. T. Hale.
A. M. Smith.

69 Battery, Weedon.
Major.—J. A. Mackenzie Grieve.
Captain.—C. D. Guinness.
Lieutenants.—D. McKay.
R. S. Hardman.
H. M. Davson.

70 Battery, Lucknow.
Major.—E. C. Hawkshaw.
Captain.—G. H. Geddes.
Lieuts.—G. M'C. Campbell.
J. Henry.
H. N. St. J. Maule.

71 Battery, Ferozepore.
Major.—C. V. B. Kuper.
Captain.—J. U. Coates.
Lieutenants.—P. A. Skipwith
G. V. Davidson.
C. Wigram.

72 Battery, Kirkee.
Major.—p.s.c. J. W. T. Spencer.
Captain.—W. D. Burrard.
Lieuts.—F. Potts.
E. W. Plummer.
T. M. Usborne.

73 Battery, Newcastle-on-Tyne.
Major.—C. M. Barlow.
Captain.—R. W. Breeks.
Lieuts.—A. S. Williams.
H. C. Russell-Oldnall.
D. R. Coates.

74 Battery, Athlone.
Major.—G. P. Owen.
Captain.—R. F. X. M. Bond.
Lieuts.—T. H. Crozier.
G. Lewis.
A. H. N. Devenish.

75 Battery, Bristol.
Major.—W. F. L. Lindsay.
Captain.—F. J. Græme.
Lieutenants.—R. Geoghegan.
M. C. P. Ward.
A. B. H. Clerke.

76 Battery, Longford.
Major.—R. A. G. Harrison.
Captain.—A. L. Hibbert.
Lieuts.—R. D. Wyldo.
A. M. R. Mallock.
B. Atkinson.

77 Battery, Aldershot.
Major.—F. M. Bland.
Captain.—C. G. Mackenzie.
Lieutenants.—C. Behrens.
C. D. Hope.
R. E. Paley.

78 Battery, Athlone.
Major.—D. C. Cartor.
Captain.—J. F. Vans-Agnew.
Lieuts.—W. H. Olivier.
G. A. S. Capo.
P. L. Foster.

79 Battery, Sheffield.
Major.—S. Watson.
Captain.—J. L. Smith.
Lieuts.—H. M. de F. Montgomery.
K. J. Kincaid-Smith.
J. W. F. Lamont.

80 Battery, Hilsea.
Major.—J. J. Porteous.
Captain.—J. L. F. Shepherd.
Lieuts.—L. A. Smith.
L. L. Parker.
C. Ravenhill.

Depots.
Lieutenant Colonels.
p.s.c. J. T. Bury, 1st Div., Woolwich.
W. S. Langley, 2nd Div., Woolwich.

Adjutants.

Riding Masters.
Lieut. J. M'Lennan, 1st Div.
Lieut. J. Learmont, 2nd Div.

Quarter Masters.
Captain A. Martin, 1st Div.
Captain J. M'Kenna, 2nd Div.

1 Battery, 1 Div., Woolwich.
Major.—F. H. Hall.
Captain.—J. Hanwell.
Lieuts.—J. A. Tyler.
W. Thwaites.

2 Battery, 1 Div., Woolwich.
Major.—J. F. Manifold.
Captain.—R. L. Heygate.
Lieuts.—C. C. Van Straubenzee.
E. G. Cheke.
F. L. Sharp.

1 Battery, 2 Div., Woolwich.
Major.—F. T. M. Beaver.
Captain.—H. A. Brendon.
Lieuts.—J. H. W. Tapp.
C. F. P. Parry.
S. F. Metcalfe.

2 Battery, 2 Div., Woolwich.
Major.—H. M. Sandbach.
Captain.—O. H. Kilner.
Lieuts.—F. Prendergast.
E. P. England.
K. D. Bell.

Mountain Artillery.

Lieutenant Colonels.
A. E. Duthy, Umballa.
Colonel J. Keith, DSO. Rawul Pindee.
H. R. L. Morgan, CB. Quetta.

Adjutant.
Capt. C. T. Robinson, Quetta.

1 Battery, Umballa.
Major.—C. P. Triscott, DSO.
Captain.—M. F. Fegen.
Lieutenants.—R. E. Stuart.
H. L. N. Beynon.
F. Lyon.

2 Battery, Umballa.
Major.—O. S. Smyth, DSO.
Capt.—C. P. Fendall, DSO.

Lieuts.—F. C. Poole.
A. D. Freeland.
E. H. B. Craster.

3 Battery, Rawul Pindee.
Major.—J. D. Cunningham.
Captain.—H. D. Grier.
Lieuts.—F. R. Patch.
W. H. Jones.
C. W. J. Orr.

4 Battery, Newport, Mon.
Major.—G. W. R. Fulton.
Captain.—C. O. Smeaton.
Lieuts.—A. A. McHardy.
A. W. Grepe.
W. J. Fowler.

5 Battery, Quetta.
Major.—W. F. Cleeve.

Captain.—p.s.c. H. E. Stanton, DSO.
Lieuts.—H. de L. Walters.
A. Ellershaw.

6 Battery, Mandalay.
Major.—A. Keene, DSO.
Captain.—F. L. Donaldson.
Lieuts.—F. H. Metcalfe.
C. E. Phipps.
H. M. Thomas.

7 Battery, Rawul Pindee.
Major.—E. Gunner.
Captain.—J. E. Harvey.
Lieuts.—T. E. Marshall.
G. R. M. Church.
E. P. Carter.

8 Battery, Rawul Pindee.
Major.—J. C. Shirres.

Captain.—F. W. S. Stanton
Lieuts.—C. J. Blunt.
A. S. Miller.
H. C. Moultrie.

9 Battery, Darjeeling.
Major.—F. A. Bowles.
Captain.—G. C. Dowell.
Lieuts.—J. F. Fisher.
H. G. Brett.
W. F. T. O'Connor.

10 Battery, Natal.
Major. — H. Montgomery-Campbell.
Captain.—C. M. Gonne.
Lieuts.—R. H. F. M'Culloch.
J. G. Dennistoun.
H. G. Moor.

Garrison Artillery.

EASTERN DIVISION.
Dover.

Armament Major.
J. de W. L. Clarke, Gibraltar.

Quarter Master.
Lt. T. F. Cooper, Gibraltar.

Adjutant.
Capt. S. J. Chamier, Bombay.

Staff at Home.
Lieutenant Colonels.
F. Howard, Shoeburyness.
J. G. Uppleby, Sheerness.
H. G. F. Siddons, Dover.
F. M. Turner, Harwich.

Armament Majors.
W. E. L. Balfour, Dover.
A. H. Carter, Tilbury Fort.

District Officers.
Capt. E. Dawson, Tower of London.
Capt. H. Orchard, Chatham.
Capt. W. Osborne, Harwich.
Lieut. R. Clarke, Newhaven.
Lieut. W. C. Mason, Gravesend.

Adjutant.
Capt. C. J. Fisher, Dover.

Quarter Master.
Lt. W. Lawrence, Sheerness.

Staff Abroad.
Lieutenant Colonels.
P. L. Macgregor, Gibraltar.
H. Barron, Gibraltar.
G. M. Stevens, Bombay.

1 Company, Delhi.
Major.—W. Hanna.
Captain.—P. T. Cooper.
Lieuts.—V. de V. Hunt.
G. T. Brierley.
C. E. Blanford.

2 Company, Shoeburyness.
Major.—A. R. Fraser.
Capt.—J. M'C. Maxwell.
Lieuts.—C. G. Vereker.
E. L. Tomkins.
W. P. L. Davies.

3 Company, Bombay.
Major.—M. W. P. Block.
Captain.—E. E. Norris.
Lieutenants.—A. J. Peile.
C. W. Stülpnagel.
A. J. Thompson.

4 Company, Fort St. George, Madras.
Major.—N. Maxwell.
Captain.—E. S. Brooke.
Lieuts.—E. R. Phillips.
G. G. W. Corrie.
W. M. Ogg.

5 Company, Gibraltar.
Major.—p.s.c. Bt. Lt. Col. J. Adyo.
Captain.—H. St. G. Ross.
Lieutenants.—A. C. Boyd.
S. F. Alderson.
D. E. Forman.

6 Company, Sheerness.
Major.—C. N. Simpson.
Captain.—G. Humphreys.
Lieuts.—J. W. Matthews.
D. Deane.

7 (Siege Train) Company, Dover.
Major.—G. N. H. Barlow.
Captain.—W. H. Onslow.
Lieutenants.—R. A. Craig.
H. C. Moorhouse.
C. R. B. Owen.

8 Company, Calcutta.
Major.—S. D. Rainsford.
Captain.—T. ff. Chamberlain
Lieuts.—W. A. C. Pilkington.
J. O'Kinealy.
A. J. S. Taylor.

9 Company, Gibraltar.
Major.—H. B. Gundry.
Captain.—H. E. Bampfylde.
Lieuts.—E. S. de V. Bland Hunt.
F. M. Rickard.

10 Company, Dover.
Major.—C. E. Jervois.
Captain.—W. W. Griffin.
Lieuts.—R. K. Scott.
L. N. Gooding.
G. H. Stobart.

11 Company, Landguard Fort.
Major.—R. F. M'Crea.
Captain.—H. J. Du Cane, Staff College.
Lieutenants.—A. P. H. Desborough.
W. E. Manley.
B. R. Brewin.

12 Company, Campbellpore.
Major.—A. B. Purvis.
Captain.—
Lieuts.—F. A. Easton.
J. H. Massie.
B. J. M. Locke.

13 Company, Rawul Pindee.
Major.—A. H. P. Turner.
Captain.—
Lieuts.—H. W. Atlay.
G. Stoddart.
A. M. Kettlewell.

14 Company, Gibraltar.
Major.—A. G. S. Wade.
Captain.—G. R. Lamb.
Lieuts.—H. S. Browning.
T. O. Seagram.
Sir J. Keane, Bt.

1840   Royal Artillery.

15 Company, **Gibraltar.**
Major.—O. Rowe.
Captain.—St. J. L. H. Du Plat-Taylor.
Lieuts.—C. de Sausmarez.
H. E. Molesworth.
A. J. H. Keyes.

16 Company, **Egypt.**
Major.—J. P. Fell.
Captain.—W. C. Hunter-Blair.
Lieuts.—A. G. Smith.
C. H. W. Owen.
S. F. Stallard.

17 Company, **Gibraltar.**
Major.—W. L. White.
Captain.—E. C. Cameron.
Lieuts.—H. C. Hall.
P. P. E. de B. Radcliffe.
E. C. W. D. Walthall.

18 Company, **Shoeburyness.**
Major.—R. M. B. F. Kelly.
Captain.—P. H. M. Dorehill.
Lieuts.—A. H. Kane.
R. B. Fife.
P. K. Lewes.

19 Company, **Sheerness.**
Major.—H. G. C. B. Weir.
Captain.—E. F. Hall.
Lieuts.—A. R. Oldfield.
D. F. Nicholl.
G. V. Clarke.

20 Company, **Sheerness.**
Major.—E. C. Wace, DSO.
Captain.—W. A. Persse.
Lieuts.—J. Chrystie.
C. M'I. Ritchie.
F. E. de C. Chevallier.

21 Company, **Gibraltar.**
Major.—W. C. Anderson.
Captain.—A. T. Baker.
Lieuts.—R. M. B. Ruthven.
B. G. Buchanan.
G. G. Thatcher.

22 Company, **Gibraltar.**
Major.—F. H. Ward.
Captain.—B. F. Drake.
Lieuts.—C. F. Bishop.
M. W. H. M'Cheane.
P. Perceval.

23 Company, **Aden.**
Major.—J. H. Rosseter.
Captain.—A. H. Block.
Lieuts.—H. J. Eaton-Evans.
G. A. S. Gordon.
H. A. Koebel.

24 Company, **Bombay.**
Major.—
Captain.—A. C. Currie.
Lieuts.—W. L. J. Carey.
H. W. G. Keddie.
L. B. Montrésor.

25 Company, **Dover.**
Major.—G. H. Bittleston.
Captain.—R. A. K. Montgomery, at Staff Coll.
Lieuts.—G. B. Mackenzie.
M. L. Wilkinson.
W. Loring.

26 (Siege Train) Company, **Roorkee.**
Major.—E. J. K. Priestley.
Captain.—H. Rouse.
Lieuts.—A.M.N. Mackenzie.
H. G. Sargeaunt.
C. R. Kelly.

Depots.
Lieutenant Colonels.
A. J. Pearson, Woolwich.
F. F. Ditmas, Dover.
W. V. Gregory, Great Yarmouth.

Adjutants.
Captain R. G. Morriman, DSO, Dover.
Captain J. P. Du Cane, Great Yarmouth.

District Officer.
Lieut. G. A. C. D. Wingfield, Great Yarmouth.

Depot, **Dover.**
Major.—W. H. Darby.
Captain.—R. E. L. Radcliffe.
Lieuts.—W. E. Wingfield.
W. E. Wailes.
J. K. Kendall.

Sub Depot, **Great Yarmouth.**
Capt.—T. L. Coxhead, DSO.
Lieuts.—C. H. Ziegler.
O. O. Adair.

Affiliated Militia Artillery.—Kent, Norfolk, Suffolk and Sussex Artillery.

SOUTHERN DIVISION.
Portsmouth.
STAFF AT HOME.
Lieutenant Colonels.
p.s.c. G. C. Wynne, Portsmouth.
p.s.c. H. H. Crookenden, Portsmouth.
W. W. Smith, Golden Hill.
J. R. S. O. Hewitt, Londonderry.
J. J. Congdon, Weymouth.
H. B. Kingscote, Cork.

Armament Majors.
C. L. Casey, Fareham.
R. W. P. Robertson, Portsmouth.

District Officers.
Major T. D. Richey, Leith Fort.
Major A. J. Lindsay, Dublin.
Capt. E. Aldridge, Portsmouth.
Lieut. W. P. Furner, Cork.
Lieut. A. R. Malcolm, Portsmouth.
Lieut. J. A. Williams, Aberdeen.

Adjutant.
Captain G. W. Biddulph, Portsmouth.

Quarter Masters.
Capt. G. Cook, Portsmouth.
Lieut. W.T. Whitley, Gosport.
Lieut. W. C. Perry, Cork.

STAFF ABROAD.
Lieutenant Colonels.
C. J. Blake, Ceylon.
R. E. Mundy, Malta.
p.s.c. de C. Daniell, Malta.
A. S. Griffiths, Malta.
W. H. Auchinleck, Rangoon.
R.H.W. Plunkett, Singapore
T. R. Disney, Roorkee.
Colonel W. Hunter, Aden.

Armament Majors.
A. H. Browne, Singapore.
R. A. Rigg, Ceylon.

District Officer.
Capt. G. Webster, Malta.

Quarter Master.
Capt. R. J. Wishart, Malta.

1 Company, **Cork.**
Major.—C. A. Howard.
Captain.—L. H. Ducrôt, at Staff College.
Lieuts.—A. C. Williams.
L. T. Ashworth.
R. S. Hamilton.

2 Company, **Malta.**
Major.—T. W. Powles.
Captain.—M. Peake.
Lieuts.—W. D. C. Trimnell.
A. R. Izat.
W. A. S. Gemmell.

3 Company, **Aden.**
Major.—W. J. Hicks.
Captain.—H. M. Slater.
Lieuts.—J. E. H. Young.
C. A. Fisher.
S. H. Jacob.

4 Company, **Golden Hill.**
Major.—A. L. Lane.
Captain.—A. T. Cuming.
Lieuts.—L. L. H. Osborn.
C. G. Pritchard.
R. N. Lockhart.

5 Company, **Attock.**
Major.—J. V. V. Baker.
Captain.—C. H. Ford.
Lieuts.—W. S. Armitage.
H. J. Cotter.
F. C. Tyler.

6 Company, **Ceylon.**
Major.—L. C. Gordon.
Captain.—J. F. Craig.
Lieuts.—W. A. W. Swettenham.
I. B. F. Currie.
A. C. S. W. Simpson.
C. M. Playfair.

7 Company, **Quetta.**
Major.—p.s.c. H.S. Dawkins.
Captain.—A. ff. Powell.
Lieutenants.—A. F. E. Stiffe.
L. B. S. Christie.
A. Thorp.

8 Company, **Malta.**
Major.—G. T. Kelaart.
Capt.—H. D, White-Thomson.
Lieuts.—J. Quain.
A. U. Stockley.
G. B. Hinton.

9 Company, **Aden.**
Major.—F. E. Kent.
Captain.—
Lieuts.—W. C. R. Farmar.
A. W. Clark-Kennedy.
H. T. Hart.

10 Company, **Cork Harbour.**
Major.—W. F. Graham.
Captain.—G. Osborn.
Lieuts.—A. E. Gordon.
C. N. Ewart.
B. D. H. Smithett.

11 Company, **Rangoon.**
Major.—
Captain.—J. S. Minter.
Lieuts.—R. G. Partridge.
G. T. Mair,
C. E. T. Rolland.

12 Company, **Hong Kong.**
Major.—W. D. Garnett-Botfield.
Captain.—E. S. Cooper.
Lieuts.—J. S. Edgar.
H. F. E. Lewin.
A. D. H. Grayson.

13 Company, **Portsmouth.**
Major.—F. J. A. Trench, at Staff College.
Captain.—S. E. G. Lawless.
Lieuts.—K. E. Haynes.
G. C. Appleyard.
A. F. Porcher.

14 Company, **Weymouth.**
Major.—Col. F. G. Slade, CB.
Captain.—W. J. Napier.
Lieuts.—A. O'C. Scott.
W. B. Anley.
E. F. Talbot Ponsonby.

15 (Siege Train) Company, **Fort Grange, Gosport.**
Major.—J. R. H. Allen.
Captain.—D. J. M. Fasson, at Staff College.
Lieuts.—J. F. Westerman.
C. Howard-Vyse.
A. C. R. Nutt.

16 Company, **Malta.**
Major.—W. C. Savile.
Captain.—F. B. R. Toms.
Lieuts.—A. R. Y. Kirkpatrick.
G. W. Rice.
A. H. Webb.

17 Company, **Portsmouth.**
Major.—G. R. Moore.
Captain.—H. F. Askwith.
Lieuts.—C. W. Collingwood.
P. L. Holbrooke.
H. P. Menres.

18 Company, **Ferozepore.**
Major.—J. O. English.
Captain.—F. R. Drake.
Lieuts.—H. M. Barnes.
G. H. M. Baker.
J. Driffield.
G. H. C. Wilkins.

19 Company, **Cork Harbour.**
Major.—R. D. Loudon.
Captain.—A. G. Norris.
Lieuts.—Hon. M.R.C. Ward.
A. H. Ollivaut.
R. H. Galwey.

20 Company, **Fort Fareham.**
Major.—T. H. J. Woodrow.
Captain.—R. P. Benson.
Lieuts.—D. F. Tulloch.
H. D. Hammond.
C. J. D. Freeth.

21 Company, **Allahabad.**
Major.—E. Ward.
Captain.—C. E. Reynolds.
Lieuts.—H. J. Kelsall.
A. C. Kennedy.
G. R. H. Nugent.

22 Company, **Malta.**
Major.—G. D. Fanshawe.
Captain.—A. S. Baker.
Lieuts.—G. C. Merrick.
H. Robinson.
A. A. Falcon.

23 Company, **Bombay.**
Major.—G. G. Simpson.
Captain.—W. W. T. Duhan.
Lieuts.—J. H. Paine.
F. O. Wyatt.
F. T. Brown.

24 (Heavy) Company, **Mooltan.**
Major.—H. O. Piers.
Captain.—R. A. Kaye.
Lieuts.—J. C. de K. Bruce-Kingsmill.
J. S. Gooch.
H. J. W. Farrell.
D. R. Poulter.
C. C. Donovan.

25 Company, **Singapore.**
Major.—J. J. Swinton.
Captains.—W. L. Warren.
M. H. B. Raby.
Lieuts.—N. D. Cochrane.
R. H. Parker.
H. R. V. de Bury.
J. T. Macdougall.
A. J. R. Greene.

26 Company, **Malta.**
Major.—T. V. W. Phillips.
Captain.—F. A. L. Powell.
Lieuts.—W. G. Blanford.
J. G. M. Watson.

27 Company, **Weymouth.**
Major.—W. S. Walford.
Captain.—C. C. Sankey.
Lieuts.—H. E. Carey.
P. Suther.
A. D. Musgrave.

28 Company, **Quetta.**
Major.—R. A. M. Henn.
Captain.—
Lieuts.—C. A. Cleghorn.
J. H. Keogh.
J. A. Dalyell.

29 Company, **Malta.**
Major.—H.C.C.D. Simpson.
Captain.—T. B. Nowlan.
Lieuts.—G. R. M. Matthew-Lanowe.
R. G. Keyworth.
A. E. B. Fair.

Royal Artillery. 184d

30 Company, **Malta.**
Major.—W. S. Churchward.
Captain.—C. S. Meeres.
Lieuts.—E. L. E. Whitehead.
F. F. Lambarde.
E. H. Stevenson.

31 Company, **Portsmouth.**
Major.—F. Saltmarshe.
Captain.—W. M. Grover.
Lieuts.—M. M. D. Morrison.
H. L. Lowry.
H. C. H. Burton.

32 Company, **Sandown, I.W.**
Major.—M. O. Hopkins.
Captain.—H. S. White.
Lieuts.—R. O. Marton.
E. E. N. Waters.
R. A. Birley.

33 Company, **Portsmouth.**
Major.—A. Eardley-Wilmot.
Captain.—C. N. Lyall.
Lieuts.—W. E. Rumbold.
G. E. Carter.
H. N. B. Hollingshead.

34 Company, **Portsmouth.**
Major.—F. A. Aylmer.
Captain.—p.s.c. N. W. H. du Boulay.
Lieuts.—H. Morrice.
W. H. Drake.
L. H. D. Broughton.

35 Company, **Hong Kong.**
Major.—C. F. Magrath.
Captain.—P. de S. Burney.
Lieuts.—W. H. Ramage-Dawson.
P. H. Cruickshank.
C. N. Buzzard.

36 Company, **Malta.**
Major.—R. C. Foster.
Captain.—H. C. Williams-Wynn.
Lieuts.—B. W. Holman.
P. P. E. de Berry.
M. J. F. Fitzgerald.

DEPOTS.
Lieutenant Colonels.
A. W. Ferrier, Fort Rowner.
J. M. Tabor, Templemore.
J. M. Alves, Leith Fort.
A. J. Dunnage, Seaforth.
G. Will, Aberdeen.

Adjutants.
Capt. H. G. Birch, Templemore.
Capt. C. D. Scott, Leith Fort.

Quarter Master.
Lieut. J. S. Clements, Templemore.

Depot, Fort Rowner, **Gosport.**
Major.—C. D. Cottrell.
Captain.—L. Bell.
Lieuts.—J. M. Macgowan.
C. E. Eady.

1st Sub Depot, **Seaforth, Liverpool.**
Captain.—W. G. Terry.
Lieuts.—A. E. C. Myers.
R. Saunders.

2nd Sub Depot, **Leith.**
Major.—A. C. T. Boileau.
Captain.—A. C. Connal.
Lieuts.—E. C. Harington.
A. McGill.
L. M. Wilson.

3rd Sub Depot, **Templemore.**
Captain.—E. Pollock.
Lieuts.—H. G. Howorth.
P. Fitz W. FitzRoy.
H. G. W. Jennison.

Affiliated Militia Artillery.
—Antrim, S.E. Coast of Scotland, Cork, Donegal, Dublin City, Edinburgh, Fife, Forfar and Kincardine, Hampshire and Isle of Wight, Lancashire, Limerick City, Mid Ulster, Tipperary, Waterford, Argyll and Bute, Wicklow, Sligo, Londonderry, and Clare.

WESTERN DIVISION.
Devonport.
STAFF AT HOME.
Lieutenant Colonels.
R. F. Williams, Devonport.
p.s.c. A. G. Walker, Devonport.
G. B. Allen, Cardiff.
W. G. Knox, CB., Pembroke Dock.

Armament Majors.
A. J. Nixon, Devonport.
B. L. Eman, Devonport.

District Officers.
Major B. D. Porterfield, Tynemouth.
Captain W. H. Popplestone, Falmouth.
Lieut. T. Y. Osmond, Paull Point.
Lieut. S. T. Smith, Plymouth.
Lieut. W. L. Beardsley, Cardiff.
Lieut. T. Lacey, Pembroke Dock.

Adjutant.
Captain T. D. Inglis, Devonport.

STAFF ABROAD.
Lieutenant Colonels.
F. C. Morgan, Bermuda.
A. W. Anstruther, Halifax, N.S.
N. Powlett, Kurrachee.
J. P. Freeth, Barrackpore.
A. W. White, Cape.
C. M. Smith, Mooltan.
P. K. L. Beaver, Allahabad.

Armament Majors.
D. F. Downing, St. Lucia.
G. F. A. Norton, Jamaica.
H. N. Jervois, Cape.

District Officers.
Lieut. J. R. F. Lightowlers.
Lieut. G. Clark, Halifax, N.S.

1 Company, **Halifax, N.S.**
Major.—A. Tracey.
Captain.—M. M. Morris.
Lieuts.—H. Crichton.
J. G. Austin.
E. V. D. Riddell.

2 Company, **Pembroke Dock.**
Major.—W. H. E. Dobie.
Captain.—Hon. R. Tyrwhitt.
Lieuts.—W. H. Hunt.
E. W. S. Brooke.
H. R. Phipps.

3 Company, **Bermuda.**
Major.—R. M. Brady.
Captain.—A. G. Scott.
Lieuts.—H. M. Innes.
W. E. Castens.
G. T. C. Dwyer.

4 Company, **Roorkee.**
Major.—C. A. Ryan.
Captain.—E. D. C. Cameron.
Lieuts.—R. H. Goodwin.
E. L. Hardcastle.
R. B. Crofton.

5 Company, **Barrackpore.**
Major.—F. J. Burridge.
Captain.—F. Vans-Agnew.
Lieuts.—A. C. Ferguson.
C. G. E. Stevens Nash.
R. H. M'Vittie.

6 Company, **Devonport.**
Major.—A. H. Callwell.
Captain.—J. H. L. Dallas.
Lieuts.—W. A. Matthews.
F. W. M. Walker.
R. G. Westropp.

7 Company, **Trimulgherry.**
Major.—F. R. Thackeray.
Captain.—C. W. Brownlow.
Lieuts.—S. G. Jobb.
C. D. Hope.
W. T. Armitage.

8 Company, **Pembroke Dock.**
Major.—*p.s.c.* R. F. Johnson.
Captain.—F. R. Maunsell, at Staff College.
Lieuts.—J. H. W. Johnstone.
W. R. Eden.
T. M. Kough.

9 (Heavy) Company, **Jhansi.**
Major.—G. G. Monck-Mason
Captain.—M. W. Noble.
Lieuts.—C. K. Busho.
E. F. Corbett.
C. M. Nuttall.

10 Company, **Guernsey.**
Major.—C. R. W. Hervey.
Captain.—E. S. Cleeve.
Lieuts.—H. M. Drake.
St. L. M. Moore.
C. F. G. Low.

11 Company, **Kurrachee.**
Major.—R. L. Haines.
Captain.—T. B. Wood.
Lieuts.—S. D. Bullen.
J. H. Lawrence Archer.
H. B. Mayne.

12 Company, **Devonport.**
Major.—T. Perrott.
Captain.—G. T. Forestier-Walker.
Lieuts.—J. J. Hanks.
C. F. Phipps.
G. E. Ellissen.

13 Company, **Devonport.**
Major.—C. M. Western.
Captain.—H. C. St. G. Molesworth.
Lieuts.—F. A. Twiss.
H. A. L. H. Wade.
A. L. B. Jacob.

14 Company, **Jamaica.**
Major.—
Capt.—H. B. Brownlow.
Lieuts.—J. W. Kempson.
G. F. Slator.
C. St. L. G. Hawkes.

15 Company (Siege Train), **Devonport.**
Major.—H. P. Hickman.
Captain.—O. Lyon.
Lieuts.—R. England.
H. C. W. Godfray.
J. F. I. H. Doyle.

16 Company, **Agra.**
Major.—E. U. Bracken.
Captain.—C. G. Watson.
Lieuts.—W. H. Bowen.
F. A. Wynter.
C. H. Wood.

17 Company, **Jersey.**
Major.—H. A. Scott.
Captain.—F. C. Fowler.
Lieuts.—W. G. Lyddon.
C. L. C. Hamilton.
S. V. Schofield.

18 Company, **Rangoon.**
Major.—R. C. E. North.
Captain.—M. S. Eyre.
Lieuts.—W. M'Gildowny.
A. S. Cotton.
H. P. R. Coode.

19 Company, **Bermuda.**
Major.—J. C. Marston.
Captain.—H. L. Gardiner.
Lieuts.—H. E. Marsh.
P. H. Parken.
C. S. S. Curteis.

20 Company, **Halifax.**
Major.—J. O. Hodgson.
Captain.—M. B. Roberts.
Lieuts.—A. C. Wilkinson.
F. B. H. Moore.
F. J. Odevaine.

21 Company, **Devonport.**
Major.—L. C. M. Blacker.
Captain.—P. B. Hanham.
Lieutenants.—F. Warren.
J. C. Hanna.
E. B. Scott.

22 Company, **Roorkee.**
Major.—F. B. Bunny.
Captain.—E. P. Lambert.
Lieuts.—C. C. Noott.
A. P. Trevor.
G. C. Sturrock.

23 Company, **St. Lucia.**
Major.—
Captain.—G. E. Bryant.
Lieuts.—S. C. Halse.
F. W. Mackenzie.
E. A. Saunders.

24 Company, **Mauritius.**
Major.—T. Mayhew.
Captain.—R. D. Anderson.
Lieuts.—W. H. W. Hope.
R. L. Muspratt Williams.
R. B. Riddell.

25 Company, **Cape Town.**
Major.—H. W. Morrieson.
Captain.—H. G. Sandilands.
Lieuts.—S. C. C. Townsend.
J. F. Tyrrell.
A. B. Forman.
G. D. Wheeler.
W. H. Moore.

DEPOTS.
Lieutenant Colonels.
Colonel J. C. Robinson, Scarborough.
A. Browne, Devonport.

Adjutant.
Captain M. L. Carletou, Devonport.

Quarter Master.
Lt. S. Coombes, Devonport.

Depot, **Plymouth.**
Major.—A. Mansel, DSO.
Captain.—D'A. B. Preston.
Lieuts.—A. M. Tyler.
J. D. Sherer.

1st Sub Depot, **Scarborough.**
Major D. C. Dean-Pitt.
Captain.—A. H. Short.
Lieuts.—A. J. Battine.
G. G. Traherne.
C. L. Peacocke.
T. Gilbertson.

2nd Sub Depot, **Woolwich.**
Captain.—J. C. Burnett.
Lieuts.—W. L. Tennant.
F. S. Butcher.
T. H. E. Anderson.

Affiliated Militia Artillery.
—Cornwall & Devon Miners, Devon, Durham, Glamorgan, Northumberland, Carmarthen, Pembroke, Yorkshire, and Cardigan.

REGIMENTAL DISTRICT STAFF,
Woolwich.
Lt. Colonel.—E. T. Browell.
Major.—L. E. Coker.
Captains.—F. J. S. Cleeve.
R. Price.
Lieuts.—J. Christian.
W. Robson.
Qr. Mr.—*Capt.* A. Seath.

ST. HELENA & SIERRA LEONE DETACHMENTS.
St. Helena.—*Capt.* B. M. Bateman. *Lieut.* C. C. Palmer.
Sierra Leone (Devonport).—*Capt.* A. L. Molesworth.
Lieut. W. C. Curme.

District Officers. [Horse Guards.

Years' Ser. F.P.	H.P.	MAJORS.	APPD. DIST. OFFICER.	LIEUT.	CAPTAIN.	BT. MAJOR.	MAJOR.
19	...	Thos. Duncan Richey,[1] *Leith Fort (Qr.Mr.* 1 Apr.76)	1 Aug. 91	25 Aug. 77	10 June 82	......	19 May 89
18	...	Bolden Dundas Porterfield, *Tynemouth*	1 Aug. 91	25 Aug. 77	16 Sept. 82	......	22 June 91
18	...	Alexander John Lindsay, *Rl. Magazine Fort, Dublin*	1 Aug. 91	24 Nov. 77	10 Jan. 86	......	1 Apr. 94
		CAPTAINS.					
15	...	Edward Aldridge,[8] *Portsmouth*	1 Aug. 91	14 Apr. 80	19 May 89		
13	...	George Webster, *Malta*	1 Aug. 91	9 Sept. 82	24 May 89		
12	...	Edward Dawson, *Tower of London*	1 Aug. 91	12 May 83	9 Mar. 91		
12	...	Henry William Albert Collins,[10] *Adjutant* 5 *Lancashire Volunteer Artillery* 10 Mar. 87	1 Aug. 91	20 June 83	9 Mar. 91		
11	...	Henry Bowman,[11] *Adj.* 1 *Monmouth Vol. Art.* 15 July 90	1 Aug. 91	2 July 84	9 Mar. 91		
11	...	Walter Osborne, *Harwich*	1 Aug. 91	18 Mar. 85	9 Mar. 91		
10	...	Arthur Bruce Chamberlin, *Adjutant* 2nd *Kent Volunteer Artillery* 20 July 93	1 Aug. 91	10 June 85	14 Apr. 91		
10	...	William Phillips, *Adjutant* 1 *Shropshire and Stafford Volunteer Artillery* 18 Nov. 89	1 Aug. 91	19 Sept. 85	2 Sept. 91		
10	...	Edward Turner, *Adj. Carmarthen Artillery (W. Div.)* 1 Oct. 92	1 Aug. 91	19 Sept. 85	2 Sept. 91		
10	...	Richard Price, *Woolwich*	1 Aug. 91	7 Nov. 85	2 Sept. 91		
10	...	Henry Orchard, *Chatham*	1 Aug. 91	7 Nov. 85	2 Sept. 91		
9	...	William Pickup, *Adj.* 9 *Lancashire Vol. Art.* 1 July 89	1 Aug. 91	7 Apr. 86	23 Aug. 92		
9	...	William Henry Popplestone, *Falmouth*	1 Aug. 91	14 Apr. 86	23 Aug. 92		
		Inspectors of Ordnance Machinery.					
11	...	Frederick Lane, *Portsmouth (Qr.Mr.* 24 Jan. 85)	1 Aug. 91	......	1 Aug. 91		
11	...	Robert Leaver Clark, *Devonport (Qr.Mr.* 24 Jan. 85)	1 Aug. 91	......	1 Aug. 91		
9	...	Wm. Edwd. Donohue, *Barrackpore (Qr.Mr.* 14 Apr. 86)	1 Aug. 91	......	1 Aug. 91		
		LIEUTENANTS.					
9	...	John Henry Chinn, *Adjutant Highland Volunteer Artillery, with rank of Captain,* 20 Nov. 91	1 Aug. 91	14 Aug. 86			
9	...	Geo. Arthur Cecil Digby Wingfield, *Gt. Yarmouth*	1 Aug. 91	14 Aug. 86			
9	...	John Russell, *Adjutant* 1 *Cumberland Vol. Art. with rank of Captain,* 1 Sept. 91	1 Aug. 91	8 Sept. 86			
8	...	Robert Montgomery Laird,[12] *Adj.* 1 *Northumberland Vol. Art. with rank of Captain,* 1 June 90	1 Aug. 91	20 July 87			
7	...	William Paine Furner, *Cork*	1 Aug. 91	12 May 88			
7	...	Thomas Young Osmond,[13] *Paull Point*	1 Aug. 91	12 May 88			
6	...	Albert Bayspoole,[14] *Adjutant* 1 *Aberdeenshire Vol. Artillery, with rank of Captain,* 20 June 94	1 Aug. 91	24 Apr. 89			
6	...	William Parker, *Adjutant Alderney Art. with rank of Captain,* 2 Apr. 90	1 Aug. 91	24 Apr. 89			
6	...	Michael J. Long, *Adjutant* 8 *Lancashire Volunteer Artillery, with rank of Captain,* 1 Apr. 90	1 Aug. 91	24 Apr. 89			
6	...	James Richard France Lightowlers, *Cape*	1 Aug. 91	10 Aug. 89			
6	...	Robert Wark,[15] *Adjutant* 2 *Lancashire Volunteer Artillery, with rank of Captain,* 12 Mar. 90	1 Aug. 91	10 Aug. 89			
6	...	Archibald M'Gill, *Leith*	1 Aug. 91	9 Oct. 89			
6	...	Joseph Henry Bell Johnston,[16] *Adj.* 2 *Durham Vol. Art. with rank of Captain,* 1 Feb. 94	1 Aug. 91	4 Dec. 89			
5	...	Sidney Thomas Smith, *Ceylon.* Ordered home	1 Aug. 91	30 Apr. 90			
5	...	Francis Chevalley,[18] *Adj.* 1 *Forfar Vol. Art. with rank of Captain,* 16 Feb. 94	1 Aug. 91	30 Apr. 90			
5	...	John Christian, *Woolwich*	1 Aug. 91	2 Aug. 90			
5	...	William Robson,[19] *Woolwich*	1 Aug. 91	2 Aug. 90			
5	...	William Joseph Beardsley,[20] *Weston-Super-Mare*	1 Aug. 91	27 Aug. 90			
5	...	Richard Saunders, *Seaforth*	1 Aug. 91	8 Oct. 90			
4	...	George Clark, *Halifax, N.S.*	1 Aug. 91	25 July 91			
4	...	William Richard Arnold, *Adjutant* 1 *Banff Volunteer Artillery, with rank of Captain,* 15 Aug. 93	1 Aug. 91	25 July 91			
4	...	Henry George William Jennison, *Devonport*	27 Jan. 92	27 Jan. 92			
4	...	Thomas Lacey, *Pembroke Dock*	27 Jan. 92	27 Jan. 92			
4	...	Thomas Gilbertson, *Sunderland*	20 Feb. 92	20 Feb. 92			
3	...	George Neal, *Adjutant,* 6 *Lancashire Vol. Artillery with rank of Captain,* 1 May 93	10 Aug. 92	10 Aug. 92			
2	...	Robert Clarke, *Newhaven*	14 Dec. 92	14 Dec. 92			
2	...	John Rowley,[21] *Adjutant Rangoon Volunteer Artillery, with rank of Captain,* 10 Nov. 93	19 Aug. 93	19 Aug. 93			
2	...	Andrew Renton Malcolm, *Portsmouth*	19 Aug. 93	19 Aug. 93			
2	...	Thomas Henry Edward Anderson, *Woolwich*	3 Feb. 94	3 Feb. 94			
2	...	John Andrews Williams, *Aberdeen*	3 Feb. 94	3 Feb. 94			
2	...	William Campbell Mason,[22] *Gravesend*	17 Feb. 94	17 Feb. 94			
		Inspectors of Ordnance Machinery.					
8	...	Thomas Carlyle, *Chatham (Qr. Mr.* 1 April 87)	1 Aug. 91	1 Aug. 91			
7	...	Richard James Edmonds, *Cork (Qr. Mr.* 25 Apr. 88)	1 Aug. 91	1 Aug. 91			
6	...	Hubert Rudd, *Malta (Qr. Mr.* 31 July 89)	1 Aug. 91	1 Aug. 91			
6	...	Henry Begbey, *Bermuda (Qr. Mr.* 4 Jan. 90)	1 Aug. 91	1 Aug. 91			
6	...	Frederick J. Hunter, *Gibraltar (Qr.Mr.* 15 Jan. 90)	1 Aug. 91	1 Aug. 91			
6	...	Frank Brown, *Ceylon (Qr. Mr.* 19 Mar. 90)	1 Aug. 91	1 Aug. 91			
5	...	Wm. Benjamin Sudds, *Edinburgh (Qr.Mr.* 30 Apr. 90)	1 Aug. 91	1 Aug. 91			
4	...	Denis Paul, *Singapore*	11 Nov. 91	11 Nov. 91			
4	...	George Milnes, *Bombay*	11 Nov. 91	11 Nov. 91			
4	...	Oscar Brown, *Kurrachee*	11 Nov. 91	11 Nov. 91			
4	...	William Lawrence Imrie, *Aden*	11 Nov. 91	11 Nov. 91			
4	...	Henry James Shipman, *St. Lucia*	11 Nov. 91	11 Nov. 91			
4	...	Frederick William Alexander Brown, *Cape*	11 Nov. 91	11 Nov. 91			
3	...	John Richard Collacott, *Jamaica*	18 May 92	18 May 92			
3	...	Edward Heaton Robinson, *Harwich*	18 May 92	18 May 92			
3	...	Charles Wallace Everett, *Halifax, N.S.*	4 Mar. 93	4 Mar. 93			
3	...	John James Truscott, *Tynemouth*	4 Mar. 93	4 Mar. 93			
3	...	John Grute, *Dover*	4 Mar. 93	4 Mar. 93			
3	...	Percy George Davies, *Hong Kong*	4 Mar. 93	4 Mar. 93			
3	...	Henry Alfred Marshall, *Rangoon*	4 Mar. 93	4 Mar. 93			
2	...	Arthur John Last, *Mauritius*	6 May 93	6 May 93			

[10] Captain Collins served with the Jowaki Afreedee Expedition in 1877-78 (Medal with Clasp). Served in the Afghan war of 1878-79, and was present at the attack and capture of Ali Musjid (Medal with Clasp).

[11] Captain Bowman served in the Egyptian war of 1882, and was present at the battle of Tel-el-Kebir (mentioned in despatches, Medal with Clasp, and Khedive's Star).

[12] Captain Laird served in the Egyptian war in 1882, and was present in the action at Kassasin on the 9th September—severely wounded (mentioned in despatches, Medal, and Khedive's Star).

[13] Lieut. Osmond served in the Egyptian war of 1882, and was present at the battle of Tel-el-Kebir (Medal with Clasp, and Khedive's Star).

[14] Lieut. Bayspoole served in the Egyptian war of 1882 (Medal, and Khedive's Star).

War Services of District Officers.

¹ Major Richey served in the second phase of the Ashanti war in 1874 (Medal).
² Captain Aldridge served in the Eastern campaign in 1854-56, and was present at the siege of Sebastopol (Medal with Clasp, and Turkish Medal). Served in the Indian Mutiny campaign in 1858 (Medal).
¹⁵ Lieut. Wark served in the Afghan war of 1878-80 (Medal).
¹⁶ Captain Johnston served throughout the Afghan war of 1878-80 with the Royal Horse Artillery, and was present at the capture of the Peiwar Kotal, in the engagement at Charasiab on the 6th October 1879, and in the operations around Cabul in December 1879 including the engagement at Killa Khazi and the investment of Sherpore (Medal with three Clasps).
¹⁸ Lieut. Chevalley served in the Afghan war of 1878-80 (Medal).
¹⁹ Lieut. Robson served throughout the Afghan war of 1878-80, and was present in the engagements at Saif-u-deen, Ahmed Kheyl, and Urzoo near Ghuznee (Medal with Clasp). Served in the Soudan campaign in 1885, and was present in the engagement at Hasheen (Medal with Clasp, and Khedive's Star).
²⁰ Lieut. Beardsley served in the Egyptian war of 1882 (mentioned in despatches, Medal with Clasp, and Khedive's Star).
²¹ Captain Rowley served in the Afghan war in 1879-80, and was present at the assault of Zawa (Medal). Served with the Mahsood Wuzeeree Expedition in 1881. Served in the Egyptian war of 1882, and was present at the battle of Tel-el-Kebir (Medal with Clasp).
²² Lieut. Mason served in the Zulu war in 1879, and took part in the pursuit of King Cetewayo (Medal).

Royal Malta Artillery.

The Royal Cypher and a Maltese Cross. "EGYPT, 1882."

LT. COLONELS.—*Joseph Speranza, 14 Feb. 91.

MAJORS.

*Paolo Bernard, 10 Nov. 85.
*Antonio Gatt, 14 Feb. 91.

*Alfred Cavarra,¹ 18 Feb. 91
*Alexander Mattei,³ 12 Oct. 92.

CAPTAINS.   [Woolwich.

*Charles Trapani,⁵ 10 Nov. 85.
*Alfred Trapani,³ 10 Nov. 85
*Achilles F. P. M. J. A. F. X. Samut, 17 Dec. 90, Ordnance Store Department.

*Achilles Baron Carbonaro, 17 Dec. 90, Long Course,
*Rinaldo Briffa, 13 Feb. 91.
*Alfred Vella,⁸ 12 Oct. 92.
*William Savona, 12 Oct. 92 (Adjutant 14 Feb. 91).

LIEUTENANTS.

*George Dallas Enriquez, 14 Jan. 85.
*Edward Savona, 20 Oct. 86.
*Henry Alexander Balbi, 14 Feb. 91.
*Louis Monreal, 23 Sept. 91.

*Walter Dunbar Vella, 12 Oct. 92.
*Joseph Francis Bernard, 15 July 94.
*Alfred William Ganado, 15 July 94.

SECOND LIEUTENANTS.

*Arthur Vella, 16 Nov. 92.

Adjutant.—*Captain W. Savona, 14 Feb. 91.
Quarter Master.—*Carmelo Grech, 5 March 84; Hon. Captain, 5 March 94.
Medical Officer.—*Surgeon Major Lorenzo Manchè, MD. 27 Feb. 75.
Blue—Facings Scarlet.

¹ Major Cavarra served in the Egyptian war of 1882 (Medal, and Khedive's Star).
³ Major Mattei and Captain A. Trapani served in the Egyptian war of 1882 (Medal, and Khedive's Star).
⁵ Captain C. Trapani served in the Egyptian war of 1882 with the Commissariat and Transport Staff (Medal, and Khedive's Star).
⁸ Captain Vella served in the Soudan campaign in 1885 as Transport Officer (Medal with Clasp, and Khedive's Star).

War Services of the Officers of the Royal Artillery.

¹ The Duke of Cambridge commanded the 1st Division of the Eastern Army throughout the campaign of 1854, including the battles of the Alma, Balaklava, and Inkerman, and siege of Sebastopol (mentioned in despatches, received the thanks of the House of Commons, Medal with four Clasps, and Turkish Medal).
³ Sir Collingwood Dickson served on the staff of Lord Raglan during the Eastern campaign of 1854-55, and was present at the affairs of Bulganac and M'Kenzie's Farm, the battles of Alma and Inkerman, capture of Balaklava, expedition to Kertch, and siege of Sebastopol (wounded 4th Feb. 1855); commanded the right siege train, and was present at the bombardments of 17th October, 9th April, and 17th June (Medal with four Clasps, C.B., Aide de Camp to the Queen and Colonel, Victoria Cross, Officer of the Legion of Honor, 2nd Class of the Medjidie, and Turkish Medal): was awarded the VC "for having, on the 17th October 1854, when the batteries of the Right Attack had run short of powder, displayed the greatest coolness and contempt of danger in directing the unloading of several waggons of the field battery which were brought up to the trenches to supply the want, and having personally assisted in carrying the powder barrels under a severe fire from the enemy." He is also a Knight of Charles the Third. 1st Class St. Fernando, and Knight of Isabella the Catholic.
⁴ Sir James William Fitzmayer served the Eastern campaign of 1854-55, including the affairs of Bulganac and M'Kenzie's Farm, battles of Alma and Inkerman, siege and fall of Sebastopol, and repulse of the sortie on the 26th

October 1854; was complimented on parade by Sir De Lacy Evans for his manner in bringing the Artillery at the Alma under "the hottest fire," and was again thanked by Sir De Lacy, and twice mentioned in his despatch on the repulse of the sortie on 26th October 1854 (Medal with three Clasps, *CB.*, Officer of the Legion of Honor, 4th Class of the Medjidie, and Turkish Medal).

⁵ General Askwith while attached to the British Embassy in Spain in 1838-39, was attached to the Spanish Army during the Carlist War. The decorations of 1st Class St. Fernando, Commander Isabella the Catholic, and Knight of Charles the Third have been conferred on him.

⁶ Sir Charles D'Aguilar served the Crimean campaign from September 1854 to March 1855, including the battle of Inkerman (horse shot) and siege of Sebastopol, in the Trenches with the siege train, and at the bombardment of 17th October (Medal with two Clasps, *CB.*, 5th Class of the Medjidie, and Turkish Medal). Served the Indian campaign of 1857-58, and commanded the Artillery of General Franks' Force at the action of Secundra, also commanded the Royal Horse Artillery at the siege and capture of Lucknow (three times mentioned in despatches, Brevet of Colonel, Medal with Clasp).

⁷ Sir John Miller Adye served the Eastern campaign of 1854-55 as Assist.Adjt.General of Royal Artillery, and was present at the affairs of Bulganac and M'Kenzie's Farm, the battles of Alma, Balaklava, and Inkerman, capture of Balaklava Castle, siege and fall of Sebastopol (Medal with four Clasps, *CB.*, Commander of the Legion of Honor, 4th Class of the Medjidie, and Turkish Medal). Served in India in 1857-58 as Assist.Adjt.General of Royal Artillery, and was present at the action of Pandoo Nuddee 26th Nov., operations before Cawnpore under General Windham, 27th 28th and 29th Nov., battle of Cawnpore and defeat of the Gwalior Contingent 6th Dec. 1857 (three times mentioned in despatches, Medal). Employed on special service with the expedition of 1863 against the tribes on the North-West Frontier of India, and was present at the storm of Laloo, capture of Umbeylah, and destruction of Mulkah (Medal with Clasp). Served as Chief of the Staff in the Egyptian war of 1882, with the rank of General, and was present at the engagements of Tel-el-Mahuta, Kassasin (9th Sept.), and in the battle of Tel-el-Kebir (twice mentioned in despatches, received the thanks of both Houses of Parliament, *GCB.*, Medal with Clasp, Grand Cross of the Medjidie, and Khedive's Star).

⁸ General H. L. Gardiner served in the operations at Prescott in Upper Canada in 1838. Also in the pursuit of Tantia Topee in Central India in 1858.

⁹ Sir Michael Biddulph served throughout the Eastern campaign of 1854-55, including the battles of Alma, Balaklava, and Inkerman, and siege and fall of Sebastopol; served as an Assistant Engineer in the trenches and as Director General of Submarine Telegraphs in the Black Sea (mentioned in despatches, Brevets of Major and Lt.Colonel, Medal with four Clasps, Knight of the Legion of Honor, 5th Class of the Medjidie, and Turkish Medal). During the Afghan war in 1878-79 he commanded the Quetta Field Force and the 2nd Division of the Candahar Field Force, and was present at the occupation of Candahar and in the engagement at Khushk-i-Nakhud; afterwards commanded the Thull Chotiali Field Force (mentioned in despatches, received the thanks of both Houses of Parliament, *KCB.*, and Medal). [See also Civil Decorations for Gallantry, "Hart's Annual Army List," p. 786.]

¹⁰ General Hon. Sir D. M. Fraser served in the Eastern campaign of 1854, including the battle of Inkerman and siege of Sebastopol (Brevet of Major, Medal with two Clasps, 5th Class of the Medjidie and Turkish Medal). Commanded a Troop of Royal Horse Artillery in the action at Hyderghur 29th Nov. 1858, defeat of a rebel force at Bujeedia, capture of Fort Mujeedia, and action at Bankee (Brevet of Lt.Colonel, Medal, and *CB.*). Served in the Afghan war in 1878-79, and took part in the second expedition to the Bazar Valley under Lieut. General Maude (mentioned in despatches, Medal).

¹¹ General Yates served in the Eastern campaign of 1854, including the affair at M'Kenzie's Farm, battles of Alma and Inkerman, siege of Sebastopol, and repulse of the sortie on the 26th October 1854 (mentioned in despatches, Medal with three Clasps, Brevet of Major, Sardinian and Turkish Medals, and 5th Class of the Medjidie). Served in the Indian campaign of 1857-58, present at the action of Secundra, commanded a troop of Horse Artillery at the siege and capture of Lucknow, and commanded the Artillery at the occupation of Fyzabad and in the action at Sultanpore on the 13th August 1858, and was present at several minor affairs throughout the Oude campaign (mentioned in despatches, Brevet of Lt.Colonel, Medal with Clasp, and *CB.*).

¹² Lt.General E. A. Williams commanded the Royal Artillery in New Zealand in 1864-66 during the Waikato, Tauranga and Wanganui campaigns, and was present at Rangiawhia, Haerini, Gate Pah, Nukumaru, and several minor affairs (twice mentioned in despatches, *CB.*, and Medal).

¹³ Lt.General G. V. Johnson served in the Crimean campaign of 1854-55, including the siege and fall of Sebastopol (Medal with Clasp, 5th Class of the Medjidie, and Turkish Medal).

¹⁴ General Pipon served in the Eastern campaign of 1854-55, including the affairs of Bulganac and M'Kenzie's Farm, the Battles of Alma and Balaklava, siege and fall of Sebastopol (Medal with three Clasps, Brevet of Major, Sardinian and Turkish Medals, and 5th Class of the Medjidie).

¹⁵ Sir Charles George Arbuthnot served in the Crimean war from May 1855, including the siege and fall of Sebastopol, in the Trenches with the siege train, and at the bombardment of 6th and 17th June—twice wounded (mentioned in despatches, Brevet of Major, Medal with Clasp, 5th Class of the Medjidie, and Turkish Medal). Served in the Afghan war of 1878-80, and commanded the expedition against the Wuzceree Khuginnis. Also commanded a Moveable Column in the operations in the Hissarik and Lughman Valleys (mentioned in despatches, *KCB.*, and Medal). Served with the Burmese Expedition in 1887 in chief command of the forces (received the thanks of the Government of India, mentioned in despatches, Medal with Clasp).

¹⁶ General F. W. Hastings served in the Crimean campaign from May 1855, including the siege and fall of Sebastopol, in the Trenches with the siege train, and at the bombardments of 6th and 17th June (Brevet of Major, Medal with Clasp, 5th Class of the Medjidie, and Turkish Medal).

¹⁷ Sir Henry Smyth served in the Crimean campaign from June 1855, including the siege and fall of Sebastopol (Medal with Clasp, and Turkish Medal).

¹⁸ Sir Robert Biddulph served throughout the Eastern campaign of 1854-55, including the battles of Alma and Balaklava, siege and fall of Sebastopol, and expedition to Kertch (Medal with three Clasps, Turkish Medal, and 5th Class of the Medjidie). Served in the Indian campaign of 1857-58, including the action of Kaleo Nuddee, siege and capture of Lucknow (as D.A.Q.M.General of Artillery), action of Jamo (as Brigade Major to the Field Force), and affair of Daoodpoore. Served as D.A.Adjutant General of the Oude Force under Sir Hope Grant from Oct. 1858 and was present in the operations in the Byswarra district, passage of the Gogra, and various actions on the Nepaul frontier, also operations there in 1859 terminating in the forcing of the Jerwah Pass (several times mentioned in despatches, Medal with Clasp). Served as Military Secretary with the expedition to China in 1860, and was present at Sinho, Tangku, capture of Taku Forts, actions near Tangchow, and surrender of Pekin (Brevet of Major, Medal with two Clasps). Was promoted Brevet Lt.Colonel for services in India.

¹⁹ Sir Henry Brackenbury served in India in 1857-58, and was present at the action of Banda and capture of Kirwee (Medal with Clasp). In the Franco-German war of 1870-71 was attached by the Government to the service of the British National Society for Aid to the Sick and Wounded, and was present with the armies till the conclusion of the Armistice. For his services in this capacity he was appointed Officer of the Legion of Honor by special decree of the French Government of National Defence, was made a Knight of the First Class of the Royal Bavarian Order of St. Michael, and received the Iron Cross from the Emperor of Germany. Accompanied Sir Garnet Wolseley to the Gold Coast in September 1873 as Assistant Military Secretary, and served throughout the Ashanti war of 1873-74, including the action of Essamen, relief of Abrakrampa, battle of Amoaful, battle of Ordahsu and capture of Coomassie (mentioned in despatches, Brevet of Major, Medal with Clasp). In 1875 was further rewarded with the Brevet of Lt.Colonel on return from special service with Sir Garnet Wolseley in Natal. Served as Military Secretary to Sir Garnet Wolseley in the latter part of the Zulu war, and throughout the operations against Sekukuni in 1879, being present at the storming of the stronghold. Performed the duties of Chief of the Staff in South Africa from the 29th Sept. 1879 to the 7th Feb. 1880 (mentioned in despatches, *CB.*, Medal with Clasp). Served in the Soudan campaign in 1885 under Lord Wolseley as Deputy Adjutant and Quarter Master General, and was present in the engagement at Kirbekan (mentioned in despatches); after the death of Major General Earle he commanded the Nile Column (mentioned in despatches, promoted Major General for distinguished service in the field, Medal with two Clasps, and Khedive's Star).

²⁰ Sir Robert Hay served as Assistant Adjutant General of Artillery with the expedition to China in 1860, and was present at Sinho, Tangku, capture of Taku Forts, actions near Tangchow, and surrender of Pekin (Brevet of Major, Medal with two Clasps).

²¹ Sir W. J. Williams served in the Crimean campaign from May 1855, including the siege and fall of Sebastopol (wounded), in Trenches with siege train, and at bombardments of 6th and 17th June (Brevet of Major, Medal with Clasp, 5th Class of the Medjidie, and Turkish Medal). Served with the Jowaki Afreedee Expedition in 1877-78 in command of the Artillery (mentioned in despatches, Medal with Clasp). Served in the Afghan war in 1878-79, and was present at the attack and capture of Ali Musjid (mentioned in despatches, Medal with Clasp).

²² Lieut.General Goodenough served in the Indian campaign of 1857-58, including the action of Pandoo Nuddee, siege and capture of Lucknow, attack and capture of Fort Birwah—severely wounded (three times mentioned in despatches, Brevet of Major, Medal with Clasp). Served in the Egyptian war of 1882 in command of the Royal Artillery, and was present at the engagements of El Magfar, Tel-el-Mahuta, Kassasin (9th Sept.), and in the battle of Tel-el-Kebir (twice mentioned in despatches, CB., Medal with Clasp, 2nd Class of the Medjidie, and Khedive's Star).

²³ Sir William Stirling served throughout the Eastern campaign of 1854-55, including the affairs of Bulganac and M'Kenzie's Farm, the battles of Alma, Balaklava and Inkerman, the siege and fall of Sebastopol, and repulse of the sortie on the 26th Oct. 1854 (Medal with four Clasps, Knight of the Legion of Honor, and Turkish Medal). Served as Brigade Major of Artillery with Rajpootana Field Force at the capture of Kotah on 30th March 1858 (Medal, and Brevet of Major). Served with the expedition to China in 1860, and was present at Sinho, actions near Tangchow, and surrender of Pekin (Medal with Clasp). Served in the Afghan war in 1878-79, and was present at the capture of the Peiwar Kotal (CB., and Medal with Clasp).

²⁵ Major General Forster served as Aide de Camp to Major General Pratt during the New Zealand war of 1860-61 (mentioned in despatches, Brevet of Major, and Medal).

²⁶ Major General King served the Eastern campaign of 1854-55, including the affairs of Bulganac and M'Kenzie's Farm, battles of Alma, Balaklava, and Inkerman, siege and fall of Sebastopol, repulse of the sortie on the 26th Oct. 1854, and was Aide de Camp to General Markham at the final assault of the Redan on the 8th September (mentioned in despatches, Medal with four Clasps, Knight of the Legion of Honor, 5th Class of the Medjidie, and Turkish Medal).

²⁷ Lieut.General Markham served the Eastern campaign of 1854, and up to January 1855, including the affair of M'Kenzie's Farm, battles of Alma and Inkerman, siege of Sebastopol, and repulse of the sortie on the 26th Oct. 1854 (Medal with three Clasps, Knight of the Legion of Honor, and Turkish Medal). Served in India in 1858, and was present at the action of Secundra on 23rd Jan. (Medal).

²⁸ Major General Smart served in India in 1857-58, and was present at the actions of Chanda and Sultanpore siege and capture of Lucknow, actions of Barree, Sirsee, and Nawabgunge (twice mentioned in despatches, Medal with Clasp).

³⁰ Major General H. Le G. Geary served in the Crimean campaign from May 1855, in the Trenches with the siege train at the siege and fall of Sebastopol, and bombardments of the 6th and 17th June and 17th August (Medal with Clasp, 5th Class of the Medjidie, and Turkish Medal). Served in the field during the Indian mutiny from October 1858 to 1859 in the Jugdespore district, and with Sir Hope Grant's and Gorruckpore Field Forces. Served throughout the Abyssinian campaign from 1st January 1868 as Brigade Major of Artillery and was present at the action of Arogee and capture of Magdala (mentioned in despatches, Brevet of Major, and Medal).

³¹ Sir H. J. Alderson served throughout the Eastern campaign of 1854-55, including the battles of Alma and Inkerman, siege and fall of Sebastopol, in the Trenches with the siege train, and bombardments of 17th October, 9th April, and 6th and 17th June (Medal with three Clasps, Knight of the Legion of Honor, and Turkish Medal).

³² Major General A. Harness served in the Kafir war in 1878-79, and was present in the engagement at the Taba ka Udoda (mentioned in despatches); also served in the Zulu war in 1879, and was present in the engagement at Ulundi (mentioned in despatches, Brevet of Lt. Colonel, CB., and Medal with Clasp).

³³ Major General J. F. Owen served with Wood's Column in the Zulu War of 1879 in command of a Mounted Gatling Battery, and was present in the engagement at Ulundi (mentioned in despatches, Brevet of Lt. Colonel, Medal with Clasp).

³⁴ Major General S. J. Nicholson served in the Soudan campaign in 1885, and was present in the engagements at Hasheen and the Tofrek zereba and at the destruction of Temai (mentioned in despatches, Brevet of Colonel, Medal with two Clasps, and Khedive's Star).

³⁷ Colonel J. B. Richardson was present with three Batteries of Royal Artillery under Colonel M'Crea in the revolution which upset the Emperor Fausti in Hayti in Jan. 1859; landed and protected the Europeans at Port au Prince, and carried off the Emperor, his family and ministers; received the thanks of the English and French Governments.

⁴⁰ Colonel P. F. Gallwey served in the Afghan war in 1878-79 in charge of the field parks of the 1st and 2nd Divisions of the Peshawur Valley Field Force, and took part in the operations against the Zakka Kheyl Afreedees in the Bazar Valley under Lt. General Maude (Medal).

⁴¹ Colonel A. E. Turner served with the Nile Expedition in 1884-85 as Deputy Assistant Adjutant General, Intelligence Department, Head Quarters Staff, and was present in the engagement at Abu Klea (mentioned in despatches, Brevet of Lt. Colonel, Medal with two Clasps, and Khedive's Star).

⁴² Colonel J. R. Slade served throughout the Afghan war of 1878-80, and took part in the Bazar Valley Expedition under Lt.General Maude, and as Adjutant of Royal Artillery with the Peshawur Valley Field Force under Lt.General S. Browne (mentioned in despatches). Afterwards served with the Candahar Field Force, and was present at the affair on the Helmand with the Wali's mutineers, in the engagement at Maiwand (where he commanded the Artillery after the death of Major Blackwood), at the siege of Candahar, and at the battle of Candahar (several times mentioned in despatches, Brevet of Major, CB., Medal with Clasp).

⁴³ Major General F. T. Lloyd served in the Egyptian war of 1882 (Medal, and Khedive's Star); served with the Soudan Expedition under Sir Gerald Graham in 1884 in command of the Royal Artillery, and was present in the engagements at El Teb and Temai (mentioned in despatches, Brevet of Lt.Colonel, two Clasps). Served during the Nile Expedition in 1884-85 as Commandant at Assiout (mentioned in despatches, CB., and Clasp).

⁴⁴ Colonel H. C. Lowes served in the Afghan war in 1878-79 (Medal).

⁴⁵ Colonel Pretyman served throughout the Afghan war of 1878-80; was Aide de Camp to Sir Frederick Roberts from November 1878 to November 1879, and was present at the capture of the Peiwar Kotal and in all the operations in the Koorum and Khost Valleys (mentioned in despatches); took part in the advance on and occupation of Cabul in 1879, and was present in the engagement at Charasiah (mentioned in despatches); was reappointed Aide de Camp Sir Frederick Roberts in March 1880, and accompanied him in the march to Candahar, and was present at the battle of Candahar (mentioned in despatches, Brevets of Major and Lieut.Colonel, Medal with three Clasps, and Bronze Decoration). Served with the Isazai Expedition in 1892 in command of the 1st Brigade.

⁴⁸ Colonel H. M. Moorsom served with the expedition to China in 1860, and was present at Sinho, Tangku, capture of Taku Forts, and surrender of Pekin (Medal with two Clasps).

⁵⁰ Colonel T. M. Hazlerigg served in the Afghan war in 1879 (Brevet of Lt.Colonel, Medal with Clasp).

⁵² Colonel Rothe served in the Afghan war in 1879-80, and was present at the capture of Ali Musjid as Adjutant of Artillery (mentioned in despatches, Medal with Clasp).

⁵⁶ Colonel J. M. Murray served in the Afghan war in 1878-79 (Medal).

⁵⁸ Colonel Noyes served with the Royal Artillery in the Egyptian war of 1882 (Medal, and Khedive's Star).

⁶⁰ Colonel Holley served with the expedition to the Soudan in 1884 under Sir Gerald Graham, and was present in the engagement at Temai (mentioned in despatches, Brevet of Lt.Colonel, Medal with Clasp, and Khedive's Star).

⁶⁷ Lt.Colonel E. R. Elles served with the Looshai Expedition in 1871-72 (Medal with Clasp). Served in the Egyptian war of 1882 as Deputy Assistant Quarter Master General Indian Contingent, and was present at the battle of Tel-el-Kebir (mentioned in despatches, Brevet of Major, Medal with Clasp, 4th Class of the Medjidie, and Khedive's Star). Served with the Hazara Expedition in 1888 as Assistant Quarter Master General (mentioned in despatches, Brevet of Lt. Colonel, Clasp).

⁷² Colonel Stewart served as Adjutant Royal Artillery in the Hazara campaign in 1868 against the tribes on the Black Mountain (mentioned in despatches, Medal). Served in the Afghan war in 1878-79 as Assistant Quarter Master General 2nd Division Candahar Field Force (mentioned in despatches, Brevet of Major, and Medal). Served

with the expedition to the Soudan in 1885 as Assistant Adjutant and Quarter Master General to the Indian Contingent, and was present in the engagements at Hasheen and the Tofrek zereba, and at the destruction of Temai (mentioned in despatches, Brevet of Lt.Colonel, Medal with two Clasps, and Khedive's Star).

74 Colonel A. G. Yeatman-Biggs served against the Taeping rebels at Shanghai in 1862, and was present at the recapture of Kahding. Served as D.A.A. and Q.M.General in the latter part of the Zulu war of 1879, and as Staff Officer to the Lydenburg Column in the operations against Sekukuni, and was present at the storming of the stronghold (Brevet of Major, Medal with Clasp). Served in the Egyptian war of 1882 as Brigade Major of Royal Artillery (mentioned in despatches, Brevet of Lt. Colonel, Medal, 4th Class of the Osmanieh, and Khedive's Star).

76 Colonel J. F. Brough served with the Looshai Expedition in 1871-72 (Medal with Clasp). Also served in the Afghan war in 1878-79 (Medal). Served with the Soudan Frontier Field Force in 1885-86 (Medal, and Khedive's Star).

84 Colonel J. C. Robinson served throughout the Kafir war of 1877-78 in command of the Colonial Artillery, and was present in the engagement at Quintana, and numerous minor affairs, including that at Malan's Mission, the attack on the Kobogaba River, and the expedition to Bomvanaland (mentioned in despatches, Brevet of Major, and Medal with Clasp). Served in the Afghan war in 1879-80, and was present under Major General Sir John Ross in the operations at Shekabad in April 1880. Accompanied Sir Frederick Roberts in the march to Candahar, and commanded a battery of Royal Artillery at the battle of Candahar (mentioned in despatches, Medal with Clasp, and Bronze Decoration).

86 Colonel G. W. M. Turnbull served with the Bikaneer Field Force in 1884-85.

88 Colonel H. Pipon served in the Afghan war in 1879, and was present in the engagement at Charasiab on the 6th October 1879, and in the operations round Cabul in December 1879 including the investment of Sherpore (mentioned in despatches); accompanied Sir Frederick Roberts in the march to Candahar, and was present at the battle of Candahar (mentioned in despatches, Medal with three Clasps, and Bronze Decoration).

89 Colonel J. F. Maurice accompanied Sir Garnet Wolseley to the Gold Coast in September 1873 on special service, and served as his Private Secretary throughout the Ashanti war of 1873-74, including the relief of Abrakrampa, battle of Amoaful, capture and destruction of Becquah (as Staff Officer to Colonel M'Leod), battle of Ordahsu and capture of Coomassie (several times mentioned in despatches, Medal with Clasp). Served as Deputy Assistant Adjutant and Quarter Master General in the operations against Sekukuni in 1879, and was present at the storming of the stronghold—severely wounded (mentioned in despatches, Brevet of Major, Medal with Clasp). Served in the Egyptian war of 1882 as Deputy Assistant Adjutant and Quarter Master General on the Head Quarters Staff, and was present at the engagements of El Magfar, Tel-el-Mahuta, and Kassasin (9th September), and in the battle of Tel-el-Kebir (mentioned in despatches, Brevet of Lt.Colonel, Medal with Clasp, 4th Class of the Osmanieh, and Khedive's Star). Served during the Nile Expedition in 1884-85 as Commandant at Assiout and at Abu Fatmeh (mentioned in despatches, Brevet of Colonel, Clasp).

90 Colonel T. R. Disney served throughout the Abyssinian campaign from the 6th Feb. 1868, and was present at the fall of Magdala (Medal).

91 Lt.Colonel W. S. Langley served throughout the Abyssinian campaign from the 13th Dec. 1867 as Adjutant to Lt.Colonel Wallace, and was present at the fall of Magdala (Medal). He served as Staff Officer of a column under Colonel Wallace at various periods during the advance on Magdala; as Acting Brigade Major of the Brigade under Brigadier Wilby, after the capture of Magdala, during the illness of the Brigade Major; was appointed Staff Officer of the 3rd column on the commencement of the march down country, and served as such and as Assistant Quarter Master General till it was broken up previous to embarkation.

94 Lt.Colonel W. F. de H. Curtis served with a Steel Mountain Battery throughout the Abyssinian campaign from the 1st Jan. 1868 and was present at the capture of Magdala (Medal).

95 Lt.Colonel J. C. Dalton served in the Afghan war in 1880 with the force under Major General Phayre in Southern Afghanistan (Medal).

98 Lt.Colonel A. J. Pearson served in the Hazara campaign in 1868 (Medal with Clasp). Also served in the Afghan war in 1878-79 (Medal). Served in the Soudan campaign in 1885 as Deputy Assistant Adjutant and Quarter Master General for Intelligence duties with the Indian Contingent, and was present in the engagement at the Tofrek zereba (Medal with two Clasps, and Khedive's Star).

103 Colonel J. Keith served in the Afghan war in 1878-79 (Medal). Served with the Sikkim Expedition in 1888 in command of Royal Artillery (mentioned in despatches, Medal with Clasp); with the Hazara Expedition in 1891 in command of Royal Artillery (mentioned in despatches, DSO, and Clasp); and with the Isazai Expedition in 1892 in command of the Artillery.

109 Lt.Colonel H. R. L. Morgan served with the Jowaki Afreedee Expedition in 1877 (Medal with Clasp). Served in the Afghan war of 1878-80, and was present at the attack on the Shutargardan, in the operations round Cabul in December 1879 including the storming of the Asmai Heights (mentioned in despatches) and the investment of Sherpore, and with the expedition to the Hissarik Valley (Brevet of Major, Medal with Clasp). Also served with the Mahsood Wuzeeree Expedition in 1881. Served with the Hazara Expedition in 1888 (Brevet of Lt.Colonel, Clasp). Served with the Zhob Field Force under Sir George White in 1890 in command of No. 7 Mountain Battery (mentioned in despatches). Served with the Hazara Expedition in 1891 in command of No. 1 Mountain Battery, Royal Artillery (mentioned in despatches, Clasp).

121 Lt.Colonel R. Corbett served in the Afghan war of 1878-80, and was present at the attack and capture of Ali Musjid and in the engagement at Ahmed Kheyl—dangerously wounded (mentioned in despatches, Brevet of Major, Medal with two Clasps).

127 Lt.Colonel E. A. Ollivant served with the Bechuanaland Expedition under Sir Charles Warren in 1884-85.

130 Lt.Colonel J. F. Bally served in the Zulu war in 1879 (Medal with Clasp).

133 Lt.Colonel Browell served in the Egyptian war of 1882 (Medal, and Khedive's Star). Served in the Soudan campaign in 1885 as Chief of the Signalling Department (mentioned in despatches, Clasp).

134 Lt.Colonels E. Lake and R. H. W. Plunkett, Majors G. R. Moore, E. B. Coke, C. J. Long, J. W. H. Potts, J. M'Donnell, T. V. W. Phillips, F. R. Thackeray and J. O. Marston, and Captain F. B. Jackson served in the Afghan war in 1879-80 (Medal).

139 Lt.Colonel J. M. Tabor served in the Egyptian war of 1882, and was present at the battle of Tel-el-Kebir (Medal with Clasp, and Khedive's Star).

140 Lt.Colonel Siddons served with the Burmese Expedition in 1885-89 including the operations of the 3rd Brigade under Brigadier Generals Lockhart and Collett (Medal with two Clasps).

142 Lt.Colonel Blaksley served in the Afghan war in 1879-80, and took part in the march to Candahar with the force under Major General Phayre (mentioned in despatches, Medal).

144 Lt.Colonel A. F. Fletcher served in the Afghan war in 1879-80 (Medal).

145 Lt.Colonel P. K. L. Beaver served in the Afghan war of 1878-80 (mentioned in despatches, Medal).

146 Lt.Colonel A. Broadfoot served with the Bhootan Expedition in 1865 (Medal with Clasp). Served in the Abyssinian campaign from February 1868 (Medal). Served in the Afghan war in 1879-80, and was present at the attack and capture of Ali Musjid, in the engagement at Charasiab on the 6th October 1879, in the advance to Cabul under Brigadier General Gough (twice mentioned in despatches), and in the engagement at Shekabad (mentioned in despatches, Brevet of Major, Medal with three Clasps). Also served with the Mahsood Wuzeeree Expedition in 1881. Served with the Burmese Expedition in 1885-86 (Clasp).

150 Colonel W. Hunter served with the Nile Expedition in 1884-85, and was present in the engagement at Abu Klea on the 16th and 17th February 1885 (mentioned in despatches, Brevet of Lt.Colonel, Medal with Clasp, and Khedive's Star).

157 Lt.Colonel J. J. Congdon served in the Soudan campaign in 1885, and was present at the destruction of Temai (mentioned in despatches, Medal with Clasp, and Khedive's Star).

161 Major J. P. Freeth served in the Afghan war in 1879-80, and was present in the operations round Cabul in December 1879 including the investment of Sherpore (Medal with Clasp).

163 Lt.Colonel H. H. Crookenden served in the Zulu war of 1879, and was present in the engagement at Ulundi (Medal with Clasp).

164 Lt.Colonel J. R. S. O. Hewitt served with the Burmese Expedition in 1885-86 (Medal with Clasp).

165 Lt.Colonel N. Powlett, Majors J. Leach, G. D. Fanshawe, F. M. Banister, H. G. Weir, P. Saltmarshe, E. H. Pickwoad, F. L. Cunliffe, E. C. F. Holland, and F. G. Stone served in the Afghan war in 1878-79 (Medal).

166 Lt. Colonel A. B. Stopford served in the Afghan war of 1878-80 as a Deputy Assistant Quarter Master General (Medal).
167 Lt. Colonel W. W. M. Smith served in the Afghan war in 1878-79 (Medal).
170 Lt. Colonels S. G. Smyth and J. A. F. Nutt, Majors W. H. Suart, J. M. S. Brunker, M. O. Hopkins, H. G. Piers, and G. G. Simpson, Captains J. S. Minter, S. G. D. Smith, W. St. P. Bunbury, N. S. Ogilvie, and G. Osborn served in the Afghan war in 1880 (Medal).
172 Lt. Colonel G. B. N. Martin served in the Egyptian war of 1882 as Aide de Camp to Brigadier General Goodenough, Commanding Royal Artillery, and was present at the battle of Tel-el-Kebir (mentioned in despatches, Brevet of Major, Medal with Clasp, 4th Class of the Medjidie, and Khedivo's Star). Served with the Nile Expedition in 1884-85 on special duty with the boats, and was present at the action of Kirbekan (two Clasps). Served with the Burmese Expedition in 1886 (Medal with Clasp).
174 Lt. Colonel A. E. Duthy served in the Afghan war in 1879-80, and was present at the attack and capture of Ali Musjid and in the engagement at Nargishai; accompanied Sir Frederick Roberts in the march to Candahar, and was present at the battle of Candahar (mentioned in despatches, Medal with two Clasps, and Bronze Decoration).
176 Lt. Colonel C. M. H. Downing served in Abyssinia from the 29th Dec. 1867 to Feb. 1868 (Medal). Served in the Afghan war in 1878-79 (Medal).
177 Lt. Colonel W. W. Smith served with the Royal Horse Artillery in the Afghan war in 1878-79 (Medal).
179 Lt. Colonel Aitken served in the Afghan war of 1878-80, and was present in the affair at Jhandola (mentioned in despatches, Medal). Also served with the Mahsood Wuzeeree Expedition in 1881. Served with the Burmese Expedition in 1886-87 (mentioned in despatches, Brevet of Lt. Colonel, Medal with Clasp).
182 Lt. Colonel W. G. Knox served throughout the Abyssinian campaign from the 13th Dec. 1867, and was stationed at Addigerat with the two guns there (Medal). Served throughout the second phase of the Ashanti war from the 17th Dec. 1873 with Rait's Artillery, including the capture of Borborassie, battle of Amoaful, battle of Ordahsu and capture of Coomassie (Medal with Clasp). Served in the Afghan war of 1878-79, first as Orderly Officer to the officer commanding Royal Artillery, and afterwards as Adjutant, and was present at the assault and capture of Ali Musjid (Medal with Clasp). Served in the Transvaal in the operations against Sekukuni in 1879, and commanded the artillery in the attack on the stronghold (mentioned in despatches, Brevet of Major, Medal with Clasp).
187 Lt. Colonel Hay served in the Egyptian war of 1882, and was present at the battle of Tel-el-Kebir (mentioned in despatches, Brevet of Major, Medal with Clasp, 4th Class of the Medjidie, and Khedive's Star).
189 Lt. Colonel H. T. S. Yates served with the Burmese Expedition in 1886-87 in command of the Northern Shan Column (mentioned in despatches, Brevet of Lt. Colonel, Medal with Clasp).
191 Lt. Colonel H. T. Curling served in the Kafir war in 1878-79, and in the Zulu war of 1879, including the engagement at Isandhlwana (Medal with Clasp). Served in the Afghan war in 1880 (Medal).
192 Lt. Colonel R. Purdy served in the Jowaki Afreedee Expedition in 1877-78 (Medal with Clasp). Served in the Afghan war of 1878-80, and was present at the attack and capture of Ali Musjid and in the operations round Cabul in December 1879 (Medal with two Clasps).
193 Lt. Colonel W. J. Fowler served in the Kafir war in 1877-78 (Medal with Clasp).
194 Major Blackburn served in the Jowaki Afreedee Expedition in 1876 (Medal with Clasp).
195 Lt. Colonel Lugard served in the Afghan war in 1878-79, and was present in the engagement at Ahmed Kheyl (mentioned in despatches, Brevet of Major, Medal with Clasp). Also served with the Mahsood Wuzeeree Expedition in 1881. Served with the Burmese Expedition in 1886-87 (mentioned in despatches, Medal with Clasp).
197 Lt. Colonel W. M. Campbell served in the Afghan war in 1879-80, and was present during the operations round Cabul in December 1879 (mentioned in despatches, Medal with Clasp). Also served with the Mahsood Wuzeeree Expedition in 1881.
198 Lt. Colonel F. O. B. Foote served in the Afghan war in 1880 (Medal). Served as Deputy Assistant Adjutant and Quarter Master General at the base of operations at Alexandria in the Egyptian war of 1882 (mentioned in despatches, Medal, 4th Class of the Medjidie, and Khedive's Star).
199 Lt. Colonel Bingham served in the Soudan campaign in 1885, and was present in the engagement at Haskeen and at the destruction of Temai (Medal with Clasp, and Khedive's Star).
201 Lt. Colonel E. H. Walker served in the Egyptian war of 1882, and was present at the battle of Tel-el-Kebir (Medal with Clasp, 4th Class of the Medjidie, and Khedive's Star).
202 Major C. M. Western served in the Afghan war in 1878-79 (Medal). Served in the Boer war of 1881.
204 Major W. L. Davidson served in the Zulu war of 1879, and was present in the engagement at Ulundi—slightly wounded (mentioned in despatches, Medal with Clasp). Served in the Afghan war in 1880 (Medal).
205 Major R. H. S. Baker served throughout the Afghan war of 1878-80 with the Royal Horse Artillery, and was present in the engagement at Jugdulluck and in the operations in Besud as Orderly Officer to Brigadier General Doran (Medal). Served in the Egyptian war of 1882 as Adjutant of Royal Artillery, and was present at the battle of Tel-el-Kebir as Adjutant of Corps Artillery (mentioned in despatches, Medal with Clasp, 4th Class of the Medjidie, and Khedivo's Star). Served with the Burmese Expedition in 1885-86 (Medal with Clasp).
206 Lt. Colonel Bigge served in the Zulu war of 1879, and was present in the engagement at Kambula (mentioned in despatches, Medal with Clasp).
210 Major Hepburne served in the expedition against the Jowaki Afreedees in 1877-78 (Medal with Clasp). Served in the Afghan war in 1878-79, and was present at the attack and capture of Ali Musjid and in the engagement at Futtehabad (Medal with Clasp).
211 Major J. W. T. Spencer served in the Boer war of 1881 with the Natal Field Force.
213 Major H. N. Jervois served in the Afghan war of 1878-80, and was present at the attack and capture of the Peiwar Kotal—where he commanded No. 1 Punjab Mountain Battery after the death of the commanding officer at the beginning of the action—in the expedition to the Khost Valley, in the engagement at Mattoon, and with the Zaimusht Expedition including the assault of Zawa (mentioned in despatches, Medal with Clasp).
216 Major Monck-Mason served in Perak with the Indian Column under Brigadier General Ross from November 1875 to February 1876 (Medal with Clasp).
217 Major Eustace served in the Afghan war of 1878-80, first as Adjutant of Royal Artillery in Southern Afghanistan, and afterwards as Aide de Camp to Sir Donald Stewart, Commanding the Forces in Northern Afghanistan (Medal).
219 Major J. V. V. Baker served in the Egyptian war of 1882, and was present at the battle of Tel-el-Kebir (Medal with Clasp, and Khedive's Star).
220 Lt. Colonel J. K. Trotter served with the Bechuanaland Expedition under Sir Charles Warren in 1884-85 in the Intelligence Department and as Commissioner in Stellaland.
224 Major C. C. Rich.—See Civil Decorations for Gallantry, "Hart's Annual Army List," p. 786.
225 Majors J. J. Swinton, F. H. Hall, T. H. J. Woodrow, and R. E. Boothby served in the Afghan war of 1878-80 (Medal).
226 Major N. P. Fowell served in the Afghan war in 1879-80, took part in the defence of Candahar, and was present at the battle of Candahar (Medal with Clasp).
228 Major H. W. Brackenbury served in the Afghan war in 1878-79, and was present at the capture of the Peiwar Kotal and in the engagement at Charasiab on the 6th October 1879 (Medal with two Clasps).
229 Major R. W. P. Robertson served in the Afghan war of 1878-80, and was present in the engagement at Baghao (mentioned in despatches, Medal).
230 Major H. V. Hunt served in the Afghan war in 1878-79 (Medal). [See also Civil Decorations for Gallantry, "Hart's Annual Army List," p. 786.]
232 Major A. N. Rochfort served in the Soudan campaign in 1885 (mentioned in despatches, Brevet of Major, Medal with Clasp, and Khedive's Star).
235 Major Woods served in the Egyptian war of 1882, and was present at the battle of Tel-el-Kebir (Medal with Clasp, and Khedive's Star).
240 Lt. Colonel Dean Pitt served in the Afghan war as Orderly Officer to Brigadier General Phayre from January to August 1879, and subsequently to the battle of Candahar in 1880 with the Royal Horse Artillery (Medal).

243 Major Newbigging served in the Bechuanaland Expedition under Sir Charles Warren in 1884-85 with the Mounted Rifles.

244 Major H. H. Pengree served in the Afghan war in 1879-80 (Medal). Served in the Egyptian war of 1882, and was present at the battle of Tel-el-Kebir (Medal with Clasp, 4th Class of the Medjidie, and Khedive's Star).

246 Major R. A. C. King served in the Afghan war in 1878-79, and was present in the engagement at Baghao (mentioned in despatches, Medal). Served throughout the Hazara Expedition in 1888 including the advance to Thakot and Allai (mentioned in despatches, Medal with Clasp).

247 Major Challenor served in the Afghan war in 1878-79 with the Candahar Column under Sir Donald Stewart (Medal).

248 Major F. A. Bowles served with the Hazara Expedition in 1891 in command of No. 9 Mountain Battery, Royal Artillery (mentioned in despatches, Medal with Clasp); and with the Isazai Field Force in 1892.

249 Major E. C. Waco served with the expedition against the Jowaki Afreedees in 1877-78 (Medal with Clasp). Served in the Afghan war of 1878-80, and was present at the attack and capture of Ali Musjid, with the expedition into the Lughman Valley, and in the advance to Cabul under Brigadier General Charles Gough (Medal with two Clasps). Served with the Burmese Expedition in 1885-87; was in command of the Hazara Mountain Battery until April 1886; was present in the engagement at Nyoungoo-Mingyan, at the surrender of Mandalay, in the expedition to Bhamo (slightly wounded), Mogoung, and against the Kachins on the Chinese Frontier, and in the engagement at Choung Pang (mentioned in despatches, DSO., and Medal with Clasp).

251 Lt. Colonel E. M. Baker served in the Afghan war of 1878-80, and took part in the advance to Candahar and Khelat-i-Ghilzie; accompanied Sir Frederick Roberts in the march to Candahar, and was present at the battle of Candahar (Medal with Clasp, and Bronze Decoration).

252 Colonel Slade served in the latter part of the Kafir war of 1878, and afterwards in the operations against Sekukuni in 1878, including the storming of Tolyana's Stadt. Commanded a division of a field battery, and acted as Ordnance Officer to the Transvaal Field Force throughout the operations. Served throughout the Zulu war of 1879 with Wood's Flying Column, and was present at the engagements of Zungin Nek, Kambula (horse shot), and Ulundi (mentioned in despatches, Medal with Clasp). Served in the Boer war of 1881 as Aide de Camp to Major General Sir Evelyn Wood. Served in the Egyptian war of 1882 as Aide de Camp to Major General Sir Evelyn Wood, Commanding the 4th Brigade (Medal, 4th Class of the Medjidie, and Khedive's Star). Served with the Soudan Expedition under Sir Gerald Graham in 1884 in the Intelligence Department, and was present in the engagements at El Teb and Temai (mentioned in despatches, Brevet of Major, two Clasps). Served with the Nile Expedition in 1884-85 as Deputy Assistant Adjutant General, Intelligence Department, and was present at the action of Kirbekan (mentioned in despatches, Brevet of Lt. Colonel, two Clasps).

253 Major M. W. Saunders served in the Afghan war in 1879-80 (Medal). Served with the Burmese Expedition n 1885-87 (mentioned in despatches, Brevet of Major, Medal with Clasp).

254 Major P. F. P. Hamilton served in the Afghan war of 1878-80, and was present in the engagements at Ahmed Kheyl and Urzoo near Ghuznee (Medal with Clasp).

255 Major H. P. Willcughby served in the Afghan war of 1878-80, first as Commissary of Ordnance 2nd Division Southern Afghanistan Field Force, and afterwards in charge of the Ordnance Field Park, Koorum Valley Field Force (Medal).

256 Major Elwes served in No. 3 Battery, 5th Brigade, with the Indian Column under Brigadier General Ross throughout the operations in Perak in 1875-7 (Medal with Clasp).

257 Major Thring served in the Egyptian war of 1882, and was present at the action at Kassasin on the 9th September, and at the battle of Tel-el-Kebir (Medal with Clasp, and Khedive's Star).

258 Majors S. A. H. Callwell and C. E. Jervois, Captains L. D. Jackson, J. W. Ormiston, F. R. M. deButts, M. S. C. Campbell, F. W. S. Stanton, and E. D. C. Cameron served with the Burmese Expedition in 1886-87 (Medal with Clasp).

259 Colonel Wodehouse served in the Zulu war of 1879, and was present in the engagement at Ulundi (Medal with Clasp). Served with the Royal Horse Artillery in the Afghan war in 1880, and was present in the engagement at Charasiab on the 25th April (mentioned in despatches, Medal). Served in the Soudan Expedition under Sir Gerald Graham in 1884, and was present in the engagements at El Teb and Temai (mentioned in despatches. Brevet of Major, Medal with Clasp, and Khedive's Star). Served in the Nile Expedition in 1884-85 with the Egyptian Army, and was present in the action of Kirbekan (two Clasps); with the Soudan Frontier Field Force in 1885-86 including the engagement at Giniss (mentioned in despatches, Brevet of Lt. Colonel, 3rd Class of the Medjidie); and in the operations on the Soudan frontier in 1889 including the engagements at Arguin and Toski (mentioned in despatches, CB., Clasp, and 2nd Class of the Medjidie). Nominated to the 2nd Class of the Osmanieh for services with the Egyptian Army.

262 Major E. N. Henriques served with a detachment of Royal Artillery in Sungbio Ujong throughout the operations in Perak in 1875-77 (Medal with Clasp).

266 Major Mansel commanded the Artillery with the Naga Expeditionary Force under Brigadier General Nation in 1879-80, and was present at the storming of Konoma (mentioned in despatches, Medal with Clasp). Served in the Mahsood Wuzeeree Expedition in 1881. Served with the Burmese Expedition in 1886-87 with the Shan Column (mentioned in despatches, two Clasps).

267 Major A. H. Howat served in the Afghan war in 1879-80, and was present in the engagement at Ali Boghan (Medal).

268 Major J. D. Cunningham served with the Zhob Valley Expedition in 1884 (mentioned in despatches). Served with the Burmese Expedition in 1885-87 (mentioned in despatches, Medal with Clasp); with the Sikkim Expedition in 1888 (Clasp); with the Miranzai Expedition in 1891 under Sir W. Lockhart, in command of the Artillery of the Force until the arrival of Lt. Colonel de Lautour (mentioned in despatches, Clasp); and with the Isazai Expedition in 1892.

269 Major H. J. Lyster served in the Afghan war of 1878-80, accompanied Sir Frederick Roberts in the march to Candahar, and was present at the battle of Candahar (Medal with Clasp, and Bronze Decoration). Also served with the Mahsood Wuzeeree Expedition in 1881.

270 Major A. M. Murray served in the Afghan war in 1878-79 (mentioned in despatches, Medal).

271 Major J. W. Hawkins served with D Battery A Brigade Royal Horse Artillery in the Afghan war of 1878-80 Medal). Served with No. 7 Screw-gun Mountain Battery 1st Brigade in the Egyptian war of 1882, and was present at the action at Kassasin (9th September) and at the battle of Tel-el-Kebir (Medal with Clasp, and Khedive's Star).

272 Major F. M. Bland served in the Soudan campaign in 1885, and was present in the engagements at Hasheen and the Tofrek zereba and at the destruction of Temai (Medal with two Clasps, and Khedive's Star).

273 Major Pole Penton served in the Afghan war in 1879-80, including the defence of For Battye, mentioned in despatches, Medal).

777 Major O. S. Smyth served in the Afghan war of 1878-80, and was present at the attack and capture of Ali Musjid, with the expedition into the Bazar Valley under Lieut. General Maude (mentioned in despatches), and in the engagement at Jugdulluck; accompanied Sir Frederick Roberts in the march to Candahar, and was present at the battle of Candahar (Medal with two Clasps, and Bronze Decoration). Served with the Burmese Expedition in 1885-86 (mentioned in despatches, DSO., and Medal with Clasp); with the Wuntho Expedition in 1801 in command of the Southern Column (mentioned in despatches, Clasp); and with the Maniporo Expedition in 1891 in command of No. 2 Mountain Battery Royal Artillery (mentioned in despatches, Clasp).

258 Major C. A. Ryan served in the Egyptian war of 1882 (Medal, and Khedive's Star).

279 Major A. H. C. Phillpotts served in the Afghan war in 1880, and took part in the march to Candahar with the force under Major General Phayre (Medal).

280 Major Vaughan Hughes served in the Afghan war in 1878-79, and was present in the engagement at Charasiah on the 6th October 1879, and in the operations round Cabul in December 1879 (Medal with two Clasps). Served in the Egyptian war of 1882, and was present at the battle of Tel-el-Kebir (Medal with Clasp, and Khedive's Star).

281 Major W. F. Cleeve served during the war in 1880 in Southern Afghanistan (Medal).

282 Major E. Gunner served in the Afghan war of 1878-80, and was present in the engagement at Charasiab on the 6th October 1879, and in the operations round Cabul in December 1879 (Medal with two Clasps).

285 Major Shirres served in the Afghan war of 1878-80, and was present at the capture of the Peiwar Kotal, at the forcing of the Sapri Pass, in the engagement at Mattoon, at the assault on the Shutargardan (mentioned in despatches), in the operations around Cabul including the investment of Sherpore, and with the expedition into the Hissarlik Valley (Medal with two Clasps). Also served with the Mahsood Wuzeeree Expedition in 1881. Served with the Akha Expedition in 1883-84 and was present in the engagement at Tanga Pani (mentioned in despatches); and with the Isazai Field Force in 1892.

286 Major H. V. Cowan served in the Afghan war of 1878-80 as Aide de Camp to the General Officer Commanding 3rd Division, and was present at the capture of the Peiwar Kotal, in the engagement at Charasiah on the 6th October 1879, and in the operations round Cabul in December 1879, including the investment of Sherpore and the storming of the Asmai Heights (Medal with three Clasps). Served in the Egyptian war of 1882 as Adjutant Royal Artillery 2nd Division, and was present at the battle of Tel-el-Kebir—severely wounded (mentioned in despatches, Brevet of Major, Medal with Clasp, 5th Class of the Medjidie, and Khedive's Star).

287 Major S. D. Rainsford served in the Afghan war in 1878-79, and was present at the attack and capture of Ali Musjid (Medal with Clasp).

289 Major J. W. M. Newton served in the Afghan war in 1879-80, and took part in the Zaimusht Expedition including the assault of Zawa (Medal).

290 Major Haggard served in the Afghan war in 1878-79 with the Koorum Valley Field Force, and was present at the attack and capture of the Peiwar Kotal, and in the engagement at Charasiab on the 6th October 1879 (Medal with two Clasps). Served with the Burmese Expedition in 1886-87 (mentioned in despatches, Medal with Clasp).

291 Major A. H. Browne served in the Afghan war in 1879-80 (Medal).

292 Major D. E. Dewar served in the Afghan war in 1880 (Medal). Served with the Soudan Frontier Field Force in 1885-86 (Medal, and Khedive's Star).

293 Colonel Creagh served in the latter part of the Zulu war of 1879 as Aide de Camp to Sir Garnet Wolseley, and took part in the pursuit of King Cetywayo. Served in the operations against Sekukuni in 1879, and was present at the capture of the stronghold (mentioned in despatches, Medal with Clasp). Served in the Egyptian war of 1882 as Aide de Camp to Sir Garnet Wolseley, and was present at the engagements of El Magfar, Tel-el-Mahuta, Kassasin (9th September), and in the battle of Tel-el-Kebir (twice mentioned in despatches, Brevet of Major, Medal with Clasp, 5th Class of the Medjidie, and Khedive's Star). Served with the Nile Expedition in 1884-85, and in the Eastern Soudan in 1885 as Aide de Camp to Lord Wolseley (mentioned in despatches, Brevet of Lt.Colonel, two Clasps).

294 Major A. C. Bailward served in the Afghan war in 1878-79, and was present in the operations round Cabul in December 1879, including the investment of Sherpore (Medal with Clasp).

295 Major F. E. A. Hunter and Captain C. E. H. Heyman served in the Egyptian war of 1882, and were present at the battle of Tel-el-Kebir (Medal with Clasp, and Khedive's Star).

296 Major H. A. D. Curtis and E. A. Burrows, Captains L. Forde, G. E. Bryant, L. G. Watkins, A. B. N. Churchill, and A. C. Currie served with the Burmese Expedition in 1885-86 (Medal with Clasp).

297 Major A. Keene served in the Afghan war of 1878-80, and took part in the march to Candahar with the force under Major General Phayre in command of two guns of No. 2 Mountain Battery (mentioned in despatches, Medal). Served with the Burmese Expedition in 1885-86 (mentioned in despatches, DSO., and Medal with Clasp).

298 Major W. A. Plant served in the Afghan war in 1879-80, took part in the defence of Candahar, and was present at the battle of Candahar (Medal with Clasp).

299 Majors Garnett-Botfield and Montgomery Campbell served in the Boer war of 1881.

301 Major C. E. Maberly served with the Nile Expedition in 1884-85 on Transport duty (Medal with Clasp, and Khedive's Star).

303 Captain T. F. T. Fowle served in the Afghan war of 1878-80, took part in the defence of Candahar, and was present at the battle of Candahar (Medal with Clasp).

304 Lt.Colonel Parsons served in the Gaika war of 1877-78, including the operations in the Perie Bush and the affair at Taba Indoda, where he commanded two mountain guns. Served throughout the Zulu war of 1879, and was present in the engagements at Isanhlwana and Ulundi (Medal with Clasp). Served in the Boer war of 1881, and was present in the engagements at Lang's Nek (mentioned in despatches) and the Ingogo River—severely wounded, and horse shot (mentioned in despatches). Served in the Egyptian war of 1882, and was present at the engagement of Tel-el-Mahuta, in the action at Kassasin (9th September), and in the battle of Tel-el-Kebir (mentioned in despatches, Brevet of Major, Medal with Clasp, 5th Class of the Medjidie, and Khedive's Star).

305 Major H. C. C. D. Simpson served with the Burmah Expedition in 1886-87 in command of a Mountain Battery of Royal Artillery (mentioned in despatches, Medal with Clasp).

307 Major H. G. H. Galton served in the Egyptian war of 1882 (Medal, and Khedive's Star).

308 Major E. W. Fleming served in the Afghan war in 1878-79 (Medal).

309 Major Bell-Irving served in the Afghan war of 1878-80, took part in the defence of Candahar, and was present at the battle of Candahar (mentioned in despatches, Medal with Clasp).

310 Major H. C. Sclater served with the Nile Expedition in 1884-85 as Staff Officer at Gemal and afterwards as Deputy Assistant Adjutant General at Head Quarters (mentioned in despatches, Brevet of Major, Medal with Clasp, and Khedive's Star). Also served with the Egyptian Frontier Field Force in 1885-86 as Deputy Assistant Adjutant and Quarter Master General, and was present in the engagement at Giniss.

311 Major O. Rowe served in the Egyptian war of 1882 (Medal, and Khedive's Star).

312 Captain H. M. Aplin served in the Egyptian war of 1882 (Medal, and Khedive's Star).

312† Major W. F. L. Lindsay served in the Egyptian war in 1882, and was present at the battle of Tel-el-Kebir (Medal with Clasp, and Khedive's Star).

313 Major Bannatine Allason served in the Afghan war in 1879-80 including the engagement at Shahjui; was Adjutant of Field Artillery in Southern Afghanistan from August 1879 till January 1880, when he was appointed Adjutant of Artillery; in April 1880 he took part in the advance to Cabul under Sir Donald Stewart as Staff Officer of Artillery, and was present in the engagements at Ahmed Kheyl (mentioned in despatches, and Urzoo near Ghuznee; accompanied Sir Frederick Roberts in the march to Candahar as Orderly Officer to Colonel Johnson, and was present in the reconnaissance on the 31st August and at the battle of Candahar (mentioned in despatches, Medal with two Clasps, and Bronze Decoration). Served in the Soudan campaign in 1885 as Brigade Major Royal Artillery, and was present in the engagements at Hasheen and in the destruction of Temai (mentioned in despatches, Medal with Clasp, and Khedive's Star).

314 Sir G. V. Thomas served in the Afghan war in 1878-79, and took part in the advance to Candahar and Khelat-i-Ghilzie (Medal). Served in the Egyptian war of 1882, and was present at the action at Kassasin on the 9th September, and at the battle of Tel-el-Kebir (Medal with Clasp, and Khedive's Star). Served in the Soudan Expedition under Sir Gerald Graham in 1884, and was present in the engagements at El Teb (horse killed) and Temai (4th Class of the Medjidie, two Clasps).

315 Major J. W. Dunlop served in the Afghan war in 1879-80, and took part in the Zaimusht Expedition (Medal). Served with the Burmese Expedition in 1886-87 (Medal with Clasp).

316 Major Norton served in the Afghan war in 1878-79. Served in the Egyptian war of 1882, and was present at the battle of Tel-el-Kebir (Medal with Clasp, and Khedive's Star). Served with the Nile Expedition in 1884-85, and was present at the actions at Abu Klea and El Gubat, in the reconnaissance to Metamneh, and in the engagement at Abu Klea Wells on the 16th and 17th February (three times mentioned in despatches, Brevet of Major, two Clasps).

318 Major R. L. Haines served in the Afghan war in 1878-79, and was present in the engagement at Ali Kheyl (Medal).

320 Major W. S. Churchward served with the Jowaki Afreedee Expedition in 1877-78 (Medal with Clasp). Served in the Afghan war of 1878-80, and was present at the attack and capture of Ali Musjid and in the engagement at Ahmed Kheyl (Medal with two Clasps). Served in the Egyptian war of 1882, and was present at the battle of Tel-el-Kebir (Medal with Clasp, and Khedive's Star).

322 Major W. A. Smith served in the Afghan war in 1880 (Medal). Served in the Egyptian war of 1882 (mentioned in despatches, Medal, 4th Class of the Medjidie, and Khedive's Star).

323 Major G. H. Bittleston served in the Afghan war in 1880 (Medal).

324 Major E. A. Lambart served in the Afghan war of 1878-80, and was present in the engagements at Ahmed Kheyl and Urzoo near Ghuznee (Medal with Clasp).
324† Major N. B. Inglefield served in the Afghan war in 1878-79 with the Royal Artillery (Medal).
325 Major F. A. Curteis served with the Soudan Frontier Field Force in 1885-86 (Medal, and Khedive's Star).
326 Major F. J. A. Trench served in the Zulu war in 1879, and was present in the engagement at Ulundi (mentioned in despatches, Medal with Clasp).
327 Major C. A. Anderson served with the Jowaki Afreedee Expedition in 1877-78 (Medal with Clasp). Served in the Afghan war of 1878-80, was present at the attack and capture of Ali Musjid, and took part in the advance to Cabul under Brigadier General Gough including the affair at Jugdulluck (mentioned in despatches, Medal with two Clasps). Served with the Burmese Expedition in 1885-86 (Clasp).
328 Major D. C. Carter served with the Soudan Expedition under Sir Gerald Graham in 1884, and was present in the engagements at El Teb and Tomai (Medal with Clasp, and Khedive's Star). Served in the Nile Expedition in 1884-85 with the Egyptian Army, and was present at the action at Kirbekan (two Clasps, 4th Class of the Medjidie).
329 Major L. Barrett served in the Egyptian war of 1882 (Medal, and Khedive's Star).
330 Major W. N. Lloyd served in the Kafir war of 1877-78, and was present during the operations in the Cis-Kei and Perie Bush in command of a division of field guns. Served throughout the Zulu war of 1879, and was present in command of the Royal Artillery of Pearson's Column at the engagement of Inyezane (mentioned in report), and during the investment of Ekowe (mentioned in report); afterwards accompanied the advance of the 1st Division (mentioned in General Crealock's despatch, Medal with Clasp). Served in the Soudan Expedition in 1884 under Sir Gerald Graham with the Cavalry Brigade, and was present in the engagement at El Teb (Medal with Clasp, and Khedive's Star); afterwards presented the Mahdi's standard, taken at Tokar, to Her Majesty the Queen at Windsor. Served with the Burmese Expedition in 1886-87, first as Adjutant to Royal Artillery; afterwards organised and equipped the Gardner Machine Gun Battery and accompanied the Expedition to the Ruby Mines in command of the Royal Artillery (mentioned in despatches, Medal with Clasp).
331 Lt.Colonel A. C. Daniell served in the Afghan war in 1879-80 (Medal).
333 Major W. H. F. Taylor served in the Zulu war in 1879 (Medal with Clasp).
334 Major J. F. Craig served in the Egyptian war of 1882, and was present at the battle of Tel-el-Kebir (Medal with Clasp, and Khedive's Star).
335 Lt.Colonel Adye served in the Afghan war in 1879 with the Koorum Valley Field Force under Major General Roberts (Medal). Served in the Egyptian war of 1882 as Aide de Camp to Sir Garnet Wolseley, and was present at the engagements of El Magfar, Tel-el-Mahuta, Kassasin (9th September), and in the battle of Tel-el-Kebir (mentioned in despatches, Brevet of Major, Medal with Clasp, 5th Class of the Medjidie, and Khedive's Star). Served with the Nile Expedition in 1884-85 and in the Eastern Soudan in 1885 as Aide de Camp to Lord Wolseley, and was present in the engagement at Abu Klea Wells on the 16th and 17th February (mentioned in despatches, Brevet of Lt Colonel, two Clasps).
337 Major W. L. White served in the Soudan campaign in 1885, and was present at the destruction of Temai (Medal with Clasp, and Khedive's Star).
338 Major W. H. O'Neill served in the Egyptian war of 1882, and was present at the battle of Tel-el-Kebir (Medal with Clasp, and Khedive's Star).
340 Major Blacker served in the Afghan war in 1878-79 (Medal).
341 Major A. Eardley Wilmot served with the Mahsood Wuzeeree Expedition in 1881.
342 Major H. B. Gundry served in the Afghan war in 1878-79, and was present at the attack and capture of Ali Musjid (Medal with Clasp).
345 Colonel Rundle served in the Zulu war of 1879 with Wood's Flying Column, and was present with the Gatling Battery in the engagement at Ulundi (mentioned in despatches, Medal with Clasp). Served with the Field Artillery in the Boer war of 1881, and took part in the defence of Potchefstroom (slightly wounded). Served with the Field Artillery in the Egyptian war of 1882, and was present at the battle of Tel-el-Kebir (Medal with Clasp, and Khedive's Star). Served during the Nile Expedition in 1884-85 on special employ with Bedouin Tribes (mentioned in despatches, Brevet of Major, 3rd Class of the Medjidie, Clasp); with the Soudan Frontier Field Force in 1885-87 including the engagements at Giniss (3rd Class of the Osmanieh) and Sarras in command of Mounted Corps as Assistant Adjutant General (mentioned in despatches, DSO.); and in the operations on the Soudan frontier in 1889 including the engagement at Toski (mentioned in despatches, Brevet of Lt.Colonel, Clasp).
346 Major T. W. Powles served in the Egyptian war of 1882, and was present at the battle of Tel-el-Kebir Medal with Clasp, and Khedive's Star).
347 Major H. M. Sandbach served in the Afghan war of 1878-80, and was present in the engagement at Shekabad (mentioned in despatches), in the operations round Cabul in December 1879, and in the engagement at Charasiab on the 25th April 1880 (Medal with Clasp). Served in the Soudan campaign in 1885, and was present in the engagement at Hasheen and at the destruction of Temai (Medal with Clasp, and Khedive's Star).
348 Major R. M. B. F. Kelly served with the second Miranzai Expedition in 1891 in command of a Mountain Battery (Medal with Clasp).
349 Major F. E. Kent served with the Hazara Expedition in 1888 (Medal with Clasp).
351 Major J. J. Porteous served in the Afghan war in 1879-80, and took part in the operations in the Mazeena Valley (Medal).
353 Major C. P. Triscott served in the Afghan war in 1879, and was present in the engagement at Charasiah on the 6th October 1879; accompanied Sir Frederick Roberts in the march to Candahar, and was present at the battle of Candahar (Medal with two Clasps, and Bronze Decoration). Served with the Burmese Expedition in 1885-87 (mentioned in despatches, DSO., and Medal with Clasp).
354 Captains J. S. Douglas and J. H. Thomson served in the Zulu war in 1879 (Medal with Clasp).
356 Captain W. H. Conolly served in the Boer war of 1881 with the Natal Field Force.
357 Major W. C. Anderson served in the Zulu war in 1879 (Medal with Clasp). Served in the Soudan campaign in 1885 as Aide de Camp to Sir Gerald Graham (mentioned in despatches, Brevet of Major, Medal with Clasp).
358 Captain Mercer served in the Afghan war in 1880 in command of two Field Guns at Khelat-i-Ghilzie, including the advance to the relief of Candahar; accompanied Sir Frederick Roberts in the march to Candahar, and was present at the battle of Candahar (Medal with Clasp, and Bronze Decoration). Served with the Burmese Expedition in 1886-87 as Staff Officer to the Lower Burmah Field Force (Medal with Clasp); and afterwards as Adjutant of Artillery Upper Burmah Field Force (mentioned in despatches). Served in the Hazara campaign in 1889, and was present in the engagement at Kotkai and in the subsequent operations with the River Column (mentioned in despatches, Clasp).
360 Captain Jervis-White-Jervis served in the Zulu war in 1879 (Medal with Clasp).
362 Captain H. M. Slater served in the Afghan war in 1879-80, and was present in the engagements at Ahmed Kheyl and Urzoo near Ghuznee (Medal with Clasp).
363 Captain C. T. Robinson served in the Afghan war of 1878-80 with the Khyber Column (Medal).
364 Captain M. F. Fegen served in the Egyptian war of 1882, and was present at the battle of Tel-el-Kebir (Medal with Clasp, and Khedive's Star). Served with the Hazara Expedition in 1891 (Medal with Clasp); and with the Isazai Expedition in 1892.
365 Captain E. B. Anderson served in the Afghan war in 1878-79 (Medal).
367 Captain W. J. A. Beatson served in the Afghan war in 1880 (Medal).
368 Captain A. W. B. Gordon served in the Egyptian war of 1882, and was present at the battle of Tel-el-Kebir (Medal with Clasp, and Khedive's Star).
369 Captain J. M. Grierson served in the Egyptian war of 1882 as Deputy Assistant Quarter Master General Intelligence Branch Indian Contingent, and was present at the action at Kassasin (9th September) and at the battle of Tel-el-Kebir (mentioned in despatches, Medal with Clasp, 5th Class of the Medjidie, and Khedive's Star). Served with the Expedition to the Soudan in 1885 as Deputy Assistant Adjutant and Quarter Master General at Head Quarters, and was present in the engagements at Hasheen and Tomai (mentioned in despatches, Clasp). Served in the expedition to the Black Mountain in 1888 as Deputy Assistant Quarter Master General 2nd Brigade Hazara Field Force (mentioned in despatches, Medal with Clasp).
370 Captain W. J. Honner served in the Afghan war in 1880 (Medal). Served with the Akha Expedition in 1883-84. Served with the Burmese Expedition in 1885-87 in command of the Hazara Mountain Battery from April 1886 (men-

tioned in despatches, Medal with Clasp); with the Hazara Expedition in 1888 in command of the Hazara Mountain Battery (Clasp), and with the first Miranzai Expedition in 1891 in command of the Hazara Mountain Battery (Clasp).

[372] Captain F. B. R. Toms served in the Egyptian war of 1882, and was present at the battle of Tel-el-Kebir (Medal with Clasp, and Khedive's Star).

[373] Captain Phipps Hornby served with the Bechuanaland Expedition under Sir Charles Warren in 1884-85.

[374] Captain M. B. G. Jackson served with the Nile Expedition in 1884-85 (Medal with Clasp, and Khedive's Star); also served in the operations of the Soudan Frontier Field Force in 1885-86, and in those in 1888 including the engagement at Gemaizah (Clasp), and in the operations in 1888 including the engagement at Gemaizah (Clasp).

[378] Captain N. D. Findlay served with the Hazara Expedition in 1888 (mentioned in despatches, Medal with Clasp).

[379] Captain E. A. Fanshawe served in the Afghan war of 1878-80 (Medal). Served in the Soudan campaign in 1885, and was present in the engagements at Hasheen and the Tofrek zereba, at that near Tofrek on the 24th March and at the destruction of Temai (Medal with two Clasps).

[380] Captain C. E. Callwell served with a battery of Royal Artillery in the Afghan war in 1880 (Medal). Served in the Boer war of 1881.

[381] Captain F. H. J. Birch served in the Afghan war in 1879-80, and was present in the affair at Jhandola (mentioned in despatches, Medal). Also served with the Mahsood Wuzeeree Expedition in 1881. Served with the Miranzai Expedition in 1891 in command of No. 3 Peshawur Mountain Battery (mentioned in despatches, Medal with Clasp).

[382] Captain F. B. Lecky served in the Egyptian war in 1882, and was present at the battle of Tel-el-Kebir (Medal with Clasp, and Khedive's Star).

[384] Captain C. B. Watkins served in the Afghan war of 1878-80 and was present in the engagements at Ahmed Kheyl and Urzoo near Ghuznee (Medal with Clasp).

[385] Captain A. ff. Powell served with the Egyptian Frontier Field Force in 1885-86 (Medal, and Khedive's Star).

[386] Captain E. J. Granet served in the Afghan war in 1879-80 (Medal). Served with the expedition to the Soudan under Sir Gerald Graham in 1884, and was present in the engagements at El-Teb and Temai (Medal with Clasp, and Khedive's Star).

[387] Captain G. V. Kemball served in the Afghan war in 1879-80 (Medal).

[388] Captain E. H. Armitage served with the Burmese Expedition in 1886-87 (mentioned in despatches, Medal with Clasp).

[389] Captain A. S. Wedderburn served in the Egyptian war of 1882, and was present at the battle of Tel-el-Kebir —horse shot (Medal with Clasp, and Khedive's Star).

[390] Captain F. E. Cooper served with No. 7 Screw-gun Mountain Battery in the Egyptian war of 1882, and was present at the battle of Tel-el-Kebir (Medal with Clasp, and Khedive's Star).

[391] Captain G. H. M'Laughlin served in the Egyptian war in 1882 (Medal, and Khedive's Star).

[391†] Captain H. J. Du Cane served with the Hazara Expedition in 1888 (mentioned in despatches, Medal with Clasp).

[392] Captain F. F. Minchin served with the Burmese Expedition in 1887-89 with the Upper Burmah Force (Medal with Clasp).

[393] Captain H. A. Inglis served in the Afghan war in 1879-80, accompanied Sir Frederick Roberts in the march to Candahar, and was present at the battle of Candahar (Medal with Clasp, and Bronze Decoration).

[394] Captain G. B. Smith served in the Afghan war in 1879-80, took part in the defence of Candahar and was present at the battle of Candahar (Medal with Clasp). Served with the Zhob Valley Expedition in 1884. Served with the Wuntho Expedition, Burmah, in 1890-91 (Medal with Clasp).

[395] Captain C. V. Hume served with the Burmese Expedition in 1886-87 as Aide de Camp to Sir Frederick Roberts (mentioned in despatches, Medal with Clasp).

[396] Captain P. H. Enthoven served in the Egyptian war of 1882, and was present at the battle of Tel-el-Kebir (Medal with Clasp, and Khedive's Star). Also served in the Soudan campaign in 1885 (Clasp).

[397] Captain H. L. Gardiner served in the Afghan war in 1879-80, took part in the defence of Candahar, and was present at the battle of Candahar (Medal with Clasp).

[397†] Captain H. Chance served with the Burmese Expedition in 1887 (Medal with Clasp).

[398] Captain C. P. Fendall served with the Burmese Expedition in 1885-86, and was present in the engagement at Myadaw on the 2nd December 1885; was Staff Officer to the Eastern Frontier Column and at Taungdwingyi till 16th September 1886 (twice mentioned in despatches, DSO., and Medal with Clasp).

[400] Captains H. C. G. Taylor, Cloeté, G. F. Herbert, and F. A. Randolph served in the Soudan campaign in 1885 (Medal with Clasp, and Khedive's Star).

[401] Captain A. Stokes served in the Boer war of 1881 with the Natal Field Force. Served with the Bechuanaland Expedition under Sir Charles Warren in 1884-85 (mentioned in despatches).

[402] Captain W. Elliot served with the Burmese Expedition in 1886-88 (mentioned in despatches, Medal with Clasp).

[402†] Captain A. M. C. Dale served in the Afghan war in 1879-80 with the Koorum Valley Field Force (Medal). Served with the Burmese Expedition in 1886-87 (Medal with Clasp).

[403] Captain A. L. Tisdall served with the Burmese Expedition in 1886-87 (mentioned in despatches, Medal with Clasp).

[404] Captain G. E. Benson served in the Soudan campaign in 1885, and was present in the engagement at Hasheen (slightly wounded) and at the destruction of Temai (Medal with Clasp, and Khedive's Star).

[405] Captains R. C. O. Stuart and A. D. Young served with the Burmese Expedition in 1885-87 (Medal with Clasp).

[405†] Captain Du Boulay served in the Nile Expedition in 1884-85, and was present at the action at Abu Klea, and in the engagements at Abu Kru, Metammeh, and Abu Klea Wells on the 16th and 17th February (Medal with two Clasps, and Khedive's Star).

[406] Captains Cooper Key, H. T. Hawkins, and R. G. Strange served in the Egyptian war of 1882 (Medal, and Khedive's Star).

[407] Captain F. H. Crampton served in the Soudan campaign in 1885, and was present at the destruction of Temai (Medal with Clasp, and Khedive's Star). Also served with the Egyptian Frontier Field Force in 1885-86, and was present in the engagement at Giniss.

[407†] Captain A. L. Carroll served in the Boer war of 1881 with the Natal Field Force, and was present at the engagement at Lang's Nek.

[408] Captain A. P. Longfield served with the Burmese Expedition in 1885-89 (Medal with two Clasps).

[409] Captain Vorcs served in the Egyptian war of 1882, and was present at the battle of Tel-el-Kebir (Medal with Clasp, and Khedive's Star). Served with the expedition to the Soudan under Sir Gerald Graham in 1884, and was present in the engagement at El Teb (two Clasps). Also served in the Soudan campaign in 1885, and was present in the engagement at Hasheen (Clasp).

[410] Captain G. F. W. St. John served in the Zhob Valley Expedition in 1890, and with the Isazai Field Force in 1892.

[411] Captain C. H. Milward served in the Egyptian war of 1882 with the siege train under Lt. Colonel Minto Elliot (Medal, and Khedive's Star).

[412] Captain C. D. King served in the Egyptian war of 1882, and was present at the battle of Tel-el-Kebir (Medal with Clasp, and Khedive's Star).

[413] Major F. R. Wingate served during the Nile Expedition in 1884-85 as Acting Aide de Camp and Military Secretary to the Major General on the Lines of Communication (mentioned in despatches, Brevet of Major, 4th Class of the Medjidie, Medal with Clasp, and Khedive's Star); also served in the operations on the Soudan frontier in 1889 including the engagement at Toski (mentioned in despatches, DSO., and Clasp), and also in the operations in 1891 including the capture of Tokar (3rd Class of the Medjidie).

[414] Captain S. M. Renny served with the Burmese Expedition in 1885-87, and was present in the engagement at Nyoungoo-Mingyan, at the surrender of Mandalay, in the expeditions to Bhanoo and Mogoung, and against the Kachins on the Chinese Frontier, and in the engagements at Choung-Pang and Paung-Yong (Medal with Clasp).

[414†] Captain E. Bickford served with the Burmese Expedition in 1885-87 (Medal with Clasp). Served with the Sikkim Expedition in 1888 (mentioned in despatches, Clasp).

[415] Captains J. Hanwell and H. R. Cook served with the Burmese Expedition in 1886 (Medal with Clasp).

War Services of the Officers of the Royal Artillery.

⁴¹⁵† Captain A. H. C. Birch served with the Burmese Expedition in 1885-86 (mentioned in despatches, Medal with Clasp). Served with the Manipore Expedition in 1891 in command of No. 8 Bengal Mountain Battery (mentioned in despatches, Clasp).

⁴¹⁶ Captain H. B. Brownlow served with the Burmese Expedition in 1886 (Medal with Clasp); and with the Hazara Expedition in 1891 in command of No. 2 Derajat Mountain Battery (mentioned in despatches, Clasp).

⁴¹⁶† Captain C. de C. Hamilton served with the Luchai Expedition in 1889 (mentioned in despatches, Medal with Clasp); and with the Isazai Field Force in 1892.

⁴¹⁷ Captain R. Morris served in the Egyptian war of 1882 on Transport Duty, and was present at the battle of Tel-el-Kebir (Medal with Clasp, and Khedive's Star).

⁴¹⁸ Captain H. G. Birch served with the Royal Artillery in the Egyptian war of 1882 (Medal, and Khedive's Star).

⁴¹⁹ Captain E. S. Brooke served with the Burmese Expedition in 1886-87 (Medal with Clasp).

⁴¹⁹† Captain H. de T. Phillips served with the Zhob Valley Expedition in 1884. Served with the Burmese Expedition in 1886-87 (Medal with Clasp). Served with the Sikkim Expedition in 1888 including the engagement at Jalep-la (Clasp).

⁴²⁰ Captain A. Crawford served in the Nile Expedition in 1884-85 with the Egyptian Army, and was present at the action at Kirbekan (Medal with two Clasps, and Khedive's Star).

⁴²⁰† Captain W. Moore Lane served with the Hazara Expedition in 1888 in command of two guns of No. 2 (Derajat) Mountain Battery (Medal with Clasp).

⁴²¹ Captain Burney served with the Royal Artillery in the Egyptian war of 1882, and was present at the surrender of Kafr Dowar (Medal, and Khedive's Star).

⁴²¹† Captain F. J. S. Cleeve served with the Hazara Expedition in 1888—dangerously wounded (Medal with Clasp).

⁴²² Captain A. Capel-Cure served in the Egyptian war of 1882, and was present at the battle of Tel-el-Kebir (Medal with Clasp, and Khedive's Star).

⁴²³ Captain F. H. S. Giles served with the Burmese Expedition in 1886-87 including the night attack on Bhamo (Medal with Clasp); and with the Hazara Expedition in 1888 (Clasp).

⁴²³† Captain M. M. Noble served with the Zhob Valley Expedition in 1884 including the affair at Pitao. Served with the Burmese Expedition in 1886-87 (Medal with Clasp).

⁴²⁴ Captain L. H. Ducrôt served in the Soudan Frontier Field Force in 1885-86 (Medal, and Khedive's Star).

⁴²⁵ Captain C. D. Scott served with the Burmese Expedition in 1886-87 (Medal with Clasp); and with the Hazara Expedition in 1888 (Clasp).

⁴²⁶ Captain H. E. Stanton served with the Burmese Expedition in 1885-87, first with a Mountain Battery, and afterwards as Attaché Intelligence Branch (mentioned in despatches, DSO., and Medal with Clasp).

⁴²⁷ Captain R. D. Anderson served with the Burmese Expedition in 1885-86 (mentioned in despatches, Medal with Clasp).

⁴²⁷† Captain M. L. Carleton served with the Hazara Expedition in 1888 (Medal with Clasp); and with the Hazara Expedition in 1891 (Clasp).

⁴²⁸ Captain Terry served with the Royal Artillery in the Egyptian war of 1882 (Medal, and Khedive's Star).

⁴²⁸† Captain T. W. G. Bryan served with the Burmese Expedition in 1886-87 including the night attack on Bhamo (Medal with Clasp); with the Hazara Expedition in 1888 (Clasp); and with the two Miranzai Expeditions in 1891 (Clasp).

⁴²⁹ Captain M. B. Bicknell served with the Soudan Frontier Field Force in 1885-86 (Medal, and Khedive's Star). Served with the Burmese Expedition in 1886-87 (mentioned in despatches, Medal with Clasp).

⁴³⁰ Captain A. H. Short served in the Soudan campaign in 1885, and was present in the engagement at Hasheen and at the destruction of Temai (Medal with Clasp, and Khedive's Star).

⁴³¹ Captain S. D. Browne.—See Civil Decorations for Gallantry, "Hart's Annual Army List," p. 786.

⁴³² Captain G. C. Dowell served with the Burmese Expedition in 1885-86 (Medal with Clasp); with the Hazara Expedition in 1888 (Clasp); with the Hazara Expedition in 1891 (Clasp); and with the Isazai Expedition in 1892.

⁴³³ Captain H. E. B. Lane served with the Burmese Expedition in 1887 (Medal with Clasp), and again in 1887-89 (Clasp).

⁴³³† Captain H. D. Grier served with the Tonhon and Wuntho Expeditions in 1889-91 (Medal with Clasp); and with the Isazai Expedition in 1892.

⁴³⁴ Captain M. Taylor served in the operations of the Soudan Frontier Field Force in 1885-86 (Medal, and Khedive's Star).

⁴³⁴† Captain E. S. Cooper served with the Burmese Expedition in 1885 (Medal with Clasp).

⁴³⁵ Captain A. W. Gay served with the Burmese Expedition in 1885-87 (Medal with Clasp).

⁴³⁶ Captain J. L. Parker served with the Burmese Expedition in 1886-87 (mentioned in despatches, Medal with Clasp); with the Hazara Expedition in 1891 (Clasp); and with the second Miranzai Expedition in 1891 (mentioned in despatches, Clasp).

⁴³⁷ Captain C. C. Smeaton served with the Bechuanaland Expedition under Sir Charles Warren in 1884-85.

⁴³⁸ Captain H. H. Butler served with the Burmese Expedition in 1885-86 (Medal with Clasp).

⁴³⁹ Captain F. L. Donaldson served with the Nile Expedition in 1884-85, and was present in the engagement at Abu Klea Wells on the 16th and 17th February (Medal with Clasp, and Khedive's Star). Also served with the Soudan Frontier Field Force in 1885-86, and was present in the engagement at Giniss. Served with the Hazara Expedition in 1888 (Medal with Clasp).

⁴³⁹† Captain C. W. Brownlow served with the Zhob Valley Expedition in 1890. Served in the Burmese Expedition in 1891-92 with the Irrawaddy Column (Medal with Clasp).

⁴⁴⁰ Captain R. A. Kaye served with the Hazara Expedition in 1891 (Medal with Clasp).

⁴⁴¹ Captain F. R. Drake served with the Hazara Expedition in 1888 (Medal with Clasp).

⁴⁴¹† Captain W. H. Robinson served with the Burmese Expedition in 1885-87 (Medal with Clasp), in 1887-89 (Clasp), and in 1890-92 (Clasp); and with the Manipore Expedition in 1891 (Clasp).

⁴⁴² Captain R. G. Morriman served with the expedition to the Tambaku Country, on the West Coast of Africa, in 1892, including the capture of Tambi (DSO., and Medal with Clasp).

⁴⁴³ Captain O. C. Williamson served with the Burmese Expedition in 1887-89—slightly wounded (Medal with two Clasps).

⁴⁴⁴ Captain A. F. Pullen served with the Burmese Expedition in 1885-87 (Medal with Clasp). Served in the operations in the Soudan in 1891 including the capture of Tokar (4th Class of the Medjidie).

⁴⁴⁴† Captain W. A. Persse served with the Manipore Expedition in 1891 (Medal with Clasp).

⁴⁴⁵ Captain J. C. Thorp served with the Burmese Expedition in 1885-87 (Medal with Clasp).

⁴⁴⁵† Captain G. E. Galbraith served with the Burmese Expedition in 1885-89 (Medal with two Clasps).

⁴⁴⁶ Captain C. N. Lyall served with the Nile Expedition in 1884-85, and was present at the action at Abu Klea—severely wounded (Medal with two Clasps, and Khedive's Star).

⁴⁴⁶† Captain L. C. Gordon served with the Burmese Expedition in 1886-87 (Medal with Clasp); and with the two Miranzai Expeditions in 1891 (Clasp).

⁴⁴⁷ Captain Logan.—See Civil Decorations for Gallantry, "Hart's Annual Army List," p. 786.

⁴⁴⁸ Captain F. C. Johnston served in the expedition to the Soudan in 1884 under Sir Gerald Graham and was present in the engagement at Temai (Medal with Clasp, and Khedive's Star). Served in the Soudan campaign of 1885, and was present in the engagement at the Tofrek zereba and at the destruction of Temai (two Clasps).

⁴⁴⁹ Captain M. S. Eyre served with the Burmese Expedition in 1885 with No. 9 Mountain Battery Cinque Ports Division, and in 1886-87 with No. 1 Mountain Battery Eastern Division (Medal with two Clasps); and with the expedition to the Black Mountain in 1888 (mentioned in despatches, Clasp).

⁴⁵⁰ Captain F. H. F. R. McMeekan served with the Miranzai Expedition in 1891 (Medal with Clasp).

⁴⁵¹ Captain W. A. Robinson served with the Burmese Expedition in 1885-87 (Medal with Clasp).

⁴⁵² Captain C. E. Lawrie served with the expedition against the Jebus, on the West Coast of Africa, in 1892—slightly wounded (mentioned in despatches, Medal with Clasp).

⁴⁵³ Captain T. L. Coxhead served with the Burmese Expedition in 1886, and was severely wounded in an engagement at Ningyan on the 10th October (mentioned in despatches, DSO., and Medal with Clasp).

⁴⁵⁵ Captain W. K. Hardy.—See Civil Decorations for Gallantry, "Hart's Annual Army List," p. 786.

War Services of the Officers of the Royal Artillery.

⁴⁵⁶ Captain J. F. Browne served with the Hazara Expedition in 1888 (Medal with Clasp); with the Zhob Valley Expedition in 1890; with the Miranzai Expedition in 1891 (Clasp); and with the Isazai Expedition in 1892.
⁴⁵⁷ Captain C. G. Watson served with the two Miranzai Expeditions in 1891 (Medal with Clasp).
⁴⁵⁸ Captain G. R. Lamb served with the two Miranzai Expeditions in 1891 (Medal with Clasp).
⁴⁵⁹ Lieut. G. S. Ogg served with the Isazai Expedition in 1892.
⁴⁶⁰ Lieut. A. W. Money served with the Zhob Valley Expedition in 1890, and with the Isazai Field Force in 1892.
⁴⁶¹ Lieut. H. W. Iles served with the Hazara Expedition in 1888 (Medal with Clasp); and with the Manipore Expedition in 1891 in command of a division of guns of No. 8 Bengal Mountain Battery (mentioned in despatches, Clasp).
⁴⁶² Lieut. H. F. Vanderzee served with the Manipore Expedition in 1891 (Medal with Clasp).
⁴⁶³ Lieut. T. E. Marshall served with the Manipore Expedition in 1891 with the Tammu Column (Medal with Clasp); with the Wuntho Expedition in 1891 (Clasp); and in the operations in the Northern Chin Hills in 1892-93 under Brigadier General Palmer (mentioned in despatches).
⁴⁶⁴ Lieut. H. B. Strange served during the rebellion in the North West Territories of Canada in 1885 as Aide de Camp to Major General Strange, Commanding Alberta Field Force, and was present in the engagement on the 28th May at Frenchman's Butte (mentioned in despatches, Medal with Clasp).
⁴⁶⁵ Lieut. Bruce Kingsmill served with the expedition to the Black Mountain in 1888 as Assistant Transport Officer 3rd Column and subsequently in the Advanced Column at Thakot and Allai (Medal with Clasp).
⁴⁶⁶ Lieut. C. E. Hill served in the Burmese Expedition in 1885-87 and again in 1887-89 with the Upper Burmah Field Force (Medal with two Clasps); with the Hazara Expedition in 1891 (Clasp); and with the Isazai Field Force in 1892.
⁴⁶⁷ Lieut. A. E. J. Perkins served with the Hazara Expedition in 1891 (Medal with Clasp).
⁴⁶⁸ Lieut. L. W. P. East served with the Miranzai Expedition in 1891 with No. 2 Derajat Mountain Battery (mentioned in despatches, Medal with Clasp), and in the operations against the Abor Tribes in the North East Frontiers of Assam in 1894 (*DSO.*).
⁴⁶⁹ Lieut. J. G. Baldwin served in the Burmese campaign in 1890-92, including the Tonhon and Wuntho Expeditions and the operations on the North-East frontier (Medal with Clasp).
⁴⁷⁰ Lieut. Lyle.—See Civil Decorations for Gallantry, "Hart's Annual Army List," p. 786.)
⁴⁷¹ Captain W. D. Nichol served with the Burmese Expedition in 1885-89 (Medal with two Clasps).
⁴⁷¹† Lieut. K. K. Knapp served with the Manipore Expedition in 1891 (Medal with Clasp).
⁴⁷² Lieut. G. G. Traherne served with the Miranzai Expedition in 1891 under Sir William Lockhart including the engagement at Sangar (Medal with Clasp).
⁴⁷³ Lieut. A. M. Smith served with the Hazara Expedition in 1891 (Medal with Clasp); and with the Isazai Field Force in 1892.
⁴⁷⁴ Lieut. H. W. M. Parker served with the Isazai Expedition in 1892.
⁴⁸² Lieut. R. St. G. Gorton served with the first Miranzai Expedition in 1891, and with the expedition against the Hunza-Nagars in 1891-92—wounded (mentioned in despatches, Medal with Clasp).
⁴⁸⁴ Lieut. F. G. Smallwood served with the Sikkim Expedition in 1888 (Medal with Clasp).
⁴⁸⁵ Lieut. D. G. Seagrim served with the Burmese Expedition in 1885-89 (Medal with two Clasps); with the Zhob Valley Expedition in 1890; and with the Isazai Field Force in 1892.
⁴⁸⁷ Lieut. W. Howel Jones served with the Miranzai Expedition in 1891 (Medal with Clasp), and with the Isazai Field Force in 1892.
⁴⁸⁸ Lieut. C. A. Molony served with the Hazara Expedition in 1891 (Medal with Clasp); and with the Hunza-Nagar Expedition in 1891 including the capture of Nilt Fort (mentioned in despatches, Clasp).
⁴⁹⁰ Lieut. F. R. Patch served in the Miranzai Expedition in 1891 under Sir William Lockhart, and was present in the engagement at Sangar—wounded (Medal with Clasp); and with the Isazai Expedition in 1892.
⁴⁹² Lieut. G. F. MacMunn served with the Burmese Expedition in 1892, and was present at the defence of Sadon—slightly wounded (mentioned in despatches, *DSO.* and Medal with Clasp).
⁴⁹³ Lieuts. E. H. B. Craster, A. W. Curtis, and H. J. Cotter served with the Isazai Expedition in 1892.
⁴⁹⁴ Lieut. J. E. L. Bruce served with the Wuntho Expedition in 1891 as Orderly Officer to Brigadier General Wolseley (mentioned in despatches, Medal with Clasp).
⁴⁹⁷ Captain Wilbond served in the China war in 1860, and was present at the capture of the Taku Forts and at the surrender of Pekin (Medal with two Clasps).
⁴⁹⁹ Captain Cook served with the Bhootan Expedition in 1865-66 (Medal with Clasp).
⁵⁰⁰ Captain Paton served in the Afghan war in 1879-80 (Medal, and Medal for distinguished conduct).
⁵⁰¹ Captain A. Martin served in the Indian Mutiny campaign in 1857-58, and was present at the actions of Pandora and Doondeakoira (Medal).
⁵⁰² Captain Firth served in the Egyptian war of 1882, and was present at the battle of Tel-el-Kebir (mentioned in despatches, Medal with Clasp, and Khedive's Star).
⁵⁰³ Lieut. W. Robinson served in the China war in 1860, and was present at the capture of the Taku Forts and at the surrender of Pekin (Medal with two Clasps).

War Services—Royal Artillery (late Bengal Artillery).

¹ General Lane served the Affghanistan campaign of 1842 under General Pollock as Commissary of Ordnance and was present at the forcing of the Khyber Pass and recapture of Cabool (Brevet of Major, and Medal). Commanded a Troop of Horse Artillery in the Gwalior campaign, including the battle of Maharajpore (Brevet of Lt. Colonel, and Bronze Star), Sutlej campaign in 1845-46, including the battles of Aliwal and Sobraon (Medal and Clasp, and *CB.*). Punjaub campaign of 1848-49, including the action of Ramnuggur, and battles of Chillianwallah and Goojerat (Medal with two Clasps).

³ Sir James Abbott served at the siege and capture of Bhurtpore in 1825-26 (Medal). Carried terms of accommodation from the Court of Kheva to the Court of Russia. Was cut down in a night attack on the banks of the Caspian Sea, and detained a prisoner, but ultimately completed the negotiation at St. Petersburg (received the thanks of H.M. Minister for Foreign Affairs, and the Dooranee Order of the 3rd Class). Reduced to submission the mountaineers of Huzara in armed rebellion against the Government. On the Sikh Governor of Huzara, with two Brigades of regular Troops, 12 guns, and the garrisons of many castles and small forts, declaring for Mcolraj, he raised the population of Huzara, and, after many small affairs, remained master of the district and of nearly all the castles; afterwards marched upon and occupied with 1,500 matchlock men, the Marquella Pass, which 16,000 Sikh Troops and 2,000 Dooranee horse were preparing to thread (received the thanks of H.M. Ministers in both Houses of Parliament, the Brevet of Major, and the Punjaub Medal, with all its Clasps). Served in the campaign on the North West Frontier of India in 1852 including the operations on the Black Mountain (Medal).

³ General Carleton commanded the Bengal Artillery Division siege train at the siege and capture of Lucknow in 1858; commanded Artillery in the action of Nawabgunge (twice mentioned in despatches, Brevet of Lt. Colonel, CB., Medal with Clasp).

⁵ General de Teissier served in the Sutlej campaign in 1846, including the battle of Sobraon (Medal). Punjaub campaign of 1848-49, including the battles of Chillinnwallah (mentioned in despatch) and Goojerat (Medal with two Clasps).

⁸ Sir William Olpherts commanded four Guns on service in Burmah in 1841; and two Guns in action at Jhirua Ghat during the insurrection in Saugor and Nerbudda territory in 1842. Commanded a Light Field Battery throughout the Gwalior campaign of 1843-44, including battle of Punniar (mentioned in despatch, Bronze Star). Raised and commanded Artillery of Bundlecund Legion in the Hill campaign in Sind under Sir Charles Napier in 1844-45. Commanded Artillery of Native Contingent against Kote Kangra. Served with Sir Colin Campbell in the Peshawur Valley in 1852 (Medal with Clasp). In Turkey and the Crimea in 1854-55-56. Commanded three Guns, which, with Detachment of 10th Foot and a few Madras Fusiliers under General Neil (in all 200 Europeans) routed three Native Regiments at Benares on 4th June 1857. Commanded a Battery with Havelock's Force in the actions at Bithoor (horse shot), Mungurwar, and Alumbagh, and first Relief of the Residency at Lucknow; acted as Brigadier of Artillery in defence of the Residency from 27th Sept. to 16th Nov. 1857 (wounded, mentioned in despatches). Commanded a Battery at the Alumbagh from 22nd Nov. 1857 to 17th March 1858, and was present in all the engagements there during that period, also at the capture of Lucknow by Lord Clyde (Brevets of Major and Lt. Colonel, CB., Victoria Cross, Medal with two Clasps): was awarded the VC "for highly distinguished conduct on the 25th September 1857, when the troops penetrated into the city of Lucknow, in having charged on horseback, with Her Majesty's 90th Regiment, when, gallantly headed by Colonel Campbell, it captured two guns in the face of a heavy fire of grape, and having afterwards returned, under a severe fire of musketry, to bring up limbers and horses to carry off the captured ordnance, which he accomplished.—*Extract from Field Force Orders of the late Major General Havelock, dated 17th October 1857.*" Commanded a Battery of Horse Artillery in Oude in 1858. Served as a Volunteer with the Frontier Expedition against the Wuzeerees in 1859-60 under Sir N. Chamberlain.

⁹ Lieut. General Cordner served in the Peshawur Mountain Train in various engagements on the Trans-Indus Frontier from 1854 to 1859 (Medal with Clasp). In the Indian Mutiny (Medal). Commanded Mountain Train Battery in the Cossyah Hill campaign of 1862-63, and also in the Bhootan campaign of 1864-65 (mentioned in despatches, Clasp).

¹¹ Lord Roberts served throughout the Indian Mutiny of 1857-58 as D.A.Q.M. General of Artillery, including the siege and capture of Delhi from the 28th June to the 20th September (wounded 14th July, horse shot 14th September), actions of Bolundshur (horse shot), Allyghur, Agra, Kunoj (horse sabred), and Bundhera where he narrowly escaped capture while reconnoitring; present in the skirmishes prior to and throughout the operations connected with the relief of Lucknow by Lord Clyde; operations at Cawnpore from 28th Nov. to 6th Dec. 1857, and do ent of the Gwalior Contingent, action of Khodagunge, reoccupation of Futtehghur, storm of Meangunge, action of Koorsee, and the various operations ending with the capture of Lucknow (thanked by the Governor General, Victoria Cross, Brevet of Major, Medal with three Clasps): received the VC under the following circumstances:—"Lieutenant Roberts' gallantry has on every occasion been most marked. On following up the retreating enemy on the 2nd January 1858, at Khodagunge, he saw in the distance two sepoys going away with a standard. Lieutenant Roberts put spurs to his horse, and overtook them just as they were about to enter a village. They immediately turned round and presented their muskets at him, and one of the men pulled the trigger, but fortunately the cap snapped, and the standard-bearer was cut down by the gallant young Officer, and the standard taken possession of by him. He also, on the same day, cut down another sepoy who was standing at bay, with musket and bayonet, keeping off a sowar. Lieutenant Roberts rode to the assistance of the horseman, and rushing at the sepoy, with one blow of his sword cut him across the face, killing him on the spot." Was employed on special service with the expedition of 1863 against the tribes on the North-West Frontier of India, and was present at the storming of Laloo, capture of Umbeylah and destruction of Mulkah (Medal with Clasp). Served in the Abyssinian campaign from January 1868, as Assistant Quarter Master General with the Bengal Brigade, and, as Senior Officer of the Department at Zoula, superintended the re-embarkation of the whole army; was selected by Sir Robert Napier as the bearer of his final despatches (Brevet of Lt. Colonel, and Medal). Served as Assistant Quarter Master General and Senior Staff Officer with the Cachar Column, Looshai Expeditionary Force, in 1871-72, and was present at the capture of the Kholel villages, and attack on the Northlang range. Commanded the Troops engaged at the burning of the village of Taikoom, 26 January 1872 (CB.). Commanded the Koorum Field Force from the commencement of the Afghan war in 1878, and was present at the storming and capture of the Peiwar Kotal and the pursuit of the Afghan army to the Shutargardan, at the affair in the Maugior Pass and during the operations in Khost (received the thanks of both Houses of Parliament, and KCB.). Commanded the Cabul Field Force during the advance on and occupation of Cabul in the autumn of 1879, and was present in the engagement at Charasiab, and throughout the operations at Sherpore during the winter of 1879-80 (CIE.). Commanded the Cabul-Candahar Field Force which marched from Cabul to Candahar in August 1880, relieved the Candahar Garrison, and on the 1st September defeated and dispersed the army under Ayub Khan (received the thanks of both Houses of Parliament, Medal with four Clasps, and Bronze Decoration). Nominated GCB. and created a Baronet for his distinguished services in India. Has been twenty-three times mentioned in despatches before the Afghan war, during which campaign he was eight times thanked by the Viceroy and Commander in Chief in India. Commanded the forces in Burmah in 1886 after the capture of Mandalay (received the thanks of the Government of India, Clasp).

¹⁸ Lieut. General Nicholl was thanked by the Governor General and mentioned in Sir Hugh Rose's despatch for services during the defence of Saugor.

²⁵ Major General Griffin served in suppression of the Indian Mutiny in 1857-58, including the battle of Agra (mentioned in despatch, Medal).

²⁷ Lieut. General Nairne served during the Indian Mutiny in 1857 (Medal). Also with the second expedition to Eusofzai, North-West Frontier, in 1863. Served in the Afghan war in 1878-79 with the Peshawur Valley Field Force (Medal). Served in the Egyptian war of 1882 in command of the Royal Horse Artillery, and was present in the two actions at Kassasin and at the battle of Tel-el-Kebir (mentioned in despatches, CB., Medal with Clasp, 3rd Class of the Medjidie, and Khedive's Star).

³⁴ Major General A. Walker served with the Bhootan Expedition in 1865-66 (Medal with Clasp).

³⁸ Colonel Ward served in the Indian Mutiny campaign in 1857-58 (Medal). Served in the campaign on the North West Frontier of India in 1863-64 (Medal with Clasp). Served in the Afghan war in 1879-80, and took part in the march to Candahar with the force under Major General Phayre (Medal).

⁴² Major General Tillard served in the Afghan war in 1879-80, and was present in the engagement at Ahmed Kheyl (mentioned in despatches); accompanied Sir Frederick Roberts in the march to Candahar and was present at the battle of Candahar (mentioned in despatches, Brevet of Lt. Colonel, Medal with two Clasps, and Bronze Decoration), Served with the Burmese Expedition in 1886-87 (mentioned in despatches, CB., and Medal with Clasp).

⁴⁶ Lieut. General Chapman served throughout the Abyssinian campaign from December 1867, having brought the "B" Battery of Mounted Ordnance from England, and was most energetic in getting it into order previous to the arrival of No. 5 Battery 21st Brigade; served with the Battery until the 9th April 1868, when he was appointed Aide de Camp to Brigadier General Petrie commanding the Artillery, and was present at the action of Arogee and fall of Magdala (mentioned in despatches, and Medal). Served in the Afghan war of 1878-80 as Deputy Adjutant and

War Services of the Officers of the Royal (late Bengal) Artillery.

Quarter Master General of the Ghuznee and Northern Afghanistan Field Forces and Cabul-Candahar Force, and was present in the engagement at Ahmed Kheyl (mentioned in despatches) ; accompanied Sir Frederick Roberts in the march to Candahar, and was present at the battle of Candahar (mentioned in despatches, Brevet of Lt. Colonel, CB., Medal with two Clasps, and Bronze Decoration). Served with the Burmese Expedition in 1885-86 (Medal with Clasp).

58 Major General Cowie served in the Afghan war of 1878-80, and took part in the advance to Cabul under Sir Donald Stewart, including the engagement at Ahmed Kheyl (mentioned in despatches) ; accompanied Sir Frederick Roberts in the march to Candahar, and was present at the battle of Candahar (mentioned in despatches, Brevet of Lt. Colonel, Medal with two Clasps, and Bronze Decoration).

71 Colonel Anderson served in the Afghan war in 1879-80 as Brigade Major Royal Artillery with the Southern Afghanistan Field Force (Medal).

72 Colonel Swinley served with the Bhootan Field Force from November 1865 to March 1866 (Medal with Clasp). Served with the Hazara Mountain Battery in the Black Mountain expedition in 1868 (Clasp). Commanded two guns of No. 2 Mountain Battery in the Jowaki Afreedee expedition of 1877-78 (mentioned in despatches, Clasp) Commanded No. 2 Mountain Battery throughout the Afghan war of 1878-80, and was present at the affair at Mattoon, in the engagement at Charasiab on 6th October 1879, and in the operations around Cabul in December 1879 including the investment of Sherpore. Was also present in the engagement at Charasiab on the 25th April 1880, and accompanied Sir Frederick Roberts in the march to Candahar, and took part in the battle of Candahar (several times mentioned in despatches, Brevets of Major and Lt. Colonel, Medal with three Clasps, and Bronze Decoration).

War Services of the Royal (late Madras) Artillery.

1 Sir Robert Cadell served on the Staff of the Turkish Army during the Russian war from October 1854, including the defence of Eupatoria, siege and fall of Sebastopol, and Omar Pacha's winter campaign in Mingrelia (mentioned in despatches, Crimean Medal with Clasp, Turkish Medal, 4th Class of the Medjidie, and Brevet of Major) Served in the Indian Mutiny campaign in Bengal, including the actions of Doomooreagunge, Baunriah, and Toolseepore (mentioned in despatches, Brevet of Lt. Colonel, Medal with Clasp).

6 Lieut. General Pearse served the Punjaub campaign of 1848-49;—was Assistant Field Engineer under General. Whish at the siege of Mooltan, and at the action of Soorujkoond, and subsequently commanding the Artillery of the Nawab of Bhawulpore under Major H. B. Edwardes; present at the capture of the city of Mooltan (mentioned in despatches for conspicuous gallantry when repelling a sortie from the fortress on 30th December 1848). Served under Major R. G. Taylor with the Force in the Derajat, which drove the Affghans from Bunnoo (Punjaub Medal with Clasp). On the 2nd Jan. 1850, at the Goombuttee Pass, at the head of the border levies defeated the tribe of Oomurzye Vizeerees who made a descent on Bunnoo. In November 1852 was in command of 4000 Cashmere Regular Troops and British Irregular Levies in the Expedition to Khagan and the Black Mountain (Medal with Clasp). Served throughout the Indian Mutiny, commanded the Cavalry of the Hurreeana Irregular Field Force of General Van Cortlandt at the actions of Aodah and Kheireeka. In command of 400 Rahtore Rajpoot Cavalry of Bickaneer,—made a forced march on the 26th June 1857, by which Hissar was relieved. Commanded a Force which stormed and captured the fortified positions of Bhatoul and Mungalce in Hurreeana. Commanded the Cavalry at Jumalpoor. Served with General Showers' Delhi Column, and was present at the occupation of the Forts of Dadree, Jhujjur, and Kanound. Commanded a body of Cavalry in Brigadier Gerrard's Delhi Column at the battle of Narnoul severely wounded). Commanded the 3rd Sikh Cavalry at the siege and capture of Lucknow in March 1858. Served with the Azimghur Field Force under Sir E. Lugard at the actions of Munnehar, Azimghur 15th April, and in the pursuit of Koer Sing including the actions of Azmitghur 17th April 1858, Munnear and Sheeapoor Ghat, and in the expedition into the Jugdespore Jungles during June and July 1858 (Medal with Clasp, and Brevet of Major).

7 Lieut.-General E. M. Playfair served in the second Burmese war in 1853 (Medal). Also served in the Indian Mutiny campaign and was often engaged with the rebels in inconsiderable actions (Medal with Clasp).

10 Lieut. General H. M'Leod served in the Afghan war in 1878-79 (Medal).

16 Colonel Hon. A. B. de Montmorency served during the suppression of the Indian Mutiny with the Gorruckpore Field Force and the Saugor Field Division from 1858 till the end of 1859 (Medal).

17 Lt. Colonel G. B. Macdonell served in the Egyptian war of 1882 (mentioned in despatches, Medal, 3rd Class of the Medjidie, and Khedive's Star).

20 Colonel Alexander served in the Zulu war of 1879, and was present in the engagement at Ulundi (mentioned in despatches, Medal with Clasp). Served in the Afghan war in 1880 (Medal).

[1] Sir Arnold Kemball served the campaign of 1838-39 in Affghanistan, including the siege and capture of Ghuznee (Medal). Campaign of 1857 in Persia (Medal with Clasp, CB., and Brevet of Major). The Governor General of India stated in his notification of the 18th June 1857 that "the valuable assistance afforded on every occasion of difficulty and danger, and especially in the brilliant expedition against Ahwaz, by Captain Kemball had been highly commended by Sir James Outram and merited the unqualified approbation and the hearty thanks of the Governor General in Council."

[4] General Aitken served with the expedition to Persia in 1856-57, and was present at the bombardment of Mohumrah (mentioned in despatches, Medal with Clasp). Served throughout the campaign in Rajpootana and Central India in 1857-59, including the action of Rewah, sieges of Awah (mentioned in despatches) and Kotah (mentioned in despatches), and subsequent operations in Central India (Medal with Clasp, and Brevet of Major).

[13] General Fuller served in suppression of the Indian mutiny, and was present at the action of Kotahkeserai and recapture of Gwalior (Medal with Clasp).

[20] Major General Caldecott served throughout the Abyssinian campaign with the Transport Train from September 1867, and commanded a Division of the Train during the latter half of the campaign (mentioned in despatches for "ability, energy, and zeal," Medal). Served in the Afghan war in 1879-80, and was present at the defence of Candahar including the sortie of Deh Khojah, and at the battle of Candahar (Brevet of Lt.Colonel, Medal with Clasp).

[25] Colonel Mortimer served throughout the Abyssinian campaign from Sept. 1867, having proceeded to Zoulla with the Reconnoitring Party; was present at the action of Arogee and capture of Magdala, and mentioned in despatches for "ability, energy, and zeal" (Medal).

Corps of Royal Engineers.

The Royal Arms and supporters, with a Cannon, and the Motto "*Ubique*" over the Gun, and "*Quo Fas et Gloria ducunt*" below it.

Head Quarters of 1 Company, Cork Harbour. 2, Egypt. 3, London. 4, Gosport. 5, Portsmouth. 6, Gibraltar. 7, Chatham. 8, Chatham. 9, Chatham. 10, Woolwich. 11, Curragh. 12, Shorncliffe. 13, Bristol. 14, Dublin. 15, Gibraltar. 16, Bedford. 17, Aldershot. 18, Halifax, N.S. 19, Southampton. 20, Gibraltar. 21, Harwich. 22, Isle of Wight. 23, Aldershot. 24, Malta. 25, Hong Kong. 26, Curragh. 27, Bermuda. 28, Malta. 29, Cape Town. 30, Plymouth. 31, Chatham. 32, Cork Harbour. 33, Cork Harbour. 34, Gravesend. 35, Bermuda. 36, Bermuda. 37, Okehampton; Half Co. Lydd. 38, Aldershot. 39, Sheerness. 40, Halifax, N.S. 41, Head Qrs. and Half Co., Ceylon: Half Co., Singapore. 42, Malta. A, B, C, D, E, F, G, M, and N Companies, Chatham. H Company, India. Telegraph Bn. 1st Division, Aldershot: 2nd Div., London. Bridging Bn.: A and B Troops, Aldershot. Mounted Detachment, Aldershot. Field Depot R.E. Troops, Aldershot. Balloon Depot and Section, Aldershot.

Colonel—Field Marshal His Royal Highness George W. F. C. Duke of Cambridge, 1 KG. KT. KP. GCB. GCSI. GCMG. GCIE. Commander in Chief, 10 May 61.

Yrs. Serv	COLONELS COMMANDANT.	SECOND LIEUT.	FIRST LIEUT.	CAPTAIN.	BREVET MAJOR.	MAJOR.	BREVET LT.COL.	LT.COL.	BREVET COLONEL.	COLONEL.	COLONEL COMM.	MAJOR GENERAL.	LIEUT. GENERAL.	GENERAL.
58	Simmons, Sir John Lintorn Arabin,3 GCB. GCMG. (Field Marshal, 21 May 90)	14 Dec. 37	15 Oct. 39	9 Nov. 46	14 July 54		12 Dec. 54	31 Jan. 60	12 Dec. 57		27 Aug. 72	6 Mar. 68	27 Aug. 72	1 Oct. 77
63	Hamilton, Robert Gorges	29 May 32	5 Dec. 35	18 Dec. 44				1 Apr. 55	1 Apr. 58		25 July 79	6 Mar. 68	1 Oct. 77	
63	Hadden, William Charles6	29 May 32	8 Feb. 36	6 Dec. 44				21 May 55	21 May 58		5 Feb. 64	6 Mar. 68	1 Apr. 80	
54	Montagu, Horace William,7 CB.	1 Jan. 42	1 May 45	17 Feb. 54	24 Apr. 58		2 Nov. 55	8 Feb. 66	2 Nov. 63		2 Aug. 73	6 Mar. 68	1 Oct. 77	1 July 81
61	Fanshawe, Charles	19 Dec. 34	23 Feb. 37	1 Apr. 46	2 Aug. 58			1 Apr. 59	1 Apr. 64		1 Mar. 68	28 June 68	1 July 78	1 July 81
54	Browne, Sir James Frankfort Manners,8 KCB.	1 Jan. 42	1 Apr. 45	7 Feb. 54	17 July 55			2 May 65	26 Dec. 64		1 June 73	22 Feb. 70	13 Aug. 81	12 Feb. 88
57	Bayly, John, CB.	19 Mar. 39	16 Sept. 41	8 Sept. 47	1 Nov. 58			26 Mar. 62	26 Mar. 67		1 Feb. 90	1 Oct. 77	23 Mar. 82	26 Apr. 82
57	Jervois, Sir William Francis Drummond,10 GCMG. CB.	19 Mar. 39	8 Oct. 41	13 Dec. 47	29 Sept. 54			1 Apr. 62	1 Apr. 67		28 June 93	1 Oct. 77	7 Apr. 82	
57	Gallwey, Sir Thomas Lionel 8th, KCMG.	19 Mar. 39	23 Nov. 41	2 Feb. 48	14 May 59			1 Apr. 62	1 Apr. 67		12 Apr. 72	1 July 78	26 Apr. 82	

Removed from the Corps, having rank as General Officers.

47	F.C. Lennox, Sir Wilbraham Oates,11 KCB. [R]	27 June 48	7 Feb. 54	25 Nov. 57	24 Mar. 58	5 July 72	26 Apr. 59	10 Dec. 73	26 Apr. 67			13 Aug. 81	12 Feb. 88	28 June 93	
40	p.s.c. Harrison, Sir Richard,12 KCB. CMG. Commanding at Devonport 15 Apr. 90		31 July 55	26 July 62	11 Oct. 64	5 Aug. 72	17 May 74	6 Aug. 81	17 May 79			20 July 88	1 Apr. 93		
41	Dawson-Scott, Robert Nicholl. Unemployed		14 Aug. 54	13 Dec. 59		5 July 72		1 Oct. 77	1 Oct. 81			1 Mar. 90	15 Feb. 94		
41	Hewett, Edward Osborne, CMG. Commandant School of Military Engineering, 1 Apr. 93	14 Aug. 54	20 Oct. 54	1 Feb. 60				21 Oct. 77	21 Oct. 81			14 June 90			
41	p.s.c. Grant, Robt.13 CB. Insp. Gen. of Fortifications and of R. Eng., with rank of Lt.-General, 18 Apr. 91	23 Oct. 54	13 Dec. 54	8 Aug. 60		5 July 72		1 July 78	1 July 82			9 May 91			
38	Warren, Sir Charles,33 GCMG. KCB. Unemployed		23 Dec. 57	20 Oct. 69		10 Apr. 78		12 Oct. 84	11 Nov. 82			1 Apr. 93			
40	Wilson, Sir Charles William,44 KCB. KCMG. Director General of Military Education, 22 Jan. 95		24 Sept. 55	20 June 64		23 May 73		19 Apr. 79	31 Dec. 82			15 Feb. 94			
39	Sanford, George Edward Langham Somerset,49 CB. CSI. Commanding Meerut District		18 Oct. 56	8 Feb. 66		10 Dec. 73		22 Nov. 79	26 Apr. 82	22 Nov. 83		1 Jan. 95			

COLONELS Re-employed and on Half-Pay List, after Completing Five Years as Lt.-Colonel R. Eng.

	COLONELS.	SECOND LIEUT.	FIRST LIEUT.	CAPTAIN.	MAJOR.	BREVET MAJOR.	LT. COL.	BREVET LT. COL.	COLONEL.	BREVET COLONEL.
	Maitland, James Makgill Heriot,36 CB. Deputy Adjutant General Royal Engineers, with temporary rank of Major General, 21 Apr. 91		20 Apr. 55	1 Apr. 62	5 July 72		1 Jan. 78	1 July	20 Dec. 79	20 Dec. 83
	Locock, Herbert, CB. Deputy Inspector General of Fortifications, War Office, Whitehall, 7 Nov. 87		7 Apr. 56	7 Jan. 65	25 Aug. 73		16 Feb. 78		31 Dec. 81	1 July 85
	Brine, Bruce. Unemployed		15 May 57	6 July 67	6 June 77		17 Dec. 78		22 May 83	22 July 85
	Le Mesurier, Frederick Augustus,67 CB.		1 Oct. 57	8 Jan. 68	1 Oct. 77		31 Dec. 78	18 Feb. 82	13 Feb. 86	13 Feb. 86
	Hogg, John Roberts. Unemployed		1 Oct. 57	4 Mar. 68	1 Oct. 77		8 Sept. 79		14 July 83	14 July 86
	Ferguson, Charles John O'Neill14		1 Oct. 57	30 July 69	1 Oct. 77				10 May 84	10 May 86
	Salmond, William,62 CB. Deputy Inspector General of Fortifications, War Office, 18 May 91		1 Oct. 57	22 July 69	16 Feb. 78			18 Nov. 82	8 Sept. 84	14 Sept. 88
	Veitch, Robert Hamilton, CB. Colonel on the Staff, Chief Engineer in Ireland, 6 Nov. 94		23 Dec. 57	30 July 69	17 Apr. 78				14 Sept. 84	14 Sept. 88
	Peters, Edward Nicolls,64 Exec. Eng., 1st Grade, D.P. Works, Central Provinces, Jubbulpore		23 Dec. 57	20 Feb. 70	31 Dec. 78				11 Nov. 84	6 May 89
	Turner, Hv. Fyers,66 Deputy Inspector General of Fortifications, War Office, 6 Nov. 94		23 Dec. 57	12 Aug. 71	1 June 79				6 May 85	6 May 89
	Athorpe, Robert, Colonel on the Staff, Commanding Royal Engineer, Home District, 1 July 93		23 Dec. 57	27 Jan. 72	8 Sept. 79				2 July 85	2 July 89
	Pellowes, James, Colonel on the Staff, Commanding Royal Engineer, Gibraltar, 12 Feb. 91		22 June 58	17 Feb. 72					2 July	2 July 89
	O'Brien, Edmund Donough Collins, Col. on the Staff, Comm. R. Eng., S. E. Dist., Dover, 31 Dec. 91		1 Oct. 58	3 Aug. 72	17 Sept. 79				22 Sept. 85	22 Sept. 89

Corps of Royal Engineers

Yrs. Ser.	Colonels Re-employed and on Half-Pay List.	Lieut.	Captain.	Brevet Major.	Major.	Brevet Lt. Col.	Lieut. Colonel.	Lt. Col. R. Eng.	Brevet Colonel.
	p.s.c. Ardagh, Sir John Charles,⁵⁹ KCIE, CB, Aide de Camp to H.R.H. the Duke of Cambridge	1 Apr. 59	3 Aug. 72	30 Nov. 78	22 Sept. 80	18 Nov. 82	17 Dec. 86		15 June 85
	Paden, William Henry, Colonel on the Staff, Commanding Royal Engineer, Edinburgh, 2 Feb. 94	2 Dec. 59	28 Aug. 72		1 July 81		1 Oct. 87		29 Aug. 93
	Wood, Elliott,¹⁰⁵ CB., Colonel on the Staff and Commanding Royal Engineer, Malta, 8 June 94	15 Jan. 64	30 Sept. 77	18 Nov. 82	21 Jan. 85	21 May 84	30 Sept. 77		1 May 88
	Nicholson, William Gustavus,⁵⁶ CB.	2 Mar. 65	16 Mar. 78	2 Mar. 81	21 Mar. 85	1 July 87			1 Jan. 91
	Woodthorpe, Robert Gosset,¹¹⁷ CB. Deputy Surveyor General of India, Bangalore	22 June 65	22 May 78	22 Nov. 79	22 June 85	18 Nov. 82			18 Nov. 86
	EṞ p.s.c. Hart, Reginald Clare,⁶⁰ Director of Military Education at Constantinople, 1 Nov. 89	23 July 70	1 July 81	18 Jan. 82	23 Nov. 87	2 Mar. 81			3 Mar. 87
	Chermside, Herbert Charles,⁶⁵ CMG. CB. Military Attaché at Constantinople, 1 Nov. 89	23 July 70	22 July 82	27 Sept.82	18 Dec. 85	15 June 85			3 Aug. 87
	Mullor, William Hutchinson,⁶⁹ Commanding Royal Engineer, Hong Kong, 15 Oct. 91	21 Dec. 58	3 Aug. 72		8 Nov. 79		1 Oct. 86		1 Oct. 90
	Slacke, William Randall, Commanding Royal Engineer, N. W. District, Chester, 1 Dec. 91	21 Dec. 58	21 July 73		9 Nov. 79		1 Oct. 86		1 Oct. 90
	Farquharson, John, OB., Southampton, Director General, Ordnance Survey	21 June 59	3 Aug. 72		1 July 81		17 Mar. 87		29 Aug. 93
	Sale, Matthew Townsend,⁸² CMG. Supdt. of Building Works, Ordnance Factories, R. Arsenal, 1 July 88	1 July 61	26 Aug. 73		1 July 81		1 July 88		30 Sept.91
	Mackworth, Sir Arthur William, Bart. ⁸⁸ Colonel on the Staff, Commanding Royal Engineer, Aldershot, 1 Apr. 94		1 Dec. 73			18 Nov. 82	8 Mar. 89		18 Nov. 86
	Brooke, Alured De Vere,⁵⁴ Colonel on the Staff, Commanding Royal Engineer, N. E. District, York	18 Dec. 61	11 Dec. 73		18 Dec. 81		19 Mar. 89		6 Jan. 94
	Fraser, Thomas,⁹¹ CB. CMG. Colonel on the Staff, Commanding R. Eng. Portsmouth, 1 Sept. 94	25 June 62	19 Aug. 74	30 Nov. 78	25 June 82	18 Nov. 82	3 May 89		15 June 85
	p.s.c. EṞ Bell, Mark Sever,⁸³ CB., Aide de Camp to the Queen. Colonel on the Staff, Commanding Royal Engineer, N.E. District, York	25 June 62	19 Aug. 74		25 June 82	28 Oct. 84	10 May 89		16 Mar. 87
	Scott, Douglas Alexander,¹²² Assistant Adjutant General for Royal Engineers, War Office, 8 June 94	8 Jan. 70	8 Jan. 82	8 Nov. 82	1 Oct. 87	15 June 85	10 July 83		15 June 89
	Moysey, Charles John,⁵⁰ CMG. Unemployed.	1 Oct. 57	2 Sept.67		1 July 81	29 Nov. 79	1 Oct. 87		29 Nov. 83
	Hepper, Albert James,⁷⁴ Member of Ordnance Committee	22 Dec. 59	25 Aug. 73		1 July 81		4 Apr. 83		20 Dec. 62
	Hill, Arthur,⁷⁷ Colonel on the Staff, Commanding Royal Engineer, Thames District, 1 Aug. 94	18 Dec. 60	25 Aug. 73	11 Nov. 78	1 July 81		22 May 88		29 Sept.93
	Nixon, Francis William,⁷⁸ Colonel on the Staff, Commanding R. Engineer, Cape of Good Hope, 4 July 94								29 Sept.93
	Drake-Brockman, Ralph Rhemius Evans, Chief Engineer for Irrigation, Madras, and Joint Secretary to Government, P.W.D. Irrigation Branch	1 Dec. 60	25 Aug. 73		1 July 81		1 July 88		22 Apr. 93
	Carey, Clement de Beauvoir⁹⁶	17 Dec. 62	27 Oct. 76	18 Nov. 82	17 Dec. 82		20 Dec. 89		6 Jan. 94
	Rathborne, William Hans,³⁰⁰ Commanding Royal Engineer, Woolwich	17 Dec. 62	23 Jan. 77		17 Dec. 82		17 Dec. 89		25 May 94
	Gehle, Henry John Wolsteyn, Colonel on the Staff, Commanding Royal Engineer, Colchester, 24 Jan. 95	21 Dec. 59	3 Aug. 72		1 July 81		27 Aug. 87		29 Aug. 93
	Lieutenant Colonels.								
32	Knocker, Herbert Paget, Commanding Royal Engineer, Newcastle-on-Tyne	24 June 63	6 June 77		24 June 83		6 May 90	6 May 90	26 July 94
32	Lee, Henry Pincke, Commanding Royal Engineer, Shorncliffe	24 June 63	6 June 77		24 June 83		2 July 90	2 July 90	
32	Todd, Killingworth Richard¹⁰¹ (Colonel, 21 May 88), Assist. Commandant School of Military Engineering	24 June 63	6 June 77		24 June 83	21 May 84	2 July 90	2 July 90	
32	Speight, William FitzHenry¹⁰² (Colonel, 15 June 89), Commanding Royal Engineer, Cork	24 June 63	6 June 77		24 June 83	15 June 85	24 Sept.90	24 Sept.90	
32	Edwards, Sir Fleetwood Isham, KCB. Assistant Private Secretary and Assistant Keeper of the Privy Purse to the Queen, Groom in Waiting and Extra Equerry to Her Majesty	30 June 63	5 July 77		30 June 83		22 Oct. 90	Oct. 90	
34	Rogers, Malcolm Wm.⁸⁵ Assist. Surv. Gen. Great Trigonometrical Survey of India, Calcutta	18 Dec. 63	11 Dec. 73	2 Mar. 81	18 Dec. 81		18 Dec. 88	5 Dec. 90	29 Sept.93
34	Sargeaunt, Richard Arthur,⁸³ Deputy Secretary to Government of India, P.W.D. Railway Branch, Simla. Leave, Europe	18 Dec. 63	11 Dec. 73		18 Dec. 81		18 Dec. 88	5 Jan. 91	29 Sept.93
34	Boileau, Lestock Francis, Executive Engineer, 1st Grade, D. P. Works, Aboo.	18 Dec. 63	11 Mar. 74		18 Dec. 81		18 Dec. 88	4 Mar. 91	29 Sept.93
34	Baird, Andrew Wilson,⁹⁰ Master of Mint, Calcutta. On Furlough	18 Dec. 63	4 Apr. 74		18 Dec. 81		18 Dec. 88	8 Apr. 91	29 Sept.93
33	Bungley, George Fletcher Ottley,⁴⁸ Executive Engineer, 1st Grade, D.P. Works, Manager Eastern Bengal Railway; Commandant Bengal State Railway Volunteers	25 June 62	15 Feb. 75		25 June 82		25 June 89	9 Apr. 91	
33	Beamish, Alfred Augustus William. On Reserve List	17 Dec. 62	9 Apr. 77		6 July 83		6 July 90	1 July 91	
33	Mascall, Francis, Commanding Royal Engineer, Plymouth	15 Jan. 64	1 Jan. 77		15 Jan. 84		15 Jan. 91	30 July 91	
33	Hill, John, Dep. Supt., 3rd Grade, Great Trigonometrical Survey of India, Poona	25 June 62	25 Sept. 75		25 June 82		25 June 89	1 Aug. 91	
33	Elsdale, Henry,¹⁰⁶ Commanding Royal Engineer, Natal	15 Jan. 64	1 Oct. 77		15 Jan. 84		15 Jan. 91	6 Aug. 91	
33	Savage, Johnson William, Commanding Royal Engineer, Curragh District, Ireland	15 Jan. 64	4 June 76	2 Mar. 81	15 Jan. 84		6 Aug. 91	6 Aug. 91	
33	Holdich, Thomas Hungerford,⁹⁷ CB. CIE. (Brevet Col., 1 Sept. 91), Dep. Supt. Topog. Sur. of India, Simla	17 Dec. 62	1 Oct. 76		17 Dec. 82	16 Feb. 87	17 Dec. 89	12 Aug. 91	
33	Gracey, Thos., Chief Eng., 3rd Cl., D.P.W. Cons. Eng. to Govt. of India for Rail, Lucknow. Leave, Europe	17 Dec. 62	1 June 77	2 Mar. 81	29 June 83		17 Dec. 89	12 Aug. 91	
32	Bisset, William Sinclair Smith,¹⁰³ CIE., Director General of Railways, Simla	29 June 63	15 June 77				8 Aug. 90	12 Aug. 91	
32	Fox, Harry Croker, Superintending Resident P.W.D. Hyderabad	21 Dec. 59	3 Aug. 77	2 Mar. 81	3 Aug. 85			12 Aug. 91	

Corps of Royal Engineers.

Yrs. Ser.	LIEUTENANT COLONELS.	LIEUT.	CAPTAIN.	BREVET MAJOR.	MAJOR.	BREVET LT.COL.	LIEUT. COLONEL.	LT.COL. R. ENG.
32	Corbett, Frank Vincent, Chief Engineer and Secretary to Bombay Govt. N.W.P. and Oude, Irrigation Branch	15 Jan. 64	1 Oct. 77	......	15 Jan. 84	......	15 Jan. 91	12 Aug. 91
32	Ottley, John Walter, C.I.E. Inspector General of Irrigation and Deputy Secretary to Government of India, } P.W. Dept. Calcutta and Simla	15 Jan. 64	1 Oct. 77	......	15 Jan. 84	......	15 Jan. 91	12 Aug. 91
32	M'Arthur, Alexander Donald, Superintending Engineer, 1st Class, D.P.W., Calcutta	16 Feb. 64	1 Oct. 77	......	16 Feb. 84	......	16 Feb. 91	12 Aug. 91
31	Greenstreet, William Lees, 107 Chief Engineer, 2nd Class, Madras. Leave, Europe	18 Oct. 64	1 Oct. 77	......	18 Oct. 84	......	18 Oct. 91	12 Aug. 91
31	Kirkwood, Hendley Paul, Ordnance Survey, Dublin	13 Jan. 64	1 Oct. 77	......	13 Jan. 84	......	13 Aug. 91	12 Aug. 91
31	Pulford, Russell Richard, Superintending Engineer, 2nd Class, D.P.W., 1st Circle, N.W.P. and Oude, Lucknow	24 Mar. 65	17 Mar. 78	......	24 Mar. 85	......	8 Sept. 91	12 Aug. 91
30	Brackenbury, Maule Campbell, 114 Exec. Engr., 2nd Grade, D.P.W.; Offg. Manager O. and R. Rail., Lucknow	22 June 65	17 Apr. 78	......	22 June 85	......	8 Sept. 91	3 Sept. 91
30	Jacob, Sydney Long, 116 Superintending Engineer, 1st Class, D.P.W., Bari Doab Circle, Umritsur	22 Dec. 64	5 May 78	......	22 Dec. 85	......	16 Sept. 91	16 Sept. 91
30	Lambert, Sydenham John, Commanding Royal Engineer, Barbadoes	15 Jan. 64	1 Oct. 77	......	15 Jan. 84	......	1 Oct. 91	1 Oct. 91
30	Macpherson, John Lawrence, 105 Commanding Royal Engineer, South Wales, Pembroke Dock	1 Mar. 64	1 Oct. 77	......	1 Mar. 84	......	1 Oct. 91	1 Oct. 91
30	Arnott, Napoleon, Deputy Director of Works, Madras	22 Dec. 65	11 July 78	......	22 Dec. 85	......	19 Oct. 91	1 Oct. 91
30	Campbell, Duncan MacNeil, Superintending Engineer, 1st Class, D.P.W., Madras. On Leave	22 Dec. 64	14 July 78	......	22 Dec. 85	......	6 Nov. 91	1 Oct. 91
30	Christie, Charles Howard Peregrine, Examiner of Accounts, D.P. Works, N.W. Provinces and Oude	17 Apr. 66	31 Dec. 78	......	17 Apr. 86	......	23 Nov. 91	2 Nov. 91
29	Turner, Samuel Compton, 121 Superintending Engineer 1st Class, Military Works Branch, Meerut. Leave, Europe	17 Apr. 66	31 Dec. 78	......	17 Apr. 86	......	6 Dec. 91	6 Dec. 91
31	Dorward, James Ford, 110 (Colonel, 15 June 86) Commanding Royal Engineer, East Sub District, Malta	19 July 65	19 July 78	......	19 July 85	15 June 85	31 Dec. 91	31 Dec. 91
31	p.s.c. Macdonald, George, Commanding Royal Engineer, West Sub District, Malta	30 Aug. 64	21 Oct. 77	......	30 Aug. 84	......	31 Dec. 91	31 Dec. 91
31	Georges, Henry Rhodes Gilbert, Commanding Royal Engineer, Gosport	18 Oct. 64	1 Oct. 77	......	18 Oct. 84	......	18 Oct. 91	31 Dec. 91
31	p.s.c. Hildebrand, Godfrey, Assistant Inspector General of Fortifications, War Office	9 Dec. 64	5 Dec. 77	18 Nov. 82	9 Dec. 84	......	31 Dec. 91	31 Dec. 91
31	Waller, Stanier, 111 Aldershot, Extra Equerry to the Queen; Commanding Royal Engineer, South Camp, Aldershot	23 Dec. 64	6 Feb. 78	......	23 Dec. 84	......	31 Dec. 91	18 Jan. 92
31	Alexander, Arthur Clifford, Commanding Royal Engineer, Sheerness	1 Apr. 66	16 Feb. 78	......	17 Apr. 86	......	18 Jan. 92	23 Mar. 92
30	Purchas, William Robert, Commanding Royal Engineer, Devon Sub. Dist. Exeter	17 Apr. 66	31 Dec. 78	......	17 Apr. 86	......	1 Oct. 92	1 Oct. 92
30	Garwood, John Frederick, 113 Superintending Engineer, 3rd Class, Military Works, Quetta	1 Apr. 66	10 Apr. 78	......	17 Apr. 86	......	4 Apr. 92	4 Apr. 92
30	Hart, Edward Chichester, Commanding Royal Engineer, Liverpool	22 June 66	22 June 78	......	22 June 86	......	3 July 92	3 June 92
30	Ielf, Richard Henry, 115 (Colonel, 9 Dec. 80), Commanding Royal Engineer, North Sub District, Gibraltar	22 June 65	17 Apr. 78	......	22 June 85	9 Dec. 85	27 July 92	27 July 92
30	Washington, Francis Palmer, Commanding Royal Engineer, Gravesend	22 Dec. 65	1 June 78	......	22 Dec. 85	......	27 Aug. 92	27 Aug. 92
30	n.r.c. Beresford, Charles Frederick Cobbe, 118 Commanding Royal Engineer, Ceylon	22 Dec. 65	4 Sept. 78	......	22 Dec. 85	......	1 Oct. 92	1 Oct. 92
30	Purchas, William Robert, Commanding Royal Engineer, Devon Sub. Dist. Exeter	17 Apr. 66	31 Dec. 78	18 Nov. 82	17 Apr. 86	......	1 Oct. 92	1 Oct. 92
29	p.s.c. Watson, Charles Moore, 119 CMG., Assistant Inspector General of Fortifications, War Office	17 Apr. 66	25 Dec. 78	......	17 Apr. 86	......	1 Oct. 92	1 Oct. 92
29	Jekyll, Herbert, 116 CMG., Private Secretary to the Viceroy, Ireland	17 July 66	31 Jan. 79	......	17 July 86	......	7 Oct. 92	7 Oct. 92
29	Broadbent, John Edward, Commanding Royal Engineer, 3rd Grade, D.P.W., Bombay	12 Feb. 67	13 Dec. 80	......	12 Feb. 87	28 July 87	13 Nov. 92	13 Nov. 92
28	Henry, George, 124 Assistant Adjutant General, Quetta, 6 Jan. 94	17 Apr. 66	31 Dec. 78	22 Nov. 79	17 Apr. 86	2 Mar. 87	23 Nov. 92	23 Nov. 92
29	Moore, Edward Crozier Sibbald, 120 CB. (Colonel, 20 Mar. 83), Commanding Royal Engineer, Halifax, N.S.	17 Apr. 66	31 Dec. 78	22 Nov. 79	17 Apr. 86	......	19 Dec. 92	5 Dec. 92
29	Ifc Leach, Edward Pemberton, 120 CB. (Colonel, 2 Mar. 83), Commanding Royal Engineer, South Sub District, Gibraltar	17 Apr. 66	25 Dec. 78	22 Nov. 79	17 Apr. 86	......	8 Jan. 93	3 Jan. 93
29	Purcell, Matthew Henry, Commanding Royal Engineer, Singapore	15 July 68	24 Jan. 79	Jan. 79	15 July 86	......	8 Jan. 93	1 Apr. 93
29	Ifc Chard, John Rouse Merriott, 122 Commanding Royal Engineer, Weymouth	15 July 68	15 July 79	......	15 July 86	......	1 Apr. 93	4 Apr. 93
27	Boyle, John du Terreau, Commanding Royal Engineer, Brighton	15 Jan. 67	13 Sept. 79	......	23 Nov. 86	......	1 Apr. 93	4 Apr. 93
29	p.s.c. Hare, William Aldworth Home, Commanding Royal Engineer, Egypt	15 Jan. 67	13 Sept. 79	21 May 84	6 Nov. 86	......	4 Apr. 93	4 Apr. 93
29	p.s.c. Green, Arthur Octavius, 123 Commanding Royal Engineer, Portsea	15 Jan. 67	13 Sept. 79	......	17 Dec. 86	......	22 May 93	22 May 93
28	de Wolski, Felician Rola, Commanding Royal Engineer, Alexandria	10 July 67	13 Sept. 79	......	17 Dec. 86	......	26 May 93	26 May 93
28	Barkie, Robert Martin, 124 Commanding Royal Engineer, Chatham	10 July 67	9 Oct. 79	15 June 85	31 Dec. 86	......	14 July 93	14 July 93
28	p.s.c. Morris, William George, CMG., School of Military Engineering, Chatham	10 July 68	9 Nov. 79	18 Nov. 82	23 July 87	26 Dec. 88	1 Aug. 93	10 July 93
28	p.s.c. Settle, Henry Hamilton, 125 DSO., Assistant Inspector General of Fortifications, War Office	10 July 68	9 Nov. 79	......	1 Oct. 87	......	10 July 93	10 July 93
28	Snart, Alexander William, Principal, College of Engineers, Madras. Leave, Europe	15 July 68	15 July 80	......	13 Nov. 87	......	11 Dec. 93	11 Dec. 93
28	Rawson, Courtney Clarke, 126 Executive Engineer 1st Grade, D.P. Works, Bellary	13 Jan. 68	1 July 81	18 Nov. 82	9 Jan. 87	......	1 Jan. 94	1 Jan. 94
27	Smith, Sidney, 128 Deputy Consulting Engineer for Railways, Lucknow	8 Jan. 68	1 July 81	......	18 Jan. 87	......	8 Mar. 94	8 Mar. 94
27	Clarke, Henry Jeremy, Examiner, 2nd Grade, D.P.W., Guernsey	8 Jan. 68	15 Dec. 79	......	18 Jan. 87	......	19 Mar. 94	19 Mar. 94
27	Day, Francis Jeremy, Commanding Royal Engineer, Jamaica	8 Jan. 68	24 Dec. 79	......	27 Mar. 87	......	28 Apr. 94	28 Apr. 94
27	Brown, Louis Faulkner, 124 Commanding Royal Engineer, Dublin District	8 Jan. 68	17 Apr. 80	......	27 Mar. 87	......	28 Mar. 94	28 Mar. 94
28	Johnston, Duncan Alexander, Ordnance Survey, Southampton	28 Dec. 68	22 Aug. 80	2 Mar. 81	27 Mar. 87	......	1 Apr. 94	1 Apr. 94
27	Clarke, Sir George Sydenham, 128 KCMG., Superintendent, Carriage Department, Royal Arsenal	15 July 68	22 Aug. 80	......	16 June 87	......	4 Apr. 94	4 Apr. 94
27	Cockburn, George Alexander, 129 Chatham	15 July 68	19 Sept. 80	......	16 June 87	......	4 Apr. 94	4 Apr. 94

Corps of Royal Engineers.

Yrs. Serv.		LIEUT.	CAPTAIN.	BREVET MAJOR.	MAJOR.	BREVET LT.COL.	LIEUT. COLONEL.	LT.COL. R. ENG.	BREVET COLONEL.
	LIEUTENANT COLONELS.								
27	Selby, Henry Oliphant, [1st] Deputy Consulting Engineer for Railways, Poona, Bombay	13 Jan. 69	1 July 81	......	17 Dec. 87	......	5 Apr. 94	5 Apr. 94	......
27	Kirke, St. George Mervyn, Commanding Royal Engineer, York Sub District, York	15 July 68	22 Sept. 80	......	1 July 87	......	3 May 94	3 May 94	......
27	Goldie, Mark Henry George, Commanding Royal Engineer, North Aldershot Sub District	15 July 68	1 July 81	......	11 July 87	......	10 May 94	10 May 94	......
27	Spratt, Frederick Thomas Nelson, [1st] Lahore	15 July 68	1 July 81	......	1 Apr. 88	......	18 May 94	18 May 94	......
27	Preston, Arthur Thomas, Commanding Royal Engineer, Isle of Wight	15 July 68	22 Jan. 81	1 July 87	23 July 87	......	21 May 94	21 May 94	......
27	Dorward, Arthur Robert Ford, [1st] DSO. Aldershot	15 July 68	1 May 81	......	1 Oct. 87	......	21 June 94	21 June 94	......
27	Hyslop, Robert Maxwell, [1st] Assistant Inspector General of Fortifications, War Office	15 July 68	1 May 81	......	1 Oct. 87	......	2 July 94	2 July 94	......
27	Yorke, Horatio Arthur, [1st] Special duty, Board of Trade, Whitehall	13 Jan. 69	3 June 81	15 June 85	1 Oct. 87	......	6 Aug. 94	6 Aug. 94	......
27	Barker, George, [1st] Assistant Inspector General of Fortifications, War Office	13 Jan. 69	21 June 81	18 Nov. 82	1 Oct. 87	......	1 Oct. 94	1 Oct. 94	......
27	Dove, Horatio, [1st] Commanding Royal Engineer, Jersey	13 Jan. 69	1 July 81	......	19 Oct. 87	......	3 Nov. 94	3 Nov. 94	......
27	p.s.c. Barker, James Campbell, Aldershot	13 Jan. 69	1 July 81	......	1 Apr. 88	......	10 Dec. 94	10 Dec. 94	......
26	p.s.c. Peacocke, William, [1st] CMG. War Office	13 Jan. 69	1 July 81	26 Feb. 87	1 Apr. 88	......	17 Dec. 94	17 Dec. 94	......
26	Orpen, Richard Theodore, [1st] Exeter	7 July 69	7 July 81	......	1 Apr. 88	......	20 Dec. 94	20 Dec. 94	......
26	Savage, George Robert Rollo, [1st] Ceylon	7 July 69	7 July 81	......	1 Apr. 88	......	24 Jan. 95	1 Jan. 95	......
26	Haslett, Pechell [1st] On passage home	7 July 69	7 July 81	......	1 Apr. 88	......	1 Mar. 95	1 May 95	......
	LIEUTENANT COLONELS on Half Pay.								
	Blood, Bindon, [so] CB., Superintending Engineer, Military Works Department, India	19 Dec. 68	25 Aug. 73	29 Nov. 79	1 July 81	18 Nov. 82	10 July 88	......	18 Nov. 86
	Cole, Henry Hardy, Sick leave	17 Dec. 62	6 June 77	......	17 Dec. 82	......	17 Dec. 89	......	......
	Champernowne, Henry, Unemployed	18 Dec. 61	10 Feb. 74	......	18 Dec. 81	......	4 Apr. 88	......	......
	Anstey, Thomas Henry, [95] Unemployed	25 June 62	12 Aug. 75	......	25 June 82	......	11 June 89	......	......
	MAJORS.								
26	Addison, George William. Special duty, Board of Trade	7 July 69	7 July 81	......	1 Apr. 88				
26	Porcelli, Alfred, Gosport	7 July 69	7 July 81	......	1 Apr. 88				
26	Thurburn, James White, [147] Executive Engineer, 2nd Grade, D. P. W., Rawul Pindee	7 July 69	7 July 81	......	1 Apr. 88				
26	Gosset, Frederic, Commanding Royal Engineer, Inverness	7 July 69	7 July 81	......	1 Apr. 88				
26	Hoskyns, Chandos, [148] Plymouth	7 July 69	7 July 81	......	4 Apr. 88				
26	Hussey, Edward Robert, Ordnance Survey, Southampton	7 July 69	7 July 81	......	22 May 88				
26	Gore, St. Geo. Corbet, [149] Dep. Supt. 3rd Grade, Great Trigonometrical Survey of India. Dehra Dhoon	8 Jan. 70	8 Jan. 82	16 Feb. 87	26 May 88				
26	Lloyd, Robert Oliver, [150] Executive Engineer, 1st Grade, D.P.W., Lucknow	8 Jan. 70	8 Jan. 82	......	1 July 88				
26	Conder, Claude Reignier, [151] Special duty, Irish Relief Works	8 Jan. 70	8 Jan. 82	......	10 July 88				
26	DeVillamil, Richard, St. Helena	8 Jan. 70	8 Jan. 82	......	14 July 88				
26	Du Boulay, Woodforde George, Woolwich	8 Jan. 70	8 Jan. 82	......	1 Aug. 88				
26	Creswell, Edmund William, Shoeburyness	8 Jan. 70	8 Jan. 82	......	16 Dec. 88				
26	Martin, Martin, [153] Glasgow	7 July 69	11 May 82	......	18 Dec. 88				
25	Main, Thomas Ryder, [155] Instructor, School of Military Engineering, Chatham	23 July 70	23 July 82	......	18 Dec. 88				
25	Sherrard, Charles William, [156] Instructor, School of Military Engineering, Chatham	23 July 70	23 July 82	......	18 Dec. 88				
25	Benny-Tailyour, Henry Waugh, Chatham	23 July 70	23 July 82	......	18 Dec. 88				
25	Pitt, William, Aldershot	23 July 70	23 July 82	......	18 Dec. 88				
25	Wilkinson, Charles, Portsmouth	23 July 70	23 July 82	......	18 Dec. 88				
25	Hart, Horatio Holt, Executive Engineer, 1st Grade, M.W. Department, Poona	23 July 70	23 July 82	......	10 Jan. 89				
25	Boddy, Owen Vidal, Superintending Engineer, 3rd Grade, Trichinopoly	23 July 70	23 July 82	......	12 Jan. 89				
25	Wilkieson, Charles Boyd, [158] Commandant Madras Sappers and Miners, Bangalore	23 July 70	23 July 82	......	28 Mar. 89				
25	Mayn, Gother Fyers, [159] Home District	23 July 70	23 July 82	15 June 85	30 Mar. 89				
25	Johnston, James Tayler, Dublin	23 July 70	23 July 82	......	1 Apr. 89				
25	Noel, William Frederick Noel, Aldershot	23 July 70	23 July 82	......	1 Apr. 89				
25	Rochfort-Boyd, Charles Augustus, [161] Chatham	23 July 70	23 July 82	......	1 Apr. 89				
25	Jessop, Henry Lethbridge, Aldershot	23 July 70	23 July 82	......	1 Apr. 89				

Corps of Royal Engineers.

MAJORS.

Name	LIEUT.	CAPTAIN.	MAJOR.
D'Aguilar, Francis Burton Grant,[126] Executive Engineer, 1st Grade, M.W.D., Meerut	1 Dec. 70	1 Dec. 82	1 Apr. 89
Skinner, Monier Williams,[162] Colchester	4 Jan. 71	4 Jan. 83	17 Apr. 89
Shone, William Terence,[163] DSO. (Brevet Lt.Colonel, 1 Sept. 91), Executive Engineer, 2nd Grade, D.P.W., Simla	4 Jan. 71	4 Jan. 83	17 Apr. 89
White, Walter Hanbury,[126] Officiating Consulting Engineer for Railways, Calcutta	4 Jan. 71	4 Jan. 83	3 May 89
Badgley, James Montague Taylor,[164] Exec. Eng., 3rd Grade, M. W. D., Madras	4 Jan. 71	4 Jan. 83	7 May 89
Duperier, Henry William,[165] Executive Engineer, 1st Grade, D. P. W., M. W. B. Leave, Europe	4 Jan. 71	4 Jan. 83	10 May 89
Bennet, Ferdinando Wallis[166] (Bt.Major :5 June 85), Aldershot	4 Jan. 71	4 Jan. 83	21 May 89
Heathcote, Alfred, Cardiff	4 Jan. 71	4 Jan. 83	11 June 89
Thompson, Richard, Liverpool	4 Jan. 71	4 Jan. 83	21 June 89
Ross of Bladensburg, Edmond James Thomas, Mauritius	4 Jan. 71	4 Jan. 83	25 June 89
Maycock, Stewart M'Murdo, Portsea	4 Jan. 71	4 Jan. 83	25 June 89
Dewing, Edward John, York	4 Jan. 71	4 Jan. 83	25 June 89
Kitchener, Sir Horatio Herbert,[167] KCMG. CB. (Bt.Major, 8 Oct. 84; Bt.Lt.Col., 15 June 85; Colonel, 11 Apr. 88), Aide de Camp to the Queen; Sirdar of the Egyptian Army, with rank of Brigadier General.	4 Jan. 71	4 Jan. 83	6 July 89
			20 July 89
Cockburn, Alexander William,[168] Sappers and Miners, Bangalore	2 Aug. 71	2 Aug. 83	20 July 89
Lake, Noel Montagu, Woolwich	2 Aug. 71	2 Aug. 83	20 July 89
Wells, Henry Lake,[169] Telegraph Service, Persia, Teheran, with rank of Lt.Colonel	2 Aug. 71	2 Aug. 83	31 July 89
Raban, Edward,[170] Superintending Engineer, Portsmouth Dockyard	2 Aug. 71	2 Aug. 83	6 Aug. 89
Scott, Buchanan,[147] CIE. Executive Engineer, 1st Grade, D. P. Works; Officiating Mint Master, Bombay	2 Aug. 71	2 Aug. 83	4 Sept 89
Wilson, George Frederick,[171] Deputy Manager N. W. Railway, Lahore	2 Aug. 71	2 Aug. 83	1 Oct. 89
Grant, Suene[172] (Bt.Major, 7 Dec. 88), Executive Engineer 1st Grade, D.P.W.Bangalore	2 Aug. 71	2 Aug. 83	3 Nov. 89
Ruck, Richard Matthews, Insp. Submarine Mining Defences, War Office, Whitehall	2 Aug. 71	2 Aug. 83	17 Dec. 89
Exham, Simeon Hardy,[173] 1st Assist. B. Works, Ord. Factories, R. Arsenal, Woolwich	2 Aug. 71	2 Aug. 83	17 Dec. 89
Glennie, Edward[174] Exec. Eng., 1st Grade, D. P. Works, M. W. Branch, Quetta	2 Aug. 71	2 Aug. 83	17 Dec. 89
Muirhead, Herbert Hugh, Esquimault	2 Aug. 71	2 Aug. 83	17 Dec. 89
Leach, Harold Pemberton,[175] DSO. (Bt.Major, 15 June 85; Bt.Lt.Colonel, 28 July 90; Bt.Colonel, 28 July 94); Commandant Bengal Sappers and Miners	2 Aug. 71	2 Aug. 83	17 Dec. 89
Chippindall, William Harold,[176] Professor Royal Military College, Sandhurst	2 Aug. 71	2 Aug. 83	17 Dec. 89
Bruce, Alfred Crawford,[177] Exec. Eng., 1st Grade, D.P.W., M.W.B. Leave, Europe	2 Aug. 71	2 Aug. 83	20 Dec. 89
Cotter, Edmond William,[178] Egypt	2 Aug. 71	2 Aug. 83	18 Jan. 90
Bor, Edward John, Clonmel	2 Aug. 71	2 Aug. 83	25 Jan. 90
M'Callum, Henry Edward,[179] CMG., Reserve List, Colonial Engineer and Surveyor General, Straits Settlements	15 Dec. 71	15 Dec. 83	1 Feb. 90
Harrison, John Henry Chenevix,[126] Adj. 2 Tower Hamlets Vol. Eng. 6 Oct. 94	15 Dec. 71	15 Dec. 83	1 Mar. 90
Kellie, James,[147] Exec. Eng., 1stGrade, D.P.W., Mil. Works Branch. Leave, Europe	15 Dec. 71	15 Dec. 83	19 Apr. 90
Von Donop, Pelham George,[181] Postal Telegraphs, London	15 Dec. 71	15 Dec. 83	6 May 90
Baddeley, William Lewis Clinton, Exec. Eng., 1st Grade, D. P. Works, Madras	15 Dec. 71	15 Dec. 83	10 May 90
Olivier, Henry Dacres, Executive Engineer, 1st Grade, D. P. Works, Ahmedabad	15 Dec. 71	15 Dec. 83	29 June 90
Smith-Rewse, Henry Whistler[183] (Bt.Major, 29 Dec. 83), Gibraltar	15 Dec. 71	15 Dec. 83	2 July 90
Blackburn, John Edward,[184] Commanding 7th Field Company, Chatham	15 Dec. 71	15 Dec. 83	2 July 90
Breton, Harry D'Arch, Whitehall	15 Dec. 71	15 Dec. 83	6 July 90
Knight, Henry Palmer, Edinburgh	15 Dec. 71	15 Dec. 83	3 Aug. 90
Goldney, William Henry, Dover	15 Dec. 71	15 Dec. 83	3 Aug. 90
Leslie, Francis Seymour, Whitehall	15 Dec. 71	15 Dec. 83	22 Sept. 90
Bowyer, Wentworth Grenville,[126] Dep. Assist. Adj. Gen. for Royal Engineers, and Secretary to Defence Committee, Army Head Quarters, Bengal. Leave, Europe	15 Dec. 71	15 Dec. 83	24 Sept. 90
Young, Carmichael Light. Ordered to Ceylon	15 Dec 71	15 Dec. 83	22 Oct. 90
p.s.c. Leverson, Julian John,[185] Home District	6 Jan. 72	6 Jan. 84	1 Jan. 91
Hippisley, Richard Lionel,[186] Aldershot	6 Jan. 72	6 Jan. 84	15 Jan. 91
Hellard, Robert Charles,[187] Woking, Aldershot	6 Jan. 72	6 Jan. 84	15 Jan. 91
Campbell, John Colin Livington,[188] Curragh	6 Jan. 72	6 Jan. 84	15 Jan. 91
Davidson, George,[126] Exec. Eng., 1stGrade, D.P.W., M.W. Branch. Leave, Europe	6 Jan. 72	6 Jan. 84	15 Jan. 91
Lister, Wastel Jameson, Executive Engineer, 2nd Grade, D. P. Works. Leave, Europe	6 Jan. 72	6 Jan. 84	16 Feb. 91
Hildebrand, Algernon, Exec. Eng. 1st Grade, D. P. Works, M. W. B. Leave, Europe	4 Jan. 71	4 Jan. 83	4 May 91
Wood, Charles Knight,[189] Malta	6 Jan. 72	6 Jan. 84	6 May 91
O'Sullivan, Gerald Hope Wildig,[190] Commandant Bombay Sappers and Miners	6 Jan. 72	6 Jan. 84	9 May 91
Blunt, Ernest,[191] Executive Engineer, 2nd Grade, M.W.D., Rawul Pindee	6 Jan. 72	6 Jan. 84	12 May 91
p.s.c. Burn-Murdoch, John,[193] Deputy Commanding Engineer, State Rails., Bombay	2 May 72	2 May 84	6 Aug. 91
Ellis, Charles Conyngham, Executive Engineer, 2nd Grade, Bareilly	2 May 72	2 May 84	12 Aug. 91
p.s.c. Sharpe, James Birch, Cape of Good Hope	2 May 72	2 May 84	13 Aug. 91
Digby, Thomas,[194] Executive Engineer, 2nd Grade, Madras Division	2 May 72	2 May 84	13 Aug. 91
Barton, Maurice Charles,[195] Superintendent Instruction, Bengal S. & M., Roorkee	2 May 72	2 May 84	8 Sept. 91
Maxwell, Ronald Charles,[196] Aldershot	2 May 72	2 May 84	16 Sept. 91
Lovo, Henry Davison, Principal Civil Engineering College at Madras. On Leave	12 Sept.72	12 Sept.84	1 Oct. 91
Sill, John Warre, Instructor Royal Military Academy, Woolwich, 26 Sept. 94	12 Sept.72	12 Sept.84	1 Oct. 91
Mackean, Kenneth,[199] Portsmouth	12 Sept.72	12 Sept.84	1 Oct. 91
Bagnold, Arthur Henry[200] (Bt.Major, 15 June 85), Instructor in Electricity, School of Military Engineering, Chatham	12 Sept.72	12 Sept.84	18 Oct. 91
Constable, Willoughby Verner,[202] North Western Railway, Lahore	12 Sept.72	12 Sept.84	19 Oct. 91
Jennings, Robert Henry,[203] H.B.M.'s Consul, Bussorah. Sick Furlough	12 Sept.72	12 Sept.84	6 Nov. 91
Foley, Algernon Campbell,[197] Commanding 23rd Field Company, Aldershot	2 May 72	2 May 84	23 Nov. 91
Darling, Charles Henry,[204] Jamaica. On Leave	12 Sept.72	12 Sept.84	6 Dec. 91
Jervois, John, Aldershot	12 Sept.72	12 Sept.84	31 Dec. 91
Rawson, Herbert Edward, Secretary, R. E. Committee, Chatham	12 Sept.72	12 Sept.84	31 Dec. 91
Mackenzie, William Jacob, Malta	12 Sept.72	12 Sept.84	31 Dec. 91
Andrews-Speed, Henry Speed,[205] Exec. Engineer, 2nd Grade, M.W.D., Umballa	12 Sept.72	12 Sept.84	31 Dec. 91
Buston, Philip Thomas[207] (Bt.Major, 7 Dec. 88), Executive Engineer, 4th Grade, D. P. Works, Lucknow	12 Sept.72	12 Sept.84	6 Jan. 92
Tyler, John Charles,[208] Bengal Sappers and Miners, Roorkee	12 Sept.72	12 Sept.84	18 Jan. 92
Sim, George Hamilton,[209] Instructor School of Military Engineering, Chatham	12 Sept.72	12 Sept.84	16 Mar. 92
Campbell, John Charles,[210] Dublin	12 Sept.72	12 Sept.84		
Finnis, Henry,[126] Executive Engineer, 2nd Grade, M.W.B., Simla	9 Jan. 73	8 Jan. 85	1 Apr. 92
Ferrier, James Archibald,[212] DSO. Executive Engineer, 3rd Grade, Simla	9 Jan. 73	8 Jan. 85	4 Apr. 92
Fullerton, John Davidson,[213] Adjutant 2 Cheshire Volunteer Engineers	9 Jan. 73	8 Jan. 85	3 May 92
Hoskyn, Chas.Reg., Dep.Account.Gen.Public Works Accounts,N.W.Prov.and Oude	9 Jan. 73	8 Jan. 85	25 May 92
Spilsbury, Edgar Chas.[214] Exec. Eng., 2nd Gr., D.P.W., M.W.D., Burmah. On Leave	9 Jan. 73	8 Jan. 85	3 June 92
Baldwin, Philip Bell,[215] Norwich	9 Jan. 73	8 Jan. 85	19 July 92
Jones, George Turner,[216] Sappers and Miners, Kirkee	9 Jan. 73	8 Jan. 85	27 July 92
Conner, William Daniel,[217] Professor Royal Military Academy	9 Jan. 73	8 Jan. 85	6 Aug. 92
Lindley, Waldemar Delmar,[218] Hong Kong	9 Jan. 73	8 Jan. 85	27 Aug. 92

Corps of Royal Engineers.

MAJORS.

Name	LIEUT.	CAPTAIN.	MAJOR.
p.s.c. Betholl, Edward Hugh,[219] Brigade Major, Royal Engineers, Dublin	9 Jan. 73	8 Jan. 85	1 Oct. 92
Attree, Frederick Wm. Town,[221] Netley	9 Jan. 73	8 Jan. 85	1 Oct. 92
p.s.c. Talbot, Hon. Milo George[223] (Bt. Major, 16 Feb. 87), Staff Captain Intelligence Branch, War Office	29 Apr. 73	8 Jan. 85	1 Oct. 92
Moir, Alexander Lechmere,[226] India	29 Apr. 73	8 Jan. 85	1 Oct. 92
p.s.c. Hickson, Samuel Arthur Einem,[223] DSO, Exec. Eng. 2nd Gr. M.W.D. Jubbulpore. On Leave, Europe	29 Apr. 73	8 Jan. 85	7 Oct. 92
Onslow, Gerald Chas. Penrice,[226] Executive Engineer, 2nd Grade, M.W.D., Chuckrata	29 Apr. 73	8 Jan. 85	21 Oct. 92
Stafford, William Francis Howard,[227] Chatham	29 Apr. 73	8 Jan. 85	5 Nov. 92
Waller, Edmund Augustus,[228] Examiner of Accounts, Southern Mahratta Railway	29 Apr. 73	8 Jan. 85	13 Nov. 92
Kenney, Arthur Herbert,[229] CMG. Okehampton	29 Apr. 73	8 Jan. 85	23 Nov. 92
Wahab, Robert Alexander,[230] Survey of India, Calcutta	29 Apr. 73	8 Jan. 85	5 Dec. 92
St. Clair, William Augustus Edmund,[231] Hilsea	29 Apr. 73	8 Jan. 85	19 Dec. 92
Tower, George Alfred,[232] School of Military Engineering	29 Apr. 73	8 Jan. 85	8 Jan. 93
Childers, Edmund Spencer Eardley[233] (Bt. Major ç Jan. 85; Bt. Lt. Colonel, 2 Apr. 93), Assistant Military Secretary to Lord Wolseley	29 Apr. 73	8 Jan. 85	1 Apr. 93
Wingfield-Stratford, Cecil Vernon, Gosport	29 Apr. 73	8 Jan. 85	1 Apr. 93
Maxwell, Cedric,[234] Egypt	29 Apr. 73	8 Jan. 85	4 Apr. 93
Coles, Walter,[235] Portsmouth	29 Apr. 73	8 Jan. 85	19 Apr. 93
Friend, Lovick Bransby, Portsmouth	11 Sept. 73	8 Jan. 85	3 May 93
Shute, Gerald Edward,[236] Ordered to India	11 Sept. 73	8 Jan. 85	22 May 93
Rainsford-Hannay, Frederick, Chester	11 Sept. 73	8 Jan. 85	26 May 93
p.s.c. Haig, Herbert de Haga,[237] Adj. 1 Newcastle-on-Tyne Vol. Eng. 24 May 92	11 Sept. 73	8 Jan. 85	1 July 93
Penrose, Cooper,[238] Assist. Insp. Sub. Defences, War Office, Whitehall	11 Sept. 73	8 Jan. 85	10 July 93
Day, John George,[239] Limerick	11 Sept. 73	8 Jan. 85	10 July 93
Porter, Geoffrey Merchead,[147] Exec. Eng., 2nd Grade, Bombay Defence Division	11 Sept. 73	8 Jan. 85	14 July 93
Jerome, Henry Joseph Walker,[240] Adjutant 1 Lanark Engineer Volunteers 1 Feb. 91	11 Sept. 73	8 Jan. 85	1 Aug. 93
Scott-Moncrieff, Geo. Kenneth,[241] Instr. School of Mil. Eng., Chatham, 1 Nov. 93	11 Sept. 73	8 Jan. 85	11 Sept. 93
p.s.c. Sinclair, Hugh Montgomerie, Aldershot	12 Feb. 74	12 Feb. 85	1 Jan. 94
Kenyon, Edward Ranulph, School of Military Engineering, Chatham	12 Feb. 74	12 Feb. 85	12 Feb. 94
Grant, Samuel Charles Norton, Ordnance Survey, Southampton	12 Feb. 74	12 Feb. 85	12 Feb. 94
Bate, Charles M'Guire,[242] Inspector of Iron Structures, War Office	12 Feb. 74	12 Feb. 85	12 Feb. 94
Middlemass, John Crawford, Pembroke Dock	12 Feb. 74	12 Feb. 85	12 Feb. 94
Peel, Frederick,[126] Exec. Eng. 2nd Gr., D.P.W., Military Works Branch, Lahore	12 Feb. 74	12 Feb. 85	12 Feb. 94
Lutyens, John Gallwey,[243] Leeds	12 Feb. 74	12 Feb. 85	12 Feb. 94
Cameron, Maurice Alexander, War Office	17 Aug. 74	17 Aug. 85	5 Apr. 94
Wrottesley, Alfred Edward, Hong Kong	17 Aug. 74	17 Aug. 85	3 May 94
Cleeve, Stewart Dalrymple,[244] Adjutant 1 Hants Engineer Militia 23 Aug. 92	17 Aug. 74	17 Aug. 85	10 May 94
MacDonnell, Alfred Creagh,[245] Curragh	17 Aug. 74	17 Aug. 85	18 May 94
Boyce, Ernest Joseph George, Ceylon	17 Aug. 74	17 Aug. 85	21 May 94
Mason, Alex. Herb.,[246] Simla, D.A.Q.M.G. Intelligence Dep. (Bt. Lt. Col. 9 June 94)	17 Aug. 74	17 Aug. 85	8 June 94
Appleton, Henry,[247] Exec. Eng., 3rd Grade, D.P.W., M.W. Branch. Leave, Europe	17 Aug. 74	17 Aug. 85	11 June 94
Dickie, John Elford,[248] Exec. Eng., 2nd Grade, D.P. Works, M.W.B., Meerut Div.	17 Aug. 74	17 Aug. 85	21 June 94
Tyler, Henry Edward, Inspector of Submarine Defences, India	17 Aug. 74	17 Aug. 85	7 July 94
Abbott, Herbert Edw. Stacy,[249] Under Sec. to Punjab Govt. P.W.D. Gen. Branch	17 Aug. 74	17 Aug. 85	6 Aug. 94
p.s.c. Foster, Hubert John,[250] D.A.A. Gen., Intelligence Department, War Office	28 Jan. 75	28 Jan. 86	20 Sept. 94
Haynes, Charles Edward,[251] Ordnance Survey, Southampton	28 Jan. 75	28 Jan. 86	1 Oct. 94
Barnet, Horace Hutton,[252] Exec. Eng., 2nd Grade, D.P.W., M.W. Branch, Bombay	28 Jan. 75	28 Jan. 86	24 Oct. 94
Ruck, Oliver Edwal,[253] Bermuda	28 Jan. 75	28 Jan. 86	3 Nov. 94
Mayne, Charles Blair,[126] Secretary Royal Engineers' Institute, Chatham	28 Jan. 75	28 Jan. 86	10 Dec. 94
Goodwyn, Henry Edward,[254] DSO. Queen's Own Sappers and Miners, Bangalore	28 Jan. 75	28 Jan. 86	12 Dec. 94
Gale, Walter Andrew, Halstead, near Sevenoaks	28 Jan. 75	28 Jan. 86	17 Dec. 94
Hawkins, Walter Francis,[255] Singapore	19 Aug. 75	19 Aug. 86	20 Dec. 94
Slater, Mortimer John,[126] Adjutant 1 West Riding of York Eng. Vols. 14 Apr. 91	19 Aug. 75	19 Aug. 86	22 Dec. 94
Randolph, Alfred Herbert,[126] Office of Inspector Gen. of Fortifications, Whitehall	19 Aug. 75	19 Aug. 86	1 Jan. 95
Jackson, Louis Charles,[147] York	19 Aug. 75	19 Aug. 86	24 Jan. 95
Littledale, Ralph Pudsay,[257] Adjutant 1 Cheshire Engineer Volunteers 1 Dec. 91	19 Aug. 75	19 Aug. 86	1 Mar. 95

CAPTAINS.

Name	LIEUT.	CAPTAIN.
Commeline, Charles Ernest,[256] Halifax, N.S.	19 Aug. 75	19 Aug. 86
Cowan, James Henry, War Office, Whitehall	2 Feb. 76	2 Feb. 87
Bond, Francis George,[261] India	2 Feb. 76	2 Feb. 87
p.s.c. Leverson, George Francis, Commanding 32nd Fortress Company, Gibraltar	2 Feb. 76	2 Feb. 87
Bowles, Frederick Gilbert,[262] G.P.O. Telegraphs, London	2 Feb. 76	2 Feb. 87
Longe, Francis Bacon,[263] Dep. Supt. 1st Grade, Topog. Surv. of India, Bangalore	2 Feb. 76	2 Feb. 87
Turton, William Harry, Adjutant 2 Lancashire Volunteer Engineers 31 May 94	14 Aug. 76	14 Aug. 87
Gordon, George Huntly Blair,[264] Home District	14 Aug. 76	14 Aug. 87
Brotherton, Thomas de la Haye,[265] Malta	14 Aug. 76	14 Aug. 87
Carr, George Anderson, Chief Instructor (S. Mining) School of Military Engineering	14 Aug. 76	14 Aug. 87
Kelly, Arthur James, Adjutant 1st London Engineer Volunteers 4 May 92	14 Aug. 76	14 Aug. 87
Stanton, Edward Charles,[266] Exec. Eng. 2nd Gr., D.P.W., M.W.B., Rangoon	14 Aug. 76	14 Aug. 87
p.s.c. Heath, Frederick Crofton[267] (Bt. Major, 26 Jan. 88), Brigade Major & Secretary S.M.E.	25 Jan. 77	25 Jan. 88
Glubb, Frederic Manley, Preston	25 Jan. 77	25 Jan. 88
Thomson, Andrew Graham[268] (Bt. Major, 26 Jan. 88), Malta	25 Jan. 77	25 Jan. 88
p.s.c. Pemberton, Ernest St. Clair,[269] Horse Guards, War Office	25 Jan. 77	25 Jan. 88
Layard, Arthur Austen Macgregor,[270] Adjutant 1 Middlesex Engineer Volunteers 1 July 89	25 Jan. 77	25 Jan. 88
p.s.c. Laffan, Henry David, Staff Captain, Intelligence Department, War Office	19 June 77	1 Apr. 88
p.s.c. Lawson, Henry Merrick[271] (Bt. Major, 2 Apr. 88), D.A.A. Gen. War Office, 29 Sept. 93	19 June 77	1 Apr. 88
Tanner, John Arthur,[272] DSO. Executive Eng., 3rd Grade, D.P.W. M.W. Branch, Calcutta	19 June 77	1 Apr. 88
Sankey, Alfred Robert Mandeville, Cork. Ordered to Jamaica	19 June 77	1 Apr. 88
Reynolds, Frank Romilly, Victoria Local Forces, Melbourne	19 June 77	1 Apr. 88
MacCarthy, Felix Denis Francis,[273] Hong Kong	19 June 77	1 Apr. 88
Paterson, Hugh Aug. Lawrence. Ordered to Ireland	19 June 77	1 Apr. 88
Irvine, James Laird,[274] Adjutant Royal Engineer Troops at Aldershot	19 June 77	1 Apr. 88
Hussey, William Clive,[275] Aide de Camp to Lieut. General Robert Grant, CB., Inspector General of Fortifications and Royal Engineers	19 June 77	1 Apr. 88
Jackson, Hugh M.,[276] Deputy Superintendent, 1st Grade, Survey of India, Calcutta	19 June 77	1 Apr. 88
p.s.c. Agar, Edward, Deputy Assistant Adjutant General, Intelligence Branch, War Office	9 Oct. 77	1 Apr. 88
Rice, Spring Robert, Adjutant School of Military Engineering 10 Aug. 92	9 Oct. 77	1 Apr. 88
Meeres, Arthur Douglas, Adjutant 1st Aberdeen Volunteer Engineers 17 Sept. 94	9 Oct. 77	1 Apr. 88
Dumbleton, Horatio Norris,[277] Home District	9 Oct. 77	1 Apr. 88
Prendergast, Theodore John Warrender, Isle of Wight	9 Oct. 77	4 Apr. 88
Massy, Hampden Hugh, Cork	9 Oct. 77	26 May 88
Adair, Henry Benjamin Naylor,[279] Adjutant Royal Anglesey Engineer Militia	9 Oct. 77	1 July 88
St. John, Charles William Robert, Lough Swilly	9 Oct. 77	1 July 88
Yolland, William, Bermuda	9 Oct. 77	1 July 88
Mantell, Alfred Montgomery,[280] Ordnance Survey, Southampton	31 Jan. 78	1 July 88
Burn-Murdoch, Paul Robt. Experimental Officer, Submarine Mining Service, Pembroke Dock	31 Jan. 78	1 July 88

CAPTAINS.	LIEUT.	CAPTAIN.
Williams, Godfrey,[281] Exec. Engineer, 2nd Grade, D.P.W., M.W. Branch, Peshawur	31 Jan. 78	10 July 88
Huskisson, William, Professor, R. M. College, Kingston, Canada	31 Jan. 78	14 July 88
Cregan, Thomas Andrew, Adjutant 1 Gloucestershire Volunteershire Engineers 30 Oct. 94	31 Jan. 78	18 July 88
Druitt, Edward, Secretary Royal Engineer Committee, Chatham	31 Jan. 78	1 Aug. 88
Chesney, Harold Frank,[278] On Leave, Europe	31 Jan. 78	19 Aug. 88
Brownrigg, Henry John Watt, Instructor Royal Military Academy 15 Aug. 93	31 Jan. 78	16 Dec. 88
Stafford, Henry Lawrence Caulfeild Howard, Instructor R. Military Academy 20 Aug. 92	31 Jan. 78	18 Dec. 88
Anderson, Francis James.[282] Penang. Col. Engineer	31 Jan. 78	18 Dec. 88
Arkwright, Leonard Arthur, Shorncliffe	31 Jan. 78	18 Dec. 88
Gubbins, Philip Charles, Belfast	31 Jan. 78	18 Dec. 88
Cairnes, William Alan,[283] Dublin	31 Jan. 78	18 Dec. 88
Stockdale, Godfrey Henry Wolley, Plymouth	31 Jan. 78	18 Dec. 88
Davidson, Stuart. Devonport	18 Dec. 78	10 Jan. 89
Leigh, Richard, Ceylon	18 Dec. 78	12 Jan. 89
Horniblow, Frank Herbert, Adjutant 2 Gloucestershire Engineer Volunteers 3 Oct. 93	18 Dec. 78	8 Feb. 89
Baker, Walter Way, War Office	18 Dec. 78	3 Mar. 89
Russell, Bruce Bremner,[284] Company Commander, Kirkee	18 Dec. 78	8 Mar. 89
Learoyd, Charles Douglas,[285] Adjutant Monmouth Engineer Militia, 14 Nov. 91	18 Dec. 78	19 Mar. 89
Norris, Stephen Leslie,[286] Edinburgh	18 Dec. 78	28 Mar. 89
Mullaly, Herbert,[287] Executive Engineer, 2nd Grade, D.P.W., M.W. Branch, Ferozepore	18 Dec. 78	30 Mar. 89
Hinde, William Henry, Portsmouth	18 Dec. 78	1 Apr. 89
Mills, Dudley Acland, Halifax, Nova Scotia. Ordered to Plymouth	18 Dec. 78	1 Apr. 89
Drummond, Arthur George, Curragh	18 Dec. 78	1 Apr. 89
Winn, John,[289] Halifax, N. S.	6 Apr. 79	1 Apr. 89
Burrard, Sidney Gerald, Dep. Supdt., 4th Grade, Topograp. Survey of India, Mussorie	6 Apr. 79	1 Apr. 89
Kelly, Francis Henry,[290] Exec. Eng., 2nd Grade, P.W.D., M.W. Branch, Jullundur	6 Apr. 79	1 Apr. 89
King, Henry Somerset,[291] Ordnance Survey, Clifton, Bristol	6 Apr. 79	1 Apr. 89
Browne, Clement Alf. Righy, Dep. Exam., 1st Grade, D.P.W. Leave, Europe	6 Apr. 79	1 Apr. 89
Russell, Walter, School of Military Engineering	6 Apr. 79	1 Apr. 89
Jeffreys, Fred. Vaughan, Aldershot	6 Apr. 79	1 Apr. 89
Roberts, Henry Bradley, Assistant Instructor (Submarine Mining), S. M. E. Chatham	6 Apr. 79	1 Apr. 89
Townshend, Ernest, Gosport	6 Apr. 79	1 Apr. 89
Sandbach, Arthur Edmund,[293] Aldershot	6 Apr. 79	1 Apr. 89
Allen, Robert Franklin,[294] Executive Engineer, 3rd Grade, M. W. Branch; Office of Inspector General of Military Works, Simla	6 Apr. 79	2 Apr. 89
Dallas, James, Executive Engineer, 3rd Grade, D. P.W., Assist. Secretary, M.W.B., Simla	30 July 79	4 Apr. 89
Stuart, Andrew Mitchell,[296] Inspector of Royal Engineers' Stores, War Office	30 July 79	17 Apr. 89
Vidal, William Sealy,[297] Chief Instructor, Submarine Mining Service, Portsmouth	30 July 79	17 Apr. 89
Norton, Charles Edward, Ordnance Survey, Derby	30 July 79	17 Apr. 89
Biggs, Henry Vero,[298] Exec. Eng., 4th Grade, Mil. Works Branch, Secunderabad	30 July 79	3 May 89
Burton, Edmund Merceron,[299] Colchester	30 July 79	7 May 89
Tuke, Martin Litchfield,[300] Commanding 31st Company, School of Military Engineering	30 July 79	10 May 89
Oldfield, Frederick Hume,[301] Ordnance Survey, Carlisle	30 July 79	21 May 89
Dopping-Hepenstal, Lambert John,[302] Cork	30 July 79	11 June 89
Grant, Alexander, Instructor of Fortification, Royal Military Academy, 1 Apr. 92	30 July 79	21 June 89
Hemming, Edward Hughes, Bombay	18 Feb. 80	25 June 89
Hodder, William Morgan,[303] School of Military Engineering, Chatham	18 Feb. 80	25 June 89
Hulcatt, Hugh,[304] Second Assistant Building Works Ordnance Factories 1 Aug. 93	18 Feb. 80	6 July 89
Maclagan, Robert Smeiton,[305] Assist. Eng., 1st Grade, P.W.D., M.W.B., Delhi	18 Feb. 80	20 July 89
Boyd, Mossom Archibald, Chief Instructor (Submarine Mining), Plymouth	18 Feb. 80	20 July 89
Hilliard, William Robert, Executive Engineer, 4th Grade, Kurrachee	18 Feb. 80	20 July 89
Swayne, Harald George Carlos,[306] School of Military Engineering	18 Feb. 80	23 July 89
Nathan, Matthew, War Office, London	19 May 80	31 July 89
Cowie, Alexander Hugh, G.P.O. Telegraphs, Exeter	19 May 80	6 Aug. 89
Thackwell, Osbert Montague Roche, School of Military Engineering, Chatham	19 May 80	10 Aug. 89
Stewart, James,[307] Assistant Engineer, 1st Grade, D.P.W., M.W. Branch, Meerut	19 May 80	4 Sept. 89
Kincaid, William Francis Henry Style,[308] serving with the Egyptian Army	27 July 80	1 Oct. 89
D'Aylmer, Fenton John,[309] Sappers and Miners, Bengal (Brevet Major, 18 Oct. 93)	27 July 80	2 Oct. 89
Capper, John Edward, Exec. Eng., 3rd Grade, M.W.B., Temp. Employ, Kashmir	27 July 80	1 Nov. 89
Haynes, Alfred Ernest,[310] School of Military Engineering, Chatham	27 July 80	3 Nov. 89
Baddeley, Charles Edward,[311] Bombay Sappers and Miners; Company Commander, Kirkee	27 July 80	17 Dec. 89
Dixon, Peter Eden, Executive Engineer, 4th Grade, D.P.W. Leave, Europe	23 Feb. 81	17 Dec. 89
Hill, Cecil,[312] Ordnance Survey, Southampton	23 Feb. 81	17 Dec. 89
Meredith, Edward Spencer, Chester	23 Feb. 81	17 Dec. 89
Petrie, Ricardo Dartnell,[313] Assistant Adjutant, Service Battalion, Chatham	23 Feb. 81	17 Dec. 89
Cowie, Charles Henry, Executive Engineer, 3rd Grade, D.P.W., Calcutta. On Furlough	23 Feb. 81	17 Dec. 89
Edmonds, James Edward, Instructor in Fortification, Royal Military Academy	26 July 81	13 Jan. 90
Morter, William Ross,[315] Executive Engineer, 4th Grade, D.P. Works, Punjab	26 July 81	25 Jan. 90
Shelley, Archibald Douglas Graham, Executive Engineer, 3rd Grade, D.P.W.; Under Secretary to Madras Government, P.W.D., Railway Branch	26 July 81	1 Feb. 90
Paske, Gordon Henry, Adjutant 1 Durham Volunteer Engineers 26 Nov. 93	26 July 81	1 Mar. 90
Glanville, Francis,[319] DSO. Queen's Own Sappers and Miners, Bangalore	26 July 81	19 Apr. 90
Ellis, William Montague, Consulting Architect, Chepah	26 July 81	6 May 90
Van Straubenzee, Arthur Hope, School of Military Engineering	30 July 81	10 May 90
Macdonald, James Ronald Leslie,[320] Simla	22 Feb. 82	7 June 90
Walton, Ellys William, Dep. Consulting Eng. to Govt. of India for Railways, Calcutta	22 Feb. 82	29 June 90
Dundee, William John Daniell, School of Military Engineering, Chatham	22 Feb. 82	30 June 90
Roper, Alexander William,[322] Gibraltar	22 Feb. 82	2 July 90
Jones, Lewis, Edinburgh	22 Feb. 82	2 July 90
Hamilton, James Edwin O'Hora. Chatham	22 Feb. 82	6 July 90
Craster, Shafto Longfield, Exec. Eng. 4th Grade, D.P.W., M.W.B., Rawul Pindee. On Leave	22 Feb. 82	3 Aug. 90
p.s.c. Heath, Gerard Moore,[324] Bengal Sappers and Miners	22 Feb. 82	3 Aug. 90
Mackenzie, Ronald Joseph Henry Louis,[325] Supdt. 4th Grade, Survey of India, Quetta	25 July 82	24 Sept. 90
Leahy, Charles Albert,[326] Ordnance Survey, Edinburgh	25 July 82	24 Sept. 90
Molony, Francis Arthur,[327] Woolwich	25 July 82	22 Oct. 90
Luard, William Du Cane,[328] Malta	25 July 82	23 Dec. 90
Cordue, William George Ranger,[329] Exec. Eng., 3rd Grade, D.P.W., M.W.B., Barrackpore	25 July 82	1 Jan. 91
Wade, James Molesworth,[330] Exec. Engineer, 3rd Grade, D.P.W., M.W. B. Leave, Europe	25 July 82	15 Jan. 91
Bythell, William John,[331] Deputy Superintendent, 2nd Grade, Survey of India, Simla	25 July 82	15 Jan. 91
Ward, Bernard Rowland. Ordered to Aldershot	25 July 82	15 Jan. 91
Stewart, William Robert, Hong Kong	1 Oct. 82	15 Jan. 91
Elliot, Gilbert Sutherland McDowell, Assistant Engineer, 1st Grade, Zhob Valley Railway Survey, Dalhousie. On Leave	1 Oct. 82	16 Feb. 91
Salvesen, Charles Emil,[333] Ordnance Survey, Clifton, Bristol	1 Oct. 82	17 Apr. 91
Godby, Charles,[334] Egyptian Army. On Leave	1 Oct. 82	4 May 91

Corps of Royal Engineers.

CAPTAINS.	LIEUT.	CAPTAIN.
Pringle, John Wallace,³³⁵ Executive Engineer, 3rd Grade, M. W. D.; Temporary Duty, Irish Relief Works. Leave, Europe	14 Feb. 83	6 May 91
Serjeant, James Robert Beza,³³⁶ Sappers and Miners, Roorkee	14 Feb. 83	9 May 91
Kent, Herbert Vaughan, Plymouth	14 Feb. 83	12 June 91
Houston, Eyre, Executive Engineer, 3rd Grade, D.P.W., Aden	14 Feb. 83	20 June 91
Morony, Burdett Edward, School of Military Engineering	14 Feb. 83	13 July 91
Brown, William Baker, Assistant Instructor (Submarine Mining), Portsmouth	14 Feb. 83	6 Aug. 91
Mould, Charles Frederick, Ordnance Survey, Chester	14 Feb. 83	12 Aug. 91
Renny-Tailyour, Thomas Francis Bruce,³³⁸ Survey of India, Burma	14 Feb. 83	13 Aug. 91
Rose, Charles Stuart,³³⁹ Exec. Eng., 4th Grade, D.P.W., M.W.B., Bangalore. Leave, Europe	14 Feb. 83	13 Aug. 91
O'Meara, Walter Alfred John,³⁴⁰ Cape Town	14 Feb. 83	8 Sept. 91
Haggitt, Edward Dashwood, Newcastle on-Tyne	14 Feb. 83	16 Sept. 91
Gordon, William Staveley,³⁴¹ Egyptian Army, Cairo	15 Feb. 83	30 Sept. 91
Lang, John Irvine, Assistant Instructor, School of Military Engineering	26 June 83	1 Oct. 91
Lawrie, Walter Gray, Assistant Instructor (Submarine Mining), S. M. E., Portsmouth	28 July 83	1 Oct. 91
Painter, Arnaud Clarke, Portland	28 July 83	18 Oct. 91
Swainson, Arthur Lake, Exec. Eng. 3rd Grade, D.P. Works, M.W. Branch, Madras	28 July 83	19 Oct. 91
Broke, Harry, Ordnance Survey, Bristol	28 July 83	6 Nov. 91
Purvis, John Spottiswoode, Belfast	28 July 83	23 Nov. 91
Bonham-Carter, Herman,³⁴³ N. W. Railway, Karachi	28 July 83	2 Dec. 91
Taylor, Ernest Frederick, Lydd	28 July 83	6 Dec. 91
Buckland, Reginald Ulick Henry,³⁴⁴ Southampton	28 July 83	31 Dec. 91
Curtis, Reginald Salmond, Aldershot	28 July 83	31 Dec. 91
Brett, Walter Percival, Instructor in Electricity, Royal Military Academy	28 July 83	31 Dec. 91
Johnston, Bruce Campbell, Weedon	28 July 83	31 Dec. 91
Johnstone, James Henry L'Estrange, War Office	15 Feb. 84	2 Jan. 92
Gibbon, James Aubrey, Exec. Eng. 4th Grade, D.P.W., M.W. Branch, Mooltan. On Leave	15 Feb. 84	6 Jan. 92
Ashworth, Perceval, Shorncliffe	15 Feb. 84	18 Jan. 92
Bullen, Edward Darley,³⁴⁵ 2nd Assistant Principal, Thomason College, Roorkee. On Leave	15 Feb. 84	15 Mar. 92
Harrison, Thomas,³⁴⁶ DSO. Sappers and Miners, Kirkee. On Furlough	15 Feb. 84	16 Mar. 92
Hunter-Weston, Aylmer Gould,³⁴⁷ Bengal Sappers and Miners, Assam	15 Feb. 84	1 Apr. 92
Reynolds, Arthur Reynold, Jamaica. Ordered home	15 Feb. 84	1 Apr. 92
Gaynor, Henry Francis, Assistant Instructor Workshops, School of Military Engineering	15 Feb. 84	1 Apr. 92
Laurence, Richard Thos. Raynes,³⁴⁹ Exec. Eng., 3rd Grade, M. W. Branch. Leave, Europe	15 Feb. 84	4 Apr. 92
Dealy, John Anderson,³⁵¹ Executive Engineer, 4th Grade, M.W.D., Madras	15 Feb. 84	25 May 92
Pery, Cecil Charles James, Ordnance Survey, Dublin	15 Feb. 84	3 June 92
Wright, Henry Brooke Hageträmer,³⁵³ Madras Sappers and Miners, Chin Hills	15 Feb. 84	12 July 92
Fowke, George Henry, Curragh	15 Feb. 84	19 July 92
Rimington, Joseph Cameron,³⁵⁴ Exec. Eng., 4th Grade, D.P.Works, Mil.Works Branch, Simla	15 Feb. 84	27 July 92
Lyons, Henry George, Egyptian Army	15 Feb. 84	6 Aug. 92
Roe, Cyril Harcourt,³⁵⁵ Sappers and Miners, Bangalore	15 Feb. 84	27 Aug. 92
Carey, Herbert Clement, Sheerness	26 June 84	1 Oct. 92
Close, Charles Frederick, School of Military Engineering, Mussoorie	5 July 84	1 Oct. 92
Laffan, Joseph de Courcy, School of Military Engineering, Chatham	5 July 84	1 Oct. 92
Harper, George Montague, Adjutant 2 West Riding of York Eng. Vols. 10 Oct. 92	5 July 84	1 Oct. 92
Tudor, Ernest Augs. Tudor, Harwich. Ordered to Mauritius	5 July 84	7 Oct. 92
Macdonogh, George Mark Watson, Submarine Mining Service, Harwich	5 July 84	21 Oct. 92
Brewin, John Palffy, Gibraltar	5 July 84	5 Nov. 92
Skey, Frederic Edward Guthrie, Bengal Sappers and Miners, Roorkee	5 July 84	13 Nov. 92
Brooker, Robert Lee Cecil,³⁵⁶ Ordnance Survey, Cork	5 July 84	23 Nov. 92
Young, Julius Ralph, Assistant Instructor, School of Military Engineering, Chatham	5 July 84	5 Dec. 92
Phillips, George Edward, War Office	5 July 84	19 Dec. 92
Simmons, George Francis Henry LeBreton,³⁵⁶† Submarine Mining Service, Sheerness	5 July 84	8 Jan. 93
Hills, Edmond Herbert, Assistant Instructor, School of Military Engineering, Chatham	5 July 84	1 Apr. 93
Baylay, Frederick, School of Military Engineering	5 July 84	1 Apr. 93
MacAdam, Walter, Paull on the Humber	5 July 84	1 Apr. 93
Speranza, Walter Stephen John J. Lawrence, Cork	5 July 84	4 Apr. 93
Edgell, Edward Arnold,³⁵⁷ Executive Engineer, 4th Grade, Pishin	9 Dec. 84	19 Apr. 93
Powell, Sidney Henry,³⁵⁸ Assistant Engineer, 1st Grade, D.P.W., Quetta	9 Dec. 84	3 May 93
Harrison, Gilbert Harwood, Cairo, Egypt	9 Dec. 84	22 May 93
Ewbank, William,³⁵⁹ Staff College	9 Dec. 84	26 May 93
Livingstone, Hubert Armine Anson, Natal	9 Dec. 84	1 July 93
Stevens, Charles Richard, Athlone, Ireland	9 Dec. 84	10 July 93
Chapman, Leonard Palmer,³⁶⁰ Executive Engineer, 4th Grade, D.P.W., M.W.B., Beloochistan	9 Dec. 84	10 July 93
Liddell, William Andrew,³⁶¹ Gravesend	9 Dec. 84	14 July 93
Schreiber, Acton Lemuel, Executive Engineer, 4th Grade, D. P. W. Wellington, Madras	9 Dec. 84	1 Aug. 93
Tulloch, John Arthur Stanford,³⁶² Madras Sappers and Miners, Mandalay	9 Dec. 84	11 Dec. 93
Evans, Usher Williamson,³⁶³ Madras Sappers and Miners, Bangalore	9 Dec. 84	1 Jan. 94
Bland, Edward Humphry,³⁶⁴ Ordnance Survey, York	9 Dec. 84	12 Jan. 94
Hedley, Walter Coote, Gibraltar	9 Dec. 84	17 Jan. 94
Stokes-Roberts, Edward Rowland Bennett,³⁶⁵ Birmingham	9 Dec. 84	8 Mar. 94
Williams, Hugh Bruce, 2nd Division Telegraph Battalion, Basingstoke	29 Apr. 85	19 Mar. 94
Fanshawe, Gerard Lewis, Falmouth	29 Apr. 85	28 Mar. 94
Euthoven, Chas. Honfrey, Assist. Instructor, School of Mil. Engineering, Chatham, 7 Sept. 93	29 Apr. 85	1 Apr. 94
Gale, Henry Richmond, South Africa	29 Apr. 85	4 Apr. 94
Close, Geoffrey Dominic,³⁶⁷ School of Military Engineering	29 Apr. 85	5 Apr. 94
Sorsbie, Robert Fox,³⁶⁸ Bangalore	29 Apr. 85	3 May 94
Lloyd, Frederic Lindsay, Western District	29 Apr. 85	10 May 94
Jones, Harry Balfour, Balloon Section, Aldershot	29 Apr. 85	18 May 94
Sherwood, Harold Joseph,³⁷⁰ Roorkee	29 Apr. 85	21 May 94
Dixon, Richard Travers, Mauritius. Ordered home	29 Apr. 85	8 June 94
Lee, Richard Philipps, Ordnance Survey, Dublin	29 Apr. 85	11 June 94
Perceval, Charles Cecil.³⁷³ On Leave	29 Apr. 85	21 June 94
Edwards, Richard Fieldin, Submarine Mining Duty, Bermuda	29 Apr. 85	7 July 94
Nanton, Herbert Colborne.³⁷⁴ Exec. Eng. 4th Grade, D.P. Works, M.W.D., Rawul Pindee	30 June 85	6 Aug. 94
Casgrain, Philippe Henri du Perron,³⁷⁵ Ordnance Survey, Bedford	30 June 85	20 Sept. 94
Ridout, Dudley Howard, Gravesend	30 June 85	1 Oct. 94
Von Hugel, Norman Guy, Plymouth	30 June 85	16 Oct. 94
Skinner, Thomas Carlyle, Dover	30 June 85	26 Oct. 94
Sloggett, Harry,³⁷⁷ Ordnance Survey, Ennis	30 June 85	3 Nov. 94
Cartwright, Geo. Strachan,³⁷⁸ Exec. Eng., 4th Grade, D.P.W, M.W. Branch. Leave, Europe	30 June 85	6 Dec. 94
Kirkpatrick, Geo. Macaulay, Aide de Camp to Major General B. L. Forster, Comdg. Thames Dist	30 June 85	12 Dec. 94
Lenox-Conyngham, Gerald Ponsonby, Dehra Dhoon	16 Sept. 85	17 Dec. 94
Tomlin, Robert Ernest, Assistant Engineer, 1st Grade, Railway Branch, Lahore	16 Sept. 85	22 Dec. 94
p.s.c. Clauson, John Eugene, Special Duty, War Office	16 Sept. 85	22 Dec. 94
Travers, George Alfred,³⁷⁹ Roorkee	16 Sept. 85	1 Jan. 95
Dunsterville, Edward Leslie, Madras Sappers and Miners	16 Sept. 85	24 Jan. 95
Bigge, Thomas Arthur Hastings, Gibraltar	6 Sept. 85	1 Mar. 95

Corps of Royal Engineers.

LIEUTENANTS.

Name	LIEUT
Tilley, William Fairbairn,[376] Assistant Engineer, 2nd Grade, D.P.W., Belgaum	30 June 85
Atkinson, Edward Henry de Vere,[381] Executive Engineer, 4th Grade, Quetta. On Leave	16 Sept. 85
Colnaghi, Dominic Henry, Malta	16 Sept. 85
Twiss, John Henry, School of Military Engineering	16 Sept. 85
Moore, Arthur Trevelyan,[382] Assistant Engineer, 1st Grade, D.P.W. Lucknow	16 Sept. 85
Prentice, Herbert, School of Military Engineering	16 Sept. 85
Johnson, Eliot Philips,[383] Bangalore	16 Sept. 85
Sclater, Bertram Lutley, Intelligence Department, War Office	16 Sept. 85
Scudamore, Walter Victor, Assistant Engineer, 1st Grade, D.P.W., Bombay. Leave, Europe	16 Sept. 85
Swiney, Alexander John Henry,[385] Executive Engineer, 4th Grade, D.P.W., M.W. Branch, Rawul Pindee	16 Sept. 85
M'Elhinny, William John,[386] Assistant Engineer, 1st Grade, Lucknow	6 Jan. 86
Duff, George Mowat,[387] Exec. Engineer, 4th Grade, D.P.W. M.W. Branch, Rawul Pindee	6 Jan. 86
Twining, Philip Geoffrey, Instructor, Royal Military College, Canada, with local rank of Captain	6 Jan. 86
Joly, Alain Chartier de Lotbinière, Bombay	6 Jan. 86
Wilson, Frederick Alfred, Kirkee	6 Jan. 86
Picton-Jones, Reginald Ernest,[388] Aden. On Furlough	6 Jan. 86
Kirby, Norborne, Burmah	6 Jan. 86
Robinson, Richard Percy, Assistant Inspector of Warlike Stores 1 Apr. 93, Manchester	6 Jan. 86
Paul, Ernest Moncreiff, Assistant Instructor, School of Military Engineering, Chatham	5 Jan. 86
Fowler, John Sharman,[390] Gilgit	6 Jan. 86
Radcliffe, Philip John Joseph, Adj. 1 Devon and Somerset Volunteer Eng. with rank of Captain	3 Feb. 85
Hutton, Gilbert Montgomerie,[391] School of Military Engineering	3 Feb. 86
Wade, Henry Molesworth St. Aubyn,[392] Ordnance Survey, Southampton	17 Feb. 86
Heycock, Charles Hensman,[393] Queen's Own Sappers and Miners, Bangalore	17 Feb. 86
Seaman, Edwin Charles, Assistant Instructor (Submarine Mining), School of Military Eng., Chatham	17 Feb. 86
Murray, Valentine, District Traffic Superintendent, Bareilly	17 Feb. 86
Babington, Stafford Charles, Cape Town	17 Feb. 86
Blair, Everard M'Leod, Assistant Instructor of Fortifications, School of Military Engineering, Chatham	17 Feb. 86
Weedon, Franklin Francis,[394] Bangalore	17 Feb. 86
Burn, James Montague, Mussorie	17 Feb. 86
Murray, James Harry Stewart, Ferozepore	17 Feb. 86
Blakeway, John Prestwich, Burmah	17 Feb. 86
Molesworth, Percy Braybrooke. On passage home	17 Feb. 86
Coffin, Campbell, Staff College	17 Feb. 86
Digby, William Trench, Curragh	17 Feb. 86
Burn, Ernest Melville Johnston, School of Military Engineering, Chatham	17 Feb. 86
Kingscote, Randolph Albert Fitzhardinge,[395] Jhansi	17 Feb. 86
Franklyn, Claude de Montmorency, Hythe	17 Feb 86
Morice, Cuthbert Charles Duguid, Poona	18 Feb 86
Stafford, Edmund Hyde Whalley Howard, Aden	18 Feb. 86
Fraser, Theodore,[396] Bangalore	18 Feb. 86
Pilcher, Arthur John, Assist. Superintendent, 2nd Grade, Indian Revenue Survey, Mussoorie	18 Feb. 86
Brooker, Edward Part, School of Military Engineering, Chatham	18 Feb. 86
Walpole, Alfred, Poona	18 Feb. 86
Vanrenen, James Ernest, Shorncliffe	18 Feb. 86
Williams, Sydney Frederick, Edinburgh	18 Feb. 86
Bullock, Frank, Assistant Engineer, School of Military Engineering	18 Feb. 86
Fair, Frederick Kendall, Kirkee	18 Feb. 86
Fraser, Howard Alan Denholm,[397] Assist. Superintendent, 1st Grade, Indian Revenue Survey, Poona	18 Feb. 86
Collins, Charles Bury, Submarine Mining Service, Halifax	18 Feb. 86
Acworth, George Pelham Aufrère, School of Military Engineering	18 Feb. 86
Campbell, George Polding, Ferozepore	12 May 86
Kennedy, John Nassau Chambers, Postal Telegraphs, Exeter	2 July 86
Versturme, Charles Hamilton, Gibraltar. Sick Leave	24 July 86
Nathan, Walter Simeon, Bangalore. Leave, Europe	24 July 86
Ainslie, Clement,[399] Bangalore	24 July 86
Ryder, Charles Henry Dudley, Simla	24 July 86
Boys, Reginald Harvey Henderson, New Cross (G.P.O.)	24 July 86
Wilson, Charles Stuart, Jamaica	24 July 86
Robertson, Charles Lonsdale, Quetta	24 July 86
Clayton, Henry Edward Gilbert, Aldershot	24 July 86
Burnaby, Charles Granet, Bermuda	24 July 86
Hunt, Edward Leslie, Cape Town	24 July 86
Kemp, Geoffrey Chicheley, Mooltan	24 July 86
Young, Edward George, Aldershot	24 July 86
Barton, Hugh John, Adjutant 1 Lanc. Vol. Eng. with rank of Captain, 21 Apr. 93	24 July 86

Name	2nd LIEUT	
Naish, Theodore Edward, Belfast	16 Feb. 87	16 Feb. 90
Ogilvie, Edward Collingwood,[401] Beloochistan	16 Feb. 87	16 Feb. 90
Mallaby, Digby Lighton,[402] Roorkee	16 Feb. 87	16 Feb. 90
Marshall, Hugh John Miles,[403] Burma	16 Feb. 87	16 Feb. 90
O'Shee, Richard Alfred Poer, Falmouth	16 Feb. 87	16 Feb. 90
Rotheram, Walter Henry, St. Lucia	16 Feb. 87	16 Feb. 90
Boileau, Frank Ridley Farrer, Sealkote	16 Feb. 87	16 Feb. 90
Waghorn, William Danvers, Bombay	16 Feb. 87	16 Feb. 90
Mair, Robert John Byford, Singapore	16 Feb. 87	16 Feb. 90
Watkins, Charles Mostyn Francis, Lucknow	16 Feb. 87	16 Feb. 90
Austin, Herbert Henry, Bengal Sappers and Miners	16 Feb. 87	16 Feb. 90
Lathbury, Henry Oscar, Meerut	15 Feb. 87	16 Feb. 90
Wathertson, Alan Edward Garrard, Assistant Instructor, School of Military Eng., Chatham	16 Feb. 87	16 Feb. 90
Dobbs, Conway Richard, Malta	16 Feb. 87	16 Feb. 90
Haig, Ernest Herman, Pembroke Dock	16 Feb. 87	16 Feb. 90
Home, George Joseph Lombard, Umballa	16 Mar. 87	16 Mar. 90
Leslie, George Arthur James, Aden	16 Mar. 87	16 Mar. 90
Harrison, William Albert, Ordnance Survey, Redhill	16 Mar. 87	16 Mar. 90
Bond, Reginald Francis George, Roorkee	23 July 87	23 July 90
Rivett-Carnac, Seymour Gordon, Ranikhet. Leave, Europe	23 July 87	23 July 90
Scholfield, George Peabody, Aldershot	23 July 87	23 July 90
Kincaid, Willie Alexander Scotland, Chutrapur, Ganjam	23 July 87	23 July 90
Liddell, John Stewart, Aldershot	23 July 87	23 July 90
Bigge, George Orde, Ceylon	23 July 87	23 July 90
Hingston, George Bennett, Allahabad. On Leave	24 July 87	23 July 90

Corps of Royal Engineers.

LIEUTENANTS.	2ND LIEUT.	LIEUT.
Crookshank, Chichester De Windt,[405] Bombay S. & M. Kirkee	23 July 87	23 July 90
Thuillier, R. Fleetwood, Rawul Pindee	23 July 87	23 July 90
Davy, Cecil William, Malta. Ordered home	23 July 87	23 July 90
Des Vœux, Henry Bertram, Malta	23 July 87	23 July 90
Rushton, Hy. Wm., Assam	23 July 87	23 July 90
Whitlock, George F. A., Gibraltar	23 July 87	23 July 90
Pike, Cecil Francis Browne, Malta	23 July 87	23 July 90
Palmer, William Legh, Comdg. Jamaica Co. Submarine Miners with local rank of Captain	23 July 87	23 July 90
Carmichael, Jas. F.H., Burmah. On Leave	23 July 87	23 July 90
Stockley, Hugh R.,[406] Roorkee	23 July 87	23 July 90
Caulfeild, St. Geo. R. S., Mauritius	23 July 87	23 July 90
Godfrey-Faussett, Edm. Godfrey, St. Lucia	17 Feb. 88	17 Feb. 91
Harvey, Edward Henry, Gibraltar	17 Feb. 88	17 Feb. 91
Cochrane, Thos. Henry, Gibraltar	17 Feb. 88	17 Feb. 91
Winsloe, Alf. Raynaud, Kamptee	17 Feb. 88	17 Feb. 91
Watson, Thos. Colclough, Lahore	17 Feb. 88	17 Feb. 91
Greer, R. Edw.,[403] Beloochistan	17 Feb. 88	17 Feb. 91
Smyth, W. Carew, E.C.Ry. Madras	17 Feb. 88	17 Feb. 91
Harvey, Robt. Napier, Halifax	17 Feb. 88	17 Feb. 91
Hare, Humphrey John, Lucknow	17 Feb. 88	17 Feb. 91
Brady, Dan., Rangoon	17 Feb. 88	17 Feb. 91
Rees, Fred. Fras Nigel,[409] Meerut	17 Feb. 88	17 Feb. 91
Bowen, C. Otway Cole, Bermuda	17 Feb. 88	17 Feb. 91
Hume, Arthur H. Bliss, Bengal Presidency	17 Feb. 88	17 Feb. 91
Gorringe, Geo. Fredk. serving with the Egyptian Army	17 Feb. 88	17 Feb. 91
Dick, George, Rawul Pindee. Sick Leave	17 Feb. 88	17 Feb. 91
Matheson, John Colin, Hong Kong	17 Feb. 88	17 Feb. 91
Grant, Philip Gordon, Lucknow	17 Feb. 88	17 Feb. 91
Swinton, Ernest Dunlop, Lucknow	17 Feb. 88	17 Feb. 91
Laurence, Gerald C. R., Bermuda	17 Feb. 88	17 Feb. 91
Fuller, Francis George, Aden	17 Feb. 88	17 Feb. 91
Coffin, Clifford. Cork	17 Feb. 88	17 Feb. 91
Smith, Geo. Ed., Halifax, N.S.	17 Feb. 88	17 Feb. 91
Shelley, Bertram A. G., Bombay	17 Feb. 88	17 Feb. 91
Watling, Francis Wyatt, Kurrachee	17 Feb. 88	17 Feb. 91
Hemming, N. M., Madras S. & M.	14 Mar. 88	14 Mar. 91
Riach, A. H. Dundas,[410] Ootacamund	1 Apr. 88	1 Apr. 91
Close, Lewis Henry, Secunderabad	1 Apr. 88	1 Apr. 91
Galloway, John Jos., Liverpool	1 Apr. 88	1 Apr. 91
Nugent, Charles Hugh Hodges, Ceylon	1 Apr. 88	1 Apr. 91
de Lotbinière, Henri Gustave July, Lahore. On Leave	28 June 88	28 June 91
Coldstream, W. Menzies, Punjab	27 July 88	27 July 91
Friederichs, Duncan A., Staff Coll.	27 July 88	27 July 91
Barkworth, John R. S. M. E.	27 July 88	27 July 91
Weekes, Henry Wilson, Kurrachee	27 July 88	27 July 91
Saunders, Fred. Wm., Attock	27 July 88	27 July 91
Scott, Geo. Theobalds. Sick Leave	27 July 88	27 July 91
Griffith, George Herbert, Meerut	27 July 88	27 July 91
Wilkinson, Chas. Wm., Bareilly	27 July 88	27 July 91
Gubbins, Frederic William Beresford, Curragh	27 July 88	27 July 91
Babington, W., Burmah. On Leave	27 July 88	27 July 91
M'Cornick, A. L. C., Beloochistan	27 July 88	27 July 91
Walker, George, Poona	27 July 88	27 July 91
Sanders, G. A. Fletcher[412] Chin Hills	27 July 88	27 July 91
Kelsall, H. Waddell, Hong Kong	27 July 88	27 July 91
Roberts, G. Bradley, Basingstoke	27 July 88	27 July 91
Girouard, Edouard P. Cranwell, Traffic Manager, R. Arsenal	28 July 88	28 July 91
Adams, Alexander, Mandalay	28 July 88	28 July 91
Lesslie. W. B., Ceylon. Ord. home	28 July 88	28 July 91
Farwell, Chas. Bowers. On Leave	28 July 88	28 July 91
Panet, Alphonse E., Bom. S. and M.	28 July 88	28 July 91
Bremner, Arthur Grant, Calcutta	28 July 88	28 July 91
Rooke, Bertram Hammersley, Madras S. and M.	15 Feb. 89	15 Feb. 92
Henniker, Alan M. Ord. Bermuda	15 Feb. 89	15 Feb. 92
Pyne, William Menzies, Jamaica	15 Feb. 89	15 Feb. 92
Muter, Robert Stanley, Belgaum	15 Feb. 89	15 Feb. 92
Falcon, Chas. Gordon, Malta	15 Feb. 89	15 Feb. 92
Westropp, Fred. M., Bombay	15 Feb. 89	15 Feb. 92
Cameron, Hugh Alan, Bareilly	15 Feb. 89	15 Feb. 92
Gwynn, C. W.[413] DSO. Comdg. R. Eng. West Coast of Africa with local rank of Captain	15 Feb. 89	15 Feb. 92
Guggisberg, Fred. G., Singapore	15 Feb. 89	15 Feb. 92
Hibbert, Wm. George, Roorkee	15 Feb. 89	15 Feb. 92
Petavel, Jas. William. On Leave	15 Feb. 89	15 Feb. 92
Dumaresq, Algernon H., Assist. Inst., School of Military Eng.	15 Feb. 89	15 Feb. 92
Thompson, Wm. M., Hong Kong	3 Mar. 89	3 Mar. 92
Macauley, George Bohun, Hythe	8 Mar. 89	8 Mar. 92
Rogers, Henry Schofield, Madras	27 June 89	27 June 92
Colvin, James M. C., Bengal	27 July 89	27 July 92
Dickson, Wm. Edm. R., Roorkee	27 July 89	27 July 92
de Vitré, Percy T. D., Hong Kong	27 July 89	27 July 92
Griffith, D. Maitland, Ferozepore	27 July 89	27 July 92
Cunningham, Allan H., Jhansi	27 July 89	27 July 92
Burne, F. H. C. Ord. to St. Lucia	27 July 89	27 July 92
Watts-Jones, Wm. Alan, Muttra	27 July 89	27 July 92
Lubbock, Guy, Madras S. and M.	27 July 89	27 July 92
Tod-Mercer, Bernard Meyrick Mercer, Rawul Pindee	27 July 89	27 July 92
Maud, Philip, Aldershot	27 July 89	27 July 92
Webber, Oswald, T. O'K., I. Wight	27 July 89	27 July 92
Wait, Hugh Godfrey Killigrew, Malta	27 July 89	27 July 92
Lees, William Edwin, Malta	27 July 89	27 July 92
Close, Francis Morton, Bombay	27 July 89	27 July 92
Oldham, Leslie Wm. Searles, Lahore	27 July 89	27 July 92
Crookshank, Sydney D'A., Surat	27 July 89	27 July 92
Beach, Wm. Henry. Ord. to India	27 July 89	27 July 92
Farquharson, Ernest Gordon, Beloochistan	27 July 89	27 July 92
Cumberlege, Arch. Farrington, Mil. Works Dept., Bellary	27 July 89	27 July 92
Meyer, James Leopold, Lahore	23 Nov. 89	23 Nov. 92
Cumming, Ernest Alf., S. M. E.	23 Nov. 89	23 Nov. 92
Knox, Robert Ferguson, Madras	23 Nov. 89	23 Nov. 92
Craven, Arthur Julius, Kirkee	23 Nov. 89	23 Nov. 92
West, Rooblie Hassan, Beloochistan	23 Nov. 89	23 Nov. 92
Outram, Fras. Davidson, Aldershot	23 Nov. 89	23 Nov. 92
Turner, Horace H., Quetta	23 Nov. 89	23 Nov. 92
Yeates, R. H. M. Quetta. On Leave	23 Nov. 89	23 Nov. 92
Halliday, Charles Ogilvie, Bombay	23 Nov. 89	23 Nov. 92
Macdonald, Ronald Hume,[414] Rawul Pindee	11 Dec. 89	11 Dec. 92
Christie, Hy. Robt. Stark, Malta	13 Feb. 90	13 Feb. 93
Johnson, Jos. F. W., Rangoon	14 Feb. 90	14 Feb. 93
Beazeley, George Adam, Bombay	14 Feb. 90	14 Feb. 93
Hopper, Harry Albert Lawless, N. W. Railway, Allahabad	14 Feb. 90	14 Feb. 93
Hildebrand, A. B. R., Meerut	14 Feb. 90	14 Feb. 93
Sheppard, Seymour Hulbert, Rawul Pindee	14 Feb. 90	14 Feb. 93
Sargeaunt, Arth. F., Singapore. Ordered home	14 Feb. 90	14 Feb. 93
Singer, Chas. William, Quetta	14 Feb. 90	14 Feb. 93
Boileau, Guy Hamilton,[415] Bombay	14 Feb. 90	14 Feb. 93
Gordon, Hen. William, Esquimault	14 Feb. 90	14 Feb. 93
Hingston, Edward, Barrackpore	14 Feb. 90	14 Feb. 93
Elkington, Geo. Edwd., Egypt	14 Feb. 90	14 Feb. 93
Walker, Herbert Jn., Lough Swilly	14 Feb. 90	14 Feb. 93
Lewis, Rich. Hull, Pembroke Dock	14 Feb. 90	14 Feb. 93
Hopkins, Norman John, Gibraltar	14 Feb. 90	14 Feb. 93
Rundle, Frank Peveril, India	14 Feb. 90	14 Feb. 93
Rolland, Alex., India	14 Feb. 90	14 Feb. 93
Traill, Wm. Stewart, Madras	29 Mar. 90	29 Mar. 93
Crosthwait, H. Leland, Roorkee	29 Mar. 90	29 Mar. 93
Campbell, H. B. D., Rawul Pindee	4 July 90	4 July 93
Leggett, E. Humphrey Manisty, School of Military Engineering	25 July 90	25 July 93
Carpenter, Chas. M., India	25 July 90	25 July 93
Elliott, Charles Allen, Lucknow	25 July 90	25 July 93
Chancellor, John R., India	25 July 90	25 July 93
Green, Eric H. E. Rawul Pindee	25 July 90	25 July 93
Hunter, Chas. G. W., Lucknow	25 July 90	25 July 93
Brunner, Chas. Wilfred, Gibraltar	25 July 90	25 July 93
Barrington, Wm. D'O., Gibraltar	25 July 90	25 July 93
MacGeorge, John B., Dalhousie	25 July 90	25 July 93
Manser, William Edward, Quetta	25 July 90	25 July 93
Stokes, Wm. Allen, Secunderabad. Sick Furlough	25 July 90	25 July 93
Jelley, Reginald F., Portsmouth	25 July 90	25 July 93
Walker, Reginald S., Plymouth	25 July 90	25 July 93
Hawksley, R. P. T., Rawul Pindee	25 July 90	25 July 93
Hearn, Gordon Risley, Madras. Leave, Europe	25 July 90	25 July 93
Tyler, Alf. Herbert, Sierra Leone	25 July 90	25 July 93
O'Donel, Manus Basil H., Malta	25 July 90	25 July 93
Faber, Sydney George, Curragh	13 Feb. 91	13 Feb. 94
Stevenson, Alex. Gavin, Woolwich	13 Feb. 91	13 Feb. 94
Woodroffe, Arth. Jas., Portsmouth	13 Feb. 91	13 Feb. 94
Manifold, Michael G. E., Aldershot	13 Feb. 91	13 Feb. 94
Rundall, Chas. Frank, Cork	13 Feb. 91	13 Feb. 94
Greenstreet, C.B.L., Rawul Pindee	13 Feb. 91	13 Feb. 94
Bonham, Chas. Barnard, S. M. E.	13 Feb. 91	13 Feb. 94
Tandy, Edw. Aldborough, Agra	13 Feb. 91	13 Feb. 94
Turner, Arth. Edw., Rawul Pindee	13 Feb. 91	13 Feb. 94
Vesey, Chas. Edw. Gore, Aldershot	13 Feb. 91	13 Feb. 94
Bunbury, Wm. Hy., Rawul Pindee	13 Feb. 91	13 Feb. 94
Gillam, R. A., Madras Sappers and Miners, Burmah	13 Feb. 91	13 Feb. 94
Barnardiston, Ernald, Umballa	13 Feb. 91	13 Feb. 94
Freeland, Henry F. E., Bellary	13 Feb. 91	13 Feb. 94
Owen, Sydney Lloyd, Cork	13 Feb. 91	13 Feb. 94
Scott, Albert Chas., Isle of Wight	13 Feb. 91	13 Feb. 94
Cusins, Albert G. Teeling, Derby	13 Feb. 91	13 Feb. 94
Pritchard, H. Lionel, Aldershot	13 Feb. 91	13 Feb. 94

Corps of Royal Engineers. 214—17

LIEUTENANTS.	2ND LIEUT.	LIEUT.	SECOND LIEUTENANTS.	2ND LIEUT.
M'Innes, Duncan Sayre, Aldershot	16 July 91	16 July 94	Gervers, Francis Richard Soutter, India ...	10 Feb. 93
Mackesy, John Pierse, S. M. E. ...	24 July 91	24 July 94	Russell, William Kelson, S. M. E.	10 Feb. 93
Polwhele, Reginald, S. M. E.	24 July 91	24 July 94	Gunter, Clarence Preston, India	10 Feb. 93
Birney, John Ramsay, Woolwich	24 July 91	24 July 94	North, Charles Napier, Malta	10 Feb. 93
Gardiner, A., Fort William, Calcutta	24 July 91	24 July 94	Cowie, Henry Edward Colvin, India	10 Feb. 93
Sewell, Jonathan W. S., Portsmouth	24 July 91	24 July 94	Armstrong, Bertie Harold Olivier	27 June 93
Tonge, Cecil R., Aden..................	24 July 91	24 July 94	Rich, Edmund Tillotson	25 July 93
Blakeney, Robert B. D., Aldershot	24 July 91	24 July 94	Hodgson, Philip Egerton	25 July 93
Cator, Edm. H. S., Aldershot	24 July 91	24 July 94	Longfield, William Elrington	25 July 93
Close, Arthur John, Bangalore ...	24 July 91	24 July 94	Kennedy, Macdougall Ralston	25 July 93
King, R. G., Fort William, Bengal	24 July 91	24 July 94	M'Clintock, Robert Lyle	25 July 93
Chamier, Arthur Tyrrell, Meerut	24 July 91	24 July 94	Crookshank, Arthur Alexander	25 July 93
Stockley, Ernest N., Allahabad ...	24 July 91	24 July 94	Jack, Evan Maclean	25 July 93
Johnston, Wm. James, S. M. E....	24 July 91	24 July 94	Craster, John Evelyn Edmund	25 July 93
Barstow, John B., Madras S. & M.	24 July 91	24 July 94	Savage, Arthur Johnson	25 July 93
Knox, George Stuart, Ceylon	24 July 91	24 July 94	Bovet, William	25 July 93
Carey, Arthur Basil, India	24 July 91	24 July 94	Newcombe, Edward Osborn Armstrong ...	25 July 93
Micklem, Henry A., Aldershot	1 Aug. 91	1 Aug. 94	Bell, Reginald William	25 July 93
Mildred, Spencer, Sheerness	6 Aug. 91	6 Aug. 94	White, Frank Augustin Kinder	25 July 93
Bannerman, A., Landguard Fort	13 Aug. 91	13 Aug. 94	Borradaile, Basil	25 July 93
Grubb, Alexander Henry Watkins, Aldershot	12 Feb. 92	12 Feb. 95	M'Harg, Alfred Alexis	25 July 93
Moir, James Philip, S. M. E.	12 Feb. 92	12 Feb. 95	Fuller, Cuthbert Graham	25 July 93
Ley, Cuthbert Hillyar, S. M. E....	12 Feb. 92	12 Feb. 95	Manley, Edgar Norman	25 July 93
Howard, Frederic Geo., Roorkee...	12 Feb. 92	12 Feb. 95	Chaldecott, William Henry	25 July 93
Hall, G. C. Miller, L. & N. W. Railway	12 Feb. 92	12 Feb. 95	Tandy, Maurice O'Connor	25 July 93
Tylden-Pattenson, E. C., Roorkee	12 Feb. 92	12 Feb. 95	Bagnall-Wild, Ralph Kirkby, Portsmouth...	25 July 93
Sandys, Edward Seton, Aldershot	12 Feb. 92	12 Feb. 95	Iles, Frederick Arthur, Portsmouth...........	27 Feb. 94
Jones, William Henry, Derby	12 Feb. 92	12 Feb. 95	Macfie, William Colvin.............................	27 Feb. 94
Garwood, Fred. Scott, Bom. S. & M.	12 Feb. 92	12 Feb. 95	Corry, John Beaumont	27 Feb. 94
Wood, Henry, Aldershot	12 Feb. 92	12 Feb. 95	Tillard, Francis Bonham	27 Feb. 94
Osborn, Oliver Edward, Plymouth	12 Feb. 92	12 Feb. 95	Mainprise, Bertie Wilmot	27 Feb. 94
Pridham, Geoffrey Robert, S.M.E.	12 Feb. 92	12 Feb. 95	Kensington, Guy Belfield	27 Feb. 94
Gillespie, R. St. John, Portsmouth	12 Feb. 92	12 Feb. 95	Clarke, Charles James	27 Feb. 94
Jelf, Richard John, Aldershot......	12 Feb. 92	12 Feb. 95	Smyth, Gerald James Watt	27 Feb. 94
			Meyrick, Harold Lothian	27 Feb. 94
			Mahon, Edward Willoughby Sandys	27 Feb. 94
SECOND LIEUTENANTS.		2NDLIEUT.	Done, Reginald John...............................	27 Feb. 94
Tighe, Clarence Digby Cecil, Halifax		12 Feb. 92	Hoysted, Desmond Murree FitzGerald ...	27 Feb. 94
Anderson, Rainy, Singapore		12 Feb. 92	Foulkes, Charles Howard	27 Feb. 94
Dumble, Wilfred Chatterton, Plymouth.....		4 July 92	Bell, Henry Lewin Gillison	27 Feb. 94
Vickers, Charles Ernest, Midland Railway		22 July 92	Montgomerie, Duncan Hector	28 Feb. 94
Biddulph, Harry, Rawul Pindee		22 July 92	Goldingham, Robt. Elphinstone Dalrymple	8 Mar. 94
Harvey, Charles Blundell, Gravesend......		22 July 92	Meyricke, Edward Gelly	19 Mar. 94
Winsloe, Herbert Edward, Burma		22 July 92	Thomson, Christopher Birdwood	28 Mar. 94
Bowdler, Basil W. Bowdler, Isle of Wight...		22 July 92	Macrory, Roland Martin	1 Apr. 94
Elliott, Gilbert Charles Edward, Lydd		22 July 92	Osborne, George Frederick Folger	27 June 94
Pearson, Hugh Drummond, Mirat		22 July 92	Pym, Ernest Harding, S. M. E., Portsmouth	24 July 91
Broughton, Theodore Delves, Gravesend ...		22 July 92	Garrett, Arthur ffolliott...........................	17 Aug. 94
Midwinter, Edw. Colpoys, L. & N. W. Railway		22 July 92	Monro, John Duncan	17 Aug. 94
Hopkins, Lewis Egertou, India		22 July 92	Elles, Malcolm Rothney	17 Aug. 94
Robertson, William, Bangalore		22 July 92	Charles, James Ronald Edmondston	17 Aug. 94
Turner, Ernest Vere, Aldershot.............		22 July 92	Turner, Frank Gordon	17 Aug. 94
Anderson, Cecil Ford, Scindo.................		22 July 92	Sowerby, Maurice Eden	17 Aug. 94
Harward, Francis Edward, Plymouth		22 July 92	Wollen, William Russell Grant	17 Aug. 94
Browne, Frederick Macdonell, S. M. E.....		22 July 92	Danford, Bertram William Young	17 Aug. 94
Brown, Claude Russell, Aldershot		22 July 92	Holme, Alfred Siegfried	17 Aug. 94
Crozier, Arthur Harry, Curragh		22 July 92	Hogg, Conrad Charles Henry....................	17 Aug. 94
Sladen, Charles St. Barbe, S. M. E.........		22 July 92	Moore, Herbert Tregosso Gwennap	17 Aug. 94
Hardcastle, Alexander, Singapore		22 July 92	Mozley, Edward Newman	20 Sept. 94
Le Mesurier, H. Grenville, Pembroke Dock		22 July 92	King, William Albert de Courcy	1 Oct. 94
Meares, Aubrey, Aldershot.....................		10 Feb. 93	Connor, Isaac Joscelyn.............................	10 Oct. 94
Wolff, Arnold Johnston, Ordered to Cape...		10 Feb. 93	Symons, Charles Bertie Owen	16 Oct. 94
Garwood, John Reginald, Plymouth		10 Feb. 93	Earle, Robert Gilmour	24 Oct. 94
Loch, Stewart Gordon, India		10 Feb. 93	Rooke, Everard Home	3 Nov. 94
Wilson, Samuel Herbert, Aldershot		10 Feb. 93	Waller, Richard Lancelot.........................	4 Nov. 94
Kelsall, Thomas Edward		10 Feb. 93	Magniac, Charles Lane	17 Nov. 94
Ogilvie, Duncan, India............................		10 Feb. 93	Meyricke, Robert Evelyn	17 Nov. 94
Henderson, Edward George, Egypt		10 Feb. 93	Heath, Charles Joseph	1 Dec. 94
Cowie, Herbert M'Cally, India		10 Feb. 93	Carden, Alan Douglas	12 Dec. 94
Thompson, Richard Lovell Brereton, Malta		10 Feb. 93	Stevens, Arthur Cornish Jeremie..............	17 Dec. 94

N.B. The Officers whose names appear in Italics are holding Civil Employment.

Deputy Adjutant General.—Maitland, Major General J. M. H. *CB*. h.p. 21 April 91.
Assistant Adjutant General.—Scott, Colonel D. A., *DSO*. 8 June 94.
Adjutant.—Rice, Captain S. R. 10 Aug. 92.

Quarter Masters.	QR. MR. & HON. LT.	Quarter Masters.	QR. MR. & HON. LT.
Goulding, William (*Hon. Captain*, 13 June 93), Portsmouth	13 June 83	Hitching, George Henry, Hong Kong ...	7 July 88
Lewis, Arthur Thomas 417 (*Hon. Captain*, 13 June 93), Gravesend..................	13 June 83	Gibson, George Gisborne, S.M.E., Chatham	29 Sept. 88
		Warburton, William, Shoeburyness	12 June 89
Hills, Alfred, Record Office, Chatham (*Hon. Captain*, 3 May 94)	3 May 84	Godfrey, Cornelius Benjamin, Exeter	22 June 89
		Michie, George, Aldershot........................	22 June 89
Walker, Crichton (*Hon. Capt.*, 27 Aug. 90; *Hon. Major*, 1 Apr. 94); Qr. Mr. S. M. E.	6 May 85	Phillips, John Campbell, Curragh	18 Dec. 89
		Blanchflower, Edward, Chatham..............	20 Sept. 90
Hooper, Frederick, Dublin	6 May 85	Stephens, Edward, Aldershot	20 Dec. 90
Symons, Thomas Cornelius (*Hon. Captain*, 27 Aug. 90), Woolwich	6 May 85	Richmond, George, Isle of Wight	9 May 91
		Payne, Charles, Athlone	9 May 91
Andrews, Francis William, Egypt	6 May 85	Law, James, Aldershot	9 May 91
Evans, James Thomas, Malta	6 May 85	Shute, William John, Plymouth	19 Apr. 93
Tucker, George, Monmouth	1 Apr. 86	Hollis, Matthew, Malta	3 May 93
Morrieon, Geo., 418 G. P. O. Telegraphs, London	2 Apr. 87	Taylor, George, Jamaica	3 May 93
Kenney, John Henry, Southampton	21 Sept. 87	Campbell, John Robert, Chatham	3 May 93
Cromie, Wm. Henry (*Army Quarter Master*, 21 Feb. 86), Intelligence Dept., War Office	25 Jan. 88	Frost, James, Isle of Wight....................	13 Dec. 93
		Thompson, Bernard Henry, Sheffield.......	5 May 94
Wall, Edw. Jas., Intell. Depart., War Office	4 Apr. 88	Wright, James Henry, Cork	5 May 94

Royal Engineer Troops.

Adjutant.—Irvine, Captain James Laird, 15 Apr. 91.
Riding Master.—John Ellis Griss, 12 Sept. 94, *Hon. Lieut.* Aldershot.
Scarlet—Facings, Blue Velvet.—*Agents,* Messrs. Cox & Co.

Royal Engineers (late Bengal Engineers).

Yrs. Serv.	Colonels Commandant.	Second Lieut.	First Lieut.	Captain.	Brevet Major.	Major.	Brevet Lt.Col.	Lieut. Colonel.	Brevet Colonel.	Colonel.	Colonel Command.	Major General.	Lieut. General.	General.
52	Fraser, Alex.,[1] CB. Unemployed	8 Dec. 43	9 Nov. 48	14 Sept. 57	......	......	......	31 Aug. 64	31 Aug. 69	1 Apr. 74	10 July 84	31 Dec. 78	18 Jan. 82	16 Sept. 86
49	Maunsell, Fred. Richard,[2] CB. Unemployed	12 June 46	15 Feb. 54	27 Aug. 58	28 Aug. 58	......	14 June 69	10 Nov. 69	10 Nov. 74	31 Dec. 78	9 Nov. 74	31 Dec. 78	12 Jan. 84	21 Feb. 87
47	Williams, Sir Edward Charles Sparshott,[3] KCIE. Railway Department, India Office	9 June 48	1 Aug. 54	27 Aug. 58	......	5 July 72	......	10 Dec. 73	10 Dec. 78	1 Feb. 82	15 Jan. 90	16 Sept. 86	1 Apr. 91	
47	Chesney, Sir George Tomkyns,[4] KCB, CSI, CIE, MP, for Oxford. Unemployed	8 Dec. 48	1 Aug. 54	27 Aug. 58	28 Aug. 58	5 July 72	14 June 69	1 Apr. 74	1 Oct. 77	10 Jan. 84	28 Mar. 90	16 Mar. 86	10 Mar. 87	1 Apr. 92
	Removed from the Corps, having rank as General Officers.													
44	Perkins, Æneas,[12] CB. Unemployed	12 Dec. 51	17 Aug. 56	12 Mar. 62	30 June 65	5 July 72	29 Dec. 74	1 Oct. 77	29 Dec. 79	......	......	10 Mar. 87	1 Apr. 91	
36	Browne, Sir James,[17] KCSI, CB. Governor General's Agent in Beloochistan [R]	11 Dec. 57	27 Aug. 58	1 July 70	5 Nov. 70	1 Oct. 77	1 Oct. 77	12 Aug. 86	1 Oct. 81	......	......	29 Mar. 90		

Lieutenant Colonels.

Yrs. Serv.		Second Lieut.	First Lieut.	Captain.	2nd Lieut.	1st Lieut.	Captain.	Brev.Maj.	Major.	Bt.Lt.Col.	Brev.Col.
37	Home, Frederic Jervis, CSI, Chief Engineer, 2nd Class, D.P.W. Leave, Europe				11 June 58	27 Aug. 58	14 Dec. 70	......	31 Dec. 78	12 Aug. 86	12 Aug. 90
37	Strahan, George. Unemployed, Dehra Dhoor					10 Dec. 58	14 Jan. 71	......	10 May 81	3 Sept. 86	8 Sept. 90
35	Tomkins, William Pericoid,[34] CIE. Director General of Military Works, Simla (Colonel, and temporary Major General, 12 Apr. 93)					8 June 60	3 Aug. 72	2 Mar. 81	1 July 81	26 May 88	
35	Strahan, Charles,[38] Deputy Surveyor General, Indian Revenue Survey, Calcutta					8 June 60	20 Aug. 72	2 Mar. 81	1 July 81	1 July 88	12 Apr. 93
35	Marshall, George Frederick Leycester, CIE. Secretary to Government of Punjab, P.W.D. Leave, Europe					8 June 60	1 Apr. 74	......	1 July 81	1 July 88	29 Sept. 93

218

Royal Engineers (late Madras Engineers).

Yrs. Serv.	Colonels Commandant.	Second Lieut.	First Lieut.	Captain.	Major.	Brevet Lt.Col.	Brevet Colonel.	Colonel.	Colonel Command.	Major General.	Lieut. General.	General.
75	Cotton, Sir Arthur Thomas, *KCSI*.[1] Europe............	16 June 20	1 May 24	5 June 29	1 Jan. 45	......	28 Nov. 54	1 Aug. 54	1 Aug. 54	14 Apr. 62	1 Mar. 67	20 Mar. 76
54	Randall, Francis Hornblow, *CSI*. Europe............	10 Dec. 41	28 June 47	1 Aug. 54	......	......	29 June 68	12 May 60	7 Oct. 76	23 Mar. 69	31 Dec. 78	28 Nov. 85
	Removed from the Corps, having rank as General Officers.											
35	Hamilton, Arthur Frank,[13] Commanding Rangoon District	......	8 June 60	9 Aug. 77	17 Apr. 78	18 Nov. 82	18 Nov. 86	......	......	17 Nov. 94	......	......

Lieutenant Colonels.

		2nd Lieut.	1st Lieut.	Captain.	Major.	Bt. Lt. Col.	Bt. Col.		Major.	Bt. Lt. Col.	Lt. Col.	Brev. Col.
37	Fraser, Alexander Thomas, Superintending Engineer, 3rd Circle, Bellary	11 June 58	27 Aug. 58	10 Nov. 69	......	......	......		7 Oct. 83	9 Jan. 86	7 Oct. 87
37	Pennycuick, John,[12] Chief Engineer, and Secretary to Government, Dept. Public Works, Ootacamund............	......	10 Dec. 58	13 Oct. 70	......	......	......		8 Dec. 83	4 Mar. 86	7 Dec. 87
35	Cumming, *William Gordon*, *CIE*. Chief Engineer, 1st Class, D.P.W., India ; Secretary to Chief Commnr., Mandalay	......	8 June 60	3 Aug. 72	30 Dec. 78	......	......		......	12 Aug. 86	12 Aug. 90

Royal Engineers (late Bombay Engineers).

Yrs. Serv.	Colonels Commandant.	Second Lieut.	First Lieut.	Captain.	Brevet Major.	Major.	Brevet Lt. Col.	Brevet Colonel.	Lieut. Colonel.	Colonel.	Colonel Commdt.	Major General.	Lieut. General.	General.
70	Turner, Henry Blois,[1] Europe............	16 June 25	17 June 25	25 Mar. 38	......	14 Oct. 51	......	......	1 Aug. 54	15 June 60	20 Mar. 76	21 Dec. 65	1 Apr. 74	21 Dec. 77
54	Kennedy, Sir Michael Kavanagh,[2] *KCSI*. Europe............	11 June 41	13 Nov. 46	1 Aug. 54	......	......	18 Feb. 61	11 July 72	18 Feb. 61	1 Mar. 67	7 Feb. 91	6 Mar. 68	21 Dec. 77	10 May 81
	Removed from the Corps, having rank as General Officer.													
40	F. C. Goodfellow, Charles Aug.,[13] Chief Engineer, 1st Class, Bombay. Leave, Europe............	8 June 55	27 Apr. 58	2 Sept. 64	15 Aug. 68	5 July 72	11 July 77	31 Dec. 78	......	......	......	15 Mar. 89	1 Apr. 92	......

Lieutenant Colonels.

		2nd Lieut.	1st Lieut.	Captain.	Major.	Bt. Lt. Col.	Lt. Col.	Bt. Col.
36	Tweenlow, *Edward D'Oyley*,[21] M. W. Department, Lahore. Leave, Europe............	9 Dec. 59	14 Jan. 71	31 Dec. 78	......	......	12 Aug. 86	12 Aug. 90
36	Cruickshank, *John Donelison*, Chief Engineer, D.P.W. Central Division, Bombay	9 Dec. 59	14 Jan. 71	4 July 79	......	......	6 Nov. 85	6 Nov. 90

Coast Battalion.

Yrs.' Ser. Full Pay	Yrs.' Ser. Half Pay	MAJOR.	LIEUT.	CAPTAIN.	MAJOR.
		CAPTAINS.			
9	...	Davis, Thomas, Greenock	2 June 86	1 Apr. 93	
9	...	Coyle, William, Dundee	2 Mar. 87	26 Nov. 93	
8	...	London, James, Liverpool	2 Apr. 87	1 Apr. 94	
8	...	Organ, James, Leith	8 Feb. 88	1 Apr. 94	
		LIEUTENANTS.			
10	...	Pring, John (*Quarter Master*, 13 June 85), Pembroke Dock	7 Mar. 86		
7	...	Montgomery, William, Woolwich	7 July 88		
7	...	Brown, William George Charteris, Staff Officer, Horse Guards, War Office	25 Aug. 88		
6	...	Giddy, William Richard George, Cardiff	8 May 89		
6	...	Martin, John, North Shields	18 Jan. 90		
5	...	Sugg, Benjamin, Falmouth	19 Nov. 90		
4	...	Brissenden, Albert, Middlesborough	1 July 91		
3	...	Robins, George, Pembroke Dock. On Leave	20 Aug. 92		
2	...	Charles Ealden, Hull	15 Nov. 92		
4	...	Bailey, John Henry (*Quarter Master*, 1 July 91), War Office, Whitehall	13 Dec. 93		

War Services of the Officers of the Royal Engineers.

[1] The Duke of Cambridge commanded the 1st Division of the Eastern Army throughout the campaign of 1854, including the battles of the Alma, Balaklava, and Inkerman (horse shot), and siege of Sebastopol (mentioned in despatches, received the thanks of the House of Commons, Medal with four Clasps, and Turkish Medal).

[3] Sir Lintorn Simmons was employed for three years in the disputed territory on the N.E. frontier of the United States in constructing works for its defence and in making military explorations. Happening to be in Turkey in 1853 he was specially employed by Lord Stratford de Redcliffe on several important services; joined Omar Pasha in March 1854; escorted the new Governor into Silistria after the former one had been killed, and was present during part of the siege of that fortress; laid out and threw up the lines of Slobodzie and Georgevo on the Danube, having entire charge of the operation with 20,000 men of all arms under his command, a Russian Army of 70,000 men being within seven miles: was present during the occupation of Wallachia and had frequent charge of reconnaissances upon the enemy's rear. Went to the Crimea in Dec. 1854 to concert with the allied Commanders in Chief as to the movements of the Turkish Army: was present at the battle of Eupatoria, laid out and threw up the entrenched camp round that place; afterwards was before Sebastopol from April 1855 until after its fall, and then went to Mingrelia and was present at the forced passage of the Ingur, where he commanded the Division which crossed the river and turned the enemy's position, capturing his works and guns: Omar Pasha in his despatch attributed the success of the day chiefly to Lt. Colonel Simmons. He served as Her Majesty's Commissioner to the Ottoman Army throughout the war and was employed in all the negotiations having reference to the movements of Omar Pasha's Army. Has received the Crimean Medal with Clasp, the Turkish Gold Medal for the Danubian campaign, the Order of Medjidie 3rd Class, and a Sword of Honor from the Turkish Government; also the 4th Class of the Legion of Honor. Was Her Majesty's Commissioner for laying out the Turco-Russian boundary in Asia, and granted the 2nd Class of the Medjidie by the Sultan, but was refused permission to accept it.

[6] Lieut.General Hadden was actively employed in Canada during the rebellion in 1837-39, and was engaged with the rebels at St. Eustache and St. Benoit.

[7] General Montagu served the Eastern campaign of 1854-55, including the battles of Alma and Inkerman; also at the siege of Sebastopol until 22nd March, when he was taken prisoner during a sortie, but exchanged, and leaving Odessa on the 2nd was again in the Crimea on the 3rd August, and again present at the siege and fall of Sebastopol (Medal with three Clasps, Brevets of Major and Lt.Colonel, Knight of the Legion of Honor, Sardinian and Turkish Medals, and 5th Class of the Medjidie).

[8] Sir James Browne served for nearly six months in the Trenches before Sebastopol; was present at the repulse of sorties on 22nd March and 5th April; was Senior Officer of Engineers at the capture and defence of Quarries on 7th June, for which service he was honourably mentioned in despatches, and received the Brevet of Major. Succeeded Colonel Tylden as Directing Engineer of the Right Attack, and in the execution of the duties of that appointment was severely wounded by a rifle-ball on 24th August, which broke the left arm, passed through shoulder, and injured jaw (Medal with Clasp, Brevets of Major and Lt. Colonel, *CB.*, Knight of the Legion of Honor, Sardinian and Turkish Medals, and 5th Class of the Medjidie).

[10] Sir William Jervois served at the Cape of Good Hope during the Kaffir war of 1846-47, and made a military sketch of 2000 square miles of Kaffirland—1100 of which he surveyed during the war (Medal).

[11] Sir Wilbraham Lennox landed in the Crimea on 30th Sept. 1854 and served uninterruptedly with the Army there until it re-embarked in June 1856: was present at the battle of Inkerman, attack and capture of the Rifle Pits on 20th Nov. 1854 (Victoria Cross), siege and fall of Sebastopol (Medal with two Clasps, Sardinian and Turkish Medals, and 5th Class of the Medjidie): was awarded the *VC* for "cool and gallant conduct in establishing a lodgment in Tryon's Rifle Pit (Sebastopol), and assisting to repel the assaults of the enemy. This brilliant operation drew forth a special order from General Canrobert." Served in the Indian campaign of 1857-58; was present at the action of Khujwa; commanded the Engineer Brigade at the relief of Lucknow by Lord Clyde (mentioned in Lord Clyde's despatch, and thanked by the Governor General in Council), and against the Gwalior Contingent ending in its defeat at the battle of Cawnpore on 6th Dec.; present at the action of Khodagunj; served at the siege of Lucknow in March 1858 (mentioned in Chief Engineer's report and received Brevet of Major); commanded the Engineers at the attack on Fort Rooya, and at the action of Alleegunj; present at the capture of Bareilly, and at the action of Dourdenkera; commanded the Engineers at the attack of Fort Oomreeah; present at the affair of Burgeedia, the capture of Fort Musjeedia, and the affair on the River Raptee near Bankeo 31st Dec. 1858 (four times mentioned in despatches, Medal with two Clasps, and Brevet of Lt. Colonel). Was sent to the German armies during the Franco-German war, and was with them from the 14th November 1870 till the 10th March 1871. Present at the siege of Paris from 11th to 15th December 1870; at the siege of Mezieres from the 24th December till its surrender on the 2nd January 1871; at the siege of Paris from the 10th January till the 4th February; and at the siege of Belfort from 7th February till the entry of the German troops on the 18th February 1871. Was Military Attaché with the Turkish Troops during the Russo-Turkish war of 1876-78 (Turkish War Medal).

[33] Lieut.General R. Grant served with the Nile Expedition in 1884-85 as Commanding Royal Engineer (mentioned in despatches, Medal with Clasp, and Khedive's Star).

[36] Major General J. M. H. Maitland served in China in 1857-59, and was present during the occupation of Canton and at the storming of Chek-Hung under Sir Charles Straubenzee. Served at the attack on the Peiho Forts on the 25th June 1859 under Rear Admiral Hope, when he was in command of the Marksmen on board a division of Gun Boats during the naval action, and in charge of the ladder party when the assault was made over the mud (specially mentioned in despatches "for gallantry, &c.," Medal). Served in the Egyptian war of 1882, and was present at the battle of Tel-el-Kebir (mentioned in despatches, *CB.*, Medal with Clasp, 3rd Class of the Medjidie, and Khedive's Star). Served with the Nile Expedition in 1884-85 (Clasp); and served in the operations of the Soudan Frontier Field Force in 1885-86 as Commanding Royal Engineer in Egypt including the engagement at Giniss.

[39] Lieut.General R. Harrison served during the Indian mutiny of 1857-59, and was present at attacks on the Alumbagh under Outram; at the siege and capture of Lucknow; throughout the Rohilcund campaign, including affairs at Fort Roolah, Alleegunge, and Bareilly; through the Oude campaign of 1858-59, including the affair at Buxarghat; and as Acting Adjutant to the Commanding Royal Engineer in India during the Trans-Gogra campaign, including

affairs a Burgudiah, Fort Mudjidea, and Bankeo (Medal with Clasp). Served during the China war of 1860, and was present at the affairs of Sinho and Tangku, and siege and capture of the Taku Forts. Was attached to the Quarter Master General's Staff during the advance on and surrender of Pekin, and present at the affairs of Senho and Uleaugho on the 18th and 23rd Sept. (mentioned in despatches, Medal with two Clasps, and Brevet of Major). Served in the Zulu war of 1879, first as Engineer at Head Quarters, afterwards as Assistant Quarter Master General, and was in charge of the Quarter Master General's Department during the second advance into Zululand, and present in the engagement at Ulundi (mentioned in despatches, and CB.). Was subsequently appointed to the command of the Flying Column. On the dissolution of that column was placed in command of the Transvaal District, conducted the reconnaissances that preceded the operations against Sekukuni, and, afterwards, maintained the supplies of the forces engaged, and made the military dispositions necessitated by the hostile attitude of the Boers (mentioned in despatches, Medal with Clasp). Served in the Egyptian war of 1882 as Assistant Adjutant General, and was Chief Staff Officer on the Lines of Communication throughout the campaign; was present in the engagement at El Magfar and at the battle of Tel-el-Kebir (mentioned in despatches, CMG., Medal with Clasp, 3rd Class of the Osmanieh, and Khedive's Star). Served with the Nile Expedition in 1885 as Assistant Adjutant General and Colonel on the Staff on the Lines of Communication (Clasp).

⁴⁴ Sir Charles Wilson served in the Egyptian war of 1882 on special service (Medal, and Khedive's Star). Served with the Nile Expedition in 1885 as Chief of the Intelligence Department, and was present at the action of Abu Klea; after the engagement at El Gubat he commanded the Desert Column in its advance to the Nile and the reconnaissance of Metammeh, and proceeded up the Nile to the vicinity of Khartoum with a small force of the Sussex Regiment and Soudanese troops in two steamers with the object of relieving Gordon (mentioned in despatches, KCB., two Clasps).

⁴⁹ Major General Sanford served in China in 1858, during the occupation of Canton, the expedition to Peiho, demolition of the forts at the mouth of the river and advance to Tientsin. Also in the campaign in the North of China in 1860 (Medal with Clasp). Also in the operations against the Taepings in 1862, including the capture of the stockades of Nanhsiang, escalade of the walled cities of Kadin, Tsinpoo, and Tsolin, and the fortified town of Najow. Served in the Jowaki Afreedee Expedition in 1878 as A.Q.M.General, Peshawur District (Medal with Clasp). Served in the Afghan war of 1878-79 as Assistant Quarter Master General of the 1st Division in the Peshawur Valley Field Force, and was present at the capture of Ali Musjid (mentioned in despatches, Brevet of Lt.Colonel, Medal with Clasp). Served with the Burmese Expedition in 1885-86 in command of Royal Engineers (received the thanks of the Government of India, mentioned in despatches, CB., and Clasp).

⁵⁶ Colonel W.G. Nicholson served in the Afghan war of 1878-80 as Field Engineer Candahar Field Force, and as Commanding Royal Engineer Thull Chotiali Field Force (mentioned in despatches), and afterwards as Field Engineer Cabul and Cabul-Candahar Field Force, and was present in the engagement at Charasiab on the 6th October 1879 and in the operations around Cabul in December 1879 including the engagement at Latabaud (mentioned in despatches); accompanied Sir Frederick Roberts in the march to Candahar, and was present at the battle of Candahar (mentioned in despatches, Brevet of Major, Medal with three Clasps, and Bronze Decoration). Served in the Egyptian war of 1882, and was present at the battle of Tel-el-Kebir (Medal with Clasp, 4th Class of the Osmanieh, and Khedive's Star). Served with the Burmese Expedition in 1886-87 as Assistant Adjutant General, Army Head Quarters (mentioned in despatches, Brevet of Lt.Colonel, Medal with Clasp).

⁵⁷ Colonel Le Mesurier served in the Boer war of 1881, and took part in the defence of Pretoria (Brevet of Lt.Colonel). Served in the Soudan campaign in 1885 in command of the Royal Engineers on the Lines of Communication (mentioned in despatches, Medal with Clasp, and Khedive's Star).

⁵⁸ Colonel Moysey served in the Zulu war of 1879, and was present in the engagement at Ulundi (mentioned in despatches, Brevet of Lt.Colonel, Medal with Clasp).

⁵⁹ Sir J. C. Ardagh served in the Egyptian war of 1882, and was present at the battle of Tel-el-Kebir (mentioned in despatches, Brevet of Lt.Colonel, Medal with Clasp, 4th Class of the Osmanieh, and Khedive's Star); served with the Soudan Expedition under Sir Gerald Graham in 1884 as Commanding Royal Engineer and Deputy Assistant Quarter Master General, Intelligence Department, and was present in the engagements at El Teb and Temai (twice mentioned in despatches, CB., and two Clasps). Served during the Nile Expedition in 1884-85 as Commandant of the Base at Cairo (mentioned in despatches, Brevet of Colonel). Was present in the engagement at Giniss, on the Upper Nile, on the 30th December 1885 (mentioned in despatches).

⁶⁰ Colonel Reginald Clare Hart served with the Khyber Column in the Afghan war from January to June 1879, first with the 2nd Division attached as a Regimental Officer to the 24th Punjab Native Infantry during the 2nd Bazar Expedition against the Zukha Khel Afreedis, and afterwards with the 1st Division. Was several times employed by the Quarter Master General's Department in making reconnaissances (mentioned in despatches, Victoria Cross, Medal) : was awarded the VC "for his gallant conduct in risking his own life in endeavouring to save the life of a private soldier. The Lieutenant General commanding the 2nd Division Peshawur Field Force reports that when on convoy duty with that Force on 31st January, 1879, Lieutenant Hart, of the Royal Engineers, took the initiative in running some 1,200 yards to the rescue of a wounded Sowar of the 13th Bengal Lancers in a river bed exposed to the fire of the enemy, of unknown strength, from both flanks, and also from a party in the river bed. Lieutenant Hart reached the wounded Sowar, drove off the enemy, and brought him under cover with the aid of some soldiers, who accompanied him on the way." Served throughout the Egyptian war of 1882 as Aide de Camp to Major General Graham, commanding the 2nd Brigade, and was present in the reconnaissance in force from Alexandria 5th August, the engagements of El Magfar and Tel-el-Mahuta, the two actions at Kassasin (as Acting Assistant Quarter Master General to Graham's force in the second action), and the battle of Tel-el-Kebir (twice mentioned in despatches, Brevet of Lt.Colonel, Medal with Clasp, 4th Class of the Osmanieh, and Khedive's Star). [See also Civil Decorations for Gallantry, "Hart's Annual Army List," p. 786.]

⁶¹ Colonel C. J. O'N. Ferguson served in the New Zealand war of 1861-66, including the actions of Katikarn and Kaitahi (Medal).

⁶² Colonel W. Salmond was employed during the Egyptian war of 1882 as Commanding Royal Engineer at the Base of Operations (mentioned in despatches, Brevet of Lt.Colonel, Medal, 4th Class of the Osmanieh, and Khedive's Star).

⁶³ Sir Charles Warren served during the suppression of the Kafir outbreak in 1877-78, with local rank of Lieut. Colonel, in command of the Diamond Fields Horse, and took part in several actions (Brevet of Lieutenant Colonel). Commanded part of the Griqualand West Field Force in the Griqua rising in 1878, including numerous engagements and skirmishes with the natives (several times mentioned in despatches; commended in the Governor's despatches for "energy, ability, and resource displayed under most trying circumstances," Medal with Clasp). Served in command of an expedition into Arabia Petraea, despatched during the Egyptian war of 1882 for the purpose of bringing to justice the murderers of Professor Palmer and his party (KCMG., Medal, 3rd Class of the Medjidie, and Khedive's Star). Commanded the forces in the Bechuanaland Expedition in 1884-85 (GCMG.).

⁶⁴ Colonel E. N. Peters served in the Afghan war in 1878-79 (Medal).

⁶⁵ Colonel H. C. Chermside served during the Russo-Turkish war in 1876-78 accompanied the Turkish troops as Military Attaché (Turkish War Medal). Served in the Egyptian war of 1882 (Medal, and Khedive's Star). Served in the expedition to the Soudan in 1884 under Sir Gerald Graham with the Intelligence Department (Clasp). Also served in the Soudan campaign in 1885 in the Egyptian Army and as Governor General of the Red Sea Littoral and Egyptian Military Commissioner (mentioned in despatches, Brevet of Lt.Colonel, 3rd Class of the Osmanich, and Clasp). Served in the operations in the Soudan in 1887, and was present in the engagement at Sarras in command of the force (Brevet of Colonel, and Class of the Medjidie).

⁶⁸ Colonel H. F. Turner served in the Soudan campaign in 1885 as Director of Telegraphs, and was present in the engagement at the Tofrek zereba (mentioned in despatches, Medal with two Clasps, and Khedive's Star).

⁶⁹ Colonel W. H. Mulloy served in the New Zealand war in 1864, including the action of Kakaramea (Medal). Served with the Nile Expedition in 1884-85 (Medal with Clasp, and Khedive's Star).

⁷⁴ Colonel A. J. Hepper served with the Nile Expedition in 1884-85 (Medal, and Khedive's Star); also served with the Soudan Frontier Field Force in command of Royal Engineers, and was present in the engagement at Giniss (DSO., and 3rd Class of the Medjidie).

⁷⁷ Colonel A. Hill served in the Afghan war of 1878-80 (Medal).

⁷⁸ Colonel F.W. Nixon served in the Kafir war in 1877-78 as Commanding Royal Engineer to the Transkei Field Force in the operations against the Galekas, and was present in the engagement at Quintana (mentioned in despatches, Brevet of Major, Medal with Clasp).

⁹⁰ Colonel Blood served in the Jowaki Afreedee Expedition in 1877–78 (Medal with Clasp). Served in the Zulu war of 1879 (Brevet of Major, Medal with Clasp). Served in the Afghan war of 1878–80 (Medal). Served in the Egyptian war of 1882, and was present at the battle of Tel-el-Kebir (mentioned in despatches, Brevet of Lt.Colonel, Medal with Clasp, 4th Class of the Osmanieh, and Khedive's Star).

⁹² Colonel M. T. Sale served throughout the Bhootan campaign of 1864–65 in command of a Company of Bengal Sappers and Miners, and as Assistant Field Engineer (Medal with Clasp).

⁹³ Sir A. W. Mackworth served in the Egyptian war of 1882 in command of the Field Telegraph Corps, and was present at the action at Kassasin on the 9th September and at the battle of Tel-el-Kebir (mentioned in despatches, Brevet of Lt.Colonel, Medal with Clasp, 3rd Class of the Medjidie, and Khedive's Star).

⁹⁴ Colonel A. de V. Brooke served in the Soudan campaign in 1885, and was present in the engagements at Hasheen and the Tofrek zereba, and at the destruction of Temai (Medal with two Clasps, and Khedive's Star).

⁹⁵ Colonel Rogers served in the Afghan war in 1878–79 with the force under Sir Donald Stewart (Brevet of Major, Medal).

⁹⁶ Colonel R. A. Sargeaunt served in the Passes during the Abyssinian campaign in charge of Water Supply and road repairs (mentioned in despatches, Medal).

⁹⁰ Colonel A. W. Baird served in the Abyssinian campaign as Traffic Manager of the Railway, and was mentioned in despatches for zeal and management in bringing safely and expeditiously troops and baggage for embarkation (Medal).

⁹¹ Colonel Fraser was specially employed in the Russo-Turkish war in 1877 as Military Officer to the Commander in Chief of the British Fleet in Besica Bay, accompanied the Turkish Commander in Chief in the campaign on the Lom, and was present at several engagements and at the bombardment of Rustchuk (Brevet of Major). Served in the Boer war of 1881 as Deputy Assistant Quarter Master General in the Intelligence Branch (mentioned in despatches, *C.M.G.*). Was afterwards Assistant Quarter Master General, and finally Assistant Military Secretary to Sir Evelyn Wood. Served in the Egyptian war of 1882 as Brigade Major of Royal Engineers, and was present in the engagements at El Magfar and Tel-el-Mahuta, in the action at Kassasin (9th September), and at the battle of Tel-el-Kebir (several times mentioned in despatches, Brevet of Lt.Colonel, Medal with Clasp, 4th Class of the Osmanieh, and Khedive's Star). Served with the Nile Expedition in 1884–85 as Assistant Adjutant General on the Lines of Communication (mentioned in despatches, Brevet of Colonel, 3rd Class of the Medjidie, Clasp).

⁹² Colonel M. S. Bell commanded the Detachment of Sappers and Miners and served as Assistant Field Engineer with the Right Column Bhootan Field Force in 1865–66, and was present at the seizure of the Monar Bridge (Medal with Clasp). Commanded the Detachment of Sappers and Miners and served as Assistant Field Engineer throughout the Hazara campaign of 1868,—the forced march of 600 miles made by the Detachment, its services, and the conduct of the Officer commanding prominently brought to notice in despatches (Medal with Clasp). Served throughout the Ashanti war of 1873–74, including the battle of Amoaful, battle of Ordahsu and capture of Coomassie (mentioned in despatches, Victoria Cross, and Medal with Clasp): was awarded the *V.C.* "for his distinguished bravery and zealous, resolute, and self-devoted conduct at the battle of Ordahsu, on the 4th February 1874, while serving under the immediate orders of Colonel Sir John Chetham McLeod, *K.C.B.*, of the 42nd Regiment, who commanded the Advanced Guard. Sir John McLeod was an eye-witness of his gallant and distinguished conduct on the occasion, and considers that this officer's fearless and resolute bearing, being always in the front, urging on and encouraging an unarmed working party of Fantee labourers, who were exposed not only to the fire of the enemy but to the wild and irregular fire of the native troops in the rear, contributed very materially to the success of the day. By his example he made these men do what no European party was ever required to do in warfare, namely, to work under fire in the face of the enemy without a covering-party." Served with the Burmese Expedition in 1886–87 on special reconnaissance duty as Deputy Quarter Master General, Intelligence Branch (Clasp).

⁹³ Lt.Colonel Boughey served in the Bhootan Expedition in 1865–66 (Medal with Clasp). Also served in the Afghan war of 1878–80 (Medal).

⁹⁵ Colonel Anstey served in the Zulu war of 1879, and was present in the engagement at Ulundi (Medal with Clasp).

⁹⁷ Colonel T. H. Holdich served in 1865–66 on special duty with a Survey Detachment in Bhootan (Medal with Clasp). Served in the Abyssinian campaign in 1868 and was engaged in carrying on the Trigonometrical Survey from the Coast to Magdala (mentioned in despatches, Medal). Served in Southern Afghanistan in 1878–79 on special survey duty (twice mentioned in despatches); served in Northern Afghanistan in 1879–80 in charge of survey operations; was present in the operations around Cabul in December 1879 and the investment of Sherpore (mentioned in despatches, Brevet of Major, Medal with Clasp). Also served in charge of survey operations in the Mahsood Wuzeeree Expedition of 1880 under Brigadier General Kennedy. Served with the Zhob Valley Expedition in 1889 and 1890 (Brevet of Colonel).

⁹⁹ Colonel C. de B. Carey served in the Egyptian war of 1882, and was present in the action at Kassasin on the 9th September (mentioned in despatches, Brevet of Major, Medal, and Khedive's Star).

¹⁰⁰ Colonel W. H. Rathborne served in the Soudan campaign in 1885 (Medal with Clasp and Khedive's Star).

¹⁰¹ Colonel K. R. Todd served in the Soudan Expedition under Sir Gerald Graham in 1884 as Commanding Royal Engineer, and was present in the engagements at El Teb and Temai (mentioned in despatches, Brevet of Lt.Colonel, Medal with Clasp, and Khedive's Star). Served with the Nile Expedition in 1884–85 (Clasp).

¹⁰² Colonel W. F. Spaight served with the Nile Expedition in 1884–85 in charge of Transport at Dal (mentioned in despatches, Brevet of Lt.Colonel, Medal with Clasp, and Khedive's Star).

¹⁰³ Lt.Colonel Bisset served in the Afghan war in 1879–80 with the Quetta Field Force (mentioned in despatches, Brevet of Major, Medal).

¹⁰⁵ Colonel E. Wood served in the Egyptian war of 1882, and was present in the reconnaissance in force from Alexandria on the 5th August and at the battle of Tel-el-Kebir (mentioned in despatches, Brevet of Major, Medal with Clasp, 4th Class of the Medjidie, and Khedive's Star); served with the Soudan Expedition under Sir Gerald Graham in 1884 in the Intelligence Department, and was present in the engagements at El Teb and Temai (twice mentioned in despatches, Brevet of Lt.Colonel, two Clasps). Also served in the Soudan campaign in 1885, and was present in the engagements at Hasheen and the Tofrek zereba (mentioned in despatches, *C.B.*, and two Clasps).

¹⁰⁶ Lt.Colonel H. Elsdale served with the Bechuanaland Expedition under Sir Charles Warren in 1884–85 in command of the Balloon Detachment.

¹⁰⁷ Major W. L. Greenstreet served with the Hazara Expedition in 1891 as Commanding Royal Engineer (mentioned in despatches, Medal with Clasp).

¹⁰⁸ Lt.Colonel Macpherson served in the Afghan war in 1879–80 as Field Engineer (Medal).

¹⁰⁹ Colonel J. F. Dorward served throughout the Egyptian war of 1882, and was present at the two actions at Kassasin and at the battle of Tel-el-Kebir (Medal with Clasp, and Khedive's Star); served with the Soudan Expedition under Sir Gerald Graham in 1884, and was present in the engagements at El Teb and Temai (mentioned in despatches, 4th Class of the Medjidie, two Clasps). Commanded the Royal Engineers who ascended the river from Halfa to Korti Pioneers of the Nile Expedition in 1884; commanded the Royal Engineers of Sir Herbert Stewart's Desert Column, and was present in the action at Abu Klea in the engagement at Gubat, in the reconnaissance to Metammeh (mentioned in despatches), and in the engagement at Abu Klea Wells on the 16th and 17th February (mentioned in despatches, Brevet of Lt.Colonel, two Clasps).

¹¹¹ Lt.Colonel Waller served in the Egyptian war of 1882 as Aide de Camp to Brigadier General Nugent, Commanding Royal Engineer, and was present at the battle of Tel-el-Kebir (mentioned in despatches, Brevet of Major, Medal with Clasp, 4th Class of the Medjidie, and Khedive's Star).

¹¹² Lt.Colonel H. Jekyll served during the Ashanti war in charge of the Telegraph until invalided on the 30th January 1874 (Medal).

¹¹³ Lt.Colonel J. F. Garwood served with the Zhob Field Force in 1890 under Sir George White as Commanding Engineer of the force (mentioned in despatches).

¹¹⁴ Lt.Colonel M. O. Brackenbury served in the operations in the Malay Peninsula in 1875–76 (Medal with Clasp). Served in the Afghan war of 1878–80, and was present at the attack and capture of Ali Musjid; accompanied Sir Frederick Roberts on the march to Candahar, and was present at the battle of Candahar (mentioned in despatches, Medal with two Clasps, and Bronze Decoration); also served with the Marri Expedition in 1880.

¹¹⁵ Colonel Jelf served with the Bechuanaland Expedition under Sir Charles Warren in 1884–85 as Director of Military Telegraphs (Brevet of Lt.Colonel).

[116] Lt.Colonel S. L. Jacob served in the Afghan war in 1879 as Field Engineer at Ali Musjid (Medal).

[117] Colonel R. G. Woodthorpe served with the Lushai Expedition in 1871-72 (Medal). Served in the Afghan war of 1878-80, and was present at the capture of the Peiwar Kotal, in the engagement at Mattoon, in the operations round Cabul in December 1879 (mentioned in despatches), and in the engagement at Shekabad (mentioned in despatches, Brevets of Major and Lt. Colonel, Medal with two Clasps). Served with the Akha Expedition in 1883-84 and with the Chitral Expedition in 1885-86. Served with the Burmese Expedition in 1886-87 on Survey duty (mentioned in despatches, CB., and Clasp).

[118] Lt.Colonel Beresford served in the Boer war of 1881. Served in the Soudan campaign in 1885 (Medal with Clasp, and Khedive's Star).

[119] Lt.Colonel C. M. Watson served in the Egyptian war of 1882 in the Intelligence Department, and was present in the engagement at Tel-el-Mahuta, at the action of Kassasin on the 9th September, and at the battle of Tel-el-Kebir (Brevet of Major, Medal with Clasp, 4th Class of the Medjidie, and Khedive's Star).

[120] Colonel E. P. Leach was specially employed on survey operations with the Looshai Expedition in 1871-72 (received the thanks of the Government of India and of the Secretary of State, Medal with Clasp). Served in the Afghan war in 1879-80, and was specially employed on survey operations; took part in the expeditions into the Bazar and Lughman Valleys—severely wounded at Maidanak (several times mentioned in despatches, Brevet of Major, and Victoria Cross); served with the Candahar Field Force in charge of survey operations and afterwards as Brigade Major Royal Engineers and Field Engineer; was present in the engagements at Girishk and Maiwand, in the defence of and sortie from Candahar, and at the battle of Candahar (received the thanks of the Government of India and twice mentioned in despatches, Brevet of Lt.Colonel, and Medal with Clasp): was awarded the VC "for having, in action with the Shinwarris, near Maidanah, Afghanistan, on the 17th March 1879, when covering the retirement of the Survey Escort who were carrying Lieutenant Barclay, 45th Sikhs, mortally wounded, behaved with the utmost gallantry in charging, with some men of the 45th Sikhs, a very much larger number of the enemy. In this encounter Captain Leach killed two or three of the enemy himself, and he received a severe wound from an Afghan knife in the left arm. Captain Leach's determination and gallantry in this affair, in attacking and driving back the enemy from the last position, saved the whole party from annihilation." Served in the Soudan campaign in 1885, and was present in the engagements at Hasheen and the Tofrek zereba and at the destruction of Temai (mentioned in despatches. CB., Medal with two Clasps, and Khedive's Star). Served with the Frontier Field Force in 1885-86 as Colonel on the Staff in command of troops at Korosko.

[121] Lt.Colonel S. C. Turner served with the Mahsood Wuzeeree Expedition in 1881 (mentioned in despatches).

[122] Lt.Colonel Chard served throughout the Zulu war of 1879, and commanded at Rorke's Drift during the gallant and successful defence of that post (mentioned in despatches, promoted Captain and Brevet Major, Victoria Cross, Medal with Clasp); together with Lieut. Gonville Bromhead, 24th Foot, was awarded the VC "for their gallant conduct at the defence of Rorke's Drift on the occasion of the attack by the Zulus on the 22nd and 23rd January 1879. The Lieutenant General commanding the troops reports that, had it not been for the fine example and excellent behaviour of these two officers under the most trying circumstances, the defence of Rorke's Drift Post would not have been conducted with that intelligence and tenacity which so essentially characterised it. The Lieutenant General adds, that its success must, in a great degree, be attributable to the two young officers who exercised the chief command on the occasion in question."

[123] Lt.Colonel A. O. Green served in the Egyptian war of 1882 on the Staff of the 2nd Division, and was present at the battle of Tel-el-Kebir (Medal with Clasp, 4th Class of the Medjidie, and Khedive's Star); served in the Soudan Expedition in 1884 under Sir Gerald Graham as Intelligence Officer, and was present in the engagement at El Teb—severely wounded (mentioned in despatches, Brevet of Major, and two Clasps).

[124] Lt.Colonel R. M. Barklie served with the Nile Expedition in 1884-85 (Medal with Clasp, and Khedive's Star).

[125] Colonel H. H. Settle served with the Nile Expedition in 1884-85 as Staff Officer at Gemai and on the Lines of Communication (mentioned in despatches, Brevet of Major, Medal with Clasp, and Khedive's Star). Served in the operations at Suakin in 1888 including the engagement at Gemaizah (mentioned in despatches, Brevet of Lt.Colonel, and Clasp); also served in the operations in 1889 including the engagement at Toski (mentioned in despatches, Clasp, and 2nd Class of the Medjidie).

[125½] Major L. F. Brown served in the Afghan war in 1879-80, and was present in the engagement at Ahmed Kheyl (mentioned in despatches, Brevet of Major, Medal with Clasp).

[126] Majors D'Aguilar, W.; H. White, J. H. C. Harrison, W. G. Bowyer, G. Davidson, H. Finnis, A. L. Mein, F. Peel, C. B. Mayne, M. J. Slater, and A. H. Randolph served in the Afghan war of 1878-80 (Medal).

[126½] Lt.Colonel G. Henry served in the Afghan war of 1878-80 (Medal). Served with the Burmese Expedition in 1885-87 as Deputy Assistant Adjutant and Quarter Master General (mentioned in despatches, Medal with Clasp). Served with the Chin-Lushai Expeditionary Force in 1889-90 as Commanding Royal Engineer (mentioned in despatches, Brevet of Lt.Colonel, and Clasp).

[127] Lt.Colonel C. H. Bagot served in the Afghan war of 1879-80, including the operations in the Koorum Valley (Medal). Served with the Bechuanaland Expedition under Sir Charles Warren in 1884-85.

[128] Sir George Clarke served in the Egyptian war of 1882 (Medal, and Khedive's Star). Served in the Soudan campaign in 1885 in the Intelligence Department and as Assistant Political Officer, and was present in the reconnaissance to Hasheen, in the engagement at Hasheen, and at the destruction of Temai (mentioned in despatches, Clasp).

[129] Lt.Colonel G. A. Cockburn served with the Nile Expedition in 1884-85 (Medal with Clasp, and Khedive's Star).

[130] Major W. W. B. Whiteford served in the Afghan war in 1879-80, and took part in the march to Candahar with the force under Major General Phayre (Medal).

[131] Lt.Colonel Rawson served as Assistant Field Engineer and in command of a company of the "Queen's Own" Sappers and Miners in the Afghan war in 1878-79, and was present in the engagement at Futtehabad (Medal).

[132] Lt.Colonel A. R. F. Dorward served in the Afghan war in 1879-80, and was present in the engagement at Kam Dakka and in the operations in the Kama district (Medal). Served with the Burmese Expedition in 1885-88 in command of the Queen's Own Sappers and Miners and as Commanding Royal Engineer (mentioned in despatches, Brevet of Major, DSO., and Medal with Clasp).

[133] Lt.Colonel R. M. Hyslop served with the Right Column of the Lushai Field Force in the campaign of 1871-72, in command of a company of Bengal Sappers and Miners (mentioned in despatches, thanks of Indian and Home Governments, Medal with Clasp). Served in the Egyptian war of 1882, and was present at the battle of Tel-el-Kebir (Medal with Clasp, and Khedive's Star).

[134] Lt.Colonel H. A. Yorke served in the Afghan war of 1878-80 (Medal). Served during the Nile Expedition in 1884-85 as Manager of the Assouan Railway (mentioned in despatches, Brevet of Major, Medal with Clasp, and Khedive's Star).

[135] Lt.Colonel G. Barker served in the Egyptian war of 1882, and was present in the engagement at Tel-el-Mahuta, in the action at Kassasin on the 9th September, and at the battle of Tel-el-Kebir (mentioned in despatches, Brevet of Major, Medal with Clasp, 4th Class of the Medjidie, and Khedive's Star). Served with the Bechuanaland Expedition under Sir Charles Warren in 1884-85 on special service.

[137] Lt.Colonel Dove served with the Bengal Sappers and Miners in the Jowaki campaign in 1877-78 (Medal with Clasp). Served in the Afghan war of 1878-80, and was present at the capture of Ali Musjid (Medal with Clasp).

[138] Lt.Colonel Sidney Smith served in the Egyptian war of 1882, and was present at the battle of Tel-el-Kebir (mentioned in despatches, Brevet of Major, Medal with Clasp, and Khedive's Star).

[141] Lt.Colonel H. O. Selby served in the Afghan war in 1879-80, and took part in the march to Candahar with the force under Major General Phayre (mentioned in despatches, Medal).

[142] Lt.Colonel F. T. N. Spratt served in the Afghan war of 1878-80, and was present at the capture of the Peiwar Kotal (mentioned in despatches), and in the engagements at Charasiab on the 6th October 1879 (mentioned in despatches), and at Mattoon; accompanied Sir Frederick Roberts in the march to Candahar, and was present at the battle of Candahar (mentioned in despatches, Medal with three Clasps, and Bronze Decoration). Served with the Burmese Expedition in 1886-87 as Director of Signalling (mentioned in despatches, Brevet of Major, Medal with Clasp).

[143] Lt.Colonel J. Cameron served in the Kafir war in 1877-78, and was present as Orderly Officer to Colonel Wood in the engagement at Taba ka Udoda (mentioned in despatches, Medal with Clasp).

144 Lt.Colonel W. Peacocke served in the Afghan war in 1878-79, and took part with the expedition into the Bazar Valley (mentioned in despatches, Medal).

145 Lt.Colonel R. T. Orpen served in the Afghan war of 1878-80 with the force under Major General Phayre (mentioned in despatches, Medal).

146 Lt.Colonel G. R. R. Savage served in the Afghan war of 1878-80 in charge of advanced Field Telegraph and Signalling arrangements with the force under Sir Donald Stewart (mentioned in despatches, Medal with Clasp).

146† Lt.Colonel P. Haslett served with the Jowaki Afreedee Expedition in 1877-78 (Medal with Clasp). Served in the Afghan war of 1878-80, and was present in the engagements at Ahmed Kheyl (mentioned in despatches) and Takht-i-Pul (Medal with Clasp).

147 Majors J. W. Thurburn, B. Scott, J. Kellie, G. M. Porter, and L. C. Jackson served in the Afghan war in 1878-79 (Medal).

148 Major Hoskyns served in the Jowaki campaign in 1877-78 (Medal with Clasp). Served in the Afghan war of 1878-80 as Assistant Field Engineer with Sir Donald Stewart's Division, and was present in the engagements at Ahmed Kheyl and Urzoo near Ghuznee (Medal with Clasp).

149 Major St. G. C. Gore served in the Afghan war of 1878-80, and was present in the engagement at Ahmed Kheyl (Medal with Clasp).

150 Major R. O. Lloyd served with the Burmese Expedition in 1885-86 as Field Engineer and was severely wounded in an engagement near Mandalay on the 8th January (mentioned in despatches, Medal with Clasp).

151 Major C. R. Conder served in the Egyptian war of 1882, and was present at the battle of Tel-el-Kebir (Medal with Clasp, 4th Class of the Medjidie, and Khedive's Star). Served with the Bechuanaland Expedition under Sir Charles Warren in 1884-85 on special service and in charge of the Topographical Department.

152 Colonel D. A. Scott served in the Afghan war of 1878-80 (Medal). Served in the Egyptian war of 1882 (Brevet of Major, Medal, and Khedive's Star). Also served with the Nile Expedition in 1884-85 as Railway Officer at Halfa and in charge of railway extensions (mentioned in despatches, Brevet of Lt.Colonel, Clasp). Also served in the operations of the Soudan Frontier Field Force in 1885-86 including the engagement at Giniss (DSO.).

153 Major Martin Martin served in the Afghan war of 1878-80, and was present in the engagement at Ahmed Kheyl (Medal with Clasp).

155 Major T. R. Main served in the Kafir war of 1877-78, and was present in the engagement at Neumaka; also served in the Zulu war in 1879, and was present in the engagement at Inyezane, at Ekowe during the investment (mentioned in despatches), and in the engagement at Ulundi (Medal with Clasp).

156 Major C. W. Sherrard served in the Zulu war in 1879 (Medal with Clasp).

158 Major C. B. Wilkieson served in the Soudan campaign in 1885 in command of the Madras Sappers and Miners, and was present in the engagements at Hasheen and the Tofrek zereba—wounded (mentioned in despatches, Brevet of Major, Medal with two Clasps, and Khedive's Star). Served with the Burmese Expedition in 1885-86 as Adjutant of Royal Engineers (mentioned in despatches, Medal with Clasp).

159 Major G. F. Mann served in the Ashanti war from 7th October 1873 until invalided on the 20th January 1874, having made the road from Dunquah to Mansu (mentioned in despatches, Medal). Served during the operations on the Malay Peninsula in 1875-76 (Medal with Clasp).

160 Major E. Dickinson served in the Egyptian war of 1882 (Medal, and Khedive's Star). Also served in the Soudan campaign in 1885, and was present in the engagements at Hasheen and the Tofrek zereba (two Clasps).

161 Major Rochfort-Boyd served in the Egyptian war of 1882 (mentioned in despatches, Brevet of Major, Medal, and Khedive's Star).

162 Major M. W. Skinner served on the Gold Coast from the 14th December 1873 until invalided on the 12th January 1874 (Ashanti Medal).

163 Lt.Colonel W. T. Shone served in the Afghan war of 1878-80 (Medal). Served with the Mahsood Wuzeeree Expedition in 1881 as Assistant Field Engineer (mentioned in despatches). Served with the Burmese Expedition in 1885-87 (mentioned in despatches, DSO., and Medal with two Clasps). Served with the Miranzai Expeditions in 1891 under Sir William Lockhart as Commanding Royal Engineer (mentioned in despatches, Brevet of Lt.Colonel, Clasp).

164 Major J. M. T. Badgley served in the Afghan war of 1878-80 (Medal). Served with the Burmese Expedition in 1885-86, and was severely wounded in an engagement on the 6th May 1886 (Medal with Clasp).

165 Major H. W. Duporier served in the Afghan war in 1879-80 (Medal).

166 Major F. W. Bennet served in the Egyptian war of 1882 (Medal, and Khedive's Star). Served in the Nile Expedition in 1884-85 with the Telegraph Department (mentioned in despatches, Brevet of Major, Clasp).

167 Sir Horatio Kitchener served with the Nile Expedition in 1884-85 as Deputy Assistant Adjutant and Quarter Master General (mentioned in despatches, Brevet of Lt.Colonel, Medal with Clasp, 2nd Class of the Medjidie, and Khedive's Star). Served in the operations near Suakin in December 1888, and was present in the engagement at Gemaizah in command of a Brigade of the Egyptian Army (mentioned in despatches, Clasp), and in the operations on the Soudan frontier in 1889 including the engagement at Toski (mentioned in despatches, CB., and Clasp).

168 Major A. W. Cockburn served with the Burmese Expedition in 1886-87 with the Queen's Own Sappers and Miners (mentioned in despatches, Medal with Clasp).

169 Lt.Colonel Wells served in the Afghan war in 1878-80. Raised a corps of Ghilzais, and with them constructed the road over the Khojuck. Was present in several minor engagements—wounded (mentioned in despatches, Medal).

170 Major E. Raban served with the expedition against the Naga Hill Tribes in 1879-80, and was present at the assault of Konoma (mentioned in despatches, Medal with Clasp).

171 Major G. F. Wilson served with the Nile Expedition in 1884-85 as Superintendent of Railway Works (mentioned in despatches, Medal with Clasp, and Khedive's Star).

172 Major S. Grant served in the Afghan war of 1878-80, and was present at the capture of the Peiwar Kotal (mentioned in despatches) and in the engagement at Charasiah on the 25th April 1880 (mentioned in despatches, Medal with Clasp). Served with the Hazara Expedition in 1888 as Field Engineer (Brevet of Major, Medal with Clasp).

173 Major S. H. Exham served in the Afghan war in 1878-79, and was present at the attack and capture of Ali Musjid (Medal with Clasp).

174 Major E. Glennie served in the Afghan war in 1879-80, and was present at the attack and capture of Ali Musjid; accompanied Sir Frederick Roberts in the march to Candahar, and was present at the battle of Candahar (Medal with two Clasps, and Bronze Decoration).

175 Colonel H. P. Leach served in the Afghan war of 1878-80, first with the 1st Division Khyber Field Force in command of a company of Bengal Sappers and Miners, and was present at the attack and capture of Ali Musjid with the expeditions into the Bazar Valley, and in the engagement at Deh Sarak (mentioned in despatches), afterwards with the Koorum Valley Field Force as Assistant Field Engineer and in command of a company of Bengal Sappers and Miners, took part in the Zaimusht Expedition under Brigadier General Tytler, and was present at the assault of Zawa (mentioned in despatches, Medal with Clasp). Served with the Nile Expedition in 1884-85 on Commissariat duty, and was present in the engagements at Abu Klea and El Gubat (Brevet of Major, Medal with two Clasps, and Khedive's Star). Served with the Chin-Lushai Expeditionary Force in 1889-90 as Commanding Royal Engineer, Chittagong Column (mentioned in despatches, Brevet of Lt.Colonel, Medal with Clasp).

176 Major W. H. Chippindall served in the Afghan war of 1879-80, and took part in the march to Candahar with the force under Major General Phayre (mentioned in despatches, Medal).

177 Major Bruce served in the Afghan war from April 1879 until invalided on 26th May 1880, as Assistant Field Engineer, first with the 2nd Division Peshawur Valley Field Force, and afterwards with the Khyber Line Force, including the operations in the Shuliman Valley and the engagement at Kam Dakka (mentioned in despatches, Medal).

178 Major E. W. Cotter served in the Ashanti war of 1873-74, and was present at the defence of the post of Quarman (Medal with Clasp). Commanded the 4th Company Bengal Sappers and Miners and was Field Engineer in the Zhob Valley Expedition in 1884. Served with the Nile Expedition and with the Nile Frontier Field Force in 1885 as Station Royal Engineer at Assouan.

179 Major H. E. M'Callum served in the operations in the Malay Peninsula in 1875 (mentioned in despatches, Medal with Clasp).

181 Major P. G. Von Donop served with the Nile Expedition in 1884-85 (Medal with Clasp, and Khedive's Star).
183 Major H. W. Smith-Rewse served in the Afghan war of 1878-80, and was present at the attack and capture of Ali Musjid (Brevet of Major, Medal with Clasp). Served in the Soudan campaign in 1885 as Brigade Major of Royal Engineers, and was present in the engagement at Hasheen (mentioned in despatches, Medal with Clasp, and Khedive's Star).
184 Major J. E. Blackburn served in the Egyptian war of 1882, and was present at the battle of Tel-el-Kebir (Medal with Clasp, and Khedive's Star). Served with the Nile Expedition in 1884-85, and was present at the action at Kirbekan (two Clasps); also served with the Soudan Frontier Field Force in 1885-86.
185 Major Leverson served in the Egyptian war of 1882 as Acting Deputy Assistant Commissary General, and was present in the action at Kassasin on the 9th September (Medal, and Khedive's Star). Served with the Bechuanaland Expedition under Sir Charles Warren in 1884-85 on special service.
186 Major R. L. Hippisley served in the Egyptian war of 1882 (Medal, and Khedive's Star).
187 Major Hollard served in the Egyptian war of 1882, and was present at the action at Kassasin on the 9th September (Medal, and Khedive's Star).
188 Major J. C. L. Campbell served in the Jowaki campaign in 1877-78 (Medal). Served in the Afghan war of 1878-80 as Adjutant Royal Engineers Khyber Line Force, and was present at the attack and capture of Ali Musjid, (Medal with Clasp). Served with the 24th Company of Royal Engineers in the Egyptian war of 1882, and was present at the action at Kassasin (9th September) and at the battle of Tel-el-Kebir (Medal with Clasp, and Khedive's Star). Served with the Bechuanaland Expedition under Sir Charles Warren in 1884-85.
189 Major C. K. Wood served with the Nile Expedition in 1884-85 on Telegraph duty (Medal with Clasp, and Khedive's Star).
190 Major G. H. W. O'Sullivan served in the Afghan war in 1879-80, and took part in the march to Candahar with the force under Major General Phayre (Medal).
191 Major E. Blunt served in the Afghan war of 1878-80 (Medal). Also served with the Mahsood Wuzeeree Expedition in 1881.
193 Major J. Burn Murdoch served in the Afghan war of 1878-80, and was present in the engagement at Charasiah on the 6th October 1879 and in the operations round Cabul in December 1879 including the storming of the Asmai Heights—wounded (mentioned in despatches, Medal with two Clasps). Served in the Egyptian war of 1882, and was present at the battle of Tel-el-Kebir (mentioned in despatches, Medal with Clasp, 5th Class of the Medjidie, and Khedive's Star).
194 Major Digby served in the Afghan war in 1879-80 in command of a company of the Queen's Own Sappers and Miners and as Assistant Field Engineer, and was present in the affair at Beaud (mentioned in despatches, Medal).
195 Major M. C. Barton served in the Afghan war in 1878-79 (mentioned in despatches, Medal). Also served with the Akha Expedition in 1883-84 (mentioned in despatches). Served with the Burmese Expedition in 1885-87 (mentioned in despatches, Medal with Clasp). Served with the Isazai Expedition as Commanding Royal Engineer.
196 Major R. C. Maxwell served in the Afghan war of 1878-80, accompanied Sir Frederick Roberts in the march to Candahar, and was present at the battle of Candahar (Medal with Clasp, and Bronze Decoration).
197 Major A. C. Foley served in the Afghan war of 1878-80, and took part in the advance to Khelat-i-Ghilzie and the occupation of Candahar (Medal). Served in the operations near Suakin in December 1888 and was present in the engagement at Gemaizah (mentioned in despatches, Medal with Clasp, and Khedive's Star).
199 Major Mackean served in the Zulu war in 1879 (Medal with Clasp).
200 Major A. H. Bagnold served in the Boer war of 1881. Served with the Nile Expedition in 1884-85 in the Telegraph Department (mentioned in despatches, Brevet of Major, Medal with Clasp).
202 Major W. V. Constable served in the Soudan campaign in 1885 (Medal with Clasp, and Khedive's Star).
203 Major R. H. Jennings served in the Afghan war in 1879-80, first in charge of a survey party, and afterwards as Political Officer (mentioned in despatches, Medal).
204 Major Darling served in the Afghan war in 1879-80 in command of a company of the Queen's Own Sappers and Miners and as Assistant Field Engineer, including the operations of the Moveable Column under Brigadier General Arbuthnot (Medal). Served in the Egyptian war of 1882 in command of a company of the Queen's Own Sappers and Miners, and was present at the battle of Tel-el-Kebir (Medal with Clasp, 5th Class of the Medjidie, and Khedive's Star); also served in the Soudan campaign in 1885 (Clasp).
206 Major Andrews Speed served with the Madras Sappers and Miners and as Assistant Field Engineer in the Egyptian war of 1882, and was present at the battle of Tel-el-Kebir (Medal with Clasp, and Khedive's Star). Served in the Burmese Expedition in 1886 (Medal with Clasp).
207 Major P. T. Buston served in the Afghan war of 1878-80, and was present in the engagement at Charasiah on the 6th October 1879 and in the operations round Cabul in December 1879 including the storming of the Asmai Heights (mentioned in despatches, Medal with Clasp). Served with the Hazara Expedition in 1888 as Field Engineer (Brevet of Major, Medal with Clasp); and with the Hazara Expedition in 1891 in command of the Bengal Sappers and Miners (mentioned in despatches, Clasp).
208 Major J. C. Tyler served in the Egyptian war of 1882, and was present at the action at Kassasin on the 9th September (Medal, and Khedive's Star).
209 Major G. H. Sim served in the Afghan war of 1878-80 (Medal). Served in the Soudan campaign in 1885 (Medal with Clasp, and Khedive's Star).
210 Major J. C. Campbell served with the Bengal Sappers and Miners in the Jowaki Afreedee Expedition in 1877-78 (Medal with Clasp). Served throughout the Afghan war of 1878-80 as Assistant Field Engineer, and in command of a company of Bengal Sappers and Miners, and was present at the attack and capture of Ali Musjid (Medal with Clasp).
212 Major J. A. Ferrier served in the Afghan war of 1878-80 (Medal). Served with the Nile Expedition in 1884-85 (Medal with Clasp, and Khedive's Star). Also served with the Soudan Frontier Field Force in 1885-86 in command at Ambigole, and was present at the attack on Ambigole Wells (DSO.).
213 Major J. D. Fullerton served in the Afghan war in 1879-80 as Acting Adjutant of the Bombay Sappers and Miners (Medal). Served with the Burmese Expedition in 1885-87 as Company Commander No. 2 Company Bombay Sappers and Miners (three times mentioned in despatches, Medal with Clasp).
214 Major E. C. Spilsbury served in the Afghan war in 1879-80, and took part in the march to Candahar with the force under Major General Phayre (Medal).
215 Major P. B. Baldwin served with the Madras Sappers and Miners and as Assistant Field Engineer in the Egyptian war of 1882, and was present at the battle of Tel-el-Kebir (Medal with Clasp, and Khedive's Star). Also served in the Soudan campaign in 1885 with the 8th (Railway) Company Royal Engineers.
216 Major G. T. Jones served in the Afghan war in 1879-80, took part in the defence of Candahar including the sortie of Deh Khojah (mentioned in despatches, and commended in General Orders by H.R.H. the Field Marshal Commanding in Chief for his gallant behaviour on the 12th August 1880), and was present at the battle of Candahar (Medal with Clasp).
217 Major Conner served in the Afghan war in 1878-79 in command of a company of the Queen's Own Sappers and Miners and as Assistant Field Engineer, and took part in the Bazar Valley Expedition (Medal).
218 Major Lindley served in the Afghan war of 1878-80 in command of a company of the Queen's Own Sappers and Miners and as Assistant Field Engineer, and took part in the Bazar Valley Expedition and in the operations of the Moveable Column under Brigadier General Arbuthnot (Medal). Served with the Madras Sappers and Miners and as Assistant Field Engineer in the Egyptian war of 1882, and was present at the battle of Tel-el-Kebir (Medal with Clasp, and Khedive's Star).
219 Major Bethell served in the Afghan war of 1878-80 (mentioned in despatches, Medal).
221 Major Attree served in the Afghan war in 1878-79 with the Queen's Own Sappers and Miners and as Assistant Field Engineer (Medal).
223 Major Hon. M. G. Talbot served in the Jowaki Afreedee Expedition in 1877-78 (Medal with Clasp). Served in the Afghan war in 1879-80, and was present at the attack and capture of Ali Musjid, in the engagement at Charasiah on the 6th October 1879, and in the operations round Cabul in December 1879; accompanied Sir Frederick Roberts in the march to Candahar, and was present at the battle of Candahar (mentioned in despatches, Medal with four Clasps, and Bronze Decoration). Also served in the Mahsood Wuzeeree Expedition in 1881.
223 Major S. A. E. Hickson served in the Afghan war of 1878-80, and took part in the march to Candahar with the force under Major General Phayre (Medal). Served in the Soudan campaign in 1885 (Medal with Clasp,

and Khedive's Star). Served with the Burmese Expedition in 1886-87 as Deputy Assistant Adjutant and Quarter Master General (mentioned in despatches, *DSO.*, and Medal with Clasp).

²²⁶ Major G. C. P. Onslow served in the Afghan war in 1879-80, and was present in the engagement at Charasiah on the 6th October 1879, and in the operations round Cabul in December 1879 including the storming of the Asmai Heights (mentioned in despatches, Medal with two Clasps). Served with the Burmese Expedition in 1885-87 (Medal with Clasp).

²²⁷ Major W. F. H. Stafford served in the Afghan war in 1878-79, and took part with the expeditions into the Lughman and Hissarik Valleys (Medal). Also served with the Mahsood Wuzeeree Expedition in 1881.

²²⁸ Major E. A. Waller served in the Afghan war in 1879-80, took part in the defence of Candahar (mentioned in despatches, and commended in General Orders by H.R.H. the Field Marshal Commanding in Chief for his gallant behaviour on the 12th August 1880), and was present at the battle of Candahar (Medal with Clasp).

²²⁹ Major A. H. Kenney served in the Afghan war of 1878-80, and was present at the capture of the Peiwar Kotal (Medal with Clasp). Served in the Nile Expedition in 1884-85, and was present at the action of Kirbekan (Medal with two Clasps, and Khedive's Star).

²³⁰ Major Wahab served in the Afghan war of 1878-80 with the Queen's Own Sappers and Miners and as Assistant Field Engineer, and took part in the Bazar Valley Expedition (Medal). Also served with the Mahsood Wuzeeree Expedition in 1881 as Assistant Field Engineer. Served with the Zhob Valley Expedition in 1884. Served with the Hazara Expedition in 1888 (mentioned in despatches, Medal with Clasp); with the Hazara Expedition in 1891 (mentioned in despatches, Clasp); and with the Isazai Field Force in 1892.

²³¹ Major W. A. E. St. Clair served in the Afghan war of 1878-80 (Medal). Served in the Soudan campaign in 1885 (Medal with Clasp, and Khedive's Star).

²³² Major G. A. Tower served with the Nile Expedition in 1884-85 (Medal with Clasp, and Khedive's Star).

²³³ Lt.Colonel Childers served in the Afghan war of 1878-80, and was present in the engagements at Takht-i-Pul and at Charasiah on the 6th October 1879 and in the operations round Cabul in December 1879; accompanied Sir Frederick Roberts in the march to Candahar, and was present at the battle of Candahar (mentioned in despatches, Medal with three Clasps, and Bronze Decoration). Served in the Egyptian war of 1882 as Aide de Camp to Sir Garnet Wolseley, and was present at the engagements of El Magfar, Tel-el-Mahuta, Kassasin (9th Sept.), and in the battle of Tel-el-Kebir (mentioned in despatches, Brevet of Major, Medal with Clasp, 5th Class of the Medjidie, and Khedive's Star). Served with the Nile Expedition in 1884-85 as Aide de Camp to Lord Wolseley (mentioned in despatches, Brevet of Lt.Colonel, Clasp).

²³⁴ Major C. Maxwell served in the Afghan war of 1878-80, including the operations round Cabul in December 1879 (Medal with Clasp). Served with the Zhob Valley Expedition in 1884.

²³⁵ Major W. Coles served in the Afghan war of 1878-80, and took part in the march to Candahar with the force under Major General Phayre (Medal). Served in the Soudan campaign in 1885 (Medal with Clasp, and Khedive's Star).

²³⁶ Major Shute served in the Afghan war in 1879-80 with the Queen's Own Sappers and Miners and as Assistant Field Engineer, and took part in the operations in Kama (Medal).

²³⁷ Major H. de H. Haig served during the rebellion in the North West Territories of Canada in 1885 as Assistant Quarter Master General, and was present in the engagement at Fish Creek and at the capture of Batoche (mentioned in despatches, Medal).

²³⁸ Major C. Penrose served in the Zulu war in 1879 (Medal).

²³⁹ Major J. G. Day served in the Afghan war of 1878-80 with the Bengal Sappers and Miners (Medal).

²⁴⁰ Major H. J. W. Jerome served in the Afghan war of 1878-80, and was present in the engagements at Ahmed Kheyl and Takht-i-Pul (Medal with Clasp).

²⁴¹ Major G. K. Scott-Moncrieff served in the Afghan war of 1878-80, and was present at the attack and capture of Ali Musjid and in the operations round Cabul in December 1879 (mentioned in despatches, Medal with two Clasps).

²⁴² Major C. M. Bate served in the Boer war of 1881. Served in the Soudan campaign in 1885 (Medal with Clasp, and Khedive's Star).

²⁴³ Major J. G. Lutyens served with the Burmese Expedition in 1886-87 (Medal with Clasp).

²⁴⁴ Major S. D. Cleeve served in the Egyptian war of 1882 (Medal, and Khedive's Star).

²⁴⁵ Major MacDonnoll served in the Afghan war in 1878-79 with the Queen's Own Sappers and Miners and as Assistant Field Engineer with the Peshawur Valley Field Force, and took part in the Bazar Valley Expedition (Medal). Served with the Rumpa Field Force in 1879-80 in command of a Company of the Queen's Own Sappers and Miners and as Superintendent of Army Signalling. Served in the Soudan campaign in 1885 with the Indian Contingent (Medal with Clasp, and Khedive's Star).

²⁴⁶ Lt.Colonel Mason served in the Afghan war of 1878-80 (Medal). Served with the Nile Expedition in 1884-85, and in the operations on the Upper Nile in 1885-86 (Medal, and Khedive's Star). Served with the Hazara Expedition in 1888 as Deputy Assistant Quarter Master General for Intelligence (mentioned in despatches, Medal with Clasp); with the Zhob Field Force in 1890 under Sir George White as Deputy Assistant Quarter Master General for Intelligence (mentioned in despatches); with the Miranzai Expedition in 1891 as Deputy Assistant Quarter Master General for Intelligence (mentioned in despatches, Brevet of Lt.Colonel, *DSO.*, and Clasp) ; with the Hazara Expedition in 1891 as Deputy Assistant Quarter Master General for Intelligence (mentioned in despatches, Clasp); with the second Miranzai Expedition in 1891 as Deputy Assistant Quarter Master General for Intelligence (mentioned in despatches, *DSO.*, and Clasp); and with the Isazai Expedition in 1892 as Deputy Assistant Quarter Master General for Intelligence.

²⁴⁷ Major H. Appleton served with the Mahsood Wuzeeree Expedition as Assistant Field Engineer. Served with the Burmese Expedition in 1886-87 (Medal with Clasp).

²⁴⁸ Major J. E. Dickie served in the Afghan war in 1879-80, and was present in the engagements at Ahmed Kheyl (mentioned in despatches) and Saif-u-deen (Medal with Clasp). Served in the Egyptian war of 1882, and was present at the battle of Tel-el-Kebir (Medal with Clasp, 5th Class of the Medjidie, and Khedive's Star). Served with the Burmese Expedition in 1885-86 (Medal with Clasp).

²⁴⁹ Major H. E. S. Abbott served in the Afghan war of 1880 as Assistant Field Engineer with the Khyber Line Force and the Khyber Brigade (Medal). Served with the Hazara Expedition in 1888 (Medal with Clasp); and with the Hazara Expedition in 1891 as Field Engineer 2nd Brigade (mentioned in despatches, Clasp).

²⁵⁰ Major H. J. Foster served in the Egyptian war of 1882, and was present at the action at Kassasin (9th September) and at the battle of Tel-el-Kebir (Medal with Clasp, and Khedive's Star).

²⁵¹ Major C. E. Haynes served in the Zulu war of 1879, and was present at the relief of Ekowe (mentioned in despatches, Medal with Clasp). Served with the Bechuanaland Expedition under Sir Charles Warren in 1884-85.

²⁵² Major H. H. Barnet served in the Afghan war of 1878-80 (Medal). Served with the Burmese Expedition in 1886-87 (mentioned in despatches, Medal with Clasp).

²⁵³ Major O. E. Ruck served in the Boer war of 1881.

²⁵⁴ Major H. E. Goodwyn served in the Afghan war of 1870-80 as Assistant Field Engineer (Medal). Served with the Madras Sappers and Miners and as Assistant Field Engineer in the Egyptian war of 1882, and was present at the battle of Tel-el-Kebir (Medal with Clasp, and Khedive's Star). Served with the Burmese Expedition in 1886-87 with the Queen's Own Sappers and Miners (mentioned in despatches, *DSO.*, and Medal with Clasp).

²⁵⁵ Major W. F. Hawkins served with the Nile Expedition in 1884-85 (Medal with Clasp, and Khedive's Star).

²⁵⁷ Major R. P. Littledale served in the Zulu war in 1879 (Medal with Clasp). Also served in the Boer war of 1881. Served with the Nile Expedition in 1884-85 (Medal with Clasp, and Khedive's Star).

²⁵⁸ Captain C. E. Commeline served in the Zulu war of 1879, and took part in the defence of Pretoria (Medal with Clasp). Served in the Boer war of 1881.

²⁶¹ Captain F. G. Bond served in the Zulu war in 1879 (Medal with Clasp). Served in the Egyptian war of 1882, and was present at the action of Kassasin (9th September) and at the battle of Tel-el-Kebir (Medal with Clasp, and Khedive's Star). Served with the Hazara Expedition in 1891 as Field Engineer 1st Brigade (mentioned in despatches, Medal with Clasp). [See also Civil Decorations for Gallantry, "Hart's Annual Army List," p. 766.]

²⁶² Captain F. G. Bowles served in the Soudan campaign in 1885, and was present at the destruction of Temai (Medal with Clasp, and Khedive's Star).

²⁶³ Captain F. B. Longe served in the Afghan war in 1879-80, and was present in the engagement at Charasiab on the 6th October 1879, and in the operations round Cabul in December 1879 (mentioned in despatches); accompanied

Sir Frederick Roberts in the march to Candahar, and was present at the battle of Candahar (Medal with three Clasps, and Bronze Decoration). Served in the Soudan campaign in 1885 in charge of the Indian Survey Party, and was present at the destruction of Temai (Medal with Clasp, and Khedive's Star).

264 Captain G. H. B. Gordon served in the Afghan war in 1879-80 with the Bengal Sappers and Miners including the engagement at Jugdulluck (Medal).

265 Captain T. de la H. Brotherton was employed in Natal during the Zulu war in 1879 (Medal). Served in the Boer war in 1881 (mentioned in despatches).

266 Captain E. C. Stanton served in the Afghan war of 1878-80 (Medal). Served with the Sikkim Expedition in 1888 (Medal with Clasp).

267 Major F. C. Heath served in the Egyptian war of 1882, and was present in the engagement at El Magfar and at the battle of Tel-el-Kebir (Medal with Clasp, and Khedive's Star). Served in the Soudan campaign in 1885 and was present in the engagement at Hasheen and at the destruction of Temai (mentioned in despatches, Brevet of Major, Clasp).

268 Major A. G. Thomson served in the Egyptian war of 1882, and was present at the battle of Tel-el-Kebir (Medal with Clasp, and Khedive's Star). Served with the expedition to the Soudan under Sir Gerald Graham in 1885 (mentioned in despatches, Brevet of Major, Clasp).

269 Captain E. St. C. Pemberton served in the Boer war in 1881. Served in the Egyptian war of 1882, and was present at the battle of Tel-el-Kebir (Medal with Clasp, and Khedive's Star).

270 Captain A. A. M. Layard served in the Soudan campaign in 1885, and was present at the engagement at Hasheen and at the destruction of Temai (Medal with Clasp, and Khedive's Star).

271 Major H. M. Lawson served in the Soudan Expedition under Sir Gerald Graham in 1884, and was present in the engagement at El Teb (Medal with Clasp, 5th Class of the Medjidie, and Khedive's Star); also served with the Nile Expedition in 1884-85, and was present at the action of Abu Klea, and in the engagements at El Gubat, Metammeh, and at Abu Klea Wells on the 16th and 17th February (mentioned in despatches, Brevet of Major, two Clasps).

272 Captain J. A. Tanner served in the Soudan campaign in 1885 (Medal with Clasp, and Khedive's Star). Served with the Burmese Expedition in 1885-88 as Adjutant of Royal Engineers (mentioned in despatches, DSO., and Medal with Clasp).

273 Captain F. D. F. MacCarthy served in the Soudan campaign in 1885, and was present in the engagement at the Tofrek zereba and at the destruction of Temai (Medal with two Clasps, and Khedive's Star).

274 Captain J. L. Irvine served in the Egyptian war of 1882, and was present at the battle of Tel-el-Kebir (Medal with Clasp, and Khedive's Star).

275 Captain W. C. Hussey served with the Bechuanaland Expedition under Sir Charles Warren in 1884-85.

276 Captain H. M. Jackson served in the Burmese campaign in 1886-87, including the Southern Shan Expedition (Medal with Clasp); and in 1888-89, when he took part in the Karenni Expedition and was slightly wounded in an engagement at Nga-Kyning (mentioned in despatches, Clasp).

277 Captain H. N. Dumbleton served with the Nile Expedition in 1884-85 (Medal with Clasp, and Khedive's Star).

278 Major H. F. Chesney served with the Hazara Expedition in 1888 as Field Engineer (mentioned in despatches, Medal with Clasp).

279 Captain H. B. N. Adair served with the Nile Expedition in 1885 (Medal with Clasp, and Khedive's Star).

280 Captain A. M. Mantell served in the Egyptian war of 1882 (Medal, 4th Class of the Osmanieh, and Khedive's Star).

281 Captain Godfrey Williams served in the Soudan campaign in 1885 (Medal with Clasp, and Khedive's Star).

282 Captain F. J. Anderson served with the Burmese Expedition in 1886 (Medal with Clasp).

283 Captain Cairnes served with the Burmese Expedition in 1885-86 (mentioned in despatches, Medal with Clasp), and with the Isazai Expedition in 1892.

284 Captain B. B. Russell served in the operations of the Zaila Field Force in 1890.

285 Captain C. D. Learoyd served in the Soudan campaign in 1885, and was present in the engagement at Hasheen (Medal with Clasp, and Khedive's Star). Served with the Burmese Expedition in 1885-86 as an Orderly Officer (mentioned in despatches, Medal with Clasp).

286 Captain S. L. Norris served in the Egyptian war of 1882, and was present in the engagement at El Magfar (Medal, and Khedive's Star).

287 Captain H. Mullaly served with the Chin-Lushai Expeditionary Force in 1889-90 as Field Engineer Chittagong Column (mentioned in despatches, Medal with Clasp).

289 Captain Winn served in the Egyptian war of 1882 (Medal, and Khedive's Star).

290 Captain F. H. Kelly served with the Burmese Expedition in 1885-87 (Medal with Clasp).

291 Captain H. S. King served in the Miranzai Expedition in 1891 with the Bengal Sappers and Miners (mentioned in despatches, Medal with Clasp).

293 Captain A. E. Sandbach served in the Egyptian war of 1882, and was present at the battle of Tel-el-Kebir (Medal with Clasp, and Khedive's Star); also served in the Soudan campaign in 1885, and was present in the engagement at Thakool (Clasp). Served with the Burmese Expedition in 1886-87 (Medal with Clasp); with the Sikkim Expedition in 1888 (Clasp); and with the Hazara Expedition in 1891 as Aide de Camp to Major General Elles, Commanding the Force (mentioned in despatches, Clasp).

294 Captain R. F. Allen served with the Manipore Expedition in 1891 as Field Engineer (mentioned in despatches, Medal with Clasp).

295 Captain A. M. Stuart served with the Nile Expedition in 1884-85 (Medal with Clasp, and Khedive's Star); also served in the operations of the Soudan Frontier Field Force in 1885-86.

297 Captain W. S. Vidal served in the Egyptian war of 1882, and was present in the action at Kassasin on the 9th September and at the battle of Tel-el-Kebir (Medal with Clasp, and Khedive's Star). Served with the Nile Expedition in 1884-85 (Clasp); also served with the Egyptian Frontier Field Force in 1885-86, including the attack on Ambigole Wells.

298 Captain H. V. Biggs served with the Burmese Expedition in 1885-87 (Medal with Clasp).

299 Captain E. M. Burton served in the Egyptian war of 1882, and accompanied Sir Charles Warren in the expedition into Arabia Petræa despatched for the purpose of bringing to justice the murderers of Professor Palmer and his party (mentioned in despatches, Medal, 5th Class of the Medjidie, and Khedive's Star). Served in the expedition to the Soudan in 1884 with the 26th Field Company of the Royal Engineers, and was present in the engagements at El Teb and Temai (two Clasps). Served in the Nile Expedition in 1884-85 with the 26th Field Company of the Royal Engineers, and afterwards with the Camel Corps, and took part in the operations of the Desert Column including the advance to Gakdul, Gubat, and Metammeh (Clasp).

300 Captain M. L. Tuke served in the Egyptian war of 1882, and was present at the action at Kassasin on the 9th September (Medal, and Khedive's Star). Served in the expedition to the Soudan under Sir Gerald Graham in 1884, and was present in the engagement at Temai (two Clasps); also served with the Nile Expedition in 1884-85 (Clasp).

301 Captain F. H. Oldfield served with the Burmese Expedition in 1888-89 (Medal with Clasp); with the Poukhan Expedition in 1889; and with the Chin-Lushai Expeditionary Force in 1889-90 (Clasp).

302 Captain Dopping-Hepenstal served in the Egyptian war of 1882 (Medal, and Khedive's Star).

303 Captain W. M. Hodder.—See Civil Decorations for Gallantry, "Hart's Annual Army List," p. 736.

304 Captain Huleatt served in the Egyptian war of 1882 (Medal, and Khedive's Star); also served in the Nile Expedition in 1884-85 with the Egyptian Army (4th Class of the Osmanieh, Clasp). Served in the operations of the Soudan Frontier Field Force in 1885-86 including the engagement at Giniss (4th Class of the Osmanieh).

305 Captain R. S. Maclagan served with the Hazara Expedition in 1888 (mentioned in despatches, Medal with Clasp); and with the Miranzai Expedition in 1891 (Clasp).

306 Captain H. G. C. Swayne served with the Chin-Lushai Expeditionary Force in 1889-90 (Medal with Clasp).

307 Captain J. Stewart served with the Burmese Expedition in 1885-86 (Medal with Clasp).

308 Captain Kincaid served with the Nile Expedition in 1884-85, and was present at the action of Kirbekan (Medal with two Clasps, and Khedive's Star).

309 Major Aylmer served with the Burmese Expedition in 1886-88 (mentioned in despatches, Medal with Clasp). Served with the Hazara Expedition in 1891 with the Bengal Sappers and Miners (mentioned in despatches,

Clasp). Served in the operations against the Hunza-Nagar‹ in 1891-92 as Commanding Royal Engineer, including the capture of the Nilt Fort—severely wounded (mentioned in despatches, Brevet of Major, VC, and Clasp); was awarded the Victoria Cross "for his conspicuous bravery in the assault and capture of the Nilt Fort on 2nd of December, 1891. This officer accompanied the storming party, burst open the inner gate with guncotton, which he placed and ignited, and though severely wounded, once in the leg and twice in the right hand, fired nineteen shots with his revolver, killing several of the enemy, and remained fighting until, fainting from loss of blood, he was carried out of action." Served with the Isazai Field Force in 1892.

310 Captain A. E. Haynes served during the Egyptian war of 1882 with the expedition into Arabia Petræa despatched for the purpose of bringing to justice the murderers of Professor Palmer and his party (mentioned in despatches, Medal, 5th Class of the Medjidie, and Khedive's Star). Served in the Bechuanaland Expedition under Sir Charles Warren in 1884-85 on special service.

311 Captain Baddeley served with the Burmese Expedition in 1886-87 (mentioned in despatches, Medal with Clasp).

312 Captain C. Hill served with the Nile Expedition in 1884-85 (Medal with Clasp, and Khedive's Star).

313 Captain Petrie served with the Zhob Valley Field Force in 1884 as Assistant Field Engineer. Served with the Burmese Expedition in 1886-88 including the expeditions to the Ruby Mines and Mainlong (mentioned in despatches, Medal with two Clasps); also served with the Chin-Lushai Expeditionary Force in 1889-90 with No. 2 Company Bengal Sappers and Miners (mentioned in despatches, Clasp).

315 Captain W. R. Morton served with the Burmese Expedition in 1885 (Medal with Clasp).

319 Captain F. Glanville served with the Burmese Expedition in 1886-88—severely wounded (mentioned in despatches, DSO., and Medal with Clasp).

320 Major J. R. L. Macdonald served with the Hazara Expedition in 1888 (mentioned in despatches, Medal with Clasp). Served in the operations in Central Africa in 1894 (Brevet of Major).

322 Captain A. W. Roper served with the Nile Expedition in 1884-85 (Medal with Clasp, and Khedive's Star).

321 Captain G. M. Heath served with the Bechuanaland Expedition under Sir Charles Warren in 1884-85.

325 Captain R. J. H. L. Mackenzie served in the Soudan campaign in 1885, and was present in the engagement at Hasheen (Medal with Clasp, and Khedive's Star). Served with the Zhob Field Force in 1890 under Sir George White (mentioned in despatches). Served with the Miranzai Expedition in 1891 (mentioned in despatches, Medal with Clasp).

326 Captain C. A. Leahy served in the operations of the Soudan Frontier Field Force in 1885-86 (Medal, and Khedive's Star).

327 Captain F. A. Molony served in the Soudan campaign in 1885 (Medal with Clasp, and Khedive's Star).

328 Captain W. Du C. Luard served with the Soudan Frontier Field Force in 1885-86 (mentioned in despatches, Medal, and Khedive's Star). Served with the expedition against the Younies, on the West Coast of Africa, in 1887-88 (mentioned in despatches, Medal with Clasp).

329 Captain W. G. R. Corduc served with the Hazara Expedition as Assistant Field Engineer (Medal with Clasp).

330 Captain J. M. Wade served with the Burmese Expedition in 1885-86 (Medal with Clasp).

331 Captain W. J. Bythell served with the Bechuanaland Expedition under Sir Charles Warren in 1884-85 on special service. Served with the Chin-Lushai Expeditionary Force in 1889-90 on Survey duty (received the thanks of the Government of India, mentioned in despatches, Medal with Clasp).

333 Captain C. E. Salvesen served with the Bechuanaland Expedition under Sir Charles Warren in 1884-85.

334 Lieut. C. Godby served in the Soudan campaign in 1885, and was present in the engagements at Hasheen and the Tofrek zereba (Medal with two Clasps, and Khedive's Star).

335 Captain J. W. Pringle served with the Burmese Expedition in 1885-86 (Medal with Clasp).

336 Captain J. R. B. Serjeant served with the Burmese Expedition in 1885-87 (Medal with Clasp).

338 Captain Renny-Tailyour served with the Burmese Expedition in 1885-88 (mentioned in despatches, Medal with two Clasps); and with the Chin-Lushai Expeditionary Force in 1889-90 on Survey duty (received the thanks of the Government of India, mentioned in despatches, Clasp).

339 Captain C. S. Rose served with the Hazara Expedition in 1891 (Medal with Clasp).

340 Captain W. A. J. O'Meara served with the Burmese Expedition in 1885-86—severely wounded (mentioned in despatches, Medal with Clasp).

341 Captain W. S. Gordon served in the operations near Suakin in December 1888, and was present with the Egyptian Army in the engagement at Gemaizah (mentioned in despatches, Medal with Clasp, and Khedive's Star); also served in the operations in the Soudan in 1889 including the engagement at Toski in command of Field Artillery (mentioned in despatches, Clasp). Granted the 4th Class of the Order of the Osmanieh for services with the Egyptian Army.

343 Captain Bonham-Carter served in the Soudan campaign in 1885 (Medal with Clasp, and Khedive's Star). Served with the Burmese Expedition in 1886-88 (Medal with Clasp).

344 Captain R. U. H. Buckland served in the Soudan campaign in 1885, and was present in the engagements at Hasheen (Medal with Clasp, and Khedive's Star); also served in the operations near Suakin in December 1888, including the engagement at Gemaizah (mentioned in despatches, 5th Class of the Medjidie, Clasp).

345 Captain E. D. Bullen served with the Burmese Expedition in 1886-87 (Medal with Clasp).

346 Captain T. Harrison served with the Burmese Expedition in 1892, and was present at the defence of Sadon (mentioned in despatches, DSO, and Medal with Clasp).

347 Captain A. G. Hunter-Weston served in the Miranzai Expedition in 1891 with the Bengal Sappers and Miners (Medal with Clasp).

349 Captain R. T. R. Laurence served with the Burmese Expedition in 1886-88 (Medal with Clasp).

451 Captain J. A. Dealy served with the Burmese Expedition in 1888 (Medal with Clasp).

353 Captain H. B. H. Wright served with the Burmese Expedition in 1886-87 with the Queen's Own Sappers and Miners (mentioned in despatches, Medal with two Clasps); in the Chin Field Force in 1888 with the Queen's Own Sappers and Miners (mentioned in despatches); and with the Chin-Lushai Field Force in 1889-90 (Clasp).

354 Captain J. C. Rimington served with the Burmese Expedition in 1886 (Medal with Clasp).

355 Captain C. H. Roe served with the Burmese Expedition in 1886-87 with the Queen's Own Sappers and Miners (Medal with Clasp).

356 Captain R. L. C. Brooker served in the operations in Zululand in 1888.

356† Captain Le Breton Simmons served with the Hazara Expedition in 1891 (Medal with Clasp).

357 Captain E. A. Edgell served with the Burmese Expedition in 1888 (Medal with Clasp).

358 Captain S. H. Powell served with the Miranzai Expedition in 1891 as Assistant Intelligence Officer (mentioned in despatches, Medal with Clasp).

359 Captain W. Ewbank served with the Burmese Expedition in 1885-87 (Medal with Clasp), and again in 1887-89 (Clasp).

360 Captain L. P. Chapman served with the Burmese Expedition in 1888 (Medal with Clasp), and with the Wuntho Expedition in 1891 (mentioned in despatches, Clasp).

361 Captain W. A. Liddell served in the operations of the Zhob Field Force in 1890.

362 Captain J. A. S. Tulloch served in the Burmese Expedition in 1885-89 with the Queen's Own Sappers and Miners, and afterwards as Orderly Officer to Brigadier General Wolseley; served as Intelligence Officer 1st Brigade from 1st Nov. 1887 to 1st April 1888, and from Aug. to Dec. 1888 as Adjutant of Royal Engineers (Medal with two Clasps); also served with the Chin Field Force in 1888-89.

363 Captain U. W. Evans served with the Chin-Lushai Field Force in 1889-90 with the Queen's Own Sappers and Miners (Medal with Clasp).

364 Captain E. H. Bland served in the Miranzai Expedition in 1891 with the Bengal Sappers and Miners (Medal with Clasp); and with the Isazai Field Force in 1892.

365 Captain Stokes-Roberts served with the Burmese Expedition in 1887 (Medal with Clasp), and with the Hazara Expedition in 1888 (Clasp).

467 Captain G. D. Close served with the Burmese Expedition in 1887 (Medal with Clasp).

368 Captain R. F. Sorsbie served with the Burmese Expedition in 1887 as Assistant Field Engineer (Medal with Clasp).

370 Captain H. J. Sherwood served with the Chin-Lushai Expeditionary Force in 1889-90 with No. 2 Company Bengal Sappers and Miners, part of the time in command of a half company (mentioned in despatches, Medal with Clasp).

373 Captain C. C. Perceval served with the Burmese Expedition in 1887-83 (Medal with Clasp). Served with the Hazara Expedition in 1888 (mentioned in despatches, Clasp); and with the Isazai Field Force in 1892.
374 Captain H. C. Nanton served during the rebellion in the North West Territories of Canada in 1885 with the Midland Battalion of Canadian Militia (Medal).
375 Captain P. H. du P. Casgrain served during the rebellion in he North West Territories of Canada in 1885 with the 9th Battalion of Militia Rifles (Medal).
376 Lieut. W. F. Tilley served with the Burmese Expedition in 1887 (Medal with Clasp).
377 Captain H. Sloggett served in the operations against the Sofas, West Coast of Africa, in 1893-94 (mentioned despatches).
378 Captain G. S. Cartwright served with the Isazai Expedition in 1892.
379 Captain A. G. Travers served in the Miranzai Expedition in 1891 with the Bengal Sappers and Miners (Medal with Clasp).
381 Lieut. de Vere Atkinson served with the Lushai Expedition in 1889 as Assistant Field Engineer; with the Chin-Lushai Expeditionary Force in 1889-90 with the Bengal Sappers and Miners (Medal with Clasp); and in the operations of the Zhob Field Force in 1890 with the Bombay Sappers and Miners.
382 Lieut. A. T. Moore served with the Isazai Expedition in 1892.
383 Lieut. E. P. Johnson served in the Chin-Lushai Field Force in 1889-90 with the Queen's Own Sappers and Miners (Medal with Clasp).
385 Lieut. A. J. H. Swiney served with the second Miranzai Expedition in 1891 (Medal with Clasp).
386 Lieut. W. J. McElhinny served with the Burmese Expedition in 1887-88 (Medal with Clasp).
387 Lieut. G. M. Duff served with the Burmese Expedition in 1887-88 (Medal with Clasp).
388 Lieut. R. E. Picton Jones served in the operations of the Zaila Field Force in 1890.
390 Lieut. J. S. Fowler served with the Isazai Expedition in 1892.
391 Lieut. G. M. Hutton served in the Chin-Lushai Field Force in 1889-90 with the Queen's Own Sappers and Miners (Medal with Clasp).
392 Lieut. H. M. St. A. Wade.—See Civil Decorations for Gallantry, "Hart's Annual Army List," p. 786.
393 Lieut. C. H. Heycock served in the Karen Field Force in 1888-89 with the Queen's Own Sappers and Miners (mentioned in despatches, Medal with Clasp); in the Chin-Lusnai Field Force in 1889-90 with the Queen's Own Sappers and Miners (Clasp); and in the Kanhow Expedition in 1891 as Intelligence Officer.
394 Lieut. F. F. Weedon served in the Burmese Expedition in 1888-89 with the Queen's Own Sappers and Mine including the operations of the Chin Field Force (Medal with Clasp).
395 Lieut. R. A. F. Kingscote served with the Chin-Lushai Expeditionary Force in 1889-90 as Assistant Field Engineer Chittagong Column (mentioned in despatches, Medal with Clasp).
396 Lieut. T. Fraser served in the Chin-Lushai Field Force in 1889-90 with the Queen's Own Sappers and Miners (Medal with Clasp); and in the Hazara Field Force in 1891 with the Bengal Sappers and Miners, part of the time in command of a Company (Clasp).
397 Lieut. H. A. D. Fraser served with the Wuntho Expedition in 1891 (mentioned in despatches, Medal with Clasp).
399 Lieut. C. Ainslie served in the Chin-Lushai Field Force in 1889-90 with the Queen's Own Sappers and Miners (Medal with Clasp); in the ope ations in the Chin Hills in 1890-92 with the Queen's Own Sappers and Miners in command of a detachment, including the engagement at Thetta (mentioned in despatches, Clasp); and in the Chin Hills in 1892 and the Shan Hills in 1893 as Attaché, Intelligence Branch (mentioned in despatches).
401 Lieut. E. C. Ogilvie served with the second Miranzai Expedition in 1891 (Medal with Clasp).
402 Lieut. D. L. Mallaby served with the Isazai Expedition in 1892.
403 Lieut. H. J. M. Marshall served in the Chin-Lushai Field Force in 1889-90 with the Queen's Own Sappers and Miners (Medal with Clasp).
405 Lieut. C. de W. Crookshank served with the second Miranzai Expedition in 1891 as Assistant Field Engineer (Medal with Clasp).
406 Lieut. H. R. Stockley served with the Hazara Expedition in 1891 (Medal with Clasp); and with the Isazai Expedition in 1892.
408 Lieut. R. E. Greer served in the operations of the Zhob Field Force in 1890.
409 Lieut. F. F. N. Rees served with the Hazara Expedition in 1891 (Medal with Clasp).
410 Lieut. A. H. D. Riach served with the Isazai Field Force in 1892.
412 Lieut. G. A. F. Sanders served in Burmah in 1893 with the Queen's Own Sappers and Miners in command of a detachment in the Kaptial Column.
413 Lieut. C. W. Gwynn served in the operations against the Sofas, West Coast of Africa, in 1893-94, as Intelligence Officer—three times wounded (mentioned in despatches, DSO. and Medal with Clasp).
414 Lieut. R. H. Macdonald served with the Isazai Expedition in 1892.
415 Lieut. G. H. Boileau served with the expedition to the Tambaka Country, West Coast of Africa, in 1892, including the capture of Tambi (mentioned in despatches); and with the expedition up the River Gambia in 1892, including the capture of Toniataba (mentioned in despatches, Medal with Clasp).
417 Captain A. T. Lewis served in the Zulu war in 1879 (Medal with Clasp). Served in the Egyptian war of 1882, and was present at the battle of Tel-el-Kebir (Medal with Clasp, and Khedive's Star); also served in the Soudan campaign in 1885 (Clasp).
418 Lieut. Morrison served in the Abyssinian war in 1867-68 (Medal).

War Services of Royal Engineers (late Bengal Engineers).

1 General Fraser served in the Sutlej campaign of 1845-46, and was present at the battle of Sobraon (Medal and Clasp). Punjaub campaign of 1848-49, as Adjutant of Sappers at the siege of Mooltan and battle of Goojerat (Medal with two Clasps). Burmese war of 1852-53, and accompanied the Column under General Steel to Tonghoo (Medal with Clasp for Pegu).
2 Lieut.General Maunsell served the Punjaub campaign of 1848-49, throughout the operations before Mooltan, including the first siege, storming of the intrenched positions on 9th and 12th September, and surrender of the fortress, also surrender of the Fort and garrison of Cheniote, and battle of Goojerat (Medal with two Clasps). In the Indian Mutiny campaign commanded Sappers and Miners at the actions on the Hindun, battle of Budlekeserai, and throughout the siege of Delhi, directed the right attack during the final operations, and was dangerously wounded when conducting the Column of assault on the Paharecpore suburb on 14th Sept. 1857. Commanded Sappers at the siege and capture of Lucknow, in the Rohilcund campaign at Rooyah, Alygunge, and Bareilly, and at Mitowlee in the Oude campaign of 1858-59 (mentioned in despatches, Medal with two Clasps, Brevet of Major, and CB.). Served in the Afghan war in 1878-79, and was present at the attack and capture of Ali Musjid (mentioned in despatches, Medal with Clasp).
3 Sir Edward Williams served as Adjutant of Engineers with the expedition to Pegu in 1852, and was present at the bombardment and capture of Martaban and Rangoon (slightly wounded), capture of Prome and occupation of Meaday (mentioned in despatches for "gallant conduct," Medal with Clasp).
6 Sir George Chesney was present at the battle of Budleekeserai, and served as Brigade Major of Engineers throughout the siege of Delhi and was twice severely wounded at the assault (mentioned in despatches, Medal with Clasp, and Brevet of Major).
12 Lieut.General Perkins served in the Indian Mutiny campaign, including the battle of Budleekeserai and siege of Delhi—wounded (Medal with Clasp). Served in the Afghan war of 1878-80, and was present at the capture of the Peiwar Kotal (mentioned in despatches), in the engagement at Charasiab on the 6th October 1879 (mentioned in despatches), and in the operations round Cabul in December 1879 including the investment of Sherpore (mentioned in despatches); accompanied Sir Frederick Roberts in the march to Candahar in command of the Royal Engineers, and was present at the battle of Candahar (mentioned in despatches, CB., Medal with four Clasps, and Bronze Decoration).

War Services of Royal Engineers (late Bengal Engineers).

[27] Sir James Browne served with the expedition against the Mahsood Wuzeerees, on the North West Frontier of India, in 1860, and was present at the storming of the Burera Pass and the capture of Kaneegurum and Mukeem (mentioned in despatches, Medal with Clasp). Served throughout the Umbeylah campaign in 1863—wounded (three times mentioned in despatches, Brevet of Major, Clasp). Served in the Afghan war in 1878-79 as Political Officer to Sir Donald Stewart, and was present at the engagement at Takht-i-Pul and in the advance to Candahar and Khelat-i-Ghilzie (several times mentioned in despatches, Medal, and C.B.). Served in the Egyptian war of 1882 in command of the Royal Engineers of the Indian Contingent, and was present at the battle of Tel-el-Kebir (mentioned in despatches, Medal with Clasp, 3rd Class of the Osmanieh, and Khedive's Star).
[36] Major General Tomkins served with the Zhob Valley Expedition in 1884.
[38] Lt. Colonel Strahan served in the Afghan war of 1878-80 (Brevet of Major, Medal).

War Services of Royal Engineers (late Madras Engineers).

[1] Sir Arthur Thomas Cotton served throughout the Burmese war of 1824-26 under Sir Archibald Campbell, and was present at the capture of Rangoon, reconnoitring in gunboats and jungle fighting near Kemundine, attack of stockades and Pagoda of Syriam, capture of Mergui and Tavoy, defence of the Lines at Rangoon and attack of the left flank of the Burmese Entrenchments, attack of the Stockade of Kokein, siege and capture of Donabew, attack of Shan Stockades and of stockades on the left bank of the Irrawaddy near Prome, capture of Melloon and jungle fight at Paghammew which terminated the war (Medal with Clasp).
[10] Colonel Filgate served as Assistant Field Engineer throughout the Chinese campaign of 1860, and was present at the action of Sinho, captures of Tangku and the Taku Forts, and surrender of Pekin (Medal with two Clasps).
[12] Colonel Pennycuick served in the Abyssinian campaign in command of H Company Madras Sappers (Medal).
[13] Major General Hamilton commanded the Madras Sappers and Miners in the Egyptian war of 1882 and was present at the battle of Tel-el-Kebir (Brevet of Lt. Colonel, Medal with Clasp, and Khedive's Star).

War Services of Royal Engineers (late Bombay Engineers).

[1] General Turner served in the expedition against Kolapore in 1827.
[2] Sir Michael Kennedy served in the Afghan war of 1878-80 as Controller General of Transport and Supply, and was present in the operations round Cabul in December 1879 (mentioned in despatches, Medal with Clasp).
[13] Lieut. General C. A. Goodfellow served with the Central India Field Force in 1857-58, and was present at the siege and capture of Ratghur, capture of Garrakota, siege and storm of Jhansi (Victoria Cross, and Medal with Clasp); was awarded the VC "for gallant conduct at the attack on the Fort of Beyt, on the 6th October 1859. On that occasion, a soldier of the 28th Regiment was shot under the walls of the fort. Lieutenant Goodfellow rushed under the walls, under a sharp fire of matchlocks, and bore off the body of the soldier, who was then dead, but whom he at first supposed to be wounded only." Was Assistant Field Engineer with the Okamundel and Kattywar Field Force in 1859. Served as Brigade Major of Royal Engineers with the Abyssinian Expeditionary Force throughout the campaign (mentioned in despatches for the "efficient manner in which he carried on the duties of his appointment," Brevet of Major, and Medal).
[21] Colonel E. D. Twemlow served in the Afghan war in 1879-80, and took part in the march to Candahar with the force under Major General Phayre (mentioned in despatches, Medal).

Continuation of Notes to the Grenadier Guards.

[35] Major Hon. H. F. White served in the Soudan campaign in 1885 (Medal with Clasp, and Khedive's Star).
[36] Major Hon. J. T. St. Aubyn served in the Soudan Expedition under Sir Gerald Graham in 1884 as Aide de Camp to Brigadier General Sir Redvers Buller, Commanding 1st Brigade, and was present in the engagements at El Teb and Temai (mentioned in despatches, Medal with Clasp, and Khedive's Star). Served in the Nile Expedition in 1884-85 as Aide de Camp to Major General Earle and after his death to Brigadier General Brackenbury, and was present at the action of Kirbekan (mentioned in despatches, Brevet of Major, two Clasps).
[37] Captain Legh served in the Soudan campaign in 1885 (Medal with Clasp, and Khedive's Star).
[38] Captain Gordon-Gilmour served in the Zulu war of 1879, and was present in the engagement at Ulundi (Medal with Clasp). Served in the Nile Expedition in 1884-85 with the Guards Camel Regiment, and was present at the actions at Abu Klea and Abu Kru (Medal with two Clasps, and Khedive's Star).
[40] Captain Scott-Kerr served in the Zulu war in 1879, and was present in the engagement at Ulundi (Medal with Clasp). Served in the Soudan campaign in 1885 (Medal with Clasp, and Khedive's Star).
[43] Captain Lane-Fox-Pitt served with the 91st Highlanders in the latter part of the Zulu war of 1879 (Medal with Clasp). Served in the Soudan campaign in 1885 (Medal with Clasp, and Khedive's Star).
[44] Captain Lindsay served with the 2nd Battalion of the Grenadier Guards in the Egyptian war of 1882, and was present at the battle of Tel-el-Kebir (Medal with Clasp, and Khedive's Star). Also served in the Soudan campaign in 1885 (Clasp).
[45] Count Gleichen served in the Nile Expedition in 1884-85 with the Camel Corps, and was present in the actions at Abu Klea and Abu Kru (Medal with two Clasps, and Khedive's Star).
[46] Captain Cotton served in the Soudan campaign in 1885 (Medal with Clasp, and Khedive's Star).
[47] Captain Taylor served in the Soudan campaign in 1885 (Medal with Clasp, and Khedive's Star).
[48] Captain Manners served with the 15th Hussars in the Boer war of 1881.
[49] Captain Pakenham served in the Soudan campaign in 1885 (Medal with Clasp, and Khedive's Star).
[51] Lieut. Davies served in the Soudan campaign in 1885 (Medal with Clasp, and Khedive's Star). Served with the Expedition against the Jebus, Lagos, on the West Coast of Africa, in 1892 (Medal with Clasp).
[53] Lieut. Lloyd served in the Soudan campaign in 1885 (Medal with Clasp, and Khedive's Star).
[56] Captain W. Holmes served in the Soudan campaign in 1885 (Medal with Clasp, and Khedive's Star).
[57] Brigade Surgeon Lt. Colonel Harrison and Surgeon Lt. Colonel Campbell.—For War Services, see Army Medical Staff.

1st Batt., Wellington Barracks.
2nd Batt., Chelsea Barracks.
3rd Batt., Tower of London.

Grenadier Guards. 229

A Company Badge. A Grenade. "BLENHEIM" "RAMILLIES" "OUDENARDE" "MALPLAQUET" "DETTINGEN" "LINCELLES" "CORUNNA" "BARROSA" "PENINSULA" "WATERLOO" "ALMA" "INKERMAN" "SEVASTOPOL" "EGYPT, 1882" "TEL-EL-KEBIR" "SUAKIN, 1885."

Years' Ser Full Pay.	Half Pay.		
		Colonel.—*His Royal Highness* George W. F. C. Duke of Cambridge,¹ *KG. KT. KP. GCB. GCSI. GCMG. GCIE. Colonel,* 3 Nov. 37; *Major General,* 7 May 45; *Lieut.General,* 19 June 54; *General,* 15 July 56; *Field Marshal,* 9 Nov. 62; *Commander in Chief,* 26 Nov. 87; *Colonel of the Grenadier Guards,* 15 Dec. 61.	
28	8/12	**Lieutenant Colonels.**—Laurence James Oliphant,² *Commanding the Regiment,* 17 July 94; *Ens. & Lt.* ᴾ17 Oct. 66; *Lt. & Capt.* ᴾ29 Dec. 69; *Capt. & Lt.Colonel,* 9 Dec. 76; *Major,* 1 Nov. 82; *Colonel,* 1 Nov. 86; *Lt.Colonel,* 26 Oct. 89.	
27	...	1 Lord Arthur Charles Wellesley, *Ens. & Lt.* ᴾ13 June 68; *Lt. & Capt.* ᴾ15 Feb. 71; *Capt. & Lt.Colonel,* 5 Apr. 79; *Major,* 1 Aug. 83; *Colonel,* 1 Aug. 87; *Lt.Colonel,* 28 Oct. 91.	
27	...	3 Edmund Antrobus,¹⁰ *Ensign & Lt.* ᴾ18 Feb. 69; *Lt. & Capt.* ᴾ17 May 71; *Capt. & Lt.Colonel,* 24 May 79; *Major,* 16 July 84; *Colonel,* 11 May 88; *Lt.Colonel,* 26 Oct. 93.	
26	...	2 Horace Ricardo,¹² *Ens. &Lt.* ᴾ17 April 69; *Lt. & Capt.* ᴾ17 May 71; *Capt. & Lt.Colonel,* 24 May 79; *Major,* 1 Apr. 85; *Colonel,* 29 Jan. 88; *Lt.Colonel,* 23 July 94.	
25	...	**Majors.**—2 Villiers Hatton, *Ensign & Lt.* ᴾ27 Aug. 70; *Lt. & Capt.* 4 Dec. 72; *Capt.& Lt.Colonel,* 5 July 82; *Major,* 31 March 86; *Colonel,* March 90.	
25	...	3 Henry Edward Colvile,¹⁶ *CB. C.M.G., on Special Service, Uganda;* *Ens. & Lt.* ᴾ1 Oct. 70; *Lt. & Capt.* 15 Mar. 72; *Capt.& Lt.Colonel,* 1 Nov. 82; *Major,* 1 July 86; *Colonel,* 2 Jan. 86.	
25	...	1 p.s.c. Ivor John Caradoc Herbert,¹⁷ *CB. Commanding the Militia in Canada, with rank of Major General,* 20 Nov. 90; *Ens. & Lt.* ᴾ5 Nov. 70; *Lt. & Capt.* 25 Nov. 74; *Bt. Major,* 18 Nov. 82; *Capt. & Lt.Colonel,* 2 May 83; *Colonel,* 18 Aug. 89; *Major,* 26 Oct. 89.	
24	...	3 Eyre Macdonnell Stewart Crabbe,¹⁹ *Lt.* 28 Oct. 71; *Capt.* 24 Nov. 83; *Bt.Major,* 15 June 85; *Major,* 1 July 90.	
23	...	1 Francis Cecil Ricardo, *Lt.* 11 Sept. 72; *Capt.* 8 June 84; *Major,* 10 Dec. 90.	
23	...	1 p.s.c. Harry James Craufurd,²² *Lt.* 29 Mar. 73; *Capt.* 9 July 84; *Major,* 28 Oct. 91.	
21	...	3 Francis Lloyd,²⁵ *Lt.* 18 Mar. 75; *Capt.* 1 Apr. 85; *Major,* 10 Aug. 92.	
21	...	2 William Arthur Ince Anderton, *Lt.* 21 Jan. 75; *Capt.* 18 Apr. 85; *Major,* 1 Apr. 93.	
19	...	1 Henry Streatfeild, *Lt.* 26 Aug. 76; *Capt.* 29 Apr. 85; *Major,* 25 July 93.	
18	...	3 Archer Parry Crawley,³³ *2nd Lt.* 13 Oct. 77; *Lt.* 28 Apr. 80; *Captain,* 16 Nov. 88; *Major,* 20 Dec. 93.	
17	...	3 Henry Goulburn, *2nd Lt.* 11 May 78; *Lt.* 1 July 81; *Capt.* 18 Oct. 89; *Major,* 23 July 94.	
17	...	2 *Hon.* Henry Frederick White,³⁵ *serving under the British South Africa Company;* *2nd Lt.* 14 Sept. 78; *Lt.* 1 July 81; *Capt.* 18 Oct. 89; *Major,* 22 Aug. 94.	
17	...	2 David Alexander Kinloch, *2nd Lt.* 11 May 78; *Lt.* 1 July 81; *Capt.* 18 Oct. 89; *Major,* 12 Sept. 94.	

		CAPTAINS.	2ND LIEUT.	LIEUT.	CAPTAIN.
17	...	1 *Hon.* John Townshend St. Aubyn³⁶ (*Bt.Major,* 2 July 90)	19 Oct. 78	1 July 81	1 July 90
17	...	1 *Hon.* Gilbert Legh³⁷	13 Nov. 78	1 July 81	2 July 90
18	...	2 Robert Gordon Gordon-Gilmour³⁸	25 Jan. 78	1 July 81	23 July 90
17	...	3 Robert Scott-Kerr⁴⁰	26 Mar. 79	1 July 81	16 Dec. 90
15	...	1 Christopher William Darby-Griffith	8 May 80	1 July 81	23 Jan. 92
15	...	1 Thomas Henry Hollis Bradford-Atkinson⁶	25 Aug. 80	1 July 81	23 Jan. 92
17	...	1 William Augustus Lane-Fox-Pitt⁴²	22 Feb. 79	1 July 81	16 Mar. 92
15	...	3 Richard Joshua Cooper⁸	26 Aug. 80	1 July 81	11 May 92
15	...	Charles Ludovic Lindsay⁴⁴ (*Depot*)	22 Jan. 81	1 July 81	10 Aug. 92
14	...	2 p.s.c. Albert Edward Wilfred, *Count Gleichen,*⁴⁵ *Extra Equerry to the Queen*		1 Oct. 81	21 Sept. 92
13	...	2 Arthur William Cotton⁴⁶		10 May 82	16 Nov. 92
14	...	2 George Godfrey Macdonald⁸		1 Oct. 81	20 Dec. 93
13	...	3 Edward Richard Taylor⁴⁷		9 Sept. 82	20 June 94
13	...	3 Charles Henry Halford		9 Sept. 82	21 July 94
16	...	2 Charles George Edmund John Manners⁴⁸	11 Feb. 80	1 July 81	23 July 94
12	...	1 Hercules Arthur Pakenham⁴⁹		14 Apr. 83	12 Sept. 94

		LIEUTENANTS.			
12	...	1 Charles Fergusson		7 Nov. 83	
12	...	Bruce Canning Vernon-Wentworth, *MP. for Brighton*		28 Nov. 83	
12	...	1 Henry Roger Crompton-Roberts		6 Feb. 84	
11	...	2 p.s.c. Francis John Davies,⁵¹ **Adjutant** 2 Aug. 93		14 May 84	
11	...	*Hon.* Walter Lewis Bagot, **Regimental Adjutant** 7 May 93		23 Aug. 84	
11	...	3 Wilfred George Howard Marshall		23 Aug. 84	
11	...	1 Arthur Henry Orlando LLoyd⁵³		23 Aug. 84	
11	...	2 *Sir* Augustus Frederick Walpole Edward Webster, *Bart.*		23 Aug. 84	
11	...	1 George Edward Pereira		23 Aug. 84	
11	...	1 Joseph Henry Russell Bailey		7 Feb. 85	
11	...	1 Henry Heywood Heywood-Lonsdale, **Adjutant** 11 Apr. 94		7 Feb. 85	
11	...	1 Godfrey Dalrymple White		7 Feb. 85	
11	...	3 George Colborne Nugent		7 Feb. 85	
10	...	Edward George Villiers *Lord* Stanley, *MP. for S.E. Lancashire*		6 May 85	
10	...	*Hon.* William Edwin Cavendish, *serving in British Central Africa with rank of Captain*		23 May 85	
10	...	Harold Goodeve Ruggles-Brise, *Adjutant Guards Depot* 1 Jan. 95		23 May 85	
10	...	1 Edward Greville Verschoyle		23 May 85	
10	...	1 Frederick Rudolph, *Visct.* Kilcoursie		29 Aug. 85	
11	...	3 Wroth Periam Christopher Lethbridge		28 Feb. 85	
9	...	2 Dudley Ferrars Loftus		19 May 86	
9	...	*Hon.* Richard Fitzroy Somerset, *Aide de Camp to Lord Wolseley* 22 Dec. 92		18 Aug. 86	
9	...	3 St. John Halford Coventry		8 Sept. 86	
9	...	2 Nathaniel John Lyon		15 Dec. 86	
8	...	2 *Lord* Edward Herbert Cecil	30 Apr. 87	16 Mar. 92	
8	...	2 *Lord* John Pakenham Cecil	4 May 87	16 Mar. 92	
8	...	1 Laurence Rowe Fisher-Rowe	14 May 87	23 Mar. 92	
8	10/12	3 George Philip Du Plat Taylor		7 Oct. 85	
8	...	2 William Murray-Threipland	28 May 87	5 May 92	
8	...	2 Noel Armar Lowry Corry	15 Feb. 88	11 May 92	

Grenadier Guards.

Years' Ser. on Full Pay	Half Pay	LIEUTENANTS	2ND LIEUT.	LIEUT.
7	...	3 Godfrey Clement Walker Heneage, **Battalion Adjutant** 1 Jan. 95	29 Dec. 88	8 June 92
8	...	1 Frederick Edward Grey Ponsonby, *Equerry in Ordinary to the Queen*	11 Feb. 88	2 July 92
6	...	1 George Frederic Molyneux-Montgomerie	31 July 89	10 Aug. 92
6	...	2 Wilfrid William Ashley	7 Aug. 89	10 Aug. 92
9	...	2 *Hon.* Grosvenor Arthur Alexander Hood	16 Feb. 87	9 Aug. 93
6	...	2 Reginald Le Normand, *Lord Ardee*	21 Sept. 89	14 Dec. 93
6	...	1 Gerard Lysley Derriman	9 Nov. 89	20 Dec. 93
6	...	3 Hugh Valdave Warrender	18 Dec. 89	27 Jan. 94
5	...	3 Claud Vere Cavendish Hobart	16 July 90	13 June 94
5	...	3 George Clement Tryon	29 Oct. 90	20 June 94
5	...	1 Wilfred Robert Abel Smith	26 Nov. 90	23 July 94

SECOND LIEUTENANTS.

5	...	3 Arthur St. Leger Glyn	7 Jan. 91	
5	...	2 Maxwell Earle	4 Mar. 91	
4	...	Frederick Edward William Hervey-Bathurst (*Depot*)	25 July 91	
4	...	2 Ernest Coleridge Hegan Kennard	10 Oct. 91	
4	...	3 Percy Archer Clive	4 Nov. 91	
4	...	2 George Lionel Bonham	12 Mar. 92	
4	...	3 Ernest Frederick Orby Gascoigne	23 Mar. 92	
4	...	1 Wilfrid Astley Blundell-Hollinshead-Blundell	23 Mar. 92	
3	...	1 Gerald Frederic Trotter	18 June 92	
3	...	3 Charles Clive Bigham	19 Oct. 92	
3	...	2 George Montague De Vere De Vere Beauclerk	17 Dec. 92	
3	...	2 Francis Lyall Fryer	30 Nov. 92	
3	...	1 Charles Edward Corkran	15 Mar. 93	
2	...	1 Edward Douglas Loch	3 May 93	
4	...	3 *Hon.* Ferdinand Charles Stanley	10 Oct. 91	
2	...	1 Edward Henry Trotter	28 June 93	
2	...	2 George Sidney Clive	21 Oct. 93	
2	...	2 Ivo Arthur Broadwood	7 Mar. 94	
1	...	2 John Sherard Reeve	2 June 94	
1	...	1 *Hon.* Edward Hugh Lygon	2 June 94	
1	...	3 *Hon.* John Francis Gathorne-Hardy	10 Oct. 94	
1	...	3 *Hon.* Alexander Victor Frederick Russell	10 Oct. 94	
1	...	1 Ambrose Yarburgh Lethbridge	20 Feb. 95	

11	...	*Quarter Masters.*—3 William Holmes,[56] 28 July 84; *Hon. Captain*, 28 July 94.
6	...	2 John Henry Hall, 8 Jan. 90; *Hon. Lieut.*
5	...	1 George Powell, 13 Nov. 90; *Hon. Lieut.*

Brig. Surg. Lt. Col.—3 Charles Edward Harrison,[57] *MB.* 19 Aug. 85; *Surgeon*, 30 Sept. 74; *Surgeon Major*, 19 Aug. 89; *Brig. Surg. Lt. Colonel*, 4 Nov. 91.

Surgeon Majors.—1 William Campbell,[57] *MB.* 12 Jan. 81; *Surgeon*, 30 Sept. 74; *Surgeon Major*, 5 Nov. 87; *Surgeon Lt. Colonel*, 30 Sept. 94.

2 William Alexander Carte, *MB.* 6 May 91; *Surgeon*, 30 May 85; *Surg. Major*, 6 May 91.

Surgeon Captains.—1 Edward Nodin Sheldrake, 7 Oct. 85; *Surgeon Captain*, 30 May 85.

3 Hugh Rayner, *MB.*, 14 April 86; *Surgeon Captain*, 30 Jan. 86.

2 Simpson Powell, *MB.* 26 Mar. 92; *Surgeon Captain*, 30 May 85 (*attached*).

Surgeon Lieut.—William Johnson Smyth, 17 Oct. 92; *Surgeon Lieut.* 27 July 92 (*attached*).

Facings Blue.—*Agents*, Messrs. Cox and Co.

1st Battalion returned from Canada, Sept. 1864. *2nd Battalion returned from Bermuda,* 1891. *3rd Battalion returned from Egypt,* 10 *Sept.* 1885.

---

[1] The Duke of Cambridge commanded the 1st Division of the Eastern Army throughout the campaign of 1854, including the battles of the Alma, Balaklava, and Inkerman (horse shot), and siege of Sebastopol (mentioned in despatches, received the thanks of the House of Commons, Medal with four Clasps, and Turkish Medal).

[2] Colonel Oliphant served in the Soudan campaign in 1885 (Medal with Clasp, and Khedive's Star).

[8] Captains Bradford-Atkinson, Cooper, and Macdonald served with the 2nd Battalion Grenadier Guards in the Egyptian war of 1882, and were present at the battle of Tel-el-Kebir (Medal with Clasp, and Khedive's Star).

[10] Colonel Antrobus served in the Soudan campaign in 1885 (Medal with Clasp, and Khedive's Star).

[12] Colonel Ricardo served in the Soudan campaign in 1885 (Medal with Clasp, and Khedive's Star).

[16] Colonel Colvile served with the Soudan Expedition under Sir Gerald Graham in 1884 in the Intelligence Department, and was present in the engagement at El Teb (mentioned in despatches, Medal with Clasp, and Khedive's Star). Served in the Nile Expedition in 1884-85 with the Intelligence Department, and was present at the action of Abu Klea (mentioned in despatches, *CB.*, and two Clasps); also served with the Egyptian Frontier Field Force in 1885-86 as Assistant Adjutant and Quarter Master General Intelligence Department, and was present in the engagement at Giniss (mentioned in despatches, Brevet of Colonel).

[17] Major General Herbert served in the Egyptian war of 1882 as Brigade Major of the 1st Brigade, and was present in the battle of Tel-el-Kebir (mentioned in despatches, Brevet of Major, Medal with Clasp, 4th Class of the Medjidie, and Khedive's Star). Served in the Nile Expedition in 1885-86 with the Guards Camel Regiment, and was present at the actions at Abu Klea and El Gubat (two Clasps).

[19] Major Crabbe served with the Auxiliary Transport in the Egyptian war of 1882 (Medal, and Khedive's Star). Served in the Nile Expedition in 1884-85 as Acting Quarter Master to the Guards Camel Regiment, and was present at the actions at Abu Klea and El Gubat (mentioned in despatches, Brevet of Major, two Clasps).

[24] Major Craufurd served with the Nile Expedition in 1884-85 on special service (Medal with Clasp, and Khedive's Star).

[25] Major Lloyd served in the expedition to the Soudan in 1884-85 as Signalling Officer to the Brigade of Guards, and was present in the engagement at Hasheen (Medal with Clasp, and Khedive's Star).

[33] Major Crawley served with the 3rd Battalion 60th Rifles in the Zulu war of 1879, and was present at the action of Gingindhlovu and relief of Ekowe (Medal with Clasp). Served in the Soudan campaign in 1885 (Medal with Clasp, and Khedive's Star).

[*For remainder of Notes, see end of Royal Engineers, p.* 228b.

1st Batt., Wellington Barracks.
2nd Batt., Dublin.

Coldstream Guards. 231

A Company Badge. "OUDENARDE" "MALPLAQUET" "DETTINGEN" "LINCELLES" "EGYPT" (with the Sphinx). "TALAVERA" "BARROSA" "PENINSULA" "WATERLOO" "ALMA" "INKERMAN" "SEVASTOPOL." "EGYPT, 1882" "TEL-EL-KEBIR" "SUAKIN, 1885."

Years' Ser. Full Pay.	Half Pay.		
29	...	Colonel.—Sir Frederick Charles Arthur Stephenson,[1] GCB. Ensign & Lieut. 25 July 37; Lieut. & Capt. P 13 Jan. 43; Capt. & Lt.Colonel, 20 June 54; Colonel, 15 Feb. 61; Major General, 6 Mar. 68; Lt. General, 23 Feb. 78; General, 12 Jan. 86; Colonel York and Lancaster Regiment, 22 Dec. 88; Colonel Coldstream Guards, 16 July 92.	
		Lieutenant Colonels.—Evelyn Edward Thomas Visct. Falmouth,[10] CB. Commanding the Regiment, 5 Feb. 95; Ens. & Lt. P22 July 66; Lt. & Capt. P5 Mar. 70; Capt. & Lt.Colonel, 16 Feb. 78; Major, 8 Dec. 84; Colonel, 27 Feb. 86; Lt.Colonel, 10 Nov. 93.	
27	...	1 Francis Aylmer Graves-Sawle,[11] Ens. P20 June 68; Ens. & Lt. P25 Nov. 68; Lt. & Capt. P7 Oct. 71; Capt. & Lt.Colonel, 10 Dec. 81; Major, 18 Apr. 85; Colonel, 18 April 89; Lt.Colonel, 29 Sept. 94.	
26	...	2 Reginald Pole-Carew,[12] CB. Ens. & Lt. P12 May 69; Lt. & Capt. 14 Aug. 72; Capt. & Lt.Colonel, 4 July 83; Major, 10 Nov. 85; Colonel, 25 Oct. 88; Lt.Colonel, 5 Feb. 95.	
24	...	Vesey John Dawson,[17] Lt. 28 Oct. 71; Capt. 25 Oct. 84; Major, 10 July 89.	
27	...	1 p.s.c. John Foster Geo. Ross of Bladensburg,[18] CB. Lt. 15 July 68; Capt. 18 Mar. 85; Major, 10 Nov. 89.	
23	...	2 Alfred Edward Codrington,[19] Lieut. 1 Feb. 73; Captain, 18 Apr. 85; Major, 4 Dec. 89.	
22	...	1 Hon. Henry Charles Legge,[20] Equerry in Ordinary to the Queen; Lieut. 31 Aug. 73; Captain, 18 Apr. 85; Brevet Major, 15 June 85; Major, 29 Sept. 90.	
22	...	p.s.c. Douglas Frederick Rawdon Dawson,[22] Military Attaché at Vienna, with rank of Lt.Colonel, 1 Apr. 90; Lt. 21 Jan. 74; Capt. 19 Sept. 85; Major, 29 July 91.	
21	...	2 Horace Robert Stopford, Lieut. 13 June 74; Captain, 19 Oct. 85; Major, 10 Nov. 93.	
20	...	p.s.c. Hon. Arthur Henry Henniker-Major,[23] Commanding Guards Depot, 1 Jan. 95; Lieut. 20 Nov. 75; Captain, 10 Nov. 85; Major, 29 Sept. 94.	
19	...	p.s.c. Herbert Conyers Surtees,[27] Lieut. 11 Sept. 76; Captain, 7 May 87; Major, 5 Feb. 95.	

		CAPTAINS.	2ND LIEUT.	LIEUT.	CAPTAIN.	BREV. MAJ.
17	...	2 George Pleydell-Bouverie[28]	19 Oct. 78	1 July 81	25 Apr. 88	
17	...	1 Hon. Arthur Grenville Fortescue[25]	13 Nov. 78	1 July 81	18 July 88	
17	...	Peter Audley David Arthur Lovell[24]	22 Feb. 79	1 July 81	4 Dec. 89	
16	...	1 Augustus John Hy. Beaumont, Marq. of Winchester[29]	27 Sept. 79	1 July 81	16 July 90	
17	5/12	Charles Porcher Wilson Kindersley, Aide de Camp to the Governor General of Canada, 7 Sept. 93	30 Jan. 78	1 July 81	29 Sept. 90	
15	...	p.s.c. Henry Gwynn Deane Shute,[30] Brigade Major, Home District, 1 Jan. 94	30 Sept. 80	1 July 81	27 Jan. 91	
13	...	Frederick Ivor Maxse		9 Sept. 82	25 Oct. 89	
15	...	2 p.s.c. Granville Roland Francis Smith	11 Aug. 80	1 July 81	29 June 91	
15	...	2 Charles Arthur Andrew Frederick[32]	30 Mar. 81	1 July 81	29 July 91	
12	...	1 George Dunbar Milligan[18]		5 Dec. 83	29 July 91	
12	...	Hon. William Lambton		6 Feb. 84	18 May 92	
12	.	p.s.c. Henry Seymour Rawlinson[33] (Depot)		6 Feb. 84	4 Nov. 91	

		LIEUTENANTS.				
12	...	2 James Adam Gordon Drummond-Hay[18]		6 Feb. 84		
12	...	2 Frederick Stanley Maude,[18] Staff College		6 Feb. 84		
11	...	2 Cecil Stanley Owen Monck, Adjutant 29 Dec. 92		23 Aug. 84		
11	...	1 John Richard Hall		31 Dec. 84		
11	...	John Trelawny Sterling, Aide de Camp to the Governor of Hong Kong 17 Apr. 92		31 Jan. 85		
11	...	1 Henry Blundell Hawkes		12 Nov. 84		
10	...	2 Sydney Earle, Staff College		9 May 85		
10	...	2 John Maurice Wingfield		10 June 85		
10	...	1 Hon. Edward Michael Pakenham		7 Oct. 85		
10	...	1 Hon. Henry Robert Baillie-Hamilton		28 Oct. 85		
10	...	2 John M'Neile		14 Nov. 85		
10	...	2 Randal Charles Edward Skeffington-Smyth		25 Nov. 85		
9	...	James Herbert Gustavus Meredyth, Lord Athlumney, serving with the Egyptian Army		4 Dec. 86		
9	...	2 Hon. John Beresford Campbell	23 Mar. 87	9 July 90		
8	...	Hugh Clement Sutton, Regimental Adjutant 1 Jan. 94	14 Sept. 87	4 Sept. 90		
8	...	1 Raymond John Marker, Adjutant 7 March 92	15 Feb. 88	29 Sept. 90		
7	...	Geoffrey Percy Thynne Feilding	25 Apr. 88	27 Nov. 90		
7	...	1 William Henry Lambton	2 May 88	1 Jan. 91		
7	...	1 John Gaspard Le Marchant, Lord Romilly	5 May 88	2 May 91		
8	...	John Ponsonby	16 Nov. 87	29 June 91		
7	...	1 Charles John Brinsley, Lord Newtown-Butler	22 Aug. 88	15 Oct. 91		
8	...	1 Guy Fremantle	11 Feb. 88	17 Apr. 92		
6	...	2 Claude Julian Hawker	22 Mar. 89	10 Aug. 92		
6	...	2 Reginald Longueville	21 Sept. 89	23 Feb. 93		
6	...	2 Cecil Edward Pereira	29 Jan. 90	6 July 93		
5	...	1 Thomas Elphinstone Case	3 May 90	8 July 93		
5	...	1 Richard Arthur Starling Benson	2 July 90	1 Jan. 94		

		SECOND LIEUTENANTS.				
5	...	2 Julian M'Carty Steele	29 Oct. 90			
5	...	Nevile Rodwell Wilkinson (Depot)	29 Oct. 90			
5	...	2 Thomas Henry Eyre Lloyd	29 Oct. 90			
5	...	2 Ronald Anthony Markham	3 Dec. 90			
5	...	2 Lawrence Challoner Garratt	3 Dec. 90			
4	...	2 Herbert William Studd	25 July 91			
4	...	1 Hon. Claud Heathcote-Drummond-Willoughby	5 Dec. 91			
4	...	1 Harry Wm. Ludovic Heathcoat Heathcoat-Amory	5 Dec. 91			
3	...	1 Eric Thomas Henry Hanbury-Tracy	25 May 92			
3	...	1 Charles Edward Wyld	8 Feb. 93			
3	...	1 Hon. Leslie d'Henin Hamilton	22 Mar. 93			
2	...	2 Hon. Guy Victor Baring	8 July 93			
2	...	2 Harry Anthony Chandos-Pole-Gell	23 Dec. 93			
1	...	1 Torquhil George Matheson	2 June 94			
1	...	2 Hon. George Arthur Charles Crichton	28 Nov. 94			
1	...	Jocelyn Henry Clive Graham	6 Mar. 95			

Quarter Masters.—1 Henry Folson,[35] 1 Apr. 85; *Hon. Lieut.*
  2 Robert Grindel, 25 July 94; *Hon. Lieut.*
Surgeon Majors.—2 James Magill,[36] *MD*, 9 Dec. 85; *Surgeon*, 3 May 76; *Surgeon Major*, 9 Dec. 85.
  1 Alexander Charles Archibald Alexander,[36] 29 July 82; *Surgeon*, 29 July 82; *Surgeon Major*, 8 Nov. 88.
Surgeon Captains.—2 Robert William Henry Jackson, *MB*. 23 Nov. 91; *Surgeon Captain*, 29 July 90 (*attached*).
  1 Michael Thomas Yarr, 3 Jan. 92; *Surgeon Captain*, 30 Jan. 86 (*attached*).
  Warren Roland Crooke-Lawless, *MD*. (*attached*).
Solicitor, Robert J. P. Broughton, 7 Jan. 62. *Facings* Blue.—*Agents*, Messrs. Cox and Co.
  1st Battalion returned from Egypt, 11 Sept. 1885. *2nd Battalion returned from Egypt*, 1882.

---

[1] Sir Frederick Stephenson served in the Eastern campaign of 1854–55, including the battles of Alma, Balaklava, and Inkerman, siege of Sebastopol and sortie on the 26th October. Was Military Secretary to the Commander in Chief in the Crimea from early in July until Nov. 1855 (Medal with four Clasps, Knight of the Legion of Honor, 4th Class of the Medjidie, and Turkish Medal). Served as Assist. Adjutant General to the expeditionary force in China from March 1857 to 14th Feb. 1860, and present at the capture of Canton in Dec. 1857; and served as Deputy Adjutant General to the force under Sir Hope Grant from 14th Feb. 1860 to 16th March 1861; present at the storming and capture of the Taku Forts, the actions of the 18th and 21st Sept., and subsequent advance on Pekin (*CB.*, Brevet of Colonel, Medal with three Clasps). Received the thanks of both Houses of Parliament for his services in connection with the Nile Expedition in 1884–85. Commanded the Egyptian Frontier Field Force in 1885–86, which defeated the enemy at Giniss (*GCB.*, and Grand Cross of the Medjidie).

[2] Colonel Sterling served with the 2nd Battalion Coldstream Guards in the Egyptian war of 1882, and was present in the engagement at Tel-el-Mahuta and at the battle of Tel-el-Kebir—slightly wounded (Medal with Clasp, 4th Class of the Osmanieh, and Khedive's Star). Served in the expedition to the Soudan in 1885 with the 1st Battalion of the Coldstream Guards, and was present in the engagement at Hasheen, at that near Tofrek on the 24th March, and at the destruction of Temai (mentioned in despatches, Clasp).

[10] Lord Falmouth served with the 2nd Battalion Coldstream Guards in the Egyptian war of 1882, and was present in the engagement at Tel-el-Mahuta and at the battle of Tel-el-Kebir (Medal with Clasp, 4th Class of the Osmanieh, and Khedive's Star). Served in the Nile Expedition in 1884–85 in command of the Guards Camel Regiment, and was present in the actions at Abu Klea and El Gubat and in the reconnaissance to Metammeh, where he commanded the whole force after the departure of Sir Charles Wilson (twice mentioned in despatches, *CB.*, and two Clasps).

[11] Colonel Graves-Sawle served in the Nile Expedition in 1884–85 with the Guards Camel Regiment, and was present at the actions at Abu Klea and Abu Kru (Medal with two Clasps, and Khedive's Star).

[12] Colonel Pole-Carew served in the Afghan war in 1879–80 as Aide de Camp to Sir Frederick Roberts, and was present at the advance on Cabul, in the engagement at Charasiab on 6th October 1879, and in the operations around Cabul in December 1879, including the investment of Sherpore; accompanied Sir Frederick in the march to Candahar, and was present at the battle of Candahar (several times mentioned in despatches, Medal with three Clasps, and Bronze Decoration). Served as Orderly Officer to H.R.H. the Duke of Connaught in the Egyptian war of 1882, and was present in the engagement at Tel-el-Mahuta and at the battle of Tel-el-Kebir (Medal with Clasp, and Khedive's Star). Served with the Burmese Expedition in 1886–87 (mentioned in despatches, *CB.*, and Medal with Clasp).

[17] Major Vesey Dawson served in the Nile Expedition in 1884–85 with the Guards Camel Regiment, and was present at the actions at Abu Klea and El Gubat and at the reconnaissance of Metammeh (Medal with two Clasps and Khedive's Star).

[18] Major Ross, Captain Milligan, and Lieuts. Drummond-Hay and Maude served in the expedition to the Soudan in 1885 with the 1st Battalion Coldstream Guards, and were present in the engagement at Hasheen, at that near Tofrek on the 24th March, and at the destruction of Temai (Medal with Clasp, and Khedive's Star).

[19] Major Codrington served in the Egyptian war of 1882 as Aide de Camp to Lieut. General Willis, Commanding 1st Division, and was present in the engagement at Tel-el-Mahuta and at the battle of Tel-el-Kebir (mentioned in despatches, Medal with Clasp, 5th Class of the Medjidie, and Khedive's Star).

[20] Major Legge served in the expedition to the Soudan in 1885 with the 1st Battalion of the Coldstream Guards, and was present in the engagement at Hasheen, at that near Tofrek on the 24th March, and at the destruction of Temai (mentioned in despatches, Brevet of Major, Medal with Clasp, and Khedive's Star).

[22] Lt. Colonel Douglas Dawson served in the Egyptian war of 1882, first with the 2nd Battalion Coldstream Guards, and afterwards with the Mounted Infantry, and was present in the engagements at Tel-el-Mahuta and Kassasin (9th September), and at the battle of Tel-el-Kebir and capture of Cairo (Medal with Clasp, 5th Class of the Medjidie, and Khedive's Star). Served in the Nile Expedition in 1884–85 with the Guards Camel Regiment, was Staff Officer to Colonel Boscawen while in command of the column, and was present at the actions at Abu Klea and El Gubat, in the reconnaissance to Metammeh, and at the attack on the wounded convoy (two Clasps).

[23] Major Hon. A. H. Henniker-Major served as Adjutant with the 2nd Battalion Coldstream Guards in the Egyptian war of 1882 (Medal, and Khedive's Star).

[24] Captain Lovell served with the 2nd Battalion Coldstream Guards in the Egyptian war of 1882, and was present in the engagement at Tel-el-Mahuta and at the battle of Tel-el-Kebir (Medal with Clasp, and Khedive's Star).

[25] Captain. Hon. A. Fortescue served with the 2nd Battalion of the Coldstream Guards in the Egyptian war of 1882, and was present in the engagement at Tel-el-Mahuta and at the battle of Tel-el-Kebir (Medal with Clasp, and Khedive's Star). Served with the Bechuanaland Expedition under Sir Charles Warren in 1884–85.

[27] Major Surtees served in the Nile Expedition in 1884–85 in command of the Turkish Mounted Infantry of the Egyptian Army and afterwards of a boat convoy (Medal with Clasp, 4th Class of the Medjidie, and Khedive's Star). Served with the Egyptian Frontier Field Force in 1885–86, and was present in the engagement at Giniss in command of the 3rd Camel Corps of the Egyptian Army (4th Class of the Osmanich).

[28] Captain Pleydell-Bouverie served with the 2nd Battalion of the Coldstream Guards in the Egyptian war of 1882, and was present in the engagement at Tel-el-Mahuta and at the battle of Tel-el-Kebir (Medal with Clasp, and Khedive's Star). Served in the Bechuanaland Expedition under Sir Charles Warren in 1884–85.

[29] Lord Winchester served with the expedition to the Soudan in 1885 as Aide de Camp to Sir John M'Neill, and was present in the engagements at Hasheen and the Tofrek zereba and at the destruction of Temai (Medal with two Clasps, and Khedive's Star).

[30] Captain Shute served with the 2nd Battalion Coldstream Guards in the Egyptian war of 1882, and was present in the engagement at Tel-el-Mahuta and at the battle of Tel-el-Kebir (Medal with Clasp, and Khedive's Star). Served in the expedition to the Soudan in 1885 with the 1st Battalion Coldstream Guards and was present in the engagement at Hasheen, at that near Tofrek on the 24th March, and at the destruction of Temai (Clasp).

[32] Captain Frederick served in the expedition to the Soudan in 1885 with the 1st Battalion of the Coldstream Guards, and was present in the engagement at Hasheen, at that near Tofrek on the 24th March, and at the destruction of Temai (Medal with Clasp, and Khedive's Star). Served with the Egyptian Frontier Field Force in 1885–86 as extra Aide de Camp to Sir Frederick Stephenson (4th Class of the Medjidie).

[34] Captain Rawlinson served with the Burmese Expedition in 1886–87 as Aide de Camp to Sir Frederick Roberts mentioned in despatches, Medal with Clasp).

[45] Lieut. Folson served in the Soudan campaign in 1885 (Medal with Clasp, and Khedive's Star).

[36] Surgeon Majors Magill and Alexander.—For War Services, see Army Medical Staff.

1st Batt., Windsor.
2nd Batt., Chelsea Barracks.

Scots Guards. 233

A Company Badge. "DETTINGEN" "LINCELLES" "EGYPT" (with the Sphinx). "TALAVERA" "BARROSA" "PENINSULA" "WATERLOO" "ALMA" "INKERMAN" "SEVASTOPOL" "EGYPT, 1882" "TEL-EL-KEBIR" "SUAKIN, 1885."

Years' Ser. Full Pay.	Half Pay.		
33	...	**Colonel.**—His Royal Highness Arthur W. P. A., *Duke of* Connaught,[1] *KG. KT. KP. GCSI. GCMG. GCIE. KCB. Colonel in Chief of the Rifle Brigade; Colonel* Scots Guards, 24 June 83.	
		Lieutenant Colonels.—William Julius Gascoigne,[2] *Commanding the Regiment*, 1 July 91; *Ensign & Lt.* P31 March 63; *Lt. & Capt.* P6 Feb. 66; *Capt. & Lt.Colonel*, 25 June 73; *Major*, 1 July 81; *Colonel*, 1 Dec. 84; *Lt.Colonel*, 31 Dec. 87.	
31	...	1 Barrington Bulkley Douglas Campbell,[10] *Ens. & Lt.* P10 May 64; *Lt. & Captain*, P18 Dec. 66; *Capt. & Lt.Colonel*, 17 May 76; *Major*, 1 Apr. 82; *Colonel*, 1 Apr. 86; *Lt.Colonel*, 24 June 91.	
29	...	2 Henry Fludyer,[13] *Ens. & Lt.* P29 May 66; *Lt. & Capt.* P21 Aug. 69; *Capt. & Lt.Colonel*, 19 Dec. 77; *Major*, 11 June 84; *Colonel*, 21 Dec. 87; *Lt.Colonel*, 23 May 92.	
29	...	**Majors.**—2 Mildmay Willson Willson,[15] *CB, Ens.& Lt.* P3 Aug. 66; *Lt.& Capt.* P3 Sept. 70 *Capt.& Lt.Colonel*, 14 Dec. 78; *Major*, 1 July 85; *Colonel*, 1 June 88.	
29	...	1 Inigo Richmond Jones,[17] *Ens. & Lt.* P18 Dec. 66; *Lt. & Capt.* P4 Feb. 71; *Capt. & Lt.Colonel*, 15 March 79; *Major*, 1 July 86; *Colonel*, 1 July 90.	
26	...	2 Arthur Broadwood,[20] *Ens. & Lt.* P5 May 69; *Lt. & Capt.* P28 Oct. 71; *Capt. & Lt.Colonel*, 20 Mar. 81; *Major*, 27 Mar. 89; *Colonel*, 2 June 92.	
27	...	1 Frederick Lorn Campbell,[21] *Ens. & Lt.* P22 Aug. 68; *Lt. & Capt.* 24 April 72; *Capt. & Lt.Colonel*, 1 Oct. 81; *Colonel*, 11 Sept. 86; *Major*, 10 June 91.	
26	...	2 Arthur Henry Paget,[22] *Ens. & Lt.* 12 June 69; *Lt. & Capt.* 29 June 72; *Capt. & Lt.Colonel*, 1 Apr. 82; *Major*, 24 June 91.	
24	...	p.s.c. Hon. North de Coigny Dalrymple,[23] *Lieut.* 28 Oct. 71; *Captain*, 15 Aug. 83; *Major*, 23 May 92.	
24	...	Archibald Spencer Drummond,[24] *Lieut.* 28 Oct. 71; *Captain*, 1 July 85; *Major*, 21 Feb. 94.	
22	...	p.s.c. Frederick William Romilly,[26] *DSO, Lieut.* 30 April 73; *Captain*, 1 Apr. 87; *Brev. Major*, 1 Jan. 88; *Major*, 12 Dec. 94.	

		CAPTAINS.	2ND LIEUT.	LIEUT.	CAPTAIN.	BREV. MAJ.
21	...	2 John Bourchier Stracey[27]		24 July 74	1 Apr. 87	
20	...	Hon. Charles Harbord, *Groom in Waiting in Ordinary to the Queen*		30 April 75	1 Apr. 87	
21	...	Chas. Crutchley,[28] *D.A.A. Gen., War Office*, 25 Mar. 89		21 Sept. 74	29 June 87	30 June 87
19	...	1 Claud Edward Stracey[29]		29 Nov. 76	20 Aug. 85	
19	...	1 John William Ainslie Drummond[31]		11 Feb. 77	23 May 88	24 May 88
18	...	2 Luke, *Lord Annaly*[27]		11 Sept. 77	8 Nov. 88	
16	...	Laurence George Drummond,[33] *Aide de Camp to Lord Methuen* 1 Apr. 92	27 Sept. 79	1 July 81	19 Dec. 88	
16	...	2 Basil Henry Scott-Murray[30]	13 Mar. 80	1 July 81	10 June 91	
15	...	2 Robert Blake Finnie[34]	4 Sept. 80	1 July 81	24 June 91	
15	...	Edward Milner,[30] *Aide de Camp to the Governor of South Australia* 18 Mar. 92	2 Feb. 81	1 July 81	4 May 92	
14	...	William Pulteney Pulteney,[2] *on special service, Uganda*	23 Apr. 81	1 July 81	4 May 92	
14	...	1 Everard Ernest Hanbury[27]		22 Oct.	4 May 92	
13	...	p.s.c. Henry Hampden Wigram[30]		10 May 82	23 May 92	
13	...	2 Gerald James Cuthbert,[30] *Adjutant* 15 Feb. 95		10 May 82	24 May 93	

		LIEUTENANTS.				
13	...	2 Baden Fletcher Smyth Baden-Powell[35]		29 July 82		
13	...	James Francis Erskine,[30] *Regimental Adjutant* 1 Apr. 92		9 Sept. 82		
12	...	1 James Buller Bradshaw		25 Aug. 83		
12	...	2 William Colquhoun Grant M'Grigor[36]		5 Dec. 83		
12	...	Frederic James Heyworth,[30] *Aide de Camp to Major General G. H. Moncrieff* 1 May 91		5 Dec. 83		
11	...	2 Sir Cuthbert Slade, *Bart.*		14 May 84		
11	...	1 William Arnold Webster Lawson		23 Aug. 84		
10	...	2 Fitzalan George John Manners		29 Aug. 85		
10	...	Berkeley John Talbot Levett, *Aide de Camp to the Governor of Bombay*		16 Dec. 85		
10	...	2 Henry Edward Dering, *Superintendent of Gymnasia, Home District*, 15 Apr. 93		30 Jan. 86		
9	...	1 Sir Ralph Barrett Macnaghten Blois, *Bart.*		28 July 86		
9	...	2 Sherard Haughton Godman	9 Mar. 87	15 May 89		
8	...	Edward Francis Clayton, *Aide de Camp to the Governor of New Zealand*, 9 Apr. 92	14 May 87	19 Mar. 90		
9	...	2 Hon. Henry Walter Trefusis (*Lieut. Gordon Highlanders* 8 Dec. 86)	28 May 87	1 Apr. 90		
8	...	2 Richard George Ireland Bolton	29 June 87	23 Oct. 90		
8	...	1 Greville John Massey Bagot-Chester	28 May 87	14 Feb. 91		
8	...	2 Charles Warden Sergison	14 Sept. 87	24 June 91		
8	...	2 James William Smith-Neill, *Adjutant* 17 Feb. 92	29 Feb. 88	18 Mar. 92		
8	...	Frederick Loch Adam, *Aide de Camp to the Governor General of India* 27 Jan. 94	24 Mar. 83	9 Apr. 92		
7	...	1 Ferdinand Henry de Kierzkowski-Steuart	9 May 88	9 Apr. 92		
7	...	2 Henry Cecil Lowther	29 Dec. 88	13 Apr. 92		
7	...	1 Archibald Stirling	23 Jan. 89	4 May 92		
7	...	Cecil Foster Seymour Vandeleur, *on special service, Uganda*	6 Feb. 89	23 May 92		
6	...	William Frank Lascelles	15 May 89	20 July 92		
6	...	2 Hon. Charles S. Heathcote-Drummond-Willoughby	22 Jan. 90	11 Aug. 94		
6	...	2 Arthur Clive Bell	29 Mar. 90	24 Oct. 94		

		SECOND LIEUTENANTS.				
5	...	2 William Sullivan Gosling	4 Mar. 91			
4	...	1 Hon. Walter Patrick Hore Ruthven (*Master of Ruthven*)	25 July 91			
4	...	1 James Alexander Gordon King	5 Dec. 91			
4	...	1 Reginald Nesbitt Wingfield Larking	5 Dec. 91			
4	...	1 John Somerled Thorp	12 Mar. 92			
4	...	1 Hon. Gavin George Hamilton	30 Mar. 92			
3	...	2 Arthur Melville Southey	23 Apr. 92			
3	...	2 John Courtown Edward Shelley	18 May 92			
3	...	1 Arthur Vernon Poynter	18 June 92			
3	...	1 Archibald Douglas Campbell	18 June 92			
3	...	1 John Campbell Heriot-Maitland	5 Oct. 92			
3	...	1 Montague Haffenden Hall	14 June 93			
2	...	2 Miles Barne	16 Aug. 93			
2	...	2 Addison Francis Baker Cresswell	15 Nov. 93			
1	...	Hon. Hugh Joseph Fraser	12 Dec. 94			
1	...	Henry Cecil Elwes	6 Mar. 95			

[35] Lieut. Baden-Powell served in the Nile Expedition in 1884-85 with the Guards Camel Regiment (Medal with Clasp, and Khedive's Star).

[36] Lieut. M'Grigor served in the expedition to the Soudan in 1885 with the 2nd Battalion of the Scots Guards, and was present in the engagement at Temai (Medal with Clasp, and Khedive's Star).

[38] Surgeon Majors Robinson and Fenn.—For War Services, see Army Medical Staff.

Years' Ser.	
Full Pay	Half Pay
4	...
3	...

Scots Guards.

Quarter Masters.—1 James Chase, 13 May 91; *Hon. Lieut.*
2 William Jamieson, 24 Aug. 92; *Hon. Lieut.*
Surgeon Majors.—2 George Somerville Robinson,[38] 31 Dec. 87; *Surgeon*, 6 March 80; *Surgeon Major*, 31 Dec. 87.
Ernest Harrold Fenn,[38] *CIE.* 26 Sept. 94; *Surgeon*, 30 Sept. 75; *Surgeon Major*, 13 May 88.
Surgeon Captains.—1 Walter Calverley Beevor, *MD.* 28 Nov. 85; *Surgeon Captain*, 2 Aug. 84.
2 Robert Ashton Bostock, 30 Nov. 87; *Surgeon Captain*, 28 July 86.
Herbert Murray Ramsay, 11 Apr. 88; *Surgeon Captain*, 30 Jan. 86.

Facings Blue.—*Agents*, Messrs. Cox and Co.
1st Battalion returned from Egypt, 1882. *2nd Battalion returned from Egypt*, 10 Sept. 1885.

[1] The Duke of Connaught served in the Egyptian war of 1882 in command of the 1st Brigade (the Guards), and was present at the battle of Tel-el-Kebir (mentioned in despatches, received the thanks of both Houses of Parliament, *CB.*, Medal with Clasp, 2nd Class of the Medjidie, and Khedive's Star).

[2] Colonel Gascoigne served with the 1st Battalion Scots Guards in the Egyptian war of 1882, and was present at the battle of Tel-el-Kebir (Medal with Clasp, and Khedive's Star). Served in the expedition to the Soudan in 1885 with the 2nd Battalion of the Scots Guards, and was present in the engagements at Hasheen and Temai (Clasp).

[10] Colonel B. B. D. Campbell served with the 1st Battalion Scots Guards in the Egyptian war of 1882, and was present at the battle of Tel-el-Kebir (Medal with Clasp, and Khedive's Star).

[13] Colonel Fludyer served with the 1st Battalion Scots Guards in the Egyptian war of 1882, and was present at the battle of Tel-el-Kebir (Medal with Clasp, and Khedive's Star). Served in the expedition to the Soudan in 1885 with the 2nd Battalion of the Scots Guards, and was present in the engagements at Hasheen and Temai (Clasp).

[15] Colonel M. W. Willson served in the Nile Expedition in 1884-85 with the Guards Camel Regiment, and was present at the actions at Abu Klea and Abu Kru (twice mentioned in despatches, *CB.*, Medal with two Clasps, and Khedive's Star).

[17] Colonel Jones served in the expedition to the Soudan in 1885 with the 2nd Battalion of the Scots Guards, and was present in the engagements at Hasheen and Temai (Medal with Clasp, and Khedive's Star).

[20] Colonel Broadwood served in the expedition to the Soudan in 1885 with the 2nd Battalion of the Scots Guards, and was present in the engagements at Hasheen and Temai (Medal with Clasp, and Khedive's Star).

[21] Colonel F. L. Campbell served in the Soudan campaign in 1885 (Medal, and Khedive's Star).

[22] Lt.Colonel Paget served in the second phase of the Ashanti war from the 17th December 1873, attached to Captain Butler's command (Medal with Clasp). Served in the expedition to the Soudan in 1885 with the 2nd Battalion of the Scots Guards, and was present in the engagements at Hasheen and Temai (Medal with Clasp, and Khedive's Star).

[23] Major the Hon. North Dalrymple served as Adjutant with the 1st Battalion Scots Guards in the Egyptian war of 1882, and was present at the battle of Tel-el-Kebir—horse shot (Medal with Clasp, 5th Class of the Medjidie, and Khedive's Star). Served in the Soudan campaign in 1885 as Brigade Major to the Brigade of Guards, and was present in the engagement at Hasheen and at that near Tofrek on the 24th March—severely wounded (Clasp).

[24] Major A. S. Drummond served with the Nile Expedition in 1884-85, and was present at the action of Abu Klea (Medal with two Clasps, and Khedive's Star).

[26] Major Romilly served in the Egyptian war of 1882 with the 1st Battalion Scots Guards, and was present at the battle of Tel-el-Kebir (Medal with Clasp, and Khedive's Star); served in the Soudan Expedition in 1884 as Aide de Camp to Sir Gerald Graham, and was present in the engagements at El Teb and Temai (mentioned in despatches, two Clasps). Served in the Nile Expedition in 1884-85 with the Guards Camel Regiment, and was present at the actions at Abu Klea and El Gubat (two Clasps); also served with the Egyptian Frontier Field Force in 1885-86 as Aide de Camp to Sir Frederick Stephenson, and was present in the engagement at Giniss (mentioned in despatches, *DSO.*).

[27] Captains Stracey, Lord Annaly, Pulteney and Hanbury served with the 1st Battalion Scots Guards in the Egyptian war of 1882, and were present at the battle of Tel-el-Kebir (Medal with Clasp, and Khedive's Star).

[28] Major Crutchley served with the 1st Battalion Scots Guards in the Egyptian war of 1882, and was present at the battle of Tel-el-Kebir (Brevet of Major, Medal with Clasp, 5th Class of the Medjidie, and Khedive's Star). Served in the Nile Expedition in 1884-85 as Acting Adjutant to the Guards Camel Regiment, and was present at the actions at Abu Klea and El Gubat—severely wounded (two Clasps).

[29] Captain Stracey served with the 2nd Battalion Manchester Regiment throughout the Egyptian war of 1882 (Medal, and Khedive's Star).

[30] Captains Scott-Murray, Milner, Wigram, and Cuthbert, Lieuts. Erskine and Heyworth served in the expedition to the Soudan in 1885 with the 2nd Battalion of the Scots Guards, and were present in the engagements at Hasheen and Temai (Medal with Clasp, and Khedive's Star).

[31] Major J. W. A. Drummond served in the expedition to the Soudan in 1885 with the 2nd Battalion of the Scots Guards, and was present in the engagements at Hasheen and Temai (mentioned in despatches, Brevet of Major, Medal with Clasp, and Khedive's Star).

[33] Captain L. G. Drummond served in the Bechuanaland Expedition under Sir Charles Warren in 1884-85 with Methuen's Horse.

[34] Captain Finnie served in the expedition to the Soudan in 1885 with the 2nd Battalion of the Scots Guards (Medal with Clasp, and Khedive's Star).

The Royal Scots (Lothian Regiment). 234

1st Batt., Chatham.
2nd Batt., Belgaum, Madras. *Formerly the 1st (The Royal Scots) Regiment.* [Regimental District No. 1.—Glencorse.

(The 3rd Battalion is formed of the Edinburgh Light Infantry Militia.)

The Royal Cypher within the Collar of St. Andrew, and the Crown over it. "BLENHEIM" "RAMILLIES" "OUDENARDE" "MALPLAQUET" "LOUISBURG" "ST. LUCIA" "EGMONT-OP-ZEE" "EGYPT" (with the Sphinx). "CORUNNA" "BUSACO" "SALAMANCA" "VITTORIA" "ST. SEBASTIAN" "NIVE" "PENINSULA" "NIAGARA" "WATERLOO" "NAGPORE" "MAHEIDPOOR" "AVA" "ALMA" "INKERMAN" "SEVASTOPOL" "TAKU FORTS" "PEKIN."

Years' Ser. Full Pay	Half Pay			ENSIGN OR 2ND LIEUT.	LIEUT.	CAPTAIN.	BREV. MAJ.	MAJOR.
		Colonel.—Henry Phipps Raymond, Ensign, 9 April 25; Lt. P17 March 27; Capt. P21 March 34; Bt.Major, 9 Nov. 46; Major, P17 Dec. 47; Lt.Colonel, P17 Jan. 51; Colonel, 28 Nov. 54; Major General, 6 Feb. 65; Lt.General, 26 May 73; General, 1 Oct. 77; Colonel 1st Foot, 11 July 77.							
35	...	Lieutenant Colonels.—2 p.s.c. Frederick de Lamare Morison,¹ Ensign, 15 Jan. 61; Lt. F8 Aug. 65; Capt. P21 June 71; Major, 1 July 81; Lt.Colonel, 21 June 91.							
31	...	1 Frederick Coningham,⁷ Ensign, 20 May 64; Lt. P13 July 67; Capt. 11 April 75; Major, 1 July 81; Lt.Colonel, 14 Aug. 91.							
		MAJORS.						
28	...	2 George Seaforth Rodon		17 April 67	P 7 Dec. 70	21 July 77	......	13 Feb. 84
27	...	1 Thomas French Ross		P 8 July 68	P27 Oct. 71	24 Nov. 77	......	21 June 85
29	...	2 William Drury Shaw		11 Dec. 66	28 Oct. 71	13 Nov. 78	......	3 Oct. 88
25	...	1 Rowland Fearnley Kyrle Money		P22 Feb. 71	28 Oct. 71	11 Feb. 80	......	27 Mar. 89
24	...	2 Alan William Low Rickards		......	30 Dec. 71	18 June 81	......	14 Aug. 91
23	...	Victor Alexander Farquharson, *Adj.* 7 Vol. Bn. Royal Scots 15 Apr. 90		......	29 May 72	18 June 81	......	15 Nov. 91
22	...	1 Egerton Payler Morgan-Payler (*Depot*)		......	12 Nov. 73	14 Aug. 81	......	18 Jan. 93
22	...	2 Charles Henry Gostling,¹³ *Adjutant* 6 Vol. Bn. Royal Scots 23 Feb. 93		......	13 June 74	29 Aug. 83	......	29 Nov. 93
		CAPTAINS.						
20	...	2 Charles William Southcott Hallett		......	20 Nov. 75	13 Jan. 85		
20	...	1 Charles Harcourt Stisted		......	11 Feb. 76	13 Jan. 85		
20	...	p.s.c. Edward Altham Altham,¹³ *Dep. Assist. Adj. Gen. Chester*, 16 Jan. 93		......	12 Feb. 76	15 Apr. 85		
20	...	2 Hamilton William Broadley (*Depot*)		......	12 Feb. 76	21 June 85		
18	...	Archibald M'Lachlan, *Adj.* Queen's Rifle Volunteer Brigade 10 July 93		8 Dec. 77	25 Sept. 78	21 June 85		
18	...	William Douglas¹⁴		30 Jan. 78	25 Nov. 78	21 June 85		
18	...	Hamilton John Goold-Adams,¹³ *CMG.* Comdg. Bechuanaland Border Police		30 Jan. 78	30 Nov. 78	14 Aug. 85		
18	...	2 Arthur Leonard Williams¹⁵		30 Jan. 78	7 Dec. 78	20 Aug. 85		
17	...	1 William Erskine Graham Login¹⁶		1 May 78	15 Nov. 79	10 Jan. 87		
17	...	2 Vincent Mackesy Birkbeck		5 Oct. 78	9 Apr. 80	31 Dec. 87		
17	...	Oliver Ramsay Brush,¹³ *Adjutant* 5 Vol. Bn. Royal Scots 26 Sept. 91		22 Jan. 79	5 Aug. 80	1 Mar. 88		
16	...	Arthur Vincent Dowdall FitzGerald		9 July 79	1 July 81	10 July 88		
15	...	2 Laurence Fleetwood Barton¹³		23 Oct. 80	1 July 81	3 Oct. 88		
13	...	2 Robert Lipton Macgregor¹¹		......	10 May 82	4 June 90		
13	...	1 William Cautley Olpherts		......	9 Sept. 82	14 Aug. 91		
13	...	2 David Gillespie Wemyss, *Adjutant* 28 Dec. 92		......	10 Mar. 83	15 Nov. 91		
12	...	Harold Hugh Francis, *Adjutant* 3 Battalion 20 Feb. 93		......	25 July 83	28 Dec. 92		
12	...	Edward Honoré Molyneux-Seel, *Adj.* Queen's Rifle Vol. Brig. 4 June 94		......	19 Dec. 83	16 Jan. 93		
12	...	1 Charles Cecil Daniel¹²		......	19 Dec. 83	26 Apr 93		
12	...	2 Harry Palairet Versturme¹⁵		......	6 Feb. 84	10 May 93		
12	...	1 Michael Henry Egan		......	6 Feb. 84	23 Sept. 93		
11	...	1 Wm. Alex. Marie Pollock-Gore¹³		......	28 Feb. 85	29 Nov. 94		
		LIEUTENANTS.						
10	...	1 Gordon Sandilands,¹³ *at Staff College*		......	9 May 85			
10	...	1 Ilay Ferrier Forrest Gardiner		......	23 Aug. 85			
10	...	1 Charles Stewart Cowie (*Depot*)		......	2 Sept. 85			
11	...	2 George Mackenzie Gunn Munro		......	28 Feb. 85			
9	...	1 Francis Lee Baird Smith		5 Feb. 87	3 June 89			
9	...	1 Robert Popham Spurway		16 Mar. 87	11 Sept. 89			
8	...	1 George Harry Davidson,¹⁷ *Adjutant* 21 Aug. 94		4 May 87	12 Oct.			
8	...	2 David Aubrey Callender¹⁸		14 Sept. 87	23 Jan. 90			
8	...	1 Harry M'Micking		14 Sept. 87	4 June 90			
8	...	1 Richard Charles Dundas¹⁹		11 Feb. 88	4 July 90			
7	...	2 Edwd. Hugh Broome Baker-Stallard-Penoyre		23 Mar. 89	15 Nov. 91			
6	...	1 Francis John Duncan		21 Sept. 89	7 Mar. 92			
6	...	2 Harry Bernard Dyson		9 Nov. 89	16 Jan. 93			
6	...	1 Thomas Stephen Charles William Broadley		4 Jan. 90	26 Apr. 93			
5	...	2 Granville George Loch		3 May 90	10 May 93			
4	...	1 John Ralli		30 May 91	22 June 92			
5	...	2 Hugh Stanley Sutherland		29 Oct. 90	23 Sept. 93			
5	...	Norman Sinclair Coghill		29 Nov. 90	29 Nov. 93			
5	...	2 Henry Edmund Palmer Nash		17 Jan. 91	25 Apr. 94			
4	...	1 Henry Percy Rudd		12 Aug. 91	30 July 94			
		SECOND LIEUTENANTS.						
4	...	2 James Henry Morison Davie		7 Nov. 91				
4	...	2 Ernest Frederick Annand		5 Dec. 91				
3	...	2 Arthur Fowler Hislop		9 Apr. 92				
3	...	2 Godfrey Harold Fenton Wingate		21 Jan. 93				
2	...	2 Gilbert Gunn		12 Apr. 93				
2	...	2 Charles Cecil Gordon		26 Apr. 93				
2	...	1 Alan James Gordon Moir		20 May 93				
2	...	1 Robert Arron Gordon		9 Sept. 93				
2	...	2 Gerald Scott Tweedie		21 Oct. 93				
2	...	1 Thomas *Lord* Denman		7 Mar. 94				
1	...	2 Garnet Wolseley Grieve Neill		2 June 94				
1	...	2 Alexander George Stuart		12 Dec. 94				
1	...	2 Richard William Duncan		12 Dec. 94				

The Royal Scots (Lothian Regiment).

Years Ser.	
Full Pay	Half Pay
12	...
4	...

Paymasters.—2 George M. G. Munro, *Lieut.* 2 *Battalion* (*acting*).
Quarter Masters.—2 William Cole Fuller, 21 Apr. 83; *Hon. Captain* 21 Apr. 93.
1 Charles Griffiths, 2 Dec. 91; *Hon. Lieut.*

Facings Blue. *Agents*, Messrs. Cox and Co.
1st Battalion returned from South Africa, 30 *Aug.* 1891. *2nd Battalion embarked for Malta,* 11 *Dec.* 1890.

[1] Lt.Colonel Morison served in the Afghan war in 1878-79 with the Koorum Valley Field Force, and was present at the capture of the Peiwar Kotal (Medal with Clasp).
[7] Lt.Colonel Coningham served in the Bechuanaland Expedition under Sir Charles Warren in 1884-85 with the 1st Battalion of the Royal Scots. Served in the operations in Zululand in 1888.
[11] Captain Macgregor served with the Bechuanaland Expedition under Sir Charles Warren in 1884-85 with the 1st Battalion of the Royal Scots. Served in the operations in Zululand in 1888.
[12] Captain Daniel served with the Bechuanaland Expedition under Sir Charles Warren in 1834-85 with the 1st Battalion of the Royal Scots. Served in the operations in Zululand in 1888.
[13] Major Gostling, Captains Altham, Goold-Adams, Brush, Barton, Versturme, and Pollock-Gore, and Lieut. Sandilands served with the Bechuanaland Expedition under Sir Charles Warren in 1884-85 with the 1st Battalion of the Royal Scots.
[14] Captain Douglas served in the Bechuanaland Expedition under Sir Charles Warren in 1884-85 as Adjutant of the 1st Battalion of the Royal Scots.
[15] Captain Williams served with the Bechuanaland Expedition under Sir Charles Warren in 1884 on special service.
[16] Captain Login served in the Afghan war in 1880 (Medal). Served in the Bechuanaland Expedition under Sir Charles Warren in 1884-85 with the 1st Battalion of the Royal Scots. Served in the operations in Zululand in 1888.
[17] Lieut. Davidson served in the operations in Zululand in 1888.
[18] Lieut. Callender served in the operations in Zululand in 1888.
[19] Lieut. Dundas served in the operations in Zululand in 1888.

Record of the Services of the 1st Battalion The Royal Scots (*Lothian Regiment*), *formerly the 1st Regiment.*

In 1633 a part of the Scottish Guards came to Scotland when Charles I. was crowned King of Scotland and was placed on the British Establishment as the Royal Regiment of Foot, returning to France immediately, where it was known as "Hepburn's Regiment." They returned to England in 1684, and on the 1st May of that year King Charles II. conferred on them the title of "The Royal Regiment of Foot." Netherlands and the Low Countries to 1697. Ireland, to 1698. Holland, to 1703. Germany and the Low Countries, to 1708 (battles of Blenheim, Ramillies, and Oudenarde). England. 1708. Low Countries, to 1713 (battle of Malplaquet). England to 1714. Ireland, to 1743. Flanders, to 1745. France and England, to 1746. Holland, to 1760. West Coast of France, 1760. Ireland, to 1762. Gibraltar, to 1775. England, to 1780. West Indies, to 1783. England, 1783. Ireland, to 1790. West Indies, to 1797 (capture of St. Lucia). Scotland, 1797. Ireland, to 1800. Scotland, 1800. West Indies. to 1812. [Two additional Battalions raised in 1804.] Entitled "The First Regiment of Foot, or Royal Scots," 1812. Canada, to 1815 (capture of Niagara). Scotland, 1815. Ireland, to 1825. Entitled "First Royal Scots Regiment of Foot," 1821. West Indies, to 1840. Gibraltar, to 1846. West Indies, to 1848. Canada. to 1851. Wales, to 1853. Turkey and the Crimea, to 1856 (battles of Alma and Inkerman, and siege of Sebastopol). England and Ireland, to 1857. Ceylon and India, to 1870. England, to 1874. Entitled "1st or Royal Scots Regiment," 1871. Scotland, to 1876. Ireland, to 1878. Malta (Half Battalion to West Indies), to 1882. West Indies, to 1884. South Africa, to 1891. England, 1891.

Record of the Services of the 2nd Battalion.

Raised in England in 1684. To Scotland, 1688. To the Netherlands, &c., 1690. To Ireland. 1698. To Holland, 1701. To England and Ireland, 1714. To the West Indies, 1741. To Scotland, 1742. To Ireland, 1749. [Called the 1st or Royal Regiment of Foot, 1751.] To Halifax, 1757. To North America, 1760 (capture of Louisburg). To the West Indies, 1761. To England, 1764. To Minorca, 1771. To England, 1775. To Gibraltar, 1784. To the Mediterranean, 1793. To Portugal, 1797. To England and Holland (battle of Egmont-op-Zee), and returned to England, 1799. To Gibraltar, 1800. To Egypt and Malta, 1801 (received the badge of "Egypt"—with the Sphinx). To Gibraltar, 1802. To West Indies, 1803. To Scotland, 1806. To India, 1807 (capture of Nagpore). (Title altered to 1st Regiment of Foot, or Royal Scots 1812; changed to 1st or Royal Regiment of Foot in 1821). To Burmah, 1825 (war of 1825-26). To India, 1826. To Scotland, 1831. To Ireland, 1833. To Canada, 1836. To West Indies, 1843. (Right Wing wrecked in 1843, taken back to Quebec, and rejoined the Left Wing at Barbadoes in 1844.) To Scotland and England, 1846. To Ireland, 1847. To Cephalonia, 1853. To the Crimea, 1855. To Malta, 1856. To Gibraltar, 1857. To China, 1858 (capture of Taku Forts, and surrender of Pekin). To England, 1861. To the Channel Islands, 1864. To Ireland, 1865. To India, 1866. (Title changed to "The Royal Scots," 1871.) To Ireland, 1880. To Scotland, 1884. To England, 1887. To Malta, 1890.

The Queen's (Royal West Surrey Regiment). 236

1st Batt., **Umballa. Bengal.**
2nd Batt., **Dover.**

Formerly the 2nd (The Queen's Royal).

Regimental District: No. 2.—Guildford.

(The 3rd Battalion is formed of the 2nd Surrey Militia.)

The Paschal Lamb, with the Mottoes "*Pristinæ virtutis memor*," and "*Vel exuviæ triumphant.*" The Royal Cypher within the Garter. "EGYPT" (with the Sphinx), "VIMIERA" "CORUNNA" "SALAMANCA" "VITTORIA" "PYRENEES" "NIVELLE" "TOULOUSE" "PENINSULA" "AFGHANISTAN" "GHUZNEE" "KHELAT" "SOUTH AFRICA, 1851-2-3" "TAKU FORTS" "PEKIN" "BURMA, 1885-87."

Years' Ser. Full Pay	Half Pay		
32	...	**Colonel.**—Sir Edward Selby Smyth,[1] KCMG. Ensign, P26 Jan. 41; Lieut. 29 May 43; Captain, P4 Aug. 48; Bt. Major, 28 May 53; Bt.Lt.Colonel, 23 Mar. 55; Colonel, 23 Mar. 58; Major : Apr. 60; Major General, 6 Mar. 68; Lt. General, 1 Oct. 77; General, 9 Mar. 82; Colonel 72 Highlanders, 11 Mar. 81; Colonel West Surrey Regiment, 29 Aug. 93.		
28	...	**Lieutenant Colonels.**—1 Edward Warren Broderick, Ensign, P28 Aug. 63; Lieut. P1 May 66; Capt. 21 July 75; Major, 10 June 82; Lt.Colonel, 29 Sept. 92.		
28	...	2 Arthur Herbert Nourse, Ensign, P7 Dec. 67; Lieut. P12 July 71; Captain, 26 Feb. 81; Major, 10 Sept. 85; Lt.Colonel, 29 Sept. 94.		

		MAJORS.	ENSIGN OR 2ND LIEUT.	LIEUT.	CAPTAIN.	BREV. MAJ.	MAJOR.
27	...	1 John Stratford Collins[6]	P 2 Jan. 69	28 Oct. 71	16 Mar. 81	......	29 Sept. 86
26	...	1 Hamilton James Elverson[7]	P 1 Sept. 69	28 Oct. 71	1 May 81	......	25 Mar. 92
26	...	2 John Richard Harloem Richards	P17 Nov. 69	28 Oct. 71	1 July 81	......	11 May 92
25	...	1 Robert Thomas Hanford-Flood	P 7 Dec. 70	28 Oct. 71	15 Apr. 82	......	29 Sept. 92
22	...	1 Edward Owen Fisher Hamilton[10]		9 Aug. 73	19 Dec. 83	......	3 July 93
22	...	1 Arthur Elias		28 Feb. 74	19 Sept. 84	......	30 Dec. 93
21	...	2 Henry Bourchier Fowler[11] (*Depot*)		13 June 74	25 Mar. 85	......	17 Apr. 94
20	...	2 William Samuel Burrell		10 Sept. 75	10 Sept. 85	......	29 Sept. 94
		CAPTAINS.					
20	...	2 Stewart Holcombe Rusbridger		20 Nov. 75	15 Feb. 86		
17	...	1 Henry Denne Robson[14]		11 Sept. 78	30 May 87		
18	...	1 Francis John Pink,[16] DSO	16 Feb. 78	8 Mar. 81	31 Mar. 88		
17	...	William Leonard Addington, *Adj.* 2 Vol. Bn. West Surrey Regt. 8 Dec. 90	29 June 78	30 Mar. 81	27 June 88		
16	...	2 Alfred Ernest Price	13 Aug. 79	1 May 81	24 July 89		
16	...	*p.s.c.* Charles Carmichael Monro	13 Aug. 79	15 May 81	24 July 89		
16	...	Wyndham Hackett Pain,[17] *Adjutant* 1 Vol. Bn. W. Surrey Regt. 16 Feb. 91	11 Oct. 79	1 July 81	29 Sept. 90		
15	...	2 *p.s.c.* Hubert Ion Wetherall Hamilton[18]	11 Aug. 80	1 July 81	8 Dec. 90		
14	...	Robert Dawson, *Adj.* 3 *Bn.* 24 Oct. 92		22 Oct. 81	24 Dec. 90		
13	...	Harold Daniel Edmund Parsons,[19] *Ordnance Store Department*		10 May 82	12 Apr. 91		
13	...	Alexander William Taylor,[20] *serving with the Egyptian Army*		10 May 82	12 Apr. 91		
13	...	Wm. Maxwell Tracy,[21] *O. S. Dept.*		9 Sept. 82	12 Apr. 91		
13	...	1 James Gurwood King-King, *Adjutant* 1 Dec. 94		10 Mar. 83	12 Apr. 91		
13	...	*p.s.c.* Gerald Francis Ellison, *Staff Capt. Intell. Dept. War Office,* 1 Sept. 94		10 May 82	15 July 91		
12	...	2 O'Brien Zouch Darrah		6 Feb. 84	11 May 92		
12	...	2 Morton Calverley Coles		6 Feb. 84	29 Sept. 92		
11	...	1 Edward Malcolmson (*Depot*)		14 May 84	23 Nov. 92		
13	...	1 Gervase Frederick Whitehead		29 July 82	30 Dec. 91		
11	...	2 Herbert Maitland Cowper		23 Aug. 84	29 Sept. 94		
11	...	1 William James Theodore Glasgow[23]		7 Feb. 85	1 Dec. 94		
		LIEUTENANTS.					
10	...	1 Dawson Warren[23]		29 Aug. 85			
10	...	2 *p.s.c.* Samuel Nattali Bevington		30 Jan. 86			
9	...	2 George Greenough Whiffin[23]		10 Nov. 86			
9	...	2 Henry Charles Pilleau	5 Feb. 87	24 July 89			
9	...	2 Arnold Frederick Sillem, *Adjutant* 27 June 94	4 May 87	16 Oct. 89			
8	...	1 Beauchamp Tyndall Pell	14 Sept. 87	7 May 90			
8	...	1 Digby Mackworth	14 Sept. 87	1 June 90			
8	...	1 Henry St. Clair Wilkins	11 Feb. 88	25 Nov. 90			
7	...	1 Wilkinson Dent Bird	22 Aug. 88	1 Dec. 90			
7	...	1 Leonard Markham Crofts	6 Mar. 89	8 Dec. 90			
7	...	1 Henry Russell Hardy	7 Aug. 89	12 Feb. 91			
6	...	George Arthur Campbell Taylor	21 Sept. 89	11 Mar. 91			
6	...	1 Hugh Edward Cotterill	21 Sept. 89	12 Apr. 91			
6	...	1 Frederic Benjamin Bissett Pickard	21 Dec. 89	26 Nov. 91			
5	...	2 Arthur Douglas Raitt (*Depot*)	28 June 90	15 Dec. 91			
5	...	1 Harry Roderick Bottomley (*Depot*)	16 July 90	6 Apr. 92			
5	...	1 Hugh Fawcett Wardon	29 Oct. 90	11 May 92			
5	...	2 Franklyn Forbes Boyd	17 Jan. 91	9 Nov. 92			
5	...	1 George Henry Neale	17 Jan. 91	23 Nov. 92			
5	...	1 Cecil Parsons	4 Feb. 91	29 Sept. 94			
5	...	1 Arthur Mudge	4 Mar. 91	16 Jan. 95			
		SECOND LIEUTENANTS.					
4	...	1 Herbert Atfield Engledue	8 Apr. 91				
4	...	1 George Edmund Reginald Kearick	18 Nov. 91				
4	...	1 William Wilfrid Bickford	5 Dec. 91				
4	...	1 Arthur Wyndham Tufnell	5 Dec. 91				
4	...	2 Henry Charles Whinfield	9 Jan. 92				
3	...	Cuthbert Vickers	12 Mar. 92				
3	...	1 Charles Edward Wilson	13 July 92				
3	...	Stewart Blakely Agnew Patterson	13 Aug. 92				
3	...	Arthur Louis Bickford	13 Aug. 92				
3	...	1 Albany Robert Cecil Savile	16 Nov. 92				
3	...	2 Hugh William Smith	17 Dec. 92				
3	...	1 Robert Joseph Atkinson Terry	13 July 92				
3	...	1 Archibald Montgomery Tringham	15 Mar. 93				
1	...	2 Roland Henry Mangles	12 Dec. 94				
1	...	1 James Atkinson Longridge	2 Feb. 95				

[7] Major Elverson served throughout the Afghan war of 1878-80 in the Transport Department. Was present at the occupation of Khelat-i-Ghilzie under Brigadier General Hughes, and in the affair at Shahjui and the operations in the Logar Valley, and in the engagements at Ahmed Kheyl and Urzoo near Ghuzni; accompanied Sir Frederick Roberts in the march to Candahar (mentioned in despatches, Medal with Clasp, and Bronze Decoration).

Yrs' Ser	
Full Pay	Half Pay
3	...
2	...

Paymasters.—2
1
Quarter Masters.—1 John James Grubb, 22 Feb. 93; *Hon. Lieut.*
2 John Griffiths, 10 Jan. 94; *Hon. Lieut.*

Facings Blue.—*Agents*, Messrs. Cox and Co.
1st Battalion embarked for Malta, 24 Dec. 1891.   2nd Battalion returned from India 23 Feb. 1894.

[1] Sir Edward Selby Smyth served as Brigade Major to the Forces in the Southern Concan and Sawant Warree country during the campaign of 1844 and 45, and was present at the attack and capture of several strong stockades, as well as in the operations before the mountain forts of Monohur, and at their final assault; also at the forcing of the Kirwattee Pass, and subsequent occupation of the country below the Ghats. Served also in the Kaffir war of 1851-52 (Medal), and mentioned in General orders for his conduct in command of a Column in action in the Fish River Bush (Brevet of Major); with the expedition north of the Orange River in 1852-53, and commanded a detached column at the action at Berea under Sir George Cathcart; afterwards as Deputy Assistant Quarter Master General of the 2nd Division; and subsequently as D. Adj.General and D. Q. M. General to the forces in South Africa from January 1854 to July 1860. Received the thanks of the Irish Government in 1867 for his services as Deputy Adjutant General during the suppression of the Fenian outbreak. While commanding the troops in Mauritius, he was twice sworn in and acted as Governor in 1870 and 1871.

[6] Major Collins served in the Burmese Expedition in 1886-89 with the 2nd Battalion Queen's Royal West Surrey Regiment under Brigadier Generals Lockhart and Collett, part of the time in command of a Company of Mounted Infantry (Medal with two Clasps).

[10] Major E. O. F. Hamilton served in the Afghan war in 1879-80, and took part in the defence of Candahar as Aide de Camp to Lieut.General Primrose, and was present in the sortie of Deh Khojah (mentioned in despatches, Medal with Clasp). Served in the Burmese Expedition in 1885-87 with the 2nd Battalion Queen's Royal West Surrey Regiment, and from April to August 1887 as Brigade Major to the 3rd Brigade (Medal with Clasp); served with the Hazara Expedition in 1891 as Superintendent of Signalling (mentioned in despatches, Clasp).

[11] Major Fowler served with the Burmese Expedition in 1888-89 with the 2nd Battalion Queen's Royal West Surrey Regiment under Brigadier General Lockhart (Medal with Clasp).

[14] Captain Robson served in the Burmese Expedition with the 2nd Battalion Queen's Royal West Surrey Regiment under Brigadier General Lockhart; was Station Staff Officer at Pyinmana from November 1886 to August 1887 (Medal with Clasp).

[16] Captain Pink served in the Afghan war in 1879-80 as Officiating Sub-Assistant Commissary General on the Khyber Line (Medal). Served with the Burmese Expedition in 1886-89 as Orderly Officer to Brigadier General Lockhart, and as Deputy Assistant Adjutant and Quarter Master General to the 3rd Brigade (mentioned in despatches, *DSO.*, and Medal with two Clasps).

[17] Captain Wyndham Pain served with the Burmese Expedition in 1885-87 (Medal with Clasp).

[18] Captain H. I. W. Hamilton served in the Burmese Expedition in 1885-87 as Adjutant of the 2nd Battalion Queen's Royal West Surrey Regiment under Brigadier General Lockhart (Medal with Clasp).

[19] Captain Parsons served in the Burmese Expedition in 1885-87 with the 2nd Battalion Queen's Royal West Surrey Regiment under Brigadier General Lockhart (Medal with Clasp); was Post Transport Officer at Pyinmana for four months, and Superintendent of Army Signalling 3rd Brigade from July 1887 to February 1888.

[20] Captain Taylor served in the Burmese Expedition in 1885-87 with the 2nd Battalion Queen's Royal West Surrey Regiment under Brigadier General Lockhart (Medal with Clasp).

[21] Captain Tracy served in the Burmese Expedition in 1885-87 with the 2nd Battalion Queen's Royal West Surrey Regiment under Brigadier General Lockhart (Medal with Clasp); served with the Mounted Infantry for seven months, and as Station Staff Officer at Pyinmana from December 1887 to February 1888 (Medal).

[23] Captain Glasgow, Lieuts. Warren and Whiffin served in the Burmese Expedition in 1885-87 with the 2nd Battalion Queen's Royal West Surrey Regiment under Brigadier General Lockhart (Medal with Clasp).

Record of the Services of the 2nd Battalion The Queen's Royal West Surrey Regiment (formerly the 2nd Regiment).

Raised in England in 1857. To Malta and the Ionian Islands, 1858. To Gibraltar, 1862. To Bermuda, 1864. To Ireland, 1865. To England, 1868. To Ireland, 1873. To England, 1876. To Malta, 1877. To India, 1878. (Entitled "2nd Battalion The Queen's Royal West Surrey Regiment," 1881.) To Upper Burmah, 1886. To India, 1888. To England, 1894.

The Buffs (East Kent Regiment). 237

1st Batt., Jullunder, Bengal.
2nd Batt., Athlone.
Formerly the 3rd (East Kent—The Buffs). [Regimental District No. 3.—Canterbury.]

(The 3rd Battalion is formed of the East Kent Militia.)

"*Veteri frondescit honore.*" The Dragon. The United Red and White Rose with the Imperial Crown. "BLENHEIM" "RAMILLIES" "OUDENARDE" "MALPLAQUET" "DETTINGEN" "DOURO" "TALAVERA" "ALBUHERA" "VITTORIA" "PYRENEES" "NIVELLE" "NIVE" "ORTHES" "TOULOUSE" "PENINSULA" "PUNNIAR" "SEVASTOPOL" "TAKU FORTS" "SOUTH AFRICA, 1879."

Colonel.—Sir Julius Augustus Robert Raines,[1] *KCB, Ensign*, 28 Jan. 42; *Lt.* 5 Apr. 44; *Capt.* P13 Apr. 52; *Bt.Major*, 24 Apr. 55; *Major*, 1 May 57; *Lt.Colonel*, 17 Nov. 57; *Colonel*, 20 July 58; *Major General*, 6 March 68; *Lieut.General*, 1 Oct. 77; *General*, 1 July 81; *Colonel* The Buffs, 23 Sept. 82.

Lieutenant Colonels.—2 Waldron Edward Roper Kelly,[9] *Ensign*, P16 Aug. 64; *Lt.* P16 Oct. 67; *Capt.* 1 April 75; *Major*, 14 Sept. 81; *Lt.Colonel*, 1 July 91.

1 George Ernest Harley, *Ensign*, P4 Oct. 64; *Lt.* P7 Dec. 67; *Capt.* 7 May 75; *Major*, 23 Dec. 81; *Lt. Colonel*, 23 May 92.

Years' Ser. Full Pay	Half Pay			ENSIGN OR 2ND LIEUT.	LIEUT.	CAPTAIN.	BREV.MAJ.	MAJOR.
			MAJORS.					
28	...	1	Robert Albert Hickson...............	P26 June 67	P29 Dec. 69	26 Feb. 76	......	4 Mar. 83
27	...	2	Arthur Charles Jackson[12]........	P 1 April 68	P29 June 70	10 Mar. 78	......	16 Apr. 84
26	...	1	Albert Edward Ommanney[13].....	P 30 Oct. 69	P27 Oct. 71	1 Nov. 78	......	30 Nov. 85
23	...	2	Julius Batt Backhouse[14]...........		15 May 72	15 Mar. 80	......	30 Nov. 85
22	...	1	*p.s.c.* Richard Stanley Hawks Moody[15]	......	9 Aug. 73	24 Oct. 80	......	14 Jan. 86
22	...	1	John William Hind[6]...............		28 Feb. 74	23 Dec. 81	......	10 Dec. 86
22	...	2	*p.s.c.* Cosmo Huntly Gordon[17]...		28 Feb. 74	19 Mar. 82	......	21 Jan. 91
21	...	2	Francis Smith[18] (*Depot*)...........		2 Dec. 74	29 Sept. 80	......	23 May 92
			CAPTAINS.					
21	...	1	Bryan Francis Holme[19]............		13 June 74	27 Sept. 83		
20	...		*p.s.c.* Alfred Jas. Whitacre Allen,[24] *D.* A. Q. M. G. for *Intell.Bengal*,5 June 92	......	12 Feb. 76	8 Jan. 85		
19	...		Arthur Horsman Coles,[25] *DSO. Adj.* 16 *Middlesex Rifle Vols.* 22 Mar. 93		11 Sept. 76	18 Apr. 85		
19	...		Hugh Blackburn,[27] *Adjutant* 1 *Lanarkshire Rifle Volunteers* 1 Jan. 94		28 Oct. 76	18 Apr. 85		
18	...	2	George Adrian Porter...............	30 Jan. 78	17 Dec. 79	24 Apr. 85		
17	...		Corry Langrishe Connellan,[28] *Adj.* 3 *Bn. Somerset Light Infantry* 1 Jan. 91		11 Nov. 78	30 Nov. 85		
17	...	2	*p.s.c.* Courtenay Bourchier Vyvyan,[29] *Brigade Major, Gibraltar* 1 Jan. 95	1 May 78	6 Jan. 80	14 Jan. 86		
17	...		Arthur Henry Tylden-Pattenson,[30] *Adj.* 1 *Vol. Battalion The Buffs* 1 Nov. 92	14 Sept. 78	1 Oct. 80	10 Dec. 86		
16	...		Archibald Francis Campbell-Johnston,[31] *Adj.* 1 *Vol. Bn. North Stafford Regt.* 2 Jan. 93	21 June 79	24 Oct. 80	1 July 87		
16	...		Edgar Evelyn Ravenhill, *Adjutant* 2 *Vol. Bn. West Kent Regt.* 11 July 90	3 July 79	1 July 81	1 July 87		
16	...	2	Robert Edw. Philips, *Adj.* 3 *Bn.* 1 Sept. 94	13 Aug. 79	1 July 81	1 July 87		
16	...	2	Douglas Abercromby Hamilton...	14 Jan. 80	1 July 81	4 Aug. 87		
15	...	2	George Victor Dauglish............	22 Jan. 81	1 July 81	1 Nov. 87		
16	...	1	Percival Forbes Brine (*Depot*).....	9 July 79	12 Mar. 81	26 June 89		
14	...	2	Edward Charles James Williams,[35] *Adjutant* 20 May 94	23 April 81	1 July 81	1 Nov. 92		
14	...		Reginald Bayard, *Army Service Corps*.....	23 April 81	1 July 81	2 Jan. 93		
13	...		Wm. Henry Booth, *Aide de Camp to Lord Frankfort de Montmorency* 26 Apr. 93		10 May 82	2 Jan. 93		
13	...	2	Alexander Rowland Eustace......		29 July 82	22 Mar. 93		
12	...	2	Naunton Henry Vertue, *Staff College*.....		6 Feb. 84	22 Mar. 93		
12	...		Charles Kendal Greene, *O. S. Dept.*.........		6 Feb. 84	26 Apr. 93		
11	...	1	Lionel George Nuttall Eales,[36] *Station Staff Officer, Jullunder*, 17 Oct. 93		23 Aug. 84	26 Apr. 93		
11	...		Edw. Cecil Morgan Parry, *Adj. Admin. Bn. Presidency Vols.* 1 Apr. 92		23 Aug. 84	4 Oct. 93		
11	...	2	Albert Vickerman...................		12 Nov. 84	4 Oct. 93		
10	...	1	Francis Denis Jack Annesley......		6 May 85	1 Jan. 94		
10	...		George Gilett Hunter, *serving with the Egyptian Army*...............		9 May 85	31 Jan. 94		
10	...	1	Arthur Lynden Bell, **Adjutant** 1 Apr. 92		9 May 85	31 Jan. 94		
10	...	2	Reginald Hughes D'Aeth, *Adj.* 2 *Volunteer Battalion* 1 Feb. 95...............		9 May 85	1 Jan. 94		
10		2	Frederick Knight Essell............		25 Nov. 85	31 Jan. 93		
			LIEUTENANTS.					
9	...	1	Bernard Richard Kinneir Tarte......		10 Nov. 86			
9	...		Henry Cecil de la Montague Hill, *Inst. Hythe School of Musketry* 4 Feb. 92		10 Nov. 86			
9	...	2	Augustus David Geddes............	5 Feb. 87	21 Nov. 89			
8	...	2	Harry Francis Sparrow (*Depot*)...	4 May 87	5 Mar. 90			
8	...	2	Richard George Armine Marriott....	4 May 87	1 Apr. 90			
8	...	1	Lewis Iggulden Backhouse Hulke (*Depot*)	14 Sept. 87	11 July 90			
8	...	1	Arthur Grant Trollope............	16 Nov. 87	20 Aug. 90			
8	...	1	Edmond Guy Tulloch Bainbridge...	11 Feb. 88	3 Dec. 90			
7	...	1	Frank William Bradley Dyne	9 May 88	24 Jan. 92			
7	...	1	Julian Hasler........................	19 Sept. 88	4 Feb. 92			
7	...	1	Charles Clermont Cobbe............	10 Nov. 88	1 Apr. 92			
6	...	1	Robert Frederick Pearson...........	3 Apr. 89	28 Sept. 92			
6	...	1	Roger Swetenham	21 Dec. 89	2 Jan. 93			
5	...	2	Robert Kenrick Price	3 May 90	22 Mar. 93			
5	...	1	William Arnold Eaton.............	8 Oct. 90	12 Apr. 93			
5	...	2	Edward Heneage Finch Hatten ...	17 Jan. 91	26 Apr. 93			
4	...	1	Robert M'Douall	9 Jan. 92	4 Oct. 93			
4	...	1	John Thomas Graves Adamson....	12 Mar. 92	4 Oct. 93			
3	...	1	William Herbert Trevor	13 July 92	13 June 94			
3½	...	1	Æneas Charles Perkins	13 Aug 92	1 Jan. 95			
			SECOND LIEUTENANTS.					
3	...	2	Fermor Godfrey-Faussett	28 Sept. 92				
3	...	2	Henry Guy Fulljames Savage Gregson...	19 Nov. 92				
3	...	1	Cyril Lachlan Porter...............	21 Jan. 93				

[6] Major Hind served throughout the operations in the Malay Peninsula in 1875-76 (Medal with Clasp).

[35] Captain Williams served with the Nile Expedition in 1884-85 (Medal with Clasp, and Khedive's Star).

The Buffs (East Kent Regiment).

Years'Ser Full Pay	Half Pay		SECOND LIEUTENANTS.	2ND LIEUT.	
3	...	2	Charles Durnford Kelynge Greenway	15 Mar. 93	
2	...	2	Colin Charles Henry Pritchard	26 Apr. 93	
2	...	1	Frederick Spencer Reeves	19 July 93	Facings Buff.—Agents, Messrs. Cox and Co.
2	...	2	Geoffrey Brouncker De Mareis Mairis	9 Sept. 93	
2	...	1	Rowland Edward Power	21 Oct. 93	1st Battalion embarked for Malta, 29 Jan. 1885.
2	...	1	Richard Bright	7 Mar. 94	2nd Battalion returned from Egypt, 29 Apr. 1886.
2	...	2	Lionel Charles Edward Knight	7 Mar. 94	
1	...	2	Francis Joyce Engelbach	20 June 94	
1	...		Charles Graham Monseil	6 Feb. 95	

Paymasters.—1 Charles C. Cobbe, Lieut. 1 Battalion (acting).
2

| 4 | ... | *Quarter Masters.*—1 Herbert Charles Cumber, 29 Apr. 91; Hon. Lieut. |
| 4 | ... | 2 George Boon, 24 June 91; Hon. Lieut. |

¹ Sir Julius Raines served throughout the Eastern campaign of 1854–55, including the affair at Bulganak, the battle of Alma (where he carried the Queen's Color as a Captain), the flank march by Mackenzie's Farm, the battles of Inkerman and Tchernaya, and repulse of the sortie of the 26th October 1854; served as an Assistant Royal Engineer in the Right Attack throughout the siege and fall of Sebastopol (severely wounded in the Trenches during the bombardment of the 17th October), and present in the Trenches at the attack of the Redan on the 18th June (Medal with three Clasps, mentioned in despatches as "having served with zeal and distinction from the opening of the campaign, Brevet of Major, Sardinian and Turkish Medals, and 5th Class of the Medjidie). Served throughout the Indian Mutiny campaign in 1857–59, commanded the troops at the assault and capture of Rowa on 6th January 1858 (received the high commendation of the Governor and the Commander in Chief of Bombay in Council for "gallantry displayed and ably conducting these operations"); commanded the Left Wing 95th Regiment at the siege and capture of Awah on 24th January; commanded the 95th at the siege and capture of Kotah, and commanded the 3rd assaulting Column on 30th March; was present at the capture of Chundaree 26th May; commanded the Infantry of Brigadier Smith's Column at the battle of Kota ke Serai; before Gwalior on the 17th June (specially mentioned in despatches by Sir Hugh Rose for "good service and assisting to take and hold the position of Kota-ka-Seria"); and in the general action, storm and capture of the city and fortress of Gwalior on 19th June (wounded by a musket-ball in the left arm, specially mentioned by Sir Hugh Rose for "gallantry and taking by assault two 18-pounders" and for "good service in turning the guns captured on the enemy"); present at the siege and capture of Pouree on 24th August 1858; and the surprise and defeat of the rebels at Koondrye on the 19th January 1859, (in addition to the above he has been four times mentioned in despatches, and marched 3,000 miles in command of the 95th Regiment in Central India, Medal with Clasp, Colonel, and CB. for distinguished service in the field). As Brigadier General commanded the expedition from Aden into the interior o Arabia in 1865–66, when the troops captured and destroyed many towns and forts, including Ussala, the Fudtholis capital, and seven cannon (received the commendation of the Commander in Chief of Bombay for the efficient manner in which those successful operations were effected). Nominated KCB. 24th May 1893.

⁹ Lt.Colonel Kelly served with the Buffs in the operations in the Malay Peninsula in 1875–76, including the actions of the 20th January and 4th February, and commanded the escort in the reconnaissance of the 22nd January (Medal with Clasp).

¹² Major Jackson served in the Zulu war in 1879, and was present in the engagement at Inyezane and at Ekowe during the investment (Medal with Clasp).

¹³ Major Ommanney served with the Buffs in the operations in the Malay Peninsula in 1875–76 (Medal with Clasp).

¹⁴ Major Backhouse served with the Buffs in the Zulu war of 1879, and was present in the engagements at Inyezane and Gingindhlovu (Medal with Clasp).

¹⁵ Major Moody served in the Zulu war in 1879 (Medal with Clasp).

¹⁷ Major C. H. Gordon served in the Zulu war in 1879, and was present in the engagement at Inyezane and in Ekowe during the investment (Medal with Clasp).

¹⁸ Major Francis Smith served in the operations against the Galekas in 1877–78. Served in the Zulu war of 1879, and was present in the engagement at Kambula—severely wounded (mentioned in despatches, Medal with Clasp).

¹⁹ Captain Holme served with the Buffs throughout the operations in the Malay Peninsula in 1875–76, including the action of the 4th February (Medal with Clasp). Served with the Nile Expedition in 1884–85 (Medal with Clasp, and Khedive's Star).

²⁴ Captain Allen served with the 3rd Buffs throughout the Zulu war of 1879, and was present in the engagements at Inyezane and Gingindhlovu (Medal with Clasp). Served with the Nile Expedition in 1884–85 as Staff Captain; was Commandant of Dal-Sarkamatts and Rail Head, and from 28th February to 22nd July he commanded the Transport Train (Medal with Clasp, and Khedive's Star).

²⁵ Captain Coles served with the Nile Expedition in 1884–85 (Medal with Clasp, and 4th Class of the Osmanieh, and Khedive's Star); in the operations of the Soudan Frontier Field Force in 1887 including the engagement at Sarras; and in the operations on the Soudan frontier in 1889 including the engagement at Toski (mentioned in despatches, DSO., and Clasp).

²⁷ Captain Blackburn served in the Zulu war of 1879, was present in the engagement at Inyezane, and was at Ekowe during the investment of that place (Medal with Clasp).

²⁸ Captain Connellan served in the Zulu war of 1879, and was present in the engagement at Inyezane and during the investment of Ekowe (Medal with Clasp).

²⁹ Captain Vyvyan served in the Zulu war in 1879, and was present in the engagement at Inyezane and at Ekowe during the investment (Medal with Clasp).

³⁰ Captain Tylden-Pattenson served in the Zulu war in 1879, and was present in the engagement at Gingindhlovu (Medal with Clasp).

³¹ Captain Campbell-Johnston served in Natal during the Zulu war in 1879 (Medal).

³⁶ Captain Eales served with the Manipore Expedition in 1891 as Signalling Officer (mentioned in despatches, Medal with Clasp).

The King's Own (Royal Lancaster Regiment). 238

1st Batt., Portsmouth.
2nd Batt., Nusseerabad, Bombay.] *Formerly the 4th (The King's Own Royal)* [Regimental District No. 4.—Lancaster.
(The 3rd and 4th Battalions are formed of the 1st Lancashire Militia.)
The Lion of England. The Royal Cypher within the Garter. "CORUNNA" "BADAJOZ" "SALAMANCA" "VITTORIA" "ST. SEBASTIAN" "NIVE" "PENINSULA" "BLADENSBURG" "WATERLOO" "ALMA" "INKERMAN" "SEVASTOPOL" "ABYSSINIA" "SOUTH AFRICA, 1879."

Years'Ser.			Ensign or 2nd Lieut.	Lieut.	Captain.	Brev.Maj.	Major.
Full Pay	Half Pay	**Colonel.**—c. Sir William Gordon Cameron,[1] KCB. Ensign, 24 May 44; Ensign and Lieut. P 12 May 47; Lt. & Capt. P 15 July 53; Bt.Major, 24 Apr. 55; Major, 23 Oct. 57; Bt.Lt.Colonel, 3 Feb. 63; Colonel, 15 Aug. 68; Major General, 25 June 78; Lt.General, 17 July 88; General, 21 Jan. 93; Colonel Lancaster Regiment, 16 Jan. 94.					
33	...	**Lieutenant Colonels.**—2 p.s.c. Edward John Lugard,[2] Ensign, 16 Jan.63; Lieut. 11 Jan. 67; Capt. 28 Oct. 76; Major, 1 July 81; Bt.Lt.Colonel, 18 Nov. 82; Colonel, 18 Nov. 86; Lt. Colonel, 24 Feb. 92.					
30	...	1 p.s.c. Edw. Robert Prevost Woodgate,[12] Ensign, 7 April 65; Lieut. P7 July 69; Capt. 2 Mar. 78; Bt.Major, 29 Nov. 79; Major, 19 Nov. 81; Lt.Colonel, 26 June 93.					
		MAJORS.					
27	...	2 Richard Hawes MacCarthy[13]	23 Jan. 69	P 3 May 71	7 Jan. 80	......	9 Mar. 86
24	...	1 John Rowlandson[16]	......	10 Jan. 72	22 Sept. 80	......	7 Oct. 91
23	...	2 p.s.c. Ernest Walter Yeatherd	......	13 Nov. 72	7 Oct. 81	15 June 85	24 Feb. 92
21	...	Archibald Hunter,[18] DSO. (Bt.Lt.Col. 17 Aug.89; Brevet Colonel, 6 Jan. 94); Gov. of the Red Sea Littoral	......	13 June 74	30 Aug. 82	......	15 June 92
20	...	1 p.s.c. John Moore Gawne,[19] Deputy Assist. Adj. Gen. Egypt, 31 Jan. 95	......	13 June 75	28 May 84	......	26 June 93
19	...	Frank Broadwood Matthews,[9] Adj. 4 Battalion 15 Jan. 91	......	15 July 76	18 Apr. 85	......	12 July 93
17	...	2 Archibald John Joseph Ross	1 May 78	6 Mar. 80	24 Mar. 86	......	2 May 94
17	...	Joseph Ignatius Bonomi[16]	11 May 78	6 Mar. 80	9 May 86	......	25 Jan. 95
		CAPTAINS.					
17	...	2 Ernest Augustus Frederic Carter[9]	11 May 78	20 Mar. 80	11 Aug. 86		
17	...	1 Alfred Bayley Ridley,[16] Aide de Camp to the Lord Lieut. of Ireland 3 Oct. 92	11 May 78	17 Apr. 80	29 Sept. 86		
17	...	Thomas Mercer Vigors, A. P. Dept.	11 May 78	21 May 80	1 Aug. 87		
17	...	1 Thomas Edmund Burke[20] (Depot)	4 Dec. 78	23 June 80	7 Oct. 87		
17	...	1 William Lancelot James[9]	4 Dec. 78	5 Dec. 80	1 Feb. 88		
17	...	2 Walter Henry Duffin, Adjutant Deolalee Depot 9 May 94	22 Jan. 79	27 Dec. 80	1 Feb. 88		
17	...	1 Thomas Cameron Fitzgerald Somerville	22 Jan. 79	1 July 81	21 May 88		
16	...	2 Alleyne Haynes (Depot)	13 Aug. 79	1 July 81	21 May 88		
16	...	Guy Audouin Carleton, D. A. A. Gen. for Musk. Bombay Army, 8 June 94	14 Jan. 80	1 July 81	21 May 88		
15	...	Antoine Dominique Thorne	23 Oct. 80	1 July 81	2 Oct. 88		
15	...	2 Charles Gerard Barton	22 Jan. 81	1 July 81	26 June 89		
13	...	Thomas Charles Hunt, Adjutant 1 Vol. Bn. Lancaster Regt. 27 July 92	......	9 Sept. 82	21 Nov. 90		
12	...	1 Godfrey Leicester Hibbert	......	6 Feb. 84	19 Aug. 91		
11	...	1 Willoughby Seymour Burton	......	14 May 84	8 Oct. 91		
11	...	Alexander James King, serving with the Egyptian Army	......	12 Nov. 84	27 July 92		
12	3 3/12	2 William Houghton	14 Jan. 80	1 July 81	18 June 88		
13	...	Henry Lynch Talbot, employed with the Perak Sikhs	......	10 Mar. 83	8 May 94		
11	...	2 Walter James Mangles	......	12 Nov. 84	2 May 94		
10	...	1 John Henry Arthur Boyce	......	6 May 85	8 June 94		
10	...	1 Charles Francis Goldie-Taubman, Adjutant 7 Aug. 93	......	9 May 85	8 June 94		
10	...	2 Leslie Falkiner John de Vere Stokes, Comdt. Poorundhur Sanitarium	......	23 May 85	25 Jan. 95		
		LIEUTENANTS.					
10	...	John Haliburton Laurie, serving with Inf.School Corps of Canadian Militia	......	2 Sept. 85			
11	...	1 William Sandbach	......	7 Feb. 85			
9	...	2 Thomas Bradford Dixon	......	28 Apr. 86			
9	...	1 James Sealy Clarke	......	25 Aug. 86			
9	...	1 Alfred Ernest Radcliffe	......	25 Aug. 86			
9	...	1 John Archibald Paton	......	25 Aug. 86			
8	...	2 Donald Maxwell M'Lachlan	4 May 87	22 Sept. 89			
8	...	1 Maurice Wrottesley Kirk	16 May 87	18 Dec. 89			
7	...	Mausel Arthur Charles Bampfylde Fenwick,[21] serving with Egyptian Army	16 May 88	22 Dec. 89			
7	...	2 Gerald Lindsay Palmes (Depot)	12 Sept. 88	22 Dec. 89			
7	...	2 Frederick Montgomerie Carleton, Adjutant 12 July 91	3 Oct. 88	1 Apr. 90			
7	...	2 Thomas John Marker	10 Nov. 88	11 June 90			
7	...	1 Edward Plunkett Burke	19 Dec. 88	11 June 90			
6	...	1 James Gordon Turing Bruce	6 July 89	21 Nov. 90			
6	...	1 John Malise Anne Graham	9 Nov. 89	19 Aug. 91			
6	...	Ernest Arthur Frederick Redl	1 Mar. 90	7 July 92			
5	...	2 Aylmer Richard Sancton Martin	4 Mar. 91	26 June 92			
5	...	Harry Leith Tomkins	29 Oct. 90	28 July 93			
5	...	Murray Ray de Buyrne James, Army Service Corps	29 Nov 90	7 Oct. 93			
4	...	Frederick Peter Charles Keily	25 July 91	30 Dec. 93			
4	...	2 James Blair Keogh	9 Sept. 91	30 Dec. 93			
4	...	1 Hugh Galloway	7 Nov. 91	2 May 94			
4	...	2 Richard Henry Edmund Pennell	7 Nov. 91	8 June 94			
2	...	2 Cecil Arthur Borrett	18 May 92	1 July 94			
3	...	1 John Henry Lloyd	13 Aug. 92	14 Oct. 94			
		SECOND LIEUTENANTS.					
3	...	2 Archibald Campbell Hobson	13 Aug. 92				
3	...	1 John Furzer Elliot	13 Aug. 92				

[9] Captains Matthews, Carter, and James served in the Zulu war of 1879 (Medal with Clasp).
[16] Majors Rowlandson and Bonomi, and Captain Ridley served in the Zulu war in 1879 (Medal with Clasp).
[18] Colonel Hunter served in the Nile Expedition in 1884-85 with the Egyptian Army (mentioned in despatches, Brevet of Major, 4th Class of the Osmanieh, 3rd Class of the Medjidie, Medal with Clasp, and Khedive's Star); with the Egyptian Frontier Field Force in 1885-86 including the engagement at Giniss—severely wounded (mentioned in despatches, DSO.); and in the operations on the Soudan frontier in 1889 including the engagement at Toski—wounded (mentioned in despatches, Brevet of Lt.Colonel, Clasp).
[19] Major Gawne served in the Zulu war of 1879 (Medal with Clasp). Served with the Bechuanaland Expedition under Sir Charles Warren in 1884-85.

Facings Blue.—*Agents*, Messrs. Cox and Co.

1st Battalion returned from West Indies, 1881. 2nd Battalion embarked for the Cape of Good Hope, 1878.

O

239 The King's Own (Royal Lancaster Regiment).

Years Ser. Full Pay	Half Pay	SECOND LIEUTENANTS.	2ND LIEUT.	
3	...	1 Francis Shand Byam Johnson (*Depot*)	19 Oct.	92
2	...	2 Edward George Evans	20 May	93
2	...	2 Algernon Thomas Henry Kemmis Betty	19 July	93
2	...	1 Eustace Montague Townend	23 Dec.	93
2	...	1 James George Constable	23 Dec.	93
2	...	2 Bertram Charles Kauntze	7 Mar.	94
1	...	1 Thomas Duncan Legh Whittington	8 Aug.	94
1	...	2 Alfred M'Nair Dykes	12 Dec.	94
1	...	William Agar Lander Lethbridge	6 Mar.	95
1	...	Francis Coventry Dudfield Davidson	6 Mar.	95

[20] Captain Burke served with the 1st Battalion Royal Irish Fusiliers in the Egyptian war of 1882, and was present at the battle of Tel-el-Kebir (Medal with Clasp, and Khedive's Star).

Paymaster.—2 Thomas J. Marker, *Lieut.* 2 *Battalion* (*acting*).
Quarter Masters.—2 John O'Neill, 11 Apr. 85; *Hon. Lieut.*
1 Thomas Batchelor, 20 Feb. 95; *Hon. Lieut.*

(Full Pay column values: 10, 1)

[1] Sir W. G. Cameron served in the Grenadier Guards during the Eastern campaign of 1854, including the battle of Alma and siege of Sebastopol as Assistant Engineer right attack. Was severely wounded on the 20th October while in command of the Volunteer Sharpshooters of the 1st Division (Medal with two Clasps, Knight of the Legion of Honor, 5th Class of the Medjidie, and Turkish Medal). Commanded the 3rd Regiment German Legion with commission of Lt.Colonel from May 1855 to November 1856, out of which time seven months in Turkey. Commanded the 1st Battalion 4th King's Own Regt. throughout the Abyssinian campaign and was present at the action of Arogee and capture of Magdala (mentioned in Lord Napier's despatches as having "won his admiration by the manner in which he has commanded his excellent Regiment, and the soldier-like spirit which by his teaching and example he has so well fostered and maintained," Brevet of Colonel, *CB.*, and Medal).

[2] Colonel Lugard served in the 4th Regiment throughout the Abyssinian campaign of 1867-68, and was employed with the Transport Train (Medal). Served in the Egyptian war of 1882 as Deputy Assistant Adjutant and Quarter Master General in the 2nd Division, and was present in the battle of Tel-el-Kebir—horse shot (mentioned in despatches, Brevet of Lt.Colonel, Medal with Clasp, 4th Class of the Osmanieh, and Khedive's Star).

[12] Lt.Colonel Woodgate served with the 4th Regt. throughout the Abyssinian campaign, and was present at the action of Arogee and capture of Magdala (Medal). Accompanied Sir Garnet Wolseley to the Gold Coast in September 1873 on special service, and served throughout the Ashanti War of 1873-74, including the action of Essaman, repulse of the Ashanti army at Abrakrampa during the 5th and 6th November 1873 (in command of the Kossoos), reconnaissances in force of the 8th and 27th November, and battle of Amoaful (mentioned in despatches, Medal with Clasp). Served in the Zulu war in 1879, and was present in the engagements at Kambula (mentioned in despatches) and Ulundi (mentioned in despatches, Brevet of Major, Medal with Clasp).

[13] Major MacCarthy served in the second phase of the Ashanti war in 1874 in the Transport Service, and was in charge of the Post at Accroful (Medal). Served in the Zulu war of 1879, and was present in the engagements at Zlobane Mountain and Kambula (Medal with Clasp).

[21] Lieut. Fenwick served in the operations in the Soudan in 1889 including the engagements at Arguin and Toski (Medal with Clasp, 4th Class of the Medjidie, and Khedive's Star).

Record of the Services of the 2nd Battalion The King's Own (Royal Lancaster Regiment),—formerly the 4th Regiment.

Raised in 1857. Proceeded to the Ionian Islands, 1859. To Malta, 1864. To Halifax, N.S., 1866. To England, 1868. To Natal, 1878. To India, 1880.

Continuation of Notes to the Northumberland Fusiliers.

[1] Lt.Colonel Way served throughout the Hazara campaign in 1888 with the 2nd Battalion Northumberland Fusiliers (Medal with Clasp).

[4] Lt.Colonel Cherry served throughout the Hazara campaign in 1888 with the 2nd Battalion Northumberland Fusiliers (mentioned in despatches, Medal with Clasp).

[14] Major H. E. Buchanan served in the Afghan war of 1878-80, and took part in the two expeditions into the Bazar Valley and in the engagement at Darunta Pass (Medal). Served throughout the Hazara campaign in 1888 as Adjutant to the 2nd Battalion Northumberland Fusiliers (Medal with Clasp).

[15] Major R. L. A. Pennington served in the Afghan war in 1878-79, and was present with the expedition into the Bazar Valley and in the engagement at Kam Dakka (Medal). Served throughout the Hazara campaign in 1888 with the 2nd Battalion Northumberland Fusiliers (Medal with Clasp).

[16] Major Malet served throughout the Afghan war of 1878-80 with the 5th Fusiliers, part of the time as Orderly Officer to Brigadier General Gib, and was present in the engagements at Kam Dakka, Deh Sarakh, and the Darunta Pass, with the two expeditions into the Bazar Valley, and with the Kama Expedition (Medal). Served with the Hazara Field Force in the expedition to the Black Mountain in 1888 (Medal with Clasp).

[18] Captain Harding served during the latter part of the Afghan war in 1880 (Medal).

[22] Captains Heard, Fletcher and Booth and Lieut. Isacke served throughout the Hazara campaign in 1888 with the 2nd Battalion Northumberland Fusiliers (Medal with Clasp).

[24] Captain Sitwell served in the Afghan war in 1880 (Medal).

[26] Captain Riddell served throughout the Hazara campaign in 1888 with the 2nd Battalion Northumberland Fusiliers (mentioned in despatches, Medal with Clasp).

1st Batt., Aldershot.
2nd Batt., Singapore.

The Northumberland Fusiliers.

Regimental District No. 5.—Peshawur. 240–1

Formerly the 5th (Northumberland Fusiliers).

(The 3rd Battalion is formed of the Northumberland Militia.)

"*Quo Fata vocant.*" St. George and the Dragon. The United Red and White Rose, with the Royal Crest. "WILHELM-STAHL" "ROLEIA" "VIMIERA" "CORUNNA" "BUSACO" "CIUDAD RODRIGO" "BADAJOZ" "SALAMANCA" "VITTORIA" "NIVELLE" "ORTHES" "TOULOUSE" "PENINSULA" "LUCKNOW" "AFGHANISTAN, 1878-80."

Years' Ser.	Full Pay	Half Pay		Ensign or 2nd Lieut.	Lieut.	Captain.	Brev.Maj.	Major.
			Colonel.—					
31		...	**Lieutenant Colonels.**—2 Wilfred FitzAllan Way,¹ *Ensign*, ᵖ18 Oct. 64; *Lt.* ᵖ22 Aug. 68; *Capt.* 15 May 78; *Major*, 25 July 83; *Lt.Colonel*, 22 Feb. 92.					
30		...	1 Henry Aitken Cherry,⁴ *Ensign*, ᵖ25 July 65; *Lt.* ᵖ27 Feb. 69; *Capt.* 7 Jan. 80; *Major*, 25 July 83; *Lt.Colonel*, 23 May 92.					
			MAJORS.					
25		...	2 Harris England Buchanan¹⁴	ᵖ 8 June 70	28 Oct. 71	9 Mar. 82	......	23 Apr. 90
23		...	1 Charles Gilbert Colvin Money	......	29 May 72	1 Sept. 82	......	9 Dec. 91
19		...	Richard Lionel Arthur Pennington,¹⁵ *Assist. Adj. General for Musketry, Madras Army*, 27 Oct. 94	......	11 Sept. 76	9 Sept. 82	......	22 Feb. 92
19		...	1 John Warre Malet¹⁶ (*Depot*)	......	29 Nov. 76	11 Oct. 82	......	23 May 92
19		...	1 George Frend¹⁷	......	29 Nov. 76	14 July 83	......	22 Apr. 93
18		...	2 Hon. Charles Lambton	......	31 May 77	25 July 83	......	21 Jan. 95
18		...	2 Thos. Graves Lowry Herbert-Armstrong	19 Dec. 77	3 April 78	24 Jan. 85	......	27 Jan. 95
18		...	William Eden Sturges, *D.A.A.Gen. for Musketry, Bengal*, 20 Apr. 94	30 Jan. 78	7 Jan. 80	4 May 85	......	30 Jan. 95
			CAPTAINS.					
17		...	1 Gerald Montrésor Harding¹⁸	11 May 78	20 Feb. 80	23 June 85		
17		...	Dudley Strathearn Stewart, *Adj. 1 Vol. Bn. Argyll and Sutherland Highlanders* 30 Nov. 93	11 May 78	1 Jan. 81	27 Jan. 86		
16		...	*p.s.c.* Thomas David Pilcher	21 June 79	1 Jan. 81	12 Feb. 86		
17		...	1 Edmund William Dashwood	22 Jan. 79	1 July 81	13 Nov. 86		
16		...	*p.s.c.* William Henry Sitwell²³	14 Jan. 80	1 July 81	10 Apr. 89		
16		...	1 St. George Charles Henry	31 Jan. 80	1 July 81	10 Apr. 89		
15		...	2 James Foster Riddell²⁴ (*Depot*)	11 Aug. 80	1 July 81	18 Nov. 89		
15		...	Edward Boaz Eagar, *Adjutant* 3 *Volunteer Battalion* 15 Jan. 91	11 Aug. 80	1 July 81	27 Jan. 90		
13		...	Josard Henry Lachlan White, *Adjutant* 2 *Volunteer Battalion* 1 Feb. 92	......	10 May 82	20 Mar. 91		
13		...	Cyril Henry Leigh James, *Adj.* 5 *Vol. Bn. Durham Lt.Infantry* 9 Nov. 91	......	9 Sept. 82	15 June 91		
13		...	2 Cecil Edw. Keith-Falconer, *at Staff Coll.*	......	27 Jan. 83	22 Feb. 92		
13		...	1 *p.s.c.* Edward Severin Heard²²	......	10 Mar. 83	11 May 92		
12		...	Wm. Albert Willmott, *Adjutant* 1 *Volunteer Battalion* 15 Dec. 92	......	25 Aug. 83	23 May 92		
10		...	Mowbray Lees Sant, *Adjutant* 3 *Battalion* 16 Feb. 93	......	6 May 85	24 Oct. 92		
10		...	1 Douglas Sapte, **Adjutant** 1 Oct. 91	......	9 May 85	24 Oct. 92		
10		...	1 Edward Walter Fletcher²²	......	23 May 85	15 Dec. 92		
10		...	2 Ferdinand George Casson	......	29 Aug. 85	17 Oct. 94		
9		...	1 Percival Spearman Wilkinson	......	28 Apr. 86	27 Oct. 94		
9		...	1 Gerard Frederick Towlerton Leather	......	28 Apr. 86	21 Jan. 95		
9		...	2 Arthur William Calvert Booth²²	......	25 Aug. 86	21 Jan. 95		
9		...	Arthur Frederick Dawkins	......	25 Aug. 86	27 Jan. 95		
			LIEUTENANTS.					
9		...	1 Arthur Edward Lowther Crofton	......	17 Nov. 86			
8		...	1 Hon. Murrough O'Brien (*Depot*)	26 Feb. 87	27 Jan. 90			
8		...	2 Clement Vincent Molyneux Sarel	14 Sept. 87	1 Apr. 90			
8		...	1 George Lake Sidney Ray	14 Sept. 87	10 Apr. 90			
8		...	2 Robert Henry Isacke²³	14 Sept. 87	10 Apr. 90			
7	4¹/₁₂		2 Arthur Gerald Milford Tozer	......	14 May 84			
7		...	2 Humphrey Loftus Bland (*Depot*)	9 Jan. 89	13 Feb. 91			
6		...	1 Samuel Herbert Enderby	21 Aug. 89	9 Nov. 91			
6		...	2 Wm. Somervell, **Adjutant** 13 Feb. 95	2 Oct. 89	22 Feb. 92			
6		...	2 Henry Sandys Ainslie	1 Mar. 90	11 May 92			
5		...	2 Spencer Charles Ferguson	16 July 90	18 Aug. 92			
7	12/12		1 Francis Colpoys Turner	14 Sept. 87	22 Oct. 90			
5		...	2 Clement Yatman	29 Oct. 90	18 Sept. 92			
4		...	1 Hugh St. Aubyn Wake	2 May 91	8 Feb. 93			
4		...	1 Henry Edmund Burleigh Leach	2 May 91	8 Feb. 93			
4		...	Robert Joseph Tucker Stewart	17 June 91	18 July 94			
4		...	2 John Arthur Coghill Somerville	9 Jan. 92	17 Oct. 94			
4		...	2 John Charles Pulleine Craster	9 Jan. 92	27 Oct. 94			
4		...	2 Arthur Jex-Blake Percival	20 Feb. 92	27 Oct. 94			
3		...	Ernest Newton Healc	9 Apr. 92	21 Jan. 95			
3		...	1 Charles Edward Fishbourne	9 Apr. 92	21 Jan. 95			
			SECOND LIEUTENANTS.					
3		...	Steuart Murray Binny	18 May 92				
3		...	1 Edward Morris Moulton-Barrett	18 June 92				
3		...	Charles Michell Aloysius Wood, *serving with the Egyptian Army*	19 Nov. 92				
3		...	1 Hugh Trevor Crispin	18 May 92				
3		...	1 Frederick Stuart Dawson	17 Dec. 92				
2		...	Stanley Smyth Flower	26 Apr. 93				
1		...	1 Charles Arthur Armstrong	10 Oct. 94				
1		...	1 Mordaunt Cyril Richards	12 Dec. 94				
1		...	1 Frank Bevan	20 Feb. 95				
1		...	1 Basil Thorold Buckley	20 Feb. 95				
1		...	2 Harry Stanley Toppin	20 Feb. 95				
1		...	Claud Henry Maitland Lennox	6 Mar. 95				

Paymasters.—1

2 Percival S. Wilkinson, *Lieut.* 2 *Battalion* (*acting*).

| 5 | ... | **Quarter Masters.**—2 James Thomson, 17 Apr. 89; *Hon. Lieut.* |
| 2 | ... | 1 James Bett, 26 July 93; *Hon. Lieut.* |

ᵇ Major Biddulph served in the Afghan war in 1880 as Superintendent of Army Signalling to the Southern Afghanistan Field Force, and in the march to Candahar with the force under Major General Phayre (Medal).

¹⁷ Major Frend served in the Afghan war of 1878-80, first as Provost Marshal 2nd Brigade and 2nd Division Peshawur Valley Field Force, and afterwards as Transport Officer to the 5th Foot (Medal). Served in the Egyptian war of 1882 (Medal, and Khedive's Star); also served in the Soudan campaign in 1885 (Clasp).

[*For remainder of Notes, see preceding page.*]

Facings White.— *Agents*, Messrs. Cox and Co.

1st Battalion returned from Bengal, 1880.

2nd Battalion embarked for Bengal, 1880.

The Royal Warwickshire Regiment.

1st Batt., Chatham.
2nd Batt., Ceylon.

Formerly the 6th (Royal 1st Warwickshire). [Regimental District No. 6.—Warwick.

(The 3rd and 4th Battalions are formed of the 1st and 2nd Warwick Militia respectively.)

The Antelope. The United Red and White Rose, with the Imperial Crown. "ROLEIA" "VIMIERA" "CORUNNA" "VITTORIA" "PYRENEES" "NIVELLE" "ORTHES" "PENINSULA" "NIAGARA" "SOUTH AFRICA, 1846-7, 1851-2-3."

Years' Ser. Full Pay	Half Pay		ENS.OR 2D LT.	LIEUT.	CAPTAIN.	BREV. MAJ.	MAJOR.
		Colonel.—Hon. Sir Francis Colborne,¹ KCB. Ensign, P1 Oct. 36; Lt. P18 Jan. 39; Capt. P24 May 44; Bt. Major, 21 Oct. 53; Bt. Lt. Colonel, 12 Dec. 54; Major, 16 Oct. 55 Colonel, 2 April 58; Major General, 6 March 68; Lt. General, 1 Oct. 77; General, 1 Apr. 82; Colonel Warwickshire Regiment, 18 July 85.					
29		**Lieutenant Colonels.**—1 Frank Longbourne, Commanding Standing Camp, Dalhousie; Ensign, P27 July 66; Lieut. P28 May 70; Captain, 1 Jan. 79; Major, 20 Sept. 84; Lt.Colonel, 24 Feb. 92.					
27		2 Edward Henry Corse-Scott, Ensign, P10 Feb. 69; Lieut. 28 Oct. 71; Capt. 30 Oct. 80; Major, 3 Mar. 86; Lt. Colonel, 3 Mar. 92.					
		MAJORS.					
26	...	2 Willoughby Edward Gordon Forbes¹⁴	P10 Nov. 69	28 Oct. 71	1 June 81	......	29 Nov. 86
22	...	1 Gregory Haines		9 Aug. 73	25 April 83	......	29 May 89
22	...	1 Morey Quayle Jones¹⁶		12 Nov. 73	25 April 83	......	21 June 90
20	...	1 Nevill Francis Augustus Maunsell¹⁵		20 Nov. 75	27 Dec. 83	......	24 Feb. 92
19	...	2 Arthur William Frank Jackson		22 May 76	12 Feb. 84	......	3 Mar. 92
20	...	Herbert Edwards Irwin		19 Jan. 76	4 June 84	......	6 Aug. 92
22	...	William Alexander Campbell, Adj. 1 Vol. Bn. Dorset Regt. 16 June 92		9 Aug. 73	30 July 84	......	25 Jan. 93
18	...	2 Henry Weston Helyar	30 Jan. 78	17 May 79	20 Sept. 84	......	3 Mar. 93
		CAPTAINS.					
17	...	1 Alex. Charles Emanuel M'Kinstry (Depot)	1 May 78	13 June 79	25 Mar. 85		
17	...	George Edward Godfrey Waller Bird, Army Pay Department	1 May 78	17 April 80	24 Feb. 86		
17	...	Cecil de Courcy Etheridge,¹⁸ Adj. 2 (South) Middlesex R.V. 16 Nov. 91	11 May 78	14 May 80	1 Mar. 86		
17	...	p.s.c. Charles James Cockburn¹⁹	11 May 78	7 July 80	3 Mar. 86		
17	...	2 Herman James Shelley Landon	22 Jan. 79	12 Feb. 81	29 Nov. 86		
17	...	Percy Rice Mockler,²⁰ Adj. 1 Vol. Bn. Yorkshire Lt. Infantry 31 Mar. 92	22 Jan. 79	12 April 81	24 Feb. 88		
16	...	2 Osborn Augustin Chambers²¹	14 Jan. 80	1 July 81	31 Oct. 86		
15	...	Grattan George O'Neil Ray, Adj. 2 Vol. Bn. Warwickshire Regt. 1 Dec. 90	23 Oct. 80	1 July 81	3 Apr. 89		
13	...	2 p.s.c. Lancelot Edward Kiggell		10 May 82	3 Apr. 89		
13	...	Herbert Russell Blyth, Adj. Burmah State Railway Volunteers, 1 Apr. 92		9 Sept. 82	29 May 89		
13	...	1 Reginald Hall		9 Sept. 82	5 July 89		
12	...	Dennis Granville, Adj. 4 Bn. 20 Sept. 93		10 May 83	5 July 89		
15	...	1 p.s.c. James Ridgeway Dyas²²	22 Jan. 81	1 July 81	4 Sept. 89		
12	...	1 Wilfred Sausmarez Carey		5 Dec. 83	18 Sept. 89		
11	...	Lewis Edward Morrice, Adjutant 3 Battalion 28 Aug. 94		14 May 84	1 Dec. 90		
11	...	2 Vere Staunton Smyth		14 May 84	1 Dec. 90		
11	...	2 Frederick George Francis Browne		7 Feb. 85	24 Feb. 92		
11	...	2 Gerald Donne Armstrong		7 Feb. 85	3 Mar. 92		
10	...	1 Robert Dundas Whigham, Adjutant 18 Jan. 92		9 May 85	3 Mar. 92		
10	...	2 Herbert Radclyffe Vaughan		25 Nov. 85	31 Mar. 92		
10	...	2 Charles Conran East (Depot)		30 Jan. 86	6 Aug. 92		
10	...	1 Guy Caldecott, Superintendent of Gymnasia, Glasgow, 16 Sept. 94		30 Jan. 86	6 Aug. 92		
10	...	1 John Ford Elkington		30 Jan. 86	25 Jan. 93		
9	...	Archibald John Stephens Maunsell, Adj. 1 Vol. Bn. Warwick Regt. 27 Dec. 93		25 Aug. 86	3 Mar. 93		
		LIEUTENANTS.					
9	...	2 Arthur Colthurst Herbert		25 Aug. 86			
9	...	2 John Frederick William Boyce		10 Nov. 86			
8	...	1 Edward Lynn Allen	14 Sept. 87	5 June 89			
8	...	Charles Edward Menzies Pyne, Aide de Camp to Sir Henry Norman 28 Jan. 94	16 Nov. 87	5 June 89			
7	...	2 Alexander Deane	6 June 88	18 Sept. 89			
7	...	1 William Melville Lauriston Lee (Depot)	22 Aug. 88	15 Oct. 90			
7	...	2 Walter Latham Loring	23 Mar. 89	1 Dec. 90			
6	...	2 Thomas Diver	26 June 89	11 Mar. 91			
6	...	2 George Taylor Young	6 July 89	7 Apr. 91			
6	...	1 Francis Alfred Earle	21 Sept. 89	8 June 91			
6	...	1 Clement Carr Wrigley	21 Sept. 89	18 Jan. 92			
6	...	2 St. John Augustus Cox	9 Nov. 89	20 Jan. 92			
5	...	2 MacGregor Greer	8 Oct. 90	13 July 92			
5	...	1 William Denziloe Sanderson	17 Jan. 91	13 July 92			
5	...	1 Augustus Edward Vincent	17 Jan. 91	6 Aug. 92			
4	...	2 William Maynard Carlisle Crowe	25 July 91	25 Jan. 93			
4	...	2 Henry Glanville-Allen Moore, Adjutant 28 Jan. 94	2 Sept. 91	3 Mar. 93			
4	...	2 Arthur Seymour Toogood	20 Feb. 92	19 Apr. 93			
4	...	Graham Walton	20 Feb. 92	3 May 93			
4	...	1 Frederick George Skipwith	12 Mar. 92	28 Jan. 94			
3	...	2 Eric Madden Murray	9 Apr. 92	25 Oct. 94			
		SECOND LIEUTENANTS.					
3	...	2 Harry Cecil Barwell	18 May 92				
3	...	2 Henry Everard Neave	18 May 92				
3	...	1 Alexander Young Spearman	18 June 92				
3	...	2 Arthur James Poole	18 June 92				
3	...	1 Charles Edward Etches	19 Nov. 92				
2	...	1 Hugh Martin Alers Hankey	22 Feb. 93				
2	...	1 Boyd Robert Horsbrugh	25 Feb. 93				
2	...	1 John Edward Speranza	26 Apr. 93				
2	...	2 George Norman Bowes Forster	20 May 93				
2	...	1 William Charles Christie	21 Oct. 93				
1	...	2 Horace Wm. Wallace Onslow Carey	2 June 94				
1	...	2 John Basil Roland Bacchus	12 Dec. 94				
12		Quarter Masters.—2 George Rance, 20 Oct. 83; Hon. Captain, 20 Oct. 93. 1 Charles Joseph Dixon, 1 May 91; Hon. Lieut.					

¹ The Hon. Sir Francis Colborne served in Canada in suppression of the rebellion in 1838-39, and was present in the action of St. Eustache. Served throughout the Eastern campaign of 1854-55, as Assistant Quarter Master General to the 3rd Division, including the battles of Alma, Balaklava, and Inkerman, siege and fall of Sebastopol (Medal with four Clasps, Brevet of Lt.Colonel, CB., Knight of the Legion of Honor, 5th Class of the Medjidie, Sardinian and Turkish Medals). Commanded the Perak Expedition in 1875-76 (Medal with Clasp).

[For remainder of Notes, see end of Royal Fusiliers, p. 243a.

Facings Blue.—*Agents*, Messrs. Cox and Co.

1st Battalion returned from Bengal, 1880.
2nd Battalion embarked for Bengal, 1878.

The Royal Fusiliers (City of London Regiment). 243

1st Batt., **Kurrachee, Bombay.**
2nd Batt., **Guernsey.**
] *Formerly the 7th (Royal Fusiliers) Regiment.* [**Regimental District No. 7.—Hounslow.**

(The 3rd, 4th, and 5th Battalions are formed of the 3rd Middlesex, the London and the 4th Middlesex Militia respectively.)

The United Red and White Rose within the Garter, and the Crown over it. The White Horse. "**MARTINIQUE**" "**TALAVERA**" "**ALBUHERA**" "**BADAJOZ**" "**SALAMANCA**" "**VITTORIA**" "**PYRENEES**" "**ORTHES**" "**TOULOUSE**" "**PENINSULA**" "**ALMA**" "**INKERMAN**" "**SEVASTOPOL**" "**KANDAHAR, 1880**" "**AFGHANISTAN, 1879-80.**"

Years' Ser. Full Pay	Half Pay						
31	...	Colonel.—Sir Richard Wilbraham,[1] KCB. 2nd Lt. P25 Mar. 28; Lt. 25 May 33; Capt. P22 July 36; Bt.Major, 31 Dec. 41; Major, P19 Jan. 44; Bt.Lt.Colonel, 11 Nov. 51; Colonel, 28 Nov. 54; Major General, 26 Jan. 66; Lt.General, 21 Mar. 74; General, 1 Oct. 77; Colonel Royal Fusiliers, 15 Sept. 81.						
26	...	Lieutenant Colonels.—2 Gardiner Frederic Guyon, Ensign, P31 Jan. 65; Lieut. 16 May 68; Capt. 7 Aug. 78; Major, 20 Dec. 82; Lt.Colonel, 11 Dec. 91.						
		1 p.s.c. Charles Lysaght Mortimer, Ensign, P1 Sept. 69; Lieut. 28 Oct. 71; Capt. 21 June 80; Major, 11 Dec. 85; Lt.Colonel, 3 Sept. 94.						

		MAJORS.	ENSIGN OR 2ND LIEUT.	LIEUT.	CAPTAIN.	BREV. MAJ.	MAJOR.
26	...	1 Robert Preston Birkett Rodick[10]	P 9 Feb. 70	28 Oct. 71	10 Sept. 80	......	19 Dec. 86
22	...	2 Charles David Myers Gall[11]		9 Aug. 73	28 Jan. 82	......	19 Dec. 86
21	...	2 Colin George Donald[12]		21 Sept. 74	30 May 83	......	3 Sept. 90
21	...	1 George Ewbank Briggs		13 June 74	16 Feb. 84	......	18 Feb. 91
16	...	Hector Archibald MacDonald,[13] DSO, serving with the Egyptian Army	7 Jan. 80	1 July 81	18 Jan. 88	......	8 July 91
20	...	1 Francis Charles Annesley		27 June 75	24 Mar. 82	......	2 Mar. 92
20	...	Graham Cludde Herbert,[17] Adj. 2 Vol. Bn. N. Staffordshire Regt. 15 Mar. 92		11 Feb. 76	24 Sept. 84	......	3 Sept. 94
19	...	2 Arthur Nugent		29 Nov. 76	31 Dec. 84	......	5 Dec. 94
		CAPTAINS.					
17	...	2 Edward Joshua Cooper (Depot)		11 Sept. 78	13 Feb. 85		
15	...	1 Francis Allix Wilkinson[21]	11 Aug. 80	1 July 81	14 May 87		
16	1 4/18	William Lachlan Forbes,[22] Adj. 1 Vol. Bn. Gordon Highlanders 15 Dec. 90	1 May 78	1 July 81	10 June 87		
15	...	Cuthbert Hy. Morrice, Adj. 3 Bn. 21 Nov. 92	23 Oct. 80	1 July 81	20 Mar. 88		
15	...	Harry Gordon Dunning,[23] DSO. on Special Service, Uganda	22 Jan. 81	1 July 81	28 Nov. 88		
16	...	1 Hon. Herbert Hiley Stafford Addington	14 Jan. 80	1 July 81	5 June 89		
13	...	1 Cecil Fowler Burton		9 Sept. 82	13 Nov. 89		
13	...	Henry Herbert Nicholson, Adj. 3 Vol. Bn. Gordon Highlanders 18 Nov. 92		9 Sept. 82	15 Dec. 90		
13	...	2 Hugh Walter George Campbell		10 Mar. 83	18 Feb. 91		
12	...	2 Stanley Bird, at Staff College		25 Aug. 83	26 Mar. 91		
16	...	Douglas Jas. Hamilton,[24] Adj. 5 Bn. 8 Dec. 91	14 Jan. 80	1 July 81	1 Jan. 91		
12	...	2 Roger Hall		25 Aug. 83	7 July 91		
12	...	1 p.s.c. Reginald John Pinney		6 Feb. 84	8 Dec. 91		
11	...	2 Charles John Stanton		14 May 84	11 Dec. 91		
11	...	2 Charles Tyrell Shipley		23 Aug. 84	2 Mar. 92		
11	...	Edward Henry Cox		12 Nov. 84	15 Mar. 92		
11	...	Cecil Francis Heyworth-Savage,[25] Adjutant 4 Battalion 17 Dec. 94		7 Feb. 85	15 Mar. 92		
11	...	1 William Bernard Hickie		7 Feb. 85	18 Nov. 92		
11	...	1 Thomas Percival England		7 Feb. 85	21 Nov. 92		
13	...	1 Steuart Menzies		10 May 82	19 Apr. 93		
11	...	2 Sydney Turing Barlow Lawford		7 Feb. 85	3 Sept. 94		
		LIEUTENANTS.					
11	...	2 Guy Louis Busson du Maurier		7 Feb. 85			
10	...	1 Walter Gilbert Barton Browne		6 May 85			
10	...	1 Fitzmaurice Thomas Favre Scoones		6 May 85			
10	...	2 Norman Reginald M'Mahon[26]		23 May 85			
10	...	George Reginald Lascelles, Aide de Camp to Sir R. Harrison 1 May 90		25 Nov. 85			
10	...	2 Richard Fowler-Butler		30 Jan. 86			
10	...	1 Charles Cattley Carr (Depot)		30 Jan. 86			
9	...	2 Henry Edward Berkeley Newenham, Adjutant 28 Feb. 94		25 Aug. 86			
9	...	2 Charles FitzClarence		10 Nov. 86			
8	...	2 James Douglas Sparks	14 Sept. 87	26 Mar. 91			
6	...	2 Henry Adolphus Smith Wright	26 Oct. 89	8 July 91			
5	...	1 Thomas Raymond Mallock, Adjutant 2 July 94	31 May 90	8 Dec. 91			
6	...	2 Vivian Henry (Depot)	9 Nov. 89	11 Dec. 91			
7	...	2 Septimus Frederick Legge	10 Nov. 88	16 Oct. 91			
5	...	1 Arthur Colin Roberts	17 Dec. 90	26 June 92			
5	...	1 Allen Victor Johnson	4 Mar. 91	26 June 92			
4	...	Rainald Owen Burne, Army Serv. Corps	2 May 91	21 Nov. 92			
4	...	2 Richard George Hely Hutchinson	13 May 91	25 Nov. 92			
6	...	2 Edward Bunbury North	5 Feb. 90	17 Mar. 92			
4	...	2 Walter Levinge Thurburn	9 Sept. 91	23 Mar. 93			
4	...	2 Mortimer Pawson Hancock	10 Oct. 91	23 June 93			
4	...	1 Arthur Henry Turing	9 Jan. 92	3 Sept. 94			
4	...	2 Alfred Harry Sanders	27 Jan. 92	1 Jan. 95			
		SECOND LIEUTENANTS.					
3	...	1 George Clement Halbot	18 May 92				
3	...	1 Reginald Cossley Batt	18 May 92				
3	...	1 Bartholomew George Price	18 June 92				
3	...	1 Thomas Kershaw Gaskell, Commandant Ghizree Sanitarium	19 Oct. 92				
3	...	1 de Courcy Ireland	17 Dec. 92				
3	...	1 Ferdinand Bigg-Wither	21 Jan. 93				
3	...	1 Cecil Rudall Overton	15 Mar. 93				
2	...	1 George David Bruce	20 May 93				
2	...	1 William Frederick Sweny	27 Sept. 93				
1	...	1 Henry Alexander Walker	12 Dec. 94				
1	...	Lionel George Tempest Stone	6 Mar. 95				

243a The Royal Fusiliers (City of London Regiment).

Years' Ser. Full Pay	Half Pay	
		Paymasters.—1 Walter G. B. Browne, Lieut. 1 Battalion (acting).
1	...	Quarter Masters.—1 Henry Reginald Bell, 18 July 94; Hon. Lieut.
1	...	2 Edward Inkerman Bell, 16 Jan. 95; Hon. Lieut.

Facings Blue.—Agents, Messrs. Cox and Co.
1st Battalion embarked for Gibraltar, 1885.   2nd Battalion returned from India, 29 March 89.

¹ Sir Richard Wilbraham served the Syrian campaign of 1840-41, including the advance on Gaza and affair near Askelon (Brevet of Major, Medal, and Turkish Medal). Served the Eastern campaign of 1854-55 as an Assistant Adjutant General, including the battle of the Alma and the siege and fall of Sebastopol (mentioned in despatches, Brevet of Colonel and Unattached Lt.-Colonel, CB., Medal with two Clasps, Officer of the Legion of Honor, 3rd Class of the Medjidie, and Turkish Medal).
¹⁰ Major Rodick served in the Afghan war in 1879-80, and was present in the engagement at Kokeran (mentioned in despatches), in the defence of Candahar, and at the battle of Candahar (Medal with Clasp).
¹¹ Major Gall served in the Afghan war in 1879-80, took part in the defence of Candahar including the sortie of Deh Khojah, and was present at the battle of Candahar (Medal with Clasp). Served in the Soudan campaign in 1885 (Medal with Clasp, and Khedive's Star).
¹² Major Donald served in the Afghan war in 1878-79 in the Transport Department (Medal).
¹³ Major MacDonald served in the Afghan war in 1879-80, and was present in the affair at Karatiga (mentioned in despatches), in the engagement at Charasiab on 6th October 1879 (mentioned in despatches), with the Maidan Expedition, in the operations around Cabul in December 1879, and in the engagement at Charasiab on 25th April 1880; accompanied Sir Frederick Roberts in the march to Cabul, and was present at the reconnaissance of 31st August and at the battle of Candahar (promoted Second Lieutenant, Medal with three Clasps, and Bronze Decoration). Served in the Boer war of 1881. Served in the operations near Suakin in December 1888, including the engagement at Gemaizah (mentioned in despatches, Medal with Clasp, and Khedive's Star), and in 1889 including the engagement at Toski (mentioned in despatches, DSO., and Clasp); was present at the capture of Tokar in 1891 (3rd Class of the Osmanieh).
¹⁷ Major Herbert served in the Afghan war in 1880, and took part in the defence of Candahar including the sortie of Deh Khojah (Medal).
²¹ Captain Wilkinson served with the Burmese Expedition in 1886-87 as Brigade Transport Officer (mentioned in despatches, Medal with Clasp).
²² Captain Forbes served in the Afghan war in 1879-80, and took part in the defence of Candahar, and was present at the battle of Candahar (Medal with Clasp). Served with the Burmese Expedition in 1885-86 (Medal with two Clasps).
²³ Captain Dunning served in the operations of the Soudan Frontier Field Force in 1887, including the engagement at Sarras (mentioned in despatches, Medal, 4th Class of the Osmanieh, and Khedive's Star); and in the operations on the Soudan frontier in 1889 including the engagement at Toski (mentioned in despatches, DSO. and Clasp).
²⁴ Captain Hamilton served with the 2nd Battalion Coldstream Guards in the Egyptian war of 1882, and was present in the engagement at Tel-el-Mahuta and at the battle of Tel-el-Kebir (Medal with Clasp, and Khedive's Star). Served in the expedition to the Soudan in 1885 with the 1st Battalion of the Coldstream Guards, and was present in the engagement at Hasheen, at that near Tofrek on the 24th March, and at the destruction of Temai (Clasp).
²⁵ Captain Heyworth Savage served with the Burmese Expedition in 1885-87 (Medal with two Clasps).
²⁶ Lieut. M'Mahon served with the Burmese Expedition in 1885-87 (Medal with Clasp).

Record of the Services of the 2nd Battalion Royal Fusiliers (City of London Regiment),—formerly the 7th Regiment.

Formed in Canada in 1795 from 1st Battalion; reduced, 1796. Again raised in 1804 in England, and proceeded to Ireland in 1808. To the Peninsula, 1809. To Jersey, 1811. To England, 1814. Absorbed into 1st Battalion, 1815. Raised again in England in 1857. To Gibraltar, 1858. To Malta, 1864. To Canada, 1865. To England, 1867. To Ireland, 1871. To India, 1873 (Afghan war in 1879-80). To England, 1889.

Continuation of Notes to the Royal Warwickshire Regiment.

¹⁴ Major Forbes served in the Afghan war in 1879-80, and was present in the engagements at Ahmed Kheyl as Orderly Officer to Brigadier General Palliser (mentioned in despatches) and Padkao Shana (mentioned in despatches, Medal with Clasp).
¹⁵ Major Maunsell served in the Afghan war in 1879-80 as Transport Officer with the Khyber Division of the Cabul Field Force (Medal).
¹⁶ Major M. Quayle Jones served with the Bechuanaland Expedition under Sir Charles Warren in 1884-85 as Major in the 4th Pioneer Regiment.
¹⁸ Captain Etheridge served in the Afghan war of 1878-80, including the operations in the Koorum Valley and with the Zaimusht Expedition (Medal).
¹⁹ Captain Cockburn served in the Nile Expedition in 1884-85 with the 1st Battalion of the Royal Sussex Regiment, and took part in the operations of the Desert Column under Sir Herbert Stewart (Medal with Clasp, and Khedive's Star).
²⁰ Captain Mockler served with the Burmese Expedition in 1885-86 as Transport Officer (mentioned in despatches, Medal with Clasp).
²¹ Captain Chambers served with the Chin-Lushai Expeditionary Force in 1889-90 as Assistant Intelligence Officer (mentioned in despatches, Medal with Clasp).
²² Captain Dyas served in the Soudan campaign in 1885 (Medal with Clasp, and Khedive's Star). Served with the Burmese Expedition in 1885-86 (mentioned in despatches, Medal with Clasp), and again in 1887-89 (Clasp).

Record of the Services of the 2nd Battalion Royal Warwickshire Regiment (formerly the 6th Royal Regiment).

Raised in England in 1857, and proceeded to Gibraltar, 1848. To Corfu, 1862. To the West Indies, 1864. England, 1867. To Ireland, 1870. To the Channel Islands, 1874. To England, 1875. To India, 1878.

The King's (Liverpool Regiment). 244

1st Batt., Halifax, N.S.
2nd Batt., Colchester.] *Formerly the 8th (The King's) Regiment.* [Regimental District No. 8.—Warrington.

(The 3rd and 4th Battalions are formed of the 2nd Lancashire Militia.)

" *Nec aspera terrent.*" The White Horse within the Garter. The Royal Cypher, with the Imperial Crown. "BLENHEIM" "RAMILLIES" "OUDENARDE" "MALPLAQUET" "DETTINGEN" "EGYPT" (with the Sphinx) "MARTINIQUE" "NIAGARA" "DELHI" "LUCKNOW" "PEIWAR KOTAL" "AFGHANISTAN, 1878-80," "BURMA, 1885-87."

Years' Ser.		
Full Pay	Half Pay	
31	19/12	**Colonel.**—George William Powlett Bingham,¹ *CB. Ensign,* P16 Feb. 38; *Lieut.* 8 April 42; *Captain,* P12 Sept. 48; *Major,* 10 Dec. 56; *Lt.Colonel,* 29 Nov. 57; *Colonel,* 29 Nov. 62; *Major General,* 28 June 68; *Lieut.General,* 19 Dec. 80; *General,* 1 July 81; *Colonel* Liverpool Regiment, 1 May 91.
22	...	**Lieutenant Colonels.**—2 Stanley Napier Roberts,³ *Ensign,* 17 July 63; *Lieut.* 11 Jan. 67; *Captain,* 25 Feb. 75; *Major,* 1 Feb. 82; *Lt.Colonel,* 28 Dec. 92.
		1 George Robert Stone, *Lieut.* 28 Feb. 74; *Capt.* 19 May 81; *Major,* 17 Dec. 84; *Lt.Colonel,* 4 Feb. 95.

			2ND LIEUT.	LIEUT.	CAPTAIN.	BREV.MAJ.	MAJOR.
		MAJORS.					
21	...	2 Standish Henry Harrison¹⁰		2 Dec. 74	1 July 81		19 Nov. 90
21	...	1 Llewellyn Salusbury Mellor¹¹		15 Jan. 75	1 July 81		26 Nov. 90
20	...	2 Henry John Robert St. George Richardson		10 Sept. 75	1 Feb. 82		16 Jan. 91
19	...	2 Percy Schletter¹² (*Depot*)		13 June 76	7 Mar. 82		22 Sept. 91
19	...	1 Arthur Charles Greaves Banning¹³		10 Sept. 76	15 April 82		20 May 92
19	...	O'Donnel Colley Grattan,¹⁴ *Adjutant* 2 *Vol. Bn. Liverpool Regt.* 19 Jan. 91		10 Mar. 77	30 Sept. 82		26 Oct. 92
18	...	Lawrence Charles Dundas,¹⁶ *DSO. D.A.A. General, Bengal,* 23 June 90	30 Jan. 78	30 Jan. 80	16 Jan. 84		28 Dec. 92
18	...	Horatio James Evans,¹⁴ *at Staff College*	30 Jan. 78	25 Feb. 80	16 Jan. 84		4 Feb. 95
		CAPTAINS.					
17	...	1 Edm. Harrington Molyneux-Seel	4 Dec. 78	17 Apr. 80	10 Dec. 84		
16	...	Valentine Augustus Milman Fowler,¹⁷ *Adj.* 3 *Bn. S. Lanc. Regt.* 1 Sept. 93	13 Aug. 79	7 July 80	27 Jan. 85		
16	...	1 Henry John Wright Guise	13 Aug. 79	25 Aug. 80	12 Apr. 86		
16	...	1 Gilbert Thomas Elliot (*Depot*)	13 Aug. 79	4 Sept. 80	1 Oct. 86		
16	...	Augustus St. John Seton,¹⁹ *Adjutant Presidency Volunteers* 28 Sept. 91	11 Oct. 79	15 Oct. 80	19 Oct. 87		
16	...	1 George Campbell	14 Jan. 80	9 Feb. 81	5 Nov. 87		
16	...	2 Stapleton Lynch Cotton²⁰	25 Feb. 80	1 July 81	10 June 88		
15	...	Arthur William Howard Tripp,²¹ *Adj.* 3 *Battalion* 1 Nov. 93	11 Aug. 80	1 July 81	25 Nov. 88		
14	...	2 Louis St. Clair Nicholson,²³ *Adjutant* 19 Oct. 91		22 Oct. 81	1 Apr. 89		
14	...	Harington Swann, *Adj.* 1 *Volunteer Battalion Liverpool Regt.* 20 May 92		28 Jan. 82	23 June 90		
14	...	2 William Henry Scales²³		22 Oct. 81	28 July 90		
11	...	2 Cleveland Edmund Greenway²¹		12 Nov. 84	19 Nov. 90		
10	...	Thomas George Powell Glynn, *Adj.* 1 *London Rifle Volunteers* 1 March 93		6 May 85	16 Jan. 91		
10	...	2 Hastings Ross-Johnson²²		6 May 85	16 Jan. 91		
12	...	2 Hugh Elliot²¹		6 Feb. 84	17 Feb. 92		
10	...	1 Hugh Walters Beaumont Johnson		29 Aug. 85	20 May 92		
10	...	1 Ralph Legh Hartley		25 Nov. 85	28 Dec. 92		
11	...	2 George Beaumont		11 Mar. 85	1 Mar. 93		
9	...	1 James Mountifort Longfield		25 Aug. 86	1 Nov. 93		
13	...	2 William Henry Goodair²⁴		27 Jan. 83	9 Mar. 92		
		LIEUTENANTS.					
8	...	2 Robert Stair Stewart	11 Feb. 88	18 Sept. 89			
8	...	1 Charles Sutton Edridge	11 Feb. 88	18 Sept. 89			
8	...	2 Humphry Stephen Woolrych	11 Feb. 88	18 Sept. 89			
8	...	2 Mortimer Stopford Adye	11 Feb. 88	15 Oct. 89			
7	...	1 William Stirling-Bannatyne	22 Aug. 88	7 May 90			
7	...	2 Arthur Henry Portal Harrisson	10 Nov. 88	31 July 90			
7	...	2 Alfred Durham Plomer (*Depot*)	23 Mar. 89	11 Aug. 90			
6	...	1 Charles John Steavenson, *Adjutant* 20 March 94	21 Dec. 89	16 Jan. 91			
6	...	Rupert Lionel Van der Gucht	29 Mar. 90	5 Aug. 91			
5	...	2 Francis Cranstoun Ommanney	8 Oct. 90	23 Jan. 92			
5	...	1 Kenneth Lyon Tupman	29 Oct. 90	23 Jan. 92			
5	...	1 Wilfred Romney Rawlinson	29 Oct. 90	17 Feb. 92			
5	...	1 Ernest Frederic Knight	29 Oct. 90	20 May 92			
5	...	2 Francis Hyslop	17 Jan. 91	28 Dec. 92			
5	...	1 Llewellyn Murray Jones	27 Jan. 91	1 Mar. 93			
5	...	1 Charles Lister Parmiter	17 Jan. 91	13 Sept. 93			
5	...	1 Vivian Telford Bailey	17 Jan. 91	1 Nov. 93			
5	...	Aubrey de Sausmarez Burton	18 Feb. 91	4 Nov. 93			
5	...	1 Francis James Austin	25 Mar. 91	1 Jan. 94			
4	...	2 Lionel Frederic Leader	10 Oct. 91	12 Sept. 94			
4	...	2 Charles Harington Harington	9 Jan. 92	4 Feb. 95			
		SECOND LIEUTENANTS.					
4	...	2 Charles Leathley Armitage	12 Mar. 92				
3	...	1 George Howard Brush	22 Feb. 93				
3	...	2 Thomas Winter Sheppard	25 Feb. 93				
3	...	2 Bernard St. John Warren Hastings	25 Feb. 93				
2	...	2 William Richard Pinwill	20 May 93				
2	...	2 Reginald Petley Fox	19 July 93				
2	...	2 Harold Alfred Denham	21 Oct. 93				
2	...	1 Francis John Langdon	23 Dec. 93				
2	...	1 George Montague Philip Hawthorn	7 Mar. 94				
2	...	2 Frank Rowland Ewart	7 Mar. 94				
1	...	1 Igino Depiro D'Amico	12 Dec. 94				
1	...	George Aubrey Howard-Vyse	6 Mar. 95				

¹² Major Schletter served in the Afghan war of 1878-80 with the 2nd Battalion of the 8th Foot, including the operations in the Koorum Valley (Medal).

¹³ Major Banning served in the Afghan war in 1878-9, and was present at the attack and capture of the Peiwar Kotal (Medal with Clasp).

¹⁴ Majors Grattan and Evans served in the Afghan war in 1878-79, took part in the operations in the Koorum Valley, and were present at the capture of the Peiwar Kotal and in the engagement at Ali Kheyl (Medal with Clasp).

244a The King's (Liverpool Regiment).

Years' Ser.		
Full Pay	Half Pay	
		Paymasters.—2
		1
14	...	*Quarter Masters.*—2 Thomas Vincent Jones,[27] 7 Jan. 82; *Hon. Captain*, 7 Jan. 92.
10	...	1 Thomas Holland Pollitt, 13 May 85; *Hon. Lieut.*

Facings Blue.—*Agents*, Messrs. Cox and Co.

1st Battalion embarked for Bermuda, 11 Feb. 1891.   2nd Battalion returned from India, 13 Nov. 92.

[1] General Bingham served with the 64th Regt. in the Persian campaign of 1856-57, including the storm and capture of Reshire, surrender of Bushire, night attack and battle of Kooshab (Medal with Clasp). Served in Bengal and N.W. Provinces in suppressing the mutiny in 1857-58; present with Havelock's Column in the actions of Futtehpore, Aoung, Pandoo Nuddee, Cawnpore, Onao, Buseerutgunge (1st and 2nd), Boorbeakechowkee, and Bithoor; commanded a convoy with provisions from Cawnpore to Alumbagh; served in defence of the Alumbagh, and afterwards in the actions at La Martiniere and the second relief of Lucknow; commanded the Regt. during the defence of Cawnpore and defeat of the Gwalior mutineers, as also in the actions of Kala Nuddee and Kerkeroulie—on General Penny being killed succeeded to the command of the whole Infantry Brigade—capture of Bareilly, Shahjehanpore, Bunnie, Mahomdie, pursuit of the enemy the following day, and occupation of Mahomdie (mentioned in despatches. *CB.*, Medal with Clasp).

[3] Lt.Colonel Roberts served throughout the Afghan war of 1878-80 with the 2nd Battalion of the Liverpool Regiment, and was present at the capture of the Peiwar Kotal (Medal with Clasp). Served in the Burmese Expedition in 1885-87 with the 2nd Battalion of the Liverpool Regiment (Medal with Clasp).

[10] Major Harrison served in the Burmese Expedition in 1885-87 with the 2nd Battalion of the Liverpool Regiment (Medal with Clasp).

[11] Major Mellor served throughout the Afghan war of 1878-80 with the 2nd Battalion of the 8th Foot, and was present in the operations in the Koorum Valley and at the capture of the Peiwar Kotal (Medal with Clasp).

[16] Major Dundas served throughout the Afghan war of 1878-80 with the 2nd Battalion of the Liverpool Regiment, and was present during the operations in the Koorum Valley and at the capture of the Peiwar Kotal (Medal with Clasp). Served with the Burmese Expedition in 1885-86 (*DSO.*, and Medal with Clasp).

[17] Captain Fowler served with the 2nd Battalion of the 8th Foot in the Afghan war of 1880 (Medal). Served in the Burmese Expedition in 1886-87 with the 2nd Battalion of the Liverpool Regiment (Medal with Clasp).

[19] Captain Seton served in the Burmese Expedition in 1885-87 with the 2nd Battalion of the Liverpool Regiment (Medal with Clasp).

[20] Captain Cotton served in the Afghan war in 1880 with the 2nd Battalion of the Liverpool Regiment (Medal). Served in the Burmese Expedition in 1885-87 with the 2nd Battalion of the Liverpool Regiment (Medal with Clasp).

[21] Captains Tripp, Greenway, and H. Elliot served in the Burmese Expedition in 1885-87 with the 2nd Battalion of the Liverpool Regiment (Medal with Clasp).

[22] Captain Ross-Johnson served in the Burmese Expedition in 1885-87 with the 2nd Battalion of the Liverpool Regiment (Medal with Clasp); and with the Chin-Lushai Expeditionary Force in 1889-90 (Clasp).

[23] Captains Nicholson and Scales served in the Burmese Expedition in 1886-87 with the 2nd Battalion of the Liverpool Regiment (Medal with Clasp).

[24] Captain Goodair served with the expedition to the Soudan in 1885, and was present in the engagements at Hasheen and the Tofrek zereba, and at the destruction of Temai (Medal with two Clasps, and Khedive's Star).

[27] Captain T. V. Jones served in the Afghan war of 1878-80 with the 2nd Battalion of the Liverpool Regiment, and was present at the capture of the Peiwar Kotal (Medal with Clasp). Served with the Burmese Expedition in 1885-87 (Medal with Clasp).

Record of the Services of the 1st Battalion King's (Liverpool) Regiment,—formerly the 8th Regiment.

Raised in 1685 and styled "Princess Anne of Denmark's Regiment." To Ireland, 1689 to 1692. England, to 1696. Netherlands, to 1697. England, to 1698. Ireland, to 1701. Low Countries, to 1714. England, to 1742. Flanders and Germany, to 1745. The Netherlands, to 1748. England, to 1750. Gibraltar, to 1752. England, to 1760. Germany, to 1763. England, to 1768. Canada, to 1785. England, to 1791. Ireland, to 1794. West Indies, to 1799. Minorca, Egypt and Gibraltar, to 1803. England, to 1805. [2nd Battalion raised, 1803.] Germany, to 1806. England, to Aug. 1807. Copenhagen, to Oct. 1807. England, to 1808. Canada, to 1815 (capture of Niagara). England, to 1816. Ireland, to 1818. Malta, to 1819. Ionian Islands, to 1824. England, to 1826. Scotland, to 1827. Ireland, to 1830. Nova Scotia, to 1833. Bermuda, from June to July, 1833. Jamaica, to 1839. Halifax, to 1841. Ireland, to 1843. England, to 1846. India, to 1860 (capture of Delhi, relief of Lucknow). England, to 1865. Ireland, to 1866. Malta, to 1868. India, to 1878. Aden, to 1879. England, to 1882. Ireland, to 1889. England, to 1891. Bermuda, 1891.

Record of the Services of the 2nd Battalion.

Raised in 1756. Numbered 63rd Foot, 1758. Raised again, 1804, and proceeded to Scotland to 1809. Holland, to 1810. Jersey, 1810. Canada, to 1815. England, 1815, when it was merged in the 1st Battalion. Again raised, 1857. Gibraltar, to 1863. Malta, to 1868. England, to 1873. Ireland, to 1876. England, to 1877. India, to 1885 (Afghan war, 1878-80—capture of the Peiwar Kotal). Burmah, to 1887. India, 1887.

Continuation of Notes to the Lincolnshire Regiment.

[1] Sir Julius Glyn served as Field Adjutant to the Force under Sir Harry Smith in the action with and defeat of the rebel Boers at Boem Plaats (horse killed). Served with the Rifle Brigade in the Kaffir war of 1852-53 (Medal). Also the Eastern campaign as a Brigade Major and Assistant Adjutant General in the Light Division, including the battles of Alma and Inkerman, and siege of Sebastopol (Medal with three Clasps, Brevets of Major and Lt.Colonel, Knight of the Legion of Honor, 5th Class of the Medjidie, and Turkish Medal). Served the Indian campaigns of 1857-59, including the defeat of the Gwalior Contingent at Cawnpore on 6th December, final capture of Lucknow, action at Nawabgunge (commanded Battalion), and subsequent operations (Medal with Clasp, and *CB.*).

[2] Lt.Colonel Huntley commanded a detachment of the 10th Regiment at the attack and capture of the Kapayan Stockades, Sunghie Ujong, Malay Peninsula, in 1874. Also served throughout the Perak Expedition in 1875-76 (Medal with Clasp). Proceeded to South Africa in November 1878, and served throughout the Zulu war of 1879, first as Transport Officer to the 2nd Division in its advance to Ulundi, and afterwards as Senior Transport Officer with Baker Russell's Column (Brevet of Major, Medal with Clasp).

[3] Lt.Colonel Verner served in the Afghan war of 1878-80, and was present in the engagements at Ahmed Kheyl and Urzoo near Ghuznee (Medal with Clasp).

Record of the Services of the 2nd Battalion Lincolnshire Regiment (formerly the 10th Regiment).

Raised in Ireland in 1858 and proceeded to the Cape of Good Hope, 1860. To India, 1864. To England, 1873. To Malta, 1878. To Gibraltar, 1881. To India, 1882.

1st Batt., Umballa, Bengal.] **The Norfolk Regiment.** [*Regimental District* No. 9.— Norwich. 245
2nd Batt., Aldershot.
Formerly the 9th (East Norfolk) Regiment.
(The 3rd and 4th Battalions are formed of the 1st and 2nd Norfolk Militia respectively.)
The figure of Britannia. "ROLEIA" "VIMIERA" "CORUNNA" "BUSACO" "SALAMANCA" "VITTORIA" "ST.
SEBASTIAN" "NIVE" "PENINSULA" "CABOOL, 1842" "MOODKEE" "FEROZESHAH" "SOBRAON" "SEVASTOPOL"
"KABUL, 1879" "AFGHANISTAN, 1879-80."

Years' Ser.							
Full Pay.	Half Pay.						
30	...	Colonel.—Thomas Edmond Knox,[1] CB. *Ens.* 26 Jan. 38; *Lt.* P24 June 42; *Capt.* 31 July 46; *Major,* P17 Aug. 52; *Lt.Colonel,* 17 Sept. 58; *Colonel,* 24 Jan. 63; *Major General,* 28 Oct. 68; *Lieut.General,* 8 May 81; *General,* 1 July 81; *Colonel* Hampshire Regiment, 11 Nov. 88; *Colonel* Norfolk Regiment, 15 Dec. 93.						
26	...	Lieutenant Colonels.—2 Charles Herbert Shepherd,[2] *DSO. Ensign,* P2 May 65 ; *Lieut.* P15 Feb. 71 ; *Capt.* 1 Sept. 80; *Major,* 10 Jan. 83; *Lt.Colonel,* 1 May 93. 1 Divie Knighton Robertson, *Ensign,* P26 Sept. P71 ; *Lieut.* 28 Oct. 71; *Capt.* 23 June 81 ; *Major,* 28 June 84 ; *Lt.Colonel,* 20 Aug. 94.						

		MAJORS.	ENSIGN OR 2ND LIEUT.	LIEUT.	CAPTAIN.	BREV.MAJ.	MAJOR.
23	...	2 Frederick Alexander Currie		3 July 72	28 Nov. 8:		28 June 84
28	...	1 Octavius Allcard	P29 May 67	28 Oct. 71	15 Feb. 81		12 Dec. 85
23	...	2 William Gibbs Straghan[7]		6 Mar. 73	21 Mar. 82		20 Aug. 90
23	...	p.s.c. John Henry Sewell,[8] *Assistant Adjutant General, Burmah,* 17 Apr.91 }		8 May 72	1 Apr. 82		5 Sept. 90
21	...	2 Lewis Horace Phillips[9] *(Depot)*		2 Dec. 74	19 July 82		19 Sept. 90
19	...	1 Ralph Henry Fenwick Lombe[10]		11 Sept. 76	21 July 82		2 Mar. 92
22	...	Otway Mayne,[11] *Adj.* 4 *Volunteer Battalion* 1 Apr. 90 }		28 Feb. 74	30 Dec. 82		1 May 9
18	...	1 James Lorne Govan[12]	30 Jan. 78	25 Aug. 80	26 Mar. 84		20 Aug. 94
		CAPTAINS.					
18	...	2 Andrew Cracroft Becher[13]	30 Jan. 78	1 Sept. 80	21 May 84		
17	...	2 William Francis Percy[14]	1 May 78	16 Nov. 80	28 June 84		
16	1 1/5	FrederickJohnDealtry Lugard,[15] *DSO. serving under Royal Niger Company* }	11 May 78	1 Jan. 81	13 Aug. 85		
17	...	2 Charles Edward Borton[16]	4 Dec. 78	15 Feb. 81	13 Aug. 85		
16	...	1 Sausmarez Dobrée Shortt *(Depot)*	31 Jan. 80	23 June 81	20 Sept. 86		
15	...	p.s.c. Henry Richard Beadon Donne,[17] *Station Staff Officer, Delhi,* 1 Nov. 94 }	11 Aug. 80	1 July 81	1 May 87		
15	...	1 Walter Hervey Besant[19]	11 Aug. 30	1 July 81	30 June 87		
15	...	H. J. Whiteside M'Kenzie Kennedy, *Adj.* 1 *Vol.Bn.Norfolk Regt.*25 Aug. 90 }	23 Oct. 80	1 July 81	30 June 87		
15	...	2 Robert Francis Cunynghame Baker	22 Jan. 81	1 July 81	1 Oct. 87		
15	...	1 Henry Yelverton Beale[20]	22 Jan. 81	1 July 81	29 Feb. 88	29 Dec. 93	
14	...	1 Godfrey Massy, *Station Staff Officer, Dugshai,* 20 Oct. 94 }		22 Oct. 81	21 July 88		
13	...	2 Arthur John Hamilton Luard[21]		10 May 82	1 May 89		
13	...	1 William Sandars Dods		10 May 82	11 Sept. 89		
13	...	William Corrie Tonge,[22] *Adjutant* 3 *Battalion* 15 Jan. 92 }		9 Sept. 82	11 Sept. 89		
13	...	1 Charles Barry Close[23]		9 Sept. 82	19 June 90		
12	...	Harry Hannam Applewhaite,*Adjutant* 2 *Vol. Bn. Norfolk Regt.* 15 May 93 }		25 Aug. 83	20 Aug. 90		
12	...	Philip Christian William Trevor,[24] *Ordnance Store Dept.* }		25 Aug. 83	25 Aug. 90		
12	...	John Marriott		5 Dec. 83	5 Sept. 90		
12	...	William Raymond Inglis, *Adjutant* 4 *Battalion* 30 June 92 }		19 Dec. 83	19 Sept. 90		
11	...	2 Evelyn Chiappini Peebles		23 Aug. 84	5 Dec. 94		
		LIEUTENANTS.					
11	...	2 Charles Ross, *serving with Egyptian Army*		12 Nov. 84			
10	...	2 George William Brownrigg Brett,[26] *Adjutant* 6 Mar. 94 }		9 May 85			
10	...	1 Gilbert Head		29 Aug. 85			
10	...	1 Evelyn William Margesson, *Adjutant* 20 Aug. 91 }		29 Aug. 85			
10	...	1 Arthur Lytton Bellamy *(Depot)*		30 Jan. 86			
10	...	1 Arthur Edward Lascelles, *Station Staff Officer, Murree,* 24 Sept. 94 }		30 Jan. 86			
10	...	2 Charles Henry Renwick		30 Jan. 86			
10	...	2 Henry George Lovinge		30 Jan. 86			
8	...	2 Edward Wingfield Verner[28]	4 May 87	18 Dec. 89			
8	...	1 Frank Leonard Northcott	8 Feb. 88	18 Dec. 89			
8	...	1 Charles Cautley Blackburn	11 Feb. 88	23 Apr. 90			
8	...	2 Colin Robert Ballard	11 Feb. 88	23 Apr. 90			
7	...	2 George Evans Bruce	22 Aug. 88	25 Aug. 90			
7	...	2 Edward Peter Strickland[30]	10 Nov. 88	29 Apr. 91			
6	...	2 Alexander Straton Campbell	21 Dec. 89	22 Nov. 91			
5	...	2 Francis de Beauvoir Bell	3 May 90	2 Dec. 91			
5	...	2 George Ernest Wilson	1 Oct. 90	12 May 92			
5	...	1 Arthur James Vavasor Durell	8 Oct. 90	28 Sept. 93			
5	...	1 Ernest Francis Knox	29 Nov. 90	6 Oct. 93			
4	...	2 John William Vincent Carroll *(Depot)*	10 Oct. 91	13 June 94			
4	...	2 Arthur Gordor Learoyd	5 Dec. 91	20 Aug. 94			
		SECOND LIEUTENANTS.					
4	...	Claude Francis John Stewart, *Army Service Corps* }	5 Dec. 91				
4	...	2 Francis Cecil Lodge	12 Mar. 92				
3	...	1 George Dodd	18 June 92				
3	...	1 John Ouseley Sherlock	13 Aug. 92				
3	...	2 Ernest Henry Denne Stracey	13 Aug. 92				
3	...	2 Robert William Hare	19 Nov. 92				
2	...	2 Percival Staverton Mathews	19 July 93				
2	...	1 William Fanshawe Loudon Gordon	19 July 93				
2	...	2 John Boyd Orr[33]	18 Oct. 93				
2	...	2 Walter Evelyn Cramer-Roberts	14 Feb. 94				
1	...	1 Noel Gilliat Thompson	2 June 94				
1	...	2 Charles Alban Grevis Shoubridge	10 Oct. 94				
1	...	1 Guy Rutherford Prescott Wheatley	20 Feb. 95				

[16] Captain Borton served in the Afghan war in 1879-80, and took part in the advance to Cabul, including the operations around Jugdulluck and the engagement at Saidabad (Medal with Clasp). Served in the Burmese Expedition in 1887-89 with the 2nd Battalion Norfolk Regiment (Medal with Clasp).

[19] Captain Besant served with the Nile Expedition in 1884-85 (Medal with Clasp, and Khedive's Star). Served with the Egyptian Frontier Field Force in 1885-86, and was present in the engagement at Giniss (4th Class of the Osmanieh for his services with the Egyptian Army); also served in the operations near Suakin in December 1888 including the engagement at Gemaizah (mentioned in despatches, Clasp, and 3rd Class of the Medjidie), and in the operations in 1891 including the capture of Tokar (3rd Class of the Osmanieh).

[21] Captain Luard served with the Burmese Expedition in 1886-87 on special service in the 4th Brigade; was Brigade Transport Officer to the Minbu Command from August 1887 to January 1888 (Medal with Clasp); also served with the first Chin Field Force in Upper Burmah in 1888-89 (Clasp).

Years'Ser.		
Full Pay.	Half Pay.	
		Paymasters.—1 George E. Bruce, *Lieut.* 1 *Battalion (acting).*
9	...	*Quarter Masters.*—1 John Connors, 1 Apr. 86; *Hon. Lieut.*
3	...	2 William Vince,[31] 1 March 93; *Hon. Lieut.*

Facings White.—*Agents,* Messrs. Holt and Co.
1st Batt. embarked for Gibraltar, 1887. *2nd Batt.* returned from Burmah, 1890.

[1] General Knox commanded the 67th Regiment throughout the campaign of 1860 in China, including the action of Sinho, taking of Tongho, and led the storming party across the main ditch at the taking of the inner Takoo Fort, when seventy-seven officers and men of the 67th were killed or wounded; also present at the surrender of Pekin—mentioned in despatches by Major General Sir Robert Napier for "having led the wing of his Regiment at the taking of the Taku Forts in the most spirited manner. . . . Among the first to enter after swimming the ditch" (*CB.*, Medal with two Clasps).

[2] Lt.Colonel Shepherd served with the Burmese Expedition in 1887-89 with the 2nd Battalion Norfolk Regiment including the operations in the Chin Hills (mentioned in despatches, *DSO.*, and Medal with Clasp); also served with the Chin-Lushai Expeditionary Force in 1889-90 (Clasp).

[5] Major Currie served in the expedition against the Jowaki Afreedees in 1877-78 (Medal with Clasp). Served with the 9th Foot in the Afghan war in 1878-79, and was present at the attack and capture of Ali Musjid as Superintendent of Army Signalling in Sir Samuel Browne's Division (Medal with Clasp).

[7] Major Straghan served in the Jowaki campaign of 1877-78 (Medal with Clasp). Served with the 9th Regiment in the Afghan war of 1879-80 (part of the time as Acting Adjutant), and took part in the advance to Cabul under Brigadier General Charles Gough, including the engagements at Jugdulluck and Saidabad and the relief of Sherpore (Medal with Clasp).

[8] Major Sewell served with the 15th Hussars in the Candahar Column in the Afghan war of 1878-80, including the advance to Khelat-i-Ghilzai; also served with the Thull-Chotiali Field Force under Major General Biddulph, and in the Column under Major General Phayre in Southern Afghanistan (Medal). Served in the Boer war in 1881. Served in the Nile Expedition in 1884-85 with the Column under Sir Herbert Stewart as Adjutant to the 1st Battalion of the Mounted Infantry, and was present at the action at Abu Klea (Medal with two Clasps, and Khedive's Star). Served in the operations in Burmah in 1889-90 with the Tonhon Expedition—severely wounded (Medal with Clasp).

[9] Major Phillips served with the expedition against the Jowaki Afreedees in 1877-78 (Medal with Clasp). Served with the 9th Foot in the Afghan war of 1878-80, including the operations in the Khyber Pass (Medal).

[10] Major Lombe served in the Jowaki campaign of 1877-78 (Medal with Clasp). Served in the Afghan war in 1879-80, took part in the advance to Cabul under Brigadier General Charles Gough (mentioned in despatches), and was present in the engagement at Saidabad (Medal with Clasp). Served with the Burmese Expedition in 1887-89 with the 2nd Battalion Norfolk Regiment including the operations in the Chin Hills (mentioned in despatches, *DSO.*, and Clasp); also served with the Chin-Lushai Expeditionary Force in 1889-90 (Clasp).

[11] Major Mayne served with the expedition against the Jowaki Afreedees in 1877-78 (Medal with Clasp). Served with the 9th Foot in the Afghan war in 1879-80, and took part in the advance to Cabul under Brigadier General Charles Gough, including the engagements at Jugdulluck and Saidabad and the relief of Sherpore (Medal with Clasp). Served with the Burmese Expedition in 1887-89 with the 2nd Battalion Norfolk Regiment and was severely wounded during the operations in the Chin Country (Clasp).

[12] Major Govan served in the Afghan war in 1879-80, took part in the march to Cabul in December 1879 under Brigadier General Charles Gough including the relief of Sherpore, and was present in the engagement at Shekabad (mentioned in despatches, Medal with Clasp).

[13] Captain Becher served in the Afghan war in 1879-80 with the 2nd Battalion of the 9th Foot, and took part in the advance to the relief of Cabul under Brigadier General Charles Gough, including the engagements at Jugdulluck and Saidabad; was afterwards Orderly Officer to Brigadier General Gough (Medal with Clasp).

[14] Captain Percy served in the Burmese Expedition in 1887-89 with the 2nd Battalion Norfolk Regiment (Medal with Clasp).

[15] Captain Lugard served with the 9th Foot in the Afghan war in 1879-80, and was present in the engagement at Saidabad (Medal). Served in the Soudan campaign in 1885 with the Indian Transport (Medal with Clasp, and Khedive's Star). Served with the Burmese Expedition in 1886-87 (mentioned in despatches, *DSO.*, and Medal with Clasp).

[18] Captain Donne served with the Burmese Expedition in 1888-89 attached to the Intelligence Branch during the expedition to the Northern Shan States, and afterwards with the Chin-Field Force (Medal with Clasp).

[20] Major Beale served in the operations in the Northern Chin Hills, Burmah, in 1892-93 (mentioned in despatches, Brevet of Major).

[22] Captain Tongo served with the Bechuanaland Expedition in 1884-85 under Sir Charles Warren on special service.

[23] Captain Close served in the Burmese Expedition in 1887-89 with the 2nd Battalion Norfolk Regiment (Medal with Clasp).

[24] Captain Trevor served in the Burmese Expedition in 1887-89 with the 2nd Battalion Norfolk Regiment (Medal with Clasp).

[26] Lieut. Brett served with the Burmese Expedition in 1887-89 including the operations in the Chin Hills (Medal with Clasp).

[28] Lieut. Verner served in the Burmese Expedition in 1887-89 with the 2nd Battalion Norfolk Regiment (Medal with Clasp).

[30] Lieut. Strickland served in the Burmese Expedition in 1887-89 with the 2nd Battalion Norfolk Regiment (Medal with Clasp).

[31] Lieut. Vince served with the Jowaki Afreedee Expedition in 1877-78 (Medal with Clasp). Served in the Afghan war in 1879-80 (Medal). Served with the Burmese Expedition in 1887-89 (Clasp).

[35] Second Lieut. Orr.—See Civil Decorations for Gallantry, "Hart's Annual Army List," p. 786.

Record of the Services of the 2nd Battalion Norfolk Regiment (formerly the 9th East Norfolk Regiment).

Raised in 1799, and proceeded to Holland. To England, 1799. To Spain, 1800. To England, 1801. Reduced, 1802. Again raised, 1804. To Portugal and Spain, 1808. To England, 1813. Reduced, 1815. Raised again, 1857. To the Ionian Islands, 1858. To Gibraltar, 1864. To Hong Kong, 1864. To Yokohama, 1866. To Ireland, 1868. To England, 1869. To India, 1874 (Afghanistan, 1879). To Burmah, 1888. To England, 1890.

1st Batt., Malta.
2nd Batt., Straits Settlements.] **The Lincolnshire Regiment.** [*Regimental District No. 10.—Lincoln.*] 246-8

Formerly the 10th (North Lincolnshire) Regiment.
(The 3rd and 4th Battalions are formed of the North and South Lincoln Militia respectively.)
"BLENHEIM" "RAMILLIES" "OUDENARDE" "MALPLAQUET" "EGYPT" (with the Sphinx). "PENINSULA"
"SOBRAON" "PUNJAUB" "MOOLTAN" "GOOJERAT" "LUCKNOW."

Years' Ser.								
Full Pay	Half Pay							
32	...	Colonel.—Sir Julius Richard Glyn,[1] KCB. Ensign, 16 July 41; Lt. P13 Oct. 43; Captain, P9 June 48; Bt. Major, 12 Dec. 54; Bt.Lt.Col. 6 June 56; Major, 5 June 57; Lt.Col. P15 Nov. 61; Colonel, 29 Oct. 62; Major Gen. 28 June 68; Lt.Gen. 5 Nov. 80; General, 1 Oct. 86; Colonel Lincolnshire Regt. 29 Nov. 90.						
31	...	Lieutenant Colonels.—2 Hongham Charles Huntley,[2] Ensign, P8 Sept. 63; Lt. P9 May 65; Captain, 31 Oct. 77; Bt.Major, 29 Nov. 79; Major, 11 Mar. 82; Lt.Colonel, 17 Feb. 92.						
		1 Thomas Edward Verner,[3] Ensign, P25 Jan. 65; Lt. P23 Mar. 66; Capt. 21 Apr. 77; Major, 1 July 81; Lt.Colonel, 11 March 92.						

		MAJORS.	**ENSIGN OR 2ND LIEUT.**	**LIEUT.**	**CAPTAIN.**	**BREV.MAJ.**	**MAJOR.**
29	...	1 Henry Robert Roberts	P19 Feb. 67	P15 Feb. 71	17 May 79	......	25 Apr. 85
25	...	2 Frank Robert Lowth[19]	P30 Nov. 70	28 Oct. 71	11 Mar. 81	......	17 Feb. 92
23	...	1 Henry Compton Sewell Goldfrap	......	30 April 73	3 May 81	......	25 Apr. 92
22	...	Beresford Robert Hamilton, *Adj.* 17 (*North*) *Middlesex R. Vols.* 1 Apr. 90	......	12 Nov. 73	18 June 81	......	8 Jan. 93
22	...	1 Henry Wiley	......	28 Feb. 74	11 Mar. 82	......	31 May 93
21	...	p.s.c. Charles Rudyerd Simpson, *Professor at the Staff College (with rank of Lt.Colonel)* 12 Sept. 94	......	21 Sept. 74	19 July 82	......	7 June 93
19	...	2 Beamish St. John Barter, *Staff College*	......	11 Sept. 76	16 Feb. 83	......	16 Dec. 93
19	...	2 Thomas Hulkes Bingham Day	......	29 Nov. 76	7 Apr. 83	......	23 Dec. 93
		CAPTAINS.					
19	...	1 Edgar Herapath	......	11 Feb. 77	1 July 84		
18	...	2 Henry Bolton Mainwaring (*Depot*)	16 Feb. 78	21 Aug. 78	18 Nov. 84		
17	...	William Cecil Welsh Rawlinson,[20] *Instructor R. M. College*, 1 Sept. 94	1 May 78	31 Aug. 78	10 Jan. 85		
17	...	George Augustus Ivatt, *Adj.* 3 *Bn.* 14 Aug. 93	1 May 78	1 Feb. 79	13 May 85		
19	...	2 Walter Latham Cox	......	11 Feb. 77	13 May 85		
17	...	Wm. Griffith Grant, *Adj.* 4 *Bn.* 20 Sept. 91	11 May 78	22 Oct. 79	3 May 86		
17	...	2 Henry Du Buisson	25 May 78	26 May 80	18 June 86		
16	...	Percy Francis Raikes Nowbury, *Adj.* 3 *Bn. Border Regiment* 3 March 90	13 Aug. 79	11 Mar. 81	18 June 87		
16	...	p.s.c. Richard Narrien Gamble,[22] *Aide de Camp to Lt.General H. Rowlands* 16 Jan. 94	13 Aug. 79	2 April 81	3 Aug. 87		
16	...	2 Frederic Charles LLoyd	14 Jan. 80	1 July 81	11 Mar. 88		
15	...	2 Arthur William Dewar, **Adjutant** 15 Dec. 92	23 Oct. 80	1 July 81	13 Aug. 88		
15	...	1 Victor George Ralph Johnson	22 Jan. 81	1 July 81	2 Mar. 92		
15	...	John Pim, *Adj.* 2 *Vol. Bn. Lincolnshire Regiment* 4 May 94	19 Feb. 81	1 July 81	11 Mar. 92		
14	...	1 Robert Pacy Maxwell	......	22 Oct.	25 Apr. 92		
13	...	1 James Forrest	......	9 Sept. 82	14 Aug. 93		
13	...	2 George Bunbury M'Andrew	......	9 Sept. 82	16 Dec. 93		
12	...	2 Arthur Sanders Vanrenen	......	12 May 83	23 Dec. 93		
12	...	1 Alfred Edward Hubbard (*Depot*)	......	25 Aug. 83	16 Jan. 94		
11	...	1 Richard Ormsby Cumberland	......	14 May 84	5 May 94		
11	...	1 Charles Gaitskell	......	28 Feb. 85	1 Sept. 94		
10	...	1 Ernest Berdoe Wilkinson,[23] **Adjutant** 14 May 94	......	25 Nov. 85	1 Sept. 94		
8	...	1 Francis Stewart Evelyn Boothby (*Depot*)	4 May 87	29 Dec. 88	12 Sept. 94		
		LIEUTENANTS.					
8	...	1 Harold Ernest Walter	4 May 87	29 Dec. 88			
8	...	1 Henry Montfort Gardner	4 May 87	29 Dec. 88			
8	...	2 Herbert Henry Harington	16 Nov. 87	14 May 90			
8	...	2 Jasper Joseph Howley	11 Feb. 88	9 July 90			
7	...	1 James Reynolds Maxwell Marsh	10 Nov. 88	13 Jan. 90			
6	...	1 William Grosvenor Harding	21 Dec. 89	11 Mar. 92			
5	...	2 Cuthbert Charles Lambert Barlow	3 May 90	25 Apr. 92			
5	...	1 Samuel FitzGibbon Cox	28 June 90	9 June 92			
5	...	1 Lancelot Edwards	17 Jan. 91	7 Oct. 92			
5	...	1 Phillip Michael Peters (*Depot*)	4 Mar. 91	10 Oct. 92			
4	...	1 Hugh Edward Richard Boxer	27 Jan. 92	14 Aug. 93			
3	...	1 Edward Abadie Plunkett	18 May 92	23 Dec. 93			
3	...	1 Herbert Bryan	18 June 92	16 Jan. 94			
3	...	1 Charles George Lyall	13 July 92	28 Mar. 94			
3	...	2 Dudley Harcourt Fleming Grant	13 Aug. 92	5 May 94			
3	...	2 Percy Orr Hazelton	13 Aug. 92	1 Sept. 94			
3	...	2 Walter Backhouse Hulke	19 Nov. 92	12 Sept. 94			
3	...	2 Henry Montague Cave Orr	19 Nov. 92	5 Dec. 94			
		SECOND LIEUTENANTS.					
2	...	2 Sidney Walter Burton	19 Nov. 92				
2	...	2 George Freshfield Davies	19 Nov. 92				
2	...	1 Edward Tatchell	9 Sept. 93				
2	...	2 Gordon Fairfax Prichard	7 Mar. 94				
2	...	1 Frederick William Stringer	7 Mar. 94				
1	...	2 Frank Douglas Gibbes	2 June 94				
1	...	1 Coverley James Rennie	10 Oct. 94				
1	...	1 Richard Henry George Wilson	10 Oct. 94				
1	...	1 Robert d'Esterre Hill	10 Oct. 94				
1	...	1 Louis Arundell Burrowes	22 Dec. 94				
1	...	1 Hamilton Hodgson	20 Feb. 95				
1	...	1 Roland Hay Morant	6 Mar. 95				

[19] Major Lowth served with the 10th Regiment in the Perak Expedition in 1875, and was present when a combined Naval and Military force attacked and captured the Stockades and five guns at Passir Sala (Medal with Clasp).

[20] Captain Rawlinson served with the Sikkim Expedition in 1888 on the Staff of Sir Steuart Bayley, Lt. Governor of Bengal, and was present in the engagement at Gnathong (Medal with Clasp).

[22] Captain Gamble served with the Bechuanaland Expedition under Sir Charles Warren in 1884-85 as Adjutant of the 3rd Mounted Rifles.

[23] Captain Wilkinson served with the Burmese Expedition in 1887-88 (Medal with Clasp).

[*For remainder of Notes, see end of Liverpool Regiment, p. 244a.*]

Facings White.—*Agents*, Messrs. Cox and Co.
1st Battalion embarked for Malta, 31 Jan. 1895.
2nd Battalion embarked for Malta, 1878.

Paymasters.—1
2

| 24 | ... | *Quarter Masters.*—2 James Templeton, 27 Sept. 71; *Hon. Captain*, 27 Sept. 81. |
| 1 | ... | 1 Thomas Fitzpatrick, 12 Dec. 94; *Hon. Lieut.* |

249 1st Batt., Nowshera, Bengal.
2nd Batt., Plymouth.] **The Devonshire Regiment.** [*Regimental District* No. 11.—Exeter.

Formerly the 11th (North Devonshire) Regiment.
(The 3rd and 4th Battalions are formed of the 2nd and 1st Devon Militia respectively.
The Castle of Exeter. "*Semper Fidelis.*" "DETTINGEN" "SALAMANCA" "PYRENEES" "NIVELLE" "NIVE" "ORTHES" "TOULOUSE" "PENINSULA" "AFGHANISTAN, 1879-80."

Years' Ser. Full Pay.	ial Pay.		Ensign or 2nd Lieut.	Lieut.	Captain.	Brev. Maj.	Major.
		Colonel.—*Sir George Harry Smith Willis*,[1] *KCB. Ensign,* P23 April 41; *Lieut.* P30 Aug. 44; *Captain*, P27 Dec. 50; *Bt. Major*, 12 Dec. 54; *Bt. Lt. Colonel*, 6 June 56; *Major*, 19 Dec. 57; *Colonel*, 26 June 62; *Major General*, 28 June 68; *Lt. General*, 8 May 80; *General*, 11 May 87; *Colonel* Devonshire Regt. 11 July 90.						
33	...	Lieutenant Colonels.—1 Philip Henry Smith, *Ensign,* P16 Jan. 63; *Lieut.* P10 July 66; *Captain*, 7 Mar. 77; *Major*, 18 Jan. 82; *Lt. Colonel*, 19 May 91.						
30	...	2 Dennett Thomas Kinder,[6] *Ensign*, 9 May 65; *Lt.* P14 Mar. 68; *Captain*, 31 Oct. 77; *Major*, 18 Nov. 82; *Lt. Colonel*, 18 Jan. 92.						

		MAJORS.					
30	...	2 Jas. Herbert Yule[8] (*Bt. Lt. Col.* 5 Oct. 92)	1 Dec. 65	P22 Aug. 68	16 Feb. 78	......	1 July 83
27	...	1 p.s.c. George Dodsworth Stawell, Commandant Murree Depot 13 Oct. 94	P 2 May 68	P 9 Feb. 70	19 May 80	......	19 May 85
26	...	1 William Prinn Noon[10]	P11 Feb. 70	28 Oct. 71	8 June 81	......	26 Oct. 85
26	...	1 James Browne	P19 May 69	28 Oct. 71	1 July 81	......	4 Feb. 91
23	...	1 p.s.c. George Mackworth Bullock	......	24 April 72	22 Feb. 82	......	19 May 91
21	...	1 Sam. K. Harries,[11] *Adj.* 4 *Bn.* 1 Mar. 92	......	26 June 74	18 Nov. 82	......	18 Jan. 92
20	...	1 Cecil William Park,[12] *Assist. Adjutant General, Madras,* 15 Nov. 93	......	5 June 75	9 Jan. 83	......	2 Mar. 92
20	...	2 Arthur Graves Spratt	......	23 May 75	20 Mar. 82	......	9 Nov. 92
		CAPTAINS.					
20	...	2 Herbert Batson	......	10 Sept. 75	1 July 83		
19	...	2 George Halford D'Oyly	......	27 June 76	20 June 84		
19	...	Thos. Arthur Harkness Davies,[13] *DSO. Dep. Assist. Adj. Gen. Burmah,* 7 Feb. 94	......	11 Sept. 76	22 Nov. 84		
18	...	Fred. Clift. Briggs,[14] *Adj.* 1 *Vol. Bn.* 1 Apr. 91	......	6 Oct. 77	24 Dec. 84		
18	...	2 Montagu Creighton Curry, **Adjutant** 10 Apr. 94	13 Oct. 77	25 July 78	5 Oct. 85		
16	...	Robert Bennett, *Ordnance Store Dept.*	13 Aug. 79	18 Dec. 80	26 Oct. 85		
16	...	2 Henry Howard Bedingfeld	13 Aug. 79	4 Feb. 80	26 Oct. 85		
16	...	p.s.c. John MacNeill Walter, *Station Staff Officer, Cawnpore,* 4 July 94	14 Jan. 80	26 Nov. 80	28 Oct. 85		
16	...	George John Ellicombe,[14] *Adjutant* 5 *Volunteer Battalion* 21 Sept. 91	11 Oct. 79	1 July 81	20 Sept. 86		
15	...	1 Mainwaring George Jacson	11 Aug. 80	1 July 81	1 Oct. 86		
15	...	1 William Boutcher Lafone	11 Aug. 80	1 July 81	18 Jan. 88		
15	...	1 Richard Hammett Kirkwood	22 Jan. 81	1 July 81	1 July 88		
15	...	2 Vancouver Alexander Richards	22 Jan. 81	1 July 81	31 Oct. 90		
14	...	1 Reginald John Hall Parlby	23 Apr. 81	1 July 81	1 Nov. 90		
14	...	Arthur John Gore, *Adj.* 3 *Bn.* 14 Nov. 92	......	28 Jan. 82	28 Jan. 91		
13	...	Philip Urban Walter Vigors, *Adjutant* 4 *Volunteer Battalion* 6 Oct. 91	......	9 Sept. 82	4 Feb. 91		
13	...	Norton James Goodwyn, *serving with the Egyptian Army*	......	9 Sept. 82	1 Apr. 91		
13	...	1 Allan Laing Peebles	......	10 Mar. 83	1 Apr. 91		
12	...	Percival George Elgood, *Adjutant* 3 *Volunteer Battalion* 1 July 93	......	25 Aug. 83	19 May 91		
12	...	1 William Theophilus Bartlett (*Depot*)	......	25 Aug. 83	6 Oct. 91		
11	...	2 Guy William George Sanders	......	23 Aug. 84	15 Apr. 92		
11	...	1 Gerald Meade Gloster, **Adjutant** 5 Dec. 94	......	12 Nov. 84	20 Oct. 92		
10	...	2 Reginald Seward Ruston	......	9 May 85	9 Nov. 92		
10	...	2 Herbert Reginald Vyvyan	......	23 May 85	14 Nov. 92		
		LIEUTENANTS.					
9	...	2 Joseph Oates Travers	......	25 Aug. 86			
9	...	2 Reynold Percy Smith	......	25 Aug. 86			
9	...	2 Edward George Williams	......	25 Aug. 86			
9	...	William Bernard Lauder, *Ordnance Store Department*	......	10 Nov. 86			
9	...	1 Louis Jean Bols	5 Feb. 87	22 Sept. 89			
7	...	1 Hurdis Secundus Lalande Ravenshaw	8 Dec. 88	18 Dec. 89			
7	...	2 Jasper Fitzgerald Radcliffe	22 Aug. 88	31 Oct. 90			
7	...	1 Charles Spencer Warwick	31 Oct. 88	31 Oct. 90			
6	...	1 John Prescott Law	6 July 89	15 Dec. 90			
6	...	2 Evelyn FitzGerald Michell Wood	9 Nov. 89	25 Mar. 91			
5	...	2 Balfour Logan (*Depot*)	28 June 90	1 Apr. 91			
5	...	1 Edward Conway Wren	28 June 90	22 Sept. 91			
5	...	2 Charles Clarkson Martin Maynard, *Supdt. of Gymnasia, Malta,* 25 Oct. 94	8 Oct. 90	8 Dec. 91			
5	...	1 Frederick John Newton Chichester	12 Nov. 90	7 Sept. 92			
5	...	1 Arthur Bourke Souter	17 Dec. 90	18 Oct. 92			
5	...	1 Edmund Merritt Morris	17 Dec. 90	20 Oct. 92			
5	...	1 Nathaniel Robert Radcliffe	17 Jan. 91	9 Nov. 92			
5	...	Edmund Lenthal Swifte	17 Jan. 91	14 Nov. 92			
5	...	1 Denis Charles Kane	17 Jan. 91	1 Jan. 93			
5	...	1 George Edmund White	4 Mar. 91	28 Jan. 94			
5	...	1 Charles Herbert Marshall	4 Mar. 91	22 Mar. 94			
5	...	1 Gwyn Thomas	4 Mar. 91	23 Nov. 94			
		SECOND LIEUTENANTS.					
4	...	1 Phillip Hampton Price-Dent	23 May 91				
4	...	2 James Edward Ignatius Masterson	15 July 91				
4	...	1 Augustus Frederick Dalzel	27 Jan. 92				
3	...	William Cortlandt Anderson	9 Apr. 92				
3	...	2 Maurice Harold Grant	17 Dec. 92				
3	...	1 Henry Norman Field	25 Feb. 93				
3	...	1 Edward Havelock Oliphant	25 Feb. 93				
3	...	2 Ernest Douglas Young	25 Feb. 93				
2	...	1 Cyril Vivian Windsor	21 June 93				
1	...	2 Walter Meredith Goodwyn	2 June 94				
1	...	2 Percival Ernest Knapp	10 Oct. 94				
1	...	2 Noël Luxmoore	12 Dec. 94				
1	...	2 John Darnley Ingles	12 Dec. 94				

Paymaster.—1 Edmund M. Morris, *Lieut.* 1 *Battalion* (acting).
6 ... Quarter Masters.—1 Henry Honner, 5 June 89; *Hon. Capt.* 16 Apr. 94.
4 ... 2 Charles Birch, 23 Sept. 91; *Hon. Lieut.*

[1] Sir George Willis served uninterruptedly throughout the Eastern campaign from April 1854 to July 1856;—with the 77th Regt. until May 1855, after which as D.A.Q.M. General at Head Quarters, and as A.Q.M. General of the 4th Division; was present at the affairs on the Bulganac and at Balnklava, battles of Alma and Inkerman, assault of the Quarries, attack of the Redan on 18th June, battle of Tchernaya, final assault of the Redan on 8th Sept., and served for upwards of seven months in the Trenches, including the repulse of several sorties, and was frequently in command in the advance Trenches (Medal with three Clasps, Brevets of Major and Lt. Colonel, Grand Officer of the Legion of Honor, Sardinian and Turkish Medals, and 5th Class of the Medjidie). Served in the Egyptian war of 1882 in command of the 1st Division and was present at the engagements of El Magfar, Tel-el-Mahuta, and Kassasin (9th Sept.), and in the battle of Tel-el-Kebir — slightly wounded (five times mentioned in despatches, received the thanks of both Houses of Parliament, KCB., Medal with Clasp, 2nd Class of the Osmanieh, and Khedive's Star).

[*For remainder of Notes, see end of the Suffolk Regiment,* p. 251.
Facings White.—*Agents,* Messrs. Cox and Co.
1st Battalion embarked for Egypt, 29 Jan. 1891. 2nd Battalion returned from India, 14 Apr. 93.

| 2nd Batt., Secunderabad, Madras. | **The Suffolk Regiment.** | Regimental District No. 12. Bury St. Edmunds. | 250 |

Formerly the 12th (East Suffolk) Regiment.

(The 3rd and 4th Battalions are formed of the West Suffolk and the Cambridge Militia respectively.)

"DETTINGEN" "MINDEN" "GIBRALTAR" the Castle, Key, and Motto, "*Montis Insignia Calpe.*" "SERINGAPATAM" "INDIA" "SOUTH AFRICA, 1851-2-3" "NEW ZEALAND" "AFGHANISTAN, 1878-80."

Years' Ser.			
Full Pay	Half Pay		
30	...	**Colonel.**—John Maxwell Perceval,[1] *CB. Ensign,* P21 June 33; *Lieut.* P18 Mar. 36; *Captain,* P18 May 38; *Major,* P14 Apr. 46; *Lt. Colonel,* P2 Apr. 50; *Colonel,* 28 Nov 54; *Major General,* 8 Aug. 64; *Lt. General,* 14 Feb. 73; *General,* 1 Oct. 77; *Colonel* 97th Foot, 21 Mar. 74; *Colonel* Suffolk Regiment, 28 Feb. 83.	
27	...	**Lieutenant Colonels.**—2 Owen Williams,[5] *Ensign,* 10 Nov. 65; *Lt.* P17 April 69; *Capt.* 7 Aug. 78; *Major,* 11 Oct. 82; *Lt. Colonel,* 1 Apr. 92.	
		1 Richard Thomas Edward Dowse, *Ensign,* 1 Aug. 68; *Lieut.* 28 May 71; *Capt.* 11 Nov. 79; *Major,* 4 June 84; *Lt. Colonel,* 9 Dec. 94.	

		MAJORS.	ENSIGN OR 2ND LIEUT.	LIEUT.	CAPTAIN.	BREV. MAJ.	MAJOR.
27	...	1 Charles Richard Townley[7]	14 Jan. 69	28 Oct. 71	10 April 80	......	9 April 85
26	...	2 p.s.c. William Randolph Routh	7 July 69	28 Oct. 71	1 Jan. 81	......	18 June 85
23	...	1 Charles Donovan Cave[9] (*Depot*)		8 June 72	3 April 82	......	26 April 86
22	...	p.s.c. Arthur John Watson,[10] *Dep.* A.A.Gen. for Inst. Bengal, 20 July 89		9 Aug. 73	14 Apr. 83	......	21 Oct. 89
20	...	1 p.s.c. Geo. Fred. Campbell Mackenzie[13]		12 Feb. 76	14 July 83	......	30 Nov. 91
20	...	1 Frederick William Scudamore[13]		22 Mar. 76	4 June 84	......	30 Dec. 93
19	...	1 Archibald Cyril Cubitt,[15] *Adj.* 5 *Admin. Bn. Cawnpore Rifle Vols.* 16 Jan. 90		11 Sept. 76	1 Dec. 84	......	18 Apr. 94
17	...	2 Frank Graham[13]	11 May 78	5 Aug. 80	18 Mar. 85	......	9 Dec. 94
		CAPTAINS.					
19	...	1 Charles Anthony Clare Deane		26 Aug. 76	16 June 84		
16	...	1 Arthur Faulconer Poulton[13]	13 Aug. 79	25 Sept. 80	9 Apr. 85		
16	...	1 Edward Arthur Kemble[18]	13 Aug. 79	12 Oct. 80	18 May 85		
16	...	William Reade De-la-Père Lloyd,[21] *Adj.* 3 *Battalion* 24 Dec. 91	14 Jan. 80	1 Jan. 81	15 May 86		
15	...	Vivian Waldegrave Hall Graham, *Adjutant* 2 *Volunteer Bn. Suffolk Regt.* 15 June 94	11 Aug. 80	1 July 81	1 Sept. 86		
14	...	2 William Freme Coleman,[22] *Adjutant* 1 Apr. 92	23 April 81	1 July 81	1 Dec. 86		
14	...	1 p.s.c. Edward Montagu[12]		22 Oct. 81	9 Mar. 89		
13	...	2 Vere Isham (*Depot*)		10 May 82	25 Sept. 89		
13	...	Leonard Julius Shadwell,[23] *Station Staff Officer, Bellary,* 3 Oct. 94		29 July 82	25 Sept. 89		
13	...	Lenox Conyngham Arbuthnot, *Adj. Bangalore Rifle Vols.* 30 Sept. 91		27 Jan. 83	27 Mar. 89		
13	...	2 Louis Hamilton Bazalgette		9 Sept. 82	16 July 90		
13	...	2 Casimir Henry Claude Van Straubenzee		9 Sept. 82	9 Dec. 90		
12	...	2 Charles Frederick Lennock,[21] *Adjutant* 4 *Battalion* 7 March 93		5 Dec. 83	1 Apr. 92		
12	...	2 William Keates		5 Dec. 83	9 Apr. 92		
12	...	1 Sydney Boyle Stotherd		30 Jan. 84	26 Apr. 93		
12	...	1 Cuthbert Montague De Gruyther,[21] *Staff College*		6 Feb. 84	18 Apr. 94		
11	...	2 William Berkeley Wallace[21]		7 Feb. 85	15 June 94		
10	...	Edward Papillon Prest,[21] *Adjutant* 1 *Volunteer Battalion* 1 Feb. 95		6 May 85	15 June 94		
10	...	1 Charles Arthur Hugh Brett,[21] *Adjutant* 10 Jan. 95		9 May 85	15 June 94		
11	...	2 William St. Lawrence Saunders		12 Nov. 84	3 Oct. 94		
10	...	2 William Gordon Thomson		9 May 85	14 Nov. 94		
10	...	1 Henry Peregrine Leader, *Supdt. of Gymnasia, Colchester,* 29 Nov. 94		2 Sept. 85	9 Dec. 94		
		LIEUTENANTS.					
10	...	1 Cecil Robert Fryer[21]		25 Nov. 85			
10	...	1 Walter Herbert Newland Glossop[21]		25 Nov. 85			
9	...	1 George Herbert Stewart Browne[21]		25 Aug. 86			
9	...	1 Alexander Braithwaite Morgan[21] (*Depot*)		25 Aug. 86			
9	...	2 Robert Burrell Unwin	5 Feb. 87	16 July 90			
8	...	1 Samuel Eyre Massy Lloyd (*Depot*)	4 May 87	9 Dec. 90			
8	...	2 Frank Gadsden Davies[21]	16 Nov. 87	10 Jan. 91			
8	...	2 Henry Frederick Hugh Clifford	11 Feb. 88	25 Feb. 91			
7	...	2 John Randolph Gorst Hopkins	10 Nov. 88	2 July 91			
7	...	2 Frank Dalzell Finlay	28 Nov. 88	31 Mar. 92			
6	...	2 Charles Douglas Parry Crooke	21 Sept. 89	1 Apr. 92			
6	...	2 John Alexander Shakespear Murray	9 Nov. 89	9 Apr. 92			
6	...	2 Arthur Wale Brown	9 Nov. 89	26 Apr. 93			
6	...	2 Hugh Barrow Rowlands	9 Nov. 89	5 Dec. 93			
6	...	2 Charles Hampden Turner	21 Dec. 89	18 Apr. 94			
5	...	2 Ernest Christie Doughty	29 Oct. 90	15 June 94			
5	...	1 Charles Philip Wynter	17 Jan. 91	3 Oct. 94			
5	...	2 Walter John William Brackenbury	4 Mar. 91	3 Oct. 94			
4	...	1 Guy Neal Landale Labertouche	9 Jan. 92	14 Nov. 94			
3	...	2 George Douglas Crooke	18 May 92	9 Dec. 94			
		SECOND LIEUTENANTS.					
3	...	1 Francis Alfred Pressland Wilkins	18 May 92				
3	...	Henry Vivian Firth	22 June 92				
3	...	1 Algernon Morland	19 July 92				
2	...	1 Herbert Edward Olivay	4 Oct. 93				
2	...	2 William Harvey Bowden	23 Dec. 93				
2	...	2 Charles Cecil Rowe Murphy	23 Dec. 93				
2	...	2 Robert John Cuming	7 Mar. 94				
1	...	1 Harry d'Arch Smith	10 Oct. 94				
1	...	1 Richard Charles Albert Whittington	10 Oct. 94				
1	...	1 Arthur Stansfield Peebles	12 Dec. 94				
1	...	2 Frederick Alexander White	12 Dec. 94				
1	...	1 Seymour James Carey	20 Feb. 95				

[21] Captains Lloyd, Lennock, De Gruyther, Wallace, Prest and Brett, Lieuts. Fryer, Glossop, Browne, Morgan, and Davies served in the Hazara Expedition in 1888 with the 1st Battalion Suffolk Regiment (Medal with Clasp).

[22] Captain Coleman served with the Nile Expedition in 1884-85 attached to the 1st Battalion of the Royal Sussex Regiment (Medal with Clasp, and Khedive's Star).

[23] Captain Shadwell served in the Hazara Expedition in 1888 as Adjutant to the 1st Battalion Suffolk Regiment (Medal with Clasp).

[25] Captain Lindop.—For War Services, see Army Pay Department.

Years' Ser.	
Full Pay	Half Pay
14	...
4	...

The Suffolk Regiment.

Paymasters.—2 Charles D. P. Crooke, *Lieut.* 2 *Battalion (acting).*
1
Quarter Masters.—2 William Norris,[30] 30 Nov. 81; *Hon. Captain,* 30 Nov. 91.
1 Andrew Smith, 19 Aug. 91; *Hon. Lieut.*

Facings White.—*Agents,* Messrs. Cox and Co.

1st Batt. returned from India, 22 March 1892. 2nd Batt. embarked for Egypt, 18 December 1889.

[1] General Perceval commanded the Reserve Battalion of the 12th Regiment in the Kaffir war of 1852-53, and for his services was nominated a *CB.* (Medal).
[5] Lt.Colonel Williams served with the 1st Battalion 12th Foot in the Afghan war in 1879-80 (Medal). Served in the Hazara Expedition in 1888 with the 1st Battalion Suffolk Regiment (mentioned in despatches, Medal with Clasp).
[7] Major Townley served as Adjutant of the 1st Battalion 12th Foot in the Afghan war of 1878-80, and was present in the engagement at Ali Boghan, the occupation of the Lughman Valley, and the expedition against the Khugianis (Medal).
[9] Major Cave served with the 1st Battalion 12th Foot in the Afghan war in 1879-80 (Medal). Served in the Hazara Expedition in 1888 as Brigade Major to the 4th Column under Brigadier General Galbraith including the engagement at Kotkai (mentioned in despatches, Medal with Clasp).
[10] Major Watson served with the Bechuanaland Expedition under Sir Charles Warren in 1884-85 as Brigade Major. Served in the Hazara Expedition in 1888 as Brigade Major to the 1st Column under Brigadier General Channer (mentioned in despatches, Medal with Clasp).
[13] Majors Mackenzie, Scudamore and Graham, and Captain Poulton served with the 1st Battalion 12th Foot in the Afghan war in 1879-80 (Medal).
[14] Captain Davies served in the Afghan war in 1879-80 with the 11th Regiment (Medal). Served with the Wuntho Expedition in 1891 in command of a detachment of the 2nd Battalion Devonshire Regiment (mentioned in despatches).
[15] Major Cubitt served in the Hazara Expedition in 1888 with the 1st Battalion Suffolk Regiment (Medal with Clasp).
[18] Captain Kemble served with the 1st Battalion 12th Foot in the Afghan war in 1880 (Medal).
[19] Captain Montagu served in the Hazara Expedition in 1888 with the 1st Battalion Suffolk Regiment (Medal with Clasp); also served with the Chin Lushai Expeditionary Force in 1889-90 as Transport Officer Northern Column Chittagong Force under Brigadier General Tregear (Clasp).
[30] Captain Norris served in the Hazara Expedition in 1888 as Quarter Master to the 1st Battalion Suffolk Regiment (mentioned in despatches, Medal with Clasp).

Record of the Services of the 1st Battalion Suffolk Regiment (formerly the 12th Regiment).

Raised in 1685, remaining in England till 1689. Ireland, to 1691. England, to 1699. Ireland, to 1703. West Indies, to 1705. England, to 1708. Flanders, to 1709 (embarked as Marines, but afterwards landed for active service). England, to 1712. Minorca, to 1719. England, to 1742. Flanders and Germany, to 1745. England and Scotland, to 1748. Holland, to 1749. Minorca, to 1752. England, to 1758. (2nd Battalion raised in 1757, and entitled the 65th Regiment in 1758). Flanders and Germany, to 1763 (battle of Minden). England, to 1769. Gibraltar, to 1783 (siege of Gibraltar). Entitled 12th East Suffolk Regiment, 1782. Ireland, to 1794 (in 1790 the greater part of the Regiment served as Marines from June to Dec.). Flanders, to 1795. (Flank Companies to the West Indies, rejoining Head Quarters in 1795). England, to 1796. East Indies, to 1810 (capture of Seringapatam). Mauritius, to 1813. Isle of Bourbon, to 1815. Mauritius, to 1817. (2nd Battalion raised in 1811, and proceeded to Ireland in 1812. To England, Flanders, France, and returned to England, 1815. To Ireland, 1816. Disbanded, 1818.) Ireland, to 1820. England, to 1823. Gibraltar, to 1834. England, to 1835. Ireland, to 1837. Mauritius, to 1847. (Entitled "1st Battalion 12th Regiment" on the raising of the Reserve Battalion in 1842.) England, to 1852. Ireland, to 1854. Australia and Tasmania, to 1863. New Zealand, to 1867 (war of 1863-65). England, to 1872. Ireland, to 1876. East Indies, 1876 (Afghan war of 1878-80; Hazara Expedition in 1888).

Continuation of Notes to the Devonshire Regiment.

[6] Lt.Colonel Kinder served in the Afghan war in 1879-80 with the 11th Regiment (Medal).
[8] Lt.Colonel Yule served in the Afghan war in 1879-80 with the 11th Regiment (Medal). Served with the Burmese Expedition in 1891-92 including the operations in the Chin Hills (Brevet of Lt.Colonel).
[10] Major Noon served in the Afghan war in 1879 with the Transport Staff, and was present at the occupation of Candahar and in the engagement at Ahmed Kheyl (Medal with Clasp).
[11] Major Harries served in the Afghan war in 1878-79 in the Transport Department with the Southern Afghanistan Field Force (Medal).
[12] Major Park served in the Afghan war in 1879-80 as Adjutant with the 2nd Battalion 11th Regiment in Southern Afghanistan (Medal).
[13] Captain Davies served in the Afghan war in 1879-80 with the 11th Regiment (Medal). Served with the Burmese Expedition in 1891-92, and took part in the Wuntho Expedition and in the operations in the Chin Hills (mentioned in despatches, *DSO.*).
[14] Captains Briggs and Ellicombe served with the 11th Regiment in the Afghan war in 1879-80 (Medal).

Record of the Services of the 2nd Battalion Devonshire Regiment (formerly the 11th Regiment).

Raised at Kingston, Yorkshire, in 1858, and proceeded to the Cape of Good Hope, 1861. To Natal, 1864. To Hong Kong and Japan, 1865. To the Cape of Good Hope, 1866. To Ireland, 1870. To Scotland, 1872. To England, 1873. To India, 1877 (Afghan war, 1879-80). To Burmah, 1890.

The Prince Albert's (Somersetshire Light Infantry). 252

1st Batt., Umballa, Bengal.
2nd Batt., Devonport.
] *Formerly the 13th (1st Somersetshire) Prince Albert's Light Infantry.* [Regimental District No. 13.—Taunton.

(The 3rd and 4th Battalions are formed of the 1st and 2nd Somerset Militia respectively.)

"DETTINGEN" "EGYPT" (with the Sphinx). "MARTINIQUE" "AVA" "AFGHANISTAN" "GHUZNEE."
A Mural Crown, superscribed "JELLALABAD" "CABOOL 1842" "SEVASTOPOL" "SOUTH AFRICA, 1878-9"
"BURMA, 1885-87."

Years' Ser. Full Pay.	Half Pay.			Ensign or 2nd Lieut.		Lieut.		Captain.		Brev. Maj.		Major.	
		Colonel.—Lord Mark Kerr,[1] GCB. Ensign, P19 June 35; Lieut. P14 Sept. 38; Captain, P26 June 40; Major, 25 July 51; Lt. Colonel, P30 Dec. 53; Colonel, 28 Nov. 54; Major General, 6 March 68; Lieutenant General, 13 July 76; General, 11 Nov. 78; Colonel 13th Light Infantry, 22 Feb. 80.												
29	...	Lieutenant Colonels.—2 John Miller Elgee Waddy,[13] Ensign, P11 Jan. 67; Lieut. P24 Nov. 69; Captain, 10 Apr. 78; Major, 8 May 85; Lt. Colonel, 14 June 94.												
26	...	1 Arthur Close Borton, Ensign, P24 July 69; Lieut. 28 Oct. 71; Captain, 9 Jan. 79; Major, 28 Dec. 86; Lt. Colonel, 8 Nov. 94.												
		MAJORS.											
26	...	2 Edward John Fownes[13]		8 Feb.	70	28 Oct.	71	8 June	79	......		28 Dec.	86
25	...	1 Edmond Joseph Gallwey[13]		P 6 July	70	28 Oct.	71	26 Feb.	80	......		28 Dec.	86
22	...	Edward Morris Poynten[14]		......		12 Nov.	73	23 May	83	......		23 Dec.	91
22	...	1 Henry Alfred Walsh[12]		......		28 Feb.	74	20 Oct.	83	15 June	85	26 Oct.	92
21	...	Anthony Lumb,[15] *Adj. 6 Volunteer Bn. Manchester Regiment* 14 Jan. 92		......		12 Feb.	75	1 April	85	......		31 Dec.	93
21	...	p.s.c. Raymond Burlton Williams,[13] *Dep. Assist. Adj. Gen., Ceylon,* 15 Nov. 93		......		13 June	74	1 April	85	......		14 June	94
20	...	2 Arthur Williamson Alsager Pollock[16]		......		20 Nov.	75	8 May	85	......		10 July	94
20	...	1 Richard Lloyd Payne,[17] DSO		......		5 Jan.	76	8 May	85	......		8 Nov.	94
		CAPTAINS.											
17	...	2 Chas. Warren Napier-Clavering[19] (*Depot*)		1 May	78	26 Feb.	80	22 July	86				
17	...	Geo. Hen. Holbeche Couchman,[20] DSO, D.A.Q.M. General, Intelligence Branch, Burmah, 18 Apr. 93		11 May	78	20 Mar.	80	1 Aug.	86				
17	...	2 Courtney Heathcote Stisted		1 May	78	20 Nov.	80	28 Dec.	86				
17	...	Herbert Rhys Lloyd,[21] *Adjutant 1 Volunteer Battalion* 5 Dec. 94		7 Aug.	78	1 July	81	31 Dec.	86				
17	...	1 Henry Wilson Lovett[22]		21 Aug.	78	1 July	81	1 May	87				
17	...	2 p.s.c. Thomas D'Oyly Snow[23]		22 Jan.	79	1 July	81	1 July	87				
15	...	1 William Charles Cox[24]		11 Aug.	80	1 July	81	15 Sept.	87				
15	...	Charles Blakeway Little,[29] D.A.A. General, Secunderabad, 14 June 92		23 Oct.	80	1 July	81	15 Sept.	87				
14	...	Herbert Cokayne Frith,[24+] serving with the Egyptian Army		......		28 Jan.	82	23 Sept.	87				
14	...	Montague Amos Foster		......		28 Jan.	82	23 Sept.	87				
13	...	Ferdinand Mansel Peacock,[25] *Adjutant 2 Volunteer Battalion* 2 July 04		......		10 May	82	1 May	89				
13	...	Douglas Grant Stewart,[26] *Adjutant 4 Battalion* 15 July 90		......		29 July	82	3 Mar.	90				
12	...	Robert Brocklehurst,[26] *Adjutant 3 Volunteer Battalion,* 4 Mar. 95		......		6 Feb.	84	14 June	90				
11	...	Stradling Louis Vaughan Crealock,[26] *Station Staff Officer, Subathoo,* 18 Jan. 94		......		10 Sept.	84	14 June	90				
11	...	1 Arthur Barton Fox[30]		......		12 Nov.	84	14 Jan.	92				
11	...	Henry Joseph Everett		......		17 Feb.	85	14 Jan.	92				
11	...	2 John Maximilian Vallentin[26]		......		7 Feb.	85	14 June	92				
10	...	Herbert Cecil Johnstone,[26] *Adj. Southern Mahratta Railway Rifles* 7 Aug. 93		......		6 May	85	31 Dec.	93				
10	...	2 Edward Hopton Swayne[31]		......		6 May	85	31 Dec.	93				
10	...	1 Leonard George Thomas Chandler		......		6 May	85	14 June	94				
10	...	1 Lionel Wodehouse Fox[32] (*Depot*)		......		29 Aug.	85	10 July	94				
10	...	2 Edward Gwyn Elger[33]		......		25 Nov.	85	8 Nov.	94				
10	...	2 Walter Pipon Braithwaite,[32] **Adjutant** 16 Nov. 92		......		30 Jan.	86	8 Nov.	94				
		LIEUTENANTS.											
9	...	1 Charles Michael Richard Rycroft		......		10 Nov.	86						
9	...	2 Edward Forbes Cooke-Hurle		5 Feb.	87	1 May	89						
9	...	2 Ernest Henderson Rowley Cooke Richard Platt (*Depot*)		5 Feb.	87	16 Oct.	89						
9	...	1 James Eads Ubsdell		5 Feb.	87	11 Nov.	89						
9	9/18	1 Albert Reginald Foord[34]		......		28 Mar.	86						
8	...	2 Amherst Blunt Whatman		4 May	87	4 Jan.	90						
8	...	2 Arthur Gerald Boyle		4 May	87	3 Mar.	90						
8	...	1 William Hartley Maud (*Depot*)		11 Feb.	88	14 June	90						
8	...	1 George Bell Roney-Dougal		11 Feb.	88	14 June	90						
7	...	Adelbert Orlando Cockayne Cust, *Aide de Camp to the Governor of Trinidad* 24 Oct. 94		9 May	88	23 Sept.	91						
7	...	1 Owen Davys Rigg		9 May	88	23 Sept.	91						
6	...	1 Charles William Compton		17 July	89	14 Jan.	92						
6	...	1 William James Bowker		21 Dec.	89	14 June	92						
6	...	1 Victor Francis Alex. Keith-Falconer **Adjutant** 30 Dec. 94		1 Mar.	90	7 Aug.	93						
6	...	2 Harold FitzWilliam Hardman		29 Mar.	90	1 Nov.	93						
5	...	1 Herbert Maxwell Martin		23 July	90	15 Dec.	93						
5	...	1 Francis Gordon Grant Thoyts		29 Oct.	90	31 Dec.	93						
5	...	2 Alfred Percival Barry		4 Feb.	91	14 June	94						
5	...	1 John Bustee Cooke Thomson		10 Oct.	91	24 Oct.	94						
4	...	1 John Audley Thicknesse		10 Oct.	91	8 Nov.	94						
4	...	1 Cecil John Troyte-Bullock		10 Oct.	91	30 Dec.	94						
		SECOND LIEUTENANTS.											
4	...	1 Francis Malcolm Evory Kennedy		10 Oct.	91								
4	...	1 Cecil Godfrey Rawling		10 Oct.	91								
4	...	1 John Rattray Nuttall		10 Oct.	91								

[11] Major Walsh served with the Mounted Infantry in the operations against Sekukuni in the Transvaal in 1878, including the storming of Tolyana's Stadt; also throughout the Zulu war of 1879, and was present in the engagements at Kambula Hill and Ulundi (Medal with Clasp). Served in the Nile Expedition in 1884-85 with the Mounted Infantry Regiment of the Camel Corps, and was present in the reconnaissance to Gakdul under Sir Herbert Stewart, at the actions at Abu Klea and Gubat, in the reconnaissance at Metammeh on the 21st January, and in the engagement at Abu Klea Wells under Sir Redvers Buller—dangerously wounded (mentioned in despatches, Brevet of Major, Medal with two Clasps, and Khedive's Star).

The Prince Albert's (Somersetshire Light Infantry).

Years ser. Full Pay.	Half Pay.		SECOND LIEUTENANTS.	2ND LIEUT.
4	...	1	Francis Thackeray Warre-Cornish	9 Mar. 92
3	...	2	John William Henry Maturin	13 Aug. 92
3	...	2	Arthur Harry Peter Luckhardt	31 Aug. 92
3	...		Robert Francis Warburton	31 Aug. 92
3	...	2	Charles Bertie Prowse	12 Oct. 92
2	...	1	Cyril Ernest Chichester	10 Jan. 94
2	...	2	Penrose Mark-Wardlaw	2 June 94
1	...	1	Montague Claude Nangle	10 Oct. 94
1	...	1	Edmund Henry Salt James	12 Dec. 94
1	...	1	Arthur Thomas Searle Dickinson	20 Feb. 95
1	...		Arthur Hamilton Yatman	6 Mar. 95

Paymaster.—1 George B. Roney-Dougal, *Lieut.* 1 *Battalion (acting).*
Quarter Masters.—2 Lawrence Donnelly,[26] 2 June 86; *Hon. Lieut.*
1 Henry Powis, 26 Oct. 92; *Hon. Lieut.*

9 ...
3 ...

Facings Blue.—*Agents,* Messrs. Cox and Co.
1st Battalion embarked for Gibraltar, 12 Nov. 91. 2nd Battalion returned from India 15 Feb. 94.

[1] Lord Mark Kerr commanded the 13th Light Infantry in the Crimea from the 30th June 1855, and was at the battle of the Tchernaya, siege and fall of Sebastopol (Medal with Clasp, Turkish Medal, and 5th Class of the Medjidie). Commanded the 1st Battalion 13th from the 3rd Oct. 1857 in suppression of the Indian mutiny. Commanded the field force of Artillery Cavalry and Infantry at the relief of Azimghur on 6th April 1858 (C.B. and thanked by the Governor General for "the gallantry and skilful management which met and broke through a very formidable opposition"). Commanded the Battalion in the escort of a large convoy of stores and ammunition into the garrison of Azimghur on 9th April and the subsequent pursuit of Koer Sing's army on 14th April; crossed the Ganges and took command of the field force in the Shahabad District. Commanded the field force of Artillery Cavalry and Infantry in the attack on and retreat from the Fort of Jugdespore (wounded). Commanded the Battalion in the Trans-Gogra campaign, including the action at Toolsepore and during December and in January 1859, in the pursuit of rebels (Medal).

[13] Lt. Colonel Waddy, Majors Fownes, Gallwey and Williams served in the operations against Sekukuni in the Transvaal in 1878, including the storming of Tolyana's Stadt; also throughout the Zulu war of 1879—Major Gallwey as Adjutant of the 1st Battalion—and were present in the engagements of Zungin Nek, Kambula Hill, and Ulundi (Medal with Clasp).

[14] Major Poynton served in the operations against Sekukuni in the Transvaal in 1878 including the storming of Tolyana's Stadt; also throughout the Zulu war of 1879, and was present in the engagements of Zungin Nek, Kambula Hill, and Ulundi (Medal with Clasp). Served in the Burmese Expedition in 1885-86 with the Tonghoo Column (Medal with Clasp).

[15] Major Lumb served with the Nile Expedition in 1884-85 (Medal with Clasp, and Khedive's Star); also served with the Soudan Frontier Field Force in 1885-86 including the engagement at Giniss.

[16] Major Pollock served in the operations against Sekukuni in the Transvaal in 1878; also throughout the Zulu war of 1879, and was present in the engagements at Zungin Nek, Kambula Hill, and Ulundi (Medal with Clasp). Served with the expedition to the Soudan in 1885 in command of the 12th company of the Commissariat and Transport Corps, as Transport Officer to the 2nd Brigade, and was present in the engagements at Hasheen and the Tofrek zereba and at the destruction of Temai (Medal with two Clasps, and Khedive's Star).

[17] Major Payne served in the operations against Sekukuni in the Transvaal in 1878, including the storming of Tolyana's Stadt; also throughout the Zulu war of 1879, and was present in the engagements of Zungin Nek, Kambula Hill, and Ulundi (Medal with Clasp). Served with the Burmese Expedition in 1885-86 with the 2nd Battalion, Somersetshire Light Infantry (mentioned in despatches, *DSO.*, and Medal with Clasp).

[19] Captain Napier-Claverlng served in the Burmese Expedition in 1885-87 with the 2nd Battalion Somersetshire Light Infantry (Medal with Clasp).

[20] Captain Couchman served with the Burmese Expedition in 1885-87 with the 2nd Battalion Somersetshire Light Infantry (twice mentioned in despatches, *DSO.*, Medal with Clasp).

[21] Captain Lloyd served in the Burmese Expedition in 1886-87 with the 2nd Battalion Somersetshire Light Infantry (Medal with Clasp).

[22] Captain Lovett served throughout the Zulu war of 1879, and was present in the engagements at Zungin Nek and Kambula Hill (Medal with Clasp). Served with the Nile Expedition in 1884-85 in the Egyptian army (mentioned in despatches, Medal with Clasp, 4th Class of the Medjidie, and Khedive's Star). Served in the Burmese Expedition in 1886-87 with the 2nd Battalion Somersetshire Light Infantry (Medal with Clasp). [See also Civil Decorations for Gallantry, "Hart's Annual Army List," p. 786.]

[23] Captain Snow served in the Zulu war of 1879 (Medal with Clasp). Served in the Nile Expedition in 1884-85 with the Mounted Infantry of the Camel Corps, and was present in the actions at Abu Klea and Abu Kru—severely wounded (Medal with two Clasps, and Khedive's Star).

[24] Captain Cox served with the Burmese Expedition in 1886-87 with the 2nd Battalion Somersetshire Light Infantry, and was slightly wounded in an engagement on the 22nd March 1887 (Medal with Clasp).

[24] Captain Frith served in the operations of the Soudan Frontier Field Force in 1885-86 with the Egyptian Army and was present in the engagement at Giniss (Medal, and Khedive's Star).

[25] Captain Peacock served with the Burmese Expedition in 1885-87 with the 2nd Battalion Somersetshire Light Infantry, and was slightly wounded in an engagement near Hlinedet on the 5th April (mentioned in despatches, Medal with Clasp).

[26] Captains D. G. Stewart, Brocklehurst, Vallentin, Crealock, and Johnstone, and Lieut. Donnelly served in the Burmese Expedition in 1886-87 with the 2nd Battalion Somersetshire Light Infantry (Medal with Clasp).

[29] Captain Little served in the Burmese Expedition in 1885-87 as Adjutant to the 2nd Battalion Somersetshire Light Infantry (Medal with Clasp).

[30] Captain A. B. Fox served with the Burmese Expedition in 1885-86, and was severely wounded in an engagement at Hinyowah on the 21st March 1886 (Medal with Clasp).

[31] Captain Swayne served in the Burmese Expedition in 1885-87 with the 2nd Battalion Somersetshire Light Infantry (Medal with Clasp); and with the Chin-Lushai Expeditionary Force in 1889-90 (Clasp).

[32] Captains L. W. Fox and Braithwaite served with the Burmese Expedition in 1886-87 with the 2nd Battalion Somersetshire Light Infantry (mentioned in despatches, Medal with Clasp).

[33] Captain Elger served with the Burmese Expedition in 1886-87 with the 2nd Battalion Somersetshire Light Infantry (Medal with Clasp).

[34] Lieut. Foord served with the Burmese Expedition in 1886-87 with the 2nd Battalion Somersetshire Light Infantry (Medal with Clasp).

Record of the Services of the 1st Battalion Prince Albert's Somersetshire Light Infantry (formerly the 13th Foot).

Raised in 1685. Scotland, to 1690. Ireland, to 1691. France, to 1692. England, to 1700. Low Countries, to 1703. Portugal, to 1704. Gibraltar, to 1705. Spain, to 1706. (Portion formed into a Regiment of Dragoons.) Re-recruited in England, 1706. Portugal, to 1711. Gibraltar, to 1728. England, to 1741. Germany, to 1745. England and Scotland, to 1746. Low Countries, to 1748.

The Prince Albert's (Somersetshire Light Infantry).

England, to 1754. Gibraltar, to 1762. England and Ireland, to 1768. Minorca, to 1775. England, to 1780. West Indies, to 1782. England, to 1783. Entitled the "First Somersetshire Regiment," 31st Aug., 1782. Ireland, to 1790. West Indies, to 1795. England, to 1797. Ireland, to 1799. England, to 1800. Egypt, to 1802. Malta, to 1803. Gibraltar, to 1805. England and Ireland, to 1807. West Indies, to 1813. Quebec, to 1815. Ireland, to 1817. Channel Islands, to 1819. Ireland, to 1822. Constituted Light Infantry, 25th Dec. 1822. India, to 1824. Burmah, to 1826. India, to 1838. Afghanistan, to 1842 (the only European Regiment at the defence of Jellalabad). Entitled "Prince Albert's Regiment of Light Infantry," 1842. India, to 1845. England, to 1847. Ireland, to 1850. Scotland, to 1851. Gibraltar, to 1854. The Crimea, to 1856. Cape of Good Hope, to 1857. India, to 1864. England, to 1866. Ireland, to 1867. Gibraltar, to 1872. Malta, to 1874. South Africa, to 1879. England, to 1891. Gibraltar, 1891.

Record of the Services of the 2nd Battalion.

Raised in England in 1858, and proceeded to the Cape of Good Hope, 1859. To Mauritius, 1863. To England, 1867. To Ireland, 1871. To Scotland, 1875. To England, 1876. To Malta, 1877. To India, 1878. [Entitled "Somersetshire Regiment," 1881. Altered to "Somersetshire Light Infantry," and afterwards to "The Prince Albert's (Somersetshire Light Infantry)," 1882.] To Burmah, 1883. To India, 1887. To England, 1894.

Continuation of Notes to the Prince of Wales' Own (West Yorkshire Regiment).

[1] General Heyland served with the 95th Regt. in the Eastern Campaign of 1854-55, including the battle of Alma (severely wounded—arm amputated), siege and fall of Sebastopol (mentioned in despatches, Medal with two Clasps, Brevet of Lt.Colonel, *CB.*, Sardinian and Turkish Medals, 4th Class of the Medjidie).
[6] Lt.Colonel Noyes served in the New Zealand war in 1864-66 (Medal). Served as Brigade Transport Officer in the Afghan war of 1878-80, and was present in the affair at Mazeena—wounded (mentioned in despatches, Medal).
[11] Lt.Colonel Gordon and Captain Lester served in the Afghan war in 1880, and were present in the affair at Mazeena and with the Kama Expedition (Medal).
[15] Major Adye served in the Afghan war of 1878-80 with the 4th Goorkhas, and was present at the attack and capture of Ali Musjid (Medal with Clasp).
[21] Major Mills served with the Bechuanaland Expedition under Sir Charles Warren in 1884-85 on special service as Acting Provost Marshal.
[23] Captain Walker served in the Afghan war in 1880, and was present in the engagement at Mazeena and with the Kama Expedition (Medal).
[24] Captain Towsey served in the operations in the South Lushai Country in 1892 with the force under Captain Shakespear (Medal with Clasp).
[25] Captain Minogue served with the Burmese Expedition in 1885-87 with the 2nd Battalion Royal Munster Fusiliers (Medal with Clasp), and again in 1887-89 (mentioned in despatches, Clasp). Served with the Chin-Lushai Expeditionary Force in 1889-90 on Transport duty (mentioned in despatches, Clasp), and again with the Lushai Expedition in 1891 on Transport duty (Clasp).

Record of the Services of the 1st Battalion of the Prince of Wales' Own (West Yorkshire) Regiment,—formerly the 14th Regiment.

Raised in Kent in 1685. To Scotland, 1689. To Flanders, 1692. To England, 1692. Expedition against French Coast and Flanders, 1693. To England, 1696. To Ireland, 1698. To Scotland, 1715. To England, 1722. To Gibraltar, 1727 (Siege). To England, 1742. To Flanders, 1745. To Scotland, 1746 (Falkirk, Culloden). To England, 1750. To Gibraltar, 1752. To England, 1759. To America, 1766. To England, 1777. To Jamaica, 1782. To England, 1791. To Holland, 1793. To England, 1795. To the West Indies, 1796. To England, 1803. To Hanover, 1803. [2nd Battalion raised in 1804 (Corunna, Walcheren, Flushing, Tarifa and Genoa). Reduced in 1817.] To England, 1806. To Ireland, 1807. To India, 1810. [3rd Battalion raised in 1813 (Waterloo and Cambray). Disbanded in 1816.] To England, 1831. To Ireland, 1832. To West Indies, 1836. To Canada, 1841. To England, 1847. To Ireland, 1850. To Malta, 1854. To the Crimea, 1855. To Malta, 1856. To Ionian Islands, 1858. To West Indies, 1860. To England, 1862. To Ireland, 1866. To India, 1867. To England, 1879. To Ireland, 1883. To England, 1891.

Record of the Services of the 2nd Battalion.

Raised in Ireland in 1857, and proceeded to New Zealand, 1860 (war of 1863-65). To Australia and Tasmania, 1866. To England, 1870. To Ireland, 1876. To India, 1878 (Afghan war, 1879-80).

[1st Batt., Gibraltar,] *Formerly the 14th (Buckinghamshire—* [*Regimental District*]
[2nd Batt., Aden.   ] *The Prince of Wales' Own) Regiment.* [No. 14.—York.]

(The 3rd and 4th Battalions are formed of the 2nd and 4th West York Militia respectively.)
The Prince of Wales' Plume. The White Horse. *"Nec aspera terrent."*—"TOURNAY" "CORUNNA"
"JAVA" "WATERLOO" "BHURTPORE" "INDIA" (with the Royal Tiger).
"SEVASTOPOL" "NEW ZEALAND" "AFGHANISTAN, 1879-80."

Years	Full Pay	Half Pay			ENSIGN OR 2ND LIEUT.	LIEUT.	CAPTAIN.	BREV.MAJ.	MAJOR.
			Colonel.—Alfred Thomas Heyland,[1] *C.B., Ensign*, P4 April 33; *Lt.* P18 July 36; *Capt.* P13 Dec. 42; *Bt.Major*, 20 June 54; *Major*, 1 Dec. 54; *Bt.Lt.Colonel*, 12 Dec. 54; *Lt.Colonel*, 5 June 55; *Colonel*, 20 Mar. 58; *Major General*, 6 Mar. 68; *Lt.General*, 1 Oct. 77; *General*, 12 April 81; *Colonel* 14th Foot, 21 Nov. 80.						
32		...	Lieutenant Colonels.—2 Arthur Walter Noyes,[8] *Ensign*, 9 Mar. 64; *Lieut.* P14 Aug. 67; *Captain*, 16 Feb. 78; *Major*, 7 Mar. 82; *Lt.Colonel*, 20 Mar. 91.						
27		...	1 Charles Steward Gordon,[11] *Ensign*, P27 June 68; *Lieut.* 28 Oct. 71; *Captain*, 24 Jan. 80; *Major*, 20 Mar. 83; *Lt.Colonel*, 7 Mar. 92.						
			MAJORS.						
29		...	2 Adolphus James Price	11 Dec. 66	21 July 71	4 Mar. 80		5 Sept. 83
23		...	2 Gerald Grant-Dalton		8 June 72	18 May 81		23 May 90
20		...	2 Capel George Adye[15]		20 Nov. 75	6 Nov. 81		10 Feb. 92
19		...	p.s.c. Fred. Walter Kitchener,[17] *D.A.A. Gen. for Inst. Poona*, 15 Aug. 91		11 Sept. 76	11 Nov. 82		7 Mar. 92
19		...	1 Edward Cyril Mills[21] (*Depot*)		29 Oct. 76	11 Nov. 82		6 May 92
18		...	2 Acheson Whitmore St. George	23 Jan. 78	28 June 78	28 Feb. 83		16 Nov. 92
18		...	1 Charles Hay Cox, *Adj.* 2 *Bn.* 26 Jan. 91	30 Jan. 78	19 Sept. 78	2 Apr. 84		13 June 94
21		...	Herbert Thomas de Cartaret Mobbs, *Adj.* 2 *Vol. Bn. Wiltshire Regt.* 2 Oct. 93		11 Feb. 75	17 Jan. 82		20 Feb. 95
			CAPTAINS.						
17		...	Hugh Alexander Vowell, *Station Staff Officer, Bhamo*, 12 Feb. 94	1 May 78	1 Nov. 78	10 Sept. 84		
17		...	p.s.c. Cecil Morris Lester,[21] *Instructor Royal Military College* 1 Sept. 92	1 May 78	19 Feb. 79	23 Dec. 85		
17		...	William Fry,[19] *Adj. Upper Burmah Vol. Rifles* 27 June 92	11 May 78	7 Jan. 80	26 Jan. 86		
17		...	2 Clement John Malcolm Heigham, *with Provisional Battalion*	4 Dec. 78	2 Oct. 80	1 Apr. 86		
17		...	2 Henry Walker[23] (*Depot*)	22 Jan. 79	1 Jan. 81	26 July 86		
17		...	2 George William Swaine	22 Jan. 79	18 May 81	20 Mar. 87		
16		...	James Corbet Yale, *Adj.* 2 *Vol. Bn. West Yorkshire Regt.* 2 Jan. 93	13 Aug. 79	1 July 81	1 Sept. 88		
15	10/16		Harold Basil Sept. Critchley-Salmon, *Army Pay Department*	1 July 79	1 July 81	4 Jan. 89		
15		...	Herbert Edward Watts, *Adjutant* 4 *Battalion* 3 Dec. 94	17 April 80	1 July 81	6 Mar. 89		
14		...	1 Thomas Rawdon Rattray Ward		22 Oct. 81	2 Dec. 89		
13		...	1 Henry O'Donnell		10 May 82	1 Apr. 90		
13		...	2 Walter de Sausmarez Cayley		10 Mar. 83	23 May 90		
11		...	Dudley Henry Alexander, *Adjutant* 3 *Vol. Bn. Bedford Regt.* 3 Sept. 94		12 Nov. 84	7 Mar. 92		
10		...	1 George Fraser Phillips, *Adjutant* 15 Aug. 94		6 May 85	27 June 92		
10		...	2 Hubert Basil Cosmo Trevor, *Supdt. of Gymnasia, Manchester*, 5 Apr. 94		6 May 85	1 Sept. 92		
10		...	2 Francis William Towsey,[24] *Adjutant* 15 Feb. 94		25 Nov. 85	16 Nov. 92		
10		...	1 Arthur James Stephen		10 Mar. 86	16 Apr. 93		
9		...	2 Francis Barrow Pearce		25 Aug. 86	25 July 93		
9		...	2 John O'Brien Minogue[25]		12 May 86	11 Oct. 93		
9		...	2 Thomas Percy Barrington	5 Feb. 87	6 Feb. 89	13 Feb. 94		
9		...	1 Godfrey George Lang	5 Feb. 87	8 May 89	13 June 94		
8		...	1 Thomas Hugh Berney	4 May 87	8 May 89	3 Sept. 94		
9		...	1 Robert Free Lush	5 Feb. 87	6 Nov. 89	2 Dec. 94		
8		...	Arthur Alexander Fisher, *serving with the Egyptian Army*	14 Sept. 87	6 Nov. 89	20 Feb. 95		
			LIEUTENANTS.						
7		...	1 George Barry Drew	22 Aug. 88	24 Sept. 90			
7		...	1 Ward Sausmarez Carey	14 Nov. 88	24 Sept. 90			
7		...	2 George Frederick Gardiner	23 Mar. 89	10 Mar. 91			
6		...	1 John Simmonds Bartrum, *with Provisional Battalion*	1 Mar. 90	11 Sept. 91			
5		...	1 Charles Ryall	3 May 90	10 Feb. 92			
5		...	2 Arthur Crawford Daly (*Depot*)	4 June 90	7 Mar. 92			
5		...	2 Edgar Patrick Carnac Purchas	23 July 90	18 May 92			
5		...	2 Conwyn Manzel-Jones	8 Oct. 90	1 July 92			
5		...	1 Wynyard Montagu Hall	17 Jan. 91	3 Aug. 92			
5		...	1 Cyril Crofton Blackburne Tew	17 Jan. 91	3 Aug. 92			
4		...	2 Charles Howard Hawes	7 Nov. 91	22 Mar. 93			
4		...	2 Eyre Walter Molyneux Purvis	30 Dec. 91	25 July 93			
4		...	2 Leighton Hume Spry	12 Mar. 92	22 Nov. 93			
4		...	1 Alexander Wighton Ingles	12 Mar. 92	1 Feb. 94			
3		...	Charles Eckford Luard	18 May 92	13 June 94			
3		...	1 Fleetwood Hugo Pellew	18 June 92	13 June 94			
2		...	Harry Townsend Fulton	9 Apr. 92	3 Sept. 94			
3		...	Albert Gardener Ames	19 Oct. 92	3 Sept. 94			
3		...	2 John Byng Pagot	19 Oct. 92	26 Sept. 94			
3		...	1 Thos. Nairne Scott Moncrieff Howard	17 Dec. 92	29 Sept. 94			
3		...	1 Reginald Garret King	21 Jan. 93	2 Dec. 94			
			SECOND LIEUTENANTS.						
2		...	2 Wynyard Feeling Lang	9 Aug. 93				
2		...	1 Maximilian David Wood	21 Oct. 93				
2		...	1 Albert Fortescue Stewart	20 Dec. 93				
2		...	2 Percival Edward Hurst Lowe	7 Mar. 94				
1		...	1 Percy Leigh Ingpen	10 Oct. 94				
1		...	1 Maxwell Hannay Logan	10 Oct. 94				
1		...	1 Almeric Arthur William Spencer	12 Dec. 94				
1		...	1 Herbert Crofton Isaac	12 Dec. 94				
1		...	1 Frank Pickford Worsley	20 Feb. 95				
1		...	1 Reginald Isacke	20 Feb. 95				
1			Bernard Anthony Thompson	6 Mar. 95				
1		...	Cyril John Deverell	6 Mar. 95				
1		...	Hubert Lionel Monrilyan	6 Mar. 95				
			Paymaster.—2 George W. Swaine, *Captain* 2 *Battalion* (*acting*).						
15		...	Quarter Masters.—2 Robert Scott, 12 Feb. 81; *Hon. Captain*, 12 Feb. 91.						
2		...	1 John Smith, 17 May 93; *Hon. Lieut.*						

[17] Major Kitchener served in the Afghan war of 1878-80 as Transport Officer Cabul Field Force, and was present in the advance on Cabul under Sir F. Roberts, in the engagement at Charasiah on the 6th October 1879, in the affair at Karez Meer, in the operations in the Chardeh Valley, at the defence of Sherpore, and with the Kama Expedition (mentioned in despatches, Medal with two Clasps).

[19] Captain Fry served in the Afghan war in 1879-80 (Medal).

[*For remainder of Notes, see preceding page.*

Facings White.—Agents, Messrs. Cox and Co.

1st Battalion embarked for Gibraltar, 8 Jan. 95. 2nd Battalion embarked for Bengal, 1878.

1st Batt., Egypt.
2nd Batt., Birr.

The East Yorkshire Regiment. [Regimental District No. 15.—Beverley.

Formerly the 15th (Yorkshire East Riding) Regiment.
(The 3rd Battalion is formed of the East York Militia.)

The White Rose. "BLENHEIM" "RAMILLIES" "OUDENARDE" "MALPLAQUET" "LOUISBURG" "QUEBEC, 1759" "MARTINIQUE" "GUADALOUPE" "AFGHANISTAN, 1879-80."

Years' Ser.			ENSIGN OR 2ND LIEUT.	LIEUT.	CAPTAIN.	BREV. MAJ.	MAJOR.
Full Pay	Half Pay						
		Colonel.—Edward Westby Donovan,[1] Ensign, 10 Jan. 40; Lieut. 14 June 42; Capt. 22 Dec. 48; Bt. Major 17 July 55; Major, 26 Oct. 55; Bt. Lt. Colonel, 26 Dec. 56; Lt. Colonel, 17 Apr. 60; Colonel, 31 Jan. 63; Major General, 28 Oct. 68; Lt. General, 18 June 81; General, 1 Apr. 87; Colonel East Yorkshire Regiment, 6 June 91.					
32	...	**Lieutenant Colonels.**—1 Henry Bellingham Le Mottée,[2] Ensign, P22 Jan. 64; Lieut. 1 Jan. 67; Captain, 12 Nov. 73; Major, 1 July 81; Lt. Colonel, 15 Aug. 91.					
30	...	2 p.s.c. Ralph Edward Allen,[3] Ensign, P7 April 65; Lieut. P12 June 69; Captain, 21 Oct. 76; Major, 26 July 82; Bt. Lt. Colonel, 9 Dec. 85; Colonel, 9 Dec. 89; Lt. Colonel, 6 Sept. 93.					
		MAJORS.					
27	...	1 Frederick Seymour Allen	P18 Nov. 68	P24 Sept. 70	15 Aug. 77	......	6 May 86
25	...	2 Frederick George Pogson[7]	P27 Aug. 70	28 Oct. 71	4 Mar. 82		3 May 91
24	...	John Robert Young, *Instructor Royal Military College* 8 Oct. 91	......	6 Mar. 72	26 July 82		5 Aug. 91
22	...	2 Walter Waterfield Ward[8] (*Depot*)	......	30 April 73	25 Jan. 84		6 Aug. 91
22	...	1 Cecil Francis Garnett[9]	......	28 Feb. 74	3 May 84		15 Aug. 91
21	...	p.s.c. Francis Seymour Inglefield, *Instructor R. M. College* 1 Sept. 92	......	13 June 74	30 June 84		2 July 92
21	...	2 Lawrence Litchfield Steele[10]	......	2 Dec. 74	1 Oct. 84		6 Sept. 93
20	...	2 George Hay Montgomerie Conran[11]	......	12 Feb. 76	1 Oct. 84		16 May 94
		CAPTAINS.					
19	...	2 Edward Frankland Gosset	......	17 May 76	2 Mar. 85		
18	...	p.s.c. Bruce Meade Hamilton,[12] *Dep. Assist. Adj. Gen., Portsmouth,* 27 Jan. 94	15 Aug. 77	9 May 78	5 May 86		
18	...	Edmund Ashton Ogle, *Adjutant 3 Battalion* 16 Sept. 93	15 Aug. 77	31 May 78	5 May 86		
18	...	Thomas Nook Bagnall, *D.A.A.Gen. Hythe School of Musketry,* 31 May 93	13 Oct. 77	1 Aug. 78	5 May 86		
18	...	1 p.s.c. Hastings St. Leger Wood,[13] DSO.	31 Oct. 77	30 Nov. 78	6 May 86		
17	...	1 Cecil Francis Harrison	7 Aug. 78	1 July 81	2 May 87		
17	...	Wilbraham Thomas Davies,[14] *Ordnance Store Dept.*	25 May 78	1 July 81	7 May 87		
18	...	Herbert Joseph Guyon, *Adjutant 1 Vol. Bn. E. Yorkshire Regt.* 19 May 92	21 July 77	26 May 80	17 Aug. 87		
16	...	Charles Henry Wray Maunsell,[15]	23 July 79	1 July 81	2 Sept. 87		
16	...	2 Charles Mulcaster Harding	6 Aug. 79	1 July 81	6 Sept. 87		
16	...	2 John Ramsay Fred. Sladen,[16] *Staff College*	14 Jan. 80	1 July 81	6 Sept. 88		
13	...	2 p.s.c. Arthur Johnstone Richardson[17]	......	9 Sept. 82	26 Feb. 89		
13	...	Henry Dowsley Stacpole,[18] *Army Pay Department*	......	9 Sept. 82	11 Mar. 89		
13	...	1 Henry Haggard (*Depot*)	......	10 Mar. 83	26 Apr. 89		
12	...	1 Leonard Henry Orde	......	5 Dec. 83	18 Dec. 89		
11	...	Frederick William Hill, *Army Pay Department*	......	14 May 84	6 Aug. 91		
11	...	Richard Erle Benson	......	14 May 84	6 Aug. 91		
10	...	1 Edward Gloster, **Adjutant** 6 May 94	......	6 May 85	8 Oct. 91		
10	...	1 Thomas Gibbons Hawkesworth Smyth	......	6 May 85	4 Feb. 92		
10	...	1 James Stuart Knox, *Staff College*	......	9 May 85	2 July 92		
10	...	1 William Southall Reid May	......	9 May 85	6 Sept. 93		
10	...	Broadley Harrison, *Ordnance Store Department*	......	23 May 85	27 Jan. 94		
9	...	2 Henry Montague Clifton Hawkes	......	10 Nov. 86	27 Jan. 94		
9	...	2 Edward William Anketell Jones	......	8 Dec. 86	16 May 94		
		LIEUTENANTS.					
9	...	1 Charles Sumner Timins	......	8 Dec. 86			
8	...	2 Beauchamp St. Clair-Ford	14 Sept. 87	18 Sept. 89			
8	...	2 Michael James Sweetman, **Adjutant** 17 Aug. 92	14 Sept. 87	Sept. 89			
8	...	2 Hubert Cecil Prichard	11 Feb. 88	18 Sept. 89			
8	...	1 William Herbert Armstrong	27 June 88	18 Sept. 89			
7	...	1 Henry Robert Prittie Perry[19]	8 Dec. 88	16 Apr. 90			
7	...	1 John Louis Justice Clarke (*Depot*)	30 Jan. 89	5 Aug. 91			
7	...	1 Walter Herbert Young	23 Mar. 89	5 Aug. 91			
7	...	2 Ernest Theodore Marshall	24 Apr. 89	6 Aug. 91			
7	...	1 John Alfred Unett (*Depot*)	8 June 89	15 Dec. 91			
6	...	1 Herman George Wellington Wayne	6 July 89	15 Dec. 91			
9	...	2 Cecil Speid Soote (*Lt. 2 Dragoons,* 29 Dec. 86)	4 Sept. 89	31 Jan. 91			
6	...	2 Harold Haines Powell	4 Sept. 89	4 Feb. 92			
7	...	1 Thomas Robert Eaton Wybault Warren-Swettenham	16 Mar. 89	20 Dec. 90			
6	...	2 Herbert Augustus Nourse Forte	9 Nov. 89	6 Sept. 93			
6	...	1 Frederick Campbell Maconchy	21 Dec. 89	27 Jan. 94			
5	...	1 John Herbert Little	25 Mar. 91	16 May 94			
4	...	1 Ernest Henry Brass	2 May 91	17 Oct. 94			
4	...	1 Charles Edward Cobb	9 Sept. 91	5 Dec. 94			
		SECOND LIEUTENANTS.					
4	...	1 Hubert Alderson-Smith	10 Oct. 91				
4	...	2 Alexander Price Conolly Herschel Wade	27 Jan. 92				
4	...	1 Frederick Heathfield Lock	27 Jan. 92				
4	...	2 Charles Joseph Tawney	20 Feb. 92				
4	...	1 Francis Garden Poole	20 Feb. 92				
3	...	1 Reginald Evelyn Atherstone Hales	18 June 92				
2	...	1 Herbert Cecil Willoughby Berthon	31 Jan. 94				

[12] Captain Hamilton served with the 15th Regiment in the Afghan war in 1880 with the force under Major-General Phayre (Medal). Served in the Boer war of 1881 as Aide de Camp to Sir George Colley, and was present in the engagement at the Ingogo River (mentioned in despatches); afterwards served as Aide de Camp to Sir Evelyn Wood until the conclusion of operations.

The East Yorkshire Regiment.

Years Ser. Full Pay	Half Pay	SECOND LIEUTENANTS.	2ND LIEUT.
2	...	1 Cecil Strachan Wood	7 Mar. 94
1	...	2 Frederic Sidney Kent	20 June 94
1	...	2 Walter Ernest Campion	12 Dec. 94
1	...	2 Brian Delves Broughton	12 Dec. 94
1	...	1 George Henville Davis	20 Feb. 95

[13] Captain Wood served in the Afghan war in 1879-80 as Transport Officer Candahar Field Force, and was present at the defence of Candahar and acted as Orderly Officer to Brigadier General Brooke in the sortie of Deh Khojah—severely wounded and horse killed (Medal). Served with the Nile Expedition in 1884-85 on special service (mentioned in despatches, Medal with Clasp, and Khedive's Star). Served with the Burmese Expedition in 1887-88 as Brigade Transport Officer and as Deputy Assistant Adjutant and Quarter Master General 2nd Brigade (mentioned in despatches, DSO., and Medal with two Clasps).

Paymasters.—1
2
Quarter Masters.—1 Francis Pidgeon, 30 Mar. 92; *Hon. Lieut.*
2 George Hedingham,[20] 19 April 82; *Hon. Captain,* 19 April 92.

4 ...
13 ...

Facings White.—*Agents*, Messrs. Cox and Co.
1st Battalion embarked for Gibraltar, 17 March 1885. 2nd Battalion returned from Aden, 2 Dec. 1888.

[1] General Donovan served with the 33rd Regiment the Eastern campaign of 1854 and up to 19th April 1855, including the battles of Alma and Inkerman, and siege of Sebastopol—severely wounded in the Trenches on the 16th of April (mentioned in despatches, Medal with three Clasps, Brevets of Major and Lt. Colonel, Knight of the Legion of Honor, 5th Class of the Medjidie, and Turkish Medal).
[2] Lt. Colonel Le Mottee served with the 2nd Battalion 15th Foot in the Afghan war in 1880 with the Candahar Field Force under Major General Phayre (Medal).
[3] Colonel Allen served with the Bechuanaland Expedition under Sir Charles Warren in 1884-85 as Deputy Assistant Adjutant and Quarter Master General (Brevet of Lt. Colonel).
[7] Major Pogson served in the Afghan war in 1879-80 as Transport Officer (Medal).
[8] Major Ward served in the Afghan war in 1880 with the 2nd Battalion 15th Foot with the Candahar Field Force under Major General Phayre (Medal).
[9] Major Garnett served in the Afghan war in 1880 with the 2nd Battalion 15th Foot with the Candahar Field Force under Major General Phayre (Medal).
[10] Major Steele served as Adjutant of the 2nd Battalion 15th Foot in the Afghan war in 1880 with the Candahar Field Force under Major General Phayre (Medal).
[11] Major Conran served in the Afghan war in 1880 with the 2nd Battalion 15th Foot with the Candahar Field Force under Major General Phayre (Medal).
[14] Captain Davies served in the Afghan war in 1880 with the 2nd Battalion 15th Foot with the Candahar Field Force under Major General Phayre (Medal).
[15] Captain Maunsell served in the Afghan war in 1880 with the 2nd Battalion 15th Foot with the Candahar Field Force under Major General Phayre (Medal).
[16] Captain Sladen served with the 2nd Battalion 15th Foot in the Afghan war in 1880 with the Candahar Field Force under Major General Phayre (Medal). Served in the Burmese Expedition in 1886-88 with the Mounted Infantry (Medal with two Clasps).
[17] Captain Richardson served in the Burmese Expedition in 1885-87 with the Mounted Infantry (Medal with Clasp).
[18] Captain Stacpole served in the Zulu war in 1879 (Medal with Clasp).
[19] Lieut. Perry served in the Burmese Expedition in 1891-92 with the Irrawaddy Column including the defence of Sadon (Medal with Clasp).
[20] Captain Hedingham served in the Hazara campaign in 1888 with the 2nd Battalion Royal Sussex Regiment (Medal with Clasp).

Record of the Services of the 1st Battalion East Yorkshire Regiment (formerly the 15th Regiment).

Raised in 1685 as the 15th Foot, and proceeded to Scotland in 1689. To Ostend, 1694. To England, 1697. To Ireland, 1698. To Holland, 1701 (battles of Blenheim, Ramillies, Oudenarde, and Malplaquet). To England, 1714. To Scotland, 1719. To England, 1728. To the West Indies, 1740. To England, 1742. To the Continent, 1745. To England, 1746. To Ireland, 1749. To England, 1755. To North America, 1758 (capture of Louisburg and of Quebec under General Wolfe). To the West Indies, 1761. To Canada, 1762. To England, 1768. To Scotland, 1771. To Ireland, 1774. To America, 1776. To the West Indies, 1778. To England, 1782. (Styled the "Yorkshire East Riding Regiment.") To Ireland, 1784. To the West Indies, 1790. To England, 1796. To Scotland, 1797. To England, 1799. To Ireland, 1802. To the West Indies, 1806 (capture of Martinique and Guadaloupe). To North America, 1817. To England, 1821. To Ireland, 1823. To Canada, 1827. To England, 1840. To Ireland, 1843. To Ceylon, 1845. To Ireland, 1855. To Gibraltar, 1856. To England, 1857. To Jersey. 1859. To Ireland, 1860. To North America, 1862. To Bermuda, 1868. To Ireland, 1870. To the Channel Islands, 1873. To England, 1874. To Ireland, 1878. To England, 1883. To Gibraltar, 1885. To the West Indies, 1886. To South Africa, 1888.

Record of the Services of the 2nd Battalion.

Raised in England in 1858. Malta, to 1863. Gibraltar, to 1868. Ireland, to 1870. Channel Islands, to 1871. England, to 1875. India, to Feb. 1888 (Afghan war, 1879-80). Aden, to Nov. 1888. England, to Nov. 1894. Ireland, 1894.

1st Batt., Peshawur, Bengal.
2nd Batt., Aldershot.] **The Bedfordshire Regiment.** [Regimental District No. 16.—Bedford.

Formerly the 16th (The Bedfordshire) Regiment.
(The 3rd and 4th Battalions are formed of the Bedford and Hertford Militia respectively.)
The United Red and White Rose. "BLENHEIM" "RAMILLIES" "OUDENARDE" "MALPLAQUET."

Years' Ser.	Full Pay	Half Pay							
30	...		Colonel.—e. John William Cox,[1] CB. Ensign, 26 June 38; Lt. 22 Apr. 40; Capt. 9 Apr. 47; Bt. Major, 15 Dec. 54; Major, 25 Jan. 56; Bt. Lt. Colonel, 20 July 58; Colonel, 4 Sept. 63; Major General, 23 Mar. 69; Lt. General, 1 Sept. 82; Colonel Bedfordshire Regiment, 15 June 93.						
27	...		Lieutenant Colonels.—1 p.s.c. Alexander Martin Paterson,[2] Ensign, 10 Oct. 65; Lieut. 9 Oct. 67; Capt. 30 Oct. 74; Major, 1 July 81; Lt. Colonel, 10 Oct. 92.						
27	...	2	Frederick John Harden,[3] Ensign, P11 April 68; Lieut. P23 Nov. 70; Capt. 25 Aug. 76; Major, 10 Oct. 84; Lt. Colonel, 1 July 94.						

			MAJORS.	ENSIGN OR 2ND LIEUT.	LIEUT.	CAPTAIN.	BREV. MAJ.	MAJOR.
27	...	2	William Henry Young	P20 June 68	P30 Nov. 70	30 Dec. 76	......	7 Mar. 88
27	...		Francis Fawkes Johnstone, *Inspector of Warlike Stores* 21 June 94	P 2 Sept. 68	P22 Feb. 71	10 Sept. 77	......	10 Oct. 88
25	...	1	Geo. Dalrymple More Nisbett[4]	P 8 June 70	28 Oct. 71	9 Mar. 79	......	23 Aug. 89
25	...	2	Justice Chapman Tilly (*Depot*)	P14 Dec. 70	28 Oct. 71	30 Apr. 79	......	1 July 90
24	...		William Henry Riddell, *District Inspector of Musketry, Cork,* 27 May 94	......	30 Dec. 71	19 June 79	......	29 Mar. 92
23	...	1	Frederick Williams Becher[5]	......	21 Sept. 72	10 Oct. 79	......	10 Oct. 92
21	...	1	p.s.c. William Aldworth,[6] DSO	......	13 June 74	30 Mar. 81	......	1 Feb. 93
21	...	1	Alfred Robert LLoyd	......	2 Dec. 74	1 Sept. 83	......	1 July 94
			CAPTAINS.					
21	...		p.s.c. Wentworth Odiarne Cavenagh, *Instructor R. Military College* 1 Feb. 89	......	11 Feb. 75	14 Jan. 85		
21	...		Affleck Alexander Fraser, *Adjutant Hyderabad Rifle Vols.* 18 Sept. 92	......	21 Sept. 75	10 Aug. 85		
20	...	1	Geo. John Ninian Logan-Home[15] (*Depot*)	......	20 Nov. 75	4 Oct. 85		
20	...	2	Charles Du Plat Richardson-Griffiths[8]	......	20 Nov. 75	4 Oct. 85		
17	...	2	Thomas Hammond	1 May 78	28 Feb. 79	1 July 87		
17	...	1	Charles Moorehead Hamilton	5 Oct. 78	12 April 79	6 July 87		
17	...	1	Edward Duroure Pickard-Cambridge[9]	22 Jan. 79	6 June 79	30 Sept. 87		
16	...	2	Henry Tufton Godden	13 Aug. 79	29 Apr. 81	7 Mar. 88		
19	...	2	John Stanley Lightfoot		29 Nov. 76	26 Nov. 88		
16	...	1	Theodore Longridge[13]	14 Jan. 80	1 July 81	1 Feb. 89		
12	...	1	Thomas Ernle Fowle		5 Dec. 83	11 Dec. 89		
12	...	1	William Thomas Wilson Scott[10]		6 Feb. 84	1 July 90		
11	...	2	Arthur Nelson[11]		23 Aug. 84	29 Apr. 92		
11	...		Arthur Frederick Pereira, *Army Pay Department*		12 Nov. 84	1 Feb. 93		
11	...		Henry Wise Unett Coates, *Adjutant* 1 Jan. 92		7 Feb. 85	1 Feb. 93		
11	...	1	John Edward Laurie Gibbs		12 Nov. 84	1 July 94		
9	...	2	Benjamin Robert Roche[13]		28 Apr. 86	9 Aug. 94		
9	...	2	Harry Clifford Franks[12]		21 July 86	7 Nov. 94		
			LIEUTENANTS.					
8	...	2	Charles Richard Jebb Griffith	14 Sept. 87	10 Apr. 89			
8	...	1	George William Dundas[13]	14 Sept. 87	3 July 89			
8	...	1	John Murray Traill[13] (*Depot*)	16 Nov. 87	31 July 89			
8	...	1	Joseph Herbert Wansbrough[13]	16 Nov. 87	31 July 89			
7	...	2	Edwyn Anthony Sylvester Ely	9 May 88	28 Aug. 89			
7	...	1	Edward George Curtis	22 Aug. 88	6 Aug. 90			
7	...	1	Robt. Percy Stares,[13] *Adjutant* 1 May 92	10 Nov. 88	6 Aug. 90			
7	...	2	Ernest Fentiman Rowe (*Depot*)	8 Dec. 88	22 Nov. 90			
7	...	1	Alexander Russel Finlay	8 Dec. 88	22 Nov. 90			
6	...	1	Stuart Goode[13]	24 Apr. 89	22 Nov. 90			
6	...	1	Cranley Charlton Onslow,[13] *Station Staff Officer, Dalhousie,* 15 Nov. 93.	9 Nov. 89	11 Aug. 91			
6	...	1	George Frederick Culler Saunders[13]	9 Nov. 89	29 Mar. 92			
6	...	1	Frederick William Crawshay	21 Dec. 89	29 Mar. 92			
6	...	1	Richard Wartyr Waldy[13]	21 Dec. 89	29 Mar. 92			
6	...	1	Kenneth Crause Wright[13]	29 Jan. 90	19 May 92			
5	...	1	Arthur Alan Collyer	28 June 90	1 Feb. 93			
5	...		George William Guy Lindesay[13]	29 Oct. 90	28 June 93			
4	...	2	Edward Ivan de Sausmarez Thorpe	20 Feb. 91	11 Nov. 93			
4	...	1	Cyril Hammond Elgee	20 Feb. 92	25 Nov. 93			
4	...	1	Hugh Ilid Nicholl	12 Mar. 92	9 Aug. 94			
3	...	1	George Percy Appleby	18 May 92	7 Nov. 94			
			SECOND LIEUTENANTS.					
3	...	1	Thomas Pelham Johnson	18 May 92				
3	...	1	John Hodson Doveton	13 Aug. 92				
3	...	2	George Edward Foster FitzGerald	17 Dec. 92				
4	...	2	Raymond Maxwell Stallard	5 Dec. 91				
3	...		Charles Edwin M'Vittie, *Army Service Corps*	15 Mar. 93				
2	...	1	Herbert Marwicke Atherstone Hales	26 Apr. 93				
2	...	2	William Edward May Wetherell	17 Jan. 94				
2	...	2	Harry Dyson Selous	7 Mar. 94				
1	...	2	Harold Palgrave Turner	2 June 94				
1	...	1	William Edwin Comber Hood	4 July 94				
1	...	1	Gerard Bannatyne Moule	10 Oct. 94				
1	...	2	Herbert Percy Strong	12 Dec. 94				
1	...		Charles Powlett Strong	6 Mar. 95				

[3] Lt. Colonel Harden served with the Isazai Expedition in 1892.
[5] Major Becher served with the Isazai Expedition in 1892.
[6] Major Aldworth served with the Burmese Expedition in 1885-86 as Aide de Camp and Acting Military Secretary to Sir Harry Prendergast (mentioned in despatches, DSO, and Medal with Clasp).
[8] Captain Richardson-Griffiths served in the Afghan war in 1879-80 with the 8th Bengal Native Infantry (Medal).
[9] Captain Pickard-Cambridge served with the Burmese Expedition in 1886-88 on special service as Orderly Officer to the Brigadier General Commanding 6th Brigade (mentioned in despatches, Medal with two Clasps). Served with the Chin-Lushai Expeditionary Force in 1889-90 as Superintendent of Army Signalling (mentioned in despatches, Clasp).
[10] Captain Scott served with the Burmese Expedition in 1888-89 (Medal with Clasp).
[11] Captain Nelson served with the expedition sent against the Yonnies, on the West Coast of Africa, in 1887-88 (Medal with Clasp).
[12] Captain Franks served with the expedition sent against the Yonnies, on the West Coast of Africa, in 1887-88 (Medal with Clasp).
[*For remainder of Notes, see end of Leicestershire Regiment, p. 257.*
Facings White.—*Agents,* Messrs. Holt and Co.
1st Battalion embarked for Malta, 12 Feb. 1890. 2nd Battalion returned from India 10 Feb. 92.

Paymasters.—2
1 Joseph H. Wansbrough, *Lieut.* 1 Battalion (*acting*).
Quarter Masters.—2 John Thomas Simkins, 11 Jan. 88; *Hon. Lieut.* 8
1 Charles Fox,[13] 4 Dec. 89; *Hon. Lieut.* 6

1st Batt., West Indies.
2nd Batt., Aldershot.] **The Leicestershire Regiment.** [*Regimental District* No. 17.—Leicester.

Formerly the 17th (Leicestershire) Regiment.
(The 3rd Battalion is formed of the Leicestershire Militia.)

"LOUISBURG" "HINDOOSTAN" (with the Royal Tiger). "AFGHANISTAN" "GHUZNEE" "KHELAT" "SEVASTOPOL" "ALI MASJID" "AFGHANISTAN, 1878-79."

Years Ser. Full Pay.	Half Pay.			2ND LIEUT.	LIEUT.	CAPTAIN.	BREV.MAJ.	MAJOR.
		Colonel.—						
30	...	Lieutenant Colonels.—1 p.s.c. Colwyn Williams Vulliamy,[1] *Ens.* 29 Sept. 65; *Lt.* [2] 18 Aug. 69; *Capt.* 22 Jan. 79; *Major,* 15 Nov. 84; *Lt.Colonel,* 5 Feb. 94.						
23	...	2 William Gregg, *Lt.* 24 July 72; *Capt.* 5 Mar. 81; *Major,* 11 Apr. 88; *Lt.Colonel,* 3 Dec. 94.						
		MAJORS.						
23	...	1 Walter Stormont Davies Liardet.........		......	17 July 72	20 Mar. 81	......	15 Aug. 88
21	...	1 Francis William Reader[6]		......	2 Dec. 74	15 Nov. 81	......	5 Feb. 90
20	...	2 Arthur Willliam M'Kinstry[7]		......	5 June 75	7 Mar. 83	......	23 Sept. 90
19	...	2 p.s.c. George Dudley Carleton............		......	11 Sept. 76	26 Mar. 84	......	15 Nov. 91
22	...	2 Richard Louis Milne,[8] *DSO. (Depot)* ...		......	31 Aug. 73	18 Mar. 85	......	18 Nov. 91
20	...	1 Edmund Richard Scott[9]		......	5 June 75	26 Mar. 84	......	18 May 92
19	...	1 Maxwell Robertson Hyslop,[10] *Adj.* 1 *Vol. Bn. Durham Lt.Inf.* 1 Dec. 93 }		......	11 Sept. 76	15 July 84	......	5 Feb. 94
19	...	1 Edward Hodding Peacock		......	26 Feb. 77	31 Oct. 84	......	3 Dec. 94
		CAPTAINS.						
18	...	James Gordon Lennox Burnett, *Adj.* 1 *Volunteer Battalion* 16 Jan. 93 }	30 Jan. 78	21 Nov. 79	24 Dec. 84			
18	...	2 p.s.c. Edward Hugh Griffith[12]	30 Jan. 78	23 Dec. 79	1 Sept. 85			
17	...	2 Benjamin Genlo Humfrey................	19 Oct. 78	15 Aug. 80	7 Oct. 85			
17	...	1 George Henry Poynta Burne.............	22 Jan. 79	5 Oct. 80	19 Jan. 86			
16	...	John Mosse,[13] *Adj.* 3 *Battalion* 25 Nov. 92	13 Aug. 79	18 Dec. 80	14 Sept. 86			
16	...	2 Cecil Henry Hunt	13 Aug. 79	5 Mar. 81	19 Nov. 86			
16	...	1 George Golbourn Tarry,[14] *Adjutant* 25 Nov. 91 }	13 Aug. 79	20 Mar. 81	1 July 87			
16	...	1 Ralph Leslie Sandwith	14 Jan. 80	1 July 81	1 July 87			
19	...	1 p.s.c. Victor Semini (*Lieut. R. Malta Fencible Art.* 28 Oct. 76) (*Depot*)... }	6 Mar. 80	1 July 81	1 July 87			
17	...	2 Vesey Thomas Bunbury[15]	22 Jan. 79	20 Oct. 80	1 July 87			
15	...	Richard Aug. Vowell, *Army Pay Dept.*	11 Aug. 80	1 July 81	15 Aug. 88			
15	...	Lionel Copley Sherer, *serving with the Egyptian Police* }	11 Aug. 80	1 July 81	5 Sept. 88			
15	...	William Fenwick,[17] *Adj.* 1 *Vol. Bn. Warwick Regt.* 1 Apr. 91 }	22 Jan. 81	1 July 81	5 Sept. 88			
14	...	1 Harry Marrion Welstead...................	......	22 Oct. 81	5 Feb. 90			
14	...	2 Frederick Henry Thomas Alexander[18]	......	22 Oct. 81	23 Sept. 90			
14	...	Wm. Locke Jones, *Ordnance Store Dept.*	......	22 Oct. 81	1 Apr. 91			
14	...	George Alfred Bulkley,[19] *Adj.* 3 *Vol. Bn. Manchester Regiment* 1 Nov. 92 }	......	22 Oct. 81	1 Apr. 91			
13	...	p.s.c. Edward Mabbott Woodward, *D.A.A. General, Malta,* 1 Nov. 93 }	......	9 Sept. 82	18 May 92			
13	...	2 William Stafford Copland, *Adjutant* 14 Jan. 95 }	......	10 Mar. 83	1 Nov. 92			
12	...	2 John Hippisley Heycock	......	12 May 83	1 Dec. 93			
10	...	Walter Sydney Melvill, *Aide de Camp to Sir J. T. N. O'Brien* 20 June 92... }	......	9 May 85	8 Jan. 94			
10	...	1 Lucius Aug. de Vere Maunsell	......	23 May 85	8 Jan. 94			
10	...	1 Francis Edward Glossop[20]	......	30 Jan. 86	8 Jan. 94			
9	...	1 Henry Leycester Croker	......	28 Apr. 86	5 Feb. 94			
		LIEUTENANTS.						
9	...	2 William Pearson[21]	......	8 Dec. 86				
9	...	Walter Patrick Hussey-Walsh.............	5 Feb. 87	16 Mar. 89				
8	...	1 Charles Edward Cox........................	5 Nov. 87	1 Dec. 89				
7	...	1 Charles Guinand Blackader	22 Aug. 88	21 Mar. 90				
7	...	1 Charles William Bengough	22 Aug. 88	21 Mar. 90				
7	...	1 George Inverarity Walsh (*Depot*)	8 Dec. 88	20 Aug. 90				
7	...	1 *Hon.* Harold Brooke Hawke	8 Dec. 88	23 Sept. 90				
7	...	1 Tom Maxwell Drew	8 Dec. 88	11 Nov. 90				
6	...	2 Herbert Gorden	21 Sept. 89	1 Apr. 91				
6	...	2 Allen Henry Wilkinson	29 Mar. 90	10 Feb. 92				
6	...	2 Henry Spencer Logan	29 Mar. 90	18 May 92				
6	...	1 William Bryce	29 Mar. 90	20 June 92				
5	...	1 Herbert Stoney Smith	17 Jan. 91	1 Jan. 93				
5	...	1 Reginald Norton Knatchbull.............	4 Mar. 91	1 Mar. 93				
4	...	2 Cecil Myles Serjeantson	2 May 91	23 Aug. 93				
4	...	2 Jepson George Mignon....................	23 May 91	1 Dec. 93				
3	...	1 Bertie Coore Dent..........................	18 June 92	1 Jan. 94				
3	...	2 Arthur Cleghorn Thomson (*Depot*) ...	18 June 92	8 Jan. 94				
3	...	1 Bertram de Weltden Weldon	13 Aug. 92	5 Feb. 94				
		SECOND LIEUTENANTS.						
3	...	2 Bertie Cunynghame Dwyer	19 Nov. 92					
3	...	2 Henry Cecil Thorold	21 Jan. 93					
3	...	1 Michael Busuttil	25 Feb. 93					
3	...	1 Harry Carleton Wilder	15 Mar. 93					
2	...	1 Edward Lacy Challenor	19 July 93					
2	...	2 James Robert Alexander Hunter Paul	9 Sept. 93					
2	...	1 Edgar Crofts Davis	9 Sept. 93					
2	...	1 Claude Henry Haig	7 Mar. 94					
2	...	1 Douglas Charles Faichnie	7 Mar. 94					
2	...	1 John Gage Lecky	7 Mar. 94					
1	...	2 Arthur Almeric Power Butler............	2 June 94					
1	...	2 Frederick Deneys Harrison	10 Oct. 94					

[19] Captain Bulkley served in the Burmese Expedition in 1888-89 with the 2nd Battalion Leicestershire Regiment in the Upper Burma Field Force (Medal with Clasp).

[20] Captain Glossop served in the Burmese Expedition in 1888 with the Chin Frontier Field Force—severely wounded (Medal with Clasp).

[21] Lieut. Pearson served in the Burmese Expedition in 1888-89 with the 2nd Battalion Leicestershire Regiment in the Upper Burma Field Force (Medal with Clasp).

Facings White.—*Agents,* Messrs. Cox and Co.

1st Battalion embarked for Bermuda, 16 September 1888. *2nd Battalion returned from Aden,* 1 December 1890.

| 14 | ... | *Quarter Masters.*—2 Thomas Halloran, 27 April 81; *Hon. Captain,* 27 Apr. 91. |
| 1 | ... | 1 William Baker, 28 Apr. 94; *Hon. Lieut.* |

[1] Lt.Colonel Vulliamy served with the 17th Regiment in the Afghan war in 1878-79, and was present at the capture of Ali Musjid and in the expeditions into the Bazar Valley (Medal with Clasp).
[6] Major Reader served in the Afghan war in 1878-79 as Orderly Officer to Brigadier General Cobbe, and was present at the storming of the Peiwar Kotal (mentioned in despatches, Medal with Clasp).
[7] Major M'Kinstry served with the 5th Punjab Infantry in the Afghan war in 1878-79, and was present in the engagement at Charasiah on the 6th October 1879 and the subsequent occupation of Cabul (Medal with Clasp).
[8] Major Milne served with the 72nd Highlanders throughout the Afghan war of 1878-80 with the Koorum, Cabul, and Cabul-Candahar Field Forces, part of the time as Acting Adjutant, and was present in the engagements at Mattoon and Charasiab, with the rear-guard of the division at Zaidabad during the night attack of 4th October 1879, and in the operations around Cabul in December 1879 (mentioned in despatches); accompanied Sir Frederick Roberts in the march to Candahar (during the latter part of it as Regimental Transport Officer), and was present at the battle of Candahar (mentioned in despatches, Medal with three Clasps, and Bronze Decoration). Served with the 1st Battalion Seaforth Highlanders in the Egyptian war of 1882, and was present at the battle of Tel-el-Kebir (Medal with Clasp, and Khedive's Star). Served with the Burmese Expedition in 1886+87 as Deputy Assistant Adjutant and Quarter Master General to the 2nd Brigade (mentioned in despatches, D.S.O., and Medal with Clasp).
[9] Major Scott served in the Burmese Expedition in 1888-89 with the 2nd Battalion Leicestershire Regiment in the Upper Burma Field Force (Medal with Clasp).
[10] Major Hyslop served with the 17th Regiment in the Afghan war in 1878-79, and was present at the capture of Ali Musjid and in the first expedition into the Bazar Valley (Medal with Clasp). Served in the Burmese Expedition in 1888-89 with the 2nd Battalion Leicestershire Regiment in the Upper Burma Field Force (Medal with Clasp).
[12] Captain Griffith served in the Afghan war of 1878-79 with the 1st Division of the Peshawur Valley Field Force and took part in the expedition into the Bazar Valley (Medal).
[13] Captain Mosse served in the Burmese Expedition in 1888-89 with the 2nd Battalion Leicestershire Regiment in the Upper Burma Field Force (Medal with Clasp).
[14] Captain Tarry served in the Soudan campaign in 1885, and was present in the engagement at the Tofrek zereba (Medal with two Clasps, and Khedive's Star).
[15] Captain Bunbury served in the Burmese Expedition in 1888-89 with the 2nd Battalion Leicestershire Regiment in the Upper Burma Field Force (Medal with Clasp).
[17] Captain Fenwick served with the Burmese Expedition in 1887-89 as Adjutant 2nd Battalion Leicestershire Regiment (Medal with Clasp).
[18] Captain Alexander served in the Burmese Expedition in 1888-89 with the 2nd Battalion Leicestershire Regiment in the Upper Burma Field Force (Medal with Clasp).

Record of the Services of the 1st Battalion Leicestershire Regiment (formerly the 17th Regiment).
Raised in 1688 by King James II., remaining in England till 1689. Ireland, to 1690. England, to 1693. Flanders, to 1699. England and Ireland, to 1701. Holland and Germany, to 1703. Portugal and Spain, to 1709. Scotland, to 1714. Ireland, to 1715. Scotland and England, to 1726. Minorca, to 1748 (detachment at Gibraltar in 1727). Ireland, to 1754. England and Ireland, to 1757. Canada, to 1761 (capture of Louisburg). West Indies, to 1763. North America, to 1767. England, to 1771. Ireland, to 1775. North America, to 1783. Nova Scotia and Newfoundland, to 1786. England and Ireland, to 1796. West Indies, to 1799. [2nd Battalion raised in 1799; reduced in 1802.] England and Holland and returned to England, 1800. Minorca, to 1802. Ireland, to 1804. England, 1804. East Indies, to 1823 (received the distinction of "Hindustan"). England, to 1826. Ireland, to 1829. England, to 1830. New South Wales, to 1836. India, to 1841 (Afghan war of 1838-42, captures of Ghuznee and Khelat). Aden, to 1845 (a detachment remaining in India). India, to 1847. England and Ireland, to 1854. Gibraltar and the Crimea, to 1856 (siege of Sebastopol). Canada, to 1865. England and Ireland, to 1870. India, to 1882 (Afghan war of 1878-89, capture of Ali Musjid). England, to 1888. Bermuda, to 1891. Halifax, N.S., 1891.

Record of the Services of the 2nd Battalion.
Raised in August 1799, and proceeded to Holland, remaining there till the end of the year. England, to 1800. Minorca, to 1802. To Ireland, and reduced at Cork, August 1802. Raised at Devonport, March 1858. England, to 1861. Ireland, 1861. Canada, to 1865. Jamaica, 1865. Canada, to 1868. Ireland, to 1869. Channel Islands, to 1870. England, to 1874. Ireland, to 1876. India, to 1888. Burmah, to 1889. Aden, to 1890. England, 1890.

Continuation of Notes to the Bedfordshire Regiment.

[1] Lt.General Cox served in the 13th Light Infantry the campaigns of 1840, 41, and 42 in Affghanistan, and was present at the assault and capture of the town and fort of Tootumdurrah, storm of Jhoolghur, night attack of Baboo Koosh Ghur, attack on Khardurrah, storming the Khoord Cabool Pass, affair of Tezeen, forcing the Jugdulluck Pass, reduction of the Fort of Mamoo Khail, heroic defence of Jellalabad and sorties on the 14th Nov. (mentioned in despatch) and 1st Dec. 1841, and 11th Mar., 24th Mar., and 1st Apr. 1842; the general action with and defeat of the besieging force under Akbar Khan before Jellalabad on the 7th April (mentioned in despatches for "gallant conduct throughout the day," and as being "the first of the party which captured them to seize two of the enemy's cannon"); the storming of the Jugdulluck heights, general action at Tezeen, and recapture of Cabool, for which he has a Medal, as also another for Jellalabad. Served in the Crimea from 30th June 1855, and was at the battle of the Tchernaya, siege and fall of Sebastopol (Medal with Clasp, 5th Class of the Medjidie, and Turkish Medal). Served in the Indian campaign, and commanded the Left Wing of the 13th Light Infantry from Aug. 1857 to Oct. 1858, and was actively employed in the Azimghur and Gorruckpore districts and southern borders of Oude, present in eight engagements, in three of which he commanded the whole force, in three others he commanded a separate Column, and in the remaining two he acted as principal Staff Officer to the force (repeatedly mentioned in despatches, Brevet of Lt.Colonel, C.B. and Medal).
[2] Lt.Colonel Paterson served as Deputy Assistant Quarter Master General at Durban during the latter part of the Zulu war of 1879 (Medal). Served with the Burmese Expedition in 1887-89 (Medal with Clasp); and with the Isazai Field Force in 1892.
[4] Major More Nisbett served in the Egyptian war of 1882 (Medal, and Khedive's Star).
[13] Captains Logan-Home and Longridge, Lieuts. Roche, Dundas, Traill, Wansbrough, Stares, Goode, Onslow, Saunders, Waldy, Wright, Lindesay and Fox served with the Isazai Expedition in 1892.

Record of the Services of the 1st Battalion Bedfordshire Regiment (formerly the 16th Regiment).
Raised in 1688, and proceeded to Holland, 1689 to 1698. Ireland, to 1701. Holland, to 1713. England and Ireland, to 1742. Holland, to 1748. England, to 1767. America, to 1781. England, to 1786. Ireland, to 1790. America, to 1791. West Indies, to 1796. England, to 1797. Scotland, to 1799. England, to 1800. Ireland, to 1804. West Indies, to Feb. 1812. England, to July 1812. Scotland, to 1813. Ireland, to 1814. England, to Aug. 1815. France, to Dec. 1815. Ireland, to 1819. Ceylon, to 1828. India, to 1840. England, to 1843. Ireland, to 1846. Gibraltar, to 1847. Corfu, to 1851. West Indies, to 1857. Ireland, to 1859. England, to 1861. America, to 1870. Ireland, to 1872. Jersey, to 1873. England, to 1877. Ireland, to 1882. England, to 1887. Ireland, to 1888. England, to Feb. 1890. Malta, to Dec. 1890. To India, 1890.

Record of the Services of the 2nd Battalion.
Raised in Ireland in 1858. To North America, 1861. To the West Indies, 1866. To England, 1869. To India 1876. To Lower Burmah, 1881. (Became 2nd Battalion Bedfordshire Regiment, 1881.) To India, 1885.

258   1st Batt., Limerick.
      2nd Batt., Juboulpore, Bengal.]   **The Royal Irish Regiment.**   [*Regimental District*
                                                                          No. 18.—Clonmel.

Formerly the 18th (The Royal Irish) Regiment.
(The 3rd, 4th, and 5th Battalions are formed of the Wexford, North Tipperary, and Kilkenny
Militia respectively.)

The Harp and Crown. The Lion of Nassau. "*Virtutis Namurcensis Præmium.*" "BLENHEIM" "RAMILLIES"
"OUDENARDE" "MALPLAQUET" "EGYPT" (with the Sphinx). "CHINA" (with the Dragon). "PEGU"
"SEVASTOPOL" "NEW ZEALAND" "AFGHANISTAN, 1879-80" "EGYPT, 1882" "TEL-EL-KEBIR" "NILE, 1884-85."

Years' Ser.				2ND LIEUT.	LIEUT.	CAPTAIN	BREV.MAJ.	MAJOR.
Full Pay	Half Pay							
27	...	**Colonel.**—Robert Walter M'Leod Fraser,¹ *Lt. Colonel*, 25 Nov. 57; *Colonel*, 25 Nov. 62; *Major General*, 28 June 68; *Lieut. General*, 3 Dec. 80; *General*, 1 July 81; *Colonel* Dublin Fusiliers, 27 May 91; *Colonel* Irish Regiment, 8 Jan. 95.						
24	...	**Lieutenant Colonels.**—2 William Wylly Lawrence,⁵ *Ensign*, P27 June 68; *Lieut.* 28 Oct. 71; *Captain*, 18 Sept. 79; *Major*, 1 Mar. 83; *Lt. Colonel*, 23 July 93.						
	...	1 John Henry Augustus Spyer,⁶ *Lieut.* 30 Dec. 71; *Captain*, 1 Jan. 81; *Major*, 3 Oct. 88; *Lt. Colonel*, 17 Dec. 94.						

		MAJORS.		2ND LIEUT.	LIEUT.	CAPTAIN	BREV.MAJ.	MAJOR.
23	...	2 John Burton Forster⁴			23 Nov. 72	26 Feb. 81		6 Feb. 89
22	...	1 p.s.c. Henry William Newton Guinness⁷			9 Aug. 73	22 May 81	15 June 85	11 Nov. 89
22	...	2 Harry Shuldham Lye,⁸ *Commandant Darjeeling Depot*, 8 Mar. 94			9 Aug. 73	23 May 81		7 May 90
22	...	Wm. John Fortescue Morgan,⁹ *A.P. Dept.*			12 Nov. 73	18 June 81		22 May 90
22	...	1 Henry Melville Hatchell¹⁰ (*Depot*)			28 Feb. 74	1 July 81		29 Apr. 91
17	...	1 Frederick James Gavin¹¹	1 May 78	9 July 79	21 May 84		2 Mar. 92
17	...	2 Alan George Chichester	4 Dec. 78	1 Jan. 80	3 Dec. 84		23 July 93
16	...	2 Chas. Herbert Lethbridge Baskerville¹⁴	13 Aug. 79	22 Dec. 80	16 May 85		17 Dec. 94
		CAPTAINS.						
16	...	1 Arthur Nairn Lysaght,¹⁵ *Adjutant* 25 Apr. 91	13 Aug. 79	29 Sept. 80	12 Feb. 86		
17	...	Archdale Irby Wilson,¹⁶ *Adjutant* 5 Battalion 1 Mar. 93	22 Feb. 79	31 Mar. 81	13 April 87		
16	...	Raymund Crawford, *Ordnance Store Dept.*	14 Jan. 80	18 June 81	22 May 87		
16	...	Beauchamp John Colclough Doran,¹⁹ *D.A.A.Gen.for Musk,Bengal*,6Nov.91	14 Jan. 80	1 July 81	22 May 87	23 May 87	
14	...	Kendal Pretyman Apthorp,²⁰ *Adjutant Oude Volunteer Rifles* 2 Aug. 94	23 April 81	1 July 81	23 July 88		
14	...	2 Alexander Stewart Orr²¹		22 Oct. 81	30 Oct. 88		
13	...	2 Walter Robert Butler Doran²²		10 May 82	26 Nov. 88		
13	...	Philip de Salis Bass,²³ *Ordnance Store Dept.*		29 July 82	11 Nov. 89		
13	...	Hen. John Downing,²⁴ *Adj.* 3 Bn. 10 Jan. 91		29 July 82	20 Nov. 89		
13	...	Alexander Bowers King,²⁵ *Adjutant* 2 *Vol. Bn. Royal Fusiliers* 15 Sept. 91		29 July 82	7 May 90		
13	...	Charles William Garraway,²⁶ *Adjutant N. Bengal Mounted Rifles* 11 July 93		27 Jan. 83	22 May 90		
13	...	Arthur Henry Morris,³⁰ *DSO. Adjutant* 4 *Battalion* 30 Oct. 93		27 Jan. 83	27 Apr. 91		
13	...	2 Thomas Louis Segrave²⁸		10 Mar. 83	29 Apr. 91		
11	...	1 Graham Owen Robert Wynne²⁹		12 Nov. 84	15 Sept. 91		
10	...	1 William Gloster³³		6 May 85	10 Feb. 92		
10	...	2 Richard Orlando Kellett,³⁴ *Adjutant* 1 Apr. 91		6 May 85	10 Feb. 92		
10	...	Ross Acheson Smyth (*Depot*)		23 May 85	12 Nov. 92		
10	...	1 Cliffe Henry Vigors		29 Aug. 85	1 Mar. 93		
9	...	1 Norton Clowes Castle		10 Nov. 86	29 Mar. 93		
9	...	1 Walter Johnston,³⁵ *Superintendent of Gymnasia, Portsmouth*		25 Aug. 86	5 Apr. 93		
8	...	2 Dudley Herbert Davis	4 May 87	20 Nov. 89	11 July 93		
8	...	Robert Nassau Alex. Flannagan, *Adj.* 4 *Bn. Connaught Rangers* 1 Jan. 95	28 Sept. 87	6 Nov. 89	11 Oct. 93		
7	...	2 Waldene FitzWilliam Hutchinson Bredin	12 Sept. 88	19 Mar. 90	12 Sept. 94		
8	...	Robert Léonce Owens, *Adj. Madras East Coast Volunteer Rifles*	21 May 87	5 Dec. 83	30 Jan. 95		
6	...	1 George Francis Reginald Forbes	6 July 89	25 Mar. 91	30 Jan. 95		
		LIEUTENANTS.						
6	...	2 Redmond Geo. Sylverius Lone Moriarty (*Depot*)		9 Nov. 89	29 Apr. 91		
6	...	1 Stratford Edward St. Leger		29 Jan. 90	12 Aug. 91		
5	...	1 Henry Newton Kelly (*Depot*)		3 May 90	12 Aug. 91		
5	...	2 James Bergmont Standly Alderson		28 June 90	26 Aug. 91		
5	...	1 John George Albert Massy		28 June 90	26 Aug. 91		
5	...	1 George Meredyth Grogan		16 July 90	26 Aug. 91		
5	...	1 Charles Edward Galwey		29 Nov. 90	15 Sept. 91		
5	...	2 Francis Langford Fosbery		4 Mar. 91	4 Jan. 92		
5	...	1 Sampson Gough French		25 Mar. 91	4 Feb. 92		
5	...	Frank M'Conaghey		25 Mar. 91	2 July 92		
4	...	1 Richard Sweetman		2 May 91	13 Sept. 92		
4	...	2 Francis Chester Macnaghten		23 May 91	13 Sept. 92		
4	...	1 William Nelson Lushington		23 May 91	13 Sept. 92		
4	...	1 Reginald Ramsay Arbuthnot		10 Oct. 91	1 Mar. 93		
4	...	2 Charles Alexander Robert Hutchinson		7 Nov. 91	29 Mar. 93		
4	...	1 Edward Francis Milner		25 Nov. 91	3 May 93		
4	...	1 Edward O'Brien		30 Dec. 91	30 May 93		
4	...	1 John Charles Henry M'Caskill		27 Jan. 92	11 July 93		
4	...	1 William Henry Willans		20 Feb. 92	28 Dec. 93		
3	...	2 Edward Herbert Sweet		9 Apr. 92	27 Mar. 94		
3	...	2 Edward Henry Edwin Daniell		9 Apr. 92	27 June 94		
3	...	2 William Hawtrey White		19 Oct. 92	2 July 94		
3	...	2 Malcolm Hammond Edward Welch		21 Jan. 93	12 Sept. 94		
		SECOND LIEUTENANTS.						
2	...	2 Fredric Mostyn Watkins		26 Apr. 93			
2	...	2 Eustace John Garrard Moffat		19 July 93			
2	...	1 Aplyn Waring Brush		9 Sept. 93			
2	...	1 Frederick Sutherland Lillie		9 Sept. 93			
2	...	2 Thomas James Willans		21 Oct. 93			
2	...	2 Charles Percy Nicolas		21 Feb. 93			

²¹ Captain Orr served in the Egyptian war of 1882, and was present at the action at Kassasin on the 9th Sept. and at the battle of Tel-el-Kebir (Medal with Clasp, and Khedive's Star). Served in the Hazara Expedition in 1888 with the 2nd Battalion Royal Irish Regiment including the engagement at Kotkai (Medal with Clasp).

³⁷ Major Hamilton served with the 18th Royal Irish throughout the New Zealand war of 1863-66, including the expeditions to Paparata and Ketemari (Medal). Served in the Egyptian war of 1882, and was present at the action at Kassasin on the 9th Sept. and at the battle of Tel-el-Kebir (mentioned in despatches, honorary rank of Major, Medal with Clasp, and Khedive's Star). Served in the Hazara Expedition in 1888 with the 2nd Battalion Royal Irish Regiment including the engagement at Kotkai (Medal with Clasp).

Years' Ser.			2ND LIEUT.
Full Pay	Half Pay	SECOND LIEUTENANTS.	
1	...	1 Langford Llanwarne Farmer.................	3 Oct. 94
1	...	2 Henry Alexander Sidney Bridge	10 Oct. 94
1	...	2 Charles de Joncourt Luxmoore	10 Oct. 94
1	...	2 Louis James Lipsett...........................	10 Oct. 94
1	...	1 Edward Martin Panter-Downes	10 Oct. 94
1	...	1 Henry William Ross Potter..................	12 Dec. 94

Paymasters.—2 Edward F. Milner, *Lieut.* 2 *Battalion (acting).*

| 27 | ... | *Quarter Masters.*—2 Thomas Hamilton,[37] 3 Feb. 69 ; *Hon. Captain*, 1 July 81 ; *Hon. Major*, 18 Nov. 87. |
| 6 | ... | 1 Fritz Philip Reger,[38] 12 Feb. 90; *Hon. Lieut.* |

Facings Blue.—*Agents*, Messrs. Cox and Co.
1*st Battalion returned from Egypt*, 9 *Sept.* 1885. 2*nd Battalion embarked for Malta*, 1884.

[3] General Fraser acted as Staff Officer to a Detachment sent from Bombay in 1837 against the rebels in Canada. Served also with the 6th Regiment in the Kaffir war of 1846-47 (Medal). He was commissioned in Oct. 1857 to raise the 2nd Battalion 6th Regiment, and having within one month raised considerably upwards of 1,000 recruits, was Gazetted on the 25th Nov. 1857 its Lieutenant Colonel. This Battalion embarked in May 1858 for service at Gibraltar.

[4] Major Forster served in the Nile Expedition in 1884-85 with the 1st Battalion of the Royal Irish Regiment (Medal with Clasp, and Khedive's Star).

[5] Lt. Colonel Lawrence served in the Transport Department throughout the Zulu war of 1879, and was present in the action of Gingindhlovu (Medal with Clasp). Served with the 18th Royal Irish in the Afghan war in 1880 (Medal).

[6] Lt. Colonel Spyer served in the Afghan war of 1878-80 (Medal). Served in the Nile Expedition in 1884-85 with the 1st Battalion of the Royal Irish Regiment (Medal with Clasp, and Khedive's Star).

[7] Major Guinness served in the Nile Expedition in 1884-85 with the 1st Battalion of the Royal Irish Regiment (mentioned in despatches, Brevet of Major, Medal with Clasp, and Khedive's Star).

[8] Major Lye served in the Afghan war in 1879-80 with the 18th Royal Irish (Medal). Served in the Egyptian war of 1882, and was present at the action at Kassasin on the 9th September and at the battle of Tel-el-Kebir (Medal with Clasp, and Khedive's Star).

[9] Major Morgan served in the Nile Expedition in 1884-85 with the 1st Battalion Royal Irish Regiment (Medal with Clasp, and Khedive's Star). Served in the Hazara Expedition in 1888 with the 2nd Battalion Royal Irish Regiment including the engagement at Kotkai (Medal with Clasp).

[10] Major Hatchell served in the Afghan war in 1879-80 with the 18th Royal Irish Regiment and as Orderly Officer to Major General Roberts (Medal). Served in the Egyptian war of 1882, and was present at the action of Kassasin on the 9th September and at the battle of Tel-el-Kebir (Medal with Clasp, and Khedive's Star)

[11] Major Gavin served in the Hazara Expedition in 1888 with the 2nd Battalion Royal Irish Regiment including the engagement at Kotkai (Medal with Clasp).

[12] Major Chichester served in the Egyptian war of 1882, and was present at the action at Kassasin on the 9th September and at the battle of Tel-el-Kebir—severely wounded (Medal with Clasp, 5th Class of the Medjidie, and Khedive's Star).

[14] Major Baskerville served in the Afghan war in 1880 with the 51st Light Infantry, and took part with the second expedition into the Lughman Valley including the engagement at Nargozi (Medal). Served with the Nile Expedition in 1885 on the Commissariat and Transport Staff.

[15] Captain Lysaght served in the Hazara Expedition in 1888 with the 2nd Battalion Royal Irish Regiment including the engagement at Kotkai (Medal with Clasp).

[16] Captain Wilson served in the Afghan war in 1880 (Medal). Served in the Nile Expedition in 1884-85 with the 1st Battalion of the Royal Irish Regiment (Medal with Clasp, and Khedive's Star).

[19] Major B. J. C. Doran served with the 18th Royal Irish in the Afghan war in 1880 (Medal). Served in the Nile Expedition in 1884-85 with the 1st Battalion of the Royal Irish Regiment (mentioned in despatches, Brevet of Major, Medal with Clasp, and Khedive's Star). Served with the Hazara Expedition in 1888, and was present in the engagement at Kotkai (Medal with Clasp). Served with the Miranzai Expedition in 1891 as Brigade Major to the 1st Brigade (mentioned in despatches, Clasp).

[20] Captain Apthorp served in the Nile Expedition in 1884-85 with the 1st Battalion Royal Irish Regiment (Medal with Clasp, and Khedive's Star). Served in the Hazara Expedition in 1888 with the 2nd Battalion Royal Irish Regiment including the engagement at Kotkai (Medal with Clasp).

[22] Captain W. R. B. Doran served in the Egyptian war of 1882, and was present at the action at Kassasin on the 9th September and at the battle of Tel-el-Kebir (Medal with Clasp, and Khedive's Star). Served with the Nile Expedition in 1884-85 with the 1st Battalion of the Royal Irish Regiment and afterwards with Native levies with the rank of Staff Captain (Clasp). Served with the Hazara Expedition in 1888 as Adjutant to the 2nd Battalion Royal Irish Regiment, and was present in the engagement at Kotkai (Medal with Clasp).

[24] Captains Bass, Downing, King, Garraway, Segrave and Wynne served in the Hazara Expedition in 1888 with the 2nd Battalion Royal Irish Regiment including the engagement at Kotkai (Medal with Clasp).

[30] Captain Morris served with the Nile Expedition in 1884-85 (Medal with Clasp, and Khedive's Star). Served with the Burmese Expedition in 1885-87 as Transport Officer (Medal with Clasp) ; and again in 1888-89 as Chief Transport Officer to the Karen Field Force (mentioned in despatches, Clasp). Served with the Chin-Lushai Expeditionary Force in 1889-90 as Chief Transport Officer to the Burma Column (received the thanks of the Government of India, mentioned in despatches, DSO., and Clasp).

[33] Captain Gloster served in the Hazara Expedition in 1888 with the 2nd Battalion Royal Irish Regiment including the engagement at Kotkai (mentioned in despatches, Medal with Clasp).

[34] Captain Kellett served in the Hazara Expedition in 1888 with the 2nd Battalion Royal Irish Regiment (Medal with Clasp).

[35] Captain Johnston served in the expedition sent against the Yonnies, on the West Coast of Africa, in 1887-88 (mentioned in despatches, Medal with Clasp). Served in the operations in the Tambaka Country, on the West Coast of Africa, in 1892, including the capture of Tambi ; and in the expedition to the Gambia in 1892, including the capture of Toniataba (mentioned in despatches, Clasp).

[38] Lieut. Reger served in the Afghan war in 1880 with the 18th Royal Irish Regiment (Medal). Served in the Nile Expedition in 1884-85 with the 1st Battalion Royal Irish Regiment (Medal with Clasp, and Khedive's Star).

The Princess of Wales' Own (Yorkshire Regiment).

1st Batt., **Jersey.**
2nd Batt., **Shwebo, Burmah.**] *Formerly the* 19th (1st *Yorkshire North Riding—Princess of Wales' Own*) *Regiment.*

Regimental District No. 1.
Richmond, Yorkshire.

(The 3rd and 4th Battalions are formed of the 5th West York and the North York Militia respectively.)

The White Rose. "MALPLAQUET" "ALMA" "INKERMAN" "SEVASTOPOL."

Colonel.—*Sir* Robert Onesiphorus Bright,[1] *KCB. Ens.* P9 June 43; *Lt.* P2 Apr. 47; *Capt.* P23 Jan. 52; *Major*, 15 Sept. 55; *Bt.Lt.Colonel*, 26 Dec. 56; *Lt.Colonel*, 28 Nov. 57; *Colonel*, 1 May 62; *Major General*, 6 March 68; *Lieut.General*, 13 Apr. 80; *General*, 1 Apr. 87; *Colonel* Yorkshire Regiment, 27 Oct. 86.

Lieutenant Colonels.—2 William Graham Waugh M'Clintock,[4] *Ensign*, 4 Aug. 65; *Lt.* P23 Jan. 69; *Capt.* 13 Mar. 78; *Major*, 4 Feb. 82; *Lt.Colonel*, 28 July 92.
1 Edward Archibald Bruce, *Ensign*, P23 Jan. 69; *Lt.* 28 Oct. 71; *Capt.* 1 Mar. 79; *Major*, 29 Sept. 82; *Lt.Colonel*, 29 Mar. 93.

Years' Ser. Full Pay.	Half Pay.		MAJORS.	2ND LIEUT.	LIEUT.	CAPTAIN.	BREV.MAJ.	MAJOR.
21	...	2	William Edmund Franklyn........		13 June 74	30 Mar. 81		20 Apr. 86
20	...	1	John William Robinson Parker		12 Feb. 76	8 June 81		2 May 90
19	...	1	Charles John Spottiswoode[6]		5 June 76	29 Sept. 82		11 May 90
19	...	2	Henry Bowles[7]		26 Feb. 77	26 Sept. 83	15 June 85	4 Mar. 92
19	...	2	Gilbert H. Fearon Mathison[9]............		10 Mar. 77	14 Nov. 83		1 Apr. 92
18	...		Edward John Bentley Buckle,[10] *Adj.* 3 *Vol. Bn. W. York Regt.* 9 Apr. 91 }	8 Dec. 77	8 Dec. 77	1 Aug. 84		28 July 92
18	...	2	James Ahmuty Fearon,[12] *Commandant Wellington Depot* 19 Nov. 94 }	23 Jan. 78	23 Jan. 78	16 Aug. 84		29 Mar. 93
18	...	1	Thomas David Kirkpatrick (*Depot*)........	8 Dec. 77	1 Jan. 78	16 Aug. 84		28 Mar. 94

CAPTAINS.

18	...	2	Edward William Mills	30 Jan. 78	13 July 78	1 Apr. 85		
17	...	1	Gerald Carlile Stratford Handcock[11]	10 Apr. 78	1 Mar. 79	24 May 85		
17	...		William Auschar Chauncy,[9] *Adjutant* 1 *Vol. Bn. Yorkshire Regt.* 20 Apr. 91 }	30 Oct. 78	21 June 79	27 July 85		
17	...		Arthur de Salis Hadow,[8] *Adjutant* 2 *Vol. Bn. Yorkshire Regt.* 15 Dec. 93 }	4 Dec. 78	11 Oct. 79	8 Nov. 85		
17	...	2	Alfred Grahame Cartwright[9]................	1 Jan. 79	11 Feb. 80	1 Sept. 86		
17	...		James Trevelyan Cotesworth,[14] *Adjutant* 3 *Battalion* 26 Oct. 91 }	22 Jan. 79	20 Mar. 80	11 Jan. 88		
16	...		Arthur Bayard Elton, *Adjutant Coorg and Mysore Vol. Rifles* 27 June 91 }	13 Aug. 79	2 Oct. 80	4 May 88		
16	...	1	Michael Harrison Orr[15]	14 Jan. 80	1 July 81	29 Sept. 88		
15	...		James Wm. Bradford Silverthorne, *Adj.* 1 *Vol. Bn. S. Lancashire Regt.* 16 Feb. 93 }	19 Feb. 81	1 July 81	31 Oct. 88		
16	...	1	Michael Lloyd Ferrar[9]	14 Jan. 80	1 July 81	2 May 90		
17	...	1	George Pearson[17]	30 Oct. 78	1 July 81	11 May 90		
15	...	1	William Lindsay Mercer[9]	22 Jan. 81	1 July 81	9 Apr. 91		
15	...	2	William Joseph Todd..........................	23 Oct. 80	1 July 81	27 June 91		
13	...	1	Edward Malcolm Esson[8].....................		10 May 82	1 Apr. 92		
13	...		Arthur Lenox Napier, *Adj.* 4 *Bn.* 1 May 94	......	9 Sept. 82	28 July 92		
13	...	2	Charles Arthur Cecil King[9]		9 Sept. 82	15 Feb. 93		
12	...	2	Francis Connop[8] (*Depot*)		6 Feb. 84	28 Mar. 94		
11	...	1	Desmond Lambert Hartley		14 May 84	17 Oct. 94		
11	...		Edward Stanislaus Bulfin		12 Nov. 84	30 Jan. 95		

LIEUTENANTS.

11	...	1	Fred. William Templetown Robinson ...		12 May 84	
11	...	1	Ernest Somervell[19]		28 Feb. 85	
10	...	2	Hardress Gilbert Holmes, *Aide de Camp to the Governor of Madras*............ }		9 May 85	
10	...		p.s.c. Cecil Lothian Nicholson		29 Aug. 85	
10	...	1	Charles William Gale, *Adjutant* 16 Jan. 93		30 Jan. 86	
9	6/12		Henry Rothes Stewart Maitland		30 Jan. 86	
10	...	2	Berkeley Cole Wilmot Williams (*Depot*)...		30 Jan. 86	
9	...	1	Leslie Michael Farrell		12 May 86	
9	...		Gerard Christian	5 Feb. 87	2 May 90	
9	...	2	Ronald D'Arcy Fife	14 Sept. 87	10 Sept. 90	
8	...	2	Edward Lovelace Vans Agnew	14 Sept. 87	9 Apr. 91	
8	...	1	Harold Futvoye Lea, *Adjutant* 19 June 91	14 Sept. 87	1 May 91	
8	...	1	Maurice Hilliard Tomlin	29 Feb. 88	19 June 91	
7	...	2	Ferdinand Harper Hodge	10 Oct. 88	13 Jan. 92	
7	...	2	Wilfrid Harry Dent	10 Nov. 88	1 Mar. 92	
6	...	1	Harry Elliott Raymond	24 Apr. 89	1 Apr. 92	
6	...	1	Arthur Francis Owen-Lewis (*Depot*)	8 June 89	28 July 92	
6	...	1	Hubert Arthur Stansfold......................	21 Dec. 89	26 July 93	
5	...		Charles Morris Kemble, *Army Service Corps* }	28 June 90	31 Dec. 93	
4	...	2	David Edward Osborne Jones...............	17 June 91	28 Mar. 94	
4	...	1	Ernest Henry Lee Warner	10 Oct. 91	26 July 94	
4	...	2	Ernest Gregorie Caffin.......................	10 Oct. 91	17 Oct. 94	

SECOND LIEUTENANTS.

4	...	2	Reginald Edwin Bond	9 Jan. 92	
4	...	2	Alexander Bredin	9 Jan. 92	
4	...	2	Herbert Albrecht Fulton.....................	27 Jan. 92	
3	...		Henry George Lyon Corbett.................	9 Apr. 92	
3	...	2	Walter Lorenzo Alexander	18 May 92	
3	...		Earls Ainslie Hosford, *Station Staff Officer, Bernardmyo* }	19 Nov. 92	
2	...	1	Edward Bouverie Pusey.......................	9 Sept. 93	
2	...	1	Ralph Elliot Noyes	21 Oct. 93	
1	...	2	John Herbert Hay Noble	12 Sept. 94	
1	...	1	William Horsburgh Lane	10 Oct. 94	
1	...	2	George Cuthbert Dillon Masterson	12 Dec. 94	
1	...	1	Edward Henry Chapman......................	20 Feb. 95	

[11] Captain Handcock served with the Soudan Frontier Field Force in 1885-86 during the operations on the Upper Nile (Medal and Khedive's Star).

[12] Major Fearon served during the Nile Expedition in 1884-85 as Adjutant 1st Battalion Yorkshire Regiment on the Line of Communications up the Nile.

[14] Captain Cotesworth served in the Soudan Expedition in 1885 with the Mounted Infantry, and was present in the engagements at Hasheen, Temai, and Takdoul (Medal with Clasp, and Khedive's Star).

[*For remainder of Notes see end of Lancashire Fusiliers, p. 261a.*

Paymasters.—2 Edward S. Bulfin, *Lieut.* 2 *Battalion* (*acting*).

Quarter Masters.—1 Charles Organ,[9] 8 Aug. 83; *Hon. Captain* 8 Aug. 93.
2 James Greer, 11 July 94; *Hon. Lieut.*

Facings White.—*Agents*, Messrs. Holt and Co.

1st Battalion returned from Egypt, 22 Sept. 1889. 2nd Batt. embarked for India, 1 Jan. 1890.

1st Batt., Curragh.
2nd Batt., Quetta, Bengal.

The Lancashire Fusiliers.

Regimental District No. 20.—Bury.

Formerly the 20th (The East Devonshire) Regiment.
(The 3rd Battalion is formed of the 7th Royal Lancashire Militia.)
"DETTINGEN" "MINDEN" "EGMONT-OP-ZEE" "EGYPT" (with the Sphinx). "MAIDA" "VIMIERA" "CORUNNA" "VITTORIA" "PYRENEES" "ORTHES" "TOULOUSE" "PENINSULA" "ALMA" "INKERMAN" "SEVASTOPOL" "LUCKNOW."

Years' Ser. Full Pay	Half Pay			Ensign or 2nd Lieut.	Lieut.	Captain.	Brev. Maj.	Major.
		Colonel.—Sir William Pollexfen Radcliffe,[1] KCB. Ensign, P12 Mar. 41; Lieut. P2 Aug. 42; Captain, P25 July 51; Bt.Major, 12 Dec. 54; Major, 29 Aug. 56; Lt.Colonel, 26 Mar. 58; Colonel, 26 Mar. 63; Major General, 28 Oct. 68; Lt.General, 9 Mar. 82; General, 1 Apr. 87; Colonel Berkshire Regiment, 30 Dec. 91; Colonel Lancashire Fusiliers, 27 Jan. 94.							
30	...	Lieutenant Colonels.—1 Frederick William Birch, Ensign, P10 Nov. 65; Lt. P14 Oct. 68; Captain, 10 Feb. 77; Major, 19 Nov. 81; Lt.Colonel, 25 Sept. 93.						
28	...	2 Cuthbert George Collingwood, Ensign, P14 Sept. 67; Lieut. P3 Sept. 70; Captain, 11 May 78; Major, 27 June 83; Lt.Colonel, 15 Oct. 94.						
		MAJORS.						
27	...	2 George Lycett Engledue May		P13 June 68	P 9 Aug. 71	22 Nov. 78	......	4 April 83
25	...	1 Richard George Bruxner Randall		P 8 June 70	28 Oct. 71	24 Jan. 80	......	10 Oct. 86
26	...	1 Ruscombe Field Westmacott[2]		P 9 Oct. 69	28 Oct. 71	23 Mar. 81	......	12 Mar. 90
21	...	Charles James Blomfield, D. A. A.Gen. Poona, 27 Oct. 92		......	11 Feb. 75	1 July 81		31 July 90
22	...	1 p.s.c. Charles Molyneux Hutton (Depot)		......	9 Aug. 73	15 Nov. 83	......	27 July 92
21	...	2 Philip Francis Tallents		......	20 Feb. 75	15 Oct. 81	......	5 Oct. 92
20	...	George Edward Capel Cure, Adj. 2 Vol. Bn. Lancashire Fusiliers 1 Sept. 92		......	20 Nov. 75	11 May 83	......	25 Sept. 93
20	...	2 Horace William Scott		......	11 Feb. 76	9 June 84		15 Oct. 94
		CAPTAINS.						
19	...	Edward Roderic Owen,[4] D.S.O.		......	11 Sept. 76	4 Aug. 84	16 Aug. 92	
19	...	1 p.s.c. Frederick Hammersley[5]		......	11 Sept. 76	2 Feb. 85	15 June 85	
19	...	Charles Digby Wallington, Adjutant 1 Volunteer Battalion 25 Jan. 94		......	28 Oct. 76	10 Oct. 86		
17	...	1 Stephen Flookton Charles		22 Jan. 79	7 July 80	9 June 88		
17	...	Brudenell Deane-Freeman		22 Jan. 79	8 July 80	1 July 88		
16	...	1 Henry Townshend Fleming		14 Jan. 80	13 April 81	12 July 88		
16	...	2 Felton Amber		14 Jan. 80	18 May 81	1 Jan. 89		
15	...	Charles Foyle Randolph, Adjutant 4 Vol. Bn. Durham Light Infantry 1 Oct. 90		11 Aug. 80	1 July 81	19 Nov. 89		
14	...	Richard Woodforde Deane, Adj. 3 Vol. Bn. Lancashire Fusiliers 8 Feb. 92		23 April 81	1 July 81	19 Mar. 90		
14	...	Robert Burton Page, Adjutant 2 Bn. B. B. & C. I. Railway Vols. 26 Nov. 91		......	22 Oct. 81	1 July 90		
14	...	1 James Henry Gideon		......	22 Oct. 81	31 July 90		
15	...	2 Capel Molyneux Brunker, Station Staff Officer, Quetta		23 Oct. 80	1 July 81	7 Feb. 88		
14	...	Hy. Stannus Hamilton, Adj. 4Bn.22Apr.91		......	22 Oct. 81	22 Apr. 91		
13	...	2 Edward Cecil Tidswell		......	10 May 82	26 Nov. 91		
13	...	p.s.c. William Frederick Walter, serving with the Egyptian Army		......	9 Sept. 82	8 Feb. 92		
12	...	Frederick David Milward, O.S.Dept.		......	12 May 83	1 Sept. 92		
12	...	2 Wilmot Foster Elmslie (Depot)		......	12 May 83	5 Oct. 92		
12	...	1 Harry Vere Benett, Adjutant 6 Dec. 92		......	25 Aug. 83	30 Nov. 92		
12	...	2 Owen Cadogan Wolley-Dod, Adjutant 15 Mar. 92		......	25 Aug. 83	30 Nov. 92		
11	...	1 Charles Lucena Robinson		......	12 Nov. 84	6 Dec. 92		
11	...	2 Charles Herbert Hicks, Paymaster Deolah Depot		......	12 Nov. 84	20 Dec. 92		
10	...	Edward Woolmer, Adjutant 3 Battalion 15 March 95		......	23 May 85	14 Dec. 92		
9	...	1 Arthur James Mitchell		......	28 Apr. 86	14 June 93		
9	...	2 Louis Lort Rhys Samson		......	25 Aug. 86	25 Jan. 94		
		LIEUTENANTS.						
9	...	1 John Nicholas Whyte			10 Nov. 86			
9	...	2 Harold Vere Selby Ormond			22 Dec. 86			
7	...	2 Harry Oswald Bishop		20 June 88	19 Mar. 90			
7	...	1 Edgar Herbert Armstrong		23 Mar. 89	1 July 90			
6	...	1 Thomas Stewart Herschel Wade		24 Apr. 89	22 Apr. 91			
6	...	2 Robert Gray Kennedy		14 Aug. 89	18 Aug. 91			
6	...	1 Wemyss Gawne Cunningham Feilden		29 Mar. 90	26 Nov. 91			
5	...	2 Walter Escott Oakshott (Depot)		29 Oct. 90	15 June 92			
5	...	2 Beresford Cecil Molyneux Carter		25 Mar. 91	1 Sept. 92			
4	...	2 Robert Thurstan Greaves		13 May 91	5 Oct. 92			
4	...	2 Percival Forbes Newnham		9 Jan. 92	7 Apr. 93			
3	...	1 Audley Reid Lempriere		9 Apr. 92	7 Apr. 93			
3	...	2 George Jasper Farmar		18 May 92	7 Apr. 93			
3	...	2 Walter Bagot Pearson		18 June 92	14 June 93			
3	...	2 Henry Percival Keelan		18 June 92	14 June 93			
3	...	Charles Fairlie Dobbs		18 June 92	14 June 93			
3	...	2 Harry Spencer Scott Harden		19 Oct. 92	8 Aug. 93			
3	...	2 Robert Bruce Blunt		19 Nov. 92	25 Jan. 94			
3	...	2 George Henry Basil Freeth		19 Nov. 92	23 May 94			
3	...	2 Kenrick Horace Lloyd		17 Dec. 92	11 Oct. 94			
		SECOND LIEUTENANTS.						
3	...	2 Edmond John Arthur		25 Feb. 93				
3	...	1 George Stopford Adams		25 Feb. 93				
3	...	2 Gilbert Macdonald Stewart		25 Feb. 93				
3	...	2 Thomas Gordon Cumming Bliss		15 Mar. 93				
2	...	1 Julian Mayne Young		20 May 93				
2	...	1 Eustace Carlile Brierley		19 July 93				
2	...	1 Harry George Burrard		9 Sept. 93				
2	...	1 John Vernon Timmis		9 Sept. 93				
2	...	1 Hamlet Bush Toller		21 Oct. 93				
1	...	1 John Frederick Vernon Thorne		28 Feb. 94				
1	...	2 Horace Hayman Wilson		2 June 94				
1	...	1 Vere Henry Ambrose Awdry		20 Feb. 95				

Years' Ser.		
Full Pay	Half Pay	
10	...	**Paymaster.**—2 George J. Farmar, *Lieut.* 2 *Battalion (acting).* **Quarter Masters.**—2 John Sullivan Cameron, 2 Jan. 86; *Hon. Lieut.*
1	...	1 George Gribble, 13 Feb, 95; *Hon. Lieut.*

Facings White.—*Agents*, Messrs. Cox and Co.
1st Battalion returned from Bermuda, 1881. *2nd Battalion embarked for Bombay*, 1881.

[1] Sir William Radcliffe served the Eastern campaign of 1854-55 with the 20th Regiment, including the battles of Alma (as Aide de Camp to acting Brigadier General Horn), Balaklava, and Inkerman, siege of Sebastopol, and affair of the 18th June (Medal with four Clasps, Brevet of Major, Sardinian and Turkish Medals, and 5th Class of the Medjidie). Served in the Indian Mutiny campaign of 1857-58, and was present at the actions of Chanda, Umeerpore, and Sultanpore, and at the siege and capture of Lucknow—wounded (sabre-cut in right hand) and twice mentioned in despatches (Medal with Clasp, and *CB*.).

[2] Major Westmacott served in the Zulu war in 1879 (Medal with Clasp).

[5] Major Hammersley served with the Nile Expedition in 1884-85 on the Lines of Communication (mentioned in despatches, Brevet of Major, Medal with Clasp, and Khedive's Star).

[4] Captain Owen served in the operations against the Jebus, Lagos, West Coast of Africa, in 1892—wounded (mentioned in despatches, Brevet of Major, *DSO*, and Medal with Clasp).

Record of the Services of the 1st Battalion Lancashire Fusiliers,—formerly the 20th (East Devonshire) Regiment.

Raised in 1688 to 1702. Spain and West Indies, to June 1704. England and Ireland, to May 1707. Portugal, to July 1713. Gibraltar, to May 1728. Ireland, to May 1741. Germany, May 1742 to November 1745 (battle of Dettingen). Scotland and England, to May 1758. Germany, to January 1763 (battle of Minden). England, to March 1763. Gibraltar, to July 1769. England, to July 1774. Ireland, to April 1776. Canada, to September 1781. England, to September 1783. Ireland, to June 1789. Canada, to June 1792. West Indies, to March 1796. England, to August 1799. Holland, to October 1799 (battle of Egmont-op-Zee). England, to June 1800. Minorca, to June 1801. Egypt, to December 1801 (badge of "Egypt"—with the Sphinx). Malta, to October 1805. Italy and Sicily, to January 1808 (battle of Maida). England, to July 1808. Portugal and Spain, to January 1809 (battles of Vimiera and Corunna). England, to July 1809. Holland, to September 1809. England, to June 1810. Ireland, to October 1812. The Peninsula and France, to June 1814 (battles of Vittoria, the Pyrenees, Orthes and Toulouse). Ireland, to March 1819. St. Helena, to April 1822. India, to May 1837. England, to June 1840. Ireland, to September 1841. Bermuda, to April 1847. Canada, to June 1853. England, to July 1854. The Crimea, to July 1856 (battles of Alma and Inkerman and siege of Sebastopol). England, to August 1857. India, to March 1867 (capture of Lucknow). England, to December 1869. Ireland, to March 1873. Bermuda, to November 1876. Nova Scotia, to November 1878. Cyprus and Malta, to January 1881. Ireland, to September 1885. England, to February 1889. Scotland, to April 1891. Ireland, 1891.

Record of the Services of the 2nd Battalion Lancashire Fusiliers.

Raised in Ireland in 1858. To England, 1861. To China, 1863. To Japan, 1864. To China, 1866. To Cape of Good Hope, 1867. To Mauritius, 1870. To Ireland, 1872. To England, 1874. To Ireland, 1879. To India, 1881.

Continuation of Notes to the Yorkshire Regiment.

[1] Sir Robert Bright served the Eastern campaign of 1854-55 with the 19th Regiment, including the battles of Alma and Inkerman, siege and fall of Sebastopol, and storming of the Redan on the 18th June and 8th September—mentioned in despatches (Medal with three Clasps, Brevet of Lt.Colonel, Knight of the Legion of Honor, 5th Class of the Medjidie, and Turkish Medal). Commanded as Brigadier General the 1st Brigade Hazara Field Force of 1868, including the expedition against the tribes on the Black Mountain (mentioned in despatches, thanked by the Government of India, *CB*., Medal with Clasp). Served in the Afghan war in 1879-80 in command of the Khyber Line Field Force, including the operations in the Hissarik Valley and the expedition against the Wuzeeree Khugianis (mentioned in despatches, received the thanks of both Houses of Parliament, *KCB*., and Medal).

[4] Lt. Colonel M'Clintock served in the Hazara campaign in 1868, including the expedition against the tribes on the Black Mountain (Medal with Clasp). Served during the Nile Expedition in 1884-85 with the 1st Battalion Yorkshire Regiment on the Line of Communications up the Nile. Served with the Soudan Frontier Field Force in 1885-86 during the operations on the Upper Nile, and was present in the engagement at Giniss (Medal, and Khedive's Star).

[7] Major Bowles served in the Nile Expedition in 1884-85 as Staff Officer at Assouan (mentioned in despatches, Brevet of Major).

[8] Major Spottiswoode, Captains Hadow, Espon and Connop served during the Nile Expedition in 1884-85 with the 1st Battalion Yorkshire Regiment on the Lines of Communication up the Nile.

[9] Major Mathison, Captains Chauncy, Cartwright, Ferrar, Mercer, and King, Lieut. Somervell, and Captain Organ served during the Nile Expedition in 1884-85 with the 1st Battalion Yorkshire Regiment on the Lines of Communication up the Nile. Served with the Soudan Frontier Field Force in 1885-86 during the operations on the Upper Nile and was present in the engagement at Giniss (Medal, and Khedive's Star).

[10] Major Buckle served during the Nile Expedition in 1884-85 with the 1st Battalion Yorkshire Regiment on the Lines of Communication up the Nile. Served with the Soudan Frontier Field Force in 1885-86 during the operations on the Upper Nile and was present in the engagement at Giniss as Assistant Provost Marshal (Medal, and Khedive's Star).

[15] Captain Orr served during the Nile Expedition in 1884-85 with the 1st Battalion Yorkshire Regiment on the Lines of Communication up the Nile. Served with the Soudan Frontier Field Force in 1885-86 during the operations on the Upper Nile (Medal, and Khedive's Star).

[17] Captain Pearson served with the Nile Expedition in 1884-85 (Medal with Clasp, and Khedive's Star).

Record of the Services of the 1st Battalion Princess of Wales's Own Yorkshire Regiment (formerly the 19th Regiment).

Raised in 1688. 1690, to Ireland (battle of the Boyne). 1692, to Flanders. 1696, to Ireland. 1697, to Flanders. 1698, to Ireland. 1702-8, on sea service. 1709, to Flanders (battle of Malplaquet, &c.). 1715, to Ireland. 1716, to England. 1718, to Scotland. 1720, to England. 1744, to Flanders (battle of Fontenoy, &c.). 1749, to England. 1750, to Gibraltar. 1753, to England. 1755, to Scotland. 1756, to England. [2nd Battalion detached and formed into the 66th Regiment, 1758.] 1761, at the capture of Belle Isle. 1762, to England and Gibraltar. 1771, to England. 1773, to Scotland. 1775, to Ireland. 1780, to America. 1782, to the West Indies. 1791, to Ireland. 1793, to Flanders. 1795, to England. 1796, to Madras and Ceylon (five companies at the capture of Seringapatam). 1810, four companies in the expedition against Mauritius. 1820, to England. 1821, to Ireland. 1826, to the West Indies. 1836, to Ireland. 1839, to England. 1840, to Ireland and Malta. 1843, to the Ionian Islands. 1845, to the West Indies. 1848, to North America. 1851, to England. 1854, to Turkey and the Crimea (battles of Alma and Inkerman and siege of Sebastopol). 1856, to England. 1857, to India. [2nd Battalion raised in 1858.] 1868, Black Mountain Expedition. 1872, to England. Entitled "The Princess of Wales' Own Yorkshire Regiment," 1875. 1877, to Bermuda. 188c, to Nova Scotia. 1884, to Malta and Egypt (action of Giniss). 1888, to Cyprus. 1889, to Egypt and England.

Record of the Services of the 2nd Battalion.

Raised in 1858. To India, 1863. Entitled "The Princess of Wales' Own," 1875. To England, 1877. To Ireland, 1881. To England, 1886. To India, 1889.

1st Batt., Aldershot.
2nd Batt., Sealkote, Bengal.] **The Royal Scots Fusiliers.** [Regimental District No. 21.—Ayr.] 262

Formerly the 21st (Royal Scots Fusiliers) Regiment.
(The 3rd Battalion is formed of the Royal Ayr and Wigtown Militia.)
The Thistle within the Circle of St. Andrew. *"Nemo me impune lacessit."* The Royal Cypher and Crown.
"BLENHEIM" "RAMILLIES" "OUDENARDE" "MALPLAQUET" "DETTINGEN" "BLADENSBURG"
"ALMA" "INKERMAN" "SEVASTOPOL" "SOUTH AFRICA, 1879" "BURMA, 1885-87."

Years' Ser. Full Pay.	Half Pay.		ENSIGN OR 2ND LIEUT.	LIEUT.	CAPTAIN.	BREV. MAJ.	MAJOR.
		Colonel.—Sir Frederick Paul Haines,[1] GCB, GOSI, CIE. 2nd Lt. P21 June 39; Lieut. P15 Dec. 40; Capt. 16 May 46; Bt.Major, 7 June 49; Bt.Lt.Colonel, 2 Aug. 50; Major, 15 Nov. 54; Colonel, 28 Nov. 54; Lt.Colonel, 24 April 55; Major General, 25 Nov. 64; Lt.General, 23 May 73; General, 1 Oct. 77; Field Marshal, 21 May 90; Colonel 104th Regiment, 16 May 74; Colonel Scots Fusiliers, 5 Oct. 90.					
33	...	**Lieutenant Colonels.**—1 Edmond Charles Browne,[5] Ensign, 23 Sept. 62; Lt. 7 July 66; Capt. 19 Oct. 74; Major, 1 July 81; Lt.Colonel, 1 July 91.					
30	...	2 Arthur John Osborne Pollock,[9] Ensign, 6 Feb. 66; Lieut. P2 Jan. 69; Capt. 2 Mar. 78; Major, 2 Feb. 85; Lt.Colonel, 25 Aug. 94.					
		MAJORS.					
28	...	1 John Henry Spurgin[11]	P15 Feb. 68	28 Oct. 71	19 Feb. 79	......	2 Nov. 85
27	...	2 William Arthur James Frere	P15 July 68	28 Oct. 71	27 Dec. 80	......	1 July 87
27	...	2 Taylor Dalrymple Wilson	P2 Jan. 69	28 Oct. 71	4 Feb. 81	......	19 Oct. 87
22	...	Edward Elliott Carr, *District Inspector of Musketry, York,* 24 Feb. 93		9 Aug. 73	14 July 83	......	10 Aug. 91
19	...	1 Alexander Houghton Abercrombie		26 July 76	21 Sept. 83	......	15 Sept. 92
20	...	1 Algernon William Collings[14] *(Depot)*		20 Nov. 75	1 Mar. 84	......	20 Feb. 93
19	...	2 George Alfred Keef[15]		11 Sept. 76	2 Feb. 85	......	26 July 94
17	...	1 William Arthur Young[18]		3 May 78	2 Nov. 85	......	21 Nov. 94
		CAPTAINS.					
19	...	Charles Tuckey, *Ordnance Store Department*		11 Sept. 76	1 Jan. 85		
17	...	1 p.s.c. Henry Hamilton Smythe[19]	1 May 78	17 July 80	3 Jan. 86		
17	...	p.s.c. Hon. Arthur Stewart Hardinge,[21] *Brigade Major, Shorncliffe,* 11 July 93	1 May 78	11 Sept. 80	25 Aug. 86	16 Aug. 92	
17	...	2 p.s.c. Richard Boileau Gaisford[22]	1 May 78	14 Sept. 80	25 Aug. 86		
17	...	1 Robert William Marmaduke Blake	4 Dec. 78	27 Dec. 80	16 Sept. 86		
17	...	Hon. Geoff. Cecil Twisleton-Wykeham-Fiennes,[25] *Adj. 3 Battalion* 16 Aug. 90	22 Jan. 79	4 Feb. 81	12 Jan. 87		
17	...	2 Herbert Stewart M'Cance Stannell[26]	22 Feb. 79	18 Apr. 81	23 Jan. 87		
17	...	2 Alex. Whitelaw Thorneycroft[27] *(Depot)*	22 Feb. 79	1 July 81	23 Jan. 87		
17	...	2 Kenneth Edw. Lean,[28] **Adjutant** 17 May 94	22 Feb. 79	1 July 81	29 June 87		
16	...	1 p.s.c. William Hely Bowes,[29] **Adjutant** 10 Sept. 94	13 Aug. 79	1 July 81	4 Oct. 87		
15	...	1 Frederick Aug. Lascelles Davidson[30]	23 Oct. 80	1 July 81	4 Apr. 88		
15	...	1 Arthur Boyer Hamilton Northcott	22 Jan. 81	1 July 81	15 Sept. 92		
14	...	2 Charles Philip Scudamore,[31] *DSO*		22 Oct. 81	15 Sept. 92		
13	...	2 Donald Mackenzie Stuart		10 Mar. 83	20 Feb. 93		
13	...	Hubert Lavie Butler, *Adjutant Galloway Rifle Volunteers* 25 Aug. 94		10 June 82	24 Feb. 93		
12	...	1 Arthur Hugh Thurburn		6 Feb. 84	21 Feb. 93		
11	...	2 Hugh Arthur Travers		7 Feb. 85	7 Feb. 94		
10	...	Herbert Scholfield Sykes, *Adjutant 1 Volunteer Battalion* 14 Nov. 94		6 May 85	25 Aug. 94		
10	...	1 William Douglas Smith[35]		29 Aug. 85	14 Nov. 94		
10	...	1 Arthur George Baird Smith[36]		29 Aug. 85	21 Nov. 94		
		LIEUTENANTS.					
9	...	Quentin Graham Kinnaird Agnew,[38] *Aide de Camp to Sir G. S. White* 8 Apr. 93		28 Apr. 86			
9	...	2 Hugh Pleydell de la Bère		25 Aug. 86			
9	...	2 James Hawkins Whitshed Pollard,[39] *Transport Officer, Waziristan Delimitation Escort*		25 Aug. 86			
9	...	George Olof Roos-Keppel,[40] *Adjutant Kurram Militia* 7 Apr. 93		25 Aug. 86			
8	...	2 Arthur Charles Herbert Macgregor	13 April 87	2 Aug. 89			
8	...	2 Walter Hayes-Sadler	4 May 87	13 Sept. 89			
8	...	1 Francis de Sausmarez Shortt[41]	28 Sept. 87	27 Aug. 90			
8	...	2 Charles Patrick Amyatt Hull, *Aide de Camp to the Viceroy of India* 19 Dec. 94	16 Nov. 87	10 Sept. 90			
8	...	1 Louis Aylmer North	14 Dec. 87	1 Nov. 90			
7	...	2 Dighton Hay Abercromby Dick *(Depot)*	11 Apr. 88	29 May 91			
7	...	2 Henry Edward Gogarty *(Depot)*	22 Aug. 88	13 Jan. 92			
6	...	1 Cecil Frederick Garnett	13 Feb. 89	18 May 92			
6	...	1 Reginald Yates Morris	23 Mar. 89	3 Aug. 92			
6	...	2 Edwin Ernest Blaine	21 Sept. 89	15 Sept. 92			
5	...	Robert Edward Archibald Hamilton	8 Nov. 90	24 Feb. 93			
5	...	George Benedict Molyneux Sarel	29 Nov. 90	7 Apr. 93			
5	...	2 John Duncan	4 Mar. 91	8 Apr. 93			
5	...	1 Athol Murray Hay Forbes	4 Mar. 91	19 June 93			
4	...	1 Herbert Hamilton Northey	25 July 91	6 July 93			
4	...	2 Arthur Hunter Buist, *Station Staff Officer, Umritsur,*	9 Sept. 91	7 Feb. 94			
4	...	1 Vernon Lewis	27 Jan. 92	20 Mar. 94			
3	...	2 Francis Edward Buchanan	10 Aug. 92	14 Nov. 94			
		SECOND LIEUTENANTS.					
3	...	1 John Clarkson Mack	28 Sept. 92				
3	...	2 Frank Hercules Walker	19 Oct. 92				
3	...	1 Philip George Stewart	8 Mar. 93				
3	...	1 Sydney Albert Mott	15 Mar. 93				
2	...	2 Harry Stuart Ravenhill	19 July 93				
2	...	2 Alban Dymoke Lewes	2 Aug. 93				
2	...	2 Hugh Montague Trenchard	9 Sept. 93				
2	...	2 Ewan Christian	21 Oct. 93				
2	...	1 William Lyon Dennistoun Baillie	7 Mar. 94				
1	...	1 Charles John Chard Barrett	10 Oct. 94				
1	...	1 Richard Knox Walsh	10 Oct. 94				
1	...	2 Herbert William Bullock	12 Dec. 94				

Years' Ser.	
Full Pay.	Half Pay.
12	...
11	...

Paymasters.—2 Herbert S. M'C. Stanuell, *Captain* 2 *Battalion* (*acting*).
Quarter Masters.—1 John Clisham, 2 Feb. 84 ; *Hon. Captain*, 2 Feb. 94.
2 Robert James Boddy,[42] 18 Oct. 84 ; *Hon. Captain*, 18 Oct. 4.
Facings Blue.—*Agents*, Messrs. Cox and Co.
1st Battalion returned from India, 1881. *2nd Battalion embarked for Natal,* 22 *February* 1879.

[1] Sir Frederick Paul Haines' services:—On the formation of the Army of the Sutlej in 1845 he was appointed to officiate as Military Secretary to the Commander in Chief in India, Sir Hugh Gough, and in that capacity he was present at the battles of Moodkee and Ferozeshah (Medal and one Clasp) ; in the latter engagement he was severely wounded by grape-shot at the attack on the enemy's works, his horse being killed under him at the same moment. At the recommendation of Lord Gough he was promoted to a Company in the 10th Foot, without purchase. As Military Secretary to his Lordship he served the Punjaub campaign of 1848-49, and was present at the affair of outposts at Ramnuggur, 22 Nov. 1848, and subsequent operations resulting in the passage of the Chenab, and the battles of Chillianwallah and Goojerat (Brevet of Major, Medal with two Clasps). Served with the 21st Fusiliers the Eastern campaign of 1854-55, including the battles of Alma, Balaclava, and Inkerman, and siege of Sebastopol (Brevet of Lt.Colonel, Medal with four Clasps, 5th Class of the Medjidie, and Turkish Medal). During the Afghan war he directed the military operations as Commander in Chief from September 1879 to September 1880 (received the thanks of both Houses of Parliament).
[5] Lt.Colonel Browne served with the Royal Scots Fusiliers in the Zulu war of 1879 (Medal with Clasp). Served in the Boer war in 1881 as Assistant Director of Transport with the Natal Field Force. Served with the Burmese Expedition in 1885-86 in command of a Mounted Corps composed of Mounted Infantry, Civilian Volunteers, and Burmans, equipped and organised by him (mentioned in despatches, Medal with Clasp).
[9] Lt.Colonel Pollock served in the Ashanti war from the 30th November 1873 (Medal with Clasp).
[11] Major Spurgin served with the 21st Fusiliers in the Zulu war of 1879 (Medal with Clasp).
[14] Major Collings served with the 21st Fusiliers in the Zulu war of 1879 (Medal with Clasp). Served in the Boer war of 1881 including the investment of Pretoria (mentioned in despatches). Served with the Burmese Expedition in 1886 (Medal with Clasp).
[15] Major Kaef served with the Mahsood Wuzeeree Expedition in 1881. Served with the Bechuanaland Expedition under Sir Charles Warren in 1884-85. Served in the Burmese Expedition in 1885-87 with the 2nd Battalion Royal Scots Fusiliers (Medal with Clasp).
[16] Major Young served in the Zulu war of 1879, and was present in the engagement at Ulundi. Afterwards served in the operations against Sekukuni (Medal with Clasp). Served in the Boer war of 1881, and was present in the engagements at Lang's Nek and the Ingogo River.
[19] Captain H. H. Smythe served in the Boer war of 1881, and was present in the engagement at Lang's Nek.
[21] Major the Hon. A. S. Harding served with the 21st Fusiliers in the Zulu war of 1879, and was present in the engagement at Ulundi; also served in the operations against Sekukuni, including the storming of the stronghold (Medal with Clasp). Served in the Boer war of 1881, and was present at the defence of Pretoria as Acting Aide de Camp to the Commandant. Served with the Burmese Expedition in 1885-87 (Medal with Clasp). Served in the operations against the Jebus, Lagos, in 1892—twice wounded (mentioned in despatches, Brevet of Major, Medal with Clasp).
[22] Captain Gaisford served in the Boer war of 1881 with the Natal Field Force. Served in the Burmese Expedition in 1885-87 as Adjutant 2nd Battalion Royal Scots Fusiliers (Medal with Clasp).
[25] Captain Fiennes served with the 21st Fusiliers in the Zulu war of 1879, and in the operations against Sekukuni, including the storming of the stronghold (Medal with Clasp).
[26] Captain Stanuell served with the 21st Fusiliers in the Zulu war of 1879, and was present in the engagement at Ulundi (Medal with Clasp). Served with the 21st Fusiliers in the Boer war of 1881, and took part in the defence of Pretoria (mentioned in despatches). Served in the Nile Expedition in 1884-85 with the Mounted Infantry of the Camel Corps, and was present in the actions at Abu Klea and Abu Kru (Medal with two Clasps, and Khedive's Star).
[27] Captain Thorneycroft served with the 21st Fusiliers in the Zulu war of 1879, and in the operations against Sekukuni, including the storming of the stronghold (Medal with Clasp). Also served in the Boer war of 1881, and took part in the defence of Pretoria.
[28] Captain Lean served with the 21st Fusiliers in the Zulu war of 1879, and in the operations against Sekukuni, including the storming of the stronghold (Medal with Clasp). Also served in the Boer war of 1881, and took part in the defence of Potchefstroom. Served in the Burmese Expedition in 1885-87 with the 2nd Battalion Royal Scots Fusiliers (Medal with Clasp).
[29] Captain Bowes served in the Burmese Expedition in 1885-87 with the 2nd Battalion Royal Scots Fusiliers (Medal with Clasp).
[30] Captain Davidson served with the Burmese Expedition in 1885-86, and was present in several engagements including the taking of the Minhla Redoubt and the capture of Mandalay (Medal with Clasp).
[32] Captain Scudamore served with the Burmese Expedition in 1886-87 with the 2nd Battalion Royal Scots Fusiliers (mentioned in despatches, DSO., and Medal with Clasp). Also served with the Hazara Field Force in the expedition to the Black Mountain in 1888 (mentioned in despatches, Clasp).
[35] Captain W. D. Smith served in the Burmese Expedition in 1885-87 with the 2nd Battalion Royal Scots Fusiliers (Medal with Clasp).
[36] Captain A. G. B. Smith served with the 2nd Battalion Royal Scots Fusiliers in the Burmese Expedition in 1885-87 (Medal with Clasp).
[38] Lieut. Agnew served with the Burmese Expedition in 1885-86 as Transport Officer (twice mentioned in despatches, Medal with Clasp).
[39] Lieut. Pollard served with the Chin-Lushai Expeditionary Force in 1890 (Medal with Clasp).
[40] Lieut. Roos-Keppel served in the Burmese Expedition in 1887 with the 2nd Battalion Royal Scots Fusiliers (Medal with two Clasps).
[41] Lieut. Shortt served in the Nile Expedition in 1884-85 with the 1st Battalion Black Watch, took part in the operations of the River Column under Major General Earle, and was present in the action of Kirbekan (Medal with two Clasps, and Khedive's Star).
[42] Captain Boddy served in the Zulu war in 1879 (Medal with Clasp). Served in the Burmese Expedition in 1885-87 with the 2nd Battalion Royal Scots Fusiliers (Medal with Clasp).

[*For the Record of the Services of the Royal Scots Fusiliers, see end of Cheshire Regiment, page* 264a.

The Cheshire Regiment.

1st Batt., Bellary, Madras.
2nd Batt., Aldershot.
] *Formerly the 22nd (The Cheshire) Regt.* [Regimental District No. 22.—Chester.

(The 3rd and 4th Battalions are formed of the 1st and 2nd Cheshire Militia respectively.)
The United Red and White Rose. "LOUISBURG" "MEEANEE" "HYDERABAD" "SCINDE."

Colonel.—David Anderson,[1] *Ensign*, 28 Dec. 38; *Lieut*. 15 May 41; *Capt*. P2 Feb. 49; *Major*, P8 July 56; *Lt.Colonel*, 5 Mar. 58; *Colonel*, 5 Mar. 63; *Major General*, 28 Oct. 68; *Lieut.General*, 15 Jan. 82; *General*, 17 July 88; *Colonel* Cheshire Regiment, 3 Mar. 94.

Years' Ser				
Full Pay	Half Pay			
29	...	Lieutenant Colonels.— 1 Arthur William Sheringham,[2] *Ensign*, P29 June 66; *Lieut*. 3 Oct. 70; *Capt*. 19 July 77; *Major*, 20 Dec. 82; *Lt.Colonel*, 14 May 91.		
32	...	2 p.s.c. Richard Charles Hare,[4] *Ensign*, P23 June 63; *Lieut*. P29 May 67; *Capt*. 17 Mar. 75; *Bt.Major*, 18 Nov. 82; *Major*, 13 Aug. 84; *Lt.Colonel*, 21 Apr. 92.		

		MAJORS.	ENSIGN OR 2ND LIEUT.	LIEUT.	CAPTAIN.	BREV.MAJ.	MAJOR.
27	...	1 John Deering	8 July 68	28 Oct. 71	1 Jan. 80	......	21 Apr. 88
23	...	2 William Frederick Curteis[5]	......	13 April 72	16 Aug. 82	......	10 Oct. 88
23	...	p.s.c. Francis William Bromfield, *Assist. Adj. Gen. Madras*, 7 Sept. 91	......	29 May 72	22 Sept. 83	......	24 Mar. 90
21	...	David Francis Lewis,[6] *serving with the Egyptian Army*	......	11 Feb. 75	20 Feb. 84	......	14 Jan. 91
25	...	2 Thomas Davison[9]	P27 Apr. 70	P27 Oct. 71	20 Feb. 84	......	28 Oct. 91
22	...	2 David Phelps Chapman[10] (*Depot*)	......	28 Mar. 74	13 Aug. 83	15 June 85	4 Nov. 91
18	...	1 William Keane Richardson	......	13 June 77	10 Sept. 84	......	21 Apr. 92
17	...	1 p.s.c. Edward Ritchie Coryton Graham	1 May 78	19 June 79	6 Sept. 85	......	24 Oct. 94
		CAPTAINS.					
17	...	2 Charles Richard Hugh Hardy[7]	11 May 78	6 Aug. 79	6 Sept. 85		
17	...	William Candler Neville,[8] *Adjutant* 3 Battalion 8 Nov. 93	5 Oct. 78	17 April 80	6 Sept. 85		
16	...	1 Reginald Parker Grove[15]	13 Aug. 79	27 Jan. 81	19 Sept. 85		
16	...	1 Edward John Lamb[11]	14 Jan. 80	1 July 81	7 Feb. 87		
15	...	Richard Armstrong,[8] *Inst. R. M. College* 1 Oct. 90	11 Aug. 80	1 July 81	19 Apr. 87		
15	...	2 Robert Joseph Cooke[8]	11 Aug. 80	1 July 81	19 Apr. 87		
13	...	1 Henry Edward Napier	......	10 May 82	23 Aug. 87		
13	...	1 Edward Thornton Taylor, *at Staff College*	......	9 Aug. 82	17 Sept. 87		
17	...	Gregory Sinclair Haines, *Adj.4 Bn.15Oct.90*	4 Dec. 78	1 July 81	16 June 87		
13	...	James Wilson Fraser, *Adjutant* 2 Vol. Bn. Gordon Highlanders 2 Apr. 94	......	9 Sept. 82	13 June 88		
14	...	James Richard Kemmis Birch,[13] *Insp. Army Signalling, Madras and Bombay*, 4 July 92	......	22 Oct. 81	15 Aug. 88		
13	...	William Frederick White,[16] *Adjutant* 3 Vol. Bn. Cheshire Regt. 2 Nov. 91	......	10 Mar. 83	11 Sept. 88		
16	...	1 Charles Higford Chapman[12]	31 Jan. 80	1 July 81	18 Feb. 87		
12	...	2 Edgar Elliott Husey	......	25 Aug. 83	16 Oct. 90		
12	...	William Hussey-Walsh,[17] *Adjutant* 1 Vol. Bn. Essex Regt. 19 Mar. 95	......	6 Feb. 84	14 Jan. 91		
11	...	1 Anthony Edw. Ranelagh Tucker (*Depot*)	......	23 Aug. 84	14 Jan. 91		
11	...	Alexander George William Tod,[8] *Ordnance Store Department*	......	12 Nov. 84	14 May 91		
12	...	2 Walter Rees Clifford[18]	......	7 Feb. 85	14 May 91		
11	...	2 Harry Fras. Kellie,[8] *Adjutant* 21 Apr. 93	......	7 Feb. 85	7 Sept. 91		
11	...	1 David Brodie Thomas[14]	......	28 Feb. 85	4 Nov. 91		
11	...	Ralph Douglas Turton, *Adjutant* 2 Volunteer Battalion 1 March 93	......	28 Feb. 85	21 Apr. 92		
10	...	2 Dudley Coryndon Boger[8]	......	9 May 85	26 Sept. 94		
10	...	2 Arthur de Courcy Scott[8]	......	9 May 85	24 Oct. 94		
		LIEUTENANTS.					
10	...	2 Arthur Brabazon Stone[8]	......	29 Aug. 85			
10	...	1 William Lionel Stretton	......	16 Dec. 85			
10	...	1 Henry Smyth[19] (*Depot*)	......	30 Jan. 86			
10	...	John Shawe-Taylor,[20] *Aide de Camp to Lt. General J. Davis*, 9 Jan. 94	......	30 Jan. 86			
9	...	1 Thos. Owen Marden,[8] **Adjutant** 8 Aug. 92	......	25 Aug. 86			
9	...	2 William Vincent Moul[8]	......	25 Aug. 86			
9	...	2 Arthur Buckley Bennet[8] (*Depot*)	......	25 Aug. 86			
9	...	1 Henry Sargeaunt[21]	......	25 Aug. 86			
9	...	2 Arthur Claud Adair	......	10 Nov. 86			
9	...	1 Charles Henry Donald Lyon-Campbell	......	8 Dec. 86			
9	...	1 Byron Leicester[8]	5 Feb. 87	16 Oct. 90			
8	...	1 William Martin-Leake[19]	4 May 87	11 Nov. 90			
8	...	1 Vincent Randolphe Pigott[19]	14 Sept. 87	14 Jan. 91			
7	...	2 John Cephas Howard	9 May 88	11 Mar. 91			
7	...	1 John Francis Wolseley	8 Aug. 88	14 May 91			
6	...	1 Allen Butler Gosset	8 May 89	7 Sept. 91			
6	...	2 Austin Samuel Cooper	9 Nov. 89	4 Nov. 91			
6	...	1 William Auchincloss	21 Dec. 89	8 Aug. 92			
5	...	2 Warren Hastings Anderson	8 Oct. 90	9 Jan. 94			
5	...	1 Thomas Gaspard Cousin	24 Dec. 90	26 Sept. 94			
5	...	1 Percy Lynes Grove	17 Jan. 91	24 Oct. 94			
		SECOND LIEUTENANTS.					
5	...	2 Cecil George Porcher	17 Jan. 91				
5	...	2 Herbert Edward Mayo	4 Feb. 91				
4	...	1 Herbert Hulseberg	9 Sept. 91				
4	...	2 Bryan Henry Chetwynd-Stapylton	9 Jan. 92				
4	...	1 Herbert Fothergill Cooke	27 Jan. 92				
3	...	1 Frederick Benjamin Young	5 Oct. 92				
3	...	2 Francis Ferguson Duffus	19 Oct. 92				
3	...	1 William Knapp Tarver	19 Nov. 92				
3	...	2 Percy North Gleig	17 Dec. 92				
3	...	2 Hugh St. John Morrell	2 June 93				
1	...	2 Charles Welman Collins	2 June 94				
1	...	1 Andrew Spotswood Ash	12 Dec. 94				
1	...	1 Reginald Seymour Thomas	12 Dec. 94				

[8] Captains Neville, Armstrong, Cooke, Tod, Kellie, Boger and Scott, and Lieuts. Stone, Marden, Moul, Bennet and Leicester served in the Burmese Expedition in 1887-89 with the 2nd Battalion Cheshire Regiment. (Medal with Clasp.)

[9] Major Davison served with the 1st Battalion Royal Irish Fusiliers in the Egyptian war of 1882, and was present at the battle of Tel-el-Kebir (Medal with Clasp, and Khedive's Star).

[12] Captain Chapman served in the Afghan war in 1879-80 with the 51st Light Infantry (Medal). Served in the Burmese Expedition during the latter part of 1887 with the 1st Battalion of the Yorkshire Light Infantry.

[13] Captain Birch served in the expedition to the Soudan in 1885 with the Mounted Infantry—severely wounded (mentioned in despatches, Medal with Clasp, and Khedive's Star).

[14] Captain Thomas served with the Chin-Lushai Expeditionary Force in 1889-90 with the 1st Battalion Cheshire Regiment (mentioned in despatches, Medal with Clasp).

Paymasters.—1 William L. Stretton, *Lieut.* 1 *Battalion (acting).*
2
Quarter Masters.—1 Alexander M'Dermott, 13 Jan. 92.
2 Albert Gregory,²² 14 June 93; *Hon. Lieut.*
Facings White.—*Agents,* Messrs. Cox and Co.
1st *Battalion embarked for Gibraltar,* 20 *Feb.* 1885. 2nd *Battalion returned from Burmah,* 8 *Feb.* 1889.

¹ General Anderson was present with the 22nd Regiment at the taking and destruction of the villages in the Boree Valley in the Peshawur district in November 1853 (Medal with Clasp).
² Lt.Colonel Sheringham served in the Burmese Expedition in 1887-89 with the 2nd Battalion Cheshire Regiment (Medal with Clasp).
⁴ Lt.Colonel Hare served in the Ashanti war of 1873-74 as Assistant Engineer, and was present at the battle of Amoaful (slightly wounded), battle of Ordahsu and capture of Coomassie (Medal with Clasp). Served in the Egyptian war of 1882 as Brigade Major of the 2nd Brigade, and was present at the engagements of El Magfar, Tel-el-Mahuta, and Kassasin (9th Sept.) (twice mentioned in despatches, Brevet of Major, Medal, 4th Class of the Medjidie, and Khedive's Star).
⁵ Major Curteis served in the Burmese Expedition in 1887-89 with the 2nd Battalion Cheshire Regiment (Medal with Clasp).
⁶ Major Lewis served in the Zulu war in 1879, and was present at Ekowe during the investment—wounded (Medal with Clasp). Served in the operations in the Soudan in 1889 including the engagements at Arguin and Toski (Medal with Clasp, 3rd Class of the Medjidie, and Khedive's Star).
⁷ Captain Hardy served in the Soudan campaign in 1885 (Medal with Clasp, and Khedive's Star).
¹⁰ Major Chapman served with the Nile Expedition in 1884-85 as Staff Officer on the Lines of Communication (mentioned in despatches, Brevet of Major, Medal with Clasp, 4th Class of the Medjidie, and Khedive's Star). Served with the Egyptian Frontier Field Force in 1885-86, and was present in the engagement at Giniss; also served in the operations near Suakin in December 1888 and was present in the engagement at Gemaizah as Assistant Adjutant General Egyptian Army (mentioned in despatches, Clasp, and 4th Class of the Osmanieh).
¹¹ Captain Lamb served with the Burmese Expedition in 1887-89 (Medal with Clasp), and with the Chin-Lushai Expeditionary Force in 1889-90 (Clasp).
¹⁵ Captain Grove served with the Burmese Expedition in 1888-89 (Medal with Clasp).
¹⁶ Captain White served with the Burmese Expedition in 1887-89 (Medal with Clasp); and with the Chin-Lushai Expeditionary Force in 1889-90 (Clasp).
¹⁷ Captain Hussey-Walsh served in the Burmese campaign in 1887-89 with the Sawlapaw Expedition, Eastern Karenni (Medal with Clasp); with the Chin Lushai Expeditionary Force in 1889-90 (Clasp); and with the Wuntho Field Force in 1891 as Intelligence Officer (Clasp).
¹⁸ Captain Clifford served with the Karen Expedition in 1888-89 as Transport Officer to the Lower Burma Column (Medal with Clasp).
¹⁹ Lieuts. Henry Smyth, Martin-Leake, and Pigott served with the Chin-Lushai Expeditionary Force in 1889-90 (Medal with Clasp).
²⁰ Lieut. Shawe Taylor served with the Burmese Expedition in 1887-89 (Medal with Clasp).
²¹ Lieut. Sargeaunt served with the Burmese Expedition in 1887-89 (Medal with Clasp); and with the Chin Lushai Expeditionary Force in 1889-90 (Clasp).
²² Lieut. Gregory served with the Burmese Expedition in 1887-89 (Medal with Clasp).

Record of the Services of the 2nd Battalion of the Cheshire Regiment (formerly the 22nd Regiment).

Raised in 1858 and proceeded to Malta, May 1859. To Gibraltar, July 1865, and to the Mauritius the same month. To England, July 1867. To India, Oct. 1873. To Burma, Oct. 1887. To England, Jan. 1889.

Record of the Services of the 1st Battalion Royal Scots Fusiliers (formerly the 21st Royal Scots Fusiliers).

Raised in Scotland, Sept. 1678. At the battle of Bothwell Brig, 1679. To England, 1688. To the Low Countries, 1689. To Scotland, 1697. To Holland, 1702 (at the battles of Blenheim, Ramilies, Oudenarde, Malplaquet, &c. &c.). At this time designated the "Royal North British Fusiliers." To Scotland, 1714 (battle of Sheriffmuir). To Ireland, 1729. To England, 1740. To Flanders, 1742 (battles of Dettingen and Fontenoy). To England and Scotland, 1745 (battle of Culloden). To Flanders, 1747. To England, 1748. At this time described as the "21st Regiment or Royal North British Fusiliers." At Gibraltar, 1751. To England, 1760. Capture of Belleisle, on the French Coast, 1761. To England, 1762. To Scotland, 1763. To America, 1765. To England, 1772. To Canada, 1776. To Scotland, 1781. To Ireland, 1781. To Nova Scotia, 1789. To the West Indies, 1793. To Scotland, 1796. To Ireland, 1800. To England, 1805. To Sicily, 1806. To Egypt, May to Oct. 1807. Returned to Sicily, 1807. To America, 1814. To England, May 1815. To Belgium and France, July 1815. To England, 1817. To the West Indies, 1819. To England, 1827. To Ireland, 1828. To England, 1831. To Tasmania and Australia, 1832. To India, 1839. To Scotland, 1848. To England, 1851. To Ireland, 1853. To Turkey and the Crimea, 1854 (battles of Alma, Balaklava, and Inkerman, siege of Sebastopol). To Malta, 1856. To the West Indies, 1860. To England, 1864. To Scotland, 1865. To Ireland, 1866. To India, 1869. Name altered to "21st Royal Scots Fusiliers," 1877. To England, 1881. To Ireland, 1886. To Scotland, 1891.

Record of the Services of the 2nd Battalion of the Royal Scots Fusiliers.

Raised as 2nd Battalion 21st Royal North British Fusiliers in Dec. 1804. To Ireland, 1806. To Scotland, 1811. To Holland, Jan. 1814 (attack on Bergen-op-Zoom). To Scotland, Nov. 1814. Disbanded, 1816. Re-formed in 1857 as 2nd Battalion Royal North British Fusiliers. To England, 1858. To Ireland, 1862. To India, 1863. To Scotland, 1873. To England, 1874. To Fort George, 1877. To Ireland, 1878. To South Africa, 1879 (Zulu war). To India, 1882. To Burmah, 1884. To India, 1887.

1st Batt., Jhansi, Bengal.
2nd Batt., Manchester.] **The Royal Welsh Fusiliers.** [Regimental District No.23.—Wrexham

Formerly the 23rd (Royal Welsh Fusiliers) Regiment.
(The 3rd and 4th Battalions are formed of the Royal Denbigh and Flint and the Royal Carnarvon and Merioneth Militia respectively.)

The Prince of Wales's Plume, "*Ich Dien.*" The Rising Sun. The Red Dragon. The White Horse. "*Nec aspera terrent.*" "BLENHEIM" "RAMILLIES" "OUDENARDE" "MALPLAQUET" "DETTINGEN" "MINDEN" "EGYPT" (with the Sphinx) "CORUNNA" "MARTINIQUE" "ALBUHERA" "BADAJOZ" "SALAMANCA" "VITTORIA" "PYRENEES" "NIVELLE" "ORTHES" "TOULOUSE" "PENINSULA" "WATERLOO" "ALMA" "INKERMAN" "SEVASTOPOL" "LUCKNOW" "ASHANTEE" "BURMA, 1885-87."

Years'Ser.	Half Pay.						
33	..	Colonel.—Charles Crutchley, 2nd Lt. P8 April 26; Lt. 22 July 30; Capt. P11 Dec. 35; Major, P22 Oct. 44; Lt.Colonel, 24 July 49; Colonel, 28 Nov. 54; Major General, 31 Jan. 64; Lt.General, 23 April 72; General, 1 Oct. 77; Colonel 23rd Fusiliers, 16 Mar. 75.					
30	...	**Lieutenant Colonels.**—1 Compton Norman,¹ Ensign, 2 Sept. 62; Lt. P12 Jan. 66; Capt. 1 June 74; Major, 24 Dec. 81; Lt.Colonel, 2 Apr. 91.					
30	...	2 Sidney Beckwith Blyth, Ensign, P1 Dec. 65; Lt. P30 Mar. 70; Capt. 4 Aug. 79; Major, 10 Apr. 85; Lt.Colonel, 1 July 91.					

			ENSIGN OR 2ND LIEUT.	LIEUT.	CAPTAIN.	BREV.MAJ.	MAJOR.
		MAJORS.					
30	...	1 Henry Woolgar Griffith, *Commandant Kussowlie Depot* 17 June 94	P 2 Mar. 66	P10 June 71	13 Sept. 79	......	21 June 85
24	...	2 Rowland Broughton Mainwaring²	......	30 Dec. 71	13 June 80	......	10 Oct. 85
21	...	2 Charles Cecil Hayford Thorold	......	13 June 74	25 Oct. 82	......	16 July 90
21	...	2 Hon. Reginald Henry Bertie	......	21 Sept. 74	10 May 83	......	2 Apr. 91
21	...	1 Frederick Morris⁴	......	2 Dec. 74	1 July 81	......	1 July 91
20	...	1 Alfred John Chamberlin Wrench	......	13 June 75	29 Oct. 81	......	6 Oct. 86
21	...	1 *Sir* Robert Augustus Wm. Colleton,⁶ *Bart.*	......	2 Dec. 74	20 Mar. 85	......	2 Apr. 89
21	...	2 Hugh James Archdale¹⁰ (*Depot*)	......	11 Feb. 75	20 Mar. 85	......	13 July 92
		CAPTAINS.					
21	...	2 John Harnage King Griffith	......	11 Feb. 75	20 Mar. 85		
18	...	2 George Ferdinand Walker	......	28 April 77	21 June 85		
19	...	Robert Henry William Dunn,¹² *Adjutant* 1 *Vol. Bn. Welsh Fusiliers* 15 Sept. 90	......	11 Nov. 76	21 June 85		
17	...	1 Hugh Thomas Lyle,¹⁴ *DSO*.	22 Jan. 79	13 Apr. 81	6 Dec. 85		
16	...	1 William Randal Hamilton Beresford¹⁵ ...	6 Aug. 79	1 July 81	9 Dec. 85		
16	...	1 Burton Henry Philips	11 Oct. 79	1 July 81	2 April 87		
15	...	Augustus Frederic Cooper,¹⁷ *Adjutant* 4 *Battalion* 1 Sept. 94	11 Aug. 80	1 July 81	17 July 89		
15	...	*p.s.c.* Arthur Willoughby George Lowry Cole,¹⁸ **Adjutant** 23 Apr. 94	11 Aug. 80	1 July 81	22 Jan. 90		
15	...	Sydney Geo. Everitt, *Adj.* 3 *Bn.* 6 Dec. 90	22 Jan. 81	1 July 81	2 July 90		
13	...	2 *Hon.* Robert White²¹	......	10 May 82	16 July 90		
13	...	1 John Lock Look (*Depot*)	......	9 Sept. 82	2 Apr. 91		
13	...	2 Evelyn Linzee Engleheart, **Adjutant** 21 Jan. 93	......	9 Sept. 82	6 Apr. 91		
13	...	Alan Percy George Gough,² *Adjutant* 2 *Vol. Bn. Welsh Fusiliers* 15 Sept. 92	......	9 Sept. 82	15 June 92		
12	...	1 Patrick Riners Mantell²⁴	......	25 Aug. 83	13 July 92		
12	...	2 Charles Edward Bancroft	......	25 Aug. 83	21 Jan. 93		
10	...	Robert Mandy Osborne Glyun, *Adjutant* 3 *Battalion Essex Regt.* 1 Nov. 94	......	6 May 85	17 Feb. 92		
11	...	2 James Hugh Gwynne²⁵	......	12 Nov. 84	23 Dec. 93		
11	...	1 George Frederic Barttelot²⁶	......	7 Feb. 85	16 May 94		
10	...	Raymond Sudeley Webber,²⁸ *serving with the Egyptian Army*	......	23 May 85	1 Nov. 94		
10	...	2 Henry Delme-Radcliffe²⁹	......	29 Aug. 85	1 Nov. 94		
		LIEUTENANTS.					
10	...	1 William Charles Hall³¹		4 Nov. 85			
10	...	2 *Sir* Horace Westropp M'Mahon, *Bart.* ...		25 Nov. 85			
10	...	1 Hugh Edward Walker³⁰		25 Nov. 85			
9	...	2 Bernard Kingscote Hanbury		26 May 86			
9	...	Henry John Madocks, *on special service, Uganda*	......	25 Aug. 86			
8	...	2 Richard Courtenay Brabazon Throckmorton (*Depot*)	24 Aug. 87	2 July 90			
8	...	1 George William David Bowen Lloyd ...	11 Feb. 88	8 Oct. 90			
7	...	1 Henry Osbert Samuel Cadogan³¹	9 May 88	28 Jan. 91			
7	...	1 Charles Hotham Montagu Doughty³⁴ ...	21 Sept. 89	23 Sept. 91			
6	...	1 Henry Meredyth Richards	11 Dec. 89	29 May 92			
6	...	1 Graham Egerton Rickman	12 Feb. 90	6 June 92			
6	...	1 Charles Edward Willes³¹ (*Depot*)	29 Mar. 90	15 June 92			
5	...	1 Charles Macpherson Dobell³¹	20 Aug. 90	13 July 92			
5	...	2 Ralph Abercrombie Berners³¹	29 Oct. 90	12 Apr. 93			
5	...	1 Randle Barnett Barker	17 Jan. 91	22 July 93			
5	...	1 Richard Gordon Beresford Lovett	4 Mar. 91	2 Aug. 93			
4	...	1 Richard William Creighton Blair	2 May 91	23 Dec. 93			
4	...	1 William Garnett Braithwaite	23 May 91	16 May 94			
4	...	1 Richard Edward Phillips Gabbett	10 Oct. 91	20 June 94			
		SECOND LIEUTENANTS.					
4	...	2 Henry Rotherham	10 Oct. 91				
3	...	Grenville Edmund Pigott, *Army Service Corps*	18 June 92				
3	...	2 Archibald Hay	13 July 92				
3	...	1 Allan Ivan Lean	28 Sept. 92				
3	...	1 Oswald Swift Flower	19 Oct. 92				
2	...	2 Edward Thomas Le Marchant	9 Sept. 93				
2	...	2 Raymond Gage De Burghs Hodge	25 Oct. 93				
2	...	1 John Brydges Cockburn	23 Dec. 93				
2	...	1 William Best	7 Mar. 94				
1	...	2 George Frederick Hayes Dickson	2 June 94				
1	...	1 Oliver de Lancey Williams	10 Oct. 94				
1	...	1 Marmaduke Henry Littledale Gale	10 Oct. 94				
1	...	2 John Arthur Higgon	10 Oct. 94				
1	...	Edward Powys Wheatly Cobb	13 Mar. 95				

Q

Years Ser.			
Full Pay	Half Pay		
5	...		
1	...		

Paymasters.—1 Richard G. B. Lovett, *Lieut.* 1 Battalion (acting).
2
Quarter Masters.—2 Arthur E. Hammond, 24 Sept. 90; *Hon. Lieut.*
1 Robert Sheffield Ransome, 20 Feb. 95; *Hon. Lieut.*
Facings Blue.—*Agents*, Messrs. Cox and Co.
1st Battalion embarked for Bengal, 1880. *2nd Battalion returned from Gibraltar*, 1880.

[1] Lt.Colonel Norman served with the Hazara Expedition in 1891 in command of the 1st Battalion Royal Welsh Fusiliers (mentioned in despatches, Medal with Clasp).
[2] Major Mainwaring embarked for the Gold Coast with the 2nd Battalion 23rd Fusiliers in 1873 (Ashanti Medal). Served in the Burmese Expedition in 1885-86 with the 1st Battalion Royal Welsh Fusiliers, and commanded the expedition from Bhamo to Mogoung in 1886 (Medal with Clasp). Served in the Hazara Expedition in 1891 with the 1st. Battalion Royal Welsh Fusiliers (Clasp).
[4] Major Morris served in the Burmese Expedition in 1885-87 with the 1st Battalion Royal Welsh Fusiliers (Medal with Clasp). Served in the Hazara Expedition in 1891 with the 1st Battalion Royal Welsh Fusiliers (Clasp).
[6] Sir Robert Colleton served with the Hazara Expedition in 1891 as Brigade Major to the 2nd Brigade (mentioned in despatches, Medal with Clasp).
[10] Major Archdale served in the Soudan campaign in 1885 (Medal with Clasp, and Khedive's Star). Served in the Burmese expedition in 1886-87 with the 1st Battalion Royal Welsh Fusiliers (Medal with Clasp).
[12] Captain Dunn served with the Burmese Expedition in 1885-86 as Adjutant to the 1st Battalion Royal Welsh Fusiliers (Medal with Clasp).
[14] Captain Lyle served with the Burmese Expedition in 1885-86 with the 1st Battalion Royal Welsh Fusiliers and was present in the expeditions to Mogoung and against the Kachins on the Chinese Frontier in 1886—severely wounded (mentioned in despatches, DSO., and Medal with Clasp). Served with the Hazara Expedition in 1891 as Orderly Officer to Brigadier General Williamson (mentioned in despatches, Clasp).
[15] Captain Beresford served with the Burmese Expedition in 1885-86 with the 1st Battalion Royal Welsh Fusiliers including the engagements at Zeedaw and Kadoe (mentioned in despatches, Medal with Clasp). Served with the Hazara Expedition in 1891 as Adjutant to the 1st Battalion Royal Welsh Fusiliers (Clasp).
[17] Captain Cooper served with the Hazara Expedition in 1891 as Transport Officer to the 1st Battalion Royal Welsh Fusiliers (Medal with Clasp).
[18] Captain Cole served in the Burmese Expedition in 1885-87 with the 1st Battalion Royal Welsh Fusiliers (mentioned in despatches, Medal with Clasp).
[21] Captain Hon. R. White served with the Nile Expedition in 1884-85 (Medal with Clasp, and Khedive's Star).
[22] Captain Gough served with the Burmese Expedition in 1885-86 with the 1st Battalion Royal Welsh Fusiliers including the engagements at Zeedaw and Kadoe, and was slightly wounded in an engagement at Tingotyi on the 16th May (twice mentioned in despatches, Medal with Clasp).
[24] Captain Mantell served in the Burmese Expedition in 1885-87 with the 1st Battalion Royal Welsh Fusiliers (Medal with Clasp). Served in the Hazara Expedition in 1891 with the 1st Battalion Royal Welsh Fusiliers (Clasp).
[25] Captain Gwynne served with the Burmese Expedition in 1885-86, and was severely wounded in an engagement at Yatha (mentioned in despatches, Medal with Clasp). Served in the Hazara Expedition in 1891 with the 1st Battalion Royal Welsh Fusiliers (Clasp).
[26] Captain Barttelot served in the Burmese Expedition in 1886-87 with the 1st Battalion Royal Welsh Fusiliers including the expedition to the relief of Thila (Medal with Clasp).
[28] Captain Webber served in the Burmese Expedition in 1886-87 with the 1st Battalion Royal Welsh Fusiliers (Medal with Clasp).
[29] Captain Delmé Radcliffe served in the Burmese Expedition in 1886-87 with the 1st Battalion Royal Welsh Fusiliers (Medal with Clasp).
[30] Lieut. Walker served in the Burmese Expedition in 1886-87 with the 1st Battalion Royal Welsh Fusiliers (Medal with Clasp).
[31] Lieuts. Hall, Cadogan, Willes, Dobell, and Berners served in the Hazara Expedition in 1891 with the 1st Battalion Royal Welsh Fusiliers (Medal with Clasp).
[34] Lieut. Doughty served in the Hazara Expedition in 1891 with the 1st Battalion Royal Welsh Fusiliers—severely wounded (Medal with Clasp).

Record of the Services of the 1st Battalion Royal Welsh Fusiliers (formerly the 23rd Regiment).

Raised in 1689, and proceeded to Flanders, 1694. To Ireland, 1697. To Flanders, 1701 (battles of Blenheim, Ramillies, Oudenarde, and Malplaquet). To England, 1713. To Flanders, 1742 (battle of Dettingen). To England, 1745. To Flanders, 1747. To England, 1748. To Minorca, 1755. To Gibraltar, 1756. To England, 1756. To Germany, 1758 (battle of Minden). To England, 1763. To America, 1763. To England, 1784. To St. Domingo, 1794. To England, 1796. To Holland, 1799. To Egypt, 1801 (received the badge of "Egypt"—with the Sphinx). To Gibraltar, 1801. To England, 1803. To Bremen, 1805. To England, 1806. To Copenhagen, 1807. To England, 1807. To Nova Scotia, Feb. 1808. To the West Indies, Dec. 1808 (capture of Martinique). To Halifax, 1809. To the Peninsula, 1810 (battles of Albuhera, Badajoz, Salamanca, Vittoria, Pyrenees, Nivelle, Orthes, and Toulouse). To England, 1814. [Second Battalion raised in 1804. To Spain, 1808 (battle of Corunna). To England, Walcheren, and returned to England, 1809. Amalgamated with 1st Battalion, 1814.] To Belgium and France, 1815 (battle of Waterloo). To England, 1818. To Gibraltar, 1823. To England, 1834. To Nova Scotia, 1838. To Canada, 1840. To West Indies, 1843. To Nova Scotia, 1847. To England, 1848. To the Crimea, 1854 (battles of Alma and Inkerman and siege of Sebastopol). To England, 1856. To India, 1857 (capture of Lucknow). To England, 1869. To India, 1880. To Burmah, 1885 (campaign of 1885-86). To India, 1887.

Record of the Services of the 2nd Battalion.

Raised at Newport (Wales) in 1858. To Malta, 1859. To Gibraltar, 1863. To Canada, 1866. To England, 1867. To West Coast of Africa and Ashanti, 1872. To England, 1873. To Gibraltar, 1874. To England, 1880. To Ireland, 1883.

1st Batt., **Egypt.**
2nd Batt., **Gosport.**
] **The South Wales Borderers.** [*Regimental District* **267**
No. 24.—**Brecon.**

Formerly the 24th (The 2nd Warwickshire) Regiment.
(The 3rd and 4th Battalions are formed of the South Wales Borderers and the Montgomery Militia respectively.)

"BLENHEIM" "RAMILLIES" "OUDENARDE" "MALPLAQUET" "EGYPT" (with the Sphinx). "CAPE OF GOOD HOPE, 1806" "TALAVERA" "FUENTES D'ONOR" "SALAMANCA" "VITTORIA" "PYRENEES" "NIVELLE" "ORTHES" "PENINSULA" "PUNJAUB" "CHILLIANWALLAH" "GOOJERAT" "SOUTH AFRICA, 1877-8-9" "BURMA, 1885-87."

Years' Ser. Full Pay	Half Pay			2ND LIEUT.	LIEUT.	CAPTAIN.	BREV. MAJ.	MAJOR.
		Colonel.—Edmund Wodehouse, *Ensign*, P24 Mar. 37; *Lieut.* P15 Jan. 41; *Capt.* P28 Apr. 46; *Major,* P8 Aug. 51; *Bt.Lt.Colonel,* 12 Dec. 57; *Lt.Colonel,* 9 Mar. 60; *Colonel,* 1 June 62; *Major General,* 6 Mar. 68; *Lieut. General,* 25 Apr. 80; *General,* 1 July 81; *Colonel* South Wales Borderers, 13 Nov. 88.							
		Lieutenant Colonels.—1 George Stanhope Banister,¹ *Ensign,* 8 July 68; *Lieut.* 28 Oct. 71 ; *Capt.* 5 Feb. 79 ; *Major,* 15 Aug. 85; *Lt.Colonel,* 9 June 92.							
27								
24		2 W⁰ Edward Stevenson Browne,³ *Ensign,* 23 Sept. 71 ; *Lieut.* 28 Oct. 7⁰; *Capt.* 19 May 80 ; *Major,* 2 Nov. 85 ; *Lt.Colonel,* 8 Apr. 93.							
		MAJORS.						
22	...	1 Henry Germain Mainwaring⁴			21 Sept. 73	7 July 80		2 Nov. 85
22	...	2 Wilfred Heaton⁵			28 Feb. 74	4 Sept. 80		28 Nov. 85
21	...	2 Ralph Arthur Penrhyn Clements,⁶ DSO. (Bt.Lt.Colonel, 1 July 87)			2 Dec. 74	4 Dec. 80		24 Feb. 86
19	...	Hon. Ulick De Rupe Burke Roche,⁹ D.A.A. Gen. Bengal, 25 Oct. 90			6 Sept. 76	18 June 81		10 Feb. 91
18	...	2 Courtney Vor Trower¹⁰ (*Depot*)			17 May 77	8 Oct. 81		4 Mar. 92
18	...	George Champney Palmes,²¹ *Adj.* 4 Vol. Bn. South Wales Borderers, 1 Oct. 91.			10 Sept. 77	9 June 82		9 June 92
17	...	2 William Weallens²²			11 May 78	23 Jan. 79	30 Sept. 82		8 Apr. 93
17	...	1 Charles Emilius Curll²³			14 Sept. 78	23 Jan. 79	5 Jan. 84		9 June 93
		CAPTAINS.						
17	...	2 John David Arthur Thomas Lloyd²³		4 Dec. 78	23 Jan. 79	15 Apr. 85		
19	...	Frederic Philip Smyly,²³ *Adj.* 2 Vol. Bn. South Wales Borderers, 1 June 90		31 Jan. 77	12 Apr. 79	15 Aug. 85		
18	...	2 Arnold Wilson Birch²³		16 Feb. 78	17 May 79	15 Aug. 85		
17	...	Reginald Campbell,²⁵ *Station Staff Officer, Sealkote,* 6 Mar. 91		26 Mar. 79	7 July 80	9 June 86		
16	...	Francis Charles King Hunter, *Adjutant* 3 Glamorgan Rifle Vols. 1 Nov. 92		2 July 79	14 Dec. 80	14 June 86		
15	...	Arthur Maitland Sugden,²⁷ *Adjutant* 3 Battalion, 4 Sept. 90.		11 Aug. 80	11 July 81	20 Sept. 86		
17	...	1 Edward Sylvester Gillman		5 Oct. 78	1 Jan. 80	25 Oct. 84		
15	...	Jonas Hamilton du Boulay Travers,²⁸ *Adjutant* 3 Volunteer Bn. 2 Feb. 91		22 Jan. 81	1 July 81	25 Feb. 89		
15	...	Douglas John Gaisford, *Adjutant* 4 Battalion 1 Feb. 92		19 Feb. 81	1 July 81	1 June 90		
13	1 10/12	2 Henry Macleod Graham³¹		11 Aug. 80	8 June 81	25 Oct. 90		
13	...	George Turner, *Adjutant* 1 Vol. Bn. South Wales Borderers 28 Apr. 93			10 Mar. 83	31 Jan. 91		
12	...	Bowen Wm. Sutton Van Straubenzee, *Instructor R. M. College* 1 Sept. 92			8 Aug. 83	2 Oct. 91		
11	...	2 George Hughes Grant³²			7 Feb. 85	3 Nov. 91		
11	...	1 Herbert Ferdinand Woodgate			7 Feb. 85	4 Mar. 92		
12	...	1 Alfred Maitland Addison			6 Feb. 84	24 Feb. 92		
11	...	1 Charles Archibald Ramsay Scott			28 Feb. 85	1 Sept. 92		
10	...	Herbert Acheson Moore,³³ O.S.Dept.			6 May 85	1 Nov. 92		
10	...	1 Arthur Henry Morris Hamilton Jones			29 Aug. 85	1 Nov. 92		
9	...	1 Hugh Gilbert Casson			25 Aug. 86	1 Nov. 92		
9	...	1 Frederick St. John Hughes, *Aide de Camp to Major General F.W. E. F. Walker* 27 Sept. 93			25 Aug. 86	2 Dec. 92		
11	...	2 Clifton Vincent Reynolds Wright³⁴			7 Feb. 85	26 Oct. 92		
9	...	1 Clayton Gascoigne Beauchamp²⁹ (*Depot*)			25 Aug. 86	11 Sept. 93		
9	...	1 Sydney Fitzwyman Cooke, **Adjutant** 31 July 93			10 Nov. 86	11 Sept. 93		
12	...	2 Henry de Clervaulx Moody²⁶			25 Aug. 83	25 Mar. 92		
		LIEUTENANTS.						
8	...	2 John Going³⁰		16 Nov. 87	31 July 89			
8	...	1 Charles Edward FitzGerald Walker (*Depot*)		16 Nov. 87	31 July 89			
9	...	2 Sydney Sheridan Bradford,³⁵ **Adjutant** 10 Oct. 94		5 Feb. 87	26 Mar. 90			
8	...	1 Victor Ferguson		16 Nov. 87	1 June 90			
8	...	Thomas Stirling Marquis,³⁹ *Ordnance Store Department*		16 Nov. 87	25 Oct. 90			
8	...	1 Henry Percy Pulleine		11 Feb. 88	10 Feb. 91			
7	...	1 Albert Canning³⁷ (*Depot*)		11 Apr. 88	6 Mar. 91			
7	...	1 Wilfred Edward Bownas Smith		9 May 88	1 Oct. 91			
6	...	2 Marcus John Barré de la Poer Beresford		6 July 89	18 Nov. 91			
5	...	1 Granville Pennefather Evans		16 July 90	12 Apr. 92			
5	...	1 Nicholas Blake Dunscombe		8 Oct. 90	9 June 92			
5	...	2 Edward Whitmore Jones		18 Feb. 91	1 Sept. 92			
4	...	2 Franklin Macaulay Gillespie		25 July 91	22 Feb. 93			
4	...	Edgar William M'Kenzie Ballantyne		25 July 91	22 Feb. 93			
4	...	Francis Gordon Arabin Wimberley		9 Sept. 91	22 Feb. 93			
4	...	2 Edward Cuninghame Margesson		5 Dec. 91	13 May 93			
4	...	1 Herbert Wykeham England Parker		27 Jan. 92	13 May 93			
4	...	Francis Geo. Courthope Mansel Morgan		12 Mar. 92	19 July 93			
4	...	2 Herbert Cleeve		9 Apr. 92	20 July 93			
3	...	1 Robert Peel Yates		13 Aug. 92	24 Oct. 93			
3	...	1 Charles John Safford		13 Aug. 92	24 Oct. 93			
3	...	2 Charles William Pearless		19 Nov. 92	24 Oct. 93			
3	...	1 James Grimwood		19 Nov. 92	28 Mar. 94			
3	...	1 Walter Ernest Lawrence		13 Aug. 92	22 May 94			

³⁶ Lieut. Canning served in the Egyptian war in 1882 (Medal, and Khedive's Star). Served in the expedition to the Soudan in 1884, and was present in the engagements at El Teb and Temai (two Clasps); also served in the Soudan campaign in 1885 (Clasp).

³⁷ Captain Tompkins served in the Kaffir war in 1877-78 including the operations against the Galekas; also served in the Zulu war in 1879, and was present in the engagement at Ulundi (Medal with Clasp).

Years Ser.				
Full Pay.	Half Pay.	SECOND LIEUTENANTS.	2ND LIEUT.	
3	...	1 Frederick William Gray	19 Nov.	92
3	...	1 Anthony Julian Reddie	19 Nov.	92
3	...	Frank Hunnard, *Army Service Corps*	17 Dec.	92
4	...	John Puckle, *Army Service Corps*	21 Jan.	92
2	...	2 William Arthur Glanmor Williams (*Depot*)	20 May	93
2	...	2 Archibald Jones Forbes (*Depot*)	20 May	93
2	...	1 William Lyttleton Lawrence	19 July	93
2	...	1 Glynne Everard Earle Welby	23 Dec.	93
2	...	2 Robert William Bradley	7 Mar.	94
2	...	2 Charles Lancaster Taylor	7 Mar.	94
2	...	1 Harry Whitehill Stevens	7 Mar.	94
1	...	2 Frederick George Lawrence	10 Oct.	94
1	...	1 Francis Innes Day	20 Feb.	95
1	...	Robert Berkeley Airey	6 Mar.	95
		Paymasters.—1		
		2		
16	...	*Quarter Masters.*—1 John James Tompkins,[37] 26 Nov. 79; *Hon. Captain*, 26 Nov. 89.		
2	...	2 William Burrows,[40] 15 Nov. 93; *Hon. Lieut.*		

Facings White.—*Agents*, Messrs. Holt and Co.
1st Battalion embarked for Egypt, 17 Dec. 1892. 2nd Battalion returned from Aden, 16 Nov. 93.

[1] Lt. Colonel Banister served in the Kafir war of 1877-78, and took part in the operations against the Galekas, and in the Zulu war of 1879 (Medal with Clasp).

[3] Lt. Colonel E. S. Browne served in the Kafir war in 1878 including the operations against the Griquas; also served in the Zulu war of 1879, and was present in the engagements at Zlobane Mountain (Victoria Cross) and Ulundi (mentioned in despatches), and in the operations against Sekukuni (Medal with Clasp): was awarded the V.C. "for his gallant conduct on the 29th March 1879, when the Mounted Infantry were being driven in by the enemy at Inhlobana, in galloping back and twice assisting on his horse (under heavy fire and within a few yards of the enemy) one of the mounted men, who must otherwise have fallen into the enemy's hands."

[4] Major Mainwaring served in the Kafir war in 1877-78 including the operations against the Galekas; also served in the Zulu war of 1879 (Medal with Clasp).

[5] Major Heaton served in the Kafir war in 1877-78, and in the Zulu war in 1879, and was present in the engagement of Ulundi (Medal with Clasp). Served with the Burmese Expedition in 1885-89 (Medal with two Clasps).

[6] Lt. Colonel Clements served in the Kafir war in 1877-78, and was present in the engagement at Neumarke; also served in the Zulu war of 1879, and was present in the engagement at Ulundi (Medal with Clasp). Served with the Burmese Expedition in 1885-89 as Brigade Major, and was present in the engagements at Obu (severely wounded), and Taindah—slightly wounded (mentioned in despatches, Brevet of Lt. Colonel, Medal with two Clasps).

[9] Major Hon. Ulick Roche served in the Kafir war in 1877-78 with the 1st Battalion of the 24th Foot, including the operations against the Gaikas and Galekas (Medal with Clasp). Served with the Burmese Expedition in 1886-89 (Medal with two Clasps).

[10] Captain Trower served in the Kafir war in 1877-78 including the operations against the Galekas and Gaikas; also served in the Zulu war in 1879 (Medal with Clasp).

[21] Major Palmes served in the Kafir war in 1877-78, and was present during the operations against the Galekas and in the engagement at Quintana (Medal with Clasp).

[22] Major Weallens served in the Zulu war in 1879, and was present in the engagement at Ulundi (Medal with Clasp).

[23] Major Curll, Captains Lloyd, Smyly, G. K. Moore and Birch served in the Zulu war of 1879 (Medal with Clasp).

[25] Captain R. Campbell served in the Zulu war in 1879 (Medal with Clasp). Served with the Burmese Expedition in 1886-89 (Medal with two Clasps).

[26] Captain Moody served in the Burmese Expedition in 1885-87 with the 2nd Battalion Queen's Royal West Surrey Regiment under Brigadier General Lockhart (Medal with Clasp).

[27] Captain Sugden served with the Burmese Expedition in 1887-89 (Medal with Clasp).

[28] Captain Travers served with the Burmese Expedition in 1887-89 (Medal with Clasp).

[29] Captain Beauchamp served with the Burmese Expedition in 1887-89 (Medal with Clasp).

[30] Lieut. Going served with the Burmese Expedition in 1887-89 (Medal with Clasp).

[31] Captain Graham served with the Burmese Expedition in 1886-89 (Medal with two Clasps).

[32] Captain Grant served with the Burmese Expedition in 1885-89 (Medal with two Clasps).

[33] Captain H. A. Moore served with the Burmese Expedition in 1885-89 (Medal with two Clasps).

[34] Captain Wright served with the expedition to the Tambaka Country in 1892 including the capture of Tambi (Medal with Clasp).

[35] Lieut. Bradford served with the Burmese Expedition in 1887-89 (Medal with Clasp).

[39] Lieut. Marquis.—See Civil Decorations for Gallantry, "Hart's Annual Army List," p. 786.

[40] Lieut. Burrows served in the Zulu war in 1879 (Medal with Clasp). Served with the Burmese Expedition in 1887-89 (Medal with Clasp).

1st Batt., York.
2nd Batt., Rawul Pindee, Bengal.

The King's Own Scottish Borderers.

[Regimental District No. 25. —Berwick-on-Tweed.]

Formerly the 25th (The King's Own Borderers) Regiment.
(The 3rd Battalion is formed of the Scottish Borderers Militia.)

The King's Crest. "*In Veritate Religionis confida.*" The Castle of Edinburgh. "*Nisi Dominus frustra.*"
The White Horse. "*Nec aspera terrent.*" "MINDEN" "EGMONT-OP-ZEE." "EGYPT" (with the Sphinx).
"MARTINIQUE" "AFGHANISTAN, 1878-80."

Years' Ser.							
Full Pay.	Half Pay.	**Colonel.**—William Craig Emilius Napier,[1] *Ensign*, 28 Aug. 35; *Lt.* P17 Nov. 37; *Capt.* P29 April 42; *Brevet Major*, 18 Feb. 48; *Brevet Lt.Colonel*, 30 May 51; *Colonel*, 28 Oct. 54; *Major*, 23 Oct. 55; *Major General*, 9 March 65; *Lieut.General*, 22 Aug. 73; *General*, 1 Oct. 77; *Colonel* King's Own Borderers, 23 Sept. 82.						
29	...	**Lieutenant Colonels.**—1 John Henry Hickman Spence Drew Hogarth,[9] *Ensign*, 5 Mar. 67; *Lt.* P28 May 70; *Capt.* 1 July 78; *Major*, 15 Dec. 85; *Lt.Colonel*, 1 Jan. 94.						
27	...	2 Henry Grey Dixon,[11] *Ensign*, P23 Dec. 68; *Lt.* P2 Aug. 71; *Capt.* 12 Feb. 79; *Major*, 17 Feb. 86; *Lt.Colonel*, 3 Dec. 94.						

			ENSIGN OR 2ND LIEUT.	LIEUT.	CAPTAIN.	BREV.MAJ.	MAJOR.
		MAJORS.					
24	...	2 p.s.c. John William Godfray	24 Sept. 71	28 Oct. 71	22 Dec. 79	......	6 June 88
24	...	1 George Thomas William Hewat	27 Sept. 71	28 Oct. 71	1 Jan. 81	......	14 June 90
23	...	1 Robert John Romanes	......	29 May 72	26 April 81	......	8 Oct. 90
22	...	2 Charles Theodore Becker[10]	......	9 Aug. 73	1 July 81	......	30 Dec. 91
22	...	1 Francis Arthur Cartwright Claughton (*Depot*)	......	28 Feb. 74	31 Oct. 83	......	27 July 92
21	...	2 George Nisbet Mayne[18]	......	13 June 74	2 June 84	......	1 Jan. 94
21	...	1 James Henry Erskine Reid[15]	......	11 Feb. 75	21 June 85	......	10 Sept. 94
19	...	2 Leonard Gordon[2]	......	6 Sept. 76	23 Sept. 85	......	3 Dec. 94
		CAPTAINS.					
18	...	Alex. Hepburne Barrington Cavaye,[16] *Dep. Assist. Adj. General, Rangoon*, 3 Oct. 94	......	31 May 77	1 Apr. 86		
19	...	Chas. Louis Woollcombe,[12] *D.A A.G. for Musketry, Bengal*, 10 May 90	......	11 Oct. 76	1 Apr. 86		
18	...	1 Montagu Grant Wilkinson[17]	30 Jan. 78	17 April 79	1 Nov. 86		
17	...	1 Alfred Worsley Pennyman[16]	1 May 78	24 May 79	1 July 87		
18	...	James Hope,[10] *Adjutant 1 Roxburgh and Selkirk Rifle Vols.* 11 Nov. 90	2 Mar. 78	17 May 79	21 Nov. 87		
17	...	2 Herwald Robert Wigram[16]	11 May 78	2 July 79	1 Feb. 88		
13	...	2 Duncan Alwyn Macfarlane,[16] *Adjutant* 31 July 93	......	6 May 82	11 Jan. 88		
18	...	James Rea, *Adj.* 3 (*Dumfries*) *Vol. Bn.* 27 Oct. 92	8 Dec. 77	3 Apr. 78	6 June 88		
16	...	1 George de Wet Verner[19]	13 Aug. 79	1 Jan. 81	1 July 88		
16	...	Reynell H. Bayley Taylor,[7] *O.S.Dept.*	13 Aug. 79	26 Feb. 81	1 Aug. 88		
16	...	1 Fitzroy Hemphill	14 Jan. 80	1 July 81	1 Aug. 88		
16	...	2 Chas. Joseph Edw. Addis M'Arthur[20]	14 Jan. 80	1 July 81	1 Feb. 89		
15	...	p.s.c. Percy Wildman-Lushington, *Instructor R. Mil. Coll.* 13 Feb. 93	23 Oct. 80	1 July 81	1 Nov. 89		
15	...	p.s.c. Alex. Beamish Hamilton,[26] *Dep. Assist.Adj.Gen.Alexandria*, 10 Dec 93	22 Jan. 81	1 July 81	11 Dec. 89		
15	...	1 James Bonham Tod Pratt,[25] *Adjutant* 25 July 94	22 Jan. 81	1 July 81	10 May 90		
15	...	2 Harold James Clifford Stanton (*Depot*)	19 Feb. 81	1 July 81	14 June 90		
14	...	Robt. Lynch Blosse,[24] *Adj.* 2 *Vol. Bn.*, *King's Own Scottish Bord.* 11 Jan. 92	23 April 81	1 July 81	10 Sept. 90		
13	...	1 Ar. Wentworth Wm. Aug. Thellusson[21]	......	9 Sept. 82	11 Jan. 92		
13	...	Walter Dennistoun Sellar,[16] *Adj.* 8 *Vol. Bn. Royal Scots* 1 Mar. 93	......	9 Sept. 82	27 July 92		
13	...	Augustus Helier Magee, *Army Pay Dep.*	......	27 Jan. 83	13 Feb. 93		
13	...	Edgar John Dent,[22] *Adjutant* 3 Battalion 1 Sept. 94	......	10 Mar. 83	13 Feb. 93		
10	...	1 Cecil Macdonald Stephenson[27]	......	25 Nov. 85	1 Mar. 93		
13	...	2 Thomas George MacLaren	......	10 Mar. 83	30 Dec. 93		
10	...	2 Archibald Stephen Koe[28]	......	30 Jan. 86	23 May 94		
9	...	2 Lionel Chorley Lascelles Davidson.....	......	10 Nov. 86	3 Dec. 94		
		LIEUTENANTS.					
10	...	1 Edward Robert Cureton[16]	......	30 Jan. 86			
8	...	2 Alfred Edward Haig[16]	14 Sept. 87	4 Dec. 89			
8	...	1 Seymour Campbell Johnston[23]	18 Jan. 88	4 Dec. 89			
7	...	1 Alexander Charles Going (*Depot*)	9 May 88	11 Dec. 89			
7	...	1 Angus George Fraser	9 May 88	10 May 90			
7	...	1 Alan Ralph Cobbold[16]	9 May 88	10 May 90			
7	...	1 David Ramsay Sladen[16] (*Depot*)	13 June 88	10 May 90			
7	...	1 Francis John Carruthers[16]	22 Aug. 88	14 June 90			
7	...	2 Herbert William Rattigan[16]	22 Aug. 88	10 Sept. 90			
7	...	Norman Ernest Playfair, *serving with the Egyptian Army*	22 Aug. 88	4 Dec. 90			
7	...	1 Thomas Byrne Sellar	29 Dec. 88	17 Apr. 91			
6	...	1 Edgar Quartus Robertson	8 June 89	4 Aug. 91			
6	...	1 Charles Baldwin Clutterbuck	1 Mar. 90	21 Jan. 93			
6	...	1 Arthur Blair	1 Mar. 90	13 Feb. 93			
5	...	1 Edward Maule Young	7 Jan. 91	1 Mar. 93			
5	...	1 Herbert Gilbert Maclachlan Amos.....	15 Oct. 90	29 Apr. 92			
4	...	Harold Hamer Grey Stansfeld	17 June 91	26 Aug. 93			
4	...	Andrew Skeen	5 Dec. 91	30 Dec. 93			
4	...	2 Godfrey Frederic Charles Baliol Scott	23 Jan. 92	30 Dec. 93			
4	...	Alfred Albert James	13 May 92	23 May 94			
3	...	2 William Henry Somerville M'Alestor...	13 July 92	23 May 94			
3	...	2 Robert Ind Chamberlain................	13 Aug. 92	3 Dec. 94			
		SECOND LIEUTENANTS.					
3	...	2 Henry Donald Neil Maclean	21 Jan. 93				
2	...	Hugh Mauritius Leet, *serving under the Royal Niger Company*	19 Apr. 93				
2	...	2 Rous Milner Limond	20 May 93				
2	...	1 George Martin Hannay	9 Sept. 93				
2	...	2 Alfred John Welch	9 Sept. 93				

[1] General Napier served as Aide de Camp to Sir Charles Napier during his campaign of 1845 against the Desert and Mountain Tribes on the right bank of the Indus. Served also at the siege of Sebastopol as Assistant Director General of the Land Transport Corps (Medal with Clasp, 5th Class of the Medjidie, and Turkish Medal).

[2] Major Gordon served with the 25th King's Own Borderers in the Afghan war in 1878-79 with the Peshawur Valley Field Force, including the Bazar Valley Expedition under Lieut. General Maude (Medal).

269a The King's Own Scottish Borderers.

Years Ser. Full Pay	Half Pay		SECOND LIEUTENANTS.	2ND LIEUT.
2	...	1	David Drummond Gunn....................	23 Dec. 93
2	...	1	Ronald Charles Gibb	7 Mar. 94
2	...	2	Humphrey Frank Pipe-Wolferstan ...	7 Mar. 94
2	...	2	James David Stirling....................	7 Mar. 94
1	...	2	Ernest Wood	2 June 94
1	...	2	Edward Sacheverell D'Ewes Coke ...	10 Oct. 94
1	...	2	Arthur Montagu Brooke	10 Oct. 94
1	...		William Munro Allan....................	6 Mar. 95

Paymasters.—1
    2 Chas. J. E. A. M'Arthur, *Captain 2 Battalion (acting).*
Quarter Masters.—1 Walter Edward Webb,[30] 8 June 92; *Hon. Lieut.*
    2 Thomas Henry Gott,[31] 26 Apr. 93; *Hon. Lieut.*

Facings Blue.—*Agents*, Messrs. Cox and Co.
1st Batt. *returned from India,* 5 Feb. 1891.   2nd Batt. *embarked for Egypt,* 19 July 1883.

[7] Major Claughton and Captain R. H. B. Taylor served with the 25th King's Own Borderers in the Afghan war in 1879-80 with the Khyber Line Force under Lieut.General Bright (Medal).
[9] Lt.Colonel Hogarth served with the 25th King's Own Borderers in the Afghan war in 1878-79 with the Peshawur Valley Field Force under Lieut.General Maude (Medal).
[10] Major Becker (as Acting Adjutant) and Captain James Hope served with the 25th King's Own Borderers in the Afghan war of 1878-80, first with the Peshawur Valley Field Force under Lieut.General Maude, and afterwards with the Khyber Line Force under Lieut.General Bright (Medal).
[11] Lt.Colonel Dixon served with the 2nd Battalion King's Own Scottish Borderers in the Afghan war of 1878-80, first with the Peshawur Valley Field Force as Orderly Officer to Brigadier General Blyth, including the Bazar Valley Expedition under Lieut.General Maude, and afterwards with the Khyber Line Force under Lieut.General Bright (mentioned in despatches, Medal). Served with the 2nd Battalion King's Own Scottish Borderers with the Suakin Field Force in December 1888 during the investment of Suakin and was present in the engagement at Gemaizah (mentioned in despatches, Medal with Clasp, Khedive's Star, and 4th Class of the Medjidie). Also served in the operations on the Soudan Frontier in 1889.
[12] Captain Woollcombe served with the 2nd Battalion King's Own Scottish Borderers in the Afghan war of 1878-80, with the Peshawur Valley Field Force under Lieut.General Maude, and afterwards with the Khyber Line Force under Lieut.General Bright (Medal). Served as Adjutant 1st Battalion King's Own Scottish Borderers in the Chin-Lushai Expedition in 1889-90 with the Burmah Column under Brigadier General Symons. (Medal with Clasp).
[15] Major Reid served in the Afghan war of 1878-80, and took part with the Bazar Valley Expedition; was present at the mutiny of the Wali's troops on the Helmund at Girishk, at the battle of Mainwand (wounded), and the defence of Candahar (mentioned in despatches, Medal).
[16] Captains Cavaye, Pennyman, Wigram, Macfarlane, and Sellar, Lieuts. Cureton, Haig, Cobbold, Sladen, Carruthers, and Rattigan served with the 2nd Battalion King's Own Scottish Borderers with the Suakin Field Force in December 1888 during the investment of Suakin and were present at the engagement at Gemaizah (Medal with Clasp, and Khedive's Star). Also served in the operations on the Soudan Frontier in 1889.
[17] Captain Wilkinson served with the Nile Expedition in 1884-85 as Transport Officer (Medal with Clasp, and Khedive's Star). Served as Adjutant to the 2nd Battalion King's Own Scottish Borderers with the Suakin Field Force in December 1888 during the investment of Suakin and was present in the engagement at Gemaizah (mentioned in despatches, Clasp).
[18] Major Mayne served with the 25th King's Own Borderers in the Afghan war in 1879-80 with the Khyber Line Force under Lieut.General Bright (Medal). Served with the Burmese Expedition in 1886-88 (mentioned in despatches, Medal with Clasp).
[19] Captain Verner served with the 25th King's Own Borderers in the Afghan war in 1879-80 with the Khyber Line Force under Lieut.General Bright (Medal). Served with the Nile Expedition in 1884-85, and was present in the engagement at Abu Klea Wells on the 16th and 17th February (Medal with Clasp, and Khedive's Star). Served with the Chin-Lushai Expeditionary Force in 1889-90 as Superintendent of Army Signallers (Medal with Clasp).
[20] Captain M'Arthur served with the 2nd Battalion King's Own Scottish Borderers in the Afghan war in 1879-80 in the Khyber Line Force under Lieut.General Bright (Medal). Served in the Soudan campaign in 1885 and was present in the engagement at the Tofrek zereba (Medal with two Clasps, and Khedive's Star). Served with the 2nd Battalion King's Own Scottish Borderers in the Chin-Lushai Expedition in 1890 with the Burmah Column under Brigadier General Symons. (Medal with Clasp).
[21] Captain Thellusson served with the Mounted Infantry with the Suakin Field Force in December 1888 during the investment of Suakin and was present in the engagement at Gemaizah (Medal with Clasp, and Khedive's Star). Also served in the operations on the Soudan Frontier in 1889.
[22] Captain Dent served with the 2nd Battalion King's Own Scottish Borderers with the Suakin Field Force in December 1888 during the investment of Suakin and was present in the engagement at Gemaizah (Medal with Clasp, and Khedive's Star); also served in the operations on the Soudan frontier in 1889 including the engagement at Toski (mentioned in despatches, 4th Class of the Medjidie, Clasp).
[23] Lieut. Johnston served in the operations on the Soudan Frontier in 1889.
[24] Captain Blosse served with the Burmese Expedition in 1889-90 (Medal with Clasp).
[25] Captain Pratt served with the Chin-Lushai Expeditionary Force in 1889-90 (Medal with Clasp).
[26] Captain Hamilton served with the Chin-Lushai Expeditionary Force in 1889-90 (Medal with Clasp).
[27] Captain Stephenson served with the Chin-Lushai Expeditionary Force in 1889-90 (Medal with Clasp).
[28] Captain Koe served with the Chin-Lushai Expeditionary Force in 1889-90 (Medal with Clasp).
[30] Lieut. Webb served in the Afghan war of 1878-80 (Medal). Served with the Chin-Lushai Expeditionary Force in 1889-90 (Medal with Clasp).
[31] Lieut. Gott served in the Soudan campaign in 1888 including the engagement at Gemaizah (Medal with Clasp, and Khedive's Star).

Record of the Services of the 2nd Battalion the King's Own Scottish Borderers (formerly the 25th Regt.).

Raised in England in 1859. England and Scotland, to 1863. Ceylon, to 1868. India, to 1875. Aden, to 1876. England, to 1879. Ireland, to 1886. Gibraltar, to 1886. England, to 1888. (Entitled "The King's Own Scottish Borderers," 1887.) Egypt, to 1888. The Soudan, to 1889 (action at Gemaizah). Egypt, to 1890. India, 1890.

1st Batt., Bareilly, Bengal.
2nd Batt., Parkhurst.] **The Cameronians (Scottish Rifles).** [Regimental District No. 26. —Hamilton.

Formerly the 26th (The Cameronian) and the 90th (Perthshire Volunteers— Light Infantry) Regiments.

(The 3rd and 4th Battalions are formed of the Royal Lanark Militia.)

"BLENHEIM" "RAMILLIES" "OUDENARDE" "MALPLAQUET" "MANDORA" "EGYPT" (with the Sphinx). "CORUNNA" "MARTINIQUE" "GUADALOUPE" "CHINA" (with the Dragon). "SOUTH AFRICA, 1846-7" "SEVASTOPOL" "LUCKNOW" "ABYSSINIA" "SOUTH AFRICA, 1877-8-9."

Years' Ser.									
Full Pay	Half Pay								
27	...	Colonel.—George Henry MacKinnon,[1] CB. 2nd Lt. 29 June 24; Ensign & Lt. P4 Nov. 24; Lt. & Capt. P21 Feb. 28; Capt. & Lt. Colonel, P24 April 40; Colonel, 11 Nov. 51; Major General, 22 Sept. 58; Lieut. General, 10 Feb. 65; General, 19 Jan. 73; Colonel 26th Foot, 21 Dec. 62.							
21	...	Lieutenant Colonels.—1 p.s.c. Percy John Hughes, Ensign, 8 July 68; Lt. 28 Oct. 71; Capt. 15 Mar. 79; Major, 23 May 83; Lt. Colonel, 10 Oct. 93.							
21	...	2 Henry de Courcy Rawlins,[5] Lieut. 23 April 74; Captain, 11 Oct. 79; Major, 30 May 83; Lt. Colonel, 15 Dec. 94.							

		MAJORS.	2ND LIEUT.	LIEUT.	CAPTAIN.	BREV. MAJ.	MAJOR.
21	...	1 p.s.c. Samuel Holt Lomax[7]		13 June 74	21 July 80		1 Jan. 86
21	...	2 Arthur Craigie FitzHarding Vincent...		11 Feb. 75	26 Feb. 81		1 Jan. 86
22	...	1 Home Johnstone Fergusson[6]		12 Nov. 73	2 Mar. 81		2 Mar. 92
19	...	1 Ernest Cooke (Depot)		15 July 76	24 Jan. 83		29 Apr. 92
18	...	2 Sydney Philip Strong[10]	30 Jan. 78	7 Aug. 78	11 Sept. 83		16 Oct. 92
17	...	Edward Douglass Kennedy, Adj. 3 } Lanarkshire Rifle Vols. 16 Nov. 91.. }		15 July 78	14 Nov. 83		10 Oct. 93
17	...	1 Cameron Charles Douglas[12]	1 May 78	31 Mar. 80	10 Oct. 85		15 Oct. 94
17	...	2 Sydney Gordon Grant[13]	1 May 78	29 Sept. 80	16 Oct. 85		15 Dec. 94
		CAPTAINS.					
17	...	2 Clement Baddeley Wood	11 May 78	1 July 81	1 Jan. 85		
17	...	Chas. Harrie Innes Hopkins,[14] Station } Staff Officer, Ferozepore, 16 Apr. 94 }	1 May 78	1 Apr. 79	2 Jan. 86		
15	...	1 Fortescue John Nason[15]	11 Aug. 80	1 July 81	17 May 86		
17	...	James Shaw,[20] Adjutant 3 Battalion } 15 Aug. 91 }	1 May 78	11 Oct. 79	17 May 86		
17	...	2 Y© p.s.c. Henry Lysons[26]	11 May 78	15 Dec. 79	23 June 86		
17	...	1 Arthur Ogilvie White[27]	11 May 78	7 Jan. 80	23 June 86		
17	...	1 Robert Black Fell[28]	11 May 78	2 June 80	13 Nov. 89		
15	...	2 Thomas Townley Macan	23 Oct. 80	1 July 81	22 June 91		
15	...	1 Allan Vesey Ussher[29] (Depot)	19 Feb. 81	1 July 81	2 Mar. 92		
13	...	1 Lionel Combe		10 Mar. 83	29 Apr. 92		
12	...	1 Conyngham Richard Cecil Ellis		5 Dec. 83	5 Apr. 93		
12	...	2 Ernest Henry Samuel Twyford[30]		5 Dec. 83	7 Mar. 94		
11	...	2 Herbert Sutherland Walker, Staff Coll.		23 Aug. 84	16 Apr. 94		
11	...	2 Leslie Dewing Blackburn, Adjutant } 20 Nov. 91 }		23 Aug. 84	16 Apr. 94		
10	...	1 Herbert Forbes Churchill		23 Aug. 84	28 Nov. 94		
11	...	2 Henry Nugent Head		7 Feb. 85	15 Dec. 94		
		LIEUTENANTS.					
11	...	1 Charles Maxwell Shurlock Henning ...		18 Feb. 85			
10	...	2 George Dalbiac Luard		7 Oct. 85			
9	...	2 Robert Wanless Smith		28 Apr. 86			
9	...	1 Archibald Offley Jenney		28 Apr. 86			
9	...	1 Wilfrid Marryat Bliss, Adjutant 29 } Oct. 94 }		25 Aug. 86			
9	...	2 Philip Rynd Robertson		25 Aug. 86			
9	...	2 John Henry Wingfield Guise		25 Aug. 86			
9	...	1 Crofton Bury Vandeleur	5 Feb. 87	22 June 91			
7	...	1 William Alston Dykes	20 June 88	16 Nov. 91			
7	...	2 Fergus Murray	23 Mar. 89	2 Mar. 92			
6	...	2 George Tupper Campbell Carter-} Campbell (Depot) }	23 Oct. 89	29 Apr. 92			
5	...	1 Ernest de Launoy Hayes	3 May 90	5 Apr. 93			
5	...	2 Maynard Francis Colchester-Wemyss	29 Oct. 90	6 Dec. 93			
5	...	Charles Gray Campbell	4 Feb. 91	7 Mar. 94			
5	...	Charles Cowan Newnham	25 Mar. 91	7 Mar. 94			
4	...	1 Arthur Ritchie (Depot)	10 Oct. 91	16 Apr. 94			
4	...	William Frank Bainbridge	7 Nov. 91	13 June 94			
4	...	1 Charles Edward Tuson	27 Jan. 92	10 Oct. 94			
4	...	2 Walmsley Donat O'Brien	12 Mar. 92	29 Oct. 94			
3	...	1 George Adams Ellis	9 Apr. 92	28 Nov. 94			
3	...	Hugh Mitchell Turton	18 June 92	15 Dec. 94			
3	...	2 Charles Walter	12 Oct. 92	15 Dec. 94			
3	...	2 Maurice Loraine Pears	17 Dec. 92	14 Jan. 95			
		SECOND LIEUTENANTS.					
2	...	2 Hesperus David Watkiss Lloyd	26 Apr. 93				
2	...	2 James Huntly Dutton	21 Oct. 93				
2	...	1 Arthur Russel Mecham	23 Dec. 93				
2	...	1 Arthur Cecil Northey	7 Mar. 94				
1	...	2 Arthur Fitzhenry Townshend	2 June 94				
1	...	1 Harold Adrian Holdich	10 Oct. 94				
1	...	1 William Hugh Barton	12 Dec. 94				
1	...	1 Richard Oakley	12 Dec. 94				
1	...	1 James Graham Chaplin	12 Dec. 94				
1	...	1 Harry More Wollstein	9 Jan. 95				
1	...	1 Samuel Lawrence	20 Feb. 95				
1	...	Frederick Lawrence Stanley Clarke..	6 Mar. 95				
1	...	Ian Stewart	6 Mar. 95				

Paymasters.—2 George D. Luard, Lieut. 1 Battalion (ac ing).

8	...	*Quarter Masters.*—1 Edward Vine, 28 Sept. 87; Hon. Lieut.	
4	...	2 William Oliphant, 6 Feb. 92; Hon. Lieut.	

Facings Rifle Green.—*Agents*, Messrs. Cox & Co.

1st Battalion embarked for India, 1 Dec. 1894. 2nd Battalion returned from India, 13 Feb. 1895.

The Cameronians (Scottish Rifles).

[1] General MacKinnon served as Assistant Quarter Master General at the Cape of Good Hope in the Kaffir war of 1846-47, and as Colonel on the Staff in command of the 2nd Division of the forces in the field in the Kaffir war of 1851-52 (Medal).

[5] Lt. Colonel Rawlins served in the Gaika war of 1878 in command of the mounted infantry of his regiment; served throughout the Zulu war of 1879 in the Second Squadron of Mounted Infantry, and was present in the engagements at Inyezane and Gingindhlovu (mentioned in despatches), and throughout the operations of Clarke's Column (Medal with Clasp).

[7] Major Lomax served as Adjutant of the 90th Light Infantry in the Gaika war of 1878, including the operations in the Waterkloof and Perie Bush, and the engagement at Taba Indoda. Also served throughout the Zulu war of 1879, and was present in the engagements at Zungin Nek, Kambula, and Ulundi (Medal with Clasp).

[8] Major Fergusson served throughout the operations in the Malay Peninsula in 1875-76 (Medal with Clasp). Served in the Afghan war in 1878-79, and took part as Transport Officer in the occupation of Candahar and Khelat-i-Ghilzie (Medal).

[10] Major Strong served with the 90th Light Infantry in the Gaika war of 1878, including the operations in the Perie Bush. Also served throughout the Zulu war of 1879, and present in the engagements at Zungin Nek, Kambula (mentioned in despatches), and Ulundi (Medal with Clasp).

[12] Major Douglas served in the Soudan Expedition under Sir Gerald Graham in 1884 as Aide de Camp to Major General Davis, Commanding 2nd Brigade, and was present in the engagements at El Teb and Temai (mentioned in despatches, Medal with Clasp, and Khedive's Star). Served with the Nile Expedition in 1884-85 with the Desert Column attached to the 19th Hussars (Clasp).

[13] Major Grant served with the Bechuanaland Expedition under Sir Charles Warren in 1884-85.

[14] Captain Hopkins served with the 90th Light Infantry in the Zulu war of 1879, and was present in the engagements at Kambula and Ulundi (Medal with Clasp).

[15] Captain Nason served in the operations in the Soudan in 1889 including the engagements at Arguin and Toski (Medal with Clasp, 4th Class of the Medjidie, and Khedive's Star).

[20] Captain Shaw served with the Hazara Expedition in 1888 as Brigade Transport Officer (Medal with Clasp).

[26] Captain Lysons served as Aide de Camp to Brigadier General Wood during the Zulu war of 1879, and was present in the engagements at Zungin Nek, Zlobane Mountain (mentioned in despatches, Victoria Cross), Kambula (again mentioned), and Ulundi (Medal with Clasp): together with Private Edmond Fowler, Scottish Rifles (since discharged), was awarded the VC under the following circumstances:—" On the 28th March 1879, during the assault of the Inhlobane Mountain, Sir Evelyn Wood ordered the dislodgment of certain Zulus (who were causing the troops much loss) from strong natural caves commanding the position in which some of the wounded were lying. Some delay occurring in the execution of the orders issued, Captain the Honourable Ronald Campbell, Coldstream Guards, followed by Lieutenant Lysons Aide-de-Camp, and Private Fowler, ran forward in the most determined manner, and advanced over a mass of fallen boulders, and between walls of rock, which led to a cave in which the enemy lay hidden. It being impossible for two men to walk abreast the assailants were consequently obliged to keep in single file, and as Captain Campbell was leading, he arrived first at the mouth of the cave, from which the Zulus were firing, and there met his death; Lieutenant Lysons and Private Fowler, who were following close behind him, immediately dashed at the cave, from which led several subterranean passages, and firing into the chasm below, succeeded in forcing the occupants to forsake their stronghold. Lieutenant Lysons remained at the cave's mouth for some minutes after the attack, during which time Captain Campbell's body was carried down the slopes." Served in the Nile Expedition in 1884-85 with the Egyptian Army (Medal with Clasp, and Khedive's Star).

[27] Captain White served with the 90th Light Infantry in the Zulu war of 1879, and was present in the engagements at Zungin Nek, Kambula, and Ulundi (Medal with Clasp).

[28] Captain Fell served with the 90th Light Infantry in the Zulu war of 1879, and was present in the engagements at Zungin Nek and Kambula (Medal with Clasp).

[29] Captain Ussher served in the operations against the Jebus, Lagos, in 1891 (mentioned in despatches, Medal with Clasp).

[30] Captain Twyford served with the Chin-Lushai Expeditionary Force in 1889 as Transport Officer (Medal with Clasp).

Record of the Services of the 1st Battalion the Cameronians (Scottish Rifles),—formerly the 26th Cameronians.

Raised in 1688 and proceeded to Flanders in 1691 till 1700. Scotland, to 1702. Netherlands, to 1713. Ireland, to 1715. Scotland, to 1716. Ireland, to 1726. Gibraltar, to 1738. Minorca, to 1748. Ireland, to 1754. Scotland, to 1757. Ireland, to 1767. North America, to 1800. England, to 1801. Egypt, to 1802. Scotland, to 1803. [2nd Battalion raised and proceeded to Ireland to 1807. Disbanded in 1813.] Germany, to 1806. England, to 1807. Ireland, to 1808. Spain, to 1809. England, 1809. Walcheren Expedition, to 1810. Jersey, to 1811. Spain, to 1812. Gibraltar, to 1821. Ireland, to 1827. England, to 1828. India, to 1840. China, to 1842. Scotland, to 1844. England, to 1845. Ireland, to 1850. Gibraltar, to 1853. Bermuda, to 1859. Ireland, to 1861. Scotland, to 1862. England, to 1865. India, to 1875. England, to 1876. Scotland, to 1878. England, to 1880. Malta, to 1881. England, to 1884. Scotland, to 1886. Ireland, 1886.

1st Batt., Kinsale.
2nd Batt., Thayetmyo, Burmah.] **The Royal Inniskilling Fusiliers.** [Regimental District. No. 27.—Omagh.] 271

Formerly the 27th (Inniskilling) and the 108th (Madras Infantry) Regiments.
(The 3rd, 4th, and 5th Battalions are formed of the Fermanagh, Tyrone, and Donegal Militia respectively.)
The Castle of Inniskilling, with St. George's Colours. The White Horse. "*Nec aspera terrent.*" "ST. LUCIA" "EGYPT" (with the Sphinx). "MAIDA" "BADAJOZ" "SALAMANCA" "VITTORIA" "PYRENEES" "NIVELLE" "ORTHES" "TOULOUSE" "PENINSULA" "WATERLOO" "SOUTH AFRICA, 1835, 1846-7" "CENTRAL INDIA."

Colonel.—Sir James Talbot Airey,¹ KCB. Ensign, 11 Feb. 30; Lieut. P3 May 33; Capt. P22 July 42; Major, 11 Nov. 51; Capt. & Lt.Colonel, 17 July 54; Colonel, 26 Dec. 59; Major General, 6 Mar. 68; Lt.General, 1 Oct. 77; General, 1 July 81; Colonel Inniskilling Fusiliers, 13 Mar. 86.

Years' Ser.			ENSIGN OR 2ND LIEUT.	LIEUT.	CAPTAIN.	BREV.MAJ.	MAJOR.
Full Pay	Half Pay						
30	...	Lieutenant Colonels.—1 Henry Crawford, Ensign, 30 Mar. 66; Lt. 22 Oct. 67; Capt. 14 Jan. 76; Major, 9 May 83; Lt.Colonel, 1 Feb. 93.					
30	...	2 Albert Philip Wodehouse, Ensign, P4 Aug. 65; Lt. P5 May 69; Capt. 12 Feb. 75; Major, 2 Feb. 85; Lt.Colonel, 1 Dec. 93.					
		MAJORS.					
27	...	1 Thomas Martin Gerard Thackeray	P25 Nov. 68	P27 Oct. 71	23 Mar. 81	......	1 Dec. 89
21	...	p.s.c. Richard Menteith Greenfield² (Brevet Lt.Colonel 29 Dec. 93)	......	13 June 74	14 Sept. 81	......	10 Aug. 90
21	...	Robert George Kekewich,³ Military Secretary, Madras, 20 June 93	......	2 Dec. 74	30 Nov. 83	15 June 85	12 Nov. 90
21	...	Hy. Cornwall Cotton Gibbings⁴	......	11 Feb. 75	10 Aug. 83	......	21 Sept. 92
19	...	1 John James Purdon (Depot)	......	11 Nov. 76	26 July 84	......	12 Oct. 92
18	...	2 Henry George Daniel⁵	5 Sept. 77	21 Mar. 78	4 Oct. 84	......	1 Feb. 93
18	...	2 John Francis William Charley	30 Jan. 78	1 Nov. 78	13 Jan. 85	......	23 Sept. 93
18	...	1 Henry M'Leod Young	30 Jan. 78	13 Nov. 78	2 Feb. 85	......	1 Dec. 93
		CAPTAINS.					
18	...	2 Francis Alexander Sanders, Station Staff Officer, Meiktila, 22 Jan. 93	16 Feb. 78	18 Nov. 78	2 Feb. 85		
17	...	1 Edward Aubrey Strachan	1 May 78	1 Feb. 79	2 Feb. 85		
17	...	Robert Lawrence Ball Steele, Adjutant 3 Battalion 29 Sept. 90	11 May 78	8 Mar. 79	1 Jan. 87		
16	...	William Charles Woollett, Army Pay Department	21 June 79	6 Mar. 80	5 Apr. 87		
16	1½	2 Peter Ridley Edward Thompson	1 May 78	12 Feb. 79	17 Aug. 85		
16	...	Richard Charles Clement Cox, Adj. 3 Vol. Bn. Liverpool Regt. 1 July 91	21 June 79	8 Dec. 80	7 May 87		
16	...	Archibald James Murray,⁶ Adjutant 4 Bn. Bedfordshire Regt. 15 Dec. 90	13 Aug. 79	1 July 81	1 July 87		
16	...	Jasper Graham Mayne, Instructor School of Musketry 1 Aug. 91	13 Aug. 79	1 July 81	10 Sept. 87		
16	...	Gerald Mackay Mackenzie, Adjutant 1 Vol. Bn. Royal Fusiliers 1 Mar. 95	13 Aug. 79	1 July 81	1 Feb. 88		
16	...	Charles John Lloyd Davidson, Adj. 4 Battalion 18 Aug. 92	13 Aug. 79	1 July 81	1 Feb. 88		
16	...	1 p.s.c. John Leathley Armitage	11 Oct. 79	1 July 81	17 Oct. 88		
16	...	1 Harry Otho Devereux Hickman,⁷ at Staff College	14 Jan. 80	1 July 81	28 Aug. 89		
15	...	Robert Whyte Melville Jackson, Ordnance Store Department	19 Feb. 81	1 July 81	22 Oct. 90		
12	...	2 George Edward Wilkinson⁹	......	19 Dec. 83	17 Jan. 91		
12	...	George Powell Stewart, Adjutant 2 Jersey Militia 17 Dec. 94	......	30 Jan. 84	6 Mar. 91		
11	...	2 Thomas Godwin Campbell Reynolds¹⁰	......	14 May 84	24 June 91		
11	...	Richard Mildmay Foot¹¹	......	7 Feb. 85	24 June 91		
11	...	1 Annesley John Hancocks	......	7 Feb. 85	1 July 91		
10	...	2 Ernest Blennerhassett Blennerhassett (Depot)	......	6 May 85	20 June 92		
10	...	1 Charles Melville Kendall	......	29 Aug. 85	12 Oct. 92		
10	...	1 Francis George Jones, Adjutant 31 Oct. 94	......	16 Dec. 85	1 Feb. 93		
10	...	2 Frederick William Hernon Sherwin	......	16 Dec. 85	1 Dec. 93		
		LIEUTENANTS.					
10	...	2 Henry Percy Hancox	......	30 Jan. 86			
10	...	Arthur Francis Hamilton Cox,¹² Adj. Discharge Depot, 1 Apr. 92	......	13 Feb. 86			
9	...	2 Charles Rodney Heastey	......	10 Nov. 86			
9	...	Claude Houston Stuart, Aide de Camp to Sir G. S. White 13 Apr. 94	5 Feb. 87	16 Jan. 89			
9	...	1 William Lionel Persée Gibton	23 Mar. 87	8 May 89			
8	...	1 Granville Eustace Matthey	4 May 87	8 May 89			
8	...	1 Charles Arthur Wilding	14 Sept. 87	11 Sept. 89			
8	...	1 Vere D'Oyly Noble	14 Sept. 87	14 Oct. 90			
8	...	1 Edward James Buckley	16 Nov. 87	22 Oct. 90			
7	...	2 Ambrose St. Quintin Ricardo	10 Nov. 88	15 Dec. 90			
6	...	1 George Peacocke (Depot)	9 Nov. 89	10 June 91			
6	...	2 Robert Campbell Pierce¹³	9 Nov. 89	10 June 91			
9	...	1 William Francis Hessey, Adjutant 15 Dec. 94	29 Mar. 90	24 June 91			
5	...	1 John Cecil Armstrong (Depot)	11 June 90	30 Sept. 91			
5	...	2 Travers Edwards Clarke	29 Oct. 90	20 June 92			
5	17/18	1 Percival Scott-Beves	10 Nov. 88	21 June 92			
5	...	2 Stafford James Somerville	29 Nov. 90	21 Sept. 92			
4	...	1 Evan Henry Llewellyn	23 May 91	21 Jan. 93			
4	...	Hugh Macdonald	17 June 91	30 Apr. 93			
4	...	1 Robie Fitzgerald Uniacke	10 Oct. 91	19 July 93			
4	...	2 Arthur Robert Burton	13 July 92	1 Dec. 93			
3	...	1 Hugh Fenwick Brooke, Army Serv. Corps	13 July 92	6 June 94			
3	...	Herbert Wareham Clinch	19 Oct. 92	6 June 94			
3	...	1 Charles George Sime	19 Nov. 92	1 Jan. 95			
4	...	Henry Adolphe Leverson	23 Jan. 92	22 Nov. 93			

Years' Ser.				2ND LIEUT.
Full Pay	Half Pay	**SECOND LIEUTENANTS.**		
3	...	1 Francis Cochrane Loftus	17 Dec.	92
3	...	2 John Wilfrid Mather	21 Jan.	93
2	...	2 George William Kenny	26 Apr.	93
2	...	2 Edward Sausmarez Carey	19 July	93
2	...	2 Robert William Hamilton Mitchell	4 Oct.	93
2	...	2 James Ronald Broun	21 Oct.	93
2	...	2 George Wheeler Morley	23 Dec.	93
2	...	2 Joseph Aloysius Byrne	23 Dec.	93
2	...	2 Alan Coast	7 Mar.	94
2	...	1 John Evans	7 Mar.	94
1	...	Archibald Hugh Arbuthnot	6 Mar.	95

Paymasters.—2 Ambrose St. Q. Ricardo, *Lieut.* 2 Battalion (*acting*).

Quarter Masters.—2

| 4 | ... | 1 Edmund Framingham, 14 Feb. 92; *Hon. Lieut.* |

Facings Blue.—*Agents*, Messrs. Cox and Co.
1st Batt. *returned from South Africa*, 21 Jan. 1889. 2nd Batt. *embarked for India*, 12 Dec. 1888.

Sir James Talbot Airey served as Aide de Camp to Major General Elphinstone in Affghanistan in 1841-42, and was present at the storming of the Khoord Cabool Pass on the 12th Oct. 1841 under Sir Robert Sale, and had his horse shot under him. He served during the insurrection at Cabool from 2nd November 1841 till January 1842; was present at the storming of the Rickarb Bashee and the neighbouring forts; also in the action on the heights on the 13th November and the battle of Beymaroo on 23rd November. Delivered up as a hostage to the Affghans on the 21st Dec. 1841, and remained a prisoner in their hands until the 17th Sept. 1842. On release joined the force proceeding to the Kohistan as second in command of Khuzzilbash Horse, under Sir John M'Caskill, and was present at the storming and capture of Istaliff (Medal). Was present with the Buffs in the Gwalior campaign of 1843, and in the battle of Punniar (Bronze Star). Served throughout the Eastern campaign of 1854-55 as Assistant Quarter Master General of the Right Division; on the 14th September 1854 captured and brought into camp at Old Fort 75 Russian waggons laden with forage and flour on their way to Sebastopol; present at the affair of Bulganack, battles of Alma (horse shot through the neck), Balaklava, and Inkerman. Served as Quarter Master General of the Expedition to Kertch under Sir George Brown in May 1855, and succeeded as senior officer to the command of the English troops on the departure of that General to Anapa; returned to Sebastopol on the 18th June; present the entire siege of Sebastopol and the attack of the Redan on the 8th September (Medal with four Clasps, *CB.*, Knight of the Legion of Honor, 4th Class of the Medjidie, and Turkish Medal).

[2] Lt. Colonel Greenfield served in the operations in the Northern Chin Hills in 1892-93 (mentioned in despatches, Brevet of Lt. Colonel).

[3] Major Kekewich served throughout the operations in the Malay Peninsula in 1875-76 (Medal with Clasp). Served with the Nile Expedition in 1884-85 as Deputy Assistant Adjutant and Quarter Master General (mentioned in despatches, Brevet of Major, Medal with Clasp, and Khedive's Star). Served in the operations near Suakin in December 1888 as Brigade Major and afterwards as Deputy Assistant Adjutant General of British troops, and was present in the engagement at Gemaizah (mentioned in despatches, 4th Class of the Medjidie, and Clasp).

[4] Major Gibbings served in the Soudan campaign in 1885 attached to the 3rd Battalion of the Grenadier Guards; was Divisional Paymaster to the whole of the Force, and was present in the engagement at Hasheen, at the attack on the convoys on the 24th and 26th March, and at the destruction of Temai (Medal with Clasp, and Khedive's Star). Also served with the Egyptian Frontier Field Force in 1885-86.

[5] Major Daniel served in the Nile Expedition in 1884-85 with the Transport and attached to the 1st Battalion of the Royal Irish Regiment (Medal with Clasp, and Khedive's Star).

[6] Captain Murray served in the operations in Zululand in 1888.

[7] Captain Hickman served with the Nile Expedition in 1884-85 (Medal with Clasp, and Khedive's Star). Served in the operations in the Soudan in December 1888 including the engagement at Gemaizah (4th Class of the Medjidie).

[9] Captain Wilkinson served in the Soudan campaign in 1885 (Medal with Clasp, and Khedive's Star).

[10] Captain Reynolds served with the Burmese Expedition in 1886-88 (Medal with two Clasps); with the Chin-Lushai Expeditionary Force in 1889-90 as Transport Officer (Clasp); and with the Manipore Field Force in 1891 as Brigade Transport Officer (Clasp).

[11] Captain Foot served in the operations in Zululand in 1888.

[12] Lieut. A. F. H. Cox served in the Soudan campaign in 1885 with the Commissariat and Transport Staff (Medal with Clasp, and Khedive's Star).

[13] Lieut. Pierce served with the Eastern Column, Burmah, in 1891-92.

1st Batt., Malta.
2nd Batt., Devonport.

The Gloucestershire Regiment.

Regimental District No. 28.—Bristol.

Formerly the 28th (North Gloucestershire) and the 61st (South Gloucestershire) Regiments.
(The 3rd and 4th Battalions are formed of the South and North Gloucester Militia respectively.)
"RAMILLIES" "LOUISBURG" "QUEBEC, 1759" "EGYPT" (with the Sphinx). "MAIDA" "CORUNNA" "TALAVERA" "BARROSA" "ALBUHERA" "SALAMANCA" "VITTORIA" "PYRENEES" "NIVELLE" "NIVE" "ORTHES" "TOULOUSE" "PENINSULA" "WATERLOO" "PUNJAUB" "CHILLIANWALLAH" "GOOJERAT" "ALMA" "INKERMAN" "SEVASTOPOL" "DELHI."

Years' Ser. Full Pay	Half Pay		ENSIGN OR 2ND LIEUT.	LIEUT.	CAPTAIN.	BREV. MAJ.	MAJOR.
		Colonel.—John William Sidney Smith,[1] *CB. Ensign*, 3 Feb. 32; *Lieut*. 4 Aug. 37; *Capt.* P7 Aug. 40; *Bt. Major*, 11 Nov. 51; *Major*, 29 Dec. 54; *Lt. Colonel*, 29 July 55; *Colonel*, 2 Sept. 58; *Major General*, 6 March 68; *Lieut. General*, 1 Oct. 77; *General*, 1 July 81; *Colonel* Gloucestershire Regiment, 20 Jan. 83.						
30	...	**Lieutenant Colonels.**—1 George Conner, *Ensign*, P2 June 65; *Lt.* P3 June 68; *Capt.* P25 Mar. 71; *Major*, 1 July 81; *Lt. Colonel*, 1 July 91.					
32	...	2 Frederic John Curtin, *Ensign*, 15 Jan. 64; *Lt.* P16 Oct. 66; *Capt.* 9 Jan. 78; *Major*, 19 Nov. 81; *Lt. Colonel*, 1 July 91.					
		MAJORS.					
29	...	1 John Henry Fitzherbert Jacson	P15 Mar. 67	28 Oct. 71	5 Oct. 80	......	22 Sept. 85
29	...	2 Thomas William Crawford Leathem	P16 Oct. 66	P20 Oct. 69	22 June 80	......	17 June 91
27	...	1 Allan Gilmore	8 July 68	28 Oct. 71	7 Aug. 81	......	1 July 91
21	...	Robert Frederick Lindsell, *District Insp. of Musketry, Ireland*, 31 May 93	......	21 Sept. 74	19 Nov. 81	......	1 July 91
22	...	Robert Wm. Peter Lodwick, *A. P. Dept.*	......	9 Aug. 73	18 June 81	......	21 Oct. 91
20	...	2 Mervyn Edward Archdale (*Depot*)	......	10 Mar. 76	10 May 83	......	13 Apr. 92
18	...	Cuthbert Johnson Baines, *Adj.* 2 *Vol. Bn. Gloucester Regt.* 7 July 90	......	28 Oct. 77	18 Oct. 84	......	11 May 94
18	...	2 Stanley Humphery	30 Jan. 78	21 April 80	17 Apr. 85	......	16 June 94
		CAPTAINS.					
17	...	Charles James Vines, *Adjutant* 1 *Vol. Bn. Gloucester Regt.* 31 Dec. 91	30 Jan. 78	22 June 80	26 June 85		
17	...	2 Herbert Capel Cure,[5] *DSO*.	11 May 78	22 Sept. 80	22 Sept. 85		
15	...	Haydon d'Aubrey Potenger Taylor, *Adjutant* 3 *Battalion* 2 Nov. 91	17 Apr. 80	29 Sept. 80	22 Sept. 85		
15	...	1 William Radcliffe Peel Wallace	17 Apr. 80	5 Oct. 80	5 May 86		
17	...	2 Clement Frederick Baxter	7 Aug. 78	30 Oct. 80	5 May 86		
16	...	1 Hugh Richard Tufnell	21 June 79	1 Dec. 80	31 May 86		
16	...	2 Hon. Robert French	13 Aug. 79	1 Dec. 80	1 Nov. 86		
15	...	Samuel Alexander James, *Adj.* 3 *Bn.* Bedford Regt. 20 March 93	23 Oct. 80	1 Jan. 81	1 July 87		
15	...	Maurice Den Keatinge, *Adj.* 4 *Bn.* 4 Aug. 90	23 Oct. 80	2 Feb. 81	1 July 87		
16	...	2 John David Jones Bishop	14 Jan. 80	1 July 81	5 Aug. 88		
14	...	Claude Moss, *Adj.* Bombay Volunteer Rifles 18 May 94	......	24 Aug. 81	1 July 91		
14	...	1 Joseph Scovell Hobbs	......	22 Oct. 81	1 July 91		
13	...	1 Cutts Humphry Hill	......	10 May 82	1 July 91		
12	...	2 Alfred Crowdy Lovett	......	25 Aug. 83	21 Oct. 91		
12	...	1 Stuart Duncan (*Depot*)	......	6 Feb. 84	31 Dec. 91		
11	...	1 Stephen Willcock[12]	......	2 July 84	31 Dec. 91		
11	...	1 Bertram Oliphant Fyffe, **Adjutant** 30 July 94	......	12 Nov. 84	12 Jan. 92		
10	...	1 Charles John Venables	......	29 Aug. 85	19 Oct. 92		
10	...	1 Henry Charles George Potts	......	29 Aug. 85	20 Mar. 93		
11	2 11/12	1 Vernon Eliott Russell	......	22 Oct. 81	1 Feb. 89		
10	...	2 James Greetham Howard Whylock	......	25 Nov. 85	18 May 94		
9	...	2 Edmund Robert St. George Holbrook, **Adjutant** 19 Oct. 94	......	25 Aug. 86	16 June 94		
		LIEUTENANTS.					
9	...	1 George Swinton Tulloh		5 Feb. 87	1 Apr. 89		
8	...	2 Keith Maitland Davie		14 Sept. 87	25 Apr. 89		
8	...	1 Richard Conner		11 Feb. 88	3 July 89		
7	...	1 Frederick Sutherland Stayner		9 May 88	5 Mar. 90		
6	...	1 Richard Price Jordan (*Depot*)		8 June 89	20 Dec. 90		
6	...	2 Harold Esmond Platt		6 July 89	17 June 91		
6	...	2 Frank Burges		21 Sept. 89	1 July 91		
6	...	1 Alan Bryant		29 Mar. 90	1 July 91		
6	...	1 Francis Courtenay Nisbet		29 Mar. 90	21 Oct. 91		
5	...	John O'Donnell Ingram, *O.S. Dept.*		3 May 90	31 Dec. 91		
5	...	2 Charles Norris Hunter		29 Nov. 90	13 Apr. 92		
5	...	2 Robert Macgregor Stewart Gardner (*Depot*)		4 Feb. 91	4 May 92		
5	...	2 Henry Leigh King Brinkley		25 Mar. 91	4 May 92		
6	...	1 Robert Maturin Manning Davy[13]		29 Jan. 90	29 June 91		
4	...	George Gawler Irving Carmichael		2 May 91	28 Mar. 93		
4	...	2 Reginald Blennerhassett Boyd		25 July 91	1 Apr. 93		
4	...	2 Charles Bayard Messiter		7 Nov. 91	27 Apr. 93		
4	...	1 Charles Stuart Knox		18 May 92	16 July 93		
3	...	Arthur Wilson Chitty		13 July 92	10 Jan. 94		
3	...	2 John Francis Bennett		13 Aug. 92	18 May 94		
3	...	Walter James Henry Hunter		13 Aug. 92	16 June 94		
3	...	Julian Frizelle		31 Aug. 92	24 Aug. 94		
3	...	1 Robert Edward Rising		19 Nov. 92	2 Sept. 94		
		SECOND LIEUTENANTS.					
4	...	Alfred Alexander Phillips Waller		27 Jan. 92			
4	...	Arthur William Donnelly Harington		27 Jan. 92			
3	...	2 Edward D'Albret Le Mottée		21 Jan. 93			
2	...	1 Raymond Coape Smith		20 May 93			
2	...	2 Joseph Robert Wethered		19 July 93			
2	...	1 William Arthur Mould Temple		19 July 93			
2	...	2 Kynaston Williams		9 Sept. 92			
2	...	1 Alfred Hutton Radice		21 Oct. 93			
2	...	2 Daniel Burges		21 Oct. 93			
2	...	1 John Egerton Rack		21 Oct. 93			

The Gloucestershire Regiment.

Years' Ser.			
Full Pay.	Half Pay.	SECOND LIEUTENANTS.	2ND LIEUT.
2	...	1 Frederick Alexander Breul	21 Oct. 93
2	...	1 Carlos Joseph Hickie	21 Oct. 93
2	...	1 William Leonard Bertram Hill	23 Dec. 93
2	...	1 Robert Ian Rawson	7 Mar. 94

Paymasters.—1
2 Harold E. Platt, *Lieut.* 2 *Battalion* (*acting*).
5 ... *Quarter Masters.*—1 Thomas Smyth, 19 Nov. 90; *Hon. Lieut.*
1 ... 2 Edward Murray, 15 Aug. 94; *Hon. Lieut.*

Facings White.—*Agents*, Messrs. Cox and Co.
1st Battalion embarked for Malta, 1 Nov. 93. 2nd Battalion returned from Aden, 28 Nov. 94.

: General J. W. Smith commanded a Detachment of the 38th Regt. in co-operation with a Naval expedition under Captain Loch in the ascent, in boats, of the river St. Juan de Nicaragua, Central America, in 1848, including the assault and capture of the port of Serapiqui, and surrender of the Forts of Castello Viejo and St. Carlos. He also accompanied Captain Loch to the town of Grenada, and was present at the deliberations and conclusions of a treaty with the Nicaraguan Commissioners. Served the Eastern campaign of 1854-55, including the battles of Alma and Inkerman, siege of Sebastopol, capture and occupation of the Cemetery and suburbs on the 18th June, and was senior Officer of the 38th at the close of the war (Medal with three Clasps, Knight of the Legion of Honor, 4th Class of the Medjidie, Turkish Medal, and *CB*.).

[5] Captain Cure served with the Burmese Expedition in 1886-87 as Transport Officer to the Ruby Mines Column (mentioned in despatches, *DSO.*, and Medal with Clasp).

[12] Captain Willcock served with the Burmese Expedition in 1886-89, and was slightly wounded in an engagement at Temaline on the 9th December 1886 (Medal with two Clasps).

[13] Lieut. Davy served with the expedition to the Tambaka Country, on the West Coast of Africa, in 1892, including the capture of Tambi (Medal with Clasp).

Record of the Services of the 1st Battalion Gloucestershire Regiment (formerly the 28th Regiment).

Raised in 1694. Disbanded in 1697. Re-formed and sent to Ireland, 1702. To Germany, 1704 (battle of Ramillies). To Portugal, 1706. To England, 1711. To Vigo, 1719. To England, 1719. To Ireland, 1720. To England, 1742. To Flanders, 1743. To Nova Scotia, 1758. To Quebec, 1759. To Havannah, 1762. To England, 1774. To America, 1776. To West Indies, 1778. To England, 1783. To Scotland, 1784. To Ireland, 1786. To Jersey, 1793. To Flanders, 1793. To Gibraltar, 1795. To Minorca, 1798. To Malta, 1800. To Alexandria, 1801. To England, 1802. [2nd Battalion formed in 1803.] To Ireland, 1804. To England, 1806. To Copenhagen, 1807. To England, 1807. To Gottenburg, 1808. To England, 1808. To Peninsula, 1808 (battles of Corunna and Talavera, siege of Badajoz). To Walcheren, 1809. To England, 1810. To Gibraltar and the Peninsula, 1811 (battles of Barrosa, Salamanca, Vittoria, and Toulouse). To Ireland, 1814. [2nd Battalion disbanded in 1814.] To Belgium, 1815 (battle of Waterloo and occupation of France). To England, 1816. To the Mediterranean, 1817. To Ireland, 1831. To England, 1834. To Australia, 1835. To India, 1842. To England, 1848. To the Crimea, 1854 (battles of Alma and Inkerman and siege of Sebastopol). To Malta, 1856. To India, 1859. To England, 1865. To Ireland, 1867. To Gibraltar, 1868. To Malta, 1872. To Hong Kong, 1875. To Straits Settlements, 1878. To Ireland, 1879. To England, 1882. To Ireland, 1888.

Record of the Services of the 2nd Gloucestershire Regiment,—formerly the 61st (South Gloucestershire Regiment).

Formed from the 2nd Battalion 3rd Buffs in 1758 and proceeded to Guadaloupe. To Jersey and Guernsey, 1762. To Ireland, 1764. To Minorca, 1771. To England, 1782. To Ireland, 1783. To Gibraltar, 1792. To Martinique, 1794. To England, 1796. To Guernsey, 1797. To the Cape of Good Hope, 1798. To Egypt, 1801 (battle of Maida). To Malta, 1803. [2nd Battalion raised 1803; disbanded, 1814.] To Messina, 1805 (received the badge of "Egypt"—with the Sphinx). To Gibraltar, 1807. To the Peninsula, 1809 (battles of Talavera, Salamanca, Pyrenees, Nivelle, Nive, Orthes and Toulouse). To Ireland, 1814. To England, 1816. To Jamaica, 1816. To England, 1822. To Ireland, 1824. To England, 1828. To Ceylon, 1834. To England, 1840. To Ireland, 1843. To India, 1845 (Punjaub campaign and battles of Chillianwallah and Goojerat, and Indian Mutiny). To Mauritius, 1859. To England, 1860. To Channel Islands, 1863. To Ireland, 1864. To Bermuda, 1866. To Canada, 1870. To Ireland, 1872. To Channel Islands, 1875. To England, 1876. To Malta, 1878. To India, 1880.

1st Batt., Rangoon.
2nd Batt., Aldershot.   **The Worcestershire Regiment.**   Regimental District No. 29.—Worcester.   273

Formerly the 29th (Worcestershire) and the 36th (Herefordshire) Regiments.
(The 3rd and 4th Battalions are formed of the 1st and 2nd Battalions Worcestershire Militia respectively.)
The United Red and White Rose. "Firm." "Ramillies" "Mysore" "Hindoostan" "Rolrìa" "Vimiera" "Corunna" "Talavera" "Albuhera" "Salamanca" "Pyrenees" "Nivelle" "Nive" "Orthes" "Toulouse" "Peninsula" "Ferozeshah" "Sobraon" "Punjaub" "Chillianwallah" "Goojerat."

Years' Ser.			
Full Pay.	Half Pay.		
29	...	**Colonel.**—Sir George Wentworth Alexander Higginson,¹ KCB., Ensign and Lieut. P14 Feb. 45; Lt. and Captain, P12 July 50; Bt. Major, 12 Dec. 54; Bt. Lt. Colonel, 2 Nov. 55; Capt. and Lt. Colonel, P10 Apr. 57; Colonel, 30 Sept. 63; Major General, 17 May 69; Lt. General, 1 Apr. 83; General, 11 Oct. 90; Colonel Worcestershire Regiment, 29 Aug. 93.	
28	...	**Lieutenant Colonels.**—2 John Francis Egerton, Ensign, P21 Aug. 66; Lt. P9 Feb. 70; Capt. 26 Nov. 79; Major, 27 Aug. 84; Lt. Colonel, 9 Oct. 93.	
		1 William Senhouse Clarke,⁹ Ensign, 8 Jan. 68; Lt. P27 Oct. 71; Capt. 1 Feb. 79; Major, 11 Aug. 86; Lt. Colonel, 18 March 95.	

Years		**MAJORS.**	ENSIGN OR 2ND LIEUT.	LIEUT.	CAPTAIN.	BREV. MAJ.	MAJOR.
24	...	2 Francis Seymour Allen....................	......	9 Mar. 72	29 June 81	......	3 Oct. 88
24	...	2 Orbell Henry Oakes (*Depot*)	......	10 Jan. 72	17 Dec. 81	......	9 Oct. 89
19	...	1 Allan Moss, *Commandant Colaba Depôt* 3 Apr. 94....................	......	19 April 76	1 Jan. 84	......	2 Mar. 91
24	...	Charles Coningham¹¹........................	......	23 Mar. 72	1 Feb. 82	......	9 Dec. 91
18	...	1 Murray Venables Hilton¹²................	30 Jan. 78	31 Aug. 78	20 Nov. 85	......	6 July 92
17	...	1 William Arbuthnot Lenox Conyngham	1 May 78	1 Feb. 79	20 Jan. 86	......	9 Oct. 93
20	...	George William Hacket Pain,¹³ *serving with the Egyptian Army*	......	20 Nov. 75	15 Feb. 86	......	16 May 94
		CAPTAINS.					
17	...	Joseph Chichester, *Adjutant 3 Battalion 8 June 91*..............	11 May 78	26 Nov. 79	19 May 86		
17	...	William Frederick James Hardisty, *Adjutant 4 Battalion 10 Aug. 93*.....	11 May 78	27 Nov. 79	7 June 86		
16	...	John Hassard Stewart Gibb¹⁴	13 Aug. 79	1 Mar. 80	1 Sept. 86		
17	...	Edward Algernon D'Arcy Thomas, *D.A.A. Gen. Bombay, 10 Feb. 91*	11 May 78	8 Sept. 80	1 Sept. 86		
17	...	Clement Maitland Edwards,¹⁵ *Adjutant 2 Vol. Bn. Worcester Regt. 13 June 92*	11 May 78	1 July 81	15 Nov. 86		
18	...	Alexander Coote Newton-King, *Adjutant 82nd Volunteer Rifles 24 Dec. 92*	30 Jan. 78	23 July 79	14 Apr. 86		
15	...	Annesley George Smith, *Army Pay Department*	23 Oct. 80	1 July 81	8 May 88		
15	...	2 Thomas Edgecomb Hickman,¹⁶ DSO. *Adjutant 15 Dec. 94*	19 Feb. 81	1 July 81	25 July 88		
13	...	Francis William Northey, *Adj. 1 Vol. Bn. Worcestershire Regt. 15 Dec. 90*	......	10 May 82	25 July 88		
18	...	1 George Nowlan Monro	16 Feb. 78	26 Feb. 81	17 Oct. 88		
13	...	2 Cecil Richard Robyns Malone	......	9 Sept. 82	21 Nov. 88		
12	...	1 Edward Ormerod Hales Wilkie	......	25 Aug. 83	8 Feb. 90		
12	...	1 Hugh de Berdt-Hovell¹⁷..................	......	6 Feb. 84	26 Mar. 90		
11	...	2 Walter Harold Lord........................	......	14 May 84	10 June 90		
11	...	1 Goodricke Thomas Peacocke	......	23 Aug. 84	10 Feb. 91		
11	...	1 Charles Christian How	......	12 Nov. 84	18 Feb. 91		
10	...	2 George White Lewis	......	29 Aug. 85	2 Sept. 91		
10	...	2 Walter Dermott Holland	......	25 Nov. 85	10 June 92		
9	...	Edward Bell, *Adjutant 3 Middlesex Rifle Volunteers 1 May 94*	......	28 Apr. 86	13 June 92		
9	...	1 Mervyn Henry Nunn	......	28 Apr. 86	6 July 92		
9	...	1 John George Ralph Swanson (*Depot*) ...	......	25 Aug. 86	24 Dec. 92		
9	...	2 Robert Muriel Sanders, *Superintendent of Gymnasia, Gibraltar, 15 Feb. 94*	......	25 Aug. 86	11 Aug. 93		
9	...	2 Coningsby Norbury	......	10 Nov. 86	9 Oct. 93		
9	...	2 de Vic Carey	5 Feb. 87	8 May 89	16 May 94		
		LIEUTENANTS.					
8	...	2 Michael Jas. Joseph Sweetman (*Depot*)	14 Sept. 87	5 Nov. 89			
8	...	1 Berkeley Hardinge Thomas	16 Nov. 87	6 Nov. 89			
7	...	1 Claude Berners Westmacott, *Adjutant 23 Nov. 92*	5 May 88	4 Dec. 89			
7	...	1 Charles Hugh Bennett (*Depot*)	9 May 88	8 Feb. 90			
7	...	2 John Paterson Strong Maitland	8 Dec. 88	10 June 90			
7	...	1 Arthur Kennedy Stubbs	23 Mar. 89	15 Dec. 90			
7	...	1 Edgar Nathaniel Loftus Brock (*Depot*)	23 Mar. 89	15 Dec. 90			
6	...	1 Burleigh Francis Brownlow Stuart	21 Dec. 89	2 Sept. 91			
6	...	1 Douglas Edward Cayley	1 Mar. 90	20 Feb. 92			
5	...	1 John Ross Gale	3 May 90	23 Mar. 92			
5	...	2 Walter Raleigh Chichester	8 June 90	6 Apr. 92			
5	...	1 Cardon Henry Seton.......................	23 July 90	13 June 92			
5	...	2 Edward Schell Cripps Hobson	17 Jan. 91	16 July 92			
4	...	2 Alexander Townsend Jackson	9 Sept. 91	24 Dec. 92			
4	...	1 Halhed Brodrick Birdwood	7 Nov. 91	1 Jan. 93			
4	...	2 Hugh John Bartholomew	5 Dec. 91	10 July 93			
3	...	1 Percyvall Hart Dyke......................	18 May 92	11 Aug. 93			
3	...	1 Maxwell Edward Dopping-Hepenstal...	18 June 92	9 Oct. 93			
3	...	1 Arthur Newton Dalgleish Fagan	22 June 92	5 May 94			
3	...	1 Arthur Dennys Gilbert Ramsay	13 July 92	16 May 94			
		SECOND LIEUTENANTS.					
3	...	1 Robert Thomas Christopher Calvert ...	13 July 92				
3	...	Henry Francis Thornhill Fisher	13 Aug. 92				
3	...	2 Ernest Charles Forbes Wodehouse, *Army Service Corps*	19 Oct. 92				
3	...	2 John Murray Reddie......................	17 Dec. 92				
3	...	2 Harry Dacres Milward	21 Jan. 93				
3	...	1 George Reginald Welstead	25 Feb. 93				

Years'Ser.			2ND LIEUT.
Full Pay	Half Pay	SECOND LIEUTENANTS.	
2	...	1 Hugh Beck...	19 Apr. 93
2	...	2 Basil Kenrick Wing Bacon..................	4 Oct. 93
2	...	2 Henry Arbuthnot Carr	21 Oct. 93
2	...	2 Perceval Charles Newsam Alderson ...	23 Dec. 93
1	...	2 Cecil Howard Palmer...........................	2 June 94
1	...	2 Henry Crawshay	19 Sept. 94
1	...	1 Bernard Ogilvie Richards	20 Feb. 95

Paymasters.—1 Arthur K. Stubbs, *Lieut.* 1 Battalion (*acting*).
2

Quarter Masters.—1 Isaac Young[21] (*Lieut. Liverpool Regt.* 19 Sept. 85), 25 Jan. 88.
10 ...
6 ... 2 James Ralston, 28 Aug. 89; *Hon. Lieut.*

Facings White.—*Agents*, Messrs. Cox and Co.
1st Battalion embarked for Bombay, 1879.
2nd Battalion returned from India, 16 December 1875.

[1] Sir George Higginson served throughout the Eastern campaign of 1854–55, as Adjutant 3rd Battalion Grenadier Guards, including the battles of Alma, Balaklava, and Inkerman (horse killed), siege and fall of Sebastopol; after which he served as Brigade Major of the Guards until the conclusion of the war (Medal with four Clasps, Brevets of Major and Lt.Colonel, Knight of the Legion of Honor, 5th Class of the Medjidie, and Turkish Medal).

[9] Lt.Colonel Clarke served in the Ashanti war in 1874 in the Transport Service, and was in charge of the Post at Sutah (Medal).

[11] Major Coningham took part in the operations of the Soudan Frontier Field Force in 1885–86 (Medal, and Khedive's Star).

[12] Major Hilton served with the Zhob Valley Expedition in 1884.

[13] Major Pain served in the operations in the Soudan in 1889 including the engagement at Toski (Medal with Clasp, 3rd Class of the Medjidie, and Khedive's Star); was present at the capture of Tokar in 1891 (3rd Class of the Osmanieh).

[14] Captain Gibb served in the Nile Expedition in 1884–85 with the Egyptian Army (Medal with Clasp, and Khedive's Star); also served with the Soudan Frontier Field Force in 1885–86, and was present at the investment of Kosheh and in the engagement at Giniss (4th Class of the Osmanieh). [See also Civil Decorations for Gallantry, "Hart's Annual Army List," p. 786.]

[15] Captain Edwards was employed with the Bikanir Field Force in 1884–85.

[16] Captain Hickman served with the Nile Expedition in 1884–85 (Medal with Clasp, and Khedive's Star); in the operations near Suakin in December 1888 including the engagement at Gemaizah (mentioned in despatches, Clasp, and 4th Class of the Osmanieh); and in the operations on the Soudan frontier in 1889 including the engagement at Toski (mentioned in despatches, *DSO.*, and Clasp).

[17] Captain H. de Berdt-Hovell.—See Civil Decorations for Gallantry, "Hart's Annual Army List," p. 786.

[21] Lieut. Young served in the Ashanti war in 1873–74 with the 42nd Royal Highlanders, and was present in the action at Amoaful (slightly wounded), the capture and destruction of Becquah, the battle of Ordahsu, and at the capture of Coomassie (Medal with Clasp). Served in the Egyptian war of 1882 with the 1st Battalion of the Black Watch, and was present at the battle of Tel-el-Kebir (mentioned in despatches, Medal with Clasp, and Khedive's Star). Served with the expedition to the Soudan under Sir Gerald Graham in 1884 with the 1st Battalion of the Black Watch, and was present in the engagements at El Teb and Temai (two Clasps). Served with the Nile Expedition in 1884–85 with the 1st Battalion of the Black Watch, and took part in the operations of the River Column under Major General Earle, including the action of Kirbekan (mentioned in despatches, promoted Lieutenant, two Clasps).

Record of the Services of the 1st Battalion Worcestershire Regiment (formerly the 29th Regiment).

Raised in 1694 and remained in England till 1698, when it was reduced, the Officers remaining on half pay till the re-forming of the Regiment in 1702. England and Ireland, to 1704. The Netherlands and Germany, to 1706;(battle of Ramillies). England and Portugal, to 1706. Alicant, to 1707 (partially reduced). England, to 1708. France and the Netherlands, to 1709. England, to 1711. Gibraltar, to 1713 (further reduced). Ireland, to 1726. Gibraltar, to 1745 (partly as Marines). America, to 1750. Ireland, to 1765. America, to 1773. England, to 1776. America, to 1787. England, to 1795 (partly as Marines). Barbadoes, to 1796. England, to 1798. Ireland, to 1799. Holland, 1799. England, to 1802. Halifax, to 1807. The Peninsula, to 1811 (battles of Roleia, Vimiera, Talavera, and Albuhera). England, to 1813. Cadiz and Gibraltar, to 1814. Halifax and England, to 1815. France, to 1819. Ireland, to 1826. Mauritius, to 1838. England, to 1840. Scotland, to 1841. Ireland, to 1842. India and Burmah, to 1859 (battles of Ferozeshah, Sobraon, Chillianwallah, and Goojerat). England, to 1862. Scotland, to 1863. Ireland, to 1865. Malta, to 1867. Canada, to 1869. West Indies, to 1873. Ireland, to 1875. Jersey, to 1876. England, to 1879. India, 1879.

Record of the Services of the 2nd Battalion,—formerly the 36th (Herefordshire) Regiment.

Raised in 1701, and proceeded to Ireland, to 1702. Expeditions to Cadiz and the West Indies, to 1703. Ireland, to 1704. Spain, to 1707. England, to 1711. Expedition to Quebec, and returned to England, to 1712. France, to 1714. Ireland, to 1715. Scotland, to 1718. Ireland, to 1719. England, to 1720. Ireland, to 1739. England, to 1744. (Detachment to the West Indies, 1740–41.) Flanders, to 1745, and returned to England. Scotland, to 1747. Flanders, to 1748, and returned to England. Gibraltar, to 1754. Scotland, to 1755. England, to 1758. [2nd Battalion raised in 1756, entitled "74th Foot" in 1758, and disbanded, 1764.] Expedition to West Coast of France, 1758. England, to 1761. West Coast of France, 1761. England, to 1764. West Indies, to 1773. England, to 1775. Ireland, to 1782. England, to 1783. East Indies, to 1798 (Mysore and Hindostan). England, to 1800. Ireland, and Expedition to Quiberon, 1800. Minorca, to 1803. Ireland, to 1806. [2nd Battalion again raised in 1804, remaining in England till 1814, when it was disbanded.] Germany and England, 1806. South America, to 1807. Ireland, to 1808. Portugal, to 1809 (battles of Roleia, Vimiera and Corunna). Expedition to Walcheren, and returned to England, 1809. The Peninsula and France, to 1814 (battles of Salamanca, Pyrenees, Nivelle, Nive, Orthes and Toulouse). Ireland, Belgium, and France, 1815. England, to 1817. Malta, to 1821. Ionian Islands, to 1825. England, to 1827. Ireland, to 1830. West Indies, to 1838. Nova Scotia, to 1840. New Brunswick, to 1842. Ireland, to 1845. England, to 1847. Ionian Islands, to 1851. West Indies, to 1857. England, to 1860. Ireland, to 1863. India, to 1875. England, to 1880. Ireland, to 1883. Jersey, to 1885. England, to 1889. Ireland, to 1893. England 1893.

1st Batt., Lucknow, Bengal.
2nd Batt., Gibraltar.] **The East Lancashire Regiment.** [Regimental District No. 30.—Burnley.] 274

Formerly the 30th (The Cambridgeshire) and the 59th (2nd Nottinghamshire) Regiments.
(The 3rd Battalion is formed of the 5th Lancashire Militia.)

"EGYPT" (with the Sphinx). "CAPE OF GOOD HOPE, 1806" "CORUNNA" "JAVA" "BADAJOZ" "SALAMANCA" "VITTORIA" "ST. SEBASTIAN" "NIVE" "PENINSULA" "WATERLOO" "BHURTPORE" "ALMA" "INKERMAN" "SEVASTOPOL" "CANTON" "AHMAD KHEL" "AFGHANISTAN, 1878-80."

Years' Ser.							
Full Pay	Half Pay						
28	...	**Colonel.**—Thomas Henry Pakenham,[1] Ensign, P12 July 44; Lt. P19 March 47; Capt. P24 Sept. 50; Bt.Major, 12 Dec. 54; Major, 9 Sept. 55; Bt.Lt.Colonel, 6 June 56; Lt.Colonel, P19 Dec. 62; Colonel, 27 March 63; Major General, 28 Oct. 68; Lt.General, 1 Apr. 82; Colonel East Lancashire Regiment, 15 Dec. 90.						
25	...	**Lieutenant Colonels.**—1 William Hunter Buller Little, Ensign, P27 Nov. 67; Lieut. P27 Oct. 71; Capt. 17 Apr. 80; Major, 12 Mar. 84; Lt.Colonel, 23 Sept. 93.						
25	...	1 Henry Theodore Penrhys Evan, Ensign, P27 Aug. 70; Lieut. 28 Oct. 71; Capt, 24 May 79; Major, 1 June 85; Lt.Colonel, 18 Mar. 95.						

			ENSIGN OR 2ND LIEUT.	LIEUT.	CAPTAIN.	BREV. MAJ.	MAJOR.
		MAJORS.					
25	...	2 Alfred George Watson[16]	3 Sept. 70	28 Oct. 71	23 June 80	......	5 Aug. 85
25	...	Archibald John Arnott Wright, *Adjutant* 3 Battalion 10 Aug. 90	P22 Oct. 70	28 Oct. 71	10 Nov. 80	......	8 Jan. 90
28	...	John Fred. Irwin,[17] *Adj.* 1 *Vol. Bn. E. Lancashire Regt.* 19 July 90	8 Jan. 68	28 Oct. 71	30 Sept. 81	......	22 Apr. 91
23	...	2 Montagu William Battye[20]	......	12 Feb. 73	8 Jan. 83	......	23 May 91
22	...	p.s.c. Percy Henry Noel Lake,[21] *Qr. Mr. Gen. Militia of Canada, with local rank of Lt. Colonel,* 14 Sept. 93	......	9 Aug. 73	31 Oct. 83	......	1 July 91
20	...	1 Walter Henry Scott	......	20 Nov. 75	12 Mar. 84	......	23 Sept. 93
		CAPTAINS.					
18	...	Bridges George Lewis, *Adjutant* 9 *Battalion Rifle Brigade* 18 Feb. 93	27 Mar. 78	31 July 79	18 Mar. 85		
17	...	1 Denis Carey	1 May 78	7 Aug. 79	18 Apr. 85		
17	...	p.s.c. William George Hamilton, *D.A.A.G. Bengal,* 26 July 90	11 May 78	23 June 80	18 Apr. 85		
17	...	1 Frank Seymour Derham	11 May 78	21 July 80	1 June 85		
17	...	Claude Arthur Bray,[24] *A. P. Dept.*	11 May 78	31 Aug. 80	5 Aug. 85		
17	...	Charles Richard Mackey O'Brien, *Adjutant* 1 *Guernsey Militia,* 9 Apr. 94	11 May 78	13 Sept. 80	28 May 87		
17	...	1 Carleton Haynes[25]	11 May 78	10 Nov. 80	28 May 87		
17	...	1 Henry Montague Browne	14 Sept. 78	12 Feb. 81	1 July 87		
17	...	Henry Lionel Gallwey, *Vice Consul Niger Coast Protectorate* 4 July 91	11 May 78	30 Mar. 81	1 Oct. 87		
17	...	1 Humphrey Martin Twynam,[26] *Station Staff Officer, Lucknow,* 5 Aug. 94	11 May 78	30 Mar. 81	1 Oct. 87		
16	...	2 Philip Bower MacAdam[27] (*Depot*)	11 Oct. 79	6 Apr. 81	28 July 90		
16	...	2 Cecil Willie Trevor Thomas Goff	14 Jan. 80	19 May 81	10 Aug. 90		
16	...	Edward Hugh Franklyn Finch, *Adj.* 3 *Punjab Volunteer Rifles* 6 Oct. 90	14 Jan. 80	1 July 81	10 Aug. 90		
16	...	Charles James Morse (*Depot*)	14 Jan. 80	1 July 81	1 Nov. 90		
16	...	Lionel Lewis Pile (*Depot*)	14 Jan. 80	1 July 81	1 Nov. 90		
15	...	John Alexander Roland Thompson, *Adj.* 5 *Bn. Inniskilling Fus.* 10 Sept. 92	22 Jan. 81	1 July 81	1 Nov. 90		
13	...	2 Henry Elliot Voyle	......	10 May 82	18 Mar. 91		
13	...	Albert Gordon Inglis, *Army Pay Department*	......	10 May 82	22 Apr. 91		
13	...	Thompson Capper	......	9 Sept. 82	22 Apr. 91		
13	...	1 Edward Revell Reade, *with Provisional Battalion*	......	9 Sept. 82	22 Apr. 91		
13	...	John Henry Hale, *O. S. Department*	......	9 Sept. 82	28 Apr. 91		
11	...	2 Henry Quinten Pinhorn	......	14 May 84	23 May 91		
11	...	2 Edward Alfred Daubeny	......	12 Nov. 84	1 July 91		
11	...	2 Henry John Martin	......	7 Feb. 85	4 July 91		
11	...	1 Francis Harrison Trent	......	7 Feb. 85	10 Sept. 92		
11	...	2 Harry Harris Were	......	7 Feb. 85	18 Feb. 93		
10	...	2 John Hamilton Anderson	......	9 May 85	1 June 93		
10	...	2 Tom Harry Finch Pearse, **Adjutant** 1 Apr. 92	......	9 May 85	1 June 93		
10	...	Robert Thomas Morland Lethbridge, *Army Pay Department*	......	30 Jan. 86	23 Sept. 93		
		LIEUTENANTS.					
9	...	1 Louis St. Gratien Le Marchant	......	10 Nov. 86			
9	...	1 Godfrey Richard Conyngham Stuart, *S.S.O. Fort William, Bengal,* 11 Dec. 94	......	10 Nov. 86			
8	...	1 Lancelot Cecil Bray Hamber, *S.S.O., Pachmarhi Depot,* 11 Nov. 94	21 May 87	20 Nov. 89			
8	...	1 Leonard Head, **Adjutant** 29 Oct. 94	11 Feb. 88	10 Aug. 90			
7	...	1 Albert Edmund Clerk (*Depot*)	8 Dec. 88	18 Mar. 91			
6	...	2 Llewellyn Bradford Carson	6 July 89	23 May 91			
6	...	Lawrence Tullock Oakley, *Adj.* 4 *Admin. Bn. N.W. Prov. Vols.* 6 May 94	15 Jan. 90	21 Oct. 91			
5	...	1 Etienne Ronald Partridge Boileau	28 June 90	21 Oct. 91			
5	...	Llewellyn William Atcherley, *Army Service Corps*	29 Nov. 90	21 Oct. 91			
5	...	George Henniker Lawrence	17 Jan. 91	27 Mar. 92			
5	...	1 Harry Maclear	18 Mar. 91	3 Apr. 92			
4	...	1 Harold Francis Wethered	2 May 91	31 Aug. 92			
4	...	2 George Edward Sharp	23 May 91	10 Sept. 92			
4	...	2 Thomas Stanton Lambert	17 June 91	13 Oct. 92			
4	...	1 Alvin Augustus Sanders	17 June 91	4 Dec. 92			
4	...	1 John Samuel Jocelyn Baumgartner	25 July 91	18 Feb. 93			
4	...	1 Cecil Delarue Mears[23]	9 Sept. 91	1 June 93			
4	...	1 Arthur Baldwyn Battye	5 Dec. 91	16 July 93			
4	...	1 Ralph Darby Cheales	27 Jan. 92	10 Sept. 93			
3	...	1 Evan Campbell Da Costa	13 July 92	1 Jan. 94			
3	...	1 William Heaton Cooper	19 Oct. 92	6 May 94			
3	...	2 Ernest Rokeby Collins	19 Nov. 92	1 July 94			

[24] Captain Bray served in the Afghan war in 1880 (Medal).

[25] Captain Haynes served in the Zulu war in 1879 (Medal with Clasp). During the Boer war of 1880 he was employed at Fort Newcastle. Served in the Afghan war in 1880 (Medal).

[26] Captain Twynam served with the 59th Regiment in the Afghan war of 1878-80, and took part in the advance on Shahjui under Lt. General Hughes and in the engagement at Ahmed Kheyl (mentioned in despatches, Medal with Clasp).

[27] Captain MacAdam served with the 59th Regiment in the Afghan war from 23rd January 1880 with the force under Sir Donald Stewart, and was present in the engagements at Ahmed Kheyl and Urzoo near Ghuznee, and in the subsequent operations in the Logar Valley (Medal with Clasp).

The East Lancashire Regiment.

Years' Ser. Full Pay	Half Pay	SECOND LIEUTENANTS.	2ND LIEUT.	
3	...	2 Francis James Tweedie	17 Dec.	92
3	...	2 James Edward Green	17 Dec.	92
3	...	1 William Henry Traill	17 Dec.	92
3	...	2 Eustace Frederick Rutter	17 Dec.	92
3	...	1 Basil Culverhouse De Gex	21 Jan.	93
3	...	2 William James Cropley Luddington	21 Jan.	93
2	...	2 Arthur Cyril Marmaduke Alington	26 Apr.	93
2	...	2 Leonard Russell	19 July	93
2	...	2 Philip Lonsdale	19 July	93
2	...	2 Cyril Edward Wilson	21 Oct.	93
2	...	1 Robert James Hilson	7 Mar.	94
2	...	2 Walter John Lambert	7 Mar.	94
1	...	1 Robert Alexander Dobbin	2 June	94
1	...	2 Walter Fairfax Richardson	2 June	94
1	...	1 Henry William Fletcher	5 May	94
1	...	2 Bertrand Henry Carter Boileau	10 Oct.	94

Facings White.—*Agents*, Messrs. Cox and Co.

1st Battalion embarked for Bengal, 1880. 2nd Battalion embarked for Gibraltar, 21 Jan. 93.

Paymasters.—1 Carleton Haynes,[25] Captain 1 Battalion (acting).

Quarter Masters.—2 Maurice Barry, 8 Aug. 94; Hon. Lieut.
1 William Holbourn, 30 Jan. 95; Hon. Lieut.

[1] Lt.General Pakenham served with the 30th Regiment in the Eastern campaign of 1854, and was slightly and also severely wounded at the battle of Alma (Medal with Clasp, Brevets of Major and Lt.Colonel, Sardinian and Turkish Medals, and 5th Class of the Medjidie).
[7] Lt.Colonel Goodwyn.—See Civil Decorations for Gallantry, "Hart's Annual Army List," p. 786.
[9] Lt.Colonel Clowes served in the Ashanti war from the 30th November 1873, and commanded the Kossoo company of Wood's Regiment at the battle of Amoaful (Medal with Clasp).
[16] Major Watson served in the Zulu war in 1879 (Medal with Clasp). Served in the Afghan war in 1880 (Medal).
[17] Major Irwin served with the 59th Regiment in the Afghan war of 1878-80 with the Candahar Column under Sir Donald Stewart, during 1878 as Orderly Officer to Brigadier General Hughes; took part in the advance on Khelat-i-Ghilzie and Ghuznee and in the subsequent operations in the Logar Valley; was present in the engagements at Shahjui, Ahmed Kheyl, and Urzoo near Ghuznee (mentioned in despatches, Medal with Clasp).
[20] Major Battye served with the 59th Regiment in the Afghan war of 1878-80 with the Candahar Column under Sir Donald Stewart, including the advance on and occupation of Khelat-i-Ghilzie, and also the second advance on. that place under Lt.General Hughes; was present in the engagements at Ahmed Kheyl and at Urzoo near Ghuznee, and in the subsequent operations in the Logar Valley, when he officiated as Deputy Assistant Commissary General to the 2nd Brigade (Medal with Clasp).
[21] Lt.Colonel Lake served in the Afghan war in 1878-79 as Assistant Field Engineer with the Southern Afghanistan Field Force (Medal). Served in the Soudan campaign in 1885 attached to the Intelligence Department, and was present in the engagements at Hasheen and the Tofrek zereba and in the advance to Temai (Medal with two Clasps, and Khedive's Star).
[23] Lieut. Mears.—See Civil Decorations for Gallantry, "Hart's Annual Army List," p. 786.

Record of the Services of the 1st Battalion East Lancashire Regiment (formerly the 30th Regiment).

Raised as Marines in 1702. Served as such afloat and ashore at capture of Gibraltar 1704 and numerous operations in Spain (capture of Barcelona, 1705), Mediterranean, France, Nova Scotia, and Canada. Appointed "30th Regiment" in 1714. Ireland, to 1724. Minorca, to 1727. Gibraltar, to 1732. Ireland, to 1743. England, to 1746. Action off Cape Finisterre, 1747 (as Marines). England, to 1747. Ireland, to 1755. England, to 1757. Attacks on the French Coast, 1758. England, to 1761. Capture of Belle Isle, 1761 (as Marines). England, to 1763. Gibraltar, to 1771. England, to 1774. Scotland, to 1775. Ireland, to 1781. North America, to 1782. Entitled the "Cambridgeshire Regiment," 1782. Jamaica, to 1791. England, to 1793. Occupation of Toulon, capture of Bastia and Calvi, and annexation of Corsica, 1794 (as Marines). Minorca, 1799. Malta, 1800 (taking of Valetta). Egypt, to 1802 (battle of Alexandria and capture of Marabout). England, to 1804. [2nd Battalion raised in England, 1803. Ireland, to 1809. Gibraltar, to 1810. Peninsula, to 1813 (battles of Badajoz. and Salamanca). England, to 1814. Holland and Belgium, to 1815 (Quatre Bras and Waterloo). France, 1815. England, to 1816. Ireland, to 1817, when it was disbanded and merged in the 1st Battalion.] Ireland, to 1804. Pomerania, to 1805. Germany, to 1806. England, to 1807. India, to 1807. Java, 1807 (as Marines). Macao, 1809. India. to 1829 (storming of Asseerghur). England, to 1831. Ireland, to 1834. Bermuda, to 1841. Nova Scotia, to 1844. Ireland, to 1846. England, to 1851. Corfu, to 1853. Gibraltar, to 1854. Crimea (battles of Alma and Inkerman, siege of Sebastopol) to 1856. Gibraltar, to 1857. Ireland, to 1860. Channel Islands, to 1861. England, 1861. Canada, to 1868. Nova Scotia, to 1869. Ireland, to 1871. Channel Islands, to 1872. England, to 1880. India, 1880. Designated "The 1st Battalion The East Lancashire Regiment," 1881.

Record of the Services of the 2nd Battalion East Lancashire Regiment (formerly the 59th Regiment).

Raised in 1755, and proceeded to America, 1763. Nova Scotia, to 1767. America, to 1775. England, to 1782. Gibraltar, to 1792. England, to 1793. Channel Islands, to 1794. Low Countries, to 1795. England, 1795. West Indies, to 1802. England, to 1808. Peninsula, to 1809. England, to 1810. Ireland, to 1811. England, to 1812. Peninsula, to 1814. Ireland, to 1815. Low Countries, to 1816. England, 1816. Ireland, 1816. India, to 1817. Ceylon, to 1818. India, to 1829. England, to 1831. Ireland, to 1834. England, to 1836. Malta, to 1841. West Indies, to 1843. England, to 1846. Ireland, to 1849. China, to 1858. Cape of Good Hope, to 1861. England and Scotland, to 1865. Ireland, to 1867. Ceylon, to 1869. India, to 1881 (Afghanistan, 1878-80). England, to 1885. Ireland, to 1893. Gibraltar, 1893.

1st Batt., Agra, Bengal.
2nd Batt., Malta.] **The East Surrey Regiment.** [*Regimental District.* No. 31.—Kingston.] 275

Formerly the 31st (The Huntingdonshire) and the 70th (Surrey) Regiments.

(The 3rd and 4th Battalions are formed of the 1st and 3rd Surrey Militia respectively.)

The United Red and White Rose. "DETTINGEN" "GUADALOUPE" "TALAVERA" "ALBUHERA" "VITTORIA" "PYRENEES" "NIVELLE" "NIVE" "ORTHES" "PENINSULA" "CABOOL 1842" "MOODKEE" "FEROZESHAH" "ALIWAL" "SOBRAON" "SEVASTOPOL" "TAKU FORTS" "NEW ZEALAND" "AFGHANISTAN, 1878-79" "SUAKIN, 1885."

Years' Ser.							
Full Pay	Half Pay						
31	...	Colonel.—Right Hon. Sir Edward Lugard,[1] GCB. *Ensign*, 31 July 28; *Lt.* P31 Oct. 31; *Capt.* 30 Dec. 43; *Bt.Major*, 3 April 46; *Bt.Lt.Colonel*, 7 June 49; *Colonel*, 20 June 54; *Major*, 13 June 55; *Major General*, 20 July 58; *Lieut.General*, 12 Jan. 65; *General*, 24 Oct. 72; *Colonel* 31st Foot, 1 June 62.						
29	...	Lieutenant Colonels.—1 *p.s.c.* Arthur FitzRoy Hart,[2] CB. Commanding the Battalion, 21 June 91; *Ensign*, 23 Dec. 64; *Lieut.* P29 May 67; *Capt.* 13 June 74; *Bt.Major*, 29 Nov. 79; *Major*, 1 July 81; *Bt.Lt.Colonel*, 18 Nov. 82; *Colonel*, 18 Nov. 86; *Lt.Colonel*, 21 June 91.						
29	...	2 Robert William Fergusson Phillips, *Ensign*, P18 Dec. 66; *Lt.* P25 Dec. 67; *Capt.* 23 Jan. 78; *Major*, 19 Nov. 81; *Lt.Colonel*, 14 Dec. 91.						

		MAJORS.	ENSIGN OR 2ND LIEUT.	LIEUT.	CAPTAIN.	BREV. MAJ.	MAJOR.
30	...	1 Fredk. Harvey Maturin[12] (*Bt.Lt.Col.* 15 June 85; *Colonel*, 15 June 89)	P22 Sept. 65	P27 Feb. 69	9 Mar. 78	......	20 May 82
28	...	2 Francis Fred. Fyler Roupell[13]	P 5 Oct. 67	P24 Sept. 70	7 Aug. 78	......	1 Aug. 82
29	...	1 George Humphrys Leatham	P23 Mar. 67	P11 April 68	2 Mar. 78	......	28 Nov. 83
22	...	2 *p.s.c.* Francis Richard Pennefather Kane (*Depot*)	......	12 Nov. 73	28 Feb. 81	......	21 June 91
22	...	2 William James Holmes Frodsham[19]	......	28 Feb. 74	30 Sept. 82	......	14 Dec. 91
21	...	2 Hugh Wodehouse Pearse[20]	......	11 Feb. 75	30 June 83	......	12 July 92
19	...	Herbert Ringwood,[22] *Adj. East Indian Railway Rifle Vols.* 7 June 92	......	11 Sept. 76	28 Nov. 83	......	11 Apr. 94
19	...	Henry Wightman Benson, *Adjutant* 3 Battalion 1 Jan. 92	......	15 July 67	10 Aug. 84	......	8 Feb. 95

		CAPTAINS.					
19	...	2 Arthur Edward Couper[21]	......	26 July 76	30 June 83		
17	...	Henry Lockhart Smith,[24] *Adjutant* 3 *Vol. Bn. E. Surrey Regt.* 14 Jan. 94	11 May 78	15 Mar. 80	25 Oct. 84		
16	...	Henry Paul Treeby, *Adjutant* 4 *Vol. Bn. E. Surrey Regt.* 1 Aug. 93	6 Aug. 79	28 May 80	5 Aug. 85		
15	...	Colin Duncan Johnstone, *Adjutant* 4 Battalion 8 Aug. 94	17 Apr. 80	21 June 80	31 Aug. 87		
16	...	1 Arthur Bruce Dunsterville,[28] *Station Staff Officer, Agra*, 25 Nov. 92	14 Sept. 78	28 Feb. 81	19 Oct. 87		
15	...	Ludlow Tonson Bowles, *Adj.* 3 *Admin. Bn. N.W.P. Rifle Vols.* 10 Aug. 91	23 Oct. 80	9 Apr. 81	14 Dec. 87		
15	...	2 Patrick Henry Augustus O'Hara	23 Oct. 80	1 July 81	14 Dec. 87		
15	...	Finch White,[28] *Adjutant* 2 *Vol. Bn. East Surrey Regt.* 1 Mar. 94	22 Jan. 81	1 July 81	1 Apr. 88		
14	...	1 Eustace Grenville Bayliss[30]	......	22 Oct. 81	29 Aug. 88		
13	...	2 Henry Stanhope Sloman,[31] *Staff Coll.*	......	10 May 82	20 Nov. 88		
13	...	1 *p.s.c.* Hugh Duncan Lawrence (*Depot*)	......	10 May 82	15 Jan. 89		
13	...	*p.s.c.* Bernard Ramsden James, *Instructor R. M. College* 1 Sept. 93	......	9 Sept. 82	1 Mar. 89		
12	...	1 Frederick Charles Boehmer[33]	......	31 Oct. 83	27 Mar. 89		
13	...	William Hastings Ellis[28]	......	27 Jan. 83	27 Mar. 89		
13	...	William Henry Gorman, *Adjutant* 1 *Surrey Rifle Volunteers* 9 Nov. 91	......	27 Jan. 83	21 June 91		
13	...	2 *p.s.c.* Bertram Reveley Mitford[34]	......	9 Sept. 82	24 June 91		
13	...	Chas. Perceval Lynden Lynden-Bell,[28] *Adj.* 4 *Vol. Bn. of Royal Scots*, 1 Feb. 93	......	10 Mar. 83	10 Aug. 91		
12	...	2 Orchart Beeton, *Adjutant* 11 Dec. 94	......	6 Feb. 84	7 June 92		
11	...	1 Arthur Joseph Hill	......	14 May 84	12 July 92		
11	...	1 Kenneth Malcolm Patrick Grant[35] (*Depot*)	......	14 May 84	1 Feb. 93		
11	...	Henry Augustus Anley, *Ordnance Store Department*	......	7 Feb. 85	28 Nov. 94		
11	...	2 Richard Norman Pochin	......	7 Feb. 85	28 Nov. 94		
9	...	Leonard Williams	......	26 May 86	6 Mar. 95		

		LIEUTENANTS.					
9	...	Lionel Charles Gostling Tufnell, *Ordnance Store Department*	......	28 Apr. 86			
8	...	1 John Raynsford Longley	4 May 87	16 Jan. 89			
7	...	Frederick Lord Aldersey Packman, *Ordnance Store Department*	9 May 88	20 Nov. 89			
7	...	1 Frank Hermann Moline	22 Aug. 88	23 Mar. 90			
7	...	2 William Naunton Roger Gilbert-Cooper, *with Provisional Battalion*	22 Aug. 88	23 Mar. 90			
7	...	1 Luke George Ionides (*Depot*)	10 Nov. 88	26 Apr. 90			
7	...	1 Harold Stuart Tew	23 Mar. 89	21 June 91			
7	...	1 Arthur George Dwyer	24 Apr. 89	10 Aug. 91			
6	...	1 Arthur Holt Wilson	9 Nov. 89	31 Oct. 91			
6	...	1 Walter Herbert Paterson	1 Mar. 90	3 Mar. 92			
5	...	1 Arthur Henry Seton Hart, *Adjutant* 1 Jan. 94	8 Oct. 90	7 June 92			
5	...	2 James FitzWalter Arcedeckne-Butler	29 Oct. 90	4 Aug. 92			
4	...	2 Arthur Christin Stewart Barchard	23 May 91	14 Apr. 93			
4	...	1 George Ross Deas Churchill	25 July 91	23 Apr. 93			
4	...	Herbert George Anderson Garsia, *Army Service Corps*	9 Jan. 92	11 May 93			
4	...	1 William Welphy Fagan	9 Jan. 92	8 July 93			
4	...	2 Henry Davidson Smalley	9 Jan. 92	11 Mar. 94			
3	...	1 Cuthbert Hanson Townsend	18 June 92	6 May 94			
3	...	2 Richard Aremburg Blennerhassett Chute	9 Apr. 92	1 July 94			
3	...	1 Henry Keith Barr	13 Aug. 92	19 Sept. 94			
3	...	1 Cecil Charles Gough Ashton	13 Aug. 92	19 Sept. 94			
3	...	2 Claude Harington Hinton	25 Feb. 93	14 Nov. 94			
3	...	Cecil Porch Porch	25 Feb. 93	28 Nov. 94			

[30] Captain Bayliss served with the expedition to the Soudan in 1885 as Signalling Officer to the 2nd Battalion of the East Surrey Regiment, and was present in the engagement at Hasheen, at the attack on the convoy on the 26th March, and in the subsequent advance to Temai; was Orderly Officer to Colonel Ralston when in command of the 2nd Brigade (Medal with Clasp, and Khedive's Star).

[32] Captain Sloman served in the expedition to the Soudan in 1885 with the Mounted Infantry, and was present in the engagement at Hasheen and at the destruction of Temai (Medal with Clasp, and Khedive's Star).

[33] Captain Boehmer served in the Jowaki Afreedee Expedition in 1877-78 with the 51st King's Own Light Infantry (Medal with Clasp). Served in the Afghan war of 1878-80, and was present at the attack and capture of Ali Musjid (Medal with Clasp).

R

275a The East Surrey Regiment.

Years' 1891 Full Pay	Half Pay		SECOND LIEUTENANTS.	2ND LIEUT.
3	...	2	Victor Henry Mottet de la Fontaine...	25 Feb. 93
3	...	2	Sidney Hugh Duxbury	25 Feb. 93
2	...	2	Francis William King-Church	26 Apr. 93
2	...	1	Edw. Sayers Talbot Goodridge..........	20 May 93
2	...	1	Harry Hatton Sproule	28 June 93
2	...	2	Victor John Birkbeck	19 July 93
2	...	2	Charles Austin Ferguson...............	21 Oct. 93
1	...	1	Charles Fayle Colquhoun	2 June 94
1	...	1	Raymond Henry Baldwin	2 June 94
1	...	1	William Thurburn Barry................	2 June 94
1	...	1	Archibald Tyrrell Robinson	2 June 94
1	...	1	Hugh Walter Davies	10 Oct. 94
1	...	2	Arthur Ernest Greatwood	10 Oct. 94
1	...	2	*Hon.* Cuthbert James	12 Dec. 94
1	...	2	Frederic George Fisher	12 Dec. 94
1	...		Roger Edward Napier North.............	6 Mar. 95

Paymasters.—1
                2
| 13 | ... | *Quarter Masters.*—1 John Alfred Keble,[37] 10 June 82 ; *Hon. Captain,* 10 June 92. |
| 5 | ... | 2 Henry M'Dermott, 6 Aug. 90 ; *Hon. Lieut.* |

Facings White.—*Agents,* Messrs. Cox and Co.
1st Battalion embarked for India, 22 Dec. 1884. 2nd Battalion embarked for Malta, 23 Feb. 893.

---

[1] Sir Edward Lugard served as a Major of Brigade throughout the campaign of 1842 in Affghanistan under General Pollock, and was present in the actions of Mazeena, Tezeen, and Jugdulluck, the occupation of Cabool, and the different engagements leading to it (Medal). He served throughout the campaign on the Sutlej;—as Deputy Assistant Adjutant General to Sir Harry Smith at the battles of Moodkee (wounded), Ferozeshah (wounded), and Sobraon;—as Adjutant General of the whole Force commanded by Sir Harry at the affair of Buddiwal, and the battle of Aliwal; and he officiated as Adjutant General of Her Majesty's Forces in India, from the battle of Sobraon to the end of the campaign, when he was appointed Assistant Adjutant General to Her Majesty's Forces in India (Medal and three Clasps). He again officiated as Adjutant General throughout the Punjaub campaign in 1848–49 ; and was present at the passage of the Chenab, and battles of Chillianwallah and Goojerat (Medal with two Clasps). Served as Chief of the Staff on the Persian expedition in 1857 (Medal with Clasp, and nominated a *KCB.*). Was promoted to the rank of Major General "for his services in the command of a Division at the capture of Lucknow, and subsequently in the command of the Azimghur Field Force" (Medal with Clasp).

[8] Colonel Hart accompanied Sir Garnet Wolseley to the Gold Coast in September 1873 on special service. Trained the Sierra Leone Company of Russell's Regiment and commanded it throughout the Ashanti war of 1873–74, taking part in the repulse of the Ashanti army at Abrakrampa during the 5th and 6th November 1873, the attack and capture of Adubiassie, battle of Amoaful, attack and capture of Becquah, advanced guard engagement of Jarbinbah (slightly wounded), battle of Ordahsu and capture of Coomassie. Attached to the Quarter Master General's Department, surveyed Cape Coast, accompanied the scouting party north of the Prah and made the surveys of the road and scenes of action from the Prah to Coomassie (twice mentioned in despatches, Medal with Clasp). Went on special service to South Africa in November 1878, and served throughout the Zulu war of 1879; first, as Staff Officer of the 2nd Regiment of Natal Native Contingent (two battalions), taking part with Pearson's Column in the engagement of Inyezane; then, as Staff Officer on the Ekowe relieving column, being present at the action of Gingindhlovu; afterwards as Brigade Major of the 2nd Brigade 1st Division; and, finally, as Principal Staff Officer of Clarke's Column (several times mentioned in despatches, Brevet of Major, Medal with Clasp). Went to South Africa on special service in January 1881, and served under Sir Evelyn Wood in the Boer war as Deputy Assistant Adjutant and Quarter Master General. Went to Egypt on special service in July 1882 and served throughout the Egyptian war as Deputy Assistant Adjutant and Quarter Master General in the Intelligence Department, being present at the reconnaissance in force from Alexandria 5th August, the engagements of El Magfar, Tel-el-Mahuta, and Kassasin 9th Sept. (slightly wounded), and in the battle of Tel-el-Kebir (mentioned in despatches, Brevet of Lt. Colonel, Medal with Clasp, 4th Class of the Osmanieh, and Khedive's Star).

[12] Colonel Maturin served with the 70th Regiment in the Afghan war in 1878–79 (Medal). Served in the expedition to the Soudan in 1885 with the 2nd Battalion of the East Surrey Regiment, and was present in the engagement at Hasheen, at the attack on the convoy on the 26th March, and in the subsequent advance to Temai (mentioned in despatches, Brevet of Lt. Colonel, Medal with Clasp, and Khedive's Star).

[13] Major Roupell served in the Afghan war in 1879 (Medal). Served in the Mahsood Wuzeeree Expedition in 1881 as Assistant Adjutant General (mentioned in despatches).

[19] Major Frodsham served in the expedition to the Soudan in 1885 as Acting Adjutant to the 2nd Battalion of the East Surrey Regiment, and was present in the engagement at Hasheen, at the attack on the convoy on the 26th March, and in the subsequent advance to Temai (Medal with Clasp, and Khedive's Star).

[20] Major Pearse served with the 70th Regiment in the Afghan war in 1878–79 under Brigadier General Biddulph, including the occupation of Candahar (Medal).

[21] Captain Couper served in the Afghan war in 1878–79 with the 70th Regiment (Medal). Served in the expedition to the Soudan in 1885 with the 2nd Battalion of the East Surrey Regiment, and was present in the engagement at Hasheen, at the attack on the convoy on the 26th March, and in the subsequent advance to Temai (Medal with Clasp, and Khedive's Star).

[22] Major Ringwood served with the 70th Regiment in the Afghan war in 1878–79, first with the Candahar Column, and afterwards with the Thull Chotiali Field Force under Major General Biddulph (Medal).

[24] Captain H. L. Smith served with the 70th Regiment in the Afghan war in 1878–79 (Medal). Served in the expedition to the Soudan in 1885 with the 2nd Battalion of the East Surrey Regiment, and was present in the engagement at Hasheen, at the attack on the convoy on the 26th March, and in the subsequent advance to Temai (Medal wit Clasp, and Khedive's Star).

[28] Captains Dunsterville, White, Ellis, and Lynden-Bell served in the expedition to the Soudan in 1885 with the 2nd Battalion of the East Surrey Regiment, and were present in the engagement at Hasheen, at the attack on the convoy on the 26th March, and in the subsequent advance to Temai (Medal with Clasp, and Khedive's Star).

[34] Captain Mitford served with the Soudan Frontier Field Force in 1886–88, and was present in the engagement at Sarras (mentioned in despatches, Medal, 4th Class of the Medjidie, and Khedive's Star); also served in the operations on the Soudan frontier in 1888 including the engagement at Gemaizah (Clasp), and again in 1889 including the engagements at Arguin and Toski (mentioned in despatches, 4th Class of the Osmanieh, and Clasp).

[35] Captain Kenneth M. P. Grant served in the expedition to the Soudan in 1885 with the 2nd Battalion of the East Surrey Regiment, and was present at the attack on the convoy on the 26th March and in the subsequent advance on Temai (Medal with Clasp), and Khedive's Star).

⁴⁷ Captain Keble served with the 31st Regiment throughout the campaign in the north of China in 1860, including the action of Sinho and storming of Tangku (Medal with Clasp for the Taku Forts). Present at the occupation of Tien Tsin 1860-62. Served during the operations against the Taepings in the vicinity of Shanghai in 1862, resulting in the taking of the stockade of Nanhsiang, capture by escalade of the walled cities of Kadin, Tsinpoo, and Tsolin, the fortified town of Najow, the affair at Nanhsiang, and relief of Kadin and Tsinpoo.

Record of the Services of the 1st Battalion East Surrey Regiment (formerly the 31st Huntingdonshire Regiment).

Raised 1702, and proceeded as Marines to Cadiz and Vigo; to England, 1702; to the Mediterranean, 1704 (capture of Gibraltar, Barcelona, Carthagena, Ivica, Majorca, Sardinia, Minorca); to England, 1711; ceased to serve as Marines, 1714; to Scotland, 1715; to Ireland, 1716; to England, 1739; to Flanders, 1742; to England, 1745; to Minorca, 1749; to England, 1752; to Scotland, 1755; to England, 1762; to West Florida, 1765; to St. Vincent, 1772; to England, 1774; to Canada, 1776; to England, 1787; to Ireland, 1792; (Flank Companies to Barbadoes, 1793;) to England, 1794; to Holland, 1794; to England, 1795; to the West Indies, 1795; to England, 1797; to Holland, 1799; to England, 1799; to Ireland, 1800; to the Isle de Huat, 1800; to Minorca, 1801; to England, 1802; to the Channel Isles, 1803; to England, 1804; [2nd Battalion (31st Regiment) raised 1804; to Channel Isles, 1807; to Ireland, 1807; to the Peninsula, 1808 (battles of Talavera, Albuhera, Vittoria, Pyrenees, Nivelle, Nive, Orthes); to Ireland, 1814; to England and disbanded, 1814;] to Sicily, 1806; to Egypt, 1807; to Sicily, 1807; to Malta, 1808; to Sicily, 1810; to Malta, 1811; to Sicily, 1811; to Genoa, 1814; to Corsica, 1814; to Sicily, 1814; to Naples, 1815; to Genoa, 1815; to Malta, 1816; to England, 1818; to Ireland, 1821; to England, 1824; to India, 1825 (Kabul 1842, and battles of Moodkee, Ferozeshah, Aliwal, and Sobraon); to England, 1846; to Ireland, 1848; to Ionian Islands, 1853; to the Crimea, 1855 (siege of Sebastopol); to Gozo, 1856; to Malta, 1857; to Gibraltar, 1857; to the Cape, 1859; to India, 1859; to China, 1860 (capture of the Taku Forts); to England, 1863; to Ireland, 1866; to Malta, 1867; to Gibraltar, 1872; to England, 1876; to Ireland, 1880; to Gibraltar, 1882; to England, 1883; to Gibraltar, 1884; to India, 1884.

Record of the Services of the 2nd Battalion,—formerly the 70th (Surrey) Regiment.

Raised as the 2nd Battalion 31st Regiment, and proceeded to Scotland, 1758; to England, 1759; to Ireland, 1763; to West Indies, 1764; to England, 1774; to Scotland, 1776; to North America, 1778; to England, 1784; to Ireland, 1787; to West Indies, 1793; to England and Gibraltar, 1795; to West Indies, 1800; to Jersey and England, 1801; to West Indies, 1803 (capture of Guadaloupe); to Scotland. 1812; to Ireland and Canada, 1813; to Ireland, 1827; to Gibraltar, 1834; to Malta, 1836; to West Indies, 1838; to Canada, 1841; to England, 1843; to Ireland, 1845; to India, 1849; to New Zealand, 1861 (war of 1863-65); to England, 1866; to Ireland, 1868; to India, 1871 (Afghan war 1878-79); entitled " 2nd Battalion East Surrey Regiment," 1881; to Egypt, 1884 (campaign of 1885); to England, 1885; to Guernsey, 1888; to Ireland, 1891; to Malta, 1893.

1st Batt., Meerut, Bengal.
2nd Batt., Newry.

Duke of Cornwall's Light Infantry.
Regimental District No. 32.—Bodmin.

Formerly the 32nd (Cornwall—Light Inf.) and the 46th (South Devonshire) Regiments.
(The 3rd Battalion is formed of the Cornwall Rangers Militia.)

The United Red and White Rose. "DETTINGEN" "DOMINICA" "ROLEIA" "VIMIERA" "CORUNVA" "SALAMANCA" "PYRENNES" "NIVELLE" "NIVE" "ORTHES" "PENINSULA" "WATERLOO" "PUNIAUB" "MOOLTAN" "GOOJERAT" "SEVASTOPOL" "LUCKNOW" "EGYPT, 1882" "TEL-EL-KEBIR" "NILE 1884-85."

Years' Ser. Full Pay	Half Pay						
32	...	Colonel.—John Thomas Hill, *Ensign*, P13 Mar. 27; *Lt.* P16 Apr. 29; *Capt.* P13 Feb. 35; *Major*, 12 Mar. 41; *Lt. Colonel*, 3 Apr. 46; *Colonel*, 20 June 54; *Major General*, 30 July 60; *Lt. General*, 14 June 69; *General*, 24 June 76; *Colonel* 75th Foot, 24 Oct. 72; *Colonel* Duke of Cornwall's Light Infantry, 8 Apr. 90.						
28	...	Lieutenant Colonels.—1 Francis Henry A. Disney-Roebuck,¹ *Ensign*, P26 Feb. 64; *Lt.* P17 Apr. 67; *Capt.* P9 Apr. 70; *Major*, 1 July 81; *Lt. Colonel*, 1 July 91.						
		2 William Barrington Browne,¹⁰ *Ensign*, 8 Jan. 68; *Lt.* P16 Mar. 70; *Capt.* 1 July 76; *Brev. Major*, 18 Nov. 82; *Major*, 26 July 85; *Lt. Colonel*, 31 July 93.						

			ENSIGN OR 2ND LIEUT.	LIEUT.	CAPTAIN.	BREV. MAJ.	MAJOR.
		MAJORS.					
30	...	1 Charles Fred. Alexander Turnbull	P 9 Mar. 66	P22 July 68	26 May 80	......	5 Apr. 86
22	...	2 Frederick George Vigor¹²	......	11 Sept. 73	1 Sept. 81	......	1 July 91
21	...	1 Henry Parry Carden¹³	......	13 June 74	8 May 83	15 June 85	1 Jan. 93
20	...	1 John Hamilton Verschoyle⁶	......	13 June 75	29 Dec. 83	......	5 Apr. 93
20	...	George Ashby Ashby,¹⁸ *Adj.* 1 *Vol. Bn.* Duke of Cornwall's Lt. Inf. 14 Nov. 92	......	20 Nov. 75	1 Jan. 86	2 Jan. 86	26 July 93
20	...	2 Wolstan Francis¹⁹	......	20 Nov. 75	17 Feb. 86	......	31 July 93
19	...	1 Edmund John Hollway²⁰	......	11 Sept. 76	2 May 86	......	18 Oct. 93
18	...	2 William Lueg Harvey²¹ (Depot)	30 Jan. 78	18 June 81	1 July 87	......	31 Aug. 94
		CAPTAINS.					
18	...	Henry Gage Morris,²⁵ *Adj.* 2 *Vol. Bn.* Duke of Cornwall's Lt. Inf. 1 Jan. 91	30 Jan. 78	1 July 81	14 Nov. 87		
17	...	Ralph James Wilbraham,²⁶ *Adjutant* 3 *Battalion* 4 Jan. 92	21 Aug. 78	1 July 81	14 Dec. 87		
16	...	2 Edward John Jenkins Teale²⁷	2 July 79	1 July 81	11 Apr. 88		
15	...	Cyril Godfrey Martyr,²⁸ *serving with the Egyptian Army, with rank of Major*	23 Oct. 80	1 July 81	14 Aug. 89		
15	...	Charles Newman Evelegh,²⁹ *Adjutant* 4 Battalion Durham Light Infantry 19 Feb. 95	19 Feb. 81	1 July 81	14 Aug. 89		
12	...	Henry Marlow Sidney,³² *serving with the Egyptian Army, with rank of Major*	......	25 Aug. 83	14 Aug. 89		
12	...	1 Rupert Stewart³³	......	25 Aug. 83	23 Apr. 90		
12	...	1 Frederic Hamilton Chapman	......	6 Feb. 84	23 May 90		
15	...	2 Frederick Gerald Griffiths Griffin	22 Jan. 81	1 July 81	14 Jan. 91		
14	1⁴/₁₂	2 Francis Mary John Dominic Rhodes	23 Oct. 80	1 July 81	20 July 88		
11	...	1 Harold Bridgwood Walker³⁵	......	14 May 84	16 Dec. 91		
11	...	2 Arthur Grant Crosse	......	23 Aug. 84	8 Mar. 92		
11	...	2 Robert Nicholas Spencer Lewin³⁶	......	23 Aug. 84	6 Jan. 93		
11	...	1 Bertram Archdall Newbury³⁷ (Depot)	......	23 Aug. 84	26 July 93		
11	...	1 Ernest Sumner Burder	......	7 Feb. 85	26 July 93		
11	...	2 George William Thursby Prowse	......	7 Feb. 85	31 July 93		
10	...	2 James Montagu Bowle Kennedy	......	9 May 85	18 Oct. 93		
10	...	1 Cecil Bradney Jervis-Edwards,³⁸ *Adjutant* 1 Mar. 93	......	29 Aug. 85	18 Oct. 93		
10	...	Geo. Brooke Millers Rawlinson	......	25 Nov. 85	19 Feb. 95		
		LIEUTENANTS.					
10	...	1 Eustace Scott Williams³⁹ (Depot)	......	27 Jan. 86			
9	...	2 John Jeffreys Bulkeley Jones-Parry	5 Feb. 87	14 Aug. 89			
8	...	1 Sutherland Henry Bradford	4 May 87	4 Jan. 90			
8	...	1 Leonard Philip Henry Bliss⁴⁰	4 May 87	26 Jan. 90			
8	...	2 Edgar Penrose Mark-Wardlaw	16 Nov. 87	23 Apr. 90			
8	...	2 Ernest Alfred Shakerley (Depot)	30 Nov. 87	23 May 90			
8	...	1 Henry Arthur Tremayne	16 Nov. 87	29 June 90			
7	...	1 Hon. Willoughby John Horace de Montmorency⁴¹	22 Aug. 88	20 Apr. 91			
7	...	1 Hon. George Bagot Molesworth, *Station Staff Officer, Chuckrata*	8 Dec. 88	13 May 91			
7	...	1 Thomas Langdon Tretbowy	23 Mar. 89	16 Dec. 91			
7	...	2 Paul Buzzard Norris, *Adjutant* 26 July 94	23 Mar. 89	23 Apr. 92			
6	...	2 Arthur St. Clair Holbrook	21 Dec. 89	3 July 92			
5	...	2 Alexander George William Grant	28 June 90	1 Mar. 93			
5	...	2 John Harold Mander	16 July 90	10 May 93			
5	...	1 Martin Newman Turner	23 July 90	26 July 93			
4	...	1 Bernard Stigand Streeten	23 May 91	31 July 93			
4	...	1 James Hubert Thos. Cornish Bowden	23 Mar. 92	5 Sept. 93			
3	...	2 Henry Thomas Cantan	18 May 92	28 Oct. 93			
3	...	1 Richard Ducat	13 Aug. 92	31 Aug. 94			
3	...	2 Paul Gregory Petavel	13 Aug. 92	19 Feb. 95			
		SECOND LIEUTENANTS.					
3	...	1 Thomas Richard Stokoe	17 Dec. 92				
3	...	2 Harold Fargus	25 Feb. 93				
3	...	1 Herbert Samuel Protheroe Simon	25 Feb. 93				
3	...	2 Thomas Herbert Francis Price	15 Mar. 93				
2	...	2 Hugh Wharton Fife	26 Apr. 93				
2	...	1 William Kenneth Hamilton Campbell	20 May 93				
2	...	1 Cecil Barrington Norton	23 Aug. 93				
2	...	1 Reginald Weston Young	9 Sept. 93				
2	...	1 Henry Harington Champernowne	23 Dec. 93				
1	...	2 Francis Arthur Dickinson	10 Oct. 94				
1	...	1 Harry John de la Condamine	30 Jan. 95				

²⁹ Captain Evelegh served with the Wuntho Expedition in 1891 in command of a detachment of Cornwall's Light Infantry (Medal with Clasp).

³⁶ Captain Lewin served in the Nile Expedition in 1884-85 with the 2nd Battalion of the Duke of Cornwall's Light Infantry (Medal with Clasp, and Khedive's Star).

³⁷ Captain Newbury served in the Nile Expedition in 1884-85 with the 2nd Battalion of the Duke of Cornwall's Light Infantry (Medal with Clasp, and Khedive's Star).

³⁸ Captain Jervis Edwards served with the Wuntho Expedition in 1891 in command of a detachment of the 1st Battalion of the Duke of Cornwall's Light Infantry (Medal with Clasp).

³⁹ Lieut. Williams served with the Bechuanaland Expedition under Sir Charles Warren in 1884-85 with the Mounted Rifles.

⁴⁰ Lieut. Bliss served with the Wuntho Expedition in 1891 (Medal with Clasp).

⁴¹ Lieut. Hon. W. J. H. de Montmorency served with the Wuntho Expedition in 1891 in command of the Mounted Infantry of the Duke of Cornwall's Light Infantry (Medal with Clasp).

Year's Ser.	Full Pay	Half Pay
	14	...
	3	...

Paymasters.—1 Thomas L. Trethewy, Lieut. 1 Battalion (*acting*).
Quarter Masters.—1 John Conway, 30 Nov. 81; Hon. Captain, 30 Nov. 91.
2 Charles John Eary, 3 Aug. 92; Hon. Lieut.

Facings White.—*Agents*, Messrs. Cox and Co.
1st Battalion embarked for Malta, 1885. *2nd Battalion returned from Egypt, June* 1886.

[1] Lt.Colonel Disney Roebuck served in the Nile Expedition in 1884-85 with the 2nd Battalion of the Duke of Cornwall's Light Infantry, and took part in the operations of the Advance Column under Major General Earle (Medal with Clasp, and Khedive's Star).

[10] Lt.Colonel Browne served in the Egyptian war of 1882, and was present in the engagements at El Magfar and Tel-el-Mahuta, at the two actions at Kassasin, and at the battle of Tel-el-Kebir (mentioned in despatches, Brevet of Major, Medal with Clasp, and Khedive's Star).

[12] Major Vigor served in the Egyptian war of 1882 (Medal, and Khedive's Star). Served in the Nile Expedition in 1884-85 with the 2nd Battalion of the Duke of Cornwall's Light Infantry, and took part in the operations of the Advance Column under Major General Earle (Clasp).

[13] Major H. P. Carden served with the 2nd Battalion Duke of Cornwall's Light Infantry throughout the Egyptian war of 1882, and was present in the engagements at El Magfar and Tel-el-Mahuta, in the actions at Kassasin on the 28th August (wounded) and 9th September, and at the battle of Tel-el-Kebir (Medal with Clasp, and Khedive's Star). Served in the Nile Expedition in 1884-85 with the 2nd Battalion of the Duke of Cornwall's Light Infantry, and took part in the operations of the Advance Column under Major General Earle (mentioned in despatches, Brevet of Major, 3rd Class of the Medjidie, Clasp).

[16] Major Verschoyle served with the 2nd Battalion Duke of Cornwall's Light Infantry throughout the Egyptian war of 1882, and was present in the engagements at El Magfar and Tel-el-Mahuta, in the two actions at Kassasin, and at the battle of Tel-el-Kebir (Medal with Clasp, and Khedive's Star).

[18] Major Ashby served as Adjutant with the 2nd Battalion Duke of Cornwall's Light Infantry throughout the Egyptian war of 1882, and was present in the engagements at El Magfar and Tel-el-Mahuta, in the two actions at Kassasin, and at the battle of Tel-el-Kebir (mentioned in despatches, Medal with Clasp, 5th Class of the Medjidie, and Khedive's Star). Served with the Nile Expedition in 1884-85 with the 2nd Battalion of the Duke of Cornwall's Light Infantry, and took part in the operations of the Advance Column under Major General Earle (mentioned in despatches, Brevet of Major, Clasp).

[19] Major Francis served with the 2nd Battalion Duke of Cornwall's Light Infantry throughout the Egyptian war of 1882, and was present at the reconnaissance in force from Alexandria on the 5th August, in the engagements at El Magfar and Tel-el-Mahuta, in the two actions at Kassasin, and at the battle of Tel-el-Kebir (Medal with Clasp, and Khedive's Star).

[20] Major Hollway served with the 2nd Battalion Duke of Cornwall's Light Infantry throughout the Egyptian war of 1882, and was present at the reconnaissance in force from Alexandria on the 5th August, in the engagement at Tel-el-Mahuta, in the two actions at Kassasin, and at the battle of Tel-el-Kebir (Medal with Clasp, and Khedive's Star).

[24] Captain Harvey served with the 2nd Battalion Duke of Cornwall's Light Infantry in the Egyptian war of 1882 and was present at the battle of Tel-el-Kebir (Medal with Clasp, and Khedive's Star). Served in the Nile Expedition in 1884-85 with the 2nd Battalion of the Duke of Cornwall's Light Infantry, and took part in the operations of the Advance Column under Major General Earle (Clasp).

[25] Captain H. G. Morris served throughout the Egyptian war of 1882 with the 2nd Battalion of the Duke of Cornwall's Light Infantry, and was present at the reconnaissance in force from Alexandria on the 5th August, in the engagements at El Magfar and Tel-el-Mahuta, in the two actions at Kassasin, and at the battle of Tel-el-Kebir (Medal with Clasp, and Khedive's Star). Served in the Nile Expedition in 1884-85 with the River Column as a Staff Captain under Major General Earle and Brigadier General Brackenbury (mentioned in despatches, Clasp); also served with the Egyptian Frontier Field Force under Major General Grenfell in 1886 as Senior Water Transport Officer.

[26] Captain Wilbraham served with the Nile Expedition in 1884-85 (Medal with Clasp, and Khedive's Star).

[27] Captain Teale served in the Nile Expedition in 1885 with the Commissariat and Transport Staff.

[28] Major Martyr served with the 2nd Battalion of the Duke of Cornwall's Light Infantry throughout the Egyptian war of 1882, and was present at the reconnaissance in force from Alexandria on the 5th August, in the engagements at El Magfar and Tel-el-Mahuta, in the two actions at Kassasin, and at the battle of Tel-el-Kebir (Medal with Clasp, and Khedive's Star). Served in the Nile Expedition in 1884-85 with the Mounted Infantry, and was present in the actions of Abu Klea and El Gubat, in the reconnaissance to Metammeh, and in the engagement at Abu Klea Wells on the 16th and 17th February (two Clasps); also served in the operations in the Soudan in 1888 including the engagement at Gemaizah (Clasp, and 4th Class of the Medjidie), and in the operations in August 1889 including the engagement at Toski (Clasp); was present at the capture of Tokar in 1891 (4th Class of the Osmanieh).

[32] Major Sidney served in the Nile Expedition in 1884-85 with the 2nd Battalion of the Duke of Cornwall's Light Infantry, and took part in the operations of the Advance Column under Major General Earle (Medal with Clasp, and Khedive's Star); was present at the capture of Tokar in 1891 (4th Class of the Medjidie).

[33] Captain Stewart served in the Nile Expedition in 1884-85 with the 2nd Battalion of the Duke of Cornwall's Light Infantry (Medal with Clasp, and Khedive's Star).

[35] Captain H. B. Walker served in the Nile Expedition in 1884-85 with the 2nd Battalion of the Duke of Cornwall's Light Infantry, and took part in the operations of the Advance Column under Major General Earle (Medal with Clasp, and Khedive's Star); also served with the Egyptian Frontier Field Force under Brigadier General Butler in 1885-86, and was present in the engagement at Giniss.

Record of the Services of the 2nd *Battalion Duke of Cornwall's Light Infantry,—formerly the* 46th. (*South Devonshire*) *Regiment.*

Raised in 1741 and numbered the 57th. To England, 1742. To Jersey, 1747. Number changed to 46th, 1748. To Ireland, 1749. To Nova Scotia, 1757. To Canada, 1760. To West Indies, 1761. To Canada, 1763. To Ireland, 1767. To America, 1776. To West Indies, 1778. To England, 1782. Received the title of South Devonshire Regiment. To Ireland, 1784. To Gibraltar, 1792. To West Indies, 1794. To England, 1796. To Ireland, 1800. To West Indies, 1808 (attack on Dominica). To England, 1811. To New South Wales, 1884. To India, 1818. To England, 1833. To Ireland, 1835. To Gibraltar, 1839. To West Indies, 1842. To Halifax, N.S., and Montreal, 1845. To Jamaica, 1846. To Nova Scotia, 1847. To England, 1848. To Ireland, 1852. To England, 1854. To the Crimea, 1854 (siege of Sebastopol). To Corfu, 1856. To India, 1858. To England, 1869. To Ireland, 1873. To Bermuda, 1876. To Gibraltar, 1880. To Egypt, 1882. To England, 1886.

The Duke of Wellington's (West Riding Regiment.)

1st Batt., Dover.
2nd Batt., South Africa.

Formerly the 33rd (Duke of Wellington's) and the 76th Regiment of Foot.

Regimental District No. 33.—Halifax.

(The 3rd and 4th Battalions are formed of the 1st and 2nd Battalions 6th West York Militia respectively.)
The Crest and Motto of the Duke of Wellington. "DETTINGEN" "MYSORE" "HINDOOSTAN" (with the Elephant). "SERINGAPATAM" "ALLY GHUR" "DELHI 1803" "LESWARREE" "DEIG" "NIVE" "PENINSULA" "WATERLOO" "ALMA" "INKERMAN" "SEVASTOPOL" "ABYSSINIA."

Years' Ser.			ENSIGN OR 2ND LIEUT.	LIEUT.	CAPTAIN.	BREV. MAJ.	MAJOR.
Full Pay.	Half Pay.						
29	...	**Colonel.**—c. William Nelson Hutchinson, *Ensign*, 24 Feb. 20; *Lt.* 25 Oct. 23; *Capt.* p17 June 26; *Major*, p4 Dec. 32; *Lt. Colonel*, p7 Sept. 41; *Colonel*, 11 Nov. 51; *Major General*, 26 Oct. 58; *Lieut. General*, 17 Aug. 65; *General*, 29 May 73; *Colonel* 33rd Foot, 1 April 63.					
		Lieutenant Colonels.—1 Cecil Conor,¹ *Ensign*, p9 Mar. 67; *Lieut.* p19 Jan. 70; *Captain*, 7 Jan. 79; *Major*, 6 Sept. 82; *Lt. Colonel*, 6 Oct. 92.					
26	...	2 Charles William Gore, *Ensign*, p24 April 69; *Lieut.* 28 Oct. 71; *Captain*, 15 Dec. 79; *Major*, 28 June 84; *Lt. Colonel*, 15 Mar. 94.					
		MAJORS.					
24	...	1 p.s.c. John Charles Duke	23 Sept. 71	28 Oct. 71	24 Aug. 81	......	25 Feb. 85
24	...	2 Vaughan Jenkins⁴ (*Bt. Lt. Colonel*, 1 Sept. 91)	......	30 Dec. 71	1 Oct. 81	......	7 May 86
21	...	1 Arthur Edward Richards Curran	......	11 Sept. 74	1 Oct. 81	......	6 Oct. 86
24	...	2 Lionel Edward Blakeney Booth¹¹	......	10 Jan. 72	6 Sept. 82	6 Sept. 82	20 Aug. 90
20	...	2 Stewart John Trench	......	6 Oct. 75	24 Jan. 83	......	26 Sept. 90
22	...	2 Percy Temple Rivett-Carnac¹²	......	3 July 73	19 Dec. 83	......	6 Oct. 92
21	...	George Herbert Chippindall,⁹ *Adj.* 2 *Vol. Bn. Durham Lt. Inf.* 1 Jan. 92	......	13 June 74	12 Nov. 83	......	13 Dec. 93
21	...	1 James Alex. Skene Thomson¹⁰ (*Depot*)	......	24 Mar. 75	24 Jan. 83	......	15 Mar. 94
		CAPTAINS.					
18	...	George Philip Berkeley Molyneux, *Army Pay Department*	8 Dec. 77	15 Dec. 79	1 Nov. 84		
16	...	2 Hayford Douglas Thorold	14 Jan. 80	1 Jan. 81	28 Oct. 85		
17	...	Francis Macleod Hastings Marshall,¹⁵ *Adj.* 2 *Vol. Bn. West Riding Regt.* 1 Feb. 92	11 May 78	12 Jan. 81	6 Oct. 86		
15	...	2 William Joseph Goold	17 Apr. 80	18 May 81	11 Apr. 87		
15	...	1 Percy Bourdillon Smithe	11 Aug. 80	1 July 81	5 Jan. 88		
15	...	Frederick Arthur Hayden, *Adjutant* 3 *Battalion* 12 Feb. 95	22 Jan. 81	1 July 81	1 Aug. 88		
15	...	1 Basil St. John Le Marchant	19 Feb. 81	1 July 81	1 Aug. 88		
15	...	Arthur William Bentley Buckle	19 Feb. 81	1 July 81	1 Aug. 88		
13	...	2 Herbert Charles Suft	......	9 Sept. 82	19 Sept. 88		
13	...	1 Charles Vesey Humphrys, *Adjutant* 9 Dec. 91	......	9 Sept. 82	19 Sept. 88		
13	...	1 Francis John De Gex	......	9 Sept. 82	17 Oct. 88		
13	...	Clarence Dalrymple Bruce, *Adjutant* 4 *Vol. Bn. Essex Regt.* 18 Nov. 93	......	9 Sept. 82	30 Nov. 88		
13	...	1 William James Anderson	......	10 May 82	6 Aug. 89		
12	...	Owen Harris, *Adj.* 2 *Vol. Bn. West Riding Regt.* 18 Feb. 92	......	30 Jan. 84	12 Feb. 90		
12	...	Arthur Ingram Stewart Godfrey, *Aide de Camp to Major General H. M. Bengough*, 1 Dec. 94	......	6 Feb. 84	31 July 90		
11	...	Oswald Albon Aldersey Taylor, *Adj.* 2 *Guernsey Militia* 2 Mar. 91	......	12 Nov. 84	12 Nov. 90		
11	...	2 Frank Harrison Ainsworth Swanson (*Depot*)	......	7 Feb. 85	11 Feb. 91		
11	...	2 William Milward Watson	......	7 Feb. 85	2 Mar. 91		
10	...	1 Samuel Charles Umfreville	......	6 May 85	2 Mar. 91		
10	...	2 Herbert William Wainman Wood	......	6 May 85	1 Feb. 92		
10	...	1 Edgar Garston Harrison	......	23 May 85	1 Feb. 92		
10	...	1 Edward Raymond Houghton¹⁶	......	23 May 85	18 Feb. 92		
11	...	Frederic Cambridge Theobald, *Army Service Corps*	......	12 Nov. 84	7 Jan. 92		
		LIEUTENANTS.					
10	...	1 Francis David Behrend	......	29 Aug. 85			
9	...	2 Robert Marshall	......	25 Sept. 86			
9	...	2 Henry Wrixon Becher, *Adjutant* 1 July 93	......	8 Dec. 86			
9	...	2 Edward Moutray Kinnaird Parsons (*Depot*)	......	8 Dec. 86			
9	...	2 Neville George Harry Turner	......	8 Dec. 86			
9	...	2 Alexander Frederic Wallis	5 Feb. 87	8 July 89			
8	...	2 James Alec Charles Gibbs	4 May 87	6 Aug. 89			
7	...	2 Thomas Sharpe Smith	10 Nov. 88	11 June 90			
7	...	1 Clement Agnew Fedden	8 Dec. 88	31 July 90			
6	...	2 William Kemp Trotter	9 Nov. 89	11 Feb. 91			
6	...	2 Percy Alexander Turner	21 Dec. 89	2 Mar. 91			
6	...	2 Norman Warden Fraser	1 Mar. 90	26 Aug. 91			
6	...	2 Francis John Thursby-Pelham	29 Mar. 90	1 Feb. 92			
6	...	1 Lawrence George Stayner	29 Mar. 90	1 Feb. 92			
6	...	1 Archibald James Macaulay Higginson	29 Mar. 90	18 Feb. 92			
5	...	1 Norman Bruce Bainbridge	3 May 90	1 Dec. 93			
5	...	1 Kenneth Anderson Macleod	29 Oct. 90	13 Dec. 93			
5	...	1 Herbert Darnton Egerton Greenwood (*Depot*)	29 Oct. 90	1 May 94			
5	...	1 Reginald Winnington Fanshawe	25 Mar. 91	7 Nov. 94			
4	...	1 Frederick John Siordet	2 May 91	30 Jan. 95			
		SECOND LIEUTENANTS.					
4	...	2 Harold Wolstenholme Cobb	23 May 91				
3	...	1 Louis Raymond Acworth (*Depot*)	18 May 92				

¹² Major Rivett-Carnac served with the expedition to the Soudan under Sir Gerald Graham in 1884 (Medal, and Khedive's Star).

¹⁵ Captain F.M.H. Marshall served in the Kafir war in 1878, including the operations against Sekukuni (Medal with Clasp).

¹⁶ Captain Houghton served in the Egyptian war of 1882 (Medal, and Khedive's Star). Served with the Burmese Expedition in 1887-88 (Medal with Clasp).

The Duke of Wellington's (West Riding Regiment).

Years' Ser. Full Pay.	Half Pay.	SECOND LIEUTENANTS.	2ND LIEUT.	
3	...	2 Arthur John Tyler	18 June	92
3	...	1 Percy Belcher Strafford	13 July	92
3	...	1 Arthur Marmaduke Whitaker	28 Sept.	92
3	...	2 Percival Coode	19 Nov.	92
3	...	2 Reginald Ernest Maffett	21 Jan.	93
2	...	2 Vincent John Tighe	7 Feb.	94
2	...	2 William Edwin Drielsma	7 Mar.	94
1	...	1 Robert Napier Bray	12 Dec.	94
1	...	William Ernest Marriott Tyndall	6 Mar	95

Facings White.—*Agents*, Messrs. Cox and Co.

1st Battalion returned from India, 18 Dec. 1889.
2nd Battalion embarked for Bermuda, 6 Oct. 1886.

| 7 | ... | *Quarter Masters.*—1 James Thomas Seaman,[14] 5 Sept. 88; *Hon. Lieut.* |
| 1 | ... | 2 Charles Hyde, 19 Sept. 94; *Hon. Lieut.* |

[1] Lt.Colonel Conor served with the 33rd Regiment throughout the Abyssinian campaign of 1867-68, and was present at the storming and capture of Magdala (Medal).
[4] Lt.Colonel Jenkins served with the Miranzai Expedition in 1891 under Sir William Lockhart as Assistant Adjutant General after Major Egerton had been wounded (mentioned in despatches, Brevet of Lt.Colonel, Medal with Clasp).
[7] Major Chippindall served with the Buffs in the operations in the Malay Peninsula in 1875-76 (Medal with Clasp).
[10] Major Thomson served with the 3rd Goorkhas in the Afghan war in 1880, and was present in the engagements at Ahmed Kheyl and Urzoo near Ghuznee, and in the subsequent operations in the Logar Valley (Medal with Clasp). Served in the Bechuanaland Expedition in 1884-85 under Sir Charles Warren with the Corps of Guides.
[11] Major Booth served in the Afghan war in 1879-80 with the force under Major General Roberts in the Koorum Valley, superintended the Transport during the advance on Cabul, and was present in the engagement at Charasiah on the 6th October 1879 (mentioned in despatches) and in the operations around Cabul in December 1879; accompanied Sir Frederick Roberts in the march to Candahar as Staff Transport Officer, and was present at the battle of Candahar (mentioned in despatches, Medal with three Clasps, and Bronze Decoration). Served with the Indian Contingent in the Egyptian war of 1882, and was present at the battle of Tel-el-Kebir (Medal with Clasp, and Khedive's Star).
[14] Lieut. Seaman served in the Abyssinian war in 1867-68, and was present at the assault and capture of Magdala (Medal).

Record of the Services of the 2nd Battalion of the Duke of Wellington's (West Riding Regiment),— formerly the 76th Regiment.

Raised in 1787 and proceeded to India, 1788. To England, 1806 (Mahratta war of 1803—granted the distinction of "Hindustan"). To Jersey, 1807. To England, 1808. To Spain, 1808 (battle of Corunna). To England, 1809. To Ireland, 1810. To Spain and France, 1813 (battle of Nive). To Canada, 1814. To Ireland, 1827. To West Indies, 1834. To Bermuda, 1840. To Halifax, Nova Scotia, 1841. To Ireland, 1842. To England, 1843. To Scotland, 1846. To England, 1847. [2nd Battalion raised 1847; disbanded, 1850.] To Ionian Islands, 1848. To Malta, 1851. To Halifax, Nova Scotia, 1853. To England, 1857. To India, 1863. To Burmah, 1868. To England, 1876. To Ireland, 1880. To England, 1885. To Bermuda, 1886. To Halifax, Nova Scotia, 1888. To West Indies, 1891.

Continuation of Notes to the South Staffordshire Regiment.

[36] Captain Sears served with the 1st Battalion South Staffordshire Regiment in the Egyptian war of 1882, and was present in the reconnaissance in force from Alexandria on the 5th August (Medal, and Khedive's Star). Served on the Staff of the Battleford Column throughout the campaign in the North West of Canada in 1885, and was present in the engagement at Cut Knife Hill; commanded a scout corps in the pursuit of Big Bear (three times mentioned in despatches, Medal).
[37] Captain Bridge served with the 1st Battalion of the South Staffordshire Regiment in the Egyptian war of 1882 (Medal, and Khedive's Star). Served with the Nile Expedition in 1884-85, and was present at the action of Kirbekan (two Clasps).
[40] Captain Glover served in the Nile Expedition in 1884-85, and was present at the action of Kirbekan (Medal with two Clasps, and Khedive's Star).
[44] Captain Barlow served with the Nile Expedition in 1884-85 (Medal with Clasp, and Khedive's Star). Served with the Soudan Frontier Field Force during the operations on the Upper Nile in 1885-86.
[45] Captain Hon. J. G. R. U. Colborne served with the Nile Expedition in 1884-85, and was present at the action of Kirbekan—severely wounded (Medal with two Clasps, and Khedive's Star). Served with the Soudan Frontier Field Force during the operations on the Upper Nile in 1885-86.
[46] Captain Billings served in the Egyptian war of 1882 (Medal, and Khedive's Star); also served with the Nile Expedition in 1884-85, and was present at the action of Kirbekan (two Clasps). Served with the Soudan Frontier Field Force during the operations on the Upper Nile in 1885-86.

Record of the Services of the 1st South Staffordshire Regiment (formerly the 38th Regiment).

Raised in 1702. On Sea Service, 1707 to 1710. To Antigua, 1710. To the West Indies, 1739. To Antigua, 1750. To England, 1765, after 58 years' foreign service. To America, 1774. To England, 1784. To Flanders, 1795. To the West Indies, 1796. [2nd Battalion raised in 1804, and disbanded in 1814—records lost.] To the Cape of Good Hope, 1805. To South America, 1806 (capture of Monte Video). To Ireland, 1807. To Spain, 1808 (battles of Roleia, Vimiera, and Corunna). To England and Ireland, 1809. To the Peninsula, 1811 (battles of Busaco, Badajoz, Salamanca, Vittoria, St. Sebastian and Nive). To Ireland and England, 1814. To the Netherlands, 1815. To England, 1815. To the Cape of Good Hope, 1818. To India, 1822. To Burmah, 1824 ("Ava"). To India, 1826. To England, 1836. To Ireland, 1837. To the Ionian Islands, 1840. To Gibraltar, 1843. To Jamaica, 1846. To Halifax, Nova Scotia, 1848. To England, 1851. To the Crimea, 1854 (battles of Alma and Inkerman and siege of Sebastopol). To England, 1856. To India, 1857 (capture of Lucknow). To England, 1872. To Ireland, 1877. To Malta, 1880. To Egypt, 1882 (war of 1882). To Malta, 1883. To Egypt and the Soudan 1884 ("Nile, 1884-85"— battle of Kirbekan). To Gibraltar, 1886. To Egypt, 1891. To England, 1893.

1st Batt., Woolwich.
2nd Batt., On Field Service, Waziristan.] **The Border Regiment.** [*Regimental District No. 34.—Carlisle.*

Formerly the 34th (The Cumberland) and 55th (Westmoreland) Regiments.
(The 3rd and 4th Battalions are formed of the Cumberland and Westmoreland Militia respectively.)
A Laurel Wreath. "ALBUHERA" "ARROYO DOS MOLINOS" "VITTORIA" "PYRENEES" "NIVELLE" "NIVE" "ORTHES" "PENINSULA" "CHINA" (with the Dragon). "ALMA" "INKERMAN" "SEVASTOPOL" "LUCKNOW."

Years' Ser. Full Pay.	Half Pay.			Ensign or 2nd Lieut.	Lieut.	Captain.	Brev. Maj.	Major.
		Colonels.—1 General *Sir* Richard Denis Kelly,[1] *KCB. Ens.* 7 Mar. 34; *Lt.* P30 July 36; *Capt.* P24 Sept. 41 *Major,* P17 Mar. 48; *Bt.Lt.Colonel,* 12 Dec. 54; *Lt.Colonel,* 9 Mar. 55; *Colonel,* 30 Jan. 58; *Major General,* 6 Mar. 68; *Lieut.General,* 1 Oct. 77; *General,* 5 Nov. 80; *Colonel* Royal Irish Regiment, 24 Jan. 86; *Colonel* 1 Battalion Border Regiment, 9 Mar. 89.							
		2 *Sir* Henry Charles Barnston Daubeney,[2] *GCB. Ensign,* 12 March 29; *Lt.* 9 Aug. 31; *Capt.*P28 Oct. 36; *Bt.Major,* 23 Dec. 42; *Major,* P25 Nov. 45; *Bt.Lt.Colonel,* 20 June 54; *Lt.Colonel,* 9 March 55; *Colonel,* 10 Sept. 57; *Major General,* 6 Mar. 68; *Lieut.General,* 1 Oct. 77; *General,* 4 March 80; *Colonel* 55th Foot, 3 Feb. 79.							
36	...	**Lieutenant Colonels.**—1 John Olphert Gage, *Ensign,* P16 Mar. 60; *Lt.* P2 Sept. 62; *Capt.* P5 Jan. 70; *Major,* 1 July 81; *Lt.Colonel,* 1 July 91.						
30	...	2 Charles George Brind, *Ensign,* P12 Jan. 66; *Lt.* P5 Jan. 70; *Capt.* 27 Feb. 80; *Major,* 20 Oct. 83; *Lt.Colonel,* 20 Oct. 93.						
		Majors.						
28	...	1 John Henry Edward Hinde	P 4 April 67	19 Jan. 70	7 Jan. 80	......	31 Mar. 86
25	...	2 Jefferson Serrell Wood	P28 May 70	P27 Oct. 71	23 June 80		15 May 89
25	...	1 Robert Williams Andrews	P 6 July 70	28 Oct. 71	6 Sept. 81		20 Oct. 89
25	...	1 Pierce Edward Hughes	P12 Nov. 70	28 Oct. 71	1 Dec. 80		19 Jan. 90
22	...	1 Arthur Dillon Denis Kelly	......	12 Nov. 73	13 Aug. 83		1 July 91
21	...	2 Gerald Hedley Ovens	......	21 Sept. 74	20 Oct. 83		9 July 91
18	...	1 Charles George Donaldson	......	15 July 77	15 May 84		28 Mar. 93
17	...	2 Hamilton Macdonald Richards	22 Jan. 79	27 Feb. 80	21 Jan. 85		20 Oct. 93
		Captains.					
17	...	2 Joseph Langton	22 Jan. 79	31 Jan. 80	15 Nov. 84		
16	...	1 John Stannus Pelly	14 Jan. 80	6 Mar. 80	1 July 85		
18	...	1 John Colin Wardlaw	8 Dec. 77	16 Aug. 80	20 Jan. 86		
17	...	Robert Henry Gage Heygate, *serving with the Egyptian Army, with rank of Major*	1 May 78	19 Sept. 80	28 Mar. 86		
15	...	Lindsay Henryson Caird, *Adjutant 1 Vol. Bn. Border Regt.* 16 May 93	7 Aug. 80	8 June 81	1 July 87		
16	...	2 John Page Wood, **Adjutant** 24 June 91	13 Aug. 79	1 July 81	19 Nov. 88		
14	...	Algernon Montgomerie Caulfeild,[8] *DSO. Adj.* 2 *Vol. Bn.* 1 Jan. 95	......	17 Dec. 81	27 Mar. 89		
15	...	Hervey Sandby Mayhew, *Dep.Assist. Adj. Gen.forMusk.Bengal,* 31 Mar.94	23 Oct. 80	1 July 81	15 May 89		
15	...	1 William Fleetwood Nash,[9] **Adjutant** 9 Jan. 94	22 Jan. 81	1 July 81	20 Oct. 89		
14	...	2 Charles Edward Hyacinth Cooch	23 Apr. 81	1 July 81	1 Jan. 90		
14	...	1 Julian Edmund Spicer Probyn	......	28 Jan. 82	19 Jan. 90		
19	...	Bartle Grant,[10] *Adjutant Rangoon Volunteer Rifles* 25 Nov. 93	......	22 May 76	14 Nov. 83		
13	...	2 David James Welsh (*Depot*)	......	10 May 82	24 June 91		
13	...	1 William John Ferguson-Davie	......	10 May 82	24 June 91		
12	...	Percy John Bellamy, *Adjutant 4 Battalion* 18 Dec. 93	......	25 Aug. 83	17 Dec. 91		
13	...	2 Henry Montague Shallett O'Brien	......	10 May 82	30 Dec. 91		
12	...	George Browne, *Adjutant Moulmein Rifle Volunteers* 19 May 92	......	5 Dec. 83	10 Mar. 93		
12	...	1 *p.s.c.* Edward Martin Dunne	......	6 Feb. 84	10 Mar. 93		
11	...	2 Reginald de Blaquière Chichester	......	14 May 84	28 Mar. 93		
11	...	2 Robert Arthur Browne,[12] *Supt. of Signalling, Waziristan Field Force*	......	23 Aug. 84	31 Mar. 94		
8	...	2 Charles Ernest Wynell-Mayow[13]	7 May 87	21 Aug. 89	7 Nov. 94		
		Lieutenants.					
9	...	2 George Herbert Ledward	......	25 Aug. 86			
9	...	2 Robert Ouseley Cuthbert Hume (*Depot*)	......	25 Aug. 86			
9	...	1 Harry Denison Tuson	......	25 Aug. 86			
9	...	2 Lewis Ironside Wood	5 Feb. 87	2 May 89			
8	...	1 Lee Oliver FitzMaurice Stack	11 Feb. 88	14 Sept. 89			
7	...	2 Arthur Lyon	22 Aug. 88	9 July 90			
7	...	2 Francis Courtenay Marsh	10 Nov. 88	9 July 90			
7	...	2 Archibald Skirving Woollery Moffat	10 Nov. 88	9 July 90			
7	...	2 James Tindal Ives Bosanquet	23 Mar. 89	3 July 91			
6	...	2 Charles Davies Vaughan	8 June 89	11 Nov. 91			
6	...	2 Ewen George Sinclair-MacLagan	21 Dec. 89	2 Mar. 92			
6	...	2 George Cecil Brooke	1 Mar. 90	21 Sept. 92			
5	...	2 Frank Evelyn Coningham	8 Oct. 90	6 Oct. 92			
5	...	2 Cecil Toogood	29 Oct. 90	21 Dec.			
5	...	2 Seignelay Gustavus Willoughby Hume	29 Nov. 90	1 Feb. 93			
4	...	2 George Fletcher Broadrick	10 Oct. 91	28 Mar. 93			
4	...	1 Colin Lawrance Macnab	10 Oct. 91	9 Aug. 93			
4	...	1 Arthur Erskine St. Vincent Pollard (*Depot*)	7 Nov. 91	16 Aug. 93			
4	...	2 Edward Savi Earle	5 Dec. 91	8 Dec. 94			
		Second Lieutenants					
4	...	2 Arthur Frederick Hamilton Pigott	27 Jan. 92				
4	...	1 Frank George Grier Morris	12 Mar. 92				
3	...	2 Harry Ernest Chapman	9 Apr. 92				
3	...	2 Charles Herford Pringle	19 Oct. 92				
3	...	1 George Ernest Warren	19 Nov. 92				
3	...	1 Percy Frederick Brunel Hawes	21 Jan. 93				
2	...	1 Arthur Robt. Seignelay Lyon-Campbell	10 May 93				
2	...	2 Arthur Brownrigg Decy Spedding	20 May 93				
2	...	1 William Lynn Allen	9 Sept. 93				
2	...	1 Arthur Lyster Longhurst	9 Sept. 93				
1	...	Louis Edm. Harington Molyneux-Seel	12 Dec. 94				
1	...	Thomas Wm. Houssemayne du Boulay	6 Mar. 95				

The Border Regiment.

Years' Ser.	
Full Pay.	Half Pay.
14	...
6	...

Paymasters.—1
2 Reginald de B. Chichester, *Lieut.* 2 *Battalion (acting).*
Quarter Masters.—1 James King, 17 Dec. 81; *Hon. Captain,* 17 Dec. 91.
2 William Richards, 24 July 89; *Hon. Lieut.*

Facings White.—*Agents,* Messrs. Cox and Co.
1st Batt. *returned from India,* 14 Dec. 1890. 2nd Batt. *embarked for Malta,* 3 Nov. 1888.

---

[1] Sir Richard Denis Kelly served with the 34th Regt. at the siege of Sebastopol in 1855; commanded the Guards in the Trenches on the 22nd March, when he was wounded and taken prisoner in a sortie of the Russians (Medal with Clasp, Brevet of Lt. Colonel, Knight of the Legion of Honor, 5th Class of the Medjidie, and Turkish Medal). Served in the Indian campaigns of 1857-59; commanded the 34th Regt. in the actions at Cawnpore on 26th, 27th (wounded), and 28th Nov. 1857, capture of Meeangunge, siege and capture of Lucknow, and relief of Azimghur; commanded the Azimghur Column in the operations in Oude in the winter of 1858-59; commanded a Field Force from Feb. to May 1859, engaged in the operations on the Nepaul Frontier, and defeated the rebels under Bala Rao near Bootwul (horse shot), capturing six guns and much baggage (thanked by the Governor General and the Commander in Chief, frequently mentioned in despatches, *CB.*, Medal with Clasp, *KCB.*, and distinguished service pension).
[2] Sir Charles Daubeney served with the 55th Regt. in the Coorg campaign, East Indies, in 1834, and was present at the assault and capture of the stockade of Kissenhully, and at the attack on the stockade of Soamwarpettah, where he had charge of one of the two guns attached to the Column, which by his perseverance and exertions he saved from capture during the retreat; served during the Chinese war of 1841-42, commanded the Light Company at the repulse of the enemy's night-attack at Chinhae, and at the storm and capture of Chapoo; served on the Staff as Major of Brigade to Sir James Schoeddeat Woosung, Shanghai, and Chin Kiang Foo—twice mentioned in despatches (Medal, Brevet Major, and *CB.*). Served the Eastern campaign of 1854, including the battles of Alma and Inkerman (wounded and horse shot), siege of Sebastopol, and repulse of the sortie of 26th October. Commanded the 55th Regiment, and subsequently the 1st Brigade 2nd Division at the battle of Inkerman. Mentioned in division orders and in the report of Sir De Lacy Evans for the battle of the Alma, and in the despatches for Inkerman. Was Gazetted to a Substantive Lieutenant Colonelcy for Inkerman on 12th Dec. 1854, but declined accepting a promotion which would have removed him from the seat of war and placed him on half pay whilst his Regiment was serving in the field. Reward for distinguished services, 1855: Medal with three Clasps, Knight of the Legion of Honor, Turkish Medal, 4th Class of the Medjidie, *KCB.* in 1871 and *GCB.* in 1884.
[7] Major Ovens served in the Afghan war in 1880 as Superintendent of Army Signalling with the Khyber Line Force and also with the Khyber Division of the Northern Afghanistan Field Force under Lieut. General Bright (Medal). [See also Civil Decorations for Gallantry, "Hart's Annual Army List," p. 786.]
[8] Captain Caulfeild served with the 66th Regiment in the Afghan war of 1878-80, and was present in the engagement on the Helmund against the Wali's mutinous troops, in the action at Maiwand (wounded) and the subsequent defence of Candahar (Medal, and Medal for distinguished conduct in the field). Served with the Burmese Expedition in 1886-88 as Brigade Transport Officer to Brigadier General Low (mentioned in despatches, *DSO.*, and Medal with two Clasps). Served with Mounted Infantry in Upper Burmah in 1889-90 (Clasp).
[9] Captain Nash served with the Tonhon Expedition, Burmah, as Staff and Treasure Chest Officer to the Momeit Column (Medal with Clasp).
[10] Captain Grant served in the Afghan war in 1879-80 (Medal).
[12] Captain R. A. Browne served with the Isazai Expedition in 1892 as Assistant Superintendent of Army Signalling.
[13] Captain Wynell Mayow served in the Egyptian war of 1882 with the 4th Dragoon Guards, and was present in the engagement at El Magfar and Tel-el-Mahuta, in the two actions at Kassasin, at the battle of Tel-el-Kebir, and the capture of Cairo (Medal with Clasp, and Khedive's Star).

Record of the Services of the 2nd Battalion The Border Regiment (formerly the 55th Regiment).

Raised at Stirling in 1755 and numbered the 57th Regiment. Became the 55th Regiment, 1757. To Halifax, N.S., 1757. To North America, 1760. 1761-75, records lost; believed to have returned to England. To North America, 1776. To West Indies, 1779. To England and Scotland, 1785. To Ireland, 1791. To Holland, 1793. To West Indies, 1795. To England, 1797. To Holland, 1799. To England, 1800. To West Indies, 1802. To England, 1812. (Detachment in West Indies, which, except one Company, rejoined Head Quarters in England, 1813.) To Holland, 1813. (Company from Jamaica rejoined Head Quarters in Holland, 1814.) To England, 1814. To Ireland, 1820. To England, 1821. To Cape of Good Hope, Dec. 1821. To India, 1830. To China, 1841 (war of 1842). To England, 1844. To Ireland, 1846. To Gibraltar, 1851. To Turkey and the Crimea, 1854 (battles of Alma and Inkerman and siege of Sebastopol). To Gibraltar, 1856. To England and Ireland, 1857. To England, 1860. To India, 1863. To England, 1877. To Malta, 1888. To India, 1890.

1st Batt., Fermoy.
2nd Batt., Dum Dum, Bengal.] **The Royal Sussex Regiment.** [*Regimental District No. 35.—Chichester.*

Formerly the 35th (Royal Sussex) and the 107th (Bengal Infantry) Regiments.
(The 3rd and 4th Battalions are formed of the 1st and 2nd Battalions Sussex Militia respectively.)
The United Red and White Rose.   "LOUISBURG"   "QUEBEC, 1759"   "MAIDA"   "EGYPT, 1882"   "NILE, 1884-85"
"ABU KLEA."

Years' Ser. Full Pay	Half Pay		Ensign or 2nd Lieut.	Lieut.	Captain.	Brev. Maj.	Major.
		Colonel.—Robert Julian Baumgartner,[1] *CB., Ens.* [P]27 Sept. 33; *Lieut.* [1]30 June 37; *Capt.* [2]23 April 41; *Major,* 23 Sept. 51; *Lt. Colonel,* 12 Dec. 54; *Colonel,* 6 April 60; *Major General,* 6 March 68; *Lieut. General,* 1 Oct. 77; *General,* 1 July 81; *Colonel Royal Sussex Regiment,* 12 Jan. 88.					
24	...	**Lieutenant Colonels.**—1 Arthur Sampson Hector Gem,[10] *Ensign,* 28 Oct. 71; *Lieut.* 28 Oct. 71; *Captain,* 10 Feb. 80; *Major,* 10 Nov. 83; *Lt. Colonel,* 6 Aug. 94.					
24	...	2 Charles Haydon Wilkinson Cafe,[11] *Ensign,* 28 Oct. 71; *Lieut.* 28 Oct. 71; *Captain,* 12 June 80; *Major,* 5 Mar. 84; *Lt. Colonel,* 2 Feb. 95.					
		MAJORS.					
24	...	2 George Harden[15]	......	30 Dec. 71	19 Feb. 81	......	6 Aug. 84
27	...	2 Walter Illingworth Haynes	[P]18 April 68	6 July 70	23 July 79	......	26 May 84
20	...	1 George Leonard Thomson (*Depot*)	......	28 May 75	26 July 82	......	18 Feb. 91
20	...	1 Benjamin Donisthorpe Alsop Donne[17]	......	10 Sept. 75	20 Oct. 83	28 Dec. 88	10 Feb. 92
19	...	John Charles Farrell, *Adjutant* 1 *Cinque Ports Rifle Vols.* 19 Jan. 91	......	6 Sept. 76	10 Nov. 83	......	26 Oct. 92
19	...	p.s.c. Jas. Chas. Young,[21] *D.A.A. Gen. for Inst. C. of G. Hope,* 23 Jan. 92	......	11 Nov. 76	5 Mar. 84	......	6 Aug. 94
22	...	1 Ribton Gore[26]	......	28 Feb. 74	5 Mar. 84	......	14 Nov. 94
17	...	Edward Wheler	22 Jan. 79	23 July 79	29 July 84	......	2 Feb. 95
		CAPTAINS.					
18	...	2 Charles Russell	......	10 Sept. 77	29 July 84		
16	...	2 Louis Eugene du Moulin[23]	14 Jan. 80	12 June 80	18 Apr. 85		
16	...	1 John Ernest Pierson[24]	13 Aug. 79	2 Oct. 80	1 Apr. 85		
16	...	1 Charles Henry Asbhurst[20]	8 Oct. 79	1 July 81	2 Feb. 87		
15	...	Henry Browse Scaife,[26] *Adjutant 3 Battalion* 24 Nov. 93	23 Oct. 80	1 July 81	11 Nov. 89		
15	...	Reginald Popys Whately,[21] *Adjutant 1 Vol. Bn. Sussex Regt.* 19 Oct. 90	23 Oct. 80	1 July 81	11 Nov. 89		
15	...	1 Osmond Cecil Le Marchant[26]	19 Feb. 81	1 July 81	6 Aug. 90		
15	...	Joseph Smythe Egginton,[29] *Adjutant 1 Vol. Bn. Derbyshire Regt.* 1 Sept. 92	19 Feb. 81	1 July 81	19 Oct. 90		
15	...	Hugh Hammond Massy O'Grady,[20] *Adj. 2 Vol. Bn. Sussex Regt.* 7 Mar. 91	19 Feb. 81	1 July 81	19 Jan. 91		
14	...	John Gerald Panton, *Adj. 2 Vol. Bn. Argyll & Suth. Highldrs.* 15 Dec. 93	......	22 Oct. 81	2 Feb. 91		
13	...	Duncan Dunbar Brogden, *Adjutant 4 Vol. Bn. Scottish Rifles* 21 Sept. 91	......	29 July 82	18 Feb. 91		
13	...	2 Charles Theobald Walsh Church[29]	......	29 July 82	21 Dec. 91		
13	...	2 Frederick St. Duthus Skinner,[29] *at Staff College*	......	9 Aug. 82	23 Jan. 92		
13	...	1 Proby Edward Payne Crawfurd[20]	......	9 Sept. 82	10 Feb. 92		
13	...	1 Arthur Robert Gilbert[29]	......	9 Sept. 82	1 Sept. 92		
12	...	1 Edmund Bulteel Hawker[31]	......	30 Jan. 84	26 Oct. 92		
12	...	2 Malcolm Hiley Burne[29]	......	30 Jan. 84	5 Apr. 93		
12	...	2 Ernest Henry Montrésor[32]	......	6 Feb. 84	6 Aug. 93		
11	...	2 Richard Alexander Kane,[33] *Adjutant* 1 Sept. 91	......	14 May 84	6 Aug. 94		
11	...	2 Norman M'Farlane	......	7 Feb. 85	23 Jan. 95		
9	...	1 Harold Jellicorse	......	10 Nov.	2 Feb. 95		
		LIEUTENANTS.					
9	...	1 James Harold Burbury	5 Feb. 87	26 Feb. 90			
9	...	1 Mostyn Eden Cookson	5 Feb. 87	6 Aug. 90			
8	...	1 Henry Scott[29]	4 May 87	19 Oct. 90			
7	...	2 John Frederick Paltock Langdon	9 May 88	2 Feb. 91			
7	...	1 Norman Atkinson Layton, *Adjutant* 24 Nov. 93	10 Nov. 88	25 Mar. 91			
7	...	2 Charles Powlett Aldridge (*Depot*)	19 Dec. 88	22 Apr. 91			
6	...	2 William Arthur Gardiner (*Depot*)	24 Apr. 89	15 July 91			
6	...	1 Thos. Faulconer Mair Wisden	28 Aug. 89	16 Sept. 91			
6	...	1 Edgar Walter Butler Green	29 Mar. 90	23 Dec. 91			
5	...	2 Edward Leslie Mackenzie	29 Oct. 90	10 Feb. 92			
5	...	2 William Lushington Osborn	29 Nov. 90	10 Feb. 92			
5	...	2 Alfred Edgar Glasgow	4 Mar. 91	13 Apr. 92			
5	...	2 Josiah Howard Hudson	4 Mar. 91	1 Sept. 92			
4	...	2 Percy Selby Cookson	25 July 91	31 May 93			
4	...	2 Bertram Rochfort Daunt	10 Oct. 91	19 Nov. 93			
4	...	Francis Aylmer Maxwell	7 Nov. 91	24 Nov. 93			
4	...	2 Sydney Drummond Worgan	9 Jan. 92	15 Dec. 93			
4	...	1 Charles James Kinahan Maguire	12 Mar. 92	30 May 94			
3	...	1 Alfred Penrose Mark-Wardlaw	9 Apr. 92	6 Aug. 94			
3	...	2 Frederic Woodall	18 May 92	23 Jan. 95			
3	...	Aubrey St. John Cooke	18 May 92	2 Feb. 95			
3	...	1 Robert Chaloner Griffin	19 Oct. 92	2 Feb. 95			
		SECOND LIEUTENANTS.					
3	...	1 Alfred Robert Davis	17 Dec. 92				
3	...	1 Richard Percival Wemyss Quin	15 Feb. 93				
2	...	2 Herbert Henry Elliott	26 Apr. 93				
2	...	2 Stuart Girdlestone Halliday	21 Oct. 93				
2	...	2 John Bartholomew Wroughton	23 Dec. 93				
2	...	1 Albert Gouldsmith	23 Dec. 93				
1	...	1 Robert Bellamy	2 June 94				
5	...	2 Robert Hugh Cotes	25 Mar. 91				
1	...	2 St. George Ross Beresford	20 Oct. 94				
1	...	1 Stanley de Vere Alexander Julius	10 Oct. 94				
1	...	Edward Martin Crawley-Boevey	6 Mar. 95				

Years' Ser.	
Full Pay.	Half Pay.
11	...
1	...

Paymasters.—2 William L. Osborn, *Lieut. 2nd Battalion (acting).*
Quarter Masters.—2 William Speak,[34] 24 Sept. 84; *Hon. Captain.* 24 Sept. 94.
1 Robert Pearce, 7 Nov. 94; *Hon. Lieut.*

Facings Blue.—*Agents*, Messrs. Cox and Co.
1st Battalion returned from Egypt, 11 Sept. 1885. 2nd Battalion embarked for Malta, 1882.

[1] General Baumgartner served in the Eastern campaign of 1854-55 with the 28th Regt., including the battles of Alma and Inkerman, siege and fall of Sebastopol, and affair on the 18th June in the Cemetery (succeeded to the command of the Regt.); was wounded in the Trenches 17th Aug. 1855 (mentioned in despatches, Medal with three Clasps, *C.B.*, Sardinian and Turkish Medals, and 4th Class of the Medjidie).

[10] Lt.Colonel Gem served in the Nile Expedition in 1884-85 with the 1st Battalion of the Royal Sussex Regiment, took part in the operations of the Desert Column under Sir Herbert Stewart, including the action at Abu Klea, and commanded a detached post at that station (Medal with two Clasps, and Khedive's Star).

[11] Lt.Colonel Cafe served in the Egyptian war of 1882, and was present at the surrender of Kafr Dowar (Medal, and Khedive's Star).

[15] Major Harden served in the Egyptian war of 1882 (Medal, and Khedive's Star). Served in the Nile Expedition in 1884-85 with the 1st Battalion of the Royal Sussex Regiment, and took part in the operations of the Desert Column under Sir Herbert Stewart, including the action at Abu Klea (two Clasps). Served in the Hazara campaign in 1888 with the 2nd Battalion Royal Sussex Regiment (Medal with Clasp).

[17] Major Donne served in the Egyptian war of 1882 with the 1st Battalion of the Royal Sussex Regiment (Medal, and Khedive's Star); also served throughout the Nile Expedition in 1884-85 on the Line of Communications with the Egyptian Army and as Commandant at Absarat (Clasp, 4th Class of the Medjidie). Served in the operations near Suakin in December 1888 and commanded the 10th Soudanese Battalion in the engagement at Gemaizah (mentioned in despatches, Brevet of Major, Clasp); also commanded the Battalion in the operations on the Nile Frontier in 1889 and was present in the engagements at Arghin and Toshki (mentioned in despatches, Clasp, and 3rd Class of the Medjidie). Has also been nominated to the 3rd Class of the Osmanieh for services in Egypt.

[20] Major Gore, Captains Ashhurst, O'Grady, and Crawfurd served in the Nile Expedition in 1884-85 with the 1st Battalion of the Royal Sussex Regiment, and took part in the operations of the Desert Column under Sir Herbert Stewart (Medal with Clasp, and Khedive's Star).

[21] Major Young and Captain Whately served in the Egyptian war of 1882 (Medal, and Khedive's Star). Served in the Nile Expedition in 1884-85 with the 1st Battalion of the Royal Sussex Regiment, and took part in the operations of the Desert Column under Sir Herbert Stewart (Clasp).

[23] Captain du Moulin served in the Hazara campaign in 1888 with the 2nd Battalion Royal Sussex Regiment (mentioned in despatches, Medal with Clasp). Served with the Chin-Lushai Expeditionary Force in 1889-90 on Transport duty (mentioned in despatches, Clasp); and with the Manipore Expeditionary Force in 1891 as Brigade Transport Officer to the Silchar Column (Clasp).

[24] Captain Pierson served throughout the Egyptian war of 1882 as Regimental Transport Officer of the left half of the 1st Battalion Royal Sussex Regiment, and was present at the surrender of Kafr Dowar and Damietta (Medal and Khedive's Star). Served in the Nile Expedition in 1884-85 as Adjutant to the 1st Battalion of the Royal Sussex Regiment, and took part in the operations of the Desert Column under Sir Herbert Stewart (Clasp).

[26] Captain Scaife served in the Egyptian war of 1882 with the 1st Battalion of the Royal Sussex Regiment, and was present at the defence of Alexandria, the surrender of Kafr Dowar, and the occupation of Damanhour (Medal, and Khedive's Star). Served in the Nile Expedition in 1884-85 as Regimental Transport Officer of the 1st Battalion of the Royal Sussex Regiment (Clasp).

[28] Captain Le Marchant served in the Egyptian war of 1882 (Medal, and Khedive's Star). Served in the Nile Expedition in 1884-85 with the 1st Battalion of the Royal Sussex Regiment, and took part in the operations of the Desert Column under Sir Herbert Stewart including the action at Abu Klea (two Clasps). Served in the Hazara campaign in 1888 with the 2nd Battalion Royal Sussex Regiment (Medal with Clasp). [See also Civil Decorations for Gallantry, "Hart's Annual Army List," p. 786.]

[29] Captains Egginton, Church, Skinner, Gilbert, and Burne, and Lieut. Scott served in the Hazara campaign in 1888 with the 2nd Battalion Royal Sussex Regiment (Medal with Clasp).

[31] Captain Hawker served with the Burmese Expedition in 1886-87 (Medal with Clasp). Served in the Hazara campaign in 1888 with the 2nd Battalion Royal Sussex Regiment (Clasp).

[32] Lieut. Montrésor served with the Nile Expedition in 1884-85 (Medal with Clasp, and Khedive's Star). Served in the Hazara campaign in 1888 with the 2nd Battalion Royal Sussex Regiment (Medal with Clasp).

[33] Lieut. Kane served in the Nile Expedition in 1884-85 with the 1st Battalion of the Royal Sussex Regiment, and took part in the operations of the Desert Column under Sir Herbert Stewart, including the actions at Abu Klea and El Gubat and the engagements at Metammeh and Abu Klea Wells (Medal with two Clasps, and Khedive's Star). Served in the Hazara campaign in 1888 with the 2nd Battalion of the Royal Sussex Regiment as Regimental Transport Officer (Medal with Clasp).

[34] Captain Speak served in the Afghan war in 1879-80 (Medal).

Record of the Services of the 1st Battalion Royal Sussex Regiment,—formerly the 35th (Royal Sussex) Regiment.

Raised in Ireland in 1701 and entitled "The Earl of Donegall's Regiment," and "The Belfast Regiment." To Cadiz and thence to the West Indies, 1702. To Gibraltar, 1704 (siege). To Spain, 1705 (capture of Barcelona). To Ireland, 1708. To Minorca, 1719. To Ireland, 1736. [2nd Battalion raised in 1748 and reduced in 1749.] Entitled the "35th Foot," 1751. To England, 1756. To North America and Nova Scotia, 1758 (capture of Louisburg). To Quebec, 1759 (battle of Quebec and capture of Montreal). To England, 1765. To Ireland, 1773. Entitled "The Prince of Orange's Own Regiment," 1774. To America, 1775 (battle of Bunker's Hill, &c.). To Brunswick, 1777. To the West Indies, 1778. Entitled "The Dorsetshire Regiment," 1782. To England, 1785. To Scotland, 1788. To Ireland, 1791. To the West Indies, 1794. To Gibraltar, 1795. To England, 1796. [2nd Battalion raised in 1799 and reduced in 1802.] To Malta, 1800. Entitled "The Sussex Regiment," 1804. To Italy, 1805 (battle of Maida). [2nd Battalion re-formed, 1805.] To Egypt (capture of Alexandria, &c.) and back to Sicily, 1807. To England, 1808. To Holland and England, 1809. To Holland, 1814. To Belgium (battle of Waterloo), Paris, and England, 1815. Reduced, 1817.] To the Ionian Islands, 1809. To Italy, 1813. To the Ionian Islands, 1815. To Malta, 1816. To England, 1817. To Ireland, 1819. To the West Indies, 1821. To England, 1832. Entitled "The 35th Royal Sussex Regiment," 1832. To Ireland, 1834. To Mauritius, 1837. To England and Ireland, 1848. To England, 1852. To the East Indies, 1853 (Indian Mutiny). To England, 1868. To Ireland, 1873. To the West Indies, 1875. To Malta, 1879. To Cyprus, 1880. To Egypt, 1882. To the Soudan, 1884 (battle of Abu Klea). To England, 1885. To Ireland, 1891.

Record of the Services of the 2nd Battalion Royal Sussex Regiment (formerly the 107th Regiment).

Raised in 1853 in Bengal (Mutiny and Central India campaigns). Proceeded to England, 1875. To Guernsey, 1879. To Ireland, 1880. (Entitled "2nd Battalion the Royal Sussex Regiment," 1881.) To Malta, 1882. To Egypt and India, 1885 (Hazara Expedition of 1888).

281 1st Batt., Ranikhet, Bengal.
2nd Batt., Curragh.
The Hampshire Regiment. [Regimental District No. 37.—Winchester.

Formerly the 37th (North Hampshire) and the 67th (South Hampshire) Regiments.
(The 3rd Battalion is formed of the Hampshire Militia.)
"BLENHEIM" "RAMILLIES" "OUDENARDE" "MALPLAQUET" "DETTINGEN" "MINDEN" "TOURNAY" "BARROSA" "PENINSULA" "INDIA" (with the Royal Tiger). "TAKU FORTS" "PEKIN" "CHARASIAH" "KABUL, 1879" "AFGHANISTAN, 1878-80" "BURMA, 1885-87."

Years' Ser. Full Pay	Half Pay			Ensign or 2nd Lieut.	Lieut.	Captain	Bvt.Maj.	Major
33	...	Colonel.—John Wellesley Thomas,¹ CB, Ensign, 7 June 39; Lieut. P7 Sept. 41; Captain, P14 May 47; Brevet Major, 3 Dec. 54; Major, 25 Apr. 55; Lt.Colonel, 31 Dec. 58; Colonel, 31 Dec. 63; Major General, 8 July 69; Lieut.General, 1 July 81; Colonel Hampshire Regiment, 15 Dec. 93.							
29	...	Lieutenant Colonels.—2 John Eyles Blundell,⁴ Ensign, 16 Jan. 63; Lieut. P20 April 67; Capt. P12 Nov. 70; Major, 1 July 81; Lt.Colonel, 29 Aug. 92.							
		1 William Henry Moberly, Ensign, 7 Aug. 66; Lieut. P30 March 67; Capt. 25 Jan. 78; Major, 8 Sept. 81; Lt.Colonel, 11 Dec. 92.							
		MAJORS.						
25	...	1 Hammond Astley Tapp⁸		P22 Mar. 71	28 Oct. 71	9 Apr. 81	......	1 Aug. 86
24	...	2 William Egginton Briggs⁹		......	27 Mar. 72	8 June 81	......	29 Aug. 86
27	...	Arthur Reginald Hennell, Dist. Insp. of Musketry, Colchester, 14 July 93		r 1 Apr. 68	28 Oct. 71	1 July 81	......	20 Dec. 90
22	...	Edward Henry LeMarchant,¹³ Inspector of Musketry, Dover, 1 Jan. 93		......	28 Feb. 74	Sept. 83	......	6 Apr. 92
18	...	1 Reginald Percy Macdonald,¹⁰ DSO		30 Jan. 78	28 Mar. 78	15 Apr. 84	......	19 May 92
17	...	2 Charles William Knox¹² (Depot)		11 May 78	15 June 79	14 Feb. 85	......	19 July 93
16	...	1 James Robert Parkinson		2 July 79	11 Oct. 79	26 Aug. 85	......	22 Apr. 94
16	...	William Henry Thackwell, Adjutant 1 Volunteer Battalion 16 Apr. 94		13 Aug. 79	17 Dec. 79	19 Sept. 85	......	6 June 94
		CAPTAINS.						
16	...	1 Arthur Dashwood Bulkeley Buckley (Depot)		27 Aug. 79	17 Apr. 80	19 Sept. 85		
16	...	Howard William Smith,¹⁴ Adjutant 3 Volunteer Battalion 1 July 90		21 June 79	10 Feb. 81	26 July 86		
16	...	p.s.c. Lewis Munro		14 Jan. 80	9 Apr. 81	26 July 86		
15	...	2 Edmund Sclater Crofts¹⁶		11 Aug. 80	1 July 81	29 Aug. 86		
15	...	1 Charles de Winton²⁰		11 Aug. 80	1 July 81	15 Apr. 89		
15	...	William George Wyld,²¹ Adjutant 4 Vol. Bn. Hampshire Regt. 23 June 90		23 Oct. 80	1 July 81	15 Apr. 89		
15	...	2 Richard Cyril Byrne Haking²²		22 Jan. 81	1 July 81	15 Apr. 89		
15	...	1 Robert Inglis Forbes²³		22 Jan. 81	1 July 81	1 July 90		
13	...	George Harvey Nicholson,²⁴ Adjutant 3 Battalion 16 Jan. 93		......	10 May 82	1 July 90		
13	...	2 Sydney Charles Fishburn Jackson,²⁵ DSO.		......	9 Sept. 82	1 July 90		
13	...	Robert HindsGill,²⁶ Ordnance Store Dept.		......	10 Mar. 83	1 July 90		
12	...	Mervyn de Montmorency,²⁷ Adj. 3 Vol. Bn. Argyll & Suth. Highlds. 1 Feb. 94		......	14 May 84	1 July 90		
11	...	2 Hugh Cochrane MacTier²⁸		......	7 Feb. 85	17 Dec. 90		
10	...	1 Frederick Hope Grant Playfair,²⁹ Adjutant 15 Dec. 92		......	20 May 85	20 Dec. 90		
12	...	Herbert Graham Westmorland, Adj. 5 Vol.Bn. Hampshire Regt. 23 Apr. 92		......	5 Dec. 83	3 May 91		
13	...	2 Henry Cecil Lowry Cole		......	9 Sept. 82	10 Feb. 92		
12	4/12	1 Thomas Godfrey Whistler (Depot)		......	25 Aug. 83	17 Aug. 91		
10	...	Richard Mordaunt Barrington,²⁹† Ordnance Store Department		......	29 Aug. 83	19 May 92		
10	...	1 Walter Hugh Trethewy³⁰		......	29 Aug. 85	19 May 92		
10	...	2 Henry di Stella Burford Burford-Hancock, Adjutant 12 June 91		......	25 Nov. 85	19 May 92		
10	...	1 Benj. Hamilton Boucher,³¹ Station Staff Officer, Ranikhet, 1 April 93		......	25 Nov. 85	29 Aug. 92		
9	...	William Prowting Roberts,³² Ordnance Store Department		......	28 Apr. 86	1 Jan. 93		
9	...	2 Norman Charles Welch³³		......	10 Nov. 86	4 July 93		
9	...	2 Arthur Carew Richards³⁴		......	8 Dec. 86	14 July 93		
8	...	1 Harold Deane Ozzard³¹		12 Oct. 87	4 Jan. 90	4 Apr. 94		
7	...	2 Edward Leigh		9 May 88	4 Jan. 90	22 Apr. 94		
		LIEUTENANTS.						
7	...	1 William Dent Bewsher		22 Aug. 88	4 Jan. 90			
7	...	Francis Jearrad Bowker, Aide de Camp to Major Gen. C.B. Knowles 10 Feb. 94		22 Aug. 88	4 Jan. 90			
7	...	1 Henry Barry Orton Coddington (Depot)		6 Mar. 89	1 Nov. 90			
7	...	1 Arthur Bellaine Ennis³⁵		6 June 88	17 Dec. 90			
6	...	2 Morris Vivian Parry		21 Sept. 89	20 Dec. 90			
6	...	1 Walter James Geddes		21 Sept. 89	19 Mar. 91			
6	...	2 Henry John Archibald Banks		9 Nov. 89	22 July 91			
6	...	2 Henry Joseph Walsham Whitaker		21 Dec. 89	1 Jan. 92			
5	...	2 Francis Stewart Kennedy Shaw (Depot)		31 May 90	19 May 92			
5	...	1 Frederick Richard Hicks		8 Oct. 90	10 Aug. 92			
5	...	1 Frank Hay Norie		4 Mar. 91	29 Aug. 92			
4	...	1 Weir de Lancey Williams		17 June 91	17 Sept. 92			
4	...	1 Nelson William Barlow		25 July 91	1 Jun. 93			
4	...	Percy Stanislaus Hicks		25 July 91	4 July 93			
4	...	1 James Craik		7 Nov. 91	14 July 93			
4	...	1 Hew Wakeman Tompson		9 Jan. 92	19 July 93			
4	...	James Robert Gaussen		20 Feb. 92	31 Jan. 94			
4	...	2 Thomas John Hounsfield		12 Mar. 92	10 Feb. 94			
3	...	1 Henry Littleton Wheeler		9 Apr. 92	4 Apr. 94			
4	...	2 Hugo William Millais		29 Apr. 91	22 Apr. 94			
4	...	2 Edwyn Harland		13 July 92	21 June 94			
3	...	1 George Hastings Parker		19 Oct. 92	13 Oct. 94			
		SECOND LIEUTENANTS.						
3	...	Charles Forster Connell		19 Oct. 92				

Years' Ser				
Full Pay	Half Pay	SECOND LIEUTENANTS.	2ND LIEUT.	
3	...	1 Seymour Arthur Dolmé-Radcliffe	17 Dec. 92	[37] Captain Hampton served in the Afghan war in 1879-80 with the 87th Regiment, and was present in the engagement at Charasiab on the 6th October 1879, and in the operations round Cabul in December 1879, including the engagements at Mir Karez and the Asmai Heights and the investment of Sherpore (Medal with two Clasps). Served in the Burmese Expedition in 1885-87 with the 2nd Battalion Hampshire Regiment including the surrender of Mandalay (Medal with Clasp).
3	...	2 Henry Richard Stirke	25 Feb. 93	
2	...	2 John Henry Deane	19 July 93	
2	...	2 Alexander Arthur Lysons Collard	9 Sept. 93	
2	...	2 Arthur Taylor Penny	9 Sept. 93	
2	...	1 Bernard Underwood Nicolay	7 Mar. 94	
1	...	1 John Grattan	18 Apr. 94	
1	...	1 Harold Lake Compton Turner	2 June 94	
1	...	1 *Hon.* Lawrence Charles Walter Palk	4 July 94	
1	...	2 Francis Sandham Geary	10 Oct. 94	
1	...	2 Thomas Faith	23 Jan. 95	
1	...	1 Alfred Montagu Hennell	20 Feb. 95	

Paymasters.—1 Walter H. Trethewy,[30] *Captain* 1 *Battalion* (acting).
2

Quarter Masters.—2 Edward Hampton,[35] 30 Nov. 81; *Hon. Captain*, 30 Nov. 91.

| 14 | ... | 1 Michael Lynch,[31] 13 May 85; *Hon. Lieut.* |
| 10 | ... | |

Facings White.—*Agents*, Messrs. Cox and Co.

1st Battalion embarked for India, 1884. *2nd Battalion returned from India,* 7 *February* 1888.

[1] Lt. General Thomas served with the 40th Regiment throughout the operations in Candahar and Afghanistan in 1841-42 (Medal inscribed "Candahar, Ghuznee, Cabul"). Also in the action of Maharajpore, 29th Dec. 1843—severely wounded (Bronze Star). Commanded Detachments of the 12th and 40th Regiments at the capture of a stockade occupied by insurgents at the Ballarat Gold Fields in Australia on the 3rd Dec. 1854, for which he received the rank of Major. Served with the 67th Regiment throughout the campaign of 1860 in North China, and was wounded while in command of a Wing employed as part of the covering and storming party at the capture of the North Taku Fort (mentioned in despatches, *CB*., Medal with two Clasps). Commanded the 67th Regiment at the second capture of Kading from the Taeping rebels in 1862.

[4] Lt.Colonel Blundell served in China during the Taeping rebellion in 1863 with the 67th Regiment (Medal). Served with the 67th Regiment in the Afghan war in 1879-80, and was present in the operations around Cabul in December 1879, including the engagements at Mir Karez, Khilla Ghazi, and the Asmai Heights and the investment of Sherpore (mentioned in despatches, Medal with Clasp). Served with the Burmese Expedition in 1885-87 as Assistant Adjutant General of the Lower Burmah Division (mentioned in despatches, Medal with Clasp). Commanded an expedition in the Kachin Hills in 1891 against the rebels Khanlaing and Prince Shaw-yan-Naing (Clasp).

[8] Major Tapp served in the Afghan war in 1879-80 with the 67th Regiment (Medal). Served with the Burmese Expedition in 1885-87 (Medal with Clasp).

[9] Major Briggs served in the Afghan war in 1879-80 with the 67th Regiment (Medal). Served with the Burmese Expedition in 1885-86 (Medal with Clasp).

[10] Major Macdonald served in the Afghan war in 1879-80 with the 67th Regiment (Medal). Served in the Burmese Expedition in 1885-87 with the 2nd Battalion Hampshire Regiment including the surrender of Mandalay (Medal with Clasp); also with the 1st Battalion Hampshire Regiment in 1887-89 including the expedition to Mogaung (mentioned in despatches, *DSO*., and Clasp).

[12] Major Knox served in the Burmese Expedition in 1887-89 with the 1st Battalion Hampshire Regiment (Medal with Clasp).

[13] Major Le Marchant served in the Afghan war of 1878-80 with the 67th Regiment (Medal).

[14] Captain Smith served with the 67th Regiment in the Afghan war in 1879-80, and was present in the operations around Cabul in December 1879, including the investment of Sherpore (Medal with Clasp). Served in the Burmese Expedition in 1885-87 with the 2nd Battalion Hampshire Regiment (mentioned in despatches, Medal with Clasp); also served in 1887-89 with the 1st Battalion (Clasp).

[16] Captain Crofts served with the Burmese Expedition in 1887 (Medal with Clasp).

[20] Captain de Winton served with the Burmese Expedition in 1887-89 with the 1st Battalion Hampshire Regiment (Medal with Clasp).

[21] Captain Wyld served with the Burmese Expedition in 1887-89 with the 1st Battalion Hampshire Regiment (Medal with Clasp).

[22] Captain Haking served with the Burmese Expedition in 1885-86 (mentioned in despatches, Medal with Clasp).

[23] Captain Forbes served with the Burmese Expedition in 1885-86 (mentioned in despatches, Medal with Clasp).

[24] Captain Nicholson served with the Burmese Expedition in 1887-89 with the 1st Battalion Hampshire Regiment, part of the time in the Intelligence Branch, Upper Burmah Field Force (Medal with Clasp).

[25] Captain Jackson served in the Burmese Expedition in 1885-88 with the 2nd Battalion of the Hampshire Regiment in the advance on Mandalay, and afterwards in command of a company of Mounted Infantry; subsequently served as Aide de Camp to Sir George White, Commanding the Burmah Field Force (mentioned in despatches, Medal with Clasp); also served with the Chin Field Force in 1888-89 as Aide de Camp to Sir George White, Commanding the Upper Burmah Field Force (mentioned in despatches, *DSO*. and Clasp). Served with the Zhob Field Force in 1890 as Aide de Camp to Sir George White, Commanding the Zhob Valley Expedition.

[26] Captain Gill served with the Burmese Expedition in 1885-86 (Medal with Clasp).

[27] Captain de Montmorency served in the Burmese Expedition in 1885-87 with the 2nd Battalion Hampshire Regiment (Medal with Clasp); also served in 1887-89 with the 1st Battalion (Clasp).

[28] Captain MacTier served with the Burmese Expedition in 1885-89 (Medal with two Clasps).

[29] Captain Playfair served with the Burmese Expedition in 1885-87 on Transport duty (Medal with Clasp), and in 1887-89 (Clasp).

[29†] Captain Barrington served with the Burmese Expedition in 1885-87 (Medal with Clasp).

[30] Captain Trethewy served with the Burmese Expedition in 1886-87 (mentioned in despatches, Medal with Clasp).

[31] Captains Boucher and Ozzard and Lieut. Lynch served in the Burmese Expedition in 1887-89 with the 1st Battalion Hampshire Regiment (Medal with Clasp).

[32] Captain Roberts served with the Burmese Expedition in 1886-87 (Medal with Clasp).

[33] Lieut. Welch served with the Burmese Expedition in 1887 (Medal with Clasp).

[34] Captain Richards served in the Burmese Expedition in 1887-89 with the 1st Battalion Hampshire Regiment—slightly wounded (Medal with Clasp).

[35] Lieut. Ennis served with the Burmese Expedition in 1889-90 (Medal with Clasp).

Record of the Services of the 2nd Battalion Hampshire Regiment (formerly the 67th Regiment).

Raised in 1756 from the 2nd Battalion 20th Regiment. Siege of Belleisle, 1761. To England, 1762. To Portugal, 1762. To Minorca, 1763. To England, 1771. To Scotland, 1773. To Ireland, 1775. Entitled "South Hampshire Regiment," 1782. To the West Indies, 1785. To Ireland, 1794. To St. Domingo, 1796. To Jamaica, 1798. To England, 1801. To Ireland and Guernsey, 1803. [Second Battalion raised in 1803. To Channel Islands, 1804. To Gibraltar and Cadiz, 1810. To Tarifa, 1811 (battle of Barrosa). To Gibraltar, 1814. To England and disbanded, 1817.] To England, 1804. To India, 1805 (badge of "India" with the Royal Tiger). To England, 1826. To Ireland, 1830. To Gibraltar, 1832. To the West Indies, 1833. To Canada, 1840. To England, 1842. To Ireland, 1844. To Gibraltar, 1848. To the West Indies, 1851. To England, 1857. To India, 1858. To China, 1859 (war of 1860, including the capture of Taku Forts and Pekin, and the operations against the Taiping rebels in 1862-63). [Right Wing to Japan, 1864 (occupation of Yokohama)]. To the Cape of Good Hope, 1865. To Ireland, 1866. To England, 1868. To British Burmah, 1872. To India, 1876 (Afghan war of 1878-80, including the battle of Charasiah, the capture of Cabul, and the investment of Sherpore). Entitled "2nd Battalion Hampshire Regiment," 1881. To Burmah, 1885 (surrender of Mandalay). To India, 1887. To England, 1888.

1st Batt., Lichfield.
2nd Batt., Egypt.
] **The South Staffordshire Regiment.** [Regimental District No. 38.—Lichfield.

Formerly the 38th (1st Staffordshire) and the 80th (Staffordshire Volunteers) Regiments.
(The 3rd and 4th Battalions are formed of the 1st Stafford Militia.)

"EGYPT" (with the Sphinx). "MONTE VIDEO" "ROLEIA" "VIMIERA" "CORUNNA" "BUSACO" "BADAJOZ" "SALAMANCA" "VITTORIA" "ST. SEBASTIAN" "NIVE" "PENINSULA" "AVA" "MOODKEE" "FEROZESHAH" "SOBRAON" "PEGU" "ALMA" "INKERMAN" "SEVASTOPOL" "LUCKNOW" "CENTRAL INDIA" "SOUTH AFRICA, 1878–9" "EGYPT, 1882" "NILE, 1884–85" "KIRBEKAN."

Years' Ser. Full Pay.	Half Pay.		2ND LIEUT.	LIEUT.	CAPTAIN.	BREV.MAJ.	MAJOR.
		Colonel.—Hon. Sir St. George Gerald Foley,[1] KCB. Ensign, P29 June 32; Lt. P27 May 36; Capt. P3 Aug. 41; Bt.Major, 19 Oct. 49; Bt.Lt.Colonel, 12 Dec. 54; Major, 22 Aug. 56; Colonel, 13 Apr. 58; Lt.Colonel, 4 Jan. 61; Major General. 6 Mar. 68; Lieut.General, 1 Oct. 77; General, 10 July 81; Colonel South Staffordshire Regiment, 15 Sept. 81.					
23	...	2 **Lieutenant Colonels.**—John Edward Hale Prior,[9] Ensign,[P21] Mar. 68; Lt. 30 Aug. 71; Capt. 18 Nov. 77; Bt.Major, 29 Nov. 79; Major, 19 July 82; Lt.Colonel, 11 Feb. 91; Colonel, 11 Feb. 95.					
22	...	1 Archibald Borthwick Horsbrugh,[12] Lieut. 28 Feb. 74; Capt. 5 April 81; Major, 11 Feb. 85; Lt.Colonel, 11 Feb. 95.					
		MAJORS.					
22	...	2 William Moore[14]	......	28 Feb. 74	4 Oct. 81	......	18 Nov. 88
21	...	1 Henry Charles Savage[16]	......	13 June 74	3 Feb. 82	......	23 Aug. 89
19	...	George Evan Lloyd,[17] DSO. Governor General of the Red Sea Littoral, with rank of Lt.Colonel	......	22 Nov. 76	20 June 83	15 June 85	1 Nov. 90
21	...	1 Martin Thackeray[18]	......	21 Sept. 74	19 July 82	......	11 Feb. 91
21	...	1 William Henry Morris Bent[19] (Depot)	......	28 Feb. 75	3 Mar. 83	......	10 May 93
19	...	2 George Backhouse Sandham	......	17 May 76	2 Oct. 83	......	2 May 94
19	...	2 Newton Seymour Allen[21]	......	6 Oct. 76	31 Oct. 83	......	27 June 94
17	...	Charles Herbert Wylly,[22] Adjutant 3 Battalion 21 Jan. 91	......	11 Sept. 78	20 Nov. 83	......	11 Feb. 95
		CAPTAINS.					
17	...	Alexander George Chesney,[23] Adjutant Royal Malta Militia 1 Feb. 90	......	11 Nov. 78	20 Nov. 83		
18	...	Herbert Aveling Raitt,[25] serving with the Egyptian Army	27 Mar. 78	9 July 79	26 Jan. 84		
17	...	Charles Owen Hore,[26] serving with Mounted Infantry, Egypt	11 May 78	8 May 80	27 Jan. 85		
17	...	2 Edward Kaye Daubeney,[27] DSO.	11 May 78	1 Dec. 80	7 Aug. 86		
17	...	George Albanus Williams,[28] Adjutant Provisional Battalion 1 May 91	22 Jan. 79	2 Feb. 81	24 Aug. 87		
P15	...	1 Harry Warry Steward[32]	23 Oct. 80	1 July 81	7 Dec. 87		
15	...	2 Ivone Kirkpatrick[33]	23 Oct. 80	1 July 81	5 May 88		
15	...	Harry Campbell Chads[34]	23 Oct. 80	1 July 81	29 Dec. 88		
15	...	Egerton Stanley Pipe-Wolferstan[35]	22 Jan. 81	1 July 81	1 Apr. 89		
14	...	James Walker Sears,[36] Adjutant 1 Vol. Bn. 7 Dec. 92	......	1 July 81	10 Apr. 89		
14	...	2 William Cyprian Bridge,[37] Staff College	......	22 Oct. 81	23 Aug. 89		
13	...	2 Ponsonby John Loftus Tottenham (Depot)	......	28 June 82	1 Dec. 89		
12	...	1 Robert Frederick Broughton Glover[40]	......	26 Mar. 84	1 Nov. 90		
11	...	1 Edward Bury Grogan	......	14 May 84	11 Feb. 91		
16	11/19	George Hearn, Ordnance Store Dept.	22 Jan. 79	1 July 81	11 Feb. 91		
11	...	Hon. Jas. Graham Raymond Ulysses Colborne,[45] Aide de Camp to Lt.Gen. Montgomery Moore, 1 June 93	......	23 Aug. 84	11 Feb. 91		
12	...	George Nuttall Going, Adjutant 4 Battalion 30 July 94	......	31 Oct. 83	1 Nov. 90		
11	...	Harry Barlow,[44] Adj. 2 Vol. Bn. South Stafford Regt. 1 Aug. 93	......	23 Aug. 84	30 Dec. 91		
11	...	2 Walter Frank Corbett (Depot)	......	28 Feb. 85	26 Feb. 92		
10	...	Hume Greenfield, Adjutant 3 Vol. Battalion 15 Jan. 94	......	9 May 85	10 May 93		
10	...	1 Digby Hildyard Barker	......	29 Aug. 85	1 June 93		
10	...	2 Robert Cosens	......	30 Jan. 86	1 Aug. 93		
10	...	1 Edward Daubeny Griffith Richards	......	30 Jan. 86	18 June 94		
8	...	2 Edward Layton	21 May 87	2 July 90	20 June 94		
8	...	1 Reginald Bethune, Visct. Garnock	16 Nov. 87	5 June 89	30 July 94		
		LIEUTENANTS.					
7	...	2 Charles Steer Davidson	16 May 88	23 Aug. 89			
7	...	2 Robert Montgomery Ovens	23 Mar. 89	25 June 90			
7	...	2 Arthur Watson	23 Mar. 89	25 June 90			
6	...	1 Henry Ernest Walshe (Depot)	8 June 89	24 Oct. 90			
6	...	1 John Thomas Medlycott	6 July 89	28 Jan. 91			
6	...	1 Edmond Vernon Cuppage	6 July 89	28 Jan. 91			
6	...	1 Swynfen John Jervis	21 Dec. 89	15 July 91			
6	...	1 Louis Cooke Kettle	29 Mar. 90	15 July 91			
5	...	1 Edward Charles Philippi Bridges	3 May 90	15 July 91			
5	...	2 Arthur Charles Buckle, Adjutant 1 Jan. 94	3 May 90	15 July 91			
5	...	2 Charles Augustus Carruthers (Depot)	28 June 90	30 Dec. 91			
5	...	2 George William Robsch Paul	29 Nov. 90	13 Apr. 92			
5	...	2 Thomas Ormsby	18 Feb. 91	23 Dec. 92			
5	...	1 Edward Richard Whishaw, Adjutant 11 Feb. 95	25 Mar. 91	10 May 93			
5	...	Pelham Maitland Home	25 Mar. 91	1 June 93			
4	...	2 George Edward Wickham Legg	2 May 91	1 Aug. 93			
4	...	1 Archibald Henry Daukes	23 May 91	5 Mar. 94			
4	...	2 Clarence Herbert Garratt	23 May 91	18 June 94			
4	...	2 Alexander Thomas Blackwood	9 Jan. 92	30 July 94			
3	...	2 Arthur David Skinner	18 June 92	9 Nov. 94			
		SECOND LIEUTENANTS.					
3	...	1 Donald Wm. Auchinbreck Campbell	18 June 9				

Years' Ser.			2ND LIEUT.	
Full Pay	Half Pay	SECOND LIEUTENANTS.		
3	...	2 Fernand Gustave Eugene Cannot	13 Aug. 92	
3	...	2 George William Robert Stacpoole	19 Oct. 92	
3	...	2 William Kingsmill Bernard	25 Feb. 93	
2	...	2 George Noel Deans	26 Apr. 93	
2	...	2 Basil Andrew Corbett	19 July 93	
2	...	1 George Marjoribanks Renny	23 Dec. 93	
2	...	1 Francis Hearle Parkin	23 Dec. 93	
1	...	2 John Frederick Loder-Symonds	2 June 94	
1	...	1 Sidney Chaytor Welchman	10 Oct. 94	
1	...	1 Vernon George Waldegrave Kell	10 Oct. 94	
1	...	2 Cecil Frederick Grant Lang	12 Dec. 94	
1	...	Godfrey Francis Evans Wardell	6 Mar. 95	

Paymasters.—1
2

11 ... *Quarter Masters.*—1 Mathew Billings,[46] 27 Aug. 84; *Hon. Captain*, 27 Aug. 94.
1 ... 2 George Richard Blogg, 23 May 94; *Hon. Lieut.*

[32] Captain Steward served in the operations of the Soudan Frontier Field Force in 1885-86 (Medal, and Khedive's Star).
[33] Captain Kirkpatrick served in the Nile Expedition in 1884-85, and was present at the action of Kirbekan (Medal with two Clasps, and Khedive's Star).

Facings White.—*Agents*, Messrs. Cox and Co.
1st Battalion embarked for Malta, 1880.
2nd Battalion embarked for Egypt, 18 Feb. 93.

[1] General the Hon. Sir St. George Foley served in the Eastern campaign in 1854-56, as Assistant Commissioner at the Head Quarters of the French Army, and was present at the battles of Alma, Balaklava, Inkerman, and Tchernaya, the siege and fall of Sebastopol (Medal with four Clasps, Brevet of Lt.Colonel, CB., Officer of the Legion of Honor, 4th Class of the Medjidie, and Turkish Medal). Served as Military Secretary to the expeditionary force in China from March 1857 to Feb. 1860; was present at the capture of Canton in Dec. 1857 (Brevet of Colonel), and other affairs in the neighbourhood. Served throughout the campaign as British Commissioner at the Head Quarters of the French Army in China from Feb. 1860 to March 1861, and was present at the storming and capture of the Taku Forts, the actions of the 18th and 21st September—in the latter commanded 200 French Mounted Artillerymen, 50 Chasseurs d'Afrique, and a squadron of' Fane's Horse—horse shot (mentioned in French despatches, and made Commander of the Legion of Honor), and subsequent advance on Pekin (good service pension, Medal with three Clasps).

[9] Colonel Prior served with a detachment of the 80th Regiment in the Perak Expedition in 1875-76 (Medal with Clasp). Proceeded on special service to South Africa at the commencement of the Zulu war in 1879; and was present with the Frontier Light Horse in the engagement at Zlobane Mountain; was Orderly Officer to Colonel Buller at the affair at Upoko River, and was present at the engagement at Ulundi and in the reconnaissance on the previous day (twice mentioned in despatches. Brevet of Major); served in the subsequent operations against Sekukuni as Staff and Orderly Officer to Colonel Harrison (Medal with Clasp).

[12] Lt.Colonel Horsbrugh served in the operations against Sekukuni in 1878 and also in 1879, and was present at the storming of the stronghold (Medal with Clasp). Served with the 1st Battalion South Staffordshire Regiment in the Egyptian war of 1882, and was present in the reconnaissance in force from Alexandria on the 5th August (Medal, and Khedive's Star). Served in the Nile Expedition in 1884-85, and was present at the action of Kirbekan —severely wounded (two Clasps).

[14] Major Moore served with the 80th Regiment in the operations against Sekukuni in 1878 and throughout the Zulu war of 1879, part of the time as District Adjutant of the Transvaal (Medal with Clasp). Served with the 1st Battalion South Staffordshire Regiment in the Egyptian war of 1882, and was present in the reconnaissance in force from Alexandria on the 5th August (Medal, and Khedive's Star). Served in the Nile Expedition in 1884-85 with the 1st Battalion of the South Staffordshire Regiment, and took part in the operations of the River Column under Major General Earle, including the action of Kirbekan (two Clasps).

[16] Major Savage served in the Kafir war in 1878 including the operations against Sekukuni (Medal with Clasp).

[17] Lt.Colonel Lloyd served with the 51st Light Infantry in the Jowaki campaign in 1877 (Medal with Clasp). Served with the 51st Light Infantry in the Afghan war in 1878-9, and was present at the attack and capture of Ali Musjid (Medal with Clasp). Served during the Nile Expedition in 1884-85 as Commandant at Tangur (mentioned in despatches, Brevet of Major, Medal with Clasp, 4th Class of the Medjidie, and Khedive's Star); also served with the Soudan Frontier Field Force in 1885-87, including the engagements at Giniss (mentioned in despatches, DSO.) and Sarras (3rd Class of the Medjidie); in the operations near Suakin in December 1888 including the engagement at Gemaizah (mentioned in despatches, Clasp); and in the operations in 1889 including the engagement at Toski (mentioned in despatches, Clasp).

[18] Major Thackeray served with the 1st Battalion South Staffordshire Regiment in the Egyptian war of 1882 (Medal, and Khedive's Star).

[19] Major Bent served with the 1st Battalion of the South Staffordshire Regiment in the Egyptian war of 1882, and was present in the reconnaissance in force from Alexandria on the 5th August (Medal, and Khedive's Star). Served with the Nile Expedition in 1884-85, and was present at the action of Kirbekan (two Clasps). Served with the Soudan Frontier Field Force during the operations on the Upper Nile in 1885-86.

[21] Major Allen served with the 1st Battalion of the South Staffordshire Regiment in the Egyptian war of 1882, and was present in the reconnaissance in force from Alexandria on the 5th August (Medal, and Khedive's Star). Served with the Nile Expedition in 1884-85, and was present at the action of Kirbekan (two Clasps).

[22] Major Wylly served with the 1st Battalion of the South Staffordshire Regiment in the Egyptian war of 1882 (Medal, and Khedive's Star); also served with the Nile Expedition in 1884-85, and was present at the action of Kirbekan (two Clasps).

[23] Captain Chesney served as Adjutant with the 1st Battalion South Staffordshire Regiment in the Egyptian war of 1882, and was present in the reconnaissance in force from Alexandria on the 5th August (mentioned in despatches, Medal, 5th Class of the Medjidie, and Khedive's Star). Served with the Nile Expedition in 1884-85 (Clasp).

[25] Captain Raitt served in the Kafir war in 1878 including the operations against Sekukuni; served in the Zulu war in 1879 and in the subsequent operations against Sekukuni including the capture of the stronghold (Medal with Clasp). Served in the Bechuanaland Expedition under Sir Charles Warren in 1885 in command of a troop of the 3rd Mounted Rifles (Diamond Fields Horse).

[26] Captain Hore served in the Egyptian war of 1882, first with the 1st Battalion South Staffordshire Regiment and afterwards with the Mounted Infantry, and was present in the reconnaissance in force from Alexandria on the 5th August, in the engagements at El Magfar, Tel-el-Mahuta, and Kassasin (9th September), and at the battle of Tel-el-Kebir (Medal with Clasp, 5th Class of the Medjidie, and Khedive's Star). Served in the Nile Expedition in 1884-85 with the Mounted Infantry, and was present at the action of Abu Klea (two Clasps).

[27] Captain Daubeney served with the 80th Regiment in the left attack against Sekukuni in 1878, in the Column under Colonel Rowlands on the Swazi border in 1879, and during the invasion of Zululand and the engagement at Ulundi (Medal with Clasp). Served with the Nile Expedition in 1884-85 (Medal with Clasp, and Khedive's Star); also served with the Egyptian Frontier Field Force in 1885-86 as Aide de Camp to Brigadier General Butler. Commanding 1st Brigade, and was present at the engagement at Giniss (DSO.).

[28] Captain Williams served in the Zulu war in 1879, and in the subsequent operations against Sekukuni (Medal with Clasp). Served with the Nile Expedition in 1884-85, and was present at the action of Kirbekan (Medal with two Clasps, and Khedive's Star).

[34] Captain Chads served with the 1st Battalion of the South Staffordshire Regiment in the Egyptian war of 1882 (Medal, and Khedive's Star). Served with the Nile Expedition in 1884-85, and was present at the action at Kirbekan (two Clasps). Served with the Soudan Frontier Field Force during the operations on the Upper Nile in 1885-86.

[35] Captain Pipe-Wolferstan served with the 1st Battalion South Staffordshire Regiment in the Egyptian war of 1882 (Medal, and Khedive's Star). Served with the Soudan Frontier Field Force during the operations on the Upper Nile in 1885-86.

[*For remainder of Notes, see end of Duke of Wellington's (West Riding Regiment), p. 277a.*

283 | 1st Batt., Wellington, Madras. | **The Dorsetshire Regiment.** | [*Regimental District* No. 39.—Dorchester.]
2nd Batt., Belfast. | |

Formerly the 39th (The Dorsetshire) and the 54th (West Norfolk) Regiments.
(The 3rd Battalion is formed of the Dorset Militia.)
"PRIMUS IN INDIA." "PLASSY" "GIBRALTAR" with the Castle, Key, and "*Montis Insignia Calpe.*" "EGYPT" (with the Sphinx). "MARABOUT" "ALBUHERA" "VITTORIA" "PYRENEES" "NIVELLE" "NIVE" "ORTHES" "PENINSULA" "AVA" "MAHARAJPORE" "SEVASTOPOL."

Years' Ser. Full Pay	Half Pay		Ensign or 2nd Lieut.	Lieut.	Captain.	Brev. Maj.	Major.
		Colonel.—Henry Ralph Browne,[1] Ensign, 3 Apr. 46; *Lt.* [P]19 Sept. 48; *Capt.* [P]28 Dec. 49; *Bt. Major*, 2 Nov. 55; *Major*, 1 Feb. 66; *Lt. Colonel*, [P]15 June 58; *Colonel*, 18 Sept. 64; *Major General*, 15 Jan. 70; *Lt. General*, 1 Jan. 85; *General*, 8 July 85; *Colonel* Dorsetshire Regiment, 24 Oct. 94.						
31	…	**Lieutenant Colonels.**—2 Caledon Philip Egerton,[11] Ensign, [P]3 Mar. 65; *Lieut.* [P]22 July 68; *Capt.* 18 Jan. 79; *Major*, 18 Nov. 82; *Lt. Colonel*, 19 Nov. 91.					
25	…	1 John Morpott Piercy, Ensign, [P]24 Dec. 70; *Lieut.* 28 Oct. 71; *Capt.* 6 April 81; *Major*, 25 Sept. 89; *Lt. Colonel*, 28 Aug. 94.					
		MAJORS.					
26	…	2 Cecil Henry Law[12]	7 July 69	28 Oct. 71	24 Jan. 83	……	21 June 90
23	…	1 Martyn John Edward Fenwick	……	3 Aug. 72	12 Sept. 83	……	21 June 90
20	…	2 Horace John James Kentish	……	10 Sept. 75	19 Mar. 84	……	31 Dec. 90
20	…	2 David Farrer (*Depot*)	……	20 Nov. 75	18 July 84	……	10 Sept. 91
19	…	p.s.c. Joseph Howard Poett,[13] *Dep. Assist. Adj. Gen., London,* 16 Dec. 92	……	11 Sept. 76	18 July 84	……	19 Nov. 91
20	…	2 Henry Blosse Lynch	……	11 Feb. 76	22 Nov. 84	……	28 Mar. 94
16	…	1 Stephen Eaton Lamb	14 Jan. 80	1 Jan. 81	14 Apr. 86	……	28 Aug. 94
22	…	John Tyrwhitt-Walker,[14] *Adj. 2 Vol. Bn. Derbyshire Regt.* 20 Mar. 93	……	28 Feb. 74	6 Jan. 86	……	13 Feb. 95
		CAPTAINS.					
19	…	Edward Hesketh Goddard, *Adjutant 2 Vol. Bn. Essex Regt.* 1 June 91	31 Jan. 77	1 Apr. 80	17 Aug. 87		
16	…	Lionel Edmund Lushington, *Adjutant 3 Battalion* 19 Sept. 94	13 Aug. 79	1 July 81	21 Nov. 87		
15	…	1 Knox Edward Harris	11 Aug. 80	1 July 81	25 Sept. 89		
16	…	1 Frederick Geale Todd-Thornton[18]	13 Aug. 79	1 July 81	1 Oct. 86		
13	…	2 p.s.c. William John Bonus	……	9 Sept. 82	21 June 90		
13	…	2 Robert Arthur Godwin-Austen	……	10 Mar. 83	5 July 90		
12	…	1 Edward Keane Ridley	……	19 Dec. 83	31 Dec. 90		
12	…	Pownoll Ramsay Phipps, *Staff Captain, Cairo,* 1 Jan. 93	……	6 Feb. 84	31 Dec. 90		
11	…	2 Arlington Augustus Chichester, at *Staff College*	……	23 Aug. 84	11 Mar. 91		
11	…	1 Henry Louis Rosher	……	7 Feb. 85	19 Nov. 91		
11	…	2 Arthur Herbert Platt	……	28 Feb. 85	12 Feb. 92		
10	…	Claude Buchanan Tugwell, *serving with Egyptian Constabulary*	……	6 May 85	6 Apr. 92		
10	…	1 Frederick Hildebrand Awdry (*Depot*)	……	6 May 85	6 Apr. 92		
10	…	2 Frederick Law Williams	……	23 May 85	15 May 92		
10	…	2 Barrington Frederick Powys Pratt-Barlow, **Adjutant,** 9 Mar. 92	……	23 May 85	15 May 92		
10	…	1 William Sykes Banks	……	9 May 85	5 May 93		
8	…	1 Joseph John Asser, **Adjutant** 11 Jan. 93	14 Sept. 87	31 July 89	5 May 93		
9	…	1 Richard Percy John Codrington	5 Feb. 87	9 Dec. 85	16 July 93		
8	…	1 Henry Septimus Hammond	14 Sept. 87	18 Sept. 89	28 Mar. 94		
7	…	2 Edward Hood Shrapnel Boxer	22 Aug. 88	19 Feb. 90	28 Aug. 94		
		LIEUTENANTS.					
7	…	2 Arthur Edward Ross Mangles	10 Nov. 88	8 Mar. 90			
7	…	1 Cecil Alured Rowley	10 Nov. 88	21 June 90			
7	…	2 William Reginald Arnold	8 Dec. 88	5 July 90			
6	…	1 Bertie St. John Clarkson	3 Apr. 89	5 July 90			
6	…	1 Edward FitzClarence	14 Aug. 89	31 Dec. 90			
6	…	2 Herbert Michael Shiel	9 Nov. 89	31 Dec. 90			
6	…	2 Richard Fitzgerald Wm. Ferris Leslie	21 Dec. 89	5 Feb. 91			
6	…	2 Henry Dacre Lowry	21 Dec. 89	11 Mar. 91			
6	…	1 Francis Fowke	21 Dec. 89	15 Dec. 91			
6	…	1 Frank Edward Allfrey	1 Mar. 90	15 Jan. 92			
5	…	1 Oliver Philip Stanhope Ingham (*Depot*)	3 May 90	12 Feb. 92			
5	…	2 Henry Barrows Household (*Depot*)	29 Oct. 90	9 Mar. 92			
5	…	2 Richard Harte Keatinge Butler	29 Oct. 90	6 Apr. 92			
5	…	1 Edward Ernest Charles Dalgliesh	29 Oct. 90	15 May 92			
5	…	Hugh Arthur Mansel	29 Nov. 90	26 Oct. 92			
5	…	2 Herbert Say Codrington	4 Mar. 91	5 May 93			
4	…	1 Horace George Thomson Costley	5 Dec. 91	1 Jan. 94			
4	…	1 Reginald Trevor Roper	27 Jan. 92	28 Mar. 94			
3	…	1 Hugh Norman Ramsay Cowie	18 May 92	29 Aug. 94			
3	…	1 Charles Sydney Herbert Waymouth	18 June 92	29 Oct. 94			
		SECOND LIEUTENANTS.					
3	…	1 Hugh Bateman Smith	13 July 92				
3	…	1 Stewart James MacTier	13 Aug. 92				
3	…	2 Clarence Weston	19 Oct. 92				
3	…	1 Cathcart Christian Hannay	19 Nov. 92				
3	…	1 Thomas Herbert Shoubridge	15 Mar. 93				
2	…	2 Henry John Russell	19 July 93				
2	…	1 James Christopher Hewett	24 Jan. 94				
2	…	2 Frederick Walter Radcliffe	7 Mar. 94				
1	…	2 Cecil Godfrey Hay	16 May 94				
1	…	1 John Maxwell Elphinstone-Dalrymple	2 June 94				
1	…	Frank William Rowland Hill	20 Feb. 95				
1	…	Archibald Ariel Mercer	6 Mar. 95				

[11] Lt. Colonel Egerton served with the Mahsood Wuzeeree Expedition in 1881 (mentioned in despatches).
[12] Major Law served in the Afghan war in 1878-79 with the Khyber Division (Medal).
[13] Major Poett served in the Afghan war in 1880 (Medal). Served with the Bechuanaland Expedition under Sir Charles Warren in 1884-85.

[*For remainder of Notes, see end of South Lancashire Regiment, p. 284a.*]

Paymasters.—2
1 Henry L. Rosher, *Captain* 1 Battalion (*acting*).
9 ... *Quarter Masters.*—2 Thomas Henry Barratt, 14 Apr. 86; *Hon. Lieut.*
11 ... 1 William Kerr, 28 Aug. 84; *Hon. Lieut.*
Facings, White.—*Agents,* Messrs. Cox and Co.
1st Battalion embarked for Malta, 8 Feb. 88. 2nd Battalion returned from Aden, 24 Dec. 86.

The Prince of Wales' Volunteers (South Lancashire Regiment). 284

1st Batt., Cork.
2nd Batt., Kamptee, Bombay. *Formerly the 40th (2nd Somersetshire) and the 82nd (Prince of Wales' Volunteers) Regiments.*   [Regimental District No. 40.—Warrington.

(The 3rd Battalion is formed of the 4th Lancashire Militia.)

The Prince of Wales's Plume. "LOUISBURG" "EGYPT" (with the Sphinx). "MONTE VIDEO" "ROLEIA" "VIMIERA" "TALAVERA" "BADAJOZ" "SALAMANCA" "VITTORIA" "PYRENEES" "NIVELLE" "ORTHES" "TOULOUSE" "PENINSULA" "NIAGARA" "WATERLOO" "CANDAHAR" "GHUZNEE and CABOOL 1842" "MAHARAJPORE" "SEVASTOPOL" "LUCKNOW" "NEW ZEALAND."

Years' Ser.			
Full Pay	Half Pay		
30	...	Colonel.—Augustus Henry Lane Fox-Pitt-Rivers,¹ *Ensign and Lt.* ᴾ16 May 45; *Lt. and Capt.* ᴾ2 Aug. 50; *Brevet Major*, 12 Dec. 54; *Capt. and Lt.Colonel*, ᴾ15 May 57; *Colonel*, 22 Jan. 67; *Major General*, 1 Oct. 77; *Lt.General*, 1 Oct. 82; *Colonel* South Lancashire Regiment, 3 March 93.	
28	5/12	Lieutenant Colonels.—2 Charles Linton, *Ensign*, ᴾ21 Nov. 65; *Lt.* ᴾ24 Sept. 70; *Capt.* 1 May 78; *Major*, 25 July 83; *Lt.Colonel*, 27 March 93.	
		p.s.c. Alexander Henry Fraser,² *Ensign*, 11 Jan. 67; *Lieut.* ᴾ15 Sept. 69; *Capt.* 31 Jan. 78; *Major*, 29 Oct. 81; *Lt.Colonel*, 21 Apr. 93.	

		MAJORS.	ENSIGN OR 2ND LIEUT.	LIEUT.	CAPTAIN.	BREV. MAJ.	MAJOR.
26	...	1 William M'Carthy O'Leary	ᴾ17 April 69	ᴾ15 Feb. 71	20 Mar. 78	......	13 Aug. 83
22	...	2 Arthur Francis George Richardson	......	5 Oct. 73	15 Mar. 80	......	13 July 87
25	...	2 Chas. Adolphus de Peyron Burroughs	ᴾ12 Oct. 70	28 Oct. 71	8 Sept. 81	......	8 Dec. 89
24	...	1 Robert Howden Kellie	......	30 Dec. 71	29 Oct. 81	......	11 Dec. 92
22	...	1 Reginald Hawkins Hall (*Depot*)	......	12 Nov. 73	15 July 83	......	27 Mar. 93
22	...	Francis Robert Millington Synge, *Adj. 4 Bn. Liverpool Regt.* 16 June 90	......	23 Nov. 73	15 July 83	......	8 Nov. 93
21	...	Edward Hay Mackenzie Elliot, *Aide de Camp to the Governor of New Zealand*	......	2 Dec. 74	4 June 84	......	26 Feb. 94
17	...	Chas. Mannoir Sumner, *Aide de Camp to Lt. General J. Davis* 3 Feb. 94	1 May 78	28 May 79	3 Nov. 85	......	7 Nov. 94
		CAPTAINS.					
22	...	2 John Robert Philip Purchas	......	26 Mar. 74	25 July 83		
17	...	1 Thomas Lamb	1 May 78	20 June 79	14 Nov. 85		
16	...	2 John Antill Moggridge	13 Aug. 79	4 Oct. 79	23 Apr. 87		
16	...	1 Eric Edmund Moffat Davison Manson	10 Oct. 79	1 July 81	2 May 87		
16	...	1 Frederick Archibald Adam	14 Jan. 80	1 July 81	13 July 87		
16	...	*p.s.c.* Hugh Pentland Shekleton, *serving with the Egyptian Army*	31 Jan. 80	1 July 81	5 Oct. 87		
15	...	1 Raymond Henry Raymond Smythies	23 Oct. 80	1 July 81	15 Nov. 87		
13	...	1 Frederick M'Iver Roome	......	27 Jan. 83	8 Dec. 89		
12	...	Donald Guy Prendergast, *serving with the Egyptian Army*	......	5 Dec. 83	22 Jan. 90		
14	...	1 Guy Edward Wentworth Withington, *Captain Inst., Hythe School of Musk.*	......	28 Jan. 82	8 May 89		
12	...	2 Cecil Stewart Filmer Ferrers	......	19 Dec. 83	7 Sept. 93		
12	...	2 George Feilden Menzies (*Depot*)	......	19 Dec. 83	8 Nov. 93		
11	...	2 Charles Gage Stewart, **Adjutant** 10 Jan. 92	......	23 Aug. 84	8 Nov. 93		
10	...	2 Frederick Annesley Dudgeon	......	29 Aug. 85	26 Nov. 93		
9	...	Robert Heylock Owen,⁴ *Adjutant 2 Volunteer Battalion* 7 Nov. 94	......	28 Apr. 86	12 Jan. 94		
9	...	2 Cecil Wanliss	......	25 Aug. 86	3 Feb. 94		
9	...	1 William Edward Saumarez-Tyler	5 Feb. 87	8 Aug. 88	26 Feb. 94		
8	...	2 Nicholas Marcus Lynch	14 Sept. 87	17 Apr. 89	1 Aug. 94		
8	...	1 Stuart Upperton	16 Nov. 87	8 May 89	7 Nov. 94		
8	...	1 Alick Francis Bundock	16 Nov. 87	31 July 89	7 Nov. 94		
		LIEUTENANTS.					
8	...	1 Horace William Plews Waters (*Depot*)	11 Feb. 88	20 Sept. 89			
8	...	2 Edmund Carleton L'Estrange	11 Feb. 88	28 Sept. 89			
7	...	1 Edward Tite James	10 Nov. 88	8 Dec. 90			
7	...	2 Chas. Grant Francis Grey Birch (*Depot*)	8 Dec. 88	21 May 90			
7	...	1 Cecil Henry Lloyd	23 Mar. 89	30 July 90			
6	...	2 Guy Charles Ashworth	24 Apr. 89	14 Jan. 91			
6	...	2 Charles Edward Lewis	8 June 89	10 Jan. 92			
6	6/12	2 Arthur de Vere Willoughby-Osborne	24 Apr. 89	15 Dec. 91			
7	...	1 Berkeley Rumbold Goren	10 Nov. 88	11 May 92			
6	...	1 Hugh de Lancey Walters	9 Nov. 89	7 Sept. 93			
6	...	1 Edward Francis Oakeley	29 Mar. 90	4 Oct. 93			
5	...	2 Eustace James Clarke-Jervoise	3 May 90	8 Nov. 93			
5	...	Christopher Stewart Fellows	3 May 90	26 Nov. 93			
5	...	1 Arthur Solly-Flood	25 Mar. 91	12 Jan. 94			
4	...	1 Frederick Melchior Raphael	10 Oct. 91	26 Feb. 94			
4	...	2 Malcolm Charles Andrew Green	5 Dec. 91	1 Aug. 94			
4	...	1 Charles Robert Sandford Woods	27 Jan. 92	22 Oct. 94			
4	...	2 Maurice Augustus Ord	27 Jan. 92	7 Nov. 94			
3	...	2 Arthur Cyril Shuttleworth	2 Nov. 92	7 Nov. 94			
3	...	1 Sidney Hill Skinner	9 Sept. 93	19 Feb. 95			
		SECOND LIEUTENANTS.					
2	...	1 John Gollibraud	21 Oct. 93				
2	...	2 Henry Carden Herbert	21 Oct. 93				
2	...	2 Frank Sinclair	7 Mar. 94				
2	...	2 Frank Beauchamp Macaulay Chatterton	7 Mar. 94				
2	...	2 William Ogilvie Grant	7 Mar. 94				
1	...	2 D'Orville Brook Dawson	2 June 94				
1	...	1 Arthur Harold Bailey	10 Oct. 94				
1	...	2 Frederick Grant Wilson	12 Dec. 94				
1	...	Richard Gardiner	6 Mar. 95				
1	...	Godfrey Douglas Henry Ewart	6 Mar. 95				

284a The Prince of Wales' Volunteers (South Lancashire Regiment).

Years' Ser.		
Full Pay	Half Pay	
		Paymasters.—1
9	...	2
		Quarter Masters.—2 Arthur Cansdale, a8 Aug. 86; Hon. Lieut.
2	...	1 James Huxford, 20 Dec. 93; Hon. Lieut.

Facings White.—Agents, Messrs. Cox and Co.
1st Battalion returned from Aden, 3 Feb. 1886. 2nd Battalion embarked for Natal, 1882.

[1] Lt. General Fox-Pitt-Rivers served in the Eastern campaign up to 15th Oct. 1854 as D.A.Q.M. General including the battle of Alma and siege of Sebastopol (Medal with two Clasps, 5th Class of the Medjidie, and Turkish Medal).
[2] Lt. Colonel Fraser served with the 33rd Regiment throughout the Abyssinian campaign of 1867-68, and was present at the storming and capture of Magdala (Medal).
[3] Captain Owen served in the Soudan campaign in 1885 with the New South Wales Contingent (Medal with Clasp, and Khedive's Star).

Record of the Services of the 1st Battalion Prince of Wales' Volunteers (South Lancashire Regiment),— formerly the 40th Regiment.

Raised in 1717, and proceeded to America (capture of Louisburg and throughout the American war). To Ostend, England, and the West Indies, 1794. To England, Holland, and returned to England, 1799. To Minorca and Malta, 1800. (Four companies to Egypt, Feb. 1801, returning to Malta, Oct. 1801; received the badge of "Egypt"—with the Sphinx). To England, 1802. To South America, 1806 (capture of Monte Video). To Ireland, 1807. To the Peninsula, 1808 (battles of Roleia, Vimiera, Talavera, Badajoz, Salamanca, Vittoria, Pyrenees, Nivelle, Orthes, and Toulouse). To Jamaica, 1814. To England and Belgium, 1815 (battle of Waterloo and Army of Occupation in France). To Scotland, 1817. To England, 1819. To Ireland, 1820. To England, 1823. To New South Wales, 1824. To India, 1828 (defence of Candahar, 1842, and capture of Ghuznee and Cabul, 1842). To England, 1845. To Ireland, 1847. To New South Wales, 1852. To New Zealand, 1860 (New Zealand war). To England, 1866. To Ireland, 1869. To India, 1872. To England, 1886. To the Channel Islands, 1890.

Record of the Services of the 2nd Battalion Prince of Wales' Volunteers (South Lancashire Regiment);— formerly the 82nd Regiment.

Raised in 1793 in two Battalions. 1st Battalion proceeded to the West Indies, 1795. [2nd Battalion to Gibraltar, 1795; afterwards to the 1st Battalion in the West Indies, when the two were amalgamated.] England, to 1800. Ireland, to 1801. Minorca, to 1802. Ireland and England, to 1807. [2nd Battalion re-formed in 1803. To the Channel Islands, 1811-15, when it was reduced.] Copenhagen, to 1807. England, to 1808. Gibraltar and the Mediterranean, to 1808. The Peninsula, to 1809 (battles of Roleia and Vimiera). England and Walcheren and returned to England, 1809. Walcheren, to 1810. Gibraltar, to 1811. The Peninsula, to 1814 (battles of Vittoria, Pyrenees, Nivelle, and Orthes). Quebec, to 1815 (capture of Niagara). England, to 1815. Ostend and England, to 1816. Ireland, to 1819. Mauritius and Isle of France, to 1831. England, to 1832. Scotland, to 1834. Ireland, to 1837. Gibraltar, to 1839. The West Indies, to 1843. North America, to 1847. Nova Scotia, to 1848. England, to 1855. The Mediterranean and the Crimea, to 1856 (siege of Sebastopol). India, to 1869 (capture of Lucknow). Aden, to 1870. England, to 1875. Ireland, to 1880. England, to 1884. Natal, to 1887. Straits Settlements, to 1889. Gibraltar, 1889.

Continuation of Notes to the Dorsetshire Regiment.

[a] General Browne served with the 9th Regt. in the Crimea from 27th Nov. 1854, including the siege and fall of Sebastopol, and assaults of the 18th June and 8th Sept. Served as Aide de Camp and subsequently as Major of Brigade to Major General Ridley, 1st Division, during the latter part of the campaign (Medal with Clasp, Brevet of Major, Knight of the Legion of Honor, 5th Class of the Medjidie, and Turkish Medal). Proceeded with Sir Hope Grant's expedition from India in 1860-61 to China. Proceeded in Command of Forces sent to Japan for protection of Treaty Ports in 1864, and received the thanks of Her Majesty's Ministers for services in that country and also the approbation of the General Officer in command of the Forces in China. Served in the Afghan war in 1879-80 with the Koorum Division, including the Zaimusht Expedition (Medal).
[14] Major Tyrwhitt-Walker served in the Egyptian war of 1882 with the 1st Battalion Royal Irish Fusiliers, and was present at the battle of Tel-el-Kebir (Medal with Clasp, and Khedive's Star).
[18] Captain Todd-Thornton served in the Egyptian war of 1882 (Medal, and Khedive's Star). Served in the expedition to the Soudan in 1884 with the Mounted Infantry in the Cavalry Brigade under Sir Herbert Stewart, and was present in the engagements at El Teb and Temai (two Clasps). Served in the Nile Expedition in 1884-85 with the Mounted Infantry Regiment of the Camel Corps, and took part in the operations of the Desert Column under Sir Herbert Stewart, including the action at Abu Klea and the engagements at Metammeh and Abu Klea Wells (two Clasps).

Record of the Services of the 1st Battalion Dorsetshire Regiment (formerly the 39th Regiment).

Raised in Ireland as the 39th Regiment in 1702. To Portugal, 1707. To Spain, 1710. To Gibraltar and Minorca, 1713. To Ireland, 1719. To Gibraltar, 1727. To Jamaica, 1730. To Ireland, 1732. To England, 1744. To Brittany, 1746. To England, 1746. To Ireland, 1748. To East Indies, 1754 ("primus in Indis," battle of Plassy). To Ireland, 1758 (a large detachment to Germany). To Gibraltar, 1769. Entitled "39th East Middlesex Regiment," 1782. To England, 1783. To Ireland, 1789. To West Indies, 1794. To Ireland, 1795. To West Indies, 1795. To South America, 1796. To England, 1803. [2nd Battalion raised in July 1803.] Entitled "1st Battalion 39th East Middlesex Regiment," July 1803. To Malta, 1805. Entitled "1st Battalion 39th Dorsetshire Regiment," 1807. To Sicily, 1810. To the Peninsula, 1811 (battles of Albuhera, Vittoria, Pyrenees, Nivelle, Nive and Orthes). To Canada, 1814. To France, 1815 (army of occupation). [2nd Battalion disbanded, 1815.] To England and Ireland, 1818. To England, 1825. To New South Wales, 1827. To the East Indies, 1832 (battle of Maharajpore). To England, 1847. To Ireland, 1850. To Gibraltar, 1854. To the Crimea, Dec. 1854 (siege of Sebastopol). To Canada, 1856. To Bermuda, 1859. To England, 1864. To Ireland, 1866. To the East Indies, 1869. Entitled "1st Battalion Dorsetshire Regiment," 1881. To England, 1882. To Malta, Sept. 1882. To England, Oct. 1882. To Malta and Egypt, 1885. To England, 1886. To Malta, 1888. To Egypt, 1889.

Record of the Services of the 2nd Battalion Dorsetshire Regiment (formerly the 54th Regiment).

Raised in 1755. To Gibraltar, 1756. Served as Marines in the Mediterranean for six months and returned to Gibraltar, to 1765. Ireland, to 1775. North America, to 1791. England, to 1793. Guernsey, to 1794. The Netherlands, to April 1795. England, to June 1795. St. Vincent, to 1796. England, to 1797. Ireland, to 1800. [2nd Battalion raised, and both Battalions to Egypt to 1802 (surrender of Marabout, and received the badge of "Egypt"—with the Sphinx. Gibraltar, 1805; 2nd Battalion disbanded.] England, to 1807. Jamaica, to 1813, where it became practically extinct. Fresh companies raised in England, and sent to North Germany, to 1813. The Netherlands and Flanders, to 1815. France, to 1816. England, to 1819. Cape of Good Hope, to 1820. India, to Jan. 1825. Burmah, to Dec. 1825 (war of 1824-25). India, to 1840. England, to 1842. Ireland, to 1846. Gibraltar and Malta, to 1848. West Indies, to 1851. Canada, to 1854. England for three weeks, and thence to Gibraltar, to 1856. England, to 1857. India, to 1866. England, to 1868. Ireland, to 1871. India, to 1885. Aden, to 1886. England, 1886.

1st Batt., Pembroke Dock.
2nd Batt., Secunderabad, Madras.

The Welsh Regiment.

[Regimental District No. 41.—Cardiff.] 285

Formerly the 41st (the Welsh) and the 69th (South Lincolnshire) Regiments.
(The 3rd Battalion is formed of the Glamorgan Militia.)
The Rose and Thistle, on the same stalk, within the Garter. The Prince of Wales' Plume. "*Gwell Angeu na Chywilydd.*" The Royal Cypher, with the Imperial Crown. "St. Vincent" "Bourbon" "Java" "Detroit" "Queenstown" "Miami" "Niagara" "Waterloo" "India" "Ava" "Candahar, Ghuznee, and Cabool, 1842" "Alma" "Inkerman" "Sevastopol."

Years' Ser.			Ensign or 2nd Lieut.	Lieut.	Captain.	Brev. Maj.	Major.
Full Pay.	Half Pay.						

Colonel.—Francis Peyton,[1] *CB. Ensign,* P29 Jan. 41; *Lieut.* P27 May 42; *Captain,* P3 Sept. 50; *Major,*
27 ... P12 May 54; *Bt.Lt.Colonel,* 26 Oct. 58; *Colonel,* 23 Oct. 63; *Major General,* 17 May 69; *Lieutenant General,* 1 Oct. 83; *General,* 30 Sept. 85; *Colonel* Welsh Regiment, 16 Jan. 94.

Lieutenant Colonels.—2 Henry Stanhope Holmes,[2] *Ensign,* P1 Aug. 68; *Lieut.* P8 June 70; *Capt.* 24 Nov.
26 ... 77; *Major,* 25 Jan. 82; *Lt.Colonel,* 12 Dec. 92.
1 John Owen Quirk,[6] *DSO. Ensign,* P1 Dec. 69; *Lieut.* 28 Oct. 71; *Capt.* 1 Dec. 80; *Major,* 18 Feb. 84; *Lt.Colonel,* 14 Apr. 93.

		Majors.					
24	...	1 p.s.c. Rees John Francis Banfield	23 Sept. 71	28 Oct. 71	8 Mar. 81	......	1 Aug. 86
22	...	FitzRoy Somerset Lanyon Penno, serving with Local Forces, Victoria, with rank of Lt. Colonel	......	9 Aug. 73	2 Feb. 81	......	13 Nov. 89
22	...	Oswald James Henry Ball	......	28 Feb. 74	1 Apr. 81	......	20 Aug. 91
24	...	2 Henry Charles Barton Gray, *Station Staff Officer, Secunderabad,* 22 Mar. 94	......	30 Dec. 71	30 Aug. 81	......	25 Nov. 91
21	...	2 Aubrey Francis White	......	13 June 74	25 Jan. 82	......	12 Dec. 92
20	...	2 William Vieris Dickinson	......	12 Feb. 76	1 Jan. 83	......	28 Dec. 92
19	...	1 James Christopher Reynolds (*Depot*)	......	6 Sept. 76	2 June 83	......	14 Apr. 93
		Captains.					
19	...	1 Robert Alexander Thresbie	......	29 Nov. 76	31 Jan. 84		
18	...	1 Francis Russell Parkinson[10]	31 Oct. 77	13 Nov. 78	18 Feb. 84		
17	...	James Sillem,[11] *serving with the Egyptian Army, with rank of Major*	11 May 78	4 July 79	11 June 84		
17	...	2 Arthur Revell Reade	11 May 78	6 Aug. 79	14 Apr. 86		
17	...	Henry D'Alton Harkness, *serving with the Egyptian Army, with rank of Major*	11 May 78	1 Nov. 79	1 Aug. 86		
17	...	1 William Carter Giffard[12]	11 May 78	13 Mar. 80	17 Aug. 86		
17	...	1 James Richard Plomer Clarke............	24 July 78	19 May 80	19 Sept. 86		
17	...	1 Thomas Lucas Woodwright Lucas......	13 July 78	11 Feb. 80	11 Aug. 86		
17	...	Julius Henry Goodwyn......................	22 Feb. 79	1 Dec. 80	4 June 87		
18	...	2 p.s.c. James Eales Caunter..................	30 Jan. 78	2 Feb. 81	31 Aug. 87		
18	...	Arthur Henry Uhthoff Tindal, *Adj. 3rd Battalion,* 15 June 92	30 Jan. 78	2 Feb. 81	7 Oct. 87		
15	...	Lancelot Shute Barrington Tristram...	8 May 80	8 Mar. 81	10 Feb. 88		
15	...	Ronald Bruce Coke, *Adjutant 2 Volunteer Battalion* 1 Jan. 95.............	23 Oct. 80	16 Mar. 81	8 June 88		
15	...	2 Richard Walt.Comyn Vyvyan, *Comdt. Poonamallee Depot,* 22 July 93	23 Oct. 80	8 June 81	8 June 88		
14	...	p.s.c. Ernest Sven David Goldschmidt, *Adj.* 1 *Volunteer Battalion* 10 Mar. 93	......	22 Oct. 81	1 July 88		
14	...	William Spottiswoode Sparkes, *serving with the Egyptian Army*	......	22 Oct. 81	5 Nov. 88		
14	...	2 Arthur Porter Nownham-Davis (*Depot*)	......	28 Jan. 82	12 Dec. 88		
12	...	2 John Henry de Albini de Moutalt Farmcot Stratford[15]	......	14 July 83	12 Oct. 89		
12	...	1 p.s.c. Robert William Perssé White.....	......	25 Aug. 83	12 Dec. 89		
12	...	2 Lawrence Harry Hawkes....................	......	25 Aug. 83	1 Feb. 90		
12	...	Edward George Wynyard,[16] *DSO., Instructor R. M. College* 22 Aug. 90	......	12 May 83	19 Mar. 90		
10	...	1 Henry George Coates Phillips	......	9 May 85	22 Aug. 90		
15	...	Henry Bannerman Phillips, *Adj.* 3 *Volunteer Battalion* 1 Feb. 95..........	12 Mar. 81	1 July 81	25 Mar. 91		
10	...	1 William Vaughton Pennefather[18]........	......	23 May 85	18 May 91		
		Lieutenants.					
10	...	1 p.s.c. Cameron Deane Shute	......	29 Aug. 85			
9	...	1 Herbert Schofield	......	8 Dec. 86			
9	...	1 Charles Henry Young[20] (*Depot*)	5 Feb. 87	17 Oct. 88			
9	...	2 Ernest Edw. Janvrin Charleton	5 Feb. 87	12 Dec. 88			
9	...	1 Charles Bernard Morland	5 Feb. 87	6 Feb. 89			
8	...	2 Arthur Geo. FitzRoy Day, **Adjutant**, 26 Feb. 92	9 Nov. 87	8 May 89			
8	...	1 Hugh Richard Westmacott.................	11 Feb. 88	12 Dec. 89			
7	...	2 Rossiter Lines[21]	11 Apr. 88	12 Dec. 89			
7	...	1 Charles Vaughan Hale[22]	9 May 88	26 Apr. 90			
7	...	2 Osborn Brace Pritchard[23]	22 Aug. 88	11 June 90			
7	...	1 Rhys Price (*Depot*)	8 Dec. 88	22 Aug. 90			
7	...	1 David Alexander Napier Lomax........	8 Dec. 88	19 Nov. 90			
7	...	2 Freke Lewis Prothero	23 Mar. 89	17 Dec. 90			
6	...	2 Henry John Bartlet Span..................	1 Mar. 90	6 Jan. 92			
6	...	2 Clarence Gorton Ross Smith	29 Mar. 90	10 Feb. 92			
6	...	2 Francis Herbert Howe (*Depot*)	29 Mar. 90	15 June 92			
6	...	1 Archer George Prothero	29 Mar. 90	13 Sept. 92			
6	...	1 Neville Travers Borton	29 Mar. 90	21 Sept. 92			
6	...	2 William Thomas Brassey Rhodes	29 Mar. 90	19 June 93			
5	...	1 Delaval Graham L'Estrange Astley, **Adjutant** 1 Jan. 94	28 June 90	23 Dec. 93			
		Second Lieutenants.					
5	...	2 Basil Tobin Ready	29 Oct. 90				
5	...	2 Archibald Ythen Cheyne	29 Nov. 90				
5	...	1 Lyall Brandreth	17 Jan. 91				

Years' Ser.				2ND LIEUT.	
Full Pay.	Half Pay.		SECOND LIEUTENANTS.		
4	...	2	John Vickris Taylor	7 Nov.	91
4	...		George Duncan Campbell, *with Hong Kong Regiment*	27 Jan.	92
4	...	1	Ernest Somerville Jackson	20 Feb.	92
3	...	2	Geo. Geoffrey Prendergast Humphreys	13 July	92
3	...	2	Roundel! Tristram Toke	28 Sept.	92
2	...	1	Edward Crawford Lloyd Fitzwilliams	9 Sept.	93
2	...	1	William Edward Armstrong Johnson	21 Oct.	93
2	...	1	George Peter Hoggan	24 Jan.	94
1	...	2	John Herbert Kerrich	10 Oct.	94
1	...	2	Lancelot Irby Oxford Robins	12 Dec.	94
1	...	2	Frederick Arthur Wyllie	20 Feb.	95

Paymasters.—2 William T. B. Rhodes, *Lieut.* 2 *Battalion (acting).*

| 9 | ... | *Quarter Masters.*—2 William Tittery Fenn,[25] 23 June 86 ; *Hon. Lieut.* |

Facings White.—*Agents*, Messrs. Cox and Co.
1*st Batt. returned from Gibraltar,* 23 Nov. 1893. 2*nd Batt. embarked for India,* 14 Sept. 1892.

[1] General Peyton served in the 98th Regt. with the expedition to the north of China in 1842, and was present at the operations in the Yangtsekiang River, the attack and capture of Chin Kiang Foo, and at the landing before Nankin (Medal). Punjaub campaign of 1848-49 (Medal). Served with the Flank Companies of the 98th Regt. at the forcing of the Kohat Pass, in the force under Sir Charles Napier and Sir Colin Campbell in Feb. 1850 (mentioned in despatches, Medal with Clasp). Commanded four Companies of the 98th Regt. in the Peshawur Expeditionary Force on the Euzofzie Frontier under Sir Sidney Cotton in April and May 1858, capture of Pungtar and Chinglee, and the affair with the Hindostance fanatics on the Heights of Sittana on 4th May (mentioned in despatches). In the Peshawur Division during the Sepoy mutiny in 1858.

[2] Lt. Colonel Holmes was present with the 69th Regiment during the repulse of an incursion of Fenians into Canada in May 1870.

[6] Lt. Colonel Quirk served in the Boer war of 1881 with the Natal Field Force. Served with the expedition to the Soudan under Sir Gerald Graham in 1884 on Transport duty, and was present in the engagements at El Teb and Temai (Medal with Clasp, and Khedive's Star). Served with the Nile Expedition in 1884-85 on the Lines of Communication as Assistant Adjutant General to the Egyptian Army (Clasp) ; also served in the operations of the Egyptian Frontier Field Force in 1885-86 as Assistant Adjutant General to the Egyptian Army, and was present in the engagement at Giniss (*DSO.*).

[10] Captain Parkinson served in the operations near Suakin in December 1888 including the engagement at Gemaizah (Medal with Clasp, and Khedive's Star).

[11] Major Sillem served in the operations of the Soudan Frontier Field Force in 1887 including the engagement at Sarras (Medal, and Khedive's Star) ; also served in the operations near Suakin in December 1888 including the engagement at Gemaizah (mentioned in despatches, Clasp, and 3rd Class of the Medjidie).

[12] Captain Giffard served in the operations near Suakin in December 1888 including the engagement at Gemaizah (mentioned in despatches, Medal with Clasp, 4th Class of the Medjidie, and Khedive's Star).

[15] Captain Stratford served in the Zulu war in 1879, and was present in the engagement at Ulundi ; also served in the subsequent operations against Sekukuni including the storming of the stronghold (Medal with Clasp). Served in the Boer war of 1881, and took part in the defence of Standerton.

[16] Captain Wynyard served in the Burmese Expedition in 1885-87 with the 2nd Battalion of the Liverpool Regiment (twice mentioned in despatches, *DSO.*, and Medal with Clasp). [See also Civil Decorations for Gallantry, "Hart's Annual Army List," p. 786.]

[18] Captain Pennefather served in the operations near Suakin in December 1888 including the engagement at Gemaizah (Medal with Clasp, and Khedive's Star).

[20] Lieut. Young served in the operations near Suakin in December 1888 including the engagement at Gemaizah (Medal with Clasp, and Khedive's Star).

[21] Lieut. Lines served with the Burmah Expedition in 1885-86 under Sir Harry Prendergast including the surrender of Mandalay (Medal with Clasp).

[22] Lieut. Hale served in the operations near Suakin in December 1888 including the engagement at Gemaizah (Medal with Clasp, and Khedive's Star).

[23] Lieut. Pritchard served in the operations near Suakin in December 1888 including the engagement at Gemaizah (Medal with Clasp, and Khedive's Star).

[25] Lieut. Fenn served in the operations near Suakin in December 1888 including the engagement at Gemaizah (Medal with Clasp, and Khedive's Star).

Record of the Services of the 2nd Battalion of the Welsh Regiment (formerly the 69th Regiment).

Originally 2nd Battalion 24th Regiment, and raised in 1756. Proceeded to Gibraltar, 1770. Home, 1775. To the West Indies, 1778. Home, 1785. To Mediterranean, 1793. To West Indies, 1796. To Holland, 1799. Home, 1799. To Jamaica, 1800. Home, 1802. To East Indies, 1805. Home, 1826. (2nd Battalion to Holland and Belgium, 1813 to 1815). To West Indies, 1831. To New Brunswick, 1839. Home, 1842. To Malta, 1847. To West Indies, 1851. Home, 1857. To East Indies, 1857. Home, 1864. To Canada, 1867. To Bermuda, 1870. To Gibraltar, 1873.

The Black Watch (Royal Highlanders).

1st Batt., Mauritius.
2nd Batt., Edinburgh.

Formerly the 42nd (Royal Highland— The Black Watch) and the 73rd (Perthshire) Regiments.

(The 3rd Battalion is formed of the Perth Militia.)

Regimental District No. 42.—Perth.

The Royal Cypher within the Garter. St. Andrew. The Royal Cypher, with the Imperial Crown. "MYSORE" "MANGALORE" "SERINGAPATAM" "EGYPT" (with the Sphinx). "CORUNNA" "FUENTES D'ONOR" "PYRENEES" "NIVELLE" "NIVE" "ORTHES" "TOULOUSE" "PENINSULA" "WATERLOO" "SOUTH AFRICA, 1846-7, 1851-2-3" "ALMA" "SEVASTOPOL" "LUCKNOW" "ASHANTEE" "EGYPT, 1882, 1884" "TEL-EL-KEBIR" "NILE, 1884-85" "KIRBEKAN."

Years' Ser. Full Pay	Half Pay		Ensign or 2nd Lieut.	Lieut.	Captain.	Brev. Maj.	Major.
		Colonel.—Hon. Robert Rollo,¹ CB. Ens. ᵖ10 Aug 32; Lt. ᵖ25 Sept. 35; Capt. ᵖ5 Nov. 41; Bt.Major, 20 June 54; Bt.Lt.Colonel, 12 Dec. 54; Major, ᵖ5 Jan. 55; Lt.Colonel, 10 Aug. 55; Colonel, 23 Feb. 58; Major General, 6 March 68; Lieut.General, 1 Oct. 77; General, 19 Dec. 80; Colonel 93rd Highlanders, 5 Apr. 80; Colonel Black Watch, 9 June 88.					
30	...	**Lieutenant Colonels.**—1 p.s.c. Richard Hugh Lambart Brickenden,¹² Ensign, 18 July 65; Lt. 11 Jan. 67; Capt. 29 Sept. 77; Major, 25 July 83; Lt.Colonel, 11 July 92.					
30	...	2 Andrew Gilbert Wauchope,¹⁴ CB. CMG. Ensign, ᵖ21 Nov. 65; Lt. 23 June 67; Capt. 14 Sept. 78; Major, 14 Mar. 84; Bt.Lt.Colonel, 21 May 84; Colonel, 21 May 88; Lt.Colonel, 20 Aug. 94.					
		MAJORS.					
26	...	1 Edward George Grogan¹⁹	ᵖ24 July 69	28 Oct. 71	19 June 79	......	4 Dec. 85
30	...	2 George Francis De Bude Davidson	ᵖ 2 Mar. 66	ᵖ19 Feb. 67	11 Nov. 70	......	11 July 86
20	...	2 John Henry Collier Coode		10 Sept. 75	17 Apr. 82	......	27 Aug. 90
20	...	Archibald Morden Carthew - Yorstoun, *Adjutant 6 (Fifeshire) Vol. Bn. Royal Highlanders* 15 May 90		20 Nov. 75	25 Oct. 82	......	29 Jan. 91
20	...	2 Alexander Gordon Duff²⁵		28 April 75	4 Dec. 85	......	3 Aug. 92
18	...	2 Ernest Maxwell Willshire *(Depot)*	13 Oct. 77	25 May 78	15 May 85	......	20 Aug. 94
17	...	2 Henry Edward Maxwell		11 Sept. 78	15 May 85	......	3 Jan. 95
		CAPTAINS.					
16	...	Charles Graham Moulton-Barrett, 4 *Vol. Bn.* 5 June 90	13 Aug. 79	26 Feb. 81	20 Oct. 85		
16	...	2 St. George Edward William Burton³⁰	13 Aug. 79	1 July 81	15 Nov. 86		
16	...	Thomas Mowbray Martin Berkeley,³² *Adj.* 1 *Vol. Bn*, 17 May 90	13 Aug. 79	1 July 81	29 Jan. 87		
17	...	Percy John Caton Livingston,³⁰ *Adj.* 3 *Battalion* 4 June 90	22 Jan. 79	1 July 81	21 Apr. 87		
17	...	John Grenfell Maxwell,³¹ *DSO. serving with Egyptian Army*	22 Mar. 79	1 July 81	28 Nov. 87	17 Aug. 89	
13	...	1 p.s.c. Norman Wm. Cuthbertson³⁶		9 Sept. 82	7 Dec. 88		
13	...	Thomas Souter,⁴² *serving with the Egyptian Army*		24 Jan. 83	17 May 90		
13	...	2 James Deane		10 Mar. 83	5 June 90		
12	...	1 Walter Gordon Wolrige-Gordon⁴⁰ *(Depot)*		12 May 83	5 June 90		
12	...	2 George Herbert Lyle Galbraith³⁰		6 Feb. 84	27 Aug. 90		
12	...	1 Hugh Rose³⁸		6 Feb. 84	22 Oct. 90		
12	...	1 David Lorraine Wilson-Farquharson³⁰		6 Feb. 84	29 Jan. 91		
11	...	1 John Stuart		14 May 84	10 Aug. 92		
11	...	1 Harrie Jennings-Bramly, *Staff College*		23 Aug. 84	3 Nov. 92		
11	...	1 William MacLaren Campbell		7 Feb. 85	9 Feb. 93		
10	...	2 *Hon.* James F. Thurlow Cumming-Bruce		29 Aug. 85	9 Feb. 93		
10	...	1 Alexander Campbell		25 Nov. 85	22 Feb. 93		
11	...	2 Herbert Cyril Orde Murray		7 Feb. 85	13 Apr. 92		
10	...	2 John George Rennie, *Adjutant* 29 May 93		30 Jan. 86	22 Mar. 93		
9	...	David Baird, *Aide de Camp to Lt.General* H. Rowlands, 1 Mar. 94		8 Dec. 86	29 May 93		
8	...	1 Edward Sidney Herbert, *Adjutant* 14 July 92	4 May 87	27 Nov. 89	27 June 94		
10	...	*Hon.* John Forbes Sempill, *Master of Sempill*³⁷		25 Nov. 85	1 Apr. 91		
		LIEUTENANTS.					
8	...	1 Alexander Colin M'Lean	4 May 87	27 Dec. 89			
8	...	Henry Scott Turner, *serving under the British South Africa Company*	31 Dec. 87	17 May 90			
8	...	2 William MacFarlan	11 Feb. 88	31 May 90			
7	...	2 Thomas Owen Lloyd *(Depot)*	9 May 88	5 June 90			
7	...	2 Erle Godfrey Elton	22 Aug. 88	13 Aug. 90			
7	...	2 Charles Herbert Philip Carter *(Depot)*	14 Nov. 88	20 Aug. 90			
7	...	1 Robert Henry Pitcairn	9 Jan. 89	27 Aug. 90			
7	...	1 Adrian Grant-Duff	23 Mar. 89	22 Oct. 90			
6	...	2 Charles Edward Stewart	10 Apr. 89	26 Oct. 90			
6	...	1 Cecil Eykyn	6 July 89	29 Jan. 91			
6	...	2 Archibald Rice Cameron	1 Mar. 90	3 Nov. 92			
6	...	2 Colin William MacRae	28 June 90	10 Aug. 92			
5	...	2 John George Harry Hamilton	8 Oct. 90	3 Nov. 92			
5	...	1 Edwin Sandys Dawes	29 Oct. 90	9 Feb. 93			
5	...	1 Henry Andrew	29 Nov. 90	22 Feb. 93			
5	...	1 John Gerrard Collins	17 Jan. 91	22 Mar. 93			
5	...	1 John Buchanan Pollok	4 Mar. 91	9 Aug. 93			
5	...	2 Frederick Guthrie Tait	29 Oct. 90	15 Apr. 93			
4	...	2 John Harvey	25 July 91	27 June 94			

³⁸ Captain Rose served in the Nile Expedition in 1884-85 with the 1st Battalion of the Black Watch, and took part with the River Column under Major General Earle, and was present at the action of Kirbekan (Medal with two Clasps, and Khedive's Star).

⁴⁰ Captain Wolrige Gordon served in the Soudan Expedition in 1884 with the 1st Battalion Black Watch, and was present in the engagement at El Teb—wounded (Medal with Clasp, and Khedive's Star). Served in the Nile Expedition in 1884-85 with the 1st Battalion of the Black Watch, took part with the River Column under Major General Earle, and was present in the engagement at Kirbekan (two Clasps).

The Black Watch (Royal Highlanders).

Full Pay	Half Pay	SECOND LIEUTENANTS.	2ND LIEUT.
4	...	1 Arthur Henry Marindin	7 Nov. 91
4	...	2 Frederick Dymoke Murray	5 Dec. 91
3	...	1 William Dick-Cunyngham	13 Aug. 92
3	...	1 William James St. John Harvey	19 Nov. 92
3	...	2 Walter Nathaniel Pike	21 Jan. 93
3	...	1 Henry Holmes Sutherland	15 Mar. 93
2	...	2 John Coulson	20 May 93
2	...	1 Colin M'Lean	20 May 93
2	...	1 James Thomas Crokatt Murray	21 Oct. 93
2	...	2 Nicholas Gifford Edmonds	21 Oct. 93
1	...	1 *Lord George Stewart-Murray*	2 June 94
1	...	1 John Douglas Glen Walker	10 Oct. 94

Paymasters.—1
2

| 12 | ... | *Quarter Masters.*—1 Charles Sinclair,⁴⁴ 28 Nov. 83 ; *Hon. Captain*, 28 Nov. 93. |
| 8 | ... | 2 William Webb, 14 May 87 ; *Hon. Lieut.* |

Facings Blue.—*Agents*, Messrs. Cox and Co.

1st Battalion embarked for Egypt, 1882. 2nd Battalion returned from Hong Kong, 1881.

---

¹ General the Hon. Robert Rollo was one of two officers sent from Malta on a special mission to Tripoli in 1846, and received the thanks of the Secretaries for Foreign Affairs and Colonies, conveyed through the Commander in Chief, for his services upon that occasion. He embarked with the 42nd Highlanders for the East, and served with the Regt. in the campaign of 1854-55; was Brigade Major from the battle of Balaklava and throughout the winter until he took command of his Regt. including the battles of Alma and Balaklava; commanded it upon the expedition to Kertch and surrender of Yenikali, and afterwards at the siege of Sebastopol and assault on the outworks on the 18th June (Medal with three Clasps, Brevet of Lt.Colonel, Knight of the Legion of Honour, 5th Class of the Medjidie, and Turkish Medal). Served as Assistant Adjutant General in Canada at the head of that Department from Nov. 1855 to Jan. 1860, and from the latter date as Military Secretary to Lieut.General Sir Fenwick Williams till that officer's retirement from the command in British North America in June 1865.

¹² Lt.Colonel Brickenden accompanied the 42nd Highlanders to the Gold Coast (Ashanti Medal).

¹⁴ Colonel Wauchope served in the Ashanti war from the 30th Nov. 1873. Commanded the Winnebah company of Russell's Regiment from the Prah to the Adansi Hills ; then served as Staff Officer to Colonel M'Leod commanding the Advanced Guard, and was present at the capture and destruction of Adubiassi, capture of Borborassie, battle of Amoaful, capture and destruction of Becquah, Advanced Guard engagement of Jarbinbah (wounded slightly), skirmishes and ambuscade affairs between Adwabin and the river Ordah, and battle of Ordahsu—severely wounded (mentioned in despatches, Medal with Clasp). Served with the 1st Battalion Black Watch in the Egyptian war of 1882, and was present at the battle of Tel-el-Kebir (Medal with Clasp, and Khedive's Star). Served in the Soudan Expedition under Sir Gerald Graham in 1884 as Deputy Assistant Adjutant and Quarter Master General, and was present in the engagement at El Teb—severely wounded (mentioned in despatches, Brevet of Lt.Colonel, two Clasps). Served in the Nile Expedition in 1884-85 with the 1st Battalion of the Black Watch, took part with the River Column under Major General Earle, and was present in the engagement at Kirbekan—very severely wounded (two Clasps).

¹⁹ Major Grogan served throughout the second phase of the Ashanti war in 1874, and was present at the battle of Amoaful, capture and destruction of Becquah, battle of Ordahsu (slightly wounded) and capture of Coomassie (Medal with Clasp).

²⁵ Major Duff served in the Egyptian war of 1882 with the 1st Battalion Black Watch, and was present at the battle of Tel-el-Kebir (Medal with Clasp, and Khedive's Star). Served in the Soudan Expedition in 1884 as Adjutant 1st Battalion Black Watch, and was present in the engagements at El Teb and Temai (two Clasps). Served in the Nile Expedition in 1884-85 as Adjutant to the 1st Battalion of the Black Watch, took part with the River Column under Major General Earle, and was present in the engagement at Kirbekan (two Clasps).

³⁰ Captains Burton, P. J. C. Livingston, Galbraith and Wilson-Farquharson served in the Nile Expedition in 1884-85 with the 1st Battalion of the Black Watch, took part with the River Column under Major General Earle, and were present in the engagement at Kirbekan (Medal with two Clasps, and Khedive's Star).

³¹ Major J. G. Maxwell served in the Egyptian war of 1882 with the 1st Battalion of the Black Watch, and was present at the battle of Tel-el-Kebir (Medal with Clasp, and Khedive's Star). Served in the Nile Expedition in 1884-85 as Staff Captain (mentioned in despatches, Clasp). Served with the Egyptian Frontier Field Force in 1885-86 as Aide de Camp to Major General Grenfell, and was present in the engagement at Giniss (*DSO.*) ; in the operations near Suakin in December 1888 including the engagement at Gemaizah as Aide de Camp to Major General Grenfell, Commanding the Suakin Field Force (mentioned in despatches, Clasp, and 4th Class of the Osmanieh) ; and in the operations on the Soudan frontier in 1889 including the engagement at Toski (mentioned in despatches, Brevet of Major, Clasp).

³² Captain Berkeley served with the Nile Expedition in 1884-85 with the 1st Battalion Black Watch (Medal with Clasp, and Khedive's Star).

³⁶ Captain Cuthbertson served in the Soudan Expedition in 1884 with the 1st Battalion Black Watch (Medal, and Khedive's Star).

³⁷ Captain the Master of Sempill served in the operations of the Soudan Frontier Field Force in 1886 with the Cameron Highlanders. Served with the Hazara Expedition in 1891 (Medal with Clasp).

⁴² Captain Souter served in the Egyptian war of 1882 with the 1st Battalion of the Cameron Highlanders, and was present at the battle of Tel-el-Kebir (mentioned in despatches, promoted Lieutenant into the Black Watch for distinguished service, Medal with Clasp, and Khedive's Star). Served in the Nile Expedition in 1884-85 with the 1st Battalion of the Black Watch, and took part with the River Column under Major General Earle, including the engagement at Kirbekan (two Clasps).

⁴⁴ Captain Sinclair served in the Egyptian war of 1882 with the 1st Battalion Black Watch, and was present at the battle of Tel-el-Kebir (Medal with Clasp, and Khedive's Star) ; also served in the Soudan Expedition in 1884 with the 1st Battalion Black Watch, and was present in the engagements at El Teb and Temai (two Clasps). Served in the Nile Expedition in 1884-85 with the 1st Battalion of the Black Watch, and took part with the River Column under Major General Earle, including the engagement at Kirbekan (two Clasps).

[*For the Record of the Services of the 1st Battalion Black Watch, see end of Oxford Light Infantry, p. 287a.*

1st Batt., Dublin.
2nd Batt., Bareilly, Bengal.] **The Oxfordshire Light Infantry.** [Regimental District 287 No. 43.—Oxford.

Formerly the 43rd (Monmouthshire Light Infantry) and the 52nd (Oxfordshire—Light Infantry) Regiments.

(The 3rd and 4th Battalions are formed of the Bucks and the Oxford Militia respectively.)
The United Red and White Rose. "QUEBEC, 1759" "MYSORE" "HINDOOSTAN" "VIMIERA" "CORUNNA" "BUSACO" "FUENTES D'ONOR" "CIUDAD RODRIGO" "BADAJOZ" "SALAMANCA" "VITTORIA" "NIVELLE" "NIVE" "ORTHES" "TOULOUSE" "PENINSULA" "WATERLOO" "SOUTH AFRICA, 1851–2–3" "DELHI" "NEW ZEALAND."

Years' Ser.							
Full Pay.	Half Pay.		ENSIGN OR 2ND LIEUT.	LIEUT.	CAPTAIN.	BREV. MAJ.	MAJOR.
34	...	Colonel—Frederick Green Wilkinson,¹ *Ensign,* P 27 Dec. 42; *Lieut,* P 13 Aug. 47; *Captain,* P 17 Oct. 51; *Major,* 9 Oct. 55; *Lt. Colonel,* 16 March 58; *Colonel,* 16 March 63; *Major General,* 28 Oct. 68; *Lt. General,* 9 Dec. 81; *Colonel* West Surrey Regiment, 15 Oct. 91; *Colonel* Oxfordshire Light Infantry, 29 Aug. 93.					
		Lieutenant Colonels.—2 William Clark,¹³ *Ensign,* P 11 Feb. 62; *Lt.* 30 Apr. 64; *Capt.* 20 Sept. 71; *Major,* 30 Nov. 81; *Bt. Lt. Colonel,* 1 July 87; *Lt. Colonel,* 27 July 91.						
30	...	1 p.s.c. James Johnstone,⁷ *Ensign,* P 20 Feb. 66; *Lt.* P 30 Sept. 68; *Capt.* 14 Feb. 74; *Major,* 15 Aug. 83; *Lt. Colonel,* 16 March 92.					
		MAJORS.					
28	...	2 Evelyn Broomfield Pocklington	P 1 May 67	P 3 Feb. 69	15 Jan. 78	......	20 May 85
25	...	1 James Arthur Strachan	5 Feb. 71	28 Oct. 71	19 Sept. 79	......	15 Jan. 86
23	...	1 Francis Hugh Plowden	......	5 Oct. 72	19 Aug. 81	......	1 Sept. 86
26	...	Hon. Arthur Edward Dalzell, *Insp. of Gymnasia, Bengal,* 15 Apr. 92	P 20 Feb. 70	28 Oct. 71	11 Mar. 82	......	11 Mar. 89
22	...	Robert Eccles,¹⁵ *Adjutant* 3 Bn. Durham Light Infantry, 2 May 92	......	28 Feb. 74	26 Mar. 84	......	27 Sept. 93
21	...	1 Frederick John Evelegh (*Depot*)	......	13 Nov. 74	23 May 85	......	13 Dec. 93
19	...	2 Reginald Whitworth Porter	......	6 Sept. 76	11 Jan. 86	......	9 Nov. 94
19	...	Horace Augustus Terry, 5 Middlesex Rifle Vols. 2 Jan. 93	......	29 Nov. 76	19 May 86	......	22 Dec. 94
		CAPTAINS.					
17	...	Augustus Ferryman Mockler-Ferryman, *Inst. R. M. College,* 17 Dec. 92	......	3 May 78	28 July 86		
18	...	1 Paul Treby Clark	20 Mar. 78	23 July 79	28 July 86		
17	...	John Hanbury-Williams,²² *Adjutant* 3 Battalion 27 Feb. 92	25 May 78	3 Apr. 80	1 Sept. 86		
17	...	2 Gerald Francis Mockler	14 Sept. 78	8 Apr. 81	6 June 82		
17	...	Henry Robert Stapleton Cotton, *Adj.* 2 Volunteer Battalion 10 Jan. 91	4 Dec. 78	1 July 81	1 Jan. 89		
14	...	Charles Russell Day, *Adjutant* 2 Vol. Bn. Middlesex Regt. 2 May 92	......	28 Jan. 82	27 July 89		
15	...	2 Denis James Bartou (*Depot*)	22 Jan. 81	1 July 81	23 Jan. 92		
13	...	2 Reginald George Hutton Hughes, *Station Staff Officer, Nynee Tal,* 22 Oct. 93	......	9 Sept. 82	27 Feb. 92		
13	...	1 Cha. Edw. Gerald Marshall Fairtlough	......	10 Mar. 83	16 Mar. 92		
12	...	2 Robert Fanshawe	......	25 Aug. 83	15 Apr. 92		
12	...	Frank Grimshaw Lagier Lamotte, *Adjutant* 1 Bucks Rifle Vols. 1 Jan. 94	......	25 Aug. 83	2 May 92		
12	...	Arthur Blyford Thruston, *on special service, Uganda*	......	6 Feb. 84	2 May 92		
11	...	Henry Rodolph Davies,²³ *Staff Capt. Intell. Branch, Bengal,* 16 Oct. 93	......	23 Aug. 84	2 May 92		
11	...	Bryan Upperton, *Aide de Camp to Maj. General R. B. H. Blundell* 2 June 91	......	12 Nov. 84	27 July 92		
11	...	2 Edward Dalrymple White, *Adjutant* 1 Nov. 91	......	7 Feb. 85	27 July 92		
11	...	2 Richard Chamberlin Luard	......	18 Mar. 85	17 Dec. 92		
10	...	1 John Davy Wright Davy	......	29 Aug. 85	2 Jan. 93		
10	...	1 Clements Parr	......	29 Aug. 85	22 Mar. 93		
10	...	Ernest Astley Edmund Lethbridge, *Adjutant* 4 Battalion 17 March 94	......	10 Oct. 85	27 Sept. 93		
9	...	1 William Owen	......	28 Apr. 86	27 Sept. 93		
9	...	2 Eardley Mostyn Childers	......	25 Aug. 86	16 Oct. 93		
9	...	2 Edward Alexander Stanton	5 Feb. 87	1 Jan. 89	17 Mar. 94		
11	...	2 George Samuel Frederick Napier, *at Staff College*	......	12 Nov. 84	30 May 94		
9	...	1 George Northcote Colvile	5 Feb. 87	3 May 89	9 Nov. 94		
		LIEUTENANTS.					
8	...	1 Percy Seymour Stanhope (*Depot*)	4 May 87	27 July 89			
8	...	1 Sir Charles Cuyler, *Bart, Adjutant* 2 Jan. 95	14 Sept. 87	30 Jan. 90			
8	...	2 Charles Coffin Pearson	14 Sept. 87	2 June 91			
8	...	2 Alexander Stewart Crum	14 Sept. 87	23 Jan. 92			
7	...	2 Roger Carmichael Robert Owen	30 May 88	27 Feb. 92			
7	...	1 Harry Lancelot Ruck-Keene	24 Apr. 89	16 Mar. 92			
6	...	2 John Lyttleton Powys	21 Sept. 89	15 Apr. 92			
6	...	2 Henry Forbes Darell-Brown	21 Dec. 89	24 July 92			
6	...	1 Cecil Henry Cobb	21 Dec. 89	24 July 92			
6	...	1 Redmond Edward Watt	26 Feb. 90	27 July 92			
5	...	1 Francis Joseph Henley	18 Feb. 91	27 July 92			
4	...	1 William Chevers Hunter	6 Jan. 92	22 Mar. 93			
4	...	2 Alexander Coburn Edwardes	27 Jan. 92	22 Mar. 93			
4	...	Hyla Napier Holden	12 Mar. 92	19 July 93			
3	...	2 Charles Joseph Wilkie	9 Apr. 92	19 July 93			
3	...	2 Duncan Robertson Napier	18 May 92	27 Sept. 93			
3	...	2 Keith Randolph Hamilton	18 May 92	16 Oct. 93			
3	...	1 Archibald James Fergusson Eden	18 June 92	17 Mar. 94			
3	...	2 Randle Montague Feilden	24 Aug. 92	18 Aug. 94			
3	...	2 Philip Barlow Osborn	28 Sept. 92	9 Nov. 94			
3	...	2 Wilfred Marriott-Dodington	19 Oct. 92	16 Jan. 95			
		SECOND LIEUTENANTS.					
3	...	1 Wilfrid Philip Bethell	19 Nov. 92				
3	...	2 Lindsay James Carter	4 Jan. 93				
3	...	1 William Lascelles Fitzgerald Blake	25 Feb. 93				
2	...	1 Lionel Folliott Scott	26 Apr. 93				

¹⁵ Major Eccles.—See Civil Decorations for Gallantry, "Hart's Annual Army List," p. 786.
²² Captain Hanbury-Williams served in the Egyptian war of 1882 as Aide de Camp to Sir E. Hamley, Commanding the 2nd Division, and was present at the battle of Tel-el-Kebir—horse shot (mentioned in despatches, Medal with Clasp, 5th Class of the Medjidie, and Khedive's Star).

287a   *The Oxfordshire Light Infantry.*

Years' Ser. Full Pay	Half Pay	SECOND LIEUTENANTS.	2ND LIEUT.
2	...	2 Henry William Bloomfield Trench.........	19 July 93
2	...	1 Stephen Frederick Hammick	24 Jan. 94
1	...	2 Charles Herbert Richards....................	2 June 94
1	...	1 Christian Cator	12 Dec. 94
1	...	1 Ashley Rowland Bright	12 Dec. 94
1	...	2 Robert Edward Salkeld	12 Dec. 94
1	...	Claud Oswald Chichester....................	6 Mar. 95
1	...	Lionel Edmund Anstey Bennett	6 Mar. 95

Paymasters.—1
2 Roger C. R. Owen, *Lieut.* 2 *Battalion* (acting).

| 14 | ... | *Quarter Masters.*—1 George Williams, 19 Nov. 81; *Hon. Captain*, 19 Nov. 91. |
| 1 | ... | 2 Benjamin Stannard, 18 July 94; *Hon. Lieut.* |

Facings White.—*Agents*, Messrs. Cox and Co.
1st Batt. returned from India, 1887.   2nd Batt. embarked for Egypt, 17 March 1885.

[1] Lt.General Wilkinson served with the 42nd Highlanders in the Crimea up to Oct. 1854, including the battle of Alma and siege of Sebastopol (Medal with two Clasps, 5th Class of the Medjidie, and Turkish Medal). Served the campaign of 1857-58 against the mutineers in India, including the action at Khodagunj, siege and fall of Lucknow, attack on the Fort of Rooyah, action of Allygunge, and capture of Bareilly (Medal with Clasp).
[7] Lt.Colonel Johnstone served in the operations near Suakin in December 1888 including the engagement at Gemaizah (mentioned in despatches, Medal with Clasp, 4th Class of the Medjidie, and Khedive's Star).
[13] Lt.Colonel Clerk served in the New Zealand war in 1864-65, and was thanked by H.R.H. the Commander in Chief on account of good service at the action of the Gate Pah—severely wounded (mentioned in despatches). Served also with expeditions in the province of Taranaki, destroying many Pahs and fortified villages (Medal). Served in the Burmese Expedition in 1886-87 as Staff Officer to the Shan Column, and with the Mounted Infantry 3rd Brigade (mentioned in despatches, Brevet of Lt.Colonel, Medal with two Clasps). Also served with the Anglo-Siam Boundary Commission and with the Wuntho and Manipore Expeditions (mentioned in despatches, Clasp).
[23] Captain Davies served with the Burmese Expedition in 1887-88 (Medal with Clasp).
[25] Major Humfrey.—For War Services, see Army Pay Department.

Record of the Services of the 1st Battalion Oxfordshire Light Infantry,—formerly the 43rd (Monmouthshire Light Infantry) Regiment.

Raised in 1741. Minorca, to 1747. Ireland, to 1757. America, to 1761. West Indies, to 1763. America, to 1764. England, to 1774. America, to 1783. England, to 1787. Ireland, to 1792. West Indies, to 1795. England, to 1797. West Indies, to 1800. England, to 1801. Channel Islands, to 1803. England, to July 1807. Denmark, to Nov. 1807. England, to 1808. The Peninsula, to 1808 (battle of Vimiera). England, to 1809 (one company remaining in the Peninsula). The Peninsula, to July 1814 (battles of Corunna, Busaco, Fuentes d'Onor, Ciudad Rodrigo, Badajoz, Salamanca, Vittoria, Nivelle, Nive, and Toulouse). England, to Oct. 1814. Gulf of Mexico, to March 1815. England and Belgium, to July 1815. France, to Oct. 1818. England, to 1819. Ireland, to 1822. Gibraltar and Portugal, to 1827. Gibraltar, to 1830. England, to 1832. Ireland, to 1834. America, to 1846. England, to 1848. Ireland, to 1851. Cape of Good Hope, to 1853. India, to 1863. New Zealand, to 1866. England, to 1868. Channel Islands, to 1869. Ireland, to 1872. India, to 1879. Burmah, to 1882. India, to 1887. England, 1887.

Record of the Services of the 2nd Battalion Oxfordshire Light Infantry (formerly the 52nd Light Infantry).

Raised in 1755 as the 54th Foot. Numbered 52nd, 1757. To Ireland, 1758. To Canada, 1765. To North America, 1774. To England, 1778. (Entitled "The Oxfordshire Regiment," 1782.) To India, 1783. To England, 1798. Formed as the 1st Light Infantry Regiment in 1803. To Sicily, 1806. To England, 1808. To Portugal, 1808 (battles of Vimiera and Corunna). To England, 1809. To the Peninsula, 1809 (battles of Busaco, Fuentes d'Onor, Ciudad Rodrigo, Badajoz, Salamanca, Vittoria, Nivelle, Nive, Orthes, and Toulouse). To England, 1814. To Belgium, 1815 (battle of Waterloo). [2nd Battalion raised in 1807, and proceeded to Copenhagen. To England, 1808. To Belgium, 1814. To England, 1815. Disbanded, 1816.] To England, 1818. To Canada, 1824. To England, 1831. To Gibraltar, 1837. To West Indies, 1838. To Canada, 1842. To England, 1848. To India, 1853 (capture of Delhi). To England, 1864. To Malta, 1868. To Gibraltar, 1873. To England, 1874. (Entitled "Oxfordshire Light Infantry," 1881.) To Gibraltar, 1884. To Egypt, 1885. To India, 1886.

Record of the Services of the 1st Battalion Black Watch,—formerly the 42nd (Royal Highland—The Black Watch) Regiment.

Independent Companies raised for service in the Highlands and styled "Black Watch," 1729. Formed into a Regiment and numbered 43rd, 1739. Scotland and England, 1743. Flanders, to 1745. England, to Sept. 1746. France, to Nov. 1746. Ireland and England, to 1747. Flanders, to 1748. England and Ireland, to 1756. (Number changed to 42nd, 1749.) America, to 1761. [2nd Battalion raised in 1758. West Indies, to 1758. America, to 1763. Reduced, 1763. Afterwards re-embodied, served in India, and formed into a Regiment in 1786, styled "The 73rd Highland Regiment of Foot."] West Indies, to 1762. America, to 1767. Ireland and Scotland, to 1776. America, to 1789. England and Scotland, to 1793. Coast of France, to Jan. 1794. England, to June 1794. Flanders, 1795. (Red Heckle conferred by King George III. for the affair at Guildermalson in 1795.) England, to 1796. (Five Companies embarked in 1795 for the West Indies, rejoining Head Quarters at Gibraltar in 1797.) Gibraltar, to 1798. Minorca, to Aug. 1800. Gibraltar, to Oct. 1800. Egypt, to 1801 ("Egypt," with the Sphinx). England and Scotland, to 1805. [2nd Battalion raised in 1803 and served in the Peninsula until consolidated with the 1st Battalion in 1812.] Gibraltar, to 1808. Peninsula, to 1809 (battles of Vimiera and Corunna). England, to July 1809. Walcheren Expedition to Sept. 1809. England and Scotland, to 1812. The Peninsula, to 1814 (battles of Fuentes d'Onor, Pyrenees, Nivelle, Nive, Orthes, and Toulouse). Ireland, to May 1815. Flanders, to Dec. 1815 (battle of Waterloo). England, Scotland and Ireland, to 1825. Gibraltar, to 1832. Malta, to 1834. Ionian Islands, to 1836. England, Scotland and Ireland, to 1840. Ionian Islands, to 1843. [Reserve Battalion formed in 1842, and served in Malta and the West Indies until consolidated with the 1st Battalion in 1850.] Malta, to 1847. West Indies, to 1851. Canada, to 1852. Scotland and England, to 1854. Turkey and the Crimea, to 1856 (battle of Alma and siege of Sebastopol). England, to 1857. India, to 1869 (capture of Lucknow). Scotland and England, to 1873. Gold Coast, to March 1874 (Ashanti war). England, to Nov. 1874. Malta and Cyprus, to 1878. Gibraltar, to 1879. England and Scotland, to 1882. Egypt and the Soudan, to 1886 (battles of Tel-el-Kebir and Kirbekan). Malta, to 1880. Gibraltar, to Jan. 1893. Egypt, to Mar. 1893. Head Quarters and Half Battalion to Mauritius, to Mar. 1893. Half Battalion to Cape Town, Apr. 1893.

1st Batt., Fermoy.
2nd Batt., Lucknow, Bengal.] **The Essex Regiment.** [Regimental District No. 44.—Warley.]

Formerly the 44th (East Essex) and the 56th (West Essex) Regiments.
(The 3rd and 4th Battalions are formed of the Essex Rifles and the West Essex Militia respectively.)
"MORO," "GIBRALTAR," with the Castle, Key, and "*Montis Insignia Calpe*," "EGYPT" (with the Sphinx),
"BADAJOZ" "SALAMANCA" "PENINSULA" "BLADENSBURG" "WATERLOO" "AVA"
"ALMA" "INKERMAN" "SEVASTOPOL" "TAKU FORTS" "NILE, 1884-85."

Years' Ser.						
Full Pay	Half Pay		ENSIGN OR 2ND LIEUT.	LIEUT.	CAPTAIN.	BREV. MAJ.	MAJOR.

Colonel.—Sir Charles William Dunbar Staveley,[1] GCB. Ensign, P 6 Mar. 35; Lt. 4 Oct. 39; Capt. P 6 Sept. 44; Major, 7 Dec. 50; Lt.Colonel, 12 Dec. 54; Colonel, 9 Mar. 58; Major General, 25 Sept. 67; Lieut.General, 29 April 75; General, 1 Oct. 77; Colonel 1st Battalion Essex Regiment, 25 July 83.

33 ... **Lieutenant Colonels.**—1 William Wood, Ensign, 31 Mar. 63; Lieut. 2 Jan. 69; Capt. 1 Apr. 75; Major, 8 Feb. 82; Lt.Colonel, 16 Sept. 91.
26 ... 2 Daniel Alexander Blest, Ensign, 7 July 69; Lieut. P 27 Oct. 71; Capt. 9 Oct. 79; Major, 3 July 82; Lt.Colonel, 8 Jan. 95.

Years		MAJORS.	ENSIGN OR 2ND LIEUT.	LIEUT.	CAPTAIN.	BREV. MAJ.	MAJOR.
21	...	2 p.s.c. Theodore Edward Stephenson	......	21 Sept. 74	1 July 81	......	27 Nov. 83
21	...	2 p.s.c. Francis Ventris[10] (Bt. Lt. Colonel 15 June 85; Colonel 15 June 89)	......	11 Feb. 75	5 Nov. 81	......	16 Dec. 83
21	...	2 Thomas Stock	......	11 Feb. 75	8 Feb. 82	......	15 Sept. 85
23	...	1 Cyril Wood	17 July 72	17 July 74	16 Aug. 82	......	21 Apr. 86
20	...	2 Frederick John Brown[19]	......	10 Sept. 75	16 Aug. 82	......	29 Apr. 91
20	...	1 Hugh Ingoldsby Massy	......	20 Nov. 75	30 Aug. 82	......	6 July 91
20	...	1 William Graydon Carter[13] (Depot)	......	10 Sept. 75	14 Mar. 83	15 June 85	16 Sept. 92

		CAPTAINS.					
19	...	2 Duncan Thomas Cruickshank[14]	......	12 Feb. 77	22 Aug. 83		
18	...	1 Charles Edward Orman[15] (Depot)	30 Jan. 78	19 Mar. 80	2 Feb. 84		
17	...	Henry Slane Fleming,[17] Commandant of Local Forces, Western Australia, with local rank of Lt. Colonel	25 Sept. 78	25 Aug. 80	30 July 84	15 June 85	
17	...	2 Henry Hyde Williamson Nason	4 Dec. 78	6 Oct. 80	10 Dec. 84		
17	...	1 John Trevor Spencer	22 Jan. 79	22 Dec. 80	15 Sept. 85		
16	...	2 p.s.c. Edward Lainson Guilding,[22]	13 Aug. 79	28 Jan. 81	15 Sept. 85		
16	...	1 Robt. John Tudway,[21] serving with the Egyptian Army, with rank of Major	13 Aug. 79	1 July 81	21 Apr. 86		
15	...	1 Henry Broadmead, Adjutant 4 Battalion 1 Nov. 92	22 Jan. 81	1 July 81	6 July 87		
14	...	2 Hugh Charles Copeman, Station Staff Officer, Bareilly, 30 Nov. 94	......	22 Oct. 81	1 July 88		
13	...	1 Launcelot Richard Carleton	......	10 May 82	1 July 88		
13	...	Percy Wilfrid Machell,[20] serving with the Egyptian Army, with rank of Major	......	10 May 82	19 Oct. 88		
13	...	2 John Cunningham[23]	......	10 May 82	19 Oct. 88		
16	...	2 William Hampden Chawner[19]	13 Aug. 79	28 June 80	2 Feb. 87		
13	...	James Frederick Macleod Prinsep[24]	......	10 May 82	6 Feb. 90		
13	...	William George Sackville Benson,[23] Army Pay Department	......	10 May 82	6 Feb. 90		
11	...	1 Henry Cowell Crawford	......	14 May 84	6 Aug. 90		
11	...	1 Frederick Gore Anley[25]	......	23 Aug. 84	6 July 91		
12	...	2 Edmund Murray Robertson (Depot)	......	25 Aug. 83	16 Sept. 91		

		LIEUTENANTS.					
11	...	1 Nevill Arthur Chas. de H.Tufnell (Depot)	......	12 Nov. 84			
11	...	Robert Francis Walters, Ordnance Store Department	......	7 Feb. 85			
11	...	1 George Bright Wallace	......	28 Feb. 85			
11	...	1 Bertram Arthur Warry	......	28 Feb. 85			
10	...	2 Henry Harris Hewitt Dowding, Staff Coll.	......	25 Nov. 85			
10	...	1 Rochfort Cade Lestock Battley	......	25 Nov. 85			
10	...	2 Owen Godfrey Godfrey-Faussett	......	30 Jan. 86			
10	...	1 Wilfrid Arthur Hebden	......	30 Jan. 86			
10	...	2 William Henry Wreford-Brown, Adjutant 2 June 91	......	30 Jan. 86			
9	...	1 William Jestyn Llewelyn Jeffreys	......	8 Dec. 86			
8	...	1 George Murray Tufnell	16 Nov. 87	2 Apr. 90			
8	...	1 Thomas Walter Milward, Adjutant 10 Aug. 92	11 Feb. 88	6 Aug. 90			
7	...	2 Edward Dalton Fawkes	......	14 Nov. 88	15 Dec. 90		
7	...	1 Hugh Roscoter Rice	......	8 Dec. 88	2 June 91		
7	...	2 William Kaye Legge	......	30 Jan. 89	6 July 91		
6	...	1 Walter Floyd Bonham	......	24 Apr. 89	16 Sept. 91		
6	...	2 Charles Wynn Barlow	......	24 Apr. 89	15 Dec. 91		
6	...	2 Charles George Lewes	......	21 Sept. 89	23 Sept. 92		
6	...	2 George Murray Home Stirling	......	9 Nov. 89	7 Oct. 92		
5	...	1 Clarence John Hobkirk	......	3 May 90	5 Apr. 93		
5	...	George Philip Roberts Beaman	......	3 May 90	4 Apr. 94		
5	...	2 Herbert Joseph Samuut	......	28 June 90	30 June 94		
6	...	2 Wm. Mountcharles Crofton Vandeleur	......	21 Dec. 89	25 Oct. 94		

		SECOND LIEUTENANTS.					
5	...	2 Frederick William Moffitt	8 Oct. 90				
5	...	1 Frederic Charles Winter	4 Mar. 91				
4	...	2 Hugo Sant-Fournier	17 June 91				
4	...	2 Charles Aitchison Smith	7 Nov. 91				
4	...	2 Herbert Charles Selwyn Heath	27 Jan. 92				
3	...	2 Charles Frederick de Bohun Boone	13 July 92				
3	...	1 Bertrand Charles Leigh	19 Oct. 92				
3	...	2 James Duncan Macpherson	19 Nov. 92				
2	...	1 Alfred Gilbert Pratt	26 Apr. 93				
1	...	1 Arthur Dowson Green	2 June 94				
1	...	2 Barnett Dyer Lompriere Gray Anley	10 Oct. 94				
1	...	Hugh Frederick Bundock	6 Mar. 95				

Years' Ser.		
Full Pay	Half Pay	
3	...	
1	...	

Paymasters.—2

Quarter Masters.—2 Moses Mead, 18 May 92; *Hon. Lieut.*
1 Thomas Piper, 10 Oct. 94; *Hon. Lieut.*

Facings White.—*Agents,* Messrs. Cox and Co.

1st Battalion returned from India, 28 *Nov.* 1884. *2nd Battalion embarked for Gibraltar,* 1882.

[1] Sir Charles Staveley served the Eastern campaign of 1854-55, including the battles of Alma and Balaklava (volunteered his services as Aide de Camp to the Duke of Cambridge), siege of Sebastopol, and attack and occupation of the Cemetery and Suburbs on the 18th June, when he succeeded to the command of the 44th Regt., and commanded it at the fall of Sebastopol (Medal with three clasps, *C.B.*, Sardinian and Turkish Medals, and 5th Class of the Medjidie). Commanded a Brigade in the campaign of 1860 in the North of China (mentioned in despatches, Medal with Clasp). Commanded the force employed against the Taepings in the vicinity of Shanghai in 1862, resulting in the attack and capture of the intrenched camp of Onkatz, of the walled cities of Kadin, Tsinpoo, Cholin, and the fortified towns of Najow and Tserpoo (made *KCB.* 1864). Served as 2nd in Command of the expedition to Abyssinia in 1867-68 and commanded the 1st Division in the action of Arroge and capture of Magdala (received the thanks of Parliament for his services and promoted Major General for distinguished services in the field, 1868; Medal).

[10] Colonel Ventris served in the Nile Expedition in 1884-85 with the 2nd Battalion of the Essex Regiment (mentioned in despatches, Brevet of Lt.Colonel, Medal with Clasp, and Khedive's Star).

[12] Major Brown served in the Nile Expedition in 1884-85 with the 2nd Battalion of the Essex Regiment (Medal with Clasp, and Khedive's Star).

[13] Major Carter served in the Nile Expedition in 1884-85 with the 2nd Battalion of the Essex Regiment (mentioned in despatches, Brevet of Major, Medal with Clasp, and Khedive's Star).

[14] Captain Cruickshank served in the Nile Expedition in 1884-85 with the 2nd Battalion of the Essex Regiment (Medal with Clasp, and Khedive's Star).

[15] Captain Orman served in the Nile Expedition in 1884-85 with the 2nd Battalion of the Essex Regiment (Medal with Clasp, and Khedive's Star).

[17] Lt.Colonel Fleming served with the Nile Expedition in 1884-85 as Staff Captain on the Head Quarters Staff (mentioned in despatches, Brevet of Major, Medal with Clasp, and Khedive's Star).

[19] Captain Chawner served in the Egyptian war of 1882, and was present at the battle of Tel-el-Kebir (Medal with Clasp, and Khedive's Star).

[20] Major Machell served in the Nile Expedition in 1884-85 with the 2nd Battalion Essex Regiment (Medal with Clasp, and Khedive's Star); served in the operations in the Soudan in 1888, including the attack on Fort Khor Mousa and the engagement at Gemaizah (4th Class of the Osmanieh, Clasp); and in the operations in 1889 including the engagement at Toski as Brigade Major No. 2 Column (Clasp); also served in the operations in 1891 including the capture of Tokar (4th Class of the Medjidie).

[21] Major Tudway served in the Nile Expedition in 1884-85 with the Mounted Infantry, and was present at the actions at Abu Klea and El Gubat (mentioned in despatches, Medal with two Clasps, and Khedive's Star); also served in the operations near Suakin in December 1888 and was present in the engagement at Gemaizah in command of Mounted Infantry (mentioned in despatches, Clasp, and 4th Class of the Medjidie).

[22] Captain Guilding served with the expedition to the Soudan under Sir Gerald Graham in 1884 (Medal, and Khedive's Star).

[23] Captains Cunningham and Benson served in the Nile Expedition in 1884-85 with the 2nd Battalion of the Essex Regiment (Medal with Clasp, and Khedive's Star).

[24] Captain Prinsep served in the Nile Expedition in 1884-85 with the 2nd Battalion of the Essex Regiment (Medal with Clasp, and Khedive's Star); also served in the operations near Suakin in December 1888 including the engagement at Gemaizah (mentioned in despatches, Clasp, and 4th Class of the Osmanieh). [See also Civil Decorations for Gallantry, "Hart's Annual Army List," p. 786.]

[25] Captain Anley served in the Nile Expedition in 1884-85 with the Mounted Infantry (Medal with Clasp, and Khedive's Star).

Record of the Services of the 2nd Battalion Essex Regiment (formerly the 56th Regiment).

Raised in 1755. Proceeded to the Havannah, 1762. Home, 1763. To Gibraltar, 1770. Home, 1783. To West Indies, 1793. Home, 1795. To West Indies, 1796. Home, 1799. To Holland, 1799. Home, 1799. (2nd Battalion raised in 1804; to India, 1807; home and disbanded in 1817.) To India, 1805. (3rd Battalion raised in 1813; proceeded to Holland, 1813; home and disbanded, 1814.) To Mauritius, 1815. Home, 1826. To West Indies, 1831. Home, 1842. To Gibraltar, 1846. (Reserve Battalion raised in 1846; proceeded to Gibraltar, 1847; incorporated with 1st Battalion, 1850.) To Bermuda, 1851. Home, 1855. To Crimea, 1855. Home, 1856. To India, 1857. Home, 1866. To India, 1871. To Aden, 1877. Home, 1878. To Gibraltar, 1882. To Egypt, 1884. To Malta, 1887.

The Sherwood Foresters (Derbyshire Regiment). 289

1st Batt., Dublin.
2nd Batt., Umballa, Bengal.] *Formerly the 45th (Nottinghamshire— Sherwood Foresters) and the 95th (Derbyshire) Regiments.* [Regimental District No. 45.—Derby.

(The 3rd Bn. is formed of the 1st and 2nd Derby Militia, the 4th Bn. of the Sherwood Foresters Militia.)
The United Red and White Rose. "LOUISBURG" "ROLEIA" "VIMIERA" "TALAVERA" "BUSACO" "FUENTES D'ONOR" "CIUDAD RODRIGO" "BADAJOZ" "SALAMANCA" "VITTORIA" "PYRENEES" "NIVELLE" "ORTHES" "TOULOUSE" "PENINSULA" "AVA" "SOUTH AFRICA, 1846-7" "ALMA" "INKERMAN" "SEVASTOPOL" "CENTRAL INDIA" "ABYSSINIA" "EGYPT, 1882."

Years' Ser.								
Full Pay	Half Pay							
33	1 5/12	**Colonel.**—Sir Daniel Lysons,[1] GCB. *Constable of the Tower*; Ensign, P26 Dec. 34; Lt. 23 Aug. 37; Captain, P29 Dec. 43; Major, P3 Aug. 49; Lt.Colonel, 21 Sept. 54; Colonel, 17 July 55; Major General, 6 March 68; Lieut.General, 2 June 77; General, 14 July 79; Colonel 45th Foot, 25 Aug. 78.							
26	...	**Lieutenant Colonels.**—2 Thomas Mercer Maxwell, Ensign, P18 Dec. 60; Lieut. P11 Aug. 63; Captain, 6 Mar. 74; Major, 14 Feb. 82; Lt.Colonel, 14 Feb. 90.							
		1 John William Thring Hume,[5] Ensign, 8 July 69; Lt. 28 Oct. 71; Captain, 18 Dec. 80; Major, 1 Dec. 84; Lt.Colonel, 1 Jan. 94.							

		MAJORS.	2ND LIEUT.	LIEUT.	CAPTAIN.	BREV.MAJ.	MAJOR.
24	...	2 Edward Cecil Dowse	......	30 Dec. 71	23 Mar. 81	......	21 July 85
21	...	1 William Bicknell Coney[3]	......	11 Feb. 75	1 Apr. 82	......	14 Feb. 90
20	...	p.s.c. H. Lockwood Smith-Dorrien,[6] DSO. A.A.Gen. Bengal, 27 Oct. 94	......	26 Feb. 76	22 Aug. 82	......	11 May 92
20	...	Arthur Dolben Bulpett, District Inspector of Musk. Aldershot, 16 Dec. 94	......	20 Nov. 75	19 Jan. 83	......	21 July 92
18	...	2 Frederick Edward Verney Taylor[3]	......	17 May 77	22 July 83	......	4 Aug. 92
17	...	Harold Carmichael Wylly,[8] D.A.A. Gen. for Musk., Bengal, 8 May 92	......	11 Sept. 78	1 May 84	......	26 May 93
17	...	1 Francis Clements Godley[9]	......	11 Sept. 78	4 Oct. 84	......	1 Jan. 94
21	...	1 Henry Crosbie[10] (Depot)	......	26 June 74	18 Jan. 82	......	11 July 94
		CAPTAINS.					
17	...	2 p.s.c. Ernest Allardice Gardiner Gosset[11]	1 May 78	12 Feb. 79	4 Oct. 84		
17	...	1 Francis Studdert Evans,[3] Adjutant 20 Mar. 93	1 May 78	21 Feb. 79	12 Nov. 84		
17	...	1 George Seymour Charles Jenkinson[12]	1 May 78	28 Feb. 79	1 Dec. 84		
16	...	p.s.c. Charles Newcomen Watts, D.A.A. General, Natal, 18 Jan. 93	13 Aug. 79	1 Jan. 81	4 June 85		
15	...	1 James Albert Reeks	11 Aug. 80	4 May 81	19 May 86		
16	...	Alfred Ashurst Etheridge[15]	13 Aug. 79	2 Feb. 81	22 Feb. 86		
15	...	Ronald Rogers Kilbee-Stuart, Adj. 1 Notts Rifle Vols. 1 May 90	22 Jan. 81	8 June 81	21 Oct. 87		
14	...	2 Ludovic Seymour Gordon-Cumming	......	22 Oct. 81	20 Feb. 89	15 Aug. 89	
14	...	George Glencairn Cunningham,[17] on special service, Uganda	......	22 Oct. 81	14 Aug. 89		
14	...	Fred. Chas. Shaw,[3] Adj. 3 Bn. 18 Aug.90	......	28 Jan. 82	14 Aug. 89		
14	...	Henry James Bowman,[18] Adjutant 4 Battalion Scottish Rifles 1 Nov. 90	......	28 Jan. 82	1 Jan. 90		
14	...	Lionel Arthur Montagu Stopford,[19] Aide de Camp to Major General J.N. Crealock 6 Dec. 93	......	28 Jan. 82	1 Jan. 90		
14	...	Grenville Edwyn Temple,[20] Adj. 4 Vol. Bn. Derbyshire Regt. 31 Mar. 92	......	28 Jan. 82	14 Feb. 90		
14	...	Herbert Augustus Iggulden,[21] Adj. Agra Volunteer Rifles 13 Jan. 93	......	28 Jan. 82	1 May 90		
15	...	2 Henry Ellison Wise,[22] Staff College	25 Aug. 80	1 July 81	26 Nov. 90		
13	...	2 Lionel Arthur Bosanquet (Depot)	......	10 Mar. 83	8 May 92		
12	...	1 Chambers Didham	......	5 Dec. 83	11 May 92		
11	...	2 John Wm. Gascoigne Roy,[23] Adjutant 2 July 91	......	12 Nov. 84	2 June 92		
10	...	Reginald Brittan, Adjutant 4 Battalion 1 Mar. 95	......	29 Aug. 85	21 July 92		
10	...	1 Philip Carteret Fall Atherley	......	6 May 85	14 Dec. 92		
10	...	2 William Raine Marshall	......	30 Jan. 86	13 Jan. 93		
10	...	2 Frederick Porter	......	25 Nov. 85	19 May 93		
8	...	1 Cyril Randell Crofton-Atkins	14 Sept. 87	1 Jan. 90	23 Sept. 93		
7	...	1 Patrick William Anderson	9 May 88	19 Apr. 90	24 Dec. 93		
7	...	2 Thomas Harold Mortimer Green	16 May 88	1 May 90	1 Jan. 94		
8	...	2 Arthur Kerr Slessor	22 Feb. 88	1 Dec. 89	11 Apr. 94		
		LIEUTENANTS.					
7	...	1 Alick Thornber England	22 Aug. 88	20 July 90			
6	...	2 Arthur Sutton Adkins	9 Nov. 89	2 July 91			
6	...	1 Leonard Alfred Bagshawe	9 Nov. 89	22 July 91			
6	...	1 William Edward Clifton Smith (Depot)	21 Dec. 89	1 Sept. 91			
5	...	2 Martin Stainforth	16 July 90	21 July 92			
5	...	2 Francis Harry Weldon (Depot)	30 July 90	21 July 92			
5	...	2 Percy George Rigby	29 Nov. 90	21 July 92			
5	...	2 John Mansfield Stradling Crealock	4 Mar. 91	21 July 92			
4	...	2 Philip Leveson Gower	9 Sept. 91	14 Dec. 92			
4	...	Thomas Louis Leeds	9 Sept. 91	14 Dec. 92			
4	...	2 Malet Peyton Phelps	10 Oct. 91	14 Dec. 92			
4	...	2 William Edmund Pye	27 Jan. 92	13 Jan. 93			
3	...	2 Sydney Ives de Kantzow	18 June 92	10 May 93			
3	...	2 Frederick Barton Maurice	18 June 92	16 May 93			
3	...	1 Frederic John Radford	13 Aug. 92	19 May 93			
3	...	2 Henry William Poyntz	13 Aug. 92	23 Sept. 93			
3	...	2 Malcolm Edward Lloyd Bruce	13 Aug. 92	23 Sept. 93			
3	...	Charles Danby Christopher, Army Service Corps	28 Sept. 92	24 Dec. 93			
3	...	2 Charles William Keene	28 Sept. 92	1 Jan. 94			
3	...	2 Charles Reynolds Mortimore	19 Nov. 92	13 July 94			
		SECOND LIEUTENANTS.					
3	...	1 John George Blackburne	19 Nov. 92				
3	...	1 Frank Casswell	7 Dec. 92				
3	...	2 Lachlan M'Kinnon	17 Dec. 92				

[21] Captain Iggulden served with the 2nd Battalion Derbyshire Regiment in the Egyptian war of 1882 (Medal, and Khedive's Star). Served in the Sikkim Expedition in 1888 with the 2nd Battalion Derbyshire Regiment, and was present in the engagements at Jeluk, Gnathong, and the Jelapla (mentioned in despatches, Medal with Clasp).

[22] Captain Wise served during the rebellion in the North West Territories of Canada in 1885 as Aide de Camp to Sir Frederick Middleton, and was present in the engagements at Fish Creek (wounded) and Batoche (mentioned in despatches, Medal with Clasp).

The Sherwood Foresters (Derbyshire Regiment).

Years' Ser. Full Pay	Half Pay	SECOND LIEUTENANTS.	2ND LIEUT.
2	...	1 Percy Matthew Dove	26 Apr. 93
2	...	1 Ralph Peyton Sadler	19 July 93
2	...	2 George Knowles	19 July 93
4	...	2 Charles Bliss	5 Dec. 91
2	...	1 Robert Vesey Savile	21 Oct. 93
2	...	1 Henry Singleton Pennell	21 Oct. 93
2	...	1 Robert James Frederick Taylor	7 Mar. 94
1	...	2 Rudolph Henry Keller	2 June 94
1	...	2 Daniel Charles Evans Gross	10 Oct. 94
32	...	*Paymasters.*—2 Thomas C. Hood,[27] 8 June 81; *Ens.* [17] Nov. 63; *Lt.* [22] June 67; *Capt.* 6 Mar. 80; *Hon. Major,* 8 June 86.	
8	...	*Quarter Masters.*—2 Albert Edward Riddell, 8 Feb. 88; *Hon. Lieut.*	
5	...	1 Edward Patterson, 25 Feb. 91; *Hon. Lieut.*	

Facings White.—*Agents,* Messrs. Cox and Co.
1st Battalion returned from India, March 1878. 2nd Battalion embarked for Gibraltar, 1881.

[1] Sir Daniel Lysons served in Canada during the rebellion in 1838–39, including the actions of St. Denis (mentioned in despatches) and St. Eustache. Was mentioned in despatches and general orders on the occasion of the wreck of the transport *Premier* on 4th November 1843; promoted in consequence. Served the Eastern campaign of 1854-55; was present at the battles of Alma (mentioned in despatches) and Inkerman, the minor affairs of Bulganac, M'Kenzie's Farm, capture of Balaklava, and throughout the whole siege of Sebastopol; led the main Column of attack on the Redan by the Light Division on the 18th June, and commanded a Brigade in the latter part of the action (slightly wounded, mentioned in despatches); was engaged in the final assault of the Redan on the 8th September (severely wounded, mentioned in despatches); commanded the 2nd Brigade Light Division from October 1855 to the end of the war (Medal with three Clasps, Brevet of Colonel, *CB.*, Officer of the Legion of Honour, Sardinian and Turkish Medals, and 3rd Class of the Medjidie).

[3] Majors Coney and Taylor, Captains Evans and Shaw served with the 2nd Battalion Derbyshire Regiment in the Egyptian war of 1882 (Medal, and Khedive's Star).

[5] Lt. Colonel Hume served in the Sikkim Expedition in 1888 with the 2nd Battalion Derbyshire Regiment, and was present in the engagement at the Jelapla (Medal with Clasp).

[6] Major Smith-Dorrien served in the Zulu war in 1879, and was present in the engagements at Isandhlwana and Ulundi (mentioned in despatches, Medal with Clasp). Served in the Egyptian war of 1882 in command of the Mounted Infantry (which he raised) with Sir Evelyn Wood's Brigade (Medal, and Khedive's Star). Served in the Soudan campaign in 1885 with the Mounted Infantry (Clasp); also served with the Soudan Frontier Field Force in 1885–86 including the investment of Kosheh and the engagement at Giniss (mentioned in despatches, *DSO.*, and 4th Class of the Medjidie). In 1887 he was nominated to the 4th Class of the Osmanieh for services with the Egyptian Army.

[8] Major Wylly served with the 2nd Battalion Derbyshire Regiment in the Egyptian war of 1882 (Medal and Khedive's Star). Served in the Sikkim Expedition in 1888 with the 2nd Battalion Derbyshire Regiment, part of the time in command of a detachment, and was present in the engagements at Jeluk, Gnathong, and the Jelapla (mentioned in despatches, Medal with Clasp).

[9] Major Godley served in the Sikkim Expedition in 1888 with the 2nd Battalion Derbyshire Regiment, and was present in the engagement at the Jelapla (Medal with Clasp).

[10] Major Crosbie served with the 81st Regiment in the Afghan war in 1878-79, and was present at the capture of Ali Musjid (Medal with Clasp).

[11] Captain Gosset served with Barrow's Mounted Infantry in the Boer war of 1881. Served as Adjutant 2nd Battalion Derbyshire Regiment in the Egyptian war of 1882 (Medal, and Khedive's Star). Served in the Sikkim Field Force in 1888 with the 2nd Battalion Derbyshire Regiment, and was present in the engagement at Gnathong (Medal with Clasp).

[12] Captain Jenkinson served with the Burmese Expedition in 1885-87, and was severely wounded in an engagement on the 9th August 1887 (Medal with Clasp).

[16] Captain Etheridge served in the Sikkim Expedition in 1888 with the 2nd Battalion Derbyshire Regiment. (Medal with Clasp).

[17] Major Cunningham served in the Egyptian war of 1882, and was present in the engagements at El Magfar and Tel-el-Mahuta, and in the action at Kassasin on the 28th August—twice wounded (mentioned in despatches, Medal, Brevet of Major, 5th Class of the Medjidie, and Khedive's Star). Served in the Nile Expedition in 1884-85 with the 2nd Battalion of the Duke of Cornwall's Light Infantry, and took part in the operations of the Advance Column under Major General Earle (Clasp); also served in the operations of the Soudan Frontier Field Force in 1887 including the engagement at Sarras, and in the operations in 1889 including the engagements at Arguin (wounded) and Toski (Clasp). Nominated to the 4th Class of the Osmanieh for services with the Egyptian Army.

[18] Captain Bowman served with the 2nd Battalion Derbyshire Regiment in the Egyptian war of 1882 (Medal, and Khedive's Star). Served in the Sikkim Expedition in 1888 with the 2nd Battalion Derbyshire Regiment, and was present in the engagements at Jeluk, Gnathong, and the Jelapla (Medal with Clasp).

[19] Captain Stopford served with the 2nd Battalion Derbyshire Regiment in the Egyptian war of 1882 (Medal, and Khedive's Star). Served in the Sikkim Expedition in 1888 as Adjutant to the 2nd Battalion Derbyshire Regiment, and was present in the engagement at the Jelapla (Medal with Clasp).

[20] Captain Temple served with the 2nd Battalion Derbyshire Regiment in the Egyptian war of 1882 (Medal, and Khedive's Star). Served in the Sikkim Expedition in 1888 with the 2nd Battalion Derbyshire Regiment, and was present in the engagements at Gnathong and the Jelapla (Medal with Clasp).

[23] Captain Roy served with the Sikkim Expedition in 1888 (Medal with Clasp).

[27] Major Hood.—For War Services, see Army Pay Department.

Record of the Services of the 2nd Battalion Sherwood Foresters (Derbyshire Regiment),—formerly the 95th Regiment.

Raised in 1823. To Malta, 1824. To the Ionian Islands, 1829. To Ireland, 1835. To Ceylon, 1838. To Hong Kong, 1847. To England, 1850. To the Crimea, 1854 (battles of Alma and Inkerman and siege of Sebastopol). To England and Ireland, 1856. To India, 1857 (Indian Mutiny—"Central India"). To England, 1870. To Ireland, 1877. To England, 1880. To Gibraltar, 1881. To Egypt, 1882. To India, 1882 (Sikkim Expedition, 1888).

[1st Batt., Poona, Bombay.]
[2nd Batt., Mhow, ?] **The Loyal North Lancashire Regt.** [Regimental District No. 47.—Preston.] 291

Formerly the 47th (Lancashire) and the 81st (Loyal Lincoln Volunteers) Regiments.
(The 3rd and 4th Battalions are formed of the 3rd Lancashire Militia.)

The Red Rose. "LOUISBURG" "QUEBEC, 1759" "MAIDA" "CORUNNA" "TARIFA" "VITTORIA" "ST. SEBASTIAN" "PENINSULA" "AVA" "ALMA" "INKERMAN" "SEVASTOPOL" "ALI MASJID" "AFGHANISTAN, 1878-79."

Colonels.—1 Sir Richard Thomas Farren,¹ KCB. Ens. 30 May 34; Lieut. 31 Jan. 40; Capt. 3 Jan. 45; Major, ²27 Dec. 50; Bt.Lt.Col. 12 Dec. 54; Lt.Col. 9 March 55; Colonel, 12 Dec. 57; Major General, 6 March 68; Lieut. General, 1 Oct. 77; General, 29 Apr. 80; Colonel North Lancashire Regt. 14 Sept. 85.

2 Henry Renny,² CSI. Ensign, ᴾ27 Dec. 33; Lieut. ᴾ7 Aug. 35; Capt. 29 May 44; Major, ᴾ17 Nov. 48; Lieut. Colonel, 27 May 53; Colonel, 28 Nov. 54; Major General, 2 Feb. 67; Lieutenant General, 5 Dec. 74; General, 1 Oct. 77; Colonel 81st Foot, 9 June 79.

Years' Ser. Full Pay	Half Pay		ENS. OR 2D LT.	LIEUT.	CAPTAIN.	BREV. MAJ.	MAJOR.
28	...	Lieutenant Colonels.—1 Frank Ryley,³ Ensign, ᴾ12 June 67; Lt. 24 Dec. 70; Capt. 7 Jan. 80; Major, 23 May 82; Lt. Colonel, 1 July 91.					
28	...	2 p.s.c. Henry Cecil Binsteed Farrant,⁴ Ensign, ᴾ4 Sept. 67; Lieut. 25 Mar. 71; Capt. 6 Mar. 80; Major, 9 July 84; Lt. Colonel, 11 Apr. 93.					
		MAJORS.					
28	...	1 p.s.c. Arthur Grey Tidy	8 Jan. 68	ᴾ24 Apr. 69	30 May 77	......	22 Nov. 84
28	...	2 Benjamin Arthur Satterthwaite¹¹	ᴾ16 Oct. 67	28 Oct. 71	26 May 80	......	28 Aug. 86
27	...	Charles Edward Sawyer,⁸ Assistant Adj. General, Bombay, 19 July 90	23 Jan. 69	28 Oct. 71	29 Sept. 80	......	14 Dec. 87
23	...	1 Spenser Jackson¹⁶	......	15 Mar. 73	2 Feb. 81	......	10 May 89
22	...	2 Edward Coxwell Morris⁹	......	9 Aug. 73	2 Feb. 81	......	31 May 90
22	...	1 Daniel de Hoghton, Commandant Khandalla Sanitarium	......	28 Feb. 74	10 July 81	......	1 July 91
21	...	1 Henry George Purdon	......	11 Sept. 74	5 Jan. 84	......	6 Mar. 91
22	...	2 John Davidson¹³ (Depot)	......	28 Feb. 74	1 Oct. 81	......	11 Apr. 93
		CAPTAINS.					
20	...	Philip Palmes,¹¹ Adj. 1 Jersey Mil. 7 Oct. 92		21 Sept. 75	23 May 82		
22	...	1 Edward Lindesay, Commandant Mount Aboo Sanitarium 21 Nov. 93	......	12 Nov. 73	15 Oct. 81		
19	...	Hugh Gastrell Leonard,¹⁰ Adjutant 3 and 4 Battalions 28 March 92		10 Sept. 76	10 Sept. 84		
17	...	1 John Randal Fraser	1 May 78	7 Jan. 80	20 Jan. 85		
21	...	Orestes John Hy. Brooker, Adjutant 3 Vol. Bn. Liverpool Regt. 3 Dec. 94	......	11 Feb. 75	27 June 85		
18	...	1 Paul Rycaut S. Churchward¹⁵ (Depot)	30 Jan. 78	26 May 80	28 Aug. 86		
17	...	2 Arthur Charles Henry Thomas¹⁷	1 May 78	29 Sept. 80	12 Feb. 87		
17	...	William Hugh Eric Murray¹⁰	22 Jan. 79	2 Oct. 80	14 May 87		
17	...	Hugh Fortesque Coleridge, Adjutant 1 Volunteer Battalion 1 May 93	22 Jan. 79	1 July 81	1 July 87		
16	...	Gerald Alfred Norcott,¹⁰ Adjutant 3 Jersey Militia 1 Oct. 91	13 Aug. 79	1 July 81	14 Dec. 87		
16	...	George William Henry Le Feuvre, Adj. 3 Bn. Lancaster Regt. 24 Mar. 91	13 Aug. 79	1 July 81	3 Feb. 88		
15	...	2 R. Sandilands Lawrence Wynell-Mayow	11 Aug. 80	1 July 81	7 Feb. 88		
15	...	George William Dowell, Adjutant 2 Volunteer Battalion 15 June 91	23 Oct. 80	1 July 81	7 Feb. 88		
14	...	Gerard Aug. Faulder, Adj. 4 Vol. Bn. West Surrey Regiment 3 July 93	......	28 Jan. 82	10 Sept. 90		
15	...	2 Douglas Paynter Stewart Reid	23 Oct. 80	1 July 81	29 Jan. 90		
13	...	2 Charles James Daniel¹⁰	......	10 May 82	7 Oct. 92		
13	...	2 John Henry Ansley	......	9 Sept. 82	12 Dec. 92		
13	...	2 Edward Gerald Costobadie	......	27 Jan. 83	12 Jan. 93		
11	...	1 Mervyn Archdall Humphrys	......	14 May 84	11 Apr. 93		
11	...	2 Roland Wycliffe Thompson, Adjutant 3 July 93	......	7 Feb. 85	1 May 93		
10	...	Francis Carleton Logan Logan, Adj. 1 Vol. Bn. W. Riding Regt. 15 Nov. 93	......	25 Nov. 85	3 July 93		
9	...	1 Russell Loscombe Stable	......	28 Apr. 86	3 July 93		
9	...	1 William ffyfe Elletson	......	28 May 86	15 Nov. 93		
9	...	1 Guy C. Knight, Adjutant 20 Oct. 94	5 Feb. 87	8 Sept. 88	11 July 94		
9	...	2 Henry George Powell	5 Feb. 87	8 Sept. 88	3 Dec. 94		
		LIEUTENANTS.					
8	...	2 Gilbert Lewes Parker	11 Feb. 88	19 July 90			
7	...	2 Ramsay Robert Feilden	9 May 88	6 Sept. 90			
7	...	1 Charles Edward Arthur Jourdain	22 Aug. 88	29 Apr. 91			
7	...	2 Walter Reginald Lloyd	22 Aug. 88	21 June 91			
7	...	1 Gerald Hopton Wylde-Browne	22 Aug. 88	15 July 91			
7	...	1 Thomas Henry O'Brien	5 Sept. 88	1 Oct. 91			
7	...	2 John Edward Pine-Coffin (Depot)	10 Nov. 88	13 Oct. 91			
6	...	1 Edward Sharpe Smith	8 June 89	30 Dec. 91			
5	...	1 John Gordon Lowndes	30 July 90	24 Aug. 92			
5	...	Norman Burrows, serving in the Niger Coast Protectorate	17 Jan. 91	7 Oct. 92			
4	...	1 Harold Arthur Robinson	2 May 91	12 Dec. 92			
4	...	1 Aubrey John O'Brien	25 July 91	12 Dec. 92			
4	...	1 George Vincent Watson (Depot)	9 Sept. 91	12 Jan. 93			
4	...	1 Percy Bosworth Hancock	7 Nov. 91	11 Apr. 93			
4	...	1 Aubrey John Carter	22 Apr. 92	1 May 93			
3	...	2 Francis Joseph Bowen	13 July 92	15 Nov. 93			
3	...	2 Robert Russell Bowlby	21 Sept. 92	15 Nov. 93			
3	...	2 Howard Alaric Gib	14 Sept. 92	11 July 94			
3	...	1 Frederick Rodolph Rothwell Greene	19 Nov. 92	3 Dec. 94			
		SECOND LIEUTENANTS.					
3	...	1 John Glennie Greig	19 Nov. 92				
3	...	2 Francis Joseph Braithwaite	21 Jan. 93				
3	...	2 Augustus Robert Wallace	21 Jan. 93				
2	...	1 Charles Henry Marion Bingham	19 July 93				
2	...	2 George Loch	19 July 93				
2	...	2 Alfred Burrows	19 July 93				
2	...	2 John Alder Burdon	23 Aug. 93				
2	...	2 Thomas M'Ghie Bridges	9 Sept. 93				
2	...	1 Francis Willoughby Woodward	21 Oct. 93				
2	...	2 Kenneth Zachary Pollock Macaulay	7 Mar. 94				
1	...	2 Cecil John Newton	10 Oct. 94				
1	...	2 Robert Mackay Cadell	6 Feb. 95				

⁸ Major Sawyer served in the Afghan war in 1878-79 as Orderly Officer to Brigadier Gen. Appleyard, and was present at the attack and capture of Ali Musjid and the Bazar Valley Expedition (Medal with Clasp).

⁹ Major Morris served in the Afghan war in 1879 as Transport Officer with the 1st Division of the Peshawur Valley Field Force (Medal). Served in the Zhob Valley Expedition in 1884 with a wing of the 1st Battalion North Lancashire Regiment.

¹⁰ Captains Leonard, Murray, Norcott and Daniel served in the Zhob Valley Expedition in 1884 with a wing of the 1st Battalion North Lancashire Regiment.

¹¹ Major Satterthwaite, and Captain Palmes served with the 81st Regiment in the Afghan war in 1878-79, and were present at the capture of Ali Musjid (Medal with Clasp).

¹³ Major Davidson served with the 81st Regiment in the Afghan war in 1878-79 (Medal). Served with the Bechuanaland Expedition under Sir Charles Warren in 1864-85.

[For remainder of Notes, see end of Northampton Regiment, page 292a.]

Facings White.—Agents, Messrs. Cox and Co.

1st Battalion embarked for Gibraltar, 1882. 2nd Battalion returned from India, 1883.

Paymasters.—1 Mervyn A. Humphrys, Captain 1 Battalion (acting).

5	...	Quarter Masters.—2 Henry John Gill, 22 Oct. 90; Hon. Lieut.		
3	...	2 Walter Bentley, 9 Nov. 92; Hon. Lieut.		

292 1st Batt., Bangalore, Madras.
2nd Batt., Colchester.]**The Northamptonshire Regiment.**[*Regimental District*
No. 48.—Northampton

Formerly the 48th (Northamptonshire) and the 58th (Rutlandshire) Regiments.
(The 3rd and 4th Battalions are formed of the Northampton and Rutland Militia.)
"LOUISBURG" "QUEBEC, 1759" "GIBRALTAR" with the Castle, Key, and "Montis Insignia Calpe." "EGYPT" with the Sphinx). "MAIDA" "DOURO" "TALAVERA" "ALBUHERA" "BADAJOZ" "SALAMANCA" "VITTORIA" "PYRENEES" "NIVELLE" "ORTHES" "TOULOUSE" "PENINSULA" "SEVASTOPOL" "NEW ZEALAND" "SOUTH AFRICA, 1879."

Years' Ser. Full Pay	Half Pay		
29	...	Colonel,—c. William Anson M'Cleverty,[1] *Ensign*, 26 March 24; *Lt.* 26 Aug. 25; *Capt.* [P]21 May 29; *Major*, [P]23 April 41; *Bt.Lt.Colonel*, 19 Dec. 45; *Colonel*, 20 June 54; *Lt.Colonel*, 2 Oct. 57; *Major General*, 4 May 60; *Lieut. General*, 22 Nov. 68; *General*, 17 March 76; *Colonel* 48th Foot, 29 April 75.		
29	...	Lieutenant Colonels.—2 Thomas Charles Orde Powlett, *Ensign*, [P]16 Oct. 66; *Lieut.* [P]14 Mar. 68; *Capt.* [P]28 Oct. 71; *Major*, 10 June 82; *Lt.Colonel*, 1 Apr. 94.		
29	...	1 Robert James Chaytor, *Ensign*, [P]6 Mar. 67; *Lieut.* [P]14 Oct. 68; *Capt.* 21 Jan. 81; *Major*, 6 Aug. 83; *Lt.Colonel*, 22 Nov. 94.		

		MAJORS.	ENS.or2D.LT.	LIEUT.	CAPTAIN.	BREV.MAJ.	MAJOR.
27	...	2 Frederick Edward Power	[P]25 April 68	[P]27 Oct. 71	20 Apr. 81	......	20 Aug. 84
26	...	1 Robert Hugh Fraser	[P]21 Aug. 69	28 Oct. 71	1 July 81	......	1 Oct. 86
25	...	p.s.c.Geo. Fitzherbert Browne,[9] *DSO.* *D. A. A.Gen., War Office*, 19 Jan. 91	6 July 70	28 Oct. 71	16 Dec. 82	......	22 Nov. 90
18	...	1 Henry Cuthbert Denny	31 Oct. 77	29 Oct. 79	20 Oct. 83	......	22 Apr. 93
18	...	p.s.c.Thos. EdwardCompton,[11] *D.A.A. Gen. Straits Settlements*, 7 Feb. 91	30 Jan. 78	15 Nov. 79	14 Nov. 83	......	8 Nov. 93
17	...	William Francis Fawcett,[12] *Adjutant* 1 *Volunteer Battalion* 22 Apr. 91	12 June 78	14 April 80	25 Mar. 84	......	1 Apr. 94
17	...	John Collinson,[13] *with the EgyptianArmy*	22 Jan. 79	8 May 80	20 Aug. 84	......	30 May 94
17	...	1 Henry Morgan[17]	22 Jan. 79	31 May 80	25 Oct. 84	......	22 Nov. 94
		CAPTAINS.					
17	...	2 Archer Clive Bolton[14] (*Depot*)	22 Feb. 79	25 Aug. 80	22 Nov. 84		
17	...	1 ⌘Alan Richard Hill,[15] *Station Staff Officer, Bangalore*, 3 May 93	22 Feb. 79	29 Jan. 81	1 Sept. 86		
15	...	Edward Fitzgerald Brereton	11 Aug. 80	12 Mar. 81	1 Sept. 86		
16	...	2 Frederick Henry Lucy[16]	14 Jan. 80	1 July 81	1 Oct. 86		
19	...	p.s.c. Harold Ar. Sandbach Barkworth		30 Nov. 76	15 Dec. 86		
15	...	2 Charles Sturrock Copland	22 Jan. 81	1 July 81	1 July 87		
16	...	2 p.s.c. Herbert Christie Prichard[18]	13 Aug. 79	1 July 81	6 Oct. 87		
16	...	Francis Bernard Lawson, *Adj.* 3 *Vol. Bn. Manchester Regt.* 8 Mar. 93	14 Jan. 80	1 July 81	22 Oct. 87		
13	...	2 Charles Stewart Prichard	......	10 May 82	2 Sept. 89		
13	...	Fred. Jas. Parker, *Adj.* 3 & 4 *Bn.* 1 Oct.92	......	10 May 82	13 Sept. 89		
13	...	1 Arthur Howel Wilfrid Norgate	......	10 May 82	22 Nov. 90		
13	...	1 Arthur Herbert Barthorp, *Staff College*	......	27 Jan. 83	22 Nov. 90		
15	...	Arthur H. Cleveland Kenney-Herbert, *Inst. R. M. College* 16 Apr. 90	......	10 Mar. 83	19 Jan. 91		
12	...	1 Arthur Parkin	......	19 Dec. 83	19 Jan. 91		
12	...	Harry Crowe Godley, *Adjutant* 3 *Vol. Bn. Norfolk Regt.* 15 Sept. 92	......	30 Jan. 84	1 Mar. 91		
10	...	John Thomas Carter, *Army Pay Dept.*					
11	...	1 George Eustace Ripley (*Depot*)	......	20 May 85	6 May 91		
11	...	2 John Andrew Chilton Wetherall	......	14 May 84	3 Oct. 91		
11	...	2 John Little	......	14 May 84	8 Nov. 92		
11	...	1 Arthur Francis Bacon	......	14 May 84	17 May 93		
11	...	2 Edward Osborne Smith	......	23 Aug. 84	28 July 93		
11	...	1 William Burnett Woodham, **Adjutant** 5 Aug. 94	......	10 Sept. 84	28 July 93		
11	...	1 Malcolm David Graham	......	12 Nov. 84	29 Sept. 93		
11	...	2 Arthur Athelwold Lloyd, **Adjutant** 20 Nov. 94	......	7 Feb. 85	8 Nov. 93		
11	...	Herbert Charles Metcalfe, *Assist. Comdt. Perak Police* 24 Oct. 92	......	7 Feb. 85	1 Apr. 94		
11	...	2 George Addison Bramwell	......	7 Feb. 85	30 May 94		
				28 Feb. 85	30 May 94		
		LIEUTENANTS.					
10	...	1 Henry Arthur Luard (*Depot*)	......	30 Jan. 86			
9	...	1 Edw. Augustine Earle Bulwer	......	28 July 86			
9	...	2 Charles Ernest Higginbotham	5 Feb. 87	16 Apr. 90			
8	...	2 Hugh de Crespigny Huntsman	4 May 87	20 May 90			
8	...	1 Harold Henry Norman	14 Sept. 87	14 Aug. 90			
8	...	2 Adrian Robert Haworth-Booth	11 Feb. 88	15 Oct. 90			
7	...	1 William John Leete (*Depot*)	16 May 88	22 Nov. 90			
7	...	2 Lewis Gray Freeland	8 Dec. 88	1 Mar. 91			
6	...	2 Philip Allen	8 June 89	9 Sept. 91			
6	...	1 Cecil Lerrier Giffard	21 Dec. 89	5 Oct. 92			
5	...	1 George Alexander Trent	3 May 90	24 Oct. 92			
5	...	1 Richard Walter Rawlins	28 June 90	17 May 93			
5	...	1 John Marshall Molesworth Collard	29 Nov. 90	28 July 93			
5	...	1 Thomas William Shene Kent	17 Jan. 91	29 Sept. 93			
4	...	2 Percy Cyrine Burrell Skinner	8 Apr. 91	8 Nov. 93			
4	...	1 Leonard George William Dobbin	23 May 91	29 Nov. 93			
4	...	James Henry Casserly	10 Oct. 91	7 Dec. 93			
4	...	2 MarmadukeOsw. Norman Rees-Webbe	10 Oct. 91	7 Dec. 93			
3	...	Alured de Laune Faunce	19 Oct. 92	1 Apr. 94			
3	...	1 Harry Robertson M'Gill	9 Nov. 92	30 May 94			
3	...	1 William Twisleton Layard	17 Dec. 92	9 Oct. 94			
		SECOND LIEUTENANTS.					
2	...	1 Guy Hastings Taylor	20 May 93				
4	...	Henry Joseph de Barry Barnett	2 May 93				
2	...	1 Harry Hugh Sidney Knox	9 Sept. 93				
2	...	1 Alexander Guthrie Thomson	21 Oct. 93				
2	...	1 John Tannoch Waddell	21 Oct. 93				
2	...	2 Durie Parsons	23 Dec. 93				
2	...	1 Horace Robert Hawley Drew	23 Dec. 93				
2	...	2 Everard Knatchbull-Hugessen	23 Dec. 93				
1	...	1 Hugh Seymour David Stuart	17 Jan. 94				
1	...	2 Charles Ryder John Mowatt	2 June 94				
1	...	2 Reginald Charles Coldwell	12 Dec. 94				
1	...	2 George Arthur Royston Pigott	20 Feb. 95				
1	...	2 James Isidore Wood-Martin	20 Feb. 95				

[12] Major Fawcett served in the Zulu war in 1879, and was present in the engagement at Ulundi (Medal with Clasp). Served in the Boer war of 1881, and was present in the engagement at Lang's Nek.

[13] Major Collinson served in the Zulu war of 1879, and was present in the engagement at Ulundi (Medal with Clasp). Served in the Boer war of 1881 in the Mounted Infantry.

[14] Captain Bolton served in the Zulu war of 1879, and was present in the engagement at Ulundi (Medal with Clasp). Served in the Boer war of 1881, and was present in the engagement at Lang's Nek.

[16] Captain Lucy served in the Boer war of 1881, and was present in the engagement at Lang's Nek—wounded (mentioned in despatches).

[18] Captain H. C. Prichard served in the Soudan campaign in 1885 attached to the New South Wales Contingent, and was present at the destruction of Temai (Medal with Clasp, and Khedive's Star).

Years'Ser.		
Full Pay	Half Pay	
7	...	
4	...	

The Northamptonshire Regiment. 292ϲ

Paymasters.—1 Leonard G. W. Dobbin, Lieut. 1 Battalion (acting).
2
Quarter Masters.—2 Joseph Perrin,[20] 24 Oct. 88; Hon. Lieut.
1 Joseph Devlin, 15 July 91; Hon. Lieut.
Facings White.—Agents, Messrs. Cox and Co.
1st Battalion embarked for India, 5 October 1892. 2nd Battalion returned from Singapore, 26 December 1892.

[1] General M'Cleverty served the campaign against the Rajah of Coorg, in April 1834, with the 48th Regiment. Commanded the Troops in New Zealand during the Native disturbances in 1847, and repulsed 400 Natives in their attack at Wanganui on the 19th July, which resulted in a peace undisturbed till 1860 (Medal).
[9] Major Browne served in the expedition against the Yonnies, on the West Coast of Africa, in 1887-88 (mentioned in despatches, DSO. and Medal with Clasp). Served in the expedition to the Tambaka Country, on the West Coast of Africa, in 1892, including the capture of Tambi—wounded (Clasp).
[11] Major Compton served with the 58th Regiment in the Zulu war of 1879, and was present in the engagement at Ulundi (Medal with Clasp). Served in the Boer war of 1880-81, and commanded a detachment of a company of the 58th Regiment in the defence of Standerton (mentioned in despatches).
[15] Captain Hill was employed in Natal during the Zulu war of 1879 (Medal). Served in the Boer war of 1881, and was present at the engagement at Lang's Nek (mentioned in despatches, and Victoria Cross): was awarded the VC "for gallant conduct at the action of Lang's Nek on the 28th January 1881, in having, after the retreat was ordered, remained behind and endeavoured to carry out of action Lieutenant Baillie, of the same Corps, who was lying on the ground severely wounded. Being unable to lift that officer into the saddle, he carried him in his arms until Lieutenant Baillie was shot dead. Lieutenant Hill then brought a wounded man out of action on his horse, after which he returned and rescued another. All these acts being performed under a heavy fire."
[17] Major Morgan served in the Zulu war in 1879, and was present in the engagement at Ulundi (Medal with Clasp). Served in the Boer war of 1881 and was present in the engagement at Lang's Nek.
[20] Lieut. J. Perrin served in the Zulu war in 1879 (Medal with Clasp).

Record of the Services of the 1st Battalion Northamptonshire Regiment (formerly the 48th Regiment).
Raised at Norwich as the 59th Foot, 1741. England, to 1745. Low Countries, to 1747. Scotland, to 1748. Low Countries, to 1748. (Became the 48th Regiment in 1748.) Ireland, to 1755. North America, to 1763. Ireland, to 1773. West Indies, to 1781. Scotland, to 1783. Ireland, to 1788. West Indies, to 1794. England, to 1795. West Indies, to 1797. England, to 1798. Gibraltar, to 1800. Malta, to 1803. England, to 1805. Gibraltar, to 1809. [2nd Battalion raised in 1803. England, to 1804. Ireland and England, to 1807. Ireland, to 1809. The Peninsula, to 1811. To England, 1814, when it was disbanded.] The Peninsula, to 1814 (passage of the Douro, battles of Talavera, Albuhera, Badajoz, Salamanca, Vittoria, Pyrenees, Nivelle, Orthes, and Toulouse). Ireland, to 1816. New South Wales, to 1824. India, to 1834. England, to 1837. Ireland, to 1838. Gibraltar, to 1844. Jamaica, to 1847. Ireland, to 1850. England, to 1853. Corfu, to 1855. The Crimea, to 1856 (siege of Sebastopol). Malta, to 1857. Gibraltar, to 1858. India, to 1865. England, to 1866. Ireland, to 1868. Malta, to 1872. India, to 1880. Ireland, to 1885. England, 1885.

Continuation of Notes to the Loyal North Lancashire Regiment.

[1] Sir Richard Farren served the Eastern campaign of 1854-55 with the 47th Regiment—present uninterruptedly with the expeditionary force from the commencement of the war with Russia to the breaking up of the Army in the Crimea at the conclusion of peace, including the battles of Alma and Inkerman, capture of Balaklava, sortie on 26th October, siege and fall of Sebastopol. Commanded the 47th Regiment at the battle of Inkerman, and uninterruptedly during the siege of Sebastopol (the Trenches) from 5th Nov. 1854 to 8th Nov. 1855, including the attacks of the 18th June and 8th September; at Inkerman he was the Senior Officer of the 2nd Brigade 2nd Division coming out of action—mentioned in despatches (Medal with three Clasps, Brevet of Lt. Colonel, CB., Officer of the Legion of Honor, Sardinian and Turkish Medals, and 4th Class of the Medjidie).
[2] General Renny commanded the 81st Regt. throughout the mutiny in India in 1857-58, a Regiment which at the commencement of the mutiny disarmed one Regiment of Native Cavalry and three Regiments of Native Infantry at Mean Meer, near Lahore; Regiments well known to be disaffected and ripe for mutiny. For this important service, and others performed by the 81st Regt. during the mutiny, he has received the order of CSI., and the Indian Mutiny Medal. Commanded the First Brigade in the Sittana expedition of May 1858 under Sir Sydney Cotton (mentioned in despatches, Medal with Clasp).
[3] Lt. Colonel Ryley served in the Afghan war in 1878-79 (Medal).
[4] Lt. Colonel Farrant served with the 81st Regiment in the Afghan war in 1878-79, and was present at the capture of Ali Musjid (Medal with Clasp).
[15] Captain Churchward served with the 81st Regiment in the Afghan war in 1878-9, and was present at the capture of Ali Musjid; subsequently served as Transport Officer with the Koorum Valley Field Force from 24th October 1879 to 24th May 1880, and with the Khyber Field Force from 25th May to 23rd August 1880 (Medal with Clasp). Served with the Bechuanaland Expedition under Sir Charles Warren in 1884-85.
[16] Major Jackson served in the Afghan war in 1878-79, and took part in the operations in the Khyber Pass (Medal).
[17] Captain Thomas served with the 81st Regiment in the Afghan war in 1878-79 (Medal).
[19] Captain Sandes.—For War Services, see Army Pay Department.

Record of the Services of the 2nd Battalion Loyal North Lancashire Regiment,—formerly the 81st (Loyal Lincoln Volunteers) Regiment.
Raised as "Loyal Lincoln Volunteers" in 1793. Ireland and England, to 1794. (30th Regiment incorporated with 81st, 1795.) Barbadoes, to March 1797. England, to Sept. 1797. Guernsey, to 1798. Cape Colony, to 1802. [2nd Battalion raised in 1803. Ireland, to 1808. The Peninsula, to 1809 (battle of Corunna). England and Holland, to 1809. England, to 1811. Jersey, to 1814. Holland, to 1816. Absorbed into 1st Battalion, March 1816.] England, to April 1803. Jersey, to Sept. 1803. England, to 1805. Malta, to 1806 (battle of Maida). Sicily and Italy, to 1812. The Peninsula and France, to 1814. Canada, to May 1815. England, to Aug, 1815. France, to 1817. Ireland, to 1822. North America, to 1829. West Indies, to 1831. England, to 1832. Ireland, to 1836. Gibraltar, to 1839. West Indies, to 1843. Canada, to 1847. England, to 1852. Ireland, to 1853. India, to 1865. England, to 1867. Ireland, to 1870. Gibraltar, to 1874. India, to 1883 (Afghan war, 1878-79). Entitled "2nd Battalion Loyal North Lancashire Regiment," 1881. England, to 1887. Jersey, to 1890. Ireland, 1890.

Princess Charlotte of Wales' (Royal Berkshire Regiment)

1st Batt., Bermuda.
2nd Batt., Devonport.

Formerly the 49th (*Princess Charlotte of Wales'*) (*Herts*) and the 66th (*Berkshire*) Regiments. (The 3rd Battalion is formed of the Berks Militia.)

Regimental District No. 49.—Reading.

"Egmont-op-Zee" "Copenhagen" "Douro" "Talavera" "Albuhera" "Vittoria" "Pyrenees" "Nivelle" "Nive" "Orthes" "Peninsula" "Queenstown" "China" (with the Dragon). "Alma" "Inkerman" "Sevastopol" "Kandahar, 1880" "Afghanistan, 1879-80" "Egypt, 1882" "Suakin, 1885" "Tofrek."

Years' Ser.							
Full Pay	Half Pay		2ND LIEUT.	LIEUT.	CAPTAIN.	BREV.MAJ.	MAJOR.
27	...	**Colonel.**—Robert William Lowry,¹ *CB. Ens.* P29 Dec. 40; *Lt.* 12 May 43; *Capt.* P18 Feb. 48; *Major*, 15 June 55; *Bt.Lt.Colonel*, 26 Dec. 56; *Lt.Colonel*, P3 Mar. 63; *Colonel*, 13 Mar. 64; *Major General*, 22 July 69; *Lt.General*, 1 Oct. 82; *Colonel* Royal Berkshire Regiment, 27 Jan. 94.					
24	...	**Lieutenant Colonels.**—1 Edward Thompson Dickson,² *Ensign*, 23 Jan. 69; *Lieut.* 14 Apr. 71; *Capt.* 30 Oct. 78; *Major*, 2 Feb. 84; *Lt.Colonel*, 30 Apr. 91.					
		2 p.s.c. Justinian Gordon Ponsonby,¹⁰ *Ensign*, 23 Sept. 71; *Lieut.* 28 Oct. 71; *Capt.* 8 Apr. 80; *Major*, 2 Feb. 84; *Lt.Colonel*, 7 Dec. 91.					
		MAJORS.					
23	...	1 p.s.c. William Augustus Collings¹²	......	16 Mar. 73	4 Oct. 80	......	28 June 84
22	...	2 Henry Somerset Hassard	......	23 Nov. 73	28 July 80	......	27 Mar. 86
20	...	2 Charles Evans-Gordon¹⁸	......	13 June 75	16 Apr. 81	......	23 Jan. 89
19	...	1 Granville De la Motte Faunce¹⁹	......	29 Nov. 76	30 Oct. 83	......	8 June 91
17	...	Charles Mackenzie Edwards,²⁰ *Adj.* 3 } Battalion 30 Oct. 90 }	22 Jan. 79	14 Nov. 79	28 June 84	......	7 Dec. 91
17	...	Elmhirst Rhodes,²¹ *DSO. Assist. Insp. of Signalling, Aldershot,* 1 Jan. 95	25 May 78	4 Mar. 80	16 Oct. 84	......	30 Aug. 93
17	...	2 Francis Charles Carter²² (*Depot*)	11 May 78	4 May 80	1 Aug. 85	......	17 Oct. 94
17	...	Ernest Henry Burney,²³ *Adj.* 4 *Bn.* } Manchester Regt. 13 Nov. 93 }	22 Jan. 79	8 Apr. 80	10 Dec. 84	......	29 Nov. 94
		CAPTAINS.					
16	...	2 Hyacinth Lynch²⁴	......	9 July 79	10 Apr. 80	15 Dec. 84	
16	...	p.s.c. Fred.Wm.NicholasM'Cracken,²⁵ *D.A.A. Gen., Barbadoes,* 13 Apr. 92 }	13 Aug. 79	28 July 80	15 Dec. 84	14 Aug. 85	
16	...	William Kerr M'Clintock²⁶	13 Aug. 79	28 July 80	6 Jan. 86		
16	...	Reginald Edward Traherne Bray²⁷	14 Jan. 80	28 July 80	13 Feb. 86		
15	...	Frank William McTier Bunny,²⁸ } *Ordnance Store Department* }	14 Jan. 80	29 Sept. 80	16 Nov. 86		
15	...	2 George Dering Remington Williams, } *at Staff College* }	11 Aug. 80	30 Mar. 81	1 Apr. 87		
15	...	Sudlow Harrison, *Adj.* 1 *Vol.Bn.* 1 Apr. 92	19 Feb. 81	1 July 81	30 Apr. 87		
15	...	1 Henry Louis Lee³⁰ (*Depot*)	19 Feb. 81	1 July 81	8 Oct. 87		
14	...	1 Charles Turner³³	......	22 Oct. 81	23 Jan. 89		
14	...	1 Ramsay Gordon Chase³¹	......	22 Oct. 81	19 Feb. 90		
13	...	Arthur John Wm. Dowell,³² *Aide de Camp to General T.C.Lyons* 14 Oct.94 }	......	10 May 82	1 Mar. 90		
13	...	1 Henry FitzHerbert³³	......	10 May 82	2 Apr. 91		
13	...	2 George Westley Richards, **Adjutant** } 4 Jan. 92 }	......	29 July 82	30 Apr. 91		
13	...	2 William Mason Inglis³⁶	......	9 Sept. 82	6 Nov. 91		
12	...	1 John Henry Willes Southey³⁷	......	12 May 83	13 Apr. 92		
12	...	2 Edward Feetham³⁸	......	12 May 83	1 June 92		
12	...	p.s.c. Hugh Gregory Fitton,⁴⁰ *serving with the Egyptian Army* }	......	6 Feb. 84	10 May 93		
11	...	1 Harcourt Ernest Taylor⁴¹	......	14 May 84	30 Aug. 93		
11	...	James Ramsay Wigan⁴²	......	12 Nov. 84	13 Nov. 93		
11	...	1 Ivon Trevor Owen	......	28 Feb. 85	13 Nov. 93		
10	...	2 Richard Graves MacDonnell	......	9 May 85	11 May 94		
10	...	1 Arthur Stephen Cave⁴³	......	29 Aug. 85	11 May 94		
		LIEUTENANTS.					
10	...	1 Charles Moore,⁴³ *Superintendent of Gymnasia, Curragh* 29 Aug. 94 }	......	29 Aug. 85			
10	...	1 George Holme Arbuthnot⁴³	......	29 Aug. 85			
10	...	2 William Clegg	......	29 Aug. 85			
10	...	1 Robert Bruce Swinton (*Depot*)	......	30 Jan. 86			
9	...	2 Sir Thomas Edward Sabine-Pasley, *Bt.*	......	25 Aug. 86			
9	...	1 Lionel Francis Abbot Barlow	......	25 Aug. 86			
9	...	1 Herbert Marshall Finch	......	10 Nov. 86			
9	...	1 Frank Wigraun Foley	......	8 Dec. 86			
9	...	John Gustavus Russell Walsh, *Ordnance Store Department* }	5 Feb. 87	6 Feb. 91			
8	...	1 William Redmond Prendergast } Kemmis Betty }	11 Feb. 88	30 Apr. 91			
8	...	2 Edward Henry Blunt	11 Feb. 88	6 Nov. 91			
6	...	1 David Blake Maurice, **Adjutant** } 29 Dec. 94 }	17 Apr. 89	3 Feb. 92			
6	...	2 Walter King Peake (*Depot*)	9 Nov. 89	1 June 92			
6	...	2 Arthur George Elton Bingley	21 Dec. 89	1 July 92			
6	...	John M'Kenzie Trower Hogg	29 Mar. 90	10 May 93			
5	...	William Hill Climo	25 Mar. 91	1 Jan. 94			
4	...	1 Alexander Scott Turner	5 Dec. 91	1 Feb. 94			
4	...	2 Piers William North	17 June 91	11 May 94			
4	...	2 Felix Forduti Ready	5 Dec. 91	28 July 94			
3	...	1 Edward John Neve	18 May 92	30 July 94			
3	...	1 Eustace Graham Lees	13 July 92	29 Dec. 94			
3	...	1 Richard Henn Collins	13 Aug. 92	8 Jan. 95			
		SECOND LIEUTENANTS.					
2	...	1 Charles Glencairn Hill	20 May 93				
2	...	2 Claude Ernest Birch	23 Aug. 93				
2	...	1 Arthur Gabell Macdonald	21 Oct. 93				
2	...	1 William Robert Ewart Annesley	21 Oct. 93				
2	...	2 Herbert Street	23 Dec. 93				
2	...	1 Richard Prentice Harvey	7 Mar. 94				
2	...	2 Arthur Henry Bathurst	7 Mar. 94				
1	...	2 Archibald Henry Buchanan-Dunlop	10 Oct. 94				
1	...	2 Charles Henry Balicl Weston	10 Oct. 94				
1	...	1 Herbert Charles Ellis	10 Oct. 94				
1	...	1 Thomas Cowper Hincks	20 Feb. 95				
1	...	1 Oscar Striedinger	20 Feb. 95				

⁴² Captain Wigan served throughout the campaign in the Eastern Soudan in 1885 with the 1st Battalion of the Berkshire Regiment, and was present in the reconnaissance to Hasheen on the 1st February, in the engagements at Hasheen and the Tofrek zereba, and the subsequent advance to and burning of Temai (Medal with two Clasps, and Khedive's Star). Served with the Egyptian Frontier Field Force in 1885-86, including the engagement at Giniss (wounded).

⁴³ Captain Cave, Lieuts. Moore and Arbuthnot served with the Egyptian Frontier Field Force in 1885-86, and were present in the engagement at Giniss (Medal, and Khedive's Star).

Years'Ser.		
Full Pay.	Half Pay.	
2	...	*Paymasters.*—1 2 *Quarter Masters.*—1 Tom Brown, 31 May 93; *Hon. Lieut.*
:	...	2 Robert Patrick Cloke, 16 Jan. 95; *Hon. Lieut.*

Facings Blue.—*Agents*, Messrs. Cox and Co.
1st Battalion embarked for Gibraltar, 1881. 2nd Battalion returned from Bengal, 1881.

[1] Lieut.General Lowry served the Eastern campaign of 1854-55 with the 47th Regiment, including the battles of Alma and Balaklava, capture of Balaklava, siege and fall of Sebastopol. Served on the Staff of the Adjutant General's Department in the Crimea and at Scutari—mentioned in despatches (Medal with three Clasps; Brevet of Lt.Colonel, 5th Class of the Medjidie, and Turkish Medal).

[2] Lt.Colonel Dickson served throughout the campaign in the Eastern Soudan in 1885 with the 1st Battalion of the Berkshire Regiment, and was present in the reconnaissance to Hasheen on the 1st February, in the engagements at Hasheen and the Tofrek zereba and the subsequent advance to and burning of Temai (Medal with two Clasps, and Khedive's Star); also served with the Egyptian Frontier Field Force in 1885-86 as Brigade Major, and was present in the engagement at Giniss.

[10] Major Ponsonby served in the Duffla Expedition in 1874-75 with the 42nd Bengal Native Infantry.

[12] Major Collings served with the Nile Expedition in 1884 as Deputy Assistant Commissary General for Transport, and throughout the campaign in the Eastern Soudan in 1885 with the 1st Battalion of the Berkshire Regiment, and was present in the reconnaissance to Hasheen on the 1st February, in the engagements at Hasheen and the Tofrek zereba and the subsequent advance to and burning of Temai (mentioned in despatches, Medal with three Clasps, and Khedive's Star).

[18] Major Evans Gordon served with the 1st Battalion Berkshire Regiment throughout the Egyptian war of 1882, and was present at the surrender of Kafr Dowar (Medal, and Khedive's Star). Served with the Nile Expedition in 1884-85 as Deputy Assistant Commissary General for Transport, and in the campaign in the Eastern Soudan in 1885 with the 1st Battalion of the Berkshire Regiment, and was present in the advance to and burning of Temai (two Clasps); also served with the Egyptian Frontier Field Force in 1885-86, and was present in the engagement at Giniss.

[19] Major Faunce served with the 66th Regiment in the Afghan war in 1879-80, and was present in the engagements at Girishk and Maiwand (mentioned in despatches), in the defence of Candahar, and at the battle of Candahar (Medal with Clasp).

[20] Major Edwards served with the 66th Regiment in the Afghan war in 1879-80, and took part in the defence of Candahar, and was present at the battle of Candahar (Medal with Clasp). Served throughout the campaign in the Eastern Soudan in 1885 with the 1st Battalion of the Berkshire Regiment, and was present in the reconnaissance to Hasheen on the 1st February, and in the engagements at Hasheen and the Tofrek zereba and the subsequent advance to and burning of Temai (Medal with two Clasps, and Khedive's Star); also served with the Egyptian Frontier Field Force in 1885-86, and was present in the engagement at Giniss.

[21] Major Rhodes served throughout the Egyptian war of 1882 with the 1st Battalion of the Berkshire Regiment, and was present at the surrender of Kafr Dowar (Medal, and Khedive's Star). Served throughout the campaign in the Eastern Soudan in 1885 with the 1st Battalion of the Berkshire Regiment, and was present at the reconnaissance to Hasheen on the 1st February as Signalling Officer to the Second Brigade, and in the engagements at Hasheen and the Tofrek zereba, and the subsequent advance to and burning of Temai (mentioned in despatches, two Clasps); also served with the Egyptian Frontier Field Force in 1885-86 as Chief of the Signalling Department at Kosheh, and was present in the engagement at Giniss—horse wounded (mentioned in despatches, DSO.).

[22] Major Carter served in the Afghan war of 1878-80 with the Khyber Line Force at Jellalabad (Medal). Served in the Hazara campaign in 1888 as Field Intelligence Officer (twice mentioned in despatches, Medal with Clasp); with the Looshai Expedition in 1889 (Clasp); and with the Hazara Expedition in 1891 as Deputy Assistant Adjutant General (mentioned in despatches, Clasp).

[23] Major Burney and Captain Turner served with the 1st Battalion Berkshire Regiment throughout the Egyptian war of 1882, and were present at the surrender of Kafr Dowar (Medal, and Khedive's Star).

[24] Captain Lynch served with the 66th Regiment in the Afghan war in 1879-80, and was present in the engagements at Girishk and Maiwand—dangerously wounded (Medal). Served throughout the campaign in the Eastern Soudan in 1885 with the 1st Battalion of the Berkshire Regiment, and was present at the reconnaissance to Hasheen on the 1st February, and in the engagements at Hasheen and the Tofrek zereba (Medal with two Clasps, and Khedive's Star).

[25] Major M'Cracken served throughout the Egyptian war of 1882 with the 1st Battalion of the Berkshire Regiment, and was present at the surrender of Kafr Dowar (Medal, and Khedive's Star). Served throughout the campaign in the Eastern Soudan in 1885 as Adjutant of the 1st Battalion of the Berkshire Regiment, and was present in the reconnaissance to Hasheen on the 1st February, in the engagements at Hasheen and the Tofrek zereba, and in the subsequent advance to and burning of Temai (mentioned in despatches, Brevet of Major, two Clasps); also served with the Egyptian Frontier Field Force in 1885-86, including the engagement at Giniss.

[26] Major M'Clintock served with the 1st Battalion Berkshire Regiment in the Egyptian war of 1882, during the latter part of the time as Transport Officer, and was present at the surrender of Kafr Dowar (Medal, and Khedive's Star). Served throughout the campaign in the Eastern Soudan in 1885 with the 1st Battalion of the Berkshire Regiment, and was present in the engagements at Hasheen and the Tofrek zereba and the subsequent advance to and burning of Temai (two Clasps); was Assistant Provost Marshal during the remainder of the campaign. Also served in the operations in the Upper Nile in 1885-86 with the 1st Battalion of the Royal Berkshire Regiment, and was present in the engagement at Giniss.

[27] Captain Bray served with the 66th Regiment in the Afghan war of 1880, and was present in the affair with the Wali's mutinous troops on 16th July, in the engagement at Maiwand and the subsequent defence of Candahar, and at the battle of Candahar (Medal with Clasp). Served with the Nile Expedition in 1884-85 (Medal with Clasp, and Khedive's Star).

[28] Captain Bunny served with the 66th Regiment in the Afghan war in 1879-80 in Southern Afghanistan (Medal).

[30] Captain Lee served with the 1st Battalion of the Berkshire Regiment throughout the Egyptian war of 1882, and was present at the surrender of Kafr Dowar (Medal, and Khedive's Star). Served with the Egyptian Frontier Field Force in 1885-86, and was present in the engagement at Giniss.

[31] Captain Chase served throughout the Egyptian war of 1882 with the 1st Battalion of the Berkshire Regiment and was present at the surrender of Kafr Dowar (Medal, and Khedive's Star). Served in the campaign in the Eastern Soudan in 1885 with the 1st Battalion of the Berkshire Regiment, and was present in the reconnaissance to Hasheen on the 1st February, and with the Mounted Infantry in the engagements at Hasheen and the advance to and burning of Temai (Clasp). Also served with the Egyptian Frontier Field Force in 1885-86, and was present in the engagement at Giniss.

[32] Captain Dowell served with the 1st Battalion of the Berkshire Regiment throughout the Egyptian war of 1882, and was present at the surrender of Kafr Dowar (Medal, and Khedive's Star). Served with the Nile Expedition in 1884-85 on Transport duty (Clasp). Also served with the Egyptian Frontier Field Force in 1885-86, and was present in the engagement at Giniss as Aide de Camp to the Brigadier General Commanding 2nd Brigade.

[33] Captain FitzHerbert served throughout the campaign in the Eastern Soudan in 1885 with the 1st Battalion of the Berkshire Regiment, and was present in the reconnaissance to Hasheen on the 1st February, in the engagements at Hasheen and the Tofrek zereba, and the subsequent advance to and burning of Temai (Medal with two Clasps, and Khedive's Star); also served with the Egyptian Frontier Field Force in 1885-86.

[36] Captain Inglis served throughout the campaign in the Eastern Soudan in 1885 with the 1st Battalion of the Berkshire Regiment, and was present at the reconnaissance to Hasheen on the 1st February, and in the engagements at Hasheen and the Tofrek zereba (Medal with two Clasps, and Khedive's Star).

T

[37] Captain Southey served throughout the campaign in the Eastern Soudan in 1885 with the 1st Battalion of the Berkshire Regiment, and was present in the reconnaissance to Hasheen on the 1st February, in the engagements at Hasheen and the Tofrek zereba, and the subsequent advance to and burning of Temai (Medal with two Clasps, and Khedive's Star). Served with the Egyptian Frontier Field Force in 1885-86 as Adjutant of the 1st Battalion of the Berkshire Regiment, including the engagement at Giniss.

[38] Captain Feetham served throughout the campaign in the Eastern Soudan in 1885 with the 1st Battalion of the Berkshire Regiment, and was present in the reconnaissance to Hasheen on the 1st February, in the engagements at Hasheen and the Tofrek zereba and the subsequent advance to and burning of Temai; afterwards served with the Camel Corps, and was present in the engagement at Takdul (Medal with two Clasps, and Khedive's Star). Also served with the Egyptian Frontier Field Force in 1885-86, including the engagement at Giniss.

[40] Captain Fitton served in the campaign in the Eastern Soudan in 1885 with the 1st Battalion of the Berkshire Regiment (Medal with Clasp, and Khedive's Star). Served with the Egyptian Frontier Field Force in 1885-86, and was present in the engagement at Giniss and at the attack on Ambigole Wells.

[41] Captain Taylor served throughout the campaign in the Eastern Soudan in 1885 with the 1st Battalion of the Berkshire Regiment, and was present in the reconnaissance to Hasheen on the 1st February, in the engagements at Hasheen and the Tofrek zereba, and the subsequent advance to and burning of Temai (Medal with two Clasps, and Khedive's Star). Served with the Egyptian Frontier Field Force in 1885-86.

Record of the Services of the 1st Battalion Princess Charlotte of Wales' (Royal Berkshire Regiment),—formerly the 49th Regiment.

Raised in 1714, but records lost to 1743. Entitled "Jamaica Volunteers," 1743. America, 1775 to 1780. England, to 1788. West Indies, to 1796. England, to Oct. 1799. Holland, to Nov, 1799 (battle of Egmont-op-Zee). England, to 1801. Served as Marines under Lord Nelson, 1801 (battle of Copenhagen). America, to 1815 (capture of Queenstown). [2nd Battalion raised in 1813.] England, to 1816. Ireland and England, to 1821. Entitled "Princess Charlotte of Wales' 49th Regiment," 1825. South Africa, to 1828. India, to 1840. China, to 1842 (war of 1840-42). India, to 1843. England, to 1845. Ireland, to 1851. Corfu, to 1853. Malta, to 1854. The Crimea, to 1856 (battles of Alma and Inkerman and siege of Sebastopol). England, to 1857. Barbadoes, to 1859. England, to 1864. Ireland, to 1865. India, to 1873. England, to 1881. Gibraltar, to 1882. Malta, to July 1882. Egypt, to 1883 (war of 1882). Gibraltar, to 1884. Entitled "1st Battalion Princess Charlotte of Wales' Royal Berkshire Regiment," 1885. Egypt and the Soudan, to 1886 (campaign of 1885—battle of Tofrek). Cyprus, to 1888 (Left Half Battalion to Malta). Malta, 1888.

Record of the Services of the 2nd Battalion Princess Charlotte of Wales' (Royal Berkshire Regiment),—formerly the 66th Regiment.

Raised in 1758 and proceeded to the West Indies, to 1792. Gibraltar, to 1795. West Indies, to 1799. Canada, to 1802. England, to 1804. [2nd Battalion raised in 1803. Ireland, to 1809. The Peninsula, to 1813 (passage of the Douro, battles of Talavera, Albuhera, Vittoria, Pyrenees, Nivelle, Nive, and Orthes). France, to 1814. Ireland, 1814. England, to 1816. St. Helena, to 1817. Absorbed in 1st Battalion, 1817.] East Indies, to 1817. St. Helena, to 1821 (attended the interment of Napoleon). England, to 1823. Ireland, to 1827. Canada, to 1840. England, to 1842. Scotland, to 1843. Ireland, to 1845. Gibraltar, to 1848. West Indies, to 1851. Canada, to 1854. Gibraltar, to 1856. England, to 1857. East Indies, to 1865. England, to 1867. Channel Islands, to 1868. Ireland, to 1870. East Indies, to 1881 (Afghan war of 1879-80, battle of Candahar). England, to 1885. Ireland, 1885.

Record of the Services of the 1st Battalion King's Own Yorkshire Light Infantry (formerly the 51st Regiment).

Raised in 1756. Expedition to Rochefort, 1757, returning same year. To Holland, 1758 (Seven Years War—battle of Minden). To United Kingdom, 1763. To Minorca, 1771. To United Kingdom, 1782. To Gibraltar, 1792. To Corsica and Ulba, 1794. To Lisbon, 1797. To East Indies, 1798. To Ceylon, 1800. To England, 1807. To Spain, 1808 (battle of Corunna). To England, 1809. Made Light Infantry, 1809. Walcheren Expedition, 1809. To the Peninsula, 1811 (battles of Fuentes d'Onor, Vittoria, Pyrenees, Nivelle, and Orthes). To Belgium and France, 1815 (battle of Waterloo). To England, 1816. Entitled "The King's Own Light Infantry," 1821. To the Mediterranean, 1821. To United Kingdom, 1834. To Australia and New Zealand, 1838. To India, 1845. To Burmah, 1852 (capture of Pegu). To England, 1854. To Malta, 1855. To England, 1856. To India, 1857. To United Kingdom, 1867. To India, 1872 (Afghan war, 1878-80, capture of Ali Musjid). To Burmah, 1885 ("Burma, 1885-7"). To England, 1887.

Record of the Services of the 2nd Battalion King's Own Yorkshire Light Infantry (formerly the 105th Light Infantry).

The 2nd European Madras Light Infantry was raised in 1839. East Indies, to 1856. Burmah, to 1858. East Indies, to 1872. Title changed to "105th Light Infantry," 1861. Aden, to 1874. England, to 1879. Ireland, to 1883. Title changed to "King's Own Yorkshire Light Infantry," 1881. England, to 1884. Malta, to 1887. East Indies, 1887.

The Queen's Own (Royal West Kent Regiment). 294

1st Batt., Meerut, Bengal.
2nd Batt., Enniskillen.

Formerly the 50th (The Queen's Own) and the 97th (The Earl of Ulster's) Regiments.

Regimental District No. 50.—Maidstone

(The 3rd and 4th Battalions are formed of the 1st and 2nd Battalions West Kent Militia respectively.)

"*Quò fas et gloria ducunt.*" "EGYPT" (with the Sphinx). "VIMIERA" "CORUNNA" "ALMARAZ" "VITTORIA" "PYRENEES" "NIVE" "ORTHES" "PENINSULA" "PUNNIAR" "MOODKEE" "FEROZESHAH" "ALIWAL" "SOBRAON" "ALMA" "INKERMAN" "SEVASTOPOL" "LUCKNOW" "NEW ZEALAND" "EGYPT, 1882" "NILE, 1884-85."

Years' Ser. Full Pay	Half Pay		2ND LIEUT.	LIEUT.	CAPTAIN.	BREV. MAJ.	MAJOR.
23	...	Colonel.—Fowler Burton,¹ *CB.*, Ensign, P30 Aug. 39; *Lieut.* 15 Apr. 42; *Capt.* P14 June 50; *Major,* 2 Nov. 55; *Bt.Lt.Colonel,* 26 Dec. 56; *Lt.Colonel,* 15 Mar. 58; *Colonel,* 10 June 62; *Major General,* 6 Mar. 68; *Lieut.General,* 25 Apr. 80; *General,* 1 July 81; *Colonel* West Kent Regiment, 5 Oct. 90. *Lt.Colonel,* 23 Dec. 92.					
27	...	Lieutenant Colonels.—1 Thomas Herbert Brock, *Lieut.* 24 July 72; *Capt.* 20 Mar. 80; *Major,* 17 Nov. 83; 2 John Cumberlege Cautley,⁵ Ensign, P13 Jan. 69; *Lieut.* P22 June 70; *Capt.* 2 Feb. 78; *Major,* 9 Sept. 84; *Lt.Colonel,* 19 Mar. 94.					
		MAJORS.					
22	...	2 p.s.c. Edward Aickin Wm. Stewart Grove⁷	......	12 Nov. 73	13 April 81	18 Nov. 82	19 Jan. 86
22	...	1 Charles William Henry Evans¹⁰	......	28 Feb. 74	17 Nov. 83	......	17 Nov. 90
19	...	2 Cholmeley Edw. Carl Branfill Harrison¹¹	......	11 Sept. 76	4 Sept. 84	......	2 Nov. 92
18	...	Arthur Templeman Morse,¹² *Adjutant* 6 Vol. Bn. Liverpool Regt. 1 Oct. 91	......	28 April 77	9 Sept. 84	......	23 Dec. 92
17	...	2 Oswald James Daniell¹³	11 May 78	8 May 79	17 Dec. 84	......	12 June 93
16	...	1 p.s.c. Wm. George Balfour Western²³	13 Aug. 79	12 July 80	6 Mar. 85	......	4 Oct. 93
17	...	George William Maunsell,²⁵ *Adj. E. Bengal State Ry. Vol. Rifles,* 31 July 93	11 May 78	17 Aug. 80	2 May 85	......	19 Mar. 94
16	...	p.s.c. Laurence Brock-Hollinshead,²⁶ *Adjutant 3rd & 4th Bns.* 26 Apr. 93	13 Aug. 79	31 Aug. 80	23 Dec. 85	......	9 May. 94
		CAPTAINS.					
17	...	2 Edward Leonard Aspinall Heygate²⁹ *(Depot)*	13 July 78	22 Dec. 80	19 Jan. 86		
17	...	2 Edwin Alfred Hervey Alderson,²⁷ *at Staff College*	4 Dec. 78	1 July 81	12 June 86		
16	...	1 Wilfred Edward Rowe²⁸	13 Aug. 79	1 July 81	16 Oct. 86		
15	...	p.s.c. Fitzgerald Wintour,³⁰ *Station Staff Officer, Fyzabad,* 10 Sept. 94	11 Aug. 80	1 July 81	2 Feb. 87	3 Feb. 87	
15	...	2 Archibald Montgomery-Campbell³¹	22 Jan. 81	1 July 81	1 July 87		
15	...	Edward Devon Caird, *Ordnance Store Department*	22 Jan. 81	1 July 81	1 July 87		
15	...	Frederick Bradford Fanshawe, *Adj.* 3 *Volunteer Battalion* 16 May 90	19 Feb. 81	1 July 81	19 Dec. 87		
13	...	Horace Mann,²³ *Adjutant 1 Volunteer Battalion,* 20 June 92	......	29 July 82	19 Mar. 90		
12	...	1 John Pelham Dalison²³	......	19 Dec. 83	16 Apr. 90		
12	...	William Richard Norton Annesley,³⁴ *DSO. Adjutant 3 Battalion Manchester Regt.* 23 Jan. 93		6 Feb. 84	15 July 91		
11	...	1 John Maudslay Maxwell²³		2 July 84	1 Oct. 91		
11	...	1 Frank Hodges³⁶		7 Feb. 85	2 Nov. 92		
11	...	1 Anthony Wood Martyn³⁵ *(Depot)*		28 Feb. 85	23 Dec. 92		
11	...	1 Rodney Charles Style³⁷		28 Feb. 85	23 Jan. 93		
10	...	1 Noel Herbert Strode Lowe		23 May 85	1 Feb. 93		
10	...	2 Hampden Lewis Clement Moody		29 Aug. 85	4 Oct. 93		
10	...	1 Edward Vincent Osborne Hewett³⁶		2 Sept. 85	19 Mar. 94		
10	...	2 Hugh Cecil Westall Beeching		30 Jan. 86	9 May 94		
10	...	2 John Lees³⁵		29 Aug. 85	16 May 94		
10	...	1 Francis Herbert Hotham		30 Jan. 86	10 Sept. 94		
		LIEUTENANTS.					
9	...	2 Stanhope Humphrey Pedley *(Depot)*		30 Jan. 86			
9	...	2 Thomas Taylor Burt		28 Apr. 86			
9	...	2 Francis William Burbury		25 Aug. 86			
9	...	1 Francis Charles Marsh		25 Aug. 86			
9	...	1 Devereux Philip Walker *(Depot)*		8 Dec. 86			
10	...	1 Edward Frederick Venables, *Adjutant* 14 Dec. 92		6 May 85			
8	...	2 Percy Umfreville, **Adjutant** 24 Jan. 94	16 Nov. 87	23 Apr. 90			
7	...	2 Arundel Martyn	9 May 88	1 Oct. 91			
7	...	1 George Marshall	30 Jan. 89	2 Jan. 92			
7	...	1 Osmond Beckett Simpson	23 Mar. 89	2 Nov. 92			
6	...	2 Matthew Perceval Buckle	10 Apr. 89	14 Dec. 92			
6	...	2 Richard John Woulfe Flanagan	26 June 89	23 Dec. 92			
6	...	2 William Hoare Bourchier Long	6 July 89	23 Jan. 93			
6	...	1 Charles George Pack-Beresford	20 Nov. 89	1 Feb. 93			
6	...	1 John Golding	29 Jan. 90	4 Oct. 93			
4	...	1 James Wilton O'Dowda	7 Nov. 91	15 Nov. 93			
4	...	1 Charles Vandeleur Molony	7 Nov. 91	24 Jan. 94			
4	...	1 Tom Parkyns Carington Smith	9 Jan. 92	19 Mar. 94			
4	...	1 Percy Morris Robinson	27 Jan. 92	9 May 94			
3	...	1 Hubert Isacke	14 Dec. 92	8 Aug. 94			
3	...	1 Percy Matcham Davies	21 Jan. 93	10 Sept. 94			
		SECOND LIEUTENANTS.					
3	...	1 Charles de Chatillon Middleton	21 Jan. 93				
4	...	Edward Arthur Fagan	2 May 91				
3	...	1 Hugh Stewart	15 Mar. 93				
2	...	1 Harry Stebbing Bush	26 Apr. 93				
2	...	1 Charles Richard Bradshaw	19 July 93				
2	...	2 Charles Edward Kitson	23 Dec. 93				
2	...	2 Barrington Shakespear Moore	23 Dec. 93				
2	...	2 Percy Hastings	7 Mar. 94				
1	...	1 Thomas Henry Clayton Nunn	2 June 94				
1	...	1 Eustace Lindsey James	4 July 94				
1	...	1 Thomas Rose Caradoc Price	10 Oct. 94				
1	...	2 Cyril Druce	10 Oct. 94				
1	...	2 Richard Berwick Hope	29 Feb. 95				

The Queen's Own (Royal West Kent Regiment).

Years' Ser. Full Pay.	Half Pay.	
		Paymasters.—1 John Golding, *Lieut.* 1 Battalion (acting).
12	...	Quarter Masters.—2 Edward Wallace Brown, 22 Aug. 83; *Hon. Captain*, 22 Aug. 93.
10	...	1 Alfred Edward Mansfield, 9 Dec. 85; *Hon. Lieut.*

Facings Blue.—*Agents*, Messrs. Cox and Co.
1st Battalion embarked for Egypt, 1882. *2nd Battalion returned from Jamaica*, 1882.

[1] General Burton served with the 97th Regt. at the siege of Sebastopol from the 20th Nov. 1854 to 5th July 1855; commanded the Light Company in the sortie on the night of the 20th Dec. 1854, and succeeded in driving the Russians out of the most forward parallel, from which the Guard had been compelled to withdraw, and retained its possession (Medal with Clasp, Brevet of Lt.Colonel, Sardinian Medal, 5th Class of the Medjidie, and Turkish Medal). Served in Bengal in suppressing the mutiny in 1857-59, with the Jounpore Field Force in the action and capture of Fort Nusrutpore (commanded the Sharpshooters of the Brigade), actions of Chanda, Ummeerpore, and Sultanpore (mentioned twice and thanked in despatch), siege and capture of Lucknow and storming of the Kaiserbagh; afterwards served in Central India (Medal with Clasp, and *CB.*).

[5] Lt.Colonel Cautley served in the Boer war in 1881 with the Natal Field Force. Served with the 1st Battalion West Kent Regiment throughout the Egyptian war of 1882, and was present at the action at Kassasin on the 9th September (Medal, and Khedive's Star).

[7] Major Grove served in the Boer war of 1881 with the Natal Field Force. Served with the 1st Battalion West Kent Regiment throughout the Egyptian war of 1882, and was present at the action of Kassasin (9th September) and at the battle of Tel-el-Kebir (Brevet of Major, Medal with Clasp, and Khedive's Star); also served with the Nile Expedition in 1884-85 as Deputy Assistant Adjutant and Quarter Master General (Clasp).

[10] Major Evans served with the 1st Battalion of the West Kent Regiment throughout the Egyptian war of 1882 (Medal, and Khedive's Star). Served in the Nile Expedition in 1884-85 with the 1st Battalion of the West Kent Regiment (Clasp); also served with the Soudan Frontier Field Force in 1885-86, and was present in the engagement at Giniss.

[11] Major Harrison served in the Boer war of 1881 with the Natal Field Force. Served throughout the Egyptian war of 1882 with the 1st Battalion West Kent Regiment (Medal, and Khedive's Star).

[12] Major Morse served with the 1st Battalion of the West Kent Regiment throughout the Egyptian war of 1882, and was present at the action at Kassasin on the 9th September (Medal, and Khedive's Star). Served in the Nile Expedition in 1884-85 with the Mounted Infantry, and was present at the action of Abu Klea and in the reconnaissance to Metammeh—wounded (two Clasps).

[13] Major Daniell served with the 1st Battalion West Kent Regiment throughout the Egyptian war of 1882 (Medal, and Khedive's Star).

[23] Major Western, Captains Mann, Dalison, and Maxwell served in the Nile Expedition in 1884-85 with the 1st Battalion of the West Kent Regiment (Medal with Clasp, and Khedive's Star).

[25] Major Maunsell served with the 1st Battalion West Kent Regiment throughout the Egyptian war of 1882, and was present at the action at Kassasin (9th September) and at the battle of Tel-el-Kebir in command of the escort to the ammunition column (Medal with Clasp, 5th Class of the Medjidie, and Khedive's Star). Served in the Boer war of 1881 with the Natal Field Force. Served with the Soudan Frontier Field Force in command of the English Camel Corps, and was present in the engagement at Giniss.

[26] Major Brock-Hollinshead served with the 1st Battalion of the West Kent Regiment in the Egyptian war of 1882 (Medal, and Khedive's Star). Served in the Nile Expedition in 1884-85 with the 1st Battalion of the West Kent Regiment (Clasp).

[27] Captain Alderson served under Sir Evelyn Wood in the Boer war of 1881 in the Mounted Infantry. Served with the Mounted Infantry in the Egyptian war of 1882, and was present in the engagements at Tel-el-Mahuta and Mahsama, in the two actions at Kassasin, and at the battle of Tel-el-Kebir and the capture of Cairo (Medal with Clasp, and Khedive's Star). Served in the Nile Expedition in 1884-85 with the Mounted Infantry, and was present at the action at Abu Klea and at the reconnaissance to Metammeh (two Clasps). [See also Civil Decorations for Gallantry, "Hart's Annual Army List," p. 786.]

[28] Captain Rowe served in the Egyptian war of 1882 with the 1st Battalion of the West Kent Regiment (Medal, and Khedive's Star). Served with the Nile Expedition in 1884-85 with the 1st Battalion of the West Kent Regiment (Clasp); also served with the Soudan Frontier Field Force in 1885-86, and was present in the engagement at Giniss.

[29] Captain Heygate served in the Boer war of 1881 with the Natal Field Force.

[30] Major Wintour served with the 1st Battalion of the West Kent Regiment in the Egyptian war of 1882 (Medal, and Khedive's Star). Served in the Nile Expedition in 1884-85 as Adjutant to the 1st Battalion of the West Kent Regiment (mentioned in despatches, Brevet of Major, Clasp); also served with the Soudan Frontier Field Force in 1885-86, and was present in the engagement at Giniss.

[31] Captain Montgomery-Campbell served in the operations near Suakin in December 1888, including the engagement at Gemaizah (Medal with Clasp, 4th Class of the Osmanieh, and Khedive's Star).

[34] Captain Annesley served in the Nile Expedition in 1884-85 with the 1st Battalion of the West Kent Regiment (Medal with Clasp, and Khedive's Star); also served with the Soudan Frontier Field Force in 1885-86, including the attack on Ambigole Wells and the engagement at Giniss (*DSO.*).

[35] Captain Martyn served with the Soudan Frontier Field Force in 1885-86, and was present in the engagement at Giniss (mentioned in despatches, Medal, and Khedive's Star).

[36] Captains Hodges and Hewett served with the Soudan Frontier Field Force in 1885-86, and were present in the engagement at Giniss (Medal, and Khedive's Star).

[37] Captain Style served with the Soudan Frontier Field Force in 1885-86 (Medal, and Khedive's Star).

[38] Captain Lees served with the expedition up the Gambia in 1891-92 (Medal with Clasp).

Record of the Services of the 2nd Royal West Kent Regiment (formerly the 97th Regiment).

Raised in 1824. To Ceylon, 1825. To England, 1836. To Ireland, 1839. To Corfu, 1841. (Reserve Battalion formed 1841-51.) To Halifax, Nova Scotia, 1849. To England, 1853. To Greece and the Crimea, 1854 (siege of Sebastopol). To England, 1856. To India, 1857 (capture of Lucknow). To England, 1866. To Ireland, 1871. To the West Indies, 1873. To Bermuda, 1875. To Halifax, Nova Scotia, 1876. To Gibraltar, 1880. To South Africa, 1881. Entitled "2nd Battalion the Queen's Own Royal West Kent Regiment," 1881. To England, 1882.

The King's Own Yorkshire Light Infantry.

1st Batt., Belfast.
2nd Batt., Poona, Bombay.] *Formerly the 51st (2nd Yorkshire West Riding* [*Reg. District No.* 51.—Pontefract.
The King's Own Light Infantry) and the 105th (Madras Light Infantry) Regiments.
(The 3rd Battalion is formed of the 1st West York Militia.)

The White Rose. "*Cede Nullis.*" "MINDEN" "CORUNNA" "FUENTES D'ONOR" "SALAMANCA" "VITTORIA" "PYRENEES" "NIVELLE" "ORTHES" "PENINSULA" "WATERLOO" "PEGU" "ALI MASJID" "AFGHANISTAN, 1878-80" "BURMA, 1885-87."

Years' Ser. Full Pay	Half Pay		ENSIGN OR 2ND LIEUT.	LIEUT.	CAPTAIN.	BREV. MAJ.	MAJOR.
29	...	Colonel.—Sir Robert Hume,¹ KCB. Ensign, ᴾ9 Apr. 47; Lieut. ᴾ30 Nov. 49; Captain, 21 Sept. 54; Bt.Major, 2 Nov. 55; Major, 20 Apr. 58; Lt.Colonel, ᶠ8 Oct. 58; Colonel, 8 Oct. 63; Major General, 17 May 69; Lt.General, 1 Aug. 83; Colonel Yorkshire Light Infantry, 14 Sept. 93.					
29	...	Lieutenant Colonels.—1 George Philip Francis Byng, Ensign, 11 Jan. 67; Lieut. 18 May 69; Capt. 14 June 76; Major, 20 May 82; Lt.Colonel, 26 Mar. 94.					
27	...	2 Thomas Johnson Seppings,⁵ Ensign, ᴾ22 July 68; Lieut. ᶠ10 June 71; Captain, 11 Aug. 78; Major, 13 June 83; Lt.Colonel, 19 July 94.					
		MAJORS.					
27	...	1 Charles Stafford Stephen Whitehill......	1 Aug. 68	6 Nov. 70	21 April 77	......	21 June 83
25	...	2 John Guyse Sparke⁸	3 Sept. 70	28 Oct. 71	4 Feb. 81	......	10 Jan. 85
20	...	1 p.s.c. Charles St. Leger Barter		10 Sept. 75	15 Mar. 81	......	26 Mar. 90
22	...	p.s.c. Sir Henry Allen Wm. Johnson,¹⁰ Bart., D. A. A. General, Bombay Army, 10 Mar. 94................................		28 Feb. 74	6 Feb. 82	......	4 July 91
19	...	1 John George Adamson (Depot)		6 Sept. 76	8 Dec. 82	......	10 Jan. 92
19	...	Henry Earle,¹⁴ DSO., Adj. 4 Vol. Bn. Suffolk Regt. 6 May 91		11 Sept. 76	14 Feb. 83	......	31 Jan. 94
17	...	Percy William Albert Altred Milton,¹⁶ S. S. Officer, Nusseerabad, 17 May 92	11 May 78	14 Dec. 78	1 Jan. 84	1 Sept. 91	26 Mar. 94
17	...	Walter Blake Butler-Creagh,¹⁷ Adj. 3 Bn. Munster Fusiliers 17 Aug. 91..	7 Aug. 78	9 Aug. 80	26 Mar. 84	......	29 July 94
		CAPTAINS.					
17	...	Chas. Hildyard Thornton Whitaker, Adj. 3 Guernsey Militia 1 Mar. 92	22 Jan. 79	30 Apr. 79	28 Apr. 84		
16	...	Lionel Dorling, Army Pay Department	13 Aug. 79	15 Nov. 79	28 May 84		
16	...	1 Bertram Witherby, Adjutant 23 May 94	13 Aug. 79	24 Jan. 80	18 Nov. 84		
18	⁴/₁₉	2 Villiers Edward Hunt		30 Nov. 76	10 Jan. 85		
15	...	2 George Frederick Ottley¹⁹	17 Apr. 80	10 Nov. 80	24 Oct. 85		
16	...	1 Alfred Richard Power²⁰	9 July 79	1 July 81	20 Jan. 86		
17	...	Chas. Mordaunt Stevens,²¹ Adj. Admin. Bn. 1 Punjab Rifle Vols. 5 June 90..	11 Sept. 78	11 Oct. 79	29 July 85		
14	...	Robert Cotton Money, Adjutant 3 Battalion 19 Nov. 91	23 April 81	1 July 81	1 July 87		
14	...	1 Henry Newport Charles Heath²⁴.......		22 Oct. 81	6 Feb. 89	7 Feb. 89	
13	...	2 John Hugh Sandham Griffith²⁵		9 Sept. 82	30 Oct. 89		
13	...	Arthur Warre Elles,²⁵ Aide de Camp to Sir W. K. Elles 27 Apr. 93		10 Mar. 83	6 May 91		
13	...	1 Leonard Alison Hall. Hamilton,²⁶ Staff College..		10 Mar. 83	4 July 91		
12	...	Lawrence Willoughby Pease,²⁷ Ordnance Store Dept................................		19 Dec. 83	10 Jan. 92		
12	...	1 Albert William Crawford M'Fall²⁸		19 Dec. 83	10 Jan. 92		
12	...	2 Percy Herbert Rogers,²⁹ Adjutant 23 July 93		30 Jan. 84	1 Mar. 92		
11	...	2 Henry Wells-Cole		23 Aug. 84	17 May 92		
11	...	2 Philip Donald Dorin de Wilton...........		28 Feb. 85	6 July 92		
10	...	2 p.s.c. Arthur George Marrable²⁵		9 May 85	23 July 93		
9		Richard Dill,³⁰ Adj. Indian Midland Railway Volunteers 24 Nov. 92		28 July 86	11 Oct. 93		
9	...	2 Hastings Curtis Folliott Scott (Depot)		25 Aug. 86	11 Oct. 93		
8	...	1 William Robert Jason Ellis²⁸	16 Nov. 87	20 Nov. 89	25 Oct. 93		
8	...	1 Robert Henry William Tulloh	18 Jan. 88	20 Nov. 89	10 Mar. 94		
8	...	1 William Thomas Potts	11 Feb. 88	24 Nov. 89	26 Mar. 94		
7	...	2 Rowan Cashel³²	15 Aug. 88	5 Feb. 90	23 May 94		
7	...	2 Reginald Coplestone Bond,²⁸ Station Staff Officer, Poona, 1 Mar. 94.........	10 Nov. 88	1 Apr. 90	19 July 94		
		LIEUTENANTS.					
7	...	1 William Maunder Withycombe (Depot)	10 Nov. 88	23 Apr. 90			
7	...	Charles Ernest Carr...........................	21 Nov. 88	7 May 90			
7	...	1 Malcolm Reginald Walker.................	8 Dec. 88	6 May 91			
7	...	David Elgar Payn, Ordnance Store Dept.	30 Jan. 89	4 July 91			
6	...	2 Thomas Percy Dowdall³⁴	15 May 89	7 Oct. 91			
6	...	1 Alan Sutherland Colquhoun................	9 Oct. 89	30 Dec. 91			
5	...	Lancelot Hugh Baldwin	3 May 90	1 Mar. 92			
5	...	1 Christopher Robert Ingham Brooke ...	28 June 90	17 May 92			
5	...	2 Edward Harold Buckle	28 June 90	16 June 92			
5	...	2 James Bruce Gregorie Tulloch	8 Oct. 90	16 June 92			
4	...	2 Charles Sydney Harris (Depot)	25 July 91	21 Dec. 92			
4	...	2 Glendower George Ottley	25 July 91	21 Dec. 92			
4	...	1 Matthew William Kemble Connolly ...	7 Nov. 91	21 Dec. 92			
4	...	Wilfred Spedding Swabey,³ Army Service Corps	12 Mar. 92	23 July 93			
3	...	Bertram Price Ellwood	18 May 92	23 July 93			
3	...	2 Lionel Maury Ross Deas....................	18 May 92	11 Oct. 93			
3	...	2 Hugh Harrison	18 May 92	25 Oct. 93			
3	...	2 Charles Allix Lavington Yate	13 Aug. 92	7 Feb. 94			
3	...	1 Herbert Edward Trevor	14 Sept. 92	26 Mar. 94			
3	...	George Henry Badcock	14 Sept. 92	18 May 94			
3	...	James Muscroft	19 Oct. 92	18 May 94			
3	...	2 Stuart Campbell Taylor	17 Dec. 92	1 July 94			
3	...	2 Alfred Fothergill Cooke	21 Jan. 93	19 July 94			
3	...	1 Raymond Edward Boulton	25 Feb. 93				
		SECOND LIEUTENANTS.					
2	...	1 John Edmund Noble, serving under the Royal Niger Company..............	23 Aug. 93				
2	...	2 Frederick Temple Thorold	21 Oct. 93				
2	...	2 Hugh Clifford Fernyhough	21 Oct. 93				

The King's Own Yorkshire Light Infantry.

Years ser. Full Pay.	Half Pay.	SECOND LIEUTENANTS.	2ND LIEUT.
2	...	2 Lionel Berkeley Holt Haworth	23 Dec. 93
2	...	2 Harold Tatum	7 Mar. 94
2	...	1 Charles Edensor Heathcote	7 Mar. 94
1	...	1 John Doull Doull	29 Aug. 94
1	...	2 Charles Ernest Alfred French Somerset Butler	10 Oct. 94
1	...	2 Gordon Charles William Gordon Hall	10 Oct. 94
1	...	2 Edward Becher Longhurst	10 Oct. 94
1	...	2 Alfred Blomefield Lane	10 Oct. 94
1	...	1 Edward Chorley Watt	12 Dec. 94
1	...	Ernest St. George Hughes	20 Mar. 95

Paymasters.—2

| 9 | ... | *Quarter Masters.*—2 William Graham Judge,[36] 28 Aug. 86; *Hon. Lieut.* |
| 2 | ... | 1 Alfred Samuel Patterson,[37] 31 Jan. 94; *Hon. Lieut.* |

Facings Blue.—*Agents*, Messrs. Cox and Co.
1st Battalion returned from Burmah, 20 Dec. 1887. *2nd Battalion embarked for Malta,* 28 Dec. 1884.

[1] Sir Robert Hume served the Eastern campaign of 1854, and up to the 13th Jan. 1855, and from the 29th May to the 30th Sept. 1855, with the 55th Regt. including the battles of Alma and Inkerman (severely wounded), siege and fall of Sebastopol, repulse of the sortie of 26th October, and assaults of the Redan on the 18th June and 8th Sept.—severely wounded, and mentioned in despatches (Medal with three Clasps, Brevet of Major, Knight of the Legion of Honour, 5th Class of the Medjidie, and Turkish Medal). Commanded the 55th Regiment in the Bhootan Expedition, including the attack and recapture of Dewangiri in 1865 (Medal with Clasp). Commanded the Southern Afghanistan Field Force from November 1880 to April 1881, including the evacuation of Candahar and Southern Afghanistan and the withdrawal of the force to India (received the thanks of Government).

[5] Lt.Colonel Seppings served with the 51st Light Infantry in the Afghan war of 1878-80, and was present at the attack and capture of Ali Musjid (Medal with Clasp).

[8] Major Sparke served with the 51st Light Infantry in the Afghan war of 1878-80, and was present at the attack and capture of Ali Musjid (Medal with Clasp). Served in the Burmese Expedition from 1886 till the close of 1887 with the 1st Battalion of the Yorkshire Light Infantry (Medal with two Clasps).

[10] Sir Henry Johnson served with the 51st Light Infantry in the Jowaki campaign in 1877 (Medal with Clasp). Served with the 51st Light Infantry in the Afghan war of 1878-80, and was present at the attack and capture of Ali Musjid and in the operations in the Bazar, Lughman, and Hissarik Valleys (Medal with Clasp). Served in the Burmese Expedition from 1886 till the close of 1887 as Adjutant of the 1st Battalion of the Yorkshire Light Infantry (two Clasps).

[14] Major Earle served with the 51st Light Infantry in the Jowaki campaign in 1877 (Medal with Clasp). Served with the 51st Light Infantry in the Afghan war of 1878-80, during the latter part of the time as Orderly Officer to Major General Bright, and was present in the operations in the Lughman and Hissarik Valleys (Medal). Served in the Egyptian war of 1882 as Aide de Camp to Major General Earle, Commanding Base and Lines of Communication, and was present in the engagements at El Magfar and Tel-el-Mahuta, in the action at Kassasin (9th September), and at the battle of Tel-el-Kebir (Medal with Clasp, 5th Class of the Medjidie, and Khedive's Star). Served in the Burmese Expedition from 1886 till the close of 1887 with the 1st Battalion of the Yorkshire Light Infantry and accompanied the Ruby Mine Column in December 1886 and the expedition to Mainloung (mentioned in despatches, *DSO.*, and two Clasps).

[16] Major Milton served with the 51st Light Infantry in the Afghan war in 1879-80 (mentioned in despatches, Medal). Served in the Burmese Expedition in 1886-87 with the 1st Battalion of the Yorkshire Light Infantry, during the latter part of the time in command of the Mounted Infantry (mentioned in despatches, Medal with Clasp). Served with the 2nd Battalion King's Own Yorkshire Light Infantry in the Zhob Field Force in 1890 under Sir George White during the Zhob and Kiderzai Expeditions and in the march to Vihowa (mentioned in despatches).

[17] Major Butler-Creagh served with the 51st Light Infantry in the Afghan war in 1879-80 (Medal). Served with the 2nd Battalion King's Own Yorkshire Light Infantry in the Zhob Field Force in 1890 under Sir George White during the Zhob and Kiderzai Expeditions and in the march to Vihowa.

[19] Captain Ottley served as Adjutant 2nd Battalion King's Own Yorkshire Light Infantry in the Zhob Field Force in 1890 under Sir George White during the Zhob and Kiderzai Expeditions and as Staff Officer to the Vihowa Column.

[20] Captain Power served in the Afghan war in 1879-80 with the 51st Light Infantry (Medal). Served in the Burmese Expedition from 1886 till the close of 1887 with the 1st Battalion of the Yorkshire Light Infantry (Medal with two Clasps).

[21] Captain Stevens served in the Nile Expedition in 1884-85 with the 1st Battalion of the Royal Irish Regiment, and took part in the operations of the Desert Column including the engagement at Abu Klea Wells on the 16th and 17th February (Medal with Clasp, and Khedive's Star).

[24] Major Heath served as Transport Officer with the 1st Battalion South Staffordshire Regiment in the Egyptian war of 1882, and was present in the reconnaissance in force from Alexandria on the 5th August (Medal, and Khedive's Star). Served with the Nile Expedition in 1884-85, and was present at the action of Kirbekan (mentioned in despatches, Brevet of Major, two Clasps). Served with the Soudan Frontier Field Force during the operations on the Upper Nile in 1885-86 as Adjutant of the 1st Battalion of the South Staffordshire Regiment.

[25] Captains Griffith, Elles and Marrable served in the Burmese Expedition from 1886 till the close of 1887 with the 1st Battalion of the Yorkshire Light Infantry (Medal with two Clasps).

[26] Captain Hamilton served in the Burmese Expedition from 1886 till the close of 1887 with the 1st Battalion of the Yorkshire Light Infantry, and for six months as Staff Officer to the Officer Commanding at Bhamo (Medal with two Clasps).

[27] Captain Pease served in the Burmese Expedition in 1885-87 (Medal with two Clasps).

[28] Captains M'Fall, Ellis and Bond served with the 2nd Battalion King's Own Yorkshire Light Infantry in the Zhob Field Force in 1890 under Sir George White during the Zhob and Kiderzai Expeditions and in the march to Vihowa.

[29] Captain Rogers served as Transport Officer to the 2nd Battalion King's Own Yorkshire Light Infantry in the Zhob Field Force in 1890 under Sir George White during the Zhob and Kiderzai Expeditions and the march to Vihowa; and with the Isazai Field Force in 1892.

[30] Captain Dill served throughout the Egyptian war of 1882, and was present at the action of Kassasin on the 9th September and at the battle of Tel-el-Kebir (Medal with Clasp, and Khedive's Star).

[32] Captain Cashel served with the 2nd Battalion King's Own Yorkshire Light Infantry in the Zhob Field Force in 1890 under Sir George White during the Zhob Expedition.

[34] Lieut. Dowdall served with the 2nd Battalion King's Own Yorkshire Light Infantry in the Zhob Field Force in 1890 under Sir George White during the Zhob and Kiderzai Expeditions and in the march to Vihowa.

[36] Lieut. Judge served as Quarter Master to the 2nd Battalion King's Own Yorkshire Light Infantry in the Zhob Field Force in 1890 under Sir George White during the Zhob and Kiderzai Expeditions and in the march to Vihowa.

[37] Lieut. Patterson served with the Jowaki Afreedee Expedition in 1877-78 (Medal with Clasp). Served in the Afghan war of 1878-80, and was present at the capture of Ali Musjid (Medal with Clasp). Served with the Burmese Expedition in 1886-87 (two Clasps).

[*For Record of Services, see end of Berkshire Regiment, page 293b.*

The King's (Shropshire Light Infantry). 297

1st Batt., Fort William, Bengal.
2nd Batt., Portland.
Formerly the 53rd (Shropshire)
and the 85th (Bucks Volunteers) (King's Light Infantry) Regiments.
(The 3rd and 4th Battalions are formed of the Shropshire and Hereford Militia respectively.)

Regimental District No. 53.—Shrewsbury.

The United Red and White Rose. "*Aucto splendore resurgo*." "NIEUPORT" "TOURNAY" "ST. LUCIA" "TALAVERA" "FUENTES D'ONOR" "SALAMANCA" "VITTORIA" "PYRENEES" "NIVELLE" "NIVE" "TOULOUSE" "PENINSULA" "BLADENSBURG" "ALIWAL" "SOBRAON" "PUNJAUB" "GOOJERAT" "LUCKNOW" "AFGHANISTAN, 1879-80" "EGYPT, 1882" "SUAKIN, 1885."

Years' Ser. Full Pay	Half Pay			Ensign or 2nd Lieut.	Lieut.	Captain.	Brev. Maj.	Major.
		Colonel.—Sir Henry Perceval de Bathe, Bt.,¹ Ens. & Lt. ᴾ1 Nov. 39; Lt. & Capt. 14 Feb. 45; Capt. & Lt. Colonel ᴾ17 Feb. 54; Colonel, 28 Nov. 54; Major General, 6 Mar. 68; Lieutenant General, 8 Oct. 76; General, 1 Jan. 79; Colonel 85th Light Infantry, 25 April 80.						
30	...	Lieutenant Colonels.—1 p.s.c. Francis Wingfield Robinson,¹³ *Ensign*, 10 Oct. 65; *Lieut.* ᴾ7 Aug. 67; *Capt.* 22 June 76; *Major*, 15 May 84; *Lt. Colonel*, 19 Aug. 93.						
27	...	2 Pulteney Henry Murray,¹⁹ *Ensign*, ᴾ27 Feb. 69; *Lieut.* 28 Oct. 71; *Capt.* 3 Apr. 80; *Major*, 21 June 85; *Lt. Colonel*, 11 Feb. 94.						
		MAJORS.						
28	...	1 Cecil Henry Collette²⁴		8 Jan. 68	28 Oct. 71	30 Sept. 82	......	19 Aug. 86
24	...	2 James Spens¹³		......	29 May 72	1 July 83	......	7 Apr. 86
22	...	1 John Hope Wynne Eyton²⁰		......	1 Feb. 74	1 July 81	15 June 85	1 Sept. 86
20	...	1 William MacLaughlin²⁶		......	23 April 75	13 Apr. 84	......	15 May 85
21	...	1 Acheson Francis Acheson Lyle		......	11 Feb. 75	11 May 84	......	30 Nov. 92
20	...	2 p.s.c. William Baume Capper²⁷		......	12 Feb. 76	15 May 84	15 June 85	19 Aug 93
20	...	Johnston Stoney Talbot,²⁸ *Instructor Staff College* 16 Dec. 92		......	6 Oct. 75	27 Aug. 84	......	4 Oct. 93
19	...	2 Philip Bulman²⁵ (*Depot*)		......	11 Sept. 76	4 Feb. 85	......	11 Feb. 93
		CAPTAINS.						
18	...	2 Arthur Havelock James Doyle³²		30 Jan. 78	19 July 80	21 June 85		
18	...	2 Herbert Vere Wilbraham³¹		30 Jan. 78	26 Feb. 81	1 Sept. 86		
17	...	Charles Tyrwhitt Dawkins,¹³ *Military Secretary, Cape of Good Hope...*		1 May 78	1 July 81	13 Sept. 86		
16	...	p.s.c. Raymond Northland Revell Reade,³¹ *Aide de Camp to Sir W. F. Butler* 17 Nov. 93		14 Jan. 80	1 July 81	19 Oct. 87		
15	...	1 James Langford Pearse²⁹		11 Aug. 80	1 July 81	31 Dec. 87		
15	...	Arthur Robert Austen,³⁵ *Adjutant 1 Hereford Rifle Volunteers* 30 Mar. 91		22 Jan. 81	1 July 81	6 Dec. 89		
13	...	2 Frederick Lionel Banon³⁶		......	9 Sept. 82	1 Jan. 90		
13	...	1 Claude William Culley Cass²⁸		......	29 July 82	1 Jan. 90		
13	...	2 Kellermann Eyre M'Mahon		......	27 Jan. 83	11 Feb. 90		
13	...	Benjamin Cotton³⁷		......	10 Mar. 83	30 Mar. 91		
12	...	Spencer Francis Judge,³⁸ *DSO, serving with the Egyptian Army*		......	12 May 83	30 Mar. 91		
11	...	1 Stephen George Moore (*Depot*)		......	14 May 84	1 Jan. 92		
13	...	1 Gilbert Howell Lenny Buchanan		......	27 Jan. 83	30 July 91		
13	...	1 Harvey Beauchamp Welman		......	9 Sept. 82	29 May 91		
11	1⅘	Ernle William Kyrle Money,³⁹ *Adjutant 1 Volunteer Bn.* 28 Mar. 94		......	25 Aug. 83	30 Mar. 91		
11	...	James Ross O'Connell, *serving with the Egyptian Army*		......	22 Nov. 84	30 Nov. 92		
10	...	Robert Astley Smith, *Adjutant 4 Battalion* 19 Sept. 93		......	6 May 85	30 Nov. 92		
10	...	2 Robert Cecil Mounsey-Heysham		......	29 Aug. 85	30 Nov. 92		
10	...	2 James Horatio Hicks⁴⁰		......	28 Nov. 85	22 Mar. 93		
10	...	2 Oscar Hyde East Marescaux, *Adjutant* 19 Sept. 93		......	29 Aug. 85	4 Oct. 93		
10	...	1 Edward Howell⁴¹		......	25 Nov. 85	11 Feb. 94		
10	...	1 John Geo. Forbes, **Adjutant** 21 Dec. 91		......	30 Jan. 86	11 Feb. 94		
9	...	2 William Scott Warley Radcliffe		......	25 Aug. 86	5 June 94		
		LIEUTENANTS.						
9	...	2 Cecil Pickford Higginson		......	10 Nov. 86			
9	...	1 Richard Avary Arthur Young Jordan		......	10 Nov. 86			
9	...	1 Charles Edmund Ruck-Keene		5 Feb. 87	1 Jan. 90			
9	...	2 John Joseph White (*Depot*)		5 Feb. 87	11 Feb. 90			
9	...	1 George Conolly Benson		5 Feb. 87	21 Feb. 90			
8	...	1 Thomas Henry Philip Helps (*Depot*)		16 Nov. 87	24 Dec. 90			
8	...	Frederic Hugh Mackenzie, *with Ordnance Store Department*		16 Nov. 87	30 Mar. 91			
8	...	1 Guy Burnett Arbouin		11 Feb. 88	3 Apr. 91			
6	...	1 Richard Rolls Gubbins		1 Mar. 90	21 Dec. 91			
6	...	1 John Arkwright Strick		1 Mar. 90	1 Jan. 92			
5	...	1 Hugh Lyle Smyth		16 Apr. 90	13 Apr. 92			
5	...	1 Godfrey Meynell		3 May 90	11 Oct. 92			
5	...	1 Clare James Garsia		3 May 90	30 Nov. 92			
5	...	1 Francis Dobbs Markham		3 May 90	22 Mar. 93			
5	...	1 Francis Ludlow Wood		3 May 90	11 Sept. 93			
5	...	2 Gerald Russell Sowray		17 Jan. 91	1 Jan. 94			
4	...	1 Edward Bourryau Luard		2 May 91	11 Feb. 94			
4	...	2 Charles Marshall		25 July 91	5 June 94			
4	...	1 William Arthur Payn		5 Dec. 91	25 Oct. 94			
3	...	2 Horace Mackenzie Smith		9 Apr. 92	22 Dec. 94			
		SECOND LIEUTENANTS.						
3	...	2 Walter Cecil Wright		18 May 92				
3	...	1 Robert Masefield		18 June 92				
3	...	2 Edward Mark Sprot		19 Nov. 92				
3	...	1 Robert Thomas Carreg		25 Feb. 93				
3	...	2 John Henry Bailey		15 Mar. 93				
3	...	1 William James Robinson		26 Apr. 93				
2	...	1 Clement Arthur Wilkinson		23 Dec. 93				
2	...	1 Clinton Wynyard Battye		7 Mar. 94				
1	...	1 Arthur Worsley Spottiswoode Pinhey		2 June 94				
1	...	1 Henry Grenville Bryant		2 June 94				
1	...	2 Charles Ernest Atchison		20 Feb. 95				
1	...	2 Percival Charles Grover		20 Feb. 95				

³⁶ Captain Banon served in the expedition to the Soudan in 1885 with the 1st Battalion Shropshire Light Infantry (Medal with Clasp, and Khedive's Star).

³⁷ Captain Cotton served in the expedition to the Soudan in 1885 with the 1st Battalion Shropshire Light Infantry (Medal with Clasp, and Khedive's Star), and in the subsequent occupation of Suakin by British troops in 1885-86. Also served in the operations in the Soudan in 1889 including the engagement at Toski (Clasp, 4th Class of the Medjidie).

Years' Ser.	298-300	The King's (Shropshire Light Infantry).
Full Pay.	Half Pay.	
14	...	*Paymasters.*—2
5	...	1
		Quarter Masters.—2 Arthur Willmott, 14 Sept. 81; *Hon. Captain*, 14 Sept. 91.
		1 John Charles Wilson, 23 July 90; *Hon. Lieut.*

Facings Blue.—*Agents*, Messrs. Cox and Co.
1st Battalion embarked for Egypt, 27 Feb. 1885.   2nd Battalion returned from India and Natal, 1881.

[1] Sir Henry Percival de Bathe served with the Scots Fusilier Guards in the Crimean campaign from 17th Nov. 1854, and was present at the siege and fall of Sebastopol (mentioned in despatches, Medal with Clasp, 5th Class of the Medjidie, and Turkish Medal).

[13] Lt.Colonel Robinson, Major Spens, and Captain Dawkins served in the Afghan war in 1879-80 with the Koorum Division, including the Zaimusht Expedition and the assault of Zawa (Medal).

[19] Lt.Colonel Murray served as Adjutant with the 1st Battalion Shropshire Light Infantry in the Egyptian war of 1882, and was present at the surrender of Kafr Dowar and Damietta (Medal, and Khedive's Star).

[20] Major Eyton served with the 1st Battalion Shropshire Light Infantry in the Egyptian war of 1882, and was present at the surrender of Kafr Dowar and Damietta (Medal, and Khedive's Star). Served in the expedition to the Soudan in 1885 with the Camel Corps, and was present in the engagement at Takdoul (mentioned in despatches, Brevet of Major, Clasp).

[24] Major Collette served with the 85th Regiment as Adjutant in the Afghan war in 1879-80, including the Zaimusht Expedition and the assault of Zawa (mentioned in despatches, Medal). Served in the occupation of Suakin by British troops in 1885-86.

[25] Major Bulman served in the Afghan war in 1879-80 with the Koorum Division, including the Zaimusht Expedition (Medal).

[26] Major MacLaughlin served with the 1st Battalion Shropshire Light Infantry in the Egyptian war of 1882, and was present at the surrender of Kafr Dowr and Damietta (Medal, and Khedive's Star). Served in the expedition to the Soudan in 1885 with the 1st Battalion Shropshire Light Infantry (Clasp), and in the subsequent occupation of Suakin by British troops in 1885-86.

[27] Major Capper served in the Afghan war in 1879-80 with the 85th Light Infantry in the Koorum Division including the Zaimusht Expedition and the assault of Zawa; was Aide de Camp to Major General Watson (Medal). Served in the Egyptian war of 1882 in the Transport Service (Medal, and Khedive's Star). Served in the Nile Expedition in 1884-85 with the Transport, and was present at the seizure of the Gakdul Wells, in the actions at Abu Klea and El Gubat, and in the reconnaissance to Metammeh (Brevet of Major, two Clasps).

[28] Major Talbot and Lieut. Cass served in the expedition to the Soudan in 1885 with the 1st Battalion Shropshire Light Infantry (Medal with Clasp, and Khedive's Star), and in the subsequent occupation of Suakin by British troops in 1885-86.

[29] Captain Pearse served with the 1st Battalion Shropshire Light Infantry in the Egyptian war of 1882, and was present at the surrender of Kafr Dowar and Damietta (Medal, and Khedive's Star). Served in the expedition to the Soudan in 1885 with the 1st Battalion Shropshire Light Infantry (Clasp), and in the subsequent occupation of Suakin by British troops in 1885-86.

[31] Captains Wilbraham and Reade served in the Afghan war in 1879-80 with the Koorum Division (Medal).

[32] Captain Doyle served in the Afghan war in 1879-80 with the Koorum Division, including the Zaimusht Expedition and the assault of Zawa (Medal). Served with the expedition against Tambi, on the West Coast of Africa, in 1892 (Medal with Clasp).

[35] Captain Austen served with the 1st Battalion Shropshire Light Infantry in the Egyptian war of 1882, and was present at the surrender of Kafr Dowar and Damietta (Medal, and Khedive's Star). Served in the expedition to the Soudan in 1885 with the 1st Battalion Shropshire Light Infantry, and was present in the engagement at Takdoul—wounded (Clasp).

[38] Captain Judge served in the occupation of Suakin by British troops in 1885-86. Served in the operations in the Soudan in December 1888 including the engagement at Gemaizah (Medal with Clasp, and Khedive's Star), and in 1889 including the engagements at Arguin and Toski (mentioned in despatches, DSO., Clasp, and 4th Class of the Osmanieh).

[39] Captain Money served in the occupation of Suakin by Britishtroops in 1885-86. Served in the Hazara Expedition in 1888 as Orderly Officer to Brigadier General Channer (Medal with Clasp).

[40] Captain Hicks served throughout the Zulu war in 1879 with the 2nd Battalion 24th Foot (Medal with Clasp), Served in the occupation of Suakin by British troops in 1886 with the 1st Battalion Shropshire Light Infantry.

[41] Captain Howell served in the occupation of Suakin by British troops in 1885-86.

Record of the Services of the 1st Battalion King's Shropshire Light Infantry,—formerly the 53rd (Shropshire) Regiment.

Raised in 1755 as the 55th Regiment. Gibraltar, to 1768. [Numbered 53rd, 1757.] Ireland, to 1776. Canada, to 1789. [Entitled "Shropshire Regiment," 1782.] England, to 1790. Served as Marines, 1791. Scotland, to 1793. Flanders, to 1795 (capture of Nieuport and battle of Tournay). England, to 1796. West Indies, to 1802 (capture of St. Lucia). [2nd Battalion raised in 1803. Ireland, to 1807. England, to 1808. Ireland, to 1809. The Peninsula, to 1814 (battles of Talavera, Salamanca, Vittoria, Pyrenees, Nivelle and Toulouse). England, to 1815. St. Helena, to 1817. Reduced, 1817.] England, to 1825. East Indies, to 1823. England, to 1826. Ireland, to 1829. Gibraltar, to 1834. Malta, to 1836. Ionian Islands, to 1840. England, to 1841. Scotland, to 1843. Ireland and England, to 1844. India, to 1860 (battles of Aliwal, Sobraon, and Goojerat, and capture of Lucknow). England, to 1864. Ireland, to 1866. Canada, to 1869. West Indies, to 1870. Bermuda, to 1875. Ireland, to 1877. Jersey, to 1878. Became 1st Battalion King's (Shropshire Light Infantry), 1881. England, to 1882. Egypt, to 1883. Malta, to 1885. Egypt, to 1887. Malta, to 1891. Egypt, 1891.

Record of the Services of the 2nd Battalion The King's Shropshire Light Infantry (formerly the 85th King's Light Infantry).

Raised in 1793 and proceded to Walcheren, 1794. England, to 1795. Jersey, to 1798. Isle of Wight, to 1799. Jersey, to 1800. Isle of Wight, to 1801. Madeira, to 1802. Jamaica, to 1803. England, to 1809. The Peninsula, to 1811 (battles of Fuentes d'Onor and Nive). England, to 1813. Spain, to 1814. America, to 1815 (battle of Bladensburg . England, to 1821. Malta, to 1827. Gibraltar, to 1828. Malta, to 1831. England, to 1833. Ireland, to 1836. Canada, to 1845. Barbadoes, to 1846. Ireland, to 1850. England, to 1853. Mauritius, to 1856. Cape of Good Hope, to 1863. England, to 1866. Ireland, to 1868. India, to 1881 (Afghan war, 1879-80). England, to 1886. Ireland, 1886.

The Duke of Cambridge's Own (Middlesex Regiment). 301

1st Batt., Aldershot.
2nd Batt., Ahmednugger, Bombay.] *Formerly the 57th (West Middlesex) and* [*Regimental District* No. 57.—Hounslow]
the 77th (East Middlesex—Duke of Cambridge's Own) Regiments.

(The 3rd and 4th Battalions are formed of the Elthorne and East Middlesex Militia respectively.)

The Plume of the Prince of Wales. The Duke of Cambridge's Coronet and Cypher. "MYSORE" "SERINGAPATAM" "ALBUHERA" "CIUDAD RODRIGO" "BADAJOZ" "VITTORIA" "PYRENEES" "NIVELLE" "NIVE" "PENINSULA" "ALMA" "INKERMAN" "SEVASTOPOL" "NEW ZEALAND" "SOUTH AFRICA, 1879."

Years' Ser.							
Full Pay.	Half Pay.	Colonel.—Sir Edward Alan Holdich,[1] KCB. Ensign, 2 July 41; Lt. 26 July 44; Capt. [2] 22 Feb. 50; Brevet Major, 2 Aug. 50; Brevet Lt. Colonel, 28 May 53; Colonel, 28 Nov. 54; Major, 26 May 58; Major General, 3 Sept. 67; Lt. General, 28 Apr. 75; General, 1 Oct. 77; Colonel 57th Foot, 11 Dec. 75.						
27	...	Lieutenant Colonels.—1 p.s.c. Henry Thomas Hughes Hallett,[7] Ensign, 13 Jan. 69; Lt. 27 Oct. 70; Capt. 8 April 75; Major, 4 Jan. 82; Lt. Colonel, 17 Dec. 91.						
24	...	2 Alfred Allan Garstin,[8] Ensign, 23 Sept. 71; Lt. 28 Oct. 71; Capt. 12 Aug. 80; Major, 14 April 83; Lt. Colonel, 18 Sept. 93.						
		MAJORS.	2ND LIEUT.	LIEUT.	CAPTAIN.	BREV. MAJ.	MAJOR.
23	...	2 Augustus West Hill[13]	......	1 Jan. 73	27 Sept. 80	......	8 May 85
22	...	1 p.s.c. James Grove White[13]	......	12 Nov. 73	2 Jan. 81	......	18 Sept. 89
22	...	2 Napoleon Joseph Rodolph Blake[14]	......	12 Nov. 73	14 Mar. 81	......	19 Mar. 90
22	...	Richard Woodroofe Graham,[13] *Army Pay Department*	......	21 Jan. 74	1 July 81	......	23 Dec. 91
21	...	Ernest Vernon Bellers,[13] *Adjutant Poona Rifle Volunteers* 17 Feb. 92	......	21 Sept. 74	23 May 84	......	18 Sept. 93
21	...	1 Francis Douglas Lumley	......	10 Mar. 75	28 June 84	......	6 Nov. 93
20	...	1 Alexander Towers-Clark[19] (*Depot*) ...	......	22 May 75	1 Jan. 85	......	21 Feb. 94
19	...	Robert Douglas Longe,[13] *Army Pay Dept.*	......	11 Sept. 76	8 May 85	......	9 Jan. 95
		CAPTAINS.					
19	...	2 p.s.c. Edward John Sharpe[21]	......	31 May 76	23 Sept. 85		
17	...	2 William Scott-Moncrieff,[13] *Adjutant* 7 Oct. 91	1 May 78	10 Mar. 80	21 Dec. 85		
17	...	1 p.s.c. Nathaniel Walter Barnardiston, *D.A.A. Gen. Colchester*, 1 Dec. 94	14 Sept. 78	11 Mar. 80	21 Dec. 85		
16	...	George Beresford Lempriere, *Adjutant* 3 Bn. Middlesex Regiment 4 May 91	21 June 79	13 Mar. 80	14 June 87		
16	...	Geo. Walter Wrey Savile, *Aide de Camp to Major Gen. H. S. Anderson* 22 Oct. 91	6 Aug. 79	15 Mar. 80	14 June 87		
16	...	1 Lionel Grant Oliver	13 Aug. 79	21 July 80	18 Sept. 87		
17	...	p.s.c. Louis William Bodé,[13] *D. A. A. Gen. Devonport*, 15 Nov. 92	11 May 78	12 Aug. 80	8 Sept. 87		
15	...	Charles Robert Dyer, *Adjutant* 4 Battalion 25 Nov. 92	11 Aug. 80	1 July 81	21 Nov. 88		
15	...	2 Reginald de Hardewicke Burton (*Depot*)	11 Aug. 80	1 July 81	17 Jan. 89		
15	...	2 Ernest Albert Bennett,[23] *with Provisional Battalion*	23 Oct. 80	1 July 81	11 May 89		
14	...	1 Henry Herriott Woolwright	......	22 Oct. 81	19 Mar. 90		
13	...	1 Francis Sapte	......	10 May 82	19 Mar. 90		
13	...	Bertram Edmund Ward, *Adj.* 3 *Vol. Bn. West Surrey Regt.* 30 May 92	......	10 May 82	19 Mar. 90		
13	...	Edmund Douglass Harvest,[24] *Army Pay Department*	......	10 May 82	1 Oct. 91		
12	...	2 p.s.c. Evelyn William Medows Norie[25]	......	25 Aug. 83	22 Oct. 91		
12	...	2 James Eyre Drummond Ward	......	30 Jan. 84	10 Nov. 91		
11	...	1 Ernest William Rokeby Stephenson ...	......	23 Aug. 84	10 Nov. 91		
11	...	1 Algernon Forbes Randolph	......	23 Aug. 84	17 Dec. 91		
11	...	2 Wallace Nelson[26]	......	23 Aug. 84	23 Dec. 91		
10	...	Henry Montague Eustace, *O.S. Dept.*...	......	29 Aug. 85	18 Sept. 92		
16	...	2 Robert Bertram Firman[27]	6 Aug. 79	1 July 87	21 Apr. 86		
10	...	2 Robert Hall Hayes[28]	......	29 Aug. 85	6 Nov. 93		
10	...	1 Jenkin Stephen Jones	......	25 Nov. 85	25 Feb. 94		
10	...	1 Frank George Mathias Rowley	......	30 Jan. 86	21 Feb. 95		
		LIEUTENANTS.					
9	...	2 William Edward Scarth Burch	......	7 July 86			
9	...	1 Robert James Ross, *Adjutant* 20 Aug. 94	......	25 Aug. 86			
9	...	2 Charles Leslie Muriel	5 Feb. 87	11 May 89			
8	...	2 William Francis Leader	19 Nov. 87	19 Mar. 89			
7	...	1 Charles Edward Pemberton	22 Aug. 88	20 Apr. 90			
7	...	1 George Gordon Grover (*Depot*)	10 Nov. 88	30 Sept 90			
7	...	1 John William Lindredge Elgee	22 Aug. 88	19 Mar. 90			
7	...	Arthur Crawford Julian Campbell, *with Hong Kong Regiment*	9 Mar. 89	1 Nov. 90			
6	...	1 Hamilton Walter Edward Finch	9 Nov. 89	1 Oct. 91			
6	...	1 Hubert George William Chandler	4 Dec. 89	22 Oct. 91			
5	...	2 Robert Archer Haviland, *with Provisional Battalion*	3 May 90	11 May 92			
5	...	1 Herbert Norwood Blakeney	29 Nov. 90	11 May 92			
5	...	2 Leslie Stuart Roome	17 Dec. 90	11 May 92			
4	...	2 John Hamilton Hall	7 Nov. 91	16 Sept. 92			
4	...	1 Gilbert Landale Cattell	27 Jan. 92	18 Sept. 93			
4	...	1 Allan Copinger Wall	20 Feb. 92	6 Nov. 93			
4	...	2 Vivian Henry Branson	20 Feb. 92	25 Feb. 94			
4	...	1 Samuel Wallace Somerville	18 June 92	11 June 94			
3	...	2 William St. Aubyn Wake	18 June 92	17 Oct. 94			
3	...	1 Hubert Edmond Foster	13 July 92	17 Oct. 94			
3	...	2 William John Phaelim Preston	31 Aug. 92	1 Dec. 95			
3	...	2 Percy George Berns	21 Sept. 92	21 Feb. 95			
		SECOND LIEUTENANTS.					
3	...	1 William Claudius Casson Ash	28 Sept. 92				
3	...	1 Charles Sydney Collison	19 Oct. 92				
3	...	2 Hugh Fletcher MacEwan	19 Nov. 92				

[19] Captain Towers-Clark served with the 57th Regiment in the Zulu campaign of 1879, including the action of Gingindhlovu and relief of Ekowe. Served afterwards to the end of the war as Orderly Officer to Lt. Colonel Clarke while commanding successively the 2nd Brigade 1st Division and "Clarke's Column." Made several road surveys, including the road in Zululand from St. Paul's to the Middle Drift of the Tugela River (Medal with Clasp).

[21] Captain E. J. Sharpe served with the 57th Regiment in the Zulu war of 1879, and was present at the action of Gingindhlovu and relief of Ekowe and throughout the operations of "Clarke's Column" (Medal with Clasp). Served in the Egyptian war of 1882 (Medal and Khedive's Star).

[23] Captain Bennett served with the Zhob Valley Expedition in 1884.

U

302-3 The Duke of Cambridge's Own (Middlesex Regiment).

Years' Ser. Full Pay.	Half Pay.	SECOND LIEUTENANTS.	2ND LIEUT.
3	...	1 George Williams Haslehust...............	19 Nov. 92
3	...	2 William Daly Ingle	17 Dec. 92
3	...	2 William St. Clair Muscroft	17 Dec. 92
2	...	2 Charles Trevor Lloyd	19 July 93
2	...	1 Hervey Noel Couchman	23 Dec. 93
2	...	1 Arthur Percival Macafee.................	23 Dec. 93
2	...	2 Frederick Alexander Galbraith............	23 Dec. 93
1	...	1 Charles Sidney Dalton Fisher	18 July 94
1	...	1 Everard Graham S. Trotter (*Depot*)......	10 Oct. 94

Paymaster.—
6 ... *Quarter Masters.*—1 James Alfred Walter,²⁶ 19 March 90 ; *Hon. Lieut.*
16 ...   2 Samuel George Miller,³¹ 27 Aug. 79 ; *Hon. Captain,* 27 Aug. 89.
Facings White.—*Agents,* Messrs. Cox and Co.
1st Battalion returned from Gibraltar, 1 Mar. 1895. *2nd Battalion embarked for Bengal,* 1880.

¹ Sir Edward Holdich served as Aide de Camp to Sir Harry Smith throughout the campaign on the Sutlej in 1845-46, including the battles of Moodkee, Ferozeshah (wounded), Buddiwal, Aliwal, and Sobraon—severely wounded (Medal and three Clasps). As Aide de Camp to Sir Harry Smith in the action with and defeat of the rebel Boers at Boom Plants (South Africa) on the 29th August 1848, and in the Kaffir campaign of 1850-51 (Medal, and Brevet of Lt.Colonel). Served with the 80th Regt. in the Burmese war in 1853, with the expedition under Sir John Cheape against the robber chief Myattoon in the Donabew district, and at the assault and capture of his stronghold on the 19th March—succeeded to the command of a Wing of Infantry (Medal for Pegu, and *CB.*) Accompanied the 80th Regt. to India in 1857, and served in the Sepoy rebellion. At the close of the operations in 1859 he succeeded Sir Alfred Horsford as Brigadier in command of the forces on the Nepaul frontier, when, in co-operation with the Nepaul troops, most of the rebel leaders and a large body of Sepoys who had taken refuge in the Nepaul Terai were captured, for which services he received the thanks of Government, and on the breaking up of the Brigade was appointed, by Lord Clyde, Deputy Adjutant General of Her Majesty's Forces in India.
⁷ Lt.Colonel Hallett served with the 57th Regiment in the latter part of the Zulu war of 1879, and throughout the operations of "Clarke's Column" (Medal with Clasp).
⁸ Lt.Colonel Garstin served as Adjutant of the 57th Regiment in the Zulu war of 1879, including the action of Gingindhlovu and relief of Ekowe, and the operations of "Clarke's Column" (Medal with Clasp). Served in the Soudan campaign in 1885 as Deputy Assistant Adjutant General on the Lines of Communication and Base (Medal with Clasp), and Khedive's Star).
¹³ Majors Hill, White, Graham, Bellers, and Longe, and Captains Scott-Moncrieff, and Bodé served with the 57th Regiment in the Zulu war of 1879, and were present at the action of Gingindhlovu and relief of Ekowe, and throughout the operations of " Clarke's Column" (Medal with Clasp).
¹⁴ Major Blake served in the latter part of the Zulu war of 1879, first with the 57th Regiment and afterwards as Garrison Adjutant at Fort Pearson (Medal with Clasp).
²⁴ Captain Harvest served in the Burmese Expedition in 1886-87 with the 23rd Madras Native Infantry (Medal with Clasp).
²⁵ Captain Norie served with the Chin-Lushai Expeditionary Force in 1889-90 in charge of the Intelligence Department (mentioned in despatches, Medal with Clasp).
²⁶ Captain Nelson served with the Burmese Expedition in 1886-87 (mentioned in despatches, Medal with Clasp).
²⁷ Captain Firman served with the Nile Expedition in 1884-85 on Transport duty, and was present at the action of Kirbekan (Medal with two Clasps, and Khedive's Star). Served in the Burmese Expedition in 1886-87 with the 1st Battalion Royal Welsh Fusiliers (Medal with Clasp).
²⁸ Captain Hayes served with the Hazara Expedition in 1891 as Brigade Transport Officer (Medal with Clasp).
³⁰ Lieut. Walter served with the 57th Regiment in the Zulu war of 1879, and was present at the action of Gingindhlovu and relief of Ekowe, and throughout the operations of "Clarke's Column" (Medal with Clasp).
³¹ Captain Miller served in the Egyptian war of 1882 with the 2nd Battalion Derbyshire Regiment (Medal, and Khedive's Star).

Record of the Services of the 1st Battalion of the Middlesex Regiment
(formerly the 57th Regiment).

Raised in 1755, and proceeded to the Mediterranean (as Marines), to 1757. Gibraltar, to 1763. Minorca, to 1767. Ireland, to 1775. America, to 1783. Nova Scotia, to 1790. England and Scotland, to 1793. Low Countries, to 1793. England, to June 1794. Low Countries, to 1795. England, to October 1795. West Indies, to 1803. (2nd Battalion raised in 1803.) England, to April 1804. Channel Islands, to October 1804. Gibraltar, to July 1809. Peninsula, to June 1814. Canada, to July 1815. (2nd Battalion reduced, Dec. 1815.) France, to November 1817. Ireland, to Sept. 1824. England, to 1825. New South Wales (embarked in 16 convict ships), to March 1831. India, to April 1846. England, to March 1848. Ireland, to Feb. 1853. Corfu, to Sept. 1854. Crimea, to May 1856. Malta, to May 1858. (A detachment at Aden from Sept. 1857 to March 1860.) India, to Nov. 1860. New Zealand, to April 1867. England, to Sept. 1871. Ireland, to Dec. 1873. Ceylon, to Feb. 1879. South Africa, to Oct. 1879. Home, Oct. 1879.

Record of the Services of the 2nd Battalion of the Middlesex Regiment
(formerly the 77th Regiment).

Raised in 1787, and proceeded to India, March 1788. To England, 1807. Embarked for the Peninsula, 1811. To Ireland, 1814. To Jamaica, 1824. To Ireland, 1834. To Malta, 1834. To Ceylon, 1842. To Jamaica, 1843. To Nova Scotia, 1846. To England, 1848. To Malta, 1854. To the Crimea, 1854. To England, 1856. To New South Wales, 1857. To India, 1858. To England, 1870 (being the first Regiment through he Suez Canal). Entitled "The Duke of Cambridge's Own Regiment of Foot," June 1876. To India, 1880.

Rifle Depot, Winchester.] **The King's Royal Rifle Corps.** 304

Formerly the 60th (The King's Royal Rifle Corps).

The 5th, 7th, 8th, and 9th Battalions are formed of the Huntingdon, 2nd Middlesex, Carlow, and North Cork Militia respectively.

"*Celer et Audax.*" "Louisburg" "Quebec, 1759" "Rolica" "Vimiera" "Martinique" "Talavera" "Busaco" "Fuentes d'Onor" "Albuhera" "Ciudad Rodrigo" "Badajoz" "Salamanca" "Vittoria" "Pyrenees" "Nivelle" "Nive" "Orthes" "Toulouse" "Peninsula" "Punjaub" "Mooltan" "Goojerat" "South Africa, 1851-2-3" "Delhi" "Taku Forts" "Pekin" "South Africa, 1879" "Ahmad Khel" "Kandahar, 1880" "Afghanistan, 1878-80" "Egypt, 1882, 1884" "Tel-el-Kebir."

Years' Ser.			2ND LIEUT.	LIEUT.	CAPTAIN.	BREV. MAJ.	MAJOR.
Full Pay.	Half Pay.	**Colonel in Chief.**—Field Marshal His Royal Highness The Duke of Cambridge,[1] K.G. K.T. K.P. G.C.B. G.C.S.I. G.C.M.G. G.C.I.E. 3 Mar. 69.					
		Colonel Commandant.—Robert Beaufoy Hawley,[2] C.B. *Ensign*, 28 Aug. 38; *Lieut.* 31 Dec. 39; *Captain*, 10 Jan. 51; *Bt. Major*, 2 Nov. 55; *Major*, 5 Sept. 56; *Lt. Colonel*, 18 May 62; *Colonel*, 18 May 65; *Major General*, 1 March 70; *Lt. General*, 18 Apr. 83; *Colonel Commandant* King's Royal Rifles, 26 Feb. 90.					
32	...	**Lieutenant Colonels.**—1 Henry Blackwood MacCall,[6] *Ensign*, 16 Feb. 64; *Lieut.* 29 Feb. 67; *Capt.* 1 Apr. 75; *Major*, 1 July 81; *Lt. Colonel*, 1 July 94.					
29	...	2 Hon. Keith Turnour,[7] *Ensign*, 2 Oct. 66; *Lieut.* 9 Feb. 70; *Captain*, 32 Oct. 78; *Major*, 19 Aug. 83; *Lt. Colonel*, 7 Jan. 94.					
28	...	3 Richard Steele Rupert Fetherstonhaugh,[9] *Ensign*, 25 Sept. 67; *Lieut.* 29 Oct. 71; *Captain*, 7 May 80; *Major*, 18 April 85; *Bt. Lt. Colonel*, 15 June 85; *Colonel*, 15 June 89; *Lt. Colonel*, 16 Apr. 94.					
24	...	4 Horatio Reginald Mends,[11] *Lieut.* 30 Dec. 71; *Captain*, 12 Jan. 81; *Major*, 9 Oct. 85; *Bt. Colonel*, 15 Oct. 94.					
		MAJORS.					
24	...	2 p.s.c. Montagu Charles Brudenell F. Walker[12]	......	6 Mar. 72	10 Feb. 81	......	9 Oct. 85
23	...	1 Geoffrey Grimwood Grimwood[13]	......	24 July 72	1 Oct. 81	......	4 Nov. 85
23	...	3 Henry Vere[14]	......	5 Oct. 72	22 Dec. 81	......	7 Jan. 86
23	...	4 Robert Henry Gunning[16]	......	26 Mar. 73	1 Aug. 83	......	5 June 90
21	...	Edward William Herbert,[17] *Assistant Military Secretary, Gibraltar*, 3 Jan. 95	......	2 Dec. 74	30 Aug. 83	21 May 84	15 Oct. 90
20	...	Robert George Buchanan-Riddell,[19] *Adj. 4 Middlesex Rifle Vols.* 12 May 90	......	20 Nov. 75	9 Sept. 84	......	10 June 92
21	...	4 p.s.c. Gerard Charles Kitson[18] (*Depot*)	......	11 Feb. 76	1 Jan. 85	......	27 July 92
20	...	3 Lord Frederick FitzGerald[21]	......	11 Feb. 76	16 Mar. 85	15 June 85	17 Aug. 92
20	...	1 Harold Gore-Browne[23]	......	11 Feb. 76	18 Apr. 85	......	4 Jan. 93
20	...	2 William Pitcairn Campbell[24]	......	10 Mar. 76	18 Apr. 85	......	4 Apr. 93
19	...	Arthur Davidson,[25] *Aide de Camp to H.R.H. the Duke of Cambridge*	......	10 Sept. 76	23 Apr. 85	23 Apr. 85	23 Sept. 93
19	...	p.s.c. Robert Calverley Alington Bewicke-Copley,[27] *Dep. Assist. Adjutant Gen., Ireland*, 25 Mar. 92	......	2 Feb. 77	9 Oct. 85	......	15 Jan. 94
17	...	Hubert Cornwall Legh,[29] *Adjutant Middlesex Rifle Vols.* 4 Nov. 91	......	6 Oct. 78	7 Jan. 86	......	14 Mar. 94
18	...	p.s.c. Edward James Montagu-Stuart-Wortley,[30] C.M.G. *Brigade Major, Malta*, 18 Aug. 93	13 Oct. 77	13 May 80	1 Mar. 86	2 Mar. 86	4 Apr. 94
18	...	Charles Arch. Townshend Boultbee, *Adjutant 7 Battalion* 20 Dec. 91	21 July 77	7 April 80	21 Apr. 86	......	16 Apr. 94
17	...	3 Dudley Granville Richard Ryder[31]	1 May 78	28 April 80	10 June 86	......	9 Jan. 95
		CAPTAINS.					
16	...	2 Geoffrey Geo. Gordon, Lord Tewkesbury[35] (*Depot*)	21 June 79	10 Feb. 81	21 June 88		
16	...	2 Fras. Alexander Fortescue,[36] *Staff Coll.*	2 July 79	10 Feb. 81	1 July 88		
16	...	3 Henry Edward Buchanan-Riddell[38]	13 Aug. 79	1 July 81	10 Oct. 88		
16	...	Thomas Edward Milborne-Swinnerton-Pilkington,[39] *Adj. 22 Middlesex Rifle Vols.* 3 Jan. 93	13 Aug. 79	1 July 81	19 Dec. 38		
16	...	3 Walpole Swinton Kays (*Depot*)	6 Aug. 79	1 July 81	29 Dec. 88		
16	...	p.s.c. Chas. Roderick Robert M'Grigor,[41] *D.A.A. Gen. Cork*, 22 June 91	13 Aug. 79	1 July 81	11 Mar. 89	12 Mar. 89	
15	...	Henry Anstruther Kinloch, *Adjutant 5 Battalion* 2 Mar. 91	8 May 80	1 July 81	11 Sept. 89		
15	...	Francis Montagu Beaumont,[43] *Aide de Camp to Sir R. Biddulph* 10 Oct. 93	14 Aug. 80	1 July 81	17 Jan. 90		
15	...	Evelyn William Thistlethwayto,[44] *Adj. 3 London Rifle Vols.* 14 March 94	14 Aug. 80	1 July 81	27 Jan. 90		
15	...	3 Robert Scarlett Bowen	21 Aug. 80	1 July 81	26 Mar. 90		
15	...	2 Hiley Reginald Addington[45]	21 Aug. 80	1 July 81	16 Apr. 90		
15	...	3 Arthur John Bonfoy St. Leger	23 Oct. 80	1 July 81	25 Apr. 90		
15	...	Wm. Horace Kennedy,[47] *Adj. 2 Vol. Bn. Bedford Regt.* 29 Nov. 90	19 Feb. 81	1 July 81	30 Apr. 90	1 May 90	
14	...	1 Horace Newton[48] (*Depot*)		22 Oct. 81	15 May 90		
13	14/12	James Evan Baillie Martin, *Dist. Insp. of Musketry, Portsmouth*	23 April 81	1 July 81	11 June 90		
13	...	2 Charles John Markham[49]		27 Sept. 82	25 June 90		
13	...	4 Gerald Neill Prendergast[50]		10 May 82	16 July 90		
13	...	1 Oliver Stewart Wood Nugent[51]		29 July 82	15 Oct. 90		
13	...	4 Frederick Brydges Major Henniker[52]		27 Jan. 83	20 Nov. 90		
13	...	1 William Henry Salmon[53]		9 Sept. 82	6 May 91		
13	...	Arthur Blewitt,[54] *Adjutant 5 Volunteer Bn. Scottish Rifles* 4 Aug. 93		27 Jan. 83	6 May 91		
12	...	3 Edward John Dewar		5 Dec. 83	1 July 91		
12	...	3 Charles Francis Sewell[55]		19 Dec. 83	21 Oct. 91		
12	...	4 Harry Francis Pakenham[56]		6 Feb. 84	10 Nov. 91		
12	...	George Coryton Lister, *A.D.C. to Lt. Governor of Bengal* 23 Aug. 91		6 Feb. 84	20 Dec. 91		
12	...	4 Cyril John Ryder		6 Feb. 84	20 Dec. 91		
12	...	Hon. Cecil Trevelyan Holland,[57] *serving with Lagos Constabulary*		10 Jan. 84	18 May 92		

U 2

The King's Royal Rifle Corps.

Years' Ser. Full Pay	Half Pay	CAPTAINS.	2ND LIEUT.	LIEUT.	CAPTAIN.
11	...	4 Craufurd Alexander Gordon Clark[58]	......	23 Aug. 84	4 Jan. 93
11	...	Sir Hunt Henry Allen Walsh,[59] *Bart. Adjutant 8 Battalion King's Royal Rifles* 1 Nov. 93	......	23 Aug. 84	15 Feb. 93
11	...	2 *p.s.c.* Thomas Lethbridge Napier Morland	......	23 Aug. 84	5 Apr. 93
11	...	4 Reginald Stewart Oxley[60]	......	23 Aug. 84	4 Aug. 93
11	...	3 Henry Charles Howard	......	12 Nov. 84	9 Sept. 93
10	...	James Kiero Watson,[61] *serving with the Egyptian Army*	......	25 April 85	23 Sept. 93
10	...	4 *Hon.* St. Leger Henry Jervis	......	6 May 85	10 Oct. 93
11	...	3 James Patrick Eden Gilmour	......	7 Feb. 85	1 Nov. 93
10	...	1 Charles Slingsby Chaplin	......	6 May 85	15 Jan. 94
10	...	Norman Nevill Bedingfeld,[62] *Adjutant 1 Middlesex Vol. Rifles* 1 Dec. 94	......	9 May 85	28 Feb. 94
10	...	4 Frank Douglas-Pennant, *Aide de Camp to the Lord Lieutenant of Ireland* 3 Oct. 92	......	24 June 85	14 Mar. 94
10	...	Cromer Ashburnham, *on special service, Uganda*	......	30 Jan. 86	14 Mar. 94
9	...	1 Stouart Welwood Hare[63]	......	5 May 86	4 Apr. 94
9	...	2 John Curteis	......	12 May 86	20 June 94
9	...	1 St. John Douglas Townshend Loftus	......	25 Aug. 86	10 Aug. 94
9	...	2 *Hon.* John Roderick Brownlow	......	4 Dec. 86	3 Jan. 95
8	...	Herbert William Christian	30 July 87	7 Jan. 90	9 Jan. 95

LIEUTENANTS.

8	...	1 Henry Charles Warre[64]	5 Oct. 87	12 Apr. 90	
8	...	1 Alan Richard Montagu Stuart-Wortley	5 Nov. 87	16 Apr. 90	
8	...	3 George Algernon James Soltau-Symons	19 Nov. 87	25 Apr. 90	
8	...	1 Edward Northey[65] (*Depot*)	7 Mar. 88	7 May 90	
8	...	3 Hugh Blomfield Nicholson	11 Feb. 88	12 May 90	
8	...	1 Mark Horace Kerr Pechell[66]	11 Feb. 88	12 May 90	
7	...	2 James Hawley Gilbert Feilden, **Adjutant** 1 Mar. 92	1 Aug. 88	15 May 90	
7	...	4 *H.H. Prince* Christian Victor Albert Ludwig Ernst Anton *of Schleswig-Holstein,*[67] *GCB.*	22 Aug. 88	25 June 90	
7	...	3 Leopold Christian Duncan Jenner, **Adjutant** 15 July 91	21 Nov. 88	20 Nov. 90	
7	...	2 Charles Gosling (*Depot*)	22 Aug. 88	25 Feb. 91	
7	...	4 Ronald James Vernon,[59] *Aide de Camp to Lt. General W. H. Goodenough* 1 Jan. 95	16 Jan. 89	25 Feb. 91	
7	...	4 Charles Legge Eustace Eustace[71]	30 Jan. 89	6 May 91	
6	...	2 John Augustus Hope	22 May 89	1 July 91	
6	...	3 Eric Pearce-Serocold (*Depot*)	9 Oct. 89	15 July 91	
6	...	3 Henry Arthur Whitby Briscoe	16 Oct. 89	23 Aug. 91	
6	...	3 John Edward Rhodes	30 Oct. 89	21 Oct. 91	
6	...	4 Charles John Sackville-West,[72] **Adjutant** 1 May 94	18 Dec. 89	4 Nov. 91	
5	...	3 Cecil William Wilson	23 Apr. 90	18 May 92	
5	...	1 Richard Byron[73]	7 May 90	23 Nov. 92	
5	...	4 Alexander John Lainson	28 June 90	4 Jan. 93	
5	...	3 Lewis Francis Philips	9 July 90	15 Feb. 93	
5	...	1 Herbert Richard Blore	29 Oct. 90	22 Feb. 93	
5	...	2 Leonard Paul Irby	29 Oct. 90	5 Apr. 93	
5	...	1 Hugh Henry Foxcroft Farmar[75]	29 Oct. 90	4 Aug. 93	
5	...	2 Charles Augustus Kerr Pechell	29 Nov. 90	9 Aug. 93	
5	...	2 Geoffrey Charles Shakerley	29 Nov. 90	9 Sept. 93	
5	...	1 Louis Bertie Cumberland[48]	17 Dec. 90	23 Sept. 93	
5	...	1 Guy Stewart St. Aubyn[48]	17 Jan. 91	23 Sept. 93	
5	...	4 William Henry Loraine Allgood[77]	17 Jan. 91	10 Oct. 93	
5	...	1 William Barnett[48]	4 Feb. 91	1 Nov. 93	
5	...	4 Richard Henry Beaumont	4 Feb. 91	14 Mar. 94	
5	...	3 *Lord* Robert William Orlando Manners[48]	4 Feb. 91	14 Mar. 94	
5	...	4 Wilfred James Long[79] (*Depot*)	4 Mar. 91	4 Apr. 94	
5	...	1 Victor Henry Sylvester Scratchley[48]	25 Mar. 91	1 May 94	
4	...	4 Gwyn Venables Hordern	10 June 91	20 June 94	
4	...	1 *Hon.* Frederick Hugh Sherston Roberts,[48] *Aide de Camp to Sir W. G. A. Lockhart*	10 June 91	22 June 94	
4	...	1 Cecil Champagné Herbert-Stepney[48]	25 July 91	10 Aug. 94	
4	...	2 Ulric Oliver Thynne	7 Nov. 91	3 Jan. 95	
4	...	2 Henry Clifford Rodes Green	18 Nov. 91	9 Jan. 95	

SECOND LIEUTENANTS.

4	...	4 *Hon.* Reginald Cathcart	25 Nov. 91		
4	...	4 William Francis George Wyndham	2 Dec. 91		
4	...	2 Mansel Loudon Porter	3 Feb. 92		
3	...	2 Edward Francis Ward	25 May 92		
3	...	1 Eardley Wilmot Brooke	9 Nov. 92		
3	...	1 Frederick Maurice Crum	8 Feb. 93		
2	...	1 Frederick William Beresford Cripps	12 Apr. 93		
2	...	2 Christopher Egerton Balfour	24 May 93		
2	...	2 Richard Chester Master	9 Aug. 93		
2	...	2 Stanley Fielder Mott	27 Sept. 93		
2	...	1 Rudolf George Jelf	4 Oct. 93		
2	...	3 Alexander Richard Mildmay	18 Oct. 93		
2	...	3 George Arthur Paget Rennie	18 Oct. 93		
2	...	3 Bertram Fitzherbert Widdrington	24 Jan. 94		
1	...	4 Dermot Howard Blundell-Hollinshead-Blundell	18 Apr. 94		
1	...	3 Charles Bernard Petre	18 Apr. 94		
1	...	4 George Ayscough Armytage	2 June 94		
1	...	2 George Frederick Barnard Hankey	10 Oct. 94		
1	...	3 Wynne Parr Lyles	10 Oct. 94		
1	...	2 Albert Ingraham Paine	10 Oct. 94		
1	...	2 John Spottiswoode	10 Oct. 94		
1	...	2 Charles Edward de Vere Beauclerk	10 Oct. 94		
1	...	1 Richard Johnstone	6 Feb. 95		
1	...	Hubert Francis Fitzwilliam Brabazon Foljambe	6 Mar. 95		
1	...	John Taylor	13 Mar. 95		

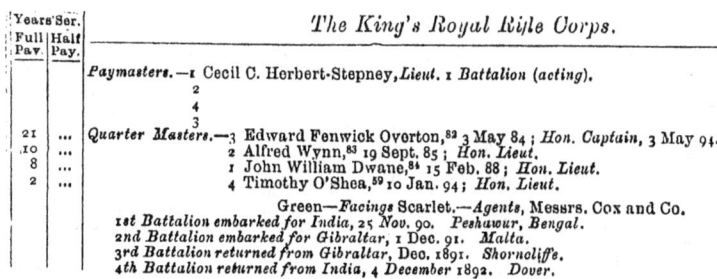

Years Ser.		
Full Pay	Half Pay	
		Paymasters.—1 Cecil C. Herbert-Stepney, *Lieut.* 1 Battalion *(acting)*.
	2	
	4	
	3	
21	...	Quarter Masters.—3 Edward Fenwick Overton,[82] 3 May 84; *Hon. Captain*, 3 May 94.
10	...	2 Alfred Wynn,[83] 19 Sept. 85; *Hon. Lieut.*
8	...	1 John William Dwane,[84] 15 Feb. 88; *Hon. Lieut.*
2	...	4 Timothy O'Shea,[59] 10 Jan. 94; *Hon. Lieut.*

Green—*Facings* Scarlet.—*Agents,* Messrs. Cox and Co.
1st Battalion embarked for India, 25 Nov. 90. *Peshawur, Bengal.*
2nd Battalion embarked for Gibraltar, 1 Dec. 91. *Malta.*
3rd Battalion returned from Gibraltar, Dec. 1891. *Shorncliffe.*
4th Battalion returned from India, 4 December 1892. *Dover.*

---

[1] The Duke of Cambridge commanded the 1st Division of the Eastern Army throughout the campaign of 1854, including the battles of the Alma, Balaklava, and Inkerman (horse shot), and siege of Sebastopol (mentioned in despatches, received the thanks of the House of Commons, Medal with four Clasps, and Turkish Medal).

[2] Lt.General Hawley served with the 89th Regiment in the Crimea from the 31st Dec. 1854, including the siege and fall of Sebastopol and attacks of the 18th June and 8th September. Served as D.A.Q.M. General at Balaklava during 1856 (Medal with Clasp, Brevet of Major, Sardinian and Turkish Medals, and 5th Class of the Medjidie).

[6] Lt.Colonel McCall served with the Isazai Expedition in 1892.

[7] Lt.Colonel the Hon. Keith Turnour served in the Red River Expedition of 1870. Also with the 3rd Battalion 60th Rifles in the Zulu war of 1879, and was present at the action of Gingindhlovu and relief of Ekowe (Medal with Clasp). Served as Garrison Adjutant at Pietermaritzburg during the Boer war in 1881. Served with the Hazara Expedition in 1891 with the 1st Battalion King's Royal Rifles (Medal with Clasp); also with the Miranzai Expedition in 1891 with the 1st Battalion King's Royal Rifles, from the 18th April in command of the Battalion, and was present in the engagements at Sangar and Mastan (mentioned in despatches, Clasp).

[9] Colonel Fetherstonhaugh served with the 3rd Battalion 60th Rifles in the Zulu war from April to September 1879 (Medal with Clasp). Served with the Nile Expedition in 1884-85 with the Mounted Infantry of the Desert Column, and was present at the actions at Abu Klea and El Gubat, and in the reconnaissance to Metammeh (mentioned in despatches, Brevet of Lt.Colonel, Medal with two Clasps, and Khedive's Star).

[11] Lt.Colonel Mends served in the Boer war of 1881.

[12] Major Walker served with the Bechuanaland Expedition in 1884-85 as Aide de Camp and Acting Assistant Military Secretary to Sir Charles Warren (mentioned in despatches). Served with the Burmese Expedition in 1891-92, including the operations in the Chin Hills as Intelligence Officer, and with the Lushai Column (Medal with Clasp).

[13] Major Grimwood served with the Manipore Expedition in 1891 (Medal with Clasp); and with the Isazai Expedition in 1892.

[14] Major Vere served with the Isazai Expedition in 1892.

[16] Major Gunning served with the 3rd Battalion 60th Rifles in the Zulu war of 1879, and was present at the action of Gingindhlovu and relief of Ekowe; afterwards served as Adjutant of the Battalion throughout the operations of "Clarke's Column" (Medal with Clasp). Served in the Burmese Expedition in 1891-92, and commanded the Baungshè Column during the operations in the Chin Hills (Medal with Clasp).

[17] Major Herbert served in the latter part of the Zulu war of 1879 with the 3rd Battalion 60th Rifles (Medal with Clasp). Served in the Soudan Expedition in 1884 with the 3rd Battalion King's Royal Rifle Corps, and was present in the engagements at El Teb and Temai (Brevet of Major, Medal with Clasp, and Khedive's Star).

[18] Major Kitson served with the Manipore Expedition in 1891 as Deputy Assistant Adjutant General (mentioned in despatches, Medal with Clasp).

[19] Major R. G. Buchanan Riddell served in the Boer war of 1881.

[21] Lord Frederick FitzGerald served as Adjutant with the 2nd Battalion 60th Rifles in the Afghan war from October 1878 to November 1880, took part in the advance on and occupation of Candahar and Khelat-i-Ghilzie, and was present in the engagements at Ahmed Kheyl and Urzoo near Ghuznee; accompanied Sir Frederick Roberts in the march to Candahar, and was present at the battle of Candahar (Medal with two Clasps, and Bronze Decoration). Served in the Marri Expedition under Brigadier General MacGregor. Served in the Boer war of 1881. Served with the 3rd Battalion King's Royal Rifle Corps in the Egyptian war of 1882, and was present in the action at Kassasin (9th September), and at the battle of Tel-el-Kebir (Medal with Clasp, and Khedive's Star). Also served with the Nile Expedition in 1884-85 as Aide de Camp to Sir Redvers Buller, Chief of the Staff (mentioned in despatches, Brevet of Major, Clasp).

[23] Major Gore-Browne served in the Miranzai Expedition in 1891 with the 1st Battalion King's Royal Rifles (Medal with Clasp); and with the Isazai Expedition in 1892.

[24] Major W. P. Campbell served in the Nile Expedition in 1884-85 with the Mounted Infantry, and was present in the engagements at Abu Klea and El Gubat (Medal with two Clasps, and Khedive's Star).

[25] Major Davidson served with the 2nd Battalion 60th Rifles in the Afghan war from October 1878 to November 1880, took part in the advance on and occupation of Candahar and Khelat-i-Ghilzie, and was present in the engagements at Ahmed Kheyl and Urzoo near Ghuznee (mentioned in despatches); served as Aide de Camp to Sir Donald Stewart at Cabul, and accompanied Sir Frederick Roberts in the march to Candahar as Aide de Camp to Major General Ross, and was present at the battle of Candahar (mentioned in despatches, Brevet of Major, Medal with two Clasps, and Bronze Decoration). Served in the Marri Expedition under Brigadier General MacGregor. Served in the Boer war of 1881 with the Natal Field Force on signalling duty. Served in the Egyptian war of 1882, and was present at the battle of Tel-el-Kebir (Medal with Clasp, 5th Class of the Medjidie, and Khedive's Star). Served with the Bechuanaland Expedition under Sir Charles Warren in 1884-85 on special service and as Acting Inspector of Army Signalling (mentioned in despatches).

[27] Major Bewicke-Copley served in the Nile Expedition in 1884-85 (Medal with Clasp, and Khedive's Star).

[29] Major Legh served with the 2nd Battalion 60th Rifles in the Afghan war from October 1878 to November 1880, took part in the advance on and occupation of Candahar and Khelat-i-Ghilzie, and was present in the engagements at Ahmed Kheyl and Urzoo near Ghuznee; accompanied Sir Frederick Roberts in the march to Candahar, and was present at the battle of Candahar (Medal with two Clasps, and Bronze Decoration). Served in the Marri Expedition under Brigadier General MacGregor. Also served in the Boer war of 1881 with the Natal Field Force.

[30] Major Montagu Stuart Wortley served in Afghanistan from October 1879 to August 1880 with the Koorum Force as Transport Officer and Assistant Superintendent of Army Signalling (Medal). Served in the Boer war of 1881 with the Natal Field Force. Served in the Egyptian war of 1882 as Orderly Officer to Sir W. O. Lanyon and to Sir Baker Russell, and was present at the battle of Tel-el-Kebir (Medal with Clasp, and Khedive's Star). Served with the Nile Expedition in 1884-85, and was present at the action of Abu Klea and in the reconnaissance to Metammeh (mentioned in despatches, two Clasps, 4th Class of the Medjidie, and *CMG.* in recognition of his services in Egypt); also served in the operations of the Egyptian Frontier Field Force in 1885-86 as Deputy Assistant Adjutant and Quarter Master General (Brevet of Major).

[31] Major Ryder served with the 3rd Battalion 60th Rifles in the latter part of the Zulu war of 1879 (Medal). Also served with the 3rd Battalion in the Boer war in 1881, and was present in the engagements at Lang's Nek and the Ingogo River. Served with the 3rd Battalion King's Royal Rifle Corps in the Egyptian war of 1882, and was present in the engagement at Tel-el-Mahuta, in the action at Kassasin (9th September), and at the battle of Tel-el-Kebir (Medal with Clasp, and Khedive's Star); also served in the Soudan Expedition in 1884 with the 3rd Battalion King's Royal Rifle Corps, and was present in the engagement at Temai (two Clasps).

[35] Lord Tewkesbury served with the 2nd Battalion 60th Rifles in the Afghan war from December 1879 to October

1880, and was present in the engagements at Ahmed Kheyl and Urzoo near Ghuznee; accompanied Sir Frederick Roberts in the march to Candahar, and was present at the battle of Candahar (Medal with two Clasps, and Bronze Decoration). Served with the 3rd Battalion in the Boer war in 1881.

³⁶ Captain Fortescue served with the 2nd Battalion 60th Rifles in the Afghan war from April to October 1880, and was present in the engagements at Ahmed Kheyl and Urzoo near Ghuznee; accompanied Sir Frederick Roberts in the march to Candahar, and was present at the battle of Candahar (Medal with two Clasps, and Bronze Decoration). Served in the Boer war in 1881 with the Natal Field Force.

³⁸ Captain H. E. Buchanan-Riddell served with the 3rd Battalion 60th Rifles in the Boer war in 1881. Served with the 3rd Battalion King's Royal Rifle Corps in the Egyptian war of 1882, and was present in the reconnaissance in force from Alexandria on 5th August, in the engagement at Tel-el-Mahuta, in the action at Kassasin (9th September), and at the battle of Tel-el-Kebir (Medal with Clasp, and Khedive's Star); also served in the Soudan Expedition in 1884 with the 3rd Battalion King's Royal Rifle Corps, and was present in the engagements at El Teb and Temai (two Clasps). Served in the Soudan campaign in 1885 (Clasp).

³⁹ Captain Pilkington served in the Boer war in 1881 as Transport Officer. Served in the Egyptian war of 1882 as Acting Aide de Camp to Sir Archibald Alison, and was present at the battle of Tel-el-Kebir (Medal with Clasp, and Khedive's Star).

⁴¹ Major M'Grigor served in the Boer war in 1881 as Adjutant of the 3rd Battalion 60th Rifles, and was present in the engagements at Lang's Nek and the Ingogo River. Served in the Egyptian war of 1882 as Adjutant 3rd Battalion King's Royal Rifle Corps, and was present in the reconnaissance in force from Alexandria on 5th August, in the engagement at Tel-el-Mahuta, the action at Kassasin (9th September), and as Orderly Officer to Brigadier Ashburnham at the battle of Tel-el-Kebir (Medal with Clasp, and Khedive's Star); also served throughout the Soudan Expedition in 1884 as Adjutant to the 3rd Battalion King's Royal Rifle Corps, and was present in the engagements at El Teb and Temai (5th Class of the Medjidie, two Clasps). Served with the expedition to the Soudan in 1885 as Aide de Camp to Major General Ewart, Commanding Lines of Communication (Brevet of Major, Clasp).

⁴³ Captain Beaumont served with the 3rd Battalion 60th Rifles in the Boer war in 1881, and was present in the engagements at Lang's Nek and the Ingogo River. Served with the 3rd Battalion King's Royal Rifle Corps in the Egyptian war of 1882, and was present in the reconnaissance in force from Alexandria on 5th August, in the engagement at Tel-el-Mahuta, in the action at Kassasin (9th September), and at the battle of Tel-el-Kebir (Medal with Clasp, and Khedive's Star); also served in the Soudan Expedition in 1884 in charge of Signallers, and was present in the engagements at El Teb and Temai (mentioned in despatches, two Clasps). Served with the Nile Expedition in 1884-85 on signalling duties, and was present at the action of Kirbekan (two Clasps).

⁴⁴ Captain Thistlethwayte served in the Boer war of 1881 (wounded).

⁴⁵ Captain Addington served in the Hazara Expedition in 1891 with the 1st Battalion King's Royal Rifles (Medal with Clasp); also served in the Miranzai Expedition in 1891 with the same Battalion including the engagements at Sangar and Mastan (Clasp).

⁴⁷ Captain Kennedy served in the Egyptian war of 1882 as Transport Officer to the 3rd Battalion King's Royal Rifle Corps, and was present in the engagement at Tel-el-Mahuta, in the action at Kassasin (9th September), and at the battle of Tel-el-Kebir (Medal with Clasp, and Khedive's Star).

⁴⁸ Captain Newton, Lieuts. Cumberland, St. Aubyn, Barnett, Lord Robert Manners, Scratchley, the Hon. F. H. S. Roberts, and Herbert-Stepney served with the Isazai Expedition in 1892.

⁴⁹ Captain Markham served with the Manipore Expedition in 1891 (Medal with Clasp); also during the operations in the Chin Hills in 1891-92.

⁵⁰ Captain Prendergast served in the Soudan Expedition in 1884 with the 3rd Battalion King's Royal Rifle Corps, and was present in the engagement at Temai (Medal with Clasp, and Khedive's Star).

⁵¹ Captain Nugent served in the Hazara Expedition in 1891 with the 1st Battalion King's Royal Rifles (Medal with Clasp); also in the Miranzai Expedition in 1891 as Extra Orderly Officer to Sir William Lockhart, Commanding the Force (mentioned in despatches, Clasp); and with the Isazai Expedition in 1892.

⁵² Captain Henriker served in the Hazara Expedition in 1891 with the 1st Battalion King's Royal Rifles (Medal with Clasp); also in the Miranzai Expedition in 1891 with the same Battalion including the engagement at Sangar (Clasp).

⁵³ Captain Salmon served in the Soudan Expedition in 1884 with the 3rd Battalion King's Royal Rifle Corps, and was present in the engagements at El Teb and Temai (Medal with Clasp, and Khedive's Star).

⁵⁴ Captain Blewitt served with the Manipore Expedition in 1891 (Medal with Clasp).

⁵⁵ Captain Sewell served in the Soudan Expedition in 1884 with the 3rd Battalion King's Royal Rifle Corps, and was present in the engagement at Temai (Medal with clasp, and Khedive's Star).

⁵⁶ Captain Pakenham served in the Hazara Expedition in 1891 with the 1st Battalion King's Royal Rifles (Medal with Clasp); also in the Miranzai Expedition in 1891 with the same Battalion including the engagements at Sangar and Mastan (Clasp).

⁵⁷ Captain Hon. C. T. Holland served in the expedition to the Soudan in 1885 with the 1st Battalion of the Coldstream Guards, and was present in the engagement at Hasheen, at that near Tofrek on the 24th March, and at the destruction of Temai (Medal with Clasp, and Khedive's Star).

⁵⁸ Captain Clark served with the Manipore Expedition in 1891 (Medal with Clasp).

⁵⁹ Sir H. H. A. Walsh, Lieuts. Vernon, and O'Shea served with the Manipore Expedition in 1891 (Medal with Clasp).

⁶⁰ Captain Oxley served with the Manipore Expedition in 1891 (Medal with Clasp).

⁶¹ Captain Watson served in the operations in the Chin Hills, Burmah, in 1891-92.

⁶² Captain Bedingfeld served with the Hazara Expedition in 1891 as Adjutant 1st Battalion King's Royal Rifles (Medal with Clasp); in the Miranzai Expedition in 1891 with the same Battalion including the engagements at Sangar and Mastan (Clasp); and with the Isazai Expedition in 1892.

⁶³ Captain Hare served in the Hazara Expedition in 1891 with the 1st Battalion King's Royal Rifles (Medal with Clasp); in the Miranzai Expedition in 1891 with the same Battalion including the engagements at Sangar and Mastan (Clasp); and with the Isazai Expedition in 1892.

⁶⁴ Lieut. Warre served in the Hazara Expedition in 1891 with the 1st Battalion King's Royal Rifles (Medal with Clasp); also in the Miranzai Expedition in 1891 with the same Battalion including the engagement at Sangar (Clasp).

⁶⁵ Lieut. Northey served in the Hazara Expedition in 1891 with the 1st Battalion King's Royal Rifles (Medal with Clasp) also in the Miranzai Expedition in 1891 with the same Battalion including the engagements at Sangar and Mastan (Clasp).

⁶⁶ Lieut. Pechell served in the Hazara Expedition in 1891 with the 1st Battalion King's Royal Rifles (Medal with Clasp); also in the Miranzai Expedition in 1891 with the same Battalion including the engagements at Sangar and Mastan (Clasp); and with the Isazai Expedition in 1892.

⁶⁷ His Highness Prince Christian of Schleswig Holstein served with the Hazara Expedition in 1891 as Orderly Officer to Major General Elles, Commanding the Force (mentioned in despatches, Medal with Clasp); in the Miranzai Expedition in 1891 with the 1st Battalion King's Royal Rifles including the engagements at Sangar and Mastan (Clasp); and in the Isazai Expedition in 1892 with the 1st Battalion King's Royal Rifles.

⁷¹ Lieut. Eustace served with the Manipore Expedition in 1891 (Medal with Clasp), and during the operations in the Chin Hills with the Lushai Column in 1891-92 (Clasp).

⁷² Lieut. Sackville West served with the Manipore Expedition in 1891 as Orderly Officer to Brigadier General Graham (mentioned in despatches, Medal with Clasp); and during the operations in the Chin Hills in 1891-92 (Clasp).

⁷³ Lieut. Byron served in the Hazara Expedition in 1891 with the 1st Battalion King's Royal Rifles (Medal with Clasp); in the Miranzai Expedition in 1891 with the same Battalion including the engagements at Sangar and Mastan (Clasp); and with the Isazai Expedition in 1892.

⁷⁴ Lieut. Farmar served in the Miranzai Expedition in 1891 with the 1st Battalion King's Royal Rifles, and was present in the engagement at Sangar (Medal with Clasp); and with the Isazai Expedition in 1892.

⁷⁷ Lieut. Allgood served in the operations in the Chin Hills in 1891-92.

⁷⁸ Lieut. Long served with the Burmese Expedition in 1891-92, including the operations in the Chin Hills with the Lushai Column (Medal with Clasp).

[82] Captain Overton served with the 3rd Battalion of the 60th Rifles in the Zulu war of 1879, and was present in the engagement at Gingindhlovu and at the relief of Ekowe (Medal with Clasp). Served in the Boer war of 1881 with the 60th Rifles. Served throughout the Egyptian war of 1882, and was present at the reconnaissance in force from Alexandria on the 5th August, in the engagement at Tel-el-Mahuta, at the action at Kassasin (9th September), and at the battle of Tel-el-Kebir (Medal with Clasp, and Khedivo's Star); also served in the Soudan Expedition in 1884 with the 3rd Battalion King's Royal Rifle Corps, and was present in the engagements at El Teb and Temai (two Clasps).

[83] Lieut. Wynn served in the Afghan war of 1878-80 with the 2nd Battalion of the 60th Rifles, and was present at the occupation of Candahar, and in the engagements at Ahmed Kheyl and Urzoo near Ghuznee; accompanied Sir Frederick Roberts in the march to Candahar, and was present at the battle of Candahar (Medal with two Clasps, and Bronze Decoration). Also served with the Marri Expedition in 1881 under Brigadier General MacGregor. Served in the Boer war of 1881 with the Natal Field Force.

[84] Lieut. Dwane served in the Hazara Expedition in 1891 with the 1st Battalion King's Royal Rifles (Medal with Clasp); also in the Miranzai Expedition in 1891 with the same Battalion including the engagement at Sangar (Clasp); and with the Isazai Expedition in 1892.

The King's Royal Rifle Corps.

Raised in 1755 as a Regiment of four Battalions, and entitled "The 62nd Royal American Regiment." Re-numbered "The 60th," 1756. 4th Battalion disbanded 1763, and 3rd Battalion, 1764. Both again raised 1775 and disbanded 1783. Raised a third time 1787 (the 3rd Battalion being the present 2nd). 5th (Rifle) Battalion raised 1797 and Rifle Companies added to other Battalions. 6th Battalion raised 1799, and 7th and 8th Battalions, 1813. 8th Battalion disbanded 1816; 7th, 1817; 6th, 1818; the 5th (Rifle) Battalion the same year, the men being drafted into the 2nd Battalion, which became "The Rifle Battalion," the 3rd Battalion being styled "Light Infantry." 1st, 4th, and 8th Battalions disbanded 1819, the 2nd becoming the 1st (Rifle Battalion) and the 3rd the 2nd (Light Infantry). Title changed to "The Duke of York's Own Rifle Corps and Light Infantry," 1824, and later in the same year "The Duke of York's Own Rifle Corps." Title again changed to "The King's Royal Rifle Corps," 1830. 3rd and 4th Battalions raised the fourth time in 1855 and 1857 respectively. The number (60th) omitted from the title, 1881.

Services of the Regiment.

Capture of Louisburg and Port du Quesne, 1758. Capture of Fort Niagara and siege and capture of Quebec, 1759 (granted the motto "Celer et Audax"). Capture of Montreal, 1760, and of Martinique and Savannah, 1762. American War of Independence, capture of Tobago, 1793, and of Martinique, St. Lucia and Guadaloupe, 1794. Surinam and battle of Bergen, 1799. Capture of the Danish West India Islands, 1807; of Martinique and Islands of Les Saintes, 1809, and of Guadaloupe, 1810. Peninsular War of 1808-14, including the battles of Roleia, Vimier and Corunna, passage of the Douro, battles of Talavera, Busaco, Fuentes d'Onor, Albuhera, Arroyo dos Molinos, siege and assault of Ciudad Rodrigo, capture of Badajoz, battle of Salamanca, siege and assault of Castle of Burgos, battles of Vittoria, Nivelle, Nive, Orthes, Toulouse and Bayonne. Punjab campaign in 1848-49, including the siege of Mooltan and battle of Goojerat. Kaffir War in 1851-53. Indian Mutiny campaign in 1857-58, including the siege, assault and capture of Delhi. China War in 1860 (Taku Forts and Pekin). Red River Expedition, 1870. Afghan war of 1878-80 (battle of Ahmed Khel, march to Candahar under Sir Frederick Roberts and battle of Candahar). Zulu war in 1879 (battle of Gingindhlovu). Boer war in 1881. Egyptian war of 1882, including the battle of Tel-el-Kebir. Soudan campaign in 1884 (El Teb and Tamai). Hazara, Miranzai and Burmese Expeditions, 1890-91.

The Duke of Edinburgh's (Wiltshire Regiment).

1st Batt., **Aldershot**.
2nd Batt., **Mandalay, Burmah.**] *Formerly the 62nd (Wiltshire) and the* [**Regimental District No. 62.—Devizes.**
99th *Duke of Edinburgh's (Lanarkshire) Regiments.*

(The 3rd Battalion is formed of the Wiltshire Militia.)

The Duke of Edinburgh's Coronet and Cypher. "NIVE" "PENINSULA" "FEROZESHAH" "SOBRAON" "SEVASTOPOL" "PEKIN" "NEW ZEALAND" "SOUTH AFRICA, 1879."

Years' Ser. Full Pay	Half Pay		ENSIGN OR 2ND LIEUT.	LIEUT.	CAPTAIN.	BREV. MAJ.	MAJOR.
		Colonel.—Sir Henry James Warre,[1] KCB, *Ensign*, 3 Feb. 37; *Lt.* 1 June 41; *Capt.* P 8 Jan. 47; *Major*, 7 Nov. 54; *Lt. Colonel*, 9 March 55; *Colonel*, 9 March 58; *Major General*, 6 March 68; *Lieut. General*, 1 Oct. 77; *General*, 26 Dec. 80; *Colonel* 99th Foot, 8 Oct. 80.					
28	...	**Lieutenant Colonels.**—1 Robert Hayne, *Ensign*, P 25 Sept. 67; *Lieut.* 26 Feb. 70; *Capt.* 11 May 78; *Major*, 10 June 82; *Lt. Colonel*, 7 Jan. 94.					
28	...	2 William Bowles Williams, *Ensign*, P 30 Oct. 67; *Lieut.* 3 April 70; *Capt.* 13 July 78; *Major*, 28 Oct. 85; *Lt. Colonel*, 19 March 94.					
		MAJORS.					
25	...	2 Henry Charles Harford[7]	P 5 Nov. 70	28 Oct. 71	30 Mar. 81	......	7 Jan. 86
28	...	1 Harry Molyneux Carter[8]	8 Jan. 68	28 Oct. 71	7 Aug. 78	......	17 Jan. 86
23	...	John Frederic Inglis, *Dist. Insp. of Musketry, Edinburgh*, 26 Oct. 93	......	12 Feb. 73	19 May 80	......	19 Mar. 90
23	28/12	*p.s.c.* Chas. Edw. de la Poer Beresford, *D.A.A. Gen. for Inst. Devonport* 1 July 92	7 July 69	28 Oct. 71	10 Jan. 83	......	4 June 90
22	...	*p.s.c.* Finlay Cochrane Beatson, *Professor at the Staff College, with rank of Lt. Colonel*, 13 Sept. 92	......	12 Nov. 73	11 Mar. 81	......	11 Oct. 93
21	...	2 Claud Henry Alexander[15]	......	21 Sept. 74	1 July 81	......	7 Jan. 94
21	...	2 Edward Cleary Hill[14]	......	2 Dec. 74	1 July 81	......	19 Mar. 94
21	...	Harry Wetherell Rowden,[16] *Adjutant 3 Battalion* 1 Sept. 90	......	2 Dec. 74	25 Oct. 81	......	8 Aug. 94
		CAPTAINS.					
18	...	Francis Richard Macmullen,[18] *Adjutant 2 Volunteer Battalion East Yorkshire Regiment* 15 Jan. 95	15 Aug. 77	13 July 78	26 April 85		
18	...	*p.s.c.* Walter Dally Jones,[19] *D.A.A. General, Gibraltar*, 11 May 91	30 Jan. 78	7 Aug. 73	26 April 85		
18	...	1 Alexander Vaughan Payne[20] (*Depot*)	30 Jan. 78	1 Feb. 79	7 Jan. 86		
18	...	Bertram Everard Winter, *Army Pay Dept.*	30 Jan. 78	28 Mar. 79	17 Jan. 86		
16	...	2 Herbert Alfred Stock	13 Aug. 79	24 June 80	22 Feb. 88		
15	...	2 Francis Slater Picot	23 Oct. 80	30 Mar. 81	1 July 88		
13	...	2 Carleton Hooper Morrison Kirkwood (*Depot*)	......	14 June 82	18 Jan. 88		
15	...	2 Hy. MacDougall Robertson Menzies	22 Jan. 81	1 July 81	7 Jan. 90		
15	...	2 Richard William Crundell Brook	22 Jan. 81	1 July 81	5 Mar. 90		
14	...	Ernest Campbell Eicko, *Army Pay Dept.*	23 April 81	1 July 81	4 June 90		
14	...	2 Ernest Herbert John Reay, *Staff Officer, Wellington Depot*, 31 July 94	......	22 Oct. 81	4 June 90		
14	...	*p.s.c.* Neville Douglas Macdonald	......	22 Oct. 81	11 June 90		
14	...	1 Louis Herbert Warden	......	22 Oct. 81	1 May 91		
14	...	2 Robert Hastings Price Snow	......	22 Oct. 81	1 May 91		
13	...	1 Walter Leslie Rocke	......	10 May 82	16 Oct. 91		
11	...	Arthur Hemming Robeson, *Adjutant 4 Vol. Bn. Cheshire Regt.* 1 May 93	......	23 Aug. 84	13 Apr. 92		
13	...	Wilfred Nash Bolton, *Instructor Royal Military College*: Sept. 94	......	10 Mar. 83	26 Feb. 93		
12	...	2 Graham Joseph Dickson	......	6 Feb. 84	26 Feb. 93		
11	...	Robert William Trim, *O. S. Dept.*	......	14 May 84	1 May 93		
11	...	1 Arthur Gordon Jeffreys	......	23 Aug. 84	1 May 93		
11	...	Thomas Wyatt Hale, *O. S. Dept.*	......	7 Feb. 85	26 Oct. 93		
11	...	Hon. Leonard Holmes-a'Court	......	28 Feb. 85	26 Oct. 93		
10	...	1 William Eyre Matcham	......	6 May 85	11 July 94		
10	...	1 Arthur Walter Hasted	......	9 May 85	8 Aug. 94		
10	...	1 James Frederick Forbes, **Adjutant** 2 Oct. 93	......	30 Jan. 86	8 Aug. 94		
9	...	Arthur Alison Stuart Barnes, **Adjutant** 10 Jan. 95	......	25 Aug. 86	15 Jan. 95		
		LIEUTENANTS.					
8	10/12	1 Reginald Holden Steward	16 Nov. 87	18 Jan. 90			
7	...	1 Edward Vincent	9 May 88	5 Mar. 90			
7	...	2 Gerard Christopher Rigby	22 Aug. 88	4 June 90			
7	...	Stephen Hungerford Pollen, *Aide de Camp to Gov. Gen. of India* 1 Apr. 93	22 Aug. 88	11 June 90			
7	...	Arth. Edw. Harington Raikes, *serving with the Forces of the Sultan of Zanzibar*	10 Nov. 88	24 Nov. 90			
6	...	1 Arthur Eyre Beadon (*Depot*)	24 Apr. 89	1 May 91			
6	...	1 Herbert Tollemache Arnold	8 June 89	29 May 91			
6	...	2 William Parry, *Station Staff Officer, Mandalay*, 6 Oct. 94	21 Dec. 89	16 Oct. 91			
6	...	2 John Reginald Wyndham (*Depot*)	1 Mar. 90	21 Oct. 91			
5	...	2 Bernard Cave-Browne-Cave	23 July 90	16 Mar. 92			
5	...	2 Stafford H. Wolferstan Tordiffe	29 Oct. 90	1 Apr. 92			
5	...	Frank Douglas Browne	29 Nov. 90	9 Apr. 92			
4	...	Clement Laurence Seton Browne	10 Oct. 91	6 Mar. 93			
4	...	2 Gonville Warneford	7 Nov. 91	12 Apr. 93			
4	...	2 Charles Henry Brownlow Lees	27 Jan. 92	2 Oct. 93			
4	...	2 Alan Melville	20 Feb. 92	18 Nov. 93			
4	...	2 Walter Sidney Brown	12 Mar. 92	29 Jan. 94			
3	...	2 Bertram Francis Percy Feilding	9 Apr. 92	7 Mar. 94			
3	...	1 Reginald George Horner	9 Apr. 92	11 July 94			
3	...	1 Hugh Edward Herdon	13 July 92	8 Aug. 94			
3	...	2 Reginald O'Bryan Taylor	13 July 92	10 Sept. 94			
3	...	2 Sidney Hunter Shaw	13 July 92	15 Jan. 95			

Years Ser.		SECOND LIEUTENANTS.	2ND LIEUT.	
Full Pay.	Half Pay.			
3	...	2 Francis Dean Davidson	13 July	92
2	...	1 George Godfrey Mussy Wheeler	20 May	93
2	...	2 Ernest Lennox Mears	19 July	93
2	...	2 Edward Evans	19 July	93
2	...	1 Arthur Harry Hutton Wilson	21 Oct.	93
2	...	1 Percy Hasler	17 Jan.	94
1	...	1 Edward Usher Bradbridge	2 June	94
1	...	2 Henry John Kreyer	11 July	94
1	...	1 Henry Paton Rogers	10 Oct.	94
1	...	1 Henry George Lynch-Staunton	12 Dec.	94
1	...	1 Allan Armstrong	20 Feb.	95

Paymasters.—2 Arthur A. S. Barnes, *Lieut.* 2 *Battalion* (acting).

| 2 | ... | *Quarter Masters.*—2 George Pepper, 23 Aug. 93; *Hon. Lieut.* |
| 1 | ... | 1 Charles Spencer Barnes, 11 Apr. 94; *Hon. Lieut.* |

Facings White.—*Agents,* Messrs. Cox and Co.
1st Battalion returned from Bengal, 1882. *2nd Battalion embarked for the Cape of Good Hope,* 1878.

[1] Sir Henry Warre, while employed on the Staff in Canada in 1845-46, examined and reported upon the river communications (2,300 miles) between Montreal and Red River Settlement, with a view to the transport of troops; also in surveying and reporting upon the various settlements in the Oregon Territory and on various Islands on the coast of the Pacific. Served in the Crimean campaign from March 1855, including the siege and fall of Sebastopol; after Colonel Shadforth was killed he commanded the 57th Regt., and was present at the assaults of the Redan on the 18th June and 8th Sept.; also at the bombardment and surrender of Kinbourn (Medal with Clasp, CB., 5th Class of the Medjidie, and Turkish Medal). Commanded the 57th on the line of posts on the Taptee River in co-operation with the Central India Field Force in 1858. Also in the war of 1861 in New Zealand, and at the assault on the rebel Maori positions on the Knitikara River on the 4th June 1863. Afterwards, as Colonel on the Staff, commanded the Troops in the province of Taranaki—under martial law—during the whole of the operations on the West Coast in 1863-66, was present and in command of the Troops in the action at Poutoko 2nd Oct. 1863, at the assaults and capture of the rebel Maori strongholds at Abuahu and Kaitaké in March 1864, and Mataitawa and To Arei in Oct. 1864, also the occupation of Opunaki and subsequent operations at Warea and Te Puru, and in command of the Field Force which was ordered to meet the troops from the South, opened the coast line of 150 miles from Taranaki to Wanganui. Was specially mentioned in Sir Duncan Cameron's despatches for his conduct during the war, and received the pension for distinguished conduct for his services in New Zealand (Medal).

[7] Major Harford served throughout the Zulu war of 1879, first as Staff Officer of the 3rd Regiment of Natal Native Contingent (two battalions), and subsequently as Second Staff Officer of "Clarke's Column".(Medal with Clasp).

[8] Major Carter was employed in the Khyber Pass on the Lines of Communication during the Afghan war in 1879 (Medal).

[14] Major Hill served in the Afghan war in 1879-80, first with the 2nd Division Peshawur Valley Field Force, and afterwards with the 2nd Division Cabul Field Force (Medal).

[15] Major Alexander served with the 99th Regiment throughout the Zulu war of 1879, and was present in the engagements of Inyezane and Gingindhlovu (Medal with Clasp).

[16] Major Rowden served with the Mounted Infantry in the Zulu war of 1879, and was present in the engagement of Inyezane and during the investment of Ekowe (mentioned in despatches, Medal with Clasp).

[18] Captain Macmullen served in the Egyptian war in 1882, and was present at the battle of Tel-el-Kebir (Medal with Clasp, and Khedive's Star).

[19] Captain Jones served with the 99th Regiment throughout the Zulu war of 1879, including the investment of Ekowe (Medal with Clasp).

[20] Captain Payne served with the 99th Regiment in the Zulu war of 1879, and was present during the investment of Ekowe (Medal with Clasp).

Record of the Services of the 1st Battalion Wiltshire Regiment (formerly the 62nd Foot).

Raised as the 2nd Battalion 4th Foot, 1756. Constituted 62nd Regiment, 1758. To Ireland, 1759. (Four Companies to North America, which returned in 1760.) To Dominica, 1763. To Ireland, 1769. To North America, 1776. To England, 1780. (Entitled " Wiltshire Regiment," 1792.) To Scotland, Feb. 1784. To Ireland, Oct. 1784. To Jamaica and San Domingo, 1790. To England, 1797. (Formed into two Battalions, 1799.) To Ireland, 1800. (2nd Battalion reduced, 1802; re-formed, 1804.) 1st Battalion to Sicily, Egypt and Italy, 1805. To North America, 1814. [2nd Battalion to England, 1805. To the Peninsula, 1813 (battle of the Nive). To Ireland and France, 1815 (Army of Occupation). To Ireland and reduced, 1816.] To Halifax, N.S., 1819. To Ireland, 1823. To India, 1830 (battles of Ferozeshah and Sobraon). To England, 1847. To Ireland, 1854. To the Crimea, 1854 (siege of Sebastopol). To Nova Scotia, 1856. To Canada, 1862. To England, 1864. To Ireland, 1867. To India, 1869. To Aden, 1880. To England, 1882. To the Channel Isles, 1886. To Ireland, 1887.

Record of the Services of the 2nd Battalion Wiltshire Regiment (formerly the 99th Regiment).

Raised at Glasgow in 1824 and proceeded to the Mauritius, 1825. Entitled the "Lanarkshire Regiment," 1832. To Ireland, 1837. To Van Diemen's Land, 1842. To New Zealand, 1845. To Ireland, 1856. To India, 1858. To China, 1860. To South Africa, 1865. To England, 1869. Entitled "Duke of Edinburgh's Regiment," 1874. To South Africa, 1878 (Zulu war of 1879). To Bermuda, 1879. To South Africa, 1881. Entitled "2nd Battalion Duke of Edinburgh's (Wiltshire Regiment)," 1881. To India, 1881.

1st Batt., Preston.
2nd Batt., Dinapore, Bengal.] **The Manchester Regiment.** [*Regimental District* No. 63.—Ashton.

Formerly the 63rd (West Suffolk) and the 96th Regiments.
(The 3rd and 4th Battalions are formed of the 6th Lancashire Militia.)
"EGMONT-OP-ZEE" "EGYPT" (with the Sphinx). "MARTINIQUE" "GUADALOUPE" "PENINSULA" "ALMA"
"INKERMAN" "SEVASTOPOL" "NEW ZEALAND" "AFGHANISTAN, 1879-80" "EGYPT, 1882."

Years' Ser.							
Full Pay	Half Pay						
28	...	Colonel.—John M'Neill Walter,¹ *CB*, Ensign, P31 July 35; Lieut., 3 July 39; Capt., 29 Sept. 47; Major, P2 Dec. 53; Lt.Colonel, P17 Oct. 56; Colonel, 17 June 61; Major General, 6 March 68; Lt.General, 21 Dec.78; General, 1 July 81; Colonel Manchester Regiment, 18 Dec. 89.					
22	...	Lieutenant Colonels.—2 John Arthur Barlow,⁵ *Ensign*, 8 Jan. 68; Lt. 18 Aug. 69; Capt. 15 Jan. 79; Major, 14 Feb.83; Lt.Colonel, 18 Mar. 92.					
		1 Basil Lloyd Anstruther, *Lieut.* 17 July 73; Capt. 13 June 79; Major, 1 Aug. 83; Lt.Colonel, 31 May 94.					

		MAJORS.	ENSIGN OR 2ND LIEUT.	LIEUT.	CAPTAIN.	BREV.MAJ.	MAJOR.
22	...	2 Charles Parker Ridley⁶	......	9 Aug. 73	13 Sept. 79	......	30 Sept. 84
21	...	1 Arthur Edmund Simpson⁹	......	21 Sept. 74	18 June 81	......	17 Jan. 90
24	...	2 Hugh Bertram Nathaniel Bewicke	28 Oct. 71	28 Oct. 78	2 Feb. 81	......	25 Jan. 89
21	...	William Peel Nash,⁹ *Adjutant 1 Vol. Bn. Manchester Regt.* 4 June 90	......	11 Feb. 75	15 Sept. 81	......	19 Aug. 91
21	...	1 Charles Tom Reay⁴	......	11 Feb. 75	18 Mar. 82	......	24 Oct. 91
19	...	2 William Bannatyne Graham,¹⁰ *Commandant Landour Depot* 12 Jan. 94	......	11 Sept. 76	9 July 84	......	18 Mar. 92
19	...	1 Henry Sherwood Smith¹⁷ (*Depot*)	......	29 Nov. 76	9 July 84	......	6 Dec. 93
17	...	1 Charles Robert Brown	......	11 Oct. 78	28 Aug. 85	......	31 May 94
		CAPTAINS.					
19	...	1 John Percy Gethin	......	11 Sept. 76	13 Aug. 84		
17	...	2 Archibald Boyd Maxwell⁹	1 May 78	19 Apr. 79	20 Nov. 86		
17	...	2 John Edward Watson¹³	11 May 78	13 June 79	10 Aug. 87		
17	...	2 John Henry Abbot Anderson¹⁴	11 May 78	21 June 79	12 Oct. 87		
17	5/19	*p.s.c.* Anthony Thos. Philip Hudson, *D.A.A. Gen. Mauritius*, 1 Mar. 95	30 Jan. 78	23 June 79	12 Oct. 87		
17	...	2 William Bertram¹⁵	4 Sept. 78	3 Sept. 79	11 Feb. 88		
16	...	2 Ralph Anstruther Henderson¹⁶	13 Aug. 79	18 June 81	2 July 88		
16	...	1 Charles Curling Melvill⁹	13 Aug. 79	1 July 81	12 Nov. 88		
16	...	Trevor Patrick Breffney Ternan,¹⁸ *DSO. on special service, Uganda*	13 Aug. 79	1 July 81	12 Nov. 88		
17	...	Claude George Henry Sitwell,¹⁹ *serving with the Egyptian Army*	14 Sept. 78	1 July 81	13 Sept. 86		
14	...	1 Robert Davenport Vizard⁹	23 April 81	1 July 81	10 Apr. 89		
14	...	Lynch Hamilton Prioleau,⁹ *Adj. 4 Vol. Bn. Manchester Regt.* 1 Feb. 92	......	22 Oct. 81	8 Nov. 89		
13	...	1 Cyril Henry Moore	......	10 May 82	17 Jan. 90		
13	...	1 Willoughby Garnons Gwatkin, *Staff Coll.*	......	10 May 82	17 Jan. 90		
13	...	2 Guy William Fitton	......	9 Sept. 82	18 Mar. 90		
12	...	1 Henry Charles Edward Westropp, *Adjutant* 18 Apr. 92	......	12 May 83	31 May 90		
11	...	2 Anthony Hugh Baldwin,²⁰ *Adjutant* 5 July 91	......	14 May 84	3 Feb. 92		
10	...	2 Herbert Lionel James	......	6 May 85	18 Mar. 92		
		LIEUTENANTS.					
9	...	1 Henry William Ernest Hitchins	......	25 Aug. 86			
9	...	1 William Herbert Williamson	......	10 Nov. 86			
9	...	1 Charles Louis Rowe Petrie	5 Feb. 87	10 Apr. 89			
8	...	1 Edmund Howard Gorges	14 Sept. 87	3 July 89			
8	...	1 Arthur William Marden	11 Feb. 88	31 July 89			
8	...	1 Arth. Wm. Valentine Plunkett²¹ (*Depot*)	14 Mar. 88	6 Nov. 89			
7	...	1 John Cane Crawford	9 May 88	18 Dec. 89			
7	...	2 Reginald Salter Weston	22 Aug. 88	17 Jan. 90			
7	...	2 Edward Vaughan	10 Nov. 88	10 Sept. 90			
6	...	1 Charles Scarborough Cottingham	24 Apr. 89	10 Sept. 90			
6	...	1 Erasmus Darwin Parker	6 July 89	10 Sept. 90			
6	...	1 Reginald Curtis Leman	21 Sept. 89	26 Sept. 90			
6	...	1 Robert James Bridgford	21 Dec. 89	3 Dec. 90			
6	...	2 Augustus Oliver Lash	1 Mar. 90	2 Mar. 92			
5	...	John Edward Stanley Maclure, *Army Pay Department*	3 May 90	18 Mar. 92			
5	...	2 Gerald Cleeve Rynd	3 May 90	19 May 92			
5	...	Herbt. Valentine Ravenscroft,²⁵ *serving with the Egyptian Army*	28 June 90	19 May 92			
5	...	2 Alfred Edward Sealy²⁶	8 Oct. 90	1 June 93			
5	...	2 Angus Menzies²⁷	8 Nov. 90	10 July 93			
5	...	1 Edward John Howard Walker (*Depot*)	29 Nov. 90	15 Apr. 94			
4	...	1 Francis Wyatt Abbot Anderson	21 Oct. 91	14 Dec. 94			
		SECOND LIEUTENANTS.					
4	...	2 Arthur Manston Houston, *Station Staff Officer, Gnatong*, 30 Nov. 93	5 Dec. 91				
4	...	2 George Courtenay King	12 Mar. 92				
4	...	1 William Patrick Eric Newbigging	23 Mar. 92				
3	...	Edward Gonville Bromhead	18 May 92				
3	...	2 Hugh Maurice Wellesley Souter	18 May 92				
3	...	2 Cyril Grey Stansfeld	13 Aug. 92				
4	...	2 Donald Archibald Dugald M'Vean	7 Nov. 91				
2	...	2 Donald Robertson Paton	9 Sept. 93				
2	...	2 Alexander Nelson Hood	21 Oct. 93				
1	...	2 Frederick Christian Hirst	20 Feb. 95				
1	...	1 Arthur George Tillard	20 Feb. 95				
1	...	2 George Augustus James Godbold	20 Feb. 95				
1	...	2 Walter Wilton Campbell Stevenson	20 Feb. 95				

* Major Reay and Captain Tenison served with the 1st Battalion Manchester Regiment in the Egyptian war of 1882 (Medal, and Khedive's Star).

Facings White.
Agents, Messrs. Cox and Co.
1st Battalion returned from Benga. 1882.
2nd Battalion embarked for Malta, 1881.

Paymasters.—1
2 Herbert L. James, *Captain 2 Battalion (acting).*
Quarter Masters.—2 Oscar Stewart-Wynne,²⁸ 16 Oct. 89; *Hon. Lieut.*
1 Alfred Jones, 19 March 90; *Hon. Lieut.*

The Manchester Regiment.

¹ General Walter served throughout the Kaffir campaign of 1846-47 as Adjutant of the 90th Light Infantry, and Field Adjutant of the 1st Division (Medal). Served with the 53rd Regiment in the Punjaub campaign in 1849, and was present at the battle of Goojerat (Medal with Clasp). Campaign of 1851-52 against the Hill Tribes on the Peshawur frontier. Served with the 35th Regiment in the Indian campaign of 1857-59; commanded the Arrah Field Force in the actions of Sirthooa, Bramineegunge, Rampoorperoiora, Jemaon, and Kareesath; subsequently a Column in the operations in Shahabad, including the actions before Nonoodhche (twice mentioned in despatches, CB., and Medal).

⁵ Lt.Colonel Bariow served in the Hazara campaign in 1888 as Deputy Assistant Adjutant General 2nd Brigade, and was present in the engagement at Kotkai (mentioned in despatches, Medal with Clasp). Served with the Miranzai Expedition in 1891 in command of a Wing of the 2nd Battalion Manchester Regiment (Clasp).

⁶ Major Ridley served throughout the Egyptian war of 1882 with the 2nd Battalion Manchester Regiment (Medal, and Khedive's Star). Served in the Miranzai Expedition in 1891 with the 2nd Battalion Manchester Regiment (Medal with Clasp).

⁹ Majors Simpson and Nash, and Captains Maxwell, Melvill, Vizard and Prioleau served with the 2nd Battalion Manchester Regiment throughout the Egyptian war of 1882 (Medal, and Khedive's Star).

¹⁰ Major Graham served in Southern Afghanistan with the 63rd Regiment in 1879-80 (Medal). Served in the Egyptian war of 1882 with the 1st Battalion Manchester Regiment (Medal, and Khedive's Star). Served in the Miranzai Expedition in 1891 with the 2nd Battalion Manchester Regiment (Medal with Clasp).

¹² Major Smith served with the 63rd Regiment as Adjutant in Southern Afghanistan in 1879-80 (Medal). Served as Adjutant with the 1st Battalion Manchester Regiment in the Egyptian war of 1882 (Medal, and Khedive's Star).

¹³ Captain Watson served throughout the Egyptian war of 1882 with the 2nd Battalion Manchester Regiment (Medal, and Khedive's Star). Served in the Miranzai Expedition in 1891 with the 2nd Battalion Manchester Regiment (Medal with Clasp).

¹⁴ Captain Anderson served in the Miranzai Expedition in 1891 with the 2nd Battalion Manchester Regiment (Medal with Clasp).

¹⁵ Captain Bertram served in the Egyptian war of 1882 with the Mounted Infantry with Sir Evelyn Wood's Brigade, and was present at the surrender of Kafr Dowar (Medal, and Khedive's Star).

¹⁶ Captain Henderson served in the Egyptian war of 1882 with the 2nd Battalion Manchester Regiment (Medal, and Khedive's Star). Served with the Burmese Expedition in 1885-87 (Medal with two Clasps).

¹⁸ Captain Ternan served with the 63rd Regiment in Southern Afghanistan in 1879-89 (Medal). Served with the 1st Battalion of the Manchester Regiment in the Egyptian war of 1882 (Medal, and Khedive's Star); with the Nile Expedition in 1884-85 with the Egyptian Army (Clasp); with the Soudan Frontier Field Force in 1885-86 including the engagement at Giniss; and in the operations on the Soudan frontier in 1889 including the engagement at Toski (mentioned in despatches, DSO., and Clasp).

¹⁹ Captain Sitwell served in the Afghan war in 1879-80 with the Koorum Division, including the Zaimusht Expedition (Medal). Served in the Egyptian war of 1882 with the 1st Battalion of the Shropshire Light Infantry, and was present at the occupation of Kafr Dowar and the surrender of Damietta (Medal, and Khedive's Star).

²⁰ Captain Baldwin served in the Miranzai Expedition in 1891 with the 2nd Battalion Manchester Regiment (Medal with Clasp).

²¹ Lieut. Plunkett served in the Miranzai Expedition in 1891 with the 2nd Battalion Manchester Regiment (Medal with Clasp).

²⁵ Lieut. Ravenscroft.—See Civil Decorations for Gallantry, "Hart's Annual Army List," p. 786.

²⁶ Lieut. Sealy served in the Miranzai Expedition in 1891 with the 2nd Battalion Manchester Regiment (Medal with Clasp).

²⁷ Lieut. Menzies served in the Miranzai Expedition in 1891 with the 2nd Battalion Manchester Regiment (Medal with Clasp).

²⁸ Lieut. Stewart Wynne served in the Miranzai Expedition in 1891 with the 2nd Battalion Manchester Regiment (Medal with Clasp).

Record of the Services of the 1st Battalion Manchester Regiment,—formerly the 63rd (West Suffolk) Regiment.

2nd Battalion 8th Foot (The King's) was constituted in England a separate Regiment, and numbered 63rd Foot, 1758. West Indies, to 1764. Ireland, to 1775. America, to 1781 (serving as Mounted Infantry). Jamaica, to 1783. Scotland, to 1786. Ireland and England, to 1793. Low Countries, to 1795. West Indies, to 1799. England and Ireland, to 1800. Ferrol, Gibraltar, and Malta, to 1803. [2nd Battalion raised in 1804; disbanded 1814.] Ireland and Madeira, to 1807. West Indies, to 1819 (capture of Martinique and Guadaloupe). England and Ireland, to 1826. Portugal, to 1828. England, 1828. New South Wales, to 1833. East Indies, to 1847. England, to 1851. Ireland, to 1854. The Crimea, to 1856 (battles of Alma and Inkerman and siege of Sebastopol). Nova Scotia and Canada, to 1865. England, to 1866. Scotland, to 1867. Ireland, to 1870. East Indies, to 1882 (Afghan war, 1879-80). Egypt, to 1882 (war of 1882). England, to 1888. Ireland, 1888.

Record of the Services of the 2nd Battalion Manchester Regiment (formerly the 96th Regiment).

Raised in 1824 and proceeded to Halifax, Nova Scotia, to 1825. Bermudas and Somers Islands, to 1828. Halifax (with detachments at Sydney, Cape Breton, Prince Edward's Isle, Annapolis Royal, and St. John's, Newfoundland), to 1835. England, to 1836. Ireland, to 1839. England, to July, 1839. New South Wales, to 1843. Van Dieman's Land (with detachments in New Zealand, Norfolk Island, and Adelaide), to 1849. East Indies, 1854. Ireland, to 1856. Gibraltar, to 1857. England, to 1860. Ireland, to 1862. England, to May 1862. Cape of Good Hope, to 1865. East Indies, to 1875. England, to 1881. Malta to 1882. Egypt, to Oct. 1882. East Indies, 1882.

The Prince of Wales' (North Staffordshire Regiment).

1st Batt., **Malta**.
2nd Batt., **Dublin**.] *Formerly the 64th (2nd Staffordshire) and the 98th (Prince of Wales') Regiments.* [*Regimental District* No. 64.—Lichfield.

(The 3rd and 4th Battalions are formed of the 2nd and 3rd Stafford Militia respectively.)

The Prince of Wales' Plume. "ST. LUCIA" "SURINAM" "CHINA" (with the Dragon). "PUNJAUB" "PERSIA" "RESHIRE" "BUSHIRE" "KOOSHAB" "LUCKNOW."

Years' Ser. Full Pay	Half Pay		ENSIGN OR 2ND LIEUT.	LIEUT.	CAPTAIN.	BREV.MAJ.	MAJOR.
22	...	**Colonel.**—1 Charles Algernon Lewis,[1] *Cornet*, [P]13 Oct. 25; *Lt.* [P]15 Aug. 26; *Capt.* [P]12 April 33; *Capt. & Lt.Colonel*, [P]30 Dec. 45; *Colonel*, 20 June 54; *Major*, 11 Jan. 58; *Lt.Colonel*, 13 Feb. 59; *Major General*, 19 June 60; *Lieut.General*, 8 March 69; *General*, 5 April 76; Colonel 64th Foot, 12 Feb. 70.						
22	...	**Lieutenant Colonels.**—1 Thomas Alfred Beale, *Lt.* 14 Aug. 73; *Capt.* 25 Aug. 80; *Major*, 22 Jan. 85; *Lt.Colonel*, 14 Sept. 92.						
22	...	2 Henry David Williams,[3] *Lt.* 9 Aug. 73; *Capt.* 6 Mar. 80; *Major*, 17 June 85; *Lt.Colonel*, 6 Mar. 95.						
		MAJORS.					
22	...	1 Thomas Currie	......	28 Feb. 74	12 Mar. 81	......	1 July 88
22	...	2 Charles Edward Bradley[4]	......	28 Feb. 74	1 July 81	......	1 July 88
22	...	1 p.s.c. Henry Beaufoy Mortimer	......	28 Feb. 74	19 Nov. 81	......	10 Oct. 88
22	...	2 Harry Stewart Bruce Hodgkinson (Depot)	......	12 Nov. 73	13 Apr. 81	......	10 Sept. 90
20	...	2 Arthur Wildman Prior[6]	......	13 June 75	14 Jan. 84	......	14 Sept. 92
19	...	1 John Watkins	......	27 June 76	1 July 84	......	15 Aug. 94
20	...	Henry Hartland Higginson[7]	......	29 Jan. 76	1 July 84	......	9 Jan. 95
		CAPTAINS.					
18	...	Edmund Walcott Newland,[10] *Army Pay Department*	30 Jan. 78	17 May 79	22 Jan. 85		
17	...	1 Charles Herbert de Kutzleben Walhouse	14 Sept. 78	24 May 79	17 June 85		
17	...	Thos. Montgomery Hawtayne,[8] *Supt. of Police at the Gambia* 21 Mar. 91	22 Jan. 79	13 Sept. 79	2 Jan. 86		
17	...	Gerard Chichester,[6] *Adj.* 4 *Bn.* 27 Feb. 93	22 Jan. 79	7 Jan. 80	2 Jan. 86		
17	...	Willoughby Fenwick Trevelyan, *Army Pay Department*	22 Jan. 79	6 Mar. 80	2 Jan. 86		
15	...	2 p.s.c. Walter Grenville Ley[6]	11 Aug. 80	12 Mar. 81	1 July 87		
15	8/12	1 Alan Mackenzie-Pendrill[10] (Depot)	6 Aug. 79	28 Apr. 80	23 Apr. 88		
17	...	2 Albert John Lindner, *Superintendent of Gymnasia, Woolwich*, 12 Jan. 95	22 Jan. 79	25 June 81	6 May 88		
16	...	2 Francis Geldard[6]	13 Aug. 79	1 July 81	4 Mar. 89		
16	...	Percy Shakespeare Dyson, *A. P. Dept.*	13 Aug. 79	1 July 81	1 Apr. 89		
13	...	Edmund Graham Snow, *O. S. Dept.*	......	10 May 82	21 Mar. 91		
13	...	2 p.s.c. William Tilston Holland	......	9 Sept. 82	16 June 91		
20	...	Arthur George, *Adj.* 3 *Bn.* 1 May 93	......	10 Sept. 75	1 Mar. 84		
13	...	1 Marshall Robinson[9]	......	28 June 82	13 Jan. 92		
12	...	1 Henry Marwood,[10] **Adjutant** 9 Jan. 93	......	6 Feb. 84	14 Sept. 92		
12	...	George Barton Smith, *Army Pay Dept.*	......	6 Feb. 84	1 Mar. 93		
11	...	2 Lionel Thomas Campbell Twyford, **Adjutant** 18 May 92	......	23 Aug. 84	1 Mar. 93		
11	...	2 Charles Grove Amphlett	......	12 Nov. 84	1 Mar. 93		
11	...	William Alexander Barnett,[10] *Adjutant Cape Colonial Vol. Rifles* 3 Feb. 94	......	7 Feb. 85	1 May 93		
12	...	1 Reginald Polo Stuart	......	6 Feb. 84	28 Oct. 93		
10	...	1 Herbert Chidgey Brine Payne[10]	......	23 May 85	30 Nov. 93		
10	...	1 Robert Harcourt Ord Capper	......	23 May 85	3 Feb. 94		
		LIEUTENANTS.					
10	...	1 Lindsay Buchanan Scott		23 May 85			
10	...	2 Charles Woodward Crofton		25 Nov. 85			
10	...	2 John Rose		30 Jan. 86			
10	...	2 Matthew Benjamin Dipnall Ffinch		30 Jan. 86			
8	...	2 Somerset Charles Godfrey Farfax Astell	4 May 87	2 Mar. 90			
8	...	Harry Seddon Prickard	11 Feb. 88	2 Mar. 90			
7	...	2 John William Saunders (Depot)	13 June 88	16 July 90			
7	...	2 Vigant William de Falbe	22 Aug. 88	15 Oct. 90			
7	...	1 Thomas Montgomerie Webb (Depot)	31 Oct. 88	15 Dec. 90			
7	...	1 Robert Schlesinger Hutchison	8 Dec. 88	6 Mar. 91			
7	...	2 Lionel Kekewich Carlyon	23 Mar. 89	8 Apr. 91			
6	...	2 Claude Edward Allan Milburne	3 July 89	16 June 91			
5	...	2 Benjamin Irby Way	3 May 90	15 Sept. 91			
5	...	2 Alfred Letchworth Law	3 May 90	11 Nov. 91			
5	...	1 William Horsman Goldfinch	28 June 90	1 May 93			
5	...	Edward Frank Harding	16 July 90	28 Oct. 93			
5	...	1 Alexander Robert Crawford Row	29 Nov. 90	28 Oct. 93			
5	...	John Cecil Cortlandt Angelo	29 Nov. 90	30 Nov. 93			
5	...	1 Morton Herbert Knaggs	25 Mar. 91	30 Nov. 93			
4	...	1 John Wilson	2 May 91	3 Feb. 94			
		SECOND LIEUTENANTS.					
4	...	2 Arthur Reginald Hoskins	23 May 91				
4	...	1 Arthur Wavell Foote	25 July 91				
4	...	1 Edward Vigor Fox	7 Nov. 91				
4	...	1 Francis Earl Johnston	5 Dec. 91				
2	...	1 Halkett Walton Money Down	13 Sept. 93				
2	...	1 James Jay Bleecker Farley	23 Sept. 93				
2	...	1 Henry Stamford Lewis Alford	21 Oct. 93				
2	...	1 Thomas Alchin Andrus	23 Dec. 93				
2	...	1 Alexander William Ralston	7 Mar. 94				
2	...	2 Alister William Stewart Ewing	7 Mar. 94				
1	...	1 William Dennistoun Sword	2 June 94				
1	...	2 William Radclyffe Dugmore	20 June 94				
		Paymasters.—2					
8	...	**Quarter Masters.**—1 Henry Francis Healy, 18 June 87; *Hon. Lieut.*					
2	...	2 John Burrage, 27 Sept. 93; *Hon. Lieut.*					

[3] Lt.Colonel Williams served with the Zhob Valley Expedition in 1884.
[4] Major Bradley served in the operations in Zululand in 1888.
[6] Major Prior, Captains Chichester, Ley, and Geldard served with the Zhob Valley Expedition in 1884.
[10] Captains Newland, Mackenzie-Pendrill, Marwood, Barnett, and Payne served in the operations in Zululand in 1888.

[*For continuation of Notes, see end of the York and Lancaster Regiment*, p. 319.

Facings White.
Agents, Messrs. Cox and Co.
1st Batt. embarked for the *West Indies*, 1884.
2nd Batt. returned from *Aden*, 30 *Mar.* 1888.

1st Batt., Cork.
2nd Batt., South Africa.] **The York and Lancaster Regiment.** [*Regimental District.* No. 65.—Pontefract. 311

Formerly the 65th (2nd York N. Riding) and the 84th (York and Lancaster) Regiments.
(The 3rd Battalion is formed of the 3rd West York Militia.)
"INDIA" (with the Royal Tiger).   The Union Rose.
"NIVE" "PENINSULA" "ARABIA" "LUCKNOW" "NEW ZEALAND" "EGYPT, 1882, 1884" "TEL-EL-KEBIR."

Years' Ser. Full Pay	Half Pay		ENSIGN OR 2ND LIEUT.	LIEUT.	CAPTAIN.	BREV. MAJ.	MAJOR.
28	...	**Colonel.**—James Henry Craig Robertson, Ensign, 2 July 29; Lieut. 30 Dec. 35; Capt. 27 Feb. 42; Bt. Major, 20 June 54; Bt. Lt. Colonel, 6 June 56; Major, 7 May 58; Colonel, 27 Sept. 65; Major General, 16 May 70; Lt. General, 1 July 81; General, 1 Apr. 91; Colonel York and Lancaster Regiment, 21 June 92.					
26	...	**Lieutenant Colonels.**—2 Reginald William Dalgety,¹ CB, Ensign, P8 June 67; Lieut. P8 Aug. 68; Capt. 12 July 74; Major, 1 July 8²; Bt. Lt. Colonel, 21 May 84; Colonel, 21 May 88; Lt. Colonel, 1 July 91.					
		1 Charles John Whitaker,¹⁵ Ensign, 8 July 69; Lieut. P4 Jan. 71; Capt. 14 Dec. 78; Major, 24 Feb. 86; Lt. Colonel, 27 Aug. 94.					
		MAJORS.					
23	...	2 Henry Boughey	P27 Nov. 67	28 Oct. 71	3 Apr. 78	......	23 Mar. 87
23	...	1 Berkeley Crosbie Quill¹⁴	......	21 Aug. 72	24 June 79	......	30 July 90
22	...	1 William Johnston Kirkpatrick¹⁷	......	28 Feb. 74	1 July 81	18 Nov. 82	27 Aug. 90
22	...	1 Frederic Percy Lousada¹⁹	......	28 Feb. 74	1 July 81	......	27 Aug. 90
19	...	1 Francis Edward Wallerstein (Depot)	......	11 Sept. 76	29 May 82	......	1 July 91
19	...	2 p.s.c. Herbert Chas. Onslow Plumer²⁶	......	11 Sept. 76	29 May 82	......	22 Jan. 93
19	...	Charles King Colhoun,¹⁸ Adjutant 3 Battalion 9 Mar. 92	......	12 Feb. 77	14 Mar. 84	......	24 May 93
17	...	2 Ernest Chamier Broughton²³	......	11 Nov. 78	29 Nov. 85	......	27 Aug. 94
		CAPTAINS.					
21	...	1 William Arthur Tebbitt²²	......	11 Feb. 75	9 Mar. 82		
18	...	1 Henry Southey Scholes¹⁸	8 Dec. 77	1 Mar. 79	24 Feb. 86		
18	...	Saumarez Frederick Grosvenor,¹⁸ Adj. 2 Volunteer Battalion 1 May 91	30 Jan. 78	29 Apr. 79	24 Feb. 86		
17	...	George Francis Robert Henderson,²⁷ Professor Staff College, with rank of Lt. Colonel, 17 Dec. 92	1 May 78	24 June 79	2 June 86	3 June 86	
17	...	Randall Chas. Annesley Howe,²⁶ Adj. 1 Vol. Bn. York & Lanc. Regt. 1 Sept. 93	19 Oct. 78	1 July 81	24 Aug. 87		
16	...	Hugo William Nairne Scott Smyth,²⁵ Ordnance Store Department	21 June 79	1 July 81	10 Sept. 87		
16	...	Edmund Charles Kyrle Money, Army Pay Department	9 July 79	1 July 81	10 Sept. 87		
16	...	Spencer Duncan Maul,¹⁸ Adj. 1 Vol. Bn. Oxford Lt. Infantry 1 Jan. 94	13 Aug. 79	1 July 81	16 July 88		
16	...	2 Edward Francis Woodford¹⁸	14 Jan. 80	1 July 81	1 Aug. 88		
13	...	2 Frederick Kershaw	......	29 July 82	25 July 89		
16	...	1 Claudius Shirley Harris	11 Oct. 79	1 July 81	18 July 88		
13	...	Arthur Steuart Palmer, O.S. Dept.	......	10 May 82	12 Feb. 90		
15	...	Charles William Brett Farrant,²⁹ Adj. 5 Vol. Bn. Manchester Regt. 2 Dec. 90	19 Feb. 81	1 July 81	19 Mar. 90		
12	...	1 Stuart Peter Rolt, Adjutant 21 Dec. 92	......	30 Jan. 84	28 Apr. 90		
12	...	1 p.s.c. Edward Honywood-Hughes	......	6 Feb. 84	7 May 90		
13	...	Arthur Montagu M'Murdo,³⁰ DSO, serving in Egyptian Slavery Dept.	......	9 Sept. 82	8 Nov. 90		
11	...	2 Harry Nicholl Byass	......	7 Feb. 85	24 Dec. 90		
10	...	2 Francis Mayne Shadwell (Depot)	......	23 May 85	11 Feb. 91		
10	...	2 Cecil Henry Kekewich	......	29 Aug. 85	2 Sept. 91		
10	...	2 Richard Eyles Galindo³¹	......	19 Sept. 85	16 Sept. 91		
10	...	2 Fred. Francis Williamson Daniell	......	29 Aug. 85	30 Sept. 91		
10	...	1 Arthur Colville Hyde	......	29 Aug. 85	27 Aug. 94		
10	...	2 Ernest Cazenove Cobbold	......	29 Aug. 85	16 Jan. 95		
		LIEUTENANTS.					
10	...	2 William Longfield Brady	......	30 Jan. 86			
12	...	John Hervey Armstrong	......	31 Oct. 83			
9	...	1 Henry Cecil East Smithett, Lieut. Instructor, Hythe School of Musketry	......	7 July 86			
9	...	1 Arthur Manning Haines	......	25 Aug. 86			
9	...	1 Edward Geo. Graham Talbot Baines (Depot)	......	25 Aug. 86			
9	...	Clifford Maunsell FitzGerald, Ordnance Store Department	5 Feb. 87	3 July 89			
8	...	1 William M'Gee Armstrong	14 Sept. 87	16 Oct. 89			
8	...	2 Arthur Geo. Burt, Adjutant 7 Jan. 92	16 Nov. 87	17 Dec. 89			
8	...	1 William Fletcher Clemson	16 Nov. 87	12 Feb. 90			
8	...	2 Somerset Edward Deane Webb (Depot)	11 Feb. 88	28 Apr. 90			
7	...	1 William Edmond John Bradshaw	22 Aug. 88	7 May 90			
7	...	2 Ernest James Woodley (Depot)	8 Dec. 88	15 Dec. 90			
7	...	2 Frederick Percy Howlett	23 Mar. 89	11 Feb. 91			
6	...	2 Thomas Tinning Gresson	9 Nov. 89	30 Sept. 91			
6	...	1 Henry Percy Thurnall	21 Dec. 89	26 Oct. 92			
6	...	1 Michael Francis Halford	8 Jan. 90	26 Oct. 92			
6	...	Clive William Justice, Aide de Camp to Major General W.C. Justice 5 Mar. 94	29 Mar. 90	9 Nov. 92			
6	...	2 George Capron	9 Nov. 89	27 Aug. 94			
5	...	2 Frederic Ellis Ashton	28 June 90	27 Nov. 94			
5	...	1 Frederick Edmund Corbett Palmer	29 Nov. 90	29 Dec. 94			
5	...	1 John Saunders Armstrong	18 Feb. 91	16 Jan. 95			
		SECOND LIEUTENANTS.					
4	...	2 Frederic Conrad Swithin Norrington	7 Nov. 91				
4	...	2 Harold Kelway Colston	7 Nov. 91				
4	...	1 Francis Edward Bradshaw Isherwood	9 Jan. 92				
3	...	2 William Ernest Sykes	19 Nov. 92				
3	...	2 Middleton Middleton	19 Nov. 92				
3	...	2 Robert James Longden	17 Dec. 92				
2	...	2 Reginald Selous	7 Mar. 94				
1	...	2 Cecil Hugh Taylor	10 Oct. 94				
1	...	2 Gerald Edward Bayley	12 Dec. 94				
1	...	1 Courtney Ernest Joseph Brown	23 Jan. 95				
1	...	Frederick Thomas Cecil Hill	6 Mar. 95				

²⁷ Lt. Col. Henderson served with the 2nd Battalion York and Lancaster Regiment throughout the Egyptian war of 1882, and was present in the engagements at El Magfar and Tel-el-Mahuta, in the two actions at Kassasin, and at the battle of Tel-el-Kebir (Brevet of Major, Medal with Clasp, 5th Class of the Medjidie, and Khedive's Star).

²⁶ Captain Howe served as Transport Officer throughout the Egyptian war of 1882, and was present in the engagements at El Magfar and Tel-el-Mahuta, in the two actions at Kassasin, and at the battle of Tel-el-Kebir (Medal with Clasp, and Khedive's Star).

²⁹ Captain Farrant served with the Burmese Expedition in 1886-88 with the 2nd Battalion Royal Munster Fusiliers (Medal with Clasp).

³⁰ Captain M'Murdo, when attached to the Egyptian Army at Suakin, commanded a detachment of Camel Corps in the attack on Osman Digna's camp at Handoub on the 17th January 1888—wounded (4th Class of the Medjidie); also served in the operations on the Soudan frontier in 1889 including the engagement at Toski (mentioned in despatches, DSO, and Clasp).

312--13 *The York and Lancaster Regiment.*

Paymasters.—1
2
Quarter Masters.—1 John Eyvoll, 17 Sept. 87; *Hon. Lieut.*
2 John Fuller, 31 Dec. 87; *Hon. Lieut.*
Facings White.—*Agents*, Messrs. Cox and Co.
1st Battalion returned from Egypt, 21 Apr. 1884. 2nd Battalion embarked for Bermuda, 1883.

[1] Colonel Dalgety served in the expedition to the Soudan under Sir Gerald Graham in 1884 with the 1st Battalion York and Lancaster Regiment, and was present in the engagements at El Teb (slightly wounded) and Temai—severely wounded (mentioned in despatches, Brevet of Lt. Colonel, Medal with Clasp, and Khedive's Star).
[14] Major Quill served with the 2nd Battalion York and Lancaster Regiment throughout the Egyptian war of 1882, and was present in the engagements at El Magfar and Tel-el-Mahuta in the two actions at Kassasin, and at the battle of Tel-el-Kebir (Medal with Clasp, and Khedive's Star).
[15] Major Whitaker served in the Afghan war in 1880 as Superintendent of Army Signalling with the Koorum Field Force (Medal).
[17] Major Kirkpatrick served with the 2nd Battalion York and Lancaster Regiment throughout the Egyptian war of 1882, and was present in the engagements at El Magfar and Tel-el-Mahuta, in the two actions at Kassasin, and at the battle of Tel-el-Kebir (Brevet of Major, Medal with Clasp, and Khedive's Star).
[18] Major Colhoun, Captains Scholes, Grosvenor, Maul, and Woodford served with the 2nd Battalion York and Lancaster Regiment throughout the Egyptian war of 1882, and were present in the engagements at El Magfar and Tel-el-Mahuta, in the two actions at Kassasin, and at the battle of Tel-el-Kebir (Medal with Clasp, and Khedive's Star).
[19] Major Lousada served with the 2nd Battalion York and Lancaster Regiment throughout the Egyptian war of 1882, and was present in the engagements at El Magfar and Tel-el-Mahuta, in the two actions at Kassasin, and at the battle of Tel-el-Kebir (Medal with Clasp, 4th Class of the Medjidie, and Khedive's Star).
[22] Captain Tebbitt served in the expedition to the Soudan under Sir Gerald Graham in 1884 with the 1st Battalion York and Lancaster Regiment, and was present in the engagements at El Teb and Temai (Medal with Clasp, 4th Class of the Medjidie, and Khedive's Star).
[23] Captains Broughton and Smyth served in the expedition to the Soudan under Sir Gerald Graham in 1884 with the 1st Battalion York and Lancaster Regiment, and were present in the engagements at El Teb and Temai (Medal with Clasp, and Khedive's Star).
[24] Major Plumer served in the expedition to the Soudan under Sir Gerald Graham in 1884 as Adjutant of the 1st Battalion York and Lancaster Regiment, and was present in the engagements at El Teb and Temai (mentioned in despatches, Medal with Clasp, 4th Class of the Medjidie, and Khedive's Star).
[31] Captain Galindo served in the Egyptian war of 1882 with the Indian Contingent (Medal, and Khedive's Star).

Record of the Services of the 1st Battalion York and Lancaster Regiment—formerly the 65th (2nd York North Riding) Regiment.

Raised as 2nd Battalion 12th Regiment in 1756. Became 65th Regiment, 1758. West Indies, to 1764. America, to 1777. England, to 1783. (A detachment served as Marines at the relief of Gibraltar, 1782.) Ireland, to 1784. America, to 1791. Nova Scotia, to 1793. West Indies, to 1795. England and Scotland, to 1800. Cape of Good Hope, to 1802. Ceylon, to 1803. East Indies, to 1809. Gulf of Persia, to 1810. Isle of France, to 1811. East Indies, to 1819. Gulf of Persia, to 1820. East India and Arabia, to 1823. England and Scotland, to 1824. Ireland, to 1829. West Indies, to 1837. Nova Scotia, to 1838. America, to 1841. England, to 1843. Ireland, to 1845. England, to 1846. New South Wales, to Nov. 1846. New Zealand, to 1865. England, to 1867. Ireland, to 1871. East Indies, to 1882. (Became 1st Battalion York and Lancaster Regiment, 1881.) Aden, to 1884. Egypt, to April 1884. England, to 1889. Ireland, 1889.

Record of the Services of the 2nd Battalion York and Lancaster Regiment (formerly the 84th Regiment).

Raised in 1758, and proceeded to India, to 1763. America and Canada, to 1783. England, to 1794. (2nd Battalion raised in 1794, reduced in 1795). Flushing, 1794. England, to 1796. Cape of Good Hope, to 1799. India, to 1819. [2nd Battalion raised in 1808. Flanders, to 1809. The Peninsula, to 1814 (battle of Nive). England, to 1819, and incorporated in 1st Battalion.] England, to 1827. Jamaica, to 1838. England, to 1842. India, to 1859 (relief of Lucknow under General Havelock). England, to 1865. Malta, to 1867. Jamaica, to 1870. Halifax, N.S., to 1871. Ireland, to 1873. Channel Islands, to 1874. England, to 1882. Egypt, Aug. to Oct. 1882. England, to Oct. 1883. Bermuda, to 1886. Halifax, N.S., to 1888. West Indies, to 1891. South Africa, 1891.

Continuation of Notes to the North Staffordshire Regiment.

[1] General Lewis served with the Grenadier Guards in the Crimea from the 13th August 1855; commanded Divisions of the Army in the Trenches, and the Grenadier Guards at the taking of Sebastopol (Medal with Clasp, Turkish Medal, and 5th Class of the Medjidie).
[7] Major Higginson served in the Soudan campaign in 1885 (Medal with Clasp, and Khedive's Star).
[8] Captain Hawtayne served in the Soudan campaign in 1885 with the Egyptian Army (Medal with Clasp, 4th Class of the Medjidie, and Khedive's Star). Served with the expedition up the River Gambia against the Native Chief, Fodey Kabba, in 1892, as Superintendent of the Gambia Police Force.
[9] Captain Robinson served with the expedition to the Gambia in 1892 under Colonel Ellis including the capture of Toniataba (Medal with Clasp).

Record of the Services of the 1st Battalion North Staffordshire Regiment (formerly the 64th Regiment).

Constituted 64th Foot in 1758, and proceeded to Island of Martinique, 1759 to 1763. England, to 1773. North America, to 1782. Jamaica, to 1784. England, to 1786. Ireland, to 1793. West Indies, to 1795 (capture of St. Lucia). England, 1795. Gibraltar, to 1796. England, 1796. Ireland, to 1799. England, to 1801. West Indies, to 1813 (capture of Surinam). Halifax, Nova Scotia, to 1815. Continent of Europe, to 1816. England, to 1818. Gibraltar, to 1827. Ireland, to 1834. Jamaica, to 1840. America, to 1843. England, to 1845. Ireland, to 1849. East Indies, to 1861 (Persian war of 1856—battles of Reshire, Bushire, and Khooshab—and Indian Mutiny, relief of Lucknow under General Havelock). England, to 1865. Ireland, to 1867. Malta, to 1872. Ireland, to 1874. Scotland, to 1875. England, to 1878. Channel Islands, to 1879. Ireland, to 1883. England, to 1884. West Indies, to 1886. South African Mauritius, 1886.

Record of the Services of the 2nd Battalion Prince of Wales' North Staffordshire Regiment (formerly the 98th Prince of Wales' Regiment).

Raised in 1824, and proceeded to Cape of Hope. To England, 1837. To China, 1841. To India, 1846. To England, 1855. To India, 1857. To England, 1867. To West Indies, 1873. To Malta, 1875. To India, 1880. To Aden, 1886. To England, 1888.

1st Batt., Buttevant.
2nd Batt., Mhow, Bombay.] **The Durham Light Infantry.** [Regimental District No. 68.—Sunderland.] 314

Formerly the 68th (Durham—Lt. Inf.) and the 106th (Bombay Lt. Inf.) Regiments.
(The 3rd and 4th Battalions are formed of the 1st and 2nd Durham Militia respectively.)
The United Red and White Rose. "SALAMANCA" "VITTORIA" "PYRENEES" "NIVELLE" "ORTHES"
"PENINSULA" "ALMA" "INKERMAN" "SEVASTOPOL" "PERSIA" "RESHIRE"
"BUSHIRE" "KOOSHAB" "NEW ZEALAND."

Years'Ser. Full Pay	Half Pay			Ensign or 2nd Lieut.	Lieut.	Captain.	Brev.Maj.	Major
28	...	**Colonel.**—Sir William Augustus Fyers,[1] KCB. *Ensign,* p 17 Oct. 34; *Lieut.* p 20 May 36; *Capt.* p 7 May 47; *Bt.Major,* 2 Nov. 55; *Bt.Lt.Colonel,* 26 Dec. 56; *Major,* 16 June 57; *Colonel,* 8 June 64; *Major General,* 23 Aug. 69; *Lieut.General,* 1 July 81; *Colonel Durham Light Infantry,* 26 May 94.							
22	...	**Lieutenant Colonels.**—1 William Gordon, *Ensign,* 8 Jan. 68; *Lieut.* p 22 April 71; *Capt.* 9 Feb. 76; *Major,* 15 Nov. 83; *Lt.Colonel,* 3 Oct. 92.							
		2 Frederick Henry Whitby, *Lieut.* 9 Aug. 73; *Capt.* 23 July 79; *Major,* 20 Jan. 84; *Lt.Colonel,* 27 Aug. 94.							
		Majors.							
29	...	1 Arthur Law Woodland..................		p 1 Feb. 67	p 32 Oct. 70	29 June 75	......	23 Mar. 84
21	...	2 Henry Donald Rosseter		......	11 Feb. 75	2 Feb. 81	......	8 Oct. 90
21	...	p.s.c. Frank Robert Crofton Carleton, Dep. Assist. Adj. Gen. War Office, 22 Aug. 94		......	21 Sept. 74	8 June 81	......	28 July 91
21	...	1 Alwyn de Blaquière Valentino Paget...		......	11 Feb. 75	24 Aug. 81	......	21 Oct. 91
21	...	1 Herbert Swayne FitzGerald[3] (*Depot*) ...		......	11 Feb. 75	5 July 82	......	31 Oct. 92
20	...	2 George Markham Davison		......	13 June 75	14 Mar. 83	......	11 Apr. 94
19	...	2 George Morley Saunders.................		......	26 Aug. 76	20 Jan. 84	......	11 Apr. 94
17	...	1 William Kingsdown Curling.............		......	24 June 78	1 Sept. 84	......	27 Aug. 94
		Captains.							
17	...	1 Thomas Roger Johnson-Smyth[4]		14 Sept. 78	30 Apr. 79	12 Feb. 85		
18	...	2 William Maxwell Menzies		15 Aug. 77	30 Oct. 79	6 Sept. 85		
16	...	2 Arthur Trelawny Payne		11 Oct. 79	17 Mar. 80	5 May 87		
18	...	Walter Charteris Ross,[9] *Adjutant* G. I. P. Railway Vols. 19 Nov. 90		29 Sept. 77	16 July 80	5 Nov. 87		
17	...	Francis Gerald Kenyon-Slaney, *Adj.* 2 Vol.Bn. Hampshire Regt. 1 Oct. 91		1 May 78	2 Feb. 81	28 Nov. 87		
16	...	1 Charles Vere Gunning.....................		9 July 79	1 July 81	5 July 88		
16	...	1 Hon. William Lyonel Vane		14 Jan. 80	1 July 81	29 Oct. 88		
15	...	p.s.c. Frederick Spencer Robb, *Brigade Major, Aldershot,* 19 Nov. 92		11 Aug. 80	1 July 81	2 Feb. 89		
15	...	1 George Clavell Mansel...................		11 Aug. 80	1 July 81	1 Apr. 89		
15	...	1 John Ernest Bush[7]........................		23 Oct. 80	1 July 81	17 Apr. 89		
15	...	Laurence Parke, *Adjutant* 5 Vol. Bn. *Cheshire Regt.* 2 Apr. 94		19 Feb. 81	1 July 81	17 Apr. 89		
15	...	Geo. Wilfred Keane, *Army Service Corps*		19 Feb. 81	1 July 81	27 Aug. 90		
15	...	Richard John Gardiner, *O. S. Dept.*.....		19 Feb. 81	1 July 81	27 Aug. 90		
14	...	2 Francis Honorius SissonSitwell (*Depot*)		......	28 Jan. 82	27 Aug. 90		
13	...	2 William Tennant Buck[7]		......	10 May 82	28 July 91		
12	...	2 Henry de Beauvoir de Lisle,[8] *DSO.* *Adjutant* 1 July 92		......	10 Mar. 83	1 Oct. 91		
12	...	Charles Edward Wilson,[7] *Adjutant* 1 Bn. B.B. & C.I.R. Vols. 23 Nov. 93		......	6 Feb. 84	1 Oct. 91		
12	...	1 Alfred William Baker[7]		......	6 Feb. 84	19 Apr. 93		
11	...	2 Nicholas Trafalgar Biddulph[5]		......	14 May 84	11 Apr. 94		
11	...	1 Ernest St. George Pratt, *Adjutant* 19 Nov. 92		......	23 Aug. 84	11 Apr. 94		
11	...	Charles Massy Mathew,[7] *Ordnance Store Department*		......	23 Aug. 84	11 Apr. 94		
10	...	1 Lincoln Edmund Cary Elwes............		......	29 Aug. 85	11 Apr. 94		
10	...	2 Charles Camac Luard[10]...................		......	2 Sept. 85	13 Feb. 95		
		Lieutenants.							
10	...	1 Bernard William Lynedoch M'Mahon...		......	25 Nov. 85			
10	...	2 Michael Derwass Goring Jones............		......	30 Jan. 86			
8	...	1 Robert Maxwell D'Arcy-Hildyard		14 Sept. 87	20 Nov. 89			
8	...	2 Edgar Assheton Iremonger, *Station Staff Officer, Colaba Depot,* 4 Apr. 94		21 Dec. 87	20 Nov. 89			
7	...	2 Robert Purdon Robertson-Glasgow (*Depot*)		22 Aug. 88	27 Aug. 90			
7	...	1 Robert Francis Bell........................		22 Aug. 88	27 Aug. 90			
7	...	1 Walter Charles Lascelles (*Depot*)		28 Nov. 88	25 Feb. 91			
7	...	1 Robert Charles Saville..................		30 Jan. 89	10 May 91			
6	...	2 Hanway Robert Cumming, *Comdt.* *Rest Camp, Khandwa*		8 June 89	28 July 91			
6	...	1 Oswald Birley Harter..................		8 June 89	15 Aug. 91			
6	...	2 Ernest Baseley Hales		8 June 89	19 Sept. 91			
6	...	1 Hubert Horatio Shirley Morant........		16 Oct. 89	19 Nov. 92			
5	...	1 Aubrey Charles Tucker		29 Nov. 90	15 Mar. 93			
5	...	Francis Owen-Lewis		18 Feb. 91	15 Mar. 93			
4	...	1 Joseph Arthur Crosthwaite		9 Sept. 91	19 Apr. 93			
4	...	Robert Holme Bankes Anderson........		10 Oct. 91	11 Apr. 94			
4	...	1 Anthony Edward Mortimer Bacon......		10 Oct. 91	11 Apr. 94			
4	...	2 Henry Benfield Des Vœux Wilkinson...		9 Jan. 92	29 July 94			
4	...	2 Horace Charles Oakes		12 Mar. 92	30 July 94			
3	...	2 Archibald Francis Stewart		28 Sept. 92	4 Aug. 94			
3	...	2 Frank Martin		28 Sept. 92	13 Feb. 95			
		Second Lieutenants.							
3	...	2 D'Arcy Wentworth Mander		17 Dec. 92				
3	...	1 Bryan Charles Fairfax		8 Mar. 93				
2	...	1 Edward Algernon Cleader Blake		26 Apr. 93				
2	...	2 Alexander Kirkland Robb		20 May 93				

The Durham Light Infantry.

Years' Ser.		SECOND LIEUTENANTS.	2ND LIEUT.
Full Pay	Half Pay		
2	...	2 William John Ainsworth	19 July 93
1	...	2 Edward Du Pré Herford Moore	2 June 94
1	...	1 George Leslie Cochrane	13 June 94
1	...	1 Charles Clarence Corbett	10 Oct. 94
1	...	2 Frederic Hugh Carter	10 Oct. 94
1	...	2 Eustace Arthur Lang	10 Oct. 94
1	...	2 Ralph Ellis Carr Hall	12 Dec. 94
1	...	John Murray Davies	6 Mar. 95

Paymasters.—2 Charles C. Luard, Lieut. 2 Battalion (acting).

Quarter Masters.—2 William John Qualtrough,[7] 1 Sept. 86; *Hon. Lieut.*
                  1 John Henry Liebrecht, 4 Oct. 93; *Hon. Lieut.*

(9 / 2)

Facings White.—*Agents*, Messrs. Holt and Co.
1st Batt. returned from India, 13 Apr. 1887.
2nd Battalion embarked for Egypt, 14 Feb. 1885.

[1] Sir William Fyers served in the 40th Regiment at the capture of Kurrachee in 1839. Commanded a Company of the 40th throughout the operations in Candahar and Affghanistan in 1841 and 1842 (Medal), and was present in the actions at Kale Shukh, Kunje Kuk, Pangwaie, Tiloo Khan, and Baba Wallie; also at the relief of Khalat-i-Ghilzee; subsequently at Killa Aziem, Goaine, Ghuznee, and occupation of Cabool; and in all the affairs in which the Candahar Division of the Army of Affghanistan, under General Nott, was engaged in its progress through the Khcord Cabool, Tezeen, Jugdulluck, and Khyber Passes. Served the Eastern campaign of 1854-55 with the 2nd Battalion Rifle Brigade, including the battle of Alma, siege and fall of Sebastopol, and attack of the Redan on the 8th September. In October 1854 he commanded a party of Rifles and 23rd Fusiliers from Piquets of the Light Division, and repulsed an attack made by the enemy's riflemen on our Piquets, and he commanded the Covering Party of 200 men on the attack of the Redan (Medal with two Clasps, Brevets of Major and Lt.Colonel, Knight of the Legion of Honor, Turkish Medal, and 5th Class of the Medjidie). Served in the Indian campaign of 1857-59, commanded 2nd Battalion (7 Companies) at Cawnpore, after effecting a junction with the force under General Windham on the 27th Nov. 1857 after effecting a forced march of 38 miles; captured two 18-pounder guns of position on the 28th November, and commanded the 7 Companies throughout the actions there under Lord Clyde, and at the subsequent capture of Lucknow (mentioned in despatches, *CB.*, Medal with Clasp).

[2] Major FitzGerald served as Adjutant with the 15th Sikhs in the Afghan war in 1880; accompanied Sir Frederick Roberts in the march to Candahar, and was present at the reconnaissance of the 31st August and at the battle of Candahar (Medal with Clasp, and Bronze Decoration). Served with the Soudan Frontier Field Force in 1885-86, and was present in the engagement at Giniss (Medal, and Khedive's Star).

[4] Captain Johnson-Smyth served with the Soudan Frontier Field Force in 1885-86, and was present in the engagement at Giniss (Medal, and Khedive's Star).

[5] Captain Biddulph served with the Soudan Frontier Field Force in 1885-86 (Medal, and Khedive's Star).

[7] Captains Bush, Buck, Wilson, Baker, and Mathew, and Lieut. Qualtrough served with the Soudan Frontier Field Force in 1885-86, and were present in the engagement at Giniss (Medal, and Khedive's Star).

[8] Captain de Lisle served with the Soudan Frontier Field Force in 1885-86 with the Mounted Infantry, including the attack on the Ambigole Wells and the engagement at Giniss (mentioned in despatches, *DSO.*, Medal, and Khedive's Star).

[9] Captain Ross served in the Afghan war in 1879-80 on Transport duty with the Koorum Field Force (Medal).

[10] Captain Luard served with the Zhob Field Force in 1890 as Assistant Superintendent of Army Signalling.

Record of the Services of the 1st Battalion Durham Light Infantry (formerly the 68th Durham Light Infantry).

Raised in 1756 as the 2nd Battalion Royal Welsh Fusiliers. Constituted 68th Foot in 1758, and proceeded to Cherbourg and St. Malo. To England, 1758. To Scotland, 1762. To Ireland, 1763. To Antigua, 1764. To England, 1773. To Scotland, 1774. To Ireland, 1776. To England, 1782. (Entitled "Durham.") To the Channel Islands, 1783. To Gibraltar, 1785. To the West Indies, 1794. To England, 1796. To Ireland, 1797. To England, 1800. To the West Indies, 1801. To England, 1806. (Made Light Infantry, 1808.) To Walcheren, 1809. To the Peninsula, 1811 (battles of Salamanca, Vittoria, Pyrenees, Nivelle, Orthes, and Toulouse). To Ireland, 1814. To Canada, 1818. To Ireland, 1829. To Scotland, 1833. To Gibraltar, 1834. To Jamaica, 1838. To Canada, 1841. To England, 1844. To Ireland, 1846. To Malta, 1851. To the Crimea, 1854 (battles of Alma and Inkerman and siege of Sebastopol). To the Ionian Islands, 1856. To England, 1857. To Burmah, 1860. To New Zealand, 1864 (war in 1864-65). To England, 1866. To India, 1872. To England, 1887. To Ireland, 1893.

Record of the Services of the 2nd Battalion Durham Light Infantry (formerly the 106th Bombay Light Infantry).

Raised at Poona as the 2nd Bombay European Light Infantry in 1840. To Belgaum, 1844. To Aden, 1846. Right Wing to Poona, 1848. To Belgaum, 1849. To Kurrachee, 1853. To Persia, 1856 (battles of Reshire, Bushire, and Khooshab). To Belgaum, 1857. To Bombay, 1860. To Neemuch, 1861. Entitled "106th (Bombay) Light Infantry," 1861. To Nusseerabad, 1864. To Meean Meer, 1867. To Umballa, 1868. To Jhansi and Nowgong, 1870. To England, 1874. To Ireland, 1880. Entitled "2nd Battalion Durham Light Infantry," 1881. To Gibraltar and Malta, 1882. To Egypt, 1885. To India, 1887.

1st Batt., Malta.
2nd Batt., Fyzabad, Bengal. } **The Highland Light Infantry.** [Regimental District No. 71.—Hamilton. **317**

Formerly the 71st (Highland—Light Infantry) and the 74th (Highlanders) Regiments.
(The 3rd and 4th Battalions are formed of the 1st Lanark Royal Militia.)

"CARNATIC" "SHOLINGHUR" "MYSORE" "HINDOOSTAN" "ASSAYE" (with the Elephant). "SERINGAPATAM" "CAPE OF GOOD HOPE, 1806" "ROLEIA" "VIMIERA" "CORUNNA" "BUSACO" "FUENTES D'ONOR" "CIUDAD RODRIGO" "BADAJOZ" "ALMARAZ" "SALAMANCA" "VITTORIA" "PYRENEES" "NIVELLE" "NIVE" "ORTHES" "TOULOUSE" "PENINSULA" "WATERLOO" "SOUTH AFRICA, 1851-2-3" "SEVASTOPOL" "CENTRAL INDIA" "EGYPT, 1882" "TEL-EL-KEBIR."

Years' Ser. Full Pay	Half Pay		ENSIGN OR 2ND LIEUT.	LIEUT.	CAPTAIN.	BREV. MAJ.	MAJOR.
		Colonel.—Walter Douglas Phillipps Patton-Bethune,¹ Ensign, P28 Sept. 38; Lt. P3 Nov. 40; Capt. P12 May 46; Major, 27 Feb. 52; Brevet Lieut.Colonel, 28 May 53; Colonel, 28 Nov. 54; Lieut.Colonel, 11 May 62; Major General, 1 Jan. 68; Lieutenant General, 14 Sept. 75; General, 1 Oct. 77; Colonel 74th Foot, 8 Oct. 76.					
27	...	Lieutenant Colonels.—2 *p.s.c.* John Harry Smith Craigie, Ensign, 8 July 68; Lieut. P17 Nov. 69; Capt. 2 Mar. 78; Major, 6 May 82; Lt.Colonel, 3 Apr. 93.					
27	...	1 Francis Maude Reid, Ensign, P8 July 68; Lieut. P27 Aug. 70; Capt. 20 Apr. 78; Major, 7 Apr. 86; Lt.Colonel, 22 Nov. 94.					
		MAJORS.					
26	...	2 Richard Dufflin Buckley Rutherford,⁵ Commdt. Nynee Tal Depot 17 Nov. 94 }	P 9 Oct. 69	28 Oct. 71	29 Apr. 79	......	24 Feb. 86
24	...	1 Edmund Spencer	28 Oct. 71	28 Oct. 71	30 Apr. 79	......	3 Apr. 89
24	...	Sir Claude Maxwell MacDonald,⁶ KCMG. Commissioner and Consul General, Niger Coast Protectorate, 1 Jan. 91 }	......	16 Mar. 72	12 Feb. 81	18 Nov. 82	14 Sept. 89
22	...	2 Henry Robert Kelham⁴	......	28 May 73	7 Jan. 82	......	31 Jan. 90
22	...	1 Carteret Walter Carey⁷ (*Depot*)	......	12 Nov. 73	25 Jan. 82	......	22 Nov. 90
21	...	Richard Eyre Goold-Adams,³ Instructor Roy. Mil. College 10 Feb. 88 }	......	13 June 74	11 Dec. 82	......	23 Nov. 92
22	...	1 James Mitchell-Innes	......	12 Nov. 73	25 Oct. 84	......	22 Nov. 94
22	...	2 Ernest Digby Mansel	......	28 Feb. 74	10 Oct. 85	......	12 Dec. 94
		CAPTAINS.					
18	...	1 John Arthur Milne Gardiner	......	12 May 77	20 Sept. 86		
20	...	¥C William Mordaunt Marsh Edwards,⁹ *Adj.* 3 *Battalion* 1 *Jan.* 92... }	......	22 Mar. 76	23 Mar. 87		
17	...	2 Ernest Alfred Crowder Garland⁴	......	11 Nov. 78	24 Jan. 88		
19	...	2 Cecil Charles Cavendish, *Station Staff Officer, Kussowlie Depot* 6 Nov. 94 ... }	......	28 Apr. 76	10 Feb. 88		
19	...	Harrison Midwood,¹² *Adjutant* 3 *Vol. Bn. Highland Light Inf.* 1 Nov. 90..}	......	11 Sept. 76	11 Sept. 88		
18	...	2 Robert Follett M. F. M. Synge¹¹	15 Aug. 77	1 July 81	15 Dec. 88		
17	...	1 Hon. Henry James Anson	11 May 78	1 July 81	3 Apr. 89		
16	...	Ingram Cosmo Conway-Gordon, *Adj.* 2 *Vol.Bn. Highland Lt. Inf.*14 Nov.92 }	21 June 79	1 July 81	6 May 89		
16	...	Alfred Granville Balfour, *Adjutant* 2 *Vol. Bn. Scottish Rifles* 1 Sept. 92 }	6 Aug. 79	1 July 81	1 Nov. 90		
16	...	John Dutton Hunt, *District Inspector of Musketry, London,* 1 Aug. 91 ...... }	13 Aug. 79	1 July 81	22 Nov. 90		
16	...	1 John Richardson	13 Aug. 79	1 July 81	22 Nov. 90		
14	...	Gordon Thomas Jas. Carey,¹² *Adj.* 3 *Vol. Bn. R. Fusiliers* 17 Dec. 92 }	......	22 Oct. 81	18 Feb. 91		
13	...	2 Spencer William Scrase-Dickins,¹³ *with Provisional Battalion*............ }	......	10 May 82	18 Feb. 91		
13	...	Fuller Whistler, *Adjutant* 1 *Volunteer Battalion* 15 June 93 .... }	......	9 Sept. 82	3 Feb. 92		
13	...	2 George Clifton I. Stockwell	......	9 Sept. 82	1 Sept. 92		
12	...	Horace Francis Kays,¹⁴ *Adjutant* 9 *Lanark Volunteer Rifles* 7 Jan. 93 }	......	5 Dec. 83	26 Oct. 92		
11	...	1 Tyrell Cartor Ross	......	23 Aug. 84	14 Nov. 92		
11	...	Alexander Francis Evans-Lombe, *Adjutant* 4 *Battalion* 1 Jan. 95 .... }	......	7 Feb. 85	14 Nov. 92		
10	...	1 Francis Myles Sandys-Lumsdaine	......	25 Nov. 85	17 Dec. 92		
9	...	2 Robert William Hawthorn Ronaldson, **Adjutant** 26 Apr. 93 .... }	......	25 Aug. 86	17 May 93		
9	...	1 Arthur Alexander Wolfe-Murray	......	25 Aug. 86	15 June 93		
9	...	2 Herbert Chaworth Fergusson	......	10 Nov. 86	22 Nov. 94		
8	...	1 Conrad Ernest Noyes	6 July 87	3 Apr. 89	1 Jan. 95		
		LIEUTENANTS.					
7	...	2 John Henry Purvis	16 May 88	18 Dec. 89			
7	...	1 Laurence Evan Maberly.........	22 Aug. 88	26 Apr. 90			
7	...	1 Alexander Frederick Lambton	22 Aug. 88	6 May 90			
7	...	1 Allan Ashton Elliott-Lockhart, with Provisional Battalion............ }	8 Dec. 88	22 Oct. 90			
7	...	2 Walter Neilson	8 Dec. 88	22 Nov. 90			
7	...	1 James William Alston Cowan (*Depot*)	30 Jan. 89	18 Feb. 91			
7	...	1 Edward Roden Hill	23 Mar. 89	4 May 91			
6	...	1 George Edward Begbie, **Adjutant** 14 Jan. 94 }	10 May 89	3 Feb. 92			
6	...	1 William Malcolm Fleming Hamilton...	14 Aug. 89	1 Sept. 92			
5	...	2 Henry James Thackeray	8 Nov. 90	14 Nov. 92			
5	...	1 George Tyrie Brand Wilson	17 Jan. 91	23 Nov. 92			
5	...	1 Edward Leyland Cooke Feilden	4 Feb. 91	24 Nov. 92			
5	...	1 Henry Geoffrey Noel de Berry	25 Mar. 91	17 Dec. 92			
4	...	1 Charles Edward Andrews	23 May 91	17 May 93			
4	...	Ranald Martin	25 July 91	15 June 93			
4	...	1 Thomas MacGregor Twynam	10 Oct. 91	25 June 93			
4	...	1 Robert John Alwynne Haldane	5 Dec. 91	14 Jan. 94			
4	...	1 Francis Charles Minshull Ford	20 Feb. 92	6 June 94			
3	...	2 John Crum Grahame (*Depot*).........	9 Apr. 92	22 Nov. 94			
3	...	2 Edward Armstrong	19 Oct. 92	1 Jan. 95			
		SECOND LIEUTENANTS.					
3	...	2 Basil Charles Mowbray	26 Oct. 92				
3	...	2 Robert Emile Shepherd Prentice	7 Dec. 92				

X

The Highland Light Infantry.

Temp.Ser.	Half	SECOND LIEUTENANTS.	2ND LIEUT.
Full Pay.	Pay.		
3	...	2 Edward Gordon Stanley Creek	15 Mar. 93
2	...	1 Arthur Neil Edmondstone Browne	20 May 93
2	...	2 Alan Colquhoun Grant	21 Oct. 93
2	...	2 Charles Robertson	21 Oct. 93
2	...	1 Robert Warren Hastings Anderson	7 Mar. 94
2	...	2 Henry John Pack-Beresford	18 July 94
1	...	2 Thomas Francis Murray	10 Oct. 94
1	...	2 Denis Wellesley Maxwell	20 Feb. 95
a	...	John James Ronald	6 Mar. 95
1	...	Edward Lewis Rolland	6 Mar. 95
1	...	Thomas Patrick Milne Home	6 Mar. 95
1	...	Henry Townsend Corbet Singleton	6 Mar. 95
22	...	*Paymasters.*—2 Robert Johnston, 10 Aug. 83; Qr. Mr. 6 Dec. 73; Lt. 12 May 75; Hon. Major, 10 Aug. 93.	
13	...	*Quarter Masters.*—1 William Bissett, 1 Apr. 82; Hon. Captain, 1 Apr. 92.	
12	...	2 Thomas Litster, 7 Feb. 83; Hon. Captain 7 Feb. 93.	

Facings Yellow.—*Agents.* Sir C. R. M'Grigor, Bt. and Co.
1st Battalion embarked for Malta, 9 Feb. 1895. 2nd Battalion embarked for India, 1 Oct. 1884.

1 General Patton-Bethune served with the 74th throughout the Kaffir war of 1851-53 (Medal), and was present in all the operations; commanded the Regiment in the Field from November 1851 until October 1852 (mentioned in despatches, Brevet of Lt. Colonel). Served in the Eastern campaign of 1854, and was present (attached to the Staff) at the battle of Balaklava and Inkerman, and was also present with the Head Quarter Staff as an amateur at the battle of the Alma, the affairs of Bulganac and M'Kenzie's Farm, and capture of Balaklava (Medal with four Clasps, 5th Class of the Medjidie, and Turkish Medal). He was on Field Service with a Madras Column during the Indian Mutiny in 1857.

2 Major Goold-Adams served in the Afghan war in 1880, and took part in the march to Candahar with the force under Major General Phayre (Medal). Served with the 2nd Battalion Highland Light Infantry in the Egyptian war of 1882, and was present at the battle of Tel-el-Kebir (Medal with Clasp, and Khedive's Star).

4 Major Kelham, Captains Garland and Litster served with the 2nd Battalion Highland Light Infantry in the Egyptian war of 1882, and were present at the battle of Tel-el-Kebir (Medal with Clasp, and Khedive's Star).

5 Major Rutherford served in the Afghan war in 1878-79 in the Transport Department (Medal). Served in the expedition to the Soudan in 1884 with the 1st Battalion York and Lancaster Regiment, and was present in the engagement at Temai (Medal with Clasp, and Khedive's Star).

6 Sir Claude MacDonald served with the 2nd Battalion Highland Light Infantry in the Egyptian war of 1882, and was present at the battle of Tel-el-Kebir (mentioned in despatches. Brevet of Major, Medal with Clasp, and Khedive's Star); also served in the Soudan Expedition in 1884 with the 1st Battalion of the Black Watch, and was present in the engagements at El Teb and Temai—slightly wounded (4th Class of the Osmanieh, two Clasps).

7 Major C. W. Carey served as Adjutant with the 2nd Battalion Highland Light Infantry in the Egyptian war of 1882, and was present at the battle of Tel-el-Kebir (Medal with Clasp, 4th Class of the Medjidie, and Khedive's Star).

9 Captain Edwards served with the 2nd Battalion Highland Light Infantry in the Egyptian war of 1882, and was present at the battle of Tel-el-Kebir—wounded (Victoria Cross, Medal with Clasp, and Khedive's Star): was awarded the V.C. "for the conspicuous bravery displayed by him during the battle of Tel-el-Kebir, on the 13th September 1882, in leading a party of the Highland Light Infantry to storm a redoubt. Lieutenant Edwards (who was in advance of his party) with great gallantry rushed alone into the battery, killed the Artillery Officer who was in charge, and was himself knocked down by a gunner with a rammer, and only rescued by the timely arrival of three men of his regiment."

11 Captain Syngo served with the 2nd Battalion Highland Light Infantry in the Egyptian war of 1882, and was present at the battle of Tel-el-Kebir—wounded (Medal with Clasp, and Khedive's Star). Served with the Burmese Expedition in 1887-92 (Medal with Clasp).

13 Captains Midwood and G. T. J. Carey served with the 2nd Battalion Highland Light Infantry in the Egyptian war of 1882, and were present at the battle of Tel-el-Kebir—severely wounded (Medal with Clasp, and Khedive's Star).

10 Captain Scrase-Dickins served in the Egyptian war of 1882 with the 2nd Battalion Highland Light Infantry, and was present at the battle of Tel-el-Kebir (Medal with Clasp, and Khedive's Star). [See also Civil Decorations for Gallantry, "Hart's Annual Army List," page 786.]

14 Captain Kays served with the Miranzai Expedition in 1891 under Sir William Lockhart as Superintendent of Signalling (mentioned in despatches, Medal with Clasp).

Record of the Services of the 2nd Battalion Highland Light Infantry (formerly the 74th Highlanders).

Raised in 1787, remaining at home till 1789. India, to 1805 (storming of Seringapatam and battle of Assaye). England and Scotland, to 1809. Ireland, to 1810. The Peninsula, to 1814 (battles of Busaco, Fuentes d'Onor, Ciudad Rodrigo, Badajoz, Salamanca, Vittoria, Pyrenees, Nivelle, Orthes, and Toulouse). Ireland, to 1818. North America, to 1828. West Indies, to 1830. Ireland, to 1834. West Indies, to 1841. Canada, to 1845. England and Scotland, to 1847. Ireland, to 1851. South Africa, to 1854. India, to 1864. England and Scotland, to 1866. Ireland, to 1868. Gibraltar, to 1872. Malta, to 1876. Straits Settlements, to 1878. Hong Kong, to 1879. Straits Settlements, to 1880. England and Scotland, to 1882. Egypt, to 1883 (war of 1882, battle of Tel-el-Kebir). England, to 1884. To India, 1884.

Seaforth Highlanders (Ross-shire Buffs, The Duke of Albany's). 318

1st. Batt., Tipperary.
2nd Batt., Ferozepore, Bengal. *Formerly the 72nd* [Regimental District No. 72.—Fort George.
(*Duke of Albany's Own Highlanders*) *and the 78th* (*Highland—Ross-shire Buffs*) *Regts*
(The 3rd Battalion is formed of the Highland Rifle Militia.)
"Cuidich'n Rhi." The late Duke of York's Cypher and Coronet. "CARNATIC" "MYSORE" "HINDOOSTAN" "ASSAYE" (with the Elephant). "CAPE OF GOOD HOPE, 1806" "MAIDA" "JAVA" "SOUTH AFRICA, 1835" "SEVASTOPOL" "PERSIA" "KOOSHAB" "LUCKNOW" "CENTRAL INDIA" "PIWAR KOTAL" "CHARASIAH" "KABUL, 1879" "KANDAHAR, 1880" "AFGHANISTAN, 1878-80" "EGYPT, 1882" "TEL-EL-KEBIR."

Years' Ser.							
Full Pay	Half Pay						

Colonel.—Sir William Parke,[1] *KCB.*, *Ensign*, P15 Dec. 40; *Lt.* P27 Sept. 42; *Capt.* 9 Jan. 49; *Major*, P1 Dec. 54; *Lt. Colonel*, P23 Nov. 55; *Colonel*, 26 Apr. 59; *Major General*, 6 March 68; *Lt. General*, 1 Oct.77; *General*, 1 Apr. 82; *Colonel* Worcestershire Regt., 25 July 83; *Colonel* Seaforth Highlanders, 29 Aug. 93.

32 ... **Lieutenant Colonels.**—2 Hugh Gough Grant,[3] *Ensign*, P28 July 63; *Lieut.* 26 Oct. 65; *Capt.* P5 Nov. 70; *Bt. Major*, 2 Mar. 81; *Major*, 30 Nov. 81; *Lt. Colonel*, 2 Sept. 91.
31 ... 1 Charles John Butler Stewart,[4] *Ensign*, P9 Aug. 64; *Lieut.* P9 Mar. 67; *Capt.* 28 May 73; *Major*, 28 Mar. 82; *Lt. Colonel*, 8 May 93.

		MAJORS.	ENSIGN OR 2ND LIEUT.	LIEUT.	CAPTAIN.	BREV. MAJ.	MAJOR.
29	...	1 Henry John Knight	P 9 Mar. 67	P24 July 69	27 Mar. 78		27 Mar. 83
28	...	1 Robert Hunter Murray[7] (*Bt. Lt. Col.*18 Nov. 82; *Bt. Col.* 10 Dec. 92) (*Depot*)	P18 Dec. 67	28 Oct. 71	8 Apr. 80	2 Mar. 81	17 Apr. 89
22	...	2 James Wyndham Hughes-Hallett[9]		26 June 73	2 Sept. 80		27 Mar. 90
19	...	1 James Alastair Campbell[10]		29 Nov. 76	22 Apr. 86		14 Feb. 91
22	...	2 Kenneth Ross MacKenzie[12]		9 Aug. 73	27 Mar. 83		2 Sept. 91
18	...	2 William de Bathe Hatton[13]		28 Apr. 77	27 Mar. 85		23 Nov. 92
18	...	1 Sydney Bellingham Jameson	3 Oct. 77	13 Nov. 78	18 Jan. 88		8 May 93
18	...	Herbert Sturges Barlow,[14] *Adjutant* 3 *Battalion* 10 May 93	8 Dec. 77	30 Apr. 79	15 Mar. 88		26 Jan. 94
		CAPTAINS.					
18	...	Seymour Charles Hale Monro,[15] *Station Staff Officer, Rawul Pindee,* 22 Jan. 94		17 May 77	25 Apr. 88	26 Apr. 88	
18	...	Harry Colquhoun Farquharson Macdonald,[16] *Adj.* 3 *Vol. Bn. R. Highldrs.*	13 Mar. 78	15 Dec. 79	10 Mar. 89		
17	...	George Mackintosh,[18] *Adjutant* 3 *Vol. Bn. Seaforth Highlanders* 1 Dec. 91	11 May 78	12 Feb. 81	8 May 89		
16	...	Granville Geo. Alg. Egerton,[19] *A.D.C.* to *Gen. A. J. Lyon-Fremantle,* 2 Feb. 94	13 Aug. 79	28 Feb. 81	15 May 89		
15	...	William Hugh Hunter,[20] *Adjutant Bengal-Nagpore Rifle Vols.* 11 Aug. 91	11 Aug. 80	11 Mar. 81	1 Aug. 89		
15	...	Alex. Redmond Bewley Warrand,[21] *Adj.* 1 *Volunteer Battalion* 7 July 90	11 Aug. 80	18 May 81	4 Sept. 89		
17	...	Alf. Chas. Seton-Christopher,[22] *Recruiting Staff Officer, Liverpool,* 15 Apr. 92	11 May 78	1 July 81	25 Oct. 89		
15	...	1 George Russell Tod[23]	23 Oct. 80	1 July 81	25 Oct. 89		
15	...	2 George Ramsay Elliot[24]	22 Jan. 81	1 July 81	25 Oct. 89		
15	...	Colin John Mackenzie,[25] *Dep. Assist. Adjutant General, Bengal,* 2 June 92	22 Jan. 81	1 July 81	25 Oct. 89	27 Apr. 92	
14	...	1 Arthur Andrew Spottiswoode[26]		22 Oct. 81	26 Oct. 89		
14	...	2 Chas. Fred. Salisbury Ewart[27] (*Depot*)		22 Oct. 81	29 Oct. 90		
13	...	2 James Rutherford Clark[28]		9 Sept. 82	29 Oct. 90		
13	...	1 Herbert Frederick Northey Hopkins[29]		29 July 82	14 Feb. 91		
12	...	Randal Frederick Alison, *A.D.C.* to *Major General C. F. Clery,* 1 Feb. 95		6 Feb. 84	11 Aug. 91		
11	...	Granville Cholmondeley Feilden, *Adj.* 1 *Sutherland Rifle Vols.* 16 July 94		12 Nov. 84	2 Sept. 91		
10	...	2 Wilfred Graham Moon[31] (*Depot*)		6 May 85	1 Dec. 91		
10	...	2 Douglas Campbell[32]		9 May 85	23 Nov. 92		
10	...	2 Hon. Douglas Forbes-Sempill[33]		29 Aug. 85	22 Jan. 94		
10	...	1 Aleck Stirling[34]		29 Aug. 85	26 Jan. 94		
9	...	2 Ernest Arnold Cowans[36]		10 Nov. 86	16 July 94		
8	...	1 George Machen Lumsden[37]	24 Sept. 87	4 Sept. 89	13 Sept. 94		
		LIEUTENANTS.					
8	...	2 Alan Charles Duncan Baillie[38]	19 Oct. 87	4 Sept. 89			
8	...	1 Malcolm Donald Murray,[39] *Adjutant* 19 Oct. 91	29 Feb. 88	4 Sept. 89			
7	...	1 Neil Campbell-Maclachlan	9 May 88	25 Oct. 89			
7	...	1 Evelyn Ridley Bradford	22 Aug. 88	11 June 90			
7	...	2 Harold Bessemer Galloway[40]	8 Dec. 88	29 Oct. 90			
6	...	1 Augustus M'Clintock	8 June 89	22 Apr. 91			
6	...	2 Frederick Hugh Gordon Cunliffe,[33] *Adjutant* 14 Nov. 92	26 June 89	11 Aug. 91			
6	...	1 Archibald Buchanan Ritchie	21 Sept. 89	2 Sept. 91			
6	...	1 Robert Seymour Vandeleur	21 Sept. 89	23 Sept. 91			
6	...	2 Timothy Fetherstonhaugh[33]	21 Dec. 89	1 Dec. 91			
6	...	1 Caryl John Ramsden	29 Mar. 90	4 May 92			
5	...	2 Alastair William Mathew Brodie[33]	8 Oct. 90	23 Nov. 92			
5	...	1 Lockhart Thomas Stockwell (*Depot*)	8 Oct. 90	10 May 93			
5	...	2 Algernon Bingham Anstruther Stewart	29 Nov. 90	1 June 93			
5	...	1 Henry Charles Barwick Hopkinson	25 Mar. 91	18 June 93			
4	...	1 Walter Thomas Gaisford	23 May 91	22 Jan. 94			
4	...	1 Andrew Holford Pitcairn	23 Sept. 91	26 Jan. 94			
4	...	1 Hugh Maxwell Blair	7 Nov. 91	16 July 94			
4	...	1 Ernest Cox	7 Nov. 91	13 Sept. 94			
		SECOND LIEUTENANTS.					
4	...	2 Charles Percy Frederick Radclyffe	12 Mar. 92				
3	...	1 Noel Arbuthnot Thomson	9 Apr. 92				
3	...	1 John Patrick Grant	13 July 92				
3	...	2 Reginald Hugh Hunter-Weston	7 Dec. 92				
2	...	2 Arthur Charles Bridgeman Alexander	20 May 93				
2	...	2 Kenneth Wyndham Arbuthnot	19 July 93				
2	...	2 Michael William Howard Lindsay	19 July 93				
2	...	2 Charles Braithwaite Chamley	9 Sept. 93				
2	...	1 Clifton Charles Orby Gascoigne	28 Feb. 94				
1	...	2 Claude Prendergast Doig	10 Oct. 94				
1	...	2 William Spencer Ollivant	10 Oct. 94				
1	...	1 Ronald Robert Stewart	24 Oct. 94				

Facings Yellow.
Agents, Messrs. Cox and Co.
1st Battalion returned from Bengal 882.
2nd Battalion embarked for Bombay 1879.

31 ... *Paymasters.*—2 William H. A. Denys,[47] 30 Nov. 82; *Ens.* P26 Apr. 64; *Lt.* P12 Oct. 67; *Capt.* 2 March 78.

Seaforth Highlanders (Ross-shire Buffs, The Duke of Albany's).

[1] Sir William Parke served in the Crimean campaign from 13th June 1855 (in command of the 72nd Highlanders from July), including the expedition to Kertch, siege and fall of Sebastopol, and assaults of 18th June and 8th Sept. (Medal with Clasp, Knight of the Legion of Honor, Sardinian and Turkish Medals, and 5th Class of the Medjidie). Served in India in 1857-59, was appointed 1st Class Brigadier, and commanded 2nd Brigade of the Rajpootana Field Force from March 1858 to July 1859, including the siege and fall of Kotah, on which occasion he commanded the leading Column of assault; subsequently throughout the leading operations in Central India in 1858-59, and pursuit of the rebel forces under Tantia Topee and Rao Sahib, who were attacked and defeated at Oodeypore in Dec. 1858 by the 2nd Brigade R.F. Force (received the thanks of the Governor General of India and of the Governor in Council of Bombay; Aide de Camp to the Queen and Colonel, CB., Medal with Clasp).

[3] Lt.Colonel Grant served in the Afghan war in 1879, and was present in the engagement at Ali Kheyl, and at the assault and capture of Zawa (mentioned in despatches, Brevet of Major, and Medal). Served as Brigade Major in the Mahsood Wuzeeree Expedition in 1881. Served in the Hazara Expedition in 1891 with the 2nd Battalion Seaforth Highlanders (Medal with Clasp).

[4] Lt.Colonel Stewart served in the Hazara Expedition in 1888 with the 2nd Battalion Seaforth Highlanders (Medal with Clasp), and in the Expedition in 1891 with the same Battalion (Clasp).

[7] Colonel Murray served with the 72nd Highlanders throughout the Afghan war of 1878-80 with the Kocrum, Cabul, and Cabul-Candahar Field Forces (till April 1880 as Adjutant); was present at the attack and capture of the Peiwar Kotal and in the engagement at Charasiah (mentioned in despatches), and in the operations around Cabul in December 1879; accompanied Sir Frederick Roberts in the march to Candahar, and was present at the battle of Candahar—severely wounded (mentioned in despatches, Brevet of Major, Medal with four Clasps, and Bronze Decoration). Served in the Egyptian war of 1882 as Brigade Major Infantry Brigade Indian Contingent, and was present at the battle of Tel-el-Kebir (Brevet of Lt.Colonel, Medal with Clasp, 4th Class of the Osmanieh, and Khedive's Star). Served throughout the Soudan campaign in 1885 on special service as Assistant to the Chief of the Staff, and was present in the engagement at Hasheen and at the destruction of Temai (mentioned in despatches, Clasp).

[9] Major Hughes-Hallett served with the 72nd Highlanders from the commencement of the Afghan war in 1878 till July 1879 with the Koorum Field Force, and was present at the attack and capture of the Peiwar Kotal (mentioned in despatches, Medal with Clasp). Served with the 1st Battalion Seaforth Highlanders in the Egyptian war of 1882, and was present in the engagement at Chalouf (mentioned in despatches), and at the battle of Tel-el-Kebir (Medal with Clasp, and Khedive's Star).

[10] Major J. A. Campbell served with the 72nd Highlanders in the Afghan war from February till December 1879 with the Koorum and Cabul Field Forces, and was present in the engagement at Charasiah (Medal with Clasp). Served with the 1st Battalion Seaforth Highlanders in the Egyptian war of 1882, and was present at the battle of Tel-el-Kebir (Medal with Clasp, and Khedive's Star).

[12] Major Kenneth Mackenzie served with the 78th Highlanders in the Afghan war in 1880 (Medal). Served with the Transport Department in Southern Afghanistan from 15th November 1879 to 14th February 1881. Served with the Hazara Expedition in 1888 (Medal with Clasp), and in that in 1891 (Clasp).

[13] Major Hatton served with the 78th Highlanders in the Afghan war in 1880 (Medal). Was Orderly Officer to the Brigadier General Commanding the 2nd Brigade Candahar Field Force from 19th December 1880 to the 21st March 1881. Served in the Hazara Expedition in 1891 with the 2nd Battalion Seaforth Highlanders (Medal with Clasp).

[14] Major Barlow served with the 78th Highlanders in the Afghan war in 1880 (Medal).

[15] Major Monro served with the 72nd Highlanders throughout the Afghan war of 1878-80 with the Koorum, Cabul, and Cabul-Candahar Field Forces, part of the time as Regimental Transport Officer, from April 1880 as Adjutant; was present at the attack and capture of the Peiwar Kotal (wounded), and in the engagement at Charasiah and the operations around Cabul in December 1879; accompanied Sir Frederick Roberts in the march to Candahar, and was present at the battle of Candahar—severely wounded (mentioned in despatches, Medal with four Clasps, and Bronze Decoration). Served with the 1st Battalion Seaforth Highlanders in the Egyptian war of 1882, and was present in the engagement at Chalouf and at the battle of Tel-el-Kebir (Medal with Clasp, and Khedive's Star). Accompanied Sir Charles Warren to South Africa in 1884, and served with the Bechuanaland Expedition in command of Volunteers (mentioned in despatches, Brevet of Major). Served in the Hazara Expedition in 1891 with the 2nd Battalion Seaforth Highlanders (Medal with Clasp).

[16] Captain Macdonald served with the 72nd Highlanders in the Afghan war from January 1879 with the Koorum, Cabul, and Cabul-Candahar Field Forces, including the Khost Expedition, the engagement at Charasiah, and the operations around Cabul in December 1879; accompanied Sir Frederick Roberts in the march to Candahar, and was present at the battle of Candahar (Medal with three Clasps, and Bronze Decoration). Served with the 1st Battalion Seaforth Highlanders in the Egyptian war of 1882, and was present at the battle of Tel-el-Kebir (Medal with Clasp, and Khedive's Star).

[18] Captain Mackintosh served in the Afghan war in 1880 with the 78th Highlanders (Medal). Served in the Hazara Expedition in 1888 as Orderly Officer to Colonel Cruickshank, Commanding the River Column and was present in the engagement at Kotkai (mentioned in despatches, Medal with Clasp).

[19] Captain Egerton served with the 72nd Highlanders in the Afghan war from November 1879 with the Cabul and Cabul-Candahar Field Forces, and was present in the operations around Cabul in December 1879 (dangerously wounded); accompanied Sir Frederick Roberts in the march to Candahar, and was present at the battle of Candahar (Medal with two Clasps, and Bronze Decoration). Served as Adjutant 1st Battalion Seaforth Highlanders throughout the Egyptian war of 1882, and was present at the battle of Tel-el-Kebir (Medal with Clasp, and Khedive's Star).

[20] Captain Hunter served in the Egyptian war of 1882 with the 1st Battalion Seaforth Highlanders, and was present at the battle of Tel-el-Kebir (Medal with Clasp, and Khedive's Star). Served in the Hazara Expedition in 1891 with the 2nd Battalion Seaforth Highlanders (Medal with Clasp).

[21] Captains Warrand and Spottiswoode served with the 1st Battalion Seaforth Highlanders in the Egyptian war of 1882, and were present at the engagement at Chalouf and at the battle of Tel-el-Kebir (Medal with Clasp, and Khedive's Star).

[22] Captain Christopher served with the 78th Highlanders in the Afghan war in 1880 (Medal); was Orderly Officer to Brigadier General Walker, Commanding 3rd Brigade Southern Afghanistan Field Force, from the 29th November 1880 till the 11th May 1881.

[23] Captain Tod served with the 1st Battalion Seaforth Highlanders as Regimental Transport Officer throughout the Egyptian war of 1882, and was present at the battle of Tel-el-Kebir (Medal with Clasp, and Khedive's Star).

[24] Captain Elliot served with the 1st Battalion Seaforth Highlanders in the Egyptian war of 1882, and was present at the battle of Tel-el-Kebir (Medal with Clasp, and Khedive's Star). Served in the Hazara Expedition in 1888 with the 2nd Battalion Seaforth Highlanders (Medal with Clasp); and in the Hazara Expedition in 1891 with the same Battalion (Clasp).

[25] Major Colin Mackenzie served with the detachment of the 2nd Battalion Seaforth Highlanders attached to the 1st Battalion Seaforth Highlanders in the Egyptian war of 1882, and was present at the battle of Tel-el-Kebir (Medal with Clasp, and Khedive's Star). Served with the Burmese Expedition in 1885-87, and again in 1887-89, as Embarkation Officer at Mandalay, Transport Officer at Myingyan, and subsequently in command of a Company of Mounted Infantry (Medal with two Clasps). Served with the Hazara Expedition in 1888 as Adjutant of the 2nd Battalion Seaforth Highlanders (mentioned in despatches, Clasp). Served in the operations against the Hunza Nagars in 1891-92 as Deputy Assistant Quarter Master General, and was present at the capture of Nilt Fort; commanded the force at the storming of the enemy's second position on 20th December 1892, and during the subsequent advance and occupation of Hunza and Nagar (mentioned in despatches, Brevet of Major, Clasp).

[27] Captain Ewart served with the detachment of the 2nd Battalion Seaforth Highlanders attached to the 1st Battalion Seaforth Highlanders in the Egyptian war of 1882, and was present at the battle of Tel-el-Kebir (Medal with Clasp, and Khedive's Star). Served with the Hazara Expedition in 1888 with the 2nd Battalion Seaforth Highlanders—severely wounded (Medal with Clasp).

[28] Captain Clark served in the Hazara Expedition in 1888 as Acting Adjutant to the Left Half Battalion 2nd Seaforth Highlanders (Medal with Clasp). Served in the Hazara Expedition in 1891 with the 2nd Battalion Seaforth Highlanders (Clasp).

[29] Captain Hopkins served in the Hazara Expedition in 1888 with the 2nd Battalion Seaforth Highlanders (Medal with Clasp).

Seaforth Highlanders (Ross-shire Buffs, The Duke of Albany's). 320

[31] Captain Moon served in the Hazara Expedition in 1888 as Transport Officer with the 2nd Column (mentioned in despatches, Medal with Clasp. Also served in the Hazara Expedition in 1891 with the 2nd Battalion Seaforth Highlanders (Clasp).

[32] Captain D. Campbell served in the Hazara Expedition in 1888 as Acting Quarter Master with the Left Half Battalion 2nd Seaforth Highlanders (Medal with Clasp).

[33] Captain Hon. D. Forbes Sempill, Lieuts. Cunliffe, Featherstonhaugh, and Brodie served in the Hazara Expedition in 1891 with the 2nd Battalion Seaforth Highlanders (Medal with Clasp).

[34] Captain Stirling served in the Hazara Expedition in 1888 with the 2nd Battalion Seaforth Highlanders (Medal with Clasp). Served in the Hazara Expedition in 1891 with the 2nd Battalion Seaforth Highlanders (Clasp).

[36] Captain Cowans served in the Hazara Expedition in 1888 as Transport Officer with the 2nd Battalion Seaforth Highlanders (Medal with Clasp). Also served in the Hazara Expedition in 1891 with the 2nd Battalion Seaforth Highlanders (Clasp).

[37] Captain Lumsden served in the Hazara Expedition in 1888 with the 2nd Battalion Seaforth Highlanders (Medal with Clasp). Served in the Hazara Expedition in 1891 with the 2nd Battalion Seaforth Highlanders (Clasp).

[38] Lieut. Baillie served in the Hazara Expedition in 1888 with the 2nd Battalion Seaforth Highlanders (Medal with Clasp). Served in the Hazara Expedition in 1891 with the 2nd Battalion Seaforth Highlanders (Clasp).

[39] Lieut. Murray served with the Hazara Expedition in 1888 (mentioned in despatches, Medal with Clasp).

[40] Lieut. Galloway served in the Hazara Expedition in 1891 with the 2nd Battalion Seaforth Highlanders (Medal with Clasp).—See also Civil Decorations for Gallantry, "Hart's Annual Army List," p. 786.

[47] Captain Denys.—For War Services, see Army Pay Department.

[50] Lieut. Glynn served in the Afghan war in 1880 with the 78th Highlanders (Medal). Served in the Hazara Expedition in 1891 with the 2nd Battalion Seaforth Highlanders (Medal with Clasp).

Record of the Services of the 1st Battalion of the Seaforth Highlanders
(formerly the 72nd Highlanders).

Raised by letter of service dated 8th January 1778. Inspected and passed 15th May 1778. Received title of 78th 18th July 1778. Proceeded to Guernsey and Jersey 12th September 1778. Proceeded to the East Indies 1st June 1781. Number changed to 72nd in 1786. Took part in the capture of Ceylon 1795. Returned to England 2nd February 1798. Embarked for the Cape of Good Hope 31st July 1805. To Mauritius 1810. To the Cape of Good Hope 1814. To India and back 1815. Returned to England 22nd December 1821. Embarked for the Cape of Good Hope 1st July 1828. Returned to England 11th April 1840. Embarked for Gibraltar 27th November 1844. To Barbadoes 1848. To Halifax, N.S., 1851. Returned to England 12th October 1854. Embarked for Malta 14th December 1854. To the Crimea 22nd May 1855. Returned to England 6th July 1856. Embarked for Bombay 4th September 1857. Returned to England 16th November 1865. Embarked for Bombay 21st February 1871. To Aden 25th February 1882. To Egypt 2nd August 1882. Returned to England 15th October 1882.

Record of the Services of the 2nd Battalion of the Seaforth Highlanders
(formerly the 78th Highlanders).

Raised by letter of service dated 7th March 1793. Inspected and passed July 1793. Proceeded to Holland September 1794. Returned to England May 1795. Proceeded to Quiberon August 1795. Returned January 1796. Proceeded to the Cape of Good Hope 1797. To Calcutta February 1797. To Bombay February 1803. To Goa February 1807. To Java August 1811. Returned to England July 1817. Proceeded to Ireland November 1817. Embarked for Ceylon April 1826. Returned to England February 1838. Embarked for India April 1842. Proceeded on active service to Persia in January 1857, returned to Bombay in May 1857, thence immediately to Bengal. Returned to England September 1859. Embarked for Gibraltar 3 August 1865. Returned to England from Nova Scotia, 21 December 1871. Embarked for India 16 February 1879.

The Gordon Highlanders.

1st Batt. Rawul Pindee, Bengal.
2nd Batt. Glasgow.

Regimental District No. 75.—Aberdeen.

Formerly the 75th (Stirlingshire) and the 92nd (Gordon Highlanders) Regiments.
(The 3rd Battalion is formed of the Royal Aberdeenshire Militia.)

"MYSORE" "SERINGAPATAM" "INDIA" (with the Royal Tiger). "EGMONT-OP-ZEE" "MANDORA" "EGYPT" (with the Sphinx). "CORUNNA" "FUENTES D'ONOR" "ALMARAZ" "VITTORIA" "PYRENEES" "NIVE" "ORTHES" "PENINSULA" "WATERLOO" "SOUTH AFRICA, 1835" "DELHI" "LUCKNOW" "CHARASIAH" "KABUL, 1879" "KANDAHAR, 1880" "AFGHANISTAN, 1878-80" "EGYPT, 1882, 1884" "TEL-EL-KEBIR" "NILE, 1884-85."

Years' Ser.							
Full Pay	Half Pay		ENSIGN OR 2ND LIEUT.	LIEUT.	CAPTAIN.	BREV.MAJ.	MAJOR.

Colonel.—Sir John Alexander Ewart,[1] KCB. *Ensign*, 27 July 38; *Lt.* 15 April 42; *Capt.* P 12 May 48; *Bt.Major*, 12 Dec. 54; *Major*, 29 Dec. 54; *Bt.Lt.Colonel*, 2 Nov. 55; *Lt.Colonel*, 16 Apr. 58; *Colonel*, 26 Apr. 59; *Major General*, 6 March 68; *Lieut. General*, 1 Oct. 77; *General*, 13 Jan. 84; *Colonel* 2nd Battalion Gordon Highlanders, 12 March 84.

29 — **Lieutenant Colonels.**—2 Robert Henry Oxley,[12] *Ensign*, P 9 Mar. 67; *Lieut.* P 15 Dec. 69; *Capt.* 28 Oct. 76; *Major*, 13 Feb. 85; *Lt.Colonel*, 1 July 91.
26 — 1 Henry Harding Mathias,[11] *Ensign*, P 17 April 69; *Lieut.* P 31 May 71; *Capt.* 8 Mar. 79; *Major*, 28 Nov. 83; *Lt.Colonel*, 14 Feb. 95.

Full	Half			ENSIGN OR 2ND LIEUT.	LIEUT.	CAPTAIN.	BREV.MAJ.	MAJOR.
			MAJORS.					
28		2	Hon. John Scott Napier[14]	P 14 Aug. 67	P 17 May 71	17 April 80	2 Mar. 81	13 May 85
26			Cha. Whittingham Horsley Douglas,[15] *Brigade Major, Aldershot*, 4 May 93	P 16 Dec. 69	P 27 Oct. 71	29 July 80	2 Mar. 81	13 May 85
22		2	Somerset E. O'Br. en Kevill-Davies[24] (*Depot*)		12 Nov. 73	18 June 81		1 July 91
19		1	George Thomas Frederick Downman[28]		29 Nov. 76	28 Nov. 83		25 Nov. 91
21			William Augustus Scott, *Adjutant* 7 *Middlesex Rifle Volunteers* 2 Nov. 91		21 Sept. 74	1 Dec. 83		10 Oct. 92
19			Forbes Macbean,[33] *Instructor Royal Military College* 1 Sept. 88		11 Nov. 76	2 July 84		23 Sept. 93
17			Charles Herbert Payne,[35] *Adjutant* 3 *Battalion* 1 May 90		11 Nov. 78	10 Oct. 85	11 Oct. 85	24 Jan. 94
19		2	Harry Wright[31]		29 Nov. 76	9 Mar. 86		14 Feb. 95
			CAPTAINS.					
18		1	*p.s.c.* Herbert Henry Burney[36]	30 Jan. 78	21 July 80	24 July 86		
17		1	Richard Dyneley Jennings-Bramly	22 Jan. 79	1 Dec. 80	1 Sept. 86		
19		2	Alexander David Fraser[37]		26 Aug. 76	8 Dec. 86		
18			Charles Reginald Sydney Douglas-Hamilton,[32] *Adjutant* 2 *Volunteer Bn. Scots Fusiliers* 1 Nov. 90	5 Sept. 77	5 Oct. 78	4 Dec. 86		
16			*p.s.c.* Henry William Denne Denne,[38] *Station Staff Officer, Mooltan*, 12 July 94	31 Jan. 80	30 Mar. 81	1 July 87		
14		1	Harry King Stewart[41]	23 Apr. 81	1 July 81	18 Dec. 87		
14		1	Claude Charles Miller-Wallnutt[42]	23 Apr. 81	1 July 81	14 Jan. 88		
16		2	George Staunton[40]	14 Jan. 80	1 July 81	18 Jan. 88		
15		2	Robert Dunbar Sinclair-Wemyss[43]	17 April 80	1 July 81	22 May 89		
14		1	John Seton Henderson[44]	23 Apr. 81	1 July 81	26 Oct. 89		
15		2	*p.s.c.* Frederick Gordon[45]	22 Jan. 81	1 July 81	1 Nov. 90		
14			Cecil Fred. Nevil Macready,[46] *Adj.* 2 *Vol.Bn. Gordon Highlanders* 1 Jan. 94		22 Oct. 81	4 Mar. 91		
14			Herbert William Jackson,[47] *serving with the Egyptian Army, with local rank of Major*		22 Oct. 81	1 Sept. 91		
14		2	Reginald Stanley Hunter-Blair[48]		22 Oct. 81	1 Sept. 91		
13			Edward Hyde Hamilton Gordon,[49] *Adj.* 15 *Middlesex Vol. Rifles* 9 Apr. 94		10 May 82	8 Apr. 92		
13		1	Slade Thomson,[50] *Station Staff Officer, Landour Depot*, 22 Jan. 94		9 Sept. 82	8 Apr. 92		
13		1	*p.s.c.* James Aylmer Lowthrop Haldane		9 Sept. 82	8 Apr. 92		
13			Tyrell Gordon Pirie, *Adjutant* 2 *London Rifle Volunteers* 1 Sept. 93		27 Jan. 83	10 Oct. 92		
13		2	Francis Hugh Neish[49]		10 Mar. 83	1 Sept. 93		
12			Alexander Penrose Murray,[52] *Vice Consul at Odessa* 31 Oct. 91		19 Sept. 83	23 Sept. 93		
11		1	Henry Percy Unincke (*Depot*)		14 May 84	23 Sept. 93		
11	10/12	2	Hector Macneal		14 May 84	9 Apr. 94		
			LIEUTENANTS.					
11			John Christie Aitken, *Aide de Camp to Maj. Gen. Lord R. D. Kerr*, 27 June 91		14 May 84			
11		1	Stewart Lygon Murray		12 Nov. 84			
11		2	Hon. Walter Robert Drummond Forbes		7 Feb. 85			
10		1	Arthur Ormond Norman		25 Nov. 85			
10		1	Ernest Beckwith Towse		16 Dec. 85			
9		2	Arth. Louis Hamilton Buchanan[53] (*Dep.*)		28 Apr. 86			
9			Eric Streatfeild, *Aide de Camp to Major General I. J. C. Herbert* 5 Dec. 90		28 Apr. 86			
9		1	Frederic Walter Kerr, *Adjutant* 31 Jan. 92		25 Aug. 86			
9		1	Desmond Adair		10 Nov. 86			
9		2	St. John Meyrick, *Aide de Camp to the Lord Lieutenant of Ireland* 3 Oct. 92		29 Dec. 86			
9		1	Walter Campbell	5 Feb. 87	5 Dec. 90			
8		1	Alan David Greenhill-Gardyne	15 Feb. 88	4 Mar. 91			
7		1	William Eagleson Gordon	6 June 88	1 Sept. 91			
7		2	Henry Alexander Bothune, *Adjutant* 1 Feb. 92	29 Dec. 88	1 Feb. 92			
6		2	Frederic Bradshaw M'Connel	6 July 89	6 Apr. 92			
6		1	Robert Adam Neilson Tytler (*Depot*)	29 Mar. 90	8 Apr. 92			
5		2	Hon. Robert Francis Carnegie	28 June 90	10 Oct. 92			
5		1	Gordon Robert Macnab	28 June 90	24 Nov. 92			
5		1	Alister Fraser Gordon	8 Oct. 90	1 Sept. 93			
5		1	Allan Sievwright Wingate	4 Mar. 91	23 Sept. 93			
4		1	Matthew Fontaine Maury Meiklejohn	17 June 91	9 Apr. 94			
4		1	George Douglas Mackenzie	9 Sept. 91	11 Apr. 94			
4		1	Kenneth Dingwall	10 Oct. 91	21 Nov. 94			

[56] Captain Carlaw served in the Egyptian war of 1882 with the 1st Battalion Gordon Highlanders, and was present at the battle of Tel-el-Kebir (Medal with Clasp, and Khedive's Star); also served in the Soudan Expedition in 1884 with the 1st Battalion Gordon Highlanders, and was present in the engagements at El Teb and Temai (two Clasps). Served in the Nile Expedition in 1884-85 with the 1st Battalion Gordon Highlanders and with the River Column under Major General Earle (Clasp).

Years'Ser.		SECOND LIEUTENANTS.	2ND LIEUT.
Full Pay	Half Pay		
4	...	1 Donald Munro Watt	7 Nov. 91
4	...	1 George Ewen Eyre Gordon Cameron...	20 Feb. 92
3	...	1 George Standish Gage Craufurd	18 June 92
3	...	2 Charles Gordon Monro	22 June 92
2	...	2 Stuart Cairns Maitland	20 May 93
2	...	2 Charles John Simpson	19 July 93
2	...	1 David Reginald Younger	23 Dec. 93
2	...	2 Henry Scrymgeour Wedderburn	23 Dec. 93
1	...	2 Alexander Lamont	2 June 94
1	...	Percy Stuart Allan	6 Mar. 95
1	...	William Muir Knox Marshall	6 Mar. 95
11	...	*Paymaster.*—1 George D. Mackenzie, *Lieut.* 1 *Battalion (acting).*	
3	...	*Quarter Masters.*—1 Henry Carlaw,[36] 16 Aug. 84; *Hon. Captain*, 16 Aug. 94.	

2 William Anderson, 31 Aug. 92; *Hon. Lieut.*
Facings Yellow.—*Agents*, Messrs. Holt and Co.
1st *Battalion embarked for Malta*, 1881. 2nd *Battalion returned from Bombay*, 1882.

---

[1] Sir John Ewart served throughout the Eastern campaign from the first landing at Gallipoli in April 1854 until the final evacuation of the Crimea in June 1856; present with the 93rd Highlanders at the battle of Alma, and until after the occupation of Balaklava; appointed a D.A.Q.M. General 26th Sept. 1854, and as such was present at the battles of Balaklava and Inkerman, and throughout the siege operations before Sebastopol up to 13th Feb. 1855, when he rejoined the 93rd on promotion; accompanied the expedition to the Sea of Azoff, and was at the capture of Kertch and Yenikali; afterwards present at the siege and fall of Sebastopol, and assaults on the 18th June and 8th Sept. (Medal with four Clasps, Brevet of Major and Lt.Colonel, Knight of the Legion of Honor, Sardinian and Turkish Medals, and 5th Class of the Medjidie). Served in Bengal during the Indian mutiny; was at an engagement near Bunnee, and afterwards at the final relief of Lucknow; held for a short time a command consisting of three squadrons of Cavalry, 5 guns, and 500 Infantry (specially named in despatches, and appointed a *CB*.); and on the 16th Nov. commanded the leading party of stormers at the assault of the Secunderbagh, on which occasion he personally captured a colour, received two sabre wounds in an encounter with the two native officers who were defending it; was again (very severely) wounded by a cannon-shot (left arm carried away) when in action with the Gwalior rebels at Cawnpore on the 1st Dec. 1857 (Medal with Clasp, Aide de Camp to the Queen, and Colonel). Commanded the 93rd Highlanders for a short period during the siege of Sebastopol, was Lt.Colonel of the 78th Highlanders for upwards of five years.

[11] Lt.Colonel Mathias served in the Nile Expedition in 1884-85 with the 1st Battalion of the Gordon Highlanders (Medal with Clasp, and Khedive's Star).

[12] Lt.Colonel Oxley served with the 92nd Highlanders in the Afghan war in 1879-80, and was present in the engagement at Charasiab on 6th October 1879 (mentioned in despatches) and in the subsequent occupation of Cabul (Medal with Clasp).

[14] Major the Hon. J. S. Napier served with the 92nd Highlanders in the Afghan war of 1878-80, and was present at the attack and capture of Ali Musjid, in the expedition into Maidan, in the operations around Cabul in December 1879 (mentioned in despatches), and in the engagement at Charasiah on the 25th April 1880 (mentioned in despatches); accompanied Sir Frederick Roberts in the march to Candahar, and was present at the reconnaissance of 31st August and at the battle of Candahar (mentioned in despatches, Brevet of Major, Medal with three Clasps, and Bronze Decoration). Served in the Boer war in 1881.

[15] Major Douglas served in the Afghan war of 1878-80 with the 92nd Highlanders, and was present in the engagement at Charasiab on the 6th October 1879 and subsequent pursuit of the Afghans, in the operations round Cabul in December 1879 including the investment of Sherpore, and in the engagement at Charasiah on the 25th April 1880 (mentioned in despatches); accompanied Sir Frederick Roberts in the march to Candahar, and was present at the reconnaissance of the 31st August and at the battle of Candahar—horse shot (mentioned in despatches, Brevet of Major, Medal with three Clasps, and Bronze Decoration). Also served in the Boer war of 1881. Served in the Soudan campaign of 1884-85 as Deputy Assistant Adjutant and Quarter Master General (mentioned in despatches, Medal with Clasp, and Khedive's Star).

[24] Major Kevill-Davies served in the Egyptian war of 1882 with the 1st Battalion Gordon Highlanders, and was present at the battle of Tel-el-Kebir (Medal with Clasp, and Khedive's Star); also served in the Soudan Expedition in 1884 with the 1st Battalion Gordon Highlanders, and was present in the engagements at El Teb and Tewai (4th Class of the Medjidie, two Clasps). Served in the Nile Expedition in 1884-85 with the 1st Battalion Gordon Highlanders and with the River Column under Major General Earle (Clasp).

[28] Major Downman served in the expedition to the Soudan in 1884 with the 1st Battalion of the Gordon Highlanders, and was present in the engagements at El Teb and Temai (Medal with Clasp, and Khedive's Star). Served in the Nile Expedition in 1884-85 with the 1st Battalion of the Gordon Highlanders and with the River Column under Major General Earle (Clasp).

[32] Captain Douglas-Hamilton served with the Carabiniers in the Afghan war in 1879-80, including the affair at Ali Boghan under Lt.Colonel Fryer, and the expeditions into the Lughman Valley and against the Wuzeeree Khugianis (Medal).

[33] Major Macbean served with the 92nd Highlanders in the Afghan war in 1879-80, and was present in the engagement at Charasiah on 6th October 1879, with the Maidan Expedition, in the operations around Cabul in December 1879, and in the engagement at Charasiah on 25th April 1880; accompanied Sir Frederick Roberts in the march to Candahar, and was present at the reconnaissance of 31st August and at the battle of Candahar (Medal with three Clasps, and Bronze Decoration). Served in the Boer war of 1881.

[34] Major Wright served with the 92nd Highlanders in the Afghan war in 1879-80, and was present in the engagement at Charasiab on 6th October 1879, with the Maidan Expedition, in the operations around Cabul in December 1879, and in the engagement at Charasiah on 25th April 1880; accompanied Sir Frederick Roberts in the march to Candahar, and was present at the reconnaissance of 31st August and at the battle of Candahar (Medal with three Clasps, and Bronze Decoration). Served in the Boer war of 1881 (mentioned in despatches).

[35] Major C. H. Payne served in the Egyptian war of 1882 with the 1st Battalion Gordon Highlanders, and was present at the battle of Tel-el-Kebir (Medal with Clasp, and Khedive's Star); also served in the Soudan Expedition in 1884 under Sir Gerald Graham with the Mounted Infantry, and was present in the engagements at El Teb and Temai (mentioned in despatches, 5th Class of the Medjidie, two Clasps). Served in the Nile Expedition in 1884-85 in command of a company of Mounted Infantry, took part in the operations of the Desert Column under Sir Herbert Stewart, and was present in the actions at Abu Klea and Abu Kru, the reconnaissance of Metammeh, and the engagement at Abu Klea Wells on the 17th February (mentioned in despatches, Brevet of Major, two Clasps).

[36] Captain Burney served in the Egyptian war of 1882 as Adjutant of the 1st Battalion of the Gordon Highlanders, and was present at the battle of Tel-el-Kebir (Medal with Clasp, 5th Class of the Medjidie, and Khedive's Star). Served in the Soudan Expedition under Sir Gerald Graham in 1884, and was present in the engagements at El Teb and Temai (two Clasps). Served in the Nile Expedition in 1884-85 with the 1st Battalion of the Gordon Highlanders and with the River Column under Major General Earle (Clasp).

[37] Captain Fraser served with the 92nd Highlanders in the Afghan war in 1879-80, and was present in the engagement at Charasiab on the 6th October 1879, with the Maidan Expedition, in the operations around Cabul in December 1879, and in the engagement at Charasiah on the 25th April 1880; accompanied Sir Frederick Roberts in the march to Candahar, and was present at the reconnaissance of 31st August and at the battle of Candahar (Medal with three Clasps, and Bronze Decoration). Served in the Boer war of 1881. Served with the Nile Expedition in 1884-85 (Medal with Clasp, and Khedive's Star).

[38] Captain Deane served in the Egyptian war of 1882 with the 1st Battalion Gordon Highlanders, and was present at the battle of Tel-el-Kebir (Medal with Clasp, and Khedive's Star); also served in the Soudan Expedition in 1884 as Transport Officer with the 1st Battalion Gordon Highlanders, and was present in the engagements at El Teb and Temai (two Clasps). Served in the Nile Expedition in 1884-85 with the 1st Battalion Gordon Highlanders and with the River Column under Major General Earle (Clasp).

[40] Captain Staunton served in the Afghan war in 1880, and accompanied Sir Frederick Roberts in the march to Candahar, and was present at the reconnaissance of 31st August and at the battle of Candahar (Medal with Clasp, and Bronze Decoration). Served in the Boer war of 1881.

[41] Captain H. K. Stewart served in the Egyptian war of 1882 with the 1st Battalion of the Gordon Highlanders, and was present at the battle of Tel-el-Kebir (Medal with Clasp, and Khedive's Star); also served in the Soudan Expedition in 1884 as Orderly Officer to Sir Redvers Buller, and was present in the engagements at El Teb and Temai (two Clasps). Served with the Nile Expedition in 1884-85 with the Mounted Infantry, took part in the operations of the Desert Column, was present in the actions at Abu Klea and Abu Kru, in the reconnaissance of Metammeh, and in the engagement at Abu Klea Wells on the 19th February (two Clasps, and 4th Class of the Medjidie).

[42] Captain Miller-Wallnutt served in the Egyptian war of 1882, and was present at the battle of Tel-el-Kebir (Medal with Clasp, and Khedive's Star); also served in the Soudan Expedition under Sir Gerald Graham in 1884, and was present in the engagements at El Teb and Temai (two Clasps). Served in the Nile Expedition in 1884-85 with the 1st Battalion Gordon Highlanders and with the River Column under Major General Earle (Clasp).

[43] Captain Sinclair-Wemyss served in the Boer war of 1881.

[44] Captain Henderson served in the Egyptian war of 1882 with the 1st Battalion Gordon Highlanders, and was present at the battle of Tel-el-Kebir (Medal with Clasp, and Khedive's Star); also served in the Soudan Expedition in 1884 with the 1st Battalion Gordon Highlanders, and was present in the engagements at El Teb and Temai (two Clasps). Served in the Nile Expedition in 1884-85 with the 1st Battalion Gordon Highlanders and with the River Column under Major General Earle (Clasp).

[45] Captain F. Gordon served in the Egyptian war of 1882, and was present at the battle of Tel-el-Kebir (Medal with Clasp, and Khedive's Star). Served in the Soudan Expedition under Sir Gerald Graham in 1884 as Adjutant of the 1st Battalion of the Gordon Highlanders, and was present in the engagements at El Teb and Temai (two Clasps).

[46] Captain Macready served in the Egyptian war of 1882, and was present at the battle of Tel-el-Kebir (Medal with Clasp, and Khedive's Star).

[47] Major Jackson served in the Egyptian war of 1882 with the 1st Battalion Gordon Highlanders (Medal, and Khedive's Star); also served in the Soudan Expedition in 1884 with the 1st Battalion Gordon Highlanders, and was present in the engagements at El Teb and Temai (two Clasps). Served in the Nile Expedition in 1884-85 with the 1st Battalion Gordon Highlanders and with the River Column under Major General Earle (Clasp); in the operations in the Soudan in 1889 including the action of Toski (4th Class of the Medjidie, Clasp); and in the operations in 1891 including the capture of Tokar (4th Class of the Osmanieh).

[48] Captain Hunter-Blair served in the Egyptian war of 1882 with the 1st Battalion Gordon Highlanders, and was present at the battle of Tel-el-Kebir (Medal with Clasp, and Khedive's Star); also served in the Soudan Expedition in 1884 with the 1st Battalion Gordon Highlanders, and was present in the engagements at El Teb and Temai two Clasps). Served in the Nile Expedition in 1884-85 with the 1st Battalion Gordon Highlanders and with the River Column under Major General Earle (Clasp).

[49] Captains E. H. H. Gordon and Neish served in the expedition to the Soudan in 1884 with the 1st Battalion of the Gordon Highlanders, and were present in the engagements at El Teb and Temai (Medal with Clasp, and Khedive's Star). Served in the Nile Expedition in 1884-85 with the 1st Battalion of the Gordon Highlanders and with the River Column under Major General Earle (Clasp).

[50] Captain Thomson served in the expedition to the Soudan in 1884 with the 1st Battalion of the Gordon Highlanders, and was present in the engagements at El Teb and Temai (Medal with Clasp, and Khedive's Star). Served in the Nile Expedition in 1884-85 with the 1st Battalion of the Gordon Highlanders (Clasp).

[52] Captain Murray served in the Soudan Expedition in 1884 with the 1st Battalion Gordon Highlanders, and was present in the engagement at El Teb (Medal with Clasp, and Khedive's Star).

[53] Lieut. Buchanan.—See Civil Decorations for Gallantry, "Hart's Annual Army List," p. 786.

Record of the Services of the 1st Battalion Gordon Highlanders—formerly the 75th (Stirlingshire) Regt.

Raised in Scotland in 1787, and proceeded to India, 1788 (storming of Seringapatam). To Scotland, 1807. To Ireland, 1810. To England, 1810. To Jersey, 1811. To Sicily, 1811. To Ionian Islands, 1814. To Gibraltar, 1821. To England, 1823. To Ireland, 1824. To England, 1830. To the Cape of Good Hope, 1830. To England, 1843. To Wales, 1844. To Ireland, 1845. To India, 1849 (capture of Delhi and relief of Lucknow under Sir Colin Campbell). To England, 1862. To Ireland, 1866. To Gibraltar, 1867. To Hong Kong, 1868. Half the Regiment to Singapore, 1869. To the Cape of Good Hope and Natal, 1870. To Ireland, 1875. To the Channel Islands, 1877. To England, 1878. To Malta, 1881. To Egypt, 1882 (war of 1882, including the battle of Tel-el-Kebir, and campaign of 1884-85). To Malta, 1885. To Ceylon, 1888.

Record of the Services of the 2nd Battalion Gordon Highlanders (formerly the 92nd Regiment).

Raised in 1794, and proceeded to the Mediterranean. Gibraltar, to 1795. Corsica, to 1796. Gibraltar, to 1798. England and Ireland, to 1799. Holland, to 1799 (battle of Egmont-op-Zee). England, to 1800. Minorca, Gibraltar and Malta, to 1801 (battle of Mandora). Egypt, to 1802 (received the badge of "Egypt," with the Sphinx), Ireland, Scotland, and England, to 1807. [2nd Battalion raised in 1803.] Denmark, to 1807. England, to 1808. Spain, England, and the Netherlands, to 1809. England, to 1810. Spain and Portugal, to 1814 (battles of Corunna, Fuentes d'Onor, Almaraz, Vittoria, Pyrenees, Nive, and Orthes). [2nd Battalion disbanded, 1814.] Ireland, to 1815. Belgium and France, to 1815 (battle of Waterloo). Scotland and Ireland, to 1819. Jamaica, to 1827. Scotland and Ireland, to 1834. Gibraltar and Malta, to 1841. Barbadoes, to 1844. Scotland, to 1846. Ireland, to 1851. Corfu, to 1853. Gibraltar, to 1855. The Crimea, to 1856. Gibraltar, to 1858. India, to 1863. England, Scotland, and Ireland, to 1868. India, to 1881 (battles of Charasiah, Cabul, and Candahar). South Africa, to 1881 (Boer war). England and Scotland, to 1885. Channel Islands, to 1887. Ireland, 1887.

Gibraltar. | **The Queen's Own Cameron Highlanders.** [Regimental District No. 79.—Inverness. 325

Formerly the 79th (Queen's Own Cameron Highlanders) Regiment.
(The 2nd Battalion is formed of the Highland Light Infantry Militia.)

The Thistle ensigned with the Imperial Crown. "EGMONT-OP-ZEE" "EGYPT" (with the Sphinx). "FUENTES-D'ONOR" "SALAMANCA" "PYRENEES" "NIVELLE" "NIVE" "TOULOUSE" "PENINSULA" "WATERLOO" "ALMA" "SEVASTOPOL" "LUCKNOW" "EGYPT, 1882" "TEL-EL-KEBIR" "NILE, 1884-85."

Years' Ser.							
Full Pay	Half Pay						
28	...	Colonel.—Sir Richard Chambre Hayes Taylor,[1] KCB., Ensign,11 Dec. 35; Lt.P29 Mar. 39; Capt.P23 Aug. 44; Major, 8 Aug. 54; Lt.Colonel, 12 Dec. 54; Colonel, 21 May 58; Major General, 6 Mar. 68; Lieut.General, 1 Oct. 77; General, 1 Apr. 83; Colonel Cameron Highlanders, 9 Sept. 87.					
		Lieutenant Colonel.—Gordon Lorn Campbell Money,[11] DSO., Aide de Camp to the Queen; Ensign, P8 Feb. 68; Lt. 28 Oct. 71; Captain, 18 Aug. 80; Major, 1 Feb. 84; Bt.Lt.Colonel, 1 Jan. 88; Lieutenant Colonel, 21 May 94; Colonel, 23 Jan. 95.					

			2ND LIEUT.	LIEUT.	CAPTAIN.	BREV.MAJ.	MAJOR.
		MAJORS.					
22	...	James Maitland Hunt[13]	......	12 Feb. 74	12 Feb. 81	18 Nov. 82	1 Dec. 86
21	...	Thomas Francis Archibald Kennedy[14]	......	27 Jan. 75	20 Jan. 86	......	22 Feb. 93
19	...	Robert Francis Ladeveze Napier[16] (Depot)	......	29 Nov. 76	14 July 83	......	4 Oct. 93
16	...	Frederick Hacket-Thompson,[17] District Insp. of Musk. Devonport, 2 Aug. 92	6 Aug. 79	22 May 80	20 Feb. 84	......	21 May
		CAPTAINS.					
17	...	Thomas Arthur Mackenzie,[18] Adjutant 2 Battalion 1 Nov. 90	22 Jan. 79	18 Aug. 80	16 Jan. 85		
17	...	Henry Huntly Leith Malcolm[19] (Depot)	2 Jan. 79	29 Sept. 80	24 Aug. 85		
16	...	Beauchamp Colclough Urquhart,[20] Aide de Camp to Gov.Gen.of Canada,7 Sept.93	14 Jan. 80	12 Feb. 81	2 Nov. 85		
15	...	Duncan Francis Davidson,[22] Adj. 5 Vol. Bn. Royal Highlanders 7 Dec. 91	23 Oct. 80	1 July 81	1 Dec. 86		
16	...	Edward Alston Pierrepoint Brooke,Adj. 5 Vol. Bn. Gordon Highlanders 24 July 91	23 July 79	1 July 81	17 Jan. 89		
15	...	Granville Eardley Forbes[25]	23 Oct. 80	1 July 81	10 July 89		
15	...	Adam Scott-Elliot[26]	23 Oct. 80	1 July 81	22 Oct. 90		
15	...	George Ross Cavaye,[27] Adjutant 1 Vol. Battalion 1 Feb. 94	23 Oct. 80	1 July 81	22 Oct. 90		
14	...	p.s.c. John Spencer Ewart,[28] Assistant Military Secretary, Malta, 5 Jan. 94	......	22 Oct. 81	24 July 91		
13	...	Malcolm Stewart Riach[29]	......	27 Jan. 83	7 Dec. 91		
12	...	Charles Findlay[29]†	......	6 Feb. 84	7 Dec. 91		
11	...	Augustus de Ségur M'Kerrell,[30] serving with the Egyptian Army	......	23 Aug. 84	2 Aug. 92		
11	...	Angus Falconer Douglas-Hamilton,[31] Adjutant 6 Vol. Bn. Gordon Highanders 1 Feb. 94	......	23 Aug. 84	7 Dec. 92		
11	...	Hon. Andrew David Murray[32]	......	12 Nov. 84	11 Mar. 93		
11	...	Walter Douglas Ewart[33]	......	7 Feb. 85	1 Apr. 93		
10	...	Henry Gordon Wolrige-Gordon[34]	......	6 May 85	7 Sept. 93		
10	...	Frederic Alexander MacFarlan,[35] Adjutant 1 Feb. 94	......	9 May 85	1 Feb. 94		
9	...	Arthur Frederick Egerton	......	28 Apr. 86	21 May 94		
		LIEUTENANTS.					
6	...	Francis Louis Scott-Kerr	17 July 89	26 Feb. 91			
6	...	Douglas Lilburn MacEwen	21 Dec. 89	24 July 92			
5	...	James Douglas M'Lachlan	25 Mar. 91	2 Aug. 92			
4	...	John Campbell	9 Jan. 92	1 Apr. 93			
4	...	Hon. Edward Oliphant Murray (Depot)	27 Jan. 92	14 June 93			
3	...	Arthur Chancellor	9 Apr. 92	7 Sept. 93			
3	...	Angus Cameron	18 May 92	12 Sept. 93			
3	...	Lawrence Oliphant Græme	18 June 92	1 Feb. 94			
3	...	Henry Robert Brown	21 Sept. 92	21 May 94			
		SECOND LIEUTENANTS.					
3	...	Neville John Gordon Cameron	17 Dec. 92				
2	...	George Cecil Minett Sorel-Cameron	5 Apr. 93				
2	...	William Wilson MacBean	9 Sept. 93				
2	...	Arthur David Nicholson	21 Oct. 93				
2	...	James Colquhoun Oliphant Blair	23 Dec. 93				
2	...	Percy Thomas Charles Baird	7 Mar. 94				
1	...	Rodolph Ladaveze Adlercron	2 June 94				
1	...	Hon. Alfred Henry Maitland	27 June 94				
		Paymaster.—					
4	...	*Quarter Master.—*William Young, 16 Apr. 91.					

Facings Blue.—*Agents,* Messrs. Holt and Co.
Embarked for Malta, 25 Feb. 1892.

[1] Sir Richard Taylor served the Eastern campaign of 1854-55 (save the interval between 9th Feb. and 15th June 1855) with the 79th Highlanders, including the battles of Alma and Balaklava, and full siege of Sebastopol (Medal with three Clasps, 5th Class of the Medjidie, and Turkish Medal). Commanded the 79th Highlanders from Feb. to 16th Nov. 1858 in the Indian campaign, including the siege and capture of Lucknow, and commanded a Brigade in Oude from Nov. 1858 to Jan. 1859 (mentioned in despatches, CB., Brevet of Colonel, Medal with Clasp).

[11] Colonel Money served in the Nile Expedition in 1884-85 with the Cameron Highlanders (Medal with Clasp, and Khedive's Star). Served throughout the operations of the Soudan Frontier Field Force in 1885-86 as Assistant Military Secretary to Sir Frederick Stephenson, and was present in the engagement at Giniss (mentioned in despatches, DSO.).

[13] Major Hunt served with the Cameron Highlanders throughout the Egyptian war of 1882, and was present at the battle of Tel-el-Kebir (mentioned in despatches, Brevet of Major, Medal with Clasp, 4th Class of the Medjidie, and Khedive's Star); also served throughout the Nile Expedition in 1884-85 with the Cameron Highlanders (Clasp). Served throughout the operations of the Soudan Frontier Field Force in 1885-86 with the Cameron Highlanders, and was present at Kosheh during its investment and in the engagement at Giniss.

[14] Major Kennedy served with the 1st Battalion Black Watch in the Egyptian war of 1882 as Regimental Transport Officer, and was present at the battle of Tel-el-Kebir (Medal with Clasp, and Khedive's Star). Served in the Soudan Expedition in 1884 as Transport Officer 1st Battalion Black Watch, and was present in the engagements at El Teb and Temai (two Clasps). Served in the Nile Expedition in 1884-85 with the 1st Battalion of the Black Watch, took part with the River Column under Major General Earle, and was present in the engagement at Kirbekan—severely wounded (two Clasps).

[16] Major Napier served throughout the Nile Expedition in 1884-85 with the Cameron Highlanders (Medal with Clasp, and Khedive's Star). Served throughout the operations of the Soudan Frontier Field Force in 1885-86 with

the Cameron Highlanders, and was present at Kosheh during its investment and in the engagement at Giniss (4th Class of the Medjidie).

[17] Major Hacket Thompson served as Transport Officer with the Cameron Highlanders throughout the Egyptian war of 1882, and was present at the battle of Tel-el-Kebir (Medal with Clasp, and Khedive's Star). Served throughout the operations of the Soudan Frontier Field Force in 1885-86 with the Cameron Highlanders, and was present at Kosheh during its investment (wounded) and in the engagement at Giniss.

[18] Captain Mackenzie served with the Cameron Highlanders throughout the Egyptian war of 1882, and was present at the battle of Tel-el-Kebir (Medal with Clasp, and Khedive's Star). Served with the Soudan Frontier Field Force in 1886.

[19] Captain Malcolm served with the Cameron Highlanders throughout the Egyptian war of 1882, and was present at the battle of Tel-el-Kebir—twice wounded (Medal with Clasp, and Khedive's Star). Served throughout the Nile Expedition in 1884-85 on special service as Staff Captain with the whaler boats (Clasp).

[20] Captain Urquhart served with the Cameron Highlanders in the Egyptian war of 1882 from the landing at Ismailia, and was present at the battle of Tel-el-Kebir (Medal with Clasp, and Khedive's Star); also served throughout the Nile Expedition in 1884-85 with the Cameron Highlanders (Clasp). Served in the operations of the Soudan Frontier Field Force in 1885-86 with the Cameron Highlanders, and was present at Kosheh during its investment and in the engagement at Giniss.

[22] Captain D. F. Davidson served with the Cameron Highlanders throughout the Egyptian war of 1882, and was present at the battle of Tel-el-Kebir (Medal with Clasp, and Khedive's Star); also served throughout the Nile Expedition in 1884-85 with the Cameron Highlanders (Clasp). Served throughout the operations of the Soudan Frontier Field Force in 1885-86 with the Cameron Highlanders, and was present at Kosheh during its investment at the reconnaissance on the 16th December, and in the engagement at Giniss.

[25] Captain Forbes served throughout the Nile Expedition in 1884-85 with the Cameron Highlanders (Medal with Clasp, and Khedive's Star). Served with the Soudan Frontier Field Force in 1886.

[26] Captain Scott-Elliot served with the Cameron Highlanders throughout the Egyptian war of 1882, and was present at the battle of Tel-el-Kebir (Medal with Clasp, and Khedive's Star); also served throughout the Nile Expedition in 1884-85 with the Cameron Highlanders (Clasp). Served throughout the operations of the Soudan Frontier Field Force in 1885-86 in command of the Cameron Division of the British Camel Corps, and was present in the engagement at Giniss.

[27] Captain Cavaye served with the Cameron Highlanders throughout the Egyptian war of 1882, and was present at the battle of Tel-el-Kebir (Medal with Clasp, and Khedive's Star); also served throughout the Nile Expedition in 1884-85 with the Cameron Highlanders (Clasp). Served in the operations of the Soudan Frontier Field Force in 1885-86 with the Cameron Highlanders, and was present at Kosheh during its investment and in the engagement at Giniss.

[28] Captain J. S. Ewart served with the Cameron Highlanders throughout the Egyptian war of 1882, and was present at the battle of Tel-el-Kebir (Medal with Clasp, and Khedive's Star); also served throughout the Nile Expedition in 1884-85 with the Cameron Highlanders (Clasp). Served throughout the operations of the Soudan Frontier Field Force in 1885-86 as Adjutant of the Cameron Highlanders, was Staff Officer at Kosheh during its investment, and was present in the engagement at Giniss (4th Class of the Medjidie).

[29] Captain Riach served throughout the Nile Expedition in 1884-85 with the Cameron Highlanders (Medal with Clasp, and Khedive's Star). Served throughout the operations of the Soudan Frontier Field Force in 1885-86 with the Cameron Highlanders, and was present at Kosheh during its investment, at the reconnaissance on the 16th December, and was Staff Officer at Kosheh Fort during the engagement at Giniss.

[29†] Captain Findlay served throughout the Nile Expedition in 1884-85 with the Cameron Highlanders (Medal with Clasp, and Khedive's Star); also served with the Soudan Frontier Field Force in 1886.

[30] Captain M'Kerrell served throughout the Nile Expedition in 1884-85 with the Cameron Highlanders (Medal with Clasp, and Khedive's Star). Served throughout the operations of the Soudan Frontier Field Force in 1885-86 with the Cameron Highlanders, and was present at Kosheh during its investment, at the reconnaissance on the 16th December, and in the engagement at Giniss.

[31] Captain Douglas Hamilton served during the latter part of the Nile Expedition in 1885 with the Cameron Highlanders (Medal with Clasp, and Khedive's Star). Served throughout the operations of the Soudan Frontier Field Force in 1885-86 with the Cameron Highlanders, and was present at Kosheh during its investment and in the engagement at Giniss.

[32] Captain Hon. A. D. Murray served during the latter part of the Nile Expedition in 1885 with the Cameron Highlanders (Medal with Clasp, and Khedive's Star). Served throughout the operations of the Soudan Frontier Field Force in 1885-86 with the Cameron Highlanders, and was present at Kosheh during its investment and in the engagement at Giniss.

[33] Captain W. D. Ewart served throughout the operations of the Soudan Frontier Field Force in 1885-86 with the Cameron Highlanders, and was present at Kosheh during its investment and in the engagement at Giniss (Medal, and Khedive's Star).

[34] Captain Wolrige-Gordon served throughout the operations of the Soudan Frontier Field Force in 1885-86 with the Cameron Highlanders, and was present at Kosheh during its investment and in the engagement at Giniss (Medal, and Khedive's Star).

[35] Captain MacFarlan served throughout the operations of the Soudan Frontier Field Force in 1885-86 with the Cameron Highlanders, and was present at Kosheh during its investment, at the reconnaissance on the 16th December, and in the engagement at Giniss (Medal, and Khedive's Star).

Record of the Services of the 1st Battalion The Queen's Own Cameron Highlanders (formerly the 79th Regiment).

Raised in 1793. Scotland, to February 1794. Ireland, to June 1794. England, to August 1794. Flanders, to May 1795. England, to July 1795. West Indies, to 1797. England, to June 1799. Guernsey, to August 1799. Holland, to October 1799 (battle of Egmont-op-Zee). England, to 1800; Spain, to March 1801. Egypt, to October 1801 (received the badge of "Egypt"—with the Sphinx). Minorca, to 1802. Scotland, to 1803. Ireland, to 1805. England, to August 1807. Denmark, to November 1807. England, to May 1808. Sweden, to July 1808. England, to August 1808. Portugal, to February 1809. England, to July 1809. Holland, to September 1809. England, to 1810. Portugal and Spain, to 1814 (battles of Fuentes d'Onor, Salamanca, Pyrenees, Nivelle, Nive, and Toulouse). Ireland, to May 1815. Belgium, to December 1815 (battle of Waterloo). France, to 1818. England, to 1820. Ireland, to 1825. Canada, to 1836. Scotland, to 1839. England, to 1841. Gibraltar, to 1848. Canada, to 1851. Scotland, to 1853. England, to May 1854. Scutari, to June 1854. Varna, to September 1854. Crimea, to 1856 (battle of Alma and siege of Sebastopol). England, to June 1857. Ireland, to July 1857. East Indies, to 1871 (capture of Lucknow). England, to 1875. Scotland, to 1879. Gibraltar, to 1882. Egypt, to 1884 (war of 1882, battle of Tel-el-Kebir). Soudan, to 1886 (campaign of 1884-85). Egypt, to 1887. England, to March 1888. Scotland, 1888.

The Royal Irish Rifles.

Regimental District No. 83.—Belfast.

Formerly the 83rd (County Dublin) and the 86th (Royal County Down) Regiments.
(The 3rd, 4th, 5th, and 6th Battalions are formed of the North Down, the Antrim, the South Down, and the Louth Militia respectively.)

The Harp and Crown. "*Quis separabit?*" "INDIA" "EGYPT" (with the Sphinx). "CAPE OF GOOD HOPE, 1806" "BOURBON" "TALAVERA" "BUSACO" "FUENTES D'ONOR" "CIUDAD RODRIGO" "BADAJOZ" "SALAMANCA" "VITTORIA" "NIVELLE" "ORTHES" "TOULOUSE" "PENINSULA" "CENTRAL INDIA."

Colonel.—Wilmot Henry Bradford,[1] *Ensign,* P24 May 33; *Lt.* P26 Aug. 36; *Capt.* P27 Aug. 41; *Major,* P8 Aug. 51; *Lt. Colonel,* 29 Dec. 54; *Colonel,* 29 Dec. 59; *Major General,* 6 Mar. 68; *Lt. General,* 1 Oct. 77; *General,* 1 July 81; *Colonel Irish Rifles,* 24 May 86.

Lieutenant Colonels.—2 Folliott Stuart Furneaux Stokes,[10] *Ensign,* P9 April 70; *Lt.* P27 Oct. 71; *Capt.* 19 Oct. 78; *Major,* 10 Oct. 85; *Lt. Colonel,* 10 Jan. 89.

1 Robert John Knox, *Ensign,* P8 Aug. 68; *Lt.* 28 Oct. 71; *Capt.* 12 May 8.1; *Major,* 26 Apr. 86; *Lt. Colonel,* 4 June 94.

Years' Ser. Full Pay	Half Pay		MAJORS.	ENSIGN OR 2ND LIEUT.	LIEUT.	CAPTAIN.	BREV. MAJ.	MAJOR.
25	...	2	Edward Guy Selby-Smyth	P 7 May 70	28 Oct. 71	28 Apr. 81	......	10 Jan. 89
24	...	1	Charles Haggard	......	27 Mar. 72	29 Nov. 81	......	3 Aug. 89
21	...	1	Henry Averell Eagar (*Depot*)	......	2 Dec. 74	18 Jan. 82	......	28 Dec. 89
21	...	2	Henry James Seton	......	2 Dec. 74	26 April 82	......	2 July 90
19	...		Arthur Thomas Swaine, *Adjutant* 6 Battalion 16 May 92	......	17 May 76	19 July 82	......	18 April 92
18	...	2	Frederick John Tobin[12]	......	12 May 77	1 Apr. 83	......	10 Jan. 93
18	...	2	Walter Adye,[13] *at Staff College*	30 Jan. 78	19 Oct. 78	14 Nov. 84	......	2 Mar. 93
17	...	2	John Southwell Brown[16]	1 May 78	12 April 79	15 Apr. 85	......	4 June 94

			CAPTAINS.					
16	...		Edward Allen, *Adjutant* 3 Bn. 1 Feb. 94	13 Aug. 79	26 Apr. 80	19 Aug. 85		
16	...	2	Robert Alleyne Stewart Buckle	13 Aug. 79	2 Oct. 80	7 Sept. 86		
17	...		Herbert Loftus Welman,[17] *Adjutant* 6 Battalion Rifle Brigade 20 Nov. 93	22 Jan. 79	12 Mar. 81	24 Jan. 87		
17	...		William Hugh Dunlop, *Adjutant* 4 Battalion 2 March 93	19 Feb. 79	9 June 80	28 May 87		
15	...		p.s.c. William Evelyn O'Leary, *serving with the Egyptian Army*	22 Jan. 81	1 July 81	28 May 87		
15	...	2	Octavius Claude John Hallum (*Depot*)	22 Jan. 81	1 July 81	4 Aug. 87		
15	...	2	William John M'Whinnie[18]	19 Feb. 81	1 July 81	25 Oct. 87		
14	...		Archibald Claude Douglas Spencer, *Adjutant* 5 Battalion 1 Feb. 95	23 April 81	1 July 81	31 Dec. 87		
13	...		Thomas Edwards, *Army Pay Dept.*		10 May 82	6 June 88		
10	...	1	FitzRoy Edmond Penn Curzon, *Adjutant* 1 Jan. 92	13 Aug. 79	1 July 81	14 Nov. 88		
12	5/12	1	Harold Martin Cliff	......	10 Mar. 83	21 Nov. 88		
12	...	2	Henry John Morphy	......	12 May 83	3 Aug. 89		
12	...	1	Kennedy Beresford	......	12 May 83	4 Sept. 89		
12	...	1	Frederick John Hamilton Bell	......	25 Aug. 83	4 Sept. 89		
12	...		Charles Edward Ramsey Harvey, *Adj. 1 Vol. Bn. Lincoln Regt.* 19 Jan. 92	......	25 Aug. 83	4 Sept. 89		
12	...	2	Godfrey Warburton Massey	......	6 Feb. 84	2 Mar. 93		
11	...		Theodore Stephen Fox-Strangways, *Staff Captain, Egypt,* 1 June 91	......	14 May 84	1 July 93		
10	...		p.s.c. Robert Abercromby Dick Rowley	......	29 Aug. 85	1 July 93		
10	...	1	George Brenton Laurie	......	2 Sept. 85	20 Nov. 93		
9	...	1	George Wm. Wallace D'Arcy Evans	......	21 July 86	13 Apr. 94		
9	2⅙	1	William George Lillingston-Johnson	......	6 Feb. 84	4 June 94		
9	...	2	Arthur Joseph Berkeley Addison	......	25 Aug. 86	20 Feb. 95		

			LIEUTENANTS.					
9	...	1	Henry Francis Rushworth Despard (*Depot*)	5 Feb. 87	18 July 88			
8	...	2	Robert Fenwick Ryan	4 May 87	18 July 88			
8	...	1	Walter Ernest Onslow Campbell Bluut	14 Sept. 87	21 Nov. 88			
8	...	1	Thomas Carson	16 Nov. 87	21 Nov. 88			
8	...	2	Arthur Robinson Kay Hall (*Depot*)	16 Nov. 87	16 Mar. 89			
8	...	2	Arthur Vavasour Weir	16 Nov. 87	3 July 89			
8	...	1	Arthur Hoskyns Festing	11 Feb. 88	3 July 89			
7	...		William Atkins, *Adj. Mounted Inf. Egypt, with rank of Capt.* 18 Apr. 91	4 July 88	3 Aug. 89			
7	...	1	Louis Hemington Noblett	22 Aug. 88	1 Oct. 89			
7	...	2	George Stanley Cary	8 Dec. 88	18 Dec. 89			
7	...	2	Brabazon Hubert Maine Fox	8 Dec. 88	2 Jan. 90			
7	...	2	William Jameson	8 Dec. 88	23 July 90			
7	...	2	Vincent Joseph Kelly	8 Dec. 88	18 July 91			
7	...	1	Michael Seymour Dudley Westropp (*Depot*)	8 Dec. 88	2 Mar. 93			
7	...	2	Edgar Jessopp Christie, *Adjutant* 3 Feb. 92	23 Mar. 89	2 Mar. 93			
6	...	1	Harry Charles Harvey	21 Sept. 89	22 Mar. 93			
6	...	1	Wilfred Philip Dimsdale	9 Nov. 89	1 July 93			
6	...	1	Philip George Wright Eckford	9 Nov. 89	20 Nov. 93			
6	...	2	Eustace Marriott Peck	21 Dec. 89	4 June 94			
6	...	1	Osbert Clinton Baker	1 Mar. 90	18 Nov. 94			
6	...	1	Wentworth Alexander King-Harman	29 Mar. 90	20 Feb. 95			

			SECOND LIEUTENANTS.					
5	...	2	Degge Wilmot-Sitwell	28 June 90				
5	...	2	Edward Chaloner Bradford	29 Oct. 90				
5	...	1	Hugh Gerald Brenan	17 Jan. 91				
4	...	2	Herbert Alexander Kennedy	25 July 91				
4	...	2	Henry Coram Wright	12 Mar. 92				
2	...	2	Gerald Macleay Molloy	19 July 93				
2	...	2	Charles Rodney Spedding	23 Dec. 93				
2	...	2	Duncan Alured Elmsly Will	7 Mar. 94				
2	...	2	Richard Algernon Craigie Daunt	7 Mar. 94				
1	...	1	James William Alston	10 Oct. 94				
1	...	1	Harry Lawrence Low	23 Jan. 95				

Years' Ser.		
Full Pay.	Half Pay.	
		Paymasters.—1
		2
4	...	*Quarter Masters.*—2 John Dwyer, 23 Jan. 92; *Hon. Lieut.*
2	...	1 Joseph Cunningham, 28 Feb. 94; *Hon. Lieut.*

Facings Dark Green.—*Agents*, Messrs. Cox and Co.
1st Battalion returned from Gibraltar, 1882. 2nd Battalion embarked for Bermuda, 1880.

¹ General Bradford served in the Eastern campaign of 1854, and up to 9th Feb. 1855 with the 2nd Battalion Rifle Brigade, including the battle of Alma and siege of Sebastopol (Medal with two Clasps, Turkish Medal, and 5th Class of the Medjidie).
¹⁰ Lt.Colonel Stokes served in the Boer war of 1881 with the Natal Field Force. Served in the Soudan campaign in 1885 (Medal with Clasp, and Khedive's Star).
¹² Major Tobin served in the Afghan war in 1879-80 with the 23rd Bombay Native Infantry, and was present in a skirmish at Sinari, near Spitungi, South Afghanistan (severely wounded), and in an affair with the Marris in the Koochali Pass (mentioned in despatches, and received the commendations of the Government and the Commander in Chief in India, Medal).
¹³ Major Adye served in the Afghan war in 1879-80, took part in the defence of Candahar, and was present in the sortie of Deh Khojah and at the battle of Candahar (Medal with Clasp). Served in the Boer war in 1881.
¹⁶ Major J. S. Brown served in the Boer war of 1881 with the Natal Field Force.
¹⁷ Captain Welman served in the Zulu war in 1879 (Medal with Clasp).
¹⁸ Captain M'Whinnie served in the operations near Suakin in December 1888 including the engagement at Gemaizah (Medal with Clasp, 4th Class of the Medjidie, and Khedive's Star).

Record of the Services of the 1st Battalion Royal Irish Rifles—formerly the 83rd (County Dublin) Regt.

Raised in 1793. To England, 1794. To the West Indies, 1795. To England, 1802. To the Cape of Good Hope, 1805 (capture of the Cape). To the Peninsula, 1809 (battles of Talavera, Busaco, Fuentes d'Onor, Ciudad Rodrigo, Badajoz, Salamanca, Vittoria, Nivelle, Orthes, and Toulouse). To Ireland, 1814. To Ceylon, 1817. To Scotland, 1829. To Ireland, 1830. To America, 1834. To England, 1843. To Ireland, 1845. To India, 1849 ("Central India"). To England, 1862. To Ireland, 1866. To Gibraltar, 1867. To India, 1870. To South Africa, 1881. To England, 1882.

Record of the Services of the 2nd Battalion Royal Irish Rifles—formerly the 86th (Royal County Down) Regiment.

Raised as Cuyler's Shropshire Volunteers in 1793. To Ireland and England, 1794. Entitled "86th, or Shropshire Volunteers," 1794. Served as Marines, 1795. To Cape of Good Hope, 1796. To India, 1799. Six companies to Egypt, 1801; returned to India, 1802. Entitled "86th, or Leinster Regiment," 1806. To Isle of Bourbon, 1810 (capture of Bourbon). To Isle of France, 1811. To India, 1812. Entitled "86th, or Royal County Down," 1814. [2nd Battalion raised and disbanded in 1814.] To England, 1819. To Ireland, 1821. To West Indies, 1827. To England, 1837. To Ireland, 1840. To India, 1842. To England, 1859. To Gibraltar, 1864. To Port Elizabeth and Mauritius, 1867. To Cape of Good Hope, 1870. To England, 1875. To Bermuda, 1880. Entitled "2nd Battalion Royal Irish Rifles," 1881. To Nova Scotia, 1883. To Gibraltar, 1886. To Egypt, 1887. To Malta, 1891.

Continuation of Notes to the Princess Victoria's (Royal Irish Fusiliers).

¹ General Ferryman commanded the 89th Regiment in the Crimean campaign from 15th Dec. 1854, including the siege and fall of Sebastopol and attacks on the 18th June and 8th Sept. (Medal with Clasp, CB., Knight of the Legion of Honour, 4th Class of the Medjidie, and Turkish Medal).
³ Major Smith served in the Soudan Expedition in 1884 with the 2nd Battalion Royal Irish Fusiliers, and was present in the engagements at El Teb and Temai (Medal with Clasp, 4th Class of the Medjidie, and Khedive's Star).
⁴ Majors Reeves, Munn, and Moore, Captains Hill, Davison, Hext, Brinckman, and Plomer served with the 2nd Battalion Royal Irish Fusiliers in the Soudan Expedition in 1884, and were present in the engagements at El Teb and Temai (Medal with Clasp, and Khedive's Star).
⁵ Major Rogers served as Adjutant with the 2nd Battalion Royal Irish Fusiliers in the Soudan Expedition in 1884, and was present in the engagements at Teb El and Temai (mentioned in despatches, Medal with Clasp, 4th Class of the Medjidie, and Khedive's Star).
⁸ Captain Kincaid served with the 1st Battalion Royal Irish Fusiliers in the Egyptian war of 1882, and was present at the battle of Tel-el-Kebir (Medal with Clasp, and Khedive's Star).
¹⁰ Captain Blood served with the 1st Battalion Irish Fusiliers in the Egyptian war of 1882, and was present at the battle of Tel-el-Kebir (Medal with Clasp, and Khedive's Star). Served with the Hazara Expedition in 1888 as Assistant Superintendent of Signalling, and Brigade (mentioned in despatches, Medal with Clasp).
¹¹ Captain Benson served with the Burmese Expedition in 1886-88 with the 2nd Battalion Royal Munster Fusiliers (Medal with Clasp).
¹² Captain Rice served with the Manipore Expedition in 1891 as Transport Officer (Medal with Clasp).
¹³ Captain Thomas served in the operations near Suakin in December 1888 including the engagement at Gemaizah (Medal with Clasp, and Khedive's Star).

Record of the Services of the 1st Battalion of the Princess Victoria's Royal Irish Fusiliers (formerly the 87th Regiment).

Raised in 1793. Proceeded to Flanders, 1794. To Bergen-op-Zoom, 1795. Home, 1796. To West Indies, 1796. Home, 1804. (2nd Battalion raised in 1804. Proceeded to Guernsey, 1807. Home, 1808. To Peninsula, 1809. Home, 1814. To Guernsey, 1814. Home, 1816. Disbanded, 1817.) To Guernsey, 1804. Home, 1805. To South America, 1806. To the Cape of Good Hope, 1807. To Mauritius, 1810. To India, 1815. To Burmah, 1825. To India, 1826. Home, 1827. To Mauritius, 1831. Home, 1843. To India, 1849. To China, 1860. Home, 1861. To Gibraltar, 1866. To Malta, 1868. To Nova Scotia, 1872. To Bermuda, 1876. Home, 1877. To Guernsey, 1880. Home, 1881. To Egypt, 1882. Home, 1882. To India, 1883.

Princess Victoria's (Royal Irish Fusiliers). 333

1st Batt., Allahabad, Bengal.
2nd Batt., Kilkenny. | *Formerly the 87th (Royal Irish Fusiliers) and the 89th (Princess Victoria's) Regiments.* | Regimental District No. 87.—Armagh.

(The 3rd, 4th, and 5th Battalions are formed of the Armagh, Cavan, and Monaghan Militia respectively.)
Princess Victoria's Coronet. "EGYPT" (with the Sphinx). "MONTE VIDEO" "TALAVERA."—An Eagle, with a Wreath of Laurel above the Harp in addition to the Plume of the Prince of Wales, in commemoration of their distinguished services on various occasions, and particularly at certain battles. "BARROSA" "TARIFA" "JAVA" "VITTORIA" "NIVELLE" "NIAGARA" "ORTHES" "TOULOUSE" "PENINSULA" "AVA" "SEVASTOPOL" "EGYPT, 1882, 1884" "TEL-EL-KEBIR."

Years' Ser. Full Pay.	Half Pay.						
31	...	\multicolumn{7}{l}{Colonel.—Augustus Halifax Ferryman,[1] CB. Ensign, p27 June 34; Lt. 30 June 37; Capt. p16 April 41; Major, p22 Dec. 43; Lt.Colonel, p24 Nov. 48; Colonel, 28 Nov. 54; Major General, 12 Feb. 63; Lieut. General, 19 Nov. 71; General, 1 Oct. 77; Colonel 40th Foot, 23 May 72; Col. Irish Fusiliers, 18 Sept. 87.}
28	...	\multicolumn{7}{l}{Lieutenant Colonels.—2 p.s.c. Evelyn Campbell Money, Ensign, 3 Jan. 65; Lieut. p27 July 66; Capt. p19 Feb. 70; Major, 21 Sept. 82; Lt.Colonel, 12 Aug. 91.}
		\multicolumn{7}{l}{1 Charles Arundel Barker, Ensign, p6 Nov. 67; Lieut. p23 June 69; Capt. 23 April 77; Major, 14 May 84; Lt.Colonel, 9 Jan. 93.}

		MAJORS.	ENSIGN OR 2ND LIEUT.	LIEUT.	CAPTAIN.	BREV.MAJ.	MAJOR.
28	...	1 George Osborne Smith[3]	13 July 67	p12 Dec. 68	6 Mar. 80	......	11 April 85
22	...	2 p.s.c. John Reeves[4]	......	21 Jan. 74	25 June 81	......	25 Jan. 88
19	...	1 Frederick Henry Munn[4]	......	11 Sept. 76	30 Mar. 83	......	1 July 88
19	...	2 Claude Rainier Rogers[5]	......	24 June 76	28 Aug. 83	......	12 Aug. 88
18	...	1 James Douglas Standen	......	28 April 77	14 May 84	......	9 Jan. 89
16	...	Alexander M'Donnell Moore,[4] *Insp. Gen. of Police, Mauritius,* 1 Oct. 92	23 July 79	1 Dec. 80	12 Aug. 85	......	5 Aug. 91
18	...	2 John Willoughby Astley Marshall[16] (*Depot*)	......	30 Nov. 77	5 Oct. 87	10 Aug. 92	19 July 9
21	9/12	2 Theodore Gordon Barclay	......	9 Aug. 73	4 Oct. 84	......	7 Nov. 94
		CAPTAINS.					
17	...	Charles Style Kincaid,[8] *Adjutant* 3 *Battalion* 24 Aug. 91	13 Nov. 78	17 May 79	20 May 86		
17	...	William Stafford Joseph Barry,[18] *Adj.* 1 *Admin.Bn.N.W.Prov.Vol.* 1 Feb.94	7 Aug. 78	30 Mar. 81	13 Oct. 86		
16	...	1 Felix Frederic Hill[4] (*Depot*)	14 Jan. 80	13 Apr. 81	25 Jan. 88		
15	...	1 William Pearson Davison[4]	3 Oct. 80	1 July 81	23 Feb. 88		
15	...	p.s.c. William Porssé Blood,[10] *Dep. Assist. Adj. Gen. Bengal,* 27 June 94	22 Jan. 81	1 July 81	18 Apr. 88		
15	...	2 Francis Marwood Hext[4]	23 Oct. 80	1 July 81	1 July 88		
15	...	2 Rowland Brinckman[4]	22 Jan. 81	1 July 81	1 July 88		
15	...	Fred. John Angell,[19] *Ord. Store Dept.*	22 Jan. 81	1 July 81	12 Aug. 88		
14	...	William Harry Perceval Plomer,[4] *Adjutant* 5 *Battalion* 24 Mar. 90	......	22 Oct. 81	7 Sept. 88		
13	...	Charles Ulric Sandys, *Adjutant* 4 *Battalion* 1 Dec. 93	......	10 May 82	9 Jan. 89		
13	...	1 Richard Meredith de Berry	......	10 Mar. 83	29 May 89		
12	...	Herbert Adolphe Coddington, *Adj.* 1 *Tower Hamlets Rifle Vols.* 2 Apr. 94	......	6 Feb. 84	8 Feb. 90		
11	...	2 William Elliot Cairnes	......	14 May 84	21 May 90		
11	...	Tom Evelyn O'Leary, *Inspector of Army Signalling, Bengal,* 1 Sept. 93	......	14 May 84	21 May 90		
11	...	1 Frederick Henry Bourne Connor	......	14 May 84	5 Aug. 91		
13	...	2 Thomas Charles Benson[11]	......	29 July 82	30 Dec. 91		
11	...	2 Gerard Beechey Howard Rice[12]	......	7 Feb. 85	25 Jan. 93		
10	...	2 Robert Waugh Leeper	......	6 May 85	1 Apr. 93		
10	...	1 Wogan Richard Festing	......	30 Jan. 86	1 Sept. 93		
9	...	1 John George Parker	......	28 Apr. 86	1 Feb. 94		
10	9/12	2 Reginald Percy Thomas[13]	......	12 Nov. 84	22 Aug. 90		
		LIEUTENANTS.					
9	...	2 Richard Tucker Gray	......	28 Apr. 86			
9	...	2 Walter Barrington Silver	......	25 Aug. 86			
9	...	1 Markham John Willoughby Pike	......	25 Aug. 86			
9	...	1 Douglas Wilfred Churcher	......	25 Aug. 86			
9	...	2 George Kilner Swettenham, *Superintendent of Gymnasia, Cork*	......	10 Nov. 86			
9	...	1 Philip Richard Wood	5 Feb. 87	10 Apr. 89			
9	...	1 Frederic Lewis Vernon Jenkins	5 Feb. 87	10 Apr. 89			
8	...	1 Arnold Robinson Burrowes, *Adjutant* 16 Sept. 91	11 Feb. 88	31 July 89			
8	...	1 Walter Francis Templer	11 Feb. 88	13 Dec. 89			
8	...	1 John Eastwood Ramsay Brush	9 May 88	18 Dec. 89			
7	...	1 Sir Henry Blyth Hill, *Bart.* (*Depot*)	10 Nov. 88	12 Nov. 89			
7	...	2 Hercules Arthur Temple Robinson, *Adjutant* 6 Feb. 94	16 Jan. 89	27 Mar. 91			
6	...	2 Charles Conyers (*Depot*)	8 June 89	16 Sept. 91			
6	...	1 Alex. Eustace Stawell Heard	21 Dec. 89	1 July 92			
5	...	2 Sydney Edward Schilling	28 June 90	1 Jan. 93			
5	...	1 Bertram Edward Crocker	23 July 90	25 Jan. 93			
5	...	1 Frederick Augustus Greer	29 Oct. 90	1 Apr. 93			
4	1/2	2 Edward Warner Shewell	18 Mar. 91	26 Apr. 94			
4	...	1 Philip Gould	8 Apr. 91	26 Apr. 94			
4	...	John William Moore Morgan, *Army Service Corps*	2 May 91	26 Apr. 94			
4	...	1 Malcolm Wilson	10 Oct. 91	9 May 94			
4	...	1 Robert Alexander Gray	10 Oct. 91	1 Jan. 95			
		SECOND LIEUTENANTS.					
3	...	2 Charles Elliot Southey	13 Aug. 92				
3	...	1 William Griffith Baynes Phibbs	19 Oct. 92				
3	...	1 Colin Dick	22 Feb. 93				
3	...	2 Hugo Mascie Taylor	15 Mar. 93				
2	...	2 Ralph Durrant Sadleir Stoney	20 May 93				
3	...	1 Richard Alexander Steel	5 Oct. 93				
2	...	1 Hugh Cracroft	7 Mar. 94				
1	...	2 Henry Ball Holmes	2 June 94				
1	...	2 Albert Lionel Westropp Hughes	2 June 94				
1	...	2 Francis Augustus Maling Welsh	2 June 94				
1	...	2 Henry Lewkonor Knight	10 Oct. 94				
1	...	Arthur Gerald Knocker	6 Mar. 95				

[16] Major Marshall served with the expedition to the Tambaka Country, on the West Coast of Africa, in 1892, including the capture of Tambi (mentioned in despatches); and with the expedition to the Gambia in 1892, including the capture of Toniataba (mentioned in despatches, Brevet of Major, Medal with Clasp).

[18] Captain Barry served with the 1st Battalion Irish Fusiliers in the Egyptian war of 1882 until invalided on 20th September (Medal, and Khedive's Star).

[19] Captain Angell served with the 2nd Battalion Royal Irish Fusiliers in the Soudan Expedition in 1884, and was present in the engagement at El Teb (Medal with Clasp, and Khedive's Star). Served with the Bechuanaland Expedition under Sir Charles Warren in 1884-85.

[*For remainder of Notes, see preceding page.*]

Facings Blue.
Agents, Messrs. Cox and Co.
1st Battalion embarked for Bengal, 1882. 2nd Battalion returned from Egypt, 21 Apr. 1884.

Paymasters.—1 John E. R. Brush, *Lieut.* 1 Battalion (*acting*).

Quarter Masters.—1 Robert Johnston, 21 Oct. 91; *Hon. Lieut.*

4 | ...

1st Batt., Portsmouth.
2nd Batt., Egypt.] **The Connaught Rangers.** [Regimental District No. 88.—Galway.

Formerly the 88th (Connaught Rangers) and the 94th Regiments.
(The 3rd, 4th, and 5th Battalions are formed of the South and North Mayo, the Galway, and the Roscommon Militia respectively.)

The Harp and Crown. "*Quis separabit?*" The Elephant. "SERINGAPATAM" "EGYPT" (with the Sphinx). "TALAVERA" "BUSACO" "FUENTES D'ONOR" "CIUDAD RODRIGO" "BADAJOZ" "SALAMANCA" "VITTORIA" "NIVELLE" "ORTHES" "TOULOUSE" "PENINSULA" "ALMA" "INKERMAN" "SEVASTOPOL" "CENTRAL INDIA" "SOUTH AFRICA, 1877-8-9."

Years' Ser.							
Full Pay	Half Pay						
30	...	Colonel.—Joseph Edwin Thackwell,[1] C.B., Ensign, P 6 June 34; Lieut. 23 Oct. 39; Captain, P 26 May 48; Major, 12 Dec. 54; Lt. Colonel, 2 Nov. 55; Colonel, 25 June 61; Major General, 6 March 68; Lt. General, 22 Dec. 78; General, 1 July 81; Colonel Connaught Rangers, 23 Dec. 89.					
29	...	Lieutenant Colonels.—1 Sir George Albert de Hochepied-Larpont,[6] Bart. Ensign, P 21 Nov. 65; Lieut. P 15 Sept. 69; Captain, 24 Nov. 77; Major, 1 July 81; Lt. Colonel, 1 July 91.					
		2 Edmund Smith Brook,[7] Ensign, P 7 Aug. 66; Lieut. P 25 Jan. 71; Captain, 3 Dec. 78; Major, 1 July 81; Bt. Lt. Colonel, 18 Feb. 82; Colonel, 18 Feb. 86; Lt. Colonel, 8 Feb. 93.					

		MAJORS.	ENSIGN OR 2ND LIEUT.	LIEUT.	CAPTAIN.	BREV. MAJ.	MAJOR.
26	...	1 Lionel Godolphin Brooke[8]	P 5 May 69	28 Oct. 71	15 April 79	......	1 July 81
25	...	2 Frederick Carpenter	P 3 Aug. 70	28 Oct. 71	30 Mar. 81	......	1 Feb. 85
20	...	1 Charles Edward Harman	......	21 Sept. 75	30 Mar. 81	......	21 Jan. 90
17	...	1 John de Courcy O'Grady[13]	......	11 Sept. 78	13 Apr. 81	......	12 Feb. 91
21	...	2 Attiwell Henry Wood[14]	......	2 Dec. 74	16 Sept. 82	......	1 July 91
21	...	Maurice George Moore,[15] *Adjutant 5 Battalion 4 May 92*	......	13 June 74	1 Nov. 82	......	8 Feb. 93
18	...	Alexander William Day Maclean,[17] *Adjutant 3 Battalion 17 Aug. 92*	30 Jan. 78	20 Aug. 79	15 Aug. 83	......	8 Feb. 93
18	...	Alfred George Goodenough Elton[21]	5 Sept. 77	20 June 79	17 Dec. 84	......	6 Sept. 93
		CAPTAINS.					
17	...	2 John James Francis Hume[20]	Feb. 79	23 June 80	30 July 85		
17	...	1 Harry Geo Adams-Connor[22] *(Depot)*	22 Feb. 79	13 July 80	27 Dec. 85		
18	...	1 James Lowry Cole Acton[23]	15 Sept. 77	27 Aug. 79	19 Feb. 87		
18	...	Nathaniel Albert Delap Barton,[25] *Adj. 12 Middlesex Rifle Vols. 2 Nov. 91*	16 Feb. 78	22 Oct. 80	7 April 87		
16	...	1 Edmund Alexander Grubbe, *Adjutant 9 Apr. 91*	9 July 79	1 July 81	1 July 87		
16	...	Coldstream James Carden[27]	9 July 79	1 Dec. 80	29 May 89		
16	...	2 Frederick George William Jones[28] *(Depot)*	6 Aug. 79	21 Dec. 80	25 Sept. 89		
16	...	Charles Hall,[30] *Ordnance Store Dept.*	13 Aug. 79	1 July 81	2 Dec. 89		
15	...	Edward Stanley Combe,[51] *Ordnance Store Department*	23 Oct. 80	1 July 81	2 Dec. 89		
15	...	2 Charles William Bowlby	22 Jan. 81	1 July 81	2 Dec. 89		
15	...	1 John Staples Molesworth Lenox Conyngham	22 Jan. 81	1 July 81	2 Dec. 89		
13	...	1 Henry Deschamps Chamier	......	10 Mar. 83	15 Jan. 90		
12	...	p.s.c. Charles Delmé-Radcliffe, *Aide de Camp to Major Gen. E. Hopton 7 Nov. 93*	......	6 Feb. 84	12 Feb. 90		
11	...	Arthur Wm. Hadden Bell, *Adjutant 9 Bn. King's R. Rifles 16 Aug. 94*	......	23 Aug. 84	24 Sept. 90		
17	...	1 Charles Herbert Davis Cass	13 July 78	2 Feb. 81	19 Jan. 88		
11	...	2 Arth. Geo. Vaughan Chichester	......	7 Feb. 85	12 Feb. 91		
10	...	2 George Higginson Ford-Hutchinson	......	9 May 85	2 Nov. 91		
12	...	p.s.c. Oswald Henry Pedley, *serving with the Egyptian Army*	......	11 Oct. 82	21 Dec. 92		
10	...	Alexander William Abercrombie,[32] *Adj. 3 Vol. Bn. Suffolk Regt. 9 Jan. 93*	......	9 May 85	21 Dec. 92		
10	...	2 Herbert Gore	......	29 Aug. 85	9 Jan. 93		
10	...	John Frederic Robertson,[33] *Adjutant Infantry Battalion, Queensland*	......	27 Jan. 86	8 Feb. 93		
9	...	2 Harry Gerald Keith Matchett	......	10 Nov. 86	14 Aug. 93		
9	...	2 George Lamont Hobbs	5 Sept. 87	7 Mar. 89	6 Sept. 93		
8	...	1 William Edward John Grylls	14 Sept. 87	6 Nov. 89	20 Dec. 93		
8	...	1 Shadwell John Murray	11 Feb. 88	20 Nov. 89	16 Aug. 94		
		LIEUTENANTS.					
7	...	George Cuthbert Digan, *serving in the Niger Coast Protectorate*	9 May 88	18 Dec. 89			
7	...	2 Harry Adair Thompson, *Adjutant 22 July 93*	27 June 88	18 Dec. 89			
7	...	1 William Charles Giffard Heneker	5 Sept. 88	12 Feb. 90			
7	...	1 William Stopford Sarsfield	19 Sept. 88	12 Feb. 90			
6	...	2 Arthur John Bromley Church, *Ordnance Store Department*	24 April 89	24 Sept. 90			
6	...	2 Francis William Lawson	6 July 89	24 Sept. 90			
6	...	2 John Claudius Henry Raven *(Depot)*	6 July 89	12 Feb. 91			
6	...	2 William Allardice Hamilton	18 Sept. 89	2 Nov. 91			
6	...	2 Claude Fulcher	9 Nov. 89	9 Aug. 92			
6	...	1 Charles Victor Isacke	1 Mar. 90	9 Jan. 93			
5	...	1 Edward Louis Laurenson *(Depot)*	28 June 90	8 Feb. 93			
5	...	1 Percy Thornton Horton	28 June 90	19 Mar. 93			
5	...	1 Archibald Swinton Hog	29 Nov. 90	21 Apr. 93			
4	...	2 Edward Fitzherbert Despard	2 May 91	11 Aug. 93			
4	...	2 Henry Robert Gordon Deacon	7 Nov. 91	14 Aug. 93			
4	...	2 Travers Hartley Falkiner	9 Jan. 92	6 Sept. 93			
4	...	1 Wilfred Arthur White	27 Jan. 92	11 Oct. 93			
4	...	2 Robert Richards Challenor	27 Jan. 92	20 Dec. 93			
3	...	2 Frederick Joseph Byrne	17 Dec. 92	7 Apr. 94			
2	...	1 Henry Francis Newdigate Jourdain	25 Feb. 93	16 Aug. 94			
2	...	2 Osmond Donald Blunt	15 Mar. 93	1 Jan. 95			
		SECOND LIEUTENANTS.					
2	...	1 Richard Percy Littleton Vigors	20 May 93				
1	...	2 Capel Hanbury Mesham	19 July 93				

[8] Major L. G. Brooke served as Adjutant with the 94th Regiment in the Zulu war of 1879, and was present in the engagement at Ulundi—slightly wounded (mentioned in despatches, Medal with Clasp).

[14] Major Wood served with the 88th Regiment throughout the Kafir war of 1877-78 (Medal with Clasp).

[30] Captain Hall served in the Boer war of 1880-81, and took part in the defence of Pretoria.

Years' Ser.		SECOND LIEUTENANTS.	2ND LIEUT.	
Full Pay	Half Pay			
2	...	1 Charles Edward Watling	21 Oct.	93
2	...	1 James Lionel Joyce Coury	21 Oct.	93
2	...	2 Kenneth Gale Crockett	21 Oct.	93
2	...	2 Robert William Harling	8 Nov.	93
2	...	1 William Nathaniel Stuart Alexander	7 Mar.	94
2	...	2 Henry Worsley Gough	7 Mar.	94
1	...	1 Addis Delacombe	6 June	94
.1	...	2 Hugh Moore Hutchinson	10 Oct.	94
1	...	2 Arthur Lorean Keogh	12 Dec.	94
.1	...	Alexander Wise	6 Mar.	95

Paymasters.—1
 2
8 ... *Quarter Masters.*—1 David M'Kelvey MacLachlan, 7 March 88 ; *Hon. Lieut.*
1 ... —2 Thomas M'Clelland, 17 Oct. 94 ; *Hon. Lieut.*
Facings Green.—*Agents*, Messrs. Cox and Co.
1st Battalion returned from Aden, 14 Dec. 91. 2nd Battalion embarked for Malta, 13 July 1889.

¹ General Thackwell served with the 22nd Regt. in the campaign in Sind, and was present at the battle of Hyderabad (Medal). Also the campaign of 1844-45 in the Southern Mahratta Country, including the investment and capture of Forts Panulla and Pownghur. Served the Eastern campaign of 1854-55 as Brigade Major to 1st Brigade 2nd Division—including the battles of Alma and Inkerman (horse shot), siege of Sebastopol and repulse of the sortie on 26th October. On 4th August 1855 he was appointed Assistant Adjutant General to the 3rd Division, and served with it until broken up in April 1856 (Medal with three Clasps, Brevets of Major and Lt.Colonel, Knight of the Legion of Honor, Sardinian and Turkish Medals, and 5th Class of the Medjidie).
⁶ Sir G. Larpent served with the 88th Regiment throughout the Kafir war of 1877-78, and the Zulu war of 1879 (Medal with Clasp).
⁷ Colonel E. S. Brook served with the 94th Regiment in the Zulu war of 1879, and was present in the engagement at Ulundi and in the subsequent operations against Sekukuni, including the storming of the stronghold (Medal with Clasp). Served in the Boer war of 1880-81 in command of the Fort at Marabastadt, which he successfully defended for a period of 92 days (mentioned in despatches, Brevet of Lt.Colonel).
¹³ Major O'Grady served with the 94th Regiment in the Zulu war of 1879, and was present in the engagement at Ulundi, and in the subsequent operations against Sekukuni including the storming of the stronghold—severely wounded (Medal with Clasp). Served in the Boer war of 1880-81 in command of the troop of Mounted Infantry 94th Regiment at Pretoria during its investment.
¹⁵ Major Moore served with the 88th Regiment throughout the Kafir war of 1877-78, and the Zulu war of 1879 (Medal with Clasp).
¹⁷ Major Maclean served with the 94th Regiment in the Zulu war of 1879, and was present in the operations against Sekukuni, including the storming of the stronghold (Medal with Clasp).
²⁰ Captain Hume served with the 94th Regiment in the Zulu war of 1879, and was present in the engagement at Ulundi, and in the subsequent operations against Sekukuni, including the storming of the stronghold (Medal with Clasp). Served in the Boer war of 1880-81, and was present in the engagement at Bronkhorst Spruit—severely wounded (mentioned in despatches).
²¹ Major Elton served with the 88th Regiment throughout the Kafir war of 1877-78, and the Zulu war of 1879 (Medal with Clasp).
²² Captain Adams-Connor served in the Boer war of 1881 as Garrison Adjutant at Newcastle.
²³ Captain Acton served with the 88th Regiment throughout the Kafir war of 1877-78, including the affair at Draaibosch (mentioned in despatches), and throughout the Zulu war of 1879 (Medal with Clasp).
²⁵ Captain Barton served with the 88th Regiment throughout the Zulu war of 1879 (Medal with Clasp).
²⁷ Captain Carden served in the Boer war of 1880-81 with the troop of Mounted Infantry 94th Regiment at Pretoria during its investment. Served in the Nile Expedition in 1884-85 with the Mounted Infantry, and was present at the action of Abu Klea (Medal with two Clasps, and Khedive's Star).
²⁸ Captain Jones served in the Boer war of 1880-81, and took part in the defence of Fort Marabastadt.
³¹ Captain E. S. Combe served in the Boer war of 1881, and took part in the defence of Potchefstroom (mentioned in despatches).
³² Captain Abercrombie served in the Burmese Expedition from 1885 till the close of 1887 with the 1st Battalion of the Yorkshire Light Infantry, including the expedition to the Ruby Mines (mentioned in despatches, Medal with two Clasps).
³³ Captain Robertson served in the Bechuanaland Expedition under Sir Charles Warren in 1884-85 with the Mounted Rifles.

Record of the Services of the 1st Battalion the Connaught Rangers (formerly the 88th Regiment).

Raised in 1793, and proceeded in 1794 to Holland. To England, 1794. To West Indies, 1795. To England, 1796. To India, 1799. To Egypt, 1801. To England, 1803. [2nd Battalion raised 1804.] To Cape of Good Hope, 1806. To Monte Video and Buenos Ayres, 1807. To England, 1807. To the Peninsula, 1808 (battles of Talavera, Busaco, Fuentes d'Onor, Ciudad Rodrigo, Badajoz, Salamanca, Vittoria, Nivelle, Orthes, and Toulouse). To Canada, 1814. To France, 1815. [2nd Battalion reduced, 1816.] To England, 1817. To Ireland, 1821. To the Ionian Islands, 1825. To England, 1836. To Ireland, 1838. To Malta, 1840. To West Indies, 1847. To Nova Scotia, 1850. To England, 1851. To the Crimea, 1854 (battles of Alma and Inkerman and siege of Sebastopol). To England, 1856. To India, 1857 (Indian Mutiny—"Central India"). To England, 1870. To Ireland, 1876. To South Africa, 1877 ("South Africa, 1877-79"). To India, 1879. To Aden, 1890. To England, 1891.

Princess Louise's (Argyll and Sutherland Highlanders).

1st Batt., Aldershot.
2nd Bn., Meean Meer, Bengal.] *Formerly the 91st (Princess Louise's Argyllshire* [Regimental District No. 91.—Stirling.
Highlanders) and the 93rd (Sutherland Highlanders) Regiments.
(The 3rd and 4th Battalions are formed of the Highland Borderers and the Renfrew Militia respectively.)
Princess Louise's Cypher and Coronet. The Boar's Head (The Campbell Crest). "*Ne Obliviscaris.*" A Cat.
"*Sans Peur.*" "Cape of Good Hope, 1806" "Rolria" "Vimiera" "Corunna" "Pyrenees" "Nivelle"
"Nive" "Orthes" "Toulouse" "Peninsula" "South Africa, 1846-7, 1851-2-3" "Alma"
"Balaklava" "Sevastopol" "Lucknow" "South Africa, 1879."

Years'Ser. Full Pay	Half Pay			2ND LIEUT.	LIEUT.	CAPTAIN.	BREV.MAJ.	MAJOR.
		Colonel.—George Erskine,[1] *Ensign,* 17 Aug. 32; *Lieut.* P3 July 36; *Captain,* P1 May 40; *Bt.Major,* 30 June 54; *Bt.Lt.Colonel,* 12 Dec. 54; *Major,* 24 Aug. 55; *Lt.Colonel,* 26 Oct. 55; *Colonel,* 12 Aug. 60; *Major General,* 6 Mar. 68; *Lieut.General,* 1 Oct. 77; *General,* 1 July 81; *Colonel* Argyll and Sutherland Highlanders, 9 June 88.							
28	...	Lieutenant Colonels.—1 Ormelie Campbell Hannay, *Ensign,* P5 Oct. 67; *Lieut.* 28 Oct. 71; *Captain,* 17 Nov. 78; *Major,* 1 Jan. 84; *Lt.Colonel,* 27 June 93.						
26	...	2 John David Fetherstonhaugh, *Ensign,* P1 Sept. 69; *Lieut.* 28 Oct. 71; *Captain,* 17 May 79; *Major,* 28 May 84; *Lieut.Colonel,* 23 July 94.						
		MAJORS.						
23	...	1 Arthur Ely Heathcote Tottenham[6]		......	1 Feb. 73	1 July 81	......	11 July 84
21	...	2 John Stirling Napier		......	P21 Jan. 74	27 Jan. 82	......	31 Mar. 90
23	...	¥C Wm. Henry Dick-Cunyngham,[15] *Dep.Assist.Adj.Gen.,Bengal* 30 Oct. 94		......	17 Feb. 73	10 Oct. 81	......	4 Mar. 91
21	...	1 Gerald Lionel Joseph Goff[6] (*Depot*)		......	10 Mar. 75	1 July 84	......	21 Sept. 92
18	...	2 John Hasluck Campbell		......	10 Sept. 77	8 Oct. 84	......	27 June 93
22	...	2 Charles Grant		......	9 Aug. 73	14 Jan. 84	......	2 Aug. 93
17	...	1 Alexander Wilson[15]		22 Feb. 79	1 July 81	13 Nov. 84	......	18 Nov. 93
16	...	1 Stanley Paterson		9 July 79	1 July 81	1 Feb. 86	......	23 July 94
		CAPTAINS.						
16	...	1 *p.s.c.* Alfred Edward John Cavendish...		14 Jan. 80	1 July 81	12 June 86		
17	...	Andrew Buchanar Blackburr, *Adj.* 5 Vol. Bn. Highland Lt. Inf.* 15 Mar. 92		11 May 78	9 Sept. 80	12 June 86		
17	...	2 *p.s.c.* Edward Brabazon Urmston		11 May 78	10 Nov. 80	27 Sept. 86		
17	11/12	William Stewart, *Adj.* 1 *Dumbartonshire Rifle Volunteers* 2 Feb. 91		......	10 Nov. 77	21 July 86		
17	...	John Gordon Wolrige-Gordon, *Adjutant* 5 *Vol. Battalion* 21 Apr. 62		22 Jan. 79	1 July 81	21 Feb. 88		
16	...	Francis Macnamara Aitken,[19] *Adjutant* 7 *Vol. Battalion* 30 Nov. 91		9 July 79	1 July 81	21 Nov. 88		
16	...	2 Sydney Loftus Robinson		23 July 79	1 July 81	21 Nov. 88		
16	...	2 Reginald L'Estrange M'Kerrell		6 Aug. 79	1 July 81	8 Mar. 89		
15	...	1 Thomas Irvine		22 Jan. 81	1 July 81	1 May 89		
15	...	Chas. Frederick Herbert Davidson,[10] *Inspector of Gymnasia, Madras and Bombay,* 7 Nov. 94		23 Oct. 80	1 July 81	1 Feb. 89		
15	...	1 Thomas Archibald Scott		22 Jan. 81	1 July 81	20 Jan. 90		
15	...	2 Alexander Francis Mackenzie		22 Jan. 81	1 July 81	31 Jan. 90		
15	...	Andrew Aytoun, *Adjutant* 3 *Battalion* 19 Sept. 92		19 Feb. 81	1 July 81	26 Feb. 90		
15	...	2 Henry D'Estampes Vallancey, *at Staff College*		22 Jan. 81	1 July 81	26 Feb. 90		
12	...	1 David Henderson, *at Staff College*		......	25 Aug. 83	26 Feb. 90		
11	...	*p.s.c.* Alan Foster, *Adjutant* 4 *Battalion* 10 Sept. 94		......	23 Aug. 84	24 July 93		
11	...	1 William Thorburn		......	23 Aug. 84	23 Aug. 93		
11	...	2 Kenneth Boswell Cameron		......	22 Nov. 84	18 Nov. 93		
11	...	1 Stafford Edmund Douglas		......	12 Nov. 84	23 July 94		
11	...	Malcolm M'Neill		......	7 Feb. 85	7 Nov. 94		
		LIEUTENANTS.						
10	...	Harry Peyton Moulton-Barrett			23 May 85			
10	...	1 Frederick Lincroft La Caze Jackson			9 May 85			
10	...	1 Herbert Augustus M'Dougal Williams (*Depot*)			14 Oct. 85			
10	...	2 Alic Sutherland, *Adjutant* 15 Jan. 95			25 Nov. 85			
10	...	1 Hugh Leslie Henderson			30 Jan. 86			
10	...	1 Robert Clements Gore			30 Jan. 86			
9	...	2 Archibald Patten			28 Apr. 86			
9	...	2 Hugh Pennycuick Gordon			25 Aug. 86			
9	...	2 Seymour Spencer Somerset Clarke			25 Aug. 86			
8	...	1 Henry Thomas Renny		17 Sept. 87	20 Jan. 90			
8	...	1 Edward Chetwood Hamilton Grant, *Adjutant* 11 June 94		25 Jan. 88	31 Jan. 90			
7	...	2 Francis James Richardson (*Depot*)		9 May 88	26 Feb. 90			
7	...	2 Duncan Darroch		22 Aug. 88	2 Feb. 91			
7	...	1 Archibald John Campbell		12 Sept. 88	25 Nov. 91			
7	...	2 Claude William Hedley Bell		5 Dec. 88	29 Mar. 93			
7	...	1 Henry Buchanan Kirk		10 Nov. 88	24 July 93			
7	...	2 Neill Malcolm, *Assist. Supdt. Army Signalling, Waziristan Field Force*		20 Feb. 89	23 Aug. 93			
7	...	1 Frederick Charles Dundas		23 Mar. 89	18 Nov. 93			
6	...	2 Kenneth Francis Crawley Marshall		24 April 89	11 June 94			
6	...	2 William John Bell Tweedie		9 Nov. 89	23 July 94			
		SECOND LIEUTENANTS.						
5	...	2 Henry Craigie Macdonald		31 May 90				
5	...	2 John Campbell		29 Oct. 90				
5	...	2 Alexander Harvey Maclean		17 Jan. 91				
4	...	2 James Johnston-Stewart		10 Oct. 91				
3	...	2 Fraser George Newall		19 Oct. 92				
2	...	1 Duncan John Glasfurd		21 Oct. 93				
2	...	1 Henry Barchard Fenwick Baker-Carr		21 Oct. 93				
2	...	2 Robert Blackall Graham		7 Mar. 94				
1	...	2 Patrick Dalmahoy McCandlish		2 June 94				
1	...	2 Henry Hugh Gordon Hyslop		10 Oct. 94				
1	...	1 Richard Phillipson Dunn Pattison		20 Feb. 95				
1	...	1 George Edward Courtenay		20 Feb. 95				

[6] Majors Tottenham and Goff served with the 91st Highlanders in the Zulu war of 1879, and were present in the action of Gingindhlovu and relief of Ekowe (Medal with Clasp).

Years' Ser.	
Full Pay.	Half Pay.
8	...
1	...

Paymasters.—1
2 Claude W. H. Bell, *Lieut.* 2 *Battalion (acting)*.
Quarter Masters.—1 William Scott, 6 July 87; *Hon. Lieut.*
2 Alexander Beattie, 27 Feb. 95; *Hon. Lieut.*
Facings Yellow.—*Agents*, Messrs. Cox and Co.
1st Battalion returned from Hong Kong, 23 Mar. 1892. 2nd Battalion embarked for India 26 Nov. 1891.

---

[1] General Erskine served with the 33rd Regiment in the Eastern campaign of 1854-55, including the battle of Inkerman and siege of Sebastopol; he commanded the piquets of the Light Division on the 14th October 1854, when they repulsed the attack made on them by the enemy (Medal with two Clasps, Brevet of Lt.Colonel, 5th Class of the Medjidie, and Turkish Medal).

[4] Lt. Colonel Hannay was employed on special service in South Africa during the latter part of the Zulu war in 1879 (Medal).

[15] Major Dick Cunyngham served in the Afghan war of 1878-80, and was present on Transport duty in the advance to Candahar and Khelat-i-Ghilzie under Sir Donald Stewart; with the Thull Chotiali Force under Major General Biddulph (mentioned in despatches); under Sir Frederick Roberts in the Koorum Valley Field Force in the 92nd Gordon Highlanders, including the engagement at Ali Kheyl; took part in the operations round Cabul in December 1879 (mentioned in despatches) including the attack on the Sherpore Pass (Victoria Cross); with the Maidan Expedition in 1880 as Acting Adjutant of a wing of the 92nd Gordon Highlanders including the engagement at Charasiah on 25th April (mentioned in despatches); accompanied Sir Frederick Roberts in the march to Candahar, and was present at the reconnaissance of the 31st August and at the battle of Candahar (mentioned in despatches, Medal with two Clasps, and Bronze Decoration): was awarded the VC "for the conspicuous gallantry and coolness displayed by him on the 13th December 1879, at the attack on the Sherpur Pass, in Afghanistan, in having exposed himself to the full fire of the enemy, and by his example and encouragement rallied the men, who, having been beaten back, were, at the moment, wavering at the top of the hill." Served in the Boer war of 1881 as Adjutant 92nd Gordon Highlanders.

[18] Major Wilson served with the 91st Highlanders in the latter part of the Zulu war of 1879 (Medal with Clasp).

[19] Captain Aitken.—See Civil Decorations for Gallantry, "Hart's Annual Army List," p. 786.

[20] Captain Davidson served with the Cameron Highlanders throughout the Egyptian war of 1882, and was present at the battle of Tel-el-Kebir (Medal with Clasp, and Khedive's Star). Served in the expedition to the Soudan in 1884 with the Gordon Highlanders, and was present in the engagements at El Teb and Temai (two Clasps); also served throughout the Nile Expedition in 1884-85 on special service as Transport Officer, and took part in the operations of the Desert Column (Clasp). Served with the Soudan Frontier Field Force in 1886 with the Cameron Highlanders.

Record of the Services of the 1st Battalion Princess Louise's Argyll and Sutherland Highlanders (formerly the 91st Highlanders).

Raised as the 98th, and proceeded to South Africa, 1795 to 1803. (Entitled "91st," 1798.) [2nd Battalion raised in 1804, and proceeded to Holland, 1813-14 (Walcheren). Reduced, 1815.] England, to 1807. Ireland, to 1808. The Peninsula, to 1809 (battles of Roleia, Vimiera, and Corunna). England, to 1812. The Peninsula, to 1814 (battles of the Pyrenees, Nivelle, Nive, Orthes, and Toulouse). Ireland, to 1815. Belgium and France, to 1818. England, to 1821. Jamaica, to 1831. England, to 1836. St. Helena, to 1839. South Africa, to 1848 (war of 1846-47). [Reserve Battalion raised in 1842, and proceeded to South Africa to 1855. England, to 1857, when it was merged in 1st Battalion.] England, to 1851. Ireland, to 1854. Malta, to 1855. Greece, to 1857. Ionian Islands, to 1858. India, to 1868 (being the first Regiment to go overland from Alexandria to Suez). Entitled "Princess Louise's," 1872. England, to 1879. South Africa, to 1885 (war of 1879). Ceylon, to 1888. Hong Kong, 1888.

Record of the Services of the 2nd Battalion Argyll and Sutherland Highlanders (formerly the 93rd Regt.).

Raised in 1800, and proceeded to Guernsey. To Scotland, 1802. To Ireland, 1803. To the Cape of Good Hope, 1805 (capture of the Cape). To England, 1814. To North America, 1814. To England and Ireland, 1815. To the Low Countries, 1819. To the West Indies, 1823. To England, 1834. To Ireland, 1836. To Canada, 1838. To Scotland, 1848. To England, 1852. To the Crimea, 1854 (battles of Alma and Balaklava, and siege of Sebastopol). To England, 1856. To India, 1857 (capture of Lucknow). To Scotland, 1870. To England, 1873. To Ireland, 1876. To Gibraltar, 1879. To England, 1881. To Scotland, 1882. To England, 1884. To Ireland, 1886. To England, 1890. To India, 1891.

Continuation of Notes to the Prince of Wales' Leinster Regiment (Royal Canadians).

[1] Lieut.General Macdonald served in the Eastern campaign of 1854 as Aide de Camp to General Pennefather, including the battles of the Alma (severely wounded) and Inkerman (severely wounded), and siege of Sebastopol (Medal with three Clasps, Brevet of Major, 4th Class of the Medjidie, and Turkish Medal).

[2] Lt.Colonel Woods served with the expedition into Griqualand West, South Africa, in 1875.

[6] Captain Foulerton served with the Sikkim Expedition in 1888 (Medal with Clasp).

[7] Captain Shakespear served with the Chin-Lushai Expeditionary Force in 1889-90 as Intelligence and Assistant Political Officer (mentioned in despatches, *DSO.*, and Medal with Clasp), and in the operations in the South Lushai Hills in command of the force.

[8] Captain Davidson served with the Lushai Expedition in 1889 as Transport Officer. Served with the Chin-Lushai Expedition in 1889-90 as Transport Officer (Medal with Clasp).

[17] Captain Dickinson served in the Burmese Expedition in 1886-87 with the 44th Goorkha Light Infantry (Medal with Clasp).

[18] Captain Browne served in the Egyptian war of 1882, and was present at the battle of Tel-el-Kebir (Medal with Clasp, and Khedive's Star).

Record of the Services of the 1st Battalion the Prince of Wales' Leinster Regiment (Royal Canadians)—formerly the 100th (Prince of Wales' Royal Canadian) Regiment.

Raised in 1760 as the "100th Highlanders." Disbanded 1763. Raised again in 1780, and served in the East Indies 1781-84, during which time it lost 39 Officers and 1,200 killed in action or died of disease. Disbanded 1785. Raised again in 1805, and in 1813 became "The 100th, or H.R.H. the Prince Regent's County of Dublin Regiment." Served in the American War in 1813-14 (capture of Fort Niagara). Disbanded 1818. Raised in Canada in 1858 as "The 100th, or Prince of Wales' Royal Canadian Regiment," and proceeded to England, to 1859. Gibraltar, to 1863. Malta, to 1866. Canada, to 1868. Scotland, to 1869. England, to 1874. Ireland, to 1876. England, to 1878. India, 1878. Became 1st Battalion "The Prince of Wales' Leinster Regiment (Royal Canadians)," 1881.

Record of the Services of the 2nd Battalion Leinster Regiment (formerly the 109th Regiment).

Raised in 1761; disbanded, 1763; again raised as the 109th (or Aberdeenshire) Regiment in 1794; disbanded 1795. Raised in 1853 as the 3rd Bombay Europeean Regiment. With Central India Field Force, 1857-59 (siege and capture of Rashghur, action of Baroda, relief of Saugor, capture of Garracota, action of Mudderpore, battle of Betwa, siege and storm of Jhansi, storm of Saharee, actions of Koonah and Muttra, battles of Galowlee and Calpee). Kurrachee, to 1864. (Became the 109th Foot, 1862.) Aden, to 1866. India, to 1877. England, to 1882. Became 2nd Battalion Leinster Regiment, 1881.) Ireland, to 1888. England, 1888.

Y

The Prince of Wales' Leinster Regiment (Royal Canadians).

1st Batt., Tipperary.
2nd Batt., Malta.

Formerly the 100th (Prince of Wales' Royal Canadian) and the 109th (Bombay Infantry) Regiments.

[Regimental District No. 100.—EIIR.

(The 3rd, 4th, and 5th Battalions are formed of the King's County, Queen's County, and Meath Militia respectively.)

The Prince of Wales' Plume. A Maple Leaf. "NIAGARA" "CENTRAL INDIA."

Years' Ser.								
Full Pay	Half Pay							
27	...	Colonel.—Alastair M'Ian Macdonald,[1] Ensign,[p]27 Mar. 46; Lieut. [p]12 Nov. 47; Capt. 6 June 54; Bt.Major, 12 Dec. 54; Major, 17 July 55; Lt.Colonel, [p]13 Jan. 60; Colonel, 13 Jan. 65; Major General, 22 Feb. 70; Lieut.General 19 Mar. 85; Colonel Leinster Regiment, 29 Nov. 94.						
		Lieutenant Colonels.—2 Adrien Samuel Woods,[2] Ensign, [p]2 Dec. 68; Lieut. 28 Oct. 71; Capt. 2 Feb. 81; Major, 18 Nov. 82; Lt.Colonel, 12 Aug. 91.						
31	10/12	1 Henry Walter Trench, Ensign, [p]16 Feb. 64; Lieut. [p]13 July 67; Capt. 23 Oct. 75; Major, 29 Sept. 82; Lt.Colonel, 3 July 93.						

		MAJORS.	2ND LIEUT.	LIEUT.	CAPTAIN.	BREV.MAJ.	MAJOR.
21	...	1 John Grogan Glancy	......	11 Feb. 75	7 Jan. 82	......	3 Mar. 86
24	...	2 Arnold Hyde Noel Urquhart Champion	......	30 Dec. 71	23 May 83	......	12 Aug. 91
18	...	2 Herbert Martin	30 Jan. 78	1 Oct. 78	6 June 83	......	21 Aug. 91
18	...	2 St. John James St. Leger	20 Mar. 78	30 Nov. 78	6 June 83	......	26 Aug. 91
21	...	Winton Seton, Adj. British Guiana Mil.	......	11 Feb. 75	1 Jan. 83	......	1 Dec. 92
18	...	James Willcocks,[4] DSO.,Deputy Assist. Adj. Gen., Bombay Army, 1 Aug. 94	30 Jan. 78	20 Oct. 78	21 Aug. 84	......	29 Sept. 93
16	...	1 Thomas Hope Stavert (Depot)	14 Jan. 80	25 Aug. 80	28 June 85	......	2 Dec. 93
19	...	p.s.c. Henry Ponting Northcott,[5] Staff Captain, Intell. Department, War Office, 24 May 93	......	12 Feb. 77	12 Feb. 86	......	17 Oct. 94
		CAPTAINS.					
17	...	1 Arthur Kerl Huddart	14 Sept. 78	20 Mar. 80	24 Nov. 84		
16	...	Cecil Walford Tribe, Ord. Store Dept.	24 Jan. 80	12 Jan. 81	3 Mar. 86		
15	...	Wm.Henry Greenwood, Ord.Store Dept.	23 Oct. 80	1 July 81	11 Aug. 86		
15	...	1 Alex. Fras. Grant Foulerton[6]	23 Oct. 80	1 July 81	29 Sept. 86		
15	...	John Shakespear,[7] DSO, on Special Duty, Lushai Country	22 Jan. 81	1 July 81	29 Sept. 86		
15	...	1 George Lamb, Adjutant 27 Dec. 92	22 Jan. 81	1 July 81	14 Aug. 87		
14	...	2 Kenneth Mackenzie Drummond	......	22 Oct. 81	10 Oct. 88		
12	...	2 Thos. St. Clair Davidson[8]	......	19 Dec. 81	12 Jan. 90		
12	...	Chas.Spencer Browne Evans-Lombe, Adj. Bermud Volunteers 1 Feb. 95	......	19 Dec. 83	24 Jan. 90		
10	...	1 Charles FitzGerald Thomas Cochrane	......	6 May 85	16 Mar. 91		
10	...	Samuel Robert Llewellyn White, Adj. 3 Battalion 5 Dec. 94	......	6 May 85	14 July 91		
10	...	Neville Hope Campbell Dickinson,[17] Ordnance Store Department	......	3 May 85	12 Aug. 91		
10	...	? Paget Edward Stuart Reeves	......	6 May 85	21 Aug. 91		
10	...	Geoffroy John Denis Browne,[18] Adjutant 5 Battalion 2 Jan. 93	......	22 July 85	13 Mar. 92		
13	...	1 Charles Logan Crutchley	......	27 Jan. 83	23 Nov. 92		
9	...	Henry Verco Platt, Adjutant 18 Middlesex Rifle Volunteers 1 Feb. 94	......	28 July 86	2 July 92		
10	...	1 Richard Trench Kirkpatrick, Staff Coll.	......	29 Aug. 85	29 Sept. 92		
10	...	Cecil Mitchell-Innes, Adj. 2 Punjab (Simla) Vol. Rifles 1 Oct. 93	......	29 Aug. 85	26 Oct. 93		
9	...	1 Theoph. Fred. Walter Ricketts	......	25 Aug. 86	26 Oct. 93		
9	...	2 Edward Frank Griffin (Depot)	......	25 Aug. 86	1 Feb. 94		
9	...	1 Arthur Frederick Magee	......	8 Dec. 86	1 Aug. 94		
13	6/12	2 Thomas Alexander Gardner Sangster	......	22 Oct. 81	18 Jan. 88		
9	...	2 Wm.Tankerville Monypenny Reeve, Adjutant 16 Mar. 95	5 Feb. 87	10 Oct. 88	10 Oct. 94		
8	...	2 Alex. Wilson Elkington Twist (Depot)	4 May 87	8 May 89	17 Oct. 94		
8	...	Ronald Gore Campbell	14 Sept. 87	3 July 89	5 Dec. 94		
		LIEUTENANTS.					
7	...	1 Charles William Dutton Pollard	22 Aug. 88	1 Apr. 90			
8	...	1 Hector Douglass Harvest	11 Feb. 88	1 Apr. 90			
7	...	1 Herbert John Coningham	10 Nov. 88	23 July 91			
7	...	1 Reginald John Ingles	10 Nov. 88	14 July 91			
7	...	Charles Kirkpatrick Anderson	23 Mar. 89	23 Sept. 91			
6	...	1 George Harry John Rooke (Depot)	9 Nov. 89	26 Nov. 91			
6	...	1 Charles Edward Hamilton Laughlin	22 Jan. 90	26 Nov. 91			
6	...	2 John Craske	1 Mar. 90	18 Dec. 91			
5	...	Albert Gerard Gavin Sharp	28 June 90	23 Nov. 92			
4	...	William St. George Chamier	9 Sept. 91	15 Apr. 93			
4	...	Wyndham Madden Pierpoint Wood	10 Oct. 91	29 Sept. 93			
4	...	2 Julian Campbell Colquhoun	5 Dec. 91	1 Oct. 93			
4	...	Aubrey Vivian Searle	20 Feb. 92	2 May 94			
4	...	Francis Charles Owens	20 Feb. 92	2 May 94			
4	...	William Johnstone Cates	20 Feb. 92	2 May 94			
4	...	2 George Moultrie Bullen-Smith	17 June 92	15 Apr. 94			
4	...	1 Francis Rogers Dugan	12 Mar. 92	1 Aug. 94			
3	...	1 Henry Edward Clonard Keating	17 Dec. 92	21 Aug. 94			
2	...	1 Arthur Willie Cummins Sherwood	26 Apr. 93	22 Aug. 94			
2	...	2 Reginald Francis Legg	20 May 93	4 Sept. 94			
2	...	2 James Kilvington Cochrane	20 May 93	6 Oct. 94			
2	...	2 George Iver Patrick Poer O'Shee	9 Sept. 93	10 Oct. 94			
2	...	2 Prendergast Bennett Carlisle	21 Oct. 93	10 Oct. 94			
2	...	2 John Dryden Mather	3 Dec. 93	17 Oct. 94			
2	...	2 Gordon Annesley Taylor	7 Mar. 94	5 Dec. 94			
		SECOND LIEUTENANTS.					
1	...	2 Henry Telford Maffett	2 June 94				
1	...	2 Frederick Ernest Whitton	2 June 94				
1	...	2 Philip Fraser Arthur Leahy	7 Nov. 94				
1	...	2 Frederick Christian Hencker	28 Nov. 94				
1	...	1 Bryan John Jones	12 Dec. 94				
1	...	1 Leonard Robert Grey Bell	12 Dec. 94				
1	...	2 James Robert Moffatt	30 Jan. 95				
1	...	Henry Gerald Rawdon Wakefield	6 Mar. 95				
1	...	Michael Francis Fox	6 Mar. 95				
1	...	Clarence Reginald Macdonald	6 Mar. 95				

Paymasters.—1 Charles W. D. Pollard, Lieut. 1 Battalion (acting).

| 13 | ... | Quarter Masters.—1 Alexander Wilkin, 10 June 82; Hon. Captain, 10 June 92. |
| 3 | ... | 2 John William Gallehawk, 1 March 93; Hon. Lieut. |

[4] Major Willcocks served in the Afghan war in 1879-80 with the Khyber and Cabul Field Forces in the Transport Train (Medal). Served as Transport Officer in the Wuzeeree Expedition of 1881 under Brigadier General Kennedy (mentioned in despatches). Served in the Soudan campaign in 1885 (Medal with Clasp, and Khedive's Star). Served with the Burmese Expedition in 1886-87 as Transport Officer and in charge of Field Commissariat and also as Acting Rond Commandant (mentioned in despatches, DSO., and Medal with two Clasps). Served with the Chin-Lushai Expedition in 1889-90 as Intelligence Officer to the Chinbok Column; also served with the Manipore Expedition in 1891 (mentioned in despatches, Clasp).

[5] Major Northcott served in the Sherbro Expedition in 1883 with the 2nd West India Regiment (mentioned in despatches). Served in the operations in Zululand in 1888 as Deputy Assistant Adjutant General.

[For remainder of Notes, see preceding page.]

Facings Blue.
Agents, Messrs. Cox and Co.
1st Battalion returned from India, 13 December 1894.
2nd Battalion embarked for Malta, 9 November 1894.

1st Batt., Curragh.
2nd Batt., Cawnpore, Bengal.] **The Royal Munster Fusiliers.** [*Regimental District* No. 101.—Tralee.] 347

Formerly the 101st (Royal Bengal Fusiliers) and the 104th (Bengal Fusiliers) Regiments.
(The 3rd, 4th, and 5th Battalions are formed of the South Cork, the Kerry, and the Royal Limerick County Militia respectively.)
The Royal Tiger. The Shamrock. "Plassey" "Condore" "Masulipatam" "Badara" "Buxar" "Rohilcund, 1774 and 1794" "Carnatic" "Sholinghur" "Guzerat" "Deig" "Bhurtpore" "Afghanistan" "Ghuznee" "Ferozeshuhur" "Sobraon" "Punjaub" "Chillianwallah" "Goojerat" "Pegu" "Delhi" "Lucknow" "Burma, 1885-87."

Years Ser. Full Pay.	Half Pay.		2ND LIEUT.	LIEUT.	CAPTAIN.	BREV. MAJ.	MAJOR.
		Colonel.—Henry Meade Hamilton,¹ CB. Ensign, P 9 Aug. 39; Lieut. P 26 Oct. 41; Capt. P BD May 49; Bt. Major, 12 Dec. 54; Major, 19 Dec. 56; Bt.Lt.Colonel, 6 June 56; Lt. Colonel, P 22 Feb. 61; Colonel, 12 Apr. 63; Major General, 9 Nov. 68; Lt. General, 1 July 81; Colonel Munster Fusiliers, 7 Apr. 92.					
26	...	**Lieutenant Colonels.**—1 David George Johnstor, Ensign, 9 Feb. 70; Lt. 28 Oct. 71; Capt. 31 Oct. 77; Major, 1 July 81; Lt. Colonel, 26 March 91.					
21	...	2 William Lloyd Brereton,⁴ Lieut. 21 Sept. 74; Capt. 22 June 81; Major, 30 Jan. 85; Lt. Colonel, 20 May 94.					
		MAJORS.					
20	...	1 Francis James Kempster,⁷ DSO. (Bt.Lt.Colonel, 5 Sept. 89)	......	10 Mar. 76	18 Nov. 82	......	4 Sept. 89
21	...	2 Edward Stokes Evans	......	13 June 74	1 July 81	......	1 Apr. 92
21	...	1 Percy Stanley Druitt (Depot)	......	21 Sept. 74	4 May 82	......	1 Apr. 92
21	...	1 Francis Henry Penny	......	2 Dec. 74	26 July 82	......	3 June 92
20	...	2 p.s.c. Benjamin Reddie Hawes⁸	......	20 Nov. 75	1 Apr. 85	......	6 Sept. 92
20	...	p.s.c. Herbert Eversley Belfield, D.A.A. Gen. Aldershot, 4 May 93	......	26 Feb. 76	20 May 85	......	1 Feb. 93
20	...	2 Charles Augustus King Hall⁹	......	29 Nov. 75	26 Sept. 83	......	8 July 93
20	...	1 Alfred Herrick Butler Clough	......	24 Mar. 76	20 May 85	......	20 May 94
		CAPTAINS.					
19	...	2 Pierce Thomas Chute¹⁰	......	29 Nov. 76	7 Dec. 87		
17	...	2 George Sumner Ormerod¹¹	11 May 78	20 Mar. 80	4 June 87		
16	...	1 Bryce Stewart,¹² Adj. 4 Bn. 1 Mar. 92	6 Aug. 79	17 April 80	3 July 87		
16	...	2 Henry Frederick Williams¹³	13 Aug. 79	7 July 80	12 Aug. 87		
16	...	2 Richard Ffennell¹⁴ (Depot)	14 Jan. 80	26 Nov. 80	27 Mar. 88		
17	...	p.s.c. Stephen Thos. Banning	1 May 78	17 Apr. 81	4 Sept. 89		
15	...	Randolph Edward Whitehead, Adjutant 1 Wiltshire Rifle Vols. 9 Nov. 91	11 Aug. 80	1 July 81	4 Sept. 89		
15	...	2 Arthur Frederick Mann¹⁵	19 Feb. 81	1 July 81	1 Aug. 90		
14	...	2 George Forbes Holland¹⁶	......	22 Oct. 81	26 Sept. 90		
13	...	1 Aymer Claud Maxwell, **Adjutant** 31 July 91	......	10 May 82	1 Nov. 90		
13	...	1 Arthur Edward Osmond Congdon¹⁷	......	10 May 82	24 June 91		
13	...	1 Wilfrid Worsley Blackden¹⁸	......	10 May 82	1 Apr. 92		
13	...	1 William Coape Oates²⁰	......	9 Sept. 82	1 Apr. 92		
13	...	James Markham Chadwick, Adjutant 5 Battalion 11 Dec. 93	......	9 Sept. 82	3 June 92		
13	...	1 George Denis Macpherson	......	9 Sept. 82	6 Sept. 92		
12	...	2 Charles Edward Spearman,²¹ Staff Coll.	......	25 Aug. 83	8 July 93		
10	...	2 Roger Courtenay Boyle,²² **Adjutant** 18 May 91	......	6 May 85	8 July 93		
10	...	1 Gerard Christopher Bowen	......	25 Nov. 85	11 Dec. 93		
9	...	1 Lionel Charles Warren	......	25 Aug. 86	20 May 94		
		LIEUTENANTS.					
8	...	2 Ernest Edward Bruno Bruno	16 Nov. 87	19 Mar. 90			
8	...	2 Henry Ernest Tizard	16 Nov. 87	1 Aug. 90			
7	...	2 Campbell Littler Hendriks	9 May 88	26 Sept. 90			
7	...	2 John Kevin O'Meagher (Depot)	22 Aug. 88	1 Nov. 90			
7	...	2 Francis Ambrose D'Oyly Goddard	8 Dec. 88	24 June 91			
5	...	2 Arthur Howe Browne	8 June 89	30 Dec. 91			
6	...	2 George Delamain Crocker	27 Nov. 89	30 Dec. 91			
6	...	1 George Ambrose Congreve Webb	29 Mar. 90	1 Apr. 92			
5	...	2 Arthur Milton Bent	3 May 90	11 Apr. 92			
5	...	2 Paul Alfred Charrier	28 June 90	13 Apr. 92			
4	...	2 Hugh Latimer Haughton	17 June 91	20 Feb. 93			
4	...	2 Albert Armstrong MacLaughlin, Station Staff Officer, Futtehghur, 20 Oct. 94	9 Sept. 91	10 May 93			
4	...	2 William Orlebar Harvey	9 Jan. 92	21 June 93			
4	...	2 Verelst Turner Worship	9 Jan. 92	8 July 93			
3	...	William John Ottley	9 Apr. 92	11 Oct. 93			
3	...	2 William Hurst Nicolson	18 May 92	28 Oct. 93			
3	...	1 Oswald Fergusson Pollok	13 July 92	11 Dec. 93			
3	...	1 Evelyn de Burgh Waddington (Depot)	13 July 92	22 Jan. 94			
3	...	1 Victor George Howard Rickard	13 July 92	18 July 94			
3	...	2 Roger Henry Monck-Mason	13 Aug. 92	19 Sept. 94			
3	...	2 Nicholas Beamish Cummin	13 Aug. 92	7 Nov. 94			
		SECOND LIEUTENANTS.					
3	...	Frank Russell Brown	21 Dec. 92				
2	...	2 Charles Frederick Moores	26 Apr. 93				
2	...	1 Arthur William Mahaffy	24 May 93				
2	...	2 Alderson Preston Berthon	9 Sept. 93				
2	...	2 Edmund Peel Thomson	21 Oct. 93				
2	...	2 Frederick Evelyn Elliot Henderson	21 Oct. 93				
2	...	1 George Thomas Bradford	21 Feb. 94				
2	...	2 Gustavus Arthur Perreau	7 Mar. 94				
2	...	1 Robert Henry Boyd Magee	29 Aug. 94				
1	...	2 Charles Harry Brownlow Jarrett	10 Oct. 94				
1	...	Bernard Joseph Fagan	6 Mar. 95				
1	...	William Arthur Hutchinson	6 Mar. 95				

⁴ Lt.-Colonel Brereton served in the Afghan war in 1878-80 with the 2nd Battalion of the 8th Foot, was present in the engagement in the Kuram Valley on the 28th November 1878, and at the capture of the Peiwar Kotal (Medal with Clasp). Served with the Burmese Expedition in 1886-88 with the 2nd Battalion Royal Munster Fusiliers (Medal with two Clasps).
⁹ Major Hall served in the Egyptian war of 1882 (Medal, and Khedive's Star). Served with the Burmese Expedition in 1886-89 with the 2nd Battalion Royal Munster Fusiliers (Medal with two Clasps).
¹² Captain Stewart served with the Burmese Expedition in 1885-88 with the 2nd Battalion Royal Munster Fusiliers (Medal with two Clasps).
¹³ Captain Williams served with the Burmese Expedition in 1886-88 with the 2nd Battalion Royal Munster Fusiliers (Medal with two Clasps).
¹⁴ Captain Ffennell served with the Burmese Expedition in 1886-89 with the 2nd Battalion Royal Munster Fusiliers, and was severely wounded in an engagement on the 14th Feb. 1887 (Medal with two Clasps).

[*For remainder of Notes, see end of Royal Dublin Fusiliers, p. 348a.*]

1	...	**Paymasters.**—2 Ernest E. B. Bruno, Lieut. 2 Battalion (acting).	
5	...	**Quarter Masters.**—1 George Thomas East, 17 Dec. 90; Hon. Lieut.	
2	...	2 Thomas Trimby,²⁴ 28 Feb. 94; Hon. Lieut.	

Facings Blue.—Agents, Messrs. Holt and Co.
1st Battalion returned from Nova Scotia, 1883. 2nd Battalion embarked for Malta, 1883.

Y 2

348 1st Batt., Sheffield.
2nd Batt., Quetta, Bengal.] **The Royal Dublin Fusiliers.** [*Regimental District* No. 102.—Naas.

Formerly the 102nd (Royal Madras Fusiliers) and the 103rd (Royal Bombay Fusiliers) Regiments.
(The 3rd, 4th, and 5th Battalions are formed of the Kildare, Royal Dublin City, and Dublin County Militia respectively.)

The Royal Tiger. *"Spectamur agendo."* "Arcot" "Plassey" "Condore" "Wyndewash" "Buxar" "Sholingur" "Nundy Droog" "Amboyna" "Ternate" "Banda" "Pondicherry" "Mahidpore" "Carnatic" "Mysore" (with the Elephant) "Guzerat" "Seringapatam" "Kirkee" "Beni Boo Ali" "Aden" "Punjaub" "Mooltan" "Goojerat" "Ava" "Pegu" "Lucknow."

Years' Ser. Full Pay	Half Pay		Ensign or 2nd Lieut.	Lieut.	Captain.	Brev. Maj.	Major.
		Colonel.—Sir John Blick Spurgin, ¹KCB. CSI. Ensign, 10 Aug. 42; Lieut. 1 June 47; Captain, 23 Nov. 56; Brevet Major, 19 Jan. 58; Brevet Lt.Colonel, 24 Mar. 58; Major, 30 July 62; Colonel, 9 Mar. 65; Major General, 1 Mar. 70; Lieut.General, 27 June 83; Colonel Dublin Fusiliers, 8 Jan. 95.					
29	...	**Lieutenant Colonels.**—2 Frederick Francis Wilder Taylor, Ensign, 29 July 66; Lt. ᴾ30 June 69; Captain, 9 June 77; Major, 1 July 81; Lt.Colonel, 21 May 92.					
29	...	1 William Carre Riddell, Ensign, 12 Jan. 67; Lieut. 25 Mar. 68; Captain, 15 Aug. 77; Major, 15 Mar. 82; Lt.Colonel, 7 June 94.					
		MAJORS.					
27	...	1 Charles Duncan Cooper	8 July 68	28 Oct. 71	1 Nov. 79	......	18 Apr. 88
22	...	2 George Arthur Mills		12 Nov. 73	26 May 80	......	21 May 88
22	...	1 Henry Tempest Hicks (*Depot*)		4 Dec. 73	10 Nov. 80	......	7 June 90
22	...	1 Spencer Godfrey Bird		28 Feb. 74	12 Mar. 81	......	21 May 92
23	...	2 Robert Charles Pentland		21 Aug. 72	6 July 82	......	17 May 93
20	...	1 William Henry Slingsby O'Neill		10 Sept. 75	29 Jan. 84	......	16 May 94
19	...	George Arthur Shadforth, *Adjutant* 3 Bn. (*Kildare Militia*) 9 Feb. 91		28 April 76	7 June 84	......	7 June 94
17	...	Frederick Paul English, *Adjutant* 3 Volunteer Bn. Welsh Regt. 15 Jan. 92	22 Jan. 79	12 Jan. 81	1 July 87	......	6 Nov. 94
		CAPTAINS.					
18	...	2 Alexander Macintosh Horrocks	8 Dec. 77	24 May 79	19 May 87		
17	...	2 Alexander Weston Gordon⁹	1 May 78	12 Mar. 81	1 July 87		
16	...	1 Elford Pearse	11 Oct. 79	8 June 81	1 July 87		
17	...	Frank Stuart Hamilton Rickards,¹⁰ *Adj.*1 *Vol.Bn.Cheshire Regt.*15Feb.92	11 May 78	22 Dec. 80	4 May 87		
16	...	Edward Hamilton Seymour, *Ordnance Store Department*	14 Jan. 80	1 July 81	15 Feb. 88		
15	...	Mark Ralph Payne Audain, *Ordnance Store Department*	23 Oct. 80	1 July 81	15 Feb. 88		
14	...	2 John Nugent Murray MacGregor	23 Apr. 81	1 July 81	1 May 88		
14	...	2 John Francis Sheppard		10 May 81	21 May 88		
15	...	2 Archibald Hawksley Rutherford (*Depot*)	22 Jan. 81	1 July 81	4 Mar. 91		
15	...	1 Edward Silver Strickland	19 Feb. 81	1 July 81	6 Mar. 91		
12	...	Arthur Hy. Bacon, *Adj.* 4 Bn. 16 Sept.92		9 Dec. 83	15 Jan. 92		
12	...	2 Cecil Bargrave Collings		30 Jan. 84	23 Aug. 92		
11	...	2 Archibald John Chapman		14 May 84	23 Aug. 92		
13	...	1 Walter Were		14 June 82	24 Aug. 92		
11	...	Richard Stewart Gage,¹³ *Adjutant* 5 Battalion 20 Dec. 94		14 May 84	16 Sept. 92		
11	...	1 Walter Bromilow		14 May 84	17 May 93		
11	...	1 Ernest Arthur Dickinson, **Adjutant** 8 Nov. 94		23 Aug. 84	23 Aug. 93		
11	...	1 Arthur Edward Mainwaring		7 Feb. 85	16 May 94		
10	...	2 Geoffrey Downing		6 May 85	7 June 94		
10	...	2 Richard Alexander Rooth, **Adjutant** 16 Dec. 93		29 Aug. 85	7 June 94		
10	...	Arthur Loveband		29 Aug. 85	20 Dec. 94		
		LIEUTENANTS.					
10	...	2 Herbert Carington Smith		2 Sept. 85			
10	...	2 Charles Albert Hensley		2 Sept. 85			
9	...	1 Alexander John Godley		25 Aug. 86			
9	...	2 George Anthony Weldon (*Depot*)		8 Dec. 86			
8	...	2 John Albert Emmanuel MacBean, *Staff College*	4 May 87	6 Mar. 89			
9	...	2 Henry Roscoe Beddoes		13 Oct. 86			
7	...	1 Arthur Forde Pilson	9 May 88	1 Apr. 90			
7	...	1 James William Royce Tomkin	22 Aug. 88	1 July 90			
7	...	2 Richard Meade Pratt Swift	22 Aug. 88	4 Mar. 91			
7	...	1 Edwyn Fetherstonhaugh	22 Aug. 88	15 Jan. 92			
7	...	2 Henry Barkly Higginson	19 Dec. 88	1 Mar. 92			
6	...	2 Maurice Lowndes	24 Apr. 89	21 May 92			
6	...	1 Athelstan Dibley	8 June 89	23 Aug. 92			
6	...	2 Malcolm Percy Eustace Lonsdale	8 June 89	16 Sept. 92			
6	...	2 Charles Oliver M'Causland	6 July 89	17 May 93			
6	...	1 Cecil Francis Romer	1 Mar. 90	23 Aug. 93			
5	...	1 Wilfrid John Venour	29 Oct. 90	16 Dec. 93			
4	...	1 Wilfred Michael Clement Moorat	10 Oct. 91	16 May 94			
4	...	2 Somerled Lorn Paterson	28 Oct. 91	7 June 94			
		SECOND LIEUTENANTS.					
4	...	2 John Deane Reece	20 Feb. 91				
3	...	2 George Chrystie	18 June 92				
3	...	Harry Trevor Naylor	18 June 92				
3	...	2 John Stewart Mortimer Harcourt	13 July 92				
3	...	2 Charles Campbell Todd	28 Sept. 92				
3	...	2 Hugh Mackenzie Shewan	19 Oct. 92				
3	...	2 Arthur Edmund Brown	21 Jan. 93				
2	...	2 Ernest Septimus Gale	28 June 93				
2	...	2 Cecil Hampfylde James Riccard	9 Sept. 93				
2	...	2 Ernest Frederick Orton	7 Mar. 94				
1	...	1 Harold John Kinsman	11 July 94				
1	...	1 Harold Whitla Higginson	10 Oct. 94				
1	...	2 Arthur Vivian Hill	10 Oct. 94				

⁹ Captain Gordon served in the Afghan war in 1880 with the 6th Bengal Light Infantry (Medal).
¹⁰ Captain Rickards served with the 88th Regiment throughout the Zulu war of 1879 (Medal with Clasp).
¹³ Captain Gage took part in the operations of the Soudan Frontier Field Force in 1885 (Medal, and Khedive's Star).

Years' Ser.		
Full Pay	Half Pay	
9	...	Paymasters.—2 Herbert C. Smith, Lieut. 2 Battalion (acting).
1	...	Quarter Masters.—1 Robert Baker, 5 May 86; Hon. Lieut.
		2 James Cyril Crump, 22 Dec. 94; Hon. Lieut.

Facings Blue.—Agents, Sir C. R. M'Grigor, Bt. and Co.
1st Battalion returned from Egypt, March 1886. 2nd Battalion embarked for Gibraltar, 9 Jan. 84.

[1] Lt.General Spurgin served with the 1st Madras Fusiliers in the Burmese war of 1852-53, including the taking of Pegu, and its subsequent defence (Medal with Clasp for Pegu). Served in suppression of the mutiny in Bengal in 1857-58; commanded the troops proceeding by steamer in July 1857 from Allahabad to Cawnpore, covering the right of Havelock's Column and engaging the enemy on two occasions, on the first landed his force repulsed the rebels and captured their 6-pounder gun; was Staff Officer to General Neill at Cawnpore, afterwards Brigade Major to the 1st Brigade and was with it during its advance and entry into Lucknow on 25th Sept., defence of the Residency and subsequent operations at the Alumbagh under Outram; also served as a Brigade Major at the capture of Kaiserbagh, and capture of Lucknow (received the thanks of the Governor General in Council, Brevets of Major and Lt.Colonel, Medal with two Clasps, a year's service for Lucknow, and CSI.).

Record of the Services of the 2nd Battalion of the Royal Dublin Fusiliers (formerly the 103rd Bombay Fusiliers, and previously the 1st Bombay European Infantry).

Raised in 1661. To India, 1662. To Persia, 1767. To Aden, 1839. To India, 1841. Styled "Fusiliers," 1843. Entitled "103rd Regiment Royal Bombay Fusiliers," 1862. To England, 1871. To Ireland, 1876. To England, 1881. Entitled "2nd Battalion Royal Dublin Fusiliers," 1881. To Gibraltar, 1884. To Egypt, 1885. To India, 1886.

Continuation of Notes to the Royal Munster Fusiliers.

[4] Lt.General Hamilton served the Eastern campaign of 1854-55 as Deputy Assistant Quarter Master General and as Assistant Quarter Master General from Oct. 1855, including the battle of Alma, capture of Balaklava, siege and fall of Sebastopol (mentioned in despatches, Medal with three Clasps, Brevets of Major and Lt.Colonel, 5th Class of the Medjidie, and Turkish Medal). Commanded the 12th Regiment during the New Zealand war of 1863-66; was present with the forces under Sir Duncan Cameron throughout the Waikato campaign and until the termination of hostilities under Sir Trevor Chute. Commanded an Expeditionary Force from Te Rore to the surrounding district; occupied and destroyed the strongly fortified positions of Pateranga and Piko Piko, and other strongholds between Te Rore and Ragland; subsequently commanded the troops in the East Coast District, and made several expeditions against the enemy, destroying the villages of Patatere, Whaiwhatawhata, Irihanga, and Whakamarama, eventually driving out all hostile natives, and establishing tranquility in this hitherto very disturbed part of the country (Medal, and CB.).

[7] Lt.Colonel Kempster served in the Afghan war in 1880 with the Khyber Line Force, and took part in the expedition into the Hissarik Valley (Medal). Served with the Bechuanaland Expedition under Sir Charles Warren in 1884-85 in command of the Corps of Guides. Served in the operations of the Soudan Frontier Field Force in 1887 including the engagement at Sarras; was Senior Staff Officer to the Column (mentioned in despatches, DSO., Medal, 3rd Class of the Medjidie, and Khedive's Star); also served in the operations near Suakin in December 1888 including the engagement at Gemaizah (mentioned in despatches, Clasp), and in the operations on the Soudan frontier in 1889 including the engagements at Arguin and Toski (mentioned in despatches, Brevet of Lt.Colonel, Clasp).

[8] Major Hawes served with the Burmese Expedition in 1885-89 with the 2nd Battalion Royal Munster Fusiliers (Medal with two Clasps).

[10] Captain Chute served with the Burmese Expedition in 1886-89 with the 2nd Battalion Royal Munster Fusiliers (Medal with two Clasps).

[11] Captain Ormerod served with the Burmese Expedition in 1886-88 as Adjutant to the 2nd Battalion Royal Munster Fusiliers (Medal with two Clasps).

[15] Captain Mann served with the Burmese Expedition in 1885-89 with the 2nd Battalion Royal Munster Fusiliers (Medal with two Clasps).

[16] Captain Holland served with the Burmese Expedition in 1887-89 (Medal with Clasp).

[17] Captain Congdon served with the Burmese Expedition in 1885-88 with the 2nd Battalion Royal Munster Fusiliers (Medal with two Clasps).

[18] Captain Blackden served with the Burmese Expedition in 1885-88 with the 2nd Battalion Royal Munster Fusiliers (Medal with two Clasps).

[20] Captain Oates served with the Burmese Expedition in 1885-89 with the 2nd Battalion Royal Munster Fusiliers (Medal with two Clasps).

[21] Captain Spearman served with the Burmese Expedition in 1885-89 with the 2nd Battalion Royal Munster Fusiliers (Medal with two Clasps).

[22] Captain Boyle served with the Burmese Expedition in 1885-89 with the 2nd Battalion Royal Munster Fusiliers (Medal with two Clasps).

[24] Lieut. Trimby served with the Burmese Expedition in 1885-89 (Medal with two Clasps).

Record of the Services of the 1st Royal Munster Fusiliers (formerly the 101st Regiment).

Raised in 1652 as a "Guard of Honour" to the East India Company in Bengal. Twice augmented in 1756, and styled the "Bengal European Battalion." Employed in Bengal, 1757 (battle of Plassey). Against the French in Madras, 1758. In Bengal and against the Dutch, 1759-80 (battle of Buxar). Augmented to three Battalions, and afterwards to three Regiments of two Battalions each, 1779. Against Hyder Ali and the French in Madras, 1781-83. In Bengal, 1784-94. Formed into two Regiments, 1798. In Rohilcund and Rajpootana, 1794-1805 (battle of Deig). Formed into one Regiment, 1803. In Bengal, 1805-10. (A detachment in China, 1808; or a against the Dutch in Java and the Molucca Islands, 1810-17; and one in the Nepaul war in 1814.) In Pindarrie war, 1817. In Bengal, 1818-26. Formed into two Regiments, 1824. In Rajpootana, 1826 (capture of Bhurtpore). 2nd European Regiment in Burma, 1825-26. Formed into one Regiment, 1830. In Afghan war, 1838-40 (Afghan war—capture of Ghuznee). Entitled the "1st Bengal European Light Infantry," 1840. In the Punjab, 1842. In the Sikh war, 1845-46 (battles of Ferozeshah, Sobraon, and Goojerat). Entitled "1st Bengal European Fusiliers," 1846. In Burma, 1852-55 (capture of Pegu). In the Indian Mutiny, 1857-58 (captures of Delhi and Lucknow). Umbeyla campaign, 1863. Entitled "101st Royal Bengal Fusiliers," 1861. To England, 1869. To Malta, 1874. To Cyprus and Canada, 1878. Entitled "1st Battalion Royal Munster Fusiliers," 1881. To Ragland, 1883.

The Rifle Brigade (The Prince Consort's Own). [Rifle Depot: Winchester

The 5th, 6th, 7th, and 9th Battalions are formed of the 2nd Tower Hamlets, the Royal Longford, the 1st Tower Hamlets, and the Westmeath Militia respectively.)

"COPENHAGEN" "MONTE VIDEO" "ROLEIA" "VIMIERA" "CORUNNA" "BUSACO" "BARROSA" "FUENTES D'ONOR" "CIUDAD RODRIGO" "BADAJOZ" "SALAMANCA" "VITTORIA" "NIVELLE" "NIVE" "ORTHES" "TOULOUSE" "PENINSULA" "WATERLOO" "SOUTH AFRICA, 1846-7, 1851-2-3" "ALMA" "INKERMAN" "SEVASTOPOL" "LUCKNOW" "ASHANTEE" "ALI MASJID" "AFGHANISTAN, 1878-79." "BURMA, 1885-87."

Years' Ser.			
Full Pay	Half Pay		

Colonel in Chief.—His Royal Highness Arthur W. P. A., *Duke of Connaught*,[1] *KG. KT. KP. GCSI. GCMG. GCIE. KCB. Personal Aide de Camp to the Queen*; *Lt.* 19 June 68; *Capt.* 1 May 71; *Major*, 7 Aug. 75; *Lieutenant Colonel*, 27 Sept. 76; *Colonel*, 29 May 80; *Major General*, 29 May 80; *Lieut. General*, 1 April 89; *General*, 1 Apr. 93; *Colonel Rifle Brigade*, 29 May 80.

Colonels Commandant.—1 Lord Alexander George Russell,[2] *CB. 2nd Lieut.* P11 July 39; *Lt.* 15 April 42; *Capt.* P7 Aug. 46; *Bt.Major*, 28 May 53; *Major*, 29 Dec. 54; *Bt.Lt.Colonel*, 6 June 56; *Lt.Colonel*, P17 Dec. 58; *Colonel*, 10 Mar. 61; *Major General*, 6 Mar. 68; *Lieut.General*, 20 Mar. 78; *General*, 7 April 86; *Colonel Liverpool Regiment*, 28 Feb. 80; *Colonel Commandant Rifle Brigade*, 1 May 91.

2 Frederick Robert Elrington,[3] *CB. 2nd Lt.* P7 June 39; *Lieut.* 23 Nov. 41; *Capt.* P22 May 46; *Bt.Major*, 12 Dec. 54; *Major*, 29 Dec. 54; *Bt.Lt.Colonel*, 26 Dec. 56; *Lt.Colonel*, P1 Sept. 57; *Colonel*, 29 Mar. 62; *Major General* 6 Mar. 68; *Lt.General* 14 Mar. 80; *General*, 1 July 81; *Colonel Bedfordshire Regiment*, 17 July 90; *Colonel Commandant Rifle Brigade*, 26 Jan. 92.

Years Ser.			Ensign or 2nd Lieut.	Lieut.	Captain.	Brev. Maj.	Major.
32	...	**Lieutenant Colonels.**—4 Lionel Richard Stopford Sackville,[16] *Ensign*, P13 June 65; *Lt.* P9, Mar. 67; *Capt.* 13 May 75; *Major*, 1 July 81; *Lt.Colonel*, 1 Dec. 91.					
31	...	1 Cecil Harley St. Paul,[20] *Ensign*, P16 Aug. 64; *Lt.* P13 Jan. 69; *Capt.* 27 Feb. 77; *Major*, 15 Oct. 81; *Lt.Colonel*, 16 Dec. 91.					
30	...	3 Hon. Montagu Curzon, *Ensign*, P10 Nov. 65; *Lt.* P19 Jan. 70; *Capt.* 2 Mar. 78; *Major*, 9 April 82; *Lt.Colonel*, 15 Oct. 93.					
29	...	2 Francis Howard,[23] *Aide de Camp to the Queen*; *Ensign*, P3 April 56; *Lt.* P28 May 70; *Capt.* 30 April 78; *Major*, 23 Apr. 82; *Bt.Lt.Colonel*, 23 Aug. 89; *Lt.Colonel*, 5 Dec. 94; *Colonel*, 30 Jan. 95.					
		Majors.					
28	...	3 Charles Hawtrey Bruce Norcott[26]	P14 Aug. 67	28 Oct. 71	1 April 79	......	1 Jan. 84
26	...	4 Walter Rupert Kenyon-Slaney	P10 Nov. 69	28 Oct. 71	14 June 80	......	1 Dec. 85
24	...	1 Hon. Edward Noel[33]	......	27 Mar. 72	20 Aug. 80	......	12 Apr. 90
22	...	2 p.s.c. Wm. Willoughby Cole Verner[37]	......	12 Nov. 73	13 Apr. 81	......	2 Dec. 91
22	...	3 Frank Stewart Whittington Raikes	......	28 Feb. 74	29 June 81	......	16 Dec. 91
21	...	John Francis Wegg-Prosser, *Adj.* 21 Middlesex Rifle Volunteers 1 Jan. 92	......	9 Aug. 74	15 Aug. 81	......	30 Dec. 91
21	...	4 Robert John Maude	......	2 Dec. 74	9 Apr. 82	......	17 Feb. 92
21	...	2 Edward Barrington Crake (*Depot*)	......	2 Dec. 74	19 Apr. 82	......	2 July 92
20	...	4 p.s.c. Francis Spencer Thornton (*Depot*)	......	13 June 75	1 June 82	......	9 Nov. 92
20	...	1 Arthur Ralph Pemberton[40]	......	11 Feb. 76	1 Jan. 84	......	7 May 93
21	...	4 Charles Theophilus Evelyn Metcalfe[41]	......	21 Sept. 74	1 Jan. 84	......	17 May 93
20	...	p.s.c. Ar. Edw. Wm. Colville,[42] *D.A.A. Gen.for Inst. Curragh*, 27 Aug. 91	......	10 Sept. 75	1 Aug. 84	......	11 Oct. 93
20	...	Charles Anthony Lamb, *Adj.* 20 Middlesex (Artists') Rifle Vols. 16 Feb. 91	......	11 Feb. 76	1 Aug. 84	......	15 Oct. 93
19	...	2 George Cockburn	......	11 Nov. 76	20 Aug. 84	......	14 Nov. 94
20	...	p.s.c. John Sherston,[44] *DSO. D.A.A. Gen.for Instruction,Bengal*,7Mar.93	......	12 Feb. 76	20 Aug. 84	......	14 Nov. 94
18	...	2 George Francis Leslie[47]	24 Nov. 77	12 April 79	3 Dec. 84	......	5 Dec. 94
		Captains.					
18	...	Henry Charles, *Visct.* Hardinge,[46] *District Inspector of Musketry, Chester*, 1 Jan. 93		30 June 77	11 April 79	20 Sept. 84	
18	...	p.s.c. Charles à Court,[48] *D.A.A. Gen. Intell. Branch, War Office*, 1 Feb. 93		30 Jan. 78	17 May 79	5 Dec. 84	
18	...	Henry Fuller Maitland Wilson,[49] *Adj.* 5 Battalion 1 Apr. 92		30 Jan. 78	30 June 79	5 Dec. 84	
18	...	2 Hon. Wenman Coke[50]		30 Jan. 78	9 July 79	18 Apr. 85	
17	...	Hon. Arthur Charles Edward Somerset, *Adjutant* 7 Battalion 11 Aug. 90		22 Feb. 79	12 Jan. 81	30 Oct. 84	
17	...	3 Hon. Chas. Cavendish Winn		1 Mar. 79	20 Jan. 81	21 Feb. 88	
17	...	Atherton Edward Jenkins, *Aide de Camp to Major General J. P. C. Glyn* 1 Oct. 94		15 Jan. 79	12 Mar. 81	1 Mar. 88	
16	...	1 Hon. Francis Michael St. Aubyn		2 July 79	13 Apr. 81	1 Apr. 88	
17	...	4 Lewis Loyd Nicol[51]		22 Feb. 79	29 June 81	9 Mar. 90	
16	...	Thomas Henry Des Vœux Wilkinson,[52] *DSO. Adjutant* 19 Middlesex Rifle Volunteers 1 Mar. 93		13 Aug. 79	1 July 81	14 Mar. 90	
16	...	3 Victor Arthur Couper[53]		13 Aug. 79	1 July 81	9 Apr. 90	
15	...	2 Arthur Fuller-Acland-Hood		23 Oct. 80	1 July 81	1 Aug. 90	
15	...	4 Hon.Edwd.Reginald Bateman-Hanbury		23 Oct. 80	1 July 81	15 Aug. 90	
15	...	p.s.c. John Steven Cowans, *Brigade Major, Aldershot*, 1 Sept. 94		22 Jan. 81	1 July 81	3 Sept. 90	
15	...	Henry Peter King-Salter, *Adjutant* 24 Middlesex Rifle Vols. 16 Mar. 91		22 Jan. 81	1 July 81	3 Sept. 90	
15	...	4 p.s.c. Hon. Chas. Granville Fortescue[54]		22 Jan. 81	1 July 81	14 Dec. 90	
15	...	William Frederic Parker, *Adj.* 3 Vol. Bn. Durham Lt.Infantry 1 Mar. 95		22 Jan. 81	1 July 81	1 Jan. 91	
15	...	G. C. Lord Bingham,[55] *Aide de Camp to H.R.H.the Duke of Connaught* 9 Oct.93		22 Jan. 81	1 July 81	1 Jan. 91	
15	...	Richard John Strachey,[56] *Staff College*		22 Jan. 81	1 July 81	12 Aug. 91	
14	...	p.s.c. Walter Edward Lascelles, *Instructor R. M. College* 10 Feb. 95		......	22 Oct. 81	12 Aug. 91	
14	...	1 Frederick Eyre Lawrence[57] (*Depot*)		......	22 Oct. 81	12 Aug. 91	
14	...	Wellesley George Pigott, *Adj.* 3 Vol. Bn. Essex Regt. 15 Feb. 92		......	25 Feb. 82	18 Nov. 91	
13	...	3 Henry Cecil Petre		......	9 Sept. 82	1 Dec. 91	
13	...	4 Albert Victor Jenner,[60] *DSO.*		......	9 Sept. 82	2 Dec. 91	
13	...	1 William Vernon Eccles[61]		......	27 Jan. 83	16 Dec. 91	
13	...	Arthur George Ferguson		......	27 Jan. 83	1 Jan. 92	
13	...	Alan Herbert Watlington Lowndes,[62] *ADC. to Governor of Ceylon* 22 Dec. 94		......	9 Sept. 82	15 Feb. 92	
12	...	2 Hubert Alcock Nepean Fyers		......	6 Feb. 84	1 Apr. 92	
12	...	4 Marcus William De la Poer Beresford		......	30 Jan. 84	8 Nov. 92	
11	...	1 Archibald Dundonald Stewart[63]		......	23 Aug. 84	23 Nov. 92	
11	...	4 Thomas Burnett Ramsay[64]		......	23 Aug. 84	23 Nov. 92	

The Rifle Brigade (The Prince Consort's Own). 357

Years' Ser Full Pay	Half Pay	CAPTAINS.	2ND LIEUT.	LIEUT.	CAPTAIN.	BREV. MAJ.
11	...	Charles Frederick Pinney, **Adjutant** 2 *Tower Hamlets Rifle Volunteers* 2 Apr. 94	......	12 Nov. 84	11 Oct. 93	
11	...	3 *Hon.* Henry Yarde-Buller	......	12 Nov. 84	15 Oct. 93	
11	...	2 p.s.c. Henry Hughes Wilson[65]	......	12 Nov. 84	6 Dec. 93	
11	...	3 Walter Norris Congreve	......	7 Feb. 85	6 Dec. 93	
11	...	4 Edward Alfred Finch Dawson	......	7 Feb. 85	4 Apr. 94	
11	...	3 *Hon.* Charles Edward Walsh, **Adjutant** 14 Feb. 93	......	11 Mar. 85	4 Apr. 94	
10	...	4 Henry Grylls Majendie,[66] **Adjutant** 27 June 91	......	9 May 85	4 Apr. 94	
10	...	3 *Hon.* Wilfred Dallas Cairns	......	13 May 85	16 May 94	
10	...	1 John Malcolm Steuart Steuart	......	6 May 85	14 Nov. 94	
10	...	4 Walter Guy Bentinck	......	9 May 85	14 Nov. 94	
10	...	4 Charles Edward Radclyffe[68]	......	25 Nov. 85	12 Dec. 94	
9	...	Lewis Frederic Green-Wilkinson,[69] *serving with the Egyptian Army*	......	14 Apr. 86	10 Feb. 95	

LIEUTENANTS.

Years' Ser Full Pay	Half Pay	LIEUTENANTS.	2ND LIEUT.	LIEUT.		
8	...	2 Leonard Robert Sunkersett Arthur[70] (*Lieut. Bedford Regt.* 28 Apr. 86)	24 Aug. 87	3 Dec. 90		
8	...	4 Douglas Elphinstone Bethune Patton-Bethune	4 May 87	1 Jan. 91		
8	...	1 Charles Russell Staveley	26 Oct. 87	11 Mar. 91		
8	...	2 Arth. Sydney Evelyn Annesley	16 Nov. 87	11 Mar. 91		
8	...	4 Philip Laurence Kington Blair Oliphant	21 Mar. 88	27 May 91		
7	...	3 Robert George Teesdale Baker-Carr, *A.D.C. to the Gov. General of India*	18 Apr. 88	27 June 21		
7	...	2 Somerset Francis Saunderson (*Depot*)	2 May 88	12 Aug. 91		
7	...	4 Hubert Edward Vernon	20 June 88	27 Aug. 91		
7	...	1 Frederick Gilbert Talbot	29 Dec. 88	18 Nov. 91		
7	...	2 Sydney Mills	23 Jan. 89	18 Nov. 91		
7	...	1 Harold Mavromichali Biddulph (*Dep.*)	10 Nov. 88	1 Dec. 91		
7	...	4 John Herbert Drax Savile	27 Mar. 89	2 Dec. 91		
7	...	1 Reginald Alexander, **Adjutant** 30 Nov. 94	23 Jan. 89	16 Dec. 91		
7	...	2 Albert Victor John Cowell	23 Mar. 89	1 Jan. 92		
6	...	2 Richard Handcock Thesiger, **Adjutant**, 20 Feb. 95	19 Mar. 90	10 Feb. 92		
5	...	2 Reginald Byng Stephens	9 Apr. 90	13 Feb. 92		
5	...	1 Charles William Cuffe Knox	3 May 90	15 Feb. 92		
5	...	2 Hew Dalrymple Ross	10 Sept. 90	23 Mar. 92		
5	...	4 Gerard Prideaux Tharp (*Depot*)	10 Sept. 90	15 June 92		
5	...	1 Llewellyn Traherne Saunderson	29 Oct. 90	15 June 92		
5	...	1 Richard Tryon	17 Jan. 91	3 Sept. 92		
5	...	4 William Henry Wemyss Steward	4 Mar. 91	23 Nov. 92		
4	...	4 *Hon.* Ar. Wm. de Brito Savile Foljambe	2 May 91	14 Feb. 93		
4	...	1 Samuel Charles Long	9 Sept. 91	18 June 93		
4	...	4 Ernest Lascelles	10 Oct. 91	8 July 93		
4	...	3 George Malcolm Nixon Harman	7 Nov. 91	11 Oct. 93		
4	...	3 *Hon.* Charles Henry Chandos Honniker-Major (*Depot*)	7 Nov. 91	15 Oct. 93		
4	...	2 George Leigh Paget	7 Nov. 91	6 Dec. 93		
4	...	1 John Edmond Gough	12 Mar. 92	6 Dec. 93		
4	...	3 George Bennet Gosling	12 Mar. 92	2 Apr. 94		
4	...	4 George Paley	12 Mar. 92	4 Apr. 94		
4	...	3 Harry Francis Darell	12 Mar. 92	16 May 94		
4	...	3 George Henry Morris	12 Mar. 92	16 May 94		
4	...	3 Beauchamp Albert Thos. Kerr-Pearse	12 Mar. 92	23 May 94		
4	...	1 *Lord* Charles Arthur Conyngham	16 Mar. 92	14 Nov. 94		
7	6/12	3 *Hon.* Villiers Richd. Bootle Wilbraham	18 Jan. 88	23 Mar. 91		
3	...	1 James Henville Throsher	9 Apr. 92	5 Dec. 94		
3	...	3 *Hon.* Chas. Fredk. Hamilton Napier	25 May 92	12 Dec. 94		

SECOND LIEUTENANTS.

Years' Ser Full Pay	Half Pay	SECOND LIEUTENANTS.	2ND LIEUT.			
3	...	2 Douglas John Propert	18 June 92			
3	...	2 Richard George Tyndall Bright	18 June 92			
3	...	1 Anthoney Drummond Boden	20 July 92			
3	...	2 Claud Victor Noble Percival	5 Oct. 92			
3	...	1 Gerard Lowther Lysley	5 Oct. 92			
3	...	3 James Dalgleish Heriot-Maitland	5 Oct. 92			
3	...	3 Ernest George Campbell	7 Dec. 92			
3	...	3 Chas. Hy. Geoffrey Mansfield Clarke	15 Feb. 93			
3	...	1 William Richard Wingfield Digby	22 Mar. 93			
2	...	4 Arthur Montague King	3 May 93			
2	...	3 Ronald Campbell Maclachlan	8 July 93			
2	...	3 *Sir* Edw. Ion Beresford Grogan, *Bart.*	19 July 93			
2	...	3 Stuart Hamilton Rickman	29 Nov. 93			
2	...	3 Matthew Gerald Edward Bell	20 Dec. 93			
2	...	3 Patrick Godfrey Ashley Cox	21 Feb. 94			
2	...	3 Gerald Montague Augustus Ellis	28 Feb. 94			
1	...	3 Auberon Claud Hegan Kennard	25 Apr. 94			
1	...	4 Alan Goring	2 June 94			
1	...	1 Geoffrey Nowell Salmon	2 June 94			
1	...	1 Elliott Derrick Le Poer Power	2 June 94			
1	...	1 Richard William Gillespie	10 Oct. 94			
1	...	3 Eustace Widdrington Bell	12 Dec. 94			
1	...	1 Thomas Close	13 Feb. 95			
1	...	Leslie Heber Thornton	6 Mar. 95			
1	...	John Theodosius Burnett-Stuart	6 Mar. 95			

Regimentals Green.—Facings Black.
Agents, Messrs. Cox and Co.
1st *Battalion embarked for Bombay*, 1880.—*Hong Kong*.
2nd *Battalion returned from Gibraltar*, 1880.—*Dublin*.
3rd *Battalion embarked for India*, 19 Oct. 1887.—*Rawul Pindee, Bengal*.
4th *Battalion returned from India*, 27 *Jan.* 1890.—*Aldershot*.

Paymasters.—1 Archibald D. Stewart, *Captain* 1 *Battalion* (acting).
3 *Hon.* Charles F. H. Napier, *Lieut.* 3 *Battalion* (acting).

		Quarter Masters.—4 Harry Hone,[71] 30 Aug. 82; *Hon. Captain*, 30 Aug. 92.				
13	...					
6	...	2 Francis Stone, 21 Aug. 89; *Hon. Lieut.*				
6	...	1 Lawrence Hoey, 11 Dec. 89; *Hon. Lieut.*				
4	...	3 John Adkins, 13 May 91; *Hon. Lieut.*				

358   *The Rifle Brigade (The Prince Consort's Own).*

[1] The Duke of Connaught served in the Egyptian war of 1882 in command of the 1st Brigade (the Guards), and was present at the battle of Tel-el-Kebir (mentioned in despatches, received the thanks of both Houses of Parliament, CB., Medal with Clasp, 2nd Class of the Medjidie, and Khedive's Star).

[2] Lord Alexander Russell served with the 1st Battalion Rifle Brigade in the Kaffir war of 1852-53 as D.A.Q.M.G. to the 1st Division, and was present at the battle of Berea—mentioned in General Orders (Medal, and Brevet of Major). Served also in the Crimea from the 11th July 1855, including the siege and fall of Sebastopol, and commanded the 1st Battalion from the 25th October 1855 until the evacuation of the Crimea (Medal with Clasp, Brevet of Lt.Colonel, Sardinian and Turkish Medals, and 5th Class of the Medjidie).

[3] General Elrington served the Eastern campaign of 1854 with the Rifle Brigade, including the battles of Alma and Inkerman, and siege of Sebastopol (Medal with three Clasps, Brevet of Major, Knight of the Legion of Honor, 5th Class of the Medjidie, and Turkish Medal).

[18] Major Sackville embarked for the Gold Coast with the 2nd Battalion Rifle Brigade, and served throughout the second phase of the Ashanti war in 1874, including the battle of Amoaful, battle of Ordahsu and capture of Coomassie (Medal with Clasp).

[20] Major St. Paul served in the Afghan war in 1878-79 with the Peshawur Valley Field Force, and was present at the attack and capture of Ali Musjid, and in the expeditions into the Kunar and Lughman Valleys (Medal with Clasp). Served with the Burmese Expedition in 1888-89 with the 4th Battalion Rifle Brigade (Medal with Clasp).

[23] Colonel Francis Howard served with the Jowaki Afreedee Expedition in 1877-78 (Medal with Clasp). Served with the 4th Battalion Rifle Brigade in the Afghan war in 1878-79, and was present at the attack and capture of Ali Musjid and with the expeditions into the Bazar and Lughman Valleys (Medal with Clasp). Served with the Burmese Expedition in 1888-89 with the 4th Battalion Rifle Brigade (mentioned in despatches, Brevet of Lt.Colonel, Clasp).

[26] Major Norcott served in the Burmese campaign in 1888-89 with the Kerenni Expedition (mentioned in despatches, Medal with Clasp).

[33] Major the Hon. E. Noel embarked for the Gold Coast with the 2nd Battalion Rifle Brigade, and served throughout the second phase of the Ashanti war in 1874, including the battle of Amoaful, advanced guard skirmishes and ambuscade affairs between Adwabin and the river Ordah, battle of Ordahsu and capture of Coomassie (Medal with Clasp). Served with a detachment of the Rifle Brigade in the expedition against the Jowaki Afreedees in 1877-78 (Medal with Clasp). Served with the Burmese Expedition in 1886-88 (Clasp).

[37] Major Verner served with the Nile Expedition in 1884-85 as Deputy Assistant Adjutant General Intelligence Department to the Desert Column under Sir Herbert Stewart, and was present at the action at Abu Klea, in the engagement at El Gubat (where he acted as guide to the square on its march to the river), in the engagement at Metammeh on the 21st January in command of Gordon's troops (mentioned in despatches), and in the action at Abu Klea Wells on the 16th February (Medal with two Clasps, and Khedive's Star). [See also Civil Decorations for Gallantry, "Hart's Annual Army List," p. 786.]

[40] Major Pemberton served with the 4th Battalion Rifle Brigade in the Afghan war in 1878-79, and was present at the attack and capture of Ali Musjid and in the expeditions into the Bazar and Lughman Valleys (Medal with Clasp).

[41] Major Metcalfe served with the Burmese Expedition in 1886-87 (Medal with Clasp).

[42] Major A. E. W. Colville served in the Afghan war in 1878-79 with the Peshawur Valley Field Force (Medal). Also served with the Mahsood Wuzeeree Expedition in 1881.

[44] Major John Sherston served in the Afghan war of 1878-80 as Aide de Camp to Sir Frederick Roberts, and was present in the engagement at Charasiah on the 6th October 1879 and subsequent pursuit of the enemy (mentioned in despatches), and in the operations around Cabul in December 1879 including the investment of Sherpore (mentioned in despatches); accompanied Sir Frederick Roberts in the march to Candahar, and was present at the battle of Candahar (mentioned in despatches, Medal with three Clasps, and Bronze Decoration). Served in the Mahsood Wuzeeree Expedition in 1881 with the 4th Battalion Rifle Brigade. Served with the Burmese Expedition in 1886-87 as Deputy Assistant Adjutant and Quarter Master General on the Head Quarters Staff (mentioned in despatches, DSO., and Medal with Clasp).

[46] Lord Hardinge served with the Nile Expedition in 1884-85, and was present at the actions at Abu Klea and El Gubat and in the reconnaissance to Metammeh (Medal with two Clasps, and Khedive's Star).

[47] Major Leslie served in the Afghan war in 1878-79 with the Peshawur Valley Field Force, and was present at the attack and capture of Ali Musjid, and with the expeditions into the Kunar and Lughman Valleys (Medal with Clasp).

[48] Captain à Court served in the Afghan war in 1878 with the Peshawur Valley Field Force, and was present at the attack and capture of Ali Musjid (Medal with Clasp).

[49] Captain Wilson served with the 4th Battalion Rifle Brigade in the Afghan war in 1878-79, and was present at the attack and capture of Ali Musjid and in the expedition into the Kunar Valley (Medal with Clasp). Served in the expedition against the Mahsood Wuzeerees in 1881.

[50] Captain the Hon. W. Coke served with the 4th Battalion Rifle Brigade in the Afghan war in 1878-79 (Medal), and in the expedition against the Mahsood Wuzeerees in 1881.

[51] Captain Nicol served in the Zulu war of 1879. and was present in the engagement at Ulundi (Medal with Clasp). Also served in the expedition against the Mahsood Wuzeerees in 1881.

[52] Captain Wilkinson served with the Mahsood Wuzeeree Expedition in 1881. Served with the Burmese Expedition in 1886-89 as Superintendent of Army Signalling 6th Brigade Upper Burmah Field Force (mentioned in despatches, DSO., and Medal with two Clasps).

[53] Captain Couper served with the Mahsood Wuzeeree Expedition in 1881. Served with the Burmese Expedition in 1889 (Medal with Clasp).

[54] Captain Hon. C. G. Fortescue served in the Burmese Expedition in 1888-89 with the 4th Battalion Rifle Brigade (Medal with Clasp).

[55] Lord Bingham served with the Bechuanaland Expedition under Sir Charles Warren in 1884-85 with the Irregular Mounted Troops.

[56] Captain Strachey served in the Burmese Expedition in 1888-89 with the 4th Battalion Rifle Brigade (Medal with Clasp).

[57] Captain Lawrence served in the Soudan campaign in 1885 with the Mounted Infantry (Medal with Clasp, and Khedive's Star).

[60] Captain Jenner served with the Burmese Expedition in 1886-87 (DSO., and Medal with Clasp).

[61] Captain Eccles served in the Burmese Expedition in 1888-89 with the 4th Battalion Rifle Brigade (Medal with Clasp).

[62] Captain Lowndes served with the Burmese Expedition in 1886-88 (Medal with Clasp).

[63] Captain A. D. Stewart served with the Burmese Expedition in 1886-88 (Medal with Clasp).

[64] Captain Ramsay served with the Burmese Expedition in 1886-88 (Medal with Clasp).

[65] Captain H. H. Wilson served with the Burmese Expedition in 1885-87—wounded in an engagement on 17th June 1887 (Medal with Clasp), and served again in 1887-89 (Clasp).

[66] Captain Majendie served with the Burmese Expedition in 1888-89 with the 4th Battalion Rifle Brigade (Medal with Clasp).

[68] Captain Radclyffe served with the Burmese Expedition in 1885-86 and was severely wounded in an engagement on the 18th December (Medal with Clasp).

[69] Captain Green Wilkinson served with the Burmese Expedition in 1886-87 (Medal with Clasp).

[70] Lieut. Arthur served with the Burmese Expedition in 1887-88 (Medal with Clasp).

[71] Captain Hope served in the Afghan war in 1878-79, and was present at the attack and capture of Ali Musjid and with the expedition into the Bazar Valley (Medal with Clasp).

The Rifle Brigade (The Prince Consort's Own).

Record of the Services of the 1st Battalion Rifle Brigade (Prince Consort's Own).

Raised in March 1800, and re-formed in August 1800. (One Company to Copenhagen, 1801.) England, to 1805. South America, Germany, and England, to 1807. South America, Denmark, and England, to 1808. South America, the Peninsula, and Sweden, to 1809. The Peninsula and England, to 1810. The Peninsula and France, to 1815. England, Belgium, and France, to 1818. England, to 1820. Ireland, to 1825. Nova Scotia and New Brunswick, to 1836. England, to 1841. Malta, to 1843. Corfu, to 1846. Cape of Good Hope, to 1850. England, to 1852. Cape of Good Hope, to Jan. 1854. England, to July 1854. The Crimea, to 1856. England, to Apr. 1861. Ireland, to Dec. 1861. Canada, to 1870. England, to 1876. Ireland, to 1878. England, to 1880. India, to 1886. Burma, to 1888. India, 1888.

Record of the Services of the 2nd Battalion Rifle Brigade (Prince Consort's Own).

Raised in 1805. To England and South America, 1806. To England, Denmark, and South America, 1807. To England, Portugal, and Spain, 1808. To England and Holland, 1809. To England and the Peninsula, 181c. To England and the Peninsula, 1813. To France and Holland, 1814. To England, Belgium, France, and Holland, 1815. To France, 1815. To England, 1818. To Ireland, 1820. To Malta, 1826. To the Ionian Islands, 1832. To Ireland, 1837. To Bermuda, 1842. To Nova Scotia, 1843. To Canada, 1846. To England, 1852. To the Crimea, 1854. To England and Ireland, 1857. To India, 1857. To England, 1867. To Ireland, 1872. To the Gold Coast, 1873 (Ashantee war). To England, 1874. To Gibraltar, 1874. To Ireland, 1880. To England, 1885. To Ireland, 1890.

Record of the Services of the 4th Battalion Rifle Brigade (Prince Consort's Own).

Raised in 1857. To Malta, 1858. To Gibraltar, 1863. To Canada, 1865. To England, 1867. To Ireland, 1872. To India, 1873. To Burmah, 1888. To England, 1889.

Continuation of Notes to the West India Regiment.

[29] Lieut. Carleton served with the expedition up the Gambia in 1891-92 (Medal with Clasp).

[30] Lieut. MacDonald served with the expedition to the Gambia in 1892 including the capture of Toniataba (Medal with Clasp); in the operations against the Sofas in 1893-94 (mentioned in despatches, Clasp); and with the expedition to the Gambia against Fodey Silah in 1894 with the 1st Battalion West India Regiment (mentioned in despatches).

[31] Lieut. Hulseberg was present during the attack of Toniataba on the 13th March 1892 (wounded), and served with the Gambia Expedition resulting in the capture of Toniataba on the 28th April (Medal with Clasp).

[32] Lieut. Cowie served with the expedition to the Tambaka Country in 1892 including the capture of Tambi, and with the expedition against the Jebus, Lagos, West Coast of Africa, in 1892 (Medal with Clasp); and in the expedition to the Gambia against Fodey Silah in 1894 with the 1st Battalion West India Regiment—slightly wounded (mentioned in despatches, Clasp).

[33] Lieut. Langlands served with the expedition to the Tambaka Country in 1892 resulting in the capture of Tambi, and also with the Gambia Expedition in 1892 including the capture of Toniataba (Medal with Clasp); and in the operations against the Sofas in 1893-94 (Clasp).

[34] Lieut. Hardyman.—See Civil Decorations for Gallantry, "Hart's Annual Army List," p. 786.

[35] Lieut. Morley served with the expedition to the Tambaka Country in 1892 including the capture of Tambi, (Medal with Clasp); and in the operations against the Sofas in 1893-94 (Clasp).

[36] Lieut. Row served with the expedition up the Gambia in 1891-92 (Medal with Clasp).

[37] Lieut. Tregear served with the expedition to the Tambaka Country in 1892 including the capture of Tambi (Medal with Clasp); and in the expedition to the Gambia against Fodey Silah in 1894 with the 1st Battalion West India Regiment (mentioned in despatches, Clasp).

[38] Lieut. Leech served in the operations against the Sofas, West Coast of Africa, in 1893-94 (Medal with Clasp); and in the expedition to the Gambia against Fodey Silah in 1894 with the 1st Battalion West India Regiment (mentioned in despatches).

[39] Lieut. Lawrenson served in the operations against the Sofas, West Coast of Africa, in 1893-94 (Medal with Clasp).

[40] Lieut. Duffey served in the expedition to the Gambia against Fodey Silah in 1894 with the 1st Battalion West India Regiment (Medal with Clasp).

[43] Captain Christie served in the expedition against the Yonnies, West Coast of Africa, in 1887-88 (Medal with Clasp). Served with the expedition to the Tambaka Country in 1892 including the capture of Tambi, and with the expedition to the Gambia in 1892 including the capture of Toniataba (Clasp).

Record of the Services of the 1st Battalion West India Regiment.

Raised in 1795 by the amalgamation of two corps—namely, the Carolina Corps, raised in North America in 1779; and Malcolm's Rangers, raised in Martinique in 1795. When first formed the Regiment consisted of ten companies and a troop of Dragoons, but the latter was abolished in 1797. At Martinique, to 1798. At St. Lucia, to 1801. At Martinique, to 1802. At St. Vincent, with detachments at Martinique, Antigua, and Grenada, to 1804. At Dominica, with detachments at St. Vincent and Grenada, to 1806. At Barbados, with detachments at Tobago and Grenada, to 1808. At Trinidad, 1809. At Martinique, with detachments at St. Lucia and Dominica, to 1813. At Guadaloupe, with detachments at Marie Galante and St. Martins, 1814. New Orleans, 1814. Guadaloupe and Barbados, 1815-16. At Antigua, with detachments at Montserrat, St. Kitts, St. Lucia, and Dominica, to 1818. At Barbados, with detachments at Antigua, St. Lucia, Dominica, Tobago and Demerara, to 1824. At Trinidad, with detachments at Barbados, St. Lucia, Dominica, Antigua, Grenada, and Tortola, to 1836. At St. Lucia, with detachments at Trinidad, Tobago, Demerara, St. Vincent, and Sierra Leone, to 1838. At Demerara, with detachments at Barbados, Trinidad, Tobago, St. Lucia, St. Vincent, Grenada, Dominica, and Sierra Leone, to 1844. At Jamaica, with detachments at Sierra Leone, Gambia, Gold Coast, Honduras, Bahamas and various West India Islands, to 1856. At Nassau, Bahamas, with detachments at Sierra Leone and Gambia, to 1860. At Barbados, with detachments at Demerara, Trinidad, St. Lucia, and Honduras, to 1863. At Nassau, with detachments at Trinidad, Honduras, and Gold Coast, to 1864. Jamaica, 1865-6. Sierra Leone, with detachments at Gold Coast and Gambia, to 1869. Jamaica, with detachments at Honduras and Nassau, to 1873. Gold Coast, 1874. Sierra Leone, with detachments at Gold Coast and Demerara, to 1877. Jamaica, with detachments at Honduras, Barbados, and Nassau, to 1880. Sierra Leone, with detachments at Gold Coast and Demerara, to 1883. Jamaica, with detachments at Honduras, Demerara, and Nassau, to 1886. Sierra Leone, with detachments at Gold Coast and Barbados, to 1889. Jamaica, with detachments at St. Lucia, Barbados and Nassau, 1889.

West India Regiment.

[1st Batt., Sierra Leone.
2nd Batt., Jamaica.

"DOMINICA" "MARTINIQUE" "GUADALOUPE" "ASHANTEE."

Years Ser.	Full Pay	Half Pay						

Colonel.—William John Chamberlayne, *Ensign,* P25 Nov. 42; *Lt.* 6 Dec. 44; *Capt.* 31 Aug. 54; *Major,* P27 Jan. 57; *Lt.Colonel* P19 Feb. 58; *Colonel,* 19 Feb. 63; *Major General,* 28 Oct. 68; *Lieut.General,* 13 July 81; *General,* 15 Jan. 82; *Colonel* West India Regiment, 26 Aug. 91.

22 ... Lieutenant Colonels.—2 James Edward Wilmot Smyth Caulfeild,¹ *Commanding the Battalion,* 24 Feb. 92; *Lt.* 14 May 73; *Capt.* 2 Feb. 78; *Major,* 1 Jan. 83; *Lt.Colonel,* 29 June 91.

21 ... 1 Arthur Bosworth, *Commanding the Battalion,* 7 March 94; *Lieut.* 11 Feb. 75; *Captain,* 1 July 81; *Major,* 3 Aug. 87; *Lt.Colonel,* 24 Feb. 92.

20 ... 1 Charles Lawford, Dale, *Lieut.* 11 Feb. 76; *Capt.* 12 Oct. 82; *Major,* 2 Feb. 87; *Lt.Colonel,* 17 Jan. 94.

20 ... 2 George Colquhoun Madden,⁵ *CB. DSO., Lieut.* 12 May 75; *Capt.* 24 Aug. 81; *Major,* 29 Jan. 88; *Lt.Colonel,* 7 March 94.

		MAJORS.	2ND LIEUT.	LIEUT.	CAPTAIN.	BREV.MAJ.	MAJOR.
20	...	1 p.s.c. Douglas Minto Allen		22 Sept. 75	16 Jan. 85	......	4 Feb. 91
20	...	1 Arthur Bor⁶		18 Dec. 75	16 Jan. 85	......	24 Feb. 92
15	...	2 Arden Lowndes Bayley⁷ (*Depot*)	11 Aug. 80	1 July 81	8 Sept. 86	......	4 Jan. 93
14	...	2 Cuthbert Dunn	18 May 81	1 July 81	26 Oct. 87	......	17 Jan. 93
14	...	2 Ralph Egerton¹⁰	18 June 81	1 July 81	11 Jan. 88	......	17 Jan. 94
17	...	1 Henry Beresford Bourke,⁹ *DSO.*		30 Nov. 78	5 Oct. 87	......	1 Apr. 94
17	...	1 Richard Joseph Norris,¹¹ *DSO.*	19 Feb. 79	1 Dec. 80	29 Jan. 88	......	1 Apr. 94
17	2½	2 Thomas Pepper Ernest Lowry		12 May 76	31 Mar. 86	......	1 Apr. 94
15	...	2 Arthur Russell Loscombe	11 Aug. 80	1 July 81	29 Jan. 88	......	1 Apr. 94
		CAPTAINS.					
13	...	2 Hugh Charles Buck		2 Dec. 82	2 Dec. 89		
16	...	James Reginald Maitland Dalrymple-Hay,¹² *Adj.* 4 *Vol. Bn. Argyll and Sutherland Highlanders* 9 Nov. 91	1 Nov. 79	1 July 81	2 Feb. 90		
13	...	2 Robert Bentley Todd		30 Aug. 82	12 Feb. 87		
13	...	2 Charles Walter Young (*Depot*)		10 Mar. 83	27 Oct. 89		
13	...	2 William Lewis Jackson		27 Jan. 83	29 June 91		
12	...	2 Wm. Beauchamp Stansfeld		21 Apr. 83	14 Sept. 91		
12	...	2 Francis Edward Ryde		6 Feb. 84	9 Nov. 91		
15	...	Edward Alfred Moulton-Barrett, *Ordnance Store Department*	11 Aug. 80	1 July 81	13 Jan. 92		
13	...	1 Alfred Cotton Way,¹⁵ *DSO., Garrison Adjutant, St. Lucia*		29 July 82	9 June 92		
13	...	Percy Thuillier Westmorland,¹⁶ *Army Pay Department*		9 Sept. 82	28 Aug. 89		
10	...	William Lancelot Tredgold,¹⁷ *Ordnance Store Department*		9 May 85	19 July 93		
10	...	Edward Stanley Curwen Kennedy, *Adjutant Jamaica Militia,* 13 Jan. 93		4 Nov. 85	19 July 93		
11	...	Oliver Caton Sherwood, *Ordnance Store Department*		23 Aug. 84	19 July 93		
11	...	1 George Oates, *Garrison Adjutant, Sierra Leone,* 9 Apr. 94		23 Aug. 84	19 July 93		
12	...	1 William Burton Watts¹⁸		14 July 83	10 Feb. 91		
11	...	Cecil Buckley Morgan, *serving under the Royal Niger Company*		23 Aug. 84	17 Jan. 94		
11	...	1 Leonard Shadwell Blackden		7 Feb. 85	1 Apr. 94		
12	...	1 Lewis Amadeus Brooks, *O. S. Dept.*		6 Feb. 84	1 Apr. 94		
9	...	2 Frederick Thomas Henstock, **Adjutant** 2 Nov. 91		25 Aug. 86	1 Apr. 94		
8	...	1 Meredith Carre Smith	24 Sept. 87	5 June 89	1 Apr. 94		
8	...	1 Frederick Bramston Luard	29 June 87	31 July 89	1 Apr. 94		
8	...	Francis Richard Lovebang	22 Feb. 88	2 Dec. 89	16 July 94		
8	...	1 David Percy Malins	23 Nov. 87	4 Jan. 90	16 July 94		
10	...	1 Arthur Whyte Melville Wilson²²		23 May 85	4 Aug. 92		
9	...	1 Norman Patrick Mellier Hadow²³ (*Depot*)		25 Aug. 86	22 Dec. 94		
8	...	1 Hepworth Arthur Hill	8 June 87	8 May 89	22 Dec. 94		
		LIEUTENANTS.					
8	...	1 Edward Baines²⁵	11 Feb. 88	4 Jan. 90			
7	...	1 Verschoyle Crawford Climo (*Depot*)	22 Aug. 88	8 Jan. 90			
7	...	2 Frederick Alexander Liston (*Depot*)	22 Aug. 88	11 June 90			
7	...	1 Noel Philip Davies²⁶	30 Jan. 89	1 Nov. 90			
6	3/12	1 Buckenham Francis Stevens²⁷ (*Depot*)	30 Jan. 89	1 Nov. 90			
7	...	1 George Dominic Price,²⁸ **Adjutant** 13 July 92	30 Jan. 89	1 Nov. 90			
7	...	2 Arthur Elphinstone Barchard, *Garrison Adjutant, Jamaica,* 1 Oct. 93	30 Jan. 89	1 Nov. 90			
7	...	2 Hugh Dudley Carleton²⁹ (*Depot*)	6 Mar. 89	1 Nov. 90			
7	...	Francis Rickman Barton, *Aide de Camp to Gov. of Barbadoes* 23 May 93	16 Mar. 89	1 Nov. 90			
6	...	1 Peter Charles Edward MacDonald³⁰	9 Oct. 89	25 Mar. 91			
6	...	1 Ernest Alexander Hulseberg³¹	29 Jan. 90	25 Mar. 91			
6	...	1 William Knightley Falcon	29 Jan. 90	25 Mar. 91			
6	...	2 John Philip Herbert Mackenzie Alone	1 Mar. 90	29 June 91			
6	...	Hugh Willoughby Marsden	1 Mar. 90	15 July 91			
6	...	Ernest Leonard Cowie³², *serving with the Gambia Police*	18 Dec. 89	14 Sept. 91			
6	...	2 James Sydney Henderson	29 Mar. 90	9 Nov. 91			
5	...	1 Percy Langlands³³	3 May 90	13 Jan. 92			
5	...	1 William Henry Hardyman³⁴	3 May 90	24 Feb. 92			
5	...	1 Francis Britton Morley³⁵	8 Oct. 90	23 Mar. 92			
5	...	1 Clement Willmore Long	29 Oct. 90	4 Jan. 93			
5	...	2 Charles Edward Daliel Oldham Rew³⁶	29 Nov. 90	4 Jan. 93			
5	...	2 James Edward Somerville Woodman	7 Jan. 91	13 Jan. 93			
5	...	Frederick Charles Tregear³⁷	4 Mar. 91	5 Apr. 93			
4	...	2 Rowland Litchford	23 May 91	2 Apr. 93			
4	...	2 Byron Henry Drury	25 July 91	23 May 93			
6	...	2 Thomas Benedict Fulton	23 Oct. 89	11 Jan. 92			
4	...	1 Arthur Clarendon Hyde	25 July 91	19 July 93			

West India Regiment.

Years' Ser. Full Pay.	Half Pay.	LIEUTENANTS.	2ND LIEUT.	LIEUT.
4	...	1 Albert Lewis Murison	10 Oct. 91	7 Sept. 93
4	...	1 Bonham Faunce	21 Oct. 91	18 Sept. 93
4	...	2 Henry Albert Thorne	13 Jan. 92	25 Oct. 93
4	...	1 Ellis Joynson Chalmer Leech[38]	10 Oct. 91	26 Oct. 93
6	...	2 Francis Lynch Blosse	22 May 89	3 Mar. 92
4	...	2 Henry Adolphe Leverson	23 Jan. 92	22 Nov. 93
4	...	1 John Plomer Bliss	9 Mar. 92	24 Nov. 93
3	...	2 Edwin Lewis Vaughan Saunders Davies	6 Apr. 92	24 Dec. 93
3	...	1 Reginald Robert Lawrenson[39]	8 June 92	1 Jan. 94
3	...	2 David Poole	10 Aug. 92	16 May 94
3	...	1 Arthur Street	12 Oct. 92	16 July 94
3	...	2 William Wallbridge Davis	25 Jan. 93	25 July 94
3	...	1 Edmund John Pomeroy	15 Mar. 93	9 Nov. 94
2	...	1 George Allan Duffey[40]	5 Apr. 93	22 Dec. 94
2	...	2 Albert Trevor De Morteval Martin	12 July 93	22 Dec. 94
6	...	George Peacocke	9 Nov. 89	10 June 91

		SECOND LIEUTENANTS.		
2	...	1 Herbert John Thompson	23 Sept. 93	
2	...	2 Sackville Edward Cecil Hamilton Beamish (*Depot*)	18 Oct. 93	
2	...	2 Arthur Tilson Magan	1 Nov. 93	
2	...	2 Walter Chill	22 Nov. 93	
2	...	1 James Haldane Stewart	29 Nov. 93	
2	...	2 Alexander Beresford Murison	13 Dec. 93	
2	...	1 Francis Edward Yeld	17 Jan. 94	
2	...	1 Frank Ernest Wilhelm Butt	17 Jan. 94	
1	...	1 Philip Edward Prideaux	25 Apr. 94	
1	...	1 Napier Edward Frederick Safford	16 May 94	
1	...	1 Samuel Howard Hingley	10 Oct. 94	
1	...	2 Colin Philip Greig	10 Oct. 94	
1	...	1 Robert Kingsbury Healing	10 Oct. 94	
1	...	1 Charles Wilberforce Maclean	10 Oct. 94	
1	...	2 George Edward Hewett	5 Dec. 94	
1	...	Harry Ewbank Menteth Hutchinson	13 Feb. 95	
1	...	1 Ernest Craig-Brown	20 Feb. 95	
1	...	Frederick Swabey	6 Mar. 95	

Paymasters.—1
2

Years			
15	...	*Quarter Masters.*—1 Henry Christie,[41] 1 Dec. 80; *Hon. Captain*, 1 Dec. 90.	
7	...	2 Eli Crane, 9 Jan. 89; *Hon. Lieut.*	
1	...	George Frederick Colley, 24 Oct. 94; *Hon. Lieut.*—Depot.	

Facings, White.—*Agents*, Messrs. Cox and Co.

---

[1] Lt.Colonel Caulfeild served in the Ashanti war in 1873-74 (Medal with Clasp).

[5] Lt.Colonel Madden served with the expedition to the Gambia in 1892 and commanded the forces at the attack of Toniataba; with the expedition against the Jebus, Lagos, West Coast of Africa, in 1892 (*DSO.* and Medal with Clasp); and with the expedition to the Gambia against Fodey Silah in 1894 with the 1st Battalion West India Regiment (mentioned in despatches, *CB.*, and Clasp).

[6] Major Bor served in operations against the the Sofas, West Coast of Africa, in 1893-94 (Medal with Clasp).

[7] Major Bayley served with the expedition up the Gambia in 1891-92 (Medal with Clasp).

[9] Major Bourke served with the expedition to the Tambaka Country in 1892 and was present at the capture of Tambi (Medal with Clasp); and in the operations against the Sofas, West Coast of Africa, in 1893-94 (mentioned in despatches, Clasp).

[10] Major Egerton served in the Commissariat Department in the Zulu war of 1879 and in the subsequent operations against Sekukuni (Medal with Clasp). Served in the Boer war of 1880-81; was present with the 94th Regiment in the engagement at Bronkhorst Spruit in the Commissariat and Transport Department—wounded (mentioned in despatches, promoted 2nd Lieutenant), and afterwards took part in the defence of Pretoria.

[11] Major Norris served with the expedition to the Tambaka Country, on the West Coast of Africa, in 1892, including the capture of Tambi (*DSO.* and Medal with Clasp).

[12] Captain Dalrymple Hay served in the Boer war of 1881, and took part in the defence of Potchefstroom.

[15] Captain Way served with the Burmese Expedition in 1885-89 (mentioned in despatches, Medal with two Clasps). Served in the operations against the Sofas, West Coast of Africa, in 1893-94 (mentioned in despatches, Medal with Clasp); and with the expedition to the Gambia against Fodey Silah in 1894 as Staff Officer to Major Fairtlough, Commanding the Troops on the West Coast of Africa (mentioned in despatches, *DSO.*, and Clasp).

[16] Captain Westmorland served with the expedition to the Gambia against Fodey Silah in 1894 with the 1st Battalion West India Regiment (mentioned in despatches, Medal with Clasp).

[17] Captain Tredgold served with the expedition to the Tambaka Country in 1892 including the capture of Tambi (Medal with Clasp).

[18] Captain Watts served in the operations against the Sofas, West Coast of Africa, in 1893-94 (Medal with Clasp); and in the expedition to the Gambia against Fodey Silah in 1894 with the 1st Battalion West India Regiment (mentioned in despatches, Clasp).

[22] Captain Wilson served in the Sikkim Expedition in 1888 with the 2nd Battalion Derbyshire Regiment, and was present in the engagement at the Jelapla (Medal with Clasp).

[23] Captain Hadow served with the expedition to the Tambaka Country in 1892 including the capture of Tambi (Medal with Clasp).

[25] Lieut. Baines was present during the attack of Toniataba on the 13th March 1892, and served with the Gambia Expedition resulting the capture of Toniataba on the 28th April (Medal with Clasp); in the operations against the Sofas, West Coast of Africa, in 1893-94 (mentioned in despatches, Clasp); and with the expedition to the Gambia against Fodey Silah in 1894 with the 1st Battalion West India Regiment (mentioned in despatches).

[26] Lieut. Davies served with the expedition to the Tambaka Country in 1892 including the capture of Tambi (Medal with Clasp).

[27] Lieut. Stevens served with the expedition to the Tambaka Country in 1892 (Medal with Clasp).

[28] Lieut. Price served in the operations against the Sofas, West Coast of Africa, in 1893-94 as Adjutant 1st Battalion West India Regiment (mentioned in despatches); and with the expedition to the Gambia against Fodey Silah in 1894 as Adjutant 1st Battalion West India Regiment and as Acting Quarter Master to the expedition (mentioned in despatches, Clasp).

[*For remainder of Notes see end of Rifle Brigade, p. 359.*

362-5 Provisional Battalion. [Shorncliffe.

Years ser. Full Pay	Half Pay		
33	1⁰/₁₀	**Lieutenant Colonel.**—Arthur Hill Sandys Montgomery,[1] 1 May 91; *Ensign,* P13 Jan. 61; *Lieut.* 5 Aug. 65; *Capt.* 23 Apr. 73; *Major,* 1 July 81; *Lt.Colonel,* 16 Oct. 89.
23	...	**Major.**—Charles Henry Kelly, 13 May 91; *Lieut.* 26 June 72; *Capt.* 18 June 81; *Major,* 13 May 91.
		Adjutant.—George Albanus Williams,[3] 1 May 91; *Captain South Staffordshire Regiment.*
.2	...	**Quarter Master.**—R. P. Norman, 17 Feb. 93; *Hon. Lieut.*

[1] Lt. Colonel Montgomery served with the Mahsood Wuzeeree Expedition in 1881.
[3] Captain Williams.—For War Services, see South Staffordshire Regiment, p. 282.

Hong Kong Regiment.

Bt.Lt.Colonel E. G. Barrow, Indian S.C.	16 Jan. 95	Commandant 11 Nov. 91.—From 7 Bengal Infantry.	[Furl.
Captain H. T. Faithfull, Indian S. C.	12 Feb. 85	2nd in Com. and Wing Comdr. 28 Nov. 91.—From 33 Bengal Inf.	
Captain J. M. A. Retallick, Indian S. C.	10 Sept. 86	Wing Commander, 22 Dec. 91.—From 45 Bengal Inf.—Furl.	
Lieut. W. C. M. Woodcock, Indian S. C.	6 May 85	Wing Officer and Adjutant, 29 Dec. 91.—From 29 Bengal Inf.	
Lieut. M. R. E. Ray, Indian Staff Corps	29 Aug. 85	Wing Officer and Qr. Mr., 13 Mar. 92.—From 7 Bengal Infantry.	
Lieut. L. E. L. C. Berger, Indian S. C.	1 Feb. 86	Wing Officer, 2 Jan. 92.—From 30 Bombay Infantry.	
Lieut E. C. Rowcroft, Indian S. C.	23 Mar. 89	Wing Officer, 9 Jan. 92.—From 35 Bengal Infantry.	
Lieut. P. G. Anderson, Indian S. C.	24 Feb. 90	Wing Officer, 5 Mar. 93.—From 24 Bengal Native Infantry.	
Lieut. A.C.J. Campbell, Middlesex Regt.	1 Nov. 90	Wing Officer, 17 Oct. 94.	
2nd Lieut. G. D. Campbell, Indian Regt.	27 Jan. 92	Wing Officer, 10 Nov. 94.	
Surgeon Captain A. L. Borradaile, MB.			
Medical Staff	......	In medical charge.	

Unattached List.

(With a view to appointment to Indian Staff Corps.)

Second Lieutenants.	2ND LIEUT.	Second Lieutenants.	2ND LIEUT.
Angus Campbell	28 Jan. 93	Harry Ernest Browne	10 Oct. 94
Henry de Courcy O'Grady	30 Aug. 93	Robert Thomas Disney Leith	10 Oct. 94
John Clayton Coldstream	30 Aug. 93	Thomas Sands Cox	10 Oct. 94
Charles Lancelot Storr	30 Aug. 93	Lionel Stuart Logan	10 Oct. 94
Kenneth Leo Warner Mackenzie	30 Aug. 93	Allan Gilbert Mayhew Hogg	10 Oct. 94
Hugh Stephenson Moberly	30 Aug. 93	Claude Edward Bateman-Champain	10 Oct. 94
Charles Augustus Vivian	30 Aug. 93	Edward Richard Wetherall	10 Oct. 94
Henry Beauchamp St. John	30 Aug. 93	Henry Walker	10 Oct. 94
Edward Willoughby Waddington	30 Aug. 93	Cecil William Carey	10 Oct. 94
Francis Deane Russell	30 Aug. 93	Patrick Barclay Sangster	28 Nov. 94
Arthur Lennard Barrett	30 Aug. 93	Walter Hesketh	28 Nov. 94
Arthur Kyffin Heyland	30 Aug. 93	Alexander Sharp	28 Nov. 94
Francis Carminowe Nicolas	30 Aug. 93	Dashwood William Harrington Humphreys	28 Nov. 94
Launcelot Hope Rix Ames	30 Aug. 93	John Gwynne Griffith	28 Nov. 94
John Ernest Blois Johnson	30 Aug. 93	Mark Synge	28 Nov. 94
Giles Rooke	30 Aug. 93	George de La Poer Beresford Pakenham	16 Jan. 95
Stair Francis Barton Dalrymple-Hay	30 Aug. 93	Arthur Francis Henderson	16 Jan. 95
Hunter Carmichael Steen	11 Oct. 93	Henry Edward ap Rhys Pryce	16 Jan. 95
John Leared Furney	23 Dec. 93	Ivan Urmston Battye	16 Jan. 95
William Maxwell Fenning	23 Dec. 93	Bertram Graham Balfour Kidd	16 Jan. 95
William Cotter Williamson Hawkes	23 Dec. 93	Percy Napier Pollock	16 Jan. 95
Harry Stephenson Garraway	23 Dec. 93	John Stirling Rivett-Carnac	16 Jan. 95
Cuthbert Prissick	23 Dec. 93	William Hugh Simpson	16 Jan. 95
Halford Le Mesurier Fellowes	31 Jan. 94	John Cunningham Moore Hoskyn	16 Jan. 95
Frederick Stewart Keen	31 Jan. 94	Charles Herbert Villiers-Stuart	16 Jan. 95
Macclesfield Heptinstall Anderson	31 Jan. 94	George Kendall Channer	16 Jan. 95
Alfred Harcourt Babington	31 Jan. 94	Gerald Steuart Palmer	16 Jan. 95
Henry Hamilton Moore	31 Jan. 94	Charles Alexander Campbell Godwin	16 Jan. 95
Henry Stuart Strong	31 Jan. 94	Addington Dawsonne Strong	16 Jan. 95
Bartholomew Denis Fitzpatrick	31 Jan. 94	Charles Valentine Keyes	16 Jan. 95
Thomas Edward Moore Lane	31 Jan. 94	Henry Stuart Tyndall	16 Jan. 95
William Desmond Villiers-Stuart	2 June 94	John Joseph Buckley	16 Jan. 95
Francis Adams	2 June 94	Lionel Forbes Ashburner	16 Jan. 95
Harry Edward Spiller Cordeaux	2 June 94	Esme Cosmo William Conway-Gordon	16 Jan. 95
Francis Taylor Duhan	10 Oct. 94	George Dighton Probyn Swinley	16 Jan. 95
Alastair Kinloch Forbes	10 Oct. 94	Robert Charles Goodfellow	16 Jan. 95
Norman Ruthven Anderson	10 Oct. 94	Bertram Robert Graham	16 Jan. 95
Spencer Burton Watson	10 Oct. 94	Jonathan Maxwell Bruce	16 Jan. 95
George Augustus Hawks	10 Oct. 94	Oliver St. John Skeen	16 Jan. 95
William Archibald Smail Walker	10 Oct. 94	Malcolm Henry Burdett Geddes	16 Jan. 95
John Lindsay Stewart	10 Oct. 94	John Lindsay Smith	16 Jan. 95
Robert Wynne Henderson	10 Oct. 94	Frederick FitzHugh Lance	16 Jan. 95
Denzil Ibbetson Michael Macaulay	19 Oct. 94	Valentine Kingston Birch	16 Jan. 95
Charles Eugene Barnes Robinson	10 Oct. 94	Hubert Cecil Luckhardt	16 Jan. 95
Harry Norman Young	10 Oct. 94		

Corps of Armourers.

Officer Commanding .... The Chief Inspector of Small Arms, Enfield Lock.
Officer Commanding Depot .... The Assistant Inspector of Small Arms, Small Arms Factory, Birmingham.
Quarter Master ....

Corps of Military Mounted Police.

Quarter Masters .... { John Lindas Emerson,[1] 19 Sept. 85; *Hon. Lieut.*—Provost Marshal, Aldershot.
{ C. Burroughs, 16 Sept. 94; *Hon. Lieut.*—Assistant Provost Marshal, Curragh.

[1] Lieut. Emerson served in the Egyptian war of 1882 (Medal, and Khedive's Star). Served with the expedition to the Soudan in 1884 and was present in the engagements at El Teb and Temai (mentioned in despatches, two Clasps, and Medal for distinguished conduct in the field); also served with the Nile Expedition in 1884-85 (Clasp).

Quarter Master not with a Regiment.

James O'Toole, 1 Apr. 88; *Hon. Lieut.* .... War Office.

Army Service Corps.

(Late the Commissariat and Transport Staff.)

Former Commissioned Rank.	COLONELS. (Late Deputy Commissaries General.)	FIRST COMMISSION ED RANK.	PRESENT RANK.	APPOINTED TO C. & T. STAFF.	STATION.
Dep.Assist.Com.Gen.	Elmes, Jonathan William[1]	16 Aug. 61	11 Dec. 88	31 Jan. 80	A. A. Gen. Western District.
Barrack Master	Goddard, Fredk. FitzClarence[20]	29 Mar. 67	11 Dec. 88	31 Jan. 80	A. A. Gen. N. Eastern Dist.
Dep.Assist.Com.Gen.	Skinner, James Tierney,[25] *CB.DSO.*	5 Aug. 64	22 Dec. 88	31 Jan. 80	A. Q. M. Gen. Head Quarters.
	LIEUTENANT COLONELS. *(Late Assist. Commissaries General.)*				
Dep.Assist.Com.Gen.	Cook, Francis John Gilbert	29 Mar. 66	11 Dec. 88	31 Jan. 80	D. A. A. Gen. Cork District.
Dep.Assist.Com.Gen.	Bridgman, Frederick Henry[24]	17 Nov. 63	11 Dec. 88	31 Jan. 80	Portsmouth.
Dep.Assist.Com.Gen.	Stewart, Thomas Brown	23 July 67	11 Dec. 88	31 Jan. 80	
Dep.Assist.Com.Gen.	Clarke, James Alleyne[16]	10 Aug. 67	11 Dec. 88	31 Jan. 80	D. A. A. Gen. Home District.
Dep.Assist.Com.Gen.	Coates, George[27]	4 Aug. 65	11 Dec. 88	31 Jan. 80	Cape of Good Hope.
Dep.Assist.Com.Gen.	Christie, Edward Tolfrey[28]	23 Oct. 66	11 Dec. 88	31 Jan. 80	Cork.
Lieut. late Mil. Train	Noake, Robert Douglas[29]	13 May 63	11 Dec. 88	31 Jan. 80	D. A. A. Gen. Woolwich.
	Richardson, Wodehouse Dillon,[32] *CB.*	13 June 72	11 Dec. 88	31 Jan. 80	D. A. A. Gen. Dublin District.
	Dunne, Walter Alphonsus[33]	9 Apr. 73	11 Dec. 88	31 Jan. 80	D. A. A. Gen. Southern Dist.
Ensign 88 Foot	Chermside, Robert Alexander[34]	8 July 68	11 Dec. 88	31 Jan. 80	Chatham.
	M'Leod, Walter Thompson[36]		11 Dec. 88	31 Jan. 80	D. A. A. Gen. Colchester.
	Fitz-Stubbs, Edwin[37]		11 Dec. 88	31 Jan. 80	D. A. A. Gen. Aldershot.
	Grattan, Ernest[38]		11 Dec. 88	31 Jan. 80	D. A. A. Gen. Malta.
Lieutenant 20 Foot	Shannon, Thomas Patrick	4 Dec. 66	11 Dec. 88	31 Jan. 80	D. A. A. Gen. Nova Scotia.
	Bannister, Charles John		11 Dec. 88	31 Jan. 80	Gibraltar.
	Nugent, Robert Arthur,[41] *CB.*	13 June 72	11 Dec. 88	31 Jan. 80	D. A. A. Gen. Scottish Dist.
	Ely, Alfred	13 June 72	11 Dec. 88	31 Jan. 80	Edinburgh.
	Bourne, Casimir Arthur	13 June 72	11 Dec. 88	31 Jan. 80	York.
	Clutterbuck, Lewis Augustus[43]	13 June 72	19 Dec. 88	31 Jan. 80	D. A. A. Gen. Gibraltar.
	Baker, Alfred Aquila[44]	13 June 72	21 May 89	31 Jan. 80	Cape Town.
	Rainsford, Marcus Edward Read[45]	13 June 72	21 May 89	31 Jan. 80	D. A. A. Gen. Egypt. [Dkyd.
	Hamilton, George Vaughan[46]	9 Apr. 73	21 May 89	31 Jan. 80	D. A. A. M. Gen. Woolwich
	Stevens, Frank Erastus	13 June 72	12 June 89	31 Jan. 80	D.A.A.Gen. Woolwich Arsnl.
	Langdon, Allan Harris[47]	13 June 72	1 Aug. 89	31 Jan. 80	London.
	Bridge, Charles Henry[48]	13 June 72	25 Aug. 89	31 Jan. 80	Aldershot.
	Wilson, John George Yule[50]	13 June 72	17 Nov. 89	31 Jan. 80	Cork.
	Collard, Arthur William[59]	13 June 72	15 June 90	31 Jan. 80	Woolwich.
	Heygate, Bernard[53]	9 Apr. 73	15 June 90	31 Jan. 80	D. A. A. Gen. Dover.
	Edwards, James Roch[54]	9 Apr. 73	15 June 90	31 Jan. 80	Natal.
	Whitley, Joseph[55]	1 Apr. 74	15 June 90	31 Jan. 80	Chester.
	Ward, Edward Willis Duncan[56]	1 Apr. 74	15 June 90	31 Jan. 80	D. A. A. Gen. Ireland.
	Boyd, John Alexander[57]	1 Apr. 75	15 June 90	23 Feb. 80	D. A. Q. M. Gen. War Office.
Captain 3 Hussars	Lea, Samuel Job[58]	6 Mar. 72	15 June 90	18 Mar. 81	Devonport.
	Smith, Edmund Philip Bowden	13 June 72	10 Oct. 90	31 Jan. 80	Gosport.
	Moore, William Francis	9 Apr. 73	15 Oct. 90	31 Jan. 80	Malta.
	Parkin, John William Brooke	9 Apr. 73	14 Nov. 90	31 Jan. 80	Straits Settlements.
	Graham, Malcolm[52]	13 June 72	10 Dec. 90	31 Jan. 80	
	Winter, Samuel Henry	9 Apr. 73	1 Aug. 91	31 Jan. 80	Aldershot.
	Hipwell, Alfred George	9 Apr. 73	8 Aug. 91	31 Jan. 80	D. A. A. Gen. Thames Dist.
	Skirving, David Scot[51]	13 June 72	1 Nov. 91	31 Jan. 80	Guernsey.
	Challice, Gerald George[61]	9 Apr. 73	1 Nov. 91	31 Jan. 80	Mauritius.
	Winter, William Robert	9 Apr. 73	1 Nov. 91	31 Jan. 80	D. A. A. Gen. Bermuda.
	Stanley, Geoffrey[62]	1 Apr. 74	24 Feb. 92	31 Jan. 80	Cyprus.
	M'Comb, Robert Brophy[63]	1 Apr. 74	6 May 92	31 Jan. 80	Ceylon.
	Hope, Lewis Anstruther[64]	1 Apr. 74	17 June 92	31 Jan. 80	D.A.A. Gen. Curragh.
	Ashley, Arthur	1 Apr. 74	3 Aug. 92	31 Jan. 80	Dublin.
	Dunne, William[67]	1 Apr. 74	1 Apr. 93	31 Jan. 80	Egypt.
	Arnold, Knighton	1 Apr. 74	1 Sept. 93	31 Jan. 80	Woolwich.
	Godfery, Masters John[68]	1 Apr. 75	15 Sept. 93	31 Jan. 80	Malta.
	Hare, Fred. Stephen Christian[69]	1 Apr. 75	14 Feb. 94	1 Apr. 80	Athlone.
	Rice, Henry Gardo[70]	1 Apr. 75	16 Mar. 94	1 Apr. 80	Ireland.
Major R. Artillery	Bunbury, Herbert Napier	15 Dec. 71	1 Apr. 94	15 Dec. 82	D.A.Q.M. Gen. War Office.
Captain York Lt. Inf.	Stoneman, James[71]	1 Apr. 75	25 June 94	1 Apr. 80	Egypt.
	Jessop, Guthrie Hylton[72]	1 Apr. 75	1 Sept. 94	7 July 82	Aldershot.
	Rogers, John[74]	1 Apr. 75	28 Oct. 94	1 Apr. 80	Egyptian Army.
	Lynn, Sydney Hume	1 Apr. 75	28 Oct. 94	1 May 80	D. A. A. Gen. Chester.
	Trench, Fred. Amelius Le Poer	1 Jan. 76	3 Feb. 95	1 May 80	Natal.
	Day, Robert Vaughan[73]	1 Jan. 76	13 Feb. 95	1 May 80	York.
	MAJORS. *(Late Assist. Commissaries General.)*				
Captain W. Kent Regt	Johnson, Frederick Francis[75]	28 Feb. 74	1 Apr. 90	18 Mar. 81	Aldershot.
	Edes, Charles Albert[76]	1 Jan. 76	2 Apr. 90	1 May 80	Bermuda.
Capt. Duke of Cornwall's Lt. Inf.	Gaussen, Edgar	1 Apr. 75	3 Sept. 90	6 Mar. 82	Jersey.
	Heath, Charles Ernest	9 Aug. 74	9 Oct. 90	18 Mar. 81	Dublin.
Captain Scots Fus.	Knocker, Cuthbert George[77]	11 Feb. 75	15 Feb. 91	18 Mar. 81	D. A. A. Gen. Barbadoes.
Capt. N. Stafford Regt.	Hadfield, Charles Arthur	2 Dec. 74	1 Apr. 91	13 Aug. 81	Curragh.
Captain Irish Regt.	Oughterson, James Charles	12 Nov. 73	1 Apr. 92	7 July 82	Aldershot.
Major Welsh Fus.	Stacpole, John[90]	21 Jan. 74	2 Apr. 92	10 Jan. 82	London.
Capt. Warwick Regt.	Clayton, Frederick Thomas[78]	29 Nov. 76	3 Apr. 92	9 June 83	Shorncliffe.
Capt. Hampshire Regt	Bourcicault, George Pensam[79]	10 Sept. 76	1 Apr. 93	1 July 83	D.A.A.Gen. C. of Good Hope.
Major Duke of Cornwall's Light Inf.	Falls, John Alexander Wright[80]	29 Nov. 76	1 Apr. 93	15 Aug. 83	Egypt.
Capt. Worcester Regt.	Erskine, Archibald James	11 Sept. 77	1 Apr. 94	24 Mar. 84	Belfast.
Captain Royal Scots	Acheson, Percival Havelock[81]	4 Dec. 78	1 Apr. 94	12 Sept. 84	Fermoy.
Capt. W. Riding Regt.	Landon, Fred. Wm. Bainbridge	13 Aug. 79	18 Apr. 94	1 Oct. 84	D. A. A. Gen. Jamaica.
Captain Irish Rifles	Monteith, Robt. Wm. Freebairn[82]	6 Aug. 79	1 Dec. 94	11 Dec. 84	Nova Scotia.
Capt. Connaught Rang	Wyncoll, Charles Edward[85]	15 Aug. 77	1 Dec. 94	30 Apr. 85	D. A. A. Gen. Malta.
	CAPTAINS. *(Late Dep. Assist. Commissaries Gen.)*				
Capt. Duke of Cornwall's Light Inf.	Steele, Frederick Willum,[83] *DSO.*	11 Nov. 76	11 Dec. 88	16 May 85	Weedon.
Capt. Leicester Regt.	Reilly, John Augustine Herbert	13 Aug. 79	11 Dec. 88	26 May 85	Parkhurst.
Lieut. Royal Artillery	Lewis, Percy John Tonson[84] *(Bt. Major, 10 Aug. 92)*	25 Feb. 81	11 Dec. 88	7 Jan. 86	Aldershot.

Army Service Corps.

Commissioned Rank.	CAPTAINS.	FIRST COMMISSIONED RANK.	PRESENT RANK.	APPOINTED TO C. & T. STAFF.	STATION.
Capt. York and Lancaster Regt.	O'Dell, Thomas John[86]	11 May 78	11 Dec. 88	1 Feb. 86	D. A. A. Gen. Portsmouth.
Capt. E. Surrey Regt.	Thomas, Arthur Havilland	11 Aug. 80	11 Dec. 88	19 Nov. 36	D. A. A. Gen. China.
Capt. W. Riding Regt.	Buist-Sparks, Fred. Braid	11 Aug. 80	11 Dec. 88	1 Jan. 87	Woolwich.
Lieut. W. York Regt.	Roberts, Arthur Noel	11 Aug. 80	11 Dec. 88	1 Feb. 87	Barbadoes.
Lieut. R. Artillery	Rawnsley, Claude	22 Feb. 82	11 Dec. 88	1 Feb. 87	
Lieut. 4 Dr. Guards	Donovan, Charles Henry Wynne[87]	2 Aug. 82	11 Dec. 88	1 Feb. 87	Colchester.
Lieut. Royal Marines	Koe, Fred. Wm. Brooke	1 Feb. 81	11 Dec. 88	1 Apr. 87	Kilkenny.
Lieut. 19 Hussars	Welch, George Osbaldeston[88]	2 Aug. 82	11 Dec. 88	18 Apr. 87	Staff Captain, Egypt.
Lieut. Gloucester Regt	Horniblow, Frederick	12 May 83	11 Dec. 88	1 July 87	D. A. A. Gen. Ceylon.
Capt. S. Lanc. Regt.	Gilpin, Frederic Charles Almon	22 Jan. 81	11 Dec. 88	20 July 87	D. A. A. Gen. Belfast.
Lieut. King's R. Rifles	Scudamore-Stanhope, Hon. E.T.[89]	22 Jan. 81	11 Dec. 88	7 Oct. 87	D. A. A. Gen. Malta.
Captain 18 Hussars	Cardew, George Hereward	9 Aug. 82	11 Dec. 88	22 Oct. 87	Bermuda.
Lieut. Gloucester Regt	Paul, Gerard Robert Clark, Adjutant 1 May 92	22 Oct. 81	1 Apr. 89		Woolwich.
Lieut. Manchestr Regt	Hill, Richard Ernest	12 May 83	12 May 89		Aldershot.
Lieut. Gloucester Regt	Morgan, Hill Godfrey	5 Dec. 83	5 Dec. 89		Egypt.
Lieut. R. Artillery	Hamnett, George Edward	15 Feb. 84	15 Feb. 90		
Lieut. 4 Hussars	Duncan, Francis Leslie	12 Nov. 84	1 Apr. 90		Jamaica.
Lieut. Bedford Regt.	p.s.c. Warner, Rowan H. Lee,[91] Adjutant 1 Jan. 95	7 Feb. 85	1 Apr. 90		Aldershot.
Lieut. R. Marines	Hobbs, Percy Eyre Francis	1 Sept. 83	2 Apr. 90		Aldershot.
Captain 20 Hussars	Hunt, Godfrey Massy Vere	7 June 79	21 Apr. 90	23 Sept. 87	China.
Lieut. Durham Lt. Inf.	Long, Sidney Selden	30 Jan. 84	23 May 90		Aldershot.
Lieut. R. Marines	French, George Arthur	1 Sept. 82	20 June 90		Sierra Leone.
Lt. York & Lanc. Regt.	Edye, Murray William Joseph	20 Aug. 85	9 Oct. 90		Inverness.
Lieut. Sussex Regt.	Blakeney, Edw. Francis John	29 Aug. 85	4 Nov. 90		Enniskillen.
Lieut. E. York Regt.	Bramhall, Edward Albert	29 Aug. 85	15 Feb. 91		Aldershot.
Lieut. R. Fusiliers	Ludlow, Edmund Ranald Owen	29 Aug. 85	1 July 91		Staff College, Sandhurst.
Lieut. Border Regt.	Sandilands, Philip Orde	10 Mar. 83	1 July 91		Pembroke Dock.
Lieut. Dublin Fus.	Dawson, Charles Herbert	23 May 85	1 July 91		Chatham.
Lieut. N. Staff. Regt.	Caldwell, Arthur Lewis	10 Mar. 83	1 July 91		Ceylon.
Lt. Worcester Regt.	King, Charles Wallis	29 Dec. 86	1 July 91		D. A. A. Gen. Home Dist.
Lieut. The Buffs	Buttanshaw, Edward Thornton	23 Aug. 84	1 July 91		Limerick.
Lieut. S. Staff. Regt.	Jack, Herbert Rowett Henry[111]	14 May 84	1 July 91		Preston.
Lieut. Essex Regt.	Buckle, Arthur Ernest	29 Aug. 85	1 July 91		Glasgow.
Lieut. Leicester Regt.	Webb, Duncan[92]	22 Oct. 81	9 Sept. 91		London.
Lieut. Devon Regt.	Sargent, Harry Neptune, Adjutant 1 Jan. 95	10 Nov. 86	7 Jan. 92		Aldershot.
Lt. N. Staff. Regt.	Longden, Arthur Edmund[93]	7 Feb. 85	3 Apr. 92		Queenstown.
Lt. Scottish Rifles	Foster, Turville Douglas	25 Aug. 86	13 May 92		Edinburgh.
Lt. Scottish Rifles	Cuming, Arthur Rufus	25 Aug. 86	4 June 92		Dublin.
Lt. York & Lanc. R.	Humphreys, Harry Lionel	25 Aug. 86	4 June 92		Newcastle-on-Tyne.
Capt. W. Riding Regt.	Boulger, John	10 Mar. 83	12 Oct. 92		Woolwich.
Lieut. Devon Regt.	Bernard, Edgar Edwin	14 Sept. 87	15 Oct. 92		Cork.
Lieut. Essex Regt.	Parker, St. John William Topp	4 May 87	15 Oct. 92		Clonmel.
Lt. King's R. Rifles.	Terry, Astley Herbert	10 Sept. 87	2 Nov. 92		Dublin.
Lieut. Leinster Regt.	Long, Arthur	16 Nov. 87	1 Jan. 93		Woolwich.
Lieut. Leicester Regt.	Colquhoun, Harry	16 Nov. 87	1 Jan. 93		Woolwich Arsenal.
Lieut. 6 Dr. Guards	Ward, William Percy Burnell	5 Feb. 87	1 Jan. 93		Exeter.
Lieut. Bedford Regt.	Mathew, Robert George	14 Mar. 88	1 Apr. 93		Portsmouth.
Lt. S. Stafford Regt.	M'Cormick, Wm. Irvine Stewart	16 Nov. 87	1 Apr. 93		Devonport.
Lieut. S. Lanc. Regt.	Hayward, Alfred Richard Lane	9 May 88	7 July 93		
Lieut. Munster Fus.	Thornton, Edw. Evelyn Danvers	11 Feb. 88	7 July 93		Curragh.
Lieut. Royal Marines	Keyes, Charles Wm. Patton	1 Feb. 86	7 July 93		Woolwich.
Lieut. 3 Hussars	Purvis, John Allen Ramsay	30 Nov. 87	7 July 93		Curragh.
Lieut. Essex Regt.	Moore, Joseph Scott	29 Aug. 85	7 July 93		Shorncliffe.
Lieut. R. Marines	Thring, Edward Clavell	1 Sept. 86	7 July 93		Sierra Leone.
Lieut. Berks Regt.	Boyce, William George Bertram	14 Sept. 87	7 July 93		Aldershot.
2nd Lt. Innis. Fus.	Welman, Arthur Pole	22 Aug. 88	1 Apr. 94		China.
Lieut. Welsh Regt.	Phelps, Arthur	8 Dec. 88	1 Apr. 94		Aldershot.
Lieut. Norfolk Regt.	Seccombe, Archibald Kennedy	30 Jan. 89	18 Apr. 94		Egypt.
Capt. Black Watch.	Gillespie, Alexander Kenneth	30 Jan. 86	14 Nov. 94		Aldershot.
Lieut. Leicester Regt.	Carter, Evan Eyare	30 Jan. 89	1 Dec. 94		Staff College, Sandhurst.
Lieut. Devon Regt.	Ryan, Charles Montgomerie	22 Aug. 88	1 Dec. 94		Gibraltar.
2nd Lt. Scot. Rifles	Hall, Douglas Keith Elphinstone	21 Nov. 88	1 Dec. 94		Curragh.
Lieut. E. Surrey R.	Dickson, Harry Wilfrid	30 Jan. 89	1 Dec. 94		York.
Lt. S. Lanc. Regt.	Davies, Henry	14 Sept. 87	1 Dec. 94		Aldershot.
Lt. E. Surrey Regt.	Dodgson, Colquhoun Scott[112]	11 Feb. 88	1 Dec. 94		Devonport.
Lieut. Irish Fusiliers	Hardy, Frederic Pelham Abbott	23 Mar. 89	9 Jan. 95		Woolwich.
	Attached as CAPTAINS.				
Capt. Durham Lt. Inf.	Keane, George Wilfred	19 Feb. 81	11 Dec. 88	24 Aug. 87	Canterbury.
Capt. E. Kent Regt.	Bayard, Reginald	23 Apr. 81	2 Jan. 93		Newport (Mon.).
	LIEUTENANTS.				
Lieut. 1 Dr. Guards.	Conway-Gordon, Gwynnedd	22 Aug. 88	1 Apr. 92		Curragh.
Lt. Durham Lt. Inf.	Grey, Charles William	29 Dec. 88	15 May 92		Curragh.
Lieut. Leicester Regt.	Hewlett, Gervase Gillham	6 Mar. 89	15 May 92		Dublin.
2nd Lt. Border Regt.	Harrison, Willoughby Hyde	15 Jan. 90	15 May 92		St. Lucia.
Lieut. Dorset Regt.	Harrison, James Molyneux	29 Dec. 89	15 Sept. 92		Egypt.
Lieut. York Lt. Inf.	Reynolds, Sidney Latimer	1 Mar. 90	15 Sept. 92		Hounslow.
2nd Lt. York Regt.	Williamson, Wm. Alex. Finiston	28 June 90	15 Sept. 92		Barbadoes.
Lieut. 5 Dr. Guards	Colquhoun, Edward Lyndon	31 Dec. 90	16 Sept. 92		Dublin.
Lt. Middlesex Regt.	Ward, Edmund Ironside	22 Aug. 88	1 Oct. 92		Woolwich.
Lt. Worcester Regt.	Taylor, Ernest Fitzwilliam	22 Aug. 88	1 Oct. 92		Manchester.
Lieut. Devon Regt.	Studdert, Edward	8 June 89	1 Oct. 92		Malta.
Lieut. Irish Fusiliers	Kaye, Richard Henry Leslie	8 June 89	1 Oct. 92		Weymouth.
Lt. Leicester Regt.	Tredgold, John Aubrey Temple	21 Sept. 89	1 Oct. 92		Jamaica.
Lieut. R. Marines	Foster, William Herbert	1 Sept. 88	15 Jan. 93		Portsmouth.
Lieut. R. Marines	Ford, Reginald	1 Feb. 89	15 Jan. 93		Aldershot.
Lieut. Lanc. Fus.	Courtney, Ed. Arthur Waldegrave	9 Nov. 89	15 Jan. 93		Dover.
Lt. Leinster Regt.	Blunt, Conrad Edward Grant	23 Nov. 89	15 Jan. 93		Egyptian Army.
Lt. Leinster Regt.	Gillespie, Ernest Carden Freeth	19 Mar. 90	15 Jan. 93		Mullingar.
Lt. Lancaster Regt.	Wilson, Frederick Maurice	28 June 90	15 Jan. 93		Shorncliffe.

Army Service Corps. 368

Commissioned Rank.	LIEUTENANTS.	FIRST COMMISSIONED RANK.	PRESENT RANK.	STATION.
2nd Lt. E. Kent Regt.	Black, John Campbell Lamont	21 Dec. 89	31 Mar. 92	York.
2nd Lt. Lanc. Regt.	Hole, Arthur William	29 Oct. 90	31 Mar. 93	Malta.
2nd Lt. Irish Fus.	Amey, Arthur	17 Jan. 91	31 Mar. 93	Portsmouth.
2nd Lt. Lanc. Regt.	Glen, Robert Nelson John	17 Jan. 91	31 Mar. 93	Chatham.
Lieut. Worcester R.	Walton, Geoffrey Frank	4 Feb. 91	31 Mar. 93	London.
Lieut. D. of C. Lt. Inf.	Standen, Robert Hargrave Fraser	29 Mar. 90	31 Mar. 93	Dundalk.
Lieut. 9 Lancers	Russell, James Walter Harold	4 Mar. 91	31 Mar. 93	Sheffield.
Lieut. S. Lanc. Regt.	Taylor, Francis Pitt Stewart	16 Oct. 89	1 Apr. 93	Devonport.
Lieut. S. Fusiliers	Coutts, Malcolm	13 Nov. 89	6 Apr. 93	Woolwich.
Lieut. Manch. Regt.	Berry, Robert Gordon John Johnston	20 Aug. 90	30 Sept. 93	Brighton.
Lieut. Shrop. Lt. Inf.	Moody, George Robert Boyd	22 Aug. 88	1 Oct. 93	Woolwich.
Lt. Liverpool Regt.	Howard, Francis James Leigh	29 Nov. 90	1 Oct. 93	Woolwich.
Lt. Leicester Regt.	Scott, Philip Clement Joseph	29 Nov. 90	1 Oct. 93	Dublin.
Lieut. Dorset Regt.	Lewis, Cecil Hallowes	18 Feb. 91	1 Oct. 93	Woolwich.
Lieut. W. India Regt.	Master, Arthur Gilbert	4 Mar. 91	1 Oct. 93	Dublin.
Lieut. E. Lanc. Regt.	Longmore, John Constantine Gordon	9 Apr. 92	1 Oct. 93	Portsmouth.
Lt. Berkshire Regt.	Gorle, Harry Vaughan	28 June 90	1 Oct. 93	Aldershot.
Lieut. Leinster Regt.	Denny, William Alfred Charles	9 Sept. 91	24 Feb. 94	Leeds.
Lieut. Leicester Regt.	Vawdrey, George	20 Feb. 92	24 Feb. 94	Shorncliffe.
2nd Lt. Irish Regt.	Armstrong, William Meredith Howard	12 Mar. 92	30 Mar. 94	Dublin.
2nd Lt. Suffolk Regt.	Delavoye, Alexander Edwin	18 June 92	30 Sept. 94	Devonport.
	On Probation.			
Lieut. R. Marines	Atkins, Alban Randell Crofton	1 Sept. 89	1 Apr. 94	Curragh.
Lieut. E. Lanc. Regt.	Atcherley, Llewellyn William	23 Nov. 90	1 Apr. 94	Aldershot.
Lieut. E. Surrey Regt.	Garsia, Herbert George Anderson	9 Jan. 92	1 Apr. 94	Shorncliffe.
Lieut. York Lt. Inf.	Swabey, Wilfred Spedding	12 Mar. 92	1 Apr. 94	Dublin.
Lieut. Lanc. Regt.	James, Murray Ray de Buyrne	29 Nov. 90	1 Apr. 94	Aldershot.
Lieut. York Regt.	Kemble, Charles Morris	28 June 90	1 Apr. 94	Aldershot.
Lieut. R. Marines	Macdonald, Charles Clanranald	1 Sept. 90	1 Oct. 94	Aldershot.
Lieut. R. Marines	Mylrea, William Percy Garland	1 Sept. 91	1 Oct. 94	Aldershot.
Lieut. R. Marines	Macdonald, Kenneth	1 Sept. 91	1 Oct. 94	Aldershot.
Lieut. R. Fusiliers	Burne, Rainald Owen	1 Sept. 91	1 Oct. 94	Aldershot.
Lieut. Derby Regt.	Christopher, Charles Danby	2 May 91	1 Oct. 94	Aldershot.
Lieut. 6 Dragoons	Atkinson, Francis Salisbury	28 Sept. 92	1 Oct. 94	Aldershot.
Lieut. Irish Fus.	Morgan, John William Moore	25 Jan. 93	1 Oct. 94	Aldershot.
Lieut. Innis. Fus.	Brooke, Hugh Fenwick	2 May 91	1 Oct. 94	Aldershot.
		13 July 92		
	SECOND LIEUTENANTS. *On Probation.*			
2nd Lt. Welsh Fus.	Pigott, Grenville Edmund	18 June 92	1 Apr. 94	Devonport.
2nd Lt. Norfolk Regt.	Stewart, Claude Francis John	5 Dec. 91	1 Oct. 94	Aldershot.
2nd Lt. Worc. Regt.	Fisher, Henry Francis Thornhill	13 Aug. 92	1 Oct. 94	Aldershot.
2nd Lt. S. W. Brdrs.	Hunnard, Frank	17 Dec. 92	1 Oct. 94	Aldershot.
2nd Lt. S. W. Brdrs.	Puckle, John	21 Jan. 92	1 Oct. 94	Aldershot.
2nd Lt. Bedford Regt.	McVittie, Charles Edwin	15 Mar. 93	1 Oct. 94	Aldershot.

QUARTER MASTERS.	FIRST COMMISSIONED RANK.	HON. LIEUT.	HON. CAPTAIN.	PRESENT RANK.	APPOINTED TO C. & T. STAFF	STATION.
Lapham, Robert John[118]	27 Mar. 78	27 Mar. 78	27 Mar. 88	11 Dec. 88	31 Jan. 80	Woolwich Dockyard.
Crumplin, William[128]	11 Dec. 78		15 June 85	11 Dec. 88	31 Jan. 80	Dublin.
Ledsham, William[130]	11 Dec. 78	11 Dec. 78	11 Dec. 88	11 Dec. 88	31 Jan. 80	Cork.
Robinson, Richard Henry[134]	11 Dec. 78	11 Dec. 78	11 Dec. 88	11 Dec. 88	31 Jan. 80	Straits Settlements.
Musgrave, William[138]	11 Dec. 78	11 Dec. 78	11 Dec. 88	11 Dec. 88	31 Jan. 80	Woolwich.
Main, James	11 Dec. 78	11 Dec. 78	11 Dec. 88	11 Dec. 88	31 Jan. 80	Birmingham.
Parsons, William[144]	11 Mar. 82		11 Mar. 92	11 Dec. 88	11 Mar. 82	Aldershot.
Brooks, Alfred[145]	10 Jan. 83		10 Jan. 93	11 Dec. 88	10 Jan. 83	Egypt.
Gardiner, Frederick[146]	16 Jan. 83		16 Jan. 94	11 Dec. 88	16 Jan. 83	Curragh.
Johnson, William[147]	17 May 84		7 May 90	11 Dec. 88	17 May 84	Malta.
Londer, Alfred Edgar[149]	25 Apr. 85	25 Apr. 85	7 May 90	11 Dec. 88	25 Apr. 85	Dublin.
Johnston, Alexander	25 Apr. 85	25 Apr. 85		11 Dec. 88	25 Apr. 85	Dublin.
Reilly, John	25 Apr. 85	25 Apr. 85		11 Dec. 88	25 Apr. 85	Aldershot.
Latten, Leonard[150]	25 Apr. 85	25 Apr. 85		11 Dec. 88	25 Apr. 85	London.
Daly, Maurice[151]	25 Apr. 85	25 Apr. 85		11 Dec. 88	25 Apr. 85	Woolwich Dockyard.
Edmondson, James Heslam[152]	15 June 85	15 June 85		11 Dec. 88	15 June 85	Devonport.
Champion, Horace Edgar[153]	15 June 85	15 June 85		11 Dec. 83	15 June 85	Aldershot.
Drage, William Henry[154]	15 June 85	15 June 85	17 Aug. 89	11 Dec. 88	15 June 85	Egyptian Army.
Haycock, William[155]	15 June 85	15 June 85		11 Dec. 88	15 June 85	Woolwich.
Lemon, George	3 Oct. 88	3 Oct. 88		11 Dec. 88	3 Oct. 88	Belfast.
Reid, Samuel	3 Oct. 88	3 Oct. 88		11 Dec. 88	3 Oct. 89	Malta.
Richardson, Richard	10 Oct. 88			11 Dec. 88	10 Oct. 88	Aldershot.
Mitchell, John Wilson	10 Oct. 88	10 Oct. 88		11 Dec. 88	10 Oct. 88	Dover.
Higgins, Peter	16 Jan. 89	16 Jan. 89				Gibraltar.
Fletcher, James	26 Oct. 89	26 Oct. 89				Bermuda.
Arthur, James	4 Mar. 91	4 Mar. 91				Aldershot.
Ward, Herbert Samuel	25 Mar. 91	25 Mar. 91				Mauritius.
Smith, Charles Edward	29 July 91	29 July 91				Nova Scotia.
Dixon, George	28 June 92	28 June 92				War Office.
Doherty, Thomas	8 Mar. 93	8 Mar. 93				Portsmouth.
Goss, William	4 Apr. 94	4 Apr. 94				Aldershot.
Cairns, Michael	22 Aug. 94	22 Aug. 94				Edinburgh.
Law, Charles Richard	22 Aug. 94	22 Aug. 94				Colchester.
Barnes, William Edward	22 Aug. 94	22 Aug. 94				Natal.
English, William	12 Dec. 94	12 Dec. 94				Shorncliffe.
Edwards, David John	12 Dec. 94	12 Dec. 94				Aldershot.
Woods, John Charles	9 Jan. 95	9 Jan. 95				Cape Town.
Chase, Herbert	22 Jan. 95	22 Jan. 95				Woolwich.
Wallace, Thomas	14 Feb. 95	14 Feb. 95				Warley.
Thornley, Robert William	6 Mar. 95	6 Mar. 95				
Gleeson, Andrew Fitzwilliam	8 Mar. 95	8 Mar. 95				

Instructor .... Lt. Colonel S. H. Winter, 1 June 92. Aldershot.
Assistant Instructor ...... Captain S. S. Long, 1 Oct. 92. Aldershot.
Riding Masters .... { Daniel Hickey, 11 Feb. 92; *Hon. Lieut.* Woolwich.
{ William Lyons, 8 Aug. 94; *Hon. Lieut.* Aldershot.

African Commissariat.

Commissioned Rank.	COMMISSARY. With Honorary rank of Lt.Colonel.	FIRST COMMISSIONED RANK.	PRESENT RANK.	STATION.
	Gore, James Casmaijor,[60] Auditor Gen. of the W. African Settlements	1 Sept. 73	2 Oct. 89	Portsmouth.
	DEPUTY COMMISSARY. With Honorary rank of Captain.			

Army Service Corps.—War Services.

[1] Colonel J. W. Elmes served in the Zulu war in 1879 (Medal with Clasp). Served in the Boer war of 1881, and was present in the engagement at Lang's Nek (mentioned in despatches, and granted the relative rank of Lt.Colonel).

[20] Colonel F. F. Goddard served in the Indian Mutiny (Medal).

[24] Lt.Colonel F. H. Bridgman served in the Kafir war in 1877-78, and in the Zulu war in 1879 (Medal with Clasp).

[25] Colonel J. T. Skinner served with the Nile Expedition in 1884-85, including the operations of the Desert Column (mentioned in despatches, granted the higher rate of pay, Medal with Clasp, and Khedive's Star); also took part in the operations of the Egyptian Frontier Field Force in 1885-86, including the engagement at Giniss (mentioned in despatches, DSO.).

[26] Lt.Colonel J. A. Clarke served in the Soudan campaign in 1885 (mentioned in despatches, Medal with Clasp, and Khedive's Star.

[27] Lt.Colonel G. Coates served in the Ashanti war under Sir Garnet Wolseley, including the battle of Amoaful (mentioned in despatches, Medal with Clasp). Served in the Zulu war of 1879, and was present in the engagement at Ulundi (mentioned in despatches, Medal with Clasp).

[28] Lt.Colonel E. T. Christie served in the New Zealand war in 1865-66 as an Ensign in the New Zealand Militia, and with the Commissariat Department in the Wanganui and Taranaki campaigns (Medal). Served in the operations in Zululand in 1888.

[29] Lt.Colonel Noake served in the Zulu war in 1879 (Medal with Clasp).

[32] Lt.Colonel Richardson served in the Ashanti war in 1873-74 under Sir Garnet Wolseley (Medal). Served in the Kafir war in 1877-78, and was present in the engagement near Draaibosch; served in the Zulu war in 1879 (promoted Deputy Commissary, Medal with Clasp). Also served in the Boer war of 1881 with the Newcastle Field Force. Served in the Egyptian war of 1882 (Medal, and Khedive's Star). Served with the Bechuanaland Expedition under Sir Charles Warren in 1884-85 as Senior Commissariat Officer (granted honorary and relative rank of Lt.Colonel).

[33] Lt.Colonel Dunne served in the Kafir war of 1877-78. Served throughout the Zulu war of 1879, first as Senior Commissariat Officer of No. 3 Column, and afterwards as Commissary of Supplies of the Flying Column; and took part in the defence of Rorke's Drift Post (mentioned in despatches, promoted Deputy Commissary). Served in the operations against Sekukuni, and was present at the storming of the stronghold (Medal with Clasp). Served in the Boer war of 1881, and took part in the defence of Potchefstroom. Served in the Egyptian war of 1882, and was present at the battle of Tel-el-Kebir (Medal with Clasp, and Khedive's Star), and in the Soudan campaign in 1885 (Clasp).

[34] Lt.Colonel R. A. Chermside served in the Zulu war of 1879 (Medal with Clasp).

[36] Lt.Colonel W. T. M'Leod served in the operations in the Malay Peninsula in 1875-76 (Medal with Clasp).

[37] Lt.Colonel E. FitzStubbs served in the Ashanti war under Sir Garnet Wolseley (Medal). Served in the Egyptian war of 1882 (Medal, and Khedive's Star).

[38] Lt.Colonel Grattan served in the Ashanti war of 1873-74 (Medal). Served in the Zulu war in 1879 (Medal with Clasp). Served in the Egyptian war of 1882 (Medal, 4th Class of the Osmanieh, and Khedive's Star).

[41] Lt.Colonel R. A. Nugent served in the Ashanti war under Sir Garnet Wolseley (Medal). Served in the Egyptian war of 1882, and was present at the battle of Tel-el-Kebir (Medal with Clasp, 4th Class of the Medjidie, and Khedive's Star); served with the Soudan Expedition under Sir Gerald Graham in 1884 as Assistant Commissary General in charge of the Commissariat and Transport Department, and was present in the engagements at El Teb and Temai (twice mentioned in despatches, CB., and two Clasps). Served with the Nile Expedition in 1884-85, and was present at the action of Abu Klea (mentioned in despatches, granted the higher rate of pay, two Clasps).

[43] Lt.Colonel Clutterbuck served in the Soudan campaign in 1885 (Medal with Clasp, and Khedive's Star).

[44] Lt.Colonel A. A. Baker served in the Ashanti war under Sir Garnet Wolseley in 1873-74 (Medal). Served in the Egyptian war of 1882, and was present at the battle of Tel-el-Kebir (Medal with Clasp, and Khedive's Star). Also served with the expedition to the Soudan under Sir Gerald Graham in 1884, and was present in the engagements at El Teb and Temai (promoted Assistant Commissary General, two Clasps). Served with the Nile Expedition in 1884-85 (mentioned in despatches, granted the higher rate of pay, Clasp).

[45] Lt.Colonel M. E. R. Rainsford served in the Ashanti war under Sir Garnet Wolseley (Medal). Served in the Boer war of 1881 with the Natal Field Force. Served in the Egyptian war of 1882 (Medal, and Khedive's Star). Served with the expedition to the Soudan under Sir Gerald Graham in 1884, and was present in the engagement at El Teb (mentioned in despatches, promoted Assistant Commissary General, two Clasps). Also served with the Nile Expedition in 1884-85, and was present at the action of Abu Klea (mentioned in despatches, granted the higher rate of pay, two Clasps).

[46] Lt.Colonel G. V. Hamilton served in the Ashanti war under Sir Garnet Wolseley, and was present at the defence of Fommanah (Medal with Clasp). Served in the Boer war of 1881. Served in the Egyptian war of 1882 (Medal, 4th Class of the Medjidie, and Khedive's Star); also served in the Soudan Expedition under Sir Gerald Graham in 1884 (mentioned in despatches, promoted Assistant Commissary General, Clasp).

[47] Lt.Colonel A. H. Langdon served with the Soudan Frontier Field Force in 1885-86, and was present in the engagement at Giniss (Medal, and Khedive's Star).

[49] Lt.Colonel C. H. Bridge served in the Egyptian war of 1882 (Medal, and Khedive's Star).

[50] Lt.Colonel J. G. Y. Wilson served in the Zulu war of 1879 (Medal with Clasp). Served with the expedition to the Soudan under Sir Gerald Graham in 1884 (Medal, and Khedive's Star).

[51] Lt.Colonel D. S. Skirving served in the Egyptian war of 1882 (Medal, and Khedive's Star); also served in the Soudan campaign in 1885 (Clasp).

[52] Lt.Colonel Malcolm Graham served in the Egyptian war of 1882, and was present at the battle of Tel-el-Kebir (Medal with Clasp, and Khedive's Star). Served with the Nile Expedition in 1884-85 (mentioned in despatches, Clasp).

[53] Lt.Colonel Heygate served in the Zulu war in 1879, including the investment of Ekowe (mentioned in despatches, Medal with Clasp). Served in the Boer war of 1881, and took part in the defence of Pretoria. Served in the Soudan campaign in 1885 (promoted Assistant Commissary General, Medal with Clasp, and Khedive's Star).

[54] Lt.Colonel J. R. Edwards served with the Nile Expedition in 1884-85 (promoted Assistant Commissary General, Medal with Clasp, and Khedive's Star).

[55] Lt.Colonel Whitley served in the Zulu war of 1879 (Medal with Clasp). Also served in the Boer war of 1881, and took part in the defence of Pretoria. Served with the Nile Expedition in 1884-85 (mentioned in despatches, promoted Assistant Commissary General, Medal with Clasp, and Khedive's Star).

[56] Lt.Colonel E. W. D. Ward served in the Soudan campaign in 1885, and was present in the engagement at the

Army Service Corps.—War Services. 368b

Tofrek zereba (mentioned in despatches, promoted Assistant Commissary General, Medal with two Clasps, and Khedive's Star).
[57] Lt.Colonel J. A. Boyd served in the Zulu war in 1879 (Medal with Clasp). Also served in the Boer war of 1881 with the Natal Field Force. Served with the Nile Expedition in 1884-85 as Senior Commissariat Officer with the River Column, and was present at the action at Kirbekan (mentioned in despatches, promoted Assistant Commissary General, Medal with two Clasps, and Khedive's Star).
[58] Lt.Colonel Lea served in the Egyptian war of 1882, and was present at the battle of Tel-el-Kebir (Medal with Clasp, 4th Class of the Medjidie, and Khedive's Star). Served with the Nile Expedition in 1884-85, and was present at the action of Kirbekan (promoted Assistant Commissary General with rank of Major in the Army, two Clasps); also served in the operations of the Soudan Frontier Field Force in 1885-86 including the engagement at Giniss.
[59] Lt.Colonel A. W. Collard served in the Soudan campaign in 1885 (Medal with Clasp, and Khedive's Star).
[61] Lt.Colonel G. G. Challice served in the Soudan campaign in 1885 (Medal with Clasp, and Khedive's Star). Also served with the Soudan Frontier Field Force in 1885-86, and was present in the engagement at Giniss.
[62] Lt.Colonel G. Stanley served in the Zulu war in 1879 (Medal with Clasp). Also served in the Boer war of 1881.
[63] Lt.Colonel M'Comb served in the Egyptian war of 1882 (Medal, and Khedive's Star). Served with the Bechuanaland Expedition under Sir Charles Warren in 1884-85, and in the operations in Zululand in 1888.
[64] Lt.Colonel L. A. Hope served in the Zulu war in 1879 (Medal with Clasp). Served with the Nile Expedition in 1884-85 (Medal with Clasp, and Khedive's Star).
[67] Lt.Colonel W. Dunne served with the Bechuanaland Expedition under Sir Charles Warren in 1884-85.
[68] Lt.Colonel M. J. Godfery served in the Boer war of 1881. Served in the Soudan campaign in 1885 (Medal with Clasp, and Khedive's Star).
[69] Lt.Colonel F. S. C. Hare served in the Soudan campaign in 1885 (Medal with Clasp, and Khedive's Star).
[70] Lt.Colonel H. G. Rice served in the Boer war of 1881. Served in the Soudan campaign in 1885 (Medal with Clasp, and Khedive's Star).
[71] Lt.Colonel J. Stoneman served in the Egyptian war of 1882 (Medal, and Khedive's Star).
[72] Lt.Colonel G. H. Jessop served in the Egyptian war of 1882 (Medal, and Khedive's Star). Also served in the Soudan Expedition in 1884 under Sir Gerald Graham, and was present in the engagement at El Teb (4th Class of the Medjidie, two Clasps).
[73] Lt.Colonel R. V. Day served in the Egyptian war of 1882 (Medal, and Khedive's Star).
[74] Lt.Colonel John Rogers served in the Egyptian war of 1882 (Medal, and Khedive's Star). Served with the expedition to the Soudan under Sir Gerald Graham in 1884, and was present in the engagements at El Teb and Temai two Clasps). Nominated to the 3rd Class of the Order of the Medjidieh for services with the Egyptian Army.
[75] Major F. F. Johnson served in the Egyptian war of 1882, and was present at the battle of Tel-el-Kebir (Medal with Clasp, 4th Class of the Medjidie, and Khedive's Star).
[76] Major C. A. Edes served in the operations in Zululand in 1888.
[77] Major Knocker served with the Commissariat and Transport Staff in the Egyptian war of 1882 (Medal, and Khedive's Star).
[78] Major Clayton served in the Bechuanaland Expedition under Sir Charles Warren in 1884-85 with the Commissariat and Transport Staff.
[79] Major Bourcicault served in the Soudan campaign in 1885 (Medal with Clasp, and Khedive's Star).
[80] Major Falls served in the Egyptian war of 1882, and was present at the action at Kassasin on the 28th August (mentioned in despatches) and at the battle of Tel-el-Kebir (mentioned in despatches, Medal with Clasp, and Khedive's Star).
[81] Major Acheson served with the Egyptian Frontier Field Force in 1885-86, and was present in the engagement at Giniss (Medal, and Khedive's Star).
[82] Major R. W. F. Monteith served in the Boer war of 1881 with the Natal Field Force.
[83] Captain F. W. Steele served with the 2nd Battalion of the Duke of Cornwall's Light Infantry throughout the Egyptian war of 1882, and was present in the reconnaissance in force from Alexandria on the 5th August, in the engagements at El Magfar and Tel-el-Mahuta, in the two actions at Kassasin, and at the battle of Tel-el-Kebir (Medal with Clasp, and Khedive's Star). Served in the Nile Expedition in 1884-85 with the 2nd Battalion the Duke of Cornwall's Light Infantry (Clasp). Served in the operations against the Sofas, West Coast of Africa, in 1893-94 (mentioned in despatches); and with the expedition to the Gambia against Fodey Silah in 1894 (mentioned in despatches, DSO.).
[84] Captain P. J. T. Lewis served in the operations on the Nile in 1889 (Medal, and Khedive's Star). Served with the expedition up the Gambia against the native chief Fodey Kabba in 1891-92; with the expedition to the Tambaku Country, on the West Coast of Africa, in 1892 (including the capture of Tambi; and with the expedition to the Gambia in 1892, including the capture of Toniataba (Brevet of Major, Medal with Clasp).
[85] Major Wyncoll served with the 88th Regiment throughout the Kafir war of 1877-78, and the Zulu war o 1879 (Medal with Clasp).
[86] Captain T. J. O'Dell served in the expedition to the Soudan under Sir Gerald Graham in 1884 with the 1st Battalion York and Lancaster Regiment, and was present in the engagements at El Teb and Temai (Medal with Clasp, and Khedive's Star).
[87] Captain C. H. W. Donovan served with the Nile Expedition in 1884-85 (Medal with Clasp, and Khedive's Star). Served in the expedition to the Tambaka Country, West Coast of Africa, in 1892 (Medal with Clasp).
[88] Captain G. O. Welch served in the Soudan Expedition in 1884 with the 19th Hussars, and was present in the engagement at Temai (Medal with Clasp, and Khedive's Star). Served in the Soudan Expedition in 1884-85 with the 19th Hussars (Clasp).
[89] Captain Hon. E. T. Scudamore-Stanhope served with the 3rd Battalion King's Royal Rifle Corps in the Egyptian war of 1882, and was present in the reconnaissance in force from Alexandria on 5th August, in the engagement at Tel-el-Mahuta, in the action at Kassasin (9th September), and at the battle of Tel-el-Kebir (Medal with Clasp, and Khedive's Star); also served in the Soudan Expedition in 1884 with the 3rd Battalion King's Royal Rifle Corps, and was present in the engagement at El Teb (two Clasps).
[90] Major Stacpole served in the Soudan campaign in 1885 (Medal with Clasp, and Khedive's Star).
[91] Captain R. H. L. Warner served with the Burmese Expedition in 1885-87 (Medal with Clasp).
[92] Captain D. Webb served in the operations against the Sofas, West Coast of Africa, in 1893-94 (mentioned in despatches); and with the expedition to the Gambia against Fodey Silah in 1894 (mentioned in despatches).
[93] Captain A. E. Longden served in the operations in Zululand in 1888.
[111] Captain Wigan.—For War Services, see Berkshire Regiment.
[112] Captain Dodgson served in the operations of the Zhob Field Force in 1890.
[114] Captain Jack served with the Nile Expedition in 1884-85, and was present at the action of Kirbekan (Medal with two Clasps, and Khedive's Star). Served with the Soudan Frontier Field Force during the operations on the Upper Nile in 1885-86.
[118] Captain Lapham served in the Ashanti war of 1873-74 (Medal with Clasp). Served in the Boer war of 1881.
[128] Captain Crumplin served in the Egyptian war of 1882 (Medal, and Khedive's Star); also served in the Nile Expedition in 1884-85 (honorary rank of Captain, Medal with Clasp).
[130] Captain Ledsham served in the Ashanti war in 1873-74 (Medal). Served in the Zulu war in 1879 (Medal).
[134] Captain R. H. Robinson served in the Egyptian war of 1882 (Medal, and Khedive's Star). Served in the Soudan Expedition under Sir Gerald Graham in 1884 (Clasp); also served with the Nile Expedition in 1884-85 (Clasp).
[138] Captain W. Musgrave served with the Bechuanaland Expedition under Sir Charles Warren in 1884-85.
[143] Captain F. L. Cassell served in the Zulu war of 1879 (Medal). Served in the Boer war of 1881, and took part in the defence of Standerton (mentioned in despatches, and promoted Quarter Master). Served in the Soudan campaign in 1885, and was present in the engagement at the Tofrek zereba (mentioned in despatches, Medal with two Clasps, and Khedive's Star).
[144] Captain Parsons served in the Zulu war in 1879 (Medal with Clasp). Served in the Boer war in 1881, and took part in the defence of Lydenburg (promoted Quarter Master). Served in the Egyptian war of 1882 (Medal, and Khedive's Star). Served with the Bechuanaland Expedition under Sir Charles Warren in 1884-85.
[145] Captain Brooks served in the Zulu war in 1879, and was present in the engagements at Kambula (slightly

Z

wounded) and Ulundi (Medal with Clasp). Served in the Egyptian war of 1882, and was present at the battle of Tel-el-Kebir (promoted to Quarter Master in the Commissariat and Transport Staff, Medal with Clasp, and Khedive's Star); also served with the Nile Expedition in 1884-85, and was present in the engagement at Kirbekan (two Clasps).

146 Captain F. Gardiner served in the New Zealand war in 1863-66, including the engagements at Nukumaru and Kakaramea and the Wanganui campaign (Medal).

147 Captain W. Johnson served in the Egyptian war of 1882 (Medal, and Khedive's Star). Also served in the Soudan campaign in 1885 (mentioned in despatches, Clasp), and in the operations near Suakin in December 1888 including the engagement at Gemaizah (honorary rank of Captain, Clasp).

149 Captain Loader served with the Nile Expedition in 1884-85 (Medal with Clasp, and Khedive's Star); also served in the operations near Suakin in December 1888 including the engagement at Gemaizah (honorary rank of Captain, Clasp).

150 Lieut. L. Latten served in the Zulu war in 1879 (Medal).

151 Lieut. M. Daly served in the Egyptian war of 1882 and was present at the two actions at Kassasin and at the battle of Tel-el-Kebir (Medal with Clasp, and Khedive's Star). Served with the Bechuanaland Expedition under Sir Charles Warren in 1884-85.

152 Lieut. Edmondson served with the Nile Expedition in 1884-85 (promoted Quarter Master, Medal with Clasp, and Khedive's Star).

153 Lieut. H. E. Champion served in the Zulu war in 1879 (Medal with Clasp). Served in the Soudan campaign in 1885 (mentioned in despatches, promoted Quarter Master, Medal with Clasp, and Khedive's Star).

154 Captain Drage served with the Nile Expedition in 1884-85 (promoted Quarter Master, Medal with Clasp, and Khedive's Star); with the Soudan Frontier Field Force in 1885-86, including the engagement at Giniss; and in the operations on the Soudan frontier in 1889 including the engagement at Toski (mentioned in despatches, honorary rank of Captain, Clasp, and 4th Class of the Medjidie).

155 Lieut. W. Haycock served with the Nile Expedition in 1884-85 (mentioned in despatches, promoted Quarter Master, Medal with Clasp, and Khedive's Star).

160 Lt.Colonel J. U. Gore served in the Ashanti war in 1873-74 under Sir Garnet Wolseley (Medal). Served in the expedition against the Yonnies, on the West Coast of Africa, in 1887-88 (Medal with Clasp).

Ordnance Store Department.

Commissioned Rank.	Commissary General of Ordnance, ranking with Major General.	First Commissioned Rank.	Present Rank.	App. to Re-organiz'd O.S. Dept.	Station.
Dep. Assist. Supdt. of Stores	Pridham, Frederick..............	5 June 60	1 Apr. 93	31 Jan. 80	Woolwich Arsenal.
	Deputy Commissaries General of Ordnance, with Honorary rank of Colonel.				
Dep. Assist. Supdt. of Stores	Taylor, Henry[1]	9 Apr. 53	26 Oct. 89	31 Jan. 80	Western District.
Dep. Assist. Supdt. of Stores	Mayo, William Robert..............	29 Apr. 59	8 Oct. 90	31 Jan. 80	Ireland.
Dep. Assist. Supdt. of Stores	Jolly, George Alfred[15]..........	20 Aug. 60	16 June 92	31 Jan. 80	Woolwich Arsenal.
	Steevens, John[18]	1 Apr. 74	1 Aug. 94	31 Jan. 80	War Office.
Dep. Assist. Supdt. of Stores	Skinner, Edmund Grey,[19] CB.......	31 July 67	1 Oct. 94	31 Jan. 80	
	Assistant Commissaries General of Ordnance, with Hon. rank of Lieut. Colonel.				
Dep. Assist. Supdt. of Stores	Vansittart, Charles Edward.........	3 Apr. 67	30 Nov. 81	31 Jan. 80	Egypt.
Dep. Assist. Supdt. of Stores	Graham, Lionel Frederick..........	3 Apr. 67	24 Aug. 83	31 Jan. 80	S. E. District.
Dep. Assist. Supdt. of Stores	St. George, Harry Hammersley[20]	31 July 67	12 Dec. 83	31 Jan. 80	Scottish District.
	Houghton, Ernest[21].............	13 June 72	21 May 84	31 Jan. 80	Pembroke Dock.
Dep. Assist. Supdt. of Stores	Bridgman, Arthur Walter...........	31 July 67	30 Dec. 84	31 Jan. 80	Malta.
	Wintle, Frank Graham,[25] DSO.....	13 June 72	15 June 85	31 Jan. 80	Aldershot.
	Mulcahy, Francis Edward[23]......	1 Jan. 76	15 June 85	1 Dec. 80	Home District.
	Markwick, Ernest Elliott[27]	13 June 72	9 Dec. 85	31 Jan. 80	Gibraltar.
	Stainforth, Richard Terrick	......	6 Jan. 86	31 Jan. 80	N. W. District.
Lieutenant Royal Artillery	Cooke, William Butterworth[24]....	15 Jan. 67	22 Mar. 86	31 Jan. 80	Bermuda.
	Leggett, Frederick Octavius	......	30 Sept. 87	31 Jan. 80	Thames District.
	Wheeler, John Langford	13 June 72	10 Oct. 88	31 Jan. 80	Dublin District.
	Clarke, Robert Fulke Noel[29]	13 June 72	6 Jan. 89	31 Jan. 80	China.
	With Hon. rank of Major.				
	Wyon, Herbert Thornton[31]	13 June 72	9 July 90	31 Mar. 80	Cork District.
	Fincham, Herbert George	9 Apr. 73	16 Aug. 90	1 Apr. 80	Halifax, N. S.
	Tate, Charles William Henry[34]..	9 Apr. 73	20 Dec. 90	1 May 80	Woolwich.
	Heath, Edward	9 Apr. 73	24 Dec. 90	1 June 80	Portsmouth.
	Jeans, Charles Gilchrist	9 Apr. 73	12 Jan. 91	17 June 80	South Africa.
	Hobbs, George Radley[24]	9 Apr. 73	13 July 91	17 June 80	Natal.
	Purchas, Charles	1 Apr. 74	1 Apr. 92	15 July 80	Purfleet.
	Atkinson, George Robert	1 Apr. 74	1 Apr. 92	29 Aug. 80	Weedon.
	Sadler, Alfred[37]	1 Jan. 76	1 Apr. 92	16 Oct. 80	Ceylon.
	Heron, Thomas[38]	1 Jan. 76	4 May 92	1 Nov. 80	Aldershot.
	Barrett, Henry Walter[24]........	1 Jan. 76	2 July 92	22 Nov. 80	Woolwich Arsenal.
	Collingwood, William George......	1 Jan. 76	14 Sept. 92	16 Dec. 80	Malta.
	Appelbe, Edward Benjamin[39].....	1 Jan. 76	21 Jan. 93	1 Dec. 80	Woolwich.
Captain Royal Artillery ...	Battersby, Thomas Preston	2 Feb. 76	1 Apr. 93	16 Jan. 83	Eastern District.
Captain Royal Artillery ...	Archdale, James Blackwood	11 Sept. 73	20 Apr. 94	18 Jan. 83	Dover.
Captain Dublin Fusiliers ...	Parkinson, Percival George	5 Sept. 77	1 Aug. 94	16 June 84	
Captain Middlesex Regt. ...	Law, Robert Theophilus Hewitt[41]	24 Mar. 76	1 Oct. 94	18 Aug. 84	Burscough.
	Deputy Assistant Commissaries General of Ordnance, with Hon. rank of Captain.				
Captain Devonshire Regt....	Stanley, Edmond Talbot[40]........	6 Oct. 77	29 Dec. 83	29 Dec. 83	Gibraltar.
Captain Cheshire Regiment	Butcher, George James............	14 Jan. 80	27 Feb. 85	27 Feb. 85	Chatham.
Captain Devon Regiment...	Bennett, Robert	13 Aug. 79	22 Apr. 85	22 Apr. 85	Portsmouth.
Captain R. Malta Artillery..	Samut, Achilles F. P. M. J. A. F. X.	1 Sept. 80	5 June 85	5 June 85	Portsmouth.
Captain Scots Fusiliers ...	Tuckey, Charles	11 Sept. 76	3 Oct. 85	3 Oct. 85	York.
Capt. York and Lanc. Regt.	Smyth, Hugo W. N. S.[44].........	21 June 79	5 Oct. 85	5 Oct. 85	Stirling.
Capt. 1 West India Regt. ...	Barrett, Edward A. Moulton	11 Aug. 80	10 Oct. 85	10 Oct. 85	
Captain Irish Regiment...	Crawford, Raymund	14 Jan. 80	21 Oct. 85	21 Oct. 85	Haulbowline.
Capt. Inniskilling Fusiliers	Jackson, Robert Whyte Melville..	19 Feb. 81	20 Mar. 86	20 Mar. 86	Malta.
Captain Dublin Fusiliers ...	Seymour, Edward Hamilton	14 Jan. 80	24 Mar. 86	24 Mar. 86	St. Helena.
Capt. Leinster Regiment ...	Greenwood, William Henry........	23 Oct. 80	31 Mar. 86	31 Mar. 86	
Captain Irish Fusiliers	Angoll, Frederick John[46]	22 Jan. 81	5 Apr. 86	5 Apr. 86	Bermuda.
Capt. S. Stafford Regt....	Hearn, George	22 Jan. 79	15 Feb. 87	15 Feb. 87	Colombo.
Captain King's Own Scottish Borderers	Taylor, Reynell H. Bayley[49]...	13 Aug. 79	2 May 87	2 May 87	Harwich.
Captain Berkshire Regt. ...	Bunny, Frank William M'T.[50]...	14 Jan. 80	11 Aug. 87	11 Aug. 87	Trincomalee.
Captain Leinster Regiment	Tribe, Cecil Walford.............	14 Jan. 80	19 Aug. 87	19 Aug. 87	Cairo.
Captain Dublin Fusiliers ...	Audain, Mark Ralph Payne	23 Oct. 80	1 Feb. 88	1 Feb. 88	Halifax, N. S.
Capt. Durham Light Inf. ...	Gardiner, Richard John	19 Feb. 81	2 Mar. 88	2 Mar. 88	Dublin.
Captain 2 Dragoons	Simpson, Francis Blake	13 Aug. 79	5 Mar. 88	5 Mar. 88	Cyprus.
Capt. Connaught Rangers	Hall, Charles[51]	13 Aug. 79	16 Apr. 88	1 Dec. 8-	Cairo.
Captain Royal Artillery ...	Taylor, Mowbray	25 July 82	27 Nov. 88	27 Nov. 88	Natal.
Capt. Connaught Rangers	Combe, Edward Stanley[52]	23 Oct. 80	14 Dec. 88	14 Dec. 88	Hong Kong.
Captain Royal Artillery ...	Perry, Hugh Whitchurch	23 Feb. 81	27 Dec. 88	27 Dec. 88	Cape Town.
Captain West Kent Regt....	Caird, Edward Devon	22 Jan. 81	26 Oct. 89	26 Oct. 89	Devonport.
Capt. Leicester Regiment...	Jones, William Locke	22 Oct. 81	8 Nov. 89	8 Nov. 89	Dover.
Capt. Yorkshire Lt. Inf......	Pease, Lawrence Willoughby[58]	19 Dec. 83	9 July 90	9 July 90	Natal.

Ordnance Store Department.

Commissioned Rank.	Deputy Assistant Commissaries General of Ordnance, with Hon. rank of Captain.	First Commissioned Rank.	Present Rank.	App. to Re-organiz'd O.S.Dept.	Station.
Capt. East Yorkshire Regt.	Davies, Wilbraham Thomas[54]	25 May 78	8 Aug. 90	8 Aug. 90	Bermuda.
Captain Hampshire Regt.	Gill, Robert Hinds[53]	10 Mar. 83	16 Aug. 90	16 Aug. 90	Barbadoes.
Captain Royal Artillery	Salmon, James Nelson	15 Feb. 84	24 Aug. 90	24 Aug. 90	Jamaica.
Capt. York & Lanc. Regt.	Palmer, Arthur Stouart	10 May 82	12 Feb. 90	26 Sept. 90	Hong Kong.
Captain West Surrey Regt.	Parsons, Harold Daniel Edmund[55]	10 May 82	8 Oct. 90	8 Oct. 90	Straits Settlements.
Captain Cheshire Regt.	Tod, Alex. George Wm.[57]	12 Nov. 84	20 Oct. 90	20 Oct. 90	Malta.
Captain West Surrey Regt.	Tracy, William Maxwell[55]	9 Sept. 82	30 Oct. 90	30 Oct. 90	Mauritius.
Lieut. West India Regt.	Sherwood, Oliver Caton	23 Aug. 84	20 Dec. 90	20 Dec. 90	Adjutant, Woolwich
Captain Irish Regiment	Bass, Philip de Salis	29 July 82	24 Dec. 90	24 Dec. 90	Jersey.
Capt. Durham Lt. Infantry	Mathew, Charles Massy[56]	23 Aug. 84	17 June 91	17 June 91	Portsmouth.
Captain 4 Dragoon Guards	Brinkley, Chas. Mich. Edgeworth	29 July 82	13 July 91	13 July 91	Aldershot.
Capt. East Yorkshire Regt.	Harrison, Broadley	23 May 85	28 July 91	28 July 91	Chatham.
Capt. N. Staffordshire Regt.	Snow, Edmund Graham	10 May 82	23 Dec. 91	23 Dec. 91	Bull Point.
Capt. 3 Dragoon Guards	Keith, Clive Skene	14 May 84	27 Apr. 92	27 Apr. 92	Colchester.
Capt. E. Lancashire Regt.	Hale, John Henry	9 Sept. 82	4 May 92	4 May 92	Guernsey.
Captain East Surrey Regt.	Anley, Henry Augustus	7 Feb. 85	2 July 92	2 July 92	Tipnor.
Captain Norfolk Regiment	Trevor, Philip Christian Wm.	25 Aug. 83	14 Sept. 92	14 Sept. 92	Aldershot.
Captain East Kent Regiment	Greene, Charles Kendal	6 Feb. 84	14 Dec. 92	14 Dec. 92	Enniskillen.
Lieut. S. Wales Borderers.	Marquis, Thomas Stirling[59]	16 Nov. 87	21 Jan. 93	21 Jan. 93	York.
Captain Leinster Regiment.	Dickinson, Neville Hope Campbell	3 May 85	1 Apr. 93	1 Apr. 93	Woolwich Arsenal.
Capt. Wiltshire Regiment.	Hale, Thomas Wyatt	7 Feb. 85	13 Sept. 93	13 Sept. 93	Dublin.
Captain Hampshire Regt.	Barrington, Richard Mordaunt[60]	29 Aug. 85	6 Dec. 93	6 Dec. 93	Dublin.
Captain Wiltshire Regt.	Trim, Robert William	14 May 84	1 Feb. 94	1 Feb. 94	York.
On Probation.					
Captain S. Wales Borderers	Moore, Herbert Acheson[61]	6 May 85	20 Apr. 94	20 Apr. 94	Gibraltar.
Captain West India Regt.	Brooks, Lewis Amadeus	6 Feb. 84	16 June 94	16 June 94	Bermuda.
Lieut. Royal Marines	Basevi, William Henry	4 Mar. 85	1 Aug. 94	1 Aug. 94	Weedon.
Capt. Lancashire Fusiliers	Milward, Frederick David	12 May 83	1 Sept. 94	1 Sept. 94	Woolwich Arsenal.
Captain West India Regt.	Tredgold, William Lancelot[62]	9 May 85	24 Oct. 94	24 Oct. 94	Devonport.

Quarter Masters.	First Commissioned Rank.	Hon. Lieut.	Hon. Captain.	Present Rank.	App. to Re-organiz'd O.S.Dept.	Station.
D'Arcy, Edward Blake[63]	27 Mar. 78	27 Mar. 78	27 Mar. 88	31 Jan. 80	31 Jan. 80	Curragh.
Morton, James[65]	27 Mar. 78	27 Mar. 78	27 Mar. 88	31 Jan. 80	31 Jan. 80	Woolwich Arsenal.
M'Caulis, William	7 Aug. 78		1 Apr. 86	31 Jan. 80	31 Jan. 80	Woolwich Dockyard.
Moore, Robert	23 Oct. 78		23 Oct. 88	31 Jan. 80	31 Jan. 80	Tower.
Tims, Frederic[63]	30 Nov. 81		30 Nov. 91	30 Nov. 81	30 Nov. 81	Woolwich Dockyard.
Ward, William Homan	17 Dec. 82		17 Dec. 92	17 Dec. 82	17 Dec. 82	Woolwich Arsenal.
Foord, William Levison Tom	4 Dec. 83		4 Dec. 93	4 Dec. 83	4 Dec. 83	Athlone.
Hunter, Charles Finch[64]	21 May 84		21 May 94	21 May 84	21 May 84	Woolwich Arsenal.
With rank of Lieutenant.						
Ledsham, James	30 Mar. 85			30 Mar. 85	30 Mar. 85	Sheerness.
Hodgson, James	30 Mar. 85			30 Mar. 85	30 Mar. 85	War Office.
Bovill, Thomas	30 Apr. 85			30 Apr. 85	30 Apr. 85	Leith Fort.
Roache, Joseph Matthew	30 Apr. 85			30 Apr. 85	30 Apr. 85	Woolwich Arsenal.
Mullen, Patrick[67]	15 June 85			15 June 85	15 June 85	Alexandria.
Warnes, Thomas John	6 Feb. 89			6 Feb. 89	6 Feb. 89	Devonport.
Heaton, Thomas	17 Apr. 89			17 Apr. 89	17 Apr. 89	Fleetwood.
Roberts, James Andrew	25 Dec. 89			25 Dec. 89	25 Dec. 89	Portsmouth.
Genders, Joshua	29 Jan. 90			29 Jan. 90	29 Jan. 90	Burscough.
Thompson, John	24 July 90			24 July 90	24 July 90	Hong Kong.
Bath, John	26 Aug. 91			26 Aug. 91	26 Aug. 91	War Office.
Cox, William	6 Apr. 92			6 Apr. 92	6 Apr. 92	Weedon.
Collins, David E.	6 Apr. 92			6 Apr. 92	6 Apr. 92	Aldershot.
Cooper, Henry	6 Apr. 92			6 Apr. 92	6 Apr. 92	Cape Town.
Brooks, James	6 Apr. 92			6 Apr. 92	6 Apr. 92	Ceylon.
Hamlin, Richard James	18 May 92			18 May 92	18 May 92	Stirling.
Andrews, Henry George	25 May 92			25 May 92	25 May 92	Alderney.
Walker, Samuel M'All	22 Dec. 94			22 Dec. 94	22 Dec. 94	Woolwich.
Hunter, James	4 Jan. 95			4 Jan. 95	4 Jan. 95	Lydd.
Swan, William	18 Mar. 95			18 Mar. 95	18 Mar. 95	

Instructor .... Assist. Commissary General of Ordnance E. B. Appelbe, 1 Feb. 95. Woolwich.
Adjutant .... Captain O. C. Sherwood, West India Regiment, 1 Apr. 93. Woolwich.

War Services.

[1] Colonel H. Taylor served in the Kafir war in 1851-53 with the 2nd Division (Medal).

[15] Colonel G. A. Jolly served on the Red River Expedition of 1870 from Canada under Sir Garnet Wolseley.

[16] Colonel J. Steevens served in the Zulu war in 1879 (promoted Deputy Commissary, Medal with Clasp). Served in the Egyptian war of 1882 as Senior Ordnance Store Officer with the 2nd Division, and was present at the battle of Tel-el-Kebir (mentioned in despatches, promoted Assistant Commissary General of Ordnance, Medal with Clasp, 4th Class of the Medjidie, and Khedive's Star).

[17] Colonel E. G. Skinner accompanied the expedition in the Malay Peninsula in 1875-76, and served in charge of the Bengal Commissariat in Larut and Sunghii Ujong (Medal with Clasp). Served in the Egyptian war of 1882, and was present in the action of Kassasin on the 9th September, and at the battle of Tel-el-Kebir (mentioned in despatches, promoted Assistant Commissary General of Ordnance, Medal, 4th Class of the Medjidie, and Khedive's Star). Served in the Soudan campaign in 1885 as Senior Ordnance Store Officer (mentioned in despatches, honorary rank of Lt. Colonel, Clasp).

[20] Lt. Colonel St. George served in the Soudan campaign in 1885 in charge of the Ordnance Depot (mentioned in despatches, Medal with Clasp, and Khedive's Star).

Ordnance Store Department.—War Services.

[21] Lt.Colonel E. Houghton served in the Boer war of 1881. Served in the Egyptian war of 1882 (Medal, and Khedive's Star); also served in the Soudan Expedition under Sir Gerald Graham in 1884 (mentioned in despatches, promoted Assistant Commissary General of Ordnance, 4th Class of the Medjidie, Clasp).

[23] Lt.Colonel F. E. Mulcahy was employed in Natal during the Zulu war in 1879 (Medal). Also served in the Boer war of 1881 at Pretoria. Served with the Nile Expedition in 1884-85 (mentioned in despatches, promoted Assistant Commissary General of Ordnance, Medal with Clasp, and Khedive's Star).

[24] Lt.Colonel W. B. Cooke, Majors Hobbs and Barrett served in the Zulu war of 1879 (Medal).

[25] Lt.Colonel F. G. Wintle served with the Nile Expedition in 1884-85 (mentioned in despatches, promoted Assistant Commissary General of Ordnance, Medal with Clasp, and Khedive's Star); also served with the Egyptian Frontier Field Force in 1885-86, including the engagement at Giniss (mentioned in despatches).

[27] Lt.Colonel E. E. Markwick served in the Zulu war in 1879 (Medal). Served in the Boer war of 1881, and took part in the defence of Pretoria. Served with the Bechuanaland Expedition under Sir Charles Warren in 1884-85 as Senior Ordnance Store Officer (promoted Assistant Commissary General of Ordnance).

[29] Lt.Colonel Clarke served with the Nile Expedition in 1884-85 (Medal with Clasp, and Khedive's Star).

[31] Major Wyon served in the Kafir war in 1878 including the operations against Sekukuni; also served in the Zulu war in 1879, and in the subsequent operations against Sekukuni (Medal). Served at Pretoria during the Boer war of 1881.

[34] Major C. W. H. Tate served in the Boer war of 1881.

[37] Major Sadler served in the Zulu war in 1879 and in the subsequent operations against Sekukuni (Medal with Clasp).

[38] Major Heron served in the Zulu war in 1879, and in the subsequent operations against Sekukuni including the capture of the stronghold (Medal with Clasp).

[39] Major Appelbe served in the Zulu war of 1879 (Medal with Clasp). Served with the Nile Expedition in 1885, and in the subsequent operations in the Eastern Soudan (Medal with two Clasps, and Khedive's Star); also served in the operations in the Soudan in 1888 including the engagement at Gemaizah (Clasp, 3rd Class of the Medjidie). Nominated to the 3rd Class of the Order of the Osmanieh for services with the Egyptian Army.

[40] Captain Stanley.—For War Services, see Devonshire Regiment.
[41] Major Law served in the Zulu war of 1879 (Medal with Clasp).
[44] Captain Hugo Smyth.—For War Services, see York and Lancaster Regiment.
[48] Captain Angell.—For War Services, see Irish Fusiliers.
[49] Captain Taylor.—For War Services, see King's Own Scottish Borderers.
[50] Captain Bunny.—For War Services, see Berkshire Regiment.
[51] Captain Hall.—For War Services, see Connaught Rangers.
[52] Captain E. S. Combe.—For War Services, see Connaught Rangers.
[53] Captain Gill.—For War Services, see Hampshire Regiment.
[54] Captain Davies.—For War Services, see East Yorkshire Regiment.
[55] Captains Tracy and Parsons.—For War Services, see West Surrey Regiment.
[56] Captain Mathew.—For War Services, see Dunham Light Infantry.
[57] Captain Tod.—For War Services, see Cheshire Regiment.
[58] Captain Pease.—For War Services, see Yorkshire Light Infantry.
[59] Captain Marquis.—See Civil Decorations for Gallantry, "Hart's Annual Army List," p. 786.
[60] Captain Barrington.—For War Services, see Hampshire Regiment.
[61] Captain Moore.—For War Services, see South Wales Borderers.
[62] Captain Tredgold.—For War Services, see West India Regiment.
[63] Captains D'Arcy and Tims served in the Egyptian war of 1882 (Medal, and Khedive's Star).
[64] Captain C. F. Hunter served in the expedition to the Soudan in 1884 under Sir Gerald Graham in the Ordnance Store Department (promoted Quarter Master, Medal, and Khedive's Star). Served in the Soudan campaign in 1885 (mentioned in despatches, Clasp).
[65] Captain Morton served in the operations in Zululand in 1888.
[67] Lieut. Mullen served with the Nile Expedition in 1884-85 (mentioned in despatches, promoted Quarter Master, Medal with Clasp, and Khedive's Star); also served in the operations near Suakin in December 1888, including the engagement at Gemaizah (Clasp).

Army Pay Department.

FORMER COMMISSION.	CHIEF PAYMASTERS (with Honorary rank of Colonel).	FIRST COM- MISSION.	PAY- MASTER.	HON. MAJOR.	STAFFPAY- MASTER.	CHIEFPAY- MASTER.	HON. COLONEL.	REGIMENT OR STATION.
Lieutenant 8 Foot	Senior, Thomas Palmer	18 Nov. 57	15 May 67	15 May 77	1 Dec. 80	24 Dec. 84	1 Nov. 87	Home District.
Ensign 24 Foot	Hughes, William	22 Mar. 64	20 Nov. 67	22 Mar. 79	1 Mar. 81	24 Mar. 85	1 Nov. 87	Southern District.
Dept. Assist. Supt. of Stores	Dragg, Thomas William[1]	3 Sept. 65	1 Apr. 78	19 Dec. 79	1 Feb. 81	1 June 85	1 Nov. 87	Gibraltar.
Lieutenant 48 Foot	Chauncey, Charles Henry[1]	18 Oct. 55	8 May 67	1 Oct. 81	1 Oct. 81	2 June 86	1 Nov. 87	Woolwich District.
Lieutenant 61 Foot	Hamilton, James Graham	18 Dec. 68	2 Dec. 68	1 Oct. 81	1 Oct. 81	1 Oct. 88	12 Nov. 87	North Western District.
Captain 4 Foot	Roberts, Edward[30]	16 Mar. 60	1 Apr. 78	1 Oct. 81	1 Oct. 81	1 Oct. 88	25 Dec. 88	Scottish District.
War Office Clerk	Gorres, Edmond Howard[33]	2 Oct. 62	1 Sept. 75	1 Oct. 81	1 Oct. 81	8 May 89	8 May 89	Ireland.
War Office Clerk	Anson, George Hamilton	2 Jan. 63	15 Apr. 77	1 Oct. 81	1 Oct. 81	5 June 89	5 June 89	Cape of Good Hope.
War Office Clerk	Treffry, Frederic	16 Mar. 66	2 Oct. 62	15 Nov. 81	15 Nov. 81	10 Sept. 90	10 Sept. 90	Egypt.
Clerk Commr. in Chief's Office	Tuck, John Johnson	1 Sept. 66	1 Apr. 78	19 Nov. 81	19 Nov. 81:	7 June 91	7 June 91	South Eastern District.
Captain 23 Foot	Whittington, George John Charles[11]	14 July 57	1 Apr. 78	1 Dec. 81	15 Nov. 81	13 Dec. 91	13 Dec. 91	Western District.
Captain 15 Foot	Barr, William Lamb[43]	17 Nov. 57	1 Apr. 78	1 Aug. 82	19 Nov. 82	4 Jan. 93	4 Jan. 93	Hong Kong.
Assistant Purveyor	Costa, Paul Dennis	3 Jan. 56	1 Apr. 78	18 May 82	1 Aug. 82	17 Mar. 93	4 Apr. 93	North Eastern District.
Captain 73 Foot	Hewson, John Iryssghi[44]	6 June 56	1 Apr. 78	1 Sept. 82	18 Sept. 82	17 Mar. 94	17 Mar. 94	Malta.
Captain 107 Foot	Playfair, William Morgan	9 Dec. 60	1 Apr. 78	20 Nov. 82	20 Nov. 82	16 Oct. 94	16 Oct. 94	Aldershot.
Captain 89 Foot	Richmond, Richard Oliffe[49]	2 July 58	1 Apr. 76	1 Apr. 83	1 Apr. 83	16 Nov. 94	16 Nov. 94	Eastern District.

FORMER COMMISSION.	STAFF PAYMASTERS (with Honorary rank of Lt. Colonel).	FIRST COM- MISSION.	PAY- MASTER.	HON. MAJOR.	STAFFPAY- MASTER.	HON. LT. COLONEL.	STATION.
Dep. Assist. Supt. of Stores	Potter, Henry[14]	7 Mar. 56	* Apr. 74	1 Apr. 74	1 Apr. 78	1 Nov. 87	Jamaica.
Lieutenant 37 Foot	Sargeant-Openshaw, Francis O.[17]	28 May 58	20 July 66	20 July 76	1 Nov. 79	1 Nov. 87	Colchester.
Lieutenant 3 Bombay Eng. Reg.	Ryder, Herbert Croft[23]		9 Feb. 64	9 Feb. 76	1 Feb. 81	1 Feb. 88	Guernsey.
Captain 8 Hussars	Ryde, James Clarke	26 Mar. 58	3 Mar. 64	1 Mar. 79	10 Mar. 81	10 Mar. 88	Ayr.
Captain 55 Foot	Hobbs, Frederick Fitz William Trench	15 July 63	1 Dec. 64	1 Dec. 79	15 Aug. 81	15 Aug. 88	Carlisle.
Lieutenant R. Canadian Rifles	Hignett, Charles Harrison[34]	28 July 63	1 Oct. 71	10 May 79	1 Oct. 81	1 Oct. 88	Gibraltar.
Assistant Purveyor	Kaye, William Robert[37]	24 Dec. 60	1 Apr. 78	8 Mar. 82	8 Mar. 82	8 Mar. 89	Cork District.
Lieutenant Q. M. G.'s Office	Creagh, Denis	6 Aug. 58	1 Jan. 68	27 Apr. 82	27 Apr. 82	27 Apr. 89	Nova Scotia.
Clerk Q.M. G.'s Office	Noyes, Augustus Finch	6 Feb. 65	28 Sept. 77	6 May 82	6 May 82	6 May 89	Lincoln.
Bt. Major 67 Foot	Raymond, Elliot Arthur[38]	18 Feb. 55	1 Apr. 78	1 June 82	1 June 82	1 June 89	Guildford.
Captain 44 Foot	Sutherland, William John Edw. Graham	11 Mar. 59	1 Apr. 78	5 June 82	5 June 82	5 June 89	Canterbury.
Captain 22 Foot	Spiller, Duncan Chisholm Oliver[42]	14 Aug. 60	1 Apr. 78	26 July 82	26 July 82	1 July 89	Stirling.
Captain 56 Foot	Bell, William[45]	31 Aug. 55	1 Apr. 78	1 Oct. 82	14 Oct. 82	14 Oct. 89	Egypt.
Captain 31 Foot	Bateman, Henry William[48]	5 Feb. 61	1 Apr. 78	1 Apr. 83	1 Apr. 83	1 Apr. 90	Newcastle-on-Tyne.
Captain 26 Foot	Wade, William Barton[52]	11 Mar. 59	1 Apr. 78	1 Apr. 83	17 Sept. 83	17 Sept. 90	London.
Captain 105 Foot	Kennedy, Walter Cranfurd	22 Aug. 65	1 Apr. 78	1 Apr. 83	1 Oct. 83	1 Jan. 91	Shorncliffe.
Captain 58 Foot	Compigné, Henry Mapleton	8 July 68	1 Apr. 78	1 Apr. 83	21 Jan. 84	21 Feb. 91	Devizes.
Captain 1 West India Regt.	Brockman, William Law[54]	24 Nov. 65	1 Apr. 78	1 Apr. 83	21 Feb. 84	27 Feb. 91	Galway.
Captain 41 Foot	Coote, Edmund Eyre[55]	4 June 61	1 Apr. 78	1 Apr. 83	16 Mar. 84	16 Mar. 91	Chester.
Captain 63 Foot	Mortimer, William Hugh[56]	21 Feb. 65	1 Apr. 78	22 June 83	22 Mar. 84	22 Mar. 91	Portsmouth.
Captain 1 Foot	Jackson, James Henry	8 Jan. 68	6 Apr. 78	6 Apr. 83	24 May 84	24 May 91	Derby.
Captain 1 Foot	Ireland, Robert Megaw	21 Mar. 68	1 Apr. 78	8 Apr. 83	24 June 84	21 June 91	Belfast District.
Captain 20 Foot	Gelston, Arthur William Hill[58]	4 Sept. 64	1 Apr. 78	14 Apr. 83	25 June 84	25 June 91	Lancaster.
Captain 54 Foot	Gahan, Melmoth Canifield	7 Apr. 64	16 Apr. 78	16 Apr. 83	10 Sept. 84	10 Sept. 91	Thames District.
Captain 1 West India Regt.	Carey, Charles Frederick	13 Dec. 61	3 June 83	3 June 83	10 Sept. 84	10 Sept. 91	Woolwich.
Captain 67 Foot	Bell, Thomas[59]	8 May 67	22 June 78	22 June 83	11 Nov. 84	11 Nov. 91	Armagh.
Captain 43 Foot	Brereton, John Sadlier	9 Aug. 66	1 July 83	1 July 83	24 Dec. 84	24 Dec. 91	Reading.
Captain 18 Foot	Longley, Arthur[60]	19 Dec. 60	9 Aug. 78	9 Aug. 83	24 Dec. 84	24 Dec. 91	Cape Town.
	Stockley, John Cator[61]	4 Apr. 66	15 Aug. 78	15 Aug. 83	1 Apr. 85	1 Apr. 92	

* Date of Commission as Paymaster or Deputy Paymaster late Pay Sub Department, Control Department.

Army Pay Department.

FORMER COMMISSION.	STAFF PAYMASTERS—continued.	FIRST COMMISSON.	PAYMASTER.	HON. MAJOR.	STAFF PAYMASTER.	REGIMENT OR STATION.
Captain 49 Foot	Fox, Thos. Chas. Armstrong[63] (Hon. Lt. Colonel, 1 Apr. 92)	24 Jan. 65	2 Sept. 78	2 Sept. 83	1 Apr. 85	Bodmin.
Captain 50 Foot	Phillips, Henry Walter[64] (Hon. Lt. Colonel, 1 Apr. 92)	7 Apr. 63	2 Sept. 78	2 Sept. 83	1 Apr. 85	Netley Hospital.
Captain 47 Foot	Burge, Benjamin Henry[65] (Hon. Lt. Colonel, 1 Apr. 92)	18 Aug. 54	6 Sept. 78	6 Sept. 83	1 Apr. 85	Winchester.
Captain 65 Foot	Crookenden, Salusbury Davenport (Hon. Lt. Col. 3 June 92)	12 Jan. 66	18 Sept. 78	18 Sept. 83	3 June 85	Barbadoes.
Captain 35 Foot	Dowdall, Aylmer Peter Gerald[70] (Hon. Lt. Colonel, 15 June 92)	29 July 62	24 June 79	24 June 84	15 June 85	Chester.
Captain 97 Foot	Healy, Michael Ryan[69] (Hon. Lt. Colonel, 30 July 92)	15 Oct. 61	8 Sept. 78	28 Sept. 83	30 July 85	Fermoy.
Captain 11 Foot	Coppinger, Thomas Stephen[61] (Hon. Lt. Colonel, 2 Sept. 92)	20 Apr. 66	1 Oct. 78	1 Oct. 83	2 Sept. 85	Birr.
Captain 19 Foot	Langford, George Edward[71] (Hon. Lt. Colonel, 6 Dec. 92)	10 Nov. 65	4 Oct. 78	4 Oct. 83	6 Dec. 85	Bristol.
Captain 41 Foot	Barnes, George West[72] (Hon. Lt. Colonel, 6 Jan. 93)	29 Apr. 59	26 Oct. 78	26 Oct. 83	6 Jan. 86	Hounslow.
Captain 26 Foot	Dougherty, Edwd. Macklon[73] (Hon. Lt. Colonel, 8 May 93)	2 June 65	26 Oct. 78	26 Oct. 83	8 May 86	Pontefract.
Captain 10 Foot	Booth, Thos. George[75] (Hon. Lt. Colonel, 17 June 93)	16 May 65	30 Oct. 78	30 Oct. 83	17 June 86	Bury.
Captain 2 W.I. Regt.	Stoker, Wm. B. Caulfeild[76] (Hon. Lt. Colonel, 10 Sept. 93)	8 May 67	6 Nov. 78	6 Nov. 83	10 Sept. 86	Natal.
Captain 98 Foot	Johnson, Osmond Moncrieff (Hon. Lt. Colonel, 16 Sept. 93)	10 Feb. 69	8 Nov. 78	8 Nov. 83	16 Sept. 86	Discharge Depot. Gosport.
Bt. Major 21 Foot	Furlong, George William[77] (Hon. Lt. Colonel, 20 Sept. 93)	5 Apr. 55	9 Nov. 78	9 Nov. 83	20 Sept. 86	Chichester.
Captain 22 Foot	Brett, Arthur[79] (Hon. Lt. Colonel 18 Nov. 93)	16 Aug. 59	2 Dec. 78	2 Dec. 83	18 Nov. 86	Devonport.
Captain 27 Foot	Caine, Henry Monteath[81] (Hon. Lt. Colonel 16 July 94)	19 Dec. 56	5 Jan. 79	5 Jan. 84	16 July 87	Jersey.
Captain 55 Foot	Taylor, Charles Wm. Joseph[21] (Hon. Lt. Colonel 31 Aug. 94)	15 Feb. 61	18 Jan. 79	18 Jan. 84	31 Aug. 87	Aberdeen.
Captain 21 Hussars	Kitson, James Edward (Hon. Lt. Colonel, 21 Dec. 94)	26 June 66	28 Jan. 79	28 Jan. 84	21 Dec. 87	War Office.
	(with the Hon. rank of Major.)					
	Dawson, Henry Coleridge[84]	18 Mar. 73	28 Jan. 79	28 Jan. 84	4 May 88	Warrington.
	Ward, Charles[85]	....	1 Feb. 79	1 Feb. 84	12 Nov. 88	Oxford.
Captain 96 Foot	D'Aguilar, John Swainson[86]	9 Feb. 70	3 Feb. 79	3 Feb. 84	19 Dec. 88	Bedford.
Captain 22 Foot	Fenton, Michael	30 Apr. 58	17 Feb. 79	17 Feb. 84	25 Dec. 88	Glencorse.
Captain 28 Foot	Moore-Lane, George Howard	10 Mar. 64	26 May 79	26 May 84	5 May 89	Bermuda.
Captain 12 Foot	Shields, George[82]	4 Dec. 72	19 June 79	19 June 84	5 June 89	Aldershot.
Captain 50 Foot	Bromfield, James[89]	15 Nov. 64	23 June 79	23 June 84	20 June 89	York.
Captain 105 Foot	Orange, John Edward[90]	4 Feb. 62	24 June 79	24 June 84	15 July 89	Taunton.
Captain 28 Foot	Webb, Francis Edward[92]	15 May 65	15 July 79	15 July 84	14 Aug. 89	Cardiff.
Bt. Major 96 Foot	Webster, Henry Francis Geo.[83]	10 Aug. 55	21 July 79	21 July 84	5 Dec. 89	Ceylon.
Captain 37 Foot	Nott, Wm. Candahar J. Farrer[94]	15 May 65	28 July 79	28 July 84	18 Dec. 89	Kingston-on-Th.
Captain 13 Hussars	Maunsell, Edward Henry	30 Nov. 60	26 Aug. 79	26 Aug. 84	6 Jan. 90	Inverness.
Captain 60 Foot	Lloyd, Thomas Prince[95]	23 July 61	5 Sept. 79	5 Sept. 84	12 Jan. 90	Dover.
Captain 102 Foot	Dowdall, Laurence Richard	21 Nov. 65	1 Oct. 79	1 Oct. 84	2 Apr. 90	Straits Settlements.
Captain 44 Foot	Churchill, Seton[68]	3 Feb. 60	31 Oct. 79	31 Oct. 84	10 Sept. 90	Lichfield.
Captain 64 Foot	Walker, John Symeon	30 Dec. 59	30 Dec. 79	27 Dec. 84	25 Dec. 90	Preston.
Captain 50 Foot	Fleury, William L.[99]	11 Jan. 59	1 Jan. 80	1 Jan. 85	11 Feb. 91	Clonmel.
Captain R. Art.	Souper, Charles Edward	18 Dec. 61	1 Jan. 80	1 Jan. 85	11 Feb. 91	Warley.
Captain 105 Foot	Ferrier, George Henry	11 Jan. 67	1 Jan. 80	1 Jan. 85	11 Feb. 91	Worcester.
Captain 107 Foot	Davidson, Thomas Reid Waugh	9 Jan. 68	5 Jan. 80	5 Jan. 85	7 June 91	Hamilton.
Captain 18 Foot	Pearson, John	20 Sept. 64	8 Jan. 80	8 Jan. 85	22 June 91	Dorchester.
Captain 20 Foot	Robinson, De la Pere[83]	24 June 62	29 Mar. 80	29 Mar. 85	9 Aug. 91	Ashton-under-Lyne.
Captain 63 Foot	Palmer, William[103]	18 Jan. 67	6 July 80	6 July 85	23 Sept. 91	London.
Captain 60 Foot	Croft, James Henry Herbert[104]	12 Nov. 58	7 July 80	7 July 85	7 Oct. 91	Exeter.
Captain 3 Foot	Ternan, R. Richards Breffney[11]	28 Oct. 71	3 Mar. 80	3 Mar. 85	13 Dec. 91	Tralee.
Bt. Major 80 Foot	Howard, Walter[98]	16 Mar. 58	13 July 80	13 July 85	17 Feb. 92	Aldershot.
Captain 28 Foot	Dempster, Thomas Carroll[100]	13 July 80	13 July 80	13 July 85	16 Mar. 92	Bury St. Edmunds.
Captain 12 Foot	Brooke, Richard O'Shaughnessy	17 Mar. 63	19 July 80	19 July 85	4 May 92	Perth.
Captain 9 Foot	Humfrey, J. Campbell Taylor[10]	28 Mar. 58	8 Aug. 80	8 Aug. 85	16 Aug. 92	Woolwich.
Captain 21 Hussars	Haynes, Frederick Hutchinson	3 Feb. 69	12 Nov. 80	12 Nov. 85	12 Oct. 92	Leicester.
Captain 10 Foot	Singer, George Hamilton[106]	7 Apr. 65	13 Nov. 80	13 Nov. 85	14 Dec. 92	Edinburgh.
Captain 57 Foot	Dewar, Gordon[107]	7 July 69	13 Nov. 80	13 Nov. 85	4 Jan. 93	Curragh.
Captain Irish Regt.	Gilbert, Herbert Henry	18 Apr. 65	27 Dec. 80	27 Dec. 85	3 Mar. 93	Norwich.
Capt. W. York. Regt.	Reid, James[108]	20 June 68	1 Jan. 81	1 Jan. 86	9 Apr. 93	Northampton.
Capt. York & Lancaster Regt.	Drury, James O'Brien[109]	27 May 62	3 Jan. 81	3 Jan. 86	24 Aug. 93	Omagh.
Capt. Essex Regt.	Reid, Ellis Ramsay[110]	3 Feb. 69	11 Mar. 81	11 Mar. 86	31 Aug. 93	Beverley.
Capt. Leicester Regt.	Parkinson, Frederick Fenton	23 Jan. 63	16 Mar. 81	16 Mar. 86	14 Nov. 93	Dublin.
Capt. K.O. Borderers	Rathborne, Hans Robert[114]	28 July 63	31 Mar. 81	31 Mar. 86	18 Dec. 93	Wrexham.
Capt. Irish Rifles	Bell, James Archibald Robert	1 Feb. 67	12 Apr. 81	12 Apr. 86	17 Mar. 94	Naas.
Capt. York & Lancaster Regt.	Angus, John[112]	1 Mar. 64	29 Apr. 81	29 Apr. 86	28 Mar. 94	Berwick.
Capt. W. Surrey Reg.	Montgomery, William	14 Mar. 65	29 Apr. 81	29 Apr. 86	18 Apr. 94	Warwick.
Major 2 Foot	Mackie, William[113]	1 May 61	2 May 81	2 May 86	4 May 94	Richmond, Yorks.
Capt. Worcester Regt.	Cowell, Henry Clayton[116]	22 Sept. 65	7 May 81	7 May 86	29 Aug. 94	Burnley.
Bt. Maj. Munster Fus	Small, William George[115]	18 Dec. 67	12 May 81	12 May 86	28 Sept. 94	Maidstone.
Capt. Dublin Fus.	Lysaght, James Douglas[94]	20 June 68	27 May 81	27 May 86	4 Oct. 94	London.
Capt. Dublin Fus.	Irving, John Charles Sarle	7 Apr. 63	30 May 81	30 May 86	16 Oct. 94	Brecon.
Capt. Border Regt.	Newbury, John Benet Thornton	20 Feb. 67	6 June 81	6 June 86	16 Nov. 94	Chatham.
Captain 34 Foot	Chisholm-Batten, James Forbes	24 Nov. 69	6 June 81	6 June 86	8 Jan. 95	Pontefract.
Captain 17 Foot	Webb, Edward A. H.[117]	13 Feb. 66	10 June 81	10 June 86	27 Feb. 95	Halifax, Yorks.
	PAYMASTERS *(with the Hon. rank of Major.)*					
Capt. Gloucestershire Regiment	Sherrard, John Meade	14 Sept. 67	7 May 81	7 May 86		Lichfield.

*Date of Commission as Deputy Paymaster late Pay Sub Department, Control Department.

Army Pay Department.

COMMISSIONED RANK.	PAYMASTERS—continued (with the Hon. rank of Major).	FIRST COMMISSION.	PAYMASTER.	HON. MAJOR.	REGIMENT OR STATION.
Capt. S. Lanc. Regt.	Hood, Thomas Cockburn[11]	17 Nov. 63	8 June 81	8 June 86	
Capt. W. York. Regt.	Robinson, Thomas Middleton	8 Feb. 68	11 Aug. 81	11 Aug. 91	Cavalry Depot.
Capt. N. Staffordshire Regiment	Robinson, Philip Albert[118]	17 Nov. 63	16 Aug. 81	16 Aug. 91	Portsmouth.
Capt. W. Kent Regt.	Yaldwyn, Percy J. Montgomerie	11 Dec. 72	23 Aug. 81	23 Aug. 91	Athlone.
Capt. Scottish Rifles	Bennett, Levett Holt[119]	12 Jan. 66	15 Sept. 81	15 Sept. 91	Aldershot.
	Hamley, Francis Gilbert	22 Sept. 73	22 Sept. 81	22 Sept. 91	Bermuda.
Capt. Munster Fus.	Maycock, Francis Mollowes	22 July 68	4 Nov. 81	4 Nov. 91	Clonmel.
Captain 13 Hussars	Lane, Henry Frederick[122]	3 Sept. 70	9 Nov. 81	9 Nov. 91	Portsmouth.
Capt. Argyll High.	Dolby, Seym. Sackville Carow[123]	24 July 73	14 Nov. 81	14 Nov. 91	Shoeburyness.
Capt. Dublin Fus.	Wynne, Skeffington John[124]	4 Feb. 69	20 Dec. 81	20 Dec. 91	Dublin.
Capt. Dublin Fus.	Dick, James Roy[128]	23 Jan. 69	6 Apr. 82	6 Apr. 92	Portsmouth.
Capt. Dublin Fus.	Burnett, William Augustus[130]	5 June 66	11 Apr. 82	11 Apr. 92	Devonport.
Capt. Cheshire Regt.	White, Loftus Otway	30 Sept. 68	16 May 82	16 May 92	Curragh.
Capt. 3 Hussars	Fuller, George Charles	2 Nov. 73	19 May 82	19 May 92	Belfast.
Capt. Connaught Rangers	Burke, William Henry	8 July 68	1 June 82	1 June 92	Warrington.
Capt. King's Own Borderers	M'Causland, John Kennedy[131]	28 Dec. 66	11 Sept. 82	11 Sept. 92	Cork.
Capt. Leinster Regt.	Denys, Wm. Henry Adolphus[132]	26 Apr. 64	30 Nov. 82	30 Nov. 92	Seaforth Highlanders (78 F.).
Capt. 6 Dragoons	Sandes, Chas.[135] (Riding Master, 6 Sept. 73)	24 Nov. 77	26 Feb. 83	26 Feb. 93	Aldershot.
	Wellesley, Gerald Valerian	9 July 75	9 July 83	9 July 93	Aldershot.
	Gaussen, John Samuel	11 Feb. 75	10 July 83	10 July 93	Belfast.
Capt. Liverpool Regt.	Johnston, Robert	6 Dec. 73	10 Aug. 83	10 July 93	Highland Light Inf. (74 F.).
Capt. Warwick Regt.	Harward, Henry Blake	14 July 67	12 Nov. 83	12 Nov. 93	Dover.
Captain Royal Fus.	Thackwell, Edw. Loftus Roche	9 Aug. 73	16 Nov. 83	16 Nov. 93	Cyprus.
Major h.p. Shropshire Lt. Inf.	Smythe, Ingoldsby Wm. Thos. Somerset[142]	2 May 67	11 Feb. 84	11 Feb. 94	Woolwich.
	Beardmore, Charles F. H.[140]	28 Sept. 77	1 Apr. 84	1 Apr. 94	Sierra Leone.
Capt. York Regt.	Simonet, John Francis	21 Feb. 70	16 May 84	16 May 94	Winchester.
Capt. York Regt.	Herapath, Edwin Loud	13 Nov. 76	24 May 84	24 May 94	Portsmouth.
Major h.p. 7 Dr. Gds.	Becher, Cecil Leycester[146]	17 Sept. 66	18 July 84	18 July 94	Dover.
Major h.p. Leicester Regiment	Brook, Matthew William	21 July 64	9 Aug. 84	9 Aug. 94	Devonport.
Capt. Argyll Hldrs.	Collings, Godfrey Disney[152]	28 Feb. 76	13 Aug. 84	13 Aug. 94	London.
Capt. W. I. Regt.	Thwaytes, Henry James	12 Aug. 75	6 Sept. 84	6 Sept. 94	London.
Capt. S. Wales Bord.	Moore, George Kenrick[154]	5 Sept. 77	3 Oct. 84	3 Oct. 94	Hong Kong.
Capt. Scottish Rifles	Low, Peter[155]	27 Mar. 73	20 Oct. 84	20 Oct. 94	London Recruiting Depot.
Capt. W. I. Regt.	Minchin, William Cyril	12 May 76	20 Oct. 84	20 Oct. 94	Belfast.
Capt. Scots Fus.	Duckett, William Morton[156]	24 Sept. 71	18 Nov. 84	18 Nov. 94	Dublin.
Capt. Gloucestershire Regt.	Trotman, William Mends Forte	13 June 68	17 Jan. 85	17 Jan. 95	Halifax, N.S.
Captain Scottish Rifles	Sheehan, Patrick Edmond Campbell[157]	5 June 76	23 Feb. 85	23 Feb. 95	Chatham.
Capt. Scots Fusiliers	Crozier, Burrard Rawson	12 Dec. 68	2 Mar. 85	2 Mar. 95	Gibraltar.

(With the Hon. rank of Captain).

COMMISSIONED RANK.	PAYMASTERS	FIRST COMMISSION.	PAYMASTER.	HON. CAPTAIN.	REGIMENT OR STATION.
Capt. York & Lancaster Regt.	Lowry, James[163]	8 Dec. 77	26 Mar. 85		Ceylon.
Capt. Manchester Regiment	Utermarck, Reginald John G.[164]	24 June 76	28 Apr. 85		London.
Capt. York & Lancaster Regt.	Nugée, Andrew Richards	28 Oct. 77	1 May 85		York.
Capt. Norfolk Regt.	Eyre, Hastings Augustus	29 Sept. 77	13 May 85		Cardiff.
Capt. Dublin Fus.	Swire, Henry	1 May 78	4 July 85		Woolwich.
Capt. York & Lancaster Regt.	Ditmas, Leonard Philip	28 Oct. 77	29 Aug. 85		Colchester.
Capt. Munster Fus.	Liptrott, John[166]	18 Dec. 66	7 Sept. 85		Discharge Depot, Gosport.
Captain Durham Lt. Infantry	Maunsell, John Drought	25 May 78	28 Sept. 85		Netley Hospital.
Captain Duke of Cornwall's Lt. In.	Carden, Henry Westenra[170]	21 Sept. 74	17 Nov. 85		
Capt. Sussex Regt.	Duberly, George	10 Sept. 76	28 Nov. 85		Colchester.
Captain S. Wales Borderers	Worlledge, Alfred Cranworth[172]	29 June 78	28 June 86		York.
Captain S. Wales Borderers	Burnett, Joseph John[173]	9 July 79	9 July 86		Jamaica.
Capt. Suffolk Regt.	Lindop, Alfred Henry[158]	2 Feb. 78	1 Sept. 86		Mauritius.
Capt. Cheshire Regt.	Stubbs, Arthur Geo. Bushby[176]	10 Sept. 75	12 Oct. 86		Shorncliffe.
Major East Lancashire Regt.	Medhurst, Charles Frederick Hastings[177]	12 Feb. 76	14 Mar. 90		Gibraltar.
Major Irish Regt.	Morgan, Wm. John Fortescue[178]	12 Nov. 73	16 May 91		Singapore.
Captain Lancaster Regiment	Vigors, Thomas Mercer	11 May 78	19 May 91		Malta.
Major Middx. Regt.	Longe, Robert Douglas[179]	11 Sept. 76	25 May 91		Halifax, N.S.
Capt Wiltshire Regt.	Winter, Bertram Everard	30 Jan. 78	16 July 91		Barbadoes.
Major Middx. Regt.	Graham, Richard Woodroofe[179]	21 Jan. 74	10 Aug. 91		Hounslow.
Capt. E. Lanc. Regt.	Bray, Claude Arthur[177]	11 May 78	25 Aug. 91		York.
Capt. Innis. Fus.	Woollett, William Charles	21 June 79	26 Sept. 91		Woolwich.
Capt. W. Rdng. Regt.	Molyneux, Geo. Philip Berkeley	8 Dec. 77	28 Sept. 91		Hounslow.
Capt. E. York Regt.	Stacpole, Henry Dowsley[180]	9 Sept. 82	1 Oct. 91		Cape Town.
Major Gloucestershire Regiment	Lodwick, Robert Wm. Peter	9 Aug. 73	12 Oct. 91		Dublin.
Capt. E. York Regt.	Hill, Frederick William	14 May 84	4 Nov. 91		Dublin.
Capt. N. Staff. Regt.	Newland, Edmund Walcott[181]	30 Jan. 78	1 Dec. 91		Pietermaritzburg.
Major Dragoon Gds.	Goold-Adams, Wm. Richard[182]	1 May 78	8 Dec. 91		Cork.
Capt. Worcstr. Regt.	Smith, Annesley George	23 Oct. 80	10 Mar. 92		Egypt.

Army Pay Department.

COMMISSIONED RANK.	PAYMASTERS—continued (with the Hon. rank of Captain).	FIRST COMMISSION.	PAYMASTER A. P. D.	REGIMENT OR STATION.
Capt. K. O. Scot. Borderers	Magee, Augustus Holier	27 Jan. 83	3 May 92	Edinburgh.
Captain Northampton Regt.	Carter, John Thomas	20 May 85	3 July 92	Hong Kong.
Captain N. Stafford Regt.	Smith, George Barton	6 Feb. 84	1 Sept.92	Newcastle-on-Tyne.
Major 18 Hussars	Patten, George Robert Brown	22 Oct. 81	12 Nov. 92	Colchester.
Captain Wilts Regiment	Eicke, Ernest Campbell	23 Apr. 81	5 Jan. 93	Aldershot.
Captain W. York Regiment	Salmonson, H. B. S. Critchley	1 July 79	16 Jan. 93	Cork.
Captain E. Lancashire Regt.	Inglis, Albert Gordon	10 May 82	1 Mar. 93	Devonport.
Captain York Lt. Infantry	Dorling, Lionel	13 Aug. 79	27 Mar. 93	Chester.
Captain Irish Rifles	Edwards, Thomas	10 May 82	1 Apr. 93	Egypt.
Captain 7 Dragoon Guards	Smerdon, Frederick Geo. Bick	9 June 85	4 Apr. 93	Canterbury.
Captain 3 Dragoon Guards	Triggs, Walter[184]	27 Mar. 86	5 Apr. 93	Ashton-under-Lyne.
Captain N. Stafford Regt.	Dyson, Percy Shakespeare	13 Aug. 79	31 Aug. 93	Winchester.
Captain Leicester Regiment	Vowell, Richard Augustus	11 Aug. 80	8 Oct. 93	Curragh.
Lieut. Manchester Regiment	Maclure, John Edward Stanley	3 May 90	15 Jan. 94	Hamilton.
Captain N. Stafford Regt.	Trevelyan, WilloughbyFenwick	22 Jan. 79	30 Jan. 94	Dublin.
Major 1 Dragoon Guards	Benbow, John Edward	22 Jan. 81	8 May 94	Dover.
Captain Bedford Regiment	Pereira, Arthur Frederick	12 Nov. 84	9 May 94	Devonport.
	On Probation.			
Captain West India Regiment	Westmorland, Percy Thuillier[185]	9 Sept. 82	12 May 94	Aldershot.
Captain Warwick Regiment	Bird, Geo. Edw. Godfrey W.	1 May 78	11 Sept.94	Devonport.
Lieut. h.p. Munster Fusiliers	Samuel, Henri Saul	10 Mar. 86	29 Sept.94	Portsmouth.
Captain 6 Dragoons	Jennings-Bramly, Guy L.[186]	31 Oct. 83	13 Oct. 94	Chatham.
Captain York & Lanc. Regt.	Money, Edmund Chas. Kyrle	9 July 79	16 Oct. 94	Cork.
Captain Essex Regiment	Benson, Wm. Geo. Sackville[187]	10 May 82	10 Nov. 94	Belfast.
Captain Middlesex Regt.	Harvest, Edmund Douglas[179]	10 May 82	21 Nov. 94	Birr.
Captain E. Lancashire Regt.	Lethbridge, Robert Thomas M.	30 Jan. 86	10 Dec. 94	York.
Lieut. 2 Dragoon Guards	O'Hara, James	30 Jan. 86	20 Jan. 95	Woolwich.
Major 15 Hussars	Leigh, *Hon.* Rupert[188]	11 Feb. 76	19 Feb. 95	Aldershot.

Uniform, Blue. *Facings*, Yellow Velvet.
Agents for Payment of Officers of Army Pay Department at Home Stations—Messrs. Cox & Co.

FORMER COMMISSION.	PAYMASTER serving under former Royal Warrants (with the hon. rank of Major).	FIRST COMMISSION.	PAYMASTER.	RANK OF MAJOR.	REGIMENT OR STATION.
Lt. 5 Beng.Eur.Reg.	Buttanshaw, William Henry		23 June 63	23 June 78	Aldershot.

[1] Colonel Drage served in the Zulu war in 1879 (Medal with Clasp). Served with the Nile Expedition in 1884-85 (mentioned in despatches, promoted Chief Paymaster, Medal with Clasp, and Khedive's Star).
[11] Colonels Chauncey and Whittington, Majors Ternan and Hood served in the Egyptian war of 1882 (Medal, and Khedive's Star).
[14] Lt.Colonel Potter served in the New Zealand war in 1863-66 (Medal). Served in the Ashanti war under Sir Garnet Wolseley (promoted Paymaster, Medal).
[17] Lt.Colonel F. O. Sargeant-Openshaw served in the Hazara campaign in 1868 including the operations against the tribes on the Black Mountain (Medal with Clasp).
[21] Lt.Colonel C. W. J. Taylor served in the Boer war in 1881.
[23] Lt.Colonel H. C. Ryder served in Natal during the Zulu war in 1879 (Medal).
[30] Colonel Roberts served as a Captain in the 4th Regiment throughout the Abyssinian campaign, and was dangerously wounded—gun-shot wound of left elbow-joint—at Arogee, in which action he commanded two Companies of the 4th King's Own, being the Baggage Guard (mentioned in despatches, Medal). Served in the Afghan war of 1878-80, and was present at the attack and capture of Ali Musjid (Medal with Clasp).
[31] Lt.Colonel Hignett served with the 81st Regiment in the Afghan war in 1878-79, and was present at the capture of Ali Musjid (Medal with Clasp).
[33] Colonel E. H. Gorges served in the Kafir war in 1877-78, including the operations against the Galekas and Gaikas; also served in the Zulu war in 1879 (Medal with Clasp).
[37] Lt.Colonel W. R. Kaye served in the Kafir war in 1877-78 (Medal).
[38] Lt.Colonel Elliott Raymond served in the Crimea with the 44th Foot subsequent to the fall of Sebastopol from the 9th September 1855 to the end of June 1856. Served in the Boer war of 1881 with the Natal Field Force as a Paymaster.
[42] Lt.Colonel Spiller commanded a Company of the 65th Regiment during the war of 1863-65 in New Zealand, and was present at the aattck on the working party at Williamson's Clearing, relief of Pokeno Piquet (mentioned in despatches), storming and capture of Pah at Rangiawhia, actions at Rangiani and Huirini, and attack and capture of Pah at Orakau (Medal). Served with the 19th Hussars in the Egyptian war of 1882 (Medal, and Khedive's Star).
[43] Colonel Barr served with the 53rd Regiment in the Indian campaign of 1858-59, including the occupation of the Goomtee and occupation of Sultanpore, passage of the Gogra at Fyzabad on 25th November, action of Toolseepore, and minor affairs (Medal). Served in the Afghan war in 1879-80, and took part in the march to Candahar with the force under Major General Phayre (Medal).
[44] Colonel J. L. Hewson served in the Afghan war of 1878-80 (Medal).
[46] Lt.Colonel W. Bell served with the Bombay Column of the Goa Field Force against the Dessai rebels from Feb. to June 1858, including several skirmishes (Medal). Served with the 1st Battalion Scots Guards in the Egyptian war of 1882 (Medal, and Khedive's Star).
[48] Lt.Colonel Bateman was attached to the Royal Artillery during the operations against the Taepings in the vicinity of Shanghai from April to Oct. 1862, resulting in the taking of the stockade at Nanhsiang, capture by escalade of the walled cities of Khadin, Tsinpoo, and Tsolin, the fortified town of Najow, affair at Nanhsiang, and second capture of Khadin. Also served as Assistant Engineer on the survey of the 30 mile circuit round Shanghai, under Lt.Colonel C. G. Gordon, from 27th Dec. 1862 to 2nd Feb. 1863. Served throughout the Egyptian war of 1882 in the Treasury Chest Office (Medal, and Khedive's Star).
[49] Colonel Richmond accompanied Sir Garnet Wolseley to the Gold Coast in September 1873 on special service, and served throughout the Ashanti war of 1873-74. Commanded the advanced guard of Houssas at the action of Essaman, and a company of Wood's Regiment at the reconnaissance in force of the 27th November (twice mentioned in despatches, promoted to an Unattached Company, Medal with Clasp).

Army Pay Department.—War Services.

⁵² Lt.Colonel Wade served with the 26th Cameronians in the Abyssinian campaign in 1868 (Medal).
⁵⁴ Lt.Colonel Brockman served in the Royal Navy in the Baltic during the Russian war in 1854-55 (Medal). Served in the Zulu war in 1879 (Medal).
⁵⁵ Lt.Colonel Coote served with the 8th Hussars in the Afghan war of 1879-80 (Medal).
⁵⁶ Lt.Colonel W. H. Mortimer served in the Egyptian war of 1882, and was present at the battle of Tel-el-Kebir (Medal with Clasp, and Khedive's Star).
⁵⁸ Lt.Colonel Gelston served in the Zulu war in 1879, and was present in the engagement at Inyezane and in Ekowe during the investment (Medal with Clasp). Served with the Egyptian Frontier Field Force in 1885-86.
⁵⁹ Lt.Colonel T. Bell served with the 14th Regiment in the Crimea subsequent to the fall of Sebastopol, from the 12th September 1855 to the 30th May 1856. Served in the 1st West India Regiment in the Ashanti war in 1873-74 (Medal with Clasp).
⁶⁰ Lt.Colonel Longley served with the 43rd Light Infantry in the New Zealand war of 1864-66, was present at the actions of Maketu and Te Ranga, and served with the expeditions in the province of Taranaki (mentioned in despatches, Medal). Served with the 85th Light Infantry in the Afghan war in 1879-80 with the Koorum Division, including the Zaimusht Expedition (Medal).
⁶¹ Lt.Colonels Stockley, Phillips, and Coppinger served in the Zulu war in 1879 (Medal).
⁶³ Lt.Colonel Fox served with the 1st Battalion Berkshire Regiment throughout the Egyptian war of 1882, and was present at the surrender of Kafr Dowar (Medal, and Khedive's Star). Served throughout the campaign in the Eastern Soudan in 1885 as Paymaster to the 1st Battalion of the Berkshire Regiment (Clasp).
⁶⁵ Lt.Colonel Burge served as Aide de Camp to Colonel Graham at the assault and capture of Canton on the 29th Dec. 1857; accompanied the Force to the Peiho in June; was also present at the assault and capture of Namtow on 11th Aug. 1858 (Medal with Clasp).
⁶⁸ Lt.Colonel Healy and Major Churchill served in the Boer war of 1881 with the Natal Field Force.
⁷⁰ Lt.Colonel A. P. G. Dowdall served with the 1st Battalion Royal Sussex Regiment in the Egyptian war of 1882 (Medal, and Khedive's Star). Served throughout the Nile Expedition in 1884-85 attached to the 1st Battalion of the Royal Sussex Regiment (mentioned in despatches, promoted Staff Paymaster, Clasp).
⁷¹ Lt.Colonel Langford served in the Hazara campaign in 1868, including the expedition against the tribes of the Black Mountain (Medal with Clasp).
⁷² Lt.Colonel Barnes served with the Bechuanaland Expedition under Sir Charles Warren in 1884-85.
⁷³ Lt.Colonel Dougherty served with the 26th Cameronians in the Abyssinian war in 1868 (Medal). Served with the 2nd Battalion York and Lancaster Regiment in the Egyptian war of 1882 (Medal, and Khedive's Star).
⁷⁵ Lt.Colonel Booth served with the 10th Regiment in the Perak Expedition in 1875. Commanded the force in the assault on the Malay Stockade of Passir Sala, and was severely wounded (Medal with Clasp). Served in the Egyptian war of 1882 (Medal, and Khedive's Star).
⁷⁶ Lt.Colonel Caulfeild Stoker served in the Ashanti war in 1873-74, including the repulse of the Ashanti army at Abrakrampa during the 5th and 6th November 1873 (Medal).
⁷⁷ Lt.Colonel Furlong was appointed to the Purveyor's Department of the Expedition which proceeded to the East in March 1854, and served in Turkey, Bulgaria, and the Crimea until April 1855, when he was Gazetted to the 21st Fusiliers, and served with the Regiment before Sebastopol until ordered to the Depôt on the 31st May 1855 (Medal with Clasp, and Turkish Medal).
⁷⁹ Lt.Colonel A. Brett served in the Soudan Expedition under Sir Gerald Graham in 1884 with the 10th Hussars (Medal, and Khedive's Star).
⁸¹ Lt.Colonel Caine served on the North-West Frontier during the Indian Mutiny in 1857-59 (Medal).
⁸² Major Shields served in the Afghan war in 1879-80 (Medal).
⁸³ Majors Webster and Robinson served with the Nile Expedition in 1884-85 (Medal with Clasp, and Khedive's Star).
⁸⁴ Major H. C. Dawson served in the Zulu war of 1879 (promoted Paymaster, Medal with Clasp).
⁸⁵ Major Ward served in the Ashanti war of 1873-4, including the defence of Fommanah (Medal with Clasp).
⁸⁶ Major D'Aguilar served in the Boer war of 1881 as Paymaster with the Advanced Force. Also served with the Bechuanaland Expedition under Sir Charles Warren in 1884-85 (mentioned in despatches); and in the operations in Zululand in 1888.
⁸⁹ Major Bromfield served in New Zealand during General Chute's campaign of 1866 (Medal).
⁹⁰ Major Orange served with the 3rd Battalion King's Royal Rifle Corps in the Egyptian war of 1882 (Medal, and Khedive's Star).
⁹² Major F. C. Webb commanded the Ladder Party at the assault of Beyt on 6th October, and served with the Okamundel Field Force in the operations before Dwarka till 11th Nov. 1859.
⁹⁴ Majors Nott and Lysaght served in the Soudan campaign in 1885 (Medal with Clasp, and Khedive's Star).
⁹⁵ Major Lloyd served with the 2nd Battalion 60th Rifles in the Afghan war of 1878-80, and took part in the advance on and occupation of Candahar and Khelat-i-Ghilzie; accompanied Sir Frederick Roberts in the march to Candahar, and was present at the battle of Candahar (Medal with Clasp, and Bronze Decoration). Served in the Boer war of 1881 with the Natal Field Force. Served during the Nile Expedition in 1884-85 with the 1st Battalion Yorkshire Regiment on the Line of Communications up the Nile. Also served with the Egyptian Frontier Field Force in 1885-86 (Medal, and Khedive's Star).
⁹⁸ Major Howard served with the 80th Regiment in the left attack during the Bhootan Expedition of 1865 (Medal). Served also in the Perak Expedition in 1875-76 (Clasp). Served throughout the operations against Sekukuni in 1878, the Zulu war of 1879, and the operations against Sekukuni in 1879, and was present at the storming of the stronghold (Brevet of Major, Medal with Clasp).
⁹⁹ Major Fleury served in the New Zealand war of 1863-65, and was present at the repulse of the enemy's attack on the Camp at Nukumaru (Medal).
¹⁰⁰ Major Dempster.—See Civil Decorations for Gallantry, "Hart's Annual Army List," p. 786.
¹⁰³ Major Palmer served in India during the mutiny of 1857-58 (Medal).
¹⁰⁴ Major Croft served in the Baltic as a midshipman during the Russian war of 1854-55 (Medal).
¹⁰⁵ Major Humfrey served with the 19th Regiment in the Hazara campaign in 1868, including the expedition against the tribes in the Black Mountain (Medal with Clasp). Served in the Jowaki campaign of 1877-78 (Clasp) Served in the Afghan war of 1878-80 in charge of the Field Treasure Chest and as Provost Marshal (Medal).
¹⁰⁶ Major Singer served with the 2nd Battalion Manchester Regiment throughout the Egyptian war of 1882 (Medal, and Khedive's Star).
¹⁰⁷ Major Dewar served in the Zulu war of 1879, first with the 57th Regiment, being present at the action of Gingindhlovu and relief of Ekowe, afterwards as Commandant of Fort Tenedos, and finally as Staff Officer at Fort Pearson (Medal with Clasp). Served with the Egyptian Frontier Field Force in 1885-86 (Medal, and Khedive's Star).
¹⁰⁸ Major J. Reid served with the Nile Expedition in 1884-85 as Paymaster.
¹⁰⁹ Major J. O'B. Drury served with the Jowaki Afreedee Expedition in 1877 (Medal with Clasp). Served in the Afghan war in 1878-79, and was present at the attack and capture of Ali Musjid (Medal with Clasp). Served with the Bechuanaland Expedition under Sir Charles Warren in 1884-85.
¹¹⁰ Major E. R. Reid served with the Bechuanaland Expedition under Sir Charles Warren in 1884-85 as District Paymaster of the force.
¹¹² Major Angus, while a Lieutenant in the 7th Royal Fusiliers, served in the Afghan war in 1878-79 as Staff Officer of Transport (Medal).
¹¹³ Major Mackie served in the Abyssinian campaign with the Transport Corps (Medal). Served in the Afghan war of 1878-79 in the Candahar Column as Staff Officer of Transport at Sukkur (Medal). Served in the Nile Expedition in 1884-85 throughout the operations of the River Column under Major General Earle and was present at the action of Kirbekan (mentioned in despatches, Medal with two Clasps, and Khedive's Star).
¹¹⁴ Major Rathborne served with the Bechuanaland Expedition under Sir Charles Warren in 1884-85.
¹¹⁵ Major Small served with the 20th Regiment in the Indian campaign in 1857-58, including the actions at Chanda, Umeerpore, Sultanpore, siege and capture of Lucknow, and affairs of Churda and Fort of Musjeedia (Medal with Clasp). Served with the 59th Regiment throughout the Afghan war of 1878-80, and took part in the advance on and occupation of Candahar and Khelat-i-Ghilzie under Sir Donald Stewart, and in the operations in

Army Pay Department.—War Services.

the Logar Valley; was present in the engagements at Ahmed Kheyl and Urzoo near Ghuznee; accompanied Sir Frederick Roberts in the march to Candahar, and was present at the battle of Candahar in charge of the field treasure chest (mentioned in despatches, Brevet of Major, Medal with two Clasps, and Bronze Decoration). Served in the operations near Suakin in December 1888 including the engagement at Gemaizah (Medal with Clasp, and Khedive's Star).

116 Major H. C. Cowell served with the Bechuanaland Expedition under Sir Charles Warren in 1884-85.

117 Major E. A. H. Webb served with the 1st Battalion 17th Regiment in the Afghan war in 1878-79 with the Peshawur Valley Field Force, and was present at the attack and capture of Ali Musjid and with the second expedition into the Bazar Valley and in the action at Cabul River (Medal with Clasp).

118 Major P. A. Robinson served in the Egyptian war of 1882 with the 2nd Battalion of the Royal Irish Regiment (Medal, and Khedive's Star). Served with the Hazara Expedition in 1888 (Medal with Clasp).

119 Major Bennett served with the 24th Regiment throughout the Zulu war of 1879, and was present in the engagement at Ulundi (Medal with Clasp).

122 Major Lane served with the 4th Dragoon Guards in the Egyptian war of 1882, and was present in the engagement at Kassasin on the 9th September (Medal, and Khedive's Star). Served in the Soudan campaign in 1885 (Clasp), and in the operations of the Egyptian Frontier Field Force in 1885-86.

123 Major Dolby served in the Soudan campaign in 1885 (Medal with Clasp, and Khedive's Star); also served with the Soudan Frontier Field Force in 1885-86.

124 Major S. J. Wynne served in the expedition to the Soudan in 1885 with the 2nd Battalion of the Scots Guards (Medal with Clasp, and Khedive's Star).

128 Major Dick served in the Zulu war and in the operations against Sekukuni in 1879 (Medal with Clasp). Served in the Hazara campaign in 1888 with the 2nd Battalion Royal Sussex Regiment (Medal with Clasp).

130 Major Burnett served in the Hazara campaign in 1868, including the expedition against the tribes on the Black Mountain (Medal with Clasp).

131 Major M'Causland served with the 25th King's Own Borderers in the Afghan war of 1878-80, first with the Peshawur Valley Field Force under Lieut.General Maude, and afterwards with the Khyber Line Force under Lieut.General Bright (Medal).

132 Major Denys served in the Hazara Expedition in 1888 as Paymaster with the 2nd Battalion Seaforth Highlanders (Medal with Clasp). Also served in the Hazara Expedition in 1891 as Paymaster with the 2nd Battalion Seaforth Highlanders (Clasp).

135 Major Sandes served in the Afghan war in 1878-79, and was present at the attack and capture of Ali Musjid and in the engagement at Futtehabad (Medal with Clasp).

140 Major C. F. H. Beardmore served in the Ashanti, war of 1873-4, including the action of Essaman and battle of Amoaful (mentioned in despatches, Medal with Clasp). [See also Civil Decorations for Gallantry, " Hart's Annual Army List," p. 786.]

142 Major Smythe served in the Afghan war in 1879-80 with the Koorum Division, including the Zaimusht Expedition (Medal).

146 Major Becher served in the Egyptian war of 1882 as Captain with the 7th Dragoon Guards, and was present in the engagements at El Magfar and Mahsama, at the action at Kassasin on the 9th September, and at the battle of Tel-el-Kebir and the capture of Cairo (Medal with Clasp, and Khedive's Star).

152 Major Collings served with the 91st Highlanders in the Zulu war of 1879, and was present in the action of Gingindhlovu and relief of Ekowe (Medal with Clasp).

154 Major Moore served in the Zulu war of 1879 (Medal with Clasp).

155 Major Low served in the Afghan war of 1879-80 (Medal).

156 Major Duckett served in the Zulu war of 1879 with the 21st Fusiliers (Medal with Clasp).

157 Major Sheehan served with the 90th Light Infantry in the Zulu war of 1879, and was present in the engagements at Zungin Nek and Kambula (Medal with Clasp). Served in the Afghan war in 1879-80 with the Khyber Line Force (Medal).

158 Captain Lindop served with the 80th Regiment in the Transvaal in November and December 1878, in the Column under Colonel Rowlands on the Swazi border as Ordnance Officer in 1879, and during the invasion of Zululand, being present in the engagement at Ulundi (Medal with Clasp).

163 Captain Lowry served with the 2nd Battalion York and Lancaster Regiment throughout the Egyptian war of 1882, and was present in the engagements at El Magfar and Tel-el-Mahuta, in the two actions at Kassasin, and at the battle of Tel-el-Kebir (Medal with Clasp, and Khedive's Star).

164 Captain Utermarck served with the 2nd Battalion Manchester Regiment throughout the Egyptian war of 1882 (Medal, and Khedive's Star).

166 Captain Liptrott served in the Ashanti war in 1874 in the Transport Service (Medal). Served in the Zulu war in 1879 (Medal with Clasp). Served with the Burmese Expedition in 1887-89 (Medal with Clasp).

170 Captain Carden served with the 2nd Battalion of the Duke of Cornwall's Light Infantry throughout the Egyptian war of 1882, and was present in the engagements at El Magfar and Tel-el-Mahuta, in the two actions at Kassasin, and at the battle of Tel-el-Kebir (Medal with Clasp, and Khedive's Star). Served with the Nile Expedition in 1884-85 (Clasp). Served with the Burmese Expedition in 1888-89 (Medal with Clasp).

172 Captain Worllodge was employed in Natal during the Zulu war in 1879 (Medal).

173 Captain Burnett served in the Zulu war of 1879 with the 99th Foot, and was present in the engagements at Inyezane and Gingindhlovu and at the relief of Ekowe (Medal and Clasp).

176 Captain Stubbs served with the 63rd Regiment in Southern Afghanistan in 1879-80 (Medal). Served with the 1st Battalion Manchester Regiment in the Egyptian war of 1882 (Medal, and Khedive's Star).

177 Major Medhurst and Captain Bray.—For War Services, see East Lancashire Regiment.

178 Major Morgan.—For War Services, see Irish Regiment.

179 Majors Graham and Long, and Captain Harvest.—For War Services, see Middlesex Regiment.

180 Captain Stacpole.—For War Services, see East Yorkshire Regiment.

181 Captain Newland.—For War Services, see North Staffordshire Regiment.

182 Major Goold-Adams served with the King's Dragoon Guards in the Zulu war of 1879 (Medal with Clasp). Served with the Hazara Expedition in 1888 as Superintendant of Army Signalling (Medal with Clasp).

184 Captain Triggs.—For War Services, see 3 Dragoon Guards.

185 Captain Westmorland.—For War Services, see West India Regiment.

186 Captain Jennings-Bramly.—For War Services, see 6 Dragoons.

187 Captain Benson.—For War Services, see Essex Regiment.

188 Major the Hon. Rupert Leigh.—For War Services, see 15 Hussars.

Army Medical Staff.

(Office, No. 18, Victoria Street, Westminster.)

[For the explanation of the qualifications of the Medical Officers, see page iii.]

DIRECTOR GENERAL.

Mackinnon, *Surgeon Major General Sir* William Alexander,[1] *KCB. FRCS.Edin.* **[R]** *Honorary Surgeon to the Queen,* 1 Feb. 93; *Assistant Surgeon,* 18 Feb. 53; *Surgeon,* 28 Jan. 62; *Surgeon Major,* 14 Sept. 66; *Deputy Surgeon General,* 1 Apr. 74; *Surgeon General,* 26 May 80; *Director General,* 7 May 89. Head Quarters.

SURGEON MAJOR GENERALS.

Bradshaw, Alexander Frederick,[2] *CB. MRCP. MRCS. LSA. Assist.Surg.* 27 May 57; *Surg.* 17 May 71; *Surg.Maj.* 1 Mar. 73; *Brigade Surgeon,* 12 Mar. 82; *Surgeon Colonel,* 28 July 8C; *Surgeon Major General,* 10 Mar. 92. India.
Lewer, Robert,[5] *LRCP.Ed. MRCS. LSA. Assist.Surg.* 1 Aug. 57; *Surgeon,* 9 Sept. 71; *Surgeon Major,* 1 Mar. 73; *Brigade Surgeon,* 1 Apr. 82; *Surgeon Colonel,* 16 Oct. 86; *Surgeon Major General,* 10 Aug. 92. Gibraltar.
Paterson, Henry Foljambe, *MD. FRCS.Ed. Assist.Surg.* 19 Oct. 57; *Surgeon,* 15 Jan. 73; *Surgeon Major,* 1 Mar. 73; *Brigade Surgeon,* 23 Apr. 83; *Surgeon Colonel,* 13 June 88; *Surgeon Major General,* 1 Apr. 93. Aldershot.
Inkson, James,[7] *MD. LRCS.Ed. Assist.Surg.* 19 Oct. 57; *Surgeon,* 1 Mar. 73; *Surgeon Major,* 1 Apr. 73; *Brigade Surgeon,* 1 May 83; *Surgeon Colonel,* 4 Sept. 88; *Surgeon Major General,* 6 June 93. Malta.
Jameson, James,[8] *MD. LRCS.Ed. Assist.Surg.* 9 Nov. 57; *Surgeon,* 1 Mar. 73; *Surgeon Major,* 1 Apr. 73; *Brigade Surgeon,* 2 May 83; *Surgeon Colonel,* 14 Sept. 88; *Surgeon Major General,* 6 July 93. Head Quarters.
Warren, John,[9] *MRCS. Assist.Surg.* 9 Nov. 57; *Surgeon,* 1 Mar. 73; *Surgeon Major,* 1 Apr. 73; *Brigade Surgeon,* 1 June 83; *Surgeon Colonel,* 24 Oct. 88; *Surgeon Major General,* 1 Aug. 93. Bombay (Poona).
Davis, James,[13] *LRCSI. LAH.Dub., Assist.Surg.* 10 Mar. 58; *Surgeon,* 1 Mar. 73; *Surgeon Major,* 1 Apr. 73; *Brigade Surgeon,* 29 Oct. 83; *Surgeon Colonel,* 19 Dec. 88; *Surgeon Major General,* 11 Jan. 94. Portsmouth.
Giraud, Charles Hervé,[15] *MRCS., Assist.Surg.* 10 Mar. 38; *Surgeon,* 1 Mar. 73; *Surgeon Major,* 1 Apr. 73; *Brigade Surgeon,* 2 Apr. 84; *Surgeon Colonel,* 7 May 89; *Surgeon Major General,* 24 Jan. 94. Netley.
Colahan, John, *MD. MRCS. Assist.Surg.* 25 May 58; *Surgeon,* 1 Mar. 73; *Surgeon Major,* 1 Apr. 73; *Brigade Surgeon,* 16 July 34; *Surgeon Colonel,* 16 Oct. 89; *Surgeon Major General,* 14 April 94. Dublin.
Walsh, Thomas,[20] *LRCSI. Principal Medical Officer, Madras; Assist.Surg.* 25 May 58; *Surgeon,* 1 Mar. 73; *Surgeon Major,* 1 Apr. 73; *Brigade Surgeon,* 16 July 84; *Surgeon Colonel,* 28 Oct. 89; *Surgeon Major General,* 18 July 94. Madras.

SURGEON COLONELS.	ASSISTANT SURGEON.	SURGEON.	SURGEON MAJOR.	BRIGADE SURGEON.	SURGEON COLONEL.	WHERE STATIONED.
Archer, Samuel,[23] *MRCS.*	5 Aug. 58	1 Mar. 73	1 Apr. 73	16 Oct. 84	23 Nov. 89	Nova Scotia.
Markey, Edward Corrigan,[27] *CB. LRCPI. LRCSI.*	1 Mar. 59	1 Mar. 73	1 Apr. 74	18 Apr. 85	11 Sept. 90	
Graves, William, *LRCSI.*	22 Sept. 58	1 Mar. 73	1 Apr. 73	25 July 85	1 Aug. 91	Bengal (Meerut).
Hamilton, John Butler,[33] *MD. BA. MRCS.* (rank of Lt.Col. 19 Jan. 80)...	19 Jan. 60	1 Mar. 73	1 Apr. 75	27 Mar. 86	30 Nov. 91	Cape of Good Hope.
Gore, Albert Aug.[41] *MD. LRCPI. LRCSI.*	1 Oct. 60	2 Sept. 68	1 Mar. 73	18 Aug. 86	13 Jan. 92	Bombay (Mhow).
Maunsell, Thomas, *LRCPI. LRCSI.*	1 Oct. 60	1 Mar. 73	17 June 75	16 Oct. 86	10 Mar. 92	Bengal (Rawul Pindee).
Preston, Alexander Francis,[48] *BA. MB. LRCSI.*	30 Sept. 63	1 Mar. 73	28 Apr. 76	30 Nov. 86	28 Mar. 92	Hong Kong.
Welch, Fras. Hen.[50] *FRCS. LSA. A.G.M.* 73	1 Apr. 61	1 Mar. 73	10 Mar. 76	24 Feb. 87	5 Apr. 92	Devonport.
Ferguson, Richard Pat.[51] *LRCP.Ed. LRCS.Ed.*	31 Mar. 62	1 Mar. 73	28 Apr. 76	13 Apr. 87	6 Sept. 92	Bengal (Umballa).
Churchill, Alexander Ferrier,[52] *BA. MB. LRCSI.*	31 Mar. 62	1 Mar. 73	28 Apr. 76	21 June 87	27 Oct. 92	Woolwich.
Maunsell, Charles Albert,[55] *MD. LRCSI.*	1 Oct. 62	1 Mar. 73	28 Apr. 76	31 Dec. 87	15 Dec. 92	Cork.
Scott, Frederick Beaufort,[57] *CMG. MD. MCh. MRCS.*	1 Oct. 62	1 Mar. 7	28 Apr. 76	23 Jan. 88	25 Dec. 92	Bengal (Quetta).
O'Dwyer, Thos. Francis,[59] *MD. LRCS.*	30 Sept. 64	1 Mar. 73	30 Sept. 76	1 Feb. 88	6 Feb. 93	Dover.
Nash, William,[65] *MD. MRCS.*	14 Apr. 63	1 Mar. 73	1 Apr. 76	2 May 88	1 Apr. 93	Egypt.
Martin, Wm. Thos.[66] *MA. MD. LRCSI.*	14 Apr. 63	1 Mar. 73	28 Apr. 76	5 May 88	6 June 93	Bengal (Lucknow).
Cuffe, Charles MacDonogh,[67] *CB. LRCP.Ed. LRCS.Ed. LAH.Dub.*	30 Sept. 63	1 Mar. 73	28 Apr. 76	1 Sept. 88	6 July 93	Bengal (Allahabad).
Atkins, Charles Alfred,[68] *LRCP. MRCS.*	30 Sept. 63	1 Mar. 73	28 Apr. 76	12 Sept. 88	1 Aug. 93	Bombay (Poona).
Muir, Henry Skey.[81] *MD. MRCS.*	31 Mar. 64	1 Mar. 73	28 Apr. 76	1 Nov. 88	23 Dec. 93	Chester.
Maxham, John William, *MD. LRCS.Ed.*	31 Mar. 64	1 Mar. 73	28 Apr. 76	19 Dec. 88	11 Jan. 94	York.
Cogan, Michael,[82] *LRCPI. LRCSI.*	31 Mar. 64	1 Mar. 73	28 Apr. 76	29 Dec. 88	24 Jan. 94	Belfast.
Churchill, Charles Fleetwood, *MB. BA. Dub. LRCSI.*	31 Mar. 64	1 Mar. 73	28 Apr. 76	6 Feb. 89	14 Apr. 94	London.
Catherwood, William Alister,[88] *MD. LRCP.Ed. LRCS.Ed.*	2 Oct. 65	1 Mar. 73	2 Oct. 77	7 Apr. 89	21 Apr. 94	Colchester.
Wilson, William Deane,[89] *MB. LRCSI.*	1 Oct. 67	1 Mar. 73	1 Oct. 79	28 Oct. 89	18 July 94	Bangalore.
Price, Wm. Sparks Martin,[93] *LRCPI. LRCSI.*	30 Sept. 64	1 Mar. 73	30 Sept. 76	7 Nov. 89	27 Feb. 95	

BRIGADE SURGEON LT.COLONELS.	ASSISTANT SURGEON.	SURGEON.	SURGEON MAJOR.	RANK OF LT.COL.	BRIG.SURG LT.COL.	
Boileau, John Peter Hamilton, *BA. Dub. MD. FRCSI.*	30 Sept. 64	1 Mar. 73	30 Sept. 76	30 Sept. 84	23 Nov. 89	Bengal.
Taylor, William, *MD. MCh.*	30 Sept. 64	1 Mar. 73	30 Sept. 76	30 Sept. 84	5 Feb. 90	China.
Riordan, Wm. Edw.[98] *LRCPI. LRCSI.*	30 Sept. 64	1 Mar. 73	30 Sept. 76	30 Sept. 84	6 May 90	
Hughes, John Henry,[100] *MD. MRCS.*	30 Sept. 64	1 Mar. 73	30 Sept. 76	30 Sept. 84	6 June 90	Straits Settlements.
Grose, Daniel Chas.[102] *LRCP.Ed. LRCSI.*	30 Sept. 64	1 Mar. 73	30 Sept. 76	30 Sept. 84	20 Aug. 90	Belfast.
Maturin, John,[103] *LRCP.Ed. LRCSI.*	30 Sept. 64	1 Mar. 73	30 Sept. 76	30 Sept. 84	11 Sept. 90	Ceylon.
O'Farrell, Thomas,[106] *MD. LRCSI.*	31 Mar. 65	1 Mar. 73	1 Mar. 77	31 Mar. 85	10 Dec. 90	Egypt.
Andrew, George,[106] *MB. MCh.*	31 Mar. 65	1 Mar. 73	1 Mar. 77	31 Mar. 85	14 Feb. 91	Madras.
Carew, Richard Hugh,[110] *DSO. LRCP. Ed. LRCSI.*	31 Mar. 65	1 Mar. 73	1 Mar. 77	31 Mar. 85	1 Aug. 91	Colchester.
White, Charles, *MRCS. LSA.*	31 Mar. 65	1 Mar. 73	1 Mar. 77	31 Mar. 85	16 Sept. 91	Portsmouth.
Harrison, Charles Edward,[112] *MB. FRCS. LSA.* H.P. 75		30 Sept. 74	19 Aug. 85		4 Nov. 91	Brigade of Foot Gds.
Evatt, Geo.Jos. Hamilton,[122] *MD. LRCSI.*	31 Mar. 65	1 Mar. 73	31 Mar. 77	31 Mar. 85	30 Nov. 91	Netley.
M'Watters, Wm.[123] *LRCPI. LRCSI.*	2 Oct. 65	1 Mar. 73	2 Oct. 77	2 Oct. 85	27 Dec. 91	Portsmouth.
Mally, Robert Nelson,[125] *LRCSI.*	2 Oct. 65	1 Mar. 73	2 Oct. 77	2 Oct. 85	27 Dec. 91	Jamaica.
O'Brien, Hen. Joseph,[156] *BA. MB. MCh.*	2 Oct. 65	1 Mar. 73	2 Oct. 77	2 Oct. 85	14 Feb. 92	Barbadoes.
Kilroy, Philip Lefeuvre, *LRCP.Ed. LRCS.Ed.*	2 Oct. 65	1 Mar. 73	2 Oct. 77	2 Oct. 85	10 Mar. 92	Dublin.
Mackinnon, Henry Wm. Alex.[139] *DSO. MRCS. LSA.*	2 Oct. 65	1 Mar. 73	2 Oct. 77	2 Oct. 85	10 Mar. 92	Aldershot.
Notter, Jas.Lane, *BA. MD. MCh. LRCSI. MRCPI. Prof. of Mil. Hygiene, Netley*	31 Mar. 66	1 Mar. 73	31 Mar. 78	31 Mar. 86	28 Mar. 92	Netley.
Comerford, Henry,[140] *MD. MCh.*	31 Mar. 66	1 Mar. 73	31 Mar. 78	31 Mar. 86	5 Apr. 92	Bermuda.
Brown, Henry Thomas,[141] *MD. LRCSI. MRCPI.*	31 Mar. 66	1 Mar. 73	31 Mar. 78	31 Mar. 86	29 May 92	Bengal.

Army Medical Staff.

BRIGADE SURGEON LT.COLONELS.	ASSISTANT SURGEON.	SURGEON.	SURGEON MAJOR.	RANK OF LT.COL.	BRIG.SURG LT.COL.	REGIMENT, OR STATION.
Rooney, Jas. Patrick, *LRCPI. LRCSI*.	31 Mar. 66	1 Mar. 73	31 Mar. 78	31 Mar. 86	16 June 92	Gibraltar.
Stevenson, Wm. Flack, *MB. MCh. Prof. Army Medical School, Netley*	31 Mar. 66	1 Mar. 73	31 Mar. 78	31 Mar. 86	3 Aug. 92	Netley.
Eaton, Robt. Coleman,[156] *LRCPI.LRCSI*	31 Mar. 66	1 Mar. 73	31 Mar. 78	31 Mar. 86	6 Sept.92	Bengal.
Burnett, Wm. Fras.,[158] *LRCP. Ed. LRCSI*.	31 Mar. 66	1 Mar. 73	31 Mar. 78	31 Mar. 86	6 Oct. 92	Madras.
Williamson, James,[159] *MB. MCh.*	2 Oct. 66	1 Mar. 73	2 Oct. 78	2 Oct. 86	27 Oct. 92	Chatham.
Steele, William Henry,[160] *MD. BA. LRCSI.*	2 Oct. 66	1 Mar. 73	2 Oct. 78	2 Oct. 86	31 Oct. 92	Devonport.
Major, Napoleon Bisdee, *MRCS. LSA*.	2 Oct. 66	1 Mar. 73	2 Oct. 78	2 Oct. 86	14 Dec. 92	Aldershot.
D℃ Reynolds, Jas. Henry,[172] *MB. MCh.*	31 Mar. 68	1 Mar. 73	23 Jan. 79	1 Apr. 87	25 Dec. 92	Shorncliffe.
O'Reilly, Thomas,[173] *LRCPI. LRCSI.*	1 Apr. 67	1 Mar. 73	1 Apr. 79	1 Apr. 87	6 Feb. 93	Gosport.
Fairland, Edwin James,[174] *LRCP. Ed. MRCS. LSA.*	1 Apr. 67	1 Mar. 73	1 Apr. 79	1 Apr. 87	16 Feb. 93	Netley.
Townsend, Edmond,[175] *MD. MCh.*	1 Apr. 67	1 Mar. 73	1 Apr. 79	1 Apr. 87	1 Apr. 93	Cork.
Supple, James Francis,[176] *LRCPI. LRCSI.*	1 Apr. 67	1 Mar. 73	1 Apr. 79	1 Apr. 87	9 Apr. 93	Jersey.
Moore, Joseph Henry,[177] *LRCP. Ed. LRCS. Ed.*	1 Apr. 67	1 Mar. 73	1 Apr. 79	1 Apr. 87	26 Apr. 93	Bombay.
Holmes, Thomas James Paul, *MB. LRCSI.*	1 Apr. 67	1 Mar. 73	1 Apr. 79	1 Apr. 87	3 May 93	Dublin.
Corbett, Rbt. de la Cour,[178] *DSO. MD. MCh.*	1 Oct. 67	1 Mar. 73	1 Oct. 79	1 Oct. 87	3 June 93	Bengal.
Pollock, Chas. Frederick,[179] *BA. MB. MCh.*	1 Oct. 67	1 Mar. 73	1 Oct. 79	1 Oct. 87	6 June 93	Bengal.
M'Namara, Wm. Henry,[180] *MD. FRCSI.*	1 Oct. 67	1 Mar. 73	1 Oct. 79	1 Oct. 87	6 July 93	Aldershot.
Gallwey, Mathew Moriarty, *MD. MCh.*	1 Oct. 67	1 Mar. 73	1 Oct. 79	1 Oct. 87	1 Aug. 93	Bombay.
Lyons, Frederick,[156] *MD. MCh.*	1 Oct. 67	1 Mar. 73	1 Oct. 79	1 Oct. 87	4 Nov. 93	Malta.
Gunning, James Davis, *LRCP. Ed. LRCS. Ed.*	1 Oct. 67	1 Mar. 73	1 Oct. 79	1 Oct. 87	6 Dec. 93	Bengal.
Barry, John, *MD. LRCS. Ed.*	1 Oct. 67	1 Mar. 73	1 Oct. 79	1 Oct. 87	11 Jan. 94	Curragh.
Riddick, John,[181] *LRCPI. LRCSI*	1 Oct. 67	1 Mar. 73	1 Oct. 79	1 Oct. 87	24 Jan. 94	Bengal.
Anderson, Alex.,[195] *LRCP. Ed. LRCS. Ed.*	1 Oct. 67	1 Mar. 73	1 Oct. 79	1 Oct. 87	14 Apr. 94	Madras.
Fraser, James,[199] *MD. MCh.*	31 Mar. 68	1 Mar. 73	31 Mar. 80	31 Mar. 88	21 Apr. 94	Mauritius.
Knox, Maurice,[201] *LRCPI. LRCSI.*	31 Mar. 68	1 Mar. 73	31 Mar. 80	31 Mar. 88	2 May 94	Bengal.
Brown, Anthony Lennon,[204] *LRCPI. LRCSI.*	31 Mar. 68	1 Mar. 73	31 Mar. 80	31 Mar. 88	18 July 94	Madras.
Macrobin, Andrew Arthur,[205] *MB. MCh.*	31 Mar. 68	1 Mar. 73	31 Mar. 80	31 Mar. 88	23 Aug. 94	Bengal.
Duke, Alex.Wm. *MD. LRCSI. LAH.Dub.*	1 Oct. 68	1 Mar. 73	1 Oct. 80	1 Oct. 88	8 Sept.94	Canterbury.
Stannard, Henry, *LRCPI. LRCSI.*	1 Oct. 68	1 Mar. 73	1 Oct. 80	1 Oct. 88	31 Oct. 94	Cape of Good Hope.
Irving, Lewis Allen, *LRCPI. LRCSI*	1 Apr. 71	1 Mar. 73	1 Apr. 83	1 Apr. 91	16 Dec. 94	Netley.
Beamish, Jas. Maybury,[221] *MA. MD. MCh. MRCS. DPH.Camb.*	1 Apr. 71	1 Mar. 73	1 Apr. 83	1 Apr. 91	27 Feb. 95	Woolwich Arsenal.

SURGEON LIEUTENANT COLONELS.	ASSISTANT SURGEON.	SURGEON.	SURGEON MAJOR.	SURGEON LT. COL.		REGIMENT, OR STATION.
Melladew, Heinrich Friedrich Lawaetz,[190] *MD. LRCS.Ed.*	31 Mar. 64	1 Mar. 73	4 Sept.80	31 Mar. 84		Royal Horse Guards.
Kirwan, Albert, *FRCS. Ed. DPH.*	31 Mar. 68	1 Mar. 73	31 Mar. 81	31 Mar. 88		York.
Corry, George,[213] *LRCP. Ed. LRCS. Ed.*	1 Oct. 68	1 Mar. 73	1 Oct. 81	1 Oct. 88		Bengal.
Bennett, Richard Dawson,[215] *LRCSI. LAH.Dub.*	1 Oct. 68	1 Mar. 73	1 Oct. 80	1 Oct. 88		Bengal.
Clery, James Albert,[222] *MB. MCh.*	1 Apr. 71	1 Mar. 73	1 Apr. 83	1 Apr. 91		
Coats, James,[223] *MB. MCh.*	1 Apr. 71	1 Mar. 73	1 Apr. 83	1 Apr. 91		Shoeburyness.
Williamson, John Gover,[156] *LRCP. MRCS. LSA.*	1 Apr. 71	1 Mar. 73	1 Apr. 83	1 Apr. 91		Dover.
Fawcett, William James,[224] *BA. MB. MCh.*	1 Apr. 71	1 Mar. 73	1 Apr. 83	1 Apr. 91		Woolwich.
Saunders, William Egerton,[225] *LRCP. MRCS.*	1 Apr. 71	1 Mar. 73	1 Apr. 83	1 Apr. 91		India.
Charlton, William Johnston, *LRCPI. LRCSI.*	1 Apr. 71	1 Mar. 73	1 Apr. 83	1 Apr. 91		India.
Anthonisz, Alfred Henry,[226] *MB. MCh.*	1 Apr. 71	1 Mar. 73	1 Apr. 83	1 Apr. 91		Bengal.
Exham, Richard, *LRCP. Ed. LRCS. Ed.*	1 Apr. 71	1 Mar. 73	1 Apr. 83	1 Apr. 91		Bengal.
M'Namara, James,[218] *MD. LRCSI.*	1 Apr. 71	1 Mar. 73	1 Apr. 83	1 Apr. 91		Dublin.
Harman, Rodolph, *MB. MCh.*	1 Apr. 71	1 Mar. 73	1 Apr. 83	1 Apr. 91		Devonport.
Leake, George Dalton Nugent,[228] *MRCS. LSA. LRCP. DPH.Camb.*	1 Apr. 71	1 Mar. 73	1 Apr. 83	1 Apr. 91		Woolwich.
Gabbett, Poole Robert, *LRCP. Ed. MRCS*	1 Apr. 71	1 Mar. 73	1 Apr. 83	1 Apr. 91		Colchester.
O'Connell, Mathew Daniel,[229] *MD. MCh. MRCPI.*	1 Apr. 71	1 Mar. 73	1 Apr. 83	1 Apr. 91		Ballincollig.
Joynt, Edward Hearne,[230] *MD. MCh.*	1 Apr. 71	1 Mar. 73	1 Apr. 83	1 Apr. 91		Sheerness.
Robinson, Robert Henry, *LRCPI. FRCSI.*	1 Apr. 71	1 Mar. 73	2 July 83	2 July 91		
Edge, John Dallas,[232] *MD. LRCSI.*	30 Apr. 71	1 Mar. 73	20 Aug. 73	30 Sept. 91		Bombay.
Dwyer, Charles Edward, *LRCPI. LRCSI.*	30 Sept.71	1 Mar. 73	30 Sept.83	30 Sept. 91		Cape of Good Hope.
Blood, Robert, *MD. MCh.*	30 Sept.71	1 Mar. 73	30 Sept.83	30 Sept. 91		Winchester.
Barrow, Henry John Waller,[243] *MRCS. LSA.*	30 Sept.71	1 Mar. 73	30 Sept.83	30 Sept. 91		Woolwich.
Bridges, William Percy, *MRCS. LSA.*	30 Sept.71	1 Mar. 73	30 Sept.83	30 Sept. 91		Weedon.
Drury, Robert,[244] *MD. LRCSI.*	30 Sept.71	1 Mar. 73	30 Sept.83	30 Sept. 91		India.
Donovan, William,[246] *LRCPI. LRCSI.*	30 Mar. 72	1 Mar. 73	30 Mar. 84	30 Mar. 92		Bengal.
Brown, Dugald Blair,[247] *LRCP. Ed. FRCS. Ed.*	30 Mar. 72	1 Mar. 73	30 Mar. 84	30 Mar. 92		Piershill.
Quill, Richard Henry,[248] *MB. MCh.*	30 Mar. 72	1 Mar. 73	30 Mar. 84	30 Mar. 92		Bombay.
Blennerhassett, Blennerhassett Montgomerie, *LRCPI. LRCSI.*	30 Mar. 72	1 Mar. 73	30 Mar. 84	30 Mar. 92		Bengal.
Slaughter, William Budd,[156] *MRCS. LSA.*	30 Mar. 72	1 Mar. 73	30 Mar. 84	30 Mar. 92		Portsmouth.
Browne, Andrew Lang, *MD. MCh.*	30 Mar. 72	1 Mar. 73	30 Mar. 84	30 Mar. 92		Woolwich.
Keys, Christopher William Moore, *MD. MCh.*	30 Mar. 72	1 Mar. 73	30 Mar. 84	30 Mar. 92		Jamaica.
Stokes, Henry Haldane,[250] *MB. MRCS.*	30 Mar. 72	1 Mar. 73	30 Mar. 84	30 Mar. 92		Netley.
Gallwey, Thomas Joseph,[251] MD. MCh.		31 Mar. 74	15 June 85	30 Sept. 93		Egyptian Army.
Pratt, William Simson,[252] *MB. MCh.*		31 Mar. 74	15 June 85	30 Sept. 93		Head Quarters.
Allin, William Briggs,[254] *MB. LRCP. Ed. LRCS.Ed.*		4 Feb. 77	15 June 85	30 Sept. 93		Bengal.
Langridge, George Thomas,[256] *LRCP. MRCS* H.P. 74		30 Sept.73	30 Sept.85	30 Sept. 93		Bengal.
Webb, William Edward,[257] *MD. MCh. LSA.*		30 Sept.73	30 Sept.85	30 Sept. 93		Gibraltar.
Mapleton, Reginald William,[258] *MB. MCh.*		30 Sept.73	30 Sept.85	30 Sept. 93		Home District.
Gubbins, William Launcelotte,[269] *BA. MB. MCh.*		30 Sept.73	30 Sept.85	30 Sept. 93		Madras.
Thomseth, Richard Gillham,[270] *LRCPI. LRCSI.*		30 Sept.73	30 Sept.85	30 Sept. 93		Hilsea.
M'Quaid, Peter John,[271] *MD. MCh. LAH.*		30 Sept.73	30 Sept.85	30 Sept. 93		India.
Ring, James,[272] *MD. MCh.*		30 Sept.73	30 Sept.85	30 Sept. 93		Bengal.
Wood, Oswald Gillespie,[275] *MD. LRCS. Ed.*		30 Sept.73	30 Mar. 86	30 Mar. 94		Ashton-under-Lyne.
Ward, Lloyd Brereton,[276] *LRCP. Ed. MRCS.*		31 Mar. 74	31 Mar. 86	31 Mar. 94		Chatham.
Miller, William Birkmyre,[277] *MA. MD. MCh.*		31 Mar. 74	31 Mar. 86	31 Mar. 94		Madras.
Martin, John,[280] *LRCS. Ed. LAH.* A.G.M. 85		31 Mar. 74	31 Mar. 86	31 Mar. 94		Dublin.
Greene, John Joseph,[281] *BA. MB. LRCS. Ed.*		31 Mar. 74	31 Mar. 86	31 Mar. 94		Golden Hill Fort.
M'Creery, Nathaniel,[282] *LRCP. Ed. LRCS. Ed.*		31 Mar. 74	31 Mar. 86	31 Mar. 94		Cape of Good Hope.
Gormley, Joseph Andrew,[283] *MD. MCh.*		31 Mar. 74	31 Mar. 86	31 Mar. 94		Cape of Good Hope.

Army Medical Staff.

Surgeon Lieutenant Colonels.	Surgeon.	Surgeon Major.	Surgeon Lt. Col.	Regiment, or Station.
Swayne, Charles Henry,[299] LRCP.Ed. LRCS.Ed. LAH. (Assistant Surgeon, 30 Mar. 72)	1 Mar. 73	18 Oct. 86	21 Aug. 94	Londonderry.
Smith, Robert,[286] MB. MCh.	30 Sept. 74	30 Sept. 86	30 Sept. 94	Aldershot.
Trevor, Francis Wollaston,[287] MB. MCh. MRCS.	30 Sept. 74	30 Sept. 86	30 Sept. 94	Bombay.
Scott, Harvie,[288] MB. LRCSI.	30 Sept. 74	30 Sept. 86	30 Sept. 94	Aldershot.
M'Gann, James,[294] LRCPI. LRCSI.	30 Sept. 74	30 Sept. 86	30 Sept. 94	Dublin.
Powell, James,[295] LRCP.Ed. MRCS.	30 Sept. 74	30 Sept. 86	30 Sept. 94	Dover.
Carter, Sidney Herbert,[296] BA. MB. LRCS.Ed.	30 Sept. 74	30 Sept. 86	30 Sept. 94	Malta.
May, William Allan, MRCS. LSA.	30 Sept. 74	30 Sept. 86	30 Sept. 94	Bengal.
Bourke, George Deane,[297] LRCPI. LRCSI.	30 Sept. 74	30 Sept. 86	30 Sept. 94	Cork.
Campbell, William,[292] MB. MCh. MRCP.Ed.	30 Sept. 74	5 Nov. 87	30 Sept. 94	Grenadier Guards.
Forrestor, James Stevenson,[302] FRCS.Ed.	30 Sept. 74	25 Oct. 94	25 Oct. 94	R. Horse Guards.

Surgeon Majors.				
Magill, James,[273] MA. MD. MCh. MRCS.		3 May 76	9 Dec. 85	Coldstream Guards.
Charlesworth, Henry,[156] MRCS. LSA.		31 Mar. 75	31 Mar. 87	Brighton.
Dorman, John Cotter,[300] MB. MCh.		31 Mar. 75	31 Mar. 87	Bengal.
Le Mottée, George Herbert, MD. MCh. MRCS. LSA.		31 Mar. 75	31 Mar. 87	
Chester, William Litchfield,[301] BA. MB. MCh. MRCPI.		31 Mar. 75	31 Mar. 87	Egypt.
Mapleton, Edward Arthur, MB. CM.		31 Mar. 75	31 Mar. 87	Bengal.
James, William Mawer, LRCP.Ed. LRCS.Ed.		30 Sept. 75	30 Sept. 87	Shorncliffe.
Robinson, George Somerville,[344] LRCP. MRCS.		6 Mar. 80	31 Dec. 87	Scots Guards.
Fenn, Ernest Harrold,[303] CIE. LRCP.Ed. MRCS.		30 Sept. 75	13 May 88	Coldstream Guards.
Alexander, Alex. C. Archibald,[304] BA. MRCS. LSA.		29 July 82	8 Nov. 88	Coldstream Guards.
Ryan, Michael Richard,[305] MD. MCh.		4 Feb. 77	4 Feb. 89	Aldershot.
Reynolds, Edward Osmund,[306] MRCS. LSA.		4 Feb. 77	4 Feb. 89	India.
Robbins, Henry John,[307] MB. MCh. LSA.		4 Feb. 77	4 Feb. 89	Home District.
Morris, John James,[308] MD. MCh.		4 Feb. 77	4 Feb. 89	
Hayes, Aylmer Ellis,[309] DSO. LRCP.Ed. MRCS.		4 Feb. 77	4 Feb. 89	Aldershot.
Williamson, John Francis,[310] MB. LCh.		4 Feb. 77	4 Feb. 89	Bengal.
Carey, John Thomas,[311] MB. MRCS. LSA.		4 Feb. 77	4 Feb. 89	Cape of Good Hope.
Rainsford, Wm. John Read,[312] LRCPI. LRCSI.		4 Feb. 77	4 Feb. 89	Aldershot.
Boulger, Isaac,[156] MRCS. LSA.		4 Feb. 77	4 Feb. 89	Dover.
Boyd, Thomas,[313] LRCPI. LRCSI.		4 Feb. 77	4 Feb. 89	Dundalk.
Johnston, Percy Herbert,[314] MD. MCh.		4 Feb. 77	4 Feb. 89	Colchester.
Emerson, Isaac Bomford,[315] LRCPI. LRCSI.		4 Feb. 77	4 Feb. 89	Madras.
Roche, Eugenius Alfred,[156] MRCS. LSA.		4 Feb. 77	4 Feb. 89	Newport.
Laffan, George,[316] MD. MCh.		4 Feb. 77	4 Feb. 89	Madras.
Bourke, Ulick Joseph,[317] LRCSI. LSA.		4 Feb. 77	4 Feb. 89	
Lamprey, Joseph John, LRCPI. LRCS.Ed.		4 Feb. 77	4 Feb. 89	Leeds.
Allen, William Henry,[318] LRCP.Ed. LRCS.Ed.		4 Feb. 77	4 Feb. 89	Queenstown.
Gunning, Robert Cardwell, LRCPI. LRCSI.		4 Feb. 77	4 Feb. 89	Chester.
Peyton, Jones Lloyd,[320] MB. LCh.		4 Feb. 77	4 Feb. 89	Bengal.
Carleton, Arthur Wellesley,[321] MB. MCh. MRCPI.		4 Feb. 77	4 Feb. 89	Madras.
Hughes, George Arthur,[322] MB. MCh.		4 Feb. 77	4 Feb. 89	
Somerville-Large, Brisbane Warren, MB. LRCP.Ed. LRCS.Ed.		4 Feb. 77	4 Feb. 89	Malta.
Johnston, William Thomas,[323] MD. LRCP.Ed.		5 Aug. 77	5 Aug. 89	Madras.
Browne, Abraham Walker,[324] LRCPI. LRCSI.		5 Aug. 77	5 Aug. 89	Limerick.
Hodson, Robert Doveton,[156] LRCP.Ed. MRCS.		5 Aug. 77	5 Aug. 89	Devonport.
Powell, Caleb K.[156] MD. MCh. MRCPI.		5 Aug. 77	5 Aug. 89	Buttevant.
Kirkpatrick, Hugh Cunningham,[156] MD. MCh.		5 Aug. 77	5 Aug. 89	Gosport.
Armstrong, John, LRCPI. LRCSI.		5 Aug. 77	5 Aug. 89	Bombay.
Kenny, William Wallace,[325] BA. MB. LRCSI.		5 Aug. 77	5 Aug. 89	Cyprus.
Ellis, Philip Mackay, LRCP. MRCS.		5 Aug. 77	5 Aug. 89	Aldershot.
O'Sullivan, Patrick Joseph, MD. MCh.		5 Aug. 77	5 Aug. 89	Curragh.
Brodie, James FitzGerald,[155] MD. MCh.		5 Aug. 77	5 Aug. 89	Bombay.
Tuthill, Phineas Barrett, BA. MD. FRCSI.		4 Feb. 77	8 Aug. 89	Dublin.
Hunt, John Percival,[319] MD. LRCP.Ed. FRCSI.		4 Feb. 77	26 Jan. 90	Woolwich.
Keays, William,[326] MRCPI. FRCSI.		3 Feb. 78	3 Feb. 90	Bengal.
Beamish, Robert Talbot,[327] MD. MCh.		3 Feb. 78	3 Feb. 90	Portland.
Parker, Walter Augustus, LRCP. MRCS.		3 Feb. 78	3 Feb. 90	Bombay.
Anderson, James, MB. MCh.		3 Feb. 78	3 Feb. 90	Aldershot.
Routh, Jules Isham, LRCP.Ed. MRCS.		3 Feb. 78	3 Feb. 90	Netley.
Grier, Henry,[329] MRCPI. LFPS.Glas.		3 Feb. 78	3 Feb. 90	Aldershot.
Power, Edward Richard,[331] MB. BCh.		3 Feb. 78	3 Feb. 90	Chatham.
Donovan, Hugh Latimer,[332] MD. MCh.		3 Feb. 78	3 Feb. 90	Tipperary.
Leader, Nicholas,[333] LRCP.Ed. FRCS.Ed.		3 Feb. 78	3 Feb. 90	Bengal.
Tidbury, James,[334] MD. MCh.		3 Feb. 78	3 Feb. 90	Malta.
Lyle, Allan Andrew, LRCPI. LRCSI.		3 Feb. 78	3 Feb. 90	Aldershot.
Charlton, Henry Arthur Herbert, LRCPI. LRCSI.		3 Feb. 78	3 Feb. 90	Bengal.
Barrington, Henry Ernest Walter, MRCS. LSA.		3 Feb. 78	3 Feb. 90	Bengal.
Stevenson, John, MB. FRCS.Ed. BSc.		4 Aug. 78	4 Aug. 90	Manchester.
Lane, William Lemon, MB. MCh.		4 Aug. 78	4 Aug. 90	Portsmouth.
Dempsey, Patrick Joseph,[156] MD. MCh.		4 Aug. 78	4 Aug. 90	India.
Wallis, Kenneth Serjeant,[336] LRCP. MRCS.		4 Aug. 78	4 Aug. 90	Bombay.
Flanagan, John William Henry,[337] LRCSI. LRCPI.		4 Aug. 78	4 Aug. 90	Preston.
Ye Lloyd, Owen Edward Pennefather,[338] LRCP.Ed. LRCS.Ed.		4 Aug. 78	4 Aug. 90	Madras.
MacNeece, James Gaussen,[339] LRCPI. LRCSI.		4 Aug. 78	4 Aug. 90	York.
O'Connell, Morgan David, LRCPI. LRCSI.		4 Aug. 78	4 Aug. 90	India.
Young, Alexander Stewart Ward, LFPS.Glas.		4 Aug. 78	4 Aug. 90	Parkhurst.
Harding, Arthur,[340] LRCP.Ed. MRCS.		4 Aug. 78	4 Aug. 90	Madras.
Falvey, John Joseph,[341] FRCSI. LAH.		4 Aug. 78	4 Aug. 90	Barbadoes.
Seymour, Charles,[343] MB. MCh. MRCS. LSA.		4 Aug. 78	4 Aug. 90	Bengal.
Young, Percy Gordon Radstock, LRCP.Ed. MRCS.		3 Feb. 78	12 Aug 90	2 Life Guards
Feltham, William Parsons, MRCS. LSA.		4 Aug. 78	27 Jan. 91	Devonport.
Carte, William Alexander, BA. MB. BCh.		30 May 85	6 May 91	Grenadier Guards.
Barker, Frederick Rowland, MB. MRCS. LSA.		6 Mar. 80	6 Mar. 92	Jamaica.
Keogh, Alfred, MD. MCh. H.P. M.G.M. 80		6 Mar. 80	6 Mar. 92	Madras.
Hill, Charles Birnie, LRCP. MRCS.		6 Mar. 80	6 Mar. 92	Bombay.
Clark, Sir James Richardson Andrew, Bart. MRCS. LSA.		16 Mar. 80	6 Mar. 92	Aldershot.
Michael, Henry James, MRCS. LSA.		6 Mar. 80	6 Mar. 92	
Dorman, Thomas, BA. MD. MCh.		6 Mar. 80	6 Mar. 92	Nova Scotia.
Inman, Arthur Walter Patrick, MB. BCh.		6 Mar. 80	6 Mar. 92	Barbadoes.
Corker, Thomas Martin, MA. MD. MCh.		6 Mar. 80	6 Mar. 92	Dublin.

Army Medical Staff.

Surgeon Majors.	Surgeon.	Surgeon Major.	Regiment, or Station.
Myles, Edmond Henry,[345] *BA. MB. BCh.*	6 Mar. 80	6 Mar. 92	Bombay.
Moffitt, Thomas Beattie, *LRCPI. LRCSI.*	6 Mar. 80	6 Mar. 92	Bengal.
Webb, Charles Alfred, *MRCS. LSA.*	6 Mar. 80	6 Mar. 92	Devonport.
Martin, Henry,[346] *MB. MCh.*	6 Mar. 80	6 Mar. 92	Surg. to Governor of Bombay.
Croly, Arthur England Johnson, *BA. LRCPI. LRCSI.*	6 Mar. 80	6 Mar. 92	Bombay.
Cusack, Robert Oriel,[350] *LRCP. MRCS.*	6 Mar. 80	6 Mar. 92	Madras.
Cowen, William Daniel Amherst, *LRCP.Ed. MRCS.*	6 Mar. 80	6 Mar. 92	Madras.
Forman, Robert Hall, *MB. MCh. LRCP.Ed. LFPS.Glas.*	6 Mar. 80	6 Mar. 92	Madras.
Flood, Samuel James, *LRCP.Ed. FRCS.Ed. LRCSI.*	6 Mar. 80	6 Mar. 92	Colchester.
Robinson, George Winsor, *LRCP. MRCS. LSA.*	6 Mar. 80	6 Mar. 92	Madras.
Watson, John, *MD. LRCP.Ed. LRCS.Ed.*	6 Mar. 80	6 Mar. 92	Bengal.
Todd, Octavius, *MB. MCh.*	6 Mar. 80	6 Mar. 92	India.
Geoghegan, Alfred Osmond, *MD. MCh.*	6 Mar. 80	6 Mar. 92	Bengal.
Day, James Dunne, *MB. BCh. FFPS.Glas.*	6 Mar. 80	6 Mar. 92	Dover.
Kavanagh, Arthur Maher, *LRCP.Ed. LRCS.Ed.*	6 Mar. 80	6 Mar. 92	Hounslow.
Harwood, John Gasson, *MRCS. LSA.*	6 Mar. 80	6 Mar. 92	Bengal.
Donaldson, Robert Dickie, *BA. MD. MCh.*	6 Mar. 80	6 Mar. 92	Bermuda.
White, Henry Lawrence Esmonde, *MRCPI. LRCSI.*	6 Mar. 80	6 Mar. 92	Bengal.
Burlton, Arthur Hyde, *LRCP.Ed. LRCS.Ed.*	6 Mar. 80	6 Mar. 92	Bengal.
North, Edward, *LRCP.Ed. LRCS.Ed.*	6 Mar. 80	6 Mar. 92	Bengal.
Poynder, George Frederick, *LRCP. MRCS.*	6 Mar. 80	6 Mar. 92	Madras
Smythe, George Frederick Alexander, *LRCP.Ed. LRCSI.*	6 Mar. 80	6 Mar. 92	India.
Battersby, Henry Lewis, *LRCPI. LRCSI.*	6 Mar. 80	6 Mar. 92	Bengal.
Hewett, Augustus, *MRCS. LSA.*	6 Mar. 80	6 Mar. 92	York.
Mulvany, Peter, *LRCP.Ed. LRCS.Ed. LAH.*	5 Mar. 80	6 Mar. 92	Jamaica.
Nicholson, James Edward, *LRCP. MRCS.*	6 Mar. 80	6 Mar. 92	Devonport.
Wolseley, William Owen, *LRCPI. LRCSI.*	6 Mar. 80	6 Mar. 92	Warley.
MacNeece, Thomas Frederick, *LRCP.Ed. LRCS.Ed.*	6 Mar. 80	6 Mar. 92	Bombay.
M'Creery, Benjamin Thos. *MB. BCh. FRCSI. MRCPI.*	6 Mar. 80	6 Mar. 92	Bengal.
O'Connor, Arthur Patrick,[347]† *LRCPI. LRCSI.*	6 Mar. 80	6 Mar. 92	Bengal.
Bolster, James M'Mullen, *LRCP.Ed. LRCS.Ed.*	6 Mar. 80	6 Mar. 92	Bengal.
Wardrop, Douglas,[348] *MB. MCh.*	6 Mar. 80	6 Mar. 92	Bengal.
Goggin, George Taylor, *LRCP.Ed. LRCS.Ed.*	6 Mar. 80	6 Mar. 92	Bombay.
Jones, John Matthew,[349] *LRCP.Ed. LRCS.Ed.*	6 Mar. 80	6 Mar. 92	Bengal.
Baker, Fausset Maher, *MB. MCh.*	6 Mar. 80	6 Mar. 92	Malta.
Asbury, Alfred, *LRCPI. LRCSI.*	6 Mar. 80	6 Mar. 92	Dublin.
Carleton, Patrick Maurice, *MD. MCh.*	6 Mar. 80	6 Mar. 92	Madras.
Maclean, Fitzroy Beresford, *LRCP.Ed. MRCS.*	6 Mar. 80	6 Mar. 92	Madras.
Barnes, Raglan Wykeham, *MRCPI. LRCS.Ed. LSA.*	6 Mar. 80	6 Mar. 92	Hounslow.
Fox, Patrick H., *LRCPI. FRCSI. LAH.*	6 Mar. 80	6 Mar. 92	Cork.
Lewis, John George Stephen, *LRCP. MRCS. LSA.*	6 Mar. 80	6 July 92	Bengal.
Hall, John Lees, *LRCP.Ed. MRCS. LSA.*	31 July 80	6 July 92	Nova Scotia.
Sylvester, George Holden, *LRCP. FRCS. DPH.*	31 July 80	31 July 92	Bengal.
Macnamara, William John, *MD.*	31 July 80	31 July 92	Gosport.
O'Sullivan, Daniel, *LRCPI. LRCSI.*	31 July 80	31 July 92	Belfast.
Milward, Edwin Oswald, *MA. LRCP.Ed. LRCS.Ed.*	31 July 80	31 July 92	Bengal.
Woods, Charles Rolleston,[359] *BA. MD. FRCSI. DPH.Camb.*	31 July 80	31 July 92	Madras.
Macnamara, Michael Francis, *LRCSI. LAH.*	31 July 80	31 July 92	Madras.
Sandiford, John Oldfield Greatrex, *MD. MCh. LAH.*	31 July 80	31 July 92	Waterford.
Love, Robert Lindsay, *BA. MD. MCh. MRCPI.*	31 July 80	31 July 92	Bengal.
Murray, Henry Walker, *MB. MRCS.*	31 July 80	31 July 92	Gibraltar.
Kerin, Michael William,[350]† *LRCSI. LAH.*	31 July 80	31 July 92	Athlone.
Peterkin, Alfred,[351] *MA. MB. MCh.*	31 July 80	31 July 92	Shorncliffe.'
Harran, James, *LRCP.Ed. LRCS.Ed. LSA.*	31 July 80	31 July 92	Bengal.
Maunsell, Edward Lewis, *LRCP.Ed. LRCS.Ed.*	31 July 80	31 July 92	Bombay.
Heffernan, William, *LRCPI. LRCSI.*	31 July 80	31 July 92	Woolwich.
Nicholson, Ranald William Edward Huntly, *LRCP.Ed. MRCS.*	31 July 80	31 July 92	Bengal.
Crofts, James Grove White, *LCh.*	31 July 80	31 July 92	Fermoy.
Dugdale, William,[351] *LRCPI. LRCSI.*	31 July 80	31 July 92	Bengal.
Irvine, Delaware Lewis,[352] *LRCP. MRCS.*	31 July 80	31 July 92	Gibraltar.
Cree, Edward Russell,[353] *MRCS. LSA.*	31 July 80	31 July 92	Bengal.
Drury, Maurice O'Connor,[354] *LRCPI. LRCSI.*	31 July 80	31 July 92	Bombay.
Nicholas, James Hamilton, *LRCPI. LRCS.Ed.*	31 July 80	31 July 92	Madras.
Franklin, Denham Francis, *LRCP.Ed. FRCS.Ed.*	31 July 80	31 July 92	Gibraltar
Saunders, Herbert, *LRCP.Ed. LRCS.Ed.*	5 Feb. 81	31 July 92	India.
Dodd, John Richard, *MB. FRCS.*	5 Feb. 81	5 Feb. 93	
Twiss, George Edward,[355] *MRCPI. FRCSI.*	5 Feb. 81	5 Feb. 93	Shorncliffe
Adams, Robert Frederick, *MB. MCh.*	5 Feb. 81	5 Feb. 93	Bombay.
Mosse, Charles George Drummond, *LRCPI. FRCSI.*	5 Feb. 81	5 Feb. 93	Bombay.
Cottell, Arthur Bowdich, *LRCP.Ed. FRCS.Ed.*	5 Feb. 81	5 Feb. 93	Gibraltar
Archer, Thomas, *MD. MCh.*	5 Feb. 81	5 Feb. 93	Bermuda.
Moberly, Herbert John Robert, *LRCP.Ed. MRCS.*	5 Feb. 81	5 Feb. 93	Cape of Good Hope.
Hart, Alfred Paul, *MB. MCh. MRCS.*	5 Feb. 81	5 Feb. 93	Bengal.
Barnes, Henry John, *LRCP.Ed. MRCS. LSA.*	5 Feb. 81	5 Feb. 93	Bombay.
Bedford, Walter George Augustus, *MB. MRCS.*	5 Feb. 81	5 Feb. 93	Staff Officer, Med. S.C., Hd. Qrs.
Jennings, Richard, *MD. MCh.*	5 Feb. 81	5 Feb. 93	Bengal.
Robinson, Stapylton Chapman Bates, *LRCP.Ed. MRCS.*	5 Feb. 81	5 Feb. 93	Malta
Ford, Richard William,[357] *LRCP.Ed. MRCS.*	5 Feb. 81	5 Feb. 93	Bermuda.
Coutts, George, *MB. MCh.*	5 Feb. 81	5 Feb. 93	Bengal.
Stoggett, Arthur Thomas, *LRCP.Ed. MRCS.*	5 Feb. 81	5 Feb. 93	Egypt.
Allport, Henry Kingston, *MD. MCh.*	5 Feb. 81	5 Feb. 93	Ceylon.
Butt, Edward, *LRCPI. FRCSI.*	5 Feb. 81	5 Feb. 93	Bengal.
Townsend, Samuel, *MD. MCh.*	5 Feb. 81	5 Feb. 93	Bengal.
Woodhouse, Tom Percy, *MRCS. LSA.*	5 Feb. 81	5 Feb. 93	Bombay.
Gibson, Joseph, *MB. BCh. MRCPI.*	5 Feb. 81	5 Feb. 93	Bengal.
Rhodes, James Havelock Alexander, *MRCS. LSA.*	5 Feb. 81	5 Feb. 93	Curragh.
Swabey, Louis William,[358] *LRCP.Ed. MRCS.*	5 Feb. 81	5 Feb. 93	Bengal.
Rowney, William,[361] *MD. MCh.*	5 Feb. 81	5 Feb. 93	Bombay.
Lucas, Thomas Rashleigh,[362] *MB. BCh.*	5 Feb. 81	5 Feb. 93	Madras.
Addison, Charles James,[363] *LRCP.Ed. LRCS.Ed. LSA.*	5 Feb. 81	5 Feb. 93	Bombay.
Kay, Alfred Goodwyn,[364] *MB. MCh. LRCS.Ed.*	5 Feb. 81	5 Feb. 93	Chatham.
Pope, William Wippell,[365] *LRCP.Ed. MRCS.*	5 Feb. 81	5 Feb. 93	Netley.
Porter, Robert, *MB. MCh.*	5 Feb. 81	5 Feb. 93	Portsdown Hill.
Mitchell, Charles Andrew Pearson,[368] *MD. MCh. FRCSI.Ed.*	5 Feb. 81	5 Feb. 93	Bombay.
Coates, George John, *MD. MCh.*	6 Mar. 80	5 Feb. 93	Tipperary.

Army Medical Staff

Surgeon Majors.	Surgeon.	Surgeon Major.	Regiment, or Station.
Tuckey, Thomas Broderick Albert,[369] LRCP.Ed. LRCS.Ed.	5 Feb. 81	5 Feb. 93	Malta.
Harris, Frederick Alfred,[370] LRCP.Ed. MRCS. LSA	5 Feb. 81	5 Feb. 93	Bombay.
Daly, Francis Augustus Bonner,[373] BA. MB. BCh. FRCSI.	5 Feb. 81	5 Feb. 93	Dublin.
Rose, Alexander Simpson,[374] MD. MCh.	5 Feb. 81	5 Feb. 93	Bengal.
Battersby, John,[375] MB. BCh. MRCPI. FRCSI.	5 Feb. 81	5 Feb. 93	Bengal.
Maconachie, James,[376] LRCP.Ed. LFPS.Glas. FRCS.Ed.	5 Feb. 81	5 Feb. 93	Bombay.
O'Keeffe, Menus William,[379] MD. MCh.	5 Feb. 81	5 Feb. 93	Belfast.
O'Donnell, Thomas Joseph,[380] LRCPI. LRCSI.	5 Feb. 81	5 Feb. 93	Bengal.
Osburne, John,[381] LRCP.Ed. LRCS.Ed.	5 Feb. 81	5 Feb. 93	India.
Hetherington, Reynolds Peyton,[382] BA. MB. BCh.	5 Feb. 81	5 Feb. 93	Madras.
Dixon, Thomas Arthur, LRCP.Ed. MRCS.	5 Feb. 81	5 Feb. 93	Bengal.
Poole, Walter Croker Thomas, BA. MB. FRCSI.	5 Feb. 81	5 Feb. 93	Madras.
Morse, Richard Edward Ricketts,[300] LRCP.Ed. MRCS.	5 Feb. 81	12 July 93	Bengal.
Davies, Arthur Mercer,[384] MRCS. LSA. DPH. M.S.M. 81	30 July 81	30 July 93	Bengal.
Hubbard, Henry William,[385] LRCP. MRCS.	30 July 81	30 July 93	Woolwich.
Noding, Thomas Edward,[386] LRCP.Ed. MRCS.	30 July 81	30 July 93	Bengal.
Yourdi, John Robert,[387] BA. MB. BCh.	30 July 81	30 July 93	Bombay.
Culling, John Chislett, MRCS. LSA.	30 July 81	30 July 93	Bombay.
Hackett, Robert Isaac Dalby,[388] MD. MCh.	30 July 81	30 July 93	Pembroke Dock.
Trewman, George Turner,[390] LRCP. MB. MRCS. LSA.	30 July 81	30 July 93	Curragh.
Johnston, Henry Halcro,[391] MB. MCh.	30 July 81	30 July 93	Leith Fort.
Wilson, Edmund Munkhouse,[392] LRCP. MRCS.	30 July 81	30 July 93	Salford.
Risk, Edmund John Erskine,[393] LRCP.Ed. MRCS.	30 July 81	30 July 93	Aldershot.
Birrell, William George,[394] MB. MCh.	30 July 81	30 July 93	Shorncliffe.
Dundon, Michael, MD. MCh.	30 July 81	30 July 93	Kinsale.
Magrath, Charles William Stanford,[400] MB. MCh.	30 July 81	30 July 93	Gosport.
Lane, Alfred Vavasour,[401] LRCPI. LRCSI.	30 July 81	30 July 93	Bombay.
Beatty, John Wm.,[402] MD. LRCPI. LRCSI.	30 July 81	30 July 93	Belfast.
Weston, George Edward,[403] LRCP.Ed. MRCS. LSA.	30 July 81	30 July 93	Gosport.
Younge, George Harrison, LRCPI. FRCSI.	30 July 81	30 July 93	Madras.
Babtie, William, MB. LRCP.Ed. LRCS.Ed.	30 July 81	30 July 93	Malta.
O'Brien, Richard Francis,[405] LRCPI. LRCSI.	30 July 81	30 July 93	India.
Thiele, Charles William, MB. MCh.	30 July 81	30 July 93	Malta.
Nichols, Frederick Peter. BA. MB. MRCS.	30 July 81	30 July 93	Madras.
M'Laughlin, John,[404] MD. LRCSI.	30 July 81	30 July 93	Maryhill.
Creagh, Stephen Henry, LRCP.Ed. MRCS.	30 July 81	30 July 93	Bermuda.
Lambkin, Francis Joseph, LRCPI. LRCSI.	30 July 81	30 July 93	Jamaica.
Reade, William Lloyd, LRCP.Ed. LRCS.Ed.	30 July 81	30 July 93	Hong Kong.
Peard, Henry James, LRCP.Ed. LRCS.Ed.	30 July 81	30 July 93	Bengal.
Rennie, Samuel James, LRCP.Ed. MRCS.	30 July 81	30 July 93	Bengal.
Carmichael, John, LRCP.Ed. LRCSI. MRCPI.	30 July 81	30 July 93	Bengal.
Creagh, George Washington Brazier, LCh.	30 July 81	30 July 93	Bengal.
Wilkinson, Francis Tichborne, LRCP. MRCS.	30 July 81	30 July 93	Aldershot.
Semple, John, LRCP.Ed. LRCSI.	30 July 81	30 July 93	
Sawyer, Richard Henry Stewart, MB. FRCSI.	5 Feb. 81	15 Aug. 93	Gibraltar.
Laffan, Richard Charles Kirby,[357] LRCP.Ed. LRCSI.	5 Feb. 81	4 Feb. 94	Newbridge.
Dick, William,[406] MB. MCh. LRCP.Ed. FRCS.Ed.	4 Feb. 82	4 Feb. 94	Netley.
Jencken, Francis John,[407] MB. BCh. MRCPI.	4 Feb. 82	4 Feb. 94	Netley.
Stuart, Henry Ogilvy,[408] MRCS. LSA.	4 Feb. 82	4 Feb. 94	Aldershot.
Treherne, Francis Harper,[409] LRCP.Ed. FRCS. Ed. DPH.Camb.	4 Feb. 82	4 Feb. 94	Surgeon to Sir G. S. White
Lougheed, Samuel Foster, MD. LRCSI.	4 Feb. 82	4 Feb. 94	Bengal.
Haslett, John Courtenay, MD. MCh. LAH.	4 Feb. 82	4 Feb. 94	Devonport.
Barratt, Herbert James, LRCP. MRCS.	4 Feb. 82	4 Feb. 94	Bengal.
James, Herbert Ellison Rhodes, LRCP. MRCS.	4 Feb. 82	4 Feb. 94	Hong Kong.
Trevor, Henry Octavius,[410] MRCS. LSA.	4 Feb. 82	4 Feb. 94	Madras.
Russell, Alexander Fraser, MA. MB. MCh.	4 Feb. 82	4 Feb. 94	Gibraltar.
Fayle, Robert James Leech, LRCPI. LRCSI.	4 Feb. 82	4 Feb. 94	Canterbury.
Jerome, John William, MRCS. LSA.	4 Feb. 82	4 Feb. 94	Ayr.
Pike, William Watson, LRCPI. LRCSI.	4 Feb. 82	4 Feb. 94	
Haywood, Lewis, MB. MCh.	4 Feb. 82	4 Feb. 94	Bengal.
Irwin, James Murray, BA. MB. MCh.	4 Feb. 82	4 Feb. 94	Gibraltar.
Nealon, Patrick Joseph,[398] MD. MCh.	4 Feb. 82	4 Feb. 94	Ceylon.
Wight, Ernest Octavius,[389] LRCP.Ed. MRCS.	4 Feb. 82	4 Feb. 94	Colchester.
Burton, Francis Henry Merceron,[412] MD. MCh. MRCS.	4 Feb. 82	4 Feb. 94	Birmingham.
Nichol, Charles Edward,[413] MB. MCh.	4 Feb. 82	4 Feb. 94	Bengal.
Morris, William Albert,[111] LRCP.Ed. LRCS.Ed. LSA.	4 Feb. 82	29 July 94	Bengal.
Westcott, Sinclair, MRCS. LRCP.Ed. M.G.M.82	29 July 82	29 July 94	Hong Kong.
Whitehead, Hayward Reader, FRCS. LRCP.Ed. DPH. M.M.82	29 July 82	29 July 94	Netley.
Skinner, Bruce Morland, LRCP.Ed. MRCS.	29 July 82	29 July 94	Bengal.
Bartlett, Charles Richard, MRCS. LSA.	29 July 82	29 July 94	
Reckitt, John Dennis Thorpe, LRCP.Ed. LRCS.Ed. MRCS. LSA.	29 July 82	29 July 94	Dover.
Marsh, Thomas Alfred Perry,[414] LRCP. MRCS. DPH.	29 July 82	29 July 94	Gibraltar.
Kirkpatrick, Roger,[396] MB. MCh. MRCS.	29 July 82	29 July 94	Bombay.
M'Gill, Harry Strickland, LRCPI. LRCSI.	29 July 82	29 July 94	
Pechell, Augustus Alexander, MB. MCh.	29 July 82	29 July 94	Madras.
Tyrrell, Charles Robert. MRCS. LSA.	29 July 82	29 July 94	Training School, Aldershot.
Hickman, James,[415] MA. DPH. LRCP. LRCS.Ed.	29 July 82	29 July 94	Colchester.
Thomson, Wilfred Burrell, LRCP.Ed. MRCS.	29 July 82	29 July 94	
Deane, Herbert Edward, LRCP.Ed. MRCS.	29 July 82	29 July 94	Aldershot.
Stuart, Sidney Offord, MRCS. LSA.	29 July 82	29 July 94	India.
Farmar-Bringhurst, Edward Dorset,[395] LRCP.Ed. FRCS.Ed.	30 July 81	16 Jan. 95	Madras.
Macpherson, William Grant, MB. MCh.Ed. M.M.83	3 Feb. 83	3 Feb. 95	Gibraltar.
Simpson, Robert John Shaw, MB. MCh.	3 Feb. 83	3 Feb. 95	Woolwich Arsenal.
Phipps, Edgar Vivian Ayre, LRCP. MRCS.	3 Feb. 83	3 Feb. 95	Bengal.
Baird, Andrew,[416] MB. MCh. FRCS.	3 Feb. 83	3 Feb. 95	Bengal.
Hamilton, Thomas William O'Hora, MB. BCh.	3 Feb. 83	3 Feb. 95	Bengal.
Semple, David, MD. MCh.	3 Feb. 83	3 Feb. 95	Netley.
Stuart, John Robert, MB. MCh.	3 Feb. 83	3 Feb. 95	Hong Kong.
Deeble, Benjamin William Chatterton, LRCP.Ed. MRCS.	3 Feb. 83	3 Feb. 95	Bengal.
Bond, Richard Pratt,[416]† LRCP. MRCS.	3 Feb. 83	3 Feb. 95	Bengal.
Thomas, George Trevor Harley, LRCP. FRCS.Ed. LSA.	3 Feb. 83	3 Feb. 95	St. Lucia.
Colman, George Maurice Hoblyn, MA. MB. MRCS. LSA.	3 Feb. 83	3 Feb. 95	Gibraltar.
	3 Feb. 83	3 Feb. 95	Jamaica.

Surgeon Captains.		Surg. Capt.	
Cross, Horatio Robert Odo,[342] LRCP.Ed. MRCS.		4 Aug. 78	1 Life Guards.

Army Medical Staff.

Surgeon Captains.	Surgeon Captain.	Regiment, or Station.
Hunter, Vero Edward, *LRCP.Ed. MRCS.*	3 Feb. 83	Hilsea.
Bruce, David, *MB. MCh.*	4 Aug. 83	Cape of Good Hope.
Bell, Edward Horace Lynden,⁴¹⁸ *MB. MCh.*	4 Aug. 83	Bermuda.
Riordan, John, *MB. MCh.*	4 Aug. 83	Malta.
Firth, Robert Hammill, *LRCP.Ed. FRCS. DPH.* A.G.M. 88 and 91, P.G.M. 89 and 92	4 Aug. 83	Netley.
Nelis, George, *LRCPI. LRCSI.*	4 Aug. 83	Bombay.
Moore, Robert Reginald Heber, *LCh.*	4 Aug. 83	Netley.
Tate, Alan Edmondson,⁴²⁰ *MRCS. LSA.*	4 Aug. 83	Bengal.
Faunce, Charles Edmund,⁴¹⁷ *MRCS. LSA.*	4 Aug. 83	Portsmouth.
Wyatt, Henry James, *LRCPI. LRCSI.*	4 Aug. 83	Bombay.
Kelly, Michael, *MA. MD. MCh.*	2 Feb. 84	Madras.
Pinching, Horace Henderson,⁴²¹ *MA. MRCS. LRCP.* P.B.M. 84	2 Feb. 84	Egyptian Sanitary Department.
Geddes, Robert James, *MB. MCh.*	2 Feb. 84	Bombay.
Kelly, William, *BA. MD. MCh.*	2 Feb. 84	Bengal.
O'Connell, David Valentine, *MD. MCh.*	2 Feb. 84	Aldershot.
Dodd, Anthony, *MRCS. LSA.*	2 Feb. 84	Woolwich.
Reid, James More, *MD. MCh.*	2 Feb. 84	Netley.
Winter, Thomas Bassell, *MRCS. LSA.*	2 Feb. 84	Bengal.
Heuston, Frederick Samuel,⁴²² *LRCPI. FRCSI.*	2 Feb. 84	Chinese Government.
Durant, Robert J. Anderson, *LRCP. MRCS.*	2 Feb. 84	York.
Gubbin, George Frederick,⁴¹⁷ *LRCP. MRCS.*	2 Feb. 84	Bermuda.
Myles, James Perceval,⁴¹⁷ *LRCP. MRCS.*	2 Feb. 84	Aldershot.
Birch, Henry Priestley,⁴¹⁷ *LRCP. MRCS.*	2 Feb. 84	Bengal.
Braddell, Monckton O'Dell,⁴²³ *BA. MB. BCh.*	2 Feb. 84	Aldershot.
Donnet, James John Conway,⁴¹⁷ *LRCP.Ed. MRCS.*	2 Feb. 84	India.
Sloggett, Henry Maxwell,⁴²⁴ *LRCP.Ed. MRCS.*	2 Feb. 84	Portsmouth.
Barefoot, John Richard,⁴²⁵† *LRCP. MRCS.*	2 Aug. 84	Portsmouth.
Clement, Robert Hampden,⁴¹⁷ *LRCPI. LRCSI.*	2 Aug. 84	Bengal.
Hunter, George Douglas,⁴²⁶ *MRCS. LSA.*	2 Aug. 84	Egyptian Army.
Beevor, Walter Calverley,⁴²⁷ *MB. MRCS.*	2 Aug. 84	Scots Guards.
Anderson, Louis Edward,⁴²⁸ *LRCPI. LRCSI. LAH.*	2 Aug. 84	Bengal.
Russell, George Blakeley,⁴²⁹ *BA. MB. BCh.*	2 Aug. 84	Madras.
Spence, Arthur E. C.,⁴³⁰ *MB. MCh. LRCP.Ed. LRCS.Ed.*	2 Aug. 84	Bengal.
Mallins, John Robert,⁴³¹ *BA. LRCPI. LRCSI.*	2 Aug. 84	Dublin.
M'Cormack, Robert James, *MD. MCh.*	2 Aug. 84	Hounslow.
Thompson, Henry Neville, *MB. BCh.*	2 Aug. 84	Bengal.
Doyle, Joseph I. Purcell, *LRCPI. LRCSI.*	2 Aug. 84	Dublin.
Manders, Neville,⁴³⁷ *LRCP. MRCS.*	2 Aug. 84	Aldershot.
Colledge, Lesley Robert,⁴²⁹ *LRCP.Ed. MRCS.*	2 Aug. 84	Mauritius.
Freyer, Samuel Foster,⁴²⁹ *MD. MCh.*	2 Aug. 84	Bengal.
Birt, Cecil,⁴²⁹ *MRCS. LRCP.* P.B.M.84, A.G.M. 94	2 Aug. 84	Bombay.
Henderson, Robert Samuel Findlay,⁴³³ *MD. MCh.*	2 Aug. 84	Bombay.
Mitchell, Henry,⁴²⁹ *MRCS. LSA.*	2 Aug. 84	2 Life Guards.
Butterworth, Samuel,⁴²⁹ *LRCP.Ed. MRCS.*	2 Aug. 84	Mauritius.
Holmes, Charles James,⁴²⁹ *MD. MCh.*	2 Aug. 84	Egypt.
Forrest, James Rocheid,⁴²⁹† *MRCS. LSA.*	2 Feb. 84	
Russell, Michael William,⁴³⁶ *MRCS. LSA.*	31 Jan. 85	Shoeburyness.
Zimmermann, Benjamin Frazier, *LRCP. MRCS.*	31 Jan. 85	Madras.
Stables, Alexander,⁴³⁸ *MB. MCh. MRCS.*	31 Jan. 85	Bengal.
Moffet, Grenville Edwin, *LA. MB. MCh.*	31 Jan. 85	Egypt.
Haines, Henry Aylmer, *MD. MCh.*	31 Jan. 85	Bengal.
Moir, John Drew,⁴³⁹ *MB. MCh.*	31 Jan. 85	Nova Scotia.
Dobson, George Magill,⁴³⁹ *MB. BCh.*	31 Jan. 85	York.
Hale, George Ernest,⁴³⁴ *DSO. LRCP.Ed. MRCS.*	31 Jan. 85	Ashton-under-Lyne.
Johnson, Cecil W.,⁴³⁹ *MB. MCh.*	31 Jan. 85	Madras.
Berryman, William Ebenezer, *LRCP.Ed. LRCS.Ed.*	31 Jan. 85	Bombay.
Lilly, Alfred Thomas Irvine, *LRCP. MRCS.*	31 Jan. 85	Bombay.
Caldwell, Robert,⁴⁴⁰ *LRCP.Ed. MRCS.*	31 Jan. 85	St. Helena.
Reilly, Charles Cooper,⁴³⁹ *LRCP. MRCS.*	31 Jan. 85	Bengal.
Duncan, Sidney Edward, *LRCP.Ed. MRCS.*	31 Jan. 85	Malta.
Perry, Allan, *MRCS. LSA. DPH.*	31 Jan. 85	Ceylon.
Cardozo, Samuel N.,⁴⁴² *LRCP. MRCS.*	31 Jan. 85	Bengal.
Scanlan, Arthur De Courcy, *MRCS. LSA.* P.B.M.85	31 Jan. 85	Bengal.
James, Henry Daniel, *LRCP. MRCS. LSA.*	31 Jan. 85	Madras.
Turner, William,⁴⁴³ *LRCP.Ed. LRCS.Ed.*	31 Jan. 85	Bengal.
Norfor, Brooke Owen William,⁴³⁹ *MB. MCh.*	31 Jan. 85	Bengal.
Hickson, Samuel, *MB. BA. BCh.Dub.* H.P.85	30 May 85	Dublin.
Fletcher, Henry James, *MB. MCh.*	30 May 85	Burnley.
Davis, Edward, *MRCS. LSA.*	30 May 85	India.
Powell, Simpson, *MB. MRCS. LSA.* P.B.M.85	30 May 85	Grenadier Guards.
Jones, Frederick William Caton,⁴⁴⁴ *MB. MRCS.*	30 May 85	Bombay.
Meek, James,⁴⁴⁵ *MD. MCh. MRCPI.*	30 May 85	Barbadoes.
Morris, Arthur Edward, *MD. MCh.*	30 May 85	Parkhurst.
FitzGerald, Arthur Ormsby, *LRCPI. LRCSI.*	30 May 85	Madras.
Elderton, Frederick Dundas, *LRCPI. LRCSI.*	30 May 85	Jamaica.
Sheldrake, Edward Nodin, *LRCP. MRCS.*	30 May 85	Grenadier Guards.
Molesworth, Robert Everard, *LRCP. MRCS.*	30 May 85	Bengal.
Long, John William Francis, *MRCS. LSA.*	30 May 85	Chatham.
Bateson, John Francis, *MB. MCh. MRCS.*	30 May 85	Egyptian Army.
Swan, William Travers, *MB. BCh.*	30 May 85	Bengal.
Macleod, Robert Lockhart Ross, *MB. MCh.*	30 May 85	India.
Curtis, James Henry, *LRCP.Ed. LRCS.Ed.*	30 May 85	Bermuda.
Adams, Gofton Gee, *LRCP. MRCS.*	30 May 85	Horfield.
Shine, James M. F. *MD. MCh.*	30 May 85	Malta.
Day, William Bullen, *MB. BCh.*	30 May 85	Malta.
Hamilton, David Rogerson,⁵⁹⁷ *MB. MCh.*	30 May 85	Bengal.
Thompson, Robert George, *MD. MCh.* M.G.M.85	30 May 85	Chatham.
Blackwell, Charles T. *LRCP.Ed. LRCS.Ed.*	30 May 85	India.
Power, Robert Ignatius, *LRCPI. LRCSI.*	30 May 85	Cork.
Kilkelly, Charles Randolph, *BA. MB. BCh. LRCSI.*	30 May 85	Aldershot.
Bean, William Henry,⁴⁴⁷ *MRCS. LSA.*	30 May 85	Madras.
Ferguson, Nicholas Charles, *MB. BCh. MRCPI.*	30 May 85	Cape of Good Hope.
Wills, Samuel Richard,⁴⁴⁸ *LRCPI. LRCSI.*	30 May 85	Bengal.
Hearn, Michael Leo, *LRCPI. LRCSI.*	30 May 85	Netley.
Hall, Richard Harris, *MD. MCh.*	30 May 85	Colchester.

A A

Surgeon Captains.	Surgeon Captain.	Regiment, or Station.
Greenway, John Henry, *MRCS. LSA*	30 May 85	Cape of Good Hope.
Hanley, Richard George, *BA. MB. BCh.*	30 May 85	Bengal.
Cree, Gerald, *MRCS. LSA.*	30 May 85	Training School, Aldershot.
Philson, Samuel Cowell,⁴⁴⁹ *LRCP. Ed. MRCS.*	30 May 85	Bengal.
Nicolls, John Michael, *BA. MB. BCh.*	30 May 85	India.
Harris, Frederick William Henry Davie, *MRCS. LSA.*	30 May 85	Training School, Aldershot.
Allen, Sydney Glenn, *LRCP. Ed. MRCS.*	1 Aug. 85	Woolwich Arsenal.
Green, James Sullivan, *BA. MB. BCh. MKQCPI.*	1 Aug. 85	Birmingham.
Lane, Cecil Alexander, *MB. MCh. LRCP. Ed.*	1 Aug. 85	Colchester.
Gordon, Philip Cecil Harcourt,⁴⁵⁴ *LRCP. Ed. LRCS. Ed.*	1 Aug. 85	Bengal.
Nash, Llewellyn Thomas Manly,⁴⁵⁵ *LRCPI. LRCSI.*	1 Aug. 85	Aldershot.
Brannigan, John Henderson, *LRCP. Ed. LRCS. Ed.*	1 Aug. 85	India.
O'Halloran, Michael, *MD. MCh.*	1 Aug. 85	Colchester.
Sparkes, Claude Stephen,⁴⁵⁶ *MRCS. LSA.*	1 Aug. 85	Egypt.
Pinches, William Hooper,⁴⁵⁷ *LRCP. Ed. MRCS.*	1 Aug. 85	Cape of Good Hope.
Tuke, George Jerry Arthur, *LRCP. Ed. LFPS. Glas.*	1 Aug. 85	Curragh.
Skerrett, Patrick B., *LRCPI. LRCSI.*	1 Aug. 85	Straits Settlements.
Greig, Frederick James,³⁹⁹ *LRCP. Ed. LRCSI.*	1 Aug. 85	Malta.
Rowan, Henry Davis,⁴⁵⁸ *MB. MCh.*	1 Aug. 85	Egypt.
Carr, Howard,⁴¹⁹ *MD. MCh.*	1 Aug. 85	Bengal.
Hathaway, Harold George,⁴⁵⁹ *MRCS. LSA.*	1 Aug. 85	Aldershot.
Dixon, Arthur Lewis Hoper	1 Aug. 85	Alderney.
Woods, Charles Greaves, *MD. MCh.*	1 Aug. 85	Straits Settlements.
Nunnerley, Phillip Jebb Rencontre,⁴⁶¹ *LRCP. MRCS.*	1 Aug. 85	Gibraltar.
Maturin, Benjamin Allen, *LRCP. Ed. LRCS. Ed.*	1 Aug. 85	Gosport.
Dillon, Henry Vincent, *LRCPI. LRCSI.*	1 Aug. 85	Madras.
Daly, Thomas, *LRCPI. LRCSI.*	1 Aug. 85	India.
Sexton, Michael John, *MD. MCh. LAH.*	1 Aug. 85	Malta.
Baylor, Henry Talbot, *LRCPI. LRCSI.*	1 Aug. 85	Bengal.
Cree, Herbert Eustace, *MRCS. LSA.*	1 Aug. 85	Bengal.
Starr, William Henderson, *LRCP. MRCS. LSA.*	1 Aug. 85	Bombay.
Sutton, Alexander Arthur, *LRCP. Ed. LFPS. Glas.*	1 Aug. 85	
Griffiths, Alfred Philip Henry, *MRCS. LSA.*	1 Aug. 85	Bengal.
Boles, William Samuel, *BA. MB. BCh.*	1 Aug. 85	Bengal.
Chavers, Herbert Longmore Grant, *LRCP. Ed. LRCS. Ed.*	1 Aug. 85	
Stoney, Frederick Joseph Wetherall, *LRCPI. FRCSI. LM. Dub.*		
Yarr, Michael Thomas, *LRCPI. LRCSI.* H.P. M.G.M. P.B.M. M.M. 86	30 Jan. 86	Coldstream Guards.
Mumby, Langton Philip, *MB. MRCS. LSA.*	30 Jan. 86	Bengal.
Melville, Charles Henderson, *MB. MCh.*	30 Jan. 86	Bombay.
Mills, Bernard Langley, *MD. LM. MCh. FRCS. Ed. MRCS. Eng.*	30 Jan. 86	Madras.
Rayner, Hugh, *MB. MRCS.*	30 Jan. 86	Grenadier Guards.
Cardew, George Schuyler, *MB. MCh. MRCS.*	30 Jan. 86	Dover.
Cocks, Horace, *MB. MCh.*	30 Jan. 86	Colchester.
Wilson, James Barnett, *MD. MCh.*	30 Jan. 86	India.
Black, John Greer, *MD. LM. MCh.*	30 Jan. 86	Gibraltar.
Kearney, John, *MD. MCh.*	30 Jan. 86	Hounslow.
Saw, Francis Albert, *MB. MRCS.*	30 Jan. 86	Chester.
Hall, Frederic William George, *MB. MCh.*	30 Jan. 85	Woolwich.
Kennedy, Arthur, *LRCPI. LRCSI.*	30 Jan. 86	Dublin.
Elkington, Henry Percival George, *MB. MRCS. LSA.*	30 Jan. 86	Tower of London.
Buchanan, John Blacker Whitla, *MB. BCh.*	30 Jan. 86	Bengal.
Adamson, Henry Mackenzie, *MB. MCh.*	30 Jan. 86	Egypt.
Ramsay, Herbert Murray, *LRCP. Ed. MRCS.*	30 Jan. 86	Scots Guards.
Lavie, Tudor Germain, *LRCP. Ed. MRCS.*	30 Jan. 86	Lichfield.
Brown, Harry Herbert,⁴⁶³ *MB. MCh.*	30 Jan. 86	Barry Links.
Corkery, Thomas Herbert, *LRCP. Ed. LFPS. Glas.*	30 Jan. 86	Gravesend.
Crooke, Warren Roland Davies, *MB. MCh.*	30 Jan. 86	Coldstream Guards.
Squire, Walter Perfect, *LRCP. Ed. MRCS.*	30 Jan. 86	Cape of Good Hope.
O'Donnell, James John, *BA. MB. BCh.*	30 Jan. 86	Bengal.
Hayman, Stanley John Wallace, *LRCP. Ed. LRCS. Ed. LFPS. Glas.*	30 Jan. 86	Canterbury.
Hayes, Julian Philip Swindell, *LRCPI. MRCS.*	30 Jan. 86	Malta.
Davidson, John Stewart, *MB. MCh.*	28 July 86	Devonport.
Will, James, *MB. MCh.*	28 July 86	Edinburgh.
Moir, James, *MB. MCh.*	28 July 86	Maryhill.
Fallon, James, *LRCP. Ed. LRCS. Ed. LAH.*	28 July 86	Mauritius.
Salvage, John Valentine, *MD. MRCS. LRCP. DSSc.*	28 July 86	Woolwich.
Fowler, John Francis Scott, *MB. MCh.*	28 July 86	Sheerness.
Aldridge, Arthur Russell, *MB. MCh.*	28 July 86	Netley.
Bostock, Robert Ashton, *LRCP. MRCS. LSA.*	28 July 86	Grenadier Guards.
Fayrer, Joseph, *MA. MB. LRCP. Ed. FRCS. Ed. LFPS. Glas.*	28 July 86	Royal Horse Guards.
Walker, Charles Pope, *MB. MRCS.*	28 July 86	Portsmouth.
MacDonald, Charles Joseph, *BA. MB. MCh.*	28 July 86	Newry.
Tatham, Charles John Willmer, *MRCS. LSA.*	28 July 86	Woolwich.
Clarkson, Thomas Harry Frederick, *LRCP. MRCS.*	28 July 86	Dover.
Austin, Herbert Ward, *LRCP. MRCS.*	28 July 86	Devonport.
Garner, Cathcart, *BA. MB. BCh.*	28 July 86	Egypt.
Wright, Robert Wallace, *LRCP. MRCS.*	28 July 86	Woolwich.
Bailey, William Frederick,⁴⁶⁵ *MD. MCh.*	28 July 86	Belfast.
Eckersley, Edwin, *MB. MCh.*	28 July 86	Woolwich.
Cottell, Reginald James Cope, *LRCP. MRCS. LSA.*	28 July 86	Woolwich.
Burrows, James Rogers, *BA. MD. MCh.*	28 July 86	Egypt.
Keatly, John, *LRCPI. LRCSI.*	28 July 86	Bengal.
Hennessy, Daniel, *MD. MCh.*	28 July 86	Birr.
Saunders, David Michael, *MD. MCh.*	28 July 86	Manchester.
Kiddle, Walter, *BA. MB. BCh. LRCPI.* P.B.M. 86	28 July 86	Woolwich.
O'Callaghan, Denis Moriarty, *LRCPI. LRCSI.*	28 July 86	Adjt. Vol. Med. Staff Corps.
Whitty, Michael Joseph, *MD. MCh.*	28 July 86	Dublin.
Cummins, Henry Alfred,⁴⁷⁰ *MD. MCh.*	28 July 86	Fermoy.
Kelly, Richard Edmund, *MD. MCh.*	28 July 86	Nova Scotia.
Donegan, James Francis,⁴³² *LRCP. Ed. LRCS. Ed.*	28 July 86	Cork.
Donaldson, John, *LRCP. Ed. LRCS. Ed. LFPS. Glas.*	28 July 86	Woolwich.
Mathias, Hugh Broderick, *MRCS. LSA.*	28 July 86	Egypt.
Bent, George, *LRCP. MRCS.*	28 July 86	Netley.
Barefoot, George Henry,⁴⁷¹ *LRCP. Ed. LRCS. Ed. LFPS. Glas.*	28 July 86	India.
Newland, Foster Reuss, *MB. BCh.*	28 July 86	India.

Army Medical Staff.

Surgeon Captains.	Surgeon Captain.	Regiment, or Station.
Windle, Reginald Joscelyn, *BA. MB. BCh.*	28 July 86	Training School, Aldershot.
Hall, Robert John Draper, *LRCP. Ed. LRCS.Ed.*	28 July 86	Madras.
Marder, Edward Swan,[472] *LRCP. MRCS.*	28 July 86	Devonport.
Allport, Charles William, *MD. MCh.*	28 July 86	Chatham.
Russell, John Joshua, *BA. MB. BCh.*	28 July 86	Kilkenny.
Edye, John Simpson, *LRCP. MRCS. LSA.*	28 July 86	Aldershot.
Scott, George, *MB. MCh.*	28 July 86	Jersey.
Browning, Thomas, *LRCPI. LRCSI.*	28 July 86	Limerick.
Bate, Albert L. F. *LRCPI. LRCSI.*	28 July 86	Dublin.
Trotter, William John, *LRCPI. LRCSI.*	28 July 86	India.
Hosie, Andrew, *MD. MCh.*	28 July 86	Woolwich.
Marks, George Frederick Handel, *MD. MCh.*	28 July 86	Dover.
Holyoake, Ralph, *LRCP. Ed. MRCS.*	28 July 86	Colchester.
Buist, Robert Napier, *MB.*	28 July 86	Bombay.
Watson, John James Carl, *BA. MD. BCh.*	28 July 86	Dublin.
Whaite, Thomas du Bédat, *MB. BCh.*	28 July 86	India.
Knaggs, Henry Thomas, *LRCPI. LRCSI.*	28 July 86	Bombay.
Le Quesne, Ferdinand Simeon,[478] *LRCP. MRCS. LSA.*	28 July 86	India.
Dowman, Willington, *LRCP. Ed. LRCS. Ed.*	28 July 86	Cork.
Morgan, Frederick James, *LRCP. MRCS.*	5 Feb. 87	Woolwich.
Horrocks, William Heaton, *MB. BSc. MRCS.* H.P. M.G.M. M.M. 87	5 Feb. 87	Bengal.
Hale, Charles Henry, *LRCP. MRCS.*	5 Feb. 87	Cape of Good Hope.
Thurston, Hugh Champneys, *LRCP. MRCS.*	5 Feb. 87	Madras.
Scott, Bertal Hopton, *MD. MCh. LRCP. Ed. MRCS.*	5 Feb. 87	Bombay.
Poole, Walter Croker, *BA. MB. BCh.*	5 Feb. 87	Bengal.
Julian, Oliver Richard Archer, *LRCP. MRCS. LSA.*	5 Feb. 87	Egypt.
Raymond, George, *BA. MB. BCh.*	5 Feb. 87	Cape of Good Hope.
Burnside, Eustace Augustus, *MRCS. LSA.*	5 Feb. 87	Malta.
M'Culloch, Thomas, *MB. MCh.*	5 Feb. 87	Dover.
Hinde, Alfred Buckley, *LRCP. MRCS.* P.D.M.87.	5 Feb. 87	Singapore.
Reily, Alexander Yates, *MB. MRCS. LSA.*	5 Feb. 87	Egypt.
Cockerill, John William,[477] *MRCS. LSA. LRCP.*	5 Feb. 87	Madras.
Ritchie, John, *MB. MCh.*	5 Feb. 87	Malta.
Hore, Harry St.George Standish, *LRCP. MRCS.*	5 Feb. 87	Malta.
Macdonald, Stuart, *MB. MCh.*	5 Feb. 87	
Corcoran, Edward, *LRCPI. LRCSI.*	5 Feb. 87	
Watson, Alexander Oswald Cowan, *MB. MCh.Ed. LRCP.Ed. LRCS.Ed.*	5 Feb. 87	
Gray, Edward Wolfenden, *BA. MB. BCh. LAH. MRCPI.*	5 Feb. 87	
Stiell, David, *MB. MCh.*	5 Feb. 87	
Salmon, Lawrence Ernest Albert, *LRCP. Ed. MRCS.*	5 Feb. 87	Aldershot.
Wade, George Augustus, *BA. MB. BCh. FRCSI.*	5 Feb. 87	Cape of Good Hope.
Minnieco, James, *MD. MCh.*	5 Feb. 87	Aldershot.
Penton, Richard Hugh, LRCP. MRCS.	5 Feb. 87	Egyptian Army.
Holt, Maurice Percy Cue, *MRCS. LSA.*	5 Feb. 87	Cape of Good Hope.
Gray, William Lewis, *MB. MCh.*	5 Feb. 87	Madras.
Browne, Edward George, *LRCPI. LRCSI.*	5 Feb. 87	Bengal.
Morgan, James Campbell, *LRCP. MRCS.*	5 Feb. 87	India.
Pocock, Herbert Innes, *LRCP. MRCS.*	5 Feb. 87	
Hilliard, George, *BA. MB. BCh.*	5 Feb. 87	Shorncliffe.
Elliott, Charles Roulston, *MD. MCh.*	5 Feb. 87	
Young, Charles Augustus, *LRCPI. LRCSI.*	5 Feb. 87	
Bullen, John Welply, *MD. MCh.*	5 Feb. 87	Bengal.
Weir, James Christopher, *MB. BCh.*	5 Feb. 87	Bengal.
Inniss, Benjamin James, *LRCP.Ed. MRCS.*	5 Feb. 87	
Thacker, Robert Christy, *LRCPI. LRCSI.*	5 Feb. 87	Aldershot.
Clark, Stephen Frazer, *MB. MCh.*	5 Feb. 87	
Hassard, Edward Moresby, *LRCP. MRCS.*	5 Feb. 87	
Smith, Henry Ernest Hill, MRCS. LSA.	27 July 87	Egyptian Army.
Graham, William Perceval Gore, MB. MRCS. M.M.87	27 July 87	Egyptian Army.
Alexander, George Forbes, *MB. MCh.*	27 July 87	Bengal.
Spong, Charles Stuart, BSc. FRCS.	27 July 87	Egyptian Army.
Leishman, William Boog, *MB. MCh.*	27 July 87	Bengal.
Thomson, James, *MA. MB. MCh.*	27 July 87	Bengal.
Rawnsley, Gerald Thomas, *MRCS. LSA.*	27 July 87	Malta.
Reilly, Charles William, *LRCP.Ed. LRCS.Ed.*	27 July 87	Bengal.
Freeman, Ernest Carrick, *LRCP. MRCS.*	27 July 87	Bengal.
Trask, John Ernest, *LRCP. MRCS.*	27 July 87	Bombay.
Blenkinsop, Alfred Percy, *LRCP. MRCS. LSA.*	27 July 87	Cape of Good Hope.
Paterson, John, *MB.*	27 July 87	Bengal.
Davoren, Vesey Henry William, *LRCPI. LRCSI.*	27 July 87	Bombay.
Wright, Alfred, LRCP.Ed. MRCS.	27 July 87	Cape Colonial Med. Service.
Copeland, Robert James, *MB. MCh.*	27 July 87	Bombay.
Girvin, John, *LRCP. MRCS.*	27 July 87	Bombay.
Luther, Anthony John, *LRCPI. LRCSI.*	27 July 87	Cahir.
Peeke, Harold Samuel, *LRCP. MRCS.*	27 July 87	Bengal.
Borradaile, Alfred Latour, *MB. MCh.*	27 July 87	Hong Kong.
Birt, Thomas, *MRCS. LSA.*	27 July 87	Bengal.
Hallaran, William, *MB. BCh.*	27 July 87	Ceylon.
Hughes, Matthew Louis, *LRCP. MRCS. LSA.* P.M.N.	1 Feb. 90	Malta.
Mould, William Thomas, *LRCP. MRCS.*	1 Feb. 90	Bengal.
Bewley, Alfred William, *LRCPI. LRCSI.*	1 Feb. 90	Bengal.
Stone, Charles Alfred, *MD. BCh.*	1 Feb. 90	Bengal.
Winter, Herbert Edmond, *LRCP. MRCS. LSA.*	1 Feb. 90	Bengal.
Moores, Samuel Guise, *LRCP. MRCS. LSA.*	1 Feb. 90	Bengal.
Way, Lewis, *LRCP. MRCS. LSA.*	1 Feb. 90	Madras.
Smith, Frederick, *LRCPI. LRCSI.*	30 Mar. 90	Singapore.
Smithson, Arthur Ernest, *BA. MB. BCh.*	29 July 90	Bengal.
Whiston, Philip Henry, LRCP. MRCS. LSA.	29 July 90	Egyptian Army.
M'Loughlin, George Somers, *MB. BS.*	29 July 90	Bengal.
Parry, Henry Jules, *MB. MRCS. LSA.*	29 July 90	Bombay.
Beveridge, Wilfred William Ogilvy, *MB. MCh.*	29 July 90	Hong Kong.
Jackson, Robert William Henry, *BA. MB. BCh.*	29 July 90	Coldstream Guards.
Mawhinny, Robert John Watt, *LRCPI. LRCSI.*	29 July 90	Bengal.
Bray, George Arthur Theodore, *LRCP. MRCS. LSA.*	29 July 90	Madras.
Forde, Bernard, *MB. MCh.*	29 July 90	York.

Army Medical Staff.

SURGEON CAPTAINS.	SURGEON CAPTAIN.		REGIMENT, OR STATION.
Ferguson, John David, *LRCPI. LRCSI*.	29 July 90		Barbadoes.
Beach, Thomas Boswall, *LRCP. MRCS. LSA*.	31 Jan. 91		Bengal.
Powell, Edgar Elkins, *LRCP. MRCS. LSA*.	31 Jan. 91		Bengal.
Healey, Coryndon W. R., *LRCPI. LRCSI*.	31 Jan. 91		Bengal.
Jennings, James Willes, *LRCPI. LRCSI*.	31 Jan. 91		Egypt.
Williams, Edgar M'Kenzie, *LRCP. MRCS*.	31 Jan. 91		Bengal.
Dowse, Henry Esmonde, *LRCP. MRCS*.	31 Jan. 91		Bengal.
Connor, John Colpoys, *MB. BCh*.	31 Jan. 91		Madras.
Carter, James Edward, *MB. BCh*.	31 Jan. 91		Ceylon.
Hardy, Frederick Wynne, *LSA*.	31 Jan. 91		Ceylon.
Clapham, John Thurlow, *LRCP. MRCS*.	31 Jan. 91		Barbadoes.
Graham, Walter Ap Samuel James, *LRCP. MRCS*.	31 Jan. 91		Barbadoes.
Shanahan, Daniel Davis, *LRCPI. LRCSI*.	31 Jan. 91		Madras.
Whitestone, Charles William Henry, *MB. BCh*.	31 Jan. 91		Madras.
Pearse, Albert, *LRCP. MRCS*.	31 Jan. 91		Bengal.
Mason, Hubert Dempster, *LRCPI. MRCS*.	31 Jan. 91		Bombay.
Dalton, Charles, *LRCPI*.	31 Jan. 91		Madras.
Porter, Frederick Joseph William, *LSA. MRCS. LRCP*.	28 July 91		Bengal.
Robinson, Oliver Long, *MRCS. LRCP*.	28 July 91		Egypt.
Stalkartt, Charles Edward Grey, *MD. MRCS. LRCP*.	28 July 91		Bombay.
Gibbard, Thomas Wykes, *MB. MRCS. LSA*.	28 July 91		Madras.
Healy, Christopher James, *MB. BCh*.	28 July 91		Bengal.
Burtchaell, Charles Henry, *MB. BCh*.	28 July 91		Bengal.
Buist, Herbert John Martin, *MB. MCh*.	28 July 91		Bengal.
Stanistreet, George Bradshaw, *MB. BCh*.	28 July 91		Bengal.
Wade-Brown, Francis Joseph, *MRCS. LRCP*.	28 July 91		Bombay.
Hardy, William Edmund, *MRCS. LRCP*.	28 July 91		Bengal.
Brogden, James England, *LRCP.Ed. LRCS.Ed. LFPS.Glas*.	28 July 91		Bengal.
Tate, Gerard William, *MB. BCh*.	28 July 91		Bengal.
Faichnie, Norman, *MB. BCh*.	28 July 91		Bombay.
Lenehan, Thomas Joseph, *MB. BCh*.	28 July 91		Bengal.
M'Dowell, Frederick, *LRCP.Ed. LRCS.Ed. LFPS.Glas*.	28 July 91		Bengal.
Begbie, Francis Warburton	28 July 91		Bengal.
MacCarthy, Ibar Ansbert Orva, *MRCS. LRCP*.	28 July 91		Egypt.
Austin, John Henry Edward, *MRCS. LRCP.Ed*.	28 July 91		Madras.
Gerrard, John Joseph, *MB. BCh*.	28 July 91		Bengal.
Jameson, James Conway, *MB. MCh*.	28 July 91		Bengal.
SURG. LT.			
Pilcher, Edgar Montagu, *MB. BCh*.	30 Jan. 92	30 Jan. 95	Bengal.
Johnson, Henry Percival, *MRCS. LRCP*.	30 Jan. 92	30 Jan. 95	Bengal.
Beyts, William George, *MRCS. LRCP*.	30 Jan. 92	30 Jan. 95	Bengal.
Stalkartt, Harold Arthur, *MB. MCh*.	30 Jan. 92	30 Jan. 95	Bengal.
Dunn, Henry Nason, *MB. BCh*.	30 Jan. 92	30 Jan. 95	Bengal.
Withers, Samuel Henry, *MB. BCh*.	30 Jan. 92	30 Jan. 95	Bengal.
Morphew, Edward Maudsley, *MRCS. LRCP*.	30 Jan. 92	30 Jan. 95	Bengal.
Anderson, Ernest Chester, *MRCS. LRCP. LSA*.	30 Jan. 92	30 Jan. 95	Bengal.
Tyacke, Nicholas, *MRCS. LRCP*.	30 Jan. 92	30 Jan. 95	Bengal.
Holt, Robert Hughtrede Edward, *MRCS. LRCP. LSA*.	30 Jan. 92	30 Jan. 95	Bengal.
Mitchell, Lionel Arthur, *MB. BCh*.	30 Jan. 92	30 Jan. 95	Bengal.
Fleming, Charles Christie, *MB. MCh*.	30 Jan. 92	30 Jan. 95	Bengal.
Hennessy, John, *MB. BCh*.	30 Jan. 92	30 Jan. 95	Bengal.
Martin, Claude Buist, *MB. MCh*.	30 Jan. 92	30 Jan. 95	Bengal.
Buchanan, George Johnstone, *MB*.	30 Jan. 92	30 Jan. 95	Bengal.
Lawson, Charles Bunbury, *MB. MCh*.	30 Jan. 92	30 Jan. 95	Bengal.
Hughes, George Edgar, *LRCSI. LRCPI*.	30 Jan. 92	30 Jan. 95	Madras.
Kelly, Joseph Francis Mary, *MB*.	30 Jan. 92	30 Jan. 95	Bengal.
Crawford, Gilbert Stewart, *LRCP.Ed. LRCS.Ed. LFPS. Glas. LM.Dub*.	30 Jan. 92	30 Jan. 95	Madras.
Alexander, John Donald, *MB. BCh*.	30 Jan. 92	30 Jan. 95	Bengal.
SURGEON LIEUTENANTS.			
Hinge, Harry Alexander, *MRCS. LRCP*.	27 July 92	.....	India.
M'Naught, James Gibson, *MA. MD. MCh. H.P.N. 92*.	27 July 92	.....	India.
Bray, Hubert Alaric, *LRCP. MRCS*.	27 July 92	.....	India.
M'Dermott, Thomas, *MB. Ch. LM.Dub*.	27 July 92	.....	India.
Slayter, Edward Wheeler, *MB. MCh*.	27 July 92	.....	India.
Thurston, Hugh Stanley, *LRCP. MRCS*.	27 July 92	.....	India.
More, Lancelot Paxton, *MB. MCh.Ed*.	27 July 92	.....	India.
Hodges, Charles O'Connor, *LRCPI. LRCSI. LM.Dub*.	27 July 92	.....	India.
Tyrrell, Arthur Frederick, *LRCP. MRCS*.	27 July 92	.....	India.
Jones, Theophilus Percy, *MB. BCh*.	27 July 92	.....	India.
Walker, George Stanley, *MB. BCh*.	27 July 92	.....	Cork.
Smyth, William Johnson, *MD. MCh*.	27 July 92	.....	Grenadier Guards.
Erskine, William Douglas, *MB. MCh*.	27 July 92	.....	India.
Thompson, Albert George, *MB. MCh*.	27 July 92	.....	India.
Chambers, Alexander Jasper, *LRCP. MRCS*.	27 July 92	.....	Bombay.
Moore, George Abraham, *MB. BCh. LM.Dub*.	27 July 92	.....	India.
Lewis, Richard Crump, *LRCPI. LRCSI. LM.Dub*.	27 July 92	.....	Bombay.
Austin, Reginald Francis Edmund, *LRCP. MRCS*.	27 July 92	.....	Bombay.
O'Reilly, Henry William Hutchinson, *MB. BCh*.	27 July 92	.....	India.
Marder, Nicholas, *LRCP. MRCS*.	27 July 92	.....	Bombay.
Condon, Edgar Hunt, *MB. MCh. LRCSI. LM.Dub*.	27 July 92	.....	Bengal.
Mansfield, Gerald Stewart, *MB. MCh*.	27 July 92	.....	Bengal.
Faichnie, Frederick George, *LRCP. MRCS*.	27 July 92	.....	Bengal.
Read, Harold William Kingcombe, *LRCP.Ed. LRCS.Ed. LFPS.Glas*.	27 July 92	.....	Bombay.
Mangan, Frederick Meredyth, *MRCS. LRCP*.	30 Jan. 93	.....	Aldershot.
Pollock, Charles Edward, *MRCS. LRCP*.	30 Jan. 93	.....	Gosport.
Taylor, William James, *MB*.	30 Jan. 93	.....	Shorncliffe.
Longhurst, Bell Wilmott, *LRCP. MRCS*.	30 Jan. 93	.....	Portland.
Rivers, John Herbert, *MRCS. LRCP*.	30 Jan. 93	.....	Pembroke Dock.
Berryman, Henry Arthur, *MRCS. LRCP*.	30 Jan. 93	.....	Jersey.
Buswell, Ferberd Richard, *MRCS. LRCP*.	30 Jan. 93	.....	Curragh.
Symons, Frank Albert, *MB*.	30 Jan. 93	.....	Fermoy.
Farmer, John Henry, *LRCSI. LRCPI*.	30 Jan. 93	.....	India.

Army Medical Staff. 386

SURGEON LIEUTENANTS.	SURGEON LIEUT.	REGIMENT, OR STATION.
Samman, Charles Thomas, *MRCS. LSA*............	30 Jan. 93	India.
Spencer, Charles George, *MB*............	29 July 93	Woolwich.
Fowler, Charles Edward Percy, *FRCS. LRCP.*............	29 July 93	York.
Goodwin, Thomas Herbert John Chapman, *MRCS. LRCP.*............	29 July 93	Newcastle.
Porter, Harry Edwin Bruce............	29 July 93	Shorncliffe.
Keble, Alfred Ernest Conquer	29 July 93	Preston.
Lattey, Arthur James, *MRCS. LRCP.*............	29 July 93	Colchester.
Collins, Denis Joseph, *MB, BCh. LAH. Dub.*............	29 July 93	Cork.
Killery, St. John Browne, *MRCS. LRCP.*............	29 July 93	Cork.
French, Herbert Cumming, *MRCS. LRCP.*............	29 July 93	Chatham.
Smith, Walter Woodbine, *MRCS. LRCP.*............	29 July 93	Dover.
Barter, William Pearson	29 July 93	Dublin.
Williams, Ernest Montgomery	29 July 93	Devonport.
M'Munn, James Robert, *LRCPI. LRCSI.*............	29 July 93	Hilsea.
Anderson, John Buckle, *MRCS. LRCP.*............	29 July 93	Chatham.
Prynne, Harold Vernon	29 Jan. 94	Gosport.
Master, Alfred Edmund, *MB.*............	29 Jan. 94	Fort George.
Dansey-Browning, George	29 Jan. 94	Barry Links.
Clark, Ernest Shaw, *MB.*............	29 Jan. 94	Woolwich.
Barnett, Kennet Bruce, *MB.*............	29 Jan. 94	Colchester.
Boyle, Michael, *MB.*............	29 Jan. 94	Aldershot.
Cameron, Kenneth Mackenzie, *MB.*............	29 Jan. 94	Aldershot.
Fleury, Charles Marlay............	29 Jan. 94	Netley.
Fox, Arthur Claude............	29 Jan. 94	Curragh.
Green, Sebert Francis St. Davids............	29 Jan. 94	Dublin.
Tibbits, Walter, *MB.*............	29 Jan. 94	Curragh.
Evans, Percy, *MB.*............	28 July 94	Portsmouth.
Milner, Arthur Edward	28 July 94	Alderney.
Morgan, Claude Kyd, *MB.*............	28 July 94	Canterbury.
Silver, John Payzant, *MB.*............	28 July 94	Devonport.
Vaughan-Williams, Herbert Wynne, *MB.*............	28 July 94	Cork.
Buist, John Martin, *MB.*............	28 July 94	Dublin.
Walker, James, *MB.*............	28 July 94	Belfast.
Dove, Frank	28 July 94	Woolwich.
Thom, George St. Clair, *MB.*............	28 July 94	Curragh.
Sweetnam, Stephen Westrope	28 July 94	Curragh.
Harrison, William Sandilands, *MB.*............	29 Jan. 95	Aldershot.
Howell, Harry Arthur Leonard	29 Jan. 95	Aldershot.
Lawson, Douglas	29 Jan. 95	Aldershot.
Steel, Edwin Bedford, *MB.*............	29 Jan. 95	Aldershot.
Profeit, Charles William, *MB.*............	29 Jan. 95	Aldershot.
Kiddle, Frederick, *MB.*............	29 Jan. 95	Aldershot.
Staddon, Henry Ernest	29 Jan. 95	Aldershot.
Whitehead, John Herbert	29 Jan. 95	Aldershot.
Murison, James Augustus, *MB.*............	29 Jan. 95	Aldershot.
Tomlinson, Lionel Philip............	29 Jan. 95	Aldershot.
Perry, Samuel James Chatterton Prittie	29 Jan. 95	Aldershot.
Heaton, Arthur Frederick	29 Jan. 95	Aldershot.

QUARTER MASTERS.

	LIEUT. OF ORDERLIES.	CAPT. OF ORDERLIES.	HON. CAPTAIN.	QUARTER MASTER.	STATION.
Osborne, Robert Toler,[482] *Hon. Major*, 7 May 90	25 June 73	7 Aug. 75	7 Aug. 75	1 July 81	Portsmouth.
O'Connor, Daniel[484]	7 Aug. 75	......	7 Aug. 85	1 July 81	Portsmouth.
McIntyre, David[488]	9 June 77	......	9 June 87	1 July 81	Edinburgh.
Lackey, Daniel[489]	9 June 77	......	9 June 87	1 July 81	Devonport.
Kennedy, Thomas Francis	9 June 77	......	9 June 87	1 July 81	Dublin.
Horn, John[491]	22 Mar. 79	......	22 Mar. 89	1 July 81	Chester.
		HON. LIEUT.			
Connor, Timothy[495]	2 July 79	2 July 79	2 July 89	1 July 81	Dublin.
Hunt, Joseph	2 July 79	2 July 79	2 July 89	1 July 81	Woolwich.
Morrison, William	17 Dec. 79	17 Dec. 79	17 Dec. 89	1 July 81	London.
Phillips, Thomas[497]	4 Sept. 80	4 Sept. 80	4 Sept. 90	1 July 81	Egypt.
M'Callum, William	18 Dec. 80	18 Dec. 80	18 Dec. 90	1 July 81	Woolwich.
Buckley, John	......	23 May 87	23 May 89	23 May 83	Portsmouth.
Merritt, George	......	10 July 89	......	10 July 89	Malta.
Gillman, David James	......	7 Aug. 89	......	7 Aug. 89	{ Training Sch. Aldershot.
Beach, Joseph Herbert Wolfe[498]	......	8 Jan. 90	......	8 Jan. 90	Cork.
Bond, Thomas	......	30 July 90	......	30 July 90	Belfast.
Thowless, Edwin	......	24 Dec. 90	......	24 Dec. 90	Natal.
Kyle, Frederick[499]	......	24 Dec. 90	......	24 Dec. 90	Netley.
Adams, Richard[500]	......	4 Feb. 91	... ...	4 Feb. 91	Hong Kong.
Hirst, James............	......	4 Feb. 91	......	4 Feb. 91	Gibraltar.
Hewitt, Martin............	......	22 Apr. 91	......	22 Apr. 91	Dover.
Arbeiter, Charles............	......	23 Sept. 91	......	23 Sept. 91	Devonport.
Goater, Benjamin............	......	23 Dec. 91	......	23 Dec. 91	Aldershot.
Lockhart, Harry	......	16 Mar. 92	......	16 Mar. 92	Chatham.
Lane, George James	......	16 Mar. 92	......	16 Mar. 92	Egypt.
Vidler, William Thomas	......	13 July 92	......	13 July 92	Shorncliffe.
Bere, Charles	......	11 Jan. 93	......	11 Jan. 93	Curragh.
Barton, William Henry............	......	9 Aug. 93	......	9 Aug. 93	York.
Lines, Edward	......	4 Oct. 93	......	4 Oct. 93	Colchester.
Tandy, John	......	16 Apr. 94	......	16 Apr. 94	Aldershot.
Freshwater, Arthur	......	22 July 94	......	22 July 94	Netley.
Crawley, Charles	......	8 Aug. 94	......	8 Aug. 94	Malta.
Brake, Timothy Francis	......	5 Sept. 94	......	5 Sept. 94	Aldershot.
Short, John Bartholomew	......	12 Sept. 94	......	12 Sept. 94	London.
Blackman, William James............	......	27 Feb. 95	......	27 Feb. 95	

Officer Commanding.—Brigade Surgeon Lt.Colonel W. H. M'Namara, *MD. FRCSI.* 22 Oct. 91.
Second in Command and Instructor.—Surgeon Major C. R. Tyrrell, 1 July 94.
Adjutant.—Surgeon Captain F. W. H. D. Harris, 29 July 94.
Commanding B Company and Assistant Instructor.—Surgeon Captain G. Cree, 1 July 94.
Commanding A Company.—Surgeon Captain R. J. Windle, *MB.* 29 July 94.
Quarter Master.—Hon. Lieut. D. J. Gillman, 1 Oct. 90.

Medical Officers serving on the West Coast of Africa.

SURGEON MAJORS.	ASSISTANT SURGEON.	SURGEON CAPTAIN.	SURGEON MAJOR.	SURGEON LT.COL.	STATION.
Sharpe, Alexander, *MD. MCh. MRCPI.*	......	5 Feb. 81	5 Feb. 93	......	
Morgan, Anthony Hickman,[317] *DSO. LRCPI.LRCSI.*	......	5 Feb. 81	5 Feb. 93	......	
Clements, William George, *MRCS. LSA.*	......	30 July 81	30 July 93	......	Sierra Leone.
SURGEON CAPTAINS.					
Wilson, George, *MB. MCh. MRCS.*	......	2 Feb. 84	......	......	Sierra Leone.
Crofts, Richard,[424]† *LRCP.Ed. LRCS.Ed.*	......	31 Jan. 85	......	......	Sierra Leone.
Maher, James,[441] *LRCP.Ed. LRCS.Ed.*	......	31 Jan. 85	......	......	Sierra Leone.
Josling, Charles Langford,[411]† *LRCP. MRCS. LSA.*	......	30 May 85	......	......	
Burke, John Fitz Gerald,[425] *LRCP.Ed. LRCS.Ed.*	......	1 Aug. 85	......	......	Sierra Leone.
Duggan, Charles William, *MB. MCh.*	......	28 July 91	......	......	

Blue *Uniform* with Black Velvet *Facings.*

APOTHECARY, *ranking with Captain* .... John Davies, 14 Apr. 68. Woolwich.

Army Medical Staff.—War Services.

[1] Sir W. A. Mackinnon served throughout the Eastern campaign of 1854-55 with the 42nd Highlanders, including the battles of Alma and Balaklava (in medical charge of the Regiment), expedition to Kertch and Yenikale, siege and fall of Sebastopol, and assault of the outworks on the 18th June and 8th September (Medal with three Clasps, Knight of the Legion of Honor, and Turkish Medal). Served as Surgeon on the personal Staff of Lord Clyde during the Indian Mutiny from April 1858 to the end of the war, and was present in the campaigns in Rohilcund, Byswarrah, and Trans-Gogra, including the actions of Bareilly, Shahjehanpore, Doondiakeira, Bergudin, Musjedia, and the Raptee (Medal). Served in the New Zealand war of 1863-66, including the capture of the rebel position at Katikara and repulse of the attack at Gilbert's Clearing (mentioned in despatches). Appointed Sanitary Officer to the New Zealand Force in Nov. 1863, and held the appointment till April 1866, when field operations ceased. In that capacity he served the campaigns in the Waikato, Tauranga, and Wanganui districts, on the headquarters Staff of Sir D. Cameron, and attached to the Quarter Master General's Department; was present in the action at Ranginwhia, assault of the Gate Pah, Tauranga (mentioned in despatches, and *CB.*), repulse of the enemy's attack on the Camp at Nukumaru, and affair at Kakaramea (Medal). Served as Principal Medical Officer in the second phase of the Ashanti war of 1873-74, including the battle of Amoaful, battle of Ordahsu and capture of Coomassie (several times mentioned in despatches, promoted Deputy Surgeon General, Medal with Clasp).

[2] Surgeon Major General A. F. Bradshaw served with the 2nd Battalion Rifle Brigade through the whole of its service in the suppression of the Indian Mutiny, including the capture of Lucknow and numerous affairs during the Oude campaign (Medal with Clasp). Served with the Zhob Valley Expedition in 1884 as Principal Medical Officer (mentioned in despatches). Served with the Hazara Expedition in 1891 as Principal Medical Officer (mentioned in despatches, *CB.*, and Medal with Clasp).

[5] Surgeon Major General R. Lower served in the Royal Navy during the operations in the Baltic and was present at the bombardment of Sweaborg (Medal). Served in the Afghan war of 1878-80 in medical charge of the 9th Lancers and as Sanitary Officer to the Cabul Field Force, and was present in the operations around Cabul in December 1879 including the investment of Sherpore; accompanied Sir Frederick Roberts in the march to Candahar, and was present at the battle of Candahar (mentioned in despatches, Medal with two Clasps, and Bronze Decoration).

[7] Surgeon Major General J. Inkson served with the Baltic Expedition of 1855, including the bombardment of Sweaborg (Medal). Served in the Indian Mutiny campaign in 1858, including the capture of Jugdespore and actions of the 17th 18th and 20th October (Medal). Served also with the Bhootan Expedition of 1865 (Medal with Clasp).

[8] Surgeon Major General J. Jameson was promoted Surgeon "in consideration of his highly meritorious services during an epidemic of yellow fever in Trinidad." Had charge of the D division of the English ambulance in the Franco-German war from October 1870 till March 1871, and was employed at the siege of Paris and in the campaign on the Loire.

[9] Surgeon Major General J. Warren served in medical charge of the 15th Hussars in the Afghan war of 1878-80, including the advance to Khelat-i-Ghilzie and with the Thull Chotiali Field Force under Major General Biddulph (Medal). Served in the Egyptian war of 1882 in charge of No. 5 Moveable Field Hospital (Medal, and Khedive's Star); also served in the Soudan campaign in 1885 (mentioned in despatches, Clasp).

[12] Surgeon Major General Davis served with the 57th Regiment in the New Zealand war in 1861 (Medal).

[13] Surgeon Major General C. H. Giraud served with a flying column in the North West Provinces of India in 1858-59, including the action at Sissaghat (Medal with Clasp). Also with the 31st Regiment during the campaign in North China in 1860, including the action of Sinho and storming of Tangku (Medal with Clasp for the Taku Forts). Served with the 31st Regiment in the operations against the Taepings in the vicinity of Shanghae, including service with the storming parties at the capture of the walled towns of Kahding, Najow, Cholin, and Tsinpoo, taking of the Stockaded fort at Nansiang, relief and recapture of Kahding. Served with the 2nd Brigade 1st Division in the Zulu war of 1879, and afterwards as Senior Medical Officer throughout the operations of "Clarke's Column" (Medal with Clasp).

[20] Surgeon Major General T. Walsh served in the Jowaki Afreedee Expedition in 1877-78 (Medal with Clasp). Served in the Afghan war in 1879-80, and was senior medical officer to the force under Brigadier General Charles Gough during the advance on Cabul in December 1879 (mentioned in despatches, Medal with Clasp). Served in the Egyptian war of 1882 as Sanitary Officer 1st Division, and was present in the engagement at Tel-el-Mahuta, at the action at Kassasin (9th September), and at the battle of Tel-el-Kebir (Medal with Clasp, and Khedive's Star).

[23] Surgeon Colonel S. Archer was attached to the 101st Fusiliers with the Busofzai Field Force on the N.W. Frontier of India in Nov. and Dec. 1863, and was present at the storming of the Conical Hill and the destruction of Umbeylah (Medal with Clasp). Served with the Nile Expedition in 1884-85 in charge of the Field Hospital at Korti (Medal with Clasp, and Khedive's Star). Served with the Soudan Frontier Field Force in 1885-86 in medical charge at Wady Halfa and of the Line of Communications to Akasheh.

[27] Surgeon Colonel E. C. Markey served in the Afghan war in 1879-80, and was present in the engagement at Saif-u-deen, in the advance to Khelat-i-Ghilzie, and in the engagement at Ahmed Kheyl; accompanied Sir Frederick Roberts in the march to Candahar, and was present at the battle of Ghadahar (mentioned in despatches, Medal with two Clasps, and Bronze Decoration). Also served with the Marri Expedition. Served with the Nile Expedition in 1884-85, and had charge of the Moveable Field Hospital with the Desert Column, and was for some time Principal Medical Officer at El Gubat (mentioned in despatches, Medal with Clasp, and Khedive's Star). Served with the Chin-Lushai Expeditionary Force in 1889-90 as Principal Medical Officer (received the thanks of the Government of India, mentioned in despatches, CB., and Medal with Clasp).

[33] Surgeon Colonel J. B. Hamilton served in the Soudan campaign as Field Director of the Lines of Communication under Brigadier General Ewart, and was present at the destruction of Temai (Medal with Clasp, and Khedive's Star). Served during the expedition to Burmah in 1886 in medical charge of the hospital ship *Tenasserim*.

[41] Surgeon Colonel A. A. Gore served at the bombardment and destruction of the Timmance town of Massougha on the Sierra Leone river on 10th December, attack on Madoukia 27th December, storm and capture of the stockaded Fotish town of Rohea on 28th Dec. 1861—mentioned in general orders for services and conspicuous bravery, and specially recommended for promotion in 1868. Served in the Ashanti war in 1873 as Sanitary Officer, and was severely wounded in the action of the 3rd November near Dunquah, and was also wounded at Quarman on the 17th November (Medal).

[48] Surgeon Colonel Preston served in medical charge of the 66th Regiment in the Afghan war in 1880, and was present at the affair at Girishk, in the engagement at Maiwand (dangerously wounded), and throughout the defence of Candahar (mentioned in despatches, promoted Surgeon Major with relative rank of Lt.Colonel, and Medal).

[50] Surgeon Colonel F. H. Welch served with the Hazara Expedition in 1888 (mentioned in despatches, Medal with Clasp).

[51] Surgeon Colonel R. P. Ferguson served in Bhootan in medical charge of the Royal Artillery during the campaign of 1864-65, and was present at the attack and capture of Bala and Buxa Dooars (Medal with Clasp). Served in the Afghan war in 1878-79 with the 2nd Division Peshawur Valley Field Force (Medal). Served in the Egyptian war of 1882 (Medal, and Khedive's Star).

[52] Surgeon Colonel A. F. Churchill served during the Nile Expedition in 1884-85 in charge of the hospital at Wady Halfa (Medal with Clasp, and Khedive's Star).

[55] Surgeon Colonel C. A. Maunsell served with the Royal Artillery during the Bhootan campaign of 1864-65, and was present at the capture of Fort Buxa, also at the taking of the Bala Pass, Tuzagon Stockade, and Fort Chamoorchee (Medal with Clasp). Served in Egyptian war of 1882 (Medal, and Khedive's Star).

[57] Surgeon Colonel F. B. Scott received the special approbation of the Madras Government, followed by that of His Royal Highness the Commander in Chief, for his services rendered while in medical charge of the 18th Hussars during a most virulent outbreak of cholera in the regiment, at Secunderabad in May 1871. Served in the Zulu war of 1879. Organised the Bearer Company; made the hospital arrangements at the Fort Pearson base for the Ekowe Relieving Column; served afterwards with the 2nd Division on the personal staff of Lord Chelmsford and in medical charge of the Head Quarters Staff; was present in the engagement at Ulundi, where his services were described by Lord Chelmsford as having been "of the greatest value;" he accompanied the 17th Lancers in their charge and pursuit of the enemy, and by rendering timely aid to a Lancer who was dangerously wounded prevented his falling into the enemy's hands, and served subsequently to the end of the war as Senior Medical Officer of Port Durnford and that line of communication between Ulundi and the Tugela (mentioned in despatches, Medal with Clasp). Served in the Egyptian war of 1882 on the personal staff of Major General the Duke of Connaught, Commanding the 1st Brigade, and was present at the battle of Tel-el-Kebir (CMG., Medal with Clasp, and Khedive's Star).

[59] Surgeon Colonel O'Dwyer served in the Egyptian war of 1882 in command of No. 2 Bearer Company, and was present at the action at Kassasin on the 9th September and at the battle of Tel-el-Kebir (mentioned in despatches, promoted Surgeon Major with relative rank of Lt.Colonel, Medal with Clasp, and Khedive's Star). Served with the Nile Expedition in 1884-85 as Secretary to the Principal Medical Officer (mentioned in despatches, Clasp).

[65] Surgeon Colonel W. Nash served in the Afghan war of 1878-80 (Medal). Served in the Egyptian war of 1882 (Medal, and Khedive's Star).

[66] Surgeon Colonel W. T. Martin served throughout the Abyssinian campaign, having been appointed to the exploring party sent to Abyssinia in Sept. 1867, and which he accompanied through various expeditions for discovering a practicable route for troops from the sea to the highlands; was afterwards Secretary to the Principal Medical Officer of the Force and present with the Head Quarters Staff at the capture of Magdala (mentioned in despatches, and Medal). Served with the Burmese Expedition in 1887 on the personal Staff of Sir Charles Arbuthnot (Medal with Clasp).

[67] Surgeon Colonel Cuffe served in the Kafir war of 1878 as Principal Medical Officer of the Transkei Column throughout the operations against the Galekas. Served throughout the Zulu campaign as Principal Medical Officer of the Northern and subsequently of Wood's Flying Column from the commencement of operations till the action of Ulundi and conclusion of the war (mentioned in despatches, CB., and Medal with Clasp). Served with the Burmese Expedition in 1887-88 (Medal with Clasp).

[68] Surgeon Colonel C. A. Atkins accompanied Sir Garnet Wolseley to the Gold Coast in September 1873; served at the attack and destruction of Essama nand Ampinee, and in Medical Charge of Russell's Regiment throughout the Ashanti war of 1873-74, including the repulse of the Ashanti army at Abrakrampa during the 5th and 6th November, capture and destruction of Adubiassie, battle of Amonful, capture and destruction of Becquah, advanced guard engagement of Jarbinbah, skirmishes and ambuscade affairs between Adwabin and the river Ordah, battle of Ordahsu and capture of Coomassie (mentioned in despatches, Medal with Clasp). Served in the Afghan war in 1879-80, and was present at the night attack at Zaidabad, in the engagement at Charasiab on 6th October 1879, and in the operations around Cabul in December 1879, including the defence of Sherporo (mentioned in despatches); accompanied Sir Frederick Roberts in the march to Candahar, and was present at the battle of Candahar (mentioned in despatches, Medal with three Clasps, and Bronze Decoration).

[81] Surgeon Colonel H. S. Muir served in the Afghan war of 1878-80, including the engagement at Shahjui (Medal).

[82] Surgeon Colonel M. Cogan served in medical charge of a detachment of the 77th Regiment in the Hazara campaign of 1868. Served in the Afghan war of 1880. Organized the Principal Base European Hospital at Candahar under the command of Major General Phayre (mentioned in despatches, and thanked by the Governor General in Council, Medal).

[88] Surgeon Colonel W. A. Catherwood served in the Ashanti war of 1873-74 (Medal with Clasp). Served in the Soudan Expedition under Sir Gerald Graham in 1884 as Principal Medical Officer at the base (mentioned in despatches, promoted Surgeon Major with relative rank of Lt.Colonel, Medal, and Khedive's Star).

[89] Surgeon Colonel W. D. Wilson served in the Afghan war of 1878-80 (Medal). Served in the Soudan Expedition under Sir Gerald Graham in 1884 as Principal Medical Officer of the Infantry Brigade, and was present in the engagements at El Teb and Temai (mentioned in despatches, promoted Surgeon Major with relative rank of Lt.Colonel, Medal with two Clasps, and Khedive's Star).

[93] Surgeon Colonel W. S. M. Price served in the Afghan war of 1878-80, and took part in the operations in

the Bazar Valley, including the engagement at Deh Sarakh (Medal). Served in the Nile Expedition in 1884-85 with the Korti Field Hospital (Medal with Clasp, and Khedive's Star).

[98] Brigade Surgeon Lt.Colonel W. E. Riordan served in the Egyptian war of 1882 and was present at the surrender of Kafr Dowar (Medal, and Khedive's Star); also served in the Soudan campaign in 1885 in charge of No. 3 Field Hospital and organized the Camel Ambulance of the force; was Senior Medical Officer of the British Troops at Suakin from 28th May to 28th November 1885 (Clasp).

[100] Brigade Surgeon Lt.Colonel J. H. Hughes served with the 2nd Field Hospital during the Ashanti war in 1873-74 (Medal with Clasp).

[102] Brigade Surgeon Lt.Colonel D. C. Grose served with the expedition from Aden into the interior of Arabia in 1865-66, was in medical charge of the Force at the action of Bir Said, and present at the subsequent operations.

[103] Brigade Surgeon Lt.Colonel John Maturin served in the Ashanti war in 1873-74 (Medal).

[106] Brigade Surgeon Lt.Colonel G. Andrew served with the 6th Regiment in the Hazara campaign of 1868, including the subsequent operations in the Black Mountain (Medal with Clasp). Served in the Afghan war of 1878-80, and took part with the expeditions into the Lughman Valley and against the Khugianis (Medal).

[110] Brigade Surgeon Lt.Colonel R. H. Carew served in the Abyssinian campaign in 1868 with the 45th Regiment, and was present at the capture of Magdala (Medal). Served with the Sikkim Expedition in 1888 as Senior Medical Officer (mentioned in despatches, DSO., and Medal with Clasp).

[112] Brigade Surgeon Lt.Colonel C. E. Harrison served with the 2nd Battalion Grenadier Guards in the Egyptian war of 1882, and was present at the battle of Tel-el-Kebir (Medal with Clasp, and Khedive's Star).

[122] Brigade Surgeon Lt.Colonel Evatt served in the Perak Expedition in 1876 (Medal with Clasp). Served in the Afghan war of 1878-80, and was present at the capture of Ali Musjid; was Senior Medical Officer with Tytler's Column in the expedition to the Bazar Valley (mentioned in Lieut.General Maude's despatch); was in charge of a Section Field Hospital on the return march to India in June 1879 (thanked by the Governor General and by the Commander in Chief in India in General Orders); afterwards served in charge of a Field Hospital with Sir Charles Gough's Brigade during the advance to Gundamuck and Cabul (Medal with two Clasps). Served with the expedition to the Soudan in 1885 in command of the 2nd Bearer Company of the Medical Staff Corps, and was present in the engagement at Hasheen and at the destruction of Temai (mentioned in despatches, Medal with Clasp, and Khedive's Star). Served with the Zhob Valley Expedition in 1890 in command of the British Field Hospital (mentioned in despatches).

[123] Brigade Surgeon Lt.Colonel W. M'Watters served in the Afghan war of 1878-80 (Medal). Served with the Hazara Expedition in 1891 (mentioned in despatches, Medal with Clasp).

[125] Brigade Surgeon Lt.Colonel R. N. Mally served in the Zulu war in 1879 in medical charge of the 2nd Battalion of the 3rd Buffs and the 3rd Battalion of the 60th Rifles and of the troops at the Black Umvolosi River (Medal with Clasp).

[137] Brigade Surgeon Lt.Colonel H. W. A. Mackinnon served in the Egyptian war of 1882, and was present at the battle of Tel-el-Kebir—slightly wounded (Medal with Clasp, and Khedive's Star). Served in the Burmese Expedition in 1885-86 with the Upper Burmah Field Force under Sir George White, part of the time as Principal Medical Officer (mentioned in despatches, DSO., and Medal with Clasp).

[140] Brigade Surgeon Lt.Colonel H. Comerford served in the Zulu war of 1879, and was present at the battle of Ulundi (Medal with Clasp). Served in the Boer war of 1881, and took part in the defence of Pretoria.

[141] Brigade Surgeon Lt.Colonel H. T. Brown served throughout the Ashanti war of 1873-74 (Medal).

[155] Brigade Surgeon Lt.Colonel W. F. Burnett served in the Zulu war of 1879 (Medal with Clasp). Served in the Afghan war from 2nd January to 28th August 1880, the greater part of the time in medical charge of the 1st Battalion 25th Regiment (Medal). Served with the Nile Expedition in 1884-85 (Medal with Clasp, and Khedive's Star).

[156] Brigade Surgeon Lt.Colonels T. O'Farrell, H. J. O'Brien, R. C. Eaton, and F. Lyons, Surgeon Lt.Colonels J. G. Williamson and W. B. Slaughter, Surgeons Major H. Charlesworth, I. Boulger, E. A. Roche, R. D. Hodson, C. K. Powell, H. C. Kirkpatrick, J. F. Brodie, and P. J. Dempsey served in the Afghan war of 1878-80 (Medal).

[159] Brigade Surgeon Lt.Colonel James Williamson served in the Ashanti war in 1873-74 (Medal).

[160] Brigade Surgeon Lt.Colonel W. H. Steele served with the 33rd Regiment in the Abyssinian Expedition of 1867-68 (Medal). Served on board H.M. Hospital Ship *Victor Emanuel* during the Ashanti war in 1873-74 (Medal).

[171] Brigade Surgeon Lt.Colonel Reynolds received the special approbation of the Commander in Chief in India followed by that of the Director General of the Army Medical Department for his services while Medical Officer of the 36th Regiment during a most virulent outbreak of cholera at Peshawur in 1869. Served in the Kafir war of 1877-78 in the Ciskei, and was present at the engagement with the Galekas at Impetu; served throughout the Zulu war of 1879, took part in the gallant and successful defence of Rorke's Drift, and was with the troops in the Laager during the engagement at Ulundi (mentioned in despatches, promoted Surgeon Major, Victoria Cross, Medal with Clasp, and Gold Medal of the British Medical Association): was awarded the VC "for the conspicuous bravery, during the attack at Rorke's Drift on the 22nd and 23rd January, 1879, which he exhibited in his constant attention to the wounded under fire, and in his voluntarily conveying ammunition from the store to the defenders of the hospital whereby he exposed himself to a cross fire from the enemy both in going and returning."

[173] Brigade Surgeon Lt.Colonel T. O'Reilly served with the Hazara Expedition in 1888 (Medal with Clasp).

[174] Brigade Surgeon Lt.Colonel E. J. Fairland served in the Abyssinian campaign from November 1867 to July 1868 (Medal).

[175] Brigade Surgeon Lt.Colonel E. Townsend served in the Abyssinian campaign from December 1867 to June 1868, and was present at the action of Arogee (Medal). Served throughout the operations in the Malay Peninsula in 1875-76, including the actions of the 4th, 14th, and 20th January, and 4th February—severely wounded (Medal with Clasp). Served in the Zulu war of 1879, and present in the engagement at Ulundi (mentioned in despatches). Served in the operations against Sekukuni in 1879, and was present at the storming of the stronghold (Medal with Clasp). Served in the Egyptian war of 1882, and was present at the battle of Tel-el-Kebir (Medal with Clasp and Khedive's Star).

[176] Brigade Surgeon Lt.Colonel J. F. Supple served in the Ashantee war of 1873-74, and was present at the attack on and defence of the Hospital at Foomanah (Medal). Served in the Afghan war of 1878-80 (Medal). Served with the Burmese Expedition in 1886-87 as Senior Medical Officer 6th Brigade (mentioned in despatches, Medal with Clasp).

[177] Brigade Surgeon Lt.Colonel J. H. Moore served in the Ashantee war of 1873-74 from the 10th October 1873, including the defence of the Hospital at Foomanah (Medal with Clasp). Served in the Afghan war in 1878-79, and took part in the occupation of Candahar and Khelat-i-Ghilzie and in the engagements at Ahmed Kheyl and Urzoo near Ghuznee (Medal with Clasp).

[178] Brigade Surgeon Lt.Colonel R. de la C. Corbett served with the Burmese Expedition in 1886-87 (mentione in despatches, DSO., and Medal with Clasp).

[179] Brigade Surgeon Lt.Colonel C. F. Pollock served in the Egyptian war of 1882 with the 42nd Highlanders (the Black Watch), and was present at the battle of Tel-el-Kebir (Medal with Clasp, and Khedive's Star).

[180] Brigade Surgeon Lt.Colonel W. H. M'Namara served in the Egyptian war of 1882 attached to the 1st Battalion Royal Irish Fusiliers, and was present at the battle of Tel-el-Kebir (Medal with Clasp, and Khedive's Star).

[181] Brigade Surgeon Lt.Colonel J. Riddick served in the Afghan war in 1880 (Medal).

[190] Surgeon Lt.Colonel H. F. L. Melladew served with the Left Division of the Dooar Field Force in Bhootan in 1865 (Medal with Clasp). Served with the British Ambulance in France during the Franco-German war from October 1870 until the declaration of the Armistice in February 1871. Served in the Nile Expedition in 1884-85 with the Desert Column including the operations during its return to Korti (Medal with Clasp, and Khedive's Star).

[195] Brigade Surgeon Lt.Colonel A. Anderson served with an Expeditionary Field Force under Colonel J. R. Mackenzie in Arabia from the 27th October to the 20th December 1873, including the investment, surrender, occupation, and destruction of the Fort at Al-Hota, and subsequent march to Zaida in pursuit of Ally Bin Mana, the chief of Houshabi. Served in the Afghan war in 1878-79 (Medal).

[199] Brigade Surgeon Lt.Colonel James Fraser served in the Zulu war in 1879, and in the subsequent operations

against Sekukuni, including the capture of the stronghold (Medal with Clasp). Served in the Boer war of 1880-81, and had medical charge of the Fort at Standerton during its investment.

²⁰¹ Brigade Surgeon Lt.Colonel M. Knox served in the Afghan war in 1878-79 (Medal).

²⁰⁴ Brigade Surgeon Lt.Colonel A. L. Brown served in the Ashanti war in 1873-74, and was present at the battle of Amoaful and advance on Coomassie (mentioned in despatches, Medal with Clasp). Served in the Kafir war in 1878 including the operations against the Gaikas, and in the Zulu war of 1879 including the engagements at Kambula and Ulundi (mentioned in despatches, Medal with Clasp). Served in the Nile Expedition in 1884-85 (Medal with Clasp, and Khedive's Star); also served in the operations of the Soudan Frontier Field Force in 1885-86 including the engagement at Giniss.

²⁰⁵ Brigade Surgeon Lt.Colonel A. A. Macrobin served with the British Ambulance in the Franco-German war from the time of its arrival in France in October 1870 until its return to England in March 1871 after the conclusion of peace, and has received the German War Steel Medal. Served with the 2nd Battalion Rifle Brigade in the second phase of the Ashanti war, in 1874, and was present at the battle of Amoaful, battle of Ordahsu and capture of Coomassie (Medal with Clasp).

²¹³ Surgeon Lt.Colonel George Corry served in the Soudan campaign in 1885 (Medal with Clasp, and Khedive's Star).

²¹⁵ Surgeon Lt.Colonel R. D. Bennett served in the Ashanti war of 1873-74 (Medal).

²¹⁸ Surgeon Lt.Colonel James M'Namara was in medical charge of the troops (detachments of Royal Artillery and 10th Foot) sent into the Native State of Sunghie Ujong, Malay Peninsula, in 1874; and was present at the attack and capture of the Kapayan stockades (Medal with Clasp). Served in the Afghan war in 1880, and was in medical charge of Brigadier General Brooke's Brigade covering the retreat from Maiwand (mentioned in despatches), took part in the defence of Candahar, and was present at the battle of Candahar (Medal with Clasp). Served in the Soudan Expedition in 1884 under Sir Gerald Graham, and was present in the engagements at El Teb and Temai (Medal with Clasp, and Khedive's Star).

²²¹ Brigade Surgeon Lt.Colonel Beamish served in the Afghan war in 1878-79 with the siege train of the 1st Division of the Cabul Expeditionary Force in Dadur and the Bolan Pass (Medal). Served with the Burmese Expedition in 1885-86 (Medal with Clasp).

²²² Surgeon Lt.Colonel J. A. Clery served during the Nile Expedition in 1884-85 in charge of the Abu Dom Field Hospital (Medal with Clasp, and Khedive's Star).

²²³ Surgeon Lt.Colonel J. Coats served in the Boer war in 1881.

²²⁴ Surgeon Lt.Colonel W. J. Fawcett served in the Soudan campaign in 1885 (Medal with Clasp, and Khedive's Star). Served with the Hazara Expedition in 1888 (mentioned in despatches, Medal with Clasp).

²²⁵ Surgeon Lt.Colonel W. E. Saunders served in the Zulu war in 1879 (Medal). Also served in the Boer war in 1881.

²²⁶ Surgeon Lt.Colonel A. H. Anthonisz served in the Egyptian war of 1882 (Medal, and Khedive's Star). Served in the Soudan campaign in 1885 (Clasp).

²²⁸ Surgeon Lt.Colonel G. D. N. Leake served in the Zulu war in 1879 (Medal). Served with the Burmese Expedition in 1885-87 (Medal with Clasp).

²²⁹ Surgeon Lt.Colonel M. D. O'Connell served in the Soudan campaign in 1885 (Medal with Clasp, and Khedive's Star).

²³⁰ Surgeon Lt.Colonel E. H. Joynt served with the Soudan Frontier Field Force in 1885-86 (Medal, and Khedive's Star).

²³⁴ Surgeon Lt.Colonel J. D. Edge was noted on the 3rd December 1872, "to be promoted Staff Surgeon, as soon as he has qualified for the superior grade, in recognition of his gallant services when engaged against the Indians at Orange Walk, British Honduras," on the 1st September 1872. Served in the Zulu war of 1879, and was present in the engagement at Gingindhlovu and at the relief of Ekowe (Medal with Clasp). Served in the Afghan war in 1879-80 and was present in the engagement at Maiwand in charge of a Field Hospital, and took part in the defence of Candahar (received the thanks of the Government of India, Medal). Served in the Egyptian war of 1882 with the Indian Contingent, and was present at the battle of Tel-el-Kebir in charge of a Field Hospital (Medal with Clasp, 4th Class of the Osmanieh, and Khedive's Star). Served with the Burmese Expedition in 1887-89 (Medal with two Clasps).

²³⁵ Surgeon Lt.Colonel H. J. W. Barrow served in the Soudan campaign in 1885 (Medal with Clasp, and Khedive's Star); also served with the Soudan Frontier Field Force in 1885-86 including the engagement at Giniss.

²⁴¹ Surgeon Lt.Colonel Drury served in the Zulu war of 1879 and in the subsequent operations against Sekukuni (Medal with Clasp). Also served in the Boer war of 1881.

²⁴⁶ Surgeon Lt.Colonel W. Donovan served in the Afghan war in 1879-80 with the Cabul Field Force, and afterwards with the Koorum Force, and took part with the Zaimusht Expedition under Brigadier General Tytler in medical charge of the 85th King's Light Infantry including the assault of Zawa (Medal). Served in the Boer war of 1881 with the Natal Field Force as a volunteer.

²⁴⁷ Surgeon Lt.Colonel D. B. Brown served in the Zulu war of 1879, and was present in the engagement at Ulundi (mentioned in despatches, Medal with Clasp). Also served in the Boer war of 1881 with the Natal Field Force. Served with the Burmese Expedition in 1885-86 under Sir Harry Prendergast in charge of the General Hospital of European Troops (Medal with Clasp).

²⁴⁸ Surgeon Lt.Colonel R. H. Quill served with the Royal Artillery in the Koorum Valley in the Afghan war of 1879-80, and had medical charge of the Depot Field Hospital during the Zaimusht Expedition under Brigadier General Tytler (Medal).

²⁵⁰ Surgeon Lt.Colonel H. H. Stokes served in the Zulu war in 1879 (Medal with Clasp). Served with the Hazara Expedition in 1891 (mentioned in despatches, Medal with Clasp).

²⁵¹ Surgeon Lt.Colonel T. J. Gallwey served in the Afghan war in 1879, and was present at the attack and capture of Ali Musjid (Medal with Clasp). Served in the Egyptian war of 1882, and was present at the battle of Tel-el-Kebir (Medal with Clasp, and Khedive's Star). Served with the Nile Expedition in 1884-85, had charge of the Debbeh Field Hospital, and took part in the operations of the Desert Column on its return to Korti (mentioned in despatches, promoted Surgeon Major, Clasp).

²⁵² Surgeon Lt.Colonel W. S. Pratt served as Assistant Surgeon with the Armée du Rhin under Marshal Bazaine in the Franco-German war of 1870-71, and was present at the actions of Gravelotte and St. Privat. Was driven into Metz with the French Army, and remained during the siege and until the surrender of the fortress from starvation. Served with the Nile Expedition in 1884-85 on the Staff of Lord Wolseley (mentioned in despatches, promoted Surgeon Major, Medal with Clasp, and Khedive's Star).

²⁵⁴ Surgeon Lt.Colonel W. B. Allin served in the Afghan war of 1878-80 (Medal). Served with the Nile Expedition in 1884-85, and had charge of the Field Hospital at Gakdul Wells (mentioned in despatches, promoted Surgeon Major, Medal with Clasp, and Khedive's Star).

²⁵⁶ Surgeon Lt.Colonel Langridge served in the Afghan war of 1878-80 with the Koorum and Cabul Field Forces, including the affair at Karatiga and the engagement at Charasiab on 6th October 1879, the capture of Cabul and subsequent cavalry pursuit, the two expeditions to Maidan, the engagement at Tukht-i-Shah, and the defence of Sherpore (Medal with two Clasps). Served in the Boer war of 1881 in medical charge of the 92nd Highlanders.

²⁵⁷ Surgeon Lt.Colonel W. E. Webb served in the Egyptian war of 1882, and was present at the battle of Tel-el-Kebir (Medal with Clasp, and Khedive's Star); also served with the Nile Expedition in 1884-85 (Clasp).

²⁵⁸ Surgeon Lt.Colonel R. W. Mapleton served with the Natal Field Force in the Boer war of 1881. Served in the Soudan campaign in 1885 (Medal with Clasp, and Khedive's Star).

²⁵⁹ Surgeon Lt.Colonel W. L. Gubbins served in the Afghan war of 1878-80, and took part with the Bazar Valley Expedition under Lieut.General Maude in medical charge of the 5th Fusiliers, and subsequently of the Head Quarters Staff; in 1879-80 he served with the Khyber Line Force under Lieut.General Bright in medical charge of the Head Quarters Staff; was also Divisional Sanitary Officer and Secretary to the Principal Medical Officer, and was present with the expeditions against the Mohmunds and into the Hissarik Valley (Medal). Served with the expedition to Burmah in 1886 (Medal with Clasp).

²⁷⁰ Surgeon Lt.Colonel Thomsett served in the Afghan war in 1878-79, and had medical charge of the Divisional Field Hospital at Thull; accompanied the expedition into the Khost country and was present in the engagement at Mattoon (Medal). Served in the Egyptian war of 1882 with No. 4 Field Hospital (Medal, and Khedive's Star).

²⁷¹ Surgeon Lt.Colonel P. J. M'Quaid served in the Afghan war in 1878-79, and was present in the engagement at Charasiab on the 6th October 1879 and in the operations round Cabul in December 1879 including the investment

of Sherpore (Medal with two Clasps). Served in the Egyptian war of 1882, and was present at the action at Kassasin on the 9th September and at the battle of Tel-el-Kebir (Medal with Clasp, and Khedive's Star).

[272] Surgeon Lt.Colonel James Ring served in the Zulu war in 1879 (Medal). Served in the Boer war of 1881, and was present in the engagements at Lang's Nek and the Ingogo River (mentioned in despatches).

[273] Surgeon Major Magill served in the Nile Expedition in 1884-5 with the Guards Camel Regiment, and was present at the action at Abu Klea—severely wounded (mentioned in despatches, Medal with two Clasps, and Khedive's Star).

[275] Surgeon Lt.Colonel O. G. Wood served in the Egyptian war of 1882, and was present at the battle of Tel-el-Kebir (Medal with Clasp, and Khedive's Star).

[276] Surgeon Lt.Colonel L. B. Ward served in the Afghan war in 1878-79, and was present at the attack and capture of Ali Musjid (Medal with Clasp).

[277] Surgeon Lt.Colonel W. B. Miller served in the Egyptian war of 1882, and was present at the action at Kassasin on the 28th August (mentioned in despatches, Medal, and Khedive's Star).

[280] Surgeon Lt.Colonel John Martin served in the Egyptian war of 1882 (Medal, and Khedive's Star). Served with the Burmese Expedition in 1886-87 as Personal Assistant to the Surgeon General (Medal with Clasp).

[281] Surgeon Lt.Colonel J. J. Greene served in the Afghan war of 1878-80 (Medal). Served with the Nile Expedition in 1884-85 (Medal with Clasp, and Khedive's Star); also served in the operations of the Soudan Frontier Field Force in 1885-86.

[282] Surgeon Lt.Colonel N. M'Creery served with the Nile Expedition in 1884-85 (Medal with Clasp, and Khedive's Star); with the Soudan Frontier Field Force in 1885-86; and in the operations near Suakin in December 1888, including the engagement at Gemaizah (mentioned in despatches, 3rd Class of the Medjidie, Clasp).

[283] Surgeon Lt.Colonel J. A. Gormley served during the operations in the Malay Peninsula in 1875-76 (Medal with Clasp). Served in the Afghan war of 1878-80 in medical charge of the 51st Light Infantry, and took part with the expeditions against the Mohmunds and into the Hissarik Valley (Medal). Served in the Boer war of 1881. Served with the Nile Expedition in 1884-85 (Medal with Clasp, and Khedive's Star).

[286] Surgeon Lt.Colonel R. Smith served in the Boer war of 1881. Served in the Soudan campaign in 1885 (Medal with Clasp, and Khedive's Star).

[287] Surgeon Lt.Colonel F. W. Trevor served in the Afghan war of 1878-80 with the Candahar Field Force, and was present in the engagement at Ahmed Kheyl; accompanied Sir Frederick Roberts in the march to Candahar, and was present at the battle of Candahar (Medal with two Clasps, and Bronze Decoration). Served with the Nile Expedition in 1884-85 (Medal with Clasp, and Khedive's Star).

[288] Surgeon Lt.Colonel H. Scott served in the Boer war of 1881.

[292] Surgeon Lt.Colonel W. Campbell served with the 1st Battalion Scots Guards in the Egyptian war of 1882, and was present at the battle of Tel-el-Kebir (Medal with Clasp, and Khedive's Star).

[294] Surgeon Lt.Colonel J. M'Gann served in the Boer war of 1881, and was present in the engagements at Lang's Nek (mentioned in despatches) and the Ingogo River (mentioned in despatches).

[295] Surgeon Lt.Colonel James Powell served with the Nile Expedition in 1884-85 in charge of Kaibur Field Hospital (Medal with Clasp, and Khedive's Star); also served in the operations of the Egyptian Field Force in 1885-86, including the engagement at Kosheh.

[296] Surgeon Lt.Colonel S. H. Carter served in the Afghan war of 1878-80, and was present in the engagement at Ahmed Kheyl (Medal with Clasp). Served in the Egyptian war of 1882, and was present at the battle of Tel-el-Kebir (Medal with Clasp, and Khedive's Star).

[297] Surgeon Lt.Colonel G. D. Bourke served with the Nile Expedition in 1884-85 (Medal with Clasp, and Khedive's Star); also served with the Egyptian Frontier Field Force in 1885-86, including the engagement at Giniss. Served with the Chin-Lushai Expeditionary Force in 1889-90 (mentioned in despatches, Medal with Clasp).

[299] Surgeon Lt.Colonel C. H. Swayne served with the Nile Expedition in 1884-85 in charge of a Field Hospital at Dongola (Medal with Clasp, and Khedive's Star). Served with the Burmese Expedition in 1886-89 (Medal with two Clasps).

[300] Surgeon Major J. C. Dorman served in the Afghan war in 1878-9, and was present in the engagement at Ali Kheyl and at the forcing of the Shutargardan (Medal). Served in the Egyptian war of 1882 (Medal, and Khedive's Star).

[301] Surgeon Major W. L. Chester served with the Nile Expedition in 1884-85 (Medal with Clasp, and Khedive's Star).

[302] Surgeon Lt.Colonel J. S. Forrester served in the Egyptian war of 1882, and was present in the engagement at Tel-el-Mahuta, in the two actions at Kassasin, and at the battle of Tel-el-Kebir (Medal with Clasp, and Khedive's Star).

[303] Surgeon Major Fenn served in the Afghan war in 1879-80 in medical charge of a battery of Royal Artillery, and was present at the affair at Zaidabad; accompanied Sir Frederick Roberts in the march to Candahar, and was present at the battle of Candahar (mentioned in despatches, Medal with Clasp, and Bronze Decoration). Served in the Soudan campaign in 1885 with the 3rd Battalion of the Grenadier Guards, and was present in the engagement at Hasheen and at the destruction of Temai (Medal with Clasp, and Khedive's Star).

[304] Surgeon Major Alexander served in the expedition to the Soudan in 1885 with the 1st Battalion of the Coldstream Guards, and was present in the engagement at Hasheen, at that near Tofrek on the 24th March, and at the destruction of Temai (Medal with Clasp, and Khedive's Star).

[305] Surgeon Major M. R. Ryan served in the Afghan war in 1878-79, and was present at the attack and capture of Ali Musjid (Medal with Clasp). Served in the Egyptian war of 1882, and was present at the battle of Tel-el-Kebir (Medal with Clasp, and Khedive's Star).

[306] Surgeon Major E. O. Reynolds served in the Egyptian war of 1882, and was present at the battle of Tel-el-Kebir (Medal with Clasp, and Khedive's Star). Served with the Hazara Expedition in 1888 (Medal with Clasp).

[307] Surgeon Major H. J. Robbins served in the Afghan war in 1878-79 with the Koorum Valley Column, took part in the Zaimusht Expedition under Brigadier General Tytler, and was present with the 85th Regiment in the assault on the heights of Zawa (Medal).

[308] Surgeon Major Morris served in the Afghan war in 1878-79 with the Koorum Field Force, and in 1879-80 with the Cabul Field Force; was present in the engagement at Charasiab and in the actions around Cabul in December 1879, including the defence of Sherpore; was in medical charge of the 92nd Highlanders in the engagement at Charasiah in April 1880 (mentioned in despatches, Medal with two Clasps).

[309] Surgeon Major A. E. Hayes served in the Afghan war of 1878-80 (Medal) Served in the operations near Suakin in December 1888 including the engagement at Gemaizah (mentioned in despatches, Medal with Clasp, 3rd Class of the Medjidie, and Khedive's Star), and in the operations on the Soudan frontier in 1889 including the engagement at Toski (mentioned in despatches, DSO., and Clasp).

[310] Surgeon Major J. F. Williamson served in the Afghan war in 1878-79, and was present in the engagement at Charasiah on the 6th October 1879, and in the operations round Cabul in December 1879 including the investment of Sherpore; accompanied Sir Frederick Roberts in the march to Candahar, and was present at the battle of Candahar (mentioned in despatches, Medal with three Clasps, and Bronze Decoration). Served in the Egyptian war of 1882, and was present at the battle of Tel-el-Kebir (Medal with Clasp, and Khedive's Star). Served with the Burmese Expedition in 1887-88 (Medal with Clasp).

[311] Surgeon Major J. T. Carey served in the Afghan war of 1878-80, and was present at the storming of the Peiwar Kotal (mentioned in despatches, Medal with Clasp). Served in the Egyptian war of 1882 (Medal, and Khedive's Star).

[312] Surgeon Major W. J. R. Rainsford served in the Afghan war in 1879-80 with the Khyber Field Force (Medal). Served in the Egyptian war of 1882 (Medal, and Khedive's Star); also served in the operations of the Soudan Frontier Field Force in 1885-86.

[313] Surgeon Major T. Boyd served in the Egyptian war of 1882, and was present at the battle of Tel-el-Kebir (Medal with Clasp, and Khedive's Star). Served with the Nile Expedition in 1884-85, and had charge of the Field Hospital at Absarat (Clasp).

[314] Surgeon Major P. H. Johnston served in the Afghan war in 1879-80, and took part with the Zaimusht Expedition including the assault of Zawa (Medal).

[315] Surgeon Major I. B. Emerson served with the 3rd Foot in the Afghan war in 1878-79 (Medal).

[316] Surgeon Major G. Laffan served with the Nile Expedition in 1884-85 (Medal with Clasp, and Khedive's Star).

[317] Surgeon Major U. J. Bourke served in the Soudan campaign in 1885, and was present in the engagement at

Hasheen, in the advance in support of the Tofrek zereba, and at the destruction of Temai (Medal with Clasp, and Khedive's Star).

³¹⁶ Surgeon Major W. H. Allen served throughout the Egyptian war of 1882, and was present at the surrender of Kafr Dowar and Damietta (Medal, and Khedive's Star). Served in the operations in Zululand in 1888.

³¹⁹ Surgeon Major J. P. Hunt served with the Soudan Frontier Field Force in 1885-86 (Medal, and Khedive's Star).

³²⁰ Surgeon Major J. L. Peyton served in the Soudan campaign in 1885 (Medal with Clasp, and Khedive's Star).

³²¹ Surgeon Major A. W. Carleton served in the Afghan war of 1878-80, and was present in the engagement at Ahmed Kheyl (Medal with Clasp). Served in the Egyptian war of 1882 (Medal, and Khedive's Star) ; also served with the Nile Expedition in 1884-85 (Clasp).

³²² Surgeon Major G. A. Hughes served in the Afghan war of 1878-80, and took part in the march to Candahar with the force under Major General Phayro (Medal). Served with the Bechuanaland Expedition in 1884-85 under Sir Charles Warren.

³²³ Surgeon Major W. T. Johnston served in the Egyptian war of 1882 in medical charge of the 1st Battalion South Staffordshire Regiment, and was present in the reconnaissance in force from Alexandria on the 5th August (Medal, and Khedive's Star). Served with the Bechuanaland Expedition in 1884-85 under Sir Charles Warren. Served with the Chin Lushai Expeditionary Force in 1889-90 in the Burmah Column (Medal with Clasp).

³²⁴ Surgeon Major A. W. Browne served in the Afghan war of 1878-80, and was present in the engagements at Ahmed Kheyl and Urzoo near Ghuznee (Medal with Clasp).

³²⁵ Surgeon Major W. W. Kenny served in the Afghan war in 1879-80 with the Khyber Line Force (Medal). Received the thanks of Sir Robert Biddulph, High Commissioner of Cyprus, for his services to the Civil Government during a virulent epidemic of fever in Nicosia in 1881. Served in the Soudan campaign in 1885, and was present in the engagement at the Tofrek zereba (Medal with two Clasps, and Khedive's Star).

³²⁶ Surgeon Major W. Kenys served in the Egyptian war of 1882 in medical charge of the 1st Battalion Royal Sussex Regiment (Medal, and Khedive's Star); also served in the Soudan campaign in 1885 with No. 2 Bearer Company, and was present in the engagements at Hasheen and Temai (Clasp).

³²⁷ Surgeon Major R. T. Beamish served with the Burmese Expedition in 1886-87 (Medal with Clasp).

³²⁹ Surgeon Major H. Grier.—See Civil Decorations for Gallantry, "Hart's Annual Army List," p. 786.

³³¹ Surgeon Major E. R. Power served in the Egyptian war of 1882 (Medal, and Khedive's Star) ; also served in the Soudan campaign in 1885 (Clasp).

³³² Surgeon Major H. L. Donovan served in the Egyptian war of 1882 (Medal, and Khedive's Star). Served in the Soudan campaign in 1885, and was present in the engagement at the Tofrek zereba (mentioned in despatches, granted the higher rate of pay, two Clasps).

³³³ Surgeon Major N. Leader served in the Egyptian war of 1882 (Medal, and Khedive's Star); also served in the Soudan campaign in 1885, and was present in the engagement at the Tofrek zereba (two Clasps).

³³⁴ Surgeon Major J. Tidbury served throughout the Egyptian war of 1882 in medical charge of the 1st Battalion of the Gordon Highlanders, and was present at the reconnaissance in force from Alexandria on the 5th August, and at the battle of Tel-el-Kebir (Medal with Clasp, and Khedive's Star).

³³⁶ Surgeon Major Wallis served in the Zulu war of 1879, and in the subsequent operations against Sekukuni including the storming of the stronghold—slightly wounded (Medal with Clasp). Served in the Boer war in 1880-81 in medical charge of the garrison at Potchefstroom during its investment (slightly wounded). Served with the Nile Expedition in 1884-85 in charge of moveable Field Hospital and was present in the reconnaisance to Metammeh (Medal with Clasp, and Khedive's Star).

³³⁷ Surgeon Major J. W. H. Flanagan served with the Southern Afghanistan Field Force in the Afghan war in 1879-80 (Medal). Served with the Zhob Valley Expedition in 1884.

³³⁸ Surgeon Major O. E. P. Lloyd served in the Zulu war in 1879 with Clarke's Column, and in the subsequent operations against Sekukuni including the storming of the stronghold, and was present at the capture of King Cetewayo (Medal with Clasp). Also served in the Boer war of 1881, and took part in the defence of Standerton. Served in the Kachin Expedition in 1892-93 with the Military Police, first as Medical Officer in charge of the North Eastern Column, and afterwards as Senior Medical Officer of the whole force, and was present at the attack on the Sima Post; commanded the Post during the attack after Captain Morton, the Officer Commanding, was killed (mentioned in despatches, ƊƆ., and Medal with Clasp): was awarded the Victoria Cross for his conspicuous bravery under the following circumstances :—" During the attack on the Sima Post by Kachins, on the 6th January last [1893], Surgeon Major Lloyd, on hearing that the Commanding Officer, Captain Morton (who had left the fort to visit a picket about 80 yards distant), was wounded, at once ran out to his assistance under a close and heavy fire, accompanied by Subadar Matab Singh. On reaching the wounded officer, Surgeon Major Lloyd sent Subadar Matab Singh back for further assistance, and remained with Captain Morton till the Subadar returned with five men of the Magwe Battalion of Military Police, when he assisted in carrying Captain Morton back to the fort, where that officer died a few minutes afterwards. The enemy were within ten or fifteen paces keeping up a heavy fire, which killed three men of the picket, and also Bugler Purna Singh. This man accompanied Captain Morton from the fort, showed great gallantry in supporting him in his arms when wounded, and was shot while helping to carry him back to the fort. (The Native Officer and five Sepoys above alluded to have been awarded the Order of Merit.)"

³³⁹ Surgeon Major J. G. MacNeece served in the Afghan war in 1879-80, took part in the defence of Candahar, and was present at the battle of Candahar (Medal with Clasp).

³⁴⁰ Surgeon Major Harding served in the Zulu war in 1879 in medical charge of the 57th Foot, and was present in the engagement at Gingindhlovu and at the relief of Ekowe (Medal with Clasp). Served in the Boer war of 1881 in medical charge of Fort Marabastadt from December 1880 till March 1881 (mentioned in despatches); subsequently at Pretoria and Standerton until the withdrawal of the British troops. Served in the Egyptian war of 1882 with No. 2 Bearer Company, and was present at the action at Kassasin on the 9th September and at the battle of Tel-el-Kebir (Medal with Clasp, and Khedive's Star). Served in the Nile Expedition in 1884-85, took part with the Desert Column under Sir Herbert Stewart, and was present at the actions at Abu Klea and Abu Kru, and in the reconnaissance before Metammeh (mentioned in despatches, two Clasps).

³⁴¹ Surgeon Major J. J. Falvey served in the Zulu war in 1879, and in the subsequent operations against Sekukuni in medical charge of a section of Moveable Field Hospital (Medal with Clasp). Served in the Boer war of 1881 in medical charge of the garrison at Lydenburg during the investment of that place (mentioned in despatches). Served in the Egyptian war of 1882 as Assistant Medical Officer Base and Lines of Communication and Medical Superintendent of the transport of the sick and wounded (Medal, and Khedive's Star). Served in the Nile Expedition in 1884-85 as Surgeon to the Heavy Camel Regiment, and was present at the action at Abu Klea; established the hospital at Abu Klea Wells, where he acted as Senior Medical Officer (two Clasps).

³⁴² Surgeon Major H. R. O. Cross served in the Zulu war in 1879 with the Mounted Infantry of the Flying Column and with the Cavalry Patrol until the capture of King Cetywayo (Medal and Clasp). Also served in the Boer war of 1881 with the Mounted Infantry of the Natal Field Force.

³⁴³ Surgeon Major C. Seymour served in the Soudan campaign in 1885 (Medal with Clasp, and Khedive's Star; also served with the Soudan Frontier Field Force in 1885-86 including the engagement at Giniss.

³⁴⁴ Surgeon Major G. S. Robinson served in the expedition to the Soudan in 1885 with the 2nd Battalion of the Scots Guards, and was present in the engagement at Hasheen and at the destruction of Temai (Medal with Clasp, and Khedive's Star).

³⁴⁵ Surgeon Major E. H. Myles served with the Burmese Expedition in 1885-87 (Medal with Clasp).

³⁴⁶ Surgeon Major H. Martin served with the Zhob Valley Expedition in 1884.

³⁴⁷ Surgeon Major S. J. Flood served with the Bikaneer Field Force in 1883-84 in medical charge of British troops. Served with the Zhob Valley Expedition under Sir O. V. Tanner in 1884 in medical charge of the 2nd Battalion of the North Staffordshire Regiment, which on its return suffered from a severe outbreak of cholera in the Bolan Pass, for his conduct during which he received the thanks of his Commanding Officer and of the Director General of the Army Medical Staff. Served in the Soudan Expedition under Sir Gerald Graham in 1884 (Medal, and Khedive's Star).

³⁴⁷† Surgeon Major A. P. O'Connor served with the Burmese Expedition in 1885-86 (Medal with Clasp).

³⁴⁸ Surgeon Major D. Wardrop served during the Kafir war in 1878 as Civil Surgeon in the operations against Sekukuni, and in the Zulu war in 1879 (Medal with Clasp).

Army Medical Staff.—War Services.

[349] Surgeon Major J. M. Jones served as Civil Surgeon during the Zulu war in 1879 (Medal with Clasp).

[350] Surgeon Major R. O. Cusack served with the Manipore Expedition in 1891 as Senior Medical Officer with the Column under Brigadier General Graham (mentioned in despatches, Medal with Clasp).

[350†] Surgeon Major M. W. Kerin served with the Burmese Expedition in 1885-86 (Medal with Clasp).

[351] Surgeon Majors A. Peterkin and W. Dugdale served in the Boer war of 1881.

[352] Surgeon Major D. L. Irvine served with the Nile Expedition in 1884-85, and was present at the action of Kirbekan (Medal with two Clasps, and Khedive's Star).

[353] Surgeon Major E. R. Cree served in the Soudan campaign in 1885 and was present in the engagements at Hasheen and the Tofrek zereba and at the destruction of Temai (Medal with two Clasps, and Khedive's Star).

[354] Surgeon Major M. O'C. Drury served in the Soudan campaign in 1885 (Medal with Clasp, and Khedive's Star). Served with the Burmese Expedition in 1886-87 (mentioned in despatches, Medal with Clasp).

[355] Surgeon Major Twiss served as Civil Surgeon in the Zulu war of 1879, and has received the Medal with Clasp. Served in the Egyptian war of 1882 in medical charge of the 1st Battalion Berkshire Regiment, and was present at the surrender of Kafr Dowar (Medal, and Khedive's Star); also served with the Nile Expedition in 1884-85 (Clasp).

[357] Surgeon Major R. W. Ford served in the Egyptian war of 1882 (Medal, and Khedive's Star).

[358] Surgeon Major Swabey served in the Egyptian war of 1882 with the 1st Field Hospital (Medal, and Khedive's Star). Served with the Soudan Expedition under Sir Gerald Graham in 1885 in medical charge of the 10th (Railway) Company of Royal Engineers (Clasp).

[359] Surgeon Major O. R. Woods served in the Manipore Expedition in 1891 with the British Field Hospital in the Column under Brigadier General Graham (Medal with Clasp).

[360] Surgeon Major E. R. Morse served in the Egyptian war of 1882 (Medal, and Khedive's Star). Served in the operations on the Soudan frontier in 1889 including the engagements at Arguin and Toski (mentioned in despatches, 3rd Class of the Medjidie, Clasp).

[361] Surgeon Major Rowney served in the Egyptian war of 1882 (Medal, and Khedive's Star). Served in the Soudan campaign in 1885 (Clasp); also served in the operations of the Soudan Frontier Field Force in 1885-86.

[362] Surgeon Major T. R. Lucas served in the Egyptian war of 1882, and was present at the action at Kassasin on the 28th August and at the battle of Tel-el-Kebir (mentioned in despatches, Medal with Clasp, and Khedive's Star); also served in the Soudan Expedition under Sir Gerald Graham in 1884 (mentioned in despatches), and was present in the engagements at El Teb and Temai (mentioned in despatches, two Clasps). Served in the Nile Expedition in 1884-85 with the Camel Bearer Company, and was present in the action at Abu Klea and in the reconnaissance to Metammeh (two Clasps); also served in the operations of the Soudan Frontier Field Force in 1885-86. Served in the operations in the Northern Chin Hills, Burmah, in 1892-93 (mentioned in despatches).

[363] Surgeon Major C. J. Addison served with the 1st Bearer Company of the Army Hospital Corps in the Egyptian war of 1882 (Medal, and Khedive's Star).

[364] Surgeon Major A. G. Kay served in the Egyptian war of 1882 (Medal, and Khedive's Star).

[365] Surgeon Major W. W. Pope served in the Egyptian war of 1882, and was present at the battle of Tel-el-Kebir (Medal with Clasp, and Khedive's Star). Served in the operations in Zululand in 1888.

[367] Surgeon Major R. C. K. Laffan served in the Egyptian war of 1882 and was present at the battle of Tel-el-Kebir (Medal with Clasp, and Khedive's Star); also served with the Nile Expedition in 1884-85 (Clasp). Nominated to the 3rd Class of the Order of the Osmanieh for his services as Inspector of Hospitals to the Egyptian Sanitary Department.

[368] Surgeon Major C. A. P. Mitchell served in the Egyptian war of 1882, and was present at the battle of Tel-el-Kebir (Medal with Clasp, and Khedive's Star). Served with the Nile Expedition in 1884-85, and was present at the action of Kirbekan (two Clasps); also served with the Soudan Frontier Field Force in 1885-86.

[369] Surgeon Major T. B. A. Tuckey served in the Egyptian war of 1882 (Medal, and Khedive's Star); also served with the Nile Expedition in 1884-85 (Clasp). Served with the Burmese Expedition in 1886 (Medal with Clasp).

[370] Surgeon Major F. A. Harris served in the Egyptian war of 1882 (Medal, and Khedive's Star).

[373] Surgeon Major F. A. B. Daly served in the Egyptian war of 1882 (Medal, and Khedive's Star). Also served with the Soudan Frontier Field Force in 1885-86.

[374] Surgeon Major A. S. Rose served in the Egyptian war of 1882 (Medal, and Khedive's Star). Served with the Soudan Expedition under Sir Gerald Graham in 1884 (Clasp). Served in the Soudan campaign in 1885 (Clasp).

[375] Surgeon Major J. Battersby served in the Egyptian war of 1882, and was present at the battle of Tel-el-Kebir (Medal with Clasp, and Khedive's Star).

[376] Surgeon Major J. Maconachie served in the Egyptian war of 1882 (Medal, and Khedive's Star). Served with the Nile Expedition in 1884-85, and was present in the action at Abu Klea (two Clasps).

[377] Surgeon Major A. H. Morgan served in the Egyptian war of 1882 (Medal, and Khedive's Star). Served with the expedition up the Gambia in 1891-92 (Medal with Clasp); in the operations against the Sofas, West Coast of Africa, in 1893-94 (mentioned in despatches); and with the expedition to the Gambia against Fodey Silah in 1894 (mentioned in despatches, DSO.).

[379] Surgeon Major W. M. O'Keeffe served in the Egyptian war of 1882, and was present at the battle of Tel-el-Kebir (Medal with Clasp, and Khedive's Star).

[380] Surgeon Major T. J. O'Donnell served in the Egyptian war of 1882 (Medal, and Khedive's Star). Served with the Bechuanaland Expedition in 1884-85 under Sir Charles Warren; and in the operations in Zululand in 1888.

[381] Surgeon Major John Osburne served in the Egyptian war of 1882, and was present at the battle of Tel-el-Kebir (Medal with Clasp, and Khedive's Star); also served in the Soudan campaign in 1885, and was present in the engagement at the Tofrek zereba (two Clasps).

[382] Surgeon Major R. P. Hetherington served in the Egyptian war of 1882 (Medal, and Khedive's Star); also served with the Nile Expedition in 1884-85 (Clasp).

[384] Surgeon Major A. M. Davies served in the Egyptian war of 1882 (Medal, and Khedive's Star). Served in the expedition to the Soudan under Sir Gerald Graham in 1884, and was present in the engagements at El Teb and Temai (two Clasps); also served with the Nile Expedition in 1884-85 (Clasp).

[385] Surgeon Major H. W. Hubbard served in the Egyptian war of 1882, and was present at the battle of Tel-el-Kebir (Medal with Clasp, and Khedive's Star).

[386] Surgeon Major T. E. Noding served in the Egyptian war of 1882 (Medal, and Khedive's Star).

[387] Surgeon Major Yourdi served in the Egyptian war of 1882, first with the Army Hospital Corps at Alexandria, and subsequently in medical charge of a battery of Royal Artillery at Ramleh (Medal, and Khedive's Star).

[388] Surgeon Major R. I. D. Hackett served in the Soudan campaign in 1885 (Medal with Clasp, and Khedive's Star).

[389] Surgeon Captain E. O. Wight served in the operations on the North East Frontier of Burmah in 1891-92.

[390] Surgeon Major G. T. Trewman served in the Soudan campaign in 1885 (Medal with Clasp, and Khedive's Star).

[391] Surgeon Major H. H. Johnston served in the Soudan campaign in 1885 (Medal with Clasp, and Khedive's Star).

[392] Surgeon Major E. M. Wilson served during the Zulu war of 1879 as Civil Surgeon (Medal with Clasp). Served with the Nile Expedition in 1884-85 (Medal with Clasp, and Khedive's Star); also served with the Egyptian Frontier Field Force in 1885-86. Served with the expedition up the River Gambia in 1891-92 (Medal with Clasp).

[393] Surgeon Major E. J. E. Risk served in the Egyptian war of 1882, and was present in the engagements at Tel-el-Mahuta and Mahsama, and at the two actions at Kassasin (Medal, and Khedive's Star).

[394] Surgeon Major W. G. Birrell served in the Soudan campaign in 1885 (Medal with Clasp, and Khedive's Star). Served with the Burmese Expedition in 1886-87 (mentioned in despatches, Medal with Clasp).

[395] Surgeon Major E. D. Farmar-Bringhurst served in the Egyptian war of 1882 (Medal, and Khedive's Star). Served in the operations in Zululand in 1888.

[396] Surgeon Major R. Kirkpatrick served with the Burmese Expedition in 1886-88 (Medal with Clasp).

[397] Surgeon Captain D. R. Hamilton served with the Burmese Expedition in 1886-88 (Medal with two Clasps).

[598] Surgeon Major P. J. Nealon served with the expedition to the Tambaka Country, West Africa, in 1892, including the capture of Tambi (Medal with Clasp).

[399] Surgeon Captain F. J. Greig served with the Hazara Expedition in 1891 (Medal with Clasp).

[400] Surgeon Major C. W. S. Magrath served in the Egyptian war of 1882, and was present at the battle of Tel-el-Kebir (Medal with Clasp, and Khedive's Star); also served with the Nile Expedition in 1884-85 (Clasp). Served with the Burmese Expedition in 1886-87 (Medal with two Clasps).

401 Surgeon Major A. V. Lane served in the Egyptian war of 1882 (Medal, and Khedive's Star); also served with the Soudan Expedition in 1884 under Sir Gerald Graham, and was present in the engagements at El Teb and Temai (two Clasps).

402 Surgeon Major J. W. Beatty served in the Egyptian war of 1882, and was present at the battle of Tel-el-Kebir (Medal with Clasp, and Khedive's Star).

403 Surgeon Major G. E. Weston served in the Egyptian war of 1882 (Medal, and Khedive's Star). Served with the Bechuanaland Expedition under Sir Charles Warren in 1884-85.

404 Surgeon Major J. M'Laughlin served in the expedition to the Tambaka Country, on the West Coast of Africa, in 1892, as Senior Medical Officer, and was present at the capture of Tambi (mentioned in despatches, Medal with Clasp). Served with the expedition up the Gambia in 1892 as Senior Medical Officer of the force, and was present at the capture of Toniataba (mentioned in despatches).

405 Surgeon Major R. F. O'Brien served with the Burmese Expedition in 1885-86 (Medal with Clasp).

406 Surgeon Major W. Dick served with the Nile Expedition in 1884-85, and was present in the action at Abu Klea (Medal with two Clasps, and Khedive's Star).

407 Surgeon Major F. J. Jencken served in the expedition to the Soudan under Sir Gerald Graham in 1884, and was present in the engagements at El Teb and Temai (Medal with Clasp, and Khedive's Star); also served with the Nile Expedition in 1884-85 (Clasp).

408 Surgeon Major H. O. Stuart served in the Afghan war in 1880 in Southern Afghanistan (Medal). Served in the expedition to the Soudan under Sir Gerald Graham in 1884 in command of detachments of the Army Hospital Corps, and was present in the engagements at El Teb and Temai (Medal with Clasp, and Khedive's Star). Served with the Nile Expedition in 1884-85, and was present at the action of Kirbekan (two Clasps).

409 Surgeon Major F. H. Treherne served in the Soudan Expedition under Sir Gerald Graham in 1884 in medical charge of the 1st Battalion Black Watch, and was present in the engagements at El Teb and Temai (mentioned in despatches, Medal with Clasp, and Khedive's Star). Served with the Nile Expedition in 1884-85, and was present at the action of Kirbekan (two Clasps).

410 Surgeon Major H. O. Trevor served with the Burmese Expedition in 1885-86 in medical charge of a Battery of Royal Artillery (Medal with Clasp).

411 Surgeon Major W. A. Morris served with the Burmese Expedition in 1886-87 (mentioned in despatches, Medal with Clasp).

412 Surgeon Major F. H. M. Burton served with the Burmese Expedition in 1885-87, including the expeditions to Bhamo, Mogaung, and against the Kachins on the frontier of China; in charge of a section of a Field Hospital at Bhamo from January 1886 to March 1887 (Medal with Clasp).

413 Surgeon Major C. E. Nichol served with the Burmah Expedition in 1885-86 (Medal with Clasp).

414 Surgeon Major T. A. Perry Marsh served in the Burmese Expedition in 1885-87 in medical charge of a Battery of Mountain Artillery, and was present in several engagements near Ningyan and Yemethen, and in the latter place during its investment in February and March 1886 (Medal with Clasp).

415 Surgeon Major J. Hickman served with the Burmese Expedition in 1886-87 in medical charge of No. 8 Battery Mountain Artillery (Medal with Clasp). Served with the expedition up the River Gambia in 1892 and was present at the capture of Toniataba (Medal with Clasp).

416 Surgeon Major A. Baird served with the Bechuanaland Expedition under Sir Charles Warren in 1884-85. Served in the operations in Zululand in 1888.

416† Surgeon Major R. P. Bond served with the Nile Expedition in 1884-85 (Medal with Clasp, and Khedive's Star); also served in the operations of the Soudan Frontier Field Force in 1885-86.

417 Surgeon Captains C. E. Faunce, J. P. Myles, H. P. Birch, J. J. C. Donnet, and R. H. Clement served with the Nile Expedition in 1884-85 (Medal with Clasp, and Khedive's Star).

418 Surgeon Captain A. E. Tate served in the Burmese Expedition in 1886-87 in medical charge of the 1st Battalion Rifle Brigade, and with No. 17 British Field Hospital (Medal with Clasp); and again in 1887-89 (Clasp).

419 Surgeon Captain H. Carr served with the Burmese Expedition in 1885-87 (Medal with Clasp); and with the second Miranzai Expedition in 1891 (Clasp).

420 Surgeon Captain E. H. Lynden Bell served with the Burmese Expedition in 1885-89 (Medal with two Clasps).

421 Surgeon Captain H. H. Pinching served with the Nile Expedition in 1884-85 (Medal with Clasp, and Khedive's Star); in the operations of the Soudan Frontier Field Force in 1885-86; and in the operations in the Soudan in 1889 including the engagement at Toski (mentioned in despatches, Clasp, and 4th Class of the Medjidie).

422 Surgeon Captain F. S. Heuston served with the Hazara Expedition in 1888 in medical charge of the 2nd Battalion Northumberland Fusiliers (Medal with Clasp).

423 Surgeon Captain M. O'D. Braddell served with the Nile Expedition in 1884-85 (Medal with Clasp, and Khedive's Star). Served with the Hazara Expedition in 1888 in medical charge of the 2nd Battalion Royal Sussex Regiment (Medal with Clasp).

424 Surgeon Captain H. M. Sloggett served with the Miranzai Expedition in 1891 (Medal with Clasp).

424† Surgeon Captain R. Crofts served with the expedition against the Jebus, Lagos, in 1892 (mentioned in despatches, Medal with Clasp).

425 Surgeon Captain J. F. Burke served in the Egyptian war of 1882 as Civil Surgeon (Medal, and Khedive's Star). Served with the Burmese Expedition in 1885-87 (Medal with Clasp).

425† Surgeon Captain J. R. Barefoot served with the Soudan Frontier Field Force in 1885-86 including the engagement at Giniss (Medal, and Khedive's Star).

426 Surgeon Captain G. D. Hunter served with the Nile Expedition in 1884-85 (Medal with Clasp, and Khedive's Star); also served in the operations of the Soudan Frontier Field Force in 1885-86. Nominated to the 4th Class of the Order of the Osmanieh for services with the Egyptian Army.

427 Surgeon Captain W. C. Beevor served in the Soudan campaign in 1885 (Medal with Clasp, and Khedive's Star).

428 Surgeon Captain L. E. Anderson served with the Nile Expedition in 1884-85, and in the subsequent operations in the Eastern Soudan in 1885 (Medal with two Clasps, and Khedive's Star).

429 Surgeon Captains G. B. Russell, L. R. Colledge, S. F. Freyer, C. Birt, H. Mitchell, S. Butterworth, and C. J. Holmes served in the Soudan campaign in 1885 (Medal with Clasp, and Khedive's Star).

429† Surgeon Captain J. R. Forrest served in the Soudan campaign in 1885 (Medal with Clasp, and Khedive's Star).

430 Surgeon Captain A. E. C. Spence served in the Soudan campaign in 1885 (Medal with Clasp, and Khedive's Star).

431 Surgeon Captain J. R. Mallins served with the Soudan Frontier Field Force in 1885-86 including the engagement at Giniss (Medal, and Khedive's Star).

432 Surgeon Captain J. F. Donegan served with the Burmese Expedition in 1887-89 with the Pounkan Column under Brigadier General Wolseley and afterwards with the Tonhon Column (Medal with Clasp).

433 Surgeon Captain R. S. F. Henderson served in the Soudan campaign in 1885, and was present in the engagement at Tofrek and at the destruction of Temai (Medal with Clasp, and Khedive's Star). Served in the Burmese war in 1886 including the operations of the Wuntho Expedition (Medal with Clasp); and in the expedition against the Tounhon Kakyens in 1889 (Clasp); also served with the Chin-Lushai Expedition on the staff of Sir Charles Arbuthnot (Clasp); also with the Wuntho Expedition in 1891 as Senior Medical Officer with Sir George Wolseley (mentioned in despatches, Clasp).

434 Surgeon Captain G. E. Hale served with the Soudan Frontier Field Force in 1885-86, and was present in the engagement at Giniss (Medal, and Khedive's Star). Served with the Burmese Expedition in 1889-91, and with the Tonhon and Wuntho Expeditions (received the thanks of the Government of India, mentioned in despatches, DSO, and Medal with Clasp).

435 Surgeon Captain L. T. M. Nash served with the Miranzai Expedition in 1891 (mentioned in despatches, Medal with Clasp); and with the Hazara Expedition in 1891 (Clasp).

436 Surgeon Captain M. W. Russell served with the Soudan Frontier Force in 1885-86 including the engagement at Giniss (Medal, and Khedive's Star). Served with the Zhob Valley and Kidderzai Expeditions in 1890 under Sir George White, including the march to Vihowa.

437 Surgeon Captain N. Manders served in the Soudan campaign in 1885 (Medal with Clasp, and Khedive's Star). Served in the Burmese Expedition under Brigadier Generals Lockhart and Collett with the Southern Shan Column

in 1887-88, and with the Karen Expedition in 1888-89, including the action at Lwékaw and minor affairs—severely wounded (Medal with two Clasps).

⁴³⁸ Surgeon Captain A. Stables served in the operations of the Soudan Frontier Field Force in 1885-86 Medal, and Khedive's Star).

⁴³⁹ Surgeon Captains J. D. Moir, G. M. Dobson, C. W. Johnson, C. C. Reilly, and B. O. W. Norfer served with the Soudan Frontier Field Force in 1885-86 (Medal, and Khedive's Star).

⁴⁴⁰ Surgeon Captain R. Caldwell served with the Soudan Frontier Field Force in 1885-86 (Medal, and Khedive's Star). [See also Civil Decorations for Gallantry, "Hart's Annual Army List," p. 786.]

⁴⁴¹ Surgeon Captain J. Maher served in the Soudan campaign in 1885 (Medal with Clasp, and Khedive's Star).

⁴⁴¹† Surgeon Captain C. L. Josling served with the expedition to the Gambia against Fodey Silah in 1894 (mentioned in despatches).

⁴⁴² Surgeon Captain S. N. Cardozo served with the Egyptian Frontier Field Force in 1885-86, including the engagement at Kosheh (mentioned in despatches, Medal, and Khedive's Star).

⁴⁴³ Surgeon Captain W. Turner served in the Soudan campaign in 1885 (Medal with Clasp, and Khedive's Star).

⁴⁴⁴ Surgeon Captain F. W. C. Jones served with the Burmese Expedition in 1886-89 (mentioned in despatches, Medal with two Clasps).

⁴⁴⁵ Surgeon Captain J. Meek served with the Sikkim Expedition in 1888 (Medal with Clasp).

⁴⁴⁷ Surgeon Captain W. H. Bean served in the Burmese Expedition in 1885-88, first under Brigadier General East and afterwards under Brigadier General Wolseley (mentioned in despatches, Medal with Clasp); also served with the Chin-Lushai Expeditionary Force in 1889-90 (mentioned in despatches, Clasp).

⁴⁴⁸ Surgeon Captain S. R. Wills served with the Hazara Expedition in 1891 (Medal with Clasp).

⁴⁴⁹ Surgeon Captain S. C. Philson served in the operations on the North East Frontier, Burmah, in 1892-93.

⁴⁵⁴ Surgeon Captain P. C. H. Gordon served with the Burmese Expedition in 1886-89 (mentioned in despatches, Medal with two Clasps).

⁴⁵⁶ Surgeon Captain C. S. Sparkes served with the Sikkim Expedition in 1888 (Medal with Clasp).

⁴⁵⁷ Surgeon Captain W. H. Pinches served with the Hazara Expedition in 1891 (Medal with Clasp).

⁴⁵⁸ Surgeon Captain H. D. Rowan served with the Hazara Expedition in 1888 including the engagement at Kotkai (Medal with Clasp).

⁴⁵⁹ Surgeon Captain H. G. Hathaway served with the Burmese Expedition in 1885-89, and accompanied the Ruby Mine Column to Mogome; was present at the capture of Mainloung in medical charge of the column under Captain H. Earle (Medal with two Clasps).

⁴⁶¹ Surgeon Captain P. J. R. Nunnerley served with the Burmese Expedition in 1886-87 (Medal with Clasp).

⁴⁶³ Surgeon Captain H. H. Brown served in the Burmese Expedition under Brigadier General Lockhart in 1885-87, and again in 1887-89 (Medal with two Clasps).

⁴⁶⁵ Surgeon Captain W. F. Bailey served in the operations in Zululand in 1888.

⁴⁷⁰ Surgeon Captain H. A. Cummins served with the Sikkim Expedition in 1888 (Medal with Clasp).

⁴⁷¹ Surgeon Captain G. H. Barefoot served with the Hazara Expedition in 1888 (mentioned in despatches, Medal with Clasp).

⁴⁷² Surgeon Captain E. S. Marder served with the Burmese Expedition in 1888-90 (Medal with two Clasps).

⁴⁷⁷ Surgeon Captain Cockerill.—See Civil Decorations for Gallantry, "Hart's Annual Army List," p. 786.

⁴⁷⁸ Surgeon Captain F. S. Le Quesne served with the Burmese Expedition in 1889 and was severely wounded during the operations in the Chin country (VC, and Medal with Clasp): was awarded the Victoria Cross for the following service:—"Displayed conspicuous bravery and devotion to duty during the attack on the village of Tartan by a Column of the Chin Field Force on the 4th May 1889 in having remained for the space of about ten minutes in a very exposed position (within five yards of the loopholed stockade from which the enemy were firing), dressing with perfect coolness and self-possession the wounds from which 2nd Lieut. Michel, Norfolk Regiment, shortly afterwards died. Surgeon Le Quesne was himself severely wounded later on whilst attending to the wounds of another officer." Served with the Chin-Lushai Expeditionary Force in 1890 (Clasp), and with the Wuntho Field Force in 1891 (Clasp).

⁴⁸² Major R. T. Osborne served in the Egyptian war of 1882, and was present at the battle of Tel-el-Kebir (honorary rank of Captain, Medal with Clasp, and Khedive's Star); also served with the Nile Expedition in 1884-85 (honorary rank of Major, Clasp).

⁴⁸⁴ Captain D. O'Connor served in the Egyptian war of 1882 (Medal, and Khedive's Star); also served with the Nile Expedition in 1884-85 (granted the higher rate of pay, Clasp).

⁴⁸⁸ Captain M'Intyre served in the Abyssinian campaign of 1867-68 (Medal).

⁴⁸⁹ Captain Lackey served with the 1st Bombay European Fusiliers at Mooltan during the Indian Mutiny in 1858 (Medal). Served with the Nile Expedition in 1884-85 (Medal with Clasp, and Khedive's Star). He has also the Medal for Long and Meritorious Service.

⁴⁹¹ Captain John Horn served in the Zulu war in 1879, and in the subsequent operations against Sekukuni including the storming of the stronghold (Medal with Clasp). Also served in the Boer war of 1881, and took part in the defence of Pretoria. Served in the Soudan campaign in 1885 (Medal with Clasp, and Khedive's Star).

⁴⁹⁵ Captain T. Connor served in the Egyptian war of 1882 (Medal, and Khedive's Star); also served with the Nile Expedition in 1884-85 (Clasp); also served in the Soudan campaign in 1885, and was present in the engagement at the Tofrek zereba (two Clasps).

⁴⁹⁷ Captain T. Phillips served in the Ashanti war in 1873-74 (Medal). Served in the Egyptian war of 1882 (Medal, and Khedive's Star).

⁴⁹⁸ Lieut. Beach served in the Egyptian war in 1882 (Medal, and Khedive's Star). Served with the Bechuanaland Expedition under Sir Charles Warren in 1884-85; and in the operations in Zululand in 1888.

⁴⁹⁹ Lieut. Kyle served with the Soudan Expedition in 1885 (Medal with Clasp, and Khedive's Star).

⁵⁰⁰ Lieut. R. Adams served with the Bechuanaland Expedition under Sir Charles Warren in 1884-85.

Army Veterinary Department.

Director General,
with the rank of Veterinary Colonel.

James Drummond Lambert,[1] *CB. FRCVS. Vet. Surg.* 12 Oct. 57; *1st Class,*[2] Sept. 68; *Insp. V. S.* 12 Mar. 81; *Principa V. S.* 28 June 90. War Office.

Veterinary Lieutenant Colonels.

George Albert Oliphant,[2] *Vet. Surg.* 22 June 60; *1st Class,* 2 Aug. 71; *Insp. V. S.* 28 June 83. London.
William Albert Russell, *Vet. Surg.* 24 June 62; *1st Class,* 4 Oct. 73; *Insp. Vet. Surgeon,* 6 Apr. 87. Woolwich.
Francis Duck,[7] *Vet. Surg.* 31 July 67; *1st Class,* 1 Aug. 77; *Insp. Vet. Surg.* 28 June 90. Bengal.
Charles Clayton,[8] *Vet. Surg.* 2 Aug. 71; *1st Class,* 21 May 84; *Insp. Vet. Surg.* 7 Aug. 90. Bombay.
Henry Thomson,[9] *Vet. Surg.* 1 Nov. 71; *1st Class,* 21 May 84; *Insp. Vet. Surg.* 8 Oct. 90. Bengal.
Alfred Ernest Queripel,[13] *Inspector General Civil Veterinary Dept. in India,* 28 May 94; *Vet. Surg.* 27 Aug. 70; *1st Class,* 2 Mar. 81; *Veterinary Lt. Colonel,* 25 Nov. 93. India.
Charles Phillips,[14] *Vet. Surg.* 27 Aug. 70; *1st Class,* 27 Aug. 82; *Veterinary Lt. Colonel,* 24 Feb. 94. Dublin.
Edward Ewing,[16] *Vet. Surg.* 8 Sept. 65; *1st Class,* 7 Mar. 76; *Veterinary Lt. Colonel,* 18 Feb. 95. Madras.
Richard Poyser,[17] *Vet. Surg.* 12 Sept. 65; *1st Class,* 8 Mar. 76; *Veterinary Lt. Colonel,* 14 Mar. 95. Bengal.

Veterinary Majors.

Walter Seymour Adams	11 Jan. 67	1 Apr. 77	Madras.	George J. Robert Rayment,[33] *FRCVS.*	24 July 72	15 Feb. 93	Bengal.
James Kettle[19]	11 Jan. 67	1 Aug. 77	Woolwich.	Geo. Digby Whitfield[36]	2 Aug. 71	1 Apr. 93	Portsmouth.
James Coleman Berne[20]	7 Aug. 67	2 Feb. 78	S. Africa.	James Kean Grainger[37]	8 June 72	1 Apr. 93	Weedon.
James Reilly[21]	7 Aug. 67	2 Feb. 78	R. Horse Gds.	James Joseph Philips[38]	24 July 72	1 Apr. 93	Bengal.
John Hammond	3 June 68	3 June 80	Egypt.	Benjamin Augustus White Powell[40]	15 Mar. 73	1 Apr. 93	Dorchester.
Benj. Lucas Glover[24]	27 Aug. 70	4 Sept. 80	Rem't. Estab.				
George Durrant[25]	2 Dec. 68	2 Dec. 80	Nwcstl.-o-T.	John Burton[41]	14 June 73	14 June 93	Shorncliffe.
John Cornelius Dwyer	23 Dec. 68	23 Dec. 80	Rem't. Estab.	Seaward Longhurst[42] *Professor Army Vet. School* 1 Dec. 92	14 June 73	14 June 93	A. V. School.
Jas. Augustus Woods[26]	24 Sept. 70	2 Mar. 81	Aldershot.				
William Walker[27]	11 Jan. 67	14 July 81	Bengal.				
Richard Rowe	14 July 69	14 July 81	Chelsea.	Frank Fairbairn Crawford[43]	14 June 73	14 June 93	Bengal.
Walter Henry Kemp	9 Feb. 70	14 July 81	Bombay.				
Stuart Murray Wilson	14 July 69	21 July 92	Exeter.	William Gladstone[45]	10 June 74	10 June 94	4 Hussars.
Robert Francis Frost	14 Jan. 71	14 Jan. 93	Curragh.	Walt. Boulton Spooner[45]	14 Feb. 74	26 Sept. 94	Sheffield.
John William Evans[30]	15 Feb. 71	15 Feb. 93	Bengal.	Samuel Gillespie[47]	10 June 74	26 Sept. 94	Bombay.
Chas. Whitney Gillard[31]	20 Sept. 71	15 Feb. 93	Woolwich.				
Iles Matthews,[32] *FRCVS.*	24 July 72	15 Feb. 93	Rem't Estab.				

Veterinary Captains.

Arthur Bostock[48]	14 Apr. 75	30 Apr. 85	Madras.	George Richard Griffith[73]	26 May 80	26 May 90	Egypt. Army
James Mills	23 June 75	23 June 85	Bombay.	John Cooper, *FRCVS.*	11 Sept. 80	11 Sept. 90	Bengal.
Thomas Flintoff[51]	23 June 75	23 June 85	2 Life Gds.	Ernest Emilius Bennett,[76] *FRCVS.*	26 Feb. 81	26 Feb. 91	Limerick.
George Frederick Davis	9 Feb. 76	9 Feb. 86	Athlone.				
John Denis Edwards[53]	4 Aug. 76	26 Aug. 86	1 Life Gds.	Richard Wm. Burke,[78] *FRCVS.*	27 July 81	27 July 91	Bengal.
William Alfred Crow[54]	1 Dec. 76	2 Oct. 86	Chatham.				
Fred. Smith	9 Dec. 76	9 Dec. 86	Aldershot.	Stephen Marsh Smith[79]	1 Oct. 81	1 Oct. 91	Bengal.
Daniel Chambers Pallin[56]	1 Apr. 77	21 Apr. 87	Madras.	Arthur Fred. Appleton	12 Sept. 83	12 Sept. 93	6 Dragoons.
Joshua Arthur Nunn[57] *CIE., DSO.*	21 Apr. 77	21 Apr. 87	Bengal.	Edwin Hills Hazelton	12 Sept. 83	12 Sept. 93	Madras.
				Layton John Blenkinsop	12 Sept. 83	12 Sept. 93	Woolwich.
John Wm. Akerman Morgan[58]	12 June 78	12 June 88	Bombay.	Richard Wellington Raymond	3 Oct. 83	3 Oct. 93	8 Hussars.
Wm. Robert Hagger[59]	13 July 78	13 July 88	Bengal.	John Armstead Braddell	19 Dec. 83	19 Dec. 03	13 Hussars.
Richard Head Ringe	5 Oct. 78	5 Oct. 88	Aldershot.	John Finlayson	12 Jan. 84	12 Jan. 94	Egypt.
Robert Pringle[60]	5 Oct. 78	5 Oct. 88	2 Dragoons.	Frank Joslen	9 May 84	9 May 94	1 Dr. Gds.
Thomas Alex. Killick[61]	30 Oct. 78	30 Oct. 88	Woolwich.	Harrie Malcolm Maxwell,[82] *FRCVS.*	11 June 84	11 June 94	Bengal.
John Burke Savage[62]	30 Oct. 78	30 Oct. 88	Cav. Depot.				
Robert Moore[63]	30 Nov. 78	30 Nov. 88	12 Lancers.	Charles Edwin Nuthall	30 July 84	30 July 94	1 Dragoons.
Francis Raymond[64]	14 Dec. 78	14 Dec. 88	Bengal.	Tom Marriott, *FRCVS.*	27 Aug. 84	27 Aug. 94	4 Dr. Gds.
John Thomas Dibben	15 Mar. 79	15 Mar. 89	17 Lancers.	Henry Thomas Pease.	27 Aug. 84	27 Aug. 94	Bengal.
Gerald Herbert Fenton[66]	5 Oct. 78	27 Apr. 89	Madras.	George Henry Evans[83]	27 Aug. 84	27 Aug. 94	Madras.
Edmund Day	17 May 79	17 May 89	9 Lancers.	Ernest Reuben Chas. Butler, *FRCVS.*	27 Aug. 84	27 Aug. 94	A.V. School.
Charles Rutherford[68]	17 May 79	17 May 89	Bengal.				
Kay Lees[69]	17 May 79	17 May 89	Colchester.	Geo. Curran Orr Fowler[85]	10 Dec. 84	10 Dec. 94	20 Hussars.
Frederick Walewski Forsdyke[70]	24 May 79	24 May 89	Bengal.	John Alfred Meredith	10 Dec. 84	10 Dec. 94	15 Hussars.
				Frank William Sharp[86]	10 Dec. 84	31 Dec. 94	Aldershot.
William Donald Gunn	13 July 78	25 Dec. 89	Bengal.	Edward Taylor[87]	4 Feb. 85	4 Feb. 95	Bengal.
Frederick John Short	24 Jan. 80	24 Jan. 90	Bengal.	Alf. Joseph Haslam,[88] *MD. MCh. FRCVS.*	4 Feb. 85	4 Feb. 95	3 Hussars.
Hy. Thos. Wm. Mann[72]	26 May 80	26 May 90	Bengal.				

Veterinary Lieutenants.

David Joseph Barry	13 May 85	6 Dr. Gds.	Francis Dillon Hunt	3 Feb. 92	Bombay.
James George O'Donel	13 May 85	14 Hussars.	Ernest Edmund Martin	3 Feb. 92	Bengal.
Alexander Edward Richardson	13 May 85	Bengal.	Harry Briscoe Knight	17 Feb. 92	Bengal.
William Reginald Walker	13 May 85	Bengal.	Hugh Augustus Sullivan	13 Apr. 92	Bengal.
Edmund James Lawson[90]	20 May 85	Egypt.	William Dunlop Smith	27 July 92	Egypt.
Harry Wilkinson	20 May 85	Madras.	Arthur England	28 Sept. 92	S. Africa.
Francis Binyoun Drage	18 July 88	Bengal.	Charles Birt Freeman	10 May 93	Bengal.
John Henry Jackson	18 July 88	10 Hussars.	Henry Thomas Sawyer	3 June 93	Bombay.
Robert James Duncan Tibaldi	10 Oct. 88	Bengal.	John Farmer	3 June 93	Bombay.
Thos. Emmanuel Watkins Lewis	28 Nov. 88	Bombay.	Alfred Smith	3 June 93	Madras.
Eugene William Larnder	28 Nov. 88	Bombay.	George Mostyn Williams	3 June 93	Bengal.
Augustus Charles Newsom	12 June 89	Bombay.	Albert Edward Clarke	3 June 93	Bengal.
Fitzpatrick Eassie[91]	11 Sept. 89	Madras.	William Nevill Wright	3 June 93	Bengal.
John Moore	18 Dec. 89	Bengal.	Hugh Cogan Harris	3 June 93	Bengal.
John Loughlin	2 July 90	Bengal.	William Allan M'Dougall	3 June 93	Bengal.
Charles Beresford Maule Harris	27 Aug. 90	Bengal.	Arthur Henry Lane	29 Nov. 93	Egypt. Army
Ernest Wilkinson	10 Sept. 90	S. Africa.	Frank Shelson Headon Baldrey.	28 Feb. 94	Bombay.
Robert Langley Cranford	22 Oct. 90	Bengal.	Frank Walter Wilson	14 Mar. 94	Aldershot.
Thomas George Peacocke	7 Jan. 91	Bombay.	Walter Francis Shore	25 July 94	Newbridge.
Walter John Tatam	18 Feb. 91	Madras.	George Kemp Walker	25 July 94	Woolwich.
Arthur Stuart Trydell	3 June 91	Madras.	Edward Patrick John Barry	25 July 94	Bengal.
Harold Price Turnbull	10 June 91	Madras.	William Edward Russell	17 Oct. 94	Canterbury.
Charles Rose	2 Sept. 91	Bengal.	Frederick Ulysses Carr	13 Mar. 95	
Henry Joseph Axe	3 Feb. 92	Bombay.	Frederick Welsley Hunt	20 Mar. 95	

Army Veterinary Department.—War Services.

¹ Veterinary Colonel Lambert served with the 17th Lancers in the Zulu war of 1879, and was present in the engagement at Ulundi (Medal with Clasp). Also served in the Boer war of 1881 as Principal Veterinary Surgeon.

² Veterinary Lt.Colonel G. A. Oliphant served in the Afghan war in 1879-80 as Principal Veterinary Surgeon with the Koorum Field Force (Medal).

⁷ Veterinary Lt.Colonel F. Duck served in the Kafir war in 1877-78 including the operations against Sekukuni; also served in the Zulu war in 1879, and was present in the engagements at Zlobane, Kambula, and Ulundi (mentioned in despatches, Medal with Clasp). Served in the Boer war in 1881. Served with the Bechuanaland Expedition under Sir Charles Warren in 1884-85 as Senior Veterinary Surgeon with the force (promoted Veterinary Surgeon 1st Class ranking with Majors).

⁸ Veterinary Lt.Colonel C. Clayton served in the Afghan war in 1879-80 (promoted Veterinary Surgeon 1st Class, and Medal). Served in the Soudan Expedition under Sir Gerald Graham in 1884 as Acting Principal Veterinary Surgeon (mentioned in despatches, promoted Veterinary Surgeon 1st Class with relative rank of Major, Medal, and Khedive's Star).

⁹ Veterinary Lt.Colonel Thomson served with the 19th Hussars in the Egyptian war of 1882, and was present in the action at Kassasin (9th September) and at the battle of Tel-el-Kebir (promoted 1st Class Veterinary Surgeon, Medal with Clasp, and Khedive's Star). Served in the Soudan Expedition in 1884 with the 19th Hussars, and was present in the engagements at El Teb and Temai (promoted 1st Class Veterinary Surgeon with relative rank of Major, two Clasps).

¹³ Veterinary Lt.Colonel A. E. Queripel served in the Afghan war in 1879-80 (promoted Veterinary Surgeon 1st Class, Medal). Served with the Nile Expedition in 1884-85, and was present at the action of Kirbekau (mentioned in despatches, promoted Veterinary Surgeon 1st Class ranking with Majors, Medal with two Clasps, and Khedive's Star).

¹⁴ Veterinary Lt.Colonel Charles Phillips served in the Zulu war in 1879 (Medal with Clasp). Served with the Nile Expedition in 1884-85 (mentioned in despatches, promoted Veterinary Surgeon 1st Class ranking with Majors, Medal with Clasp, and Khedive's Star).

¹⁶ Veterinary Lt.Colonel Ewing served with the Hazara Expedition in 1888 (mentioned in despatches, Medal with Clasp).

¹⁷ Veterinary Lt.Colonel Poyser served with the Carabiniers in the Afghan war in 1879-80, and took part in the expeditions into the Lughman Valley and against the Wuzeeree Khugianis (Medal).

¹⁹ Veterinary Major J. Kettle served in the Abyssinian war in 1867-68 (Medal).

²⁰ Veterinary Major Berne served throughout the Abyssinian campaign of 1868 (Medal). Served with the Bechuanaland Expedition under Sir Charles Warren in 1884-85.

²¹ Veterinary Major James Reilly served in the Abyssinian war in 1867-68 (Medal). Served in the Boer war of 1881.

²⁴ Veterinary Major Glover served in the Kafir war in 1878 including the operations against Sekukuni (promoted 1st Class Veterinary Surgeon); also served in the Zulu war in 1879 (Medal with Clasp).

²⁵ Veterinary Major G. Durrant served in the Boer war of 1881.

²⁶ Veterinary Major Woods served with the 9th Lancers in the Afghan war of 1878-80, and was present in the operations round Cabul in December 1879; accompanied Sir Frederick Roberts in the march to Candahar, and was present at the battle of Candahar (promoted 1st Class Veterinary Surgeon, Medal with two Clasps, and Bronze Decoration). Served in the Bechuanaland Expedition under Sir Charles Warren in 1884-85.

²⁷ Veterinary Major W. Walker served in the Afghan war in 1878-79 with the force under Sir Donald Stewart (Medal).

³⁰ Veterinary Major J. W. Evans served in the Egyptian war of 1882 with the Indian Contingent, and was present at the battle of Tel-el-Kebir (Medal with Clasp, and Khedive's Star).

³¹ Veterinary Major C. W. Gillard served in the Afghan war in 1880, and took part in the advance to Candahar (Medal). Served in the Boer war in 1881 (promoted 1st Class Veterinary Surgeon for services in Afghanistan and South Africa). Served in the Soudan campaign in 1885 (Medal with Clasp, and Khedive's Star).

³² Veterinary Major Matthews served throughout the Egyptian war of 1882 with the 4th Dragoon Guards and was present in the engagement at Tel-el-Mahuta, in the two actions at Kassasin, and at the battle of Tel-el-Kebir and the capture of Cairo (promoted Veterinary Surgeon 1st Class, Medal with Clasp, and Khedive's Star).

³³ Veterinary Major G. J. R. Rayment served in the Afghan war in 1880, including the expedition against the Atchakzais (Medal). Served in the Egyptian war of 1882, and was present in the engagement at Mahsama (promoted Veterinary Surgeon 1st Class, Medal, and Khedive's Star). Served in the Soudan campaign in 1885 (Clasp).

³⁶ Veterinary Major G. D. Whitfield served in the Egyptian war of 1882 (Medal, and Khedive's Star).

³⁷ Veterinary Major J. K. Grainger served in the Afghan war in 1880 (Medal).

³⁸ Veterinary Major J. J. Philips served in the Afghan war of 1878-80 (Medal).

⁴⁰ Veterinary Major B. A. W. Powell served with the Burmese Expedition in 1885-86 (Medal with Clasp).

⁴¹ Veterinary Major J. Burton served in the Afghan war in 1879-80 (Medal).

⁴² Veterinary Major Longhurst served with the King's Dragoon Guards in the Zulu war of 1879 (Medal with Clasp).

⁴³ Veterinary Major F. F. Crawford served with the Bechuanaland Expedition under Sir Charles Warren in 1884-85. Served in the operations in Zululand in 1888.

⁴⁵ Veterinary Major W. Gladstone served in the Soudan campaign in 1885 (Medal with Clasp, and Khedive's Star). Served with the Burmese Expedition in 1888-90 (Medal with Clasp).

⁴⁶ Veterinary Major W. B. Spooner served in the Afghan war in 1879-80, and took part in the defence of Candahar (mentioned in despatches, Medal). Served in the Egyptian war of 1882 (Medal, and Khedive's Star). Also served with the Nile Expedition in 1884-85 (Clasp).

⁴⁷ Veterinary Major Gillespie served in the Afghan war in 1878-79, took part in the operations in the Khyber Pass including the capture of the Peiwar Kotal, and was present in the engagement at Charasiah on the 6th October 1879 and in the subsequent operations around Cabul until invalided to England in November 1879 (Medal with Clasp for Charasiah).

⁴⁸ Veterinary Captain Bostock served in the Afghan war in 1880 (Medal).

⁵¹ Veterinary Captain T. Flintoff served in the Afghan war in 1879-80 (Medal).

⁵³ Veterinary Captain J. D. Edwards served in the Afghan war in 1879-80 (Medal).

⁵⁴ Veterinary Captain W. A. Crow served with the Royal Horse Artillery in the Egyptian war of 1882, and was present at the action at Kassasin (9th September) and at the battle of Tel-el-Kebir (Medal with Clasp, and Khedive's Star). Served in the two Miranzai Expeditions under Sir William Lockhart in 1891, and was present in the engagement at Tsallia and at the capture of Sangar (mentioned in despatches, Medal with Clasp).

⁵⁶ Veterinary Captain D. C. Pallin served in the Boer war of 1881.

⁵⁷ Veterinary Captain J. A. Nunn served in the Afghan war in 1879-80 (Medal). Served in the operations in Zululand in 1888. Served with the Chin-Lushai Expeditionary Force in 1889-90 with the Chittagong Column (mentioned in despatches, DSO., Medal with Clasp).

⁵⁸ Veterinary Captain Morgan served in the Zulu war in 1879 (Medal with Clasp). Served in the Afghan war in 1879-80 with the Khyber Line Force (Medal).

⁵⁹ Veterinary Captain W. R. Hagger served in the Zulu war of 1879, and was present in the engagement at Ulundi (Medal with Clasp). Served in the Afghan war in 1879-80, and was present in the engagement at Kam Dakka (Medal). Served in the Egyptian war of 1882 (Medal, and Khedive's Star). Also served in the Soudan campaign in 1885 (Clasp). Served with the Hazara Expedition in 1891 (mentioned in despatches, Medal with Clasp).

⁶⁰ Veterinary Captain Pringle served in the Afghan war in 1879-80 with the Koorum Valley Field Force under

Army Veterinary Department.—War Services.

Major General J. Watson (Medal). Served in the Wuzeeree Expedition of 1881 under Brigadier General Kennedy. Served with the Zhob Valley Expedition in 1884.
[61] Veterinary Captain Killick served in the Zulu war in 1879 (Medal with Clasp).
[62] Veterinary Captain J. B. Savage served in the Egyptian war of 1882 (Medal, and Khedive's Star).
[63] Veterinary Captain Moore served with the King's Dragoon Guards in the Zulu war of 1879. Also served in the operations against Sekukuni, and was present at the storming of the stronghold (mentioned in despatches, Medal with Clasp).
[64] Veterinary Captain Raymond served with the 17th Lancers in the Zulu war of 1879, and was present in the engagement at Ulundi (Medal with Clasp).
[66] Veterinary Captain G. H. Fenton served in the Zulu war in 1879 (Medal with Clasp). Served with the Burmese Expedition in 1888 (Medal with Clasp).
[68] Veterinary Captain Rutherford served in the Boer war of 1881. Served with the Bechuanaland Expedition under Sir Charles Warren in 1884-85.
[69] Veterinary Captain Kay Lees served with the Royal Artillery in the Afghan war in 1880-81 (Medal).
[70] Veterinary Captain Forsdyke served in the Afghan war in 1880 with the Khyber Line Field Force under Lieut. General Bright (Medal). Served in the Bozdar Expedition in 1881 under Brigadier General Wilkinson.
[72] Veterinary Captain Mann served in the Egyptian war of 1882, and was present at the battle of Tel-el-Kebir (Medal with Clasp, and Khedive's Star).
[73] Veterinary Captain G. R. Griffith served in the Egyptian war of 1882, and was present in the engagements of El Magfar and Mahsama, at the action at Kassasin (28th August), and at the battle of Tel-el-Kebir and the capture of Cairo (Medal with Clasp, and Khedive's Star). Served with the Nile Expedition in 1884-85 (Clasp); also served in the operations near Suakin in December 1888 including the engagement at Gemaizah (Clasp).
[76] Veterinary Captain Bennett served in the Egyptian war of 1882, and was present in the engagement at Tel-el-Mahuta and at the battle of Tel-el-Kebir (Medal with Clasp, and Khedive's Star). Served with the Nile Expedition in 1884-85, and was present at the action of Abu Klea (two Clasps).
[78] Veterinary Captain R. W. Burke served in the Egyptian war of 1882 (Medal, and Khedive's Star).
[79] Veterinary Captain S. M. Smith served in the Egyptian war of 1882, and was present in the engagements at Tel-el-Mahuta and Mahsama (Medal, and Khedive's Star). Also served with the Nile Expedition in 1884-85 (Clasp). Served with the Manipore Expedition in 1891 (Medal with Clasp).
[82] Veterinary Captain H. M. Maxwell served with the Hazara Expedition in 1891 (Medal with Clasp).
[83] Veterinary Captain G. H. Evans served with the Chin-Lushai Expeditionary Force in 1889-90 (mentioned in despatches, Medal with Clasp).
[84] Veterinary Captain E. R. C. Butler served with the Burmese Expedition in 1885-87 (mentioned in despatches, Medal with Clasp).
[85] Veterinary Captain G. C. O. Fowler served with the Burmese Expedition in 1887 (Medal with Clasp).
[86] Veterinary Captain F. W. Sharp served in the Soudan campaign in 1885 (Medal with Clasp, and Khedive's Star).
[87] Veterinary Captain E. Taylor served with the Wuntho Expedition in 1891 (Medal with Clasp).
[88] Veterinary Captain Haslam served with the Isazai Expedition in 1892.
[90] Veterinary Lieutenant Lawson served with the Burmese Expedition in 1885-89 (Medal with two Clasps).
[91] Veterinary Lieutenant F. Eassie served with the Manipore Expedition in 1891 (Medal with Clasp); and in the operations in the Chin Hills in 1891-92.

Continuation of Notes to the Army Chaplains' Department.

[18] The Rev. J. Corbett served in the Egyptian war of 1882 (Medal, and Khedive's Star).
[20] The Rev. J. Hackett served in the Egyptian war of 1882 (Medal, and Khedive's Star).
[21] The Rev. George Smith served in the Zulu war of 1879 as Acting Chaplain to the Forces, and was present at the defence of Rorke's Drift and in the engagement at Ulundi (Medal with Clasp). Served throughout the Egyptian war of 1882 (Medal, and Khedive's Star). Served in the Soudan Expedition under Sir Gerald Graham in 1884, and was present in the engagement at El Teb (mentioned in despatches, two Clasps). Served with the Nile Expedition in 1884-85 (Clasp); also served with the Soudan Frontier Field Force in 1885-86, and was present in the engagement at Giniss.
[22] The Rev. O. A. W. O'Neill served in the Egyptian war of 1882 (Medal, and Khedive's Star). Also served with the Nile Expedition in 1884-85 (Clasp).
[23] The Rev. E. M. Morgan served with the Nile Expedition in 1884-85 (Medal with Clasp, and Khedive's Star); also served with the Egyptian Frontier Field Force in 1885-86, including the engagement at Giniss.
[24] The Rev. C. W. Keatinge served with the Nile Expedition in 1884-85 (Medal with Clasp, and Khedive's Star).
[25] The Rev. S. P. H. Statham served in the Soudan campaign in 1885, and was present in the engagement at the Tofrek zereba (Medal with two Clasps, and Khedive's Star).
[26] The Rev. H. Kelly served in the Boer war of 1881 with the Natal Field Force.
[28] The Rev. J. Robertson served throughout the operations of the Soudan Frontier Field Force in 1885-86 as Chaplain to the Cameron Highlanders, and was present at the investment of Kosheh the reconnaissance of the 16th December, and the engagement at Giniss (Medal, and Khedive's Star).

Army Chaplains' Department.

Chaplain General to the Forces (ranking as Major General).—Rev. John Cox Edghill, MA., DD., *Chaplain Tower of London, Hon. Chaplain to the Queen, and Hon. Chaplain to the Duke of Cambridge,* 8 Feb. 85.

Chaplains to the Forces of the First Class, ranking as Colonels.

Name	Date	Station	Name	Date	Station
Rev. W. H. Bullock[1]	15 June 85	Halifax, N.S.	Rev. Robert Stewart Patterson[12]	14 Apr. 92	Egypt
Rev. Robert Brindle[7] (R.C.)	15 June 85	Aldershot	Rev. James Bellord[13] (R.C.)	18 Nov. 92	Colchester
Rev. Franc Sadleir, MA.	14 Mar. 87	Dover	Rev. Geo. Kirkwood[14] (*Presb*)	{ 9 Jan. 64 / 3 Dec. 88 }	{ Edinburgh }
Rev. C. A. Solbé,[9] BA.	1 Dec. 90	London	Rev. Thomas Foran[15] (R.C.)	24 Oct. 94	Bermuda
Rev. Alfred J. Townend, BA.	1 Dec. 90	Sandhurst	Rev. Alfred Mulim, MA.	1 Dec. 94	Malta
Rev. Joseph H. Sutton Moxly	11 Mar. 92	Warley			

Chaplains to the Forces (2nd Class), ranking as Lt. Colonels.

Name	Date	Station	Name	Date	Station
Rev. Eras. Harpur Goodwin, BA.	15 May 90	Dublin	Rev. Tho. Patterson Mullins, BA.	16 Jan. 93	Gibraltar
Rev. Reginald F. Collins[16] (R.C.)	15 June 90	Netley	Rev. William Le Grave (R.C.)	18 Jan. 93	Portsmouth
Rev. Fred. J. Bateman	16 Oct. 90	Netley	Rev. John Hackett,[20] BA.	2 Mar. 93	Cyprus
Rev. Walter Hebdon Milner	27 Nov. 90	Aldershot	Rev. H. H. Beattie, LLD.	13 Mar. 93	London
Rev. John King Lethbridge, M.A.	3 Dec. 90	Pembroke Dk.	Rev. Henry Arthur Darnell	3 July 93	London
Rev. Joseph Corbett[18] (R.C.)	1 Apr. 91	Woolwich	Rev. Timothy Twomey (R.C.)	13 July 93	Egypt
Rev. Riddall Morrison	16 June 91	Manchester	Rev. Henry Kelly[26] (R.C.)	11 Jan. 94	Dover
Rev. Charles Gregson, MA.	6 Jan. 92	Woolwich	Rev. Albert Springett Norfolk	18 Feb. 94	Gosport
Rev. David Nickerson, MA.	10 Jan. 92	Dublin	Rev. Fras. Aubrey Darnell, MA.	9 Aug. 94	Hilsea
Rev. Edward John Hardy, BA.	13 Sept. 92	Plymouth	Rev. George Smith[21]	10 Feb. 95	Malta.

Chaplains to the Forces (3rd Class), ranking as Majors.

Name	Date	Station	Name	Date	Station
Rev. O. A. W. O'Neill,[22] BA.	10 Aug. 90	Egypt	Rev. Edward H. F. Jenner, BA.	6 June 92	London
Rev. Rob. Edmund Kavanaugh	12 Feb. 91	Aldershot	Rev. Charles Freeman O'Reilly	18 June 92	Woolwich
Rev. Emman. Maria Morgan[23]	31 July 91	Gibraltar	Rev. Charles Walter Kentinge[24]	1 Apr. 93	Shorncliffe
Rev. Charles Josiah Hort	1 Sept. 91	Gibraltar	Rev. Wm. Sidney Randall, BA.	29 Sept. 93	Woolwich
Rev. Thos. Felton Falkner, MA.	15 Sept. 91	Aldershot	Rev. S. P. H. Statham,[25] BA.	17 Oct. 93	Shorncliffe
Rev. P. F. Raymond, MA.	8 Jan. 92	Colchester	Rev. W. Bernard Lyon Alexander	9 Apr. 94	Aldershot

Chaplains to the Forces (4th Class), ranking as Captains.

Name	Date	Station	Name	Date	Station
Rev. Fred. George Wright	7 Apr. 85	Malta	Rev. Ernest F. Newman, MA.	1 Jan. 89	Caterham
Rev. Chas. Henry Murphy, MA.	8 Apr. 85	Bermuda	Rev. Reginald Moseley, BA.	27 June 89	London
Rev. William Berkeley Dowding	28 Oct. 83	York	Rev. Joshua Brough, MA.	13 Mar. 90	Dublin
Rev. Wm. Foster Ray Buckle, BA.	16 Apr. 85	Natal	Rev. John Alexander Hatton	1 Mar. 91	Cork
Rev. Edward Ryan	1 May 83	Malta	Rev. Wm. Francis Sorsbie, MA.	11 Sept. 90	Malta
Rev. Frederic Bethune Norman Lee, MA.	19 Jan. 84	Gosport	Rev. Marcus Wellesley Churchward, MA.	19 Sept. 90	Shoeburyness
Rev. Arthur Augustus Lynn Gedge, BA.	1 May 85	Gibraltar	Rev. William John Ward, BA.	1 Oct. 90	Chatham
Rev. James Robertson[28]	8 Apr. 84	Dublin	Rev. Edward Herbert Pulling	27 Nov. 90	Canterbury
Rev. John Morrow Simms, BA.	29 Mar. 87	Dover	Rev. Maurice Jones, BA.	1 Nov. 90	Malta
Rev. Robert Armitage, BA.	1 Oct. 86	Barbadoes	Rev. Harwood Little, BA.	31 May 90	Dover
Rev. Joseph Barnaby Charles Murphy, MA.	22 Feb. 87	Portsmouth	Rev. Chas. Fredk. Baines, MA.	31 Jan. 91	Dublin
Rev. Sydney William Wentworth Wilkin	1 Oct. 87	Egypt	Rev. Ewen Geo. FitzRoy Macpherson, BA.	1 Mar. 92	Curragh
Rev. Willoughby Chas. Haines	5 Nov. 87	Winchester	Rev. E. W. M. Norris, BA.	1 Mar. 92	Colchester
Rev. Lewis Joseph Matthews	10 Oct. 84	Gosport	Rev. Richd. John Deane Oliver MA.	12 Mar. 92	Aldershot
Rev. Willoughby Chase Parr, MA.	10 Oct. 88	Chatham	Rev. Francis Bickerstaffe-Drew, BD.	27 Jan. 92	Devonport
Rev. Alf. Wm. Brown Watson, BA.	4 Sept. 88	Egypt	Rev. Thomas Henderson Chapman, BD.	13 May 88	Aldershot
Rev. Geo. Hubert Andrews, MA.	1 Nov. 87	Duke of York's R. M. School	Rev. Hy. Biddulph Bush, BA.	1 Jan. 93	Aldershot
			Rev. James Benoy, BA.	1 Jan. 93	Shorncliffe
Rev. Edward Parke Smith, MA.	9 Jan. 89	Preston	Rev. John Turnbull Bird	31 Jan. 91	Curragh
Rev. Thomas Hy. Foulkes, MA.	1 Mar. 89	Devonport	Rev. Henry Tudway Coney, BA.	20 May 93	Aldershot

War Services.

[1] The Rev. W. H. Bullock served in the Soudan campaign in 1885 as Senior Chaplain to the force (mentioned in despatches, promoted Chaplain 1st Class, Medal with Clasp, and Khedive's Star).

[7] The Rev. R. Brindle served in the Egyptian war of 1882 (Medal, and Khedive's Star). Served with the Soudan Expedition under Sir Gerald Graham in 1884, and was present in the engagements at El Teb and Temai (mentioned in despatches, promoted Chaplain of the 2nd Class, two Clasps, and 4th Class of the Osmanieh). Also served in the Nile Expedition in 1884-85 as Senior Chaplain with the force (mentioned in despatches, promoted Chaplain of the 1st Class, Clasp). Was present in the engagement at Giniss, on the Upper Nile, on the 30th December, 1885 (mentioned in despatches).

[9] The Rev. C. A. Solbé served in the Egyptian war of 1882 (Medal, and Khedive's Star).

[12] The Rev. R. S. Patterson was in Turkey in the Imperial Ottoman service during the war in the East. Served as a Lieutenant in the Canadian Volunteer Rifles at the time of the Trent affair, and also in the first Fenian raid. Accompanied, as Chaplain, the Red River expeditionary force of 1870 under Sir Garnet Wolseley to Fort Garry Proceeded to the Gold Coast in September 1873, and served there until the capture of Coomassie (Medal).

[13] The Rev. J. Bellord served in the Zulu war of 1879, and was present in the engagement at Ulundi (Medal with Clasp). Served in the Boer war in 1881. Served throughout the Egyptian war of 1882, and was present at the battle of Tel-el-Kebir—slightly wounded (promoted Chaplain 3rd Class, Medal with Clasp, and Khedive's Star).

[14] The Rev. G. Kirkwood served in the Ashanti war in 1873 (Medal). Served in the Zulu war in 1879 (Medal with Clasp).

[15] The Rev. T. Foran served in the Zulu war in 1879 (Medal). Served in the Soudan campaign in 1885 (Medal with Clasp, and Khedive's Star).

[16] The Rev. R. F. Collins served in the Egyptian war of 1882 with the 1st Battalion of the Royal Irish Fusiliers, and was present at the battle of Tel-el-Kebir (Medal with Clasp, and Khedive's Star). Served in the Soudan campaign in 1884-85, took part in the defence of Suakin, and was present in the engagements at Hasheen and the Tofrek zereba and at the destruction of Temai (mentioned in despatches, promoted Chaplain of the 3rd Class, two Clasps).

[For remainder of Notes, see preceding page.

Royal Marine Forces.

"**GIBRALTAR**."—The Globe, with the motto "*Per Mare, per Terram.*" The Crown—The Anchor and Laurel.—Her Majesty's Cypher.
Post in the Line, next to the Berkshire Regiment. Officers whose names are printed in *Italics* are on the Supernumerary list.
Royal Marine Office, 21, *Northumberland Avenue, W.C.*

HONORARY COLONEL.—*His Royal Highness Alfred Ernest Albert, Duke of Edinburgh (reigning Duke of Saxe Coburg-Gotha), KG. KT. KP. GCB. GCSI. GCMG. GCIE. Personal Aide de Camp to the Queen,* 9 Dec. 82.

GENERALS.	2nd LIEUT.	1st LIEUT.	CAPTAIN.	BREVET MAJOR.	MAJOR.	LIEUT. COLONEL.	2nd COMMANDANT.	COLONEL.	COL. 2nd COMDT.	COL. COMMANDANT.	MAJOR GENERAL.	LIEUT. GENERAL.	GENERAL.
Meade, John Michael De Courcy[1]	20 Feb. 49	27 Dec. 52	1 Aug. 60	23 Apr. 73	1 Oct. 77	25 Dec. 77		3 Dec. 81	3 Dec. 81	4 July 83	7 Nov. 85	22 June 87	8 Sept. 89
Thorpe, Francis William[7]	28 June 49	15 Aug. 53	26 Apr. 61	17 May 74	1 Oct. 77	1 Apr. 78		1 Apr. 82	13 Apr. 82	13 Apr. 85	1 Feb. 86	23 Mar. 89	20 Nov. 89
Hallidy, Francis Edward,[8] Royal Marine Artillery	27 Dec. 52	14 Mar. 54	8 Oct. 63	1 Apr. 75		5 Apr. 80		5 Apr. 84	3 Sept. 86	5 Oct. 86	22 Nov. 86	21 May 88	6 Aug. 93

LIEUTENANT GENERALS.

Mairis, Geoffrey[8]	27 Dec. 52	24 Feb. 54	27 Aug. 62	4 Nov. 76	1 Oct. 77	13 Apr. 79		4 June 82	4 June 82	4 June 85	9 May 86	8 Sept. 89	
Jones, Howard Sutton,[9] CB.	3 Aug. 53	10 Nov. 54	11 Dec. 63	1 Oct. 77	1 Oct. 77	7 July 79		18 Nov. 82	14 Apr. 83	7 Nov. 85	18 July 86	20 Nov. 89	
Le Grand, Frederick Gasper[10]	20 Mar. 54	1 Mar. 55	5 Nov. 64	1 Oct. 77		4 July 80		4 July 83	4 July 83	1 Feb. 86	15 Apr. 87	20 Nov. 89	
Tuson, Henry Brasnell,[12] CB. Royal Marine Artillery; } Deputy Adjutant General 29 Aug. 93	19 Apr. 54	22 June 55	28 Nov. 65			5 July 80		18 Nov. 82	18 Nov. 82	22 Nov. 86	21 May 88	6 Aug. 93	
p.s.c. Suther, Cuthbert Collingwood (Bt. Lt. Col. 26 Oct. 83)	26 Oct. 55	4 May 59	3 Aug. 67		1 Oct 77	5 July 79	5 Apr. 86	26 Oct. 87	21 May 88	21 May 91	6 Aug. 93	29 Aug. 93	

MAJOR GENERALS.

Graham, Samuel James,[11] CB.	20 Mar. 54	1 Mar. 55	5 Nov. 64		1 Oct. 77	6 Aug. 80		6 Aug. 84	13 Apr. 85	9 May 86	22 June 87		
Barnes, Ardley Henry Falwasser[13]	20 Mar. 54	22 June 55	20 June 65			24 Jan. 82	7 Nov. 85	7 Nov. 85		13 July 86	29 Aug. 88		
Munro, Gustavus Francis.	19 Apr. 54	22 June 55	10 Sept. 65			13 Apr. 82	5 Jan. 86	5 Jan. 86		5 Apr. 87	23 Mar. 89		
Walsh, Arthur Huntly Hill[4] (Bt. Lt. Colonel, 19 Apr. 82)	19 Apr. 54	22 June 55	10 Nov. 65		1 Oct. 77	4 June 82	1 Feb. 86	1 Feb. 86		1 Feb. 86	22 June 87	8 Sept. 89	
Cairncross, John[15] (Bt. Lt. Colonel, 19 Apr. 82)	19 Apr. 54	8 July 55	17 Nov. 65			2 Dec. 77	25 Jan. 83	1 Feb. 86	1 Feb. 86		1 Feb. 86	8 Sept. 89	
French, Arthur,[16] CB. (Bt. Lt. Colonel, 18 Nov. 82)	4 Feb. 58	8 Dec. 58	19 Oct. 67			10 Oct. 79	22 Nov. 86	1 Feb. 86	18 Nov. 86	19 May 91	6 Aug. 93	29 Aug. 93	

Royal Marine Artillery.

Yrs. Serv.	COLONEL COMMANDANT.	2nd LIEUT.	1st LIEUT.	CAPTAIN.	BREVET MAJOR.	MAJOR.	BT. LT. COLONEL.	LIEUT. COLONEL.	COLONEL.	COL. 2nd COMDT.	COL. COMMANDANT.
37	Ogle, **Frederick Amelius**,[1] CB.	29 July 58	20 Apr. 60	30 July 68		5 Apr. 80	18 Nov. 82	31 Dec. 86	18 Nov. 86	6 Aug. 93	29 Aug. 93

COLONELS 2nd COMMANDANT.

| 36 | Poore, Francis Haywood, *Extra Equerry in Waiting to the Duke of Edinburgh* | 14 Apr. 59 | 13 Sept. 60 | 1 Mar. 70 | | 1 July 81 | 14 Apr. 87 | 22 June 87 | | | 6 Aug. 93 |

LIEUTENANT COLONELS.

36	Pengelley, George Farquharson	23 Dec. 59	18 May 65	10 Nov. 74	1 July 81	5 Sept. 83	23 Dec. 87	19 May 91	22 Nov. 86		
27	Tucker, William Guise,[6] CB		1 July 61	24 June 68	24 Mar. 79	18 Nov. 82	21 May 84		1 Dec. 86		
34	p.s.c. Hall, Burnett Greive		3 Aug. 67	1 Apr. 76	4 Feb. 80	4 Feb. 86	1 July 89	21 May 91	31 Dec. 88		
31	Campbell, William,[14] *1. Aide de Camp to the Queen*		3 Aug. 67	20 Mar. 77	11 July 82	5 Apr. 86	27 June 92	22 June 93	29 Aug. 93		

MAJORS.

29	Crooke, Edward Rea Milner[17]			8 Dec. 66	3 Aug. 67	12 Sept. 77	15 June 85	22 Nov. 86			
28	p.s.c. Leefe, John Beckwith			22 June 67	3 Aug. 67	17 Sept. 77		1 Dec. 86			
28	Burrowes, Alexander Leslie Scott[19]				6 Dec. 68	21 May 78		31 Dec. 86			
27	Rawstorne, George Albert Lawrence[21]				24 June 68	21 July 79		22 June 87			
27	Wheeler, Edward[20]				24 June 68	1 Jan. 79		12 Sept. 87			
27	Milne, Benjamin Arthur				24 June 68	2 Oct. 79		25 Jan. 88			
27	Shakespear, Arthur Bucknall[22]				24 June 68	12 June 80		29 May 88			
26	Cheetham, Charles Joseph[23]				5 Nov. 69	8 June 80		12 Oct. 88			
26	Moore, Thomas[24]				5 Apr. 69	5 July 80		7 May 90			
25	Connolly, Lawrence Richard[25]				18 Feb. 71	15 Sept. 80		12 June 91			
25	Le Quesne, Augustus Simeon, *Adjutant Dublin City Artillery*, 23 Nov. 91				18 Feb. 71	29 Sept. 80		2 July 92			
23	Swinburne, Thomas Robert,[26] *Instructor of Gunnery*, 23 May 90				15 July 72	21 Jan. 84		2 May 93			
23	Grant, James Walter[27]				15 July 72	15 July 84					
23	Raitt, George Dalhousie Churchill,[28] *Instructor of Gunnery*, 21 May 93				15 July 72	15 July 84	15 July 93	6 Aug. 91			

Royal Marine Artillery.

Yrs. Ser.	CAPTAINS.	2nd LIEUT.	LIEUT.	CAPTAIN.	BREVET MAJOR.
23	Nicholls, William Charles, *Staff Officer*, 23 Oct. 94	......	15 July 72	15 July 84	15 July 93
22	p.s.c. Eastman, William Inglefield	......	1 Oct. 73	8 Jan. 85	1 Oct. 94
23	Alexander, Robert Homfray[29]	......	19 July 72	21 May 84	
21	Bor, James Henry	......	1 Oct. 74	1 Oct. 85	
21	Latham, Arthur Granville[30]	......	1 Oct. 74	1 Oct. 85	
20	Pease, Leonard Thales	......	1 Oct. 75	4 Feb. 86	
19	Gaitskell, Walter James[31]	......	1 Sept. 76	23 Mar. 86	
19	Orford, Alfred,[32] *Instructor of Gunnery*, 31 Mar. 94	......	1 Sept. 76	25 Mar. 86	
19	Trotter, Warren Francis,[33] *Instructor of Gunnery*, 9 Aug. 92	......	1 Sept. 76	5 Apr. 86	
19	Talbot, Harry Lynch[34]	......	1 Sept. 76	15 June 86	
19	Bishop, Charles Louis Nepean,[35] *Adjutant 1 Essex Artillery Volunteers (Eastern Division, Royal Artillery)*, 15 Sept. 91	......	1 Sept. 76	1 Aug. 86	
18	p.s.c. Drake, Henry Dowrish,[36] *Dep. Assist. Adj. Gen. and Dep. Assist. Adj. Gen. for Instruction, Portsmouth*, 16 July 90	......	19 Sept. 77	1 Dec. 86	
17	Kappey, Frederick George,[37] r	......	1 Sept 78	31 Dec. 86	
17	Pym, Harry Reginald Lockyer[38] (*Depot, Walmer*)	......	1 Sept. 78	12 Sept. 87	
16	p.s.c. Aston, George Grey[39]	......	1 Sept. 79	25 Jan. 88	
16	Brittan, Edward Pole,[40] *Member of Admiralty Intelligence Committee* ...	......	1 Sept. 79	12 Oct. 89	
16	p.s.c. Purie, Archibald, *Adjutant Antrim Artillery (Southern Division, Royal Artillery)*, 1 Aug. 94	......	1 Sept. 79	7 May 90	
15	Campbell, Gunning Morehead[42]	......	1 Sept. 80	23 Mar. 91	
15	Slessor, Herbert[43]	......	1 Sept. 80	12 June 91	
15	Cox, Aubrey Hamilton	......	1 Sept. 80	1 Sept. 91	
14	p.s.c. Conway-Gordon, Lewis	......	1 Sept. 81	6 Feb. 92	
14	Barton, Alured Yarker	......	1 Sept. 81	2 July 92	
14	Hire, Ashton Hope	......	1 Sept. 81	1 Sept. 92	
13	Mackay, Henry Forbes	......	1 Sept. 82	1 Sept. 93	
13	p.s.c. Rose, John Markham	......	1 Sept. 82	1 Sept. 93	
13	Harkness, William Bathurst	......	1 Sept. 82	1 Sept. 93	
12	Dobrée, De Saumarez	......	1 Sept. 83	1 Sept. 94	
12	Whiffin, Walter John, *Assistant to Professor of Fortification, R.N. College*, 1 Jan. 92	......	1 Sept. 83	1 Sept. 94	
12	Templer, Frederick Napier	......	1 Sept. 83	1 Sept. 94	
12	Barnes, George Edward	......	1 Sept. 83	1 Sept. 94	
12	Homer, John Leonard, *Assistant Instructor of Gunnery*, 1 Oct. 92	......	1 Sept. 83	1 Sept. 94	
12	Francis, Charles Arthur William	......	1 Sept. 83	1 Sept. 94	
	LIEUTENANTS.				
11	Osmaston, Cecil Alvend FitzHerbert, **Adjutant** 12 Feb. 94	......	1 Sept. 84		
11	Oldfield, Humphrey	......	1 Sept. 84		
11	Gaitskell, Sydney	......	1 Sept. 84		
11	Cottingham, Edward Roden	......	1 Sept. 84		
11	Harris, Gerald Noel Anstice	......	1 Sept. 84		
10	Poole, Gerald Robert	......	1 Sept. 85		
10	Brooke, Charles Louis	......	1 Sept. 85		
10	Brown, Richard Cradock	......	1 Sept. 85		
10	Ussher, Percy John	......	1 Sept. 85		
9	Phillipps, Picton	......	1 Sept. 86		
9	Pym, Frederick Harry Norris	......	1 Sept. 86		
9	Peacock, Pryce	......	1 Sept. 86		
9	Worthington, Hugo	......	1 Sept. 86		
9	Dixon, William	......	1 Sept. 86		
9	Homfray, John Robert Henry	......	1 Sept. 86		
8	Henderson, Edgar	1 Sept. 87	1 Sept. 87		
8	Geddes, Ernest David Eckford	1 Sept. 87	1 Sept. 87		
8	Binney, Arthur Frederick	1 Sept. 87	1 Sept. 87		
8	French, Fitzstephen John Fetherston	1 Sept. 87	1 Sept. 87		
8	Dyer, Thomas Woodford Peachy	1 Sept. 87	1 Sept. 87		
7	Dibblee, Frederick Lewis	1 Sept. 88	1 Sept. 88		
5	M'Carthy, Edward	1 Sept. 90	1 July 91		
5	Rombulow-Pearse, Alfred Bertie	1 Sept. 90	1 July 91		
5	Lumsden, Frederick William	1 Sept. 90	1 July 91		
5	Wyley, John Deane Newbank	1 Sept. 90	1 July 91		
4	Brough, John	1 Sept. 91	1 July 92		
3	Nugent, Thomas George Hodges	1 Sept. 92	1 July 93		
3	Schreiber, Arthur Thomas	1 Sept. 92	1 July 93		
3	Spurway, Humphry Weston	1 Sept. 92	1 July 93		
3	Foulis, Archibald Primrose Liston	1 Sept. 92	1 July 93		
	SECOND LIEUTENANTS.				
2	Senior, Guy	1 Sept. 93			
2	Beyts, Herbert William Hope	1 Sept. 93			

Quarter Masters.—Muir, John, 3 Dec. 81 ; *Hon. Captain*, 3 Dec. 91 ; *Hon. Major*, 17 Mar.
    Hill, Arthur, 17 Mar. 95 ; *Hon. Lieut.* 17 Mar. 95.
Paymaster.—Kelly, Henry Holdsworth, 15 Feb. 83; 2nd Lt. 2 May 59; Lt. 26 Apr. 61 ; *Capt.* 23 Feb. 72 ; *Major*, 1 July 81 ; *Hon. Lt.Colonel*, 15 Feb. 90.
Staff Officer.—Nicholls, Major W.C., 23 Oct. 94.
Barrack Master.—Allen Alexander,[18] 2 July 92 ; 2nd Lt. 13 Dec. 65; *1st Lt.* 3 Aug. 67 ; *Capt.* 8 May 77 ; *Bt.Major*, 11 July 82 ; *Major*, 15 June 86.
Fleet Surgeon.—Mahon, E. E., *CB*, 20 Aug. 94.
Surgeons.—Moore, John, BA. MD. 21 May 94.
    Iliowicz, H. F., 2 Sept. 94.
Chaplain.—York, Rev. W. E., 1 Oct. 94.

Blue—*Facings* Scarlet. | *Head Quarters*—*Eastney Barracks*, near Portsmouth.

Royal Marine Light Infantry.

Div.	Yrs. Ser.	COLONELS COMMANDANT.	2nd LIEUT.	1st LIEUT.	CAPTAIN.	BREVET MAJOR.	MAJOR.	BT. LT. COLONEL.	LIEUT. COLONEL.	BREVET COLONEL.	2nd COMMANDANT.	COL. COMMANDANT.
Ply.	40	Way, Nowell FitzUpton,[1] CB.	23 Nov. 55	7 May 59	8 June 68	......	6 Aug. 80	23 Nov. 83	17 May 85	23 Nov. 87	23 Mar. 89	8 Sept. 92
Por.	39	Philips, Joseph,[13] CB.	24 Dec. 56	12 July 59	19 June 72	29 Nov. 79	26 Aug. 80	21 July 81	21 June 85	11 July 86	8 Sept. 92	20 Nov. 92
Cha.	37	Colwell, George Harrie Thorn,[23] CB.	11 Aug. 58	20 Apr. 60	14 Nov. 72	......	1 July 81	30 May 84	7 Nov. 85	21 May 88	20 Nov. 89	23 Mar. 95

COLONELS SECOND COMMANDANTS.

Div.	Yrs. Ser.		2nd LIEUT.	1st LIEUT.	CAPTAIN.	BREVET MAJOR.	MAJOR.	BT. LT. COLONEL.	LIEUT. COLONEL.	BREVET COLONEL.	2nd COMMANDANT.	COL. COMMANDANT.
Por.	36	Rose, Edward Lee,[14]	14 Apr. 59	22 Dec. 60	24 Mar. 74	......	1 July 81		1 Feb. 86	1 Feb. 90	23 Mar. 92	
Ply.	36	Byram, Edward Willoughby Grenville,[20]	12 May 59	26 Dec. 61	30 Nov. 75	......	11 July 81	11 May 87	8 Aug. 88	......	8 Sept. 92	
Deal	36	Morris, John Ignatius,[21]	12 May 59	15 Jan. 62	6 Dec. 75	......	1 May 82	12 May 87	24 Nov. 88	......	20 Nov. 92	
Cha.	36	Bird, Frederic Vincent Godfrey, *Assistant Adjutant General* 29 Aug. 93	29 Mar. 60	10 Dec. 65	27 Sept. 77	1 July 81	4 June 82	29 Mar. 88	8 Sept. 89	29 Aug. 93	23 Mar. 95	
Cha.	36	Sweny, John Alfred	20 Sept. 59	29 Dec. 62	4 May 77	1 July 81	24 Jan. 82	17 Nov. 87	20 Nov. 87	28 Dec. 93	23 Mar. 95	

LIEUTENANT COLONELS.

Div.	Yrs. Ser.		2nd LIEUT.	1st LIEUT.	CAPTAIN.	BREVET MAJOR.	MAJOR.	BT. LT. COLONEL.	LIEUT. COLONEL.	BREVET COLONEL.
Ply.	35	Armstrong, William Gage	2 Jan. 61	5 Nov. 64	2 Dec. 77	2 Jan. 82	14 Sept. 82	2 Jan. 89	2 Jan. 90	6 Jan. 94
Por.	35	Campbell, William Frederick	2 Jan. 61	13 Nov. 64	25 Dec. 77	31 Dec. 82	31 Dec. 82	21 Apr. 89	21 Apr. 90	25 May 94
	34	Soafe, Charles Harington, *Deputy Assistant Adjutant General*, 28 Sept. 92	4 Feb. 63	19 Sept. 65	30 Mar. 78	4 Feb. 83	10 Feb. 83	4 Feb. 90	25 Apr. 91	
Cha.	33	Fagan, Christopher Sullivan Feltrim	31 Dec. 63	23 Aug. 66	5 July 78	......	1 Sept. 83	1 Sept. 90	1 Feb. 91	
Por.	33	Wright, William Purvis	28 Dec. 63	12 Aug. 66	2 Sept. 78	......	8 Sept. 83	8 Sept. 90	1 Feb. 92	
Cha.	31	Crosbie, Adolphus Brett,[28]	28 Dec. 64	3 Aug. 67	3 Dec. 78	17 Dec. 79	28 May 84	28 May 91	18 July 92	
Por.	31	Schomberg, Herbert St. George,[30]	24 Jan. 63	13 Feb. 67	17 Apr. 79	11 July 81	8 May 85	8 Sept. 91	8 Sept. 92	
Por.	32	Baldwin, Frederick,[32]	1 Jan. 64	3 Aug. 66	31 May 79	1 Jan. 85	17 May 85	1 Jan. 92	28 Sept. 92	
Ply.	31	Kirchhoffer, Robert Brooke,[38]	28 Dec. 64	21 Dec. 67	4 Oct. 79	7 Nov. 85	7 Nov. 85	7 Nov. 92	29 Aug. 93	
Cha.	30	Dowding, Townley Ward,[40]	28 Dec. 65	3 Aug. 67	15 Nov. 79	1 Sept. 80	11 Dec. 85	11 Dec. 92	11 Sept. 93	
Deal	31	Coffin, Roger Pine,[43]	28 Dec. 64	3 Aug. 67	21 June 80	18 Nov. 82	28 May 86	28 Dec. 92	5 Dec. 93	
Ply.	30	Corbet, Arthur Domville,[47] CB.	13 Dec. 65	3 Aug. 67	11 Sept. 80	......	29 Sept. 86	29 Sept. 93	25 Nov. 94	

MAJORS.

Div.	Yrs. Ser.		2nd LIEUT.	1st LIEUT.	CAPTAIN.	BREVET MAJOR.	MAJOR.	BT. LT. COLONEL.
Cha.	30	Chapman, Arthur Emerson	28 June 65	3 Aug. 67	26 Aug. 80	28 June 86	29 Sept. 86	29 June 93
Cha.	29	Bridge, Thomas Field Dunscomb,[48] r.	26 June 66	3 Aug. 67	6 May 81	15 June 85	23 Sept. 87	26 June 94
Por.	29	Edye, Lourenço,[49] *Member of Naval Intelligence Department, Admiralty*	8 Dec. 66	3 Aug. 67	1 July 81	8 Dec. 87	29 Aug. 88	8 Dec. 94
Por.	29	Burrowes, Algernon St. Leger,[50]	8 Dec. 66	3 Aug. 67	1 July 81	15 June 85	24 Nov. 88	8 Dec. 94
Por.	28	Robbins, Herbert Eyre,[51]	22 June 67	3 Aug. 67	1 July 81	1 July 81	8 Feb. 89	
Deal	28	Gordon, Cosmo George,[52]	22 June 67	22 June 67	1 July 81	22 June 88	8 Feb. 89	
Cha.	28	p.s.c. Adair, Wm. Thompson, *Professor of Fortification, R.N. College*		6 Dec. 67	1 July 81	6 Dec. 88	3 May 89	
Por.	28	Pyne, Edward Ernest,[53]		6 Dec. 67	1 July 81	6 Dec. 88	3 June 89	
Por.	28	Thompson, Howard Stanley		6 Dec. 67	1 July 81	17 June 89	28 Sept. 89	
Ply.	28	Nepean, Alfred Oliver De Blaquiere		6 Dec. 67	1 July 81	28 Dec. 88	28 Dec. 89	
Cha.	27	Newington, Frank Alexander,[55]		24 June 68	1 July 81	24 June 89	10 Mar. 90	
Ply.	27	Denny, Richard		24 June 68	1 July 81	24 June 89	17 Apr. 90	
Por.	27	Quill, John Jerome,[57]		24 June 68	1 July 81	24 June 89	21 Apr. 90	
Cha.	25	Hearle, Parkins,[59]		16 Dec. 67	1 July 81	16 Dec. 89	25 Apr. 90	
C.lus.	25	Kitching, Charles William Ross,[60]		1 Oct. 70	21 July 82	......	16 July 90	
Ply.	22	Skipwith, Grey		1 Oct. 73	26 Jan. 84	......	1 Aug. 90	
Deal	22	Houghton, Albert Evelyn		7 Jan. 71	1 Feb. 84	......	10 Aug. 90	
Ply.	21	Evans, Thomas Julian Penrhys		1 July 74	17 May 84	......	9 Jan. 91	
Ply.	21	Roche, Thomas Horatio de Montmorency,[62]		1 July 74	18 May 84	......	27 Sept. 91	
Ply.	21	Robyns, John Wilmot,[63] r.		1 Oct. 71	23 July 84	......	21 Oct. 91	
Ply.	21	Wilkinson, Edward Grant		1 July 74	19 July 84	......	1 Feb. 92	

Royal Marine Light Infantry.

Div.	Yrs. Ser.	MAJORS.	2nd LIEUT.	1st LIEUT.	CAPTAIN.	BREVET MAJOR.	MAJOR.
Ply.	20	Onslow, George Thorpe,[64] *Inst. of Musketry*, 24 Jan. 94	......	1 Jan. 76	22 Sept. 84	......	3 Feb. 92
Ply.	21	Eagles, Henry Cecil	......	1 July 74	19 Jan. 85	......	3 June 92
Por.	20	p.s.c. Gatliff, Albert Farrar, *Inst. R.Mil.Coll.* 16 Aug.90	......	27 Jan. 76	23 Mar. 85	......	18 July 92
Por.	20	Wylde, Edward Andrée, *Inst. of Gunnery*, 15 Sept. 90	......	27 Jan. 76	13 Apr. 85	......	8 Sept. 92
Ply.	20	Horniblow, Arthur Edmund	......	27 Jan. 76	17 May 85	......	28 Sept. 92
Deal	20	Darling, James Bruce,[65] *Inst. of Musketry*, 4 Apr. 92	......	27 Jan. 76	17 May 85	......	18 Nov. 92
Cha.	20	Lang, Percy Owen	......	27 Jan. 76	4 June 85	......	20 Nov. 92
Por.	18	Kysh, Douglas John[66]	......	24 Nov. 77	15 June 85	......	1 July 93
Por.	20	Parish, Charles Wellesley	......	27 Jan. 76	21 June 85	......	29 Aug. 93
Deal	19	M'Causland, Edwin Loftus,[67] *Staff Officer*, 19 Dec. 90	......	1 Sept. 76	8 Aug. 85	......	11 Sept. 93
Ply.	19	Money, Herbert Cecil,[68] *Inst. of Gunnery*, 27 Sept. 91	......	1 Sept. 76	28 Aug. 85	......	11 Sept. 93
Ply.	19	Cotter, Francis Gibson[69]	......	1 Sept. 76	6 Oct. 85	......	6 Oct. 93
Deal	19	Congdon, Ernest Charles Lambert	......	1 Sept. 76	1 Nov. 85	......	5 Dec. 93
Ply.	19	Johnstone, James Robert[70]	......	1 Sept. 76	7 Nov. 85	......	1 May 94
Ply.	19	Barrett, Dacre Lennard, *Inst. of Gunnery*, 5 Nov. 94	......	1 Sept. 76	11 Dec. 85	......	11 July 94
Cha.	19	Cochran, Archibald Gell[71]	......	1 Feb. 77	5 Jan. 86	......	5 Nov. 94
	18	Langford, William John, *Adjutant a Volunteer Bn.,* East Lancashire Regiment 15 Jan. 91	......	19 Sept.77	1 Feb. 86	......	25 Nov. 94
	18	Kelly, Hy. Chas. Thos., *Adj.* 4 Vol. Bn. L'pool Regt. 8 July 93	......	19 Sept.77	4 Feb. 86	......	15 Dec. 94
Deal	18	Plumbe, John Hulke, *Inst. of Gymnastics, R.M. Depot*	......	19 Sept.77	5 Mar. 86	......	22 Jan. 95
Por.	18	Maclurcan, John Lewis Rooke[72]	......	19 Sept.77	2 Apr. 86	......	25 Jan. 95
		CAPTAINS.		2nd LIEUT.	1st LIEUT.	CAPTAIN.	BREVET MAJOR.
Por.	18	Fraser, Hobart Charles	......	......	19 Sept.77	9 May 86	
Por.	18	p.s.c. Daniell, John Frederic, *Staff Officer*, 29 June 91	......	......	31 Jan. 78	28 May 86	
Deal	18	Peile, Schofield Patten[73]	......	......	31 Jan. 78	18 July 86	
	18	Johnson, Frederick Colpoys Ormsby, *Adjutant 1 Volunteer Battalion Bedfordshire Regiment* 1 June 92	......	......	31 Jan. 78	25 July 86	
Cha.	17	Cumming, William Sydney	......	......	1 Sept.78	20 Sept. 86	
Por.	17	Clavell, Richard Keppel Winterton Rose	......	......	1 Sept.78	29 Sept. 86	
Ply.	17	Brittan, Chas. Gisborne, *Staff Officer, Plymouth Division*, 1 May 94	......	......	1 Sept.78	5 Nov. 86	
Cha.	17	Oldfield, John Rawdon Hodge[74]	......	......	1 Sept.78	15 Nov. 86	
Ply.	17	Hadley, Leonard Joseph	......	......	1 Sept.78	21 Jan. 87	
Por.	17	Matson, Charles George	......	......	1 Sept.78	1 Mar. 87	
Cha.	17	Willis, Charles Hope,[75] *Staff Officer, Chatham Division*, 6 Aug. 94	......	......	1 Feb. 79	8 Dec. 87	
Por.	17	Roberts, Herbert Hodder	......	......	1 Feb. 79	23 Dec. 87	
Ply.	17	Percy, Robert FitzGerald	......	......	1 Feb. 79	7 Apr. 88	
Ply.	17	Swanton, James Hutchinson[77]	......	......	1 Feb. 79	17 June 88	
Ply.	17	Tate, Henry Pennell	......	......	1 Feb. 79	26 Aug. 88	
Ply.	17	White, Frederick[78]	......	......	1 Feb. 79	26 Aug. 88	
Cha.	17	Palmer, William Henry[79]	......	......	1 Feb. 79	29 Aug. 88	
Ply.	16	Field, Cyril,[80] r.	......	......	1 Sept.79	24 Nov. 88	
Por.	16	Raitt, Francis Jolliffe	......	......	1 Sept.79	22 Jan. 89	
Por.	16	Harvest, William Sidney Smith[82]	......	......	1 Sept.79	8 Feb. 89	
Por.	16	Bernard, John[81]	......	......	1 Sept.79	8 Feb. 89	
Por.	16	Clarke, Charles[83]	......	......	1 Sept.79	8 Feb. 89	
Cha.	16	Cotterill, Harry Gordon[84]	......	......	1 Feb. 80	23 Mar. 89	
Ply.	16	Kennedy, Charles Henry	......	......	1 Feb. 80	3 May 89	
	16	Luke, Edward Vyvyan,[85] *Adj.* 1 Vol. Bn. W. York Regt. 21 Sept. 91	......	......	1 Feb. 80	17 June 89	
	16	Peters, Leonard Christopher, *Adj.* 2 Vol. Bn. Devon Regt. 16 Nov. 91	......	......	1 Feb. 80	18 Aug. 89	
Por.	15	Montgomery, Richard Hugh	......	......	1 Sept.80	8 Sept.89	
Por.	15	Anderson, Graham D'Arcy	......	......	1 Sept.80	28 Sept. 89	
Por.	15	Huggins, Michael Alfred Colin, r.	......	......	1 Sept.80	17 Oct. 89	
Ply.	15	Scott, Fitzroy Tufton Holt	......	......	1 Sept.80	20 Nov. 89	
Ply.	15	Byrne, Gervis Taylor, r.	......	......	1 Sept.80	28 Dec. 89	
Deal	15	Drury, William Price	......	......	1 Sept.80	2 Jan. 90	
Cha.	15	Prendergast, Frederick Lenox[86]	......	......	1 Sept.80	10 Mar. 90	
Deal	15	Urmston, Archibald George Brabazon	......	......	1 Sept.80	10 Mar. 90	
Cha.	15	Crowther, Edward Samuel Dashwood	......	......	1 Feb. 81	17 Apr. 90	
Por.	15	Holman, Herbert William Liddell,[86a] *Staff College*	......	......	1 Feb. 81	21 Apr. 90	
Ply.	15	Robertson, Francis Andrew, r.	......	......	1 Feb. 81	22 Apr. 90	1 June 90
	14	David, Ernest Frederic,[87] *serving with the Egyptian Army*	......	......	1 Sept.81	31 May 90	
Cha.	14	Byne, Roland Martin	......	......	1 Sept.81	31 May 90	
Por.	14	Vincent, Arthur Gustave	......	......	1 Sept.81	16 July 90	
Ply.	14	Marchant, Alfred Edmund[88]	......	......	1 Sept.81	1 Aug. 90	
Por.	14	Gordon, Charles Louis	......	......	1 Sept.81	10 Aug. 90	
Ply.	14	Roe, Edward Charles Bartlett,[89] *Adjutant* 30 Mar. 91	......	......	1 Sept.81	16 Aug. 90	
Cha.	15	Grant, William Arthur Churchill	......	......	1 Sept.80	1 Sept.91	
Ply.	14	Couchman, Bertram Cornish	......	......	1 Sept.81	16 Nov. 91	
Ply.	14	Wolfe, George Cecil Burleigh	......	......	1 Sept.81	1 Feb. 92	
Cha.	13	White, H. Southey Neville,[90] *Member of Naval Intel. Dep, Admiralty*	......	......	1 Sept.82	1 June 92	
Por.	13	Curtoys, Charles Ernest Edward[91]	......	......	1 Sept.82	18 July 92	
Cha.	13	Logan-Home, Henry Waldeve,[92] *serving in the Niger Coast Protectorate*	......	......	1 Sept.82	8 Sept.92	
Cha.	13	Hailes, David Augustus	......	......	1 Sept.82	8 Sept.92	
Deal	13	Trotman, Charles Newsham,[93] *Adjutant* 15 Dec. 91	......	......	1 Sept.82	28 Sept.92	
Ply.	13	Cox, Gerald Aylmer	......	......	1 Sept.82	20 Nov. 92	
Ply.	13	Abrahall, John Hoskyns,[95] *Assist. Instructor of Musketry*,	......	......	1 Feb. 83	8 July 93	
Por.	13	Chown, Ernest Edward	......	......	1 Feb. 83	29 Aug. 93	
Ply.	13	Binney, Walter Erskine	......	......	1 Feb. 83	11 Sept.93	
Cha.	13	Goddard, James Rainey[96]	......	......	1 Feb. 83	11 Sept.93	
Cha.	13	Parsons, Cunliffe M'Neilo	......	......	1 Feb. 83	6 Oct. 93	
Por.	13	Curteis, Herbert St. Leger	......	......	1 Feb. 83	28 Nov. 93	
Cha.	13	Shubrick, Charles Louis	......	......	1 Feb. 83	5 Dec. 93	
Cha.	13	Saumarez, Richard James	......	......	1 Feb. 83	6 Jan. 94	
Por.	13	Mercer, David, *Adjutant* 2 Apr. 91	......	......	1 Feb. 83	20 Jan. 94	
Cha.	12	Henderson, Cecil	......	......	1 Sept.83	1 Feb. 94	
Deal	12	Orlebar, Evelyn Henry	......	......	1 Sept.83	1 Apr. 94	
Cha.	12	Eady, Frederick William Edward	......	......	1 Sept.83	1 Apr. 94	
Por.	12	Daniel, Edward Yorke, *Assist. Instructor of Musketry*, 12 Jan. 94	......	......	1 Feb. 84	16 Aug. 94	
Cha.	12	Connolly, Arthur Matthew	......	......	1 Feb. 84	5 Nov. 94	
Cha.	11	Luard, Frank William	......	......	1 Sept.84	5 Nov. 94	
Cha.	11	Matthews, Godfrey Estcourt, *Adjutant* 10 Sept. 91	......	......	1 Sept.84	15 Dec. 94	
Por.	11	Gibsone, Hugh John Craig, *Assist. Instructor of Musk.*, 11 Aug. 93	......	......	1 Sept.84	15 Jan. 95	
Cha.	11	Bayliff, Richard Lane	......	......	1 Sept.84	25 Jan. 95	
Cha.	...	Beaumont, G. Lancaster, *Member of Naval Intel. Dpt. Admiralty*	......	......	1 Sept.84	20 Feb. 95	

Royal Marine Light Infantry. 401

Div.	LIEUTENANTS.	LIEUT.	Div.	LIEUTENANTS.	2ND LIEUT.	LIEUT.
Cha.	Beith, Robert Douglas, *Supdt. of Gymnasia, Thames District,* 12 Apr. 93	1 Sept. 84	Deal	Edwards, Frederick Charles...	1 Sept. 90	1 July 91
Deal	Athow, Frank, *Assistant Instructor of Musketry,* 15 Nov. 93	1 Feb. 85	Ply.	Finlaison, John Bruce	1 Sept. 90	1 July 91
			Cha.	Mylrea, *Wm. Percy Garland, Army Service Corps*	1 Sept. 90	1 July 91
Ply.	Lywood, Edwin Gifford, *Assistant Instructor of Musketry,* 12 Oct. 94	1 Feb. 85	Por.	Bridges, Francis Doveton	1 Sept. 90	1 July 91
			Por.	Colquhoun, Robt. Crosthwaite	1 Sept. 90	1 July 91
Por.	Pym, John Beville	1 Feb. 85	Deal	Bowes, Arthur Edward	1 Sept. 90	1 July 91
	Basevi, *Wm. Henry, Ordnance Store Dept.*	4 Mar. 85	Cha.	Kitcat, Arthur do Winton	1 Sept. 90	1 July 91
Ply.	Bendyshe, Richard Nelson	1 Sept. 85	Ply.	Pryce-Browne, Wm. Herbert	1 Sept. 90	1 July 91
Por.	Palmer, Harry Douglas, *Instructor of Musketry, Malta,* 18 June 94	1 Sept. 85	Cha.	Darley, Henry La Touche	1 Sept. 90	1 July 91
Ply.	Brabazon, Anthony Heyland	1 Sept. 85		Brogden, *John Silvester, serving under the Royal Niger Company*	1 Sept. 90	1 July 91
Deal	Ward, John Harry	1 Sept. 85				
Deal	Evelegh, Edmund George	1 Sept. 85	Por.	Boyle, Francis Rayner	1 Sept. 90	1 July 91
Deal	Graham, Hamilton Maximillian Christian William	1 Sept. 85	Ply.	Dalton, Cecil William Robert	1 Sept. 90	1 July 91
			Cha.	Robinson, Guy Vandeleur	1 Sept. 90	1 July 91
Deal	Parker, James Henry	1 Feb. 86	Cha.	Abrahall, Christopher Henry Hoskyns	1 Sept. 90	1 July 91
Ply.	Godfrey, Frederick Rowlandson	1 Feb. 86				
Ply.	Johnston-Stewart, William Maxwell	1 Feb. 86	Deal	Bockett-Pugh, Edw. Harding	1 Sept. 90	1 July 91
Cha.	Eagle, Francis Elwyn Bunbury	1 Feb. 86	Por.	Lloyd, Henry Talbot Rickard	1 Sept. 90	1 July 91
Cha.	Stroud, Edward James, *Assistant Instructor of Gunnery,* 2 Nov. 92	1 Sept. 86	Por.	Wray, Edmund	1 Sept. 91	1 July 92
			Por.	Story, Edward Kenmir	1 Sept. 91	1 July 92
Cha.	Evans, Horace Carlyon	1 Sept. 86		Hopwood, Herbert Reginald	1 Sept. 91	1 July 92
Ply.	Wylde, Arthur William	1 Sept. 86	Cha.	Hawkins, Thomas Henry	1 Sept. 91	1 July 92
Cha.	Hobbs, Fred. Manoli Baltuzzi, *Supdt. of Gymnasia, Devonport,* 16 Sept. 93	1 Sept. 86		Macdonald, *Kenneth, Army Service Corps*	1 Sept. 91	1 July 92
Cha.	Frankis, Walter William	1 Sept. 86	Ply.	Miller, Leander William	1 Sept. 91	1 July 93
Cha.	Connolly, William Edward Gunnell	1 Sept. 86	Cha.	Naylor, Henry William Letts	1 Sept. 92	1 July 93
			Ply.	Howard, Henry Martin	1 Sept. 92	1 July 93
	2ND LIEUT.		Por.	O'Sullivan, Hugh Dermod Evan	1 Sept. 92	1 July 93
Por.	Lambert, John Hamilton	1 Feb. 87 24 Mar 88				
Por.	Harris, William Albert	1 Feb. 87 24 Mar. 88	Cha.	Burnard, Frank Evelyn Chichester	1 Sept. 92	1 July 93
Por.	Marchant, John	1 Feb. 87 24 Mar. 88				
Por.	Smith, Wilfred Noel Edmund	1 Sept. 86	Por.	Harvey, Francis John Wm.[100]	1 Sept. 92	1 July 93
Por.	Watson, Charles Stanbrough	1 Sept. 87 28 Sept. 88	Por.	Grattan, Arthur Phayre	1 Sept. 92	1 July 93
Por.	Smith, Wilfred Hugh Moore	1 Sept. 87 28 Sept. 88	Por.	Clark, J. Arthur Myles Ariel	1 Sept. 92	1 July 93
Ply.	Garrett, John Raymond	1 Sept. 87 28 Sept. 88	Cha.	Buckle, Herbert Stewart	1 Sept. 92	1 July 93
Por.	Collard, Charles Edwin	1 Sept. 87 28 Sept. 88	Ply.	Way, Nowell FitzEdward Greville	1 Sept. 92	1 July 93
Ply.	Blumberg, Herbert Edward, *Assist. Inst. of Gunnery,* 23 May 93	1 Feb. 88 1 Apr. 89	Cha.	Brownjohn, Charles Woodland	1 Sept. 92	1 July 93
			Ply.	Cator, Robert	1 Sept. 92	1 July 93
Cha.	Crowther, John Ernest	1 Feb. 88 1 Apr. 89	Cha.	Dustan, John William	1 Sept. 92	1 July 93
Deal	Phillips, Frank Truscott	1 Feb. 88 1 Apr. 89	Por.	Cumberlege, Henry Charles Faithfull	1 Sept. 93	1 July 94
	Harding, Maynard Ffolliott	1 Feb. 88 1 Apr. 89				
Por.	Drake-Brockman, Charles Edward Fitzroy	1 Feb. 88 1 Apr. 89	Por.	Jones, Walter Thos. Cresswell	1 Sept. 93	1 July 94
			Por.	Luard, Traut Bramston	1 Sept. 93	1 July 94
Ply.	Prynne, Reginald Parkins	1 Feb. 88 1 Apr. 89	Cha.	Little, William Campbell	1 Sept. 93	1 July 94
Cha.	Noble, John Brecknock	1 Feb. 88 27 Sept. 89	Ply.	Scott, Neville Anderson Woodward	1 Sept. 93	1 July 94
Cha.	Tupman, John Arthur	1 Sept. 88 27 Sept. 89				
Ply.	Rombulow-Pearse, Arthur Egmont	1 Sept. 88 27 Sept. 89	Por.	Shine, John Piercey	1 Sept. 93	1 July 94
			Ply.	Morse, Allan Stewart	1 Sept. 93	1 July 94
Ply.	Coke, Ernest Sacheverell	1 Sept. 88 27 Sept. 89	Cha.	Esson, William	1 Sept. 93	1 July 94
Cha.	Strouts, Bernard Murton	1 Sept. 88 27 Sept. 89	Cha.	Rigby, John Cecil Heagren	1 Sept. 93	1 July 94
Ply.	Ommanney, Edmund Manaton Carpenter	1 Sept. 88 27 Sept. 89	Cha.	Thoroton, Charles Julian	1 Sept. 93	1 July 94
			Ply.	Simmons, Percy Walter	1 Feb. 94	1 Jan. 95
Por.	Farquharson, Harry Douglas, *Assistant Instructor of Gunnery,* 8 Dec. 94	1 Sept. 88 27 Sept. 89	Ply.	Nelson, Francis Arthur	1 Feb. 94	1 Jan. 95
			Por.	Cartwright, Fras. John Winsor	1 Feb. 94	1 Jan. 95
			Por.	Deed, John Cyril	1 Feb. 94	1 Jan. 95
Por.	Meister, Richard Henry Julius	1 Feb. 89 28 Mar. 90	Por.	Molloy, Percy	1 Feb. 94	1 Jan. 95
Ply.	Armstrong, St. George Bowes	1 Feb. 89 28 Mar. 90	Cha.	Coles, Herbert Jefferis	1 Feb. 94	1 Jan. 95
Cha.	Gardner, Francis Stewart	1 Feb. 89 28 Mar. 90	Por.	Willis, Richard Ffolliott	1 Feb. 94	1 Jan. 95
Cha.	Anderson, Gilbert Ironside	1 Feb. 89 28 Mar. 90	Cha.	Strong, Frederic Lewis Harford	1 Feb. 94	1 Jan. 95
Ply.	Hutchison, Alex. Richard Hamilton	1 Feb. 89 28 Mar. 90				
Ply.	Mullins, George Jas. Herbert	1 Feb. 89 28 Mar. 90		**SECOND LIEUTENANTS.**		
Por.	Whitmarsh, John Francis Victor Silver	1 Feb. 89 28 Mar. 90		Grover, John		1 Sept. 94
				Manley, George Errington Drummond		1 Sept. 94
Por.	Robertson, Claude William	1 Sept. 89 1 July 90				
Ply.	Halliday, Lewis Stratford Tollemache	1 Sept. 89 1 July 90		Headlam, Thomas Emerson		1 Sept. 94
				Heard, Samuel Ferguson		1 Sept. 94
Ply.	Crooker, Herbert James	1 Sept. 89 1 July 90		Muller, George Fison		1 Sept. 94
	Atkins, *Alban Randell Crofton, Army Service Corps*	1 Sept. 89 1 July 90		Webb, George Theodosius Wynne		1 Sept. 94
Cha.	Morres, Elliot Hody	1 Sept. 89 1 July 90		Little, Arthur Greenway		1 Sept. 94
Ply.	Heriot, Granville Mackey	1 Sept. 89 1 July 90		French, Arthur Harwood		1 Sept. 94
Ply.	Barker, Edward Henry Payne	1 Sept. 89 1 July 90		Hall, Fras. Hamilton Howard		1 Feb. 95
Deal	Bourchier, Philip Lennox Walter	1 Sept. 89 1 July 90		Heycock, Alf. Geo. Sydney		1 Feb. 95
				Wilson, Leslie Orme		1 Feb. 95
Ply.	Macdonald, *Charles Clanrana, Army Service Corps*	1 Sept. 90 1 July 91		Mayhew, Charles Lawson		1 Feb. 95
				Simpson, William George		1 Feb. 95
Cha.	Drage, Gilbert	1 Sept. 90 1 July 91		Nixon, James Ryder		1 Feb. 95
Por.	Doig, Richard Osborn Maclean	1 Sept. 90 1 July 91		Walthall, Brian Jas. Delves		1 Feb. 95
Por.	Morgan, Reginald Hallward	1 Sept. 90 1 July 91		Saunders, Frederick John		1 Feb. 95
				Burge, Norman Ormsby		1 Feb. 95

(Royal Naval College.)

GENERAL STAFF.

Deputy Adjutant General.—Tuson, Lieut. General H. B. *CB.* 29 Aug. 93.
Assistant Adjutant General.—Bird, Colonel F. V. G. 29 Aug. 93.
Deputy Assistant Adjutant General.—Scafe, Colonel C. H. 28 Sept. 92.
Quarter Masters.—Davies, Thomas William, 5 June 84; *Hon. Major,* 1 Feb. 89;
Hoare, John James, 1 April 89; *Hon. Major,* 24 Sept. 91.

Royal Marine Light Infantry.

PAYMASTERS.

Cha. Gritton, Henry, 1 Aug. 90; 2nd Lt. 31 Dec. 62; 1st Lt. 28 June 66; Capt. 2 July 78; Major, 1 Sept. 83.
Deal Innes, Edward Selby,[26]r. 27 Sept. 91; 2nd Lieut. 31 Mar. 63; 1st Lieut. 23 Oct. 66; Captain, 9 Oct. 78; Brevet Major, 11 July 82; Major, 26 Jan. 84.
Ply. Dick, Charles Baker Goodrich, 1 July 93; 2nd Lt. 8 Dec. 86; 1st Lt. 3 Aug. 67; Capt. 1 July 81; Bt.Major, 8 Dec. 87; Major, 7 Apr. 83.

BARRACK MASTERS.

Ply. Norcock, Henry John Lawrence,[99] 6 Oct. 85; 2nd Lt. 12 Oct. 60; 1st Lt. 7 July 64; Captain, 1 Oct. 77; Brevet Major, 12 Oct. 81; Major, 11 Sept. 82; Hon. Lt.Colonel, 6 Oct. 92.
Deal Hungerford, Thomas Everard,[24] 21 Jan. 87; 2nd Lt. 26 June 60; Lt. 5 Feb. 64; Captain, 1 Oct. 77; Bt.Major, 1 July 81; Major, 5 Aug. 82; Hon. Lt.Colonel, 21 Jan. 94.
Por. Linrdot, Augustus Bury, 27 Sept. 91; 2nd Lt. 24 June 63; Lieut. 10 Nov. 66; Captain, 19 Oct. 78; Major, 11 Feb. 84; Bt.Lt.Colonel, 11 Feb. 91.
Tyers, Sydney, 3 June 92; 2nd Lt. 24 June 63; Lieut. 15 Jan. 67; Capt. 12 Apr. 79; Bt.Major, 24 June 84; Major, 12 Aug. 87; Bt.Lt.Colonel, 24 June 91.

QUARTER MASTERS.

Cha. Brown, Valentine,[102] 1 Sept. 79; Hn.Major, 8 Aug. 89. | Por. Burtenshaw, John,[103] 4 July 83; Hon. Capt. 4 July 93.
Deal Rowe, William Arthur Samuel,[103] 27 Apr. 82; Hon. | Cha. Powell, Francis, 18 July 88; Hon. Lieut.
  Captain, 27 Apr. 92. | Deal Harding, George Foster, 8 Aug. 89; Hon. Lieut.
Por. Murphy, James, 1 July 82; Hon. Captain, 1 July 92. | Ply. Powell, William, 25 Dec. 90; Hon. Lieut.
Ply. Syms, Edwin Albert,[101] 31 Mar. 83; Hon.Capt. 31 Mar. 93 |

FLEET SURGEONS.

Por. Grant, Robt., M.D. M.B., 15 May 92. || Deal Stone, J. N., 23 July 92.

STAFF SURGEON.

Horatio S. R. Sparrow, 8 Feb. 95.

SURGEONS.

Deal Doyne, H. W. G., 13 Mar. 93. | Por. Lilly, F. J., 28 May 94.
Por. Gunn, B. C. E. F., 25 Aug. 93. | Ply. Jenkins, J., 28 Aug. 94.
Ply. Bassett-Smith, P. W., 15 Nov. 93. |

CHAPLAINS.

Cha. Dixon, Rev. William, LL.D., 26 Apr. 92. || Deal Bovry, Rev. J. H., M.A., 1 Sept. 93.
Por. Law, Rev. W., 1 Oct. 94. ||

Scarlet—*Facings* Blue. *Agent,*
Office, 21, *Northumberland Avenue, W.C.*

Naval Ordnance Department.

(Transferred from Ordnance Store Department under Order in Council 9 May 1891.)

Assistant Commissaries General of Ordnance. With Hon. rank of Lieut.Colonel.	Dep. Assist. Com. Gen. of Ord.	Assist. Com. Gen. of Ord.	Deputy Com. Gen. of Ord.	Station.
Baker, Robert Barrington[1]	31 Jan. 80	4 July 87	......	Plymouth.
de Salis, Edward John	31 Jan. 80	1 Oct. 87	......	Portsmouth.
St. Quintin, Arthur Newton	31 Jan. 80	23 Dec. 87	......	Woolwich.
Hain, Herbert Andrew David[2]	31 Jan. 80	30 Nov. 88	......	Chatham.
With Hon. rank of Major.				
Arnold, Francis Havard	1 Apr. 80	8 Aug. 90	......	Priddy's Hard.
Wright, William Frederick[3]	1 May 80	8 Oct. 90	......	Woolwich.
Bruno, Hugh Watson Bruno	17 June 80	17 June 91	......	Portsmouth.
Ozanne, Charles Hainekin	11 Sept. 80	1 Apr. 92	......	Admiralty.
Edyvean, Frederick George	1 Dec. 80	1 Apr. 93	......	Bull Point.
Aplin, Hugh Morgan (*Lt. R. Art.* 28 Jan. 75; *Capt. R. Art.* 1 Jan. 84)	20 Apr. 82	1 Apr. 93	......	Upnor.
Deputy Assistant Commissaries General of Ordnance.				
Brabazon, William Beaufort (*2nd Lt.* 44 *F.* 13 Aug.79; *Lt. Essex Regt.* 1 July 81; *Capt. Essex Regt.* 13 Apr.87)	27 Apr. 85	......	......	
		Quarter Master.	Hon. Capt.	
Quarter Masters.				
Cox, William Smith[5]	......	27 Mar. 78	18 July 83	Marchwood.
Harris, George[6]	......	30 Sept. 81	10 Jan. 83	Woolwich.
Sheppard, Charles Lee[7]	......	30 Mar. 85	15 June 85	Woolwich.

[1] Lt.Colonel Baker served in the Ashanti war under Sir Garnet Wolseley (Medal).
[2] Lt.Colonel Hain served in the Soudan campaign in 1885 (Medal with Clasp, and Khedive's Star).
[3] Lt.Colonel Wright served with the Nile Expedition in 1884-85 (Medal with Clasp, and Khedive's Star).
[5] Captain Cox served in the Zulu war in 1879 and in the operations against Sekukuni in 1880 (Medal with Clasp, honorary rank of Captain). Served in the Boer war in 1881. Served in the Bechuanaland Expedition in 1884-85.
[6] Captain Harris served in the Zulu war in 1879, and in the subsequent operations against Sekukuni (Medal). Served in the Boer war of 1881. Served in the Egyptian war of 1882 (mentioned in despatches, honorary rank of Captain, Medal, and Khedive's Star). Served with the Bechuanaland Expedition under Sir Chas. Warren in 1884-85.
[7] Captain Sheppard served in the Egyptian war in 1882 (Medal, and Khedive's Star). Served with the Nile Expedition in 1884-85 (mentioned in despatches, granted honorary rank of Captain, Clasp).

War Services of General Officers of Royal Marine Forces.   402a

[1] General Meade served the Eastern campaign of 1854-55 with the R.M. Brigade, including the battle of Balaklava and siege of Sebastopol (Medal with two Clasps, 5th Class of the Medjidie, and Turkish Medal). Served on the China Expedition of 1857-59, including the blockade of the Canton river, operations before and capture of the city, afterwards as Quarter Master of the 2nd Battalion. Served with the expedition to the north of China in 1860, including the action of Sinho, taking of Tangku, storm and capture of the North Taku Forts, and subsequent operations (Medal with three Clasps).

[6] General F. E. Halliday served with the Baltic Expedition in 1855, and in the flotilla of mortar boats during the bombardment of Sweaborg (Medal).

[7] General Thomas served with the R.M. Battalion at Eupatoria in 1854, and with the Brigade in the Crimea during the siege and fall of Sebastopol, and was also at the surrender of Kinbourn (Medal with Clasp, 5th Class of the Medjidie, and Turkish Medal).

[8] Lieut.General Mairis served the Eastern campaign of 1854-55 with the R.M. Brigade, including the battle of Baiaklava and siege of Sebastopol (Medal with two Clasps, 5th Class of the Medjidie, and Turkish Medal). Served with the expedition to the Baltic until the declaration of peace in 1856. Served in China with the expeditionary force in 1858-59; also the campaign of 1860, including the action of Sinho, the taking of Tonghoo, storm and capture of the North Takoo Fort (severely wounded in the left shoulder, and mentioned in despatches), and subsequent operations as Acting Quarter Master (Medal with two Clasps).

[9] Lieut.General H. S. Jones served with the Baltic Expedition in 1854 (Medal). Commanded the Brigade of Royal Marines in the Egyptian war of 1882, and was present in the engagement at Tel-el-Mahuta, in the two actions at Kassasin, and at the battle of Tel-el-Kebir (twice mentioned in despatches, CB., Medal with Clasp, Khedive's Star, 2nd Class of the Medjidie, and Aide de Camp to the Queen).

[10] Lieut.General F. G. LeGrand served at the siege of Sebastopol from 1854 until its fall; was also at the capture of Kertch, and occupation of Yeni Kalé, and at the surrender of Kinbourn (Medal with Clasp, and Turkish Medal). Served in the Egyptian war of 1882 (Medal, 3rd Class of the Medjidie, and Khedive's Star).

[11] Major General Graham served with the Baltic Expeditions in 1854 and 1855, including the destruction of telegraph stations on 29th June, and the shelling a large body of troops on 1st July (Medal). Served in the Egyptian war of 1882 (mentioned in despatches, CB., Medal, 4th Class of the Osmanieh, and Khedive's Star).

[12] Lieut. General Tuson served in China in 1858-60, and commanded a Detachment on an expedition against pirates from 26th Aug. to 5th Sept. 1858 (mentioned in despatches), and was present at the capture and destruction of 100 junks and 236 guns. Was also present at the attack on the Peiho Fort on 25th June 1859, the capture of the Peiho Forts in 1860, and subsequent operations (Medal with Clasp). Served in the Egyptian war of 1882, and commanded the Royal Marine Artillery in the reconnaissance in force from Alexandria on the 5th August, and was present in the engagements at El Magfar and Tel-el-Mahuta, in the two actions at Kassasin, and at the battle of Tel-el-Kebir (twice mentioned in despatches, Aide de Camp to the Queen, CB., Medal with Clasp, 3rd Class of the Medjidie, and Khedive's Star.) Served with the Soudan Expedition under Sir Gerald Graham in 1884 in command of the Royal Marines, and was present in the engagement at El Teb (twice mentioned in despatches, 3rd Class of the Osmanieh, two Clasps).

[13] Major General Barnes served in the operations in the Canton river in 1856-58; was in Macao Fort when attacked by junks on 4th January, at the destruction of war junks in Fatsham Creek, landed to destroy a village, storm and capture of Canton (mentioned in despatches, Medal with two Clasps).

[14] Major General Walsh served with the Baltic Expedition of 1855 (Medal); and also with the Baltic Expedition of 1856 until the declaration of peace.

[15] Major General Cairncross served with the Baltic Expedition in 1855 (Medal).

[16] Major General A. French served in the Egyptian war of 1882 (Brevet of Lt.Colonel, Medal, and Khedive's Star).

War Services.—Royal Marine Artillery.

[1] Colonel Ogle was landed from H.M.S. Brisk in command of a detachment of Royal Marines for the protection of Cape Coast Castle during the mutiny of the Gold Coast Artillery in October 1862, and received a vote of thanks from the Colonial Government. Served in China in H.M.S. Rodney from September 1867 to September 1869; commanded the Royal Marine Artillery of the Battalion of Royal Marines from the Squadron at the occupation of Yangchow in Nov. 1868; served with the Battalion at the attack and capture of three walled villages in January 1869 (mentioned in despatches). Served with the Battalion of Royal Marine Artillery throughout the Egyptian war of 1882, and was present in the engagements at El Magfar and Tel-el-Mahuta (slightly wounded), in the actions at Kassasin on the 28th August (mentioned in despatches) and 9th September, and at the battle of Tel-el-Kebir (Brevet of Lt.Colonel, Medal with Clasp, 4th Class of the Osmanieh, and Khedive's Star).

[6] Lt.Colonel W.G. Tucker served in the Egyptian war of 1882, and was present in the reconnaissance in force from Alexandria on the 5th August, in the engagements at El Magfar and Tel-el-Mahuta, in the two actions at Kassasin, and at the battle of Tel-el-Kebir (twice mentioned in despatches, Brevet of Major, Medal with Clasp, 4th Class of the Medjidie, and Khedive's Star). Served in the Soudan Expedition under Sir Gerald Graham in 1884, and was present in the engagement at El Teb (three times mentioned in despatches, promoted Major, two Clasps).

[14] Colonel W. Campbell served in the Ashanti war of 1873-74 (Medal). Served in the Egyptian war of 1882, and was present at the bombardment of the Alexandria Forts, and subsequently served on shore till the end of the war, including the occupation of Port Said and the surrender of Fort Gemileh (Brevet of Major, Medal with Clasp, and Khedive's Star).

[15] Major A. Allen served in the Ashanti war in 1873, including the engagements at Elmina, and action at Essaman (mentioned in despatches, Medal). Served in the Egyptian war of 1882, and was present at the bombardment of Alexandria (Brevet of Major, Medal with Clasp, and Khedive's Star). Served with the Soudan Expedition under Sir Gerald Graham in 1884, and was present in the engagements at El Teb (slightly wounded) and Temai (4th Class of the Osmanieh, two Clasps).

[17] Lt.Colonel E. R. M. Crooke served in the Soudan campaign in 1884-85, took part in the defence of Suakin, and was present at the destruction of Temai (mentioned in despatches. Brevet of Major, Medal with Clasp, and Khedive's Star).

[19] Lt.Colonel A. L. S. Burrowes served in the Zulu war in 1879, and was present in the engagement at Gingindhlovu and at the relief of Ekowe (Medal with Clasp). Served in the Egyptian war of 1882, and was present in the reconnaissance in force from Alexandria on the 5th August, in the two actions at Kassasin, and at the battle of Tel-el-Kebir (Medal with Clasp, and Khedive's Star).

[20] Lt.Colonel E.Wheeler served in the Egyptian war of 1882, and was present in the engagements at El Magfar and Tel-el-Mahuta, in the two actions at Kassasin, and at the battle of Tel-el-Kebir (Medal with Clasp, and Khedive's Star).

[21] Lt.Colonel G. A. L. Rawstorne served in the Egyptian war of 1882, and was present in the engagements at El Magfar and Tel-el-Mahuta, at the two actions at Kassasin (mentioned in despatches), and at the battle of Tel-el-Kebir (Medal with Clasp, and Khedive's Star).

[22] Lt.Colonel A. B. Shakespear served in the Nile Expedition in 1884-85 with the Egyptian Army (Medal with Clasp, and Khedive's Star). Served in the operations in the Soudan in December 1888 including the engagement at Gemaizah (Clasp), and again in 1889 including the engagement at Toski (mentioned in despatches, Clasp). Promoted Brevet Lt.Colonel in recognition of his services in various operations in the Soudan 28 July 1891.

[23] Major Cheetham proceeded to the Gold Coast with Colonel Festing's detachment of Marines in May 1873, and served in the Ashanti war till invalided in September (Medal). Served in the Egyptian war of 1882 (Medal, 4th Class of the Medjidie, and Khedive's Star).

[24] Major T. Moore served in the Ashanti war in 1873, and was present in the engagements at Essaman and Abrakrampa (Medal).

[25] Major L. R. Connolly served with the expedition to the Soudan under Sir Gerald Graham in 1884 (Medal, and Khedive's Star).

[26] Major T. R. Swinburne served in the Egyptian war of 1882, and was present in the engagement at Nefiche (mentioned in despatches, Medal, and Khedive's Star). Served in the Soudan campaign in 1884-85, and was present in the engagement at Hasheen and at the destruction of Tomai (Medal with Clasp).

[27] Major J.W. Grant served in the Egyptian war of 1882, and was present in the engagement at El Magfar, at the two actions at Kassasin, and at the battle of Tel-el-Kebir (Medal with Clasp, and Khedive's Star).

War Services.—Royal Marine Artillery.

[28] Major G. D. C. Raitt served in the Egyptian war of 1882, and was present at the bombardment of Alexandria (Medal with Clasp, and Khedive's Star).

[29] Major R. H. Alexander served in the Egyptian war of 1882 with the Royal Marine Artillery, and was present in the reconnaissance in force from Alexandria on the 5th August (Medal, and Khedive's Star).

[30] Captain Tatham served in the Egyptian war of 1882, and was present at the bombardment of Alexandria (Medal with Clasp, and Khedive's Star).

[31] Captain W. J. Gaitskell served in the Egyptian war of 1882 (Medal, and Khedive's Star).

[32] Captain Orford served in the Egyptian war of 1882, and was present in the engagement at El Magfar and at the battle of Tel-el-Kebir (Medal with Clasp, and Khedive's Star). Served in the Soudan campaign in 1884-85, and was present in the engagement at Hasheen and at the destruction of Temai (Clasp).

[33] Captain W. F. Trotter served in the Egyptian war of 1882, and was present at the bombardment of Alexandria (Medal with Clasp, and Khedive's Star).

[34] Captain H. L. Talbot served in the Egyptian war of 1882, and was present at the bombardment of Alexandria, in the reconnaissance in force of the 5th August, in the engagements at El Magfar and Tel-el-Mahuta, at the two actions at Kassasin (mentioned in despatches), and at the battle of Tel-el-Kebir (Medal with two Clasps, 5th Class of the Medjidie, and Khedive's Star).

[35] Captain C. L. N. Bishop served in the Egyptian war of 1882 (Medal, and Khedive's Star).

[36] Captain H. D. Drake.—See Civil Decorations for Gallantry, "Hart's Annual Army List," p. 786.

[37] Captain Kappey served in the Egyptian war of 1882 (Medal, and Khedive's Star).

[38] Captain H. R. L. Pym served in the Egyptian war of 1882, and was present at the two actions at Kassasin (mentioned in despatches), and at the battle of Tel-el-Kebir (Medal with Clasp, and Khedive's Star).

[39] Captain G. G. Aston served with the expedition to the Soudan under Sir Gerald Graham in 1884, and was present in the engagement at Temai (Medal with Clasp, and Khedive's Star).

[40] Captain E. P. Brittan served with the expedition to the Soudan under Sir Gerald Graham in 1884, and was present in the engagement at El Teb (Medal with Clasp, and Khedive's Star).

[42] Captain G. M. Campbell served in the Soudan campaign in 1885 (Medal with Clasp, and Khedive's Star).

[43] Captain H. Slessor served in the Soudan campaign in 1884-85, and was present in the engagements at Hasheen and the Tofrek zereba and at the destruction of Temai (Medal with two Clasps, and Khedive's Star).

War Services.—Royal Marine Light Infantry.

[1] Colonel N. F. Way served in the Soudan campaign in 1885 in command of Royal Marines, and was present in the engagements at Hasheen and the Tofrek zereba, at that near Tofrek on the 24th March, and at the destruction of Temai (mentioned in despatches, CB., Medal with two Clasps, and Khedive's Star).

[12] Colonel Joseph Philips served in the Zulu war in command of the Royal Marines in 1879, and was present in the engagement at Gingindhlovu (mentioned in despatches, Brevet of Major, Medal). Served in the Egyptian war of 1882, and was present at the bombardment of the Alexandria Forts (Brevet of Lt. Colonel, Medal with Clasp, 4th Class of the Osmanieh, and Khedive's Star).

[13] Colonel Colwell served in the Soudan Expedition under Sir Gerald Graham in 1884, and was present in the engagements at El Teb and Temai (mentioned in despatches, Brevet of Lt.Colonel, Medal with Clasp, and Khedive's Star).

[14] Colonel E. L. Rose served with the expedition to the Soudan under Sir Gerald Graham in 1884 in command of Royal Marines in Forts Carysfort and Euryalus at Suakin (Medal, and Khedive's Star).

[20] Colonel Byam served in the Ashanti war of 1873-74 as Adjutant to the Royal Marine Battalion (Medal).

[21] Colonel J. I. Morris served in the Soudan campaign in 1885 in command of the Sandbag Camp; was Assistant Provost Marshal at Suakin, and was present in the reconnaissance to Hasheen and Handoub (Medal with Clasp, and Khedive's Star).

[24] Lt.Colonel Hungerford served in the Soudan campaign in 1884-85 as Paymaster with the Royal Marines, and took part in the defence of Suakin including the operations round that place (Medal with Clasp, and Khedive's Star).

[26] Major E. S. Innes served in the Egyptian war of 1882, and was present at the bombardment of the Alexandria Forts (Brevet of Major, Medal with Clasp, and Khedive's Star).

[28] Lt.Colonel Crosbie served in China in H.M.S. *Rodney* from September 1867 to September 1869; was landed from the Squadron at the occupation of Yangchow in November 1868; also served in a Battalion at the attack and capture of three walled villages in January 1869 (mentioned in despatches). Was landed from H.M.S. *Active* on the 27th November 1873, and served throughout the second phase of the Ashanti war in command of the Royal Marines, including the battle of Amoaful, battle of Ordahsu (slightly wounded) and capture of Coomassie (mentioned in despatches, Medal with Clasp). Commanded the Marines of H.M.S. *Active* on the expedition up the river Congo in August and September 1875, and was mentioned in despatches (Brevet of Major).

[30] Lt.Colonel Schomberg served in the Egyptian war of 1882, and was present at the bombardment of Alexandria (Brevet of Major, Medal with Clasp, and Khedive's Star). Served in the expedition to the Soudan under Sir Gerald Graham in 1884, and was present in the engagements at El Teb and Temai (4th Class of the Osmanieh, two Clasps).

[33] Lt.Colonel F. Baldwin served in China in H.M.S. *Rodney* from September 1867 to September 1869; landed from the Squadron at the occupation of Yangchow in November 1868; also served in a Battalion at the attack and capture of three walled villages in January 1869 (mentioned in despatches). Served in the Egyptian war of 1882, and commanded the Royal Marines of the East India Squadron at the occupation of Suez (Medal, 4th Class of the Medjidie, and Khedive's Star); also served with the expedition to the Soudan under Sir Gerald Graham in 1884, and was present in the engagement at Temai as Adjutant of the Royal Marine Battalion (mentioned in despatches, two Clasps).

[37] Colonel Sandwith served throughout the Egyptian war of 1882 as Deputy Assistant Adjutant and Quarter Master General, first at Alexandria, and afterwards on the Base and Lines of Communication (mentioned in despatches, Brevet of Major, Medal, 4th Class of the Medjidie, and Khedive's Star). Served with the Nile Expedition in 1884-85 as Deputy Assistant Adjutant and Quarter Master General, Provost Marshal, and Commandant and was present at the action of Kirbekan (mentioned in despatches, Brevet of Lt.Colonel, two Clasps).

[38] Lt.Colonel Kirchhoffer served in the Egyptian war of 1882, and was present in the engagement at Nefiche and with the Naval Brigade in the action at Tel-el-Mahuta (Medal, and Khedive's Star).

[40] Lt.Colonel Dowding served in the Kafir war in 1877-78 in command of the Royal Marines of the Naval Brigade, and was present in the Transkei operations and in the engagements at Neumarke, Quintana, and the Perie Bush; also served in the Zulu war of 1879 in command of the Royal Marines of H.M.S. *Active*, and was present in the engagement at Inyezane and in Ekowe during the investment (mentioned in despatches, promoted Captain and Brevet Major, Medal with Clasp).

[43] Lt.Colonel Coffin served in the Egyptian war of 1882 and was present in the engagements at El Magfar, Tel-el-Mahuta, and Mahsama, at the two actions at Kassasin, and at the battle of Tel-el-Kebir (mentioned in despatches, Brevet of Major, Medal with Clasp, and Khedive's Star). Served in the Soudan campaign in 1885, and was present in the engagements at Hasheen and the Tofrek zereba (two Clasps).

War Services.—Royal Marine Light Infantry.

⁴⁷ Lt. Colonel A. D. Corbet served with the expedition up the River Gambia against Fodey Silah in 1894 (mentioned in despatches, promoted Lt. Colonel, CB.).

⁴⁸ Lt. Colonel Bridge served in the Soudan campaign in 1885, and was present in the engagements at Hasheen and the Tofrek zereba, at that near Tofrek on the 24th March, and at the destruction of Temai (mentioned in despatches, Brevet of Major, Medal with two Clasps, and Khedive's Star).

⁴⁹ Lt. Colonel L. Edye served in the Egyptian war of 1882, and was present in the engagements at Malaha Junction, El Magfar, Tel-el-Mahuta, and Mahsama, at the two actions at Kassasin, and at the battle of Tel-el-Kebir (Medal with Clasp, and Khedive's Star). Served with the Royal Marine Battalion in the Soudan campaign in 1884-85, and was present in the engagements at Hasheen and the Tofrek zereba and at the destruction of Temai (two Clasps).

⁵⁰ Lt. Colonel Burrowes served in the Egyptian war of 1882, and was present in the engagement at Tel-el-Mahuta, and, as Adjutant of the Battalion, in the action at Kassasin (9th Sept.), and in the battle of Tel-el-Kebir (Medal with Clasp, and Khedive's Star). Served in the Soudan campaign in 1885 in command of the Mounted Infantry of the Royal Marines, and was present in the engagement at Hasheen and at the destruction of Temai (mentioned in despatches, Brevet of Major, Clasp).

⁵¹ Major H. E. Robbins served in the Soudan campaign in 1885 as Deputy Assistant Adjutant and Quarter Master General at the base of operations at Suez (Medal, and Khedive's Star).

⁵² Major C. G. Gordon served with the expedition to the Soudan in 1884-85, took part in the defence of Suakin, and was present in the engagements at Hasheen and the Tofrek zereba, at the attack on the convoy on the 24th March, and at the destruction of Temai (Medal with two Clasps, and Khedive's Star).

⁵³ Major Pyne served in the Ashanti war of 1873-74 (Medal). Served in the Soudan campaign in 1885, and was present in the engagements at Hasheen and the Tofrek zereba, at that near Tofrek on the 24th March, and at the destruction of Temai (Medal with two Clasps, and Khedive's Star).

⁵⁵ Major F. A. Newington.—See Civil Decorations for Gallantry, "Hart's Annual Army List," p. 786.

⁵⁷ Major Quill was present with the force under Colonel Festing at the defeat of the Ashantis in the two engagements at Elmina on the 13th June 1873, and was mentioned in despatches as having "skirmished his men with great alacrity, and merited much praise" (Medal).

⁵⁹ Major Hearle served in the Ashanti war of 1873-74. Was sent in October as Special Commissioner to the King of Denkera, and served as Assistant Engineer from the middle of November to the end of the war, and was present at the battle of Amoaful (Medal with Clasp).

⁶⁰ Major C. W. R. Kitching served in the Soudan campaign in 1885, and was present in the engagements at Hasheen and the Tofrek zereba, at that near Tofrek on the 24th March, and at the destruction of Temai (Medal with two Clasps, and Khedive's Star).

⁶² Major T. H. de M. Roche served in the Egyptian war of 1882, and was present in the engagement at Tel-el-Mahuta, at the two actions at Kassasin, and at the battle of Tel-el-Kebir (Medal with Clasp, and Khedive's Star).

⁶³ Major J. W. Robyns served in the Zulu war in 1879, and was present in the engagement at Gingindhlovu and at the relief of Ekowe (Medal with Clasp). In 1880 he was present at the bombardment of Batonga, on the West Coast of Africa, and commanded the Royal Marines at the destruction of those villages (mentioned in despatches). Also served in the Boer war of 1881.

⁶⁴ Major G. T. Onslow served in the Soudan campaign in 1884-85, took part in the defence of Suakin, and was present in the engagements at Hasheen and the Tofrek zereba, at that near Tofrek on the 24th March, and at the destruction of Temai (Medal with two Clasps, and Khedive's Star).

⁶⁵ Major J. B. Darling served in the Egyptian war of 1882, and was present in the reconnaissance in force from Alexandria on the 5th August, in the engagement at Tel-el-Mahuta, and at the battle of Tel-el-Kebir (Medal with Clasp, and Khedive's Star); also served in the Soudan campaign in 1885, and was present in the engagements at Hasheen and the Tofrek zereba, at that near Tofrek on the 24th March, and at the destruction of Temai (two Clasps).

⁶⁶ Major Kysh served in the Egyptian war of 1882, and was present in the engagement at Tel-el-Mahuta, in the two actions at Kassasin, and at the battle of Tel-el-Kebir (Medal with Clasp, and Khedive's Star). Served in the expedition to the Soudan under Sir Gerald Graham in 1884, and was present in the engagements at El Teb and Temai (two Clasps); also served in the Soudan campaign in 1884-85 on Signalling duties (mentioned in despatches, promoted Captain, Clasp).

⁶⁷ Major E. L. M'Causland served in the Egyptian war of 1882, and was present in the engagement at Tel-el-Mahuta, in the two actions at Kassasin, and at the battle of Tel-el-Kebir—severely wounded (Medal with Clasp, and Khedive's Star).

⁶⁸ Major Money served with the Royal Marines in the Egyptian war of 1882, and was present in the action at Kassasin on the 28th August, and in the battle of Tel-el-Kebir (Medal with Clasp, and Khedive's Star). Also served at Suakin during the expedition to the Soudan in 1884.

⁶⁹ Major F. G. Cotter served in the Soudan campaign in 1885, took part in the defence of Suakin, and was present in the engagements at Hasheen and the Tofrek zereba, at that near Tofrek on the 24th March, and at the destruction of Temai (Medal with two Clasps, and Khedive's Star).

⁷⁰ Major J. R. Johnstone served in the Egyptian war of 1882 (Medal, and Khedive's Star).

⁷¹ Major A. G. Cochran served in the Egyptian war of 1882 as Transport Officer at Ramleh while the Battalion was at Alexandria, and was present in the engagement at Malaha Junction, at the action at Kassasin on the 9th September, and at the battle of Tel-el-Kebir (Medal with Clasp, and Khedive's Star).

⁷² Major Maclurcan served in the Soudan campaign in 1884-85, took part in the defence of Suakin, and was present in the engagements at Hasheen and the Tofrek zereba, and at that near Tofrek on the 24th March—wounded (Medal with two Clasps, and Khedive's Star).

⁷³ Captain S. P. Peile served in the Egyptian war of 1882, and was present in the engagements at El Magfar and Tel-el-Mahuta (Medal, and Khedive's Star).

⁷⁴ Captain J. R. H. Oldfield served in the Egyptian war of 1882 (Medal, and Khedive's Star). [See also Civil Decorations for Gallantry, "Hart's Annual Army List," p. 786.]

⁷⁶ Captain C. H. Willis served in the Egyptian war of 1882, including the occupation of Alexandria and the defence of Fort Mex (Medal, and Khedive's Star).

⁷⁷ Captain J. H. Swanton served in the Egyptian war of 1882, and was present at the bombardment of the Alexandria Forts (Medal with Clasp, and Khedive's Star).

⁷⁸ Captain Frederick White served in the Egyptian war of 1882, and was present at the bombardment of the Alexandria Forts (Medal with Clasp, and Khedive's Star). Also served in the expedition to the Soudan under Sir Gerald Graham in 1884, and was present in the engagements at El Teb and Temai (5th Class of the Medjidie, two Clasps).

⁷⁹ Captain W. H. Palmer served in the Egyptian war of 1882, and was present in the engagements at Tel-el-Mahuta and Mahsama, in the two actions at Kassasin, and at the battle of Tel-el-Kebir (Medal with Clasp, and Khedive's Star).

⁸⁰ Captain C. Field served in the Egyptian war of 1882, and was present in the engagements at Malaha Junction and Tel-el-Mahuta, at the two actions at Kassasin, and at the battle of Tel-el-Kebir (Medal with Clasp, and Khedive's Star).

⁸¹ Captain J. Bernard served in the Egyptian war of 1882, and was present in the engagements at Malaha Junction, Tel-el-Mahuta, and Mahsama, at the two actions at Kassasin, and at the battle of Tel-el-Kebir (Medal with Clasp, and Khedive's Star).

⁸² Captain W. S. S. Harvest served with the Royal Marines in the Egyptian war of 1882, and was present in the reconnaissance in force from Alexandria on 5th August, in the engagements at El Magfar and Tel-el-Mahuta, the action at Kassasin (9th September), and at the battle of Tel-el-Kebir (Medal with Clasp, and Khedive's Star).

⁸³ Captain C. Clarke served in the Egyptian war of 1882 (Medal, and Khedive's Star).

⁸⁴ Lieut. H. G. Cotterill served in the Egyptian war of 1882, and was present at the occupation of Port Said, in the engagement at Nefiche, and at the two actions at Kassasin (Medal, and Khedive's Star).

⁸⁵ Captain E. V. Luke served in the Egyptian war in 1882, and was present in the engagements at Tel-el-Mahuta and Mahsama, in the action at Kassasin on the 9th September, and at the battle of Tel-el-Kebir (Medal with Clasp, and Khedive's Star).

⁸⁶ Captain F. L. Prendergast served in the expedition to the Soudan under Sir Gerald Graham in 1884, and was present in the engagements at El Teb and Temai (Medal with Clasp, and Khedive's Star).

86† Captain H. W. L. Holman served in the Soudan campaign in 1884-85, took part in the defence of Suakin, and was present in the engagements at Hasheen and the Tofrek zereba, the attack on the convoy on the 24th March, and the destruction of Temai (Medal with two Clasps, and Khedive's Star).

87 Major E. F. David served in the Soudan campaign in 1884-85, took part in the defence of Suakin, and was present in the engagements at Hasheen and the Tofrek zereba, at that near Tofrek on the 24th March, and at the destruction of Temai (Medal with two Clasps, and Khedive's Star). Served in the operations near Suakin in December 1888 including the engagement at Gemaizah—slightly wounded (Brevet of Major, Clasp, and 4th Class of the Medjidie).

88 Captain A. E. Marchant served in the Soudan campaign in 1884-85, took part in the defence of Suakin, and was present in the engagements at Hasheen and the Tofrek zereba, and at that near Tofrek on the 24th March—wounded (Medal with two Clasps, and Khedive's Star).

89 Captain E. C. B. Roe served in the Soudan campaign in 1884-85, and took part in the defence of Suakin (Medal with Clasp, and Khedive's Star).

90 Captain H. S. N. White served in the Nile Expedition in 1884-85 with the Royal Marines attached to the Guards Camel Regiment, and was present at the actions at Abu Klea and Abu Kru (Medal with two Clasps, and Khedive's Star).

91 Captain Curtoys served in the Soudan campaign in 1884-85, took part in the defence of Suakin, and was present in the engagements at Hasheen and the Tofrek zereba, at that near Tofrek on the 24th March, and at the destruction of Temai (Medal with two Clasps, and Khedive's Star).

92 Captain Logan-Home served with the expedition to the Soudan under Sir Gerald Graham in 1884 with the Royal Marines at Port Said and Suakin, and took part in the defence of Forts Carysfort and Euryalus (Medal, and Khedive's Star).

93 Captain C. N. Trotman served in the Soudan campaign in 1884-85, took part in the defence of Suakin, and was present in the engagements at Hasheen and the Tofrek zereba, at that near Tofrek on the 24th March, and at the destruction of Temai (Medal with two Clasps, and Khedive's Star).

95 Captain Abrahall served in the operations against Vitu, East Africa, in 1890.

96 Captain J. R. Goddard served in the Soudan campaign in 1884-85, and took part in the defence of Suakin and the destruction of Temai (Medal with Clasp, and Khedive's Star).

99 Lt.Colonel Norcock served with the Battalion sent out for service in Japan in 1864-66, and was present at the bombardment of the batteries at the Straits of Simonosaki, the entrance of the inland sea of Japan, the assault capture and destruction of the five batteries, stockade, magazines, and barracks, and during the shore operations from the 5th to the 8th Sept. 1864.

100 Lieut. F. J. W. Harvey served with the expedition to the Gambia against Fodey Silah in 1894 in charge of a detachment of Royal Marines (Medal with Clasp).

102 Major Valentine Brown served throughout the campaign in China in 1857-61, and was present at the capture of Canton in 1857 and at the taking of the Taku Forts in 1860 (Medal with two Clasps). Has received the Medal for Long Service and Good Conduct.

103 Captain Rowe served in the China war in 1857-60, and was present at the blockade of the Canton River, at the action of Fatshan, and at the capture of the Taku Forts (Medal with three Clasps).

104 Captain Syms served in the Soudan campaign in 1884-85, and took part in the defence of Suakin (Medal with Clasp, and Khedive's Star).

105 Captain Burtenshaw served in the Egyptian war of 1882, and was present in the engagement at Tel-el-Mahuta, at the two actions at Kassasin, and at the battle of Tel-el-Kebir (Medal with Clasp, and Khedive's Star). Also served in the Soudan campaign in 1885, took part in the defence of Suakin, and was present in the engagements at Hasheen and the Tofrek zereba (horse shot), and at the destruction of Temai (two Clasps).

HER MAJESTY'S LOCAL INDIAN FORCES.

GENERAL.

	2ND LIEUT., CORNET, OR ENSIGN.	LIEUT.	CAPTAIN.	MAJOR.	LIEUT. COLONEL.	COLONEL.	MAJOR GENERAL.	LIEUT. GENERAL.	GENERAL.
F & Gough, Sir Charles John Stanley,¹ KCB. Bengal Cavalry	20 Mar. 48	1 Sept. 49	9 June 57	20 July 58	24 Jan. 67	28 Nov. 75	2 July 85	5 June 89	1 Apr. 94

LIEUTENANT GENERALS.

Lockhart, Sir Wm. Stephen Alexander,³ KCB. CSI. Bengal Inf.; Commanding Punjab Frontier Force	4 Oct. 58	9 June 59	16 Dec. 68	9 June 77	6 Apr. 79	6 Apr. 83	1 Sept. 91	1 Apr. 94	
Rowband, Henry,² Bengal Infantry	29 Sept. 57	17 Sept. 58	29 Jan. 69	1 Oct. 75	30 Aug. 76	1 July 81	5 Apr. 93	1 Nov. 94	
Stewart, Sir Richard Campbell,³ KCB. Madras Cavalry; Commanding Secunderabad District	4 Aug. 53	28 Nov. 54	1 Jan. 62	4 Dec. 71	22 Dec. 77	22 Dec. 81	30 July 93	8 Jan. 95	

MAJOR GENERALS.

M'Nair, Henry Archibald, Bengal Infantry	20 Sept. 58	11 July 61	1 Nov. 68	16 July 76	1 Apr. 77	1 July 81	30 Sept. 93	
Steward, Charles Samuel,³⁴ Madras Cavalry	4 Oct. 54	30 Sept. 55	21 Apr. 61	11 May 72	24 May 77	1 July 81	5 Oct. 93	
Low, Sir Robert Cunliffe,⁴⁴ KCB. Bengal Cavalry; Commanding Oude District	28 Aug. 54	29 Sept. 55	15 Feb. 65	8 Feb. 72	8 Feb. 82	5 Oct. 93		
Inglis, Robert Hastie,³⁷ Bengal Infantry	28 June 56	22 Oct. 58	19 Oct. 65	1 Oct. 75	12 Mar. 77	3 Oct. 81	5 Oct. 93	
May, James,⁴⁶ CB. Bengal Infantry	20 Feb. 59	1 Jan. 60	1 Nov. 68	20 Feb. 70	10 June 79	9 Aug. 83	10 Feb. 94	
Prinsep, Arthur Haldimand,⁴⁰ CB. Bengal Cavalry [R]	20 Oct. 56	23 Jan. 57	17 Nov. 63	18 Apr. 74	21 July 80	21 July 84	1 Apr. 94	
Galloway, John Mawby Clossy,⁶³ Madras Cavalry [R]	1 Sept. 57	10 Mar. 58	31 May 64	13 Aug. 74	15 Dec. 80	15 Dec. 84	10 May 94	
							25 May 94	

COLONELS.

F & Sartorius, Reginald William,⁶⁷ CMG. Bengal Infantry. Residing out of India	20 Jan. 58	18 May 58	1 Nov. 68	1 Apr. 74	12 Sept. 78	27 Feb. 85	
Peacock, Henry Phipson,⁶⁹ Bengal Cavalry	20 Sept. 56	9 Jan. 57	6 May 65	23 July 76	1 July 82	20 Sept. 86	
Moore, Charles Alfred,⁷⁰ Bombay Cavalry; Pension Paymaster, Southern Concan	4 Nov. 56	1 Jan. 58	4 May 63	10 Apr. 74	14 July 80	6 Nov. 86	
Morris, Robert,⁷⁵ Bengal Cavalry	4 Aug. 57	18 May 58	8 Aug. 65	16 Dec. 76	8 Jan. 83	8 Jan. 87	
Henderson, Philip Durham, CSI. Madras Cavalry; Resident, Mysore, and Chief Commissioner, Coorg	20 Nov. 57	13 Sept. 59	28 Apr. 64	8 July 74	5 Oct. 80	8 Jan. 87	
Erskine, George Elphinstone,⁷⁷ Bombay Cavalry; Commissioner of Kumaon Division, Oude	4 Nov. 57	4 Apr. 60	4 Nov. 69	4 Nov. 77	4 Nov. 83	4 Nov. 87	
Stenhouse, William, Madras Infantry. Elected to reside in Europe	11 Dec. 58	1 Jan. 62	1 Dec. 70	1 Oct. 77	26 Nov. 75	26 Nov. 87	
Halliday, George Thomas,⁷⁸ Bengal Cavalry; Officiating Colonel on the Staff, Cawnpore	20 Dec. 58	4 Feb. 59	24 June 69	1 Jan. 84	1 Jan. 84	4 Jan. 88	
Beadon, Cecil,⁷³ Madras Cavalry. Residing out of India	20 Apr. 58	4 Feb. 58	22 June 62	29 Aug. 73	20 Apr. 81	20 Apr. 88	
Hooper, Willoughby Wallace,⁸⁰ Madras Cavalry. Permitted to reside in Europe	11 Dec. 58	21 Dec. 59	1 Nov. 68	1 June 75	16 July 81	16 July 88	
Woodhouse, Harvey, Bengal Infantry. Permitted to reside out of India	11 Dec. 58	11 Feb. 61	1 Oct. 68	4 Oct. 84	4 Oct. 88		
Walker, James Grant Duff,⁸¹ Madras Cavalry. Residing out of India	4 Oct. 58	12 Apr. 59	4 Oct. 67	27 Oct. 84	27 Oct. 88		
Hogg, George Crawford,⁸² Bombay Cavalry; Quarter Master General of the Bombay Army	27 Oct. 58	16 Oct. 58	27 Oct. 70	27 Oct. 84	27 Oct. 88		
Currie, Algernon, Bombay Cavalry; Assistant Adjutant General, Sind	27 Oct. 58	25 Dec. 60	27 Oct. 70	28 Oct. 78	28 Oct. 84	28 Oct. 88	
Currie, Fendall, Bengal Cavalry; Commissioner, Fyzabad Division	20 Nov. 58	29 Mar. 59	14 Sept. 70	20 Nov. 78	20 Nov. 84	20 Nov. 88	

General List of Officers of Bengal Cavalry.

	CORNET.	LIEUT.	BREVET CAPTAIN.	CAPTAIN.	BREVET MAJOR.	MAJOR.	BT. LT. COLONEL.	LIEUT. COLONEL.	COLONEL.	MAJOR GENERAL.
Biscoe, William Walters,¹ Colonel on the Staff, Moolan	4 Feb. 60	1 Jan. 72	4 Feb. 72	31 Dec. 72		4 Feb. 80	2 Mar. 81	4 Feb. 86	2 Mar. 85	8 Jan. 95

LIEUTENANT COLONELS.

Roberts, Arthur William, Political Agent, 1st Class, Rajpootana, 'Mount Aboo	20 Feb. 59	12 July 59		25 Oct. 66	28 Mar. 77	20 Feb. 79	16 July 83	20 Feb. 85	20 Feb. 89	
Jennings, Robert Melvill,⁶ Deputy Adjutant General, Bengal Army	20 May 59	12 May 60		15 Jan. 68	1 Oct. 77	20 May 79	28 Nov. 82	18 Nov. 85	18 Nov. 86	
Cowper, Herbert Henry Paterson, Controller of Military Accounts, Poona	20 Sept. 59	4 Sept. 60		4 Apr. 68		4 Sept. 79		4 Sept. 85	4 Sept. 89	
Lang, Richard Tickell Montgomery, Deputy Commissioner, 1st Class, Umritsur, Punjab	12 Oct. 59	9 Dec. 60		6 Apr. 71		12 Oct. 79		12 Oct. 85	20 Oct. 89	
Jackson, George D'Aguilar,⁷ Executive Engineer, 1st Grade, D.P.W., M.W. Branch	20 Nov. 59	1 Jan. 62		20 Nov. 71		20 Nov. 79		20 Nov. 85	20 Nov. 89	

General List of Officers of Bengal Infantry.

MAJOR GENERALS.	ENSIGN.	LIEUT.	CAPTAIN.	BREVET MAJOR.	MAJOR.	BT. COLONEL.	LIEUT. COLONEL.	COLONEL.	MAJOR GENERAL.
Waller, John Edmund[2]	4 July 59	20 Feb. 61	16 Dec. 68	.....	4 July 79	.....	2 Mar. 85	2 Mar. 85	1 Aug. 94
Strong, Dawsonne Melancthon[3]	10 Dec. 59	13 Oct. 60	29 June 69	.....	22 Nov. 79	.....	2 Mar. 81	2 Mar. 85	26 Aug. 94
Atkinson, John Richard Breeks[4]	7 June 61	30 July 62	1 Mar. 70	.....	22 Nov. 79	.....	2 Mar. 81	2 Mar. 85	15 Sept. 94
Eardley-Wilmot, Revell[5]	4 Mar. 60	1 Jan. 62	29 Oct. 69	.....	4 Mar. 80	2 Mar. 81	4 Mar. 86	2 Mar. 85	12 Feb. 95
LIEUTENANT COLONELS.									
Quin, Thomas James,[8] Deputy Commissioner, 2nd Class, Hurdui District, N.W. Provinces	4 Mar. 59	11 May 60	19 Oct. 68	28 Oct. 77	1 Jan. 79	1 Jan. 84	4 Mar. 85	4 Mar. 89	
Parker, Neville Fraser,[9] Residing out of India	9 Apr. 59	25 July 60	1 Nov. 68	22 Dec. 77	9 Apr. 79	1 Jan. 84	9 Apr. 85	1 Jan. 88	
Marsh, Frank Hale Berwick[11]	20 May 59	19 Sept. 60	1 Nov. 68	2 May 78	20 May 79	10 June 84	20 May 85	10 June 88	
Tregear, Vincent William,[12] CB. Residing in India	11 June 59	7 Nov. 60	1 Nov. 68	23 July 78	1 June 79	4 Aug. 84	16 June 85	4 Aug. 88	
Marshall, Herbert Seymour.[14] Residing out of India	16 June 59	2 Dec. 60	10 Nov. 68	14 Sept. 78	16 June 79	25 Nov. 84	16 June 85	25 Nov. 88	
Marriott, Edwin Metcalfe Leslie.[16] Residing out of India	9 July 59	20 Feb. 61	16 Dec. 68	.....	9 July 79	.....	9 July 85	9 July 89	
Reade, George Edward. Residing out of India	15 July 59	1 Mar. 61	16 Dec. 68	.....	15 July 79	.....	15 July 85	15 July 89	
Inglis, David William[18] Residing out of India	20 Aug. 59	5 May 61	29 Jan. 69	13 Aug. 79	20 Aug. 79	.....	20 Aug. 85	20 Aug. 89	
Chatterton, Frank William,[19] CIE. Comdt. Administrative Battalion Presidency Volunteers; Honorary Aide de Camp to the Governor General	20 Sept. 59	6 July 61	29 Jan. 69	.....	20 Sept. 79	.....	20 Sept. 85	20 Sept. 89	
Hastings, Francis Eddowes,[24] CB. Commandant 2 Sikh Infantry	10 Dec. 59	2 Oct. 61	2 June 69	.....	10 Dec. 79	2 Mar. 81	10 Dec. 85	10 Dec. 89	
Mainwaring, Edward Phillipson.[26] Residing out of India	20 Dec. 59	14 Nov. 61	23 June 69	.....	20 Dec. 79	.....	20 Dec. 85	20 Dec. 89	
Thomas, Francis Henry. Residing out of India	4 Jan. 60	1 Jan. 62	25 Aug. 69	.....	4 Jan. 80	.....	4 Mar. 86	4 Mar. 90	
Prendergast, Charles Lewis,[31] Commandant 28 Bengal Infantry	4 Mar. 60	1 Jan. 62	29 Oct. 69	.....	4 Mar. 80	.....	4 Mar. 86	4 Mar. 90	
Carruthers, Joseph George Thomson,[34] Commandant 21 Bengal Infantry	8 June 60	1 Jan. 62	27 Nov. 69	.....	25 May 80	.....	25 May 86	8 June 90	
Ramsay, Herbert Maynard, District Superintendent of Police, 1st Grade, Moznifferpore, Bengal	4 Aug. 60	1 Jan. 62	27 Nov. 69	20 July 80	4 Aug. 80	.....	4 Aug. 86	4 Aug. 90	
Tyler, Robert Francis Christopher Alexander[43]	2 Oct. 60	1 Jan. 62	27 Nov. 69	21 Sept. 80	2 Oct. 80	2 Mar. 81	2 Oct. 86	2 Oct. 90	
Bruce, Andrew McCrae.[45] Residing out of India	4 Nov. 60	1 Jan. 62	27 Nov. 69	.....	4 Nov. 80	.....	4 Nov. 86	4 Nov. 90	
Tucker, Louis Henry Emile,[47] CIE. Inspector General of Police, and Under Secretary to Punjab Government Police Department	19 Dec. 60	1 Jan. 62	28 Nov. 69	18 Dec. 80	19 Dec. 80	.....	19 Dec. 86	19 Dec. 90	
Harrison, William Pringle,[50] Deputy Commissioner, 1st Grade, Kheree, N.W. Provinces	4 Jan. 61	6 Feb. 62	1 Jan. 70	1 Jan. 81	4 Jan. 81	.....	4 Jan. 87	.....	
Farwell, Walter Charles.[51] Residing in India	20 Jan. 61	17 Mar. 62	1 Jan. 70	31 Dec. 80	20 Jan. 81	.....	20 Jan. 87	.....	
Grigg, Edward Evans, Deputy Commissioner, 1st Grade, Seetapore, N.W. Provinces	7 June 61	25 July 62	1 Jan. 70	30 May 81	7 June 81	.....	7 June 87	.....	
Ransford, Charles. Residing out of India	7 June 61	30 July 62	1 Mar. 70	.....	7 June 81	.....	7 June 87	.....	
Smyth, Edwall Walter.[57] Commandant 25 Bengal Infantry	7 June 61	30 July 62	1 Mar. 70	.....	7 June 81	.....	7 June 87	28 Dec. 93	
Scott, William Walter Hopton,[58] Commandant 11 Bengal Lancers	7 June 61	30 July 62	1 Mar. 70	.....	7 June 81	.....	7 June 87	.....	
Percy-Smith, Percy Wyndham,[59] Commandant Brinpoorah Irregular Force	8 June 61	30 July 62	1 Mar. 70	.....	8 June 81	.....	8 June 87	29 Aug. 93	
McNeale, James Agnew,[60] Commandant 8 Bengal Cavalry	8 June 61	30 July 62	9 May 70	.....	8 June 81	.....	8 June 87	.....	
Thomas, Charles Frederick, Controller of Military Accounts, Calcutta	8 June 61	30 July 62	26 May 70	.....	8 June 81	.....	8 June 87	29 Aug. 93	
Wylie, Henry, CSI.[73] Political Agent, 1st Class; Resident in Nepaul	4 Oct. 61	4 Oct. 62	13 Dec. 70	1 July 81	4 Oct. 81	.....	4 Oct. 87	29 Aug. 93	
Meiklejohn, William Hope,[75] CMG. Commandant 20 Bengal Infantry	4 Dec. 61	11 Dec. 62	24 May 71	1 July 81	4 Dec. 81	.....	4 Dec. 87	29 Aug. 93	
Bigg-Wither, Archibald Cuthbert, Superintendent Engineer, 1st Grade, D. P. W. Shillong, Assam; Secretary to the Chief Commissioner	2 Jan. 62	25 Jan. 63	1 July 71	1 July 81	2 Jan. 82	.....	2 Jan. 88	.....	
Lawrence, Henry John, Divisional Judge, 2nd Grade, Punjab	4 Jan. 62	10 Mar. 63	18 July 71	1 July 81	4 Jan. 82	.....	4 Jan. 88	.....	
Loch, William,[74] Principal of the Mayo College, Ajmere	4 Jan. 62	13 Mar. 63	1 July 71	1 July 81	4 Jan. 82	.....	4 Jan. 88	.....	
Wenyss, Binfield.[75] Residing out of India	20 Jan. 62	24 Mar. 63	18 July 71	20 Jan. 82	20 Jan. 82	.....	20 Jan. 88	20 Aug. 93	

General List of Officers of Madras Cavalry.

LIEUTENANT COLONELS.	CORNET.	LIEUT.	BREVET CAPTAIN.	CAPTAIN.	BREVET MAJOR.	MAJOR.	BT. COLONEL.	LIEUT. COLONEL.	COLONEL.
Law, Victor Edward, 1st Class Political Agent	20 Apr. 59	20 Apr. 60	.....	16 July 64	28 Apr. 75	20 Apr. 79	.....	20 Apr. 85	20 Apr. 86
Hope, Hugh Richard,[1] Secretary to Government, Military Dept., with rank of Brigadier Gen. 31 Oct. 91	4 Nov. 60	4 Jan. 62	.....	15 Dec. 70	.....	4 Nov. 80	.....	4 Nov. 86	1 July 87
Bailer, Frederick William, District Superintendent of Police, Bulandshar, N. W. Provinces	4 Dec. 61	1 Jan. 62	.....	15 Aug. 71	.....	4 Dec. 81	.....	4 Dec. 86	4 Dec. 90
Warner, William Bannatyne,[2] Colonel on the Staff, Bhamo	1 July 61	1 July 62	1 July 73	4 Oct. 74	.....	1 July 81	17 May 86	1 July 87	17 May 90
McLeod, Donald James Sim,[3] DSO. Assistant Adjutant General, Secunderabad	20 July 67	20 July 62	20 July 73	4 Nov. 74	.....	20 July 81	.....	20 July 87	12 Aug. 93

404a

General List of Officers of Madras Infantry.

	ENSIGN.	LIEUT.	BREVET CAPTAIN.	CAPTAIN.	MAJOR.	BT.LT. COLONEL.	LIEUT. COLONEL.	COLONEL.
LIEUTENANT COLONELS.								
Hutchins, Alfred George. Residing out of India	20 Feb. 59	20 Feb. 60		10 Apr. 70	20 Feb. 79	18 Feb. 85	20 Feb. 85	20 Feb. 89
Bergbie, Elphinstone Waters,[4] DSO. Deputy Adjutant General of the Madras Army	4 Apr. 59	25 Apr. 61		8 Mar. 71	4 Apr. 79		4 Apr. 85	4 Apr. 89
Rankine, William Lancaster,[5] Assistant Adjutant General, Belgaum	4 Apr. 59	13 Sept. 61	4 Apr. 71	9 Sept. 71	4 Apr. 79		4 Apr. 85	4 Apr. 89
Smalley, Frederick. Residing out of India	20 May 59	1 Oct. 61	20 May 71	9 Sept. 71	20 May 79		20 May 85	20 May 89
Cox, Robert Emilius, Commandant Neilgherry Volunteer Rifles	16 June 59	1 Jan. 62	16 June 71	23 Oct. 71	16 June 79		16 June 85	16 June 89
Shelley, Henry Richard Superintendent of Army Clothing, Madras	20 July 59	1 Jan. 62	20 July 71	7 Dec. 71	20 July 79		20 July 85	20 July 89
Weston, George Edward.[6] Residing out of India	4 Aug. 59	1 Jan. 62	4 Aug. 71	23 Mar. 72	4 Aug. 79		4 Aug. 85	4 Aug. 89
Anderson, Alfred.[7] Residing out of India	20 Oct. 59	1 Jan. 62	20 Oct. 71	8 Apr. 73	20 Oct. 79		20 Oct. 85	20 Oct. 89
Anderson, Arthur William Leslie.[8] Residing out of India	4 Dec. 59	1 Jan. 62	4 Dec. 71	13 Apr. 73	4 Dec 79		4 Dec. 85	4 Dec. 89
MacNeill, James Graham Robert Douglas,[9] CB. Residing out of India	22 Dec. 59	1 Apr. 62	22 Dec. 71	13 Apr. 73	22 Dec. 79		22 Dec. 85	22 Dec. 89
Chaplin, Allan, Deputy Judge Advocate General, Ootacamund	12 Nov. 60	10 Dec. 62	12 Nov. 72	1 Jan. 74	12 Nov. 80		12 Nov. 86	12 Nov. 90
Shaw, Alexander John. Residing out of India	20 Dec. 60	23 Mar. 63	20 Dec. 72	1 Jan. 74	20 Dec. 80		20 Dec. 86	20 Dec. 90

General List of Officers of Bombay Cavalry.

	CORNET.	LIEUT.	BREVET CAPTAIN.	CAPTAIN.	MAJOR.	BT.LT. COLONEL.	LIEUT. COLONEL.	COLONEL.
LIEUTENANT COLONELS.								
Pent, Walter Scott. Residing out of India	27 June 59	6 Feb. 61	27 June 71	28 Jan. 75	27 June 79		27 June 85	27 June 89
Fagan, Joseph G. Residing out of India	27 Dec. 59	10 June 61	27 Dec. 71	4 Mar. 75	27 Dec. 79		27 Dec. 85	27 Dec. 89

General List of Officers of Bombay Infantry.

	ENSIGN.	LIEUT.	BREVET CAPTAIN.	CAPTAIN.	MAJOR.	BT.LT. COLONEL.	LIEUT. COLONEL.	COLONEL.	MAJOR GENERAL.
MAJOR GENERAL.									
Nicolson, Malcolm Hassells,[1] CB. Commanding Deesa District	9 Dec. 59	4 Jan. 62		31 Oct. 69	9 Dec. 79	2 Mar. 81	2 Mar. 85		1 Nov. 94
LIEUTENANT COLONELS.									
Hibbert, John.[1] Residing out of India	27 Feb. 59	21 Feb. 61		1 Mar. 69	27 Feb. 79	27 Feb. 85	27 Feb. 89		
Mockler, Edward, Political Resident, Turkish Arabia	2 Aug. 59	1 Jan. 62		14 Oct. 69	2 Aug. 79	2 Aug. 85	2 Aug. 89		
Mander, Frederick Day.[3] Residing out of India	2 Aug. 59	1 Jan. 62		14 Oct. 69	2 Aug. 79	2 Aug. 85	2 Aug. 89		
Rutherford, James. Residing out of India	4 Aug. 59	1 Jan. 62		14 Oct. 69	4 Aug. 79	4 Aug. 85	4 Aug. 89		
Willoughby, James Fortnom.[7] Residing out of India	27 Jan. 59	30 Oct. 62		4 Feb. 71	27 Jan. 81	27 Jan. 87	29 Aug. 93		
Prideaux, Robert Austice, Deputy Judge Advocate General, Poona	27 Mar. 61	1 Dec. 62		4 Feb. 71	27 Mar. 81	27 Mar. 87			
Jackson, Freeman Henry, Political Superintendent, Palanpore	7 June 61	5 Feb. 63		4 Feb. 71	7 June 81	7 June 87			
Browne, Charles Michael. Residing out of India	8 June 61	19 Sept. 63		4 Feb. 71	8 June 81	8 June 87			
Hore, Walter Stuart[10] (Bt. Major, 1 July 81), Commandant 20 Bombay Infantry	12 Sept. 61	29 Feb. 64		21 Feb. 71	12 Sept. 81	12 Sept. 87	29 Aug. 93		
Stevens, Malcolm Wilkinson[2] (Bt. Major, 1 July 81), Commandant 3 Bombay Cavalry	27 Dec. 61	16 July 64		19 Aug. 71	27 Dec. 81	27 Dec. 87			

Her Majesty's Local Indian Forces.—War Services.

¹ Sir Charles Gough served throughout the Punjaub campaign of 1848-49, including the action of Ramnuggur, passage of the Chenab, and battles of Sadoolapore, Chillianwalla, and Goojerat (Medal with two Clasps). Served in the Indian mutiny campaign of 1857-58; with the Guide Corps at siege and capture of Delhi; commander Guide Cavalry in affairs at Khurkonda on 15th, and Rhotuck on 17th and 13th August; engaged in the cavalry affair in rear of the Camp on 11th September. Served with Brigadier Showers' Column in the Delhi and Jhujjur districts. Was engaged in the action of Narnole on the 16th November. Served with Hodson's Horse at the actions of Gungeeree, Putteallee, Mynpoorie, and Shumshabad (wounded). Commanded a Squadron of Hodson's Horse at the action of Meangunge; present throughout the siege and capture of Lucknow (Medal with two Clasps, Victoria Cross, and Brevet of Major): was awarded the VC—"1. For gallantry in an affair at Khurkowdah, near Rhotuck, on the 15th August 1857, in which he saved his brother, who was wounded, and killed two of the enemy. 2. For gallantry on the 18th August when he led a Troop of the Guide Cavalry in a charge, and cut down two of the enemy's sowars, with one of whom he had a desperate hand-to-hand combat. 3. For gallantry on the 27th January 1858, at Shumshabad, where, in a charge, he attacked one of the enemy's leaders, and pierced him with his sword, which was carried out of his hand in the melée. He defended himself with his revolver, and shot two of the enemy. 4. For gallantry on the 23rd February 1858, at Meangunge, where he came to the assistance of Brevet Major O. H. St. George Anson, and killed his opponent, immediately afterwards cutting down another of the enemy in the same gallant manner." Served with the Bhootan Expedition in 1864-65 (Medal with Clasp). Served in the Afghan war of 1878-80, and was present at the attack and capture of Ali Musjid, and in the engagement at Futtehabad (mentioned in despatches); commanded a force of all arms which proceeded from Gundamuck to the relief of Cabul in December 1879 (mentioned in despatches), and commanded a brigade in the engagement at Saidabad (mentioned in despatches, KCB., Medal with two Clasps).

³ Sir William Lockhart served with the 5th Fusiliers in Oude in December 1858 and January 1859. Served throughout the Bhootan campaign of 1864-66 as Adjutant 14th Bengal Lancers (Medal with Clasp). Served as Aide de Camp to Brigadier General Morewether commanding Cavalry Brigade in the Abyssinian campaign, and was present at Arogee and the fall of Magdala (mentioned in despatches, Medal). Was present at the capture of Lambada during the Dutch war in Acheen in 1875-77 (mentioned in despatches, Dutch War Medal with Clasp). Served as D.A.Q.M. General 2nd Brigade with Hazara Field Force in the Black Mountain Expedition in 1868 (mentioned in despatches, Clasp). Served in the Afghan war in 1879-80 as Road Commandant in the Khyber from September to November 1879, and afterwards as Assistant Quarter Master General to Major General Roberts's Division, and was present in the operations around Cabul in December 1879, including the investment of Sherpore (mentioned in despatches, CB., Medal with Clasp). Served with the Burmese Expedition in 1886-87 in command of a Brigade (received the thanks of the Government of India, mentioned in despatches, KCB., and Clasp). Commanded the two Miranzai Expeditions in 1891 (received the thanks of the Government of India and of the Commander in Chief in India, promoted Major General for distinguished service in the field, Clasp); and also commanded the Isazai Expedition in 1892. [See also Civil Decorations for Gallantry, "Hart's Annual Army List," p. 786.]

²³ Lieut.General H. Rowband served with the Bhootan Expedition in 1864-65 (Medal with Clasp). Served in the Afghan war of 1878-80, and was present at the attack and capture of Ali Musjid (Medal with Clasp).

³⁴ Major General C. S. Steward was employed during the Indian Mutiny, and was present at the action of Itrowlea with Kooer Sing's rebel force on the 21st March 1858 (wounded), and at the sortie from the fort of Azimghur 27th March, also at the taking of Jugdespore and at the engagements of Beliea, Peeroo, twice at Muttahee, Dullepore, Ceswah, Rujapore Gamur, and the final ejectment of the rebels from the Jugdespore Jungles between May and June 1858 (Medal).

³⁷ Major General R. H. Inglis served with the Bhootan Expedition in 1865-66 (Medal with Clasp). Served in the Afghan war in 1879 (Medal).

³⁹ Sir Richard Stewart served with a party of the Mysore Silladar Horse attached to the Kurnool Movable Column and was present at the attack on Shorapore on the 8th February 1858, on which occasion he was dangerously wounded by two sword cuts; also commanded a detachment of the 4th Cavalry Hyderabad Contingent with Brigadier Hill's Field Force in the Taptee Valley, in Berar, and in the Deccan from November 1858 till March 1859 (Medal). Served with the Burmese Expedition in 1886-87 in command of a Brigade sent to the Ruby Mines (received the thanks of the Governor General in Council, mentioned in despatches, CB., Medal with Clasp).

⁴⁴ Sir Robert Low served in the Sonthal campaign in 1855. Served throughout the Indian Mutiny campaign of 1857-59 present at the actions of Budlee-ke-Serai and Nudjufghur, and siege and capture of Delhi; pursuit of the rebels and taking of Fort Jhujjur; siege and capture of Lucknow; and as Brigade Major to the Agra Field Force under Brigadier Showers in pursuit of rebels in Central India (twice mentioned in despatches, Medal with two Clasps). Served with the Eusofzie Expedition in 1863 (Medal with Clasp). Served in the Afghan war of 1878-80, and was present with the expedition into the Bazar Valley (mentioned in despatches) and at the assault of Zawa; accompanied Sir Frederick Roberts in the march to Candahar as Chief Director of Transport, and was present at the battle of Candahar (mentioned in despatches, CB., Medal with Clasp, and Bronze Decoration). Served with the Burmese Expedition in 1885-88 in command of a Brigade (received the thanks of the Government of India, mentioned in despatches, KCB., and Clasp).

⁴⁶ Major General J. May served with the Volunteer Cavalry at Lucknow, and was present at the action of Chinhut 30th June 1857, also throughout the defence of the Residency acting as a Subaltern of Artillery and subsequently as Assistant Field Engineer. Served afterwards with the force at the Alumbagh and was present in the various actions (wounded), and accompanied Lord Clyde's Force at the final capture of Lucknow (Medal with two Clasps, and a year's service). Served with the Bhootan Expedition in 1864-65, and was present at the capture of Dalimkote and Chamoorchee (mentioned in despatches, Medal with Clasp). Served with the Burmese Expedition in 1886-87 (mentioned in despatches, Clasp).

⁶⁰ Major General A. H. Prinsep was present at the mutiny of his Regiment, the 6th Bengal Light Cavalry, at Sealkote on the 9th July 1857 and was wounded. He afterwards served against the rebels in the Gogaria Jungles and was present at the final siege and capture of Lucknow (Medal with Clasp). Served in the campaign on the North-West Frontier of India in 1863 (Medal). Served in the Afghan war in 1878-79, and was present at the attack and capture of Ali Musjid (mentioned in despatches, Medal with Clasp).

⁶² Major General J. M. C. Galloway was employed during the Indian Mutiny in Shahabad, and was engaged at Kheree 7th October, Burhampoor 14th October, Kheree Saugor 16th October, Jugdespore 18th October, and Seekreta and Koath Khaz 20th October 1858, and in Bundlecund during the whole of 1859 (Medal with Clasp). Served with the Burmese Expedition in 1886 (Medal with Clasp).

⁶⁷ Colonel R. W. Sartorius served in the Indian Mutiny campaign in 1858-59, and was present at the relief of Azimghur and during the operations in the Goruckpore district (Medal). Served with the Bhootan Expedition in 1864-65 (Medal with Clasp). Served in the Ashanti war in 1873-74 (Brevet of Major, Victoria Cross, CMG. and Medal): was awarded the VC "for having during the attack on Abogoo, on the 17th January 1874, removed from under a heavy fire Sergeant Major Braimah Doctor, a Houssa Non-Commissioned Officer, who was mortally wounded, and placed him under cover." Also served in the Afghan war in 1878-79 (Medal).

⁶⁹ Colonel H. P. Peacock served in the Indian Mutiny campaign in 1857-59, and was present at the siege and capture of Lucknow (Medal with Clasp).

⁷⁰ Colonel C. A. Moore commanded a detachment of the 2nd Bombay Light Cavalry at the taking of Rewal, present at the taking of Awah; served with the Field Force in Central India in 1858; present during the operations in the Mahee Kanta in 1858; and at the night attack of the Khosias at Bbyrannah and during the operations at Nuggur Parker; present during the operations in Kattywar, and at the taking of the Burda Hills and defeat of the Wagheers at that place in 1859 (Medal with Clasp). Served with the 3rd Light Cavalry during the Abyssinian campaign of 1867-68, and commanded the Regiment at the storming and capture of Magdala (mentioned in despatches, Medal).

Her Majesty's Local Indian Forces.—War Services. 404c

73 Colonel C. Beadon, prior to entering the Indian Army, served five years as a Midshipman in the Royal Navy, was on board H.M. ship *Algiers* at the bombardment and fall of Bomarsund during the Baltic campaign of 1854 under Sir Charles Napier (Medal). Served afterwards in the same ship during the siege and fall of Sevastopol between the 23rd October 1854 and December 1855, and was present at the taking of Kertch and Kinbourn (Medal with Clasp). Was engaged in the operations against Canton in 1856-57 on board H.M. ships *Calcutta* and *Elk* (Medal). Served on the River Ganges as a Volunteer during the late mutiny in the H.E.I. Company's gunboat *Jumna*.

75 Colonel R. Morris served with the 2nd Dragoon Guards in the Indian Mutiny campaign in 1858, and was present at the siege and capture of Lucknow and subsequent operations at Koorsee (Medal with Clasp). Served in the Afghan war in 1880 (Medal).

77 Colonel G. E. Erskine served with the Rajpootana Field Force under Brigadier M. W. Smith in 1858-59.

78 Colonel G. T. Halliday served with the Hazara Expedition in 1888 (Medal with Clasp).

80 Colonel W. W. Hooper served with a squadron of his regiment on field service in the Deccan from the 16th November 1858 to the 5th April 1859, including the march of fifty miles without a halt on the 28th February in pursuit of and defeat of the enemy and taking several prisoners (Medal). Served with the Burmese Expedition in 1885-86 (Medal with Clasp).

81 Colonel J. G. D. Walker served with his regiment in the campaign in Bundlecund under Brigadier Wheler in 1859. Served with the Burmese Expedition in 1887-88 (mentioned in despatches, Medal with Clasp).

82 Colonel G. C. Hogg served in the Afghan war in 1879-80, and was present in the engagement at Girishk, and in the defence of Candahar including the sortie of Deh Khojah (several times mentioned in despatches, Medal).

General List of Officers of Bengal Infantry.—War Services.

1 Major General Biscoe served in the Afghan war in 1879-80, and was present in the engagements at Khelat-i-Ghilzie and Sir-i-Asp (mentioned in despatches, Brevet of Lt.Colonel, Medal). Served with the Miranzai Expedition in 1891 in command of the Cavalry of the Force (mentioned in despatches, Medal with Clasp).

2 Major General J. E. Waller served with the Bhootan Expedition in 1865-66, and was present at the destruction of the Bala Stockades (Medal with Clasp). Served in the Afghan war of 1878-80, and was present in the engagement at Ahmed Kheyl and in the advance on Cabul under Sir Donald Stewart (mentioned in despatches, Brevet of Lt.Colonel, Medal with Clasp). Served with the Hazara Expedition in 1891 (Clasp), and with the second Miranzai Expedition in 1891 (Clasp).

3 Major General D. M. Strong served in the Abyssinian war in 1868 (Medal). Served in the Afghan war in 1879-80, and was present in the engagement at Kam Dakka (mentioned in despatches, Brevets of Major and Lt.Colonel, and Medal).

4 Major General J. R. B. Atkinson served in the Afghan war of 1878-80, and was present in the engagements at Saif-u-deen, Ahmed Kheyl, and Patkao Shana (several times mentioned in despatches, Brevet of Lt.Colonel, Medal with Clasp).

5 Major General R. Eardley-Wilmot served in the Bhootan campaign in 1864-66—slightly wounded (mentioned in despatches, Medal with Clasp). Served with the expedition against the Jowaki Afreedees in 1877-78 (mentioned in despatches, Clasp). Served in the Afghan war of 1878-80, and was present at the attack and capture of Ali Musjid, in the engagement at Charasiah on the 6th October 1879, and in the operations round Cabul in December 1879 including the investment of Sherpore (mentioned in despatches, Brevet of Lt.Colonel, Medal with three Clasps).

6 Colonel R. M. Jennings served in the campaign on the North West Frontier of India in 1863-64, and was present at the action of Shubkudder (Medal with Clasp). Served in the Egyptian war of 1882, and was present at the battle of Tel-el-Kebir (mentioned in despatches, Brevet of Lt.Colonel, Medal with Clasp, 4th Class of the Osmanieh, and Khedive's Star). Served with the Hazara Expedition in 1888 (Medal with Clasp).

7 Colonel G. D'A. Jackson served in the Afghan war in 1878-79 (Medal).

8 Colonel T. J. Quin served with the Bhootan Expedition in 1865, and was present at the capture of Dewangiri (Medal).

9 Colonel N. F. Parker served in the Hazara campaign in 1868 (Medal). Also served in the Afghan war in 1878-79 (Medal).

11 Colonel F. H. B. Marsh served in the campaign on the North-West Frontier of India in 1863 and was present at the capture of Umbeyla (mentioned in despatches, Medal with Clasp). Served in the Abyssinian war in 1868 (Medal).

12 Colonel V. W. Tregear served in the Afghan war in 1879-80 on the Khyber line of communications (Medal). Commanded the Lushai Expedition in 1889, and served with the Chin-Lushai Expeditionary Force in 1889-90 in command of the Chittagong Column with rank of Brigadier General (received the thanks of the Government of India, *C.B.*, and Medal with Clasp).

14 Colonel H. S. Marshall served in the Afghan war of 1878-80, and was present in the operations in the Khost Valley, in the engagements at Mattoon and at Charasiah on the 6th October 1879, and in the operations around Cabul in December 1879 (mentioned in despatches, Medal with two Clasps).

16 Colonel E. M. L. Marriott served with the Looshai Expedition in 1871-72 (mentioned in despatches, Medal with Clasp). Also served in the Afghan war in 1878-79 (Medal).

18 Colonel D. W. Inglis served in the Afghan war of 1878-80, took part in the advance on Ghuznee, and was present in the engagements at Ahmed Kheyl and Urzoo near Ghuznee; accompanied Sir Frederick Roberts in the march to Candahar, and was present at the battle of Candahar (mentioned in despatches, Medal with two Clasps, and Bronze Decoration). Served in the Soudan campaign in 1885 (mentioned in despatches, Brevet of Lt.Colonel, Medal with Clasp, and Khedive's Star).

19 Colonel F. W. Chatterton served in the campaign on the North-West Frontier of India in 1863, including the capture of Umbeyla (Medal with Clasp). Also served with the Bhootan Expedition in 1865—slightly wounded (Clasp).

24 Colonel F. E. Hastings served in the Afghan war of 1878-80, and was present in the engagements at Ahmed Kheyl and Urzoo near Ghuznee; accompanied Sir Frederick Roberts in the march to Candahar, and was present at the battle of Candahar (twice mentioned in despatches, Brevet of Lt.Colonel, Medal with two Clasps, and Bronze Decoration). Served with the Hazara Expedition in 1888 (mentioned in despatches, Medal with Clasp); and with the Zhob Valley Expedition in 1890.

26 Colonel E. P. Mainwaring served in the Hazara campaign in 1868 (Medal with Clasp), and in the Looshai Expedition in 1871-72 (Clasp). Served in the Afghan war of 1878-80, and was present at the attack and capture of Ali Musjid, in the operations in the Jugdulluck Pass, in the engagement at Saifabad, and in the operations round Cabul in December 1879; accompanied Sir Frederick Roberts in the march to Candahar, and was present at the battle of Candahar (mentioned in despatches, Medal with three Clasps, and Bronze Decoration). Also served in the Marri Expedition.

31 Colonel Prendergast served in the expedition to the Cossyah and Jynteah Hills in 1862-63. Served in the Afghan war in 1879-80 (Medal). Served with the Chin Lushai Expedition in 1889-90 (Medal with Clasp), and with the Hazara Expedition in 1891 (Clasp).

34 Colonel J. G. T. Carruthers served in the Abyssinian campaign in 1867-68 (Medal). Served in the Afghan war in 1878-79, and was present in the engagement at Mattoon (Medal).

40 Colonel R. F. C. A. Tytler served in the Afghan war of 1878-80, and was present at the engagements at Ahmed Kheyl (mentioned in despatches) and Urzoo near Ghuznee (Brevet of Lt.Colonel, Medal with Clasp).

C C

45 Colonel A. M. Bruce served in the Bhootan Expedition in 1865-66 (Medal with Clasp). Served in the expedition against the Jowaki Afreedees in 1877-78 (Clasp). Served in the Afghan war in 1879, and took part in the assault of Zawa (Medal), and in the Mahsood Wuzeeree Expedition in 1881 (mentioned in despatches). Also served with the Zhob Valley Expedition in 1884. Served with the Hazara Expedition in 1888 (Clasp). Served with the Miranzai Expedition in 1891 in command of the 1st Column (mentioned in despatches, Clasp).
47 Colonel L. H. E. Tucker served in the campaign on the North West Frontier of India in 1863, including the forcing of the Umbeyla Pass (mentioned in despatches, Medal with Clasp); served with the expedition against the Jowaki Afreedees in 1877-78 (mentioned in despatches, Clasp). Served in the Afghan war of 1878-80, and was present at the attack and capture of Ali Musjid, with the second expedition into the Bazar Valley (mentioned in despatches), and in the advance to Cabul under Brigadier General Charles Gough (mentioned in despatches, Medal with two Clasps).
50 Lt.Colonel W. P. Harrison served in the China war in 1860, and was present at the capture of the Taku Forts (Medal).
51 Lt.Colonel W. C. Farwell served with the Jowaki Afreedee Expedition in 1877-78 (Medal with Clasp). Served in the Afghan war of 1878-80, and was present at the attack and capture of Ali Musjid, in the engagement at Charasiah on the 6th October 1879 (mentioned in despatches), and in the operations round Cabul in December 1879 including the storming of the Asmai Heights (mentioned in despatches); accompanied Sir Frederick Roberts in the march to Candahar, and was present at the battle of Candahar (mentioned in despatches, Medal with four Clasps, and Bronze Decoration). Served with the Burmese Expedition in 1886-88 (Clasp).
57 Colonel E. W. Smyth served with the Bhootan Expedition in 1865-66 (Medal with Clasp). Served in the Afghan war in 1879 (Medal).
58 Lt.Colonel W. W. H. Scott served in the Abyssinian war in 1868, and was present at the capture of Magdala (mentioned in despatches, Medal).
59 Colonel P. W. Smith served in the campaign on the North-West Frontier of India in 1863, and was present at the storming of Lalloo and at the capture of Umbeyla (Medal with Clasp). Served in the Afghan war in 1880 (Medal).
60 Lt.Colonel J. A. M'Neale served in the Afghan war of 1878-80 (Medal).
73 Colonel W. H. Meiklejohn served in the Hazara campaign in 1868, including the operations on the Black Mountain (Medal with Clasp); and with the expedition against the Jowaki Afreedees in 1877-78 (mentioned in despatches, Clasp). Served with the 20th Bengal Native Infantry in the Afghan war of 1878-80, and was present at the attack and capture of Ali Musjid and with the Znimusht Expedition (Medal with Clasp). Also served with the Mahsood Wuzeeree Expedition in 1881. Served with the 20th Bengal Native Infantry in the Egyptian war of 1882, and was present at the battle of Tel-el-Kebir (mentioned in despatches, Medal with Clasp, 4th Class of the Osmanieh, and Khedive's Star).
74 Lt.Colonel W. Loch served in the campaign on the North-West Frontier of India in 1863-64, and was present at the forcing of the Umbeyla Pass (Medal with Clasp).
75 Colonel B. Wemyss served in the Afghan war in 1879-80 on the Khyber line of communications (Medal).
78 Colonel Wylie served with the 7th Royal Fusiliers in the Umbeyla campaign of 1863, and was present at the capture of the Conical Hill and the taking of Umbeyla (Medal with Clasp); also served with the Bhootan Expedition in 1865 (Clasp). Served with the 10th Bengal Lancers throughout the Abyssinian war of 1868 (Medal). Served in the Hazara campaign in 1868 including the expedition to the Black Mountain (Clasp). Served throughout the Afghan war of 1878-80 as Political Officer in charge of the Afghan country north of Quetta, was present with two expeditions against the Kakar and Atchakzai tribes, and as Chief Political Officer took part in the march to Candahar with the force under Major General Phayre (mentioned in despatches, received the thanks of Her Majesty's Government and of the Government of India, CSI., and Medal).

General List of Officers of Madras Infantry.—War Services.

1 Brigadier General Hope served in the Afghan war in 1879-80 (Medal). Served with the Burmese Expedition in 1886-89 (mentioned in despatches, Brevet of Colonel, Medal with two Clasps).
2 Colonel W. B. Warner served in the Afghan war in 1879-80, and took part in the march to Candahar with the force under Major General Phayre (mentioned in despatches, Medal). Served with the Burmese Expedition in 1885-89 (mentioned in despatches, Brevet of Lt.Colonel, Medal with Two Clasps).
3 Colonel D. J. S. M'Leod served with the Burmese Expedition in 1886-87 (mentioned in despatches, DSO., and Medal with Clasp).
4 Colonel Begbie was employed in the Commissariat Department with the Abyssinian Expedition in 1867-69 (mentioned in despatches, Medal). Also served in the Duffla Expedition in 1874-75 as Superintendent of Army Signalling (mentioned in despatches). Served with the Burmese Expedition in 1885-86 as Superintendent of Army Signalling (mentioned in despatches, received the thanks of the Government of India, Medal with Clasp).
5 Colonel Ranking served with the Burmese Expedition in 1887-88 (Medal with Clasp).
6 Colonel Weston served with the Burmese Expedition in 1887-90 (Medal with Clasp).
7 Colonel Anderson served with the Burmese Expedition in 1889 (Medal with Clasp).
8 Colonel A. W. L. Anderson served with the Burmese Expedition in 1885-87– severely wounded (Medal with Clasp).
9 Colonel J. G. R. D. MacNeill served with the Burmese Expedition in 1885-86 as Deputy Assistant Adjutant and Quarter Master General for Intelligence duties, and acted as guide to the Column in the attack on the Minhla Redoubt—severely wounded (mentioned in despatches, CB., and Medal with two Clasps).

General List of Officers of Bombay Infantry.—War Services.

1 Major General M. H. Nicolson served in the Afghan war in 1879-80, and was present in the engagements at Ahmed Kheyl (mentioned in despatches) and Urzoo near Ghuznee (Brevet of Lt.Colonel, Medal with Clasp). Served in the Abyssinian war in 1867-68, and was present at the action of Arogee and at the capture of Magdala (Medal). Served with the Zhob Field Force in 1890 under Sir George White in command of No. 2 Column (mentioned in despatches).
1 Colonel J. Hibbert served in the Afghan war in 1880 as Executive Commissariat Officer at Sibi, on the Line of Communication, also at Candahar and Quetta (Medal). Served in the Burmese war in 1887 as Assistant Principal Commissariat Officer at Mandalay from the 22nd July to the 27th September (Medal with Clasp).
3 Colonel F. D. Mauder served in the Afghan war in 1879-80 as General Transport Officer on the Line of Communications in Southern Afghanistan (Medal).
7 Colonel J. F. Willoughby served in the Abyssinian war of 1867-68, and was present at the storming of Magdala (Medal). Served in the Afghan war in 1880, took part in the defence of Candahar, and was present at the battle of Candahar (Medal with Clasp).
10 Colonel W. S. Hore served with the Commissariat Department in the Abyssinian campaign of 1867-68 (Medal).
12 Lt.Colonel M. W. Stevens served in the Afghan war in 1879-80 as Transport Officer, Cavalry Brigade, and was present in the engagement at Ahmed Kheyl (Medal with Clasp).

INDIAN STAFF CORPS.

Last Regiment.	Yrs. Serv.		2nd Lieut., Cornet, or Ensign.	Lieut.	Brevet Captain.	Captain.	Brevet Major.	Major.	Brevet Lt. Col.	Lieut. Colonel.	Brevet Colonel.	Major General.	Lieut. General.	General.
		GENERALS.												
60 Be. N.I.	48	Lumsden, Sir Peter Stark,[1] *GCB. CSI*	10 Dec. 47	23 May 54		18 Feb. 61	19 Feb. 61	10 Dec. 67	21 Aug. 66	1 Dec. 73	16 Mar. 70	1 July 78	8 Jan. 87	17 Aug. 90
4 Foot	46	Gordon, John James Hood,[2] *CB.* Assistant Military Secretary for Indian Affairs, Horse Gds. 3 Oct. 90	P 21 Aug. 49	9 Jan. 54		2 Dec. 59	30 Nov. 60	22 Aug. 65	23 Mar. 69	21 Aug. 75	23 Feb. 77	20 Dec. 86	3 Jan. 91	1 Apr. 94
19 Hussars	42	F/C Gough, Sir Hugh Henry,[3] *KCB.*	4 Sept. 53	9 Aug. 55		4 Jan. 61	5 Jan. 61	4 Sept. 73	30 Mar. 64	4 Sept. 79	1 Oct. 77	6 Feb. 87	13 June 91	16 May 94
		LIEUTENANT GENERALS.												
5 Bo. N.I.	42	Hogg, Adam George Forbes,[4] *CB.*	4 Jan. 54	21 Apr. 57		4 Jan. 66	15 Aug. 68	4 Jan. 74	11 July 77	1 Jan. 80	17 Dec. 79	1 July 81	1 Apr. 90	10 June 93
43 Bo. N.I.	45	Anderson, Horace Searle,[5] *CB.* Com. Mhow District	6 Apr. 50	18 Sept. 53		29 Nov. 59	2 Jan. 70	6 Apr. 70		6 Apr. 76	6 Apr. 81	6 Feb. 82	1 Apr. 90	20 Sept. 94
45 Bo. N.I.	45	La Touche, Cecil D'Urban[7]	23 July 50	23 Nov. 56		29 July 62		29 July 70		29 July 76	1 July 81	1 July 81	13 June 91	20 Sept. 94
70 Be. N.I.	45	Harris, Philip Henry Farrell,[8] *CB.*	23 Dec. 50	23 Nov. 56		20 Dec. 62		20 Dec. 70			1 July 81	17 Apr. 82	22 Oct. 92	22 Sept. 94
		MAJOR GENERALS.												
47 M. N.I.	45	Grant, Seafield Falkland Murray Treasure[9]	20 Jan. 51	5 Oct. 55	20 Jan. 63	16 July 64		20 Jan. 71		20 Jan. 77	1 July 81	25 Apr. 92		
13 Bo. N.I.	40	Beville, George Francis,[10] *CB.* [R]	4 Sept. 55	4 Jan. 58		4 Sept. 67	15 Aug. 68	4 June 78	11 July 77	4 June 78	11 July 81	23 Sept. 92		
27 Be. N.I.	41	McQueen, Sir John Withers,[11] *KCB.*	4 Apr. 54	4 June 57		4 Apr. 66		4 Apr. 72	4 Apr. 72	4 Apr. 80	4 Apr. 80	3 Dec. 81	10 Dec. 92	
79 Foot	41	Mackey, William Henry[12]	11 Aug. 54	8 Dec. 54		6 Dec. 59	4 Jan. 70	4 Apr. 74	1 Oct. 77	1 Aug. 80	3 Feb. 82	10 Dec. 92		
95 Foot	36	F/C Chaucer, George Nicholas,[13] *CB.* Commanding Rohilcund District, Bengal Army [R]	4 Sept. 59	25 May 61		4 Sept. 71	12 Apr. 76	4 Sept. 79	22 Nov. 79	4 Sept. 85	21 Nov. 83	27 Apr. 93		
7 Foot	42	p.s.c. Little, Henry Alexander,[14] *CB.*	16 Mar. 55	P 29 May 57		P 14 Oct. 68	31 Mar. 69	31 Mar. 78	1 Oct. 77	16 May 82	13 May 82	10 June 93		
5 K.R.	39	Palmer, Sir Arthur Power,[15] *KCB.* Commanding Allahabad District, Bengal Army [R]	20 Feb. 57	30 Apr. 58		20 Feb. 69		20 Feb. 77	20 Feb. 77	20 Feb. 83	22 Nov. 83	10 June 93		
70 Be. N.I.	42	Middleton, Charles Smith,[16] *CB. CIE.*	14 Dec. 53	23 Nov. 56		14 Dec. 65		14 Dec. 73	22 Nov. 75	14 Dec. 79	22 Nov. 83	2 Sept. 93		
27 M. N.I.	41	Faunce, Edmund,[17] *CB.*	4 Sept. 55	4 Jan. 58		20 Dec. 60		4 Sept. 75	22 Nov. 79	4 Sept. 81	20 Nov. 83	12 Nov. 93		
21 Be. N.I.	41	Campbell, Robert Byng Patricia Price,[18]† *CB.*	4 Sept. 55	2 Sept. 57		4 Sept. 67		4 Sept. 75	22 Nov. 79	4 Sept. 81	20 Nov. 83	19 Nov. 93		
79 Foot	39	Chapman, Hamilton[19]	15 July 56	23 Nov. 56		15 July 68		15 July 76	22 Nov. 79	15 July 82	20 Nov. 83	20 Dec. 93		
17 Be. N.I.	38	Ross, Alexander George,[19] *CB.* [R]	20 Nov. 57	4 Nov. 59		20 Nov. 69		4 Nov. 77	22 Nov. 79	4 Nov. 83	20 Jan. 83	1 Apr. 94		
34 Be. N.I.	42	Hennessy, George Robertson,[20] *CB.*	4 Feb. 54	11 Dec. 57		4 Feb. 66		4 Feb. 74		4 Feb. 80	4 Feb. 84	9 June 94		
22 Bo. N.I.	41	Boyd, Julius Middleton[21]	6 Sept. 54	23 Nov. 56		P 6 Sept. 66	12 Sept. 66	6 Sept. 74		6 Sept. 80	4 Sept. 84	20 Sept. 94		
55 Bo. N.I.	41	La Touche, William Puget[22]	20 Jan. 55	31 Mar. 58		20 Jan. 67		20 Jan. 75		20 Jan. 81	20 Jan. 85	24 Sept. 94		
19 Bo. N.I.	41	Browne, Swinton John,[23] *CB.*												
55 Bo. N.I.	41	Jacob, William[24]												
5 F.R.	39	Lance, Frederick,[25] *CB.* Commanding Presidency District, Bengal Army [R]	13 June 56	14 Sept. 57		13 June 68		13 June 76	2 Mar. 81	13 June 82	2 Mar. 85	24 Dec. 94		
5 F.R.	39	Smith, Joseph Barnard[26]	25 June 56	30 Apr. 58		26 June 68		26 June 76	2 Mar. 81	26 June 82	2 Mar. 85	3 Mar. 55		
		LIEUTENANT COLONELS.												
56 Be. N.I.	41	Matthews, Charles Richard,[27] Residing out of India	20 Mar. 55	30 Sept. 58		20 Mar. 67		20 Mar. 75		20 Mar. 81	20 Mar. 85			
56 Foot	40	Swinhoe, Charles,[28] Residing out of India	4 Sept. 55	8 Sept. 57		27 July 67		27 July 75		27 July 81	27 July 85			
30 M. N.I.	40	St. John, Frederick Charles,[31] Colonel on the Staff, Bellary	20 Jan. 56	17 Aug. 59		20 Jan. 68		20 Jan. 76		20 Jan. 82	20 Jan. 86			
8 M. N.I.	39	Rolland, Alexander Tulloch,[32] Residing out of India	4 Apr. 56	26 Jan. 57		4 Apr. 68		4 Apr. 76		4 Apr. 82	4 Apr. 86			
35 M. N.I.	39	Higginson, Theophilus,[33] *CB.* Residing out of India	26 June 56	24 July 58		26 June 68		26 June 76		26 June 82	26 June 86			
13 Bo. N.I.	39	Birt, George Corrie,[34] *CB.* Commanding Mandalay District, Burmah, with rank of Major General [R]	20 Sept. 56	17 Oct. 57		20 Sept. 68		20 Sept. 76		20 Sept. 82	30 Sept. 86			
13 Bo. N.I.	39	Tweedie, Maurice,[5] Deputy Inspector General of Police, Allahabad, Oude	20 Sept. 56	17 May 59		20 Sept. 68		20 Sept. 76		20 Sept. 82	30 Sept. 86			
49 M. N.I.	39	Wroughton, William Nesbitt, Residing out of India	23 Sept. 56	28 Apr. 58		23 Sept. 68		23 Sept. 76		23 Sept. 82	23 Sept. 86			

Indian Staff Corps.

Last Regiment.	Serv. Yrs.	LIEUTENANT COLONELS.	2ND LIEUT. CORNET, OR ENSIGN.	LIEUT.	BREVET CAPTAIN.	CAPTAIN.	BREVET MAJOR.	MAJOR.	BREVET LT. COL.	LIEUT. COLONEL.	BREVET COLONEL.
29 Bo. N.I.	39	Jopp, John,[36] *CB*. Brigadier General Commanding Aden District; *Aide de Camp to the Queen* [R]	20 Oct. 56	4 Aug. 60	......	20 Oct. 68	......	20 Oct. 76	......	20 Oct. 82	20 Oct. 86
38 Be. N.I.	39	Clifford, Robert Cecil Richard,[37] *CB*. Colonel on the Staff, Cawnpore [R]	13 Dec. 56	6 June 57	......	13 Dec. 68	......	13 Dec. 76	2 Mar. 81	13 Dec. 82	2 Mar. 87
3 E.R.	39	Jarrett, Henry Sullivan,[38] *CIE*. Residing out of India.	13 Dec. 56	1 July 57	......	13 Dec. 68	......	13 Dec. 76	......	13 Dec. 82	13 Dec. 86
16 Be. N.I.	39	Grey, Leopold John Herbert,[39] *CSI*. Residing out of India.	13 Dec. 56	15 Sept. 57	......	13 Dec. 68	......	13 Dec. 76	2 Mar. 81	13 Dec. 82	2 Mar. 87
51 Be. N.I.	39	Pratt, Henry Marsh,[40] *CB*. [R] Permitted to reside out of India.	13 Dec. 56	30 Apr. 58	......	13 Dec. 68	......	13 Dec. 76	......	13 Dec. 82	2 Mar. 87
12 Bo. N.I.	39	Jacob, George Adolphus. Permitted to reside in Europe	13 Dec. 56	20 May 58	......	13 Dec. 68	......	13 Dec. 76	......	13 Dec. 82	13 Dec. 86
22 M. N.I.	39	Underwood, Thomas Ormsby	13 Dec. 56	1 Oct. 59	......	13 Dec. 68	......	13 Dec. 76	......	13 Dec. 82	13 Dec. 86
27 M. N.I.	39	Porteous, Charles Arkcoll.[41] Residing out of India.	13 Dec. 56	8 June 61	......	13 Dec. 68	......	13 Dec. 76	......	13 Dec. 82	13 Dec. 86
21 Be. N.I.	39	Sanderson, Henry Bristow.[42] *CIE*.	13 Dec. 56	8 June 57	......	13 Dec. 68	......	13 Dec. 76	......	13 Dec. 82	13 Dec. 86
19 M. N.I.	39	Atkins, George.[44] Residing out of India.	20 Dec. 56	30 Apr. 58	......	20 Dec. 68	......	20 Dec. 76	......	20 Dec. 82	20 Dec. 86
12 Bo. N.I.	39	Chambers, Charles James Osborn[43]	20 Dec. 56	20 Sept. 59	......	20 Dec. 68	......	20 Dec. 76	......	20 Dec. 82	20 Dec. 86
47 M. N.I.	39	Wilson, William Henry,[44] Commissioner of Police, Bombay	20 Dec. 56	2 May 61	......	20 Dec. 68	......	20 Dec. 76	......	20 Dec. 82	20 Dec. 86
52 M. N.I.	39	Furlong, Malcolm.[45] Residing out of India.	4 Jan. 57	14 Feb. 59	......	4 Jan. 69	......	4 Jan. 77	......	4 Jan. 83	4 Jan. 87
25 Be. N.I.	39	Strover, George Augustus. Residing out of India.	20 Jan. 57	7 Jan. 59	......	20 Jan. 69	......	20 Jan. 77	......	20 Jan. 83	20 Jan. 87
38 M. N.I.	39	Vertue, William. Residing out of India.	20 Jan. 57	2 Mar. 60	......	20 Jan. 69	......	20 Jan. 77	......	20 Jan. 83	20 Jan. 87
10 Bo. N.I.	39	Ewart, Charles Henry.[46] Residing out of India.	20 Feb. 57	30 Apr. 58	......	20 Feb. 69	......	20 Feb. 77	......	20 Feb. 83	20 Feb. 87
42 M. N.I.	39	Prendergast, James Henry,[49] Brigadier General Comdg. Southern Dist., Madras	3 Mar. 57	21 Sept. 58	......	3 Mar. 69	......	3 Mar. 77	......	3 Mar. 83	3 Mar. 87
39 M. N.I.	39	Newport, Charles Peter.[51] Residing out of India.	4 Mar. 57	28 Nov. 58	......	4 Mar. 69	......	4 Mar. 77	......	4 Mar. 83	4 Mar. 87
40 M. N.I.	39	FitzGerald, Charles John Oswald.[52] *CB*. Residing out of India	4 Mar. 57	27 Nov. 59	......	4 Mar. 69	......	4 Mar. 77	......	4 Mar. 83	4 Mar. 87
8 M. N.I.	39	Oakes, George Henry. Residing out of India.	4 Mar. 57	2 Sept. 60	......	4 Mar. 69	......	4 Mar. 77	......	4 Mar. 83	4 Mar. 87
	39	Sewell, Henry Fane Haylett.[54] Supdt. of Family Payments and Pensions, Madras	20 Mar. 57	2 Feb. 60	......	20 Mar. 69	......	20 Mar. 77	......	20 Mar. 83	20 Mar. 87
3 I Foot	38	Hesketh, Robert Walter. Residing out of India	20 Mar. 57	2 Feb. 60	......	20 Mar. 69	......	20 Mar. 77	......	20 Mar. 83	20 Mar. 87
6 M. N.I.	38	Vanderzee, Francis Henry.[55] Residing out of India	7 Apr. 57	18 Feb. 59	......	7 Apr. 69	......	7 Apr. 77	......	7 Apr. 83	7 Apr. 87
4 Bo. N.I.	38	Gordon, James Henry,[56] *CB. DSO*. Residing out of India.	20 Apr. 57	24 June 59	......	20 Apr. 69	......	20 Apr. 77	......	20 Apr. 83	7 Apr. 87
40 Be. N.I.	38	Codrington, George Henry Forbes. Residing out of India.	13 June 57	10 Jan. 59	......	13 June 69	......	13 June 77	......	13 June 83	13 June 87
28 Be. N.I.	38	Szczepanski, Henry Chas. Antony,[57] Dep. Commr. 1st Cl. Hyderabad Assigned Dist.	13 June 57	18 May 58	......	13 June 69	......	13 June 77	......	13 June 83	13 June 87
20 M. N.I.	38	Scott, Thomas Augustus. Residing out of India.	13 June 57	18 May 58	......	13 June 69	......	13 June 77	......	13 June 83	13 June 87
19 Bo. N.I.	38	Malden, Robert Vaughan.[58] Residing out of India.	13 June 57	2 Dec. 58	......	13 June 69	......	13 June 77	......	13 June 83	13 June 87
42 M. N.I.	38	Swifte, Joshua Waddington. Residing out of India.	13 June 57	16 Jan. 59	......	13 June 69	......	13 June 77	......	13 June 83	13 June 87
23 Bo. N.I.	38	Gatacre, John,[59] *CB*. Commanding Nagpore District, Bombay Army	13 June 57	15 Aug. 60	......	13 June 69	......	13 June 77	......	13 June 83	13 June 87
52 M. N.I.	38	FitzPatrick, Francis Skelton.[60] Residing out of India.	13 June 57	25 May 60	......	13 June 69	......	13 July 77	......	13 July 83	11 July 87
2 E.R.	38	Kilgour, Frederick, Deputy Inspector General of Police, Northern Range, Madras	13 June 57	2 June 60	......	13 June 69	......	13 July 77	......	13 July 83	11 July 87
38 Be. N.I.	38	Seton, Sir William Samuel,[61] *Bart*. Residing out of India.	11 July 57	18 May 58	......	20 July 69	......	20 July 77	......	20 July 83	20 July 87
34 Be. N.I.	38	Hills, George Scott.[63] Residing out of India	20 July 57	18 May 58	......	4 Aug. 69	......	4 Aug. 77	......	4 Aug. 83	4 Aug. 87
1 E.R.	38	Waterfield, Henry Gordon.[61] Colonel on the Staff, Ferozepore	4 Aug. 57	18 May 58	......	4 Aug. 69	......	4 Aug. 77	......	4 Aug. 83	4 Aug. 87
105 Foot	38	Luxmoore, Coryndon Thos. Putt.[63] Residing out of India.	4 Aug. 57	13 June 59	......	4 Aug. 69	......	4 Aug. 77	......	4 Aug. 83	4 Aug. 87
17 Bo. N.I.	38	Blair, Henry William. Residing out of India.	4 Aug. 57	18 Nov. 59	......	4 Aug. 69	......	4 Aug. 77	......	4 Aug. 83	4 Aug. 87
6 E.R.	38	Miles, Samuel Barrett. Residing out of India	20 Aug. 57	2 Jan. 61	......	20 Aug. 69	......	20 Aug. 77	2 Mar. 81	20 Aug. 83	20 Aug. 87
22 Be. N.I.	38	Cologan, John Francis FitzGerald.[64] *CB*. Residing out of India.	4 Sept. 57	17 June 58	......	4 Sept. 69	......	4 Sept. 77	2 Mar. 81	4 Sept. 83	2 Mar. 87
Artillery	38	Sartorius, George Conrad,[65] *CB*. Colonel on the Staff, Nusseerabad	20 Sept. 57	15 Aug. 58	......	20 Sept. 69	......	20 Sept. 77	......	20 Sept. 83	22 July 86
32 Bo. N.I.	38	Pennington, Charles Richard,[69] *CB*. Commanding a District, Bengal Army	4 Oct. 57	1 Oct. 58	......	4 Oct. 69	......	4 Oct. 77	......	4 Oct. 83	1 Oct. 87
13 Bo. N.I.	38	Crawford, Richmond Irvine,[70] Collector and Magistrate of Kurrachee	4 Oct. 57	18 May 58	......	4 Oct. 69	......	4 Oct. 77	2 Mar. 81	4 Oct. 83	2 Mar. 85
74 Be. N.I.	38	Dodd, Charles Albert.[71] Residing out of India	4 Oct. 57	18 May 58	......	4 Oct. 69	......	4 Oct. 77	......	4 Oct. 83	4 Oct. 87
49 Be. N.I.	38	Brereton, Willoughby Thomas.[72] Nair Brigade	4 Oct. 57	18 Feb. 61	......	4 Oct. 69	......	4 Oct. 77	......	4 Oct. 83	4 Oct. 87
27 Be. N.I.	38	Horsford, Norman Macleod Thomas,[73] Chief Commissioner, Andaman and Nicobar Islands, and Superintendent of Port Blair.	10 Oct. 57	17 Feb. 61	......	10 Oct. 69	......	10 Oct. 77	......	10 Oct. 83	10 Oct. 87
5 M. N.I.	38	Cox, Henry William Holmes, Commissioner of Police, Madras	20 Nov. 57	26 May 58	......	20 Nov. 69	......	20 Nov. 77	......	20 Nov. 83	20 Nov. 87
33 Foot	38	Philips, James.[74] Residing out of India.	P 27 Nov. 57	31 Oct. 59	......	27 Nov. 69	......	27 Nov. 77	......	27 Nov. 83	27 Nov. 87
20 Hussars	38	Hogg, Theodore William, Deputy Commissioner, 1st Class, Sangor, Central Prov.	4 Dec. 57	18 May 58	......	4 Dec. 69	......	4 Dec. 77	......	4 Dec. 83	4 Dec. 87

Indian Staff Corps.

Last Regiment.	Yrs. Serv.	LIEUTENANT COLONELS.	2ND LIEUT. CORNET, OR ENSIGN.	LIEUT.	BREVET CAPTAIN.	CAPTAIN.	BREVET MAJOR.	MAJOR.	BREVET LT. COL.	LIEUT. COLONEL.	BREVET COLONEL.
1 E.R.	38	Tabuteau, Thomas Rooke,[76] Commandant Bangalore Rifle Volunteers	11 Dec. 57	1 Jan. 62	.....	11 Dec. 69	.....	11 Dec. 77	.....	11 Dec. 83	11 Dec. 87
Artillery	38	Wilkins, William Henry, Assistant Surveyor General, Revenue Survey, Calcutta	12 Dec. 57	27 Aug. 56	.....	12 Dec. 69	.....	12 Dec. 77	.....	12 Dec. 83	11 Dec. 87
Artillery	38	Grierson, John. Residing out of India	12 Dec. 57	27 Aug. 58	.....	12 Dec. 69	.....	12 Dec. 77	.....	12 Dec. 83	12 Dec. 87
10 M. N.I.	38	Shaw, Elphinstone. Residing out of India	12 Dec. 57	11 July	.....	12 Dec. 69	.....	12 Dec. 77	.....	12 Dec. 83	12 Dec. 87
3 E.R.	38	Chrystie, George,[77] Deputy Inspector General of Police, Southern Range, Madras	12 Dec. 57	1 Feb. 60	.....	12 Dec. 69	.....	12 Dec. 77	.....	12 Dec. 83	12 Dec. 87
91 Foot	38	Spearman, Horace Ralph, Commissioner, 1st Grade, Tenasserim Division, Burmah	18 Dec. 57	1 Feb. 60	.....	18 Dec. 69	.....	18 Dec. 77	.....	18 Dec. 83	18 Dec. 87
65 Be. N.I.	38	Macpherson, James Duncan,[78] Residing out of India	18 Dec. 57	1 Aug. 59	.....	18 Dec. 69	.....	18 Dec. 77	.....	18 Dec. 83	18 Dec. 87
24 Be. N.I.	38	Jacob, Herbert Bruce,[79] Pension Paymaster, Southern Konkan	19 Dec. 57	13 Dec. 58	.....	19 Dec. 69	.....	19 Dec. 77	.....	19 Dec. 83	18 Dec. 87
10 M. N.I.	38	Cotton, Thomas James,[80] Residing out of India	4 Jan. 58	9 Sept. 59	.....	4 Jan. 70	.....	20 Dec. 77	.....	20 Dec. 83	20 Dec. 87
40 M. N.I.	38	Protheroe, Montague,[81] CB. CSI. Brigadier General Commanding Hyderabad Contingent ; Aide de Camp to the Queen	4 Jan. 58	9 Mar. 60	.....	4 Jan. 70	.....	4 Jan. 78	.....	4 Jan. 84	4 Jan. 87
14 Bo. N.I.	38	Cahill, Charles John Stannion	20 Jan. 58	21 Feb. 59	.....	20 Jan. 70	.....	20 Jan. 78	.....	20 Jan. 84	17 May 86
48 Be. N.I.	38	Atkins, Robert.[82] Residing out of India	4 Feb. 58	7 June 58	.....	4 Feb. 70	.....	4 Feb. 78	.....	20 Jan. 84	4 Feb. 88
2 Be. N.I.	38	Marett, James Richard,[83] District Judge, 3rd Grade, Seetapore, Oude	4 Feb. 58	25 Dec. 58	.....	4 Feb. 70	.....	4 Feb. 78	.....	4 Feb. 84	4 Feb. 88
3 E.R.	38	Whitlock, Charles James Toller,[84] Superintendent of Police, Central Range	20 Feb. 58	9 Mar. 60	.....	4 Feb. 70	.....	4 Feb. 78	.....	20 Feb. 84	4 Feb. 88
39 M. N.I.	38	Magrath, Hy. Marsh Septimus, Magist. and Pres.of the Municipal Comm. Bangalore	4 Mar. 58	1 Feb. 59	.....	4 Mar. 70	.....	4 Mar. 78	.....	4 Mar. 84	4 Mar. 88
33 M. N.I.	38	Eyre, Edmund Henry,[85] CB. Quarter Master General of the Madras Army, with rank of Brigadier General	4 Mar. 58	1 Jan. 62	.....	4 Mar. 70	.....	4 Mar. 78	.....	4 Mar. 84	1 July 87
104 Foot	38	Bunbury, William Reeves,[86] Residing out of India	31 Mar. 58	27 Mar. 63	.....	31 Mar. 70	.....	31 Mar. 78	.....	31 Mar. 84	31 Mar. 88
37 Be. N.I.	37	Michell, James William Abbot,[87] Commanding at Dinapore	4 Apr. 58	25 Jan. 61	.....	4 Apr. 70	.....	4 Apr. 78	.....	4 Apr. 84	4 Apr. 88
Artillery	37	Mackenzie, Kenneth Jas. Loch, CIE. Judicial Commr., Hyderabad Assigned Dists.	11 June 58	27 Aug. 58	.....	11 June 70	.....	11 June 78	.....	11 June 84	11 June 88
Artillery	37	Macdougall, James William, Deputy Comur.. 1st Class, Betul, Central Provinces	11 June 58	27 Aug. 58	.....	11 June 70	.....	11 June 78	.....	11 June 84	11 June 88
Artillery	37	Trevor, Geo. Herb., CB. Resident, 1st Cl., and Gov. General's Agent in Rajpootana	11 June 58	27 Aug. 58	.....	11 June 70	.....	11 June 78	.....	11 June 84	11 June 88
Artillery	37	Bowie, Mathew Morton, Comr r. Narbudda Div., Hoshungabad, Central Prov.	12 June 58	27 Aug. 58	.....	12 June 70	.....	12 June 78	.....	12 June 84	11 June 88
30 Bo. N.I.	37	Carpendale, Montagu Maxwell.[88] Permitted to reside in Europe	12 June 58	2 June 59	.....	12 June 70	.....	12 June 78	.....	12 June 84	2 June 88
8 Bo. N.I.	37	Morse, Henry Charles.[89] Residing out of India	12 June 58	1 Oct. 58	.....	12 June 70	.....	12 June 78	.....	12 June 84	12 June 88
34 M. N.I.	37	Haschell, David Thompson. Residing out of India	12 June 58	19 July 60	.....	12 June 70	.....	12 June 78	.....	12 June 84	12 June 88
42 M. N.I.	37	Grove, Alexander Sinclair.[90] DSO. Assistant Adjutant General, Burmah	12 June 58	1 Oct. 61	.....	12 June 70	.....	12 June 78	.....	12 June 84	12 June 88
104 Foot	37	Evans, Horace Moule,[91] CB. Colonel on the Staff, Fyzabad	12 June 58	1 Oct. 61	.....	12 June 70	.....	12 June 78	.....	12 June 84	12 June 88
28 Bo. N.I.	37	Cuningham, Charles Alexander,[92] Secretary to Bombay Government, Military, &c., Departments, with rank of Brigadier General	20 June 58	2 Jan. 59	.....	20 June 70	.....	20 June 78	2 Mar. 81	20 June 84	2 Mar. 85
60 Be. N.I.	37	Clifford, Richard Melville,[93] Assistant Adjutant General, Peshawur	20 June 58	26 July 61	.....	20 June 70	.....	20 June 78	.....	20 June 84	20 June 88
17 M. N.I.	37	Hallett, Hy. Honywood H.,[94] Deputy Commissioner, 2nd Class, Central Provinces.	25 June 58	22 Oct. 58	.....	25 June 70	.....	25 June 78	.....	25 June 84	25 June 88
49 M. N.I.	37	Hoskins, William Henry, 1st Grade Superintendent of Police, Madras	4 July 58	2 Jan. 59	.....	4 July 70	.....	4 July 78	.....	4 July 84	4 July 88
66 Be. N.I.	37	Young, George.[95] Residing out of India	20 July 58	31 July 60	.....	20 July 70	.....	20 July 78	.....	20 July 84	20 July 88
41 M. N.I.	37	Rowlandson, Michael Alexander.[96]	20 Aug. 58	20 Apr. 60	.....	20 Aug. 70	.....	20 Aug. 78	.....	20 Aug. 84	20 Aug. 88
20 M. N.I.	37	Goldie, James Ord. Residing out of India	20 Aug. 58	17 June 60	.....	20 Aug. 70	.....	20 Aug. 78	.....	20 Aug. 84	20 Aug. 88
103 Foot	37	Vallings, Adolphus.[97] Residing out of India	4 Sept. 58	1 Jan. 60	.....	4 Sept. 70	.....	4 Sept. 78	.....	4 Sept. 84	4 Sept. 88
16 M. N.I.	37	Elton, Henry Strachan.[98] Residing out of India	20 Sept. 58	24 May 59	.....	20 Sept. 70	.....	20 Sept. 78	.....	20 Sept. 84	20 Sept. 88
1 M. N.I.	37	Doveton, John Chadwick. Residing out of India	20 Oct. 58	14 Feb. 61	.....	20 Oct. 70	.....	20 Oct. 78	.....	20 Oct. 84	1 July 87
1 Be. N.I.	37	Parker, William Jackson	20 Oct. 58	1 Oct. 58	.....	20 Oct. 70	.....	20 Oct. 78	.....	20 Oct. 84	20 Oct. 88
107 Foot	37	Willis, James L. N. Residing out of India	4 Nov. 58	26 Aug. 60	.....	4 Nov. 70	.....	4 Nov. 78	.....	4 Nov. 84	4 Nov. 88
17 M. N.I.	37	Butler, James William Smith.[99] Residing out of India	13 Nov. 58	21 June 61	13 Nov. 70	12 June 71	.....	13 Nov. 78	.....	13 Nov. 84	13 Nov. 88
42 M. N.I.	37	Stewart, Hopton Scott,[99a] Commanding Madras Volunteer Guards	20 Nov. 58	26 Apr. 61	.....	20 Nov. 70	.....	20 Nov. 78	.....	20 Nov. 84	20 Nov. 88
30 Ba. N.I.	37	Coiils, Francis William,[100] CB. Permitted to reside out of India.	4 Dec. 58	1 Oct. 58	.....	4 Dec. 70	.....	4 Dec. 78	.....	4 Dec. 84	4 Dec. 88
Artillery	37	Jacob, Samuel Swinton, CIE. Superintending Engineer, 1st Grade, Joypore	10 Dec. 58	29 Mar. 59	.....	10 Dec. 70	.....	10 Dec. 78	.....	10 Dec. 84	10 Dec. 85
Artillery	37	Major, Francis Ward. Residing out of India	.....	10 Dec. 58	.....	10 Dec. 70	.....	10 Dec. 78	.....	10 Dec. 84	10 Dec. 88
16 Be. N.I.	37	Godfrey, Charles Willis, Superintendent, Revenue Survey, Konkan	11 Dec. 58	29 Mar. 59	.....	11 Dec. 70	.....	11 Dec. 78	.....	11 Dec. 84	11 Dec. 88
2 Bo. N.I.	37	Lane, Clayton Turner, Insp. General of Police and Jails, Hyderabad Assigned Dists.	11 Dec. 58	15 Mar. 59	.....	11 Dec. 70	.....	11 Dec. 78	.....	11 Dec. 84	11 Dec. 88
58 Be. N.I.	37	Brooke, William Saurin. Residing out of India	11 Dec. 58	15 July 59	.....	11 Dec. 70	.....	11 Dec. 78	2 Mar. 81	11 Dec. 84	2 Mar. 85
43 Be. N.I.	37	Syn, John Munro,[102] CB. Residing out of India	11 Dec. 58	20 Aug. 59	.....	11 Dec. 70	.....	11 Dec. 78	2 Mar. 81	11 Dec. 84	2 Mar. 85
	37	Handcock, Arthur Gore,[102] CB. Colonel on the Staff, Delhi								11 Dec. 84	2 Mar. 85

Indian Staff Corps.

Last Regiment.	Ser- vice, yrs.	Lieutenant Colonels.	2nd Lieut. Cornet, or Ensign.	Lieut.	Brevet Captain.	Captain.	Brevet Major.	Major.	Brevet Lt. Col.	Lieut. Colonel.	Brevet Colonel.
25 M. N.I.	37	Ludlow, Edmund Samuel, [105] *CIE.* Deputy Commissioner, 2nd Class, Berar; Inspector General of Police under Nizam's Government	11 Dec. 58	1 Sept. 60	......	11 Dec. 70	......	11 Dec. 78	......	11 Dec. 84	11 Dec. 88
103 Foot	37	Nutt, Henry Lowther, Political Superintendent, Sawant Warree; Commandant Sawant Warree Local Corps.	11 Dec. 58	30 July 62	......	11 Dec. 70	......	11 Dec. 78	......	11 Dec. 84	11 Dec. 88
73 Be. N.I.	37	Hawes, Alex. James Donnelly, [105] *DSO.* Permitted to reside out of India	6 Jan. 59	9 Nov. 60	......	6 Jan. 71	......	6 Jan. 79	......	6 Jan. 85	6 Jan. 89
65 Be. N.I.	37	Thomas, Robert Mosely Bryce, [105] *DSO.* Inspector General of Police, Central Provinces	6 Jan. 59	9 Nov. 60	......	6 Jan. 71	......	6 Jan. 79	......	6 Jan. 85	6 Jan. 89
37 M. N.I.	37	Bruce, Elliott Armstrong, [105] Commissary General, Eastern Circle	6 Jan. 59	4 Aug. 61	......	6 Jan. 71	......	6 Jan. 79	......	6 Jan. 85	1 July 87
58 Foot	37	Bromhead, Sir Benjamin Parnell, *Bart.* [110] *CB.* Gov. of Aitchison College, Lahore	18 Jan. 59	7 Mar. 63	......	18 Jan. 71	......	18 Jan. 79	......	18 Jan. 85	18 Jan. 89
73 Bo. N.I.	37	Senior, Henry William John, [115] Residing out of India	4 Mar. 59	9 Mar. 61	......	4 Mar. 71	......	4 Mar. 79	......	19 Mar. 85	4 Mar. 89
76 Bo. N.I.	37	Westmacott, Richard, [114] *CB. DSO.* Assistant Adjutant General, Poona	19 Mar. 59	20 Feb. 61	......	19 Mar. 71	......	19 Mar. 79	......	19 Mar. 85	19 Mar. 89
Infantry	36	Salmon, William Arthur, Political Superintendent, Palampore	12 April 59	14 May 61	......	12 Apr. 71	......	12 Apr. 79	......	12 Apr. 85	12 Apr. 89
Artillery	36	Waterhouse, James, Superintendent 2nd Grade, Calcutta	......	10 June 59	......	10 June 71	......	10 June 79	......	10 June 85	10 June 89
Artillery	36	Hancock, George Edward, Political Agent, Kolapore, &c., and Officiating President of the Rajasthanic Court, Kattywar	......	10 June 59	......	10 June 71	......	10 June 79	......	10 June 85	10 June 89
Infantry	36	Hay, James, [115] Permitted to reside out of India.	11 June 59	22 Nov. 60	......	11 June 71	......	11 June 79	......	11 June 85	11 June 89
Infantry	36	Fagan, James Lawrie, [116] Assistant Commissary General, 2nd Class, Jubbulpore	11 June 59	9 July 61	......	11 June 71	......	11 June 79	......	11 June 85	11 June 89
Infantry	36	Byng, Thomas Richard, [117] Residing out of India	11 June 59	1 Jan. 62	......	11 June 71	......	11 June 79	......	11 June 85	11 June 89
Artillery	36	Wilmer, John Randal, Supdt. and Grade, Topographical Survey of India	22 June 59	22 June 59	22 June 71	22 June 71	......	22 June 79	......	22 June 85	22 June 89
107 Foot	36	Garbett, Colin Hubert, Deputy Commissioner, 1st Grade, Hazeerabagh, Bengal	......	4 Feb. 61	......	7 June 71	......	27 June 79	......	27 June 85	27 June 89
Infantry	36	Peart, George Richard, [119] Commandant Bhopaul Battalion	12 Aug. 59	1 Jan. 62	......	12 Aug. 71	......	12 Aug. 79	......	12 Aug. 85	12 Aug. 89
11 Foot	36	Lillingston, Edw. Gordon. [120] Permitted to reside out of India	30 Aug. 59	17 Nov. 63	......	30 Aug. 71	......	30 Aug. 79	......	30 Aug. 85	30 Aug. 89
72 Hussars	36	Pitcher, Duncan George, Director of Land Records, Gwalior State, Central India	3 Sept. 59	1 Jan. 62	3 Sept. 71	3 Sept. 71	......	3 Sept. 79	......	3 Sept. 85	3 Sept. 89
Infantry	36	Gunthorpe, Edw. Jas, [121] Dist. Supdt. of Police, 3rd Class, Hyderabad Assigned Dists.	7 Sept. 59	7 Sept. 59	7 Sept. 71	7 Sept. 71	......	7 Sept. 79	......	7 Sept. 85	7 Sept. 89
38 Foot	36	Skinner, George John, [125] *DSO.* Residing out of India	10 Sept. 59	22 Dec. 63	......	1 Dec. 75	......	10 Sept. 74	......	16 Sept. 85	10 Sept. 89
Infantry	36	Marshall, Charles Henry Tilson, Divisional Judge, 1st Grade, Punjab	12 Oct. 59	23 July 61	12 Oct. 71	12 Oct. 73	......	12 Oct. 79	......	12 Oct. 85	12 Oct. 89
Infantry	36	Reynolds, Edward Swatman, [125] Residing out of India	27 Oct. 59	1 Jan. 62	......	27 Oct. 71	......	27 Oct. 79	27 Mar. 81	27 Oct. 85	2 Mar. 85
Infantry	36	Campbell, John Edward, Deputy Conservator of Forests, 1st Grade, N. W. Provs.	10 Dec. 59	26 Sept. 61	......	10 Dec. 71	30 Dec. 79	10 Dec. 79	......	10 Dec. 85	10 Dec. 86
21 Foot	36	Wingate, Thomas Oliver, Executive Engineer, 1st Grade, D.P.W., M.W. Branch	30 Dec. 59	22 Dec. 63	......	30 Dec. 71	......	30 Dec. 79	......	30 Dec. 85	30 Dec. 86
Infantry	36	Skinner, Evelyn Swinton, Deputy Judge Advocate General, Rawul Pindee	4 Jan. 60	7 Mar. 62	......	4 Jan. 72	......	4 Jan. 80	......	4 Jan. 86	4 Jan. 90
Infantry	36	Prideaux, William Francis, [127] *CSI.* Resident at Jeypore.	12 Mar. 60	27 May 62	......	12 Mar. 72	......	12 Mar. 80	......	12 Mar. 86	12 Mar. 90
Artillery	35	Scott, Walter, Commandant 5 Bombay Infantry	4 May 60	......	......	4 May 72	......	4 May 80	18 Nov. 82	4 May 86	18 Nov. 86
Infantry	35	Toker, Allistor Champion, [129] *CB.* Superintendent of Army Clothing, Bengal	......	8 June 60	8 June 72	8 June 72	......	8 June 80	......	8 June 86	8 June 89
Artillery	35	Wilson, Fred. Alexander, [131] and Class Resident; Political Resident, Persian Gulf	......	1 July 60	16 July 72	4 July 72	......	4 July 80	......	4 July 86	4 July 90
Infantry	35	Rivaz, Vincent, [122] Residing out of India	16 July 60	22 Aug. 65	......	4 July 72	......	16 July 80	......	16 July 86	16 July 90
105 Foot	35	Cowie, Thomas Renny, District and Sessions Judge, 2nd Grade, Fyzabad, Oude	7 Sept. 60	17 Mar. 65	......	7 Sept. 72	......	2 Sept. 80	15 June 85	2 Sept. 86	15 June 89
Artillery	35	Money, Elliot Alexander, Commandant 3 Bengal Cavalry	......	30 Dec. 62	......	2 Oct. 72	......	2 Oct. 80	......	2 Oct. 86	2 Oct. 90
20 Hussars	35	Shakespear, Geo. Robt. James, [135] Assistant Adjutant General, Mil.Dept.	12 Nov. 60	12 Nov. 60	12 Nov. 72	12 Nov. 72	......	12 Nov. 80	......	12 Nov. 86	12 Nov. 90
Infantry	35	Lecky, George. Residing out of India.	......	30 Dec. 62	......	19 Dec. 72	......	19 Dec. 80	......	19 Dec. 86	2 Mar. 85
Artillery	35	Steuman, Edward, [139] *CB.* Quarter Master General in India, with rank of Major Gen.	19 Dec. 60	1 Jan. 62	......	19 Dec. 72	......	19 Dec. 80	......	19 Dec. 86	19 Dec. 90
Infantry	35	Shepherd, Charles Edward, Deputy Consulting Engineer, Lucknow	19 Dec. 60	1 Jan. 62	......	19 Dec. 72	......	19 Dec. 80	......	19 Dec. 86	19 Dec. 90
19 Hussars	35	Temple, John Alex., Deputy Commissioner, 1st Class, Jubbulpore, Central Provs.	29 Dec. 60	15 Oct. 69	20 Dec. 72	20 Dec. 72	......	29 Dec. 80	......	20 Dec. 86	20 Dec. 90
6 Foot	35	Dalrymple, Robert Graeme Elphinstone, [140] Residing out of India.	29 Dec. 60	5 Oct. 62	......	29 Dec. 72	......	29 Dec. 80	......	29 Dec. 86	29 Dec. 90
21 Hussars	35	Ebden, Francis Thomas, [142] Residing out of India	15 Jan. 61	4 Oct. 66	......	15 Jan. 73	......	15 Jan. 81	......	15 Jan. 87	15 Jan. 87
79 Foot	35	Carey, Horace Richard Le Marchant, [143] Exam. of Public Works Accounts, Calcutta	4 Feb. 61	2 Dec. 64	......	4 Feb. 73	......	4 Feb. 81	......	4 Feb. 87	4 Feb. 87
Infantry	35	Lawrence, William Alexander, [144] Commandant 17 Bengal Cavalry	24 May 61	4 July 65	......	24 May 73	......	24 May 81	......	24 May 87	16 May 87
		Turner, Augustus Henry, [145] Commanding Wazi[r]istan Delimitation Escort, with rank of Brigadier General.									
Infantry	34	T. G. Hammond, Arthur George, [146] *CB. DSO.* Commandant Corps of Guides; Aide de Camp to the Queen	7 June 61	14 May 62	......	7 June 73	......	7 June 81	......	7 June 87	1 Sept. 91
Infantry	34	Molloy, Edward, [148] Residing out of India	7 June 61	19 June 62	......	7 June 73	2 Mar. 81	7 June 81	......	7 June 87	2 Aug. 93
Infantry	34	Sandeman, John Edward, [147] Superintendent, 1st Grade, Revenue Survey, Calcutta	7 June 61	19 May 62	......	7 June 73	......	7 June 81	......	7 June 87	20 Aug. 93

408

Indian Staff Corps.

Last Regiment.	Yrs. Serv.	LIEUTENANT COLONELS.	2ND LIEUT. CORNET, OR ENSIGN.	LIEUT.	BREVET CAPTAIN.	CAPTAIN.	BREVET MAJOR.	MAJOR.	BREVET LT. COL.	LIEUT. COLONEL.	BREVET COLONEL.
109 Foot	34	Abbott, Henry Byam, Resident, Western States of Rajpootana	7 June 61	30 July 62		7 June 73	2 Mar. 81	7 June 81		7 June 87	23 Aug. 89
Infantry	34	Hughes, Charles Frederick, 150 Commissary General, Madras	7 June 61	31 Jan. 63		7 June 73	2 Nov. 79	7 June 81	27 Jan. 86	8 June 87	27 Jan. 90
Infantry	34	Cook, James, 151 Residing out of India	8 June 61	30 July 62		8 June 73		8 June 81		8 June 87	1 Sept. 91
Infantry	34	Brownlow, Celadon Charles, 152 Commandant 1 Punjab Infantry	8 June 61	30 July 62		8 June 73	2 Mar. 81	8 June 81		8 June 87	28 Dec. 93
Infantry	34	Cummins, James Turner, 153 DSO. Commandant 2 Lancers Hyderabad Contingent	8 June 61	24 July 63	8 June 73	1 Jan. 74		4 June 83		8 June 87	
109 Foot	34	Mayhew, Alfred Hercules, Collector and Magistrate, Shikarpore	8 June 61	23 May 65		8 June 73		8 June 81		8 June 87	
106 Foot	34	Hunter, Frederick Mercer, CB, CSI. Political Agent, Mahi Kanta	8 June 61	25 July 65		8 June 73		8 June 81		12 June 87	29 Aug. 93
Infantry	34	Tandy, Henry Strafford, 154 Assistant Adjutant General, Bombay Army	12 June 61	4 Oct. 63		12 June 73		1 July 81		1 July 87	
Artillery	34	Stace, Edward Vincent, CB. Political Agent, Cutch		1 July 62	1 July 73	16 Nov. 74		27 Aug. 81		27 Aug. 87	29 Aug. 93
106 Foot	34	M‘Nair, Alfred Lionel, 155 Residing out of India	27 Aug. 61	26 Oct. 64		1 Oct. 73	2 Nov. 79	1 Oct. 81		1 Oct. 87	2 Mar. 55
Infantry	34	Badcock, Alex. Robert, 156 CB, CSI. Com. Gen. in Chief, with local rank of Major Gen.	1 Oct. 61	1 Oct. 64		1 July 74		20 Oct. 81		20 Oct. 87	
7 Foot	34	Browne, William Henry	20 Jan. 58	17 July 63		1 Nov. 74	8 Dec. 77	22 Oct. 85	24 Feb. 84	22 Oct. 87	24 Feb. 88
10 Hus.	38	Biddulph, John, 157 Governor General's Agent, Baroda		18 May 58	20 Oct. 73	20 Jan. 75		26 Nov. 81		26 Nov. 87	26 May 91
45 Foot	34	Watling, John Thomas, 158 Deputy Adjutant General, Bombay Army	26 Nov. 61	2 July 64		1 Nov. 74		14 Apr. 83	17 May 86	27 Nov. 87	17 May 90
109 Foot	34	Simpson, George, 159 Deputy Quarter Master General, Madras Army	27 Nov. 61	13 Oct. 64	27 Nov. 73	24 Apr. 81	27	1 Dec. 81		8 Dec. 87	28 Aug. 93
103 Foot	34	Hogg, Arthur Melvill. Residing out of India	12 Dec. 61	14 June 64		1 Dec. 74		18 Dec. 81	1 July 87	18 Dec. 87	5 Oct. 92
Art.	34	Rennick, Robert Henry Francis 160		18 Dec. 61	18 Dec. 73	26 Mar. 74		18 Dec. 81		18 Dec. 87	28 Aug. 93
Art.	34	Warburton, Robt. 161 CSI, Assist. Commr., 1st Grade, Punjab ; Polit. Officer, Khyber		18 Dec. 61		18 Dec. 74	2 Mar. 81	4 Mar. 82		4 Mar. 88	21 Sept. 92
21 Hus.	34	Deane, Thomas, 170 Director of the Army Remount Department	4 Mar. 62	24 Aug. 68		6 May 74		6 May 82		6 May 88	29 Sept. 93
103 Foot	33	Burne, Jasper. Residing out of India	6 May 62	17 Nov. 66		10 June 74	2 Mar. 81	10 June 82		10 June 88	29 Sept. 93
36 Foot	33	Ellis, William Veruer, 163 Commandant 14 Bengal Infantry	10 June 62	15 Nov. 64		29 July 74		29 July 82		29 July 88	23 Aug. 89
21 Foot	33	Clark-Kennedy, Alexander, 173 Assistant Commissary General, 1st Class	28 July 62	9 Dec. 64		29 Aug. 74		29 Aug. 82		1 Aug. 88	
Art.	33	Vaurenen, Jacob Pieter Deneys, 170 Commandant 6 Bengal Cavalry		2 Sept. 62		1 Sept. 74	22 Nov. 79	1 Sept. 82		1 Sept. 88	29 Sept. 93
28 Foot	33	Rogers, George Walters, 177 DSO. Residing out of India		17 May 64	17 May 73	23 Sept. 74		23 Sept. 82		23 Sept. 88	29 Sept. 93
54 Foot	33	Paterson, Henry. 178 Residing out of India	2 Dec. 62	2 Dec. 65		2 Dec. 74	2 Mar. 81	2 Dec. 82		2 Dec. 88	29 Sept. 93
93 Foot	33	Bishop, Edward Harry, 180 Commandant 1 Battalion 5 Goorkha Regiment ; Aide de *Camp to the Queen*.	9 Jan. 63	6 Jan. 66		9 Jan. 75	2 Mar. 81	9 Jan. 83	9 July 87	9 Jan. 89	1 Feb. 93
35 Foot	33	Gascele, Alfred, 181 CB, Commandant 1 Battalion 5 Goorkha Regiment ;										
35 Foot	33	Wood, Henry Mackenzie Macdonald, Divisional Judge, Umballa, Punjab		11 Oct. 66		17 Jan. 75		17 Jan. 83		17 Jan. 89	
82 Foot	33	Thompson, William Oliver, 183 Commandant 3 Sikh Infantry	18 Mar. 63	12 Oct. 66		18 July 75		18 Mar. 83		18 Mar. 89	
21 Foot	33	Davidson, John, 185 Commandant 3 Punjab Cavalry	24 Mar. 63	24 Mar. 66		24 Mar. 75	2 Nov. 79	24 Mar. 83		31 Mar. 89	1 Feb. 95
82 Foot	33	Abbott, George Massol, 186 Residing out of India		31 Mar. 63		31 Mar. 75	2 Mar. 81	31 Mar. 83		31 Mar. 89	
21 Foot	33	Quin, Edward 188	12 May 63	3 Apr. 67		12 May 75		12 June 83	7 Dec. 88	23 June 89	7 Dec. 91
55 Foot	33	Patch, Robert, 189 Commissary General, Western Circle	12 June 63	27 July 66		23 June 75		23 June 83		23 June 89	
3 Dr. Gds.	33	Hodgson, George Robert, Superintendent of Police, Central Range, Madras	23 June 63	26 Apr. 67		1 July 75		1 July 83	15 June 85	1 July 89	15 June 89
Art.	32	p.s.c. Gollen, Sir Edwin Henry Hayter, 190 KCIE. Secretary to Government of India, Military Department, with local rank of Major General		1 July 63	1 July 75	16 July 75		16 July 83		16 July 89	
82 Foot	32	Graves, Henry Affleck, 191 Executive Engineer, 2nd Grade, D.P.W. M.W. Branch		17 July 66		17 July 75		17 July 83		18 July 89	
19 Foot	32	Hutchinson, James Bird, Commissioner, Lahore, Punjab	28 Aug. 63	20 Jan. 68		28 Aug. 75	2 Mar. 81	28 Aug. 83		28 Aug. 89	15 Jan. 95
104 Foot	32	Campbell, Lorn Robert, Henry Dick, 194 Commandant 38 Bengal Infantry	11 Sept. 63	2 Mar. 68		11 Sept. 75		11 Sept. 83		11 Sept. 89	6 Jan. 94
Infantry	32	Hunt, Henry Vere, 195 Assistant Commissary General, 2nd Class, Peshawur	11 Sept. 63	3 Apr. 67		11 Sept. 75		11 Sept. 83		11 Sept. 89	25 May 94
1 3 Foot	32	Stoddart, Charles Henry, 196 Commandant 16 Bengal Infantry	11 Sept. 63	28 Aug. 67		11 Sept. 75		11 Sept. 83		11 Sept. 89	
64 Foot	32	Kelly, James Graves, 197 Commandant 32 Bengal Cavalry	2 Oct. 63	9 Feb. 67		2 Oct. 75		2 Oct. 83		2 Oct. 89	
1 Foot	32	Watts, John Briscoe, 198 Commandant 0 Bengal Infantry	16 Oct. 63	18 Sept. 67		16 Oct. 75		16 Oct. 83	1 July 87	16 Oct. 89	23 Feb. 55
12 Foot	32	Haites, Walter, 199 Commandant 0 Bengal Infantry	16 Oct. 63	24 Nov. 63		24 Nov. 75		24 Nov. 83		1 Nov. 89	26 July 94
2 Dr Gs.	32	Barron, Frank, Deputy Commissioner, 1st Grade, Gonda, Oude	15 Jan. 64	18 Sept. 67		15 Mar. 76		24 Nov. 83		8 Jan. 90	25 May 94
7 Hus.	32	Bartou-Bennet, John Robert, 200 Assist. Commissary General, 1st Class, Umballa		3 Feb. 64			2 Mar. 8	15 Mar. 84		15 Jan. 90	
ErC Vousden, William John, 202 Commandant 5 Punjab Cavalry		2 Feb. 64				2 Mar. 84					
35 Foot	32	Ryfke, Arthur, 203 Commandant 8 Bengal Infantry	2 Feb. 64	29 Aug. 68	1 Jan. 76	1 Feb. 76		2 Feb. 84		2 Feb. 90	16 Feb. 90
4 Foot	32	Harvey-Kelly, Harvey Hamilton, 204 Assist. Com. Gen., 2nd Class, Secunderabad	16 Feb. 64	28 Aug. 68	25 May 71	25 May 76		6 Feb. 84	16 Aug. 89	16 Feb. 85	25 May 94
55 Foot	32	Carruthers, John Thomas, 205 Commandant 16 Bombay Infantry										
19 Foot	32	Miller, John Francis James, 209 Supt. Eng., 2nd Grade, D.P. Works, Umritsur, Punjab	1 Mar. 64	8 Sept. 68		1 Mar. 76		1 Mar. 84		1 Mar. 90	

Indian Staff Corps.

Last Regiment.	Yrs. Serv.	Lieutenant Colonels.	2nd Lieut. Cornet, or Ensign.	Lieut.	Brevet Captain.	Captain.	Brevet Major.	Major.	Brevet Lt. Col.	Lieut. Colonel.	Brevet Colonel.
108 Foot	32	Cooke, Crawfold Boyd,[209] Commissioner, Pegu Division, Burmah	8 Mar. 64	3 Apr. 67	....	8 Mar. 76	....	8 Mar. 84	....	8 Mar. 90	....
109 Foot	31	Hervey, Hugh De la Motte,[211] Commandant 13 Bengal Lancers	5 Apr. 64	5 Apr. 67	....	5 Apr. 76	....	5 Apr. 84	....	5 Apr. 90	....
Art.	31	Hunter, John Muir, President Rajasthanic Court, Katywar	....	12 Apr. 64	....	12 Apr. 76	....	12 Apr. 84	....	12 Apr. 90	....
Art.	31	Gerard, Montagu Gilbert,[213] CB. Commandant 1 Central India Horse	....	19 Apr. 64	....	19 Apr. 76	....	19 Apr. 84	2 Mar. 81	19 Apr. 90	2 Mar. 85
21 Foot	31	Proudfoot, James George. Residing at Aurungabad	6 Apr. 64	3 May 67	....	26 Apr. 76	....	26 Apr. 84	....	26 Apr. 90	....
58 Foot	31	Browne, William Henry,[214] Commandant 18 Bengal Infantry	....	4 Sept. 68	3 May 76	15 Oct. 77	....	3 May 84	....	3 May 90	....
8 Foot	31	Sawyer, George Westrenen, Controller of Military Accounts, Madras	28 June 64	20 May 67	....	14 Mar. 74	....	28 June 84	....	3 June 90	....
56 Foot	31	Leckie, Frederick William Vans,[214] Commandant 19 Bombay Infantry	5 July 64	1 June 65	....	6 July 76	....	3 Jan. 84	....	5 July 90	26 July 94
3 Foot	31	Rennick, Albert de Clancy, Deputy Commissioner, 3rd Grade, Rhotuck, Punjab	6 July 64	18 July 68	....	26 July 76	....	6 July 84	....	6 July 90	....
59 Foot	31	Jones, William Henry Dawes,[218] Commandant 2 Bombay Lancers	26 July 64	21 Aug. 67	....	9 Aug. 76	....	26 July 84	....	26 July 90	....
36 Foot	31	Gordon, Stannus Verner, Commandant 23 Bengal Infantry	9 Aug. 64	22 May 68	....	9 Sept. 76	....	9 Aug. 84	....	9 Aug. 90	....
83 Foot	31	Heath, Lewis Forbes,[219] Commandant 10 Bombay Infantry	9 Sept. 64	11 Jan. 67	....	9 Sept. 76	....	9 Sept. 84	....	9 Sept. 90	....
104 Foot	31	Halkett, William George Craigie,[220] Commandant 31 Bengal Infantry	9 Sept. 64	16 Apr. 66	....	9 Sept. 76	....	9 Sept. 84	....	9 Sept. 90	....
42 Foot	31	Boileau, Henry, Deputy Commissioner, 2nd Grade, Julpigoree, Bengal	12 Jan. 65	12 Jan. 66	....	13 Sept. 76	....	13 Sept. 84	....	13 Sept. 90	....
33 Foot	31	Fraser, Edward Alexander, Political Agent, Cashmere	13 Sept. 64	29 May 67	....	11 Oct. 76	....	11 Oct. 84	....	20 Sept. 90	....
11 Foot	31	Barr, David William Keith,[221] Resident, Cashmere	P.1 Oct. 64	1 Oct. 67	....	30 Dec. 76	....	30 Dec. 84	....	11 Oct. 90	....
77 Hus.	31	Martelli, Norton Charles, Political Agent, 1st Class, Eastern States, Rajpootana	30 Dec. 64	7 May 68	....	3 Jan. 77	....	3 Jan. 85	....	30 Dec. 90	....
21 Hus.	31	Dyce, George Hugh Coles,[223] Commandant 33 Madras Infantry	3 Jan. 65	8 Sept. 68	31 Jan. 77	12 May 77	....	31 Jan. 85	....	3 Jan. 91	....
24 Foot	31	Walker, Charles Warren,[227] Commandant 25 Madras Infantry	P.31 Jan. 65	1 Jan. 67	....	18 Apr. 77	....	18 Apr. 85	....	31 Jan. 91	....
12 Foot	30	Gordon, Alexander Evans, Deputy Commissioner, 1st Grade, Bengal, Lohardugga	18 Apr. 65	2 Apr. 69	....	25 July 77	....	25 Apr. 85	....	18 Apr. 91	....
102 Foot	30	Morse, Walter John,[220] Commandant 17 Bombay Infantry	25 July 65	3 Sept. 68	....	26 May 77	....	26 May 85	....	25 Apr. 91	....
92 Foot	30	Massy, Charles Francis,[222] Deputy Commissioner, 1st Grade, Umballa	25 May 65	14 Aug. 67	....	26 May 77	....	26 May 85	....	26 May 91	29 Aug. 93
37 Foot	30	Swetenham, Robert Alexander.[225] Residing in India	26 May 65	23 June 68	....	2 June 77	....	2 June 85	....	26 May 91	....
45 Foot	30	Humfrey, John,[234] 1st Inspector General of Police, Bombay	2 June 65	4 Nov. 68	....	10 June 77	....	10 June 85	....	2 June 91	....
59 Foot	30	Forjett, Frederick Hutchinson	10 June 65	30 Mar. 70	....	18 June 77	....	18 June 85	7 Dec. 88	30 June 91	7 Dec. 91
22 Foot	30	Young, George Frederick,[237] CSI. Inspector General, Imperial Service Troops	18 June 65	8 Mar. 69	....	30 June 77	18 Nov. 82	30 June 85	....	30 June 91	....
46 Foot	30	Grant, James,[230] Commandant 4 Bombay Infantry	30 June 65	31 Mar. 68	....	4 July 77	....	30 June 85	....	30 June 91	....
2 Dr. Gds.	30	Newill, Joseph Henry, Political Agent, 2nd Class	4 July 65	7 Nov. 68	....	1 July 77	4 Aug. 85	4 July 85	....	4 July 91	....
38 Foot	30	Burton, Francis Charles,[240] Commandant 2 Bengal Lancers	1 July 65	30 May 69	....	18 July 77	2 Mar. 81	1 July 85	....	11 July 91	....
12 Foot	30	Miley, James Aloysius, Accountant General, Military Department	18 July 65	18 May 69	....	25 July 77	22 Nov. 79	18 July 85	....	18 July 91	....
21 Foot	30	Holiday, Thomas Francis,[241] Commissary General, Poona	25 July 65	24 July 68	....	4 Aug. 77	....	25 July 85	....	25 July 91	....
49 Foot	30	Wilson, Edward Hales,[242] Commandant 34 Bengal Infantry	4 July 65	13 July 69	....	8 Aug. 77	....	4 Aug. 85	....	4 Aug. 91	....
26 Foot	30	Gilchrist, Robert Alexander,[243] Commandant 3 Lancers Hyderabad Contingent	8 Aug. 65	8 Aug. 69	....	1 Sept. 77	....	8 Aug. 85	....	8 Aug. 91	....
21 Foot	30	Robertson, Donald, Resident at Gwalior	8 Aug. 65	11 Jan. 67	....	7 Nov. 77	....	1 Sept. 85	....	1 Sept. 91	....
19 Foot	30	Johnstone, William George Currie.[244] Residing out of India	1 Sept. 65	28 July 70	....	1 Dec. 77	....	22 Sept. 85	1 July 87	22 Sept. 91	....
95 Foot	30	Kirkwood, James Nicholson Sotion, Commandant 6 Inf. Hyderabad Contingent	7 Nov. 65	8 Aug. 69	....	1 Dec. 77	....	7 Nov. 85	....	7 Nov. 91	....
10 Foot	30	Porteous, James Edward,[245] Commissary General, Madras Infantry	1 Sept. 65	18 May 69	....	1 Dec. 77	....	21 Nov. 85	....	21 Nov. 91	....
24 Foot	30	Cooke, William,[246] Assistant Commissary General, 1st Class	22 Sept. 65	1 Jan. 68	....	8 Dec. 77	2 Mar. 81	1 Dec. 85	....	1 Dec. 91	....
58 Foot	30	Fenwick, George Carew [247] Commandant 1 Madras Infantry	7 Nov. 65	1 Oct. 66	....	1 Dec. 77	....	1 Dec. 85	....	1 Dec. 91	....
25 Foot	30	Cuninghame, David Stanley,[248] Commandant 5 Bengal Infantry	1 Dec. 65	18 July 68	....	5 Jan. 78	....	1 Dec. 85	....	8 Dec. 91	....
6 Foot	30	Birch, Wm. James Alexander,[249] Commandant 4 Bengal Infantry	8 Dec. 65	14 Dec. 69	....	12 Jan. 78	....	19 Dec. 85	....	19 Dec. 91	....
55 Foot	30	Thomson, Thomas George, Commandant 1 Bombay Infantry	19 Dec. 65	12 Jan. 66	....	12 Jan. 78	....	12 Jan. 86	....	12 Jan. 92	....
Art.	30	Macpherson, Andrew Kennedy, Cantonment Magistrate, Meean Meer, Punjab	5 Jan. 66	12 Jan. 66	....	12 Jan. 78	2 Mar. 81	12 Jan. 86	....	12 Jan. 92	....
109 Foot	30	Hill, William,[250] Officiating Assistant Adjutant General for Musketry, Bengal Army	....	31 Mar. 67	....	12 Jan. 78	....	12 Jan. 86	....	30 Jan. 92	....
Art.	30	Black, William Campbell,[251] Commandant 1 Bombay Infantry	....	8 Dec. 66	....	30 Jan. 78	....	30 Jan. 86	....	30 Jan. 92	....
49 Foot	30	Salmon, Chas. Arthur, Deputy Commissioner, 1st Grade, Prome District, Burmah	....	14 Dec. 69	....	30 Jan. 78	....	30 Jan. 86	....	12 Jan. 92	....
106 Foot	30	Cresswell, Benjamin Chamney,[252] Commandant 39 Bengal Infantry	30 Jan. 66	8 Dec. 66	....	30 Jan. 78	....	30 Jan. 86	....	30 Jan. 92	....
19 Foot	30	Graves, Benjamin Chamney,[252] Commandant 39 Bengal Infantry	30 Jan. 66	7 Sept. 68	....	30 Jan. 78	....	30 Jan. 86	....	30 Jan. 92	....
49 Foot	30	Wetherall, William Alexander, Commandant 22 Bombay Infantry	13 Feb. 66	8 Dec. 66	....	13 Feb. 78	....	13 Feb. 86	....	13 Feb. 92	....
106 Foot	30	Bingham, Edward Henry,[253] Commandant 13 Bombay Infantry	....	7 Sept. 68	....	7 Feb. 78	....	7 Feb. 86	....	13 Feb. 92	....
19 Foot	30	Butler, James, Deputy Commissioner, 1st Grade, Henzada District, Burmah	20 Feb. 66	9 July 68	....	20 Feb. 78	....	20 Feb. 86	....	20 Feb. 92	....

410

Indian Staff Corps.

Last Regiment.	Years' Service.	Lieutenant Colonels.	2nd Lieut., Cornet, or Ensign.	Lieut.	Brevet Captain.	Captain.	Brevet Major.	Major.	Brevet Lt.-Col.	Lieut. Colonel.	Brevet Colonel.
26 Foot	30	Bishop, Leslie Trevor,²⁵⁶ Commandant 2 Punjab Cavalry	2 Mar. 66	1 Mar. 69	......	2 Mar. 78	2 Mar. 81	2 Mar. 86	......	2 Mar. 92	......
104 Foot	30	Loch, William,²¹⁵ 2nd Class Polit. Assistant, Rajpootana; Polit. Agent, Bikaneer	2 Mar. 66	14 May 68	......	2 Mar. 78	......	2 Mar. 86	......	2 Mar. 92	......
38 Foot	30	Jenkins, Thomas Morris, Deputy Commissioner, and Grade, Toungoo, Burmah	2 Mar. 66	19 June 69	......	2 Mar. 78	......	2 Mar. 86	......	2 Mar. 92	......
109 Foot	30	Macintire, Andw. Hy. Mil. Sec. to Maharajah of Mysore; in charge Amrat Mahal Dept.	9 Mar. 66	30 Sept. 68	......	9 Mar. 78	......	9 Mar. 86	......	9 Mar. 92	......
38 Foot	30	Richardson, George'Lloyd Reilly,²⁵⁷ CIE, Commandant 18 Bengal Lancers	23 Mar. 66	5 Mar. 69	......	23 Mar. 78	23 Mar. 81	23 Mar. 86	......	23 Mar. 92	......
38 Foot	30	Lydiard, Arthur Coombe Gordon,²⁵⁸ Commandant 1 Bengal Infantry	3 Mar. 66	19 Feb. 69	......	3 Apr. 78	......	3 Apr. 86	......	3 Apr. 92	......
105 Foot	29	Woodhouse, Henry Opie,²²⁹ Commandant 9 Bengal Infantry	10 April 66	22 Aug. 68	......	10 Apr. 78	......	10 Apr. 86	......	10 Apr. 92	......
93 Foot	29	Maitland, Pelham James,²⁶¹ Dep. Secretary, Government of India, Military Dept.	2 May 66	8 Feb. 70	......	2 May 78	......	2 May 86	16 Feb. 87	2 May 92	......
45 Foot	29	Garrett, Annesley John,²⁶² Military Secretary to the Resident at Hyderabad	29 May 66	8 Oct. 68	......	29 May 78	......	29 May 86	......	29 May 92	11 Aug. 92
lt. Art.	29	Sealy, Charles William Henry, Assistant Political Resident, Aden, and Political Agent for the Somali Coast		17 July 66	......	17 July 78	......	17 July 86	......	17 July 92	......
37 Foot	29	Begbie, Francis Richard,²⁶³ Commandant 2 Battalion 2 Goorkha Regiment	20 July 66	7 May 69	......	20 July 78	......	20 July 86	......	20 July 92	......
1 Foot	29	Yaldwyn, Alfred George,²⁶⁵ Assistant Commissary General, 2nd Class, Lucknow	14 Sept. 66	2 Dec. 69	......	14 Sept. 78	......	14 Sept. 86	......	14 Sept. 92	......
102 Foot	29	Rind, Alex. Thomas Seton Abercromby,³⁶⁶ CMG. Commissary Gen. for Transport	2 Oct. 66	18 Jan. 70	......	2 Oct. 78	2 Mar. 81	2 Oct. 86	......	2 Oct. 92	......
95 Foot	29	FG. Creagh, O'Moore,²⁶⁷ Commandant 9 Bombay Infantry	2 Oct. 66	16 Feb. 70	......	2 Oct. 78	22 Nov. 79	2 Oct. 86	......	2 Oct. 92	......
12 Foot	29	p.s.c. Sawyer, Herbert Anthony,²⁶⁸ Commandant 45 Bengal Infantry	2 Oct. 66	17 Aug. 70	......	1 July 77	......	1 July 86	......	2 Oct. 92	......
12 Foot	29	Gouldsbury, Dudley Elphinstone,²⁶⁹ Cantonment Magistrate, Jullunder, Punjab	16 Oct. 66	17 Apr. 69	......	16 Oct. 78	......	16 Oct. 86	......	16 Oct. 92	......
49 Foot	29	Lyster, William Henry,²⁷⁰ Commandant 14 Bombay Infantry	16 Oct. 66	6 July 70	......	16 Oct. 78	......	16 Oct. 86	......	16 Oct. 92	......
10 Foot	29	Maltby, Francis Crichton,²⁷¹ Commandant 5 Madras Infantry	16 Oct. 66	14 Oct. 70	......	16 Oct. 78	......	16 Oct. 86	......	16 Oct. 92	......
106 Foot	29	Wyllie, William Hutt Curzon,²⁷² CIE, Resident, Meywar	30 Oct. 66	5 Oct. 68	......	30 Oct. 78	......	30 Oct. 86	......	30 Oct. 92	......
106 Foot	29	Jamieson, Alister William, 2nd in Command and Wing Commander 7 Bengal Inf.	9 Nov. 66	18 Nov. 68	......	9 Nov. 78	......	9 Nov. 86	......	9 Nov. 92	......
19 Foot	29	Rolland, Stuart Erskine,²⁷⁴ Commandant 26 Madras Infantry	9 Nov. 66	9 Dec. 68	......	9 Nov. 78	......	9 Nov. 86	1 July 87	9 Nov. 92	......
104 Foot	29	Vincent, Henry Alexander,²⁷⁵ 2nd in Com. and Squad. Comdr., 1 Central India Horse	9 Nov. 66	9 Feb. 70	......	9 Nov. 78	......	9 Nov. 86	......	9 Nov. 92	......
37 Foot	29	Neville, Josiah Philip Crampton,²⁷⁶ Commandant 74 Bengal Lancers	9 Dec. 66	4 Dec. 68	......	9 Dec. 78	......	9 Dec. 85	......	9 Dec. 92	......
107 Foot	29	Leslie, Sir Charles Henry,²⁷⁷ Bart. Commandant 2 Battalion 4 Goorkhas	11 Dec. 66	6 Jan. 68	......	11 Dec. 78	......	11 Dec. 86	......	11 Dec. 92	......
92 Foot	29	Anson, Geo. Wemyss, Dep. Comm.²⁷⁸ and Gr. Gonda, N.W.P.; Agent Bulrampore Estate	11 Jan. 67	22 Jan. 68	......	11 Jan. 79	......	11 Jan. 87	......	11 Jan. 93	......
62 Foot	29	Baxtye, Frederick Drummond,²⁷⁹ 2nd in Com. and Wing Comdr. Corps of Guides.	11 Jan. 67	29 June 69	......	11 Jan. 79	......	11 Jan. 87	......	11 Jan. 93	......
108 Foot	29	Gompertz, Bowes Thorpe Montague, Assist. Commissary Gen., 2nd Class, Madras	11 Jan. 67	2 Dec. 69	......	11 Jan. 79	......	11 Jan. 87	......	11 Jan. 93	......
59 Foot	29	James, Montague,²⁸⁰ Residing out of India	11 Jan. 67	18 Mar. 70	......	11 Jan. 79	......	11 Jan. 87	......	11 Jan. 93	......
41 Foot	29	Money-Simons, John James,²⁸¹ 2nd in Command and Wing Commander 24 Ben. Inf.	11 Jan. 67	26 Apr. 70	......	11 Jan. 79	......	11 Jan. 87	......	11 Jan. 93	......
Art.	29	Talbot, Adelbert Cecil, CIE. Deputy Secretary to the Govt. of India, Foreign Dept.	15 Jan. 67	15 Jan. 67	......	15 Jan. 79	2 Mar. 81	15 Jan. 87	......	15 Jan. 93	......
109 Foot	29	Reid, Alexander John Forsyth,²⁸⁴ Commandant 29 Bengal Infantry	18 Jan. 67	6 May 71	......	18 Jan. 79	18 Jan. 81	18 Jan. 87	7 Dec. 88	18 Jan. 93	6 Jan. 94
103 Foot	29	Greenaway, Thomas,²⁵⁷ Commandant 6 Madras Infantry	12 Feb. 67	1 Jan. 67	......	12 Feb. 79	......	12 Feb. 87	......	12 Feb. 93	......
14 Hus.	29	Channer, Bernard²⁸⁸ DSO, Commandant 2 Bengal Infantry	23 Feb. 67	14 Mar. 68	......	23 Feb. 79	......	13 Feb. 87	......	13 Feb. 93	......
108 Foot	29	Aberich-Mackay, James Lavingston,²⁸⁹ 2nd in Com. and Squad. Comdr. 8 Ben. Cav.	13 Feb. 67	10 Sept. 69	......	13 Feb. 79	......	13 Feb. 87	......	13 Feb. 93	......
107 Foot	29	Anderson, Edward Brooke,²⁹⁰ Commandant 24 Madras Infantry	14 Feb. 67	14 Apr. 69	......	14 Apr. 79	......	14 Apr. 87	......	9 Mar. 93	......
38 Foot	29	Rose, Henry Metcalfe,²⁹¹ DSO, Commandant 27 Bengal Infantry	18 Mar. 67	24 May 67	......	18 Mar. 79	......	8 Mar. 87	......	8 Mar. 93	......
107 Foot	29	Macbay, William George Wolfe,²⁹² Assistant Commissary General, 1st Class, Simla	8 Mar. 67	13 July 70	......	23 Mar. 79	18 Nov. 82	23 Mar. 87	......	23 Mar. 93	......
8 Foot	29	Christopher, Leonard William,²⁹² Commandant 26 Bombay Infantry	23 Mar. 67	15 Aug. 69	......	3 Apr. 79	......	3 Apr. 87	......	3 Apr. 93	......
11 Foot	29	Keighley, Charles Marsh,²⁹⁴ DSO, Assist. Commissary General, and Class, Quetta	20 Apr. 67	19 Apr. 70	......	20 Apr. 79	......	20 Apr. 87	......	20 Apr. 93	......
108 Foot	28	Welch, Frederick Gibson Tyrrell,²⁹⁵ Commandant 3 Bombay Infantry	1 May 67	7 June 67	......	1 May 79	3 Mar. 81	3 May 87	......	3 Apr. 93	......
39 Foot	28	Dening, Lewis,²⁹⁶ DSO, Commandant 26 Bengal Infantry	8 June 67	18 Jan. 70	......	8 June 79	......	8 June 87	1 Sept. 91	20 May 93	......
19 Foot	28	Egerton, Charles Comyn,²⁹⁷ DSO, 2nd in Com. and Squadron Comdr. 3 Punjab Cav.	8 June 67	19 Oct. 67	......	8 June 79	......	8 June 87	......	8 June 93	......
88 Foot	28	Mercer, Charles Archibald,²⁹⁸ Commandant 1 Battalion 4 Goorkha Regiment	8 June 67	18 Jan. 70	......	8 June 79	......	8 June 87	......	9 June 93	......
19 Foot	28	Goldney, Thomas Holloway,²⁵⁹ Commandant 35 Bengal Infantry	9 June 67	2 July 69	......	9 June 79	......	9 June 87	......	9 June 93	......
88 Foot	28	Martin, Gerald Ward³⁰⁰ Assay Master, Bombay Mint	22 June 67	18 May 69	......	22 June 79	......	6 July 87	......	22 June 93	......
105 Foot	28	Maltby, Francis Grant,³⁰¹ Commandant 1 Infantry Hyderabad Contingent	6 July 67	14 May 69	......	6 July 79	......	6 July 87	......	6 July 93	......
77 Foot	28	Hutchinson, Henry Doveton, Commandant 2 Battalion 3 Goorkhas	10 July 67	6 July 67	......	10 July 79	......	10 July 87	......	10 July 93	......
Art.	28	Ditmas, Frederick Robertson,³⁰³ Commandant 13 Bengal Lancers	13 July 67	17 Jan. 70	......	13 July 79	13 July 81	13 July 87	......	13 July 93	......
93 Foot	28	Elliott, George Hambley,³⁰⁴ 2nd in Command and Squadron Comdr. 3 Bengal Cav.	17 July 67	17 Aug. 70	......	17 July 79	......	17 July 87	......	17 July 93	......
55 Foot	28	Walker, John Newman,³⁰⁵ Commandant 3rd Class, Chin Hills Command	20 July 67	17 Jan. 71	......	20 July 79	......	20 July 87	......	20 July 93	......
45 Foot	28	Rawlinson, Spencer Rich.³⁰⁶ DSO, Assist. Com. Gen. 3rd Class, Bengal Cav.	20 July 67	22 July 69	......	20 July 79	......	20 July 87	......	20 July 93	......
11 Foot	28	Chalmers, Edward Willock,³⁰⁷ 2nd in Command and Squadron Comdr. 7 Ben. Cav.	14 Aug. 67	25 Feb. 71	......	14 Aug. 79	......	14 Aug. 87	......	14 Aug. 93	......

Indian Staff Corps.

Last Regiment.	Serv. Yrs.	LIEUTENANT COLONELS.	2ND LIEUT., CORNET, OR ENSIGN.	LIEUT.	BREVET CAPTAIN.	CAPTAIN.	BREVET MAJOR.	MAJOR.	BREVET LT. COL.	LIEUT. COLONEL.	BREVET COLONEL.
92 Foot	28	Montgomery, James Alex. Lawrence, Deputy Commr. 1st Grade, Rawul Pindee, Punjab	14 Sept. 67	9 Oct. 69		14 Sept. 70		14 Sept. 87		14 Sept. 93	
36 Foot	28	Thornton, Arthur Parry, Political Agent, 2nd Class, Oomrawuttee and Tonk	14 Sept. 67	28 Sept. 71		14 Sept. 79		14 Sept. 87		14 Sept. 93	
50 Rifles	28	Brander, Arthur James, 309 Commandant 19 Bengal Infantry	6 Nov. 67	28 Oct. 71		6 Nov. 79		6 Nov. 87		6 Nov. 93	
49 Foot	28	Yate, Charles Edward, 310 CSI. CMG. Political Agent, 1st Class; Offg. Resident and Governor General's Agent, Khorasan and Seistan	9 Nov. 67	22 Mar. 72		9 Nov. 79		9 Nov. 87		9 Nov. 93	
96 Foot	28	Pollard, Benjamin Horatio, 312 Commandant 20 Madras Infantry	25 Dec. 67	18 Jan. 70		25 Dec. 79		25 Dec. 87		25 Dec. 93	
R. Art.	28	Adamson, Charles Henry Ellison, 313 CIE. Commissioner, Sagaing, Burmah	8 Jan. 68	14 Feb. 70		8 Jan. 80		8 Jan. 88		8 Jan. 94	
96 Foot	28	H/G p.s.c. Ridgeway, Richard Kirby, 314 Commandant 44 Bengal Infantry	8 Jan. 68	22 Feb. 70		8 Jan. 80		8 Jan. 88		8 Jan. 94	
12 Foot	28	Eliot, Geffery Lawrence, 315 Commanding General, Simla	8 Jan. 68	7 July 70		8 Jan. 80		8 Jan. 88		8 Jan. 94	
108 Foot	28	Peile, Frederick Babington, 316 2nd in Com. and Wing Comdr. 2 Bombay Infantry	8 Jan. 68	8 Sept. 70		8 Jan. 80		8 Jan. 88		8 Jan. 94	
37 Foot	28	Lynch, James Beverley, 317 Commandant 12 Bengal Cavalry	8 Jan. 68	3 Oct. 70		8 Jan. 80		8 Jan. 88		8 Jan. 94	
108 Foot	28	Gordon, Robert, 318 Commandant 22 Bengal Infantry	8 Jan. 68	23 Aug. 70		8 Jan. 80		8 Jan. 88		8 Jan. 94	
62 Foot	28	Fenton, Herbert Edward, 320 Commandant 7 Bombay Lancers	22 Jan. 68	9 Feb. 70		22 Jan. 80		22 Jan. 88		22 Jan. 94	
25 Foot	28	Elliot, Edward Locke, 321 DSO. Commandant 7 Bombay Lancers	22 Jan. 68	18 Nov. 70		1 Feb. 80		1 Feb. 88		1 Feb. 94	
37 Foot	28	Hingston, Clayton William James, 322 Commandant to Bengal Infantry	1 Feb. 68	28 Oct. 71		15 Feb. 80		15 Feb. 88		15 Feb. 94	
96 Foot	28	Mills, Arthur M'Leod, Commandant 37 Bengal Infantry	15 Feb. 68	28 Oct. 71		22 Feb. 80		22 Feb. 88		22 Feb. 94	
66 Foot	28	Abbott, Henry Alexius, 324 Commandant, Quetta and Pishin	22 Feb. 68	28 May 71		14 Mar. 80		14 Mar. 88		14 Mar. 94	
66 Foot	28	Gaisford, Gilbert, 325 Political Agent, Quetta and Pishin	14 Mar. 68	74 Mar. 71		14 Mar. 80	2 Mar. 81	14 Mar. 88	2 Aug. 88	14 Mar. 94	
96 Foot	28	Ternan, Henry Brefney, Commandant 12 Bombay Infantry	3 June 68	7 Dec. 70		3 June 80		3 June 88		3 June 94	
41 Foot	28	Raikes, Frederick Duncan, 327 CIE. Deputy Commissioner, 1st Grade, Sagaing, Burmah	3 June 68	20 July 70		8 July 80		3 June 88		3 June 94	
19 Foot	27	Macgregor, Charles Reginald, 328 DSO. Commandant 42 Bengal Infantry	8 July 68	8 Aug. 70		8 July 80		8 July 88		8 July 94	
108 Foot	27	Newall, Wm. Potter, 329 2nd in Com. and Wing Commander 1 Battalion 2 Goorkha Regt.	8 July 68	31 Aug. 70		8 July 80		8 July 88		8 July 94	
66 Foot	27	Grey, William Francis Hungerford, Dep. Commissioner, 1st Grade, Yemethin, Burmah	8 July 68	18 Dec. 70		8 July 80		8 July 88		8 July 94	
76 Foot	27	Mansel, Charles Grenville, Squadron Commander 3 Punjab Cavalry	8 July 68	15 July 71		8 July 80		8 July 88		8 July 94	
104 Foot	27	Bingham, Chas. Thos. Conservator of Forests, 3rd Grade, Tenasserim, Burmah	8 July 68	27 Oct. 71		8 July 80	1 July 87	8 July 88		8 July 94	
109 Foot	27	Parrott, Benjamin Alex. Napier, 331 Commissioner, Southern Division, Burmah	8 July 68	28 Oct. 71		8 July 80		9 July 88		9 July 94	
104 Foot	27	Pryce, Douglas Davidson, 332 Commandant 9 Madras Infantry	9 July 68	30 Mar. 70		10 July 80	2 Mar. 81	10 July 88		10 July 94	
39 Foot	27	Sage, Charles Arthur Ross, 333 Commandant 2 Battalion 1 Goorkhas	10 July 68			2 Oct. 76	15 June 85	22 July 88		23 July 94	
39 Foot	27	Burgess, Francis Forsyth Robert, Military Accountant, 2nd Class, Poona	22 July 68								
3 Foot	27	Dempster, Cathcart, 334 Commandant 4 Sikh Infantry	23 July 68	2 Nov. 71		23 July 80		23 July 88		23 July 94	
107 Foot	27	Bruce, Edward, 335 Commandant 19 Bengal Lancers	8 July 68	11 Apr. 71		2 Aug. 80		2 Aug. 88		22 Aug. 94	
104 Foot	27	Spencer, Thomas Edward, 336 2nd in Com. and Wing Commander 17 Bengal Infantry	23 July 68	21 Nov. 70		2 Aug. 80		22 July 88			
1 Foot	27	Abbott, Frank, 337 Commandant 7 Bombay Lancers	22 Aug. 66	15 Dec. 69		2 Sept. 80		2 Sept. 88		16 Sept. 94	
17 Foot	27	Radcliffe, Geo. Bulstrode Edmund, 338 Assistant Commissary General, 2nd Class, Mhow	2 Sept. 68	28 Oct. 71		16 Sept. 80		16 Sept. 88		30 Sept. 94	
1 Hus.	27	Halkett, Henry Craigie, 339 2nd in Com. and Wing Commander 32 Bengal Infantry	16 Sept. 68								
1 Hus.	27	Howlett, Arthur, 340 Commandant 12 Madras Infantry	30 Sept. 68	28 Oct. 71		30 Sept. 80		30 Sept. 88		30 Sept. 94	
25 Foot	27	Graves, Somerset Henry Paul, Commandant 40 Bengal Infantry	7 Nov. 58	6 May 71		7 Nov. 80		7 Nov. 88		7 Nov. 94	
106 Foot	27	Hay, Henry, 342 2nd in Command and Squadron Commander 1 Bombay Lancers	13 Jan. 69	28 Mar. 71		13 Jan. 81		13 Jan. 89		13 Jan. 95	
106 Foot	27	Muir, Archibald Mungo, 343 Political Agent, 2nd Class	13 Jan. 69	28 Oct. 71		13 Jan. 81		13 Jan. 89		13 Jan. 95	
76 Foot	27	Broome, William Arthur, 344 Commandant 27 Bombay Infantry	4 Feb. 69	28 Oct. 71		3 Feb. 81		3 Feb. 89		3 Feb. 95	
1 Hus.	27	Gray, Malcolm Alexander, Deputy Commissioner, 3rd Grade, Shillong, Assam	4 Feb. 69	28 Oct. 71		4 Feb. 81		4 Feb. 89		4 Feb. 95	
106 Foot	27	Holiday, James Ramsay, 346 Deputy Superintendent, 3rd Grade, Revenue Survey, Poona	6 Feb. 69	27 Apr. 71		6 Feb. 81		6 Feb. 89		6 Feb. 95	
106 Foot	27	Deane, George Williams, 347 2nd in Com. and Squad. Commander 13 Bengal Lancers	6 Feb. 69	28 Oct. 71		6 Feb. 81		10 Feb. 89		10 Feb. 95	
76 Foot	27	Snell, Francis William, 2nd in Command Sawant Warree Local Corps	10 Feb. 69	28 Oct. 71		10 Feb. 81		10 Feb. 89		10 Feb. 95	
83 Foot	27	Mackenzie, Thomas Harding, 349 2nd in Com. and Wing Commander 2 Bombay Infantry	27 Feb. 69	28 Oct. 71		27 Feb. 81		27 Feb. 89		27 Feb. 95	
		MAJORS.									
4 Hus.	26	Wilson, William Bernard, 355 Assistant Judge Advocate General, Secunderabad	24 Apr. 69	28 Oct. 71		24 Apr. 81	1 July 87	24 Apr. 89			
5 Lanc.	26	Monteith, Edward Vernon Peshall, 356 Commandant 6 Bombay Cavalry	5 May 69	28 Oct. 71		5 May 81		5 May 89			

Indian Staff Corps.

Last Regiment.	Yrs. Srv.	MAJORS.	2ND LIEUT. CORNET, or ENSIGN.	LIEUT.	BREVET CAPTAIN.	CAPTAIN.	BREVET MAJOR.	MAJOR.	BREVET LT. COL.
26 Foot	26	Lamb, Henry Campbell,³⁵⁷ 2nd in Command and Squadron Commander 4 Bengal Cavalry	5 May 69	28 Oct. 71		5 May 81	1 July 87	5 May 89	
85 Foot	26	Schalch, Vernon Ansdell,³⁵⁸ Commandant 11 Bengal Infantry	29 May 69	28 Oct. 71		29 May 81		29 May 89	
36 Foot	26	Eyre, Gervas Selwyn,³⁵⁹ Deputy Commissioner, 2nd Grade, Burmah	12 June 69	27 Oct. 71		12 June 81		12 June 89	
49 Foot	26	p.s.c. Saife, Edmund,³⁶⁰ Deputy Judge Advocate General, Army Head Quarters	30 June 69	28 Oct. 71		30 June 81		30 June 89	
108 Foot	26	Orr, William John, Assistant Commissary General, 2nd Class	7 July 69	19 Apr. 71		7 July 81		7 July 89	
58 Foot	26	Bell, Alexander William Croker, 2nd in Command and Wing Commander 14 Bombay Infantry	7 July 69	28 Oct. 71		7 July 81		7 July 89	
10 Foot	26	Dobbs, George Cadell,³⁶² Assistant Commissary General, 1st Class	7 July 69	28 Oct. 71		7 July 81		7 July 89	
85 Foot	26	Macpherson, Duncan Alexander Allan,³⁶³ Controller of Military Accounts, Ravul Pindee	7 July 69	28 Oct. 71		7 July 81		7 July 89	
11 Foot	26	Reilly, Bradshaw Lewis Philip,³⁶⁴ Assistant Commissary General, and Class, Bombay	7 July 69	28 Oct. 71		7 July 81		7 July 89	
6 Foot	26	Muir, Charles Wemyss,³⁶⁵ C.I.E. 2nd in Command and Squadron Commander 17 Bengal Cavalry	7 July 69	28 Oct. 71		7 July 81		7 July 89	
109 Foot	26	Macpherson, Thomas Robert Matheson, District Superintendent of Police, Poona	8 July 69	28 Oct. 71		8 July 81		8 July 89	
109 Foot	26	Bignell, Edward Duncan Fred,³⁶⁷ Commandant Meywar Bheel Corps	14 July 69	28 Oct. 71		14 July 81		14 July 89	
16 Lanc.	26	Austin, George Brougham, Commandant 3 Bengal Infantry	14 July 69	28 Oct. 71		14 July 81		14 July 89	
62 Foot	26	Money, Geo. Edward,³⁶⁸ 2nd in Command and Squadron Commander 1 Central India Horse	18 Aug. 69	28 Oct. 71		18 Aug. 81 16 Feb. 87		12 Aug. 89	
104 Foot	26	Clibborn, John, Principal of Thomason Civil Engineering College, Roorkee	18 Aug. 69	28 Oct. 71		18 Aug. 81		18 Aug. 89	
107 Foot	26	Ferris, William Butler, Assistant Governor General's Agent, Baroda	21 Aug. 69	28 Oct. 71		21 Aug. 81		21 Aug. 89	
1 Foot	26	p.s.c. Barrow, Arthur Frederick, C.M.G. Commandant 12 Bengal Infantry	21 Aug. 69	28 Oct. 71		21 Aug. 81		21 Aug. 89	
58 Foot	26	Lucas, Hugh Claude Edward,³⁷¹ 2nd in Command and Wing Commander 28 Bengal Infantry	10 Nov. 69	28 Oct. 71		10 Nov. 81		10 Nov. 89	
1 Foot	26	Porter, Atwell Robert,³⁷² 2nd in Command and Wing Commander 19 Bombay Infantry	17 Nov. 69	28 Oct. 71		17 Nov. 81		17 Nov. 89	
5 Lanc.	25	Kellie, Edward Charnier,³⁷³ Commandant 6 Bengal Cavalry	24 Nov. 69	28 Oct. 71		24 Nov. 81		24 Nov. 89	
76 Foot	25	Gordon, John Charles Frederick,³⁷⁴ Commandant and Squadron Commander 2 Bengal Lancers	1 Dec. 69	28 Oct. 71		1 Dec. 81		1 Dec. 89	17 Jan. 71
5 Lanc.	25	Garbett, Chas. Henry Vincent, 2nd in Command 9 Bombay Infantry	7 Dec. 69	28 Oct. 71		7 Dec. 81		7 Dec. 89	
3 Foot	26	Proudfoot, Andrew William, Commandant and Squadron Commander 1 Bengal Cavalry	8 Dec. 69	28 Oct. 71		8 Dec. 81		8 Dec. 89	
1 Hus.	26	Mitchell, St. John Fancourt,³⁷⁶ 2nd in Command 16 Bengal Cavalry	8 Dec. 69	28 Oct. 71		8 Dec. 81		8 Dec. 89	
11 Hus.	25	Alexander, Aubrey De Vere,³⁷⁷ Commandant 7 Bengal Cavalry	15 Dec. 69	28 Oct. 71		15 Dec. 81		15 Dec. 89	
R. Art.	26	Trotter, Robert Francis,³⁷⁸ Squadron Commander 7 Bengal Cavalry	5 Jan. 70	27 Oct. 71		5 Jan. 82		5 Jan. 90	6 Jan. 90
R. Art.		Young, Edward Archibald,³⁷⁹ Assistant Adjutant General, Lahore. (Colonel 6 Jan. 94)		8 Jan. 70				8 Jan. 90	
44 Foot	26	Fenton, Layard Livingstone, Superintendent of Surveys under Rajasthanic Court	8 Feb. 70	28 Oct. 71		8 Feb. 82		8 Feb. 90	
45 Foot	26	Kennedy, Willoughby Pitcairn,³⁸² Administrator, Rajpipla State	8 Feb. 70	28 Oct. 71		8 Feb. 82		8 Feb. 90	
105 Foot	26	Mason, Henry Macan,³⁸³ Commandant 4 Lancers Hyderabad Contingent	8 Feb. 70	28 Oct. 71		8 Feb. 82	11 July 87	8 Feb. 90	
107 Foot	26	Stevenson, Francis,³⁸⁴ 2nd in Command and Wing Commander 19 Bombay Infantry	8 Feb. 70	28 Oct. 71		8 Feb. 82		8 Feb. 90	
19 Foot	26	Pearson, Alfred Astley,³⁸⁵ Commandant 21 Bombay Infantry	19 Feb. 70	28 Oct. 71		19 Feb. 82		19 Feb. 90	
55 Foot	25	Hawkes, George,³⁸⁶ Commandant 2 Battalion 5 Goorkhas	27 Apr. 70	28 Oct. 71		27 Apr. 82		27 Apr. 90	
108 Foot	25	Hadow, Reginald Campbell,³⁸⁷ 2nd in Command and Wing Commander 15 Bengal Infantry	7 July 70	6 June 71		7 July 82		6 July 90	
39 Foot	25	Barclay, Ernest Armond,³⁸⁸ Assistant Commissary General, 2nd Class, Poona	6 July 70	28 Oct. 71		6 July 82		6 July 90	
96 Foot	25	Nicholetts, Charles Oldfield,³⁸⁹ Commandant 5 Bombay Infantry	6 July 70	6 June 71		6 July 82		6 July 90	
17 Foot	25	Sadler, James Hayes, Assistant to the Governor General's Agent at Baroda	6 July 70	28 Oct. 71		6 July 82		6 July 90	
17 Foot	25	Mein, John Edmund,³⁹¹ Commandant 5 Punjab Infantry	20 July 70	28 Oct. 71		20 July 82		20 July 90	
89 Foot	25	Harris, William Octavius,³⁹² 2nd in Command and Wing Commander 20 Bengal Infantry	3 Aug. 70	28 Oct. 71		3 Aug. 82		3 Aug. 90	
65 Foot	25	Welch, Malcolm Edw. Haleman Owen, Commandant 23 Madras Infantry	27 Aug. 70	28 Oct. 71		27 Aug. 82		27 Aug. 90	
74 Foot	25	Wheatley, Henry Spencer,³⁹¹ 2nd in Command 4 Lancers Hyderabad Contingent 2 Battalion 3 Goorkhas	3 Sept. 70	28 Oct. 71		3 Sept. 82		3 Sept. 90	
50 Foot	25	Young, Harry Howlett,³⁹⁵ Commandant 27 Madras Infantry	3 Sept. 70	28 Oct. 71		3 Sept. 82		3 Sept. 90	
25 Foot	25	Kenny, Edward Evans,³⁹⁶ Assistant Commissary General, 2nd Class, Rangoon	3 Sept. 70	28 Oct. 71		30 May 83		1 Oct. 90	
63 Foot	25	Gastroll, George Davidson Campbell,³⁹⁷ 2nd in Command and Wing Commander 8 Bengal Infantry	1 Oct. 70	28 Oct. 71		1 Oct. 82		1 Oct. 90	
63 Foot	25	Garstin, George Lindsay,³⁹⁸ 2nd in Command and Squadron Commander 9 Bengal Lancers	2 Oct. 70	28 Oct. 71		2 Oct. 82		5 Nov. 90	
17 Foot	25	Anderson, William Robert Le Geyt,³⁹⁹ Military Accountant, 1st Class, Calcutta	5 Nov. 70	28 Oct. 71		5 Nov. 82		5 Nov. 90	
39 Foot	25	Angelo, John William Edward,⁴⁰⁰ 2nd in Command and Wing Commander 12 Bengal Infantry	12 Nov. 70	28 Oct. 71		12 Nov. 82		12 Nov. 90	
65 Foot	25	Francis, George Frankland,⁴⁰¹ Commandant 5 Bombay Cavalry	12 Nov. 70	28 Oct. 71		12 Nov. 82		12 Nov. 90	
12 Foot	25	Weller, Alexander Thomas,⁴⁰² 2nd in Command 9 Bombay Infantry	12 Nov. 70	23 Oct. 71		12 Nov. 82		12 Nov. 90	
108 Foot	25	Bough, Guilium Scott,⁴⁰³ Commandant 21 Madras Infantry	12 Nov. 70	28 Oct. 71		12 Nov. 82		12 Nov. 90	
		Wray, John Willoughby, Assistant Political Agent, Southern Mahratta Country, Jagheers							
5 Lanc.	25	Masters, Alexander,⁴⁰⁵ 2nd in Command and Squadron Commander 7 Central India Horse	30 Nov. 70	28 Oct. 71		30 Nov. 82		30 Nov. 90	

Indian Staff Corps.

Last Regiment.	Yrs. serv.	Majors.	2ND LIEUT. CORNET, OR ENSIGN.	LIEUT.	BREVET CAPTAIN.	CAPTAIN.	BREVET MAJOR.	MAJOR.	BREVET LT.-COL.
56 Foot	25	Alexander, Frederick Gordon, 407 2nd in Command and Wing Comdr. 10 Bombay Inf.	7 Dec. 70	28 Oct. 71		7 Dec. 82		7 Dec. 90	
Royal Artillery	25	Leigh, Henry Percy Poingdestre, 409 *CIE*, Dep. Commissioner, 3rd Cl., Kohat, Punjab.	a Jan. 71	4 Jan. 71		4 Jan. 83		4 Jan. 91	
21 Foot	25	Temple, Richard Carnac, 410 *CIE*, President, Municipal Committee, Rangoon	4 Jan. 71	4 Jan. 71		4 Jan. 83		4 Jan. 91	
65 Foot	25	Vivian, Frederick Guy, 2nd in Command and Wing Comdr. 38 Bengal Infantry	4 Jan. 71	4 Jan. 71		4 Jan. 83		4 Jan. 91	
8 Foot	25	McRae, Henry Napier, 412 2nd in Command and Wing Comdr. 45 Bengal Infantry	4 Jan. 71	4 Jan. 71		4 Jan. 83		4 Jan. 91	
77 Foot	24	Maisey, Frederick Charles, 413 Commandant 30 Bengal Infantry	25 Mar. 71	25 Mar. 71		25 Mar. 83		25 Mar. 91	
19 Foot	24	Hogge, Charles, 414 2nd in Command and Wing Comdr. 33 Bengal Infantry	23 Sept. 71	23 Sept. 71		23 Sept. 83	7 Dec. 88	23 Sept. 91	
83 Foot	24	Wingate, George, Assistant Commissary General, 2nd Class, Rawul Pindee	23 Sept. 71	23 Sept. 71		23 Sept. 83		23 Sept. 91	
75 Foot	24	Radford, Oswald Claude, 417 Commandant 4 Punjab Infantry	23 Sept. 71	23 Sept. 71		23 Sept. 83	7 Dec. 88	23 Sept. 91	
11 Foot	24	Montanaro, Alfred, 418 2nd in Command and Wing Comdr. 14 Bengal Infantry	23 Sept. 71	23 Sept. 71		23 Sept. 83		23 Sept. 91	
45 Foot	24	MacMullen, William Henry Fothergill, 412 Judge Advocate General in India	26 Sept. 71	26 Sept. 71		26 Sept. 83	7 Dec. 88	26 Sept. 91	
36 Foot	24	Sorell, Francis Sheffield, 420 Commandant 5 Infantry Hyderabad Contingent	28 Oct. 71	14 Oct. 71		14 Oct. 83		14 Oct. 91	
108 Foot	24	Pulley, Charles, 421 Commandant 1 Battalion 3 Goorkha Regiment	28 Oct. 71	28 Oct. 71		28 Oct. 83		28 Oct. 91	
54 Foot	24	Browne, Lambart John, 422 2nd in Command and Wing Commander 18 Bengal Inf.	28 Oct. 71	28 Oct. 71		28 Oct. 83		28 Oct. 91	
25 Foot	24	Henderson, Percy Edward, 423 Assistant Commissioner, 1st Grade, Nowgong, Assam	28 Oct. 71	28 Oct. 71		28 Oct. 83	1 July 87	28 Oct. 91	
72 Foot	24	Jameson, Robert Feild, 424 Commandant 5 Punjab Infantry	28 Oct. 71	28 Oct. 71		28 Oct. 83		28 Oct. 91	
44 Foot	24	Haughton, John, Commandant 36 Bengal Infantry	28 Oct. 71	28 Oct. 71		28 Oct. 83		28 Oct. 91	
108 Foot	24	Browne, Arthur Geo. Frederic, 25 *DSO*, 2nd in Con. and Wing Comdr. 2 Bn. 4 Goorkhas.	28 Oct. 71	28 Oct. 71		28 Oct. 83		28 Oct. 91	
1 Foot	24	Wapshare, Arthur, Cantonment Magistrate, Deesa	28 Oct. 71	28 Oct. 71		28 Oct. 83		28 Oct. 91	
Royal Artillery	24	Coats, George Henry B. 428 2nd in Command and Wing Commander 25 Bengal Infantry				15 Dec. 83		15 Dec. 91	
68 Foot	24	Bird, William John Butterworth, Deputy Accountant Gen. Govt. of India, Military Dept.	15 Dec. 71	15 Dec. 71		15 Dec. 83		15 Dec. 91	
15 Hussars	24	Stewart, Norman Robert 430 (*Colonel*, 28 Mar. 90), Commandant Mhairwara Battalion	29 Oct. 71	29 Oct. 71		29 Oct. 79	2 Mar. 83	30 Dec. 91	15 June 85
13 Hussars	24	Campbell, Alex. William Dennistoun, 431 Cantonment Magistrate, 1st Cl., Lucknow, Oude	30 Dec. 71	30 Dec. 71		30 Dec. 83		30 Dec. 91	
89 Foot	24	Wheler, Charles Stuart, 432 2nd in Command and Squadron Commander 6 Bengal Cavalry	30 Dec. 71	30 Dec. 71		30 Dec. 83		30 Dec. 91	
36 Foot	24	Barrow, Edmund George, 434 Commandant Hong Kong Regiment	30 Dec. 71	30 Dec. 71		30 Dec. 83		30 Dec. 91	
68 Foot	24	Smith, Allan, 2nd in Command and Wing Commander 22 Bombay Infantry	30 Dec. 71	30 Dec. 71		30 Dec. 83		30 Dec. 91	
92 Foot	24	Mansel, William Grenville, Wing Commander 7 Bengal Infantry	30 Dec. 71	30 Dec. 71		30 Dec. 83	16 Feb. 87	30 Dec. 91	
14 Foot	24	Cooke-Collis, Maurice Crosby, 436 Wing Commander 34 Bengal Infantry	30 Dec. 71	30 Dec. 71		30 Dec. 83	16 Feb. 87	30 Dec. 91	16 Jan. 95
65 Foot	24	Gambier, Claude Frederic, 437 2nd in Command and Squadron Commander 5 Punjab Cav.	30 Dec. 71	30 Dec. 71		30 Dec. 83		30 Dec. 91	
2 Foot	24	Hewett, William Selwood, 438 Cantonment Magistrate, 2nd Class, Meerut	30 Dec. 71	30 Dec. 71		30 Dec. 83	1 Sept. 91	30 Dec. 91	
73 Foot	24	Mainwaring, Francis George Lawrence, 439 2nd in Com. and Wing Comdr. 29 Bengal Inf.	30 Dec. 71	30 Dec. 71		30 Dec. 83		30 Dec. 91	
107 Foot	23	Mein, Alexander Bowes, 440 Commandant 21 Bombay Infantry	30 Dec. 71	30 Dec. 71		30 Dec. 83		30 Dec. 91	
11 Foot	23	Gibbs, Mossom Inniss, 441 Commandant 31 Bengal Infantry	30 Dec. 71	30 Dec. 71		30 Dec. 83		30 Dec. 91	
37 Foot	23	FitzGerald, Charles Mordaunt, 442 Assistant Commissary General, 3rd Class, Bareilly	10 Jan. 72	10 Jan. 72		10 Jan. 84		10 Jan. 92	
89 Foot	23	Bunny, Arthur Cautley, 443 Commandant 1 Sikh Infantry	3 Feb. 72	3 Feb. 72		3 Feb. 84		3 Feb. 92	
49 Foot	23	Des Voeux, Charles Hamilton, 2nd in Com. and Wing Commander 13 Bengal Infantry	17 Feb. 72	17 Feb. 72		17 Feb. 84		17 Feb. 92	
53 Foot	23	Hayne, Arthur Gorham Howard, 445 Station Staff Officer, Pallaveram	9 Mar. 72	9 Mar. 72		9 Mar. 84		9 Mar. 92	
62 Foot	23	Fulton, Robert, 446 Commandant 1 Battalion 1 Goorkha Regiment	27 Mar. 72	27 Mar. 72		27 Mar. 84	28 July 90	27 Mar. 92	
83 Foot	23	Randall, Frank Montague, 448 *DSO*, 2nd in Com. and Wing Comdr. 1 Battalion 4 Goorkhas	24 Apr. 72	24 Apr. 72		24 Apr. 84		24 Apr. 92	
21 Foot	23	Gwatkin, Frederick Stapleton, 449 Squadron Commander, 3rd Class; Pay Examiner, Rawul Pindee	24 Apr. 72	24 Apr. 72		24 Apr. 84	1 Sept. 91	24 Apr. 92	
Royal Artillery	23	Renny, George Blakiston, 450 Military Accountant, 3rd Class, Rajpootana; Military Department	2 May 72	2 May 72		2 May 84		2 May 92	
8 Foot	23	Buckland, Philip Arnold, 452 Wing Commander 15 Bengal Infantry	8 May 72	8 May 72		8 May 84		8 May 92	
70 Foot	23	Allen, Bedford Morant, 453 2nd in Command and Wing Commander 2 Sikh Infantry	29 May 72	29 May 72		29 May 84		29 May 92	
7 Foot	23	Sandys, Edwin Capel Currie, 454 Assistant Commissary General, 2nd Class, Mean Meer	8 June 72	8 June 72		8 June 84		8 June 92	
King's Royal Rifles	23	Raveneshaw, Charles Withers, 455 Polit. Agent and 2nd Class, Mysore; Sec. to Chief Commr. Coorg	17 July 72	17 July 72		17 July 84		17 July 92	
14 Foot	23	Field, William Caldwell Faure, 456 Assistant Accountant General, Military Department	24 July 72	24 July 72		24 July 84	16 Feb. 87	24 July 92	
10 Hussars	23	Pears, Thos. Caldwell, 456 Political Assist. 3rd Class, Rajpootana; Political Agent, Ulwur	31 Aug. 72	31 Aug. 72		31 Aug. 84	15 June 85	31 Aug. 92	
63 Foot	23	Temple, Henry Marindale, Political Agent, Kelat							
6 Foot	23	Bolton, Harry John, 457 2nd in Command and Wing Commander 42 Bengal Infantry	11 Sept. 72	11 Sept. 72		11 Sept. 84		11 Sept. 92	
	23	Heath, Harry Heptinstall Rose, 458 2nd in Com. and Squadron Comdr. 2 Bengal Lancers							
	23	Reilly, Rawdon Edward Denny, 459 Commandant 8 Bombay Infantry							
	23	Lean, William Walker, 460 2nd in Command and Squadron Commander 5 Bengal Cavalry							

Indian Staff Corps.

Last Regiment.	Yrs. Serv.	Majors.	2nd Lieut, Cornet, or Ensgn.	Lieut.	Brevet Captain.	Captain.	Brevet Major.	Major.	Brevet Lt. Col.
8 Foot.	23	Money, George Alfred,⁴⁶¹ 2nd in Command and Squadron Commander 18 Bengal Lancers.		11 Sept. 72		11 Sept. 84		11 Sept. 92	
3 Hussars.	23	MacIvor, Ivar,⁴⁶² *C.I.E.* Political Agent, 3rd Class; Revenue Commissioner, Beloochistan		19 Oct. 72		19 Oct. 84		19 Oct. 92	
67 Foot.	23	Torrie, Lawrence Jameson, Commandant 22 Madras Infantry.		19 Oct. 72		19 Oct. 84		19 Oct. 92	
51 Foot.	23	MacLeod, Roderick William,⁴⁶³ Wing Commander 29 Bengal Infantry.		19 Oct. 72		19 Oct. 84		19 Oct. 92	
43 Foot.	23	Plowden, Walter Francis Courtenay Chichelé,⁴⁶⁴ Squadron Commander 5 Bengal Cavalry		2 Nov. 72		2 Nov. 84		2 Nov. 92	
6 Lancers.	23	Bairnsfather, Peter Robert,⁴⁶⁵ 2nd in Command and Squad. Commander 14 Bengal Lancers		2 Nov. 72		2 Nov. 84		2 Nov. 92	
39 Foot.	23	Macausland, Redmond Conyngham S.⁴⁶⁶ Cant. Magistrate, 1st Class, Peshawur, Punjab.		13 Nov. 72		13 Nov. 84		13 Nov. 92	
72 Foot.	23	Monteith, John,⁴⁶⁷ 2nd in Command and Squadron Commander 7 Bombay Lancers		13 Nov. 72		13 Nov. 84		13 Nov. 92	
14 Foot.	23	Marrett, Henry Richard,⁴⁶⁸ Superintendent of the Hussar Cattle Farm.		13 Nov. 72		13 Nov. 84		13 Nov. 92	
12 Foot.	23	Adye, Goodson,⁴⁷⁰ Commandant 1 Lancers Hyderabad Contingent		13 Nov. 72		13 Nov. 84		13 Nov. 92	
70 Foot.	23	Hawkes, Hy., Montague Pakington,⁴⁷¹ Assist. Commissary General, 2nd Class, Rawul Pindee		23 Nov. 72		23 Nov. 84		23 Nov. 92	
65 Foot.	23	p.s.c. Durand, Algernon George Arnold,⁴⁷² *C.B.* Military Sec. to Governor General of India		21 Dec. 72	13 Nov. 89	21 Dec. 84		21 Dec. 92	27 Apr. 92
83 Foot.	23	Mayne, Richard Charles Graham,⁴⁷³ Commandant 30 Bombay Infantry		21 Dec. 72		21 Dec. 84		21 Dec. 92	
56 Foot.	23	Pringle, Alexander,⁴⁷⁴ 2nd in Command and Squadron Commander 2 Bombay Lancers		30 Dec. 72		30 Dec. 84		30 Dec. 92	
4 Hussars.	23	Wood, Edward James Fandon,⁴⁷⁵ Commandant 10 Bengal Lancers		1 Jan. 73		1 Jan. 85		1 Jan. 93	
83 Foot.	23	Read, Hastings,⁴⁷⁶ 2nd in Command and Wing Commander 4 Bengal Infantry		15 Jan. 73		15 Jan. 85		15 Jan. 93	
3 Hussars.	23	Roberts, Charles James,⁴⁷⁷ Squadron Commander 16 Bengal Cavalry		8 Feb. 73		8 Jan. 85		8 Feb. 93	
67 Foot.	23	O'Mealy, William Arthur D'Oyly,⁴⁷⁸ 2nd in Com. and Squadron Comdr. 1 Punjab Cavalry		8 Feb. 73		8 Jan. 85		8 Feb. 93	
14 Foot.	23	Molesworth, Edward Hogarth,⁴⁷⁹ Commandant 43 Bengal Infantry		24 Feb. 73		8 Jan. 85		24 Feb. 93	
39 Foot.	23	Sturt, Robert Ramsay Napier,⁴⁸⁰ Commandant 2 Punjab Infantry.		9 Mar. 73		8 Jan. 85		9 Mar. 93	
8 Foot.	23	Thornhill, Henry Beaufoy,⁴⁸¹ Cantonment Magistrate, Chuckrata		23 Apr. 73		8 Jan. 85		8 May 93	
67 Foot.	22	Montresor, Edward Henry Hopton,⁴⁸² Squadron Commander 4 Bengal Cavalry.		29 May 73		8 Jan. 85		29 May 93	
77 Foot.	22	Young, William Hope,⁴⁸³ Mil. Accountant, 3rd Class; Examiner Commt. Accounts, Madras		24 July 73		8 Jan. 85		24 July 93	
51 Foot.	22	White, Frederick Power Lawrence, Wing Commander 1 Bengal Infantry		3 Aug. 73		8 Jan. 85		3 Aug. 93	
6 Foot.	22	Garstside-Tipping, Robert Francis,⁴⁸⁵ Commandant 1 Bengal Cavalry		9 Aug. 73		8 Jan. 85		9 Aug. 93	
80 Foot.	22	Tonnochy, Valens Congreve,⁴⁸⁶ 2nd in Command and Wing Commander 4 Sikh Infantry		9 Aug. 73		8 Jan. 85		9 Aug. 93	
89 Foot.	22	Meade, Malcolm John, Political Agent, Bhopaul, Central India.		9 Aug. 73		8 Jan. 85		9 Aug. 93	
89 Foot.	22	Meade, John de Courcy Dashwood,⁴⁸⁷ Squadron Commander 8 Bengal Cavalry		9 Aug. 73		8 Jan. 85		9 Aug. 93	
17 Foot.	22	Passy, Harry Everard, Military Accountant, 3rd Class.		9 Aug. 73		8 Jan. 85		9 Aug. 93	
17 Foot.	22	Masters, Edward Steuart,⁴⁸⁸ 2nd in Command and Wing Commander Bhopaul Battalion.		9 Aug. 73		8 Jan. 85		9 Aug. 93	
43 Foot.	22	Lawford, Eustace Edward Melville,⁴⁸⁹ Commandant 1 Madras Lancers		9 Aug. 73		8 Jan. 85	1 July 88	9 Aug. 93	
62 Foot.	22	Egerton, Francis William, Assistant Commissioner, 1st Class, Loodhiana, Punjab		9 Aug. 73		8 Jan. 85		9 Aug. 93	
17 Foot.	22	Nedham, Edward Montgomerie,⁴⁹⁰ Cantonment Magistrate, Kampdee, Central Provinces		9 Aug. 73		8 Jan. 85		9 Aug. 93	
72 Foot.	22	Beason, Stuart Brownlow,⁴⁹¹ Squadron Commander 11 Bengal Lancers.		9 Aug. 73		8 Jan. 85		9 Aug. 93	
17 Foot.	22	Monteith, Arthur Mackworth,⁴⁹² Squadron Commander 7 Bombay Lancers.		9 Aug. 73		8 Jan. 85		9 Aug. 93	
12 Foot.	22	Robinson, George Henry,⁴⁹³ 2nd in Command and Wing Commander 1 Bn. 1 Goorkhas.		9 Aug. 73		8 Jan. 85		9 Aug. 93	
Royal Artillery	22	Radcliffe, Arthur Wilbraham Twining,⁴⁹⁴ Wing Commander 14 Bengal Infantry.		9 Sept. 73		8 Jan. 85		9 Sept. 93	
Royal Marine Artillery	22	Renny, Alexander MacWhirter,⁴⁹⁵ 2nd in Com. and Squadron Commander 7 Bengal Cavalry		1 Oct. 73		8 Jan. 85	2 Aug. 88	1 Oct. 93	
Royal Marine Artillery	22	Hall, Lewis Montgomery Murray,⁴⁹⁶ 2nd in Com. and Wing Commander 2 Bn. 2 Goorkhas		1 Oct. 73		8 Jan. 85		1 Oct. 93	
10 Hussars	22	Woon, John Blaxoll,⁴⁹⁷ Wing Officer 40 Bengal Infantry		11 Sept. 73		8 Jan. 85		11 Sept. 93	
49 Foot.	22	Montresor, Welby Francis, Squadron Commander 17 Bengal Cavalry		19 Oct. 73		8 Jan. 85		19 Oct. 93	
72 Foot.	22	Candy, James Molesworth, Wing Commander 14 Bombay Infantry		2 Nov. 73		8 Jan. 85		2 Nov. 93	
West Surrey Regiment	22	Lambert, William,⁴⁹⁸ Squadron Commander 3 Punjab Cavalry		12 Nov. 73		8 Jan. 85		12 Nov. 93	
68 Foot.	22	Dawson, Harry Leonard,⁴⁹⁹ Squadron Commander 9 Bengal Lancers		12 Nov. 73		8 Jan. 85		12 Nov. 93	
66 Foot.	22	Yate, William Gordon,⁵⁰⁰ Squadron Commander 1 Bengal Cavalry.		12 Nov. 73		8 Jan. 85		12 Nov. 93	
Middlesex Regiment	22	Fenton, Alexander Bulstrode,⁵⁰¹ Commandant 2 Madras Lancers		12 Nov. 73		8 Jan. 85		12 Nov. 93	
83 Foot.	22	Lyde, Malcolm Thomas,⁵⁰² 2nd in Com. Kolapore Inf. and ex officio Assist. Pol. Agent, Kolapore		21 Jan. 74		29 Apr. 85		21 Jan. 94	
Royal Artillery	22	Cadell, Herv Francis, Military Accountant, 2nd Class		12 Feb. 74		12 Feb. 85		12 Feb. 94	
2 West India Regiment	22	Faithfull, Henry Turner,⁵⁰³ Wing Commander 33 Bengal Infantry		12 Feb. 74		12 Feb. 85		12 Feb. 94	
11 Foot.	22	Hastings, Warren, Deputy Commissioner, 3rd Class, Hyderabad		28 Feb. 74		28 Feb. 85		28 Feb. 94	
67 Foot.	22	Ramsay, Henry Lushington,⁵⁰⁴ Political Officer with Ayoob Khan		28 Feb. 74		28 Feb. 85		28 Feb. 94	
11 Foot.	22	O'Bryen, James Lourghan,⁵⁰⁵ 2nd in Command and Wing Commander 3e Bengal Infantry		28 Feb. 74		28 Feb. 85		28 Feb. 94	
67 Foot.	22	Sparling, James Philip,⁵⁰⁶ Assistant Commissary General, 3rd Class, Lahore.		28 Feb. 74		28 Feb. 85		28 Feb. 94	

Indian Staff Corps.

Last Regiment.	Yrs. Sv.	Majors.	2nd Lieut., Cornet, or Ensign.	Lieut.	Brevet Captain.	Captain.	Brevet Major.	Major.	Brevet Lt.Col.
11 Foot	22	Ryland, Henry George,[507] Assistant Commissary General, 4th Class, Lucknow		28 Feb. 74		28 Feb. 85		28 Feb. 94	
98 Foot	22	Preston, Frederick George,[508] Commandant 28 Madras Infantry		28 Feb. 74		28 Feb. 85		28 Feb. 94	
54 Foot	22	Deane, Harold Arthur,[509] Assistant Commissioner, 2nd Grade, Peshawur, Punjab		28 Feb. 74		28 Feb. 85		28 Feb. 94	
51 Foot	22	Macdonald, Charles Edward Wylde,[510] Squadron Commander 6 Bengal Cavalry		28 Feb. 74		28 Feb. 85		28 Feb. 94	
109 Foot	22	Hastings, Edward Spence,[511] DSO, Commandant 32 Madras Infantry		28 Feb. 74		28 Feb. 85		28 Feb. 94	
45 Foot	22	Worledge, John Franklin,[512] 2nd in Command and Wing Commander 35 Bengal Infantry		28 Feb. 74		28 Feb. 85		28 Feb. 94	
22 Foot	22	Massy, Harry Stanley,[513] 2nd in Command and Squadron Commander 19 Bengal Lancers		28 Feb. 74		28 Feb. 85		28 Feb. 94	
70 Foot	22	p.s.c. Jones, Alfred Edwin,[514] Assist. Secretary, Military Department, Government of India		28 Feb. 74		28 Feb. 85		28 Feb. 94	
3 Foot	22	Drury, Francis Macdonald,[515] Wing Commander 30 Bengal Infantry		26 Mar. 74		26 Mar. 85		26 Mar. 94	
65 Foot	22	Dennys, Charles John,[516] Cantonment Magistrate, 1st Class, Rawul Pindee, Punjab		26 Mar. 74		26 Mar. 85		26 Mar. 94	
15 Foot	22	Dun, Edward Wm.[517] DSO, Wing Commander 20 Bengal Infantry		28 Mar. 74		10 Mar. 85		10 June 94	
East Surrey Regiment	21	Jones, Juxon Henry,[518] Commandant 2 Madras Infantry		10 June 74		10 June 85		10 June 94	
45 Foot	21	Herbert, Charles,[519] Political Agent, 3rd Class; Political Agent in Kotah		13 June 74		13 June 85		13 June 94	
3 Foot	21	Ozzard, Hudson Henry,[520] Wing Officer 14, Bengal Infantry		13 June 74		13 June 85		13 June 94	
5 Foot	21	Collins, George Atkins,[521] 2nd in Command and Wing Commander Mhairwarra Battalion		13 June 74		13 June 85		13 June 94	
108 Foot	21	Aslett, William Charles,[522] Commandant 8 Bombay Infantry		13 June 74		13 June 85		13 June 94	
45 Foot	21	Peyton, Lumley Scobell,[523] Squadron Commander 14, Bengal Lancers		13 June 74		13 June 85		13 June 94	
Inniskilling Fusiliers	21	p.s.c. Bayly, Alfred William Lambart,[524] DSO, 2nd in Com. and Wing Comdr. 26 Bombay Inf.		13 June 74		13 June 85		13 June 94	
3 Foot	21	Jameson, William Henry,[525] Wing Commander 23 Bengal Infantry		13 June 74		13 June 85		13 June 94	
2 Foot	21	Adye, Arthur,[526] Commandant 4 Infantry Hyderabad Contingent		13 June 74		13 June 85		13 June 94	
17 Foot	21	Pollock, John Archibald Henry,[527] 2nd in Command and Wing Commander 3 Sikh Infantry		13 June 74		13 June 85		13 June 94	
16 Foot	21	Fasken, Charles Grant Mansell,[528] Wing Commander 2 Sikh Infantry		13 June 74		13 June 85		13 June 94	
Gloucestershire Regiment	21	Beckham, Lionel Grafton,[529] Commandant 25 Bombay Infantry		27 June 74		27 June 85		27 June 94	
17 Foot	21	Stuart, Charles John Lewis[530]		11 July 74		11 July 85		11 July 94	
51 Foot	21	Welchman, Edim Walter St. George,[531] Commandant 2 Infantry, Hyderabad Contingent		9 Aug. 74		9 Aug. 85	7 Nov. 85	9 Aug. 94	1 July 87
11 Foot	21	Chamberlain, Neville Francis Fitzgerald,[532] Squadron Commander 1 Central India Horse		9 Aug. 74		9 Aug. 85		9 Aug. 94	
		(Brevet Colonel, 6 Jan. 94)							
22 Foot	21	Spankie, John Patrick Walker,[533] Cantonment Magistrate, 1st Grade, Ranikhet, N.W. Prov.		9 Aug. 74		9 Aug. 85		9 Aug. 94	10 Aug. 94
109 Foot	21	Peile, Solomon Charles Frederick,[534] Assistant Commissary General, 3rd Class; Inspector General of Military Police, Burmah							
Royal Artillery	20	p.s.c. Duff, Beauchamp,[535] Deputy Assistant Adjutant General at Head Quarters		17 Aug. 74		8 May 86		17 Aug. 94	
65 Foot	21	Westmorland, Charles Henry,[536] 2nd in Command and Wing Comdr. 6 Bengal Infantry		21 Sept. 74		21 Sept. 85	23 Aug. 89	21 Sept. 94	
72 Foot	21	Gordon, Stewart Douglas,[537] Squadron Commander 19 Bengal Lancers		21 Sept. 74		21 Sept. 85		21 Sept. 94	
Yorkshire Light Infantry	21	Preston, Jenico Edward,[538] DSO, Commandant 33 Madras Infantry		21 Sept. 74		21 Sept. 85		21 Sept. 94	
8 Foot	21	Hawkins, Frederick,[539] DSO, Assistant Military Secretary, Teheran		21 Sept. 74		21 Sept. 85		21 Sept. 94	
33 Foot	21	Picot, Henry Philip,[540] 2nd in Command and Wing Commander 3 Bombay Infantry		21 Sept. 74		21 Sept. 85		21 Sept. 94	
81 Foot	21	Birdwood, William Spiller,[541] 2nd in Command and Wing Commander 37 Bengal Infantry		21 Sept. 74		21 Sept. 85		21 Sept. 94	
40 Foot	21	Marshall, William Simpson,[542] 2nd in Command and Wing Commander Squad. Comdr. 6 Bombay Cav.		21 Sept. 74		21 Sept. 85		21 Sept. 94	
6 Foot	21	Faithfull, William Conrad,[543] 2nd in Command and Wing Commander 1 Bengal Infantry		21 Sept. 74		21 Sept. 85		21 Sept. 94	
Royal Marine Artillery	21	Butler, John Blandford Rateclyffe,[544] 2nd in Command and Squadron Commander 6 Bengal Cavalry		1 Oct. 74		1 Oct. 85		1 Oct. 94	
Royal Marines	21	Hayes, Clarence Henry,[545] 2nd in Command and Squadron Commander 16 Bengal Cav.		1 Oct. 74		1 Oct. 85		1 Oct. 94	
40 Foot	21	Stockley, Vesey Mangles,[546] 2nd in Command and Wing Commander 17 Bengal Infantry		5 Oct. 74		5 Oct. 85		5 Oct. 94	
Irish Rifles	21	Enriquez, Albert Dallas,[546] 2nd in Command and Wing Commander 17 Bengal Infantry		5 Sept. 77		14 Nov. 85		14 Nov. 94	
		(Lt. R. Malta Fenc. Art., 14 Nov. 74)							
34 Foot	21	Martin, Alfred Robert,[549] 2nd in Command and Wing Commander 1 Battalion 5 Goorkhas		2 Dec. 74		2 Dec. 85	1 Sept. 91	2 Dec. 94	
25 Foot	21	Sinclair, Alfred Law,[547] DSO, 2nd in Command and Wing Commander 27 Bombay Infantry		2 Dec. 74		2 Dec. 85		2 Dec. 94	
16 Foot	21	Lamb, John,[548] 2nd in Command and Wing Commander 2 Bengal Infantry		2 Dec. 74		2 Dec. 85		2 Dec. 94	
72 Foot	21	Fairbrother, William Tomes,[552] 2nd in Command and Wing Commander 13 Bengal Inf.		11 Feb. 75		11 Feb. 86		11 Feb. 95	
14 Foot	21	Ramsay, John George,[553] Deputy Assistant Adjutant General, Punjab Frontier Force		11 Feb. 75		11 Feb. 86		11 Feb. 95	
18 Foot	21	Williamson, Andrew Pennell,[554] 2nd in Command and Squadron Comdr. 5 Punjab Cavalry		11 Feb. 75		11 Feb. 86		11 Feb. 95	
7 Foot	21	Minchin, Hugh Dillor Massy,[555] Squadron Commander 1 Bombay Infantry		11 Feb. 75		11 Feb. 86	29 Dec. 93	11 Feb. 95	
21 Foot	21	Presgrave, Edward Robert John,[556] DSO, Commandant to Madras Infantry		11 Feb. 75		11 Feb. 86		11 Feb. 95	

Indian Staff Corps.

Last Regiment.	Yrs. Serv.	MAJORS.	2ND LIEUT. CORNET, OR ENSIGN.	LIEUT.	BREVET CAPTAIN.	CAPTAIN.	BREVET MAJOR.	MAJOR.	BREVET LT. COL.
Black Watch	21	Blyth, Frederick Augustus, 2nd in Command and Squad. Commander 10 Bengal Lancers		11 Feb. 75		11 Feb. 86		11 Feb. 95	11 Feb. 95
109 Foot	21	Barrett, Alfred Lloyd,³⁵⁷ DSO. 2nd in Command and Wing Commander 43 Bengal Infantry		11 Feb. 75		11 Feb. 86		11 Feb. 95	11 Feb. 95
North Staffordshire Regt.	21	Parker, John William,³⁵⁸ Commandant 16 Madras Native Infantry		11 Feb. 75		11 Feb. 86		11 Feb. 95	11 Feb. 95
63 Foot	21	Fagan, Christopher George Forbes,³⁵⁹ Political Assistant 3rd Class ; Assistant Resident and Superintendent of Operations for the Suppression of Thuggee and Dacoity		11 Feb. 75		11 Feb. 86		11 Feb. 95	
12 Foot	21	Richardson, William St. John,³⁶⁰ Military Accountant, 4th Class, Calcutta		11 Feb. 75		11 Feb. 86	16 Feb. 87	11 Feb. 95	
109 Foot	21	Drummond, Francis Henry Rutherford,³⁶¹ Squadron Commander 11 Bengal Lancers		11 Feb. 75		11 Feb. 86		11 Feb. 95	
70 Foot	21	Shawe, Robert Baker,³⁶² Wing Commander 16 Bengal Infantry		11 Feb. 75		11 Feb. 86		11 Feb. 95	
43 Foot	21	Burn, Arthur George,³⁶³ Commandant 14 Madras Infantry		10 Mar. 75		10 Mar. 86		10 Mar. 95	
		CAPTAINS.							
Border Regiment	20	Marriott, Edward Frere¹		21 Sept. 74		21 Sept. 85			
2 Foot	20	Alban, Clifton Frederick Samuel,¹ 2nd in Command and Wing Commander 7 Bombay Inf.		13 June 75		13 June 86			
67 Foot	20	Jones, Richard Godfrey,² 2nd in Command and Squadron Commander 1 Madras Lancers		13 June 75		13 June 86			
33 Foot	20	Thatcher, John Frederick Charles,³ 2nd in Com. and Wing Commander 20 Bombay Inf.		13 June 75		13 June 86			
East Lancashire Regiment	20	Boulderson, Henry Allan Balfour,³ Commandant 17 Madras Infantry		13 June 75		13 June 86			
33 Foot	20	Lyons-Montgomery, Hugh Fred.,⁴ Assist. Commissary General, 3rd Class, Rawul Pindee		13 June 75		13 June 86			
33 Foot	20	Lushington, Edw. Chas. Mortimer,⁵ 2nd in Com. and Wing Comdr. 2 Inf. Hyderabad Cont.		27 June 75		27 June 86			
South Yorkshire Regiment	20	Pollock, Frederick George,⁶ 2nd in Com. and Squadron Commander 7 Bengal Cavalry		9 Aug. 75		9 Aug. 86			
56 Foot	20	Prichard, George Penry Montague, Commandant 7 Madras Infantry		9 Aug. 75		9 Aug. 86			
2 West India Regiment	20	Clothier, Robert Freebairn,⁷ Deputy Assistant Adjutant General, Chin Hills		12 Aug. 75		12 Aug. 86			
1 West India Regiment	20	Lawson, Herbert,⁸ Commandant 13 Madras Infantry		12 Aug. 75		12 Aug. 86			
Royal Artillery	20	Davison, Kenneth Stuart, Deputy Assistant Adjutant General, Meerut		19 Aug. 75		19 Aug. 86			
Border Regiment	20	Martin, Edward William Fane,⁹ 2nd in Com. and Wing Comdr. 1 Battalion 1 Goorkhas		Sept. 75		Sept. 86			
15 Foot	20	Phillips, Charles Reginald,¹⁰ Wing Commander 19 Bombay Infantry		Sept. 75		Sept. 86	1 Sept. 91		
44 Foot	20	Barrett, Arthur Arnold,¹¹ 2nd in Command and Wing Commander 2 Battalion 5 Goorkhas		Sept. 75		Sept. 86			
Derbyshire Regiment	20	Swann, John Christopher,¹² Deputy Assistant Adjutant General, Bombay		Sept. 75		Sept. 86			
3 Foot	20	Tate, Hugh Boddam,¹³ Squadron Commander 15 Bengal Lancers		Sept. 75		Sept. 86			
67 Foot	20	Ramsden, Herbert Frecheville Smyth,¹⁴ Military Accountant, 3rd Class ; Assistant Secretary to Government of India, Military Department		Sept. 75		Sept. 86			
68 Foot	20	Goad, Howard,¹⁵ Superintendent of Reserve Depot, Saharanpore		Sept. 75		Sept. 86	1 July 87		
25 Foot	20	Nixon, John Eccles, Deputy Assistant Adjutant General for Instruction, Chuckrata		Sept. 75		Sept. 86			
25 Foot	20	Retallick, John Mark Anthony,¹⁶ Wing Officer 45 Bengal Infantry		Sept. 75		Sept. 86			
44 Foot	20	Bell, James Alexander, Commandant Deolee Irregular Force		Sept. 75		Sept. 86			
25 Foot	20	Travers, Eaton Aylmer,¹⁷ Wing Commander 1 Battalion 2 Goorkhas		Sept. 75		Sept. 86	2 Nov. 88		
85 Foot	20	Godfray, Herbert,¹⁸ 2nd in Command and Wing Commander 9 Bombay Infantry		Sept. 75		Sept. 86			
15 Foot	20	Chase, William St. Lucien,¹⁹ Wing Commander 28 Bombay Infantry		Sept. 75		Sept. 86			
44 Foot	20	Hutchins, Herbert Leonard,²⁰ Assistant Commissary General, 3rd Class, Mandalay		Sept. 75		Sept. 86			
68 Foot	20	Seymour, Henry William,²¹ 2nd in Command and Wing Commander 16 Bombay Infantry		Sept. 75		Sept. 86			
17 Foot	20	Brownlow, Cecil Barry,²² 2nd in Command and Wing Commander 1 Punjab Infantry		Sept. 75		Sept. 86			
33 Foot	20	P.S.C. Poynder, Charles Eliot,²³ 2nd in Command and Wing Commander 25 Madras Infantry		Sept. 75		Sept. 86			
9 Foot	20	Williams, Geo. Augustus,²⁴ Military Accountant, 4th Class ; Junior Pay Examiner, Calcutta		Sept. 75		Sept. 86			
89 Foot	20	Cook, Walter,²⁴ Commandant 30 Madras Infantry		Sept. 75		Sept. 86			
Madras Staff Corps	20	Gray, William du Gard,²⁵ 2nd in Command and Wing Commander 4 Punjab Infantry		Sept. 75		Sept. 86	1 Sept. 91		
21 Foot	20	Teversham, Richard Kinloch,²⁵ DSO. Commandant 3 Madras Infantry		Sept. 75		Sept. 86			
34 Foot	20	Batten, Alan Coddington,²⁶ Deputy Assistant Adjutant General, Bundelcund		Sept. 75		Sept. 86			
48 Foot	20	Wilson, John Francis,²⁷ 2nd in Command and Wing Commander 22 Madras Infantry		Sept. 75		Sept. 86			
9 Foot	20	Cunliffe, Ernest William,²⁷ 2nd in Command and Wing Commander 6 Punjab Infantry		Sept. 75		Sept. 86			
25 Foot	20	Bradshaw, Laurence Julius Elliott,²⁷ Wing Commander 35 Bengal Infantry		Sept. 75		Sept. 86			
65 Foot	20	Fyen, George Eusébe,²⁸ 2nd in Command and Wing Commander 30 Bombay Infantry		21 Sept. 75		21 Sept. 86			
Suffolk Regiment	20	Smith, John Graham,²⁸ Assistant Commissary General, 4th Class		11 Sept. 75		11 Sept. 86			
34 Foot	20	Younghusband, George William,²⁹ Squadron Commander 14 Bengal Lancers		11 Sept. 75		11 Sept. 86			
68 Foot	20	Burn, Alex. Edward Pelham,²⁹ Wing Commander 25 Bengal Infantry		11 Sept. 75		21 Sept. 86			

Indian Staff Corps.

Last Regiment.	Yrs. Serv.	Captains.	2nd Lieut. Cornet, or Ensign.	Lieut.	Brevet Captain.	Captain.	Brevet Major.
Royal Marine Artillery	20	Farrant, Harland FitzLyddon,[30] Commandant 11 Madras Infantry		1 Oct. 75		1 Oct. 86	
1 West India Regiment	20	Peirse, Charles Edward,[31] 2nd in Command and Squadron Commander 5 Bombay Cavalry		13 Nov. 75		13 Nov. 86	
72 Foot	20	Downing, John George,[32] Military Accountant, 2nd Class ; Pay Examiner, Poona		20 Nov. 75		20 Nov. 86	
83 Foot	20	Mansfield, Herbert,[33] Assistant Commissary General, 3rd Class		20 Nov. 75		20 Nov. 86	2 Nov. 88
59 Foot	20	Gordon, John Wood,[33] 2nd in Command and Wing Commander 17 Bombay Infantry		20 Nov. 75		20 Nov. 86	
Royal Marines	20	Paul, Ernest Theodore,[34] Deputy Assistant Adjutant General, Assam		1 Jan. 76		1 Jan. 87	
Royal Marines	20	Taylor, William Willoughby,[35] Wing Commander 45 Bengal Infantry		1 Jan. 76		1 Jan. 87	
1 West India Regiment	20	O'Donnell, George Boodrie,[36] Assistant Political Resident, Aden		1 Jan. 76		1 Jan. 87	
Royal Marines	20	Williamson, Cyril Venn Wilton, Assistant Commissary General, 3rd Class, Meerut		27 Jan. 76		27 Jan. 87	
Royal Marines	20	Powell, Charles Herbert, Wing Commander 2 Battalion 1 Goorkhas		27 Jan. 76		27 Jan. 87	
Royal Marines	20	Baillie, Robert, Wing Commander 20 Bombay Infantry		27 Jan. 76		27 Jan. 87	
Royal Marines	20	Abud, Henry Mallaby, Assistant Political Resident, Aden		27 Jan. 76		27 Jan. 87	
Dorsetshire Regiment	20	Quentin, Walter, Wing Commander 4 Bombay Infantry		27 Jan. 76		27 Jan. 87	
54 Foot	20	Hickman, Devereux Walter,[37] Wing Officer 34 Bengal Infantry		11 Feb. 76		11 Feb. 87	
Cheshire Regiment	20	Garrett, Robert Vernon, Assistant Director of Land Records and Agriculture, Hyderabad		11 Feb. 76		11 Feb. 87	
Shropshire Regiment	20	Goldsmid, George Steuart,[38] Wing Commander 8 Bengal Infantry		11 Feb. 76		11 Feb. 87	
	20	Rivett-Carnac, Ernest Henry,[39] Squadron Commander 19 Bengal Lancers		11 Feb. 76		11 Feb. 87	
43 Foot	20	p.s.c. Geoghegan, Thomas Patrick,[40] 2nd in Com. and Squadron Comdr. 3 Bombay Cavalry		12 Feb. 76		12 Feb. 87	
6 Foot	20	Currie, John William,[41] Private Secretary to the Lieutenant Governor of Bengal		12 Feb. 76		12 Feb. 87	
72 Foot	20	Scallon, Robert Irwin,[42] DSO, 2nd in Command and Wing Commander 23 Bombay Infantry		12 Feb. 76		12 Feb. 87	
72 Foot	20	Delamain, Frank Gun,[43] Squadron Commander 11 Bengal Lancers		12 Feb. 76		12 Feb. 87	
Royal Marines	20	Gott, George Arthur, Commandant Governor's Body Guard		23 Feb. 76		23 Feb. 87	
1 West India Regiment	20	Lyster, Arthur Walker,[44] 2nd in Command and Wing Commander 1 Battalion 3 Goorkhas		8 Mar. 76		8 Mar. 87	
12 Foot	20	Ashby, John Shuckburgh,[45] Assistant Political Agent, Kattywar		22 Mar. 76		22 Mar. 87	
6 Foot	20	Ravenshaw, Harold Alexander,[46] 2nd in Command and Wing Commander 26 Bengal Infantry		24 Mar. 76		24 Mar. 87	
66 Foot	19	Walter, George Egbert,[47] Wing Commander 19 Bombay Infantry		15 Apr. 76		15 Apr. 87	
21 Foot	19	Stevens, Charles Frederick, Commandant 15 Madras Infantry		19 Apr. 76		19 Apr. 87	
34 Foot	19	Huggins, Ponsonby Glenn,[48] DSO, 2nd in Command and Wing Officer 21 Madras Infantry		28 Apr. 76		28 Apr. 87	
15 Foot	19	Sandwith, John Robert,[49] 2nd in Command and Wing Commander 8 Bombay Infantry		13 May 76		13 May 87	
Bedfordshire Regiment	19	Craster, James Cecil Balfour,[50] Squadron Commander 5 Bengal Infantry		25 May 76		25 May 87	
17 Foot	19	Mazera, Joseph Scott Gowrie, Commandant 8 Madras Infantry		15 July 76		15 July 87	
67 Foot	19	Evans-Gordon, William Eden, Political Agent, 3rd Class		12 Feb. 76		10 Aug. 87	
Lancaster Regiment	19	Penrose, Edward Rawdon,[51] 2nd in Command and Squadron Commander Meywar Bheel Corps		14 Aug. 76		14 Aug. 87	
Royal Artillery	19	Pollard, William Charles,[52] Squadron Commander 15 Bengal Lancers		26 Aug. 76		26 Aug. 87	
Seaforth Highlanders	19	Swiney, George Walter Brandon,[55] 2nd in Command and Wing Commander 2 Punjab Infantry		1 Sept. 76		1 Sept. 87	
Royal Marines	19	Atkinson, Francis Garnett,[56] Squadron Commander 13 Bengal Lancers		1 Sept. 76		1 Sept. 87	
East Surrey Regiment	19	Lumsden, Henry Richmond, William,[57] 2nd in Command and Wing Commander 3 Bengal Infantry		6 Sept. 76		6 Sept. 87	
18 Foot	19	Downes, William Knox,[58] DSO, 2nd in Command and Wing Commander 11 Bombay Infantry		10 Sept. 76		10 Sept. 87	
66 Foot	19	Leslie, Albert Edmond,[59] Wing Commander 2 Bombay Infantry		10 Sept. 76		10 Sept. 87	
16 Foot	19	Wyllie, John Alfred, Cantonment Magistrate, Rangoon		10 Sept. 76		10 Sept. 87	
51 Foot	19	Mason, Henry Espine Monck,[60] 2nd in Command and Wing Commander 17 Madras Infantry		10 Sept. 76		10 Sept. 87	
83 Foot	19	Tinley, Gervase Francis Newport,[61] Squadron Officer 1 Bombay Lancers		10 Sept. 76		10 Sept. 87	
67 Foot	19	Deane, Frederick Bernard, 2nd in Command and Squadron Commander 2 Madras Lancers		10 Sept. 76		10 Sept. 87	
73 Foot	19	Harris, Charles Walter,[62] Wing Commander 4 Bengal Infantry		11 Sept. 76		11 Sept. 87	
Duke of Cornwall's Lt. Inf.	19	MacMullen, George Reade,[63] Wing Commander 6 Punjab Infantry		11 Sept. 76		11 Sept. 87	
North Lancashire Regt.	19	Burne, Newdigate Addington Knightley, Wing Commander 23 Bengal Infantry		11 Sept. 76		11 Sept. 87	
12 Foot	19	Onslow, Richard Cranley,[64] Squadron Commander 10 Bengal Lancers		11 Sept. 76		11 Sept. 87	
5 Lancers	19	Dressner, Charles John Bernhard Hough, Squadron Commander 1 Central India Horse		11 Sept. 76		11 Sept. 87	
62 Foot	19	Wallace, Alexander,[65] 2nd in Command and Wing Commander 27 Bengal Infantry		11 Sept. 76		11 Sept. 87	
Irish Regiment	19	Lindsell, Philip Barber,[66] Squadron Commander 15 Bengal Lancers		11 Sept. 76		11 Sept. 87	
Dorsetshire Regiment	19	Bowring, George,[67] Wing Commander 17 Bengal Infantry		11 Sept. 76		11 Sept. 87	
63 Foot	19	Parsons, James Henry,[68] Squadron Commander 7 Bengal Cavalry		11 Sept. 76		11 Sept. 87	

418

Indian Staff Corps.

Last Regiment.	Yrs. Serv.	Captains.	2nd Lieut. Cornet, or Ensign.	Lieut.	Brevet Captain.	Captain.	Brevet Major.
39 Foot	19	Watson, George Herbert,[69] Cantonment Magistrate, Ferozepore	......	11 Sept. 76	......	11 Sept. 87	......
The Buffs	19	De Brath, Ernest,[70] Assistant Secretary, Military Department, Government of India	......	11 Sept. 76	......	11 Sept. 87	......
The Buffs	19	Cakes, George Edward Hyde, Adjutant Kholapore Infantry Corps	......	11 Sept. 76	......	11 Sept. 87	......
70 Foot	19	Wharry, Herbert,[71] Assist. Com. General 3rd Class; Brigade Commt. Officer Waziristan Delimitation Escort	......	11 Sept. 76	......	11 Sept. 87	......
70 Foot	19	Grover, Malcolm Henry Stanley,[72] Squadron Commander 2 Punjab Cavalry	......	11 Sept. 76	......	11 Sept. 87	......
80 Foot	19	Adams, Robert Bellew,[73] 2nd in Command and Squadron Commander Corps of Guides	......	22 Sept. 76	......	22 Sept. 87	......
12 Foot	19	Yate, Arthur Campbell,[74] 2nd in Command and Wing Commander 29 Bombay Infantry	......	6 Oct. 76	......	6 Oct. 87	......
1 West India Regiment	19	Balfour, Joseph Hume,[75] Squadron Commander 13 Bengal Lancers	......	6 Oct. 76	......	6 Oct. 87	......
8 Foot	19	Wilmer, Algernon Henry,[76] 2nd in Command and Wing Commander 19 Bengal Infantry	......	11 Oct. 76	......	11 Oct. 87	......
York and Lancaster Regt.	19	Maxwell, George William,[77] Commandant 29 Madras Infantry	......	28 Oct. 76	......	28 Oct. 87	......
40 Foot	19	Middleton, Herbert John James,[78] Squadron Commander 3 Bengal Cavalry	......	28 Oct. 76	......	28 Oct. 87	......
East Kent Regiment	19	Watson, George Frederick,[79] Assistant Commissary General, 3rd Class	......	28 Oct. 76	......	28 Oct. 87	......
62 Foot	19	Andrews, Robert Charles, 2nd in Command and Wing Commander 19 Madras Infantry	......	11 Nov. 76	......	11 Nov. 87	......
33 Foot	19	Stevens, Charles, Squadron Commander 1 Madras Lancers	......	29 Nov. 76	......	29 Nov. 87	......
34 Foot	19	Yeilding, William Richard,[80] DSO, Assistant Commissary General, 3rd Class, Meerut	......	30 Nov. 76	......	30 Nov. 87	28 July 90
54 West India Regiment	19	Bond, Wensly James Hodson,[81] Assistant Commissary General, 3rd Class Lancers Hyderabad Contingent	......	25 Jan. 77	......	25 Jan. 88	......
Royal Artillery	19	Meade, John William Babington,[82] 2nd in Com. and Squadron Commander 3 Madras Infantry	......	11 Feb. 77	......	11 Feb. 88	......
1 West India Regiment	19	Haughton, Thomas Hutchinson,[83] 2nd in Command and Wing Commander 8 Madras Infantry	......	11 Feb. 77	......	11 Feb. 88	......
39 Foot	19	Congreve-Schneider, Stewart Melvill,[84] Assistant Political Agent, Kattywar	......	12 Feb. 77	......	12 Feb. 88	......
40 Foot	19	Eardley-Wilmot, Henry,[85] Squadron Commander 2 Madras Lancers	......	12 Feb. 77	......	12 Feb. 88	......
54 Foot	18	Prior, Herbert Morris, Military Accountant, 2nd Class; Junior Pay Examiner, Calcutta	......	12 Feb. 77	......	12 Feb. 88	......
73 Foot	18	Inglis, Ernest,[86] Assistant Commissioner, 2nd Grade, Hoshiarpore, Punjab	......	3 May 77	......	3 May 88	......
15 Foot	18	Aspinall, Hugh Harry Hayworth,[87] 2nd in Command and Wing Commander 5 Madras Infantry	......	20 May 77	......	22 Mar. 88	......
44 Foot	18	Melvill, Henry,[88] Military Accountant, 2nd Class; Examiner Commissariat Accounts, Poona	......	29 Nov. 76	......	14 June 88	......
Scots Fusiliers	18	Lowry, William Robert,[89] 2nd in Command and Wing Commander 28 Madras Infantry	......	14 June 77	......	14 June 88	......
59 Foot	18	Gordon, Louis Augustus,[90] Squadron Commander 2 Bombay Lancers	......	14 June 77	......	24 June 88	......
63 Foot	18	Foss, Kenneth Mackenzie,[91] 2nd in Command and Wing Commander 26 Madras Infantry	......	24 June 77	......	......	......
34 Foot	18	Willes, George Frederick,[92] Squadron Officer 15 Bengal Lancers	5 Sept. 77	14 Nov. 79	......	5 Sept. 88	29 Dec. 91
Border Regiment	18	Bidanlph, Stephen Francis,[93] Squadron Commander 19 Bengal Lancers	......	10 Sept. 77	......	10 Sept. 88	......
12 Foot	18	Keary, Henry D'Urban,[95] DSO, Commandant 31 Madras Infantry	......	10 Sept. 77	......	10 Sept. 88	......
63 Foot	18	Vansittart, Eden,[96] Wing Commander 2 Battalion 5 Goorkhas	......	11 Sept. 77	......	11 Sept. 88	......
54 Foot	18	Jones, Frank Lewis, Commandant 3 Madras Lancers	......	11 Sept. 77	......	11 Sept. 88	......
65 Foot	18	Forbes, Arthur William,[97] 2nd in Command and Squadron Commander 4 Bombay Cavalry	......	11 Sept. 77	......	11 Sept. 88	......
22 Foot	18	Welman, George Arthur,[98] 2nd in Command and Wing Commander 13 Madras Infantry	......	11 Sept. 77	......	11 Sept. 88	......
66 Foot	18	Burton, Charles William Westbrooke,[99] 2nd in Command and Wing Commander 8 Madras Infantry	......	19 Sept. 77	......	19 Sept. 88	5 Oct. 90
Suffolk Regiment	18	Carpendale, John Maxwell,[100] Squadron Commander 8 Bengal Cavalry	......	9 Oct. 77	......	9 Oct. 88	......
Royal Marines	18	Stevens, George Borlase,[101] Assistant Adjutant General, Bangalore	13 Oct. 77	25 Feb. 80	......	13 Oct. 88	......
Royal Artillery	18	Carleton, Henry Augustus,[102] 2nd in Command and Squadron Commander 12 Bengal Cavalry	......	28 Oct. 77	......	28 Oct. 88	......
Devonshire Regiment	18	Dobbin, William James Knowles,[103] Wing Commander 1 Sikh Infantry	......	11 Nov. 77	......	11 Nov. 88	......
83 Foot	18	Baker, Louis Samuel Hyde,[104] Squadron Commander 1 Punjab Cavalry	......	11 Nov. 77	......	11 Nov. 88	......
59 Foot	18	Atkinson, George Charles, 2nd in Command and Wing Commander 3 Madras Infantry	......	11 Nov. 77	......	11 Nov. 88	......
2 Foot	18	Elaston, Henry,[105] 2nd in Command and Wing Commander 11 Madras Infantry	......	11 Nov. 77	......	11 Nov. 88	......
65 Foot	18	Iremonger, Robert George,[106] 2nd in Command and Wing Commander 33 Madras Infantry	......	11 Nov. 77	......	11 Nov. 88	......
70 Foot	18	Clark-Kennedy, Arthur Harry,[107] Assistant Commissary General, 3rd Class, Madras	......	29 Nov. 77	......	29 Nov. 88	......
8 Foot	18	Porter, Robert Edward,[108] 2nd in Command and Wing Commander 2 Madras Lancers	......	29 Nov. 77	......	30 Nov. 88	......
70 Foot	18	Westlake, Almond Paul,[109] DSO, Squadron Commander 1 Madras Lancers	......	29 Sept. 77	......	19 Dec. 88	......
2 West India Regiment	18	Mackintosh, William Charles Henry,[110] Assistant Commissary General, 3rd Class, Belgaum	1 July 81	......	......	19 Dec. 88	......
77 Foot	18	Gordon, William David,[111] Wing Commander 36 Bengal Infantry	18 Dec. 80	1 Feb. 79	......	23 Jan. 89	......
Hampshire Regiment	18	Carbonaro, Ernest,[112] (2nd Lieut. *Malta Fencible Art.* 19 Dec. 77; Lieut. 1 Sept. 80), Wing Officer 17 Bengal Inf.	23 Jan. 78	1 Feb. 79	......	23 Jan. 89	......
Derbyshire Regiment	18	Taylor, Robert Byre Sullivan, Wing Commander 38 Bengal Infantry	30 Jan. 78	22 Mar. 78	......	30 Jan. 89	......
Leinster Regiment	18	Gastrell, Everard Thuillier, Inspecting Officer, Kashmir Imperial Service Troops, Jammoo	30 Jan. 78	22 Mar. 78	......	30 Jan. 89	......
Royal Scots	18	Pakenham, William Wingfield Vernes, Wing Officer 19 Madras Infantry	......	18 Nov. 76	......	......	......

Indian Staff Corps.

Last Regiment.	Serv. Yrs.	Captains.	2nd Lieut. Cornet, Ensign.	Lieut.	Brevet Captain.	Captain.	Brevet Major.
Wiltshire Regiment	18	Whistler, Albert Edward,[114] 2nd in Command and Wing Commander 2 Bengal Infantry	30 Jan. 78	3 Apr. 79	....	30 Jan. 89	
South Wales Borderers	18	O'Donnell, Hugh,[115] DSO, Wing Commander 44 Bengal Infantry	30 Jan. 78	12 Apr. 79	....	30 Jan. 89	
Leicestershire Regiment	18	Priestley, Frederick Joseph Blakiston, Squadron Commander 4 Bengal Cavalry	30 Jan. 78	6 Aug. 79	....	30 Jan. 89	
Manchester Regiment	18	Angelo, Frederick William Pakenham,[117] Squadron Commander 9 Bengal Lancers	30 Jan. 78	8 Aug. 79	....	30 Jan. 89	
Leinster Regiment	18	Judge, Charles Bellew,[118] Wing Commander 1 Battalion 2 Goorkhas	30 Jan. 78	8 Sept. 79	....	30 Jan. 89	
East Surrey Regiment	18	Rodwell, Ernest Hunter,[119] Wing Commander 2 Punjab Infantry	30 Jan. 78	13 Sept. 79	....	30 Jan. 89	
Cheshire Regiment	18	Rastray, Ruilion Hare,[120] Wing Commander 22 Bengal Infantry	30 Jan. 78	1 Jan. 80	....	30 Jan. 89	
17 Foot	18	Cole, Robert Arthur, 2nd in Command and Squadron Commander Erinpoorah Irregular Force	30 Jan. 78	10 Mar. 80	....	30 Jan. 89	
Liverpool Regiment	18	Edwards, John Burnard,[121] Squadron Commander 1 Central India Horse	30 Jan. 78	17 Mar. 80	....	30 Jan. 89	
100 Foot	18	Carr, Arthur Nisbet,[122] Squadron Commander 3 Bengal Cavalry	30 Jan. 78	27 Mar. 80	....	30 Jan. 89	
Royal Fusiliers	18	Shipley, Mordaunt Lee,[123] Squadron Officer 13 Bengal Lancers	30 Jan. 78	27 Aug. 80	....	30 Jan. 89	
Essex Regiment	18	Boswell, William Legh,[124] Wing Commander 33 Bengal Infantry	30 Jan. 78	4 Sept. 80	....	30 Jan. 89	
Irish Fusiliers	18	Cahusac, William Fremantle, 2nd in Command and Wing Commander 21 Bombay Infantry	30 Jan. 78	9 Sept. 80	....	30 Jan. 89	
West Surrey Regiment	18	Crawley, George Burridge,[127] Cantonment Magistrate, 1st Grade, Allahabad, N. W. Provinces	30 Jan. 78	4 Dec. 80	....	30 Jan. 89	
2 Foot	18	Marrett, Edward Uvedale,[128] Assistant Commissioner, 4th Grade, Burmah	30 Jan. 78	29 Feb. 80	....	31 Jan. 89	
Royal Artillery	18	Western, John Sutton Edward,[129] Squadron Commander 1 Punjab Cavalry	....	12 Feb. 78	....	12 Feb. 89	
7 Foot	18	Chapman, Francis Robert Henry,[130] Superintendent of Army Schools, Bombay Presidency	....	12 Feb. 78	....	12 Feb. 89	
Yorkshire Regiment	18	Davies, John, Assistant Political Agent, Mahi Kanta	6 Feb. 78	21 Aug. 78	....	16 Feb. 89	
1 Dragoon Guards	13	Younghusband, Francis Edward, CIE, Officiating Political Assistant, 1st Class; Political Officer in Chitral	....	10 May 82	....	18 Feb. 89	
18 Foot	18	Georges, Henry Wallace Edgcome,[132] 2nd in Command and Squadron Commander 3 Madras Lancers	....	26 Feb. 78	....	26 Feb. 89	
9 Foot	17	Shaw, George Jocelyn,[133] 2nd in Command and Wing Commander 6 Madras Infantry	....	1 Apr. 78	....	1 Apr. 89	
Yorkshire Light Infantry	17	Kreyer, Frederick August Christian,[133] Wing Officer 16 Bombay Infantry	1 May 78	2 Oct. 78	....	1 May 89	
Durham Light Infantry	17	Purdon, David William,[134] 2nd in Command and Wing Commander 6 Infantry Hyderabad Contingent	1 May 78	1 Nov. 78	....	1 May 89	
Cheshire Regiment	17	Hodgson, Godfrey Beckett,[135] Deputy Superintendent, 1st Grade, Survey of India	1 May 78	13 Nov. 78	....	1 May 89	
Cheshire Regiment	17	Allen, Walter Harding,[136] Deputy Assistant Commissary General, 1st Class, Peshawur	1 May 78	3 Jan. 79	....	1 May 89	
Yorkshire Light Infantry	17	Thackwell, Colquhoun Grant Roche,[137] Assistant Commissary General, 4th Class	1 May 78	29 Jan. 79	....	1 May 89	
Cheshire Regiment	17	Davies, Henry Samuel Price, Assistant Commissioner, 2nd Grade, Punjab	1 May 78	29 Jan. 79	....	1 May 89	
Hampshire Regiment	17	Tuite, Mark Antony,[139] 2nd in Command and Wing Commander 23 Madras Infantry	1 May 78	5 Mar. 79	....	1 May 89	
Irish Rifles	17	Thomson, William David,[140] Squadron Commander 1 Bengal Cavalry	1 May 78	15 Mar. 79	....	1 May 89	
West Yorkshire Regiment	17	Christie, James Harry, Wing Officer 35 Bengal Infantry	1 May 78	25 Apr. 79	....	1 May 89	
Black Watch	17	Melvill, Philip James, Political Agent, 3rd Class, Rajpoolana; Assistant Commissioner, Ajmere	1 May 78	15 May 79	....	1 May 89	
West Yorkshire Regiment	17	Lowry, Frederic James Sharples,[142] Wing Officer 29 Bombay Infantry	1 May 78	9 June 79	....	1 May 89	
Wiltshire Regiment	17	Johnson, Thomas George,[143] 3rd Grade Deputy Commissioner, Burmah	1 May 78	15 June 79	....	1 May 89	
King's Own Borderers	17	Taylor, Douglas James Orr,[144] Wing Commander 6 Punjab Infantry	1 May 78	19 Sept. 79	....	1 May 89	
Oxfordshire Light Infantry	17	Kerrich, George Steuart,[145] Squadron Commander 1 Madras Lancers	1 May 78	24 Sept. 79	....	1 May 89	
East Surrey Regiment	17	Hunter, John Gunning,[146] 2nd in Command and Wing Commander 10 Bengal Infantry	1 May 78	17 Nov. 79	....	1 May 89	
Manchester Regiment	17	Waldron, Henry Francis Kelly,[147] Squadron Commander 16 Bengal Cavalry	1 May 78	4 Dec. 79	....	1 May 89	
Wiltshire Regiment	17	Reid, Lestock Hamilton,[148] Wing Commander 27 Bengal Infantry	1 May 78	7 Jan. 80	....	1 May 89	
North Lancashire Regiment	17	Young, Charles Frederic Gordon,[149] 2nd in Command and Wing Commander 6 Bengal Infantry	1 May 78	15 Mar. 80	....	1 May 89	
Leicestershire Regiment	17	Young, Julian Henry,[150] Assistant Commissary General, 3rd Grade, Agra	1 May 78	1 Apr. 80	....	1 May 89	
Suffolk Regiment	17	p.s.c. Younghusband, George John,[151] Wing Commander Corps of Guides	1 May 78	19 May 80	....	1 May 89	
Devonshire Regiment	17	Hutchinson, Francis Patrick,[152] Wing Commander 2 Battalion 2 Goorkhas	1 May 78	20 May 80	....	1 May 89	
Oxfordshire Light Infantry	17	Sanlez, Philip Homar,[153] Wing Commander 16 Bombay Infantry	1 May 78	22 May 80	....	1 May 89	
East Yorkshire Regiment	17	Vidal, Leonard Hugh,[154] Wing Commander 28 Bombay Infantry	1 May 78	2 June 80	....	1 May 89	
Devonshire Regiment	17	Dobbs, Alexander Hugh,[155] 2nd in Command and Wing Commander 16 Madras Infantry	1 May 78	1 July 80	....	1 May 89	
Somersetshire Lt. Infantry	17	Aplin, Philip John Hanham,[156] Wing Commander 7 Bombay Infantry	1 May 78	16 Aug. 80	....	1 May 89	
Dublin Fusiliers	17	Phayre, Arthur,[157] Squadron Commander 5 Bombay Cavalry	1 May 78	4 Sept. 80	....	1 May 89	
Norfolk Regiment	17	Templer, Henry, Squadron Commander 5 Punjab Cavalry	1 May 78	16 Oct. 80	....	1 May 89	
York and Lancaster Regt.	17	King, Henry Thomas, Deputy Assistant Adjutant General for Musketry, Secunderabad	1 May 78	1 Dec. 80	....	1 May 89	
Irish Fusiliers	17	Ommanney, George Stewart,[158] Wing Commander 1 Battalion 1 Goorkhas	1 May 78				
	17	Parkin, Henry,[159] Deputy Inspector of Police Supply and Clothing, Burmah					
	17	Dobbie, Herbert Hugh, Wing Commander 30 Bengal Infantry					

Indian Staff Corps.

Last Regiment.	Yrs. Serv.	CAPTAINS.	2nd LIEUT.	LIEUT.	BREVET CAPTAIN.	CAPTAIN.	BREVET MAJOR.
East Yorkshire Regiment	17	Piers, William Barrington, 1st Wing Commander 10 Bombay Infantry	1 May 78	1 Jan. 81		1 May 89	
Border Regiment	17	Wilmot, Irton Bardley, Squadron Commander 18 Bengal Lancers	1 May 78	30 Apr. 81		1 May 89	
Bedfordshire Regiment	17	Johnstone, Robert Fitz-Roy Maclean, 2nd in Command and Squadron Commander 4 Lancers Hyderabad Cont.	11 May 78	9 Mar. 79		11 May 89	
Irish Rifles	17	Armstrong, Oliver Carleton, 164 Squadron Commander 14 Bengal Infantry	11 May 78	23 Apr. 79		11 May 89	
Lincolnshire Regiment	17	Richardson, Francis Bernard Walter, 165 Wing Commander 3 Bengal Infantry	11 May 78	17 May 79		11 May 89	
North Staffordshire Regt.	17	Steele, St. George Loftus, 166 Squadron Commander 1 Bengal Lancers	11 May 78	1 Jan. 79		11 May 89	
Hampshire Regiment	17	Hight, Edward Lancelot, 167 Wing Commander 1 Punjab Infantry	11 May 78	1 Aug. 79		11 May 89	
West Yorkshire Regiment	17	Mitchell, George Warder, Wing Commander 21 Bombay Infantry	11 May 78	25 Feb. 80		11 May 89	
39 Foot	17	M'Carthy, George Alexander, 169 Wing Commander 19 Bengal Infantry	11 May 78	6 Mar. 80		11 May 89	
Northamptonshire Regt.	17	Lewis, David Silvanus, 2nd in Command and Wing Commander 7 Madras Infantry	11 May 78	13 Mar. 80		11 May 89	
Wiltshire Regiment	17	Justice, Charles Le Gendre, 170 Wing Commander 13 Bengal Infantry	11 May 78	1 Apr. 80		11 May 89	
Seaforth Highlanders	17	Robertson, Edmund Elliot, 171 Squadron Commander 2 Central India Horse	11 May 78	3 Apr. 80		11 May 89	
Leinster Regiment	17	Broome, Ralph Champneys, Squadron Officer 13 Bengal Lancers	11 May 78	14 Apr. 80		11 May 89	
West Yorkshire Regiment	17	Hogge, Arthur Fountaine, 172 Wing Officer 34 Bengal Infantry	11 May 78	14 Apr. 80		11 May 89	
Middlesex Regiment	17	James, Herbert, 173 Assistant Commissary General, 4th Class, Quetta	11 May 78	1 Apr. 80		11 May 89	
Warwickshire Regiment	17	Ostrehan, Francis George Rodney, 174 Wing Commander 9 Bengal Infantry	11 May 78	1 Apr. 80		11 May 89	
Cheshire Regiment	17	Rose, Hugh, 175 Wing Commander 2 Battalion 3 Goorkha Regiment	11 May 78	2 May 80		11 May 89	
Suffolk Regiment	17	Newell, William Joseph, 177 Wing Commander 11 Bengal Infantry	11 May 78	5 May 80		11 May 89	
Leicestershire Regiment	17	Medley, Ernest James, 178 Squadron Commander 17 Bengal Cavalry	11 May 78	30 May 80		11 May 89	
Warwickshire Regiment	17	Carpendale, Percy Maxwell, 179 Wing Commander 21 Bengal Infantry	11 May 78	2 June 80		11 May 89	
Suffolk Regiment		p.s.c. Watkis, Henry Buickley Burlton, Wing Commander 31 Bengal Infantry	11 May 78	7 Aug. 80		11 May 89	
Hampshire Regiment	17	Giles, William, 181 Wing Officer 21 Bengal Infantry	11 May 78	1 Aug. 81		11 May 89	
Hampshire Regiment	17	Lloyd, Arthur Malcolm, 182 Wing Officer 24 Madras Infantry	11 May 78	20 Aug. 80		11 May 89	
Derbyshire Regiment	17	Fagan, Henry Horace Frederick, 183 Squadron Commander 10 Bengal Lancers	25 May 78	14 Sept. 80		25 May 89	
Hampshire Regiment	17	Hall, Herbert Sidney George, Assistant Commissary General, 4th Class, Meerut	25 May 78	28 Sept. 80		25 May 89	
Shropshire Regiment	17	O'Donoghue; Montague Ernest, 185 2nd in Command and Wing Commander 15 Madras Infantry	12 June 78	2 Nov. 80		12 June 89	
Devonshire Regiment	17	Thomson, Mowbray Townshend, 186 Wing Commander 1 Battalion 4 Goorkhas	11 May 78	8 Dec. 80		29 July 89	
1 Dragoon Guards	17	Pirie, Charles Patrick William, 187 Squadron Commander 18 Bengal Lancers	11 May 78	12 May 81		31 Mar. 89	
Manchester Regiment	17	Wright, Ernest Leonard, 188 2nd in Command and Wing Commander 2 Lancers Hyderabad Contingent	11 May 78	1 July 81		21 Aug. 89	
Oxford Light Infantry	18	Mein, Frederick Blundell, 189 Wing Officer 5 Punjab Infantry	25 May 78	12 Mar. 81		14 Sept. 89	
Somerset Light Infantry	17	Stewart, William Hall Macintosh, 190 Political Assistant, 1st Class, Gilgit	25 May 78	1 Mar. 80		5 Oct. 89	
Argyll & Suth. Highlanders		Unwin, Gaston Bouverie, Squadron Commander 1 Punjab Cavalry	12 June 78	1 Feb. 82		5 Oct. 89	
Madras Staff Corps		Wright, Hedley, 192 Squadron Commander 11 Bengal Lancers	28 Jan. 78	28 Feb. 82		5 Oct. 89	
Wiltshire Regiment		Carnegy, Philip Mainwaring, 193 Wing Commander 1 Battalion 4 Goorkhas	21 Aug. 78	31 Mar. 80		12 Nov. 89	
Wiltshire Regiment	17	Fryer, Geo. Willoughby Smith, Assist. Mil. Accountant, 1st Class; Examiner Commissariat Accounts, Rangoon	21 Aug. 78	26 May 80		4 Dec. 89	
83 Foot	17	Loch, Granville Henry, 194 Wing Commander 1 Battalion 3 Goorkhas	14 Sept. 78	26 Nov. 79		4 Dec. 89	
Cheshire Regiment	17	Westropp, George Ralph Collier, 196 Assistant Commissary General, 3rd Class	4 Oct. 78	23 Apr. 80		18 Dec. 89	
West Riding Regiment	17	Montgomery, Thomas Roger Arundel Gazer, Wing Officer 21 Bombay Infantry	5 Oct. 78	1 Aug. 81		18 Dec. 89	
Somerset Light Infantry	17	Rich, William Harry Derville, 197 Assistant Commissary General, 4th Class, Ohin Hills	5 Oct. 78	1 July 81		18 Dec. 89	
Somerset Light Infantry		O'Donnell, Alexander Clement, 198 2nd in Command and Grade, Shwegyin District, Burmah		1 Nov. 79		18 Dec. 89	
Irish Fusiliers		Pritchard, Alfred Bassett, Assistant Commissary General, and Grade, Shwegyin District, Burmah		1 Sept. 80		18 Dec. 89	
Lincolnshire Regiment		Shakespear, George Cortlandt Childe, 2nd in Command and Wing Commander 1 Infantry Hyderabad Cont.	4 Dec. 78	21 Dec. 79		6 Jan. 90	
Royal Artillery		Hollway, James Clinton, 200 Wing Commander 7 Bombay Infantry	4 Dec. 78	7 Aug. 80		6 Jan. 90	
East Yorkshire Regiment	17	Jones, George Goring John Sutton, 201 2nd in Command and Squadron Commander Deolee Irregular Force	4 Dec. 78	1 Sept. 80		22 Jan. 90	
Bedfordshire Regiment	18	Turner, James Gibbon, Squadron Commander 2 Bengal Lancers	4 Dec. 78	18 Dec. 79		30 Jan. 90	
Bedfordshire Regiment		Grantham, Charles Fulford, Squadron Commander 4 Bombay Cavalry	22 Jan. 79	22 June 79		22 Jan. 90	
Bedfordshire Regiment		Burlton, Reginald Dennis, 203 Squadron Officer 2 Madras Lancers	22 Jan. 79	1 July 79		22 Jan. 90	
South Lancashire Regiment		Oswald, Frank, 2nd in Command and Squadron Commander 1 Lancers Hyderabad Contingent	22 Jan. 79	4 Oct. 79		22 Jan. 90	
Sussex Regiment		Fordyce, Alexander Dingrwall, 204 Wing Commander 3 Bombay Infantry	22 Jan. 79	1 Feb. 80		22 Jan. 90	
Irish Regiment		M'Swiney, Edward Frederick Henry, 205 DSO, Squadron Commander 4 Lancers Hyderabad Contingent	22 Jan. 79	1 Feb. 80		22 Jan. 90	
		Yate, Frederick Herbert, Squadron Officer 5 Punjab Cavalry	22 Jan. 79	1 Jan. 80		22 Jan. 90	
	17	Moore, George Henry John, 2nd in Command and Wing Commander Mhairwarra Battalion	22 Jan. 79	3 Mar. 80		22 Jan. 90	

Indian Staff Corps.

Last Regiment.	Yrs. Serv.	Captains.	2nd Lieut.	Lieut.	Brevet Captain.	Captain.	Brevet Major.
King's Own Borderers	17	Hutchinson, James William Caldwell, 207 Wing Officer 6 Punjab Infantry	22 Jan. 79	25 May 80	......	22 Jan. 90	
North Lancashire Regiment	17	Phillips, Walter Ernest, 208 Wing Commander 28 Bengal Infantry	22 Jan. 79	14 July 80	......	22 Jan. 90	
Somersetshire Lt. Infantry	17	Kerrich, Leonard Wilkinson Cleveland, Commandant Governor's Body Guard	22 Jan. 79	1 Sept. 80	......	22 Jan. 90	
Scots Fusiliers	17	Swanston, Nowell Sherson, 209 Assistant Commissary General, 4th Class, Bangalore	22 Jan. 79	13 Sept. 80	......	22 Jan. 90	
Yorkshire Regiment	17	Macartney, Henry Frederick Tucker, 210 Wing Commander 10 Bengal Infantry	22 Jan. 79	25 Sept. 80	......	22 Jan. 90	
Duke of Cornwall's Lt. Inf.	17	Legh, Piers Richard, Wing Officer 16 Bombay Infantry	22 Jan. 79	2 Oct. 80	......	22 Jan. 90	
Leicestershire Regiment	17	Thompson, William Anson, 211 Squadron Commander 1 Bombay Lancers	22 Jan. 79	16 Oct. 80	......	22 Jan. 90	
Irish Fusiliers	17	Fry, Charles Irwin, 212 Wing Officer 4 Bombay Infantry	22 Jan. 79	1 Dec. 80	......	22 Jan. 90	
Cheshire Regiment	17	Hancock, Frank Herbert, 213 Wing Commander 26 Bengal Infantry	22 Jan. 79	1 Jan. 81	......	22 Jan. 90	
Warwickshire Regiment	17	Brown, George Rodney, Wing Officer 1 Battalion 4 Goorkhas	22 Jan. 79	23 Apr. 81	......	22 Jan. 90	
East Yorkshire Regiment	17	Hodges, Henry Francis Edward, 214 Wing Officer 3 Bombay Infantry	22 Jan. 79	17 May 81	......	22 Jan. 90	
Royal Scots	17	Chenevix-Trench, George Frederick, Political Assistant, 2nd Class	22 Jan. 79	8 June 81	......	22 Jan. 90	
Oxfordshire Light Infantry	17	Rideout, Frederick Charles Wood, 215 Assistant Commissary General, 4th Class, Wellington	22 Jan. 79	1 July 81	......	22 Jan. 90	
Oxford Light Infantry	17	Howell, Llewellyn James, Squadron Officer 16 Bengal Cavalry	22 Jan. 79	1 July 81	......	22 Jan. 90	
East Yorkshire Regiment	17	Sherard, Ralph Woodchurch, 217 Squadron Commander 5 Bombay Cavalry	22 Jan. 79	1 July 81	......	22 Jan. 90	
Seaforth Highlanders	17	Brown, James Andrew, Wing Commander 37 Bengal Infantry	22 Jan. 79	1 July 81	......	22 Jan. 90	
Royal Marines	17	Kellie, Archibald Henry, 218 Wing Commander 2 Madras Infantry	......	1 Feb. 79	......	1 Feb. 90	
Argyll & Suth. Highlanders	17	Wyllie, Frederick, 219 Squadron Commander 2 Lancers Hyderabad Contingent	2 Feb. 79	7 Dec. 80	......	2 Feb. 90	
West India Regiment	17	Broome, Robert Dennis, Wing Officer 9 Bombay Infantry	8 Mar. 79	1 Feb. 81	......	8 Mar. 90	
Hampshire Regiment	-7	Cardew, Yorstoun, Morden Ewart, 220 2nd in Command and Squadron Commander 4 Bombay Cavalry	26 Mar. 79	16 Oct. 81	......	26 Mar. 90	
Bombay Staff Corps	16	Custance, Hugh Lionel, 221 Wing Officer 36 Bengal Infantry	17 May 79	19 Sept. 80	......	7 June 90	
Yorkshire Light Infantry	16	Merewether, Henry Arthur, 222 Squadron Commander 7 Bengal Cavalry	21 June 79	4 Feb. 81	......	21 June 90	
Irish Rifles	16	Burrows, George Vernon, 223 2nd in Command and Wing Commander 14 Madras Infantry	21 June 79	9 July 80	......	21 June 90	
South Wales Borderers	16	Williams, Reginald, 224 2nd in Command and Wing Commander 25 Bombay Infantry	21 June 79	30 Oct. 80	......	21 June 90	
Hampshire Regiment	16	Shaw, David George Levinge, 225 Squadron Commander 1 Punjab Cavalry	21 June 79	29 Apr. 81	......	21 June 90	
York and Lancaster Regt.	16	Stewart, William, Squadron Commander 10 Bengal Lancers	21 June 79	1 July 81	......	21 June 90	
Connaught Rangers	16	Fraser, William Forbes Mackenzie Ian, 227 Wing Commander 18 Bengal Infantry	2 July 79	1 Feb. 81	......	2 July 90	
Yorkshire Light Infantry	16	Strachey, John, 228 Wing Commander 11 Bengal Infantry	7 July 79	16 Oct. 81	......	7 July 90	
Leicestershire Regiment	16	Walker, Percy Gerald, Wing Officer 20 Bengal Infantry	9 July 79	1 July 81	......	9 July 90	
Connaught Rangers	16	Alexander, Richard Stuart, 230 Squadron Commander 7 Bengal Cavalry	9 July 79	9 Oct. 81	......	9 July 90	
Scots Fusiliers	16	Dawson, Francis William, Assistant Resident, Travancore and Cochin; Commandant Resident's Escort	23 July 79	1 July 81	......	23 July 90	
Scottish Rifles	16	Colomb, Richard Pasley, 231 Assistant Commissioner 2nd Class, Oomrawuttee, Berar	23 July 79	9 Oct. 80	......	23 July 90	
West Riding Regiment	16	Campbell, Frederick, 232 Deputy Assistant Adjutant General for Musketry, Allahabad	6 Aug. 79	1 July 81	......	6 Aug. 90	
South Lancashire Regiment	16	Bremner, Harry John, 234 Wing Commander 15 Madras Infantry	13 Aug. 79	15 Mar. 80	......	13 Aug. 90	
Leinster Regiment	16	Weller, George Herbert, Squadron Officer 14 Bengal Lancers	13 Aug. 79	5 May 80	......	13 Aug. 90	
Munster Fusiliers	16	Banken, George Patrick, 235 Wing Commander 24 Bengal Infantry	13 Aug. 79	26 May 80	......	13 Aug. 90	
N. Staffordshire Regiment	16	Campbell, Colin Powys, Squadron Commander 2 Central India Horse	13 Aug. 79	9 June 80	......	13 Aug. 90	
King's Own Scot. Borderers	16	Fleming, John Muncrieson, 236 Deputy Superintendent, 2nd Grade, Revenue Survey, Calcutta	13 Aug. 79	2 July 80	......	13 Aug. 90	
Leinster Regiment	16	Battiscombe, William Wilson, Wing Officer 9 Bombay Infantry	13 Aug. 79	7 July 80	......	13 Aug. 90	
Wiltshire Regiment	16	Dennys, William Annesley Burton, 237 Wing Officer 26 Bengal Infantry	13 Aug. 79	14 July 80	......	13 Aug. 90	
Dorsetshire Regiment	16	Lampen, John, 238 Wing Commander 5 Bengal Infantry	13 Aug. 79	1 Aug. 80	......	13 Aug. 90	
Wiltshire Regiment	16	Dobbie, William Hugh, 239 2nd in Command and Wing Commander 32 Madras Infantry	13 Aug. 79	4 Sept. 80	......	13 Aug. 90	3 Jan. 94
South Lancashire Regiment	16	Perkins, Norman Chichester, Assistant Commissioner, 1st Grade, Burmah	13 Aug. 79	9 Sept. 80	......	13 Aug. 90	
Northamptonshire Regt.	16	Plumer, Thomas Hall, 2nd in Command and Wing Commander 5 Infantry Hyderabad Contingent	13 Aug. 79	27 Sept. 80	......	13 Aug. 90	
Irish Rifles	16	Alban, William Gore, 241 Wing Commander 26 Bombay Infantry	13 Aug. 79	25 Oct. 80	......	13 Aug. 90	
Irish Rifles	16	Vaux Agnew, John, 240 Squadron Commander 3 Madras Lancers	13 Aug. 79	9 Nov. 80	......	13 Aug. 90	
Dorsetshire Regiment	16	Kettlewell, Edward Alexander, 242 2nd in Command and Wing Commander 5 Punjab Cavalry	13 Aug. 79	18 Dec. 80	......	13 Aug. 90	
Warwickshire Regiment	16	Edwards, Charles Grant Franco, 243 Squadron Commander 5 Punjab Cavalry	13 Aug. 79	18 Dec. 80	......	13 Aug. 90	
Leinster Regiment	16	Twigg, Robert Henry, 244 Wing Commander 12 Bengal Infantry	13 Aug. 79	26 Dec. 80	......	13 Aug. 90	
Cheshire Regiment	16	Hamilton, Henry, Wing Officer 2 Battalion 4 Goorkhas	13 Aug. 70	1 Jan. 81	......	13 Aug. 90	27 Apr. 92
Devonshire Regiment	16	Dunlop-Smith, James Robert, Assistant Commissioner, 2nd Grade, Sealkote, Punjab	13 Aug. 79	2 Feb. 81	......	13 Aug. 90	
	16	Light, Reginald Hough, 245 Wing Commander 17 Bombay Infantry	13 Aug. 79	8 Feb. 81	......	13 Aug. 90	

Indian Staff Corps.

Last Regiment.	Yrs. Serv.	Captains.	2nd Lieut.	Lieut.	Brevet Captain.	Captain.	Brevet Major.
Leinster Regiment	16	Repton, Frederick William,²⁴⁷ Assistant Commissary General, 4th Class, Calcutta	13 Aug. 79	12 Feb. 81		13 Aug. 90	
Leicestershire Regiment	16	Egerton, Raleigh Gilbert,²⁴⁸ Squadron Commander Corps of Guides	13 Aug. 79	19 Feb. 81		13 Aug. 90	
East Surrey Regiment	16	Anderson, Rolland Frederick Hart, Assistant Judge Advocate General, Poona	13 Aug. 79	26 Feb. 81		13 Aug. 90	
Irish Regiment	16	Maxwell, Richard Money,²⁴⁹ Wing Commander 6 Bengal Infantry	13 Aug. 79	26 Feb. 81		13 Aug. 90	3 Feb. 95
Cheshire Regiment	16	Bairnsfather, Thomas Henry, Wing Officer 29 Bengal Infantry	13 Aug. 79	3 Mar. 81		13 Aug. 90	
Yorkshire Regiment	16	Mackenzie-Kennedy, Edward Charles William,²⁵⁰ 2nd in Command and Wing Commander 1 Madras Infantry	13 Aug. 79	30 Mar. 81		13 Aug. 90	
Warwickshire Regiment	16	Newmarch, Lindsay Sherwood, Assistant Governor General's Agent, Central India	13 Aug. 79	1 June 81		13 Aug. 90	
Devonshire Regiment	16	Smith, James Herbert,²⁵¹ Wing Officer 13 Madras Infantry	13 Aug. 79	8 June 81		13 Aug. 90	
West Surrey Regiment	16	Thuillier, Willoughby, Wing Officer 21 Bengal Infantry	13 Aug. 79	18 June 81		13 Aug. 90	
Yorkshire Regiment	16	Searle, Alfred Ernest Stuart,²⁵² Wing Officer 14 Bombay Infantry	13 Aug. 79	18 June 81		13 Aug. 90	
York and Lancaster Regt.	16	Carter, Edward James, Assistant Commissary General, 4th Class	13 Aug. 79	1 July 81		15 Aug. 90	
South Lancashire Regt.	16	Cooper, Lewis Ernest, Wing Officer 5 Punjab Infantry	13 Aug. 79	1 July 81		13 Aug. 90	
West Riding Regiment	16	Burton, Edmund Boteler,²⁵³ Squadron Officer 17 Bengal Cavalry	13 Aug. 79	1 July 81		13 Aug. 90	
Dorsetshire Regiment	16	Rowcroft, George Francis,²⁵⁴ Wing Officer 15 Bengal Infantry	13 Aug. 79	1 July 81		13 Aug. 90	
Dorsetshire Regiment	16	Prior, William,²⁵⁴ Wing Officer 13 Bengal Infantry	13 Aug. 79	1 July 81		13 Aug. 90	
Leicestershire Regiment	16	Kerr, Mark Ancrum, Wing Commander 4 Bengal Infantry	13 Aug. 79	1 July 81		13 Aug. 90	
Seaforth Highlanders	16	Macintyre, Donald Charles Frederick,²⁵⁷ Wing Officer 1 Battalion 2 Goorkhas	13 Aug. 79	1 July 81		13 Aug. 90	
Worcestershire Regiment	16	Browning, Arthur Robertson,²⁵⁸ 2nd in Command and Wing Commander 4 Punjab Infantry	13 Aug. 79	1 July 81		13 Aug. 90	
Leicestershire Regiment	16	Beale, Anthony,²⁵⁹ 2nd in Command and Wing Commander 5 Bombay Infantry	13 Aug. 79	1 July 81		13 Aug. 90	
East Lancashire Regiment	16	Billings, Clement Henry, Wing Officer 11 Bengal Infantry	13 Aug. 79	1 July 81		13 Aug. 90	
Royal Scots	16	Heyman, Charles Henry Cockburn,²⁶⁰ Wing Officer 21 Bombay Infantry	13 Aug. 79	1 July 81		13 Aug. 90	
Northumberland Fusiliers	16	Colvin, John Russell Colquhoun,²⁶¹ Political Assistant 1st Class, N.W.P.; Political Officer Rampore State	13 Aug. 79	1 July 81		13 Aug. 90	
Manchester Regiment	15	Wickham, William James Richard,²⁶² Assistant Commissary General, 3rd Class	13 Aug. 79	1 July 81		13 Aug. 90	
Bedfordshire Regiment	16	Sutton, Henry George,²⁶³ 2nd in Command and Wing Commander 27 Madras Infantry	13 Aug. 79	1 July 81		13 Aug. 90	
Bedfordshire Regiment	16	Vaughan, Percy Balderston,²⁶⁴ Wing Officer 35 Bengal Infantry	13 Aug. 79	1 July 81		13 Aug. 90	
Black Watch	16	Gough, Stanley Charles,²⁶⁵ Squadron Commander 5 Bengal Cavalry	11 Oct. 79	1 July 81		11 Oct. 90	
Leinster Regiment	16	Owen, Eldred Owen, Squadron Coron Commander 5 Bombay Cavalry	11 Oct. 79	1 July 81		11 Oct. 90	
Worcestershire Regiment	16	Pond, Alexander Donald Charters,²⁶⁶ Wing Commander 12 Bengal Infantry	1 Nov. 79	12 Feb. 81		1 Nov. 90	
Bedfordshire Regiment	16	Ffrench, Arthur, Wing Commander 11 Madras Infantry	15 Nov. 79	8 June 80		15 Nov. 90	
Border Regiment	16	Tennant, Claude Cambridge,²⁶⁷ Assistant Commissary General, 4th Class, Bhamo	26 Nov. 79	26 Sept. 80		26 Nov. 90	
Leinster Regiment	16	Hogge, George Sapte, 2nd in Command and Wing Commander 12 Bombay Infantry	14 Jan. 80	2 Oct. 80		14 Jan. 91	
North Lancashire Regiment	16	p.s.c. Brander, Herbert Ralph,²⁶⁸ Wing Commander 32 Bengal Infantry	14 Jan. 80	1 Dec. 80		14 Jan. 91	
North Lancashire Regiment	16	Cracroft, Bernard Walter, Assistant Commissary General, 4th Class, Calcutta	14 Jan. 80	1 Dec. 80		14 Jan. 91	
King's Own Scot. Borderers	16	Davidson, Charles, Wing Officer 2 Punjab Infantry	14 Jan. 80	26 Apr. 81		14 Jan. 91	
Irish Rifles	16	Borradaile, Harry Benn,²⁷⁰ Wing Officer 32 Bengal Infantry	14 Jan. 80	28 Apr. 81		14 Jan. 91	
Leinster Regiment	16	Welman, Harvey, Wing Commander 13 Bombay Infantry	14 Jan. 80	23 May 81		14 Jan. 91	
Connaught Rangers	16	Thompson, David Montgomery,²⁷¹ Assistant Commissary General, 4th Class, Cawnpore	14 Jan. 80	1 July 81		14 Jan. 91	
East Lancashire Regiment	16	Murray, George, Squadron Commander 3 Punjab Cavalry	14 Jan. 80	1 July 81		14 Jan. 91	
Shropshire Light Infantry	16	Crowther, Robert Theodore, Wing Officer 23 Bengal Infantry	14 Jan. 80	1 July 81		14 Jan. 91	
South Lancashire Regiment	16	Mardall, Charles Ernest,²⁷³ Military Accountant, 4th Class; Presidency Pay Master, Bombay	14 Jan. 80	1 July 81		14 Jan. 91	
Connaught Rangers	16	Phillott, Douglas Craven,²⁷⁴ Squadron Officer 3 Punjab Cavalry	14 Jan. 80	1 July 81		14 Jan. 91	
Yorkshire Light Infantry	16	Hatch, Arthur Vincent,²⁷⁴ Wing Officer 2 Battalion 1 Goorkhas	14 Jan. 80	1 July 81		14 Jan. 91	
Connaught Rangers	16	Codrington, Edward William,²⁷⁵ Wing Officer 3 Sikh Infantry	14 Jan. 80	1 July 81		14 Jan. 91	
Manchester Regiment	16	Cowley, James William,²⁷⁶ Wing Commander 43 Bengal Infantry	14 Jan. 80	1 July 81		14 Jan. 91	
Northumberland Fusiliers	16	Little, William Rutherford, Wing Officer 21 Bengal Infantry	14 Jan. 80	1 July 81		14 Jan. 91	
Worcestershire Regiment	16	Southey, Robert,²⁷⁷ Wing Commander 30 Bombay Infantry	14 Jan. 80	1 July 81		14 Jan. 91	
South Lancashire Regiment	16	Aitken, Arthur Edward,²⁷⁸ Wing Officer 19 Bombay Infantry	14 Jan. 80	1 July 81		14 Jan. 91	
Argyll & Suth. Highlanders	16	Campbell, Frank James Brook, Wing Officer 37 Bengal Infantry	14 Jan. 80	1 July 81		14 Jan. 91	
Warwickshire Regiment	16	M'Intyre, Hugh David,²⁷⁹ 2nd in Command and Wing Commander 8 Madras Infantry	14 Jan. 80	1 July 81		14 Jan. 91	
Irish Rifles	16	Robinson, John Graham, Wing Officer 1 Battalion 2 Goorkhas	14 Jan. 80	1 July 81		14 Jan. 91	
Norfolk Regiment	16	Browne, Willoughby Brooking,²⁸⁰ Wing Commander 6 Madras Infantry	14 Jan. 80	1 July 81		14 Jan. 91	
Devonshire Regiment	16	Mullins, Willoughby Brooking,²⁸¹ Wing Commander 27 Bengal Infantry	14 Jan. 80	1 July 81		14 Jan. 91	
	16	Wood, Percy Arthur Noding St. Leger,²⁸³ Wing Officer 7 Bombay Infantry	14 Jan. 80	1 July 81		14 Jan. 91	

Indian Staff Corps.

Last Regiment.	Yrs. Serv.	CAPTAINS.	2nd LIEUT.	LIEUT.	BREVET CAPTAIN.	CAPTAIN.
Cheshire Regiment	16	Parsons, Clement George, Assistant Commissioner, 2nd Class, Punjab	14 Jan. 80	1 July 81		14 Jan. 91
Bedfordshire Regiment	16	Cave, Henry Charles Edward, Assistant Commissary General, 4th Class, Poona	14 Jan. 80	1 July 81		14 Jan. 91
King's Own Borderers	16	Cox, Herbert Vaughan, 324 Wing Commander 21 Madras Infantry	14 Jan. 80	1 July 81		14 Jan. 91
Suffolk Regiment	16	Caulfeild, Francis William John, Wing Commander 5 Bombay Infantry	14 Jan. 80	1 July 81		31 Jan. 91
North Staffordshire Regt.	16	Bradley, Frederick Gardner, 285 Wing Commander 5 Madras Infantry	31 Aug. 80	23 Aug. 81		31 Jan. 91
North Lancashire Regt.	16	Smith, Thomas Hugh, Squadron Commander 12 Bengal Cavalry	2 Feb. 81	2 Feb. 81		31 Jan. 91
1 West India Regiment	16	Hitchins, Charles Henry Macintire, Wing Commander 14 Madras Infantry	31 Mar. 81	23 Mar. 81		31 Jan. 91
1 West India Regiment	16	Errington, Richard, 286 Wing Commander 8 Bombay Infantry	31 Jan. 80	8 May 81		31 Jan. 91
East Surrey Regiment	16	Hamilton, George Frederick Dashwood, 287 Deputy Assistant Commissary General, 1st Class; Hussar Castle Farm	31 Jan. 80	1 Feb. 80		1 Feb. 91
Royal Marines	16	Wapshare, Richard, 288 Squadron Commander 3 Lancers Hyderabad Contingent		1 Feb. 80		1 Feb. 91
Royal Marines	16	Hartigan, Edward Ross, 289 Wing Officer 2 Bombay Infantry		1 Feb. 80		1 Feb. 91
Royal Artillery	16	Shewen, Mansel Travers, 290 2nd in Command and Wing Commander 4 Infantry Hyderabad Contingent		18 Feb. 80		18 Feb. 91
Dorsetshire Regiment	16	Anderson, Clinton Cortlandt, 291 Wing Officer 26 Bengal Infantry	25 Feb. 80	9 June 81		25 Feb. 91
Oxfordshire Light Infantry	16	Montgomery, Charles Arnulph Shrewsbury, 292 2nd in Command and Wing Commander 1 Bombay Infantry	25 Feb. 80	1 July 81		25 Feb. 91
Manchester Regiment	16	Holloway, Edward Leigh, Wing Commander 4 Madras Infantry	25 Feb. 80	1 July 81		25 Feb. 91
East Surrey Regiment	16	O'Brien, Donatus J. Thomond, 293 Wing Officer 15 Bengal Infantry	17 Apr. 80	4 May 81		17 Apr. 91
Leinster Regiment	15	Priestley, Henry Wood, 294 Wing Commander 42 Bengal Infantry	17 Apr. 80	4 May 81		17 Apr. 91
Lancaster Regiment	15	Vaughan, Henry Bathurst, 295 Wing Officer 7 Bengal Infantry	17 Apr. 80	1 July 81		17 Apr. 91
King's Own Borderers	15	Tritton, Charles, 296 Wing Officer 25 Bombay Infantry		10 May 82		10 May 91
Suffolk Regiment	15	Wadeson, Frederick William George, Squadron Commander 4 Bombay Cavalry	11 Aug. 80	29 Mar. 81		11 Aug. 91
Leinster Regiment	15	E C Grant, Charles James William, 297 Wing Commander 12 Madras Infantry (*Brevet Major*, 11 May 91)	11 Aug. 80	1 July 81		11 Aug. 91
Middlesex Regiment	15	Cowper, Maitland, Squadron Commander 10 Bengal Lancers	11 Aug. 80	1 July 81		11 Aug. 91
1 West India Regiment	15	Wilson, William Augustine Mitchell, 299 Deputy Assistant Adjutant General, Bombay	11 Aug. 80	1 July 81		11 Aug. 91
Irish Regiment	15	Lewin, Wilfred Hale, 300 Wing Commander 2 Infantry Hyderabad Contingent	11 Aug. 80	1 July 81		11 Aug. 91
Liverpool Regiment	15	p.s.c. Loch, Harry Frere, Wing Commander 1 Bengal Infantry	11 Aug. 80	1 July 81		11 Aug. 91
Middlesex Regiment	15	Elliot, Lawrence Edward, Assistant Commissioner, 1st Grade, Burmah	11 Aug. 80	1 July 81		11 Aug. 91
Suffolk Regiment	15	Cronin, John Jos., Assistant Commissioner, 1st Class, Calcutta	11 Aug. 80	1 July 81		11 Aug. 91
The Buffs	15	Grey, Edward, 301 Deputy Assistant Commissary General and Wing Commander 29 Madras Infantry	11 Aug. 80	1 July 81		11 Aug. 91
East Lancashire Regt.	15	Rippon, George, 302 2nd in Command and Wing Commander 19 Bengal Lancers	11 Aug. 80	1 July 81		11 Aug. 91
Madras Staff Corps	15	Templer, Charles Bertram, Squadron Officer 7 Bengal Lancers	11 Aug. 80	1 July 81		11 Aug. 91
Middlesex Regiment	15	Martindale, Cecil S. de Butts, District Judge, 2nd Class, Ferozepore, Punjab	11 Aug. 80	1 July 81		11 Aug. 91
Essex Regiment	15	Quin, Thomas, 304 Wing Commander 4 Sikh Infantry	11 Aug. 80	1 July 81		11 Aug. 91
Worcestershire Regiment	15	Thornton, Hugh, Wing Commander 9 Madras Infantry	11 Aug. 80	1 July 81		11 Aug. 91
Welsh Fusiliers	15	p.s.c. Jackson, John, Wing Commander 1 Central India Horse	11 Aug. 80	1 July 81		11 Aug. 91
South Wales Borderers	15	Cawood, George Crane, 306 Squadron Officer 7 Bengal Cavalry	11 Aug. 80	1 July 81		11 Aug. 91
East Surrey Regiment	15	Thwaytes, Edmund Charles, Wing Commander 24 Madras Infantry	11 Aug. 80	1 July 81		11 Aug. 91
Warwickshire Regiment	15	Peyton, Algernon George, 307 Squadron Commander 9 Bengal Lancers	11 Aug. 80	1 July 81		11 Aug. 91
Royal Scots	15	Cooper, Edward Edmonstone, Wing Officer 1 Battalion 4 Goorkhas	11 Aug. 80	1 July 81		11 Aug. 91
Oxfordshire Light Infantry	15	Kemball, Arnold Henry Grant, 308 2nd in Command and Wing Commander 1 Battalion 5 Goorkhas	11 Aug. 80	1 July 81		11 Aug. 91
King's Own Scot. Borderers	15	Acton, Henry Lowry Barnwell, Squadron Commander 1 Madras Lancers	11 Aug. 80	1 July 81		11 Aug. 91
Royal Fusiliers	15	Hamilton, Alexander, Wing Officer 25 Bengal Infantry	11 Aug. 80	1 July 81		11 Aug. 91
West Surrey Regiment	15	Atkinson, George Duncan, 310 Squadron Commander 1 Bombay Lancers (*Brevet Major*, 3 Jan. 91)	11 Aug. 80	1 July 81		11 Aug. 91
South Wales Borderers	15	Malcolm, Pulteney, 311 Wing Officer 2 Battalion 4 Goorkhas	11 Aug. 80	1 July 81		11 Aug. 91
Bombay Staff Corps	15	Tulloch, John Walter Graham, 313 2nd in Command and Wing Commander 24 Bombay Infantry	11 Aug. 80	1 July 81		11 Aug. 91
Suffolk Regiment	15	Melville, John Swinton, 314 Wing Officer 4 Bengal Infantry	11 Aug. 80	1 July 81		11 Aug. 91
8 Hussars	15	Grant, Francis Charles, Squadron Commander 1 Central India Horse	11 Aug. 80	1 July 81		11 Aug. 91
Royal Marines	15	Jackson, Cecil, Squadron Commander 3 Bengal Cavalry	11 Sept. 80	1 Sept. 81		11 Sept. 91
Scottish Rifles	15	Macdonald, Clarence Herbert, 315 2nd in Command and Wing Commander 3 Infantry Hyderabad Contingent	11 Sept. 80	1 Sept. 81		11 Sept. 91
Seaforth Highlanders	15	Cookson, George Arthur, Squadron Commander 16 Bengal Cavalry	23 Oct. 80	1 July 81		23 Oct. 91
Norfolk Regiment	15	Burne, Knightley Poyntz, 316 Wing Commander 38 Bengal Infantry	23 Oct. 80	1 July 81		23 Oct. 91
Devonshire Regiment	15	Comins, Henry, 317 Wing Officer 1 Bengal Infantry	23 Oct. 80	1 July 81		23 Oct. 91
		Bower, Hamilton, Squadron Officer 17 Bengal Cavalry				

Indian Staff Corps.

Last Regiment.	Yrs. Serv.	CAPTAINS.	2ND LIEUT.	LIEUT.	BREVET CAPTAIN.	CAPTAIN.
Lancaster Regiment	15	Mosse, William Oliver Matless, Wing Officer 20 Bombay Native Infantry	23 Oct. 80	1 July 81		23 Oct. 91
Worcester Regiment	15	Dawson, Charles Hutton, Wing Officer Meywar Bheel Corps	23 Oct. 80	1 July 81		23 Oct. 91
Middlesex Regiment	15	Smart, Edward de Sausmarez, 318 Wing Commander 1 Battalion 5 Goorkhas	23 Oct. 80	1 July 81		23 Oct. 91
Munster Fusiliers	15	p.s.c. Kenny, Henry Torrens, Squadron Officer 2 Bombay Lancers	23 Oct. 80	1 July 81		23 Oct. 91
Dorsetshire Regiment	15	Strickland, William Alexander Wickedé, Assistant Commissioner, 1st Grade, Kyaukse District, Burmah	23 Oct. 80	1 July 81		23 Oct. 91
Border Regiment	15	Norman, William Wylie, Squadron Officer 2 Punjab Cavalry	23 Oct. 80	20 July 81		23 Nov. 91
Lancaster Regiment	15	Belli-Bivar, Charles Elphinstone, Squadron Commander 7 Bombay Lancers	11 Aug. 80	31 July 81		22 Jan. 92
Northamptonshire Regt.	15	Dallas, Charles Mowbray, 319 Assistant Commissioner, 2nd Grade, Mozufferngger, Punjab	22 Apr. 81	1 May 81		22 Jan. 92
Welsh Regiment	15	Wood, Ernest Perceval, Wing Officer 20 Madras Infantry	22 Jan. 81	3 June 81		22 Jan. 92
Sussex Regiment	15	Rynd, Frederick Cecil, 320 Deputy Assistant Commissary General, 1st Class, Madras	22 Jan. 81	29 June 81		22 Jan. 92
Leinster Regiment	15	Young, Arthur Thomas, 321 Wing Officer 2 Madras Infantry	22 Jan. 81	1 July 81		22 Jan. 92
West Surrey Regiment	15	Keane, Charles Robert, 2nd in Command and Wing Commander 31 Madras Infantry	22 Jan. 81	1 July 81		22 Jan. 92
Suffolk Regiment	15	Mayne, Augustus Blair, Squadron Commander 2 Central India Horse	22 Jan. 81	1 July 81		22 Jan. 92
Irish Fusiliers	15	Godfrey, Stuart Hill, Assistant British Agent, Gilgit	22 Jan. 81	1 July 81		22 Jan. 92
Dorsetshire Regiment	15	Ducat, Charles Merewether, 322 Squadron Commander 4 Bombay Cavalry	22 Jan. 81	1 July 81		22 Jan. 92
Yorkshire Light Infantry	15	Nurse, Charles George, 323 Wing Officer 13 Bombay Infantry	22 Jan. 81	1 July 81		22 Jan. 92
Scottish Rifles	15	Gordon, Philip James, 324 Assistant Superintendent, 1st Grade, Topographical Survey of India, Mandalay	22 Jan. 81	1 July 81		22 Jan. 92
South Wales Borderers	15	Johnson, Charles Edward, 325 Wing Officer 36 Bengal Infantry; employed in British Central Africa (Bt. Major, 14 Nov. 94)	22 Jan. 81	1 July 81		22 Jan. 92
Leinster Regiment	15	Colomb, Francis Cracroft, 326 Wing Officer 42 Bengal Infantry	22 Jan. 81	1 July 81		22 Jan. 92
North Lancashire Regt.	15	Rainey, Robert Maximilian, 327 2nd in Command and Wing Commander 12 Madras Infantry	22 Jan. 81	1 July 81		22 Jan. 92
East Lancashire Regiment	15	Whittall, Fras. Vaughan, Wing Officer 1 Infantry Hyderabad Contingent	22 Jan. 81	1 July 81		22 Jan. 92
Dorsetshire Regiment	15	Hobbs, Simpson Hackett, Beresford, 328 Squadron Officer 14 Bengal Lancers	22 Jan. 81	1 July 81		22 Jan. 92
Suffolk Regiment	15	Browning, Herbert Arros, Assistant Commissioner, 1st Grade, Sagaing, Burmah	22 Jan. 81	1 July 81		22 Jan. 92
Border Regiment	15	Phillips, Alfred Lucian, 329 Deputy Assistant Commissary General, 1st Class, Murree	22 Jan. 81	1 July 81		22 Jan. 92
Incshire Regiment	15	Herbert, Lionel, Squadron Commander 1 Central India Horse	22 Jan. 81	1 July 81		22 Jan. 92
Scots Fusiliers	15	Dick, Arthur Robert, Officiating Squadron Commander 3 Punjab Cavalry	22 Jan. 81	1 July 81		22 Jan. 92
Oxford Light Infantry	15	Trevor, Harry, 330 Wing Officer 15 Bengal Infantry	22 Jan. 81	1 July 81		22 Jan. 92
North Lancashire Regt.	15	Eales, Cecil Moncrieff, 331 Wing Officer 2 Punjab Infantry	22 Jan. 81	1 July 81		22 Jan. 92
West Yorkshire Regiment	15	Thring, Richard Henry Dugdale, 332 Squadron Commander 1 Madras Lancers	22 Jan. 81	1 July 81		22 Jan. 92
Liverpool Regiment	15	Rawlins, George William, 333 Squadron Commander 12 Bengal Cavalry	22 Jan. 81	1 July 81		22 Jan. 92
Suffolk Regiment	15	Williams, Arthur Blount, Cuthbert, Deputy Assistant Commissary General, 1st Class, Allahabad	22 Jan. 81	1 July 81		22 Jan. 92
West Riding Regiment	15	Cuppage, William Adam, 334 Wing Officer 5 Bengal Infantry	22 Jan. 81	1 July 81		22 Jan. 92
East Yorkshire Regiment	15	Fayrer, James Outram Spens, 335 Wing Commander 2 Battalion 5 Goorkhas	22 Jan. 81	1 July 81		22 Jan. 92
Bedford Regiment	15	Chesney, Kellow, 336 Squadron Commander 8 Bengal Lancers	22 Jan. 81	1 July 81		22 Jan. 92
Welsh Regiment	15	Kemball, Charles Arnold, Deputy Commissioner, Thull Chotiali, and Political Agent, Loralai	22 Jan. 81	1 July 81		22 Jan. 92
Yorkshire Light Infantry	15	Peyton, Westropp Joseph, 337 CMG, Squadron Commander 26 Bombay Cavalry	22 Jan. 81	1 July 81		22 Jan. 92
Irish Fusiliers	15	Hazelgrove, Harry Seymour, Wing Commander 12 Bombay Infantry	22 Jan. 81	1 July 81		22 Jan. 92
Liverpool Regiment	15	Row, George Russell, 338 Wing Officer 44 Bengal Infantry	22 Jan. 81	1 July 81		22 Jan. 92
Leinster Regiment	15	Williams, Frederic Thesiger, 339 Wing Commander 26 Madras Infantry	22 Jan. 81	1 July 81		22 Jan. 92
South Wales Borderers	15	Dodgson, Harcourt Leicester, 340 Wing Commander 2 Bengal Infantry	22 Jan. 81	1 July 81		22 Jan. 92
Liverpool Regiment	15	Johnstone, Augustus Anderson Jervis, Wing Officer 5 Punjab Infantry	22 Jan. 81	1 July 81		22 Jan. 92
Welsh Regiment	15	Stainforth, Lesley Charles Hamilton, Wing Commander 38 Bengal Infantry	22 Jan. 81	1 July 81		22 Jan. 92
Inniskilling Fusiliers	15	Caulfeild, Gordon Napier, 341 DSO, 2nd in Command and Wing Commander 10 Madras Infantry	31 Jan. 81	1 July 81		22 Jan. 92
Yorkshire Regiment	15	Shakespear, Leslie Waterfield, 342 Wing Officer 2 Battalion 5 Goorkhas	22 Jan. 81	1 July 81		22 Jan. 92
Royal Marines	15	Jones, Jenkin, Squadron Commander 2 Punjab Cavalry	22 Jan. 81	1 July 81		22 Jan. 92
Royal Marines	15	Graves, Acton Alexander, Wing Officer 20 Bombay Infantry	22 Jan. 81	1 July 81		22 Jan. 92
Royal Marines	15	Newnham, Arthur T. Herbert, Wing Officer 10 Bombay Infantry	22 Jan. 81	1 Feb. 81		1 Feb. 92
Royal Marines	15	Ransom, James Mann, Wing Officer 12 Bombay Infantry	22 Jan. 81	1 Feb. 81		1 Feb. 92
Royal Marines	15	Mardall, William Stratford, Squadron Officer 17 Bengal Cavalry	19 Feb. 81	1 July 81		19 Feb. 92
Royal Marines	15	Townshend, Charles Vere Ferrers, 344 Squadron Officer 1 Central India Horse	19 Feb. 81	1 July 81		19 Feb. 92
Northumberland Fusiliers	15	Radcliff, Samuel Garnett, 345 Wing Commander 33 Madras Infantry	19 Feb. 81	1 July 81		19 Feb. 92
Irish Rifles	15	Brown, Charles Allen, Wing Officer 8 Bombay Infantry	19 Feb. 81	1 July 81		19 Feb. 92
		Formby, Reginald Frederick Robert, Squadron Commander 3 Madras Lancers	19 Feb. 81	1 July 81		19 Feb. 92

Indian Staff Corps.

Last Regiment.	Yrs. Serv.	Captains.	2nd Lieut.	Lieut.	Brevet Captain.	Captain.
Gloucestershire Regiment	15	Rooke, Alfred Shipton, Wing Officer 2 Battalion 5 Goorkhas	19 Feb. 81	1 July 81	...	19 Feb. 92
West Kent Regiment	15	Lowry, Henry Ward,³⁴⁶ Deputy Assistant Commissary General, 1st Class, Meiktila	19 Feb. 81	1 July 81	...	19 Feb. 92
Dublin Fusiliers	15	Dawes, William Myers,³⁴⁷ Wing Commander 28 Madras Infantry	19 Feb. 81	1 July 81	...	19 Feb. 92
Sussex Regiment	15	Reed, Edmund Martin,³⁴⁸ Squadron Commander 2 Madras Lancers	19 Feb. 81	1 July 81	...	19 Feb. 92
North Lancashire Regt.	14	Grimston, Rollo Estouteville, Squadron Commander 6 Bengal Cavalry	23 Apr. 81	1 July 81	...	23 Apr. 92
Irish Rifles	14	Tighe, Michael Augustus, Political Agent, Bhopal	23 Apr. 81	1 July 81	...	23 Apr. 92
Welsh Regiment	14	Wimble, Walter Ernest,³⁴⁹ Deputy Assistant Commissary General, 1st Class, Bangalore	23 Apr. 81	1 July 81	...	23 Apr. 92
Dorsetshire Regiment	14	Holland, Harry Francis, Wing Commander 24 Bengal Infantry	23 Apr. 81	1 July 81	...	23 Apr. 92
Dorsetshire Regiment	14	Kratt, John Thorold, 2nd in Command and Wing Commander 39 Bengal Infantry	23 Apr. 81	1 July 81	...	23 Apr. 92
Wiltshire Regiment	14	Fryer, Leslie Charles,³⁵¹ Wing Officer 45 Bengal Infantry	23 Apr. 81	1 July 81	...	23 Apr. 92
Cheshire Regiment	14	Boileau, Herbert Edward, Squadron Commander 5 Bengal Cavalry	23 Apr. 81	1 July 81	...	23 Apr. 92
Royal Scots	14	Logan-Home, Ferdinand Cospatric, Squadron Officer 3 Madras Lancers	23 Apr. 81	1 July 81	...	23 Apr. 92
Wiltshire Regiment	14	Barlow, Francis Johr Herbert,³⁵² Squadron Officer Corps of Guides	23 Apr. 81	1 July 81	...	23 Apr. 92
Hampshire Regiment	14	Johnstone, Beresford Assheton, Deputy Assistant Adjutant General for Musketry, Burmah	23 Apr. 81	1 July 81	...	23 Apr. 92
Lancashire Fusiliers	14	Hawks, George William Shafto,³⁵³ Wing Commander 23 Madras Infantry	23 Apr. 81	1 July 81	...	23 Apr. 92
East Lancashire Regt.	14	Rich, Charles Lionel Mainwaring,³⁵⁴ Wing Officer Corps of Guides	23 Apr. 81	1 July 81	...	23 Apr. 92
Manchester Regiment	14	Davis, Cecil, Squadron Commander 1 Bengal Cavalry	23 Apr. 81	1 July 81	...	23 Apr. 92
West Yorkshire Regiment	14	Clements, Charles Henry,³⁵⁵ Assistant Commissary General, 4th Class, Mandalay	23 Apr. 81	1 July 81	...	23 Apr. 92
Munster Fusiliers	14	Turner, George Harvey, Wing Officer 26 Bombay Infantry	23 Apr. 81	1 July 81	...	23 Apr. 92
Royal Artillery	14	Stratton, Wallace Christopher Ramsay, Political Agent, Southern Beloochistan	23 Apr. 81	26 July 81	...	26 July 92
Royal Marines	14	Lloyd, Charles Edward,³⁵⁶ Deputy Assistant Commissary General, 1st Class	...	1 Sept. 81	...	1 Sept. 92
Gloucestershire Regiment	14	Daly, Hugh,³⁵⁷ CIE, Assistant Secretary, Government of India, Foreign Department	22 Oct. 81	22 Oct. 81	...	22 Oct. 92
Lancashire Fusiliers	14	Cruikford, John Archibald Houison,³⁵⁸ Wing Officer 7 Bombay Infantry	22 Oct. 81	22 Oct. 81	...	22 Oct. 92
Warwickshire Regiment	14	Brown, Harry Troup, Deputy Assistant Commissary General, 1st Class	22 Oct. 81	22 Oct. 81	...	22 Oct. 92
Irish Regiment	14	Macdonald, Frederick Weston Peile, Political Assistant, 2nd Class	22 Oct. 81	22 Oct. 81	...	22 Oct. 92
Irish Fusiliers	14	Cartwright, Charles Marling, Squadron Commander 6 Bombay Cavalry	22 Oct. 81	22 Oct. 81	...	22 Oct. 92
Oxford Light Infantry	14	Holloway, Benjamin,³⁵⁹ Squadron Officer 2 Madras Cavalry	22 Oct. 81	22 Oct. 81	...	22 Oct. 92
West Surrey Regiment	14	Edwards, FitzJames Maine, Squadron Commander 3 Bombay Cavalry	22 Oct. 81	22 Oct. 81	...	22 Oct. 92
Berkshire Regiment	14	Delamain, Walter Sinclair,³⁶⁰ Wing Officer 23 Bombay Infantry	22 Oct. 81	22 Oct. 81	...	22 Oct. 92
Warwickshire Regiment	14	Wingate, Alfred Woodrow Stanley, Squadron Officer 14 Bengal Lancers	22 Oct. 81	22 Oct. 81	...	22 Oct. 92
Irish Regiment	14	Jermyn, Turenne, Wing Officer 2 Sikh Infantry	22 Oct. 81	22 Oct. 81	...	22 Oct. 92
West Yorkshire Regiment	14	Carpendale, William Maxwell,³⁶² Squadron Commander 8 Bengal Cavalry	22 Oct. 81	22 Oct. 81	...	22 Oct. 92
Norfolk Regiment	14	Eliott, Francis Hardinge, Assistant Commissioner, 3rd Grade, Burmah	22 Oct. 81	22 Oct. 81	...	22 Oct. 92
Somerset Light Infantry	14	Crommelin, Charles Yule, Wing Officer 1 Battalion 1 Goorkhas	22 Oct. 81	22 Oct. 81	...	22 Oct. 92
West Riding Regiment	14	Duncan, Frank,³⁶³ Wing Officer 23 Bengal Infantry	22 Oct. 81	22 Oct. 81	...	22 Oct. 92
Berkshire Regiment	14	Harris, Arthur Philip Desborough,³⁶⁴ Wing Officer 11 Bengal Infantry	22 Oct. 81	22 Oct. 81	...	22 Oct. 92
Leinster Regiment	14	Nicholls, Arthur,³⁶⁵ Wing Officer 2 Punjab Infantry	22 Oct. 81	22 Oct. 81	...	22 Oct. 92
Somerset Light Infantry	14	Warren, Richard Pennefather, Wing Commander 9 Bengal Infantry	22 Oct. 81	22 Oct. 81	...	22 Oct. 92
Somerset Light Infantry	14	Barton, Henry Gerard, Wing Officer 4 Sikh Infantry	22 Oct. 81	22 Oct. 81	...	22 Oct. 92
Welsh Regiment	14	Mason, Sydney Moore,³⁶⁶ Squadron Commander 4 Lancers Hyderabad Contingent	22 Oct. 81	22 Oct. 81	...	22 Oct. 92
Gloucester Regiment	14	Price, Charles Henry Uvedale,³⁶⁷ Wing Commander 27 Bombay Infantry	22 Oct. 81	22 Oct. 81	...	22 Oct. 92
Northampton Regiment	14	Stewart, James Marshall,³⁶⁸ Wing Officer 1 Battalion 5 Goorkhas	22 Oct. 81	22 Oct. 81	...	22 Oct. 92
Duke of Cornwall's Lt. Inf.	14	Hudson, Havelock, Squadron Officer 19 Bengal Lancers	22 Oct. 81	22 Oct. 81	...	22 Oct. 92
Lancaster Regiment	14	Holland, Percy,³⁶⁹ Wing Officer 5 Punjab Infantry	22 Oct. 81	22 Oct. 81	...	22 Oct. 92
Gloucestershire Regiment	14	Crawford, George Ranier,³⁷⁰ Wing Officer 28 Bengal Infantry	22 Oct. 81	22 Oct. 81	...	22 Oct. 92
West Riding Regiment	14	Ross, Claye Ross, Wing Officer 14 Bengal Infantry	22 Oct. 81	22 Oct. 81	...	22 Oct. 92
East Lancashire Regiment	14	Mathias, Leonard John, Deputy Assistant Commissary General, 1st Class, Bombay	22 Oct. 81	22 Oct. 81	...	22 Oct. 92
Northampton Regiment	14	Woods, Albert Edward, Deputy Commissioner, 4th Grade, Naga Hills, Assam	22 Oct. 81	22 Oct. 81	...	22 Oct. 92
Sussex Regiment	14	Hatherell, William George,³⁷² Wing Officer 22 Bombay Infantry	22 Oct. 81	22 Oct. 81	...	22 Oct. 92
Duke of Cornwall's Lt. Inf.	14	Ievers, Oliver Goldsmith,³⁷³ Assistant Commissioner, Berar	22 Oct. 81	22 Oct. 81	...	22 Oct. 92
Essex Regiment	14	Bernard, Edward Henry,³⁷⁴ Wing Officer 6 Punjab Infantry	22 Oct. 81	22 Oct. 81	...	22 Oct. 92
Oxford Light Infantry	14	Churchill, Folliott,³⁷⁵ Wing Officer 4 Madras Infantry	22 Oct. 81	22 Oct. 81	...	22 Oct. 92

Indian Staff Corps.

427

Last Regiment.	Yrs.' Serv.	Captains.	2nd Lieut.	Lieut.	Brevet Captain.	Captain.
Liverpool Regiment	14	Brett, Walter Edward, 376 Wing Officer 6 Madras Infantry		22 Oct. 81		22 Oct. 93
Worcester Regiment	14	Lincoln, Sydney Woodward, 377 Assistant Commissary General, 4th Class, Kurrachee		28 Jan. 82		28 Jan. 93
East Yorkshire Regiment	14	Maconchy, Ernest William Stuart King, 378 DSO, Wing Officer 4 Sikh Infantry		28 Jan. 82		28 Jan. 93
Bedfordshire Regiment	14	Taylor, Hugh Neufville, 380 DSO, Wing Commander 30 Madras Infantry		28 Jan. 82		28 Jan. 95
Suffolk Regiment	14	Pressey, Arthur, 381 Wing Officer 4 Bengal Infantry		28 Jan. 82		28 Jan. 93
Suffolk Regiment	14	Poingdestre, Alfred, 382 Adjutant Malwah Bheel Corps		28 Jan. 82		28 Jan. 93
Derbyshire Regiment	14	Thornhill, John, 383 2nd in Command and Wing Commander 6 Madras Infantry		28 Jan. 82		28 Jan. 93
Munster Fusiliers	14	Denne, Arthur Robert, 384 Wing Officer 2 Madras Infantry		28 Jan. 82		28 Jan. 93
Royal Artillery	14	Green, George Edward Tempest, 385 Assistant Commissioner, 3rd Grade, Myaungmya District, Burmah		22 Feb. 82		22 Feb. 93
Liverpool Regiment	14	Pinhey, Alexander Fleetwood, Political Agent, Ulwur		10 May 82		10 May 93
Lancaster Regiment	13	Prichard, Charles Hamerton, Political Assistant, 2nd Class, Rajpootana		10 May 82		10 May 93
Seaforth Highlanders	13	p.s.c. Shore, Offley Bohun Stovin Fairless, Squadron Officer 18 Bengal Lancers		10 May 82		10 May 93
West Yorkshire Regiment	13	Whyte, Charles William Frederick, Wing Officer 17 Bombay Infantry		10 May 82		10 May 93
Oxford Light Infantry	13	Mathews, John Rocke, 387 Squadron Officer 2 Madras Lancers		10 May 82		10 May 93
East Yorkshire Regiment	13	Thomson, David Birdwood, 388 Wing Officer 8 Bombay Infantry		10 May 82		10 May 93
Scots Fusiliers	13	Johnston, Harley M'Alpine, 389 Squadron Officer 15 Bengal Lancers		10 May 82		10 May 93
Royal Scots	13	De Lisle, George de Saussmarez, Wing Commander 3 Bombay Infantry		10 May 82		10 May 93
Lincoln Regiment	13	Fasken, William Henry, Squadron Commander 10 Bengal Lancers		10 May 82		10 May 93
West Yorkshire Regiment	13	Schneider, Claude Vyvian, Squadron Officer 1 Central India Horse		10 May 82		10 May 93
Devonshire Regiment	13	Colgrave, Edwin Charles Barnes, Wing Commander 39 Bengal Infantry		10 May 82		10 May 93
Derbyshire Regiment	13	Campbell, Alexander Augustus Elphinstone, Deputy Assistant Adjutant General for Musketry, Abbottabad		10 May 82		10 May 93
Leinster Regiment	13	Mocatta, Daniel Edward, Wing Officer 1 Battalion 1 Goorkhas		10 May 82		10 May 93
Warwickshire Regiment	13	Thomas, Francis Herbert Sullivan, 391 Deputy Assistant Commissary General, 1st Class, Bangalore		10 May 82		10 May 93
Cheshire Regiment	13	Lang, Arthur George Boileau, Wing Officer 1 Punjab Infantry		10 May 82		10 May 93
2nd Cheshire Regiment	13	Minchin, Charles Frederick, 392 Squadron Officer 1 Punjab Infantry		10 May 92		10 May 93
Oxford Light Infantry	13	Hodson, George Benjamin, 393 Wing Commander Corps of Guides		10 May 82		10 May 93
Irish Regiment	13	Bond, Chetwynd Rokeby Alfred, Wing Officer 35 Bengal Infantry		10 May 82		10 May 93
Liverpool Regiment	13	Leslie, William Clarence Colebrook, 394 Cantonment Magistrate, 2nd Class, Benares		10 May 82		10 May 93
Irish Regiment	13	Broome, George Simpson, 395 Wing Commander 29 Bombay Infantry		10 May 82		10 May 93
Irish Fusiliers	13	Daly, Henry Dermot, 396 Wing Commander 32 Madras Infantry		10 May 82		10 May 93
Liverpool Regiment	13	Conran, William Loraine, 397 Wing Officer 1 Bombay Infantry		10 May 82		10 May 93
N. Lancashire Regiment	13	Loudon, Francis Arthur, 398 Wing Officer 25 Madras Infantry		10 May 82		10 May 93
K. O. Scottish Borderers	13	Hall, George James Cadell, Squadron Commander 12 Bengal Cavalry		10 May 82		10 May 93
York & Lancaster Regt.	13	Blakeney, William Edward Albemarle, 399 Squadron Officer 3 Bengal Cavalry		10 May 82		10 May 93
Northumberland Fusiliers	13	Cooke, William Nevinson Macdonald, 400 Wing Officer 8 Madras Infantry		10 May 82		10 May 93
Border Regiment	13	Le Bailly, Alexander Cortlandt, 401 Wing Officer 17 Bombay Infantry		10 May 82		17 May 93
Royal Artillery	13	Griffiths, Charles, 402 Squadron Commander 16 Bengal Cavalry		10 May 82		10 May 93
Suffolk Regiment	13	Hamilton, Claude Leslie, Squadron Officer 3 Bengal Cavalry		25 July 82		25 July 93
Cheshire Regiment	13	Dillon, George Frederick Horace, 403 Wing Commander 40 Bengal Infantry		29 July 82		29 July 93
Irish Regiment	13	Maxwell, Frederick Doveton, Deputy Commissioner, 4th Grade, Burmah		29 July 82		29 July 93
East Surry Regiment	13	Bretherton, George Howard, 405 Deputy Assistant Commissary General, 1st Class; on special duty, Gilgit		29 July 82		29 July 95
Essex Regiment	13	Wimberley, Charles Irvine, Squadron Commander 8 Bengal Cavalry		29 July 82		29 July 93
10 Hussars	13	Jones, Aubrey Arbuthnot, 406 Squadron Commander 1 Lancers Hyderabad Contingent		2 Aug. 82		2 Aug. 93
4 Dragoon Guards	13	Nicholson, Ralph Wise, 407 Deputy Assistant Commissary General, 1st Class, Mhow		2 Aug. 82		2 Aug. 93
6 Dragoon Guards	13	Shakespear, William Frederic, Squadron Commander 6 Bengal Cavalry		9 Sept. 82		9 Sept. 93
Dorsetshire Regiment	13	Stirling, William George Hay, 408 Squadron Officer 1 Madras Lancers		9 Sept. 82		9 Sept. 93
Devonshire Regiment	13	Archer, Charles, Political Agent, Zhob		9 Sept. 82		9 Sept. 93
Worcestershire Regiment	13	Gurdon, Philip Richard Thornhagh, Assistant Commissioner, 1st Grade, Assam		9 Sept. 82		9 Sept. 93
Essex Regiment	13	Jacob, Claud William, 410 Wing Commander 24 Bombay Infantry		9 Sept. 82		9 Sept. 93
Scots Fusiliers	13	Hawkes, Thomas Bate, 411 Wing Commander 22 Madras Infantry		9 Sept. 82		9 Sept. 93
North Lancashire Regt.	13	Erck, John Caillard, 412 Wing Officer 23 Madras Infantry		9 Sept. 82		9 Sept. 93
	13	Savage, William Henry, Wing Commander 1 Battalion 3 Goorkhas		9 Sept. 82		9 Sept. 93

Indian Staff Corps.

Last Regiment.	Yrs. Sety.	Captains.	2nd Lieut.	Lieut.	Brevet Captain.	Captain.
Oxford Light Infantry	13	Oswald, William Alexander,⁴³ Wing Officer 33 Madras Infantry		9 Sept. 82		9 Sept. 93
Scottish Rifles	13	Campbell, Charles Ferguson, Squadron Commander 6 Bengal Cavalry		9 Sept. 82		9 Sept. 93
South Wales Borderers	13	Arbuthnot, George Herbert,⁴¹⁴ Squadron Officer 3 Madras Lancers		9 Sept. 82		9 Sept. 93
Border Regiment	13	Woodward, John Alfred Hudson, Wing Officer 37 Bengal Infantry		9 Sept. 82		9 Sept. 93
Cheshire Regiment	13	Barnsay, John, Political Agent, Bundelcund		9 Sept. 82		9 Sept. 93
Irish Regiment	13	Herbert, Lionel Norton, Wing Officer 22 Bengal Infantry		9 Sept. 82		9 Sept. 93
Border Regiment	13	M'Kay, Thompson,⁴¹⁵ Wing Officer 40 Bengal Infantry		9 Sept. 82		9 Sept. 93
Irish Regiment	13	Ryall, Edward Charles, Wing Officer 1 Battalion 4 Goorkhas		9 Sept. 82		9 Sept. 93
East Lancashire Regiment	13	Giles, Albert,⁴¹⁶ Wing Officer 13 Bengal Infantry		9 Sept. 82		9 Sept. 93
East Yorkshire Regiment	13	Melliss, Charles John, Wing Officer 9 Bombay Infantry		9 Sept. 82		9 Sept. 93
Suffolk Regiment	13	Campbell, Henry William,⁴¹⁷ Squadron Officer 8 Bengal Lancers		9 Sept. 82		9 Sept. 93
North Stafford Regiment	13	Birdwood, George Christopher M'Dowall,⁴¹⁸ Squadron Officer 1 Bombay Lancers		9 Sept. 82		9 Sept. 93
Berkshire Regiment	13	Kaye, James Lovett,⁴¹⁹ Political Assistant, 3rd Class; Assistant Resident in Cashmere		9 Sept. 82		9 Sept. 93
N. Lancashire Regiment	13	Brownrigg, George Alexander,⁴²⁰ Wing Officer 28 Bombay Infantry		9 Sept. 82		9 Sept. 93
Leinster Regiment	13	Leslie, Thomas Dowrglasse, Squadron Officer 3 Madras Lancers		9 Sept. 82		9 Sept. 93
Bengal Staff Corps	13	Crawford, Claude Melville,⁴²¹ Wing Officer 2 Battalion 5 Goorkhas		9 Sept. 82		9 Sept. 93
East Yorkshire Regiment	13	Merewether, Herbert Duncan, Assistant Political Resident, Aden		9 Sept. 82		9 Sept. 93
Essex Regiment	13	Beames, David, Wing Officer 19 Bengal Infantry		9 Sept. 82		9 Sept. 93
Yorkshire Light Infantry	13	Priestley, George William, Wing Officer 2 Infantry Hyderabad Contingent		9 Sept. 82		9 Sept. 93
East Yorkshire Regiment	13	O'Bryen, Charles William,⁴²² Wing Officer 27 Bengal Infantry		9 Sept. 82		9 Sept. 93
Cheshire Regiment	13	Holland, Guy Lushington,⁴²³ Wing Officer 34 Bengal Infantry		27 Jan. 83		27 Jan. 94
Liverpool Regiment	13	Sullivan, Rupert Edward,⁴²⁴ Deputy Assistant Commissary General, 1st Class, Bellary		27 Jan. 83		27 Jan. 94
Somerset Light Infantry	13	Whiffin, Henry Edward,⁴²⁵ Wing Officer 13 Bengal Lancers		27 Jan. 83		27 Jan. 94
East Surrey Regiment	13	Young, William Bensley,⁴²⁶ Wing Officer 5 Madras Infantry		27 Jan. 83		27 Jan. 94
Essex Regiment	13	Horsbrugh, Robert Patrick,⁴²⁷ Assistant Commissioner, 2nd Class, Khamgaon, Hyderabad		1 Feb. 83		1 Feb. 94
7 Dragoon Guards	13	Buchanan, Kenneth James,⁴²⁸ Wing Officer 4 Sikh Infantry		1 Feb. 83		1 Feb. 94
Royal Marines	13	Baker, Donald, Deputy Assistant Commissary General, 1st Class, Meerut		14 Feb. 83		14 Feb. 94
Royal Artillery	13	Baynes, Charles Edward, Squadron Officer 2 Bombay Lancers		14 Feb. 83		14 Feb. 94
Royal Marines	13	Davidson, Walter Lloyd,⁴²⁹ Wing Officer 17 Bengal Infantry		28 Feb. 83		28 Feb. 94
Royal Artillery	13	Kennedy, Hugh,⁴³⁰ Squadron Officer 3 Punjab Cavalry		25 July 82		7 Mar. 94
Royal Artillery	13	Brockman, Percy William Drake, C.I.E. Political Agent, 3rd Class		10 Mar. 83		10 Mar. 94
Liverpool Regiment	13	M'Mahon, Arthur Henry,⁴³¹ C.I.E. Political Agent, 3rd Class		10 Mar. 83		10 Mar. 94
West Riding Regiment	13	Lindesay, Alexander Lunsdaine,⁴³² Wing Officer 24 Bengal Infantry		10 Mar. 83		10 Mar. 94
Connaught Rangers	13	de Wilton, Albert Walter,⁴³² Wing Officer 1 Bengal Infantry		10 Mar. 83		10 Mar. 94
Norfolk Regiment	13	Smith, John Manners,⁴³³ C.I.E. Assistant Governor General's Agent, Beloochistan		10 Mar. 83		10 Mar. 94
South Lancashire Regt.	13	Comminee, Francis Henry Bagot, Wing Officer 2 Bengal Lancers		10 Mar. 83		10 Mar. 94
East York Regiment	13	Hoghton, Frederick Aubrey, Wing Commander 1 Bombay Infantry		10 Mar. 83		10 Mar. 94
Dorsetshire Regiment	13	Schofield, Charles, Wing Commander 4 Punjab Infantry		10 Mar. 83		10 Mar. 94
Oxford Light Infantry	13	Cardew, Francis Gordon,⁴³⁵ Squadron Officer 10 Bengal Lancers		10 Mar. 83		10 Mar. 94
Manchester Regiment	13	Johnson, Arthur Cyril Beaumont,⁴³⁶ Wing Officer 1 Battalion 1 Goorkhas		10 Mar. 83		10 Mar. 94
Lincolnshire Regiment	13	Hartigan, Arthur Edwin Stewart, Squadron Commander 6 Bombay Cavalry		10 Mar. 83		10 Mar. 94
S. Lancashire Regiment	13	Andrews, Louis James,⁴³⁷ Wing Commander 17 Madras Infantry		10 Mar. 83		10 Mar. 94
Worcestershire Regiment	13	Betham, Robert Mitchell,⁴³⁸ Wing Officer 8 Bombay Infantry		10 Mar. 83		10 Mar. 94
Oxford Light Infantry	13	Falcon, Robert Morgan,⁴³⁹ Wing Officer 4 Sikh Infantry		10 Mar. 83		10 Mar. 94
Welsh Regiment	13	Swayne, Eric John Eagles,⁴⁴⁰ Wing Officer 16 Bengal Infantry		10 Mar. 83		10 Mar. 94
Durham Light Infantry	13	Mead, Harold Richard,⁴⁴¹ Wing Officer 16 Bombay Infantry		10 Mar. 83		10 Mar. 94
Lincolnshire Regiment	13	Gayer, Edward Alexander,⁴⁴² Deputy Assistant Commissary General, 2nd Class, Port Blair		10 Mar. 83		10 Mar. 94
Cheshire Regiment	13	Wilkieson, Claude William,⁴⁴³ Wing Officer 4 Madras Infantry		10 Mar. 83		10 Mar. 94
Norfolk Regiment	13	Fisher, John, Wing Officer 28 Bengal Infantry		10 Mar. 83		10 Mar. 94
Irish Rifles	13	Stewart, James Fearnley, Squadron Officer 14 Bengal Lancers		10 Mar. 83		10 Mar. 94
Scottish Rifles	13	Bruce, Arthur Francis,⁴⁴⁴ Wing Officer 2 Goorkhas		10 Mar. 83		10 Mar. 94
Yorkshire Regiment	13	Fischer, Thomas Adam,⁴⁴⁵ Wing Officer 19 Madras Infantry		10 Mar. 83		10 Mar. 94
Lancashire Fusiliers	13	Baugh, Mackenzie Walcott,⁴⁴⁶ Wing Officer 3 Bombay Infantry		19 Mar. 83		10 Mar. 94

Indian Staff Corps.

Last Regiment.	Yrs. Sery.	CAPTAINS.	2nd LIEUT.	LIEUT.	BREVET CAPTAIN.	CAPTAIN.
Leicestershire Regiment	13	Crocker, Sydney Francis, 447 Squadron Officer 9 Bengal Lancers		10 Mar. 83		10 Mar. 94
Welsh Regiment	13	Knatchbull, George Wyndham Chichester, 448 Wing Officer 22 Bombay Infantry		10 Mar. 83		10 Mar. 94
Derbyshire Regiment	13	Impey, Lawrence, Political Assistant, 2nd Class		10 Mar. 83		10 Mar. 94
Northamptonshire Regt.	13	de Vismes de Ponthieu, Raoul Guy Richard, Wing Commander 10 Bombay Infantry		10 Mar. 83		10 Mar. 94
Leicestershire Regiment	13	London, John Archer, 449 Wing Commander 13 Madras Infantry		10 Mar. 83		10 Mar. 94
Devonshire Regiment	13	Carruthers, Robert Alexander, Squadron Officer 11 Bengal Lancers		10 Mar. 83		10 Mar. 94
Oxford Light Infantry	13	Connell, Charles Edward Halkett, Wing Officer 5 Madras Infantry		10 Mar. 83		10 Mar. 94
Bombay Staff Corps	13	Baitt, Henry George Bowen, Wing Officer 7 Bengal Infantry		10 Mar. 83		10 Mar. 94
Inniskilling Fusiliers	13	Mainwaring, Charles Vaughan, 451 Wing Commander 29 Madras Infantry		10 Mar. 83		10 Mar. 94
Essex Regiment	13	Leonard, Alfred Wilberforce, 452 Wing Officer 4 Infantry Hyderabad Contingent		10 Mar. 83		10 Mar. 94
Scottish Rifles	13	Vanrenen, Adrian John Hetron, Squadron Officer 8 Bengal Cavalry		10 Mar. 83		10 Mar. 94
Sussex Regiment	13	Brown, Robert James Reid, 453 Wing Officer 1 Bengal Infantry		10 Mar. 83		10 Mar. 94
Suffolk Regiment	13	Sillery, Charles Cecil Archibald, 454 Wing Officer 6 Punjab Infantry		12 May 83		12 May 94
2 West India Regiment	13	Manduit, Frank Rowley Metcalfe Charles De Rittich, Assistant Commissioner, Amraoti		12 May 83		12 May 94
Oxford Light Infantry	12	Philipps, Ivor, 455 Wing Officer 1 Battalion 5 Goorkhas		12 May 83		12 May 94
2 Lancashire Regiment	12	Binsteed, Charles Henry Frederic, Squadron Officer 1 Madras Lancers		12 May 83		12 May 94
Cheshire Regiment	12	Faulknor, Augustus Arthur Malcolm Maude, Wing Officer 2 Bengal Infantry		12 May 83		12 May 94
N. Staffordshire Regiment	12	Woodyatt, Nigel Gresley, Wing Officer 2 Battalion 3 Goorkhas		12 May 83		12 May 94
Norfolk Regiment	12	Pair, Gilbert Walter, 457 Assistant Commissary General, 4th Class, Deesa		28 July 83		28 July 94
Royal Artillery	12	Shewers, Herbert Lionel, Assistant Commissioner Thull Chohah		25 Aug. 83		25 Aug. 94
North Lancashire Regt.	12	Chalfecott, Algernon Winn, Squadron Officer 1 Punjab Cavalry		25 Aug. 83		25 Aug. 94
South Wales Borderers	12	Fowler, Francis John, 458 DSO, Wing Officer 27 Bombay Infantry		25 Aug. 83		25 Aug. 94
Devonshire Regiment	12	Kirkpatrick, William, 459 Wing Officer 1 Punjab Infantry		25 Aug. 83		25 Aug. 94
Munster Fusiliers	12	Townsend, Edward Copleston, Assistant Commissioner, 3rd Grade, Magwe District, Burmah		25 Aug. 83		25 Aug. 94
Connaught Rangers	12	Roberts, Hereward Llewellyn, Squadron Officer 1 Bengal Cavalry		25 Aug. 83		25 Aug. 94
Yorkshire Light Infantry	12	p.s.c. Selwyn, Charles Henry, 460 Squadron Officer 12 Bengal Cavalry		25 Aug. 83		25 Aug. 94
South Wales Borderers	12	Amesbury, Frederick Cholmeley Dering, Officiating Wing Officer 3 Bengal Infantry		25 Aug. 83		25 Aug. 94
Munster Fusiliers	12	Field, Charles William, 461 Wing Officer 26 Bengal Infantry		25 Aug. 83		25 Aug. 94
West Surrey Regiment	12	Maxwell, William Lockhart, 461 Squadron Commander 10 Bengal Lancers		25 Aug. 83		25 Aug. 94
Worcestershire Regiment	12	Millar, William Henry, 462 Wing Officer 27 Bengal Infantry		25 Aug. 83		25 Aug. 94
Dorsetshire Regiment	12	Hardy, Thomas Henry, Wing Commander 5 Infantry Hyderabad Contingent		25 Aug. 83		25 Aug. 94
Worcestershire Regiment	12	Douglas, James Archibald, Squadron Commander 2 Bengal Lancers		25 Aug. 83		25 Aug. 94
Leinster Regiment	12	Tighe, Michael Joseph, 463 DSO, Wing Officer 27 Bombay Infantry		25 Aug. 83		25 Aug. 94
Lincolnshire Regiment	12	Moseley, Robert John Dennys, 464 Wing Officer 15 Bengal Infantry		25 Aug. 83		25 Aug. 94
Worcestershire Regiment	12	Knight, Wyndham Charles, Squadron Officer 4 Bengal Cavalry		25 Aug. 83		25 Aug. 94
Border Regiment	12	Sutherland, John Campbell, 465 Wing Officer 17 Bengal Infantry		25 Aug. 83		25 Aug. 94
Hampshire Regiment	12	Banbury, Walter Edward, 466 Wing Officer 25 Madras Infantry		23 Aug. 83		23 Aug. 94
N. Staffordshire Regiment	12	Bourchier, Arthur Charles Francis, Wing Officer 2 Infantry Hyderabad Contingent		25 Aug. 83		25 Aug. 94
Scottish Rifles	12	Hatch, Alfred Edmund, 467 Wing Officer 29 Bombay Infantry		25 Aug. 83		25 Aug. 94
Durham Light Infantry	12	Davidson, Robert Venour, 468 Wing Officer 13 Bengal Infantry		25 Aug. 83		25 Aug. 94
West Yorkshire Regt.	12	Searle, Charles Thomas Arnold, Wing Officer 30 Bengal Infantry		25 Aug. 83		25 Aug. 94
Lancashire Fusiliers	12	Hudson, Wemyss, Wing Officer 20 Madras Infantry		25 Aug. 83		25 Aug. 94
Hampshire Regiment	12	Anderson, Horace Robert Francis, Assistant Commissary General, 4th Class, Aden		25 Aug. 83		25 Aug. 94
Bedfordshire Regiment	12	Jackson, Robert Postance, 470 Deputy Assistant Commissary General, 1st Class, Kussowlie		25 Aug. 83		25 Aug. 94
Yorkshire Light Infantry	12	Eckford, John James Haldane Black, 471 Wing Officer 1 Bengal Infantry		25 Aug. 83		25 Aug. 94
South Wales Borderers	12	Ewart, Richard Henry, Deputy Assistant Commissary General, 1st Grade, Burma		1 Sept. 83		1 Sept. 94
Royal Marines	12	Aplin, Stephen Lushington, 473 Assistant Commissioner, 4th Grade, Burma		1 Sept. 83		1 Sept. 94
Royal Marines	12	Orpen, Ralph Churnside Osborne, Wing Officer 5 Punjab Infantry		20 Oct. 83		1 Oct. 94
2 West India Regiment	12	Daun, Henry Churnside Beaumont, Wing Officer 10 Bombay Infantry		5 Dec. 83		5 Dec. 94
Worcestershire Regiment	12	Palmer, Henry Ingham Everest, 474 Squadron Officer 5 Punjab Cavalry		5 Dec. 83		5 Dec. 94
Scottish Rifles	12	Webster, Thomas, 475 Wing Officer 12 Bengal Infantry		5 Dec. 83		5 Dec. 94
Leinster Regiment	12	Stevens, Morton, Wing Officer 13 Bengal Infantry		5 Dec. 83		5 Dec. 94

Indian Staff Corps.

Last Regiment.	Yrs. Serv.	CAPTAINS.	2nd LIEUT.	LIEUT.	BREVET CAPTAIN.	CAPTAIN.
York Light Infantry	12	Sanders, Gerhardt L'Homneu, Deputy Assistant Commissary General, 1st Class; Brigade Commissariat Officer, Reserve Brigade, Waziristan Delimitation Escort	......	5 Dec. 83	......	5 Dec. 94
Berkshire Regiment	12	Barratt, William Cross,⁴⁷⁷ Wing Officer 1 Sikh Infantry	......	5 Dec. 83	......	5 Dec. 94
Derbyshire Regiment	12	Cole, Edward Hearle,⁴⁷⁸ Squadron Officer 11 Bengal Lancers	......	19 Dec. 83	......	19 Dec. 94
Durham Light Infantry	12	Shaw, Alexander James,⁴⁷⁹ Officiating Wing Officer 26 Madras Infantry	......	19 Dec. 83	......	19 Dec. 94
Durham Light Infantry	12	Cooper, Edmund Saffery,⁴⁸⁰ Wing Officer 31 Bengal Infantry	......	19 Dec. 83	......	19 Dec. 94
Sussex Regiment	12	Somerset, Charles Wyndham,⁴⁸¹ Wing Officer 12 Bengal Infantry	......	30 Jan. 84	......	30 Jan. 95
Sussex Regiment	12	Finch, Colin, Squadron Officer 1 Bengal Cavalry	......	30 Jan. 84	......	30 Jan. 95
Scots Fusiliers	12	Renton, Robert Ross,⁴⁸² Wing Officer 18 Bengal Infantry	......	30 Jan. 84	......	30 Jan. 95
Sussex Regiment	12	Venner, Charles Frederick Venner Sidebottom,⁴⁸³ Wing Officer 10 Bengal Infantry	......	30 Jan. 84	......	30 Jan. 95
Royal Marines	12	Keown, John Charrier, Wing Officer 4 Bombay Infantry	......	1 Feb. 84	......	1 Feb. 95
Northumberland Fusiliers	12	Clay, Charles Herbert,⁴⁸⁴ Wing Officer 43 Bengal Infantry	......	6 Feb. 84	......	6 Feb. 95
Warwickshire Regiment	12	Willoughby, Michael Edward, Squadron Commander 2 Bengal Lancers	......	6 Feb. 84	......	6 Feb. 95
Seaforth Highlanders	12	Elphinstone, Arthur Percy Archibald,⁴⁸⁵ Wing Officer 7 Bombay Infantry	......	6 Feb. 84	......	6 Feb. 95
Irish Fusiliers	12	Hair, Thomas Wolseley,⁴⁸⁶ Assistant Commissioner Hyderabad	......	6 Feb. 84	......	6 Feb. 95
Irish Fusiliers	12	Tod, John Kelso,⁴⁸⁷ Squadron Officer 7 Bengal Cavalry	......	6 Feb. 84	......	6 Feb. 95
N. Lancashire Regiment	12	Henderson, Thomas Hume,⁴⁸⁸ Wing Officer 13 Bombay Infantry	......	6 Feb. 84	......	6 Feb. 95
Irish Rifles	12	Bradshaw, Frederick Ewart, Assistant Commissioner, 3rd Grade, Punjab	......	6 Feb. 84	......	6 Feb. 95
Liverpool Regiment	12	Wake, Edward St. Aubyn, Squadron Officer 10 Bengal Lancers	......	6 Feb. 84	......	6 Feb. 95
Warwickshire Regiment	12	Robertson, George Alan,⁴⁸⁹ Squadron Officer 15 Bengal Lancers	......	6 Feb. 84	......	6 Feb. 95
Cheshire Regiment	12	Roche, Henry John, Wing Officer 6 Bengal Infantry	......	6 Feb. 84	......	6 Feb. 95
Scots Fusiliers	12	Walton, William Crawford,⁴⁹⁰ Wing Officer 4 Bombay Infantry	......	6 Feb. 84	......	6 Feb. 95
Liverpool Regiment	12	Grimston, Sylvester Bertram,⁴⁹¹ Squadron Officer 18 Bengal Lancers	......	6 Feb. 84	......	6 Feb.·95
Gloucestershire Regiment	12	Pollard, James Herbert, Wing Officer Bhopaul Battalion	......	6 Feb. 84	......	6 Feb. 95
N. Staffordshire Regiment	12	Ayerst, William,⁴⁹² Wing Officer 20 Bombay Infantry	......	6 Feb. 84	......	6 Feb. 95
Liverpool Regiment	12	Colomb, George Henry Cooper,⁴⁹³ Wing Officer 1 Battalion 4 Goorkhas	......	6 Feb. 84	......	6 Feb. 95
Cheshire Regiment	12	Brookfg, Harry Trifcott,⁴⁹⁴ Wing Officer 21 Madras Infantry	......	6 Feb. 84	......	6 Feb. 95
	12	Ross, Charles Edmond,⁴⁹⁵ Assistant Resident at Hyderabad and General Superintendent of Operations for the Suppression of Thuggee and Dacoity	......	6 Feb. 84	......	6 Feb. 95
Scottish Rifles	12	Burne, Knightley Owen, Wing Officer 1 Sikh Infantry	......	6 Feb. 84	......	6 Feb. 95
Scottish Rifles	12	Cox, Percy Zachariah, Assistant Political Resident, Aden	......	6 Feb. 84	......	6 Feb. 95
Inniskilling Fusiliers	12	Foster, Lonis Maurice,⁴⁹⁷ Wing Officer 28 Bombay Infantry	......	6 Feb. 84	......	6 Feb. 95
Cheshire Regiment	12	Egerton, Charles Philip, Assistant Commissioner, 3rd Grade, Punjab	......	6 Feb. 84	......	6 Feb. 95
Dorsetshire Regiment	12	Bendon, Guy Cecil, Assistant Commissioner, 3rd Grade, Punjab	......	6 Feb. 84	......	6 Feb. 95
Suffolk Regiment	12	Medley, Allen George, Squadron Officer 19 Bengal Lancers	......	6 Feb. 84	......	6 Feb. 95
Sussex Regiment	12	Graham, Stuart Bruce,⁴⁹⁹ Wing Officer 14 Madras Infantry	......	6 Feb. 84	......	6 Feb. 95
Bedfordshire Regiment	12	Johnson, Thomas Shaw,⁵⁰⁰ Wing Officer 33 Madras Infantry	......	6 Feb. 84	......	6 Feb. 95
N. Lancashire Regiment	12	Watson, Edward Yerbury,⁵⁰¹ Deputy Assistant Commissary General, 1st Class	......	6 Feb. 84	......	6 Feb. 95
Oxford Light Infantry	12	Cox, Francis William Henry,⁵⁰² Wing Officer 12 Madras Infantry	......	6 Feb. 84	......	6 Feb. 95
Worcestershire Regiment	12	Mennie, John Oliver, Wing Officer 30 Bombay Infantry	......	6 Feb. 84	......	6 Feb. 95
S. Staffordshire Regiment	12	Murray, Cyril F. Tyrrell,⁵⁰³ Deputy Assistant Commissary General, 1st Class	......	6 Feb. 84	......	6 Feb. 95
Hampshire Regiment	12	Warden, Alfred Walter,⁵⁰⁴ Squadron Officer 3 Lancers Hyderabad Contingent	......	6 Feb. 84	......	6 Feb. 95
N. Staffordshire Regiment	12	Douglas, Montagu William, Assistant Commissioner, Sealkote, Punjab	......	6 Feb. 84	......	6 Feb. 95
Gloucestershire Regiment	12	Erskine, Keith David, Political Assistant 1st Class, Rajpootana	......	6 Feb. 84	......	6 Feb. 95
Border Regiment	12	Warde, Hugh North, Assistant Commissioner 2nd Grade, Burmah	......	6 Feb. 84	......	6 Feb. 95
Devonshire Regiment	12	Soady, George Joseph Fitz M.,⁵⁰⁵ Wing Officer 19 Bengal Infantry	......	6 Feb. 84	......	6 Feb. 95
South Wales Borderers	12	Henegan, John,⁵⁰⁶ DSO, Wing Officer 10 Madras Infantry	......	6 Feb. 84	......	6 Feb. 95
West Riding Regiment	12	Bayley, S. Farquharson, Political Assistant, 3rd Class	......	6 Feb. 84	......	6 Feb. 95
Leinster Regiment	12	Windle, Ernest te V.,⁵⁰⁷ Squadron Officer 15 Bengal Lancers	......	6 Feb. 84	......	6 Feb. 95
Munster Fusiliers	12	Campbell, William Neville,⁵⁰⁸ Squadron Commander 2 Punjab Cavalry	......	6 Feb. 84	......	6 Feb. 95
Derbyshire Regiment	12	Baird, John M'Donald,⁵⁰⁹ Wing Officer 24 Bengal Cavalry	......	6 Feb. 84	......	6 Feb. 95
East Lancashire Regiment	12	Barnes, James Petit, Squadron Officer 6 Bengal Cavalry	......	6 Feb. 84	......	6 Feb. 95
Royal Fusiliers	12	Williams, Charles Stanley,⁵¹⁰ Wing Officer 43 Bengal Infantry	......	6 Feb. 84	......	6 Feb. 95
Somerset Light Infantry	12	Peach, Edmund,⁵¹¹ Wing Officer 3 Madras Infantry	......	6 Feb. 84	......	6 Feb. 95

Indian Staff Corps.

Last Regiment.	Yrs. Serv.	LIEUTENANTS.	2nd LIEUT.	LIEUT.
Yorkshire Light Infantry...	11	Warren, Percy Bliss,⁵¹² Wing Officer 3 Bengal Infantry........	......	14 May 84
Welsh Regiment	11	Pearse, Sydney Arthur,⁵¹³ Wing Officer 17 Madras Infantry...	......	14 May 84
Middlesex Regiment	11	Wynch, Fred. John Henry,⁵¹⁴ Wing Officer 37 Benga. Inf.	......	14 May 84
Irish Regiment	11	Lilly, George William,⁵¹⁵ Wing Officer 3 Madras Infantry	......	14 May 84
Suffolk Regiment................	11	Montagu, Arthur Henry, Wing Officer 21 Bengal Infantry ...	......	14 May 84
East Surrey Regiment	11	Brasier-Creagh, George Percy,⁵¹⁶ Squad. Officer 9 Bengal Lan.	......	14 May 84
Sussex Regiment	11	Thomas, Hubert St. George,⁵¹⁷ Wing Officer 19 Madras Inf. ...	......	14 May 84
Norfolk Regiment................	11	Boileau, Colin Campbell,⁵¹⁸ Squad. Officer 5 Bengal Cavalry	......	14 May 84
Wiltshire Regiment.............	11	Ffrench, Thomas, Wing Officer 27 Madras Infantry.............	......	14 May 84
Devonshire Regiment.........	11	Murray, Henry Brooke,⁵¹⁹ Wing Officer 34 Bengal Infantry ...	......	14 May 84
Royal Scots	11	Baldwin, Archibald Colin,⁵²⁰ Wing Officer 30 Madras Inf........	......	14 May 84
Durham Light Infantry	11	Ward, George Alexander,⁵²¹ Wing Officer 30 Madras Inf........	......	2 July 84
Royal Artillery	11	Richards, Edw. Willoughby, Dep. Assist. Com. Gen., 1st Class	......	5 July 84
Royal Artillery	11	Boudier, Edw. Wm., Squadron Officer 17 Bengal Cavalry	......	5 July 84
N. Staffordshire Regiment..	11	Lewis, Charles Henry, Squadron Comdr. 5 Bombay Cavalry	......	30 July 84
Devonshire Regiment.........	11	M'Conaghey, Allen, Squadron Officer 2 Bengal Lancers	......	23 Aug. 84
Royal Scots	11	Jackson, Ernest Montague,⁵²³ Wing Officer 28 Madras Inf. ...	......	23 Aug. 84
Dorsetshire Regiment	11	Watson, Edward Hurlock,⁵²⁴ Wing Officer 33 Bengal Inf........	......	23 Aug. 84
Gloucestershire Regiment...	11	Bradley, Hugh Vachell,⁵²⁵ Wing Officer 2 Bn. 2 Goorkhas ...	......	23 Aug. 84
Highland Light Infantry ...	11	Crichton, Richmond Trevor, Assist. Supdt. 1st Grade, Revenue Survey..	......	23 Aug. 84
Connaught Rangers	11	Barrow, George de Symons, Squad. Officer 4 Bengal Cavalry	......	23 Aug. 84
1 West India Regiment	11	Burton, Reginald George, Wing Officer 1 Inf. Hyd. Cont.	......	23 Aug. 84
Middlesex Regiment............	11	Hay, Henry Thomas Horatio, Wing Officer 11 Madras Inf. ...	......	23 Aug. 84
Cheshire Regiment.............	11	Cubitt, Wm. Martin, Attaché Govt. of India, Foreign Dept. ...	......	23 Aug. 84
Norfolk Regiment	11	Chatterton, John Balsir,⁵²⁶ Wing Officer 42 Bengal Infantry...	......	23 Aug. 84
Highland Light Infantry ...	11	Baynes, Douglas Dyneley, Squadron Officer 12 Bengal Cav....	......	23 Aug. 84
K. O. Scottish Borderers ...	11	Napier, Hon. Hen. Dundas, Squadron Officer 2 C. I. Horso...	......	23 Aug. 84
East Yorkshire Regiment...	11	Clowes, Henry, Dep. Assist. Com. Gen., 1st Class, Kamptee...	......	23 Aug. 84
Durham Light Infantry......	11	p.s.c. Tweddell, Francis,⁵²⁷ Wing Officer 28 Bengal Infantry ...	......	23 Aug. 84
Hampshire Regiment..........	11	Bernard, Herbert Clifford,⁵²⁸ Wing Officer 32 Madras Infantry	......	23 Aug. 84
1 West India Regiment	11	Dewing, Robert Henry,⁵²⁹ Wing Officer 16 Madras Infantry ...	......	23 Aug. 84
East Lancashire Regiment	11	Jones, Herbert John,⁵³⁰ Wing Officer 14 Bengal Infantry	......	23 Aug. 84
East Yorkshire Regiment...	11	Hill, James Pennell, Wing Officer 20 Bombay Infantry	......	23 Aug. 84
Oxford Light Infantry	11	Prendergast, Chas. Gordon,⁵³¹ Wing Officer 4 Punjab Infantry	......	23 Aug. 84
East Yorkshire Regiment...	11	Carnegy, Charles Gilbert,⁵³² Wing Officer 21 Bombay Infantry	......	23 Aug. 84
Hampshire Regiment..........	11	Gordon, Ramsay F. C., Squadron Officer 15 Bengal Lancers	......	23 Aug. 84
Suffolk Regiment.................	11	Ryder, Wilfred Ironside,⁵³³ Wing Officer 2 Bn. 1 Goorkhas ...	......	23 Aug. 84
N. Lancashire Regiment ...	11	Edwardes, Stanley Malcolm, Wing Officer 2 Bombay Infantry	......	23 Aug. 84
Sussex Regiment...............	11	Dunsterville, Lionel Chas., Wing Officer 20 Bengal Infantry	......	23 Aug. 84
Highland Light Infantry ...	11	Macnabb, Donald J. C., Assist. Commr. 3rd Grade, Burmah	......	23 Aug. 84
Devonshire Regiment..........	11	Evans, George Milford, Wing Officer 8 Bengal Infantry........	......	23 Aug. 84
East Yorkshire Regiment...	11	Young, Frank Popham, Assist. Commr. 3rd Grade, Punjab.....	......	23 Aug. 84
Suffolk Regiment.................	11	Audain, Guy Mortimer, Wing Officer 5 Inf. Hyderabad Cont.	......	23 Aug. 84
Sussex Regiment...............	11	Newbold, Ambrose Wm.⁵³⁵ Wing Officer 22 Madras Infantry	......	23 Aug. 84
Border Regiment...............	11	Goodenough, Herbert Lane, Wing Officer Bhopal Battalion...	......	23 Aug. 84
Royal Marines	11	Whyte, John Frederick, Wing Officer 4 Sikh Infantry	......	1 Sept. 84
4 Hussars.........................	11	Barry, John Fred.⁵³⁷ Dep. Assist. Com. Gen. 2nd Class	......	25 Oct. 84
Gloucester Regiment	11	Marlow, Benjamin William,⁵³⁸ Wing Officer 23 Madras Infantry	......	12 Nov. 84
Welsh Regiment	11	Hendley, Charles Edward,⁵³⁹ Wing Officer 21 Madras Infantry	......	12 Nov. 84
East Yorkshire Regiment...	11	Herbert, Claude, Wing Officer 1 Battalion 1 Goorkhas	......	12 Nov. 84
Scots Fusiliers	11	Bailey, Charles,⁵⁴⁰ Squadron Officer 16 Bengal Cavalry	......	12 Nov. 84
Cheshire Regiment.............	11	Hill, Joseph Robert, Wing Officer 20 Bombay Infantry	......	12 Nov. 84
Manchester Regiment.........	11	Fane, Vere Bonamy, Squadron Officer 1 Punjab Cavalry	......	12 Nov. 84
Warwickshire Regiment ...	11	Hilliard, Harold Nash, Dep. Assist. Com. Gen. 1st Class	......	12 Nov. 84
Irish Regiment	11	Pritchard, Henry Edward, Wing Officer 22 Madras Infantry	......	12 Nov. 84
Cheshire Regiment.............	11	Battye, Arthur Henry,⁵⁴¹ Wing Officer 2 Bn. 4 Goorkhas	......	12 Nov. 84
Middlesex Regiment............	11	Mercer, Wm. Hugh Welch,⁵⁴² Wing Officer 26 Madras Infantry	......	12 Nov. 84
South Lancashire Regiment	11	Rainsford, John Aug. G.,⁵⁴³ Wing Officer 32 Madras Infantry	......	22 Nov. 84
Royal Artillery	11	Young, Fredk. de Budé,⁵⁴⁴ Squadron Officer 6 Bengal Cavalry	......	9 Dec. 84
Royal Marines	11	Miles, Philip John,⁵⁴⁵ Wing Officer 4 Punjab Infantry	......	1 Feb. 85
Royal Marines	11	Poulter, Creighton M'Crea, Wing Officer 29 Madras Infantry	......	1 Feb. 85
Royal Marines	11	Dennys, Alex. Harry, Wing Officer 23 Bombay Infantry	......	1 Feb. 85
West Yorkshire Regiment	11	Muspratt, Francis Clifton, Wing Officer 30 Bengal Infantry...	......	7 Feb. 85
West Yorkshire Regiment	11	Younghusband, Leslie N. Squad. Officer 19 Bengal Lancers	......	7 Feb. 85
Devonshire Regiment..........	11	Fowler, Charles Astley,⁵⁴⁶ Wing Officer 22 Bengal Infantry....	......	7 Feb. 85
Connaught Rangers	11	Moore, Fred. Lewis, Squadron Officer 3 Bengal Cavalry	......	7 Feb. 85
East Yorkshire Regiment,..	11	Chitty, Walter Willis, Wing Officer 19 Bombay Infantry......	......	7 Feb. 85
Middlesex Regiment............	11	Wilkins, Ernest George Rule, Wing Officer 16 Bombay Inf. ...	......	7 Feb. 85
Middlesex Regiment............	11	Williams, Arthur Henry,⁵⁴⁷ Wing Officer 12 Madras Infantry	......	7 Feb. 85
Hampshire Regiment..........	11	Lye, Robert Cobb,⁵⁴⁸ Wing Officer 23 Bengal Infantry	......	7 Feb. 85
Dorsetshire Regiment	11	Grant, Arthur,⁵⁴⁹ Wing Officer 2 Battalion 4 Goorkhas........	......	7 Feb. 85
Leinster Regiment	11	Bingley, Alfred Horsford, Wing Officer 7 Bengal Infantry.....	......	7 Feb. 85
West Surrey Regiment	11	Ditmas, Alfred Robertson,⁵⁵⁰ Wing Officer 9 Madras Infantry	......	7 Feb. 85
Border Regiment	11	Waller, Edmund,⁵⁵¹ Wing Officer 19 Bengal Infantry	......	7 Feb. 85
Devonshire Regiment..........	11	Murray, Frank,⁵⁵² Wing Officer 20 Bengal Infantry	......	7 Feb. 85
Shropshire Light Infantry	11	Foley, Reginald Edw.⁵⁵³ Wing Officer 45 Bengal Infantry ...	......	7 Feb. 85
Northampton Regiment......	11	Drew, Arthur Blanchard H.,⁵⁵⁴ Wing Officer 29 Bengal Inf. ...	......	7 Feb. 85
East Kent Regiment	11	Pilleau, Arthur Langston, Squadron Officer 2 Bombay Lancers	......	7 Feb. 85
West Surrey Regiment	11	Edwards, Roderick Mackenzie,⁵⁵⁵ Wing Officer 18 Bengal Inf...	......	7 Feb. 85
Dorsetshire Regiment	11	Watson, Harry Davis,⁵⁵⁶ Wing Officer 1 Bn. 2 Goorkhas	......	7 Feb. 85
Hampshire Regiment..........	11	Carrick, Ethelbert William,⁵⁵⁷ Wing Officer 32 Madras Inf.....	......	7 Feb. 85
Yorkshire Light Infantry ...	11	Smith, Frederic Alex.⁵⁵⁸ Wing Officer 2 Bengal Infantry	......	7 Feb. 85
Dorsetshire Regiment	11	Harrison, Thomas Aylett, Wing Officer 25 Bombay Infantry	......	7 Feb. 85
Durham Light Infantry......	11	Berkeley, Robert Bruce,⁵⁶⁰ Wing Officer 44 Bengal Infantry...	......	7 Feb. 85
Yorkshire Light Infantry ...	11	Richardson, Herbert Lance, Wing Officer 14 Bengal Infantry	......	7 Feb. 85
Irish Regiment	11	Low, Robert Balmain,⁵⁶² Squadron Officer 9 Bengal Lancers	......	7 Feb. 85
West Yorkshire Regiment	11	Vincent, Wm. Torrens, Dep. Assist. Com. Gen. 1st Class	......	7 Feb. 85
Leicestershire Regiment ...	11	Stuart, Donald Forbes,⁵⁶⁴ Wing Officer 11 Bengal Infantry...	......	7 Feb. 85
Liverpool Regiment............	11	Waymouth, Hugh Newcome,⁵⁶⁵ Wing Officer 43 Bengal Inf.....	......	7 Feb. 85
East Surrey Regiment	11	Ormsby, Vincent Alexander, Wing Officer 1 Bn. 3 Goorkhas	......	7 Feb. 85
Leicestershire Regiment ...	11	Erskine, Charles Ellis Hay, Wing Officer 36 Bengal Infantry	......	7 Feb. 85
Manchester Regiment	11	Jephson, John Noble, Wing Officer 5 Bengal Infantry	......	7 Feb. 85

Indian Staff Corps.

Last Regiment.	Yrs. Serv.	Lieutenants.	2nd Lieut.	Lieut.
Worcester Regiment	11	Griffin, Cecil Pender Griffiths, Squad. Officer 1 Bengal Cav...	......	7 Feb. 85
Lincolnshire Regiment	11	D'C Boisragon, Guy Hudleston,⁵⁶⁸ Wing Officer 1 Bn. 5 Goorkhas	......	7 Feb. 85
Dorsetshire Regiment	11	Stainforth, Herbert Graham, Squad. Officer 4 Bengal Cav. ...	......	7 Feb. 85
West York Regiment	11	Taylor, Neville Cracroft, Squad. Officer 14 Bengal Lancers ...	......	7 Feb. 85
East Surrey Regiment	11	Coles, Colin Hennessey Read, Wing Officer 37 Bengal Inf. ...	......	7 Feb. 85
South Lancashire Regiment	11	Nelson, Frederic Justin,⁵⁶⁹ Squad. Officer 4 Lancers Hyd. Cont.	......	28 Feb. 85
Yorkshire Regiment	11	Paxton, Archibald F. P.,⁵⁷⁰ Wing Officer 17 Madras Infantry	......	28 Feb. 85
Yorkshire Light Infantry	11	Dobbie, Chas. Fras., Wing Officer 4 Bengal Infantry	......	28 Feb. 85
Welsh Regiment	11	Moore, Arthur G. W., Squadron Officer 2 Madras Lancers	......	28 Feb. 85
West Yorkshire Regiment	10	Robin, Nicholas Edmund,⁵⁷¹ Wing Officer 7 Bengal Infantry	......	6 May 85
Welsh Fusiliers	10	Edwards, Charles Augustus,⁵⁷² Wing Officer 35 Bengal Inf. ...	......	6 May 85
Liverpool Regiment	10	Woodcock, Wm. C. M.,⁵⁷³ Wing Officer 29 Bengal Infantry	......	6 May 85
East Surrey Regiment	10	Eustace, Alexander Henry,⁵⁷⁴ Wing Officer 2 Sikh Infantry	......	6 May 85
Gloucestershire Regiment	10	Walters, Herbert Flamstead, Wing Officer 24 Bengal Inf. ...	......	6 May 85
Border Regiment	10	Ryatt, Francis Willie,⁵⁷⁵ Wing Officer 2 Battalion 5 Goorkhas	......	6 May 85
Middlesex Regiment	10	Batten, Frederick Graeme, Wing Officer 1 Madras Infantry ...	......	6 May 85
Connaught Rangers	10	Smith, Clarence T. W., Wing Officer 30 Bengal Infantry	......	6 May 85
Sussex Regiment	10	Webber, Fras. Peirson,⁵⁷⁶ Wing Officer 3 Bengal Infantry	......	6 May 85
East Surrey Regiment	10	Swiney, Ernest R. R.,⁵⁷⁷ Wing Officer 9 Bengal Infantry	......	6 May 85
Oxford Light Infantry	10	Budd, Norman A. H.,⁵⁷⁸ Wing Officer 12 Bombay Infantry ...	......	9 May 85
Derbyshire Regiment	10	Burlton, Philip S. M., Assist. Commr. 3rd Grade, Lahore	......	9 May 85
East Lancashire Regiment	10	Campbell, Alan James,⁵⁷⁹ Wing Officer 15 Madras Infantry	......	9 May 85
Bengal Staff Corps	10	Rawlinson, Chas. Brooke, Assist. Comr., Peshawur, Punjab	......	9 May 85
Cheshire Regiment	10	Hughes, Francis T. O., Wing Officer Erinpoora, Irreg. Force	......	9 May 85
12 Lancers	10	Birdwood, Wm. Riddell,⁵⁸⁰ Squadron Officer 11 Bengal Lanc.	......	9 May 85
Dublin Fusiliers	10	Kendall, John,⁵⁸¹ Wing Officer 7 Madras Infantry	......	9 May 85
West India Regiment	10	Lowis, Harry Elliot, Wing Officer 10 Bombay Infantry	......	9 May 85
Sussex Regiment	10	Tottenham, Robert Loftus, Wing Officer 25 Bengal Infantry	......	9 May 85
Yorkshire Light Infantry	10	Norie, Charles Edw. de M., Wing Officer 1 Bn. 2 Goorkhas	......	9 May 85
Dorsetshire Regiment	10	Gilbert, Gerald Edwin Lloyd,⁵⁸² Wing Officer 34 Bengal Inf...	......	9 May 85
Irish Fusiliers	10	Swanston, Chas. Oliver, Squad. Officer 18 Bengal Lancers	......	9 May 85
Bedfordshire Regiment	10	Wright, Ernest Granville,⁵⁸³ Wing Officer 10 Bengal Infantry	......	9 May 85
Worcestershire Regiment	10	Seddon, Thomas Young, Wing Officer 34 Bengal Infantry	......	9 May 85
Durham Light Infantry	10	Lockhart-Mure, Wm. Craven,⁵⁸⁴ Squad. Comdr. 4 Bombay Cav.	......	9 May 85
Inniskilling Fusiliers	10	Beresford, Jas. Hugh Brownlow,⁵⁸⁵ Wing Officer 3 Sikh Inf.	......	23 May 85
Northampton Regiment	10	Lowther, Henry, Wing Officer 1 Inf. Hyderabad Contingent	......	23 May 85
Dublin Fusiliers	10	Cowie, Wm. Alex. Lomer, Wing Officer 15 Bengal Infantry...	......	23 May 85
East York Regiment	10	Morris, Gordon Suth., Squadron Officer 2 Lancers Hyd. Cont.	......	23 May 85
Leinster Regiment	10	Roberts, Montgomery Browne, Wing Officer 39 Bengal Inf.	......	23 May 85
York and Lancaster Regt.	10	Allenby, Aug. Heathcote,⁵⁸⁶ Wing Officer 13 Madras Infantry	......	23 May 85
South Lancashire Regiment	10	Young, Thomas Simpson,⁵⁸⁷ Wing Officer 22 Madras Infantry	......	23 May 85
Welsh Regiment	10	Colquhoun, Herbert W. C., Wing Officer 24 Madras Infantry	......	23 May 85
York Light Infantry	10	Roome, Henry Napier, Squadron Officer 7 Bombay Lancers	......	23 May 85
Hampshire Regiment	10	Burlton, W. Erle Ferdinand,⁵⁸⁸ Dep. Assist. Com. Gen. 1st Class	......	23 May 85
Suffolk Regiment	10	Walker, William George, Wing Officer 1 Bn. 4 Goorkhas	......	29 Aug. 85
West Yorkshire Regiment	10	Drummond, Edm. Johnston,⁵⁸⁹ Wing Officer 2 Bn. 2 Goorkhas	......	29 Aug. 85
Leicestershire Regiment	10	Harvey, Ambrose Blacklock,⁵⁹⁰ Wing Officer 16 Bengal Inf. ...	......	29 Aug. 85
East Lancashire Regiment	10	Fox-Strangways, Harold S., Assist. Commr. 3rd Grade, Punjab	......	29 Aug. 85
2 West India Regiment	10	Trydell, Botét,⁵⁹¹ Wing Officer 10 Madras Infantry	......	29 Aug. 85
East Yorkshire Regiment	10	Frazer, Geo. Stanley, Wing Officer 6 Inf. Hyderabad Cont. ...	......	29 Aug. 85
Wiltshire Regiment	10	Davies, Fred. George Hugh, Squadron Officer Corps of Guides	......	29 Aug. 85
Highland Light Infantry	10	Bannerman, Arthur D'A. G., Squad. Officer 1 C.I. Horse	......	29 Aug. 85
Derbyshire Regiment	10	Spence, Philip T. A., Assist. Gov. Gen.'s Agent, Beloochistan	......	29 Aug. 85
Worcester Regiment	10	Beville, Chas. Hamilton,⁵⁹³ Dep. Assist. Com. Gen. 1st Class	......	29 Aug. 85
Manchester Regiment	10	Dennys, Herbert Travers, Dist. Supt. of Police, 5th Gr. Punjab	......	29 Aug. 85
King's Royal Rifles	10	Parker, Harry P. E., Wing Officer 29 Bombay Infantry	......	29 Aug. 85
South Wales Borderers	10	Reid, Chas. Lestock Onslow,⁵⁹⁴ Assist. Commissioner, Burma	......	29 Aug. 85
Border Regiment	10	Rea, Frederic Wm., Wing Officer 4 Inf. Hyderabad Cont. ...	......	29 Aug. 85
Connaught Rangers	10	Fagan, Hugh Rollo,⁵⁹⁵ Wing Officer 1 Punjab Infantry	......	29 Aug. 85
Worcester Regiment	10	Widdicombe, Fred. Serington, Wing Officer 16 Bombay Inf...	......	29 Aug. 85
West Surrey Regiment	10	Dyer, Reginald E. H.,⁵⁹⁶ Wing Officer 29 Bengal Infantry	......	29 Aug. 85
South Wales Borderers	10	Cockerill, Robert Charles,⁵⁹⁷ Wing Officer 16 Madras Infantry	......	29 Aug. 85
Cheshire Regiment	10	Davies, Charles Hugh,⁵⁹⁸ Wing Officer 3 Sikh Infantry	......	29 Aug. 85
Border Regiment	10	Wintle, FitzHardinge, Wing Officer 30 Bengal Infantry	......	29 Aug. 85
Lancaster Regiment	10	Brownlow, Howe Montgomery, Wing Officer 39 Bengal Inf...	......	29 Aug. 85
South Wales Borderers	10	King, Henry,⁶⁰⁰ Wing Officer 33 Bengal Infantry	......	29 Aug. 85
Wiltshire Regiment	10	Thompson, Cyril Powney, Assist. Commr., 3rd Grade, Punjab	......	29 Aug. 85
East Yorkshire Regiment	10	Tighe, Stanislaus Michael, Wing Officer 20 Bengal Infantry	......	29 Aug. 85
Bedfordshire Regiment	10	Walton, Herbert,⁶⁰¹ Wing Officer 3 Bengal Infantry	......	29 Aug. 85
Yorkshire Light Infantry	10	Barton, Arthur Elliott,⁶⁰² Assist. Commr. 3rd Grade, Punjab	......	29 Aug. 85
Leicestershire Regiment	10	Obbard, Owen James,⁶⁰³ Assist. Commr., 4th Grade, Burmah	......	29 Aug. 85
Devonshire Regiment	10	Baldock, Charles Blair, Wing Officer Mhairwara Battalion ...	......	29 Aug. 85
Northumberland Fusiliers	10	Cole, Henry Walter George,⁶⁰⁴ Assist. Commr. 3rd Grade, Assam	......	29 Aug. 85
Manchester Regiment	10	Cooper, Harry Ashley,⁶⁰⁵ Wing Officer 1 Sikh Infantry	......	29 Aug. 85
Duke of Cornwall's Lt. Inf.	10	Walker, Launcelot Henry,⁶⁰⁶ Wing Officer 15 Madras Infantry	......	29 Aug. 85
Bedfordshire Regiment	10	Williams, Hugh Edward,⁶⁰⁷ Wing Officer 25 Madras Infantry	......	29 Aug. 85
K. O. Scottish Borderers	10	Lane, Horace Powys, Wing Officer 3 Inf. Hyderabad Cont. ...	......	29 Aug. 85
Manchester Regiment	10	Cadell, Alexander,⁶⁰⁸ Wing Officer 38 Bengal Infantry	......	29 Aug. 85
Worcester Regiment	10	Hunter, Malcolm Russell, Wing Officer 8 Bombay Infantry ...	......	29 Aug. 85
Norfolk Regiment	10	Ray, MacCarthy Reagh Emmet, Wing Officer 7 Bengal Inf...	......	29 Aug. 85
Irish Regiment	10	Geoghegan, Stannus, Wing Officer 31 Madras Infantry	......	29 Aug. 85
N. Lancashire Regiment	10	Rennick, Frank,⁶⁰⁹ Wing Officer 40 Bengal Infantry	......	29 Aug. 85
East Kent Regiment	10	Kaye, William John Pettitt, Wing Officer 30 Bengal Infantry	......	29 Aug. 85
Northumberland Fusiliers	10	Howell, Auberon Arthur, Assist. Commr. 2nd Grade, Assam...	......	29 Aug. 85
Irish Fusiliers	10	Gough, Chas. Hugh Henry, Squad. Officer 12 Bengal Cav. ...	......	29 Aug. 85
Dorsetshire Regiment	10	Hildebrand, Wm. Hatton,⁶¹⁰ Wing Officer 27 Bengal Infantry	......	29 Aug. 85
Yorkshire Light Infantry	10	Elsmie, George E. D.,⁶¹¹ Squadron Officer 5 Punjab Cavalry...	......	29 Aug. 85
West Kent Regiment	10	Nepean, Herbert E. C. B.,⁶¹² Wing Officer 5 Madras Infantry	......	29 Aug. 85
Inniskilling Fusiliers	10	Ward, Trimnell Martin, Wing Officer 4 Inf. Hyd. Cont.	......	29 Aug. 85
N. Staffordshire Regiment	10	Harris, Edw. Wm., Wing Officer 3 Madras Infantry	......	29 Aug. 85
Royal Marines	10	Luck, Churchill Arthur, Squadron Commander 2 Punjab Cav.	......	1 Sept. 85
Royal Marines	10	Le Mesurier, Eugène, Squadron Officer 6 Bombay Cavalry ...	......	1 Sept. 85
West India Regiment	10	Venour, Walter Edwin,⁶¹⁴ Wing Officer 5 Punjab Infantry	......	2 Sept. 85
Dorsetshire Regiment	10	Parker, Neville Thornton, Wing Officer 6 Bengal Infantry ...	......	25 Nov. 85

Indian Staff Corps. 433

Last Regiment.	Yrs. Serv.	LIEUTENANTS.	2nd-LIEUT.	LIEUT.
N. Lancashire Regiment ...	10	Morton, Edward Ross, Wing Officer 31 Bengal Infantry	......	25 Nov. 85
Hampshire Regiment	10	Buist, David Simson,⁶¹⁸ Squad. Officer 2 Lancers Hyd. Cont.	......	25 Nov. 85
Leicestershire Regiment ...	10	Sullivan, Edward Langford, Wing Officer 36 Bengal Infantry	......	25 Nov. 85
Hampshire Regiment	10	Bower, Denis Mahoney, Wing Officer 2 Bengal Infantry	......	25 Nov. 85
Dorsetshire Regiment	10	Bell, Ralph Maitland,⁶¹⁵ Wing Officer 24 Madras Infantry	......	25 Nov. 85
Devonshire Regiment	10	Dunlop, Henry Hinton, Squad.Officer 2 Lanc. HyderabadCont.	......	25 Nov. 85
Hampshire Regiment	10	Shewell, Percy Garratt,⁶¹⁷ Assist. Mil. Accountant, 1st Class ...	......	25 Nov. 85
Lincolnshire Regiment ...	10	Vesey, Herbert Charles,⁶¹⁸ Wing Officer 2 Sikh Infantry	......	25 Nov. 85
Yorkshire Light Infantry ...	10	Peterson, Frederick Hopewell,⁶¹⁹ Wing Officer 32 Bengal Inf.	......	25 Nov. 85
Lincolnshire Regiment	10	Herbert, Douglas, Assistant Commr. Hailakandi, Assam......	......	25 Nov. 85
Northamptonshire Regt. ...	10	Vickers, Hilton,⁶²¹ Wing Officer 23 Madras Infantry	......	25 Nov. 85
Inniskilling Fusiliers	10	Browne, Alex. J. W., Squadron Officer 3 Bombay Cavalry ...	......	16 Dec. 85
Oxford Light Infantry	10	Johnston, Herbert William, Wing Officer 7 Madras Infantry	......	30 Jan. 94
Warwick Regiment	10	Andrew, David Clapham Adrian, Wing Officer 21 Bengal Inf.	......	30 Jan. 86
N. Staffordshire Regiment	10	Beville, Fras. Granville, Assist. Political Agent, Bussorah ...	......	30 Jan. 86
Middlesex Regiment	10	Elliot, Chas. Riversdale, Squad. Officer 3 Lancers Hyd. Cont.	......	30 Jan. 85
Derbyshire Regiment	10	James, William Bernard, Squad. Officer 2 Bengal Lancers ...	......	30 Jan. 86
N. Lancashire Regiment	10	Jacob, Arthur Le Grand,⁶²² Wing Officer 30 Bombay Infantry	......	30 Jan. 86
3 Dragoon Guards	10	Edwards, Henry Charles, Squadron Officer 4 Bengal Cavalry	......	30 Jan. 86
South Wales Borderers ...	10	Anwyl-Passingham, Robt. T.,⁶²³ Wing Officer 12 Madras Inf.	......	30 Jan. 86
N. Staffordshire Regiment	10	Sartorius, George C. F.,⁶²⁴ Wing Officer 19 Bombay Infantry	......	30 Jan. 86
Border Regiment	10	Leeds, Lionel Nelson,⁶²⁵ Squadron Officer 5 Punjab Cavalry	......	30 Jan. 86
Oxford Light Infantry	10	Ducat, Hugh Charles Claude,⁶²⁶ Wing Officer 2 Bn. 4 Goorkhas	......	30 Jan. 86
Devonshire Regiment	10	Wall, Edward Watkin, Squadron Officer 17 Bengal Cavalry	......	30 Jan. 86
Derbyshire Regiment	10	Campbell, Leslie W. Y., Wing Officer 8 Madras Infantry	......	30 Jan. 86
Durham Light Infantry	10	Purvis, Herbert J. E., Squadron Officer 3 Bombay Lancers...	......	30 Jan. 86
Leicestershire Regiment ...	10	Domenichetti, Francis Henry,⁶¹⁷ Wing Officer 28 Madras Inf.	......	30 Jan. 86
Manchester Regiment	10	Tytler, Harry Christopher,⁶²⁸ Wing Officer 11 Bengal Infantry	......	30 Jan. 86
20 Hussars	10	Jollie, Francis,⁶²⁹ Squadron Officer 3 Madras Lancers	......	30 Jan. 86
Middlesex Regiment	10	Mullaly, Alex., Dep. Assist. Com. Gen. 2nd Class, Umballa...	......	30 Jan. 86
Bedfordshire Regiment	10	Humfrey, Benj. John H., Adj. Madras Governor's Body Guard	......	30 Jan. 86
South Wales Borderers ...	10	Parker, James,⁶³⁰ Wing Officer 26 Bombay Infantry	......	30 Jan. 36
Worcestershire Regiment...	10	Campbell, Geo. Patrick, Wing Officer 25 Bengal Infantry ...	......	30 Jan. 86
North Lancashire Regt.....	10	Baldwin, Guy Melfort,⁶³¹ Squadron Officer Corps of Guides ...	......	30 Jan. 86
Lincolnshire Regiment	10	Walling, Arthur Tremearne,⁶³² Wing Officer 5 Bengal Infantry	......	30 Jan. 86
Munster Fusiliers	10	Carey, Octavius William,⁶³³ Wing Officer 28 Bengal Infantry	......	30 Jan. 86
Warwickshire Regiment ...	10	Drever, James William,⁶³⁴ Wing Officer 11 Madras Infantry...	......	30 Jan. 86
Yorkshire Light Infantry ...	10	Halliday, Hugh Maclean, Assist. Commr., 3rd Grade, Assam	......	30 Jan. 86
18 Hussars	10	Arnold, Arthur Seymour, Squadron Officer 1 Madras Lancers	......	30 Jan. 86
West Riding Regiment	10	Strachey, Bertram, Wing Officer 2 Bn. 2 Goorkhas	......	30 Jan. 86
West Riding Regiment	10	Marson, Henry W. A., Wing Officer 8 Bengal Infantry	......	30 Jan. 86
Leinster Regiment	10	Widdicombe, Geo. Templer,⁶³⁶ Wing Officer 9 Bengal Inf.	......	30 Jan. 86
Irish Rifles	10	Lowry, James Herbert,⁶³⁷ Wing Officer 8 Madras Infantry ...	......	30 Jan. 86
N. Lancashire Regiment ...	10	Carnegy, Harry George, Assist. Polit. Supdt. Kolapore	......	30 Jan. 86
West Yorkshire Regiment...	10	Campbell, Aylmer M'Iver, Squad. Officer 3 Punjab Cavalry	......	30 Jan. 86
Leinster Regiment	10	Kingston, Fred. Anderson, Wing Officer 2 Bn. 3 Goorkhas	......	30 Jan. 86
S. Staffordshire Regiment...	10	Errington, Walter Henry, Wing Officer 1 Bombay Infantry...	......	30 Jan. 86
Duke of Cornwall's Lt. Inf.	10	Southey, Wm. Melvill, Wing Officer 27 Bombay Infantry......	......	30 Jan. 86
Bedfordshire Regiment	10	Stevens, Stephen Repton,⁶³⁸ Wing Officer 33 Madras Infantry	......	30 Jan. 86
Essex Regiment	10	Wallace-Dunlop, Arthur, Wing Officer 23 Bengal Infantry ...	......	30 Jan. 86
Norfolk Regiment	10	Bateman-Champain, ArthurPat., Wing Officer 2 Bn.3 Goorkhas	......	30 Jan. 86
Lancashire Fusiliers	10	Wodehouse, Frederic Wm.,⁶³⁹ Adjutant Kolapore Inf. Corps	......	30 Jan. 86
Cheshire Regiment	10	Chesney, Napier Elles,⁶⁴⁰ Wing Officer 2 Bn. 5 Goorkhas	......	30 Jan. 86
Royal Marines	10	Kappey, Max Albert Burns, Wing Officer 26 Madras Inf.....	......	1 Feb. 86
Royal Marines	10	Magrath, Hen. Aug. F., Wing Officer 1 Sikh Infantry	......	1 Feb. 86
Royal Marines	10	Berger, Ernest L. C., Wing Officer 30 Bombay Infantry	......	1 Feb. 86
Royal Marines	10	Hurly, Maurice Randall, Wing Officer 33 Madras Infantry...	......	1 Feb. 86
Royal Scots	10	Taylor, ArthurWm. Neufville,⁶⁴¹ Wing Officer10 Madras Inf.	......	13 Feb. 86
Royal Artillery	10	Cook, Charles Chesney, Squadron Officer 2 Punjab Cavalry...	......	13 Feb. 86
Royal Artillery	10	Home, James Murray, Wing Officer 2 Bn. 2 Goorkhas	......	13 Feb. 86
7 Dragoon Guards	10	MacGeorge, Henry King, Squad. Officer 6 Bombay Cavalry	......	3 Mar. 86
S. Lancashire Regiment.....	9	Armstrong, Arthur Knox, Squad. Officer 1 Lanc. Hyd. Cont.	......	28 Apr. 86
Warwickshire Regiment....	9	Leveson-Gower, Chas. C., Squad. Officer 1 Bombay Lancers	......	28 Apr. 86
Warwickshire Regiment....	9	Thacker, Henry Joseph, Wing Officer 8 Bengal Infantry ...	......	28 Apr. 86
South Wales Borderers	9	Rooke, Benjamin P. S.,⁶⁴² Squad Officer 5 Bombay Cavalry...	......	28 Apr. 86
Cheshire Regiment	9	Palin, Philip Charles,⁶⁴³ Wing Officer 14 Bengal Infantry......	......	28 Apr. 86
Gloucestershire Regiment...	9	Hawkins, George Arthur, Wing Officer 4 Bengal Infantry ...	......	19 May 86
Royal Artillery	9	Burrard, Charles, Wing Officer 21 Bombay Infantry	......	24 July 86
Royal Artillery	9	Smith, Owen Annesley, Wing Officer 27 Bengal Infantry	......	24 July 86
Royal Artillery	9	Robinson, George Tracey, Wing Officer 33 Bengal Infantry..	......	24 July 86
Royal Artillery	9	Burlton, Alfred Ralph, Dep. Assist. Com. Gen. 2nd Class ...	......	24 July 86
Lancaster Regiment	9	Rowlandson, Alf. Turner,⁶⁴⁴ Wing Officer 26 Bombay Infantry	......	25 Aug. 86
E. Lancashire Regiment	9	Lucas, Frederic George,⁶⁴⁵ Wing Officer 2 Bn. 5 Goorkhas ...	......	25 Aug. 86
East Yorkshire Regiment...	9	Begbie, Arundel Sinclair, Wing Officer 16 Bengal Infantry...	......	25 Aug. 86
Wiltshire Regiment	9	Badcock, Francis F.,⁶⁴⁶ DSO, Wing Officer 2 Bn. 5 Goorkhas	......	25 Aug. 86
Derbyshire Regiment	9	Lewarne, Nicholas Albert,⁶⁴⁷ Wing Officer 15 Bengal Inf. ...	......	25 Aug. 86
Leinster Regiment	9	Senior, Henry William R., Wing Officer 44 Bengal Infantry...	......	25 Aug. 86
Suffolk Regiment	9	Grant, Ian Hope, Wing Officer 29 Bengal Infantry	......	25 Aug. 86
Oxford Light Infantry	9	Harman, Richard,⁶⁴⁸ DSO, Wing Officer 4 Sikh Infantry ...	......	25 Aug. 86
Wiltshire Regiment	9	Hall, Ernest Stanley, Wing Officer 30 Bengal Infantry	......	25 Aug. 86
Middlesex Regiment	9	Turner, Fred.Wm. Chas., Squad. Officer 1 Lancers Hyd. Cont.	......	25 Aug. 86
East Surrey Regiment	9	Wood, Ernest J. Macfarlane, Wing Officer 6 Inf. Hyd. Cont.	......	25 Aug. 86
7 Dragoon Guards	9	Daunt, Walter Dickens, Squad. Officer 1 Central India Horse.	......	25 Aug. 86
Gloucestershire Regiment...	9	Walker, Henry George, Wing Officer 12 Bombay Infantry ...	......	25 Aug. 86
Lincolnshire Regiment	9	Brandreth, Edgar, Squadron Officer 13 Bengal Lancers	......	25 Aug. 86
Wiltshire Regiment	9	Symonds, Chas. W. H., Assist. Supdt. 2nd Gr. Survey of India	......	25 Aug. 86
Berkshire Regiment	9	Swan, Charles Tarrant,⁶⁵⁰ Wing Officer 4 Madras Infantry...	......	25 Aug. 86
Liverpool Regiment	9	Gordon, M'Leod James, Squadron Officer 4 Bombay Cav......	......	25 Aug. 86
Manchester Regiment	9	Barwell, Arthur Ross, Wing Officer 9 Bengal Infantry	......	25 Aug. 86
Yorkshire Light Infantry ...	9	Waller, Fred. C. Livingston, Wing Officer Deolee Irreg. Force	......	25 Aug. 86
Warwickshire Regiment ...	9	Tomkins, William Edward,⁶⁵¹ Wing Officer 38 Bengal Inf. ...	......	25 Aug. 8
Yorkshire Light Infantry ...	9	Vincent, Frank Lloyd, Squadron Officer 7 Bombay Lancers	......	25 Aug. 86
Border Regiment	9	Moore, Harry Alexander,⁶⁵² Wing Officer 45 Bengal Infantry	......	25 Aug. 86
Border Regiment	9	Hallowes, Francis William, Dep. Assist. Com. Gen. 2nd Class	......	25 Aug. 86

Indian Staff Corps

Last Regiment.	Yrs. Serv.	Lieutenants.	2nd Lieut.	Lieut.
Gloucestershire Regiment	9	Peart, Denis George, Wing Officer 2 Bombay Infantry		25 Aug. 86
Worcestershire Regiment	9	Hodgson, Walter George, Wing Officer 17 Madras Infantry		25 Aug. 86
Gloucestershire Regiment	9	Lock, Fred. R. E., Wing Officer 2 Bombay Infantry		25 Aug. 86
South Wales Borderers	9	Manning, William Henry,653 Wing Officer 1 Sikh Infantry		25 Aug. 86
Middlesex Regiment	9	Schneider, Reginald P. C., Wing Officer 12 Bombay Infantry		25 Aug. 86
West Kent Regiment	9	Brown, Walter Henry, Wing Officer 25 Madras Infantry		25 Aug. 86
Somerset Light Infantry	9	Lewis, Robert Montrésor, Assist. Commr. Rajanpore, Punjab		25 Aug. 86
K. O. Scottish Borderers	9	Pritchard, Harry Torriano, Wing Officer 3 Bengal Infantry		25 Aug. 86
Bedfordshire Regiment	9	Wood, Cyril Edward,654 Wing Officer 17 Bengal Infantry		25 Aug. 86
Worcestershire Regiment	9	Richards, James Saurin, Wing Officer 3 Inf. Hyd. Cont.		25 Aug. 86
Cheshire Regiment	9	Walton, Lewin Barlow, Wing Officer 26 Bengal Infantry		25 Aug. 86
Wiltshire Regiment	9	Watson, Alfred Carnac, Wing Officer 11 Bengal Infantry		25 Aug. 86
Dublin Fusiliers	9	Sexton, John J. O'B., Wing Officer 10 Bombay Infantry		25 Aug. 86
Connaught Rangers	9	Hogg, Theodore C.M.T.,656 Squadron Officer 8 Bengal Cavalry		25 Aug. 86
West India Regiment	9	Argles, Owen Charles,657 Wing Officer 5 Bengal Infantry		25 Aug. 86
Irish Regiment	9	Macnamara, Wilfred C. F. R., Wing Officer 13 Bombay Inf.		25 Aug. 86
Manchester Regiment	9	Gurdon, Bertrand E. M., Durbar Assist. British Agent, Gilgit		25 Aug. 86
Leinster Regiment	9	Merewether, John Walter Beresford, Wing Officer 43 Ben. Inf.		25 Aug. 86
South Lancashire Regiment	9	Grey, Wm. George, Wing Officer 3 Madras Infantry		25 Aug. 86
Hampshire Regiment	9	Chalmers, Robert C. H.,658 Wing Officer 5 Inf. Hyd. Cont.		25 Aug. 86
Lincolnshire Regiment	9	Bell, Lindesay Maxwell, Wing Officer 16 Bengal Infantry		25 Aug. 86
Royal Marines	9	Windham, Chas. Joseph, Wing Officer 5 Bombay Infantry		1 Sept. 86
Devonshire Regiment	9	Andrew, Albert, Squad. Officer 1 Lancers Hyderabad Cont.		9 Sept. 86
7 Hussars	9	Peacock, Henry Barnes, Squadron Officer 3 Bengal Cavalry		13 Oct. 86
Scots Fusiliers	9	Malcolm, William Leith, Wing Officer 31 Bengal Infantry		27 Oct. 86
Northumberland Fusiliers	9	Lugard, Edward Jas.,660 DSO, Wing Officer 42 Bengal Inf.		10 Nov. 86
Irish Fusiliers	9	Ricketts, Henry Carew,661 Squad. Officer 15 Bengal Lancers		10 Nov. 86
Highland Light Infantry	9	Forbes, Lindsay Anstruther, Wing Officer 39 Bengal Inf.		10 Nov. 86
N. Staffordshire Regiment	9	Tanner, Charles O. O., Wing Officer 29 Bombay Infantry		10 Nov. 86
Sussex Regiment	9	Fleming, Henry Lawrence, Wing Officer 36 Bengal Infantry		10 Nov. 86
Middlesex Regiment	9	Forster, Philip Byron Bohun,662 Wing Officer 2 Sikh Infantry		10 Nov. 86
Yorkshire Light Infantry	9	Williams, Cecil Howard,663 Wing Officer 31 Madras Infantry		10 Nov. 86
Yorkshire Light Infantry	9	Sangster, Alfred Bruce,664 Assist. Polit. Resident, Aden		10 Nov. 86
Highland Light Infantry	9	Stewart, Fras. Thornton, Wing Officer 45 Bengal Infantry		10 Nov. 86
N. Lancashire Regiment	9	Jamieson, Aubrey James, Wing Officer 6 Bengal Infantry		10 Nov. 86
East Yorkshire Regiment	9	Benn, Harry Gordon, Squadron Officer 3 Bombay Cavalry		10 Nov. 86
Lincolnshire Regiment	9	MacAndrew, Hy. J. Milnes, Squad. Officer 5 Bengal Cavalry		10 Nov. 86
Bedfordshire Regiment	9	Orchard, John Waller,665 Wing Officer 15 Madras Infantry		10 Nov. 86
Dublin Fusiliers	9	Bolton, Arthur Hely, Wing Officer 13 Bombay Infantry		10 Nov. 86
East Yorkshire Regiment	9	Jacob, Wm. Swinton, Wing Officer 16 Bombay Infantry		8 Dec. 86
Border Regiment	9	Laing, Fred. Charles, Wing Officer 12 Bengal Infantry		8 Dec. 86
Border Regiment	9	Napier, Hon. Arthur Fullarton, Squad. Officer 12 Bengal Cav.		8 Dec. 86
West Riding Regiment	9	Hickley, Alfred Charles,666 Wing Officer 1 Bn. 3 Goorkhas		8 Dec. 86
Inniskilling Fusiliers	9	Denne, Richard Wm. Arthur, Wing Officer 19 Madras Infantry		8 Dec. 86
Somerset Light Infantry	9	Kirkwood, Thomas Moore, Wing Officer 4 Inf. Hyd. Cont.		8 Dec. 86
East Yorkshire Regiment	9	Stuart, Alex. Percy D. C., Wing Officer 25 Bombay Infantry		8 Dec. 86
Essex Regiment	9	Dunolly, Kenneth J. G., Wing Officer 5 Madras Infantry		8 Dec. 86
Shropshire Light Infantry	9	Howe, Rupert Bohun Blunt, Wing Officer 6 Madras Infantry		8 Dec. 86
1 Dragoon Guards	9	Smithett, Arthur C. H.,667 Squad. Officer 15 Bengal Lancers		29 Dec. 86
Manchester Regiment	9	Southey, Henry Herbert, Squadron Officer 7 Bombay Lancers	5 Feb. 87	28 Nov. 87
Suffolk Regiment	9	Patterson, Harry M'Neale, Squad. Officer 5 Bengal Cavalry	5 Feb. 87	10 Dec. 87
Hampshire Regiment	9	Nurse, Henry Harvey, Wing Officer 22 Bombay Infantry	5 Feb. 87	30 Dec. 87
Hampshire Regiment	9	Scott, Walter Cleland, Wing Officer 38 Bengal Infantry	5 Feb. 87	2 Jan. 88
Connaught Rangers	9	Eardley-Howard, Wm. Sebastian,670 Wing Officer 29 Ben. Inf.	16 Mar. 87	21 Jan. 88
Worcestershire Regiment	9	Creagh, Arthur H. D., Wing Officer 21 Bombay Infantry	5 Feb. 87	22 Jan. 88
East Surrey Regiment	9	Powell, Nathaniel J. H.,671 Wing Officer 23 Bengal Infantry	30 Mar. 87	24 Jan. 88
S. Staffordshire Regiment	9	Carter, John R. B. G., Wing Officer 8 Bombay Infantry	5 Feb. 87	29 Jan. 88
S. Lancashire Regiment	9	Ross, John William, Offg. Wing Officer 23 Madras Infantry	5 Feb. 87	29 Jan. 88
Connaught Rangers	8	Maxwell, Hamilton George, Squad. Officer 16 Bengal Cavalry	7 May 87	29 Jan. 88
Worcestershire Regiment	9	Chitty, Ernest R. I., Wing Officer 5 Bombay Infantry	5 Feb. 87	1 Feb. 88
Worcestershire Regiment	9	Ducat, Claude Tulloch, Squadron Officer 1 Bombay Lancers	16 Mar. 87	2 Feb. 88
West Yorkshire Regiment	8	Des Vœux, Herbert, Assist. Commr. 4th Grade, Burmah	28 Sept. 87	5 Feb. 88
Oxford Light Infantry	9	Taylor, Francis Heale,673 Wing Officer 3 Sikh Infantry	5 Feb. 87	11 Feb. 88
Oxford Light Infantry	9	Hill, John,674 Wing Officer 15 Bengal Infantry	5 Feb. 87	11 Feb. 88
Welsh Regiment	9	Priestley, Charles E. N., Squadron Officer 2 Madras Lancers	5 Feb. 87	21 Feb. 88
Welsh Regiment	9	Bruce, Frederick, Wing Officer 1 Madras Infantry	5 Feb. 87	21 Feb. 88
Lincolnshire Regiment	8	Jacob, Harold Fenton, Wing Officer 14 Bombay Infantry	14 Sept. 87	22 Feb. 88
Dorsetshire Regiment	8	Mockler, Guy H. G., Wing Officer 30 Madras Infantry	14 Sept. 87	22 Feb. 88
Manchester Regiment	8	Brown, Henry George, Wing Officer 3 Bombay Infantry	14 Sept. 87	22 Feb. 88
Warwickshire Regiment	8	Fraser, Nicol Grahame,675 Squadron Officer 4 Bombay Cavalry	4 May 87	23 Feb. 88
Gloucestershire Regiment	8	Wintour, Evelyn, Squadron Officer 3 Madras Lancers	14 Sept. 87	23 Feb. 88
N. Lancashire Regiment	8	Prendergast, Wm. Henry,676 Wing Officer 20 Bengal Infantry	4 May 87	24 Feb. 88
Dorsetshire Regiment	8	Savi, Robert J. T.,677 Wing Officer 30 Madras Infantry	14 Sept. 87	25 Feb. 88
Warwickshire Regiment	8	Warner, Wm. Ward, Squadron Officer 3 Lancers Hyd. Cont.	4 May 87	26 Feb. 88
Yorkshire Regiment	9	Sillery, John Jocelyn Doyne, Wing Officer 25 Bombay Inf.	5 Feb. 87	27 Feb. 88
Yorkshire Regiment	8	Twigg, Edward Francis, Wing Officer 24 Bombay Infantry	5 Feb. 87	28 Feb. 88
Scots Fusiliers	9	Cunningham, Percy Henry,678 Wing Officer 1 Bombay Inf.	13 Apr. 87	29 Feb. 88
Bedfordshire Regiment	8	Oakes, George Richard, Wing Officer 28 Madras Infantry	4 May 87	29 Feb. 88
West India Regiment	8	Robinson, Godfrey Walker,679 Wing Officer 27 Bengal Infantry	14 Sept. 87	29 Feb. 88
Border Regiment	8	Clarke, Arthur C. S., Squadron Officer 18 Bengal Lancers	20 July 87	2 Mar. 88
Duke of Cornwall's Lt. Inf.	8	Fraser, Walter Simon, Offg. Squad. Officer 19 Bengal Lancers	23 Mar. 87	3 Mar. 88
K. O. Scottish Borderers	8	Stanton, Hubert Lionel,681 Wing Officer 3 Bengal Infantry	5 Feb. 87	9 Mar. 88
Leicestershire Regiment	8	Adye, Daniel Richard, Wing Officer 6 Inf. Hyd. Cont.	14 Sept. 87	10 Mar. 88
South Wales Borderers	9	Hennessy, John Patrick C., Dep. Assist. Com. Gen. 2nd Class	5 Feb. 87	22 Mar. 88
East Kent Regiment	8	Lethbridge, Fras. W.,682 Offg. Wing Officer 2 Bn. 5 Goorkhas	28 Sept. 87	22 Mar. 88
Royal Marines	8	Drake-Brockman, David Henry, Wing Officer 6 Bengal Inf.	1 Feb. 78	24 Mar. 88
Welsh Regiment	8	Allen, Hugh Morris, Squadron Officer 5 Punjab Cavalry	14 Sept. 87	25 Mar. 88
Manchester Regiment	8	Shakespear, Frank, Offg. Squadron Officer 4 Bengal Cavalry	9 Nov. 87	30 Mar. 88
Leicestershire Regiment	8	Chaplin, Ronald Eustace, Squad. Officer 8 Bengal Cavalry	16 Nov. 87	31 Mar. 88
West India Regiment	9	Stotherd, Edw. Aug. Wood,683 Squad. Officer 4 Lan. Hyd. Cont.	5 Feb. 87	1 Apr. 88
Munster Fusiliers	8	Burton, Frederic Nuthall,684 Wing Officer 27 Madras Infantry	14 Sept. 87	1 Apr. 88
Manchester Regiment	8	Chichester, Alfred G. de V., Wing Officer 28 Bengal Infantry	16 Nov. 87	1 Apr. 88
Northamptonshire Regt.	8	Beddek, Edward Escott, Wing Officer 2 Madras Infantry	14 Sept. 87	2 Apr. 88
N. Lancashire Regiment	8	Lester, Claude Dallas,685 Wing Officer 17 Bombay Infantry	14 Sept. 87	7 Apr. 88

Indian Staff Corps.

Last Regiment.	Yrs.' Serv.	LIEUTENANTS.	2nd LIEUT.	LIEUT.
Liverpool Regiment	9	Codrington, Hubert Walter,686 Wing Officer Corps of Guides	30 Mar. 87	9 Apr. 88
Essex Regiment	9	Holmes, Gilbert Vallentin, Wing Officer 4 Madras Infantry ...	5 Feb. 87	12 Apr. 88
Scots Fusiliers	8	Roome, Reginald Eckford, Squad. Officer 6 Bombay Cav. ...	14 Sept. 87	20 Apr. 88
N. Lancashire Regiment ...	8	Smith, George R. de H., Squadron Officer 2 C. I. Horse	16 Nov. 87	21 Apr. 88
Warwickshire Regiment ...	9	Wikeley, James Masson,687 Squad. Officer 17 Bengal Cavalry	5 Feb. 87	4 May 88
6 Dragoon Guards	9	Barton, Thomas Steward, Squad. Officer 3 Bengal Cavalry...	5 Feb. 87	8 May 88
6 Dragoon Guards	9	Browne, Alfred Percy, Squadron Officer 1 C. I. Horse	5 Feb. 87	10 May 88
1 Dragoon Guards	9	Waterfield, Arthur C. M.,688 Squadron Officer 11 Bengal Lan.	5 Feb. 87	21 May 88
Dublin Fusiliers	9	Roddy, Henry Hugh,689 Wing Officer 42 Bengal Infantry	5 Feb. 87	13 May 88
K. O. Scottish Borderers ...	9	Kennion, Roger Lloyd, Squadron Officer 2 C. I. Horse	5 Feb. 87	9 June 88
Highland Light Infantry ...	9	Wallis, Hugh Ryves,690 Wing Officer 34 Bengal Infantry	30 Mar. 87	29 June 88
Hampshire Regiment	9	Grant, Fras. Douglas, Wing Officer 6 Punjab Infantry	5 Feb. 87	2 July 88
Suffolk Regiment	8	Saulez, Edmund, Wing Officer 8 Bombay Infantry	14 Sept. 87	13 July 88
East Surrey Regiment	9	Thompson, Harry A. H., Wing Officer 2 Bn. 1 Goorkhas ...	5 Feb. 87	31 July 88
West Yorkshire Regiment...	9	Tweddell, Henry, Wing Officer 4 Bengal Infantry	5 Feb. 87	2 Aug. 88
Cheshire Regiment	8	James, Montague Gifford, Wing Officer 42 Bengal Infantry	14 Sept. 87	17 Aug. 88
Liverpool Regiment	8	Macquoid, Chas. E. E. F. K., Squadron Officer 1 Lan.Hyd.Cont	11 Feb. 88	26 Aug. 88
Somerset Light Infantry ...	8	Keays, Robert William C., Wing Officer 28 Madras Infantry	14 Sept. 87	31 Aug. 88
21 Hussars	8	Harward, Arthur J. N., Wing Officer 10 Bengal Infantry ...	5 Oct. 87	1 Sept. 88
6 Dragoon Guards	8	Stack, Chas. Spottiswoode,693 Squad. Officer 3 Bombay Cav...	11 Feb. 88	13 Sept. 88
East Lancashire Regt.	8	Caruana, Alfred Joseph,694 Wing Officer 2 Punjab Infantry ...	6 July 87	15 Sept. 88
Gloucestershire Regiment...	8	Britten, Thomas Xavier, Wing Officer 10 Bombay Infantry...	14 Sept. 87	21 Sept. 88
Durham Light Infantry ...	8	Birch, Fred.Wm.,Dep.Assist.Com.Gen. 2nd Class, Mecan Meor	11 Feb. 88	21 Sept. 88
Royal Marines	8	Tribe, Charles Walter, Wing Officer 38 Bengal Infantry ...	1 Sept. 87	28 Sept. 88
Gloucestershire Regiment ...	8	Lucas, Harold M. A., Dep. Assist. Com. Gen. 2nd Class	11 Feb. 88	14 Oct. 88
Worcestershire Regiment ...	9	Vaughan, Richard Randal, Wing Officer 22 Bengal Infantry	5 Feb. 87	17 Oct. 88
Bedfordshire Regiment	9	Dale, George Arthur, Wing Officer 19 Bengal Infantry	5 Feb. 87	17 Oct. 88
West India Regiment	9	Rainey, Edmund Flower, Wing Officer 12 Madras Infantry ...	5 Feb. 87	17 Oct. 88
Bedfordshire Regiment	8	Firth, Edward William Anson, Wing Officer 9 Madras Inf. ...	4 May 87	17 Oct. 88
Norfolk Regiment	9	Vaughan, Robert Edward, Dep. Assist. Com. Gen. 2nd Class	5 Feb. 87	27 Oct. 88
Oxford Light Infantry	8	Bruce, Hon. Chas. Granville,696 Wing Officer 1 Bn. 5 Goorkhas	4 May 87	29 Oct. 88
Scots Fusiliers	8	Thomason, Arch. Fawcett, Wing Officer 21 Bengal Infantry...	16 Nov. 87	30 Oct. 88
Devonshire Regiment	9	Grove, Henry Montgomery, Squad. Officer 1 Bengal Cavalry	5 Feb. 87	1 Nov. 88
York & Lancaster Regiment	9	Gunning, Charles John, Wing Officer 1 Madras Infantry	5 Feb. 87	8 Nov. 88
East Yorkshire Regiment...	11	Camilleri, John Mary,697 Wing Officer 13 Bengal Infantry	14 Jan. 85	21 Nov. 88
Inniskilling Fusiliers	8	Coape-Smith, Henry,698 Squadron Officer 11 Bengal Lancers	5 Feb. 87	21 Nov. 88
Cheshire Regiment	8	Peterson Cecil Herbert	5 Feb. 81	21 Nov. 88
Cheshire Regiment	8	Macmullen, Frederic C. K., Squad. Officer 12 Bengal Cav. ...	11 Feb. 88	4 Dec. 88
West Surrey Regiment	8	Williamson, Michael,699 Wing Officer 21 Bengal Infantry	4 May 87	7 Dec. 88
Durham Light Infantry ...	8	Dunsford, Francis P. S., Wing Officer 15 Bengal Infantry ...	16 Nov. 87	11 Dec. 88
Gloucestershire Regiment..	8	Bruce, Wm. Alex. M., Wing Officer 26 Bombay Infantry ...	14 Sept.87	23 Dec. 88
West Surrey Regiment	8	Nisbett, William Gibbon, Wing Officer 32 Madras Infantry...	16 Nov. 87	4 Jan. 8
West India Regiment	8	Lindsay, Henry A. P., Dep. Assist. Com. Gen. 2nd Class	5 Feb. 87	16 Jan. 89
Lancashire Fusiliers	9	Stone, William Richard, Wing Officer 25 Madras Infantry ...	16 Nov. 87	21 Jan. 89
King's Own Scottish Bord.	8	Johnson, Gilbert Ward,701 Squadron Officer 3 Punjab Cavalry	14 Sept.87	28 Jan. 89
Dublin Fusiliers	8	Griffith, Wm. W. G., Squadron Officer 2 Bombay Lancers	16 Nov. 87	29 Jan. 89
7 Dragoon Guards	8	ffrench-Mullen, John L.Wm., Squad. Officer 13 Bengal Lancers	14 Sept.87	30 Jan. 89
Yorkshire Light Infantry...	9	Renton, Colin Campbell,702 Wing Officer 6 Inf. Hyd. Cont. ...	5 Feb. 87	4 Feb. 89
West Yorkshire Regiment	9	Badcock, Alex. James, Dep. Assist. Com. Gen. 2nd Class	5 Feb. 87	5 Feb. 89
West India Regiment	8	Bentinck, Reg. Joseph, Squad. Officer 4 Lancers Hyd. Cont.	5 Feb. 87	6 Feb. 89
3 Dragoon Guards	8	Lane, Henry Arthur, Squadron Officer 2 Lancers Hyd. Cont...	14 Sept.87	9 Feb. 89
South Lancashire Regiment	8	Boome, Edward Herbert,703 Nair Brigade	16 Nov. 87	11 Feb. 89
1 Dragoon Guards	9	Scharlieb, Wm. Karl, Squadron Officer 5 Bengal Cavalry	5 Feb. 87	26 Feb. 89
Leinster Regiment	8	Bowen, Charles Eustace, Wing Officer 1 Madras Infantry	16 Nov. 87	26 Feb. 89
Worcestershire Regiment...	8	Bell, Henry Phillipps. Wing Officer 11 Madras Infantry	4 May 87	27 Feb. 89
South Lancashire Regiment	8	Morris, Godfrey Maxwell,704 Wing Officer 22 Madras Infantry	14 Sept.87	27 Feb. 89
Duke of Cornwall's Lt. Inf.	8	Barnett, Carew, Wing Officer 31 Madras Infantry	16 Nov. 87	28 Feb. 89
Duke of Cornwall's Lt. Inf.	8	Ware, Frank C. W., Squadron Officer 7 Bombay Lancers ...	16 Nov. 87	28 Feb. 89
Connaught Rangers	8	Ridgway, Richard T. I., Wing Officer 40 Bengal Infantry ...	14 Sept.87	3 Mar. 89
West Surrey Regiment	8	Solbé, Chas. E. de Lisle,705 Wing Officer 3 Sikh Infantry	16 Nov. 87	3 Mar. 89
Northamptonshire Regt. ...	8	Powell, Wm. Bowen, Wing Officer 9 Madras Infantry	14 Sept. 87	12 Mar. 89
Irish Regiment	8	Sutton, Fras. G. Hill,706 Wing Officer 10 Madras Infantry...	16 Nov. 87	17 Mar. 89
Manchester Regiment	7	Leslie, Clement S. D.,707 Wing Officer 2 Bombay Infantry ...	25 July 88	22 Mar. 89
Devonshire Regiment	9	Rowcroft, Ernest Cave, Wing Officer 35 Bengal Infantry...	5 Feb. 87	23 Mar. 89
Gloucestershire Regiment...	8	Bailey, Wm. Aug., Cantonment Magistrate, Cawnpore	31 Dec. 87	24 Mar. 89
6 Dragoon Guards	8	Howell, Ernest A.R., Assist. Commt. Officer, Waziristan...	11 Feb. 88	30 Mar. 89
E. Lancashire Regiment ...	8	Turner, Henry Hamilton Fyers, Squad. Officer 2 Ben. Lancers	14 Sept.87	1 Apr. 89
Royal Marines	8	Murray, Edw. R. Blakiston, Offg. Wing Officer 29 Madras Inf.	1 Feb. 88	1 Apr. 89
West Kent Regiment	8	How, Arthur Pemberton, Wing Officer 1 Madras Infantry	11 Feb. 88	2 Apr. 89
Lancaster Regiment	8	Dickson, John Herbert, Wing Officer 5 Bombay Infantry ...	11 Feb. 88	2 Apr. 89
Argyll and Suth. Highrs. ...	8	Anderson, Allan Meyrick.708 Wing Officer 21 Madras Infantry	4 May 87	4 Apr. 89
Irish Fusiliers	9	M'Crea, Alfred Coryton,709 Wing Officer 37 Bengal Infantry	19 Jan. 87	10 Apr. 89
Irish Fusiliers	8	Harvest, Herbert de Vere, Wing Officer 9 Madras Infantry ...	14 Sept.87	10 Apr. 89
East Surrey Regiment	8	White, Ion Grove, Squadron Officer 16 Bengal Cavalry	28 Sept. 87	10 Apr. 89
Suffolk Regiment	8	Fraser, Walter Andrew, Wing Officer 22 Bengal Infantry ...	16 Nov. 87	20 Apr. 89
Lancashire Fusiliers	8	Newnham, Walter Fawcett, Squadron Officer 4 Bombay Cav.	14 Sept. 87	30 Apr. 89
N. Lancashire Regiment ...	8	Cockcraft, Charlton Macleod, Dep. Assist. Com. Gen. 2nd Class	14 Sept.87	2 May 89
Devonshire Regiment	8	Turner, Alfred G. B., Squadron Officer 13 Bengal Lancers...	5 Feb. 87	6 May 89
Worcestershire Regiment...	8	Beatty, Lionel Nicholson, Squad. Officer 1 Bombay Lancers	4 May 87	8 May 89
West Yorkshire Regiment	8	Bliss, Charles Ernest, Wing Officer 1 Bn. 3 Goorkhas	14 Sept.87	8 May 89
Lincolnshire Regiment	8	Pirrie, Francis William, Wing Officer 4 Bengal Infantry ...	14 Sept.87	8 May 89
Lancaster Regiment	8	Watling, Gordon, Wing Officer 16 Bengal Infantry	14 Sept.87	12 May 89
Northumberland Fusiliers	8	Webb, Algernon Edward,710 Wing Officer 3 Bengal Infantry	16 Nov. 87	14 May 89
Highland Light Infantry ...	8	Rose, John Latham, Wing Officer 2 Bn. 1 Goorkhas	16 Nov. 87	15 May 89
N. Lancashire Regiment ...	8	Thornton, Chas. Edw., Squad. Officer 16 Bengal Cavalry ...	16 Nov. 87	28 May 89
Liverpool Regiment	8	Porteous, Chas. M'Leod,71 Wing Officer 9 Bengal Infantry ...	16 Nov. 87	30 May 89
West India Regiment	8	Boddam, Ernest B. C.,712 Wing Officer 2 Sikh Infantry	19 Oct. 87	5 June 89
West India Regiment	8	Eliott-Lockhart, Percy C., Wing Officer Corps of Guides ...	23 Nov. 87	5 June 89
Leicestershire Regiment ...	8	Obbard, Edw. Naismith, Wing Officer 10 Bengal Infantry ...	14 Sept.87	7 June 89
Bedfordshire Regiment ...	8	Daniell, Frank Wm., Wing Officer 8 Bengal Infantry	11 Feb. 88	20 June 89
West Surrey Regiment ...	8	Cockerill, Geo. Kynaston,714 Wing Officer 28 Bengal Infantry	11 Feb. 88	26 June 89
Durham Light Infantry ...	8	Lloyd, Wm. Edm. Eyre, Wing Officer 4 Inf. Hyd. Cont. ...	11 Feb. 88	26 June 89
S. Staffordshire Regiment	8	Hodding, James Sweet,715 Wing Officer 20 Madras Infantry...	11 Feb. 88	26 June 89
Royal Artillery	9	Fordyce, Hy. Lawrence Dingwall, Wing Officer 23 Mad. Inf.	16 Nov. 87	28 June 89

E E

Indian Staff Corps.

Last Regiment.	Yrs. Serv.	LIEUTENANTS.	2nd LIEUT.	DEBUT.
Worcestershire Regiment...	7	Cobham, Horace Walter, Squadron Officer 5 Bombay Cavalry	9 May 88	29 June 89
7 Hussars	7	Orr, John Loch, Squadron Officer 1 Lancers Hyd. Cont.	16 May 88	30 June 89
Leinster Regiment	8	Vanderzee, John Herbert, Wing Officer 3 Inf. Hyd. Cont.	14 Sept.87	3 July 89
Durham Light Infantry ...	8	Ford, Charles A. W., Wing Officer 4 Bombay Infantry	14 Sept.87	3 July 89
Border Regiment	8	Pennington, Arthur Watson, Squad. Officer 9 Ben. Lancers...	11 Feb. 88	3 July 89
S. Lancashire Regiment ...	8	Bell, Richard Carmichael, Squad. Officer 2 Central India Horse	16 Nov. 87	5 July 89
Warwickshire Regiment ...	8	Longden, Arthur Berridge, Wing Officer 37 Bengal Infantry	11 Feb. 88	5 July 89
Border Regiment	8	Climo, Skipton Hill, Wing Officer 24 Bengal Infantry	11 Feb. 88	11 July 89
Manchester Regiment	8	Eastmead, Charles Sidney, Wing Officer 2 Bn. 3 Goorkhas....	11 Feb. 88	18 July 89
Bedfordshire Regiment......	8	Vaughan, E. Gyles,717 Dep.Assist.Com. Gen. 2nd Class Kalewa	11 Feb. 88	26 July 89
Norfolk Regiment	8	Brakspear, William Rae, Wing Officer 2 Bn. 3 Goorkhas	14 Sept.87	27 July 89
Warwickshire Regiment ...	8	Jackson, Robert Pilkington, Wing Officer 13 Madras Infantry	11 Feb. 88	31 July 89
Dublin Fusiliers	8	Martin, Edw. Victor, Wing Officer 18 Bengal Infantry	16 Nov. 87	31 July 89
Warwickshire Regiment ...	8	Vanrenen, Geo. Rainier, Wing Officer 16 Bengal Infantry....	11 Feb. 88	31 July 89
Bedfordshire Regiment......	8	Stevens, Nathaniel M. C., Wing Officer 21 Madras Infantry...	11 Feb. 88	31 July 89
West India Regiment	8	Baker, Harold Robert, Wing Officer 13 Madras Infantry	15 Feb. 88	31 July 89
Irish Fusiliers	8	Annesley, Arthur S. R., Wing Officer 33 Bengal Infantry...	11 Feb. 88	1 Aug. 89
Norfolk Regiment	8	Heffernan, Herbert Wm., Wing Officer 19 Madras Infantry ...	11 Feb. 88	10 Aug. 89
Lincolnshire Regiment	8	Donnan, William, Wing Officer 19 Madras Infantry	1: Feb. 88	12 Aug. 89
Inniskilling Fusiliers	7	Scott, Bernard, Assistant Military Accountant, Madras ...	9 May 88	26 Aug. 89
Oxford Light Infantry ...	8	Faunce, Robert deLaune,718 Squad. Officer 1 Madras Lancers...	17 Sept.87	27 Aug. 89
Cheshire Regiment	9	Davies, Charles Henry, Wing Officer 3 Sikh Infantry.........	5 Feb. 87	1 Sept.89
Hampshire Regiment......	8	Robson, Charles Grœme,719 Wing Officer 10 Bengal Infantry	11 Feb. 88	1 Sept.89
Seaforth Highlanders	8	Wilson, James Alban, Wing Officer 44 Bengal Infantry	16 Nov. 87	4 Sept. 89
Middlesex Regiment	7	Harrington, John Lane, Wing Officer 14 Bombay Infantry ...	26 June 88	11 Sept.89
East Surrey Regiment ...	8	Parr, Harington Owen,720 Wing Officer 7 Bengal Infantry...	16 Nov. 87	18 Sept. 89
Liverpool Regiment	8	Lyne, Charles Virgil Nunez, Wing Officer 16 Madras Infantry	11 Feb. 88	18 Sept. 89
Oxford Light Infantry ...	7	Bagshawe, Fred. Wm., Wing Officer 8 Madras Infantry	22 Aug. 88	19 Sept. 89
8 Hussars	8	M'Conaghey, Harry, Squadron Officer 7 Bengal Cavalry	14 Sept. 87	23 Sept. 89
Dorsetshire Regiment	8	Gardon, Arch. Ross Hervey,721 Wing Officer Corps of Guides...	11 Feb. 88	25 Sept. 89
Dorsetshire Regiment	8	Fenner, Claude Cambridge, Wing Officer 6 Punjab Infantry ...	11 Feb. 88	25 Sept. 89
Derbyshire Regiment.........	8	Hamilton, Arch. Samuel,722 Offg. Wing Officer 4 Sikh Inf. ...	11 Feb. 88	3 Oct. 89
Shropshire Light Infantry	8	Searle, Percy Cormack, Wing Officer 9 Bombay Infantry.....	11 Feb. 88	3 Oct. 89
Dorsetshire Regiment	8	Major, Francis Forbes, Wing Officer 1 Infantry Hyd. Cont. ...	11 Feb. 88	10 Oct. 89
Essex Regiment	8	Fisher, Frederick, Wing Officer 7 Bombay Infantry............	11 Feb. 88	20 Oct. 89
Essex Regiment	8	Brooke, Harry Morris M., Wing Officer 20 Madras Infantry ...	11 Feb. 88	22 Oct. 89
East Surrey Regiment	7	Henslowe, Francis J. Deloraine, Squad. Officer 2 Punjab Cav.	22 Aug. 88	24 Oct. 89
8 Hussars	8	Petre, Bernard James, Offg. Squad. Officer 2 Madras Lancers	30 Nov. 87	26 Oct. 89
Berkshire Regiment	8	Quinn, John James Patrick, Wing Officer 28 Madras Infantry	11 Feb. 88	26 Oct. 89
South Lancashire Regiment	3	Troup, Hugh Rose, Wing Officer 26 Madras Infantry	11 Feb. 88	26 Oct. 89
S. Staffordshire Regiment	7	Rampini, Fred. Charles, Dep. Assist. Com. Gen. 2nd Class ...	22 Aug. 88	27 Oct. 89
West Riding Regiment ...	8	Beale, Willy, Wing Officer 17 Bombay Infantry	29 Feb. 88	31 Oct. 89
Dorsetshire Regiment	8	Sherer, John Corrie, Squadron Officer 3 Punjab Cavalry ...	11 Feb. 88	3 Nov. 89
K. O. Scottish Borderers ...	8	Beadon, William,723 Wing Officer 4 Sikh Infantry............	14 Sept.87	4 Nov. 89
21 Hussars	8	Evans, William Noble, Squad. Officer 10 Bengal Lancers ...	5 Oct. 87	6 Nov. 89
West Yorkshire Regiment	8	Bell, John Beatson,724 Wing Officer 32 Bengal Infantry	11 Feb. 88	6 Nov. 89
Manchester Regiment	7	Pearson, Hugh Fred. Archie,725 Wing Officer 23 Bengal Infantry	22 Aug. 88	6 Nov. 89
Northamptonshire Regt. ...	8	Johnstone, Francis Herbert, Wing Officer 11 Madras Infantry	14 Sept.87	16 Nov. 89
Irish Regiment	8	Foord, Edward Russell, Wing Officer 23 Madras Infantry ...	11 Feb. 88	17 Nov. 89
West Kent Regiment.........	7	Dallas, Julian Stuart. Wing Officer 23 Madras Infantry	9 May 88	18 Nov. 89
Hampshire Regiment.........	7	Pigou, Fred. Hugo, Wing Officer 1 Infantry Hyd. Cont.	22 Aug. 88	19 Nov. 89
Yorkshire Light Infantry...	9	Benn, Robert Arthur E.,727 Squad. Officer 5 Bombay Cavalry	5 Feb. 87	20 Nov. 89
York Light Infantry	8	Lloyd-Jones, Fred. Llewellyn, Wing Officer 13 Bombay Inf. ...	11 Feb. 88	20 Nov. 89
West Riding Regiment ...	8	White, William Edward, Wing Officer 1 Bengal Infantry ...	16 Nov. 87	25 Nov. 89
West Riding Regiment ...	8	Bagley, Richard George, Wing Officer 3 Bengal Infantry ...	9 May 88	25 Nov. 89
Cheshire Regiment	8	Clarke, Geo. Lecot Philip, Wing Officer 9 Madras Infantry ...	14 Sept. 87	27 Nov. 89
West Yorkshire Regiment	8	Hitchins, Harold Edmund, Wing Officer 1 Bengal Infantry ...	11 Feb. 88	2 Dec. 89
West Yorkshire Regiment	8	Limond, Alexander,728 Wing Officer 6 Punjab Infantry	11 Feb. 88	2 Dec. 89
West Riding Regiment......	8	Norman, Henry Erasmus,729 Wing Officer 2 Madras Infantry	16 Nov. 87	4 Dec. 89
Worcestershire Regiment...	8	Windsor, Wm. John, Wing Officer 19 Bengal Infantry	11 Feb. 88	4 Dec. 89
Irish Rifles	7	Playfair, Alan, Wing Officer 15 Madras Infantry	22 Aug. 88	4 Dec. 89
Sussex Regiment	7	Beynon, Wm. G. L.,730 Wing Officer 1 Bn. 3 Goorkhas.........	5 Feb. 87	11 Dec. 89
Inniskilling Fusiliers.........	7	Dew, Armine Brereton,731 Wing Officer Corps of Guides.........	10 Nov. 87	16 Dec. 89
Leinster Regiment	7	Perkins, John C. C., Wing Officer 10 Bengal Infantry	16 Nov. 87	18 Dec. 89
Leinster Regiment	8	Blockley, Fred.Colin Campbell, Squad.Officer 8 Bengal Cav.	11 Feb. 88	18 Dec. 89
Irish Fusiliers	7	Scott, Thomas Edwin, Wing Officer 3 Sikh Infantry	9 May 88	18 Dec. 89
Lancashire Fusiliers	7	Dalyell, Hugh Kenneth, Squadron Officer 3 Lancers Hyd. Cont.	22 Aug. 88	18 Dec. 89
Derbyshire Regiment	7	Barnard, Andrew E., Squad. Officer 4 Lancers Hyd. Cont. ...	11 Feb. 88	1 Jan. 90
West Surrey Regiment ...	7	Randall, John, Wing Officer 23 Bengal Infantry	22 Aug. 88	1 Jan. 90
Bedfordshire Regiment......	8	Jeffcoat, Fred. H. H., Wing Officer 7 Madras Infantry	16 Nov. 87	4 Jan. 90
Dublin Fusiliers	8	Price, Cyril Uvedale,732 Wing Officer 30 Bombay Infantry......	11 Feb. 88	4 Jan. 90
Lincolnshire Regiment ...	7	Hughes, Victor, Wing Officer 35 Bengal Infantry	9 May 88	4 Jan. 90
Bedfordshire Regiment......	7	Doveton, Albert Mangles, Wing Officer 1 Bombay Infantry...	22 Aug. 88	4 Jan. 90
York Light Infantry	7	Clay, Stanley, Wing Officer 43 Bengal Infantry	22 Aug. 88	5 Jan. 90
Middlesex Regiment	7	Roberts, Archibald, Wing Officer 24 Bengal Infantry.........	3 Oct. 88	6 Jan. 90
Wiltshire Regiment	7	Codrington, Ernest, Wing Officer 26 Madras Infantry.........	14 Sept.87	7 Jan. 90
Welsh Fusiliers	7	Crosthwaite, John Graham, Assist. Commr. Ferozepore, Punjab	22 Aug. 88	13 Jan. 90
Wiltshire Regiment	7	Whitehead, John Holberton, Wing Officer 33 Madras Infantry	22 Aug. 88	13 Jan. 90
N. Lancashire Regiment ...	7	Hay, Arthur, Offg. Wing Officer 7 Bombay Infantry	9 May 88	14 Jan. 90
Middlesex Regiment	7	Prince, Wm. Chas. Stuart, Wing Officer 13 Madras Infantry	16 Nov. 87	22 Jan. 90
Berkshire Regiment	7	Gray, Fred. Wm. B., Wing Officer 4 Punjab Infantry	22 Aug. 88	22 Jan. 90
Royal Artillery	7	Murray, Alan Beville, Wing Officer 31 Madras Infantry.........	17 Feb. 88	2 Feb. 90
Derbyshire Regiment	8	Black, Walter Clarence, Wing Officer 12 Bengal Infantry ...	11 Feb. 88	14 Feb. 90
Dublin Fusiliers	7	Staunton, Wm. Beauchamp, Wing Officer 22 Madras Infantry	22 Aug. 88	15 Feb. 90
Irish Regiment	8	Shea, John Stuart Mackenzie, Offg. squad.Officer 15 Ben. Lan.	11 Feb. 88	18 Feb. 90
Dublin Fusiliers	8	Pierce, Frederick George, Wing Officer 9 Madras Infantry ...	11 Feb. 88	23 Feb. 90
Munster Fusiliers	7	Talbot, John,734 Squadron Officer 7 Bombay Lancers	14 Sept.87	24 Feb. 90
Leicestershire Regiment ...	7	Anderson, Patrick Graham, Wing Officer 24 Bengal Infantry	11 Feb. 88	24 Feb. 90
4 Dragoon Guards	8	Sheppard, George Sidney, Squad. Officer 9 Bengal Lancers	29 Dec. 88	26 Feb. 90
Devonshire Regiment	3	Rattray, Charles, Wing Officer 26 Bengal Infantry	11 Feb. 88	27 Feb. 90
Leicestershire Regiment ...	7	Watson, Lionel Arthur, Wing Officer 31 Bengal Infantry......	22 Aug. 88	2 Mar. 90
Devonshire Regiment	8	Jones, Harry Harvey, Dep. Assist. Com. Gen. 2nd Class	14 Sept. 87	7 Mar. 90
Worcestershire Regiment...	7	Gordon, John L. R., Offg. Wing Officer 15 Bengal Infantry...	22 Aug. 88	7 Mar. 90
Durham Light Infantry ...	8	Wilmot, Ernest Eardley, Offg. Wing Officer 3 Bengal Inf. ...	11 Feb. 88	12 Mar. 90

Indian Staff Corps.

Last Regiment.	Yrs. Serv.	LIEUTENANTS.	2nd LIEUT.	LIEUT.
Shropshire Light Infantry	7	Chatterton, George D. D., Offg. Wing Officer 1 Sikh Infantry	8 Dec. 88	13 Mar. 90
Royal Artillery		Sandford, Harry Coddington,754 Wing Officer 1 Punjab Infantry	27 July 88	17 Mar. 90
Munster Fusiliers	7	Davis, Edward Newnham, Wing Officer 3 Inf. Hyd. Cont.	10 Nov. 88	18 Mar. 90
Somerset Light Infantry	8	Shewell, Arthur Poole, Wing Officer 23 Bombay Infantry	16 Nov. 87	19 Mar. 90
Middlesex Regiment	8	Grace, Charles H. C., Wing Officer 5 Bombay Infantry	16 Nov. 87	19 Mar. 90
Liverpool Regiment	8	Blois-Johnson, Thos. Gordon, Wing Officer 22 Bengal Inf.	14 Mar. 88	19 Mar. 90
Liverpool Regiment	7	Vallings, Henry Alan, Offg. Wing Officer 24 Bengal Infantry	9 May 88	19 Mar. 90
Devonshire Regiment	7	Lash, Henry Andrew, Offg. Squad. Officer 1 Cent. India Horse	9 May 88	19 Mar. 90
West India Regiment	7	Wallis, Francis Joseph, Wing Officer 15 Madras Infantry	22 Aug. 88	19 Mar. 90
Leicestershire Regiment	7	Trotter, Frank Wallace D., Wing Officer 3 Bombay Infantry	22 Aug. 88	21 Mar. 90
Leicestershire Regiment	7	Cooper, Wm. George, Squadron Officer 4 Bombay Cavalry	22 Aug. 88	21 Mar. 90
N. Lancashire Regiment	8	Jacques, Francis Aug., Wing Officer 14 Bengal Infantry	16 Nov. 87	22 Mar. 90
Derbyshire Regiment	8	Walker, William Robert, Wing Officer 15 Madras Infantry	11 Feb. 88	23 Mar. 90
East Surrey Regiment	7	Elderton, Murray Trent, Offg. Wing Officer 8 Bombay Inf.	10 Nov. 88	23 Mar. 90
Berkshire Regiment	8	Wooldridge, Wm. Hugh, Wing Officer 24 Bombay Infantry	16 Nov. 87	23 Mar. 90
York Light Infantry	7	Anderson, Henry Lawrence, Wing Officer 5 Bengal Infantry	22 Aug. 88	26 Mar. 90
Welsh Regiment	7	Ricketts, Lancelot Hamilton, Wing Officer 12 Madras Infantry	8 Dec. 88	26 Mar. 90
Wiltshire Regiment	7	Down, Cecil Patton	22 Aug. 88	1 Apr. 90
Leinster Regiment	8	Gabb, Chris. Wm. W., Squad. Officer 2 Bombay Lancers	30 Nov. 88	1 Apr. 90
Suffolk Regiment	8	Kauntze, Cedric Richard, Wing Officer 5 Madras Infantry	16 Feb. 88	2 Apr. 90
Irish Rifles	6	Clery, Carleton Buckley Laming, Wing Officer 25 Bombay Inf.	24 Apr. 89	2 Apr. 90
Welsh Fusiliers	7	Ford, Harry Burroughs, Wing Officer 31 Bengal Infantry	14 Mar. 88	4 Apr. 90
Welsh Regiment	7	Harington, Herbert Hastings, Wing Officer 32 Madras Inf.	8 Dec. 88	4 Apr. 90
3 Dragoon Guards	9	Molyneux, Edward M. J., Squad. Officer 12 Bengal Cavalry	5 Feb. 87	8 Apr. 90
Irish Fusiliers	7	Waterfield, Bertram Clarke, Assistant Commissioner, Punjab	9 Sept. 88	14 Apr. 90
Norfolk Regiment	7	Richardson, Chas. Wm. Grant,736 Wing Officer 19 Bengal Inf.	11 Feb. 88	23 Apr. 90
Border Regiment	7	Elsmie, Alex. M. Spears, Wing Officer 2 Punjab Infantry	30 Jan. 89	3 May 90
Lancaster Regiment	7	Mears, Arthur, Wing Officer 2 Madras Infantry	30 Jan. 89	3 May 90
Hampshire Regiment	7	Thatcher, Francis Alexander737	23 Jan. 89	5 May 90
West Riding Regiment	7	Lillingston, William Edward Gordon, Squadron Officer, 1 Lancers Hyderabad Contingent	8 Dec. 88	8 May 90
Manchester Regiment	7	Gaisford, James, Wing Officer 25 Bengal Infantry	22 Aug. 88	9 May 90
West Yorkshire Regiment	7	Codrington, Harry de Burgh, Dep. Assist. Com. Gen. 2nd Class	28 Nov. 88	10 May 90
East Surrey Regiment	7	Cooke, Augustus Hodson, Wing Officer 1 Inf. Hyd. Cont.	5 Dec. 88	14 May 90
South Wales Borderers	8	Hood, Ernest Frederick,738 Wing Officer 7 Bengal Infantry	21 Dec. 87	29 May 90
Warwickshire Regiment	7	Hill, Frank Barton, Wing Officer 34 Bengal Infantry	6 June 88	6 June 90
Liverpool Regiment	7	Blakeway, Denys Brooke, Assist. Commr. 3rd Grade, Moolan	22 Aug. 88	14 June 90
Devonshire Regiment	7	Ricketts, Percy Edward, Squad. Officer 28 Bengal Cavalry	22 Aug. 88	17 June 90
Irish Regiment	7	Nethersole, Fred. Ralph, Assist. Comdt. Burma Mil. Police	30 Jan. 89	18 June 90
Royal Artillery	9	Saunders, Arthur Rivers, Squad. Officer 2 Lancers Hyd. Cont.	16 Feb. 87	23 June 90
Liverpool Regiment	7	Ralph, Alfred Colyer, Wing Officer 8 Bengal Infantry	22 Aug. 88	23 June 90
S. Staffordshire Regiment	7	Keyworth, Walter, Wing Officer 14 Madras Infantry	23 Mar. 89	25 June 90
Lancashire Fusiliers	7	Shaw, Herbert Stuart, Wing Officer 42 Bengal Infantry	10 Nov. 88	7 July 90
Manchester Regiment	7	Gunning, Orlando Geo.740 Offg. Wing Officer 35 Bengal Inf.	22 Aug. 88	9 July 90
Manchester Regiment	7	Stewart, John Alexander, Offg. Wing Officer 7 Bengal Inf.	22 Aug. 88	9 July 90
Border Regiment	7	Garden, Alex. Harry,741 Wing Officer 32 Bengal Infantry	22 Aug. 88	9 July 90
Manchester Regiment	7	Condon, James Knighton, Wing Officer 18 Bengal Infantry	22 Aug. 88	9 July 90
Liverpool Regiment	7	Fraser, Frederick John, Offg. Wing Officer 5 Bengal Infantry	12 Sept. 88	9 July 90
Irish Fusiliers	7	Gough, George Broomfield,742 Wing Officer 20 Bengal Infantry	10 Nov. 88	9 July 90
Border Regiment	7	Jackson, Cyril Compton, Wing Officer Bhopal Battalion	10 Nov. 88	9 July 90
South Wales Borderers	7	Lightfoot, Thos. Williams, Wing Officer 8 Bengal Infantry	22 Aug. 88	9 July 90
Warwickshire Regiment	7	Macdonald, Norman Alex., Wing Officer 14 Bengal Infantry	22 Sept. 88	10 July 90
Royal Artillery	8	Cameron, Donald Hay, Squadron Officer 2 C. I. Horse	23 July 87	23 July 90
East Surrey Regiment	7	Tayler, Wm. Fothergill Cooke, Squad. Officer 1 Punjab Cav.	30 Jan. 89	24 July 90
Lancashire Fusiliers	7	Maxwell, Laurence Lockhart, Squad. Officer 2 Ben. Lancers	23 Mar. 89	31 July 90
Border Regiment	6	M'Barnet, Alex. Edward, Offg. Squad. Officer 5 Punjab Cav.	3 July 89	20 Aug. 90
Durham Light Infantry	7	Lees, Clarence Edward, Wing Officer 34 Bengal Infantry	22 Aug. 88	27 Aug. 90
Gordon Highlanders	7	Lee, Alex. Wm. Henry, Wing Officer 16 Madras Infantry	30 Jan. 89	28 Aug. 90
Highland Light Infantry	6	Forteath, Fred. Wm. Hughes, Wing Officer 3 Bombay Inf.	8 June 89	30 Aug. 90
Manchester Regiment	7	Stevens, John Lucius Cary,745 Wing Officer 20 Bengal Inf.	30 Jan. 89	10 Sept. 90
Manchester Regiment	7	Hughes, Edw. Malcolm,746 Offg. Squad. Officer 14 Ben. Lan.	30 Jan. 89	10 Sept. 90
Middlesex Regiment	7	Strahan, George Aubrey, Wing Officer 29 Madras Infantry	8 Dec. 88	11 Sept. 90
Royal Fusiliers	7	Turner, Wm. Derington, Wing Officer 2 Bn. 2 Goorkhas	1 Mar. 87	17 Sept. 90
West Yorkshire Regiment	8	Moore, Chas. H. J., Dep. Assist. Com. Gen. 2nd Class, Mandalay	11 Feb. 88	24 Sept. 90
West Yorkshire Regiment	7	Hutchinson, Chas. R. Maclagan, Wing Officer Bn. 4 Goorkhas	9 May 88	24 Sept. 90
West Yorkshire Regiment	7	Haldane, Chas. Levenax, Wing Officer 8 Madras Infantry	10 Nov. 88	24 Sept. 90
Connaught Rangers	6	Moore, Frederick T. T., Offg. Squad. Officer 2 Bengal Lan.	8 June 89	24 Sept. 90
Connaught Rangers	6	Moore, Alexander, Wing Officer 6 Madras Infantry	6 July 89	24 Sept. 90
Warwickshire Regiment	8	Pinney, John O. Digby, Squadron Officer 1 C. I. Horse	8 June 89	25 Sept. 90
Gloucestershire Regiment	7	Grove, James Scott, Offg. Squad. Officer 1 Bengal Cavalry	8 Dec. 88	1 Oct. 90
Gloucestershire Regiment	7	Douglas, Walter Binny, Wing Officer 8 Bengal Infantry	30 Jan. 89	1 Oct. 90
Irish Rifles	7	Carter, Godfrey Lambert, Offg. Wing Officer 2 Sikh Infantry	8 Dec. 88	5 Oct. 90
Warwickshire Regiment	7	Macpherson, Roderick Geo.,748 Offg. Wing Officer 19 Ben. Inf.	12 Sept. 88	15 Oct. 90
Irish Regiment	7	Cruddas, Hugh Wilson, Assist. Comdt. Burmah Mil. Police	30 Jan. 89	15 Oct. 90
Irish Regiment	7	Andrew, Frederick Annesley, Wing Officer 11 Bengal Inf.	23 Mar. 89	15 Oct. 90
Irish Regiment	7	Hill, Wm. Alfred, Wing Officer 11 Bengal Infantry	24 Apr. 89	15 Oct. 90
West Kent Regiment	6	Copeland, Frederick, Wing Officer 30 Madras Infantry	8 June 89	19 Oct. 90
Scottish Rifles	8	Bayley, Edward Charles, Offg. Squad. Officer 15 Bengal Lan.	14 Sept. 87	25 Oct. 90
West Riding Regiment	7	Hanmer, Lambert A. G., Squad. Officer 1 Punjab Cavalry	23 Mar. 89	25 Oct. 90
Gloucestershire Regiment	6	Bannerman, Wyndham P., Squadron Officer 1 Bom. Lancers	24 Apr. 89	29 Oct. 90
7 Dragoon Guards	7	Humfrey, Frederick George Clinton, with 12 Bengal Cavalry	22 Aug. 88	31 Oct. 90
Hampshire Regiment	7	Thompson, Ivan Frank Ross, Wing Officer 26 Bengal Inf.	10 Nov. 88	1 Nov. 90
Highland Light Infantry	7	Anderson, William Christian, Wing Officer 1 Bn. 1 Goorkhas	8 Dec. 88	1 Nov. 90
Derbyshire Regiment	7	Kaye, Cecil, Wing Officer 21 Bengal Infantry	6 Mar. 89	1 Nov. 90
Derbyshire Regiment	7	Munn, Reginald George, Offg. Wing Officer 36 Bengal Inf.	23 Mar. 89	1 Nov. 90
Oxford Light Infantry	6	Payne, Edward Henry, Wing Officer 20 Madras Infantry	21 Sept. 89	8 Nov. 90
Wiltshire Regiment	7	Alexander, Henry Sterling, Wing Officer 16 Madras Inf.	23 Mar. 89	13 Nov. 90
York & Lancaster Regiment	7	Clark, Charles H. Baldwin,750 Wing Officer 26 Madras Inf.	23 Mar. 89	13 Nov. 90
N. Staffordshire Regiment	7	Ainslie, Henry Perceval, Wing Officer 3 Madras Infantry	22 Aug. 89	17 Nov. 90
Lancaster Regiment	7	Tennant, Edward, Squadron Officer 3 Lancers Hyd. Cont.	30 Jan. 89	17 Nov. 90
Irish Fusiliers	6	Maxwell, Alex. Gordon, Squadron Officer 6 Bengal Cavalry	21 Sept. 89	1 Dec. 90
Leicestershire Regiment	6	Cocq, Chas. Alex. Roosmale, Wing Officer 3 Bombay Inf.	6 July 89	13 Dec. 90
Lincolnshire Regiment	8	Kemball, John Shaw, Offg. Wing Officer 23 Bengal Inf.	11 Feb. 88	15 Dec. 90

Indian Staff Corps.

Last Regiment.	Yrs. Serv.	Lieutenants.	2nd Lieut.	Lieut.
King's Own Scottish Bords.	7	Bell, George Henry,[751] Wing Officer 38 Bengal Infantry	22 Aug. 88	15 Dec. 90
Lancashire Fusiliers	7	Burton, Richard Watkins, Wing Officer 5 Inf. Hyd. Cont.	23 Mar. 89	16 Dec. 90
15 Hussars	6	Tancred, Thomas Selby,[752] Squadron Officer 1 C. I. Horse	11 Sept.89	17 Dec. 90
West Yorkshire Regiment	7	Barff, Reg. Merton, Wing Officer 45 Bengal Infantry	8 Dec. 88	18 Dec. 90
Gloucestershire Regiment	6	Darley, James Russell, Wing Officer 9 Bombay Infantry	6 July 89	20 Dec. 90
West Surrey Regiment		Plowden,Trevor Chichele, Assist. Commr. 3rd Class, Amraoti	23 Mar. 89	24 Dec. 90
Royal Scots	6	Carden, John Rutter, Offg. Wing Officer 15 Bengal Infantry	4 Sept.89	3 Jan. 91
West Yorkshire Regiment	6	Champain, Hugh F. Bateman, Offg. Adjutant 1 Bn.1 Goorkhas	21 Sept. 89	3 Jan. 91
3 Dragoon Guards	8	Holland-Prior, Pomeroy, Squad. Officer 13 Bengal Lancers	16 Nov. 87	14 Jan. 91
Lincolnshire Regiment	7	Money, Ernest Douglas, Wing Officer 1 Bn. 1 Goorkhas	9 May 88	14 Jan. 91
East Surrey Regiment	7	Smith, Guy de Herriez, Offg. Wing Officer 45 Bengal Inf.	8 Dec. 88	14 Jan. 91
Royal Fusiliers	6	Cummins, Harry Ashley Vane, Wing Officer 2 Inf. Hyd. Con.	21 Sept.89	15 Jan. 91
Liverpool Regiment	6	Young, Malcolm Græme, Wing Officer Meywar Bheel Corps	24 Apr. 89	16 Jan. 91
Liverpool Regiment	6	Cheyne, Reg. Edmonstone, Offg. Squad. Officer 8 Ben. Cav.	21 Sept.89	16 Jan. 91
Liverpool Regiment	6	Dallas, Alex. Egerton, Wing Officer 6 Punjab Infantry	21 Sept. 89	16 Jan. 91
Liverpool Regiment	6	Wardell, Warren Henry,[753] Wing Officer 39 Bengal Infantry	21 Dec. 89	16 Jan. 91
Inniskilling Fusiliers	7	West, Geo. W. Maxwell, Wing Officer 1 Bn. 3 Goorkhas	23 Mar. 89	5 Feb. 91
West Surrey Regiment	7	Travers, Robert Eaton, Offg. Wing Officer 2 Bn. 4 Goorkhas	23 Mar. 89	12 Feb. 91
Gloucestershire Regiment		Geoghegan, Francis Edw. Wing Officer 13 Bombay Infantry	23 Mar. 89	12 Feb. 91
Gloucestershire Regiment	6	West, Alex. Arthur, Wing Officer 5 Bombay Infantry	8 June 89	12 Feb. 91
Royal Artillery		Morris, Donald Ogilvy, Wing Officer 3 Inf. Hyd. Cont.	17 Feb. 88	17 Feb. 91
Northumberland Fusiliers	6	MacLean, Hector L. Stewart,[754] Wing Officer Corps of Guides	24 Apr. 89	17 Feb. 91
Sussex Regiment	7	Davis, Chas. M'Mullin, Wing Officer 24 Bengal Infantry	10 Nov. 88	18 Feb. 91
Worcestershire Regiment	6	Cassels, Gilbert Robert, Wing Officer 35 Bengal Infantry	24 Apr. 89	18 Feb. 91
Lancashire Fusiliers	6	Nuttall, Mansfield Elliot, Wing Officer 12 Bombay Infantry	27 May 89	27 Feb. 91
Worcestershire Regiment		Hannyngton, John Arth., Wing Officer 29 Bombay Infantry	8 June 89	2 Mar. 91
Lincolnshire Regiment		Baker, Cecil Norris, Wing Officer 2 Bengal Infantry	19 Sept.88	4 Mar. 91
Inniskilling Fusiliers	6	Lawrenson, Thomas G. P., Wing Officer 6 Madras Infantry	27 Nov. 89	8 Mar. 91
Warwickshire Regiment	6	Ewart, Chas. Geo. Edmundson, Squad. Officer 5 Bengal Cav.	10 Apr. 89	11 Mar. 91
East Lancashire Regiment		Amesbury, Wheaten L. R., Wing Officer 6 Bengal Infantry	10 Nov. 88	18 Mar. 91
East Lancashire Regiment	7	Hornby, Montague Leyland, Wing Officer 24 Bombay Inf.	30 Jan. 89	18 Mar. 91
East Lancashire Regiment	7	Bunbury, Wm. Clement Hanmer, Wing Officer 40 Ben. Inf.	30 Jan. 89	18 Mar. 91
N. Staffordshire Regiment		Lavie, Leslie J. Germaine, Wing Officer 20 Madras Infantry	23 Mar. 89	21 Mar. 91
N. Lancashire Regiment		Marriott, Leslie Hawthorne, Wing Officer 6 Madras Infantry	9 May 89	24 Mar. 91
Devonshire Regiment	6	Holman, Herb. Campbell,[755] Squad. Officer 16 Bengal Cav.	21 Sept. 89	25 Mar. 91
Bedfordshire Regiment	6	Samborne, Frederick Carey Stukeley Palmer, Officiating Wing Officer 13 Bengal Infantry	23 Oct. 89	25 Mar. 91
Devonshire Regiment	6	Field, Charles Douglas, Wing Officer 28 Madras Infantry	1 Mar. 90	25 Mar. 91
Highland Light Infantry	7	Brand, Herbert, Wing Officer 5 Bombay Infantry	23 Mar. 89	29 Mar. 91
East Yorkshire Regiment	7	Firth, Richard Anson, Wing Officer 10 Madras Infantry	8 Dec. 88	2 Apr. 91
Irish Regiment		Alexander, Arthur Vickers, Wing Officer 14 Madras Infantry	21 Dec. 89	5 Apr. 91
Welsh Fusiliers	6	Smith, William Frank,[756] Dep. Assist. Com. Gen. 2nd Class	21 Sept. 89	6 Apr. 91
Connaught Rangers	6	Keily, Edward Wm., Offg. Wing Officer 25 Madras Infantry	9 Nov. 89	7 Apr. 91
Wiltshire Regiment	7	Knox, Stuart Geo., Offg. Wing Officer Merwara Battalion	19 Sept. 88	14 Apr. 91
S. Staffordshire Regiment	6	Greig, Piercy, Wing Officer 27 Madras Infantry	9 Nov. 89	15 Apr. 91
Connaught Rangers	6	Hudson, Arthur Keith, Offg. Squad. Officer 17 Bengal Cav.	9 Nov. 89	15 Apr. 91
S. Staffordshire Regiment	6	Raven, Alex. Wm. Nicholas, Wing Officer 14 Madras Infantry	21 Dec. 89	15 Apr. 91
East Lancashire Regiment		Bethune, Hector, Wing Officer 32 Bengal Infantry	30 Jan. 89	28 Apr. 91
Irish Regiment	6	Ralph, Arthur Jeffreys, Wing Officer 7 Madras Infantry	8 June 89	29 Apr. 91
Irish Regiment		Beatty, Guy Arch. Hastings, Squad. Officer 9 Bengal Lancers	21 Dec. 89	29 Apr..91
Hampshire Regiment		Carleton, Henry Anthony, Offg. Wing Officer 31 Madras Inf.	24 Apr. 89	3 May 91
South Wales Borderers	7	Jones, Edm. Gunning, Offg. Wing Officer 16 Madras Inf.	10 Nov. 88	8 May 91
Royal Artillery		Thornhill, Clement Bensley, Cantonment Magist., Nowgong	4 Dec. 89	15 May 91
Devonshire Regiment	5	Morris, George Mortimer, Wing Officer 24 Madras Infantry	28 June 90	19 May 91
East Lancashire Regiment	6	Blair, Arthur Kennedy, Offg. Wing Officer 36 Bengal Inf.	9 Nov. 89	19 May 91
East Lancashire Regiment		King, Stewart William, Wing Officer 17 Bombay Infantry	21 Dec. 89	23 May 91
Royal Artillery		Reid, George Elliot, Offg. Squad. Officer 1 Madras Cavalry	15 Feb. 89	28 May 91
Scots Fusiliers	6	Kindersley, Maitland FitzRoy, Squad. Officer 11 Ben. Lan.	6 July 89	30 May 91
Scots Fusiliers	7	Nethersole, Alfred Ralph,[758] Wing Officer 27 Madras Infantry	2 Aug. 88	3 June 91
Hampshire Regiment	7	Cassels, Kenneth Scougall, Wing Officer 43 Bengal Infantry	23 Oct. 89	12 June 91
Dublin Fusiliers	7	Grimshaw, Ewing Wrigley, Wing Officer 24 Madras Infantry	10 Nov. 88	14 June 91
1 Dragoon Guards	6	Cooke, Samuel Arthur, Squadron Officer 2 C. I. Horse	1 Mar. 90	14 June 91
N. Lancashire Regiment	6	Glasfurd, Alex. Inglis R., Wing Officer 4 Inf. Hyd. Cont.	29 Mar. 90	17 June 91
Border Regiment	6	Paul, Robert Sears, Wing Officer 26 Bombay Infantry	30 Jan. 89	23 June 91
2 Dragoon Guards	7	Alexander, James Leslie, Squad. Officer 2 Bombay Cavalry	19 Sept.88	24 June 91
Sussex Regiment	6	MacTier, Henry Mackinnon, Wing Officer 39 Bengal Inf.	21 Dec. 89	2 July 91
7 Dragoon Guards	6	Young, Wilfred Edward, Squad. Officer 10 Bengal Lancers	21 Sept. 89	4 July 91
Royal Fusiliers	8	Flood, Fred. Frere Solly, Wing Officer 29 Bengal Infantry	14 Sept.87	7 July 91
Bedfordshire Regiment	6	Garratt, Harry Sumner, Wing Officer 26 Bombay Infantry	9 Nov. 89	10 July 91
Royal Artillery	7	Cobbe, Henry Hercules, Squadron Officer 13 Bengal Lancers	27 July 88	11 July 91
Lancaster Regiment	7	Raymond, Radcliffe Herb., Offg. Squad. Officer, 4 Bom. Cav.	21 Sept.89	14 July 91
Manchester Regiment	6	Harington, Henry Andrew, Wing Officer 26 Bengal Infantry	9 Nov. 89	14 July 91
Middlesex Regiment		Moberly, Guy, Wing Officer 8 Madras Infantry	21 Sept.89	15 July 91
Suffolk Regiment	6	Carter, Charles Murray, Offg. Wing Officer 14 Bengal Inf.	23 Oct. 89	18 July 91
Worcestershire Regiment	6	Harold, Charles Frederick, Wing Officer 27 Bombay Inf.	21 Sept. 89	19 July 91
Suffolk Regiment	6	Smith, Frederic Vincent, Offg. Squad. Officer 4 Ben. Cav.	15 May 89	27 July 91
Hampshire Regiment	6	Brown, Walter Medlicott, Wing Officer 1 Bn. 3 Goorkhas	21 Dec. 89	26 July 91
1 Dragoon Guards	7	Morris, Robert Lee, Offg. Squadron Officer 3 Bengal Cavalry	30 Jan. 89	31 July 91
Bedfordshire Regiment		Rolland, George Murray, Wing Officer 1 Bombay Infantry.	9 Nov. 89	2 Aug. 91
N. Lancashire Regiment	6	Hawks, Fred. Welman, Dep. Assist. Com. Gen. 2nd Class	21 Sept.89	4 Aug. 91
18 Hussars		Gaussen, Charles Louis, Aide de Camp to Lt. Gov. of Bengal	23 Oct. 89	5 Aug. 91
Dublin Fusiliers	6	Pock, John Herbert, Wing Officer 27 Bombay Infantry	24 Apr. 89	10 Aug. 91
Irish Regiment	5	O'Reilly, Charles Myles, Offg. Wing Officer 3 Madras Inf.	3 May 90	13 Aug. 91
Royal Artillery	6	Fisher, Wm. Annesley, Offg. Squad. Officer 3 Bombay Cav.	27 July 89	14 Aug. 91
Norfolk Regiment	6	Palcologus, Wm. Constantine, Wing Officer 28 Bengal Inf.	23 Mar. 89	14 Aug. 91
Leinster Regiment	6	Lyon, John Wilmot Harley, Wing Officer 25 Madras Infantry	6 July 89	22 Aug. 91
Border Regiment	6	Maclachlan, Thomas Robertson, Wing Officer 40 Bengal Inf.	23 Mar. 89	26 Aug. 91
Worcestershire Regiment	6	Drever, Thomas Ian, Wing Officer 25 Madras Infantry	9 Nov. 89	29 Aug. 91
K. O. Scottish Borderers	6	Cumberlege, Chas. John, Wing Officer 23 Bombay Infantry	9 Nov. 89	29 Aug. 91
Wiltshire Regiment	5	Gough, Hugh A. Keppel, Offg. Wing Officer 2 Bn. 2 Goorkhas.	4 June 90	31 Aug. 91
Scottish Rifles		Hocken, Chas. Aug. Fred., Offg. Squad. Officer 5 Bom. Cav.	1 Mar. 90	1 Sept. 91
Connaught Rangers	6	Bedford, Jas. Blackburn, Offg. Squad. Officer 14 Ben. Lancers	24 Apr. 89	4 Sept. 91
East Kent Regiment	5	Macpherson, Neil, Offg. Wing Officer 1 Bn. 2 Goorkhas	4 June 90	14 Sept. 91
Welsh Fusiliers	6	Johnson, Clarence A. K.,[760] Offg. Squad. Officer 1 Ben. Cav.	21 Sept.89	15 Sept. 91

Indian Staff Corps.

Last Regiment.	Yrs. Serv.	LIEUTENANTS.	2nd LIEUT.	LIEUT.
Lancashire Fusiliers	6	Lane, Frank Macdonald, Wing Officer 28 Bombay Infantry	1 Mar. 90	20 Sept. 91
West Yorkshire Regiment	5	Harrison, Wm. Chris. Warde, Wing Officer 7 Madras Inf.	28 June 90	20 Sept. 91
Suffolk Regiment	5	Perry, George Edgar John, Wing Officer 6 Inf. Hyd. Cont.	3 May 90	21 Sept. 91
Leinster Regiment	6	Brownlow, d'Arcy Charles, Wing Officer 21 Bengal Infantry	21 Sept. 89	23 Sept 91
Northumberland Fusiliers	5	Vivian, Arthur Granville, Offg. Squad. Officer 5 Punjab Cav.	3 May 90	25 Sept. 91
Yorkshire Regiment	5	Clay, Spencer, Offg. Wing Officer Meywar Bheel Corps	3 May 90	26 Sept. 91
Oxford Light Infantry	7	Moberley, Fred. Jas.,[761] DSO. Wing Officer 37 Bengal Inf.	22 Aug. 88	4 Oct. 91
Royal Artillery		Crocker, Alfred Gilbert, Squad. Officer 2 Punjab Cavalry	15 Feb. 89	5 Oct. 91
Irish Fusiliers	6	Gregory, Charles Levinge, Offg. Squad. Officer 19 Ben. Lan.	9 Nov. 89	7 Oct. 91
Lancaster Regiment		Fagan, Lucius Emilius, Wing Officer 6 Madras Infantry	21 Dec. 89	9 Oct. 91
Royal Scots	7	Ferguson-Davie, Arthur Fras., Wing Officer 3 Sikh Infantry	22 Aug. 88	12 Oct. 91
Northamptonshire Regt.	6	Alexander, Chas. Henry, Squad. Officer 6 Bombay Cavalry	29 Mar. 90	12 Oct. 91
S. Lancashire Regiment	6	Ward, Cyril Harding, Offg. Wing Officer 4 Bengal Infantry	21 Dec. 89	13 Oct. 91
Connaught Rangers	6	Pritchard, Aubrey Gordon, Squad. Officer 2 Ben. Lancers	21 Dec. 89	13 Oct. 91
Derbyshire Regiment	6	Wheeler, John Charles Massy, Wing Officer 28 Bengal Inf.	15 Jan. 90	15 Oct. 91
Connaught Rangers	6	Roe, Bernhard Oswald, Assist. Commr, 2nd Gr., Hoshiarpore	9 Nov. 89	20 Oct. 91
Norfolk Regiment	6	Becher, George Arthur, Squad. Officer 8 Bengal Cavalry	27 Apr. 89	21 Oct. 91
Manchester Regiment	6	Finnis, John Fortescue, Offg. Wing Officer 3 Sikh Infantry	21 Dec. 89	21 Oct. 91
East Lancashire Regiment	5	O'Meara, Chas. Albert Edmond, Offg. Wing Officer 2 Ben. Inf.	17 Jan. 91	21 Oct. 91
Connaught Rangers		Nicholson, Wm. Cumberland, Wing Officer 3 Madras Inf.	21 Dec. 89	31 Oct. 91
Connaught Rangers	6	Poole, Wm. Thos. Conway, Offg. Wing Officer 8 Bengal Inf.	1 Mar. 90	31 Oct. 91
South Wales Borderers	5	Basevi, Wm. Henry Francis, Wing Officer 31 Madras Inf.	22 Aug. 88	3 Nov. 91
Norfolk Regiment		Lloyd, John Herbert, Wing Officer 2 Bombay Infantry	9 Nov. 89	10 Nov. 91
Irish Regiment	6	Edwardes, John Grahame, Offg. Wing Officer 1 Bn. 5 Goorkhas	29 Nov. 90	24 Nov. 91
K. O. Scottish Borderers	5	Carwithen, Edw. Terry, Offg. Wing Officer Erinpoora Irregular Force	4 June 90	26 Nov. 91
Middlesex Regiment	5	Bliss, Jas. Arthur, Wing Officer 21 Madras Infantry	3 May 90	4 Dec. 91
Dublin Fusiliers	5	Barratt, Ernest Bird, Wing Officer 23 Madras Infantry	28 June 90	7 Dec. 91
S. Staffordshire Regiment	5	Creagh, Edward Cottingham, Wing Officer 4 Punjab Inf.	3 May 90	9 Dec. 91
West Yorkshire Regiment		Colan, Wm. Robert Boyle, Wing Officer 8 Madras Infantry	3 May 90	14 Dec. 91
East Surrey Regiment	6	Rawlins, Arthur Kennedy, Wing Officer 24 Bengal Infantry	21 Dec. 89	15 Dec. 91
Border Regiment		Carnegy, Richard Lloyd, Wing Officer 9 Bengal Infantry	8 June 89	17 Dec. 91
Warwickshire Regiment	5	Johnson, Chas. Rich., Offg. Wing Officer 1 Bn. 5 Goorkhas	9 Nov. 89	18 Dec. 91
S. Lancashire Regiment	6	Lovell, Arthur Neville, Offg.Squad. Officer 2 Lan.Hyd. Cont.	21 Dec. 89	21 Dec. 91
Warwickshire Regiment	5	Norman, Walter Henry,[762] Squad. Officer 11 Bengal Lancers	8 Oct. 90	22 Dec. 91
Cheshire Regiment	6	Nightingale, Manners R. W., Wing Officer 2 Bn. 5 Goorkhas	1 Mar. 90	23 Dec. 91
Sussex Regiment		Elliott, Alfred Charles, Assist. Commr., 3rd Grade, Delhi	9 Apr. 90	31 Dec. 91
Leinster Regiment	5	Kelly, George Henry F., Offg. Wing Officer 23 Bengal Inf.	1 Mar. 90	12 Jan. 92
South Wales Borderers	6	Bousfield, Edmund Emerson, Wing Officer 15 Madras Inf.	21 Sept. 89	13 Jan. 92
Wiltshire Regiment	5	Sanford, Geo. Batthyany, Offg. Wing Officer 2 Bn. 4 Goorkhas	8 Oct. 90	17 Jan. 92
West Yorkshire Regiment	6	Cullen, Ernest Henry Scott, Offg. Wing Officer 32 Ben. Inf.	1 Mar. 90	21 Jan. 92
Liverpool Regiment	5	Hickie, William Bradley, Offg. Wing Officer 28 Bengal Inf.	29 Oct. 90	23 Jan. 92
Hampshire Regiment	5	Tillard, Arthur Basil, Offg. Wing Officer 1 Bn. 3 Goorkhas	24 Dec. 90	30 Jan. 92
Royal Artillery	5	Pottinger, Robert Southey, Wing Officer 19 Bombay Inf.	27 July 89	4 Feb. 92
Border Regiment	6	Hay, Lenox Theobald, Squadron Officer 5 Bengal Cavalry	9 Nov. 89	5 Feb. 92
Bedfordshire Regiment	5	Stevenson, William Fred. Wing Officer 23 Bombay Infantry	29 Oct. 90	6 Feb. 92
Seaforth Highlanders	6	Ketchen, Sotheby Douglas Brodie,[763] Officiating Wing Officer 1 Bn. 5 Goorkhas	1 Mar. 90	11 Feb. 92
Royal Artillery	7	Barnes, Ernest, Squadron Officer 2 Punjab Cavalry	15 Feb. 89	15 Feb. 92
Royal Artillery	7	Parsons, Fred. Chas. Alf., Assist. Comdt. Burmah Mil. Police	15 Feb. 89	15 Feb. 92
Scottish Rifles	6	Davis, Gronow John, Offg. Wing Officer 24 Bengal Infantry	1 Mar. 90	16 Feb. 92
Durham Light Infantry	6	Young, David Coley, Offg. Wing Officer 1 Bn. 4 Goorkhas	21 Sept. 89	17 Feb. 92
Middlesex Regiment		Bailey, Arthur Wellesley, Wing Officer 38 Bengal Infantry	16 Apr. 90	17 Feb. 92
Manchester Regiment	6	Thomas, Frederick Wm., Offg. Wing Officer 26 Madras Inf.	1 Mar. 90	19 Feb. 92
Derbyshire Regiment	6	Rattray, Haldane Burney, Offg. Wing Officer 45 Bengal Inf.	1 Mar. 90	24 Feb. 92
Lancashire Fusiliers	5	Moore, George D. M., Wing Officer 28 Bombay Infantry	3 May 90	1 Mar. 92
Oxford Light Infantry	7	Drage, Godfrey, Offg. Wing Officer 30 Madras Infantry	23 Mar. 89	2 Mar. 92
Lincolnshire Regiment		Byers, Cyril Bertram, Wing Officer 12 Bengal Infantry	15 May 89	2 Mar. 92
Royal Fusiliers	5	Young, Henry Geo., Squadron Officer 10 Bengal Lancers	8 Oct. 90	2 Mar. 92
South Wales Borderers	5	Cobbe, Alex. Stanhope, Offg. Wing Officer 32 Bengal Inf.	21 Sept. 89	4 Mar. 92
Norfolk Regiment	5	Goldthorp, Fras. Herbert, Offg. Squad. Officer 3 Punjab Cav.	28 June 90	4 Mar. 92
Inniskilling Fusiliers	5	Nangle, Kenlis Edward, Wing Officer 3 Inf. Hyd. Cont.	8 Oct. 90	5 Mar. 92
Lancashire Fusiliers	5	Bryce, David Greig, Offg. Wing Officer 16 Madras Infantry	28 June 90	7 Mar. 92
Royal Artillery	6	Lang, Ewen Montgomery, Offg. Qr. Mr. 1 Bn. 1 Goorkhas	27 July 89	9 Mar. 92
Worcestershire Regiment	5	Wooldridge, H. Cheselden, Wing Officer 9 Bombay Infantry	26 Apr. 90	9 Mar. 92
Lincolnshire Regiment	6	Battye, Richmond Moffat, Squad. Officer 6 Bengal Cavalry	27 Nov. 89	10 Mar. 92
Lincolnshire Regiment	6	Peck, Arthur Wharton, Squadron Officer 2 Punjab Cavalry	1 Mar. 90	10 Mar. 92
Wiltshire Regiment	5	Ross, Fleetwood George Campbell	9 July 90	14 Mar. 92
N. Lancashire Regiment	5	Greig, William Best, Wing Officer 22 Madras Infantry	29 Oct. 90	16 Mar. 92
East Lancashire Regiment	5	Browne, Edgar Thornburgh, Offg.Wing Officer 6 Mad. Inf.	4 Feb. 91	27 Mar. 92
Bedfordshire Regiment	5	Kennedy, Jas. Robt., Wing Officer 3 Inf. Hyd. Cont.	9 Nov. 89	29 Mar. 92
Lincolnshire Regiment	6	Winter, Clifford Boardman, Wing Officer 25 Bengal Inf.	1 Mar. 90	30 Mar. 92
Munster Fusiliers	5	Walker, Francis Spring, Wing Officer 22 Bombay Infantry	29 Mar. 90	1 Apr. 92
Bedford Regiment	6	Mackenzie, Charles, Squadron Officer 13 Bengal Lancers	21 Dec. 89	5 Apr. 92
Munster Fusiliers	6	Browning, Theodore Charles, Wing Officer 2 Inf. Hyd. Cont.	29 Mar. 90	5 Apr. 92
King's Own Scottish Bord.	5	Ormiston, Thomas Lane, Wing Officer 24 Madras Infantry	8 Oct. 90	5 Apr. 92
Munster Fusiliers	5	Newell, Herbert Andrews, Wing Officer 28 Madras Infantry	29 Nov. 90	5 Apr. 92
Middlesex Regiment	5	Berthon, Henry Warwick, Wing Officer 5 Bombay Infantry	8 Oct. 90	14 Apr. 92
21 Hussars	7	da Costa, Oscar Michael John, Squad. Officer 5 Bombay Cav.	30 Jan. 89	15 Apr. 92
Suffolk Regiment	5	Beville, Harry G. P., Offg. Wing Officer 5 Inf. Hyd. Cont.	9 Nov. 89	15 Apr. 92
Berkshire Regiment	5	Ward, George Louis Stuart, Wing Officer 44 Bengal Inf.	3 May 90	16 Apr. 92
Inniskilling Fusiliers	5	Kennedy, William Magill, Assist. Commissioner, Assam	28 June 90	21 Apr. 92
Gloucestershire Regiment	5	Jacob, Arthur Leslie, Wing Officer 30 Bombay Infantry	24 Mar. 91	21 Apr. 92
Somerset Light Infantry	5	Ross, Harry, Wing Officer 7 Bombay Infantry	31 May 90	24 Apr. 92
Derbyshire Regiment	6	Beacon, Henry Cecil, Wing Officer 17 Madras Infantry	1 Mar. 90	1 May 92
Oxford Light Infantry	6	Prentis, Walter Sladen, Wing Officer 29 Madras Infantry	21 Sept. 89	2 May 92
Norfolk Regiment	5	Scott, Herbert Courteney, Wing Officer 11 Madras Infantry	29 Oct. 90	2 May 92
Yorkshire Light Infantry	5	Lukin, R. C. Wellesley, Offg. Squad. Officer 9 Bengal Lanc.	3 May 90	11 May 92
Northumberland Fusiliers	5	Lawson, Oswald Head, Offg. Wing Officer 26 Bengal Inf.	3 May 90	11 May 92
Middlesex Regiment	5	Prideaux, Francis Beville, Offg. Wing Officer 31 Bengal Inf.	3 May 90	11 May 92
East Surrey Regiment	5	Nicholas, Stephen Henry Edm. Wing Officer 14 Mad. Cont.	8 Oct. 90	19 May 92
West Surrey Regiment	5	Langtry, Hy. Vivian Montague, Offg.WingOfficer 28 Bom. Inf.	4 Feb. 91	21 May 92
Northumberland Fusiliers	5	Drummond, Arthur B., Offg. Wing Officer 39 Bengal Inf.	3 May 90	23 May 92
7 Dragoon Guards	5	Smith, Alick Le Fleming, Offg. Squad.Officer 4 Bengal Cav.	3 Dec. 90	24 May 92

Indian Staff Corps.

Last Regiment.	Yrs. Serv.	LIEUTENANTS.	2nd LIEUT.	LIEUT.
Somerset Light Infantry	5	Davidson, Sisley Richard, Offg. Wing Officer 27 Madras Inf.	16 Apr. 90	3 June 92
Munster Fusilierrs	5	Hill, Harold Charles, Wing Officer 10 Bombay Infantry	29 Oct. 90	3 June 92
Gloucestershire Regiment	5	Eastwood, Robt. John Camac, Wing Officer 30 Bom. Inf.	11 Mar. 91	3 June 92
Bedfordshire Regiment	6	Jones, Leslie Cockburn,764 Offg. Squad. Officer 7 Ben. Cav.	1 Mar. 90	11 June 92
Dublin Fusiliers	5	Hurley, Henry Kellett, Offg. Wing Officer 14 Bengal Inf.	16 July 90	13 June 92
Somerset Light Infantry	6	Kirkpatrick, Edward, Offg. Wing Officer 2 Punjab Infantry	1 Mar. 90	14 June 92
Lancashire Fusiliers	5	French, Wm. Cotton, Offg. Wing Officer 2 Bn. 3 Goorkhas	29 Oct. 90	15 June 92
Yorkshire Light Infantry	5	Phillips, Richard Sylvester, Offg. Wing Officer 2 Sikh Inf.	28 June 90	16 June 92
Cheshire Regiment	5	Cooke, Hugh Wm. Fothergill, Wing Officer 24 Bengal Inf.	4 Mar. 91	22 June 92
N. Lancashire Regiment	5	Godfrey, Charles, Offg. Wing Officer 7 Bombay Infantry	2 May 91	26 June 92
West Yorkshire Regiment	5	Musgrave, Walter Wm. F.C., Offg. Wing Officer 12 Mad. Inf.	8 Oct. 90	27 June 92
South Wales Borderers	5	Malden, Travers Edw., Wing Officer 17 Bengal Infantry	29 Oct. 90	1 July 92
Liverpool Regiment	5	Pocock, Philip Fredk., Wing Officer 19 Bombay Infantry	25 Mar. 91	6 July 92
Durham Light Infantry	5	Bridges, Arthur Holroyd, Offg. Wing Officer 9 Bombay Inf.	25 Mar. 91	8 July 92
East Surrey Regiment	5	Haydon, William Pitt, Wing Officer 22 Bombay Infantry	29 Oct. 90	12 July 92
Bedfordshire Regiment	5	Strange, Arthur James, Offg. Wing Officer 42 Bengal Inf.	28 June 90	19 July 92
Derbyshire Regiment	5	Gabbett, Alex. Cecil, Offg. Wing Officer 28 Madras Inf.	8 Oct. 90	21 July 92
Derbyshire Regiment	5	Leslie, Philip Norman, Offg. Squad. Officer 4 Lan. Hyd. Cont.	29 Nov. 90	21 July 92
Lancashire Fusiliers	5	Hancock, Fras. De Berckem, Wing Officer 23 Bombay Inf.	4 Mar. 91	25 July 92
King's Own Scottish Bord.	6	Swan, John Stewart, Offg. Wing Officer 1 Bengal Infantry	21 Dec. 89	27 July 92
Scottish Rifles	5	Milne, James William, Wing Officer 22 Madras Infantry	4 Mar. 91	31 July 92
King's Own Scottish Bord.	6	Spens, Alex. Hieron O., Offg. Squad. Officer 2 C. I. Horse	1 Mar. 90	3 Aug. 92
Welsh Fusiliers	5	Tarver, Alex. Leigh, Wing Officer 24 Bombay Infantry	29 Oct. 90	6 Aug. 92
Lincolnshire Regiment	5	Riddell, Henry James, Offg. Wing Officer 4 Bengal Inf.	8 Oct. 90	9 Aug. 92
Hampshire Regiment	5	Scott, Hopton Arthur, Wing Officer 11 Madras Infantry	4 Feb. 91	10 Aug. 92
Middlesex Regiment	5	Bailey, Gilbert, Wing Officer 4 Bombay Infantry	29 Oct. 90	17 Aug. 92
King's Royal Rifles	5	M'Leod, Torquil John,765 Offg. Wing Officer 2 Bn. 1 Goorkhas	29 Oct. 90	26 Aug. 92
Cheshire Regiment	5	Butler, Alex. Hazelwood, Offg. Wing Officer 5 Madras Inf.	4 Feb. 91	28 Aug. 92
Norfolk Regiment	5	Barclay, Patrick Chas. R., Offg. Wing Officer 20 Bom. Inf.	29 Nov. 90	2 Sept. 92
Scottish Rifles	5	Guthrie-Smith, W. Marshall, Offg. Wing Officer 10 Mad. Inf.	4 Mar. 91	3 Sept. 92
3 Dragoon Guards	6	Swinhoe, Edmund Arthur, Offg. Squad. Officer 2 Ben. Lanc.	23 Oct. 89	5 Sept. 92
Munster Fusiliers	5	Bourne, Walter Fitzgerald, Wing Officer 10 Bombay Inf.	29 Oct. 90	6 Sept. 92
Devonshire Regiment	5	Ayerst, Chas. Egerton, Offg. Wing Officer 2 Bombay Inf.	8 Oct. 90	7 Sept. 92
Devonshire Regiment	5	Chisholm, John H. G. Seton, Offg. Squad. Officer 3 Ben. Cav.	29 Oct. 90	7 Sept. 92
Liverpool Regiment	5	Teed, Arthur S. Hollond, Offg. Wing Officer 12 Bengal Inf	29 Nov. 90	13 Sept. 92
Duke of Cornwall's Lt. Inf.	4	Tregear, Vincent F. W., Offg. Wing Officer 4 Inf. Hyd. Cont.	25 May 91	24 Sept. 92
West Surrey Regiment	5	Baillie, Hubert, Offg. Wing Officer 43 Bengal Infantry	7 Jan. 91	29 Sept. 92
Connaught Rangers	6	Kemball, Alick Gurdon, Offg. Wing Officer 23 Bengal Inf.	1 Mav. 90	8 Oct. 92
Gloucestershire Regiment	4	Burn, George Callander, Wing Officer 13 Madras Infantry	25 July 91	11 Oct. 92
Lincolnshire Regiment	4	Irvine, Andrew Alex., Offg. Wing Officer 3 Bengal Inf.	17 June 91	12 Oct. 92
Dorsetshire Regiment	5	Tristram, Charles Edward, Wing Officer 29 Madras Inf.	25 Mar. 91	16 Oct. 92
Gloucestershire Regt.	4	Smith, Fred. Manners, Offg. Wing Officer 1 Bengal Inf.	2 May 91	19 Oct. 92
Highland Light Infantry	5	Campbell, Ian Hamilton, Offg. Squad. Officer 7 Bengal Cav.	3 Sept. 90	26 Oct. 92
Sussex Regiment	5	Buck, Cecil Henry, Offg. Squad. Officer 6 Bengal Cavalry	25 Mar. 91	26 Oct. 92
West Kent Regiment	5	Rouse, Arch. Henry T., Offg. Wing Officer 1 Madras Inf.	28 June 90	30 Oct. 92
York and Lancaster Regt.	5	Bidwell, Reginald Frank, Wing Officer 20 Madras Infantry	28 June 90	31 Oct. 92
Shropshire Light Infantry	5	Hole, Henry Lewis, Offg. Wing Officer 19 Madras Infantry	3 May 90	2 Nov. 92
Liverpool Regiment	4	Jackson, Keith Hungerford, Offg. Squad. Officer 19 Ben. Lan.	17 June 91	6 Nov. 92
Liverpool Regiment	4	Barlow, Murray H. P., Offg. Wing Officer 2 Bn. 5 Goorkhas	10 Oct. 91	10 Nov. 92
Irish Regiment	4	Orr, Sutherland Alex. M., Offg. Squad. Officer 2 Lan. Hyd. Cont.	10 Oct. 91	12 Nov. 92
7 Dragoon Guards	4	Henderson, Maxwell H., Squad. Officer 4 Lanc. Hyd. Cont.	4 Mar. 91	17 Nov. 92
Royal Fusiliers	4	Stephen, Arthur Sandeman, Offg. Wing Officer 36 Ben. Inf.	25 Mar. 91	18 Nov. 92
Worcestershire Regt.	4	Fox, Lionel Whitelaw, Offg. Wing Officer 21 Madras Inf.	2 May 91	23 Nov. 92
Lancashire Fusiliers	4	M'Taggart, Wm. A. T., Offg. Squad. Officer 1 Bombay Lan.	7 Nov. 91	10 Dec. 92
Lancashire Fusiliers	4	Sargent, Hy. Gresham Forbes, Wing Officer 14 Bom. Inf.	25 May 91	14 Dec. 92
West Riding Regiment	4	Grimley, Walter Macdonnell, Offg. Wing Officer 11 Ben. Inf.	3 May 90	17 Dec. 92
Duke of Cornwall's Lt. Inf.	5	Orman, Frank Leslie,767 Offg. Wing Officer 10 Madras Inf.	3 May 90	6 Jan. 93
Royal Scots	4	Preston, George Allen, Offg. Wing Officer 40 Bengal Inf.	9 Sept. 91	14 Jan. 93
South Wales Borderers	4	Lindsay, Alex. Bertram, Offg. Wing Officer 1 Bn. 2 Goorkhas	7 Nov. 91	18 Jan. 93
East Surrey Regiment	5	James, Fras. Polglase, Offg. Wing Officer 21 Bengal Inf.	28 Feb. 91	1 Feb. 93
King's Royal Rifles	5	Prevost, George Herbert,768 Wing Officer 25 Bombay Inf.	28 June 90	7 Feb. 93
Wiltshire Regiment	5	Ommanney, A. Hammond, Offg. Wing Officer Corps of Guides	5 Dec. 91	13 Feb. 93
Royal Artillery	5	Crawford, John Halket, Offg. Squad. Officer 2 Bom. Lan.	1 Nov. 90	3 Mar. 93
Oxford Light Infantry	4	Stewart, Arch. Campbell, Offg. Squad. Officer Corps of Guides	27 Jan. 92	21 Mar. 93
West Kent Regiment	5	Riddell, Henry Vansittart, Offg. Wing Officer 4 Bom Inf.	3 May 90	5 Apr. 93
Middlesex Regiment	4	Macpherson, Arch. Duncan. Offg. Squad. Officer 2 Punjab Cav.	7 Nov. 91	6 Apr. 93
N. Lancashire Regiment	4	Mitchell, Wilfrid James, Offg. Wing Officer 24 Bombay Inf.	28 Oct. 91	11 Apr. 93
E. Lancashire Regiment	4	Downes, Oliver Longcroft, Offg. Squad. Officer 7 Bom. Lan.	5 Dec. 91	11 Apr. 93
Norfolk Regiment	5	Thomson, Alex. Hy. Gouger, Offg. Wing Officer 20 Ben. Inf.	29 Nov. 90	14 Apr. 93
King's Own Scottish Bord.	4	Browne, Herbert J. P., Offg. Wing Officer 2 Bn. 5 Goorkhas	5 Dec. 91	14 Apr. 93
Suffolk Regiment	5	Rice, Harry Arthur H., Offg. Wing Officer 1 Sikh Infantry	4 Feb. 91	22 Apr. 93
Norfolk Regiment	4	Fenn, Edwin H. McB., Offg. Squad. Officer 2 Bombay Lan.	5 Dec. 91	22 Apr. 93
Inniskilling Fusiliers	5	Moores, Clarence Mann, Offg. Wing Officer 27 Bombay Inf.	17 Jan. 91	30 Apr. 93
Durham Light Infantry	4	Loring, Charles Buxton, Offg. Squad. Officer 7 Bombay Lan.	7 Nov. 91	6 May 93
18 Hussars	4	Claridge, Percy S. F., Offg. Squad. Officer 3 Madras Lan.	5 Dec. 91	12 May 93
Northamptonshire Regt.	5	Crawford, Arthur Gossett, Offg. Wing Officer 24 Mad. Inf.	29 Nov. 90	13 May 93
Inniskilling Fusiliers	5	Preston, Eyre Evans, Offg. Wing Officer 16 Bombay Inf.	25 July 91	16 May 93
King's Own Scottish Bord.	4	Pennington, Wm. Herbert, Offg. Squad. Officer 12 Ben. Cav.	22 Feb. 91	18 May 93
Welsh Regiment	4	Scott, William, Offg. Wing Officer 12 Bombay Infantry	7 Nov. 91	24 May 93
Northamptonshire Regt.	4	Cox, Arthur Ditmas, Offg. Wing Officer 11 Madras Inf.	29 Oct. 90	29 May 93
Leinster Regiment	4	Kirkwood, Andrew Torton, Wing Officer 29 Mad. Inf.	9 Sept. 91	15 June 93
Bedfordshire Regiment	5	Minchin, Alfred Beckett,769 Wing Officer 25 Bengal Inf.	4 Mar. 91	28 June 93
N. Lancashire Regiment	4	Codrington, Hopton Osbert, Offg. Wing Officer 4 Bom. Inf.	29 Jan. 92	3 July 93
Yorkshire Light Infantry	4	Cotten, William Lewis, Wing Officer 5 Inf. Hyd. Cont.	27 Jan. 92	12 July 93
Middlesex Regiment	4	Jackson, Herbert Wm., Offg. Wing Officer 26 Madras Inf.	5 Dec. 91	23 Aug. 93
Irish Rifles	4	Knox, Alf. Wm. Fortescue, Offg. Wing Officer 19 Mad. Inf.	2 May 91	18 Nov. 93
Lancashire Fusiliers	3	Dundas, Patrick Henry, Wing Officer 6 Bengal Infantry	3 Sept. 92	3 Dec. 94
Northamptonshire Regt.	3	Johnes, Cyril Ivo Fyers O., Offg. Squad. Officer 1 Madras Lan.	3 Sept. 92	3 Dec. 94
Hampshire Regiment	3	Cadell, James Dalmahoy, Offg. Wing Officer 2 C. I. Horse	3 Sept. 92	3 Dec. 94
Durham Light Infantry	3	Abbey, W. Bulmer Tait, Offg. Wing Officer 7 Bombay Lan.	3 Sept. 92	3 Dec. 94
Northamptonshire Regt.	3	Hughes, John Edward, Offg. Squad. Officer 2 Madras Lan.	3 Sept. 92	3 Dec. 94
Lancashire Fusiliers	3	Stewart, Walter FitzAlan, Offg. Wing Officer 10 Bombay Inf.	3 Sept. 92	3 Dec. 94
Border Regiment	3	Brodhurst, Bernard M. L., Offg. Wing Officer 1 Bn. 4 Goorkhas	3 Sept. 92	3 Dec. 94
Hampshire Regiment	3	Corlett, John Stebbing, Offg. Squad. Officer 13 Bengal Lan.	3 Sept. 92	3 Dec. 94

Indian Staff Corps.

Last Regiment.	Yrs.' Serv.	LIEUTENANTS.	2ndLIEUT.	LIEUT.
2 Dragoon Guards............	3	Ricketts, Robt. Lumsden, Offg. Squad. Officer 10 Bengal Lan.	3 Sept. 92	3 Dec., 94
Durham Light Infantry	3	Parker, Geo. Marcus Godfrey, Wing Officer 14 Bombay Inf.	3 Sept. 92	3 Dec. 94
Northamptonshire Regt......	3	Harbord, Cyril Rodney, Wing Officer 5 Inf. Hyderabad Cont.	3 Sept., 92	3 Dec. 94
Suffolk Regiment	3	Pratt, E. G. W. Offg. Wing Officer 3 Inf. Hyderabad Cont...	3 Sept. 92	3 Dec. 94
West Kent Regiment	3	Hall, Robt. Macpherson, Offg. Squad. Officer 13 Bengal Lan.	3 Sept. 92	3 Dec. 94
Manchester Regiment.........	3	Stewart, John Henry Keith, Offg. Wing Officer 39 BengalInf.	3 Sept. 92	3 Dec. 94
		SECOND LIEUTENANTS.		2ndLIEUT.
Suffolk Regiment	3	Magrath, Beauchamp Henry B., Offg. Wing Officer 16 Madras Infantry		3 Sept. 92
Bedfordshire Regiment	3	Rice, Sheridan Knowles B., Offg. Wing Officer 35 Bengal Infantry......		3 Sept. 92
Derbyshire Regiment	3	Corbyn, Edwyn C., Officiating Squadron Officer 18 Bengal Lancers...		3 Sept. 92
Leinster Regiment.............	3	Dudgeon, Ralph de Seton, Wing Officer 25 Bombay Infantry		3 Sept. 92
Lancashire Fusiliers	3	Watts, George A. Ross, Squadron Officer 2 Bombay Lancers..............		3 Sept. 92
East Lancashire Regt.	3	Barwell, Edward Egerton, Wing Officer 4 Punjab Infantry		3 Sept. 92
Welsh Fusiliers..................	3	Keen, William John, Officiating Wing Officer 37 Bengal Infantry		19 Nov. 92
West Yorkshire Regiment	3	Costello, Edmond William, Officiating Wing Officer 22 Bengal Infantry		19 Nov. 92
Irish Regiment	3	Browne, Leslie Swinton, Officiating Wing Officer 38 Bengal Infantry		19 Nov. 92
Welsh Regiment	3	Marshall, Henry Turnbull, Officiating Wing Officer 1 Bengal Infantry		19 Nov. 92
Manchester Regiment.........	3	Bolland, Theodore Julian, Officiating Wing Officer 16 Bengal Infantry		23 Nov. 92
Suffolk Regiment	3	Bogle, John Savile, Officiating Wing Officer Corps of Guides............		23 Nov. 92
West Kent Regiment	3	de Labilliere, Edw. G. D., Officiating Wing Officer 38 Bengal Infantry		23 Nov. 92
N. Lancashire Regiment ...	3	Krickenbeek, Ronald E. E., Officiating Wing Officer 4 Bombay Inf. ...		30 Nov. 92
Highland Light Infantry ...	3	Loch, Edward Campbell, Officiating Wing Officer 17 Bengal Infantry...		21 Jan. 93
Devonshire Regiment.........	3	Bowring, John Bellasis, Officiating Wing Officer 2 Punjab Infantry ...		28 Jan. 93
Cheshire Regiment	3	Elliott, Reginald W. S., Officiating Wing Officer 8 Madras Infantry ...		28 Jan. 93
Northamptonshire Regt......	3	Rice, Sydney Mervyn, Officiating Wing Officer 4 Madras Infantry ...		28 Jan. 93
Cheshire Regiment	3	Hope, Adrian Victor W., Officiating Wing Officer 27 Madras Infantry.		28 Jan. 93
Argyll and Suth. Highldrs.	3	Murray, Walter Godfrey Patrick, Officiating Wing Officer 29 Bengal Inf.		28 Jan. 93
Lancaster Regiment	3	Hewlett, Alan, Officiating Wing Officer 2 Bombay Lancers..............		28 Jan. 93
Yorkshire Light Infantry ...	3	Palin, Randle Harry, Wing Officer 30 Bombay Infantry		28 Jan. 93
Welsh Regiment	3	Knollys, Robert Walter E., Officiating Wing Officer 5 Punjab Infantry		28 Jan. 93
Welsh Regiment................	3	Byland, Sidney Veale, Officiating Wing Officer 5 Madras Infantry ...		28 Jan. 93
21 Hussars	3	Taylor, Edward Moore, Officiating Squadron Officer 2 Madras Lancers		28 Jan. 93
Yorkshire Light Infantry ...	3	Light, William Alfrey, Wing Officer 24 Bombay Infantry................		28 Jan. 93
Cheshire Regiment	3	Perrin, Charles Louis, Officiating Wing Officer 27 Madras Infantry ...		28 Jan. 93
Unattached List	3	Hawkes, Robert, Officiating Wing Officer 1 Bengal Infantry		28 Jan. 93
Northamptonshire Regt......	3	Scott-Elliot, Chas. Reg., Officiating Wing Officer 4 Madras Infantry ...		28 Jan. 93
King's Royal Rifles............	3	Wylie, Gordon Macleod, Offg. Wing Officer 2 Battalion 2 Goorkhas ...		28 Jan. 93
Essex Regiment.................	3	Peacock, Edward Barnes, Officiating Wing Officer 31 Bengal Infantry		28 Jan. 93
Welsh Regiment	2	Ross, Ralph James, Officiating Wing Officer 4 Madras Infantry		19 Apr. 93
Unattached List	2	Harrison, Arthur H. P., Offg. Wing Officer 33 Bengal Infantry		28 June 93
Unattached List	2	Davidson-Houston, Chas. E. D., Offg. Wing Officer 21 Madras Infantry		28 June 93
Unattached List	2	Holbrooke, Bernard F. R., Offg. Wing Officer 2 Bombay Infantry		28 June 93
Unattached List	2	Pritchard, Frank Vernon Leslie, Offg. Squad. Officer 1 Madras Lancers		9 Aug. 93

[1] Sir Peter Lumsden served with the force employed in various expeditions against the frontier tribes in 1852-56; served as D. A. Qr. Master General at the action of Punjhao 15th April 1852; at Nowadund, Pranghur, Iskakot, and operations in the Ranezai Valley in May 1852; against the Boree Afreedees in 1853; to Shah Mooseh Kheyl against the Mohmund Tribe in 1854; expedition against the Meranzaie tribe in April 1855, including the cavalry affair at Dursummund; against the Bussy Khelut Alum in November 1855; in Meranzaie and Kooran expeditions in November 1856 (received the special thanks of the Local and the Supreme Governments). Served in a Special Military Mission to Affghanistan in 1857-58, and received the thanks of the Supreme Government (Medal with Clasp). In July 1848 he joined the Gwalior Force under General R. Napier, and was present at Ranode and subsequent pursuit in Central India (mentioned in despatches, Medal). Accompanied the expedition to China in 1860, and was present at the actions of Sinho and Tangchow, assault and capture of the Taku Forts, and advance on Pekin (mentioned in despatches, Medal with two Clasps, and Brevet of Major). With Bhootan Field Force in 1865 (Clasp).

[2] General J. J. H. Gordon served in the Indian campaign of 1857-58 with the Jounpore Field Force attached to the 97th Regt.; at the actions of Nusrutpore, Chanda, Umeerpore, and Sultanpore, at the siege and capture of Lucknow and storming the Kaiser Bagh (Medal with Clasp); and from Sept. 1858 to April 1850 as Field Adjutant to Colonel Turner commanding the Troops on the Grand Trunk road, and Field Force during the operations in Shahabad, final attack on Jugdespore, action of Noandee, and subsequent pursuit (mentioned in despatches, Brevet of Major). Served with the Jowaki Afreedee Expedition in 1877-78 (mentioned in despatches, Medal with Clasp). Served in the Afghan war in 1878-79 in command of the Koorum Field Force and of the Koorum Brigade, and was present at the capture of the Peiwar Kotal (mentioned in despatches), and took part in the Zaimusht Expedition including the assault of Zawa (CB. Medal with Clasp). Also served in the Mahsood Wuzeeree Expedition in 1881 in command of the 2nd Column (mentioned in despatches, received the thanks of the Government of India). Served with the Burmese Expedition in 1886-87 in command of a Brigade and conducted the operations which succeeded in opening up the country between Manipore and Kendat (received the thanks of the Government of India, mentioned in despatches, Clasp).

[3] Sir Hugh Gough served as Adjutant of Hodson's Horse throughout the siege of Delhi (wounded). Commanded a Wing of the Regiment in the actions of Bolundshur, Allyghur, and Agra, relief of Lucknow by Lord Clyde, battle of Cawnpore, affairs at Seraighat and Khodagunge, siege and capture of Lucknow (severely wounded, and two horses killed), and action of Ranode (mentioned in despatches on several occasions for "distinguished bravery," and thanked by the Governor General of India, Brevet of Major, Victoria Cross, and Medal with three Clasps): received the VC under the following circumstances:—"Lieutenant Gough, when in command of a party of Hodson's Horse, near Alumbagh, on the 12th November 1857, particularly distinguished himself by his forward bearing in charging across a swamp, and capturing two guns, although defended by a vastly superior body of the enemy. On this occasion he had his horse wounded in two places, and his turban cut through by sword cuts, whilst engaged in combat with three sepoys. Lieutenant Gough also particularly distinguished himself near Jellalabad, Lucknow, on the 25th February 1858, by showing a brilliant example to his regiment, when ordered to charge the enemy's guns, and by his gallant and forward conduct he enabled them to effect their object. On this occasion he engaged himself in a series of single combats, until at length he was disabled by a musket-ball through the leg, while charging two sepoys with fixed bayonets. Lieutenant Gough on this day had two horses killed under him, a shot through his helmet and another through his scabbard, besides being severely wounded." Commanded the 12th Bengal Cavalry in the Abyssinian campaign in 1868, and was present at the capture of Magdala (mentioned in despatches, CB., and Medal). Served throughout the Afghan war of 1878-80. Commanded the Cavalry of the Koorum Force in 1878-79, and was present at the capture of the Peiwar Kotal, in the pursuit of the Afghans over the Shutargardan, in the affair in the Maugior Pass, and during the operations in Khost. Served with the Cabul Field Force in 1879-80 as Brigadier-General of Communications, and was present in the engagement at Charasiab, and in the various operations around Cabul in December 1879 (wounded); accompanied Sir Frederick Roberts in the march to Candahar in command of the Cavalry Brigade, and was present at the reconnaissance of 31st August in command of the troops engaged and in the cavalry pursuit on the following day (frequently mentioned in despatches, KCB., Medal with four Clasps, and Bronze Deccration).

[4] Lieut.General A. G. F. Hogg served as Adjutant of the 1st Sind Horse in the Persian campaign of 1857 (Medal with Clasp). In 1858-59 he served with the forces in Khandeish and the Nizam's country; and with his Regiment at Canton during the China war of 1860. Served throughout the Abyssinian campaign as Deputy Assistant Quarter Master General, and was present at the action of Arogee and capture of Magdala (mentioned in despatches, Medal, and Brevet of Major). Served in the Afghan war in 1879-80 as Director of Transport with the Bombay Reserve Brigade on the Candahar line, and was present during the investment of Shorpore and in the operations round Cabul in December 1879 (mentioned in despatches, Brevet of Colonel, Medal with Clasp).

[5] Lieut.General H. P. Hawkes served in the Abyssinian war of 1867-58 as Assistant Commissary General (mentioned in despatches, Brevet of Major, Medal). Served in the operations in the Malay Peninsula in 1875 as Assistant Commissary General with the Laroot Column (Medal). Served with the Burmese Expedition in 1886-87 as Acting Commissary General in Chief (received the thanks of the Government of India, mentioned in despatches, CB., and Clasp).

[6] Lieut.General H. S. Anderson served in the Persian Expeditionary Force in 1867, and was present at the bombardment and capture of Mohumra (Medal with Clasp). Also in Khandeish against the attempted invasion of the Deccan by the rebel army under Tantia Topee in 1858-59. Served in the Afghan war of 1878-80 in command of the 1st Bombay Native Infantry, and was present in the affair at Girishk, in the engagement at Maiwand (severely wounded), and at the siege of Candahar (mentioned in despatches, Medal). Served with the Burmese Expedition in 1886-87 in command of a Brigade (received the thanks of the Governor General of India in Council, mentioned in despatches, CB., and Clasp).

[7] Lieut.General C.D'U.La Touche served with the Persian Expeditionary Force in 1856-57, including the attack on Reshire, capture of Bushire, destruction of the enemy's magazines at Chakota, at Borazjoon, and battle of Khooshab (Medal with Clasp). Served with the Satpoora Field Force in the action fought with the insurgent chiefs and rebels in the Satpoora Hills on the 11th April 1858. Served in the Afghan war in 1880, and took part in the defence of Candahar (mentioned in despatches); commanded a sortie of all arms on Khairabad, and was present at the sortie of Deh Khojah (mentioned in despatches) and at the battle of Candahar (Medal with Clasp).

[8] Lieut.General P. H. F. Harris served with the China Expeditionary Force in 1858-59, and was present in the White Cloud Expedition against the Braves in June 1858 (Medal). Served in the Afghan war of 1878-80, and was present in the engagement at Ali Kheyl (mentioned in despatches, Medal). Served with the Burmese Expedition in 1885-86, and was present at the attack on the Minhla Redoubt and commanded the Garrison at Mingyan (mentioned in despatches, CB., and Medal with Clasp).

[9] Major General S. F. M. T. Grant was employed with the Southern Mahratta Field Force from 5th March 1858 in command of a detachment of the 4;th Madras N.I., and from May to December 1858 served with the North Canara Field Force employed against the rebels under the Sawunt Warrie Dessaes, and commanded for eight months the outpost of Coissee on the Goa Frontier, occupied by the 47th Detachment and a detachment of the 35th Madras Native Infantry (Medal).

[10] Major General G. F. Boville served at the assault and capture of Kotah, with the column in pursuit of the Gwalior rebels under Tantia Topee; employed throughout the Oude campaign for the reduction of the province; present in the attack on and expulsion of the enemy from their strongly fortified position of Rampoor Kussia on the 3rd November 1858, accompanying the support of the storming party; present at the surrender of the fort of Amethee, and subsequently with Lord Clyde's Force at the occupation of Sunkerpoor, and pursuit of the rebels under Beni Mahadeo, resulting in the action of Dhoondia Keria and capture of the fort of Buxar on the 24th November 1858; with the column detached after the action to drive the enemy across the river Goomptee; served throughout the operations in the Trans-Gogra district, including the advance on and occupation of Baraitch; action with the Nana's force at Churdah, and occupation of the fort on the 26th December 1858 ;. capture of the fort of Mujeediah on the 27th December, and defeat of the Nana and Begum at Banki, and final expulsion of the rebels from Oude across the river Raptee on the 31st December 1858 (Medal with Clasp). Served throughout the Abyssinian campaign in 1867-68 as Brigade Major of the 1st Brigade 1st Division, and was present at the action of Arogee and capture of Magdala (mentioned in despatches, Brevet of Major, and Medal). Served in the Afghan war in 1879-80 as

Deputy Judge Advocate and Provost Marshal, took part in the defence of Candahar, and was present at the battle of Candahar (mentioned in despatches, Medal with Clasp).

11 Sir J. W. M'Queen served throughout the Indian Mutiny campaign of 1857-58; served with the 4th Punjaub Infantry at the siege assault and capture of Delhi; present with Greathed's Column in the actions of Booundshuhur, Allyghur, Aksabad, Agra, and Kanouge; also in the advance to the relief of Lucknow, including action at Marigunge (slightly wounded), affairs near the Alumbagh and Dilkoosha, and storming of the Secunderbagh severely wounded); afterwards present at Cawnpore, and in the advance on Futtehghur including the action at Kala Nuddee and several minor affairs. Commanded the 4th Punjaub Infantry during the Oude and Rohilcund campaign in April and May 1858, including the capture of Bareilly (mentioned in despatches, Medal with two Clasps). Served with the force under Brigadier General Chamberlain against the Cabool Kheyl Wuzeerees in December 1859 and January 1860; also with that against the Mahsood Wuzeerees in April and May 1860 (Medal with Clasp). Was present with Colonel Keyes' force in the attack on the Bezooties at Gara in March 1869. Served in the Jowaki Afreedee expedition in 1877-78 (mentioned in despatches, Clasp). Served in the Afghan war of 1878-80 with the Koorum Field Force, and commanded the 5th Punjab Infantry in the attack on the Peiwar Kotal (mentioned in despatches, Brevet of Lt. Colonel, and CB.). Took part with Sir Frederick Roberts' Division in the advance on and occupation of Cabul, and was present in the engagement at Charasiah (mentioned in despatches, Medal with two Clasps). Served with Brigadier General Gordon's force in the Mahsood Wuzeeree Expedition in May 1881. Commanded the Hazara Expedition in 1888 (KCB., and Clasp).

12 Major General W. H. Mackesy served in the Crimea from 16th Aug. 1855, and was present at the siege and fall of Sebastopol, including assault of the 8th Sept., and acted as Assistant Engineer to the Highland Brigade (Medal with Clasp, and Turkish Medal). Served in the Indian campaign of 1858-59, including the siege and capture of Lucknow; also acted as Assistant Field Engineer from Nov. 1858, and was engaged with the 4th Company Royal Engineers in all the actions and at the taking and destruction of various fortifications from Allahbad to the Nepaul country (Medal with Clasp).

13 Major General G. N. Channer served in the Umbeyla campaign of 1863 and was present at the actions of the 16th and 17th December (Medal with Clasp). Afterwards served with General Wilde's Column in Jadoon Country in 1864. Looshai field operations in 1871-72. Served with the 1st Goorkhas in the Malay Peninsula in 1875-76, with the Malacca Column in operations in Sunghie Ujong, Terrachee, and Srimenanti; led the advanced party at the surprise and capture of Malay Stockades in Bukit Putus Pass (mentioned in despatches, Victoria Cross, Brevet of Major, Medal with Clasp): received the VC "for having with the greatest gallantry been the first to jump into the Enemy's Stockade, to which he had been despatched with a small party of the 1st Ghoorkha Light Infantry, on the afternoon of the 20th December 1875, by the Officer commanding the Malacca Column to procure intelligence as to its strength, position, &c. Major Channer got completely in rear of the Enemy's position, and finding himself so close that he could hear the voices of the men inside, who were cooking at the time, and keeping no look-out, he beckoned to his men, and the whole party stole quietly forward to within a few paces of the Stockade. On jumping in, he shot the first man dead with his revolver, and his party then came up, and entered the Stockade, which was of a most formidable nature, surrounded by a bamboo palisade; about seven yards within was a log-house, loop-holed, with two narrow entrances, and trees laid latitudinally, to the thickness of two feet. The officer commanding reports that if Major Channer, by his foresight, coolness, and intrepidity, had not taken this Stockade, a great loss of life must have occurred, as from the fact of his being unable to bring guns to bear on it, from the steepness of the hill, and the density of the jungle, it must have been taken at the point of the bayonet." Served with the expedition against the Jowaki Afreedees in 1877 (Clasp). Served with the 29th Punjab Infantry in the Afghan war of 1878-80 with the Koorum Field Force, and was present in command of the Regiment at the attack and capture of the Peiwar Kotal (mentioned in despatches, Brevet of Lt. Colonel, Medal with Clasp). Served with the Expedition to the Black Mountain in 1888 in command of the 1st Brigade (mentioned in despatches, CB., and Clasp).

14 Major General H. A. Little served with the 17th Regiment in the Crimea, subsequent to the fall of Sebastopol, from the 26th Nov. 1855, till the evacuation in June 1856. Served as Adjutant of the 1st Battalion 7th Fusiliers in the Indian N.W. frontier war of 1863 with the Eusafyze Field Force, present at the defence of the Sungahs at the Umbeyla Pass and at the attack on and storming of the Conical Hill and destruction of Lalloo on the 15th Dec., also in the action of Umbeyla and destruction of the village at the foot of the Bonair Pass on 16th Dec., which ended in the complete rout of the enemy and the submission of the hill tribes on 17th Dec. (Brevet of Major, Medal with Clasp). Served as Chief Staff Officer (Deputy Adjutant and Quarter Master General) of the Southern Afghanistan Field Force from November 1880 till its withdrawal from Candahar and Southern Afghanistan. Served with the Burmese Expedition in 1886-87, and again in 1888-89 (mentioned in despatches, CB., and two Clasps).

15 Sir Arthur Palmer served throughout the Indian Mutiny campaign of 1857-59. Raised a Regiment of Sikhs 600 strong for service in Oude in March 1858. Joined Hodson's Horse at Lucknow in June 1858, and was present with it at the action of Nawabgunga, Barabunki (horse killed), and minor affairs in the Oude campaign until its conclusion on the Neapul frontier (wounded). Detached for several months in command of a Squadron, and frequently engaged with the enemy (Medal, mentioned in despatches). Served in the campaign on the North-West Frontier of India in 1863-64, and was present in the engagement at Shubkudder (Medal with Clasp). Served as Adjutant of the 10th Bengal Lancers in Abyssinia—services brought to the notice of Her Majesty's Government by Lord Napier of Magdala (Medal). Served as Aide de Camp to General Stafford in the Duffla Expedition of 1874-75 (mentioned in despatches). Served in the Afghan war of 1878-80, and was present at the capture of the Peiwar Kotal (mentioned in despatches) and with the expedition into the Khost Valley (Brevet of Lt. Colonel, Medal with Clasp). Served in the Soudan campaign in 1885 in command of the 9th Bengal Cavalry (mentioned in despatches, CB., Medal with Clasp, and Khedive's Star). Commanded the force in the operations in the Northern Chin Hills, Burmah, in 1892-93 (received the thanks of the Government of India, mentioned in despatches).

16 Major General C. S. Maclean served at the siege and capture of Delhi in 1857. Subsequently present at the actions of Boolundshuhur, Coel, Acrabad, and Agra—severely wounded (Medal with Clasp). Served with the China Expeditionary Force of 1860, and was present at the action of Sinho, capture of the Taku Forts, actions of Chankiawan and Tangchow, and surrender of Pekin (Medal with two Clasps). Served in the Afghan war of 1878-80, and was present in the engagements at Takht-i-Pul, Ahmed Kheyl, Urzoo near Ghuznee, and Padkao Shana (several times mentioned in despatches, Brevet of Lt. Colonel, CB., Medal with Clasp). Also served in the Mahsood Wuzeeree Expedition in 1881.

17 Major General E. Faunce was employed in the suppression of the mutiny in India in 1857-58, and accompanied the detachment from the Dorundah Field Force under the command of Major G. G. Macdonnell to act against the insurgents of Palimow; was present with the force for restoring and maintaining peace in the Chota Nagpore district in 1857-58 (Medal). Served with the Burmese Expedition in 1888-89 in command of the 2nd Brigade (mentioned in despatches, CB., and Medal with Clasp).

17† Major General R. B. P. P. Campbell served with the 1st Bengal European Fusiliers at the siege and capture of Delhi in 1857, and with the 2nd European Fusiliers in the subsequent operations in the Meerut, Jhujjur, and Rawaree districts. Was attached to the faithful remnants of his 11th Native Infantry, and engaged in rescuing the Rohilcund refugees. Served with the 2nd Punjaub Cavalry at the siege and capture of Lucknow, action of Koorsee, capture of Kooya, action of Allygunge, capture of Bareilly, action of Rohunpore, and against the rebels in the Terai (Medal with two Clasps). Served with the expeditionary force under Brigadier General Chamberlain against the Cabool Kheel Wuzeerees in 1859-60 (Medal with Clasp). Commanded a detached squadron of the Corps of Guides Cavalry throughout the Hazara campaign of 1868, including the Black Mountain Expedition (mentioned in despatches). Commanded the Corps of Guides throughout the Jowaki Afreedee Expedition in 1877-78 (mentioned in despatches, Clasp). Commanded the troops engaged in the operations against the Ranizai village of Skhakat on 14th March 1878 (received the thanks of Government); and was also with the Corps of Guides at the attack on the Utman Kheyl villages on 21st March 1878. Served in the Afghan war of 1878-79, and was present at the capture of Ali Musjid and in the engagements around Cabul in December 1879, and at Charasiab (mentioned in despatches, Brevet of Lt. Colonel, Medal with two Clasps).

18 Major General H. Chapman was at Meean Meer on the outbreak of the mutiny in 1857; served with the 1st Bengal European Fusiliers in the actions of Narnoul, Gungeree, Pattialee, and Mynpooree; commanded a detachment of

Alexander's horse in several minor affairs in the Etawah district in 1858, actions of Oreyah (charger twice wounded), and Dewsa ; pursuit of the rebels through Rajpootana and Central India; Bundlecund campaign of 1859-60 (mentioned in despatches, Medal). Served in the Afghan war of 1878-80, and was present in the engagement at Baghao (mentioned in despatches, Brevet of Lt. Colonel, and Medal).

[19] Major General A. G. Ross served in the Indian Mutiny campaign of 1858-59, and was present with the 35th Foot at Arrah, and with the 79th Highlanders in the Oude campaign, including the capture of the fort of Rampore Kussia and the passage of the Gogra at Fyzabad (Medal). Raised the Lahore Mule Train in September and October 1867, and commanded it through the Abyssinian campaign of 1868, was present at the operations before and capture of Magdala (mentioned in despatches, Medal). Served with the 1st Sikh Infantry in the Jowaki campaign in 1877-78 (mentioned in despatches, Medal with Clasp); in the Afghan war in 1878-79, including the capture of Ali Musjid (Brevet of Lt. Colonel, Medal with Clasp) ; and in the Mahsood Wuzeeree Expedition in 1881. Served with the Zhob Field Force in 1890 under Sir George White in command of a Contingent of the Punjab Frontier Force (mentioned in despatches).

[20] Major General G. R. Hennessy served in the Indian Mutiny campaign in 1857 with the 93rd Highlanders, and was present in the engagements at Bunthera, Maharajgunge, and Alumbagh, and at the relief of Lucknow under Lord Clyde. Served in the 75th Regiment in the force under Sir James Outram, and was present in the action at Guillic and throughout the occupation of the Alumbagh, and took part in various actions, including those of 12th January (wounded) and 16th January 1858 (Medal with Clasp for the relief of Lucknow). Commanded the Humeerpore Military Police Battalion in the Bundelcund campaign in 1859-60, and was engaged in several affairs with the rebels (repeatedly thanked by the Government of India, the Government of the North West Provinces, and the Commander in Chief in India). Commanded the 15th Sikhs in the Afghan war of 1878-80, and was present with Sir Donald Stewart's Division in the advance to and occupation of Candahar, and in the engagements at Ahmed Kheyl and Urzoo near Ghuznee (mentioned in despatches) ; accompanied Sir Frederick Roberts in the march to Candahar in August 1880, and took part in the reconnaissance of the 31st August and the battle of Candahar (twice mentioned in despatches, Medal with two Clasps, and Bronze Decoration). Served in the Soudan campaign in 1885 in command of the 15th Bengal Infantry, and was present in the engagements at Hasheen and the Tofrek zereba, and at the destruction of Temai (mentioned in despatches, C.B., Medal with two Clasps, and Khedive's Star).

[21] Major General J. M. Boyd served in the Abyssinian war in 1868 (Medal). Served in the Afghan war in 1880, and took part in the march to Candahar with the force under Major General Phayre (mentioned in despatches, Medal).

[22] Major General W. P. La Touche served with the Light Battalion in the Persian Expeditionary Force in 1857, and was present at the bombardment and capture of the fort of Mohumra and pursuit of the Persian army (Medal with Clasp). Was present at the action of Hulgallee as Adjutant with the Southern Mahratta Horse in November 1857; present at the action of Sharapoor as 2nd in Command with the Southern Mahratta Horse in February 1858; acted as Staff Officer to the Field Forces at the occupation of Jamkhundee in March and Nurgoond in June 1858 (Medal).

[23] Major General S. J. Browne served with the 5th Punjaub Infantry during the Oude campaign of 1858-59, and was present at the passage of the Raptee and capture of the enemy's guns at Sitkaghat; commanded a detachment of the Regiment at Darzee Talas—horse shot (Medal). Served with the 6th Punjaub Infantry throughout the Umbeyla campaign of 1863 (Medal with Clasp). Served throughout the expedition against the Jowaki Afreedees in 1877-78 (Clasp). Commanded the 6th Punjab Infantry in the Mahsood Wuzeeree Expedition in 1881.

[24] Major General W. Jacob served as Interpreter to the 72nd Highlanders at the siege and capture of Kotah (Medal with Clasp). Also served in the Afghan war in 1880 (Medal).

[25] Major General F. Lance served against the rebels in Rohilcund in 1858; was present at the defence of the Jail at Shahjehanpore, and in the affairs of Mohunrudpore and Nooria, and action at Sisseahghat—severely wounded by a musket ball above the left ankle and horse shot (mentioned in despatches, Medal). Served in the Afghan war in 1879-80, and was present in the engagements at Ahmed Kheyl and Urzoo near Ghuznee (mentioned in despatches, Medal with Clasp). Also served in the Mahsood Wuzeeree Expedition in 1881.

[26] Colonel C. M'Inroy served in the Indian Mutiny campaign in 1857-59, and was present with General Whitlock's Force at the surrender of Kirwee ; joined the Sikh Mounted Police (Metge's Sikh Horse) attached to Brigadier McDuff's Brigade in 1858, and commanded the same from January 1859 ; was present in the action at Sahao (mentioned in despatches); commanded in Cavalry actions of Maharajpore, Jaccoli, and Mow Mahoni ; commanded escort to the guns during the action at Girwassah (mentioned several times in despatches, Medal with Clasp). Employed in disarming the Banda district in 1859-60. Commanded a Division of the Transport Train in the Abyssinian campaign in 1868 (thanked in despatches for the "extent and value of his assistance," Medal). Served in the Egyptian war in 1882 and was present at the battle of Tel-el-Kebir (Medal with Clasp, and Khedive's Star). Served with the Burmese Expedition in 1885-86, and in 1888-89 as Principal Commissariat Officer in Upper Burmah (Medal with two Clasps).

[27] Colonel C. R. Matthews served in the China war in 1858, and was present at the capture of Canton (Medal).

[29] Colonel C. Swinhoe served in the Afghan war in 1880 (Medal).

[30] Colonel H. G. Saunders served during the Indian Mutiny campaign of 1857-58 including the action of the 5th July 1857 near Agra with the Neemuch mutineers, and affair at Shereghat (Medal).

[31] Colonel F. C. St. John served in the Afghan war of 1878-80 (Medal). Served with the Burmese Expedition in 1885-86 (Medal with Clasp).

[32] Major General J. B. Smith served in the campaign on the North West Frontier of India in 1863 with the 2nd Eusofzie Expedition, and was present at the forcing of the Umbeyla Pass (Medal with Clasp); also served with the Looshai Expedition in 1871-72 (Clasp). Served in the Afghan war of 1878-80 Brevet of Lt. Colonel, Medal).

[33] Colonel T. Higginson served on the North-West Frontier of India in the expedition against the Bezotee Tribe in February 1869, and was mentioned in despatches and thanked by the Government of India. Served also with the Moranzio Valley Field Force in April 1869. Served in the Afghan war in 1878-9 with the Courtland Column, and was present in the affair at Baghao (mentioned in despatches, Medal). Commanded the 1st Punjab Infantry in the Wuzeeree Expedition in 1881.

[34] Major General G. C. Bird served in the North Canara campaign from March to December 1858, and was present in various skirmishes and pursuits (Medal). Served in the Afghan war of 1878-80 as Brigade Major to the Cavalry Brigade Ghuznee Field Force, and was present in the engagements at Ahmed Kheyl (mentioned in despatches), and Padkao Shana (mentioned in despatches, Brevet of Lt. Colonel, Medal with Clasp).

[35] Colonel M. Tweedie was present at the assault and capture of Kotah ; served with Brigadier Parke's Column during part of the pursuit of Tantia Topee ; employed during the latter part of the Oude campaign with the Oude Mounted Police under Lord Clyde; present at the occupation of Shurkerpoor, the stronghold of Raja Beni Madho ; served with Colonel Carmichael's Column to drive the enemy across the Gogra ; served under Lord Clyde during the greater part of the Trans-Gogra campaign, including the advance on and occupation of Baraitch, action with the Nana's Force at Churdah, and occupation of the fort on the 26th December 1858 ; served with the Oude Police Force on the Nepaul Frontier from April to the 2nd of October 1859, after the return of the regular forces from the frontier (Medal with Clasp).

[36] Brigadier General J. Jopp served with the force under Brigadier Coghlan which captured and destroyed the fort of Sheik Othman in the vicinity of Aden in 1858. Served in the Abyssinian war in 1868 (Medal). Served in the Afghan war in 1879-80 as Assistant Quarter Master General, and took part in the march to Candahar with the force under Major General Phayre (mentioned in despatches, Medal).

[37] Colonel R. C. R. Clifford served with the left wing of the 54th Foot in pursuit of the mutineers of the 34th and 73rd Native Infantry from Dacca to Chittagong in 1857. Served the winter campaign of 1858 in Oude, and was present at the first attack on the fort of Tyroul on the 21st March (Medal). Served in the Jowaki Afreedes Expedition in 1877 (Medal with Clasp). Served in the Afghan war of 1878-80, and was present in the engagement at Ahmed Kheyl (mentioned in despatches, Brevet of Lt. Colonel, Medal with Clasp). Served in the Wuzeeree Expedition in 1881.

[38] Colonel H. S. Jarrett was present at the outbreak of the Native Troops at Mooltan on the 31st August 1858, and commanded a troop of the 6th Irregular Cavalry in pursuit of the mutineers (Medal). Served with the 3rd Punjaub Cavalry in the Expeditionary Force under Brigadier General Chamberlain against the Mahsood Wuzeereea

in 1860, and was present at the action of the Barrara Pass and capture of Makeen (Medal with Clasp). Engaged with the same Regiment in the blockade of the same tribe on the Tak frontier in 1861-62. Served also in all the actions and operations of the Eusofzaie Field Force of 1863, as Aide de Camp to Sir Neville Chamberlain, and afterwards to Sir John Garvock, and was thanked in despatches by both those generals (Clasp for Umbeyla).

39 Colonel L. J. H. Grey served in the Indian Mutiny campaign of 1857-59, and was present in the actions of Boolundshuhur and Allyghur, skirmish of Ackerabad, actions of Gungaree and Puttialee, attack of the forts of Koheia and Kololee, operations on the Gogra, final advance to the Nepaul Hills, action at Sitka Ghat and capture of the enemy's guns, and various skirmishes in the Nepaul Hills (Medal).

40 Colonel H. M. Pratt was present at the mutiny of the 51st Native Infantry at Peshawur on the 28th August 1857. Served the campaign of 1860 in China, including the action of Sinho, capture of Tangku and of the Taku Forts, and actions of Chankiawhan and Tungchow, and surrender of Pekin (Medal with two Clasps). Served in the Afghan war of 1878-80, and was present at the capture of the Peiwar Kotal, in the engagement at Charasiah on the 6th October 1879, and in the operations around Cabul in December 1879 including the investment of Sherpore (mentioned in despatches); accompanied Sir Frederick Roberts in the march to Candahar, and was present at the battle of Candahar (twice mentioned in despatches, Brevet of Lt.Colonel, Medal with four Clasps, and Bronze Decoration). Served with the Hazara Expedition in 1888 (CB., and Medal with Clasp).

41 Colonel C. A. Porteous was employed in the suppression of the Indian Mutiny in 1857-59, and was present at Kanta, at Bunnee with the force forming the rear guard of the Commander in Chief's Army during the capture of Lucknow, present at Bansee on the 22nd and 28th September 1858, at Chittrah on the 30th September 1858, at two other affairs on the 9th and 20th October 1858, and at Doomeragunge on the 13th September 1858; served with the force under Major General Whitlock in Bundlecund, and present with the detachment which proceeded in March 1859 under Brigadier Faddy against Runmust Singh (Medal with two Clasps).

42 Colonel H. B. Sanderson served in the Indian Mutiny campaign in 1857-59, and was present at the relief of Azimghur, in the engagement at Toolsepore, and in the operations on the Nepaul frontier (Medal).

42† Colonel G. Atkins served at Peshawur during the Indian Mutiny campaign in 1857-58. Served in the campaigns on the North-West Frontier of India in 1858 and 1863 (Medal with Clasp). Served with the Zhob Valley Expedition in 1884. Also served with the Burmese Expedition in 1886-87 (Clasp).

43 Colonel C. J. O. Chambers served in the suppression of the mutiny in Bengal with Major General Whitlock's Force in 1858, was present with the reserve during the action at Girwassah 16th December 1858. Engaged with the rebels in the Ballaput Jungle 26th August 1859 (Medal).

44 Colonel Wilson took part in the operations against the insurgent Dessaies in the North Canara and Bedee districts in 1858 (Medal).

45 Colonel M. Furlong was present at the capture of Copul on the 1st June 1858. With the Bellary Field Force under Colonel Spottiswoode.

46 Colonel C. H. Ewart served throughout the operations before Delhi in 1857, including the battle of Budleekeserai, and final assault and capture of Delhi (Medal with Clasp).

49 Colonel J. H. Prendergast served during the Rumpa Rebellion in 1879-80. Served in the operations on the North-East Frontier, Burmah, in 1891-92.

50 Colonel A. Ollivant served during the Indian Mutiny campaign of 1857-59, including a skirmish at Madrock, action near Agra with the Neemuch mutineers on the 5th July, battle of Agra on the 10th Oct. 1857; Bundlecund campaign in 1858-59, attack on Serowlie, and affair with Burgem Singh (Medal).

51 Colonel C. P. Newport was at the siege and capture of Kotah; with Brigadier Smith's Brigade during all its operations in Central India; at the recapture of Chandaree, battle of Kotah-ke-Serai, battle and capture of Gwalior, siege and capture of Powree and subsequent pursuit of the rebels, action of Koondrye and at Buorda, and at the actions of Geonapoora and Goripooric (Medal with Clasp). Served in the Abyssinian war in 1867-68 (Medal).

53 Colonel C. J. O. Fitzgerald was employed on Field service in the Raichore Doab from 4th June to 5th August 1858. Served in the Afghan war in 1880 with the Candahar Field Force (Medal). Served with the Burmese Expedition in 1886-88 (mentioned in despatches, CB., and Medal with two Clasps).

54 Colonel H. F. H. Sewell was actively employed during the mutiny against the insurgents in the Sumbulpoor districts in 1858.

55 Colonel F. H. Vanderzee served with the Burmese Expedition in 1885-86 (Medal with Clasp).

56 Colonel J. H. Gordon served with the Burmese Expedition in 1885-86 in command of the 23rd.Madras Native Infantry (mentioned in despatches, DSO., and Medal with Clasp).

57 Colonel H. C. A. Szczepanski served during the Indian Mutiny campaign of 1857-58, including the actions of the 25th, 26th, and 27th November 1857, and subsequent operations at Cawnpore, action of Kalee Nuddee, and pursuit of the rebels in Bundlecund (Medal).

58 Colonel R. V. Malden served in the Central India campaign in 1858-59 with the field force under Sir John Michel and was present at the actions of Rajghur, Mungrowlee, and Sindwaho, and the affair at Kurai (Medal with Clasp). Accompanied the 3rd Sind Horse to Abyssinia and was present throughout the campaign of 1867-68 (Medal). Also served in the Afghan war in 1879 (Medal).

59 Colonel J. Gatacre served with his regiment in Khandeish in 1858, with a detachment of his regiment with the Oojein Field Force in 1859-60, and in the Chinese war in the Commissariat Department from July 1860 to March 1861 (Medal). Served in the Afghan war in 1879-80 (Medal). Served with the Burmese Expedition in command of the Kanlé Column in 1886-87, and afterwards of the expedition to Gungaw (mentioned in despatches, CB., and Medal with Clasp).

60 Colonel F. S. FitzPatrick was employed on Field service in the Raichore Doab from 4th June to 5th August 1858. Served in the Afghan war in 1879-80 (Medal). Served with the Burmese Expedition in 1886-87 (Medal with two Clasps).

61 Sir William Seton served with the Persian Expeditionary Force in 1856-57 as a Midshipman in the Indian Navy, and was present at the landing at Hallilah Bay, at the capture of Bushire, and at the bombardment of Mohumrah (Medal with Clasp). Served in the Afghan war in 1880, took part in the defence of Candahar, and was present at the battle of Candahar (Medal with Clasp).

63 Colonel G. S. Hills served in the Afghan war in 1879-80, and was present in the engagement at Mattoon, and in the operations around Cabul in December 1879 including the investment of Sherpore (mentioned in despatches, Medal with Clasp).

64 Colonel H. G. Wtterfield served with the 82nd Foot in the Indian Mutiny campaign of 1857-58, including the operations at Cawnpore in November under General Windham, and defeat there of the Gwalior.Contingent on the 6th December 1857; actions of Kalee Nuddee and Khankur, defence of the Jail at Shahjehanpore and operations subsequent to its relief, capture of the forts of Bunnai, Mahomdee, and Shahabad, and action of Bunkagaon. Served with the 66th Goorkhas in the Oude campaign of 1858-59, including the actions of Pusgaon and Russoolpore, attack and capture of the fort of Mittowlee, and action of Biswa (Medal). Served with the Hazara Expedition in 1888 (mentioned in despatches, Medal with Clasp).

65 Colonel C. T. P. Luxmoore served in the suppression of the mutiny in Bengal in 1857-58. With Sir J. Outram's Corps of Observation at the Alumbagh, and at the capture of Lucknow; served with Sir Hope Grant's Division during his campaign in Oude, from June to December 1858; present at the passage of the Goomtee river at Sultanpore and other minor affairs; and with Major Raikes' Field Column which engaged and repulsed the enemy at Shahpore, Oude, on the 13th October (Medal with Clasp).

66 Colonel J. C. Stewart served in the Indian Mutiny campaign in 1858, including the capture of Meeangunge, siege and capture of Lucknow, and affairs of Barree and Nuggur (Medal with Clasp). Served in the Jowaki Afreedee expedition in 1878 (Medal with Clasp). Served in the Afghan war of 1878-80, and was present at the affair at Mattoon (mentioned in despatches), in the engagement at Charasiab on 6th October 1879, and in the operations around Cabul in December 1879, including the investment of Sherpore (mentioned in despatches, Brevet of Lt.Colonel, Medal with two Clasps). Served with the Burmese Expedition in 1887-88 (Clasp).

67 Colonel J. F. F. Cologan served in the Indian Mutiny campaigns of 1857-59, and was present at the siege and capture of Lucknow in March 1858, siege and capture of Calpee, action of Gowlowlie, attack and capture of Forts Dehayn and Tiroul, occupation of Bhyspore, and operations of Brigadier Kelly's Force in the

Azimghur and Goruckpore districts in 1858-59 (Medal with two Clasps). Served in the Afghan war in 1879-80, first as Staff Officer and afterwards as Paymaster of the Transport, Khyber Line (mentioned in despatches, received the thanks of the Imperial Government, Brevet of Lt.Colonel, Medal). Served with the Burmese Expedition in 1887-88 including the operations of the 3rd and 4th Brigades under Brigadier Generals Collett and Low respectively (Medal with Clasp).

68 Colonel G. C. Sartorius served in the Afghan war in 1878-79 (Medal). Served in the Egyptian war in 1882 (Medal, and Khedive's Star). Served with the Burmese Expedition in 1886-88 (mentioned in despatches, Brevet of Colonel, CB., and Medal with Clasp).

69 Colonel C. R. Pennington served with the 23rd Welsh Fusiliers in the Indian Mutiny campaign, and was present at the siege of Lucknow and in the operations in Oude (mentioned in despatches, Medal with Clasp). Served with the 13th Bengal Lancers in the Umbeyla campaign in 1863 (Medal with Clasp). Served with the 13th Bengal Lancers in the Afghan war in 1879-80 on the Khyber Line, and took part with the Zaimusht Expedition including the assault of Zawa (mentioned in despatches, Brevet of Lt.Colonel, and Medal). Served with the 13th Bengal Lancers in the Egyptian war of 1882, and was present at the action at Kassasin on the 9th September (mentioned in despatches, and at the battle of Tel-el-Kebir (Medal with Clasp, 4th Class of the Osmanieh, and Khedive's Star).

70 Colonel R. I. Crawford served in the pursuit of the Gwalior rebels under Tantia Topee, the Rao Saheb, and the Nawab of Banda in June, July and August 1858; present at the action at Sanganeer on the 8th, and the battle of Bunass on the 14th August 1858; accompanied Brigadier Parke's pursuing Column from August 1858 to January 1859; commanded the party detached to bring in the Nawab of Banda on his surrender (Medal).

71 Colonel C. A. Dodd served in the Indian Mutiny campaign of 1858 with the 23rd Fusiliers, including the action of Kalee Nuddee, siege and capture of Lucknow, and subsequent operations in Oude. Joined the Oude Police Force on 1st Dec. 1858, and served during the Trans-Gogra campaign (Medal with Clasp).

72 Colonel W. T. Brereton served in the Rumpa Rebellion in 1879-80. Served with the Burmese Expedition in 1888-89 (Medal with Clasp).

73 Colonel N. M. T. Horsford served in the Indian Mutiny campaign of 1858, including the siege and capture of Lucknow, action of Nawabgungo, and subsequent operations in Oude (Medal with Clasp).

74 Colonel J. Philips served in the Afghan war in 1878-79 (Medal).

76 Colonel T. R. Tabuteau served with the 1st Madras Fusiliers in the suppression of the Bengal mutiny in 1858, including the Oude campaign and an affair at the fort of Koli (Medal). Served with the 3rd Bombay Native Infantry in the Abyssinian Expedition in 1868 (Medal).

77 Colonel G. Chrystie was employed on field service in the Saugor and Nerbudda Territories, in the suppression of the Indian Mutiny from 20th June 1858; served with the Field Detachment under Brigadier Wheeler and Colonel Reece in the Saugor districts in November and December 1858, and in Bundlecund in January and February 1859.

78 Colonel J. D. Macpherson served in the Oude campaign, and was present at the capture of the fort of Tiroul on the 16th July 1858 (Medal). Served in the Hazara campaign in 1868 (mentioned in despatches, Medal). Served in the Afghan war in 1879-80, accompanied Sir Frederick Roberts in the march to Candahar, and was present at the battle of Candahar (mentioned in despatches, Medal with Clasp, and Bronze Decoration). Also served with the Marri Expedition.

79 Colonel H. B. Jacob accompanied a detachment of his regiment which formed part of Colonel Lockhart's Force in the Field Division of Bundlecund under Brigadier F. Wheeler.

80 Colonel T. J. Cotton served with the Burmese Expedition in 1885-86 (Medal with Clasp).

81 Colonel M. Protheroe served in the Abyssinian war in 1867-68 (Medal). Served in the Afghan war of 1878-80 as Aide de Camp to Lieut.General Sir Donald Stewart, Commanding Candahar Field Force, and took part in the operations in the Kama District and at Besud; accompanied Sir Frederick Roberts in the march to Candahar, and was present at the battle of Candahar (mentioned in despatches, CSI., Medal with Clasp, and Bronze Decoration). Served with the Burmese Expedition in 1885-89 as Deputy Assistant Adjutant and Quarter Master General (mentioned in despatches, promoted Colonel, CB., and Medal with two Clasps); and with the Chin-Lushai Expeditionary Force in 1889-90 (Clasp).

82 Colonel R. Atkins served with the Suraon Field Force in 1859; and on the Nepaul Frontier in 1859-60 (Medal). Served in the Afghan war in 1879 with the Thull Chotiali and Vitakri Field Forces (Medal). Served with the Hazara Expedition in 1888 (Medal with Clasp).

83 Colonel J. R. Marett served with the Bhootan Expedition in 1865, and was present at the capture of the Chamoorchee Stockades (Medal with Clasp).

84 Colonel C. J. T. Whitlock was employed with the Saugor Field Division in the Saugor and Nerbudda Territories, in the suppression of the Indian Mutiny from 31st October 1858; served as Aide de Camp to Major General Whitlock commanding the division from 6th April 1859 to the breaking up of the force on 31st December 1859 (Medal).

85 Colonel E. H. Eyre served with the Zhob Valley Expedition in 1884. Served with the Burmese Expedition in 1885-86 (mentioned in despatches, Brevet of Colonel, Medal with Clasp).

86 Colonel W. R. Bunbury served in the Afghan war of 1878-80, and was present in the engagement at Ali Kheyl (Medal).

87 Colonel J. W. A. Michell served with the Bhootan Expedition in 1864-66, and was present at the capture of Dewangiri (Medal with Clasp). Served with the Sikkim Expedition in 1888 as 2nd in Command of the expedition (mentioned in despatches, Clasp).

88 Colonel M. M. Carpendale served in the Afghan war in 1880, and took part in the march to Candahar with the force under Major General Phayre (Medal).

89 Colonel H. C. Morse served in the Afghan war in 1879-80 with the Southern Afghanistan Field Force and was present in the engagement on the Khojak range in command of the front attack—wounded (Medal).

90 Colonel A. S. Grove served in the Afghan war of 1880 (Medal). Served with the Burmese Expedition in 1886-89 (mentioned in despatches, DSO., and Medal with two Clasps).

91 Colonel H. M. Evans served with the Duffla Expedition in 1874-75 (mentioned in despatches). Served in the operations against the Nagas in 1879-80, and was present at the assault of Konoma (mentioned in despatches, Brevet of Lt.Colonel, Medal with Clasp). Served with the Manipore Expedition in 1891 in command of the 43rd Goorkha Rifles (mentioned in despatches, Clasp).

92 Colonel C. A. Cuningham served in the Afghan war in 1880 as Assistant Adjutant General of Division, and afterwards as Assistant Adjutant General on the Line of Communications (Medal).

93 Colonel Clifford served in the Hazara campaign in 1868 as Adjutant of the 16th Bengal Cavalry (Medal with Clasp). Served in the Soudan campaign in 1885 as 2nd in command of the 9th Bengal Lancers, and was present in the engagement at Hasheen and at the destruction of Temai and Takdoul (Medal with Clasp, and Khedive's Star).

94 Colonel H. H. Hallett served with Major General Whitlock's Field Force in Bundlecund from April to 30th December 1859.

95 Colonel George Young served with the Bhootan Expedition in 1865-66 (Medal with Clasp); in the Hazara campaign in 1868 (Clasp); and in the operations in the Malay Peninsula in 1875-76 (Clasp). Served in the Afghan war in 1880 (Medal).

96 Colonel M. A. Rowlandson served in the Abyssinian war in 1867-68 as Sub Assistant Commissary General (Medal). Served in the Egyptian war of 1882, and was present at the battle of Tel-el-Kebir (Medal with Clasp, 4th Class of the Osmanieh, and Khedive's Star).

97 Colonel A. Vallings served with the 6th Foot against the Hill Tribes in Sikkim in 1861. Served with the 1st Punjaub Infantry in the Umbeyla campaign of 1863 (mentioned in despatches, Medal with Clasp). Served in the Afghan war in 1878-79, and was present in the engagement at Baghao (mentioned in despatches, Medal). Served in the Mahsood Wuzeeree Expedition in 1881.

98 Lt.Colonel H. S. Elton served with the Burmese Expedition in 1886-88 (mentioned in despatches, Brevet of Colonel, Medal with two Clasps).

99 Colonel J. W. S. Butler served with the Burmese Expedition in 1886-88 (Medal with Clasp). [See also Civil Decorations for Gallantry, "Hart's Annual Army List," p. 786.]

100 Colonel H. S. Stewart served in the Afghan war in 1879-80 (Medal).
102 Colonel F. W. Collis served in the Abyssinian war in 1868 (Medal). Served in the Afghan war in 1879, and was present in the operations in the Khost Valley, and at the forcing of the Shutargardan (twice mentioned in despatches, Brevet of Lt.Colonel, Medal). Also served with the Mahsood Wuzeeree Expedition in 1881.
103 Colonel J. M. Sym served in the campaign on the North-West Frontier of India in 1863, and was present at the capture of Umbeyla (Medal with Clasp); also served in the Hazara campaign in 1868, including the operations on the Black Mountain (Clasp). Served in the Afghan war in 1879-80, and was present in the engagement at Charasiah on the 6th October 1879, in the operations around Cabul in December 1879 including the storming of the Asmai Heights (mentioned in despatches); accompanied Sir Frederick Roberts in the march to Candahar, and was present at the battle of Candahar (mentioned in despatches, Brevet of Lt.Colonel, Medal with three Clasps, and Bronze Decoration); also served with the Atchakzai and Marri Expeditions in 1880. Served with the Hazara Expedition in 1888 in command of a Column (mentioned in despatches, CB., and Clasp). Served with the Miranzai Expedition in 1891 in command of the 1st Column (mentioned in despatches, Clasp).
104 Colonel A. G. Handcock served with the Bhootan Expedition in 1865-66 (Medal with Clasp). Served in the Afghan war of 1878-80 as Assistant Adjutant General to the Northern and Southern Afghanistan Field Forces, and was present in the engagement at Ahmed Kheyl (mentioned in despatches, Brevet of Lt.Colonel, Medal with Clasp).
105 Colonel E. S. Ludlow served with the Saugor Field Division in 1859.
108 Colonel A. J. D. Hawes served in the Sikkim Expedition of 1861. Served with the 4th Punjaub Infantry at the surprise of the Bezzotee village of Gara in February 1869. Served with the Jowaki Expedition in 1877-78 (mentioned in despatches, Medal with Clasp). Served in the Afghan war in 1879, and took part in the Zaimusht Expedition including the assault of Zawa (Medal). Also served with the Zhob Valley Expedition in 1884. Served with the Hazara Expedition in 1888 (DSO., and Clasp).
109 Colonel E. A. Bruce served in the Afghan war of 1878-80 with the Vitakri and Lower Koorum Field Forces (Medal). Served with the Burmese Expedition in 1885-87 as Executive Commissariat Officer (mentioned in despatches, Brevet of Colonel, Medal with Clasp).
110 Sir Benjamin Bromhead served in the Afghan war of 1878-80, and took part in the two expeditions into the Bazar Valley (mentioned in despatches, Medal). Served in the Soudan campaign in 1885 (Medal with Clasp, and Khedive's Star). Served with the Sikkim Expedition in 1888—severely wounded, right hand amputated CB., and Medal with Clasp); and with the Hazara Expedition in 1891 in command of the 32nd Bengal Infantry (mentioned in despatches, Clasp).
113 Colonel H. W. J. Senior served in the campaign on the North-West Frontier of India in 1863, and was present at the forcing of the Umbeyla Pass (Medal with Clasp). Served in the Hazara campaign in 1868, including the operations against the tribes on the Black Mountain (Clasp). Also served in the Afghan war in 1878-79 (Medal). Served with the Burmese Expedition in 1885-87 (mentioned in despatches, Clasp). [See also Civil Decorations for Gallantry, "Hart's Annual Army List," p. 786.]
114 Colonel R. Westmacott served with the 28th Foot with the Okamundel Field Force in 1858, and was present at the storming and capture of Beyt, reconnaissance before, siege, and occupation of Dwarka. Served in the Afghan war in 1879-80, and took part in the march to Candahar with the force under Major General Phayre (mentioned in despatches, Medal). Served in the Soudan campaign in 1885, and was present in the engagements at Hasheen and the Tofrek zereba and at the destruction of Temai (Medal with two Clasps, and Khedive's Star). Served with the Chin-Lushai Expeditionary Force in 1889-90 in command of the 28th Bombay Native Infantry (mentioned in despatches, DSO., and Medal with Clasp).
115 Colonel J. Hay served with the 4th Goorkhas throughout the Umbeyla campaign of 1863, including assault and capture of the Conical Hill and the villages of Lalloo and Umbeyla (Medal with Clasp). Served throughout the Hazara Expedition of 1868 (Clasp). Served also with the Looshai Expeditionary Force in 1871-72 (Clasp). Served in the Afghan war in 1878-80, and was present at the attack and capture of Ali Musjid, and in the engagement at Saidabad (mentioned in despatches, Medal with Clasp).
116 Colonel J. L. Fagan served in the Afghan war in 1879-80, and took part in the march to Candahar with the force under Major General Phayre (mentioned in despatches, Medal).
117 Colonel T. R. Byng served with the Burmese Expedition in 1888-89 (Medal with Clasp).
119 Colonel G. R. Peart served in the Afghan war in 18-8-79 (Medal).
120 Colonel E. G. Lillingston served in the campaign on the North-West Frontier of India in 1863, and was present at the forcing of the Umbeyla Pass (Medal with Clasp).
122 Colonel E. J. Gunthorpe served in the Abyssinian war in 1867-68 (Medal).
123 Colonel G. J. Skinner served in the Afghan war in 1879-80, and took part with the expedition against the Marris (Medal). Served with the Chin-Lushai Expeditionary Force in 1839 in command of the Northern Column (received the thanks of the Government of India, mentioned in despatches, DSO., and Medal with Clasp); and with the second Miranzai Expedition in 1891 (Clasp).
125 Colonel E. S. Reynolds was employed during the Afghan war of 1878-80 as Assistant Governor General' Agent for Beloochistan (Brevet of Lt. Colonel, Medal).
127 Colonel W. F. Prideaux served in the Abyssinian war in 1868 (Medal).
129 Colonel A. C. Toker served with the Bhootan Expedition in 1865-66 (Medal with Clasp). Served in the Egyptian war of 1882 as Deputy Assistant Adjutant General of the Indian Contingent, and was present at the battle of Tel-el-Kebir (mentioned in despatches, Brevet of Lt.Colonel, 4th Class of the Osmanieh, Medal with Clasp, and Khedive's Star). Served with the Burmese Expedition in 1886-87, and commanded a force on the Upper Chindwin (mentioned in despatches, CB., and two Clasps).
131 Colonel F. A. Wilson served with the Bhootan Expedition in 1864-65, and was present at the capture of Buxar and the Bala Stockade (Medal with Clasp); also served in the Hazara campaign in 1868 including the operations on the Black Mountain (Clasp).
134 Colonel V. Riyaz served in the Hazara campaign in 1868, including the operations on the Black Mountain (Medal with Clasp). Served in the Afghan war of 1878-80, and was present in the engagement at Jhandola (mentioned in despatches, Medal), and with the Mahsood Wuzeeree Expedition in 1881. Served in the Hazara Expedition in 1891 in command of the 37th Bengal Infantry (mentioned in despatches, Clasp).
135 Colonel G. R. J. Shakespear served in the Soudan campaign in 1885 as Chief Transport Officer with the Indian Contingent (mentioned in despatches, Brevet of Lt.Colonel, Medal with Clasp, and Khedive's Star). Served in the Hazara Expedition in 1891 as Assistant Adjutant General (mentioned in despatches, Medal with Clasp).
136 Colonel M. J. King Harman served in the Hazara campaign in 1868, including the operations on the Black Mountain (Medal with Clasp); also served with the Looshai Expedition in 1871-72 (mentioned in despatches, Clasp).
139 Major General E. Stedman served in the Hazara campaign in 1868 (Medal with Clasp). Served in the Afghan war of 1878-80, and was present in the second expedition into the Bazar Valley and in the engagement at Jugdulluck (mentioned in despatches); accompanied Sir Frederick Roberts in the march to Candahar, and was present at the battle of Candahar (mentioned in despatches, Brevet of Lt.Colonel, Medal with Clasp, and Bronze Decoration). Served with the Burmese Expedition in 1886-89, and had command of the operations in the Shan States (mentioned in despatches, CB., and two Clasps).
140 Colonel R. G. E. Dalrymple served in the Abyssinian campaign, and was present at the capture of Magdala (Medal).
142 Colonel F. T. Ebden served in the operations in Okamundel and Kattywar in 1865-66. Served in the Afghan war in 1879-80 (Medal). Served with the Burmese Expedition in 1885-88 (Medal with Clasp).
143 Lt.Colonel H. R. Le M. Carey served in the Hazara campaign in 1868 (Medal with Clasp).
144 Colonel W. A. Lawrence served in the Afghan war of 1878-80, and was present in the engagements at Ahmed Kheyl (mentioned in despatches) and Urzoo near Ghuznee (Brevets of Major and Lt.Colonel, Medal with Clasp)
145 Brigadier General Turner served in the Hazara campaign in 1868 (Medal with Clasp). Served in the Afghan war of 1878-80, and was present at the capture of the Peiwar Kotal, at the forcing of the Shutargardan, and in the engagement at Charasiah on the 6th October 1879 (mentioned in despatches, Medal with two Clasps). Also served in the Mahsood Wuzeeree Expedition in 1881. Served with the Zhob Field Force in 1890 under Sir George White (men-

Indian Staff Corps.—War Services of Field Officers.

tioned in despatches). Served with the Miranzai Expedition in 1891 in command of a Column (mentioned in despatches, Brevet of Colonel, Clasp).

¹⁴⁶ Colonel A. G. Hammond served with the Corps of Guides throughout the Jowaki Afreedee Expedition in 1877-78 under General Keyes (mentioned in despatches, Medal with Clasp). Present in the operations against the Ranizai village of Skbakat on 14th March 1878, and also in the attack on the Utman Kheyl villages on 21st March 1878. Served with the Corps of Guides in the Afghan war of 1878-80, and was present at the capture of Ali Musjid and in the engagements around Cabul in December 1879, and at Charasiab (mentioned in despatches, Victoria Cross, Medal with two Clasps): was awarded the VC "for conspicuous coolness and gallantry at the action on the Asmai Heights, near Kabul, on the 14th December 1879, in defending the top of the hill with a rifle and fixed bayonet, against large numbers of the enemy, while the 72nd Highlanders and Guides were retiring; and again, on the retreat down the hill, in stopping to assist in carrying away a wounded Sepoy, the enemy being not sixty yards off, firing heavily all the time." Served with the Hazara Expedition in 1888 (DSO., and Clasp), and with the Hazara Expedition in 1891 in command of the 2nd Brigade (mentioned in despatches, CB., and Clasp).

¹⁴⁷ Colonel J. E. Sandeman served in the Hazara campaign in 1868, including the operations on the Black Mountain (Medal).

¹⁴⁸ Colonel E. Molloy served with the force employed in the Cossiah and Jynteah hills during the rebellion of 1862-63. Served with the Bhootan Expedition in 1865, and was present at the capture of the Bala Stockade (Medal with Clasp); and in the Hazara campaign in 1868 (Clasp). Served in the Afghan war of 1878-80, and accompanied Sir Frederick Roberts in the march to Candahar, and was present at the battle of Candahar (twice mentioned in despatches, Brevet of Major, Medal with Clasp, and Bronze Decoration). Also served with the Marri Expedition in 1881. Served in the Hazara Expedition in 1891 in command of the 2nd Battalion 5th Goorkhas (mentioned in despatches, Clasp), and with the Isazai Field Force in 1892 in command of the 2nd Battalion 5th Goorkhas.

¹⁵⁰ Colonel C. F. Hughes served in the Afghan war in 1879-80, and was present in the engagement at Ahmed Kheyl (Brevet of Major, Medal with Clasp). Served with the Burmese Expedition in 1886-87 (mentioned in despatches, Brevet of Lt.Colonel, Medal with two Clasps).

¹⁵¹ Colonel James Cook served in the campaign on the North-West Frontier of India in 1863, and was present at the capture of Umbeyla (Medal with Clasp). Served in the Afghan war of 1878-80, and was present at the attack and capture of Ali Musjid, and with the first expedition into the Bazar Valley under Lieut. General Maude (mentioned in despatches, Brevet of Major, Medal with Clasp). Also served with the Mahsood Wuzeeree Expedition in 1881. Served in the Soudan campaign in 1885 as Brigade Major with the Indian Contingent (mentioned in despatches, Medal with Clasp, and Khedive's Star).

¹⁵² Colonel C. C. Brownlow served in the campaign on the North-West Frontier of India in 1863, including the capture of Umbeyla (Medal with Clasp), and in the campaign against the Jowaki Afreedees in 1877-78 (Clasp). Served in the Afghan war in 1879 (Medal). Served with the Miranzai Expedition in 1891 in command of the 3rd Column (mentioned in despatches, Brevet of Colonel, Clasp).

¹⁵³ Colonel J. T. Cummins served in the Afghan war of 1878-80, and was present in the operations in the Bazar Valley, and acted as Staff Officer Koorum Valley Transport (Brevet of Major, and Medal). Served during the Egyptian war in 1882 as 2nd in Command of the Punjab Mule Corps for British Forces; also served in the Soudan campaign in 1885, and was present in the advance to and destruction of Temni (Medal with Clasp, and Khedive's Star). Served with the Burmese Expedition in 1886-89 (mentioned in despatches, DSO., and Medal with two Clasps).

¹⁵⁶ Colonel H. S. Tandy served in the Afghan war in 1880, and took part in the march to Candahar with the force under Major General Phayre (Medal). Served with the Burmese Expedition in 1886-88 (Medal with two Clasps).

¹⁵⁸ Colonel A. L. M'Nair served in the Abyssinian war in 1867-68 (Medal). Also served in the Afghan war in 1878 (Medal).

¹⁵⁹ Major General A. R. Badcock served in the Bhootan Expedition in 1864-65 (Medal with Clasp), in the Hazara campaign in 1868 (Clasp), and throughout the operations in the Malay Peninsula in 1875-76 (mentioned in despatches, and received the thanks of the Government of India, Clasp). Served in the Afghan war in 1879-80, and was present at the forcing of the Peiwar Kotal (mentioned in despatches), in the affair at Killa Kazi, and in the operations around Cabul in December 1879 (mentioned in despatches); accompanied Sir Frederick Roberts in the march to Candahar in command of the Commissariat Department, and was present at the battle of Candahar (twice mentioned in despatches, Brevet of Lt.Colonel, CB., Medal with three Clasps, and Bronze Decoration).

¹⁶¹ Lt.Colonel W. H. Browne served with the 101st Fusiliers in the Indian North-West Frontier war of 1863, and was present at the storm and capture of the Crag Piquet (Medal with Clasp). Served in the Afghan war in 1878-79 (Medal).

¹⁶² Colonel J. Biddulph served in the Indian Mutiny campaign in 1858-59, and was present at the action of Doundeakera, taking of the Forts of Chanda and Musjeedia, and action on the banks of the Raptee (Medal).

¹⁶³ Colonel J. T. Watling served in the Afghan war in 1879-80 as Deputy Assistant Quarter Master General on the Line of Communication, and took part in the march to Candahar with the force under Major General Phayre (mentioned in despatches, Medal).

¹⁶⁴ Colonel G. Simpson served with the Burmese Expedition in 1885-88 as Brigade Major (mentioned in despatches, Brevet of Lt.Colonel, Medal with two Clasps).

¹⁶⁵ Colonel R. Warburton served in the Abyssinian campaign in the Transport Train (Medal). Served in the Afghan war in 1879-80 (Brevet of Major, and Medal).

¹⁶⁶ Colonel R. H. F. Rennick served in the Abyssinian campaign with the Army Works Corps (Medal). Served with the 39th Bengal Native Infantry in the Khyber Pass in the Afghan war in 1879-80 (Medal). Served with the Burmese Expedition in 1886-89, including the expedition up the Chindwin River under Colonel Toker (mentioned in despatches, Brevet of Lt.Colonel, Medal with two Clasps). Served with the Manipore Expedition in 1891 in command of the Silchar Column (received the thanks of the Government of India, mentioned in despatches, Clasp), and in the operations in the Chin Hills in 1891-92 (Brevet of Colonel).

¹⁷⁰ Colonel T. Deane served in the Afghan war in 1879-80, and was present in the operations round Cabul in December 1879, including the engagements of Takht-i-Shah and the Asmai Heights and the investment of Sherpore (mentioned in despatches, Medal with Clasp).

¹⁷³ Colonel W. V. Ellis served in the Afghan war of 1878-80 with the Candahar Column, including the advance to Khelat-i-Ghilzie, and the engagements at Saif-u-deen, Ahmed Kheyl (mentioned in despatches), and Urzoo near Ghuznee; accompanied Sir Frederick Roberts in the march to Candahar, and was present at the battle of Candahar (mentioned in despatches, Brevet of Major, Medal with two Clasps, and Bronze Decoration). Served with the Hazara Expedition in 1888 (mentioned in despatches, Medal with Clasp).

¹⁷⁵ Colonel A. Clark Kennedy served in the Egyptian war of 1882 (Medal, and Khedive's Star). Served with the Burmese Expedition in 1887-88 (mentioned in despatches, Brevet of Colonel, Medal with Clasp), and with the Chin-Lushai Expeditionary Force in 1889-90 (mentioned in despatches, Clasp).

¹⁷⁶ Colonel J. P. D. Vanrenen served in the Afghan war in 1879-80, and was present in the engagement at Mazeena (Medal).

¹⁷⁷ Colonel G. W. Rogers served with the Looshai Expedition in 1871-72 (Medal with Clasp). Served in the Afghan war of 1878-80, and was present at the attack and capture of Ali Musjid, with the expedition into the Bazar Valley, including the engagement at Deh Sarakh as Orderly Officer to Brigadier General Tytler (mentioned in despatches), and in the operations round Cabul in December 1879; accompanied Sir Frederick Roberts in the march to Candahar and was present at the battle of Candahar (Brevet of Major, Medal with three Clasps, and Bronze Decoration). Served with the Sikkim Expedition in 1888 (DSO., and Clasp).

¹⁷⁸ Colonel H. Paterson served in the Abyssinian war in 1867-68 (mentioned in despatches, Medal). Served in the Afghan war of 1878-80, and was present at the capture of the Peiwar Kotal, at the forcing of the Sapri Pass, in the operations in the Khost Valley, in the engagement at Charasiab on the 6th October 1879, and in the engagement at Saidabad; accompanied Sir Frederick Roberts in the march to Candahar, and was present at the battle of Candahar (mentioned in despatches, Brevet of Major, Medal with three Clasps, and Bronze Decoration).

Indian Staff Corps.—War Services of Field Officers. 442g

180 Colonel E. B. Bishop served in the Afghan war in 1879-80, and was present in the engagement at Ahmed Kheyl as Orderly Officer to Brigadier General Hughes (mentioned in despatches, Brevet of Major, Medal with Clasp). Served with the Burmese Expedition in 1886-87 (mentioned in despatches, Brevet of Lt.Colonel, Medal with Clasp).

181 Colonel Gaselee served with the 93rd Highlanders in the Umbeyla campaign of 1863 (Medal with Clasp). Served as Staff Officer to the Director of Transports on the Highlands throughout the Abyssinian campaign in 1868. and was present at the capture of Magdala (mentioned in despatches, Medal). Served with the Hazara Field Force in 1868. Served with the 4th Punjaub Infantry at the surprise of the Bezotee village of Gara on the 25th Feb. 1869 (mentioned in despatches, and thanked by the Governor General). Served with the 4th Punjaub Infantry throughout the Jowaki Afreedee expedition of 1877-78 (mentioned in despatches, Clasp). Served throughout the Afghan war of 1878-80 in the Quarter Master General's Department, and was present at the affair at Shahjui and in the engagements at Ahmed Kheyl and Oorzoo near Ghuzni (mentioned in despatches); accompanied Sir Frederick Roberts in the march to Candahar, and was present at the reconnaissance on 31st August and at the battle of Candahar (mentioned in despatches, Brevet of Major, Medal with two Clasps, and Bronze Decoration). Served with the Zhob Valley Expedition in 1884 (mentioned in despatches). Served with the Hazara Expedition in 1891 in command of the 4th Sikh Infantry (mentioned in despatches, *CB*., and Clasp); and with the Isazai Expedition in 1892.

183 Colonel W. O. Thompson served in the Afghan war in 1878-79 (Medal). Also served with the Mahsood Wuzeeree Expedition in 1881. Served with the Hazara Expedition in 1888 (Medal, with Clasp); and with the Miranzai Expedition in 1891 in command of the 3rd Sikhs (mentioned in despatches, Clasp).

184 Lt.Colonel J. Davidson served with the expedition against the Jowaki Afreedees in 1877-78 (mentioned in despatches, Medal with Clasp). Served in the Afghan war in 1878-79, and was present at the attack and capture of Ali Musjid and in the engagement at Futtehabad (mentioned in despatches, Brevet of Major, and Medal with Clasp). Also served with the expedition against the Mahsood Wuzeerees in 1881 (mentioned in despatches).

185 Lt.Colonel G. M. Abbott served in the Abyssinian campaign in 1868, and was present at the action of Arogee and at the capture of Magdala (Medal). Served in the Afghan war in 1879-80, and was present in the engagements at Ahmed Kheyl (mentioned in despatches) and Padkao Shana (twice mentioned in despatches, Brevet of Major, Medal with Clasp).

186 Lt.Colonel Sandilands served with the 6th Punjab Infantry throughout the Jowaki Afreedee Expedition in 1877-78 (Medal with Clasp). Served in the Mahsood Wuzeeree Expedition in 1881. Served with the Miranzai Expedition in 1891 in command of the 6th Punjab Infantry (mentioned in despatches, Clasp).

188 Lt.Colonel F. Quin served with the 33rd Regiment throughout the Abyssinian campaign of 1867-68, and was present at the storming and capture of Magdala (Medal). Served in the Afghan war in 1880 (Medal). Served with the Burmese Expedition in 1885-86 (Medal with Clasp).

189 Colonel Patch served with the 55th Regt. on the Bhootan Expedition in 1865 (Medal with Clasp). Served in the Afghan war in 1879-80 with the Peshawur Valley Field Force (Medal). Served with the Hazara Expedition in 1888 (Brevet of Lt.Colonel, Clasp). Served with the Miranzai Expedition in 1891 under Sir W. Lockhart as Chief Commissariat Officer (received the thanks of the Government of India, mentioned in despatches, Clasp).

190 Sir Edwin Collen served throughout the Abyssinian campaign from the 6th Feb. 1868, and was employed on Special Survey Duty from the 23rd March until the end (Medal). Served in the Afghan war in 1880 (Medal). Served in the Soudan campaign in 1885 as Assistant Military Secretary to Sir Gerald Graham (mentioned in despatches, Brevet of Lt.Colonel, Medal with Clasp, and Khedive's Star).

191 Lt.Colonel H. A. Graves served in the Afghan war in 1878-79 (Medal).

194 Colonel L. H. R. D. Campbell served as Orderly Officer to Major General Wilde commanding the Hazara Field Force in 1868, including the expedition against the tribes on the Black Mountain (Medal with Clasp). Served in the Afghan war in 1878-79, and was present at the affairs in the Kundil Pass and at Baghao (mentioned in despatches, Medal), and with the expedition against the Mahsood Wuzeerees in 1881.

195 Colonel C. H. Stoddart served in the Afghan war in 1879-80 with the Jellalabad Field Force and afterwards with the Koorum Valley Field Force (Medal). Served with the Burmese Expedition in 1885-89 in the operations under Brigadier Generals East and Wolseley, and commanded the Column which recaptured Thonzé on the 18th August 1887 (mentioned in despatches, Medal with two Clasps).

196 Lt.Colonel J. G. Kelly served with the Hazara Expedition in 1891 (Medal with Clasp); and with the second Miranzai Expedition in 1891 (Clasp).

197 Colonel H. V. Hunt served in the Afghan war in 1879-80, and was present in the engagement at Charasiab on the 6th October 1879, and in the operations round Cabul in December 1879 including the investment of Sherpore (mentioned in despatches, Medal with two Clasps).

198 Lt.Colonel Watts served in the Jowaki Afreedee Expedition in 1877-78, and was present at the affair at Jummoo (Medal with Clasp). Served in the Afghan war in 1879-80, and was present in the engagement at Charasiab on 6th October 1879, and at the subsequent occupation of Cabul (Medal with Clasp).

199 Colonel W. Hailes served in the Afghan war in 1879-80 as Deputy Assistant Quarter Master General Reserve Division; also at Peshawur (mentioned in despatches, Medal). Served with the Burmese Expedition in 1885-85, and was severely wounded in an engagement near Tummoo (mentioned in despatches, Brevet of Lt.Colonel, Medal with Clasp).

201 Colonel Burlton-Bennett served with the Looshai Expedition in 1871-72 (mentioned in despatches, Medal with Clasp), and in the expedition against the Jowaki Afreedees in 1877-78 (twice mentioned in despatches, Clasp). Served in the Afghan war in 1878-79, and was present at the attack and capture of Ali Musjid (Medal with Clasp). Served with the Zhob Field Force in 1890 (mentioned in despatches).

202 Colonel Vousden served in the Jowaki Afreedee Expedition of 1877-78, and was present at the affair at Jummo (Medal with Clasp). Served in the Afghan war of 1878-80, and was present at the affairs at Karatiga and Mattoon, in the engagement at Charasiab on 6th October 1879, and in the operations around Cabul in December 1879, including the investment of Sherpore (three times mentioned in despatches, Brevet of Major, Victoria Cross, and Medal with two Clasps): was awarded the VC "for the exceptional gallantry displayed by him on the 14th December 1879, on the Koh Asmai Heights, near Kabul, in charging, with a small party, into the centre of the line of the retreating Kohistani force, by whom they were greatly outnumbered, and who did their utmost to close round them. After rapidly charging through and through the enemy backwards and forwards, several times, they swept off round the opposite side of the village and joined the rest of the troops." Served with the two Miranzai Expeditions in 1891 (mentioned in despatches, Clasp).

203 Colonel A. Fishe served in the Afghan war in 1879-80 (Medal).

204 Colonel J. T. Carruthers served with the 4th Foot throughout the Abyssinian campaign, including the action of Arogee and capture of Magdala (Medal). Served in the Afghan war in 1880 (Medal).

206 Lt.Colonel Harvey Kelly served with the Burmese Expedition in 1887-89 as Assistant Commissary General for Transport; was Brigade Transport Officer in the operations of the 3rd Brigade under Brigadier General Wolseley (mentioned in despatches, Brevet of Lt.Colonel, Medal with two Clasps); with the Poukhan Expedition in 1889 as Assistant Commissary General under Brigadier General Wolseley (Clasp); and in the operations in the Chin Hills and on the North East Frontier of Burmah in 1891-92 as Principal Commissariat Officer under Major General Stewart.

208 Lt.Colonel J. F. J. Miller served with the 19th Foot in the Hazara campaign in 1868, including the expedition against the tribes on the Black Mountain (Medal with Clasp). Also served in the Afghan war in 1879-80 (Medal).

209 Lt.Colonel C. B. Cooke served with the Burmese Expedition in 1885-87 (Medal with Clasp).

211 Lt.Colonel H. de la M. Hervey served in the Afghan war of 1878-80, and was present in the engagements at Takht-i-Pul, Saif-u-deen, Ahmed Kheyl, and Urzoo near Ghuznee (mentioned in despatches, Medal with Clasp). Also served in the Mahsood Wuzeeree Expedition in 1881. [See also Civil Decorations for Gallantry, " Hart's Annual Army List," p. 786.]

213 Colonel M. G. Gerard served in the Abyssinian campaign with the Transport Train from the 13th March 1868 (mentioned in despatches for " ability, energy, and zeal," and Medal). Served in the Afghan war of 1878-80, and was present with the second expedition into the Bazar Valley under Lieut.General Maude (mentioned in despatches), and in the advance to Cabul under Brigadier General Charles Gough (mentioned in despatches);

accompanied Sir Frederick Roberts in the march to Candahar, and was present at the battle of Candahar (mentioned in despatches, Brevet of Lt.Colonel, Medal with two Clasps, and Bronze Decoration). Served in the Egyptian war of 1882 as Deputy Assistant Adjutant and Quarter Master General Cavalry Division, and was present at the reconnaissance in force from Alexandria on the 5th August and at the battle of Tel-el-Kebir (mentioned in despatches, CB., Medal with Clasp, 3rd Class of the Medjidie, and Khedive's Star).

²¹⁴ Lt.Colonel W. H. Browne served in the Afghan war in 1879-80 with the Koorum Field Force (Medal). Served with the Burmese Expedition in 1886-89 including the expedition up the Chindwin River under Colonel Toker (Medal with two Clasps), and with the Manipore Expedition in 1891 (Clasp).

²¹⁵ Colonel F. W. V. Leckie served in the Afghan war in 1879-80, and was present in the engagement at Kokeran (mentioned in despatches), at the defence of Candahar including the sortie of Deh Khojah, and at the battle of Candahar (Medal with Clasp).

²¹⁶ Lt.Colonel W. H. D. Jones served in the Afghan war of 1878-80 (Medal).

²¹⁸ Lt.Colonel S. V. Gordon served in the Afghan war of 1878-80, and took part in the operations in the Khost Valley, in the engagement at Charasiab on the 6th October 1879, in the operations around Cabul in December 1879 (mentioned in despatches), and in the engagement at Saidabad; accompanied Sir Frederick Roberts in the march to Candahar, and was present at the battle of Candahar (mentioned in despatches, Brevet of Major, Medal with three Clasps, and Bronze Decoration)

²¹⁹ Lt.Colonel L. F. Heath served in the Abyssinian campaign of 1867-68 as Aide de Camp to Major General Malcolm (mentioned in despatches, Medal).

²²⁰ Lt.Colonel W. G. Craigie-Halkett served in the Afghan war in 1879-80, and was present in the engagement at Kam Dakka (Medal). Also served in the Mahsood Wuzeeree Expedition in 1881.

²²² Lt.Colonel D. W. K. Barr served the Abyssinian campaign in 1868 with the Transport Train (Medal).

²²⁴ Lt.Colonel G. H. C. Dyce served in the Hazara campaign in 1868, including the operations on the Black Mountain (Medal with Clasp). Served in the Afghan war of 1878-80, and was present in the engagement of Mattoon and at the forcing of the Shuturgardan (mentioned in despatches, Medal). Served with the Mahsood Wuzeeree Expedition in 1881. Served with the Burmese Expedition in 1886-87 (mentioned in despatches, Clasp).

²²⁵ Lt.Colonel S. D. Turnbull served in the Afghan war in 1879-80 (Medal). Served with the Akha Expedition in 1883-84 (mentioned in despatches). Served with the Hazara Expedition in 1888 (Medal with Clasp).

²²⁷ Lt.Colonel C. W. Walker served with the Burmese Expedition in 1885-86 as Deputy Assistant Adjutant and Quarter Master General, and was slightly wounded in an engagement near Mandalay on the 12th December (mentioned in despatches, Medal with Clasp).

²³⁰ Lt.Colonel W. J. Morse served in the Afghan war in 1880 (Medal).

²³² Lt.Colonel C. F. Massy served with the Transport Train in the Abyssinian campaign in 1868 (Medal). Also served in the Afghan war in 1879 (Medal).

²³³ Colonel R. A. Swetenham served with the Looshai Expedition in 1871-72 (Medal with Clasp), and with the Jowaki Afreedee Expedition in 1877 (Clasp). Served in the Afghan war in 1879-80, and was present at the attack and capture of Ali Musjid (Medal with Clasp). Served with the Burmese Expedition in 1886-88 (Brevet of Lt.Colonel, Clasp); with the Hazara Expedition in 1891 (Clasp); and with the Miranzai Expedition in 1891 in command of the 27th Bengal Infantry (mentioned in despatches, Clasp).

²³⁴ Lt.Colonel J. Humfrey served with the 45th Foot in the Abyssinian campaign in 1868 (Medal).

²³⁶ Lt.Colonel J. Grant served in the Afghan war in 1879-80, and took part in the affair on the Helmund against the Wali's mutineers; was present in the engagement at Maiwand (severely wounded), and at the siege of Candahar (Medal).

²³⁷ Colonel G. F. Young served in the Afghan war in 1879-80 as Transport Officer and as Deputy Assistant Quarter Master General, Khyber Brigade, and was present in the engagement at Kam Dakka (mentioned in despatches, Medal). Also served in the Mahsood Wuzeeree Expedition in 1881 as Deputy Assistant Quarter Master General and Brigade (mentioned in despatches). Served with the Hazara Expedition in 1888 (Brevet of Lt.Colonel, Medal with Clasp).

²³⁸ Colonel H. Melliss served with the 33rd Regiment throughout the Abyssinian war in 1868, and was present at the capture of Magdala (Medal). Served in the Egyptian war of 1882 as Assistant Quarter Master General of the Indian Contingent, and was present at the battle of Tel-el-Kebir (mentioned in despatches, Brevet of Major, Medal with Clasp, 4th Class of the Medjidie, and Khedive's Star). Served with the Burmese Expedition in 1885, as Military Attaché to the Naval Commander in Chief (Medal with Clasp).

²⁴⁰ Lt.Colonel F. C. Burton served in the Afghan war of 1878-80 (Brevet of Major, Medal).

²⁴¹ Lt.Colonel T. F. Hobday served in the Afghan war in 1878-79 with the Candahar Field Force (Brevet of Major, Medal).

²⁴² Lt.Colonel E. H. Wilson served with the Hazara Expedition in 1888 (Medal with Clasp).

²⁴³ Lt.Colonel R. A. Gilchrist served with the 26th Cameronians in the Abyssinian campaign in 1868 (Medal).

²⁴⁴ Lt.Colonel W. G. C. Johnstone served with the Burmese Expedition in 1887-88 (Medal with Clasp).

²⁴⁵ Lt.Colonel J. E. Porteous served in the Abyssinian war in 1867-68 (Medal). Served in the Afghan war in 1879-80, and took part with the Kama Expedition including the engagement at Kam Dakka (Medal). Served in the operations in the Chin Hills, Burmah, in 1891-92.

²⁴⁶ Lt.Colonel W. Cooke served with the Koorum Valley Field Force in the Afghan war in 1879 in charge of the Commissariat, and was present in the engagement at Ali Kheyl, at the forcing of the Shutargardan, in the engagement at Charasiah on the 6th October 1879, and in the operations round Cabul in December 1879 (Medal with two Clasps). Served with the Burmese Expedition in 1885-87 with the Commissariat Department at Rangoon (received the thanks of the Government of India, mentioned in despatches, Brevet of Lt.Colonel, Medal with Clasp).

²⁴⁷ Lt.Colonel G. C. Fenwick served in the Afghan war in 1879-80 including the operations in the Besud Valley (Medal). Served with the Burmese Expedition in 1885-87 (Medal with Clasp).

²⁴⁸ Lt.Colonel D. S. Cuninghame served in the Afghan war of 1878-80, and was present in the engagements at Takht-i-Pul, Ahmed Kheyl (mentioned in despatches), Urzoo near Ghuznee, and Padkao Shana (mentioned in despatches, Brevet of Major, Medal with Clasp). Served with the Mahsood Wuzeeree Expedition in 1881. Served with the second Miranzai Expedition in 1891 (Medal with Clasp).

²⁴⁹ Lt.Colonel W. J. A. Birch served in the Afghan war in 1878-79, and was present at the attack and capture of Ali Musjid (Medal with Clasp).

²⁵⁰ Lt.Colonel W. Hill served with the Looshai Expedition in 1871-72 (Medal with Clasp). Served in the Afghan war of 1878-80, and was present at the attack and capture of Ali Musjid, and in the engagement at Charasiah on the 6th October 1879 (mentioned in despatches); accompanied Sir Frederick Roberts in the march to Candahar, and was present at the battle of Candahar (Brevet of Major, Medal with two Clasps, and Bronze Decoration).

²⁵¹ Lt.Colonel W. C. Black served in the Burmese campaign in 1885-88 with the 23rd Bombay Light Infantry (Medal with Clasp).

²⁵² Lt.Colonel B. C. Graves served in the Afghan war in 1879-80 on the line of communications in the Khyber (Medal).

²⁵³ Lt.Colonel E. H. Bingham served in the Afghan war of 1878-80 with the Quetta Field Force, and took part in the Zaimusht Expedition (Medal).

²⁵⁵ Lt.Colonel W. Loch served in the Afghan war in 1879-80, and took part in the march to Candahar with the force under Major General Phayre (mentioned in despatches, Medal).

²⁵⁶ Lt.Colonel L. T. Bishop served in the expedition against the Jowaki Afreedees in 1877 (Medal with Clasp). Served in the Afghan war of 1878-80 as Deputy Assistant Quarter Master General to the Ghuznee Field Force, and was present in the engagements at Ahmed Kheyl (mentioned in despatches) and Padkao Shana (mentioned in despatches, Brevet of Major, Medal with Clasp).

²⁵⁷ Lt.Colonel G. L. R. Richardson served in the Afghan war in 1879-80 (Brevet of Major, Medal). Served in the Egyptian war of 1882, and was present at the battle of Tel-el-Kebir—severely wounded (Medal with Clasp, and Khedive's Star). Served with the Zhob Field Force under Sir George White in command of the 18th Bengal Lancers (mentioned in despatches).

²⁵⁸ Lt.Colonel A. O. G. Lydiard served in the Afghan war in 1879-80, and was present in the engagement at Kam Dakka and with the expedition into the Hissarik Valley (Medal).

Indian Staff Corps.—War Services of Field Officers. 442*i*

²⁵⁹ Lt. Colonel H. O. Woodhouse served in the Afghan war in 1880 on the line of communications with Cabul (Medal).
²⁶¹ Colonel P. J. Maitland served in the Afghan war in 1878-79, and was present in the engagement at Khushk-i-Nakhud (mentioned in despatches, Medal).
²⁶² Lt. Colonel A. J. Garrett served in the Afghan war in 1879-80, took part in the defence of Candahar and was present at the battle of Candahar—wounded (Medal with Clasp).
²⁶³ Lt. Colonel F. R. Begbie served in the campaign against the Jowaki Afreedees in 1877 (Medal with Clasp). Served in the Afghan war in 1878-79, and was present at the attack and capture of Ali Musjid (Medal with Clasp). Also served in the Mahsood Wuzeeree Expedition in 1881. Served with the Chin-Lushai Expeditionary Force in 1889-90 with the 2nd and Battalion 2nd Goorkhas (mentioned in despatches, Clasp).
²⁶⁵ Lt. Colonel A. G. Yaldwin served in the Afghan war in 1879-80 (Medal).
²⁶⁶ Lt. Colonel A. T. S. A. Rind served in the Afghan war in 1879-80, accompanied Sir Frederick Roberts in the march to Candahar, and was present at the battle of Candahar (twice mentioned in despatches, Brevet of Major, Medal with Clasp, and Bronze Decoration). Served in the Egyptian war of 1882 (Medal, and Khedive's Star).
²⁶⁷ Lt. Colonel O. Creagh served in the Afghan war in 1878-79 as Deputy Assistant Quarter Master General and afterwards as Assistant Quarter Master General, and was present in the engagement at Kam Dakka, with the expedition into the Bazar Valley, and in the engagement at Ali Kheyl (mentioned in despatches, Brevet of Major, Victoria Cross, and Medal); received the VC under the following circumstances:—"On the 21st April 1879 Captain Creagh was detached from Dakka with two companies of his battalion to protect the village of Kam Dakka, on the Cabul River, against a threatened incursion of the Mohmunds, and reached that place the same night. On the following morning the detachment, 150 men, was attacked by the Mohmunds in overwhelming numbers, about 1500; and the inhabitants of Kam Dakka having themselves taken part with the enemy, Captain Creagh found himself under the necessity of retiring from the village. He took up a position in a cemetery not far off, which he made as defensible as circumstances would admit of, and this position he held against all the efforts of the enemy, repeatedly repulsing them with the bayonet until three o'clock in the afternoon, when he was relieved by a detachment sent for the purpose from Dakka. The enemy were then finally repulsed, and being charged by a troop of the 10th Bengal Lancers, under the command of Captain D. M. Strong, were routed and broken, and great numbers of them driven into the river. The Commander in Chief in India has expressed his opinion that but for the coolness, determination, and gallantry of the highest order, and the admirable conduct which Captain Creagh displayed on this occasion, the detachment under his command would, in all probability, have been cut off and destroyed." Served with the Zhob Field Force in 1890 under Sir George White in command of the 29th Bombay Infantry (mentioned in despatches).
²⁶⁸ Lt. Colonel H. A. Sawyer served with the Burmese Expedition in 1887-89 (Medal with Clasp).
²⁶⁹ Lt. Colonel D. E. Gouldsbury served in the Afghan war of 1878-80, and was present in the engagements at Ahmed Kheyl and Urzoo near Ghuznee (Medal with Clasp).
²⁷⁰ Lt. Colonel W. H. Lyster served in the Afghan war in 1880 (Medal).
²⁷¹ Lt. Colonel F. C. Maltby served with the Burmese Expedition in 1887-88 including the operations of the 3rd Brigade under Brigadier Generals Lockhart and Collett (Medal with Clasp); and with the Chin Lushai Expeditionary Force in 1889-90 (Clasp).
²⁷² Lt. Colonel W. H. C. Wyllie served in the Afghan war in 1878-80, and took part in the march to Candahar with the force under Major General Phayre (mentioned in despatches, CIE., and Medal).
²⁷⁴ Lt. Colonel S. E. Rolland served with the Burmese Expedition in 1885-87 (mentioned in despatches Brevet of Lt. Colonel, Medal with Clasp).
²⁷⁵ Lt. Colonel H. A. Vincent served with the 33rd Foot throughout the Abyssinian campaign of 1867-68, and was present at the storming and capture of Magdala (Medal).
²⁷⁶ Lt. Colonel J. P. C. Neville served in the Afghan war of 1878-80, and was present in the engagement at Charasiah on the 6th October 1879, and in the operations around Cabul in December 1879 (mentioned in despatches, Brevet of Major, Medal with two Clasps).
²⁷⁷ Sir Charles Leslie served with the Chin-Lushai Expeditionary Force in 1889-90 in command of a Half Battalion 2nd Battalion 4th Goorkhas (mentioned in despatches, Medal with Clasp). Served with the Manipore Expedition in 1891 in command of the 2nd Battalion 4th Goorkha Rifles (mentioned in despatches, Clasp).
²⁷⁹ Lt. Colonel F. D. Battye served with the Corps of Guides throughout the Jowaki Afreedee expedition in 1877-78 under General Keyes (Medal with Clasp). Also present at the operations against the Ranizai village of Skhakut on the 14th March 1878, and in the attack on the Utman Kheyl villages on 21st March 1878. Served with the Corps of Guides in the Afghan war of 1878-80, and was present at the capture of Ali Musjid, and in the operations around Cabul in December 1879 (severely wounded at the storming of the Asmai Heights), and in the engagement at Charasiah on the 25th April 1880 (mentioned in despatches, Medal with two Clasps). Served with the Hazara Expedition in 1891 in command of the Queen's Own Corps of Guides (mentioned in despatches, Clasp).
²⁸⁰ Lt. Colonel M. James served in the Afghan war in 1879-80 including an engagement at Hurnui (Medal).
²⁸¹ Lt. Colonel J. J. Money-Simons served in the Afghan war of 1878-80 with the Thull Chotiali Field Force, and was present in the engagements at Jugdulluck and Saidabad; accompanied Sir Frederick Roberts in the march to Candahar, and was present at the battle of Candahar (Medal with Clasp, and Bronze Decoration).
²⁸⁴ Colonel A. J. F. Reid served in the Afghan war of 1878-80, was present at the capture of the Peiwar Kotal severely wounded), and took part in the Zaimusht Expedition including the assault of Zawa (Brevet of Major, Medal with Clasp). Served with the Hazara Expedition in 1888 (Brevet of Lt. Colonel, Medal with Clasp). Served with the Miranzai Expedition in 1891 in command of the 29th Bengal Infantry (mentioned in despatches, Clasp).
²⁸⁷ Lt. Colonel T. Greenaway served with the Burmese Expedition in 1886-89 (Medal with two Clasps).
²⁸⁸ Lt. Colonel B. Channer served in the Afghan war in 1879-80 (Medal). Served with the Burmese Expedition in 1885-87 (DSO. and Medal with Clasp), and with the Lushai Expedition in 1889 (Clasp).
²⁸⁹ Lt. Colonel Aberigh-Mackay served in the Afghan war in 1880 (Medal).
²⁹⁰ Lt. Colonel E. B. Anderson served with the Burmese Expedition in 1885-86 as Brigade Transport Officer (Medal with Clasp).
²⁹¹ Lt. Colonel H. M. Rose served in the Afghan war in 1879-80 on the line of communications with the Khyber (Medal). Served with the Burmese Expedition in 1886-87 (mentioned in despatches, DSO., and Medal with two Clasp); with the Hazara Expedition in 1891 (Clasp); and with the second Miranzai Expedition in 1891 (Clasp).
²⁹² Lt. Colonel L. W. Christopher served in the Afghan war of 1878-80 (Medal). Served in the Egyptian war of 1882 (Medal, and Khedive's Star).
²⁹³ Lt. Colonel Machay served in the Egyptian war of 1882 with the 2nd Belooch Regiment, and was present at battle of Tel-el-Kebir (mentioned in despatches, Brevet of Major, Medal with Clasp, and Khedive's Star). Served with the Burmese Expedition in 1888 (Medal with Clasp).
²⁹⁴ Lt. Colonel C. M. Keighley served in the Afghan war in 1878-79, and took part in the expedition into the Bazar Valley and in the advance on Cabul (Medal). Also served in the Mahsood Wuzeeree Expedition in 1881. Served with the Hazara Expedition in 1888 (DSO., and Medal with Clasp).
²⁹⁵ Lt. Colonel F. G. T. Welch served in the Afghan war in 1880 (Medal). Served with the Burmese Expedition in 1886-87 (mentioned in despatches, Medal with two Clasps).
²⁹⁶ Lt. Colonel L. Dening served in the Afghan war in 1878-79 (Medal). Served with the Burmese Expedition in 1886-88 (mentioned in despatches, DSO., and Medal with Clasp).
²⁹⁷ Lt. Colonel C. C. Egerton served in the Afghan war in 1879-80, accompanied Sir Frederick Roberts in the march to Candahar, and was present at the battle of Candahar (mentioned in despatches, Medal with Clasp, and Bronze Decoration). Served with the Hazara Expedition in 1888 as Assistant Adjutant General (mentioned in despatches, Medal with Clasp). Served with the two Miranzai Expeditions under Sir William Lockhart in 1891 as Assistant Adjutant General—severely wounded (mentioned in despatches, Brevet of Lt. Colonel, Clasp).
²⁹⁸ Lt. Colonel C. A. Mercer served in the Hazara campaign in 1868 (Medal with Clasp); and in the Looshai Expedition in 1871-72 (Clasp). Served in the Afghan war of 1878-80, and was present at the attack and capture of Ali Musjid, in the operations round Cabul in December 1879, and in the engagement at Saidabad; accompanied Sir Frederick Roberts in the march to Candahar, and was present at the battle of Candahar (mentioned in despatches, Medal with three Clasps, and Bronze Decoration). Also served with the Marri Expedition in 1880.
²⁹⁹ Lt. Colonel T. H. Goldney served with the Sikkim Expedition in 1888 (mentioned in despatches, Medal with Clasp).

F F

300 Lt. Colonel G. W. Martin served in the Afghan war in 1879-80 with the Koorum and Cabul Field Forces, and was present in the engagement at Ali Kheyl, and in the operations around Cabul in December 1879 including the investment of Sherpore (mentioned in despatches, Medal with Clasp). Also served in the Mahsood Wuzeeree Expedition in 1881.

301 Lt. Colonel Maltby served with the Transport Department throughout the Afghan war of 1878-80 (Medal). Served with the Burmese Expedition in 1886-88 with the 2nd Infantry Hyderabad Contingent (Medal with two Clasps).

302 Lt. Colonel F. R. Ditmas served in the Afghan war in 1879 with the Vitakri Field Force (mentioned in despatches, Medal).

304 Lt. Colonel G. H. Elliott served in the Afghan war in 1879-80, accompanied Sir Frederick Roberts in the march to Candahar, and was present at the battle of Candahar (mentioned in despatches, Brevet of Major, Medal with Clasp, and Bronze Decoration). Served in the Soudan campaign in 1885 with the Transport Department of the Indian Contingent (mentioned in despatches, Medal with Clasp, and Khedive's Star). [See also Civil Decorations for Gallantry, "Hart's Annual Army List," p. 786.]

305 Lt. Colonel J. N. Walker served in the Afghan war in 1880 as Brigade Major to the Candahar Line of Communications (Medal). Served with the Zhob Valley Expedition in 1884 as Deputy Assistant Adjutant General.

306 Lt. Colonel S. R. Rawlinson served with the Burmese Expedition in 1885-87 (mentioned in despatches, DSO., and Medal with Clasp).

307 Lt. Colonel E. W. Chalmers served in the expedition against the Jowaki Afreedees in 1877 (Medal with Clasp). Served in the Afghan war of 1878-80 (Medal). Served with the Burmese Expedition in 1886-88 (mentioned in despatches, Clasp).

309 Lt. Colonel A. J. Brander served in the Afghan war of 1878-80, first with the Candahar Field Force, and afterwards with the Northern Afghanistan Field Force (Medal). Served with the Hazara Expedition in 1891 (Medal with Clasp); and with the second Miranzai Expedition in 1891 (Clasp).

310 Lt. Colonel C. E. Yate served in the Afghan war in 1880 as Political Officer at Khelat-i-Ghilzie, accompanied Sir Frederick Roberts in the march to Candahar, and was present at the battle of Candahar (Medal with Clasp, and Bronze Decoration).

312 Lt. Colonel B. H. Pollard served with the Burmese Expedition in 1888 (Medal with Clasp).

313 Lt. Colonel C. H. E. Adamson was employed on civil duty during the Burmese Expedition in 1885-89 (received the thanks of the Government of India, mentioned in despatches, Medal with Clasp).

314 Lt. Colonel R. K. Ridgeway served in the operations against the Naga Hill tribes in 1879-80, and was severely wounded at the assault of Konoma (mentioned in despatches, Victoria Cross, and Medal with Clasp); was awarded the VC "for conspicuous gallantry throughout the attack on Konoma, on the 22nd November 1879, more especially in the final assault, when, under a heavy fire from the enemy, he rushed up to a barricade and attempted to tear down the planking surrounding it, to enable him to effect an entrance, in which act he received a very severe rifle shot wound in the left shoulder." Served with the Manipore Expedition in 1891 in command of the 44th Goorkha Rifles (mentioned in despatches, Clasp).

315 Lt. Colonel G. L. Eliot served with the Duffla Expedition in 1874-75, and with the Jowaki Afreedee Expedition in 1877-78 (Medal). Served in the Afghan war in 1878-79 (Medal).

316 Lt. Colonel F. B. Peile served with the Zhob Valley Expedition in 1884.

317 Lt. Colonel J. B. Lynch served in the Afghan war of 1878-80, and was present at the capture of the Peiwar Kotal, in the engagement at Charasiab on the 6th October 1879, and in the operations round Cabul in December 1879 including the investment of Sherpore (Medal with three Clasps).

318 Lt. Colonel R. Gordon served with the Jowaki Afreedee Expedition in 1877-78 (Medal with Clasp). Served with the Miranzai Expedition in 1891 (Clasp).

320 Lt. Colonel H. E. Penton served with the Burmese Expedition in 1885-89 (Medal with two Clasps).

321 Lt. Colonel E. L. Elliot served in the Afghan war in 1878-79 (Medal). Served with the Burmese Expedition in 1885-89 (mentioned in despatches, DSO., and Medal with two Clasps).

322 Lt. Colonel C. W. J. Hingston served with the Burmese Expedition in 1888-89 (mentioned in despatches, Medal with Clasp), and with the Chin-Lushai Expeditionary Force in 1889-90 (Clasp).

324 Lt. Colonel H. A. Abbott served in the Afghan war of 1878-80, and was present in the engagements at Ahmed Kheyl and Urzoo near Ghuznee; accompanied Sir Frederick Roberts in the march to Candahar, and was present at the battle of Candahar (mentioned in despatches, Medal with two Clasps, and Bronze Decoration). Served in the Soudan campaign in 1885, and was present in the engagements at Hasheen and the Tofrek zereba and at the destruction of Temai (mentioned in despatches, Brevet of Major, Medal with two Clasps, and Khedive's Star). Served with the Miranzai Expedition in 1891 in command of the 15th Sikhs (mentioned in despatches, Medal with Clasp).

325 Lt. Colonel G. Gaisford served with the expedition against the Jowaki Afreedees in 1877-78 (mentioned in despatches, Medal with Clasp). Served in the Afghan war of 1878-80, and was present in the engagement of Kam Dakka (mentioned in despatches, Medal). Served with the Zhob Field Force under Sir George White in 1890 as Political Officer (mentioned in despatches).

327 Lt. Colonel F. D. Raikes served with the Burmese Expedition in 1885-87 on special Political duty (received the thanks of the Government of India, mentioned in despatches, Medal with Clasp); also served with the Burmese Expedition in 1887-89 (Clasp), and with the Chin-Lushai Expeditionary Force in 1889-90 (Clasp).

328 Colonel C. R. Macgregor served as Adjutant with the 44th Bengal Native Infantry in the Duffla Expedition in 1874-75; also served with the 44th Bengal Native Infantry in the Naga Expedition in 1875 (mentioned in despatches, and received the thanks of the Government of India), and with the expedition against the Angami Naga Hill tribes in 1877-78 (received the thanks of the Governor General of India). Served as Deputy Assistant Quarter Master General to the Naga Field Force in 1879-80 (mentioned in despatches, Brevet of Major, Medal with Clasp). Served in the Afghan war in 1880, accompanied Sir Frederick Roberts in the march to Candahar as Brigade Transport Officer, and acted as Orderly Officer to Brigadier General Macgregor at the battle of Candahar (mentioned in despatches, Medal with Clasp, and Bronze Decoration). Also served with the Marri Expedition in 1880 under Brigadier General Macgregor (mentioned in despatches). Served with the Akha Expedition in 1884 (mentioned in despatches). Served with the Burmese Expedition in 1886-89 in command of the 44th Goorkha Light Infantry (mentioned in despatches, Brevet of Lt. Colonel, DSO., and Clasp). Served with the Wuntho Expedition in 1891 in command of the Northern Column (mentioned in despatches).

329 Lt. Colonel W. P. Newall served in the Afghan war of 1878-80, and was present in the operations around Cabul in December 1879 (Medal with Clasp).

331 Lt. Colonel B. A. N. Parrott served with the Burmese Expedition in 1885-87 on civil duties (received the thanks of the Government of India, mentioned in despatches, Medal with Clasp).

332 Lt. Colonel C. A. R. Sage served in the Burmese Expedition in 1886-87 (mentioned in despatches, Brevet of Major, Medal with Clasp), and with the Sikkim Expedition in 1888 (Clasp).

334 Lt. Colonel C. Dempster served with the Mahsood Wuzeeree Expedition in 1881. Served with the Hazara Expedition in 1891; organized the base and lines of communication (mentioned in despatches, Medal with Clasp). Served with the Isazai Expedition in 1892.

335 Lt. Colonel E. Bruce served in the Afghan war in 1879-80, and was present in the engagements at Ahmed Kheyl and Urzoo near Ghuznee (mentioned in despatches, Brevet of Major, Medal with Clasp).

336 Lt. Colonel T. E. Spencer served with the Nile Expedition in 1884-85 (mentioned in despatches, Brevet of Major, Medal with Clasp, and Khedive's Star). Served with the Burmese Expedition in 1888-89 (mentioned in despatches, Medal with Clasp).

337 Lt. Colonel F. Abbott served in the Afghan war of 1878-80 as Orderly Officer to Brigadier General Nuttall in the advance on Candahar and afterwards as Brigade Major to the Vitakri Field Force (Medal).

338 Lt. Colonel G. B. E. Radcliffe served in the Soudan campaign in 1885 (Medal with Clasp and Khedive's Star). Served with the Burmese Expedition in 1887-89 (Medal with two Clasps).

339 Lt. Colonel H. C. Halkett served in the Afghan war in 1878-79, first with the Candahar Field Force, and afterwards on the line of communications in the Khyber (Medal), and with the Mahsood Wuzeeree Expedition in 1881. Served with the Sikkim Expedition in 1888 (mentioned in despatches, Medal with Clasp).

Indian Staff Corps.—War Services of Field Officers.

³⁴⁰ Lt.Colonel A. Howlett served with the Manipore Expedition in 1891 in command of the 12th Madras Infantry (mentioned in despatches, Medal with Clasp).

³⁴¹ Lt.Colonel H. Hay served with the Zhob Valley Expedition in 1884. Served with the Burmese Expedition in 1885-89 (Medal with two Clasps).

³⁴² Lt.Colonel A. M. Muir served in the Afghan war of 1878-80, and was present in the engagement at Takht-i-Pul, at the defence of Candahar, and at the battle of Candahar (Medal with Clasp).

³⁴⁴ Lt.Colonel W. A. Broome served in the Afghan war of 1878-80 as Adjutant 2nd Beloochh Regiment, and was present in the engagement at Takht-i-Pul and at the occupation of Candahar and Girishk (Medal). Served with the 2nd Belooch Regiment in the Egyptian war of 1882, and was present at the battle of Tel-el-Kebir (Medal with Clasp, and Khedive's Star). Served with the Burmese Expedition in 1886-89 as Second in Command of the 1st Belooch Battalion Light Infantry; took part in the operations against the Karen Tribes in 1887-88, and served with the Karen Field Force under Brigadier General Collett in 1888-89 including the engagement at Nga-Kyne, the forcing of the Nanko Defile, and the capture of Sawlon (Medal with two Clasps).

³⁴⁶ Lt.Colonel J. R. Hobday served with the Candahar Field Force in the Afghan war in 1879 (Medal). Served with the Burmese Expedition in 1886-87 on Survey duty (mentioned in despatches, Brevet of Major, Medal with Clasp), and in 1887-89 (Clasp); accompanied the special expedition in Upper Burmah along the Chinese Frontier in 1890-91 (mentioned in despatches).

³⁴⁷ Lt.Colonel G. W. Deane served with the 13th Bengal Lancers in the Afghan war of 1878-80 (Medal). Served with the 13th Bengal Lancers in the Egyptian war of 1882, and was present at the battle of Tel-el-Kebir (mentioned in despatches, Medal with Clasp, and Khedive's Star). Served with the Burmese Expedition in 1887-88 as Deputy Assistant Adjutant and Quarter Master General 1st Brigade Upper Burmah Field Force (mentioned in despatches, Medal with Clasp).

³⁴⁹ Lt.Colonel S. H. Mackenzie served in the Afghan war in 1880 (Medal).

³⁵⁰ Lt.Colonel J. F. D. Fordyce served in the Afghan war in 1878-79 (Medal).

³⁵¹ Lt.Colonel H. S. Maxwell served in the operations against the Naga Hill Tribes in 1879-80, and was present at the assault of Konoma (mentioned in despatches, and received the thanks of the Governor General in Council and of the Commander in Chief in India, Medal with Clasp). Served with the Akha Expedition in 1883-84 (mentioned in despatches). Served with the Manipore Expedition in 1891 as Chief Political Officer (received the thanks of the Governor General in Council and of the Commander in Chief in India, mentioned in despatches, Clasp).

³⁵³ Lt.Colonel A. J. P. Nuthall served with the Burmese Expedition in 1886-89 (Medal with two Clasps).

³⁵⁴ Lt.Colonel E. D. N. Smith served in the Afghan war of 1878-80, and was present in the engagement at Khushk-i-Nakhud (mentioned in despatches), at the defence of Candahar including the sortie of Doh Khojah, and at the battle of Candahar (Medal with Clasp).

³⁵⁵ Major W. B. Wilson served in the Afghan war of 1878-80, and was present at the capture of the Peiwar Kotal, in the engagement at Charasiab on the 6th October 1879, and in the operations round Cabul in December 1870, Medal with three Clasps). Served with the Burmese Expedition in 1886-87 (mentioned in despatches, Brevet of Major, and Medal with Clasp).

³⁵⁶ Major E. V. P. Monteith served in the Afghan war in 1879-80, and was present in the engagement on the Helmund with the Wali Shere Ali's mutinous troops, in the affair at Khaizabad, at the defence of Candahar (mentioned in despatches), and at the battle of Candahar (Medal with Clasp).

³⁵⁷ Major H. C. Lamb served in the Afghan war in 1879-80 (Medal).

³⁵⁸ Major V. A. Schalch served in the Afghan war of 1878-80, and was present in the engagement at Ali Kheyl (Medal). Served with the Burmese Expedition in 1885-86 as a Brigade Major (mentioned in despatches, Brevet of Major, Medal with Clasp), and with the Hazara Expedition in 1891 (Clasp).

³⁵⁹ Major G. S. Eyre served in the Afghan war in 1878-79, as Assistant Superintendent of Transport, Koorum Valley Field Force, and was present at the attack and capture of the Peiwar Kotal as Acting Orderly Officer to Colonel M'Queen (Medal with Clasp). Served with the Burmese Expedition in 1885-87 as Civil Officer (received the thanks of the Government of India, mentioned in despatches, Medal with Clasp). [See also Civil Decorations for Gallantry, "Hart's Annual Army List," p. 786.]

³⁶⁰ Major E. Balfe served in the Hazara Expedition in 1891 as Provost Marshal and Judge Advocate (mentioned in despatches, Medal with Clasp).

³⁶² Major G. C. Dobbs served in the Afghan war in 1879-80, was present in the engagement at Maiwand, and took part in the defence of Candahar (Medal).

³⁶³ Major D. A. A. Macpherson served with the Burmese Expedition in 1885-86 as Field Paymaster (mentioned in despatches, Medal with Clasp).

³⁶⁴ Major B. L. P. Reilly served in the Afghan war of 1878-80, and was present in the engagements at Khushk-i-Nakhud and Ahmed Kheyl (mentioned in despatches, Medal with Clasp). Served in the Egyptian war of 1882 (Medal, and Khedive's Star). Also served with the Zhob Valley Expedition in 1884.

³⁶⁵ Major C. W. Muir served in the Afghan war in 1880 (Medal). Served in the Soudan campaign in 1885 as Aide de Camp to Colonel Hudson, Commanding Indian Contingent, and was present in the engagements at Hasheen and the Tofrek zereba, and in the operations at Tamai (mentioned in despatches, Medal with two Clasps, and Khedive's Star). Served with the Burmese Expedition in 1885-87 (Medal with Clasp).

³⁶⁷ Major E. D. F. Bignell served in the Afghan war in 1880 (Medal).

³⁶⁹ Major G. E. Money served in the Afghan war in 1878-79 with the Koorum Field Force, and took part with the expedition into the Khost Valley (Medal).

³⁷¹ Major H. C. E. Lucas served in the Afghan war in 1878-79 (Medal). Served in the Soudan campaign in 1885 (Medal, and Khedive's Star).

³⁷² Major A. R. Porter served in the Afghan war in 1879 (Medal). Served with the Hazara Expedition in 1891 (Medal with Clasp).

³⁷³ Major E. C. Kellie served in the Afghan war in 1880 (Medal). Served with the Burmese Expedition in 1885-88 as Deputy Assistant Adjutant and Quarter Master General 4th Brigade (mentioned in despatches, Medal with two Clasps).

³⁷⁴ Major J. C. F. Gordon served with the Mahsood Wuzeeree Expedition as Deputy Assistant Quarter Master General 2nd Column. Served in the Egyptian war of 1882, and was present at the battle of Tel-el-Kebir (mentioned in despatches, Medal with Clasp, and Khedive's Star).

³⁷⁵ Lt.Colonel St. J. F. Michell served with the Burmese Expedition in 1887-89 on special service beyond the Indian frontier (Brevet of Lt.Colonel, Medal with Clasp). Served with the Manipore Expedition in 1891 as Assistant Quarter Master General (mentioned in despatches, Clasp).

³⁷⁷ Major A. de V. Alexander served with the Khyber Field Force in the Afghan war in 1879-80 (Medal).

³⁷⁸ Major R. F. Trotter served with the Jowaki Afreedee Expedition in 1877-78 (Medal). Served in the Afghan war in 1879-80, and was present at the attack and capture of Ali Musjid (Medal with Clasp).

³⁷⁹ Major E. A. Young served in the Afghan war of 1878-80, and was present in the advance to Candahar and Kholat-i-Ghilzie and in the engagement at Ahmed Kheyl—severely wounded and horse shot (Medal with Clasp).

³⁸⁰ Colonel G. H. More Molyneux served in the Afghan war of 1878-80 (Medal). Served in the Soudan campaign in 1885 attached to the Intelligence Department (Medal with Clasp, and Khedive's Star). Served with the Burmese Expedition in 1885-89 as Assistant Adjutant General (mentioned in despatches, Brevet of Lt.Colonel, Medal with Clasp).

³⁸² Major W. P. Kennedy served during the Afghan war in 1880 as Assistant Governor General's Agent in Beloochistan (Medal).

³⁸³ Major H. M. Mason served with the Burmese Expedition in 1886-87 (Medal with two Clasps).

³⁸⁴ Major F. Stevenson served in the Afghan war in 1879-80, and was present in the engagements at Ahmed Kheyl (mentioned in despatches) and Urzoo near Ghuznee; accompanied Sir Frederick Roberts in the march to Candahar, and was present at the battle of Candahar (Medal with two Clasps, and Bronze Decoration).

³⁸⁵ Major A. A. Pearson served in the Afghan war in 1880 (Medal). Served with the Burmese Expedition in 1886-87 as Deputy Assistant Adjutant and Quarter Master General 3rd Brigade Upper Burmah Field Force (mentioned in despatches, Brevet of Major, Medal with Clasp).

³⁸⁶ Major G. Hawkes served in the Rumpa Rebellion in 1880. Served with the Hazara Expedition in 1888

F F 2

(Medal with Clasp); in the Hazara Expedition in 1891 with the 2nd Battalion 5th Goorkhas (Clasp); and with the Isazai Expedition in 1892.

387 Major R. C. Hadow served in the Afghan war of 1878-80, and was present in the engagements at Ahmed Kheyl and Urzoo near Ghuznee; accompanied Sir Frederick Roberts in the march to Candahar, and was present at the battle of Candahar (Medal with two Clasps, and Bronze Decoration). Served in the Soudan campaign in 1885 and was present at the engagement at the Tofrek zereba and at the destruction of Temai (Medal with two Clasps, and Khedive's Star). Served with the second Miranzai Expedition in 1891 (Medal with Clasp).

388 Major E. A. Barclay served in the Afghan war in 1879-80 (Medal). Served with the Burmese Expedition in 1887-89 (mentioned in despatches, Medal with two Clasps).

389 Major C. C. Nicholetts served in the Afghan war in 1879-80 (Medal). Served with the Burmese Expedition in 1885-89 (mentioned in despatches, Medal with two Clasps).

391 Major J. E. Mein served with the expedition against the Jowaki Afreedees in 1877-78 (Medal with Clasp). Served with the 5th Punjab Infantry in the Afghan war of 1878-80, and was present in the operations around Cabul in December 1879 (Medal with Clasp). Also served with the Mahsood Wuzeeree Expedition in 1881. Served with the second Miranzai Expedition in 1891 (Clasp).

392 Major W. O. Harris served in the expedition against the Jowaki Afreedees in 1877-78 (Medal with Clasp). Served with the 20th Bengal Native Infantry in the Afghan war of 1878-80, and was present at the attack and capture of Ali Musjid, in the advance to Gundamuck, and with the Zaimusht Expedition including the assault of Zawa (Medal with Clasp). Also served with the Mahsood Wuzeeree Expedition in 1881. Served with the 20th Bengal Native Infantry in the Egyptian war of 1882, and was present at the battle of Tel-el-Kebir (Medal with Clasp, and Khedive's Star).

394 Major H. S. Whentley served in the Afghan war of 1878-80, and was present in the advance to Cabul under Brigadier General Charles Gough, and at the relief of Sherpore; accompanied Sir Frederick Roberts in the march to Candahar, and was present at the battle of Candahar (mentioned in despatches, Medal with two Clasps, and Bronze Decoration).

395 Major H. H. Young served with the Burmese Expedition in 1886 (Medal with Clasp).

396 Major E. E. Kenny served with the Burmese Expedition in 1886-87 (Medal with two Clasps).

397 Major G. D. C. Gastrell served in the Afghan war in 1879-80, and took part in the expedition into the Hissarik Valley (Medal).

398 Major G. L. Garstin served in the Afghan war in 1880 (Medal). Served in the Soudan campaign in 1885 (Medal with Clasp, and Khedive's Star).

399 Major W. R. Le G. Anderson served in the Egyptian war of 1882 (Medal, and Khedive's Star).

400 Major J. W. E. Angelo served in the Afghan war in 1878-79, and took part in the advance to Candahar and Khelat-i-Ghilzie (Medal). Served with the Burmese Expedition in 1886-87 (Clasp).

401 Major G. F. Francis served in the Afghan war in 1873-79 (Medal). Served with the Zhob Valley Expedition in 1884. Served in the Soudan campaign in 1885, and was present in the engagements at Hasheen and the Tofrek zereba, at various attacks on convoys, and at the destruction of Temai (Medal with two Clasps, and Khedive's Star).

402 Major G. S. Baugh served with the Burmese Expedition in 1885-89 (Medal with two Clasps).

403 Major A. T. Weller served in the Afghan war in 1880 on the Khyber line of communications (Medal). Served with the Burmese Expedition in 1886-87 (Medal with Clasp); with the Lushai Expedition in 1889 (mentioned in despatches; and with the Chin-Lushai Expeditionary Force in 1889-90 with the 9th Bengal Native Infantry (mentioned in despatches, Clasp).

405 Major A. Masters served in the Afghan war in 1879-80, and took part with the Kama Expedition; accompanied Sir Frederick Roberts in the march to Candahar, and was present at the battle of Candahar (Medal with Clasp, and Bronze Decoration).

407 Major F. G. Alexander served in the Afghan war in 1878-79 (Medal).

409 Major H. P. P. Leigh served with the Miranzai Expedition under Sir William Lockhart in 1891 as Political Officer (received the thanks of the Government of India, mentioned in despatches, Medal with Clasp).

410 Major R. C. Temple served in the Afghan war in 1878-79, and took part in the advance on Khelat-i-Ghilzie (Medal). Served with the Burmese Expedition in 1885-87 (Medal with Clasp).

412 Major H. N. McRae served in the Afghan war of 1878-80, and was present at the attack and capture of Ali Musjid, in the two expeditions into the Bazar Valley (mentioned in despatches), in the expedition to Jugdulluck and in that at Charasiah on the 25th April 1880 (Medal with Clasp). Served with the Zhob Valley Expedition in 1884. Served with the Hazara Expedition in 1888 (Brevet of Major, Medal with Clasp). [See also Civil Decorations for Gallantry, "Hart's Annual Army List," p. 786.]

413 Major F. C. Maisey served in the Afghan war of 1878-80, and was present at the capture of the Peiwar Kotal, in the engagement at Kam Dakka and with the Kama Expedition (Medal with Clasp). Also served with the Mahsood Wuzeeree Expedition in 1881. Served with the Miranzai Expedition in 1891 with the 29th Bengal Infantry—wounded (mentioned in despatches, Medal with Clasp).

414 Major C. Hogge served in the Afghan war of 1878-80, and was present in the engagement at Mazeena (Medal). Served with the Hazara Expedition in 1888 (Brevet of Major, Medal with Clasp).

416 Major J. W. Hogge served in the Afghan war in 1878, and was present at the attack and capture of Ali Musjid (Medal with Clasp). Also served with the Mahsood Wuzeeree Expedition in 1881. Served with the Hazara Expedition in 1888 (Medal with Clasp).

417 Major O. C. Radford served with the Jowakee Afreedee Expedition in 1877-78 (mentioned in despatches, Medal with Clasp). Served in the Afghan war in 1879, and took part in the Zaimusht Expedition including the assault of Zawa (Medal). Served with the Zhob Valley Expedition in 1884. Served with the Hazara Expedition in 1888—wounded (Brevet of Major, Clasp).

418 Major A. Montanaro served in the Afghan war in 1879-80 on the Khyber line of communications (Medal). Served with the Burmese Expedition in 1886-89 (Medal with two Clasps).

419 Major W. H. F. MacMullen served in the Afghan war in 1879-80 (Medal).

420 Major F. S. Sorell served with the Burmese Expedition in 1886-88 (mentioned in despatches, Medal with two Clasps).

421 Major C. Pulley served in the Afghan war of 1878-80, and was present in the engagements at Ahmed Kheyl and Urzoo near Ghuznee (Medal with Clasp). Served with the Burmese Expedition in 1886-87, and was slightly wounded in an engagement on the 25th November 1886 (mentioned in despatches, Brevet of Major, Medal with Clasp).

422 Major L. J. Browne served in the Afghan war in 1878-79, and was present at the attack and capture of Ali Musjid (Medal with Clasp). Served with the Burmese Expedition in 1887-88, including the operations of the 4th Brigade under Brigadier General Low (Medal with Clasp).

423 Major P. E. Henderson served with the Jowaki Expedition in 1877-78 (Medal). Served in the Afghan war in 1878-79 (Medal), and with the expedition against the Naga Hill Tribes in 1879-80 (Clasp).

424 Major R. F. Jameson served in the Afghan war of 1878-80 as Adjutant and Quarter Master 5th Punjab Infantry with the Koorum Field Force, and was present at the affair on the 22nd November 1878 and at the capture of the Peiwar Kotal, the engagement at Charasiab on 6th October 1879, and in the various operations around Cabul in December 1879, and the subsequent defence of Sherpore (Medal with three Clasps). Served as Adjutant and Quarter Master 5th Punjab Infantry in the Mahsood Wuzeeree Expedition under Brigadier General Gordon in 1881.

426 Major A. G. F. Browne served in the Afghan war in 1878-79 (Medal). Served with the Burmese Expedition in 1886 (Medal with Clasp). Served with the Chin-Lushai Expeditionary Force in 1889-90 as Superintendent of Signalling (mentioned in despatches, *DSO.* and Clasp).

428 Major Coats served in the Afghan war of 1878-80 with the Candahar Column, including the advance to Khelat-i-Ghilzie, the engagement at Saif-u-deen, and in the engagements at Ahmed Kheyl and Urzoo near Ghuznee; accompanied Sir Frederick Roberts in the march to Candahar and was present at the battle of Candahar (Medal with two Clasps, and Bronze Decoration).

430 Colonel N. R. Stewart served in the Afghan war of 1878-80, and was present in the engagements at Ahmed Kheyl and Urzoo near Ghuznee (mentioned in despatches, Brevet of Major, Medal with Clasp). Served with the

Nile Expedition in 1884-85 as Deputy Assistant Adjutant and Quarter Master General with the Indian Contingent (mentioned in despatches, Brevet of Lt. Colonel, Medal with Clasp, and Khedive's Star).

⁴³¹ Major A. W. D. Campbell served with the 15th Hussars in the Candahar Column in the Afghan war of 1878-79 including the advance to Khelat-i-Gilzai (Medal).

⁴³² Major C. S. Wheler served in the Egyptian war of 1882, and was present at the battle of Tel-el-Kebir (Medal with Clasp).

⁴³¹ Lt. Colonel E. G. Barrow served in the Afghan war in 1878-79 with the column under Sir Samuel Browne, and was present at the attack and capture of Ali Musjid (Medal with Clasp). Served in the Egyptian war of 1882 as Deputy Assistant Quarter Master General with the Indian Contingent, and was present at the battle of Tel-el-Kebir (Medal with Clasp, 5th Class of the Medjidie, and Khedive's Star).

⁴³⁵ Major M. C. Cooke-Collis served with the Corps of Guides throughout the Jowaki Afreedee Expedition in 1877-78 under General Keyes (Medal with Clasp). Also present at the operations against the Ranizai village of Skhakat on the 14th March 1878, and in the attack on the Utman Kheyl villages on 21st March 1878. Served with the Corps of Guides in the Afghan war of 1878-80, and was present at the capture of Ali Musjid, the investment of Sherpore in December 1879, and in the engagement at Charasiah on 25th April 1880 (Medal with two Clasps). Served with the Hazara Expedition in 1891 (Clasp).

⁴³⁷ Major Gambier served in the Jowaki Afreedee Expedition of 1877-78 (Medal with Clasp). Served in the Afghan war of 1878-80, and was present in the affair at Mattoon, in the engagement at Charasiah on 6th October 1879, and in the operations around Cabul in December 1879 including the investment of Sherpore—wounded (Medal with two Clasps). Served with the Miranzai Expedition in 1891 as Brigade Major to the 3rd Column (mentioned in despatches, Brevet of Major, Clasp).

⁴³⁸ Major W. S. Hewett served in the Afghan war of 1878-80, and was present in the engagement at Ahmed Kheyl (Medal with Clasp).

⁴³⁹ Major F. G. L. Mainwaring served in the Afghan war of 1878-80 (Medal).

⁴⁴⁰ Major A. B. Mein served in the Afghan war in 1879-80 (Medal).

⁴⁴¹ Major M. I. Gibbs served in the Afghan war in 1879-80, and was present in the engagement at Kam Dakka (Medal).

⁴⁴² Major C. M. FitzGerald served in the Afghan war of 1878-30, and was present in the engagements at Mattoon and at Charasiab on the 6th October 1879; accompanied Sir Frederick Roberts in the march to Candahar, and was present at the battle of Candahar (Medal with two Clasps, and Bronze Decoration). Served with the Akha Expedition in 1883-84 (mentioned in despatches). Served with the Manipore Expedition in 1891 as Chief Commissariat Officer (mentioned in despatches, Medal with Clasp).

⁴⁴³ Major A. C. Bunny served in the expedition against the Jowaki Afreedees in 1877-78 (Medal with Clasp). Served in the Afghan war in 1879, and took part in the operations in the Lughman Valley (mentioned in despatches, Medal). Also served in the Mahsood Wuzeeree Expedition in 1881 (mentioned in despatches). Served with the Zhob Valley Expedition in 1890.

⁴⁴⁵ Major A. G. H. Hayne served with the Burmese Expedition in 1886-87 (Medal with Clasp).

⁴⁴⁶ Major R. Fulton served with the Sikkim Expedition in 1888 (Medal with Clasp).

⁴⁴⁸ Major F. M. Rundall served with the Burmese Expedition in 1886-87 (Medal with Clasp); in the Chin-Lushai Expeditionary Force in 1889-90 with the Burma Column (Clasp); in the operations in the Chin Hills in 1890-91 in command of the Kanhow Expedition (DSO.); and with the Manipore Expedition in 1891 (mentioned in despatches, Clasp).

⁴⁴⁹ Major F. S. Gwatkin served in the Afghan war in 1878-79 and was present with the two expeditions to the Bazar Valley, in the engagement at Deh Sarak, and with the Zaimusht Expedition (Medal). Served in the Egyptian war of 1882, and was present in the action at Kassasin (9th September) and at the battle of Tel-el-Kebir (Medal with Clasp, and Khedive's Star); also served in the Soudan campaign in 1885 (Clasp). Served with the Chin-Lushai Expeditionary Force in 1889-90 as Staff Officer to Brigadier General Tregear (mentioned in despatches, Brevet of Major, Medal with Clasp). Served in the Manipore Expedition in 1891 as Assistant Adjutant General (mentioned in despatches, Clasp).

⁴⁵⁰ Major G. B. Renny served in the Afghan war in 1879-80 (Medal).

⁴⁵¹ Major B. M. Allen served in the Afghan war in 1879 (Medal), and in the Mahsood Wuzeeree Expedition in 1881 attached to the Signalling Department.

⁴⁵² Major P. A. Buckland served in the Afghan war in 1879-80, and was present at the capture of the Peiwar Kotal (Medal with Clasp).

⁴⁵³ Major E. C. C. Sandys served in the Afghan war in 1879-80, including the operations in the Mazeena Valley (Medal). Served with the Miranzai Expedition in 1891 under Sir William Lockhart as Chief Commissariat Officer (mentioned in despatches, Brevet of Major, Medal with Clasp).

⁴⁵⁴ Major W. C. F. Field served with the Zhob Valley Expedition in 1884. Served with the Burmese Expedition in 1887 (Medal with Clasp).

⁴⁵⁵ Major C. W. Ravenshaw served in the Afghan war in 1880 (Medal).

⁴⁵⁶ Major T. C. Pears served with the Thull Chotiali Field Force in the Afghan war in 1878-79, and was present in the engagement at Baghao (mentioned in despatches, Medal).

⁴⁵⁷ Major H. J. Bolton served in the Afghan war of 1878-80, and was present at the attack and capture of Ali Musjid and in the advance to Cabul under Brigadier General Charles Gough (mentioned in despatches); accompanied Sir Frederick Roberts in the march to Candahar, and was present in the battle of Candahar (Medal with three Clasps, and Bronze Decoration). Also served with the Marri Expedition in 1881.

⁴⁵⁸ Major H. H. R. Heath served with the Jowaki Expedition in 1877-78 (mentioned in despatches, Medal with Clasp). Served in the Afghan war in 1878-79, and was present at the attack and capture of Ali Musjid and in the engagement at Deh Sarak (mentioned in despatches, Medal with Clasp). Served with the Hazara Expedition in 1891 (Clasp).

⁴⁵⁹ Major R. E. D. Reilly served in the Afghan war in 1880, and was present at the battle of Candahar (Medal with Clasp). Served in the Soudan campaign in 1885 with the 28th Bombay Native Infantry, and was present in the engagements at Hasheen and the Tofrek zereba and at the destruction of Temai (mentioned in despatches, Brevet of Major, Medal with two Clasps, and Khedive's Star).

⁴⁶⁰ Major W. W. Lean served in the Afghan war of 1878-80, and was present at the capture of the Peiwar Kotal, in the engagement at Charasiab on the 6th October 1879, and in the operations around Cabul in December 1879, including the investment of Sherpore (Medal with three Clasps).

⁴⁶¹ Major G. A. Money served in the Afghan war in 1879-80 (Medal), and in the Mahsood Wuzeeree Expedition in 1881. Served with the Zhob Field Force under Sir George White in 1890 (mentioned in despatches).

⁴⁶² Major I. MacIvor served with the Zhob Field Force under Sir George White in 1890 as Political Officer (mentioned in despatches).

⁴⁶³ Major R. W. MacLeod served in the expedition against the Jowaki Afreedees in 1877-78 (Medal with Clasp). Served in the Afghan war in 1878-79, and was present at the capture of the Peiwar Kotal, and with the Zaimusht Expedition including the assault of Zawa (Medal with Clasp). Served with the Hazara Expedition in 1888 (mentioned in despatches, Clasp). Served in the Miranzai Expedition in 1891 with the 29th Punjab Infantry—wounded (Clasp).

⁴⁶⁴ Major Plowden served with the 6th Punjab Infantry in the Jowaki campaign in 1877. Served with the 2nd Sikh Infantry in the Afghan war of 1878-80, including the march to Cabul under Sir Donald Stewart, the occupation of Ghuznee, and the engagement at Ahmed Kheyl (Medal with Clasp).

⁴⁶⁵ Major P. R. Bairnsfather served in the Jowaki Afreedee Expedition in 1877-78 (Medal with Clasp). Served in the Afghan war of 1878-80, and was present in the engagement at Charasiab on the 6th October 1879, and in the operations around Cabul in December 1879 (Medal with two Clasps).

⁴⁶⁶ Major R. C. S. Macausland served in the Afghan war in 1878-79, and was present at the attack and capture of Ali Musjid, and with the first expedition into the Bazar Valley (Medal with Clasp).

⁴⁶⁷ Major J. Monteith served in the Afghan war in 1879-80, and was present in the engagement at Girishk, in the defence of Candahar including the sortie of Deh Khojah, and at the battle of Candahar (several times mentioned in despatches, Medal with Clasp). Served in the Soudan campaign in 1885 (Medal with Clasp, and Khedive's Star). Served with the Zhob Field Force in 1890.

468 Major H. R. Marrett served in the Afghan war of 1878-80 (Medal).
470 Major G. Adye served in the Afghan war in 1879-80, and was present at the forcing of the Shutargardan, in the engagement at Ali Kheyl, and in the operations around Cabul in December 1879 including the investment of Sherpore; accompanied Sir Frederick Roberts in the march to Candahar, and was present at the battle of Candahar (Medal with two Clasps, and Bronze Decoration).
471 Major H. M. P. Hawkes served in the Afghan war in 1879-80, accompanied Sir Frederick Roberts in the march to Candahar, and was present at the battle of Candahar (mentioned in despatches, Medal with Clasp, and Bronze Decoration).
472 Colonel A. G. A. Durand served in the Afghan war of 1878-80 with the Khyber Field Force, accompanied Sir Frederick Roberts in the march to Candahar, and was present at the battle of Candahar (Medal with Clasp, and Bronze Decoration). Served in the operations in the Hunza-Nagar country in 1891-92 in command of the troops, including the capture of the Nilt Fort—severely wounded (received the thanks of the Government of India, Brevet of Lt.Colonel, CB., and Medal with Clasp).
473 Major R. C. G. Mayne served in the Afghan war in 1879-80, and was present in the engagement at Sir-i-Asp; accompanied Sir Frederick Roberts in the march to Candahar, and was present at the battle of Candahar (Medal with Clasp, and Bronze Decoration). Served in the Egyptian war of 1882, and was present at the battle of Tel-el-Kebir (Medal with Clasp, and Khedive's Star). Served in the operations of the Zhob Field Force in 1890.
474 Major A. Pringle served in the Afghan war in 1880 (Medal).
475 Major E. J. F. Wood served with the 17th Bengal Cavalry throughout the Jowaki campaign of 1877-78 (Medal with Clasp). Served in the Afghan war of 1878-80, first with the 19th Bengal Lancers, including the advance on and occupation of Candahar and Khelat-i-Ghilzie, afterwards with the 10th Bengal Lancers, and was present in the affair at Jugdulluck as Staff Officer to Colonel Norman during the operations against the Ghilzies (mentioned in despatches, Medal).
476 Major H. Read served in the Afghan war in 1879-80 (Medal). Served with the Burmese Expedition in 1887-88 (mentioned in despatches, Medal with Clasp).
477 Major C. J. Robarts served in the Afghan war in 1879-80, and was present in the engagement at Charasiab on the 25th April 1880 (Medal). Served with the 2nd Bengal Cavalry in the Egyptian war of 1882, and was present in the action at Kassasin (9th September) and at the battle of Tel-el-Kebir and the capture of Cairo (Medal with Clasp, and Khedive's Star).
478 Major W. A. D. O'Mealy served with the Mahsood Wuzeeree Expedition in 1881.
479 Major E. H. Molesworth served in the Afghan war in 1879-80, and was present with the Zaimusht Expedition (Medal). Served with the Akha Expedition in 1883-84 (mentioned in despatches).
480 Major R. R. N. Sturt served in the Afghan war in 1878-79, and was present at the capture of the Peiwar Kotal (Medal with Clasp), and with the Mahsood Wuzeeree Expedition in 1881. Served with the Miranzai Expedition in 1891 with the 2nd Punjab Infantry (mentioned in despatches, Medal with Clasp); and with the Zhob Valley Field Force in 1890.
481 Major H. B. Thornhill served in the Afghan war in 1878-79 (Medal).
482 Major E. H. H. Montresor served in the Afghan war in 1879-80 (Medal).
483 Major W. H. Young served in the Afghan war of 1878-80, and was present in the engagement at Mattoon and at the forcing of the Shutargardan (Medal). Also served with the Mahsood Wuzeeree Expedition in 1881. Served in the Hazara Expedition in 1891 in charge of the treasure chest (mentioned in despatches, Medal with Clasp).
484 Major R. F. Gartside-Tipping served in the Afghan war in 1879-80, including the operations in the Koorum Valley (Medal). Served with the Miranzai Expedition in 1891 (Medal with Clasp).
486 Major V. C. Tonnochy served with the Mahsood Wuzeeree Expedition in 1881 (mentioned in despatches). Served with the Burmese Expedition in 1886-89 (Medal with two Clasps); and with the Isazai Field Force in 1892.
487 Major J. de C. Meade served in the Afghan war in 1880 (Medal).
488 Major E. S. Masters served in the Afghan war in 1878-79 (Medal).
489 Major E. E. M. Lawford served with the 1st Madras Cavalry in the Afghan war of 1879-80, and was present in the engagement at Girishk, at the defence of Candahar, and at the battle of Candahar (Medal with Clasp). Served with the Burmese Expedition in 1886-87 (Medal with Clasp); and in the operations of the Chin Field Force in 1889 (Clasp).
490 Major E. M. Nedham served in the Afghan war in 1878-79, and was present at the attack and capture of Ali Musjid and with the second expedition into the Bazar Valley (Medal with Clasp). Served with the Burmese Expedition in 1886-89 (Medal with two Clasps).
491 Major S. B. Beatson served in the Jowaki Afreedee Expedition in 1877-78 (Medal with Clasp). Served in the Afghan war of 1878-80, and was present at the attack and capture of Ali Musjid (Medal with Clasp). Served in the Egyptian war of 1882 (Medal, and Khedive's Star). Served with the Burmese Expedition in 1886-87 as Military Secretary and with the Mounted Infantry (mentioned in despatches, Brevet of Major, and Clasp).
492 Major A. M. Monteith served in the Afghan war of 1878-80, and was present in the engagements at Takht-i-Pul and Maiwand (wounded), took part in the defence of Candahar and was present at the battle of Candahar (mentioned in despatches, Medal with Clasp).
493 Major G. H. Robinson served in the Afghan war of 1878-80 with the Thull Chotiali and Khyber Line Field Forces, and took part in the expeditions into the Hissarik and Lughman Valleys (Medal). Served with the Sikkim Expedition in 1888 (mentioned in despatches, Medal with Clasp).
494 Major Radcliffe served with the 14th Sikhs throughout the Jowaki campaign in 1877-78 (Medal with Clasp).
495 Major A. M. Renny served in the Afghan war in 1880, and took part with the Zaimusht Expedition (Medal). Served with the Burmese Expedition in 1886-87 (Medal with two Clasps).
496 Major L. M. M. Hall served with the Chin-Lushai Expeditionary Force in 1889-90 with the 2nd Battalion 2nd Goorkhas (mentioned in despatches, Medal with Clasp).
497 Major J. B. Woon served in the Afghan war in 1879-80 with the Candahar Field Force (Medal).
498 Major W. Lambert served in the Afghan war in 1879-80, and was present in the engagement at Charasiah on the 6th October 1879 (mentioned in despatches), and in the operations around Cabul in December 1879; accompanied Sir Frederick Roberts in the march to Candahar, and was present at the battle of Candahar (Medal with three Clasps, and Bronze Decoration). Also served in the Marri Expedition in 1880. Served with the Hazara Expedition in 1888 as Provost Marshal (mentioned in despatches, Medal with Clasp).
499 Major H. L. Dawson served in the Soudan campaign in 1885 (Medal with Clasp, and Khedive's Star).
500 Major W. G. Yate served in the Afghan war of 1878-80, took part in the advance on Khelat-i-Ghilzie and Ghuznee under Sir Donald Stewart, and was present in the engagements at Ahmed Kheyl and Urzoo near Ghuznee; accompanied Sir Frederick Roberts in the march to Candahar, and was present at the battle of Candahar (Medal with two Clasps, and Bronze Decoration).
501 Major A. B. Fenton served with the Burmese Expedition in 1884-89 as Brigade Major and as Deputy Assistant Quarter Master General for Intelligence (mentioned in despatches, Brevet of Major, Medal with two Clasps); and with the Chin-Lushai Expeditionary Force in 1889-90 as Deputy Assistant Quarter Master General for Intelligence (Clasp).
502 Major M. T. Lyde served with the 57th Regiment in the latter part of the Zulu war of 1879, and throughout the operations of "Clarke's Column" (Medal with Clasp). Served with the 15th Bombay Native Infantry in the latter part of the Afghan war in 1880, and at the occupation of the Marree country (Medal).
503 Major H. T. Faithfull served in the Afghan war of 1878-80, and was present at the advance on the Helmund and in the engagements at Ahmed Kheyl and Urzoo near Ghuznee (Medal with Clasp).
504 Major H. L. Ramsay served in the Afghan war in 1878-79, and was present in the operations around Cabul in December 1879 including the investment of Sherpore (mentioned in despatches, Medal with Clasp).
505 Major J. L. O'Bryen served in the Afghan war of 1878-80, and was present with the expeditions into the Lughman Valley (Medal). Served with the Burmese Expedition in 1886-87 (Medal with Clasp).
506 Major J. P. Sparling served in the Afghan war of 1878-80, and was present at the capture of the Peiwar Kotal, in the engagement at Charasiah on the 6th October 1879, and in the operations round Cabul in December 1879 (Medal with three Clasps). Served with the Hazara Expedition in 1888 (Medal with Clasp).
507 Major H. G. Ryland served in the Afghan war of 1878-80 (Medal).

508 Major F. G. Preston served with the Burmese Expedition in 1885-87 (Medal with two Clasps).
509 Major H. A. Deane served in the Afghan war in 1879-80, and was present at the engagements at Ahmed Kheyl and Urzoo near Ghuznee (mentioned in despatches, Medal with Clasp).
510 Major C. E. W. Macdonald served in the Afghan war of 1878-80 (Medal). Served in the Egyptian war of 1882, and was present at the two actions at Kassasin and at the battle of Tel-el-Kebir (Medal with Clasp, and Khedive's Star). Served with the Bechuanaland Expedition under Sir Charles Warren in 1884-85.
511 Major E. S. Hastings served in the Afghan war of 1878-80, and was present with the Kama Expedition as General Transport Officer (Medal). Served in the Boer war of 1881 with the Natal Field Force. Served with the Burmese Expedition in 1885-87 (mentioned in despatches, DSO., and Medal with Clasp); with the Chin-Lushai Expeditionary Force in 1889-90 (Clasp); and with the Manipore Expedition in 1891 (Clasp).
512 Major J. F. Worlledge served with the 12th Bengal Native Infantry in the Afghan war in 1878-79 with the Candahar Column under Sir Donald Stewart (Medal). Served in the Egyptian war of 1882 as Officiating Adjutant 7th Bengal Infantry, and was present at the battle of Tel-el-Kebir (Medal with Clasp, and Khedive's Star).
513 Major H. S. Massy served with the expedition against the Jowaki Afreedees in 1877-78 (Medal with Clasp). Served in the Afghan war of 1878-80, and was present in the engagements at Ahmed Kheyl (wounded), Urzoo near Ghuznee, and Patkao Shana (Medal with Clasp). Served with the Burmese Expedition in 1886-88 as Signalling Officer (mentioned in despatches, Clasp).
514 Major A. E. Jones served in the Afghan war of 1878-80, and was present at the attack and capture of the Peiwar Kotal, in the operations in the Khost Valley, in the engagement at Charasiah on the 6th October 1879, and in the operations round Cabul in December 1879 including the investment of Sherpore; accompanied Sir Frederick Roberts in the march to Candahar, and was present at the battle of Candahar (Medal with four Clasps, and Bronze Decoration). Also served in the Mahsood Wuzeeree Expedition in 1881. Served with the Miranzai Expedition in 1891 (Medal with Clasp); with the Manipore Expedition in 1891 (Clasp); and with the Isazai Expedition in 1892.
515 Major F. M. Drury served in the Afghan war in 1879-80 (Medal). Served in the Soudan campaign in 1885, and was present in the engagement at the Tofrek iereba—wounded (mentioned in despatches, Medal with two Clasps, and Khedive's Star). Served with the Chin-Lushai Expeditionary Force in 1889-90 (Medal with Clasp); and in the Manipore Expedition in 1891 with the 2nd Battalion 4th Goorkha Rifles—severely wounded (mentioned in despatches, Clasp).
516 Major C. J. Dennys served in the Afghan war of 1878-80, and was present in the engagements at Mattoon and at Charasiah on the 6th October 1879, and in the operations around Cabul in December 1879 (Medal with two Clasps).
517 Major E. W. Dun served with the expedition against the Jowaki Afreedees in 1877-78 (Medal with Clasp). Served with the Burmese Expedition in 1886-87 in charge of the Intelligence Branch (mentioned in despatches, DSO., and Clasp). Served with the Manipore Expedition in 1891 as Assistant Quarter Master General for Intelligence to the Silchar Column (mentioned in despatches, Clasp).
518 Major J. H. Jones served in the Afghan war in 1879-80 (Medal). Served with the Burmese Expedition in 1886-87 (Medal with Clasp); and with the Chin-Lushai Expeditionary Force in 1889-90 (Clasp).
519 Major C. Herbert served in the Afghan war in 1879-80, and took part in the Zaimusht Expedition (Medal). Served with the Burmese Expedition in 1886-87 (Medal with Clasp).
520 Major Ozzard served throughout the operations in the Malay Peninsula in 1875-76. Served in the Afghan war in 1878-79 (Medal).
521 Major G. A. Collins served in the Afghan war in 1879, and was present with the Zaimusht Expedition (Medal).
522 Major W. C. Aslett served in the Afghan war in 1879-80, and was present in the engagement at Girishk, at the defence of Candahar, and at the battle of Candahar (Medal with Clasp). Served with the Burmese Expedition in 1885-87 (Medal with Clasp).
523 Major L. S. Peyton served in the Afghan war in 1879-80 (Medal).
524 Major A. W. L. Bayly served in the Afghan war in 1879-80, and was present at the defence of Candahar and in the battle of Candahar (Medal with Clasp). Served with the expedition to the Soudan in 1885 and was present at the destruction of Temai (Medal with Clasp, and Khedive's Star). Served with the Burmese Expedition in 1886-87 as Deputy Assistant Adjutant and Quarter Master General (mentioned in despatches, DSO. and Medal with two Clasps).
525 Major W. H. Jameson served in the Afghan war of 1878-80, and took part with the Zaimusht Expedition including the assault of Zawa (Medal). Served in the Hazara Expedition in 1891 with the 32nd Bengal Infantry (mentioned in despatches, Medal with Clasp).
526 Major A. Adye served in the Afghan war of 1878-80 with the Cabul and the Koorum Field Forces (Medal).
527 Major J. A. H. Pollock served with the Jowaki Afreedee Expedition in 1877-78 (Medal with Clasp). Served in the Afghan war in 1878-79, and was present at the attack and capture of Ali Musjid (Medal with Clasp), and with the Mahsood Wuzeeree Expedition in 1881.
528 Major C. G. M. Fasken served in the Afghan war of 1878-80, and was present in the engagements at Ahmed Kheyl and Urzoo near Ghuznee; accompanied Sir Frederick Roberts in the march to Candahar, and was present at the battle of Candahar (Medal with two Clasps, and Bronze Decoration). Served with the Hazara Expedition in 1888 (Medal with Clasp).
529 Major L. G. Beckham served with the 8th Bombay Native Infantry in the Afghan war in 1880, and took part in the march to Candahar with the force under Major General Phayre (Medal). Also served with the Marri Expedition in 1881. Served with the Burmese Expedition in 1885-8/ with the 1st Brigade Burmah Field Force (Medal with Clasp), and again in 1887-89 (Clasp).
530 Major C. J. L. Stuart served with the Jowaki Afreedee Expedition in 1877 (Medal with Clasp. Served in the Afghan war in 1879-80, and was present in the engagement at Ahmed Kheyl—severely wounded (Medal with Clasp).
531 Major E. W. S. Welchman served with the Jowaki Afreedee Expedition in 1878 (Medal with Clasp). Served in the Afghan war in 1879-80, and was present in the engagement at Kam Dakka (mentioned in despatches, Medal). Served with the Burmese Expedition in 1886-88 (Medal with Clasp).
532 Colonel N. F. F. Chamberlain served in the Afghan war of 1878-80, and was present at the capture of the Peiwar Kotal as Orderly Officer to Major General Roberts (mentioned in despatches), in the engagement at Charasiah on the 6th October 1879 (mentioned in despatches), and in the operations round Cabul in December 1879 (mentioned in despatches); accompanied Sir Frederick Roberts in the march to Candahar, and was present at the battle of Candahar—slightly wounded (Medal with three Clasps, and Bronze Decoration). Served with the Burmese Expedition in 1886-87 as Deputy Assistant Adjutant and Quarter Master General (mentioned in despatches, Brevet of Lt. Colonel, Medal with Clasp).
533 Major J. P. W. Spankie served in the Afghan war of 1878-80, and was present with the expedition against the Khugianis and with that into the Hissarik Valley (Medal).
534 Lt. Colonel S. C. F. Peile served in the Afghan war in 1878-79 (Medal). Served during the Burmese Expedition in 1886-87 with the Commissariat Department at Rangoon (mentioned in despatches, Medal with Clasp); and in the operations in the Kachin Hills in 1892-93 (Brevet of Lt. Colonel).
535 Major B. Duff served in the Afghan war of 1878-80 (Medal).
536 Major C. H. Westmorland served in the Afghan war in 1878-79, and was present at the attack and capture of Ali Musjid and with the second expedition into the Bazar Valley (Medal with Clasp). Served with the Burmese Expedition in 1888-89 (mentioned in despatches, Brevet of Major, Medal with Clasp).
537 Major S. D. Gordon served in the Afghan war in 1878-79, and was present in the engagements at Ahmed Kheyl (slightly wounded) and Padkao Shana (mentioned in despatches, Medal with Clasp). Served in the Egyptian war of 1882, and was present at the battle of Tel-el-Kebir (Medal with Clasp, 5th Class of the Medjidie, and Khedive's Star).
538 Major J. E. Preston served with the 51st Light Infantry in the Jowaki campaign in 1877 (Medal with Clasp). Served in the Afghan war in 1880 with the Khyber Line Force (Medal). Served with the Burmese Expedition in 1885-89, and was severely wounded in an attack on Lamaing Post on the 27th June 1886 (mentioned in despatches, DSO., and Medal with two Clasps); and in the operations in 1892 in command of the Eastern Column.
539 Major F. Hawkins served in the Afghan war in 1879-80, and took part in the operations against the Mohmunds (Medal). Served with the Zhob Valley Expedition in 1884. Served with the Burmese Expedition in 1885-87 (Medal with Clasp).

Indian Staff Corps.—War Services of Field Officers.

540 Lt.Colonel H. P. Picot served in the Afghan war of 1878-80, and was present at the capture of the Peiwar Kotal (mentioned in despatches), in the engagement at Ali Kheyl, and with the Zaimusht Expedition including the assault of Zawa (Medal with Clasp). Served with the Miranzai Expedition in 1891 on Commissariat duty (mentioned in despatches, Medal with Clasp).

541 Major W. S. Birdwood served in the Afghan war in 1879-80 (Medal). Served with the Zhob Valley Expedition in 1884.

542 Major W. S. Marshall served in the Afghan war of 1878-80 with the Ghuznee Field Force, and was present in the engagement at Ahmed Kheyl (Medal with Clasp).

543 Major W. C. Faithfull served in the Afghan war of 1878-80, and was present at the attack and capture of Ali Musjid, the advance to Gundamuck, and the operations in the Koorum Valley (Medal with Clasp). Served in the Mahsood Wuzeeree Expedition in 1881.

544 Major J. B. R. Butler served in the Afghan war in 1880 (Medal).

545 Major V. M. Stockley served with the 2nd Bengal Cavalry in the Egyptian war of 1882, and was present in the action at Kassasin (9th September) and at the battle of Tel-el-Kebir and the capture of Cairo (Medal with Clasp, and Khedive's Star).

546 Major A. D. Enriquez served in the Afghan war of 1878-80 (mentioned in despatches, Medal).

547 Major A. L. Sinclair served with the Burmese Expedition in 1886-88 (mentioned in despatches, DSO., and Medal with Clasp).

548 Major J. Lamb served in the Afghan war in 1879-80, and took part in the advance on Cabul under Brigadier General Charles Gough (mentioned in despatches, Medal with Clasp). Served with the Zhob Field Force under Sir George White in 1890 as Deputy Adjutant General (mentioned in despatches).

549 Major A. R. Martin served with the expedition against the Jowaki Afreedees in 1877-78 (Medal with Clasp) Served in the Afghan war of 1878-80, and was present at the capture of the Peiwar Kotal, at the forcing of the Sapri Pass (mentioned in despatches), in the engagement at Charasiab on the 6th October 1879 (twice mentioned in despatches), and in the operations around Cabul in December 1879; accompanied Sir Frederick Roberts in the march to Candahar, and was present at the battle of Candahar (mentioned in despatches, Medal with four Clasps, and Bronze Decoration). Served with the Hazara Expedition in 1888 (Clasp); and with the Miranzai Expedition in 1891 in command of the 1st Battalion 5th Goorkhas (mentioned in despatches, Brevet of Major, Clasp).

552 Major Fairbrother served in the Afghan war of 1878-80, first in the Khyber Column with the Mhairwarra Battalion, and was present with the expedition to the Bazar Valley and in the engagement at Kam Dakka; afterwards in the Kurrum Column with the 29th Punjab Infantry, and was present with the Zaimusht Expedition under Brigadier General Tytler, and took part in the attack and capture of the stronghold of Zawa (Medal). Served with the Sikkim Expedition in 1888 (mentioned in despatches, Medal with Clasp).

553 Major J. G. Ramsay served in the Afghan war of 1878-80, and took part in the second expedition into the Bazar Valley under Lieut.General Maude; accompanied Sir Frederick Roberts in the march to Candahar, and was present at the battle of Candahar (Medal with Clasp, and Bronze Decoration).

554 Major Williamson served in the Afghan war of 1878-80 (Medal).

555 Major H. D. M. Minchin served in the Afghan war in 1880, took part in the defence of Candahar including the sortie of Deh Khojah, and was present at the battle of Candahar (Medal with Clasp). Served with the Burmese Expedition in 1885-87 (Medal with Clasp).

556 Major E. R. J. Presgrave served in the Afghan war in 1879-80 (Medal). Served with the Burmese Expedition in 1886-89 (Medal with two Clasps); with the Manipore Expedition in 1891 with the 12th Madras Infantry (mentioned in despatches, Clasp); and in the operations in the Northern Chin Hills in 1892-94 (mentioned in despatches, Brevet of Major, and DSO.).

557 Major A. L. Barrett served with the expedition against the Naga Hill Tribes in 1879-80 (Medal with Clasp). Also served with the Akha Expedition in 1883-84. Served with the Burmese Expedition in 1885-88, and was slightly wounded in an engagement near Lamaing on the 2nd September 1886 (DSO., and Clasp).

558 Major J. W. Parker served in the Afghan war of 1878-80 including the engagement at Besud (Medal). Served with the Burmese Expedition in 1885-89 including the attack on Nga-Mingyan's Stockade (Medal with two Clasps).

559 Major C. G. F. Fagan served in the Afghan war in 1879-80 (Medal).

560 Major W. St. J. Richardson served in the Afghan war in 1879-80 (Medal).

561 Major F. H. R. Drummond served in the Afghan war of 1878-80, and was present in the engagement at Jugdulluck and in the advance to the relief of Sherpore under Brigadier General Charles Gough (twice mentioned in despatches, Medal with Clasp).

562 Major R. B. Shawe served in the Afghan war in 1880 with the Southern Afghanistan Field Force (Medal). Served with the Burmese Expedition in 1886-89 (Medal with two Clasps).

563 Major A. G. Burn served with the Burmese Expedition in 1887 (Medal with Clasp).

War Services of Captains.

1 Captain E. F. Marriott served in the Afghan war of 1878-80, and took part with the expedition against the Wuzeeree Khugianis (Medal).

1½ Captain C. F. S. Alban served in the Afghan war in 1879-80, took part in the defence of Candahar and was present at the battle of Candahar (Medal with Clasp). Served with the Burmese Expedition in 1885-87 (Medal with Clasp).

2 Captain R. G. Jones served in the Afghan war in 1879-80 (Medal). Served with the Burmese Expedition in 1886-89, and was severely wounded during the operations against the Chins (mentioned in despatches, Medal with two Clasps).

Captain H. A. B. Boulderson served in the Afghan war of 1878-80 with the 59th Regiment, took part in the advance to and occupation of Khelat-i-Ghilzie under Sir Donald Stewart, and was present in the engagements at Ahmed Kheyl and Urzoo near Ghuznee and in the subsequent operations in the Logar Valley; accompanied Sir Frederick Roberts in the march to Candahar with the 25th Punjab Native Infantry, and was present at the reconnaissance on the 31st August and at the battle of Candahar (Medal with two Clasps, and Bronze Decoration). Served with the Burmese Expedition in 1885-87 (Medal with Clasp).

4 Major Lyons Montgomery served in the Afghan war of 1878-80, and was present in the engagements at Mattoon and at Charasiab on the 6th October 1879 and in the operations round Cabul in December 1879; accompanied Sir Frederick Roberts in the march to Candahar, and was present at the battle of Candahar (mentioned in despatches, Medal with three Clasps, and Bronze Decoration). Served in the Hazara Expedition in 1891 as Chief Commissariat Officer (mentioned in despatches, Brevet of Major, Medal with Clasp).

5 Captain E. C. M Lushington served with the Burmese Expedition in 1886-87 (Medal with two Clasps).

6 Captain F. G. Pollock served with the 51st Light Infantry in the Jowaki campaign in 1877 (Medal with Clasp). Served in the Afghan war of 1878-80, and was present in the engagement at Baghao and with the expedition into the Hissarik and Lughman Valleys (Medal). Served with the Burmese Expedition in 1887-88 (mentioned in despatches, Clasp).

7 Captain R. F. Clothier served with the Burmese Expedition in 1886-88 (Medal with two Clasps).

8 Captain H. Lawson served with the Burmese Expedition in 1887-88 (Medal with Clasp).

⁹ Captain E. W. F. Martin served in the Afghan war in 1879-80, and took part in the expedition into the Hissarik Valley (Medal).
¹⁰ Captain C. R. Phillips served in the Afghan war in 1879-80, took part in the defence of Candahar, and was present at the battle of Candahar (Medal with Clasp).
¹¹ Captain A. A. Barrett served in the Afghan war in 1879-80, and was present at the forcing of the Shutargardan, and in the operations around Cabul in December 1879 including the investment of Sherpore; accompanied Sir Frederick Roberts in the march to Candahar, and was present at the battle of Candahar (Medal with two Clasps, and Bronze Decoration). Served with the Hazara Expedition in 1888 (Medal with Clasp); and with the second Miranzai Expedition in 1891 (Clasp).
¹² Captain J. C. Swann served in the Soudan campaign in 1885 (Medal with Clasp, and Khedive's Star). Served with the Burmese Expedition in 1885-87 (Medal with Clasp).
¹³ Captain H. B. Tate served in the Afghan war in 1878-79, and was present at the attack and capture of Ali Musjid and with the second expedition into the Bazar Valley (Medal with Clasp).
¹⁴ Major H. F. S. Ramsden served in the Afghan war in 1878-79 (Medal). Served in the Soudan campaign in 1885 (Medal with Clasp, and Khedive's Star). Served with the Burmese Expedition in 1885-86 as Field Paymaster (received the thanks of the Government of India, mentioned in despatches, Brevet of Major, Medal with Clasp).
¹⁵ Captain H. Goad served in the Afghan war in 1879-80, and was present in the engagement at Jugdulluck (Medal).
¹⁶ Captain J. M. A. Retallick served in the Afghan war of 1878-80, and was present in the expedition into the Bazar Valley and in the engagement at Charasiab on the 6th October 1879 (mentioned in despatches, Medal with Clasp).
¹⁷ Major E. A. Travers served in the Afghan war of 1878-80, and was present in the advance on Khelat-i-Ghilzie, and in the operations around Cabul in December 1879; accompanied Sir Frederick Roberts in the march to Candahar, and was present at the battle of Candahar (Medal with two Clasps, and Bronze Decoration). Served with the Sikkim Expedition in 1888 as Deputy Assistant Adjutant General (mentioned in despatches, Brevet of Major, Medal with Clasp); and with the Manipore Expedition in 1891 (Clasp).
¹⁸ Captain H. Godfray served in the Afghan war in 1879-80 (Medal).
¹⁹ Captain W. S. Chase served in the Afghan war in 1879-80, took part in the defence of Candahar including the sortie of Deh Khojah (mentioned in despatches), and was present at the battle of Candahar (Victoria Cross, Medal with Clasp); together with Private James Ashford, Royal Fusiliers, he received the V℃ "for conspicuous gallantry on the occasion of the sortie from Kandahar, on the 16th August 1880, against the village of Deh Khoja, in having rescued and carried for a distance of over 200 yards, under the fire of the enemy, a wounded soldier, Private Massey, of the Royal Fusiliers, who had taken shelter in a block-house. Several times they were compelled to rest, but they persevered in bringing him to a place of safety. Private Ashford rendered Lieutenant Chase every assistance, and remained with him throughout." Served with the Zhob Valley Expedition in 1884 as Deputy Assistant Quarter Master General (mentioned in despatches). Served with the Chin-Lushai Expeditionary Force in 1889-90 with the 28th Bombay Native Infantry (mentioned in despatches, Medal with Clasp).
²⁰ Captain H. L. Hutchins served with the Burmese Expedition in 1885-87 (mentioned in despatches, Medal with two Clasps).
²¹ Captain H. W. Seymour served in the Afghan war in 1880 as Aide de Camp to Major General Phayre, and was wounded at the defence of the Camp of Kuch (Medal).
²² Captain C. B. Brownlow served in the Afghan war of 1878-80 (Medal), and with the expedition against the Mahsood Wuzeerees in 1881. Served with the two Miranzai Expeditions in 1891 (Medal with Clasp).
²³ Captain C. E. Poynder served with the Burmese Expedition in 1887-89 (mentioned in despatches, Medal with two Clasps).
²⁴ Captain G. A. Williams served in the Afghan war in 1878-79, and took part in the expedition into the Bazar Valley under Lieut.General Maude (mentioned in despatches, Medal).
²⁴† Captain W. Cook served with the 1st Battalion 17th Foot throughout the Afghan war in 1878-79, and was present at the assault and capture of Ali Musjid and the subsequent operations in the Bazar Valley, in the operations around Cabul in December 1879 including the investment of Sherpore—severely wounded in the engagement in the Chardeh Valley; accompanied Sir Frederick Roberts in the march to Candahar, and was present at the battle of Candahar (mentioned in despatches, Medal with three Clasps, and Bronze Decoration).
²⁵ Major W. du G. Gray served in the Afghan war in 1879-80 with the Khyber Field Force as Transport Officer (Medal). Served in the Hazara campaign in 1888, and was present in the engagement at Kotkai (mentioned in despatches, Medal with Clasp). Served with the Miranzai Expedition in 1891 as Brigade Major to the 2nd Column (mentioned in despatches, Brevet of Major, Clasp).
²⁵† Captain R. K. Teversham served with the Burmese Expedition in 1886-87 (mentioned in despatches, DSO., and Medal with Clasp).
²⁶ Captain Batten served in the Jowaki Afreedee Expedition of 1877-78 (Medal with Clasp). Served in the Afghan war of 1878-80, and was present at the affair at Shahjui (mentioned in Colonel Kennedy's report), and in the engagements at Ahmed Kheyl and Urzoo near Ghuznee, and at the occupation of Ghuznee (mentioned in despatches); accompanied Sir Frederick Roberts in the march to Candahar and was present at the battle of Candahar (Medal with two Clasps, and Bronze Decoration).
²⁶† Captain J. F. Wilson served with the Burmese Expedition in 1885-86 (Medal with Clasp).
²⁷ Captain Cunliffe served in the Afghan war of 1878-80, including the operations in the Khyber Pass (Medal), and with the expedition against the Mahsood Wuzeerees in 1881.
²⁷† Captain L. J. E. Bradshaw served in the Afghan war of 1878-80, and was present in the engagements at Jugdulluck (mentioned in despatches) and Shekabad (mentioned in despatches); accompanied Sir Frederick Roberts in the march to Candahar, and was present at the battle of Candahar (Medal with Clasp, and Bronze Decoration). Served with the Hazara Expedition in 1891 as Brigade Major 1st Brigade (mentioned in despatches, Medal with Clasp). Served with the Hazara Expedition in 1891 (mentioned in despatches, Medal with Clasp). Served in the operations in the Hunza-Nagar country in 1891-92, part of the time in command of the force (mentioned in despatches, Clasp).
²⁸ Captain G. E. Even served in the Afghan war in 1879-80 on Transport duty (Medal). Served with the Chin-Lushai Expeditionary Force in 1889-90 (Medal with Clasp).
²⁸† Captain J. G. Smith served in the Afghan war in 1879-80, and was present in the expedition into the Lughman Valley and with that against the Khugianis (Medal).
²⁹ Captain G. W. Younghusband served with the Jowaki Afreedee Expedition in 1877-78 (Medal with Clasp). Served in the Afghan war of 1878-80, and was present in the engagements at Takht-i-Pul, Shahjui, Ahmed Kheyl and Urzoo near Ghuznee (Medal with Clasp).
²⁹† Captain A. E. P. Burn served in the Afghan war of 1878-80 (Medal). Served with the Burmese Expedition in 1886-87 (Medal with Clasp).
³⁰ Captain H. F. Farrant served with the Burmese Expedition in 1885-87 (Medal with Clasp).
³¹ Captain J. G. Downing served with the 72nd Highlanders from the commencement of the Afghan war in 1878 till 18th June 1879 with the Koorum Field Force, including the Khost Expedition and the engagement at Mattoon(Medal).
³² Major H. Mansfield served in the Afghan war of 1878-80, and was present at the attack and capture of Ali Musjid, and with the Zaimusht Expedition including the assault of Zawa (mentioned in despatches, Medal with Clasp). Served with the Sikkim Expedition in 1888 (Brevet of Major, Medal with Clasp).
³³ Captain J. W. Gordon served in the Afghan war in 1880, and took part in the march to Candahar with the force under Major General Phayre (Medal).
³⁴ Captain E. T. Paul served in the Egyptian war of 1882, and was present at the battle of Tel-el-Kebir (Medal with Clasp, and Khedive's Star).
³⁵ Captain W. W. Taylor served with the Zhob Valley Expedition in 1884. Served with the Hazara Expedition in 1888 (Medal with Clasp).
³⁶ Captain G. B. O'Donnell served with the Zhob Valley Expedition in 1884 in the Intelligence Branch.
³⁷ Captain D. W. Hickman served with the Zhob Valley Expedition in 1884. Served with the Burmese Expedition in 1886-87 (Medal with Clasp); also with the Miranzai Expedition in 1891 under Sir William Lockhart as Deputy Assistant Adjutant General (mentioned in despatches, Clasp).
³⁸ Captain G. S. Goldsmid served with the Hazara Expedition in 1888 (Medal with Clasp).
³⁹ Captain E. H. Rivett-Carnac served with the 85th Regiment in the Afghan war in 1879-80, and was present with

the Zaimusht Expedition including the assault of Zawa (Medal). Served in the Egyptian war of 1882 as Orderly Officer to Brigadier General Wilkinson, Commanding the Cavalry Brigade of the Indian Contingent, and was present at the action at Kassasin (9th September) and at the battle of Tel-el-Kebir (Medal with Clasp, 5th Class of the Medjidie, and Khedive's Star).

⁴⁰ Captain T. P. Geoghegan served in the Afghan war in 1879-80, and was present in the engagement at Girishk (mentioned in despatches), in the defence of Candahar including the sortie of Deh Khojah (mentioned in despatches), and at the battle of Candahar (Medal with Clasp).

⁴¹ Captain J. W. Currie served with the Burmese Expedition in 1886-87 (Medal with two Clasps).

⁴⁴ Captain R. I. Scallon served in the Afghan war in 1879-80, and was present in the engagements at Khelat-i-Ghilzie and Sir-i-Asp; accompanied Sir Frederick Roberts in the march to Candahar, and was present at the battle of Candahar (Medal with Clasp, and Bronze Decoration). Served in the Burmese Expedition in 1885-88 with the 23rd Bombay Light Infantry; was Staff Officer to the Kanlé Column in 1886-87, and afterwards in command of the Myaing outpost and subsequently of the Myaing-Yaw Column (DSO., and Medal with two Clasps).

⁴⁵ Captain F. G. Delamain served in the Afghan war of 1878-80 with the Candahar and Khyber Field Forces (Medal). Served with the Hazara Expedition in 1891 (Medal with Clasp); and with the Isazai Expedition in 1892.

⁴⁶ Captain A. W. Lyster served with the Burmese Expedition in 1886-87 (Medal with Clasp).

⁴⁷ Captain J. S. Ashby served in the Afghan war in 1880 (Medal).

⁴⁸ Captain H. A. Ravenshaw served with the Candahar Column in the Afghan war in 1878-79 (Medal). Served with the Burmese Expedition in 1885-88 (Medal with Clasp).

⁴⁹ Captain G. E. Walter served in the Afghan war in 1879-80 (Medal).

⁵⁰ Captain P. G. Huggins served in the Afghan war in 1878-79 (Medal). Served with the Burmese Expedition in 1885-89, and was present at the capture of Minhla Redoubt and at the surrender of Mandalay (mentioned in despatches, DSO., and Medal with two Clasps).

⁵¹ Captain J. R. Sandwith served in the Afghan war in 1880, and took part in the march to Candahar with the force under Major General Phayre (Medal).

⁵² Captain J. C. B. Craster served in the Afghan war of 1878-80 with the Koorum Field Force, including the advance from Ali Kheyl to Cabul and the engagement at Charasiah on 6th October 1889 (Medal with Clasp). Served with the Burmese Expedition in 1887-89 with the Upper Burmah Field Force under Sir George White, including the engagement at Salak Hill on 3rd December 1887 (Medal with Clasp).

⁵³ Captain E. R. Penrose served in the Zulu war in 1879 (Medal with Clasp). Served with the Burmese Expedition in 1885-88 (Medal with Clasp).

⁵⁴ Captain W. C. Pollard served in the Afghan war of 1878-80 (Medal), and with the Mahsood Wuzeeree Expedition in 1881. Served with the Burmese Expedition in 1886-87 (mentioned in despatches, Medal with two Clasps); and with the Hazara Expedition in 1888 (mentioned in despatches, Clasp).

⁵⁵ Captain Swiney served with the 72nd Highlanders from the commencement of the Afghan war in 1878 till August 1880 with the Koorum and Cabul Field Forces, and was present in the engagement at Charasiab and in the operations around Cabul in December 1879 (Medal with two Clasps). Served in the Zhob Valley Expedition in 1890.

⁵⁶ Captain F. G. Atkinson served with the 13th Bengal Lancers in the Egyptian war of 1882, and was present at the battle of Tel-el-Kebir and the capture of Cairo (Medal with Clasp, and Khedive's Star).

⁵⁷ Captain H. R. W. Lumsden served in the Afghan war of 1878-80 (Medal). Served with the Sikkim Expedition in 1888—severely wounded (mentioned in despatches, Medal with Clasp).

⁵⁸ Captain W. K. Downes served in the Afghan war in 1879-80 (Medal). Served with the Burmese Expedition in 1885-87, and was present at the storming of the Minhla redoubt (mentioned in despatches, DSO., Medal with Clasp).

⁵⁹ Captain A. E. Leslie served with the Zhob Valley Expedition in 1884.

⁶⁰ Captain H. E. M. Mason served with the Burmese Expedition in 1885-89 (Medal with two Clasps).

⁶¹ Captain G. F. N. Tinley served with the Zhob Valley Expedition in 1884. Served with the Burmese Expedition in 1885-89 (mentioned in despatches, Medal with two Clasps).

⁶² Captain C. W. Harris served in the Afghan war in 1879-80 (Medal). Served with the Burmese Expedition in 1886-87 (mentioned in despatches, Medal with Clasp).

⁶³ Captain G. R. MacMullen served with the Burmese Expedition in 1887-88 (Medal with Clasp), and with the Miranzai Expedition in 1891 (Clasp); and in the operations in the Kachin Hills in 1892-93.

⁶⁴ Captain R. C. Onslow served in Afghan war of 1878-80, was present in the engagement at Jugdulluck (Medal).

⁶⁵ Captain A. Wallace served in the Afghan war in 1879-80 (Medal). Served with the Burmese Expedition in 1886-88 (Medal with two Clasps); with the Hazara Expedition in 1891 (Clasp); and with the 2nd Miranzai Expedition in 1891 (Clasp).

⁶⁶ Captain P. B. Lindsell served in the Afghan war of 1878-80 with the Cabul Field Force in the Transport Department, including the relief of Sherpore under Brigadier General Charles Gough (Medal with Clasp).

⁶⁷ Captain G. Bowring served with the Burmese Expedition in 1888-90 (Medal with Clasp).

⁶⁸ Captain J. H. Parsons served in the Afghan war in 1880, and took part with the Aitchakzai Expedition (Medal). Served with the Burmese Expedition in 1885-86—dangerously wounded (Medal with Clasp).

⁶⁹ Captain G. H. Watson served in the Afghan war in 1880 in the Khyber Line of Communication (Medal).

⁷⁰ Captain de Brath served in the Afghan war in 1880 and was present in the engagement at Mazeena (Medal); also served with the Mahsood Wuzeeree Expedition in 1881 (twice mentioned in despatches). Served with the Hazara Expedition in 1891 (Medal with Clasp).

⁷¹ Captain H. Wharry served with the Miranzai Expedition in 1891 under Sir William Lockhart as Divisional Transport Officer (mentioned in despatches, Medal with Clasp).

⁷² Captain M. H. S. Grover served with the Thull Chotiali Field Force in the Afghan war of 1878-80 (Medal). Served in the Soudan campaign in 1885 with the 9th Bengal Cavalry (Medal with Clasp, and Khedive's Star).

⁷³ Captain R. B. Adams served in the Afghan war in 1879-80, and was present in the operations round Cabul in December 1879, including the storming of Takt-i-Shah and the Asmai Heights, and in the engagement at Charasiah on the 25th April 1880 (Medal with Clasp).

⁷⁴ Captain A. C. Yate served in the Afghan war in 1880, and took part in the march to Candahar with the force under Major General Phayre (Medal). Served with the Burmese Expedition in 1886-88; was Intelligence Officer with the Northern Shan Column, 1887-88 (Medal with two Clasps).

⁷⁵ Captain J. H. Balfour served with the 13th Bengal Lancers in the Afghan war of 1878-80, and was present at the capture of the Peiwar Kotal (Medal with Clasp). Served in the Egyptian war of 1882, and was present at the battle of Tel-el-Kebir and the capture of Cairo (Medal with Clasp).

⁷⁶ Captain A. H. Wilmer served with the Hazara Expedition in 1891 (Medal with Clasp); and with the second Miranzai Expedition in 1891 (Clasp).

⁷⁷ Captain G. W. Maxwell served with the Burmese Expedition in 1887-89 (Medal with Clasp).

⁷⁸ Captain H. J. J. Middleton served in the Zulu war in 1879, and was present in the engagement at Inyezane and at Ekowe during the investment (Medal with Clasp).

⁷⁹ Captain G. F. Watson served with Burmese Expedition in 1886-87 (mentioned in despatches, Medal with Clasp); and in the operations in the Northern Chin Hills in 1892-93 (mentioned in despatches).

⁸⁰ Captain W. R. Yeilding served in the Afghan war in 1879-80 with the 1st Sikhs and 1st Goorkhas, and took part in the expedition to the Logar Valley; accompanied Sir Frederick Roberts in the march to Candahar, and was present at the battle of Candahar (Medal with Clasp, and Bronze Decoration). Also served with the Marri Expedition in 1880, and with the Mahsood Wuzeeree Expedition in 1881. Served in the Hazara campaign in 1888 as Divisional Transport Officer with the Head Quarters of the Force (mentioned in despatches, DSO., and Clasp).

⁸¹ Major W. J. H. Bond served with the Burmese Expedition in 1886-87 as Executive Commissariat Officer, (mentioned in despatches, Medal with Clasp). Served with the Chin-Lushai Expeditionary Force in 1889-90 as Chief Commissariat Officer to the Chittagong Column (received the thanks of the Government of India, mentioned in despatches, Brevet of Major, Clasp).

⁸² Captain J. W. B. Meade served in the Afghan war of 1878-80, and was present in the engagements at Ahmed Kheyl and Urzoo near Ghuznee (Medal with Clasp).

⁸³ Captain T. H. Haughton served with the Burmese Expedition in 1889 (Medal with Clasp).

Indian Staff Corps.—War Services of Captains.

[84] Captain S. M. Congreve Schneider served with the Zhob Valley Expedition in 1884.
[85] Captain H. Eardley Wilmot served in the Afghan war in 1879-80 (Medal). Served with the Burmese Expedition in 1886 (Medal with Clasp).
[86] Captain E. Inglis served with the Hazara Expedition in 1888 (mentioned in despatches, Medal with Clasp).
[87] Captain H. H. H. Aspinall served with the Burmese Expedition in 1886-89 (Medal with two Clasps).
[88] Captain H. Melvill served in the Afghan war in 1879-80, took part in the defence of Candahar, and was present at the battle of Candahar (Medal with Clasp).
[89] Captain W. H. Lowry served with the Burmese Expedition in 1885-89 (Medal with two Clasps).
[90] Captain L. A. Gordon served in the Afghan war in 1880 as Transport Officer and as Orderly Officer to Brigadier General Burrows (Medal).
[91] Captain K. M. Foss served during the Rumpa Rebellion in 1879-80 (received the thanks of the Government of India). Served in the Burmese Expedition in 1886-87 with the 6th Brigade (mentioned in despatches, Medal with Clasp).
[92] Captain G. F. Willes served in the Afghan war of 1878-80 (Medal).
[93] Captain S. F. Biddulph served in the Afghan war in 1878-79 as Aide de Camp to Major General Biddulph (Medal).
[93] Major H. D'U. Keary served in the Afghan war in 1880 including the engagement at Kam Dakka (Medal). Served with the Burmese Expedition in 1885-87 (mentioned in despatches, Medal with Clasp). Served with the Wuntho Expedition in 1891 in command of the Shwebo Military Police (received the thanks of the Government of India, mentioned in despatches, DSO., and Clasp); also served in the operations in the Northern Chin Hills in 1892-93 (Brevet of Major).
[96] Captain E. Vansittart served with the Mahsood Wuzeeree Expedition in 1881. Served with the Hazara Expedition in 1891 with the 2nd Battalion 5th Goorkhas (Medal with Clasp).
[97] Captain A. W. Forbes served in the Afghan war in 1880 (Medal).
[98] Captain G. A. Welman served with the Burmese Expedition in 1886-89 (Medal with two Clasps).
[99] Captain G. W. W. Burton served with the Burmese Expedition in 1888-89 (Medal with Clasp); and with the Chin-Lushai Expeditionary Force in 1889-90 as Staff Officer (mentioned in despatches, Clasp).
[100] Captain J. M. Carpendale served in the Afghan war of 1878-80, and took part in the operations in the Lughman Valley (Medal).
[101] Major G. B. Stevens served with the Burmese Expedition in 1886-88 with the Mounted Infantry throughout the operations of the 1st Brigade, and as Staff Officer and Assistant Inspector of Mounted Infantry Upper Burma Field Force (mentioned in despatches, Medal with two Clasps); with the Lushai Expedition in 1888-89 in command of a detachment of the 4th Madras Pioneers (mentioned in despatches); and throughout the operations in the Chin Hills in 1890-92 and commanded the Kauhaw Column (twice mentioned in despatches, Brevet of Major).
[102] Captain H. A. Carleton served in the Afghan war of 1878-80, and was present in the engagement at Ahmed Kheyl; accompanied Sir Frederick Roberts in the march to Candahar, and was present at the battle of Candahar (Medal with two Clasps, and Bronze Decoration).
[103] Captain W. J. K. Dobbin served with the Mahsood Wuzeeree Expedition in 1881. Served with the Zhob Valley Expedition in 1890.
[104] Captain Hyde Baker served in the Afghan war in 1879-80, and was present in the engagement at Charasiah on 25th April 1880. Accompanied Sir Frederick Roberts in the march to Candahar, and was present at the battle of Candahar—slightly wounded (Medal with Clasp, and Bronze Decoration). Served in the Marri Expedition under Brigadier General MacGregor in November 1880.
[105] Captain H. Elston served with the Burmese Expedition in 1886-87 (Medal with Clasp).
[106] Captain R. W. Iremonger served with the Burmese Expedition in 1888-89 (Medal with Clasp).
[107] Major A. H. Clark-Kennedy served in the Afghan war in 1879-80, including the engagement at Kam Dakka (Medal). Served with the Burmese Expedition in 1888-89 (Medal with Clasp); and with the Chin-Lushai Expeditionary Force in 1889-90 as Principal Commissariat Officer (received the thanks of the Government of India, mentioned in despatches, Brevet of Major, Clasp).
[108] Captain H. E. Porter served with the Burmese Expedition in 1885-86 as Transport Officer (mentioned in despatches, Medal with Clasp).
[109] Captain A. P. Westlake served in the Afghan war in 1879-80 (Medal). Served with the Burmese Expedition in 1886-89 (mentioned in despatches, DSO., and Medal with two Clasps).
[110] Captain W. C. H. Mackintosh served with the Burmese Expedition in 1886-87 (Medal with Clasp).
[111] Captain W. D. Gordon served in the Afghan war in 1879-80, and was present at the forcing of the Shutargardan, and in the operations around Cabul in December 1879, including the investment of Sherpore; accompanied Sir Frederick Roberts in the March to Candahar, and was present at the battle of Candahar (Medal with two Clasps, and Bronze Decoration). Also served with the Marri Expedition in 1880.
[112] Captain E. Carbonaro served in the Soudan campaign in 1885 with the 17th Bengal Native Infantry, and was present in the engagements at Hasheen and the Tofrek zereba—horse shot (Medal with two Clasps, and Khedive's Star).
[114] Captain A. E. Whistler served in the Egyptian war of 1882 (Medal, and Khedive's Star). Served with the Burmese Expedition in 1885-87 (Medal with Clasp).
[115] Captain H. O'Donnell served in the Zulu war in 1879 (Medal with Clasp). Served with the Burmese Expedition in 1888-91 (mentioned in despatches, DSO., and Medal with Clasp); commanded the Mogaung Field Force—wounded (Clasp). Served with the Wuntho Expedition in 1891 in command of the Mogaung Column (mentioned in despatches).
[117] Captain F. W. P. Angelo served in the Soudan campaign in 1885 (Medal with Clasp, and Khedive's Star).
[118] Captain C. B. Judge served with the Hazara Expedition in 1888 (mentioned in despatches, Medal with Clasp).
[119] Captain E. H. Rodwell served in the Afghan war in 1878-79 (Medal). Also served with the Mahsood Wuzeeree Expedition in 1881.
[120] Captain R. H. Rattray served in the Afghan war in 1880 (Medal).
[121] Captain J. B. Edwards served in the Afghan war of 1878-80, took part in the operations in the Koorum Valley and was present at the capture of the Peiwar Kotal (Medal with Clasp).
[122] Captain A. N. Carr served in the Egyptian war of 1882 (Medal, and Khedive's Star).
[123] Captain M. L. Shipley served in the Afghan war in 1879-80 with the Transport Department (Medal).
[124] Captain W. L. Boswell served with the Burmese Expedition in 1886-88 (Medal with Clasp).
[125] Captain W. E. Bunbury served in the Afghan war in 1880 (Medal); also served with the Mahsood Wuzeeree Expedition in 1881.
[127] Captain G. B. Crawley served in the Afghan war in 1880 (Medal).
[128] Captain E. U. Marrett served in the Afghan war in 1880 (Medal).
[129] Captain J. S. E. Western served with the Mahsood Wuzeeree Expedition in 1881. Served with the Hazara Expedition in 1888 as Aide de Camp to Sir John M'Queen, Commanding the Force (mentioned in despatches, Medal with Clasp).
[130] Captain F. R. H. Chapman served in the Afghan war in 1880 (Medal).
[132] Captain H. W. E. Georges served with the Burmese Expedition in 1886-87 (Medal with two Clasps).
[133] Captain F. A. C. Kreyer served in the Afghan war in 1878-79 including the two expeditions into the Bazar Valley (Medal).
[134] Captain D. W. Purdon served with the Burmese Expedition in 1887-88 (Medal with Clasp).
[135] Captain G. B. Hodgson served in the Afghan war in 1880 (Medal).
[136] Captain W. H. Allen served in the Afghan war in 1879-80, including the engagement at Mazeena (Medal). Also served with the Mahsood Wuzeeree Expedition in 1881. Served in the Soudan campaign in 1885 (Medal with Clasp, and Khedive's Star). Served with the Lushai Expedition in 1889 (mentioned in despatches); with the Chin-Lushai Expeditionary Force in 1889-90 as Brigade Transport Officer (mentioned in despatches, Medal with Clasp); and with the Isazai Expedition in 1892.
[137] Captain C. G. R. Thackwell served in the Afghan war of 1878-80, and took part with the Hissarik and Lughman Valley Expeditions, and was severely wounded in an engagement near Jugdulluck (Medal). Also served in the Mahsood Wuzeeree Expedition in 1881. Served with the 20th Bengal Native Infantry in the Egyptian war of 1882, and was present at the battle of Tel-el-Kebir (Medal with Clasp, and Khedive's Star).

Indian Staff Corps.—War Services of Captains.

138 Captain G. J. Shaw served with the Burmese Expedition in 1888-89 (Medal with Clasp).

139 Captain M. A. Tuite served with the 67th Regiment in the Afghan war of 1878-80, and was present in the engagement at Charasiab on the 6th October 1879, and in the operations around Cabul in December 1879 including the investment of Sherpore (Medal with two Clasps).

140 Captain W. D. Thomson served with the Manipore Expedition in 1891 (Medal with Clasp)

142 Captain F. J. S. Lowry served in the operations of the Zhob Field Force in 1890.

143 Captain T. G. Johnson served in the Zulu war in 1879 (Medal with Clasp).

144 Captain D. J. O. Taylor served with the 25th King's Own Borderers in the Afghan war of 1878-80, first with the Peshawur Valley Field Force under Lieut.General Maude, and afterwards with the Khyber Line Force under Lieut.General Bright (Medal). Served with the 2nd Miranzai Expedition in 1891 (Medal with Clasp).

145 Captain G. S. Kerrich served in the Afghan war in 1879-80 (Medal). Served with the Burmese Expedition in 1886-89 (Medal with two Clasps).

146 Captain J. G. Hunter served in the Afghan war in 1878-79 with the 70th Regiment, first with the Candahar Column under Sir Donald Stewart, and afterwards with the Thull Chotiali Field Force under Major General Biddulph (Medal). Served with the Burmese Expedition in 1885-87, and again in 1887-89, as Adjutant 10th Bengal Native Infantry, and took part in the operations of the 1st Brigade under Brigadier Generals East and Wolseley, and in the Pagyi District under Colonel Symons (Medal with two Clasps). Served in the Chin-Lushai Expedition in 1889-90 with the 10th Bengal Native Infantry in the Column under Brigadier General Symons, and had charge of the attack on the village of Hanta (mentioned in despatches, Clasp).

147 Captain H. F. K. Waldron served in the Afghan war of 1878-80 (Medal).

148 Captain L. H. Reid served with the 63rd Regiment in Southern Afghanistan in 1879-80 (Medal). Served with the Burmese Expedition in 1886, and was severely wounded in an engagement on the 14th Dec. (Medal with Clasp); with the Hazara Expedition in 1891 (Clasp); and with the second Miranzai Expedition in 1891 (Clasp).

149 Captain C. F. G. Young served in the Zulu war of 1879, and was present in the engagement at Gingindhlovu (Medal with Clasp).

150 Captain J. H. Young served in the Afghan war in 1878-79 on the Khyber Line of Communications, and in the Koorum Valley (Medal).

151 Captain G. J. Younghusband served in the Afghan war of 1878-80, and was present at the attack and capture of Ali Musjid, with the second expedition into the Bazar Valley, and in the engagement at Futtehabad (Medal with Clasp). Served in the Soudan campaign in 1885 (Medal with two Clasps, and Khedive's Star). Served with the Burmese Expedition in 1886-87 (Medal with Clasp).

152 Captain F. P. Hutchinson served in the Afghan war in 1879-80, including the operations in the Lughman Valley (Medal). Served with the Chin-Lushai Expeditionary Force in 1889-90 (Medal with Clasp).

153 Captain P. H. Saulez served in the Afghan war in 1879-80 (Medal).

154 Captain L. H. Vidal served in the Egyptian war of 1882 (Medal, and Khedive's Star).

155 Captain A. H. Dobbs served with the Burmese Expedition in 1888-89 (Medal with Clasp).

156 Captain P. J. H. Aplin served in the Afghan war in 1879-80 (Medal). Served with the Burmese Expedition in 1885-89 (Medal with two Clasps).

157 Captain A. Phayre served in the Afghan war of 1878-80 (Medal).

159 Captain G. S. Ommanney served with the 9th Foot in the Afghan war in 1879-80, and was present in the engagement at Saidabad (Medal). Served with the Sikkim Expedition in 1888 (Medal with Clasp).

160 Captain H. Parkin served with the Zhob Valley Expedition in 1884. Served with the Burmese Expedition in 1886-87 (mentioned in despatches, Medal with Clasp); and in the operations in the Kachin Hills in 1892-93.

161 Captain W. B. Piers served in the Afghan war of 1878-80, and took part in the march to Candahar with the force under Major General Phayre (Medal).

163 Captain R. F. M. Johnstone served with the Burmese Expedition in 1888-89 (Medal with Clasp).

164 Captain O. C. Armstrong served with the Burmese Expedition in 1888 (Medal with Clasp).

165 Captain F. B. W. Richardson served with the Chin-Lushai Expeditionary Force in 1889-90 (Medal with Clasp).

166 Captain St. G. L. Steele served with the 2nd Bengal Cavalry in the Egyptian war of 1882, and was present in the action at Kassasin (9th September) and at the battle of Tel-el-Kebir and the capture of Cairo (Medal with Clasp, and Khedive's Star). Served with the Manipore Expedition in 1891 as Brigade Major to the Silchar Column (mentioned in despatches, Medal with Clasp).

167 Captain E. L. Hight served with the 67th Regiment in the Afghan war of 1878-80, and was present in the engagement at Charasiah on the 6th October 1879, and in the operations around Cabul in December 1879 including the investment of Sherpore (Medal with two Clasps). Served with the two Miranzai Expeditions in 1891 (Medal with Clasp).

169 Captain G. A. M'Carthy served in the Afghan war in 1880 (Medal).

170 Captain C. Le G. Justice served in the Zulu war in 1879, and was present in the engagement at Gingindhlovu (Medal with Clasp). Served with the Sikkim Expedition in 1888 (Medal with Clasp).

171 Captain Robertson served with the 72nd Highlanders in the Afghan war from January 1879 with the Koorum, Cabul, and Cabul-Candahar Field Forces, including the Khost Expedition, the engagement at Charasiah, and the operations around Cabul in December 1879; accompanied Sir Frederick Roberts in the march to Candahar, and was present at the battle of Candahar (Medal with three Clasps, and Bronze Decoration).

172 Captain A. F. Hogge served with the Mahsood Wuzeeree Expedition in 1881. Served with the Hazara Expedition in 1888 (Medal with Clasp).

173 Captain James served with the 57th Regiment in the Zulu war of 1879, and was present at the action of Gingindhlovu and relief of Ekowe, and throughout the operations of "Clarke's Column" (Medal with Clasp). Served in the Afghan war in 1879-80 (Medal). Served with the Hazara Expedition in 1888 (mentioned in despatches, Medal with Clasp).

174 Captain F. G. R. Ostrehan served in the Afghan war in 1880 (Medal).

175 Captain H. Rose served with the Burmese Expedition in 1886-87 (Medal with Clasp); and in the operations in the Lushai country in 1891-92 with the Nwengal Column.

177 Captain W. J. Newell served in the Afghan war in 1879-80 (Medal), and with the Mahsood Wuzeeree Expedition in 1881. Served with the Burmese Expedition in 1888-89 (Medal with Clasp); and with the Hazara Expedition in 1891 (Clasp).

178 Captain E. J. Medley served in the Afghan war of 1878-80, including the expedition against the Wuzeeree Khugianis (Medal).

179 Captain P. M. Carpendale served in the Afghan war in 1880 with the Koorum Valley Field Force (Medal), and with the expedition against the Mahsood Wuzeerees in 1881.

181 Captain W. Giles served in the Afghan war in 1879-80, and was present in the expedition to the Lughman Valley and with that against the Khugianis (Medal).

182 Captain A. M. Lloyd served with the 67th Regiment in the Afghan war in 1879-80 (Medal).

183 Captain H. H. F. Fagan served with the 67th Regiment in the Afghan war of 1878-80, and was present in the engagement at Charasiah on the 6th October 1879, and in the operations around Cabul in December 1879 including the investment of Sherpore (Medal with two Clasps).

185 Captain M. E. O'Donoghue served with the 67th Regiment in the Afghan war in 1879-80 (Medal). Served with the Burmese Expedition in 1886-89 (Medal with two Clasps).

186 Captain M. T. Thomson served with the 85th Regiment in the Afghan war in 1879-80, and took part in the Zaimusht Expedition under Brigadier General Tytler, including the assault of Zawa (Medal).

187 Captain C. P. W. Pirie served with the 11th Regiment in the Afghan war in 1879-80 (Medal).

188 Captain E. L. Wright served with the King's Dragoon Guards in the Zulu war of 1879 and in the subsequent operations against Sekukuni (Medal with Clasp).

189 Captain F. B. Mein served in the Afghan war in 1880 (Medal).

190 Captain W. H. M. Stewart served with the expedition against the Hunza-Nagars in 1891-92 as Political Officer (mentioned in despatches, Medal with Clasp).

192 Captain Hedley Wright served with the Hazara Expedition in 1891 (Medal with Clasp).

193 Captain P. M. Carnegy served with the 67th Regiment in the Afghan war of 1878-80, and was present in the engagement at Charasiah on the 6th October 1879, and in the operations around Cabul in December 1879, including the investment of Sherpore (mentioned in despatches, Medal with two Clasps). Served with the Burmese Expedition in 1885-86, and was severely wounded in an engagement at Yatha (mentioned in despatches, Medal with Clasp); with the Chin-Lushai Expeditionary Force in 1889-90 (Clasp); and with the Manipore Expedition in 1891 with the 2nd Battalion 4th Goorkha Rifles—severely wounded (mentioned in despatches, Clasp).

194 Captain G. H. Loch served in the Afghan war in 1880 (Medal). Served with the Burmese Expedition in 1886-87 (Medal with Clasp); and in the operations in Lushai in 1892 with the Eastern Sonai Column.

195 Captain G. R. C. Westropp served in the Afghan war in 1879-80 as Assistant Superintendent of Transport (Medal). Served with the Zhob Valley Expedition in 1884 as Commissariat Officer. Served with the Chin-Lushai Expeditionary Force in 1889-90 on Transport duty (received the thanks of the Government of India, mentioned in despatches, Medal with Clasp).

197 Captain W. H. D. Rich served with the Burmese Expedition in 1885-88 (mentioned in despatches, Medal with Clasp).

198 Captain A. C. O'Donnell was employed in Natal during the Zulu war of 1879 (Medal). Served with the Hazara Expedition in 1888 (mentioned in despatches, Medal with Clasp).

199 Captain C. J. Corfield served with the 25th King's Own Borderers in the Afghan war in 1879-80 with the Khyber Line Force under Lieut. General Bright (Medal). Served with the Hazara Expedition in 1888 (mentioned in despatches, Medal with Clasp).

200 Captain J. C. Hollway served with the Burmese Expedition in 1885-89 (Medal with two Clasps).

201 Captain G. G. J. S. Jones served with the 57th Regiment in the latter part of the Zulu war of 1879, and throughout the operations of "Clarke's Column" (Medal with Clasp).

203 Captain Burton served with the Burmese Expedition in 1885-86 (mentioned in despatches, Medal with Clasp).

204 Captain A. D. Fordyce served with the Burmese Expedition in 1886-87 (Medal with Clasp).

205 Captain E. F. H. M'Swiney served in the Afghan war in 1880 (Medal). Served with the Burmese Expedition in 1886-87 (DSO., and Medal with Clasp).

207 Captain J. W. C. Hutchinson served with the 25th King's Own Borderers in the Afghan war of 1878-80, first with the Peshawur Valley Field Force under Lieut. General Maude, and afterwards with the Khyber Line Force under Lieut. General Bright (Medal). Served with the second Miranzai Expedition in 1891 (Medal with Clasp).

208 Captain W. E. Phillips served in the Afghan war in 1880 (Medal). Served with the Hazara Expedition in 1891 (Medal with Clasp).

209 Captain N. S. Swanston served with the Burmese Expedition in 1886-87 with the Toungoo Column and the 3rd Brigade (Medal with Clasp). Served with the Chin-Lushai Expeditionary Force in 1889-90 as Chief Commissariat Officer (mentioned in despatches, Clasp).

210 Captain H. F. T. Macartney served with the Hazara Expedition in 1891 (Medal with Clasp).

211 Captain W. A. Thompson served with the Burmese Expedition in 1885-89 (Medal with two Clasps).

212 Captain C. I. Fry served with the Zhob Valley Expedition in 1884. Served in the Soudan campaign in 1883 (Medal with Clasp, and Khedive's Star).

213 Captain F. H. Hancock served with the Mahsood Wuzeeree Expedition in 1881. Served with the Burmese Expedition in 1886-88 (Medal with Clasp).

214 Captain H. F. E. Hodges served in the Afghan war in 1879-80 (Medal).

216 Captain F. C. W. Rideout served with the Burmese Expedition in 1887-88 (Medal with Clasp).

217 Captain R. W. Sherard served in the Afghan war in 1879-80 (Medal).

218 Captain A. H. Kellie served in the Egyptian war of 1882, and was present in the engagement at Mahala-Junction and at the battle of Tel-el-Kebir (Medal with Clasp, and Khedive's Star). Served with the Burmese Expedition in 1886 (Medal with Clasp); and with the Chin-Lushai Expeditionary Force in 1889 (Clasp).

219 Captain Wyllie served with the 91st Highlanders in the latter part of the Zulu war of 1879 (Medal with Clasp). Served with the Burmese Expedition in 1887-88 (mentioned in despatches, Medal with Clasp).

220 Captain M. E. Carthew-Yorstoun served in the Zulu war of 1879 (Medal with Clasp).

221 Captain H. L. Custance served in the Soudan campaign in 1885, and was present in the engagements at Hasheen and the Tofrek zereba and at the destruction of Temai (Medal with two Clasps, and Khedive's Star).

222 Captain H. A. Merewether served with the 51st Light Infantry in the Afghan war in 1880 (Medal). Served with the Burmese Expedition in 1886-88 (Medal with two Clasps).

223 Captain G. V. Burrows served in the Boer war of 1881 with the Natal Field Force. Served with the Burmese Expedition in 1885-86 as Assistant Provost Marshal and as Staff Officer of Mounted Infantry (mentioned in despatches, Medal with two Clasps).

224 Captain R. Williams served with the Burmese Expedition in 1885-89 (Medal with two Clasps).

225 Captain D. G. L. Shaw served in the Afghan war in 1879-80, including the operations round Cabul (Medal with Clasp). Served with the Zhob Valley Expedition in 1890.

227 Captain W. F. M. I. Fraser served with the Burmese Expedition in 1886-89 including the expedition up the Chindwin River under Colonel Toker (Medal with two Clasps).

228 Captain J. Strachey served with the Burmese Expedition in 1885-87 (mentioned in despatches, Medal with Clasp).

230 Captain R. S. Alexander served with the Burmese Expedition in 1886-88 (Medal with two Clasps).

231 Captain R. P. Colomb served with the Burmese Expedition in 1886-87 (Medal with Clasp).

232 Captain W. P. Anderson served with the Chin-Lushai Expedition in 1889-90 (Medal with Clasp).

233 Captain F. Campbell served with the Hazara Expedition in 1888 (Medal with Clasp).

234 Captain H. J. Bremner served with the Burmese Expedition in 1885-88 (Medal with two Clasps).

235 Captain G. P. Ranken served with the Burmese Expedition in 1886-87 (mentioned in despatches, Medal with two Clasps); and with the Hazara Expedition in 1888 (Clasp).

236 Captain J. M. Fleming served with the 25th King's Own Borderers in the Afghan war in 1879-80 with the Khyber Line Force under Lieut. General Bright (Medal).

237 Captain W. A. B. Dennys served with the Burmese Expedition in 1886-88 (Medal with Clasp).

238 Captain J. Lampen served with the Mahsood Wuzeeree Expedition in 1881. Served with the Burmese Expedition in 1886-89 (Medal with two Clasps).

239 Captain W. H. Dobbie served with the Burmese Expedition in 1885-86 (mentioned in despatches, Medal with Clasp).

240 Captain J. Vans Agnew served with the Burmese Expedition in 1888 in the Intelligence Branch (Medal with Clasp).

241 Major W. G. Abam served in the Soudan campaign in 1885 (Medal with Clasp, and Khedive's Star). Served with the Burmese Expedition in 1887-89 (Medal with Clasp); with the Momrik Expedition in 1891 (Clasp); and in the operations against the Kachins in 1892-93 in command of the Kaukkwè Column and of the combined Military Police Columns at the relief of Sima (received the thanks of the Government of India, Brevet of Major).

242 Captain E. A. Kettlewell served with the Burmese Expedition in 1885-87 (Medal with Clasp).

243 Captain C. G. F. Edwards served with the two Miranzai Expeditions in 1891 (Medal with Clasp).

244 Major R. H. Twigg served with the Akha Expedition in 1883-84. Served with the Burmese Expedition in 1886-87 (Medal with Clasp); also served in the operations in the Hunza-Nagar Country in 1891-92 as Deputy Assistant Adjutant General (mentioned in despatches, Brevet of Major, Clasp).

246 Captain R. H. Light served with the 11th Regiment in the Afghan war in 1879-80 (Medal).

247 Captain F. W. Repton served with the Sikkim Expedition in 1888 (mentioned in despatches, Medal with Clasp).

248 Captain R. G. Egerton served with the Hazara Expedition in 1888 (Medal with Clasp).

249 Major R. M. Maxwell served with the 18th Royal Irish in the Afghan war in 1879-80 (Medal). Served in the operations against the Abor tribes on the North East Frontier of Assam in 1894 (Brevet of Major).

250 Captain Mackenzie-Kennedy served with the Burmese Expedition in 1885-87 (Medal with Clasp); and with the Hazara Expedition in 1891 (Clasp).

251 Captain J. H. Smith served with the 11th Regiment in the Afghan war in 1879-80 (Medal). Served with the Burmese Expedition in 1886-89 (Medal with two Clasps).

253 Captain A. E. S. Searle served with the Burmese Expedition in 1885-86 (Medal with Clasp).

254 Captain E. B. Burton served with the 4th Sikhs in the Mahsood Wuzeeree Expedition in 1881 under Brigadier

Indian Staff Corps.—War Services of Captains.

General Konnedy. Served with the 7th Bengal Native Infantry in the Egyptian war of 1882, and was present at the battle of Tel-el-Kebir (Medal with Clasp, and Khedive's Star). Served with the Burmese Expedition in 1886-87 on Transport duty (mentioned in despatches, Medal with Clasp).

²⁵⁵ Captain G. F. Rowcroft served in the Soudan campaign in 1885, and was present in the engagement at Hasheen and at the destruction of Temai (Medal with Clasp, and Khedive's Star).

²⁵⁶ Captain W. Prior served with the Sikkim Expedition in 1888 (Medal with Clasp); and with the Manipore Expedition in 1891 (Clasp).

²⁵⁷ Captain D. C. F. Macintyre served in the Afghan war in 1880 (Medal). Served in the Manipore Expedition in 1891 in command of the Assam Military Police (mentioned in despatches, Medal with Clasp).

²⁵⁸ Captain A. R. Browning served with the Zhob Valley Expedition in 1884. Served with the Hazara Expedition in 1888 (Medal with Clasp).

²⁵⁹ Captain A. Beale served with the Burmese Expedition in 1885-89 (Medal with two Clasps).

²⁶⁰ Captain C. H. C. Heyman served with the Burmese Expedition in 1886-88 (Medal with two Clasps).

²⁶¹ Captain J. R. C. Colvin served in the Soudan campaign in 1885 (Medal with Clasp, and Khedive's Star).

²⁶² Captain W. J. R. Wickham served in the Soudan campaign in 1885 as Staff Officer to the Director of Indian Transport with the Home Forces (Medal with Clasp, and Khedive's Star). Served with the Hazara Expedition in 1888 (Medal with Clasp).

²⁶³ Captain H. G. Sutton served with the Burmese Expedition in 1885-89 (Medal with two Clasps).

²⁶⁴ Captain P. B. Vaughan served with the Akha Expedition in 1883-84.

²⁶⁵ Captain S. C. Gough served in the Afghan war in 1879-80 with the 67th Regiment (Medal).

²⁶⁶ Captain A. D. C. Pond served with the Burmese Expedition in 1886-89 (mentioned in despatches, Medal with two Clasps). Served with the Wuntho Expedition in 1891 in command of the Ye-u Battalion (mentioned in despatches, Clasp).

²⁶⁷ Captain C. C. Tennant served with the Burmese Expedition in 1886-87 (Medal with Clasp).

²⁶⁸ Captain H. R. Brander served with the Hazara Expedition in 1891 (Medal with Clasp).

²⁷⁰ Captain H. B. Borradaile served with the Burmese Expedition in 1885-89 (Medal with two Clasps).

²⁷¹ Captain D. M. Thompson served with the 18th Royal Irish in the Afghan war in 1880 (Medal). Served with the Sikkim Expedition in 1888 (Medal with Clasp).

²⁷² Captain C. E. Mardall served in the Afghan war in 1879-80 with the Koorum Division (Medal).

²⁷³ Captain D. C. Phillott served with the Hazara Expedition in 1891 as Field Intelligence Officer and Deputy Assistant Quarter Master General for Intelligence (Medal with Clasp).

²⁷⁴ Captain A. V. Hatch served with the Sikkim Expedition in 1888 (Medal with Clasp).

²⁷⁵ Captain E. W. Codrington served with the 63rd Regiment in Southern Afghanistan in 1879-80 (Medal). Served with the 1st Battalion Manchester Regiment in the Egyptian war of 1882 (Medal, and Khedive's Star). Served with the Hazara Expedition in 1888 (Medal with Clasp); and with the Miranzai Expedition in 1891 (Clasp).

²⁷⁶ Captain J. W. Cowley served with the Akha Expedition in 1883-84. Served with the Burmese Expedition in 1886-88 (Medal with Clasp). Served in the Manipore Expedition in 1891 in command of the 43rd Goorkha Rifles (mentioned in despatches, Clasp).

²⁷⁷ Captain R. Southey served with the Hazara Expedition in 1888 (Medal with Clasp), and in the operations of the Zhob Field Force in 1890.

²⁷⁸ Captain A. E. Aitken served in the Soudan campaign in 1885, and was present in the engagements at Hasheen and the Tofrek zereba, and at the destruction of Temai (Medal with two Clasps, and Khedive's Star).

²⁷⁹ Captain H. D. M'Intyre served with the Burmese Expedition in 1886-89 (Medal with two Clasps).

²⁸⁰ Captain W. Browne served in the Boer war of 1881 with the Natal Field Force. Served with the Burmese Expedition in 1888-89 (Medal with Clasp).

²⁸¹ Captain W. B. Mullins served with the Burmese Expedition in 1886-87 (Medal with Clasp).

²⁸² Captain P. A. N. St. L. Wood served with the 11th Regiment in the Afghan war in 1879-80 (Medal). Served with the Burmese Expedition in 1886-89 (Medal with two Clasps).

²⁸³ Captain H. V. Cox served with the 75th King's Own Borderers in the Afghan war in 1879-80 with the Khyber Line Force under Lieut. General Bright (Medal). Served with the Burmese Expedition in 1885-89 (mentioned in despatches, Medal with two Clasps).

²⁸⁵ Captain F. G. Bradley served with the Burmese Expedition in 1885-86 (Medal with Clasp).

²⁸⁶ Captain R. Errington served with the Burmese Expedition in 1885-87 (Medal with Clasp).

²⁸⁷ Captain G. F. D. Hamilton served with the Hazara Expedition in 1888 (Medal with Clasp).

²⁸⁸ Captain R. Wapshare served with the Burmese Expedition in 1886-88 (mentioned in despatches, Medal with two Clasps).

²⁸⁹ Captain E. R. Hartigan served with the Burmese Expedition in 1887 (Medal with Clasp).

²⁹⁰ Captain M. T. Shewen served in the Egyptian war of 1882, and was present at the occupation of Alexandria and Port Said, and at the surrender of Fort Ghemil (Medal, and Khedive's Star). Served with the Burmese Expedition in 1885-87 (Medal with Clasp).

²⁹¹ Captain C. C. Anderson served with the Burmese Expedition in 1886-88 (Medal with Clasp).

²⁹² Captain C. A. S. Montgomery served with the Burmese Expedition in 1886-87 (Medal with Clasp).

²⁹³ Captain D. J. T. O'Brien served with the 63rd Regiment in Southern Afghanistan in 1879-80 (Medal). Served with the 1st Battalion Manchester Regiment in the Egyptian war of 1882 (Medal, and Khedive's Star). Served in the Soudan campaign in 1885, and was present in the engagements at Hasheen and the Tofrek zereba, and at the destruction of Temai (two Clasps).

²⁹⁴ Captain H. W. Priestley served with the Manipore Expedition in 1891, temporarily in command of the 42nd Goorkha Rifles (mentioned in despatches, Medal with Clasp).

²⁹⁵ Captain H. B. Vaughan served with the 7th Bengal Infantry in the Egyptian war of 1882 (Medal, and Khedive's Star).

²⁹⁶ Captain C. Tritton served with the Burmese Expedition in 1887-89 (Medal with Clasp).

²⁹⁷ Major C. J. W. Grant served with the Burmese Expedition in 1885-86 (Medal with Clasp). Served in the Manipore Expedition in 1891 with the 12th Madras Infantry and was present at the attack and capture of Thobal—severely wounded and horse shot (mentioned in despatches, Victoria Cross, promoted Captain and Brevet Major, Clasp). Was awarded the Victoria Cross "for the conspicuous bravery and devotion to his country displayed by him in having, upon hearing on March 27, 1891, of the disaster at Manipur, at once volunteered to attempt the relief of the British captives with eighty Native soldiers, and having advanced with the greatest intrepidity, captured Thobal, near Manipur, and held it against a large force of the enemy. Lieut. Grant inspired his men with equal heroism by an ever-present example of personal daring and resource."

²⁹⁹ Captain W. A. M. Wilson served in the Burmese Expedition in 1885-88 with the 23rd Bombay Light Infantry; was Staff Officer to the Expedition to Gungaw (twice mentioned in despatches, Medal with two Clasps). Served with the Hazara Expedition in 1891 (Clasp).

³⁰⁰ Captain W. H. Lewin served with the Burmese Expedition in 1886-88 (Medal with two Clasps).

³⁰¹ Captain E. Grey served with the Sikkim Expedition in 1888 (Medal with Clasp).

³⁰² Captain G. Rippon served with the Burmese Expedition in 1887-89 (Medal with Clasp); in the Wuntho Expedition in 1891 with the Southern Column (Clasp); with the Manipore Expedition in 1891 as Deputy Assistant Quarter Master General to the Tammu Column (mentioned in despatches, Clasp); and in the operations in the Northern Chin Hills in 1891-92 as Transport Officer, during the latter part of the time as Transport Officer with the Burma Lushai Relief Column (Clasp).

³⁰⁴ Captain T. Quin served with the 1st Battalion Manchester Regiment in the Egyptian war of 1882 (Medal, and Khedive's Star). Served with the Hazara Expedition in 1888 (Medal with Clasp); and with the Miranzai Expedition in 1891 (Clasp).

³⁰⁵ Captain W. A. Watson served in the Soudan campaign in 1885 with the Camel Corps (mentioned in despatches, Medal with Clasp, and Khedive's Star).

³⁰⁶ Captain G. C. Cawood served with the Burmese Expedition in 1887-88 (Medal with Clasp).

³⁰⁷ Captain A. G. Peyton served in the Soudan campaign in 1885 (Medal with Clasp, and Khedive's Star).

³⁰⁸ Captain A. H. G. Kemball served with the Hazara Expedition in 1888 (Medal with Clasp); in the Hazara Expedition in 1891 with the 2nd Battalion 5th Goorkhas (Clasp); and with the Isazai Expedition in 1892.

310 Major G. D. Atkinson served with the Zhob Valley Expedition in 1884. Served with the Burmese Expedition in 1885-89 (Medal with two Clasps); also served in the operations against the Kachins in 1892-93 (Brevet of Major).
311 Captain P. Malcolm served with the Chin-Lushai Expeditionary Force in 1889-90 (Medal with Clasp). [See also Civil Decorations for Gallantry, "Hart's Annual Army List," p. 786.]
313 Captain J. W. G. Tulloch served with the Zhob Field Force under Sir George White in 1890 as Executive Commissariat Officer to the Force (mentioned in despatches). Served with the Hazara Expedition in 1891 as Head of the Transport Department (mentioned in despatches, Medal with Clasp).
314 Captain J. S. Melville served with the Burmese Expedition in 1885-87 (Medal with Clasp).
315 Captain C. H. Macdonald served with the Burmese Expedition in 1885-87 (Medal with Clasp).
316 Captain K. P. Burne served with the 1st Battalion Seaforth Highlanders in the Egyptian war of 1882, and was present at the battle of Tel-el-Kebir (Medal with Clasp, and Khedive's Star). Served in the Burmese Expedition in 1886-87 with the Kubo Valley Field Force (mentioned in despatches, Medal with Clasp).
317 Captain H. Comins served with the Zhob Valley Expedition in 1884. Served with the Burmese Expedition in 1887-88 (Medal with Clasp).
318 Captain E. de S. Smart served with the Hazara Expedition in 1888 (Medal with Clasp); with the second Miranzai Expedition in 1891 (Clasp); and with the Isazai Field Force in 1892.
319 Captain C. M. Dallas served with the Miranzai Expedition in 1891 as Assistant Political Officer (mentioned in despatches, Medal with Clasp).
320 Captain F. C. Rynd served with the Burmese Expedition in 1885-86 and was wounded in an engagement at Thyetgone on the 16th August 1886 (Medal with Clasp).
321 Captain A. T. Young served with the Burmese Expedition in 1885-89 and was slightly wounded in the engagement at Minhla (Medal with two Clasps).
322 Captain C. M. Ducat served with the Burmese Expedition in 1885-89 (Medal with two Clasps).
323 Captain C. G. Nurse served with the 2nd Battalion Royal Irish Fusiliers in the Soudan Expedition in 1884 and was present in the engagement at El Teb and Temai (Medal with Clasp, and Khedive's Star). Served in the operations of the Zaila Field Force in 1890.
324 Captain P. J. Gordon served with the Hazara Expedition in 1888 (Medal with Clasp).
325 Major C. E. Johnson served in the operations in Nyassaland, Central Africa, in 1892-94 (Brevet of Major).
326 Captain F. C. Colomb served with the Burmese Expedition in 1885-89 (Medal with two Clasps).
327 Captain R. M. Rainey served with the Zhob Valley Expedition in 1884. Served with the Burmese Expedition in 1885-89 (mentioned in despatches, Medal with two Clasps). Conducted the Chin Bok operations in 1889-90 as Commandant of the Chin Levy Military Police (mentioned in despatches, Clasp). Served with the Manipore Expedition in 1891 (Clasp); and in the operations in Burmah in 1891-92 as Staff Officer to the Baungshè Column.
328 Captain S. H. B. Hobbs served with the Isazai Expedition in 1892.
329 Captain A. L. Phillips served with the Chin-Lushai Expeditionary Force in 1889-90 as Assistant Commissariat Officer (Medal with Clasp). Served with the Hazara Expedition in 1891 as Executive Commissariat Officer (Clasp).
330 Captain H. Trevor served in the Soudan campaign in 1885, and was present in the engagements at Hasheen and the Tofrek zereba, and at the destruction of Temai (Medal with two Clasps, and Khedive's Star). Served with the Burmese Expedition in 1887 (Medal with Clasp). [See also Civil Decorations for Gallantry, "Hart's Annual Army List," p. 786.]
331 Captain C. M. Eales served with the second Miranzai Expedition in 1891 (Medal with Clasp).
332 Captain R. H. D. Thring served with the Burmese Expedition in 1886-89 (Medal with two Clasps).
333 Captain G. W. Rawlins served with the 20th Bengal Native Infantry in the Egyptian war of 1882 (Medal, and Khedive's Star).
334 Captain W. A. Cuppage served in the Burmese Expedition in 1886-87 with the 5th Bengal Light Infantry, and was severely wounded in an engagement in the Shan Hills (mentioned in despatches, Medal with Clasp).
335 Captain J. O. S. Fayrer served with the Hazara Expedition in 1888 (Medal with Clasp); with the Hazara Expedition in 1891 (Clasp); and with the second Miranzai Expedition in 1891 (Clasp).
336 Captain K. Chesney served with the Burmese Expedition in 1886-87 (mentioned in despatches, Medal with Clasp). Served with the Zhob Field Force in 1890 under Sir George White (mentioned in despatches).
337 Captain W. J. Peyton served in the Eastern Soudan in 1885, and took part in the operations for the withdrawal of the Egyptian Garrison from Harrar (CMG.).
338 Captain G. R. Row served with the Akha Expedition in 1883-84 (mentioned in despatches). Served with the Burmese Expedition in 1886-87 (Medal with Clasp), and again in 1888-89 with the Chin Field Force (Clasp).
339 Captain F. T. Williams served with the 2nd Battalion Royal Irish Fusiliers in the Soudan Expedition in 1884, and was present in the engagments at El Teb and Temai (Medal with Clasp, and Khedive's Star). Served with the Burmese Expedition in 1885-87 (Medal with two Clasps).
340 Captain H. L. Dodgson served with the Burmese Expedition in 1885-87 (mentioned in despatches, Medal with Clasp).
341 Captain G. N. Caulfeild served with the Burmese Expedition in 1885-87 (Medal with Clasp); also served in the operations in the Northern Chin Hills in 1892-93 (DSO.).
342 Captain L. W. Shakespear served with the Chin-Lushai Expeditionary Force in 1889-90 (Medal with Clasp). [See also Civil Decorations for Gallantry, "Hart's Annual Army List," p. 786.]
344 Captain C. V. F. Townshend served in the Nile Expedition in 1884-85 with the Royal Marines attached to the Guards Camel Regiment, and was present at the actions at Abu Klea and El Gubat (Medal with two Clasps, and Khedive's Star). Served with the expedition against the Hunza-Nagars in 1891-92 (mentioned in despatches, Medal with Clasp).
345 Captain S. G. Radcliff served with the Burmese Expedition in 1887-89 (Medal with Clasp).
346 Captain H. W. Lowry served with the Burmese Expedition in 1887-89 (Medal with Clasp).
347 Captain W. M. Dawes served with the Burmese Expedition in 1886 (Medal with Clasp).
348 Captain E. M. Reed served in the Egyptian war of 1882 (Medal, and Khedive's Star). Served with the Burmese Expedition in 1888-89 (Medal with Clasp).
349 Captain W. E. Wimble served with the Burmese Expedition in 1885-87 (Medal with Clasp).
351 Captain L. C. Fryer served with the Burmese Expedition in 1886-87, and was severely wounded in the engagement on the 7th November 1886 (mentioned in despatches, Medal with Clasp).
352 Captain F. J. H. Barton served in the Hazara Expedition in 1891 as Orderly Officer to Brigadier General Hammond, Commanding the 2nd Brigade; commanded the Khyber Rifles in the engagements of the 25th and 27th March (mentioned in despatches, Medal with Clasp).
353 Captain G. W. S. Hawks served with the Burmese Expedition in 1888 (Medal with Clasp).
354 Captain C. L. M. Rich served with the Hazara Expedition in 1888 (Medal with Clasp); and with the Hazara Expedition in 1891 (Clasp).
355 Captain C. H. Clements served with the Burmese Expedition in 1887-89 in the operations of the 1st Brigade under Brigadier General East (mentioned in despatches, Medal with two Clasps).
356 Captain C. E. Lloyd served in the Soudan campaign in 1884-85 as Staff Officer to the Governor General of the Red Sea Littoral during the defence of Suakin, and was present in the engagements at Hasheen and the Tofrek zereba, and at that near Tofrek on the 24th March (Medal with two Clasps, and Khedive's Star). Served with the Burmese Expedition in 1885-86 (Medal with Clasp).
357 Captain H. Daly served in the Burmese Expedition in 1886-87 as Political Assistant, Upper Chindwin (mentioned in despatches, Medal with Clasp).
358 Captain J. A. H. Craufurd served with the Burmese Expedition in 1885-87 (Medal with two Clasps).
359 Captain B. Holloway served with the Burmese Expedition in 1885-86 (mentioned in despatches, Medal with Clasp).
360 Captain W. S. Delamain served with the 1st Battalion Berkshire Regiment throughout the Egyptian war of 1882, and was present at the surrender of Kafr Dowar (Medal, and Khedive's Star). Served with the Burmese Expedition in 1885-88 (Medal with two Clasps). Served in the operations of the Zaila Field Force in 1890.
361 Captain W. M. Carpendale served with the Burmese Expedition in 1885-87 (Medal with Clasp).

Indian Staff Corps.—War Services of Captains.

[363] Captain F. Duncan served with the Hazara Expedition in 1888 (Medal with Clasp). Served with the expedition against the Hunza-Nagars in 1891-92 as Transport Officer (mentioned in despatches, Clasp).
[364] Captain A. P. D. Harris served with the Burmese Expedition in 1885-87 (mentioned in despatches, Medal with Clasp).
[365] Captain A. Nicholls served with the 1st Battalion Berkshire Regiment throughout the Egyptian war of 1882, was present at the surrender of Kafr Dowar (Medal, and Khedive's Star). Served with the Zhob Valley Expedition in 1890. Served with the two Miranzai Expeditions in 1891 (Medal with Clasp).
[366] Captain S. M. Mason served with the Burmese Expedition in 1888-89 (mentioned in despatches, Medal with two Clasps).
[367] Captain C. H. U. Price served with the Burmese Expedition in 1886-88, and was severely wounded in an engagement on the 24th February 1887 (Medal with two Clasps).
[368] Captain J. M. Stewart served with the Hazara Expedition in 1888 (Medal with Clasp); with the Chin-Lushai Expeditionary Force in 1889-90 as Orderly Officer to Brigadier General Symons (mentioned in despatches, Clasp); with the Hazara Expedition in 1891 (Clasp); and with the second Miranzai Expedition in 1891 (Clasp).
[369] Captain P. Holland served in the Egyptian war of 1882, and was present in the engagements at El Magfar and Tel-el-Mahuta, at the two actions at Kassasin, and at the battle of Tel-el-Kebir (Medal with Clasp, and Khedive's Star). Served with the Burmese Expedition in 1885-87 (twice mentioned in despatches, Medal with two Clasps).
[370] Captain G. R. Crawford served with the Lushai Expedition in 1889; and with the Hazara Expedition in 1891 (Medal with Clasp).
[372] Captain W. G. Hatherell served with the Burmese Expedition in 1885-89 (Medal with two Clasps); and with the Chin-Lushai Expeditionary Force in 1889-90 (Clasp).
[373] Captain O. G. Ievers served in the Egyptian war of 1882 (Medal, and Khedive's Star). Served with the Burmese Expedition in 1887 (Medal with Clasp).
[374] Captain E. H. Bernard served in the Nile Expedition in 1884-85 with the 2nd Battalion of the Essex Regiment (Medal with Clasp, and Khedive's Star). Served with the Burmese Expedition in 1886-87 (Medal with Clasp); and with the second Miranzai Expedition in 1891 (Clasp).
[375] Captain F. Churchill served with the Burmese Expedition in 1885-87 (Medal with Clasp).
[376] Captain W. E. Brett served with the Burmese Expedition in 1886-88 (Medal with two Clasps).
[377] Captain S. W. Lincoln served with the Burmese Expedition in 1886-89 including the repulse of the attack on Lingadaw (Medal with two Clasps); and with the Miranzai Expedition in 1891 (Clasp).
[378] Captain E. W. S. K. Maconchy served in the Hazara Expedition in 1888 as Transport Officer (Medal with Clasp); in the Hazara Expediton in 1891 with the 4th Sikh Infantry—wounded (mentioned in despatches, Clasp, and DSO.); and with the Isazai Expedition in 1892.
[380] Captain H. N. Taylor served in the operations in the Northern Chin Hills, Burmah, in 1892-93 (mentioned in despatches, DSO.).
[381] Captain A. Pressey served with the 1st Battalion West Kent Regiment throughout the Egyptian war of 1882, and was present at the action at Kassasin on the 9th September (Medal, and Khedive's Star). Served with the Hazara Expedition in 1891 (Medal with Clasp).
[382] Captain A. Poingdestre served with the 1st Battalion South Staffordshire Regiment in the Egyptian war of 1882 and was present in the reconnaissance in force from Alexandria on the 5th August (Medal, and Khedive's Star).
[383] Captain J. Thornhill served with the Burmese Expedition in 1888-89 (Medal with Clasp).
[384] Captain A. R. Denne served with the Burmese Expedition in 1885-87—severely wounded (Medal with two Clasps); with the Chin-Lushai Expeditionary Force in 1889-90 (Clasp); and in the operations on the North East Frontier of Burmah in 1891-92 with the Irrawaddy Column (Clasp).
[385] Captain G. E. T. Green served with the Burmese Expedition in 1885-89 (Medal with Clasp).
[387] Captain J. R. Mathewes served with the Burmese Expedition in 1886 (Medal with Clasp).
[388] Captain D. B. Thomson served in the Soudan campaign in 1885, and was present in the engagements at Hasheen and the Tofrek zereba—slightly wounded (Medal with two Clasps, and Khedive's Star). Served with the Chin-Lushai Expeditionary Force in 1889-90 (Medal with Clasp).
[389] Captain H. M'A. Johnston served with the Hazara Expedition in 1888 (Medal with Clasp).
[391] Captain F. H. S. Thomas served in the Burmese Expedition in 1886 (Medal with Clasp); also served with the Chin-Lushai Expeditionary Force in 1889-90 as Assistant Commissariat Officer Northern Column (mentioned in despatches, Clasp); and with the Manipore Expedition in 1891 as Chief Commissariat Officer under Brigadier General Graham (mentioned in despatches, Clasp).
[392] Captain C. F. Minchin served with the Hazara Expedition in 1888 (Medal with Clasp).
[393] Captain G. B. Hodson served in the Afghan war in 1880 (Medal). Served with the 1st Battalion South Staffordshire Regiment in the Egyptian war of 1882, and was present in the reconnaissance in force from Alexandria on the 5th August (Medal, and Khedive's Star). Served with the Burmese Expedition in 1885-87 (mentioned in despatches, Medal with Clasp).
[394] Captain W. C. C. Leslie served with the 2nd Battalion York and Lancaster Regiment throughout the Egyptian war of 1882, and was present in the engagements at El Magfar and Tel-el-Mahuta, in the two actions at Kassasin and at the battle of Tel-el-Kebir (Medal with Clasp, and Khedive's Star).
[395] Captain G. S. Broome served in the Egyptian war of 1882, and was present at the surrender of Kafr Dowar and Damietta (Medal, and Khedive's Star).
[396] Captain H. D. Daly served in the Egyptian war of 1882, and was present at the battle of Tel-el-Kebir (Medal with Clasp, and Khedive's Star). Served with the Burmese Expedition in 1886-87 (mentioned in despatches, Medal with Clasp).
[397] Captain W. L. Conran served with the 1st Battalion Royal Irish Fusiliers in the Egyptian war of 1882, and was present at the battle of Tel-el-Kebir (Medal with Clasp, and Khedive's Star). Served with the Burmese Expedition in 1885-88 in command of the Mounted Infantry of the 23rd Bombay Light Infantry (Medal with Clasp).
[398] Captain F. A. Loudon served with the Burmese Expedition in 1885-87 (Medal with two Clasps).
[399] Captain W. E. A. Blakeney served in the Egyptian war of 1882, and was present at the surrender of Kafr Dowar and Damietta (Medal, and Khedive's Star).
[400] Captain W. N. M. Cooke served with the 2nd Battalion York and Lancaster Regiment in the Egyptian war of 1882, and was present in the engagement at Tel-el-Mahuta (Medal, and Khedive's Star).
[401] Captain A. C. Le Bailly served with the 2nd Battalion York and Lancaster Regiment throughout the Egyptian war of 1882, and was present in the engagements at El Magfar and Tel-el-Mahuta, in the two actions at Kassasin, and at the battle of Tel-el-Kebir (Medal with Clasp, and Khedive's Star).
[402] Captain C. Griffiths served with the 2nd Battalion York and Lancaster Regiment throughout the Egyptian war of 1882, and was present in the engagements at El Magfar and Tel-el-Mahuta, in the two actions at Kassasin, and at the battle of Tel-el-Kebir (Medal with Clasp, and Khedive's Star).
[403] Captain E. B. Lang served with the Burmese Expedition in 1885-86 (Medal with Clasp).
[404] Captain G. F. H. Dillon served with the Burmese Expedition in 1886-87 including the operations of the 2nd Brigade under Brigadier General Cox (mentioned in despatches, Medal with Clasp); also served with the Lushai Expedition in 1889 as Assistant Superintendent of Army Signalling.
[405] Captain G. H. Bretherton served with the Miranzai Expedition in 1891 on Commissariat duty (mentioned in despatches, Medal with Clasp).
[406] Captain A. A. Jones served with the Burmese Expedition in 1886 (Medal with Clasp).
[407] Captain R. W. Nicholson served in the Soudan Expedition in 1884 with the 19th Hussars, and was present in the engagements at El Teb and Temai (Medal with Clasp, and Khedive's Star). Served in the Nile Expedition in 1884-85 with the 19th Hussars (Clasp).
[408] Captain W. G. H. Stirling served with the Burmese Expedition in 1886-89 (Medal with two Clasps); and with the Wuntho Expedition in 1891 (mentioned in despatches, Clasp).
[410] Captain C. W. Jacob served in the operations of the Zhob Field Force in 1890.
[411] Captain T. B. Hawks served with the Burmese Expedition in 1886 (Medal with Clasp).
[412] Captain J. C. Erck served with the Burmese Expedition in 1887 (Medal with Clasp).
[413] Captain W. A. Oswald served with the Burmese Expedition in 1885-87 (Medal with two Clasps).
[414] Captain G. H. Arbuthnot served with the Burmese Expedition in 1886-87 (Medal with Clasp).

Indian Staff Corps.—War Services of Captains.

⁴¹⁵ Captain T. McKay served with the Hazara Expedition in 1888 (Medal with Clasp).
⁴¹⁶ Captain A. Giles served with the Sikkim Expedition in 1888 (Medal with Clasp); and with the Manipore Expedition in 1891 in command of a detachment of the 13th Bengal Infantry (mentioned in despatches, Clasp).
⁴¹⁷ Captain H. W. Campbell served with the Zhob Valley Expedition in 1890.
⁴¹⁸ Captain G. C. M'D. Birdwood served with the Burmese Expedition in 1885-89 (Medal with two Clasps).
⁴¹⁹ Captain J. L. Kaye served throughout the campaign in the Eastern Soudan in 1885 with the 1st Battalion of the Berkshire Regiment, and was present in the reconnaissance to Hasheen on the 1st February (Medal with Clasp, and Khedive's Star).
⁴²⁰ Captain G. A. Brownrigg served with the Chin-Lushai Expeditionary Force in 1889-90 with the 28th Bombay Native Infantry, and was severely wounded in a skirmish on the 23rd February 1890 (mentioned in despatches, Medal with Clasp).
⁴²¹ Captain C. M. Crawford served with the Burmese Expedition in 1887-89 (Medal with Clasp). Served in the Hazara Expedition in 1891 with the 2nd Battalion 5th Goorkhas (Clasp); and with the Isazai Expedition in 1892.
⁴²² Captain C. W. O'Bryen served with the Burmese Expedition in 1886-88 in command of Mounted Infantry (mentioned in despatches, Medal with two Clasps); with the Hazara Expedition in 1891 (Clasp); and with the second Miranzai Expedition in 1891 (Clasp).
⁴²³ Captain G. L. Holland served with the Sikkim Expedition in 1888 (mentioned in despatches, Medal with Clasp).
⁴²⁴ Captain R. E. Sullivan served with the Burmese Expedition in 1885-86 (Medal with Clasp).
⁴²⁵ Captain H. E. Whiffin served in the expedition to the Soudan in 1885 with the 2nd Battalion of the East Surrey Regiment, and was present in the engagement at Hasheen and the subsequent advance to Temai (Medal with Clasp, and Khedive's Star).
⁴²⁶ Captain W. B. Young served in the Nile Expedition in 1884-85 with the 2nd Battalion of the Essex Regiment (Medal with Clasp, and Khedive's Star). Served with the Burmese Expedition in 1885-86 (Medal with Clasp).
⁴²⁷ Captain R. P. Horsbrugh served with the Burmese Expedition in 1886-88 (Medal with Clasp).
⁴²⁸ Captain K. J. Buchanan served with the Burmese Expedition in 1887-89 (Medal with Clasp); and with the Isazai Expedition in 1892.
⁴²⁹ Captain W. L. Davidson served with the Burmese Expedition in 1889-90 (Medal with Clasp).
⁴³⁰ Captain H. Kennedy served with the Burmese Expedition in 1885-89 (Medal with two Clasps). Served with the Zhob Valley Expedition in 1890.
⁴³¹ Captain A. H. McMahon served with the Zhob Valley Expedition in 1890.
⁴³² Captain W. de Wilton served with the Burmese Expedition in 1885-87 (Medal with Clasp).
⁴³³ Captain J. M. Smith served in the operations in the Hunza-Nagar Country in 1891-92 as Political Officer, including the capture of the Nilt Fort (mentioned in despatches, Victoria Cross, Medal with Clasp): was awarded the Victoria Cross "for his conspicuous bravery when leading the storming party at the attack and capture of the strong position occupied by the enemy near Nilt, in the Hunza-Nagar Country, on the 20th December, 1891. The position was, owing to the nature of the country, an extremely strong one, and had barred the advance of the force for seventeen days. It was eventually forced by a small party of fifty rifles, with another of equal strength in support. The first of these parties was under the command of Lieut. Smith, and it was entirely owing to his splendid leading, and the coolness, combined with dash, he displayed while doing so, that a success was obtained. For nearly four hours, on the face of a cliff which was almost precipitous, he steadily moved his handful of men from point to point, as the difficulties of the ground and showers of stones from above gave him an opportunity, and during the whole of this time he was in such a position as to be unable to defend himself from any attack the enemy might choose to make. He was the first man to reach the summit, within a few yards of one of the enemy's sungars, which was immediately rushed, Lieut. Smith pistolling the first man."
⁴³⁵ Captain F. Cardew served with the Burmese Expedition in 1886-87 as Intelligence Officer 4th Brigade (Medal with Clasp).
⁴³⁶ Captain A. C. B. Johnson served with the Sikkim Expedition in 1888 (Medal with Clasp).
⁴³⁷ Captain L. J. Andrews served with the Burmese Expedition in 1887-89 as Transport Officer (Medal with two Clasps).
⁴³⁸ Captain R. M. Botham served with the Zhob Valley Expedition in 1884.
⁴³⁹ Captain R. W. Falcon served with the Burmese Expedition in 1887-89 (Medal with two Clasps); and with the Isazai Expedition in 1892.
⁴⁴⁰ Captain E. J. E. Swayne served with the Burmese Expedition in 1886-87 (Medal with Clasp).
⁴⁴¹ Captain H. R. Mead served with the Soudan Frontier Field Force in 1885-86, and was present in the engagement at Giniss (Medal, and Khedive's Star).
⁴⁴² Captain E. A. Gayer served with the Burmese Expedition in 1885-88 (Medal with two Clasps).
⁴⁴³ Captain C. W. Wilkieson served with the Burmese Expedition in 1886-89 (Medal with two Clasps).
⁴⁴⁴ Captain A. F. Bruce served with the Hazara Expedition in 1891 (Medal with Clasp).
⁴⁴⁵ Captain T. A. Fischer served with the Burmese Expedition in 1885-89 (Medal with two Clasps).
⁴⁴⁶ Captain M. W. Baugh served with the Burmese Expedition in 1886-88 (Medal with two Clasps).
⁴⁴⁷ Captain S. F. Crocker served with the Burmese Expedition in 1886-87 (Medal with Clasp).
⁴⁴⁸ Captain G. W. C. Knatchbull served with the Burmese Expedition in 1885-87 (Medal with Clasp).
⁴⁴⁹ Captain J. A. Loudon served with the Burmese Expedition in 1886-89 (Medal with two Clasps).
⁴⁵¹ Captain C. V. Mainwaring served with the Burmese Expedition in 1887-88 (mentioned in despatches, Medal with two Clasps).
⁴⁵² Captain A. W. Leonard served in the Nile Expedition in 1884-85 with the 2nd Battalion of the Essex Regiment (Medal with Clasp, and Khedive's Star). Served with the Burmese Expedition in 1885-89 (Medal with two Clasps).
⁴⁵³ Captain R. J. R. Brown served with the Burmese Expedition in 1885-87 (mentioned in despatches, Medal with Clasp).
⁴⁵⁴ Captain C. C. A. Sillery served with the Burmese Expedition in 1885-87, and was severely wounded in the attack on the Minhla Redoubt (mentioned in despatches, Medal with Clasp); and with the second Miranzai Expedition in 1891 (Clasp).
⁴⁵⁶ Captain L. Philipps served with the Burmese Expedition in 1885-89 (Medal with two Clasps); with the second Miranzai Expedition in 1891 (Clasp); and with the Isazai Field Force in 1892.
⁴⁵⁷ Captain G. W. Palin served with the Zhob Valley Expedition in 1884; and with the Isazai Field Force in 1892.
⁴⁵⁸ Captain F. J. Fowler served with the Burmese Expedition in 1887-89 (mentioned in despatches, *DSO.*, and Medal with Clasp). Served with the Zhob Valley Expedition in 1884.
⁴⁵⁹ Captain W. Kirkpatrick served with the Burmese Expedition in 1885-87 (Medal with Clasp).
⁴⁶⁰ Captain C. H. Selwyn served with the Burmese Expedition in 1886-87 (Medal with Clasp).
⁴⁶¹ Captain C. W. Field served with the Burmese Expedition in 1886-88 (Medal with Clasp).
⁴⁶¹† Captain W. L. Maxwell served with the Burmese Expedition in 1886-87 including the operations of the 1st Brigade under Brigadier Generals East and Wolseley respectively; and with the Wuntho Expedition under Brigadier General Cox (Medal with two Clasps). Served with the second Miranzai Expedition in 1891 (Clasp).
⁴⁶² Captain W. H. Millar served with the Burmese Expedition in 1886-88 (Medal with two Clasps); with the Hazara Expedition in 1891 (Clasp); and with the second Miranzai Expedition in 1891 (Clasp).
⁴⁶³ Captain M. J. Tighe served with the Burmese Expedition in 1886-88 (mentioned in despatches, *DSO.*, and Medal with Clasp).
⁴⁶⁴ Captain R. J. D. Moseley served with the Miranzai Expedition in 1891 (Medal with Clasp).
⁴⁶⁵ Captain J. C. Sutherland served with the Burmese Expedition in 1889 (Medal with Clasp).
⁴⁶⁶ Captain W. E. Banbury served with the Burmese Expedition in 1885-87 (Medal with Clasp).
⁴⁶⁷ Captain A. E. Hatch served with the Zhob Valley Expedition in 1884; and in the operations of the Zhob Field Force in 1890.
⁴⁶⁸ Captain R. V. Davidson served with the Sikkim Expedition in 1888 (Medal with Clasp).
⁴⁷⁰ Captain R. P. Jackson served with the Burmese Expedition in 1885-86 (Medal with Clasp).
⁴⁷¹ Captain J. J. H. B. Eckford served with the Burmese Expedition in 1886-88 (Medal with Clasp).
⁴⁷² Captain C. Hamilton served with the Burmese Expedition in 1885-87 (Medal with Clasp).
⁴⁷³ Captain S. L. Aplin served with the Burmese Expedition in 1887-88 (Medal with Clasp); and with the Chin-Lushai Expedition in 1889-90 (Clasp).

Indian Staff Corps.— War Services of Captains and Lieutenants.

[474] Captain H. I. F. Palmer served with the second Miranzai Expedition in 1891 (Medal with Clasp).
[475] Captain T. Webster served with the Burmese Expedition in 1886-88 (Medal with two Clasps).
[477] Captain W. C. Barratt served throughout the campaign in the Eastern Soudan in 1885 with the 1st Battalion of the Berkshire Regiment, and was present in the reconnaissance to Hasheen on the 1st February, in the engagements at Hasheen and the Tofrek zereba and the subsequent advance to and burning of Temai (Medal with two Clasps, and Khedive's Star).
[478] Captain E. H. Cole served in the Burmese Expedition in 1886-87 with the 7th Bengal Cavalry including the operations of the 1st Brigade under Brigadier Generals East and Wolseley (Medal with two Clasps).
[479] Captain A. J. Shaw served with the Burmese Expedition in 1885-87 (Medal with Clasp).
[480] Captain E. S. Cooper served with the Soudan Frontier Field Force in 1885-86, and was present in the engagement at Giniss (Medal, and Khedive's Star). Served with the Hazara Expedition in 1888 (Medal with Clasp).
[481] Captain C. W. Somerset served with the Burmese Expedition in 1886-89 (Medal with two Clasps).
[482] Captain R. R. Renton served in the Burmese Expedition in 1886-87 including the operations round Hlindet, Yemethen, and Nyingan, and the operations of the 1st and 3rd Brigades under Brigadier General Wolseley and Brigadier General Lockhart respectively (Medal with two Clasps); and with the Manipore Expedition in 1891 (Clasp).
[483] Captain C. F. V. S. Venner served in the Nile Expedition in 1884-85 with the 1st Battalion of the Royal Sussex Regiment, and took part in the operations of the Desert Column under Sir Herbert Stewart (Medal with Clasp, and Khedive's Star). Served with the Burmese Expedition in 1887-89, and took part in the operations of the 1st Brigade under Brigadier Generals East and Wolseley respectively (Medal with two Clasps), and with the Chin-Lushai Expeditionary Force in 1890 with the Burma Column (Clasp).
[484] Captain C. H. Clay served in the Burmese Expedition in 1886-87 (Medal with Clasp).
[485] Captain A. P. A. Elphinstone served with the Burmese Expedition in 1885-89 (Medal with two Clasps).
[486] Captain T. W. Haig served with the Burmese Expedition in 1887-88 (Medal with Clasp).
[487] Captain J. K. Tod served with the Burmese Expedition in 1886-88 as Orderly Officer to Brigadier General East (mentioned in despatches, Medal with two Clasps).
[488] Captain T. H. Henderson served with the Burmese Expedition in 1885-87 (Medal with Clasp).
[489] Captain G. A. Robertson served with the Hazara Expedition in 1888 (Medal with Clasp).
[490] Captain W. C. Walton served with the Burmese Expedition in 1885-86 (Medal with Clasp).
[491] Captain S. B. Grimston served with the Burmese Expedition in 1886-87 (Medal with Clasp).
[492] Captain Ayerst served with the Burmese Expedition in 1885-89, and was slightly wounded in an engagement near Mingaon (mentioned in despatches, Medal with two Clasps).
[493] Captain G. H. C. Colomb served with the Burmese Expedition in 1885-87 (Medal with Clasp).
[494] Captain H. T. Brooking served with the Burmese Expedition in 1885-89 (mentioned in despatches, Medal with two Clasps).
[495] Captain C. E. Ross served with the Burmese Expedition in 1886-89 (Medal with two Clasps).
[497] Captain L. M. Foster served with the Chin-Lushai Expeditionary Force in 1889-90 (Medal with Clasp).
[499] Captain S. B. Graham served in the Nile Expedition in 1884-85 with the 1st Battalion of the Royal Sussex Regiment, and took part in the operations of the Desert Column under Sir Herbert Stewart (Medal with Clasp, and Khedive's Star). Served with the Burmese Expedition in 1887 (Medal with Clasp).
[500] Captain T. S. Johnson served with the Burmese Expedition in 1886-88 (Medal with two Clasps).
[501] Captain E. Y. Watson served with the Burmese Expedition in 1886-87 (mentioned in despatches, Medal with Clasp); and with the Chin-Lushai Expeditionary Force in 1889-90 (Clasp).
[502] Captain F. W. H. Cox served with the Burmese Expedition in 1885-88 including the operations under Brigadier Generals East and Wolseley (mentioned in despatches, Medal with two Clasps). Also served with the Manipore Expedition in 1891 with the 12th Madras Infantry—severely wounded (mentioned in despatches, Clasp).
[503] Captain C. F. T Murray served with the second Miranzai Expedition in 1891 (Medal with Clasp).
[504] Captain A. W. Warden served with the Burmese Expedition in 1885-86 (Medal with Clasp).
[505] Captain G. J. F. Soady served with the Hazara Expedition in 1891 (Medal with Clasp); and with the second Miranzai Expedition in 1891 (Clasp).
[506] Captain J. Hanegan served with the Burmese Expedition in 1886-89 (Medal with two Clasps); also served in the operations in the Northern Chin Hills in 1892-93 (DSO.).
[507] Captain E. de V. Wintle served with the Hazara Expedition in 1888 (Medal with Clasp).
[508] Captain W. N. Campbell served with the Burmese Expedition in 1886-87 (mentioned in despatches, Medal with Clasp).
[509] Captain J. M'D. Baird served with the Burmese Expedition in 1888 in the Intelligence Department (Medal with Clasp); with the Hazara Expedition in 1888 in the Intelligence Department (Clasp); with the Hazara Expedition in 1891 (Clasp); and with the expedition against the Hunza-Nagars in 1891-92 (mentioned in despatches, Clasp).
[510] Captain C. S. Williams served with the Burmese Expedition in 1886-87 (Medal with Clasp); with the expedition against the Hunza-Nagars in 1891-92 as Commissariat Officer (mentioned in despatches, Clasp).
[511] Captain E. Peach served with the Burmese Expedition in 1885-87—wounded (Medal with Clasp).
[512] Lieut. P. B. Warren served with the Chin-Lushai Expeditionary Force in 1889-90 (Medal with Clasp).
[513] Lieut. S. A. Pearse served with the Burmese Expedition in 1885-89 (Medal with two Clasps).
[514] Lieut. F. J. H. Wynch served with the Hazara Expedition in 1888 (Medal with Clasp).
[515] Lieut. G. W. Lilly served with the Burmese Expedition in 1885-88 (Medal with two Clasps).
[516] Lieut. G. P. Brasier Creagh served in the Miranzai Expedition in 1891 as Orderly Officer to Sir William Lockhart (mentioned in despatches, Medal with Clasp).
[517] Lieut. H. St. G. Thomas served in the Nile Expedition in 1884-85 with the 1st Battalion of the Royal Sussex Regiment, and took part in the operations of the Desert Column under Sir Herbert Stewart (Medal with Clasp, and Khedive's Star). Served with the Burmese Expedition in 1886-89 (Medal with two Clasps).
[518] Lieut. C. C. Boileau served with the Burmese Expedition in 1886 (Medal with Clasp).
[519] Lieut. H. B. Murray served with the Hazara Expedition in 1888 (Medal with Clasp).
[520] Lieut. A. C. Baldwin served with the Bechuanaland Expedition in 1884-85. Served with the Burmese Expedition in 1887 (Medal with Clasp).
[521] Lieut. G. A. Ward served with the Burmese Expedition in 1886-88 (Medal with Clasp).
[523] Lieut. E. M. Jackson served with the Burmese Expedition in 1886-87 (mentioned in despatches, Medal with Clasp).
[524] Lieut. E. H. Watson served with the Hazara Expedition in 1888 (Medal with Clasp).
[525] Lieut. H. V. Bradley served with the Lushai Expedition in 1889 (Medal with Clasp); and with the Manipore Expedition in 1891 (Clasp).
[526] Lieut. J. B. Chatterton served in the Burmese Expedition in 1885-87 with the 2nd Brigade under Brigadier General Cox (mentioned in despatches, Medal with Clasp).
[527] Lieut. F. Tweddell served with the Soudan Frontier Field Force in 1885-86, and was present in the engagement at Giniss (Medal, and Khedive's Star).
[528] Lieut. H. C. Bernard served with the Burmese Expedition in 1885-89 (Medal with two Clasps); and with the Manipore Expedition in 1891 (Clasp).
[529] Lieut. R. H. Dowing served with the Burmese Expedition in 1887-89 (Medal with two Clasps).
[530] Lieut. H. J. Jones served in the Nile Expedition in 1884-85 with the 1st Battalion of the Royal Irish Regiment (Medal with Clasp, and Khedive's Star). Served with the Hazara Expedition in 1888 (Medal with Clasp).
[531] Lieut. C. G. Prendergast served with the Burmese Expedition in 1885-87 (Medal with Clasp).
[532] Lieut. C. G. Carnegy served with the Burmese Expedition in 1886-88 (Medal with Clasp).
[533] Lieut. W. I. Ryder served with the Sikkim Expedition in 1888 (mentioned in despatches, Medal with Clasp).
[536] Lieut. A. W. Newbold served in the Nile Expedition in 1884-85 with the 1st Battalion of the Royal Sussex Regiment, and took part in the operations of the Desert Column under Sir Herbert Stewart (Medal with Clasp, and Khedive's Star). Served with the Wuntho Expedition and in the operations in the Kachin Hills, Burmah, in 1891-93 (Medal with Clasp).

Indian Staff Corps.—War Services of Lieutenants.

⁵³⁷ Lieut. J. F. Barry served in the Boer war in 1881. Served with the Burmese Expedition in 1886-87 (Medal with Clasp).
⁵³⁸ Lieut. B. W. Marlow served with the Burmese Expedition in 1886 (Medal with Clasp).
⁵³⁹ Lieut. C. E. Hendley served with the Burmese Expedition in 1885-89 (Medal with two Clasps).
⁵⁴⁰ Lieut. C. Bailey served with the Burmese Expedition in 1885-87 (Medal with Clasp).
⁵⁴¹ Lieut. A. H. Battye served with the Burmese Expedition in 1886-87 (Medal with Clasp); with the Chin-Lushai Expedition in 1889-90 (Clasp); and with the Manipore Expedition in 1891 (Clasp).
⁵⁴² Lieut. W. H. W. Mercer served with the Burmese Expedition in 1886-87, and was severely wounded in an engagement on the 27th March 1887 (Medal with Clasp). [See also Civil Decorations for Gallantry, "Hart's Annual Army List," p. 786.]
⁵⁴³ Lieut. J. A. G. Rainsford served with the Burmese Expedition in 1886-87 (Medal with Clasp).
⁵⁴⁴ Lieut. F. de B. Young served with the Hazara Expedition in 1888 (Medal with Clasp).
⁵⁴⁵ Lieut. P. J. Miles served with the Hazara Expedition in 1888 (Medal with Clasp).
⁵⁴⁶ Lieut. C. A. Fowler served with the Miranzai Expedition in 1891.
⁵⁴⁷ Lieut. A. H. Williams served with the Burmese Expedition in 1886-87 (Medal with Clasp); and with the Manipore Expedition in 1891 (Clasp).
⁵⁴⁸ Lieut. R. C. Lye served with the Burmese Expedition in 1885-87, and was slightly wounded in an engagement at Oungdaw (mentioned in despatches, Medal with Clasp); and with the Miranzai Expedition in 1891 (Clasp).
⁵⁴⁹ Lieut. A. Grant served with the Chin-Lushai Expeditionary Force in 1889-90 (Medal with Clasp); and with the Manipore Expedition in 1891 (Clasp).
⁵⁵⁰ Lieut. A. R. Ditmas served with the Burmese Expedition in 1887-88 (Medal with Clasp).
⁵⁵¹ Lieut. E. Waller served with the Hazara Expedition in 1891 (Medal with Clasp); and with the second Miranzai Expedition in 1891 (Clasp).
⁵⁵² Lieut. F. Murray served with the Burmese Expedition in 1885-89 (Medal with Clasp).
⁵⁵³ Lieut. R. E. Foley served in the occupation of Suakin by British troops in 1885-86. Served with the Hazara Expedition in 1888 (Medal with Clasp); and with the Manipore Field Force in 1891 as Transport Officer to the Kohima Column (Clasp).
⁵⁵⁴ Lieut. A. B. H. Drew served with the Hazara Expedition in 1888 (Medal with Clasp); and with the two Miranzai Expeditions in 1891 (Clasp).
⁵⁵⁵ Lieut. R. M. Edwards served with the Burmese Expedition in 1886-89, including the operations of the 3rd Brigade under Brigadier General Lockhart and the expedition up the Chindwin River under Colonel Toker (Medal with two Clasps). Also served with the Manipore Expedition in 1891 (Clasp).
⁵⁵⁶ Lieut. H. D. Watson served with the Sikkim Expedition in 1888 (Medal with Clasp).
⁵⁵⁷ Lieut. E. W. Carrick served with the Burmese Expedition in 1885-89 (Medal with two Clasps); and with the Manipore Expedition in 1891 (Clasp).
⁵⁵⁸ Lieut. F. A. Smith served with the Chin-Lushai Expeditionary Force in 1889-90 (Medal with Clasp).
⁵⁵⁹ Lieut. R. B. Berkeley served with the Burmese Expedition in 1886-87 (Medal with Clasp).
⁵⁶² Lieut. R. B. Low served with the Lushai Expedition in 1889.
⁵⁶⁴ Lieut. D. F. Stuart served with the Burmese Expedition in 1885-87 (Medal with Clasp).
⁵⁶⁵ Lieut. Waymouth served with the Burmese Expedition in 1885-87 (Medal with Clasp).
⁵⁶⁸ Lieut. G. H. Boisragon served with the Hazara Expedition in 1888 (Medal with Clasp); with the Hazara Expedition in 1891 (Clasp); and with the two Miranzai Expeditions in 1891, in the first expedition as Orderly Officer to the General Officer in command (Clasp). Served in the operations in the Hunza-Nagar Country in 1891-92, including the capture of the Nilt Fort (Victoria Cross, Clasp): was awarded the Victoria Cross "for his conspicuous bravery in the assault and capture of the Nilt Fort on 2nd December 1891. This officer led the assault with dash and determination, and forced his way through difficult obstacles to the inner gate, when he returned for reinforcements, moving intrepidly to and fro under a heavy cross-fire until he had collected sufficient men to relieve the hardly-pressed storming party and drive the enemy from the fort."
⁵⁶⁹ Lieut. F. J. Nelson served with the Bechuanaland Expedition under Sir Charles Warren in 1884-85. Served with the Burmese Expedition in 1886-87 (mentioned in despatches, Medal with Clasp); and on the North-Eastern Frontier of Burmah in 1891-92, including the operations against the Kachins, in command of the Sinkan Column—severely wounded (Clasp).
⁵⁷⁰ Lieut. A. F. P. Paxton served during the Nile Expedition in 1884-85 with the 1st Battalion Yorkshire Regiment on the Lines of Communication up the Nile. Served with the Soudan Frontier Field Force in 1885-86 during the operations on the Upper Nile, and was present in the engagement at Giniss (Medal, and Khediye's Star. Served with the Burmese Expedition in 1887-89 (Medal with two Clasps).
⁵⁷¹ Lieut. N. E. Robin served with the Sikkim Expedition in 1888 (Medal with Clasp).
⁵⁷² Captain C. A. Edwards served in the Burmese Expedition in 1886-87 with the 1st Battalion Royal Welsh Fusiliers (Medal with Clasp).
⁵⁷³ Lieut. W. C. M. Woodcock served with the Burmese Expedition in 1885-87 including the operations of the 6th Brigade under Brigadier General Low (Medal with Clasp); and with the two Miranzai Expeditions in 1891 (Clasp).
⁵⁷⁴ Lieut. A. H. Eustace served with the Hazara Expedition in 1888 (Medal with Clasp); and with the Hazara Expedition in 1891 as Field Intelligence Officer (Clasp).
⁵⁷⁵ Lieut. F. W. Evatt served with the Hazara Expedition in 1888 (Medal with Clasp); in the Hazara Expedition in 1891 with the 2nd Battalion 5th Goorkhas (Clasp); with the first Miranzai Expedition in 1891 (Clasp); and with the Isazai Expedition in 1892.
⁵⁷⁶ Lieut. F. P. Webber served with the Chin-Lushai Expeditionary Force in 1889-90 (Medal with Clasp).
⁵⁷⁷ Lieut. E. R. R. Swiney served with the Burmese Expedition in 1886-87 including the operations of the 3rd Brigade under Brigadier Generals Lockhart and Collett respectively (Medal with two Clasps); with the Lushai Expeditionary Force in 1889; and with the Zhob Valley Field Force in 1890.
⁵⁷⁸ Lieut. N. A. H. Budd served with the Chin-Lushai Expedition in 1889-90 (Medal with Clasp). Served in the operations against the Sultanate of Vitu under Admiral Fremantle (mentioned in despatches).
⁵⁷⁹ Lieut. A. J. Campbell served with the Burmese Expedition in 1889 (Medal with Clasp).
⁵⁸⁰ Lieut. W. R. Birdwood served with the Hazara Expedition in 1891 (Medal with Clasp).
⁵⁸¹ Lieut. J. Kendall served with the Burmese Expedition in 1887-88 (Medal with two Clasps).
⁵⁸² Lieut. G. E. L. Gilbert served with the Hazara Expedition in 1888 (Medal with Clasp).
⁵⁸³ Lieut. E. G. Wright served with the Burmese Expedition in 1886-89 (Medal with two Clasps); and with the Chin-Lushai Expeditionary Force in 1889-90 (Clasp).
⁵⁸⁴ Lieut. Lockhart-Mure served with the Soudan Frontier Field Force in 1885-86, and was present in the engagement at Giniss (Medal, and Khedive's Star).
⁵⁸⁵ Lieut. J. H. B. Beresford served with the Burmese Expedition in 1886-87 (Medal with Clasp). Served in the Hazara campaign in 1888 (Clasp).
⁵⁸⁶ Lieut. A. H. Allenby served with the Burmese Expedition in 1886-89 (Medal with two Clasps).
⁵⁸⁷ Lieut. T. S. Young served with the Burmese Expedition in 1887-88 (Medal with Clasp).
⁵⁸⁸ Lieut. W. E. F. Burlton served with the Burmese Expedition in 1885-89 (Medal with two Clasps).
⁵⁸⁹ Lieut. S. J. Drummond served with the Chin-Lushai Expeditionary Force in 1889-90 (Medal with Clasp).
⁵⁹⁰ Lieut. A. B. Harvey served with the Burmese Expedition in 1886-89 (Medal with two Clasps).
⁵⁹¹ Lieut. B. Trydell served with the Burmese Expedition in 1888 (Medal with Clasp); and with the Wuntho Field Force in 1891 (Clasp).
⁵⁹³ Lieut. C. H. Beville served in the Hazara Expedition in 1891 with the Commissariat Department (mentioned in despatches, Medal with Clasp).
⁵⁹⁴ Lieut. C. L. O. Reid served with the Burmese Expedition in 1885-89 (Medal with two Clasps).
⁵⁹⁵ Lieut. H. R. Fagan served with the Miranzai Expedition in 1891 (Medal with Clasp).
⁵⁹⁶ Lieut. R. E. H. Dyer served with the Burmese Expedition in 1886-87 (Medal with Clasp). Served with the Hazara Expedition in 1888 (Clasp).
⁵⁹⁷ Lieut. R. C. Cockerill served with the Burmese Expedition in 1888-89 (Medal with Clasp).
⁵⁹⁸ Lieut. C. H. Davies served in the Hazara Expedition in 1888 (Medal with Clasp).

600 Lieut. H. King served with the Burmese Expedition in 1885-88 (mentioned in despatches, Medal with Clasp).
601 Lieut. H. Walton served with the Sikkim Expedition in 1888 (Medal with Clasp).
602 Lieut. A. E. Barton served in the Burmese Expedition in 1887 with the 1st Battalion of the Yorkshire Light Infantry (Medal with Clasp).
603 Lieut. O. J. Obbard served with the Burmese Expedition in 1887 (Medal with Clasp).
604 Lieut. H. W. G. Cole served with the Hazara Expedition in 1888 (Medal with Clasp). Served with the Chin-Lushai Expeditionary Force in 1889-90 as Staff Officer Chittagong Column (mentioned in despatches, Clasp). Served with the Manipore Expedition in 1891 in command of the Surma Valley Military Police (mentioned in despatches, Clasp).
605 Lieut. H. A. Cooper served with the Hazara Expedition in 1888 (Medal with Clasp).
606 Lieut. L. H. Walker served with the Burmese Expedition in 1887-90 (Medal with two Clasps).
607 Lieut. H. E. Williams served with the Burmese Expedition in 1885-89 (Medal with two Clasps).
608 Lieut. A. Cadell served with the Chin-Lushai Expeditionary Force in 1889-90 (Medal with Clasp).
609 Lieut. F. Rennick served with the Hazara Expedition in 1888 (Medal with Clasp).
610 Lieut. W. H. Hildebrand served with the Burmese Expedition in 1887-88 (Medal with Clasp); and with the Chin-Lushai Expeditionary Force in 1889-90 as Hill-Coolie Transport Officer (mentioned in despatches, Clasp).
611 Lieut. G. E. D. Elsmie served with the Burmese Expedition in 1885-89 (Medal with two Clasps); and with the two Miranzai Expeditions in 1891 (Clasp).
612 Lieut. H. E. C. B. Nepean served with the Soudan Frontier Field Force in 1885-86, and was present in the engagement at Giniss (Medal, and Khedive's Star). Served with the Burmese Expedition in 1887-89 (Medal with Clasp).
614 Lieut. W. E. Venour served with the Chin-Lushai Expeditionary Force in 1889-90 (Medal with Clasp).
615 Lieut. D. S. Buist served with the Burmese Expedition in 1885-89 (Medal with two Clasps).
616 Lieut. R. M. Bell served with the Burmese Expedition in 1887-88 (Medal with Clasp).
617 Lieut. P. G. Shewell served with the Burmese Expedition in 1885-87 (Medal with Clasp).
618 Lieut. H. C. Vesey served with the Burmese Expedition in 1887-88 (Medal with Clasp), and with the Hazara Expedition in 1888 (Clasp).
619 Lieut. F. H. Peterson served with the Sikkim Expedition in 1888 (Medal with Clasp); and with the Hazara Expedition in 1891 (Clasp).
621 Lieut. H. Vickers served with the Chin-Lushai Expeditionary Force in 1889-90 (Medal with Clasp).
622 Lieut. A. Le G. Jacob served in the operations of the Zhob Field Force in 1890.
623 Lieut. Anwyl-Passingham served with the Burmese Expedition in 1886-89 (Medal with two Clasps).
624 Lieut. G. C. F. Sartorius served with the Burmese Expedition in 1886-89 (Medal with two Clasps).
625 Lieut. L. N. Leeds served with the two Miranzai Expeditions in 1891 (Medal with Clasp).
626 Lieut. H. C. C. Ducat served with the Sikkim Expedition in 1888 (Medal with Clasp); with the Chin-Lushai Expeditionary Force in 1889-90 (Clasp); and with the Manipore Expedition in 1891 (Clasp).
627 Lieut. F. H. Domenichetti served with the Burmese Expedition in 1888-89 (Medal with Clasp).
628 Lieut. H. C. Tytler served with the Sikkim Expedition in 1888 (mentioned in despatches, Medal with Clasp), and in the operations in Lushai in 1892 with the Eastern Sonai Column.
629 Lieut. F. Jollie served in the operations on the Soudan frontier in 1889, including the engagement at Toski (Medal with Clasp, 4th Class of the Medjidie, and Khedive's Star.)
630 Lieut. J. Parker served with the Burmese Expedition in 1886-87 (Medal with Clasp).
631 Lieut. G. M. Baldwin served with the Hazara Expedition in 1888 (Medal with Clasp).
632 Lieut. A. T. Walling served with the Burmese Expedition in 1886-87 (Medal with Clasp); and with the Manipore Expedition in 1891 (Clasp).
633 Lieut. O. W. Carey served with the Burmese Expedition in 1885-89 (Medal with two Clasps).
634 Lieut. J. W. Drever served with the Burmese Expedition in 1887-89 (Medal with Clasp).
636 Lieut. G. T. Widdicombe served with the Lushai Expedition in 1888-89; with the Chin-Lushai Expeditionary Force in 1889-90 (Medal with Clasp); and with the expedition against the Hunza-Nagars in 1891-92 (mentioned in despatches, Clasp).
637 Lieut. J. H. Lowry served with the Burmese Expedition in 1888-89 (Medal with Clasp).
638 Lieut. S. R. Stevens served with the Burmese Expedition in 1888-89 (Medal with Clasp).
639 Lieut. F. W. Wodehouse served with the Chin-Lushai Expeditionary Force in 1889-90 (Medal with Clasp).
640 Lieut. N. E. Chesney served with the Hazara Expedition in 1888 (Medal with Clasp); and in the Hazara Expedition in 1891 with the 2nd Battalion 5th Goorkhas (Clasp).
641 Lieut. A. W. N. Taylor served with the Nile Expedition in 1884-85, and was present in the engagements at Abu Klea and El Gubat and in the reconnaissance to Metammeh (Medal with two Clasps, and Khedive's Star).
642 Lieut. B. P. S. Rooke served with the Burmese Expedition in 1886-87 (Medal with Clasp).
643 Lieut. P. C. Palin served with the Burmese Expedition in 1887-89 (Medal with Clasp), and with the Hazara Expedition in 1888 (Clasp).
644 Lieut. A. T. Rowlandson served in the operations of the Zhob Field Force in 1890.
645 Lieut. F. G. Lucas served in the Hazara Expedition in 1891 with the 2nd Battalion 5th Goorkhas (Medal with Clasp).
646 Lieut. F. F. Badcock served with the Hazara Expedition in 1891 as Brigade Transport Officer 2nd Brigade (mentioned in despatches, Medal with Clasp); also served in the operations in the Hunza-Nagar Country in 1891-92, including the capture of the Nilt Fort—wounded (DSO. and Clasp).
647 Lieut. N. A. Lewarne served in the Sikkim Expedition in 1888 with the 2nd Battalion Derbyshire Regiment, and was present in the engagement at the Jelapla (Medal with Clasp). Served with the second Miranzai Expedition in 1891 (Clasp).
648 Lieut. R. Harman served with the Hazara Expedition in 1891 with the 4th Sikh Infantry—severely wounded (mentioned in despatches, DSO., and Medal with Clasp).
649 Lieut. C. T. Swan served with the Lushai Expedition in 1889 (Medal with Clasp); and in the operations in Burmah in 1891-92 with the Tlang-tlang and Tashon Columns.
651 Lieut. W. E. Tomkins served with the Chin-Lushai Expeditionary Force in 1889-90 (Medal with Clasp).
652 Lieut. H. A. Moore served with the Hazara Expedition in 1888 (Medal with Clasp).
653 Lieut. W. H. Manning served with the Burmese Expedition in 1887-89 as Intelligence Officer (Medal with Clasp); with the Miranzai Expedition in 1891 (Clasp); and with the Hazara Expedition in 1891 (Clasp).
654 Lieut. C. E. Wood served with the Burmese Expedition in 1889-90 (Medal with Clasp).
655 Lieut. T. C. M. T. Hogg served with the Hazara Expedition in 1888 (Medal with Clasp).
657 Lieut. O. C. Argles served with the expedition against the Yonnies, on the West Coast of Africa, in 1887-88 (Medal with Clasp).
658 Lieut. R. C. H. Chalmers served with the Hazara Expedition in 1888 (Medal with Clasp).
660 Lieut. E. J. Lugard served in the operations against the Chins in 1888-89 under Brigadier General Faunce (Medal with Clasp); in the Chin-Lushai Expeditionary Force in 1889-90 with the 42nd Goorkha Light Infantry (mentioned in despatches, DSO., and Clasp); and with the Manipore Expedition in 1891—slightly wounded (Clasp).
661 Lieut. H. C. Ricketts served with the Hazara Expedition in 1888 (Medal with Clasp).
662 Lieut. P. B. B. Forster served with the Hazara Expedition in 1888 (Medal with Clasp); and with the Zhob Valley Expedition in 1890.
663 Lieut. C. H. Williams served in the Burmese Expedition in 1885-89 (Medal with two Clasps).
664 Lieut. A. B. Sangster served in the Burmese Expedition in 1885-89 (Medal with two Clasps).
665 Lieut. J. W. Orchard served with the Burmese Expedition in 1889 (Medal with Clasp).
666 Lieut. A. C. Hickley served with the Hazara Expedition in 1888 (Medal with Clasp).
667 Lieut. A. C. H. Smithett served with the Hazara Expedition in 1888 (Medal with Clasp).
670 Lieut. W. S. Eardley-Howard served with the Hazara Expedition in 1888 (Medal with Clasp).
671 Lieut. N. J. H. Powell served with the two Miranzai Expeditions in 1891 (Medal with Clasp).
672 Lieut. F. H. Taylor served with the Hazara Expedition in 1888 (Medal with Clasp); in the Hazara Expedition in 1891 attached to the 4th Sikh Infantry (mentioned in despatches, Clasp); with the Miranzai Expedition

in 1891 (Clasp); and with the expedition against the Hunza-Nagars in 1891-92, including the capture of the Nilt Fort (mentioned in despatches, Clasp).

⁶⁷⁴ Lieut. J. Hill served with the Lushai Expedition in 1889; and with the second Miranzai Expedition in 1891 (Medal with Clasp).

⁶⁷⁵ Lieut. N. G. Fraser served with the Chin-Lushai Expeditionary Force in 1889-90 (Medal with Clasp).

⁶⁷⁶ Lieut. W. H. Prendergast served with the Hazara Expedition in 1888 (Medal with Clasp).

⁶⁷⁷ Lieut. R. J. T. Savi served with the Burmese Expedition in 1883-89 (Medal with Clasp).

⁶⁷⁸ Lieut. P. H. Cunningham served in the Soudan campaign in 1885, and was present in the engagements at Hasheen and the Tofrek zereba and at the destruction of Temai (Medal with two Clasps, and Khedive's Star); also served in the operations of the Soudan Frontier Field Force in 1885-86 including the engagement at Giniss.

⁶⁷⁹ Lieut. G. W. Robinson served with the Hazara Expedition in 1891 (Medal with Clasp); and with the second Miranzai Expedition in 1891 (Clasp).

⁶⁸¹ Lieut. H. L. Stanton served with the Chin-Lushai Expeditionary Force in 1889-90 (Medal with Clasp).

⁶⁸² Lieut. F. W. Lethbridge served in the Hazara Expedition in 1891 with the 2nd Battalion 5th Goorkha (Medal with Clasp).

⁶⁸³ Lieut. E. A. W. Stotherd served with the Burmese Expedition in 1888-89 (Medal with Clasp).

⁶⁸⁴ Lieut. F. N. Burton served with the Burmese Expedition in 1887-89 (Medal with Clasp).

⁶⁸⁵ Lieut. C. D. Lester served in the operations of the Zaila Field Force in 1890.

⁶⁸⁶ Lieut. H. W. Codrington served in the Hazara Expedition in 1891 attached to the 3rd Sikh Infantry (mentioned in despatches, Medal with Clasp).

⁶⁸⁷ Lieut. J. M. Wikeley served with the Chin-Lushai Expeditionary Force in 1889-90 (Medal with Clasp).

⁶⁸⁸ Lieut. A. C. M. Waterfield served with the Hazara Expedition in 1888 (Medal with Clasp); and with the Hazara Expedition in 1891 (Clasp).

⁶⁸⁹ Lieut. H. H. Roddy served in the operations in Lushai in 1892 with the Eastern Sonai Column.

⁶⁹⁰ Lieut. H. R. Wallis served with the Hazara Expedition in 1888 (Medal with Clasp).

⁶⁹³ Lieut. C. S. Stack served with the second Miranzai Expedition in 1891 as Transport Officer (Medal with Clasp).

⁶⁹⁴ Lieut. A. J. Caruana served with the Zhob Valley Expedition in 1890. Served with the two Miranzai Expeditions in 1891 (Medal with Clasp).

⁶⁹⁶ Lieut. Hon. C. G. Bruce served with the Burmese Expedition in 1889 (Medal with Clasp); with the Hazara Expedition in 1891 as Orderly Officer (Clasp); and with the Miranzai Expedition in 1891 as Orderly Officer to Sir William Lockhart (mentioned in despatches, Clasp).

⁶⁹⁷ Lieut. J. M. Camilleri served with the Manipore Expedition in 1891 (Medal with Clasp).

⁶⁹⁸ Lieut. H. Coape Smith served with the Hazara Expedition in 1891 (Medal with Clasp); and with the Isazai Expedition in 1892.

⁶⁹⁹ Lieut. M. Williamson served in the Burmese Expedition in 1887-88 with the 2nd Battalion West Surrey Regiment in the operations under Brigadier General Collett (Medal with Clasp).

⁷⁰¹ Lieut. G. W. Johnson served with the Burmese Expedition in 1889 (Medal with Clasp).

⁷⁰² Lieut. C. C. Renton served in the Burmese Expedition in 1887 with the 1st Battalion of the Yorkshire Light Infantry (Medal with Clasp).

⁷⁰³ Lieut. E. H. Boome served with the Chin-Lushai Expedition in 1889-90 (Medal with Clasp).

⁷⁰⁴ Lieut. G. Maxwell Morris served with the Chin-Lushai Expeditionary Force in 1889-90 (Medal with Clasp); and with the Eastern Column, Burmah, in 1891-92.

⁷⁰⁵ Lieut. C. E. De L. Solbe served with the Burmese Expedition in 1888-89 (Medal with Clasp).

⁷⁰⁶ Lieut. F. G. H. Sutton served in the operations in the Northern Chin Hills, Burmah, in 1892-93.

⁷⁰⁷ Lieut. C. S. D. Leslie served in the Nile Expedition in 1885 (Medal, and Khedive's Star); also served with the Soudan Frontier Field Force in 1885-86 including the engagements at Kosheh and Giniss.

⁷⁰⁸ Lieut. A. M. Anderson served with the Burmese Expedition in 1889-92 with the Tonhon Column as Staff Officer to the North-Eastern Column (Medal with Clasp).

⁷⁰⁹ Lieut. A. C. M'Crea served in the operations in the Northern Chin Hills, Burmah, in 1892-93.

⁷¹⁰ Lieut. A. E. Webb served with the Hazara Expedition in 1888 (Medal with Clasp).

⁷¹¹ Lieut. C. M'L. Porteous served with the Chin-Lushai Expeditionary Force in 1889-90 (Medal with Clasp); and with the Isazai Field Force in 1892.

⁷¹² Lieut. E. B. C. Boddam served with the Zhob Field Force under Sir George White in 1890, and with the Isazai Expedition in 1892.

⁷¹⁴ Lieut. G. K. Cockerill served with the Hazara Expedition in 1891 (Medal with Clasp).

⁷¹⁵ Lieut. J. S. Hodding served with the Wuntho Expedition in command of Mounted Infantry of the 20th Madras Infantry.

⁷¹⁷ Lieut. E. G. Vaughan served with the Chin-Lushai Expeditionary Force in 1889-90 (Medal with Clasp).

⁷¹⁸ Lieut. R. de L. Faunce served with the Burmese Expedition in 1888-89 (mentioned in despatches, Medal with Clasp).

⁷¹⁹ Lieut. C. G. Robson served with the Burmese Expedition in 1888-89 (Medal and Clasp), and with the Chin-Lushai Expeditionary Force in 1889-90 (Clasp).

⁷²⁰ Lieut. H. O. Parr served in the operations in the Northern Chin Hills, Burmah, in 1892-93 (mentioned in despatches).

⁷²¹ Lieut. A. R. H. Garden served with the Hazara Expedition in 1891 (Medal with Clasp).

⁷²² Lieut. A. S. Hamilton served with the Hazara Expedition in 1891 (Medal with Clasp); and with the Isazai Expedition in 1892.

⁷²³ Lieut. W. Beadon served with the Chin-Lushai Expedition in 1889-90 (Medal with Clasp); and with the Isazai Expedition in 1892.

⁷²⁴ Lieut. J. B. Bell served with the Hazara Expedition in 1891 (Medal with Clasp).

⁷²⁵ Lieut. H. F. A. Pearson served with the two Miranzai Expeditions in 1891 (Medal with Clasp).

⁷²⁷ Lieut. R. A. E. Benn served in the Burmese Expedition in 1887 with the 1st Battalion of the Yorkshire Light Infantry (Medal with Clasp).

⁷²⁸ Lieut. A. Limond served with the second Miranzai Expedition in 1891 (Medal with Clasp).

⁷²⁹ Lieut. H. E. Norman served with the Chin-Lushai Expeditionary Force in 1889-90 (Medal with Clasp).

⁷³⁰ Lieut. W. G. L. Beynon served in the Hazara campaign in 1888 with the 2nd Battalion Royal Sussex Regiment (Medal with Clasp).

⁷³¹ Lieut. A. B. Dew served with the Hazara Expedition in 1891 (Medal with Clasp).

⁷³² Lieut. C. U. Price served in the operations of the Zhob Field Force in 1890.

⁷³⁴ Lieut. J. Talbot served with the Burmese Expedition in 1885-89 (Medal with two Clasps).

⁷³⁵ Lieut. H. C. Sandford served in the operations in Burmah in 1892 with the North East Column (Medal with Clasp).

⁷³⁶ Lieut. Richardson served with the Burmese Expedition in 1887-89 including the operations in the Chin Hills (Medal with Clasp).

⁷³⁷ Lieut. F. A. Thatcher served with the Burmese Expedition in 1889-90 (Medal with Clasp).

⁷³⁸ Lieut. E. F. Hood served with the Burmese Expedition in 1887-89 (Medal with Clasp).

⁷⁴⁰ Lieut. O. G. Gunning served with the Miranzai Expedition in 1891 with the 2nd Battalion Manchester Regiment (Medal with Clasp).

⁷⁴¹ Lieut. A. H. Garden served with the Hazara Expedition in 1891 (Medal with Clasp).

⁷⁴² Lieut. G. B. Gough served with the second Miranzai Expedition in 1891 (Medal with Clasp).

⁷⁴⁵ Lieut. J. L. C. Stevens served in the Miranzai Expedition in 1891 with the 2nd Battalion Manchester Regiment (Medal with Clasp).

⁷⁴⁶ Lieut. E. M. Hughes served in the Miranzai Expedition in 1891 with the 2nd Battalion Manchester Regiment (Medal with Clasp).

⁷⁴⁸ Lieut. R. G. Macpherson served with the Hazara Expedition in 1891 (Medal with Clasp); and with the second Miranzai Expedition in 1891 (Clasp).

⁷⁵⁰ Lieut. C. H. B. Clark.—See Civil Decorations for Gallantry, "Hart's Annual Army List," p. 786.

751 Lieut. G. H. Bell served with the 2nd Battalion King's Own Scottish Borderers with the Suakin Field Force in December 1888 during the investment of Suakin and was present at the engagement at Gemaizah (Medal with Clasp, and Khedive's Star). Also served in the operations on the Soudan Frontier in 1889.

752 Lieut. T. S. Tancred served with the two Miranzai Expeditions in 1891 (Medal with Clasp).

753 Lieut. W. H. Wardell served in the operations in the Northern Chin Hills, Burmah, in 1892-93 (mentioned in despatches).

754 Lieut. H. L. S. MacLean served with the Hazara Expedition in 1891 (Medal with Clasp).

755 Lieut. H. C. Holman served with the Wuntho Expedition in 1891—slightly wounded (mentioned in despatches, Medal with Clasp).

756 Lieut. W. F. Smith served in the Hazara Expedition in 1891 with the 1st Battalion Royal Welsh Fusiliers (Medal with Clasp).

758 Lieut. F. R. Nethersole served in the operations in the Kachin Hills, Burmah, in 1892-93.

760 Lieut. C. A. K. Johnson served in the Hazara Expedition in 1891 with the 1st Battalion Royal Welsh Fusiliers (Medal with Clasp).

761 Lieut. F. J. Moberly served in the operations in Gilgit in 1893, and was slightly wounded in the engagement at Chilas (mentioned in despatches, DSO.).

762 Lieut. W. H. Norman served with the Isazai Expedition in 1892.

763 Lieut. S. D. B. Ketchen served in the Hazara Expedition in 1891 with the 2nd Battalion Seaforth Highlanders (Medal with Clasp).

764 Lieut. L. O. Jones served with the Isazai Field Force in 1892.

765 Lieut. T. J. M'Leod served in the Miranzai Expedition in 1891 with the 1st Battalion King's Royal Rifles, and was present in the engagements at Saugar and Mastan (Medal with Clasp).

767 Lieut. F. L. Orman.—See Civil Decorations for Gallantry, "Hart's Annual Army List," p. 786.

768 Lieut. G. H. Prevost served with the Manipore Expedition 1891 in (Medal with Clasp).

769 Lieut. A. B. Minchin served with the Isazai Expedition in 1892.

N.B. War Services should be communicated to the Editor of "Hart's Army List," and addressed to him at 50, Albemarle Street, London, W.

Governor General's Body Guard (Raised in 1773). 443

"JAVA"—"AVA"—"MAHARAJPORE"—"MOODKEE"—"FEROZESHUHUR"—"ALLIWAL"—"SOBRAON."

Head Quarters at Dehra Dhoon. *Uniform, Scarlet. Facings, Dark Blue.*

RANK, NAMES, AND CORPS.	ARMY RANK.	REMARKS.
Captain J. G. Turner, Staff Corps	18 Dec. 89	Commandant, 6 Jan. 94.—From 2 Bengal Lancers.
Lieut. W. R. Birdwood, Staff Corps	9 May 85	Adjutant, 24 May 93.—From 11 Bengal Lancers.
Brig. Surg. Lt.Colonel B. Franklin	1 Jan. 94	In medical charge, 15 Dec. 94.

Establishment.—Commandant; Adjutant; 1 Subadar; 2 Jamadars; 7 Havildars; 7 Naicks; 3 Farriers; 2 Trumpeters; 98 Troopers.

1st Bengal Cavalry (late 1st Irregular Cavalry—Skinner's Horse.—Raised in 1803).

"BHURTPORE"—"CANDAHAR, 1842"—"AFGHANISTAN, 1879-80."

Head Quarters at Meerut. *Uniform, Yellow. Facings, Black.*

Major R.F.Gartside-Tipping,Staff Corps	3 Aug. 93	Commandant, 10 Sept. 94.
Bt.Lt.Colonel St. J. F. Michell, Staff C.	17 Jan. 91	2nd in Command and Squadron Commander, 20 Feb. 93.—Assistant Adjutant General, Presidency District.
Major C. H. Hayes, Staff Corps	1 Oct. 94	2nd in Command and Squadron Commander, 10 Sept. 94.
Captain W. D. Thomson, Staff Corps	1 May 89	Squadron Commander, 22 Feb. 88.—Offg. Cant. Mag. Allahabad.
Captain C. Davis, Staff Corps	23 Apr. 92	Squadron Commander, 4 Aug. 91.
Captain H. L. Roberts, Staff Corps	25 Aug. 94	Squadron Commander. Squadron Commander, 6 May 87.
Captain O. Finch, Staff Corps	30 Jan. 95	Squadron Officer and Adjutant, 22 Feb. 88.
Lieut. C. P. G. Griffin, Staff Corps	7 Feb. 85	Squadron Officer, 25 April 90.
Lieut. H. M. Grove, Staff Corps	1 Nov. 88	Squadron Officer, 10 Sept. 94.—Sick Furlough.
Lieut. J. S. Grove, Staff Corps	1 Oct. 90	Officiating Squadron Officer.—Sick Furlough.
Lieut. C. A. K. Johnson, Staff Corps	15 Sept. 91	Officiating Squadron Officer.
Surgeon Captain G. T. Mould	31 Mar. 88	In medical charge, 4 Aug. 92.—Furlough.
Surgeon Major H. Hamilton, MD.	31 Mar. 88	Officiating in medical charge.

2nd Bengal Lancers (late 2nd Irregular Cavalry.—Raised in 1809).

"ARRACAN"—"SOBRAON"—"PUNJAB"—"EGYPT, 1882,"—"TEL-EL-KEBIR."

Head Quarters at Bareilly. *Uniform, Blue. Facings, Light Blue.*

Lt.Colonel F. C. Burton, Staff Corps	11 July 91	Commandant, 20 Feb. 93.
Major C. H. V. Garbett, Staff Corps	17 Nov. 89	2nd in Command and Squadron Commander, 13 May 92.
Captain K. S. Davison, Staff Corps	19 Aug. 86	Squadron Commander, 22 Dec. 89.—D. A. A. Gen. Meerut.
Captain St. G. L. Steele, Staff Corps	11 May 89	Squadron Commander, 22 Feb. 88.
Captain J. G. Turner, Staff Corps	18 Dec. 89	Squad. Commander, 1 Jan. 91.—Comdt. Gov. Gen.'s Body Guard.
Captain F. H. B. Commeline, Staff Corps	10 Mar. 94	Squadron Commander, 1 Jan. 91.—Furlough.
Captain J. A. Douglas, Staff Corps	25 Aug. 94	Squadron Commander, 6 Jan. 94.—Intelligence Officer, Reserve Brigade, Waziristan Delimitation Escort.
Captain M. E. Willoughby, Staff Corps	6 Feb. 95	Squadron Commander, 6 Jan. 94.—Furlough.
Lieut. A. M'Conaghey, Staff Corps	23 Aug. 84	Squadron Officer, 5 May 88.—Assistant Political Agent, Zhob.
Lieut. W. B. James, Staff Corps	30 Jan. 86	Squadron Officer and Adjutant, 1 Jan. 91.
Lieut. H. H. F. Turner, Staff Corps	1 Apr. 89	Squadron Officer, 6 Oct. 92.
Lieut. L. L. Maxwell, Staff Corps	31 July 90	Squadron Officer, 28 Sept. 93.—Waziristan Field Force.
Lieut. A. G. Pritchard, Staff Corps	13 Oct. 91	Squadron Officer, 6 Jan. 94.—Furlough.
Lieut. F. T. T. Moore, Staff Corps	24 Sept. 90	Officiating Squadron Officer.
Lieut. E. A. Swinhoe, Staff Corps	5 Sept. 92	Officiating Squadron Officer.
Surgeon Captain A. W. Dawson, MB	1 Apr. 86	In medical charge, 15 May 90.

3rd Bengal Cavalry (late 4th Irregular Cavalry—2nd Regiment Skinner's Horse.—Raised 6 Dec. 1814).

"AFGHANISTAN"—"GHUZNEE"—"KHELAT"—"MAHARAJPORE"—"MOODKEE"—"FEROZESHUHUR"—"ALLIWAL"—"KANDAHAR, 1880"—"AFGHANISTAN, 1879-80."

Head Quarters at Fyzabad. *Uniform, Blue. Facings, Yellow.*

Colonel E. A. Money, Staff Corps	16 July 90	Commandant, 24 March 92.—Furlough.
Lt.Colonel G. H. Elliott, Staff Corps	13 July 93	2nd in Command and Squad. Comdr., 1 Nov. 88.—Offg. Comdt.
Captain H. J. J. Middleton, Staff Corps	28 Oct. 87	Squadron Commander, 1 Nov. 88.—Sick Furlough.
Captain A. N. Carr, Staff Corps	30 Jan. 89	Squadron Commander, 1 Nov. 88.—Offg. and in Command.
Captain O. Jackson, Staff Corps	11 Aug. 91	Squadron Commander, 1 July 92.—Sick Furlough.
Captain W. E. A. Blakeney, Staff Corps	10 May 93	Squadron Officer, 15 Feb. 87.—Offg. Squadron Commander.
Captain C. L. Hamilton, Staff Corps	10 May 93	Squadron Officer, 12 Aug. 89.—Offg. Squadron Commander.
Lieut. F. L. Moore, Staff Corps	7 Feb. 85	Squadron Officer and Adjutant, 6 July 89.—Sick Furlough.
Lieut. H. B. Peacock, Staff Corps	13 Oct. 86	Squadron Officer, 20 Aug. 92.—Assist. Gov. Gen.'s Agent, Aboo.
Lieut. T. S. Barton, Staff Corps	8 May 88	Squadron Officer, 20 Aug. 92.—Furlough.
Lieut. R. L. Morris, Staff Corps	31 July 91	Officiating Squadron Officer and Adjutant.
Lieut. A. G. S. Chisholm, Staff Corps	7 Sept. 92	Officiating Squadron Officer.
Surg. Captain F. Wyville-Thomson, MB.	30 Sept. 86	In medical charge, 26 Sept. 93.
Surgeon Lieut. E. S. Peck	29 Jan. 94	Officiating in medical charge.

Each Regiment of Bengal Cavalry consists of 8 Troops, with the following Establishment:—Commandant; 4 Squadron Commanders; 4 Squadron Officers; 1 Medical Officer; 4 Risaldars; 4 Risaidars; 1 Wordie Major; 8 Jamedars; 8 Kote Defedars; 56 Dafedars; 8 Trumpeters; 536 Privates.

443a **4th Bengal Cavalry** (*late 6th Irregular Cavalry.—Raised in 1840*).

Granted an Honorary Standard for Service in Sind, 1844, with the device—" *a lion passant regardant.*"
" **AFGHANISTAN**, 1879-80."
Head Quarters at Cawnpore. *Uniform, Scarlet. Facings, Blue.*

RANK, NAMES, AND CORPS.	ARMY RANK.	REMARKS.
Major H. C. Lamb, Staff Corps	5 May 89	Commandant,
Major E. H. H. Montresor, Staff Corps	8 Jan. 93	2nd in Command and Squadron Commander, 15 Jan. 92.
Major W. G. Yate, Staff Corps	12 Nov. 93	Squadron Commander, 15 June 86.
Captain F. J. B. Priestley, Staff Corps	30 Jan. 89	Squadron Commander, 10 May 87.
Captain W. C. Knight, Staff Corps	25 Aug. 94	Squadron Commander, 15 Jan. 92.
Lieut. G. de S. Barrow, Staff Corps	23 Aug 84	Squadron Officer, 18 Sept. 85.
Lieut. H. G. Stainforth, Staff Corps	7 Feb. 85	Squadron Officer, 24 July 87.—Waziristan Field Force.
Lieut. H. C. Edwards, Staff Corps	30 Jan. 86	Squadron Officer and Adjutant, 4 Aug. 87.—Sick Furlough.
Lieut. F. Shakespear, Staff Corps	30 Mar. 88	Squadron Officer, 22 May 90.
Lieut. F. V. Smith, Staff Corps	21 July 91	Officiating Squadron Officer.
Lieut. A. Le F. Smith, Staff Corps	24 May 92	Officiating Squadron Officer.
Surgeon Captain W. W. White, *MD.*	1 Oct. 87	In medical charge, 11 May 92.

5th Bengal Cavalry (*late 7th Irregular Cavalry.—Raised 28 April 1841*).

"**PUNJAB**"—"**MOOLTAN**"—"**AFGHANISTAN**, 1879-80."
Head Quarters at Nowgong. *Uniform, Scarlet. Facings, Dark Blue.*

RANK, NAMES, AND CORPS.	ARMY RANK.	REMARKS.
Lt.Colonel J. P. D. Vanrenen, S. C.	8 Aug. 88	Commandant, 17 Nov. 91.
Major W. W. Lean, Staff Corps	11 Sept. 92	2nd in Command and Squadron Commander, 24 Nov. 93.
Major W. F. C. C. Plowden, Staff Corps	19 Oct. 92	Squadron Commander, 5 Mar. 88.—Cant. Mag. Fyzabad.
Captain S. C. Gough, Staff Corps	11 Oct. 90	Squadron Commander, 13 May 90.—Furlough.
Captain H. E. Boileau, Staff Corps	23 Apr. 92	Squadron Commander, 17 Nov. 91.—Commandant and District Supdt. of Police, Port Blair and the Nicobars.
Captain E. B. Lang, Staff Corps	25 July 93	Squadron Commander, 24 Nov. 93.—Station Staff Officer.
Lieut. C. C. Boileau, Staff Corps	14 May 84	Squadron Officer, 21 Nov. 88.—Surma Valley Military Police.
Lieut. H. J. M. Macandrew, Staff Corps	10 Nov. 86	Squadron Officer and Adjutant, 13 May 90.
Lieut. H. M. Patterson, Staff Corps	10 Dec. 87	Squadron Officer, 17 Nov. 91.
Lieut. W. K. Scharlieb, Staff Corps	26 Feb. 89	Squadron Officer, 30 Aug. 92.—Burmah Military Police.
Lieut. C. G. E. Ewart, Staff Corps	11 Mar. 91	Squadron Officer, 24 Nov. 93.
Lieut. L. T. Hay, Staff Corps	5 Feb. 92	Squadron Officer, 19 Nov. 93.—Furlough.
Lieut. H. N. Holden, Oxford Lt. Inf.	19 July 93	Officiating Squadron Officer.
Surgeon Captain F. W. Gee, *MB.*	31 Mar. 88	In medical charge, 16 July 94.

6th (*The Prince of Wales's*) **Bengal Cavalry** (*late 8th Irregular Cavalry.—Raised 31 Jan. 1842*).

Plume of the Prince of Wales.
"**PUNNIAR**"—"**MOODKEE**"—"**FEROZESHUHUR**"—"**SOBRAON**"—"**EGYPT**, 1882"—"**TEL-EL-KEBIR**."
Head Quarters at Jullundur. *Uniform, Blue. Facings, Red.*
Honorary Colonel.—Field Marshal *H.R.H.* Albert Edward, *Prince of Wales and Duke of Cornwall,*
KG, KT, KP, GCB, GCSI, GCMG, GCIE.

RANK, NAMES, AND CORPS.	ARMY RANK.	REMARKS.
Major J. C. F. Gordon, Staff Corps	10 Nov. 89	Commandant, 20 Nov. 92.
Major C. S. Wheler, Staff Corps	30 Dec. 91	2nd in Command and Squadron Commander, 20 Nov. 92.
Major C. E. W. Macdonald, Staff Corps	28 Feb. 94	Squadron Commander, 30 March 86.
Captain E. T. Paul, Staff Corps	1 Jan. 87	Squadron Commander, 18 July 87.—Dep. Assist. Adj. General.
Captain R. E. Grimston, Staff Corps	23 Apr. 92	Squadron Commander, 20 Nov. 92.—A. D. C. to the Viceroy.
Captain W. F. Shakespear, Staff Corps	9 Aug. 93	Squadron Commander, 20 Nov. 92.
Captain C. F. Campbell, Staff Corps	9 Sept.93	Squadron Commander, 23 Apr. 94.
Captain J. P. Barnes, Staff Corps	6 Feb. 95	Squadron Officer, 2 June 88.
Lieut. F. de B. Young, Staff Corps	9 Dec. 84	Squadron Officer, 9 Apr. 91.—Staff College, Sandhurst.
Lieut. A. G. Maxwell, Staff Corps	1 Dec. 90	Squadron Officer and Adjutant, 20 Nov. 92.
Lieut. R. M. Battye, Staff Corps	10 Mar. 92	Squadron Officer, 23 Apr. 94.—Furlough.
Lieut. C. H. Buck, Staff Corps	26 Oct. 92	Officiating Squadron Officer.
Surg. Lt.Colonel P. F. O'Connor, *MD.*	31 Mar. 95	In medical charge, 23 Aug. 82.

7th Bengal Cavalry (*late 17th Irregular Cavalry.—Raised 24 Jan. 1846*).

"**PUNJAB**"—"**BURMA**, 1885-87."
Head Quarters at Lucknow. *Uniform, Red. Facings, Dark Blue.*

RANK, NAMES, AND CORPS.	ARMY RANK.	REMARKS.
Lt.Colonel J. B. Watts, Staff Corps	2 Oct. 89	Commandant, 20 June 92.
Lt.Colonel E. W. Chalmers, Staff Corps	14 Aug. 93	2nd in Command and Squadron Commander, 9 Feb. 88.—Sundt. Remount Rearing Depot, Hussur. [Ranikhet.
p.s.c. Major A. M. Renny, Staff Corps	11 Sept.93	2nd in Com. and Squad. Comdr., 1 Feb. 90 —D. A. A. Gen. for Inst,
Captain F. G. Pollock, Staff Corps	9 Aug. 86	2nd in Command and Squadron Commander, 2 Apr. 92.—Furl.
Captain J. H. Parsons, Staff Corps	11 Sept.87	Squadron Commander, 26 Feb. 92.—Offg. 2nd in Command.
Captain H. A. Merewether, Staff Corps	7 June 90	Squadron Commander, 1 Feb. 90. [Ahmednugger.
Captain R. S. Alexander, Staff Corps	9 July 90	Squadron Commander, 2 Apr. 92.—Offg. Supdt. Reserve Depot,
Captain C. C. Cawood, Staff Corps	11 Aug. 81	Squadron Officer, 10 Aug. 86.
Captain J. K. Tod, Staff Corps	6 Feb. 95	Squadron Officer, 1 Feb. 90.
Lieut. H. M'Conaghey, Staff Corps	23 Sept.89	Squadron Officer, 20 Aug. 92.
Lieut. I. H. Campbell, Staff Corps	26 Oct. 92	Officiating Squadron Officer and Adjutant.
Lieut. L. C. Jones, Staff Corps	11 June 92	Officiating Squadron Officer.—Furlough.
Lieut. G. H. Badcock, York Lt. Inf.	18 May 94	Officiating Squadron Officer.
Brigade Surgeon Lt.Colonel W. Finden	2 Nov. 91	In medical charge, 17 Nov. 90.

8th Bengal Cavalry (late 18th Irregular Cavalry.—Raised 24 Jan. 1846). 443b

"AFGHANISTAN, 1878-80."
Head Quarters at Allahabad. *Uniform, Blue. Facings, Scarlet.*

Rank, Names, and Corps.	Army Rank.	Remarks.
Lt.Colonel J. A. M'Neale, Gen.List, Inf.	8 June 87	Commandant, 12 Sept. 88.
Lt.Colonel J. L. Aberigh-Mackay, S. C.	13 Feb. 93	2nd in Command and Squadron Commander, 7 Nov. 88.
Major J. de C. D. Meade, Staff Corps...	9 Aug. 93	Squadron Commander, 18 Sept. 85.
Captain J. M. Carpendale, Staff Corps	11 Sept. 88	Squad. Comdr., 3 Jan. 89.—Assist. Judge Adv. Gen. Allahabad.
Captain W. M. Carpendale, Staff Corps	22 Oct. 92	Squadron Commander, 21 July 92.
Captain C. I. Wimberley, Staff Corps...	29 July 93	Squadron Commander, 27 May 93.
Captain A. J. H. Vanrenen, Staff Corps	10 Mar. 94	Squadron Officer, 3 Jan. 89.—Furlough.
Lieut. T. C. M. T. Hogg, Staff Corps ...	25 Aug. 86	Squadron Officer, 11 Dec. 91.—Burmah Military Police.
Lieut. R. E. Chaplin, Staff Corps.........	31 Mar. 88	Squadron Officer and Adjutant, 11 Dec. 91.
Lieut. F. C. C. Bleckley, Staff Corps...	18 Dec. 89	Squadron Officer, 16 Sept. 92.
Lieut. G. A. Becher, Staff Corps	21 Oct. 91	Squadron Officer, 24 July 93.—Furlough.
Lieut. R. E. Cheyne, Staff Corps	16 Jan. 91	Officiating Squadron Officer.
Lieut. J. R. Gaussen, Hampshire Regt.	31 Jan. 94	Officiating Squadron Officer.
Surgeon Captain J. T. Daly	1 Apr. 86	In medical charge, 22 April 93.

NOTE.—The Cavalry Regiments of the Punjab Frontier Force, viz.—Guide Cavalry, and 1st, 2nd, 3rd and 5th Punjab Cavalry—take rank immediately after the 8th Regiment of Bengal Cavalry.

9th Bengal Lancers (late 1st Hodson's Horse.—Raised in 1857).

"DELHI"—"LUCKNOW" (*Relief and Capture*)—"SUAKIN," 1885."
Head Quarters at Rawul Pindee. *Uniform, Blue. Facings, White.*

		Commandant,
Major G. L. Garstin, Staff Corps	3 Sept. 90	2nd in Command and Squadron Commander, 1 Feb. 93.
Major H. L. Dawson, Staff Corps	12 Nov. 93	Squadron Commander, 16 Feb. 86 [H. F. Grant.
Captain F. W. P. Angelo, Staff Corps...	30 Jan. 89	Squadron Commander, 10 Dec. 88.—Brig. Major to Major Gen.
Captain A. G. Peyton, Staff Corps......	11 Aug. 91	Squadron Commander, 1 Feb. 93.
Captain S. F. Crooker, Staff Corps......	10 Mar. 94	Squadron Officer, 26 April 88.—Officiating Squad. Commander.
Lieut. G. P. B. Creagh, Staff Corps	14 May 84	Squadron Officer and Adjutant, 26 April 88.
Lieut. R. B. Low, Staff Corps	7 Feb. 85	Squadron Officer, 10 Dec. 88.—A.D.C. to Major Gen. R. C. Low.
Lieut. A. W. Pennington, Staff Corps...	3 July 89	Squadron Officer, 6 Jan. 92.
Lieut. G. S. Sheppard, Staff Corps	26 Feb. 90	Squadron Officer, 1 Feb. 93.—Military Accounts Department.
Lieut. G. A. H. Beatty, Staff Corps	29 Apr. 91	Squadron Officer, 29 June 93.
Lieut. R. C. W. Lukin, Staff Corps	11 May 92	Officiating Squadron Officer.
Surgeon Lt.Colonel E. Palmer	30 Mar. 62	In medical charge, 19 Nov. 86.

10th (The Duke of Cambridge's Own) Bengal Lancers (late 2nd Hodson's Horse.—Raised in 1857).

"DELHI"—"LUCKNOW" (*Relief and Capture*)—"ABYSSINIA"—"AFGHANISTAN, 1878-80."
Head Quarters at Jhelum. *Uniform, Blue. Facings, Scarlet.*
Honorary Colonel.—Field Marshal H.R.H. The Duke of Cambridge, KG. KT. KP. GCB. GCSI. GCMG. GCIE.

Major E. J. F. Wood, Staff Corps	1 Jan. 93	Commandant, 14 Oct. 94.
Major F. A. Blyth, Staff Corps	11 Feb. 95	2nd in Command and Squadron Commander, 14 Oct. 94.—
Captain R. C. Onslow, Staff Corps	11 Sept. 87	Squadron Commander, 2 Mar. 90.—Assistant Judge Advocate General, Meerut.
Captain H. H. F. Fagan, Staff Corps...	11 May 89	Squadron Commander, 2 Mar. 90.
Captain W. Stewart, Staff Corps	21 June 90	Squadron Commander, 1 Oct. 91. [Troops.
Captain M. Cowper, Staff Corps	11 Aug. 91	Squadron Comdr., 14 Oct. 94.—Special duty, Imperial Service
Captain W. H. Fasken, Staff Corps	10 May 93	Squadron Commander, 14 Oct. 94.—Special duty, Imperial Service Troops. [of Council.
Captain F. G. Cardew, Staff Corps	10 Mar. 94	Squadron Comdr. 5 Dec. 94.—Personal Assist. to Mil. Member.
Captain W. L. Maxwell, Staff Corps ...	25 Aug. 94	Squadron Commander, 17 Dec. 94.
Captain E. St. A. Wake, Staff Corps ...	6 Feb. 95	Squadron Officer, 1 Oct. 91.—Cant. Mag., Barrackpore, &c.
Lieut. W. N. Evans, 21 Hussars	6 Nov. 89	Squadron Officer, 2 May 92.
Lieut. W. E. Young, Staff Corps	4 July 91	Squadron Officer, 17 Nov. 94.
Lieut. H. G. Young, Staff Corps	2 Mar. 92	Squadron Officer, 17 Nov. 94.
Lieut. R. L. Ricketts, Staff Corps	3 Dec. 94	Officiating Squadron Officer. [in India.
Surgeon Major C. H. Beatson...............	16 May 89	In medical charge, 21 Dec. 86.—Sec. to P. M. O. H.M.'s Forces
Surgeon Captain W. H. E. Woodwright	1 Oct. 87	Officiating in medical charge.

11th (Prince of Wales's Own) Bengal Lancers (late 1st Sikh Cavalry).

Raised in 1857.—Plume of the Prince of Wales.
"LUCKNOW" (*Capture*)—"TAKU FORTS"—"PEKIN"—"ALI MUSJID"—"AFGHANISTAN, 1878-79."
Head Quarters at Nowshera. *Uniform, Blue. Facings, Red.*
Honorary Colonel.—Field Marshal H.R.H. Albert Edward, *Prince of* Wales *and Duke of* Cornwall,
KG. KT. KP. GCB. GCSI. GCMG. GCIE.

Lt.Colonel W.W.H. Scott, Gen. List, Inf.	7 June 87	Commandant, 13 June 91.
Major H. R. Heath, Staff Corps	16 Feb. 87	2nd in Command and Squadron Commander, 13 June 91.
Major S. B. Beatson, Staff Corps.........	1 July 87	Squadron Commander, 18 Sept. 85.—Furlough.
Major F. H. R. Drummond, Staff Corps.	16 Feb. 87	Squadron Comdr. 6 July 88.—Employed under Foreign Dept.
Captain F. G. Delamain, Staff Corps ...	12 Feb. 87	Squadron Commander, 20 Aug. 89.
Captain H. Wright, Staff Corps.........	12 June 89	Squadron Commander, 20 Aug. 89.
Captain A. Carruthers, Staff Corps ...	10 Mar. 94	Squadron Officer, 11 Mar. 86.—Burmah Military Police.
Captain E. H. Cole, Staff Corps.........	19 Dec. 94	Squadron Officer, 10 Aug. 89.
Lieut. W. R. Birdwood, Staff Corps ...	9 May 85	Squadron Officer, 10 Aug. 89.—Adj. Gov. Gen.'s Body Guard.
Lieut. A. C. M. Waterfield, Staff Corps...	12 May 88	Squadron Officer and Adjutant, 4 June 91.
Lieut. H. Coops-Smith, Staff Corps...	21 Nov. 88	Squadron Officer, 24 July 93.—Aide de Camp to the Gov. Gen.
Lieut. M. F. Kindersley, Staff Corps ...	15 Sept. 92	Squadron Officer, 18 Dec. 93.—Burmah Military Police.
Lieut. W. H. Norman, Staff Corps	22 Dec. 92	Squadron Officer, 18 Dec. 93.
Lieut. G. B. M. Sarel, Scots Fusiliers...	7 Apr. 93	Officiating Squadron Officer.
Surgeon Major W. A. Mawson	31 Mar. 88	In medical charge, 16 July 91.—Furlough.
Surgeon Lieut. G. T. Birdwood, *MB*...	20 July 93	Officiating in medical charge.—Waziristan Field Force.

443c **12th Bengal Cavalry** (*late 2nd Sikh Cavalry*).—Raised 20 Oct. 1857.
"Abyssinia"—"Peiwar Kotal"—"Charasia"—"Kabul, 1879"—"Afghanistan, 1878-80."
Head Quarters at Sealkote. *Uniform, Blue. Facings, Blue.*

Rank, Names, and Corps.	Army Rank.	Remarks.
Lt.Colonel J. B. Lynch, Staff Corps	8 Jan. 94	Commandant, 1 April 91. [Gen. Secunderabad-
Major W. B. Wilson, Staff Corps	1 July 87	2nd in Com. and Squad. Comdr. 1 Apr. 91.—Assist. Judge Adv.
Captain H. Goad, Staff Corps	10 Sept. 86	2nd in Com. and Squad. Comdr. 1 Apr. 93.—Supt. Reserve Depot,
Captain H. A. Carleton, Staff Corps	9 Oct. 88	2nd in Com. and Squad. Comdr. 1 Apr. 93. [Saharanpore.
Captain T. H. Smith, Staff Corps	31 Jan. 91	Squadron Commander, 1 June 38.—Furlough.
Captain G. W. Rawlins, Staff Corps	22 Jan. 92	Squadron Commander, 2 Apr. 89.—Assist. Inst. Army Signalling.
Captain G. J. C. Hall, Staff Corps	10 May 93	Squadron Commander, 1 April 93.
p.s.c. Captain C. H. Selwyn, Staff Corps	25 Aug. 94	Squadron Officer, 1 June 88.—Officiating Staff Captain, Intelligence Branch, Quarter Master General's Department.
Lieut. D. D. Baynes, Staff Corps	23 Aug. 84	Squadron Officer, 12 Aug. 89.
Lieut. C. H. H. Gough, Staff Corps	29 Aug. 85	Squadron Officer, 2 Apr. 89.—Aide de Camp to Sir G. S. White.
Lieut. Hon. A. F. Napier, Staff Corps	8 Dec. 86	Squadron Officer, 8 April 93.—Employed under Foreign Dept.—Sick Furlough.
Lieut. E. M. J. Molyneux, Staff Corps	8 Apr. 90	Squadron Officer, 8 April 93.—Furlough.
Lieut. F. C. K. Macmullen, Staff Corps	4 Dec. 88	Squadron Officer and Adjutant, 4 Aug. 93.
Lieut. W. H. Pennington, Staff Corps	18 May 93	Officiating Squadron Officer.
Surgeon Lt.Colonel W. A. Simmonds	31 Mar. 95	In medical charge, 3 Nov. 81.

13th (*Duke of Connaught's*) **Bengal Lancers** (*late 4th Sikh Cavalry*).—Raised 1858.
"Afghanistan, 1878-80"—"Egypt, 1882,"—"Tel-el-Kebir."
Head Quarters at Peshawur. *Uniform, Dark Blue. Facings, Scarlet.*
Honorary Colonel.—General H.R.H. Arthur William Patrick Albert, *Duke of* Connaught and Strathearn,
KG. KT. KP. GCSI. GCMG. GCIE. KCB.

Rank, Names, and Corps.	Army Rank.	Remarks.
Lt.Colonel H. De la M. Hervey, Staff C.	5 Apr. 90	Commandant, 9 Sept. 93.
Lt.Colonel G. W. Doane, Staff Corps	13 Jan. 95	2nd in Command and Squadron Commander, 1 April 90.
Major F. S. Gwatkin, Staff Corps	28 July 90	Squadron Commander, 18 Sept. 85.
Captain F. G. Atkinson, Staff Corps	1 Sept. 87	Squadron Commander, 1 Oct. 88.
Captain J. H. Balfour, Staff Corps	6 Oct. 87	Squadron Commander, 1 July 89.
Captain M. L. Shipley, Staff Corps	30 Jan. 89	Squadron Officer, 22 Mar. 84.
Captain R. C. Broome, Staff Corps	11 May 89	Squadron Officer, 8 May 85.—Supdt. Remount Depot, Ahmednugger.
Captain H. E. Whiffin, Staff Corps	27 Jan. 94	Squadron Officer, 11 May 89.—Burmah Military Police.
Lieut. E. Brandreth, Staff Corps	25 Aug. 86	Squadron Officer, 1 April 90.—Assist. Supdt. Remount Depot,
Lieut. A. G. B. Turner, Staff Corps	6 May 89	Squadron Officer, 24 Feb. 91. [Saharanpore.
Lieut. J. L. W. ffrench-Mullen, S. C.	30 Jan. 89	Squadron Officer, 6 May 93.
Lieut. P. Holland-Pryor, Staff Corps	14 Jan. 91	Squadron Officer and Adjutant, 9 May 93.—Transport Officer, Reserve Brigade, Waziristan Delimitation Escort.
Lieut. H. H. Cobbe, Staff Corps	11 July 91	Squadron Officer, 24 July 93.—Burmah Military Police.
Lieut. C. Mackenzie, Staff Corps	5 Apr. 92	Squadron Officer, 5 Apr. 92.
Lieut. J. S. Corlett, Staff Corps	3 Dec. 94	Officiating Squadron Officer.—Furlough.
Lieut. R. M. Hall, Staff Corps	3 Dec. 94	Officiating Squadron Officer.
Surgeon Major W. Conry, MB.	31 Mar. 89	In medical charge, 2 Aug. 84.—Sick Furlough.
Surgeon Lieut. G. M. C. Smith, MB.	27 July 92	Officiating in medical charge.

14th Bengal Lancers (*late Murray's Ját Horse.—Raised in 1857*).
"Charasia"—"Kabul, 1879"—"Afghanistan, 1878-80."
Head Quarters at Saugor. *Uniform, Dark Blue. Facings, Scarlet.*

Rank, Names, and Corps.	Army Rank.	Remarks.
Lt.Colonel J. P. C. Neville, Staff Corps	11 Dec. 92	Commandant, 29 Aug. 94.
Major P. R. Bairnsfather, Staff Corps	2 Nov. 92	2nd in Command and Squadron Commander, 29 Aug. 94.
Major L. S. Peyton, Staff Corps	13 June 94	Squadron Commander, 3 Feb. 86.
Captain G. W. Younghusband, Staff C.	21 Sept. 86	Squadron Commander, 15 Oct. 86.
Captain O. C. Armstrong, Staff Corps	11 May 89	Squadron Commander, 29 Aug. 94.
Captain G. H. Weller, Staff Corps	13 Aug. 90	Squadron Officer, 18 Sept. 85.
Captain S. H. B. Hobbs, Staff Corps	22 Jan. 92	Squadron Officer, 18 Sept. 85.
Captain A. W. S. Wingate, Staff Corps	22 Oct. 92	Squadron Officer, 3 Feb. 86.
Captain J. F. Stewart, Staff Corps	10 Mar. 94	Squadron Officer, 8 July 92.—At Saugor.
Lieut. N. C. Taylor, Staff Corps	7 Feb. 85	Squadron Officer and Adjutant, 8 July 92.
Lieut. E. M. Hughes, Staff Corps	10 Sept. 90	Officiating Squadron Officer.
Lieut. J. B. Bedford, Staff Corps	14 Sept. 91	Officiating Squadron Officer.—Sick Furlough.
Surgeon Captain R. J. Marks	31 Mar. 87	In medical charge, 30 July 91.—Furlough.
Surgeon Lieut. J. Gould	29 July 93	Officiating in medical charge.

15th Bengal Lancers (*Cureton's Mooltanee Cavalry*).—Raised 14 Jan. 1858.
"Afghanistan, 1878-80."
Head Quarters at Mooltan. *Uniform, Blue. Facings, Scarlet.*

Rank, Names, and Corps.	Army Rank.	Remarks.
Lt.Colonel F. R. Ditmas, Staff Corps	10 July 93	Commandant, 16 June 92.
Lt.Colonel S. D. Turnbull, Staff Corps	3 Jan. 91	2nd in Command and Squadron Commander, 1 Apr. 90.
Captain H. R. Tate, Staff Corps	10 Sept. 86	Squadron Commander, 3 Mar. 89.—Employed under Foreign
Captain W. O. Pollard, Staff Corps	14 Aug. 87	Squadron Commander, 1 Apr. 91. [Dept.
Captain P. B. Lindsell, Staff Corps	11 Sept. 87	Squadron Commander, 10 May 90.
Captain G. F. Willes, Staff Corps	24 June 88	Squadron Officer, 19 Apr. 83.
Captain H. M'A. Johnston, Staff Corps	10 May 93	Squadron Officer, 6 Dec. 85.—Adj. Surma Valley Light Horse.
Captain G. A. Robertson, Staff Corps	6 Feb. 95	Squadron Officer and Adjutant, 25 July 88.—Furlough.
Captain E. de V. Wintle, Staff Corps	6 Feb. 95	Squadron Officer, 1 Aug. 88.
Lieut. R. F. C. Gordon, Staff Corps	23 Aug. 84	Squadron Officer, 6 July 89.—Burmah Military Police.
Lieut. H. C. Ricketts, Staff Corps	10 Nov. 86	Squadron Officer, 10 May 90.
Lieut. A. C. H. Smithett, Staff Corps	29 Dec. 86	Squadron Officer, 17 May 91.—Officiating Adjutant.
Lieut. C. Bayley, Scottish Rifles	25 Oct. 90	Officiating Squadron Officer.—Furlough.
Lieut. J. S. M. Shea, Staff Corps	18 Feb. 90	Officiating Squadron Officer.
Surgeon Captain E. Hudson	1 Apr. 86	In medical charge, 21 Mar. 90.

16th Bengal Cavalry.—*Raised in 1857, disbanded in 1882, re-formed in 1885.* 443d

Head Quarters at Loralai. *Uniform, Blue. Facings, Blue.*

Rank, Names, and Corps.	Army Rank.	Remarks.
Major A. de V. Alexander, Staff Corps...	8 Dec. 89	Commandant, 4 Nov. 93.—Furlough.
Major V. M. Stockley, Staff Corps	5 Oct. 94	2nd in Command and Squadron Commander, 4 Nov. 93.
Major C. J. Robarts, Staff Corps	8 Jan. 93	Squadron Commander, 18 Sept. 85.—Cant. Magistrate, Dinapore.
Captain H. F. K. Waldron, Staff Corps	1 May 89	Squadron Commander, 2 Feb. 92.
Captain L. J. Howell, Staff Corps	22 Jan. 90	Squadron Commander, 29 Apr. 93.—Furlough. [Dept.
Captain G. A. Cookson, Staff Corps	11 Sept. 91	Squadron Commander, 4 Nov. 93.—Employed under Foreign
Captain C. Griffiths, Staff Corps	10 May 93	Squadron Commander, 4 Nov. 93.—With Afghanistan Boundary
Lieut. C. Bailey, Staff Corps	12 Nov. 84	Squadron Officer and Adjutant, 2 Feb. 92. [Commission.
Lieut. H. G. Maxwell, Staff Corps	29 Jan. 88	Squadron Officer, 16 May 88.—Burmah Military Police.
Lieut. C. E. Thornton, Staff Corps	22 May 89	Squadron Officer, 20 Apr. 92.
Lieut. I. G. White, Staff Corps	10 Apr. 89	Squadron Officer, 28 July 93.
Lieut. H. C. Holman, Staff Corps	25 Mar. 91	Squadron Officer, 18 Dec. 93.—Russia, to study.
Lieut. E. S. St. Quintin, 19 Hussars	31 Jan. 94	Officiating Squadron Officer.
Lieut. H. A. Gib, N. Lanc. Regt.	11 July 94	Officiating Squadron Officer.
Surgeon Major H. C. Hudson	2 Apr. 93	In medical charge, 30 May 87.—Waziristan Field Force.

17th Bengal Cavalry.—*Raised in 1858, disbanded in 1882, re-formed in 1885.*

"AFGHANISTAN, 1879-80."

Head Quarters at Umballa. *Uniform, Blue. Facings, White.*

Rank, Names, and Corps.	Army Rank.	Remarks.
Colonel W. A. Lawrence, Staff Corps	16 May 87	Commandant, 19 Dec. 88.—Furlough.
Major C. W. Muir, CIE. Staff Corps	7 July 89	2nd in Command and Squadron Comdr., 12 Sept. 90.—Offg. Comdt.
Major R. F. Trotter, Staff Corps	8 Dec. 89	Squadron Commander, 18 Sept. 85.—Furlough.
Major W. F. Montresor, Staff Corps	19 Oct. 93	Squadron Commander, 18 Sept. 85.—Offg. 2nd in Command.
Captain E. J. Medley, Staff Corps	11 May 89	Squadron Commander, 12 Sept. 90.—Attaché Adjutant General's Department, Calcutta.
Captain E. B. Burton, Staff Corps	13 Aug. 90	Squadron Officer, 18 Sept. 85.
Captain H. Bower, Staff Corps	23 Oct. 91	Squadron Officer, 18 Sept. 85.—D. A. Q. M. Gen. Intell. Branch.
Captain W. S. Mardall, Staff Corps	1 Feb. 92	Squadron Officer, 14 Apr. 87.
Lieut. E. W. Boudier, Staff Corps	5 July 84	Squadron Officer and Adjutant, 12 Sept. 90.
Lieut. E. W. Wall, Staff Corps	30 Jan. 86	Squadron Officer, 16 Jan. 91.—Sick Furlough.
Lieut. J. M. Wikeley, Staff Corps	4 May 88	Squadron Officer, 10 June 93.
Lieut. A. K. Hudson, Staff Corps	15 Apr. 91	Officiating Squadron Officer.
Surgeon Captain D. G. Marshall, MB.	31 Mar. 88	In medical charge, 31 Aug. 92.—Furlough.

18th Bengal Lancers (*late 2nd Mahratta Horse.*—*Raised 26 Aug. 1858).*

"AFGHANISTAN, 1879-80."

Head Quarters at Ferozepore. *Uniform, Red. Facings, Blue.*

Rank, Names, and Corps.	Army Rank.	Remarks.
Lt.Col. G. L. R. Richardson, CIE. S. C.	23 Mar. 92	Commandant, 20 Nov. 91.
Major G. A. Money, Staff Corps	11 Sept. 92	2nd in Command and Squadron Commander, 20 Nov. 91.
Captain J. E. Nixon, Staff Corps	10 Sept. 86	Squadron Comdr. 15 May 87.—D.A.A. Gen. for Inst., Chuckrata.
Captain I. Eardley-Wilmot, Staff Corps	1 May 89	Squadron Commander, 22 Feb. 88.—Furlough.
Captain C. P. W. Pirie, Staff Corps	11 May 89	Squadron Commander, 25 July 88.
Captain K. Chesney, Staff Corps	22 Jan. 92	Squadron Commander, 13 May 89.
p.s.c. Captain C. B. S. F. Shore, Staff C.	10 May 93	Squadron Officer, 8 May 85.—Offg. Squadron Commander.
Captain H. W. Campbell, Staff Corps	9 Sept. 93	Squadron Officer, 4 Sept. 87.—Burmah Military Police.
Captain S. B. Grimston, Staff Corps	6 Feb. 95	Squadron Officer and Adjutant, 22 Feb. 88.
Lieut. C. O. Swanston, Staff Corps	9 May 85	Squadron Officer, 13 May 89.
Lieut. A. C. S. Clarke, Staff Corps	2 Mar. 88	Squadron Officer, 20 Nov. 91.
Lieut. P. E. Ricketts, Devon Regt.	15 Aug. 90	Squadron Officer, 28 Sept. 93.
2nd Lieut. E. C. Corbyn, Staff Corps	3 Sept. 92	Officiating Squadron Officer.
Surg. Major W. A. Sykes, DSO. MB.	1 Apr. 94	In medical charge, 20 Oct. 88.—Waziristan Field Force.

19th Bengal Lancers (*late Fane's Horse.*—*Raised 14 Jun. 1860).*

"TAKU FORTS"—"PEKIN"—"AHMED KHEL"—"AFGHANISTAN, 1878-80."

Head Quarters at Meean Meer. *Uniform, Blue. Facings, French Grey.*

Rank, Names, and Corps.	Army Rank.	Remarks.
Lt.Colonel E. Bruce, Staff Corps	10 July 94	Commandant, 22 Aug. 93.
Major E. A. Young, Staff Corps	15 Dec. 89	2nd in Com. and Squad. Comdr., 9 Oct. 82.—A.A. Gen. Lahore.
Major H. S. Massy, Staff Corps	28 Feb. 94	2nd in Command and Squadron Commander, 10 Oct. 93.
Major S. D. Gordon, Staff Corps	21 Sept. 94	Squadron Commander, 28 Aug. 92.
Captain E. H. Rivett-Carnac, Staff Corps	12 Feb. 87	Squadron Commander, 28 Aug. 92.
Captain F. Biddulph, Staff Corps	5 Sept. 88	Squadron Commander, 1 Nov. 93.
Captain C. B. Templer, Staff Corps	11 Aug. 91	Squadron Officer, 16 Dec. 85.
Captain H. Hudson, Staff Corps	22 Oct. 92	Squadron Officer, 27 Apr. 86.
Captain A. G. Medley, Staff Corps	6 Feb. 95	Squadron Officer, 10 Feb. 88.—Russia, for study.
Lieut. L. N. Younghusband, Staff Corps	7 Feb. 85	Squadron Officer and Adjutant, 1 Nov. 88.
Lieut. W. S. Fraser, Staff Corps	3 Mar. 88	Officiating Squadron Officer.—Furlough.
Lieut. C. L. Gregory, Staff Corps	7 Oct. 91	Officiating Squadron Officer.—Sick Furlough.
Lieut. K. H. Jackson, Staff Corps	6 Nov. 92	Officiating Squadron Officer.
Surgeon Captain M. A. Ker	31 Mar. 87	In medical charge, 2 Dec. 90.—Waziristan Field Force.
Surgeon Captain J. N. Macleod, MB.	30 Jan. 94	Officiating in medical charge.

444

No. 7 Bengal Mountain Battery.—*Raised* 15 *Sept.* 1886.
"BURMA, 1885-87." At Dehra Dhoon.

Rank, Names, and Corps.	Army Rank.	Remarks.
Captain R. W. Fuller, Royal Artillery...	14 Jan. 89	Commandant, 10 Nov. 90.
Lieut. O. K. Tancock, Royal Artillery	17 Feb. 86	Subaltern, 22 Jan. 91.
Lieut. M. A. C. Crowe, Royal Artillery	17 Feb. 86	Subaltern, 20 July 92.
Lieut. J. B. Mackintosh, R. Artillery ...	27 July 91	Officiating Subaltern.

No. 8 Bengal Mountain Battery.—*Raised* 15 *Sept.* 1886.
"BURMA, 1885-87." On Field Service, Waziristan.

Captain A. H. C. Birch, Royal Artillery	1 Apr. 89	Commandant, 7 Apr. 91.
Lieut. K. K. Knapp, Royal Artillery ...	18 Feb. 86	Subaltern, 23 June 91.
Lieut. W. St. C. Bland, Royal Artillery	23 July 90	Subaltern, 7 Nov. 91.
Lieut. A. T. Crawford, Royal Artillery	17 Feb. 91	Subaltern, 31 Jan. 92.

Establishment.—Commandant; 3 Subalterns; 1 Subadar; 2 Jamadars; 1 Havildar Major; 1 Pay and Quarter Master Havildar; 6 Havildars; 6 Naicks; 2 Trumpeters; 88 Gunners; 3 Havildars of Drivers; 6 Naicks of Drivers; 138 Drivers; 1 Farrier; 1 Salootrie: Total Officers and Men, 226.

Corps of Bengal Sappers and Miners.—*Raised in* 1803.
Designation changed by G. G. O. of 20 March 1851.

"CABOOL, 1842"—"FEROZESHUHUR"—"PUNJAB"—"MOOLTAN"—"GOOJERAT"—"DELHI"—"LUCKNOW" (*Relief and Capture*)—"ALI MUSJID"—"CHARASIA"—"KABUL, 1879"—"AHMED KHEL"—"AFGHANISTAN, 1878-80"—"BURMA, 1885-87."

Head Quarters at Roorkee. *Uniform, Scarlet. Facings, Dark Blue.*

1st Company, Roorkee.	4th Company, Roorkee.	A Company, Roorkee.
2nd Company, on Field Service, Waziristan.	5th Company, on Field Service, Waziristan.	B Company, Roorkee.
3rd Company, Roorkee.	6th Company, Roorkee.	

Bt. Colonel H. P. Leach, DSO. R. Eng.	28 July 94	Commandant, 30 June 93.
Major M. C. Barton, Royal Engineers	8 Sept. 91	Superintendent of Park, 26 Apr. 94.
Major J. C. Tyler, Royal Engineers ...	18 Jan. 92	Superintendent of Instruction, 30 Aug. 93.
Captain H. J. Sherwood, Royal Eng. ...	21 May 94	Adjutant, 28 Oct. 92.
B̶t̶. Bt. Major F. J. Aylmer, R. Eng.	18 Oct. 93	Company Commander, 16 Dec. 85.—4th Company.
Captain G. M. Heath, Royal Engineers	3 Aug. 90	Company Commander, 20 Dec. 93.—B Company.—Attaché Army Head Quarters.
Captain J. R. B. Serjeant, Royal Eng...	9 May 91	Company Commander, 1 Dec. 87.—1st Company.
Captain A. G. Hunter-Weston, R. Eng.	1 Apr. 92	Company Commander, 29 Apr. 90.—2nd Company.
Captain F. E. G. Skoy, Royal Engineers	13 Nov. 92	Company Commander, 22 Dec. 92.—A Company.
Captain C. C. Perceval, R. Engineers...	21 June 94	Company Commander, 18 Dec. 91.—6th Company.—Furlough.
Lieut. G. A. Travers, Royal Engineers	16 Sept. 85	Company Commander, 3 May 92.—5th Company.
Lieut. J. S. Fowler, Royal Engineers...	6 Jan. 86	Company Officer, 24 May 92.—On special duty, Gilgit.
Lieut. D. L. Mallaby, Royal Engineers	16 Feb. 90	Company Officer, 29 Oct. 91.—3rd Company.—Offg. Comp. Comdr.
Lieut. H. R. Stockley, R. Engineers ...	23 July 90	Company Officer, 17 Apr. 90.—4th Company.—With 5th Comp.
Lieut. W. E. R. Dickson, R. Engineers	27 July 92	Company Officer, 17 Nov. 91.—1st Company.—With 2nd Comp.
Lieut. A. H. Cunningham, R. Eng.	27 July 92	Company Officer, 15 July 92.—3rd Company.
Lieut. B. M. M. Tod-Mercer, R. Eng.....	27 July 92	Company Officer, 18 Dec. 91.—6th Comp.—Offg. Comp. Comdr.
Lieut. R. H. Macdonald, R. Engineers	11 Dec. 90	Company Officer, 30 May 90.—A Company.—Govt. Tel. Dept.
Lieut. S. H. Sheppard, Royal Engineers	14 Feb. 93	Company Officer, 29 July 93.—5th Company.
Lieut. E. H. E. Green, Royal Engineers	25 July 93	Company Officer and Quarter Master, 23 Aug. 93.—B Company.—
Lieut. H. H. Austin, Royal Engineers	16 Feb. 90	Company Officer.—5 Company.
Surgeon Lt. Colonel J. Young, MB. ..	30 Mar. 92	In medical charge, 15 March 90.

Establishment.—8 Companies (6 General Service Companies; A Depot Company—special for Bridging, Telegraph, Submarine Mining, Field Printing, and Photo Services; B Depot Company—Recruits); Commandant; Adjutant; Superintendent of Park; Superintendent of Instruction; 8 Company Commanders; 8 Company Officers; 1 Medical Officer; 1 Warrant Officer attached to the Park; 1 Regimental Sergeant Major (Assistant Superintendent of Instruction); 1 Quarter Master Sergeant; 4 Company Sergeant Majors; 24 British Non-Commissioned Officers; 8 Subadars; 15 Jamadars; 49 Havildars; 78 Naicks; 1,152 Sappers; 15 Buglers: a total of 1,368 of all ranks.

1st Bengal Infantry (*late 21st N.I.—Neelwur-ki-Paltan.—Raised* 1776).
Linked with 3rd Regiment.—Regimental Centre, Allahabad.

"LASWARRIE"—"BHURTPORE"—"BURMA, 1885-87."
Head Quarters at Jubbulpore. *Uniform, Red. Facings, White.*

Lt. Colonel A. C. G. Lydiard, Staff Corps	3 Apr. 92	Commandant, 15 Dec. 93.
Major F. Hawkins, Staff Corps	21 Sept. 94	2nd in Command and Wing Commander, 13 Dec. 92.—Furl.
p.s.c. Captain H. F. Loch, Staff Corps...	11 Aug. 91	Wing Commander, 13 Dec. 92.
Captain H. Comins, Staff Corps	23 Oct. 91	Wing Officer, 29 July 84.—Officiating 2nd in Command.
Captain A. W. de Wilton, Staff Corps..	10 Mar. 94	Wing Officer, 12 Nov. 88.—Officiating Wing Commander.
Captain J. J. H. B. Eckford, Staff Corps	25 Aug. 94	Wing Officer, 15 Jan. 91.
Lieut. W. E. White, Staff Corps	25 Nov. 89	Wing Officer and Adjutant, 9 Oct. 92.
Lieut. H. E. Hitchins, W. York Regt. ...	2 Dec. 89	Wing Officer, 24 Dec. 90.—Furlough.
Lieut. J. S. Swan, Staff Corps...............	27 July 92	Officiating Wing Officer.
Lieut. F. M. Smith, Staff Corps	19 Oct. 92	Officiating Wing Officer.
Lieut. H. T. Marshall, Staff Corps	19 Nov. 92	Officiating Wing Officer.
2nd Lieut. R. Hawkes, Staff Corps	28 Jan. 93	Officiating Wing Officer.
Surgeon Major E. Cretin, MB.	30 Mar. 90	In med. charge, 24 Aug. 85.—In charge Cant. Hosp., Jubbulpore.

Each Regiment of Bengal Infantry consists of 8 Companies (excepting the 27th and 28th Regiments, which have an additional Company, composed of Afridis), with the following Establishment:—Commandant; 2 Wing Commanders; 5 Wing Officers; 1 Medical Officer; 8 Subadars; 8 Jamadars; 40 Havildars; 40 Naicks; 16 Drummers; 800 Sepoys; 912 Natives of all Ranks. The Goorkha Regiments are also allowed an establishment of 912 of all ranks.

2nd (Queen's Own) Bengal Infantry (Lt. Inf.–late 31 N.I.–Broon-ki-Paltan—Raised 1798).—Linked with 4th and 16th Regiments.—Regimental Centre, Agra.

The Royal Cypher within the Garter.
"Delhi"—"Laswarrie"—"Deig"—"Bhurtpore"—"Khelat"—"Afghanistan"—"Maharajpore"—
"Punjab"—"Chillianwallah"—"Goojerat"—"Central India"—"Afghanistan, 1879-80"—"Burma, 1885-87."
Head Quarters at Silchar. Wing at Debrooghur. *Uniform, Red. Facings, Blue.*
Honorary Colonel.—Field Marshal H.R.H. Albert Edward, *Prince of* Wales *and Duke of* Cornwall,
KG. KT. KP. GCB. GCSI. GCMG. GCIE.

Rank, Names, and Corps.	Army Rank.	Remarks.
Lt. Colonel B. Channer, DSO. Staff C....	13 Feb. 93	Commandant, 1 May 94.—And Commanding at Silchar.
Captain A. E. Whistler, Staff Corps	30 Jan. 89	2nd in Command and Wing Commander, 1 May 94.
Captain H. L. Dodgson, Staff Corps	22 Jan. 92	Wing Commander, 1 May 94.
Captain C. Hamilton, Staff Corps...........	23 Aug. 94	Wing Officer, 1 July 86.—Offg. Wing Commander, Debrooghur.
Lieut. F. A. Smith, Staff Corps	7 Feb. 85	Wing Officer and Adjutant, 5 Sept. 88.
Lieut. D. M. Bower, Staff Corps	25 Nov. 85	Wing Officer, 1 Sept. 90.—Sick Furlough.
Lieut. F. P. S. Dunsford, Staff Corps.....	11 Dec. 88	Wing Officer and Quarter Master, 4 June 90.
Lieut. E. G. Vaughan, Staff Corps	26 July 89	Wing Officer, 16 Aug. 94.—Dep. Assist. Com. Gen. 2nd Class.
Lieut. C. N. Baker, Staff Corps	4 Mar. 91	Wing Officer, 16 Aug. 94.—Sick Furlough.
Lieut. C. A. E. O'Meara, Staff Corps	21 Oct. 91	Officiating Wing Officer, Debrooghur.
Surgeon Lt. Colonel T. Robinson, MB...	1 Oct. 89	In medical charge, 29 Nov. 92.—Furlough.
Surgeon Lieut. J. Mulvany.................	29 July 93	Officiating in medical charge.

3rd Bengal Infantry (late 32nd N.I.—Guthrie-ki-Paltan.—Raised in 1798).—Linked with 1st Regiment.—Regimental Centre, Allahabad.

"Bhurtpore"—"Afghanistan, 1879-80."
Head Quarters at Cawnpore. *Uniform, Red. Facings, Black.*

Rank, Names, and Corps.	Army Rank.	Remarks.
Major G. B. Austin, Staff Corps............	8 July 89	Commandant, 26 Nov. 92.
Captain H. R. W. Lumsden, Staff Corps	6 Sept. 87	2nd in Command and Wing Commander, 20 Jan. 93.—Furlough.
Captain F. B. W. Richardson, Staff C....	11 May 89	Wing Commander, 10 Jan. 90.—Officiating 2nd in Command.
Captain W. P. Anderson, Staff Corps...	6 Aug. 90	Wing Officer, 24 Oct. 83.—Furlough.
Lieut. P. B. Warren, Staff Corps	14 May 84	Wing Officer, 30 July 86.—Officiating Wing Commander.
Lieut. F. P. Webber, Staff Corps	6 May 85	Wing Officer, 14 May 89—Officiating Adjutant.
Lieut. H. Walton, Staff Corps	29 Aug. 85	Wing Officer and Quarter Master, 4 Dec. 91.
Lieut. H. T. Pritchard, Staff Corps	25 Aug. 86	Wing Officer, 10 Jan. 90.—Offg. Polit. Assist. 3rd Cl., Rajpootana.
Lieut. H. L. Stanton, Staff Corps........	9 Mar. 88	Wing Officer, 10 Jan. 90.—Burmah Military Police.
Lieut. A. E. Webb, Staff Corps	14 May 89	Wing Officer, 5 May 92.—Dep. Assist. Com. Gen., Calcutta.
Lieut. R. G. Bagley, Staff Corps	25 Nov. 89	Wing Officer, 5 Jan. 94.
Lieut. E. Eardley-Wilmot, Staff Corps...	12 Mar. 90	Officiating Wing Officer.
Lieut. A. A. Irvine, Staff Corps	12 Oct. 92	Officiating Wing Officer.
Surgeon Major S. Hassan	2 Oct. 92	In medical charge, 13 Aug. 87.—Furlough.
Surgeon Lieut. T. W. A. Fullerton, MB.	27 July 92	Officiating in medical charge.—Waziristan Field Force.

4th (Prince Albert Victor's) Bengal Infantry (late 33rd N.I.—Hilliard-ki-Paltan.—Raised 1798).—Linked with 2nd and 16th Regiments.—Regimental Centre, Agra.

"Laswarrie"—"Bhurtpore"—"Cabul, 1842"—"Ferozeshuhur"—"Sobraon"—"Afghanistan, 1879-80"—"Burma, 1885-87."
Head Quarters at Dinapore. *Uniform, Red. Facings, Black.*

Rank, Names, and Corps.	Army Rank.	Remarks.
Lt. Colonel T. G. Thomson, Staff Corps	8 Dec. 91	Commandant, 13 Feb. 92.
Major M. Read, Staff Corps.................	8 Jan. 93	2nd in Command and Wing Commander, 26 Apr. 92.—Furlough.
Captain C. W. Harris, Staff Corps	10 Sept. 87	Wing Commander, 10 Dec. 89.—Officiating 2nd in Command.
Captain J. S. Melville, Staff Corps	11 Aug. 91	Wing Officer, 6 Sept. 83.—Officiating Wing Commander.
Captain A. Pressey, Staff Corps...........	28 Jan. 93	Wing Officer, 19 Aug. 86.
Lieut. C. F. Dobbie, Staff Corps	28 Feb. 85	Wing Officer and Quarter Master, 27 Feb. 89.—Furlough.
Lieut. H. Tweddell, Staff Corps............	2 Aug. 88	Wing Officer and Adjutant, 15 Jan. 91.
Lieut. F. W. Pirrie, Staff Corps............	8 May 89	Wing Officer, 18 Nov. 90.
Lieut. C. H. Ward, Staff Corps	13 Oct. 91	Officiating Wing Officer.
Lieut. H. J. Riddell, Staff Corps...........	10 Aug. 92	Officiating Wing Officer and Quarter Master.
Surgeon Captain B. K. Basu, MD.	1 Apr. 86	In medical charge, 29 May 90.

5th Bengal Infantry (Lt.Inf.–late 42 N.I.-Jhansin-ki-Paltan.–Raised 1803)—Linked with 12th Regiment.—Regimental Centre, Bareilly.

"Arracan"—"Afghanistan"—"Candahar"—"Ghuznee"—"Cabul, 1842"—"Moodkee"—"Ferozeshuhur"—"Sobraon"—"Afghanistan, 1879-80"—"Burma, 1885-87."
Head Quarters at Allahabad. *Uniform, Red. Facings, Yellow.*

Rank, Names, and Corps.	Army Rank.	Remarks.
Lt. Colonel W. J. A. Birch, Staff Corps..	1 Dec. 91	Commandant, 29 June 91.
Captain J. C. B. Craster, Staff Corps ...	13 May 87	2nd in Command and Wing Commander, 10 Mar. 94.
Captain J. Lampen, Staff Corps............	13 Aug. 90	Wing Commander, 21 May 92.	Sim
Captain A. D. C. Pond, Staff Corps ...	1 Nov. 90	Wing Officer, 27 Feb. 85.—Intell. Branch, Qr. Mr. Gen's Dept.,
Captain W. A. Cuppage, Staff Corps ...	22 Jan. 92	Wing Officer, 8 May 85.
Captain P. W. D. Brockman, S. Corps...	25 July 93	Wing Officer, 12 June 88.
Lieut. J. N. Jephson, Staff Corps.........	7 Feb. 85	Wing Officer and Quarter Master, 14 May 89.
Lieut. A. T. Walling, Staff Corps.........	30 Jan. 86	Wing Officer, 6 June 89.
Lieut. O. C. Argles, Staff Corps...........	25 Aug. 86	Wing Officer, 21 May 92.—Furlough.
Lieut. H. L. Anderson, Staff Corps	26 Mar. 90	Wing Officer, 2 Feb. 94.—Furlough.
Lieut. F. J. Fraser, Staff Corps............	9 July 90	Officiating Wing Officer.
Surgeon Captain U. N. Mukerji, MD....	1 Oct. 84	In medical charge, 14 July 88.

444b **6th Bengal Infantry** (*Lt. Inf. late 43 N.I.—Kyne-ki-dahini Paltan—
Raised 1803).—Linked with 10th and 13th Regiments.—Regimental Centre, Meerut.*
"NAGPORE"—"AFGHANISTAN"—"CANDAHAR"—"GHUZNEE"—"CABUL, 1842"—"MAHARAJPORE"—"SOBRAON"—
"ALI MUSJID"—"AFGHANISTAN, 1878-79."
Head Quarters at Fort William. *Uniform, Red. Facings, White.*

Rank, Names, and Corps.	Army Rank.	Remarks.
Colonel W. Hailes, Staff Corps	12 Feb. 95	Commandant, 23 Feb. 91. [bad Cont.
Major C. H. Westmorland, Staff Corps	23 Aug. 89	2nd in Com. and Wing Comdr. 4 May 92.—A. A. Gen. Hydern-
Captain C. F. G. Young, Staff Corps	1 May 89	2nd in Command and Wing Commander, 31 Dec. 92.—Furlough.
Bt. Major R. M. Maxwell, Staff Corps	13 Feb. 95	Wing Commander, 31 Dec. 92.
Captain H. J. Roche, Staff Corps	6 Feb. 95	Wing Officer and Adjutant, 29 Sept. 86.—Furlough.
Lieut. N. T. Parker, Staff Corps	25 Nov. 85	Wing Officer, 4 Aug. 87.—Dep. Assist. Com. Gen. 2nd Class.—Furl.
Lieut. A. J. Jamieson, Staff Corps	10 Nov. 86	Wing Officer and Quarter Master, 18 May 89.
Lt. D. H. Drake-Brockman, Staff Corps	24 Mar. 88	Wing Officer, 1 June 92.—Dep. Assist. Com. Gen. 2nd Class.
Lieut. W. L. R. Amesbury, Staff Corps	18 Mar. 91	Wing Officer, 22 Aug. 91.
Lieut. F. G. A. Wimberley, S. Wales Bord.	22 Feb. 93	Wing Officer, 30 Aug. 94.
Lieut. P. H. Dundas, Staff Corps	3 Dec. 94	Wing Officer, 25 Feb. 94.
Surg. Lt. Col. F. W. Wright, DSO. MB.	3 Dec. 94	In medical charge, 10 Dec. 94.

7th (*The Duke of Connaught's Own*) **Bengal Infantry**
(*late 47th N.I.—Craum-ki-Paltan.—Raised in* 1824).—*Linked with 8th and 11th Regiments.—
Regimental Centre, Lucknow.*
"MOODKEE"—"FEROZESHUHUR"—"ALLIWAL"—"SOBRAON"—"CHINA, 1858-59"—"EGYPT, 1882"—
"TEL-EL-KEBIR."
Head Quarters at Lucknow. *Uniform, Red. Facings, Yellow.*
Honorary Colonel.—General H.R.H. Arthur W.P.A. *Duke of* Connaught, KG, KT, KP, GCSI, GCMG, GCIE, KCB.

Lt. Colonel A. W. Jamieson, Staff Corps	9 Nov. 92	Commandant, 6 March 92. [Regt.
Major E. G. Barrow, Staff Corps	16 Feb. 87	2nd in Com. and Wing Comdr. 6 Mar. 92.—With Hong Kong
Major W. G. Mansel, Staff Corps	30 Dec. 91	2nd in Command and Wing Commander, 16 Apr. 92.
Captain H. B. Vaughan, Staff Corps	17 Apr. 91	Wing Commander, 7 July 92.
Captain H. G. B. Raitt, Staff Corps	10 Mar. 94	Wing Officer, 16 Dec. 88.—Furlough.
Lieut. A. H. Bingley, Staff Corps	7 Feb. 85	Wing Officer and Adjutant, 15 Feb. 88.
Lieut. N. E. Robin, Staff Corps	6 May 85	Wing Officer and Quarter Master, 5 Sept. 88.
Lieut. M. R. E. Ray, Staff Corps	29 Aug. 85	Wing Officer, 31 Dec. 89.—With Hong Kong Regiment.
Lieut. H. O. Parr, Staff Corps	18 Sept. 89	Wing Officer, 21 May 92.
Lieut. E. F. Hood, Staff Corps	20 May 90	Wing Officer, 7 July 92.—Sick Furlough.
Lieut. J. A. Stewart, Staff Corps	9 July 90	Officiating Wing Officer.
Surgeon Major P. Mullane, MD	2 Apr. 93	In medical charge, 30 May 87.

8th Bengal Infantry (*late 59th Native Infantry.—Raised in* 1815).—
Linked with 7th and 11th Regiments.—Regimental Centre, Lucknow.
"SOBRAON"—"AFGHANISTAN, 1879-80."
Head Quarters at Saugor. Detachment at Gantak. *Uniform, Red. Facings, White.*

Colonel Arthur Fishe, Staff Corps	25 May 94	Commandant, 3 Oct. 89.—Furlough.
Major G. D. C. Gastrell, Staff Corps	3 Sept. 90	2nd in Command and Wing Comdr., 3 Oct. 89.—Offg. Comdt.
Captain R. W. MacLeod, Staff Corps	19 Oct. 92	Officiating 2nd in Command.—From 29 Bengal Infantry.
Captain G. S. Goldsmid, Staff Corps	11 Feb. 87	Wing Commander, 31 Oct. 93.
Lieut. G. M. Evans, Staff Corps	23 Aug. 84	Wing Officer and Adj., 29 Apr. 87.—Offg. Wing Comdr. Gantak.
Lieut. H. W. A. Marson, Staff Corps	30 Jan. 86	Wing Officer, 19 July 87.—Furlough.
Lieut. H. J. Thacker, Staff Corps	28 Apr. 86	Wing Officer, 4 Jan. 89.—Dep. Assist. Com. Gen., 1st Class.
Lieut. J. P. O. Hennessy, Staff Corps	22 Mar. 88	Wing Officer, 13 March 91.—Dep. Assist. Com. Gen., 2nd Class.
Lieut. F. W. Daniell, Staff Corps	20 June 89	Wing Officer, 19 June 91.—Cant. Mag., Saugor, and Offg. S.S.O.
Lieut. A. C. Ralph, Staff Corps	23 June 90	Wing Officer and Quarter Master, 21 Aug. 91.—Offg. Adjutant.
Lieut. T. W. Lightfoot, Staff Corps	15 July 90	Wing Officer, 30 Sept. 91.—Furlough.
Lieut. W. B. Douglas, Staff Corps	1 Oct. 90	Wing Officer, 27 May 92.—At Gantak.
Lieut. W. T. C. Poole, Staff Corps	31 Oct. 91	Officiating Wing Officer.
Surgeon Captain G. B. French	30 Sept. 86	In medical charge, 15 May 90.—Furlough.
Surgeon Lieut. D. R. Green, MD	27 July 92	Officiating in medical charge.

9th (*Goorkha Rifle*) **Bengal Infantry** (*late 63rd Native Infantry.—Raised
in* 1823).—*Linked with 39th Regiment.—Regimental Centre, Lansdowne.*
"BHURTPORE"—"SOBRAON"—"AFGHANISTAN, 1879-80."
Head Quarters at Lansdowne. *Uniform, Dark Green. Facings, Black.*

Lt. Colonel H. O. Woodhouse, Staff Corps	10 Apr. 92	Commandant, 15 Sept. 93.
Major A. T. Weller, Staff Corps	12 Nov. 90	2nd in Command and Wing Commander, 15 Sept. 93.
Captain F. G. R. Ostrehan, Staff Corps	11 May 89	Wing Commander, 15 Sept. 93.—Dist. Recruiting Officer, Delhi.
Captain R. P. Warren, Staff Corps	22 Oct. 92	Wing Commander, 15 Sept. 93.—Furlough.
Lieut. E. R. R. Swiney, Staff Corps	6 May 85	Wing Officer and Adjutant, 10 Sept. 87.
Lieut. G. T. Widdicombe, Staff Corps	30 Jan. 86	Wing Officer and Quarter Master, 22 Apr. 89.
Lieut. A. R. Barwell, Staff Corps	25 Aug. 86	Wing Officer, 10 Dec. 92.
Lieut. C. M'L. Porteous, Staff Corps	30 May 89	Wing Officer, 20 June 92.
Lieut. R. L. Carnegy, Staff Corps	17 Dec. 92	Wing Officer, 24 Oct. 93.—Furlough.
Lieut. J. M'K. T. Hogg, Berkshire Regt.	10 May 93	Officiating Wing Officer.
Surgeon Lt. Colonel A. H. Williams, MB.	30 Mar. 92	In medical charge, 17 Oct. 76.

10th Bengal Infantry (*late 65th Native Infantry.—Raised in* 1823).— 444c
Linked with 6th and 13th Regiments.—Regimental Centre, Meerut.
"CHINA, 1858-59"—"BURMA, 1885-87."
Head Quarters at Barrackpore. *Uniform, Red. Facings, Yellow.*

RANK, NAMES, AND CORPS.	ARMY RANK.	REMARKS.
Lt.Colonel C. W. J. Hingston, Staff C...	22 Jan. 94	Commandant, 3 June 93.
Captain J. G. Hunter, Staff Corps	1 May 89	2nd in Command and Wing Commander, 30 Dec. 92.
Captain H. F. T. Macartney, Staff Corps	22 Jan. 90	Wing Commander, 26 Dec. 93.
Captain C. F. V. S. Venner, Staff Corps	30 Jan. 95	Wing Officer and Adjutant, 21 June 86.—Furlough.
Lieut. E. G. Wright, Staff Corps	9 May 85	Wing Officer and Quarter Master, 27 June 87.—Furlough.
Lieut. E. N. Obbard, Staff Corps	10 June 89	Wing Officer, 4 June 90.—Officiating Adjutant. [Bombay.
Lieut. A. J. N. Harward, Staff Corps	1 Sept. 88	Wing Officer, 27 May 91.—Dep. Assist. Com. Gen. 2nd Class,
Lieut. C. G. Robson, Staff Corps	1 Sept. 89	Wing Officer, 2 Feb. 94.—Officiating Quarter Master and S.S.O.
Lieut. J. C. C. Perkins, Staff Corps	18 Dec. 89	Wing Officer, 24 July 93.—Assist. Mil. Accountant, Calcutta.
Lieut. H. de B. Codrington, Staff Corps	10 May 90	Wing Officer. 1 Sept. 94.—Dep. Assist. Com. Gen., 2nd Class.
Lieut. W. F. Bourne, Staff Corps	6 Sept. 92	Wing Officer, 1 Sept. 94.
Lieut. C. G. Campbell, Scottish Rifles...	7 Mar. 94	Officiating Wing Officer.
Surgeon Captain K. Prasad, *MB.*	31 Mar. 88	In medical charge, 31 Aug. 92.—Civil Employ, Burmah.
Surgeon Lieut. V. G. Drake-Brockman	30 Jan. 93	Officiating in medical charge.

NOTE.—The 1st Goorkha Regiment, when acting with other Bengal Native Troops, takes rank after the 10th Native Infantry.

11th Bengal Infantry (*late 70th Native Infantry.—Raised in* 1825).—
Linked with 7th and 8th Regiments.—Regimental Centre, Lucknow.
"PUNJAB"—"CHILLIANWALLAH"—"GOOJERAT"—"CHINA, 1858-59"—"AFGHANISTAN, 1878-80"—"BURMA, 1885-87."
Head Quarters at Dorunda. Wing at Baxa. *Uniform, Red. Facings, Yellow.*

Major V. A. Sobalch, Staff Corps	1 July 87	Commandant, 3 June 93.
Captain W. K. Downes, *DSO.* Staff C,	10 Sept. 87	2nd in Command and Wing Commander, 14 Mar. 92.—Baxa.
Captain W. J. Newell, Staff Corps	11 May 89	Wing Comdr., 14 Mar. 92.—Dist. Recruiting Officer, Lucknow.
Captain J. Strachey, Staff Corps	2 July 90	Wing Commander, 12 Apr. 92.
Captain C. H. Billings, Staff Corps	13 Aug. 90	Wing Officer, 1 July 82. [Infantry.
Captain A. P. D. Harris, Staff Corps	22 Oct. 92	Wing Officer, 30 Oct. 85.— Insp. Officer, Punjab Imp. Service
Lieut. D. F. Stuart, Staff Corps	7 Feb. 85	Wing Officer and Adjutant, 5 Nov. 87.
Lieut. H. C. Tytler, Staff Corps	30 Jan. 86	Wing Officer, 26 Feb. 89.—Officiating Quarter Master.
Lieut. A. C. Watson, Staff Corps	25 Aug. 86	Wing Officer and Quarter Master, 1 Apr. 80.—Furlough.
Lieut. R. E. Vaughan, Staff Corps	27 Oct. 88	Wing Officer, 2 Apr.89.—Dep.Assist.Com. Gen.2nd Class.—Furl.
Lieut. F. A. Andrew, Staff Corps	15 Oct. 90	Wing Officer, 13 Nov. 91.—Baxa.
Lieut. W. A. Hill, Staff Corps	15 Oct. 90	Wing Officer, 14 Mar. 92.—Sick Furlough.
Lieut. W. M. Grimley, Staff Corps	17 Dec. 92	Officiating Wing Officer.
Surgeon Captain J. M. Cadell, *MB.*	1 Oct. 85	In medical charge, 1 June 89.—Offg. Civil, Sultanpore.
Surgeon Lieut. L. Rogers, *MB.*	29 July 92	Officiating in medical charge.

12th (*The Kelat-i-Ghilzai*) Bengal Infantry (*late Regiment of Kelat-i-Ghilzai.—Raised in* 1838).—*Linked with 5th Regt.—Regimental Centre, Bareilly.*
"KELAT-I-GHILZAI, 1842"—"CANDAHAR"—"GHUZNEE"—"CABUL, 1842"—"MAHARAJPORE"—"AFGHANISTAN, 1878-79"—"BURMA, 1885-87."
Head Quarters at Bareilly. *Uniform, Red. Facings, White.*

p.s.c. Major A. F. Barrow, *CMG.* S.C.	16 Feb. 87	Commandant, 13 June 92.
Major J. W. E. Angelo, Staff Corps	2 Oct. 90	2nd in Command and Wing Commander, 13 June 92.
Bt.Major R. H. Twigg, Staff Corps	27 Apr. 92	Wing Commander, 15 Jan. 94.
		Wing Commander.
Captain T. Webster, Staff Corps	5 Dec. 94	Wing Officer and Quarter Master, 18 May 86.—Furlough.
Captain C. W. Somerset, Staff Corps	30 Jan. 95	Wing Officer and Adjutant, 28 June 86.
Lieut. F. C. Laing, Staff Corps	8 Dec. 86	Wing Officer, 10 Feb. 91.
Lieut. W. C. Black, Staff Corps	14 Feb. 90	Wing Officer, 25 July 92.—Russia, to study.
Lieut. C. B. Byers, Staff Corps	2 Mar. 92	Wing Officer, 15 Dec. 92.
Lieut. A. S. H. Teed, Staff Corps	13 Sept. 92	Officiating Wing Officer.
Surgeon Major D. B. Spencer	31 Mar. 92	In medical charge, 29 Sept. 86.

13th (*The Shekhawattee*) Bengal Infantry (*late Shekhawattee Battalion.—Raised in* 1835).—*Linked with 6th and 10th Regiments.—Regimental Centre, Meerut.*
"ALLIWAL"—"AFGHANISTAN, 1879-80."
Head Quarters at Fyzabad. *Uniform, Red. Facings, Dark Blue.*

Lt.Colonel E. H. Bingham, Staff Corps	13 Feb. 92	Commandant, 28 Aug. 93.
Major W. T. Fairbrother, Staff Corps	11 Feb. 95	2nd in Com. and Wing Commander, 28 Aug. 93.—Debrooghur.
Captain C. Le G. Justice, Staff Corps	11 May 89	Wing Commander, 28 Aug. 93. [Dist.
Captain W. Prior, Staff Corps	13 Aug. 90	Wing Officer, 15 Nov. 83.—Offg. Dist. Recruiting Officer, Hindu
Captain A. Giles, Staff Corps	9 Sept. 93	Wing Officer, 1 March 86.—Officiating Wing Commander.
Captain R. V. Davidson, Staff Corps	25 Aug. 94	Wing Officer, 9 July 86.
Captain M. Stevens, Staff Corps	5 Dec. 94	Wing Officer, 28 Aug. 93.—Officiating Quarter Master.
Lieut. J. M. Camilleri, Staff Corps	21 Nov. 83	Wing Officer and Quarter Master, 19 Jan. 89.—Sick Furlough
Lieut. F.C. S. P. Samborne, Staff Corps	25 Mar. 91	Officiating Wing Officer and Adjutant.
2nd Lieut. C. Vickers, W. Surrey Regt.	12 Mar. 92	Officiating Wing Officer. [Agency.
Surgeon Captain F. P. Maynard	1 Oct. 87	In medical charge, 2 July 91.—Officiating Supdt. Behar Opium
Surgeon Lieut. G. Y. C. Hunter	30 Jan. 93	Officiating in medical charge.

444d **14th** (*The Ferozepore Sikhs*) **Bengal Infantry** (*late Regiment of Ferozepore.*
—Raised 30 July 1846).—Linked with 15th and 45th Regiments.—Regimental Centre, Ferozepore.
"LUCKNOW" (*Defence and Capture*)—"ALI MUSJID"—"AFGHANISTAN, 1878-79."
Head Quarters at **Ferozepore**. *Uniform, Red. Facings, Yellow.*

RANK, NAMES, AND CORPS.	ARMY RANK.	REMARKS.
Colonel W. V. Ellis, Staff Corps	29 Sept. 93	Commandant, 1 Oct. 88.—Furlough.
p.s.c. Major J. W. Hogge, CIE. Staff Corps	23 Sept. 91	2nd in Command and Wing Comdr., 17 Feb. 91.—Offg. Comdt.
Major A. W. T. Radcliffe, Staff Corps	9 Aug. 93	Wing Commander, 3 Jan. 89.—Officiating 2nd in Command.
Major H. H. Ozzard, Staff Corps	13 June 94	Wing Officer, 24 May 79.—Cantonment Mag., Roorkee.—Furl.
Captain C. R. Ross, Staff Corps	22 Oct. 92	Wing Officer, 17 Feb. 85.—Offg. Wing Commander.—At Gilgit.
Lieut. H. J. Jones, Staff Corps	23 Aug. 84	Wing Officer, 16 Apr. 87.—At Gilgit.
Lieut. H. L. Richardson, Staff Corps	7 Feb. 85	Wing Officer, 11 Feb. 89.
Lieut. P. O. Palin, Staff Corps	28 Apr. 86	Wing Officer and Adjutant, 22 Oct. 89.
Lieut. F. A. Jacques, N. Lanc. Regt.	22 Mar. 90	Wing Officer and Quarter Master, 19 June 91.
Lieut. N. A. Macdonald, Staff Corps	19 July 90	Wing Officer, 28 Oct. 91.
Lieut. C. M. Carter, Staff Corps	17 July 91	Officiating Wing Officer.
Lieut. H. K. Harley, Staff Corps	13 June 92	Officiating Wing Officer.—At Gilgit.
Surgeon Captain G. B. Irvine	31 Mar. 87	In medical charge, 1 Dec. 91.

15th (*The Ludhiana Sikhs*) **Bengal Infantry** (*late Regiment of Ludhiana.*—
Raised 30 July 1846).—Linked with 14th and 45th Regiments.—Regimental Centre, Ferozepore.
"CHINA, 1860-62"—"AHMED KHEL"—"KANDAHAR, 1880"—"AFGHANISTAN, 1878-80"—"SUAKIN, 1885"—"TOFREK."
Head Quarters at **Peshawur**. *Uniform, Red. Facings, Green.*

RANK, NAMES, AND CORPS.	ARMY RANK.	REMARKS.
Lt. Colonel H. A. Abbott, Staff Corps	15 Feb. 94	Commandant, 1 April 90.
Major R. C. Hadow, Staff Corps	27 Apr. 90	2nd in Command and Wing Commander, 1 Apr. 90.
Major P. A. Buckland, Staff Corps	24 Apr. 92	Wing Commander, 1 April 90.—Officiating Assistant Secretary, Government of India, Military Department.
Captain G. F. Rowcroft, Staff Corps	13 Aug. 90	Wing Officer, 16 Nov. 81.—Officiating Wing Commander.
Captain D. J. T. O'Brien, Staff Corps	25 Feb. 91	Wing Officer, 20 June 84.
Captain H. Trevor, Staff Corps	22 Jan. 92	Wing Officer, 26 Dec. 84.—Furlough.
Captain R. J. D. Moseley, Staff Corps	25 Aug. 94	Wing Officer, 13 Feb. 87.—Burmah Military Police.
Lieut. W. A. L. Cowie, Staff Corps	23 May 85	Wing Officer, 4 Aug. 87.—Burmah Military Police.
Lieut. N. A. Lewarne, Staff Corps	25 Aug. 86	Wing Officer and Quarter Master, 8 Oct. 90.—Offg. Adjutant.
Lieut. J. Hill, Staff Corps	11 Feb. 88	Wing Officer, 13 Aug. 90.—Officiating Quarter Master.
Lieut. J. L. R. Gordon, Staff Corps	7 Mar. 90	Officiating Wing Officer.—Furlough.
Lieut. J. R. Carden, Staff Corps	3 Jan. 91	Officiating Wing Officer.
Surgeon Captain C. N. O. Wimberley, MB	31 Mar. 90	In medical charge, 11 Aug. 94.

NOTE.—The 2nd, 3rd, and 4th Goorkha Regts., when acting with other Bengal Native Troops, rank after 15th N.I. When Regiments of the Punjab Frontier Force are acting with other Bengal Native Troops, they take rank according to the dates on which they were raised, thus :—The Corps of Guides Infantry, the 1st, 2nd, 3rd, and 4th Sikh Infantry, and the 1st, 2nd, 4th, 5th, and 6th Punjab Infantry, after the 15th Native Infantry and the 3rd Goorkha Regiment.

16th (*The Lucknow*) **Bengal Infantry** (*late Regt. of Lucknow.*
Raised 8 Dec. 1857).—Linked with 2nd and 4th Regiments.—Regimental Centre, Agra.
On the Colours and Appointments the design of a "Turreted Gateway."—"LUCKNOW" (*Defence*)—
"AFGHANISTAN, 1879-80"—"BURMA, 1885-87."
Head Quarters at **Alipore**. *Uniform, Red. Facings, White.*

RANK, NAMES, AND CORPS.	ARMY RANK.	REMARKS.
Colonel C. H. Stoddart, Staff Corps	25 May 94	Commandant, 5 March 90.
Major A. Montanaro, Staff Corps	14 Oct. 91	2nd in Command and Wing Commander, 5 March 90.
Major R. B. Shawe, Staff Corps	11 Feb. 95	Wing Commander, 5 March 90.—Sick Furlough.
Captain E. J. E. Swayne, Staff Corps	10 Mar. 94	Wing Officer, 30 Mar. 86.—Officiating Wing Commander.
Lieut. A. B. Harvey, Staff Corps	29 Aug. 85	Wing Officer and Adjutant, 4 Aug. 87.
Lieut. A. S. Begbie, Staff Corps	25 Aug. 86	Wing Officer and Quarter Master, 11 Apr. 89.—Sick Furlough.
Lieut. L. M. Bell, Staff Corps	25 Aug. 86	Wing Officer, 6 Nov. 89.—Officiating Quarter Master.
Lieut. G. Watling, Staff Corps	12 May 89	Wing Officer, 3 Apr. 91.
Lieut. G. R. Vanrenen, Staff Corps	31 July 89	Wing Officer, 20 Aug. 90.—Furlough.
2nd Lieut. T. J. Bolland, Staff Corps	23 Nov. 92	Officiating Wing Officer.
Surgeon Captain E. R. W. C. Carroll	1 Apr. 85	In medical charge, 11 July 91.—Officiating Civil, Shillong.
Surgeon Lieut. C. R. Stevens	29 July 93	Officiating in medical charge.

17th (*The Loyal Purbiya*) **Bengal Infantry** (*late Loyal Purbiya Regiment.*
Raised in 1858).—Linked with 18th Regiment.—Regimental Centre, Benares.
"AFGHANISTAN, 1879-80"—"SUAKIN, 1885"—"TOFREK."
Head Quarters at **Agra**. *Uniform, Red. Facings, White.*

RANK, NAMES, AND CORPS.	ARMY RANK.	REMARKS.
Lt. Colonel T. E. Spencer, Staff Corps	22 July 94	Commandant, 12 Mar. 92.
Major A. D. Enriquez, Staff Corps	14 Nov. 94	2nd in Command and Wing Commander, 18 May 92.
Captain G. Bowring, Staff Corps	11 Sept. 87	Wing Commander, 26 May 92.
Captain E. Carbonaro, Staff Corps	19 Dec. 88	Wing Officer, 20 Dec. 84.
Captain W. L. Davidson, Staff Corps	14 Feb. 94	Wing Officer, 12 Oct. 88.
Captain J. C. Sutherland, Staff Corps	25 Aug. 94	Wing Officer, 8 Dec. 86.—Station Staff Officer, Meerut.
Lieut. C. E. Wood, Staff Corps	25 Aug. 86	Wing Officer and Quarter Master, 12 Oct. 88.—Offg. Adjutant.
Lieut. F. R. Nethersole, Staff Corps	18 June 90	Wing Officer, 22 Dec. 92—Burmah Military Police.
Lieut. T. E. Madden, Staff Corps	1 July 92	Wing Officer, 16 May 94.—Officiating Quarter Master.
2nd Lt. A. L. Bickford, W. Surrey Regt.	13 Aug. 94	Officiating Wing Officer.
2nd Lieut. E. C. Loch, Staff Corps	21 Jan. 93	Officiating Wing Officer.
Surgeon Major G. Money Shewan, MB	31 Mar. 92	In medical charge, 22 Apr. 93.

18th Bengal Infantry (*late Alipore Regiment.—Raised* 29 *June.* 1795). 444e
Linked with 17th Regiment.—Regimental Centre, Benares.
"BURMA, 1885-87."
Head Quarters at **Benares.** *Uniform, Red. Facings, Black.*

RANK, NAMES, AND CORPS.	ARMY RANK.	REMARKS.
Lt.Colonel W. H. Browne, Staff Corps	3 May 90	Commandant, 2 Apr. 94.
Major L. J. Browne, Staff Corps	28 Oct. 91	2nd in Command and Wing Commander, 2 Apr. 94.
Captain W. F. M. I. Fraser, Staff Corps	2 July 90	Wing Commander, 2 Apr. 94.—Sick Furlough.
Captain R. R. Renton, Staff Corps	30 Jan. 95	Wing Officer and Adjutant, 29 Aug. 87.—Offg.Wing Commander.
Lieut. R. M. Edwards, Staff Corps	7 Feb. 85	Wing Officer and Quarter Master, 14 July 87.—Offg. Adjutant.
Lieut. E. V. Martin, Staff Corps	31 July 89	Wing Officer, 30 Aug. 92.
Lieut. J. K. Condon, Staff Corps	9 July 90	Wing Officer, 22 March 93.—Officiating Quarter Master.
Lieut. C. K. Anderson, Leinster Regt.	23 Sept. 91	Wing Officer, 15 May 94.
Lt. G. Pennefather-Evans, S. Wales Bord.	12 Apr. 92	Officiating Wing Officer.
Surgeon Lieut. J. J. Bourke, *MB*	30 Jan. 93	In medical charge. Officiating in medical charge.—Waziristan Field Force.

19th (*Punjab*) Bengal Infantry (*late 7th Punjab Infantry.—Raised in* 1857).—*Linked with* 22nd *and* 24th *Regiments.—Regimental Centre, Mooltan.*
"AHMED KHEL"—"AFGHANISTAN, 1878-80."
Head Quarters at **Dera Ismail Khan.** *Uniform, Red. Facings, Dark Blue.*

RANK, NAMES, AND CORPS.	ARMY RANK.	REMARKS.
Lt.Colonel A. J. Brander, Staff Corps	6 Nov. 93	Commandant, 24 Jan. 94.—Furlough.
Captain A. H. Wilmer, Staff Corps	6 Oct. 87	2nd in Command and Wing Commander, 24 Jan. 94.—Offg.Comdt.
Captain G. A. M'Carthy, Staff Corps	11 May 89	Wing Commander, 24 Jan. 94.—Officiating 2nd in Command.
Captain D. Beames, Staff Corps	9 Sept. 93	Wing Officer, 23 July 86.—Officiating Wing Commander.
Captain G. J. F. Soady, Staff Corps	6 Feb. 95	Wing Officer and Adjutant, 10 Sept. 87.—Furlough.
Lieut. E. Waller, Staff Corps	7 Feb. 85	Wing Officer, 15 June 89.—Officiating Civil Employ.
Lieut. G. A. Dale, Staff Corps	17 Oct. 88	Wing Officer and Quarter Master, 22 Oct. 89.
Lieut. W. J. Windsor, Staff Corps	4 Dec. 89	Wing Officer, 2 July 91.
Lieut. C. W. G. Richardson, Staff Corps	23 Apr. 90	Wing Officer, 30 June 94.
Lieut. R. G. Macpherson, Staff Corps	15 Oct. 90	Officiating Wing Officer and Adjutant.
Lieut. H. L. Tomkins, Lancaster Regt.	28 July 93	Officiating Wing Officer.
Surgeon Captain W. H. Gray	31 Mar. 88	In medical charge, 4 Oct. 92.—Furlough.
Surgeon Lieut. R. G. Turner	29 July 93	Officiating in medical charge.

20th (*The Duke of Cambridge's Own Punjab*) Bengal Infantry—
(*late 8th Punjab Inf.*)—*Raised in* 1857.—*Linked with* 21st *and* 26th *Regts.—Regtl. Centre, Jhelum.*
"TAKU FORTS"—"PEKIN"—"ALI MUSJID"—"AFGHANISTAN, 1878-80"—"EGYPT, 1882,"—"TEL-EL-KEBIR."
On Field Service, **Waziristan.** Depot at **Meean Meer.** *Uniform, Drab. Facings, Green.*
Honorary Colonel.—Field Marshal *H.R.H. the Duke of* Cambridge, *KG. KT. KP. GCB. GCSI. GCMG. GCIE.*

RANK, NAMES, AND CORPS.	ARMY RANK.	REMARKS.
Col. W. H. Meiklejohn, *CMG.* Gen.List	29 Aug. 93	Commandant, 26 Jan. 89.
Major W. O. Harris, Staff Corps	6 July 90	2nd in Command and Wing Commander, 20 Aug. 92.—Furlough.
Major E. W. Dun, *DSO.* Staff Corps	28 Mar. 94	Wing Commander, 20 Aug. 92.
Captain P. G. Walker, Staff Corps	9 July 90	Wing Officer, 28 March 82.
Lieut. L. C. Dunsterville, Staff Corps	23 Aug. 84	Wing Officer and Adjutant, 11 May 89.
Lieut. F. Murray, Staff Corps	7 Feb. 85	Wing Officer and Quarter Master, 27 June 87.
Lieut. S. M. Tighe, Staff Corps	29 Aug. 85	Wing Officer, 19 Apr. 88.—Burmah Military Police.
Lieut. W. H. Prendergast, Staff Corps	24 Feb. 88	Wing Officer, 9 July 90.—Burmah Military Police.
Lieut. G. B. Gough, Staff Corps	9 July 90	Wing Officer, 25 July 92.— Dep. Assist. Com. Gen. 2nd Class.
Lieut. J. L. C. Stevens, Staff Corps	10 Sept. 90	Wing Officer, 8 March 93.
Lieut. J. Kemball, Staff Corps	15 Dec. 90	Officiating Wing Officer.—From 27 Bengal Infantry.
Lieut. A. G. G. Sharp, Leinster Regt.	23 Nov. 92	Officiating Wing Officer.
Lieut. J. C. C. Angelo, N. Stafford Regt.	30 Nov. 93	Officiating Wing Officer.
Surgeon Lt.Colonel W. E. Griffiths	1 Oct. 92	In medical charge, 4 Oct. 92.

21st (*Punjab*) Bengal Infantry (*late 9th Punjab Infantry*).—
Raised 27 *Aug.* 1857.—*Linked with* 20th *and* 26th *Regiments.—Regimental Centre, Jhelum.*
"ABYSSINIA"—"AFGHANISTAN, 1878-80."
Head Quarters at **Kurram.** Detachments at **Kohat, Sultan Kot,** &c. Depot at **Lucknow.** *Uniform, Drab. Facings, Red.*

RANK, NAMES, AND CORPS.	ARMY RANK.	REMARKS.
Colonel J. G. T. Carruthers, Gen. List.	8 June 90	Commandant, 27 Apr. 89. [Parachenar.
Major W. C. Faithfull, Staff Corps	21 Sept. 94	2nd in Command and Wing Commander, 27 Apr. 89.—At Fort
Captain P. M. Carpendale, Staff Corps	11 May 89	Wing Commander, 11 May 89.—At Kohat.
Captain W. Giles, Staff Corps	11 May 89	Wing Officer, 15 Sept. 82.—With 31 Bengal Infantry.
Captain W. Thuillier, Staff Corps	13 Aug. 90	Wing Officer, 3 Feb. 83.—At Lucknow. [Hills.
Captain W. R. Little, Staff Corps	14 Jan. 91	Wing Officer, 18 July 83.—Comdt. Assam Mil. Police Bn., Naga
Lieut. A. H. Montagu, Staff Corps	14 May 84	Wing Officer and Adjutant, 6 Oct. 86.—Furlough.
Lieut. D. C. A. Andrew, Staff Corps	30 Jan. 86	Wing Officer, 27 June 87.—Burmah Military Police.
Lieut. M. Williamson, Staff Corps	7 Dec. 88	Wing Officer, 2 Nov. 90.—Officiating Adjutant. [Bandipore.
Lieut. A. F. Thomason, Staff Corps	30 Oct. 88	Wing Officer, 21 Aug. 91.—Dep. Assist. Com. Gen., 2nd Class,
Lieut. C. Kaye, Staff Corps	1 Nov. 90	Wing Officer, 15 Dec. 92.—Furlough.
Lieut. D.A.C.Brownlow, Leinster Regt.	23 Sept. 91	Wing Officer and Quarter Master, 15 Feb. 92.—At Lucknow.
Lieut. F. P. James, Staff Corps	1 Feb. 93	Officiating Wing Officer.—At Kohat.
Surgeon Captain C. H. Bedford, *MD.*	30 Sept. 89	In medical charge, 26 Sept. 93.

H H

444f **22nd** (*Punjab*) **Bengal Infantry** (*late 11th Punjab Infantry*).—
Raised 1 Aug. 1857.—Linked with 19th and 24th Regiments.—Regimental Centre, Mooltan.
"CHINA, 1860-62"—"AFGHANISTAN, 1879-80."
Head Quarters at Fort Sandeman. *Uniform, Red. Facings, Blue.*

RANK, NAMES, AND CORPS.	ARMY RANK.	REMARKS.
Lt.Colonel R. Gordon, Staff Corps	8 Jan. 94	Commandant, 12 July 92.
Major J. Lamb, Staff Corps	2 Dec. 94	2nd in Command and Wing Commander, 14 Nov. 92.
Captain R. H. Rattray, Staff Corps	30 Jan. 89	Wing Commander, 14 Nov. 92.—Furlough.
Captain L. N. Herbert, Staff Corps	9 Sept.93	Wing Officer, 10 Aug. 86.—Furlough.
Lieut. C. A. Fowler, Staff Corps	7 Feb. 85	Wing Officer and Adjutant, 25 Oct. 86.
Lieut. R. R. Vaughan, Staff Corps	17 Oct. 88	Wing Officer, 20 May 92.—Offg. Cant. Magistrate, Jhansi.
Lieut. W. A. Fraser, Staff Corps	20 Apr. 89	Wing Officer, 21 Aug. 91.
Lieut. T. G. Blois-Johnson, Staff Corps	19 Mar. 90	Wing Officer, 8 July 92.—Furlough.
Lieut. G. J. Davis, Staff Corps	15 Feb. 92	Officiating Wing Officer.
2nd Lieut. E. W. Costello, Staff Corps	19 Nov. 92	Officiating Wing Officer.
Surgeon Captain H. B. Luard, MB	31 Mar. 90	In medical charge, 26 Sept. 93.—Offg. Agency Surgeon, Gilgit.
Surgeon Captain G. H. Frost, MB	28 July 91	Officiating in medical charge.

23rd (*Punjab*) **Bengal Infantry** (*Pioneers—late 15th Punjab Infantry*).
Raised in 1857.—Linked with 32nd and 34th Regiments.—Regimental Centre, Mecan Meer.
"TAKU FORTS"—"PEKIN"—"ABYSSINIA"—"PEIWAR KOTAL"—"CHARASIA"—"KABUL, 1879"—"KANDAHAR, 1880"—"AFGHANISTAN, 1878-80."
Head Quarters at Jhelum. *Uniform, Drab. Facings, Chocolate.*

Lt.Colonel S. V. Gordon, Staff Corps	9 Aug. 90	Commandant, 23 June 93. [Govt. of India, Mil. Dept.
p.s.c. Major A. E. Jones, Staff Corps	28 Feb. 94	2nd in Command and Wing Commander,23 June 93.—Assist.Sec.
Major W. H. Jameson, Staff Corps	13 June 94	2nd in Command and Wing Commander, 18 Nov. 93.
Captain N. A. K. Burne, Staff Corps	11 Sept.87	Wing Commander, 18 Nov. 93.—With 30 Madras Infantry.
Captain R. T. Crowther, Staff Corps	14 Jan. 91	Wing Officer, 26 May 84.—District Recruiting Officer, Umritsur.
Captain F. Duncan, Staff Corps	22 Oct. 92	Wing Officer, 23 June 86.—On special duty, Gilgit.
Lieut. R. C. Lye, Staff Corps	7 Feb. 85	Wing Officer and Quarter Master, 27 Aug. 89.—Assist. District Recruiting Officer, Sikh District.
Lieut. A. Wallace Dunlop, Staff Corps	30 Jan. 86	Wing Officer, 9 Apr. 90.—Officiating Wing Commander.
Lieut. N. J. H. Powell, Staff Corps	24 Jan. 88	Wing Officer, 4 Dec. 91.
Lieut. H. F. A. Pearson, Staff Corps	6 Nov. 89	Wing Officer and Adjutant, 21 May 92.
Lieut. J. Randall, Staff Corps	1 Jan. 90	Wing Officer, 7 Oct. 92.
Lieut. G. H. F. Kelly, Staff Corps	12 Jan. 92	Officiating Wing Officer.
Lieut. A. G. Kemball, Staff Corps	8 Oct. 92	Officiating Wing Officer and Quarter Master.
Surgeon Captain W. B. Lane	29 Sept.88	In medical charge, 13 May 93.

24th (*Punjab*) **Bengal Infantry** (*late 16th Punjab Infantry*).—
Raised 5 June 1857.—Linked with 19th and 22nd Regiments.—Regimental Centre, Mooltan.
"KANDAHAR, 1880"—"AFGHANISTAN, 1878-80."
Head Quarters at Delhi. *Uniform, Red. Facings, White.*

Colonel G. F. Young, Staff Corps	7 Dec. 91	Commandant. [Gen. at Head Qrs. 2nd in Com. and Wing Commander, 5 May 87.—Assist. Qr. Mr.
Lt.Colonel J.J.Money-Simons,StaffCorps	11 Jan. 93	2nd in Command and Wing Commander, 4 Nov. 90.
Major J. G. Ramsay, Staff Corps	11 Feb. 95	Wing Comdr., 4 Nov. 90.—D.A.A.Gen.,Punjab Field Force.—Furl.
Captain G. P. Ranken, Staff Corps	13 Aug. 90	Wing Comdr. 4 Nov. 90.—Dist. Recruiting Officer, Peshawur.
Captain H. F. Holland, Staff Corps	23 Apr. 92	Wing Commander, 24 Jan. 91.
Captain A. L. Lindesay, Staff Corps	10 Mar. 94	Wing Officer, 8 Nov. 86.
Captain J. M. Baird, Staff Corps	6 Feb. 95	Wing Officer and Quarter Master,18 Sept.89.—Specialduty,Gilgit.
Lieut. F. W. Hallowes, Staff Corps	25 Aug. 86	Wing Officer, 31 May 89.—Dep. Assist. Com. Gen., 2nd Class.
Lieut. S. H. Climo, Staff Corps	11 July 88	Wing Officer and Adjutant, 1 Apr. 90.
Lieut. P. G. Anderson, Staff Corps	24 Feb. 90	Wing Officer, 21 Aug. 91.—With Hong Kong Regiment.
Lieut. A. Roberts, Staff Corps	6 Jan. 91	Wing Officer, 19 Dec. 90.—Assist. Recruiting Officer, Umritsur.
Lieut. C. M'M. Davis, Sussex Regiment	18 Feb. 91	Wing Officer, 19 Dec. 93.—Burmah Military Police.
Lieut. A. K. Rawlins, Staff Corps	15 Dec. 91	Wing Officer, 16 March 94.
Lieut. H. W. F. Cooke, Staff Corps	22 June 92	Wing Officer, 8 Aug. 94.
Lieut. H. A. Vallings, Staff Corps	19 Mar. 90	Officiating Wing Officer.
Lieut. F. A. Maxwell, Sussex Regt	24 Nov. 93	Officiating Wing Officer.
Lieut. A. Skeen,K.O. Scottish Bords	30 Dec. 93	Officiating Wing Officer.
Surgeon Captain H. F. Whitchurch	31 Mar. 88	In medical charge, 11 May 92.—Temporary duty, Gilgit.
Surgeon Lieut. A. S. Harriss	29 Jan. 94	Officiating in medical charge.

25th (*Punjab*) **Bengal Infantry** (*late 17th Punjab Infantry*).—
Raised in 1857.—Linked with 27th, 28th and 33rd Regiments.—Regimental Centre, Rawul Pindee.
"AHMED KHEL"—"KANDAHAR, 1880"—"AFGHANISTAN, 1878-80."
Head Quarters at Sealkote. *Uniform, Red. Facings, White.*

Colonel E. W. Smyth, Gen. List, Inf.	28 Dec. 93	Commandant, 15 Oct. 89.
Major G. H. B. Coats, Staff Corps	28 Oct. 91	2nd in Command and Wing Commander, 1 Feb. 91.
Captain A. E. P. Burn, Staff Corps	21 Sept.85	Wing Comdr., 1 Feb. 91.—Assist. Judge Adv. Gen., Rangoon.
p.s.c. Captain W. E. Bunbury, S. C.	30 Jan. 89	Wing Comdr., 28 Sept. 93.—D.A.A. Gen. Nerbudda District.
Captain A. Hamilton, Staff Corps	11 Aug. 91	Wing Officer, 20 Dec. 84.—Dist.Recruiting Officer,Rawul Pindee.
Captain A. A. E. Campbell, Staff Corps	10 May 93	Wing Officer, 5 Nov. 85.—D.A.A.Gen. for Musketry, Abbottabad.
Lieut. R. L. Tottenham, Staff Corps	9 May 85	Wing Officer and Quarter Master, 10 July 87.
Lieut. G. P. Campbell, Staff Corps	30 Jan. 86	Wing Officer, 14 July 88.—Assistant Recruiting Officer.
Lieut. J. Gaisford, Staff Corps	9 May 92	Wing Officer and Adjutant, 16 Apr. 92.—Furlough.
Lieut. C. B. Winter, Staff Corps	30 Mar. 92	Wing Officer, 30 Nov. 93.—Furlough.
Lieut. A. B. Minchin, Staff Corps	28 June 93	Wing Officer, 20 Apr. 94.
Surgeon Captain A. C. Younan, MB	1 Oct. 85	In medical charge, 8 March 89.

26th (*Punjab*) **Bengal Infantry** (*late 18th Punjab Infantry*).— 444g

Raised in June 1857.—Linked with 20th and 21st Regiments.—Regimental Centre, Jhelum.
"AFGHANISTAN, 1878-79"—"BURMA, 1885-87."
Head Quarters at **Jhelum.** Two Companies at **Mooltan.** *Uniform, Drab. Facings, Red.*

RANK, NAMES, AND CORPS.	ARMY RANK.	REMARKS.
Lt.Colonel L. Dening, DSO, Staff Corps	11 May 93	Commandant, 11 May 94.
Captain H. A. Ravenshaw, Staff Corps	24 Mar. 87	2nd in Command and Wing Commander, 11 May 92.—Furlough.
Captain F. H. Hancock, Staff Corps	22 Jan. 90	Wing Commander, 11 May 92.—Furlough.
Captain W. A. B. Dennys, Staff Corps	13 Aug. 90	Wing Officer, 23 Oct. 84.—Adj. 2 Admin. Bn. N.W.P. Vols.
Captain C. C. Anderson, Staff Corps	18 Feb. 91	Wing Officer, 23 Oct. 84.—At Mooltan.
Captain C. W. Field, Staff Corps	25 Aug. 94	Wing Officer, 11 June 86.—Cantonment Magistrate, Mooltan.
Lieut. L. B. Walton, Staff Corps	25 Aug. 86	Wing Officer and Adjutant, 22 Jan. 91.
Lieut. C. Rattray, Staff Corps	15 Aug. 90	Wing Officer and Quarter Master, 26 Aug. 91.
Lieut. I. F. R. Thompson, Staff Corps	1 Nov. 90	Wing Officer, 30 Dec. 91.
Lieut. H. A. Harington, Staff Corps	14 July 91	Wing Officer, 15 Dec. 92.
Lieut. O. H. Lawson, Staff Corps	11 May 92	Officiating Wing Officer.
Lieut. G. Walton, Warwick Regt.	24 May 93	Officiating Wing Officer.
Surgeon Captain J. K. Close, MD.	1 Oct. 87	In medical charge, 11 May 92.

27th (*Punjab*) **Bengal Infantry** (*late 19th Punjab Infantry*).—

Raised 19 June 1857.—Linked with 25th, 28th and 33rd Regiments.—Regimental Centre, Rawul Pindee.
"CHINA, 1860-62"—"ALI MUSJID"—"AFGHANISTAN, 1878-80"—"BURMA, 1885-87."
Head Quarters at **Jullundur.** *Uniform, Drab. Facings, Red.*

RANK, NAMES, AND CORPS.	ARMY RANK.	REMARKS.
Lt.Colonel H. M. Rose, DSO, Staff C...	8 Mar. 93	Commandant, 26 Sept. 93.
Captain A. Wallace, Staff Corps	11 Sept. 87	2nd in Command and Wing Commander, 18 Nov. 94.
Captain L. H. Reid, Staff Corps	1 May 89	Wing Commander, 18 Nov. 94.—Cantonment Magistrate, Agra.
Captain W. B. Mullins, Staff Corps	14 Jan. 91	Wing Commander.
Captain C. W. O'Bryen, Staff Corps	9 Sept. 93	Wing Officer, 27 June 87.—Officiating Wing Commander.
Captain W. H. Millar, Staff Corps	25 Aug. 94	Wing Officer, 19 Apr. 88.—Furlough.
Lieut. W. H. Hildebrand, Staff Corps	29 Aug. 85	Wing Officer and Adjutant, 27 Feb. 89.
Lieut. O. A. Smith, Staff Corps	24 July 86	Wing Officer, 27 May 93.
Lieut. G. W. Robinson, Staff Corps	29 Feb. 88	Wing Officer and Quarter Master, 29 Sept. 90.
Lieut. J. S. Kemball, Staff Corps	15 Dec. 90	Officiating Wing Officer.—With 20 Bengal Infantry.
Surgeon Major J. Shearer, MB.	2 Oct. 92	In medical charge, 8 June 87.—Waziristan Field Force.

28th (*Punjab*) **Bengal Infantry** (*late 20th Punjab Infantry*).—

Raised 1 July 1857.—Linked with 25th, 27th and 33rd Regiments.—Regimental Centre, Rawul Pindee.
"CHARASIA"—"KABUL, 1879"—"AFGHANISTAN, 1878-80."
Head Quarters at **Ferozepore.** *Uniform, Red. Facings, Emerald Green.*

RANK, NAMES, AND CORPS.	ARMY RANK.	REMARKS.
Colonel C. L. Prendergast, Gen.List, Inf.	4 Mar. 90	Commandant, 10 Aug. 92.—Furlough.
Major A. R. Porter, Staff Corps	21 Aug. 89	2nd in Command and Wing Comdr., 10 Aug. 92.—Offg. Comdt.
Captain W. E. Phillips, Staff Corps	22 Jan. 90	Wing Commander, 10 Aug. 92.—Offg. 2nd in Command.
Captain G. R. Crawford, Staff Corps	22 Oct. 81	Wing Officer, 15 Mar. 86.—Officiating Wing Commander.
Captain A. F. Bruce, Staff Corps	10 Mar. 94	Wing Officer, 21 Apr. 87.—Assist. Political Agent, Quetta.
p.s.c. Lieut. F. Tweddell, Staff Corps	23 Aug. 84	Wing Officer, 1 Aug. 89.—Russia.
Lieut. O. W. Carey, Staff Corps	30 Jan. 86	Wing Officer, 4 Feb. 92.
Lt. A. G. de V. Chichester, Staff Corps	1 Apr. 88	Wing Officer, 7 Oct. 92.
Lieut. G. K. Cockerill, Staff Corps	26 June 89	Wing Officer, 19 Aug. 92.—Officiating Quarter Master.
Lieut. W. C. Palæologus, Staff Corps	15 Aug. 91	Wing Officer, 7 Oct. 92.—Burmah Military Police.
Lieut. J. C. M. Wheeler, Staff Corps	15 Oct. 91	Wing Officer, 14 Aug. 92.—Furlough.
Lieut. W. B. Hickie, Staff Corps	23 Jan. 92	Officiating Wing Officer.
Surgeon Lt.Colonel Z. A. Ahmed, MD.	1 Oct. 92	In medical charge, 23 July 84.

29th (*Punjab*) **Bengal Infantry** (*late 21st Punjab Infantry*).—

Raised 12 July 1857.—Linked with 30th and 31st Regiments.—Regimental Centre, Peshawur.
"PEIWAR KOTAL"—"AFGHANISTAN, 1878-80."
Head Quarters at **Meerut.** *Uniform, Red. Facings, Blue.*

RANK, NAMES, AND CORPS.	ARMY RANK.	REMARKS.
Colonel A. J. F. Reid, Staff Corps	6 Jan. 94	Commandant, 26 Nov. 89.
Major F. G. L. Mainwaring, Staff Corps	30 Dec. 91	2nd in Command and Wing Commander, 31 July 91.
Major R. W. MacLeod, Staff Corps	19 Oct. 92	Wing Commander, 9 Sept. 86.—With 8 Bengal Infantry.
Captain T. H. Bairnsfather, Staff Corps	13 Aug. 90	Wing Officer, 15 Sept. 82.—Offg. Cantonment Mag., Umballa.
Lieut. A. B. H. Drew, Staff Corps	7 Feb. 85	Wing Officer and Adjutant, 27 June 87.
Lieut. W. C. M. Woodcock, Staff Corps	6 May 85	Wing Officer, 18 Sept. 89.—With Hong Kong Regiment.
Lieut. R. E. H. Dyer, Staff Corps	23 Aug. 85	Wing Officer and Quarter Master, 28 Apr. 88.
Lieut. T. H. Grant, Staff Corps	25 Aug. 86	Wing Officer, 9 Aug. 93.
Lieut. W. S. E. Howard, Staff Corps	21 Jan. 88	Wing Officer, 22 Oct. 89.—Burmah Military Police.
Lieut. F. F. Solby-Flood, Staff Corps	7 July 91	Wing Officer, 6 Oct. 92.—Furlough.
2nd Lieut. A. James, K.O. Scot. Brdrs.	28 Jan. 93	Wing Officer.
2nd Lieut. W. G. P. Murray, Staff Corps	28 Jan. 93	Officiating Wing Officer.
Surgeon Captain D. T. Lane, MD.	1 Oct. 87	In medical charge, 5 May 93.—Offg. Chonawan Central Jail.

444h **30th (Punjab) Bengal Infantry** (late 22nd Punjab Infantry).—
Raised in June, 1857.—Linked with 29th and 31st Regiments.—Regimental Centre, Peshawur.
"AFGHANISTAN, 1879-80."
Head Quarters at Rawul Pindee. Uniform, Red. Facings, White.

RANK, NAMES, AND CORPS.	ARMY RANK.	REMARKS.
Major F. G. Maisey, Staff Corps	23 Sept. 91	Commandant, 12 Dec. 93.
Major J. L. O'Bryon, Staff Corps	28 Feb. 94	2nd in Command and Wing Commander, 12 Dec. 93.
Captain H. H. Dobbie, Staff Corps	1 May 89	Wing Commander, 12 Dec. 93.—D.A.A.Gen. for Musk., Meerut.
Major F. M. Drury, Staff Corps	26 Mar. 94	Wing Commander, 1 Apr. 94.
Lieut. F. C. Muspratt, Staff Corps	7 Feb. 85	Wing Officer and Adjutant, 28 Feb. 87.—Furlough.
Lieut. C. T. W. Forth, Staff Corps	6 May 85	Wing Officer, 23 Jan. 80.
Lieut. F. Wintle, Staff Corps	29 Aug. 85	Wing Officer and Quarter Master, 21 Mar. 90.—Assist. Recruiting Officer, Dhurmsala.
Lieut. W. J. P. Kaye, Staff Corps	29 Aug. 85	Wing Officer, 23 May 87.—Furlough.
Lieut. E. S. Hall, Staff Corps	25 Aug. 86	Wing Officer, 19 Apr. 91.—Officiating Adjutant. Officiating Wing Officer.
Lieut. A. H. G. Thompson, Staff Corps	14 Apr. 93	Officiating Wing Officer.
Surgeon Captain C. E. L. Gilbert	31 Mar. 87	In medical charge, 4 Apr. 91.—Waziristan Field Force.

31st (Punjab) Bengal Infantry (late 23rd Punjab Infantry).—
Raised in 1857.—Linked with 29th and 30th Regiments.—Regimental Centre, Peshawur.
"AFGHANISTAN, 1879-80."
Head Quarters at Peshawur. Uniform, Red. Facings, White.

Lt. Colonel W. G. C. Halkett, Staff C.	9 Sept. 90	Commandant, 15 May 91.—Furlough.
Major M. I. Gibbs, Staff Corps	30 Dec. 91	2nd in Command and Wing Comdr. 15 Dec. 93.—Offg. Comdt.
Captain W. Giles, Staff Corps	21 May 89	Officiating 2nd in Command.—From 21 Bengal Infantry.
p.s.c. Captain H. B. B. Watkis, Staff Corps	11 May 89	Wing Commander, 15 Dec. 93.—Attaché, Army Head Quarters, Simla.—Officiating D. A. A. Gen., Simla.
Captain F. S. Cooper, Staff Corps	19 Dec. 94	Wing Officer, 2 Dec. 88.—Sick Furlough.
Lieut. E. R. Morton, Staff Corps	25 Nov. 85	Wing Officer and Adjutant, 5 June 91.—Furlough.
Lieut. W. L. Malcolm, Staff Corps	27 Oct. 86	Wing Officer and Quarter Master, 24 Aug. 91.—Offg. Adjutant.
Lieut. H. B. Ford, Staff Corps	4 Apr. 90	Wing Officer, 7 Jan. 94.
Lieut. L. A. Watson, Staff Corps	2 Mar. 90	Wing Officer, 7 Mar. 94.—Officiating Quarter Master.
Lieut. F. B. Prideaux, Staff Corps	11 May 92	Officiating Wing Officer.
2nd Lieut. E. B. Peacock, Staff Corps	28 Jan. 93	Officiating Wing Officer.
Surgeon Captain J. G. Jordan, M.B.	30 Sept. 86	In medical charge, 19 July 90.—Officiating Civil, Backergunge. Officiating in medical charge.

32nd (Punjab) Bengal Infantry (Pioneers—late 24th Punjab Infantry).
Raised in 1857.—Linked with 23rd and 34th Regiments.—Regimental Centre, Meean Meer.
"Aut viam inveniam aut faciam." "DELHI"—"LUCKNOW" (Relief and Capture)—"AFGHANISTAN, 1878-80."
Head Quarters at Bunji (Gilgit Command). Depot at Umballa. Uniform, Red. Facings, Dark Blue.

Lt. Colonel J. G. Kelly, Staff Corps	11 Sept. 89	Commandant, 14 July 92.
Lt. Colonel H. C. Halkett, Staff Corps	2 Aug. 91	2nd in Command and Wing Commander, 15 Oct. 91.
p.s.c. Captain E. De Brath, Staff Corps	11 Sept. 87	Wing Comdr. 13 June 93.—Assist. Sec. Govt. of India, Mil. Dept.
p.s.c. Captain H. R. Brander, Staff Corps	14 Jan. 91	Wing Commander, 13 June 93.
Captain H. B. Borradaile, Staff Corps	14 Jan. 91	Wing Officer, 17 Feb. 85.—Officiating Wing Commander.
Lieut. F. H. Peterson, Staff Corps	25 Nov. 85	Wing Officer and Adjutant, 11 Oct. 87.
Lieut. A. R. Burlton, Staff Corps	24 July 86	Wing Officer, 4 Dec. 91.—Dep. Assist. Com. Gen. 2nd Class.
Lieut. J. B. Bell, Staff Corps	6 Nov. 89	Wing Officer and Quarter Master, 31 Dec. 91.—At Umballa.
Lieut. A. H. Garden, Staff Corps	9 July 90	Wing Officer, 21 May 92.
Lieut. H. Bethune, Staff Corps	22 Apr. 91	Wing Officer, 13 June 93.
Lieut. E. H. S. Cullen, Staff Corps	21 Jan. 92	Officiating Wing Officer.
Lieut. A. S. Cobbe, Staff Corps	4 Mar. 92	Officiating Wing Officer.
2nd Lieut. M. F. Cooke, Cheshire Regt.	27 Jan. 92	Officiating Wing Officer.
Surgeon Captain E. Jennings	30 Mar. 89	In medical charge, 29 Sept. 93.—Officiating Civil, Rungpore.
Surgeon Captain S. B. Smith	28 July 91	Officiating in medical charge.

NOTE.—The 5th Goorkha Regiment, when acting with other Bengal Native Troops, takes rank after the 32nd Native Infantry.

33rd (Punjabi Mahomedan) Bengal Infantry.—Raised in 1857.
Linked with 25th, 27th and 28th Regiments.
"BURMA, 1885-87."
On Field Service, Waziristan. Uniform, Red. Facings, White.

Lt. Colonel G. H. C. Dyce, Staff Corps	30 Dec. 90	Commandant, 17 Jan. 91.
Major C. Hogge, Staff Corps	7 Dec. 88	2nd in Command and Wing Commander, 1 Mar. 91.
Major H. T. Faithfull, Staff Corps	12 Feb. 94	Wing Commander, 27 Jan. 91.—With Hong Kong Regiment.
Captain W. L. Boswell, Staff Corps	30 Jan. 89	Wing Commander, 28 Nov. 91. Wing Officer.
Lieut. E. H. Watson, Staff Corps	23 Aug. 84	Wing Officer and Adjutant, 13 Feb. 91.
Lieut. H. King, Staff Corps	29 Aug. 85	Wing Officer and Quarter Master, 13 Apr. 91.—Furlough.
Lieut. T. Robinson, Royal Artillery	24 July 86	Wing Officer, 14 Mar. 94.
Lieut. A. S. R. Annesley, Staff Corps	1 Aug. 89	Wing Officer, 15 Jan. 92.—Dep. Assist. Com. Gen., 2nd Class.
2nd Lt. A. H. P. Harrison, Staff Corps	28 June 93	Officiating Wing Officer.
Surgeon Captain H. E. Banatvala	1 Apr. 84	In medical charge, 1 Jan. 91.—Officiating Civil, Betul.
Surgeon Lieut. W. H. Orr	31 Jan. 93	Officiating in medical charge.

34th (Punjab) Bengal Infantry (Pioneers).—Raised in 1858, disbanded in 1881, re-formed 23 March 1887.—Linked with 23rd and 32nd Regts.—Regimental Centre, Meean Meer.

Head Quarters at Meean Meer. Uniform, Red. Facings, Dark Blue.

Rank, Names, and Corps.	Army Rank.	Remarks.
Lt. Colonel E. H. Wilson, Staff Corps	25 July 91	Commandant, 24 Oct. 88. 2nd in Command and Wing Commander.
Major M. C. Cooke-Collis, Staff Corps	30 Dec. 91	Wing Commander, 27 May 91.
Captain D. W. Hickman, Staff Corps	11 Feb. 87	Wing Officer, 1 July 87.—D.A.A. Gen. Sirhind District.
Captain A. F. Hoggo, Staff Corps	11 May 89	Wing Officer, 25 May 87.
Captain G. L. Holland, Staff Corps	27 Jan. 94	Wing Officer, 9 June 87.
Lieut. H. B. Murray, Staff Corps	14 May 87	Wing Officer, 29 May 87.—Sick Furlough.
Lieut. G. E. L. Gilbert, Staff Corps	9 May 85	Wing Officer and Adjutant, 10 Oct. 87.
Lieut. T. Y. Seddon, Staff Corps	9 May 85	Wing Officer and Quarter Master, 18 Nov. 90.
Lieut. H. R. Wallis, Staff Corps	29 June 88	Wing Officer, 4 May 92.—Burmah Military Police.
Lieut. F. B. Hill, Warwick Regiment	6 June 91	Wing Officer, 4 May 92.
Lieut. C. E. Lees, Staff Corps	27 Aug. 90	Wing Officer, 19 Dec. 93.
Surgeon Captain W. H. B. Robinson	1 Apr. 86	In medical charge, 21 March 90.—Waziristan Field Force.

35th (Sikh) Bengal Infantry.—Raised in 1858, disbanded in 1882, re-formed 23 March 1887.—Linked with 36th Regiment.—Regimental Centre, Jullunder.

Head Quarters at Nowgong. Uniform, Red. Facings, Yellow.

Rank, Names, and Corps.	Army Rank.	Remarks.
Lt. Colonel T. H. Goldney, Staff Corps	9 June 93	Commandant, 26 Apr. 92.
Major J. F. Worlledge, Staff Corps	28 Feb. 94	2nd in Command and Wing Commander, 26 Nov. 94.
Captain L. J. E. Bradshaw, Staff Corps	10 Sept. 86	Wing Commander, 26 Apr. 92.
Captain J. H. Christie, Staff Corps	1 May 89	Wing Officer, 30 May 87.—Cantonment Magistrate, Sealkote.
Captain P. B. Vaughan, Staff Corps	13 Aug. 90	Wing Officer, 11 June 87.
Captain C. R. A. Bond, Staff Corps	10 May 93	Wing Officer, 29 April 87.—A.D.C. to Major General Sanford.
Lieut. C. A. Edwards, Staff Corps	6 May 85	Wing Officer, 26 Sept. 88.
Lieut. E. C. Rowcroft, Staff Corps	23 Mar. 89	Wing Officer, 3 April 90.—With Hong Kong Regiment.
Lieut. V. Hughes, Staff Corps	4 Jan. 90	Wing Officer and Adjutant, 12 July 92.—Furlough.
Lieut. O. G. Gunning, Manch. Regt.	9 July 90	Wing Officer, 17 Nov. 94.—Officiating Quarter Master.
Lieut. G. R. Cassels, Staff Corps	18 Feb. 91	Wing Officer, 15 Mar. 93.—Furlough.
Lieut. G. W. G. Lindesay, Bedford Regt.	28 June 93	Officiating Wing Officer.
2nd Lieut. S. K. B. Rice, Staff Corps	3 Sept. 92	Officiating Wing Officer.
Surgeon Captain S. H. Henderson, MB.	30 Sept. 86	In medical charge, 16 Aug. 91.—Officiating Supdt. Central Jail, Allahabad.
Surgeon Lieut. R. H. Maddox, MB.	27 July 92	Officiating in medical charge.—And Bundelkund Polit. Agency.

36th (Sikh) Bengal Infantry.—Raised in 1858, disbanded in 1882, re-formed 23 Apr. 1887.—Linked with 35th Regiment.—Regimental Centre, Jullunder.

Head Quarters at Peshawur. Uniform, Red. Facings, Yellow.

Rank, Names, and Corps.	Army Rank.	Remarks.
Major J. Haughton, Staff Corps	28 Oct. 91	Commandant, 25 June 94.
Major C. H. Des Vœux, Staff Corps	10 Jan. 92	2nd in Command and Wing Commander, 15 Aug. 91.
Captain W. D. Gordon, Staff Corps	19 Dec. 88	Wing Commander, 25 Nov. 94.
Captain H. L. Custance, Staff Corps	17 May 90	Wing Officer, 9 June 87.—Sick Furlough.
Captain C. E. Johnson, Staff Corps	22 Jan. 92	Wing Officer, 16 June 87.
Captain C. T. A. Searle, Staff Corps	25 Aug. 94	Wing Officer, 22 June 87.
Lieut. C. E. H. Erskine, Staff Corps	7 Feb. 85	Wing Officer, 1 June 87.—Offg. Adj. Rangoon Bn. Military Police.
Lieut. E. L. Sullivan, Staff Corps	25 Nov. 85	Wing Officer and Adjutant, 15 Aug. 91.
Lieut. H. L. Fleming, Staff Corps	10 Nov. 86	Wing Officer, 25 Nov. 94.
Lieut. R. G. Munn, Staff Corps	1 Nov. 90	Officiating Wing Officer.
Lieut. A. K. Blair, Staff Corps	23 Mar. 91	Officiating Wing Officer.
Lieut. A. S. Stephen, Staff Corps	18 Nov. 92	Officiating Wing Officer.
Surgeon Captain F. C. Clarkson	30 Sept. 86	In medical charge, 2 Dec. 90.—Officiating Civil, Nadia.
Surgeon Lieut. C. B. Prall	30 Jan. 93	Officiating in medical charge.

37th (Dogra) Bengal Infantry.—Raised in 1858, disbanded in 1882, re-formed 20 Apr. 1887.—Linked with 38th Regiment.—Regimental Centre, Sealkote.

Head Quarters at Kohat. Uniform, Red. Facings, Yellow.

Honorary Colonel.—H. H. Maharajah Sir Pratap Singh, GCSI. Indra Mahendra, Bahadoor, Sipar-i-Saltanat of Jummoo and Cashmere.

Rank, Names, and Corps.	Army Rank.	Remarks.
Lt. Colonel A. M. Mills, Staff Corps	1 Feb. 94	Commandant, 28 April 94.
Major W. S. Marshall, Staff Corps	21 Sept. 94	2nd in Command and Wing Commander, 28 Apr. 94.
Captain J. A. Brown, Staff Corps	22 Jan. 90	Wing Commander, 28 Apr. 94.
Captain F. J. B. Campbell, S. Lan. Regt.	14 Jan. 91	Wing Officer, 7 June 87.—Furlough.
Captain J. A. H. Woodward, Staff Corps	9 Sept. 93	Wing Officer, 25 June 87.—Station Staff Officer and Cantonment Magistrate, Nowshera.
Lieut. F. J. H. Wynch, Staff Corps	14 May 84	Wing Officer and Adjutant, 15 June 87.
Lieut. C. H. R. Coles, Staff Corps	7 Feb. 85	Wing Officer and Quarter Master, 15 June 87.
Lieut. A. C. M'Crea, Staff Corps	10 Apr. 89	Wing Officer, 27 May 91.
Lieut. E. B. Longden, Staff Corps	5 July 89	Wing Officer, 7 Oct. 92.—Furlough.
Lieut. F. J. Moberly, DSO. Staff Corps	4 Oct. 91	Wing Officer, 5 March 92.—On special duty, Gilgit.
2nd Lieut. W. J. Keen, Staff Corps	19 Dec. 93	Officiating Wing Officer.
Surgeon Captain A. T. Bown	1 Oct. 84	In medical charge, 9 July 87.

38th (*Dogra*) Bengal Infantry.—*Raised in* 1858.
Linked with 37th Regiment.—Regimental Centre, Sealkote.
On Field Service, **Waziristan**. *Uniform, Red. Facings, Yellow.*

RANK, NAMES, AND CORPS.	ARMY RANK.	REMARKS.
Colonel L. R. H. D. Campbell, Staff C....	15 Jan. 95	Commandant, 15 Jan. 91.—Furlough.
Major F. G. Vivian, Staff Corps.........	4 Jan. 83	2nd in Command and Wing Comdr. 7 Jan. 91.—Offg. Comdt.
aptain R. E. S. Taylor, Staff Corps ...	23 Jan. 89	Wing Comdr. 15 Jan. 91.—Offg. Cant. Mag. N.W.P. and Oude.
Captain K. P. Burne, Staff Corps	23 Oct. 91	Wing Comdr., 1 June 94.—Dist. Recruiting Officer, Sealkote.
Captain L. C. H. Stainforth, Staff Corps	22 Jan. 92	Wing Commander, 1 June 94.—Officiating 2nd in Command.
Lieut. A. Cadell, Staff Corps	29 Aug. 85	Wing Officer and Adjutant, 22 Jan. 92.—Offg. Wing Commander.
Lieut. W. E. Tomkins, Staff Corps	25 Aug. 86	Wing Officer and Quarter Master, 1 Feb. 91.—Offg. Adjutant.
Lieut. W. C. Scott, Staff Corps	9 Jan. 88	Wing Officer, 17 May 92.—Assistant Inspecting Officer Punjab States, Imperial Service Troops.
Lieut. C. W. Tribe, Staff Corps............	28 Sept. 88	Wing Officer, 22 Apr. 92.—Furlough.
Lieut. G. H. Bell, Staff Corps...............	15 Dec. 90	Wing Officer, 2 April 94.
Lieut. H. W. Cruddas, Staff Corps	15 Oct. 90	Wing Officer, 1 Aug. 94.—Burmah Military Police.
Lieut. A. W. Bailey, Staff Corps	17 Feb. 92	Wing Officer, 1 Aug. 94.—Officiating Quarter Master.
2nd Lieut. S. B. A. Patterson, Staff C....	13 Aug. 92	Officiating Wing Officer.
2nd Lieut. L. S. Browne, Staff Corps ...	19 Nov. 92	Officiating Wing Officer.
2nd Lieut. E. G. D. de Labilliere, S. C.	23 Nov. 92	Officiating Wing Officer.
Surgeon Lt.Colonel W. M. Courtney ...	1 Oct. 89	In medical charge, 15 Jan. 91.—Furlough.
Surgeon Lieut. C. Milne	30 Jan. 93	Officiating in medical charge.

39th (*Garwhal Rifle*) Bengal Infantry.—*Raised in* 1858.
Linked with 9th Regiment.—Regimental Centre, Lansdowne.
"AFGHANISTAN, 1878-80."
Head Quarters at **Lansdowne**. *Uniform, Dark Green. Facings, Black.*

RANK, NAMES, AND CORPS.	ARMY RANK.	REMARKS.
Lt.Colonel B. C. Graves, Staff Corps ...	30 Jan. 92	Commandant, 8 Dec. 93.—Commanding at Lansdowne.
p.s.c. Major B. Duff, Staff Corps	17 Aug. 94	2nd in Command and Wing Commander, 24 Oct. 93.—Dep. Assist. Adj. Gen., Simla.
Captain A. C. O'Donnell, Staff Corps ...	5 Oct. 89	2nd in Command and Wing Commander, 24 Oct. 93.—Adjutant Assam Valley Admin. Bn.—Furlough.
Captain J. T. Evatt, Staff Corps............	23 Apr. 92	2nd in Command and Wing Commander, 24 Oct. 93.
Captain D. E. Mocatta, Staff Corps......	10 May 93	Wing Commander, 24 Oct. 93.
Lieut. M. B. Roberts, Staff Corps	23 May 85	Wing Officer, 24 Dec. 87.—Sick Furlough.
Lieut. H. M. Brownlow, Staff Corps	29 Aug. 85	Wing Officer, 25 Mar. 88. [India.
Lieut. L. A. Forbes, Staff Corps	10 Nov. 86	Wing Officer, 17 May 89.—Boundary Settlement Officer, Central
Lieut. W. H. Wardell, Staff Corps	16 Jan. 91	Wing Officer, 4 Aug. 93.—Furlough.
Lieut. H. M. MacTier, Staff Corps	2 July 91	Wing Officer, 24 Oct. 93.—Officiating Adjutant.
Lieut. A. B. Drummond, Staff Corps ...	23 May 92	Officiating Wing Officer.
Lieut. J. H. K. Stewart, Staff Corps.....	3 Dec. 94	Officiating Wing Officer.
Surgeon Lt.Colonel C. J. M'Cartie, *MD*.	30 Sept. 94	In medical charge, 15 Jan. 91.

40th (*Pathan*) Bengal Infantry.—*Raised in* 1858.
Head Quarters at **Quetta**. *Uniform, Drab. Facings, Green.*

RANK, NAMES, AND CORPS.	ARMY RANK.	REMARKS.
Lt.Colonel S. H. P. Graves, Staff Corps	2 Sept. 94	Commandant, 22 Jan. 91.
Major J. B. Woon, Staff Corps	1 Oct. 93	2nd in Command and Wing Commander, 1 Apr. 91.
Captain G. F. H. Dillon, Staff Corps ...	29 July 83	Wing Commander, 30 Dec. 92.—Waziristan Field Force.
Captain T. M'Kay, Staff Corps	9 Sept. 93	Wing Officer, 1 June 91.—Officiating Wing Commander.
Lieut. F. Rennick, Staff Corps	29 Aug. 85	Wing Officer and Quarter Master, 19 Dec. 91.
Lieut. R. T. I. Ridgway, Staff Corps ...	3 Mar. 89	Wing Officer and Adjutant, 2 May 91.
Lieut. W. C. B. Bunbury, Staff Corps ...	18 Mar. 91	Wing Officer, 6 April 93.
Lieut. T. R. Maclachlan, Staff Corps ...	26 Aug. 91	Wing Officer, 2 Feb. 94.
Lieut. G. A. Preston, Staff Corps.........	14 Jan. 92	Officiating Wing Officer.
Surgeon Captain W. Vost, *MD*.	31 Mar. 87	In medical charge, 21 Feb. 91.—Offg. Civil and Jail, Baraitch.
Surgeon Lieut. W. H. Ogilvie, *MB*. ...	30 Jan. 93	Officiating in medical charge.

42nd (*Goorkha Rifle*) Bengal Infantry (*late* 1st *Assam Lt. Infantry*.—
Raised 16 *May* 1817).—*Linked with* 43rd *and* 44th *Regiments.—Regimental Centre, Shillong.*
"BURMA, 1885-87."
Head Quarters at **Shillong**. *Uniform, Dark Green. Facings, Black.*

RANK, NAMES, AND CORPS.	ARMY RANK.	REMARKS.
Colonel C. R. Macgregor, *DSO*. Staff C.	3 Dec. 94	Commandant, 11 Dec. 93.
Major H. J. Bolton, Staff Corps	17 July 92	2nd in Command and Wing Commander, 1 Oct. 92.
Captain H. W. Priestley, Staff Corps ...	25 Feb. 91	Wing Commander, 6 Dec. 92. [Intell. Branch.
Captain F. C. Colomb, Staff Corps	22 Jan. 92	Wing Officer, 16 Jan. 84.—Paid Attaché, Qr. Mr. Gen.'s Dept.
Lieut. J. B. Chatterton, Staff Corps ...	23 Aug. 84	Wing Officer and Adjutant, 27 Mar. 89.
Lieut. E. J. Lugard, *DSO*. Staff Corps	10 Nov. 86	Wing Officer, 1 Aug. 89.
Lieut. H. H. Roddy, Staff Corps...........	13 May 88	Wing Officer, 17 Nov. 91.—Dep. Assist. Com. Gen. 2nd Class.
Lieut. M. G. James, Staff Corps	17 Aug. 88	Wing Officer, 20 Aug. 92.
Lieut. H. S. Shaw, Staff Corps............	1 July 90	Wing Officer, 12 Nov. 93.
Lieut. A. J. Strange, Staff Corps	19 July 92	Officiating Wing Officer.
Surgeon Capt. J. Chaytor-White, *MD*.	30 Sept. 89	In medical charge, 17 Aug. 93.—Offg. Civil, N. W. P. and Oude.
Surgeon Captain H. S. Wood, *MB*.	28 July 91	Officiating in medical charge.

43rd (*Goorkha Rifle*) **Bengal Infantry** (*late 2nd Assam Lt. Infantry*.— 445
Raised 13 April 1835).—*Linked with 42nd and 44th Regiments.—Regimental Centre, Shillong.*
"BURMA, 1885-87."
Head Quarters at **Kohima**. *Uniform, Dark Green. Facings, Black.*

RANK, NAMES, AND CORPS.	ARMY RANK.	REMARKS.
Major E. H. Molesworth, Staff Corps ...	24 Feb. 93	Commandant, 31 Mar. 94.—With 44 Bengal Infantry.
Major A. L. Barrett, *DSO*. Staff Corps...	11 Feb. 95	2nd in Com. and Wing Comdr. 11 Dec. 93.—Offg. Commandant.
Captain J. W. Cowley, Staff Corps	14 Jan. 91	Wing Commander, 27 June 94.—Officiating 2nd in Command.
Captain C. H. Clay, Staff Corps	6 Feb. 95	Wing Officer, 11 Apr. 86.
Captain C. S. Williams, Staff Corps.....	6 Feb. 95	Wing Officer, 4 Aug. 87.—Officiating Wing Commander.
Lieut. H. N. Waymouth, Staff Corps ...	7 Feb. 85	Wing Officer, 7 June 90.—Assist. Mil. Accountant, 2nd Class.
Lieut. J.W.B. Merewether, Staff Corps ..	25 Aug. 86	Wing Officer, 1 Oct. 92.—Offg. 2nd in Com. Kolapore Inf. Corps.
Lieut. S. Clay, Staff Corps	5 Jan. 90	Wing Officer and Quarter Master, 15 Dec. 92.—Furlough.
Lieut. K. S. Cassels, Staff Corps	12 June 91	Wing Officer, 2 Feb. 93.—Officiating Adjutant.
Lieut. H. Baillie, Staff Corps	29 Sept. 92	Officiating Wing Officer and Quarter Master.
2nd Lt. R.F. Warburton, Somerset Lt.Inf.	31 Aug. 92	Officiating Wing Officer.
Surg. Capt. F. H. Burton-Brown, *MB*.	28 July 91	In medical charge, 10 Dec. 94.

44th (*Goorkha Rifle*) **Bengal Infantry** (*late Sylhet Lt. Infantry*.—
Raised 19 Feb. 1824).—*Linked with 42nd and 43rd Regiments.—Regimental Centre, Shillong.*
"BURMA, 1885-87."
Head Quarters at **Manipore**. *Uniform, Dark Green. Facings, Black.*

¥ℂ p.s.c. Lt.Col. R. K. Ridgeway, S. C.	8 Jan. 94	Commandant, 1 Jan. 91.—Furlough.
Major E. H. Molesworth, Staff Corps ...	24 Feb. 93	Officiating Commandant.—From 43 Bengal Infantry.
Captain H. O'Donnell, *DSO*. Staff Corps	30 Jan. 89	2nd in Command and Wing Comdr., 31 Mar. 94.—Furlough.
Captain M. A. Ker, Staff Corps	13 Aug. 90	Wing Commander, 31 Dec. 94.—Offg. 2nd in Command.
Captain G. R. Row, Staff Corps	22 Jan. 92	Wing Officer, 22 May 83.—Comdt. Luckimpore Mil. Police Bn.
Lieut. R. B. Berkeley, Staff Corps.........	7 Feb. 85	Wing Officer, 29 Nov. 86. — Boundary Settlement Offices, Western Malwa.
Lieut. H. W. R. Senior, Staff Corps	25 Aug. 86	Wing Officer and Adjutant, 18 Sept. 89.—Offg. Wing Commander.
Lieut. J. A. Wilson, Staff Corps............	4 Sept. 89	Wing Officer, 14 May 91.—Officiating Adjutant.
Lieut. L. H. Baldwin, Yorkshire Lt.Inf.	1 Mar. 92	Wing Officer, 18 May 94.—Officiating Quarter Master.
Lieut. G. L. S. Ward, Staff Corps	16 Apr. 92	Wing Officer, 25 Oct. 93.—Officiating Comdt. Naga Hills Police.
2nd Lt. J. R. Nuttall, Somerset Lt. Inf.	10 Oct. 91	Wing Officer, 29 June 94. In medical charge.
Surgeon Lieut. E. R. Parry, *MB*..........	30 Jan. 93	Officiating in medical charge.

45th (*Rattray's Sikhs*) **Bengal Infantry** (*late 1st Bengal Police Battalion*.
—Rattray's Sikhs). (*Raised in 1856.*—Added to the Bengal Army in 1864.)—
Linked with 14th and 15th Regiments.—Regimental Centre, Ferozepore.
"DEFENCE OF ARRAH"—"BEHAR"—"ALI MUSJID"—"AFGHANISTAN, 1878-80."
Head Quarters at **Jhansi**. *Uniform, Red. Facings, White.*

p.s.c. Lt.Colonel H. A. Sawyer, S. C. ...	2 Oct. 92	Commandant, 6 Apr. 92.
Major H. N. McRae, Staff Corps	7 Dec. 88	2nd in Command and Wing Comdr. 6 Apr. 92.—Furlough.
Captain J. M. A. Retallick, Staff Corps	10 Sept. 86	Wing Commander, 6 Apr. 92.—With Hong Kong Regiment.
Captain W. W. Taylor, Staff Corps	1 Jan. 87	Wing Commander, 24 June 92.
Captain L. C. Fryer, Staff Corps	23 Apr. 92	Wing Officer, 10 Aug. 86.—Furlough.
Lieut. R. E. Foley, Staff Corps	7 Feb. 85	Wing Officer, 8 July 87.—Officiating Wing Commander.
Lieut. H. A. Moore, Staff Corps	25 Aug. 86	Wing Officer and Adjutant, 8 May 91.
Lieut. F. T. Stewart, Staff Corps	10 Nov. 86	Wing Officer and Quarter Master, 21 May 92.
Lieut. R. M. Barff, Staff Corps	18 Dec. 90	Wing Officer, 24 June 92.—Furlough.
Lieut. G. de H. Smith, Staff Corps	14 Jan. 91	Officiating Wing Officer.
Lieut. H. B. Rattray, Staff Corps.........	1 Mar. 92	Officiating Wing Officer. In medical charge.
Surgeon Lieut. H. Burden	29 Jun. 94	Officiating in medical charge.

1st Goorkha (*Rifle*) **Regiment** (*Light Infantry—late 66th or Goorkha Lt. Inf.—*
Raised 24 Apr. 1815.) *The Regimental Centres of Goorkha Battalions are at their own Stations.*
"BHURTPORE"—"ALIWAL"—"SOBRAON"—"AFGHANISTAN, 1878-80."
FIRST BATTALION.
On Field Service, **Waziristan**. *Uniform, Dark Green. Facings, Scarlet.*

Major R. Fulton, Staff Corps	17 Feb. 92	Commandant, 1 Sept. 94.
Major G. H. Robinson, Staff Corps	9 Aug. 93	2nd in Command and Wing Commander, 6 Feb. 93.
Captain G. S. Ommanney, Staff Corps	1 May 89	Wing Commander, 1 Sept. 94.—With 2 Battalion.
Captain C. H. Powell, Staff Corps......	27 Jan. 87	Officiating Wing Commander.—From 2 Battalion.
Captain C. Y. Crommelin, Staff Corps ...	22 Oct. 92	Wing Officer, 1 Jan. 86.
Captain A. G. B. Lang, Staff Corps.....	10 May 93	Wing Officer, 29 March 86. Wing Officer and Adjutant.
Lieut. C. Herbert, Staff Corps	12 Nov. 84	Wing Officer and Quarter Master, 27 Apr. 93.
Lieut. E. D. Money, Staff Corps..........	14 Jan. 91	Wing Officer, 1 Sept. 94.
Lieut. W. C. Anderson, Staff Corps ...	1 Nov. 90	Wing Officer.
Lieut. H. F. B. Champain, Staff Corps	3 Jan. 91	Officiating Adjutant.
Lieut. E. M. Lang, Staff Corps	9 Mar. 92	Officiating Quarter Master.
Surgeon Lt.Colonel A. B. Seaman	1 Oct. 89	In medical charge, 20 March 93.

1st Goorkha (Rifle) Regiment (Light Infantry).

SECOND BATTALION.—*Raised* 19 Feb. 1886.
Head Quarters at **Dhurmsala**. *Uniform, Dark Green. Facings, Scarlet.*

Rank, Names, and Corps.	Army Rank.	Remarks.
Lt.Colonel C. A. R. Sage, Staff Corps ...	8 July 94	Commandant, 5 Mar. 94.
Captain E. W. F. Martin, Staff Corps...	10 Sept. 86	2nd in Command and Wing Commander, 1 Sept.94.—Furlough.
Captain G. S. Ommanney, Staff Corps	1 May 89	Officiating 2nd in Command.—From 1 Battalion.
Captain C. H. Powell, Staff Corps	27 Jan. 87	Wing Commander, 6 Feb. 93.—With 1 Battalion. [Comdr.
Captain A. V. Hatch, Staff Corps.........	14 Jan. 91	Wing Officer, 19 Feb. 86.—Station Staff Officer.—Offg. Wing
Captain A. C. B. Johnson, Staff Corps	10 Mar. 94	Wing Officer, 19 Feb. 86.
Lieut. W. I. Ryder, Staff Corps.........	23 Aug. 84	Wing Officer, 18 Dec. 90.
Lieut. H. A. H. Thompson, Staff Corps	31 July 88	Wing Officer and Quarter Master, 8 Aug. 93.
Lieut. J. L. Rose, Staff Corps............	15 May 89	Wing Officer and Adjutant, 4 Aug. 93.
Lieut. T. J. M'Leod, Staff Corps	26 Aug. 92	Officiating Wing Officer.
Surgeon Lt.Colonel R. N. Stoker	30 Sept. 94	In medical charge, 6 Mar. 86.

2nd (Prince of Wales' Own) Goorkha (Rifle) Regiment (The Sirmoor Rifles).—
Late Sirmoor Rifle Regiment.—Raised 24 *April* 1815.
Plume of the Prince of Wales.
"Bhurtpore"—"Alliwal"—"Sobraon"—"Delhi"—"Kadul, 1879"—"Kandahar, 1880"—
"Afghanistan, 1878-80."
FIRST BATTALION.
Head Quarters at **Dehra Dhoon**. *Uniform, Dark Green. Facings, Scarlet.*
Honorary Colonel.—Field Marshal *H.R.H.* Albert Edward, *Prince of* Wales *and Duke of* Cornwall,
KG. KT. KP. GCB. GCSI. GCMG. GCIE.

Rank, Names, and Corps.	Army Rank.	Remarks.
Lt.Colonel W. P. Newall, Staff Corps...	3 June 94	Commandant 2nd in Command and Wing Comdr. 24 Dec. 87.—Offg. Comdt.
Bt.Major E. A. Travers, Staff Corps ...	2 Nov. 88	Wing Commander, 24 Jan. 91.—D.A.A. Gen. Rawul Pindee.
Captain C. B. Judge, Staff Corps	30 Jan. 89	Wing Commander, 24 Jan. 91.—Officiating 2nd in Command.
Captain D. C. F. Macintyre, Staff Corps	13 Aug. 90	Wing Officer, 14 May 83.—Officiating Wing Commander.
Captain J. G. Robinson, Staff Corps ...	14 Jan. 91	Wing Officer, 11 Sept. 83.—With 2 Battalion.
Captain J. Fisher, Staff Corps	10 Mar. 94	Wing Officer, 6 Mar. 86.
Lieut. H. D. Watson, Staff Corps.........	7 Feb. 85	Wing Officer and Adjutant, 31 Jan. 94.
Lieut. C. E. de M. Norie, Staff Corps ..	9 May 85	Wing Officer and Quarter Master, 31 July 89.
Lieut. N. Macpherson, Staff Corps	14 Sept. 91	Officiating Wing Officer.
Lieut. A. B. Lindsay, Staff Corps.........	18 Jan. 93	Officiating Wing Officer.
Surgeon Lt.Colonel W. R. Murphy, *DSO.*	30 Mar. 92	In medical charge, 8 Dec. 94.

SECOND BATTALION.—*Raised* 19 Feb. 1886.
Head Quarters at **Dehra Dhoon**. *Uniform, Dark Green. Facings, Scarlet.*

Rank, Names, and Corps.	Army Rank.	Remarks.
Lt.Colonel F. R. Bogbie, Staff Corps ...	20 July 92	Commandant, 22 July 92.
Major L. M. M. Hall, Staff Corps	1 Oct. 93	2nd in Command and Wing Commander, 22 July 92.
Captain F. P. Hutchinson, Staff Corps	1 May 89	Wing Commander, 22 July 92.
Captain L. W. Shakespear, Staff Corps	22 Jan. 92	Wing Officer, 15 Apr. 86.—Furlough.
Lieut. H. V. Bradley, Staff Corps	23 Aug. 84	Wing Officer and Adjutant, 11 Feb. 86.—Furlough.
Lieut. E. J. Drummond, Staff Corps ...	29 Aug. 85	Wing Officer, 6 Aug. 90.—Furlough.
Lieut. B. Strachey, Staff Corps............	30 Jan. 86	Wing Officer and Quarter Master, 24 Jan. 91.
Lieut. J. M. Home, Staff Corps............	18 Feb. 86	Wing Officer, 31 Jan. 94.—Officiating Adjutant.
Lieut. W. D. Turner, Staff Corps	17 Sept.90	Wing Officer, 7 Oct. 92.
Captain J. G. Robinson, Staff Corps ...	14 Jan. 91	Officiating Wing Officer.—From 1 Battalion.
Lieut. H. A. K. Gough, Staff Corps	31 Aug. 91	Officiating Wing Officer.—On special duty, Gilgit.
2nd Lieut. G. M. Wylie, Staff Corps ...	28 Jan. 93	Officiating Wing Officer.
Surgeon Major A. Duncan, *MD.*	30 Mar. 90	In medical charge, 10 Dec. 94.

3rd Goorkha (Rifle) Regiment (Raised 24 April 1815).
"Delhi"—"Ahmed Khel"—"Afghanistan, 1878-80"—"Burma, 1885-87."
FIRST BATTALION.
Head Quarters at **Almora**. *Uniform, Dark Green. Facings, Black.*

Rank, Names, and Corps.	Army Rank.	Remarks.
Major C. Pulley, Staff Corps	1 July 87	Commandant, 26 Apr. 94.—Commanding at Almora.
Captain A. W. Lyster, Staff Corps	8 Mar. 87	2nd in Command and Wing Commander, 26 Apr. 94.
Captain G. H. Loch, Staff Corps	21 Aug. 89	Wing Comdr., 26 Apr. 94.—Comdt. Surma Valley Military Police.
Captain W. H. Savage, Staff Corps	9 Sept.93	Wing Commander, 26 Apr. 94.
Lieut. V. A. Ormsby, Staff Corps.........	7 Feb. 85	Wing Officer and Adjutant, 15 Jan. 91.—Station Staff Officer.
Lieut. A. C. Hickley, Staff Corps.........	8 Dec. 86	Wing Officer and Quarter Master, 15 Jan. 91.
Lieut. W. G. L. Beynon, Staff Corps ...	11 Dec. 89	Wing Officer, 28 Nov. 91.—On special duty, Gilgit.
Lieut. C. E. Bliss, Staff Corps.............	8 May 89	Wing Officer, 12 July 92.
Lieut. G. W. M. West, Staff Corps......	5 Feb. 91	Wing Officer, 26 Apr. 94.
Lieut. W. M. Brown, Staff Corps.........	26 July 91	Wing Officer, 20 Aug. 94.
Lieut. J. G. Edwardes, Staff Corps	24 Nov. 91	Officiating Wing Officer.
Lieut. A. B. Tillard, Staff Corps	30 Jan. 92	Officiating Wing Officer.
Brig.Surg.Lt.Col.J.C.G.Carmichael, *MD*	1 Apr. 88	In medical charge, 13 Feb. 83.—Furlough. Officiating in medical charge.

SECOND BATTALION.—*Raised Jan.* 1887.
Head Quarters at **Lansdowne**. *Uniform, Dark Green. Facings, Black.*

Rank, Names, and Corps.	Army Rank.	Remarks.
Lt.Colonel H. D. Hutchinson, S. C.	6 July 93	Commandant, 15 Jan. 91.
Major H. S. Wheatley, Staff Corps	3 Aug. 90	2nd in Command and Wing Comdr., 28 Jan. 91.—Furlough.
Captain H. Rose, Staff Corps...............	11 May 89	Wing Commander, 11 June 92.—Officiating 2nd in Command.
Captain N. G. Woodyatt, Staff Corps ...	12 May 94	Wing Officer, 15 Jan. 91.—Offg. Wing Commander.—S.S.O.
Lieut. F. A. Kingston, Staff Corps	30 Jan. 86	Wing Officer and Adjutant, 27 Mar. 91.
Lieut. A. P. Bateman-Champain, S. C.	30 Jan. 86	Wing Officer and Quarter Master, 15 Jan. 91.
L'eut. W. R. Brakspear, Staff Corps ...	18 Dec. 89	Wing Officer, 28 June 91.
Lieut. C. S. Eastmead, Staff Corps	31 July 89	Wing Officer, 15 Jan. 91.
Lieut. W. C. French, Staff Corps.........	15 June 92	Officiating Wing Officer.—Furlough.
Surgeon Lt.Colonel F. A. Smyth	1 Oct. 89	In medical charge, 29 Jan. 91.—Furlough.
Surgeon Lieut. A. O. Hubbard	27 July 92	Officiating in medical charge.

Corps under the Orders of the Government of India. 446

4th Goorkha (*Rifle*) Regiment (late Extra Goorkha Regt.).—Raised 6 Aug. 1857.
"ALI MUSJID"—"KABUL, 1879"—"KANDAHAR, 1880"—"AFGHANISTAN, 1878-80."

FIRST BATTALION.
On Field Service, Waziristan. *Uniform, Dark Green. Facings, Black.*

RANK, NAMES, AND CORPS.	ARMY RANK.	REMARKS.
Lt.Colonel C. A. Mercer, Staff Corps ...	8 June 93	Commandant, 19 Aug. 90.
Major F. M. Rundall, DSO. Staff Corps	9 Mar. 92	2nd in Command and Wing Commander, 19 Aug. 90.
Captain M. T. Thomson, Staff Corps ...	11 May 89	Wing Commander, 19 Aug. 90.
Captain G. R. Brown, Staff Corps	22 Jan. 90	Wing Officer, 12 June 83.—Furlough.
Captain E. E. Couper, Staff Corps	11 Aug. 91	Wing Officer, 22 July 84.
Captain E. C. Ryall, Staff Corps	9 Sept.93	Wing Officer, 6 March 86.
Captain G. H. C. Colomb, Staff Corps ...	6 Feb. 95	Wing Officer and Adjutant, 16 Sept. 87.
Lieut. W. G. Walker, Staff Corps	29 Aug. 85	Wing Officer and Quarter Master, 19 Aug. 90.—Furlough.
Lieut. D. C. Young, Staff Corps	17 Feb. 92	Officiating Wing Officer.—Furlough.
Lieut. B. M. L. Brodhurst, Staff Corps	3 Dec. 94	Officiating Wing Officer.
Surgeon Major G. S. Griffiths	30 Sept.86	In medical charge, 7 Sept. 93.

SECOND BATTALION.—Raised 10 April 1886.
Head Quarters at Bukloh. *Uniform, Dark Green. Facings, Black.*

RANK, NAMES, AND CORPS.	ARMY RANK.	REMARKS.
Lt.Colonel Sir C. H. Leslie, Bt. Staff C.	11 Jan. 93	Commandant, 11 Aug. 92.
Major A.G. F. Browne, DSO. Staff Corps	28 Oct. 91	2nd in Command and Wing Commander, 14 Oct. 93.—Furlough.
Captain P. M. Carnegy, Staff Corps ...	27 July 89	Wing Commander, 31 Oct. 93.
Captain H. Hamilton, Staff Corps	13 Aug. 90	Wing Officer, 22 May 86.—Assist. Military Accountant, 2nd Class.
Captain P. Malcolm, Staff Corps	11 Aug. 91	Wing Officer, 1 May 86.—Offg. D.A.A.Gen. Meerut District.
Lieut. A. H. Battye, Staff Corps	12 Nov. 84	Wing Officer and Adjutant, 10 Aug. 92.
Lieut. A. Grant, Staff Corps	7 Feb. 85	Wing Officer, 20 July 89.—Furlough.
Lieut. H. C. C. Ducat, Staff Corps......	30 Jan. 86	Wing Officer and Quarter Master, 13 Dec. 89.
Lieut. C. R. M. Hutchinson, Staff Corps	24 Sept.90	Wing Officer, 31 Oct. 93.
Lieut. R. E. Travers, Staff Corps......	12 Feb. 91	Officiating Wing Officer.
Lieut. G. B. Sanford, Staff Corps	17 Jan. 92	Officiating Wing Officer.
Lieut. R. E. A. Hamilton, Scots Fus. ...	24 Feb. 93	Officiating Wing Officer.
Surgeon Lt.Colonel A. S. Reid, MB	30 Mar. 92	In medical charge, 24 Oct. 87.

NOTE.—These Regiments, when acting with other Bengal Native Troops, rank—the 1st Goorkhas after the 10th Native Infantry; the 2nd, 3rd, and 4th Goorkhas after the 15th Native Infantry.

₊ The 5th GOORKHA REGIMENT, being attached to the Punjab Frontier Force, is placed following the 6th Punjab Infantry, four pages farther on.

PUNJAB FRONTIER FORCE.
Head Quarters at Abbottabad.
Raised, 18 May 1849. Remodelled, 15 Feb. 1851. *Designation changed,* 19 Sept. 1865.

NOTE.—When Regiments of the Punjab Frontier Force are acting with other Bengal Native Troops, they take rank according to the dates on which they were raised, thus—The Guide Cavalry, and 1st, 2nd, 3rd, and 5th Punjab Cavalry rank immediately after the 8th Bengal Cavalry; the Corps of Guides Infantry, the 1st, 2nd, 3rd, and 4th Sikh Infantry, and the 1st, 2nd, 4th, 5th, and 6th Punjab Infantry after the 15th Native Infantry and the 3rd Goorkhas; the 5th Goorkhas after the 32nd Native Infantry.

STAFF.

Lieut.General Sir W. S. A. Lockhart, KCB. CSI. Bengal Infantry	1 Apr. 94	Commandant, 1 Apr. 92.—Commanding Waziristan Field Force
Bt. Major A. R. Martin, Staff Corps	1 Sept.91	Aide de Camp, Assistant Adjutant General, 1 Feb. 92.—From 1 Bn. 5 Goorkhas—Waziristan Field Force.
Captain J. G. Ramsay, Staff Corps	11 Feb. 86	Dep. Assist. Adj. Gen., 13 Apr.93.—From 24 Bengal Inf.—Furl.
Captain M. H. S. Grover, Staff Corps ...	11 Sept.87	Officiating Dep. Assist. Adj. General.—From 2 Punjab Cavalry.—Waziristan Field Force.
Captain A. A. E. Campbell, Staff Corps	10 May 93	Dep. Assist. Adj. Gen. for Musk. 13 May 94.—From 25 Bengal Inf.
Surgeon Colonel L. D. Spencer, MD. ...	24 Oct. 92	Principal Medical Officer, 21 Nov. 93.—Waziristan Field Force.

FOUR REGIMENTS OF PUNJAB CAVALRY.

1st (Prince Albert Victor's Own) Punjab Cavalry (Raised 18 May 1849).
"DELHI"—"LUCKNOW" (*Relief and Capture*)—"AHMED KHEL"—"AFGHANISTAN, 1878-80."
Head Quarters at Dera Ismail Khan. *Uniform, Dark Blue. Facings, Red.*

RANK, NAMES, AND CORPS.	ARMY RANK.	REMARKS.
Lt.Colonel D. S. Cuninghame, Staff C.	1 Dec. 91	Commandant, 29 Oct. 94.
Major W. A. D. O'Mealy, Staff Corps...	8 Jan. 93	2nd in Command and Squadron Commander, 29 Oct. 94.—Waziristan Field Force.
p.s.c. Captain J. S. E. Western, Staff C...	12 Feb. 89	Squadron Commander, 11 Feb. 90.—Waziristan Field Force.
Captain G. B. Unwin, Staff Corps	25 May 89	Squadron Commander, 15 Dec. 93.—Waziristan Field Force.
Captain D. G. L. Shaw, Staff Corps ...	21 June 90	Squadron Commander, 29 Oct. 94.—Waziristan Field Force.
Captain C. F. Minchin, Staff Corps......	10 May 93	Squadron Officer, 11 Feb. 90.—Political Assist. 3rd Class, Punjab.
Captain A. W. Chaldecott, Staff Corps	28 July 94	Squadron Officer and Adj., 19 Sept.90.—Waziristan Field Force.
Lieut. V. B. Fane, Staff Corps	12 Nov. 84	Squadron Officer, 1 April 91.—Waziristan Field Force.
Lieut. W. F. C. Tayler, Staff Corps	24 July 90	Squadron Officer, 15 Dec. 93.—Sick Furlough.
Lieut. L.A. G. Hanmer, Staff Corps......	29 Oct. 90	Squadron Officer, 29 Oct. 94.
Lt.E.W.M'K.Ballantyne, S.Wales Bord	22 Feb. 93	Officiating Squadron Officer.—Waziristan Field Force.
Lieut. R. St. C. Battine, 16 Lancers	23 May 91	Officiating Squadron Officer.—Waziristan Field Force.
Surgeon Major P. de H. Haig...............	30 Sept.87	In medical charge, 8 July 81.—Waziristan Field Force.

2nd Punjab Cavalry (Raised April 1849).
"DELHI"—"LUCKNOW" (*Relief and Capture*)—"AHMED KHEL"—"AFGHANISTAN, 1878-80."
Head Quarters at Dera Ghazee Khan. *Uniform, Scarlet. Facings, Dark Blue.*

RANK, NAMES, AND CORPS.	ARMY RANK.	REMARKS.
Lt.Colonel L. T. Bishop, Staff Corps ...	2 Mar. 92	Commandant, 28 March 94.
Major C. J. L. Stuart, Staff Corps.........	27 June 94	2nd in Command and Squadron Commander, 28 March 94.
Captain A. C. Batten, Staff Corps	10 Sept.86	Squadron Commander, 11 Aug. 87.—D.A.A. Gen. Bundelcund.
Captain M. H. S. Grover, Staff Corps...	11 Sept.87	Squadron Commander, 16 Aug. 89.—Offg. D.A.A.Gen. Punjab Field Force.—Waziristan Field Force.
Captain W. W. Norman, Staff Corps ...	23 Oct. 91	Squadron Commander, 24 Mar. 92.—Comdt. Zhob Levy Corps.
Captain J. Jones, Staff Corps...............	22 Jan. 92	Squadron Commander, 24 March 92.
Captain W. N. Campbell, Staff Corps...	6 Feb. 93	Squadron Commander, 24 March 92.—Burmah Military Police.
Lieut. C. A. Luck, Staff Corps	1 Sept.85	Squadron Commander, 8 Sept. 94.
Lieut. C. C. Cook, Staff Corps............	16 Feb. 86	Squadron Officer, 27 May 93.—Officiating Squadron Comdr.
Lieut. F. J. D. Henslowe, Staff Corps ...	24 Oct. 89	Squadron Officer, 24 March 92.—Adj. and 2nd in Command, Zhob Levy Corps.
Lieut. A. G. Crocker, Staff Corps.........	5 Oct. 91	Squadron Officer, 10 Oct. 94.
Lieut. E. Barnes, Staff Corps...............	15 Feb. 92	Squadron Officer, 8 Sept. 94.
Lieut. A. W. Peck, Staff Corps	10 Mar. 92	Squadron Officer, 20 May 93.—Officiating Adjutant.
Lieut. A. D. Macpherson, Staff Corps ...	6 Apr. 93	Officiating Squadron Officer.
Surgeon Captain J. Garvie	31 Mar. 87	In medical charge, 5 Feb. 91.

446a *Corps under the Orders of the Government of India.*

3rd Punjab Cavalry (Raised 18 May 1849).
"KANDAHAR, 1880"—"AFGHANISTAN, 1879-80."
On Field Service, **Waziristan.** *Uniform, Blue. Facings, Red.*

Rank, Names, and Corps.	Army Rank.	Remarks.
Lt.Colonel J. Davidson, Staff Corps	24 Mar. 89	Commandant, 25 Nov. 92.—Furlough.
Lt.Colonel C. C. Egerton, DSO. Staff C.	1 Sept.91	2nd in Com. and Squad. Comdr. 25 Nov. 92.—Offg. Commandant.
Lt.Colonel C. G. Mansel, Staff Corps	8 July 94	Squadron Commander, 5 Aug. 87.—Offg. 2nd in Command.
Major W. Lambert, Staff Corps	12 Nov. 93	Squadron Commander, 1st Sept. 89.—Assistant Judge Advocate
Captain L. S. Hyde Baker, Staff Corps	28 Oct. 88	Squadron Commander, 25 Nov. 89. [General, Megan Meer.
Captain G. Murray, Staff Corps	14 Jan. 91	Squadron Commander, 25 Jan. 93.
Captain A. R. Dick, Staff Corps	22 Jan. 92	Officiating Squadron Commander.
Captain D. C. Phillott, Staff Corps	14 Jan. 91	Squadron Officer, 5 Aug. 87.—Furlough.
Captain H. Kennedy, Staff Corps	28 Feb. 91	Squadron Officer, 19 May 91.—Furlough.
Lieut. A. M'I. Campbell, Staff Corps	30 Jan. 86	Squadron Officer and Adjutant, 25 Nov.92.
Lieut. G. W. Johnson, Staff Corps	28 Jan. 89	Squadron Officer, 5 Jan. 93.—Burmah Military Police.
Lieut. J. C. Sherer, Staff Corps	3 Nov. 89	Squadron Officer, 24 July 94.
Lieut. F. H. Goldthorp, Staff Corps	12 May 92	Officiating Squadron Officer.
Surgeon Major S. F. Bigger, MB.	30 Mar. 90	In medical charge, 13 April 86.

5th Punjab Cavalry (Raised 18 May 1849).
"DELHI"—"LUCKNOW" (*Relief and Capture*)—"CHARASIA"—"KABUL, 1879"—"AFGHANISTAN, 1878-80."
Head Quarters at **Rajanpore.** *Uniform, Dark Green. Facings, Scarlet.*

𝔙ℭ Colonel W. J. Vousden, Staff Corps	26 July 94	Commandant, 22 June 90.
Major C. F. Gambier, Staff Corps	1 Sept.91	2nd in Command and Squadron Commander, 16 Oct. 94.
Major A. P. Williamson, Staff Corps	11 Feb. 95	2nd in Command and Squadron Commander, 16 Oct. 94. Squadron Commander,
Captain H. Templer, Staff Corps	1 May 89	Squadron Commander, 4 Mar. 89.
Captain C. G. F. Edwards, Staff Corps	13 Aug. 90	Squadron Commander, 29 Mar. 90.
Captain F. H. Yate, Staff Corps	22 Jan. 90	Squadron Officer, 13 Aug. 84.
Captain H. I. E. Palmer, Staff Corps	5 Dec. 94	Squadron Officer, 4 Mar. 89.
Lieut. G. E. D. Elsmie, Staff Corps	29 Aug. 85	Squadron Officer and Adjutant, 4 Mar. 89.
Lieut. L. N. Leeds, Staff Corps	30 Jan. 86	Squadron Officer, 29 Mar. 90.
Lieut. H. M. Allen, Staff Corps	25 Mar. 88	Squadron Officer, 18 Nov. 91.
Lieut. A. E. M'Barnet, Staff Corps	24 Aug. 90	Officiating Squadron Officer.—Furlough.
Lieut. A. G. Vivian, Staff Corps	25 Sept. 91	Officiating Squadron Officer.
Lieut. F. M'Conaghey, Irish Regiment	2 July 92	Officiating Squadron Officer.
Surgeon Major C. B. Hunter	31 Mar. 91	In medical charge, 14 Jan. 89.—Offg. Civil and Jail, Seonee.
Surgeon Lieut. H. G. Melville, MB.	27 July 92	Officiating in medical charge.—Waziristan Field Force.

Establishment of each Regiment of Punjab Cavalry.—8 Troops; Commandant; 4 Squadron Commanders; 4 Squadron Officers; 1 Medical Officer; 4 Risaldars; 4 Risaidars; 1 Wordie Major; 8 Jamadars; 8 Kote Dafedars; 56 Dafedars; 8 Trumpeters; 536 Sowars.

Corps of Guides (*Queen's Own*) (*Cavalry and Infantry.—Raised for General Service 14 Dec. 1846*).—*Infantry Regimental Centre, Hoti Mardan.*
The Royal Cypher within the Garter. "PUNJAB"--"MOOLTAN"—"GOOJERAT"—"DELHI"—"ALI MUSJID"—"KABUL, 1879"--"AFGHANISTAN, 1878-80."
At **Mardan.** *Uniform, Drab. Facings, Red.*
Honorary Colonel—Field Marshal **H.R.H. Albert Edward,** *Prince of Wales and Duke of Cornwall,*
KG. KT. KP. GCB. GCSI. GCMG. GCIE.

𝔙ℭ Col. A. G. Hammond, CB. DSO. S.C.	12 Feb. 90	Commandant, 1 Feb. 91.
Lt.Colonel F. D. Battye, Staff Corps	11 Jan. 93	2nd in Command and Wing Commander, 17 Feb. 91.
Captain R. B. Adams, Staff Corps	11 Sept.87	2nd in Command and Squadron Commander, 17 Feb. 91.
p.s.c. Capt. G. J. Younghusband, Staff C.	1 May 89	Squadron Commander, 22 Feb. 88.
Captain G. R. Egerton, Staff Corps	13 Aug. 90	Squadron Commander, 17 Feb. 91.—Waziristan Field Force.
Captain F. Campbell, Staff Corps	13 Aug. 90	Wing Commander, 27 May 91.—D. A. A. General for Musketry. Wing Commander.
Captain F. J. H. Barton, Staff Corps	23 Apr. 92	Squadron Officer, 27 Oct. 86.
Lieut. F. G. H. Davies, Staff Corps	29 Aug. 85	Squadron Officer and Adjutant, 27 Sept. 87.
Lieut. G. M. Baldwin, Staff Corps	30 Jan. 86	Squadron Officer, 31 Dec. 91.—Offg. Squadron Commander.
Lieut. H. L. S. MacLean, Staff Corps	17 Feb. 91	Squadron Officer, 4 Dec. 91. [derabad.
Captain C. L. M. Rich, Staff Corps	23 Apr. 92	Wing Officer, 10 April 85.—Offg. Assist. Judge Adv.Gen., Secun-
Captain G. B. Hodson, Staff Corps	10 May 93	Wing Officer, 27 Sept. 87.—Furlough.
Lieut. H. W. Codrington, Staff Corps	2 Apr. 89	Wing Officer and Adjutant, 2 Apr. 89.
Lieut. P. C. Eliott-Lockhart, Staff Corps	5 June 89	Wing Officer and Quarter Master, 31 Aug. 92.
Lieut. A. R. H. Garden, Staff Corps	25 Sept.89	Wing Officer, 17 Feb. 91.—Sick Furlough.
Lieut. A. B. Dew, Staff Corps	16 Dec. 89	Wing Officer, 27 May 91.—On special duty, Gilgit.
Lieut. A. J. Ommanney, Staff Corps	13 Feb. 93	Wing Officer, 30 Nov. 94.
Lieut. A. C. Stewart, Staff Corps	21 Mar. 93	Offg. Squadron Officer and Offg. A.D.C. to Sir R. C. Stewart. Officiating Wing Officer.
2nd Lieut. J. S. Bogle, Staff Corps	23 Nov. 92	Officiating Squadron Officer.
Surgeon Captain A. J. Macnab	31 Mar. 90	In medical charge, 10 Nov. 94.—And Civil, Mardan.

Establishment.—Commandant; 5 Wing and Squadron Commanders; 9 Wing and Squadron Officers; 1 Medical Officer. *Cavalry.*—6 Troops, with 3 Risaldars; 3 Risaidars; 1 Wordie Major; 6 Jamadars; 6 Kote Dafedars; 42 Dafedars; 6 Trumpeters; 394 Sowars; 8 Camel Sowars; 1 Native Doctor. *Infantry.*—8 Companies, with 8 Subadars; 8 Jamadars; 40 Havildars; 40 Naicks; 16 Buglers; 2 Native Doctors; 800 Sepoys.

ARTILLERY.
At Edwardesabad. **No. 1 Kohat Mountain Battery.**
Linked with Nos. 2, 3 and 4 Mountain Batteries.
"PEIWAR KOTAL"—"KABUL, 1879"—"AFGHANISTAN, 1878-80."

Captain G. F. W. St. John, R. Artillery	22 Oct. 88	Commandant, 8 July 90.—Furlough.
Captain O. C. Williamson, R. Artillery	1 Jan. 92	Officiating Commandant.
Lieut. A. W. Money, Royal Artillery	29 Apr. 85	Subaltern, 75 Apr. 89.—Sick Furlough.
Lieut. T. R. C. Hudson, Royal Artillery	29 Apr. 85	Subaltern, 6 Dec. 94.—From No. 4 Mountain Battery.
Lieut. D. G. Seagrim, Royal Artillery	24 July 86	Subaltern, 26 Apr. 90.
Lieut. R. E. Home, Royal Artillery	17 Feb. 91	Officiating Subaltern.

Corps under the Orders of the Government of India. 447

At Kohat. **No. 2 Derajat Mountain Battery.**
Linked with Nos. 1, 3 and 4 Mountain Batteries.
"CHARASIA"—"KABUL, 1879"—"KANDAHAR, 1880"—"AFGHANISTAN, 1878-80."

Rank, Names, and Corps.	Army Rank.	Remarks.
Captain J. L. Parker, Royal Artillery...	7 Oct. 91	Commandant, 29 Nov. 93.
Lieut. H. E. J. Brake, Royal Artillery ...	18 Feb. 86	Subaltern, 1 Apr. 93.—With Punjab Garrison Battery.
Lieut. R. H. Hare, Royal Artillery	24 July 86	Subaltern, 5 Nov. 91.—With Section in Kurram Valley.
Lieut. J. A. Stewart, Royal Artillery ...	16 Feb. 90	Subaltern, 7 Oct. 91.

On Field Service, Waziristan. **No. 3 Peshawur Mountain Battery.**
Linked with Nos. 1, 2 and 4 Mountain Batteries.
"AFGHANISTAN, 1878-79."

Captain F. H. J. Birch, Royal Artillery	24 Mar. 86	Commandant, 21 Sept. 87.
Lieut. G. R. Lamb, Royal Artillery	29 Apr. 85	Subaltern, 16 July 88.—Furlough.
Lieut. G. M'K. Franks, Royal Artillery	23 July 91	Subaltern, 13 Dec. 91.
Lieut. R. P. Molesworth, Royal Artillery	23 July 90	Subaltern, 30 Nov. 92.
Lieut. J. E. L. Bruce, Royal Artillery	15 Feb. 92	Subaltern, 29 Oct. 93.

At Abbottabad. **No. 4 Hazara Mountain Battery.**
Linked with Nos. 1, 2 and 3 Mountain Batteries.
"ALI MUSJID"—"KABUL, 1879"—"AFGHANISTAN, 1878-80"—"BURMA, 1885-87."

Captain T. W. G. Bryan, Royal Artillery	13 Nov. 88	Commandant, 18 Dec. 91.—Furlough.
Captain F. H. S. Giles, Royal Artillery	29 Oct. 91	Officiating Commandant.—From Punjab Garrison Battery.
Lieut. T. R. C. Hudson, Royal Artillery	29 Apr. 85	Subaltern, 25 March 91.—With No. 1 Mountain Battery.
Lieut. R. St. G. Gorton, Royal Artillery	18 Feb. 86	Subaltern, 29 Jan. 90.
Lieut. H. A. Reid, Royal Artillery	18 Feb. 86	Subaltern, 13 Apr. 91.
Lieut. A. Le M. Bray, Royal Artillery...	17 Feb. 91	Subaltern, 7 Jan. 93.

At Kohat. **Punjab Garrison Battery.**

Captain F. H. S. Giles, Royal Artillery	29 Oct. 91	Commandant, 22 March 94.—With No. 4 Mountain Battery.
Lieut. H. E. J. Brake, Royal Artillery...	18 Feb. 86	Officiating Commandant.—From No. 2 Mountain Battery.

Establishment of Nos. 1 and 3 Mountain Batteries.—1 Commandant; 3 Subalterns; 1 Subadar; 2 Jamadars; 1 Havildar Major; 1 Pay and Quarter Master Havildar; 6 Havildars; 6 Naicks; 2 Trumpeters; 88 Gunners; 3 Havildars of Drivers; 6 Naicks of Drivers; 138 Drivers; 1 Farrier; 1 Salootri.
Establishment of Nos. 2 and 4 Mountain Batteries.—Commandant; 3 Subalterns; 1 Subadar; 2 Jamadars; 1 Havildar Major; 1 Pay and Quarter Master Havildar; 6 Havildars; 6 Naicks; 80 Gunners; 2 Trumpeters; 3 Havildars of Drivers; 6 Naicks of Drivers; 112 Drivers; 1 Farrier; 1 Salootrie.
Establishment of the Punjab Garrison Battery.—Commandant; 1 Subadar; 1 Jamadar; 6 Havildars; 6 Naicks; 1 Trumpeter; 60 Gunners.
Note.—One Subadar Major and one Trumpet Major are allowed for the Artillery of the Force.

FOUR REGIMENTS OF SIKH INFANTRY.—Raised 10 Dec. 1846.

1st Sikh Infantry.—*Linked with 3rd and 4th Sikh Infantry.—Regimental Centre, Edwardesabad*
"PUNJAB"—"ALI MUSJID"—"AFGHANISTAN, 1878-79."
On Field Service, Waziristan. *Uniform, Drab. Facings, Yellow.*

Major A. C. Bunny, Staff Corps.............	30 Oct. 91	Commandant, 11 May 94.—And Comdg. at Edwardesabad. 2nd in Command and Wing Commander.
Captain W. J. K. Dobbin, Staff Corps...	13 Oct. 88	Wing Commander, 30 Nov. 92.—Officiating 2nd in Command.
Captain W. C. Barratt, Staff Corps	5 Dec. 94	Wing Officer, 20 May 87.—Officiating Wing Commander.
Captain K. O. Burne, Staff Corps	6 Feb. 95	Wing Officer, 30 Sept. 87.
Lieut. H A. Cooper, Staff Corps	29 Aug. 85	Wing Officer and Quarter Master, 22 Oct. 88.—Offg. Adjutant. Station Staff Officer, Edwardesabad.
Lieut. H. A. F. Magrath, Staff Corps	1 Feb. 86	Wing Officer, 13 Oct. 90.—Officiating Quarter Master.
Lieut. W. H. Manning, Staff Corps	25 Aug. 86	Wing Officer, 27 Sept. 91.—Furlough.
Lieut. G. D. L. Chatterton, Staff Corps	13 Mar. 90	Officiating Wing Officer.
Lieut. H. A. H. Rice, Staff Corps	22 Apr. 93	Officiating Wing Officer.
Surgeon Captain H. Fooks	1 Apr. 86	In medical charge, 30 July 89.

2nd (or Hill) Sikh Infantry.—*Raised in 1846.*
Linked with 2nd and 6th Punjab Infantry.—Regimental Centre, Kohat.
"PUNJAB"—"AHMED KHEL"—"KANDAHAR, 1880"—"AFGHANISTAN, 1878-80."
Head Quarters at Dera Ghazee Khan. Left Wing at Dera Ismail Khan. Detachments at Droog, &c.
Uniform, Drab. Facings, Red.

Colonel F. E. Hastings, C.B. Gen. List, Inf.	7 Mar. 85	Commandant, 1 Apr. 91.—Furlough.
Major B. M. Allen, Staff Corps	24 Apr. 92	2nd in Command and Wing Commander, 1 Apr. 91.—Offg. Comdt.
Major C. G. M. Fasken, Staff Corps	13 June 94	Wing Commander, 29 June 89.—Offg. 2nd in Command.
Captain C. Davidson, Staff Corps	14 Jan. 91	Officiating Wing Commander at Dera Ismail Khan.—From 2 Punjab Infantry.
Captain T. Jermyn, Staff Corps	22 Oct. 92	Wing Commander, 23 May 84.—Officiating Wing Commander.
Lieut. A. H. Eustace, Staff Corps	6 May 85	Wing Officer and Adjutant, 30 Sept. 87.—Furlough.
Lieut. H. C. Vesey, Staff Corps	25 Nov. 85	Wing Officer, 11 May 88.—At Droog.
Lieut. P. B. B. Forster, Staff Corps	10 Nov. 86	Wing Officer and Quarter Master, 29 June 89.
Lieut. E. B. O. Boddam, Staff Corps ...	5 June 89	Wing Officer, 18 Sept. 91.—With 2 Battalion 5 Goorkhas.
Lieut. G. L. Carter, Staff Corps	5 Oct. 90	Officiating Wing Officer.
Lieut. R. S. Phillips, Staff Corps	10 June 92	Officiating Wing Officer at Dera Ismail Khan.
2nd Lieut. C. P. Wynter, Suffolk Regt	17 Jan. 91	Officiating Wing Officer at Droog.
Surgeon Major J. W. Rodgers	2 Apr. 93	In medical charge, 7 Nov. 86.

3rd Sikh Infantry.—*Raised in 1847.*
Linked with 1st and 4th Sikh Infantry.—Regimental Centre, Edwardesabad.
"KABUL, 1879"—"KANDAHAR, 1880"—"AFGHANISTAN, 1879-80."
On Field Service, Waziristan. *Uniform, Drab. Facings, Black.*

Colonel W. O. Thompson, Staff Corps	1 Feb. 95	Commandant, 1 Feb. 91.
Major J. A. H. Pollock, Staff Corps	13 June 94	2nd in Command and Wing Commander, 13 Sept. 92.—Furl.
Captain W. Cook, Staff Corps...............	10 Sept. 86	Wing Commander, 22 Mar. 93.—With 30 Madras Infantry.
Captain E. W. Codrington, Staff Corps	14 Jan. 91	Wing Commander, 22 Mar. 93.—Offg. 2nd in Command.
Captain T. Quin, Staff Corps...............	11 Aug. 91	Officiating Wing Commander.—From 4 Sikh Infantry.
Lieut. J. H. B. Beresford, Staff Corps ...	23 May 85	Wing Officer and Adjutant, 23 Dec. 87.
Lieut. F. H. Taylor, Staff Corps............	11 Feb. 88	Wing Officer and Quarter Master, 14 Dec. 89.
Lieut. C. H. Davies, Staff Corps	1 Sept. 89	Wing Officer, 27 June 92.
Lieut. C. E. De L. Solbé, Staff Corps ...	3 Mar. 89	Wing Officer, 1 Nov. 92.—Furlough.
Lieut. H. E. Scott, Staff Corps	18 Dec. 89	Wing Officer, 11 May 93.
Lt. A. F. Ferguson-Davie, Staff Corps	12 Oct. 91	Wing Officer, 11 May 93.
Lieut. J. F. Finnis, Manchester Regt....	21 Oct. 91	Officiating Wing Officer.
Surgeon Major A. W. Mackenzie, M.D.	31 Mar. 89	In medical charge, 4 Sept. 90.

Corps under the Orders of the Government of India.

4th Sikh Infantry.—Raised in 1846.

Linked with 1st and 3rd Sikh Infantry.—Regimental Centre, Edwardesabad.

"Pegu"—"Delhi."

Head Quarters at Edwardesabad. Uniform, Drab. Facings, Emerald Green.

RANK, NAMES, AND CORPS.	ARMY RANK.	REMARKS.
Lt.Colonel C. Dempster, Staff Corps ...	9 July 94	Commandant, 27 Sept. 92.
Major V. C. Tonnochy, Staff Corps	9 Aug. 93	2nd in Command and Wing Commander, 27 Sept. 92.
Captain T. Quin, Staff Corps	11 Aug. 91	Wing Commander, 26 Feb. 93.—With 3 Sikh Infantry.
Captain C. B. Reid, Staff Corps...........	22 Oct. 92	Wing Officer, 4 Jan. 84.—Officiating Wing Commander.
Captain H. G. Burton, Staff Corps	22 Oct. 92	Wing Officer, 16 Sept. 86.
Captain E.W. S. K. Maconchy, DSO.S.C.	28 Jan. 93	Wing Officer, 29 Nov. 86.—Commandant Kuram Militia.
Captain K. J. Buchanan, Staff Corps ...	1 Feb. 94	Wing Officer, 30 Sept. 87.—Furlough.
Captain R. W. Falcon, Staff Corps......	10 Mar. 94	Wing Officer, 30 Sept. 87.—Offg. Dist. Recruiting Officer, Sikh [Dist.
Lieut. J. F. Whyte, Staff Corps...........	1 Sept. 84	Wing Officer, 6 July 88.—Attaché Foreign Department.
Lieut. R. Harman, DSO. Staff Corps ...	25 Aug. 86	Wing Officer, 1 Mar. 90.—Officiating Adjutant.
Lieut. W. Beadon, Staff Corps	4 Nov. 89	Wing Officer, 24 Oct. 92.—Officiating Quarter Master.
Lieut. A. S. Hamilton, Staff Corps	3 Oct. 89	Officiating Wing Officer.—With Indian Contingent, British Central Africa.—Furlough. Officiating Wing Officer.
Surgeon Captain B. J. Singh	31 Jan. 91	In medical charge, 16 July 94.

Establishment of each Regiment of Sikh Infantry.—8 Companies—Commandant; 2 Wing Commanders; 5 Wing Officers; 1 Medical Officer; 8 Subadars; 8 Jamadars; 40 Havildars; 40 Naicks; 16 Drummers; 800 Sepoys.

SIX REGIMENTS OF PUNJAB INFANTRY.

1st Punjab Infantry.—Raised in 1849.

Linked with 4th and 5th Punjab Infantry.—Regimental Centre, Dera Ismail Khan.

"Delhi"—"Afghanistan, 1878-79."

Head Quarters at Abbottabad. Uniform, Dark Green. Facings, Red (piping).

RANK, NAMES, AND CORPS.	ARMY RANK.	REMARKS.
Colonel C. C. Brownlow, Staff Corps ...	1 Sept. 91	Commandant, 1 Apr. 91.—Furlough.
Captain C. B. Brownlow, Staff Corps ...	10 Sept. 86	2nd in Command and Wing Comdr., 16 Nov. 93.—Offg. Comdt.
Captain E. L. Hight, Staff Corps.........	11 May 89	Wing Commander, 16 Nov. 93.—Sick Furlough. Wing Officer.
Captain W. Kirkpatrick, Staff Corps ...	25 Aug. 94	Wing Officer, 30 Sept. 87.—Furlough.
Lieut. H. R. Fagan, Staff Corps	29 Aug. 85	Wing Officer and Adjutant, 27 May 91.
Lieut. H. C. Sandford, Staff Corps	17 Mar. 90	Wing Officer and Quarter Master, 27 May 93.
Lieut. R. Martin, Highland Lt. Inf.......	15 June 93	Wing Officer, 2 Apr. 94.
Lieut. C. L. S. Browne, Wiltshire Regt.	6 Mar. 93	Officiating Wing Officer.
2nd Lieut. H. M. Turton, Scottish Rifles	18 June 93	Officiating Wing Officer.
Surgeon Captain F. R. Ozzard	30 Mar. 89	In medical charge, 6 Mar. 93.

2nd Punjab Infantry.—Raised in 1849.

Linked with 2nd Sikh Infantry and 6th Punjab Infantry.—Regimental Centre, Kohat.

"Delhi"—"Lucknow" (Relief and Capture)—"Peiwar Kotal"—"Afghanistan, 1878-79."

On Field Service, Waziristan. Uniform, Drab. Facings, Black.

RANK, NAMES, AND CORPS.	ARMY RANK.	REMARKS.
Major R. R. N. Sturt, Staff Corps	9 Mar. 93	Commandant, 1 June 94.
Captain G. W. B. Swiney, Staff Corps...	26 Aug. 87	2nd in Command and Wing Commander, 1 June 94.
Captain E. H. Rodwell, Staff Corps	30 Jan. 89	Wing Commander, 1 June 94.
Captain C. Davidson, Staff Corps	14 Jan. 91	Wing Officer, 15 Dec. 86.—With 2 Sikh Infantry.
Captain C. M. Eales, Staff Corps	22 Jan. 92	Wing Officer, 22 Aug. 87.
Captain A. Nicholls, Staff Corps	22 Oct. 92	Wing Officer, 26 Sept. 88.—Furlough.
Lieut. A. J. Caruana, Staff Corps	15 Sept. 88	Wing Officer and Adjutant, 18 Sept. 91.—Furlough.
Lieut. P. G. Shewell, Staff Corps	25 Nov. 85	Wing Officer, 13 Mar. 93.—Assist. Mil. Accountant, 1st Class.
Lieut. A. M. S. Elsmie, Staff Corps	3 May 90	Wing Officer and Quarter Master, 7 Nov. 93.
Lieut. E. Kirkpatrick, Staff Corps	14 June 92	Officiating Wing Officer.
2nd Lieut. J. B. Bowring, Staff Corps...	28 Jan. 93	Officiating Wing Officer.
Surgeon Captain A. H. Nott, MB.........	1 Oct. 87	In medical charge, 6 Sept. 91.—Officiating Civil, Hazeerabagh.
Surgeon Lieut. E. A. R. Newman, MB.	29 July 93	Officiating in medical charge.

4th Punjab Infantry.—Raised in 1849.

Linked with 1st and 5th Punjab Infantry.—Regimental Centre, Dera Ismail Khan.

"Delhi"—"Lucknow" (Relief and Capture)—"Afghanistan, 1879-80."

On Field Service, Waziristan. Uniform, Drab. Facings, Blue.

RANK, NAMES, AND CORPS.	ARMY RANK.	REMARKS.
Major O. C. Radford, Staff Corps.........	7 Dec. 88	Commandant, 5 Jan. 94.
Bt. Major W. du G. Gray, Staff Corps ...	1 Sept. 91	2nd in Command and Wing Commander, 5 Jan. 94.—D.A.A. Gen. Nerbudda.—Furlough.
Captain A. R. Browning, Staff Corps ...	13 Aug. 90	2nd in Command and Wing Commander, 5 Jan. 94.
Captain C. Schofield, Staff Corps	10 Mar. 94	Wing Commander, 5 Jan. 94.
Lieut. C. G. Prendergast, Staff Corps...	23 Aug. 84	Wing Officer and Adjutant, 10 Jan. 88.
Lieut. P. J. Miles, Staff Corps...............	1 Feb. 85	Wing Officer and Adjutant, 1 April 91—On special duty, Gilgit.
Lieut. F. W. B. Gray, Staff Corps.........	22 Jan. 90	Wing Officer, 5 Jan. 94.
Lieut. E. C. Creagh, Staff Corps	9 Dec. 91	Wing Officer, 5 Jan. 94.
Lieut. E. L. Swifte, Devon Regiment ...	1 Jan. 93	Wing Officer, 22 March 94.
2nd Lieut. E. E. Barwell, Staff Corps ...	3 Sept. 92	Wing Officer, 7 March 94.
Surgeon Captain W. H. W. Elliot	31 Mar. 87	In medical charge, 30 June 90.—Furlough.
Surgeon Lieut. G. Lamb, MB...............	29 June 94	Officiating in medical charge.

Corps under the Orders of the Government of India. 449.

5th Punjab Infantry.—*Raised in* 1849.

Linked with 1st *and* 4th *Punjab Infantry.—Regimental Centre, Dera Ismail Khan.*

"Peiwar Kotal"—"Charasia"—"Kabul, 1879"—"Afghanistan, 1878-80."

Head Quarters at Samana. *Uniform, Drab. Facings, Green.*

Rank, Names, and Corps.	Army Rank.	Remarks.
Major R. F. Jameson, Staff Corps	28 Oct. 91	Commandant, 16 Apr. 94.— And Commanding at Samana. 2nd in Command and Wing Commander.
Major F. P. L. White, Staff Corps	24 July 93	Wing Commander, 12 Aug. 90.—Officiating 2nd in Command.
Captain F. B. Mein, Staff Corps	11 May 89	Wing Officer, 1 Sept. 82.
Captain L. E. Cooper, Staff Corps	13 Aug. 90	Wing Officer, 11 Jan. 84.—Officiating Wing Commander.
Captain A. A. J. Johnstone, Staff Corps	22 Jan. 92	Wing Officer, 28 Feb. 85.—Officiating Staff Captain, Intelligence Branch, Quarter Master General's Department.
Captain P. Holland, Staff Corps	22 Oct. 92	Wing Officer, 30 Sept. 87.—Staff Captain, Quarter Master General's Department, Intelligence Branch.
Captain R. C. O. Creagh, Staff Corps	1 Sept. 94	Wing Officer, 12 Nov. 88.—Officiating Quarter Master.
Lieut. W. E. Venour, Staff Corps	2 Sept. 85	Wing Officer and Adjutant, 18 July 90.
Lieut. B. O. Roe, Staff Corps	20 Oct. 91	Officiating Quarter Master.
2nd Lieut. R. W. E. Knollys, Staff Corps	28 Jan. 93	Officiating Wing Officer. In medical charge.

6th Punjab Infantry.—(*Transferred from Bombay Presidency in* 1849. *Designation changed,* 4 *Aug.* 1856.)—*Linked with* 2nd *Sikh Infantry and* 2nd *Punjab Infantry.* —*Regimental Centre, Kohat.*

"Ready, Aye Ready." On Field Service, Waziristan. *Uniform, Drab. Facings, Red.*

Major J. E. Mein, Staff Corps	6 July 90	Commandant, 2 Mar. 92.
Captain E. W. Cunliffe, Staff Corps	10 Sept. 86	2nd in Command and Wing Comdr., 2 Mar. 92. [Burmah.—Furl.
Captain G. R. MacMullen, Staff Corps	11 Sept. 87	Wing Commander, 2 Mar. 92.—Dep. Insp. Gen. of Mil. Police.
Captain D. J. O. Taylor, Staff Corps	1 May 89	Wing Commander, 2 June 92.—Furlough.
Captain J. W. C. Hutchinson, Staff Corps	22 Jan. 90	Wing Officer, 9 July 86.
Captain E. H. Bernard, Staff Corps	22 Oct. 92	Wing Officer, 30 Sept. 87.—Cantonment Magistrate, Mandalay.
Captain C. C. A. Sillery, Staff Corps	10 Mar. 94	Wing Officer, 6 Aug. 90.—Burmah Military Police.
Lieut. F. D. Grant, Staff Corps	2 July 88	Wing Officer, 30 July 90.—Assist. Mil. Accountant, 3rd Class,
Lieut. C. C. Fenner, Staff Corps	25 Sept. 89	Wing Officer, 18 Mar. 93.—Furlough. [Calcutta.
Lieut. A. Limond, Staff Corps	2 Dec. 89	Wing Officer, 7 Oct. 92.—Officiating Adjutant.
Lieut. A. E. Dallas, Staff Corps	16 Jan. 91	Wing Officer, 19 Aug. 93.—Prob. Commissariat Department.
Lieut. F. D. Browne, Wiltshire Regt.	9 Apr. 92	Wing Officer, 2 Apr. 94.—Officiating Quarter Master.
Lieut. J. C. H. M'Caskill, Irish Regt.	11 July 93	Officiating Wing Officer.
Lieut. W. H. Williams, Irish Regt.	28 Dec. 93	Officiating Wing Officer.
Surgeon Lt.Colonel J. T. B. Bookey	30 Mar. 92	In medical charge, 31 Mar. 76.—With 1 Battalion 5 Goorkhas.

Establishment of each Regiment of Punjab Infantry.—8 Companies—Commandant; 2 Wing Commanders; 5 Wing Officers; 1 Medical Officer; 8 Subadars; 8 Jamadars; 40 Havildars; 40 Naicks; 16 Drummers; 800 Sepoys.

5th Goorkha (*Rifle*) Regiment.—*Raised in* 1858.

"Peiwar Kotal"—"Charasia"—"Kabul, 1879"—"Kandahar, 1880"—"Afghanistan, 1878-80."

FIRST BATTALION.—*Raised* 22 *May* 1858.—*Regimental Centre, Abbottabad.*

On Field Service, Waziristan. *Uniform, Dark Green. Facings, Black.*

Colonel A. Gaselee, CB. Staff Corps	1 Feb. 93	Commandant, 27 Sept. 92. [Punjab Frontier Force.
Major A. R. Martin, Staff Corps	1 Sept. 91	2nd in Command and Wing Commander, 1 April 91.—A. A. Gen.
Captain A. H. G. Kemball, Staff Corps	11 Aug. 91	2nd in Command and Wing Commander, 1 Mar. 94.—Furlough.
Captain E. de S. Smart, Staff Corps	23 Oct. 91	Wing Commander, 1 Feb. 92.—Furlough.
Captain J. O. S. Fayrer, Staff Corps	22 Jan. 92	Wing Officer, 10 Oct. 84.—Officiating 2nd in Command.
Captain J. M. Stewart, Gloucester Regt.	22 Oct. 92	Wing Officer, 12 Dec. 85.—D.A.Q.M.Gen. Waziristan Delim. Escort.
Captain I. Philipps, Staff Corps	12 May 94	Wing Officer, 10 Nov. 86.—Staff College, Sandhurst.
2C Lieut. G. H. Boisragon, Staff Corps	11 Feb. 92	Wing Officer and Quarter Master, 7 Apr. 87.
Lieut. C. H. Davies, Staff Corps	29 Aug. 85	Wing Officer, 1 Aug. 87.—Officiating Adjutant.
Lieut. *Hon.* C. G. Bruce, Staff Corps	20 Oct. 88	Wing Officer, 29 Mar. 94.
Lieut. S. D. B. Ketchen, Staff Corps	11 Feb. 92	Officiating Wing Officer.
Lieut. C. R. Johnson, Staff Corps	18 Dec. 91	Officiating Wing Officer.
Lieut. H. J. P. Browne, Staff Corps	14 Apr. 93	Officiating Wing Officer.
Surgeon Major J. A. Nelis, *MB*	31 Mar. 89	In medical charge, 20 Aug. 86.—Furlough.
Surgeon Lt. Colonel J. T. B. Bookey	30 Mar. 92	Officiating in medical charge.—From 6 Punjab Infantry.

SECOND BATTALION.—*Raised* 10 *Nov.* 1886.—*Regimental Centre, Abbottabad.*

Head Quarters at Abbottabad. *Uniform, Dark Green. Facings, Black.*

Major G. Hawkes, Staff Corps	19 Feb. 90	Commandant, 10 Nov. 93.
Captain A. A. Barrett, Staff Corps	10 Sept. 86	2nd in Command and Wing Commander, 10 Nov. 93.
Captain E. Vansittart, Staff Corps	10 Sept. 88	Wing Comdr. 25 July 91.—Dist. Recruiting Officer, Goruckpore.
Captain J. O. S. Fayrer, Staff Corps	22 Jan. 92	Wing Commander, 1 Mar. 94.—With 1 Battalion.
Captain A. S. Rooke, Staff Corps	19 Feb. 92	Wing Officer, 10 Nov. 86.—Cantonment Magistrate, Mhow.
Captain C. M. Crawford, Staff Corps	9 Sept. 93	Wing Officer, 10 Nov. 86.
Lieut. F. W. Evatt, Staff Corps	6 May 85	Wing Officer and Adjutant, 29 April 89.—Assist. Supt. of Army Signalling, Waziristan Delimitation Escort.
Lieut. N. E. Chesney, Staff Corps	30 Jan. 86	Wing Officer, 25 July 91.—Burmah Military Police.
Lieut. F. G. Lucas, Staff Corps	25 Aug. 86	Wing Officer and Quarter Master, 21 May 92.—Furlough.
Lieut. F. F. Badcock, *DSO*. Staff Corps	25 Aug. 86	Wing Officer, 18 July 92.—Waziristan Field Force.
Lieut. M. R. W. Nightingale, Staff Corps	23 Dec. 91	Wing Officer, 13 Feb. 94.—Furlough.
Lieut. E. B. C. Boddam, Staff Corps	5 June 89	Officiating Wing Officer and Adjutant.—From 2 Sikh Infantry.
Lieut. M. H. P. Barton, Staff Corps	10 Nov. 92	Officiating Wing Officer.
Surgeon Major G. Duncan, *MB*.	1 Apr. 94	In medical charge, 17 Nov. 86.—Waziristan Field Force.

Corps under the Orders of the Government of India.

THE CENTRAL INDIA HORSE.

Raised for service ordinarily in Central India, but available on emergency for General Service.
The Two Regiments of Beatson's Horse incorporated with the Central India Horse, 16 April and 8 Sept. 1860.
The Regiment of Meade's Horse incorporated with the Central India Horse on 16 Feb. 1861.
"AFGHANISTAN, 1879-80."—"KANDAHAR, 1880."
1st Regiment at Goonah. 2nd Regiment at Agar, W. Malwa. *Uniform, Drab. Facings, Maroon.*

RANK, NAMES, AND CORPS.	ARMY RANK.	REMARKS.
Colonel M. G. Gerard, *CB*. Staff Corps	2 Mar. 85	Commandant, 18 May 93.
Lt.Colonel H. A. Vincent, Staff Corps	9 Nov. 92	2nd in Command and Squadron Commander, 3 Feb. 89.—Political Agent, Bundelkund, and Supdt. Rewah State. [Goona.
2 Major A. Masters, Staff Corps	30 Nov. 90	2nd in Command and Squad. Comdr., 16 July 91.—Polit. Assist.,
1 Major G. E. Money, Staff Corps	14 July 89	2nd in Command and Squadron Commander, 1 Apr. 92.
2 *p.s.c.* Lt.Col. A.G. A. Durand, *CB. S.C.*	13 Nov. 89	Squadron Commander, 14 March 87.—Mil. Sec. to Viceroy.
1 Colonel N. F. F. Chamberlain, Staff C.	6 Jan. 94	Squadron Comdr., 18 Sept. 85.—Mil. Sec. to Kashmir Govt.
2 Captain E. E. Robertson, Staff Corps	11 May 89	Squadron Commander, 21 Oct. 86.
1 Captain J. B. Edwards, Staff Corps	30 Jan. 89	Squad. Comdr. 14 Mar. 87.—Insp. Officer, Imperial Def. Cav. C. I.
1 Captain W.A. Watson, Staff Corps	11 Aug. 91	Squadron Commander, 17 Apr. 88.—A.D.C. to Sir G. S. White.
1 Captain L. Herbert, Staff Corps	22 Jan. 92	Squadron Commander, 17 July 89.—Interp. to Sir G. S. White.
1 Captain F. C. Grant, Staff Corps	11 Aug. 91	Squadron Commander, 17 July 89.—Furlough.
2 Captain C. P. Campbell, Staff Corps	13 Aug. 90	Squadron Commander, 14 Apr. 91.—Senior Mil. Assist., Brit. Agent and Insp. Officer, Kashmir Troops at Gilgit.
2 Captain A. B. Mayne, Staff Corps	22 Jan. 92	Squadron Commander, 26 Oct. 91.—Offg. Civil Employ, Kotah.
1 Captain C. J. B. H. Dressner, Staff C.	11 Sept. 87	Squadron Commander, 1 Apr. 92.
1 Captain C.V.F.Townshend, Staff Corps	1 Feb. 90	Squadron Officer, 17 July 89.—Employed in Gilgit.
1 Captain E. C. B. Cotgrave, Staff Corps	10 May 93	Squadron Officer, 18 March 87.—Assist. Inspecting Officer, C. I. States, Imperial Service Cavalry. [Qr.Mr.Gen.'s Dept.
2 Lieut. *Hon.* H. D. Napier, Staff Corps	23 Aug. 84	Squadron Officer, 17 Apr. 88.—Staff Capt. Intelligence Branch,
1 Lieut. A.D.G. Bannerman, Staff Corps	29 Aug. 85	Squadron Officer, 11 March 90.—Assist. Agent to Gov. Gen. C.I.
1 Lieut. W. D. Daunt, Staff Corps	3 Aug. 86	Squadron Officer, 11 March 90. [Horse.—Furlough.
1 Lieut. A. P. Browne, Staff Corps	10 May 88	Squadron Officer and Adjutant, 11 March 90.—Staff Officer, C. I.
2 Lieut. R. L. Kennion, Staff Corps	9 June 88	Squadron Officer, 26 Oct. 91.—Boundary Settlement Officer,
2 Lieut. G. R. de H. Smith, Staff Corps	21 Apr. 88	Squadron Officer and Adjutant, 1 Apr. 92. [Bhopawur.
2 Lieut. D. H. Cameron, Staff Corps	23 July 90	Squadron Officer, 21 Apr. 93.
2 Lieut. R. C. Bell, Staff Corps	5 July 89	Squadron Officer, 7 Apr. 94.
1 Lieut. J. C. D. Pinney, Staff Corps	25 Sept. 90	Squadron Officer, 1 Nov. 92.—Sick Furlough.
1 Lieut. T. S. Tancred, Staff Corps	17 Dec. 90	Squadron Officer, 8 Nov. 93.
2 Lieut. S. A. Cooke, 1 Dragoon Gds.	14 June 91	Squadron Officer, 29 Nov. 93.
1 Lieut. H. A. Lash, Staff Corps	19 Mar. 90	Officiating Squadron Officer.
2 2nd Lt. A. S. Capper, Royal Artillery	24 July 91	Officiating Squadron Officer.
2 Lt. A. H. O. Spence, Staff Corps	3 Aug. 92	Officiating Squadron Officer.
2 Lieut. J. D. Cadell, Staff Corps	3 Dec. 94	Officiating Squadron Officer.
1 Surg. Capt. T. W. Shaw, *MB*.	30 Sept. 89	Officiating in medical charge, and of Goona Polit. Agency.
1 Surg.Capt.C.M.Moore,*MD*.Bom.Est.	30 Mar. 89	In medical charge, 26 Mar. 94.—And Western Malwa Pol. Agency. Officiating in medical charge.

Establishment of each Regiment.—4 Squadron Commanders; 4 Squadron Officers; 1 Medical Officer; 4 Risaldars; 4 Risaidars; 1 Wordie Major; 8 Jamadars; 8 Kote Dafedars; 56 Dafedars; 8 Trumpeters; 536 Sowars.

Deolee Irregular Force (*Cavalry—Lancers, and Infantry*).—Raised in 1857.
"AFGHANISTAN, 1879-80."
At Deolee. *Uniform, Dark Green. Facings, Scarlet.*

Captain J. A. Bell, Staff Corps	10 Sept. 86	Commandant, 11 Apr. 90.—And Cantonment Magistrate, Deolee.
Captain C. G. J. S. Jones, Staff Corps	4 Dec. 89	2nd in Command and Squadron Commander, 18 Nov. 94.
Lieut. F. C. L. Waller, Staff Corps	25 Aug. 86	Wing Officer and Adjutant, 30 Aug. 87.—Station Staff Officer.
Surg.Capt.H.N.V.Harington,Madr.Est.	2 Oct. 80	In medical charge, 6 Aug. 84.—Civil Surgeon, Bikaneer.
Surgeon Captain H. R. Woolbert, *MB.*	1 Oct. 85	Officiating in medical charge.—And in medical charge Oomrawuttee and Tonk Political Agency.

Establishment.—Commandant; 1 Squadron Commander; 1 Wing Officer; Medical Officer; 2 Native Doctors. *Cavalry*—2 Troops, with 2 Risaldars; 2 Jamadars; 18 Dafedars; 2 Trumpeters; 138 Sowars; 2 Camel Sowars; or 164 of all ranks. *Infantry*, 8 Companies, with 8 Subadars; 8 Jamadars; 40 Havildars; 40 Naicks; 16 Drummers; 600 Sepoys: 712 of all ranks. *Non-effective Native Staff*, Subadar Major; 1 Havildar Major; 1 Native Adjutant; 1 Drill Naick; 8 Colour Havildars; 8 Pay Havildars; 1 Drum Major; 1 Fife Major.

Erinpoorah Irregular Force (Raised 12 June 1860).
At Erinpoorah (Rajpootana). *Uniform, Dark Green. Facings, Scarlet.*

Colonel P. W. Smith, Gen. List, Inf.	29 Aug. 93	Commandant, 22 Jan. 89.
Captain R. A. Cole, Staff Corps	30 Jan. 89	2nd in Command and Squadron Commander, 22 Jan. 89.
Lieut. F. T. C. Hughes, Staff Corps	9 May 85	Wing Officer and Adj., 22 Jan. 89.—Station Staff Officer.—Furl.
Lieut. E. T. Carwithen, Staff Corps	26 Nov. 91	Officiating Wing Officer and Adjutant.—From 29 Bengal Inf.
Surg.Maj.W. H. Neilson, *MB.* Madr.Est.	30 Sept. 94	In medical charge, 10 May 84.—And Offg. Ulwur Agency.
Surg. Lieut. J. G. Hulbert, *MB.*	27 July 92	Officiating in medical charge.

Establishment.—Commandant; Squadron Commander; Wing Officer; 1 Medical Officer; 2 Native Doctors. *Cavalry*—2 Troops, with 2 Risaldars; 2 Jamadars; 18 Dafedars; 2 Trumpeters; 136 Sowars; 4 Camel Sowars; or 164 of all ranks. *Non-effective Native Staff*—2 Pay Dafedars. *Infantry*—8 Companies, with 8 Subadars; 8 Jamadars; 40 Havildars; 40 Naicks; 16 Drummers; 600 Privates; or 712 of all ranks. *Non-effective Native Staff*—1 Subadar Major; 1 Native Adjutant; 1 Drill Havildar; 1 Drill Naick; 8 Colour Havildars; 8 Pay Havildars; 1 Drum Major; 1 Fife Major.

Resident's Escort—Katmandhoo (Nepaul) (*Raised* 5 *April* 1816).

Establishment.—1 Native Doctor; 1 Subadar; 1 Jamadar; 5 Havildars; 5 Naicks; 2 Buglers; 80 Sepoys.

Corps under the Orders of the Government of India. 449b

BHEEL CORPS.

Malwah Bheel Corps (Raised 24 Feb. 1840).

Head Quarters at Sirdarpore (Central India). *Uniform, Green. Facings, Scarlet.*

Rank, Names, and Corps.	Army Rank.	Remarks.
Major G. A. Collins, Staff Corps	13 June 94	Commandant, 1 Nov. 94.
Captain A. Poingdestre, Staff Corps	28 Jan. 93	Adjutant, 7 July 89.
Surgeon Lt. Colonel J. Duke	30 Mar. 92	In medical charge, 27 Nov. 84.—And Bhopawur Polit. Agency.

Establishment.—Commandant; Adjutant; 1 Medical Officer; 2 Native Doctors; 1 Subadar Major; 7 Subadars; 8 Jamadars; 40 Havildars; 40 Naicks; 16 Buglers; 500 Privates.

Meywar Bheel Corps (Raised 15 July 1840).

Head Quarters at Kherwarah (Rajpootana). *Uniform, Rifle Green. Facings, Scarlet.*

Major E. D. F. Bignell, Staff Corps	7 July 89	Commandant, 18 Nov. 94.—And Political Supdt. Hilly Tract, Meywar.
Captain E. R. Penrose, Staff Corps	10 Aug. 87	2nd in Command and Wing Commander, 18 Nov. 94.—And 2nd Assistant Resident, Meywar.
Captain C. H. Dawson, Staff Corps	23 Oct. 91	Wing Officer and Adjutant, 26 Nov. 86.
Lieut. M. G. Young, Staff Corps	16 Jan. 91	Wing Officer, 26 Oct. 94.
Lieut. S. Clay, Staff Corps	26 Sept. 91	Officiating Wing Officer.
Surgeon Captain R. Shore, *MD.*	29 Sept. 83	In medical charge, 4 Mar. 93.

Establishment.—Commandant; Wing Commander; 2 Wing Officers; 1 Medical Officer; 1 English Writer; 2 Thakoors; 2 Native Doctors; 1 Subadar Major; 7 Subadars; 8 Jamadars; 40 Havildars; 40 Naicks; 1 Bugle Major; 15 Buglers; 600 Privates.

Bhopaul Battalion (late Bhopaul Levy.—Raised Jan. 1859, for General Service).
"AFGHANISTAN, 1878-79."
Head Quarters at Sehore. *Uniform, Drab. Facings, Chocolate.*

Colonel G. R. Peart, Staff Corps	12 Aug. 89	Commandant, 4 Nov. 86.
Major E. S. Masters, Staff Corps	9 Aug. 93	2nd in Command and Wing Commander, 17 Oct. 94.
Captain J. H. Pollard, Staff Corps	6 Feb. 95	Wing Officer and Adjutant, 24 Apr. 89.—Furlough.
Lieut. H. L. Goodenough, Staff Corps	23 Aug. 84	Wing Officer, 13 Sept. 91.—Assistant Political Agent, Manipore.
Lieut. C. C. Jackson, Staff Corps	9 July 90	Wing Officer, 23 Nov. 94.—Officiating Adjutant.
Lieut. S. R. Davidson, Staff Corps	3 June 92	Officiating Wing Officer.—From 27 Madras Infantry.
Surg. Major A. H. C. Dane, *MD.* Bom. Est	31 Mar. 87	In medical charge, 5 Dec. 84.

Establishment.—Commandant; Wing Commander; 2 Wing Officers; 1 Medical Officer; 1 Subadar Major; 9 Subadars; 10 Jamadars; 50 Havildars; 50 Naicks; 20 Drummers; 2 Native Doctors; 800 Sepoys.

Mhairwarra Battalion (late Mhairwarra Local Battalion.—Raised 16 June 1822).
"CENTRAL INDIA," "AFGHANISTAN, 1878-79."
Head Quarters at Ajmere. *Uniform, Scarlet. Facings, Yellow.*

Colonel N. R. Stewart, Staff Corps	28 Mar. 90	Commandant, 15 Apr. 90.
Captain G. H. J. Moore, Staff Corps	22 Jan. 92	2nd in Command and Wing Commander, 1 Nov. 94.
Lieut. C. B. Baldock, Staff Corps	29 Aug. 85	Wing Officer and Adjutant, 27 Nov. 94.
Lieut. S. G. Knox, Staff Corps	14 Apr. 91	Officiating Wing Officer.—Asst. Polit. Agent, Bussorah.
Surgeon Major D. ffrench-Mullen	31 Mar. 89	In medical charge, 24 Mar. 93.—And Civil, Ajmere.

Establishment.—Commandant; Wing Commander; Wing Officer; Medical Officer; 8 Subadars; 8 Jamadars; 40 Havildars; 40 Naicks; 16 Drummers; 600 Sepoys. *Non-effective Native Staff*—1 Subadar Major; 1 Drill Havildar; 1 Drill Naick; 1 Drum Major; 1 Fife Major; 8 Pay Havildars; 8 Colour Havildars.

HYDERABAD CONTINGENT.

The Contingent consists of 4 *Regiments of Cavalry,* 4 *Field Batteries of Artillery, and* 6 *Regiments of Infantry.*
Head Quarters, Bolarum.

STAFF.

Brig. Gen. M. Protheroe, *CB. CSI.* Staff Corps; Aide de Camp to the Queen	17 May 86	Commandant, 26 Oct. 90.
Bt. Major C. H. Westmorland, Staff C...	23 Aug. 89	Assistant Adjutant General, 17 June 92.—From 6 Bengal Inf.

1st Lancers.

At Mominabad.] "CENTRAL INDIA."

Major G. Adye, Staff Corps	13 Nov. 92	Commandant, 24 Jan. 92.—Furlough. 2nd in Command and Squadron Comdr.
Captain A. A. Jones, Staff Corps	29 July 93	Squadron Commander, 29 July 93.—Officiating 2nd in Command.
Lieut. A. K. Armstrong, Staff Corps	28 Apr. 86	Squadron Officer, 27 Mar. 90.—Furlough.
Lieut. F. W. C. Turner, Staff Corps	25 Aug. 86	Squadron Officer and Adjutant, 27 Mar. 90.
Lieut. A. Andrew, Staff Corps	8 Sept. 86	Squadron Officer, 1 Apr. 91.—Officiating Squadron Commander.
Lieut. C. E. E. F. K. Macquoid, Staff C.	26 Aug. 88	Squadron Officer, 24 Jan. 92.
Lieut. J. L. Orr, Staff Corps	30 June 89	Squadron Officer, 1 Apr. 91.—Burmah Military Police.
Lieut. W. E. G. Lillingston, Staff Corps	8 May 90	Squadron Officer, 1 Feb. 94.
Lieut. P. S. Hicks, Hampshire Regt.	1 July 93	Officiating Squadron Officer.
Surg. Major C. Mullins, *MB.* Madr. Est.	30 Sept. 90	In medical charge, 3 Dec. 86.
Surg. Capt. C. A. Johnston, *MB.* Mad. Est.	31 Mar. 90	Officiating in medical charge.

2nd Lancers.
At Bolarum.]

Rank, Names, and Corps.	Army Rank.	Remarks.
Colonel J. T. Cummins, DSO. Staff Corps	28 Dec. 93	Commandant, 14 Oct. 89.—Offg. Deputy Adj. Gen., Madras.
Captain E. L. Wright, Staff Corps	11 May 89	2nd in Command and Squad. Comdr., 16 Dec. 91.—Offg Comdt.
Captain F. Wyllie, Staff Corps	22 Feb. 90	Squadron Commander, 9 Jan. 92.—Offg. 2nd in Command.
Lieut. G. S. Morris, Staff Corps	23 May 85	Squadron Officer, 24 May 92.—Offg. Squadron Commander.
Lieut. D. S. Buist, Staff Corps	25 Nov. 85	Squadron Officer, 1 Apr. 91.—Offg. Squadron Commander.
Lieut. H. H. Dunlop, Staff Corps	25 Nov. 85	Squadron Officer and Adjutant, 22 Feb. 90.
Lieut. H. A. Lane, Staff Corps	9 Feb. 89	Squadron Officer, 9 Jan. 92.—Personal Assist. Resdt. Hyderabad.
Lieut. A. R. Saunders, Staff Corps	23 June 90	Squadron Officer, 24 Mar. 93.
Lieut. S. A. M. Orr, Staff Corps	12 Nov. 92	Officiating Squadron Officer.
Lieut. A. N. Lovell, Staff Corps	21 Dec. 91	Officiating Squadron Officer.
Surgeon Major G. J. Kellie, Ben. Est.	31 Mar. 89	In medical charge, 1 Dec. 94.

3rd Lancers.
At Aurungabad.] "CENTRAL INDIA"—"BURMA, 1885-87."

Rank, Names, and Corps.	Army Rank.	Remarks.
Lt. Colonel R. A. Gilchrist, Staff Corps	4 Aug. 91	Commandant, 4 Apr. 90.
Captain J. W. B. Meade, Staff Corps	25 Jan. 88	2nd in Command and Squadron Commander, 14 Aug. 91.—Furl.
Captain R. Wapshare, Staff Corps	1 Feb. 91	Squadron Commander, 1 Apr. 91.—Offg. 2nd in Command.
Captain A. W. Warden, Staff Corps	6 Feb. 95	Squadron Officer, 22 Feb. 90.—Offg. Squadron Commander.
Lieut. C. R. Elliot, Staff Corps	17 Feb. 86	Squadron Officer and Adjutant, 27 Mar. 90.
Lieut. W. W. Warner, Staff Corps	26 Feb. 88	Squadron Officer, 6 June 91.
Lieut. H. K. Dalyell, Staff Corps	30 Dec. 89	Squadron Officer, 1 Dec. 92.
Lieut. E. Tennant, Staff Corps	21 Nov. 90	Squadron Officer, 1 Apr. 93.
Lieut. A. B. Souter, Devon Regiment	18 Oct. 9e	Officiating Squadron Officer.
Surg. Major R. James, MB. Madr. Est.	31 Mar. 91	In medical charge, 26 Apr. 89.

4th Lancers.
At Hingoli.] "CENTRAL INDIA."

Rank, Names, and Corps.	Army Rank.	Remarks.
Major H. M. Mason, Staff Corps	8 Feb. 90	Commandant, 6 June 91.
Capt. R. F. M. Johnstone, Staff Corps	11 May 89	2nd in Command and Squadron Commander, 11 Apr. 93.
Capt. E. F. H. M'Swiney, DSO. Staff Corps	22 Jan. 90	Squadron Commander, 1 Apr. 91.—Dep. Assist. Qr. Mr. Gen. Waziristan Field Force.
Captain S. M. Mason, Staff Corps	22 Oct. 92	Squadron Commander, 11 Apr. 93.—Furlough.
Lieut. F. J. Nelson, Staff Corps	28 Feb. 85	Squadron Officer and Adjutant, 12 June 89.—Aide de Camp to Lieut. Governor N. W. P. and Oude.
Lieut. E. A. W. Stotherd, Staff Corps	1 Apr. 88	Squadron Officer, 18 Nov. 88.—Offg. Squadron Commander.
Lieut. R. J. Bentinck, Staff Corps	6 Feb. 89	Squadron Officer, 1 Apr. 89.
Lieut. A. E. Barnard, Derbyshire Regt.	1 Jan. 90	Squadron Officer, 1 Dec. 92.
Lieut. M. H. Henderson, Staff Corps	17 Nov. 92	Squadron Officer and Adjutant, 1 Sept. 94. [From 3 Mad. Lan.]
Captain T. D. Leslie, Staff Corps	30 Sept. 94	Squadron Officer, 10 Aug. 94.— Offg. Squadron Commander.
Lieut. P. N. Leslie, Staff Corps	21 July 92	Officiating Squadron Officer.
Brig. Surg. Lt. Colonel J. F. Sargent, Madras Establishment	31 May 90	In medical charge, 1 Dec. 94.

Establishment of each Regiment of Cavalry.—Commandant; 3 Squadron Commanders and 2nd in Command; 4 Squadron Officers; 1 Medical Officer; 14 Native Commissioned Officers; 48 Dafedars; 4 Camel Gunners; 7 Trumpeters; 478 Troopers; Total 551. 1 Apothecary; 1 Hospital Assistant.
Note.—The horses are *Silladaree* or private property.

No. 1 Field Battery.
At Bolarum.] "MAHIDPOOR"—"NOWAH"—"CENTRAL INDIA."

Rank, Names, and Corps.	Army Rank.	Remarks.
Captain A. G. Johnson, Royal Artillery	12 Apr. 90	Commandant, June 94.
Lieut. H. S. Langhorne, R. Artillery	16 Sept. 85	Subaltern, 1 March 90.—Furlough.
Lieut. H. F. Head, Royal Artillery	18 Feb. 86	Supernumerary Subaltern, 1 March 90.

No. 2 Field Battery.
At Aurungabad.] "CENTRAL INDIA."

Rank, Names, and Corps.	Army Rank.	Remarks.
Captain A. B. Shute, Royal Artillery	5 Feb. 86	Commandant, 26 Apr. 84.
Lieut. F. M. Davidson, Royal Artillery	16 Sept. 85	Subaltern, 1 Oct. 89.—With 4 Field Battery.
Lieut. R. F. Brewster, Royal Artillery	18 Feb. 86	Supernumerary Subaltern, 26 Dec. 90.

No. 3 Field Battery.
At Hingolee.]

Rank, Names, and Corps.	Army Rank.	Remarks.
Captain F. J. Winter, Royal Artillery	12 May 88	Commandant, 18 Nov. 90.
Lieut. G. S. Worsley, Royal Artillery	30 June 85	Subaltern, 6 Oct. 90.
Lieut. G. G. Woods, Royal Artillery	15 Feb. 92	Officiating Subaltern.

No. 4 Field Battery.
At Ellichpore.] "CENTRAL INDIA."

Rank, Names, and Corps.	Army Rank.	Remarks.
Captain L. H. Parry, Royal Artillery	3 Sept. 91	Commandant, 15 Nov. 90.—Furlough. Officiating Commandant.
Lieut. R. G. Ouseley, Royal Artillery	17 Feb. 86	Subaltern, 15 Nov. 90.—Furlough.

Establishment of each Battery.—1 Commandant; 1 Subaltern. *Gunners*—2 Native Commissioned Officers; 12 Non-Commissioned Officers; 2 Buglers; 56 Gunners. *Drivers*—4 Non-Commissioned Officers; 36 Syce Drivers; 18 Bullock Drivers; 1 Farrier Salootrie; 1 Hospital Assistant: Total, 132. *Ordnance*—2 6-pounder Guns; 2 12-pounder Howitzers. The four Batteries are linked together.

1st Infantry.—*Linked with 2nd and 3rd Infantry.*
At Hingolee.] "MAHIDPOOR"—"NOWAH."

Rank, Names, and Corps.	Army Rank.	Remarks.
Lt. Colonel F. G. Maltby, Staff Corps	6 July 93	Commandant, 26 Mar. 90.
Captain G. C. C. Shakespear, Staff C.	12 Nov. 89	2nd in Command and Wing Comdr. 20 Aug. 91.—Offg. Comdt.
Captain F. V. Whittall, Staff Corps	22 Jan. 92	Wing Comdr., 20 June 92.—Station Staff Officer, Bolarum. Wing Commander.
Lieut. R. G. Burton, Staff Corps	23 Aug. 84	Wing Officer and Quarter Master, 28 July 89.—Offg. Wing Comdr.
Lieut. H. Lowther, Staff Corps	23 May 85	Wing Officer and Adjutant, 12 Dec. 88.
Lieut. F. F. Major, Staff Corps	10 Oct. 89	Wing Officer, 26 June 91.—Furlough.
Lieut. F. H. Pigou, Staff Corps	19 Nov. 89	Wing Officer, 1 Apr. 93.
Lieut. A. Hodson-Cooke, Staff Corps	14 May 90	Wing Officer, 11 Jan. 91.
Lieut. E. H. Payne, Staff Corps	8 Nov. 90	Officiating Wing Officer.
Lieut. C. F. Dobbs, Lancashire Fus.	14 June 93	Officiating Wing Officer.
Surg. Major F. J. Doyle, Madras Estab.	2 Oct. 92	In medical charge, 21 Mar. 87.

Corps under the Orders of the Government of India. 45r

2nd Infantry.—*Linked with 1st and 3rd Infantry.*

At Bolarum.] "Mahidpoor"—"Nowah"—"Burma, 1885-87."

Rank, Names, and Corps.	Army Rank.	Remarks.
Major E. W. St. G. Welchman, Staff Corps	11 July 94	Commandant, 15 Sept. 94.
Capt. E. C. M. Lushington, Staff Corps	27 June 86	2nd in Command and Wing Comdr., 26 Mar. 90.—With 4 Inf.
Captain W. H. Lewin, Staff Corps	11 Aug. 91	Wing Commander, 1 Dec. 94.
Captain G. W. Priestley, Staff Corps	9 Sept. 93	Wing Officer, 1 Oct. 89.
Captain A. C. F. Bourchier, Staff Corps	25 Aug. 94	Wing Officer, 13 May 89.—Officiating 2nd in Command.
Lieut. H. A. V. Cummins, Staff Corps	15 Jan. 91	Wing Officer, 1 Jan. 93.
Lieut. S. H. E. Nicholas, Staff Corps	19 May 92	Wing Officer and Adjutant, 4 Aug. 93.
Lieut. T. C. Browning, Staff Corps	5 Apr. 92	Wing Officer, 17 Sept. 93.—Officiating Quarter Master.
Lieut. H. G. W. Chandler, Midd'x Regt.	22 Oct. 91	Officiating Wing Officer.
Surg. Capt. C. H. L. Palk, Mad. Estab'	28 July 91	In medical charge, 20 Dec. 93.

3rd Infantry.—*Linked with 1st and 2nd Infantry.*

At Ellichpore.] "Nowah"—"Central India"—"Burma, 1885-87."

Rank, Names, and Corps.	Army Rank.	Remarks.
Lt. Colonel W. H. Salmon, Staff Corps	12 Jan. 92	Commandant, 16 Nov. 87.
Captain C. H. Macdonald, Staff Corps	1 Sept. 91	2nd in Command and Wing Commander, 1 Dec. 94.—Furlough.
Lieut. H. P. Lane, Staff Corps	29 Aug. 86	Wing Officer and Adjutant, 2 Dec. 89.
Lieut. J. S. Richards, Staff Corps	25 Aug. 86	Wing Officer, 21 June 90.
Lieut. J. H. Vanderzee, Staff Corps	3 July 89	Wing Officer and Quarter Master, 21 June 90.—Offg. Wing Comdr.
Lieut. E. N. Davis, Staff Corps	18 Mar. 90	Wing Officer, 24 Jan. 92.—Officiating Adjutant.
Lieut. D. O. Morris, Staff Corps	17 Feb. 91	Wing Officer, 1 Apr. 93.—Assist. Commr. 3rd Class, Oomrawuttee.
Lieut. J. R. Kennedy, Staff Corps	29 Mar. 92	Wing Officer, 1 Apr. 93.
Lieut. K. E. Nangle, Staff Corps	5 Mar. 92	Wing Officer, 11 Oct. 93.—Officiating Quarter Master.
Lieut. E. G. W. Pratt, Staff Corps	3 Dec. 94	Officiating Wing Officer.
Surgeon Major H. G. L. Wortabet, MD.	31 Mar. 91	In medical charge, 18 Jan. 84.—Furlough.
Surg. Capt. E. H. Wright, Madras Est.	31 Mar. 90	Officiating in medical charge.

4th Infantry.—*Linked with 5th and 6th Infantry.*

At Aurungabad.] "Nagpoor."

Rank, Names, and Corps.	Army Rank.	Remarks.
Major A. Adye, Staff Corps	13 June 94	Commandant, 1 July 93.—Furlough.
Capt. E. C. M. Lushington, Staff Corps	27 June 86	Officiating Commandant.—From 2 Infantry.
Captain M. T. Shewen, Staff Corps	1 Feb. 91	2nd in Command and Wing Commander, 31 Oct. 94. Wing Commander.
Captain A. W. Leonard, Staff Corps	10 Mar. 94	Wing Officer, 12 Sept. 88.—Officiating Wing Commander.
Lieut. F. W. Rea, Staff Corps	29 Aug. 85	Wing Officer and Quarter Master, 22 May 90.—Offg. Wing Comdr.
Lieut. T. M. Ward, Staff Corps	29 Aug. 85	Wing Officer, 14 Nov. 91.
Lieut. T. M. Kirkwood, Staff Corps	8 Dec. 86	Wing Officer and Adjutant, 1 Nov. 89.
Lieut. W. E. E. Lloyd, Staff Corps	26 June 89	Wing Officer, 1 Apr. 91.—Sick Furlough.
Lieut. A. J. R. Glasfurd, Staff Corps	17 June 91	Wing Officer, 1 Apr. 93.
Lieut. V. F. W. Tregear, Staff Corps	24 Sept. 92	Officiating Wing Officer. Officiating Wing Officer.
Surg. Major C. L. Swaine, MD. Mad. Est.	31 Mar. 88	In medical charge, 20 Dec. 93.

5th Infantry.—*Linked with 4th and 6th Infantry.*

At Raichore.] "Central India."

Rank, Names, and Corps.	Army Rank.	Remarks.
Major F. S. Sorell, Staff Corps	28 Oct. 91	Commandant, 27 May 90.
Captain T. H. Plumer, Staff Corps	13 Aug. 90	2nd in Command and Wing Commander, 16 June 93.—Furlough.
Captain T. H. Hardy, Staff Corps	25 Aug. 94	Wing Commander, 26 Aug. 94.—Officiating 2nd in Command.
Lieut. G. M. Audain, Staff Corps	23 Aug. 84	Wing Officer and Quarter Master, 23 June 89.
Lieut. R. C. H. Chalmers, Staff Corps	25 Aug. 86	Wing Officer, 9 Oct. 91.
Lieut. R. W. Burton, Staff Corps	16 Dec. 90	Wing Officer and Adjutant, 1 Apr. 93.—Offg. Wing Commander.
Lieut. W. L. Cotton, Staff Corps	12 July 93	Wing Officer, 23 Feb. 94.—Officiating Quarter Master.
Lieut. C. R. Harbord, Staff Corps	3 Dec. 94	Wing Officer, 29 May 94.
Lieut. H. G. P. Beville, Staff Corps	15 Apr. 92	Officiating Wing Officer.
Surg. Major H. Greany, MD. Madr. Est.	1 Oct. 93	In medical charge, 25 Aug. 91.

6th Infantry.—*Linked with 4th and 5th Infantry.*

At Jaulna.]

Rank, Names, and Corps.	Army Rank.	Remarks.
Lt. Col. J. N. S. Kirkwood, Staff Corps	1 Sept. 91	Commandant, 1 July 87.
Captain D. W. Purdon, Staff Corps	1 May 89	2nd in Command and Wing Commander, 1 July 93.
Lieut. G. S. Frazer, Staff Corps	29 Aug. 85	Wing Officer and Adjutant, 12 Nov. 89.—Furlough.
Lieut. E. J. M. Wood, East Surrey Regt.	25 Aug. 86	Wing Officer and Qr. Mr., 22 May 90.—Offg. Wing Commander.
Lieut. D. R. Adye, Staff Corps	10 Mar. 88	Wing Officer, 10 June 90.—Sick Furlough.
Lieut. C. C. Renton, Staff Corps	4 Feb. 89	Wing Officer, 1 Apr. 91.—Offg. Adjutant and Quarter Master.
Lieut. G. E. J. Perry, Staff Corps	21 Sept. 91	Wing Officer, 1 Apr. 93.—Sick Furlough.
Lieut. H. Macdonald, Inniskilling Fus.	30 Apr. 93	Wing Officer, 21 Sept. 94.
Lieut. C. E. Luard, West York Regt.	13 June 94	Officiating Wing Officer.
Lieut. J. Muscroft, York Lt. Inf.	1 July 90	Officiating Wing Officer.
2nd Lt. A. St. J. Cooke, Sussex Regt.	18 May 92	Officiating Wing Officer.
Surgeon Lieut. G. M. Bidie	30 Jan. 93	In medical charge, 24 Feb. 94.—Sick Furlough.
Surg. Lieut. E. H. Sharman, Madr. Est.	29 July 93	

Establishment of each Regiment of Infantry.—Commandant; 2 Wing Commanders and 2nd in Command; 5 Wing Officers; 1 Medical Officer; 17 Native Commissioned Officers; 81 Non-Commissioned Officers; 1 Drum Major; 8 Drummers; 1 Fife Major; 7 Fifers; 4 Buglers; 732 Privates. Total, 851. 1 Apothecary; 1 Hospital Assistant.

Bengal Medical Department.

[For the explanation of the qualifications of the following Officers, see page iii.]

SURGEON MAJOR GENERAL.	ASSISTANT SURGEON.	SURGEON MAJ. GEN.	REMARKS.
Rice, William Roche,[1] *CSI. MD. MRCS.* [R]	20 Nov. 6	29 Mar. 90	Sanitary Commissioner with the Govt. of India

SURGEON COLONELS.		SURGEON COLONEL.	
Pilcher, Jesse Griggs, *FRCS. LAH.Dub.* ...	1 Oct. 66	29 Mar. 90	Insp. General of Civil Hospitals, N.W.P. & Oude.
Cleghorn, James,[6] *MD. LRCS.Ed.*	31 Mar. 65	13 Aug. 91	Insp. General of Civil Hospitals, Punjab.—Furl.
Harvey, Robert,[7] *DSO. MD. MCh. Hon. Surgeon to the Governor General* [R]	31 Mar. 65	2 Sept. 91	Inspector General of Civil Hospitals, Bengal.
Spencer, Lionel Dixon, *MD. MRCS.*	31 Mar. 65	24 Oct. 92	Punjab Frontier Force.
Thomson, George,[8] *MB. MCh.*	2 Oct. 65	1 Apr. 93	Lahore District.
Ross, George Cumberland, *LRCP. LRCS.*	2 Oct. 65	1 Jan. 94	Administrative Medical Officer and Sanitary Commissioner, Central Provinces.
Warburton, William Pleace, *MD. MCh. FRCSI.*	31 Mar. 65	17 Jan. 94	Assam District.—Officiating Bundelkhund and Nerbudda Districts.
Raye, Daniel O'Connell, *MD. FRCSI. Hon. Surgeon to the Governor General*	31 Mar. 66	2 Apr. 94	Bundelkhund and Nerbudda Districts.
Stephen, Arthur,[15] *MA. MB. MCh.*	30 Sept. 67	19 May 94	Presidency District.—Officiating P. M. O. and Sanitary Commissioner, Assam District.

BRIGADE SURGEON LIEUTENANT COLONELS.	BRIGADE SURGEON.	RANK OF LT. COL.	
King, George, *CIE. MB. MCh.*	2 Oct. 65	2 Apr. 89	2 Oct. 85	Supdt. Royal Botanic Gardens at Calcutta, and *ex officio* Prof. of Botany, Calcutta Med. College.
Purves, Henry Black, *LRCP.Ed. LRCS.Ed.*	2 Oct. 65	16 June 89	2 Oct. 85	Civil, Howrah.
Massy, George, *LKQCPI. MRCS.*	2 Oct. 65	29 Mar. 90	2 Oct. 85	Civil and Jail, Murree.
Jameson, Robert,[19] *MD. LRCS.Ed.*	2 Oct. 65	1 Mar. 91	2 Oct. 85	Deputy Sanitary Commissioner, 1st Circle, N.W. Provinces.

		BRIG. SURG. LT. COL.		
Mullen, Thomas ffrench, *MD. MCh.*	1 Oct. 66	2 Sept. 91	1 Oct. 86	Civil, Bikaneer. — Offg. Residency Surg. Western States, Rajpootana.
Finden, Woodforde,[13] *LRCP.Ed. MRCS.* ...	1 Oct. 66	2 Nov. 91	1 Oct. 86	7 Bengal Cavalry.
Lethbridge, Alfred Swaine, *CSI. MD. MCh. MRCS,*	30 Sept. 67	9 Apr. 92	......	Gen. Supdt. of operations for suppression of Thuggee and Dacoity.—Member of Gov. Gen.'s Council.
Newman, John Henry,[16] *MD. MCh.*	30 Sept. 67	1 June 92	......	Residency Surgeon and Chief Medical Officer, Rajpootana.
Cunningham, David Douglas, *CIE. MD. MCh.Ed.* H.P. 68 *Hon. Surg. to Gov. Gen.*	1 Apr. 68	24 Oct. 92	......	Professor of Physiology, Medical College, Calcutta.
Cameron, Archibald, *MB. MCh.*	1 Apr. 68	1 Apr. 93	......	Civil and Jail, Allahabad.
Carmichael, James Charles Gordon,[18] *MD. MCh.*	1 Apr. 68	2 Apr. 93	......	1 Battalion 3 Goorkhas.
Hutcheson, George, *MD. MCh. LRCP.Ed. LRCS.Ed.*	1 Oct. 68	27 June 93	......	Sanitary Commissioner, N.W. Prov. and Oude.
Sanders, Richard Careless, *MD. FRCS.Ed. MRCS. LSA.*	1 Apr. 69	4 Oct. 93	......	Ophthalmic Surgeon, &c., Calcutta Medical College.
Franklin, Benjamin, *MRCS. LSA. Hon. Surgeon to the Governor General*	1 Apr. 69	1 Jan. 94	......	Surgeon to the Viceroy.
Davis, Geo. M'Bride,[24] *MD.MCh. LAH.Dub.*	1 Apr. 69	17 Jan. 94	......	P.M.O. Waziristan Delimitation Escort.
Nicholson, Francis Cobham,[25] *MB. MCh.*	1 Oct. 69	1 Apr. 94	......	Civil, Patna.
Hendley, Thomas Holbein, *CIE. LRCP. MRCS. LSA.*	1 Oct. 69	2 Apr. 94	......	Residency Surgeon, Jeypore.
Johnstone, Hugh, *MD. MCh.*	30 Sept. 67	19 May 94	......	Civil and Port Health Officer, Rangoon.
Gregg, William Henry,[26] *MB. MCh. MRCP.*	1 Oct. 69	20 June 94	......	Sanitary Commissioner, Bengal.
Seaman, Albert Baird,[27] *MB. LRCP.Ed. MRCS.*	1 Oct. 69	22 Oct. 94	......	1 Battalion 1 Goorkhas.

SURGEON LIEUTENANT COLONELS.		SURGEON LT. COL.	
Evers, Benj. *MD. LRCP.Ed. LRCS. Ed.* ...	1 Apr. 68	1 Apr. 88	Civil, Raepore.—Offg. Supdt. Central Jail.
Calthrop, Christopher William,[22] *MD. MRCS. LRCPI. LSA.* H.P. 69	1 Apr. 69	1 Apr. 89	Medical Storekeeper, Meean Meer.
Gupta, Kali Pada, *MB. MA. LRCP.Ed. LRCS.Ed.*	1 Apr. 69	1 Apr. 89	Civil, Backergunge.—Officiating Civil, Hooghly.
Smyth, Frederick Aug.[28] *LM.Dub. L.Ch.*	1 Oct. 69	1 Oct. 89	2 Battalion 3 Goorkhas.
Courtney, William Michael,[30] *FRCSI. LAH.Dub.*	1 Oct. 69	1 Oct. 89	38 Bengal Infantry.
Rutledge, Edward Butler, *MRCS. LSA.*	1 Oct. 69	1 Oct. 89	Civil, Budaun.—Offg. Civil & Jail, Deyrah Dhoon.
Robinson, Thomas,[31] *MB. MCh.*	1 Oct. 69	1 Oct. 89	2 Bengal Infantry.

Bengal Medical Department.

SURGEON LIEUTENANT COLONELS.	ASSISTANT SURGEON.	SURGEON LT. COL.	REMARKS.
Martin, Daniel Nicholns, *MD. MCh.*	1 Oct. 69	1 Oct. 89	Civil, Sumbulpore.—Officiating Civil, Saugor.
Roe, William Alex. Crauford, *LRCP.Ed. FRCS.Ed.*	1 Oct. 69	1 Oct. 89	Sanitary Commissioner, Punjab.
Meadows, Charles John Walford,[33] *MRCS. LSA.*	1 Oct. 69	1 Oct. 89	Civil, Moorshedabad.—Offg. Civil, Burdwan.
Deane, Andrew, *MD. FRCSI. LAH.Dub.* ...	1 Oct. 69	1 Oct. 89	Residency Surgeon, Cashmere.
Murray, William Flood, *MB. MCh.*	1 Oct. 69	1 Oct. 89	Civil, Shahabad.
M'Connell, James Frederick Parry, *MB. MCh. MRCS.* H.P. 70	1 Apr. 70	1 Apr. 90	Prof. of Mat. Med. and Clin. Med. and *ex officio* 2nd Physician, Med. Coll. Hosp., Calcutta.
O'Brien, Joseph,[34] *MA. MD. LRCP.Ed. LRCS.Ed.*	1 Apr. 70	1 Apr. 90	Professor of Surgery, Med. College, Calcutta, and *ex officio* 1st Surgeon, College Hospital.
M'Donnell, James O'Malley, *MD. MCh. FRCS.*	1 Apr. 70	1 Apr. 90	Civil and Jail, Rohtuck.
Crombie, Alex. *MD. LRCS.Ed.* H.P. 71	30 Mar. 72	30 Mar. 92	Surg. Supdt. Presidency Gen. Hospital, Calcutta.
Murphy, William Reed,[35] *DSO. LRCSI. LRCPI.* H.P. 72	30 Mar. 72	30 Mar. 92	1 Battalion 2 Goorkhas.
Joubert, Charles Henry, *MB. FRCS.*	30 Mar. 72	30 Mar. 92	Professor of Midwifery, Medical College, and Obstetric Physician, Eden Hospital, Calcutta.
Russell, Edgar Geer, *MB. B.Sc. MRCS. LSA.*	30 Mar. 72	30 Mar. 92	Civil, Dacca.
Scully, John, *LRCP. MRCS.*	30 Mar. 72	30 Mar. 92	Assay Master, Calcutta Mint.
Hall, Geoffrey Craythorne, *LRCP.Ed. MRCS.*	30 Mar. 72	30 Mar. 92	Superintendent, Central Jail, Allahabad.
Reid, Adam Scott,[36] *MB. MCh.*	30 Mar. 72	30 Mar. 92	2 Battalion 4 Goorkhas.
Fasken, William Andrew Durnford, *MD. MRCS.*	30 Mar. 72	30 Mar. 92	Civil, Kheree.—Officiating Civil, Futtehghur.
Lawrie, Edward, *MB. MRCS.*	30 Mar. 72	30 Mar. 92	Residency Surgeon, Hyderabad.
Zorab, John Manook, *MB. MCh.*	30 Mar. 72	30 Mar. 92	Civil, Cuttack.
Dutt, Russick Lall, *MD. MRCS. LSA.*	30 Mar. 72	30 Mar. 92	Civil, Hoogly.
Bookey, John T. Brownrigg,[37] *LRCP.Ed. LRCSI.*	30 Mar. 72	30 Mar. 92	6 Punjab Infantry.
Young, James,[38] *MB.MCh.Ed.* P.B.M., M.M., H.P., M.G.M. 83	30 Mar. 72	30 Mar. 92	Bengal Sappers and Miners.
Duke, Joshua,[40] *MRCS. LSA.*	30 Mar. 72	30 Mar. 92	Malwah Bheel Corps.
M'Conaghey, John, *MD. MCh.*	30 Mar. 72	30 Mar. 92	Civil, Benares.—Offg. Civil and Jail, Lucknow.
Palmer, Edward,[41] *LRCPI. LRCSI.*	30 Mar. 72	30 Mar. 92	9 Bengal Lancers.
Williams, Alfred Henry,[42] *MB. MCh. MRCS.*	30 Mar. 72	30 Mar. 92	Bengal Infantry.
Holmes, Robert Andrew King, *BA. MD. MRCS.*	30 Mar. 72	30 Mar. 92	Superintendent, Jails, Lucknow.
Moriarty, Matthew Denis, *BA. MB. FRCSI.*	1 Oct. 72	1 Oct. 92	Civil, Bijnore.—Officiating Civil and Jail, Meerut.
Price, Gordon, *MD. MCh.*	1 Oct. 72	1 Oct. 92	Civil, Burdwan.—Officiating Civil, Moorshedabad.
Bovill, Edward, *MB. MCh. FRCS.*	1 Oct. 72	1 Oct. 92	Civil, Chumparun.
O'Brien, Bartholomew, *MD. MCh.*	1 Oct. 72	1 Oct. 92	Civil, Allahabad.
Ahmed, Zalnoor Allee,[43] *MD. LRCP.Ed. LFPS.Glas.*	1 Oct. 72	1 Oct. 92	28 Bengal Infantry.
Griffiths, Wm. Edwin,[44] *MRCS. LSA*	1 Oct. 72	1 Oct. 92	20 Bengal Infantry.

		SURGEON.	
Wilkie, David, *MB. MCh.* H.P. 73		1 Apr. 73	1 Apr. 93	Statistical Officer to Govt. of India in Sanitary, &c., Departments.
Macdonald, Denis Peter, *MD. MCh. LRCSI.*		1 Apr. 73	1 Apr. 93	Senior Medical Officer, Port Blair.
Baker, Oswald, *LRCP.Ed. LRCS.Ed.*		1 Apr. 73	1 Apr. 93	Junior, Civil, and Superintendent Lunatic Asylum, Rangoon.
Wright, Frederick Wm.[46] *DSO. MB. MCh.*		1 Apr. 73	1 Apr. 93	6 Bengal Infantry.
Willcocks, Alexander John, *MD. MRCS.* *Hon. Surgeon to the Governor General* ...		30 Sept. 73	30 Sept. 93	Civil and Lunatic Asylum, Agra.
M'Kay, Henry Kellock,[47] *MRCS. LSA.* ...		30 Sept. 73	30 Sept. 93	Civil, Jubbulpore.
Swaine, Frederick Robert, *MB. MCh.*		30 Sept. 73	30 Sept. 93	Civil and Jail, Lohardugga.
Browne, Samuel Haslett, *MD. MCh.*		31 Mar. 74	31 Mar. 94	Principal, Lahore Medical School.
Mair, Edward, *MB. MCh.*		31 Mar. 74	31 Mar. 94	Superintendent Central Jail, Bareilly.
Armstrong, James, *MB. MCh.*		31 Mar. 74	31 Mar. 94	Civil, Alighur.—Offg. Civil and Jail, Cawnpore.
Fullerton, John Campbell,[50] *BA. MB. MCh.*		31 Mar. 74	31 Mar. 94	Beloochistan Political Agency.—Furlough.
Warden, Charles James Hislop, *LRCP. MRCS.*		31 Mar. 74	31 Mar. 94	Medical Storekeeper to Government, Calcutta.
Stoker, Rd. Nugent,[51] *LRCPI. LRCSI.*		30 Sept. 74	30 Sept. 94	2 Battalion 1 Goorkhas.
Bomford, Gerald, *MD. LRCP. MRCS. LSA.*		30 Sept. 74	30 Sept. 94	Principal, Medical College, Calcutta, and *ex-officio* 1st Physician, Med. Coll. Hospital.
M'Cartie, Charles Joseph,[52] *MD. MCh.* ...		30 Sept. 74	30 Sept. 94	39 Bengal Infantry.
Ranking, George Spiers Alex. *BA. MD. MRCS. LSA.* H.P. 75		31 Mar. 75	31 Mar. 95	Secretary to the Board of Examiners.
Murray, Robert Davidson,[54] *MB. MCh.* ...		31 Mar. 75	31 Mar. 95	Civil, Gya.—Officiating Civil, Chittagong.
Comins, Dennis Wood Deane,[55] *LRCP. MRCS.*		31 Mar. 75	31 Mar. 95	Inspector General of Jails, Bengal.
O'Connor, Patrick Fenélon,[56] *MD. MCh.* ...		31 Mar. 75	31 Mar. 95	6 Bengal Cavalry.
Moran, James,[57] *BA. MD. MCh.*		31 Mar. 75	31 Mar. 95	Civil, Seetapore.—Offg.Civil and Jail, Goruckpore.
Simmonds, William Allason,[58] *LRCP. MRCS. LSA.*		31 Mar. 75	31 Mar. 95	12 Bengal Cavalry.
Macrae, Roderick, *MB. MCh.*		31 Mar. 75	31 Mar. 95	Civil, Pooree.—Officiating Civil, Gya.
Bate, Thomas Elwood Lindesay, *LRCPI. LRCSI.*		31 Mar. 75	31 Mar. 95	Inspector General of Prisons, Punjab.
Borah, Shibram,[60] *MB. LRCP.Ed. LFPS. Glas.*		31 Mar. 75	31 Mar. 95	Civil, Seebsaugor.

SURGEON MAJORS.		SURGEON MAJOR.	
Weir, Patrick Alex.,[61] *MA. MB. MCh.Ab.* H.P. 76		30 Sept. 75	30 Sept. 87	Residency Surg. and *ex officio* Assist. Resident, Nepaul.—Offg. Agency Surg., Beloochistan.
Freyer, Peter Johnston, *BA. MD. MCh.*		30 Sept. 75	30 Sept. 87	Civil, Saharunpore.—Officiating Civil, Benares.

Surgeon Majors.	Surgeon.	Surgeon Major.	Remarks.
Haig, Percy de Haga,[64] *LRCP. MRCS*	30 Sept. 75	30 Sept. 87	1 Punjab Cavalry.
Lewtas, John,[65] *MD. MRCS. LSA.*	30 Sept. 75	30 Sept. 87	Civil, Chittagong.—Offg. Statistical Officer to Govt. of India, Sanitary and Med. Depts.
O'Neill, John,[66] *MD. MCh.*	30 Sept. 75	30 Sept. 87	Civil, Goordaspore.—Furlough.
Toutes, Arthur, *MD. MRCS. LSA.* H.P. 76	31 Mar. 76	31 Mar. 88	Civil, Midnapore.—Sick Furlough.
Mawson, Wm. Arthur,[67] *LRCP. MRCS.*	31 Mar. 76	31 Mar. 88	11 Bengal Lancers.
Dantra, Sorabshaw Hormasji, *MD. MCh.*	31 Mar. 76	31 Mar. 88	Civil, Mandalay.
Hamilton, Henry,[68] *BA. MD. MCh.*	31 Mar. 76	31 Mar. 88	Officiating 1 Bengal Cavalry.
Doyle, Bernard,[69] *MB. MCh.*	31 Mar. 76	31 Mar. 88	Civil, Peshawur.
Cobb, Robert, *MD. LRCP. MRCS.*	31 Mar. 76	31 Mar. 88	Civil, Darjeeling.
Stephens, Augustus Edwd. Rich,[70] *LRCP. MRCS.*	31 Mar. 76	31 Mar. 88	Civil, Jessore.
Gadge, William Hotson, *LRCP. MRCS.*	31 Mar. 76	31 Mar. 88	Civil, Gondah.—Officiating Civil, Nynee Tal.
Moorhead, James, *MA. MD. MRCS.*, H.P. M.G.M. 77	30 Sept. 76	30 Sept. 88	Civil, Bengal.—On deputation Joint Civil, Simla.
Owen, Charles William,[71] *CMG. CIE. LRCP. MRCS.*	30 Sept. 76	30 Sept. 88	Medical Adviser to H. H. Maharaja of Patiala.
Griffiths, Gilbert Saunders,[72] *MRCS. LSA.*	30 Sept. 76	30 Sept. 88	1 Battalion 4 Goorkhas.
Owen, William,[73] *BA. MD. LRCSI.*	31 Mar. 77	31 Mar. 89	Superintendent Opium Factory, Behar.
Conry, Walter,[74] *MB. LRCP.Ed. LRCS.Ed.*	31 Mar. 77	31 Mar. 89	13 Bengal Lancers.
Kellie, George Jerome,[75] *LRCP. MRCS.*	31 Mar. 77	31 Mar. 89	2 Lancers Hyderabad Contingent.
Basu, Dharmadas, *LRCP.Ed. LFPS. Glas.*	31 Mar. 77	31 Mar. 89	Civil, Mymensingh.—Furlough.
Mackenzie, Alexander William,[76] *MB. MCh.*	31 Mar. 77	31 Mar. 89	3 Sikh Infantry.
Mullane, Jeremiah,[77] *MD. MCh.*	31 Mar. 77	31 Mar. 89	Civil, Debrooghur.
ffrench-Mullen, Douglas, *MD. MCh.*	31 Mar. 77	31 Mar. 89	Merwara Battalion.
Nelis, James Alexander,[78] *MB. LCh.*	31 Mar. 77	31 Mar. 89	1 Battalion 5 Goorkhas.
Crofts, Aylmer Martin,[79] *LRCP.Ed.LRCS.Ed.*	31 Mar. 77	31 Mar. 89	Residency Surgeon, Gwalior. [Agencies.
Crofts, James,[80] *MD. MCh.*	31 Mar. 77	31 Mar. 89	In. med. charge of Kotah and Jhullawur Political
Coates, William,[81] *MD. MCh.*	31 Mar. 77	31 Mar. 89	Civil, Lahore.
Bentson, Chas. Hy.[82] *LRCP.Ed. LRCS.Ed.*	30 Sept. 76	16 May 89	10 Bengal Lancers.
Thomson, Samuel John,[83] *MRCS. LSA.* H.P. M.G.M. 78	1 Oct. 77	1 Oct. 89	Deputy Sanitary Commissioner, N.W. Provinces, 2nd Circle.—Furlough.
Campbell, Robert Neil,[84] *MB. MCh.*	1 Oct. 77	1 Oct. 89	Civil and Jail, Gowhatty.
Brander, Edward Salisbury,[85] *MB. MCh. LRCP.Ed. LRCS.Ed.*	1 Oct. 77	1 Oct. 89	Civil, Jounpore.—Officiating Civil and Jail, Minpoorie.
Chatterjie, Fakir Chundra,[86] *MB. MCh.*	1 Oct. 77	1 Oct. 89	Civil, Unao.—Offg. Civil and Jail, Pilibheet.
Emerson, George Augustus,[87] *MB. MCh.*	1 Oct. 77	1 Oct. 89	Civil, Mirzapore.
Mullen, Jarlath ffrench, *MD. MCh.* H.P. 77	30 Mar. 78	30 Mar. 90	Civil, Rajshahye.—Officiating Civil, Burdwan.
Cretin, Eugene,[89] *MB. LRCP. FRCS. LSA.* H.P. M.G.M. 78	30 Mar. 78	30 Mar. 90	1 Bengal Infantry.
Duncan, Andrew,[90] *MD. FRCS. LSA.* P.B.M. 78, P.G.M. 86	30 Mar. 78	30 Mar. 90	2 Battalion 2 Goorkhas.
Nicholson, George Frederick, *MD. LRCSI.*	30 Mar. 78	30 Mar. 90	Medical Officer to the Rajah of Jhind.
Bigger, Saml. Ferguson,[92] *MB. MRCS.LSA.*	30 Mar. 78	30 Mar. 90	3 Punjab Cavalry.
Robertson, George Scott,[93] *CSI. MRCS.LSA.*	30 Mar. 78	30 Mar. 90	British Agent, Gilgit.
Nixon, Geo. Michael,[94] *MB. MCh.*	30 Mar. 78	30 Mar. 90	Civil, Moradabad.—Offg. Civil and Jail, Jhansi.
Sweeny, Terence Humphrys,[95] *LRCPI. FRCSI.* H.P. P.B.M. 79	30 Sept. 78	30 Sept. 90	Civil, Bareilly.—Offg. Civil and Jail, Fyzabad.
Barry, Daniel Francis,[96] *MD. MCh.* M.G.M. 79	30 Sept. 78	30 Sept. 90	Civil, Bulandshuhur.—Offg. Civil and Jail, Seetapore.
Harris, Geo. Francis Angelo, *LRCP. MRCS.*	30 Sept. 78	30 Sept. 90	Civil, Nagpore.
Anderson, John,[98] *MB. MCh.*	30 Sept. 78	30 Sept. 90	Civil, Minpoorie.—Offg. Civil, Bareilly.
Bamber, Charles James,[99] *LRCP. MRCS.*	30 Sept. 78	30 Sept. 90	Civil, Rawul Pindee.
O'Dwyar, Malachi,[100] *BA. MB. BCh.*	30 Sept. 78	30 Sept. 90	Civil and Jail. Jullundur.
Perry, Francis Frederic, *LRCP. MRCS.* H.P. M.G.M. P.B.M. 79	31 Mar. 79	31 Mar. 91	Professor of Surgery, Lahore Medical School.—Furlough.
Little, Stephen,[101] *MD. MCh.*	31 Mar. 79	31 Mar. 91	Civil, Mooltan.
Gimlette, Geo. Hart Desmond,[102] *MD.MCh. MRCS.LSA.*	31 Mar. 79	31 Mar. 91	Agency Surgeon at Bhaugelcund.
Hunter, Christian Bernard,[103] *LRCP. MRCS.*	31 Mar. 79	31 Mar. 91	5 Punjab Cavalry.
Smith, Julian Carter Carington,[104] *MB. MCh.*	31 Mar. 79	31 Mar. 91	Civil, Shahjehanpore.—Officiating Civil and Jail, Bara Bankee.
Dennys, George Wm. Patrick, *LRCP. MRCS.*	31 Oct. 79	31 Oct. 91	Civil, Delhi.
Macnamara, John William Unthank, *MD. LRCSI. LAH.Dub.*	31 Oct. 79	31 Oct. 91	Civil and Jail and Lunatic Asylum, Tezpore.
Sykes, Joseph,[105] *LRCP.Ed. LFPS.Glas.*	31 Oct. 79	31 Oct. 91	Civil, Ghazeepore.—Offg. Civil, Mussoorie.
Tuohy, John Francis, *MD. MCh.*	31 Oct. 79	31 Oct. 91	Civil, Fyzabad.—Offg. Civil & Jail, Saharanpore.
Lukis, Chas. Pardey,[106] *MRCS.LSA.* P.B.M. 80	31 Mar. 80	31 Mar. 92	Civil, Futtehghur.—Officiating Civil and Jail, Shahjehanpore.
Whitwell, Robert Richard Harvey, *MB. MCh.*	31 Mar. 80	31 Mar. 92	Civil, Bhaugulpore.
Waddell, Lawrence Austine,[108] *MB. MCh.*	31 Mar. 80	31 Mar. 92	Deputy Sanitary Commissioner, Darjeeling Circle, Bengal.—Furlough.
Shewan, George Money,[109] *MB.*	31 Mar. 80	31 Mar. 92	17 Native Infantry.
Spencer, Dhanjibhai Barjooji,[110] *LFPS.Glas. LSA.*	31 Mar. 80	31 Mar. 92	12 Native Infantry.
Clarke, James,[111] *MD. MCh.*	31 Mar. 80	31 Mar. 92	Civil, Nuddea.—Offg. Professor of Surgery, Lahore Medical College.
Vaid, Cooverjee Cawasjee,[112] *LRCP.Ed. LFPS.Glas.*	31 Mar. 80	31 Mar. 92	Civil, Nynee Tal.—Officiating Civil, Kheri.
Pank, Philip Durrell, *LRCP.Ed. LRCS.Ed.*	31 Mar. 80	31 Mar. 92	Residency Surgeon, Meywar.
Mulroney, Thomas Richard, *MD. MCh. LRCP.Ed. LRCS.Ed. MRCS.*	31 Mar. 80	31 Mar. 92	Civil and Jail, Umritsur.
Macdonald, Thomas Rankin,[113] *MB. MCh. LRCS.Ed.*	31 Mar. 80	31 Mar. 92	Civil, Saran.
Giles, George Michael Jas., *MB. FRCS.LSA.* H.P. P.B.M. 81	2 Oct. 80	2 Oct. 92	Officiating Civil and Jail, Bijnore.
Sedgefield, Arthur Rbt. Wyatt, *MB. MRCS.*	2 Oct. 80	2 Oct. 92	Superintendent Opium Factory, Ghazeepore.
Dobson, Edwin Francis Horatio, *MB. MCh.*	2 Oct. 80	2 Oct. 92	Civil, Shillong.
Shearer, Johnston,[114] *MA. MB. MCh.*	2 Oct. 80	2 Oct. 92	27 Bengal Infantry.
Hassan, Syed,[115] *MB. LRCP. MRCS.*	2 Oct. 80	2 Oct. 92	3 Bengal Infantry.
Banerji, Hem Chandra,[117] *LRCP. Ed. LFPS. Glas.*	2 Oct. 80	2 Oct. 92	Civil and Jail, Sylhet.
Naudi, Sambhu Chandra,[116] *MB. MCh.*	2 Oct. 80	2 Oct. 92	Wing at Buxar.

Bengal Medical Department.

SURGEON MAJORS.	SURGEON.	SURGEON MAJOR.	REMARKS.
Peck, Francis Samuel,[118] *LRCP.Ed. MRCS.*	2 Oct. 80	2 Oct. 92	Civil, Mozufferpore.
Deane, William,[119] *LRCP.Ed. LRCSI.*	2 Oct. 80	2 Oct. 92	Civil, Azimghur.—Offg. Civil and Jail, Moradabad.
Hawkins, Frederick Daly Cæsar, *LRCP.Ed. MRCS.*	2 Apr. 81	2 Apr. 93	Civil, Goruckpore.—Officiating Civil, Etawah.
Cunningham, John Adams, *MD. MCh.*	2 Apr. 81	2 Apr. 93	Civil, Simla.
Hudson, Harry Chalmers,[120] *LRCPI. LRCSI.*	2 Apr. 81	2 Apr. 93	16 Bengal Cavalry.
Silcock, Alexander, *BA. MB. BCh. MRCPI.*	2 Apr. 81	2 Apr. 93	Civil, Belaspore.
Mullane, Patrick,[121] *MD., MCh.*	2 Apr. 81	2 Apr. 93	7 Bengal Infantry.
Rodgers, John Wm.,[121]† *LRCP.Ed. LRCS.Ed*	2 Apr. 81	2 Apr. 93	2 Sikh Infantry.
Maclaren, James Farquharson, *MB. MCh.*	2 Apr. 81	2 Apr. 93	Civil, Sultanpore.—Offg. Civil & Jail, Ghazeepore.
Young, Louis Tarleton,[122] *BA. MB. BCh. Dub. LCh.* H.P. M.S.M. P.B.M. 82	1 Oct. 81	1 Oct. 93	Civil, Umballa.
Gibbons, Jas. Barry, *LRCSI. LRCPI.* M.M. 82	1 Oct. 81	1 Oct. 93	Supt. Campbell Med. School & Hospital, Sealdah.
Grant, Donald St. John Dundas,[123] *MB. BCh.*	1 Oct. 81	1 Oct. 93	{ Chemical Examiner, Punjab, and Professor Medical College, Lahore.
Crawford, Dirom Grey, *MB. MCh. Hon. FRCSI.*	1 Oct. 81	1 Oct. 93	Civil, Monghyr.
Charles, Richard Havelock, *MD. MCh. LRCS.Ed.* H.P. P.B.M. 82	1 Apr. 82	1 Apr. 94	{ Professor of Anatomy, Medical Coll., Calcutta, and *ex officio* 2nd Surg. College Hospital.
Duncan, George,[124] *MB. MCh. LRCS.Ed.,*	1 Apr. 82	1 Apr. 94	2 Battalion 5 Goorkhas.
Sykes, Wm. Ainley,[125] *DSO. MB. LRCP. MRCS.*	1 Apr. 82	1 Apr. 94	18 Bengal Lancers.
Leahy, Albert Wm. Denis, *FRCS.LSA.* H.P. 83	30 Sept. 82	30 Sept. 94	Civil, 24-Pergunnahs.
Weir, Richard Rose, *MB. MCh.Ab.* P.B.M. 83	30 Sept. 82	30 Sept. 94	Jails, Futtehghur.
Jameson, Granville,[126] *MB. MCh. MRCS.*	31 Mar. 83	31 Mar. 95	Civil, Tipperah.—Officiating Civil, Malda.

SURGEON CAPTAINS.		SURGEON CAPTAIN.	
Pratt, Jas. John, *MRCS. LRCP.Ed.* H.P. M.M. 84		29 Sept. 83	Civil, Banda.—Offg. Civil and Jail, Gondah.
Shore, Robert, *MD. LFPS.Glas.*		29 Sept. 83	Meywar Bheel Corps.
Walsh, John Henry Tull,[126] *MRCS. LRCP.* H.P. M.G.M. M.M. 84		1 Apr. 84	{ 1st Resident Surgeon, Presidency General Hospital.—Furlough.
Hendley, Harold,[129] *MRCS. LSA.*		1 Apr. 84	Civil, Kangra.
Banatvala, Hormasjie Edaljie,[130] *MD. LRCP. MRCS.*		1 Apr. 84	33 Bengal Infantry.
Fink, George Herbert, *MRCS., LSA.*		1 Apr. 84	Civil, Jhansi.
Alpin, William George Patrick, *MD. LRCP. MRCS*		1 Apr. 84	{ Civil, Moozuffernugger.—Officiating Civil and Jail, Hardoi.
Leslie, John Tasman Waddell, *MB. MCh.Ab.* H.P. M.G.M. 85		1 Oct. 84	{ Sec. to Surg. Gen. and Sanitary Commr. with Govt. of India.
Prain, David, *MB. MCh. LRCS.Ed.*		1 Oct. 84	Curator of Herbarium, Calcutta.
Bown, Arthur Thomas, *LRCP. MRCS.*		1 Oct. 84	27 Bengal Infantry.
Mukerji, Upendra Nath, *MD. MCh. MRCS.*		1 Oct. 84	5 Bengal Infantry.
Price, William Locking,[132] *MB. MCh.*		1 Oct. 84	Officiating Civil, Chindwara.
Drury, Francis James,[133] *BA. MB. BCh.*		1 Apr. 85	{ Resident Surgeon, Med. Coll. Hospital, Calcutta, and Professor of Pathology, Medical College.
Dyson, Herbert Jekyl,[134] *FRCS. LSA.* M.M. 85		1 Apr. 85	Deputy Sanitary Commissioner, Punjab.
Rogers, Frederick Arthur,[135] *DSO. LRCP. MRCS.*		1 Apr. 85	Civil, Bogra.—Officiating Civil, Tipperah.
Carroll, Edward Richard Wm. Chas.,[136] *LRCP. MRCS.*		1 Apr. 85	16 Bengal Infantry.
Woolbert, Henry Robert, *MB. MRCS.*		1 Oct. 85	Med. Officer, Meshed.—Offg. Deolee Irreg. Force.
Baker, George Henry,[137] *MRCS. LSA.*		1 Oct. 85	Civil, Cawnpore.—Offg. Civil and Jail, Banda.
Grainger, Thomas,[138] *MD. MCh.*		1 Oct. 85	Civil, Khoolna.
Adie, Joseph Rosamond,[139] *MB. MRCS.*		1 Oct. 85	Civil, Purneah.—Sick Furlough.
Younan, Arthur Charles,[140] *MB. MCh.*		1 Oct. 85	25 Bengal Infantry.
Alcock, Alfred William, *MB. MCh.*		1 Oct. 85	Superintendent of Museum, Calcutta.
Cadell, John Macfarlane,[142] *MB. MCh.*		1 Oct. 85	11 Bengal Infantry. [N.W.P.
Thorold, William Grant, *LRCP. MRCS.* H.P. M. 86.		1 Apr. 86	Dep. San. Commr., 3rd Circle.—Offg. 2nd Circle.
Hehir, Patrick,[143] *MD. LRCP.Ed. FRCS.Ed. MRCS. LSA. DPH.Camb.* M.G.M. 86		1 Apr. 86	Staff Surgeon, Nizam's Troops.
Pisani, Lionel John,[144] *MRCS. LSA.*		1 Apr. 86	Civil, Roy Bareilly.—Offg. Civil & Jail, Jaunpore.
Basu, Basanta Kumar, *MD. MCh.*		1 Apr. 86	4 Bengal Infantry. [Offg. Civil, Jessore.
Sinha, Narendra Prasanna, *MRCP. MRCS.*		1 Apr. 86	Deputy Sanitary Commissioner, W. B. Circle.—
Edwards, William Rice, *MD. MRCS.*		1 Apr. 86	Civil, Quetta.
Mactaggart, Charles, *MA. MB. MCh.*		1 Apr. 86	Superintendent of Jails, Agra. [Coll. Calcutta.
Evans, John Fenton, *MB. MCh.*		1 Apr. 86	Chemical Examiner & Prof. of Chemistry, Med.
Bell, George James Hamilton,[145] *MB. MCh.*		1 Apr. 86	Superintendent, Insein Jail.
Daly, Joseph Thomas, *MB. MCh. MRCPI.*		1 Apr. 86	8 Bengal Cavalry.
Fooks, Henry,[146] *MRCS. LSA.*		1 Apr. 86	1 Sikh Infantry.
Hudson, Ernest,[147] *FRCS. LSA.*		1 Apr. 86	15 Bengal Lancers.
Dawson, Arthur William, *MB. MRCS.*		1 Apr. 86	2 Bengal Lancers.
Robinson, Wm. Hy. Banner,[148] *LRCPI. LRCSI.*		1 Apr. 86	34 Bengal Infantry.
Macnamara, Robert Joseph, *MD. MCh.*		30 Sept. 86	Mooltan Central Jail. [Offg. 1st Resdt. Surgeon
Pilgrim, Herbert Wilson, *MB. MRCS. LSA.*		30 Sept. 86	2nd Resdt. Surgeon, Presidency General Hospital.—
French, George Brooke, *LRCP. MRCS.*		30 Sept. 86	8 Bengal Infantry.
Thomson, Francis Wyville, *MA. MB. MCh.*		30 Sept. 86	3 Bengal Cavalry.
Brown, Edwin Harold, *LRCP. LRCS.Ed.*		30 Sept. 86	Civil, Durbhunga.
Bensley, Charles Norman, *MB. MCh.*		30 Sept. 86	Civil and Jail, Toungoo.
Henderson, Selby Herriot, *MB. MCh.*		30 Sept. 86	35 Bengal Infantry.
Scotland, David Wilson, *MB. MCh.*		30 Sept. 86	Officiating Jails, Benares.
Green, Chas. Robert Mortimer,[150] *LRCP. MRCS.LSA.*		30 Sept. 86	Civil, Maubhoom.—Furlough.
Sellick, James Henderson, *MB. MRCS.*		30 Sept. 86	Civil, Sagaing.—Offg. Civil and Jail, Myingyan.
Hare, Edward Christian, *LRCP. MRCS.*		30 Sept. 86	Civil, Chanda.—On special duty, Assam.
Clarkson, Frank Cecil, *LRCP. MRCS.*		30 Sept. 86	36 Bengal Infantry.
Jordan, John Gregory, *MB. MCh.*		30 Sept. 86	31 Bengal Infantry.
Morris, Herbert Mackinlay, *LRCP. MRCS.*		30 Sept. 86	Officiating Civil, Goojerat.
Russell, Allan Rupert Postance, *MB. MCh.*		30 Sept. 86	Civil, Yemethin.—Offg. Civil and Jail, Toungoo.
Morwood, James,[151] *MD. MCh.*		30 Sept. 86	Civil, Meerut.—Offg. Civil and Jail, Basti.
Hall, Edmund Alexander William, *MB. MCh.*		30 Sept 86	Officiating Civil, Maunbhoom.
Elliot, William Henry Wilson,[152] *MRCS. LSA. MB.*		31 Mar. 87	4 Punjab Infantry.
Murray, James,[153] *MB. MCh.Ab.* P.B.M. 87		31 Mar. 87	Professor, Lahore Medical College.
Clark, William Ronaldson, *MB. MCh.*		31 Mar. 87	Civil, Ferozepore.
Braide, George Frederick William, *MB. MRCS.*		31 Mar. 87	Central Jail, Lahore.
Marks, Robert John, *MRCS. LSA.*		31 Mar. 87	14 Bengal Lancers.
Sunder, Charles Edward,[155] *MB. MRCS. LSA.*		31 Mar. 87	Resident Surgeon, Eden Hospital, Calcutta.
Ker, Malcolm Albert, *MB. MCh.*		31 Mar. 87	19 Bengal Lancers.
Buchanan, Andrew, *MA. MD. MCh,*		31 Mar. 87	Superintendent Central Jail, Nagpore.
Fischer, Lewis Gordon, *MB. MCh.,*		31 Mar. 87	Civil, Baraitch.—Offg. Civil and Jail, Budaun.
Vost, William, *MB. MCh. MRCS.*		31 Mar. 87	10 Bengal Infantry.

SURGEON CAPTAINS.	SURGEON CAPTAIN	REMARKS.
Garvie, John, *MB. MCh.*	31 Mar. 87	2 Punjab Cavalry.
Gilbert, Clarence E. L.,[156] *MB. MCh. LRCPI. MRCS.*	31 Mar. 87	30 Bengal Infantry.
Manifold, Courtenay Clarke, *MB. MCh.*	31 Mar. 87	Medical Officer, Rampore State.
Irvine, Gerard Beatty, *LRCPI. LRCSI.*	31 Mar. 87	14 Bengal Infantry.
Roberts, Alfred Ernest, *MB. MCh. MRCS. M.G.M.* 88	1 Oct. 87	Civil, Dehra Dhoon—Offg. Civil and Jail, Alighur.
Davidson, David Macdonald, *MB. MCh. Ab. H.P. P.B.M. M.M.* 88	1 Oct. 87	Civil, Goordaspore.
Maynard, Frederic Pinsent, *MB. LRCP. MRCS.*	1 Oct. 87	13 Bengal Infantry.
Lamont, John Charles, *MB. MCh. MRCS.*	1 Oct. 87	Professor of Anatomy, Lahore Medical College.
Nott, Arthur Holbrook,[158] *MB. LRCP. MRCS.*	1 Oct. 87	2 Punjab Infantry.
Coleman, Albert, *MB. MCh.*	1 Oct. 87	Superintendent Central Jail, Montgomery.
White, William Westropp,[159] *MD. MCh.*	1 Oct. 87	4 Bengal Cavalry.
Lane, Daniel Thomas, *MD. MCh.*	1 Oct. 87	29 Bengal Infantry.
Macwatt, Robert Charles, *MB. MCh.*	1 Oct. 87	Superintendent Central Jail, Raepore.—Officiating [Civil, Saugor.
Woodwright, Wm. Hy. Edwd.,[160] *LRCPI. LRCSI.*	1 Oct. 87	Officiating 10 Bengal Lancers.
Buchanan, Walter James, *BA. Dub. MB. BCh. LM.*	1 Oct. 87	General duty, Presidency General Hospital.
Close, Joseph Kinnear,[161] *MD. MCh.*	1 Oct. 87	26 Bengal Infantry.
Marshall, Daniel Grove,[162] *MB. MCh. Ed. H.P. P.B.M. M.M.* 88	31 Mar. 88	17 Bengal Cavalry.
Moir, David Macbeth, *M.A. MB. MCh. MRCP. M.G.M.* 88	31 Mar. 88	{ Dep. San. Commr. Metrop. and E. Bengal Circle. —Offg. 2nd Res. Surg. Pres. Gen. Hosp. Calcutta.
Whitchurch, Harry Frederick, *LRCP. MRCS.*	31 Mar. 88	24 Bengal Infantry.
Roberts, James Reid,[163] *MB. LRCP. FRCS.*	31 Mar. 88	Agency Surgeon, Gilgit.—Furlough.
Gee, Frederick William, *MB. MRCS. LSA.*	31 Mar. 88	5 Bengal Cavalry.
Prasad, Kanta, *MB. MCh. LRCP. Ed. LRCS. Ed. LFPS. Glas.*	31 Mar. 88	10 Bengal Infantry.
O'Gorman, Patrick Wilkins, *LRCP. Ed. LRCS. Ed. LFPS. Glas.*	31 Mar. 88	Officiating Civil, Midnapore.
Gray, William Henry, *MB. MCh.*	31 Mar. 88	19 Bengal Infantry.
Mould, George Thomas, *LRCP. MRCS.*	31 Mar. 88	1 Bengal Cavalry.
Drake-Brockman, Herbert Edward, *MRCS. LRCP. H.P. M.G.M. P.B.M.* 89	29 Sept. 88	Civil, Etawah.—Officiating Civil, Muttra.
Lane, William Byam, *LRCP. MRCS.*	29 Sept. 88	23 Bengal Infantry.
Lumsden, Philip James, *MB. MCh.*	29 Sept. 88	Residency Surgeon, Persian Gulf.
Ozzard, Fairlie Russell,[164] *LRCP. MRCS.*	30 Mar. 89	1 Punjab Infantry.
Anderson, Andrew Rivers Steele, *BA. MB. DPH. MRCS.*	30 Mar. 89	Surgeon Naturalist, Marine Survey of India.
Calvert, John Telfer, *MB. LRCP. MRCS. DPH.*	30 Mar. 89	Officiating Civil, Mymensingh.
Jennings, Edgar, *MRCS. LSA.*	30 Mar. 89	32 Bengal Infantry.
Hendley, Arthur Gervase, *LRCP. MRCS.*	30 Mar. 89	Sick Furlough.
Melville, Henry Bruce, *MB. MCh.*	30 Mar. 89	North Lushai.—Officiating Civil, Azimghur.
Vaughan, Joseph Charles Stoelke, *MB. MCh.*	30 Sept. 89	Officiating Dep. San. Commr. West. Bengal Circle.
Duke, Alexander Leonard, *MB. MCh.*	30 Sept. 89	Officiating Agency Surgeon, Meshed.
Chaytor-White, Joshua, *MB. MCh.*	30 Sept. 89	42 Bengal Infantry.
Elphick, Harry William, *MB. LRCP. MRCS.*	30 Sept. 89	Officiating Civil and Jail, Moozuffernugger.
Bedford, Charles Henry, *MD. MCh. DSc. MRCS. FSA. Scot.*	30 Sept. 89	21 Bengal Infantry.
Macnab, Allan James,[166] *LRCP. MRCS.*	31 Mar. 90	Corps of Guides.
Smith, Henry, *MD. MCh.*	31 Mar. 90	Medical Officer, Muskoff Bolan Railway.
Luard, Hugh Bixby,[167] *BA. MB. DPH. LRCP. MRCS.*	31 Mar. 90	22 Bengal Infantry.
Wimberley, Charles Neil Campbell, *MB. MCh.*	31 Mar. 90	15 Bengal Infantry.
Hore, Ernest Wickham, *MB. LRCP. MRCS.*	31 Mar. 90	Medical charge, Loralai Outposts.
Crawford, James Muir, *MB. MCh. LRCP. Ed. LRCS. Ed. LFPS. Glas.*	31 Jan. 91	Officiating Civil, North West Provinces.
Wolfe, John William, *MB. BCh.*	31 Jan. 91	Offg. Sec. to Insp. Gen. of Jails, &c., Burmah.
Singh, Bawa Jiwan, *MRCS. LRCP.*	31 Jan. 91	4 Sikh Infantry.
Barber, Hugh Robert Campbell, *MB.*	31 Jan. 91	Civil, Sealkote.
James, Charles Henry, *LRCP. MRCS.*	31 Jan. 91	Officiating Central Jail, Montgomery.
O'Kinealy, Frederick, *MRCS. LRCP.*	31 Jan. 91	Resident Surg. Medical College Hosp. Calcutta.
Cassidy, Christopher Clemons, *LRCP. Ed. LRCS. Ed. LFPS. Glas.*	31 Jan. 91	Officiating Civil, Purneah.
Buist-Sparks, Arthur Wm. Treminhere, *MB. MCh.*	31 Jan. 91	General duty, Presidency General Hospital.
Burton-Brown, Frederic Hewlett, *MB. BCh.*	28 July 91	43 Bengal Infantry.
Deare, Benjamin Hobbs, *MRCS. LRCP.*	28 July 91	{ Officiating Deputy Sanitary Commissioner, Northern Bengal Circle.
Oldham, Benjamin Curwen, *MRCS. LRCP.*	28 July 91	{ Officiating Dep. San. Commr. Metropolitan and Eastern Bengal Circle.
Bird, Robert, *MCRS. LRCP. MD.*	28 July 91	General duty, Presidency General Hospital.
Smith, Sidney Browning, *MRCS. LRCP.*	28 July 91	Officiating 32 Bengal Infantry.
Henvey, William,[169] *MRCS. LRCP.*	28 July 91	Offg. Residency Surg. Turkish Arabia, Bagdad.
Lumsden, John Stuart Shepherd, *MB. MCh.*	28 July 91	Superintendent Bannoo Jail.—Waziristan Field
Frost, George Hewitt, *MB. BCh.*	28 July 91	Officiating 22 Bengal Infantry. [Force.
Wilkinson, Edmund, *MRCS. LRCP.*	28 July 91	Waziristan Field Force.
Ewens, George Francis William, *MRCS. LRCP. MD. LSA. DPH. Camb.*	28 July 91	Sikkim.
Duer, Charles, *MRCS. LRCP. MB.*	28 July 91	
Wood, Henry Stotesbury, *MB. MCh.*	28 July 91	Officiating 42 Bengal Infantry.
	SURG. LT.	
Seton, Bruce Gordon, *MRCS. LRCP.*	30 Jan. 92	Waziristan Field Force.

SURGEON LIEUTENANTS.	SURG. LT.	
Haig, Patrick Balfour, *MB. MCh. LRCP. MRCS.*	27 July 92	
Fullerton, Thomas William Archer, *MB. BCh.*	27 July 92	Officiating 3 Native Infantry.
Maddox, Ralph Henry, *MB. MCh. MRCS.*	27 July 92	Officiating 35 Bengal Infantry.
Hugo, Edward Victor, *MB. MRCS. LRCP.*	27 July 92	Waziristan Field Force.
Melville, Harry George, *MB. MCh.*	27 July 92	Waziristan Field Force.
Hubbard, Arthur Oldham, *MRCS. LRCP.*	27 July 92	Officiating 2 Battalion 3 Goorkhas.
Robson-Scott, Chas. Geo., *MB. MCh. LRCP. MRCS.*	27 July 92	Waziristan Field Force.
Smith, Herbert Austen, *MB. BCh. MRCS. LRCP.*	27 July 92	Furlough.
Green, Douglas Richard, *MB.*	27 July 92	Officiating 8 Bengal Infantry.
Smith, George M'Iver Campbell, *MB. MCh.*	27 July 92	Officiating 13 Bengal Lancers.
Earle, Hubert Malins, *MRCS. LRCP.*	27 July 92	Med. Officer, Lawrence Mil. Asylum, **Sanawar**
Hulbert, Joseph George, *MB. BCh. MRCS. LRCP.*	27 July 92	Officiating Erinpoorah Irregular Force.
Milne, Charles, *MB. MCh.*	30 Jan. 93	Officiating 38 Bengal Infantry.
Drake-Brockman, Vivian Godfrey, *MRCS. LRCP.*	30 Jan. 93	Officiating 10 Bengal Infantry.
Young, William, *MB. MCh.*	30 Jan. 93	Civil, North Lushai.

Surgeon Lieutenants.	Surg. Lt.	Remarks.
Bourke, John Joseph, *MB. BCh*.	30 Jan. 93	Officiating 18 Bengal Infantry.
Hunter, George Yeates Cobb, *MRCS. LRCP*.	30 Jan. 93	Officiating 13 Bengal Infantry.
Chatterton, Bernard Robert, *MB. BCh.*	30 Jan. 93	Wing 42 Bengal Infantry.
Prall, Cedric Barkley, *MRCS. LRCP.*	30 Jan. 93	Officiating 36 Bengal Infantry.
Williams, Charles Edward, *MB. BCh.*	30 Jan. 93	
MacLeod, John Norman, *MB. MCh.*	30 Jan. 93	Officiating 19 Bengal Lancers.
Ogilvie, Walter Holland. *MB. MCh.*	30 Jan. 93	Officiating 40 Bengal Infantry.
Langston, Thomas Alfred Ollivant, *MRCS. LRCP.*	30 Jan. 93	
Heard, Richard, *MB. BCh.*	30 Jan. 93	Waziristan Field Force.
Parry, Edgar Rowe, *MB. MCh.*	30 Jan. 93	Officiating 44 Bengal Infantry.
Orr, Walter Hood, *MRCS. LRCP.*	30 Jan. 93	
More, Paxton St. Clair, *MB. MCh.*	30 Jan. 93	Sick Furlough.
Stevens, Cecil Robert, *MD. LRCP. FRCS.*	29 July 93	Officiating 16 Bengal Infantry.
Barry, Cecil Charles Stuart, *MRCS. LRCP.*	29 July 93	
Rogers, Leonard, *MD. LRCP. FRCS.*	29 July 93	Officiating 1 Bengal Infantry.
Newman, Ernest Alan Robt., *MB. BCh. LRCP. MRCS.*	29 July 93	Officiating 2 Punjab Infantry.
Birdwood, Gordon Travers, *MB. BCh. LRCP. MRCS.*	29 July 93	Officiating 11 Bengal Lancers.
Gould, Jay, *MB.*	29 July 93	
Turner, Reginald George, *MRCS. LRCP.*	29 July 93	Officiating 19 Bengal Infantry.
Davidson, James, *MB. MCh.*	29 July 93	Waziristan Field Force.
Mulvany, John, *MRCS. LRCP.*	29 July 93	Officiating 2 Bengal Infantry.
Lamb, George	29 Jan. 94	Waziristan Field Force.
Burden, Henry	29 Jan. 94	Officiating 45 Bengal Infantry.
Fisher, John	29 Jan. 94	Medical charge, Civil Buxa, Julpigoree.
Peck, Edward Surman	29 Jan. 94	Officiating 3 Bengal Lancers.
Evans, Charles Harford	29 Jan. 94	Civil, Dera Ismail Khan.—Waziristan Field Force.
Harriss, Stanley Arthur	29 Jan. 94	
MacLeod, Ewan Cameron	29 Jan. 94	Civil, Rajanpore.
Thomson, Charles	29 Jan. 94	
Ramsay, George	28 July 94	Presidency District.
Sutherland, David Waters	28 July 94	Punjab Frontier Force.
Selby, William	28 July 94	Meerut District.
Granger, Thomas Arthur	28 July 94	Meerut District.
Grmfield, Harold John Kinahan	28 July 94	Lahore District.
Mant, John Wemyss	28 July 94	Rawul Pindee District.
Hoorhead, Arthur Henry	28 July 94	Waziristan Field Force.
Rayward, William Davey	28 July 94	Lahore District.
Sussell, Archibald William Forbes	28 July 94	Oude District.
Scott-Moncrieff, William Elmsley	28 July 94	Rawul Pindee District.
Milne, Charles John	29 Jan. 95	
Stevens, Algernon Francis	29 Jan. 95	
Bensley, Clement Henry	29 Jan. 95	
Watling, Francis Hammond	29 Jan. 95	
McMillan, John Duncan	29 Jan. 95	
Gwyther, Arthur	29 Jan. 95	
Morgan, Edgar John	29 Jan. 95	
Ward, Alfred Edward Joseph	29 Jan. 95	
Carr, William	29 Jan. 95	
Hamilton, John Archaibld	29 Jan. 95	

War Services.

¹ Surgeon Major General W. R. Rice served in the Indian Mutiny campaign in 1857 (Medal).

⁶ Surgeon Colonel J. Cleghorn served with the Bhootan Expedition in 1865-66 (Medal).

⁷ Surgeon Colonel R. Harvey served with the Bhootan Expedition in 1865-66 (Medal with Clasp); with the Looshai Expedition in 1871-72 (Clasp); and with the Miranzai Expedition in 1891 under Sir William Lockhart as Principal Medical Officer (mentioned in despatches, *DSO.*, and Clasp).

⁸ Surgeon Colonel G. Thomson served in the Afghan war in 1878-79 (Medal).

¹⁰ Brigade Surgeon Lt. Colonel R. Jameson served in the Abyssinian war in 1868 (Medal).

¹³ Brigade Surgeon Lt. Colonel W. Finden served in the Afghan war of 1878-80, accompanied Sir Frederick Roberts in the march to Candahar, and was present at the battle of Candahar (mentioned in despatches, Medal with Clasp, and Bronze Decoration). Served with the Burmese Expedition in 1887-88 (Medal with Clasp), and with the Miranzai Expedition in 1891 (Clasp).

¹⁵ Surgeon Colonel A. Stephen served in the Abyssinian war in 1868 (Medal).

¹⁶ Brigade Surgeon Lt. Colonel J. H. Newman served in the Abyssinian war in 1868 (Medal). Served in the Afghan war in 1878-79, and took part in the two expeditions into the Bazar Valley (Medal).

¹⁸ Brigade Surgeon Lt. Colonel J. C. G. Carmichael served with the Mahsood Wuzeeree Expedition in 1881. Served in the Egyptian war of 1882, and was present at the battle of Tel-el-Kebir (Medal with Clasp, and Khedive's Star). Served with the Burmese Expedition in 1886-87 (mentioned in despatches, Medal with Clasp).

²² Surgeon Lt. Colonel C. W. Calthorp served in the Afghan war in 1879-80, and was present in the engagement at Ali Kheyl and in the operations around Cabul in December 1879 including the investment of Sherpore (Medal with Clasp).

²⁴ Brigade Surgeon Lt. Colonel G. M. Davis served with the Mahsood Wuzeeree Expedition in 1881.

²⁵ Brigade Surgeon Lt. Colonel F. C. Nicholson served with the Looshai Expedition in 1871-72 (Medal with Clasp).

²⁶ Brigade Surgeon Lt. Colonel W. H. Gregg served with the Looshai Expedition in 1871-72 (Medal with Clasp).

²⁷ Brigade Surgeon Lt. Colonel A. B. Seaman served in the Afghan war in 1879-80 (Medal). Served with the Burmese Expedition in 1885-86 including the capture of Minhla (Medal with Clasp), and with the Lushai Expedition in 1889 as Principal Medical Officer to the force (mentioned in despatches).

²⁸ Surgeon Lt. Colonel F. A. Smyth served with the Burmese Expedition in 1886-87 (Medal with two Clasps).

³⁰ Surgeon Lt. Colonel W. M. Courtney served with the Duffla Expedition in 1873-74. Served with the Burmese Expedition in 1886-87 in medical charge of No. 18 Field Hospital with the 4th Brigade Upper Burmah Field Force (Medal with Clasp); was Senior Medical Officer in charge of the General Hospital, Chin-Lushai Force, under Brigadier General Symons in 1889-90 (Clasp).

³¹ Surgeon Lt. Colonel T. Robinson served in the Afghan war in 1879, and was present with the Zaimusht Expedition including the assault of Zawa (Medal). Served also with the Mahsood Wuzeeree Expedition in 1881.

³³ Surgeon Lt. Colonel C. J. W. Meadows served with the Looshai Expedition in 1871-72 (mentioned in despatches, Medal with Clasp).

³⁴ Surgeon Lt. Colonel J. O'Brien served with the expedition against the Naga Hill Tribes in 1879-80, and was present at the assault of Konoma (Medal with Clasp).

35 Surgeon Lt.Colonel W. R. Murphy served in the Afghan war of 1878-80, and was present in the engagement at Saif-u-deen, at the occupation of Candahar, and in the engagements at Ahmed Kheyl, Urzoo near Ghuznee, and Padkao Shana (mentioned in despatches, Medal with Clasp). Served with the Hazara Expedition in 1888 (mentioned in despatches, Medal with Clasp). Served with the Chin-Lushai Expeditionary Force in 1889-90 as Principal Medical Officer to the Chittagong Column (received the thanks of the Government of India, mentioned in despatches, *DSO.*, and Clasp).

36 Surgeon Lt.Colonel A. S. Reid served in the Afghan war in 1879-80 (mentioned in despatches, Medal). Served with the Chin-Lushai Expeditionary Force in 1889-90 (Medal with Clasp).

37 Surgeon Lt.Colonel Bookey served with the 6th Punjab Infantry in the Jowaki Afreedee Expedition in 1877-78 (Medal with Clasp), and in the Mahzood Wuzeeree Expedition in 1881. Served with the Burmese Expedition in 1886-88 (mentioned in despatches, Clasp) ; with the Hazara Expedition in 1888 (mentioned in despatches, Clasp) ; and with the Miranzai Expedition in 1891 (mentioned in despatches, Clasp).

38 Surgeon Lt.Colonel J. Young served with the Burmese Expedition in 1885-86 (Medal with Clasp).

40 Surgeon Major J. Duke served in the Afghan war in 1879-80, and was present in the engagement at Charasiah on the 6th October 1879 and in the operations around Cabul in December 1879 including the storming of the Asmai Heights (mentioned in despatches); accompanied Sir Frederick Roberts in the march to Candahar, and was present at the battle of Candahar (Medal with three Clasps,and Bronze Decoration). Also served with the Marri Expedition in 1881.

41 Surgeon Lt.Colonel E. Palmer served with the Hazara Expedition in 1891 (mentioned in despatches, Medal with Clasp).

42 Surgeon Lt.Colonel A. H. Williams served in the Afghan war in 1880 (Medal). Served with the Burmese Expedition in 1886-87 (Medal with Clasp).

43 Surgeon Lt.Colonel Z. A. Ahmed served with the Hazara Expedition in 1891 (Medal with Clasp).

44 Surgeon Lt.Colonel W. E. Griffiths served in the Afghan war in 1878-79, and was present in the engagement at Served with the Hazara Expedition in 1888 (Clasp).

46 Surgeon Lt.Colonel F. W. Wright served in the Afghan war of 1878-80, and was present in the engagement at Jugdulluck and in that at Charasiah on the 6th October 1879; accompanied Sir Frederick Roberts in the march to Candahar, and was present at the battle of Candahar (Medal with two Clasps, and Bronze Decoration). Served with the Burmese Expedition in 1886-87 (mentioned in despatches, *DSO.*, and Medal with Clasp).

47 Surgeon Lt.Colonel H. K. M'Kay served in the Afghan war of 1878-80, and was present in the engagement at Mazeena (Medal). Also served in the Mahsood Wuzeeree Expedition in 1881.

50 Surgeon Lt.Colonel J. C. Fullerton served in the Afghan war of 1878-80, and was present in the engagement at Takht-i-Pul (Medal).

51 Surgeon Lt.Colonel R. N. Stoker served in the Afghan war in 1879 (Medal). Served with the Sikkim Expedition in 1888 (Medal with Clasp).

52 Surgeon Lt.Colonel C. J. M'Cartie served in the Afghan war in 1879-80, and was present in the engagements at Saif-u-deen and Shahjui—wounded (mentioned in despatches, Medal).

54 Surgeon Lt.Colonel R. D. Murray served with the Burmese Expedition in 1886-87 (mentioned in despatches, Medal with Clasp).

55 Surgeon Lt.Colonel D. W. D. Comins served in the Afghan war in 1878-79 with the Candahar Field Force, and was present in the engagement at Charasiah on the 6th October 1879, at the capture of Cabul, the action at Lataband, and the relief of Sherpore (twice mentioned in despatches, Medal with two Clasps).

56 Surgeon Lt.Colonel P. F. O'Connor served in the Afghan war of 1878-80, and was present in the engagements at Ahmed Kheyl and Urzoo near Ghuznee, and at Patkao Shana (mentioned in despatches, Medal with Clasp). Served in the Egyptian war of 1882, and was present at the battle of Tel-el-Kebir (Medal with Clasp, and Khedive's Star). Served with the Burmese Expedition in 1886-87 (mentioned in despatches, Medal with Clasp).

57 Surgeon Lt.Colonel J. Moran served in the Afghan war in 1878-79 (Medal).

58 Surgeon Lt.Colonel W. A. Simmonds served in the Afghan war of 1878-80, and was present in the engagement at Charasiah on the 6th October 1879, and in the operations around Cabul in December 1879 (Medal with two Clasps). Served with the Burmese Expedition in 1885-86 (Medal with Clasp).

60 Surgeon Lt.Colonel S. Borah served with the expedition against the Naga Hill Tribes in 1879-80 (Medal with Clasp).

61 Surgeon Major P. A. Weir served in the Afghan war in 1879-80 (Medal).

64 Surgeon Major P. de H. Haig served in the Afghan war of 1878-80 with the Peshawur Valley Field Force (Medal).

65 Surgeon Major Lewtas served in the Afghan war of 1878-80 with the Guides Cavalry, and was present at the taking of Ali Musjid, the action of Futtehabad, the storming of the Takht-i-Shah heights near Cabul on 13th December 1879, and at the storming of the Asmai heights on the 14th December (mentioned in despatches) ; was present throughout the operations at Sherpore, and in the engagement at Charasiah on 25th April 1880 (mentioned in despatches, Medal with two Clasps).

66 Surgeon Major J. O'Neill served in the Ashanti war of 1873-74 (Medal).

67 Surgeon Major Mawson served in the Afghan war of 1878-80, and was present at the attack and capture of Ali Musjid, in the engagement at Charasiah on the 6th October 1879, and in the operations round Cabul in December 1879 (Medal with three Clasps).

68 Surgeon Major H. Hamilton served in the Afghan war of 1878-80, and was present in the engagement at Charasiah on the 6th October 1879 and subsequent pursuit of the enemy, in the operations round Cabul in December 1879 including the investment of Sherpore, and in the engagement at Saidabad; accompanied Sir Frederick Roberts in the march to Candahar, and was present at the battle of Candahar (mentioned in despatches, Medal with three Clasps, and Bronze Decoration). Served with the Chin-Lushai Expeditionary Force in 1889-90 (Medal with Clasp).

69 Surgeon Major B. Doyle served in the Afghan war in 1879-80 (Medal).

70 Surgeon Major A. E. R. Stephens served in the Afghan war of 1878-80, and was present at the action of Ahmed Kheyl (Medal with Clasp). Served with the Hazara Expedition in 1888 (Medal with Clasp).

71 Surgeon Major C. W. Owen served in the Afghan war in 1879-80, and was present in the engagement at Charasiah on the 6th October 1879 (mentioned in despatches), and in the operations around Cabul in December 1879—slightly wounded at the engagement at the Chardeh Valley (mentioned in despatches, *CIE*., Medal with two Clasps). Served in the Egyptian war of 1882, and was present at the battle of Tel-el-Kebir (Medal with Clasp, and Khedive's Star).

72 Surgeon Major G. S. Griffiths served in the Afghan war of 1878-80, and was present in the engagement at Baghao (Medal). Served with the Zhob Valley Expedition in 1884. Served with the Sikkim Expedition in 1888 (Medal with Clasp).

73 Surgeon Major W. Owen served in the Afghan war of 1878-80, and was present in the engagements at Ahmed Kheyl and Urzoo near Ghuznee (Medal with Clasp).

74 Surgeon W. Conry served with the Burmese Expedition in 1885-87 (Medal with Clasp).

75 Surgeon Captain G. J. Kellie served with the Burmese Expedition in 1888-89 (Medal with Clasp).

76 Surgeon Major A. W. Mackenzie served in the Afghan war of 1878-80, and was present in the engagement near Charasiah in April 1880; accompanied Sir Frederick Roberts in the march to Candahar, and was present at the battle of Candahar; took part in the expedition to the Atchakzai country under Brigadier General Baker (Medal with Clasp, and Bronze Decoration). Served with the Mahsood Wuzeeree Expedition in 188:. Served with the two Miranzai Expeditions in 1891 (Medal with Clasp).

77 Surgeon Major J. Mullane served in the Afghan war of 1878-80, and was present in the advance to Ghuznee under Sir Donald Stewart, and in the engagements at Ahmed Kheyl and Urzoo; accompanied Sir Frederick Roberts in the march to Candahar. and was present at the battle of Candahar (Medal with two Clasps, and Bronze Decoration).

78 Surgeon Major J. A. Nelis served in the Afghan war of 1878-80, and was present in the engagements at Ahmed Kheyl and Urzoo near Ghuznee; accompanied Sir Frederick Roberts in the march to Candahar, and was present at the battle of Candahar; also served with the Atchakzai and Marri Expeditions (Medal with two Clasps, and Bronze Decoration). Served with the Mahsood Wuzeeree Expedition in 1881. Served with the Hazara Expedition

in 1888 (Medal with Clasp); with the second Miranzai Expedition in 1891 (Clasp); and with the Isazai Expedition in 1892.

[79] Surgeon Major A. M. Crofts served in the Afghan war of 1878-80 at Candahar and with the Khyber Brigade (Medal). Served in the Egyptian war of 1882, and was present at the battle of Tel-el-Kebir (Medal with Clasp and Khedive's Star).

[80] Surgeon Major James Crofts served in the Afghan war of 1878-80, and was present in the engagement at Ali Kheyl (Medal).

[81] Surgeon Major W. Coates served in the Afghan war of 1878-80, and was present at the attack and capture of Ali Musjid, in the engagement at Charasiah on the 6th October 1879, and in the operations round Cabul in December 1879 (mentioned in despatches); accompanied Sir Frederick Roberts in the march to Candahar, and was present at the battle of Candahar (Medal with four Clasps, Bronze Decoration). Also served with the Mahsood Wuzeeree Expedition in 1881.

[82] Surgeon Major C. H. Beatson served with the Manipore Expedition in 1891 (mentioned in despatches, Medal with Clasp).

[83] Surgeon Major S. J. Thomson served in the Afghan war in 1880 (Medal).

[84] Surgeon R. N. Campbell served in the operations against the Naga Hill tribes in 1879-80, and was present at the assault of Konoma (Medal with Clasp). Served with the Akha Expedition in 1883-84.

[85] Surgeon E. S. Brander served in the Afghan war in 1879-80 with the 41st Bengal Native Infantry in the Khyber Line Force (Medal).

[86] Surgeon Major F. C. Chatterjee served with the Burmese Expedition in 1886-87 (Medal with Clasp).

[87] Surgeon G. A. Emerson served in the Soudan campaign in 1885 (Medal with Clasp, and Khedive's Star).

[89] Surgeon Major E. Cretin served in the Afghan war in 1880, and was present in the engagement at Kam Dakka, in the Lughman Valley Expedition, and the engagement at Hissarik (Medal). Served with the Burmese Expedition in 1885-87 (Medal with Clasp).

[90] Surgeon Major Andrew Duncan served in the Afghan war of 1878-80, and was present in the engagement at Mattoon and in that at Charasiab on the 6th October 1879—severely wounded (Medal with Clasp).

[92] Surgeon Major Bigger served in the Afghan war in 1879-80, and was present in the Zaimusht Expedition including the assault of Zawa (Medal). Served with the Chin-Lushai Expeditionary Force in 1889-90 with the Chittagong Column (mentioned in despatches, and Medal with Clasp).

[93] Surgeon Major G. S. Robertson served during the expedition against the Hunza-Nagars in 1891-92 as Chief Political Officer (mentioned in despatches, Medal with Clasp).

[94] Surgeon Major G. M. Nixon served with the Burmese Expedition in 1886-87 (Medal with Clasp).

[95] Surgeon Major T. H. Sweeny served in the Afghan war in 1879-80, and was present in the operations around Cabul in December 1879 including the investment of Sherpore (Medal with Clasp).

[96] Surgeon Major D. F. Barry served with the expedition against the Naga Hill Tribes in 1879-80 (Medal with Clasp).

[98] Surgeon Major J. Anderson served in the Afghan war in 1879-80, and was present in the engagement at Jugdulluck (Medal).

[99] Surgeon Major C. J. Bamber served with the expedition against the Mahsood Wuzeerees in 1881. Served with the Burmese Expedition in 1886-87 (Medal with Clasp).

[100] Surgeon Major M. O'Dwyer served in the Afghan war in 1879 (Medal).

[101] Surgeon Major S. Little served in the Afghan war in 1879-80, and took part with the expedition into the Hissarik Valley (Medal). Also served with the Mahsood Wuzeeroe Expedition in 1881.

[102] Surgeon Major G. H. D. Gimlette served in the Egyptian war of 1882, and was present at the battle of Tel-el-Kebir (Medal with Clasp, and Khedive's Star).

[103] Surgeon Major C. B. Hunter served in the Afghan war in 1879-80 (Medal). Served with the Zhob Valley Expedition in 1890. Served with the two Miranzai Expeditions in 1891 (Medal with Clasp).

[104] Surgeon Major J. C. C. Smith served in the Afghan war in 1879-80 (Medal). Served with the Burmese Expedition in 1886-87 (Medal with Clasp).

[105] Surgeon Major J. Sykes served in the Egyptian war of 1882, and was present at the battle of Tel-el-Kebir (Medal with Clasp, and Khedive's Star).

[106] Surgeon Major C. P. Lukis served with the Mahsood Wuzeeree Expedition in 1881, and with the Zhob Valley Expedition in 1884.

[108] Surgeon Major L. A. Waddell served with the Burmese Expedition in 1886-87 (Medal with Clasp).

[109] Surgeon Major G. Money Shewan served in the Egyptian war of 1882, and was present at the battle of Tel-el-Kebir (Medal with Clasp, and Khedive's Star). Served with the Burmese Expedition in 1886-87 (Medal with Clasp).

[110] Surgeon Major D. B. Spencer served in the Soudan campaign in 1885, and was present in the engagements at Hasheen and the Tofrek zereba and at the destruction of Temai (Medal with two Clasps, and Khedive's (Star). Served with the Burmese Expedition in 1886-88 (Medal with Clasp).

[111] Surgeon Major J. Clarke served with the Akha Expedition in 1883-84.

[112] Surgeon Major C. C. Vaid served with the Burmese Expedition in 1885-87 (Medal with Clasp).

[113] Surgeon Captain T. R. Macdonald served in the Egyptian war in 1882, and was present at the battle of Tel-el-Kebir (Medal with Clasp, and Khedive's Star).

[114] Surgeon Major J. Shearer served in the Egyptian war of 1882 (Medal, and Khedive's Star). Served with the Burmese Expedition in 1887-88 as Senior Medical Officer of the Southern Shan Column (Medal with two Clasps); with the Hazara Expedition in 1891 (Clasp); and with the second Miranzai Expedition in 1891 (Clasp).

[115] Surgeon Major S. Hassan served with the Burmese Expedition in 1886-87 (Medal with Clasp); with the Chin-Lushai Expeditionary Force in 1889-90 (Clasp); and with the Miranzai Expedition in 1891 (Clasp).

[116] Surgeon Major S. C. Nandi served with the Burmese Expedition in 1886-88 (Medal with Clasp).

[117] Surgeon Major H. C. Banerji served with the Burmese Expedition in 1886-87 (Medal with Clasp). Served with the Manipore Expedition in 1891 (mentioned in despatches, Clasp).

[118] Surgeon Major F. S. Pack served with the Burmese Expedition in 1886-87 (Medal with Clasp).

[119] Surgeon Major W. Deane served with the Akha Expedition in 1883-84. Served with the Burmese Expedition in 1886-87 (Medal with Clasp).

[120] Surgeon Captain H. C. Hudson served in the Soudan campaign in 1885 (Medal with Clasp, and Khedive's Star). Served with the Burmese Expedition in 1886-88 (Medal with two Clasps). Served with the Manipore Expedition in 1891 (mentioned in despatches, Clasp).

[121] Surgeon Captain P. Mullane served with the Burmese Expedition in 1885-87 (Medal with Clasp).

[121†] Surgeon Major J. W. Rodgers served with the Hazara Expedition in 1888 (Medal with Clasp).

[122] Surgeon Major L. T. Young served with the Akha Expedition in 1883-84.

[123] Surgeon Major D. St. J. D. Grant served with the Akha Expedition in 1883-84.

[124] Surgeon Major G. Duncan served with the Hazara Expedition in 1888 (Medal with Clasp); and in the Hazara Expedition in 1891 with the 2nd Battalion 5th Goorkhas (Clasp).

[125] Surgeon Major W. A. Sykes served with the Burmese Expedition in 1886-87 (mentioned in despatches, DSO. and Medal with two Clasps). Served with the Zhob Valley Expedition in 1890.

[126] Surgeon Major G. Jameson served in the Soudan campaign in 1885 (Medal with Clasp, and Khedive's Star).

[128] Surgeon Captain J. H. T. Walsh served with the Burmese Expedition in 1885-87 (Medal with Clasp).

[129] Surgeon Captain H. Hendley served in the Soudan campaign in 1885 (Medal with Clasp, and Khedive's Star). Served with the Burmese Expedition in 1886-88 (Medal with Clasp).

[130] Surgeon Captain H. E. Banatvala served with the Burmese Expedition in 1886-87 (Medal with Clasp).

[132] Surgeon Captain W. L. Price served with the Burmese Expedition in 1887-88 (Medal with Clasp).

[133] Surgeon Captain F. J. Drury served with the Burmese Expedition in 1886-88 (Medal with Clasp).

[134] Surgeon Captain H. J. Dyson served with the Burmese Expedition in 1886-88 (Medal with Clasp).

[135] Surgeon Captain F. A. Rogers served with the Burmese Expedition in 1886-87 (mentioned in despatches, Medal with Clasp); also served with the Chin-Lushai Expeditionary Force in 1889-90 with the 42nd Goorkha Light Infantry (mentioned in despatches, DSO., and Clasp).

[136] Surgeon Captain E. R. W. Carroll served with the Burmese Expedition in 1886-87 (Medal with Clasp).

[*For remainder of Notes to the Bengal Medical Department, see end of Madras Medical Department, p. 5064.*]

460–94

Bengal Veterinary Department.

Veterinary Lt.Colonel.	Vet. Surgeon.	1st Class Vet. Surg.	Present Rank.	Remarks.
Kettlewell, George	5 Dec. 54	10 Mar. 69	1 Oct. 77	Madras Army, Ootacamund.

Bengal Ecclesiastical Establishment.

The Most Reverend Edward Ralph Johnson, DD. Lord Bishop of Calcutta and Metropolitan in India and the Island of Ceylon, 14 Dec. 76.
The Rev. Welbore MacCarthy, Archdeacon of Calcutta and Commissary, 12 Aug. 92.
The Rev. Herbert Octavius Moore, MA. Domestic Chaplain to the Lord Bishop of Calcutta, 7 Nov. 91.
Arthur Mountjoy Dunne, Esq., Registrar of the Archdeaconry of Calcutta, and Sec. to the Lord Bishop, and Registrar of the Diocese of Lahore, 1 Sept. 94.
The Right Reverend Henry James Matthew, MA. Lord Bishop of Lahore, 22 Dec. 87.—Furlough.
The Rev. Arthur Nathanial Wadham Spens, Archdeacon and Commissary of Lahore, 1 Oct. 92.
The Right Rev. Arthur Clifford, MA. Lord Bishop of Lucknow, 21 Jan. 93.
The Ven. Brook Deedes, MA. Archdeacon of Lucknow, 25 Jan. 93.
J. E. Howard, Esq., Registrar of the Diocese of Lucknow, 23 Jan. 93.

Yr. of Appt.	Senior Chaplains.	Remarks, &c.	Yr. of Appt.	Junior Chaplains.	Remarks, &c.
1873	Rev. Edw. Montifort Beasley, BA.	Fyzabad.	1885	Rev. Montague C. Sanders, MA.	Furlough.
1873	Rev. Welbore MacCarthy	Archdeacon of Calcutta.	1885	Rev. Henry Jas. Spence Gray, MA	Lahore.
1874	Rev. William Henry Bray	Furlough.	1885	Rev. Herbert Octavius Moore, MA	Domestic Chaplain to the Bishop.
1874	Rev. Albert William Rebsch, BA.	Furlough.	1885	Rev. Charles Herbert Reynolds	Furlough.
1875	Rev. Andrew N. Wadham Spens	Archdeacon of Simla.	1885	Rev. Walter Kitchin	Chuckrata.
			1885	Rev. S.L. Graham Sandberg, BA.	Subathoo.
1875	Rev. Edmund Jermyn, MA.	Furlough.	1886	Rev. R. Augustine Storrs, BA.	Mooltan.
1876	Rev. Wm. Fred. Armstrong, BA.	Kurrachee.	1887	Rev. Henry Barry Hyde, MA.	Kussowlie.
1876	Rev. Kingston Egan Barrow, MA	Benares.	1887	Rev. Wm. A. Grant Luckman, BA.	Furlough.
1876	Rev. Arthur George Arthur Robarts, MA.	Darjeeling.	1887	Rev. Charles Arthur Mason, BA.	Allahabad Cant.
			1887	Rev. Gerald Edward Nicolls, BA.	Peshawur.
1877	Rev. Brook Deedes, MA.	Archdeacon of Lucknow.	1887	Rev. Clement Henry Barlow, MA	Nagpore.
			1887	Rev. Wm. Fras. Thompson, MA.	Nynee Tal.
1877	Rev. Clement Glover Moore, BA.	Ranikhet.	1888	Rev. George M. Davies, MA.	Barrackpore.
1877	Rev. Charles Swynnerton	Waziristan.	1888	Rev. Barclay Kitchin	Bankipore.
1878	Rev. Charles Walter Hume, MA.	Hazara.	1888	Rev. George Adam Ford, BA.	Civil Lines, Lucknow
1879	Rev. Hy. Coleridge Spring, BA.	Futtehghur.	1888	Rev. Henry James Long, MA.	Umballa.
1879	Rev. Thomas Francis Dale	Furlough.	1889	Rev. Herbert Taylor Ottley	Kidderpore.
1879	Rev. Walter Adolphus Hamilton	Roorkee.	1889	Rev. Charles Richard Therold Winckley	Nowgong.
1879	Rev. Robert John Langford, MA.	Lucknow Canton.			
1879	Rev. Ferguson John Montgomery, MA.	Sealkote.	1889	Rev. Piercy Griffith Bruce Austin	Shillong.
			1889	Rev. Theodore Edw. F. Cole	Jubbulpore.
1880	Rev. L. Freemantle Philips, MA.	Muttra.	1889	Rev. Edmond John Warlew	Quetta.
1880	Rev. Theophilus C. Shepherd, MA	Dalhousie.	1890	Rev. Frederick James Clarke	Dera and Landour
1880	Rev. Josiah O'Farrell Willcocks, MA.	Kamptee.	1890	Rev. Jas. Middleton Macdonald	Cuttack.
			1890	Rev. William John Wickins	St. James', Calcutta.
1880	Rev. Arthur Edward Stone	Fort William.	1890	Rev. William Boycott Handford	Meean Meer.
1880	Rev. J. Irwin Browne Cockin, BA.	Meerut.	1890	Rev. Herbert Wheler Bush	Delhi.
1881	Rev. Oscar Daniel Watkins, MA.	Mussoorie.	1890	Rev. William Gore Burroughs, BA	Dagshai.
1881	Rev. Ralph Allen Cumine, MA.	Bareilly.			
1881	Rev. Vivian Wm. Kinsman	Saugor.	1890	Rev. Charles Jasper Palmer	St. Paul's Cathedral.
1881	Rev. Henry Wager Griffith, MA.	Furlough.	1891	Rev. Hugh Robert Coulthard	Umritsur.
1882	Rev. John Moulson, BA.	Rawul Pindee.	1891	Rev. Lawrence Hosier Levmit	Howrah.
1882	Rev. Arthur Bridge	Jullunder.	1891	Rev. Henry Naish	Nowshera.
1882	Rev. Francis B. Sandberg, BA.	Kurrachee.	1891	Rev. Leonard Klugh	Jhansi.
1883	Rev. Arthur Kitchin, MA.	St. Thomas' Chch., Calcutta.	1892	Rev. H. W. T. Plowman	Hyderabad, Sind.
			1893	Rev. Fredk. Wm. Chamberlain.	Moradabad.
1883	Rev. William Ellison, MA.	Furlough.	1893	Rev. Robert Mansel Kirwan	Cawnpore.
1884	Rev. Jas. Frank Warden Gompertz,[1] BA.	Seetapore.	1893	Rev. Albt. Edw. Brown Constable	Puchmaree.
			1893	Rev. Percy Hugh Chapman	Bareilly.
1884	Rev. Talbot Monckton Milnes Griffiths, BA.		1894	Rev. Sydney Septimus Scott	Dinapore.
			1894	Rev. J. Greensill Skittowe Syme	Berhampore.
1884	Rev. Charles Albert Gillmore	Rawul Pindee.	1894	Rev. Walter Paul Gray Field	Junior Chaplain, St. Paul's, Calcutta.
1884	Rev. Alfred Saunders Dyer, MA.	Mhow.			
1884	Rev. Fras. Edw. Davy Cobbold	Ferozepore.	1894	Rev. Horace Barbut Cogan	Dum Dum.
			1894	Rev. Walter Lilley P. Shaw	

[1] The Rev. J. F. W. Gompertz served in the Burmese Expedition in 1886-87 with the Upper Burmah Field Force. (Medal with two Clasps).

CHURCH OF SCOTLAND.

Yr. of Appt.	Senior Chaplain.			Assistant Chaplains.	
1879	Rev. Alexander Ferrier, MA.	Senior Chaplain of St. Andrew's Ch. Calcutta.—Furl.	1889	Rev. Thomas Scott, MA.	Scots Fusiliers.
	Chaplain.		1892	Rev. George Johnstone Ofree, MA. BD.	Allahabad.
1880	Rev. John Taylor, MA.	Fyzabad.	1892	Rev. John Cameron, MA. BD.	Ferozepore.

Governor's Body Guard. 495
"Seetabuldee."
Head Quarters at **Madras.** *Uniform, Scarlet. Facings, Blue. Lace, Gold.*

RANK, NAMES, AND CORPS.	ARMY RANK.	REMARKS.
Captain L. W. C. Kerrich, Staff Corps...	22 Jan. 90	Commandant, 1 Jan. 90.—From 3 Lancers.
Lieut. B. J. H. Humfrey, Staff Corps...	30 Jan. 86	Adjutant, 2 Apr. 91.
Brig. Surg. Lt.Colonel H. J. Hazlett ...	7 Mar. 99	In medical charge, 13 Feb. 93.

Establishment.—Commandant; Adjutant; Medical Officer; 1 Hospital Assistant; 2 Subadars; 2 Jamadars; 1 Havildar Major; 7 Havildars; 6 Naicks; 1 Farrier Major; 2 Farrier Havildars; 2 Shoeing Smiths; 2 Trumpeters; 100 Troopers; 8 Recruit and Pension Boys, and 100 Horses. *Native Artificers.*—1 Superintendent; 1 Smith; 2 Chucklers; 1 Hammerman; 1 Bellows Boy.

1st Madras Lancers (*Raised in October* 1787—*formerly the* 5th *Regt.*).
"MYSORE"—"SERINGAPATAM"—"AVA"—"AFGHANISTAN, 1879-80."—"BURMA, 1885-87."
Head Quarters at Secunderabad. *Uniform, French Grey. Facings, Buff. Lace, Silver.*

Major E. E. M. Lawford, Staff Corps....	9 Aug. 93	Commandant. 28 July 94.
Captain R. G. Jones, Staff Corps	13 June 86	2nd in Command and Squadron Commander, 10 Aug. 94.—Insp. Officer, Mysore State, Imperial Service Cavalry.
Captain C. Stevens, Staff Corps	11 Nov. 87	Squadron Commander, 1 Jan. 92.—D.A.A. General, Belgaum.
Captain A. P. Westlake, *DSO.* Staff C...	29 Nov. 88	Squadron Commander, 26 July 89.—Superintendent Remount Depot, Haupore.
Captain G. S. Kerrich, Staff Corps	1 May 89	Squadron Commander, 11 July 90.
Captain H. L. B. Acton, Staff Corps ...	11 Aug. 91	Squadron Commander, 4 Aug. 93.
Captain R. H. D. Thring, Staff Corps ...	22 Jan. 92	Squadron Comdr., 4 Aug. 93.—Offg. D. A. A. G. Secunderabad.
Captain W. G. H. Stirling, Staff Corps	9 Sept. 93	Squadron Officer, 26 Feb. 92.—Sick Furlough.
Captain C. H. F. Binsteed, Staff Corps	12 May 94	Squadron Officer, 26 Feb. 92.
Lieut. A. S. Arnold, Staff Corps...........	30 Jan. 86	Squadron Officer, 4 Aug. 93.
Lieut. R. de L. Faunce, Staff Corps	27 Aug. 89	Squadron Officer and Adjutant, 28 July 93.
Lieut. C. E. N. Priestley, Staff Corps...	21 Feb. 88	Officiating Squadron Officer.—From 2 Madras Lancers.
2nd Lieut. N. B. G. Strong, 21 Hussars	18 June 92	Officiating Squadron Officer.
Lieut. C. J. F. O. Johnes, Staff C	3 Dec. 94	Officiating Squadron Officer.
2nd Lt. F. V. L. Pritchard, Staff Corps	9 Aug. 93	Officiating Squadron Officer.
Brigade Surgeon Lt.Colonel J. North...	1 July 93	In medical charge, 3 Feb. 82.—Furlough.

2nd Madras Lancers (*Stevenson Pater.*—*Received into the British Service* 1784).
"CARNATIC"—"SHOLINGHUR"—"MYSORE"—"SERINGAPATAM"—"BURMA, 1885-87."
Head Quarters at Bangalore. *Uniform, French Grey. Facings, Buff. Lace, Silver.*

Major A. B. Fenton, Staff Corps	2 Aug. 88	Commandant, 19 Apr. 92.—Furlough.
Captain F. B. Deane, Staff Corps.........	10 Sept. 87	2nd in Command and Squadron Comdr. 23 Apr. 94.—Offg. Comdt.
Captain H. Eardley-Wilmot, Staff Corps	12 Feb. 88	Squadron Commander, 27 Sept. 89.—Offg. 2nd in Command.
Captain R. D. Burlton, Staff Corps	22 Jan. 90	Squadron Commander, 1 Jan. 92.
Captain E. M. Reed, Staff Corps	19 Feb. 92	Squadron Commander, 27 Apr. 94.—D. A. A. G. Bangalore.
Captain B. Holloway, Staff Corps.......	22 Oct. 92	Squadron Officer, 23 July 86.
Captain J. R. Mathewes, Staff Corps...	10 May 93	Squadron Officer, 22 Dec. 87.—Officiating Adjutant.
Lieut. A. G. W. Moore, Staff Corps...	28 Feb. 85	Squadron Officer, 28 July 93.—Furlough.
Lieut. C. E. N. Priestley, Staff Corps ...	21 Feb. 88	Squadron Officer, 27 Apr. 94.—With 1 Madras Lancers.
Lieut. B. J. Petre, Staff Corps	26 Oct. 89	Officiating Squadron Officer.—Furlough.
Lieut. J. E. Hughes, Staff Corps.........	3 Dec. 94	Officiating Squadron Officer.
2nd Lieut. E. M. Taylor, Staff Corps ...	28 Jan. 93	Officiating Squadron Officer.
Surgeon Major E. P. Youngerman, *MB.*	1 Oct. 93	In medical charge, 12 Feb. 92.

3rd Madras Lancers (*Murray.*—*Raised at Arcot in May* 1784 *as the* 2nd *Regt.*).
"MYSORE"—"SERINGAPATAM"—"MAHIDPORE."
Head Quarters at Secunderabad. *Uniform, French Grey. Facings, Buff. Lace, Silver.*

Captain F. L. Jones, Staff Corps	10 Sept. 88	Commandant, 11 Aug. 93.
Captain H. W. E. Georges, Staff Corps	12 Feb. 89	2nd in Command and Squadron Commander, 18 Aug. 93.
Captain L. W. C. Kerrich, Staff Corps ...	22 Jan. 92	Squadron Commander, 1 Jan. 92.—Commandant Governor's Body Guard.
Captain J. Vans Agnew, Staff Corps ...	13 Aug. 90	Squadron Commander, 11 Aug. 93.
Captain R. F. R. Formby, Staff Corps	19 Feb. 92	Squadron Commander, 11 Aug. 93.—Furlough.
Captain F. C. Logan-Home, Staff Corps	23 Apr. 92	Squadron Officer, 5 April 83.
Captain G. H. Arbuthnot, Staff Corps...	9 Sept. 93	Squadron Officer, 24 Apr. 86.—Aide de Camp to the Governor.
Lieut. F. Jollie, Staff Corps.................	30 Jan. 86	Squadron Officer, 17 March 93.—Furlough.
Lieut. E. Wintour, Staff Corps	23 Feb. 88	Squadron Officer and Adjutant, 15 Jan. 94.
Lieut. F. F. Fenton, 11 Hussars	10 Aug. 92	Officiating Squadron Officer.
Lieut. P. S. F. Claridge, Staff Corps ...	12 May 93	Officiating Squadron Officer.
Surgeon Major H. Armstrong	30 Mar. 90	In medical charge, 13 Apr. 91.

Each Regiment of Cavalry consists of 8 *Troops with the following Establishment:*—Commandant; 4 Squadron Commanders; 4 Squadron Officers; 1 Medical Officer; 2 Hospital Assistants; 3 Subadars; 8 Jamadars; 1 Havildar Major; 40 Havildars; 40 Naigues; 1 Trumpet Major; 8 Trumpeters; 1 Farrier Major; 8 Farrier Havildars; 4 Shoeing Smiths; 4 Veterinary Pupils; 502 Troopers; 16 Recruit and 14 Pension Boys; 1 Second Tindal; 4 Regimental Lascars; 4 Puckallies; 2 Toties; and Horses 87 per cent. of the effective strength of the Establishment. *Native Artificers.*—1 Superintendent; 1 Maistry Smith; 1 Maistry Chuckler; 1 Smith; 1 Hammerman; 1 Bellows-boy; 4 Chucklers.

Corps of Madras Sappers and Miners (*Queen's Own*),

The Royal Cypher within the Garter.

"CARNATIC"—"SHOLINGHUR"—"MYSORE"—"SERINGAPATAM"—"EGYPT" (with the Sphinx)—"ASSAYE"—"JAVA"—"NAGPORE"—"MAHIDPORE"—"AVA" (with the Dragon)—"MEEANEE"—"HYDERABAD"—"PEGU"—"PERSIA"—"LUCKNOW"—"CENTRAL INDIA"—"TAKU FORTS"—"PEKIN"—"ABYSSINIA"—"AFGHANISTAN, 1878-80"—"EGYPT, 1882"—"TEL-EL-KEBIR"—"SUAKIN, 1885"—"TOFREK"—"BURMA, 1885-87."

Head Quarters at Bangalore.

A Depot Company,—Bangalore.
B Company,—Bangalore.
No. 1 Company,—Bangalore.
No. 2 Company,—Secunderabad.
No. 3 Company,—Falam.
No. 4 Company,—Bangalore.
No. 5 Company,—Bangalore.
No. 6 Company,—Bangalore.

Detachment (Telegraph Section),—Sealkote. Burmah Company,—Fort Dufferin.

Honorary Colonel—Field Marshal *H.R.H.* Albert Edward, *Prince of* Wales and *Duke of* Cornwall, *KG. KT. KP. GCB. GCSI. GCMG. GCIE.*

RANK, NAMES, AND CORPS.	ARMY RANK.	REMARKS.
Major C. B. Wilkieson, R. Engineers	15 June 85	Commandant, 28 Oct. 90.
Major H. E. Goodwyn, *DSO.* R. Eng	12 Dec. 94	Superintendent of Instruction, 28 Oct. 90.
Major A. W. Cockburn, R. Engineers	20 July 89	Superintendent Park and Train, 7 March 90.
Lieut. T. Fraser, Royal Engineers	18 Feb. 86	Adjutant, 6 Sept. 93.
Captain H. B. H. Wright, R. Engineers	27 July 92	Company Commander, 28 Dec. 88.—4 Company.—Furlough.
Captain C. H. Roe, Royal Engineers	27 Aug. 92	Company Commander, 13 April 89.—1 Company.
Captain J. A. S. Tulloch, R. Engineers	1 Jan. 94	Company Commander, 31 Aug. 89.—Burmah Company.
Captain U. W. Evans, R. Engineers	12 Jan. 94	Company Commander, 28 Feb. 90.—6 Company.
Captain R. F. Sorsbie, Royal Engineers	3 May 94	Company Commander, 28 Oct. 90.—2 Company.
Captain E. L. Dunsterville, R. Engineers	24 Jan. 95	Company Commander, 15 Jan. 91.—3 Company.
Lieut. E. P. Johnson, Royal Engineers	16 Sept. 85	Company Commander, 15 June 93.—5 Company.
Lieut. C, H. Heycock, R. Engineers	17 Feb. 86	Company Commander, 21 March 94.—B Company.
Lieut. F. F. Weedon, R. Engineers	17 Feb. 86	Company Commander, 2 Nov. 94.—A Company.
Lieut. O. Ainslie, Royal Engineers	24 July 86	Company Officer, 28 Feb. 90.—6 Company.—Offg. Comp. Comdr
Lieut. H. J. M. Marshall, R. Engineers	16 Feb. 87	Company Officer, 25 Feb. 91.—4 Company.
Lieut. N. M. Hemming, R. Engineers	14 Mar. 91	Company Officer, 2 Nov. 94.—1 Company.
Lieut. W. Babington, Royal Engineers	27 July 91	Company Officer, 15 June 93.—Furlough.
Lieut. G. A. F. Sanders, R. Engineers	27 July 91	Company Officer and Quarter Master, 25 March 92.—5 Company.
Lieut. B. H. Rooke, Royal Engineers	15 Feb. 92	Company Officer, 15 June 93.—2 Company.
Lieut. W. S. Traill, Royal Engineers	29 Mar. 93	Company Officer, 2 July 93.—B Company.
Lieut. R. A. Gillam, Royal Engineers	29 July 94	Company Officer, 6 Sept. 93.—3 Company.
Lieut. J. B. Barstow, Royal Engineers	24 July 94	Company Officer.—A. Company.—Telegraph Study, Lahore.
2nd Lieut. W. Robertson, R. Engineers	22 July 92	Officiating Company Officer.—B Company.
Surgeon Lt.Colonel W. E. Johnson, *MD.*	30 Mar. 92	In medical charge, 23 May 90.

Establishment :—The Corps consists of 8 Companies (6 Service Companies numbered 1 to 6, and 2 Depot Companies lettered A and B) : Commandant; Superintendent of Instruction; Superintendent Park and Train; Adjutant ; 1 Medical Officer; 8 Company Commanders; 8 Company Officers; Warrant Officer ; Sergeant Major; Quarter Master Sergeant; 4 Company Sergeant Majors; 6 Sergeants ; 9 First Corporals ; 9 Second Corporals ; 2 Hospital Assistants ; 8 Subadars ; 15 Jamadars ; 49 Havildars ; 78 Naicks ; 15 Buglers ; 1,152 Sappers ; 42 Recruit Boys.

1st Madras Infantry—*Pioneers* (*Shaik Modeen—Porannah—formerly* 1st

Battalion 1st *Regiment.—Raised at Fort St. George in* 1758).—*Linked with* 4th & 21st *Regiments.—Regimental Centre, Bangalore.*

"CARNATIC"—"MYSORE"—"SERINGAPATAM"—"SEETABULDEE"—"NAGPORE"—"AVA"—"PEGU"—"CENTRAL INDIA"—"AFGHANISTAN, 1879-80"—"BURMA, 1885-87."

Head Quarters at **Kalewa.** *Uniform, Red. Facings, White. Lace, Gold.*

Lt.Colonel G. C. Fenwick, Staff Corps	21 Nov. 91	Commandant, 16 March 94.
Captain E. O. C. W. M. Kennedy, Staff C.	13 Aug. 90	2nd in Command and Wing Commander, 16 June 93.
Captain B. A. Johnstone, Staff Corps	23 Apr. 92	Wing Commander, 9 Mar. 94.—D. A. A. Gen. for Musk., Burmah.
Lieut. F. G. Batten, Staff Corps	6 May 85	Wing Officer and Adjutant, 26 Sept. 87.
Lieut. F. Bruce, Staff Corps	21 Feb. 88	Wing Officer and Quarter Master, 16 Jan. 91.
Lieut. C. J. Gunning, Staff Corps	25 July 89	Wing Officer, 26 Feb. 92.
Lieut. C. E. Bowen, Staff Corps	26 Feb. 89	Wing Officer, 26 Feb. 92.
Lieut. A. P. How, Staff Corps	1 Apr. 89	Wing Officer, 28 Apr. 93.
Lieut. A. H. T. Rouse, Staff Corps	30 Oct. 92	Officiating Wing Officer.
Surgeon Major D. P. Warliker	30 Mar. 90	In medical charge, 27 June 90.

2nd Madras Infantry (*Mootoo Naik—formerly* 1st *Battalion* 2nd

Regiment.—Raised at Madras in 1759).—*Linked with* 15th & 26th *Regiments.—Regimental Centre, Secunderabad.*

"CARNATIC"—"MYSORE"—"ASSAYE"—"NAGPORE"—"CHINA"—"*The Dragon.*"

Head Quarters at Belgaum. *Uniform, Red. Facings, Green. Lace, Gold.*

Major J. H. Jones, Staff Corps	10 June 94	Commandant, 1 June 93.
Captain T. H. Haughton, Staff Corps	11 Feb. 88	2nd in Command and Wing Commander, 1 June 93.—D. A. A. Gen. Burmah.
Captain A. H. Kellie, Staff Corps	1 Feb. 90	Wing Commander, 1 June 93.
Captain A. T. Young, Staff Corps	22 Jan. 92	Wing Officer, 12 May 90.
Captain A. R. Denne, Staff Corps	28 Jan. 93	Wing Officer, 26 Aug. 87.
Lieut. E. F. Beddek, Staff Corps	2 Apl. 88	Wing Officer and Quarter Master, 1 Feb. 91.
Lieut. H. E. Norman, Staff Corps	4 Dec. 89	Wing Officer and Adjutant, 21 Nov. 90.
Lieut. A. Mears, Staff Corps	3 May 90	Wing Officer, 28 July 93.—Furlough.
Lieut. H. R. Hopwood, R. Marines	1 July 92	Officiating Wing Officer.
Lt. G. G. J. Carmichael, Gloucester R.	20 Mar. 93	Officiating Wing Officer.
Surgeon Captain T. C. Moore	31 Mar. 87	In medical charge, 4 Jan. 94.

Each Regiment of Native Infantry consists of 8 Companies with the following Establishment:—Commandant; 2 Wing Commanders; 5 Wing Officers; Medical Officer; 2 Hospital Assistants; 8 Subadars; 8 Jamadars; 1 Havildar Major; 40 Havildars; 40 Naicks; 16 Drummers; 720 Privates; 24 Recruit Boys; 18 Pension Boys; 1 2nd-Tindal; 4 Lascars; 8 Puckallies; 1 Choudry; and 2 Toties. The 20th Regiment Native Infantry has an additional Jamadar to carry an Honorary Colour.

3rd Madras (or Palamcottah) Light Infantry (Turin—formerly 1st Battalion 497 3rd Regiment.—Raised at Madras in 1759).—Linked with 23rd and 31st Regiments.—Regimental Centre, Trichinopoly.

"Now or Never"—"Carnatic"—"Sholinghur"—"Mysore"—"Mahidpore"—"Ava"—"Burma, 1885-87."
Head Quarters at Myingyan. Detachment at Kalewa. Uniform, Red. Facings, Green. Lace, Gold.

Rank, Names, and Corps.	Army Rank.	Remarks.
Captain R. K. Teversham, DSO, Staff C.	10 Sept. 86	Commandant, 6 June 94.
Captain G. C. Atkinson, Staff Corps	28 Oct. 88	2nd in Command and Wing Commander, 6 June 94.—Furlough.
Captain E. Peach, Staff Corps	6 Feb. 95	Wing Officer, 3 Aug. 88.—Staff College, Sandhurst.
Lieut. G. W. Lilly, Staff Corps	14 May 84	Wing Officer and Quarter Master, 23 Dec. 86.—Offg. Wing Comdr.
Lieut. E. W. Harris, Staff Corps	29 Aug. 85	Wing Officer, 26 July 89.
Lieut. W. G. Grey, Staff Corps	25 Aug. 86	Wing Officer, 23 Oct. 89.
Lieut. H. P. Ainslie, Staff Corps	17 Nov. 90	Wing Officer, 14 Aug. 91.—Offg. Adjutant and S.S.O.
Lieut. W. C. Nicholson, Staff Corps	31 Oct. 91	Wing Officer, 28 Apr. 93.—Cantonment Magistrate, Myingyan.
Lieut. G. A. C. Taylor, West Surrey Regt.	11 Mar. 91	Officiating Wing Officer.
Lieut. C. M. O'Reilly, Staff Corps	12 Aug. 91	Officiating Wing Officer.
Surgeon Major M. H. Smith	1 Mar. 88	In medical charge, 6 Jan. 81.

4th Madras Infantry—Pioneers (Baillie—formerly 1st Battalion 4th Regt.

Raised at Madras in 1759).—Linked with 1st and 21st Regiments.—Regimental Centre, Bangalore.
"Carnatic"—"Sholinghur"—"Mysore"—"Assaye"—"Afghanistan, 1879-80."
Head Quarters at Trichinopoly. Uniform, Red. Facings, White. Lace, Gold.

Rank, Names, and Corps.	Army Rank.	Remarks.
Lt.Colonel J. E. Porteous, Staff Corps	22 Sept. 91	Commandant, 5 Nov. 91.
Bt.Major G. B. Stevens, Staff Corps	5 Oct. 92	2nd in Command and Wing Comdr., 5 Nov. 91.—Assist. Adj. Gen.
Captain E. L. Holloway, Staff Corps	25 Feb. 91	Wing Commander, 5 Nov. 91.—Officiating D.A.A.Gen. for Musk., Secunderabad.
Captain F. Churchill, Staff Corps	22 Oct. 92	Wing Officer, 23 May 86.
Captain C. W. Wilkieson, Staff Corps	10 Mar. 94	Wing Officer, 23 Nov. 88.—Officiating Adjutant.
Lieut. C. T. Swan, Staff Corps	25 Aug. 86	Wing Officer and Adjutant, 5 Nov. 91.—Furlough.
Lieut. G. V. Holmes, Staff Corps	12 Apr. 88	Wing Officer, 9 July 90.
		Wing Officer,
2nd Lieut. S. M. Rice, Staff Corps	28 Jan. 93	Officiating Wing Officer.
2nd Lieut. C. R. Scott-Elliot, Staff Corps	28 Jan. 93	Officiating Wing Officer and Quarter Master.
2nd Lieut. R. J. Ross, Staff Corps	19 Apr. 93	Officiating Wing Officer.
Surgeon Major M. J. Kelawala	2 Oct. 92	In medical charge, 5 Oct. 88.

5th Madras Infantry (Shaik Kudawund—formerly 1st Bn. 5th Regiment.

Raised near Madras in December 1759).—Linked with 16th and 27th Regiments.—Regimental Centre, Madras.
"Carnatic"—"Sholinghur"—"Mysore"—"Pegu"—"Burma, 1885-87."
Head Quarters at Secunderabad. Uniform, Red. Facings, Yellow. Lace, Gold.

Rank, Names, and Corps.	Army Rank.	Remarks.
Lt.Colonel F. C. Maltby, Staff Corps	16 Oct. 92	Commandant, 23 Aug. 90.
Captain H. H. H. Aspinall, Staff Corps	22 Mar. 88	2nd in Command and Wing Commander, 11 May 94.—Furlough.
Captain F. G. Bradley, Staff Corps	31 Jan. 91	Wing Commander, 16 Jan. 91.—Adj. S. Indian Railway Vols.
Captain W. B. Young, Staff Corps	27 Jan. 94	Wing Officer, 7 Aug. 85.
Captain C. E. H. Connell, Staff Corps	10 Mar. 94	Wing Officer, 26 March 91.
Lieut. H. E. C. B. Nepean, Staff Corps	29 Aug. 85	Wing Officer and Adjutant, 1 Feb. 91.
Lieut. K. J. G. Dunolly, Staff Corps	8 Dec. 86	Wing Officer and Quarter Master, 22 Nov. 89.
Lieut. C. R. Kauntze, Suffolk Regt.	2 Apr. 90	Wing Officer, 27 Oct. 93.
Lieut. A. H. Butler, Staff Corps	28 Aug. 92	Officiating Wing Officer.
2nd Lieut. S. V. Byland, Staff Corps	28 Jan. 93	Officiating Wing Officer.
Surgeon Major J. Scott, MB	1 Apr. 94	In medical charge, 21 Dec. 94.

6th Madras Infantry (Mackenzie—formerly 1st Battalion 6th Regiment.

Raised at Trichinopoly in July 1761).—Linked with 14th Regiment.—Regimental Centre, Bellary.
"Carnatic"—"Sholinghur"—"Mysore"—"Seringapatam"—"Bourbon"—"China"—"The Dragon."
Head Quarters at Madras. Uniform, Red. Facings, White. Lace, Gold.

Rank, Names, and Corps.	Army Rank.	Remarks.
Lt.Colonel T. Greenaway, Staff Corps	12 Feb. 93	Commandant, 27 Sept. 92. [Gen., Madras District.—Furl.
Captain G. J. Shaw, Staff Corps	1 Apr. 89	2nd in Command and Wing Commander, 27 Sept. 92.—D.A.A.
Captain J. Thornhill, Staff Corps	28 Jan. 93	2nd in Command and Wing Commander, 9 June 93.—Furlough.
Captain W. Browne, Staff Corps	14 Jan. 91	Wing Officer, 1 Feb. 83.
Captain W. E. Brett, Staff Corps	22 Oct. 92	Wing Officer, 20 Apr. 94.
Lieut. R. B. B. Howe, Shropshire Lt. Inf.	8 Dec. 86	Wing Officer, 29 March 90.
Lieut. A. Moore, Staff Corps	24 Sept. 90	Wing Officer and Adjutant, 24 April 91.
Lieut. L. H. Marriott, Staff Corps	24 Mar. 91	Wing Officer, 9 June 93.—D. A. Com. Gen. 2nd Class, Lucknow.
Lieut. T. G. P. Lawrenson, Staff Corps	8 Mar. 91	Wing Officer, 7 July 93.—D. A. Com. Gen. 2nd Class.
Lieut. L. E. Fagan, Staff Corps	9 Oct. 91	Wing Officer and Quarter Master, 12 Oct. 94.
Lieut. E. T. Browne, Staff Corps	22 Mar. 92	Officiating Wing Officer.
Lieut. T. L. Leeds, Derbyshire Regt.	14 Dec. 92	Officiating Wing Officer.
Surgeon Major E. Ferraud	30 Sept. 87	In medical charge, 1 July 82.—Furlough.

7th Madras Infantry (Cooke—formerly 1st Battalion 7th Regiment.

Raised at Trichinopoly, August 1761).—Linked with 19th and 24th Regiments.—Regimental Centre, Belgaum.
"Carnatic"—"Mysore"—"Ava."
Head Quarters at Belgaum. Uniform, Red. Facings, Yellow. Lace, Gold.

Rank, Names, and Corps.	Army Rank.	Remarks.
Captain G. P. M. Prichard, Staff Corps	9 Aug. 86	Commandant, 16 Oct. 93.
Captain D. S. Lewis, Staff Corps	11 May 89	2nd in Command and Wing Commander, 28 Oct. 94.
Captain H. Thornton, Staff Corps	11 Aug. 91	Wing Commander, 25 May 94.
Lieut. J. Kendall, Staff Corps	9 May 85	Wing Officer, 10 June 87.—Adjutant Malabar Vol. Rifles.
Lieut. H. W. Johnston, Staff Corps	30 Jan. 86	Wing Officer and Adjutant, 21 Oct. 87.
Lieut. F. H. H. Jeffcoat, Staff Corps	4 Jan. 90	Wing Officer, 1 July 92.—Furlough.
Lieut. A. J. Ralph, Staff Corps	29 Apr. 91	Wing Officer and Quarter Master, 1 July 92.
Lieut. W. C. W. Harrison, Staff Corps	20 Sept. 91	Wing Officer, 20 July 94.
Lieut. R. L. Van der Gucht, Liverp'l. Regt.	5 Aug. 91	Officiating Wing Officer.
Surgeon Major J. A. Burton	2 Oct. 92	In medical charge, 30 Sept. 87.

8th Madras Infantry (*formerly* 1st Battalion 8th Regiment.

Raised near Madras in September 1761).—Linked with 17th and 25th Regiments.—
Regimental Centre, Bangalore.
"CARNATIC"—"SHOLINGHUR"—"SERINGAPATAM"—"ASSAYE."
Head Quarters at **Bangalore**. *Uniform, Red. Facings, White. Lace, Gold.*

RANK, NAMES, AND CORPS.	ARMY RANK.	REMARKS.
Captain J. S. G. Maneras, Staff Corps...	22 May 87	Commandant, 7 Oct. 94.
Captain O. W. W. Burton, Staff Corps ...	11 Sept. 88	2nd in Command and Wing Commander, 14 Aug. 91.
Captain H. D. M'Intyre, Staff Corps	14 Jan. 91	Wing Commander, 14 Aug. 91.
Captain W. N. M. Cooke, Staff Corps ...	10 May 93	Wing Officer, 29 Jan. 86.
Lieut. T. W. Y. Campbell, Staff Corps...	30 Jan. 86	Wing Officer and Adjutant, 14 Oct. 89.
Lieut. J. H. Lowry, Staff Corps	30 Jan. 86	Wing Officer, 14 Sept. 88.—Station Staff Officer, Vellore.
Lieut. F. W. Bagshawe, Staff Corps.......	19 Sept. 89	Wing Officer, 16 Oct. 93.
Lieut. C. L. Haldane, Staff Corps........	24 Sept. 90	Wing Officer and Quarter Master, 1 July 92.—Furlough.
Lieut. G. Moberly, Staff Corps	15 July 91	Wing Officer, 1 July 92.—Sick Furlough.
Lieut. W. R. B. Colan, Staff Corps	14 Dec. 91	Wing Officer, 30 June 93.—Officiating Quarter Master.
Lieut. P. A. Charrier, Munster Fus........	13 May 92	Officiating Wing Officer.—Sick Furlough.
Lieut. L. R. G. Walker, Inniskilling Fus.	30 Apr. 93	Officiating Wing Officer.
2nd Lieut. R. W. S. Elliott, Staff Corps	28 Jan. 93	Officiating Wing Officer.
Surgeon Major F. R. Divecha	31 Mar. 92	In medical charge, 2 Oct. 85.

9th Madras Infantry (*Kelly—formerly* 1st Battalion 9th Regiment.

Raised at Madura in 1765).—Linked with 11th and 28th Regiments.—Regimental Centre, Madras.
A Galley with the Motto "KHOOSHKEE WU TUREE"—"CARNATIC"—"SHOLINGHUR"—"MYSORE"—"AVA"—"PEGU."
Head Quarters at **Thayetmyo**. Detachment at **Mindat Sakan**.
Uniform, Red. Facings, Green. Lace, Gold.

Lt. Colonel D. D. Pryce, Staff Corps......	8 July 94	Commandant, 1 Dec. 90.
Captain J. Jackson, Staff Corps............	11 Aug. 91	2nd in Command and Wing Commander, 1 July 92. [Furl.
Lieut. A. R. Ditmas, Staff Corps	7 Feb. 85	Wing Officer, 25 April 90.—Dep. Assist. Com. Gen., 2nd Class.—
Lieut. E. W. A. Firth, Staff Corps	17 Oct. 88	Wing Officer and Adjutant, 6 Dec. 89.
Lieut. W. B. Powell, Staff Corps	10 Mar. 89	Wing Officer, 21 Nov. 90.—At Mindat Sakan.
Lieut. H. de V. Harvest, Staff Corps ...	10 Apr. 89	Wing Officer, 17 Dec. 90.
Lieut. G. L. P. Clarke, Staff Corps	27 Nov. 89	Wing Officer, 14 Sept. 91.
Lieut. F. G. Pierce, Staff Corps............	23 Feb. 90	Wing Officer, 1 July 92.—With 27 Madras Infantry.
Lieut. R. J. T. Stewart, North'd Fus.....	18 July 94	Officiating Wing Officer.—S. S. O. Thayetmyo.
Surgeon Major R. H. Cama.................	31 Mar. 92	In medical charge, 23 July 86.

10th Madras Infantry (*1st Burma Rifles*).—*Thusmee.—Raised at Vellore, in June* 1766.

"CARNATIC"—"MYSORE"—"AMBOOR"—"ASSAYE"—"AVA"—"BURMA, 1885-87."
Head Quarters at **Tiddim**. Detachments at **Fort White, No. 3 Stockade, &c**. *Uniform, Dark Green. Facings, Black.*

Major E. R. J. Presgrave, DSO. Staff Corps	29 Dec. 93	Commandant, 7 June 93.
Capt. G. N. Caulfield, DSO. Staff Corps	22 Jan. 92	2nd in Command and Wing Commander, 25 May 94.
Captain J. Henegan, DSO. Staff Corps	6 Feb. 95	Wing Officer, 9 May 90.
Lieut. B. Trydell, Staff Corps..............	29 Aug. 85	Wing Officer and Quarter Master, 9 May 90.—Sick Furlough.
Lieut. A. W. N. Taylor, Staff Corps......	13 Feb. 86	Wing Officer and Adjutant, 9 May 90.—S. S. O. Tiddim.
Lieut. F. G. H. Sutton, Staff Corps	17 Mar. 89	Wing Officer, 24 July 91.
Lieut. R. A. Firth, Staff Corps	2 Apr. 91	Wing Officer, 28 Apr. 93.—Furlough.
Lieut. F. L. Orman, Staff Corps	6 Jan. 93	Officiating Wing Officer.—With 6 Madras Infantry.
Lieut. W. M. Guthrie-Smith, Staff Corps	3 Sept. 92	Officiating Wing Officer.—Fort White.
Surgeon Captain C. Donovan, MD.......	28 July 91	In medical charge, 13 Jan. 93.

11th Madras Infantry (*Macneile—Syed Homed—formerly* 2nd Battalion 9th Regiment.—Raised at Ongole in January 1767).—Linked with 9th and 28th Regiments.—Regimental Centre, Madras.

"SERINGAPATAM."
Head Quarters at **Vizianagram**. *Uniform, Red. Facings, Green. Lace, Gold.*

Captain H. F. Farrant, Staff Corps	1 Oct. 86	Commandant, 28 Nov. 93.
Captain H. Elston, Staff Corps	11 Nov. 88	2nd in Command and Wing Commander, 12 Jan. 94.
Captain A. Ffrench, Staff Corps...........	15 Nov. 90	Wing Commander, 27 Jan. 93.
Lieut. T. T. H. Hay, Staff Corps..........	23 Aug. 84	Wing Officer and Adjutant, 24 Apr. 86.—S. S. O.—Furlough.
Lieut. J. W. Drever, Staff Corps..........	30 Jan. 86	Wing Officer, 12 May 90.—Burmah Police.
Lieut. H. P. Bell, Staff Corps...............	27 Feb. 89	Wing Officer, 21 Nov. 89.
Lieut. F. H. Johnstone, Staff Corps.....	16 Nov. 89	Wing Officer, 28 Apr. 93. [Madras.
Lieut. B. Scott, Staff Corps.................	26 Aug. 89	Wing Officer, 13 May 93.—Assist. Mil. Accountant, 3rd Class,
Lieut. H. A. Scott, Staff Corps	10 Aug. 92	Wing Officer, 28 Apr. 93.—With 6 Madras Infantry.
Lieut. H. C. Scott, Staff Corps............	2 May 92	Wing Officer and Quarter Master, 20 July 94.
Lieut. A. D. Cox, Staff Corps	29 May 93	Officiating Wing Officer.
Surgeon Major M. E. Reporter	1 Oct. 89	In medical charge, 26 Nov. 86.

12th Madras Infantry (*2nd Burma Battalion*).—*Barim.—Raised at Cuddalore in February* 1767.

"CARNATIC"—"SHOLINGHUR"—"AVA"—"BURMA, 1885-87."
Head Quarters at **Mandalay**. *Uniform, Red. Facings, White. Lace, Gold.*

Lt. Colonel A. Howlett, Staff Corps......	22 Aug. 94	Commandant, 9 May 90.
Captain R. M. Rainey, Staff Corps	22 Jan. 92	2nd in Command and Wing Commander, 9 June 93.
℣℃ Bt. Major C. J. W. Grant, Staff Corps	11 May 91	Wing Commander, 9 June 93.—Adjutant Neilgherry Vol. Rifles.
Captain F. W. H. Cox, Staff Corps	6 Feb. 95	Wing Officer, 9 May 90.
Lieut. A. H. Williams, Staff Corps	7 Feb. 85	Wing Officer and Adjutant, 9 May 90.
Lieut. R. T. Anwyl-Passingham, S. C....	30 Jan. 86	Wing Officer, 9 May 90.
Lieut. E. F. Rainey, Staff Corps	17 Oct. 88	Wing Officer, 26 June 91.—Furlough.
Lieut. L. H. Ricketts, Staff Corps	26 Mar. 90	Wing Officer and Quarter Master, 20 Apr. 94.
Lieut. W. W. F. C. Musgrave, Staff C.	27 June 92	Officiating Wing Officer.
Surgeon Captain W. G. Pridmore	28 July 91	In medical charge, 22 Dec. 93.

13th Madras Infantry (*Alcock—formerly 2nd Bn. 3rd Regiment*). 499
—*Raised at Madras in 1776*).—*Linked with 20th and 22nd Regiments.—Regimental Centre, Pallaveram.*
"CARNATIC"—"SHOLINGHUR"—"MYSORE"—"SERINGAPATAM."—"BURMA, 1885-87."
Head Quarters at Cannanore. *Uniform, Red. Facings, White. Lace, Gold.*

Rank, Names, and Corps.	Army Rank.	Remarks.
Captain H. Lawson, Staff Corps	12 Aug. 86	Commandant, 26 May 94.
Captain G. A. Welman, Staff Corps	11 Sept. 88	2nd in Command and Wing Commander, 8 May 93.
Captain J. A. London, Staff Corps	10 Mar. 94	Wing Commander, 8 Nov. 94.—With 8 Madras Inf. [Furlough.
Captain J. H. Smith, Staff Corps	13 Aug. 90	Wing Officer, 7 June 83.—Canton. Mag. St. Thomas's Mount.—
Lieut. A. H. Allenby, Staff Corps	23 May 85	Wing Officer, 1 Nov. 89.—Officiating Quarter Master.
Lieut. R. P. Jackson, Staff Corps	31 July 89	Wing Officer and Adjutant, 22 Aug. 90.—Furlough.
Lieut. W. C. S. Prince, Staff Corps	22 Jan. 90	Wing Officer and Quarter Master, 22 Aug. 90.—Furlough.
Lieut. H. R. Baker, Staff Corps	31 July 89	Wing Officer, 17 Apr. 91.—Officiating Adjutant.—S. S. O.
Lieut. G. C. Burn, Staff Corps	11 Oct. 92	Wing Officer, 12 Oct. 94.
Lieut. H. W. Marsden, W. India Regt.	15 July 91	Officiating Wing Officer.
2nd Lieut. W. C. Anderson, Devon Regt.	9 Apr. 92	Officiating Wing Officer.
Surgeon Major N. Chatterjie, MD.	31 Mar. 89	In medical charge, 23 Nov. 82.

14th Madras Infantry (*Wahab—formerly 2nd Battalion 6th Regiment*).
Raised at Vellore 10th December 1776).—Linked with 6th Regiment.
Regimental Centre, Bellary.
"CARNATIC"—"SHOLINGHUR"—"MYSORE"—"MAHIDPORE"—"CHINA"—"BURMA, 1885-87"—"*The Dragon*"—
"TUKYAR-O-WUFADAR," *or* "READY AND TRUE."
Head Quarters at Moulmein. *Uniform, Red. Facings, White. Lace, Gold.*

Rank, Names, and Corps.	Army Rank.	Remarks.
Major A. G. Burn, Staff Corps	10 Mar. 95	Commandant, 11 Feb. 94.
Captain G. V. Burrows, Staff Corps	21 June 90	2nd in Command and Wing Commander, 1 June 94.
Captain C. H. M. Hitchins, Staff Corps	31 Jan. 91	Wing Commander, 8 June 94.—Adj. Madras Volunteer Guards.
Captain S. B. Graham, Staff Corps	6 Feb. 95	Wing Officer, 23 Dec. 86. Wing Officer.
Lieut. F. C. Rampini, Staff Corps	27 Oct. 89	Wing Officer, 18 Sept. 91.—Dep. Assist. Com. Gen. 2nd Class.
Lieut. W. Keyworth, Staff Corps	25 June 90	Wing Officer and Adjutant, 1 July 92.—Furlough.
Lieut. A. V. Alexander, Staff Corps	5 Apr. 91	Wing Officer and Quarter Master, 1 July 92.—Offg. Adjutant.
Lieut. A. W. N. Raven, Staff Corps	15 Apr. 91	Wing Officer, 7 July 93.—S.S.O., and Cant. Mag., Moulmein.—
2nd Lt. H.J.deB.Barnett,Northamp.Reg	2 May 91	Officiating Wing Officer. [Offg. Qr. Mr.
2nd Lt. C. F. Connell, Hampshire Regt.	19 Oct. 92	Officiating Wing Officer.
Brig. Surgeon Lt.Colonel P. R. Martin.	7 May 91	In medical charge, 9 Nov. 78.

15th Madras Infantry (*Davis—formerly 2nd Battalion 4th Regiment*).
Raised at Tanjore in December 1776).—Linked with 2nd and 26th Regiments.—
Regimental Centre, Secunderabad.
"CARNATIC"—"SHOLINGHUR"—"MYSORE"—"AFGHANISTAN, 1879-80"—"BURMA, 1885-87."
Head Quarters at Madras. *Uniform, Red. Facings, Yellow. Lace, Gold.*

Rank, Names, and Corps.	Army Rank.	Remarks.
Captain C. F. Stevens, Staff Corps	19 Apr. 87	Commandant, 8 Apr. 93. [D.A.A.G., Belgaum.
Captain M. E. O'Donoghue, Staff Corps	11 May 89	2nd in Command and Wing Commander, 9 June 93.—Offg.
Captain H. J. Bremner, Staff Corps	13 Aug. 90	Wing Commander, 26 Feb. 92.
Lieut. A. J. Campbell, Staff Corps	9 Apr. 85	Wing Officer, 12 May 89.—With 26 Madras Infantry.
Lieut. L. H. Walker, Staff Corps	29 Aug. 85	Wing Officer, 12 May 90.
Lieut. J. W. Orchard, Staff Corps	10 Nov. 86	Wing Officer, 26 Feb. 92.—Burmah Military Police.
Lieut. F. J. Wallis, Staff Corps	19 Mar. 90	Wing Officer, 26 Feb. 92.—Burmah Military Police.
Lieut. W. R. Walker, Staff Corps	23 Mar. 90	Wing Officer and Quarter Master, 23 June 93.—Offg. Adjutant.
Lieut. A. Playfair, Staff Corps	4 Dec. 89	Wing Officer, 8 Dec. 93.—Silchar Military Police.
Lieut. E. E. Bousfield, Staff Corps	13 Jan. 92	Wing Officer, 12 Oct. 94.—Officiating Quarter Master.
Lt. A. J. M. Higginson, W. Riding Regt.	18 Feb. 92	Officiating Wing Officer.
Lieut. H. A. Mansel, Dorset Regt.	28 Oct. 92	Officiating Wing Officer.
2nd Lt. S. M. Binny, Northumber'd Fus.	18 May 92	Officiating Wing Officer.
Surgeon Major J. J. Moran, MD.	30 Mar. 90	In medical charge, 17 Nov. 93.

16th Madras Infantry (*Lane—formerly 2nd Battalion 5th Regiment*).
Raised at Trichinopoly 10th December 1776).—Linked with 5th and 27th Regiments.—
Regimental Centre, Madras.
"CARNATIC"—"SHOLINGHUR"—"MYSORE"—"SERINGAPATAM"—"AVA"—"BURMA, 1885-
Head Quarters at Bellary. *Uniform, Red. Facings, Yellow. Lace, Gold.*

Rank, Names, and Corps.	Army Rank.	Remarks.
Major J. W. Parker, Staff Corps	11 Feb. 95	Commandant, 30 Dec. 93.
Captain A. H. Dobbs, Staff Corps	1 May 89	2nd in Command and Wing Commander, 16 Nov. 94. Wing Commander.
Lieut. R. H. Dewing, Staff Corps	23 Aug. 84	Wing Officer, 10 June 87.
Lieut. R. C. Cockerill, Staff Corps	29 Aug. 85	Wing Officer, 14 Sept. 88.—Furlough.
Lieut. C. V. N. Lyne, Staff Corps	18 Sept. 89	Wing Officer and Quarter Master, 12 May 90.
Lieut. A. W. H. Lee, Staff Corps	28 Aug. 90	Wing Officer and Adjutant, 23 Oct. 91.
Lieut. H. S. Alexander, Staff Corps	13 Nov. 90	Wing Officer, 26 Feb. 92.
Lieut. E. G. Jones, Staff Corps	8 May 91	Officiating Wing Officer.
Lieut. D. G. Bryce, Staff Corps	7 Mar. 92	Officiating Wing Officer.
2nd Lt. B. H. B. Magrath, Staff Corps	3 Sept. 92	Officiating Wing Officer.
Surgeon Major E. R. Da Costa	2 Apr. 93	In medical charge, 21 Dec. 94.

17th Madras Infantry (*Butler—formerly 2nd Battalion 1st Regiment*).
Raised in 1777).—Linked with 8th and 25th Regiments.—Regimental Centre, Bangalore.
"CARNATIC"—"SHOLINGHUR"—"NAGPORE"—"BURMA, 1885-87."
Head Quarters at Rangoon. *Uniform, Red. Facings, White. Lace, Gold.*

Rank, Names, and Corps.	Army Rank.	Remarks.
Capt. H. A. B. Bouldersnon, Staff Corps	13 June 86	Commandant, 30 Mar. 94.
Captain H. E. M. Mason, Staff Corps	10 Sept. 87	2nd in Command and Wing Commander, 13 Feb. 93.
Captain L. J. Andrews, Staff Corps	10 Mar. 94	Wing Commander, 30 Mar. 94.—Furlough.
Lieut. S. A. Pearse, Staff Corps	14 May 84	Wing Officer, 10 June 87.—Station Staff Officer.
Lieut. A. F. P. Paxton, Staff Corps	25 Feb. 85	Wing Officer, 3 Aug. 88.
Lieut. W. G. Hodgson, Staff Corps	25 Aug. 86	Wing Officer and Adjutant, 15 Mar. 89.
Lieut. H. C. Beadon, Staff Corps	1 May 92	Wing Officer and Quarter Master, 23 June 93.
Lieut. W. J. Ottley, Munster Fus.	11 Oct. 92	Officiating Wing Officer.
Lieut. G. P. R. Beaman, Essex Regt.	4 Apr. 92	Officiating Wing Officer.
Surgeon Major W. F. Thomas	31 Mar. 91	In medical charge, 11 June 86.—On other duty.
Surgeon Lieut. Bhola Nath	29 July 93	Officiating in medical charge.

19th Madras Infantry (*Muirhead—formerly 2nd Bn. 7th Regiment.*
Raised at Trichinopoly in 1777.)—*Linked with 7th and 24th Regiments.—Regimental Centre, Belgaum.*
"CARNATIC"—"SHOLINGHUR"—"MYSORE"—"SERINGAPATAM"—"PEGU"—"CENTRAL INDIA."
Head Quarters at Berhampore. Wing at Cuttack. *Uniform, Red. Facings, Yellow. Lace, Gold.*

RANK, NAMES, AND CORPS.	ARMY RANK.	REMARKS.
Captain R. C. Andrews, Staff Corps	28 Oct. 87	Commandant 2nd in Command and Wing Commander. 10 Nov. 94.
Captain W.V. Pakenham, Staff Corps	30 Jan. 89	Wing Commander, Wing Officer, 1 July 82.
Captain T. A. Fischer, Staff Corps	10 Mar. 94	Wing Officer, 17 Nov. 93.—Burmah Military Police.
Lieut. H. St. G. Thomas, Staff Corps	14 May 84	Wing Officer and Adjutant, 21 Oct. 87.—Furlough.
Lieut. R. W. A. Denne, Staff Corps	8 Dec. 86	Wing Officer, 17 Nov. 83.
Lieut. H. W. Heffernan, Staff Corps	25 Apr. 90	Wing Officer and Quarter Master, 21 Nov. 90.
Lieut. W. Donnan, Staff Corps	12 Aug. 89	Wing Officer, 6 Mar. 91.—Station Staff Officer, Cuttack.
Lieut. M. F. Harding, Royal Marines	1 Apr. 85	Officiating Wing Officer.—Station Staff Officer, Berhampore.
Lieut. H. L. Hole, Staff Corps	2 Nov. 92	Officiating Wing Officer.
Lieut. A. W. F. Knox, Staff Corps	18 Nov. 93	Officiating Wing Officer.
Surgeon Major R. Ross	2 Apr. 93	In medical charge, 17 Nov. 93.—Furlough.
Surgeon Lieut. R. K. Mitter	30 Jan. 92	Officiating in medical charge.

20th Madras Infantry (*Bagot—formerly 2nd Battalion 2nd Regiment.*
Raised at Tanjore in 1777).—*Linked with 13th and 22nd Regiments.—Regimental Centre, Pallaveram.*
"CARNATIC"—"SHOLINGAPUR"—"MYSORE"—"SERINGAPATAM."
Head Quarters at Secunderabad. *Uniform, Red. Facings, Green. Lace, Gold.*

RANK, NAMES, AND CORPS.	ARMY RANK.	REMARKS.
Lt.Colonel B. H. Pollard, Staff Corps	25 Dec. 93	Commandant, 8 May 93.
Captain E. P. Wood, Staff Corps	22 Jan. 92	2nd in Command and Wing Commander, 8 May 93.
Captain W. Hudson, Staff Corps	25 Aug. 94	Wing Officer, 12 Oct. 94.
Lieut. H. M. M. Brooke, Staff Corps	22 Oct. 89	Wing Officer, 16 Oct. 93.—Dep. Assist. Com. Gen. 2nd Class.
Lieut. J. S. Hodding, Staff Corps	26 June 89	Wing Officer, 19 Apr. 92.
Lieut. L. J. G. Lavie, Staff Corps	21 Mar. 01	Wing Officer, 15 May 93.—Officiating Adjutant.
Lieut. E. H. Payne, Staff Corps	8 Nov. 90	Wing Officer and Qr. Mr., 12 May 93.—With 1 Inf. Hyd. Cont.
Lieut. R. F. Bidwell, Staff Corps	31 Oct. 92	Wing Officer, 19 Jan. 94.—Officiating Quarter Master.
Lieut. A. V. Searle, Leinster Regiment	2 May 94	Officiating Wing Officer.
Surgeon Major C. H. Bennett, MD	1 Oct. 89	In medical charge, 8 March 83.

21st Madras Infantry (*Roberts—formerly 1st Battalion 11th Regiment.*
Raised at Chicacole in 1786).—*Linked with 1st and 4th Regiments.—Regimental Centre, Bangalore.*
"MYSORE"—"SERINGAPATAM"—"NAGPORE"—"AFGHANISTAN, 1878-80"—"BURMA, 1885-87."
Head Quarters at Bangalore. *Uniform, Red. Facings, White. Lace, Gold.*

RANK, NAMES, AND CORPS.	ARMY RANK.	REMARKS.
Major G. S. Baugh, Staff Corps	12 Nov. 90	Commandant, 24 Oct. 91.—Furlough.
Captain P. G. Huggins, DSO. Staff C.	19 Apr. 87	2nd in Command and Wing Commander, 24 Oct. 91.
Captain H. V. Cox, Staff Corps	14 Jan. 91	Wing Commander, 24 Oct. 91.—With Imp. Service Troops.
Captain H. T. Brooking, Staff Corps	6 Feb. 95	Wing Officer and Adjutant, 19 Oct. 88.
Lieut. C. E. Hendley, Staff Corps	12 Nov. 84	Wing Officer, 2 Apr. 91.
Lieut. A. M. Anderson, Staff Corps	4 Apr. 89	Wing Officer, 27 Oct. 93.
Lieut. N. M. C. Stevens, Staff Corps	31 July 89	Wing Officer and Quarter Master, 27 May 92.
Lieut. J. A. Bliss, Staff Corps	4 Dec. 91	Wing Officer, 8 June 94.
Lieut. L. W. Fox, Staff Corps	23 Nov. 92	Officiating Wing Officer.
2nd Lt. C. E. D. D. Houston, Staff C.	28 June 93	Officiating Wing Officer.
Surgeon Captain D. H. M'D. Graves	28 July 91	In medical charge, Officiating in medical charge.

22nd Madras Infantry (*Dalrymple—formerly 2nd Battalion*
11th Regiment.—Raised at Ellore in 1788).—Linked with 13th and 20th Regiments.
—Regimental Centre, Pallaveram.
"MYSORE"—"SERINGAPATAM"—"AVA."
Head Quarters at Secunderabad. *Uniform, Red. Facings, White. Lace, Gold.*

RANK, NAMES, AND CORPS.	ARMY RANK.	REMARKS.
Major L. J. Torrie, Staff Corps	19 Oct. 92	Commandant, 18 Jan. 93.
Captain J. F. Wilson, Staff Corps	10 Sept. 86	2nd in Command and Wing Commander, 18 Jan. 93.
Captain T. B. Hawks, Staff Corps	9 Sept. 93	Wing Commander, 18 Jan. 93.
Lieut. A. W. Newbold, Staff Corps	23 Aug. 84	Wing Officer, 17 May 89.—Burmah Military Police.
Lieut. H. E. Pritchard, Staff Corps	12 Nov. 84	Wing Officer, 20 July 91.—Burmah Military Police.
Lieut. T. S. Young, Staff Corps	23 May 85	Wing Officer, 25 May 94.
Lieut. G. M. Morris, Staff Corps	27 Feb. 89	Wing Officer, 17 June 92.—Sick Furlough.
Lieut. W. B. Greig, Staff Corps	16 May 92	Wing Officer and Quarter Master, 28 Apr. 93.
Lieut. J. W. Milne, Staff Corps	31 July 92	Wing Officer and Adjutant, 27 Oct. 93.
Lieut. J. H. Hudson, Sussex Regt.	1 Sept. 92	Officiating Wing Officer.
Surgeon Major D. F. Dymott, MB	31 Mar. 92	In medical charge, 1 Dec. 93.—Offg. Dist. Med. and San. Officer. [Salem.
Surgeon Captain W. Molesworth	31 Mar. 90	Officiating in medical charge.

23rd Madras (*or Wallajahbad*) **Light Infantry** (*Tolfry—formerly 1st Battalion*
12th Regiment.—Raised at Madras in 1794).—Linked with 3rd and 31st Regiments.
—Regimental Centre, Trichinopoly.
"NOW OR NEVER"—"SERINGAPATAM"—"NAGPORE"—"BURMA, 1835-87."
Head Quarters at Trichinopoly. *Uniform, Red. Facings, Green. Lace, Gold.*

RANK, NAMES, AND CORPS.	ARMY RANK.	REMARKS.
Major M. E. H. O. Welch, Staff Corps	20 July 90	Commandant, 6 May 91.
Captain M. A. Tuite, Staff Corps	1 May 89	2nd in Command and Wing Commander, 14 Aug. 91.
Captain G. W. S. Hawks, Staff Corps	23 Apr. 92	Wing Commander, 14 Aug. 91.
Captain J. C. Erck, Staff Corps	9 Sept. 93	Wing Officer, 11 Feb. 87.—Burmah Military Police.
Lieut. B. W. Marlow, Staff Corps	12 Nov. 84	Wing Officer, 17 May 90.—Assist. Mil. Account. 1st Class.
Lieut. H. Vickers, Staff Corps	25 Nov. 85	Wing Officer and Quarter Master, 18 May 88.—Offg. Adj.—S.S.O.
Lieut. E. R. Foord, Staff Corps	17 Nov. 89	Wing Officer, 9 Sept. 92.—Sick Furlough.
Lieut. J. S. Dallas, Staff Corps	18 Nov. 89	Wing Officer, 13 Oct. 93.
Lieut. E. B. Barratt, Staff Corps	7 Dec. 91	Wing Officer, 20 July, 94.
Lieut. J. W. Bolton, Staff Corps	29 Jan. 88	Officiating Wing Officer.
Lieut. E. F. Harding, N. Stafford Regt.	28 Oct. 93	Officiating Wing Officer.—With 6 Madras Infantry.
Surgeon Major G. M. E. M'Kee	2 Oct. 92	In medical charge, 16 Oct. 85.—Furlough.
Surgeon Lieut. C. R. Pearce	23 July 94	Officiating in medical charge.

24th Madras Infantry (*McDonald—formerly 2nd Bn. 12th Regiment.*)

Raised at Vellore in 1794).—Linked with 7th and 19th Regiments.—Regimental Centre, Belgaum.
"SERINGAPATAM"—"ASSAYE"—"BOURBON."
Head Quarters at Bangalore. *Uniform, Red. Facings, Green. Lace, Gold.*

Rank, Names, and Corps.	Army Rank.	Remarks.
Lt. Colonel E. B. Anderson, Staff Corps	19 Feb. 93	Commandant, 8 Dec. 92.
Captain H. E. Porter, Staff Corps	11 Nov. 88	2nd in Command and Wing Commander, 8 Dec. 92.
Captain E. C. Thwaytes, Staff Corps	11 Aug. 91	Wing Commander, 8 Dec. 92.
Captain A. M. Lloyd, Staff Corps	11 May 89	Wing Officer, 1 July 82.—Burmah Police.
Lieut. H.W. C. Coiquhoun, Staff Corps	23 May 85	Wing Officer, 7 June 89.—Furlough.
Lieut. R. M. Bell, Staff Corps	25 Nov. 85	Wing Officer, 29 Aug. 90.— Dep. Assist Com. Gen. 2nd Class.
Lieut. E. W. Grimshaw, Staff Corps	14 June 91	Wing Officer and Quarter Master, 9 Sept. 92.
Lieut. G. M. Morris, Staff Corps	19 May 91	Wing Officer, 28 Apr. 93.
Lieut. A. G. Crawford, Staff Corps	15 May 93	Officiating Wing Officer.
Lieut. W. St. G. Chamier, Leinster Regt.	15 Apr. 93	Officiating Wing Officer.
Surgeon Lt.Colonel T. Mayne	30 Mar. 92	In medical charge, 4 Nov. 87.

25th Madras Infantry (*Kenny—formerly 1st Battalion 13th Regiment.*)

Raised at Trichinopoly in 1794).—Linked with 8th and 17th Regiments.—Regimental Centre, Bangalore.
"BURMA, 1885-87."
Head Quarters at Madras. *Uniform, Red. Facings, Green. Lace, Gold.*

Rank, Names, and Corps.	Army Rank.	Remarks.
Lt. Colonel C. W. Walker, Staff Corps	31 Jan. 91	Commandant, 28 Aug. 91.
p.s.c. Captain C. E. Poynder, Staff Corps	10 Sept. 86	2nd in Command and Wing Commander, 30 Jan. 91.—Dep. Assist. Adjutant General for Instruction, Bangalore.
Captain H. T. King, Staff Corps	1 May 89	Wing Commander, 18 Sept. 91.—D. A. A. General for Musketry, Secunderabad.
Captain F. A. Loudon, Staff Corps	10 May 93	Wing Officer, 23 July 86.
Captain W. E. Banbury, Staff Corps	25 Aug. 94	Wing Officer, 23 July 86.—Garrison Qr. Mr. Fort St. George.
Lieut. H. E. Williams, Staff Corps	29 Aug. 85	Wing Officer, 1 Feb. 92.
Lieut. W. H. Brown, Staff Corps	25 Aug. 86	Wing Officer and Adjutant, 20 June 90.—Furlough.
Lieut. W. R. Stone, Staff Corps	21 Jan. 89	Wing Officer, 1 Feb. 92.—Station Staff Officer, Chin Hills.
Lieut. J. W. H. Lyon, Staff Corps	22 Aug. 91	Wing Officer, 1 July 92.—Officiating Quarter Master.
Lieut. T. I. Drever, Staff Corps	29 Aug. 91	Wing Officer, 1 July 92.
Lieut. E. W. Keily, Staff Corps	7 Apr. 91	Officiating Wing Officer.
Surgeon Major J. Hoey	31 Oct. 91	In medical charge, 4 Jan. 94.

26th Madras Infantry (*Innes—formerly 2nd Battalion 13th Regiment.*)

Raised at Tanjore in 1794).—Linked with 2nd and 15th Regiments.—Regimental Centre, Secunderabad.
"NAGPORE"—"KEMENDINE"—"AVA"—"PEGU"—"BURMA, 1885-87."
Head Quarters at Rangoon. Detachment at Port Blair. *Uniform, Red. Facings, Green. Lace, Gold.*

Rank, Names, and Corps.	Army Rank.	Remarks.
Lt.Colonel S. E. Rolland, Staff Corps	1 July 87	Commandant, 27 Sept. 90.—Offg. Colonel on the Staff, Chin Hills.
Captain K. M. Foss, Staff Corps	14 June 88	2nd in Command and Wing Comdr., 3 Nov. 93.—Offg. Comdt.
Captain F. T. Williams, Staff Corps	22 Jan. 92	Wing Comdr., 1 July 92.—Offg. D. A. A. Gen. Chin Hills.
Lieut. W. H. W. Mercer, Staff Corps	12 Nov. 84	Wing Officer, 1 Aug. 87.—Port Blair.
Lieut. M. A. B. Kappey, Royal Marines	1 Feb. 86	Wing Officer, 19 Dec. 89.—Sick Furlough.
Lieut. E. Codrington, Staff Corps	7 Jan. 90	Wing Officer, 28 Apr. 93.—Burmah Military Police.
Lieut. H. R. Troup, Staff Corps	8 Dec. 89	Wing Officer, 20 June 90.—Dep. Assist. Com. Gen., 2nd Class. Wing Officer and Adjutant.
Lieut. C. H. B. Clark, Staff Corps	13 Nov. 90	Wing Officer and Quarter Master, 14 Apr. 92.—S.S.O. Port Blair.
Lieut. T. L. Ormiston, Staff Corps	5 Apr. 92	Wing Officer, 7 July 93.—Offg.Cantonment Magistrate St. Thomas' Mount.
Captain A. J. Shaw, Staff Corps	19 Dec. 94	Officiating Wing Officer.—Furlough.
Lieut. F. W. Thomas, Staff Corps	19 Feb. 92	Officiating Wing Officer and Adjutant.
Lieut. H. W. Jackson, Staff Corps	23 Aug. 93	Officiating Wing Officer.
2nd Lt. H. T. Fulton, W. Yorkshire Regt.	9 Apr. 92	Officiating Wing Officer.—Port Blair.
Surgeon Lt.Colonel J. Backhouse	1 Apr. 89	In medical charge, 13 March 91.

27th Madras Infantry (*Lindsay—formerly 1st Battalion 14th Regiment.*)

Raised at Trichinopoly in 1798).—Linked with 5th and 16th Regiments.—Regimental Centre, Madras.
"MAHIDPORE"—"LUCKNOW"—"BURMA, 1885-87."
Head Quarters at Madras. Detachment at St. Thomas' Moun*t*. *Uniform, Red. Facings, Yellow. Lace, Gold.*

Rank, Names, and Corps.	Army Rank.	Remarks.
Major H. H. Young, Staff Corps	27 Aug. 90	Commandant, 2 June 91.—Furlough. [Belgaum District.—Furl.
Captain R. F. Clothier, Staff Corps	12 Aug. 86	2nd in Command and Wing Comdr., 1 July 92.—Offg. A. A. Gen.
Captain H. B. Sutton, Staff Corps	13 Aug. 90	2nd in Command and Wing Commander, 1 July 92.
Lieut. T. Ffrench, Staff Corps	14 May 84	Wing Officer and Quarter Master, 12 May 90.
Lieut. F. N. Burton, Staff Corps	1 Apr. 88	Wing Officer, 12 May 90.—St. Thomas' Mount.
Lieut. A. R. Nethersole, Staff Corps	3 June 91	Wing Officer and Adjutant, 22 July 92.
Lieut. P. Greig, Staff Corps	15 Apr. 91	Wing Officer,
Lieut. S. R. Davidson, Staff Corps	3 June 92	Officiating Wing Officer.—With Bhopal Battalion.
2nd Lieut. H. V. Firth, Suffolk Regt.	22 June 92	Officiating Wing Officer.
2nd Lieut. A. V. W. Hope, Staff Corps	28 Jan. 93	Officiating Wing Officer.—St. Thomas' Mount.
2nd Lieut. C. L. Perrin, Staff Corps	28 Jan. 93	Officiating Wing Officer.
Surgeon Captain I. P. Doyle, *DSO*	30 Sept. 86	In medical charge, 17 Nov. 93.

28th Madras Infantry (*Martin—formerly 2nd Battalion 14th Regiment.*)

Raised at Vellore in 1798).—Linked with 9th and 11th Regiments.—Regimental Centre, Madras.
"MAHIDPORE" — "NAGPORE" — "AVA."
Head Quarters at Quilon. Detachments at Trichoor and Trivandrum. *Uniform, Red. Facings, Yellow. Lace, Gold*

Rank, Names, and Corps.	Army Rank.	Remarks.
Major F. G. Preston, Staff Corps	28 Feb. 94	Commandant, 14 Aug. 91.
Captain W. H. Lowry, Staff Corps	20 May 88	2nd in Command and Wing Commander, 14 Aug. 91.
Captain W. M. Dawes, Staff Corps	19 Feb. 92	Wing Commander, 14 Aug. 91.
Lieut. E. M. Jackson, Staff Corps	23 Aug. 84	Wing Officer and Adjutant, 10 June 87.—S. S. O. Quilon.
Lieut. F. H. Domenichetti, Staff Corps	30 Jan. 86	Wing Officer, 12 May 90.—Burmah Military Police. [Furlough.
Lieut. H. L. D. Fordyce, Staff Corps	28 June 89	Wing Officer, 16 Oct. 93.—Dep. Assist. Com. Gen., 2nd Class.—
Lieut. G. R. Oakes, Staff Corps	29 Feb. 88	Wing Officer and Quarter Master, 18 Oct. 89.—Sick Furlough.
Lieut. R. W. C. Keays, Staff Corps	31 Aug. 88	Wing Officer, 1 Feb. 92.—Assist. Mil. Accountant.—Sick Furl.
Lieut. J. J. P. Quinn, Staff Corps	26 Oct. 89	Wing Officer, 14 Aug. 91.
Lieut. C. D. Field, Staff Corps	25 Mar. 91	Wing Officer, 7 July 93.
Lieut. H. A. Newell, Staff Corps	5 Apr. 92	Wing Officer, 27 Oct. 93.
Lieut. A. C. Gabbett, Staff Corps	21 July 92	Officiating Wing Officer.—Station Staff Officer, Trichoor.
Surgeon Major M. S. Eyre, *MD*	30 Sept. 88	In medical charge, 8 Mar. 83.

29th (*7th Burma Battalion*) **Madras Infantry** (*Macleod—formerly* 1st Battalion 15th Regiment.—*Raised at Masulipatam in 1798*).
Head Quarters at **Meiktila.** *Uniform, Red. Facings, White. Lace, Gold.*

Rank, Names, and Corps.	Army Rank.	Remarks.
Captain G. W. Maxwell, Staff Corps	11 Oct. 87	Commandant, 16 Oct. 93.
Captain G. Rippon, Staff Corps	11 Aug. 91	2nd in Command and Wing Commander, 16 Oct. 93.
Captain C. V. Mainwaring, Staff Corps	10 Mar. 94	Wing Commander, 16 Oct. 93.—Furlough.
Lieut. C. McC. Poulter, Staff Corps	1 Feb. 85	Wing Officer and Adjutant, 16 Oct. 93.—Offg. Wing Commander.
Lieut. W. R. Staunton, Staff Corps	15 Feb. 90	Wing Officer, 2 Feb. 94.—Officiating Adjutant.
Lieut. G. A. Strahan, Staff Corps	11 Sept. 90	Wing Officer and Quarter Master, 16 Oct. 93.
Lieut. W. S. Prentis, Staff Corps	2 May 92	Wing Officer, 16 Oct. 93.—Furlough.
Lieut. C. E. Tristram, Staff Corps	16 Oct. 92	Wing Officer, 16 Oct. 93.
Lieut. E. R. B. Murray, Staff Corps	1 Apr. 89	Officiating Wing Officer.
Lieut. A. T. Kirkwood, Staff Corps	15 June 93	Officiating Wing Officer.
Brigade Surgeon Lt.Colonel J. Smith	12 Oct. 90	In medical charge, 1 Apr. 89.—Sick Furlough.
Surgeon Lieut. T. Stodart	29 July 93	Officiating in medical charge.

30th (*5th Burma Battalion*) **Madras Infantry** (*Crewe—formerly* 2nd Battalion 15th Regiment.—*Raised at Masulipatam in 1799*).
"AVA"—"AFGHANISTAN, 1878-80"—"BURMA, 1885-87."
Head Quarters at **Bhamo.** *Uniform, Red. Facings, White. Lace, Gold.*

Rank, Names, and Corps.	Army Rank.	Remarks.
Captain W. Cook, Staff Corps	10 Sept. 86	Commandant, 1 Feb. 92.—From 3 Sikh Infantry.
Captain N. A. K. Burne, Staff Corps	11 Sept. 87	2nd in Com. and Wing Comdr. 1 Feb. 92.—From 23 Bengal Inf.
Captain H. N. Taylor, *DSO*, Staff Corps	28 Jan. 93	Wing Commander, 1 Feb. 92.
Lieut. A. C. Baldwin, Staff Corps	14 May 84	Wing Officer, 1 Feb. 92.
Lieut. G. A. Ward, Staff Corps	2 July 84	Wing Officer, 1 Feb. 92.—Officiating Adjutant.
Lieut. G. H. C. Mockler, Staff Corps	22 Feb. 88	Wing Officer, 1 Feb. 92.
Lieut. R. J. T. Savi, Staff Corps	25 Feb. 88	Wing Officer and Adjutant, 1 Feb. 92.
Lieut. F. Copeland, Staff Corps	19 Oct. 90	Wing Officer and Quarter Master, 1 Feb. 92.
Lieut. G. Drage, Staff Corps	2 Mar. 92	Officiating Wing Officer. Officiating Wing Officer.
Surgeon Lt.Colonel W. G. King, *MB*	31 Mar. 94	In medical charge, 12 Feb. 92.—On other duty.
Surgeon Captain J. Entrican, *MD*	28 July 91	Officiating in medical charge.

31st (*6th Burma Battalion*) **Madras Light Infantry** (*Jeannerrett—formerly* 1st Battalion 16th Regiment.—*Raised at Trichinopoly 1 January 1800*).
"NOW OR NEVER"—"MAHIDPORE."
Head Quarters at **Haka.** Detachment at **Falam.** *Uniform, Red. Facings, Green. Lace, Gold.*

Rank, Names, and Corps.	Army Rank.	Remarks.
Bt.MajorH. D'U.Keary, *DSO*, StaffCorps	29 Dec. 93	Commandant, 1 Feb. 92.
Captain C. R. Keate, Staff Corps	22 Jan. 92	2nd in Command and Wing Commander, 26 Jan. 94.—At Falam. Wing Commander.
Lieut. S. Geoghegan, Staff Corps	29 Aug. 85	Wing Officer and Adjutant, 1 Feb. 92.
Lieut. C. H. Williams, Staff Corps	10 Nov. 86	Wing Officer and Quarter Master, 1 Feb. 92.
Lieut. C. Barnett, Staff Corps	28 Feb. 89	Wing Officer, 1 Feb. 92.—Furlough.
Lieut. A. B. Murray, Staff Corps	2 Feb. 90	Wing Officer, 27 May 92.—Station Staff Officer, Haka.
Lieut. W. H. F. Basevi, Staff Corps	3 Nov. 91	Wing Officer, 2 Mar. 94.—Station Staff Officer, Falam.
Lieut. H. A. Carleton, Staff Corps	3 May 91	Officiating Wing Officer.
2nd Lt. E. G. Bromhead, Manchester Regt.	18 May 92	Officiating Wing Officer.
Surgeon Major A. G. E. Newland	2 Apr. 93	In medical charge, 17 Nov. 93.

32nd (*4th Burma Battalion*) **Madras Infantry** (*Dyce—formerly* 2nd Battalion 16th Regiment.—*Raised at Madura 1 January 1800*).
"AVA."
Head Quarters at **Fort Stedman.** Detachments at **Loikaw, Bampon, &c.** *Uniform, Blue. Facings, Scarlet.*

Rank, Names, and Corps.	Army Rank.	Remarks.
Major E. S. Hastings, *DSO*, Staff Corps	28 Feb. 94	Commandant, 1 Jan. 91.
Captain W. H. Dobbie, Staff Corps	13 Aug. 90	2nd in Command and Wing Commander, 1 Jan. 91.—Furlough.
Captain H. D. Daly, Staff Corps	10 May 93	Wing Commander, 1 Jan. 91.
Lieut. H. C. Bernard, Staff Corps	23 Aug. 84	Wing Officer and Adjutant, 1 Jan. 91.—S.S.O. Fort Stedman.
Lieut. J. A. G. Rainsford, Staff Corps	22 Nov. 84	Wing Officer, 16 Mar. 94. [Branch, Burma.
Lieut. E. W. Carrick, Staff Corps	7 Feb. 85	Wing Officer and Qr. Mr. 1 Jan. 91.—Unpaid Attaché Intell.
Lieut. W. G. Nisbett, Staff Corps	4 Jan. 89	Wing Officer, 5 June 91.—Loikaw.
Lieut. H. H. Harington, Welsh Regt.	22 Aug. 90	Wing Officer, 1 Jan. 91.—Bampon.
Surgeon Major M. P. Kharegat	2 Oct. 92	In medical charge, 9 Mar. 92.

33rd (*3rd Burma Battalion*) **Madras Infantry** (*Wahab—formerly* 1s Battalion 17th Regiment).
"COCHIN."
Head Quarters at **Mandalay.** *Uniform, Red. Facings, Yellow. Lace, Gold.*

Rank, Names, and Corps.	Army Rank.	Remarks.
Major J. E. Preston, *DSO*, Staff Corps	21 Sept. 94	Commandant, 12 Feb. 91.
Captain R. G. Iremonger, Staff Corps	11 Nov. 88	2nd in Command and Wing Commander, 6 March 91.
Captain S. G. Radcliff, Staff Corps	19 Feb. 92	Wing Commander, 24 Apr. 91.
Captain W. A. Oswald, Staff Corps	9 Sept. 93	Wing Officer, 9 May 90.
Captain T. S. Johnson, Staff Corps	6 Feb. 95	Wing Officer and Adjutant, 9 May 90.
Lieut. S. R. Stevens, Staff Corps	30 Jan. 86	Wing Officer and Quarter Master, 9 May 90.
Lieut. M. R. Hurly, Staff Corps	1 Feb. 86	Wing Officer, 9 May 90.—Furlough.
Lieut. J. H. Whitehead, Staff Corps	13 Jan. 90	Wing Officer, 17 Apr. 91.
2nd Lt. H. G. L. Corbett, York Regt.	9 Apr. 92	Officiating Wing Officer.
Surgeon Captain P. C. H. Strickland	1 Oct. 87	In medical charge, 31 Aug. 94.

Madras Medical Department. 504

[For the explanation of the qualifications of the following Officers, *see* page iii.]

SURGEON MAJOR GENERAL.	ASSISTANT SURGEON.	SURGEON MAJ. GEN.	REMARKS.
Sibthorpe, Charles,[1] *FRCPI. LRCSE*......	1 Apr. 70	18 May 54	Surgeon General with the Madras Government.
SURGEON COLONELS.		**SURG. COL.**	
McVittie, Charles Edwin,[2] *LRCP.Ed. FRCSI.*	31 Mar. 66	13 Mar. 91	Southern District.
Hunt, Samuel Bradshaw, *LRCP.Ed. LRCSI.*	31 Mar. 65	1 Mar. 93	Rangoon District.
Bateman, Daniel Frederick,[4] *LRCP.Ed. LRCS.Ed.*	31 Mar. 65	1 July 93	Mandalay District and Chin Hills Command.
BRIGADE SURGEON LIEUTENANT COLONELS.		**BRIG. SURG LT. COL.**	**RANK OF LT. COL.**
Sargent, James Forbes, *MRCS. LSA.*	1 Oct. 66	31 May 90	......	2 Lancers Hyderabad Contingent.
McGann, Terence J., *FRCS.Ed. LRCP.Ed. LAH.Dub.*	1 Apr. 67	25 July 90	......	Senior Surgeon and Sanitary Commissioner with the Mysore Govt.
Smith, James, *LRCP.Ed. LRCS.Ed.*	1 Apr. 67	12 Oct. 90	1 Oct. 87	29 Madras Infantry.
Hackett, Arthur Luke, *LRCP.Ed. LRCS.Ed.*	1 Apr. 67	28 Jan. 91	......	2nd District, Madras. [Guard."
Hazlett, Henry James, *LRCPI. LRCSI.*	1 Apr. 67	7 Mar. 91	1 Apr. 87	3rd District, Madras, including "Body
Martin, Patrick Richard,[9] *MD. MCh.*	1 Apr. 68	7 May 91	1 Apr. 88	14 Madras Infantry.
Blenkinsop, Frederick Henry,[12] *MRCS. LSA.*	1 Oct. 68	23 May 92	1 Oct. 88	Officiating P.M.O. Secunderabad District and Hyderabad Contingent.
Price, William, *MD. MCh.*	1 Apr. 69	1 Mar. 93	......	Senior Physician, General Hospital, and Principal Medical College, Madras.
Sinclair, David, *MB. MCh.*	1 Oct. 69	18 May 93	......	Inspector General of Prisons, Sanitary Commissioner, and Chief of Civil Medical Dept. Burmah.
North, John,[13] *MRCS. LSA.*	1 Oct. 69	1 July 93	......	1 Madras Lancers.
Fawcett, Edward,[15] *LRCPI. FRCSI.*	1 Oct. 69	4 Apr. 94	......	Staff Surgeon, Secunderabad.
SURGEON LIEUTENANT COLONELS.		**SURGEON LT. COL.**	
Hyde, Henry, *LRCPI. MRCS.*	1 Oct. 66	1 Oct. 86	Dist. Med. and San. Officer, Tinnevelly—Acting South Arcot, and Supdt. of Jail, Cuddalore.
Mookerjee, Preo Nath,[14] *LRCP.Ed. LRCS.Ed.*	1 Apr. 68	1 Apr. 88	Civil Surgeon, Sagairg.
Fitzpatrick, John Francis, *MD. MCh. MRCPI. LAH.Dub.*	1 Apr. 68	1 Apr. 88	District Medical and Sanitary Officer, Coimbatore.—Hon. Surgeon, N. V. Rifles.
Backhouse, Joseph, *LRCPI. FRCSI.*	1 Apr. 69	1 Apr. 89	26 Madras Infantry.
Laing, James Anderson, *MB. MCh. LRCS.Ed.*	1 Apr. 70	1 Apr. 90	Sanitary Commissioner, Madras.—Furlough.
Cook, Henry David, *MB. MCh.*	1 Apr. 70	1 Apr. 90	Surgeon, 1st District, and Medical Inspector of Emigrants.
Branfoot, Arthur Mudge, *MB. LRCP. MRCS.*	30 Mar. 72	30 Mar. 92	Superintendent Lying-in Hospital and Professor of Midwifery, Medical College.—Furlough.
Johnson, William Edward, *MD. MCh.*	30 Mar. 72	30 Mar. 92	Sappers and Miners.
Dobie, Stanley Locker,[16] *LRCP.Ed. MRCS. LSA.*	30 Mar. 72	30 Mar. 92	Principal Medical Storekeeper, Madras.
Bevan, George Fred., *LRCPI. LRCSI.*	30 Mar. 72	30 Mar. 92	Secretary and Statistical Officer to P.M.O. Madras Army.
Dobson, Andrew Francis, *BA. MB. LRCSI.*	30 Mar. 72	30 Mar. 92	Residency Surgeon, Bangalore.
Little, Charles, *MD. MCh. LRCSI.*	30 Mar. 72	30 Mar. 92	Sanitary Commissioner, &c., Hyderabad Assigned Districts.
Mayne, Thomas, *MRCS. LSA.*	30 Mar. 72	30 Mar. 92	24 Madras Infantry.
Rogers-Harrison, Aug. Nap., *LRCP. MRCS.*	1 Oct. 72	1 Oct. 92	District Med. and San. Officer, Salem,—Funl.
Esmonde-White, Henry FitzLawrence Plunkett French, *MRCPI. FRCSI.*	1 Oct. 72	1 Oct. 92	Physician to the Maharajah of Travancore.
Browne, Wm. Richard, *MD. MCh.*	1 Apr. 73	1 Apr. 93	Surgeon, General Hospital, Madras, and Professor of Surgery, Madras Medical College.
Leapingwell, Arthur Henry, *LRCP.Ed. LRCS.Ed.*	1 Apr. 73	1 Apr. 93	District Medical and Sanitary Officer, and Superintendent of Jail, Vizagapatam.
Allison, Hazlett, *MD. MCh.*	30 Sept. 73	30 Sept. 93	Fort Surgeon, Fort St. George, Medical Inspector of Seamen, Professor of Anatomy, Medical College, &c.
Wilkins, Thomas Jas. Hackett,[17] *LRCP.Ed. LRCS.Ed.*	30 Sept. 73	30 Sept. 93	District Medical and Sanitary Officer, Ganjam, and Superintendent of Jail, Berhampore.
Benson, Percy Hugh, *MB. MCh. MRCS.* ...	31 Mar. 74	31 Mar. 94	Chemical Examiner to the Mysore Government. —Civil Surg. & Supdt. of Jail, Mysore.
Lancaster, John, *MB. LRCP.Ed. LRCS.Ed.*	31 Mar. 74	31 Mar. 94	District Med. and San. Officer, N. Arcot.—Civil Surg., Coonoor, with charge of Kotagheree.
King, Walter Gawen, *MB. MCh.*	31 Mar. 74	31 Mar. 94	30 Madras Infantry.
O'Hara, William, *LRCP.Ed. LRCS.Ed.*	30 Sept. 74	30 Sept. 94	District Medical and Sanitary Officer, and Supdt. of Jail, Bellary.—District Medical and Sanitary Officer, Trichinopoly.
Thomas, George Tucker, *LRCP. MRCS.* ...	31 Mar. 75	31 Mar. 95	Civil Surgeon, Moulmein.
Sturmer, Arthur James, *LRCP. MRCS.*	31 Mar. 75	31 Mar. 95	District Medical and Sanitary Officer, Kistna.— Acting Supdt. Lying-in Hospital and Prof. of Midwifery, Medical College, Madras.
Adams, Archibald,[18] *MD. MCh. FRCSI.* ...	31 Mar. 75	31 Mar. 95	Med. Officer, Western Rajpootana States.—Offg. Res. Surg. & Chief Med. Officer, Rajpootana.
SURGEON MAJORS.		**SURGEON MAJ.**	
Ferrand, Edward,[19] *LRCP.Ed. MRCS.*	30 Sept. 75	30 Sept. 87	6 Madras Infantry.
Pedroza, Fras. Hookins,[20] *BA. LRCP.Ed. LRCS.Ed.*	30 Sept. 75	30 Sept. 87	Madras District.
Maitland, John, *MB. MCh. MD.*	31 Mar. 75	31 Mar. 88	Surg. 4th District.—Professor of Medical Jurisprudence, &c., Madras Medical College.
Walker, George Lemon, *MD. MCh. LM.*	31 Mar. 76	31 Mar. 88	District Medical and Sanitary Officer, Tanjore. —Civil Surgeon, Ootacamund, and in charge of Army Head Quarters, &c.
Swaine, Charles Lethbridge,[22] *MB. MCh.*	31 Mar. 76	31 Mar. 88	4 Infantry Hyderabad Contingent.
Smith, Maurice Henry,[23] *LRCP.Ed. MRCS.*	31 Mar. 76	31 Mar. 88	3 Madras Infantry.
Lee, Wm. Alexander, *LRCPI. LRCSI.*	30 Sept. 76	30 Sept. 88	District Medical and Sanitary Officer, and Superintendent of Jail, Mangalore.

K K 2

SURGEON MAJORS.	SURGEON.	SURGEON MAJOR.	REMARKS.
Eyre, Montague Stokes, *MB. MCh.*	30 Sept. 76	30 Sept. 88	28 Madras Infantry.
Nailer, Henry Augustus Fitzroy, *MB. LRCP.Ed. LRCS.Ed.*	31 Mar. 77	31 Mar. 89	District Medical and Sanitary Officer, Chingleput.
Elcum, Donald,[24] *MRCS. LSA.*	31 Mar. 77	31 Mar. 89	Superintendent Lunatic Asylum, Madras.
Chatterjie, Nityananda,[25] *LRCP.Ed. LFPS.Glas.*	31 Mar. 77	31 Mar. 80	13 Madras Infantry.
Bennett, Charles Henry, *MD. MCh.*	1 Oct. 77	1 Oct. 89	20 Madras Infantry.
Thornhill, William Henry,[26] *BA. MD. MCh. LRCPI. LRCS.Ed.*	1 Oct. 77	1 Oct. 89	District Medical and Sanitary Officer, and Superintendent of the Jail, Nellore.
Reporter, Maneckjee Eduljee,[27] *LRCP. LRCS.Ed.*	1 Oct. 77	1 Oct. 89	11 Madras Infantry.
Pope, Thomas Henry, *MD. MCh.*	30 Mar. 78	30 Mar. 90	Superintend Ophthalmic Hospital, Madras, and Professor of Ophthalmic Surgery, &c., Madras Medical College.
Pemberton, Robert, *MRCS. LSA.*	30 Mar. 78	30 Mar. 90	Civil Surgeon, Guntoor.—Acting Civil, Cochin.
Warliker, Damodar Purshotum,[28] *MRCS. LSA.*	30 Mar. 78	30 Mar. 90	1 Madras Infantry.
Moran, James Joseph,[29] *MD. MCh.*	30 Mar. 78	30 Mar. 90	15 Madras Infantry.
Quayle, William Adair, *MD. MCh.*	30 Mar. 78	30 Mar. 90	Civil and Superintendent of the Jail, Nimar.
Armstrong, Henry, *LRCPI. LRCSI.*	30 Mar. 78	30 Mar. 90	3 Madras Lancers.
Mallins, Clement, *MA. MD. MCh. MRCPI.*	30 Sept. 78	30 Sept. 90	1 Lancers Hyderabad Contingent.
Damla, Edulji Manekji, *LRCS.Ed. LSA.*	30 Sept. 78	30 Sept. 90	M. I. Depot, Pallaveram.
Carruthers, Herbert St. Clare,[30] *LRCP.Ed. LRCS.Ed.*	30 Sept. 78	30 Sept. 90	District Medical and Sanitary Officer, Rajahmundry.—Dist. Med. and San. Officer, Calicut.
Thomas, William Frederick,[31] *MRCS. LSA.*	31 Mar. 79	31 Mar. 91	17 Madras Infantry.
Wortabet, Henry Geo. Luther,[32] *MD. MCh.*	31 Mar. 79	31 Mar. 91	3 Infantry Hyderabad Contingent.
Frenchman, Edulji Palanji, *LRCP.Ed. LFPS.Glas.*	31 Mar. 79	31 Mar. 91	Civil Surgeon and Superintendent of Jail, Bassein.
James, Richard, *MB. MCh.*	31 Mar. 79	31 Mar. 91	3 Lancers Hyderabad Contingent.
Sarkies, Sarkies Carrapiet, *LRCP.Ed. LRCS.Ed. MRCS.*	31 Mar. 79	31 Mar. 91	Civil Surgeon, Cannanore.
Bain, David Stuart Erskine, *MRCS. LSA.*	31 Mar. 79	31 Mar. 91	Civil Surgeon, Coorg. [Officer, Rajahmundry.
Marsden, James Cort, *MRCS. LSA.*	31 Oct. 79	31 Oct. 91	Civil Surgeon, Cocanada.—Dist. Med. and San.
Reeves, Francis Casement, *LRCPI. LRCSI.*	31 Oct. 79	31 Oct. 91	Dist. Medical and Sanitary Officer, Malabar.—District Medical and Sanitary Officer, and Superintendent of Jail, Madura.
Poynder, John Leopold, *LRCP. MRCS. LSA.*	31 Oct. 79	31 Oct. 91	Civil Surgeon and Supdt. of Jail, Sambalpore.
Hoey, John,[34] *LRCPI. LRCSI.*	31 Oct. 79	31 Oct. 91	25 Madras Infantry.
Dymott, Donald Frederick,[35] *MB. MRCS.*	31 Mar. 80	31 Mar. 92	22 Madras Infantry.
Cama, Rustam Hormasji,[36] *LRCP.Ed. MRCS.*	31 Mar. 80	31 Mar. 92	9 Madras Infantry.
Browning, Winthrop Benj., *LRCP. LRCSI.*	31 Mar. 80	31 Mar. 92	Dist. Medical and Sanitary Officer, and Supdt. of Jail, Madura.—Surgeon to the Governor.
Henderson, Cecil, *LRCP. MRCS. LSA.*	31 Mar. 80	31 Mar. 92	Civil Surgeon, and Supdt. of Jail, Hoshungabad.
Divecha, Framji Ruttonji, *LRCP.Ed. LFPS.Glas.*	31 Mar. 80	31 Mar. 92	8 Madras Infantry.
Thompson, Croasdaile Miller, *MB. BCh. LCh.*	31 Mar. 80	31 Mar. 92	Secretary to the Surgeon General —District Medical and Sanitary Officer, Tanjore.
Rundle, Cubitt Sindall, *MB. MCh.*	31 Mar. 80	31 Mar. 92	Civil Surgeon, Thayetmyo.
Evans, James William,[38] *MRCS. LSA.*	31 Mar. 80	31 Mar. 92	Civil Surgeon, Cochin.—District Medical and Sanitary Officer, and Supdt. of Jail, Bellary.
VanGeyzel, John Lawrence, *MB. MCh.*	2 Oct. 80	2 Oct. 92	Chemical Examiner, Madras, and Professor of Chemistry, Medical College.
Harington, Hastings Norman V., *LRCP.Ed. LRCS.Ed.*	2 Oct. 80	2 Oct. 92	Deoloe Irregular Force.
M'Kee, Gerard Macklin Eccles,[39] *LRCP. MRCS.*	2 Oct. 80	2 Oct. 92	23 Madras Infantry.
Sarjana, Kavasji Cursetji,[40] *LRCS.Ed. LSA.*	2 Oct. 80	2 Oct. 92	District Medical and Sanitary Officer, Tinnevelly.
Hakim, Hormasji Merwanji,[41] *LRCS.Ed. LSA.*	2 Oct. 80	2 Oct. 92	Civil Surgeon, Tellicherry. — Acting District Medical and Sanitary Officer, Anantapore.
Burton, John Adolphus, *LRCP.Ed. LRCS.Ed.*	2 Oct. 80	2 Oct. 92	7 Madras Infantry.
Doyle, Fras. Joseph, *LRCPI. LRCSI.*	2 Oct. 80	2 Oct. 92	1 Infantry Hyderabad Contingent.
Kelawala, Manekshaw Jamshedji,[42] *LRCS.Ed. LSA.*	2 Oct. 80	2 Oct. 92	4 Madras Infantry.
Kharegat, Mervanji Pestanji,[43] *BA. LRCP.Ed. LRCS.Ed.*	2 Oct. 80	2 Oct. 92	32 Madras Infantry.
Newland, Arthur Geo. Edward,[44] *LRCP.Ed. LRCS.Ed.*	2 Apr. 81	2 Apr. 93	31 Madras Infantry.
Patch, Arthur Theophilus Lodge,[45] *MB.*	2 Apr. 81	2 Apr. 93	District Surgeon and Supdt. of Jail, Kurnool.
Ross, Ronald,[46] *MRCS. LSA.*	2 Apr. 81	2 Apr. 93	19 Madras Infantry.
Adams, Charles,[47] *BA. MB. BCh. FRCSI.*	2 Apr. 81	2 Apr. 93	Civil Surgeon, Chittoor.—District Medical and Sanitary Officer, Vellore.
Da Costa, Edw. Ronald, *LRCS.Ed. LRCP.Ed.*	2 Apr. 81	2 Apr. 93	16 Madras Infantry.
Kanga, Jamshedji Karshedji, *LRCS.Ed. LSA.*	2 Apr. 81	2 Apr. 93	Furlough.
O'Hara, Alfred James,[48] *LRCP.Ed. LRCS.Ed.*	2 Apr. 81	2 Apr. 93	Dist. Med. and San. Officer, and Supdt. of Jail, Cuddapah.—Acting Dist. Med. & San. Officer, South Canara and Supdt. of Jail, Mangalore.
Roe, Robert Bradley, *MRCS. LSA.*	1 Oct. 81	1 Oct. 93	Civil Surgeon and Supdt. of Jail, Oomrawuttee.
Smyth, John,[50] *MD. MCh.*	1 Oct. 81	1 Oct. 93	Resident Surgeon, General Hospital, and Prof. of Pathology, Medical College.
Greany, Hugh, *MD. MCh.*	1 Oct. 81	1 Oct. 93	5 Infantry Hyderabad Contingent.
Youngerman, Edw. Pottingall,[51] *MB. MCh.*	1 Oct. 81	1 Oct. 93	2 Madras Lancers.
Reilly, Edwin Wm.,[52] *LRCP.Ed. LRCS.Ed.*	1 Apr. 82	1 Apr. 94	Civil Surgeon, Akola.
Scott, James, *MB.*	1 Apr. 82	1 Apr. 94	5 Madras Infantry.
Davis, Robt. Evans Stuart,[53] *MB. BCh.*	30 Sept. 82	30 Sept. 94	Superintendent and Medical Officer, Rangoon.
Neilson, William Henry, *MB. MCh.*	30 Sept. 82	30 Sept. 94	Erinpoorah Irregular Force.
Evans, Arthur Owen, *LRCP. MRCS.*	31 Mar. 83	31 Mar. 95	Civil Surgeon, Superintendent of Jail, and Port Health Officer, Akyab.
SURGEON CAPTAINS.		SURGEON CAPTAIN.	
Bannerman, William Burney,[54] *MB. MCh.*	29 Sept. 83		Inspector of Vaccination and Dep. Sanitary Commr.—Furl.
Thomson, Henry,[55] *MB. MCh.*	29 Sept. 83		Dist. Med. & San. Officer, South Arcot, and Supdt. of Jail Cuddalore.—Acting Sec. to Surg. Gen. with Madras Gov.
Hall, Gilbert Capel, *MRCS. LSA.*	30 Sept. 86		Additional Med. Officer, Gen. Hosp., Madras.—Sick Furl.

Madras Medical Department.

Surgeon Captains.	Surgeon Captain.	Remarks.
Castor, Richd. Henderson,[17] *LRCP. MRCS.*	30 Sept. 86	Civil Surgeon, Myingyan.
Maidment, Fred. Geo. *LRCP.Ed.LFPS.Glas.*	30 Sept. 86	Sick Furlough.
Doyle, Ignatius Purcell,[59] *DSO. LRCPI. LRCSI*	30 Sept. 86	27 Madras Infantry.
Crawford, Frederick Jas. *BA. MD. MCh.* ...	31 Mar. 87	2nd Surgeon, General Hospital, and Professor of Pharmacy, &c., Medical College, Madras.
Simpson, David,[60] *MA. MB. MCh.*	31 Mar. 87	District Medical and Sanitary Officer, Anantapore.
Robertson, Robert, *MB. MCh.*	31 Mar. 87	Acting Assistant Physician General Hospital, and Professor of Hygiene, Medical College, Madras.
Moore, Thos. Charles, *LRCP,Ed. LRCSI.* ...	31 Mar. 87	2 Madras Infantry.
Dewes, Frederick Joseph,[61] *LRCP. MRCS.*	1 Oct. 87	Civil, Minbu.
Pinto, Jos. Orphino, *LRCP.Ed. LRCS.Ed. LFPS.Glas.*	1 Oct. 87	Madras District.
Strickland, Percy C. Hutchison, *LRCP. MRCS. LSA.*	1 Oct. 87	Officiating 33 Madras Infantry.
Stewart,Thos.Wm.,[62]*LRCP.Ed. LRCS,Ed. LFPS.Glas.*	1 Oct. 87	Civil Surgeon, Toungoo.
Grant, Allan Ewen,[63] *MB. MCh.*	31 Mar. 88	Assist. Physician, General Hospital, and Prof. of Hygiene, Madras Medical College.—Sick Furlough.
Pereira, Frank Chas., *LRCP.Ed. LRCS.Ed. LFPS.Glas.*	31 Mar. 88	Acting Civil Surgeon, Cannanore.
Williams, Chas. Louis,[64] *MD. MCh. MRCS.*	30 Sept. 89	Officiating Resident Surgeon, General Hospital.—Professor of Pathology, Medical College, Madras.
Vickers, Wilfrid Constant, *MB. MCh.*	30 Sept. 89	Civil Surgeon, Cocoanda.
Sutherland, William Dunbar,[65] *MB. MCh.* ...	30 Sept. 89	Civil Surgeon, Dumoh.
Carr-White, Percy, *MB. MCh.*	31 Mar. 90	Staff Surgeon, Bangalore.
Wright, Edmund Hasell, *LRCP. MRCS.*	31 Mar. 90	Officiating 3 Infantry Hyderabad Contingent.
Molesworth, Wm., *MB. LRCP. MRCS.*	31 Mar. 90	Officiating 22 Madras Infantry.
Fearnside, Clarence Forbes, *MA. MB. MCh.*	31 Mar. 90	Acting District Medical and Sanitary Officer and Superintendent of Jail, Cuddapah.
Johnston, Charles Arthur, *MB. MCh.*	31 Mar. 90	Officiating 1 Lancers Hyderabad Contingent.
Giffard, Gerald Godfray, *LRCP. MRCS.* ...	31 Mar. 90	Acting Additional Medical Officer, Gen. Hospital, Madras.
Entrican, James, *MD. MCh.*	28 July 91	Officiating 30 Madras Infantry.
Pridmore, Walter George, *MRCS. MB.*	28 July 91	12 Madras Infantry.
Donovan, Charles, *MD. BCh.*	28 July 91	10 Madras Infantry.
Penny, Jeremiah, *MRCS. LRCP.*	28 July 91	Sick Furlough.
Graves, Douglas Henry M'Donell, *MB. MCh.*	28 July 91	Officiating 21 Madras Infantry.
Dallas, Stuart Alex. Chas. *MRCS. LRCP.*	28 July 91	Civil Surgeon, Chanda, Central Provinces.
Palk, Charles Henry Leet, *MB. MCh.*	28 July 91	2 Infantry Hyderabad Contingent.
Surgeon Lieutenants.	**Surg. Lt.**	
Elliot, Robert Henry, *LRCP. FRCS.*	30 Jan. 92	Officiating Professor of Biology, Presidency Coll., Madras.
Mitter, Robert King, *LRCP.Ed.LRCS.Ed. LFPS.Glas.*	30 Jan. 92	Officiating 19 Madras Infantry.
Armstrong, Wilfrid Ernest Arbuthnot, *LRCP. MRCS.*	30 Jan. 92	Officiating Residency Surgeon and *ex-officio* Assistant Resident, Nepaul.
Gabbett, Pulteney Charles, *LRCP. MRCS.*	27 July 92	Officiating Wing 6 Madras Infantry.
Macrae, John Lewis, *MB. MCh.*	27 July 92	In medical charge Detachment Native Infantry and Station Hospital, Port Blair.
Bidie, Geo., *LRCP.Ed.LRCS.Ed.LFPS.Glas.*	30 Jan. 93	6 Infantry Hyderabad Contingent.
Morton, John Plowden, *MB. MCh.*	30 Jan. 93	Chin Hills Command.
Sharman, Eric Harding, *LRCP. MRCS.* ...	29 July 93	Officiating 6 Infantry Hyderabad Contingent.
Stodart, Thomas, *MB. MCh.*	29 July 93	Officiating 29 Madras Infantry.
Bhola Nauth	29 July 93	Officiating 17 Madras Infantry.
Foulkes, Thomas Howard, *LRCP. MRCS.*	29 July 93	Mandalay District and Chin Hills Command.
Berry, Alfred Eugene	29 Jan. 94	Mandalay District and Chin Hills Command.
Fraser, Herbert St. John	29 Jan. 94	Mandalay District and Chin Hills Command.
Pearce, Charles Ross	28 July 94	Officiating 23 Madras Infantry.
Wall, Frank	29 Jan. 95	
Mathew, Charles Montague	29 Jan. 95	

[1] Surgeon Colonel C. Sibthorpe served in the Afghan war in 1879-80 with the Peshawur Valley Field Force (Medal). Served with the Burmese Expedition in 1885-86 in medical charge of the Head Quarters Staff (mentioned in despatches, promoted Brigade Surgeon, Medal with Clasp).

[2] Surgeon Colonel C. E. M'Vittie served in the Afghan war in 1879-80 (Medal). Served with the Burmese Expedition in 1886-88 (mentioned in despatches, Medal with two Clasps).

[4] Surgeon Colonel D. F. Bateman served with the Burmese Expedition in 1885-86 (Medal with Clasp).

[9] Brigade Surgeon Lt.Colonel P. R. Martin served with the Burmese Expedition in 1886-88 (Medal with two Clasps).

[12] Brigade Surgeon Lt.Colonel F. H. Blenkinsop served with the Burmese Expedition in 1885-87 (Medal with Clasp).

[13] Brigade Surgeon Lt.Colonel J. North served in the Afghan war in 1880 (Medal). Served with the Burmese Expedition in 1886-87, including the operations under Brigadier General R. C. Low (Medal with two Clasps).

[14] Surgeon Lt.Colonel P. N. Mookerjee served with the Burmese Expedition in 1888-89 (Medal with Clasp); and with the Manipore Expedition in 1891 (Clasp).

[15] Brigade Surgeon Lt.Colonel E. Fawcett served with the Burmese Expedition in 1886-87 (mentioned in despatches, Medal with Clasp).

[16] Surgeon Lt.Colonel S. L. Dobie served in the Afghan war of 1878-80 in medical charge of the 1st Madras Cavalry (Medal). Served at Suakin in 1885-86 with the Indian Contingent in medical charge of No. 2 Field Hospital.

[17] Surgeon Lt.Colonel T. J. H. Wilkins served with the Burmese Expedition in 1885-86 (Medal with Clasp).

[18] Surgeon Major A. Adams, while a Surgeon in the Royal Navy, served in the Ashantee war in 1873-74 with the Royal Marines (Medal).

[19] Surgeon Major E. Ferrand served with the Burmese Expedition in 1886-89 (Medal with Clasp).

[20] Surgeon Major F. H. Pedrosa served with the Burmese Expedition in 1886-89 (Medal with Clasp).

[22] Surgeon Major C. L. Swaine served with the Burmese Expedition in 1885-89 (Medal with two Clasps).

[23] Surgeon Major M. H. Smith served with the Burmese Expedition in 1885-87 (Medal with Clasp); and with the Chin-Lushai Expeditionary Force in 1889-90 (Medal).

[24] Surgeon Major D. Elcum served in the Afghan war in 1880 (Medal). Served with the Burmese Expedition in 1886-87 (mentioned in despatches, Medal with Clasp).

[25] Surgeon Major N. Chatterjee served with the Burmese Expedition in 1886-89 (Medal with two Clasps).

[26] Surgeon Major W. H. Thornhill served in the Afghan war in 1879-80 (Medal). Served with the Burmese Expedition in 1886-88 (Medal with Clasp).

[27] Surgeon Major M. E. Reporter served with the Burmese Expedition in 1886-88 (Medal with two Clasps).

[28] Surgeon Major D. P. Warliker served with the Burmese Expedition in 1886-88 (Medal with two Clasps).

[29] Surgeon Major J. J. Moran served in the Afghan war in 1880 (Medal). Served with the Chin-Lushai Expeditionary Force in 1889-90 (Medal with Clasp).

Madras Medical Department.—War Services.

30 Surgeon Major H. St. C. Carruthers served in the Afghan war in 1879-80 (Medal).
31 Surgeon Major W. F. Thomas served with the Burmese Expedition in 1886-88 (Medal with two Clasps).
32 Surgeon Major H. G. L. Wortabet served in the Afghan war in 1880 (Medal). Served with the Burmese Expedition in 1886-88 (Medal with two Clasps).
34 Surgeon Major J. Hoey served in the Egyptian war of 1882, and was present at the battle of Tel-el-Kebir (Medal with Clasp, and Khedive's Star). Served with the Burmese Expedition in 1885-86 (Medal with Clasp), and again in 1886-87 (Clasp).
35 Surgeon Major D. F. Dymott served with the Burmese Expedition in 1885-86 (Medal with Clasp).
36 Surgeon Major R. H. Cama served with the Burmese Expedition in 1885-86 (Medal with Clasp).
38 Surgeon Major J. W. Evans served in the Egyptian war of 1882, and was present at the battle of Tel-el-Kebir (Medal with Clasp, and Khedive's Star).
39 Surgeon Major G. M. E. M'Kee served with the Burmese Expedition in 1885-87 (Medal with Clasp).
40 Surgeon Major K. C. Sanjana served with the Burmese Expedition in 1886-87 (Medal with Clasp).
41 Surgeon Major H. M. Hakim served with the Burmese Expedition in 1885-89 (Medal with two Clasps).
42 Surgeon Major M. J. Kelawala served with the Burmese Expedition in 1886-88 (Medal with two Clasps).
43 Surgeon Major M. P. Kharegat served with the Burmese Expedition in 1886-87 (Medal with Clasp).
44 Surgeon Major A. G. E. Newland served with the Burmese Expedition in 1886-89 (Medal with Clasp); with the Manipore Expedition in 1891 (Clasp); and in the operations on the North-Eastern Frontier of Burmah in 1891-92, with the Baungshe, Tiang-tlang and Tashon Columns.
45 Surgeon Major A. T. L. Patch served with the Burmese Expedition in 1887-90 (Medal with Clasp).
46 Surgeon Major R. Ross served with the Burmese Expedition in 1886 (Medal with Clasp).
47 Surgeon Major C. Adams served with the Burmese Expedition in 1885-87 (Medal with Clasp).
48 Surgeon Major A. J. O'Hara served with the Burmese Expedition in 1886-88 (Medal with Clasp).
49 Surgeon Major J. Smyth served in the Soudan campaign in 1885 in medical charge of the Queen's Own Sappers and Miners, and was present in the engagements at Hasheen and the Tofrek zereba and at the destruction of Temai—wounded (Medal with two Clasps, and Khedive's Star).
51 Surgeon Major E. P. Youngerman served with the Burmese Expedition in 1885-86 (Medal with Clasp).
52 Surgeon Major E. W. Reilly served with the Burmese Expedition in 1886-89 (Medal with two Clasps).
53 Surgeon Captain R. E. S. Davis served with the Burmese Expedition in 1886-87 (mentioned in despatches, Medal with Clasp).
54 Surgeon Captain W. B. Bannerman served with the Burmese Expedition in 1885-89 (Medal with two Clasps).
55 Surgeon Captain H. Thomson served with the Burmese Expedition in 1886-87 (Medal with two Clasps).
57 Surgeon Captain R. H. Castor served with the Wuntho Expedition in 1891 (mentioned in despatches, Medal with Clasp).
58 Surgeon Captain M. J. T. J. Blancard served with the Burmese Expedition in 1887-88 (Medal with two Clasps).
59 Surgeon Captain I. P. Doyle served with the Burmese Expedition in 1888-89 (mentioned in despatches, *DSO*, and Medal with Clasp).
60 Surgeon Captain D. Simpson served with the Chin-Lushai Expeditionary Force in 1889-90 (Medal with Clasp); and with the Manipore Expedition in 1891 (Clasp).
61 Surgeon Captain F. J. Dewes served with the Burmese Expedition in 1888-89 (Medal with Clasp); and with the Chin-Lushai Expeditionary Force in 1889-90 (Clasp).
62 Surgeon Captain T. W. Stewart served with the Burmese Expedition in 1888-90 (Medal with Clasp).
63 Surgeon Captain A. E. Grant served with the Chin-Lushai Expeditionary Force in 1889-90 (Medal with Clasp).
64 Surgeon Captain C. L. Williams served in the operations on the North-East Frontier of Burmah in 1891-92.
65 Surgeon Captain W. D. Sutherland served in the operations on the North-East Frontier of Burmah in 1891-92.

Continuation of War Services of the Bengal Medical Department.

137 Surgeon Captain G. H. Baker served with the Burmese Expedition in 1886-87 (Medal with Clasp).
138 Surgeon Captain T. Grainger served with the Sikkim Expedition in 1888 (Medal with Clasp).
139 Surgeon Captain J. R. Adie served with the Burmese Expedition in 1885-87 (Medal with Clasp).
140 Surgeon Captain A. C. Younan served with the Burmese Expedition in 1886-87 (Medal with Clasp).
142 Surgeon Captain J. M. Cadell served with the Burmese Expedition in 1886-89 (Medal with two Clasps); and with the Hazara Expedition in 1891 (Clasp).
143 Surgeon Captain P. Hehir served with the Burmese Expedition in 1886-87 (Medal with Clasp).
144 Surgeon Captain L. J. Pisani served with the Hazara Expedition in 1888 (Medal with Clasp).
145 Surgeon Captain G. J. H. Bell served with the Lushai Expedition in 1889 (Medal with Clasp).
146 Surgeon Captain H. Fooks served with the Zhob Valley Expedition in 1890.
147 Surgeon Captain E. Hudson served with the Chin-Lushai Expeditionary Force in 1889-90 with the Chittagong Column (mentioned in despatches, Medal with Clasp).
148 Surgeon Captain W. H. B. Robinson served with the Burmese Expedition in 1888-89 in the Chin Hills (mentioned in despatches, Medal with Clasp).
150 Surgeon Captain C. R. M. Green served with the Hazara Expedition in 1888 (Medal with Clasp).
151 Surgeon Captain J. Morwood served with the Hazara Expedition in 1888 (Medal with Clasp).
152 Surgeon Captain W. H. W. Elliot served with the Hazara Expedition in 1888 (Medal with Clasp).
153 Surgeon Captain J. Murray served with the Hazara Expedition in 1888 (Medal with Clasp).
155 Surgeon Captain C. E. Sunder served with the Sikkim Expedition in 1888 (Medal with Clasp).
156 Surgeon Captain C. E. L. Gilbert served with the Sikkim Expedition in 1888 (Medal with Clasp); with the Manipore Expedition in 1891 (Clasp); and with the Isazai Field Force in 1892.
158 Surgeon Captain A. H. Nott served with the two Miranzai Expeditions in 1891 (Medal with Clasp), and in the operations of the Zhob Valley Expedition in 1890.
159 Surgeon Captain W. W. White served with the Hazara Expedition in 1891 (Medal with Clasp).
160 Surgeon Captain W. H. E. Woodwright served with the Hazara Expedition in 1888 (Medal with Clasp).
161 Surgeon Captain J. K. Close served with the Sikkim Expedition in 1888 (Medal with Clasp).
162 Surgeon Captain D. G. Marchall served with the Burmese Expedition in 1891-92 (Medal with Clasp), and with the Isazai Expedition in 1892.
163 Surgeon Captain J. R. Roberts served with the expedition against the Hunza-Nagars in 1891-92 as Principal Medical Officer (mentioned in despatches, Medal with Clasp).
164 Surgeon Captain F. R. Ozzard served with the two Miranzai Expeditions in 1891 (Medal with Clasp).
166 Surgeon Captain A. J. Macnab served with the Hazara Expedition in 1891 (Medal with Clasp).
167 Surg on Captain H. B. Luard served with the expedition against the Hunza-Nagars in 1891-92 (mentioned in despatches, Medal with Clasp).
169 Surgeon Captain W. Henvey served with the Isazai Expedition in 1892.

Madras Veterinary Department.

VETERINARY LT. COLONEL.	DATE OF PRESENT RANK.	REMARKS.

Madras Ecclesiastical Establishment.

The Right Reverend Frederick Gell, *DD*. Lord Bishop of Madras, 27 Nov. 61.
The Rev. Samuel Morley, Domestic Chaplain to the Bishop, 2 Oct. 84.
The Venerable William Weston Elwes, *MA*. Archdeacon of Madras, 13 Apr. 93.
F. Rowlandson, Esq., *BA*. Registrar of the Diocese and Secretary to the Lord Bishop, 1 Dec. 75.

Year of Appt.	SENIOR CHAPLAINS.	REMARKS.	Year of Appt.	SENIOR CHAPLAINS.	REMARKS.
1870	*Ven.* Wm. Weston Elwes, *MA*...	St. George's Cathedral.—Archdeacon and Commissary.	1880	*Rev.* Robt. Henry Durham, *DD*	Ootacamund.
			1881	*Rev.* Chas. Edw. Whiteley, *MA*.	Berhampore.- Furl.
			1881	*Rev.* John English	Offg. Berhampore.
			1882	*Rev.* Edward Gibson	Wellington.
1874	*Rev.* Alfred Charles Taylor, *MA*.	Garrison, Fort St. George.—Furl.	1883	*Rev.* Edward Tyroll Beatty	Vizagapatam.
1874	*Rev.* Harry Arch. Williams, *MA*.	Holy Trinity, Bangalore.—Furl.	1883	*Rev.* Clement Henry Lakin Wright, *MA*.	Secunderabad.
1875	*Rev.* Daniel Wilson Kidd, *BA*...	Cannanore.	1884	*Rev.* Alexander James Jones	Trimulgherry.
1875	*Rev.* Samuel Morley	Domestic Chaplain to Bishop.			
1875	*Rev.* Walter Wace, *MA*.	St. Thomas' Mount.			
1876	*Rev.* Charles Henry Polly, *MA*.	Offg. Garrison, Fort St. George		JUNIOR CHAPLAINS.	
1877	*Rev.* Frank Penny, *BA*	St. Mark's, Bangalore.	1885	*Rev.* Chas. Herbert Malden, *MA*.	Mysore and Mercara.
1878	*Rev.* William Scott, *BA*	South Black Town.	1886	*Rev.* Fras. Ewen Cameron, *BA*.	Offg. Trichinopoly.
1878	*Rev.* R. Joseph Brandon, *LL.D.*	Offg. North Black Town.	1885	*Rev.* Fredk. Charles Hill, *MA*...	Bolarum.—Furl.
			1886	*Rev.* Fras. Nelson Crowther, *BA*.	Calicut.
1879	*Rev.* James Sharp	Offg. St. John's, Bangalore.	1886	*Rev.* Arthur Bird, *BA*.	Offg. Bolarum.
1879	*Rev.* Forster Clarke Gittens, *MA*.	Coimbator.	1886	*Rev.* Charles Philip Croker Nugent	Furlough.
1879	*Rev.* Charles John Etty	Holy Trinity, Bangalore.	1887	*Rev.* Harry Clince Parker,[1] *MA*.	St. George's Cathedral.
1879	*Rev.* John Wilberforce Cassels, *MA*	Poonamallee.	1887	*Rev.* Arthur Henry Barrett Brittain, *BA*.	Offg. Joint Chaplain, Vepery.
1880	*Rev.* John Black, *MA*.	Vepery, Madras.	1888	*Rev.* Harry Bathurst Norman, *BA*.	Coconada.—Furl.
1880	*Rev.* Rich. Parry Burnett, *MA*.	Coonoor.	1888	*Rev.* Walter Geo. Barry, *AKC*...	Bellary.
1880	*Rev.* Arth. Acheson Williams, *MA*.	Vellore.	1889	*Rev.* Arthur A. Sharp, *MA*.	Cuddalore.—Sick Furlough.

CHURCH OF SCOTLAND.

	SENIOR CHAPLAIN.	REMARKS.
1878	*Rev.* William Forest Archibald	Officiating Secunderabad.
	CHAPLAINS.	
1885	*Rev.* James Nicholl Ogilvie, *MA*...	St. Andrew's, Bangalore.
1889	*Rev.* Robert Horne Stevenson, *MA*.	Officiating St. Andrew's, Bangalore.
1893	*Rev.* John Heron, *MA*	Joint Chaplain, St. Andrew's, Madras.

War Services.

[1] The Rev. H. C. Parker served with the Burmese Expedition in 1887-89 (Medal with Clasp).

Rangoon Ecclesiastical Establishment.

The Right Rev. John Miller Strachan, *DD. MD*. Bishop of Rangoon, 1 May 82.
The Ven. Charles Henry Chard, Archdeacon and Commissary of Rangoon, 17 Dec. 93.
John Dakeyne Heaton, *MA. LLM.* (*Barrister-at-Law*), Registrar of the Diocese and Archdeaconry, 1 Jan. 89.

Year of Appt.	SENIOR CHAPLAINS.	REMARKS.	Year of Appt.	JUNIOR CHAPLAINS.	REMARKS.
1879	*Ven.* Charles Henry Chard	Archdeacon and Commissary.	1889	*Rev.* Chas. Henry Richards, *MA*.	Meiktila.
			1889	*Rev.* James Low, *MA*.	Port Blair.
			1890	*Rev.* Henry Guise Beatson Cowley	Thayetmyo.
	JUNIOR CHAPLAINS.		1891	*Rev.* Chas. Page Cory, *MA*.	Cantonments, Rangoon.
1885	*Rev.* Joseph Perry Dyer, *MA*...	Fort Dufferin, Mandalay.	1893	*Rev.* James Henry Collins	Bhamo.
1885	*Rev.* Arthur Henry Finn	Port Blair.—Furl.	1894	*Rev.* John Horndon Parry, *BA*	Shwebo.
1887	*Rev.* David George Lathom Browne, *BA*.	Schwebo.—Furl.			

Governor's Body Guard (Raised 22 March 1865).
Head Quarters at Ganesh Khind. *Uniform, Scarlet. Facings, Blue. Lace, Gold.*

Rank, Names, and Corps.	Army Rank.	Remarks.
Lieut. C. C. Leveson-Gower, Staff Corps	28 Apr. 86	Commandant, 5 May, 94.—From 1 Lancers.

Establishment.—Commandant, 1 Risaldar, 1 Risaidar, 1 Kote Dafedar, 5 Dafedars, 1 Trumpeter, 1 Farrier, 60 Sowars.

1st (Duke of Connaught's Own) Bombay Lancers (Raised 5 Nov. 1817).
"Ghuznee"—"Affghanistan"—"Punjaub"—"Mooltan"—"Central India"—"Burma, 1885-87."
Head Quarters at Neemuch. Detachment at Nusseerabad. *Uniform, Dark Green. Facings, Scarlet.*
Honorary Colonel—General H.R.H. Arthur W. P. A. Duke of Connaught, KG. KT. KP. GCSI. GCMG. GCIE. KCB. Rifle Brigade.

Lt.Colonel E. L. Elliot, DSO, Staff Corps	22 Jan. 94	Commandant, 6 Dec. 89.
Lt.Colonel H. Hay, Staff Corps	16 Sept. 94	2nd in Command and Squadron Commander, 6 Dec. 89.—Acting Pension Paymaster, S. Konkan.
Major H. D. M. Minchin, Staff Corps	11 Feb. 95	Squadron Commander, 4 June 86.—Cant. Mag. Belgaum.
Captain G. F. N. Tinley, Staff Corps	10 Sept. 87	Squadron Commander, 23 Oct. 85.—At Nusseerabad.
Captain W. A. Thompson, Staff Corps	22 Jan. 90	Squadron Commander, 4 Dec. 91.
Bt. Major G. D. Atkinson, Staff Corps	14 Oct. 94	Squadron Commander, 14 Oct. 94.
Captain G. C. M. Birdwood, Staff Corps	9 Sept. 93	Squadron Officer, 1 Oct. 86.—Supdt. Remount Depot, Kurnool.
Captain C. V. Schneider, Staff Corps	10 May 93	Squadron Officer, 22 June 88.—Furlough.
Lieut. C. C. Leveson-Gower, Staff Corps	28 Apr. 86	Squadron Officer, 12 Apr.93.—Comdt. Governor's Body Guard.
Lieut. C. T. Ducat, Staff Corps	2 Feb. 88	Squadron Officer, 30 Aug. 89.—Boundary Settlement Officer, C.I.
Lieut. L. N. Beatty, Staff Corps	8 May 89	Squadron Officer and Adjutant, 1 Apr. 93.—Furlough.
Lieut. W. P. Bannerman, Staff Corps	29 Oct. 90	Squadron Officer.
Lieut. W. A. M'Taggart, Staff Corps	10 Dec. 92	Officiating Squadron Officer.
Lieut. C. F. Templer, Royal Artillery	15 Feb. 92	Officiating Squadron Officer.
Surgeon Major C. B. Maitland	31 Mar. 92	In medical charge, 22 Jan. 92.—Furlough.
Surgeon Captain E. G. R. Whitecombe	31 Jan. 91	Officiating in medical charge.

2nd Bombay Lancers (Raised 5 Nov. 1817).
"Central India"—"Afghanistan, 1879-80."
Head Quarters at Poona. *Uniform, Dark Green. Facings, White.*

Lt.Colonel W. H. D. Jones, Staff Corps	26 July 90	Commandant, 1 June 94.
Major A. Pringle, Staff Corps	30 Dec. 92	2nd in Command and Squadron Commander, 1 June 94.
Captain L. A. Gordon, Staff Corps	14 June 88	Squadron Commander, 26 July 89.
p.s.c. Captain H. T. Kenny, Staff Corps	23 Oct. 91	Squadron Commander, 6 Sept. 89. Squadron Commander,
Captain C. E. Baynes, Staff Corps	14 Feb. 94	Squadron Officer, 20 Sept. 89.—A. D. C. and Interp. to C. in C., (Bombay.
Lieut. A. L. Pilleau, Staff Corps	7 Feb. 85	Squadron Officer and Adjutant, 13 July 88.
Lieut. W. W. G. Griffith, Staff Corps	29 Jan. 89	Squadron Officer, 28 Nov. 90.—Offg. Squadron Commander.
Lieut. C. W. W. Gabb, Staff Corps	1 Apr. 90	Squadron Officer, 17 Feb. 93.—Extra A. D. C. to Gov. of Bombay.
2nd Lieut. G. A. R. Watts, Staff Corps	3 Sept. 92	Squadron Officer, 24 Dec. 93.
Lieut. J. H. Crawford, Staff Corps	3 Mar. 93	Officiating Squadron Officer and Commander.
Lieut. E. H. M'B. Fenn, Staff Corps	24 Apr. 93	Officiating Squadron Officer.
2nd Lieut. A. Hewlett, Staff Corps	28 Jan. 93	Officiating Squadron Officer.
Surgeon Major R. W. S. Lyons, MD	1 Apr. 94	In medical charge, 27 July 88.—Acting Civil Surgeon, &c., Rutnagherry.
Surgeon Captain A. J. Heath, MD	31 Mar. 90	Officiating in medical charge.

3rd Bombay Light Cavalry (Queen's Own) (Raised 4 May 1820).
"Ghuznee"—"Cabool, 1842"—"Hyderabad"—"Persia"—"Reshire"—"Khooshab"—"Bushire"—
"Central India"—"Abyssinia"—"Kandahar, 1880"—"Afghanistan, 1879-80."
Head Quarters at Deesa. Squadron at Rajkote. *Uniform, Dark Green. Facings, Scarlet.*
Honorary Colonel—Field Marshal H.R.H. Albert Edward, Prince of Wales and Duke of Cornwall, KG. KT. KP. GCB. GCSI. GCMG. GCIE.

Lt.Colonel M. W. Stevens, Gen. List	27 Dec. 87	Commandant, 1 June 92.
p.s.c. Captain T. P. Geoghegan, Staff C.	12 Feb. 87	2nd in Command and Squadron Commander, 1 June 92.—Furl.
Captain A. Phayre, Staff Corps	1 May 89	Squadron Commander, 16 Aug. 89.—Offg. 2nd in Com.—At Rajkote.
Captain G. A. Gott, Staff Corps	23 Feb. 87	Squadron Commander, 16 Aug. 89.
p.s.c. Capt. F. J. M. Edwards, Staff Corps	22 Oct. 92	Squadron Commander, 23 May 90.
Lieut. A. J. W. Browne, Staff Corps	16 Dec. 85	Squadron Officer, 17 May 89.—Officiating Squadron Commander.
Lieut. H. J. E. Purvis, Staff Corps	30 Jan. 86	Squadron Officer and Adjutant, 4 Oct. 93.
Lieut. H. G. Benn, Staff Corps	10 Nov. 86	Squadron Officer, 15 Feb. 89.
Lieut. C. S. Stack, Staff Corps	13 Sept. 88	Squadron Officer, 11 May 90.
Lieut. J. L. Alexander, Staff Corps	24 June 91	Squadron Officer, 6 July 94.—At Rajkote.
Lieut. W. A. Fisher, Staff Corps	14 Aug. 91	Officiating Squadron Officer.
Lieut. R. H. B. Anderson, Durham Lt. Inf.	11 Apr. 94	Officiating Squadron Officer.
Surgeon Captain H. F. Cleveland	30 Sept. 89	In medical charge, 8 June 94.

4th (Prince Albert Victor's Own) Bombay Cavalry (Poona Horse) (Raised 15 July 1817).
"Corygaum"—"Ghuznee"—"Affghanistan"—"Candahar"—"Meeanee"—"Hyderabad"—"Persia"—
"Reshire"—"Khooshab"—"Bushire"—"Kandahar, 1880"—"Afghanistan, 1879-80."
Head Quarters at Siroor. *Uniform, Dark Green. Facings, French Grey.*

Lt.Colonel H. R. D. Thomas, Staff Corps	10 Feb. 95	Commandant, 3 June 93.—And Commanding at Siroor.
Captain A. W. Forbes, Staff Corps	11 Sept. 88	2nd in Command and Squadron Comdr. 9 Dec. 92.—Inspecting Officer, Kattywar Imperial Service Troops.
Capt. M. E. Carthew Yorstoun, Staff Corps	26 Mar. 90	2nd in Command and Squadron Commander, 9 Dec.92.—Sick Furl.
Captain F. W. G. Wadeson, Staff Corps	17 Apr. 91	Squadron Commander, 18 Dec. 91.—Comdt. Aden Troop.
Captain C. F. Grantham, Staff Corps	6 Jan. 90	Squadron Commander, 28 July 93.—Offg. 2nd in Command.
Captain C. M. Ducat, Staff Corps	22 Jan. 90	Squadron Commander, 16 Jan. 91.—At Staff College.
Lieut. W. C. L. Mure, Staff Corps	9 May 85	Squadron Commander, 23 Feb. 94.
Lieut. M. J. Gordon, Staff Corps	25 Aug. 86	Squadron Officer and Adjutant, 13 Dec. 89.
Lieut. N. G. Fraser, Staff Corps	16 Feb. 88	Squadron Officer, 2 May 90.—Officiating Squadron Comdr.
Lieut. W. F. Newnham, Staff Corps	30 Apr. 89	Squadron Officer, 20 Feb. 91.—Officiating Squadron Comdr.
Lieut. W. G. Cooper, Staff Corps	21 Mar. 90	Squadron Officer, 9 Dec. 92.—Sick Furlough.
Lieut. R. H. Raymond, North'n Regt.	7 Dec. 93	Officiating Squadron Officer.
Lieut. B. P. Ellwood, York Lt. Infantry	23 July 93	Officiating Squadron Officer.
2nd Lieut. A. F. Hislop, Royal Scots	9 Apr. 94	Officiating Squadron Officer.
Surgeon Major A. K. Stewart, MD	31 Mar. 88	In medical charge, 3 Nov. 77.

Each Regiment of Bombay Cavalry consists of 8 Troops, with the following Establishment:—Commandant; 4 Squadron Commanders; 4 Squadron Officers; 1 Medical Officer; 1 Risaldar Major; 3 Risaldars; 1 Wordie Major; 4 Risaidars; 8 Jamadars; 1 Kote Dafedar Major; 1 Farrier Major; 8 Kote Dafedars; 32 Dafedars; 8 Trumpeters; 40 Naiks; and 518 Sowars.

5th Bombay Cavalry (Sind Horse) (Raised August 1839). 524

"Cutchee"—"Meeanee"—"Hyderabad"—"Punjaub"—"Mooltan"—"Goojerat"—"Persia"—"Central India"—"Afghanistan, 1878-79."

Head Quarters at Jacobabad. *Uniform, Dark Green. Facings, White.*

Rank, Names, and Corps.	Army Rank.	Remarks.
Major G. F. Francis, Staff Corps	5 Nov. 90	Commandant, 8 Apr. 94.—And Commanding at Jacobabad.
Captain C. E. Peirse, Staff Corps	13 Nov. 86	2nd in Command and Squadron Commander, 8 Apr. 94.—Offg. Cantonment Magistrate, Jacobabad.
Captain R. W. Sherard, Staff Corps	22 Jan. 90	Squadron Commander, 8 Nov. 89.—Furlough.
Captain E. O. Owen, Staff Corps	11 Oct. 90	Squadron Commander, 21 Oct. 92.—Offg. Assist. Judge Advocate General, Meean Meer.
Lieut. C. H. Lewis, Staff Corps	30 July 84	Squadron Commander, 8 Apr. 94.—Escort Duty, Kurrachee.
Lieut. B. P. S. Rooke, Staff Corps	28 Apr. 86	Squadron Officer and Adjutant, 1 Mar. 89.
Lieut. R. A. E. Benn, Staff Corps	20 Nov. 89	Squad. Officer, 21 Oct. 92.—Intell. Officer, Afghan Beloochistan.
Lieut. H. W. Cobham, Staff Corps	29 June 89	Squadron Officer, 1 July 92.—Officiating Squadron Commander.
Lieut O. M. J. da Costa, Staff Corps	15 Apr. 92	Squadron Officer, 20 Apr. 94.—Furlough.
Lieut. C. A. F. Hocken, Staff Corps	1 Sept. 91	Officiating Squadron Officer.
Lieut. E. O'Brien, Irish Rifles	30 May 93	Officiating Squadron Officer.
2nd Lieut. R. N. Benwell, 2 Drag. Gds.	10 Oct. 91	Officiating Squadron Officer.
Surgeon Captain J. G. Hojel, MB.	31 Mar. 88	In medical charge, 10 June 92.—Sick Furlough.
Surgeon Captain J. B. Jameson, MB.	31 Mar. 90	Officiating in medical charge, and Civil, Jacobabad.

6th Bombay Cavalry (Jacob's Horse) (Raised 17 Jan. 1846).

"Cutchee"—"Meeanee"—"Hyderabad"—"Punjaub"—"Mooltan"—"Goojerat"—"Afghanistan, 1879-80."

Head Quarters at Fort Sandeman. Detachments at Jacobabad, &c. *Uniform, Dark Green. Facings, Primrose.*

Major E. V. P. Monteith, Staff Corps	5 May 89	Commandant, 1 Mar. 94.
Major J. B. R. Butler, Staff Corps	1 Oct. 94	2nd in Command and Squadron Commander, 1 March 92.
Captain C. F. Grantham, Staff Corps	6 Jan. 90	Squadron Commander, 2 Dec. 92.—With 4 Bombay Cavalry.
Captain C. M. Cartwright, Staff Corps	22 Oct. 92	Squadron Commander, 28 July 93.—Furlough.
Captain A. E. S. Hartigan, Staff Corps	10 Mar. 94	Squadron Commander, 25 Aug. 93.—At Jacobabad. [of Kelat.
Lieut. E. Le Mesurier, Staff Corps	1 Sept. 85	Squadron Officer, 2 May 90.—Military Adviser to H.H. the Khan
Lieut. H. K. MacGeorge, Staff Corps	3 Mar. 86	Squadron Officer, 2 Dec. 92.
Lieut. R. E. Roome, Staff Corps	20 Apr. 88	Squadron Officer and Adjutant, 22 Nov. 89.
Lieut. C. H. Alexander, Staff Corps	12 Oct. 91	Squadron Officer, 20 Oct. 93.—Offg. Squadron Commander. Officiating Squadron Officer.
2nd Lt. H. T. Naylor, Dublin Fusiliers	18 June 92	Officiating Squadron Officer at Mir Ali Khel.
Brig. Surg. Lt.Colonel A. Barry, MD.	26 Feb. 88	In medical charge, 13 May 92.

7th Bombay Lancers (Belooch Horse) (Raised 21 Oct. 1885).

Head Quarters at Sibi. Detachments at Kelat, Chaman, Peshin, and Quetta. *Uniform, Dark Green. Facings, White.*

Lt. Colonel F. Abbott, Staff Corps	22 July 94	Commandant, 4 Nov. 92.—Sick Furlough. [Comdt.
Major J. Monteith, Staff Corps	13 Nov. 92	2nd in Command and Squadron Commander, 4 Nov. 92.—Offg.
Major A. M. Monteith, Staff Corps	9 Aug. 93	Squadron Commander, 4 June 86.—Offg. 2nd in Command.
Captain C. E. B. Bivar, Staff Corps	23 Nov. 91	Squadron Commander, 21 July 93.—Furlough.
Captain W. J. Peyton, CMG, Staff Corps	22 Jan. 92	Squadron Commander, 28 July 93.
Lieut. H. N. Roome, Staff Corps	23 May 85	Squadron Officer, 18 Jan. 89.—Offg. Squadron Commander.
Lieut. F. L. Vincent, Staff Corps	25 Aug. 85	Squadron Officer and Adjutant, 20 Sept. 89. [At Quetta.
Lieut. H. H. Southey, Staff Corps	28 Nov. 87	Squadron Officer, 30 Aug. 89.—Offg. Squadron Commander.—
Lieut. J. Talbot, Staff Corps	24 Feb. 90	Squadron Officer, 27 Jan. 93.—Furlough.
Lieut. F. C. W. Ware, Staff Corps	28 Feb. 89	Squadron Officer, 25 Nov. 92.
Lieut. O. L. Downes, Staff Corps	11 Apr. 93	Officiating Squadron Officer.
Lieut. C. B. Loring, Staff Corps	6 May 93	Officiating Squadron Officer.
2nd Lt. C. T. Mathew, 5 Lancers	11 Mar. 91	Officiating Squadron Officer.
Lieut. W. B. T. Abbey, Staff Corps	3 Dec. 94	Officiating Squadron Officer.
Surgeon Captain J. L. T. Jones, MB.	24 Feb. 90	In medical charge, 4 Sept. 91.—Acting Civil Surgeon, Kaira.
Surgeon Captain A. Street, MB.	31 Mar. 90	Officiating in medical charge.—From 1 Bombay Infantry.

Aden Troop (Raised 23 Oct. 1867).

Head Quarters at Khormaksar. *Uniform, Dark Green. Facings, White. Throat Plume, Yellow.*

Captain F. W. G. Wadeson, Staff Corps	17 Apr. 91	Commandant, 14 July 93.—From 4 Cavalry.

Note.—The Effective Establishment of the Aden Troop consists of 1 Commandant, 1 Risaldar, 2 Risaidars, 1 Kote Dafedar, 1 Quarter Master Dafedar, 1 Pay Dafedar, 8 Dafedars, 1 Trumpeter, 2 Farriers, 83 Sowars.

Native Artillery.

No. 5 Mountain Battery—"Punjaub"—"Mooltan"—"Abyssinia"—"Burma, 1885-87." No. 6 Mountain Battery—"Afghanistan, 1878-80."

No. 5 Mountain Battery at Bhamo; Detachment at Sadon. No. 6 Mountain Battery at Loralai; Detachment at Fort Sandeman. *Uniform, Dark Blue. Facings, Scarlet.*

Captain F. R. M'C. de Butts, R. Art.	20 June 90	Commanding No. 5 Mountain Battery, 21 Aug. 91.
Lieut. C. E. Forestier-Walker, R. Art.	24 July 86	Subaltern, 22 Aug. 90.
Lieut. E. C. Pottinger, Royal Artillery	13 July 90	Subaltern, 21 Aug. 91.
Lieut. R. H. Massie, Royal Artillery	27 July 91	Subaltern, 8 Apr. 92.
Captain G. B. Smith, Royal Artillery	29 Aug. 87	Commanding No. 6 Mountain Battery, 21 June 89.
Lieut. J. G. Baldwin, Royal Artillery	16 Sept. 85	Subaltern, 2 Aug. 89.—Furlough.
Lieut. L. J. Chapman, Royal Artillery	23 July 90	Subaltern, 21 Aug. 91.—At Fort Sandeman.
Lieut. H. S. de Brett, Royal Artillery	15 Feb. 92	Subaltern, 26 Jan. 94.
Lieut. H. W. M. Parker, Royal Artillery	17 Feb. 91	Officiating Subaltern.

Establishment of a Native Mountain Battery.—1 Commandant, 3 Subalterns, 1 Subedar, 2 Jamadars, 8 Havildars, 6 Naiks, 2 Trumpeters, 80 Gunners. Total, 103. *Drivers' Establishment.*—3 Havildars, 6 Naiks, 112 Drivers with an increase of 12 on service, 1 Salootrie, 1 Shoeing Smith.

Corps of Sappers and Miners.

"BENI-BOO-ALI"—"GHUZNEE"—"AFFGHANISTAN"—"KHELAT"—"PUNJAUB"—"MOOLTAN"—"GOOJERAT"—"PERSIA"—"RESHIRE"—"KHOOSHAB"—"BUSHIRE"—"CENTRAL INDIA"—"ABYSSINIA"—"KANDAHAR, 1880."
"AFGHANISTAN, 1878-80"—"BURMA, 1885-87."

Head Quarters at Kirkee. *Uniform, Scarlet. Facings, Blue.*

| 1st Company.—Aden. | 3rd Company.—Kirkee. | A (Depot) Company.—Kirkee. |
| 2nd Company.—Kirkee. | 4th Company.—Quetta. | |

RANK, NAMES, AND CORPS.	ARMY RANK.	REMARKS.
Major G. H. W. O'Sullivan, R.Engineers	9 May 91	Commandant, 30 Oct. 91.
Major G. T. Jones, R. Engineers	27 Aug.92	Superintendent of Instruction, Park and Train, 2 Dec. 90.
Lieut. F. K. Fair, R. Engineers	18 Feb. 86	Adjutant, 16 Oct. 91.
Captain B. B. Russell, R. Engineers	30 Mar. 89	Company Commander, 7 Feb. 88.—4 Company.
Captain C. E. Baddeley, R. Engineers	17 Dec. 89	Company Comdr. 29 May 88.—No. 2 Company.—S.S.O. Kirkee.
Captain T. Harrison, DSO. R. Engineers	16 Mar. 92	Company Commander, 16 Oct. 91.—A Company.—Furlough.
Lieut. F. A. Wilson, Royal Engineers	6 Jan. 86	Company Commander, 22 Nov. 89.—No. 3 Company.
Lieut. C. W. Singer, Royal Engineers	14 Feb. 93	Company Commander, 1 Aug. 93.—No. 1 Company.
Lieut. C. E. W. Crookshank, R. Eng.	23 July 87	Company Officer, 16 Nov. 92.—No. 2 Company.
Lieut. A. E. Panet, Royal Engineers	28 July 91	Company Officer, 13 Dec. 91.—Telegraph duty, Punjab.
Lieut. G. H. Boileau, Royal Engineers	14 Feb. 93	Company Officer and Quarter Master, 16 Aug. 93.—A Company.
Lieut. C. R. Tonge, Royal Engineers	24 July 94	Company Officer, 17 Feb. 94.—1 Company. [Offg.Comp.Comdr.
2nd Lieut. F. S. Garwood, R. Engineers	12 Feb. 92	Company Officer, 11 Apr. 94.—4 Company.
Surgeon Lt.Colonel W. A. Barren	31 Mar. 94	In medical charge, 13 Jan. 93.—Furlough.
Surgeon Captain T. W. Irvine, MB.	28 July 91	Officiating in medical charge.

NOTE.—The Effective Establishment of the Corps of Sappers and Miners consists of 4 Service Companies and 1 Depot Company, with 1 Commandant, 1 Superintendent of Instruction Park and Train, 1 Adjutant, 5 Company Commanders, 5 Company Officers, a Warrant Officer, 1 Sergeant Major, 1 Quarter Master Sergeant, 3 Company Sergeant Majors, 3 Sergeants, 5 First Corporals, 5 Second Corporals, 5 Subedars, 9 Jamadars, 29 Havildars, 47 Naiques, 726 Privates, 9 Buglers, and 12 Boys.

1st Bombay Infantry (*Grenadiers—Raised* 12 *November* 1779).—
Linked with 8th and 9th Regiments.—Regimental Centre, Ahmednugger.

"MANGALORE"—"MYSORE"—"HYDERABAD"—"KANDAHAR, 1880"—"AFGHANISTAN, 1878-80"—"BURMA, 1885-87."
Head Quarters at Baroda. Detachment at Surat. *Uniform, Red. Facings, White.*

Lt.Colonel W. C. Black, Staff Corps	12 Jan. 92	Commandant, 26 Apr. 91.—And Commanding at Baroda.
Captain J. C. Swann, Staff Corps	10 Sept.86	2nd in Command and Wing Commander, 16 Sept. 94.—D.A.A. Gen. Bombay.
Captain C. A. S. Montgomery, Staff C.	25 Feb. 91	2nd in Command and Wing Commander, 13 June 93.—Cant.
Captain F. A. Hoghton, Staff Corps	10 Mar. 94	Wing Commander, 16 Sept. 94.—Furlough. [Mag., Baroda.
Lieut. W. H. Errington, Staff Corps	30 Jan. 86	Wing Officer and Quarter Master, 6 Dec. 89.—Offg. Wing Comdr.
Lieut. P. H. Cunningham, Staff Corps	29 Feb. 88	Wing Officer, 4 Oct. 89.—Station Staff Officer, Surat.
Lieut. A. M. Doveton, Staff Corps	4 Jan. 90	Wing Officer, 9 Nov. 93.—Officiating Quarter Master.
Lieut. G. M. Rolland, Staff Corps	2 Aug. 91	Wing Officer and Adjutant, 30 Sept. 92.—S. S. O. Baroda.
Lieut. H. Ross, Staff Corps	24 Apr. 92	Wing Officer, 9 Nov. 94.—Prob. Commissariat Department.
2nd Lt. E. N. Heale, Northumb. Fus.	9 Apr. 92	Officiating Wing Officer.
Surgeon Captain A. Street, MB.	31 Mar. 90	In medical charge.
Surg. Lieut. H. M. Moore	28 July 94	Officiating in medical charge.

2nd (*Prince of Wales' Own*) Bombay Infantry (*Grenadiers—*
Raised 18 *September* 1788).—*Linked with* 12*th and* 13*th Regiments.—Regimental Centre, Poona.*
"EGYPT" (with the Sphinx)—"KIRKEE"—"KOREGAUM"—"ABYSSINIA."
Head Quarters at Poona. *Uniform, Red. Facings, White.*
Honorary Colonel.—Field Marshal H.R.H. Albert Edward, *Prince of* Wales *and Duke of* Cornwall,
KG. KT. KP. GCB. GCSI. GCMG. GCIE.

Lt.Colonel F. B. Peile, Staff Corps	8 Jan. 94	Commandant, 22 March 89.
Lt.Colonel T. H. Mackenzie, Staff Corps	3 Feb. 95	2nd in Command and Wing Commander, 26 July 89.
Captain A. E. Leslie, Staff Corps	10 Sept.87	Wing Commander, 1 Feb. 89.
Captain E. R. Hartigan, Staff Corps	1 Feb. 91	Wing Officer, 3 Sept. 86.
Lieut. D. Baker, Staff Corps	1 Feb. 87	Wing Officer, 5 Apr. 89.—Sick Furlough.
Lieut. S. M. Edwardes, Staff Corps	23 Aug. 84	Wing Officer and Adjutant, 29 Apr. 87.—On special duty, Gilgit.
Capt. A. A. M. M. Faulknor, Staff Corps	12 May 94	Wing Officer, 29 Apr. 87.—Offg. Canton. Magis., Quetta. [kund.
Lieut. D. G. Peart, Staff Corps	25 Aug. 86	Wing Officer, 28 June 89.—Boundary Settlement Officer, Bundel-
Lieut. F. R. E. Lock, Staff Corps	25 Aug. 86	Wing Officer, 16 Dec. 92.—Offg. Quarter Master. [Bombay.
Lieut. C. S. D. Leslie, Staff Corps	22 Mar. 89	Wing Officer, 13 Mar. 91.—Dep. Assist. Com. Gen. 2nd Class.
Lieut. J. H. Lloyd, Staff Corps	10 Nov. 91	Wing Officer and Adjutant, 30 June 93.
Lieut. C. E. Ayerst, Staff Corps	14 Sept. 92	Officiating Wing Officer.
2nd Lt. B. F. R. Holbrooke, Staff Corps	28 June 93	Officiating Wing Officer, 14 Dec. 94.—With 7 Bombay Lancers.
Surgeon Captain C. T. Hudson	30 Mar. 89	In medical charge, 3 Nov. 93.

3rd Bombay Infantry (*Light Infantry—Raised* 18 *September* 1788).—
Linked with 5*th and* 10*th Regiments.—Regimental Centre, Sattara.*

"MYSORE"—"SEEDASEER"—"SERINGAPATAM"—"BENI-BOO-ALI"—"PUNJAUB"—"MOOLTAN"—"GOOJERAT"—"ABYSSINIA."
Head Quarters at Mhow. Detachment at Asseerghur. *Uniform, Red. Facings, Black.*

Lt.Colonel F. G. T. Welch, Staff Corps	20 Apr. 93	Commandant, 25 Dec. 93.
Major W. S. Birdwood, Staff Corps	21 Sept.94	2nd in Command and Wing Commander 24 Feb. 93.
Captain A. D. Fordyce, Staff Corps	22 Jan. 90	Wing Commander, 8 Mar. 94.—Canton. Magistrate, Neemach.
Captain G. de S. De Lisle, Staff Corps	10 May 93	Wing Commander, 8 Mar. 94.—On Recruiting Service, Sattara.
Captain H. F. E. Hodges, Staff Corps	22 Jan. 90	Wing Officer, 21 July 93.—Offg. Wing Comdr.—Offg. Comdt.
Captain M. W. Baugh, Staff Corps	10 Mar. 94	Wing Officer, 8 Nov. 89. [Asseerghur.
Lieut. H. G. Brown, Staff Corps	23 Feb. 88	Wing Officer, 1 Nov. 93.—Officiating Quarter Master.
Lieut. F.W. D. Trotter, Staff Corps	21 Mar. 90	Wing Officer, 4 Mar. 92.
Lieut. F. W. H. Forteath, Staff Corps	30 Aug. 90	Wing Officer, 14 April 93.—Dep. Assist. Com. Gen. 2nd Class.
Lieut. C.A. Roosmale-Cocq, Staff Corps	13 Dec. 90	Wing Officer, 4 May 94.—Sick Furlough.
Lieut. A. W. Chitty, Gloucester Regt.	10 Jan. 94	Officiating Wing Officer.
Surgeon Major A. F. Sargent	1 Oct. 89	In medical charge, 14 Sept. 83.

NOTE.—The Effective Establishment of a Native Infantry Regiment consists of Eight Companies with 1 Commandant, 2 Wing Commanders, 5 Wing Officers, 1 Medical Officer, 8 Subedars, 8 Jamadars, 40 Havildars, 40 Naiks, 10 Drummers, 720 Sepoys, or 832 of all Ranks (Native). *Non-effective Native Staff.*—1 Subedar Major, 1 Native Adjutant, 1 Drill Havildar, 1 Drill Naik, 8 Pay Havildars, 1 Drum Major, 1 Fife Major.

4th Bombay Infantry (*Raised* 18 *September* 1788). 525*a*
—Regimental Centre, Poona.
(*First Battalion The Bombay Rifle Regiment.*)
"MYSORE"—"SERINGAPATAM"—"BOURBON"—"BENI-BOO-ALI"—"PUNJAUB"—"MOOLTAN"—"PERSIA"—
"RESHIRE"—"KHOOSHAB"—"BUSHIRE"—"CENTRAL INDIA"—"KANDAHAR, 1880"—"AFGHANISTAN, 1879-80."
Head Quarters at Poona. *Uniform, Rifle Green. Facings, Red.*

RANK, NAMES, AND CORPS.	ARMY RANK.	REMARKS.
Lt.Colonel J. Grant, Staff Corps	30 June 91	Commandant, 12 June 91.
Captain W. Quentin, Staff Corps	27 Jan. 87	2nd in Command and Wing Commander. Wing Commander, 24 Aug. 88.—Officiating 2nd in Command.
Captain C. I. Fry, Staff Corps	22 Jan. 90	Wing Officer, 4 Feb. 87.—Officiating Wing Commander.
Captain J. C. Keown, Staff Corps	1 Feb. 95	Wing Officer, 10 May 89.—Officiating Quarter Master.
Captain W. C. Walton, Staff Corps	6 Feb. 95	Wing Officer and Adjutant, 19 June 91.
Lieut. A. B. Sangster, Staff Corps	10 Nov. 86	Wing Officer, 26 July 89.
Lieut. C. A. W. Ford, Staff Corps	3 July 89	Wing Officer and Quarter Master, 26 Aug. 92.—Asst. Insp. Army [Signalling.
Lieut. G. Bailey, Staff Corps	17 Aug. 92	Wing Officer, 2 Mar. 94.
Lieut. W.H.O. Codrington, Staff Corps	3 July 93	Officiating Wing Officer.
Lieut. H. V. Riddell, Staff Corps	5 Apr. 93	Officiating Wing Officer.
2nd Lieut. R. E. Kriekenbeek, S. C.	30 Nov. 92	Officiating Wing Officer.
Surgeon Captain G. H. Bull, *MD.*	30 Mar. 90	In medical charge, 27 Jan. 93.

5th Bombay (*Light*) Infantry (*Raised* 18 *September* 1788).—
Linked with 3*rd and* 10*th Regiments.—Regimental Centre, Sattara.*
"MYSORE"—"SEEDASEER"—"SERINGAPATAM"—"BENI-BOO-ALI"—"KAHUN"—"CHINA, 1860-62"—
"AFGHANISTAN, 1879-80"—"BURMA, 1885-87."
Head Quarters at Quetta. Detachments at Kelat, Shellabagh, &c. *Uniform, Red. Facings, Black.*

RANK, NAMES, AND CORPS.	ARMY RANK.	REMARKS.
Major C. O. Nicholetts, Staff Corps	6 July 90	Commandant.
Captain A. Beale, Staff Corps	13 Aug. 90	2nd in Command and Wing Commander.
Captain E. A Kettlewell, Staff Corps	13 Aug. 90	Wing Commander, 24 Dec. 94.
Captain F. W. J. Caulfeild, Staff Corps	14 Jan. 91	Wing Commander, 3 Jan. 95. [paul.
Lieut. C. J. Windham, Staff Corps	1 Sept. 86	Wing Officer, 22 July 92.—Boundary Settlement Officer, Bho-
Lieut. E. R. L. Chitty, Staff Corps	1 Feb. 88	Wing Officer and Adjutant, 28 Mar. 90.
Lieut. C. H. C. Grace, Staff Corps	19 Mar. 90	Wing Officer and Quarter Master, 15 July 92.
Lieut. J. H. Dickson, Staff Corps	2 Apr. 89	Wing Officer, 1 May 91.—Dep. Assist. Com. Gen. 2nd Class.
Lieut. H. Brand, Staff Corps	29 Mar. 91	Wing Officer, 11 Nov. 92.—At Kelat.
Lieut. A. A. West, Staff Corps	12 Feb. 91	Wing Officer, 14 Oct. 92.—Commanding at Shellabagh.
Lieut. H. W. Berthon, Staff Corps	14 Apr. 92	Wing Officer, 28 Sept. 94.
Surgeon Captain S. E. Prall, *MB.*	29 Sept. 88	In medical charge, 24 Mar. 93.—Acting Civil, Bejapore.
Surgeon Lieut. T. Jackson, *MB.*	27 July 92	Officiating in medical charge.

7th Bombay Infantry (*Raised* 18 *September* 1788).—
Regimental Centre, Mhow.
"MYSORE"—"SEEDASEER"—"SERINGAPATAM"—"BENI-BOO-ALI"—"BURMA, 1885-87."
Head Quarters at Raipore. Wing at Sumbulpore. *Uniform, Red. Facings, White.*

RANK, NAMES, AND CORPS.	ARMY RANK.	REMARKS.
Lt.Colonel H. E. Penton, Staff Corps	8 Jan. 94	Commandant, 3 Mar. 93.—And Commanding at Raipore.
Captain C. F. S. Alban, Staff Corps	13 June 86	2nd in Command and Wing Comdr., 3 Mar. 93.—Sick Furlough.
Captain P. J. H. Aplin, Staff Corps	1 May 89	Wing Comdr., 15 June 94.—Offg. 2nd in Comd. & Comdg. at Sumbul-
Captain J. C. Hollway, Staff Corps	4 Dec. 89	Wing Officer, 9 Jan. 85.—Offg. Wing Commander. [pore.
Captain J. A. H. Craufurd, Staff Corps	22 Oct. 92	Wing Officer, 10 Apr. 85.
Captain P. A. N. St. L. Wood, Staff C.	14 Jan. 91	Wing Officer, 27 Aug. 86.
Capt. A. P. A. Elphinstone, Staff Corps	6 Feb. 95	Wing Officer and Adjutant, 30 Sept. 87.—S. S. O. Raepore.
Lieut. F. Fisher, Staff Corps	20 Oct. 89	Wing Officer and Quarter Master, 10 July 91.
Lieut. A. Hay, Staff Corps	14 Jan. 90	Officiating Wing Officer.
Lieut. C. Godfrey, Staff Corps	26 June 92	Officiating Wing Officer.—Station Staff Officer, Sumbulpore.
Lieut. F. C. Owens, Leinster Regt.	2 May 94	Officiating Wing Officer.
Surgeon Major H. P. Jervis	1 Oct. 89	In medical charge, 10 July 85.
Surgeon Lieut. P. P. Kilkelly, *MB.*	29 July 93	In medical charge of Wing, Sumbulpore.

8th Bombay Infantry (*Raised in* 1768).—
Linked with 1*st and* 9*th Regiments.—Regimental Centre, Ahmednugger.*
"MYSORE"—"HYDERABAD"—"AFGHANISTAN, 1879-80."
Head Quarters at Ahmednugger. Detachment at Malegaon. *Uniform, Red. Facings, White.*

RANK, NAMES, AND CORPS.	ARMY RANK.	REMARKS.
Major W. C. Aslett, Staff Corps	13 June 94	Commandant, 16 Sept. 94.—Furlough. [Comdt.
Captain J. R. Sandwith, Staff Corps	28 Apr. 87	2nd in Command and Wing Commander, 16 Sept. 94.—Offg.
Captain R. Errington, Staff Corps	31 Jan. 91	Wing Commander, 5 Feb. 92.—Offg. 2nd in Command.
Captain C. A. Brown, Staff Corps	19 Feb. 92	Wing Officer, 16 Apr. 86.—Officiating Wing Commander, Cantonment Magistrate and Commanding at Malegaon.
Captain R. M. Betham, Staff Corps	10 Mar. 94	Wing Officer, 16 Apr. 86.—S.S.O. & Cant. Mag., Ahmednugger.
Lieut. M. R. Hunter, Staff Corps	29 Aug. 85	Wing Officer, 27 April 88.—Sick Furlough.
Lieut. J. R. B. G. Carter, Staff Corps	29 Jan. 88	Wing Officer and Adjutant, 5 Apr. 89.—Furlough.
Lieut. E. Saulez, Staff Corps	13 July 88	Wing Officer and Quarter Master, 7 Mar. 90.
Lieut. M. T. Elderton, Staff Corps	23 Mar. 90	Officiating Wing Officer and Adjutant.
Lieut. C. S. Fellows, S. Lanc. Regt.	26 Nov. 93	Officiating Wing Officer.
Surgeon Captain C. J. Sarkies, *MB.*	29 Sept. 83	In medical charge, 11 Oct. 89.—Sick Furlough.
Surgeon Captain B. D. Basu	31 Jan. 91	Officiating in medical charge, and Civil Surgeon, Ahmednugger.

9th Bombay Infantry (*Raised* 18 *September* 1788).—
Linked with 1*st and* 8*th Regiments.—Regimental Centre, Ahmednugger.*
"MYSORE"—"SERINGAPATAM"—"PUNJAUB"—"MOOLTAN"—"AFGHANISTAN, 1879-80."
Head Quarters at Quetta. *Uniform, Red. Facings, Black.*

RANK, NAMES, AND CORPS.	ARMY RANK.	REMARKS.
Major A. W. Proudfoot, Staff Corps	24 Nov. 89	Commandant, 29 Jan. 91.
Captain H. Godfray, Staff Corps	10 Sept. 86	2nd in Command and Wing Commander, 29 Jan. 91.
Captain R. D. Broome, Staff Corps	8 Mar. 90	Wing Commander, 9 Oct. 91.
Captain W. Battiscombe, Staff Corps	13 Aug. 90	Wing Officer, 12 June 85.
Captain C. J. Melliss, Staff Corps	9 Sept. 93	Wing Officer, 1 Oct. 86.
Lieut. P. C. Searle, Shropshire Lt. Inf.	3 Oct. 89	Wing Officer, 8 May 92.—Station Staff Officer, Kamptee.
Lieut. J. R. Darley, Staff Corps	20 Dec. 90	Wing Officer, 12 Aug. 92. Wing Officer,
Lieut. H. C. Wooldridge, Staff Corps	9 Mar. 92	Wing Officer and Adjutant, 9 Nov. 94.—Offg. Quarter Master.
Lieut. E. H. Bridges, Staff Corps	8 July 92	Officiating Wing Officer.
Surgeon Major C. F. Willis, *MB.*	31 Oct. 91	In medical charge, 11 Aug. 84.

525b   **10th Bombay (*Light*) Infantry** (*Raised* 14 *October* 1797).
—*Linked with* 3rd *and* 5th *Regiments.*—*Regimental Centre, Sattara.*
"CENTRAL INDIA"—"ABYSSINIA"—"AFGHANISTAN, 1879-80."
Head Quarters at **Sattara**. *Uniform, Red. Facings, Black.*

RANK, NAMES, AND CORPS.	ARMY RANK.	REMARKS.
Lt. Colonel L. F. Heath, Staff Corps	9 Sept. 90	Commandant, 12 May 91.—Sick Furlough.
Major F. G. Alexander, Staff Corps	7 Dec. 90	2nd in Command and Wing Comdr., 31 July 91.—Offg. Comdt.
Captain W. B. Piers, Staff Corps	1 May 89	Wing Commander, 30 May 90.—Offg. 2nd in Command.
Captain A. T. H. Newnham, Staff Corps	22 Jan. 92	Wing Officer, 13 May 85.
Captain R. G. R. de V. de Ponthieu, S.C.	10 Mar. 94	Wing Officer, 7 Jan. 87.—On special duty, Gilgit.
Captain H. C. B. Dann, Staff Corps	20 Oct. 94	Wing Officer, 18 Oct. 89.—Furlough.
Lieut. J. J. O'B. Sexton, Staff Corps	25 Aug. 86	Wing Officer and Quarter Master, 1 March 89.
Lieut. T. X. Britten, Staff Corps	21 Sept. 88	Wing Officer and Adjutant, 20 Dec. 89.—S.S.O. Sattara.
Lieut. H. C. Hill, Staff Corps	3 June 92	Wing Officer.
Lieut. F. P. C. Keily, Lancaster Regt.	30 Dec. 93	Officiating Wing Officer.
Lieut. W. F. Stewart, Staff Corps	3 Dec. 94	Officiating Wing Officer. [Registration District.
Surgeon Captain H. C. L. Arnim	31 Mar. 88	In medical charge, 30 Sept. 92.—Acting Dep. San. Commr. Sind
Surgeon Lieut. B. H. F. Leumann, *MB.*	29 Jan. 94	Officiating in medical charge.

12th Bombay Infantry (*Raised* 15 *January* 1798).—
Linked with 2nd *and* 13th *Regiments.*—*Regimental Centre, Poona.*
"KIRKEE"—"MEEANEE"—"HYDERABAD"—"CENTRAL INDIA."
Head Quarters at **Kamptee**. Detachment at **Seetabuldee**. *Uniform, Red. Facings, Yellow.*

RANK, NAMES, AND CORPS.	ARMY RANK.	REMARKS.
Lt. Colonel H. B. Ternan, Staff Corps	22 Feb. 94	Commandant, 5 Sept. 94.
Captain G. S. Hogge, Staff Corps	14 Jan. 91	2nd in Command and Wing Commander, 5 Sept. 94.
Captain H. S. Hazelgrove, Staff Corps	22 Jan. 92	Wing Commander, 5 Sept. 94.
Captain J. M. Ransom, Staff Corps	1 Feb. 92	Wing Officer, 18 Feb. 87.—On Recruiting Service, Nusseerabad.
Lieut. N. A. H. Budd, Staff Corps	9 May 85	Wing Officer and Quarter Master, 11 Nov. 87.
Lieut. H. G. Walker, Staff Corps	25 Aug. 86	Wing Officer, 5 July 89.
Lieut. R. P. C. Schneider, Staff Corps	25 Aug. 86	Wing Officer, 1 Nov. 89.—Officiating Adjutant.
Lieut. M. E. Nuttall, Staff Corps	18 Aug. 91	Wing Officer, 29 Dec. 93—Sick Furlough.
Lieut. F. Owen-Lewis, Durham Lt. Inf.	15 Mar. 93	Officiating Wing Officer.
Lieut. W. Scott, Staff Corps	24 May 93	Officiating Wing Officer.—S. S. O. Seetabuldee.
Surgeon Major H. B. Briggs	30 Sept. 90	In medical charge, 14 Aug. 85.—Sick Furlough.
Surgeon Lieut. H. Bennett, *MB.*	29 Jan. 94	Officiating in medical charge.

13th Bombay Infantry (*Raised* 6 *March* 1800).—
Linked with 2nd *and* 12th *Regiments.*—*Regimental Centre, Poona.*
"EGYPT" (with the Sphinx)—"KIRKEE"—"BENI-BOO-ALI"—"CENTRAL INDIA"—"AFGHANISTAN, 1879-80."
Head Quarters at **Aden**. Detachments at **Berbera**, &c. *Uniform, Red. Facings, Yellow.*

RANK, NAMES, AND CORPS.	ARMY RANK.	REMARKS.
Lt. Colonel J. N. Walker, Staff Corps	20 July 93	Commandant, 2 Mar. 90.
Lt. Colonel A. J. P. Nuthall, Staff Corps	10 Feb. 95	2nd in Command and Wing Commander, 5 Sept. 90.
Captain H. Welman, Staff Corps	14 Jan. 91	Wing Commander, 10 Mar. 93.—Furlough.
Captain C. G. Nurse, Staff Corps	22 Jan. 92	Wing Officer, 15 Sept. 93.—Offg. Wing Comdr. and Adjutant.
Captain T. H. Henderson, Staff Corps	6 Feb. 95	Wing Officer, 1 Aug. 91.—Military Accounts Dept.
Lt. W. C. F. R. Macnamara, Staff Corps	25 Aug. 86	Wing Officer, 28 Sept. 94.
Lieut. A. H. Bolton, Staff Corps	10 Nov. 86	Wing Officer, 4 Oct. 89—Officiating Quarter Master.
Lieut. F. L. Lloyd-Jones, Staff Corps	10 Nov. 89	Wing Officer and Quarter Master, 7 Oct. 92.—Furlough.
Lieut. F. E. Geoghegan, Staff Corps	12 Feb. 91	Wing Officer, 21 July 93.—Prob. Commissariat Department.
Lieut. E. A. F. Redl, Lancaster Regt.	7 July 92	Officiating Wing Officer.
Surgeon Lt. Colonel S. B. Halliday	1 Apr. 87	In medical charge, 18 May 78.

14th Bombay Infantry (*Raised* 6 *March* 1800).—
Linked with 16th *and* 17th *Regiments.*—*Regimental Centre, Ahmedabad.*
Head Quarters at **Deesa**. *Uniform, Red. Facings, Yellow.*

RANK, NAMES, AND CORPS.	ARMY RANK.	REMARKS.
Lt. Colonel W. H. Lyster, Staff Corps	16 Oct. 92	Commandant, 19 Dec. 91. [Deesa District.
Major A. W. C. Bell, Staff Corps	7 July 89	2nd in Command and Wing Comdr. 4 Nov. 92.—Offg. A.A.G.
Major J. M. Candy, Staff Corps	2 Nov. 93	Wing Commander, 26 July 89.—Offg. 2nd in Command.
Captain A. E. S. Searle, Staff Corps	13 Aug. 90	Wing Officer, 15 Oct. 93.
Lieut. E. G. R. Wilkins, Staff Corps	7 Feb. 85	Wing Officer and Adjutant, 19 Aug. 87.
Lieut. H. F. Jacob, Staff Corps	22 Feb. 88	Wing Officer 21 June 89.—Officiating Assistant Political Superintendent, Palanpore.
Lieut. J. L. Harington, Staff Corps	11 Sept. 89	Wing Officer, 20 March 91.—Offg. Assist. Polit. Resident, Aden.
Lieut. H.G.F. Sargent, Staff Corps	14 Dec. 92	Wing Officer, 28 Sept. 94.—Officiating Quarter Master.
Lieut. G. M. G. Parker, Staff Corps	3 Dec. 94	Wing Officer, 2 Feb. 94.
2nd Lieut. W. A. Light, Staff Corps	28 Jan. 93	Officiating Wing Officer.—From 24 Bombay Infantry, Officiating Wing Officer.
Surgeon Captain G. S. Thomson, *MB.*	31 Mar. 88	In medical charge, 27 Jan. 93.

16th Bombay Infantry (*Raised* 6 *March* 1800).—
Linked with 14th *and* 17th *Regiments.*—*Regimental Centre, Ahmedabad.*
"AFGHANISTAN, 1879-80."
Head Quarters at **Ahmedabad**. Detachment at **Sudra**. *Uniform, Red. Facings, Yellow.*

RANK, NAMES, AND CORPS.	ARMY RANK.	REMARKS.
Colonel J. T. Carruthers, Staff Corps	25 May 94	Commandant, 11 June 88.—And Commanding at Ahmedabad.
Captain H. W. Seymour, Staff Corps	10 Sept. 86	2nd in Command and Wing Commander, 3 Oct. 90.
Captain P. H. Saulez, Staff Corps	1 May 89	Wing Comdr., 3 Oct. 90.—Offg. Cant. Mag., Poona and Kirkee.
Captain F. A. C. Kroyer, Staff Corps	1 May 89	Wing Officer, 22 Nov. 89.—Officiating Wing Commander.—Acting Cantonment Magistrate Ahmedabad.
Captain P. R. Legh, Staff Corps	22 Jan. 90	Wing Officer, 4 Nov. 92.
Captain H. R. Mead, Staff Corps	10 Mar. 94	Wing Officer, 24 Aug. 88.—Station Staff Officer, Ahmedabad.
Lieut. F. S. Widdicombe, Staff Corps	29 Aug. 85	Wing Officer and Quarter Master, 18 May 88.
Lieut. W. S. Jacob, Staff Corps	8 Dec. 86	Wing Officer, 8 Aug. 90.—Officiating Adjutant.
Lieut. E. F. Preston, Staff Corps	16 May 93	Officiating Wing Officer.
2nd Lt. H. W. D. Harington, Gloucester Regiment	27 Jan. 92	Officiating Wing Officer.
Surgeon Major G. E. Fooks	2 Oct. 92	In medical charge, 24 March 93.

17th Bombay Infantry (Raised 21 December 1800).—
Linked with 14th and 16th Regiments.—Regimental Centre, Ahmedabad.
Head Quarters at Bhooj. *Uniform, Red. Facings, Yellow.*

Rank, Names, and Corps.	Army Rank.	Remarks.
Lt. Colonel W. J. Morse, Staff Corps	25 Apr. 91	Commandant, 5 Oct. 93.—And Commanding at Bhooj.
Captain J. W. Gordon, Staff Corps	20 Nov. 86	2nd in Command and Wing Commander, 5 Oct. 93.—Furlough.
Captain R. H. Light, Staff Corps	13 Aug. 90	Wing Commander, 5 Oct. 93.—Officiating 2nd in Command.
Captain O. W. F. Whyte, Staff Corps	10 May 93	Wing Officer, 30 Jan. 85.—Officiating Wing Commander and Cant. [Mag., Bhooj.
Captain A. C. Le Bailly, Staff Corps	10 May 93	Wing Officer, 8 Nov. 89.
Lieut. C. D. Lester, Staff Corps	7 Apr. 88	Wing Officer and Adjutant, 17 July 91.—Furlough.
Lieut. W. Beale, Staff Corps	31 Oct. 89	Wing Officer and Qr. Mr., 30 Mar. 93.—Acting Assist. Polit. Superintendent, Palanpore.
Lieut. S. W. King, Staff Corps	23 May 91	Wing Officer, 10 Nov. 93.—Officiating Adjutant.—S. S. O. Officiating Wing Officer.
Surgeon Captain W. S. P. Ricketts, *M.B.*	30 Mar. 89	In medical charge, 27 Jan. 93.

19th Bombay Infantry (Raised 1 November 1817).—
Linked with 20th and 22nd Regiments.—Regimental Centre, Nusseerabad.
"Ghuznee"—"Affghanistan"—"Punjaub"—"Mooltan"—"Goojerat"—"Kandahar, 1880"—"Afghanistan, 1878-80."
Head Quarters at Mhow. Detachment at Indore. *Uniform, Red. Facings, Yellow.*

Colonel F. W. V. Leckie, Staff Corps	26 July 94	Commandant, 10 May 89.
Major F. Stevenson, Staff Corps	8 Feb. 90	2nd in Command and Wing Commander, 27 Dec. 89.—Furlough.
Captain C. R. Phillipps, Staff Corps	10 Sept. 86	Wing Comdr., 27 Dec. 89.—Dep. Assist. Adj. Gen., Aden.—Furl.
Captain G. E. Walter, Staff Corps	15 Apr. 87	Wing Commander, 12 July 89.—Offg. 2nd in Com.—S.S.O. and Commanding at Indore.
Captain A. E. Aitken, Staff Corps	14 Jan. 91	Wing Officer, 8 Feb. 94.—Officiating Wing Commander.—Station Staff Officer, Mhow.
Lieut. W. W. Chitty, Staff Corps	7 Feb. 85	Wing Officer and Adjutant, 27 Apr. 88.—Sick Furlough.
Lieut. H. E. Lowis, West India Regt.	9 May 85	Wing Officer and Quarter Master, 7 Nov. 90.—Offg. Adjutant.
Lieut. C. G. F. Sartorius, Staff Corps	30 Jan. 86	Wing Officer, 28 Apr. 83. [Local Corps.
Lieut. R. S. Pottinger, Staff Corps	4 Feb. 92	Wing Officer, 30 June 93.—Offg. 2nd in Com., Sawant Warree
Lieut. P. F. Pocock, Staff Corps	6 July 92	Wing Officer.
Lieut. W. M. P. Wood, Leinster Regt.	29 Sept. 93	Officiating Wing Officer.
2nd Lieut. E. A. Fagan, W. Kent Regt.	2 May 91	Officiating Wing Officer.
Surgeon Major A. F. Ferguson, *M.B.*	2 Oct. 92	In medical charge, 11 May 94.

20th Bombay Infantry (Raised 1 November 1817).—
Linked with 19th and 22nd Regiments.—Regimental Centre, Nusseerabad.
"Persia"—"Reshire"—"Bushire"—"Khooshab."
Head Quarters at Nusseerabad. Detachment at Neemuch. *Uniform, Red. Facings, Yellow.*

Colonel W. S. Hore, Gen. List, Inf.	29 Aug. 93	Commandant, 25 May 88.—Furlough.
Captain J. F. C. Thatcher, Staff Corps	13 June 86	2nd in Command and Wing Commander, 19 May 89.—Furlough.
Captain R. Baillie, Staff Corps	27 Jan. 87	Wing Commander, 25 May 88.—Offg. 2nd in Com. at Neemuch.
Captain W. O. M. Mosse, Staff Corps	23 Oct. 91	Wing Officer, 28 May 86.—Station Staff Officer, Neemuch.
Captain A. A. Graves, Staff Corps	22 Jan. 92	Wing Officer, 4 Nov. 92.—Offg. Wing Commander.
Captain W. Ayerst, Staff Corps	6 Feb. 95	Wing Officer, 23 Oct. 91.—At Neemuch.
Lieut. J. P. Hill, Staff Corps	23 Aug. 84	Wing Officer, 4 Nov. 87.—Furlough.
Lieut. J. R. Hill, Staff Corps	12 Nov. 84	Wing Officer and Adjutant, 22 June 88.
Lieut. C. M. Cockcraft, Staff Corps	22 May 89	Wing Officer, 2 Jan. 91.—Dep. Assist. Com. Gen. 2nd Class.
Lieut. N. B. Dunscombe, S. Wales Bordrs.	9 June 92	Officiating Wing Officer.
Lieut. P. C. R. Barclay, Staff Corps	2 Sept. 92	Officiating Wing Officer.
Surgeon Major J. Macgregor, *M.D.*	31 Mar. 88	In medical charge, 9 Dec. 87.—Sick Furlough.
Surgeon Lieut. V. B. Bennett, *M.B.*	28 July 94	Officiating in medical charge.

21st Bombay Infantry (or Marine Battalion) (Raised 3 January 1777).
Regimental Centre, Bombay.
An Anchor and Laurel Wreath, with Motto in Hindoostanee corresponding with "Per Mare, per Terram."
"Persian Gulf"—"Beni-Boo-Ali"—"Burmah"—"Aden"—"Hyderabad"—"Punjaub"—"Abyssinia."
Head Quarters at Bombay. Detachments in the Persian Gulf. *Uniform, Red. Facings, Emerald Green.*

Major A. B. Mein, Staff Corps	30 Dec. 91	Commandant, 28 Jan. 94.
Captain W. F. Cahusac, Staff Corps	30 Jan. 89	2nd in Command and Wing Commander, 8 Mar. 94.
Captain G. W. Mitchell, Staff Corps	11 May 89	Wing Commander, 21 Dec. 92.
Capt. T. E. A. G. Montgomery, Staff Corps	5 Oct. 89	Wing Officer, 15 June 83.
Captain C. H. C. Heyman, Staff Corps	13 Aug. 90	Wing Officer, 14 Feb. 90.
Lieut. C. G. Carnegy, Staff Corps	23 Aug. 84	Wing Officer and Adjutant, 25 July 90.—Sick Furlough.
Lieut. F. G. Beville, Staff Corps	30 Jan. 86	Wing Officer, 8 Feb. 89.—Polit. Assist. 1st Class, Bussoorah.
Lieut. C. Burrard, Staff Corps	24 July 86	Wing Officer, 28 Aug. 91.
Lieut. A. H. D. Creagh, Staff Corps	23 Jan. 88	Wing Officer and Quarter Master, 13 Mar. 90.—Offg. Adjutant. Officiating Wing Officer and Quarter Master.—And in charge of Native Details.
Lieut. J. H. Casserly, Northmptn. Reg.	7 Dec. 93	Officiating Wing Officer.
2nd Lt. A. A. P. Waller, Gloucester Reg.	27 Jan. 92	Officiating Wing Officer.
Surg. Lt. Colonel J. S. Wilkins, *D.S.O.*	31 Mar. 94	In medical charge, 14 Dec. 94.

22nd Bombay Infantry (Raised 1 January 1818).—
Linked with 19th and 20th Regiments.—Regimental Centre, Nusseerabad.
Head Quarters at Bombay. Detachment at Tanna. *Uniform, Red. Facings, Emerald Green.*

Lt. Colonel W. A. Wetherall, Staff Corps	30 Jan. 92	Commandant, 8 Nov. 89.
Major A. Smith, Staff Corps	30 Dec. 91	2nd in Command and Wing Commander, 8 Nov. 89. Wing Commander.
Captain W. G. Hatherell, Staff Corps	22 Oct. 92	Wing Officer, 27 Aug. 86.—Officiating Wing Commander.
Captain C. W. Knatchbull, Staff C.	10 Mar. 94	Wing Officer, 3 June 87.—Offg. Supdt. Army Schools, Bombay Wing Officer. [Pres.
Lieut. H. H. Nurse, Staff Corps	30 Dec. 87	Wing Officer and Adjutant, 19 July 89.
Lieut. F. S. Walker, Staff Corps	1 Apr. 92	Wing Officer and Quarter Master, 27 Oct. 90.
Lieut. W. P. Haydon, Staff Corps	12 July 92	Wing Officer, 14 Dec. 94. Officiating Wing Officer.
Surgeon Major P. J. Damania	30 Mar 90	In medical charge, 19 Dec. 84.

527

23rd Bombay Infantry (Raised 4 May 1820).
(Second Battalion The Bombay Rifle Regiment.)
Regimental Centre, Poona.
"KIRKEE"—"PERSIA"—"AFGHANISTAN, 1879-80"—"BURMA, 1885-87."
Head Quarters at Rajkote. *Uniform, Rifle Green. Facings, Red.*

RANK, NAMES, AND CORPS.	ARMY RANK.	REMARKS.
Major E. C. Kellie, Staff Corps	21 Aug. 89	Comdt., 1 Nov. 91.—And Comdg. at Rajkote. [Bombay Dist.
Captain R. I. Scallon, *DSO.* Staff Corps	12 Feb. 87	2nd in Com. and Wing Comdr., 26 Feb. 92.—Offg. D.A.A.G.
Captain W. A. M. Wilson, Staff Corps	11 Aug. 91	Wing Comdr., 26 Feb. 92.—D.A.A. Gen. for Musketry, Mhow.
Captain W. S. Delamain, Staff Corps	22 Oct. 92	Wing Officer, 17 July 91.—Officiating 2nd in Command.
Lieut. A. H. Dennys, Staff Corps	1 Feb. 85	Wing Officer, 4 July 90.—Furlough.
Lieut. A. P. Shewell, Staff Corps	19 Mar. 90	Wing Officer and Quarter Master, 16 Oct. 91.—Furlough.
Lieut. C. J. Cumberlege, Staff Corps	29 Aug. 91	Wing Officer and Adjutant, 5 May 93.—Station Staff Officer.
Lieut. W. F. Stevenson, Staff Corps	26 Feb. 92	Wing Officer, 15 Sept. 93.—Officiating Wing Commander.
Lieut. F. de B. Hancock, Staff Corps	25 July 92	Wing Officer, 29 June 94.—Sick Furlough.
Lieut. N. S. Coghill, Royal Scots	30 Nov. 93	Officiating Wing Officer and Quarter Master.
Surgeon Captain W. E. Jennings, *MB.*	1 Oct. 87	In medical charge, 29 Jan. 92.—Furlough.
Surgeon Lieut. W. C. Sprague, *MD.*	30 Jan. 92	Officiating in medical charge.

24th Beloochistan Infantry (Raised 4 May 1820).—
Linked with 26th Regiment.
"ADEN"—"CENTRAL INDIA"—"AFGHANISTAN, 1879-80."
Head Quarters at Chaman. *Uniform, Drab. Facings, Red.*

Major A. A. Pearson, Staff Corps	1 July 87	Commandant, 5 Nov. 93.—Furlough. [Comdg. at Chaman.
Captain J. W. G. Tulloch, Staff Corps	11 Aug. 91	2nd in Command and Wing Comdr., 5 Nov. 93.—Offg. Comdt. and
Captain C. W. Jacob, Staff Corps	9 Sept. 93	Wing Commander, 5 Nov. 93.—Officiating 2nd in Command.
Lieut. H. F. Walters, Staff Corps	6 May 85	Wing Officer, 1 July 91.—S. S. O.—Offg. Wing Commander.
Lieut. E. F. Twigg, Staff Corps	27 Feb. 88	Wing Officer and Quarter Master, 1 July 91.
Lieut. W. H. Wooldridge, Staff Corps	25 Mar. 90	Wing Officer and Adjutant, 1 Oct. 93.
Lieut. M. L. Hornby, Staff Corps	18 Mar. 91	Wing Officer, 21 July 93.—Orderly Officer Waziristan Delimitation Escort.
Lieut. A. L. Tarver, Staff Corps	6 Aug. 92	Wing Officer.
2nd Lieut. W. A. Light, Staff Corps	28 Jan. 93	Wing Officer, 1 Apr. 94.—With 14 Bombay Infantry.
Lieut. W. J. Mitchell, Staff Corps	11 Apr. 93	Officiating Wing Officer.
Surgeon Major H. D. Masani	31 Mar. 89	In medical charge, 6 May 92.

25th Bombay Infantry (Raised 24 May 1820).
(Third Battalion The Bombay Rifle Regiment.)
Regimental Centre, Poona.
"MEEANEE"—"HYDERABAD"—"CENTRAL INDIA"—"ABYSSINIA"—"BURMA, 1885-87."
Head Quarters at Poona. *Uniform, Rifle Green. Facings, Red.*

Major L. G. Beckham, Staff Corps	13 June 94	Commandant, 12 May 94.
Captain R. Williams, Staff Corps	21 June 90	2nd in Command and Wing Commander, 12 May 94.
Captain F. R. H. Chapman, Staff Corps	12 Feb. 89	Wing Commander, 25 Dec. 93.—Superintendent of Army Schools, Bombay Presidency.—Sick Furlough.
Captain C. Tritton, Staff Corps	17 Apr. 91	Wing Officer, 15 Sept. 93.
Captain W. L. Conran, Staff Corps	10 May 93	Wing Officer, 7 Sept. 88.—Assistant Inspecting Officer, Rajpootana States, Imperial Service Infantry.
Lieut. T. A. Harrison, Staff Corps	7 Feb. 85	Wing Officer, 16 Aug. 89.—Assist. Mil. Accountant, 2nd Class.
Lieut. A. P. D. C. Stuart, Staff Corps	8 Dec. 86	Wing Officer, 2 Feb. 94.—Officiating Wing Commander.
Lieut. J. J. D. Sillery, Staff Corps	27 Feb. 88	Wing Officer and Adjutant, 7 Oct. 92.
Lieut. C. B. L. Clery, Staff Corps	2 Apr. 90	Wing Officer, 23 Oct. 91.—Burmah Military Police.
2nd Lieut. R. Dudgeon, Staff Corps	3 Sept. 92	Wing Officer, 5 March 94.
Lieut. G. H. Prevost, Staff Corps	7 Feb. 93	Wing Officer, 28 Sept. 94.—Officiating Quarter Master. Officiating Wing Officer.
Lieut. A. de S. Burton, Liverpool Regt.	4 Nov. 93	Officiating Wing Officer.
Surgeon Major A. V. Anderson, *MB.*	1 Apr. 94	In medical charge, 8 Feb. 89.—Acting Deputy Sanitary Commissioner, Central Registration District.

26th Beloochistan Infantry (Raised 9 March 1825).—
Linked with 24th Regiment.
"PERSIA"—"KHOOSHAB."
Head Quarters at Peshin. *Uniform, Drab. Facings, Red.*

Lt. Colonel W. G. W. Macbay, Staff Corps	23 Mar. 93	Commandant, 1 Nov. 92.—Furlough.
p.s.c. Major A. W. L. Bayly, *DSO.* S. C.	13 June 94	2nd in Command and Wing Commander, 1 Nov. 92.—Sick Furl.
Major W. G. Alban, Staff Corps	3 Jan. 94	Wing Comdr., 7 July 93.—Offg. Comdt. and Comdg. at Peshin.
Captain G. H. Turner, Staff Corps	23 Apr. 92	Wing Comdr., 1 Nov. 92.—Furlough.
Lieut. J. Parker, Staff Corps	30 Jan. 86	Wing Officer and Quarter Master, 1 Nov. 92.—Offg. 2nd in Comd.
Lieut. A. T. Rowlandson, Staff Corps	25 Aug. 86	Wing Officer and Adjutant, 1 Oct. 93.—Station Staff Officer.
Lieut. W. A. M. Bruce, Staff Corps	23 Dec. 88	Wing Officer, 4 Nov. 92.—Dep. Assist. Com. Gen. 2nd Class.
Lieut. R. S. Paul, Staff Corps	23 June 91	Wing Officer, 25 Nov. 92.
Lieut. H. S. Garratt, Staff Corps	10 July 91	Wing Officer, 28 Apr. 93.—Officiating Quarter Master.
Surgeon Captain G. W. Jenney, *MB.*	30 Mar. 89	In medical charge, 7 Apr. 93.—And Civil, Peshin.

27th Bombay Infantry, or 1st Belooch Regiment (*Light Infantry*)
(Raised 8 May 1844).—*Linked with 29th and 30th Regiments.—Regimental Centre, Kurrachee.*
"DELHI"—"ABYSSINIA"—"AFGHANISTAN, 1879-80"—"BURMA, 1885-87."
Head Quarters at Loralai. *Uniform, Dark Green. Facings, Red.*

Lt. Colonel W. A. Broome, Staff Corps	30 Sept. 94	Commandant, 16 Dec. 92.—And Commanding at Loralai.
Major A. L. Sinclair, *DSO.* Staff C.	2 Dec. 94	2nd in Command and Wing Commander, 16 Dec. 92.
Captain C. H. U. Price, Staff Corps	22 Oct. 92	Wing Commander, 16 Dec. 92.—S.S.O.
Captain M. J. Tighe, *DSO.* Staff Corps	25 Aug. 94	Wing Officer, 19 Nov. 86.
Captain F. J. Fowler, *DSO.* Staff Corps	25 Aug. 94	Wing Officer and Adjutant, 21 Jan. 87.—With Afghan-Beloochistan Boundary Commission.
Lieut. W. M. Southey, Staff Corps	30 Jan. 86	Wing Officer and Adjutant, 11 Sept. 91.
Lieut. C. F. Harold, Staff Corps	19 July 91	Wing Officer and Quarter Master, 7 Apr. 93.—Sick Furlough.
Lieut. J. H. Peck, Staff Corps	10 Aug. 91	Wing Officer, 28 Sept. 94.—Officiating Quarter Master.
Lieut. C. M. Moores, Staff Corps	30 Apr. 93	Officiating Wing Officer.
Surgeon Major S. T. Avetoom	2 Apr. 93	In medical charge, 27 July 88.

28th Bombay Infantry (*Pioneers*).—(Raised 21 January 1846).

Regimental Centre, Kirkee.

"*Progredior.*" "KANDAHAR, 1880"—"AFGHANISTAN, 1879-80"—"SUAKIN, 1885"—"TOFREK."
Head Quarters at **Kirkee**. *Uniform, Red. Facings, Yellow.*

Rank, Names, and Corps.	Army Rank.	Remarks.
Major R. E. D. Reilly, Staff Corps	15 June 85	Commandant, 24 Feb. 93.
℔ Captain W. St.L. Chase, Staff Corps	10 Sept. 86	2nd in Command and Wing Commander, 24 Feb. 93.—Furlough.
Captain L. H. Vidal, Staff Corps	1 May 89	Wing Commander, 24 Feb. 93.—Offg. D.A.A. Gen. Aden District.
Captain D. B. Thomson, Staff Corps	10 May 93	Wing Officer, 16 July 86.—Officiating Wing Commander.
Captain L. M. Foster, Staff Corps	6 Feb. 95	Wing Officer and Adjutant, 18 Feb. 87.—Furlough.
Captain G. A. Brownrigg, Staff Corps	9 Sept. 93	Wing Officer, 22 July 87.
Lieut. F. M. Lane, Staff Corps	20 Sept. 91	Wing Officer, 5 Jan. 94.—Officiating Adjutant.
Lieut. G. D. M. Moore, Staff Corps	1 Mar. 92	Wing Officer, 23 Nov. 94.
Lieut. H. V. M. Langtry, Staff Corps	21 May 92	Officiating Wing Officer and Quarter Master.
Surgeon Captain T. W. Shaw, MB.	30 Sept. 89	In medical charge, 5 Oct. 94.—Officiating 1 Central India Horse.
Surgeon Lieut. F. E. Swinton	27 July 92	Officiating in medical charge.

29th (*The Duke of Connaught's Own*) Bombay Infantry, *or* 2nd Belooch Regt.

(*Raised 6 May* 1846).—*Linked with* 27*th and* 30*th Regiments.*—*Regimental Centre, Kurrachee.*

"PERSIA"—"RESHIRE"—"BUSHIRE"—"KHOOSHAB"—"KANDAHAR, 1880"—"AFGHANISTAN, 1879-80"—
"EGYPT, 1882" "TEL-EL-KEBIR."

Head Quarters at **Hyderabad**. Detachment at **Jacobabad**. *Uniform, Dark Green. Facings, Red.*

Hon. Colonel.—General H.R.H. Arthur W. P. A. Duke of Connaught, KG, KT, KP, GCSI, GCMG, GCIE, CB.

℔ Lt. Colonel O'M. Creagh, Staff Corps	2 Oct. 92	Commandant, 15 Apr. 90.—And Commanding at Hyderabad.
Captain A. C. Yate, Staff Corps	22 Sept. 87	2nd in Command and Wing Commander, 16 Apr. 94.—Furlough.
Captain G. S. Broome, Staff Corps	10 May 93	Wing Commander, 16 Apr. 94.—Officiating 2nd in Command. Station Staff Officer and Cantonment Magistrate, Hyderabad.
Captain F. J. S. Lowry, Staff Corps	1 May 89	Wing Officer, 22 Feb. 84.—Furlough.
Captain A. E. Hatch, Staff Corps	25 Aug. 94	Wing Officer, 18 Feb. 87.—Officiating Wing Commander.
Lieut. H. P. E. Parker, Staff Corps	29 Aug. 85	Wing Officer, 16 May 90.—At Jacobabad.
Lieut. C. O. O. Tanner, Staff Corps	10 Nov. 86	Wing Officer and Adjutant, 1 Aug. 90.
Lieut. J. A. Hannyngton, Staff Corps	2 Mar. 91	Wing Officer, 16 Apr. 94.—Officiating Quarter Master.
2nd Lieut. W. N. Hay, Royal Artillery	24 July 91	Officiating Wing Officer.
Surgeon Major H. Adey	1 Oct. 89	In medical charge, 18 March 81.

30th Bombay Infantry, *or* 3rd Belooch Battalion (*late Jacob's Rifles*)

—*Raised* 30 *June* 1858.—*Linked with* 27*th and* 29*th Regiments.*—*Regimental Centre, Kurrachee.*

"AFGHANISTAN, 1878-80."

Head Quarters at **Kurrachee**. *Uniform, Dark Green. Facings, Red.*

Major R. C. G. Mayne, Staff Corps	21 Dec. 92	Commandant, 10 Apr. 94.
Captain G. E. Even, Staff Corps	21 Sept. 86	2nd in Command and Wing Commander, 21 Oct. 92.—Furlough.
Captain R. Southey, Staff Corps	14 Jan. 91	Wing Commander, 7 July 93.—Officiating 2nd in Command.
Captain J. O. Mennie, Staff Corps	6 Feb. 95	Wing Officer, 25 Feb. 87.—A. D. C. to Brig. Gen. J. Jopp.
Lieut. A. Le G. Jacob, Staff Corps	30 Jan. 86	Wing Officer and Adjutant, 18 Jan. 89.—Offg. Wing Commander and Cantonment Magistrate, Kurrachee.
Lieut. E. L. C. Berger, Staff Corps	1 Feb. 86	Wing Officer, 21 Aug. 91.—With Hong Kong Regiment.
Lieut. C. U. Price, Staff Corps	4 Jan. 90	Wing Officer, 9 Oct. 91.—Furlough.
Lieut. A. L. Jacob, Staff Corps	21 Apr. 92	Wing Officer and Quarter Master, 7 July 93.—Offg. Adjutant.
Lieut. R. J. C. Eastwood, Staff Corps	3 June 92	Wing Officer, 23 Feb. 94.—Officiating Quarter Master and in charge of Native Details.
2nd Lt. R. H. Palin, Staff Corps	28 Jan. 93	Wing Officer, 9 Nov. 94.
Surgeon Major M. B. Braganza	2 Apr. 93	In medical charge, 6 May 92.

Bombay Medical Department.

[For the explanation of the qualifications of the following Officers, *see* page iii.]

SURGEON MAJOR GENERAL.	ASSISTANT SURGEON.	SURGEON MAJ. GEN.	REMARKS.
Turnbull, Peter Stephenson,[1] *MD*.	1 Oct. 60	26 Feb. 93	With the Government of Bombay.
SURGEON COLONELS.		SURG. COL.	
Cook, Henry, *MD. LRCS. Ed.*	31 Mar. 65	18 Sept. 90	Nagpore District.
Hughes, David Erskine, *MD. FRCS. Ed.*	31 Mar. 66	15 Sept. 92	Bombay, Deesa and Aden Districts.
Bowman, Robert,[15] *LRCPI. LRCS.*	31 Mar. 66	26 Feb. 93	Sind District.

BRIGADE SURGEON LIEUTENANT COLONELS.		BRIG. SURG LT. COL.	RANK OF LT. COL.	
Barry, Andrew,[13] *MD. FRCS. Ed.*	31 Mar. 65	26 Feb. 88	31 Mar. 85	6 Bombay Cavalry.
Banks, Samuel O'Brien,[16] *MRCPI. FRCSI.*	1 Oct. 66	19 Nov. 89	1 Oct. 86	Presidency Surgeon, 2nd District, and Marine Surgeon.
Maconachie, George Archibald,[17] *MD. MCh. MRCP.*	1 Apr. 67	1 May 90	1 Apr. 87	Ophthalmic Surgeon, and Principal and Prof. of Ophthalmic Medicine, &c., Grant Med. College.
Bainbridge, George, *LRCP. MRCS. LSA.*	1 Apr. 67	18 Sept. 90	1 Apr. 87	Civil Surgeon, Kurrachee.
Arnott, James,[19] *MD. MCh.*	1 Apr. 67	30 Apr. 91	1 Apr. 87	Physician, St. George's Hospital.
Hay, George William Robertson, *MD. LRCS. Ed.*	1 Apr. 68	3 Dec. 92	1 Apr. 88	Secretary to P. M. O. Bombay Army.
Peters, Charles Thomas,[28] *MB. LRCP. Ed. LRCS. Ed.*	1 Apr. 69	26 Feb. 93	1 Apr. 89	Civil Surgeon, Bejapore.
MacRury, Collin William, *FRCS. Ed. LRCP. Ed.*	1 Apr. 69	12 Apr. 93	1 Apr. 89	Sanitary Commissioner for Government of Bombay.
Salaman, Selim Myer, *MD. MCh. MRCS.*	1 Oct. 69	7 May 94	1 Oct. 89	Superintendent Yerrowda Central Jail.

SURGEON LIEUTENANT COLONELS.		SURGEON LT. COL.	
Haliday, Saunders Barton,[21] *LRCP. Ed. MRCS.*	1 Apr. 67	1 Apr. 87	13 Bombay Infantry.
Jayakar, Atmaram S. Grandin, *LRCP. MRCS.*	30 Sept. 67	30 Sept. 87	Civil Surgeon, Muscat. — Officiating Political Agent, Muscat.
Barker, Frederick Charles, *MD. FRCSI.*	1 Oct. 69	1 Oct. 89	Kattywar Political Agency, &c.
Caldecott, Randolph, *LRCP. Ed. MRCS.*	1 Oct. 69	1 Oct. 89	Residency Surgeon and Civil Administrative Medical Officer, Central India.
Waters, George, *LRCP. Ed. LRCS. Ed.*	1 Oct. 69	1 Oct. 89	Presidency Surgeon, 3rd District, with medical charge of Jails, House of Correction, and Byculla Schools.
M'Conaghy, William, *MD. LRCSI.*	1 Oct. 69	1 Oct. 89	Civil Surgeon, Supdt. B. J. Medical School and Superintendent Lunatic Asylum, Poona.
Weir, Thomas Stephenson, *LRCPI. LRCSI.*	1 Apr. 70	1 Apr. 90	Bombay.—Health Officer to the Municipality.
Bartholomeusz, Matthew Lorenz,[30] *MB. MCh.*	30 Sept. 73	30 Sept. 93	Civil Surgeon and Supdt. B. J. Medical School and Lunatic Asylum, Ahmedabad.—Furl.
Wilkins, James Sutherland,[31] *DSO. LRCP. MRCS.*	31 Mar. 74	31 Mar. 94	21 Bombay Infantry.
Barren, William Alexander,[32] *LRCP. Ed. LRCS. Ed.*	31 Mar. 74	31 Mar. 94	Sappers and Miners.
Parakh, Dhanjisha Navroji, *LRCP. MRCS.*	30 Sept. 74	30 Sept. 94	Surgeon Goculdass Tejpal Native General Hosp.
Dane, Arthur Hy. Cole,[34] *MD. LRCPI. FRCSI.*	31 Mar. 75	31 Mar. 95	Bhopaul Battalion.
Greany, John Philip, *MD. MCh.*	31 Mar. 75	31 Mar. 95	Civil Surgeon, Belgaum.—Furlough.
Burroughs, George Edward Elton,[35] *LRCPI. MRCS. LSA.*	31 Mar. 75	31 Mar. 95	Sick Furlough.
M'Cloghry, James,[36] *LRCPI. FRCSI.*	31 Mar. 75	31 Mar. 95	Civil Surgeon, Broach.—Acting Civil and Supdt. B. J. Medical School and Lunatic Asylum, Ahmedabad.

SURGEON MAJORS.		SURGEON.	SURGEON MAJOR.	
Clarkson, John Wilkins,[37] *LRCP. MRCS.*		30 Sept. 75	30 Sept. 87	Dep. Sanitary Commr., Western Registration Dist.
Parker, Joseph,[38] *MD. MCh.*		30 Sept. 75	30 Sept. 87	Medical Storekeeper, Bombay.
MacGregor, John,[39] *MD. MCh.*		31 Mar. 76	31 Mar. 88	20 Bombay Infantry.
Stewart, Alexander Kenneth,[40] *MB. MCh. LRCS. Ed.*		31 Mar. 76	31 Mar. 88	4 Cavalry.
Henderson, William George Hume,[41] *LRCPI. FRCSI.*		31 Mar. 76	31 Mar. 88	Civil Surgeon and Superintendent Lunatic Asylum and Medical School, Hyderabad.
Dalal, Kharshedji Ardeshir, *MB. MCh.*		31 Mar. 76	31 Mar. 88	Civil Surgeon, Dhoolia.
Boyd, Henry Walker Butler, *LRCPI. FRCSI.*		31 Mar. 76	31 Mar. 88	Superintendent Colaba Lunatic Asylum.
Channer, Osborne Henry,[44] *MB. MCh*		30 Sept. 76	30 Sept. 88	Deputy Sanitary Commissioner, Southern Registration Districts. [School, Poona.
Young, Edward William, *MD. LRCS. Ed.*		30 Sept. 76	30 Sept. 88	Staff Surgeon, and Med. Officer R. C. Orphanage
M'Calman, Hugh, *MD. MCh.*		30 Sept. 76	30 Sept. 88	Civil Surgeon and Superintendent Lunatic Asylum, Dharwar.
Hatch, Wm. Keith,[45] *MB. MCh. FRCS.*		31 Mar. 77	31 Mar. 89	Senior Med. Officer, Jamsetjee Jejeebhoy Hosp., and Prof. of Surg., &c., Grant Med. College.
Masani, Hormasji Dadabhoi,[46] *LRCP. MRCS.*		31 Mar. 77	31 Mar. 89	24 Bombay Infantry.
Kirtikar, Kanoba Ranchhoddas,[47] *LRCP. MRCS.*		31 Mar. 77	31 Mar. 89	Civil Surgeon, Tanna.
Manser, Robert,[48] *MRCS. LSA.*		1 Oct. 77	1 Oct. 89	1st Physician Jamsetjee Jejeebhoy Hosp. & Prof. of Medicine, &c., Grant Medical College.
Adey, Henry,[49] *MB. MCh.*		1 Oct. 77	1 Oct. 89	20 Bombay Infantry.
Street, Alfred William Fredk.,[50] *DSO. LRCP. MRCS.*		1 Oct. 77	1 Oct. 89	Deputy Sanitary Commissioner, Central Registration District.—Furlough.
Jervis, Hy. Pruce,[51] *LRCS. Ed. LSA.*		1 Oct. 77	1 Oct. 89	7 Bombay Infantry.
Davidson, D. Chas. *LRCP. Ed. LRCS. Ed.*		1 Oct. 77	1 Oct. 89	Civil Surgeon, Sattara.
Peacocke, James Chas. Harding, *LRCPI. LRCSI.*		1 Oct. 77	1 Oct. 89	Dep. Sanitary Commr., Sind Registration Districts.—Acting Civil Surgeon, Belgaum.
Nariman, Kaikhoso Sorabji,[52] *LRCS. Ed. LSA.*		1 Oct. 77	1 Oct. 89	Civil, Surat.
Sargent, Arthur Francis,[53] *MRCS. LSA.*		1 Oct. 77	1 Oct. 89	3 Bombay Infantry.
Monks, Charles,[54] *LRCPI. LRCSI.*		30 Mar. 78	30 Mar. 90	Superintendent, Mahableshwur.

Bombay Medical Department.

Surgeon Majors.	Surgeon.	Surgeon Major.	Remarks.
Damania, PhirozshaJamsetjee,[55] LRCS. Ed. LSA.	30 Mar. 78	30 Mar. 90	22 Bombay Infantry.
Bull, George Henry,[56] MD. MCh.	30 Mar. 78	30 Mar. 90	4 Bombay Infantry.
MacCartie, Frederick Fitzgerald,[57] MB. BCh.	30 Mar. 78	30 Mar. 90	Health Officer, Port of Bombay.
Lowdell, Charles George Walton, LRCP. MRCS.	30 Sept. 78	30 Sept. 90	Civil Surgeon, Nassick.
Briggs, Harry Beecham,[58] MB.MRCS.LSA.	30 Sept. 78	30 Sept. 90	12 Bombay Infantry.
Carson, Walter Peter,[59] MB. LRCSI.	30 Sept. 78	30 Sept. 90	Port Surgeon, Aden.
Faulkner, Alexander Samuel,[60] FRCS.Ed. MRCPI. MRCS	30 Sept. 78	30 Sept. 90	Agency Surgeon, Ulwur.—Sick Furlough.
Willis, Chas. Fancourt,[61] MD. MRCP.Ed. MRCS.	31 Oct. 79	31 Oct. 91	9 Bombay Infantry.
Dimmock, Henry Peers, LRCP. MRCS.	31 Mar. 80	31 Mar. 92	Obstetric Physician, Jamsetjee Jejeebhoy Hospital, and Prof. of Midwifery, Grant Med. Coll., and Presidency Surgeon, 1st District.
Maitland, Chas. Bradley,[63] LRCP.Ed.MRCS.	31 Mar. 80	31 Mar. 92	1 Bombay Lancers.
Ferguson, Alex. Fredk.[64] MB. MCh. MD.	2 Oct. 80	2 Oct. 92	19 Bombay Infantry.
Mistri, Kavasji Hormasji,[65] LRCS.Ed. LSA.	2 Oct. 80	2 Oct. 92	Civil, Godhra.
Fooks, George Ernest,[66] MRCS. LSA.	2 Oct. 80	2 Oct. 92	16 Bombay Infantry.
Anderson, Joseph William Townsend, LRCP.Ed. LRCS. Ed. LSA.	2 Oct. 80	2 Oct. 92	Civil Surgeon, Aden.
Milne,Alexander,MA. MB. MCh.Ab. P.B.M. 81	2 Apr. 81	2 Apr. 93	Deputy Assay Master, Calcutta Mint.
Baker, Richard John, MD. LRCSI.	2 Apr. 81	2 Apr. 93	Residency Surgeon, Turkish Arabia, Bagdad.
Corkery,Wm.Alf.[67] LRCP. Ed. LFPS.Glas.	2 Apr. 81	2 Apr. 93	Civil Surgeon, Sukkor.
Braganza, Moscardi Bellarmin,[68] LFPS. Glas. LSA.	2 Apr. 81	2 Apr. 93	30 Bombay Infantry.
Avetoom, Sarkies Thaddeus,[69] LRCP.Ed. LRCS.Ed.	2 Apr. 81	2 Apr. 93	27 Bombay Infantry.
Stevenson, Henry Wickham, MRCS. LSA.	2 Apr. 81	2 Apr. 93	Civil Surgeon, Ahmednugger.
Lyons, Robert William Steele, MD. MCh.	1 Apr. 82	1 Apr. 94	2 Bombay Lancers.
Barry, John Patrick,[70] BA. MB. LRCSI.	1 Apr. 82	1 Apr. 94	Superintendent, Matheran.
Anderson, Alexander Vass,[71] MB. MCh.	1 Apr. 82	1 Apr. 94	25 Bombay Infantry.
Burke, William Henry,[72] BA. MB. BCh.	30 Sept. 82	30 Sept. 94	Assistant Civil Surgeon, Poona.
M'Crimmin, John,[73] LRCPI. LRCSI.	30 Sept. 82	30 Sept. 94	Civil Surgeon, Rutnagherry.
Collie, Mackintosh Alex. T., MB. MCh. LRCP.Ed. LRCS.Ed.	31 Mar. 83	31 Mar. 95	Resident Surgeon, St. George's Hosp., Bombay, and Prof of Materia Medica, &c., G. M. Coll.
Quicke, William Henry,[74] MRCS. LSA.	31 Mar. 83	31 Mar. 95	2nd Surgeon, Jamsetjee Jejeebhoy Hospital, and Professor of Anatomy and Curator of Museum, Grant Medical College.

Surgeon Captains.		Surgeon Captain.	
Sarkies, Carrapiet John, MB. MCh.		29 Sept. 83	8 Bombay Infantry.
Grayfoot, Blenman Bahot, LRCP.Ed. LRCS.Ed. LFPS.Glas. MRCS.		30 Sept. 86	Secretary to Surg. Gen. with Govt. of Bombay.
Dyson, Thomas Edward, MB. MCh.		30 Sept. 86	Dep. Sanitary Commissioner, Goozerat Registration District.
Meyer, Charles Hardwick Louw, MD. MRCS. H.P. M.G.M. '87		31 Mar. 87	Prof. of Physiology, Histology and Hygiene, Grant Medical College.
Childe, Letterstedt Frederick, BA. MB. MRCS.		31 Mar. 87	2nd Phys.& RegistrarJamsetjee JejeebhoyHosp. and Prof. of Pathology, &c. Grant Med. Coll.
Herbert, Herbert,[76] LRCP. MRCS.		31 Mar. 87	Civil, Kaira.
Barry, Thomas David Collis, LRCPI. MRCS.		31 Mar. 87	Chemical Analyser to Govt. and Professor of Chemistry, &c., Grant Medical College, &c.
Jones, John Lloyd Thomas, MB. MRCS.		1 Oct. 87	7 Bombay Lancers.
Jennings, William Ernest, MB. MCh.		1 Oct. 87	23 Bombay Infantry.
Hojel, James Graham, BA. MB. BCh. MRCPI.		31 Mar. 88	5 Bombay Cavalry.
Arnim, Henry Charles Loffler, LRCP. MRCS.		31 Mar. 88	10 Bombay Infantry.
Thomson, George Sloane, MB. MCh.		31 Mar. 88	14 Bombay Infantry.
Prall, Samuel Esmond, MB. LRCP. MRCS.		29 Sept. 88	17 Bombay Infantry.
Ricketts, William Symonds Percival, MB. MCh.		30 Mar. 89	17 Bombay Infantry.
Moore, Charles Malcolm, MD.		30 Mar. 89	2 Central India Horse.
Jenney, George William, MB. MCh.		30 Mar. 89	26 Bombay Infantry.
Hudson, Charles Tilson, LRCP. MRCS.		30 Mar. 89	2 Bombay Infantry.
Smith, John Blackburn, BA. MB. MCh.		30 Sept. 89	Civil Surgeon, Shikarpore.
Cleveland, Henry Francis, LRCP. MRCS. LSA.		30 Sept. 89	3 Bombay Cavalry.
Shaw, Townsend Wharton, MB. BCh.		30 Sept. 89	28 Bombay Infantry.
Jackson, James, MB.		31 Mar. 90	Superintendent Central Prison, Hyderabad, Sind.
Street, Ashton,[78] MB. FRCS.		31 Mar. 90	1 Bombay Infantry.
Heath, Alan Jasper, MB. LRCP. MRCS.		31 Mar. 90	Officiating 2 Bombay Lancers.
Jameson, John Bland, MB. MCh.		31 Mar. 90	Officiating 5 Bombay Cavalry.
Whitcombe, Ernest Gerald Robert, LRCP.Ed. LRCS.Ed. LFPS.Glas.		31 Jan. 91	Officiating 1 Bombay Lancers.
Basu, Baman Das, LSA. MRCS.		31 Jan. 91	Officiating 8 Bombay Infantry.
Irvine, Thomas Walter, MB. MCh.		28 July 91	Officiating Sappers and Miners.
Sprague,William Carr, MD. MCh. LRCP. MRCS.		30 Jan. 95	Officiating 23 Bombay Infantry.

Surgeon Lieutenants.		Surgeon Lieut.	
Swinton, Francis Edward, LRCP. MRCS.		27 July 92	Officiating 28 Bombay Infantry.
Barnett, Sidney Harvey, MB. MCh.		27 July 92	General duty, Sind District.
Jackson, Thomas, MB. BCh.		27 July 92	Officiating 5 Bombay Infantry.
Kilkelly, Patrick Percy, MB. BCh.		29 July 93	Wing 7 Bombay Infantry.
Leumann, Bernard Henry Frederick		29 Jan. 94	Officiating 10 Bombay Infantry.
Bennett, Hugh		29 Jan. 94	Officiating 12 Bombay Infantry.
Bennett, Vivian Bosse		28 July 94	Officiating 20 Bombay Infantry.
Moore, Hugh Myddelton		28 July 94	Officiating 1 Bombay Infantry.
Johnston, Dudley Cator		28 July 94	General Duty, Sind District.
Evans, Samuel		29 Jan. 95	
M'Donald, James Harding		29 Jan. 95	

[1] Surgeon Major General P. S. Turnbull served in the Abyssinian war in 1867-68 and was present at the action of Arogee and at the storming of Magdala (Medal).
[13] Brigade Surgeon Lt.Colonel A. Barry served in the Abyssinian war in 1867-68 (Medal). Served in the Afghan war in 1880, and took part in the march to Candahar with the force under Major General Phayre (Medal).
[15] Surgeon Colonel Bowman served in the Abyssinian war of 1867-68 in medical charge of the 3rd Sind Horse (Medal).
[16] Brigade Surgeon Lt.Colonel S. O. Banks served in the Abyssinian campaign in 1867-68, and was present at the capture of Magdala (Medal).
[17] Brigade Surgeon Lt.Colonel G. A. Maconachie served with the 3rd Sind Horse in the Abyssinian war in 1867-68 (Medal).
[19] Brigade Surgeon Lt.Colonel J. Arnott served with the Field Hospital during the Abyssinian war in 1867-68 (Medal). Served in the Afghan war in 1879-80 as Principal Medical Officer of the Reserve Brigade in the Bolan Pass, and in medical charge of the Head Quarters Staff at the defence of Candahar (mentioned in despatches), and was present in the sortie of Deh Khojah (mentioned in despatches) and at the battle of Candahar (Medal with Clasp).
[21] Surgeon Lt.Colonel S. B. Haliday served in the Abyssinian war in 1867-68 as Assistant Surgeon of a Hospital Ship (Medal). Served in the Afghan war in 1879-80 in medical charge of the 13th Bombay Native Infantry (Medal).
[28] Brigade Surgeon Lt.Colonel C. T. Peters served with the Zhob Valley Expedition in 1884. Served with the Burmese Expedition in 1885-87 (Medal with two Clasps).
[30] Surgeon Lt.Colonel M. L. Bartholomeusz served in the Afghan war in 1880 (Medal).
[31] Surgeon Lt.Colonel J. S. Wilkins served in the Afghan war in 1880, and took part in the march to Candahar with the force under Major General Phayre (Medal). Served with the Burmese Expedition in 1886-87 (mentioned in despatches, Medal with two Clasps).
[32] Surgeon Lt.Colonel W. A. Barren served in the Afghan war in 1880 in medical charge of the 4th Bombay Native Infantry (Medal). Served with the Burmese Expedition in 1886-88 (Medal with two Clasps).
[34] Surgeon Lt.Colonel A. H. C. Dane served in the Afghan war in 1879-80, and was present in the engagements at Girishk, in the defence of Candahar including the sortie of Deh Khojah, and at the battle of Candahar (mentioned in despatches, Medal with Clasp).
[35] Surgeon Lt.Colonel G. E. E. Burroughs served in the Afghan war of 1878-80, and was present in the engagements at Khushk-i-Nakhud (mentioned in despatches) and Girishk, at the defence of Candahar, and at the battle of Candahar (Medal with Clasp).
[36] Surgeon Lt.Colonel J. M'Cloghry served in the Afghan war of 1878-80 in Southern Afghanistan (Medal).
[37] Surgeon Major J. W. Clarkson served in the Afghan war in 1880 in Southern Afghanistan (Medal). Served with the Burmese Expedition in 1887-88 (Medal with Clasp).
[38] Surgeon Major J. Parker served with the Burmese Expedition in 1886-89 (Medal with two Clasps).
[39] Surgeon Major John MacGregor served with the Burmese Expedition in 1885-87 including the expeditions to Mogaung, against the Kachins on the frontier of China and against the Shans near Mandalay (mentioned in despatches, Medal with two Clasps).
[40] Surgeon Major A. K. Stewart served in the Afghan war in 1880, took part in the defence of Candahar including the sortie of Deh Khojah (twice slightly wounded), and was present at the battle of Candahar (Medal with Clasp).
[41] Surgeon W. G. H. Henderson served with the Burmese Expedition in 1887-88 (mentioned in despatches, Medal with Clasp).
[44] Surgeon Major O. H. Channer served in the Afghan war in 1879-80 in Southern Afghanistan (mentioned in despatches, Medal).
[45] Surgeon Major W. K. Hatch served in the Afghan war in 1880 in Southern Afghanistan (Medal).
[46] Surgeon Major H. D. Masani served in the Afghan war in 1879 as Sanitary Officer in the Bolan Pass (Medal). Served in the operations of the Zhob Field Force in 1890.
[47] Surgeon Major K. R. Kirtikar served in the Afghan war in 1879-80, and was present in the engagement at Girishk and at the defence of Candahar (Medal).
[48] Surgeon Major R. Manser served in the Afghan war in 1879-80, and took part in the defence of Candahar (Medal).
[49] Surgeon Major H. Adey served in the Afghan war in 1879-80 in Southern Afghanistan (Medal). Served in the Egyptian war in 1882, and was present at the battle of Tel-el-Kebir (Medal with Clasp, and Khedive's Star).
[50] Surgeon Major A. W. F. Street served in the Afghan war of 1878-80, and was present in the engagement with the Wali's mutinous troops in July 1880, in the defence of Candahar, and at the battle of Candahar (Medal with Clasp). Served with the Burmese Expedition in 1886-87 (mentioned in despatches, DSO., and Medal with Clasp).
[51] Surgeon Major H. P. Jervis served with the Burmese Expedition in 1885-87 (Medal with Clasp).
[52] Surgeon Major K. S. Nariman served with the Burmese Expedition in 1885-87 (Medal with Clasp).
[53] Surgeon Major A. F. Sargent and Surgeon Captain W. H. Quicke served with the Zhob Valley Expedition in 1884.
[54] Surgeon Major Monks served in the Afghan war in 1880 with the Southern Afghanistan Field Force (Medal).
[55] Surgeon Major P. J. Damania served in the Afghan war in 1880 with the Base Hospital at Candahar, and in medical charge of the Depot Hospital at Gulistan (Medal). Served with the Burmese Expedition in 1885-87 (Medal with Clasp).
[56] Surgeon Major G. H. Bull served with the Burmese Expedition in 1885-89 (Medal with two Clasps).
[57] Surgeon Major F. F. MacCartie served in the Afghan war in 1880 (Medal).
[58] Surgeon Major H. B. Briggs served with the Burmese Expedition in 1885-87 (Medal with Clasp).
[59] Surgeon Major W. P. Carson served in the Afghan war in 1880 (Medal). Served with the Burmese Expedition in 1885-87 (Medal with Clasp).
[60] Surgeon Major A. S. Faulkner served in the Afghan war in 1879-80 with the Southern Afghanistan Field Force (Medal).
[61] Surgeon Major C. F. Willis served in the Egyptian war of 1882 with the Cavalry Field Hospital, Indian Contingent, and was present at the battle of Tel-el-Kebir and at the capture of Cairo (Medal with Clasp, and Khedive's Star).
[63] Surgeon Major C. B. Maitland served in the Egyptian war of 1882 (Medal, and Khedive's Star). Served with the Burmese Expedition in 1886-88 (Medal with two Clasps).
[64] Surgeon Major A. F. Ferguson served with the Burmese Expedition in 1885-87 (Medal with Clasp).
[65] Surgeon Major K. H. Mistri served with the Burmese Expedition in 1886-88 (Medal with Clasp).
[65] Surgeon Major G. E. Fooks served with the Zhob Valley Expedition in 1884.
[67] Surgeon Major W. A. Corkery served with the Burmese Expedition in 1885-87 (Medal with Clasp).
[68] Surgeon Major M. B. Braganza served with the Burmese Expedition in 1885 (Medal with Clasp).
[69] Surgeon Major S. T. Avetoom served in the Soudan campaign in 1885 (Medal with Clasp, and Khedive's Star). Served with the Burmese Expedition in 1888-89 (Medal with Clasp).
[70] Surgeon Major J. P. Barry served with the Burmese Expedition in 1886-87 (mentioned in despatches, Medal with Clasp).
[71] Surgeon Major A. V. Anderson served with the second Miranzai Expedition in 1891 (Medal with Clasp).
[72] Surgeon Major W. H. Burke served with the Burmese Expedition in 1886-87 (Medal with Clasp).
[73] Surgeon Major John Crimmin served with the Burmese Expedition in 1886-89 (mentioned in despatches, Victoria Cross, and Medal with two Clasps): was awarded the VC for the following act of bravery:—"Lieutenant Tighe, 27th Bombay Infantry (to the Mounted Infantry of which Corps Surgeon Crimmin was attached), states that in the action near Lwekaw, Eastern Karenni, on the 1st January, 1889, four men charged with him into the midst of a large body of the enemy who were moving off from the Karen left flank, and two men fell to the ground wounded He saw Surgeon Crimmin attending one of the men about 200 yards to the rear. Karens were round the party in every direction, and he saw several fire at Surgeon Crimmin and the wounded man. A Sepoy then galloped up to Surgeon Crimmin, and the latter joined the fighting line which then came up. Lieutenant Tighe further states that very shortly afterwards they were engaged in driving the enemy from small clumps of trees and bamboo, in which the Karens took shelter. Near one of these clumps he saw Surgeon Crimmin attending a wounded

Bombay Medical Department.—War Services.

man. Several Karens rushed out at him; Surgeon Crimmin thrust his sword through one of them, and attacked a second, a third Karen then dropped from the fire of a Sepoy, upon which the remaining Karens fled."
[74] Surgeon Major W. H. Quicke served with the Zhob Valley Expedition in 1884 including the engagement at Dowlatzai. Served with the Burmese Expedition in 1885-86 (Medal with Clasp).
[75] Surgeon Captain H. Herbert served in the operations of the Zaila Field Force in 1890.
[78] Surgeon Captain A. Street served with the second Miranzai Expedition in 1891 (Medal with Clasp).

Bombay Veterinary Department.

Veterinary Lt. Colonel.	Veterinary Surgeon.	Date of Present Rank.	Remarks.

Bombay Ecclesiastical Establishment.

The Right Reverend Louis George Mylne, *MA. DD.* Bishop of Bombay, 6 July 1876.—Sick Furlough.
Venerable Alexander Goldwyer Lewis, *BA. BD.* Archdeacon and Commissary, 13 Oct. 1890.
John Cuthbert Greenside Bowen, Esq. Registrar of the Diocese, 19 Nov. 94.

Year of App		Stations, etc.
	Senior Chaplains. *Monthly Salary, Rupees 800.*	
1875	*Ven.* Alex. Goldwyer Lewis, *BA. BD.*	Archdeacon and Commissary.
1876	*Rev.* William Wingate, *MA*	Deolalee.
1876	*Rev.* Arthur Wilfred Baynham, *MA.*	Ahmednugger.
1878	*Rev.* George Gothard, *MA.*	Satara and Mahableshwur.
1878	*Rev.* Henry Nathaniel Midwinter, *MA.*	Officiating at Aden.
1878	*Rev.* Charles Hume Badham, *BA.*	St. Paul's, Poona.
1879	*Rev.* George Herbert Lewis, *BA.*	Presidency Chaplain.
1880	*Rev.* Elias Jenkins Bowen, *MA.*	Belgaum.
1884	*Rev.* Philip Bruce Horne, *MA.*	St. Mary's, Poona.
	Junior Chaplains. *Monthly Salary, Rupees 500.*	
1885	*Rev.* William Worters Baillie, *BA.*	Dharwar.
1885	*Rev.* Edward Stephenson Hall, *MA.*	Deesa and Aboo.
1885	*Rev.* William Edward Scott, *BA.*	Domestic Chaplain to the Bishop.
1886	*Rev.* Francis Nathaniel Hill, *BA.*	Officiating Senior Presidency Chaplain, Bombay.
1887	*Rev.* John Henry Beck, *MA.*	Sick Furlough.
1887	*Rev.* Philip Sydney Grove, *BA.*	Furlough.
1887	*Rev.* William Babington Preston, *BA.*	Nusseerabad.
1888	*Rev.* John Annand Sellar, *MA.*	Ghorpadee, Poona.
1889	*Rev.* Henry Thomas Higginson Rountree	Neemuch.
1889	*Rev.* Lancelot Melvill Haslope, *MA.*	Kirkee.
1889	*Rev.* Sidney Leigh Lye, *BA.*	Garrison Chaplain, Bombay.
1889	*Rev.* Philip Raikes Harrison	Ahmedabad.
1890	*Rev.* Alfred York Browne	Steamer Point, Aden.
1891	*Rev.* William Arthur Dickins	Sick Furlough.
1892	*Rev.* Charles E. Cambridge de Coetlogon	Colaba.
1892	*Rev.* Cyril Maybew	Byculla.
1893	*Rev.* Horatio William Nelson, *BA.*	Aden Camp.

CHURCH OF SCOTLAND.

	The Senior Chaplain. *Monthly Salary, Rupees 980.*	
	Senior Chaplains. *Monthly Salary, Rupees 800.*	
1875	*Rev.* Thomas H. Greig.	St. Andrew's, Bombay.—Furlough.
1878	*Rev.* Andrew Bullock Watson, *MA.*	Officiating St. Andrew's, Bombay.
1878	*Rev.* James Hutton Mackay, *MA.*	Poona and Kirkee.
1882	*Rev.* James Henderson, *MA.*	Kurrachee.
	Junior Chaplains. *Monthly Salary, Rupees 500.*	

INDEX TO THE ACTIVE LIST.

Abadie, George H. F. ... 158
— Harry Bertram 153
— Henry Richard 17
Abbey, Walter B. T. 440
Abbott, Frank 47, 412
— George Masson ...40, 409
— Henry Alexius......47, 412
— Henry Byam 40, 409
— Herbert E. Stacy...68, 209
— Sir James 179
Abdy, Anthony John 65, 169
Abercrombie, Alex. H.63, 262
— Alexander William ... 334
Aberigh-Mackay, James Livingston 45, 411
Abrahall, Chris. H. H. ... 401
— John H. 400
Abud, Henry M. 418
Acheson, Percival H. 67, 366
Acland-Troyte, Hugh L. 162
a'Court, Charles........... 356
— Leonard Holmes 308
Acton, Hy. L. Barnwell ... 424
— James Lowry Cole ... 334
— Thomas H. E. 61, 169
Acworth, G. P. Aufrère 212
— Louis Raymond 277
Adair, Arthur C. 264
— Charles Osborn 174
— Desmond 321
— Henry Benjamin N.... 209
— Hugh Robert 172
— William Thompson 52, 399
Adam, Clement Geo. M. 156
— Fred. Archibald 284
— Frederick Loch........ 233
Adams, Alexander 213
— Archibald 504
— Charles 505
— Francis 362
— George Stopford 261
— Gofton Gee 382
— Hamilton John Goold 231
— Henry E. F. Goold 172
— Henry Coker 24
— John C. 401
— Richard 386
— Robert Bellew 419
— Robt. Frederick 380
— Robert Henry 144
— Walter Seymour 395
— William Augustus ... 147
Adamson, C. H. E. ..46, 412
— Henry Mackenzie 383
— John George........59, 295
— John Thomas Graves 237
Addington, Hon. H. Wm.171
— Hon. Herbert H. S. ... 243
— Hiley Reginald 304
— Wm. Leonard 230
Addison, Alfred M. 267
— Arthur Jos. Berkeley 329
— Charles James 380
— George William ...51, 207
— Thomas, ... 295
Adey, Henry 529
Adie, Joseph Rosmond 455
Adkins, Arthur S. 289
— John 357
Adlercron, Rodolph L. ... 325
Adye, Arthur 68, 416
— Capel Geo. 59, 253
— Daniel Richard 434
— John 46, 169
— Sir J. Miller.............. 164
— Goodson 63, 415
— Mortimer Stopford ... 244
— Walter 65, 329
Agar, Edward............... 209
Agnew, Chas. Hamlyn... 149
— Patrick A. Vans........ 357
— Quentin G. Kinnaird 262
Ahmed, Zahoor A. 453
Aikenhead, Frank......... 174
Ainslie, Clement 212
— Henry Percival......... 437

Ainslie, Henry Sandys 240
Ainsworth, Wm. John... 315
Airey, Sir James T. 271
— Robert Berkeley 268
Airlie, Earl of 50, 152
Aitken, Arthur E. 423
— Francis M. 337
— John Christie........... 321
— William 40, 166
Alban, Clifton Fred. S... 417
— William Gore 67, 422
Alcock, Alfred Wm. 455
Alderson, Edwin A. H. 294
— Sir Henry James 6, 164
— James B. Standly ... 258
— Perceval C. Newsam...273
— Samuel Frank 177
Alderson-Smith, H. 254
Aldridge, Arthur R. 383
— Charles Powlett 279
— Edward 186
John Bartelot 176
Aldworth, William ... 65, 255
Alexander, Alex.Chas.A. 379
— Arthur Chas. B. 318
— Arthur Clifford ...43, 206
— Arthur Vickers 438
— Aubrey de Vere ...53, 413
— Major Charles H. 68, 169
— Lieut. Charles Henry 439
— Claud Henry........67, 308
— Dudley Henry 253
— Ernest Wright 176
— Frederick Freeman 453
— Fred. Gordon 57, 414
— Fred. Henry Thomas 256
— George Forbes......... 384
— Gerald D'Arragon ... 170
— Harvey 152
— Henry Sterling 437
— James Leslie............ 438
— John Donald 385
— Reginald 357
— Richard Stuart 422
— Robert................24, 180
— Robert Gustavus...50, 145
— Robert Homfray 68, 398
— Walter Lorenzo 259
— Hon. Walter Philip 50, 144
— Rev. W. Bernard Lyon 386
— Wm.Nathaniel Stuart 335
— William Patrick 174
Alford, Fred. Lewis 175
— Henry S. Lewis 370
Alington, Arthur C. M. 274
Alison, Randal Frederick 318
Allan, Percy Stuart 322
— William Munro 269
Allatt, Hy. T. Ward...... 5
Allcard, Octavius......50, 245
Allen, Alexander ...49, 308
— Alfred J. W. 237
— Bedford Morant ...61, 414
— Douglas M. 57, 360
— Edward 329
— Edward Lynn 295
— Francis S. 52, 273
— Fred. Edw. Halstead 174
— Fred. Seymour...50, 254
— George Burges...46, 166
— Hugh Morris 434
— John Richard H....58, 168
— Newton Seymour 68, 234
— Philip 292
— Ralph Edward....24, 254
— Robert Franklin....... 210
— Sydney Glenn 383
— Walter Harding 420
— William Henry 379
— William Jefferies B... 176
— William Lynn 278
Allenby, Augustus H. ... 432
— Edmund H. H. 148
Alleyne, James 174
Allfrey, Frank Edward 283
Allgood, Wm. Hy. L. ... 303

Allhusen, Fred. Hy...... 151
Allin, Wm. B. 378
Allison, Hazlett 504
Allport, Chas. Wm. 384
— Henry K. 380
Alone, John P. H. M. ... 360
Alpin, Wm. Geo. P. 455
Alston, James William 329
Altham, Edward A. 234
Alves, John Morison 43, 166
Amber, Felton............... 261
Amos, Albert G. 253
— Launcelot Hope Rix 362
— Oswald Henry 134
Amesbury, Fred. C. D... 429
— Wheaten L. Raleigh 438
Amey, Arthur 333, 368
Amos, Herbert G. M..... 269
Amphlett, Charles Grove 310
Anderson, Abdy F. 155
— Acland A. G. 138
— Adam R. Steele........ 456
— Alexander 378
— Alex. Dugwall......28, 179
— Alexander Vass 530
— Alfred 24, 404a
— Allan Meyrick 435
— Arthur W. Leslie 24, 404a
— Austin Thomas........ 175
— Cecil Ford 214
— Charles Alex........65, 169
— Charles Kirkpatrick 346
— Clinton Cortlandt ... 424
— David 264
— David Murray 150
— Edmund Bullar 170
— Edward Brooke ...45, 411
— Ernest Chester........ 385
— Francis James 210
— Fras. Wyatt Abbot ... 309
— George Whitefield ... 318
— Graham D'Arcy....... 400
— Gilbert Ironside 401
— Henry Lawrence 437
— Horace Robert Fras. 429
— Horace Searle......5, 405
— James 379
— James Douglas 173
— John 454
— John Buckle 386
— John Hamilton 274
— John Henry Abbot ... 391
— Joseph Wm. Townsend 530
— Louis Edward 382
— Macclesfield H. 362
— Norman Ruthven..... 362
— Patrick Graham 436
— Patrick William 289
— Rainy....................... 214
— Robert Douglas 172
— Robt. Holme Bankes 314
— Robert Warren H..... 317
— Rolland Fred. Hart... 423
— Rowland J. Percy 153
— Thomas Henry Edw. 185
— Warren Hastings..... 264
— 2nd Lt. William........ 177
— Qr. Mr. William 322
— William Campbell ... 157
— Major W. Christian 50, 169
— Lt. William Christian 437
— William Cortlandt ... 249
— William James 277
— William Paul 422
— William R. Le G...57, 413
Anderson-Pelham, Hon. D. R. H. 152
Anderton, Wm. A. 1. 65, 229
Andrew, Albert 434
— David C. Adrian 433
— Fred. Annesley 437
— George 377
— Henry 286
— William Bennet 137
Andrews, Chas. Edw. ... 317
— Francis William 214

Andrews, Rev. George Hubert 396
— Henry George 370
— Louis James 428
— Robert Charles 419
— Robert Williams ...53, 278
Andrews-Speed, H.S 59, 208
Andrus, Thos. Alchin... 310
Angell, Fred. John. 333, 369
Angelo, Fred. W. P. 420
— J. C. Cortlandt 310
— John Wm. Edward 57, 413
Angus, John 372
Anley, Barnett D. L. G. 288
— Frederick Gore 288
— Henry Augustus 275, 370
— William Bower........ 177
Annaly, Luke, Lord..... 233
Annand, Ernest Fred ... 234
Annesley, Arthur L. Lyttelton 5
— Arthur S. R. 436
— Arthur Sydney E. ... 437
— Francis Charles ...59, 243
— Francis Denis Jack 237
— Jas. Howard A........ 160
— Wm. Robt. Ewart ... 293
— Wm. R. Norton 294
Ansell, George K 148
Ansley, John Henry ... 291
Anson, Geo. Hamilton ... 371
— George Wemyss... 45, 411
— Hon. Henry Jaw's ... 317
Anstey, Thos.Henry 28, 207
Anstice, John C. A. 148
Anstruther,Alex.W. 46, 166
— Basil Lloyd 47, 309
— Charles James 159
Anthonisz, A. H. 378
Antrobus, Edmund ...22, 229
Aplin, Hugh Morgan 169, 402
— Philip John Hanham 420
— Stephen Lushington. 429
Appelbe, Edw. B. 369
Apperley, H. Wynne ... 27
Appleby, Geo. Percy ... 255
Appleton, Arthur Fred. 395
— Henry 68, 209
Applewhaite, Harry H. 245
Appleyard, George C. ... 170
Apthorp, Dudley R....58, 161
— Frederick East........ 41
— Kendal Preyman..... 258
Arbeiter, Charles 386
Arbouin, Guy Burnett... 297
Arbuthnot, Alex. George 178
— Archibald Hugh 271
— Sir Charles G. 164
— Dalrymple 174
— George Herbert 428
— George Holme 293
— Kenneth Wyndham 318
— Lenox Conyngham... 250
— Reginald Ramsay ... 258
Arcedeckne-Butler, J.F. 275
Archdale, Hugh Jas. 61, 255
— James Blackwood ... 369
— Mervyn Edward ...61, 229
Archer, Charles........... 427
— Samuel 377
— Thomas 380
Archer-Shee, Martin ... 161
Archibald, Rev. W.F. ... 407
Ardagh, Sir John C. 16, 205
Ardee, Reg. Le N. Lord 230
Arderne, David Davies 176
Argles, Owen Chas...... 434
Arkwright, Cyril 147
— Leonard A. 210
Armitage, Chas. L. 244
— Edw. Hume 170
— John Leathley 271
— Rev. Robert............ 306
— William Stuart........ 174
— William Thompson 178
Armstrong, Allan 308

Index—Active List. 542

Armstrong, Arth. Knox 433
— Arthur Reginald 161
— Bertie Harold O. 214
— Charles Arthur........ 240
— Edgar Herbert........ 260
— Edward 317
— Gerald Denne 242
— Henry 505
— James 453
— John 379
— John Cecil 271
— John Hervey 311
— J. Saunders 311
— Oliver Carleton 421
— Richard 264
— St. George Bewes 401
— Thos. G. L. Herbert69, 240
— Wilfrid E. Arbuthnot 506
— Rev. Wm. Fred. 460
— William Gage 28, 399
— William Herbert 254
— William M'Gee 311
— W. M. Howard 368
Armytage, Geo. A. 305
Arnim, H. Chas. L. 530
Arnold, Alfred James ... 145
— Arthur Seymour 433
— Francis Howard 402
— Herbert Tollemache 308
— Knighton 46, 366
— William Reginald ... 283
— William Richard 185
Arnott, James 529
— Napoleon 43, 206
Aron, Eugene Felix S... 145
Arthur, Edm. John 261
— James 368
— Leon. R. S........... 357
Arthy, Walter 175
Asbury, Alfred 380
Ash, Andrew Spotswood 264
— William C. Casson ... 301
Ashburner, Lionel Forbes 362
Ashburnham, Cromer ... 305
Ashby, George A. ..50, 276
— John S. 418
Asher-Tooth, Thos. 158
Ashhurst, Chas. Hen. ... 279
Ashley, Arthur 44, 366
— James 135
— Wilfrid Wm. 230
Ashmore, Edwd. Bailey 177
Ashton, Cecil O. Gough 275
— Fred. Elis 311
Ashworth, Guy Charles 284
— Leonard Temple 176
— Perceval 211
Askwith, Henry Francis 173
— John B. H. 172
— W. Harrison 164
Aslett, Wm. Chas. ...68, 416
Aspinall, Hugh H. H. ... 419
— Robert Lowndes 157
Aspinwall, James Henry 140
Asser, Joseph J. 283
Astell, Somerset C. G. F. 310
Astley, Delaval G. L'E. 285
Aston, George Grey ... 398
Atcherley, Llewellyn Wm. 274, 368
Atchison, Charles Ernest 297
Atherley, Philip C. F. ... 289
Atherton, Thos. Jas. ..65, 154
Athlumney, Lord 231
Athorpe, Robert 24, 204
Athow, Frank......... 401
Atkins, Alban Randell 368, 401
— Chas. Alfred 377
— George..........19, 406
— Robert...........21, 407
— William 329
Atkinson, Ben. 177
— E. H. De Vere 212
— Francis Garnett 418
— Francis Salisbury148, 368
— Frederick Dayot 410
— George Charles 419
— George Duncan...67, 424
— George Robert 365
— John R. Brooks 7, 404
— Thomas Henry H. B. 229
Atlay, Hugh W. 178
Attree, Fred. Wm. T. 63, 209
Auchincloss, William ... 264
Auchinleck, William H.41, 165
Audain, Guy Mortimer. 431
— Mark Ralph P. ...348, 369

Auld, Robert 28
Austen, Arthur Robt. ... 297
Austin, Francis James .. 244
— Geo. Brougham ..53, 413
— Herbert Henry...... 212
— Herbert Ward 383
— John Gardiner 177
— John Henry Edward 385
— Rev. Piercy G. B.... 460
— Reginald F. E. 335
Avetoom, Sarkies T. ... 530
— F. Hildebrand 283
Awdry, Vere H. A. 261
Axe, Henry Joseph 395
Ayerst, Chas. Egerton... 440
— William 430
Aylmer, Edm. K. G. 65, 161
— Fenton John.....66, 210
— Frederick A......50, 167
— Henry Leycester...57, 158
Ayre, Percy T. 176
Aytoun, Andrew 337
Babington, Alfred H.... 362
— David Melville 172
— Jas. Melville......43, 158
— Stafford Charles 212
— Walter 213
Babtie, William 381
Bacchus, John Basil R. 242
Backhouse, Joseph 505
Bacon, Anthony E. M... 314
— Arthur Francis...... 292
— Arthur Henry 348
— Basil Kenrick Wing 273
— Francis Temple..... 153
Badcock, Alex. James.. 435
— Alex. R. 16, 409
— Francis Frederick ... 433
— George Henry 295
Baddeley, Chas. Edw. ... 210
— Paul Fred. M....... 41
— Wm. Lewis O. ... 55, 208
Badgley, J. Mont. T. 52, 208
Badham, Rev. C. Hume... 532
Bagley, Richard Geo. .. 436
Bagnall, Thomas Nook 254
Bagnall-Wild, Ralph K. 214
Bagnold, Arth. Henry 50, 208
Bagot, Chas. Hervey 47, 206
— Hon. Walter Lewis... 229
Bagot-Chester, Greville
 J. M. 233
Bagshawe, Fred. Wm... 436
— Leonard Alfred 289
Bagwell-Purefoy, Edwd. 158
— Henry 140
Bailey, Arthur Harold... 284
— Arthur W 439
— Charles 440
— Gilbert 440
— Henry Vincent 147
— Lieut. John Henry .. 220
— 2nd Lt. John Henry 297
— Joseph Henry Russell 229
— Vivian Telford 244
— William 153
— Wm. Augustus 435
— William Fred....... 383
Baillie, Thos. Maubourg 6
Baillie, Alan C. D....... 318
— Frederick David 146
— George 176
— Hubert 421
— Robert 418
— Wm. L. Dennistoun... 262
— Rev. Wm. Worters . 532
Bailloni, Arthur C.G. 61, 244
Bain, David S. Erskine 505
Bainbridge, Edmond27, 166a
— Edm. Guy Tulloch ... 237
— George 529
— Norman Bruce 497
— Percy Agnew 173
— William Frank 270
Baines, Rev. Chas. Fred. 396
— Cuthbert Johnson 67, 272
— Edward 360
— Edw. Geo. G. Talbot . 370
Baird, Andrew 381
— Andrew Wilson ...27, 205
— David 286
— Sir Jas. Gardiner, Bt. 1
— John M'Donald 430
— Percy Thomas Chas. 325
Bairnsfather, P. Robt. 63, 415
— Thomas Henry 423
Baker, Alfred Aquila 40, 365

Baker, Alfred Willam... 314
— Arthur Slade........ 172
— Aug. Theodore 171
— Cecil Norris 438
— Donald 428
— Eden Moyle ... 45, 166a
— Fausset Maher 380
— George 18
— George Duff 170
— George Henry 455
— Godfrey H. Massy... 176
— Harold Robert 436
— James V. V. 5c, 167
— Joseph 160
— Louis S. Hyde 419
— Osbert Clinton 329
— Oswald 453
— Richard John 530
— Robert 349
— Robert Barrington ... 402
— Robt. Francis C. 245
— Rob. Henry S. ...50, 167
— Walter Way 210
— William 256
Baker-Carr, Henry B. F. 337
— R. G. T. 357
Baker-Stallard-Penoyre,
   Edw. Hugh Broome. 234
Balbi, Henry Alex. 189
Bald, Ernest H. Campbell 157
— Francis Evelyn Campbell 157
Baldock, Charley Blair 432
— Thomas Stanford 53, 168
Baldroy, Frank S. H.... 395
Baldwin, Anthony Hugh 309
— Archibald Colin 431
— Frederick 43, 399
— John Gray 174
— Guy Melfort 433
— Lancelot Hugh 295
— Philip Bell 61, 208
— Raymond Henry 275
Balfe, Edmund 53, 413
Balfour, Alfred G. 317
— Arthur Mackintosh ... 172
— Christopher Egerton 305
— Joseph Hume 419
— Kenneth Robert 143
— Wm. Edw. L....58, 168
Balguy, John Henry.... 170
Ball, Oswald Jas. Hy.58, 285
Ballantyne, E. W. M'K.. 267
Ballard, Chas. N. Bruere 175
— Colin Robert 245
Bally, John Ford ...43, 166a
Balmain, Jas. A. S. 157
Bamber, Charles James 454
Bamfield, Harold J. K. 457
Bampfylde, Henry Edw. 173
Banatvala, Hormusjie E. 455
Banbury, Walter Edward 429
Bancroft, Chas. Edw. ... 265
Banfield, Rees J. Fras. 50, 285
Banister, Fitzg. M....52, 167
— George Stanhope 44, 267
Banks, Henry J. A. 267
— Samuel O'Brien..... 529
— William Sykes 283
Bannatine-Allason, R.59, 168
Bannatyne, Wm. Stirling 154
Bannerman, Alexander 214
— Arth. D'Arcy Gordon 432
— William Burney 505
— Wyndham Philip ... 437
Banning, Arthur C.G. 61, 244
— Stephen Thomas ... 347
Bannister, Chas. John40, 366
Banon, Frederick Lionel 297
Banting, Wm. Robert... 143
Barber, Hugh R. C..... 68
Barchard, Arthur C. S. 275
— Arthur E........... 450
Barclay, Art. Hayward 160
— Cameron 152
— Ernest Armond ...55, 413
— Patrick Charles R. ... 440
— Theodore 6, 333
Barefoot, Geo. Henry ... 383
— John Richard 382
Barff, Reginald M. 438
Baring, Everard 152
— Hon. Guy Victor ... 231
Barker, Chas. Arundel 45, 333
— Digby Hilliard 282
— Edward Hy. Payne... 401

Barker, Francis William
 James 41
— Fred. Charles 529
— Fred. Edw. Lloyd... 171
— Fred. Rowland 379
— George..........48, 207
— George Digby 5
— James Campbell ..48, 207
— J. Stewart S. ...53, 167
— Randle Barnett 265
Barklie, Robt. Martin 46, 206
Barkworth, H. A. S. ... 292
— John Raymond 213
Barlow, B. F. P. Pratt... 283
— Charles M. ...66, 169
— Charles Wynn 288
— Rev. Clement H. ... 460
— Cuthbert C. Lambert 246
— George N. H. ...63, 169
— Harry 282
— Herbert Sturges ...67, 318
— Hilaro Wm. Wellesley 171
— John Arthur.....44, 309
— John Frederick 176
— Lionel F. Abbot 293
— Murray H. Pratt ... 440
— Nelson William 281
Barnard, Andrew Edw. 436
— Sir Charles Loudon... 397
— John H. 25
— William Osborne ... 16
Barnardiston, Ernald ... 213
— Nathaniel W. 301
Barne, Miles 232
Barnes, Ardlo' H. F. 5, 397
— Arth. Alison Stuart 5, 308
— Charles Spencer 308
— Chris. Chevallier 178
— Ernest 439
— George Edward..... 398
— George West 372
— Henry John 380
— Henry Marshall 175
— James Petit 430
— Percy George 301
— Raglan Wykeham ... 380
— Reg. Walter Ralph... 146
— William Edward ... 368
Barnet, Horace H. ...68, 209
Barnett, Carew 435
— Henry J. de Barry ... 292
— Konnet Bruce 386
— William 305
— Wm. Alexander 310
Barr, D. W. Keita....41, 410
— Henry Keith 275
— William Cross 371
Barratt, Ernest Bird ... 439
— Herbert James 381
— Thomas Henry 283
— William Cross 430
Barren, Wm. Alex. 529
Barrett, Alfred L ...69, 417
— Arthur Arnold 417
— Arthur Leonard 352
— Ch. Graham Moulton 286
— Charles John Chard 261
— Dacre Lennard...68, 209
— Edw. Alf. Moulton 360, 369
— Edw. M. Moulton ... 240
— Harry F. Moulton ... 337
— Henry Walter 369
— Leonard.........65, 169
Barrington, H. E. W. ... 379
— Richard Mordaunt 281, 370
— Thomas Percy 253
— William D'Olier ... 213
Barron, Harry......47, 166a
— Notterville Guy..... 174
Burrow, Rev. Alf. Henry 505
— Arthur Fredk. 51, 413
— Etienne George ..48, 414
— Frank 41, 409
— George de Symons... 431
— Henry John Willee... 378
— Rev. Kingston E. ... 461
Barrows, William 154
Barry, Alfred Percival .. 252
— Andrew 523
— Cecil Charles Stuart. 457
— Daniel Francis 456
— David Joseph 395
— Edward Patrick John 395
— Jo'n 378
— John Frederick 131
— John Patrick 530
— Maurice 274
— Stanley Leonard ... 152

Index—Active List.

Barry, Thomas David C. 530
— Rev. Walter Geo. 507
— Wm. Stafford J. 333
— William Thurburn ... 275
Barstow, John B. 214
Barter, Beamish St J. 66, 246
— Charles St. L. 55, 293
— William Pearson 386
Bartholomeusz, M. L.... 529
Bartholomew, Hugh J. 273
Barthorp, Arthur H..... 292
Bartlett, Chas. Richard 381
— William Theophilus... 240
Barton, Alured Y 398
— Arthur Elliott 432
— Charles Gerard 238
— Denis James 287
— Francis John Herbert 426
— Francis Rickman....... 360
— Geoffry 18
— Hugh John 212
— Laurence Fleetwood 234
— Maurice Charles ...58, 208
— Nath. Albert D......... 334
— Thomas Steward 435
— William Henry 386
— William Hugh 270
Bartrum, John S. 253
Barttelot, Geo. Frederic 265
Barwell, Arthur Ross... 433
— Edward Egerton 441
— Harry Cecil 242
Basevi, William Henry 370,401
— William Henry Fras. 439
Basing, G. L. Lord 143
Baskerville, C. H. L....69, 258
Bass, Philip de S. 258
Basu, Baman Das........ 530
— Basanta Kumar 455
— Dharmadas............... 454
Batchelor, Thomas 239
Bate, Albert L. F. 384
— Charles M'Guire ...67, 209
— Thomas E. L............. 453
Bateman, B. Montague 173
— Daniel Fred. 504
— Rev. Fred. J. 396
— George M. Yunge...... 172
— Henry William 372
Bateman-Champain, C.E. 362
Bates, Charles Loftus ... 136
Bateson, John Fras....... 382
Bath, John 370
Bathurst, Arthur Henry 293
Batson, Herbert............ 249
Batt, Reginald C. 243
Batten, Alan C. 417
— Frederick Graeme ... 432
Battenberg, H.R.H. Prince
  Henry Maurice of... 27
Battersby, Henry Lewis 380
— John 381
— Thomas Preston 568
Battine, Alex. James ... 175
— Cecil William 142
— Reginald St. Clair ... 158
Battiscombe, Charles ... 173
— William Wilson......... 422
Battley, R. Cade L. 288
Battye, Ar. Baldwyn ... 274
— Arthur Henry 431
— Clinton Wynyard 297
— Fred. Drummond 45, 411
— Ivan Urmston 362
— Lionel R. Jas. S. 155
— Montagu Wm......58, 274
— Richmond Moffatt... 439
Baugh, Guillum Scott 57, 413
— Mackenzie Walcott... 428
Baumgartner, John S. J. 274
— R. J. 279
Baxter, Clement Fred.... 272
Bayard, Reginald ...237, 367
Bayford, Edm. H......... 160
Baylay, Frederick......... 211
Bavley, Arden L......63, 360
— Edward Charles 437
— Gerald Edward 311
— Steuart Farquharson 430
— Thomas Elliott 162
Bayliff, Richard Lane... 400
Bayliss, Eustace G. 275
Baylor, Henry Talbot... 383
Baytv, Abingdon Robert 176
— Alfred William L. 68, 416
— John 204
— Richard Kerr 18
— William Head............ 24

Baynes, Charles Edward 428
— Douglas Dynoley 431
Barnham, Rev. A. W.... 532
Bayspoole, Albert......... 185
Bazalgette, Louis H...... 250
Beach, Joseph. H. Wolfe 386
— Thomas Boswall 385
— William Henry......... 213
Beadon, Arthur Eyre ... 308
— Cecil...................21, 403
— Charles Edward 167
— Guy Cecil 430
— Henry Cecil 439
— William 436
Beale, Anthony 423
— Henry Yelverton...66, 245
— Thomas Alfred 44, 310
— Willy 436
Bealo-Browne, D. J. E. 151
Beaman, George P. R.... 288
Beames, David 428
Beamish, Alf. A. W. 41, 205
— James M................... 378
— Robert Talbot 379
— Sackville E. C. H. ... 361
Bean, William Henry ... 382
Beardmore, Chas. F. H. 373
Beardsley, Wm. Joseph 185
Beasley, Rev. Edw. M.... 460
Beatson, Chas. Henry... 454
— Finlay C. 66, 308
— Stuart Brownlow 51, 415
— Wm. John Arnold ... 170
Beattie, Alexander 338
— Rev. H. H. 396
Beatty, Rev. Edw. T. ... 507
— Guy Arch. H............. 438
— John William............ 381
— Lionel Nicholson 435
Beauchamp, Clayton G. 267
— Horace G. P. 66, 162
Beauclerk, Chas. E. de V. 305
— G. M. de V. de V...... 230
Beaumont, E. de Grey... 158
— Francis Montagu....... 304
— George 244
— Godfrey Lancaster ... 401
— Miles, Lord...........46, 162
— Richd. Henry 305
Beaver, Fred. T. M. 51, 167
— Philip Keith L. ...42, 166
Beazeley, George Adam 213
Becher, Andrew Cracroft 245
— Cecil Leycester 373
— Fred. Williams......63, 255
— George Arthur 439
— Henry Wrixon 277
Beck, Charles Edward 45, 154
— Hugh 273
— Rev. J. H. 532
Becke, Archibald Frank 177
Becker, O. Theodore 59, 269
Beckett, Chas. Edw. 44, 137
Beckham, Lionel Grafton
  ....68, 416
Beddek, Edw. Escott ... 434
Beddoes, Henry Roscoe 348
Bedford, Chas. Henry ... 456
— Jas. Blackburn 438
— Walter George Aug.... 380
Bedingfeld, E. Gordon... 150
— Henry H.................... 249
— Norman Nevill 305
Beeching, Hugh Cecil
  Westall.................. 294
Beeton, Orchart.......... 276
Beever, Henry Holt ... 170
Beevor, Walter Calverley 382
Begbey, Henry 185
Begbie, Arundel Sinclair 433
— Elphinstone Waters 23,404a
— Francis Richard....44, 411
— Francis Warburton... 385
— George Edward 317
Behrend, Francis David 277
Behrens, Clive 176
Beith, Robert Douglas... 401
Belfield, Herbert E. ...65, 347
— Sydney 172
Belford, Ernest Aug. 43, 159
Belk, William 139
Bell, Arthur Wm. C. ...53, 413
— Arthur Clive 213
— Arthur Lynden......... 237
— Arth. Wm. Hadden... 334
— Chas. Percival L....... 275
— Charles Thornhill ... 172
— Claude Wm. Hedley 337

Bell, Edward 273
— E. H. Lynden........... 382
— Edward Inkerman ... 243
— Ernest Fitzroy 151
— Eustace Widdrington 357
— Frns. de Beauvoir ... 245
— F. John Hamilton ... 329
— George Henry 438
— Geo. Jas. Hamilton... 455
— Henry L. Gillison ... 214
— Henry Phillipps 435
— Henry Reginald 243
— Henry Urmston 147
— James Alex. 417
— James Archibald R.... 372
— John Beatson............ 436
— Kenneth Dowie....... 174
— Leonard 170
— Leonard Robert Grey 346
— Lindesay Maxwell ... 434
— Mark Sever 19, 205
— Matthew G. Edw...... 357
— Maurice Douglas 176
— Ralph Maitland........ 433
— Reginald William ... 214
— Richard Carmichael 436
— Robert Francis......... 314
— Thomas 371
— Colonel William....... 1
— Staff Paym. William... 371
Bell-Irving, Andrew 58, 168
— Hector 438
Bell-Smyth, J. Ambard 136
Bellairs, Norman Edw. B. 175
Bellamy, Arthur Lytton 245
— Percy John 278
— Robert 279
Bellers, Ern. Vernon 66, 301
Bellew, Robert W. D.... 158
Bellhouse, John........... 175
Bellord, Rev. James 396
Benbow, John Edw. 68, 136, 374
Bendyshe, Rich. Nelson 401
Benett, Harry V. 261
Bengough, Chas. Wm..... 256
— Harcourt M. 7
Benn, Harry Gordon ... 434
— Robert Arthur Edw... 378
Bennet, Ferdinando W. 49, 208
Bennett, Arthur Buckley 264
— Charles Henry 505
— Charles Hugh 273
— Ernest Albert........... 301
— Ernest Emilius......... 395
— Hugh 530
— John Francis 272
— Levett Holt............... 373
— Lionel Edmd. Anstey 287
— Richard Dawson 378
— Robert 249, 369
— Vivian Boase........... 530
Benoy, Rev. James 396
Bensley, Chas. Norman 455
— Clement Henry 457
Benson, Fred. William... 45
— George Conolly....... 297
— George Elliott 171
— Henry W. 69, 275
— Percy Hugh 504
— Richard A. Stanley... 231
— Richard Erle 254
— Rion Philip 172
— Starling Meux.......... 25
— Thomas Charles 333
— Wm. Geo. Sackville 288, 374
Bent, George 383
— Wm. Henry Morris 65, 282
— Reginald Joseph 435
— Walter Guy.............. 357
Bentley, Walter 291
Benwell, Albert........... 175
— Reginald Limond ... 137
Bere, Charles 386
Beresford, Arthur W. P. 174
— Chas. E. de la Poer 55, 308
— Chas. Fred. Cobbe 44, 206
— St. George Ross 279
— James H. Brownlow... 432
— Hon. John G. H. H.... 149
— Kennedy................... 25
— Marcus John Barré
  De la Poer 267
— Marcus W. De la Poer 356
— Lord W. L. de la Poer 266
— W. Randal Hamilton 265
Borger, Ernest L. Corbett 433
Berkeley, Frederick Geo. 17
— Robert Bruce 431

Berkeley, Thomas M.
  Martin 286
Berkley, James 172
Bernard, Edgar E....249, 367
— Edward Henry......... 426
— Herbert Clifford 431
— John 400
— Joseph Francis 186
— Paolo 50, 186
— William Kingsmill ... 282
Berne, James Coleman... 395
Berners, Ralph A........ 265
Berney, Thos. Hugh ... 253
Berry, Alfred Eugene ... 506
— Robert G. J. J. 368
Berryman, Hon. Arthur 385
— William Eben.......... 382
Berthon, Alderson P.... 347
— Henry W. 439
— Herbert Cecil W...... 254
Bortie, Hon. Reg. H....58, 265
Bertram, William 309
Besant, Walter Fervey 245
Best, Philip George...... 176
— William 265
Betham, Robert M. 428
Bothell, Edward Hugh 63, 209
— Henry Arthur 171
— Wilfrid Philip 287
Bethune, Edward Cecil 141
— Hector 438
— Henry Alex. 321
Bett, James 240
Betty, Alf. T. Hy. K. ... 265
— Algernon T. H. K. ... 239
— Wm. R. P. K. 293
Bevan, Frank.............. 240
— George Frederick..... 504
Beveridge, Wilfred W.O. 384
Beville, Chas. Hamilton 432
— Francis Granville ... 433
— George Francis ...6, 405
— Harry G. Peyton 439
Bewington, John 178
— Samuel Nattali 236
Bewes, Arthur Edw. ... 401
Bewicke, Hugh B. N.52, 309
Bewicke-Copley, R.C.A.
  ....67, 304
Bowley, Alfred William 384
Bowsher, Wm. Dent...... 281
Beynon, Henry L. N. ... 174
— Wm. George L. 436
Beyts, Herbert Wm. Hope 398
— William George 385
Bickerstaffe-Drew, Rev.
  Francis................... 396
Bickford, Arthur Louis 236
— Edward 171
— William Wilfrid 238
Bicknell, Maldion Byron 172
Biddulph, Geo. Warren 217
— Harold Mavromichali 357
— Harry 214
— Hope 174
— John 21, 409
— Michael 176
— Sir Michael A. S...... 164
— Nicholas Trafalgar ... 314
— Sir Robert 4, 164
— Stephen Francis 419
Bidie, George............. 506
Bidgood, Thos. E. W. ... 173
Bidwell, Reg. Frank ... 440
Bigg-Wither, Ferdinand 243
Bigge, Arthur John...46, 166a
— George Orde 212
— Thos. Arth. Hastings. 211
Bigger, Samuel F......... 454
Biggs, Henry Vero 210
Bigham, Chas. C. 230
Bignoll, E. D. Fred..53, 413
Billings, Clement H..... 423
— Mathew 285
Bindloss, Wm. Robert... 137
Bingham, Hon. Cecil Edw. 133
— Charles Hy. Marion 385
— Charles Thomas ...47, 412
— Edmund G. Hy....44, 166a
— Edward Henry ...43, 410
— Hon. Fras. Richard... 173
— George C. Lord........ 356
— George Wm. Powlett 244
Bingley, Alfred Horsford 431
— Arthur George E. ... 293
Binney, Arthur Fred.... 398
— Walter E. 400
Binning, George, Lord 48, 135

Index—Active List.

Binny, Stouart M. 240
— Steuart Scott. 161
Binsteed, Chas. H. F. ... 429
Birch,Alex.HarryColvin 171
— Arnold Wilson 267
— Arthur Charles 176
— Charles 249
— Charles Grant F. G.... 284
— Claude Ernest 293
— Downward P. Lea ... 172
— Edward Alfred 452
— Fred. Henry John ... 170
— Major Fred. Wm. 46, 261
— Lt. Frederick William 435
— Henry George 171
— Henry Priestley 382
— Jas. Fred. Noel......... 173
— James R. Kemmis ... 264
— Valentine Kingston .. 352
— William Jas. Alex. 43, 410
Bird, Rev. Arthur......... 507
— Fred. V. Godfrey 27, 399
— George Corrie 16, 405
— Geo.Edw.G. Waller242,374
— John Turnbull 396
— Robert 456
— Spencer Godfrey...61, 348
— Stanley 243
— Wilkinson Dent 236
— Wm. John B. 59, 414
Birdwood,Geo.Chris. M. 428
— Gordon Travers 457
— Halhed Brodrick 273
— William Riddell 432
— Wm. Spiller 68, 416
Birkbeck, Victor John... 275
— Vincent M. 234
— William Henry 130
Birley, Richard Arch.... 178
Birney, John R. 214
Birrell, William Geo. ... 381
Birt, Cecil 382
— Thomas 384
Biscoe,Albert S.Tyndale 171
— Julian D. T. Tyndale 153
— Vincent Robert 29
— William Walters ... 7, 403
Bishop, Charles 151
— Charles Frederick ... 175
— Charles L. N. 398
— Edward Barry 40, 409
— Harry Oswald 261
— John David Jones ... 272
— Leslie Trevor ...44, 411
Bisset, Wm. S. Smith 41, 205
Bissett, William......... 317
Bittleston, Geo. H. ...61, 169
Bivar, C. E. Belli- 425
Black, Rev. John 261
— John Campbell L. 237, 368
— John Greer 383
— Walter Clarence 436
— William Campbell 43, 410
— Wilsone 6
Blackader, Chas. G. 256
Blackburn, Andrew B.... 337
— Charles Cautley 245
— Hugh 237
— John Edward 55, 208
— Leslie Dewing 270
— Peter 49, 160a
Blackburne, John G. 290
Blackden, Leon. Shad. 360
— Wilfrid W. 347
Blacker, Lath. C. M. 66, 169
— Stewart Ward William 174
Blackett, E. Umfre ...55, 168
Blackman, Wm. James 386
Blackwell, Chas. T. 382
Blackwood, Alex. Thos. 284
Blagrove, Henry John 53, 155
Blaine, Edwin Ernest... 262
Blair, Arthur 269
— Arthur Kennedy 438
— Everard M'Leod 212
— Henry William ...21, 406
— Hugh Maxwell 318
— James C. O. 325
— Reginald S. Hunter... 321
— Richd.Wm.Creighton 265
— Walter Chas. Hunter 171
Blake, Charles John 46, 166
— Edward Algernon C. 315
— Martin Pierce 16
— Napoleon J. R........55, 301
— Robert Wm. M. 262
— Wm. L. Fitzgerald ... 287

Blakeney, Edward F. J. 367
— Herbert Norwood ... 301
— Robert Byron D. ... 214
— William Edward A.... 427
Blakeway, Denys B. ... 437
— J. Prestwich 213
— Thomas Wootton ... 141
Blaksley, Edward 44, 166
Blanchflower, Edward . 214
Bland, Edw. Humphry 211
— Fred. Milbank 55, 167
— Humphrey Loftus ... 240
— William St. Colum... 175
Bland-Hunt,E.S.de Vere 176
Blandy, Wm. Poyntz ... 43
Blane, Chas. Forbes..... 170
Blanford, Chas. Edw. ... 178
— William Geo. 175
Bleckley, Fred. C. C. ... 436
Blenkinsop, Alf. Percy... 384
— Frederick Henry 504
— Layton John 395
Blennerhassett, B. M. 378
— Ernest Blennerhassett 271
Blest, Daniel Alex. ...48, 288
Blewitt, Arthur 304
— Charles Turner......... 170
— William Edward...58, 168
Bliss, Charles 290
— Charles Ernest......... 435
— James Arthur 439
— John Plomer 361
— Leonard P. H. 276
— Thomas G. Cumming 261
— Wilfrid Marryat 270
Blissett, Henry F. 368
Block, Arthur Hugh..... 170
— Maurice W. P. 68, 169
Blogg, George Richard 282
Blois, Sir R. B. Macn.Bt. 233
Blois-Johnson,T.Gordon 437
Blomfield,Charles Jas. 55, 261
Blood, Bindon 18, 207
— Robert 378
— William Persse......... 333
Blore, Herbert Richard 305
Blosse, Fras. Lynch..... 361
— Robert Lynch 269
Blount, Charles H. ...63, 169
— George Percy Cosmo 178
Blount, Charles H. 115
— Robert Frederick ... 115
Blumberg, Herbert E.... 401
Blundell, R. B. H. 6
— John Eyles 44, 281
— Wilfrid A. B. H. 230
Blundell - Hollinshead -
Blundell, D. H. 305
Blunt, Charles Jasper ... 174
— Conrad Edw. G. 367
— Edward Henry 293
— Edward W............... 171
— Ernest 58, 208
— Rev. James H. T. 532
— Osmond Donald 334
— Robert Bruce........... 261
— Walter Ernest O. C. ... 329
Blyth, Fred. Aug. ... 69, 417
Bockett, Pugh Edw. H. 401
Boddam, Ernest B. C. 435
Boddy, Owen Vidal...52, 207
— Robert James........... 263
Bodé, Louis Wm. 301
Boden, Anthoney D..... 337
Boehmer, Fred. Chas.... 275
Boger, Dudley C........... 264
Boggs, Arthur Addison 173
Bogle, John du T. ...45, 206
Boileau, Arthur C. T. 68, 169
— Bertrand Hy. Carter 274
— Colin Campbell......... 431
— Etienne R. Partridge 274
— Frank R. Farrer 212
— Guy Hamilton 213
— Henry 41, 410
— J. Peter Hamilton ... 377
— Lestock Francis ... 27, 205
Boisragon, Guy H. 432
Boles, Wm. Samuel 383
Bolland, Theo. J. 441
Bols, Louis Jean 249
Bolster, James M. 380
Bolton, Archer C......... 292

Bolton, Arthur Hely ... 434
— Harry John 61, 414
— Richard A. L. M...... 155
— Richard. G. Ireland... 233
— Wilfred Nash........... 308
Bomford, Gerald......... 453
Bond, Chetwynd R. A... 427
— Francis George......... 209
— Henry Hendley 177
— Ralph F. X. M. 171
— Reginald Coplestone 296
— Reginald Edwin 259
— Reginald Fras. Geo. 212
— Richard Pratt 381
— Thomas 386
— Wensly J. H. 55, 419
Bonham, Chas. Barnard 213
— George Lionel 230
— Walter F. 288
Bonomi, J. Ignatius 69, 238
Bonus, William John ... 283
Bookey, John Thos. B. ... 453
Boome, Edw. Herbert ... 435
Boon, George 273
Boone, Chas.Fred.de B. 288
Booth, Arthur Wm. C. ... 240
— Hon. Geo. L. Sclater 141
— Lionel Edward B. 49, 277
— Thomas George......... 372
— William Henry......... 237
Boothby, Francis S. E. 246
— Reginald Evelyn ...59, 168
Bootle-Wilbraham, Hon.
V. R. 357
Bor, Arthur 59, 360
— Edward John 55, 208
— James Henry 398
Borah, Shibram........... 453
Borradaile, A. Latour ... 384
— Basil...................... 423
— Harry Benn 423
Borrett, Cecil Arthur ... 238
— Herbert Charles 17
Borton, Arthur Close 48, 252
— Sir Arthur 245
— Charles Edward 245
— Neville Travers 285
Bosanquet, Jas.Tindal I. 278
— Lionel A. 289
Bostock, Arthur........... 305
— Robert Ashton 383
Boswell, William Legh 420
Bosworth, Arthur.....44, 360
Boulton, Raymond Edw. 295
Bourchier, Arthur C. F. 429
— Philip Lennox W. ... 401
Bourcicault, Geo. P...63, 267
Bourke, Geo. Deane..... 379
— Henry Beresford...67, 360
— John Joseph 457
— Paget John............. 130
— Ulick Joseph. 17
Bourne, Casimir Arth.40, 366
— Frank 268
— Walter FitzGerald ... 440
Bousfield, E. Emerson 490
Bouverie, Geo. Pleydell 231
— Hon. J. Pleydell 44
Bovet, William 214
Bovill, Edward 453
— Thomas 289
Bowden, James H. T. C. 276
— William Harvey 250
Bowdler, Basil W. B. ... 214
Bowen, Charles Eustace 435
— Charles Otway Cole... 213
Rev. Elias Jenkins ... 532
— Francis Joseph......... 262
— Gerard Chris. 347
— Herbert Walter 529
— John Cuthbert G..... 532
— Robert Cole............. 288
— Robert Scarlett......... 304
Bower, Denis Mahoney 433
— Hamilton................ 424

Bowers, Maunsell ... 45, 140
Bowes, William Hely ... 262
Bowie, Math. Morton 22, 407
Bowker, Fras. Jearrad 281
— William James 252
Bowlby, Chas. Wm....... 334
— Robert Russell 295
Bowles, A. Montagu..... 42
— Fred.. Aug............51, 167
— Fred. Gilbert........... 209
— Henry 49, 259
— Ludlow Tonson........ 275
Bowly, David............. 163
Bowman, Henry 186
— Henry James........... 289
— Robert 529
Bown, Arthus Thomas 455
Bowring, Arthur H..... 176
— George 418
— John Bellasis 441
Bowyer,Wentworth G.57,208
Boxer, Edw. Hood S. ... 283
— Hugh Edwd. Richd. 246
Boyce, Ernest J. G...67, 209
— Harry Augustus 176
— John Fred. Wm....... 242
— John Henry A. 238
— Wm. Geo. Bertram 293, 307
Boyd, Alex. Charles ... 175
— Franklyn Forbes...... 236
— Henry W. B. 529
— John Alex. 41, 360
— Julius Middleton ...7, 405
— Mossom Archibald ... 210
— Reg. Blennerkassett 272
— Stuart Ogilvy 177
— Thomas 379
— William Henry........ 174
Boyes, John Edward ... 19
Boyle, Arthur Gerald ... 252
— Francis Rayner 401
— Michael 386
— Roger Courtenay..... 347
Boys, Reginald H. H. ... 212
Brabazon, Auth.Heyland 401
— John Palmer......24, 146
— William Beaufort..... 402
Brackenbury, Henry ... 130
— Sir Henry...........4, 164
— Herbert Wm........51, 167
— Manle Campbell ...43, 206
— Walter John William 250
Bradbridge, Edward U. 308
Braddell, John A. 395
— Moncketon O'Dell ... 382
Bradford,Edw.Chaloner 329
— Evelyn Ridley 318
— George Thomas 347
— Sutherland Henry ... 276
— Sydney Sheridan...... 267
— Wilmot Henry 329
Bradley, Chas. Edw. 52, 310
— Fred. Gardner 424
— Hugh Vachell 431
— Robert William 268
Bradshaw, Alex. F. 377
— Charles Richard 294
— Frederick Ewart 430
— James Butler 233
— Laurence Julius E. ... 417
— William Edm. J. 311
Brady, Daniel............. 213
— Robt. Maziere 57, 168
— Wm. Longfield 311
Braganza, Moscardi B. 530
Braid, Arthur Reade ... 172
Braide, Geo. F. W. 455
Braithwaite, Fras. J. ... 291
— Walter P................. 252
— William Garnett 265
Brake, Herbert Edw. J. 174
— Timothy Francis 386
Brakspear, William Rae 436
Bramhall, Edward....... 115
— Edward Albert 367
Bramly, Alfred Jennings 161
— Alwyn Wm. Jennings 144
— Guy L. Jennings 148, 374
— Harrie Jennings 286
— R. D. Jennings........ 321
Bramwell, Geo. Addison 292
— Henry Duncombe ... 157
Brand, Herbert 438
— Hon. Thomas Walter 152
Brander, Arthur Jas. 46, 412
— Edw. Salisbury 453
— Herbert Ralph 42

Brandon, Rev. R. J. 507	Broadrick, Fred. B. D. 174	Brown, Louis Faulkner 47, 206	Bruce, Frederick... 434
Brandreth, Edgar 433	— George Fletcher 278	— Oscar 185	— George David... 243
— Lyall............ 285	Broadwood, Arthur...26, 233	— Richard Cradock ... 398	— George Evans 345
Braufoot, Arth. Mudge 504	— Ivo Arthur............ 230	— Robert Jas. Reid 429	Hon. James F. T. C. 286
Brannigan, John H...... 383	— Robert George 154	— Thomas 138	— James G. Turing...... 238
Branson, Vivian Henry 301	Brock, Edgar N. Loftus 273	— Tom 293	— John Eliot L. 176
Brass, Ernest Henry ... 254	— Henry J. 175	— Valentine 401	— Jonathan Maxwell ... 362
Bray, A. Le Mesurier ... 175	— Matthew William...... 373	— Walter Henry 434	— Malcolm Edw. Lloyd. 289
— Claude Arthur 373	— Thomas Herbert...45, 294	— Walter Medlicott 438	— Thomas 177
— George Arthur Theo... 384	Brocklehurst, J. F....42, 135	— Walter Sydney 308	— William Alex. M. 435
— Hubert Alaric 385	— Robert 252	— William Baker 217	Bruuker, C. Molyneux... 261
— Reginald Edw. T....... 293	Brockman, Charles E. F. 401	— Wm. Geo. Charteris.. 223	— Jas. Milford S... 55, 168
— Robert Napier 277	— William Law 371	— William H. Wreford.. 268	Brunner, Chas. Wilfred 213
— Rev. Wm. Henry 460	Broderick, E. Warren 44, 236	Browne, Abraham W. ... 379	Bruno, Ern. Edw. Bruno 347
Breakey, Arthur John... 172	Brodhurst, B. M. L. 440	— Alex. John Wogan ... 433	— Hugh Watson Bruno 402
Bredin, Alexander 259	Brodie, Alastair Wm. B. 318	— Alfred Percy 435	Brush, Aplyn Waring .. 258
— Waldene FitzWm. H. 258	— James FitzGerald...... 379	— Andrew Lang............ 378	— George Howard 244
Brooks, Richard Wm. ... 172	Brogan, Thomas Henry 178	— Andrew Smythe M. ... 6	— John E. Ramsay 333
Bremner, Arthur Grant 213	Brogden, Duncan Dunbar 279	— Arthur Geo. Fred. 59, 414	— Oliver Ramsay 234
— Donald 173	— James England............ 385	— Arthur Henry 57, 168	Bryan, Hon. Geo. Leopold 152
— Harry John............ 412	— John Silvester 401	— Arthur Howe............ 347	— Herbert 246
— Henry 162	Broke, Harry 21	— Arthur Neil E. 317	— Thomas Wm. Guy ... 171
Brennu, Hugh G. 329	Bromfield, Fra. Wm. 55, 264	— Augustus 42, 166	Bryant, Alan 272
Brendon, Herbert A. ... 172	— James 372	— Charles Michael... 40, 404a	— Gilbert Edward...... 171
Brennan, Charles 271	Bromhead, Sir B. P. Bt. 23, 407	— Clement A. R. 210	— Henry Grenville 297
Brereton, Ed. Fitzgerald 292	— Charles James 23	— Clement L. S. 308	Bryce, David Greig 439
— John Sadleir 371	— Edw. Gonville 309	— Clement Metcalfe 221	— William............ 256
— William Lloyd...... 47, 347	Bromilow, Walter 348	— Rev. D. G. Lathom... 507	Buccleuch, W. F. Duke of 1
— Willoughby Thos. 21, 406	Brook, Edmund Smith 13, 334	— Edgar Thornburgh...... 289	Buchan, G. C. Fordyce 174
Bretherton, George H. ... 427	— Richard W. Crundell 308	— Edmond Charles...42, 262	Buchanan, Andrew 455
Breton, Chas. Travers... 148	Brooke, A. De Vere ...28, 206	— Edward George 384	— Arthur L. H. 321
— Harry D'Arch......55, 208	— Arthur Montagu 269	— Edw. Stevenson ...45, 257	— Bertram George 177
Brett, Arthur 372	— Charles Louis 398	— Frank Douglas 308	— Francis Edward 262
— Arth. Henry W.... 53, 163	— Chris. R. Ingham 295	— Frank Wm. N. Wogan 145	— George Johnston...... 385
— Chas. Arth. Hugh ... 250	— Eardley Wilmot 305	— Fred. George Francis 242	— Gilbert Howell L....... 207
— Geo. Wm. Brownrigg 245	— Edw. Alston P............ 325	— Fred. Macdonell 214	— Harris England ...55, 240
— Herbert George 175	— Edward Sabine 171	— Fred. William 115	— Henry James 5
— Walter Edward......... 427	— Edward Wm. Saurin 178	— Geoffrey J. Denis...... 346	— John B. Waith............ 383
— Walter Percival......... 211	— George Cecil 278	— George 278	— Kenneth James......... 428
Breul, Fred. Alex. 272	— Harry Morris M. 436	— Geo. Fitzherbert ...57, 232	— Walter James 456
Brewin, Bertram R....... 177	— Hugh Fenwick... 271, 368	— Geo. Herbert Stewart 250	Buchanan-Dunlop, A. H. 293
— John Palffy 211	— Lionel Godolphin...49, 334	— H. D............40, 166a	
Brewster, R. Ferdinand 174	— Rich. O'Shaughnessy 372	— Harold Gore ...63, 304	Buck, Cecil Henry 440
Brickenden, R. H. L. 44, 286	— Ronald George 149	— Harry Ernest 352	— Hugh Charles 360
Bridge, Rev. Arthur...... 460	— Victor Reginald 151	— Henry Donald 28	— William Tonnans 314
— Chas. Henry 41, 366	— William Saurin 23, 407	— Hy. Montague 279	Buckland, Philip A....61, 414
— Tho. F. Dunscomb 47, 399	Brooker, Edward Part... 212	— Henry Ralph ... 6, 283	— Reginald Ulick H. ... 211
— William Albert......... 27	Brooker, Orestes J. H.... 291	— Herbert José P............ 440	Buckle, Archie Stewart 175
— William Cyprian 282	— Robert Leo Cecil 21	— Sir James............6, 218	— Arthur Charles 282
Bridges, Arch. Holroyd 440	Brooking, Harry Triscott 430	— Major James......57, 249	— Arthur Ernest 367
— Edw. Cha. Philippi ... 282	Brooks, Alfred 368	— Colonel James 16	— Arthur W. B............ 273
— Francis Doveton 401	— James 370	— Sir Jas. F. Manners ... 204	— Christopher Reginald 172
— George Tom M. 177	— Lewis Amadeus...360, 370	— James Frederick 177	— Edward Harold 295
— Thomas McGhie 291	Brooksbank, R. Gylby... 156	— Lambart John 59, 414	— Edw. John Bentley 61, 259
— Wm. Percy 378	Broome, George Simpson 427	— Leslie Swinton 441	— Herbert Stewart 401
Bridgford, Robt Jas. ... 309	— Guy Saville Fred. ... 176	— Robert Arthur 278	— Matthew Perceval 294
Bridgman, Arthur W. ... 369	— Ralph Champneys 421	— Samuel H. 453	— Robert Alleyne S....... 329
— Fred. Henry 40, 265	— Robert Dennis 422	— Samuel Swinton 176	— Rev. W. F. Ray 396
Brierley, Eustace Carlile 261	— William Arthur ... 48, 412	— Sherwood Dighton ... 174	Buckley, Arthur D. B. ... 281
— Geoffrey T. 177	Brotherhood, M 163	— Swinton John ... 7, 405	— Basil Thorold 207
Briffa, Rinaldo 180	Brotherton, T. de la H.... 209	— Walter G. Barton...... 243	— Edw. Duncombe Hen. 171
Briggs, Charles James... 136	Brough, James Fox...28, 165	— William 423	— Edward James 271
— Fred. Clifton 249	— John 393	— Wm. Barrington...46, 276	— John 386
— George Ewbank...57, 243	Broughton, Bryan D. ... 254	Lt. Col. Wm. Henry 40, 409	— John Joseph 362
— Harry Beecham...... 530	— Ern. Chamier... 68, 311	Lt. Col. Wm. Henry 41, 410	Budd, Norman A. Hay 432
— Wm. Egginton...51, 281	— Legh Harley Delves 177	— Wm. Rich. 504	Budworth, Chas. E. D. 175
Bright, Ashley Rowland 287	— Theodore Delves 214	Browne-Clayton, Rbt. C. 147	Buist, Arthur Hunter ... 262
— Richard 237	Broun, James Ronald ... 271	Browning, Arthur R. ... 423	— David Simson 423
— Richard G. T. 357	Browell, Edwd. Thos. 41, 166	Hanworth Stephens 177	— Herbert John Martin 365
— Sir R. O. 259	— William Basil 176	— Herbert Arrott 425	— John Martin 386
— Reginald Arthur 176	Brown, Anthony Lennon 378	— Theodore Charles 439	— Robert Napier 258
Brinckman, Rowland ... 333	— Arthur Edmund 348	— Thomas 384	Buist-Sparks, Art. W. T. 456
Brind, Charles Geo. ...46, 278	— Arthur Wale 250	— Winthrop Benjamin 505	— Frederick Braid 367
— Edw. Agincourt 27	— Charles Allen............ 425	Brownjohn, C. W............ 401	Bulfin, Edw. Stanislaus 259
— John Thomas 98	— Charles Robert ...68, 309	Brownlow, Cecil Barry 417	Balkley, George Alfred 256
Brindle, Rev. Robert...... 396	— Claude Russell 214	— Celadon Charles ...26, 429	Bull, George Henry...... 530
Brine, Bruce 19, 204	— Courtney Ernest Jos. 311	— Charles William 172	Bullen, Edward Darley 212
— Percival Forbes......... 7	— Dugald Blair 378	— d'Arcy Charles............ 439	— John B. Symes 46, 157
Brinkley, Chas. M. E. 139, 370	— Edward............ 130	— Henry Blaikie 171	— John Welply 284
— Henry Leigh King ... 272	— Edward Douglas 160	— Howe Montgomery... 432	— Stephen Darley 175
Brinton, John Chaytor 134	— Edward Wallace 294	Hon. J. Roderick 305	Bulton-Smith, Geo. M. . 346
Briscoe, Alex. Villiers ... 171	— Edwin Harold 455	— William Vesey 18	Buller, Frederick Wm. 26, 404
— Edward William 169	— Francis Joseph 385	Brownrigg, Geo. Alex.... 428	Hon. Henry Yarde ... 357
— Henry Arthur W....... 305	— Frank 185	— Henry John Watt...... 210	— James Hornby 130
Briso, Harold G. Ruggles 229	— Frank Russell 347	— Henry Studholme ... 28	Rt. Hon. Sir Redvers
Brissenden, Albert 220	— Frank Tatton 178	— Metcalfe Studholme 44	Henry 5
Brittain, Rev. A. H. B. ... 507	— Fred. John 58, 288	Bruce, Alan G. Cameron 150	Bullock, Frank 212
Brittan, Cha. Gisborne... 400	— Fredk. Wm. Alex. ... 185	— Alfred Crawford ...53, 208	— Geo. Muckworth ...58, 249
— Edward Pole 398	— George Rodney 422	— Andrew McCrae... 26, 404	— Herbert William 262
— Reginald 289	— Harry Herbert 383	— Arthur Francis............ 428	— Rev. W. H. 396
Britton, Thos. X. 435	— Harry Troup 426	Hon. Chas. Granville 435	Bulman, Philip 67, 297
Brittlebank, Joseph. ... 141	— Henry George 434	— Chas. Maurice Dundas 177	Bulpett, Arthur D. ...61, 289
Broadbent, John Edw. 44, 206	— Henry Robert 325	— Clarence Dalrymple 277	Bulwer, Edw. A. E....... 292
Broadfoot, Archibald 43, 166	— Henry Thomas 377	— David 382	— Sir Edward G. 4
Broadhurst, Arthur B.... 156	— Howard Clifton...... 154	— Edward 47, 412	Bunbury, Herbert N. 47, 366
Broadley, Hamilton W. 154	— James Andrew 259	— Edw. Archibald ...45, 259	— Vesey Tuos. 256
— Thomas S. Chas. Wm. 234	— John Southwell ...48, 379	— Edward Maunsell...... 148	— Wm. E. Ewin 420
Broadmead, Henry 283	— Lewis George... 510	— Elliott Armstrong 21, 408	— W. H. C. Hanmer 438

Index—Active List.

Bunbury, William Hy... 213
— Wm. Reeves 21, 407
— Wm. St. Pierre 170
Bundock, Alick Fras. ... 284
— Hugh Frederick 288
Bunny, Arth. Cautley 59, 414
— Frank Wm. M'Ti 293, 369
— Frederick Brice ...53, 167
Bunting, Thomas King 112
Burbury, Fras. Wm 294
— James Harold 279
Burch, Wm. E. S. 301
Burden, Henry 457
Burder, Ernest Sumner 276
Burdett, Sir Francis, Bt. 159
Burdon, John Alder 291
— Walter B. Chandless ... 150
Burge, Benjamin Henry 372
— Norman Ormsby 401
Burges, Daniel 272
— Frank 272
Burgess, Fra. F. R....47, 412
Burgmann, Geo. John 24, 165
Burke, Edward Plunkett 238
— John FitzGerald 387
— Richard William 393
— Thomas Edmund 238
— Paym. William Henry 373
— Surg. Capt. Wm. Henry 530
Burlton, Alfred Ralph... 433
— Arthur H. 380
— Philip Sykes Murphy 432
— Reginald Dennis...... 421
— William E. Ferdinand 432
Burlton-Bennett, J.R 28, 409
Burn, Alex. Edw. P...... 417
— Arthur George ...69, 417
— Charles Rosdew 143
— Ernest M. Johnston... 212
— George Callander 440
— James Montague 212
Burn-Murdoch, John 58, 268
— John Francis 61, 143
— Paul Robert 209
Burnaby, Charles G. 212
Burnard, Frank E. C.... 401
Burne, Fras. Henry G. ... 212
— George H. P. 256
— Jasper..............27, 409
— Knightley Owen 430
— Knightley Poyntz 424
— Malcolm Hiley 279
— Newdigate A. K. 418
— Rainald Owen ... 243, 368
Burnett, Charles John... 16
— Charles Kenyon 160
— Jas. Gordon Lennox 256
— John Chaplyn 173
— Joseph John 373
— Rev. Richard P. 507
— Sidney Harvey....... 530
— William Augustus ... 373
— William Francis 378
Burnett-Stuart John T. 357
Burney, Ernest Henry 69, 293
— Ernle K. Amyatt 27
— Herbert Henry 321
— Percy de Sausmarez.. 171
Burns, John William ... 145
Burns-Lindow, Isaac W. 150
Burnside, E. Aug....... 384
Burrage, John 310
Burrard, Charles 433
— Harry George 261
— Sidney Gerald 210
— William Dutton 172
Burrell, Wm. Samuel 68, 236
Burridge, Fras. John 49, 166a
Burroughs, C. 362
— C. A. de P. 53, 284
— George Edward E. ... 529
— Rev. Wm. Gore 460
Burrowes, A. Robinson 333
— A. St Leger......48, 399
— Alex. Leslie Scott 46, 397
— Henry Gray 170
— Louis Arundell 246
Burrows, Alfred 291
— Edmund A. 61, 169
— George Vernon 422
— James Rogers 383
— Norman 16
Burt, Arthur George ... 31
— Charles Henry 134
— John Marshall 171
— Thomas Taylor 294
Burtchnell, Chas. Henry 335
Burtenshaw, John 451

Burton, Albert 55, 168
— Arthur Robert 271
— Aubrey de Sausmarez 214
— Benjamin 58, 163
— Cecil Fowler 243
— Charles Wm. W. 419
— Edmund Boteler 423
— Edmund Merceron ... 210
— Fowler 294
— Francis Charles ...42, 410
— Fras. Hy. M. 381
— Fredk. Nuthall 434
— Gerard Septimus..... 28
— Harry Chas. Hay..... 176
— Henry Gerard 426
— Hubert 65, 168
— John 395
— John Adolphus 505
— Reginald de H. 301
— Reginald George 431
— Richard Watkins 438
— Samuel 398
— St. George Edw. Wm. 286
— Sidney Walter 246
— Willoughby Seymour 238
Burton-Brown, Frederic
Hewlett............... 456
Bury, John Thomas 42, 166
Bush, Harry S. 294
— Henry Biddulph 395
— Herbert Wheeler 457
— John Ernest 314
Bushe, Lt. Chas. Kendal 137
— 2nd Lt. Chas. Kendal 176
— Thomas Francis 170
Bushman, Hy. Augustus 176
Buston, Philip Thos. 52, 208
Busuttil, Michael 256
Buswell, Ferberd R..... 385
Butcher, Arthur E. A. .. 171
— Frederick Spurrell... 175
— George James.....264, 369
— Henry Townsend 65, 169
Butler, Alex. Hazelwood 440
— Arthur Almeric P. ... 256
— Arthur Townley 174
— Chas. E.A.F.Somerset 296
— Ernest Reuben C. ... 395
— Fra. John P. 63
— Henry Hugh 172
— Hubert Lavie 262
— James 44, 411
— James W. S. 22, 407
— John B. R. 68, 416
— Richard Fowler 243
— Richd. H. Keatinge... 283
— Robert Fowler 17
— Sir Wm. Fras. 6
— William J. Chesshyro 141
Butler-Creagh, W. B. 68, 295
Butlin, Wm. Brooks..... 25
Batt, Edward 385
— Frank Ern. Wilhelm 361
Buttanshaw, Edw. T. .. 367
— William Henry 374
Butterworth, Samuel ... 382
Buxton, J. Walton F. ... 40
Buzzard, Chas. Norman 177
Byam, E. W. G. 26, 399
— William 17
Byass, Harry N. 311
Byers, Cyril B. 439
Byland, Sidney Veale... 441
Byne, Roland M. 400
Byng, Hon. C. C. G. 23
— Geo. Philip Fras. 47, 295
— Hon. Julian E. G. 152
— Thomas Richard ...23, 408
Byrne, Fred. Joseph ... 335
— Gervis Taylor 400
— Joseph Aloysius 271
Byron, John 177
— Richard 303
Bythell, William John... 210
Cadell, Alexander...... 432
— Harry Ernest 174
— Hew Francis......67, 415
— James Dalmahoy ... 440
— John Francis 172
— John Macfarlane 455
— Sir Robert 180
— Robert Mackay 291
Cadge, Wm. H. 454
Cadogan, Henry O. S... 265
Caffin, Ernest G. 259
Cahill, Charles J. S. 21, 407
Cahusac, Wm. Fremantle 420

Caillard, Wm. M. C. duQ. 147
Caine, Henry Monteath 372
Caird, Edw. Devon 294, 369
— Lindsay Heuryson ... 278
Cairncross, John 6, 397
Cairnes, James Elliot ... 177
— William Alan........ 210
— William Elliot 334
Cairns, Michael 568
— Hon. W. Dallas....... 357
Caldecott, Fras. Jas....7, 180
— Guy 242
— Randolph............ 529
Caldwell, Arthur L. 310, 367
— J. Fletcher 17
— Robert 382
Callender, David A..... 234
Calley, Henry......... 172
— Thomas C. P. 67, 133
Callwell, Albert Henry 52, 167
— Charles Edward 170
Calthorpe, Hon.S.J.G. .. 140
Calthrop, Christopher W. 452
Calvert, Chas. Arch..... 143
— George 174
— John Tolfer 456
— Robt. T. Chris 456
Cama, Rustam Hormasji 503
Cambier, Ernest F....41, 165
CAMBRIDGE, H.R.H.Duke
of, 4, 159, 164, 204, 229, 304
— Edward D. P. 255
Cameron, Angus 325
— Archibald 452
— Archibald Rice 286
— Donald Hay 437
— Ewan Cornwallis ... 173
— Ewan Duncan 174
— Ewen Donald Charles 173
— Rev. Francis Ewen ... 507
— George E. E. Gordon 322
— Hillyard H. A. 44
— Hugh Alan........... 213
— James 48, 207
— Rev. John 460
— John Sullivan 261
— Kenneth Boswell ... 337
— Kenneth Mackenzie.. 386
— Maurice Alex....67, 209
— Neville J. Gordon ... 325
— Sir William Gordon.. 238
Camilleri, John M...... 435
Campbell, Alan James.. 432
— Capt. Alexander ... 286
— Alex. A. Elphinstone 427
— Alexander Sereton .. 245
— Alex. Wm. D. 59, 414
— Angus 362
— Archibald Douglas... 233
— 2nd Lieut. Arch. John 161
— Lieut. Arch. John ... 337
— Arthur Crawford J... 301
— Aylmer M'Iver 433
— Barrington B. D. 18, 233
— Chas. H. D. Lyon ... 264
— Charles Ferguson ... 428
— Charles Gray 270
— Charles Lionel K. ... 158
— Claud Herbert 141
— Colin Powys 421
— David G. Mushiet.... 151
— Donald Wm. A. 282
— Douglas 318
— Duncan MacNeil...43, 206
— Edmund Arthur 173
— Ernest George 357
— Frank James Brook.. 423
— Frederick............ 422
— Fred. Lorn......18, 233
— George 244
— George Duncan 285
— George Patrick 433
— George Polding 212
— Gordon M'Clelland... 176
— Gunning Morehead.. 398
— Harold B. D. 213
— Henri Montgomery.. 173
— Henry William 428
— Herbert Montgomery 171
— Hugh Walter Geo. ... 243
— Hugo Montgomery 67, 169
— Ian Hamilton 440
— James Alastair...57, 318
— 2nd Lieut. John..... 325
— 2nd Lieut. John..... 337
— John Beresford 231
— John Charles 61, 208
— John C. L. 57, 208

Campbell, John Edw. 24, 408
— John Hasluck 65, 337
— John Robert 214
— Kenneth J. R. 141
— Leslie Warner Y..... 433
— LornR. Henry Dick 29, 409
— MalcolmSydenhamC. 172
— Napier George 180
— Reginald 267
— Robert Byng P. P. 7, 405
— Robert Neil.......... 454
— Ronald Gore 346
— Walter 321
— Surg. Major William 379
— Col. Wm. 27, 397
— Wm. Alex..........65, 242
— William Fred. .. 28, 399
— Wm. Kenneth H..... 276
— William MacLaren ... 286
— Wm. Mussen 44, 166a
— Wm. Nevile 430
— William Pitcairn...65, 304
Campbell - Maclachlan,
Neil 318
Campion, Walter Ernest 254
Candy, J. Molesworth 66, 415
Canning, Albert....... 257
Cannot, Fernand G. E. 282
Cansdale, Arthur 284
Cant, Ernest Pettitt ... 139
Cautan, Henry Thos. ... 276
Cape, Geo. Augustus S. 176
— Herbert Anderson ... 160
Capper, Alfred Stewart 177
— John Edward........ 210
— Robert Harcourt Ord 310
— Thompson........... 274
— William Baume ...50, 297
Capron, George 311
Carandini, Frank J. ...65, 147
Carbonaro, Achilles B. ... 186
— Ernest 419
Carbutt, Edw. Goddard 177
Carden, Alan Douglas 214
— Coldstream J......... 334
— Henry Parry.....49, 276
— Henry Westenra 373
— John Rutter 438
— Louis Peile 171
Cardew, Francis Gordon 428
— George Ambrose ... 174
— George Hereward ... 367
— George Schuyler ... 383
Cardozo, Samuel N..... 382
Carew, Bampfylde L. ... 139
— Geo. Albert Ludo.... 149
— Ponsonby May L..... 162
— Richard Hugh 377
Carey, Arthur Basil... 214
— Carteret W......57, 317
— Charles Frederick.... 371
— C. de Beauvoir ...28, 205
— Cecil William 362
— Denis 274
— de Vic 273
— Edward Sausmarez... 271
— Ernest Adolphus ... 17
— George G. Sandeman 174
— Gordon Thos. Jas..... 317
— H.R. Le Marchant 40, 408
— Harold Eustace...... 177
— Herbert Clement ... 211
— Horace William W.
Onslow 169
— John Thos. 379
— Octavius William ... 433
— Seymour James 250
— Walter Louis John ... 177
— Ward Sausmarez 253, 368
— Wilfred Sausmarez .. 242
— Wm. H. villiand..... 175
Carlaw, Henry 322
Carleton, Arth. W. 379
— Frank R. 58, 314
— Fred. Montgomerie... 238
— George Dudley....59, 256
— Guy Audouin........ 238
— Henry Alex. 179
— Henry Anthony 438
— Henry Augustus 419
— Hugh Dudley 360
— Launcelot Richard ... 288
— Montgomery L....... 172
— Patrick Maurice 380
Carlisle, Prendergast B. 346
Carlyle, Thomas 185
Carlyon, Lionel K...... 310
Carmichael, George G. T. 277

Index—Active List.

Carmichael, J.C. Gordon 452
— James F. H. 213
— John 381
Carnaghan, John 178
Carnegie, Hon. R. F. ... 321
Carnegy, CharlesGilbert 431
— Harry George 433
— Philip Mainwaring ... 421
— Richard Lloyd 439
Carpendale, John M...... 419
— Montagu Maxwell 22, 407
— Percy Maxwell 421
— William Maxwell 426
Carpenter, Charles M.... 213
— Frederick 49, 334
Carr, Arthur Nisbet 420
— Charles Cattley 243
— Charles Ernest 295
— Edward Elliott....58, 262
— Frederick Ulysses ... 395
— George Anderson ... 209
— Henry Arbuthnot..... 273
— Howard 383
— Robert Cattley 171
— William 457
Carr-White, Percy 506
Carreg, Robert Thomas 297
Carrington, Edmund ... 25
— Sir Fredk. 7
Carrick, Ethelbert Wm. 431
Carroll, Arthur Lyons... 171
— Edw. Rich. W. C. ... 455
— James Henry......... 115
— John Wm. Vincent... 245
Carruthers, CharlesAug. 282
— Frns. John 269
— Herbert St. Clare..... 505
— John Thomas 28, 409
— Joseph George Thomson 25, 404
— Robert Alexander ... 429
Carson, Llewellyn B..... 274
— Inspector Thomas.... 115
— Lieut. Thomas 323
— Walter P. 530
Carte, Thomas Elliott... 171
— William 128
— William Alex. 379
Carter, Alfred Henry 61, 169
— Aubrey John......... 291
— Beresford C.Molyneux 261
— Charles Herbert P.... 286
— Charles Murray 438
— Duncan Campbell 65, 169
— Edward James 423
— Ernest Aug. Frederic 238
— Ernest Pasley 173
— Evan Eyare 367
— Francis Charles 293
— Frederick Hugh 315
— Gerard Edward 177
— Godfrey Lambert.... 437
— Gordon 133
— Harry Molyneux....50, 308
— Herman Bonham ... 211
— James Edward 385
— John R. B. Graham. 434
— John Thomas....292, 374
— Leslie Fitz William ... 155
— Lindsay James....... 287
— Sidney H. 379
— William 155
— William Graydon....49, 288
Carter-Campbell,G.T.C. 270
Cartwright, Alfred G. ... 259
— Charles Marling 426
— Francis John Winsor 401
— Garnier Norton. 275
— George Strachan 211
Caruana, Alfred Joseph 435
Carwithen, Edw. Terry 439
— Geo. T. L. 21
Cary, Francis Walter ... 24
— George Stanley...... 329
Case, Charles 415
— Thos. Elphinstone ... 231
Casement, Roger 173
Casey, Chas. Leslie...52, 167
Casgrain,P.H.duPerron 211
Cashel, Rowan 295
Cass, Chas. Herbert D. 334
— Claude Wm. Culley. 297
Cassan, Ernest 52, 167
Cassels, Gilbert R. 438
— Rev. J. W. 507
— Kenneth Scougall ... 438
Casserly, James Henry 292
Cassidy, Chris. C....... 456
Casson, Ferdinand Geo. 240
— Hugh Gilbert........ 267
Casswell, Frank 290
Castens, Wm. Ernest ... 178
Castle, Norton Clowes.. 258
Castor, Richard H. 506
Cates, Geo. Edw. H..... 419
— William Johnstone... 346
Cathcart,Hon. Reginald 305
Catherwood, Wm. A. ... 277
Cator, Christian 287
— Edmund H. Style.... 214
— Robert 401
Cattell, Gilbert L......... 301
Caulfeild, Alg. M........ 278
— Charles T. 172
— Fras. W. J. 424
— Gordon Napier 425
— JamesEdwardW.S.42, 360
— St. Geo. R. Sanderson 213
Caunter, Jas. Eales 285
Cautley, John C. 47, 294
Cavarra, Alfred 57, 186
Cavaye, Alex. H. B. ... 269
— George Ross 325
— William Fred........ 21
Cave, Arthur Stephen... 293
— Bernard Cave Browne 308
— Chas. Donovan ...50, 250
— George Noble 411
— Henry Charles Edw. 424
Cavenagh,WentworthO. 255
Cavendish, Alfred E. J. 337
— Cecil Charles......... 317
— Hon. William Edwin 229
Cavendish - Bentinck,
  Lord W. A. 152
Cawood, George Crane 424
Cayley,Arthur Macaulay 175
— Douglas Edward ... 273
— W. de Sausmarez ... 253
Cayzer, John S. 142
Cecil, Lord Edw. H...... 229
— Lord J. Pakenham... 229
Chads, Harry Campbell 282
Chadwick,Jas.Markham 347
Chaldecott, Alg. Winn.. 298
— William Henry 214
Challenor, Edw. Lacy... 256
— Geo. Richards....51, 167
— Robert Richards ... 335
Challice, Gerald Geo. 43, 366
Chalmer, Reginald ... 29
Chalmers, Edw. W. 46, 411
— Robert C. Hilliard ... 434
Chamberlain, Rev. F. W. 460
— Neville F. FitzG...28, 416
— Robert Ind........... 269
— Thomas Ffoster..... 170
Chamberlayne, Wm. J... 360
Chamberlain, Arthur B... 186
Chambers, Alexander J. 385
— Charles James O. 19, 406
— Osborn Augustin ... 242
— Robert Yeld 413
Chamier, Arthur Tyrrell 214
— George Daniel 171
— Henry Deschamps... 334
— Saunders James 173
— William St. George.. 346
Champain, Charles B.... 318
Champain,A.P.Bateman 433
— Hugh Fred.Bateman 438
Champernowne, H. 28, 207
— Henry Harington ... 276
Champion, A. N. H. U.58, 346
— Arthur Duncan 163
— Horace Edgar 368
Chance, Harry 170
Chancellor, Arthur ... 325
— John Robert 629
Chandler, H. Geo. Wm. 301
— Leonard G. T. 252
Chandos-Pole-Goll,H.A. 231
Channer, Bernard... 45, 411
— George Kendall ... 362
— Geo. N. 6, 405
— Osborne H........... 529
Chaplin, Allan 26, 404a
— Chas. Slingsby 147
— James Graham 270
— Reginald Spencer ... 152
— Ronald Eustace...... 434
Chapman, Arch. John ... 348
— Arthur Emerson ...46, 399
— Charles Higford...... 264
— David Phelps ...49, 264
— Edwd. Fras. 5, 179
Chapman, Edw. Henry 259
— Francis Robert H. ... 420
— Sir Fred. E. 204
— Frederic Hamilton... 276
— Hamilton..........7, 405
— Harry Ernest......... 278
— Herbert Alex......... 170
— Lawrence Joseph.... 175
— Leonard Palmer ... 211
— Lionel James A....49, 166a
— Rev. P. H. 460
— Rev. Thos.Henderson 396
— Rev. Chas. Henry 507
— Jno. R. M. 45, 206
Charles, Jas. Ronald E. 214
— Richard Havelock ... 455
— Stephen Flockton ... 261
— Rev. Williams........ 457
Charleston, Ernest E. J. 285
— Charley, JohnFras.W.66,271
— Charlton, Claud E. C. G. 177
— Hy. Arthur Herbert 379
— Wm. Johnston 378
Charrier, Paul Alfred ... 347
Charteris, Edm. Butler 135
Charters, Frank H. ... 155
Chartres, Richd. C. 176
Chase, Herbert 368
— James 733
— Ramsay Gordon ... 293
— William St. L. 417
Chatter, Vernon 28
Chatterje,FakirChundra 454
— Nityananda 529
Chatterton,BernardRbt. 457
— Frank B. Macaulay... 284
— Frank Wm. 24, 404
— George D. Latham ... 437
— John Balsir 431
Chauncey, Chas. Henry 371
Chauncy, Wm. Auschar 258
Chawner,Wm. Hampden 288
Chaworth-Musters,H.C. 145
Chaytor, Robt. Jas....48, 292
Cheales, Ralph Darby... 274
Cheetham, Chas. J....51, 398
Cheke, Edw. Geo. 175
Chepmell, C. Herries ... 174
Chermside, Herb. C....21, 205
— Robert Alex. 40, 366
— Cherry, Hy. Aitkin 44, 240
Chesnaye, G. Cochet.... 452
Chesney, Alex. Geo. ... 282
— Sir Geo. Tomkyns...4, 218
— Harold Frank......... 210
— Kellow 425
— Napier Elles 433
Chester, Wm. L. 379
Chesterfield, Earl of ... 130
Chetwode, Philip W. ... 161
Chetwynd - Stapylton,
  Bryan Henry 264
Chevalley, Francis 185
Chevallier,Fras. E. deC. 178
Chevers, Herbert L. G. 383
Cheyne, Arch. Ythen ... 285
— ReginaldEdmonstone 438
Chichester, Alan Geo. 65, 258
— Alfred G. de Vaud ... 434
— Arlington Augustus 283
— Arthur G. Vaughan... 334
— Claud Oswald 287
— Cyril Ernest 252
— Fred. John Newton.. 249
— Gerard 310
— Joseph 273
— Reginald de Blaquière 178
— Walter Raleigh 273
Childe, L. Fred.......... 530
Childers, Eardley M..... 287
— Edm. S. Eardley....45, 209
Chill, Walter 361
Chinn, John Henry ... 185
Chippindall, G. Herbt.66,277
— Wm. Harold 53, 208
Chisholm, John H. G. S. 440
Chisholm - Batten, J.
  Forbes 372
Chisholme, J. J. Scott47, 193
Chitty, Arthur Wilson... 272
— Ernest R. Inglis ... 434
— Walter Willis......... 431
Chown, Ernest Edw. ... 400
Chree, Rev. Geo. J. ... 460
Christian, Ewan 262
— Gerard 259
— Herbert William ... 305
Christie, C. H. P. 43, 206
— Edgar Jessopp 329
— Edward T.........40, 366
— Henry 361
— Henry R. Stark...... 213
— Herbert W. Andrew 175
— James Harry........ 420
— Lindsay Bruce Stark 176
— William Charles ... 242
Christopher, A.C. Seton 318
— Charles Danby... 289, 368
— Leonard William 45, 411
Chrystie, Col. George 21, 407
— 2nd Lt. George...... 348
— John 177
Church, Arth. Geo. Hay 18
— Arthur J. B. 334
— Bernard Elliot 158
— Chas.Theobald Walsh 29
— George Ross M...... 174
— John Fletcher 155
Churcher, Douglas W... 333
Churchill, Alex. F. 377
— Arthur Ben. Norton.. 171
— Arth. Gillespie......63, 154
— Charles Fleetwood ... 377
— Folliott 426
— George Ross Deas ... 275
— Herbert Forbes...... 270
— Mackenzie 28
— Seton 372
— Winston L. P. 146
Churchward, Rev. M. W. 396
— Paul R. S. 291
— Walter Stanbury...61, 169
Chute, Pierce T. 347
— Richard A. S. 275
Clanchy, Frank 333
Clapham, John Thurlow 385
Claridge,PercyShelleyF. 440
Clark, Chas. H. Baldwin 437
— Charles Watson ... 175
— CraufurdAlex.Gordon 305
— Ernest Shaw......... 386
— George............... 185
— James Richardson A. 379
— James Rutherford... 318
— Joseph A. M. A. ... 401
— Paul Treby......... 287
— Robert Leaver ... 185
— Stephen Frazer ... 384
— William 49, 287
— Wm. Ronaldson ... 455
Clarke, Albert Edw..... 395
— Arthur C. Stanley ... 434
— Qr. Mr. Charles ... 159
— Capt. Charles....... 400
— Charles C. Wiseman. 171
— Charles Hy. G. Mansfield 357
— Charles James 214
— Charles M. 5
— Rev. Fred. James.... 460
— Fred. L. Stanley ... 270
— George Calvert ... 144
— George L. Philip ... 436
— Sir Geo. Sydenham 47, 206
— George Vernon...... 177
— Henry 46, 206
— Hen. Calvert Stanley 178
— James 454
— James Alleyne ...40, 366
— James Richard P. ... 285
— James Sealy........ 238
— John de W. Lardner69, 169
— John Louis J. 254
— John Walrond 130
— Lionel A. Graham ... 174
— Robert 185
— Robert F. N. 309
— Seymour Spencer S. 337
— Somerset M. Wiseman 5
— Tom 178
— Travers Edwards... 271
— Walter William ... 115
— William Senhouse J... 48
— Clarke-Jervoise,Eus.Jas. 284
— Clarkson,Bertie St.John 283
— Frank Cecil 455
— John Wilkins 529
— Thos. H. Frederick... 383
Claughton, Fra. A. C. 61, 269
Clauson, John Eugene.. 211
Clavell, Rich. K. W. R. 400
Clay, Bertie Gordon..... 140
— Charles Herbert ... 430
— Neville S. Bertie ... 173
— Spencer 439

Index—Active List. 548

Clay, Stanley	436
Clayton, Charles	395
— Edward Francis	233
— Emilius	27, 165
— Fred. Thos.	61, 366
— Henry E. Gilbert	212
Cleeve, Egerton Stewart	173
— Frederick J. S.	171
— Herbert	267
— Stewart Dalrymple	67, 209
— Wm. Fred.	55, 168
Clegg, William	293
Cleghorn, Chas. Angus	176
— James	452
Clement, Reynold A.	130
— Robert Hampden	382
Clements, Chas. Henry	426
— John Samuel	178
— Ralph Arthur P.	40, 267
— William George	387
Clemson, Wm. Fletcher	311
Clerk, Albert Edmund	274
— Charles James	163
— Godfrey	5
— Henry	52, 137
Clerke, Augustus B. H.	176
Clery, Carleton B. L.	437
— Cornelius F.	7
— James Albert	378
Cleveland, Hen. Fras.	530
Clibborn, John	53, 413
Cliff, Harold Martin	329
Clifford, Rev. Arthur	460
— Henry Frederick H.	250
— Rich. Melville	22, 407
— Robert Cecil R.	16, 406
— Walter Rees	264
Climo, Skipton Hill	436
— Verschoyle C.	360
— William Hill	293
Clinch, Herbert W.	271
Clisham, John	263
Clive, Edward Henry	5
— George Sidney	230
— Percy Archer	230
Cloeté, Evelyn R. H. J.	172
Cloke, Robert Patrick	293
Close, Arthur John	214
— Charles Barry	245
— Charles Frederick	211
— Francis Morton	213
— Frederick Macdonald	170
— Geoffrey Dominic	211
— Joseph Kinnear	456
— Lewis Henry	213
— Maxwell Arch	55, 155
— Thomas	357
Clothier, Robert F.	417
Clough, Alfred H. B.	67, 347
Clowes, Ernest Wm.	133
— Henry	431
— Henry Arthur	133
— Peter Legh	50, 150
Clutterbuck, Charles B.	269
— Edmund Ricardo	146
— Lewis Augustus	40, 366
Coast, Alan	271
Coates, Douglas R.	175
— George	40, 366
— George John	380
— Henry Wise Unett	255
— John Unett	172
— Reginald Carylon	175
— William	454
Coats, James	378
— George Henry B.	59, 414
Cobb, Cecil Henry	287
— Charles Edward	254
— Edward P. Wheatly	265
— Harold Wolstenholme	277
— Robert	454
Cobbe, Alex. Stanhope	439
— Charles Clermont	237
— Henry Hercules	438
Cobbold, Alan Ralph	209
— Ernest Cazenove	311
— Rev. F. E. Davy	460
Cobham, Horace W.	436
Cochran, Archibald G.	68, 400
— Francis	25
Cochrane, C. FitzG. T.	346
— George Leslie	315
James Kilvington	346
— Norman Denneys	176
— Thomas Henry	213
— Wm. Fras. Dundonald	45
Cockburn, Alex. Wm.	53, 208
— Charles James	242
Cockburn, George	69, 356
— George Alexander	49, 206
— James George	19
— John Brydges	265
— Wm. Alex. Crawford	137
— Wm. Fredk.	170
Cockcraft, C. Macleod	435
Cockerill, Geo. Kynaston	435
— John William	384
— Robert Charles	432
Cockin, Rev. J. I. B.	460
Cocks, Horace	383
Cocq, Charles Alex. R.	437
Coddington, H. B. Orton	281
— Herbert Adolphe	333
Codrington, Alfd. Edw.	53, 231
— Edw. William	423
— Ernest	436
— George Henry F.	19, 406
— Harry de Burgh	437
— Herbert Say	283
— Hopton Osbert	440
— Hubert Walter	435
— Richard Percy John	283
— William Robert	153
Coffin, Campbell	213
— Clifford	213
— Roger Pine	45, 399
Cogan, Rev. Horace B.	460
— Michael	377
Coghill, Charles Edw.	171
— Norman Sinclair	234
Coke, Edward B.	56, 407
— Edw. Sacheverell D'E.	269
— Ernest Sacheverell	401
— John Talbot	24
— Ronald Bruce	285
— Thos. William, Visct.	26
Hon. Wenman	356
Coker, Lewis Edm.	51, 167
Colan, Wm. Robt. Boyle	439
Colahan, John	377
Colborne, Hon. Sir Fra.	242
— Hon. Francis L. L.	132
— Hon. J. G. R. Ulysses	282
Colchester-Wemyss, M.F.	270
Coldstream, John C.	362
— William M.	213
Coldwell, Reg. Charles	292
Cole, A. W. G. Lowry	265
— Edward Hearle	430
— Frederick Temple	171
— Henry Cecil Lowry	281
— Henry Hardy	41, 207
— Henry Walter George	432
— Henry Wells	295
— Robert Arthur	420
— Rev. T. E. F.	460
Coleman, Albert	456
— William Freme	250
Coleridge, Hugh F.	291
Coles, Arthur H.	237
— Colin Hennessey R.	432
— Herbert Jefferis	401
— Morton Calverley	236
— Walter	65, 209
Coley-Bromfield, J. C.	175
Colhoun, Charles K.	65, 311
Collacott, John Richard	185
Collard, Alex. A. Lysons	281
— Arthur William	41, 366
— Charles Edwin	401
— John Marshall M.	292
Colledge, Leslie Robert	382
Collen, Sir Ed. H.H.	24, 409
Colleton, Sir R. A. W. Bt. 61,	265
Collette, Cecil Henry	50, 297
Colley, George Fred.	361
Collie, Mackintosh A. T.	530
Collings, Alg. Wm.	65, 262
— Cecil Bargrave	348
— Godfrey Disney	337, 373
— Wm. Augustus	49, 293
Collingwood, Clennell W.	177
— Cuthbert G.	48, 261
— Henry	25
— William George	369
Collins, Anthony	130
— Charles Bury	212
— Charles Welman	460
— David E.	370
— Denis Joseph	386
— Ernest Rokeby	274
— George Atkins	68, 416
— James	395
— John Gerrard	286
— John Robert	17
Collins, John Stratford	51, 236
— Rev. Reginald F.	390
— Richard Henn	293
— Thos. Gerrard	159
— William Fellowes	144
— William Henry	136
— Wm. Henry Albert	186
Collinson, John	67, 292
Collis, Francis William	16, 407
— Wilfrid E. Russell	147
Collison, Chas. S.	301
Collyer, Arthur Alan	255
Colman, George M. H.	381
Colnaghi, Dominic H.	212
Cologan, J. F. FitzG.	18, 406
Colomb, Fras. Cracroft	425
— George Henry Cooper	430
— Richard Pasley	422
Colquhoun, Alan S.	293
— Charles Fayle	275
— Edward Lyndon	367
— Harry	367
— Herbert W. C.	432
— Julian Campbell	34
— Robert Crosthwaite	401
Colston, Harold K.	311
Colvile, Geo. Northcote	287
— Henry Edward	18, 229
Colville, Arthur E.W.	66, 356
Colvin, Forrester F.	151
— Jas. Morris C.	213
— John Russell C.	423
Colwell, Geo. H. T.	22, 399
Combe, Boyce	153
— Boyce Albert	16
— Edward Stanley	334, 369
— Kenneth	174
— Lionel	270
Comerford, H.	377
Comins, Dennis W. D.	453
— Henry	424
Commeline, Chas. Ern.	209
— Francis Henry Bagot	428
Compigné, H. Mapleton	371
Compton, Charles Wm.	252
— Lord Douglas J. Cecil	151
— Thomas Edward	66, 292
Comyn, Edward Walter	174
Conder, Claude R.	52, 207
Condon, Edgar Hunt	385
— Jas. Knighton	437
Coney, Rev. Henry T.	396
— William Bicknell	55, 289
Congdon, Arthur E. O.	347
— Ernest C. L.	66, 400
— John James	44, 166
Congreve, Walter Norris	357
Coningham, Charles	59, 273
— Frank Evelyn	278
— Frederick	43, 234
— Henry	175
— Herbert John	346
Connal, Alex. C.	172
CONNAUGHT, H.R.H. the Duke of	1, 42, 356
Connell, Chas. Edw. H.	429
— Charles Forster	281
Connellan, Cory L.	237
Conner, George	42, 272
— Richard	272
— William Daniel	61, 208
Connolly, Arthur M.	400
— Lawrence R.	55, 397
— Matthew Wm. Kemble	295
— Wm. Edw. Gunnell	401
— William Hallett	169
Connop, Francis	259
Connor, Fred. Henry B.	333
— Harry G. Adams	334
— Isaac Joscelyn	214
— John Colpoys	385
— Timothy	360
Connors, John	245
Conolly, Edw. Michael	178
— Thomas	144
Conor, Cecil	44, 277
Conran, George H. M.	67, 254
— William Loraine	427
Conry, Jas. Lionel J.	335
— Walter	454
Constable, Rev. A. E. B.	460
— James George	239
— Willoughby V.	59, 208
Conway, John	276
Conway-Gordon, Esme	
Cosmo William	362
— G.	367
Conyers, Charles	333
Conyngham, Lord C. A.	357
— Gerald P. L.	211
— Jno. Staples M. L.	334
— Wm. Arbuthnot L.	66, 273
Cooch, Charles	130
— Chas. Edw. Hyacinth	278
Coode, Henry P. R.	178
— John H. C.	57, 286
— Percival	277
Cook, Charles Chesney	433
— Edwin Berkeley	133
— Francis J. Gilbert	40, 366
— George	178
— Henry	529
— Henry David	504
— Henry Rex	172
— James	25, 409
— Walter	417
Cooke, Alf. Fothergill	295
— Aubrey St. John	279
— Augustus Hodson	437
— Crawford Boyd	41, 410
— Ernest	61, 270
— Herbert Fothergill	264
— Hugh Wm. Fothergill	440
— Robert Joseph	264
— Samuel Arthur	438
— Sydney Fitzwyman	207
— Thomas Arthur	13
— William	40, 410
— William Butterworth	369
— William Nevinson M.	427
— William Smith	27
Cooke-Collis, M. C.	59, 414
Cookson, George Arthur	210
— Mostyn Eden	279
— Percy Selby	279
— Philip Blencowe	133
— William Whicher	172
Coombes, Samuel	178
Cooper, Alfred	115
— Aug. Frederic	265
— Austin Samuel	264
— Chas. Duncan	51, 348
— Edmund Saffery	430
— Edward Joshua	229
— Edward Shewell	172
— Francis Edward	170
— Harry	41
— Harry Ashley	432
— Henry	370
— John	395
— Lewis Ernest	423
— Philip Templer	173
— Richard Joshua	229
— Robert	142
— Thomas Francis	178
— William George	437
— William Heaton	274
— Rev. William W. G.	506
Coote, Chas. H. Eyre	69, 153
— Edmund Eyre	371
Copeland, Frederick	437
— Robert J.	384
Copeman, Hugh Chas	288
Copland, Chas. Sturrock	292
— William Stafford	256
Coppinger, Thomas S.	372
Corbet, Arth. Domville	46, 399
— Bertram D.	133
Corbett, Basil Andrew	282
— Charles Clarence	315
— Chas. Harold	160
— Edwy Frank	177
— Frank Vincent	42, 206
— Hy. George Lyon	259
— Rev. Joseph	396
— Richard	43, 165
— Rob. de la Cour	378
— Walter Frank	282
Corbyn, Edwyn C.	441
— Hector	173
Corcoran, Edward	384
Cordeaux, Harry Edw. S.	362
— Wm. Wilfrod	163
Cordner, Jas. Edw.	179
Cordue, W. Geo. Ranger	210
Corfield, Chas. John	421
Corker, Thomas M.	379
Corkery, Thos. Herbert	383
— William Alfred	530
Corkran, Chas. Edw.	230
Corlett, John S.	440
Cornish, F. T. Warre	252
Cornish-Bowden, J.H.T.	276
Corrie, Alf. Thomas	398
— George Gowan Wyatt	177
— Wm. Fras. Taylor	175

Index—Active List.

Corry, George	378
— Hon. H. Wm. Lowry	21
— John Beaumont	214
— Noel Armar Lowry	229
Corse-Scott, Edw. Hy.	44, 242
Cory, Rev. Chas. Page	507
Cosens, Robert	282
Costa, Paul Dennis	371
Costello, Edmond Wm.	441
Costley, Horace G. T.	283
Costobadie, Edw. Gerald	291
— Henry Holmes	44, 166
Cotes, Robert Hugh	279
Cotesworth, James T.	259
Cotgrave, Edwin C. B.	427
Cottell, Arthur B.	380
— Reginald Jas. Cope	383
Cotter, Edmond Wm.	55, 208
— Francis Gibson	66, 400
— Harry John	176
Cotterell, John R. G.	133
Cotterill, Harry E.	400
— Hugh Edward	236
Cottingham, Chas. S.	309
— Edward Roden	398
— Henry Langrishe	176
Cotton, Arthur Stedman	178
— Sir Arthur T.	219
— Arthur William	229
— Benjamin	297
— Charles Leonard	138
— Henry Robert S.	287
— Richard Godman T.	44, 291
— Robert Benjamin	28
— Stapleton Charles	130
— Stapleton Lynch	444
— Thomas James	21, 407
— Wellington R. P. Stapleton	161
— William Lewis	440
Cottrell, Charles D.	61, 109
Couchman, Bertram C.	400
— George H. H.	252
— Hervey Noel	302
Coulson, John	286
Coulthard, Rev. Hugh R.	460
Couper, Arthur Edw.	275
— Edward Edmonstone	424
— Victor Arthur	356
Courage, Miles Rafe F.	177
Courtenay, Edw. Jas.	9
— Edw. Reginald	52, 153
— George Edward	337
— Michael Hudson	174
Courtney, Edw. A. W.	367
— Wm. Michael	452
Cousin, Thos. Gaspard	264
Coutts, George	380
— Malcolm	368
Coventry, Charles	159
— St. John Halford	229
Cowan, Henry Vivian	49, 168
— James Henry	209
— James Wm. Alston	317
Cowans, Ernest Arnold	356
— John Steven	356
Cowell, Albert V. J.	257
— Henry Clayton	372
Cowen, Hon. D. A.	380
Cowie, Alexander Hugh	210
— Alexander John	453
— Charles Henry	210
— Charles Stewart	234
— Crombie	6, 179
— Ernest Leonard	360
— Henry Edw. Colvin.	214
— Herbert M'Cally	214
— Hugh Norman Ramsay	283
— Thomas Rennie	25, 408
— Wm. Alex. Lomer	432
Cowley, Rev. Hy. G. B.	507
— James William	423
Cowper, Herbert H. P.	24, 403
— Herbert Maitland	236
— Maitland	2
Cox, Arthur Ditmas	440
— Arth. Fras. Hamilton	271
— Aubrey Hamilton	398
— Charles Edward	256
— Charles Hay	68, 253
— Edward Henry	243
— Ernest	318
— Francis W. Henry	430
— George	19
— Gerald Aylmer	2
— Hen. Wm. Holmes	21, 406
— Herbert Vaughan	424
— John	178
Cox, John William	255
— Patrick G. Ashley	357
— Percy Zechariah	430
— Richard Charles C.	271
— Robert Emilius	24, 404a
— Robert Frederick	161
— St. John Augustus	242
— Samuel FitzGibbon	246
— Thomas Sands	362
— Walter Latham	246
— William	370
— William Charles	252
— William Smith	402
Coxhead, Jas. Alfred	52, 167
— T. Langhorne	173
Coyle, William	223
Crabbe, Eyre M. S.	49, 229
Crabbie, John	144
Cracroft, Bernard Walter	423
— Hugh	333
Cradock, Montagu	141
Craig, John Francis	66, 169
— Robert Annesley	176
Craig-Brown, Ernest	281
Craigie, J. H. Smith	45, 317
Craik, James	281
Crake, E. Barrington	61, 356
Cramer-Roberts, W. E.	245
Crampton, Fiennes H.	171
— Philip J. R.	171
Crane, Eli	361
Cranford, Robert L.	395
Craske, John	346
Craster, Edm. Henry B.	176
— James C. Balfour	418
— John Chas. Pulleine	240
— John Evelyn Edm.	214
— Shafto Longfield	210
Craufurd, George S. G.	322
— Harry James	59, 229
— John Arch. Houison	426
— Wm. Reg. Houison	41
Craven, Arthur Julius	213
Crawford, Alfred Temple	175
— Archibald	171
— Arthur Gossett	440
— Dirom Grey	453
— Claude Molville	428
— Frank F.	395
— Frederick James	506
— G. A.	116
— George Rainier	426
— Gilbert Stewart	385
— Henry	45, 271
— Henry Cowell	288
— James Muir	456
— John Cane	309
— John Halket	309
— Raymund	258, 309
— Richmond Irvine	21, 406
Crawfurd, Proby E. P.	279
Crawley, Archer P.	66, 229
— Charles	386
— Eustace	154
— George Burridge	420
— Leonard Russell	140
— Thos. Gorges	23
Crawley-Boevey, Edward Martin	279
Crawshaw, John R.	162
Crawshay, Fred. Wm.	255
Creagh, Arthur Gethin	26, 168
— Arthur H. Dopping	434
— Denis	371
— Edward Cottingham	439
— George Percy Brasier	431
— G. Washington Brazier	431
— O'Moore	44, 411
— Ralph Chas. Osborne	429
— Stephen Henry	387
— Walter	47, 142
Crealock, John M. S.	289
— John North	6
— Stradling L. Vaughan	210
Cree, Edward Russell	380
— Gerald	383
— Herbert Eustace	51
Creek, Edw. Gordon S.	317
— Edw. Stanley	25
Cregan, Thos. Andrew	210
Cresswell, A. F. B.	210
— Charles A.	43, 410
Creswell, Edm. Wm.	52, 207
Cretin, Eugene	454
Crichton, Hon. Geo. A. C.	231
— Henry William Visct.	135
— Hew	176
Crichton, Richmond T.	431
Crimmin, John	530
Cripps, Arthur Wm.	428
— Fred. Wm. Beresford	305
Crispin, Hugh Trevor	240
Critchley, Edw. Asheton	146
Crocker, Alfred Gilbert	242
— Bertram Edward	333
— George Delamain	347
— Herbert James	401
— Sydney Fras.	429
Crockett, Kennett Gale	335
— Sydney Laurence	175
— W. Macandrew	174
Croft, James H. Herbert	372
Crofton, Arthur E. L.	240
— Charles Woodward	310
— Malby Edward	48
— Morgan Samuel	24
— Richard Martin	63, 169
— Robert Benjamin	178
Crofton-Atkins, C. R.	289
Crofts, Aylmer Martin	454
— Edmund Sclater	281
— James	454
— James Grove White	380
— Leonard Markham	236
— Richard	387
Croker, Henry Leycester	256
Croly, Arthur E. J.	380
Crombie, Alex.	453
Cromie, William Henry	214
Crommelin, C. Yule	426
Cronin, John Joseph	424
Crooke, Chas. D. Parry	250
— Ed. Rea Milner	46, 397
— George Douglas	250
— Warren R. Davies	383
Crookenden, Hy. H.	46, 166
— Salusbury Davenport	372
Crookshank, Arthur Alex.	214
— C. de Windt	213
— Sydney D'Aguilar	213
Crosbie, Adolph. B.	42, 399
— Charles	139
— Henry	68, 289
Cross, Horatio R. O.	381
Crosse, Arthur Grant	276
Crosthwait, Herbert L.	213
Crosthwaite, Jno. Graham	436
— Joseph Arthur	314
Crow, William Alfred	395
Crowe, John Henry W.	172
— Mordaunt Abingdon C.	174
— Wm. M. Carlisle	242
Crowther, Edward S. D.	400
— Rev. F. Nelson	507
— John Ernest	401
— Robert Theodore	423
Crozier, Arthur Harry	214
— Burrard R.	262, 373
— Thomas Henry	175
Cruddas, Hugh W.	437
Cruickshank, Duncan T.	288
— Hugh Alexander	176
— J. Donaldson	26, 219
— Percy Hamilton	178
Crum, Fred. Maurice	305
Crump, James Cyril	349
Crumplin, William	368
Crutchley, Gen. Charles	265
— Major Charles	51, 233
— Charles Logan	346
Cubitt, Arch. Cyril	67, 250
— Thomas Astley	177
— William Martin	431
Cuffe, C. MacDonogh	377
Cullen, Ernest H. Scott	439
Culling, John C.	381
Cumber, Herbert Chas.	237
CUMBERLAND, H.R.H. the Duke of, KG.	5
Cumberland, Louis Bertie	305
— Richard Ormsby	246
— William	142
Cumberlege, Arch. F.	213
— Charles John	438
— Henry Chas. Faithfull	401
Cumine, Rev. R. A.	460
Cuming, A. Edwin	367
— Arthur Thomas	173
— Robert John	250
Cummin, Nicholas B.	347
Cumming, Ernest Alfred	213
— Hanway R.	314
— Ludovic S. Gordon	289
— William Gordon	25, 219
— Wm. Sydney	400
Cummings, Wilfrid Heron	170
Cummins, Harry A. V.	438
— Henry Alfred	383
— James Turner	27, 409
Cuningham, Chas. A.	22, 407
Cuninghame, Dav. S.	43, 410
— John A. Smith	57, 134
— William Cuninghame	130
Cunliffe, Ernest Wm.	417
— Foster Lionel	57, 168
— Fred. Hugh Gordon	318
Cunningham, Allau H.	213
— David Douglas	452
— George Glencairn	53, 289
— John	288
— John Adams	455
— J. Dacres	53, 167
— John	330
— Lawrence	142
— Percy Henry	434
Cunyngham, W.H.D.	57, 337
Cuppage, Edm. Vernon	282
— William Adam	425
Cure, Alfred Capel	171
— George Edw. C.	66, 261
— Herbert Capel	272
Cureton, Edward Robert	269
Curling, H. Thomas	48, 166a
— William K.	68, 314
Curll, Cha. Emilius	65, 267
Curme, Wm. Charles	174
Curran, Ar. Edw. R.	51, 277
Currie, Algernon	22, 403
— Arthur Cecil	172
— Fendall	22, 403
— Fred. Alex.	49, 245
— Ivor Bertram Fendall	177
— John William	418
— Thomas	52, 310
Curry, Montagu Creighton	249
Curreis, Cyril S.	178
— Francis Algernon	63, 169
— Herbert St. Leger	400
— John	305
— Reg L. Herbert	22
— William F.	52, 264
Curtin, Frederic John	42, 272
Curtis, Arthur William	176
— Edward George	255
— Harry Alex. D.	57, 108
— James Henry	382
— John G. Cockburn	45
— Reginald Salmond	211
— William Fred. de H.	41, 165
Curtoys, Chas. E. E.	400
Curzon, Ernest C. P.	160
— Fitzroy Edm. Penn.	329
— Hon. Montagu	46, 356
— Nathaniel William	5
— Wm. Southwell	18, 105
Cusack, Robert Oriel	380
Cusins, Albert G. T.	213
Cust, Adelbert O. C.	252
Custance, Hugh Lionel	422
Cutbill, H. Duppa Alfred	28
Cuthbert, Gerald Jas.	2
Cuthbertson, Norman W.	286
Cutlar-Fergusson, Robt.	233
Cuyler, Sir Chas. Bart.	287
da Costa, Edw. Ronald	505
— Evan Campbell	274
— O. M. John	439
D'Aeth, Geo. G. Hughes	237
— Reginald Hughes	237
D'Aguilar, Sir C. L.	164
— Fra. B. Grant	52, 208
— John Swainson	372
Dalal, K. A.	529
Dalby, John	177
Dale, Alfred Morris Cecil	17
— Charles L.	46, 360, 374
— George Arthur	435
— Rev. Thos. Fras.	460
Dalgety, Fredk. John	157
— Henry Barkly	149
— Reginald William	22, 311
Dalgliesh, Edward E. C.	283
Dalison, John Pelham	294
Dallas, Alex. Egerton	438
— Alister Grant	158
— Charles Mowbray	425
— James	210
— John Hen. Langford	170
— Julian Stuart	436
— Stuart Alex. Chas.	590
Dalrymple, G. R. E.	214
— Hon. North de C.	61, 233

Index—Active List. 550

Dalrymple, R. G. Elphinstone............25, 408
— William Liston......... 16
Dalrymple-Hay, S. F. B. 362
Dalton, Cecil William R. 401
— Charles............... 385
— James Cecil........41, 166a
Daly, Arthur Crawford.. 253
— F. A. Bonner......... 381
— Henry Dermot....... 427
— Hugh................. 426
— Joseph Thomas...... 455
— Maurice.............. 368
— Thomas............... 383
Dalyell, Hugh Kenneth 436
— John Arthur......... 178
Dalzel, Aug. Fre†...... 249
Dalzell, Hon. Arth. E. 52, 287
Damania, Phiroszha J. 530
D'Amico, Igino Depiro 244
Damla, Edulji M....... 505
D'inby, William Edwin. 142
Dane, Arthur H. C..... 529
Danford, Bertram W. Y. 214
Dangar, Henry P....... 155
Daniel, Charles Cecil .. 234
— Charles James...... 291
— Edward Yorke...... 290
— Henry George....65, 271
Daniell, Arthur C... 65, 169
— De Courcy....... 47, 166
— Edward Henry E.... 258
— Frank William...... 435
— Frederick Fran. W... 311
— John Alan Le Norreys 153
— John Frederic...... 400
— Oswald Jas........ 65, 294
Dann, Hy. Churnside B. 429
Dansey-Browning, Geo. 386
Dántrā, S. H........... 454
Darby, Wm. Henry 59, 168
Darbyshire, Percy H.... 140
D'Arcy, Edw. Blake... 370
D'Arcy-Hildyard, R. N. 314
Darell, Harry Francis.. 359
Darell-Brown, H. F.... 287
Darley, George Roe.... 170
— Henry La Touche... 401
— James Russell...... 438
Darling, Chas. H.†...59, 208
— James Bruce....63, 400
Darnell, Rev. F. A..... 395
— Rev. Hen. A........ 396
Darrah, O'Brien Zouch 236
Darroch, Duncan...... 337
Darwin, C. Waring.... 47
Dashwood, Edmd. Wm. 240
Daubeney, Sir H. C. B. 278
— Edward Kaye....... 282
Daubeny, Edwd. Alfred 274
— James............... 295
Dauglish, George Victor 237
Daukes, Arch. Henry... 282
Dauncey, Thursby H. E. 163
Daunt, Bertram Rochfort 279
— Richard Algernon C. 329
— Walter D............ 433
Davey, F. Griffiths... 137
— Horace Scott....... 160
David, Ernest Fred. 55, 400
Davidson, Arthur.... 49, 304
— Arthur Noel........ 177
— Charles............. 423
— C. F. Herbert....... 337
— Charles Steer....... 282
— Chris. Middlemass .. 130
— C. John Lloyd...... 271
— David Chas......... 529
— David Macdonald... 456
— Duncan Fras........ 325
— Francis C. Dudfield. 239
— Francis Dean....... 303
— Francis Middleton.. 174
— Fred. Aug. Lascelles 262
— George.......... 57, 208
— Geo. F. De Bude ..50, 286
— George Harry...... 233
— Gordon Villiers.... 175
— Henry Edward..... 17
— Surg. Lieut. James.. 457
— Lt. Col. James...45, 150
— Major John.... 65, 291
— Lt. Colonel John ..40, 409
— John Robert B...... 170
— John Stewart...... 383
— Lionel Chorley L.... 269
— Robert Vernour.... 429
— Sisley Richard..... 446

Davidson, Stuart....... 210
— Thomas Reid Waugh 372
— Thomas St. Clair.... 346
— Walter Lloyd....... 428
— William Leslie...49, 166a
Davidson-Houston, C. E.
D....................... 441
Davie, James Henry M. 234
— Keith Maitland..... 272
— Wm. J. Ferguson... 278
Davies, Arthur Mercer.. 381
— Charles Henry...... 436
— Charles Hugh...... 432
— Edwin L. V. Saunders 361
— Ernest Wilson...... 174
— Francis John....... 229
— Frank Gadsden..... 250
— Frederick Geo. Hugh 432
— George Freshfield .. 246
— Rev. George M...... 460
— Henry.............. 367
— Henry Faushawe... 5
— Henry Rodolph..... 287
— Hy. Samuel Price .. 420
— Hugh Walter....... 275
— Captain John....... 420
— Apothecary John... 337
— John Murray....... 315
— Noel Philip......... 350
— Percy George....... 185
— Percy Matcham.... 294
— Thomas Arthur H... 215
— Thomas Reid....... 425
— Thomas William... 401
— Walter P. Lionel... 177
— Wilbraham Thos. 254, 370
Davis, Alfred Robert... 279
— A. P. Newnham... 285
— Cecil............... 426
— Charles M'Mullin... 438
— Dudley Herbert... 258
— Edgar Crofts....... 256
— Edward............ 382
— Edward Newnham.. 437
— Ernest Horace..... 174
— George Frederick... 395
— George Henville... 254
— George McBride... 452
— Gronow John...... 439
— James.............. 377
— John................ 5
— John William...... 401
— Robert Evans Stuart 505
— Thomas............ 223
— William Wallbridge 361
Davison, G. Markham 67, 314
— Kenneth Stuart.... 417
— Colonel Thomas.... 23
— Major Thomas...59, 264
— William Pearson... 333
Davoren, Vesey H. W... 384
Davson, Harry Miller... 177
Davy, Cecil William .. 213
— John Davy Wright .. 287
— Robert M. Manning.. 418
Dawes, Edwin Sandys.. 285
— William Myers..... 426
Dawkins, Arthur Fred. 240
— Charles Tyrwhitt... 297
— Henry Stopford ..63, 169
— John Wyndham Geo. 171
Dawnay, Hon. John ... 152
Dawson, Arthur Wm... 455
— Charles Herbert... 367
— Charles Hutton.... 425
— Cuthbert P......63, 137
— D'Orville Brook.... 284
— Douglas F. R....58, 231
— Edward............ 186
— Edward Alfred Finch 357
— Francis Wm........ .
— Frederick Stuart... 240
— Harry Leonard...66, 415
— Henry Coleridge... 372
— Henry Finch....... 58
— Henry Philip ...46, 166a
— John................ 23
— Joseph Temperley... 178
— Robert............. 236
— Vesey John.....53, 231
— Wm. Hutchison R... 177
Day, Arthur G. Fitzroy 285
— Chas. Russell....... 287
— Edmund............ 395
— Francis Innes...... 268
— Francis Jeremy ..46, 206
— James Dunne..... 330
— John George ...65, 259

Day, Robert Vaughan 48, 366
— Thomas H. B. 69, 246
— William Bulien..... 382
Deacon, Edmund..... 136
— Henry Robert Gordon 334
Dealy, John Anderson.. 211
Deane, Alexander..... 242
— Andrew............. 453
— Rev. Barry O'Meara.. 506
— Charles A. C........ 250
— Dennis.............. 178
— Fredk. Bernard..... 418
— George Williams .. 48, 412
— Harold Arthur 67, 416
— Herbert Edward... 381
— James............... 236
— John Henry........ 281
— Rich. Woodforde... 261
— Thomas........... 26, 409
— William............. 453
Deans, George Noel.... 282
Deare, Benjamin Hobbs 456
— Henry Foulkes..... 150
Deas, Lionel M. Ross... 295
Deasy, Henry H. Peter 158
de Bathe, Sir Henry Percival, Bart........... 297
N.................... 150
— Maximilian........ 150
de Berniere, Hon. J. deB. 28
de Berry, Geo. J. Lewes 172
— Henry Geoffrey N... 371
— Philip P. Evelyn... 177
— Richard Meredith... 333
De Brath, Ernest..... 419
de Brett, Harry Simonds 176
de Burgh, Ulick G. C. 57, 142
de Bury, Henry R. V... 177
De Butts, Fred. R. M... 172
Decie, Cyril Prescott ... 174
de Coetlogon, Rev. C. E. C. 532
de Crespigny, T. O. W. C. 157
Deeble, Benjamin W. C. 381
Deed, John Cyril..... 401
Deedes, Rev. Brook ... 460
Doering, John......51, 264
deFalbe, Vigant William 310
De Gex, Basil C....... 274
— Fras. John......... 277
De Gruyther, Cuthbert Montague............ 250
de Hoghton, Daniel ..58, 291
de Jersey, Colebrooke... 171
— William Grant....55, 108
de Kantzow, C. Adol... 405
— Sidney Ives........ 289
deKierzkowski-Steuart,
F. H.................. 233
De la Bère, Hugh Pleydell 262
de Labilliere, E. G. D... 441
de la Condamine, Harry
John.................. 276
Delacombe, Addis..... 335
de la Fontaine, V. H. M. 275
Delaforce, Edwin F..... 176
Delamain, Frank G..... 418
— Walter Sinclair..... 426
Delavoye, Alex. Edw. 250, 368
— Alex. Marin........ 26
DeLisle, G. deSausmarez 427
— Henry De Beauvoir... 314
Delmé-Radcliffe, S. A... 281
de Lotbinière, H. G. J... 213
de Moleyns, Hon F. R.
W. Eveleigh......... 146
de Montmorency, Hon.
A. B............... 19, 180
— Mervyn............ 281
— Raymond H. J. 163
— Willoughby J. R.... 276
Dempsey, Patrick Jos.. 379
Dempster, Cathcart 47, 412
— Thos. Carroll........ 372
Denham, Harold A..... 244
Dening, Lewis......45, 411
Denman, Thomas, Lord 234
Denne, Alured B....... 172
— Arthur Robt........ 177
— Henry Wm. Denne... 321
— Richard William A... 395
Dennis, Meade J. C..... 173
Dennistoun, Jas. G..... 177
Denny, Ernest W...... 155
— Henry Cuthbert ..65, 292
— Richard............ 53, 399
— Wm. Alfred Chas. 340, 365
Dennys, Alex. Harry... 431
— Charles John......67, 416
— George Wm. P...... 454

Dennys, Hector Travers 432
— Wm. Annesley Burton 422
Dent, Bertie Coore 256
— Edgar John........ 269
— Frank Wilkinson... 175
— John William 68, 139
— Wilfrid Harry...... 259
Denys, W. Hy. Adolphus 373
De Pledge, Harold Geo. 161
De Prée, Hugo Douglas 176
dePonthieu, R. G. R. deV. 429
Derham, Frank Seymour 274
Dering, Henry Edward 233
de Ros, Geo. de R...... 132
de Rougemont, Cecil H. 174
Dorriman, Gerald L.... 230
de Salis, Edw. John ... 402
de Sausmarez, Cecil... 176
Desborough, Arth. P. H 175
Despard, Edw. Fitzh.... 335
— Henry F. R........ 329
Des Vœux, Chas. H. ..59, 414
— Fred. Henry Arthur 141
— Henry Bertram.... 213
— Herbert............ 434
de Teissier, H. Price ... 179
Devenish, Arthur Henry
N.................... 177
Deverell, Cyril J....... 253
de Villamil, Richard 52, 207
de Vitré, Percy T. D.... 213
Devlin, Joseph......... 292
Dew, Armine B....... 436
Dewar, Arthur Wm..... 246
— David Erskine ... 57, 168
— Edward John...... 304
— Gordon.............. 372
— James Edward..... 137
DoWend, Douglas C.... 26
Dowes, Fred. Joseph ... 506
de Wilton, Albert W.... 423
— P. Donald Dorin ... 529
Dewing, Edw. John....53, 208
— Robert Henry..... 431
de Winton, Charles ... 281
— Richard Stretton... 176
de Wolski, F. Roh ...46, 206
Dibben, John Thomas... 395
Dibble, Harry......... 149
Dibblee, Fred. Lewis ... 398
Dibley, Athelstan...... 348
Dick, Arthur Robert... 425
— C. B. Goodrich...51, 431
— Colin............... 333
— Dighton Hay A...... 262
— George............. 213
— James Roy......... 373
— William............ 381
Dick-Cunyngham, Wm. 286
Dickens, John......... 179
Dickie, John Elford ..63, 209
Dickin, John Lloyd ... 42
Dickins, S. W. Scrase-.. 317
— William Arthur..... 532
Dickinson, Arthur T. S. 252
— Edward.........52, 207
— Ernest Arthur..... 348
— Francis Arthur..... 276
— Neville H. Campbell 346, 370
— Thos. Malcolm..... 173
— William V.......63, 285
Dickson, Bertram..... 178
— Sir Collingwood... 164
— Edward Thomson 42, 293
— George Fred. Hayes 265
— Graham Joseph..... 308
— Harry Wilfrid ...275, 367
— John Baillie B....... 23
— John Herbert...... 435
— Wm. Edmund Ritchie 213
— Wm. Thomas...... 149
Didham, Chambers..... 289
Dietz, Bernard R...... 142
Digan, Geo. Cuthbert... 334
Digby, Hon. Everard C. 25
— Thomas.........58, 208
— Wm. R. Wingfield .. 357
— William Treach.... 213
Dill, Richard......... 295
Dillon, George Fred. H. 427
— Henry Vincent..... 383
Dimmock, Henry Peers 530
Dinsdale, Wilfred P.... 329
Dingwall, Kenneth ... 321
Dinwiddie, David..... 593
Disney, Robert....... 505
— Thomas Robert ... 28, 165
Ditmas, Alf. Robertson 431

Index—Active List.

551

- Ditmas, Francis Fred. 41, 165
- — Fred. Robertson ...46, 411
- — Leonard Philip 373
- Divecha, Framji Rattonji 505
- Diver, Thomas 242
- Dixon, Arthur L. Hoper 383
- — Charles Joseph 242
- — Clive Macdonnell...... 158
- — Edward George....... 176
- — George................ 368
- — George Frederick 403
- — Henry Grey 48, 205
- — Peter Eden............ 210
- — Richard Travers 211
- — Thomas Arthur........ 381
- — Thomas Bradford 238
- — William 358
- Dobbie, Charles Francis 432
- — Herbert Hugh 420
- — William Hugh 422
- Dobbin, Leonard Geo. Wm 292
- — Robert Alexander ... 274
- — William J. Knowles... 419
- Dobbs, Alex. Hugh 420
- — Charles Fairlie 261
- — Conway Richard 212
- — George Cadell 53, 413
- Dobell, Charles Macp... 265
- Dobie, Stanley Locker.. 504
- — Wm. Hugh Edw...57, 168
- Dobrée, De Sausmarez 398
- Dobson, And. Fras. 504
- Edwin Francis H. ... 454
- — George Magill 382
- — Arth. H. Wolley 171
- — Owen C. Wolley 261
- Dodd, Anthony 382
- — Charles Albert ...21, 406
- — George................ 245
- — John Richard.......... 380
- Dodgson, Colquhoun S. 367
- — Harcourt Leicester ... 425
- — Heathfield Butler...... 172
- Dods, Wm. Sandars..... 245
- Doherty, Thomas 368
- Doig, Claude P........... 318
- — Richard O. M. 401
- Dolby, Seymour S. C. ... 373
- Dolton, Edward John ... 367
- Domenichetti, Fras. H... 433
- Donald, Colin Geo... 57, 243
- Donaldson, Chas. Geo. 65, 278
- — Frederick Leverton... 172
- — John 383
- — John Wm. Edward ... 176
- — Robt. D. 380
- Donaldson-Hudson, R.C. 154
- Done, Reginald John ... 214
- Donegan, Jas. Fras...... 383
- Donnan, William 436
- Donne, B. D. A. 52, 279
- — Henry Rich. Beadon 245
- — John Robert 141
- Donnelly, Lawrence..... .
- — Robert 178
- Donnet, Jas. J. Conway 382
- Donohue, Wm. Edward 185
- Donovan, Charles........ 506
- — Charles Creaghe 176
- — Charles H. W. 367
- — Donovan.............. 506
- — Edward Westby 254
- — Hugh Latimer 379
- — William 378
- Dooner, Wm. Toke...... 27
- Doran, B. J. C. 51, 258
- — Walter Robert B...... 258
- Dorehill, Philip H. M. ... 172
- Dorling, Francis 29
- — Lionel 295, 374
- Dorman, John C. 379
- — Thomas 379
- Dorrien, H. L. Smith 61, 289
- Dorward, A. R. F....47, 207
- — James Ford 24, 206
- Dougall, Walter 141
- Dougherty, Edw. M..... 50
- Doughty, Charles H. M. 265
- — Ernest Christie ....
- Douglas, Arch. Philip... 174
- — Cameron Charles 68, 270
- — Charles W. H. 49, 321
- — George Prescott 137
- — James Archibald 429
- — James Stewart........ 170
- — John Douglas 44, 169
- — Montagu Wm. 430
- — Sir R. Percy, Bt. 310

- Douglas, Sholto William 176
- — Stafford Edmund...... 337
- — Walter Binny 437
- Doull, John Doull........ 296
- Dove, Frank 386
- — Horatio 48, 207
- — Percy Matthew........ 290
- Doveton, Albert M. 436
- — John Chadwick ... 22, 407
- — John Hodson.......... 255
- Dowdall, Aylmer P. G.... 372
- — Laurence Richard ... 372
- — Thomas Percy........ 295
- Dowding, Hy. Harris H. 286
- — Townley Ward ... 45, 399
- Rev. Wm. Berkeley... 396
- Dowell, Arth. John Wm. 293
- — George Cecil 172
- — George William 291
- Dowman, Willington ... 364
- Down, Cecil Patton 437
- — Halkett Walton Money 310
- Downes, Joseph.......... 249
- — Leonard Sawbridge 177
- — Oliver Longcroft 440
- — William Knox 418
- Downing, C. M. H. ...46, 166
- — David Fitzgerald...59, 168
- — Geoffrey 348
- — Henry John 258
- — John George 418
- Bownman, Geo. T. F.59, 321
- Dowse, Edw. Cecil .. 50, 289
- — Henry Esmonde 385
- Richard Thos. Edw. 48, 250
- Doyle, Arth. Havelock J. 297
- — Bernard 454
- — Francis Joseph 505
- du Maurier, Guy L. B. ... 243
- — Ignatius Purcell 506
- — John Fras. Innes H. ... 177
- — Joseph Ignatius P.... 382
- D'Oyly, Geo. Halford ... 249
- Doyne, Mordaunt B..... 147
- — Philip Kavanagh 44, 139
- — Wm. Markham 163
- Drage, Francis Binyoun 395
- — Gilbert................ 401
- — Godfrey 439
- — Thomas William 371
- — William Henry 368
- Drake, Bernard Francis 172
- — Francis Richard 172
- — Henry Dowrish 398
- — Henry Manning 176
- — William Hacche 178
- — Wyndham 135
- Drake-Brockman, D. H. 452
- — Herbert Edw. 456
- — Percy William 25
- — Ralph R. E. 27, 207
- — Vivian Godfrey....... 456
- Draper, Frederick........ 178
- Dressner, C. J. B. H. ... 210
- Drover, James William 433
- — Thomas Ian 432
- Drew, Arth. Blanshard H. 431
- — George Barry 253
- — Horace Robt. Hawley 292
- — Tom Maxwell 256
- Drielsma, Wm. Edwin... 277
- Driffield, John 177
- Druce, Cyril............. 294
- Druitt, Edward 210
- — Percy Stanley 61, 347
- Drummond, Arch. Spen. 67, 233
- — Arthur Berkeley 439
- — Arthur George 210
- — Edmund Johnston ... 432
- — Fra. Henry R.....51, 417
- — John Wm. A. 51, 293
- — Kenneth Mackenzie... 346
- Drury, Byron Henry ... 360
- — Francis James 455
- — Francis Macdonald 67, 416
- — James O'Brien 372
- — Laurence George 233
- — Maurice O'Connor ... 380
- — Robert 378
- — William Price.......... 400
- Drysdale, Sir Wm. 151
- Duberly, George 373
- Du Boulay, D. de la M. 58, 142
- — Noel Wilmot H....... 171
- — Thos. W. Houssemayne 28
- — Woodforde George 52, 207
- Du Buisson, Henry...... 246

- DuCane, Hubert John... 170
- — John Philip 173
- — Ducat, Charles M. 125
- — Claude Tulloch........ 434
- — Hugh Charles Claude 433
- — Richard 276
- — Duck, Francis.......... 395
- — Duckett, Wm. Morton ... 373
- Duckworth, Arthur C. 144
- Ducrôt, Louis Hay 171
- Dudgeon, Fred. Annesley 284
- — Ralph de Seton........ 441
- Duer, Charles........... 456
- Duff, Alex. Gordon ...61, 286
- — Beauchamp....... 68, 416
- — Charles Edward ...65, 150
- — Frederick William ... 151
- — George Graham Kayll 176
- — George Mowat 212
- Duffey, George Allan ... 361
- — Duffin, Walter Henry ... 230
- Duffus, Edward John... 174
- — Fras. Ferguson....... 264
- — Græme Sym 172
- Dugan, Francis Rogers 340
- Dugdale, Herbert Crowe 158
- — William 380
- Duggan, Chas. Wm. ... 387
- Dugmore, W. Radclyffe 310
- Duhan, Francis Taylor 362
- — Wm. W. Taylor 171
- Duke, Alex. Leonard ... 456
- — Alex. W. 378
- — John Charles.......49, 277
- — William 380
- Duleep Singh, Prince
- Victor A. J. 143
- Dumaresq, Algernon H. 213
- Dumble, Wilfred C. 214
- Dumbleton, Horatio N... 209
- du Moulin, Louis E. 279
- Dun, Edw. Wm.......67, 416
- Dunbar, Lewis Maxwell 140
- — William Mathew 130
- Duncan, Andrew 454
- — Francis John.......... 234
- — Francis Leslie 367
- — Frank 426
- — George 455
- — Colonel John 16
- — 2nd Lieut. John....... 262
- — Richard William 234
- — Sidney Edward 382
- — Stuart 272
- Duncombe, C. Wilmer ... 6
- Dundas, Fred. Charles.. 337
- — George William 255
- — Henry H. Philip 157
- — Henry Lawrence 25
- — Lawrence Charles 63, 244
- — Patrick Henry 440
- — Richard Chas. 234
- Dundee, Wm. J. Daniell 210
- Dundon, Michael 381
- Dundonald, Earl of ...24, 134
- Dunlop, Archibald Saml. 173
- — Arthur Wallace....... 433
- — Henry Cleland ...59, 168
- — Henry Hinton 433
- — James William ...61, 168
- — Wm. Hugh 329, 367
- Dunn, Cuthbert 65, 365
- — Henry Nason 385
- — Robert Henry W. 265
- Dunnage, Arth Jas. 46, 166
- Dunne, Edward Martin 278
- — John Hart 4
- — Walter A. 40, 365
- — William 45, 366
- Dunning, Harry Gordon 243
- Dunolly, Kenneth J. G. 434
- Dunscombe, N. Blake ... 268
- Dunsford, Fras. P. S. ... 435
- Dunsterville, Arthur B. 275
- — Edward Leslie 211
- — Lionel Charles 431
- — Knightley S......61, 169
- Duperier, Henry Wm. 52, 208
- Durand, Alg. G. A. ...44, 415
- Durant, Robert J. A. ... 382
- Durell, Arthur J. V..... 245
- Durham, Philip F.... 61, 152
- Rev. Robert Henry ... 507
- Durrant, George......... 395
- Dury, Alexander Wm. ... 47
- Dustan, John W. 401
- Duthy, Arch. Edward 46, 166

- Dutt, Russick Lall........ 453
- Dutton, Hon. Charles ... 40
- — Jas. Huntly 270
- Duxbury, Sidney H...... 275
- Dwane, John William ... 305
- Dwyer, Arthur Geo...... 275
- — Bertie Cunynghame 256
- — Charles Edward 378
- — George Toulmin C... 178
- — John.................. 330
- — John Cornelius....... 395
- — Philip Fogarty........ 145
- Dyas, James Ridgeway 242
- Dyce, George H. Coles ... 48
- Dyer, Rev. Alfred S...... 460
- — Charles Robert 301
- — John Edw. Frederick 142
- Rev. Joseph Perry ... 507
- — Reginald Edw. Harry 432
- — Thomas W. B. 398
- Dyke, George Hart 48
- — Percyvall Hart 273
- Dykes, Alfred McNair... 249
- — Lionel E. B. 173
- — William Alston....... 270
- Dymott, Donald F. 505
- Dyne, Frank W. B. 237
- Dyson, Harry Bernard 230
- — Herbert Jekyll 455
- — P. Shakespeare ...312, 374
- — Thomas Edward 530
- Dyson-Laurie, Julius D. 17
- Eadon, Frank Henry ... 163
- Eady, Chas. Edward ... 176
- — Frederick W. E. 400
- Eagar, Edward Bonz ... 240
- — Henry Averell 53, 329
- — Robert John 283
- Eagle, F. E. Bunbury ... 401
- Eagles, Henry Cecil 61, 400
- Ealden, Charles.......... 220
- Eales, Cecil Moncrieff... 425
- — Lionel Geo. Nuttall... 237
- Eames, Rev. W. Leslie.. 533
- Eardley-Wilmot, Arth. 66, 169
- — Ernest 314
- — Henry 419
- Earle, Cecil Arthur 175
- — Edward Savi.......... 278
- — Francis Alfred 242
- — Frederick John....... 453
- — Henry 67, 295
- — Hubert Malins 456
- — Maxwell 230
- — Robert Gilmour 214
- Eary, Chas. John 276
- Eassie, Fitzpatrick 395
- East, Cecil James 5
- — Charles Conran 242
- — George Thomas 347
- — Lionel Wm. Pellew... 174
- Eastman, Wm. Ingle-
  field.............. 68, 398
- Eastmead, Chas. Sidney 436
- Easton, Fred. Arthur ... 176
- Eastwood, Hugh de C.... 136
- — John C. B. 154
- — Robert John Camac 440
- Eaton, Hon. Herb. Fras. 19
- — James Bird........... 529
- — Robert Coleman 378
- — William Arnold 237
- Eaton-Evans, H. J. 176
- Ebden, Fras. Thos....26, 408
- Eccles, Cuthbert J...... 158
- — Robert............66, 287
- — William Vernon 356
- Eckersley, Edwin........ 383
- Eckford, John J. H. B... 429
- — John 366
- — Philip George W 329
- Eden, Arch. Jas. F...... 287
- — Wm. Alexander ... 43, 166
- — William Rushbrooke 177
- Edes, Charles Albert 55, 366
- Edgar, John Stewart ... 177
- Edge, John Dallas 378
- Edgell, Edw. Arnold ... 211
- Edghill, Rev. J. C. 396
- Edinburgh, H.R.H. the
  Duke of 397
- Edlmann, Ernest E...... 175
- Edmonds, James Edw... 210
- — Nicholas Gifford 286
- Edmonds, James 185
- — Richard James....... ..
- Edmondson, James H. 368
- Edridge, Chas. Sutton... 244
- Edwardes, Alex. Coburn 287
- — John Grahame 439

Edwardes, Stanley Malcolm	431	Ellis, Chas. C. 58, 208	Eustace, Alex. Rowland 237	Fairholme, Wm. Ernest 170
— *Hon.* William	134	— Chas. H. Fairfax 22	— Charles Legge E....... 305	Fairland, Edwin Jas. ... 378
Edwards, A. Hamilton M.	136	— Conyngham R. C. ... 270	— Fra. John Wm. ...57, 167	Fairclough, Chas. E.G.M. 287
— Arthur Clement	178	— George Adams 270	— Fred. Adolphus D. O. 140	Faith, Thomas 281
— Cecil Bradney Jervis	276	— Gerald Montague Aug. 357	— Henry Montague...... 301	Faithfull, Hy. Turner 67, 415
— Charles Aug............	432	— Herbert Charles 293	Evans, Arthur Owen 506	— Wm. Conrad 62, 416
— Chas. Grant F.	422	— Philip Mackay 379	— Charles Harford 457	Falcon, Arch. Anthony 178
— Chas. Mackenzie...59,	293	— Walter Treslove 45	— Chas. Wm. Henry 57, 294	— Chas. Gordon 213
— Clement Maitland......	273	— William Hastings ... 271	— Cuthbert................. 177	— Robert Morgan........ 428
— David John.............	368	— William Montague ... 210	— Edward 308	— Wm. Knightley 360
— FitzJames Maine	426	— Wm. Robert Jason ... 295	— Edward George......... 239	Falconer, C. E. Keith ... 240
— *Sir* Fleetwood I. ...41,	205	— William Verner ...27, 409	— Edward Stokes......61, 347	Falkiner, Travers H. ... 334
— Frederick Charles ...	401	Ellison, George Paget... 151	— Francis Studdert 289	Falkner, *Rev.* T. F. 326
— Graham Thos. George	162	— Gerald Francis 236	— Geo. Alfred Penrhys 66, 149	Fallon, James............. 383
— Henry Charles	433	— Ralph Henry Carr ... 143	— George Henry 395	— John Chris. Joseph... 214
— James	178	— Richard George......... 132	— George Milford 431	Falls, John Alex. W. 51, 366
— James Roch 41,	366	— Richard Todd 134	— Geo. Wm. Wallace D'A. 329	Falmouth, *Visct.* 18, 231
— John Burnard...........	420	— *Rev.* William 460	— Granville Pennefather 268	Falvey, John Joseph...... 379
— John Denis	395	Ellisson, Gustav Edm. ... 178	— Henry Theo. P. ...48, 274	Fane, Fred. John 17
— Lancelot	246	Ellwood, Bertram Price 295	— Horace Carlyon......... 401	— Vere Bonamy 431
— Richard Feilding......	211	Elmes, Jonathan Wm. 23, 366	— Horace Moule ...16, 407	Fanshawe, Charles 204
— Roderick Mackenzie...	431	Elmslie, Alex. M. Spears 437	— Horatio James ... 69, 244	— Edw. Arthur 170
— Thomas 329,	374	— Fred. B. 63, 169	— James Thomas 214	— Frederick Bradford... 294
— William Egerton	178	— Wilmot Foster 261	— James William 505	— George Dalrymple 50, 167
— William M. M.	317	Elphick, Harry Wm. ... 456	— John...................... 271	— Gerard Lewis........... 211
— William Rice............	455	Elphinstone, Arth. P. A. 430	— John Fenton 455	— Hew Dalrymple... 66, 161
Edye, John Simpson ...	384	Elphinstone-Dalrymple,	— John William 395	— Reginald Winnington 277
— Lourenco 48,	399	J. M. 283	— Leopold Exxel 403	— Robert 287
— Murray W. Joseph ...	367	Elrington, Fred. R. 356	— Percy 386	Faustone, Frederick ... 144
Edyvean, Fred. Geo. ...	402	Elrington-Bisset, Maurice 210	— Samuel 530	Fargus, Harold 276
Egan, Michael Henry ...	234	Elsdale, Henry 42, 205	— Thos. Julian P. ... 57, 399	Farley, James J. B. 310
Egerton, Arthur Fredk.	325	Elsmie, Geo. Edw. D. ... 432	— Usher Williamson ... 211	Farmar, George Jasper 261
— Caledon Philip ...43,	283	Elston, Henry............ 419	— William 177	— Hugh H. F. 305
— Charles Comyn ...43,	411	Elton, Alfred G. G. ...66, 334	— William Noble 436	— William Cecil R. 175
— Charles Philip	430	— Arthur Bayard 259	Evans-Gordon, Charles	— Wm. Lawrance......... 172
— Francis Wm. 66,	415	— *Rev.* Edw. Daubeny... 457	52, 293, 374	Farmar-Bringhurst, E. D. 381
— George Algernon	161	— Erle Godfrey 286	— Wm. Eden 418	Farmer, Fra. Colebrooke
— Granville Geo. A......	318	— Fred. Algernon G. Y. 174	Evatt, Francis Willie ... 432	55, 168
— John Francis.........46,	273	— Henry Strachan ...21, 407	— George J. H. *M D*...... 377	— John 395
— Raleigh Gilbert	423	Elverson, Hamilton J. 61, 236	— John Therold............ 426	— John Henry 385
— Ralph 67,	360	Elwes, Ernest Veness 52, 167	Evelegh, Chas. Newman 276	— Langford Llanwarne 258
Egginton, Joseph S.......	279	— Henry Cecil 233	— Edmund George 401	Farquhar, Hercules Thos. 176
Eicke, Ernest C.....308,	374	Lincoln E. Cary 314	— Fred. John 66, 287	Farquharson, Charles
Elcum, Donald	505	— Walter V. J. Cary 176	Even, George E............ 417	H.................. 63, 138
Elderton, Fred. Dundas	382	— *Rev.* William Weston 507	Everett, Chas. Wallace 185	— Ernest Gordon 213
— Murray Trent	437	Elworthy, Chas. K. 141	— Henry Joseph 252	— Harry Douglas 401
Eley, William Gardiner	156	Ely, Alfred 40, 366	— William 27	— John 27, 205
Elgee, Cyril Hammond	255	— Edwyn A. Sylvester... 255	Everitt, Sydney George 265	— Victor Alex. 59, 234
— John W. I...............	301	Eman, Bowes Leslie 53, 168	Evers, Benjamin......... 452	Farrant, Chas. Wm. Brett 311
Elger, Edward Gwyn ...	252	Emerson, Geo. Augustus 454	Eversley, C. *Visct.*......... 1	— Harland Fitz L......... 418
Elgood, Percival Geo. ...	249	— Isaac Bomford 379	Ewart, Chas. F. Salisbury 318	— Henry C. B. 45, 291
Elias, Arthur 66,	236	Emerson, John Lindas.	— Charles George E...... 438	— Robt. Kincaid 175
— Robert	27	Emery, Wm. Basil 16	— Charles Henry ...19, 406	Farrell, Henry J. Wm. ... 174
Eliot, Geffery Lawr. 46,	412	Empson, Chas. Anglesea 41	— Charles Nicholson ... 177	— John Charles......63, 279
Eliott, Francis H.........	426	Enderby, Samuel H. ... 240	— Frank Rowland 244	— Leslie Michael 259
— Laurence Edw..........	424	Engelbach, Fras. Joyce 237	— Godfrey D. Henry ... 284	Farren, *Sir* Rich. T......... 291
Eliott-Lockhart, Allan A.	317	England, Alick Thornber 289	— *Sir* John Alex. 321	Farrer, Philip........ 58, 283
— Percy Clare	435	— Arthur 395	— John Spencer 325	Farrington, Hastings D. O. 17
Elkington, Chas. Jarvie	213	— Edward Lutwyche ... 7	— Richard Henry 429	Farwell, Chas. Bowers 213
— George Edward	213	— Edward Parker......... 174	— Walter Douglas 325	— Walter Charles....40, 404
— H. Percival George ...	383	— Raymond 176	Ewbank, William 211	Fasken, Chas. G. M. 68, 416
— John Ford	242	— Thomas Percival 243	Ewens, Geo. F. Wm. 456	— Wm. A. D. 453
— Robert James Goodall	174	Engledue, Herb. Atfield 236	Ewing, Alister W. S. ... 310	— William Henry......... 427
Ellershaw, Arthur	175	Engleheart, E. L. 265	— Edward 395	Fasson, Disney J. M. ... 173
— Wilfrid	177	English, Aug. John...51, 156	— James Alex. Orr 158	Faulder, Gerard Aug.... 291
Elles, Arthur Warre......	295	— Charles Ernest 171	Exeter, *Marquis of*......... 1	Faulkner, Alex. S........... 530
— Edmund Roche ...26,	165	— Frederick Paul...68, 348	Exham, Richard 378	Faulknor, Aug. A. M. M. 429
— Malcolm Rothney ...	4	— *Rev.* John 507	— Simeon Hardy ...53, 208	Faunce, Alured De Laune 292
— *Sir* William Kidston	6	— Joseph Oxley ...65, 169	Eykyn, Cecil 286	— Bonham 361
Elletson, William ffyffe...	291	— William 368	Eyre, Edmund Henry 21, 407	— Charles Edmund 382
Ennis, Arthur B.	213	— Gervas Selwyn ...53, 413	— Edmund 7, 405	
Ellice, Robert Frederick	174	Enriquez, Albert D... 69, 416	— Hastings Aug.... 245, 373	— Granville de la M. 58, 293
Ellicombe, Geo. John ...	249	— George Dallas 186	— Montague Stokes 505	— Robert de Lance 436
Elliot, Adam Scott	325	Enthoven, Cha. Henfrey 211	— Morland Stanhope ... 173	Faussett, E. G. Godfrey 214
— Alex. J. Hardy	141	— Percy H. 170	Eyre-Williams, Edw. ... 18	— Owen G. Godfrey...... 288
— Charles Riversdale ...	433	Entrican, James......... 506	Eyton, John Hope W. 49, 297	— Percival G. Godfrey 175
— Edmund Halbert......	132	Entwistle, Thos. Geo. ... 134	Eyvoll, John 312	Fawcett, Edward 504
— Edward Hay M....67,	284	Erck, John C............... 427	Faber, Sydney George 213	— Jas. Farish Malcolm 63, 147
— Edward Locke...47,	412	Erle, Christopher 144	Fagan, Arthur Newton 273	— Percy Harrison......... 174
— George Ramsay	318	Errington, Richard 424	— Bernard Joseph 347	— William Francis ...67, 292
— Gilbert S. M'D	210	— Walter Henry 433	— *Rev.* C. C. T. 457	— William James 378
— Gilbert Thomas	244	Erroll, *Earl of* 9	— Chris. G. Forbes...69, 417	Fawkes, Edward Dalton 288
— Harry Macintire	175	Erskine, Arch. Jas. ...67, 366	— Chris. S. F. 41, 399	— Lionel Grimston 41, 166a
— Hugh....................	244	— Charles Ellis Hay...... 431	— Edward Arthur 294	Fayle, Robert J. Leech... 381
— John Furzer	238	— George 287	— Henry Horace Fred. 421	Fayrer, James O. S......... 425
— Robert Henry	506	— George Elphinstone 21, 403	— Hugh Rollo 432	— Joseph 383
— William	171	— James Francis 233	— James Lawtie......21, 408	Fearnside, Clarence F... 506
— Wm. Hy. Wilson	455	— Keith David 430	— Joseph 25, 404a	Fearon, Jas. Ahmuty 65, 259
Elliott, Alfred Charles...	439	— William Douglas 385	— Lucius Emilius 439	Fedden, Clement Aguew 277
— Charles Allen	213	Essell, Fred. Knight ... 237	— William Welply......... 275	Feetham, Edward......... 293
— Chas. Roulston	213	Esson, Edw. Malcolm ... 259	Faichnie, Douglas C. ... 256	Fegen, Magrath Fogarty 163
— Edward Draper...18,	179	— William 401	— Fred. Geo. 385	Feilden, Cecil Wm. M. ... 144
— George Hambley...46,	411	Etches, Chas. Edw. 242	— Norman 385	— Edward Leyland C...... 317
— Gilbert Chas. Edward	144	Eteson, H. Carlton W... 172	Fair, Arthur E. B. 178	— Granville Cholm....... 318
— Herbert Henry	279	Etheridge, Alf. Ashurst... 289	— Fred. Kendall 212	— James Hawley Gilbert 305
— Hugh Ernest	146	— Cecil de Courcy......... 242	— James George 163	— Ramsay Robert 291
— *Rev.* J. A.	460	Etty, *Rev.* Charles John 507	Fairbrother, Wm. T. 69, 416	— Rundle Montague ... 287
— Reginald Wm. Sydney	441	Eustace, Alex. Henry ... 432	Fairfax, Bryan C........... 314	— Robert Basil 173

Index—Active List.

Feilden, Wemyss Gawne C.... 262
Feilding, Bertram F. P. 308
— Geoffrey P. T. 231
— *Hon.* Wm. H. A. 4
Fell, John Percy 58, 168
— Robert Black 270
Fellowes, Halford Le M. 362
— James 24, 204
— Peregrine H. 397
Fellows, Chris. Stewart 284
Feltham, Wm. Parsons 379
Fendall, C. Pears 170
Fenn, Edwin Glass 22
— Edwin Harold M'B... 440
— Ernest Harrold...233, 379
— William Tittery 285
Fenner, Claude C. 436
Fenning, Wm. Maxwell 362
Fenton, Alex. B. 52, 415
— Frank Ford 153
— Gerald Herbert 395
— Layard L. 53, 413
— Michael 372
Fenwick, Geo. Carew 43, 410
— Henry Thomas 135
— Mansel A. C. B. 238
— Martyn J. Edward 55, 283
— William 256
Ferguson, Alex. Fred. 530
— Algernon Fras. H. 134
— Arthur George 356
— Charles Austin 275
— Chas. J. O'Neill... 21, 204
— James William 138
— John David 385
— Nicholas Charles 382
— Richard Patrick 377
— Spencer Charles 240
— Victor 267
— Victor John Fergus 69, 135
Ferguson-Davie, A. F. 439
Fergusson, Arthur Chas. 177
— Charles 229
— Herbert Chaworth 317
— Horne Johnstone...59, 270
— John Adam 45
— William Jas. Smyth.. 130
Fernie, Francis Hood.. 136
Fernyhough, Hugh C... 295
Ferrand, Edward 504
Ferrar, Henry M. 173
— Michael L. 259
Ferrers, Cecil S. F. 284
Ferrier, *Rev.* Alex. 460
— Alex. Walter 42, 165
— George Henry 372
— Jas. Arch 61, 208
Ferris, Wm. Butler ...53, 413
Ferryman, A. H. 333
Festing, Arthur Hoskyns 329
— Wogan Richard 333
Fetherstonhaugh, Edwyn 348
— John David 47, 337
— Rich. Steele Rupert 24, 304
— Timothy 318
Ffennell, Richard 347
Ffinch, Matthew B. D... 310
Ffolliott, William 378
Ffrench, Arthur 423
— Thomas 431
ffrench-Mullen, J. L. W. 435
Field, Cecil Duncan 160
— Charles Douglas 438
— Charles Wm. 429
— Cyril 400
— Henry Norman 249
— Wm. C. Faure 61, 414
— *Rev.* Walter P. Gray... 460
Fielden, Harold 149
Fielding, Joshua 139
Fiennes, G. C. Twisleton Wykeham 262
— H. E. Twisleton Wykeham 151
Fife, Aubone G. 130
— Hugh Wharton 276
— Robert Bainbridge 176
— Ronald D'Arcy 259
Fincastle, Alex. E. *Visct.* 158
Finch, Colin 430
— Edward H. F. 270
— George Forbes C. 178
— Hamilton W. Edw. 301
— Herbert Marshall 293
Fincham, Herbert Geo. 369
Finden, Woodforde 452
Findlay, Charles 325

Findlay, Neil Douglas... 170
Fink, George Herbert 455
Finlaison, John Bruce 401
Finlay, Alex. Russel 255
— Frank Dalzell 250
Finlaison, John 395
Finn, *Rev.* Arthur Henry 460
— Harry 68, 163
Finnie, Robert Blake 233
Finnis, Henry 61, 208
— John Fortescue 439
Firman, Robert Bertram 301
Firth, Edw. Wm. Anson 435
— Henry Vivian 250
— Richard Anson 438
— Robert Hammill 382
— Samuel 178
Fishbourne, Chas. Edw. 240
Fischer, Lewis Gordon 455
— Thomas Adam 428
Fisher, Arthur 28, 409
Fisher, Arthur Alex. 253
— Charles Alex. 177
— Charles John 172
— Chas. Sidney Dalton 302
— Fra. Torriano 172
— Frederic George 275
— Frederick 436
— Henry Francis T. 273, 368
— *Lieut.* John 428
— *Surg. Lieut.* John 457
— John Francis 175
— Ralph B. W. 57, 152
— William Annesley 438
Fitton, Guy William 309
— Hugh Gregory 293
FitzClarence, Charles 243
— Edward 283
FitzGeorge, Aug. C. F. 25
— George W. Adolphus 21
FitzGerald, A. V. D. 234
— Arthur Ormsby 382
— Chas. J. Oswald...19, 406
— Chas. Mordaunt ..59, 414
— Clifford Maunsell 311
— *Lord* Fred 50, 304
— George Alfred 174
— Geo. Edw. Foster 255
— Gerald 147
— Gerald James 135
— Herbert Swayne..63, 314
— Maurice 139
— Mordaunt John F. 178
— Percy Desmond 153
FitzGibbon, John A. 177
FitzHenry, C. Brittain... 149
Fitz Herbert, Henry 293
Fitzherbert, E. Herbert 46
FitzMaurice, Robert 174
Fitzmayer, *Sir* Jas. Wm. 164
FitzPatrick, Barthol. D. 362
— Francis S. 21, 406
— John Francis 504
— Thomas 246
FitzRoy, Philip Fitz W. 176
Fitz Stubbs, Edwin... 40, 366
Fitz Wygram, *Sir* F. W. J., *Bart.* 157
Fixott, James Laing 53, 168
Flanagan, J. Wm. Henry 379
— Richd. John Woulfe... 294
— Robert Nassau Alex. 258
Fleming, Chas. Christie 385
— Edward Wm.....58, 168
— Frederick 178
— George 395
— Henry Lawrence 434
— Henry Slane 50, 288
— Henry Townshend 261
— John Murchison 422
— Peter Fraser 144
Fletcher, Alfd. Foulger 42, 166a
— Edward Walter 240
— Henry Arthur 130
— Henry James 382
— Henry William 274
— James 368
— Walter Blunt ...53, 167
Fleury, Chas. Marlay.. 386
— William L. 372
Flint, Edw. Montagu 52, 167
— John 139
Flintoff, Thomas ...134, 395
Flood, Arthur Solly..... 214
— Fred. Frere Solly..... 438
— Robt. Thos. Hanford 63, 246
— Samuel James 380
Flower, Philip Henry... 173

Flower, Oswald Swift 265
— Stanley Smyth 240
Fludyer, Henry 21, 233
Foley, Algernon C. ...59, 208
— Frank Wigram 293
— Reginald Edward 431
— *Hon. Sir* St. G. G. 282
Foljambe, Hubert F. F. B. 305
— A. W. de B. S. 357
Follett, Henry Spencer 142
— Robert W. Webb 21
— Spencer W. 69, 151
Folson, Henry 232
Fooks, George Ernest 530
— Henry 455
Foord, Albert Reginald 252
— Edward Russell 436
— William L. Tom 370
Foot, Richard Mildmay 271
Foote, Arthur Wavell 310
— F. O. Barrington 44, 166a
— Henry Bruce 172
Foran, *Rev.* Thomas 396
Forbes, Alastair Kinloch 362
— Athol Murray H. 262
— Archibald Jones 268
— Arthur 175
— Arthur William 43
— Geo. Fras. Reginald 258
— George Wentworth 65, 136
— Granville Eardley 325
— James Frederick 308
— James Stewart 151
— John George 297
— Lindsay Anstruther 434
— Robert Inglis 281
— *Hon.* Walter R. D. 321
— William Lachlan 243
— Willoughby E. G. 51, 242
Ford, Beauchamp St. C. 254
— Charles A. W. 436
— Charles Hopewell 173
— Francis C. Minshull 317
— *Rev.* George A. 460
— Harry Burroughes 437
— Reginald 367
— Richard 356
— Richard William 380
Forde, Bernard 384
— Lionel 170
Fordyce, Alex. D. 421
— Henry L. Dingwall 435
— John Fraser D. 48, 412
Forjett, Frederick H. 42, 410
Forman, Arthur B. 178
— Douglas Evans 177
— Robert H. 380
Formby, Reginald F. R. 425
Forrest, Geo. A. Wm. 44
— James 246
— James Rocheid 382
— William Chas. 153
Forrester, James S. 133, 379
Forsdyke, Fred. W. 395
Forster, Bowes Lennox 5, 164
— Geo. Norman Bowes 242
— John Burton......52, 258
— Philip B. Bohun 434
Forte, Hbt. Aug. Nourse 254
Forteath, F. W. Hughes 437
Fortescue, *Hon.* A. G. 231
— *Hon.* Chas. Granville 356
— Francis Alexander 304
— Henry 66, 159
— *Hon.* Lionel H. D. 159
— Forth, Clarence T. W. 432
Fosbery, Fras. Langford 258
Foss, Kenneth M. 419
Foster, Alan 337
— Charles Edward 17
— *Sir* Charles John 158
— Hubert Edmond 301
— Hubert John......68, 209
— John Raffray 170
— Louis Maurice 430
— Montague Amos 252
— Percival Lloyd 177
— Philip 173
— Raymond Charles 63, 169
— Turville Douglas 270, 367
— William Herbert 367
— William Yorke 171
— Foulerton, Alex. F. Grant 346
— Foulis, Arch. P. L. 398
— Foulkes, Chas. Howard 214
— Henry Drury 177
— *Rev.* T. H. 396

Foulkes, Thos. Howard 506
Fowell, Newtn. Plomer 51, 167
Fowke, Francis 283
— George Henry 211
Fowle, John 163
— Thomas Ernle 255
— Trenchard F. T. ...58, 168
Fowler, Charles Astley.. 431
— Charles Edw. Percy.. 386
— Francis Charles 173
— Francis John 429
— George Curran Orr 395
— Henry B. 67, 236
— John Francis S. 363
— John Sharman 212
— Valentine A. M. 244
— William James... 48, 166a
— Willoughby Jones 177
Fownes, Edward John 51, 252
Fox, Arthur Barton 252
— Arthur Claude 386
— Brabazon H. Maine... 319
— Charles 255
— Edward Vigor 310
— George Malcolm 28
— Harry Croker 41, 205
— Lionel Whitelaw 440
— Lionel Wodehouse 252
— Michael Francis 346
— Patrick H. 380
— Reginald Petley 244
— Robert Fanshawe 172
— Thos. C. Armstrong 32
Fox-Pitt, Wm. Aug. Lane 229
Fox-Pitt-Rivers, Aug. Hy. Lane 284
Framingham, Edmund 271
Frampton, William John 76
Francis, Allan O. 146
— Charles A. William... 398
— Geo. Frankland ... 57, 413
— Harold Hugh 234
— Owen Lyall 141
— Wolstan 56, 276
Frankfort de Montmorency, *Lord* 6
Frankis, Walter Wm. 401
Franklin, Benjamin 452
— Denham Francis 380
Franklyn, Claude de M. 212
— Wm. Edmund 50, 259
Franks, Geo. Despard 161
— George M'Kenzie 175
— Harry Clifford 255
Fraser, Affleck Alex. 255
— Alex. David 321
— Alexander Henry 45, 284
— Alexander Thos....21, 219
— Angus George 269
— Arthur Reginald...50, 167
— C. Cranfurd 150
— *Hon. Sir* D. Macdowall 164
— Edward Alexander 41, 410
— Frederick John 437
— Herbert St. John 506
— Hobart Charles 400
— Howard A. Denholm 212
— Hugh Cranfurd 133
— *Hon.* Hugh Joseph 233
— James 378
— James Keith 5
— James Wilson 264
— John Randal 291
— Keith Alex. 149
— Lyons David 175
— Nicol Grahamo 434
— Norman Warden 277
— Robert Hugh 51, 292
— Robert Walter M'Leod 258
— Theodore 25
— Thomas 16, 205
— Walter Andrew 435
— Walter Simon 434
— Wm. Aug. Cumming 163
— Wm. Forbes M. I. 422
Frazer, George Stanley 432
Freckleton, Geo. Wm. 334
Frederick, C. Arthur A. 231
Freeland, Anthony D. 175
— Henry Fras. Edw. 213
— Lewis Gray 292
Freeman, B. Deane 262
— Charles Birt 395
— Ernest Carrick 384
Freeth, Chas. John D. 177
— Francis Edward 173
— George Hy. Basil 261
— James Plomer .. 45, 166

Index—Active List. 554

Fremantle, Sir A. J. Lyon 4
— Gay 231
French, Arthur 6, 397
— Fitzstephen J. F. 398
— Col. Geo. Arthur 26, 165
— Capt. George Arthur 367
— George Brooke 455
— Herbert Cumming 386
— Houston 134
— John Denton P. 273
— Hon. Robert 272
— Sampson Gough 258
— William Cotton 440
Frenchman, Edulji P. 505
Frend, George 65, 240
Frere, Wm. Arth. Jas. 51, 262
Freshwater, Arthur 386
Frewen, Stephen 59, 158
Freyer, Peter J 453
— Samuel Foster 382
Friederichs, B. Alex. 213
Friend, Lovick B. 65, 209
Frith, Herbert C. 252
— Reginald C. Cokayne- 157
— Warren Hastings 51, 167
Frizelle, Julian 284
Frodsham, W. J. H. 59, 275
Frost, George Howitt 456
— James 214
— Robert Francis 395
Fry, Charles Irwin 422
— William 253
Fryer, Cecil Robert 250
— Francis Lyall 230
— Fred. Arth. Bashford 148
— George W. Smith 421
— Major Gen. John 6
— 2nd Lieut. John 149
— Leslie Charles 426
Fulcher, Claude 334
Fuller, Chas. Bowdler 180
— Cuthbert Graham 214
— Francis George 213
— Geo. Chas. 373
— John 312
— Richard Woodfield 171
— William Cole 235
Fullerton, J. Campbell 453
— John Davidson 61, 208
— Thomas Wm. Archer 456
Fulton, Geo. Wade R. 57, 168
— Harry Townsend 253
— Herbert Albrecht 259
— Robert 59, 414
— Thomas Benedict 360
Furlong, Geo. Wm. 372
— Malcolm 19, 406
Furner, Wm. Paine 185
Furney, John Leared 362
Furse, Wm. Thomas 173
Fyers, Hubert A. N. 356
— Sir Wm. Augustus 314
Fyffe, Bertram Oliphant 272
Gabb, Christopher W. W. 247
Gabbett, Alex. Cecil 440
— Poole Robert 378
— Pulteney Charles 506
— Richd. Edw. Phillips 265
Gage, Æila Molyneux B. 156
— John Olphert 42, 278
— Moreton Foley 142
— Richard Stewart 348
Gahan, Melmoth Caulfield 371
Gaisford, Douglas John 267
— Gilbert 47, 412
— James 437
— Richard Boileau 262
— Walter Thomas 318
Gaine, C. H. Brydges 146
Gaitskell, Charles 246
— Sydney 398
— Walter James 398
Galbraith, Fred. Alex. 302
— G. H. L. 286
— Gerald Edward 173
— William 7
Gale, Charles William 259
— Ernest Septimus 348
— Henry Richmond 211
— John Ross 273
— Marmaduke Hy. L. 265
— Walter Andrew 68, 209
Galindo, Richard Eyles 337
Gall, Chas. David M. 51, 243
Gallehawk, John Wm. 346
Galloway, Frank Lennox 175
— Harold B. 318
— Hugh 238

Galloway, John Joseph 213
— John M. C. 7, 403
Gallwey, Edmond Jos. 51, 252
— Henry Lionel 274
— Matthew M. 378
— Patrick Fitzgerald 22, 165
— Thos. Joseph 378
— Sir Thos. Lionel J. 204
Galton, Hubert G. H. 58, 168
Galwey, Chr. Edward 258
— Reginald Hugh 177
Gambier, Claude Fred. 58, 414
Gamble, Richard Narrien 246
Ganado, Alfred Wm. 186
Garbett, Cha. H. V. 53, 413
— Colin Hubert 24, 408
Garden, Alex. Harry 437
— Arch. Ross H. 436
Gardiner, Alec 214
— Frederick 368
— George Frederick 253
— Henry Laurence 170
— Henry Lynedoch 164
— Ilay Ferrier Forrest 234
— John Arthur M. 317
— Richard 284
— Richard John 314, 369
— William Arthur 279
Gardner, Fras. Stewart 401
— Henry Montfort 246
— Robert 152
— Robert Macgregor S. 272
Garland, Ernest A. C. 217
Garner, Cathcart 383
Garnett, Cecil Francis 58, 254
— Cecil Frederick 262
— Reginald 25
Garnett-Botfield, W. D. 57, 168
Garnock, R. B. Visct. 282
Garrard, James R. L. 140
Garratt, Clarence H. 282
— Fras. Sudlow 141
— Harry Sumner 438
— Lawrence Challoner 231
Garraway, Chas. Wm. 258
— Harry Stephenson 362
Garrett, Annesley J. 44, 411
— Arthur Mollioit 214
— John Raymond 401
— Robert Vernon 418
— Thos. Horsfall H. 41
Garsia, Clare James 297
— Herb. G. Anderson 275, 368
Garstin, Alfred Allan 46, 301
— Geo. Lindsay 57, 413
— Henry Edward 177
Gartside-Tipping, E. A. 17
— Robert Francis 66, 415
Garvie, John 456
Garwood, Fred. Scott 214
— John Fred. 44, 206
— John Reginald 214
Gascoigne, Clifton C. O. 318
— Ernest F. O. 230
— William Julius 16, 233
Gaselee, Alfred 26, 409
Gaskell, Thomas K. 243
Gastrell, Everard T. 419
— Geo. Davidson C. 57, 413
Gatacre, John 21, 406
— William Forbes 18
Gathorne-Hardy, Hon. J. F. 230
Gatliff, Albert Farrar 61, 400
Gatt, Antonio 57, 186
Gaunt, Cecil Robert 139
Gausson, Chas. Louis 438
— Edgar 57, 366
— James Robert 281
— John Samuel 373
— Gavin, Fred. James 59, 258
Gawne, John Moore 65, 238
Gay, Arthur William 24
— Robert, Edw. Alex. 428
Gaynor, Henry Francis 261
Geach, Gerald B. 139
Geary, Fras. Sandham 281
— Henry Le Guay 6, 164
Geddes, Aug. David 237
— Ernest D. Eskford 398
— George Hessing 173
— John Gordon 173
— Malcolm H. Burdett 362
— Robert James 382
— Walter James 231
Gedge, Rev. A. A. L. 336
Geo, Fred. William 436

Gehle, H. J. Wolsteyn 27, 207
Geldard, Francis 310
Gell, Rt. Rev. Fred. 507
Gollibrand, John 284
Gelston, Arthur W. Hill. 371
Gem, Arthur S. H. 47, 279
Gemmell, Wm. A. S. 178
Genders, Joshua 370
Geoghegan, A. O. 380
— Francis Edward 438
— Robert 175
— Stannus 432
— Thos. Patrick 418
George, Arthur 310
Georges, H. R. Gilbert 43, 206
— Henry W. E. 420
Gerard, Montagu G. 16, 410
— R. T. Lord 1
German Emperor, H. M. William II. 143
Gerrard, John Joseph 385
Gervers, Fras. R. S. 214
Geslin, John Percy 309
Gib, Howard Alaric 291
Gibb, John Hassard S. 273
— Richard Charles 269
Gibbard, Thos. Wykes 385
Gibbes, Frank Douglas 246
Gibbings, Hen. C.C. 58, 271
Gibbins, Ralph B. H. 163
Gibbon, James Aubrey 211
Gibbons, James Barry 455
Gibbs, James Alec Chas. 277
— John Edward Laurie 255
— Mossom Innis 59, 414
Gibson, Rev. Edward 507
— Geo. Gisborne 112
— Joseph 380
Gibsone, Hugh J. Craig 400
Gibton, Wm. L. Perssé 271
Gideon, Jas. Henry 261
Giddy, William R. G. 223
Giffard, Cecil Lerrier 292
— Gerald Godfray 506
— William Carter 285
Gifford, Robert 140
Gilbert, Arthur Robert 279
— Clarence Edwin Lloyd 456
— Gerald Edwin Lloyd 432
— Herbert Henry 372
Gilbert-Cooper, W. N. R. 275
Gilbertson, Thomas 185
Gilchrist, Robert Alex. 43, 410
Gildea, Thos. Stanhope 27
Giles, Albert 428
— Francis Henry Synge 172
— Geo. Michael J. 454
— William 421
Gill, Fred. Andrew 138
— H. J. 291
— Robert Hinds 281, 370
— Reynold Alex. 213
Gillan, Rev. G. G. 457
Gillard, C. Whitney 395
Gillespie, A. Kenneth 285, 367
— Ernest C. Freath 367
— Franklin Macaulay 205
— James Carnegie 42, 166
— Richard William 357
— Rollo St. John 214
— Samuel 395
Gillies, Mark M. 25
Gilligan, William Arthur 19
Gillman, David Jas. 386
— Edward Sylvester 257
— Webb 176
Gillmore, Rev. Charles A. 460
Gillson, Godfrey 176
Gilmore, Allan 58, 272
Gilmour, Jas. Patrick R. 305
Gilpin, Frederic C. Almon 207
Gimlette, Geo. H. D. 454
Gipps, Sir Reginald 5
Giraud, Charles Herve 377
Girouard, Edouard P. C. 213
Girvin, John 384
Gittens, Rev. F. C. 250
Gladstone, William 395
Glancy, John Grogan 50, 346
Glanville, Arthur George 174
— Francis 210
Ghaslurd, Alex. I. R. 438
— Duncan John 255
Glasgow, Alfred Edgar 279
— John C. R. 29
— Wm. James Theodore 300
G.eeson, Andrew P. 363
Gleichen, Count A. E. W. 223

Gleig, Percy N. 264
Glen, Archibald 25
— Robert N. John 238, 368
Glencross, William 27
Glennie, Edward 53, 208
— Farquhar 25, 267
Glossop, Bertram R. M. 140
— Francis Edward 250
— Walter H. Newland 250
Gloster, Edward 254
— Gerald Meade 249
— William 258
Glover, Benj. Lucas 395
— Robert F. B. 282
Glubb, Fred. Manley 209
Glyn, Arthur St. Leger 231
— J. Plump. Carr 5
— Sir Julius Richard 246
Glynn, Martin 318
— Robert M. Osborne 265
— Thos. G. Powell 214
Goad, Howard 417
Goater, Benjamin 386
Godbold, George Aug. J. 309
Godby, Charles 210
Goddard, Edward H. 283
— Fras. Ambrose D'O. 347
— Fred. FitzClarence 23, 366
— James Rainey 403
Godden, Henry Tufton 255
Godfrey, Masters John 46, 366
Godfray, Hugh C. W. 177
— Sir James, Knt. 1
— John William 51, 269
— Herbert 417
Godfrey, Arthur I. S. 277
— Charles 440
— Charles Willis 23, 407
— Cornelius Benjamin 24
— Fredk. Rowlandson 401
— Stuart Hill 425
Godfrey-Faussett, E. G. 211
— Fermor 237
— Owen Godfrey 288
— Percival G. 174
— Godley, Alex. John 25
— Francis O. 66, 289
— Harry Crowe 292
Godman, Sherard H. 233
Godwin, Chas. A. C. 362
— Charles Henry Young 377
Godwin-Austen, R. Arth. 283
Goff, Algernon H. S. 217
— Cecil Willie T. T. 274
— Gerald L. J. 63, 337
— Wm. Ernest Davis 138
Gogarty, Henry Edw. 262
Goggin, George T. 380
Going, Alexander Chas. 269
— John 267
— George Nuttall 282
Goldfinch, Wm. Horsman 310
Goldfrap, Henry C. S. 61, 246
Goldie, Adrian Hope 175
— James Ord 22, 407
— Mark Henry George 47, 207
— John 294
Goldney, T. Holbrow 46, 411
— William Rous 55, 203
Goldschmidt, Ernest S. D. 285
Goldsmid, Albert E. Williamson 28
— Geo. Stewart 418
Goldsmith, Edm. Woods 395
— Edward P. T. 29
Goldthorp, Fras. Herbert 439
Gompertz, Alfred C. M. 63
— Bowes T. M. 45, 411
— Rev. J. F. Warden 460
Gonne, Charles Melville 17
Gooch, John Sherlock 173
Goodair, Wm. Henry 24
Goode, Richard John 178
— Stuart 255
Goodenough, Herb. Lane 431
— W. Howley 5, 164
Goodeve, Hen. Hills 211
Goodfellow, C. Aug. 5, 219
— Robert Charles 24
Gooding, Lancelot N. 177
Goodrich, Henry Selwyn 285
Goodridge, Edw. S. T. 275
Goodwin, Rev. Er as. H. 390
— Robert Hamilto 177
— Thos. H. J. Chapman 380
Goodwyu, Hy. Edw. 69, 207
— James Edward 42
— Julius Henry 235

M M

Index—Active List.

Goodwyn, Norton James 249
— Walter Meredith 249
Goold, William Joseph... 277
Goold-Adams,Hamilton J.. 234
— Henry Edward Fane 170
— Richard E............63, 317
— Wm. Richard 65, 373
Gordon, Alex. Evans 42, 410
— Alex. Hamilton 471
— Alex. Weston 348
— Alfred Ernest 177
— Alister Fraser 321
— Arthur W. Bolton 170
— Charles Cecil............ 234
— Charles Louis............ 400
— Charles Steward ..44, 253
— Cosmo George ...51, 399
— Cosmo Huntly ...57, 237
— Edward Hyde H. 321
— Edward Robertson ... 137
— Frederick 321
— Geo. Alex. Stewart ... 177
— George Huntly Blair 209
— Henry G. Wolrige 325
— Henry William......... 213
— Herbert 256
— Hugh Pennycuick ... 337
— Ingram C. Conway... 317
— James Henry.......19, 406
— James Redmond P. ... 157
— John Charles Fred..53, 413
— John G. Wolrige 337
— John James H.......4, 405
— John Lewis R........... 436
— John Maxwell 154
— John Wood............. 418
— Lawrence Christian... 173
— Lawrence Geo. F...... 173
— Leonard 69, 269
— Lewis Conway......... 398
— Lochinvar A. C. 173
— Louis Aug. 419
— M'Leod James 433
— Neil Fraser.............. 175
— Philip Cecil H........... 383
— Philip James 425
— Ramsay Fred.Clayton 431
— Robert..............46, 412
— Robert Ayron 234
— Stannus, Venner ...41, 410
— Stewart Douglas...68, 416
— Walter G. Wolrige ... 286
— Colonel William....... 25
— Major William....45, 314
— William David 419
— William Eagleson ... 321
— Wm. F. Loudon 245
— William Neville........ 174
— William Staveley...... 211
Gordon-Gilmour,Robert
Gordon 229
Gordon-Lennox, Ld.A.C 19
Gore, Albert A. 377
— Arthur John 249
— Charles Olitherow ... 130
— Charles William ..47, 277
— Edward Arthur 6
— Hon. Henry A. O. 93, 153
— Herbert 334
— Jas. Casmajor 368
— Ribton 69, 279
— Robert Clements 337
— St. George Corbet 51, 297
— St. John Corbet...66, 140
— Wm. A. Marie Pollock 234
Goren, Berkeley R. 284
Gorges, Chief Pu. m. Edm.
Howard 371
— Lieut. Edm. Howard 309
Goring, Alan 333
— Walter 145
Gorle, Harry V. 293, 368
Gorman, Wm. Henry ... 275
Gormley, Jos. A. 378
Gorringe, George Fred. 213
Gorton, Reginald St. G. 174
Gosling, Charles........... 205
— George Bennet 357
— Seymour Frederick... 177
— William Sullivan 233
Goss, William 368
Gosselin, Bertrand 176
— John Haslett 160
Gosset, Allen Butler ... 264
— Edw. F. 254
— Ernest Allardice G... 289
— Frederic 51, 207
— Matthew W. E......... 19

Gostling, Chas. Henry 66, 234
Gothard, Rev. Geo. 532
Gott, Geo. Arthur 418
Gotto, Harold Ralph ... 175
Gough, Alan Percy G.... 265
— Bloomfield........49, 151
— Charles Hugh Henry 432
— Sir Charles John S. 4, 403
— George Bloomfield ... 437
— Hon. Geo. Hugh ...24, 156
— Henry Worsley........ 335
— Hubert De le Poer ... 158
— Hugh Aug. Keppel ... 438
— Sir Hugh Henry ...4, 405
— Hugh Sutlej 22, 160
— John Edmond 357
— Stanley Charles 423
Goulburn, Cuthbert E... 170
— Henry 68, 229
— Gould, Jay 457
— Philip 333
Goulding, William 214
Gouldsbury, Dudley E.45,411
Gouldsmith, Albert 279
Govan, James Lorne 68, 245
Gower, C. C. Leveson... 433
— Philip Leveson 289
Grace, Charles H. C. ... 437
Grasey, Thomas......41, 205
Greme, Fred. James ... 169
— Lawrence Oliphant... 325
— Robert Charles 27
Graham, Bertram R. ... 362
— Charles Lanfear 146
— Edw. Ritchie C.....62, 264
— Frank 69, 250
— Frederic 136
— George Leslie 163
— Hamilton M. C. Wm. 401
— Lt. Col. Henry 45
— Captain Henry 162
— Henry Macleod 267
— Jocelyn H. Clive 231
— John Malise Anne ... 238
— Lancelot 173
— Lionel Frederick 309
— Malcolm 42, 366
— Malcolm David 292
— Richard N. ...59, 301, 373
— Robt. Blackall 337
— Samuel James 5, 397
— Stuart Bruce............ 430
— Vivian W. Hall......... 250
— Walter Ap S. James 585
— Walter Ferrier......51, 167
— Wm. Bannatyne....61, 309
— William P. Gore 384
Grahame, John Crum... 317
Grainger, James Kean... 395
— Thomas 455
— Francis, Edward John ... 170
— Granger, Thos. Arthur 457
Grant, Alan Colquhoun 317
— Alexander 210
— Alex. Geo. Wm....... 276
— Allan Ewen 506
— Arthur 431
— Bartle 150
— Charles 66, 337
— Charles James Wm.
  58, 424
— Donald St. John D.... 455
— Dudley H. Fleming... 246
— Edward C. Hamilton 337
— Francis Charles 424
— Francis Douglas 435
— George Hughes 267
— Henry Fane 22
— Ian Hope............... 433
— James 42, 410
— James Walter 65, 397
— John Patrick........... 318
— John Wemyss 457
— Kenneth Malcolm P. 275
— Maurice Harold 249
— Philip Gordon 213
— Robert 6, 204
— Samuel Chas. N....67, 209
— Seafield F. M. T. ...5, 405
— Sueno 52, 208
— Sydney Gordon ...69, 270
— Wm. Arthur Churchill 400
— William Griffith 246
— William Ogilvie 284
Grant-Dalton, Gerald 55, 253
Grant-Duff, Adrian 286
Grey, Charles Wm. 314, 307
Grantham, Charles F... 423

Granville, Bevil............ 130
— Dennis 242
Grattan, Arthur P. 401
— Ernest 40, 366
— John 281
— O'Donnel C. 63, 244
Graves, Acton Alex..... 425
— Benj. Charney 43, 410
— Douglas Henry M'D. 506
— Francis John 24
— Henry Affleck 40, 409
— Somerset H. Paul 47, 412
— William 377
Gray, Chas. Lloyd R. ... 176
— Edw. Wolfenden 384
— Frederick William ... 268
— Fred Wm. Barton ... 436
— Henry Chas. B. ...59, 285
— Rev. H. J. Spence ... 460
— Malcolm Alex......48, 412
— Philip Easson 173
— Richard Tucker 333
— Robert Alexander ... 333
— Wm. du Gard ...58, 417
— William Henry 456
— William Lewis 384
Grayfoot, B. Buhot 530
Grayson, Ambrose D. H. 178
Greany, Hugh............ 505
— John P. 529
Greathed, Hervey....... 150
— Robert Napier 176
Grentrex, Ferd. Wm. 67, 143
Greatwood, Arth. Ernest 275
Greaves, Sir G. Richards 5
— Robert Thurstan 261
Grech, Carmelo.......... 186
Green, A. Qotavius...45, 206
— Arthur Dowson 288
— Charles R. Mortimer 455
— Douglas Richard..... 456
— Edgar W. Butler 179
— Eric Henry Ernest ... 212
— Francis Egerton 154
— George 115
— George Edward T. ... 427
— Gilbert Victor 176
— Hy. Clifford Rodes ... 305
— James Edward 274
— James Sullivan 383
— Malcolm C. Andrew... 284
— Sebert F. St. Davids 386
— Thomas H. Mortimer 289
Greenaway, Thomas 45, 411
Greene, Albert J. R. ... 177
— Charles Kendal. 237, 370
— Fred. Rodolph R..... 291
— John Joseph 378
Greenfield, Hume 282
— Richard M. 46, 271
Greenhill-Gardyne,A.D. 321
— George, Walter N..... 154
Greenstreet, Chas. B. L. 213
Greenway, Chas. D. K. 237
— Cleveland Edmund ... 244
— John Henry 383
Greenwood,HerbertD.E. 277
— William Henry 346, 369
— William Mortimer ... 519
— George William 175
— James 259
— MacGregor............ 242
— Richard Edward 213
Greetham, Fred. Wm. V. 157
Gregg, William 48, 256
— William Henry 454
Gregory, Albert......... 264
— Charles Levinge 439
— William Villeneuve 43, 165
Gregson, Rev. Chas. ... 396
— Henry G. F. Savage ... 290
Grehan, Francis 245
Greig, Colin Philip 361
— Frederick James 383
— John Glennie.......... 291
— Piercy 202
— Rev. T. H............... 532
— William Best 439
Grenfell, Sir Fra. Wallace 6
— Harold Maxwell 133
Grepe, Arthur W......... 175
Gresson, Thomas T..... 311
— Henry A. F. C. F. S... 160
— Henry A. F. C. F. S... 160
Greville, Hon. C. B, Fulke 149
— Henry A. F. C. F. S... 160
Guise, Henry J. W....... 244
— Ronald H. Fulke 113
— Edward 424

Grey, Leopold J. H. 19, 406
— Raleigh 148
— William Francis H. 47, 412
— William George 434
Gribble, George 261
Grier, Harry Dixon 172
— Henry 379
Grierson, Jas. Moncrieff 170
— John 21, 407
Grieve, Frank............ 19
— John A. Mackenzie 55, 168
Griffin, Cecil P. Griffiths 432
— Edward Christian 6, 179
— Edward Frank 346
— Frederick Gerald C.. 276
— Henry Lysaght........ 174
— Robert Chaloner 279
— William Waudby ... 171
Griffith, Charles R. J. ... 255
— Chris. William Darby 229
— David Maitland 213
— Edward Hugh 256
— George Herbert 213
— George Richard 395
— Rev. H. W. 460
— Henry Woolgar ...50, 265
— John Gwynne 362
— John H. King......... 265
— John Hugh Sandham 295
— Wm. Walter Gilbert. 435
Griffiths, Alfred P. Hy. 383
— Algernon Sydney 48, 166a
— Capt. Charles......... 427
— Qr. Mr. Charles 235
— Cha. D. Richardson... 255
— Gilbert Saunders..... 454
— Henry Harcourt 23
— John 236
— Rev. T. M. Milnes ... 400
— William Edwin 453
Grigg, Edward Evans 40, 404
Grimley, Walter M. 440
Grimshaw, Ewing W... 438
Grimston, Rollo E...... 426
— Sylvester B. 430
Grinwood,Geoffrey G.59, 304
— James 267
Grindel, Robert 232
Griss, John Ellis 214
Gritton, Henry.......49, 401
Grogan, Charles M. ... 139
— Edward Bury 282
— Edward George ...50, 289
— Sir Edward I. Beres-
  ford 357
— George Meredyth... 258
Grose, Daniel Charles ... 377
— Daniel Chas. Evans. 299
— James 178
Grosvenor, Saumarez F. 311
Grove, Alex. Sinclair 22, 407
— Coleridge 17
— Edward A. W. S. 49, 294
— Ernes t Williams 176
— Henry Montgomery 435
— James Scott 437
— Percy Lynes 264
— Rev. Philip Sydney... 532
— Reginald Parker 264
Grover, George Gordon 301
— John 401
— Malcolm H. S......... 419
— Percival Charles 297
— William Montague ... 173
Grubb, Alex. H. W....... 214
— John James 236
Grubbe, Edmund Alex. 334
Grute, John.............. 185
Grylls, Wm. E. J. 334
Gubbin, George Fred... 382
Gubbins,Frederick Wm.
Beresford 213
— Philip Charles 210
— Richard Rolls 297
— Russell Dunmore... 172
— Wm. Launcelotte.... 378
Guest, Hon. C. H. C. ... 143
— Frank Chas. 274
Guggisberg, F. G. 213
Guilding, Edward L.... 288
Guille, Henry S. Le M. 172
Guinness, Charles D... 170
— Eustace 170
— Henry Wm. N....49, 258
Guise, Henry J. W....... 244
— Howard 277
— John H. Wingfield ... 270
Gundry, Henry B. ...66, 169

Index—Active List.

Gunn, David D............ 269
— Gilbert 234
— William Donald........ 395
Gunner, Edward 55, 168
Gunning, Chas. Vere ... 314
— Charles John............ 435
— James Davis... 378
— Orlando George 437
— Robert Cardwell 379
— Robt. Henry........55, 304
Gunter, Clarence Preston 214
— Howel 42
Gunthorpe, Edw. Jns. 24, 408
Gunton, Thomas W. ... 111
Gupta, Kali Pada 452
Gurdon, Bertrand E. M. 434
— Philip Richard T. ... 427
— William 172
Guthrie-Smith, W. M.... 440
Guyon, Gardiner Fred. 43, 243
— Herbert Joseph......... 254
Gwatkin, F. Stapleton. 55, 414
— Willoughby Garnons. 309
Gwyn, Ham. Weston ... 397
— Reg. Preston Jermy 147
Gwynn, Chas. Wm. 213
Gwynne, James Hugh... 265
Gwyther, Arthur 457
Gzowski, Casimir S...... 1
Haag, Emil Carr 160
Hackett, Arthur Luke... 504
— Rev. John................ 396
— Robert Isaac D......... 381
Hadden, Chas. Fred 55, 168
— William Charles 204
Hadfield, Charles Ar. 58, 366
Hadley, Henry 361
— Leonard Jos............. 400
Hadow, Arthur de S.... 259
— Norman P. Mellier ... 360
— Reg. Campbell ...55, 413
Haggard, Charles ... 53, 329
— Claude Mason....57, 168
— Henry 254
— John 173
Hagger, William Robert 395
Haggitt, Edward D...... 211
Haig, Alfred Edward ... 269
— Claude Henry 256
— Douglas 149
— Ernest Herman........ 212
— Herbert de Haga...65, 209
— Noil Wolseley 148
— Patrick Belfour 456
— Percy de Haga 454
— Roland.................. 158
— Thomas Wolseley 430
Hailes, David Aug. 406
— Walter 29, 409
Hain, Herbert A. D..... 402
Haines, Arthur M........ 311
— Sir Fred. Paul...... 4, 262
— Gregory 53, 242
— Gregory Sinclair 264
— Henry Aylmer 30
— Robert Lewis 61, 169
— Rev. Willoughby Chas. 396
Hakim, Hormasji M.... 505
Haking, Richard C. B... 281
Halbot, Geo. Clement ... 243
Haldane, Chas. Levenax 437
— Jas. Aylmer Lowthrop 321
— Robert J. Alwynne... 317
Hale, Charles Henry ... 384
— Charles Vaughan..... 285
— Edmund Thomas..... 177
— George Ernest 382
— John Henry ...274, 370
— Robert 154
— Thomas Wyatt ... 308, 370
Hales, Ernest B. 314
— Herbert Marwicke A. 255
— Reg. Evelyn N 254
Halford, Charles Henry 229
— Michael Francis 311
Haliburton, Sir A. L. ... 2
Haliday, Saunders B.... 529
Halkett, Hy. Craigie 47, 412
— William G. Craigie 41, 410
Hall, Arthur R. Kay ... 330
— Burnett Greive ...40, 397
— Charles............334, 369
— Charles Aug. Kay 65, 347
— Douglas 133
— Douglas Keith E. 270, 367
— Edm. Alex. Wm. 455
— Rev. Edw. Stephenson 532
— Ernest Frederick..... 173

Hall, Ernest Stanley ... 433
— Francis H. Howard... 401
— Francis Henry ... 52, 267
— Fred. Wm. Geo. 383
— Geoffrey C............. 453
— George Clifford Miller 204
— George Jas. Cadell ... 427
— Gilbert Capel........... 505
— Gordon Chas. Wm. G. 296
— Henry 46
— Henry Constable..... 177
— Herbert Sydney G.... 421
— John Hamilton 301
— John Henry 230
— John Lees 380
— John Richard.......... 231
— Julian Hamilton 5
— Lewis M. M. 66, 415
— Montague Haffenden 243
— Ralph Ellis Carr 315
— Reginald 242
— Reginald H..........65, 284
— Richard Harris........ 382
— Robert J. Draper..... 384
— Robert Macpherson.. 441
— Roger 243
— Thomas Erskine A.. 6
— William Charles 265
— Wynyard Montagu ... 253
Hallaran, William....... 384
Hallett, Cha. William S. 254
— Henry T. Hughes 43, 301
— Henry H. H............. 407
— James W. Hughes 61, 318
Halliday, Chas. Ogilvie 213
— Francis Edward ... 4, 397
— George Thomas ... 21, 403
— Hugh Maclean......... 433
— Lewis S. Tollemache 401
— Stuart Girdlestone... 279
Hallorn, Thomas......... 256
Hallowes, Fras. Wm. ... 433
— Henry Jardine 17
Hallum, Octavia C. J... 329
Halpin, William.......... 347
Halse, Stanley Clarence 177
Haly, Richard H. O'G. 18
Hambor, L. C. Bray..... 274
Hambro, Perceval O.... 157
Hamilton, Alexander ... 424
— Alexander Beamish. 269
— Angus F. Douglas ... 325
— Archibald Samuel ... 436
— Arthur Cochrane ... 141
— Arthur Frank ... 7, 219
— Arthur Richard Cole 149
— Beresford R. ... 63, 246
— Bruce Meade 254
— Charles M. 255
— Charles R. S. Douglas 321
— Lord Claud John ... 1
— Claud Lorn Campbell 177
— Claude 429
— Claude de Courcy... 171
— Claude Leslie 427
— David Rogerson 382
— Douglas Abercromby 237
— Douglas James 243
— Edmund Charles ... 145
— Edw. Owen F. 65, 236
— Hon. Gavin George... 233
— George F. Dashwood 424
— George Vaughan...40, 366
— Gilbert H. C.......66, 156
— Captain Henry 422
— Surg. Major Henry ... 454
— Henry Blackburne ... 25
— Henry Meade.......... 347
— Hon. Hy. R. Baillie... 231
— Henry Stannus 261
— Hubert Ion Wetherall 236
— Ina S. Monteith 26
— Jas. A. E. Marquis of 133
— Jas. Edwin O'Hora... 210
— James Graham 371
— James Stevenson ... 148
— J. Butler 377
— John Archibald 457
— John George Harry. 286
— John James............ 29
— Keith Rudolph........ 287
— Leonard Anson H. ... 295
— Hon. Leslie d'Henin. 231
— Percy Douglas 174
— Peter Fisher P. ...52, 167
— Robert Edw. Arch.... 262
— Robert Gorges........ 204
— Robert Sydney........ 176

Hamilton, Thomas 258
— Thos. W. O'Hora ... 381
— Rev. Walter Adolphus 450
— William Allardice ... 335
— William George...... 274
— William M. Fleming 371
Hamilton-Russell, Hon.
  A. 143
Hamley, Francis G..... 373
Hamlin, Richard James 370
Hammersley, Fred. 50, 261
Hammick, Sir St. Vin-
  cent A. Bt. 26
— Stephen Frederick ... 287
Hammond, Arthur E. ... 266
— Arthur Geo.......25, 408
— Rev. Baldwin 457
— Davrell T. 334
— Harry Durham....... 177
— Henry Septimus ... 283
— John 325
— Peter Henry 44, 1660
— Thomas 255
Hamnett, George Edw. 307
Hampton, Edward 281
Hanbury, B. Kingscote 265
— Hon. E. R. Bateman 356
— Everard Ernest....... 233
— Hon. W. S. Bateman. 134
Hanbury-Tracy, Hon. Al-
  gernon H. C. 135
— Eric T. H. 231
— Hancock, Francis de B. 410
— Frank Herbert 422
— George Edward ...23, 408
— Hon. di S. B. Burford 281
— Mortimer Pawson ... 243
— Percy Bosworth 291
Hancocks, Annesley J. 271
Hancox, Henry Percy... 271
Handcock, A. Gore ...16, 407
— Gerald Carlile S. 259
Handley, Arthur 172
Hanford, John C......24, 161
Hanham, Phelips Brooke 170
Hankey, George F. B... 305
— Hugh M. Alers 242
— John C. G. A. 177
— Sydney Thornhill ... 134
Hanks, John James...... 177
Hanley, Rich. Geo. 383
— Hanmer, Lambert A. G. 437
Hanna, John Connor ... 177
— William 65, 169
Hannay, Cath. Christian 283
— George Martin 269
— Ormelie C. 46, 337
— Ramsay W. R.... 50, 1660
Hannyngton, J. A. 438
Hansard, Arthur C....58, 168
Hanwell, Joseph 172
Harbord, Hon. Chas. ... 235
— Cyril Rodney......... 441
Harbottle, Robt. Cecil. 160
Harcourt, John S. M.... 348
Hardcastle, Alexander. 214
— Edward Lewis 178
— J. Herschel............. 252
Harden, Frederic Jn. 47, 255
— George............49, 279
— Harry Spencer Scott 261
Harding, Arthur 172
— Charles Mulcaster ... 254
— Edward Frank 22
— George Foster 401
— Gerald Montrésor ... 210
— Maynard Ffolliott ... 401
— William 115
— William Grosvenor 246
Hardinge, Hon. Arthur
  Stewart 63, 262
— Henry Charles, Visct. 356
— Henry 130
Hardisty, Wm. F. J..... 273
Hardman, Harold F. ... 252
— J. Wreford J. 143
— Reginald Stanley.... 176
Hardy, Charles R. Hugh 264
— Rev. Edwd. John ... 396
— Fred. Pelham A. 367
— Frederick Wynne ... 385
— Harry Fred. H........ 156
— Henry Russell 236
— Thomas Henry 293
— William Edward 385
— William Kyle 173
Hardyman, W. H. 360
Hare, Edw. Christian ... 455

Hare, Fred. S Christian
  47, 366
— Humphrey John..... 213
— Richard Charles ...44, 254
— Robert Hugh........... 174
— Robert William 245
— Steuart Welwood..... 305
— Wm. A. Home ...45, 206
Harford, Henry Chas. 50, 308
Harington, Arthur W. D. 272
— Charles Harington ... 244
— Elliott C................. 177
— Fred. William 25
— Hastings Norman V. 505
— Henry Andrew 438
— Herbert Hastings ... 437
— Herbert Henry 246
Harkness, Henry D'Alton 285
— Thomas Robert...... 170
— William Bathurst.... 398
Harland, Edwyn 281
Harley, Geo. Ernest ...44, 237
— Henry Kellett......... 440
Harling, Robt. Wm. ... 335
Harmon, Antony E. W. 138
— Chas. Edw. ... 55, 334
— George M. Nixon ... 357
— James Fredk. ... 42, 166
— Montague J. King 26, 408
— Ramsay St. Clair..... 176
— Richard 433
— Rodolph 378
Harness, Arthur 7, 104
Harold, Chas. Fred..... 438
Harper, Geo. Montague 211
— Leonard Llewellyn... 175
Harpur, Edm. H. 177
Harran, James 380
Harries, Saml. Keith 59, 249
Harrington, John Lane 436
Harris, Arthur P. D..... 428
— C. Beresford Maule... 395
— Charles Sidney....... 293
— Charles Walter 418
— Claudius Shirley ... 311
— Edward William ... 432
— Francis Anderson ... 425
— Frederick Alfred 381
— Frederick Wm. H. D. 383
— George 402
— Geo. Fras. Angelo ... 454
— Gerald Noel Anstice. 398
— Hugh Cogan 395
— James Edward 25
— Knox Edward 283
— Owen 277
— Philip H. Farrell ... 5, 403
— Richard Han. W. H. ... 50
— Thomas 45
— William Albert 204
— William Octavius 55, 413
Harrison, Ar. Estcourt 173
— Arthur H. Pryce 441
— Aug. Napoleon Rogers 504
— Broadley..........254, 370
— Cecil Francis 254
— Charles Edward 377
— Cholmeley E. C. B. 63, 294
— Edgar Garston......... 277
— Esme Stuart Erskine 153
— Frederick Deneys ... 2,6
— Gilbert Harwood ... 211
— Halford Claude V. ... 172
— Hugh 293
— James Molyneux ... 367
— John Collinson 144
— John Henry C....55, 208
— Rev. Philip Raikes ... 532
— Sir Richard.........5, 204
— Robert Arthur G....58, 168
— Standish Henry ...57, 244
— Sudlow................ 293
— Thomas 211
— Thomas Aylett 431
— William Albert 212
— Wm. Chris. Warde ... 439
— William Pringle...40, 404
— Willoughby Hyde 278, 367
Harriss, Stanley A. ... 457
Harrison, Arthur H. P. 244
— Hart, Alfred Paul 380
— Arthur Fitz Roy...18, 275
— Arthur Henry Seton 275
— Henry C. 270
— Henry Travers....... 177
— Horatio Holt.......52, 207

M M 2

Index—Active List.

Hart, Israel 158
— Reginald Clare ... 19, 205
Harter, Oswald B. 314
Wartigan, Arthur E. S. ... 428
— Edward Ross 424
Hartley, Desmond L. ... 259
— Ralph Legh 244
Harvest, Edmund D. 301, 374
— Hector Douglass 340
— Hector Horatio 174
— Herbert de Vere 435
— William S. S. 400
Harvey, Ambr. Blacklock 432
— Charles Bateson 152
— Charles Blundell 214
— Chas. Edw. Ramsey ... 329
— Charles Lacon 23
— Edward Henry 213
— Fras. John Wm. 401
— Harry Charles 330
— John 286
— John Edward 170
— Richard Prentice 293
— Robert 452
— Robert Napier 213
— Wm. Jas. St. John ... 28c
— William Lueg ... 68, 276
— William Orlebar 347
Harward, Arthur J. N. 435
— Francis Edward 214
— Henry Blake 373
Harwood, John G. 380
Haslam, Alfred Joseph 395
Haslehurst, Geo. W. ... 302
Hasler, Julian 237
— Percy 308
Haslett, John C. 331
— Pechell 48, 207
Haslope, Rev. L. M. 532
Hassan, Syed 454
Hassard, Edw. Moresby 384
— Henry Somerset ... 50, 293
Hasted, Arthur Walter 308
Hastings, Bernard St. J. W 244
— Edward Spence ... 67, 416
— Francis Eddowes ... 16, 404
— Francis William 164
— Percy 294
— Warren 67, 415
Hatch, Alfred Edmund 429
— Arthur Vincent 423
— William Keith 529
Hatchell, David Thompson 22, 407
— George 7
— Henry M 58, 258
Hathaway, Harold Geo. 383
Hatherell, Wm. Geo. 426
Hatton, Edw. H. Finch 237
— R e. John Alexander 396
— Villiers 25, 229
— William de Bathe ...63, 318
Haughton, Hugh L. 347
— John 59, 414
— Thomas H. 419
Haviland, Robert A. 302
Hawes, A. B. 116
— Alexander J. D. ...23, 408
— Benjamin Reddie 63, 307
— Charles Howard 253
— Percy Fred. Brunel ... 278
Hawke, Hon. H. B. 256
Hawker, Claude J. 231
— Edmund Bulteel 279
Hawkes, Corlis St. L. G. 178
— George 55, 528
— Henry Blundell 231
— Henry Montague C. 254
— Henry Montague P.63, 415
— Lawrence Harry 285
— Robert 441
— William Cotter W. ... 362
Hawkins, Frederick 68, 416
— Frederick Daly C. 455
— George Arthur 433
— Henry Theodore 171
— John William ...53, 167
— Thomas Henry 401
— Walter Francis ... 69, 209
Hawks, Fredk. Welman 438
— George Augustus ... 286
— George William S. ... 426
— Thomas Bate 427
Hawkshaw, Edward
  Crichton 58, 168
Hawksley, Randal P. T. 213
Hawley, Francis H. T. ... 144
— Robert B. 304

Haworth, Cyril H. 147
— Lionel Berkeley Holt 296
Haworth-Booth, A. R. ... 292
Hawtayne, Thos. M. ... 310
Hawthorn, George M. P. 244
Hay, Archibald 265
— Arthur 416
— Cecil Godfrey 283
— Edward Owen ...48, 166a
— George W. R. 529
— Henry 47, 412
— Henry Thos. Horatio 431
— 2nd Lieut. James 176
— Colonel James 23, 408
— J. A. G. Drummond 231
— Jas. R. M. Dalrymple 360
— Lenox Theobald 140
— Sir Robert John ... 4, 164
— Westwood Norman ... 177
Haycock, William 368
Hayden, Fredk. Arthur ... 277
Haydon, William Pitt. ... 440
Hayes, Aylmer Ellis ... 379
— Clarence Henry ... 68, 416
— Ernest de Launoy ... 270
— Julian P. Swindell ... 383
— Robert Hall 301
Hayman, S. J. Wallace 383
Haymes, Robt. L. 177
Hayne, A. Gorham H. 59, 414
— Robert 46, 308
Haynes, Alfred Ernest ... 210
— Aloyne 238
— Car cton 274
— Charles Edward 68, 209
— Frederick Hutchinson 372
— Kenneth Edward 176
— Walter Illingworth 50, 279
Hayward, Alfred R. L. 284, 367
— William Davey 457
Haywood, Lewis 381
Hazelgrove, Harry S. ... 425
Hazelton, Edwin H. 395
Hazlerigg, T. Maynard 16, 165
Hazlett, Henry James ... 594
Head, Charles Octavius 175
— Gilbert 245
— Harry Francis 174
— Henry Nugent 270
— Leonard 281
Headlam, John E. W. ... 173
— Thomas Emerson ... 401
Heale, Ernest N. 240
Healey, Coryndon W. R. 385
Healing, Robert K. 361
Henly, Christopher J. ... 385
— Henry Francis 310
— Michael Ryan 372
Heard, Alex. E. S. 333
— Edward Severin 240
— Richard 457
— Samuel Ferguson ... 401
Hearla, Parkins 33, 399
Hearn, George 282, 369
— Gordon Risley 213
— Michael Leo 382
Heastey, Charles R. 271
Heath, Alan Jasper 159
— Charles Ernest ...57, 366
— Charles Joseph 214
— Edward 369
— Francis William 174
— Fred. Crofton 51, 209
— Gerard Moore 401
— Harry H. Rose 51, 414
— Hen. Newport Chas. 52, 293
— Herbert C. Selwyn ... 288
— Lewis Forbes 41, 410
Heathcoat - Amory, H.
  W. L. 231
Heathcote, Alfred ... 53, 208
— Charles Edensor 295
Heathcote - Drummond-
  Willoughby, Hon. C. 231
Heaton, Arthur Fred ... 386
— J. A. D. 507
— Thomas 370
— Wilfred 50, 267
Hebden, Wilfrid A. 288
Hedingham, George 254
Hedley, Walter Coote ... 211
Heffernan, Herbert Wm. 435
— Nesbitt B. 171
— William 380
Hogan, Edward 51, 140
Hehir, Patrick 455
Heigham, Clement J. M. 253

Hellard, Robt. Chas . 57, 209
Helps, Thos. H. P. 297
Hely-Hutchinson, R. G. 243
Helyar, Arthur B. 170
— Charles W. H. 42, 145
— Henry Weston 65, 242
Hemming, Edw. Hughes 210
— Fred. Wilson 40, 140
— Norman Mackenzie.. 213
Hemphill, Fitzroy 269
Henderson, Ar. Francis 152
— Carlisle V. 161
— Surgeon Capt. Cecil ... 505
— Capt. Cecil 400
— David 337
— Edgar 398
— Edward George 214
— Fred. Evelyn Elliot. 347
— Geo. Fra. Robert... 50, 311
— George James 176
— Henry O. Page- ... 68, 148
— Hugh Leslie 337
— Rev. James 532
— James Sydney 361
— John Acheson 150
— John Seton 360
— Kenneth Gregg 16
— Maxwell Hume........ 440
— Percy Edward 59, 414
— Philip D. 19, 403
— Ralph Anstruther ... 309
— Robt. Samuel F. 382
— Robert Wynne 362
— Selby Herriot 455
— Thomas Hume 430
— Wm. George Hume.. 529
Hendley, Arthur G. 456
— Charles Edward 431
— Fred. George 115
— Harold 455
— Thomas Holbein 452
— Hendriks Campbell L. 347
Honeage, Alfred R. 140
— Godfrey C. Walker ... 230
— Henry Granville 154
Henegan, John 430
Heneker, Fred. C. 346
— William O. G. 334
Henley, Francis Jos. ... 287
Henn, Richard A. M. 65, 169
Hennell, Alfred Montagu 281
— Arthur Reg. 57, 281
— Reginald 132
Hennessy, Daniel 383
— G. Robertson 7, 405
— John 385
— John Patrick C. 434
Henniker, Alan Major... 213
— Fred. B. M. 305
Henniker - Major, Hon.
  C. H. C. 357
Henning, Charles M. S. 270
— Philip Walter B 176
Henriques, Edw. N.....52, 167
Henry, George 41, 206
— Gilbert Frank 151
— John 176
— St. George Charles ... 240
— Vivian 243
— William 156
Henshaw, Clinton Grant 171
Hensley, Charles Albert 348
Henslowe, Fras. J. D. ... 436
Henson, Christopher ... 170
Henstock, Fred. Thos. ... 360
Henvey, William 456
Hepburne, Rob. G.W. 50, 167
Hepenstall, L. J. Dopping 210
— Maxwell E. Dopping 273
Hepper, Alb. Jas. ... 26, 207
— Harry A. Lawless ... 213
— Lionel Lees 176
Herapath, Edgar 246
— Edwin Loud ... 259, 373
Herbert, A. Colthurst ... 247
— Charles 68, 416
— Claude 431
— Douglas 433
— Edmund Arthur 240
— Edward B. 69, 159
— Edward Sidney 208
— Edward William...49, 304
— George 243
— George Frederick ... 172
— Graham Cludde... 68, 243
— Henry Carden 284
— Herbert 530
— Ivor John C...........24, 229

Herbert, Lionel 425
— Lionel Norton 428
— Percy T. Colthurst ... 175
Herbert-Stepney, O. C. 305
Hercy, Eust. Lovelace... 17
Herdon, Hugh Edw. ... 308
Heriot, Granville Mackey 401
Heriot-Maitland, Jas. D. 357
— John C. 233
Heron, Thomas 369
Herron, Robert Douglas 137
Hervey, Const. R. Wm. 52, 167
— Hugh DeLaMotte....41, 410
Hervey-Bathurst, F.E.W. 230
Hesketh, Alg. Ernest ... 158
— Robert Walter 19, 406
Hessey, Wm. Fras. 271
Hetherington, R. P. 381
Houston, Fred. Samuel 382
Howat, Arthur H. ...53, 167
— Geo. Thos. Wm....55, 269
Hewetson, Alex. Wm. ... 176
Hewett, Augustus 380
— Edward O. 6
— Edw. Vincent Osborne 294
— George Edward 361
— James Christopher ... 283
— William Selwood...59, 414
Hewitt, J. R. Silver O. 46, 166a
— Martin 386
Hewlett, Alan 441
— Gervase G. 256, 367
Hewson, John Lysaght 371
Hext, Fras. Marwood ... 333
— Lyonel John 176
Heycock, Alfred G. S. ... 401
— Charles Hensman ... 212
— John H. 256
Hoygate, Bernard.. 41, 366
— Edward Lionel A. ... 294
— Richard Lionel 170
— Robt. Henry Gage ... 278
Heyland, Alf. T. 253
— Arthur Kyffin 362
Heyman, Cecil Edw. H. 169
— Chas. Henry Cockburn 423
Heysham, R. C. Mounsey 297
Heywood — Lonsdale,
  Henry H. 229
Heyworth, Fred. James 233
Heyworth-Savage, Cecil
  J. 243
Hibbert, Arch. Louis ... 170
— Godfrey Leicester ... 238
— John 23, 404a
— William George 213
Hichens, Thos. S. 175
Hickey, Daniel 368
Hickie, Arthur Francis ... 174
— Carlos Joseph 272
— William Barnard 243
— William Bradley 439
Hickley, Alfred Charles 434
Hickman, Devoreux W. 4:8
— Harry Otho D. 271
— James 381
— Thomas Edgecomb ... 273
Hicks, Chas. Herbert ... 261
— Fredk. Richard 281
— Henry Tempest ... 55, 348
— James Horatio 297
— Percy Stanislaus 281
— William John 61, 169
Hickson, Robt. Albert 49, 237
— Samuel 382
— Samuel Arth. E... 63, 290
— Higgin, Chippingdall H. 148
Higginbotham, Chas. E. 292
Higgins, Peter 308
Higginson, Arch. J. M. 277
— Cecil Pickford 297
— Sir Geo. W. Alex. ... 273
— Harold Whitla 348
— Henry Barkly 348
— Henry H. 69, 310, 367
— Henry Shakespear ... 179
— Theophilus ... 18, 405
Higgon, John Arthur ... 265
Higgs, Henry Charles ... 163
Hignet, Edw. Lancelot ... 421
Hignett, Chas. Harrison 371
Hildebrand, Algernon 58, 208
— Arthur B. Ross 213
— Charles Phayre 403
— Godfrey 43, 206
— Wm. Hatton 432

Index—Active List.

Hildyard, Harold C. T. 177
— Hy. John T. 19
— Robert M. D'Arcy 314
Hill, Alan Richard 292
— Arthur 27, 207
— Qr.Mr. Arthur 308
— Arthur Joseph 275
— Arthur Vivian 348
— Augustus James 130
— Augustus West 49, 301
— Cecil 210
— Charles Birnie 379
— Charles Edward 174
— Charles Glencairn 293
— Cutts Humphry 272
— Edward Cleary 67, 308
— Edward Roden 317
— Eustace Tickell 161
— Felix Frederic 333
— Frank Barton 437
— Frank Wm. Rowland 283
— Frederick Thos. Cecil 311
— Rev. Francis N. 532
— Rev. Fred. Chas. 507
— Frederick William 254, 373
— Harold Charles 440
— Sir Henry Blyth, Bart. 333
— Henry C. de la M. 237
— Hepworth Arthur 360
— Howard Berkeley 175
— James Pennell 431
— Lt. Colonel John 40, 235
— Lieut. John 434
— John Thomas 276
— Joseph Robert 431
— Richard Ernest 367
— Robert d'Esterre 246
— Thomas Alex. 63, 154
— William 43, 410
— William Alfred 437
— Wm. Leonard Bertram 272
Hill-Trevor, Hon.A.W. 47, 133
— Hon. Nevill Windsor 134
Hilliard, George 384
— Harold Nash 431
— William Edward 43
— William Robert 210
Hills, Alfred 214
— Edmund Herbert 211
— George Scott 21, 406
Hilson, Robert Jas. 274
Hilton, James Foord 24
— Murray Venables 61, 273
Hincks, Thomas Cowper 293
Hind, John William 51, 237
Hinde, Alfred Buckley 384
— John Henry Edw. 50, 278
— Wm. Fred. Honywood 154
— William Henry 210
Hine-Haycock, V. R. 177
Hinge, Harry Alex. 385
Hingley, Saml. Howard 361
Hingston, Clayton W. J. 47, 412
— Edward 213
— George Bennett 212
Hinton, Claude H. 275
— Godfrey B. 176
Hippisley, Wm. H. 65, 144
— Rich. L. 57, 208
Hipwell, Alfred Geo. 43, 366
Hire, Ashton Hope 308
Hirst, Frederick C. 309
— James 386
Hislop, Arthur Fowler 234
Hitching, George H. 214
Hitchins, Charles H. M. 424
— Harold Edmund 436
— Henry William Ernest 309
Hoare, Herbert 140
— John James 401
— Reginald 146
Hobart, Claud V. C. 230
— George 46, 399
Hobbs, F. FitzWm. T. 371
— Frederick M. B. 401
— George Lamont 334
— George Radley 369
— Herbert T. De C. 69, 253
— Joseph Scovell 272
— Percy Eyre Fras. 23
— Simpson Hackett B. 425
Hobday, Edm. A. P. 170
— Thomas Francis 42, 410
— James Ramsay 48, 412
Hobkirk, Clarence John 288
Hoblyn, Edw. Florance 172
Hobson, Arch. Campbell 238
— Edw. Schell C. 273

Hobson, Fred. Taylor 17
— Gerald Walton 154
— John Alexander 176
Hocken, Charles A. F. 438
Hodder, Wm. Morgan 210
Hodding, James Sweet 435
Hodge, Ferd. Harper 259
— Raymond Gage de B. 265
— Wm. Buller Chapell 154
Hodges, Charles O'C. 385
Hodges, Frank 294
— Henry F. E. 422
Hodgins, Charles Richd. 174
— Jacob 113
Hodgkinson, Charles 140
— Harry S. B. 57, 310
— John 147
Hodgson, George Robt. 10, 403
— Godfrey Beckett 420
— Hamilton 246
— Henry West 157
— James 370, 168
— James Owen 59, 168
— Philip Egerton 214
— Walter George 434
Hodson, Geo. Benjamin 427
— Robert Doveton 379
Hoey, John 505
— Lawrence 357
Hog, Arch. Swinton 335
Hogarth, J. H. H. S. D. 46, 269
Hogg, A. G. Forbes 5, 405
— Allan G. Mayhew 434
— Arthur Melville 40, 409
— Conrad Chas. Henry 214
— George Crawford 22, 403
— John M'Kenzie Trower 293
— John Roberts 21, 204
— Theodore C. M. Trower 434
— Theodore William 21, 406
Hoggan, George Peter 285
Hogge, Arth. Fountaine 421
— Charles 52, 414
— George Sapte 423
— John William 58, 414
Hoghton, Fred. A. 428
Hojel, James Graham 530
Holbech, Walter Hy. 130
Holbourn, William 274
Holbrook, A. St. Clair 276
— Edm. Robt. St. George 272
Holbrooke, Bernard F. R. 441
— Philip L. 177
Holden, Ernest Frank 139
— Henry Capel L. 63, 169
— Hyla Napier 287
Holdich, Sir E. A. 301
— Harold Adrian 202
— Thos. Hungerford 26, 205
Holdsworth, Geo. Lewis 149
— Henry Lewis 440
Holford, George L. 133
— James Henry Edward 149
Holland, A. Gambier 53, 157
— Hon. Cecil Trevelyan 304
— Ellis Chas. F. 57, 168
— Ernest Charles 148
— George Forbes 347
— Guy Lushington 428
— Harry Francis 426
— Percy 426
— Walter Dermott 273
— William Tilston 310
Holland-Prior, P. 438
Holley, Edmund Hunt 22, 163
Hollinshead, Hy. N. B. 178
— L. Brock 67, 294
Hollis, Matthew 214
Holloway, Benjamin 425
— Edward Leigh 424
— William Octavius 176
Hollway, Edm. John 66, 276
— James Clinton 421
Holman, Bertram Wm. 177
Holme, Alfred Siegfried 214
— Bryan Francis 237
Holmes, Chas. Jas. 382
— Gilbert Vallentin 435
— Hardress Gilbert 259
— Henry Ball 333
— Henry Stanhope 45, 285
— Robert Andr. K. 453
— Thomas James Paul 378
— William 230
Holt, Maurice Percy Cue 384

Holt, Robt. Hughtrede E. 385
— William John 18
Holyoake, Ralph 384
Home, Arch. F. 153
— C. A. Earl of 1
— David John 16
— FerdinandCospatricL. 425
— Frederick Jervis 25, 21
— Geo. Joseph Lombard 212
— Henry W. Logan 401
— James Murray 433
— Pelham Maitland 282
— Robert Elton 175
— Thos. Patrick Milne 317
— Hon. W. S. Douglas 17
— Homer, J. Leonard 398
— Homfray, John Robert H. 308
— Hone, Harry 357
— Honnor, Henry 249
— William James 176
— Hood, A. Fuller-Acland 350
— Alex. Nelson 309
— Ernest Frederick 437
— Hon. Grosvenor A. A. 230
— Hon. Neville Albert 177
— Thomas Cockburn 373
— William E. Comber 255
— Hooke, Henry Hodson 24
— Hooper, Frederick 214
— Stuart Huntley 175
— Willoughby W. 21, 403
— Hope, Adrian V. W. 441
— Charles Dunbar 178
— Graham Archibald 177
— Hugh Richard 21, 404
— James 269
— John Augustus 305
— Lewis A. 44, 366
— Michael Berwick 295
— Wm. Henry Webley 176
— Hopkins, Cha. Harrie I. 270
— Herbert F. Northey 318
— John Randolph G. 250
— Joseph 139
— Lewis Egerton 214
— Manley Ogden 55, 168
— Norman John 213
— Hopkinson, Henry C. B. 318
— J. Farthing 141
— Hopton, Edward 6
— Hopwood, Herbert Reg. 401
— Hordern, Gwyn V. 305
— Hore, Charles Owen 282
— Ernest Wickham 456
— Harry St. George S. 384
— Walter Stuart 27, 404a
— Horn, John 386
— Hornby, Edm. J. Phipps 170
— Leyland 23
— Montague Leyland 438
— Horne, Henry Sinclair 171
— Rev. Philip Bruce 532
— Horner, Reg. George 308
— Horniblow, Arthur E. 63, 400
— Frank Herbert 210
— Frederick 367
— Horrocks, Alex. M. 348
— William Heaton 384
— Horsbrugh, Arch. B. 43, 282
— Boyd Robert 242
— Robert Patrick 428
— Horsfall, Rev. Thomas 533
— Horsford, N. M. T. 21, 406
— Hort, Rev. Chas. Josiah 396
— Horton, Percy T. 335
— Sydney George 172
— Hosier, Earls A. 384
— Hosie, Andrew 384
— Hoskins, Arthur R. 310
— William Henry 22, 407
— Hoskyn, Chas. Reg. 61, 208
— Jn. Cunningham Moore 362
— Hoskyns, Chandos 51, 208
— Hotham, Francis Herbert 294
— John 51, 167
— Houghton, A. Evelyn 55, 399
— Edward Raymond 277
— Ernest 369
— William 238
— Housfield, Thos. John 281
— Household, Henry B. 283
— Houston, Arth. Manston 309
— Eyre 211
— Hovell, Hugh de Berdt 273
— How, Arth. Pemberton 435
— Howard, Cecil Arthur 61, 169

Howard, Hon. Chris. Edw. 150
— Francis 29, 356
— Francis John Charles 150
— Francis Jas. Leigh 244, 368
— Frederic 44, 166
— Frederick George 214
— Henry Charles 325
— Henry Martin 401
— John Cephas 264
— J. E. 460
— Thos. N. S. Moncrieff 253
— Walter 372
— W. Sebastian Eardley 434
— Howard-Vyse, Cecil 177
— Edward 145
— George Aubrey 244
— Howe, Fras. Herbert 285
— Joseph Swann 269
— R. W. P. Earl 134
— Rupert B. Blunt 214
— Randall Chas. A. 311
— Howell, Auberon Arthur 431
— Edward 297
— Ernest Alf. Russell 435
— Harry Arthur Leonard 386
— Llewellyn James 422
— Howlett, Arthur 47, 412
— Frederick Percy 310
— Howley, Jasper Joseph 246
— Howorth, Henry G. 176
— Hoysted, Desmond M. F. 214
— Hubbard, Alfred Edw. 246
— Arthur Oldham 456
— Henry Wm. 381
— Huddart, Arth. Kerl. 346
— Hudson, Anthony T. P. 309
— Arthur Keith 438
— Charles Tilson 530
— Ernest 455
— Harry Chalmers 455
— Havelock 426
— Josiah Howard 279
— Thos. Roe Chris. 174
— Wemyss 429
— Huggins, M. A. Colin 400
— Ponsonby Glenn 418
— Hughes, Albert Lionel W. 333
— Arbuthnott J. 66, 169
— Charles Frederick 24, 409
— David Erskine 529
— Edward Malcolm 437
— Edward Honywood 311
— Ernest St. George 296
— Fra. T. Cunynghame 432
— Frederick St. John 268
— George Arthur 379
— George Edgar 385
— Henry Andrew 137
— Henry Bodvel Lewis 156
— John Edward 440
— John Henry 377
— Matthew Louis 384
— Michael James 134
— Percy John 46, 270
— Pierce Edward 55, 271
— Reginald George H. 287
— Victor 436
— William 371
— Hughes-Hallett, J.W. 55, 318
— Hugo, Edw. Victor 456
— Hulbert, Jos. Geo. 456
— Huleatt, Hugh 210
— Hulke, Lewis I. B. 237
— Walter Backhouse 246
— Hull, Chas. P. A. 262
— Hulse, Harold H. 147
— Hulseberg, Ernest A. 362
— Herbert 264
— Hulton, Fred. C. L. 210
— Hume, Arthur H. Bliss 213
— Rev. C. N. 533
— Charles Vernon 170
— Charles Wheler 130
— Rev. Chas. W. 460
— John James Fras. 334
— John Wm. Tarring 46, 289
— Sir Robert 295
— Robert O. Cuthbert. 278
— Seignelay G. W. 278
— Humfrey, Benj. Geale 256
— Benjamin John H. 433
— Frederick G. Clinton 437
— John 42, 410
— Geo. C. Taylor 45, 372
— Humphery, Stanley 68, 272
— Humphrey, Jas. Wm. 117
— Humphreys, Dashwood W. H. 362

Hu nphreys, Gardiner... 173
— George Geoffrey P. ... 285
— Harry Lionel 367
Humphrys, Chas. Vesey 277
— Mervyn Archdall...... 291
Hungerford, T. Everard 49
Hunnard, Frank ... 268, 368
Hunt, Cecil Henry 256
— Edward Leslie 212
— Francis Dillon 395
— Frederick Welsley ... 395
— Godfrey Massy V....... 367
— Henry Vaughan... 51, 167
— Henry Vere 28, 409
— James Maitland ...49, 325
— John Dutton 317
— John Lombard 28
— John Percival........... 379
— Joseph 386
— Samuel Bradshaw ... 504
— Thomas Charles 237
— Vere de Vere............ 177
— Villiers Edward 295
— William Holdsworth 175
Hunter, Archibald... 28, 238
— Charles Finch 370
— Chas. Geo. Woodburn 213
— Charles Norris 272
— Christian B. 454
— Francis Chas. King... 267
— Fred. Ernest A......57, 168
— Frederick Joseph ... 185
— F. Mercer.......... 40, 409
— George Douglas......... 382
— George Gillett 237
— George Yeates Cobb 457
— James 370
— John Gunning 420
— John Muir 41, 410
— Malcolm Russell 432
— Vere Edward............ 382
— Walter James Henry 272
— William Chevers...... 287
— William Hugh 318
— Woodburn 23, 166
Hunter-Weston, Aylmer G. 211
— Reginald Hugh......... 318
Huntley, Hougham C. 43, 246
Huntsman, Hugh de C. 292
Hurle, Edw. F. Cooke... 252
Hurly, Maurice Randall 433
Husey, Edgar Elliott ... 264
Huskisson, Samuel Geo. 301
— William..................... 210
Hussey, Arthur H.......... 172
— Charles Edward 27
— Edward Robert ... 51, 207
— William Clive 209
Hutcheson, George 452
Hutchins, Alf. Geo....22, 404a
— Herbert Leonard 417
Hutchinson, Alex. J. R. 423
— Chas. Alex. Robert... 258
— Chas. Hammond 172
— Chas. Roderick M'L. 437
— Coote Synge 161
— Francis Patrick......... 420
— Fred. Pierrepont 175
— Geo. Higginson Ford 334
— Hy. Ewbank Menteth 361
— Henry Doveton ... 46, 411
— Hugh Moore 335
— James Bird 41, 409
— James William O. 422
— William Arthur 347
— William F. Moore..23, 165
— Wm. Nelson 277
Hutchison, Alex. R. H. 401
— Craufuird George G. 163
— Robert Schlesinger... 310
Hutson, Herbert Edw.... 289
Hutt, *Sir* George 116
Hutton, C. Molyneux 61, 261
— Edward Thos. Henry 1, 26
— Gilbert Montgomerie 212
Huxford, James 284
Hyde, Arthur Clarendon 360
— Arthur Colville......... 311
— Charles 277
— Henry 504
— *Rev.* Hen. Barry 460
Hyslop, Francis............ 244
— Henry Hugh Gordon 337
— Maxwell R.......... 67, 256
— Robert Maxwell... 47, 207
Ing). G. William Haigh 174
Ievers, Oliver Goldsmith 426
Iggulden, Herbert Aug. 289
Ilderton, Chas. Edw. 29
Iles, Frederick Arthur.. 214
— Henry Wilson 173
Imbert-Terry, A. F. A... 142
Impey, Laurence 429
Imrie, Wm. Lawrence... 185
Ingham, Chas. St. Maur 178
— Oliver P. S. 283
Ingle, *Rev.* Geo. Hy...... 460
— William Daly............ 302
Inglefield, F. Seymour 61, 254
— Norman Bruce ...63, 169
Ingles, Alex. Wighton... 253
— John Darnley 249
— Reginald J.............. 346
Inglis, Albert Gordon 274, 374
— David William 24, 404
— Ernest 419
— Henry Alves 170
— John Fred.............55, 308
— Robert Hastie.........7, 403
— Thomas Drummond . 170
— William Mason 293
— William Raymond ... 245
Ingpen, Percy L. 255
Ingram, John O'Donnell 277
Inkson, James............. 377
Inman, Arthur W. P....... 379
Innes, Cecil Mitchell ... 346
— Edward Selby 45
— Hector Munro 177
Inniss, Benj. Jas. 384
Ionides, Luke George... 275
Irby, Leonard Paul 305
Ireland, de Courcy 243
— Robert Megaw 371
Iremonger, E. Asshcton 314
— Robert George 419
Irvine, Andrew Alex. ... 440
— Delaware Lewis 380
— Gerard Beatty 456
— James Laird 209
— Thomas 337
— Thomas Walter......... 530
Irving, John Chas. Sarle 372
— Lewis Allen............. 378
Irwin, Herb. Edwards 61, 242
— James Murray 381
— John Fredk..........58, 274
— William 115
— William John 40, 162
Isaac, Herbert Crofton 253
Isaacson, Henry de S. 22, 165
Isacke, Charles Victor... 334
— Hubert..................... 294
— Reginald 253
— Robert Henry 240
Isham, Vere 250
Isherwood, Fras. Edw. B. 311
Ivatt, George Aug. 246
Izat, Alex. Rennie 178
Jack, Evan Maclean ... 214
— Herbert R. H. 282, 367
Jackson, Alex. T. 273
— Arthur Charles......49, 237
— Arthur W. F. 61, 242
— Cecil 424
— Chris. Goddard......... 142
— Cyril Compton 437
— Edmund Sylvester ... 148
— Ernest Montague...... 431
— Ernest Somerville ... 285
— Francis Benjamin...... 170
— Frederick George 22
— Frederick L. La Caze 337
— Freeman Henry...40, 404a
— George D'Aguilar 24, 403
— Herbert Kendall 170
— *Lieut.* Herbert Wm.... 440
— *Capt.* Herbert William 321
— Hugh Milbourne 209
— James..................... 530
— James Henry 371
— John 424
— John Henry 395
— Keith Hungerford ... 440
— Landon Dealtry......... 172
— Louis Charles...... 69, 209
— Montague B. Gosset... 170
— Ralph Stapleton Ward 153
— Robert Pilkington ... 436
— Robert Postance 429
— Robt. Wm. Henry...... 384
— R. Whyte M. 271, 369
— Spenser 52, 291
— Sydney C. Fishburn... 281
— Thomas 530
— William Lewis 360
Jacob, Arthur L. B....... 178
— Arthur Le Grand 433
— Arthur Leslie........... 439
— Arthur Otway 162
— Claud William 427
— George Adolphus ..19, 406
— Harold Fenton 434
— Herbert Bruce 21, 407
— Samuel Swinton ...23, 407
— Stephen Hector 178
— Sydney Long 43, 206
— Walter Henry Bell ... 176
— William 7, 405
— William Swinton...... 434
Jacques, Fras. Aug........ 437
Jacson, John H. F....50, 272
— Mainwaring George... 249
Jaffray, Edward W. 155
James, Alfred Albert ... 269
— Bernard R............... 275
— Charles Henry 456
— *Hon.* Cuthbert 275
— Cyril Henry Leigh ... 240
— Edmund Henry Salt 252
— Edward Tito 284
— Eustace L. Haweis ... 294
— Francis Polglase 410
— Henry Daniel............ 382
— Herbert 421
— Herbert Ellison R. ... 381
— Herbert Lionel 309
— John Edgcumbe 176
— Montague 45, 411
— Montague Gifford... .. 435
— Murray Ray de B. 238, 368
— Richard 505
— Samuel Alexander ... 272
— William Bernard 433
— William Lancelot...... 238
— William Mawer......... 379
— Wm. Reg. Wallwyn... 171
— William Wybergh ... 162
Jameson, Granville 455
— James 377
— James Conway 385
— John Bland.............. 531
— Robert 452
— Robert Feild........... 59, 414
— Sydney Bellingham 65, 318
— William 329
— William Henry ...68, 416
Jamieson, Alister Wm. 45, 411
— Aubrey James 434
— Elliot Michael 254
— William 233
Jardine, James Bruce... 147
Jarrett, Chas. Harry B. 347
— Hy. Sullivan 19, 406
Jarvis, William 178
Jayakar, Atmaram S. G. 529
Jeans, Chas. Gilchrist... 369
Jebb, Sydney Gladwyn 176
Jeffcoat, Fred. H. H. ... 436
— Henry J. Powell 177
Jeffcock, Jas. W. G. P. 148
Jeffreys, Arthur Gordon 308
— Fred. Vaughan 210
— Henry Byron..........53, 167
— Patrick Douglas 26
— William J. Llewelyn 288
Jekyll, Herbert 44, 206
Jelf, Richard Henry..24, 206
— Richard John 214
— Rudolf George 305
Jellett, John Hewett...... 170
Jelley, Reg. Frank 213
Jellicorse, Harold 279
Jencken, Fras. J. 381
Jenkins, Atherton Edw. 357
— Fred Lewis Vernon... 333
— Thomas Morris......44, 411
— Vaughan................43, 277
Jenkinson, George S. C. 289
— Henry Law Acland ... 172
Jenner, Albert Victor ... 356
— *Rev.* Edw. H. F. 396
— Leopold Christian D. 305
— Walter Kentish Wm. 151
Jenney, Arch. Offley ... 270
— George William 530
Jennings, Edgar 456
— Herbert Alex. Kaye... 172
— James Willes........... 385
— Richard 380
— Robert 210
— Robert H. 59, 208
— Robert Melvill......18, 403
— Walton.................... 175
Jennings, Wm. Ernest... 530
Jennings-Bramly, A. ... 161
Jennison, Hy. G. W. ... 185
Jenour, Arthur Stawell 174
Jephson, John Noble ... 431
Jermyn, *Rev.* Edm......... 460
— Turenne 426
Jerome, Henry Jos. W. 66, 209
— John William 381
Jerrard, Aug. G. A....... 139
— F. Barthol. Jos.......... 28
Jervis, Henry Pruce...... 529
— *Hon.* St. Leger Henry 305
— Swynfen John 282
— Walter Neil......... 46, 166
Jervis-White-Jervis, J. H. 169
Jervois, Cha. Edwyn 68, 169
— Henry Napier 50, 167
— John 59, 208
— *Sir* W. F. Drummond 204
Jervoise, J. Purefoy E. 24
Jessel, Herbert M. 159
Jessop, H. Lethbridge 52, 207
Jessop, Guthrie Hylton 47, 366
Joudwine, Hugh S. 172
Jocelyn, Julian R. J. 46, 166a
Johnes, Cyril I. F. O.... 440
Johnson, Allen Victor... 243
— Arthur Cyril B. 428
— Arthur Graham......... 172
— Cecil Willoughby 382
— Chas. B. Bulkeley .. 144
— Charles Edward ...69, 425
— Charles Richard 439
— Clarence A. Keatinge 438
— Cuthbert Fra. 148
— Cyril Maxwell R....... 174
— *Rt. Rev.* E. R............. 460
— *Sir* Edwin Beaumont 179
— Eliot Philips 212
— Francis Shand Byam 239
— Frank Ernest............ 171
— Fred Colpoys Ormsby 400
— Fred. Francis 55, 366
— Frederick Luttmann... 45
— George Vanderheyden 164
— Gilbert Ward........... 435
— Hastings Ross 244
— *Sir* Hy. A. Wm. *Bt.* 58, 295
— Henry Percival......... 385
— Hugh W. Beaumont 245
— John Ernest Blois ... 362
— John Owens 154
— Joseph F. Walter...... 213
— Osmond Moncrieff ... 372
— Richard Francis... 52, 167
— Ronald Marr 177
— Thomas George......... 420
— Thomas Pelham 255
— Thomas Shaw 430
— Victor George Ralph. 246
— William 368
— Wm. Edw. 504
— Wm. Edw. Armstrong 285
Johnston, Alexander ... 368
— Arch. F. Campbell 237, 367
— Bruce Campbell 211
— Charles Arthur......... 506
— David George 42, 347
— Dudley Cater........... 530
— Duncan Alexander 47, 206
— Francis Earle 310
— Frederick Campbell.. 174
— George Napier 175
— Gordon Campbell...... 174
— Harley M'Alpine 427
— Henry Halcro 381
— Herbert William 433
— James Tayler 52, 207
— James Thomason...... 170
— Joseph Henry Bell ... 185
— Percy Herbert 370
— Robert 373
— Seymour Campbell... 269
— Thomas Kelly Evans 170
— Walter 258
— William James 214
— Wm. Thomas 379
Johnston-Stewart, Jas... 337
Johnstone, Aug. A. Jervis 425
— Beresford Assheton... 426
— Charles Melville 141
— Colin D. 275
— Francis Buchanan ... 173
— Fras. Fawkes 52, 255
— Fras. Herbert........... 436
— Henry Arthur 149
— Herbert Cecil........... 259

Index—Active List. 560

Johnstone, Hope 175
— Hugh 452
— James 44, 287
— James Hy. L'Estrange 211
— James Henry Waller 177
— James Robert 67, 400
— Norman Marshall ... 153
— Richard 305
— Robert Fitz Roy M... 421
— Wm. George Currie 43, 410
Jollie, Francis 433
Jolly, Geo. Alfred 369
Joly, Alain C. de L. 212
Jones, *Rev.* Alex. J. 507
— Alfred 309
— Alfred Edwin 67, 416
— A.H.M.Hamilton 267
— Arthur M. Bulkeley ... 162
— Aubrey Arbuthnot ... 427
— Bryan John 346
— David Edw. Osborne 259
— Douglas Forde 26
— Edmund Gunning ... 438
— Edward Whitmore ... 267
— Edward Wm. A. 254
— Francis George....".... 271
— Frank Lewis 419
— Fred. George W. 334
— Fred. Wm. Caton...... 382
— Geo. Augustus 456
— Geo. Goring John S... 421
— Geo. Turner 61, 208
— Harry Balfour 211
— Harry Harvey 436
— Herbert John 431
— Howard Sutton 4, 397
— Inigo Richmund ...25, 233
— Jenkin 425
— Jenkin Stephen......... 301
— John Lloyd Thos. 530
— John Matthew 380
— Juxon Henry 68, 416
— Leslie Cockburn 440
— Lewis 210
— Llewellyn Murray ... 244
— Martin 153
— *Rev.* Maurice 396
— Michael Derwass G... 314
— Morey Quayle 55, 242
— Reginald E. Picton ... 212
— Richard Godfrey 417
— Tertius 174
— Theophilus Percy 385
— Thos. Fred. Newcome 139
— Thomas Henry 117
— Thomas Vincent 244
— Walter Dally 308
— Walter Hover 174
— Walter T. Cresswell 401
— William H. Dawes 41, 410
— William Henry 214
— William Locke... 256, 369
Jones-Vaughan, HughT. 19
Jopp, John......... 18, 406
— Stephen J. M. 45
Jordan, John Gregory... 455
— R. A. A. Y. 297
— Richard Price 272
Joslen, Frank......... 395
Josling, Chas. Langford 387
Josselyn, Jas. Edw. 45, 166
Joubert, Cha. Henry....... 453
Jourdain, Chas. E. A. ... 291
— Hy. 'Fras. Newdigate 334
Joynt, Edward Hearne 378
Judge, Charles Bellew 420
— Spencer Francis 297
— William Graham 296
Julian, Oliver Rich. A. 384
Julius, Stanley de V. A. 279
Jupp, William R. 115
Justice, Chas. Le Gendre 421
— Olive William 311
— William Olive......... 6
Kane, Arthur Hyde 176
— Denis Charles 249
— Francis R. P. 58, 276
— Richard Alexander... 279
Kanga, Jamshedji K. 505
Kappey, Fred. George... 398
— Max Albert Burns ... 433
Kauntze, Bertram C. ... 239
— Cedric R. 437
Kavanagh, Arthur M. ... 421
— Cha.Teler M'Murragh 152
— *Rev.* Robert Edmund 396
Kay, Alf.Goodwyn 380
— William Heape 176

Kaye, Cecil 437
— James Levett 428
— Ralph Arthur 172
— Richard H.Leslie...... 367
— William John Pettitt 432
— William Robert......... 371
Kays, Horace Francis... 317
— Walpole Swinton 304
Keane, Geo. Wilfred 314, 367
— Sir John, *Bart.* 178
Kearney, John 383
Keary, Hy. D'Urban 66, 419
Keato, Charles Robert... 425
Keates, William 250
Keating, Hy. Edw. C. ... 346
Keatinge, *Rev.* C. Walter 396
— Maurice Den 272
Keatly, John 383
Keays, Robert Wm. C... 435
— William 379
Keble, Alf. E. Conquer 386
— John Alfred 379
Keddie, Herbert W. G. 178
Keef, Geo. Alfred ...68, 262
Keelan, Henry Percival 261
Keen, Fred. Stewart ... 352
— Wm. John 441
Keene, Alfred 57, 168
— Charles Edm. Ruck... 297
— Charles William 289
Keighley, C. Marsh...45, 411
Keily, Edw. Wm. 438
— Fred. Peter Charles 238
Keir, John Lindesay 63, 169
Keith, Clive Skene 138, 370
— James 28, 165
Keith-Falconer, V. F. A. 252
Kekewich, Cecil Henry 311
— Robert George... 49, 271
Kelaart,Gerald Talbot 57,168
Keláwálá,Manekshaw J. 505
Kelham. Henry Robert 55, 317
Kell, Vernon G. W. 282
Keller, Rudolph Hy. ... 290
Kellett,Richard Orlando 258
Kellie, Arch. Henry 422
— Edward Chamier...53, 413
— George Jerome 454
— Harry Francis 264
— James 55, 208
— Robt. Howden ... 63, 284
Kelly, Arthur D. D....58, 278
— Arthur James 209
— Charles Henry......58, 362
— Courtenay Russell ... 177
— Edward 288
— Francis Henry 210
— Geo. Hy. Fitzmaurice 439
— Harvey H. H. 41, 409
— *Rev.* Henry 690
— Henry Chas. Thos. 69, 400
— Henry Edw. Theodore 176
— Henry Newton 258
— Henry Holdsworth ... 393
— James 508
— James Graves 41, 409
— Joseph Fras. M. 385
— Michael 382
— *Sir* Richd. D. 278
— Richard Edm. 383
— Richard M. B. F. ...67, 169
— Vincent Jones 329
— Waldron E. Roper 42, 237
— William 381
— William Freeman...... 22
— Kelly-Kenny, Thos. ... 17
Kelsall, Harry Joseph... 174
— Hope Waddell 213
— Thomas Edward 214
Kelsey, Walter Fred. ... 130
Kemball, Alick Gurdon 440
— Arnold Henry G. 424
— Chas. Arnold 425
— George Vero 170
— John Shaw......... 437
Kemble, C. Morris...259, 368
— Edward Arthur 250
— William Edward 178
Kemmis,Wm.H. Olphert 173
Kemp, Geoffrey C. 212
— Walter Henry 395
Kempson, J. Wedgwood 176
Kempster, Frs. Jas....41, 347
Kendall, Chas. Melville 271
— John 432
— John Kaye 175
Kenna, Paul A. 163
Kennard, Arthur M. 174

Kennard,Auberon Claud
— Hegan 357
— Ern. Coleridge Hegan 230
— Henry Gerard Egan 140
— Lionel Edward 157
Kennedy, Alex. Clark 24, 409
— Alex. W. Clark 177
— Alfred Alexander.... 145
— Andrew Campbell ... 177
— Arthur 383
— Arthur H. Clark ...55, 419
— Charles Henry 400
— Chas. Henry Scott ... 28
— Claude 46
— Edw. Charles Wm. M. 423
— Edw. Douglass ... 66, 270
— Edw. S. Curwen 360
— Fra. Malcolm Evory 252
— Herbert Alex. 329
— Herbert J. W. M. 243
— Hugh 428
— James Montagu B. ... 276
— James Robert 439
— John Nassau C. 212
— Macdougall Ralston 214
— *Sir* Michael Kavanagh 219
— Robert Gray 261
— Thos. Francis Arch. 65,325
— Thomas Francis 386
— Walter Craufurd 371
— William Horace 304
— William Magill 439
— Willoughby Pitcairn 55,413
Kenney, Arth.Herbert 63,209
— John Henry 214
Kenney-Herbert, A. H. C. 292
Kennion, Roger Lloyd... 435
Kenny, Edw. Evans 57, 413
— George William 271
— Henry Torrens 425
— Wm. Wallace 379
Kenrick, Geo. Edm. R. ... 236
— Herbert Wm. M. 153
Kensington, Guy Belfield 214
— Wm. *Lord* 132
Kent, Fred. Edmond 67, 109
— Frederic Sidney 254
— Herbert Vaughan 211
— Percival Naylor 138
— Thomas Wm. Shene 292
Kentish, Horace J. J. 57, 283
Kenyon,Edw.Raeulph67,209
— Lionel Richard......... 157
Kenyon-Slaney, Fra. G. 314
— Walter Rupert 50, 356
Keogh, Alfred 379
— Arthur Lorcan 335
— James Blair 238
— John Henry 178
Keown, John Charrier... 430
Koppel, Edw. George... 130
Ker, Malcolm Albert ... 455
Kerin, Michael Wm. 380
Kerr, Charles Robert 41, 348
— Frederick Walter...... 322
— *Lord* Mark 252
— Mark Ancrum 423
— *Lord* Ralph D. 6
— Robert Scott 229
— William 283
— William Frederick ... 26
Kerr-Pearse,Beauchamp
  A. T. 357
Kerrich, George Steuart 420
— John Herbert......... 285
— Leonard W. C. 42
— Walter Edmund 171
Kerrison, Edm. R. A. 59, 168
Kershaw, Frederick 311
Ketchen, Sotheby
  Douglas B. 439
Kettle, James 395
— Louis Cooke 282
Kettlewell, Arch. M. 178
— Edw. Alex. 229
— George 457
Kevill-Davies, Somerset
  E. O'B. 58, 321
Key, Aston M. Cooper... 171
Keyes, Alf. J. H. 178
— Charles Valentine ... 362
— Ch. Wm. Patton...367, 401
Keys, Chris. W. M. 378
Keyser, Fred. Charles ... 18
Koyworth, Robert G. ... 177
— Walter 437
Kharegat, M. P. 505
Kidd, Bertram G. B. ... 362

Kidd, *Rev.* Daniel W. ... 507
Kiddle, Frederick......... 386
— Walter, *MB.* 383
Kidston, Alex. Ferrier ... 22
Kiggell, Lancelot E. 242
Kilcoursie, *Visct.* 229
Kilgour, Frederick... 21, 406
— Henry 48
Kilkelly, Charles R. 382
— Patrick Persy 580
Killery, St. John B. 386
Killick, Thomas Alex.... 395
Kilner, Charles H. 173
Kilroy, Philip Lefeuvre 377
Kinahan, Edward H. ... 163
Kincaid, Chas. Style ... 333
— Wm. Fras. Hy. Style 210
— Willie Alex. Scotland 212
Kincaid-Smith, K. John 177
— Thomas Malcolm H. 131
Kinder, Dennett Thos. 437 249
Kindersley, C. P. Wilson 231
— Maitland FitzRoy...... 438
King, Alex. Bowers 258
— Alex. C. Newton 273
— Alexander James 238
— Algernon D'Aguilar... 172
— Arthur Montague...... 357
— Augustus Carter...68, 147
— Charles Arthur Cecil 259
— Charles Dickson 171
— Charles Edward 17
— Charles Wallis 367
— George 452
— George Courtenay ... 309
— Henry 432
— Henry Somerset 210
— Henry Thomas 420
— James 278
— James Alex. Gordon... 213
— Reginald Garret 253
— Rbt. Ambrose Cecil 51, 167
— Robert George 214
— Stewart William 438
— Walter Gawen 504
— William Albert de C. 214
— William Henry......... 163
King-Church, Fras. W. 275
King-Harman, W. Alex. 329
King-King, James Q. ... 236
Kingscote, Henry B. 41, 165
— Howard 23
— Randolph A. Fitz H. 212
Kingsmill, J. C. de K. B. 174
Kingston, F. Anderson 433
Kinloch, Alex. A. A. ... 16
— David Alex. 68, 229
— Henry Anstruther ... 304
Kinsman, Harold John 348
— *Rev.* Vivian W. 60
Kirby, Arthur Durham 175
— Norborne 212
— Stuart Rodger 141
Kirchhoffer, Robert B. 45, 399
Kirk, *Rev.* C. 532
— Henry Buchanan...... 337
— John Chartres 174
— Maurice Wrottesley 238
— William 137
Kirkby, *Rev.* Marsh 457
Kirke, Hy. Lushington 173
— St. Geo. Mervyn...47, 207
Kirkpatrick, Alex. R. Y. 175
— Edward 410
— George Macaulay...... 211
— Hugh C. 379
— Henry Pownall 156
— Ivone 282
— Richard Trench 346
— Roger 381
— Thomas David ...67, 259
— William 429
— Wm. Johnston ...49, 311
Kirkwood, Andrew T.... 440
— Carleton H. M. 308
— *Rev.* George 396
Hendley Paul 43, 206
— Jas. Nicholson S. 43, 410
— Richard Hammett...... 249
— Thomas Moore 434
Kirtikar, Kanoba R. 529
Kirwan, Albert 379
— Bertram Richard 176
— *Rev.* Mansel Robt. ... 460
Kitcat, Arthur de W. ... 401
Kitchener, Fred. W...51, 253
— Henry F. O. 46
— *Sir* Horatio 21, 298

Name	Page	Name	Page	Name	Page	Name	Page
Kitchin, Rev. A	460	Lambert, Jos. Alex.	52, 137	LaTouche Wm. Puget	7, 405	Ledward, Geo. Herbert	278
— Rev. Barclay	460	— Sydenham J.	43, 206	Latten, Leonard	368	Lee, Alex. Wm. Henry	437
— Rev. W.	460	— Thomas Stanton	274	Lattey, Arthur James	386	— Arth. Hamilton	175
Kitching, Chas. W.R.	55, 399	— Walter	170	Lauder, Wm. Bernard	249	— Arth. V. H. Vaughan	135
Kitson, Chas. Edw.	294	— Walter John	66	Laughlin, Chas. Edw. H.	346	— Edw. H. Hanning	29
— Gerard Charles	61, 304	— William	66, 415	Laurence, Gerald C. R.	213	— Ellis	28
— James Edward	372	Lambkin, Fras. Joseph	381	— Richard Thomas R.	211	— Francis	146
Klugh, Rev. Leonard	460	Lambton, Alex. Fredk.	317	Laurenson, Edw. Louis	335	— Rev. Fred. B. N. N.	396
Knaggs, Henry Thos.	384	— Hon. Charles	69, 240	Laurie, George Brenton	329	— George Arthur	22
— Morton Herbert	310	— Hon. William	231	— John Haliburton	238	— Harry Romer	160
Knapp, K. Kenmure	174	— William Henry	231	Lavie, Leslie J. G.	438	— Henry Louis	293
— Percival Ernest	249	Laming, Henry T.	160	— Tudor Germain	383	— Henry Pincke	4, 205
Knatchbull, Geo. W. C.	429	Lamont, Alexander	322	Law, Alf. Letchworth	310	— Richard Philipps	211
— Reginald Norton	256	— John Charles	456	— Cecil Henry	55, 283	— William Alexander	504
Knatchbull - Hugessen, Everard	292	— John William F.	177	— Charles Richard	368	— Wm. M. Lauriston	242
Knight, Ernest Frederic	244	Lamotte, Frank G. L.	287	— Edwin	47	— William Hanning	17
— Guy Cuningham	291	Lampen, John	422	— James	214	Leech, Ellis J. C.	361
— Harry Briscoe	395	Lamprey, Joseph John	379	— John Prescott	249	Leeds, Lionel N.	433
— Henry John	49, 318	Lancaster, John	504	— Robert T. H.	301, 369	— Thomas Louis	289
— Henry Lewkenor	333	Lance, Frederick	7, 405	— Victor Edward	23, 404	Leefe, Jn. Beckwith	46, 397
— Henry Palmer	55, 208	— Frederick FitzHugh	352	Lawford, E. E. M.	66, 415	Leeke, Ralph	24, 229
— Lionel Chas. Edward	237	Landon, Fred. W. B.	67, 366	— Sidney Turing Barlow	243	Leeper, Robert Waugh	333
— Wyndham Chas.	429	Lane, Alfred Blomefield	266	Lawless, Skerrett E. G.	171	Lees, Chas. H. Brownlow	308
Knocker, Arthur G.	333	— Alfred Luther	51, 167	Lawley, Hon. R. T.	65, 149	— Clarence Edw.	437
— H. Paget	28, 205	— Alfred Vavasour	381	Lawrence, Fred. Eyre	356	— Eustace Graham	293
— Cuthbert George	57, 366	— Arthur Henry	395	— Frederick George	268	— John	294
Knollys, Henry	27, 166	— Cecil Alexander	383	— Freeling Ross	156	Kay	395
— Robt. Walter Edm.	441	— Chris. Wm. Moore	170	— George Henniker	274	— William Edwin	213
Knowles, Chas. B.	7	— Clayton Turner	23, 407	— Henry John	40, 404	Leet, Hugh M.	269
— George	290	— Daniel Thomas	456	— Hon. Herbert Alex.	159	Leete, William John	232
Knox, Alfred Wm. F.	440	— Frank Macdonald	439	— Hugh Duncan	275	Leetham, William	140
— Arthur Rice	173	— Frederick	186	— Richard O. B.	47, 136	Le Feuvre, Geo. Wm. H.	291
— Charles Edmond	24	— Frederick Cecil	175	— Samuel	270	Le Gallais, Philip W. J.	150
— Charles Stuart	267	— Geo. Howard Moore	372	— Walter Ernest	267	Legg, Geo. Edw. W.	282
— Charles William	65, 281	— George James	386	— William	178	— Reginald Francis	346
— Ernest Francis	245	— Henry Arthur	435	— William Alexander	19, 408	Legge, Hon. Heneage	23
— Eustace Chaloner	160	— Henry Frederick	373	— William Lyttleton	268	— Hon. Henry Chas.	50, 231
— George Stuart	214	— Herbert Edw. Bruce	172	— William Wylly	46, 258	— Norton	162
— Harry Hugh Sidney	292	— Horace Powys	432	Lawrence-Archer, Jas. H.	176	— Septimus Fred.	243
— James Stuart	254	— J. Theophilus	179	Lawrenson, Edw. Louis	335	— William Kaye	288
— Maurice	378	— Ronald Bertram	18	— Reginald Robert	361	Leggett, Charles G.	26
— Robert Ferguson	213	— Samuel Willington	170	— Thomas Geo. P.	438	— Edward H. Manisty	213
— Robert John	47, 329	— Thomas Edw. Moore	362	Lawrie, Charles Edward	173	— Frederick O.	369
— Stuart George	438	— William Byam	456	— Edward	453	Legh, Hon. Gilbert	229
— Thomas Edmond	245	— William Horsburgh	259	— Walter Gray	211	— Hubert C.	67, 304
— William George	43, 166	— William Lemon	379	Lawson, Algernon	144	— Piers Richard	422
Knox-Gore, W. A. G. S.	61, 169	— William Moore	171	— Charles B.	385	Le Grand, F. Gaspar	4, 397
Koe, Arch. Stephen	269	Lang, Arthur Geo. Boileau	427	— Charles F.	26	Le Grave, Rev. Wm.	396
— Fred. William B.	401	— Cecil Fred. Grant	282	— Douglas	386	Lehmann, Fred. Hope	153
Koebel, Hy. Arthur	178	— Elliot Brownlow	427	— Edmund James	395	Leicester, Byron	264
Kortright, Mounteney	145	— Eustace Arthur	315	— Francis Bernard	292	Leigh, Bertrand Chas.	288
Kough, Thos. Macgregor	178	— Ewen Montgomery	439	— Francis William	254	— Edward	281
Kroyer, Fred. August O.	420	— Godfrey George	253	— Henry Merrick	51, 209	— Henry Percy P.	57, 414
— Henry John	303	— Rev. Jas. Paisley	507	— Herbert	417	— Captain Richard	210
Krickenbeck, R. E. E.	441	— John Irvine	211	— Oswald Head	439	— Col. Richard	19
Kuper, Chas. Victor B.	58, 162	— Percy Owen	63, 400	— Wm. Arnold Webster	233	— Hon. Rupert	67, 157, 374
Kyle, Frederick	386	— Rich. T. Montgomery	24, 403	Layard, Arthur A. M.	209	Leishman, Wm. Boog	384
Kysh, Douglas John	65, 400	— Wynyard Feeling	253	— William Twistleton	292	Leith, Robt. Thos. D.	362
Lubalmondiere, Julian A.	170	Langdale, Philip	150	Laye, Joseph Henry	28	Leman, Reg. Curtis	309
Labertouche, Guy N. L.	250	Langdon, Allan H.	41, 366	Layton, Edward	282	Le Marchant, Basil St. J.	277
Lachlan, Ernest M.	173	— Francis John	244	— Norman Atkinson	272	— Edw. Henry	61, 281
Lackey, Daniel	380	— John Fred. P.	279	Lea, Harold Futvoye	259	— Edward Thomas	265
Lacey, Thomas	185	— Paul Perram	175	— Samuel Job	49, 366	— H. St. J. V. Le M. T.	24, 165
Laffan, George	379	Langford, Geo. Edward	372	Leach, Edmund	7	— Louis St. Gratien	274
— Henry David	209	— Rev. Robt. John	460	— E. Pemberton	16, 206	— Osmond Cecil	279
— Joseph de Courcy	211	— William John	69, 400	— Harold Pemberton	29, 208	Le Mesurier, Eugene	432
— Richard Chas. Kirby	381	Langhorne, Harold Ste.	174	— Henry Edmund B.	240	— Fred. Augustus	18, 204
Latone, Edgar Mortimore	146	Langlands, P.	360	— John	49, 166	— Herbert Grenville	284
— Herbert Arthur	138	Langley, John Penrice	170	— Reginald P.	59, 168	Lemon, George	368
— Wm. Boutcher	240	— Lionel	52, 208	Leader, Henry P.	250	LeMottée, Edw. D'Albret	272
Laing, David	151	— William Savage	41, 165	— Lionel Frederick	244	— Henry B.	43, 254
— Fred. Charles	434	Langridge, Geo. Thos.	378	— Nicholas	379	— George Herbert	379
— James	158	Langston, Thos. A. O.	457	— William Francis	301	— Reginald Edw. Arthur	176
— James Anderson	504	Langton, Herb. Fras.	136	Leahy, Albert W. D.	455	Lempriere, Audley Reid	261
Lainson, Alex. John	305	— Joseph	278	— Charles Albert	210	— Geo. Beresford	301
Laird, Gordon	175	— Theobald Michael	163	— Henry Gordon	175	— Henry Anderson	142
— Robert Montgomery	185	Langtry, Henry	17	— Philip Fraser A.	346	Lenehan, Thos. Joseph	385
Lake, Edward	42, 160	— Henry V. Montague	439	Leake, Geo. D. Nugent	275	Lennock, Charles Fred.	250
— Hubert Atwell	174	Langworthy, George	142	— William Martin	268	Lennox, Amyot M. Aug.	174
— Noel Montagu	53, 208	Lapham, Robert John	368	— Lean, Alan Ivan	265	— Claud H. Maitland	240
— Percy Henry N.	58, 274	Large, Brisbane W. S.	380	— Kenneth Edward	262	— Sir Wilb. Oates	4, 204
Lamb, Charles A.	66, 356	Larking, Reginald N. W.	233	— Wm. Walter	63, 414	Leonard, Alfred W.	204
— Edward John	264	Larnder, Eugene W.	395	Leapingwell, Art. Hy.	504	— Hugh Gastrell	291
— Captain George	346	Larpent, Sir Geo. Albert de Hochepied, Bt.	42, 334	Learmont, John	178	Le Pelley, Edw. Carey	76
— Surg. Lieut. George	457	Lascelles, Alfred	177	Learoyd, Arthur G.	245	Le Quesne, Aug. S.	58, 397
— George Rothney	173	— Arthur Edward	245	— Charles Douglas	210	— Ferdinand Simeon	384
— Hy. Campbell	52, 413	— Ernest	357	Leatham, George H.	49, 275	Lermit, Lawrence H.	460
— Henry Hodge	140	— George Reginald	243	— Thomas William O.	58, 212	Leslie, Albert Edmond	418
— John	69, 416	— Walter Charles	315	Leather, Gerard F. T.	240	— Sir Charles H. Bt.	45, 411
— Stephen Eaton	68, 283	— Walter Edward	356	Le Bailly, Alex. C.	427	— Clement Stanley D.	435
— Thomas	284	— William Frank	233	Leckie, Fred. W. Vans	29, 410	— Francis Seymour	57, 208
Lambarde, Fras. F.	175	Lash, Aug. Oliver	309	Lecky, Frederick B.	170	— George	164
Lambart, Hon. Arthur	170	— Henry Andrew	437	— John Gage	256	— George Arthur Jas.	212
— Edgar Alan	61, 169	Last, Arthur John	185	— Robert St. Clair	179	— George Francis	69, 356
Lambert, Edward Parry	173	Lathbury, Henry O.	212	Lodsham, James	370	— John Henry	170
— James Drummond	395	LaTouche, C. D'Urban	5, 405	— William	368	— John T. Waddell	455
— John Hamilton	401					— Philip Norman	440

Index—Active List. 562

Leslie, Richd. F. Wm. F. 283	Lindsay, Hon. Robert Hamilton... 144	Loder, Eustace ... 154	Lowndes, Alan H. W. ... 356
— Thomas Dowglasse... 428	— Walter F. L........ 59, 168	— Loder-Symonds, John F. 282	— John Gordon 291
— William Clarence C.... 427	— Lindsell, Philip Barber.. 418	— Lodge, Fras. Cecil 245	— John Henry 130
Lesslie, Wm. Breck 213	— Robert Fred. 58, 272	— Lodwick, Robt. W. P.59, 373	— Maurice 318
Lester, Cecil Morris 253	Lines, Edward 386	— Loftus, Dudley Ferrars 229	Lowry, Fred.J.Sharples 420
— Claude Dallas 434	— Rossiter 285	— Fras. Cochrane 271	— Henry Dacre......... 285
L'Estrange, E. Carleton 284	Linton, Charles 45, 284	— St. John D. Townshend 305	— Henry Ward 426
Lethbridge, Alf. S. 452	— John 402	Logan, Balfour 249	— Herbert Leslie 176
— Ambrose Yarburgh... 230	Lipsett, Louis Jas......... 258	— David Finlay H. 173	— James 373
— Ernest Astley E....... 287	Liptrott, John 373	— Fras. Carleton Logan 291	— James Herbert 433
— Francis Washington 434	Lister, George Coryton 304	— Henry Spencer 256	— Robert William...... 293
— John Guy Baron 145	— Wastel Jameson...57, 208	— Lionel Stuart......... 352	— Thomas Pepper E. 67, 360
— Rev. J. King 396	Liston, Fred. Alex. 360	— Maxwell Hannay 253	— William Henry 419
— Robert T.Moriand274, 374	Litchford, Rowland 360	Logan-Home, G. J. N.... 255	Lowth, Frank Robert 59, 246
— Sydney............... 175	Lithgow, H.Lancaster.. 175	— Henry Waldeve......... 400	Lowther, Henry......... 432
— Wm. Agar Lander ... 239	Litster, Thomas......... 317	Login, Wm. Erskine G. 234	— Henry Cecil 233
— Wroth Periam C. 229	Little, Arthur Greenway 401	Lomax, David Alex. N... 285	Luard, Arthur J. H. 245
Leumann, Bernard H.F. 530	— Charles 504	— Samuel Holt.......50, 270	— Charles Camac....... 314
Leveson, Chas. Hen. ... 160	— Charles Blakeaway... 252	Lombe,Alex.Fras.Evans 317	— Charles Eckford 253
Leverson, George F...... 209	— Rev. Harwood 396	— Charles S. B. Evans... 346	— Edward Bourryau ... 297
— Henry Adolphe 271	— Henry Alex. 6, 406	— Ralph H. F...... 59, 245	— Frank William 400
— Julian Wm. 57, 208	— John 292	London, James 223	— Frederick Bramston 360
Levett, Berkeley J. T. ... 233	— John Herbert......... 254	Long, Arthur 346, 367	— George Dalbiac 270
Levinge, Henry George 245	— Malcolm Orme......68, 151	— Charles James.....50, 167	— Henry Arthur......... 292
Levita, Cecil Bingham... 174	— Stephen 454	— Clement Willmore ... 360	— Hugh Bixby 456
— Harry Plumridge... 136	— William Campbell ... 401	— Rev. Henry J. 460	— Richard Chamberlin 287
Lewarne, Nicholas Albert 343	— W. Hunter Buller 46, 274	— John Wm. Francis ... 382	— Trant 400
Lewer, Robert 737	— Wm. Herherford...... 423	— Michael John 185	— William Du Cane ... 210
Lewes, Alban Dymoke 262	Littledale, Herbt. C.T. 49, 139	— Samuel Charles 357	Lubbock, Guy............ 213
— Charles George...... 288	— Ralph P............69, 299	— Sidney Selden 293	Lucas, Frederic George 433
— George Alban 41	Liveing, Chas. Hawker 177	— Wilfred James 305	— Harold Maude Alfred 45
— Henry Colebrooke 17, 164	Livesay, William 2	— William Edward 146	— Hugh C. Edw. 53, 413
— John 170	Livingston, Percy J. C. 286	— Wm. Hoare B.......... 294	— Thos. Lucas W. 285
— Price Kinnear 176	Livingston, H.A.Anson 211	Longbourne, Frank 44, 242	— Thos. Rashleigh ... 380
Lewin, Henry F. E....... 178	Livingstone-Learmouth,	Longden, Arth.Berridge 436	Luck, Arthur P. 26
— Robert Nicholas 276	Lennox C............... 176	— Arthur Edmund 367	— Churchill Arthur ... 432
— Wilfred Halo 424	Llewellyn, Evan Henry 271	— Robert James 311	— George 6
Lewis, Rev. Alex. G....... 532	Lloyd, Alfred Robert 68, 255	Longe, Francis B.......... 209	Luckhardt, Arthur H. P. 252
— Arthur Thomas...... 214	— Arthur Athelwold ... 292	— Robert Douglas69,301, 373	— Hubert Cecil 362
— Bridges George 274	— Arthur H. Orlando ... 229	Longfield, Alf. Purcell... 171	Luckman, Rev. W. A. G. 460
— Cecil Hallowes ... 283, 368	— Arthur Malcolm 421	— James Mountifort...... 244	Lucy, Fred. Henry 292
— Charles Algernon ... 310	— Cecil Henry 284	— Mountifort John C.... 134	Luddington, Wm.Jas.C. 274
— Charles Edward 284	— Charles Edward 426	— Richard William 138	Ludlow, Edmund R. O. 367
— Charles Henry 431	— Charles Trevor......... 302	— William Elrington ... 214	— Edmund S. 23, 408
— David Francis ...57, 264	— Francis 63, 229	Longford, Thos. Earl of 134	Lugard, Rt. Hon. Sir E. 275
— David Silvanus 421	— Francis Thomas ...22, 165	Longhurst, Arthur L.... 278	— Edward James 434
— Ernest Hastings 163	— Frederic Charles 246	— Bell Willmott 385	— Edward John ...19, 238
— Gerald 176	— Frederick Lindsay ... 217	— Edward Becher......... 296	— Frederick J. Dealtry 245
— Rev. George Herbert 532	— George Evan 49, 282	— Seaward 395	— Henry Travers... 44, 1664
— George White......... 273	— Geo. Wm. D. Bowen 265	Longley, Arthur 371	Luke, Edward Vyvyan... 400
— James Frederick 45, 206	— Henry T. Rickard ... 401	— John Raynsford 275	— Thomas Mawe 177
— John Geo. Stephen ... 380	— Herbert Rhys......... 252	Longmore, John C. G. 274, 368	Lukin, Robert C. W. ... 439
— Percy John Tonson 63, 366	— Hesperus B. Watkiss 270	Longridge, J. Atkinson 236	Lukis, Chas. Pardey...... 454
— Richard Crump 385	— Horace Giesler......... 177	— Theodore 255	Lumb, Anthony 66, 252
— Richard Hull 213	— John D. A. T. 267	Longueville, Reginald... 231	Lumley, Francis D. 66, 301
— Thos. E. Watkins...... 395	— John Hardress 139	Lousdale, Philip 274	— Hon. Osbert V. G. A. 153
— Vernon 262	— John Henry 238	— Malcolm P. E. 348	Lumsdaine, F.M.Sandys 317
Lewtas, John 454	— John Herbert......... 439	Lord, Norman 305	Lumsden, Fred. Wm. ... 398
Ley, Cuthbert Hillyar ... 214	— Kenrick Horace 261	— Walter Harold	— George M. 318
— Walter Grenville 310	— Maurice Brickdale ... 173	Loring, Charles Buxton 440	— Henry Richmond W. 48
Leyland, H. S. Naylor... 134	— Owen Edward P...... 379	— Walter Latham......... 242	— J. S. Shepherd......... 456
Liardet, Aug. Bury...42, 401	— Robert Oliver ...52, 207	— William 177	— Philip James 456
— Walter S. D. 52, 256	— Samuel Eyre Massy... 250	Loscombe, A. Russell 67, 360	— Sir P. S. 4, 405
Liddell, Arthur Robert 139	— Thomas Henry Eyre 231	Loudon, Fras. Arthur ... 427	Lund, Fred. Thwaites... 151
— John Stewart 212	— Thomas Owen 286	— John Archer 429	Lush, Robert Free......... 253
— Robert Spencer 17	— Thomas Prince 372	— Robert Dunn......57, 168	Lushington, A. P. D. 63, 138
— William Andrew 211	— Walter Reginald 291	Lougheed, S. F............ 381	— Edw. Chas. M. 417
Liebert, Bernhard Robt. 149	— Wilford Neville ...65, 169	Loughlin, John 395	— Lionel Edmund 283
Liebrecht, John Henry 315	Lousada, F. Percy ...57, 311	— Percy Wildman 269
Ligertwood, T.............. 128	— Wm. Edmund Eyre... 435	Lovat, S. J. Lord 133	— Stephen 173
Light, Reginald Hough 422	— Wm.Reade De-la-Pere 250	Love, Henry Davison 57, 208	— William Nelson 258
— William Alfrey........ 441	Lloyd-Jones, Fred. L. ... 426	— Robert Lindsay......... 255	Luther, Anthony J. 384
Lightfoot, J. Stanley ... 255	Lloyd-Thomas, Thos. C. 178	Loveband, Arthur 348	Lutyens, JohnGallwey67,209
— Thomas Williams...... 437	Loader, Alfred Edgar... 368	— Francis Richard 399	Luxmooro, C. T. P....21, 406
Lillie, Fred. Sutherland 258	Loch, Edw. Campbell... 441	Lovell, Arthur Neville... 439	— Charles de Joncourt 258
Lillington, Edw. G. 24, 408	— Edward Douglas 230	— John 45	— Noël 249
— William Edw. Gordon 437	— George............... 291	— Peter A. D. A. 173	Lyall, Chas. George...... 246
Lillingston - Johnson,	— Granville Geo. 234	Lovett, Alfred Crowdy... 272	— Chas. Noel 173
William George ... 329	— Granville Henry 421	— Henry Wilson 252	Lyde, Malcolm Thos. 59, 415
Lilly, Alfred Thos. Irvine 382	— Harry Frere 424	— Richard G. Beresford 265	Lydiard, A.C.Gordon 44, 411
— George William......... 431	— Stewart Gordon 214	Low, Alexander 146	Lyddon, William Geo.... 176
Limerick, Earl of........ 1	— Lt. Col. William ...40, 404	— Chas. Fred. Gemley... 255	Lye, H. Shuldham ...55, 258
Limond, Alex. 436	— Lt. Col. William......41, 411	— Francis Simon 134	— Robert Cobb 431
— Rous Milner 269	Lock, Fred. Heathfield 254	— Harry Lawrence 329	Rev. Sidney Leigh ... 532
Limont, John C. 456	— Fred. Robert Edw. ... 434	Rev. James 507	Lygon, Hon. Edw. H. ... 230
Lincoln, Sydney W....... 427	— John Lock 265	— Peter 270, 379	Lyle, Acheson F. A.....63, 297
Lindesay, Alex. L......... 428	Locke, Brian J. M. 177	— Robert Balmain 431	— Allan Andrew 379
— Edward 291	Lockett, Wm. Jeffery ... 156	— Sir R.Cunliffe......7, 403	— George Samuel B. ... 373
— George William Guy 255	Lockhart, Harry 386	Lowdell, Chas. G. W. ... 530	— Henry Duntze......... 174
Lindley, John Edward... 143	— Robt. D. Eliott 27, 165	Lowe, Sir Drury C. Drury 5, 159	— Hugh Thomas 265
— Waldemar D........63, 208	— Robt. Norman 177	— Francis Manley	Lynch, A. H. Comick ... 22
Lindner, Albert John ... 310	— Sir Simon M., Bt...44, 133	— Noel Herbert Streds 294	— Henry Blosse......57, 283
Lindop, Alf. Hen. 373	— William Eliott... 21, 180	— Percival Edw. Hurst 253	— Hyacinth 293
Lindsay, Alex. Bertram 440	— Sir Wm. S. Alex. ...5, 403	— Wm. Henry Muir 61, 142	— James Baverley ...46, 412
— Alexander John ...67, 186	Lockyer, Edm. S. Braitu-	Lowis, Harry Elliot 432	— Michael 281
— Chas. Ludovic 229	waite..........28, 165	— Walter Nevill....44, 166a	— Nicholas Marcus ... 284
— Henry Arthur Peyton 435	Locock, Herbert 17, 204	— Panton Shakespear... 176	Lynch-Staunton, Hy. G. 303
— Michael Wm. Howard 318		— Robert Montrésor ... 434	Lyne, Charles V. N..... 436

Index—Active List.

Name	Page
Lyons, Samuel Parr	17, 164
— Wynne Parr	305
Lynn, Sydney H.	48, 366
Lyon, Arthur	278
— Charles	173
— Edward	165
— Francis	175
— John Wilmot Harley	438
— Nathaniel John	229
Lyon-Campbell, Arthur Robert S.	278
— C. H. D.	264
Lyons, Frederick	378
— Henry George	211
— Robert W. S.	530
— Thomas Casey	4
— William	368
Lyons-Montgomery, Hugh Fred.	58, 417
Lysaght, Arthur N.	258
— James Douglas	372
Lysley, Gerald L.	357
Lysons, Sir Daniel	289
— Henry	270
Lyster, Arthur W.	418
— Henry John	53, 167
— William Henry	45, 412
Lyttelton, Hon. N. G.	19
Lywood, Edwin Gifford	401
M'Alester, Wm. Hy. S.	269
M'Andrew, G. Bunbury	246
M'Arthur, A. Donald	42, 206
— Charles	397
— Charles J. E. A.	209
M'Barnet, Alex. Edw.	437
M'Cafferty, Charles	178
M'Callum, Geo. Kelly	130
— Henry Edw	55, 208
— William	386
M'Calman, Hugh	529
M'Calmont, Hugh	16
M'Candlish, Patrick B.	337
M'Canlis, William	370
M'Carthy, Edward	398
— George Alex.	421
M'Cartie, Chas. J.	453
M'Caskill, John C. H.	258
M'Causland, Charles Oliver	348
— Edwin Loftus	66, 400
— John Kennedy	373
M'Cheane, M. W. H.	177
M'Clellan, Herbert T.	139
M'Clelland, Thomas	335
M'Cleverty, James	24
— William Anson	292
M'Clintock, Augustus	318
— Robert Lyle	214
— Wm. G. Waugh	44, 259
— William	27, 165
— William Kerr	293
M'Cloghry, James	529
M'Clorg, Alexander	504
M'Comb, Robt. Brophy	44, 366
M'Combie, Alexander William	178
M'Conaghey, Allen	431
— Frank	258
— Harry	436
— John	453
M'Conaghy, Wm.	529
M'Connel, Fred. B.	321
M'Connell, J. F. P.	453
M'Cormack, Robt. Jas.	382
M'Cormick, Andrew L.C.	213
— Wm. I. S.	368
M'Corquodale, Robt. H.	138
M'Cracken, Frederick Wm. Nicholas	50, 293
M'Crea, Alfred Coryton	435
— Richard Francis	69, 169
M'Creery, Benj. T.	380
— Nathaniel	378
M'Cullock, Robert H. F.	175
— Thomas	384
M'Dermott, Alexander	264
— Henry	275
— Thomas	385
M'Donald, Jn. Haldane	530
M'Donnell, Jas. O'Malley	453
— John	52, 167
M'Douall, Robert	237
M'Dougal, J. Brown	26
M'Dougall, Wm. A.	395
M'Dowell, Frederick	385
M'Elhinny, Wm. John	212
M'Fall, Albert Wm. C.	295
M'Farlane, Norman	279
M'Gann, Terence Joseph	504
— James	379
M'Gildowny, Wm.	176
M'Gill, Archibald	185
— Harry Robertson	292
— Harry S.	381
M'Governe, Robt. Wm.	115
M'Grigor, Chas. R. R.	52, 304
— Wm. Colquhoun Grant	233
M'Hardy, A. Anderson	175
M'Harg, Alfred A.	214
M'Ilroy, Henry	115
M'Innes, Duncan S.	214
M'Intyre, David	386
— Hugh David	423
M'Kay, Donald	174
— Henry Kellock	453
— Thompson	428
M'Kean, Alex. C.	29, 148
M'Kee, Gerard M. E.	505
M'Kenna, John	178
M'Kerrell, Aug. de Ségur	325
— Reginald L.	337
M'Kinnon, Lachlan	290
M'Kinstry, Alex. C. F.	242
— Arthur W.	57, 256
M'Lachlan, Albert C.	160
— Archibald	234
— Donald Maxwell	238
— James Douglas	325
M'Laren, George G.	454
— Wm. Henry	50, 143
M'Laughlin, Albert A.	347
— George Hall	170
— Hubert James	63, 147
— David John	504
— John	381
M'Lean, Alex. Colin	286
— Colin	286
— John Alexander	147
M'Lennan, John	178
M'Leod, Donald J.S.	27, 404
— Harry	5, 180
— Reginald G. M.	170
— Torquil John	440
— Walter T.	40, 366
— William Kelty	172
M'Loughlin, Geo. S.	384
M'Mahon, Arthur H.	428
— Bernard Wm. L.	314
— Francis Yorke	143
— Sir Horace Westropp	265
— Kellermann Eyre	297
— Norman Reginald	243
M'Meekan, Fras. H.F.R.	173
M'Micking, Harry	234
M'Millan, John Duncan	457
M'Munn, Jas. Robert	386
M'Murdo, Arthur M.	311
M'Nair, Alfred Lionel	40, 409
— Edward John	403
— Henry Arch.	7, 403
M'Nalty, Chas. Edwd. I.	138
M'Namara, J.	377
— William H.	378
M'Naught, Jas. Gibson	385
M'Neale, Jas. Agnew	40, 404
M'Neile, Donald Hugh	176
— John	231
— Henry Donald	143
M'Neill, Capt. Malcolm	139
— Lieut. Malcolm	337
M'Quaid, Peter John	378
M'Queen, Sir J. Withers G.	406
M'Rae, Henry Napier	52, 414
M'Swiney, Edw. F. H.	421
— William Daniel	142
M'Swiny, Myles O'C.	401
M'Taggart, M. F.	147
— William A. T.	440
M'Vean, Donald A. D.	309
M'Vittie, Surg. Col. Chas. Edwin	504
— 2nd Lt. Chas. Edwin	255, 368
— Robert Henry	177
M'Watters, William	377
— Whinnie, Wm. John	320
Maberly, Chas. Evan	58, 168
— Laurence Evan	317
MacAdam, Philip Bower	274
— Macan Evan	211
Macafee, Ar. Percival	302
Macalpine-Leny, R. Leny	158
Macan, Thomas Townly	270
MacAndrew, Henry J.M.	434
Macartney, Henry F. T.	422
Macaulay, Denzil I. M.	362
Macaulay, Kenneth Z. P.	295
Macauley, George Bohun	213
Macausland, R. C. S.	62, 415
Macbay, William G.W.	45, 411
Mac Bean, Forbes	66, 321
— John Albert E.	348
— Wm. Alleyne	172
— William Wilson	325
MacCall, Henry B.	42, 304
MacCartie, Fred. F.	529
MacCarthy Felix D. F.	209
— Ibar Ausbert Orva	385
— Morgan John	174
— Richard Hawes	50, 238
— Rev. Welbore	460
Macdonald, Alastair M'I.	346
— Arthur Gabell	293
— Charles C.	368, 401
— Chas. Edward Wylde	67, 416
— Charles Joseph	383
— Clarence Herbert	424
— Clarence Reginald	346
— Sir Claude M.	49, 317
— Denis Peter	453
— Fred. Weston Peile	426
— George	48, 206
— George Godfrey	229
— Harry Colquhoun F.	318
— Hector Archibald	58, 243
— Henry Craigie	337
— Hugh	271
— Rev. Jas. Middleton	460
— James R. Leslie	69, 210
— Kenneth	368, 401
— Neville D.	308
— Norman Alexander	437
— Peter Chas. Edward	360
— Ranald Hume	213
— Reginald James	175
— Reginald Percy	61, 281
— Stuart	384
— Thomas Rankin	454
Macdonell, Geo. Bean	21, 180
MacDonnell, Alfred Creagh	67, 209
— Richard Graves	293
Macdonogh, G. Mark W.	211
MacDougall, Donald	59, 142
— James Taylor	177
— James William	22, 407
MacEwan, Hugh F.	301
MacEwen, Douglas L.	325
— Maurice Lilburn	158
MacFarlan, Daniel M.	178
— Frederick Alexander	325
— William	286
Macfarlane, Duncan A.	269
Macfie, William Colvin	214
MacGeorge, Henry King	433
— John Buxton	213
— Wm. Henry	42, 141
Macgowan, Geo. Lionel	176
— James Murray	174
— Robert Stuart	173
MacGregor, Arthur C. H.	262
— Chas. Reginald	29, 412
— John	529
— John Nugent Murray	348
— Malcolm John R.	6
— Philip Leighton	43, 166
— Robert Lipton	234
Machell, Percy W.	28
Macintire, Arch. Hon.	44, 411
Macintyre, Donald C. F.	423
Mac Ivor, Ivar	63, 415
Mack, John Clarkson	262
Mackay, Henny Forbes	398
— Rev. James	460
— Rev. J. H.	532
Mackean, Kenneth	58, 208
Mackenzie, Alex. Francis	330
— Alex. William	454
— Allan	310
— Arthur M. Nutt	176
— Charles	439
— Colin	61, 318
— Colin John	61, 318
— Cortlandt Gordon	173
— Edward Leslie	279
— Frederic Hugh	297
— Frederick William	148
— George Birnie	207
— George Douglas	321
— George F. C.	59, 250
— Gerald Mackay	117
— James Alex. F.H.S.	29, 151
— John Edmund	142
— Kenneth J. Loch	22, 407
— Kenneth L. Warner	362
Mackenzie, Kenneth R.	58, 318
— Ronald Joseph H. L.	210
— Thomas Arthur	325
— Thos. Harding	48, 412
— William Jacob	59, 208
Mackenzie-Pendrill, Alan	310
Mackeson, Wm. James	65, 140
Mackesy, John Pierse	214
— William Henry	6, 406
Mackie, William	375
MacKinnon, G. H.	270
Mackinnon, Henry Wm. Alexander	377
— William Henry	23
— Sir William Alex.	377
Mackintosh, George	318
— John Burn	175
— William Charles H.	419
Mackworth, Sir A. W. Br.	19, 205
— Digby	236
Maclachlan, David M'K.	335
— Donald	163
— Ronald Campbell	357
— Thos. Robertson	438
Maclagan, Robert S.	20
Maclaren, J. Farquharson	455
MacLaren, Kenneth	155
— Thomas George	269
MacLaughlin, William	52, 297
Maclean, Alex. Harvey	337
— Alex. Wm. Day	65, 334
— Allan	23
— Chas. Smith	6, 405
— Charles Wilberforce	361
— Fitzroy Beresford	380
— Hector Lachlan S.	438
— Henry Donald Neil	269
— Maclear, Harry	274
MacLeod, Ewan Cameron	457
— John Norman	457
— Kenneth Anderson	277
— Robert L. Ross	65, 382
— Roderick Wm.	63, 415
Maclurcan, John L. R.	69, 400
Maclure, John Edw. S.	309, 374
MacMahon, Geo. F. W.	59, 445
— John Joseph	191
— Percy Alexander	52, 167
MacMillan, John St. C.	175
Macmullen, Fred. C. K.	435
— Francis Richard	308
— George Reade	41
— William Henry F.	59, 414
MacMunn, George F.	175
Macnab, Allan James	456
— Colin Lawrance	278
— Gordon Robert	321
Macnabb, Donald J. C.	431
Macnaghten, Edm. F.	158
— Ernest Brandon	177
— Francis Chester	258
Macnamara, John W. U.	454
— Robert Joseph	455
— Wilfred C. F. R.	434
— William John	380
Macneal, Hector	321
MacNeece, James G.	379
— Thos. Fred.	380
Macneill, J. G. R. D.	24, 494
Maconachie, Geo. A.	529
— James	529
Maconchy, E. W. S. K.	427
— Fred. Campbell	254
Macpherson, A. Kennedy	43, 410
— Archibald Duncan	21
— Duncan Alex. A.	53, 413
— Rev. Ewen Geo. F.	399
— George Denis	347
— Colonel Jas. Duncan	21, 407
— 2nd Lt. Jas. Duncan	288
— John Lawrence	43, 206
— Neil	438
— Roderick George	437
— Thos. R. Matheson	53, 413
— William Grant	381
Macquoid, C. E. F. K.	435
Macrae, Colin William	286
— John Lewis	506
— Roderick	453
Macready, Cecil F. N.	321
Macrobin, A. A.	371
Macrory, R. M.	128
MacRury, C. William	529
Mactaggart, Charles	455
MacTier, Henry M.	438

Index—Active List. 564

MacTier, H. Cochrane... 281
— Stewart James 283
MacWalter, Robert 155
Macwatt, Robert C. ... 456
Madden, George C.... 47, 360
— Gerald Hugh Chas.... 145
— Travers Edward 440
Maddox, Ralph H. 456
Madocks, Henry John... 265
— Wm. Robarts Napier 176
Maffett, Henry Telford 346
— Reginald E. 277
Magan, Arthur T. 361
Magee, Arthur Fred. ... 346
— Aug. Helier 269, 374
— Robert Henry Boyd.. 347
Magill, James 379
Magniac, Charles Lane 214
Magrath, B. Hy. Butler 441
— Charles Fred. 68, 169
— Chas. Wm. S. 381
— Henry Aug. F. 433
— Henry Marsh S. 21, 407
Maguire, C. J. Kinahan 279
— Constantine 17
Mahaffy, Arthur Wm.... 347
Maher, James 387
Mahon, Bryan Thomas 150
— Edward Willoughby 214
— Reginald Henry 170
Mahony, Frederick H... 114
Maidman, Geo. Ed. John 421
Maidment, Fred. George 506
Main, James 368
— Thomas Ryder......52, 207
Mainprise, Bertie W. ... 214
Mainwaring, Arthur Edw 348
— Charles Vaughan 429
— Edward Phillipson 24, 404
— Fra. G. Lawrence 59, 414
— Henry Bolton 246
— Henry Germain ...50, 267
— Rowland B. 50, 265
Mair, Edward 453
— George Tagore 178
— Robert John Byford 212
— Wm. Crosbie S. 23
Mairis, Geoffrey 4, 397
— Geoffrey B. De M. 237
Maisey, Fred. Charles 58, 414
Maitland, *Hon.* A. H. ... 325
— Chas. Bradley 530
— D. Makgill Crichton 7
— Henry Rothes Stewart 259
— Jas. Makgill H. ...16, 204
— John 504
— John Paterson S. 273
— Pelham James...... 27, 411
— Stuart Cairns 322
Majendie, Hy. Grylls ... 357
Major, *Hon.* A. H. Henniker 68, 231
— Francis Forbes 436
— Francis Ward........23, 407
— Frederic 115
— Napoleon Bisdee 378
Malcolm, Andrew R. ... 185
— *Sir* George 513
— Henry Huntley L..... 325
— Neill 337
— Pulteney 424
— William Leith 434
Malcolmson, John Grant 130
— Edward 236
Malden, *Rev.* C. H. 507
— Robert Vaughan...19, 406
Malet, John Warre ...61, 240
Malim, *Rev.* Alfred 396
Maling, Arthur Irwin ... 158
Malins, David P. 360
Mallaby, Digby Lighton 212
Malleson, Wilfrid 174
Mallins, Clement 505
— John Robert 382
— William 41, 165
Mallock, A. M. Raymond 176
— Thomas Raymond ... 243
Mally, Rob. Nelson 377
Malone, Cecil R. R. 273
Maltby, Fra. Crichton 45, 411
— Francis Grant ... 46, 411
Manché, Lorenzo 186
Mander, D'Arcy W....... 314
— Frederick Day ...24, 404a
— John Harold 276
Manders, Neville 382
Manera, Joseph S. G. ... 418
Mangan, Fred. M. 385
Mangles, Arthur Edw. R. 283
— Roland Henry 236
— Walter James 238
Manifold, Courtney C.... 456
— John Forster.........69, 169
— Michael G. Egerton... 213
Manley, Edgar Norman 214
— Francis Capel 26
— Geo. Errington Drummond 401
— Reginald Harwood... 177
— William Edward 177
— William Geo. Henry 176
Mann, Arthur Fred. 347
— Gother Fyers.........52, 207
— Henry Thos. Wm....... 395
— Horace 294
Manners, Chas. G. E. J. 229
— Fitzalan Geo. John ... 233
— *Lord* Robert Wm. O... 305
Manning, Wm. Henry... 434
Mansel, Alfred 53, 167
— Charles Grenville 47, 412
— Ernest Digby 69, 317
— George Clavell 314
— Hugh Arthur 283
— William Grenville 59, 414
Mansel-Jones, Conwyn 253
Mansell, John Herbert... 173
Manser, Robert 529
— William Edward 213
Mansfield, Alfred Edw. 294
— Gerald Stewart......... 385
— *Hon.* Hy. Wm. 143
— Herbert 52, 418
Manson, Eric E. M. D.... 284
Mantell, Alfred M. 209
— Patrick Riners 265
Manton, Herbert Roberts 162
Mapleton, Edw. A. 379
— Reginald Wm. 378
Mappin, Geo. Fred. 139
Marchant, Alfred E. 400
— John 401
Mardall, Chas. Ernest... 423
— William Stratford...... 425
Marden, Arthur Wm. ... 309
— Thomas Owen 264
Marder, Edw. Swan ... 384
Nicholas 385
Marescaux, Oscar H. E. 297
Marett, James Rich...21, 407
Margesson, Edward C.... 267
— Evelyn Wm. 245
Marindin, Arthur Henry 286
Mark-Wardlaw, Alfred Penrose 279
— Edgar Penrose 276
— Penrose 252
Marker, R. John 231
— Thomas John............ 238
Markey, Edward C. 377
Markham, Charles John 304
— Edwin 5, 164
— Francis Dobbs 297
— Ronald Anthony 231
Marks, Geo. Fred. H. 384
— Robert John 455
Markwick, Ernest E. ... 369
Marley, Wm. Peverell... 140
Marling, Percival Scrope 160
Marlow, Benjamin Wm. 431
Marquis, T. Stirling 267, 370
Marrable, Arthur Geo.... 295
Marrett, Edw. Uvedale 420
— Henry Richard..... 63, 415
Marriott, Edward Frere 417
— Edwin M. L. 24, 404
— John 245
— Leslie Hawthorne .. 438
— Richard George A. ... 237
— Tom 395
Marriott-Dodington, W. 287
Marsden, Hugh W. 360
— James Cort............... 505
— Richard Travers 176
Marsh, F. Hale Berwick 22, 404
— Francis Charles 294
— Francis Courtenay ... 278
— Harry Graham 161
— Hopton Eliott 173
— James Reynolds M.... 246
— *2nd Lt.* Jeremy Taylor 139
— Thos. Alf. Perry 381
Marshall, Charles 297
— Chs. Henry Tilson 24, 408
— Charles Herbert 249
Marshall, Daniel Grove 456
— Ernest Theodore 254
— Francis Macleod H... 277
— Fred 143
— George 294
— Geo. F. Leycester 27, 218
— George Henry ...28, 166a
— Hawtrey Charles 173
— Henry Alfred 185
— Henry Turnbull 441
— Herbert S. 22, 404
— Hugh John Miles 212
— John W. Astley ...63, 333
— Kenneth F. C. 337
— Robert 277
— Thomas Edward 174
— Wilfred Geo. Howard 229
— Wm. Muir Knox 322
— William Thomas 161
— Wm. Raine 289
— William Simpson 68, 416
Marsham, *Hon.* Regd. H. 149
Marson, Hy. Wyndham A. 433
Marston, Jeffery Chas. 69, 169
Martel, Charles P. 171
Martelli, Norton Chas. 41, 410
Marter, William Maurice 136
Martin, Albert T. de M. 361
— Alexander 178
— Alfred Robert 58, 416
— Aylmer R. Sancton... 238
— Claude Buist 385
— Daniel Nicholas 453
— Edward Victor 436
— Edward Wm. F. 417
— Ernest Edmund 395
— Frank 314
— George Blake N. ...46, 166
— Gerald Ward......... 46, 411
— Henry 380
— Henry John 274
— Herbert 58, 346
— Herbert Maxwell...... 252
— James 128
— James Evan Baillie... 304
— *Lieut.* John 220
— *Surg. Major* John...... 378
— Martin 52, 207
— Patrick Richard 504
— Ranald 317
— Rowland Hill 45, 163
— Wm. Thomas 377
Martindale, C. S. de Butts 424
Marton, Richard O. 177
Martyn, Anthony W. ... 294
— Arundel 294
Martyr, Cyril Godfrey... 276
Marwood, Henry 310
Masani, Hormasji D. 529
Mascall, Francis 42, 205
Masefield, Robert 297
Mason, Alex. Herbert 47, 209
— *Rev.* Chas. Arthur ... 460
— George 398
— Henry Espine M. 418
— Henry Macan 55, 413
— Hubert Dempster ... 385
— Sydney Moore 426
— William Campbell ... 185
Massey, Godf. Warburton 329
Massie, John Hamon ... 177
— Roger H. 175
Massy, Charles Fra. 42, 410
— Edward Charles 175
— George 452
— Godfrey 245
— Hampden Hugh 209
— Harry Stanley 67, 416
— Hugh Ingoldsby.... 58, 288
— John George Albert... 258
— Percy Hugh H.... 65, 141
— William George... 69, 169
— Wm. G. D. 5, 139
Master, Alfred Edm. ... 380
— Ar. Gilbert 360, 368
— Richard Chester 305
— William Chester 130
Masters, Alexander...57, 413
— Edw. Steuart 56, 415
Masterson, George C. D. 259
— James Edward I. 249
— John 415
Matcham, William Eyre 308
Matchett, Harry G. K. ... 334
Mather, John Dryden.... 346
— John W. 271
Matheson, John..... 43, 206
— John Colin 213
Matheson, Torquhil G... 231
Mathew, Chas. Massy 314, 370
— Charles Montague ... 506
— Charles Theobald...... 147
— Robert George 367
Mathew-Lannowe, B. H. H 139
— G. R. M. 177
Mathewes, John R. 427
Mathews, Percival S. ... 245
Mathias, Hy. Harding 48, 321
— Hugh Brodie 383
— Leonard John 426
Mathison, Gilbert H. F. 61, 259
Matson, Charles George 400
Mattei, Alexander ...63, 186
Matthew, *Rev.* H. J. 460
Matthews, Alfred 170
— Charles Richard ...16, 405
— Frank B. 65, 238
— George 136
— Godfrey Estcourt...... 400
— Iles 395
— John Williams 174
— *Rev.* Lewis Joseph ... 396
— Llewellin Washington 140
— William Arthur......... 175
Matthey, Granville E. ... 271
Maturin, Benjamin A.... 383
— Fred. Harvey.........23, 275
— John 377
— John Wm. Henry...... 252
Maud, Philip 213
— William Hartley 252
Maude, Eustace Addison 144
— Fred. Stanley 231
— Henry Noel St. John 177
— Robert John 59, 356
Mauduit, F. R. M. C. DeR. 429
Maul, Spencer Duncan 311
Maunsell, Arch. J. Stephens 242
— Chas. A. 377
— Charles H. Wray 254
— Edward Henry 372
— Edward Lewis 380
— Francis Richard 171
— Frederick Guy 173
— George William ...67, 294
— John Drought 373
— Lucius Augustus de V. 256
— Manuel Chas. 173
— Nevill Francis A....59, 242
— Thomas 377
Maurice, David Blake... 293
— Frederick Barton...... 289
— John Frederick ...17, 165
Mawbey, Henry Way ... 397
Mawhinny, Robert J. W. 384
Mawson, Wm. Arthur ... 454
Maxham, John W. 377
Maxse, Fred. Ivor......... 231
Maxwell, Alex. Gordon. 437
— Archibald Boyd......... 309
— Aymer Claud 347
— Cedric 65, 209
— Charles James 144
— Denis Wellesley 317
— Francis Aylmer 279
— Frederick Doveton ... 427
— George William........ 419
— Hamilton George 434
— Harrie Maxwell......... 395
— Henry Edward ... 69, 286
— Henry St. Patrick 48, 412
— James M'Call 173
— John Grenfell 53, 286
— John Maudslay......... 294
— Lawrence L. 437
— Nigel 63, 169
— Richard Money... 69, 423
— Robert Pacy 246
— Ronald Charles......58, 208
— Thomas Mercer ... 41, 289
— William Lockhart...... 429
May, Edward Sinclair 59, 168
— George Lycett E. ...49, 261
— James 7, 403
— William Allan........... 379
— Wm. Southall Reid... 254
Maycock, Francis M. ... 373
— Stewart M. 53, 208
Mayhew, Alfred H. ...40, 409
— *Rev.* C. 532
— Charles Lawson......... 401
— Hervey Sandby 278
— Thomas 49, 166a
Maynard, Chas. C. M.... 249

Index—Active List.

Maynard, Fred. Pinsent 456
Mayne, Augustus Blair 425
— Charles Blair 69, 209
— George Nisbet 66, 269
— Herbert Blair 177
— Jasper Graham 271
— Otway 65, 245
— Richard Charles G. 63, 415
— Thomas 504
Mayo, Herbert Edward 264
— William Robert......... 369
Mayow, Robert S. L. W. 291
Mead, Rev. George 396
— Harold Richard 426
— Moses 288
Mende, John M. de O. 4, 397
— John de Courcy D. 66, 415
— John Wm. B. 419
— Malcolm John 66, 415
Meadows, C. J. Walford 453
Meares, Aubrey............ 214
— Hugh Poynder 177
Mears, Arthur 437
— Cecil Delarue............ 274
— Ernest Lennox 308
Mecham, Ar. Russel 270
— John Russell 42
Medd, Henry 255
Medhurst, C.F.H. 373
Medley, Allen George ... 430
— Ernest James 421
Medlycott, John Thos... 282
Meek, James 382
Meeking, Bertram C.C.S. 152
Meeres, Arthur Douglas 209
— Charles Stuart 171
Meiklejohn, Mat. F. M. 321
— William Hope 27, 404
Mein, Alex. Bowes ... 59, 414
— Alex. Lechmere... 63, 209
— Frederick Blundell ... 421
— John Edmund 55, 413
Meister, R. H. J. 401
Melladew, Heinrich F. L. 378
Melliss, Charles John ... 428
— Howard 42, 410
Mellor, Llewellyn S... 57, 244
Melvill, Chas. Curling... 309
— Henry 419
— Philip James 420
— Walter Sydney 256
Melville, Alan 308
— Charles Henderson... 383
— Harry George 456
— Henry Bruce 456
— John Swinton 424
Melvin, Alexander 422
Mends, Horatio Reg. 48, 304
Mennie, John Oliver ... 430
Menzies, Angus........... 309
— George Feilden 284
— Henry M. R. 308
— Steuart 243
— William Maxwell 314
Mercer, Arch. Aird........283
— Charles Arch......... 46, 411
— David 400
— Harvey Frederic 169
— Herbert 138
— Wm. Hugh Welch ... 431
— Wm. Lindsay 259
Meredith, Edw. Spencer 210
— John Alfred 395
Merewether, Hy. Arthur 422
— Herbert Duncan 428
— John W. Beresford ... 434
Merrick, Geo. Charleton 177
Merriman, Reg. Gordon 173
Merritt, George 386
Mesham, Capel H. 334
Messiter, Chas. Bayard. 272
Metcalfe, Charles Theo.
Evelyn............... 65, 356
— Fenwick Henry 175
— Herbert Charles 292
— Sydney Fortescue ... 176
Mothuen, Paul S., Lord.. 6
Meyer, Chas. Hardwick L. 530
— James Leopold 213
Meynell, Godfrey 297
Meyrick, Fred. Charlton 157
— Harold Lothian 214
— St. John 321
Meyricke, Edward Gelly 214
— Robert Evelyn 278
Michael, Henry James ... 379
Michell, Jas. Wm. A. 21, 407
— St. John Fancourt 42, 413

Michie, George 214
Micklem, Henry A. 214
Middlemass, J. Crawford
.... 67, 209
Middleton, Chas. de O. 294
— Herbert J. J. 295
— Middleton 311
— Oswald R. 17
— Wm. Crawford 69, 144
Midwinter, Edw. Colpoys 214
— Rev. H. N. 532
Midwood, Harrison 317
Mignon, Jepson George 256
Milbanke, John P. 152
Milburne, C. E. A. 310
Mildinay, Alex. Richd. 305
— C. B. St. John 172
— Herbert Alex. St. John 130
Mildred, Spencer 214
Miles, Charles Napier 66, 133
— Herbert Scott Gould... 27
— Philip John 431
— Samuel Barrett ...21, 406
Miley, James Aloysius 42, 410
Millais, Hugo Wm. Reid 281
Millar, William Henry... 429
Miller, Alan Stewart..... 175
— Alfred Douglas 144
— Denis Menezes 156
— John Francis Jas. 41, 409
— Leander William 401
— Wm. Birkmyre 378
Milles, Hon. Lewis A. ... 158
Milligan, Geo. Dunbar 231
Mills, Arthur M'Leod 51, 412
— Bernard Langley 383
— Dudley Acland 210
— Edward Cyril 61, 253
— Edward William 259
— George Arthur..... 51, 348
— James 395
— Rev. M. E. 457
— Sydney 357
— William Holroyd 172
— Milne, Alexander 317
— Benj. Arthur...... 48, 397
— Charles................... 456
— Charles John........... 457
— George Francis 174
— James William 440
— Richard Louis... 59, 256
— Milner, Arthur Edward 386
— Edward 233
— Edward Francis 258
— George Francis 133
— Rev. Walter Hebden... 395
Milnes, George 185
Milton, Percy Wm. A.A.58, 295
Milward, Clement H. ... 171
— Edwin Oswald 295
— Frederick D. 261, 370
— Harry Dacres 273
— Thomas Walter 288
Milward-Jones, R. A. ... 139
Minchin, Alfred Beckett 440
— Charles Fred. 427
— Fred. Falkiner 170
— Hugh Dillon M. ...69, 416
— William Cyril ...360, 373
Minnies, James 384
Minogue, John O'Brien 253
Minter, John Surtees ... 169
Mistri, Kavasji H......... 530
Mitchell, Alex. Ian 138
— Arthur James 261
— Charles Andrew P. ... 380
— Geo. Warder 421
— Henry 172
— Henry Wilmot......67, 156
— John Wilson 368
— Lionel Arthur 214
— Robt. Wm. Hamilton 271
— Wilfrid James 440
Mitchell-Innes, Cecil... 346
— James 69, 317
Mitford, Bertram R..... 275
— Herbert, Master King. 66
Moberly, Cuthbert von E. 159
— Frederick James....... 439
— Guy 438
— Herbert John R. 380
— Hugh Stephenson ... 362
— William Henry ... 45, 281
Mocatta, Daniel E. 427
Mockler, Edward ... 24, 404
— Gerald Francis 287
— Guy Henry G. 434
— Percy Rise 343

Moffat, Archibald S. W. 273
— Eustace Jno. Garrard 258
Moffat, James Robert ... 346
Moffet, Grenville E. 382
Moffitt, Fred. Wm. 288
— Thomas B. 380
Moggridge, John Antill 284
Moir, Alan James G. ... 234
— Chas. Fred. Wm. 29
— David Macbeth........ 456
— James 383
— James Philip............ 214
— John Drew 382
Moir-Byres, Patrick..... 144
Molesworth, A. Ludovic 171
— St. Aubyn 28, 165
— Edward Hogarth...63, 415
— Hon. George Bagot... 276
— Herbert Crofton S. ... 172
— Herbert Ellicombe ... 177
— Hickman C. 170
— Percy Braybrooke ... 213
— Richard Pigot 175
— Robert Everard 382
— William 506
Moline, Frank H.......... 275
Möller, Bernhard D. 50, 160
Molloy, Edward 40, 408
— Gerald Macleay 329
— Percy...................... 40:
Molony, Chas. Vandeleur 294
— Clement Arthur 174
— Francis Arthur 210
— Trevor C. Wheler ... 175
Molyneux, Edw. Mary
    Joseph 437
— Geo. Philip B.....277, 373
— Hon. Osbert Cecil... 134
Molyneux-Montgomerie,
    G. F. 230
Molyneux - Seel, Louis
    E. W. 278
Monck, Cecil Stanley O. 231
Monck-Mason, G. G....50, 167
— Roger H. 347
Moncrieff, George Hay... 5
— William Scott. 301
Money, Arthur Wigram 173
— Chas. G. Colvin ...59, 240
— Edm. Chas. Kyrle 311, 374
— Elliot Alex. 25, 408
— Ernest Douglas 438
— Ernle William Kyrle 297
— Evelyn Campbell...43, 333
— George Alfred ... 63, 415
— George Edward ... 53, 413
— Gordon Lorn Camp-
    bell 29, 323
— Herbert Cecil ... 66, 400
— Robert Cotton 295
— Rowland F. K......52, 234
Money-Simons, J. J....45, 411
Monkhouse, W. Percival 177
Monks, Charles 529
Monreal, Louis 6
Monro, Chas. Carmichael 236
— Charles Gordon....... 322
— George Nowlan 273
— John Duncan........... 273
— Seymour C. Hale...51, 318
Monsell, Charles Graham 237
Montagu, Arthur Henry 431
— Edward 250
— Horace Wm. 204
Montagu-Douglas-Scott,
    Lord G. W. 152
Montanaro, Alfred ...58, 414
— Arthur Forbes 171
Monteith, Arthur M. 66, 415
— Edw. V. Peshall ...52, 412
— John 63, 415
— Robert, William F. 69, 366
Montgomerie, Duncan H. 214
Montgomery, Alex. J. 52, 167
— Archibald Armar 292
— Arthur Hill Sandys 841, 362
— Rev. Ferguson J. 450
— Charles Arnulph S. ... 424
— Hugh Maude de F. ... 176
— Hugh Wyndham 159
— James A. Lawrence 46, 412
— Richard Hugh 400
— Robert Arthur ... 44, 166a
— Thomas Robert A. G. 421
— Paymaster William ... 372
— Lieut. William 220
— William Edward 7

Montresor, Edw. H. H. 65, 415
— Ernest Henry 279
— Louis Basset 178
Montressor, Welby F. 66, 415
Mondy, Geo. Robt. B. 297, 308
— Hampden Lewis C. ... 294
— Henry de C. 203
— Rich. S. H. 50, 237
Mookerjee, Preo Nath... 504
Moon, Wilfred Graham 318
Moor, Hatherley George 176
Moorat, Wilfred M. C... 348
Moore, Alexander 437
— Alexander G. M. ... 5, 160
— Alex. M'Donnell... 58, 333
— Arthur Guy W. 432
— Arthur Thomas 544
— Arthur Trevelyan ... 212
— Barrington Shakespr. 294
— Charles 293
— Charles Alfred ...18, 403
— Charles Hesketh G... 437
— Charles Malcolm 530
— Rev. Clement Glover 466
— Cyril Henry 309
— Edw. Crozier S. ...45, 206
— Edw. Du Pré Herford 315
— Frank Beaumont H... 177
— Frederick Lewis 431
— Fred. Thornton Trevor 437
— George Abraham ... 385
— George Henry J. 421
— George Kenrick ...267, 373
— Geo. D. Maxwell 439
— George Robert 50, 167
— Harry Alex. 433
— Henry 42
— Hy. Glanville Allen... 242
— Henry Hamilton ... 362
— Herbert Acheson 267, 370
— Herbert Tregosse G. 214
— Rev. H. O. 460
— Hugh Myddleton 530
— John 395
— Joseph Henry 378
— Joseph Scott 367
— Maurice George ...65, 334
— Qr. Mr. Robert....... 370
— Vet. Capt. Robert ... 395
— Robert Reginald H... 382
— Robert Thornton ... 174
— St. Leger Montgomery 175
— Stephen George...... 297
— Thomas 53, 397
— Thomas Charles 506
— William 52, 289
— William Francis... 41, 369
— William Henry 178
Moores, Charles Fred... 347
— Clarence Mann 440
— Samuel Guise 384
Moorhead, Arthur Hy. 457
— James 454
Moorhouse, Harry C. ... 177
Moorsom, Chas. John ... 6
— Henry Manvers... 21, 165
Moran, James 453
— Jas. Joseph............. 505
Morant, Hubert H. S.... 315
More, Lancelot P........ 385
— Paxton St. Clair 457
More-Molyneux, G. H. 28, 413
Moren, James Alex...... 174
Morgan,'Alex. B.......... 250
— Anthony Hickman ... 387
— Cecil Buckley 360
— Claude Kyd 386
— Edgar Johns 457
— Rev. Emmanuel M.... 396
— Francis G. C. Mansel 267
— Frederick Cyril... 45, 166a
— Frederick James 384
— Harrison R. Lewin 40, 165
— Henry 69, 292
— Hill Godfrey 367
— James Campbell 384
— John Wm. Akerman 395
— John Wm. Moore 333, 368
— Reginald Hallward... 401
— Wm. John F. 55, 258, 373
Morgan-Payler, Egerton
    Payler 65, 234
Moriarty, Mat. Denis ... 453
— Redmond G.S. Lone.. 258
Morice, Cuthbert C. D. 212
Morison, F. de Lamare
.... 42, 234
Morland, Algernon 250

Index—Active List. 556

Morland, Charles H. 285
— Thos. Lethbridge N. 305
Morley, Clervaux... 27, 105
— Francis Britton... 360
— George Wheeler 271
— Robert Wilton 139
— *Rev.* Samuel 507
Morony, Burdett Edw. 211
Morphew, Edward M... 385
Morphy, Henry John... 329
Morrell, Hugh St. J... 264
Morres, Elliot Hody... 401
Morrice, Cuthbert H. ... 243
— Herbert 175
— Lewis Edward 242
Morrieson, Henry W. 67, 169
Morris, Arth. Edward... 382
— Arthur Henry 258
— Augustus Williams... 29
— Charles Henry...68, 417
— Charles Jas. Ussher 174
— Donald Ogilvy 438
— Edmund Merritt 249
— Edward Coxwell...55, 22
— Frank George Grier 278
— Frederick 58, 265
— George Henry 357
— George Mortimer 43
— Godfrey Maxwell 435
— Gordon Sutherland... 432
— Henry Gage 276
— Herbert Mackinlay... 455
— John Ignatius ...26, 399
— John James 379
— Maurice Morgan 170
— Reginald Yates 262
— *Captain* Robert 171
— *Colonel* Robert....19, 403
— Robert Cochrane 176
— Robert Lee 438
— Samuel Guise 385
— William Albert 381
— William George... 46, 206
Morrison, Colquhoun Grant 140
— George 214
— John C. D. 130
— Maskell M. Downie 175
— Richard Hobart ...53, 160
— *Rev.* Riddall 396
— William 386
Morse, Allan Stewart... 401
— Arthur Francis 148
— Arthur T. 63, 294
— Charles James 274
— Henry Charles....22, 407
— Richd. Edw. Ricketts 381
— Walter John 42, 410
Mortimer, C. Lysaght 47, 243
— Francis James ...22, 181
— Henry Beaufoy...52, 310
— William Hugh 371
Mortimore, Chas. R. ... 290
Morton, Chas. Falkiner 17
— Edward Ross 433
— Gerald de Courcy 18
— James 370
— John Plowden 506
— William Ross 210
Morwood, James 455
Moseley, Andrew J. ... 161
— *Rev.* Reginald 396
— Robert J. D. 429
Mosley, Arthur Rowland 148
Moss, Allan 57, 253
— Claude 272
Mosse, C. G. Drummond 380
— John 256
— Wm. Oliver Matless... 425
Mostyn, *Hon.* R. E. M. ... 172
Mott, Sydney Albert 262
— Stanley Fielder ... 395
Moul, Wm. Vincent 264
Mould, Chas. Fred. 211
— George Thomas 456
— William Thomas 384
Moule, Gerard B. 255
Moulson, *Rev.* J. 460
Moultrie, Hugh C. 175
MountEdgcumbe,*Earl of*
Mourilyan, Hubert L... 253
Mowatt, Chas. R. John 292
Mowbray, Basil C. 317
Moxly, *Rev.* J. H. S. 396
Moysey, Chas. John...16, 204
Mozley, Edward N. 214
Mudge, Arthur 236

Mugford, Frederick 156
Muir, Archibald M. 47, 412
— Charles Wemyss...53, 413
— Henry Skey 377
— John 398
Muirhead,Herbert H. 53, 208
Mukerji, Upendra Nath 455
Mulcahy, Francis Edw. 369
Mullaly, Alexander 433
— Herbert 210
Mullane, Jeremiah 454
— Patrick 455
Mullen, Douglas ffrench 454
— Jarlath Ffrench 454
— John L. W. ffrench ... 142
— Patrick 370
— Thomas Ffrench 452
Mullens, Richard Lucas 158
Muller, George Fison ... 401
Mullins, Arthur John ... 171
— Geo. James H. 401
— *Rev.* T. Patterson 396
— Willoughby Brooking 423
Mulloy,W.Hutchinson 26,205
Mulroney, Thos. R. 454
Mulvany, John 457
— Peter 380
Mumby, Langton P. 383
Mummery, Wm. Edgar 160
Mundy, Basil St. John... 157
— Rodney Edw. 43, 166
Munn, Fredk. Henry 51, 333
— Reginald George 437
Munro, Geo. Mackenzie G. 234
— Gustavus Francis... 5, 397
— Lewis 281
Murdoch, Robert H 178
— William W. 18, 165
Mure, Wm. C. Lockhart 432
Muriel, Chas. Leslie 301
Murison, Albert Lewis... 361
— James Augustus 386
Murphy, Chas. C. R. ... 250
— *Rev.* Chas. Hy. 396
— Fred. James 155
— James 401
— James Andrew 143
— *Rev.* Joseph B. C. 396
— Moore 114
— Wm. Reed 453
Murray, Alan Beville ... 185
— Alex. Penrose 321
— *Hon.* Andrew David... 325
— Anthony Hepburn 23, 179
— Archibald James 271
— Arth. Alex. Wolfe 317
— Arthur Mordaunt 53, 167
— Basil Henry Scott 233
— Charles Wyndham... 130
— Cyril Francis Tyrrell 430
— Edward 295
— Edward James 178
— *Hon.* Edwd. Oliphant 325
— Edward R. Blakiston 435
— Eric Madden 242
— Fergus 270
— Frank 431
— Frederick Dymoke 286
— George 423
— Henry Brooke 431
— Henry Walker 380
— Herbert C. Orde 286
— James 455
— James Harry S. 212
— Jas. Murray 25, 165
— Jas. Thos. Crokatt ... 286
— James Wolfe...52, 167
— John 156
— *Qr.Mr.* John 178
— John A. Shakespear 250
— Kenelm Digby 19
— Malcolm Donald 318
— Pulteney Henry ...47, 297
— Robert D. 453
— Robert Hunter...26, 318
— Shadwell John 334
— Stewart Lygon 321
— Thomas 115
— Thomas Francis 317
— Valentine 212
— Walter Godfrey P. ... 441
— Walter Graham 145
— Wm. Flood 453
— Wm. Hugh Eric 291
Muscroft, James 295
— Wm. St. Clair 302
Musgrave, Arthur D. ... 178
— Walter W. F. C. 443

Musgrave, William 368
Muspratt, Francis C. ... 431
Muspratt-Williams, Reginald Lawford 176
Mussenden,Fras. Wm... 150
Muter, Robert Stanley... 213
— St. John A. D. 173
Myers, Alfred Edw. C. ... 177
Myles, Edmond H. 380
— James Perceval 382
Mylne, *Rt. Rev.* Louis G. 532
Mylrea, Wm. P. G....368, 401
Nailer, Henry A. F. ... 505
Nairne, C. Edw. 6, 179
— Edward Spencer 175
Naish, *Rev.* Henry 460
— Theodore E. 212
Nandi, Sambhu C. 454
Nangle, Kenlis Edward 439
— Montague Claude 252
Nanton, Herbert C. 211
Napier, Hon. A. Fullarton 434
— Arthur Lenox 252
— *Hon.* Charles F. H. 357
— Duncan Robertson ... 287
— George Samuel Fred. 287
— Henry Edward 264
— *Hon.* James Pearse ... 44
— *Hon.* J. Scott 49, 321
— John Stirling 55, 337
— Robert Fra. L. 66, 325
— William C. E. 269
— William John 173
Napier-Clavering, Chas.
— Warren 252
Nariman, Kaikhoso S. 529
Nash, Henry Edm. P. ... 234
— Llewellyn T. Manly... 383
— William 377
— William Fleetwood ... 278
— William Peel 58, 309
Nason, Fortescue John 270
— Henry Hyde W. 288
Nathan, Fred. Lewis 170
— Matthew 211
— Walter Simeon 212
— Nauth, Bhola 506
— Naylor, Harry Trevor... 343
— Henry Wm. Lotts ... 401
Neal, George 179
Neale, George Henry ... 236
Nealon, Patrick J. 381
— Henry Everard 212
Nedham, E. Montgomerie 66, 416
Needham, Charles 19
— Neeld, Audley Dallas 48, 134
— Mortimer G. 50, 159
— Neill, Garnet W. G. 214
— Neilson, Walter 317
— William Henry 505
— Noish, Colin G. 171
— Francis Hugh 321
Nelis, George 382
— James Alex. 454
Nelson, Arthur 255
— Edgar Forbes 170
— Francis Arthur 401
— Frederic Justin 432
— Horace Sydney 177
— Wallace 301
Nepean, A. Oliver do Blaquiere 52, 393
— Herbert E. C. Bayley 432
Nesbitt, Edward 28
— Nethersole, Alf. R. ... 438
— Frederick Ralph 437
Neve, Edw. John 293
Neville, Josiah P. C. 45, 411
— William Candler 254
Nevinson, Tom St. A. B. Lennard 176
Newall, Fraser G. 337
— Wm. Potter 47, 412
Newbigging, P. C. E.51, 167
— Wm. Patrick Eric 309
Newbold, Ambrose Wm. 431
Newbould, Hy. Jas. F. 146
Newbury, B. Archdall... 276
— J. B. Thornton 372
— Percy F. R. 246
Newcombe, Edw. O. A. 214
Newdigate, Hy.R.Legge 5
Newell,HerbertAndrews 439
— Wm. Joseph 421
Newenham, Henry E. B. 243
Newill, Joseph Henry 42, 410

Newington, F. Alex. 53, 397
Newland, Arthur Geo. E. 505
— Edmund Walcott 310, 373
— Foster Reuss 383
Newlett, Alan 441
Newman, E. A. R. 457
— *Rev.* E. F. 395
— Edward Harding 177
— John Henry 451
Newmarch, L. S. 423
Newnham, Arthur T. H. 425
— Charles Cowan 270
— Percival Forbes 261
— Walter Fawcett 435
Newport, Cha. Peter 19, 405
Newsom, Aug. Chas. 375
Newton Cecil John 291
— Horace 304
— John W. Marsdin 57, 168
Newtown-Butler, *Lord*... 231
Nichol, Charles Edward 331
— William Dale 174
Nicholas, Chas. Percy ... 258
— Jas. Hamilton 382
— John 178
— Stephen Henry E. 439
Nicholetts, C.Oldfield 55, 413
Nicholl, Donald Fitz Roy 177
Nicholl, Hugh Ilfid 255
Nicholls, Arthur 426
— William Charles...65, 398
Nichols, Fred. Peter 381
Nicholson, Arthur D. 325
— Cecil L. 259
— Fras. Cobham 452
— George Fred. 454
— George Harvey 281
— Graham Hy. Whalley 175
— Henry Herbert 243
— Hugh Blomfield 305
— James Edward 330
— John Sanctuary 149
— Louis St. Clair 241
— Ralph Wise 427
— Ranald Wm. E. H. 383
— Stuart James 16, 164
— Walter Adams 175
— William Cumberland 439
— Wm. Cyril Alwynne 174
— Wm. Gustavus 26, 205
Nickalls, Norman T. 159
Nickerson,*Rev.*David ... 396
Nicol, Lewis Loyd 355
Nicolas, Francis C. 362
— *Rev.* Percy 457
Nicolay, Bernard U. 281
Nicolls, Edm. Gustavus 170
— *Rev.* Gerald E. 460
— John Michael 383
— Oliver H. Atkins 6, 164
Nicolson, Malcolm H.7, 404a
— William Hurst 347
Nightingale, Manners Ralph W. 439
Nisbet, Francis C. 272
Nisbett, Geo. D. More 53, 255
— Wm. Gibbon 255
Nixon,ArundelJames49,166a
— Francis William... 27, 207
— Fred. Eckersall 175
— George Michael 454
— James Ryder 401
— John Eccles 417
— Noake, Robert Douglas40, 366
Noble, Geo. John Wm... 155
— John Brocknock 401
— John Edmund 295
— John Herbert Hay ... 259
— Montagu Mark 172
— Vere D'Oyly 271
Noblett, Louis H. 329
Noding, Thos. Edw. 381
Noel, Henry Cecil 159
— *Hon.* Edward 53, 350
— Edward A. 130
— Wm. Fred. Noel ...52, 207
Nolan, Andrew Ballow 138
Noon, Wm. Prian ...52, 249
Noott, Cuthbert C. 175
Norbury, Connagby ... 273
Norcock, Henry John L. 49
Norcott, Charles H. B. 49, 356
— Gerald Alfred 291
Norfolk, *Rev.* A. Springett 395
Norfor,BrookeOwenWm. 382
Norgate, Arthur H. W. 24
Norie, Charles E. de M. 432
— Evelyn Wm. Medows 301

Norie, Frank Hay ... 281
Norman, Arthur Ormond 321
— Compton ... 42, 265
— Harold Henry ... 292
— *Rev.* H. Bathurst ... 507
— Henry Erasmus ... 436
— R. P. ... 362
— Walter Henry ... 439
— William Wylie ... 425
Norrington, Fred. C. S. 311
Norris, Arthur Gambier 173
— *Rev.* E. W. B. ... 396
— Ernest Edward ... 173
— Paul Buzzard ... 276
— Richard Joseph ... 67, 360
— Stephen Leslie ... 210
— William ... 251
North, Charles Napier ... 214
— Dudley ... 22
— Edward ... 380
— Edward Bunbury ... 243
— John ... 504
— Louis Aylmer ... 262
— Piers William ... 293
— Roger Chas. Edw. 49, 166a
— Roger Edw. Napier ... 275
Northcott, Arthur B. H. 262
— Frank Leonard ... 245
— Henry P. ... 68, 346
Northey, Arthur Cecil ... 270
— Edward ... 305
— Francis William ... 273
— Herbert Hamilton ... 262
Norton, Cecil B. ... 276
— Charles Edward ... 210
— Chas. Ernest Graham 149
— Gilbert F. A. ... 50, 168
— Henry Hume ... 153
Norwood, Wm. Blakeney 174
Nott, A. Holbrook ... 456
— William C. J. F. ... 372
Notter, Jas. L. ... 377
Nourse, Arth. Herbert 47, 236
Nowlan, Thos. Bowman 172
Noyes, Arthur Walter 42, 253
— Augustus Finch ... 371
— Conrad Ernest ... 317
— Ralph Elliot ... 259
— *Rev.* William Charles 457
Nugee, Andrew R. ... 311, 373
Nugent, Andrew ... 142
— Arthur ... 69, 243
— *Rev.* Chas. P. C. ... 507
— Charles H. Hodges ... 213
— George Colborne ... 229
— Geo. Roubiliac H. ... 178
— Oliver Stewart Wood 305
— Robt. Arthur ... 40, 366
— Thos. Geo. Hodges ... 398
Nunn, Joshua Arthur ... 395
— Mervyn Henry ... 273
— Thos. Hy. Clayton ... 294
Nunnerley, P. Jebb R. 383
Nurse, Charles George ... 425
— Henry Harvey ... 434
Nuthall, Alf. Jas. P. 48, 412
— Charles Edwin ... 395
— William Frederick ... 43
Nutt, Arthur Chas. R. ... 177
— H. Lowther ... 23, 408
— James Anson F. ... 46, 166
Nuttall, Charles M. ... 177
— John Rattray ... 252
— Mansfield E. ... 438
Oakeley, Edw. Fras ... 284
Oakes, George Henry 19, 406
— George Richard ... 434
— Horace Charles ... 314
— Montague P. Rowland 147
— Orbell Henry ... 53, 273
— Reginald ... 52, 167
Oakley, Lawrence T. ... 274
— Richard ... 270
Oakshot, Walter E. ... 261
Oates, George ... 360
— William Coape ... 347
Obbard, Edw. Naismith 435
— Owen James ... 432
O'Brien, Aubrey J. ... 291
— Bartholomew ... 453
— Chas. Richard M. ... 274
— Donatus Jas. Thos. ... 424
— Edmund D. Collins 24, 204
— Edm. Donough J. ... 138
— Edward ... 258
— Egerton Aug. Stafford 150
— Henry Joseph ... 377
— Henry Montague S. ... 278
O'Brien, Joseph ... 453
— *Hon.* Murrough ... 240
— Richard Francis ... 381
— Thomas Henry ... 291
— Walmsley Donat ... 270
O'Bryen, Chas. Wm. ... 428
— James Loughnan ... 67, 415
O'Callaghan, D. D. T. 28, 165
— Denis Moriarty ... 383
Occleston, Sidney V. ... 153
O'Connell, David V. ... 382
— James Ross ... 297
— Matthew D. ... 378
— Morgan David ... 379
O'Connor, Arthur P. ... 380
— Daniel ... 386
— George ... 69, 148
— Patrick F. ... 453
— Wm. Fredk. Travers 176
O'Dell, Thomas John ... 367
Odevaine, Ferdinald J. 178
Odlum, Richard ... 156
O'Donel, James George 395
— Manus Basil Hugh ... 213
O'Donnell, Alex. C. ... 421
— George B. ... 418
— Henry ... 253
— Hugh ... 420
— James J. ... 383
— Thomas Joseph ... 381
O'Donoghue, Mont. E. ... 421
O'Dowda, James Wilton 294
O'Dwyer, Malachi ... 454
— T. Francis ... 377
O'Farrell, Thomas ... 377
Ogg, George Sim ... 173
— William Mortimer ... 178
Ogilvie, Duncan ... 214
— E. Collingwood ... 212
— Norman Stuart ... 170
— Walter Holland ... 457
— *Rev.* Wm. Nicholl ... 507
Ogilvy, Angus H. R. ... 155
Ogle, Edmund Ashton 24, 254
— Frederic Amelius ... 19, 397
O'Gorman, N. Purcell ... 46
— Patrick Wilkins ... 456
O'Grady, Hy. de Courcy 362
— Hugh H. M. ... 279
— John de Courcy ... 57, 334
O'Halloran, Mich. ... 383
O'Hara, Alfred James ... 505
— James ... 137, 374
— Patrick Henry Aug. ... 275
— William ... 504
O'Keeffe, Menus W. *MD.* 381
O'Kinealy, Frederick ... 456
— James ... 177
Oldfield, Arthur R. ... 176
— Christopher G. ... 172
— Frederick Hume ... 210
— Henry Elliott ... 170
— Humphrey ... 398
— John R. Hodge ... 400
— Leopold Chas. Louis 177
Oldham, Benjamin C. ... 456
— Frank Trevor ... 175
— Henry Hugh ... 130
— Leslie Wm. Searles ... 213
O'Leary, Tom Evelyn ... 333
— William Evelyn ... 329
— Wm. M'Carthy ... 49, 284
Oliphant, Edw. Havelock 249
— Geo. Albert ... 395
— Lawrence James ... 78, 229
— Philip L. K. Blair ... 357
— William ... 270
Oliver, Lionel Grant ... 301
— *Rev.* Richard John D. 396
Olivey, Herbert Edw. ... 250
Olivier, Henry Dacres 55, 208
— William Henry ... 174
Ollivant, Alfred ... 178
— Alfred Henry ... 177
— Edward Albert ... 43, 166
— John Spencer ... 177
— William Spencer ... 318
Olpherts, *Sir* William ... 179
— William Cautley ... 234
O'Malley, Chas. Loughlin 178
— George Hunter ... 45, 166
O'Meagher, John Kevin 347
O'Mealy, Wm. A. D. ... 65, 415
O'Meara, Chas. A. Edm. 439
— Walter A. J. ... 211
Ommanney, Albt. Edw. 50, 237
— Arthur Hammond ... 440
— Edmund M. Carpenter 401
Ommanney, F. Cranstoun 244
— George Stewart ... 420
O'Neill *Qr. Mr.* John ... 239
— *Surg. Major* John ... 454
— *Rev.* O. A. W. ... 396
— William H. S. ... 67, 348
— Wm. Heremon ... 66, 169
O'Nial, Albert Francis ... 493
Onslow, A. Hughes- ... 152
— Cranley Charlton ... 255
— George Manners ... 21
— George Thorp ... 59, 400
— Gerald Chas. P. ... 63, 209
— Richard Cranley ... 418
— William Henry ... 173
Orange, John Edw. ... 372
Orchard, Henry ... 186
— John Waller ... 434
Ord, Maurice Aug. ... 284
Orde, Leonard Henry ... 254
O'Reilly, *Rev.* Chas. F. 396
— Chas. Myles ... 438
— Hy. Wm. Hutchinson 385
— Thomas ... 378
Orford, Alfred ... 398
Organ, Charles ... 259
— James ... 223
Orlebar, Evelyn H. ... 400
Orman, Charles Edward 288
— Frank Leslie ... 440
Ormerod, Geo. Sumner 347
Ormiston, Jas. Walker ... 172
— Thomas Lane ... 439
Ormond, Harold V. S. ... 261
Ormsby, John Becher ... 26
— Thomas ... 282
— Vincent Alexander ... 431
Orpen, Richard Theo. 48, 207
Orr, Alex. Stewart ... 258
— Charles Wm. James ... 176
— Hy. Montague Cave 246
— John Boyd ... 245
— John Loch ... 436
— Michael Harrison ... 259
— Sutherland A. Mackay 440
— Walter Hood ... 457
— William John ... 53, 413
Orton, Ernest Fred. ... 348
Osborn, George ... 170
— Lestock L. Hatton ... 176
— Oliver Edward ... 214
— Philip Barlow ... 287
— Wm. Lushington ... 279
Osborne, E. F. Fitzroy 158
— George F. F. ... 214
— Robert T. ... 386
— Walter ... 186
Osburne, John ... 381
O'Shea, Timothy ... 306
O'Shee, George I. P. P. ... 346
— Richard A. P. ... 212
Osmaston, Cecil A. F. ... 398
Osmond, Thos. Young 185
Ostrehan, F. Geo. Rodney 421
O'Sullivan, Daniel ... 380
— Gerald Hope Wildig 58, 208
— Hugh Dermod E. ... 401
— Patrick Joseph ... 379
Oswald, Julian ... 69, 158
— St. Clair ... 145
— William Alex. ... 428
O'Toole, James ... 362
Ottley, George Fred ... 295
— Glendower George ... 295
— *Rev.* Herbert T. ... 460
— John Walter ... 42, 206
— William John ... 347
Oughterson, Jas. C. ... 61, 366
Ouseley, Ralph Glynn ... 174
Outram, Fras. Davidson 213
Ovens, Gerald Hedley 58, 278
— Robert Montgomery 282
Overton, Cecil R. ... 243
— Edw. Fenwick ... 305
— Harry Rudall ... 177
Owen, Charles Cunliffe 172
— Chas. Harold Wells ... 177
— Chas. Rd. Blackstone 176
— Charles William ... 454
— Edw. Roderic ... 63, 261
— Eldred Owen ... 423
— Frederick Cunliffe ... 175
— George Pridham ... 51, 167
— Henry O'Brien ... 57, 168
— Henry Mostyn ... 141
— Ivon Trevor ... 293
— John Fletcher ... 7, 164
— Richard ... 63, 163
Owen, Robert Heylock ... 284
— Roger Carmichael R. 287
— Sydney Lloyd ... 213
— *Lieut.* William ... 287
— *Surg. Major* William 454
Owen-Lewis, A. Fras. ... 259
— Francis ... 314
Owens, Francis Charles 346
— Robert Léonce ... 258
Oxley, Reginald Stewart 305
— Robert Henry ... 42, 321
Ozanne, Chas. H. ... 402
Ozzard, Fairlie R. ... 456
— Harold Deane ... 281
— Hudson Henry ... 68, 416
Pack-Beresford, C. G. ... 294
— Henry John ... 317
Packard, H. Norrington 176
Packman, Fred. Lord A. 275
Page, George ... 153
— Louis Cecil ... 150
— Robert Burton ... 261
Paget, Alwyn de B. V. 58, 314
— Arthur Henry ... 40, 233
— George Leigh ... 357
— Harold ... 49, 149
— John Byng ... 253
— Victor Fred. Wm. Aug. 172
— Wellesley Lynedoch H. 170
Pain, George Wm. H. 67, 273
— Wyndham Hackett ... 236
Paine, Albert I. ... 305
— Jas. Henry ... 176
Painter, Arnaud C. ... 211
Pakenham, *Hon.* Edw. M. 231
— George de la P. Beresford ... 362
— Harry Francis ... 304
— Hercules Arthur ... 229
— Wm. Wingfield Verner 419
Paleologus, Wm. C. ... 438
Paley, Edw. Groves 46, 160
— George ... 357
— Raymond Edward ... 178
Palin, Gilbert Walter ... 429
— Philip Charles ... 433
— Randle Harry ... 441
Palk, Chas. H. Leet ... 506
— *Hon.* Lawrence C. Walter ... 281
Pallin, Daniel C. ... 395
Palmer, *Sir* Arth. Power 6, 405
— Arthur Steuart ... 311, 370
— *Rev.* C. J. ... 457
— Cecil Charles ... 177
— Cecil Howard ... 273
— Cyril Eustace ... 176
— Edward ... 453
— Fred. Edm. Corbett ... 311
— Gerald Steuart ... 362
— Harry Douglas ... 401
— Henry Ingham E. ... 429
— Hugh Robert ... 174
— *Sir* Roger W. H. *Bart.* 162
— William ... 372
— William Henry ... 400
— William Legh ... 213
Palmes, George C. ... 61, 267
— Gerald Lindsay ... 238
— Philip ... 291
Panet, Alphonse E. ... 213
Pank, Philip Durrell ... 454
Panton, John Gerald ... 279
Panter-Downes, Edw. M. 258
Parakh, Dhanjisha N. ... 529
Paris, Archibald ... 398
Parish, Chas. W. ... 66, 400
Park, Cecil William ... 59, 249
Parke, Laurence ... 314
— Roger Kennedy ... 45, 138
— *Sir* William ... 318
Parken, Philip Hugh ... 175
Parker, Arthur ... 147
— Denham ... 136
— Erasmus Darwin ... 309
— Frederick James ... 292
— Frederick Thomas ... 140
— George ... 151
— George Hastings ... 281
— George Marcus G. ... 441
— Gilbert Lewes ... 291
— Harry P. England ... 432
— Hy. Wm. Manwaring 175
— Herb. W. England ... 267
— *Rev.* Harry C. ... 507
— James ... 433
— James Henry ... 401
— John George ... 333

Index—Active List. 568.

Parker, John Lewes...... 172
— John Wm............ 69, 417
— John Wm. R. 55, 259
— Joseph 529
— Lionel Lewis 176
— Neville Fraser......21, 404
— Neville Thornton...... 432
— Robert Hamilton...... 176
— St. John W. Topp 288, 367
— Walter Augustus 379
— William 185
— William Frederic.... 356
— William Jackson ...22, 407
Parkin, Arthur 272
— Francis Hearle......... 282
— Henry 420
— John Wm. Brooke 41, 366
Parkinson, Fran. Russell 283
— Frederick F. 372
— James Robert 67, 281
— Percival George 369
Parlby, Reginald J. Hall 249
Parmiter, Chas. Lister 244
Parnell, Hon. Henry...... 6
Parr, Clements 287
— Harington Owen 436
— Henry Hallam 20
— Rev. Willoughby C.... 393
Parrott, Ben. Alex. H. 47, 412
Parry, Claud Fred. P.... 176
— Edgar Rowe 457
— Edward Cecil M. 237
— Henry Jules 384
— James Bacchus......... 173
— Rev. John Horndon... 507
— John J. B. Jones 276
— Llewellyn Humffreys 172
— Morris Vivian 281
— William 308
Parsons, Cecil............... 236
— Chas. Sim B.......49, 168
— Clement George 424
— Cunliffe M'Neile 400
— Durie.................... 292
— Edw. H. Thornbrough 175
— Edward M. Kinnaird 277
— Fred. Charles Alfred 439
— Harold Dan. Edm 236, 370
— James Henry 418
— Lawrence W. 50, 167
— William 368
Partridge, Richard G. ... 176
Paske, Gordon H. 210
Pasley, Montagu W. S... 173
— Sir T. E. Sabine, Bt... 293
Passingham, Robert
  Townshend Anwyl- 433
Passy, Harry Everard.66, 415
Patch, Arthur T. L. 505
— Francis Robert......... 175
— Robert 116, 409
Paterson,Alex.Martin 44, 255
— Edward Hamilton ... 170
— Ewing 148
— Harry Foljambe 377
— Henry 27, 409
— Hugh Aug. Lawrence 209
— John.................... 384
— Somerled Lorn 348
— Stanley............ 68, 337
— Walter Herbert 275
Paton, Donald R. 309
— George 18
— John Archibald......... 238
— William 178
Patten, Archibald......... 338
— Geo. R. B. ... 68, 160, 374
— Wm. Henry......27, 205
Pattenson, A. H. Tylden 237
Patterson, Alfred S. 296
— Charles D. 132
— Edward 290
— Henry M'Neale........ 434
— Rev. Robert S. 396
— Stewart B. Agnew ... 236
Pattison, Richard P. D. 337
Patton-Bethune,Douglas
  E. Bethune 57
— Herbert B. 145
— Walter Douglas 317
Paul, Denis 185
— Ernest Moncrieff 212
— Ernest Theodore 418
— Gerard Robert C. 367
— Geo. William Rebsch 282
— James R. A. Hunter 256
— Robert Sears........... 438
Paulet, Francis Edw.... 163

Paulson, John 178
Pavy, Francis 130
Paxton, A. Fra. Piakney 432
Payn, David Elgar 295
— Sir William 255
— William Arthur 297
Payne, Alex. Vaughan... 308
— Arthur Trelawny 314
— Charles 290
— Charles Herbert ...5c, 321
— Edward Henry......... 437
— Henry 147
— Herbert Chidgey B... 310
— Richard Lloyd......69, 252
Paynter, Camborne H... 148
Peach, Edmund 430
Peacock, Ed. Hodding 69,256
— Rev. Frank ....
— Edward Barnes......... 441
— Ferdinand Mansel ... 252
— Henry Barnes 434
— Henry P............18, 403
— Pryce 209
Peacocke, Chas. Leslie 174
— George................. 361
— Goodricke Thomas ... 273
— J. C. Harding......... 529
— Thos. George 395
— William 48, 207
Peake, Malcolm 173
— Walter King 293
Pearce, Charles Ross ... 506
— Fras. Barrow 253
— Robert 280
Pearce-Serocold, E...... 305
Peard, Henry James ... 381
Pearless, Chas. Wm.... 276
Pears, Maurice L......... 270
— Thos. Caldwell....61, 414
Pearse, Albert 385
— Elford 348
— Geo. Godfrey......... 180
— Hugh Wodehouse 61, 275
— James Langford...... 297
— Sydney Arthur 431
— Tom Harry Finch ... 274
Pearson, Alf. Astley 51, 414
— Rev. Arthur Charles 460
— Arthur James ... 41, 165
— Charles Coffin 287
— Sir Charles Knight... 5
— Francis Campbell 58, 146
— George 259
— Hugh Drummond ... 214
— Hugh Fred. Archie. 436
— Hugh Pearce 16
— John 372
— Robert Frederick...... 237
— Walter Bagot......... 261
— William 256
Peart, Denis George.... 434
— George Rich.......24, 408
Pease, Henry Thomas... 395
— Lawrence W. ...295, 369
— Leonard Thales......... 398
— Peat, Walter Scott...24, 404
Pechell, Aug. Alex. 381
— Chas. Aug. Kerr 305
— Mark Horace Kerr... 305
Peck, Arthur Wharton 439
— Edward Surman 457
— Eustace M............... 329
— Francis Samuel 455
— John Herbert........... 438
Pedder, Ernest Wm. N. 155
Pedley, Oswald H. 334
— Stanhope Humphrey 294
Pedroza, Francis H...... 504
Peebles, Allan L. 249
— Arthur Stansfield...... 250
— Evelyn Chiappini..... 245
Peeke, Harold Samuel... 384
Peel, Arthur................ 21
— Edw. John Russell ... 176
— Frederick...... 67, 209
— Reginald Arthur H... 134
— William Croughton... 138
Poile, Alfred James 175
— Fred. Babington 46, 412
— Schofield Patten 400
— Solomon Chas. F....47, 416
Peirse, Chas. Edward... 418
Pell, Beauchamp T....... 236
Pellew, Fleetwood Hugo 253
Pelly, Rev. C. H. 507
— Henry Joseph........... 513
— John Stannus........... 278
Pemberton, Arthur R.65, 356
— Charles Edward 301

Pemberton, E. St. Clair 209
— Robert 505
Pengelley, George F. 40, 397
Pengree, Hy. Hewitt 51, 167
Pennant, Frank Douglas 305
Pennefather, W. V. 285
Pennell, Henry Lee ...68, 136
— Henry Singleton 290
— Richd. Henry Edm.... 238
Pennethorne, Henry E. 175
Pennington, A. Watson 245
— Chas. Richard 10, 406
— Richard L. Arthur 59, 240
— William Herbert 440
Penno, FitzRoy S. L. 35, 285
Penny, Arthur Taylor... 281
— Rev. Frank 507
— Francis Henry .. 61, 347
— Jeremiah 506
Pennycuick, John....21, 219
Pennyman, Alf. Worsley 269
Penrose, Cooper ...65, 209
— Edward R. 418
Pentland, Robert Chas.65,348
— Herbert Edward...46, 412
— Richard Hugh 384
Pepper, George 308
Percival, Charles Cecil.. 211
— Claude John 173
— Edward M. 171
— John Maxwell 250
— Philip 177
Perceval, Ar. Jex-Blake 240
— Claud V. Noble........ 357
Percy, Robt. Fitz Gerald 40
— William Francis 245
— Wm. Frank Graham 161
Pereira, Arch. Fred. 255, 374
— Cecil Edward........... 231
— Frank Charles 506
— George Edward........ 290
Perkins, Arthur J. E. ... 174
— Æneas............... 5, 218
— Æneas Charles 237
— Charles George........ 140
— John C. 139
— John Chas. Campbell 436
— Norman Chichester... 422
Perreau,ArthurMontagu 176
— Gustavus Arthur...... 347
Perrin, Chas. Louis 441
— Joseph 292
Perrott, Thomas 50, 167
— William H. Willy...... 174
Perry, Allan 382
— Charles Smith 19
— Francis Frederic 454
— George 378
— George Edgar John... 439
— Henry Robert P. 254
— Hugh Whitchurch 171, 369
— S.J.ChattertonPrittie 386
— William Change 178
— Persse, William Arthur 173
— William Horsley 137
Pery, Cecil Charles J.... 211
Petavel, Jas. Wm......... 213
— Paul Gregory 276
Peterkin, Arthur H. 380
Peters, Cecil Wyburn 49, 146
— Charles T. 529
— Edward Nicolls....22, 204
— John Weston P........ 142
— Leonard Chris. 400
— Phillip Michael........ 246
Peterson, F. Hopewell... 435
— Cecil Herbert 435
— Petre, Bernard James... 435
— Charles Bernard 305
— Henry Cecil 225
— Petrie, Charles L. Rowe 309
— Ricardo Dartnell 210
Peyton, Algernon George 424
— Charles Talbot......... 210
— Francis 285
— Jones Lloyd 379
— Lumley Scobell ...68, 416
— William Eliot 400
Phayre, Arthur 420
Phelps, Arthur......285, 367
— Malet Peyton 289
Phibbs, Wm. G. Baynes 310
Philipps, Ivor 429
Philips, Burton Henry... 265
— Francis Charles 139
— James 21, 405

Philips, Jas. Joseph...... 395
— Joseph 13, 399
— Robert Edward......... 237
— Phillipps, Charles......... 174
— Picton 398
— Phillips, Alfred Lucian 425
— Charles 395
— Charles Reginald...... 417
— Ernest Robert 175
— Frank Truscott......... 401
— George Edward........ 211
— George Fraser 253
— Henry Bannerman ... 285
— Henry George Coates 285
— Henry Walter 372
— Herb. de Touffreville 171
— John Campbell 214
— Rev. Lionel F. 460
— Lewis Francis 305
— Lewis Horace....57, 245
— Richard Sylvester ... 440
— Robt. W. Fergusson 43, 275
— Major Gen. Thomas... 7
— Qr. Mr. Thomas 386
— Thomas Brocklehurst 155
— Thomas Richmond ... 174
— Thomas V. W.....59, 168
— Walter Ernest 422
— William 186
— Phillipson, Richard W.B. 142
— Phillott, Douglas C...... 423
— Phillpotts,A.H.Croker 53,168
— Louis Murray 176
— Philson, Samuel Cowell 383
— Phipps, Charles Edw... 174
— Charles Foskett 177
— Edgar Vivian A. 381
— Henry Ramsay........ 178
— Pownoll Ramsay 283
— Pickard, F. B. B. 236
— Pickup, William......... 185
— Pickwond,Edwin Hay 53, 167
— Picot, Francis Slater ... 308
— Henry Philip 68, 416
— Pidgeon Francis 254
— Pierce, Fred. George... 436
— Robert Campbell...... 271
— Piercy, Benj. Herbert ... 154
— John Morpott....47, 283
— Piers, Hy. Octavius...61, 169
— Wm. Barrington 421
— Pierson, John Ernest... 279
— Pigott, Arthur F. H. ... 278
— C. Berkeley 49, 163
— Grenville Edmund 26 5,368
— Vincent Randolphe... 264
— Wellesley George 356
— Pigou, Fred. Hugo 436
— Pike, Cecil Fras. B. ... 213
— Markham J. W........ 333
— Walter Nathaniel...... 286
— William Watson 381
— Pilcher, Arthur John ... 212
— Edgar Montagu 385
— Jesse Griggs............ 452
— Thomas David 240
— Pile, Lionel Lewis 274
— Pilgrim, Herbert W.... 455
— Pilkington, Fred. C.... 157
— Herbert W. Malony... 360
— Thos. Edw. Milborne-
  Swinnerton............ 304
— W. Alex. Cunningham 176
— Pilleau, Arthur Langston 431
— Henry Charles 236
— Pilloy, William.......... 159
— Pilson, Arthur F. 348
— Pim, Edward Hugh... 175
— John 246
— Pinches, Wm. Hooper... 383
— Pinching, B. Henderson 182
— Pine-Coffin, John E.... 291
— Pinhey, Alex. F. 427
— Arthur Worsley S. ... 297
— Pinhorn, Henry Quinten 274
— Pink, Francis John ... 236
— Pinney, Charles Fredk. 357
— John Chas. Digby ... 437
— Pinto, Joseph O. 506
— Pinwill, Wm. Richd... 244
— Pipe-Wolferstan, H. F. 209
— Piper, Thomas 288
— Pipon, Henry.......28, 165
— Philip Gosset.......... 164
— Pirie, Arthur Murray ... 163
— Chas. Patrick Wm. ... 421
— Duncan Vernon....... 145

Index—Active List.

Pirie, Tyrell Gordon...... 321
Pirrie, Francis Wm...... 435
Pisani, Lionel J............ 455
Pitcairn, Andw. Holford 318
— Robt. Henry 286
Pitcher, Duncan Geo. 24, 408
Pitman, Alfred C........ 174
— Thomas Tait 153
Pitt, Douglas C. Dean 31, 167
— Thomas M. Stanhope 143
— William 52, 207
Plant, Wm. Arthur ...57, 168
Platt, Arthur Herbert ... 286
— Ernest H. R. C. R. ... 252
— Harold Esmond 272
— Henry Verco 346
Playfair, Alan............ 436
— Charles Murray 177
— Elliot Minto 180
— Fredk. H. Grant 281
— Frederick Lyon...... 173
— *Hon.* Geo. James 45, 166a
— Norman Ernest....... 269
— William Morgan 371
Plomer, Alfred Durham 244
— Wm. H. Percival 333
Plowden, Fran. Hugh 51, 287
— Trevor Chichele 438
— Walter F. C. C. ... 63, 415
Plowman, *Rev.* H. W. T. 460
Plumbe, John Hulke 69, 400
Plumer, Herbert C.O.65, 311
— Thomas Hall 422
Plummer, Edm. Waller 176
— Plunkett, Arthur W. V. 309
— Edward Abadie 246
— Robt. Hastings W. 43, 166
Pochin, Richd. Norman 275
Pocklington, Evelyn B.
.... 49, 287
— George Henry 130
— Harry Evelyn S...... 157
Pocock, Herbert Innes... 384
— Philip Frederick 440
Poett, Joseph H. 59, 283
Pogson, Fred. George58, 254
Poignand, George 28
Poingdestre, Alfred..... 427
Pole-Carew, Reg. 22, 231
Pollard, Arthur E....... 278
— Benj. Horatio 46, 412
— Chas. William Dutton 346
— James Hawkins W.... 262
— James Herbert 430
— Wm. Charles 418
Pollard-Urquhart, Fras.
Edw. Romulus ...50, 167
Pollen, Stephen H....... 308
Pollitt, Thomas H. 244
Pollock, A. J. Osborne 47, 262
— Arthur W. A. 68, 252
— Arthur Julius 172
— Charles Edward ... 385
— Charles Fred........ 378
— Evelyn 171
— Fred. George........ 417
— John Arch. Henry 68, 416
— Percy Napier........ 362
Pollok, John Buchanan 286
— Oswald Fergusson ... 347
— Wm. P. Morris 160
Polwhele, Reginald 214
Pomeroy, Edm. John ... 361
— *Hon.* Ralph Legge... 140
Pond, Alex. Donald C. 423
Ponsonby, Edw. F. T.... 177
— F. Edward G......... 230
— *Rt. Hon.* Sir H. F. ... 1
— John 231
— Justinian G. 43, 293
Poole, Arthur Edward... 152
— Arthur Jas.... 242
— David 361
— Francis Garden 254
— Frederick Cuthbert... 175
— Gabriel Roland R..... 45
— Gerald Robert 398
— Walter Croker 384
— Walter Croker T..... 381
— Wm. Thos. Conway 439
Poore, Fra. Harwood 27, 397
— Robert Montagu 149
Pope, Thomas Henry ... 505
— William Wippell 380
Popplestone, Wm. H.... 185
Porcelli, Ernest.....51, 207
Porch, Cecil P........... 275
Porcher, Alec Francis 177

Porcher, Cecil George ... 264
Portal, Bertram Percy... 159
Porteous, Charles A. 19, 406
— Charles M'Leod 435
— James Edward......43, 410
— John James 67, 169
Porter, Atwell Robt. 53, 413
— Cyril Lachlan 237
— Frederick 289
— Fred. Joseph Wm..... 385
— Geoffrey M. 65, 209
— George Adrian 237
— Harry Edwin Bruce 386
— Herbert Alfred 161
— Herbert Edward ... 419
— Mansel Loudon 305
— Reginald W. 69, 287
— Robert 380
— Thomas Cole 50, 141
Porterfield, Bolden D. 58, 186
Potter, Henry 371
— Henry Wm. Ross ... 258
Pottinger, Eldred Chas. 175
— Robert Southey 439
Potts, Frederick 174
— Henry Charles George 227
— John Wm. H. 52, 167
Poulter, Creighton M'Crea 431
— Douglas Ryley 176
Poulton, Arthur F. 250
Povah, John Richard ... 45
Powell, Albert Lawrence 161
— Atherton ff......... 170
— Baden F. S. Baden... 233
— Benj. Aug. W. 395
— Caleb K............. 379
— Charles Herbert ... 418
— Edgar Elkins....... 385
— Edw. Weyland Martin 176
— Fred. Acton Lambert 171
— George 230
— Harold Haines 542
— Henry George 291
— Henry Lloyd 174
— James 379
— John Joseph Charles 178
— Nathaniel J. H....... 434
— Robt. S. S. Baden- 61, 155
— Sidney Henry 211
— Simpson 382
— *Rev.* William Bassett 506
— William Bowen..... 435
Power, Altred Rich 295
— Chas. Herford 278
— Edward Richard ... 379
— Elliott D. Le Poer ... 357
— Frederick Edward 49, 292
Powis, Henry........... 252
Powles, Thomas Wm.67, 169
Powlett, Norton 42, 166
— Thos. Charles Orde 47, 292
Powys, John L.......... 287
Poynder, Chas. Eliot ... 417
— George Frederick ... 380
— John Leopold 505
Poyntz, Arthur Vernon 233
Poynton, Edw. Morris 59, 252
Poyntz, Henry Wm..... 289
Poyser, Richard........ 455
Prain, David 455
Prall, Cedric B......... 457
Prasad, Kanta 456
Pratt, Alfred Gilbert ... 288
— Arth. Spencer ...58, 169
— Ernest G. Wilberforce 176
— Ernest St. George ... 314
— Henry Arthur 173
— Henry Marsh 16, 406
— Jas. Bonham Tod... 269
— James John......... 455
— Wm. Simson 378
Prendergast, Chas L. 25, 424
— Charles Gordon 431
— Donald Guy 284
— Frederick 174
— Frederick Lenox 400
— Gerald Neill........ 305
— James Henry 19, 406
— Theodore John W. ... 209
— William Henry 434
Prentice, Herbert 212
— Robert E. Shepherd 317
Prentis, Walter S. 439
Presgrave, Edwd. R. J. 66, 416
Pressey, Arthur 427

Prest, Edw. Papillon ... 250
Preston, Alex. Fras...... 377
— Arthur Thomas ... 47, 207
— D'Arcy Brownlow ... 171
Eyre Evans 440
— Fred. George 67, 416
— George Allen 440
— George Berthon 137
— Jenico Edward ... 68, 416
— *Rev.* Wm. Babington 532
— Wm. John Phaelim... 301
Pretyman, Geo. Tindal 18, 165
Prevost, George Herbert 440
— George William 156
Price, Adolphus J. ...49, 253
— Alfred Ernest.....236, 369
— Bartholomew George 243
— Charles Henry U..... 426
— Cyril Uvedale....... 436
— George Dominic 361
— Geo. Richardson...51, 167
— Gordon............ 453
— Rhys.............. 285
— Richard 185
— Robert Kenrick 237
— Thos. Herbert Fras... 276
— Thos. Rose Caradoc 294
— William 504
— William Locking.... 455
— Wm. Sparks M....... 377
Price-Dent, Phillip H.... 249
Prichard, Chas. Stewart 292
— Geo. Penry M. 417
— Gordon Fairfax 246
— Herbert Christie 292
— Hubert Cecil 398
— Prickard, Harry S. ... 310
Prickett, Thomas 42
Prideaux, Francis B. ... 439
— Philip Edward...... 387
— Robert A....... 40, 404a
— William Francis ...25, 206
— Pridham, Frederick ... 369
— Geoffrey Robert 214
Pridmore, Walter George 506
Priestley, Chas. E. Nixon 434
— E. J. Kenworthey 55, 168
— F. J. Blakiston 420
— George William 428
— Henry Wood 424
Prince, Wm. C. S. 436
Pring, John 223
Pringle, Alexander ...63, 415
— Chas. Herford 278
— Geo. Octavius Shaw... 174
— John Wallace....... 211
— Robert 395
Prinsep, A. Haldimand 7, 403
Prioleau, Lynch H..... 309
Prior, Arthur W. 63, 310
— George Upton 16
— Herbert M.......... 419
— John Edw. Hale ... 29, 282
— William 423
Prissick, Cuthbert 361
Pritchard, Alfred B..... 421
— Aubrey Gordon 439
— C. Hamerton 427
— Olive Gordon 439
— Colin Chas. Henry ... 237
— Frank Vernon L...... 441
— Harry Lionel 213
— Harry Torriano 434
— Henry Edward 431
— Osborn Brace....... 285
Probyn, Dighton Gordon 176
Profait, Charles William 386
Propert, Douglas John 357
Prothero, Archer Geo. ... 285
— Freke L........... 285
Protheroe, Montague 18, 407
Proudfoot, Andrew W.53, 413
— James George 41, 410
Prowse, Chas. Bertie ... 252
— Geo. W. Thursby.... 276
Pryce, Doug. Davidson 47, 412
— Henry E. ap Rhys ... 362
Pryce-Browne, Wm. H. 401
Prynne, Harold Vernon 386
— Reginald P......... 401
Puckle, John 268, 368
Pulford, Russell R... 43, 206
Pullen, Arthur Fox 172
Pulley, Charles.....51, 414
Pulleine, Henry P...... 267

Pulling, *Rev.* Edw. Herb. 396
Pulteney, Wm. Pulteney 233
Purcell, Matthew H. 45, 209
Purchas, Charles 369
— Edgar Patrick Carnac 253
— John R. Philip 284
— William Robert ... 44, 206
Purdon, David Wm...... 420
— Henry Geo........58, 291
— John James 63, 271
Purdy, Robert 48, 166a
Purves, Henry Black ... 452
Purvis, Alex. R. 58, 163
— Eyre Walter Molyneux 251
— Herbert John Edw.... 433
— John Allen R. ... 145, 367
— John Henry 317
— John Spottiswoode ... 211
Pusey, Edw. Bouverie... 259
Pye, Wm. Edmund 289
Pym, Edward Lawes 12, 397
— Fred. Harry Norris... 398
— H. Reginald Lookyer 398
— John Beville 401
— Samuel 28, 165
Pyne, Chas. E. Menzies 241
— Edward Ernest... 52, 399
— William Menzies ... 213
Quain, John 176
Qualtrough, Wm. John 315
Quayle, W. Adair 505
Quentin, Walter 418
Queripel, Alfred Ernest 395
Quicke, F. Churchill ... 136
— Wm. Henry.......... 509
Quill, Berkeley Crosbie 55, 311
— John Jerome.....51, 399
— Rich. Henry 378
Quin, Edward 40, 409
— Richd. P. Wemyss ... 279
— Thomas 424
— Thomas James.....23, 404
— W. H. Wyndham....65, 158
Quinn, John Jas. P..... 213
Quinton, Francis W. D. 174
Quirk, John Owen... 45, 285
Raban, Edward 53, 208
Raby, Montague H. B. 173
Radcliff, Samuel Garnett 425
Radcliffe, Alfred Ernest 238
— Arthur W. T....66, 415
— Charles Delmé 334
— Frederick Walter.... 283
— Geo. B. Edmund...47, 412
— Henry Delmé........ 265
— Frederick Walter ... 283
— Jasper Fitzg........ 249
— Nathaniel Robert.... 244
— Percy P. de Blaquiere 178
— Philip J. Joseph 212
— Robert E. Lowndes... 173
— Robert Parker 164
— William C. Allred.... 172
— Sir Wm. Pollexfen ... 261
— William Scott Warley 297
Radolyffe, Chas. Edw. 357
— Chas. Percy Fred..... 357
Radford, Frederick John 289
— Oswald Claude...52, 414
Radice, Alfred Hutton 272
Raikes, Arthur Edw. H. 308
— Frank S. W......59, 356
— Frederick Duncan 47, 412
Railston, H. Edward..... 44
Raines, *Sir* Julius A. R. 237
Rainey, Edm. Flower ... 435
— Robert Maximilian... 425
Rainsford, John Aug. G. 437
— Marcus Edw. R. ...40, 306
— Stephen Dickson...55, 168
— William John Read... 379
Rainsford-Hannay, F.65, 209
— Ramsay Wm. 42, 166a
Raitt, Arthur Douglas... 236
— Francis J........... 204
— G. Dalhousie C. ...65, 397
— Henry Geo. Bowen ... 429
— Herbert Avoling 282
Ralli, Antonio Stephen... 154
— John 234
Ralph, Alfred Colyer ... 437
— Arthur Jeffreys...... 433
Ralston, Alex. William... 310
— James 273
— Wm. Henry......... 7
Rampini, Fred. Chas.... 436
Ramsay, Arthur D. G.... 273
— George 457

Ramsay, Henry Lushington 67, 415	Reddie, John Murray 273	Rice, George William 175
— Herbert Maynard 25, 404	Redfern, Peter Y. 175	— Gerard B. Howard 333
— Herbert Murray 353	Redl, E. A. Fred. 238	— Harry A. Harington 440
— John 428	Reece, John Deane 348	— Henry Garde 47, 366
— John George 69, 416	Reed, Edmund Martin 426	— Hugh Rosoetor 283
— Thomas Burnett 356	— Hamilton Lyster 175	— Sheridan Knowles B. 441
— William Alexander 49, 146	Rees, Fred. Fras. Nigel 213	— Sidney Mervyn 441
Ramsden, Caryl John 318	Rees-Webbe, M. O. N. 292	— Spring Robert 209
— Henry 177	Reeve, John Sherard 230	— William Roche 454
— Herbert F. S. 51, 417	— William T. M. 346	Rich, Charles Carroll 50, 167
Rance, George 242	Reeves, Fras. Casement 505	— Charles Lionel M. 426
Randall, John 436	— Frederick Spencer 237	— Edmund Tillotson 214
— Rich. G. Bruxner 51, 261	— John 51, 333	— Harold Hampden 171
— Rev. Wm. Sidney 396	— Paget Edw. Stuart 346	— W. Harry Derville 421
Randolph, Alfred H. 69, 209	Reger, Fritz P. 258	Richard, Rev. O. H. 209
— Algernon Forbes 301	Reid, Adam Scott 453	Richards, Arthur Carew 281
— Charles Foyle 261	— Alex. John Forsyth 28, 411	— Arthur W. M. 144
— Francis Arthur 173	— Charles Clements 426	— Bernard Ogilvio 273
Ranken, George Patrick 422	— Chas. Lestock Onslow 432	Rev. Chas. Hen. 507
Rankin, Chas. Herbert 149	— Doug. Paynter S. 291	— Charles Herbert 267
Ranking, W. Lancaster 23, 404	— Ellis Ramsay 372	— E. Danbeny Griffith 282
— G. Spiers A. 453	— Francis Maude 48, 317	— Edw. Willoughby 431
Ransford, Charles 40, 404	— George Elliot 438	Geo. Westley 293
Ransom, James Mann 426	— Harrie Archbold 46, 149	— Hamilton Macd. 66, 278
Ransome, Robert S. 266	— Harold Arthur 174	— Harold Coston 160
Raper, Allan Graeme 23	— James 374	— Henry Moredyth 265
Raphael, Fred. M. 284	— James Henry E. 68, 269	— James Saurin 434
Rathborne, Hans Robert 372	— James More 382	— John Richard H. 61, 236
— Wm. Hans. 28, 205	— John Leslie 141	— Mordaunt Cyril 240
Rattigan, Herbert Wm. 269	— John Watt 174	— Vancouver Alexander 249
Rattray, Charles 436	— Lestock Hamilton 420	— William 278
— Haldane Burney 439	— Samuel 298	Richardson, Alex. Edw. 395
— Rullion Hare 420	Reilly, B. Lewis Philip 53, 413	— Arthur Fra. George 51, 234
Raven, Alex. Wm. N. 438	— Charles Cooper 382	— A. Johnstone 254
— John C. H. 335	— Charles William 384	— Charles William 171
Ravenhill, Collingwood 176	— Edwin William 505	— Chas. William Grant 427
— Edward H. G. 28	— James 395	— Fras. Bernard Walter 421
— Edgar Evelyn 237	— John 308	— Francis James 337
— Fred. Thornhill 174	— John Aug. Herbert 306	— Frederick 178
— Harold William 178	— Rawdon Edward D. 50, 414	— Geo. Lloyd Reilly 44, 411
— Harry Stuart 262	Reily, Alex. Yates 384	— Henry J. R. S. 57, 244
Ravenscroft, Herbert V. 309	Reiss, Edw. Leopold 141	— Herbert Lance 431
Ravenshaw, Chas. W. 61, 414	Rennick, A. de Clancy 41, 410	— James Jardine 153
— Harold Alex. 418	— Frank 432	— John 317
— Hurdis S. Lalaude 249	— Robert H. Francis 26, 409	— John Booth 17, 165
Rawling, Cecil Godfrey 252	Rennie, Coverley J. 246	— Lionel James 156
Rawlins, Arthur Kennedy 439	— George A. Paget 305	— Richard 368
— George William 425	— John George 286	— Robert Mervyn 156
— Henry de C. 48, 270	— Samuel James 381	— Walter Fairfax 274
— Richard Walter 292	Renny, Alex. MacW. 66, 411	— Wm. Keane 61, 264
— Sebastian White 18	— George Blakiston 61, 414	— Wm. St. John 69, 417
Rawlinson, Chas. Brooke 432	— George Marjoribanks 284	— Wodehouse D. 40, 366
— George Brooke M. 276	— Henry 291	Richey, Thos. Duncan 53, 186
— Henry Seymour 231	— Henry Thomas 337	Richmond, George 214
— Spencer Rich. 46, 411	— Sidney Mercer 171	— Richard Olifte 371
— Wilfred Romney 244	Renny-Tailyour, H. W. 52, 207	Rickard, Frank Martin 177
— Wm. Cecil Welch 246	— Thos. Fras. Bruce 211	— Victor Geo. Howard 347
Rawnsley, Claude 367	Renton, Colin Campbell 435	Rickards, Alan W. Low 58, 234
— Gerald Thomas 384	— Robert Ross 430	— Edward 137
Rawson, Court. Clarke 46, 206	— William Gordon 159	— Frank Stuart H. 348
— Herbert Edward 59, 208	Renwick, Charles Henry 245	Ricketts, Henry Carew 434
— Robert Ian 272	Reporter, Maneckjee E. 505	— Lancelot Hamilton 437
Rawstorne, Geo. A. L. 47, 397	Repton, Fred. Wm. 423	— Percy Edward 437
— Lawrence 149	Retallick, John M. A. 417	— Robert Lumsden 411
Ray, Geo. L. Sidney 240	Rettie, Wm. J. Kerr 175	— Theophilus Fred. W. 346
— Grattan Geo. O'Neil 242	Rew, Alex. R. C. 310	— William Symonds Perceval 530
— MacCarthy R. Emmet 437	— Chas. E. D. O. 360	Rickman, Graham E. 265
Raye, D. O'Connell 452	Reynolds, Arth. Reynold 211	— Stuart Hamilton 357
Rayment, G. Jos. Robert 395	— Cecil Edward 169	Riddell, Albert Edward 290
Raymond, Elliott A. 371	— Rev. O. H. 460	— Edw. Vausittart Dick 178
— Francis 395	— Edward Osmund 379	— Henry Edw. Buchanan 304
— George 384	— Edw. Swatman 16, 408	— Henry James 440
— Harry Elliott 259	— Frank Romilly 209	— Henry Vansittart 410
— Henry Phipps 234	— James C. 65, 285	— James Foster 240
— Rev. P. F. 396	— James Henry 378	— Robert Barnham 177
— Radcliffe Herbert 438	— Philip Guy 140	— Robt. G. Buchanan 61, 304
— Richard Wellington 395	— Sidney Latimer 367	— Robert Vansittart 26, 218
Rayner, Hugh 383	— Thomas G. Campbell 271	— William Carre 47, 348
Rea, Frederick Wm. 432	Rhodes, Bernard M. 171	— William Henry 61, 255
— James 269	— Elmhirst 66, 293	Riddick, John 378
Read, Harold W. K. 385	Fra. William 24	Rideout, Fred. Chas. W. 422
— Hastings 63, 415	— James Havelock Alex. 380	Ridgeway, R. Kirby 46, 412
Reade, Arthur Revell 285	— John 146	Ridgway, Richard T. L. 435
— Edward Revell 274	— John Edward 305	Ridley, Alfred Bayley 238
— George Edward 24, 404	— William Thomas B. 285	— Chas. Parker 49, 309
— Piercy Nevill G. 176	Riach, Arthur H D. 213	— Edward Keane 283
— Raymond N. R. 297	— John 146	— Henry Matthew 55, 149
— William Lloyd 381	— Malcolm S. 288	Ridout, Dudley Howard 211
Reader, Francis Wm. 55, 256	Ricardo, Ambrose St. Q. 271	Rigan, Charles M. 348
Ready, Basil Tobin 285	— Francis Cecil 57, 220	Rigby, Gerard Chris 308
— Felix Fordati 293	— Harry Wm. Ralph 159	— John Cecil Heagren 401
Reay, Charles Tom 59, 299	— Henry George 170	— Percy George 289
— Ernest Herbert John 308	— Horace 21, 229	Rigg, Owen Davys 252
Rebsch, Rev. A. W. 460	— Louis Ferdinand 150	— Robt. Addison 55, 168
Reckitt, John D. T. 381	— Wilfred Francis 135	Riley, Thomas 112
Reddie, Anthony J. 268	Riccard, Cecil B. J. 316	Rimington, Jos. Cameron 211
		— Michael F. 148

Rind, A'ex. Thomas Seton Abercromby 44, 411	
Ring, James 378	
Ringe, Richard Hoad 395	
Ringwood, Herbert 67, 275	
Riordan, John 382	
— William Edward 377	
Ripley, George Eustace 292	
Rippon, George 424	
Rising, Robert Edw. 272	
Risk, Edm. John E. 381	
Ritchie, Archibald B. 318	
— Arthur 270	
— Charles MacIver 178	
— James 41	
— James Frederick 161	
— John 384	
— John Robert 173	
Ritherdon, Robt Augustus 486	
Rivaz, Vincent 25, 408	
Rivers, John H. 385	
Rivett-Carnac, Ernest H. 418	
— John Stirling 362	
— Percy T. 63, 277	
— Seymour-Gordon 212	
Roache, Joseph Matthew 370	
Robarts, Rev. Alf. G. A. 460	
— Charles James 65, 415	
Robb, Alex. Kirkland 314	
— Frederick Spencer 314	
Robbins, Henry J. 379	
— Herbert Eyre 57, 40?	
Roberts, Rev. A. G. A. 457	
— Alfred Ernest 456	
— Archibald 436	
— Arthur Colin 243	
— Arthur Noel 367	
— Arthur William 23, 403	
— Charles Percy 177	
— Edward 371	
— Edw. R. B. Stokes 211	
— Hon. Fred. H. Sherston 305	
— Fred. S. Lord 4, 179	
— George Bradley 213	
— Henry Bradley 210	
— Henry Robert 49, 246	
— Hy. Roger Crompton 210	
— Herbert Hodder 400	
— Hereward Llewelyn 429	
— Hugh Bradley 175	
— James Andrew 370	
— James Reid 456	
— Michael Bradley 173	
— Montgomery Browne 432	
— Stanley Napier 45, 244	
— William Prowting 281	
Robertson, Charles 317	
— Charles C. 176	
— Charles L. 212	
— Claude William 401	
— Divie Knighton 47, 145	
— Donald 43, 410	
— Edgar Quartus 269	
— Edm. Elliot 421	
— Edmund Murray 288	
— Francis Andrew 400	
— George Alan 430	
— George Scott 454	
— Rev. James 396	
— Jas. Henry Craig 311	
— John Frederic 334	
— Patrick Francis 43	
— Philip Rynd 270	
— Robert 506	
— Robert William P. 51, 167	
— William 214	
— William Robert 138	
Robertson-Glasgow, R. P. 314	
Robeson, Arth, Hemming 308	
Robin, Nicholas E. 432	
Robins, George 285	
— Lancelot Irby Oxford 285	
Robinson, Arch. Tyrrell 275	
— Chas. Eugene Barnes 362	
— Charles Lucena 261	
— Charles T. 170	
— Charles Walker 7	
— De la Pere 372	
— Edward Heaton 185	
— Francis Wingfield 46, 297	
— Frederick W. Templetown 259	
— George Henry 66, 415	
— George Somerville 379	
— George Tracey 174	
— George Winor 380	
— Godfrey Walker 434	
— Guy Vandeleur 401	

N N

Index—Active List.

Robinson, Harold Arth. 291
— Henry 177
— Hercules Arthur T. . 333
— John Corsane ...28, 165
— John Graham 423
— Marshall 310
— Oliver Long 385
— Percy Morris 294
— Philip Albert 373
— Richard Henry 368
— Richard Percy 217
— Robert Henry 378
— StapyltonChapmanB. 380
— Stratford Watson..... 176
— Sydney Loftus 337
— Thomas 452
— Thomas Middleton .. 373
— Walter Henry 172
— William 178
— William Arthur.......... 173
— Wm. Henry Banner... 455
— William James 297
Robson, Charles Græme 436
— Henry Denne 236
Robson-Scott, Chas. G. 456
Robyns, JohnWilmot 59, 399
Roche, Benjamin Robert 255
— Eugenius Alfred 379
— Henry John 430
— James Stamers 163
— John E. F. H. ... 52, 138
— Thos. H. de M. ... 58, 399
— Hn.UlickDeR.Burke57,267
Rochfort,Alex.Nelson49, 167
Rochfort-Boyd, Charles
  Augustus.....49, 207
Rocke, Walter Leslie ... 308
Roddy, Henry Hugh ... 435
Rodgers, John William 455
Rodick,R.Preston B. 51, 243
Rodon, Geo. Seaforth49, 234
Rodwell, Ernest Hunter 420
— Reginald Mandeville 171
Roe, Bernard Oswald ... 439
— Cyril Harcourt 217
— Edward Charles B.... 400
— Robert Bradley 503
— Wm. Alex. Cranford 453
Roebuck,Fra.H.A.D. 42, 276
Rogers, Claude R. ...52, 333
— Frederick Arthur..... 455
— George Walters ...27, 409
— GeorgeWm.Nisbet ... 19
— Henry Paton 308
— Henry Schofield 213
— John 48, 366
— John Middleton 143
— Leonard 457
— Malcolm William ..27, 205
— Percy Herbert 295
— Walter James 173
Rolfe, Rev. A. Neville ... 460
Rolland, Alexander ... 213
— Alexander T..........18, 405
— Chas. Edw. Tulloch... 178
— Edward Lewis 317
— George Murray 438
— Stuart Erskine ...40, 411
Rollo, Hon. Robert 286
Rolph, William Mogg ... 28
Rolt, Charles Edward ... 173
— Stuart Peter 311
Romanes, Robt. John 57,269
Rombulow-Pearse, A.E. 401
— Alfred Bertie 398
Romer, Cecil Fras. 348
Romilly, Frederick W.51,233
— Hon. J. G. LeM. 231
Ronald, John James ... 317
Ronaldson, Robert Wm.
  Hawthorn.......... 317
Roney-Dougal, Geo. B... 252
Rooke, Alf. Shipton..... 426
— Benjamin P. Simpson 433
— Bertram Hammersley 213
— Cres. Keane O.......... 24
— Everard Home 214
— George Harry John.. 346
— Giles 362
— Harry William ...27, 165
Roome,FrederickM'Iver 284
— Henry Napier 432
— Leslie Stuart 301
— Reginald Eckford ... 435
Rooney, Jas. Patrick ... 378
Roos-Keppel, Geo. Olof 210
Rooth, Richard Alex. ... 348
Roper, Alex. Wm. 210

Roper, Reginald Trevor 263
Rorke, John 285
Rose, Alexander S. 381
— Charles 395
— Charles Ernest 135
— Charles Stuart 211
— Edward Lee.... 25, 339
— Henry Metcalfe ...45, 411
— Hugh (Black Watch) 286
— Hugh (Indian S. C.) 421
— John 310
— John Latham 435
— John Markham 398
Rosher, Henry Louis ... 283
Ross, Alex. Geo. ... 7, 405
— Arch. John Joseph67, 238
— Charles 245
— Charles Edmund 430
— Claye Ross 426
— Edm. James Thomas,
  of Bludensburg ...53, 208
— Fleetwood Geo. 439
— George Cumberland... 452
— Harry 439
— Hew Dalrymple 357
— Horatio St. George ... 173
— James Clarke 371
— Sir John 4
— John Foster Geo., of
  Bludensburg.....53, 231
— John Leith 29
— John William 434
— Rev. Malcolm Munro 533
— Ralph James 411
— Robert James 301
— Ronald 505
— Thomas French ...50, 234
— Tyrell Carter 317
— Walter Charteris 314
Rosseter, Ja..Hurley 51, 167
— Henry Donald.....57, 314
Rotheram, WalterHenry 212
Rotherham, Henry ... 255
Rotton, John Guy 396
Rough, W.EdwardM. 49, 142
Rountree. Rev. H. T. H. 532
Roupell, Fra. Fred.F.49, 275
Rouse, Arch. H. Tylden 440
— Hubert 173
Routh, Jules Isham ... 379
— William Randolph 50, 250
Row, George Russell ... 425
Rowan, Hen. Davis ... 38
— Terence England...57, 168
Rowband, Henry ... 5, 403
Rowcroft, Claude H. 177
— Ernest Cave 435
— George Francis 423
Rowden. H. Wetherell 68,308
Rowe, Ernest Fentiman 255
— Laurence R. Fisher. 229
Octavius 59, 168
— Richard 395
— Wilfred Edward 294
— Wm. Arthur Samuel.. 401
Rowlands, Hugh 4
— Hugh Barrow 250
Rowlandson, Alf.Turner 433
— F. 247
— John 59, 237
— Michael Alexander 22, 407
Rowley, Cecil Alured ... 282
— Charles Robert 22
— Frank G. Mathias..... 301
— John 185
— Robert A. Dick 329
Rowney, William 380
Roy, John W. Gascoigne 289
Royston, Pigott George
  Arthur 292
Ruck, John Egerton ... 272
— Oliver Edwd..........68, 209
— Rd. Matthews.....53, 208
Ruck-Keene, H. L. 287
— Robert Francis 176
Rudd, Henry Percy ... 234
— Hubert 185
Rugge-Price, C. Fred... 175
Ruggles, George 115
Rumbold, Wm. Edwin.. 176
Rundall, Charles Frank 213
— Frank Montague...61, 414
Rundle, Cubitt S. 505
— Frank Peverill 225
— George RichardTyrell 170
— Henry M. L..... 28, 169
Rusbridger, S. H. 236, 374
Rushton, Henry Wm.... 213

Russell, Alex. F 381
— Lord Alex. George ... 356
— Hon. Alex. Victor F. 230
— Allan R. Postance ... 455
— Arch. Wm. Forbes ... 457
— Sir Baker C.......... 5, 155
— Bruce Bremner.......... 210
— Chas. Charles... 44, 166a
— Captain Charles.......... 279
— Edgar G. 403
— Edm. S. E. Wilmot... 175
— Francis Deane 362
— Francis Shirley 17
— George Blakeley 382
— Henry 178
— Henry Cairns Oldnall 174
— Henry John 283
— James W. Harold..... 368
— John 185
— John Cecil 16
— John Joshua 384
— Leonard 274
— Michael William 382
— Vernon Elliott.......... 272
— Walter 210
— William Albert 395
— William Edward 393
— William Kelson 214
— Ruston, Reginald S. ... 249
Rutherford, Arch. H. ... 348
— Charles 395
— James 24, 40 1a
— Rich.DuffinBuckley 50,317
Ruthven, R.M.Berming-
  ham 174
— Hon.W.P.H.Master of 233
Rutter, Eustace F. 274
Ruttledge, Edw. Butler 452
Ruxton. Fred. Chas. 17
Ryall, Charles. 253
— Edw. Chas. 428
Ryan, Chas. Aloysius 53, 167
— Chas. Montgomerie249,358
— Rev. Edward 396
— Michael R. 379
— Robert Fenwick 329
Rycroft, Chas. M. R..... 252
— Wm. Henry 142
Ryde, Francis R........... 360
Ryder, Cmas. H. Dudley 212
— Cyril John 304
— Dudley G. R. 69, 304
— Francis John 138
— Herbert Croft.......... 371
— Wilfred Ironside 431
Ryland,Henry George 67,416
Ryley, Frank.......... 42, 291
Rynd, Fred. Cecil 425
— Gerald Cleeve.......... 309
Sackville,Lionel R. S. 43, 356
Sackville-West, Cons. J. 305
Sadleir, Rev. F. 395
Sadler, Alfred.......... 369
James Hayes ... 55, 413
— Ralph Peyton........... 290
— Walter Hayes........... 202
Safford, Charles John ... 267
— Napier E. Fredk.......... 361
Sage, Charles A.Ross 47, 412
St. Aubyn, Guy Stewart 305
— Hon. John T..........55,229
St. Clair, Jas. Latimer C. 41
— W. Aug. Edm. ... 63, 209
St.George,AchesonW.63,253
— Harry H. 309
St. John, Chas. Wm. R. 249
— Frederick Charles18, 405
— George Francis Wm. 171
— Henry Beauchamp... 362
St. Leger, Arthur J. B. 304
— St. John James ... 58, 361
— Stratford Edward ... 255
St. Paul, Cecil Harley 43, 367
St. Quintin, Arthur N... 402
— Ernest Snowdon 161
— Thomas Astell 25
Salaman, Selim Myer ... 529
Sale, Mat. Townsend 26, 205
Salkeld, Robt. Edward 287
Salmon, Geoffrey N. ... 57
— James N. 173, 370
— Lawrence E. Albert 384
— William Arthur ...23, 408
— William Harry ...43, 410
— William Henry 304
Salmond, William ... 18, 204
Salmonson, H. B. S. 9
Critchley 253, 374

Salt, Thomas Anderdon 153
Salter, Henry P. King... 356
Saltoun, Lord 229
Saltmarshe, Philip...53, 167
Salvage, John V. 383
Salvesen, Charles Emil. 210
Samborne, Fred. C. S.P. 438
Samman, Charles Thos. 450
Sammut, Herbert Joseph 288
Samson, Louis L. R. ... 261
Samuel, Henri Saul..... 374
Samut, A. F. P. M. J.
  A. F. X. 185, 369
Sandars, Edw. C 176
Sandbach, Arthur E. ... 210
— Henry M. 67, 169
— William 238
Sandberg, Rev. F. B. ... 460
— Rev. S. L. G. 460
Sandeman,JohnEdw.27, 408
— John Glas 130
— Victor Staunton ... 159
Sanders, Alfred Harry 243
— Alvin Aug. 274
— Francis Alex. 271
— George Herber 175
— Gerard Arthur F..... 213
— Gerhardt L'Honneux 430
— Guy William George 249
— Rev. M. C. 460
— Richard Careless 452
— Robert Muriel 273
Sanderson, H.Bristow19,406
— William Denziloe..... 242
Sandes, Charles 373
Sandford,H.Coddington 437
San Jham, George B.67, 282
Sandiford, J. O.Greatrex 380
Sandlands, Gordon 234
— Henry George 173
— Philip Orde.........278, 367
Sandwith, John Robert. 418
— Lincoln 150
— Ralph Leslie 256
Sandys, ArthurAbney57, 139
— Charles Ulric 333
— Edward Seton 214
— Edwin Capel C. ...58, 414
— William Bain R. 175
Sanford, Geo.Batthyany 439
— George E. L. S ... 7, 204
Sangster, Alfred Bruce 434
— Patrick Barclay 362
— Thos. Alex. Gardner 346
Sanjana, Kavasji C..... 505
Sankey, Alfred R. M.... 209
— Cyril Charles.......... 172
Sant, Mowbray Lees ... 240
Sant-Fournier, Hugo ... 288
Sapte, Douglas 240
— Francis 301
Sarel, Clement V. M. ... 240
— Geo. Benedict M..... 262
Sargeant-Openshaw,F.O.371
Sargenant, A. Frederic 213
— Henry 264
— Herbert Gaussen 177
— Richard A. 27, 205
Sargent, Arthur Fra. ... 529
— Harry Neptune 367
— Hy. Gresham Forbes 410
— James Forbes 504
Sarkies, Carrapiet John 530
— Sarkies C. 505
Sarsfield, Wm. Stopford 334
Sartorius, Euston Henry 19
— George Chas. Fras. ... 433
— George Conrad....21, 406
— Reginald Wm.....18, 403
Satterthwaite, Benjamin
  Arthur 51, 2 1
Saulez, Edmund 435
— Philip Homan 420
Saumarez, Richard J... 400
Saunders, Arthur Aug.
  ....41, 166a
— Arthur Rivers 437
— David Michael 383
— Edward Aldborough 178
— Frederick John 401
— Frederick William ... 213
— George Fred. Cullen... 255
— George Morley.....67, 314
— Herbert 380
— John William 310
— Macan Wm........51, 167
— Richard 185
— William Egerton ... 378

Index—Active List.

Saunders, William Power	175
— William St. Lawrence	250
Saunders - Knox - Gore, Cecil Henry	137
Saunderson, L. T.	357
— S. Fras.	357
Savage, Arthur R. B.	175
— Arthur Johnson	214
— George Robt. Rollo	48, 207
— Henry Charles	53, 282
— John Burke	395
— Johnson William	43, 205
— William Henry	427
Savi, Robert J. T.	434
Savile, Albany R. C.	236
— George Walter Wrey	301
— John Herbert Drax.	357
— Robert Vesey	290
— Walter Clare	58, 163
Saville, Robt. Chas.	314
Savona, Edward	186
— William	186
Savory, Albert	146
Saw, Fras. Albt.	383
Saward, Michael H.	24, 179
Sawle, Fra. A. Graves	23, 231
Sawyer, Chas. Edw.	51, 291
— George Westrenen	41, 410
— Henry Thomas	395
— Herbert Anthony	44, 411
— Richard H. Stewart	381
Saxe-Weimar, *His Serene Highness Prince* Wm. Augustus Edward *of*...	133
Sayer, Jas. R. S.	130
Sayers, *Rev.* J. J. Brydges	506
Scafe, C. Harington	28, 399
Scaife, Henry Browse	279
Scales, Wm. Henry	244
Scallon, Robert I.	418
Scanlan, Arthur de C.	382
Schalch, Vernon A.	51, 413
Scharlieb, Wm. Karl	435
Schilling, Syduey Edw.	333
Schleswig - Holstein, *H.R.H. Prince* F. C. O. A. *of*	4
— *H.H. Prince* Christian V. A. L. E. A. *of*	305
Schletter, Percy	58, 244
Schneider, Claude V.	427
— Reg. Percy Congreve	434
— Stewart M. Congreve	419
Schofield, Charles	428
— Harry Norton	173
— Herbert	285
— Sydney Vaughan	178
Scholes, Henry Southey	311
Scholfield, Geo. Peabody	212
Schomberg, H. St. Geo.	42, 399
Schreiber, Acton Lemuel	211
— Arthur Thomas	398
— Charles Shuldham	133
Schwabe, Geo. Salis.	17
Sclater, Bertram L.	212
— Henry Crichton	50, 168
Sclater-Booth, *Hon.* W. D.	175
Scoboll, Henry J.	144
Scoones, Fitzmaurice T. F.	243
Scotland, David W.	455
Scott, Albert Charles	213
— Alex. Fras.	175
— Arch. Galbraith	172
— Arch. O'Connor	176
— Arthur Binny	171
— Arthur de Courcy	264
— Bernard	436
— Bertal Hopton	384
— Buchanan	53, 208
— Chas. Archibald R.	267
— Charles Darracott	172
— Chas. Henry	43, 166a
— Charles Inglis	138
— Douglas Alex.	24, 205
— Edmund Richard	61, 256
— Edward Baliol	177
— Edward H. Corse	53, 242
— Edw. Wm. Woodward	163
— Fitzroy Tufton H.	400
— Fred. Beaufort	377
— George	384
— Geo. Theobalds.	213
— Godfrey F. G. Baliol	269
— Harvie	379
— Hastings C. Folliott.	295
— Henry	279
— Herbert Courtenay	439
— Hopton Arthur	440
Scott, Horace Wm.	68, 261
— Hugh Aboukir	52, 167
— James	505
— James S. R.	63, 145
— Lindsay Buchanan	310
— Lionel Folliott	287
— Neville A. Woodward	401
— Philip Clement J.	256, 368
— Richard Alex	67, 137
— Robert	253
— Robert Kellock	177
— Robert N. Dawson	5
— *Sir* Samuel Edw., *Bt.*	135
— *Rev.* Sydney S.	460
— *Rev.* Thomas	236
— Thos. Archibald	337
— Thomas Aug.	20, 406
— Thomas Edwin	436
— Walter	25, 408
— Walter Cleland	434
— Walter Henry	66, 274
— 2nd *Lt.* William	440
— *Qr. Mr.* William	338
— *Rev.* William	507
— Wm. Aug.	63, 321
— *Rev.* William Edward	532
— Wm. Thomas Wilson	255
— William W. Hopton	40, 404
Scott-Beves, Percival	271
Scott-Elliot, Chas. R.	441
— William	153
Scott-Kerr, Francis L.	325
Scott-Moncrieff, G. K.	66, 209
— William Elmsley	457
Scratchley, Victor H. S.	305
Scriven, John Barclay.	147
Scudamore, Chas. Philip	252
— Fred. Wm	66, 250
— Walter Victor	212
Scully, John	453
Seager, William	178
Seagram, Tom Ogle.	174
Seagrim, Dudley G.	174
Sealy, Alfred Edw.	309
— Chas. Wm. Henry	44, 411
Seaman, Albert Baird	452
— Edwin Charles	212
— James Thomas	277
Searight, Hugh Fforde	136
Searle, Alfred E. S.	423
— Aubrey Vivian	346
— Chas. Thomas Arnaud	429
— Percy Cormack	436
Sears, James Walter	282
Seath, Alexander	178
— Alexander George	395
Seccombe, Arch. K.	245, 367
Seddon, Edw. M'Mahon	175
— Thomas Young	432
Sedgefield, Arthur R. W.	454
Seel, Edm. H. Molyneux	244
— Edw. H. Molyneux	234
Segrave, Thomas Louis	258
Selby, Henry Oliphant	47, 207
— William	457
Selby-Smyth, Edw. Guy	52, 329
Seligman, Herbert S.	177
Sellar, David P.	139
— *Rev.* John Annand	532
— Thomas Byrne	269
— Walter D.	269
Sellick, J. Henderson	455
Selous, Harry Dyson	255
— Reginald	311
Selwyn, Chas. N.	429
Semini, Victor	256
Sempill, *Hon.* D. Forbes	318
Semple, *Hon. J. F. Master of Sempill*	286
Semple, David	381
— John	381
Senior, Guy	398
— Henry Wm. John	23, 408
— Henry Wm. Richd.	433
— Thomas Palmer.	371
Seppings, T. Johnson	47, 295
Sergison, Charles W.	233
Serjeant, Jas. Robert B.	211
Serjeantson, Cecil M.	256
Seton, Augustus St. John	244
— Bruce Gordon	456
Cardon Henry	273
— Henry James	55, 329
— *Sir* Wm. Samuel, *Bt*	21, 406
— Winton	63, 146
Settle, Hy. Hamilton	27, 205
Sewell, Charles Francis	304
Sewell, Henry Fane H.	19, 406
— John Henry	57, 245
— Jonathan Wm. S.	214
Sexton, John Jos. O'Brien	434
— Michael John	383
Seymour, Charles	379
— Edw. Hamilton	348, 369
— Henry Wm.	417
— *Lord* Wm. F. Ernest.	5
— Wm. Henry	137
Shadforth, Geo. A.	68, 348
Shadwell, Francis Mayne	311
— Leonard Julius	250
Shaftesbury, *Lord*	152
Shairp, Alex.	362
Shakerley, Ernest Alf.	276
— Geoffrey Chas.	305
Shakespear, Arthur B.	42, 397
— Frank	434
— George C. C.	422
— George Joseph	178
— Geo. Robt. James	23, 408
— John	346
— Leslie W.	425
— Wm. Fred.	427
Shanahan, Daniel Davis	385
Shannon, Thos. Patrick	40, 366
Sharman, Eric Harding	506
Sharp, *Rev.* A. A.	507
— Albert Gerard Gavin	316
— Frank William	393
— Frederick Leonard	174
— George Edward.	274
— *Rev.* James	507
Sharpe, Alex.	337
— Edward John	301
— James Birch	58, 208
Sharpin, *Rev.* G. W.	533
Shaw, Alexander Jas.	430
— Alexander John	26, 404
— Clements R bert	411
— David George L.	422
— Elphinston	21, 407
— Francis S. Kennedy.	281
— Frederic Charles.	289
— George Jocelyn	420
— Herbert Stuart	437
— James	270
— Sidney Hunter	308
— Townsend Wharton.	531
— William Drury	52, 234
— Shawyer, Alf. Chas.	148
— Shea, John Stuart M.	436
— Shearer, Johnston	454
— Shearme, Frank.	134
— Sheehan, P E. C.	270, 373
— Shekleton, Hugh P.	284
— Sheldrake, Edw. Nodin	382
— Shelley, Arch. D. G.	210
— Bertram A. Graham	213
— Henry Richard	24, 404
— John Courtown Edw.	233
— Shepherd, Chas. Edw.	25, 408
— Charles H.	45, 245
— J. Laurance F.	173
— *Rev.* Theoph. C.	460
— Sheppard, Charles Lee.	401
— George Sidney	436
— Herbert Cecil	17.
— John Francis	233
— Seymour Hulbert	213
— Thomas Winter	244
— Sherard, R. Woodchurch	422
— Sherer, Jas. Donnelly.	176
— John Corrie	436
— Lionel Copley	256
Sheringham, Arthur W.	42, 264
Sherlock, John Ouseley	245
Sherrard, Chas. Wm.	52, 207
— John Meade	372
Sherston, John	69, 356
— William Maxwell	160
Sherwin, Frd. W. Hernon	271
Sherwood, Arthur W. C.	346
— Harold Joseph	211
— Oliver Caton	360
Shewan, George	454
— Hugh Mackenzie	348
Shewell, Arthur Poole.	256
— Edward Warner	333
— Harry W. M.	270
— Percy Garratt	433
Shewen, Mansel T.	424
Shiel, Herbert M.	283
Shields, George	372
Shine, Jas. M. F.	382
— John Piercey	401
Shipley, Charles Tyrell	243
— Mordaunt Lea	420
— Reg. Youge	246
Shipman, Henry James	185
— William	178
Shirreff, Geo. F. F.	53, 167
Shirres, John Chivas	55, 168
Shone, Wm. T.	43, 208
Shore, Offley Bohun S. F	427
— Robert	455
— Walter Francis	395
Short, Anthony H.	172
— Frederick John	395
— John Bartholomew	336
— William Ambrose	176
Shortt, Alex. Graham	174
— Francis de Sausmarez	252
— Sausmarez Dobree	245
Shoubridge, Chas. A. G.	245
— Thomas H.	283
Showers, Herbert Lionel	429
Shubrick, Chas. Louis	400
Shute, Arth. Blagdon	170
— Cameron Deane	285
— *Sir* Chas. C.	148
— Gerald Edward	65, 209
— Henry Gwyun Deane	231
— William John	214
Shuttleworth, Arthur C.	284
Sibthorpe, Charles	504
Siddons, Henry G. F.	42, 166
Sidney, *Hon.* Algernon	57, 168
— Henry Marlow	276
Silcock, Alexander	455
Sill, John Warre	58, 208
Sillem, Arnold Fred.	236
— James	285
Sillery, Chas. C. A.	429
— John Jocelyn D	144
Silver, John Payzaut	386
— Walter Barrington	333
Silverthorne, Jas. W. B.	25
Sim, Geo. Hamilton	61, 208
Sime, Chas. Geo.	271
Simkins, John Thos.	255
Simmonds, Percy R.	170
— William A.	453
Simmons, Geo. F. H. Le B.	211
— *Sir* J. L. A.	4, 204
— Percy Walter	401
Simnus, *Rev.* J. M.	396
Simon, Herbert S. P.	276
Simonds, Cecil Barrow	174
Simonet, John Francis	373
Simpson, Arth. C. S. Ward	178
— Arthur Edmund	55, 309
— Charles John	322
— Charles Napier	59, 168
— C. Rudyerd	63, 246
— David	506
— Francis Blake	144, 369
— George	25, 409
— George Gregory	67, 169
— H. C. O. D.	58, 168
— John Murray	59
— Osmond Beckett	244
— Robert	173
— Robert John S.	381
— William George	401
— William Hugh	362
Simpson-Baikie, H. A. D.	175
Sinclair, Alf Law.	69, 410
— Charles	236
— David	504
— Frank	284
— Hugh Montgomerie	66, 239
Sinclair-MacLagan, E. G.	278
Singer, Charles William	213
— George Hamilton	372
Singh, Bawa Jiwan	456
Singleton, Henry T. C.	317
Sinha, Narendra P.	455
Siordet, Fred. John	277
Sitwell, Claude G. Hen.	309
— Fras. Honorius S.	314
— William Henry	240
Skeen, Andrew	265
— Oliver St. John	362
Skeffington, *Hon.* W. J. C.	159
Skelmersdale, *Lord*	139
Skerrett, Patrick B.	383
Skey, Fred. E. G.	211
Skinner, Arthur David	282
— Bruce M.	381
— Edmund Grey	369
— Evelyn Swinton	25, 408
— Frederick St. Duthus	279
— George John	24, 403

N N 2

Index—Active List.

Name	Page	Name	Page	Name	Page	Name	Page
Skinner, James Tierney	366	Smith, J. Robt. Dunlop	422	Somerset, C. Wyndham	430	Stack, Lee Oliver Fitz M.	278
— Monier Williams ...52,	208	— John	253	— Hon. Richard Fitz Roy	229	Stacpoole, Henry D. 254,	373
— Percy Cyriac B.	292	— John Blackburn	530	Somervell, Ernest	259	— John 57,	366
— Sidney Hill	284	— John Graham	417	— William	240	Stacpoolo, Geo. Wm. R.	282
— Thomas Carlyle	211	— John Leslie	171	Somerville, John A. C.	240	Staddon, Henry Ernest	386
Skipwith, Fred. Geo.	242	— John Lindsay	362	— Samuel Wallace	301	Stafford, Edmund H. W. H.	212
— Grey	55, 399	— John Manners	428	— Stafford James	271	— Henry L. C. H.	210
— Philip Armfield	175	— J. Wm. Sidney	272	— Thomas Cameron F.	238	— Wm. Fra. Howard 63,	209
Skirving, David Scot 43,	366	— Joseph Barnard ... 7,	405	Somerville-Large, B. W.	379	Stainforth, Herbert G.	432
Slacke, Wm. Randal. 26,	205	— Josh. Waddington	492	Soote, Cecil Speld.	254	— Lesley C. H.	425
Slade, *Sir* Cuthbert, *Bt.*	233	— Julian C. Carington	454	Sorel-Cameron, G. C. M.	325	— Martin	289
— Fred. George 24,	167	— Lionel Abel	176	Sorell, Fra. Sheffield 59,	414	— Richard T.	369
— John Ramsay 25,	165	— Lonsdale R. Douglas	141	Sorsbie, Robert Fox	211	Stalkartt, Chas. Edw. G.	385
Sladen, Chas. St. Barbe	214	— Maurice Henry	504	— *Rev.* Wm. Fras.	396	— Harold A.	385
— David Ramsay	269	— Meredith Carre	360	Souper, Charles Edward	372	Stallard, Raymond M.	255
— John Ramsay F.	254	— Owen Annesley	433	Souter, Arthur Bourke	249	— Stacy Frampton	178
Slater, Henry Martyn	169	— Percy Wyndham...27,	404	— Hugh Maurice W.	309	Stamer, Lovelace	158
— Mortimer John... 69,	209	— Philip Henry.........42,	249	— Thomas	286	Standbridge, Edm. B. 44,	166
Slator, George Francis	171	— Raymond Coape	272	Souther, Arthur Melville	233	Standen, Jas. Douglas 52,	333
Slaughter, Wm. Budd.	378	— Rennell Percy	171	— Charles Elliot	333	— Robert H. Fraser	308
Slayter, Edward W.	385	— Reynold Percy	249	— Henry Herbert	434	Stanford, Henry Bedell	171
Slee, Percy Henry	172	— Robert	379	— John Henry W.	293	Stanhope, *Hon.* Evelyn	
Slessor, Arthur Kerr	289	— Robert Astley	247	— Robert	423	T. Scudamore	367
— Herbert	398	— Robert Wanless	270	— Wm. Melvill	433	— Percy Seymour	287
Sloane-Stanley, R. F. A.	158	— Ronald Kincaid	146	Sowerby, Maurice E.	214	Stanistreet, George B.	385
Sloe, Cyril Harcourt	213	— Sidney..........46,	206	Sowray, Gerald R	297	Stanley, Cecil V. S.	154
Sloggett, Arthur T.	380	— Sidney Browning	456	Spaight, Wm. Fitz H. 24,	205	— Edmund Talbot	369
— Harry	212	— Sidney Thomas	185	Spann, Henry J. B.	285	— Edw. G. Villiers *Lord*	229
— Henry Maxwell	382	— Stanley George Drew	401	Spankie, J. Patrick W. 68,	416	— *Hon.* Ferdinand Chas.	230
Sloman, Henry S.	275	— Stephen Marsh	395	Sparke, John Guveo 49,	295	— *Rt. Hon. Lord*	1
Small, Alexander	178	— Steuart Bogle	136	Sparkes, Claude S.	383	— Geoffrey 44,	366
— William George	372	— Sydenham C. U.	170	— John Geo.	26	— *Hon.* George Fred.	177
Smalley, Frederick...23,	404	— Thomas Hugh	424	— Wm. Spottiswoode	285	— Herbert F. Wentworth	151
— Henry Davidson	275	— Thomas Parkyns	178	Sparks, James Douglas.	243	Stannard, Benjamin	287
Smallwood, Frank G.	274	— Thomas Sharpe	277	Sparling, Jas. Philip 67,	415	— Henry	378
Smart, Alex. Wm....46,	207	— Thomas Woodford	115	Sparrow, H. Fras.	237	Stannus, Gerald W. J.	
— Edward deSausmarez	423	— Tom Parkyns C.	294	— Richard	142	Fitzgerald	161
— George Joseph... 6,	164	— W. Wm. Marriott 43,	166	Speak, William	280	Stansfeld, Cyril Grey	309
Smenton, Chas. O.	172	— Walter Woodbine	386	Spearman, Alex. Young	242	— Harold H. G.	209
Smerdon, Fred. G. B. 142,	374	— Wilfred Hugh Moore	401	— Chas. Edw	317	— Hubert Arthur	259
Smith, Alfred	395	— Wilfrid Edw. Bownas	267	— Horace R. 21,	407	— James Rawdon	174
— Alick Le Fleming	439	— Wilfrid Lionel Brook	171	Spedding, Arthur B. D.	278	— William Beauchamp	360
— Allan 59,	414	— Wilfred Noel Edm.	440	— Charles Rodney	329	Stanton, Charles John	243
— Andrew	251	— Wilfred Robt. Abel	230	— Edw. Wilfrid	175	— Edward Alexander	257
— Annesley George 273,	373	— William Apsley ... 61,	169	Spence, A. E. Cecil	382	— Edward Charles	209
— Archibald Geo.	176	— William Douglas	262	— Alex. Hierom O.	440	— Francis Henry Guy	178
— Arthur George Baird	262	— William Dunlop	395	— Edw. K. E.	419	— Frederick W. Starkey	172
— Arth. M. de L. Cowper	174	— Wm. E. Clifton	290	— John	40	— Harold James Clifford	269
— Arthur Murray	174	— William Frank	438	— Philip T. Augustine.	432	— Henry Ernest	172
— Charles Aitchison	288	— William Hugh U.	175	Spencer, Almeric A. W.	253	— Hubert Lionel	434
— Charles Edward	368	— Wm. Whitmore... 49,	106	— Almeric George	25	Stannell, H. S. M.	262
— *Sir* Charles Holled	23	Smith-Bingham, O. B. B.	138	— Arch. Claude Douglas	329	Stapleton, *Hon.* Miles 43.	162
— Charles Mitchell...42,	166	Smith-Neill, James Wm.	233	— Charles George	386	Stapylton, Granville J. C.	177
— Clarence Gorton Ross	285	Smith-Rowse, H. W....49,	208	— Dhanjibhai Burjooji.	454	— Miles John	163
— *Rev.* Clement	506	Smithe, Percy Bourdillon	277	— Edmund 52,	31	Stares, Robert P.	255
— David Noble	157	Smithett, Arthur C. H.	434	— Harrison	177	Starkey, Lewis Edward	146
— Edmund Perceval	173	— Bertie D. Hamilton	177	— Herbert Ennes.	155	Starr, W. Henderson	383
— Edmund Philip B. 41,	366	— Henry C. E.	311	— John Trevor	288	Statham, *Rev.* S. P. H.	396
— Edward Arthur ...53,	168	Smithson, Arthur E.	384	— John W. T. 50,	167	Staunton, George	321
— Edw. D. Newnham 48,	412	— Walter C	155	— Lionel Dixon	414	— W. Beauchamp	436
— Edward Locke C.	530	Smyly, Fred. Philip	267	— Thomas Edward...47,	414	Staveley, Charles Russell	357
— Edward Osborne	292	Smyth, Benjamin	115	Spens, *Rev.* A. N. W.	460	— *Sir* Charles W. D.	288
— *Rev.* Edward Parke.	396	— Charles Coghlan	277	— James 50,	297	— William Cathcart.	173
— Edward Pelham	175	— *Sir* Edward Selby	318	Speranza, John Edward	242	Stavert, Thos. Hope 66,	346
— Edward Sharpe	291	Etwall Walter 27,	404	— Joseph..........42,	286	Stawell, George D. ...49,	249
— Francis 61,	237	— Fred. Augustus	454	— Walter S. J. J. L.	211	Stayner, Frederick S.	272
— Francis Lee Baird	237	— George Abraham	176	Spiller, Duncan C. Oliver	371	— Lawrence George	277
— *Surg. Capt.* Frederick	384	— Gerald James Watt.	214	Spilling, John Kinder	24	Steavenson, Chas. John	244
— *Vet. Capt.* Frederick	395	— Henry	264	Spilsbury, Edgar Chas. 61,	208	Stedman, Edward ...16,	408
— Frederic Alexander	431	— *Sir* Henry Aug.	164	Spong, Charles Stuart.	384	— Frederick Savignac	531
— Frederick Manners.	440	— Hugh Lyle	297	Spooner, Walter B.	395	Steel, Edwin Bedford	386
— Frederic Vincent.	438	— Hugo Wm. N. S. 311,	369	Spottiswoode, Arthur A.	318	— James Nisbet	450
— F. Yorke	532	— John	505	— Chas. J. 55,	259	— Richard Alexander	333
— *Rev.* George	396	— Nevill Maskelyne	137	— John	305	Steele, Fred. William	366
— George Barton ...310,	374	— Owen Stuart.....53,	168	Spragge, Chas. Hy. 27,	166	— George Frederick.	143
— George Edward	213	— R. C. E. Skeffington.	247	Sprague, Wm. Carr	530	— Julian M'Carty	256
— Geo. M'Iver C.	456	— Robert Napier	163	Spratt, Arthur Graves 63,	249	— Lawrence L. 66,	254
— George Osborne... 49,	333	— Ross Acheson	258	— Edw. Jas. Henry	242	— Robert L. B.	271
— George Rainier de H.	435	— Samuel Gardiner 45,	166	— Fred. Thos. Nelson 47,	207	— St. George Loftus	421
— Gilbert Boys	170	— T. G. Hawkesworth.	254	Spring, *Rev.* Henry		— William Henry	378
— Granville Roland Fra.	231	— Thomas	230	Coleridge	460	Steen, Hunter C.	362
— Guy de Herriez	438	— Thos. R. Johnson.	314	Sprot, Alexander.....53,	141	Steevens, John	369
— Harry d'Arch.	250	— Vere Staunton	242	— Edward Mark	297	Stenhouse, William ...21,	63
— Henry	456	— William Carew	213	Sproule, Harry H.	275	Stepher, Arthur	452
— Henry Coupe	435	— William Johnson	253	Spry, Leighton Hume.	279	— Arthur James	253
— Hy. Ernest Hill	384	Smythe, George F. A.	380	Spurgin, *Sir* John Blick	348	— Arthur Sandeman	440
— Henry Lockhart	275	— Henry Hamilton	262	— John Henry 50,	262	— Robert Campbell	156
— Henry Sherwood...66,	309	— Ingoldsby W. T. S.	370	Spurrell, Robert John.	147	Stephens, Augustus E. R.	454
— Herbert Austen	456	Smythies, Raymond H. R.	284	Spurway, H. Weston	398	— Edward	214
— Herbert Carington	348	Snell, Francis Wm....48,	412	— R. Popham	234	— William	178
— Herbert Guthrie	173	Snow, Edm. Graham 310,	370	Spyer, John H. Aug. 48,	258	Stephenson, Cecil M.	269
— Herbert Stoney	256	— Robert Hastings P.	383	Squire, W. Perfect	383	— Ernest Wm. Rokeby	301
— Horace Mackenzie	297	— Thos. D'Oyly	252	Stable, Russell Loscombe	291	— *Sir* Fred. C. A.	231
— Howard William	254	Soady, G. J. Fitz-M.	430	Stables, Alex.	382	— Theodore Edward 49,	288
— Hugh Bateman	283	Solbe, *Rev.* C. A.	396	Stace, Edw. Vincent 40,	409	Sterling, John Barton	17
— Hugh William	178	— Chas. Edw. de Lisle	435	Stacey, Cyril	156	John Trelawny	231
— James	504	Soltau-Symons, G. A. J.	305	Stack, Charles Edw.	403	Stern, Hy. Julius J.	153
— James Herbert	423	Somerse, *Hon.* A. C. E.	357	— Charles Spottiswoode	435	Steuart, J. M Steuart	357

Stevens, Algernon F. 457	Stiell, David 384	Strickland, Edw. Peter 245	Swanson, John G Ralph 273
— Arthur C. J. 214	Stiffe, Arch F. E. 174	— Edward S. 348	Swanston, Charles Oliver 432
— Buckenham F. 360	Still, Rev. Alexander ... 460	— Percy C. Hutchison... 506	— Nowell Sherson 422
— Charles 419	Stirke, Hy. Richd........ 281	— Wm. Alex. Wickede... 425	Swanton, James H. 400
— Lt. Charles Frederick 174	Stirling, Alock 318	Striedinger, Oscar 291	Swayne, Chr. Henry ... 379
— Capt. Chas. Frederick 418	— Archibald 233	Stringer, Fred. Wm 246	— Edward Hopton 252
— Charles Mordaunt ... 293	— Charles 176	Strong, Addington Daw-	— Eric John Eagles...... 428
— Charles Richard 211	— George Murray Home 288	sonne 362	— Harald Geo. C. 210
— Cecil Robert 457	— James David 269	— Charles Powlett 255	Sweeny, Terence H. 454
— Frank E. 42, 306	— James Wilfred......58, 168	— Dawsonne M. 7, 404	Sweet, Edw. Herbert ... 258
— George Borlase ...63, 419	— Sir William 5, 164	— Frederic Lewis H. ... 401	Sweetman, Michael J.... 254
— George Morton ...43, 160	— William Geo. Hay ... 427	— Henry Stuart......... 362	— Michael James J...... 73
— Harry Cavaye 404	Stisted, Charles H. 234	— Herbert Percy 255	— Richard 258
— Harry Whitehill 268	— Courtenay Heathcote 252	— Norman B. Glegg..... 163	Sweetnam, Stephen
— John 178	Stobart, Geo. Herbert... 178	— Sydney Philip......63, 270	Westrope 336
— John Lucius Cary..... 437	— William Eden 140	— William 175	Sweny, John Alfred 23, 399
— Malcolm Wilkinson	Stock, Herbert Alfred .. 308	Stroud, Edward James.. 401	— William Frederick ... 243
40, 404	— Thomas 50, 288	Strouts, Bernard M..... 401	Swetenham, Robert
— Morton 429	Stockdale, Godfrey H.W. 210	Strover, Geo. Aug....19, 405	Alexander.........27, 410
— Nathaniel M. Comins 436	— Herbert Edward 174	Stuart, Alex.P.D.Carmutt 434	— Roger 237
— Stephen Repton 433	Stockley, Arthur Uniacke 176	— Alex. George 234	Swettenham, Geo. Kilner 233
— Thomas 178	— Charles More......... 22	— Alex. Ramsay 170	— Wm. Alex. Whybault 178
Stevens-Nash, C. G. E. 176	— Ernest Norman...... 214	— Andrew Mitchell ... 210	Swift, R. Meade P. 343
Stevenson, Alex. Gavin 213	— Hugh Roderick 273	— Burleigh Fras. B. ... 273	Swifte, Edm. Lenthal .. 249
— Edward Hall 177	— John Cator 370	— Chas. John Lewis 68, 416	— Joshua W. 19, 405
— Francis 55, 413	— Vesey Mangles ...63, 416	— Clande Houston 271	Swinburne, Thos. Robt. 61, 397
— Henry Wickham. 530	Stockwell, Chas. M. 16	— Donald Forbes 431	Swiney, Alex. J. Henry 212
— John 379	— Clifton de N. Orr ... 17	— Donald Mackenzie ... 262	— Ernest Robt. Rainier 432
— Nathaniel 5	— Geo. Clifton Inglis ... 317	— Godfrey R. Conyngham 274	— Geo. Clayton 17
— Robert 40	— Lockhart Thomas ... 318	— Henry Ogilvy 381	— George Walter B. ... 418
— Robert Crawford 172	Stodart, Thomas 505	— Hugh Seymour David 172	— Gilbert Mars R. A. ... 161
— Rev. R. Horne 507	Stodart, Chas. Hen. 28, 409	— John 286	Swinhoe, Charles.....17, 405
— Thomas Ronnie....... 6	— George 178	— John Robert 381	— Edmund Arthur 440
— Walter Wilton Camp-	Stoker, Richard N....... 453	— Ralph Esme 175	Swinley, George.......18, 179
bell 309	— Wm. B. Caulfeild..... 372	— Reginald Polo 310	— Geo. Dighton Probyn 362
— William Flack 378	Stokes, Alfred 171	— Robert Charles O. ... 171	Swinton, Ernest Dunlop 213
— William Frederick ... 439	— Follicott Stuart F. 45, 329	— Ronald R. Kilbee ... 289	— Francis Edward 530
Stevenson-Hamilton, Jas. 148	— Henry Haldane 378	— Sidney Offord 381	— John James.......50, 167
Steward, Chas. Saml. 7, 403	— Leslie Falkiner J. deV. 238	Stuart-Wortley, A. R. M. 304	— Robert Bruce 293
— Harry Warry 373	— William Allen 213	Stubbs, Arthur G. B. ... 373	Swire, Henry 373
— Reginald Holden 308	Stokoe, Thomas Richard 276	— Arthur Kennedy 273	Sword, Wm. Dennistoun 310
Stewart, Albert F. 253	Stone, Ar. Brabazon..... 264	Studd, Herbert Wm. ... 210	Swynnerton, Rev. Chas. 460
— Alex. Kenneth........ 529	— Rev. Arthur E. 460	Studdert, Edward 367	Sykes, Clement Arthur 176
— Alg. Bingham A. 318	— Charles Alfred 384	Studdy, T. J. Ch. A. 22, 179	— Harold Platt 137
— Archibald Campbell 442	— Francis 357	Stalpnagel, Chas. Wm. 177	— Herbert Scholfield .. 262
— Archibald Dundonald 356	— Francis Gleadowe 65, 169	Sturges, Wm. Elen 69, 240	— Joseph 454
— Archibald Francis ... 314	— Geo. Robt. 48, 244	Sturmer, Arthur J. 504	— Percy Molesworth ... 137
— Bryce 347	— John Graham 41	Sturrock, George C..... 177	— William 138
— Lt.Chas. Edw.(R.Art.) 175	— Lionel Geo. Tempest 243	Sturt, Robert R. N... 65, 415	— Wm. Ataley 455
— Lt. Charles Edward	— William Richard 435	Style, Rodney Charles... 294	— William Ernest 311
(Black Watch) 286	Stoneman, James......67, 344	Suart, Wm. H. 51, 167	Sylvester, George Holden 380
— Charles Gage......... 284	Stoney, F. J. Wetherall 383	Su ids, Wm. Benj........ 185	Syrn, John Munro ...16, 407
— Charles J. Butler 45, 248	— Ralph D. Sadleir 333	Sudley, A. J. C. G. Visct. 135	Symon, Walter C. 177
— Claude Frns. John 245, 368	Stopford, A. Bouverie 42, 160a	Suft, Herbert Charles ... 277	Symonds, Charles Wm.
— Cosmo Gordon 175	— Hon. Fred. William... 47	Sugden, A. Maitland ... 267	Herbert 433
— Davison Bruce 176	— Horace Robert ...66, 231	Sugg, Benjamin 220	— Rev. Geo. D. 457
— Sir Donald M. Bart. .. 4	— Lionel Arthur M..... 289	Sullivan, G. D. Filmer 52, 157	— George Davey 174
— Douglas Grant 252	Storr, Charles L. 362	Sullivan, Edw. Langford 433	Symons, Adolpho 153
— Dudley Strathearn ... 240	Storrs, Rev. R. A. 460	— Hugh Augustus 393	— Charles Bertie Owen 214
— Francis Thornton..... 434	Story, Edw. Kenmir ... 401	— Rupert Edward...... 428	— Frank Albert......... 385
— George Powell 271	Stothert, Edw. A. Wood 434	Sumner, Chas. Mannoir 69, 284	— Thomas Cornelius ... 214
— Gilbert Macdonald ... 261	— Sydney Boyle 250	Sunder, Chas. Edward.. 455	— William Penn 21
— Harry King........... 321	Stracey, Claud. Edw. ... 233	Sunderland, D. Pearce... 146	Syms, Edwin Albert ... 401
— Hopton Scott 22, 407	— Sir Edw. Paulet, Bt... 134	— Marsden Samuel J.... 23	Synge, Fra. Robt. M...66, 284
— Houston M. Shaw.... 159	— Ernest H. Denne 243	Supple, James Fras..... 370	— Mark 362
— Hugh 294	— Henry Hardinge D... 7	Surtees, Herbert C. 69, 231	— Robert F. M. F. M... 317
— Ian 270	— John Bourchier 233	Suther, Cuthbert C. ...23, 391	Szczepanski, H.C.A. 19, 405
— James 210	Strachan, Edw. Aubrey 271	— Percival 178	Tabor, Albert M. 145
— James Ainslie......... 130	— Jas. Arthur 50, 287	Sutherland, Alic. 337	— John Minnitt 42, 165
— James Anthony....... 174	— Rt. Rev. John Miller 507	— David Waters 457	Tabuteau, Thos. Rokeet, 407
— James Calder 16, 406	Strachey, Bertram...... 433	— Henry Holmes 289	Tagart, Francis D. to 55, 160
— James Fearnley 428	— John 422	— Hugh Stanley 234	— Harold Arthur Lewis 157
— James Haldane 361	— Richard John 356	— John Campbell 449	Tailby, Thos. M. Jones. 153
— James Logan 149	Strafford, Percy B. 277	— William Dunbar 506	Tait, Fred. Guthrie 286
— James Marshall....... 426	Straghan, Wm. Gibbs 55, 244	— Wm. John Edward G. 371	Talbot, Adelbert Cecil 45, 411
— John Alexander 130	Strahan, Charles 27, 218	Sutton, Alex. Arthur ... 383	— Lord Edmund B.... 59, 153
— John Henry Keith ... 441	— George 26, 218	— Evelyn Willoughby . 149	— Fred. Gilbert 357
— John Lindesay 362	— George Aubrey 437	— Francis Goodwin Hill 435	— George J. F. 69, 169
— Norman Robert ... 25, 414	Strange, Arthur James. 440	— Henry George 423	— George R. FitzRoy ... 176
— Philip George 294	— Harry Bland 174	— Hugh Clement 231	— Harry Lynch 398
— Sir Richd. Campbell 5, 403	— Robert George 171	Swabey, Frederick 361	— Henry Lynch 238
— Robert Joseph Tucker 240	Strangways, H. S. Fox.. 432	— Louis William 380	— H. C. 228
— Robert MacGregor 21, 165	— Theodore Stephen Fox 329	— Wilfred Spedding 295, 358	— John 436
— Robert Stuir 244	Stratford, Cecil V. Wing-	Swaine, Arthur T.....61, 329	— Johnston S. 66, 297
— Ronald Robert 318	field 66, 210	— Charles Edward ...43, 153	— Hon. Milo George 51, 209
— Rupert 276	— J. H. de A. de M. F. 285	— Charles L. 504	— Hon. Reginald A. J. 18
— Thomas Brown......40, 365	Stratton, Wallace C. R. 426	— Frederick Robt. 453	Talland, Frank 162
— Thomas William 506	Streatfeild, Eric 321	— George William 253	Tallents, Philip Fra. 63, 261
— Walter FitzAlan 440	— Henry 65, 229	— Leopold V. 17	Tancock, Osborne K. ... 174
— Hon. Walter John.... 18	Street, Alf. Wm. Fred... 529	Swainson, Arthur Lake. 211	Tancred, Thos. Angus ... 174
— Captain Wm. (Argyll	— Arthur 361	Swan, Charles Tarrant 433	— Thomas Selby 438
Highlanders) 337	— Ashton 531	— John Stewart........ 401	Tandy, Edward Ord..... 452
— Capt. Wm. (Ind. S. C.) 422	— Edward Lee 23	— William 370	— Henry Strafford...40, 409
— William Hall M. 421	— Herbert 293	— William Travers 253	— John 386
— Wm. Maxwell Johnston 401	Streeten, Bernard S. ... 276	Swann, Clarence J. H... 177	— Maurice O'Conner ... 213
— William Robert 210	Stretton, W. de Courcy 172	— Harington 292	Tanner, Charles Oriel O. 434
— William Scott 145	— William Lionel 264	— John Christopher.... 417	— John Arthur 209
Stewart-Murray, LordG. 286	Strick, John Arkwright 297	Swanson, Frank H. A. 277	Tapp, Hammond A....50, 281

Index—Active List.

app, James H. William	174
Tarry, Geo. Golbourn	256, 367
Tarte, Bernard R. Kinneir	237
Tarver, Alex. Leigh	440
— William Knapp	264
Tatam, Walter John	395
Tatchell, Edward	246
Tate, Alan E.	382
— Chas. Wm. Henry	369
— Gerard William	385
— Henry Pennell	400
— Hugh Boddam	417
Tatham, Arthur G.	398
— Charles J. Willmer	383
Tatum, Harold	296
Tubman, Chr s. F. Goldie	238
Twiney, Charles Joseph	254
— Edw. P. A.	170
Tayler, Wm. Fothergill C.	457
Taylor, Alex. Wm.	236
— Rev. Alfred Chas.	507
— Arch. John Scriven	178
— Arthur H. Mendle	163
— Arthur Wm. Neuville	433
— Cecil Hugh	311
— Cecil Salusbury	174
— Charles Lancaster	268
— Charles Wm. Joseph	372
— Douglas James Orr	420
— Edward	395
— Edward More	411
— Edward Richard	230
— Edward Thornton	264
— Ernest Fitzwilliam	367
— Ernest Frederick	211
— Francis Heale	434
— Frns. Pitt Stewart	368
— Fred. Edw. V.	61, 239
— Frederick F. Wilder	44, 348
— George	214
— Geo. A. Campbell	236
— Rev. George Ledwell	457
— G. Philip Du Plat	127
— Gordon Annesley	316
— Guy Hastings	292
— Harcourt Ernest	293
— Haydon d'A. P.	272
— Henry	369
— Henry Clarence Grant	170
— Herbert Wodehouse	174
— Hugh Neufville	427
— Hugo Mascie	333
— John	305
— Rev. John	460
— John Shawe	264
— John Vickriss	285
— Mowbray	172, 369
— Neville Cracroft	433
— Oswald Albon A.	277
— Philip Beauchamp	170
— Reginald O'Bryan	308
— Reynell H. B.	269, 369
— Sir R. C. Hayes	325
— Robert Eyre S.	419
— Robert James Fred.	290
— St. John L. H. Du Plat	173
— Stuart Campbell	295
— William	377
— William H. F.	66, 169
— William James	385
— William Willoughby	418
Teale, Edward J. J.	276
Tebbitt, Wm. A.	311
Teck, H. H. the Duke of	6
— H. S. H. Prince Alexander of	149
— H. S. H. Prince Adolphus of	159
— H. S. H. Prince Francis of	143
Teed, Arthur S. H.	440
Teevan, George James	101
Temple, C. Pilcher	25
— Grenville Edwyn	289
— Henry M.	61, 414
— John	32, 167
— John Alexander	26, 408
— Richard Carnac	57, 414
— William Arthur M.	272
Templer Chas. Bertram	424
— Cyril Frank	175
— Fred. Napier	398
— Henry	420
— Walter Francis	333
Templeton, James	246
Tennant, C. Cambridge	423
— Edward	437
— Hy L ncelot	174
Tennant, T. B. Everest	481
Ternan, Hy. Brettney	47, 412
— Richard R. B.	372
— Trevor Patrick B.	309
Terry, Astley Herbert	367
— Horace Auc.	69, 287
— Robt. J. Atkinson	236
— William Gordon	172
Teversham, R. K.	417
Tew, Cyril Crofton B.	253
— Harold S.	275
Tewkesbury, Geoffrey G. G. Lord	304
Thacker, Henry Joseph	433
— Robert Christy	384
Thackeray, Fred. R.	66, 169
— Henry James	317
— Martin	57, 282
— Thomas M. Gerard	53, 271
Thackwell, C. G. R.	420
— Charles Joseph	160
— Edward Loftus R.	373
— Joseph Edwin	334
— Osbert Montague R.	210
— William Henry	68, 281
Tharp, Gerard Prideaux	357
Thatcher, Fras. Alex.	437
— Gerald Gane	178
— John Fred. Charles	417
Thellusson, A. W. W. A.	269
Theobald, F. Cambridge	277
Thesiger, Hon. C. W.	5, 147
— Richard Handcock	357
Thicknesse, John A.	252
Thiele, Chas. W.	381
Thistlethwayte, Evelyn William	304
Thom, George St. Clair	386
Thomas, Arthur C. H.	291
— Arthur Haviland	367
— Berkeley Hardinge	273
— Charles Fred.	27, 404
— David Brodie	254
— E. C.	115
— Edward Algernon D.	273
— Francis Henry	25, 401
— Francis Herbert S.	427
— Francis Wm.	4, 397
— Frederick William	439
— Geo. Trevor H.	381
— George Tucker	504
— Sir Godfrey V. Bart.	61, 108
— Gwyn	249
— Henry Melville	176
— Henry Robt. Dacres	48, 412
— Hubert St. George	431
— John Wellesley	281
— Reginald Percy	333
— Reginald Seymour	204
— Robt, Mosely Bryce	23, 405
— William Fred.	505
— William Godfrey	29
Thomason, Arch. F.	435
Thompson, Albert Geo.	385
— Andrew Green	50, 168
— Aubrey Julian	178
— Bernard Anthony	253
— Bernard Henry	214
— Gen. Charles William	150
— Capt. Charles William	142
— Cronsdale Miller	505
— Cyril Powney	432
— David Montgomery	423
— F. Hacket	67, 325
— Harry Adair	334
— Harry Arth. Hale	11, 179
— Henry Neville	382
— Herbert John	361
— Howard Stanley	52, 399
— Ivan Frank Ross	457
— John	370
— John Alexander R.	274
— Noel Gilliat	245
— Peter R. Edward	271
— Richard	53, 208
— Richd. L. Brereton	214
— Robert George	382
— Roland Wycliffe	291
— William Anson	422
— Wm. Arthur Murray	173
— William David	420
— William George	395
— William Henry	18
— William Maxwell	213
— William Oliver	40, 409
— Rev. W. F.	460
Thomsett, Rich. Gil ham	378
Thomson, Alex. Fred. R.	175
Thomson, Alex. Guthrie	292
— Alex. Henry Gougor	440
— A. Graham	51, 209
— Arthur Cleghorn	256
— Charles	457
— C. B.	178
— Charles FitzGerald	45
— C. F. S. Anstruther	69, 134
— Charles William	27, 165
— David Birdwood	427
— Edmund Peel	347
— Francis Wyville	455
— George	45
— George Leonard	57, 279
— George Sloane	530
— Vet. Lt. Col. Henry	391
— Surgeon Capt. Henry	505
— James	384
— James Alex. Skene	67, 277
— Jocelyn Home	170
— John Bustee Cooke	252
— Mowbray Townshend	421
— Noel Arbuthnot	318
— Samuel John	454
— Slade	321
— Thomas George	43, 410
— Wilfred Burrell	381
— William Anstruther	135
— William Brooke	412
— William Dixon	135
— Wm. Gordon	250
— Thorburn, William	337
— Thorne, Antoine D.	238
— Henry Albert	361
— James	178
— John F. Vernon	261
Thorneycroft, Alex. W.	262
Thornhill, Clement Bensley	438
— Henry Beaufoy	65, 415
— John	427
— Wm. Henry	505
Thornley, Robert Wm.	368
Thornton, Arth. Parry	46, 412
— Charles Edward	435
— Edward Evelyn D.	367
— Fran. Spencer	63, 356
— Fred. Geale Todd	283
— Hugh	424
— James Aylmer	174
— Leslie Heber	357
— Sidney Vernon	170
Thorold, Chas. Cecil H.	55, 265
— Frederick Temple	295
— Hayford Douglas	277
— Henry Cecil	256
— William Grant	455
Thoroton, Charles J.	401
— Wm. Henry	505
— Austin	177
— John Claude	172
— John Somerled	233
Thorpe, Edw. Ivan de S.	255
Thowless, Edwin	386
Thoyts, Fras. Gordon G.	252
— Harry Newman Morgan	150
Threipland Wm. Murray	229
Thresher, Jas. Henville	357
Thrashie, Robert A.	285
Thring, Edw. Clavell	367
— Richard H. D.	425
— Wm. Powlett	52, 167
Throckmorton, R. C. B	205
Tnrupp, Francis Morton	175
Thruston, Arth. Blyford	287
Thuillier, Sir H. E. L.	179
— Henry Fleetwood	213
— Sir Henry R.	21, 218
— Willoughby	423
Thurburn Arthur Hugh	262
— James White	51, 207
— Walter Levinge	243
Thurnall, Henry	311
Thursby-Pelham, F. J.	277
Thurston, Hugh C.	281
— Hugh Stanley	385
Thwaites, William	175
Thwaytes, Edmund Chas.	424
— Henry J.	373
Thynne, Reginald T.	6
Tibaldi, Robert J. D.	295
Tibbits, Walter	386
Tickell, Edward James	152
Tidbury, James	379
Tidswell, Edward Cecil	261
Tidy, Arthur Grey	49, 291
Tighe, Clarence D. C.	214
Tighe, Francis Alfred	175
— Michael Augustus	426
— Michael Joseph	429
— Staub lans Michael	432
— Vincent John	277
Tillard, Arthur B.	439
— Arthur George	309
— Francis Bonham	214
— J. Arthur	6, 179
Tillbrook, P. Lim.	130
Tilley, Wm. Fairbairn	212
Tilly, Justice C.	55, 255
Tilney, Norman E.	177
— Wm. Arthur	159
Timins, C. Sumner	254
Timmis, John Vernon	261
Tims, Frederic	370
Tindal, Arthur H. U.	285
Tinker, Edward	171
Tinley, Gervase F. N.	418
Tippinge, Ernest Alfred Gartside	173
Tisdall, Arthur Lance	171
Tizard, Henry E.	347
Tobin, Fred. John	65, 329
Tod, Alex. Geo. Wm.	264, 370
— George Russell	318
— John Kelso	430
Tod-Mercer, B. M. M.	213
Todd, C. Campbell	348
— Killingworth R.	22, 205
— Octavius	380
— Robert Bentley	138
— Wm. Joseph	250
Toke, Roundell Tristram	285
Toker, Alliston C.	19, 408
Toller, Hamlet B.	261
Tolmer, Barrett Lennard	28
Tolson, Wilfred	22
Tomblings, Edw. G.	150
Tomes, Arthur	454
Tomkin, Jas. W. Royce	348
Tomkins, Ernest Leith	175
— Harry Leith	238
— William Edward	433
— Wm. Percival	27, 216
Tomkinson, Henry	42, 143
Tomlin, Maurice Hillard	259
— Robert Ernest	211
Tompkins, John James	268
Tomlinson, Lionel Philip	386
Tompson, How Wakeman	281
— Toms, Francis B. R.	170
T nzo, Cecil Richard	214
— William Corrio	245
T nuochy, Valens C.	66, 415
Toogood, Arth. Seymour	242
— Cecil	278
Toppin, Harry Stanley	240
Tordiffe, Stafford H. W.	308
Torin, Ernest R. Hope	44, 155
Torkington, Henry	41, 166
Torrie, Lawrence J.	63, 415
Tothill, Francis W. G.	170
Tottenham, Arth. E. H.	49, 337
— Charles Bosvile	156
— Ponsonby John Loftus	152
— Robert Loftus	432
Toulson, Clement P.	139
Tower, Conyors	138
— George Alfred	65, 209
— William Maitland	145
Towers-Clark, Alex.	67, 301
Townend, Rec. A. J.	396
— Eustace Montague	239
Townley, Charles R.	49, 250
Townsend, C. C.	170
— Cuthbert Hanson	275
— Edmond	378
— Edward Copleston	429
— Samuel	380
— Samuel C. Chetwode	176
Townshend, A. Fitzhenry	270
— Chas. V. F.	425
— Ernest	380
— George Robert	59, 168
Towse, Ernest Beckwith	321
Towsey, Francis Wm.	253
Tozer, Arthur G. M.	250
Tracey, Arthur	61, 169
Tracy, Wm. Maxwell	236, 370
Traherne, Geo. Gilbert	174
Traill, John Murray	255
— William Henry	274
— William Stewart	213
Trapani, Alfred	186
— Charles	186
Trask, John Ernest	384

Index—Active List.

Travers, Eaton Aylmer 52, 417	Tufnell, L. Chas. Gostling 275	Tylden, William 55, 168	Vaughan, P. Balderston 423
— George Alfred 211	— Nevill Arthur C. de H. 288	Tylden-Pattenson, E. C. 214	— Richard Randal 435
— Hugh Arthur............ 262	Tufton, Hon. John Sackville R. 133	Tyler, Alfred Herbert... 213	— Robert Edward 435
— Hugh Price 140		— Arthur John 277	— Thomas Tweed ...55, 163
— Jonas Hamilton du B. 267	Tugwell, Cl. Buchanan 283	— Arthur Malcolm 174	Vaughan-Hughes, Ernest 55, 168
— Joseph Oates 249	Tuite, Mark Antony..... 420	— Charles William 173	
— Robert Eaton............ 438	Tuke, George Jerry A. 383	— Francis Cameron...... 178	Vaughan-Williams, Herbert Wynne........... 386
Tredgold, John A. T. ... 367	— Martin L. 290	— Henry Edward...63, 209	
— Wm. Lancelot......360, 370	Tullibardine, Marquis of 135	— James Arbuthnot...... 174	Vawdrey, George 368
Treeby, Henry Paul 275	Tulloch, Alex. Bruce...... 18	— John Charles......59, 208	Vella, Alfred 186
Treffry, Frederic 371	— Donald Fiddes 176	— Ralph Edward 175	— Arthur 186
Trefusis, Hon. Hy. W.... 233	— Jas. Bruce Gregorie .. 295	— Trevor Bruce 26, 165	— Walter Dunbar 186
Tregear, Fred. Charles 360	— John Arthur S.......... 211	— W. E. Saumerez 284	Venables, Charles John 272
— Vincent F. W. 440	— John Walter Graham 424	Tyndall, Henry Stuart 362	— Edward Frederick ... 294
— Vincent Wm...........22, 404	— Tom Gregorie 175	Tyrell, Rev. Edw. 306	Venner, Charles F. V.
Treherne, Fras. Harper 381	Tulloh, Geo. Swinton ... 272	— Wm. Ernest Marriott 277	Sidebottom 430
Tremaine, Richard 171	— Robert Henry Wm.... 295	Tyrrell, Arthur Fredk.... 385	Venour, Walter Edwin 432
Tremayne, Hon. Arthur 276	Tuohy, John Fra........... 454	— Chas. Robert 381	— Wilfrid John 343
— J. Hearle.................. 155	Tupman, John A. 401	— Gerald Ernest 177	Ventris, Francis...... 24, 288
Trench, Charles 17	— Kenneth Lyon 244	— John Frederick......... 177	Vere, Henry 50, 304
— Fred. A. Le Poer...48, 366	Tupper, Gas. Le Marchant 164	Tyrwhitt, Hon. Rupert 170	Vereker, Chas. G........ 176
— Fred. John A. 65, 169		Tyrwhitt-Walker, J. 69, 233	— Hon. J. E. P. 170
— Geo. Fred. Cheuevix 422	— Jasper Selwyn 42	Tytler, H. Christopher 433	Verner, Edw. Wingfield 245
— Henry Walter......46, 346	Turing, Arthur Henry... 243	— Robert Adam Neilson 321	— George de Wet 269
— Henry Wm. Bloomfield 287	Turnbull, Cha. Fred.A.50, 276	— Robert F. C. A....16, 404	— Thomas Edward....44, 245
— Stewart John 57, 277	— George Wilmot M. 28, 165	Ubsdell, James Eads ... 252	— Wm. V. Cole......59, 356
Trenchard, Hugh M. ... 262	— Harold Price 335	Umfreville, Percy 294	Verney, Hon. Hy. Peyto 149
Trent, Francis Harrison 274	— P. Stephenson 529	— Samuel O................... 277	Vernon, Granville...... 28
— George Alexander ... 292	— Sydney Drummond 42, 410	Underwood, Joseph Wm. 146	— Hubert Edward 357
Trethewy, Thomas L. ... 276	Turner, Alex. Scott 293	— Thomas Ormsby...19, 405	— Ronald James 305
— Walter Hugh............ 281	— Alfred Edw. 23, 165	— Walter John 172	Verschoyle, E. Greville 229
Trevelyan, W. F. ... 310, 374	— Alfred G. Burn 435	Unett, John Alfred 254	— Jno. Ham 65, 276
Trevor, Arthur P. 177	— Alfred H. P. 61, 167	Uniacke, Henry Percy... 321	Versturme, Charles H. 212
— Francis W................. 379	— Archer L. M............... 170	— Herbert C. Campbell 174	— Hy. Palairet............ 234
— George Herbert ...22, 407	— Arthur Edward......... 213	— Norman Fyfe............ 161	Vertue, Naunton Henry 237
— Harry 425	— Augustus Henry...26, 408	— Robie Fitzgerald 271	— William 19, 405
— Henry Octavius......... 381	— Benjamin 141	Unthank, Clement W. O. 145	Vesey, Chas. Edw. Gore 213
— Herbert Edward 205	— Charles..................... 293	Unwin, Gaston B.......... 421	— Chas. Nicholas O..... 150
— Hubert B. Cosmo...... 252	— Charles Hampden ... 230	— Robert Burrell 250	— Herbert Charles ... 433
— Philip C. Wm. ...245, 370	— Edward 185	Upcher, Russell 18	Votch, Robt. Hamilton22, 204
— William Herbert 237	— Ernest Vere 214	Upperton, Bryan 287	— William Francis 22
Trevor-Boothe, Arthure	— Francis Charles 240	— Stuart 284	Vickerman, Albert 237
Lockwood 146	— Frank Gordon 214	Uppleby, John Geo ...42, 166	Vickers, Chas. Ernest... 214
Trewman, Geo. T. 381	— Fred. Cooper 42	Urmston, Archibald G.B. 400	— Cuthbert 236
Tribe, Cecil Walford 346, 369	— Fred. Mansel 48, 156a	— E. Brabazon 337	— Hilton 433
— Charles Walter 435	— Frederick Wm. Chas. 433	Urquhart, B. Colclough 325	— Wilfrid Constant ... 505
Triggs, Walter 138, 374	— George 267	— Edward Wm. L. 377	Vidal, Leonard Hugh ... 426
Trim, Robert William 308, 370	— George Harvey......... 426	— Walter A. 58, 163	— William Sealy 210
Trimby, Thomas 347	— Harold LakeCompton 231	Usborne, Thos. Masters 174	Vidler, Wm. Thomas ... 385
Trimnell, Wm. D C...... 178	— Harold Palgrave 255	Usmar, Geo. Alleyne ... 178	Vigne, Robert Austen... 172
Tringham, Archibald M. 256	— Henry Blois 179	Usher, Allan Vesey 270	Vigor, Fred. George 53, 275
Tripp, Arth. W. Howard 244	— Henry Fyers.........23, 224	— Edward 144	Vigors, Cliffe Henry ... 253
Triscott, Charles P....68, 169	— Henry Hamilton F.... 435	— Percy John 393	— Philip C. W. 243
Tristram, Chas. Edw..... 440	— Henry Scott 286	Utermarck, Reginald	— Richd. Percy L......... 334
— L. S. B 285	— Horace Harrison 213	J. G. 309, 373	— Thomas Mercer...233, 373
— Miles Haltou............ 154	— James Gibbon 421	Utterson, Archibald H. 56	Villiers, Charles Hyde . 135
Tritton, Charles 424	— Martin Newman 276	Vaid, Cooverjee Cawasjee 454	Villiers-Stuart, Chas. H. 352
Trollope, A. G............. 237	— Neville George Harry 277	Vallancey, H.d'Estampes 337	— William D. 372
Trotman, C. Newsham ... 400	— Percy Alexander 277	Valentin, John M. 252	Vince, William 245
— Wm. Mends Forte 272, 373	— Reginald George 457	Valling, A. tolphus...22, 407	Vincent, Arth. Gustave 400
Trotter, Alg. Richard ... 134	— Samuel Compton...43, 206	— Henry Alan 437	— Arth. C. FitzH......50, 270
— Edward Henry......... 230	— William 382	Vance, Horatio Page ... 132	— Aug. Edward 242
— Everard G. Stanley ... 302	— Wm. Derington......... 409	Van Cortlandt, Arthur	— Berkeley 177
— Frank W. D. 437	Turnour, Hon. Keith 46, 304	James Ramsay...63, 145	— Edward 308
— Gerald Frederic 230	Turton, Hugh M. 270	Vandeleur, Cecil Fosters. 233	— Frank Lloyd 433
— Henry 16	— Ralph Douglas 264	— Crofton Bury............ 270	— Henry Alex. 45, 411
— James Keith 43, 166a	— William Harry 209	— Robert Seymour 268	— Henry Osmin 172
— Philip Durham 23	Tuson, Chas. Edward ... 270	— Wm. MountCharles C. 283	— William Torrens 431
— Robert Francis.....53, 413	— George Edward 158	Van der Gucht, Rupert L. 244	Vines, Charles James ... 272
— Warren Francis 398	— H. Brasnell 5, 397	Vanderzee, Fra. Hy....19, 406	Vivian, Arthur Granville 439
— William John 384	— Harry Denison 278	— Henry Frank............ 174	— Charles Augustus ... 362
— William Kemp 277	Tuthill, Charles H. 136	— John Herbert............ 436	— Frederick Guy 57, 414
Troup, Hugh Rose 436	— Phineas B. 379	Vane, Hon. Wm. Lyonel 374	Vizard, Robt. Davenport 309
Trower, Courtney Vor.61, 207	Tweddell, Francis 431	Van Gayzel, John L. ... 503	Von Donop, Pelham G.55, 208
Troyte-Bullock, Cecil J. 252	— Henry 435	Vanrenen, Adrian J. H. 429	— Stanley Brenton 171
Trumin, Wm. Robinson 19	— Wm. Walter Maurice 163	— Arthur Sanders 216	Von Hugel, Norman G. 211
Truscott, John Jas. 185	Tweedie, Fras. James ... 274	— George Rainier 436	von Schröder, William
Trusler, James 178	— Gerald Scott 234	JacobPieterDenays40, 409	Henry 151
Trydell, Arthur Stuart... 395	— John L. 22	— James Ernest............ 212	Vores, Charles H. S. ... 171
— Botét.......................... 432	— Maurice 18, 405	Vans-Agnew, Edward Lovelace 259	Vost, William.......... 455
Tryon, George C. 230	— William John Bell ... 337		Vousden, Wm. John 28, 409
Tuck, John Johnson...... 371	— Wm. Walter Maurice 163	— Francis 173	Vowell, Hugh Alex. ... 253
Tucker, A. E. Ranelagh 264	Twemlow, E. D'Oyley 25, 219	— John 171	— Richard Augustus 256, 374
— Aubrey Charles 314	Twigg, Edw. Francis ... 434	— John Fraser 170	Voyle, Henry Elliot ... 274
— Charles..................... 7	— Robert Henry.....61, 422	Vansittart, Charles E.... 369	Vulliamy, Colwyn Williams 47, 255
— George 214	Twining, P. Geoffrey ... 212	— Eden 419	
— Louis Henry Emile 26, 404	Twiss, Francis Arthur 177	Van Straubenzee, A. H. 210	Vyvyan, Courtenay B.... 237
— William Guise 43, 397	— George Edward......... 380	— Bowen Wm. Sutton... 267	— Herb. Reginald 249
Tuckey, Charles......262, 369	— John Henry 212	— Casimir Cartwright... 174	— Richard Walter C. ... 285
— Thos. Broderick A.... 381	Twist, Alex. W. E. 346	— Casimir Henry C. ... 250	Wace, Ernest C.......51, 167
Tudor, Ernest Augustus	Twomey, Rev. Timothy 396	— Turner 17	— Richard 23
Tudor............................. 211	Twyford, Ernest H. S.... 270	Vaughan, Chas. Davies 17	— Rev. Walter 507
— Henry Hugh 176	— Lionel Thos. C.......... 310	— Edward 309	Waddell, Charles Claudo 155
Tidway, Robert John ... 288	Twynam, Humphrey M. 274	— Edward Gyles 436	— Lawrence Nicholas 454
Tufnell, Arth. Wyndham 236	— Thomas MacGregor... 317	— Henry Bathurst 424	Waddington, Edward W. 362
— Edward 130	Tyacke, George 173	— Herbert R. 242	— Evelyn de B............ 347
— George Murray......... 288	— Nicholas 385	— John 149	— P. M. 176
— Hugh Richard 272	Tyers, Sydney 42, 401	— Joseph Chas. Stoelke 456	Wadly, J. M. Elgee 47, 252

Index—Active List.

Wade, Alex. P. C. H. 254
— Arthur G. S. ...50, 167
— George Augustus 384
— Harry A. L. H. 178
— H. Molesworth St. A. 212
— James Molesworth 210
— T. Stewart Herschel 261
— William Barton 371
Wadeson, Fred. W. G. 424
Wadham, William 357
Wagborn, Wm. Danvers 212
Wahab, Robert Alex.63, ... 209
Wailes, Wm. Eteson 175
Wait, Hugh G. K. 213
Waite, Albert Wm. 152
— William John 149
Wake, Edw. St. Aubyn 430
— Hugh St. Aubyn 240
— William St. Aubyn 301
Wakefield, Henry G. R. 346
Waldron, Francis......55, ... 168
— Henry Fra. Kelly 420
Waldy, Richard W. 255
WALES, H. R. H. the Prince of
1, 4, 133, 134, 135, 152
Walford, Neville Lloyd 28
— Wm. Sworder ......51, ... 167
Walhouse,Chas. H. de K. 310
Walker, Albert Lancelot 7
— Alexander ......7, ... 179
— Alex. Lamond 173
— Arthur Greenwood 42, ... 166
— Chas. E. FitzGerald 267
— Charles Pope 383
— Charles Warren ...42, ... 410
— Claude E. Forestier 174
— Crichton 214
— Devereux Philip 294
— Edgar Holford......44, ... 166
— Edmond Somerville F. 171
— Edw. John Howard 309
— Edward Wm. May 170
— Francis Spring 439
— Frank Hercules 262
— F. W. E. F. 5
— Qr.Mr. George 178
— Lieut. George 213
— George Ferdinand 265
— George Kemp 395
— George Lemon 504
— George Stanley 385
— George T. Forestier 173
— Harold Bridgwood 270
— Harold Maxwell 133
— Capt. Henry 253
— 2nd Lt. Henry 362
— Henry Alexander 243
— Henry C. C. ......52, ... 167
— Henry George 432
— Herbert John 213
— Herbert Sutherland 27
— Hugh Edward 265
— James 38
— James Grant D. ...22, ... 403
— JohnChas.Arthington 101
— John Douglas Glen 286
— John Newman ... 46, ... 411
— John Symeon 372
— Launcelot Henry 432
— Malcolm Reginald 295
— Melville 172
— Montagu C. B. F....50, ... 304
— Percy Gerald 422
— Reginald Selby 213
— Samuel McAll 370
— Thomas ......24, ... 181
— William 395
— William Arch. Small 362
— William George 432
— William Reginald 395
— William Robert 437
Walkey, Rowland ... 27, ... 165
Wall, Allan Copinger 301
— Edward James 214
— Edward Watkin 433
— Frank 506
Wallace, Alexander 418
— Augustus Robert 291
— John Tannoch 292
— Chas. Tennant 19
— George Bright 288
— Robert Hugh ... 43, ... 166
— Thomas 368
— Wm. Berkeley 250
— William R. P. 272
Wallack, Henry Jobling 130
Waller, Alfred A. P. 272

Waller, Edmund ......65, ... 431
— Edmund Aug. ......63, ... 209
— Fred. C. Livingston 433
— John Dawson H. 170
— John Hampden 130
— John Edmund ......7, ... 404
— Richard Lancelot 214
— Stanier 43, 206
Wallerstein,Fra.Edw.58, ... 311
— Walling, A. Tremearne 433
Wallington, Charles D. 261
Wallis, Alex. Fred. 277
— Edward Snell 259
— Francis Joseph 437
— Hugh Ryves 435
— Kenneth S. 379
Wallnutt,Claude Charles Miller 321
Walpole, Alfred 212
Walsh, Art. H. Hill... 6, ... 397
— Hon. Charles Edw. 357
— Fred. Wm. Henry 177
— George Inverarity 256
— Henry Alfred ......49, ... 252
— Hunt Henry A. 305
— John G. Russell 293
— John Henry Tull 455
— Richard Knox 262
— Thomas 377
— Walter P. Hussey 256
— William Hussey 264
Walshe, Henry E. 282
Walter, Charles 270
— George Egbert 418
— Harold Ernest 246
— James Alfred 302
— General John M'Neill 309
— Capt. John MacNeill 249
— Richard Lionel 149
— Stephen 138
— William Frederick 318
Walters, Herbert Flamstead 432
— Hubert de Lansey 175
— Hugh de Laucey 284
— Robert Francis 288
Wallscourt H. H. ... 64, ... 169
Walthall, Brian J. D. 401
— Edw. C. W. D. 178
Walton, Ellys William 210
— Geoffrey Frank ...273, ... 368
— Graham 242
— Herbert 432
— Lewin Barlow 434
— Wm. Crawford 430
Wanliss, Cecil 284
Wansbrough, Joseph H. 255
Wapshare, Arthur ...59, ... 414
— Richard 424
Warburton, Robert ...40, ... 403
— Robert Francis 252
— William 214
— Wm. Peace 454
Ward, A. Clitherow...40, ... 205
— Alfred Edw. J seph 457
— Arthur Edward ...43, ... 411
— Bernard Rowland 210
— Bertram Edmund 301, ... 368
— Charles 372
— Cyril Harding 439
— Edward ......53, ... 167
— Edmund Ironside 367
— Edward Francis 305
— Edw. Willis D. ...41, ... 366
— Francis William... 18, ... 179
— Frederick Houlton 69, ... 169
— George Alexander 431
— George Louis Stuart 439
— Harry Dudley O. 177
— Herbert Samuel 368
— J. E. Drummond 301
— John Harry 401
— Lloyd Brereton 378
— Hon. Maxwell R. C. 175
— Montagu C. Pearson 175
— Hon. Reginald 135
— 2nd Lieut. Thomas 137
— Qr. Mr. Thomas 178
— Thomas Rawdon R. 253
— Trimnell Martin 432
— Walter W. ......58, ... 254
— William Homan 370
— William John 395
— Wm.Percy Burnell 368
Warde,Henry Murray A. 46
— Hugh North 430
Wardell, Godfrey F. E. 282
— Warren Hy. 438

Warden, Alf. Walter 430
— Charles J. H. 453
— Hugh Fawcett 236
— Louis Herbert 308
— Richard Edward 173
Wardlaw, John Colin 278
Wardrop, Alex. Ernest 177
— Douglas 380
— Frederick Meyer 23
— Wardroper, Edwin 26
Ware, Frank C. W. 435
Waring, Henry 172
— Richard 176
— William Wheat 153
Warliker, Damodar P. 505
Warlow, Rev. George 506
— Rev. Edmund John 460
Warneford, Gonville 252
Warner, Charles Algernon Simeon 159
— Ernest Henry Lee 259
— Rowan H. Lee 367
— Wm. Bannatyne 25, ... 404
— William Ward 434
Warrand, Alex. Redmond Bewley 318
Warre, Henry Charles 305
— Sir Henry James 185
Warren, Sir Charles ...6, ... 204
— Dawson 236
— Frank 177
— George Ernest 278
— John 377
— Lionel Charles 347
— Percy Bliss 431
— Richard Pennefather 426
— William Lewis 173
Warren - Swettenham, Thos, R. E. Wybault 254
Warrender, Hugh V. 230
Warry, Arthur 165
— Bertram Arthur 288
Warwick, Chas. Spencer 249
Washington, Cecil F. G. 176
— Francis Palmer... 44, ... 206
Waterfield, Arthur C. M. 435
— Bertram Clarke 437
— Henry Gordon ...21, ... 406
Waterhouse, James 23, ... 408
Waterman, George 147
Waters, Edm. E. Nash 177
— George 529
— Horace William Plews 284
— Wallscourt H. H. ..61, ... 169
Wathen, Edw. Owen 147
Watherston, Alan E. G. 212
Watkin, Henry George 145
— H. S. Spiller 41
Watkins, Chas. Bell 170
— Chas. Mostyn F. as. 212
— Fredric Mostyn 258
— John 68, 318
— Leonard George 171
Watkis, Hon. B. Burlton 421
Watling, Charles Edw. 335
— Francis Hammond 457
— Francis Wyatt 213
— Gordon 435
— John Thomas ... 26, ... 409
Watson, Alex. O. C....41, ... 384
— Alfred Carnac 434
— Alfred George ...50, ... 274
— Rev. Alf. Wm. Brown 396
— Arthur 282
— Arthur John ...51, ... 250
— Rev. A. B. 532
— Charles Moore ....44, ... 206
— Charles Stanbrough 401
— Chris. Godfrey 173
— Edward Hurlock 301
— Edw. Yerbury 430
— George Fred. 199
— George Herbert 419
— George Vincent 291
— Guy Hartley 140
— Harry Davis 431
— James Kiero 305
— John 380
— John Capron 174
— John Edward 309
— John G. Maitland 176
— John Jas. C. 384
— Lionel Arthur 258
— Robert Samuel ... 44, ... 166
— Solomon ......51, ... 167
— Spencer Burton 362
— Thos. Colclough 213

Watson, Thomas James 417
— William Arthur 424
— Wm. Donald Paul 144
— William Milward 277
Watt, Donald Munro 322
— Redmond Edw. 287
Watts, Chas. D. Raynsford 176
— Charles N. 289
— Edward Chorley 296
— Geo. Annesley Ross 441
— Herbert Edward 253
— John Briscoe......41, ... 409
— Ponsonby William 42
— William Burton 360
Watts-Jones, Wm. A. 213
Wauchope, A. G.....22, ... 286
Wavell, Arch. E. 28
Way, Alfred Cotton 360
— Benjamin Irby 310
— Lewis 384
— Nowell Fitz E. G. 401
— Nowell FitzUpton 21, ... 399
— Wilfred Fitz Allan 44, ... 240
Waymouth, Chas. S. H. 283
— Ernest G. 175
— Hugh Newcome 431
Wayne, Herman Geo. W. 254
Weallens, William... 65, ... 267
Webb, Algernon Edward 435
— Andrew Henry 177
— Charles Alfred 380
— Charles S. Chapman 400
— Duncan 367
— Edw. Arthur H. 372
— Francis Edward 372
— G. Ambrose Congreve 347
— Geo. Theodosius W. 401
— Humphrey Lakin 143
— Roderick Beauclerk 143
— Somerset E. Denne 311
— Thomas Montgomerie 254
— Walter Edward 269
— William 286
— Wm. Edward 378
Webber,Francis Peirson 432
— James Webber 23
— Oswald Thomas O'K. 213
— Raymond Sudeley 265
Webster, Sir Aug. F. W. E. Bt. 229
— George 186
— Henry F. George 372
— Thomas 429
Wedderburn, Alex. S. 170
— Henry Scrymgeour 322
Weelon, Franklin F. 212
Weekes, Henry W. 213
Wegg - Prosser, John Francis ......59, ... 356
Weigall, GeorgeEdward 171
Weir, Arthur Vavasour 330
— Harry George ......53, ... 167
— James Chris. 384
— Patrick Alex. 453
— Richard Rose 455
— Tho. Stephenson 529
Welby, Alf. C. Earle....44, ... 144
— Glynne E. Earle 268
Welch, Alfred John 269
— Francis Henry 377
— Frederick G. T. ......45, ... 411
— Geo. Osbaldeston 367
— Malcolm E. H. O....55, ... 413
— Malcolm H. Edw. 258
— Norman Charles 281
Welchman, E.W.St.G.58, ... 416
— Sidney Chaytor 281
— Weldon, Bertram de W. 256
— Francis Harry 289
— George Anthony 348
Wellby,MontaguSinclair 160
Weller, Alex. Thos. ...57, ... 413
— George Herbert 422
Wellesley, Lord Ar.C. 21, ... 229
— Gerald Valerian 373
— Richard A. Colley 175
— Richard Colley 174
Wells, Henry Lake ...45, ... 208
Welman, Arthur Pole 271, ... 367
— George Arthur 419
— Harvey 423
— Harvey Beauchamp 297
— Herbert Loftus 329
Welsh, David James 278
— Francis Aug. Maling 333
Welstead, Geo. Reginald 273
— Harry M. 250

Index—Active List. 578

Wemyss, Binfield	27, 404
— David Gillespie	234
— Fras. *Earl of*	1
— Francis C.	130
— Robert D. S.	321
— Robert E. Fitzmayer	177
Wentworth, B. C. Vernon	229
Were, Harry Harris	274
— Walter	348
West, Alex. Arthur	438
— Ernest Edw.	147
— George Wm. Maxwell	438
— Rooblio Hassan	213
Westcott, Sinclair	381
Westerman, Joseph F.	176
Western, Charles M.	49, 166a
— Charles M.T.	61, 168
— John S. E.	420
— Wm. Geo. Balfour	66, 294
Westlake, Almond P.	419
Westmacott, Claude B.	273
— H. Richard	285
— Richard	23, 408
— Ruscombe Field	55, 261
Westmorland, Ch. H.	53, 416
— Herbert Graham	281
— P. Thuillier	360, 374
Weston, Chas. Hy. Balliol	293
— Clarence	283
— *Col.* George Edw.	24, 404a
— *Surg. Capt.* Geo. Edw.	381
— Reginald Salter	309
— Thos. Barnes	52, 162, 374
Westropp, Fred. Malcolm	213
— George R. Collier	421
— Henry Chas. Edw.	309
— Michael S. Dudley	323
— Richard Gibbings	177
Wetherall, Edw. Richard	362
— John And. C.	292
— William Alex.	431, 410
Wethered, Harold F.	274
— Joseph Robert	272
Wetherell, Robt. W. M.	17
— William Edward May	255
Whaite, Thomas du B.	384
Wharry, Herbert	419
Whately, Reginald Pepys	279
Whatman, Amherst B.	252
— William Douglas	162
Wheatley, Guy R. P.	245
— H. Spencer	55, 413
— Philip	177
Wheeler, *Rev.* Charles E.	457
— Edgar Lockyer	178
— Edward	47, 397
— Geo. Godfrey Massy	303
— Guy Danvers	177
— Henry Littleton	281
— John C. Massy	439
— John Langford	369
Wheler, Chas. Stuart	59, 414
— Edward	69, 279
Whiffin, George G.	236
— Henry Edward	428
— Walter John	398
Whigham, Robt. Dundas	242
Whinfield, Henry Chas.	236
Whishaw, Edw. Richard	282
Whistler, Albert Edw.	420
— Fuller	317
— Thomas Godfrey	281
Whiston, Philip Henry	384
Whitaker, Arthur M.	277
— Charles John	47, 311
— Chas. Hildyard T.	295
— Hen. Joseph W.	281
— James	162
Whitby, Fred. Henry	47, 314
Whitchurch, H. Fred.	456
Whitcombe, Ernest G. R.	530
White, Arthur Ogilvie.	270
— Arthur Wellesley	40, 166
— Aubrey Francis	63, 285
— Charles	377
— Edward Dalrymple.	287
— Finch	275
— Frank Aug. Kinder.	214
— Frederick	400
— Frederick Alexander	250
— Fred. Benj. Price	18
— Fred. Power L.	65, 415
— Geoffrey H. Anthony	176
— George Edmund	249
— George Francis	173
— *Sir* G. Stewart	5
— Godfrey Dalrymple.	229
— Hans Stannard	170
White, H. A. Pilkington	174
— *Hon.* Henry Fred.	68, 229
— Henry Lawrence E.	380
— Henry Fitz L. P. F. E.	504
— Herbert Southey N.	400
— Ion Grove	435
— James Grove	53, 301
— John Joseph	297
— Joseph Henry L.	240
— Joshua Chaytor	456
— Loftus Otway	370
— *Sir* Robert	163
— *Hon.* Robert	265
— Robert Wm. Perssé.	285
— Samuel R. Llewellyn	346
— W. Hanbury	52, 208
— Wilfred Arthur	335
— William Edward	436
— William Frederick	264
— William Hawtrey	258
— William Lewis	66, 169
— Wm. Westropp	456
White-Thomson, H. D.	173
Whitehead, Edmd. L'E.	176
— Gervase F.	236
— Hayward Reader	381
— John Herbert	386
— John Holberton	436
— Randolph Edward	347
Whitehill, Cha. S.	49, 295
Whitehorne, Arth. H.	50, 167
Whiteley, *Rev.* C. E.	507
Whitestone, Chas. W. H.	385
Whitfield, Geo. Digby	395
Whitla, Valentino Geo.	137
Whitley, Joseph	41, 366
— Wm. Thomas	178
Whitlock, Chas. Jas. T.	21, 407
— George Fred. Ashford	213
Whitmarsh, John F.V.S.	401
Whittall, Fras. Vaughan	425
Whitting, John Everard	18
Whittington, Geo. J. Ch.	371
— Richard Chas. Albert	250
— Thomas Duncan Legh	239
Whitton, Fred. Ernest.	346
— J. M'Gregor	28
Whitty, Michael J.	383
Whitwell, Robt. Rich. H.	454
Whylock, Jas. G. H.	272
Whyte, Chas. Wm. Fred.	427
— John Frederick	431
— John Nicholas	277
Wickham, Charles B.	42, 166
— Wm. James Richard.	423
Widdicombe, Fred. S.	432
— George Templer	433
Widdrington, Bertram F.	305
Wiehe, Fras. Geo. A.	47
Wigan, Jas. Ramsay	293
Wiggin, Edgar Askin	155
Wight, Ernest O.	381
Wigram, Clive	173
— Henry Hampden	233
— Herwald Robert	269
Wikeley, Jas. Masson.	435
Wilberforce, Herbert Wm.	137
Wilbond, James	178
Wilbraham, Herbert V.	297
— Ralph James	276
— *Sir* R.	243
Wilder, Harry C.	256
Wilding, Charles A.	271
Wiley, Henry	65, 246
Wilford, Edmund P.	47
Wilfred, Marriott-Dod-ington	287
Wilken, John	178
Wilkie, Charles Joseph	287
— David	453
— Edward Ormerod H.	273
Wilkieson, Chas. Boyd	49, 207
— Claude Wm.	428
Wilkin, Alexander	346
Wilkins, Ernest G. Rule	431
— Fras. A. Pressland	250
— Geo. Hubert Carey	178
— Henry St. Clair	236
— James Sutherland	529
— Thomas J. Hackett.	504
— William Henry	21, 407
Wilkinson, Allen H.	256
— Arthur	28
— Arthur Clement	176
— Charles	52, 207
— Charles Wm.	213
— Clement Arthur	297
Wilkinson, Edmund	456
— Edward Grant	59, 399
— Ernest	396
— Ernest Berdoe	246
— Francis Allix	243
— Francis Tichborne	381
— Frederick Green	287
— George Edward	271
— Harry	395
— Henry B. Des Voeux	314
— Henry Clement	5
— Lewis Fred. Green	357
— Lionel Thomson V.	329
— Maurice Lean	177
— Montagu Grant	260
— Nevile R.	231
— Percival Spearman.	240
— Roland L. Clennell	140
— Thomas Henry Des V.	356
— Will, Duncan A. E.	420
— George	41, 166
— James	383
— *Rev.* Josiah O.	460
— Wilcox, Walter T.	140
Willes, Charles Edw.	265
— George Fred.	249
Willett, A. J. Saltren	173
Williams, Alfred Henry	453
— *Rev.* Arthur Acheson	507
— Arthur Blount C.	425
— Arthur Cecil	175
— Arthur Henry	431
— Arthur Leonard	234
— Arthur Stuart	176
— Berkeley C. Wilmot.	299
— Cecil Howard	434
— Charles Aug. Muspratt	171
— Charles Edward	457
— Charles Louis	506
— Charles Stanley	430
— Coventry	155
— Edgar M'Kenzie	385
— Edward Arthur	160
— Edward Arthur	164
— Edward Charles Jas.	237
— Edward George	249
— Ernest Montgomery.	386
— Eustace Scott	276
— Frederick Law	283
— Fred. Thesiger	425
— George	239
— George Albanus.	362
— George Augustus	417
— George D. Remington	293
— George Mostyn	395
— Godfrey	239
— Godfrey Trevelyan	153
— *Rev.* Harry Arch.	507
— Henry David	48, 310
— Henry Frederick	347
— Henry John	136
— Herbert A. M'Dougal	337
— Hubert B. Ogilvy	162
— Hugh Bruce	211
— Hugh Edward	434
— John Andrews	185
— John Hanbury	160
— Kynaston	272
— Leonard	229
— Lewis Owen	153
— Masterman Stanley	175
— Oliver de Laucey	265
— Owen	44, 250
— Raymond B.	63, 250
— Reginald	422
— Richard Francis	43, 166
— Sydney Fred.	212
— Thomas	178
— Weir de Lancey	281
— William A. Glanmor	268
— William Hugh	67, 169
— *Sir* William John	65, 164
Williamson, And. P.	69, 416
— Cyril Venn Wilton	77, 378
— James	378
— John Francis	379
— John Gover	378
— Michael	429
— Oswald Charles	172
— Wm. Alex. Finiston	367
Williamson, Wm. Herb.	309
Willis, Chas. Fancourt.	531
— Charles Hope	400
— Edward Henry	178
— *Sir* Geo. H. Smith.	249
— Harry Richard Jas.	145
— James L. N.	22, 407
— Richard ffolliott	401
— Willmott, Arthur	298
— William Albert	240
Willoughby, *Hon.* Claude Henry C.	151
— *Hon.* C. S. Heathcote-Drummond	233
— Herbert Percival.	52, 167
— James Fortnom	27, 404a
— *Sir* John C. *Bt.*	69, 135
— Michael Edward	430
— Robert Frederick	45
Willoughby-Osborne, A. de V.	284
Wills, Samuel Richard.	382
Willson, Mildmay W.	22, 233
Willshire, E. Maxwell	68, 286
Wilmer, Algernon H.	419
— John Randal	24, 408
Wilmot, Arthur Eardley-	67, 171
— Ernest Eardley	436
— Irton Eardley	421
— Wilmot, John Charles	140
— Revell Eardley	7, 404
— W. Ascheton Eardley	25
Wilmot-Sitwell, Degge	329
Wilson, Adam B. Boyd	161
— Alexander	66, 338
— Archdale Irby	258
— Arthur H. Hutton	308
— Arthur Holt	275
— A. Whyte Melville	360
— *Rev.* A. Newton	457
— Cecil William	305
— 2nd *Lt.* Charles Edwd.	236
— *Capt.* Charles Edward	314
— Charles Henry L. F.	170
— Charles Holmes	176
— Charles Stuart	212
— *Sir* Chas. Wm.	7, 204
— Charles Wm. Henry	25
— Cyril Edward	274
— Edmund Munkhouse	381
— Edward Hales	42, 410
— Edwin Bryce	147
— Frank Walter	395
— Fred. Alexander	25, 408
— Frederick Alfred	212
— Frederick Grant	284
— Frederick Maurice	307
— George	387
— George Ernest	245
— George Fred.	53, 208
— George Tyrie Brand	317
— Gordon Chesney	135
— Henry Brooke	25
— Henry Fuller M.	356
— Henry Hughes	357
— Herbert Stanley	177
— Horace Hayman	261
— James Alban	436
— James Barnett	383
— John	310
— John Charles	298
— John Francis	417
— George Jno. Yule	41, 369
— Joseph Reginald	174
— Lancelot Machell	177
— Leslie Orme	401
— Malcolm	333
— Richard Hy. Francis Wharton	50, 152
— Richard Hy. George	246
— Samuel Herbert	214
— Stuart Murray	395
— Taylor Dalrymple	51, 262
— Wm. Augustus Mitchell	424
— Wm. Bernard	51, 412
— Wm. Deane	377
— Wm. Henry	19, 406
Wilson — Farquharson, David Lorraine	286
Wiltshire, Herbert	162
Wimberley, Chas. Irvine	427
— Chas. Neil Campbell	456
— Fras. Gordon Arabin	268
Wimble, Walter Ernest	426
Winchester, *Marq. of*	231
Winckley, *Rev.* C. R.	460
Windham, Charles Jsph.	434

Index—Active List.

- Windle, Reg. J. ... 384
- Windsor, Cyril Vivian... 249
- Wm. John ... 436
- Wing, Fred. D. V. ... 171
- Wingate, Alfred W. S... 426
- — Allan Sievwright..... 321
- — Fras. Reginald ... 52, 171
- — George................58, 414
- — Godfrey H. F. ... 234
- — Thomas Oliver.....25, 408
- — Rev. William 532
- Wingfield, Geo. A. Cecil Digby................... 185
- — John Maurice............ 231
- — Mervyn E. G. R. 134
- — Walter Clopton......... 120
- — William Edward 174
- Wingfield-Stratford, C. V. 65, 209
- Winn, Hon. Charles Cavendish 357
- — John 210
- Winsloe, Alf. Raynaud... 213
- — Herbert Edward 214
- Winter, Bertram E. 308, 373
- — Clifford Boardman ... 439
- — Frederic Charles 288
- — Frederic John 171
- — Herbert Edmond 384
- — Samuel Henry 43, 366
- — Thomas Bassell......... 382
- — Wm. Robt............43, 366
- Wintle, Ernest de Vaynes 430
- — FitzHardinge............ 432
- — Frank G. 369
- — Henry Russell 403
- Wintour, Evelyn 434
- — Fitzgerald 51, 294
- Winwood, Hon. J. Hoyte 174
- — William Quintyne ... 140
- Wisden, Thos. F. Mair 279
- Wise, Alexander 335
- — Fras. Hubert............ 155
- — Henry Ellison 289
- Wishart, Richard James 176
- Witham, Francis 142
- Wither, Arch. C. Bigg 40, 404
- Witherby, Bertram 295
- Withers, Samuel H 385
- Withington, Guy E. W... 284
- Withycombe, Wm. M... 295
- Wodehouse, Alb. Philip 46, 271
- — Edmund 267
- — Ernest Chas F.......... 273
- — Frederic William 433
- — Josceline Heneage 25, 167
- Wolfe, George Cecil B. 400
- — John William 456
- Wolferstan, Egerton Stanley Pipe 282
- Wolff, Arnold J............ 214
- Wollen, Wm. R. Grant.. 214
- Wollstein, Harry More 270
- Wolseley, G. J. Visct. ... 4
- — Sir George Benjamin 6
- — John Francis............ 264
- — William Owen 480
- Wolseley-Jenkins, C. B. H............. 49, 161
- Wombwell, Reg. Arthur 143
- Wood, Alex. Vaughan L. 147
- — Attiwell Henry.....58, 334
- — Cecil Strachan 254
- — Charles Hastings...... 177
- — Charles Knight ... 58, 208
- — Chas. M. Aloysius ... 240
- — Clement Baddeley ... 270
- — Creighton 171
- — Cyril 50, 288
- — Cyril Edward 434
- — David Edward.....63, 150
- — Edw. Alexander 7
- — Edw. Jas. Fandon 63, 415
- — Elliott 22
- Wood, Ernest 269
- — Ernest J. Macfarlane 433
- — Ernest Perceval 425
- — Evelyn FitzGerald M. 249
- — Francis Ludlow....... 297
- — Hastings St. Leger ... 254
- — Henry 214
- — Sir H. Evelyn........... 4
- — Hon. Mackenzie M. 40, 409
- — Henry Stotesbury ... 456
- — Herbert Wm. Wainman 277
- — Jefferson Serrell... 52, 278
- — John Lockhart 160
- — John Page 278
- — John Wm. Massey ... 143
- — Lewis Ironside 278
- — Manners Charles...44, 152
- — Maximilian David ... 253
- — Oswald G. 378
- — Percy Arthur N. S. ... 423
- — Philip Richard 333
- — Thomas Birchall 173
- — William 43, 288
- — Wyndham M. P. 346
- Woodall, Frederic 279
- Woodcock, Hen. Stephen 174
- — Wm. Cha. Marmaduke 432
- Woodford, Edw. Fras..... 311
- Woodgate, E. R. P. ...46, 238
- — Herbert Ferdinand ... 267
- Woodham, Wm. Burnett 292
- Woodhouse, Harvey 22, 403
- — Henry Opie 44, 411
- — Tom Percy 380
- Woodifield, A. Hudson... 174
- Woodland, Arth. Law 49, 314
- Woodley, Ernest Jas. 311
- Woodman, James E. S. 360
- Wood - Martin, James Isidore 292
- Woodmass, Montagu G. E. 161
- Woodroffe, Arthur Jas. 213
- Woodrow, Thos. H. J. 57, 168
- Woods, Adrien Saml. 43, 346
- — Albert Edward 426
- — Charles Greaves 383
- — Chas. Robt. Sandford 284
- — Charles Rolleston...... 380
- — George Greville 175
- — Hans Charles M....51, 167
- — Henry 363
- — James Aug............... 395
- — John Charles............ 368
- Woodthorpe, R. Gosset 16, 205
- Woodward, Ed. Mabbott 256
- — Fras. Willoughby...... 291
- — John Alfred Hudson... 428
- Woodwright, Fra.B.L.68, 139
- Woodyatt, Nigel G. 429
- Woolbert, Henry Robert 455
- Wooldridge, Herb. C..... 439
- — Wm. Hugh 437
- Woollcombe, Charles L. 269
- Woollett, Wm. Chas. 271, 373
- Woolright, Henry H. ... 301
- Woolmer, Edward....... 261
- Woolrych, Humphry S. 244
- Woon, John Blaxell...66, 415
- Worgan, Sydney D. 279
- Worlledge, Alfred C. ... 373
- — J. Franklin......... 67, 416
- Wormald, Frank 152
- — Frederick William ... 144
- Worship, Verelst T....... 347
- Worsley, Frank P. 253
- — George Stanley......... 174
- Wortabet, Hen. G. L. ... 505
- Worthington, Hugo 398
- Wortley, Edw. James Montagu Stuart 50, 504
- Wragg, William............ 133
- Wray, Edmund............ 401
- — John Cecil 173
- Wray J. Willoughby 57, 413
- Wren, Edward Conway 249
- Wrench, Alf. J. Cham. 51, 265
- Wright, Alfred 384
- — Arch. J. Arnott ...53, 274
- — Rev. Clement H. L.... 507
- — Clifton Vincent R. ... 267
- — Edmund Hasell 506
- — Ernest Granville 432
- — Ernest Leonard......... 421
- — Rev. Frederick Geo... 396
- — Frederick William ... 453
- — George 170
- — Godfrey C. de C. 154
- — Harry 69, 321
- — Hedley 421
- — Henry Adolphus S.... 243
- — Henry Brooke H. ... 211
- — Henry Coram............ 329
- — James Henry............ 214
- — Kenneth Crause 255
- — Robert Wallace......... 383
- — Walter Cecil 297
- — William Frederick ... 64
- — William Nevill 395
- — William Purvis 41, 399
- Wrigley, Clement Carr 242
- Wrottesley, Alfred E. 67, 209
- — Hon. William............ 139
- Wroughton, John B....... 279
- — Wm. Nesbitt........18, 405
- Wyatt, Chas. Edwyn ... 130
- — Francis Ogilvy......... 177
- — Henry James............ 382
- Wyld, Chas. Edward ... 231
- — William George........ 261
- Wylde, Arthur Wm...... 401
- — Edw. Andrée 63, 400
- — Robert Darell 176
- Wylde-Browne, G. H. 491
- Wyley, John Deane N... 398
- Wylie, Gordon Macleod 441
- — Henry 27, 404
- — Frederick 42
- — John Alfred 418
- — W. Hutt Curzon ...45, 411
- Wyllie, Frederick Arth. 285
- Wylly, Charles H. ... 69, 282
- — Harold C. 65, 289
- Wynch, Fredk. John Hy. 431
- Wyncoll, Chas. Edw. 69, 366
- Wyndham, Hon. C. H... 133
- — Guy Percy 158
- — John Reginald 308
- — Walter G. C. 49, 163
- — Wm. Francis George 305
- Wynell-Mayow, Chas. E. 278
- — R. Sandilands L. 291
- Wynn, Alfred 305
- — Henry C. W. 173
- Wynne, Arthur S. 23
- — George Clement ...43, 166
- — Graham Owen Robert 258
- — John George Erskine 171
- — Oscar Stewart........... 309
- — Richard John Arthur 136
- — Skeffington John 373
- — Wynter, Chas. Philip ... 250
- — Fras. Arthur 176
- — Hugh Talbot 177
- Wynyard, Edw. George 285
- — Montagu 42
- — Rowley 58, 168
- Wyon, Herbert Thornton 36
- Yaldwyn, Alf. Geo. ...44, 411
- — Percy James M........ 373
- Yale, James Corbet 253
- Yardley, John W. 148
- Yarr, Michael Thomas 383
- Yate, Arthur C. 419
- — Chas. Allix Lavington 295
- — Cha. Edw. 46, 412
- — Frederick Herbert ... 421
- — William Gordon....66, 415
- Yates, Henry Peel 164
- — H. Townley Scott 40, 166a
- — Robert Peel 267
- — Samuel Pearson 153
- Yatman, Arthur H. 252
- — Clement 240
- Yeates, Robert H. M.... 213
- Yeatherd, Ernest W...59, 238
- Yeatman-Biggs, A. G. 19, 165
- Yeilding, Wm. R. 419
- Yeld, Francis Edward... 361
- Yolland, William 209
- York, Edward 143
- — Robert 290
- Yorke, Fred. Aug....47, 166a
- — Horatio Arthur ...47, 207
- — Ralph Maximilian ... 153
- Yorstoun, A. M. C. ... 56, 286
- — Morden E. Carthew... 422
- Younan, Arthur Chas. ... 455
- Young, Alex. S. Ward .. 379
- — Arthur Davidson ... 172
- — Arthur Thomas 425
- — Carmichael Light 57, 208
- — Chas. Augustus 384
- — Chas. Fred. Gordon... 420
- — Charles Henry 285
- — Charles Walter......... 360
- — David Coley 419
- — Edward Archibald 53, 413
- — Edward Gordon 212
- — Edward Maule 209
- — Edward William 529
- — Ernest Douglas......... 249
- — Francis Henry 173
- — Frank Popham 431
- — Frederick Benjamin 204
- — Frederick De Budé .. 431
- — George................22, 407
- — George Frederick...26, 410
- — George Taylor 242
- — Harry Howlett ... 57, 413
- — Harry Norman 362
- — Henry Alfred............ 175
- — Henry George 439
- — Henry M'Leod 66, 271
- — Hugh Gerald S......... 161
- — Isaac 273
- — James 453
- — James Charles 68, 279
- — Jn. Edgar Harington 177
- — John Robert 58, 254
- — Julian Henry............ 420
- — Julian Mayne 261
- — Julius Ralph............ 211
- — Louis Tarleton 455
- — Malcolm Graeme 438
- — Norman Edward 172
- — Percy Gordon R. 379
- — Reginald Weston 276
- — Telford Mackenzie ... 158
- — Thomas Simpson 432
- — Walter Herbert......... 254
- — Wilfred Edward 438
- — Qr.Mr. William 325
- — Surg.Lt. William 456
- — William Arthur ...69, 262
- — William Bensley 428
- — William Henry....51, 255
- — William Hope......65, 415
- Younge, Geo. Harrison 381
- Younger, David Reg. ... 322
- Youngerman, E. P. 505
- Younghusband, Fra. E. 420
- — George John 420
- — George William 417
- — Leslie Napier 431
- Yourdi, John R............. 381
- Yule, James Herbert 44, 249
- — William Andrew 47
- Ziegler, Charles Henry 176
- Zigomala, Pandia J...... 161
- Zimmermann, B. Frazier 382
- Zorab, John M............. 452

HON. ARTILLERY COMPANY OF LONDON. 579
(Incorporated 25 Aug. 1537.) The Armoury House, Finsbury, London, E.C.

Captain General and Colonel.
H.R.H. Albert Edw., *Prince of Wales & Duke of Cornwall*, KG. KT. KP. GCB. GCSI. GCMG. GCIE. ...14 June 93

Lt.Colonels.
R. R. B. A. A., *Earl of Denbigh and Desmond, p. late Capt. R. Artillery* .... 4 Mar. 93
H.B.Wm. Henry Baker, p. ...27 Mar. 95

Majors.
Francis J. Stohwasser, p.s.
Hon. Lt.Colonel 6 Sept.90
L. R. C. Boyle, p.s.late R.N.18 Apr. 94

Captains.
John Pash, p. Hon. Major 9 Jan. 86
Walter E. Williams, p.s.
Hon. Major .... 8 May 89
Richard Birkett, p.s..........14 June 90
William Evans, p. [t] ...... 7 Jan. 92

John C. Sanderson, p. ......25 Apr. 91
F.B. Frank Burman Bell, p. 29 Aug. 91
Alfred Fyson, p. (t)............ 2 Jan. 95

Lieutenants.
F.B. Henry Joseph Ford, p. 2 Oct. 86
George Arthur Marshall, p.30 July 87
George Tho. Carpenter,p.s. 6 Sept. 90
Charles Hammond,p.s....... 4 July 91
Percy Willats Leggatt, p.s. 18 Dec. 91
John Stanley Kent, p.s.......18 Dec. 91
H.B. Geo. Thomas Lewis, p. 19 Dec. 91
Henry John Bertram, p.s...23 July 92
Frank Farrington, p.s. (S) 23 July 92
F.B.Richard White, p........23 July 92
H.B. Thomas Perkins, p. ...11 Nov. 93
Wm. Freke M. Williams, p. 2 Jan. 95
FleetwoodErnestVarley(t)
Instructor of Musketry ... 2 Jan. 95

Second Lieutenants.
Charles Grierson Lowe, p.s. 4 May 91
George Frederick Smith, p.25 Nov. 93

Herbert Charles Duncum... 3 Feb. 94
Edward Treffry, p...............23 June 94
John Major Wright ....29 Aug. 94
Tom Robinson.....................30 Jan. 95
Charles Clement Hodges...20 Feb. 95
Adjutant.—J. O. Wray, Capt.
Royal Artillery............. 1 Dec. 94
Quarter Master. — William
Hy.Hayward.p.Hon.Capt.17 May 90
Chaplain. — Rev. William
Rogers, MA................... 9 May 77
*Med.Off.—Surg.Maj.*Walter
Culver James, MD. p.s ... 6 Oct. 88
F.B. *Surg.Capt.* Thomas E.
F. M'Geagh, MD. p. ......11 Aug. 88
L.C. *Surg.Capt.* Richard Jas.
Reece, MB. p.s. ....10 Aug. 89
Surg.Capt. Hy.Geo.Read,p.19 Aug. 93
Vet. Lieuts. — H.B. Henry
Durant Gibbings............. 8 Feb. 90
David R. C. Tennant........21 Apr. 94

F.B. signifies Field Battery; H.B. Horse Artillery Battery; L.C. Light Cavalry. Scarlet—Facings Blue.

MILITIA ARTILLERY.

⁎ For an alphabetical Table of Contents to the Militia Artillery, see p. vi.

EASTERN DIVISION.

Kent Artillery.
(*Formerly the Kent Artillery Militia.*)
Head Quarters, Dover.

Honorary Colonel.
Sir Walter George Stirling,
Bart., *late Capt. R. Art*... 8 Mar. 90

Lieutenant Colonel.
Edw. L. F. Jennings, p.s.
Hon. Colonel .... 8 Mar. 90

Major.
Thompson Hunter, p.s. (I),
Hon. Lt.Colonel .... 8 Mar. 90

Captains.
B. Lewis-Barned, p.s. (S)
Hon. Major................28 May 84
Henry Arthur H. Farnaby-Lennard, DL. ....10 Mar. 88
Jas. Arthur Tapley, p.s. (I),
Instructor of Artillery ...18 May 89
Robert Arthur Crawford Christie, p.s. ret. pay 12 Lancers, Hon. Major 17 Sept.90
Count Dudley B.M. Gurowski de Wczele, p.s..............14 Mar. 91
Wm. Richd. Jones-Byron, ret. pay 3 *Hussars*............14 Dec. 92

Lieutenants.
Robert de Bray Hussell, p.s. (I) ....11 June 90
Charles E. Schlesinger, p.s. (S) (I) ....11 May 92

Second Lieutenants.
Nigel Martin Smith .... 4 Oct. 93
Philip Joseph Paterson......14 Mar. 94
Edward Hawtin Phillips... 3 Apr. 94
Harold Everard Hambro 19 Sept. 94
Adjt. & Capt.—R. G. Merriman,DSO.Capt.R.Artillery1 Mar. 95
Qr. Master.— W. Jarvis,
Qr. Mr. R. Art., Hon. Lt.24 Nov. 86
Med. Off.—Surgeon Lt.Col.
Clement Cuthbert Walter 1 Mar. 73

The Prince of Wales' Own Norfolk Artillery.
(*Formerly the Prince of Wales' Own Norfolk Artillery Militia.*)
Head Quarters, Yarmouth.

Honorary Colonel.
Field Marshal *His Royal Highness the Prince of Wales*,KG.KT.KP.GCB.
GCSI. GCMG. GCIE......28 Oct. 71

Lieutenant Colonel.
Thos. William Visct. Cole,[5]
Colonel h.p. Scots Guards21 Feb. 94

Majors.
Fra. D'Arcy Wm. C. Newcome, Hon. Lt.Colonel ...23 Jan. 95

Captains.
Sir Reg.Wm.Proctor Beauchamp,Bart.,Hon.Major24 Dec. 84
Hon. Assheton E. Harbord14 Dec. 89
Sir S. B. Crossley, Bart. ... 2 Apr. 92
Philip Bennet .... 7 Jan. 93
Thos. Leigh Hare, *late Lt.*
Scots Guards ....21 July 94
John Cator...................... 6 Feb. 95

Lieutenants.
Edw. Henry Evans-Lombe, p.s. (I), *Aide de Camp to Col. Bulwer, Com. Norfolk Brig. Inf. Vols.* ....14 Apr. 86
Anthony John Thornhill... 2 Apr. 92
Hugh Augustus Bagot-Chester ....30 July 92
Hon. George Keppel, *late Lt. Gordon Highlanders*...17 Oct. 94
Wyndham Cremer Cremer 21 Nov. 94
Henry Bowyer Sparke......13 Mar. 95

Second Lieutenants.
Cyril Harry Walter ....11 Nov. 93
Adjt. & Capt.— J.P. Du Cane,
Capt. R. Artillery ....16 Feb. 94
Qr.Master.— H. Russell, Qr.
Mr. R. Art., Hon. Major., 6 Apr. 87
Med.Off.—

Suffolk Artillery.
(*Formerly the Suffolk Artillery Militia.*)
Head Quarters, Ipswich.

Honorary Colonel.
F. W. B. *Lord* Rendlesham.12 Feb. 87

Lieutenant Colonel.
Howard Whitbread, *late Lt.
2 Lt. Drs. British German Legion*; Hon. Colonel ......19 Nov. 81

Major.
Lionel Tillotson, Hon. Lt.
Colonel, ret. pay R. Art. 16 Mar. 89

Captains.
Edward Charles Moor, p.s....26 May 79
Charles John Easton, Hon.
Major, *Instructor of Artillery* ....23 Apr. 80
A. Waller Cobbold, p.s........26 June 86
Ranulphus J. Carthew, p.s. 2 May 88
Robt. Chas. H. Lampen,p.s.18 Nov. 93

Lieutenants.

Second Lieutenants.
Geo.E. J. Annesley West,p.s. 1 Mar. 93
Thos. Edward Carew Hunt23 Dec. 93
Adj. & Capt.—W. Gurdon,
Captain Royal Artillery...23 Nov. 51

Qr. Must.—T. Ward, Qr. Mr.
R. Art. Hon. Capt. ....26 June 72
Med. Off.—

Sussex Artillery.
(*Formerly Royal Sussex Art. Militia.*)
Head Quarters, Eastbourne.

Honorary Colonel.
James Hayes Sadler .... 5 Aug. 82

Lieutenant Colonel.
A. R. Margary,p.s. (H), (I),
Hon. Colonel ....30 Jan. 92

Major.
Fairfax Rhodes, p.s. [t] Hon.
Lt. Colonel ....27 Feb. 92

Captains.
Rushton Webber Adamson13 Apr. 87
Herbert Haworth Peel, p.s.
(I), *Inst. of Artillery* ...... 9 Jan. 92
Freeman Thomas .... 27 Feb. 92
Reg.C.M.GillettGridley, p.s.
(I) ....28 Mar. 94
Chas.Hamilton R.Pelly, p.s.27 Feb. 95

Lieutenants.
Claud Lonsdale, p.s. ....26 Nov. 92
Frns. Jas. Maitland, p.s. (I) 26 Nov. 92
George Frederic Thompson 17 Feb. 94

Second Lieutenants.
Geoffery Nicolas Charlton 26 Feb. 94
Charles Harold Bennett ...12 Dec. 94
Everard Archer Dealtry ...16 Jan. 95
Adjt. & Capt.—A.M. Balfour,
Capt. R. Artillery .... 1 Jan. 94
Med. Off.—

SOUTHERN DIVISION.

Antrim Artillery.
(*Formerly the Antrim Artillery Militia.*)
Head Quarters, Carrickfergus.

Honorary Colonel.
Sir Edw. Selby Smyth,[1]
KCMG., W. Surrey Regt. 7 Jan. 92

Lt.Colonel Commandant.
Eldred Thomas Pottinger,[2]
late Capt.R.(Bombay) Art.
Hon. Colonel ....11 Oct 90

Majors.
Jas. L. Alison, Hon. Lt.Col.25 May 89
Edward J. Kinsey (I.) ... 8 Aug. 91

Militia Artillery.

CAPTAINS.
George Edward Elmitt, *p.s.*,
(I), (t), *Inst. of Artillery* 4 June 92
Arthur Heywood a' Beckett,
p.s. (I) ....16 July 92
Walter Wm. Masters ....15 Mar. 93
George Hamilton Fenner,
p.s. [t] ....16 Sept. 93
James Boyd G. Smith (T) 16 Sept. 92
Edw. Ernest Robinson.... 16 July 94

LIEUTENANTS.

SECOND LIEUTENANTS.
red. C. Herbert Campbell 19 Apr. 94
William Aguilar Allpress 25 July 94
John Hall Hedley .... 3 Oct. 94
Richard Jellard Ford......... 6 Feb. 95
Adjutant.—Arch. Paris, *Capt.*
R. Marine Artillery ..... 1 Aug. 94
Qr. Master.—J. Wilbond,
Qr. Mr. R. Art.; Hon. Capt. 11 June 81
Med. Off.—

South-East of Scotland Artillery.

(*Formerly the Haddington, Berwick Linlithgow, and Peebles Art. Militia.*)
Head Quarters, Dunbar.

HONORARY COLONEL.
Archibald Dickson.............25 Feb. 91

LIEUTENANT COLONEL.
T. A. Houstoun-Boswall-
Preston, *Hon. Colonel*......12 Nov. 92

MAJOR.
John C. Innes ....24 Dec. 92

CAPTAINS.
Chas. Thompson Menzies, *p.s.* 8 Aug. 83
Napier Macleod Wylie, *p.s.*
(I), *Hon. Major, Inst. of Artillery* ....21 Dec. 87
Wm. H. S. Heron-Maxwell,[3]
Hon. Col. late Capt. R. Fus.
Hon. Major..................22 Dec. 88
Harry Hope, *p.s* ....31 May 90
William Jas. Oliver, *late
Capt. R. Artillery* ....22 Aug. 91
Robert Walter Purvis, *p.s.*...19 June 93

LIEUTENANTS.
Douglas Morrison Oliver,
p.s...................18 Apr. 94
Bertram Vaughan-Arbuckle,
p.s...................18 Apr. 94

SECOND LIEUTENANTS.
David Wm. Milne-Home... 5 Sept. 94
Alan Sim Murray .... 19 Sept. 94
Adjt. & Capt.—H. C. G.
Taylor, *Capt. R. Artillery* 6 Jan. 92
Qr. Master.—J. Murray, *Qr.*
Mr. R. Art.; Hon. Lieut.....15 Oct. 92
Med. Off.—

Cork Artillery.

(*Formerly the West Cork Artillery and the Royal Cork City Artillery.*)
Head Quarters, Fort Elizabeth, Cork.

HONORARY COLONEL.
J. F. *Earl* Bandon, *DL. JP.* 31 July 78

LIEUTENANT COLONEL.
Thos. Ainslie Lunham, *p.s.*
Hon. Colonel ....19 Aug. 85

MAJORS.
Wm. Taylor,[4] *ret. pay R.
Artillery, Hon. Lt. Col.* .... 25 Apr. 88

CAPTAINS.
John Craig, *Hon. Major* ...22 Sept. 83
John R. Seymour Lemon,
p.s...................26 Nov. 92
John Frederick Ord, *p.s.* (I)
Instructor of Artillery ... 7 June 93
Chas. G. Cathcart Hemphill,
p.s...................19 Dec. 94

LIEUTENANTS.
Daniel S. P. O'Riordan, *p.s.* 22 Feb. 90
John Lysaght ....10 Jan. 91
Edm. Harold Duke Southby,
p.s...................4 Mar. 93
Arthur Cary, *p.s.*............ 4 Mar. 93
John Walter M'Kenna, *p.s.* 28 Nov. 94

SECOND LIEUTENANTS.
Arthur Quain ....24 Oct. 94
Fras. Chas. Deane Burton 19 Dec. 94
Adjt. & Capt.—H. R. Cook,
Captain R. Artillery ......27 June 92
Qr. Master.—T. Stevens, *Qr.
Mr. R. Art.; Hon. Lieut.* 25 July 91

Donegal Artillery (The Prince of Wales').

(*Formerly the Prince of Wales' Donegal Artillery Militia.*)
Head Quarters, Letterkenny.

HONORARY COLONEL.

LIEUTENANT COLONEL.
Harry H. Aug. Stewart, *p.s.*
ret. pay 9 *F.*; *Hon. Colonel* 23 Mar. 89

MAJORS.
T. E. Batt, (I), *Inst. of Art.* 8 June 89
Joseph George Griffith, *p.s.* 21 Apr. 94

CAPTAINS.
William Daniel Swiney...... 1 Apr. 88
William Bernard Reed, *p.s.* 1 Apr. 88
D. B. T. Todd-Thornton, *p.s.* 19 May 88
John Robert Baillie, *p.s.* (t) 29 May 89
George Castriot De Rinzy,
Inspector of Police, British Guiana ....28 June 90
John E. C. Jas. Cochrane,
p.s. (I), *Inst. of Artillery* 23 Dec. 91
Richard Abercrombie Irvine,
p.s. (I) (II), *Assist. Insp.
Gold Coast Constabulary* .. 2 Apr. 92

LIEUTENANTS.
Charles Kemp Dawson, *p.s.* 15 Nov. 90
Louis Morgan Dyson, *p.s.*... 6 Feb. 92
Harold Dewhurst ....12 Aug. 93
Wm. Nathaniel Sawer, *p.s.*,
late Lt. 2 *Middlesex Vol. Art.* 10 Oct. 94

SECOND LIEUTENANTS.
Harold Despard Twigg ...13 Feb. 95
Adjt. & Capt.—H. E. Bampfylde, *Captain R. Artillery* 23 Oct. 93
Qr. Master. — J. Paulson,
Qr. Mr. R. Art.; Hon. Lieut. 26 Oct. 85

Dublin City Artillery.

(*Formerly Dublin City Art. Militia.*)
Head Quarters, Dublin.

LIEUTENANT COLONEL.
W. J. N. Magill, *Hon. Col. p.s.* 31 Aug. 78

MAJOR.
Wykeham C. Dickenson,
Hon. Lt. Colonel.............. 8 Dec. 81

CAPTAINS.
Arthur Wm. Thompson, *p.s.*
Hon. Major ....22 Aug. 77
Wm. L. Smythe, *p.s.* (I), *Inst.
of Artillery, Hon. Major*... 5 Nov. 79
Edw. John M. Briscoe, *p.s.* 27 June 88
Ferdinand R. H. Merrick, *p.s.* 10 Sept. 92
Howard John Sawer, *p.s.* ...25 Nov. 93

LIEUTENANTS.
John Berchmans Crean ...10 Sept. 91

SECOND LIEUTENANTS.

Adjt. & Capt.—A. S. Le
Quesne, *Major R. Marine Artillery* ....23 Nov. 91

Edinburgh Artillery.

(*Formerly the Duke of Edinburgh's Own Edinburgh Artillery Militia.*)
Head Quarters, Edinburgh.

HONORARY COLONEL.
H.R.H. the Duke of Edinburgh (reigning *Duke of Saxe-Coburg-Gotha*), *KG. KT. KP. GCB. GCSI. GCMG. GCIE.* ....24 June 74

LIEUTENANT COLONEL.
Alan John Colquhoun, *late
Lt.* 42 *F.*; *Hon. Colonel*...20 Aug. 87

MAJOR.
James Reid Peploe, *p.s.* (I) 22 Oct. 87

CAPTAINS.
Robert S. Marshall, *p.s.* (I),
Adj. British Guiana Police 21 Mar. 85
William Scott, *p.s.* (I) ...... 8 May 86
Algernon Mercer, *p.s.* (I)
Instructor of Artillery......12 Feb. 87
A. Annerly Corder, *p.s.* [t] 8 May 86
Hen. Douglas Larymore,[9] *p.s.*
(t) (H), *Assist. Inspector
Gold Coast Constabulary*... 7 Feb. 91
Joseph Edward Lee, *p.s. late
Maj.* 1 *Newcastle-on-Tyne
Art. Vols., Hon. Major*......14 Mar. 91
Robert Alex. Christison, *p.s.* 4 Apr. 94
Gilbert Lumley Johnstone
p.s. (H) (I) ....20 Feb. 95

LIEUTENANTS.
C. W. N. Brown-Constable 7 Mar. 91

SECOND LIEUTENANTS.
Brownlow H. H. Muthow-
Lannowe, *p.s.*...............30 Apr. 91
Henry Maurice M'Leod, *p.s.* 11 Mar. 92
Charles Rushton Turner ...23 Oct. 93
Keith Lyon Buist............... 3 Feb. 94
Hugh Fawcus ....17 Oct. 94
Thos. J. Melville Keegan 13 Mar. 95
Adj. & Capt.—C. D. Scott,
Capt. R. Artillery ....25 Nov. 90
Qr. Master.—
Med. Off.—

Fife Artillery.

(*Formerly the Fife Artillery Militia.*)
Head Quarters, Cupar.

HONORARY COLONEL.
John Balfour, *Vice Lt. JP.
late of Gr. Gds.*..............23 Feb. 55

LIEUTENANT COLONEL.
William Baird, *p.s. Hon. Col.* 19 May 88

MAJOR.
George Murray Boothby,
late Capt. Royal Artillery 23 June 94

CAPTAINS.
Robert Davidson, *p.s.* (I),
Inst. of Artillery ......30 Jan. 84
Arthur Moubray ....21 May 90
Alfred G. Goodwin, *p.s.* ... 4 May 92
Wm. Cossley Atherton, *late
Lt. Royal Navy, Hon. Major* 10 Dec. 92

LIEUTENANTS.
Bertie E. Arthur Pritchard,
p.s...................15 Aug. 94

SECOND LIEUTENANTS.
Gwynn Churchill Preston 13 Mar. 95
Adjt. & Capt.—E. B. Anderson, *Capt. R. Artillery* ... 1 Feb. 91
Qr. Master. —
Med. Off.—

Militia Artillery.

Forfar and Kincardine Art.
(*Formerly the Forfar and Kincardine Artillery Militia.*)
Head Quarters, Montrose.

HONORARY COLONEL.
Sir Reg. H. Alex. Ogilvy, Bt., *p.s.*, Aide de Camp to the Queen ....19 Sept. 94

LT.COLONEL.
C. N., *Lord Carnegie, p.s.*, Hon. Colonel ....28 Nov. 94

MAJORS.
Hon. Chas. Maule Ramsay, late Lt. R. Artillery ...... 4 Oct. 90

CAPTAINS.
Geo.Robertson Chaplin,*p.s.* serving under the British South African Company ...28 Nov. 83
Alexander D. Seton (t), *p.s.* (1), *Inst.of Art., Hon.Major* 8 Jan. 87
Wm. Fred. Forsyth-Grant, *p.s.* (I) .... 6 Jan. 94

LIEUTENANTS.
Alex.C.Fownes-Luttrell,*p.s.*21 May 92
Wm. Hamilton Ritchie, *p.s.* 6 Feb. 92
Sydney James Gammell ...26 Sept.94

SECOND LIEUTENANTS.
Adjt. & Capt.—H. C. Molesworth, *Captain R. Art.* 1 June 91
Qr.Master.—Wm.Robinson, *Qr.Mr. R.Art.; Hon.Lieut.* 9 Sept.85
Med. Off.—

Hampshire and Isle of Wight Artillery.
(*Duke of Connaught's Own.*)
(*Formerly the Hampshire Art. Militia and the Isle of Wight Art. Militia.*)
Head Quarters, Sandown, I.W.

HONORARY COLONELS.
General H.R.H. the Duke of Connaught, *KG. KT. KP. GCSI. GCMG. GCIE. KCB.* ....24 July 75
Henry, *Duke of Wellington, late Grenadier Guards* ...22 Nov. 84

LIEUTENANT COLONEL.
Maitland Moore-Lane, *late Lt.Col. R. Art. Hon. Col.* 20 July 89

MAJORS.
Wm. L. Nicholl Clayton,*p.s.* (t), *Hon. Lt.Colonel* .... 5 Aug. 85
John M. F. Hunt, *p.s., Hon. Lt.Colonel* .... 1 Feb. 90

CAPTAINS.
JohnArthurLainson,*p.s.*(t) *Hon. Major* ....10 Apr. 80
Wm. H.G. Gordon, *p.s.* (t), *Hon. Major* ....19 Nov. 81
CharlesWestrow Hulse,*p.s. Hon. Major* ....25 Apr. 85
Geoffrey Warburton,*p.s.*(I) 6 Feb. 86
Wm. R. Reeve-Tucker, *p.s.* (T), (H), *serving with Lagos Constabulary* ....14 Apr. 90
Ashley Paget W. Williams, *p.s. serving with Bechuanaland Police* ....25 July 91
Hon. Gordon Watson, *p.s.* (I), *Inst. of Artillery* ...... 1 Mar. 93

LIEUTENANTS.
Robert Olliver Harrild ...20 Jan. 94
Herbert St.Geo.Cobbold,*p.s.*20 Jan. 94
ErnestRokebyRobinson,*p.s.*20 Jan. 94
Godfrey Maule Nicholson, *p.s.* ....13 Mar. 95

SECOND LIEUTENANTS.
Cecil E. G. Woollcombe-Adams ....27 Apr. 94

Adjt.& Capt.—H.B.Stanford, *Capt. R. Artillery* .... 3 Nov. 90
Qr.Master.—
Med. Off.—

Lancashire Artillery.
(*Formerly the Royal Lancashire Artillery Militia.*)
Head Quarters, Seaforth.

HONORARY COLONEL.
James Clifton Brown ......14 July 88

LT.COLONEL.
Stanley Arnold, *Hon. Col.* 14 July 88

MAJOR.
Wm. Hall Walker, (I).........28 July 88

CAPTAINS.
Francis C. Batson, *p.s. Hon. Major* ....26 June 80
R. C. Drury, *p.s.* (t), (I), *Inst. of Art., Hon. Major*.17 Aug. 81
Alfred James Budd,*p.s.* (I)18 Aug. 86
Leonard Walter Pead, *p.s.* [t], *Hon. Major* ...... 6 Nov. 86
Greville E. Joseph,*p.s.* [t]...13 Nov. 86
Wm. Hen. Edwardes,*p.s.*(t) 3 Oct. 88

LIEUTENANTS.
Eustace Theodore Heaven 27 Nov. 89
Reginald Sutcliffe Wilson, *p.s.* .... 4 Oct. 93
Austin Clement Alexander, *p.s.* .... 4 Oct. 93
Clare Basil Schreiber, *p.s.* 4 Oct. 93
Harold Shaw ....29 Aug. 94
Harold Findlay ....29 Aug. 94

SECOND LIEUTENANTS.
Frank Sydney Pershouse...10 Feb. 94
William Raymond Heaven 24 Feb. 94
Dudley Baines Forwood ...19 Dec. 94
Adj.& Capt.—G.D.Chamier, *Capt. R. Artillery* ....12 Jan. 91
Qr. Master.—J. Cox, *Qr. Mr. R. Art.; Hon. Lieut.*18 May 92
Med. Off.—

Limerick City Artillery.
(*Formerly the Limerick City Artillery Militia.*)
Head Quarters, Limerick.

HONORARY COLONEL.
S. P., *Visct.* Gort.................30 Nov. 65

LT.COLONEL.
Wm. D. Maunsell, *p.s.* [t] *Hon. Colonel* .... 2 Dec. 93

MAJOR.
Wm. A. Bentley, *p.s.* [t], (I)..................................13 Jan. 94

CAPTAINS.
Mountiford Westropp,*p.s.* 25 Apr. 88
Arthur Edwin Kershaw,*p.s. Chief Commandant Cyprus Constabulary* .... 2 Mar. 89
Warren De la F.Wright,*p.s.*11 Apr. 90
Austin F. Budden, *p.s., late Major* 1 *Kent Art. Vols. Hon. Major* ....19 July 90
Henry James Hillyard, *p.s.* 28 May 92

LIEUTENANTS.
Claud Lefroy, *p.s.* ....26 Oct. 89
John Jermyn Nicholson, *p.s.* (I), *Inst. of Artillery* 27 Feb. 92

Harold Galway Warren,*p.s.* 3 Mar. 92
William Ross Brown .... 3 Mar. 94
Joseph Lindsey Curtis ......21 Nov. 94
Jas. Robert Bury-Barry ...21 Nov. 94

SECOND LIEUTENANTS.
RaymondEdwardsHarman24 Feb. 94
Walter H. Cavour Hungerford ....22 Aug. 94
Basil Roche-Kelly ....17 Oct. 94
Adjt. & Capt.—J. J. MacMahon, *Capt. R. Artillery*15 Jan. 94
Qr. Master.— J. Edwards, *Qr.Mr. R. Art.; Hon.Lt.*21 May 87
Med. Off.—

Mid-Ulster Artillery.
(*Formerly Mid-Ulster Art. Militia.*)
Head Quarters, Dungannon.

HONORARY COLONEL.
Hon. Wm. Stuart Knox, *late Major* 21 F ....26 Mar. 67

LIEUTENANT COLONEL.
Robert J. P. Saunders, *late Lt. R. Art., Hon. Colonel* 16 Feb. 89

MAJOR.
J. S. Irwin, *Hon. Lt.Col....* 8 June 89

CAPTAINS.
William Browne, *Hon. Maj.*27 Sept.80
Wm. RyanLyle,*p.s Hon.Maj.*17 May 84
Cecil Balfour Phipson, *p.s.* (I), *Instructor of Artillery* 18 Mar. 91
Thos. A. H. Knox-Browne 27 Apr. 93

LIEUTENANTS.
Edw.M.R.Emmott-Rawdon20 June 85
Augustin James Digan, *p.s.*24 Sept.92
HenryHowellHewlings,*p.s.*24 Sept.92
Robert Jackson Adams, *p.s.* 3 Feb. 94

SECOND LIEUTENANTS.
Ynyr Richard P. Burges ...27 Apr. 93
Frederick Hugh Crawford 3 Feb. 94
Adjt. & Capt.—J. B. Parry, *Captain R. Artillery* ......20 Feb. 95
Med. Off.—*Surg. Lt.Colonel* Wm. Twigg, *MD.* .... 1 Mar. 73

Tipperary Artillery.
(*Formerly the Duke of Clarence's Munster Artillery, South Tipperary Militia.*)
Head Quarters, Templemore.

LT.COLONEL.
James A. Prendergast, *p.s. Hon. Colonel* ....10 Dec. 92

MAJORS.
Wm. C. Chadwick .... 6 May 93

CAPTAINS.
Fred.J.S.Lecky,*Hon. Major* 5 Sept. 83
John Godfrey Phillips,*p.s.*28 Apr. 86
David Ernest Shine ....23 May 92
John Hopkinson Phillips ...15 May 93
Ambrose Austin Lane, *p.s.* 22 July 93

LIEUTENANTS.
Wm. Frederick Houghton 21 May 92
Howard Mount S. Lovering, *p.s.* (I), *Inst. of Artillery* 11 June 94

SECOND LIEUTENANTS.
Thomas Moreton Sheppard23 Sept.93
Adjt. & Capt.—H. G. Birch, *Captain R. Artillery*.........26 Jan. 90
Qr. Master.—

Militia Artillery.

Waterford Artillery.
(Formerly the Waterford Art. Militia.)
Head Quarters, Waterford.
HONORARY COLONEL.
Marquis of Waterford, *KP.*
  late Capt. 1 *Life Guards*...13 May 76
LT. COLONEL.
Henry A. Hewetson, *p.s.*
  Hon. Colonel .... 8 Mar. 90
MAJORS.
Henry W. F. Chapman,*p.s.*
  Hon. Lt. Colonel .... 8 Oct. 92
CAPTAINS.
Robert Thomas Carew, Jun.19 Jan. 89
Laurence Grattan Esmonde,
  p.s. .... 3 June 89
Loftus A. Bryan, *p s.* (I),
  Instructor of Artillery ...15 June 91
L. W. Bonaparte Wyse, *p.s.*
  (I) ....10 Sept. 92
Henry C. Villiers Stuart ... 5 Nov. 92
LIEUTENANTS.
SinclairF.Kirkwood, *p.s.*(I) 8 Apr. 93
CalverleyJas.Jn.Lyster,*p.s.* 8 Apr. 93
Wm. Robert Penrose, *p.s.* 11 Nov. 93
Geo. F. Stratford Tuke, *p.s.* 26 May 94
Napoleon G. A. E. Bona-
  parte-Wyse .... 20 Feb. 95
SECOND LIEUTENANTS.
James Ferguson............28 Oct. 93
ErnestDesmondFarrellGee 9 Dec. 93
Adjt. & Capt.—C. H. Mil-
  ward, *Capt. R. Artillery* 10 Jan. 93
Qr. Master.—
Med. Off.—

Argyll and Bute Artillery.
(Formerly Argyll and Bute Art. Militia.)
Head Quarters, Campbeltown.
HONORARY COLONEL.
Smollett M. Eddington, *DL.*
  JP. late Lt. & Adj. 78 *F.* 22 Oct. 84
LIEUTENANT COLONEL.
John Younger,[11] *late Colonel*
  R. Artillery .... 2 Dec. 93
MAJOR.
Fra. A. Walker-Jones, *p.s.* 21 Nov. 91
CAPTAINS.
James Thos. Nichol, *p.s.*(t),
  (I), *Inst. of Artillery, Hon.*
  Major .... 5 Nov. 81
DuncanC.BurnsMacdonald,
  p.s. ....20 Aug. 87
Joseph Buckle ....22 Oct. 87
Alasdair Stewart Robert-
  son, *p.s.* ....16 Aug. 90
LIEUTENANTS.
T.P.U.J.Harvey Blake, *p.s.* 4 Aug. 88
Reginald Wm. F. Fullarton:6 July 92
Joseph Fox Tarratt, *p.s.* ... 3 Feb. 94
David Lee Crawford, *p.s.*... 3 Feb. 94
SECOND LIEUTENANTS.
Edwin William Cushen......20 Mar. 95
Adjt. & Capt.—A. G. Scott,
  Captain R. Artillery ......15 Nov. 93
Qr. Mr.—G. A. Usmar, *Qr.*
Mr. R. Art., Hon. Lieut. 26 Sept.88
Med. Off.—

Wicklow Artillery.
Formerly the Wicklow Artillery Militia.)
Head Quarters, Wicklow.
HONORARY COLONEL.
Charles Geo. Tottenham,[6]
  late Scots Guards...........17 Aug. 81
LT. COLONEL.
Henry E.W. de Robeck, *ret.*
  pay, R. Artillery ....25 Apr. 92
MAJOR.
Wm. Heighington, *p.s.* (I),
  Hon. Lt. Colonel ....17 May 92
CAPTAINS.
Richard Thos. Welch, *p.s.*
  (I), [*t*], *Hon. Maior, In-
  structor of Artillery*......18 Apr. 77
Harry Perry Ringwood, *p.s.*
  *Deputy Registrar, Irish
  Land Commission* ....18 Apr. 88
John G. Latham Nott, *p.s.* 2 May 92

H. S. W. Pennington, *p.s.* 1 May 93
Thos. Edw. M. Madden, *p.s.*23 May 93
Chas.CarlyleMacdowell,*p.s.* 7 Nov. 94
LIEUTENANTS.
Henry Joseph Harrington 16 June 94
Theodore M. Archdale, *p.s.*16 June 94
SECOND LIEUTENANTS.
Thomas Ord................30 Mar. 94
John Henry Breslin ....30 Jan. 95
William Tyndall Black...... 6 Feb. 95
George Stratford Burton ...20 Feb. 95
Adjt. & Capt.—M.J.C.Dennis,
  Captain R. Artillery ...... 1 June 94
Qr. Master.—A. Small, *Qr.*
  Mr. R. Art.; Hon. Lieut. 20 July 87
Med. Off.—

Sligo Artillery.
(The Duke of Connaught's Own.)
*(Formerly the Duke of Connaught's Own
  Sligo Artillery Militia.)*
Head Quarters, Sligo.
HONORARY COLONEL.
H.R.H. The Duke of Con-
  naught and Strathearn,
  *KG. KT. KP. GCSI.
  GCMG. GCIE. KCB* ...... 3 June 91
LIEUTENANT COLONEL.
Wm. G. Wood-Martin, *late
  Lt.* 44 *F. p.s. Hon. Colonel* 21 Apr. 83
MAJOR.
James Campbell, *Hon. Lt.
  Colonel*................ 9 June 83
CAPTAINS.
Gerrard Macklin Eccles......24 July 86
Robert W. G. Hillas,[7] *late
  Capt. Somerset Lt. Inf.* ..18 July 91
John D. A. Roberts,*ret. pay
  Royal Artillery* ....18 June 90
ArthurHarold W.Saunders-
  Knox-Gore,*p.s.*................ 4 Nov. 93
LIEUTENANTS.
SECOND LIEUTENANTS.
Cecil Pomeroy Russell, *p.s.* 14 Jan. 93
Dawson Dean R.H.Heather20 Mar. 95
Capt.&Adjt.—T. E. W. Bid-
  good, *Major R. Artillery*20 Aug. 94
Paymaster.—AlbertH.Knox 2 Feb. 55
Med. Off.—

Londonderry Artillery.
*(Formerly the Londonderry Artillery
  Militia, and previously the London-
  derry Light Infantry.)*
Head Quarters, Londonderry.
HONORARY COLONEL.
Sir H. H. Bruce, *Bt. late Cor.
  & Sub Lt.* 1 *Life Guards* ...16 Jan. 78
LIEUTENANT COLONEL.
John Lawrence,[8] *late Capt.*
  90 *Foot, p.s., Hon. Colonel* 20 Aug. 92
MAJOR.
David W. Stevenson, (*H*),
  (I), *Hon. Lt. Colonel*............17 Sept.92
CAPTAINS.
Alex. Boyle, *Hon. Major* ...29 Jan. 81
Wm. Quin, *Hon. Major* ......23 June 83
Stewart A. M. Bruce, *p.s.*
  Hon. Major.....................22 May 86
Hargrave B. de Hamel, *p.s.*13 Aug. 92
Erskine Eyre West...........17 Sept.92
William Irvine Leathem ...24 Apr. 93
LIEUTENANTS.
Charles William Adair, *p.s.*27 July 89
John Godfrey W. Hime,*p.s.*16 May 91
Alexander Duff Moore ......11 Oct. 91
Wm. Hovenden Ffolliott ...22 Apr. 93
Henry Alexander Cowper,
  p.s. (I), *Inst. of Artillery* 5 May 94
Robt.Joseph Starkie Byrne,
  p.s........................... 5 May 94
SECOND LIEUTENANTS.
Walter H. Fred. Hughes ...16 Feb. 94
Sidney Smith ....16 Jan. 95
Ernest G. Meade Swifte ...27 Mar. 95
Adjt. & Capt.—A. L. Tisdall,
  Capt. Royal Artillery ...15 Mar. 92
Qr. Master.—J. Dickens, *Qr.
Mr. R. Art.; Hon. Lieut.* 6 Dec. 90
Med. Off.—

Clare Artillery.
*(Formerly the Clare Artillery Militia
  and previously the Clare Infantry.)*
Head Quarters, Ennis.
HONORARY COLONEL.
E. D. *Lord* Inchiquin ......26 Apr. 82
LT. COLONEL.
Daniel M. Massy,*Hon.Colonel* 1 Aug. 93
MAJOR.
Matthew Joseph Kenny ... 8 Aug. 94
George O'Callaghan-West-
  ropp, (*H*), (t), *retired pay
  Irish Rifles*......................20 Feb. 89
Wm. Mansel Bowen, *p.s.*(I),
  Instructor of Artillery ... 4 June 92
Gerald A. Ward Holtz ...27 Aug. 92
Philip Anthony Dwyer, *p.s.* 17 Feb. 94
LIEUTENANTS.
Robt.W.Harrison Moreland 9 July 90
Chas.Pat.Mahon-Hagan,*p.s.*13 June92
Rupert Henn Griffith, *p.s.* 12 June 93
SECOND LIEUTENANTS.
Gerald Corlett Parker, *p.s.* 27 May 93
John G. Morris M'Ostrich... 7 Feb. 94
Adjt.&Capt.—L. P. Carden,
  Capt. Royal Artillery ...... 2 Jan. 94
Qr. Master.—W. Anderson,
  Qr.Mr. R. Art., ...30 Apr. 90
Paymaster.—C.M.Parkinson 6 Jan. 55

WESTERN DIVISION.
Cornwall and Devon Miners Artillery.
*(Formerly the Royal Cornwall & Devon
  Miners Artillery Militia.)*
Head Quarters, Falmouth.
HONORARY COLONEL.
Sir Colman Rashleigh, *Bart.
  CB. DL. JP.*................ 4 Apr. 83
LT. COLONEL.
Colman Battie Rashleigh,
  JP., Hon. Colonel ....24 Dec. 92
MAJOR.
Thos. Moor A. Horsford, *JP.
  p.s.; Hon. Lt.Colonel* ...... 5 Aug. 93
CAPTAINS.
Francis John Hext, *JP.* (I),
  Hon. Major............10 May 82
Harry J. Y. Jamieson, *JP.
  Hon. Major* ....18 Apr. 85
Robert M. Nowell-Usticke18 July 91
LIEUTENANTS.
William Deane Preston,*p.s.* 8 May 93
William Edward Copeland14 Nov. 94
A. F. Bealey, (P) *late Capt.
  Falmouth Div. Eng. Vols.*22 Mar. 90
SECOND LIEUTENANTS.
William Guthrie Bedford... 2 Sept.93
Rodney Lewis Bourchier...21 Mar. 94
Ralph Halford Thompson 16 June 94
Adj. & Capt.—F. M. Close,
  Captain R. Art. ....25 Mar. 91
Med.Off.—

Devon Artillery.
(Formerly the Devon Artillery Militia.)
Head Quarters, Devonport.
HONORARY COLONEL.
Sir Geo. S. Stucley, *Bart.* 1 Jan. 73
LIEUTENANT COLONEL.
Wm.Gorges Lowther,[9]*t ret.
  pay R. Artillery,Hon. Col.* 5 May 94
MAJOR.
Owen Willmer White........29 Apr. 94
CAPTAINS.
Charles George Nottage ...17 Oct. 85
Roger Miller, *p.s.* (I) .... 8 May 85
Oscar Knocker Dibb, *p.s.* (I),
  Inst. of Artillery 27 June94
John Wright Guise........... 9 Jan. 95

Militia Artillery. 583

LIEUTENANTS.
G. Edwards Bulmer, *p.s.*(I),27 Sept. 90
Frederic Dalton .... 8 Aug. 94
SECOND LIEUTENANTS.
John Stanley Riccard ......29 Aug. 94
Wilfrid Bliss Spender 5 Sept.94
Frederick Thomas Ord......30 Jan. 95
Reginald William Pearson 6 Feb. 95
Adjt.& Capt.—M.L.Carleton,
Captain R. Artillery ......16 Feb. 95
Med. Off.—

Durham Artillery.
(*Formerly the Durham Artillery Militia.*)
Head Quarters, Hartlepool.
HONORARY COLONEL.
У℃ *Lt. General Sir Henry*
M. Havelock-Allan,[10] *Bt.,*
KCB., retired list, Com.
Tyne and Tees Brig. Inf.
Vols. .... 7 May 87
LT.COLONEL.
Arthur Robson, *Hon. Colonel* 12 June 86
MAJOR.
Harold P. Ditmas, *p.s.*[t](I)
Hon. Lt. Colonel .... 5 Nov. 87
T.C.M'Kenzie *Hon.Lt.Col.* 12 Dec. 94
CAPTAINS.
John Cook H. M. Jones, *p.s.*21 June 86
Chas. Septimus Berthon (I),
p.s. Inst. of Artillery, Hon.
Major ....25 Apr. 88
Hugh W.H.Elwes,*p.s.*(t)...15 Dec. 88
Wm. Edwd.Bailey,*late Capt.*
*2 Vol. Bn. W. Riding Regt.*28 Sept. 89
Reginald Leigh Broad, *p.s.* 21 May 91
John F. Clarkson, *p.s.* (t) ...12 Dec. 94
LIEUTENANTS.
Charles Lillington Hall ...17 July 93
James Gowans.................30 June 94
George Chas. Grazebrook 30 June 94
Albert S. Leigh Broad, *p.s.*30 June 94
Hugh Sidney Streatfeild,
late Capt. 4 Vol. Bn. East
Surrey Regt. ....21 Nov. 94
Walter Norman Grope ......12 Dec. 94
SECOND LIEUTENANTS.
Herbert Walter Sleddon ... 4 Oct. 93
Alex. Gordon M'Kenzie ...22 Aug.94
Adjt. & Capt.—A. E. Harri-
son, *Capt. R. Artillery* ... 5 Jan. 95
Qr.Master.— G. J. Shake-
spear,*Hon.Lieut.; Qr.Mr.*
R. Art. ....14 Apr. 86
Med. Oy.—*Surg. Lt. Colonel*
James Rawlings............ 1 Dec. 91

Glamorgan Artillery.
(*Formerly the Royal Glamorgan*
Artillery Militia.)
Head Quarters, Swansea.
LIEUTENANT COLONEL.
ohn Roper Wright............28 Nov. 94
MAJOR.

CAPTAINS.
John Morris (I), *Inst. of*
Art.; Hon. Major .... 1 May 82
Robert B. Robertson ....18 July 83
Chas. Cecil P. Stoughton,[12]
Capt. ret. pay 14 Hussars 31 Dec. 87
Eliezer Jones Evans ......29 Aug. 91
LIEUTENANTS.
George W. A. Lloyd ......19 Apr. 90
Lorn E. H. Humfrey, *p.s.*
(II), *Assistant Inspector*
Lagos Constabulary ....27 Aug. 90
Kenneth Lambert Bath ...24 Oct. 91
Rowland M. Daniel, *p.s.* ... 4 June 94
Sampson Geo. V. Harris,
late Lt. 1st Cumberland
Volunteer Artillery ....24 Oct. 94
SECOND LIEUTENANTS.

Adjt. & Capt.—E. D. H.
Buckley, *Capt. R. Art* ... 2 Dec. 91
Med. Off.—

Northumberland Artillery.
Formerly Northumberland Art. Militia.)
Head Quarters, Berwick-on-Tweed.
HONORARY COLONEL.
Charles John Reed, *CB*......10 Nov. 88

LT.COLONEL.
Henry Best Hans Hamilton,
Hon. Colonel ....10 Nov. 88
MAJOR.
Charles C. Edwards,[13] *Hon.*
Lt. Colonel, p.s. ....12 Jan. 89
CAPTAINS.
Jasper M. Richardson, *p.s.*
(t), *Hon. Major* ....15 May 75
Fra. Douglas Blake, *p.s.*,
Hon. Major ....17 Nov. 80
Peter Swanston, *p.s.* (I),
Hon. Major .... 3 July 86
Frederick Aug.S.Steele,*p.s.*12 Jan. 89
Mathias Hugh Dunn, *p.s.*... 6 May 92
Alfred James Foster, *p.s.*(T)11 June 92
LIEUTENANTS.
George Elliot A. Pyle, *p.s.* 6 July 82
Fras.Jsph.Humphreys, *p.s.* 8 Mar. 90
Robt. B. M'Leod Cameron 22 Oct. 92
Hector Macdonald, *p.s.*......22 Mar. 93
Henry Alwyn Bros, *p.s.*...... 7 Oct. 93
SECOND LIEUTENANTS.
Bertram Allgood .... 7 Mar. 93
John E. Kyrie Oldfield, *p.s.*22 Mar. 93
J. Donald Pepper-Staveley 3 Mar. 94
John Carnaby Collingwood 14 Apr. 94
Adj.& Capt.—R.G. Strange,
Captain R. Artillery ......20 Mar. 91
Qr. Master.—W. Seager,
*Hon. Lt.; Qr. Mr. R. Art.*11 Nov. 91
Med. Off.—

Carmarthen Artillery.
(*Formerly the Royal Carmarthen*
Artillery Militia.)
Head Quarters, Carmarthen.
HONORARY COLONEL.
У℃ *Lt. General Sir James*
Hills-Johnes,[18] *GCB. ret.*
pay Royal Artillery ....25 Feb. 91
LT.COLONEL.
Visct. Emlyn, *Hon. Colonel*...24 Sept.92
MAJOR.
Sir Jas. H. Williams-Drum-
mond, *Bt. late Lt. Gr. Gds.* 6 May 93
CAPTAINS.
Wm. Henry B. Morris, *late*
Lt. R. Art. ....27 Apr. 87
Fras. B. Dalrymple,[14]*Major*
*late R. Art. Hon. Major*16 June 90
Andrews George Parker ...21 Mar. 91
Grismond Philipps, *p.s.* (I),
Inst. of Artillery ....14 Nov. 91
Ernald E. Richardson, *p.s.* 15 Mar. 93
F. D. Williams-Drummond,
p.s............................. 6 May 93
LIEUTENANTS.
William Kennedy ....23 Mar. 89
Fredk. Colpoys Keane, *p.s.* 2 July 90
Herbert Davies-Evans, *p.s.*22 May 91
Hon. Hugh F. V. Campbell,
p.s.............................12 Mar. 92
Charles Leyshon Dillwyn-
Venables-Llewelyn..........29 July 93
George Powell Roch 26 Sept.94
SECOND LIEUTENANTS.
Hon. Walter Fitzuryan Rice 7 Nov. 94
Hon, Ralph Alex, Campbell 27 Mar. 95
Adjt. & Capt.—E. Turner,
Dist. Officer, R. Artillery 1 Sept. 92
Qr.Master.— T. Williams,
Qr.Mr.R.Art.; Hon.Lieut. 6 Apr. 92
Med. Off.—

Pembroke Artillery.
(*Formerly Royal Pembroke Art. Militia.*)
Head Quarters, Fort Hubberstone.
HONORARY COLONEL.

LIEUTENANT COLONEL.
Fra. Perrott Edwardes,*Hon.*
Colonel .... 6 Oct. 88
MAJOR.
Wm. Charles Cope, (I) ......17 Oct. 91

CAPTAINS.
Hugh Russell, *p.s.* .... 4 Sept. 86
Lewis Peskett,*p.s.* (I), *Inst.*
of Artillery ....24 Nov. 88
Chas. Joshua Jos. Harris,
p.s .... 5 Aug. 93
LIEUTENANTS.
Frederick Wm. Green , *p.s.* 25 Feb. 91
Ralph Dunn, (T), [t], *late*
Capt. 2 Vol. Bn. Manchester
Regt. ....20 Jan. 94
Wm. Thomson Barton, *p.s.*
*late Capt. 1 Banff Vol.Art.*10 June 93
SECOND LIEUTENANTS.
Adjt. & Capt.—H. E. B. Lane,
Capt. Royal Artillery ......13 Mar. 93
Med.Off.—

Yorkshire Artillery.
(*Formerly Yorkshire Art. Militia.*)
Head Quarters, Scarborough.
HONORARY COLONEL.
Arthur Brooksbank,[15] *late*
Capt. 38 F. JP. ....23 Nov. 89
LT.COLONEL.
p.s.c. Jas. Digby Legard,[16]
late Capt. R. Artillery,
Hon. Colonel ....23 Nov. 89
MAJORS.
Charles Francis Fellows,
p.s. Hon. Lt. Colonel.........29 Mar. 90
CAPTAINS.
Robert Lesley, *p.s.* (I) ......10 May 79
Simon C. Scrope, *p.s.* .... 2 Apr. 87
George F. Marwood, *p.s.* ... 9 Apr. 90
Wm. Edwin Fell, *p.s.*, (I),
Instructor of Artillery ... 4 Nov. 91
Richard Marshall, *p.s.* (I)...15 Mar. 93
Henry A. Cholmley Darley 2 Jan. 95
LIEUTENANTS.
Anthony Gerard Salvin,*p.s.*14 Jan. 93
John Cecil Yorke, *p.s.* ......14 Jan. 93
Edw. A. F. Whittall Herbert,
p.s............................15 May 93
Yarburgh Lloyd-Greame...23 Jan. 95
Verney Asser ....23 Jan. 95
D'Arcy Legard ....23 Jan. 95
SECOND LIEUTENANTS.
Joseph Robinson Pease...... 5 Dec. 94
Thomas Owen Lloyd ....19 Dec. 94
Gilbert Thompson ....13 Feb. 95
Adjt. & Capt.—J. M. Burt,
Capt. R. Artillery ....15 Jan. 95
Qr.Master.—S. Frith, *Qr.*
Mr. R. Art. Hon. Capt. ...11 Nov. 90
Med. Off.—

Cardigan Artillery.
(*Formerly Royal Cardigan Art.Militia.*)
Head Quarters, Aberystwith.
HONORARY COLONEL.
John Lewes,[17] *late* 10*Dragns.*11 Aug. 88
LIEUTENANT COLONEL.
Thomas Lloyd, *p.s.Hon.Col.*26 Oct. 87
MAJOR.
John J. Bonsall ....12 Nov 87
CAPTAINS.
Hugh Edward Bonsall, *p.s.*
(I) ....16 Apr. 87
John Williams Cunliffe (t) 4 May 87
Michael Bowring Castle, *p.s.*16 Mar. 89
James Barry Taunton, *p.s.*13 Apr. 89
Edw. Chester Rogerson, *p.s.*18 Apr. 94
William Jenks, *p.s.*, (I), *Inst.*
of Artillery .... 7 May 94
LIEUTENANTS.
Edw. W. David Evans, *p.s.*29 Dec. 86
Harry Gordon Hodgkinson 28 Sept.89
Hy. Robt. Skynner Stradling 15 July 93
Thos. O. Ramsay Sladen,*p.s.* 4 Apr. 94
Rhodri V.L.Lloyd-Philipps,
p.s.............................. 7 May 94
John Lloyd Hughes .... 7 May 94
SECOND LIEUTENANTS.
Adjt. & Capt.—S. Tushing-
ton, *Captain R. Artillery* 16 Feb 95
Qr.Mr.—W. Stephens, *Qr.*
Mr. R. Art.; Hon. Lieut. 6 Apr. 92
Med. Off.—

ENGINEER MILITIA.
Fortress Forces, Royal Engineers.

Royal Anglesey.
Head Quarters, Beaumaris.
HONORARY COLONEL.
Thos. L. Hampton Lewis,[19]
late Capt. 5 Dragoon Gds.17 Oct. 91
LIEUTENANT COLONEL.
L. F. W. Dwyer, *p.s.* (*H*),
Capt.ret.pay 106 Fusiliers 7 Nov. 91
CAPTAINS.
R. ap Hugh Williams, DL.
Hon. Major ....29 Apr. 84
William Glynne Massey......24 Apr. 89
Francis Hooper Rawlins,
(*H*), *p.s.* ....12 Nov. 92
LIEUTENANTS.
Thomas Fanning Evans ... 9 May 92
John Hy. Pritchard Rayner 4 Apr. 94
SECOND LIEUTENANTS.
Robert May Wetherell ......13 Mar. 93
Sir Thos. L. Hughes Neave,
Bart. ....15 July 93
John L. Hampton-Lewis ...12 Apr. 94
Arundel Neave ....10 Oct. 94
Adjutant.—H. B. N. Adair,
Captain R. Engineers 10 Sept.91
Med. Off.—

Blue Facings.

Royal Monmouthshire.
Head Quarters Monmouth.
HONORARY COLONEL.
Godfrey C., *Lord* Tredegar[20] 9 Dec. 85
LT. COLONEL.
Wm. E. C. Curre, *p.s.*......... 6 Feb. 95
MAJORS.
Edward L. Lister, *p.s.* ......13 Dec. 90
CAPTAINS.
Wm. Ferdinand Batt.........16 Apr. 84
Geo. F. Henry, *Lord* Raglan,[21]
*p.s. ret. pay Grenadier
Guards, Hon. Major* ......23 Apr. 87
Hon. G.W.R. Somerset,*p.s.*16 Nov. 89
Henry E. Morgan Lindsay,[22]
Capt.ret. pay,R.Engineers,
Hon. Major .... 2 Dec. 91
Courtenay C.E.Morgan,*p.s.*30 Dec. 91
C.M.Crompton-Roberts,*p.s.*14 May 92
Fras.H.Green-Wilkinson*p.s.* 4 Mar. 93
Chas. J. Helbert Helbert,
p.s., late Lt. Welsh Fus.... 2 Sept.93

LIEUTENANTS.
Edw.W.J.P.H. Smythe,*p.s.*13 May 9?
Fras. J. Denis M'Donnell,
p.s. .... 3 June 91
Charles Bathurst, *p.s.*.......... 4 June 92
Geo.M. Lagier Lamotte,*p.s.*
(*H*),*Inst. of Musketry*...... 4 June 9?
Frederic John Lawrence ...15 Apr. 93
Charles Jerome Vaughan...15 Apr. 93.
Arthur R. P. *Visct.* South-
well, *p.s.* 2 Sept.93
SECOND LIEUTENANTS.
Hon. Henry Allen Rolls ...27 Aug. 92
Reginald J. S. Price ....14 Apr. 93
Chas. T. H. Kemys-Tynte 6 Jan. 94
Herbert Millingchamp
Vaughan ....20 Jun. 94
Richard Henry Edwards ...17 May 94
Edw. Douglas M. H. Cooke 6 July 94
Robert Llewellyn Matthews27 Mar. 95
Adjutant.—C. D. Learoyd,
Capt. R. Engineers ....14 Nov. 9?
Qr.Master.—G. Tucker, *Qr.*
Mr. R. Engineers, Hon. Lt. 1 Apr. 86
Med. Off.—

Blue Facings.

Submarine Miners, Royal Engineers.

Portsmouth Division.
(Gosport.)
MAJOR.
T. E. A. Jones, (P), (*H*)......25 Feb. 88
CAPTAINS.
William Hawley, *p.s.*........... 4 Mar. 93
LIEUTENANTS.
William Arch.Yockney (P) 25 Mar. 93
SECOND LIEUTENANTS.
SpencerLewisMortimer,*p.s.*, 4 Mar. 93
Percy N. Buckley ....12 Aug. 93
Adjt —

Needles Division.
(Fort Victoria, Isle of Wight.)
MAJOR.
LeonardNormanBarrow (P)19 Aug. 93
CAPTAIN.
A. F.W. H. Somerset-Leeke,
(*H*), (P), *Inst. of Musketry* 8 July 93
LIEUTENANTS.
Osbert Joseph Blundell, *p.s.*25 Mar. 93
George Jones Mitton, *p.s.* 28 Nov. 94
SECOND LIEUTENANTS.

Plymouth Division.
(Plymouth, Devonport & Anchorage.)
MAJOR.
R. Penrose Pilgrim, (*t*) (P) 4 May 89
CAPTAINS.
Richard D. Lee James, (*H*),
(P), *Inst. of Musketry* ...... 2 June 88
Charles Percy Dean, (P),
late Capt. Canadian Art. 10 Jan. 91
LIEUTENANTS.
Geo. Percy A. Phillips, (P) 5 Mar. 94
Chas.OsbornSpringfield(P)19 Sept.9¡
John Harvey Prior 16 Sept.93
SECOND LIEUTENANTS.
Francis Gerard Callaghan 8 Aug. 94

Thames Division.
(Gravesend.)
MAJOR.
Charles Purvis Boyd, (P)... 8 June 89
CAPTAINS.
Albert Gybbon Spilsbury,
(P) (*H*), *Hon. Major* ... 15 Apr. 89
Chas. Grundy Holland,
p.s. (*H*) .... 5 June 89
LIEUTENANTS.
Franz Vernon Beste, *p.s.* ...13 Jan. 94
Lionel Norton Blackwell
(*Lt.* 4 *Bn. Shropshire Lt.*
Inf. 21 Sept. 89) ....27 Feb. 95
SECOND LIEUTENANTS.
Arthur Midgley Kettlewell 10 Mar. 94

Medway Division.
(Sheerness.)
MAJOR.
Rich. Colley Wellesley, (P),
Hon. Lt. Colonel .... 4 June 90
CAPTAINS.
Ernest W. Guinness, (P) ... 4 July 91
Robert Murray Lawes, *p.s.* 4 July 91
LIEUTENANTS.
Henry Mansford, *p.s.*, *In-
structor of Musketry* ......10 June 93
Adrian Edw. G. Graces (P),
serving in the Niger Coast
Protectorate ....16 June 94
SECOND LIEUTENANTS.
Charles G. Manners-Sutton 6 Mar. 95

Harwich Division.
(Harwich.)
MAJOR.
Fras.W. Panzera,[t],(P),(I),
serving under Govt. of British
Bechuanaland ....1 Apr. 90
Geo. Blakemore Robbins,[23]
*ret. pay Argyll and Suth-
erland Highlanders, Hon.
Lt.Colonel* ....25 Feb. 93
CAPTAIN.
Francis Gumley, *p.s.* (*H*)... 5 July 90
LIEUTENANTS.
Edw. Beckles Bartley, (*H*),
(P), *Instructor of Musketry* 21 July 88
Arthur Ratcliffe Willis,(P),
(*T*), (*Lt.* 3 *Bn. Cheshire*
Regt. 28 July 88) ....24 May 93
SECOND LIEUTENANTS.
Philip Stansfeld Huth ..... 13 Mar. 95

Milford Haven Division.
(Pembroke Dock.)
MAJOR.
Henry Davis, *p.s.*..............12 Nov. 89
CAPTAINS.
Phillip A. Alexander, *p.s.* 4 Oct. 90
LIEUTENANTS.
Ern. Percy S. Roupell(P),(t),
*employed under the Commis-
sioners for the Niger Coast
Protectorate* .... 8 Mar. 90
T. P. Cooke Cumming, (P),
(*H*), *Sub Insp. of Consta-
bulary, British Honduras* 27 June 85
Chas.FrederickAndrew,*p.s.*27 Jan. 94
Donald Osborn Springfield,
(P), (*H*), *Inst. of Musketry* 7 Apr. 91
Richd. John Carey Oakes 17 Feb. 94

Western Division.
(Plymouth.)
MAJOR.
Chicholy S. Baker ....12 Nov. 89
CAPTAINS.
T. M. Holmes, (P), (*H*), (*t*),
Hon. Major ....8 Aug. 83
Alf. R. Galsworthy, (P) ...11 May 92
LIEUTENANTS.
Geo. Edward Northey, (*H*),
(P), *Inst. of Musketry* ...18 July 91
SECOND LIEUTENANTS.
Chas. EustaceConstable,(P),20 Feb. 92
Aug. Egerton Skynner, *p.s.*19 May 92
Richard B. Tonson Rye ...20 Mar. 95

Humber Division.
(Peull-on-Humler.)
HONORARY LT. COLONEL.
Sir Albert Kaye Rollit, *Knt.*
MP. .... 2 Nov. 91
MAJOR.
Wm. Henry Wellsted,*p.s.*(*t*)
Hon. Lt. Colonel .... 2 Nov. 91
CAPTAINS.
CharlesHargittJohnson,(F) 2 Nov. 91
Jas. Forster, *p.s.*, *Hon. Maj.* 2 Nov. 91
LIEUTENANTS.
CharlesA.Sebastian-Smith,
p.s. (*t*) ....30 Mar. 93
Edgar William Mayor, *p.s.*
(*H*), *Inst. of Musketry* ... 1 Apr. 9?
SECOND LIEUTENANTS.
John Reginald Riddell, *p.s.*
(*H*) ....19 Mar. 92
John Geo. Smithson, *p.s.* ... 2 Sept.93

Falmouth Division.
(Falmouth.)
HONORARY LT. COLONEL.
Arthur Tremayne ....12 Jan. 93
MAJOR.
John Mead, *p.s.*................12 Jan. 93
CAPTAINS.
John E. Prower, late Lt Col.
Canadian Militia (*H*), (P) 4 Apr. 93
Herbert Reg. Ryder,(P) (*H*) 5 Apr. 93
LIEUTENANTS.
Sir George Johnson (*t*) *p.s.*
(*H*), *Inst. of Musketry* ... 4 July 91
John T. D'Arcy Hutton,
(P), (*Lt. York Art. West.*
Div. 4 May 91) .... 2 Dec. 93
SECOND LIEUTENANTS.
Herbert Cecil Fanshawe ...28 Oct. 93
Arthur Percy Wainwright 5 Apr. 92

MILITIA INFANTRY.

*** For an Alphabetical Table of Contents to Militia Infantry, see p. vi.

The Royal Scots (Lothian Regiment).

3RD BATTALION.
(*Formerly the Edinburgh, or Queen's Regiment of Light Infantry.*)
Head Quarters, Glencorse.

HONORARY COLONEL.
Schomberg Henry, Marq. of Lothian, KT. DL. .... 2 Feb. 89

LT. COLONEL.
George Grant Gordon,[2] CB. (*H*), *late Lt. Col. Scots Guards; Hon. Col., Treasurer of the Household to H.R.H. Prince Christian* 2 Feb. 89

MAJORS.
Mackay John Scobie,[3] (*H*), *late Lt.* 42 F. *Hon.Lt. Col.* 27 June 85
Edward James Grant,[4] (*H*), *Capt. ret. pay Irish Regt.*17 Feb. 94
Harcourt Sawyer, p.s. ....31 Oct. 94

CAPTAINS.
Percy Newby Salmond, p.s. (*H*) .... 9 July 87
Thos. Clarence E. Goff,p.s.,14 Apr. 90
Lord H. F. Montagu-Douglas-Scott, p.s..........18 Oct. 90
Cyril Pelham Foley, p.s. ...26 Aug. 93
Lord Herbert A. Montagu-Douglas-Scott ....24 Feb. 94
John F.G.S. Visct. Brackley, p.s. ....10 Mar. 94
Charles Peever B. Wood ...18 Nov. 93
Robert Dundas,[5]*Hon.Major, late Scots Guards* ....19 Dec. 94

LIEUTENANTS.
Richard Brinsley Sheridan 21 Oct. 93
Dudley Henry Forbes, p.s. 21 Oct. 93
Giles S. H. *Lord* Stavordale 21 Oct. 93
Lord Chas. George Francis Fitzmaurice ....21 Oct. 93
John T. Carpenter-Garnier, p.s. ....18 Apr. 94
William Henry B. Robinson Pease, p.s. ....18 Apr. 94
Schomberg Henley Eden, p.s. ....26 May 94
Halliburton F. Dallas-Yorke 13 Feb. 95

SECOND LIEUTENANTS.
Reginald Badd Trotter .... 1 Mar. 94
John Spencer Cavendish...10 Mar. 94
Walter Jos. Maxwell Scott 14 Apr. 94
Arctas Akers Douglas ......28 Nov. 94
Adjt. & Capt.—H. H. Francis, *Capt.* 1 *Battalion* ....20 Feb. 93
Qr. Master.—Walter F. Horniblow,[7] *Hon. Lieut.* ......23 June 86
Med. Off.—*Surg. Lt. Colonel* Robert Lucas, *MD.* .... 1 Dec. 91
Blue Facings.

The Queen's Royal West Surrey Regt.

3RD BATTALION.
(*Formerly the 2nd Royal Surrey Militia.*)
Head Quarters, Guildford.

HONORARY COLONEL.

LT. COLONEL.
J. Davis, p.s. [t], *Hon. Col.* 14 Feb. 85

MAJORS.
Godfrey Fox Webster, p.s. *Capt. retired pay* 20 F.Hon. *Lt. Colonel* .... 2 Nov. 89
F. H. Fairtlough, p.s.(H), [t] 7 May 91

CAPTAINS.
Tudor Lloyd-Harries, p.s.... 7 July 83
Campbell Edw. Fraser, p.s. 30 July 87
Wellington A. D. Shelton, p.s. 13 Aug.87
Reginald Edward Pole, p.s., *Hon. Major* ....14 Apr. 88
John F. W. Blake Taylor, p.s. 12 Oct. 89
Albert George Shaw, p.s.... 7 May 91
Fras. Hugh Geo. Hercy, p.s. 12 Mar. 92
Alex. Bruce Siddons Fraser 4 Apr. 94
Walter William Shaw .....26 Apr. 94

LIEUTENANTS.
T. B. Houghton Thorne, p.s. 20 Jan. 94
Humphrey Mackworth, p.s. 20 Jan. 94
Peter Robert Denny, p.s. ...27 Feb. 95
Maurice W. Grey Bell, p.s. 27 Feb. 95
Arth. Wilmot Rickman, p.s. 27 Feb. 95
Gerald Bertram Byrne......27 Feb. 95
Chas. Campbell Hook, p.s. 27 Feb. 95

SECOND LIEUTENANTS.
Harry Thornton Reed ......20 Jan. 94
Henry Winchester Richards 2 Feb. 94
Richard Vernon Guest Brettell .... 6 Feb. 94
Ralph Seymour ....10 Mar. 94
Geoffrey William Poynder 26 Sept. 94
George Frederick Cardew 28 Nov. 94
Alex. Wellesley Timmis ...20 Feb. 95
Adjt. & Capt.—R. Dawson, *Capt.* 1 *Battalion* ....24 Oct. 92
Qr. Master.—John S. Dyke,[1] *Hon. Lieut.* ....13 Nov. 86
Med. Off.—

Blue Facings.

The Buffs (East Kent Regt.).

3RD BATTALION.
(*Formerly the East Kent Militia.*)
Head Quarters, Canterbury.
The Motto "*Invicta*" under a White Horse. "*Mediterranean.*"

HONORARY COLONEL.
General Chas. Wm. Powlett Bingham, CB., Liverpool Regiment ....26 Apr. 73

LT. COLONEL COMMANDANT.
Sir Herbert C. Perrott, *Bart.*, p.s., *Hon. Colonel*...31 Oct. 93

MAJORS.
Harry S. Blaydes, p.s. ...... 2 Apr. 92
Theo. F. Brinckman .... 2 Dec. 93

CAPTAINS.
James Collier, (*H*) ....30 Apr. 84
Alex. David Stevenson, p.s. (*H*) ....30 Apr. 84
Charles Mordaunt M'Killop 16 Dec. 85
Herbert Graystone............12 Mar. 92
Malcolm James Russell Dundas, p.s. .... 3 Feb. 94
Charles Vipan, p.s. (*H*) ...12 June 92
Philip Francis Fletcher ...26 Sept.94

LIEUTENANTS.
Cha. Geo. Dering Haslewood 27 Feb. 92
Arthur Reginald Harris ...22 Apr. 93
J. R. Holden ....22 Apr. 93

SECOND LIEUTENANTS.
Roger Archibald Reith.... 17 Dec. 92
Jno. Wm. Hamilton Seppings 13 Apr.93
Bernhard Puckle Steinman 16 Sept.9 3
Wm. Hales Wilkie Young 28 Oct.
Edward Aubrey Schön......14 Apr. 94
James Edward Shaw ...... 3 Oct. 94
Vivian T. Dampier Palmer 24 Oct. 94
Trevor I. Nevitt Mears ... 9 Jan. 95
Charles Fitz G. Hamilton Trueman .... 6 Mar. 9
Adjt. & Capt.—R. E. Philips, *Captain* 1 *Battalion*......... 1 Sept.94
Qr. Masters.—James Wilson Colley,[1] *Hon. Captain* ... 2 Fe¹. 82
Med. Off.—

Buff Facings.

The King's Own (Royal Lancaster Regiment).

3RD AND 4TH BATTALIONS.
(*Formerly the 1st Royal Lancashire Militia.*)
Head Quarters, Lancaster.
"*Mediterranean.*"

HONORARY COLONEL.
Right Hon. Fred. A. *Earl of* Derby, GCB. *Aide de Camp to the Queen; late Lt. and Capt. Grenadier Guards* ....27 Feb. 86

LT. COLONEL COMMANDANT.
George B. H. Marton, DL. JP., *Hon. Colonel*...........20 Mar. 86

LT. COLONEL.
Joseph Lawson Whalley, JP., *Hon. Colonel* ....26 Nov. 87

MAJORS.
Ralph John Aspinall, JP. DL., *Hon. Lt. Colonel*............26 Nov. 87
Bordrigge North North,[1] JP. (t).......................23 Dec. 91
William Kemmis, JP. ......23 Dec. 91
Charles Edward Every-Halsted, JP. 12 Sept.94

CAPTAINS.
Jas. Meredith Maurice, (*H*) *Instructor of Musketry* ...19 Jan. 87
Russell N. Darbishire, p.s. (*H*) ....22 Sept. 88
George Joseph Taaffe........13 Apr. 89
Herbert Ramsay Feilden, *ret. pay Lancashire Fusiliers, Hon. Major* ....19 Mar. 90
William Henry Feilden......13 June 89
Richard Norman De la Bère, *Instructor of Musketry* ...30 July 92
Henry Hastings Jones, JP. p.s. ....30 July 92
Felix V. S. Churchill, *ret. pay Gloucester Regiment* 19 Oct. 92
Frederick George Parsons 4 Apr. 94
William Wilson-Wilson, (t) 23 June 94

LIEUTENANTS.
James Samuel M'Call ...... 7 Jan. 91
Richd. Trappes-Lomax, JP. 21 July 94
Fisher Henry Froke Evans 21 July 94
Hon. Algernon F. Stanley 21 July 94

SECOND LIEUTENANTS.
Thos. Teece Whitehurst ... 6 Jan. 94
Manuel Leigh Henry......... 9 Feb. 94
Harold Saml. Oppenheimer 14 Nov. 94
Adjts. & Capts.—F. B. Matthews, *Major* 1 *Bn.* ....15 Jan. 91
G. W. H. Le Feuvre, *Capt. North Lancashire Regiment* 24 Mar. 91
Qr. Master.—Bernard Daly, *Hon. Lieut.*..................27 Feb. 95
Med. Off.—

Blue Facings.

Northumberland Fusiliers.

3RD BATTALION.
(*Formerly the Northumberland Militia.*)
Head Quarters, Alnwick.

HONORARY COLONEL.
The Duke of Northumberland KG. *late Capt. Gren. Gds.* 1 Aug. 74

LT. COLONEL.
Henry G. *Earl* Percy, p.s., *Aide de Camp to the Queen, and Colonel*...................17 Feb. 75

MAJORS.
Anthony Marshall, *Hon. Lt. Colonel* .... 2 July 83
Lord Algernon M. A. Percy (*H*), *late Lt. Gren. Gds., late of* 3 *Bn.* Berkshire *Regt.* ... 9 Apr. 81

CAPTAINS.
Lord Lionel Cecil, *Hon. Major* ....26 May 79
William Orde ....23 Nov. 81
Roddam J. Roddam, p.s. ... 5 Aug. 85
Lawrence M. Crossman ...18 Aug. 86
Percy Horace G. Cotton, p.s. (*H*), (*T*) .... 3 Aug. 89
Hon. Ronald C. Jervis ...... 3 May 90
Edward Joicey...............21 Mar. 91
Robert Scott..................18 Feb. 93
William Maxwell .... 5 May 94

O O

Militia Infantry.

LIEUTENANTS.
Algernon E. Calvert Grey 4 June 87
Alexander Browne............13 Sept. 90
George Anthony Woods ...13 Sept. 90
Montague Browne............13 Sept. 90
Richard Foulis Roundell... 5 Mar. 92
Charles Selborne Roundell 5 Mar. 92
John Westmacott .... 9 June 94
Percival C. Fenwicke-
  Clennell .... 9 June 94
Clement Sawrey-Cookson 9 June 94

SECOND LIEUTENANTS.
William Matthew Burrell... 2 Mar. 93
John R. Hutton-Squire ...10 Mar. 94
Edw. Pius Arthur Riddell 12 Apr. 94
Alan Wm. Berkley Spencer 5 Dec. 94
Frederick Raymond Coates 2 Jan. 95
Adjt. & Capt.—M. L. Sant,
  Captain 2 Battalion.........18 Feb. 93
Qr. Master.—Jns. Sampson
  Cartwright, *Hon. Capt....*16 Apr. 84
Med. Off.—

White Facings.

The Royal Warwickshire Regt.

3RD BATTALION.
(*Formerly the 1st Warwick Militia.*)
Head Quarters, Warwick.
"*The Bear and Ragged Staff.*"

HONORARY COLONEL.
Rt. Hon. W. H., *Lord* Leigh 2 June 6

LT. COLONEL.
Wm. Alex. Pennington, *JP*.
  Hon. Colonel ....17 Oct. 94

MAJORS.
Barklie Cairns M'Calmont,
  late Captain 1 Battalion...21 Nov. 94
Geo. Le Mesurier Gretton,[1]
  p.s. [t] .... 5 Dec. 94

CAPTAINS.
Simon William Creagh......18 Nov. 82
Arthur Edmd. Thursby, *p.s.* 16 Apr. 84
Geo. Thomas Congreve, *p.s.* 9 Jan. 86
Jas. Douglas S. D. Archer,
  p.s., Hon. Major............. 3 Apr. 88
Wm. Dalrymple Strachan, *p.s.* 4 June 90
Fred. Edw. Hervey Parratt,
  p.s. (*H*), *Inspector Sierra*
  Leone Frontier Police......23 Dec. 91
George Robert Powell, *p.s.* 10 Mar. 94
Henry E. Du Cane Norris,
  p.s., (*H*) ....21 Nov. 94
Fras. Sheffield Webster, *p.s.*
  (*Lt. 4 Bn.* 5 May 88) ......19 Dec. 94

LIEUTENANTS.
Launcelot M. Fane Gladwin 4 June 92
Edward Mervyn Baker......18 Apr. 94
Fred. Hy. Walter Carden...18 Apr. 94
Alfred Burt, *p.s.* .... 2 Jan. 95
James George Whish .... 2 Jan. 95
Stanhope Alfred Bruce..... 2 Jan. 95

SECOND LIEUTENANTS.
Philip Eustace Besant ....24 Oct. 94
Chandos W. Rogers Bridges 6 Feb. 95
Cameron O'B. Harford
  Methuen..................... 9 Feb. 95
Adjutant & Captain.—L. E.
  Morrice, *Captain 2 Battalion* ....28 Aug. 94
Qr. Master (*with rank of Qr. Mr. in the Army*).— Henry
  Cragg, *Hon. Lieut.* .... 7 May 91
Med. Off.—

Blue Facings.

4TH BATTALION.
(*Formerly the 2nd Warwick Militia.*)
Head Quarters, Warwick.

HONORARY COLONEL.
Geo. D. Steele Perkins ...... 6 Oct. 88

LT. COLONEL
James Gildea, *Hon. Colonel* 22 Oct. 90

MAJORS.
Harry L. B. M'Calmont, *DL*.
  late Lt. Scots Guards ...18 Jan. 90
Harry W. Schofield .... 6 Aug. 92

CAPTAINS.
John E. R. Campbell, *DL*.
  p.s., Hon. Major ....19 Jan. 84
Archd. Kelso, *Hon. Major* 21 May 87
Alex. J. B. Redmayne, *Hon.*
  Major ....19 Jan. 89
Abel Edgar Morrall, *p.s.* (*H*) 6 Dec. 90
Grey D'E. H. Fullerton,
  late Lt. 13 Hussars ....15 Oct. 91
Edward Wilson Dawes, *ret.*
  pay 4 Dragoon Guards ...18 Apr. 94
John B. Ludford-Astley ... 1 Aug. 94
Chas. Harold L. Barnett ... 1 Aug. 94

LIEUTENANTS.
Chandos Leigh................24 Dec. 92
George Gem ....23 June 93
Harry C. Trevor Parker ...17 Feb. 94
Percy John Foster ....17 Feb. 94
Frederick John Gossett ...17 Feb. 94

SECOND LIEUTENANTS.
Henry Sheppard H.
  Cavendish ....13 Jan. 94
Arthur Hill ....10 Feb. 94
John Egerton Leigh ....10 Feb. 94
Chas. Albert Leslie French 10 Feb. 94
Claude Wreford Brown ...20 Feb. 95
Adjt. & Capt.—D. Granville,
  Captain 1 Battalion.........20 Sept. 93
Qr. Master.—William Hall,
  Hon. Lieut. .... 9 Nov. 92
Med. Off.—

Blue Facings.

The Royal Fusiliers (City of London Regiment).

3RD BATTALION.
(*Formerly the Royal Westminster Militia.*)
Head Quarters, Hounslow.
"*Mediterranean.*"

HONORARY COLONEL.
Rt. Hon. G. H. *Earl* Cadogan 24 Feb. 36

LT. COLONEL.
Charles Edward Lang, *ret.*
  pay Devon Regt. Hon. Col. 9 Dec. 93

MAJORS.
Henry Burgess Weatherall 5 Oct. 92
Graham R. Pearce,[6] *p.s.* (*H*),
  (t), *ret. pay Manchester*
  Regiment ....21 Apr. 94

CAPTAINS.
Alfred Lund ....17 Mar. 88
H. A. *Visct.* Chelsea, *MP*. ...31 May 92
Herbert Cartwright Bell ...22 Oct. 92
Wm. Albert Gillam, (*H*), *p.s.*, 27 Aug. 92
Edw. Burgess Weatherall,
  (*H*), *Inst. of Musketry*...27 Feb. 95

LIEUTENANTS.
William Jones Walker .....13 June 92
Francis Cannon ....26 Nov. 92
John Keyworth .... 3 Feb. 94
Harold William Compton... 3 Mar. 94
Thos. Chas. Bedford Holland 13 Mar. 95
Arthur Hy. Daniel Britton,
  p.s.............................17 Mar. 95

SECOND LIEUTENANTS.
Edw. W. E. G. Sealy-Vidal 10 Oct. 94
Pandia Schilizzi ....20 Mar. 95
Adjt. & Capt.—C. H. Morrice,
  Captain 1 Battalion ....21 Nov. 94
Qr. Master.—John Dillick
  Bennell, *Hon. Lieut.* ......26 Mar. 90
Med. Off.—

Blue Facings.

4TH BATTALION.
(*Formerly the Royal London Militia.*)
Head Quarters, Artillery Place, Finsbury.

HONORARY COLONEL.
Sir Reginald Hanson, *Bart.*
  MP. ....21 Oct. 82

COLONEL.
Lorenzo Geo. Dundas,[1] (*H*),
  late Capt. 92 F. .... 5 Jan. 81

LT. COLONEL.
Ambrose Humphrys Bircham,[2] *ret. pay King's R.*
  Rifles. ....23 Nov. 89

MAJOR.
Cha. E. R. W. Mortimer,
  late Lt. 9 *F.; Hon. Lt. Col.* 17 May 93

CAPTAINS.
Chas. L. Griesbach,[5] *CIE. p.s.*,
  Hon. Major, employed on the
  Geological Survey of India 5 Jan. 81
Henry Norton B. Good, (*H*),
  Hon. Major ....12 June 80
John Henry Helpman, *p.s.*
  Hon. Major ....30 Jan. 86
Robert H. R. Helpman ......28 Apr. 86
Frederick Randall Harrison 3 Sept. 87
Henry Harrison Parry, *p.s.*
  (*H*) ....25 Apr. 88
Arthur Charles Tompkins. 27 July 89
Edw. Ernest Henry Atkin 11 Jan. 90
Frederick Charles Richmond-Parry ....19 Dec. 91
Francis Stanhope Hanson 8 Feb. 93
J. Chabot Low, *p.s.* (*H*), [t]17 May 93

LIEUTENANTS.
Coote R. Hely-Hutchinson,
  (*H*), *Inst. of Musketry* ...18 Feb. 91
Wm. Vernon Harcourt ......18 Feb. 91
Fletcher Wm. Barnes, *late*
  Lieut. 1 *Guernsey Militia* 9 June 91
Gordon M'Leod Johnson ... 9 Jan. 92
Granville Edm. W. Money[8] 8 Feb. 93
Fras. Cyril Dunn-Gardner 3 Feb. 93
John Hubert Griffin ....17 May 93
Llewellyn E. Richmond-
  Parry .... 3 June 93
Reginald Spencer Lord..... 3 June 93
Charles Edwin Fenner, (t) 9 Jan. 95

SECOND LIEUTENANTS.
Ernest Mawbey Birch ......15 May 93
Henry Fox Adams ....22 July 93
Spencer James Langton ... 3 May 94
Dare Heber-Percy H. Reade 9 Jan. 95
Wm. E. R. Richmond-Parry 13 Feb. 95
Adj. & Captain.—C. F. Heyworth, *Captain 1 Battalion* 17 Dec. 94
Qr. Master.—Wm. Simpson,
  Hon. Lieut. .... 6 Nov. 86
Med. Off.—

Blue Facings.

5TH BATTALION.
(*Formerly the Royal South Middlesex Militia.*)
Head Quarters, Hounslow.

HONORARY COLONEL.
Hon. Chas. E. Edgcumbe,
  p.s., late Capt. & Lt. Col.
  Grenadier Guards ....11 Feb. 88

LT. COLONEL.
Walter Andrew Wynter,[3]
  Bt. Major late West Riding
  Regiment, Hon. Colonel ...29 Apr. 91

MAJORS.
Fenwick B. de S. La Terrière,[4]
  ret. pay 18 *Hussars* ......24 Nov. 88
Henry N. Pendleton, *Hon.*
  Lt. Colonel ....28 May 92

CAPTAINS.
George Dibley, *p.s.* (*H*), *Hon.*
  Major ....25 Mar. 85
Maydwell Parsons, *p.s.* .....13 May 85
Chas. Aprilis Sutton Warde,
  late Lieut. 7 *Dragoon Gds.* 8 June 85
Walter Sidney Livesay......25 May 86
Geo. Carr Forster, *p.s.* (*H*),
  Instructor of Musketry ...27 Aug. 90
Christopher Heseltine ......24 Dec. 92
Geoffrey Baskerville, *p.s.*... 9 Dec. 93
Somerset F. Gough-Calthorpe, *p.s.* .... 9 Dec. 93

LIEUTENANTS.
Fras. Eastwood Eastwood,
  (*H*) .... 6 Dec. 90
Guy Dickson ....29 July 93
Jas. J. Raymond Mallock 27 Jan. 94
Wm. Jocelyn R. Wingfield 27 Jan. 94
Alfred Chas. Hugh Dixon... 9 June 94
Norman Dudley Horsford 20 Feb. 95
Geo. Sutherland Guyon ...20 Feb. 95

Militia Infantry. 587

SECOND LIEUTENANTS.
Hugo Frank Henry ....17 Feb. 94
G.DouglasBaillie Hamilton21 Nov. 94
James B. Lindsay Deane... 9 Jan. 95
C.J.Fitz R. Rhys Wingfield13 Mar. 95
Adjt. & Capt.—D. J. Hamil-
ton, *Capt. R. Fusiliers* ... 8 Dec. 91
Qr. Master.—George Her-
bert, *Hon. Captain* ....15 Mar. 90
Med. Off.—

Blue Facings.

The King's (Liverpool Regt.).
3RD AND 4TH BATTALIONS.
Formerly the Duke of Lancaster's Own Rifles.)
Head Quarters, Warrington.
HONORARY COLONEL.
Sir Thos. George Fermor
Hesketh, Bart...........12 Sept.94
LT.COLONEL COMMANDANT.
Cha. C. Woodward,[1] *Hon.
Colonel* 19 Sept.94
LIEUTENANT COLONEL.
John M.Batten(*H*),*Bt.Major
ret. pay* 8 *F. Hon. Colonel* 17 Oct. 94
MAJORS.
Peter Priestley, *p.s.*, *Hon.
Lt.Colonel* .... 6 June 85
William Hudson Hand, *p.s.
late Lt.* 37 *F.*..............26 Oct. 90
Hon. Walter Maxwell, *p.s.* 28 May 90
William Henry Parkinson,
Hon. Lt.Colonel ....17 Oct. 94
Walter Geo. R. Chichester-
Constable ....12 Dec. 94
CAPTAINS.
T. Prichard Sheraton,*p.s.*..21 Apr. 86
Edmund Culpeper Weston,
p.s. [t],(*H*), *Inst. of Musk.
Hon. Major* ....18 June 87
Edw. Henry Beaman, jun. 25 May 89
Samuel Reddy ....25 May 89
Charles Edward Terry ......15 June 89
John Woolley Allen, *p.s.* ... 7 July 90
Wm. Norman L. Davidson 18 Oct. 90
Fred.Wm. Proctor, p.s. (S),
*Capt. ret. pay W. Riding
Regt.* ....11 Feb. 91
John Beresford Jobling ... 1 June 91
Henry Greaves Walker,*p.s.*18 July 91
James Binney .... 5 Oct. 92
Thomas Caldwell Connell 4 Oct. 93
LIEUTENANTS.
Roger Fitzhardinge Gage... 2 June 88
Charles Gerald Gordon, *p.s.*
(*H*), *Assistant Inspector
Lagos Constabulary* .... 9 Apr. 90
Harry Norman Packer 13 Sept.90
Samuel Devereux Norris ...18 July 91
Arthur James Oxley ....18 July 91
Henry Littlehales Barker,
(*H*), (t) *late Lt. W. Kent
Regt. Inst. of Musketry* ..11 May 92
Hugh Lewis Sharpe ....20 Jan. 94
Francis Julian Whalley....20 Jan. 94
Disney Younger Watt.......20 Jan. 94
Walter Ernest Stuart......20 Jan. 94
SECOND LIEUTENANTS.
Robert Tyndall ....16 Dec. 93
Francis John Joslin ......23 Dec. 93
Louis John Wyatt .... 6 Jan. 94
Bertram William Collier...14 Feb. 94
Walter Mansel Parker .....24 Feb. 94
Hugh Gordon Watson ....10 Mar. 94
Hugh Frederick Byrne......10 Mar. 94
Henry Johnston Dunlop ... 6 Apr. 94
Charles Latimer Thomas...26 Sept.94
Herbert SeymourHusted...13 Feb. 95
John Bennett Hearsey.....13 Feb. 95
Walter S. Wilfrid Browne 13 Feb. 95
Lionel Knox D'Arcy.......14 Feb. 95
John Tyson Wigan ....14 Feb. 95
Adjts. & Capts.— F. R. M.
Synge,*Major S.Lanc.Regt.*16 June 90
A.W. H. Tripp, *Capt. 1 Bn.* 1 Nov. 93
Qr. Masters.—David Clarke,
Hon. Lieut. ....11 Dec. 86
Med. Off.—

Blue Facings.

The Norfolk Regiment.
3RD BATTALION.
(*Formerly the 1st Norfolk Militia.*)
Head Quarters, Norwich.
HONORARY COLONEL.

LT.COLONEL.
Fred. Willock Garnett, *late
Lt.* 85 *F.*, *Hon.Colonel* ...17 Mar. 88
MAJORS.
Fred. Hambleton Custance,
*late Capt. & Lt.Col. Gren.
Guards*, *Hon. Lt.Colonel*:.. 5 Oct. 81
Sir K. H. Kemp, *Bt.* ....28 Mar. 94
CAPTAINS.
S. Arthur Snow,*Hon. Major* 25 Apr. 82
Henry H. F. Eden, p.s. (*H*)
Hon. Major................. 3 Feb. 87
Lionel Garrick Trevor (*H*) 28 Feb. 91
*Hon.*A.E.J.Henniker-Major 18 Feb. 93
Algernon Harold Baillie(*H*)18 Feb. 93
Sidney Lennard Barrett,
Instructor of Musketry ...25 Nov. 93
Richard Ludwig Bagge ...18 Apr. 94
LIEUTENANTS.
Lovel Wodehouse Gurney22 Feb. 93
John Cecil Hylton-Jolliffe...29 Apr. 93
Edgar Cooper Cooper-
Brown, *p.s.*...............22 July 93
Reginald Seager Hunt .....25 Nov. 93
Hector Fitzroy Maclean ... 28 Apr. 94
Leopold Hy. VivianForster19 Sept.94
Harry P. Gott Crosse, *late
Hon. Capt. Cadet Corps
with 1 Vol. Batt.; Acting
Adjutant 1 Cadet Bn.*......16 Jan. 95
Percy John Finch ....20 Feb. 95
SECOND LIEUTENANTS.
Alwyne Mason ....25 Nov. 93
Percy Neeld Worthington. 31 Jan. 95
Francis Edward Walter ... 1 Feb. 95
Albemarle BertieEdw.Cator 2 Feb. 95
Adj. & Capt.—W. C. Tonge,
Capt. 1 Battalion ....13 Jan. 92
Qr. Master.—Wm. Halpin,[2]
Hon. Captain..............20 Sept.82
Med. Off.—

White Facings.

4TH BATTALION.
Formerly the 2nd Norfolk Militia.)
Head Quarters, Norwich.
HONORARY COLONEL.

LT.COLONEL.
Thomas Wm. Haines, *JP.*,
Hon. Colonel ....24 Apr. 89
MAJORS.
Sir Charles Harvey, *Bt.
Hon. Lt.Colonel* .... 5 May 88
Horace Walpole, *late Capt.
60 F.*, *Hon. Lt.Colonel* ...18 May 89
CAPTAINS.
John Edward Fryer, *p.s.*,
Hon. Major................10 Mar. 75
Owen Hunt Fisher ....22 Apr. 86
Harold Wm. Thatcher,[1] *ret.
pay Shropshire Lt.Infantry,
Hon. Major*................13 Apr. 87
Charles Remington Mills...28 July 88
John Henry Steward.......28 July 88
James Mackenzie Leith, *p.s.*
[t], (*H*),(*I*), *Hon. Major* 28 Nov. 83
Cecil J. Cramer-Roberts ... 2 Apr. 90
George N. Latham, *p.s.* ...25 Feb. 95
LIEUTENANTS.
Charles Surtees Robinson 16 Jan. 92
WoodburnA. R. Bartleman 27 Feb. 92
Arch. Rowsell Brakspear 25 Feb. 93
SECOND LIEUTENANTS.
John C. Harding Newman 3 May 93
Ryves Alex. Mark Currie...13 Feb. 94
Frederic George Dayley ...16 Feb. 94
Henry Fowler ....17 May 94
Lloyd N. Jones-Bateman ...10 Oct. 94
Adj.& Capt.—W. R. Inglis,
Captain 2 Battalion .....30 June 92
*Qr. Master (with rank of Qr.
Mr. in the Army)*—Fras.
Grehan,[4] *Hon. Captain*... 1 Dec. 80
Med. Off.—

White Facings.

The Lincolnshire Regiment.
3RD BATTALION.
(*Formerly the Royal North Lincoln Militia.*)
Head Quarters, Lincoln.

HONORARY COLONEL.
Rt.Hon.William John, *Visct.*
Oxenbridge, *DL. Aide de
Camp to the Queen* ....29 Mar. 90
LIEUTENANT COLONEL.
Edw. Walter Willson.........27 Feb. 95
MAJORS.
Charles Arthur Swan, (*H*) 2 July 92
CAPTAINS.
Christopher W. A. Nevile,
Hon. Major................ 1 Sept.83
Sutton Harvey Lowe, ((*H*),
Inst. of Musketry..........14 June 90
Alf. James Reed, *late Capt.
3 Brig. E. Div. R. Art.*... 5 Aug. 91
George Henry Dymoke ...15 June 92
Herbert James Torr ....10 Dec. 92
George Edward Honeage...24 June 93
Edward Mason Grantham 21 July 94
Cecil Harry St. L. Howard 8 Aug. 94
LIEUTENANTS.
Arthur Wellesley Wilson... 5 Aug. 91
Chas. E. Frederick Rich ...24 June 93
George Hugh H. Allott.....24 June 93
Basil Hepburn Hastie...... 7 July 94
John B. Redfern Russell... 7 July 94
Gordon Halswelle.......... 7 July 94
SECOND LIEUTENANTS.
Robert Neal King ....14 Oct. 93
Hugh Francis Blair, *p.s.* ... 2 Dec. 93
Stephen Massingberd ......14 Apr. 94
Joseph Billiat ....15 Aug. 94
Owen Daly Atkinson.......24 Oct. 94
Adjt. & Capt.—G. A. Ivatt,
Captain 1 *Battalion*......14 Aug. 93
Qr.Master—Joseph Cowen,
Hon. Lieut. 30 Sept.91
Med. Off.—

White Facings.

4TH BATTALION.
(*Formerly the Royal South Lincoln Militia.*)
Head. Quarters, Grantham.
HONORARY COLONEL.
Earl Brownlow, *late Ens. &
Lt. Grenadier Guards*...... 3 Mar. 58
LT.COLONEL COMMANDANT.
Lord William Cecil,[1] *late
Capt. Grenadier Guards,
Groom in Waiting to the
Queen* ....16 Apr. 90
MAJORS.
Eustace Beaumont Burna-
by, *ret. pay* 2 *Battalion,
Hon. Lt.Colonel* ....14 May 90
Sir Jas. de Hoghton, *Bart.*,
ret. pay Lincoln Regt.....13 Feb. 95
CAPTAINS.
Harry Austin L. Young ...19 Sept.85
Richard Gleed .... 7 Jan. 88
Thomas WilliamPinder,((*H*)17 Aug. 89
Fras. H. Smeathman Huxton,
*employed under the Royal
Niger Company* ....23 Aug. 90
William Alfred Cragge ....23 Aug. 90
Arthur Anthony W. Bailey 23 Aug. 90
James Henry Part .... 1 Mar. 94
Henry Thomas Timson..... 3 Mar. 94
LIEUTENANTS.
Edward Kyme Cordeaux,
(*H*) ....11 May 91
John George Thorold ......14 May 91
Cecil H. Anderson-Pelham 29 Apr. 93
Hugo Meynell FitzHerbert 19 June 93
John Albert Cole,*Instructor
of Musketry* ....23 Dec. 93
Cosmos Chas. Richd. Nevill 3 Mar. 94
Charles Eustace Hutton ...21 Nov. 94
SECOND LIEUTENANTS.
Montague R. A. Cholmeley 2 Dec. 93
Evelyn Fountaine Villiers 16 Mar. 94
Sir Berkeley Geo. D. Shef-
field, *Bart.*...............14 Nov. 94
Bertram Wm. Arnold Keppel19 Dec. 94
Adjt. & Capt.—W. G. Grant,
Captain 1 *Battalion* ......20 Sept. 91
Qr. Master.—C. Young,*Hon.
Captain* ....15 Aug. 82
Med. Off.—*Surg. Lt.Colonel*
Geo. Wm. Shipman ...... 1 Dec. 91

White Facings.

O O 2

Militia Infantry.

The Devonshire Regiment.

3RD BATTALION.
(*Formerly the 2nd Devon Militia.*)
Head Quarters, Plymouth.

HONORARY COLONEL.
Rt. Hon. Chas. Seale Hayne,
MP. p.s. (H), JP, Paymaster General ....10 Oct. 94

LT. COLONEL.
Henry Howorth, late Lt.
88 F. Hon. Colonel ....28 Nov. 94
Fra. Hender Mounsteven,
p.s. (H), late Lt. Royal
Marines; Hon. Lt. Colonel 9 Jan. 95

MAJORS.

CAPTAINS.
John I. Scarbrough, p.s.,
  Hon. Major .... 3 Mar. 80
Richard A. M. Stevens,
  Hon. Major .... 26 May 83
Robt. Keate, p.s., Hon. Major 19 Nov. 87
George S. S. Lowe, (H) p.s.
  Hon. Major .... 3 Mar. 88
John H. How, p.s Hon. Major 9 Feb. 89
Henry Limbrey Toll ....16 Mar. 89
Gerald N. Pitts Langdon... 6 Feb. 95

LIEUTENANTS.
Melville Richmond Brown 14 Dec. 89
Chas. George Carew Elers,
  (H)Instructor of Musketry 14 Dec. 89
Bertram Vernon Mitford... 9 May 92
George Lambert, p.s. .... 7 May 94

SECOND LIEUTENANTS.
Henry Jas. Lucius Cary ...18 Feb. 92
Hon. John R. Lopes Yarde-
  Buller ....28 Jan. 93
Hubert Jas. Cecil Rostron 24 Feb. 94
Lionel Culme Soltau-
  Symons ....13 Mar. 95
Adj. & Capt.—A. J. Gore,
  Captain 1 Battalion.........14 Nov. 92
Qr. Master.—Thomas Reynolds, Hon. Captain ... 1 Feb. 85
Med. Off.—Surg. Lt. Col.
Connell Whipple .... 1 Dec. 91
White Facings.

4TH BATTALION.
(*Formerly the 1st Devon Militia.*)
Head Quarters, Exeter.

LT. COLONEL.
Henry Walrond, p.s. (H), (t),
JP., Hon. Colonel ....27 May 93

MAJORS.
Hon. John S. Trefusis,
  Hon. Lt. Colonel .... 8 May 86

CAPTAINS.
Hon. Edw. Arthur Palk, JP.,
  Hon. Major .... 5 Nov. 81
J. Stafford Goldie Harding,
  p.s. JP., Hon. Major ...... 5 Nov. 81
George Wrigley ....21 May 86
Sutherland Dumbreck[1] ...21 May 86
Dennis Fortescue Boles ...14 Apr. 88
Walter Eldred Warde, p.s.(t) 5 Dec. 88
Christopher T. P. Keene,[2]
  Capt. ret. pay King's Own
  Scottish Borderers, Hon.
  Major ....24 July 89
Chas. Douglas Caird, p.s. (H)25 Jan. 90

LIEUTENANTS.
John FitzLloyd Horner, (H),
  Instructor of Musketry ... 4 Dec. 86
Richard Wells Arthur ......27 May 89
Henry Arthur Sealy Bridge 27 May 89
Reginald Maitland Snow(t)27 May 89

SECOND LIEUTENANTS.
Evelyn William Pierrepont
  Uniacke ....22 Feb. 94
Reginald F. Wm. Hill ......14 Mar. 94
Charles Alexander Bryce...14 Mar. 94
Francis Bryce .... 5 Dec. 94
Norman M. L. Earl of Rothes 6 Mar. 95
Adjt. & Capt.—S. K. Harrier,
  Major 2 Battalion........... 1 Mar. 92
Qr. Master.—John Carr,[5]
  Hon. Captain ....16 Aug. 84
Med. Off.—Surg. Lt. Colonel
  Mark Farrant .... 1 Dec. 91
White Facings.

The Suffolk Regiment.

3RD BATTALION.
(*Formerly the West Suffolk Militia.*)
Head Quarters, Bury St. Edmunds.

HONORARY COLONEL.
The Marquess of Bristol........10 Jan. 65

LT. COLONEL.
Montague Cha. Browning,[1]
late Capt. 87 F., Hon. Colonel 24 Sept. 81

MAJORS.
Geo. Villiers Turner,[2] ret. pay
  York Lt. Inf. Hon. Lt. Col. 22 Apr. 91
Reuben Norton, late Durham
  Lt. Inf. Hon. Lt. Colonel...20 Apr. 93

CAPTAINS.
Henry Tansley Luddington 1 Apr. 87
Ernest Wm. Chas. Squirl... 8 Feb. 90
George O. Mead, (t), (H)...22 May 90
Gerald Arthur Burton ......29 Apr. 91
Hamilton Luard Begbie,
  late Capt. Worcester Regt.,
  Hon. Major ....19 Nov. 92
Montagu Berthon Burnand 17 May 92
Herbert Ogilvie Francis,[3]
  p.s. ....17 May 93
Chas. L. Andrewes Skinner,
  late Lieut. 4 Hussars ......23 Nov. 89

LIEUTENANTS.
Arthur Wyndham Gelston 9 Jan. 92
Chas. Augustine Fonnereau 4 Nov. 93
Philip Wm. T. H. Wortham 4 Nov. 93
Russell Kendall Brittain ...21 Nov. 94
John Gerald Healy..........21 Nov. 94

SECOND LIEUTENANTS.
Samuel J. B. Barnardiston 12 Sept. 94
William Oxenham Cautley 21 Nov. 94
Herbert Wm. Duckworth 21 Feb. 95
Arthur Grant Ross Crawford 6 Mar. 95
Adjt. & Capt.—W. R. D. Lloyd,
  Capt. 1 Battalion ....24 Dec. 91
Qr. Master.—J. T. Potter,
  Hon. Lieut. .... 7 Feb. 94
Med. Off.—

White Facings.

4TH BATTALION.
(*Formerly the Cambridge Militia.*)
Head Quarters, Ely.

HONORARY COLONEL.
H.R.H. G. W. F. C. Duke
  of Cambridge, KG. KT.
  KP. GCB. GCSI. GCMG.
  GCIE...........................30 July 92

LT. COLONEL.
Harry Frost, DL. Hon. Col. 29 Nov. 90

MAJORS.
Wm. Browne Ferris, (H),
  ret. pay 12 F., Hon. Lt. Col. 4 May 89
Herbert D. Fryer .... 7 Jan. 91

CAPTAINS.
Hon. Alex. G. Yorke ....22 Jan. 79
Robert S. Bacchus, Hon.
  Major ....26 June 82
Hy. W. Hurrell, Hon. Major 26 June 82
Francis W. E. Beldam, Hon.
  Major ....22 July 93
Alan Sidney W. Stanley ...23 Apr. 85
Chas. Wentworth Stanley...23 Apr. 85
Sir R. C. Percy Gethin, Bt.,
  p.s. (H) .... 9 Apr. 86
Albert Julian Pell, DL.(H),
  Instructor of Musketry ... 9 Apr. 90
Walter Hamond Francis ...28 Mar. 94

LIEUTENANTS.
Alexander Cross Hall, p.s. 3 May 90
Alf. Shafto Barthropp, p.s.24 Jan. 91
Frederick Gustave Bagnell 6 May 93
Patrick M'Causland ....22 July 93
Maurice Patk. Macnaghten 23 Dec. 93
Reginald Hignett Wilford 10 Oct. 94
Lionel E. Loraine Triscott 16 Jan. 95
Henry Hampden English...27 Feb. 95

SECOND LIEUTENANTS.
James George Black ....23 Jan. 95
Herbert Carter Chapman 30 Jan. 95
Adjt. & Capt.—C. F. Lennock, Captain Suffolk Regt. 7 May 95
Qr. Master.—Arthur James,[5]
  Hon. Lieut. .... 7 Apr. 86
Med. Off.—Surg. Lt. Colonel
  Fred. Fawssett, jun..MD. 1 Dec. 91
White Facings.

The Prince Albert's (Somersetshire Light Infantry).

3RD BATTALION.
(*Formerly the 1st Somerset Militia.*)
Head Quarters, Taunton.

HONORARY COLONEL.

LT. COLONEL.
Henry Cornish Henley, JP.,
  Hon. Colonel .... 26 Feb. 79

MAJORS.
John Hammet Bendon, p.s.
  Hon. Lt. Colonel .... 10 Oct. 91
Henry P. Gore-Langton,[1]
  late Lieut. 72 Foot ...... 6 Aug. 92

CAPTAINS.
Hamilton Alex. Kinglake,
  Capt. ret. pay Lanc. Fus.,
  Hon. Major ....16 Jan. 89
Edw. Brinsley Rawlins, p.s.24 Aug. 89
Hastings Edw. Hicks, Comdg.
  Gambia Frontier Police 25 May 91
Edw. Reginald John Talbot 29 Aug. 91
Clement Phipps Tudway,
  (H), Inst. of Musketry ...11 May 92
Theobald Leonard Walsh,
  (H), p.s. (t) ....20 Dec. 84
Hon. Chas. Pepys Courtenay 22 Feb. 93
Sidney E. O. Owen-Swaffield 11 June 94

LIEUTENANTS.
Clement Brady Upperton... 8 Apr. 93
Hon. Chandos G. Gore-
  Langton .... 5 Aug. 93
John Darley Colley .... 7 Oct. 93
Alg. Wm. S. Lord Langton 10 Feb. 94
Chas. J. Matthew Kenrick 10 Feb. 94
Bethune Minet Patton ...... 5 Sept. 94
Charles Carus Maud .... 5 Sept. 94
Wm. John Wilmot Kerr ... 5 Sept. 94

SECOND LIEUTENANTS.
John Neville Hood Walrond 11 Feb. 94
Ronald H. M. Capel Miers 27 Mar. 94
Fletcher Hayes Henderson-
  Cleland .... 5 June 94
Edw. J. Forrester Vaughan 26 Sept. 94
Adjt. & Capt.—C. L. Connellan, Capt. East Kent Regt. 1 Jan. 91
Qr. Master.—Chas. Jas.
  Leyster, Hon. Lieut.........24 Oct. 94
Med. Off.—

Blue Facings.

4TH BATTALION.
(*Formerly the 2nd Somerset Militia.*)
Head Quarters, Taunton.

HONORARY COLONEL.
William Pinney, DL. JP....12 Mar. 70

LT. COLONEL COMMANDANT.
Wm. Long, JP, late Lt.
  46 F. p.s., Hon. Colonel...17 May 89

MAJOR.
Evan Hy. Llewellyn, JP.
  Hon. Lt. Colonel ....11 Mar. 91

CAPTAINS.
Alfred James Riley, p.s.,
  Hon. Major ....31 Mar. 75
Wm. G. S. Sainsbury, (H),
  p.s., Inst. of Musketry,
  Hon. Major ....15 June 83
John Wm. Henry Webb, p.s.,
  (t), late Lt. 2 Bn. Somerset
  Lt. Infantry .... 2 Aug. 84
Saml. H. Woodhouse, p.s. (t) 5 Oct. 87
Charles Beague St. John-
  Mildmay, p.s. 1 et. pay R.
  Art. ....30 Apr. 90
Chas. Sinclair Shepard [6]
  DSO. Major ret. 1 cyRoyal
  Fusiliers; Brig. Major W.
  Counties Brig. Vol. Inf... 5 Aug. 91
Hy. Norris Glynn Hindi, late
  Lieut. 1 Bn. ....24 Oct. 91

LIEUTENANTS.
Percy Neville ....26 Sept. 85
Roger Harbin Manley ...... 4 Nov. 91

Militia Infantry.

Arthur Llewellyn .... 8 Mar. 93
Robt. Guy Incledon Chichester .... 25 Apr. 93
Ernest A. Braggo Warry ... 2 Sept.93
Harry Erling Sykes ....22 Aug. 94
Philip Humphry Morres ... 6 Feb. 95

Second Lieutenants.
Bertie Fielding Knox Leet 27 Mar. 93
Charles Chamier Lance ... 4 Nov. 93
Robert Nelson Dobson......15 Aug. 94
Stuart Hay .... 30 Jan. 95
Adjt. & Capt.—D.G. Stewart,
Capt. 1 *Battalion* ....15 July 90
Qr. Master.—Frank Sturt,
from 2 Battalion, Hon. Capt. 1 Apr. 86
Med. Off.—

Blue Facings

The Prince of Wales' Own (West Yorkshire Regt.).

3RD BATTALION.
(*Formerly the 2nd West York Militia.*)
Head Quarters, York.
"*Mediterranean.*"

Honorary Colonel.
H.R.H. G. F. E. A. *Duke of York, KG.* ....30 July 92

Lt. Colonel.
Geo. J. Hay, *p.s. DL. JP.,
Hon. Colonel* ....12 May 79

Majors.
John Rickaby, *p.s., Hon. Lt.
Colonel* .... 3 Mar. 88
Henry Trafford-Rawson,
(*b*), *Hon. Lt. Colonel*........12 May 93

Captains.
R. W. Hine-Haycock, (*H*),
Hon. Major ....15 Mar. 82
Abraham M. Sagar-Musgrave, p.s., *Hon. Major* 22 Jan. 87
John Musgrave Benson, *p.s.*22 Jan. 87
Francis Boynton .... 3 Mar. 88
Josph. Straker, *p.s.*(*H*), [*t*],
(S).................... 9 Mar. 89
John Stott, *p.s.*...............16 July 90
Arthur Sale Whiteley, *p.s.* 18 Feb. 94
Fred. Anastasius Saunders,
p.s. .... 3 Feb. 94

Lieutenants.
Wm. Fras. Elcocke Massey,
p.s. ....18 Feb. 93
Charles Benwell, *p.s.* (*H*)
Inst. of Musketry ...... 1 Mar. 93
Geoffroy Francis Dixon,*p.s.*29 May 93
Walter D. Surtees, *p.s.*........29 May 93
George Marsden, *p.s.*...... 4 Nov. 93
Wm. Edm. L. Stewart, *p.s.*12 May 94

Second Lieutenants.
Francis Edm. Lane-Fox ...20 Mar. 93
Howard N. B. Burlton, *p.s.*12 May 93
Aug. Fred. S. Leggatt, *p.s.*21 Oct. 93
Arthur Laidley Brown ......10 Feb. 94
William Ernest Watson... 19 Dec. 94
Balfour Macnaghten ......13 Feb. 95
Adjt. & Capt.—C. H. Cox,
Capt. 2 *Battalion* ......26 Jan. 91
Qr. Master—Francis Pye,
Hon. Lieut. .... 7 Apr. 86
Med. Off.—*Surg. Lt. Colonel*
James Ramsay, MD.......14 May 93
White Facings.

4TH BATTALION.
(*Formerly the 4th West York Militia.*)
Head Quarters, York.

Honorary Colonel.
George Philip Fawkes, (*H*),
late Capt. 63 *F.* ....22 Dec. 88

Lieutenant Colonel.
Chas. R. Prideaux-Brune,¹
*p.s. ret. pay Rifle Brigade,
Hon. Colonel* .... 7 Oct. 93

Majors.
William H. Gott ....22 Apr. 93
John T. Lee .... 2 June 94

Captains.
Alfred Charles Bennett, *p.s.
Hon. Major* ....25 Nov. 82
Henry C. Bulkeley, *Hon. Maj.*28 Feb. 85
Henry Stuart Murray, *Hon.
Major* ....13 Apr. 89
Sir Wm. Henry Mahon, *Bt.*25 Apr. 89
James B. Garforth Tottie, (*H*) 3 May 90

George S. Garland Scaife,
*serving in the Niger Coast
Protectorate* ....22 Apr. 93

Lieutenants.
D'Arcy Edw. Swainston
Strangwayes, (*H*), *Inst.
of Musketry* ....23 July 92
John Philip N. Swainston
Strangwayes............23 July 92
John Lawrence Scarlett ...23 July 92
George Wilmer Herbert ...15 May 93
Henry Reay Yorke...........15 May 93
Charles Ernest Jobling ...15 May 93
Harold Charles Hart........15 May 93
Harry O. Lavallin Puxley 23 Jan. 95

Second Lieutenants.
Oswald Bethell Walker ...10 Mar. 94
Edw. John Chas. Leeming24 Oct. 94
Harold J. Moysey-Thompson12 Dec. 94
Charles Temple Morris ...13 Feb. 95
Adjt. & Capt.—H. E. Watts,
Captain 1 *Battalion*......... 3 Dec. 91
Qr. Master (*with rank of Qr.
Mr. in the Army*)—Thomas
Wilson, *Hon. Lieut.*........23 July 90
Med. Off.—*Surg. Lt. Colonel*
James Walker .... 1 Dec. 91
White Facings.

The East Yorkshire Regt.

3RD BATTALION.
(*Formerly the East York Militia.*)
"*White Rose of York.*"
Head Quarters, Beverley.

Honorary Colonel.
Wm. Henry Grimston,¹ *late
Capt.* 13 *F. JP*............... 1 Nov. 90

Lt. Colonel Commandant.
*p.s.c.*Chas. Kennedy Brooke,
ret. pay 1 *Bn.* ; *Hon. Col.* 15 Nov. 90

Majors.
John H. Burstall,² *late Lt.*
60 *F., Hon. Lt. Colonel* ... 4 May 89
R. T. Ringrose ....18 Apr. 91

Captains.
Fras. Fraser, *Hon. Major*...20 May 82
Herbert John Whittle, *p.s.* 10 June 82
James B.W. Wilson,*p.s.* (*H*)
Hon. Major ....18 Apr. 85
Harold Robinson Pease, (*H*)23 June 85
Alfred St. Hill Gibbons, (*H*)16 Dec. 85
Fred. Charles Strickland-Constable, (*H*), *ret. pay
Royal Horse Guards* ......20 May 90
Alfred Arthur Jolley, *p.s.
(H)*, [*t*] .... 2 Apr. 91
Asbe Windham, (*H*), *Instructor of Musketry* ...... 6 May 91

Lieutenants.
H.G. de Lavalotte Ferguson,
p.s. ....10 Apr. 86
Jno. Bush, [*f*] *late Capt.* 1 *Vol.
Bn. Somerset Lt. Inf.* ......24 Oct. 91
E. N. Buchanan Boyd, *p.s.
(H),serving with Gold Coast
Constabulary*............24 Oct. 91
Digby Francis Wrangham 17 May 93
Edward Starkey Wade......17 May 93
Noël Tayleur ....10 Mar. 94

Second Lieutenants.
Philip T. Snerling Maxsted20 Aug. 92
Henry R. Seguier Brown....22 Oct. 92
Ernest Gadesden Fellows 8 July 93
Cecil Robert ffordo.......... 6 Jan. 94
Edward Rammell Little ...26 Sept. 94
Arthur Henry Wilson ...... 21 Jan. 95
Guy Greville Wilson ....20 Feb. 95
Adjt. & Capt.—E. A. Ogle,
Capt. 1 *Battalion* 16 Sept.93
Paymaster.—John William
F. Sandwith, *late Capt.
Bombay Army*............15 Nov. 55
Qr. Master (*with rank of Qr.
Mr. in the Army*).—Wm.
Alfred Webb, *Hon. Lieut.*10 Apr. 89
White Facings.

The Bedfordshire Regiment.

3RD BATTALION.
(*Formerly the Bedford Light Infantry.*)
Head Quarters, Bedford.

Honorary Colonel.
Sir John M. Burgoyne,
*Bart., late Gren. Guards*20 Jan. 94

Lt. Colonel.
Alfred H. Lucas, *Hon. Col.*19 Aug 91

Majors.
Herbrand A., *Duke of Bedford* .... 7 Oct. 93
Geo. O'Neil Segrave, (*H*),
ret. pay Yorkshire Regt.... 17 Mar. 94

Captains.
Walter de Pradine Cazenove,
p.s. .... 2 Apr. 87
Henry Patrick Macan, (*H*),
Instructor of Musketry ...28 Jan. 88
Gerald M. de L. Davrell, *p.s.* 18 Mar. 91
*Sir Fred.W.F.G. Frankland,
Bart.p.s.*(*H*),*serving under
the Brit. S. Africa Company*29 Aug. 91
Edward Arthur Haggard,¹
ret. pay Army Serv. Corps 2 Nov. 92
Bertie Philip Newbolt ......20 Jan. 94
Simon James Symons, *n.s.* 20 Jan. 94

Lieutenants.
Frederick Edward Bishop 23 Mar. 92
Sir Alg. Kerr B. Osborn, *Bart.* 7 May 92
Arthur Norman White ...... 4 Feb. 93
Shelley L. Laurence Scarlett 10 Mar. 94
Rowland Ernest Alston ...10 Mar. 94
Arthur Northen ....10 Mar. 94
Wm. R. Algernon Chaine 10 Mar. 94
Arthur Bushe Lemon ......16 Jan. 95

Second Lieutenants.
Edward Pugh Attpress.....17 Mar. 94
George Ryefield Taylour...17 Mar. 94
William John Topham......17 Mar. 94
Gustavus Francis Higgins 30 Jan. 95
Adjt. & Capt.—S. A. James,
Capt. Gloucester Regt. ...20 Mar. 93
Qr. Master.—Archibald Hislop, *Hon. Captain* ...... 7 Nov. 83
Med. Off.—*Surg. Lt. Colonel*
Rowland H. Coombs, MD. 1 Dec. 91
White Facings.

4TH BATTALION.
(*Formerly the Hertford Militia.*)
Head Quarters, Hertford.

Honorary Colonel.
The Marquis of Salisbury,
KG. ....11 June 68

Lt. Colonel.
James Edw. Hubert, *Visct.*
Cranborne, *MP.* ....29 Oct. 92

Majors.
Edgar R. S. Sebright,
*Equerry in Waiting to
H.R.H.the Duchess of Teck*26 Nov. 92
Henry R. Solly...............15 May 93

Captains.
Charles, *Visct.* Marsham, *DL.* 3 July 86
Henry Jenney, (*H*) ....11 Apr. 88
Charles H. B. Heaton-Ellis 11 May 89
Hubert Fred Barclay, (*H*) 10 Aug. 89
Lord Henry FitzGerald...... 5 Oct. 89
Charles Percy Boulton ...11 May 91
G. Sholto Douglas, (*H*), (S),
late Capt. Scottish Rifles...22 Feb. 93
Edwin Philip Smith ....15 July 93

Lieutenants.
Edward John Whitfield ... 6 Sept. 90
Hon. Douglas H. Marsham,
*serving with Bechuanaland
Border Police* ....29 Nov. 90
Arthur Holford .... 3 Feb. 94
Egerton Griffith Carrol, (*H*),
Inst. of Musketry .... 7 May 94
Henry du Bois O'Neill ......27 June 94
Montagu Collet Norman ...27 June 94
Robt.Walter Maxwell Brine30 Jan. 95

Second Lieutenants.
Arthur A. Dorrien-Smith .. 8 Aug. 94
Robert Septimus Darnell 17 Oct. 94
Aynsley Eyre Greenwell ...21 Jan. 95
Leonard E. Alex. J iques...21 Jan. 95
Arthur Vincent Utterbuck 27 Feb. 95
Adjt. & Capt.—A. J. Murray,
*Capt. Inniskilling Fusiliers*15 Dec. 90
Qr. Master.—Henry Medd,
Hon. Capt. 17 Sept.87
Med. Off.—*Surg. Lt. Colonel*
L. F. Osbaldeston .... 1 Dec. 91
White Facings.

The Leicestershire Regt.

3RD BATTALION.
(*Formerly the Leicestershire Militia.*)
Head Quarters, Leicester.

Honorary Colonel.
Rt. Hon. J. J. R., *Duke of
Rutland, KG. GCB*........11 Aug. 83

590   *Militia Infantry.*

LT.COLONEL.
Wm. Pearson,¹ *JP, DL, late
Capt.* 45 *F. Hon. Colonel*...28 May '92
MAJORS.
Edw. G. Broadley Palmer 14 June'92
A. T. T. Lord Braye, *JP,
DL.* 20 Feb.95
CAPTAINS.
Maclaine K. D. Whitting...25 June 84
George Espec J. Manners 21 Apr. 86
Clement Kemble Penche ...10 May '90
Daniel Burton W. Mouncey,
 p.s. (H), Inst. of Musketry 27 Jan. '91
Mansfield Turner, jun...... 7 Nov. 85
Philip Reginald Fuller......28 May 92
Robert Samuel Phillips (*H*)20 Aug. 92
LIEUTENANTS.
Robert Henry Collis .... 4 Jan. 93
Arthur L. Crisp Clarke...... 4 Jan. 93
Edw. Athelstane L. Powell 9 Dec. 93
Cyril Owen Ibbetson .... 9 Dec. 93
Canning Turner ....27 Jan. 94
Chas. Hy. Dayrell Palmer 27 Jan. 94
Harold Delacour Beanvish 17 Mar. 94
Roger C. Hans Sloane-
 Stanley ....12 May 94

SECOND LIEUTENANTS.
Donald Holmes M'Gregor 1 Mar. 93
Thomas Frewen .... 8 Mar. 93
Hy. E. Visct. Kingsborough 10 Mar. 94
Gregory Morgan Knight ... 11 July 94
John A. Cuthbert Quilter ...20 Mar. 95
Adjt. & Capt.—John Mosse,
 Captain 1 *Battalion* ...25 Nov. 92
Qr. Master. — Robt. Harri-
son, *Hon. Lieut*............13 Feb. 86
Med. Off.—

White Facings.

The Royal Irish Regiment.
3RD BATTALION.
(*Formerly the Wexford Militia.*)
Head Quarters, Wexford.
HONORARY COLONEL.
Henry S. *Lord* Templemore 2 Sept.93
LT.COLONEL.
Morgan Geo. Lloyd, *late
Cornet* 1 *Dr. Gds. p.s. (H),
JP., Hon. Colonel*............30 Mar. 85
MAJORS.
Henry Arthur Boyse, *p.s.*... 9 Jan. 84
James W. M. *Visct.* Stopford 13 July 91
CAPTAINS.
Owen L. F. Lloyd .... 9 June 79
Chas. Edw. Wogan-Browne,
 p.s. (H), Inst. of Musketry 4 Aug. 88
Hon. B. L. H. Stopford,¹
 ret. pay Irish Fusiliers ...25 June 90
Hon. Arthur H. Chichester; 3 Apr. 92
William Worth Deane ......24 Dec. 92
Jervald H. Pomeroy Colley,
 *Aide de Camp to the
 Governor of Jamaica* ......18 Nov. 93
Arthur Wm. P. M'Dermott 17 May 94
Clarence Percival Warden 5 Dec. 94

LIEUTENANTS.
William Perry .... 6 Mar. 86
David Malcomson ....12 June 93
Robert Murdoch ....12 June 93
Fred. James Robt. Hughes 26 May 94
Hon. H. R. T. G. Fitzmaurice-
 Deane-Morgan ....26 May 94
Henry Vincent Shortland ...26 May 94

SECOND LIEUTENANTS.
Richard G. S. Macbeth ......13 Jan. 94
Louis Charles Sprague ... 3 Mar. 94
Morgan Crofton Lloyd ......12 Mar. 94
djt. & Capt.—H. J. Down-
ing, *Captain* 1 *Battalion*...10 Jan. 91
r. Mr.—G. W. Hawkesby,
Hon. Captain ....29 Nov. 79
Met. Off.—

Blue Facings.

4TH BATTALION.
(*Formerly the North Tipperary Light
Infantry.*)
Head Quarters, Clonmel.
HONORARY COLONEL.
G. Ponsonby, *Visc.* Lismore,
 Lt. of the County, late Cor.
 17 *Lancers* .... 11 Jan. 55
LT.COLONEL.
Fitzgibbon Trant, *late Lt.*
 64 *F. Hon. Colonel* ....22 Nov. 90
MAJORS.
Claude Richard J. Cane,³
 late Capt. R. Artillery......12 Nov. 92
Wm. A. deWarrenne Waller 29 Aug. 94
CAPTAINS.
Chas. S. Hamilton, *p.s.; Hon.
 Major* ....19 July 76
Alex. Lindsay Carnegie ...19 Jan. 84
John Francis Trant,⁴ *Lieut.
 retired pay* 2 *W. I. Regt.* 11 Aug. 86
Edward Herbert Lawrie ...29 Aug. 90
John Rolleston Wolfe ...... 6 May 91
Richard MinchinWelch, (*H*) 11 May 92
Henry Hugh Hutchinson...26 Sept. 94
Arthur Bingham Crabbe,⁵
 ret. pay 8 *Hussars* ....17 Oct. 94

LIEUTENANTS.
Seatic F. M. O'Donnell, *p.s.
 (H), serving with Gold
 Coast Constabulary* ....11 Dec. 86
John Charles Metge ....11 May 92
John Hall Murray ....11 May 92
George Washington Biggs,
 (*H*), *Instructor of Musketry* 11 May 92

SECOND LIEUTENANTS.
Philip Urban Vigors .... 4 Oct. 93
Adjt. & Capt.—A. H. Morris,
 DSO. Capt. 1 *Battalion* ...30 Oct. 93
Qr. Master.—Wm. Griffiths,⁷
Hon. Captain ....14 Nov. 85
Med. Off.—

Blue Facings.

5TH BATTALION.
(*Formerly the Kilkenny Fusiliers.*)
Head Quarters, Kilkenny.
HONORARY COLONEL.
James E. W. T. *Marquis of
 Ormonde, KP. late Capt.*
 1 *Life Guards* .... 7 Jan. 80
LT.COLONEL.
John Nugent Cahill......... 9 Dec. 93
MAJORS.
Walter T. Butler ....13 Apr. 92
Robert C. Knox, (*H*) ......13 Jan. 94
CAPTAINS.
Morley S. M. Dennis........26 May 84
Ernest H. Goldie-Taubman
 p.s. ....29 Oct. 91
George Lionel J. Sargent...16 Sept 93
Daniel George Howlett...16 Sept.93
Hen. Reynolds O'Meagher 16 Sept.93
Joseph Armstrong 16 Sept.93
LIEUTENANTS.
George Smith, *Instructor of
 Musketry*.................. 3 Dec. 93
Rudolph M'Kee .... 3 Dec. 93
Daniel Joseph Smithwick 26 June 94

SECOND LIEUTENANTS.
Augustus Edward Carr ...23 Apr. 93
William Daniel Byrne ... 27 May 93
Archibald Frederick Penny 10 Mar. 94
John Willcocks ....13 May 95
Adjt. & Capt.—A. T. Wil-
son, *Capt.* 1 *Battalion* ... 1 Mar. 93
Qr. Mr.—Cornelius M'Kee,
 Hon. Captain ....15 May 82
Med. Off.—

Blue Facings.

The Princess of Wales' Own (Yorkshire Regiment).
3RD BATTALION.
(*Formerly the 5th West York Militia.*)
Head Quarters, Richmond.

HONORARY COLONEL.
Robert Gunter,¹ *MP. late
 Capt.* 4 *Dragoon Guards*...22 May 86
LT.COLONEL.
Fred. Compton Howard,²
 *ret. pay Rifle Brigade, Hon.
 Colonel*....................15 May 93
MAJORS.
James Hoole, (*H*), *Hon.
 Lt.Colonel* .... 10 Apr. 90
John W. Lodge, *Hon.Lt.Col.* 18 May 91
CAPTAINS.
Wm. E. C. Ellis, *p.s.* ....24 Mar. 86
Morton Jas. Baring Tomlin 10 Apr. 86
Michael G. McNamara ......16 May 87
Hon. Alex. Hugh Wil-
loughby, *Aide de Camp to
 Col. Legard, Com. East
 York Brig. Vol. Inf.* ......25 Mar. 91
Hon. G. Algernon Lascelles,
 *Aide de Camp to the Gover-
 nor of Madras* 16 May 92 18 May 91
Sidney Ernald Ralph Lane 14 June 92
George W. Lowsley Hoole-
 Lowsley-Williams .... 5 June 94
Henry de Teissier,³ *ret. pay*
 8 *Hussars, Inst. of Musk.* 28 July 94
Basil Chas. Hood, *ret.pay* 2 *Bn.* 30 Jan. 95

LIEUTENANTS.
Robt. Benyon Nevill Gunter 25 Apr. 91
Henry Francis Wickham...22 Oct. 92
William Henry Ingilby ...22 Oct. 92
Wilfrith Gerald Key Green 23 Sept. 93
Matthew Robert Liddon ...17 Mar. 94
Fred. Albert H. Palmer ...18 Apr. 94
Aug. Ernest Cathcart ......19 Sept. 94

SECOND LIEUTENANTS.
Benjamin William Bogle ... 9 Mar. 94
Chas. F. Cracroft Jarvis ...21 Mar. 94
Wm. Robt. Hodgson Iles....10 May 94
Roger Stephen Tempest ... 8 Aug. 94
Durham Simpson Matthews 30 Jan. 95
Adjt. & Capt.—J. T. Cotes-
 worth, *Capt.* 1 *Battalion* 26 Oct. 91
Qr. Master.—George Croft,
Hon. Captain.............. 4 Oct. 84
Med.Off.—

White Facings.

4TH BATTALION.
(*Formerly the North York Rifles.*)
Head Quarters, Richmond.
HONORARY COLONEL.
Robert George Hopkinson,
 JP. Hon. Colonel ....29 Aug. 91
LT.COLONEL.
F. P. *Visct.* Falkland, *ret.
 pay Sussex Regt. Hon.Col.* 3 Oct. 91
MAJORS.
James Wm. Richardson,
 Hon. Lt.Colonel ....5 Dec. 85
Robert Hutton-Squire, *Hon.
 Lt.Colonel* .... 5 June 89
CAPTAINS.
Walter Wynne Northcott,
 [*] ....23 June 84
Bernard Gauntlett Harrison 6 Nov.86
James Whaley Fryer, *p.s.*... 1 Feb. 90
Thomas Knowles Ashworth 7 June 93
Chas. Edward Bagnall, *p.s.* 3 July 93
John Charles Rivis ....27 June 94
Reg. Edw. Fras. S. Dudding,
 (*H*), *Inst. of Musketry* ...27 June 94

LIEUTENANTS.
Edward Henry Chapman 12 May 94
Fras. Herbert English
 Torbett ....12 May 94
Percy Chapman ....12 May 94
Charles Elliot ....12 May 94
Alex. Wm. Lewis Trotter 12 May 94

SECOND LIEUTENANTS.
Anthony Courage .... 3 Mar. 94
Robert Harold Merry ...... 6 Apr. 94
Harry Jacob Smith .... 7 Apr. 94
Geo. Demetrius Katinakis 25 June 94
Charles Rupert Wright......31 Oct. 94
Thos. Wolryche Stansfeld 9 Jan. 95
Adjt. & Capt.—A. L. Napier,
 Captain 2 *Battalion*....... 1 May 94
Qr. Master.—Jos. Downes,
 Hon. Captain............. 5 June 89
Med. Off.—*Surg. Lt.Colonel*
Thos. Carter .... 2 June 93

Militia Infantry.

The Lancashire Fusiliers.
3RD AND 4TH BATTALIONS.
(Formerly 7th Royal Lancashire Rifles.)
Head Quarters, Bury.

HONORARY COLONEL.
Thomas Haie, *late Capt. 88 F.* 2 July 92
LT. COLONEL COMMANDANT.
Thomas Brindley ....18 July 92
LT. COLONEL.
Fred. Finch Mackenzie ...18 July 92

MAJORS.
William Worthington Biggs,
 Hon. Lt. Colonel............... 1 Apr. 91
Fred. Chas. Romer, *p.s.(H)*,
 (S),[t] Hon. Lt. Colonel ... 1 Apr. 9;
James Osmond Nelson ...... 4 Mar. 93
John F. C. Hamilton,[1] *ret.*
 pay South Stafford Regt....17 Oct. 94

CAPTAINS.
Fred. Maitland Balfour (*H*),
 late Lieut. 90 Foot, Hon.
 Major ....25 July 85
Frederick W. Mallins ....18 Sept. 86
Francis Joseph Radcliffe... 9 Mar. 89
Henry Alex. Schank (*H*),
 Instructor of Musketry ...16 Nov. 89
Thomas Hutchings............9 Jan. 92
Godfrey Armitage, *late 2nd*
 Lt. 6 Dragoon Guards ...21 Jan. 93
Walter Henry Davenport... 2 Sept. 93
Leonard Broke Willoughby,
 p.s..............................12 May 94
Herbert Richard Cobbett...29 Aug. 94
Wm. Dixon Haddock Green,
 ret. pay K. R. Rifles ......23 Jan. 95

LIEUTENANTS.
Darwin Harry Parker ......14 July 90
Robert Wharton Ford, *p.s.* 14 July 92
Hon. Richard F. Molyneux 13 Aug. 92
Bertram Gordon Snell.......21 Oct. 93
Ernest Frederick Wallace,
 (*H*), *Instructor of Musketry* 21 Oct. 93
Guy Brooke Morris ....21 Oct. 93

SECOND LIEUTENANTS.
Robert Armstrong O'Neill 28 Jan. 93
John Ernest Chalmers ... 9 Feb. 93
Evelyn H. M. P. Pearson... 4 Aug. 93
Geo. Fred. Wallace Brindley 16 Dec. 93
Percy James Bailey .... 6 Jan. 94
John Victor Hermon ...... 3 Feb. 94
William Henry Abell ...... 3 Feb. 94
Harold Bowyer Roffey...... 3 Feb. 94
Richard Jebb Dennis ......30 Jan. 95

Adjts. & Capts.—
E. Woolmer, *Captain* 1 Bn, 15 Mar. 95
H. S. Hamilton, *Capt.* 1 Bn. 22 Apr. 91
Qr. Master.—Edw. Michael
 Collins, *Hon. Lieut.* ......19 May 86
Med. Off.—

White Facings.

The Royal Scots Fusiliers.
3RD BATTALION.
(Formerly the Prince Regent's Royal Ayr and Wigtown Militia.)
Head Quarters, Ayr.

HONORARY COLONEL.
A. P., *Earl of Galloway, KT.*
 late Capt. R. Horse Gds.
 p.s. ....24 June 91
LT. COLONEL.
Wm. Hugh Campbell, *p.s.*
 Hon. Colonel ....11 July 91

MAJORS.
John M. Mathie Morton,
 Hon. Lt. Colonel ....22 Dec. 88
Hon. H. H. Dalrymple ......13 July 91

CAPTAINS.
Reginald Curtis Toogood,[1]
 Capt. retired pay ....26 May 86
George James Fergusson
 Buchanan ....14 May 87
R. L. Nugent-Dunbar, *p.s.* 4 June 87
Lewis N. H. D'Aeth,[2] *Capt.*
 retired pay 1 *Battalion* ...15 Feb. 88
Fullarton James, *p.s.*........22 Dec. 88
Hugh Scott, *p.s.*..............14 July 90
Charles G. S. M'Alester, *p.s.*13 July 91
Ralph G. Riddell-Carre, *p.s.* 13 May 93

Geo. P. Macneil Warner, *p.s.* 19 Oct. 89
John Henry Mugliston, (*H*),
 Instructor of Musketry ... 9 Aug. 90
John Edwards Vaughan,[3]
 p.s. late Lt. 2nd Bn........15 May 91
Ivo D. Walker-Heneage ...11 July 91
Arch. *Earl of Cassillis* ...... 9 July 92
Charles Walter Villiers ...26 May 94
Dominick Sidney Browne, *p.s.* 26 May 94
Arth. M. Mitchell Campbell 20 Mar. 95

SECOND LIEUTENANTS.
Thomas Allen Rose ....13 May 93
Hon. Edward Geo. Boyle... 31 Oct. 94
Alex. Hamilton Dunlop ...13 May 94
John Stewart Duckett ...... 1 Feb. 95
Adjt. & Capt.—*Hon.* G. C.
 Twistleton - Wykeham-
 Fiennes, *Capt.* 1 *Bn.* ......16 Aug. 90
Qr. Master.—Wm. Jas. Hancock, *Hon. Captain* ......31 Aug. 82
Med. Off.—

Blue Facings.

The Cheshire Regiment.
3RD BATTALION.
(Formerly the 1st Royal Cheshire Light Infantry.)
Head Quarters, Chester.

HONORARY COLONEL.
Charles Hosken France-
 Hayhurst,[2] *DL. JP. late*
 Lt. 77 F. ....21 May 92
LT. COLONEL.
Arthur Hill...................21 May 92

MAJORS.
Frank Kirkman Loyd, (*H*),
 [*t*], *late Capt. Inniskilling*
 Fusiliers; Hon. Lt. Colonel 13 Apr. 89
George Frederick Scott, *p.s.* 5 May 94

CAPTAINS.
Charles Percy Lees, *p.s.* ...28 July 88
Lea Jones(*H*), *p.s. Hon. Maj.* 24 Nov. 88
Ed. Kinnersly Williamson... 12 Oct. 89
Edward Townshend Logan 4 May 91
Robert Alexander Greg, (*H*),
 Instructor of Musketry ...25 Nov. 93
Charles F. C. Luxmoore ...27 June 94

LIEUTENANTS.
Geo. Perceval Dodsworth... 13 Feb. 92
Edw. Waldegrave Griffith 19 Nov. 92
Fred. Cha. France-Hayhurst 19 Nov. 92
Wm. Hy. Luttman-Johnson 25 Nov. 93
Frederick Henry Tennyson 29 Aug. 94
Chas. Hy. Kemble Chauncy 29 Aug. 94
Lord Gerald Richard Grosvenor...........................30 Jan. 95

SECOND LIEUTENANTS.
Wm. Thos. Chorley Davidson 10 Mar. 94
Edward Gordon Wilder ...28 Apr. 94
Thos. G. Bayley-Worthington............................27 June 94
George Richard Hennessy 6 Mar. 95
Adjt. & Capt.—W. C. Neville,
 Captain 1 *Battalion* .... 8 Nov. 93
Quarter Master.—Frederick
 Howard, *Hon. Captain* ...14 Apr. 83
Med. Off.—

White Facings.

4TH BATTALION.
(Formerly the 2nd Royal Cheshire Militia.)
Head Quarters, Macclesfield.

HONORARY COLONEL.
Sir Henry Brougham Loch,[1]
 GCB. GCMG. Governor
 Cape of Good Hope .... 7 June 84
LT. COLONEL.
John Moutray Read, *late*
 Capt. 13 *F. Hon. Colonel* 23 Dec. 93

MAJORS.
John A. Arnott .... 5 June 93
Charles Harrop Beck........ 8 Aug. 94

CAPTAINS.
Joseph F. Holliday, p.s.
Hon. Major ....18 Oct. 84
Henry Millett Nicholls ...... 3 Dec. 84
Charles William Willis, *p.s.*
 (*H*) [*t*] *Inst. of Musketry* 9 Oct. 85
W. A. Bromley-Davenport 9 Oct. 86
William Woodward .... 5 Aug. 93
William M'Kay, *p.s.* (*H*) ...12 Aug. 93

LIEUTENANTS.
John Kells Ingram........... 6 Aug. 92
Charles Gosset Mayall...... 6 Aug. 92
Hy. de la Poer Beresford... 2 Sept. 93
Austin Macaulay .... 2 Sept. 93
Maxton Moore .... 2 Sept. 93
Fra. E. Brind Mainwaring 2 Sept. 93
Beresford Moutray Read ...22 Aug. 94
Ion Richd. S. Shinkwin ...16 Jan. 95

SECOND LIEUTENANTS.
Austin Claude Girdwood... 24 Feb. 94
Geoffrey Turner D. Hickman 17 Oct. 94
Reginald Charles Warren 6 Feb. 95
Adjt. & Capt.—G. S. Haines,
 Captain 1 *Battalion*........15 Oct. 89
Qr. Master.—R. M'Kay,
 Hon. Lieut...................24 Jan. 94
Med. Off.—*Surgeon Lt. Col.*
 James B. Hughes .... 1 Dec. 91

White Facings.

The Royal Welsh Fusiliers.
3RD BATTALION.
(Formerly the Royal Denbigh and Merioneth Rifles.)
Head Quarters, Wrexham.

HONORARY COLONEL.
Sir Robert Alfred Cunliffe,
 Bart. late Lt. & Capt.
 Scots Guards, p.s. ....12 May 86
LT. COLONEL.
Samuel Sandbach, *p.s.*......21 Nov. 94

MAJORS.
Chas. R. Mostyn-Owen......19 Mar. 92

CAPTAINS.
Rumley Fred. Godfrey ......14 Apr. 87
Charles Henry Lord, *p.s.(H),*
 [*t*], *Hon. Major, Inst. of*
 Musketry.....................23 Nov. 81
Chas. J. C. Touzel, *p.s.* (*H*) 17 Mar. 88
Edward Lloyd *Hon. Major* 28 Apr. 86
Basil Edwin Phillips, (*H*)...24 Apr. 89
M. R. D'Albuquerque Anderson, *p.s.*................... 4 May 92
Thomas M'Keown..........21 July 94

LIEUTENANTS.
Robert Ormus Campbell ...25 Feb. 91
Fredryck Van C. Philips...25 May 91
Bernard Granville ....10 Sept. 92
Horace Dixon Mayhew.....10 Sept. 92
Hugh Russell Elliott ....21 Jun. 93
Geo. Fred. Myddelton West 4 June 94
Walter Lloyd ....26 Sept. 94
Adrian D. Philip Hughes... 16 Jan. 95

SECOND LIEUTENANTS.
Rowland Percy S. Elderton 9 Dec. 93
Walter Leslie Rigby ....14 Nov. 94
William Noel Cunliffe ...... 9 Jan. 95
Adjt. & Capt.—S. G. Everitt,
 Capt. 1 *Battalion* .... 6 Dec. 90
Qr. Master. —Joseph E. A.
 Barr, *Hon. Lieut.*.......... 5 Oct. 92

Blue Facings.

4TH BATTALION.
(Formerly the Royal Carnarvon Rifles.)
Head Quarters, Carnarvon.
"The Plume of the Prince of Wales."
"Ich Dien."

HONORARY COLONEL.
G. S. G. *Lord* Penrhyn ...... 6 Mar. 95
LT. COLONEL.
Henry Platt, *p.s. DL., Hon.*
 Colonel ....22 Oct. 84

MAJORS.
Owen L. J. Evans ....25 Apr. 88
Hon. Henry R. H. Lloyd-
 Mostyn, *late Sub Lieut.*
 23 *F.* ....14 Nov. 94

CAPTAINS.
Francis W. Turner, *Hon.*
 Major ....14 Mar. 83
Howell R. Jones-Williams 7 Jan. 85
Griffith Radcliffe Owen......28 Mar. 90
Arthur Hamilton Pryce ...20 Sept. 90
Richd. Edw. Lloyd Richards,
 p.s..............................21 Nov. 91
William Buckley ... . 6 Feb. 92
Ernest F. C. Evanson, Consular Assistant, Niger Coast Protectorate ....10 Feb. 93
Lionel John Theobald, (*H*),
 Inst. of Musketry ....10 Feb. 93
A. R. P. Macartney-Filgate 2 Jan. 95

Militia Infantry.

LIEUTENANTS.
Sylvanus Reynolds............ 19 Sept. 91
Wm. Douglas Jones .... 3 Oct. 91
Eric Jas. Walter Platt ...... 12 Mar. 92
Arthur Edward Lewis ...... 8 Apr. 93
Charles Patrick Holroyd .. 3 Mar. 94
Wm. Edw. Strange Butson 2 Jan. 95
Arthur Frampton .... 2 Jan. 95
SECOND LIEUTENANTS.
Frederick Henry Lloyd ...14 Mar. 94
Hon. Chas. R. Clegg-Hill...28 Nov. 94
Foster Swotenham............ 6 Mar. 95
Adjt. & Capt.—Aug. F. Cooper,
 Capt. 2 Battalion .... 1 Sept. 94
Qr. Master.—Henry Edward
 White, *Hon. Captain* ......10 Dec. 84
Med. Off.—

Blue Facings.

The South Wales Borderers.
3RD BATTALION.
(*Formerly the Royal South Wales Borderers Militia.*)
Head Quarters, Brecon.
HONORARY COLONEL.
Arthur *Lord* Ormathwaite,
 late Capt. 1 *Life Guards*...30 Dec. 76
LIEUTENANT COLONEL.
Wm. Jones Thomas,[1] *DL.*
 JP. late Capt. 2 *Dr. Gds.*
 Aide de Camp to the Queen,
 and Colonel .... 4 Oct. 76
MAJORS.
John James, *Hon. Lt. Colonel* 22 Mar. 84
James Aug. Fra. Snead,
 Hon. Lt. Colonel .... 7 May 87
CAPTAINS.
Herbert Arthur Franklin 28 Feb. 85
Charles Healy ....25 Sept. 86
Thomas Williams Jones,*p.s.*10 Sept. 87
Chas. S. D. O. Oldham, (*H*),
 [S], (t), *ret. pay* 4 *Dr. Gds.*
 Hon. Major .... 3 Apr. 89
Stuart Williams Morgan ...16 Aug. 90
Baldwin John St. George,(*H*)
 (t), *ret. pay* 4 *Dragoon Gds.* 4 July 91
Hy. J. Vaughan Phillips,*p.s.* 2 Dec. 93
Hy. Read Darley (*H*), (t),
 ret. pay 4 *Dragoon Guards*14 Feb. 94
Harry Hickman Bromfield 29 Aug. 94
LIEUTENANTS.
Walter Herbert Jeffreys ...11 Apr. 91
Cecil Hamilton Armitage (*H*),
 serving with Gold Coast
 Constabulary ....11 Apr. 91
Richard Descou Stevens ... 8 Apr. 93
Guy Maxwell-Heron .... 8 Apr. 93
David Hughes Morgan ...... 8 Apr. 93
Richard Francis Gunter ...23 Dec. 93
Alexander Fred. Douglas... 5 May 94
James Reginald Harris,......10 Oct. 94
Frank Henry Foote ....10 Oct. 94
SECOND LIEUTENANTS.
James Miller Gibson-Watt 5 Sept. 94
Douglas Maitland King ...17 Oct. 94
George Lewis-Lloyd ....12 Dec. 94
Robin Begbie Clifton ......20 Mar. 95
Adjt. & Capt.—A. M. Sugden,
 Capt. 2 Battalion .... 4 Sept. 90
Qr. Mr.—Moore Murphy,
 Hon. Captain.................. 1 May 93
Med. Off.—

White Facings.

4TH BATTALION.
(*Formerly the Royal Montgomery Rifles.*)
Head Quarters, Welshpool.
HONORARY COLONEL.
John Heyward Heyward...25 June 79
LT. COLONEL.
Robert John Harrison,*Hon.*
 Colonel ....16 Apr. 87
MAJOR.
Arthur Agg Gardner,
 Hon. Lt. Colonel ....21 May 87
CAPTAINS.
William Charles Hunter,
 Hon. Major ....30 June 81
Chas. Edw. Ramsbottom-
 Isherwood,*p.s. Hon. Major* 17 Oct. 83
Edward H. A. Tolcher (*H*),
 v.s. Instructor of Musketry 9 July 87
John Lomax ....25 May 91
Ferdinand Louis Genth ...22 Aug. 94

LIEUTENANTS.
Fiennes Maurice Colvile ...15 July 91
Wilfrid Chas. N. Hastings 5 July 93
Hugh Robert E. Harrison 1 Aug. 94
Charles Fred. Woodward 3 Oct. 94
SECOND LIEUTENANTS.
Lumley Owen W. Jones ... 6 Feb. 95
Philip Edwin Hopwood ... 6 Feb. 95
William Charles Worth ... 6 Feb. 95
Lechmere Howell Tudor...27 Feb. 95
Adjt. & Capt.—D. J. Gaisford,
 Captain 1 *Battalion*......... 1 Feb. 92
Qr. Master.—John Tigar,
 Hon. Captain ....13 Apr. 89
Med. Off.—

White Facings.

King's Own Scottish Borderers.
3RD BATTALION.
(*Formerly the Scottish Borderers Mil.*)
Head Quarters, Dumfries.
HONORARY COLONEL.
Sir Geo. Gus. Walker, *KCB.*
 p.s.(*H*),[t], *JP.* .... 5 July 93
LT. COLONEL.
Archibald Hume, *p.s.* (*H*),
 [t], *Hon. Colonel* ....10 July 93
MAJORS.
Jas. K. Maxwell Witham,
 p.s. (*H*), *Hon. Lt. Colonel* 19 Nov. 87
Claud V. E. Laurie,*p.s.*(*H*)[t]17 Oct. 94
CAPTAINS.
John Mackie, *p.s. Hon. Maj.* 7 June 84
John P. K. Handay, *p.s. Hon.*
 Major ....19 Apr. 85
Sir Alex. D. Grierson, *Bt.*
 (*H*) [t], *p.s.*...............10 July 86
W. C. Critchley-Salmonson,
 p.s..........................18 Aug. 88
Wm. Sholto Douglas,*p.s.*(*H*)30 June 91
Harold Wm. Alex. Fins.
Crichton-Browne, *p.s.* ...13 Jan. 94
Arth D. Ripley Pott, *p.s.* (t)28 Mar. 94
W. D. Young-Herries, *p.s.*
 (*T*) (*H*), *Inst. of Musketry*17 Oct. 94
LIEUTENANTS.
James Bruce Wilkie,*p.s.* (t) 17 Nov. 90
James Lewis Greig, *p.s.*......13 Dec. 90
Wm. L. Campbell Allan, *p.s.*25 Feb. 93
Henry Keswick, *p.s.*........25 Feb. 93
William M'Call, *p.s.* ...... 1 Aug. 94
George Gordon Moir, *p.s.*... 1 Aug. 94
SECOND LIEUTENANTS.
Herbert Philip Timms, *p.s.* 7 Nov. 91
James Hay Maxwell, *p.s.*...16 Jan. 92
Hon. Arch. Jas. M. St. Clair,
 Master of Sinclair ...... 29 Jan. 94
Pat. A. Vansittart Stewart 14 Apr. 94
Jas. Chas. Walter Connell 24 Oct. 94
Adjt. & Capt.—E. J. Dent,
 Capt. 2 Battalion .... 1 Sept. 94
Qr. Master.—John Swann
 Howe,[1] *Hon. Lieut.*,........21 Oct. 94
Med. Off.—

Blue Facings.

Cameronians (Scottish Rifles).
3RD AND 4TH BATTALIONS.
(*Formerly 2nd Royal Lanark Militia.*)
Head Quarters, Hamilton.
HONORARY COLONEL.
Sir D. C. R. Carrick
 Buchanan, *KCB, DL, JP.*
 late Cornet 2 *Dragoons* ...31 Oct. 85
LT. COLONEL COMMANDANT.
Jas. Ross Gray Buchanan,
 late Capt. ret. pay 14 *F.*
 Hon. Colonel ....12 Dec. 91
LIEUTENANT COLONEL.
Arthur Henry Courtenay,
 Hon. Colonel ....12 Dec. 91
MAJORS.
Geo. Farie, *late Capt.* 74 *F.*,
 Hon. Lt. Colonel .... 9 July 84
James J. Bailey, *p.s.* [*t*] .... 4 June 87
J. A. H. Thomson-Carmichael12 Dec. 91

CAPTAINS.
H. FitzJohn Townshend,
 (*H*), *late Lieut.* 27 *F.* ......16 Sept. 93
William Charles Douglas...26 Sept. 82
Fred. Harcourt Stovenson 29 Oct. 87
Henry Chavasse ....29 Oct. 87
Daniel Fras. M. Macqueen,
 p.s. (*H*), *Inst. of Musketry*29 Oct. 87
Frederick Brentnall ....18 Apr. 90
Harold Mills Clifford, *p.s.*(t)
 (*H*), *Instructor of Musketry*27 Aug. 90
Kenneth Rodas Devaynes
Shaw .... 5 May 91
Ernest Dorrington Drabble22 Aug. 91
William Hustler Hopkins 22 Aug. 91
Alfred John Bowman ......23 Mar. 92
Henry V. J. M'Cann Neal,
 (*H*), *Assistant Inspector*
 Lagos Constabulary ....23 Apr. 92
Kenneth MacIver Morrison23 Apr. 92
Ernest William Hepworth 6 Aug. 93
Arthur R. C. Littledale ......17 June 93
James Campbell Gardner...17 May 94
Rich. Landale Cumberland28 May 94
John Arthur Briggs, *ret.*
 pay 2 *Battalion* ....28 Nov. 94
LIEUTENANTS.
Lawrence Johnstone .... 7 Feb. 91
Henry M. M'Neill-Hamilton17 Oct. 91
Vivian J. Forbes Smith ... 6 May 93
John Stewart Wood .... 6 May 93
Tom Henry Newall .... 6 May 93
Reginald Montg. H. Morant 6 May 93
John Craigie Norwell, *p.s.*
 (*H*) .... 1 Aug. 94
Donld. M'Pherson M'Tarnet 1 Aug. 94
SECOND LIEUTENANTS.
John Robert Fraser ....21 Jan. 93
Geo. Arch. Swinton Home 4 Nov. 93
George Douglas Lumsden 21 Feb. 94
Guy Arthur Geo. Haig ......24 Mar. 94
Charles Napier Lambton... 5 Apr. 94
Alen Sidney Jas. Crawford 5 Sept. 94
Francis Alex. Chetwood
 Hamilton ....13 Feb. 95
Adjts. & Capts.—H. J. Bowman, *Capt. Derbyshire*
 Regiment .... 1 Nov. 90
Jas. Shaw, *Capt.* 2 *Battalion*15 Aug. 91
Qr. Master.—Geo. Wishart,[1]
 Hon. Lieut. ....13 Apr. 87
Med. Off.—*Surg. Lt. Colonel*
 Alex. M. Adams. ...... 1 Dec. 91

Dark Green Facings.

The Royal Inniskilling Fusiliers.
3RD BATTALION.
(*Formerly the Fermanagh Light Inf.*)
Head Quarters, Enniskillen.
HONORARY COLONEL.
Lowry Egerton, *Earl of*
 Enniskillen .... 8 Jan. 87
LT. COLONEL.
W. B. Neville, *p.s. Hon. Col.* 6 June 92
MAJOR.
John Gerard C. Irvine, (*H*) 6 June 92
CAPTAINS.
Arthur Percival Tod Collum 22 May 89
Edward Simon White ......27 Feb. 92
Jas. M. Townsend Reilly,*late*
 Major 2 *Guernsey Militia,*
 Hon. Major ....17 Sept. 92
Armar, *Visct.* Corry ....12 Aug. 93
Ernest Joseph Feist, *p.s.*...16 Sept. 93
Fitzherbert Wheatly Bloomfield ....24 Oct. 94
LIEUTENANTS.
Robert Pakenham Walsh,
 (*H*), *Inst. of Musketry* ...25 Jan. 82
John Rogers Heard .. ..18 Apr. 94
Henry Alexander Johnson 18 Apr. 94
Henry de Courcy Denny... 18 Apr. 94
SECOND LIEUTENANTS.
Edward Wm. Atkinson ...13 May 93
John Hy. M. Visct. Cole ...23 Jan. 95
Francis Knox Pomeroy ...13 Feb. 95
Augustus Rich. Hennessy 13 Mar. 95
Adjt. & Capt.—R. L. B. Steele,
 Capt. 1 *Battalion* ....29 Sept. 90
Qr. Master.—
Med. Off.—

Blue Facings.

Militia Infantry.

4TH BATTALION.
Formerly the Royal Tyrone Fusiliers.)
Head Quarters, Omagh.

HONORARY COLONEL.
Jas. Alf. Visct. Charlemont,
CB. *Comptroller of the Household to the Lord Lieutenant of Ireland*......25 Apr. 85

LT. COLONEL.
Lewis Mansergh Buchanan,[1]
late Lt. 38 F.; *Hon.Colonel* 27 Dec. 87

MAJORS.
Charles Murray Alexander,
Hon. Lt.Colonel............19 May 84
Henry Irvine, *Hon. Lt.Col.* 4 Feb. 88

CAPTAINS.
Hon. Geo. Saml. Alexander,
Hon. Major ....29 Apr. 74
Rowley Alex. Miller, *p.r*.,
Hon. Major ....13 May 76
Hon. Chas. Alexander, *p.s.*
Hon.Major...... 8 Jan. 79
Jas. Alex., *Earl of Caledon*,[3]
Capt. ret. pay 1 *Life Gds.*,
Hon. Major............ 7 July 80
Wm. Edw. Carver, *Hon. Major* ....18 Jan. 82
John Knox M'Clintock,(H)29 May 86

LIEUTENANTS.
James Gildea Browne ...... 7 Mar. 85
Robt. Lyon Moore, *p.s.*(H) 14 July 88
Jas. H. Davidson-Houston,(H) (t), *Sub Inspector of Constabulary, British Honduras* 16 Aug. 90
Lewis Ernest Buchanan ...21 Mar. 91
Walter Vaughan Jones......21 Mar. 91
Randolph George Gethin,
(H), *Inst. of Musketry*......7 Apr. 94

SECOND LIEUTENANTS.
Chas. Tristram Beresford ...24 Oct. 92
James Taylor Lowry......... 7 Feb. 94
Ambrose Upton Gledstanes 23 Jan. 95
Francis William Swifte ... 6 Mar. 95
Adjt. & Capt.—C. J. L. Davidson, *Capt.* 1 *Bn.* ...18 Aug. 92
Paymaster.—
*Qr. Master.—*Wm. George Williams, *Hon. Captain*......11 Mar. 85
Med. Off.—

Blue Facings.

5TH BATTALION.
(*Formerly the Prince of Wales' Own Donegal Militia.*)
Head Quarters, Lifford.

HONORARY COLONEL.
Lord Claud J. Hamilton,
Aide de Camp to the Queen 17 Jan. 91

LT. COLONEL.
Baptist Johnston Barton,[4]
late Lt. 33 F.; *Hon.Col*. ...21 Feb. 91

MAJORS.

CAPTAINS.
Wm. R. Collum, *p.s.* ....25 Feb. 82
George Percy Lloyd ......24 Nov. 83
William Deane-Freeman Thompson ....16 June 88
Maxwell John Carpendale 26 May 90
George Edw. Sutcliffe (t)...15 Mar. 93

LIEUTENANTS.
Charles A.P.H. Macartney-Filgate...................22 Nov. 90
Chas. Fredk. Stewart, (H), *Instructor of Musketry* ...25 Mar. 91
Robert Johnston............23 Jan. 92
Andrew E. Hamilton Mitcheil ....10 Mar. 94
Richd. Fras. E. E. Cochrane 23 May 94

SECOND LIEUTENANTS.
James Norman Crawford 4 Oct. 93
Edward Clinton Baddeley 21 Feb. 94
Edmund Armstrong Crofts 20 Mar. 95
Adjt. & Capt. — J. A. R. Thompson, *Captain East Lancashire Regiment* 10 Sept.92
Paymaster.—
Qr.Mr.—JamesWhite, *Hon. Lieut.* ....31 Aug. 87
Med. Off.—

Blue Facings.

The Gloucestershire Regiment.

3RD BATTALION.
(*Formerly the Royal South Gloucester Light Infantry.*)
Head Quarters, Bristol.

HONORARY COLONEL.
F. Wm. F. Lord FitzHardinge, *late Capt. Royal Horse Guards* ....26 May 68

LT. COLONEL.
WilliamAlexanderHill, *p.s.*, [t], *Hon. Colonel* ....16 Oct. 86

MAJORS.
Sir Wm. F. G. Guise, *Bt.p.s.*
Hon. Lt.Colonel............27 Nov. 86
Lionel SeymourBenson,*p.s.*
Hon. Lt.Colonel............15 Nov. 90

CAPTAINS.
Christopher D. Guise, p.s.
[t], *Hon. Major* .... 3 May 84
W. E. Parry Burges, *p.s.* [t] 6 May 84
Gilbert Robert H. Collis,
p.s. [t] ....22 July 85
David J. *Earl of Northesk,p.s.*18 Aug.88
Edw. Dodwell Crichton, *p.s.*18 Aug. 88
Russell James Kerr, *p.s.* [t]26 Oct. 89
Chandos B. Lee Warner,
p.s. (t)..................... 6 Feb. 92
Hon. Douglas George Carnegio, *p.s.*..................23 Mar. 92
Walter H. de Burgh Griffith,
p.s.(H)(t)*Inst. of Musketry* 5 Aug. 93

LIEUTENANTS.
Geo. Herbert Burges, *p.s.* 25 Mar. 91
Robert Lionel Marshall,*p.s.*19 Mar. 92
Cecil J. Herbert Spence,*p.s.*15 Oct. 92
Geo. Templeton Brett, *p.s.*
(H) ....15 Oct. 92
Alfred Irvine Menzies, *p.s.* 19 July 93
Harold A. David Richards,
p.s.........................18 Nov. 93
Stephen Edw. H. Atkinson,
p.s........................... 7 Apr. 94
Hugo Gerald de Bathe ......16 Jan. 95

SECOND LIEUTENANTS.
Wm. Aug. SpencerEdwards 24 Feb. 94
William Hooker Lyall ......24 Feb. 94
Walter Hayle Walshe, *p.s.*
late Lt. 3 Bn. York and Lancaster Regiment ......29 Mar. 94
Hubert Charles Guise ......12 Apr. 94
Adjt. & Capt.—H. d'A. P. Taylor, *Capt.* 1 *Battalion* 2 Nov. 91
Qr. Master.—Geo. Johnson,
Hon. Captain.................12 Dec. 83
Med. Off.—

White Facings.

4TH BATTALION.
(*Formerly the Royal North Gloucester Militia.*)
Head Quarters, Cirencester.

HONORARY COLONEL.
Sir R.N.F. Kingscote,*KCB.*
late Lt. Col. Scots Guards,
Extra Equerry to H.R.H.
the Prince of Wales, and Commissioner of Woods and Forests ....20 Jan. 62

LT. COLONEL.
T. Wm. Chester Master,
MP., Hon. Colonel .... 16 Oct. 86

MAJORS.
William Playne Marling ...24 Feb. 94
Seymour H., *Earl Bathurst*,
p.s...........................17 Mar. 94

CAPTAINS.
William Hicks Beach ......28 July 88
Arthur Leopold Paget, (H),
Hon. Major ....28 July 88
Henry Selwyn Goodlake,
ret.pay Lancashire Fusiliers 29 Jan. 90
Jesse Devenish Gouldsmith 13 May 91
John W.S.Wingfield-Digby,
(H),*Instructor of Musketry*14 Apr. 94
Hon. Allen Benj. Bathurst 23 Jun. 95

LIEUTENANTS.
John Seager B.Ingham,*p.s.* 5 Mar. 92
John Edwin Hardon .... 5 Mar. 92
Godfrey H. Upton Miller ...21 Jan. 93
Charles Henry Harding,*p.s.*17 Mar. 94
Chas. Edw. Frank Henry*p.s.*17 Mar. 94
Henry Needham .... 5 May 94
James George Wynn Tetley 23 Jan. 95
Fred. Geo. *Earl of Guildford* 13 Feb. 95

SECOND LIEUTENANTS.
Henry Martin Shingleton Smith ....21 Mar. 94
Clifford R. Templeman Aunesley ....12 Sept 94
Phillips Saumarez Vassall 9 Jan. 95
Robt. H. Dick-Cunyngham 30 Jan. 95
Adjt. & Capt.—M. D. Keatinge, *Capt.* 1 *Battalion*... 4 Aug. 90
Qr. Master.—B. N. Spraggett, *Hon. Captain* ....29 Oct. 81
Med. Off.—

White Facings.

The Worcestershire Regt.

3RD AND 4TH BATTALIONS.
(*Formerly the Worcester Militia.*)
Head Quarters, Worcester.

HONORARY COLONEL.
T. Coningsby N. Norbury,[1]
CB. DL. JP. *late Capt.* 6 *Drs.* ....18 Oct. 90

LT. COLONEL COMMANDANT.
Richard Prescott Decie, *p.s.*
late Capt. R. Engineers,
Hon. Colonel ....19 Apr. 90

LT. COLONEL.
Hon. Gillum Webb, *p.s. late Capt.* 36 F., *Hon.Colonel*...14 May 90

MAJORS.
Alfred Winsmore Hooper,
Hon. Lt.Colonel............. 5 July 86
Edward Hugh Bearcroft,
Hon. Lt.Colonel............16 Apr. 90
John R. M. Anderson, (H) 5 June 93
Hugh Edm. E. Everard,(H),
(T), *p.s., late Lt.* 1 *Bn.*
Hon. Lt.Colonel .... 2 July 94

CAPTAINS.
Robert Holden,[2] *p.s. Adj.*
1 *Cadet Bn. West Surrey Regiment, Hon. Major* ...27 June 83
Octavius Scarlett Vale,(H),
p.s. Inst. of Musketry ......22 Mar. 84
Maurice Hon. Berkeley,*p.s.*29 May 84
Shirley A. Stephenson-Fetherstonhaugh,*p.s.*(H) 1 June 86
Alfred Henry Hudson,*p.s.*,
Hon. Major ....11 July 87
Harry S. Richardson, *Capt.*
ret. pay 12 *Lancers* ....15 Feb. 88
Fras. W. Montagu-Douglas-Scott,[3] (t),*late Lt. Oxford*
Lt. Inf. ....23 Aug. 90
Oscar Tolley Mence, *p.s.* ... 5 May 91
Arthur Gordon Steward, *p.s.*(H) June 91
Edw. Thos. Foakes, *p.s.*(t) 16 May 92
Hon. Charles J. Coventry,
serving with Bechuanaland Mounted Police .... 6 Aug. 92
Chas. G. Irving Edmondes,
p.s........................... 3 Sept 92
William Frederick Holroyd Morgan, *p.s.* .... 5 Nov. 92
Ferd. D. Wm. Lea-Smith...17 June 93
Alfred Ernest Speer ....29 July 93
Percival Henry A. Leggett,
(H), *Inst. of Musketry* ...17 Feb. 94
William W. Stanley Clarke 22 Aug. 94

LIEUTENANTS.
Constantine T. F. Dillon ...13 June 92
Christian de Falbe, *late Lt.*
2 *Battalion* ....27 Nov. 94

Fred. Pellatt Elkington ...28 Nov. 94
Pryse Lloyd ....28 Nov. 94
Robt. Edw. L. Townsend ...28 Nov. 94
Charles Henry Bailey ......28 Nov. 94
Henry Wilding ....28 Nov. 94
John Hy. Morris Arden......28 Nov. 94
Upton Fitz-Herbert Ruxton 28 Nov. 94
John Harington ....28 Nov. 94
Jas. L. Meredith Elkington 28 Nov. 94
Henry De la P., *Earl of Tyrone*..................28 Nov. 94
Robert A. C. L. Leggett ...28 Nov. 94
Edward Major Kingsmill...28 Nov. 94
Edw. Fras. Herbert Evans 28 Nov. 94
SECOND LIEUTENANTS.
Jas. B. Falkner Cartland...17 Mar. 94
Geo. Checkland Williams... 5 Apr. 94
Archibald Herbert Leggett 15 Aug. 94
John Fras. S. Winnington 30 Jan. 95
John Feilding H. Kane ...30 Jan. 95
Thos.Chas.Jones-Williams 27 Feb. 95
Oswald Walter Brinton ...13 Mar. 95
Adjts. & Capts.—J. Chichester, *Capt. 2 Bn.* .... 8 June 91
W.F.J.Hardisty,*Capt.2 Bn.*10 Aug. 93
Qr. Masters.—John Moore,
 Hon. Captain ....23 Oct. 78
Med. Offs.—Surgeon Lt.Col.
 G. E. Hyde .... 1 Dec. 91
Surgeon Lt.Colonel Herbert
 G. Budd .... 1 Dec. 91
White Facings.

The East Lancashire Regt.

3RD BATTALION.
(*Formerly 5th Royal Lancashire Militia.*)
Head Quarters, Burnley.
HONORARY COLONEL.
Sir John Hardy Thursby,
 Bart. late Lt. 90 F. ....30 July 79
LT.COLONEL.
John Erdeswick Butler-
 Bowdon, *p.s. Hon.Colonel* 19 Dec. 91
MAJORS.
Hubert Slater, *p.s., Hon.
Lt.Colonel* ....24 Jan. 91
R.H. Mine-Redhead (*H*), [*t*] 13 Apr. 92
CAPTAINS.
Hugh E. Wilbraham, (*H*),
 *ret. pay S. Lancashire Regt.
Hon. Major* ....23 Apr. 87
Clement James M'Coan,*p.s.*
 (*H*), *Instr. of Musketry*...28 July 88
William Alfred Jupp ....23 May 91
Ernest Arthur Snow,(*H*),*ret.
pay South Lancashire Regt.* 5 Aug. 91
Chas. E. A.T. Trevor-Battye 13 Apr. 92
Wm. Craufurd Hurrell......17 Oct. 85
*Chas. H. Newman Ringer,
employed in the Niger Coast
Protectorate* ....20 May 93
Edm. A. Le Gendre Starkie 28 Apr. 94
John M'Mahon Roberts,
 late Lt. 14 *Hussars* ...... 5 May 94
LIEUTENANTS.
Joseph Dudley Cloran ... 3 June 93
Kenneth Davidson Mac-
 kenzie .... 3 June 93
Stuart E. Bloxam Richards 3 June 93
SECOND LIEUTENANTS.
Henry Joseph Nugent...... 4 Nov. 93
Chas. Fred. M. Recaño ...13 Jan. 94
James Leslie Cross..........31 Jan. 94
Martyn Brooke Webb ...24 Feb. 94
Joseph Haywood .... 4 June 94
Joshua Percival Horton ... 9 Jan. 95
Adjt. & Capt.—A. J. A.
 Wright, *Major 2 Battalion* 10 Aug. 90
Qr. Master.—John Holbourne, *Hon. Lieut.* ...... 7 Dec. 92
White Facings.

The East Surrey Regiment.

3RD BATTALION.
(*Formerly the 1st Royal Surrey Militia.*)
Head Quarters, Kingston.
HONORARY COLONEL.
LT.COLONEL.
Thomas Warne Lemmon,
 Hon. Colonel ....26 Feb. 87
MAJORS.
Edward Clifton Griffith,
 Hon. Lt.Colonel 22 Sept.88
John Roper Parkington ... 3 Jan. 91

CAPTAINS.
John Charles Worthington 21 July 85
James Cazalet Crofton,*Hon.
 Major* .... 6 Aug. 87
Walter Boynton .... 7 Jan. 88
Fras. Lee Sanders, *p.s.* (*H*),
 Instructor of Musketry ...21 Jan. 88
Lachlan R. Mackintosh
 Rate ....31 May 93
John Henrique Dunn...... 21 Oct. 93
LIEUTENANTS.
Henry Archibald Bellville 20 Nov. 86
John William P. Russell ...13 Apr. 89
Leslie Winton White........12 June 93
Henry Ardwick Burgess...12 June 93
Harold Rowley Wood .....13 Feb. 95
Chas. Arch. M. Howard ...13 Feb. 95
Jones Charles Lamprey ...13 Feb. 95
SECOND LIEUTENANTS.
Charles Raymond Roberts-
 West.......................17 Oct. 94
Edward Last Kelsey........31 Oct. 94
Edw. A. Elphinstone-Dalrymple......................14 Nov. 94
Robert Stewart Tute......... 9 Jan. 95
Cecil Arbuthnot Law ...... 8 Jan. 95
Fras. Edward Till .... 6 Feb. 95
Henry John des Vœux ......13 Mar. 95
Adj.& Capt.—H.W. Benson,
 Major 2 Battalion......... 1 Jan. 92
Qr. Master.—Fras. Nadin,
 Hon. Lieut. 9 Sept.85
Med. Off.—

White Facings.

4TH BATTALION.
(*Formerly the 3rd Royal Surrey Militia.*)
Head Quarters, Kingston on Thames.
HONORARY COLONEL.
James Le Geyt Daniell...... 8 Oct. 92
LT.COLONEL.
Bernard Gilpin Haines,[1]
 late Lt. 18 *F. Hon. Colonel* 31 Oct. 94
MAJORS.
Francis S. G. Moon, *p.s.,
 Hon. Lt.Colonel*............12 Nov. 87
CAPTAINS.
Wm. H. Bulpett, (*H*), *p.s.,
 Hon. Major* ....11 Jan. 82
Gerald Edw. Maude, *p.s.* (t),
 (*H*), *Inst. of Musketry,
 Hon. Major* .... 3 May 84
George Frederick Davis ...13 Nov. 86
E.A. Uvedale Price, *p.s.* (*H*) 24 May 88
Howard Vyse Welch .... 8 Apr. 90
Wm. Vere Reeve Fane ......27 June 90
William Knox, *ret. pay* 21
 Hussars ....11 Nov. 90
Henry Eley, (*H*), *ret. pay
 Liverpool Regiment* ....19 Nov. 90
Fred. L. Chas. Thomas, *late
 2 Bn. East Surrey Regt.
 Hon. Major* ....21 Jan. 93
LIEUTENANTS.
*Fras. R. Bircham Parmeter,
 Assist. Inspector Gold Coast
 Constabulary* ....28 Jan. 91
Geo. Hamilton Alexander,
 (*H*) .... 7 Apr. 94
Hon. Fred. Edward Guest 7 Apr. 94
Edward Barnard Hankey 7 Apr. 94
Charles Alan C. Perkins ... 7 Apr. 94
SECOND LIEUTENANTS.
George Ess .... 5 May 93
William Henry Tucker Hill 6 Jan. 94
Harold V. Barnard Byles....27 Jan. 94
Elliot P. Philipson-Stow ...17 Mar. 94
Ronald Macclesfield Heath 8 Aug. 94
Robert Francis Peel .... 9 Jan. 95
Edward Seymour ....30 Jan. 95
Harry Michael Thomson... 6 Feb. 95
William Aubrey Spooner...27 Feb. 95
Herbert Maddick, *late Lt.* 3
 Vol. Bn. E. Surrey Reg. 13 Mar. 95
Adj.& Capt.—C.D. Johnstone,
 Capt. East Surrey Regt..... 8 Aug. 94
Qr. Master.—William Leven
 Proudfoot, *Hon. Captain* 19 May 83
Med.Off.—*Surg.Lt.Col.*Matthew Owen Coleman,*MD*, 1 Dec. 94
White Facings.

The Duke of Cornwall's Light Infantry.

3RD BATTALION.
(*Formerly the Royal Cornwall Rangers
 —Duke of Cornwall's Own Rifles.*)
Head Quarters, Bodmin.
HONORARY COLONEL.
Field Marshal *H.R.H.* the
 *Prince of Wales, KG.KT.
 KP. GCB. GCSI.GCMG.
 GCIE.*.....................28 Apr. 75
LT.COLONEL.
Hon. Charles Geo. C. Eliot,
 *late Lt. & Capt. Gr. Gds.
 Hon. Colonel* ....29 June 89
MAJORS.
Thomas E. J. Lloyd, *DL.,
 Hon. Lt.Colonel* .... 4 May 85
Hugh Halse Ley, [*t*] *Hon.
 Lt.Colonel* ....10 Aug. 89
CAPTAINS.
Hugh C. Fownes Luttrell,
 *M.P. retired pay late Rifle
 Brigade, Hon. Major* ...... 6 July 87
Henry John Greame Lloyd,[1]
 late Lt. 2 Battalion ....22 Oct. 87
Arthur Francis Salmon (*T*) 5 Nov. 87
Gerald Marcell Conran......12 Nov. 87
John G. Orlebar Aplin, (*H*),
 *Assistant Inspector, Gold
 Coast Constabulary* .... 4 Apr. 88
Piers Alex. H. *Viscount
 Valletort*...................23 Mar. 91
John Colloryan Michell ... 9 Jan. 95
LIEUTENANTS.
Stuart James Bevan, *p.s.*... 4 May 92
Reginald W. Cassan Fenton 13 May 93
James Edw. Salusbury
 Trelawny ....17 Feb. 94
Herbert Augustine Carter 7 May 94
Geo. S. Harcourt Aldham 7 May 94
SECOND LIEUTENANTS.
Arthur Derry .... 4 Nov. 93
Wilfred Wm. Maitland Gott 3 May 94
Claude D. Disney-Roebuck 26 Sept. 94
Robt.S.Jno. Norris Hawker 27 Feb. 95
Adj. & Capt.—R. J. Wilbraham,*Capt.* 1 *Battalion* 4 Jan. 92
Qr. Master.—Henry C. Hart,[2]
 Hon. Captain ....10 June 82
Med. Off.—

White Facings.

The Duke of Wellington's (West Riding Regiment).

3RD BATTALION.
(*Formerly the 6th West York Militia.*)
Head Quarters, Halifax.
HONORARY COLONEL.
Henry, *Duke of* Wellington,
 late of Grenadier Guards 10 Apr. 86
LT.COLONEL COMMANDANT.
LT.COLONEL.
Gerald Stovell .... 20 Feb. 95
MAJORS.
Alex. Keith Wyllie,*p.s.*......12 May 88
Hen. E. Heydemann,p.s. [*t*] 20 May 95
CAPTAINS.
Robert N. D. Bruce, *Hon.
 Major* ....28 Nov. 83
Alfred Wm. Adams, [*t*] ...28 Nov. 83
Edw. Feetham Coates, *p.s.
 Hon. Major* ....28 Nov. 83
Ernest Lucas Cordes ....18 Oct. 84
Gurnell E. Hammond, *p.s.*
 [*t*] ....26 Nov. 84
Brian Trengrove Williams[1] 28 Feb. 85
George Edwd. Moke-Norrie,
 p.s. [*t*] (*H*)...............26 May 88
Horace James Johnston,*p.s.*14 July 90
Arthur Edward Burgett ...16 June 94
LIEUTENANTS.
Chas. Alan C. de Trafford 6 Feb. 92
Harry Robt. Hildyard, *p.s.*10 July 93
Charles Percival Foster ...10 July 93
Arthur P. Wm. Rickman...16 June 94
Cecil Pellew Bradshaw ...16 June 94

Militia Infantry.

SECOND LIEUTENANTS.
Maurice Gordon Heath......11 Nov. 93
Herbert Cleland Nicolay ...23 Dec. 93
Basil Sholto A. Douglas-
 Hamilton ....20 Jan. 94
Edward Gerald Ingham ... 3 Feb. 94
Henry Montagu Digby...... 7 Feb. 94
Herbert Wm. A. Collum ...17 Feb. 94
Lucius Charles Hope .... 6 Mar. 94
Arch. José Campbell Mur-
 doch ....20 Feb. 95
Adjt. & Capt.—F.A.Hayden,
 Capt. West Riding Regt.,..12 Feb. 95
Qr.Mr.—Wm. Fitz Patrick,[2]
 Hon. Captain ....11 Feb. 85
*Med.Off.—Surg.Lt.Col.*John
 Hodgson Wright............ 1 Dec. 91
White Facings.

The Border Regiment.
3RD BATTALION.
(*Formerly Royal Cumberland Militia.*)
Head Quarters, Carlisle.

HONORARY COLONEL.
H. C. *Earl of* Lonsdale......14 Feb. 91

LT.COLONEL.
James Robert Bain ....28 May 92

MAJORS.
G. F. A. H. Le Fleming...... 4 Feb. 91
Henry P. G. Blencowe ...... 3 June 92

CAPTAINS.
Spencer Broadbent, *Hon.*
 Major ....25 Nov. 82
Arthur G. Singleton Hunt 4 Feb. 91
Noble Fleming Jenkins,
 ret. pay 2 Battalion.........24 June 91
John Fell Woodburne ......18 June 92
Alfred H. Collingwood, (t)... 5 Oct. 92
Rhys Wm.Wykeham Jones,[1]
 retired pay Sussex Regt. ...26 Oct. 92
John Congreve................31 May 94
Wm. Plunkett MacBride..12 Aug. 93

LIEUTENANTS.
John Norman .... 7 Nov. 91
William Verner Ellis......... 7 Nov. 91
*Hon.*Alf.Edw.C.J.Stourton18 Feb. 93
John Cecil Latham Bott ...24 Feb. 94
Cecil Aubrey Escombe...... 6 Mar. 95
Alfred John Markham...... 6 Mar. 95
Robt.Walker H.Woodburne 6 Mar. 95
Hew S. Campbell Ross...... 6 Mar. 95

SECOND LIEUTENANTS.
Edward Mivian Moore......13 Mar. 95
Adjt. & Capt.—P. F. R. New-
 bury, *Capt. Lincoln Regt.* 3 Mar. 90
Qr.Master. — James Edw.
 Bonner, *Hon. Lieut.* ...... 1 Apr. 85
Med.Off.—
White Facings.

4TH BATTALION.
(*Formerly the Royal Westmoreland Light Infantry.*)
Head Quarters, Carlisle.

HONORARY COLONEL.
Louis C. Salkeld, *retired* ...10 Feb. 94

LIEUTENANT COLONEL.
Henry Paul Mason, (*H*)...... 4 May 92

MAJOR.
Arthur W. D. Lewis, *p.s.* ...14 May 92

CAPTAINS.
Geo. A. Mounsey-Heysham11 Feb. 88
Geo. Algernon Draffen, *p.s.* 2 Nov. 89
Robert Thomas Harland ...18 Feb. 91
William Scott Fulton, (*H*)30 Jan. 92
John C. Pengelly Manuell,
 Hon. Major 1 *Cadet Bn.*
 Norfolk Regt. .... 9 Apr. 92
Thomas Ricketts Morse,[3]
 p.s. late Surg. Capt. Army
 Medical Staff ....15 Mar. 93

LIEUTENANTS.
Maurice J. Draffen Cockle 29 Dec. 88
LauncelotSalkeldBramwell21 Jan. 93
John Henry Wybergh ......71 Jan. 93
John David B. Erskine ...10 Feb. 94
George Herbert Pedler......10 Feb. 94
Seymour Clarke Bull......... 4 June 94

SECOND LIEUTENANTS.
Ernest St. George Anson...12 Feb. 94
Deane Orford Shute ....13 Feb. 94
George Petre Wymer......... 6 Feb. 95
Adjt. & Capt.—P. J. Bellamy.
 Capt. 2 Battalion............18 Dec. 93
Qr. Master.—John Henry
 Jones, *Hon. Lieut.* ....12 Dec. 94
Med. Off.—
White Facings.

The Royal Sussex Regiment.
3RD BATTALION.
(*Formerly the Royal Sussex Light Inf.*)
Head Quarters, Chichester.

HONORARY COLONEL.
LT.COLONEL COMMANDANT.
The Earl of March, JP.
 late Lt. & Capt. Gr. Gds.,
 Hon. Colonel ....28 June 76

LIEUTENANT COLONEL.
Sir Craven Chas. Goring,[1]
 Bart. p.s., late Capt. 33 F.,
 p.s.; *Hon. Colonel*............20 Aug. 87

MAJORS.
Henry Colville Bridger, (*H*),
 p.s., Hon. Lt.Colonel ...... 6 Nov. 86
Charles B.Godman,*p.s.Hon.*
 Lt.Colonel .... 6 July 89

CAPTAINS.
Chas. Percival Henty, *p.s.*
 Hon. Major..................23 Feb. 81
Harvey T. B. Combe, *p.s.*
 Hon. Major...................23 Feb. 81
Charles R. A. Leslie, *Hon.*
 Major 13 Sept.84
Joseph Godman ....12 Mar. 87
Stephenson Robert Clarke.12 Mar. 87
Henry William Sheffield
 Adair, *p.s.* ....12 Mar. 87
Robt.Law.Thornton, *p.s.*(t)17 Aug. 89
HerbertGranvilleGrant,*p.s.*12 Feb. 90
Charles Henry von Roemer 8 Mar. 92
Arthur Reginald Hurst, *p.s.*14 Apr. 93

LIEUTENANTS.
William Molyneux Clarke.12 Feb. 90
Chas. H. *Lord* Settrington 12 Feb. 90
Charles Arthur Fletcher ...15 Nov. 90
Pelham Rawstorn Papillon15 Nov. 90
Fiennes Wm. Edw. Blake 2 July 92
Frank Thomas Wisden...... 9 Sept.93
Cecil G. H. Akers Hankey 9 Sept.93
Robert Kenrick Evered ...12 Sept.94
Edward Campion ....12 Sept. 94
Algernon E. Venning ......12 Sept. 94

SECOND LIEUTENANTS.
Fred. Tyrell Godman.........10 Apr. 93
Arthur Patrick Wisden......14 Apr. 93
Hon. Esmé C. Gordon-
 Lennox........................... 3 Feb. 94
Samuel Davenport............14 Nov. 94
Merrik Raymond Burrell... 5 Dec. 94
Adj. & Capt.—H. B. Scaife.
 Capt. 1 Battalion ....24 Nov. 93
Paymaster.—W. F. Perry ...24 Feb. 60
Qr.Master.—Thos. Kinloch,
 Hon. Captain .... 1 Apr. 83
Med. Off.—Surg. Lt.Colonel
 J. M. Percival .... 1 Dec. 91
Blue Facings.

The Hampshire Regiment.
3RD BATTALION.
(*Formerly the Hampshire Militia.*)
Head Quarters, Winchester.

HONORARY COLONEL.

LT.COLONEL.
George Hope Lloyd-Ver-
 ney, *p.s. late Lt. 74 F.*
 Hon. Colonel ....15 Aug. 91

MAJORS.
Richard Edw. F. Howard-
 Brooke, *late Lt.* 37 *F.*,
 Hon. Lt.Colonel ....27 Oct. 88
AlfredJ.Bowyer-Smijth,*p.s.*
 Hon. Lt.Colonel 5 Sept.91

CAPTAINS
Henry F. B. Archer, *p.s.*,
 Hon. Major ....29 Oct. 81
William W. *Visct.* Wolmer,
 MP. JP. p.s...................29 July 85
HydeS.Whalley-Tooker,*JP.*14 Apr. 86
Fras. Chas. Baring, *p.s.* ...12 Feb. 87
William Graham Nicholson 3 Mar. 88
Wm. Barrow Simonds ......27 Oct. 88
Philip Pester Phelps, (*H*),
 Inst. of Musketry .... 5 Apr. 90
SirRich.NelsonRycroft, *Bt.*
 (t) (*H*) *p.s., late Lt. Rifle*
 Brigade ....11 Apr. 91
Geo. J. Hardress Stevenson 4 May 91
James Heron Walker......... 9 Feb. 94
Maurice Raymond Portal(*H*),
 serving with Bechuanaland
 Border Police .... 4 Apr. 94

LIEUTENANTS.
John Evelyn Bazalgette ... 4 May 91
Harold Edw. Lepel Glass,
 p.s. ....18 Mar. 93
Frederic Edgar Silva, *p.s.* 8 Apr. 93
Thomas Fawcett Burra, *p.s.* 2 Sept.93
Chas.Wm. Hy.Crichton,*p.s.* 2 Sept.93
Charles Edward St.. John
 Harris, *p.s.*..................... 9 Dec. 93
Rich. FitzGerald Glyn, *p.s.* 1 Aug. 94
Robert C. L. Stapleton-
 Bretherton .... 1 Aug. 94
Henry Edward Walcott,*p.s.*23 Jan. 95
Philip Edw. Hardwick ......13 Feb. 95

SECOND LIEUTENANTS.
Edmond Cecil Russell, *p.s.* 8 Feb. 94
Martin Gurdon-Rebow, *p.s.* 9 Feb. 94
Harry Wm. Morgan Willis14 Nov. 94
Algernon Charles Cox ......19 Dec. 94
Arthur Hope Travers ......13 Feb. 95
Adjt.& Capt.—G.H. Nichol-
 son, *Captain 1 Battalion*...16 Jan.. 94
Qr. Mr.—Patrick M'Evoy,
 Hon. Captain..................12 June 89
Med. Off.—
White Facings.

The South Staffordshire Regt.
3RD AND 4TH BATTALIONS.
(*Formerly the King's Own 1st Stafford Militia.*)
Head Quarters, Lichfield,.
"*Mediterranean.*"

HONORARY COLONEL..
Hon. Wellington Patt. Man-
 versChetwynd Talbot,*late*
 of 7 Fusiliers, Serj.at Arms
 in Ordinary to the Queen.. 26 Apr.73

LT.COLONEL COMMANDANT.
Walter George Webb, *Hon.*
 Colonel .... 1 Apr. 89

LT.COLONEL.
Michael A. W. Broun........10 Dec. 92

MAJORS.
Alexander Finlay .... 4 July 85
Francis Charrington ....16 Apr. 91
Septimus J. A. Denison, (*H*)
 Infantry School Corps,
 Canadian Militia .... 4 Jan. 93
Geo. Wm. Hargreuve, *ret.*
 pay 5 Foot, Hon. Lt.Colonel 1 May 93

CAPTAINS.
Edward V.D.Pearse, *p.s.* (t),
 (*H*) .... 3 Dec. 84
Noville C. B. Chamberlain,
 p.s...............................23 Jan. 86
BassettThorneSeckbam,*p.s.*31 May 86
Edward Wm.Tennant, *p.s.* 7 May 87
Francis E. Devereux Hick-
 man, (*H*) *p.s.*................21 Sept. 87
Hon. Richd. W. Chetwynd,
 (*H*) .... 5 Apr. 88
Lionel Erskine Hall 19 Sept.01
John Challenor ....23 Apr. 92
Harry Cecil Wrigley.........23 Apr. 92
John Henry HerveyV.Lane11 Apr. 93

Militia Infantry.

Harold Harvey Smith ......11 Mar. 93
Gwyn Williams ....29 Apr. 93
Herbert J. S. Saunders-
  Davies ....28 Mar. 94
George Campbell Grahame28 Mar. 94
Geo. P. Elystan Evans......28 Mar. 94

LIEUTENANTS.
Bertram Noel Foster........ 4 June 92
Philip Granville Mason ...14 Jan. 93
Charles Carroll Macnamara14 Jan. 93
Douglas Thorne Seckham 14 Jan. 93
Arthur G. Mossop ....21 Mar. 94
Lionel Boyd Moss ....18 Apr. 94
James Saumarez Cameron 18 Apr. 94
HoraceCaryHarrisMarriotti8 Apr. 94
Robt. Miles Collins Moss...18 Apr. 94
Philip Chas. L. Routledge 18 Apr. 94
Cecil T. Vincent Fosbery...18 Apr. 94
Henry Owen Knox..........27 June 94
George Harrison Townson27 June 94
Herbert Erskine Oates ....27 June 94
Lupert Le Grice Elers ....27 June 94

SECOND LIEUTENANTS.
Gilbert Edward Talbot ...13 Jan. 94
Percie E. B. Fitzwarine
  Smith ....13 Jan. 94
Hugh Hoskyns Bury........ 3 Mar. 94
Charles Peter Berthon ....15 Mar. 94
Bernard Nugent Shaw......25 Apr. 94
Geo. Alfred Osborne Lane 24 May 94
Alf. Richard Hugh Rycroft25 May 94
Cyril German Danks ...... 6 Feb. 95
Stephen E. Wright Thomp-
  son ....13 Feb. 95
Adjts. & Capts.—C.H.Wylly,
  Major 2 Battalion ....21 Jan. 91
G. N. Going, *Capt. 1 Bn.* ...30 July 94
Qr. Master.—Jas. Penketh,
  Hon. Lieut. ....15 Feb. 93
Med. Off.—

White Facings.

The Dorsetshire Regiment.

3RD BATTALION.
(*Formerly the Dorset Militia.*)
Head Quarters, Dorchester.

HONORARY COLONEL.
Edward H. T. Lord Digby,[1]
  late Coldstream Guards ...25 Apr. 91

LT.COLONEL.
Angus Wm. Hall,[2] *CB.* [t],
  *JP., late Capt. 58 F. and
  Adjt. Depot Batt.; Hon.
  Colonel* ....24 May 73

MAJORS.
RichardCha.Wm.Bingham,
  Hon. Lt. Colonel ....16 Feb. 81
John Henry Austen, *Hon.
  Lt.Colonel* .... 8 May 86

CAPTAINS.
Herbert Carey Geo. Batten,
  Hon. Major ....22 Apr. 84
Robert Erasmus Saunders,
  *late Lt. R. Fusiliers; Hon.
  Major* ....11 Oct. 84
Edward Castleman Smith,
  (*H*), (t), *Hon. Major* ...... 7 Aug. 86
FrederickCharlesWingrove12 May 90
John Herbert Devenish ... 6 Feb. 92
Denzil Hughes-Onslow,*ret.
  pay 2 Bn* .... 6 Apr. 92

LIEUTENANTS.
Vivian E. Archer-Burton...16 Mar. 89
Chas. Robt. E. Radclyffe,
  *Instructor of Musketry;
  late Lt. 1st Life Guards* ... 3 Feb. 94
Eric Andrew Bridge ....19 May 94
Robt. Edw. McIllree Lomer 2 June 94

SECOND LIEUTENANTS.
George Reginald Stephens 19 Nov. 92
Hugh Valentine Fison ......27 Jan. 94
John Hy. Strode Batten...21 July 94
Edw. Alexander Pope ......21 July 94
Egbert Napier ....20 Feb. 95
Adjt. & Capt.—L. E. Lush-
  ington, (*Capt. 2 Battalion*)19 Sept.94
Qr. Master.—Wm. Clinch,[3]
  Hon. Captain .... 1 Apr. 86
Med. Off.— Surgeon Lt.Col.
  Decimus Curme .... 1 Dec. 91

White Facings.

Prince of Wales' Volunteers (South Lancashire Regiment).

3RD BATTALION.
(*Formerly the Duke of Lancaster's Own Light Infantry.*)
Head Quarters, Warrington.

HONORARY COLONEL.
John Southcote Mansergh 4 Nov. 93

LT.COLONEL.
Frederic Wm. O'Malley,*ret.
  pay 71 F., Hon. Colonel* ...25 Nov. 85

MAJORS.
Rob. Ireland Blackburne,
  Hon. Lt.Colonel ....13 Feb. 92
Edward Joynson,(*H*), *Hon.
  Lt.Colonel* ....13 Aug. 92

CAPTAINS.
Montagu H. Hall, [t]..........15 Mar. 82
Alexander Francis Tarbet,[1]
  *Assistant Inspector, Lagos
  Constabulary* .... 3 Apr. 86
Edw. Kermode Heath, (*H*),
  p.s. Inst. of Musketry 10 Sept.87
Charles Marson, (t) ....17 May 90
Hugh Fulthorpe Gooch ...13 Feb. 92
ArthurGeo.WalterSkirrow,
  ret. pay 2 Battalion .... 1 Aug. 94

LIEUTENANTS.
Harold James Tilney........17 Sept.92
Herbert Craven Stuart......21 Oct. 93
George Postlethwaite ..... 5 Sept. 94
Louis William Herbert...... 5 Sept. 94

SECOND LIEUTENANTS.
Russell Ernest C. Edye......23 Sept.93
Mowbray L. S. Owen Cole.. 3 Feb. 94
Nelson Graham Anderson23 June 94
George Norman Simms ... 7 Nov. 94
Francis Wood ....12 Dec. 94
Thos. Douglas Pilkington 6 Feb. 95
Nigel Lucius S. Lysons ... 6 Feb. 95
Robert Cecil Trousdale ...13 Feb. 95
Adjt. & Captain—V. A. M.
  Fowler, *Captain Liverpool
  Regiment* 1 Sept.93
Qr.Master.—Frank Hawes,
  Hon. Captain .... 7 May 83
Med. Off.—

White Facings.

The Welsh Regiment.

3RD BATTALION.
(*Formerly the Royal Glamorgan Light Infantry.*)
Head Quarters, Cardiff.

HONORARY COLONEL.
Hubert C. Gould, *JP. late
  Lt.* 31*F., p.s.* ....15 Mar. 84

LT.COLONEL.
James C. Revell Reade,
  JP. p.s.(*H*),[t],*lateCornet,
  14 Hussars; Hon. Colonel* 23 Oct. 86

MAJORS.
Alfred Thrale Perkins, *JP.*
  (*H*), *late Capt. 21 F., Hon.
  Lt.Colonel* ....28 May 84
William Watts, [t] *p.s.* ..... 5 May 94

CAPTAINS.
EdmundPlunkettDashwood,
  p.s. (*H*), *Inst.of Musketry,
  Hon. Major* .... 2 May 85
Clifford John Cory .... 2 May 88
Philip Septimus Dowson...19 Jan. 89
Samuel Moreton Thomas...16 Mar. 89
William Forrest, *p.s.* ....13 July 91
Ernest William Pickering 19 Mar. 92
Alfred Thrale Perkins ..... 5 July 93
Chas.D.Carleton-Smith,(*H*)11 Nov. 93
Chas. Morton Hastings, *late
  and Lt. S. Wales Borderers*17 Feb. 94
John Wheeler Aldridge,
  p.s. (t) ....18 Apr. 94
Richard Wentworth Taylor26 Sept.94
Hy. Frank W. Poppelwell,
  p.s., (*H*), [t] (*S*) ....24 Oct. 94

LIEUTENANTS.
Douglas How .... 9 June 94
Richard Grenside Hooper 9 June 94
Bertram Falls Perkins......14 Nov. 94

SECOND LIEUTENANTS.
Richd. G. Douglas Nivison 9 Dec. 93
Richd. John Enys Sincock28 Apr. 94
JohnThos.Llewelyn Davies12 Dec. 94
Arnold Jeffreys Marten ....13 Feb. 95
Adjt. & Capt.—A. H. U.
  Tindal, *Capt. 1 Battalion* 15 June 92
Qr. Master—Thos. Tinnock,
  Hon. Lieut. ....10 May 93
Med. Off.—

White Facings.

The Black Watch (Royal Highlanders).

3RD BATTALION.
(*Formerly the Royal Perth Rifles.*)
Head Quarters, Perth.

HONORARY COLONEL.
H.R.H. Alfred E. A.*Duke of
  Edinburgh*(reigning*Duke
  of Saxe-Coburg-Gotha),
  KG. KT. KP,GCB.GCSI.
  GCMG. GCIE. Personal
  Aide de Camp to the Queen* 21 June 87

LT.COLONEL COMMANDANT.

LT.COLONEL.
D. M. Smythe,[1] *late Lt.*79 *F.*18 Nov. 93

MAJORS.
Hon. W. C. W. Rollo,
  Master of Rollo, p.s. ....20 Jan. 94
Lord Alex. Kennedy,[2] *late
  Bt.Major 1 Battalion* ......10 Mar. 94

CAPTAINS.
Alex. Blair Stewart, *p.s.
  Hon. Major* ....11 June 79
Jas. S. Robertson,*p.s.*(*H*),
  Hon. Major ....30 Dec. 85
Wm. Angel Scott,[3] *late Lt.
  Cameron Highlanders,Brig.
  Maj. Surrey Brig. Vol.Inf.
  Hon. Major* ....10 Mar. 88
Robert W. P. Clarke-Camp-
  bell-Preston, *p.s. Aide de
  Camp to the Governor of
  New Zealand* ....13 July 89
John Lewis Macandrew,
  p.s. (*H*) 30 June90
John. MacRae,*ret.pay 1 Bn.* 22 Oct. 90
Alex. Holdewier O. Dennis-
  toun, *p.s.* ....13 June 91
Carolus H. GrahamStirling,
  p.s. ....20 Jan. 94
Hon. Alex. David Murray,
  p.s. ....14 July 94

LIEUTENANTS.
Gilbert Compton Elliot.... 7 July 90
John Hewley Outhwaite ...19 Mar. 92
Arch. Glen Kidston ....19 Mar. 92
Edw.A.Stewart-Richardson19 Mar.92
James Geo. Eliott Wood...15 Apr. 93
Wm. Huntly, *Visct.* Strath-
  allan .... 4 July 94
G. F. A. *Earl of* Yarmouth,
  DL. .... 4 July 94
William Keith Murray ......19 Dec. 94

SECOND LIEUTENANTS.
Fras. Haliburton Scott ......10 Feb. 94
Ronald T. Graham Murray 7 May 94
Thos. E. L. Hill-Whitson... 8 May 94
Philip George Anstruther 12 Dec. 94
Adjt.—P. J. C. Livingston,
  Captain 2 Battalion .... 4 June 90
Qr. Master.—James Robert-
  son Hay, *Hon. Captain* ...20 Oct. 83

Blue Facings.

Oxfordshire Light Infantry.

3RD BATTALION.
(*Formerly the King's Own Royal Bucks Militia.*)
Head Quarters, High Wycombe.

HONORARY COLONEL.
Walter Caulfield Pratt, *JP.
  late Capt.* 67 *F.* .... 8 Dec. 80

LT.COLONELS.
Chas. R. Lord Carrington,
  *GCMG. p.s.late Capt.R.H.
  Guards, Lord Chamberlain* 4 May 81
Edward Dyke Lee, *Hon.Col.* 16 Jan. 86

MAJORS.
Henry Edward Burney,*Hon.
  Lt. Colonel* ....17 June 82
Charles Meeking, *p.s.*,*Hon.
  Lt.Colonel* .... 1 Aug. 94

The Essex Regiment.

CAPTAINS.
Arthur Wm. Hervey Good(*H*)13 May 85
William Terry ....24 May 88
George Frederick Paske,
  p.s. (*H*), *Inst. of Musketry* 22 Mar. 90
E. W. *Earl of* Orkney ...... 8 Mar. 93
Charles Spencer Hall ...... 8 Mar. 93
Fras.GuyDelaval Thoroton 7 May 94
Charles Francis Kynaston
  Mainwaring ....31 Oct. 94
Philip Vivian Rose............ 6 Feb. 95

LIEUTENANTS.
Edward Wm. Wallington ... 4 July 85
Albert Norman Henderson 28 Nov. 91
Edw. Noel Napier Bartlett 14 Jan. 93
Ernest Bernard Clark ...... 8 Mar. 93
Bernard J. Merlin Walsh...31 Oct. 94
Ellis Haldane Chinnery ...31 Oct. 94
Fras. Joseph Scott-Murray31 Oct. 94
Lewis Duval Hall ....31 Oct. 94
Sir Robt. John Dashwood,
  Bart. ....20 Feb. 95

SECOND LIEUTENANTS.
Stavely Napier Gore .... 6 Mar. 94
Lancelot Edw. Seth Ward 5 Dec. 94
Arthur Douglas Knapp ...30 Jan. 95
Adjt. & Capt.—J. Hanbury-
  Williams, *Capt. Oxford
  Light Infantry* ....27 Feb. 92
Qr. Master.—Robert M'Coy,
  Hon. Captain..............13 Feb. 86
Med. Off.—

White Facings.

4TH BATTALION.
(*Formerly the Oxfordshire Militia.*)
Head Quarters, Oxford.
"*Mediterranean.*"

HONORARY COLONEL.
*Hon.*Alg. S. Arth. Annesley,
  late Lt. 16 *Lancers, p.s.* ...12 Dec. 91

LT. COLONEL.
Charles Rivers Bulkeley,
  (*H*), *Hon. Colonel*............28 Nov. 91

MAJORS.
Arthur Bott Cook,*Hon. Lt.
  Colonel* ....16 Dec. 85
Frank Willan, (*t*), *Hon.
  Lt. Colonel* ....19 Dec. 91

CAPTAINS.
Warner J. L. Heriot, *Hon.
  Major* ....26 May 77
Sir Geo. J. E. Dashwood,
  Bart. (*H*), *late Lt. and
  Capt. Scots Guards, Hon.
  Major* ....31 May 80
Chas. H. B. Williams,¹ *Hon.
  Major* ....26 Jan. 84
Charles John Boyle,⁴(*H*),*late
  Capt. 2 Bn., Hon. Major* 30 Dec. 85
HughC.Fortescue,*Hon.Maj.* 6 May 91
Thomas C. T. Warner, *MP.
  Hon. Major* ....19 Dec. 91
Fred. Edward Withington,
  (*H*), *Inst. of Musketry*......14 Apr. 92
J.H.Upton-Cottrell-Dormer30 Jan. 95

LIEUTENANTS.
*Robert Wentworth Doyne,
  serving under the British
  South Africa Company* ... 7 May 90
James Blyth .... 1 Feb. 91
Richard Pulteney Pulteney 19 Dec. 91
Wm. C. De M. *Visct.* Milton 8 Apr. 93
Maurice W. G. Rowley-
  Conwy....................... 9 Dec. 93
Robt. Hy. Watkin Brewis 27 Jan. 94
OliverNeedham Holt-Need-
  ham..........................27 Jan. 94
Angus John M'Neill ....17 Oct. 94
Thos. Hy. Rivers Bulkeley16 Jan. 95

SECOND LIEUTENANTS.
Robt. Bingham Brassey ... 6 Jan. 94
Alastair Hamilton .... 6 Jan. 94
Lionel E. H. Marmaduke
  Darell ....14 Apr. 94
Hy. Wm. E. *Earl of* Kerry 8 Jan. 95
W. Reg. Shute Barringtono Jan. 95
Adjt. & Capt.—E. A. E.
  Lethbridge, *Capt.* 1 *Bn.*...17 Mar. 94
Qr. Master.—Geo. A. Hirst,
  Hon. Captain ....21 June 83
Med. Off.—

White Facings.

The Essex Regiment.
3RD BATTALION.
(*Formerly the Essex Rifles.*)
Head Quarters, Warley.

HONORARY COLONEL.
Edgar John Disney,(*H*),*DL.
  JP. late Capt.* 7 *F.*......... 8 Mar. 90

LIEUTENANT COLONEL.
Tyssen Sowley Holroyd,¹
  late Capt. 23 *F.; Hon. Col.*12 Aug. 93

MAJORS.
Geo.B.C.Lyons,*Hon.Lt.Col.*26 May 90
Henry C. Masterman.........21 Oct. 93

CAPTAINS.
John Herbert Greenhalgh,
  (*H*) ....25 Sept. 86
Arthur J. Galsworthy ......26 Apr. 90
John Bernard O'Reilly......26 May 90
Wm.Coesvelt M. Kortright 20 May 91
Thos.Alfred Pamplin Green23 May 92
Edward Samuel Penrose...23 May 92
Percy Tatham ....26 Mar. 93
Chas.L.Vaughan-Arbuckle18 Nov. 93

LIEUTENANTS.
Walter George Arkwright 23 May 92
Walter Spoor Brindle ......14 Jan. 93
Richd. Wm. Winter Bayley 9 Sept. 93
Claude Arthur Worthington 6 Jan. 94
Cecil Frank M'Causland ...12 May 94
Edward Matthews .... 5 Sept. 94
Gerald Patrick O. Carnegy 5 Sept. 94
Roderick Murrie Burgoyne26 Sept.94

SECOND LIEUTENANTS.
Douglas Stewart George ...14 Feb. 94
George Nelson Sheffield... 11 Apr. 94
Lionel Hunter Escombe...28 Nov. 94
Arth. D. Nairne Merriman23 Jan. 95
Adjt. & Capt.—Robert M.O.
  Glynn, *Capt. Welsh Fus.* 1 Nov. 94
Qr. Master.—George S.
  Ames, *Hon. Lieut.*...........13 Feb. 95
Med.Off.—

White Facings.

4TH BATTALION.
(*Formerly the West Essex Militia.*)
Head Quarters, Warley.

HONORARY COLONEL.
Samuel B. Ruggles-Brise,
  CB. DL. JP.late 1 *Dr. Gds.*20 Feb. 89

LT. COLONEL.
Fred. Smart Walker, *Hon.
  Colonel*.....................10 Feb. 94

MAJORS.
Alf. Tufnell Robson(*H*), *late
  Lt.*92*Foot, Hon.Lt.Colonel* 2 Mar. 89
Edw. Charles Bond, *Hon.
  Lt.Colonel* .... 4 Apr. 94

CAPTAINS.
Geo. P. Townsend, *Hon.Maj.*27 July 81
James Hiscutt Crossman...11 May 85
Cecil Hodgson Colvin,⁶(*H*),
  Instructor of Musketry ... 4 June 87
Charles F. D. Sperling......16 Mar. 89
George Alan Kirk ....26 Apr. 91
Mansel W. Jones-Mortimer 28 Apr. 93
Edm. Leveson Calverley,(t),
  (*H*) .... 4 Apr. 94
John Edw. Chas. Blakeney,
  (*t*) ....27 Feb. 95

LIEUTENANTS.
Chas.NevillF.Gostling,(*H*) 19 July 90
Gerald Stanley Caldecott...18 June 92
Arthur Groome Howes......10 Dec. 92
Richard Hedley Robinson 10 Dec. 92
Richd. Fras. Knight Gooch15 July 93
Charles Vernon Ommanney 4 Apr. 94
Arthur Crosby Halahan ... 8 Aug. 94
Alex. Phayre Churchill ...27 Feb. 95

SECOND LIEUTENANTS.
Richard Edmund Shepherd10 Apr. 94
Ivone Guy Chas. Hunter...22 Aug. 94
Robert Minturn Claryes
  Ruxton ....13 Feb. 95
Adjt. & Capt.—Hy. Broad-
  mend, *Captain* 1 *Battalion* 1 Nov. 92
Qr. Master.—Daniel M.
  Bailey, *Hon. Lieut.*.......10 Sept 90
Med. Officer—

White Facings.

The Sherwood Foresters (Derbyshire Regiment).
3RD BATTALION.
(*Formerly the* 1*st and* 2*nd Derby
  Militia.*)
Head Quarters, Derby.

HONORARY COLONELS.
Rt. Hon. S. C. *Duke of
  Devonshire, KG.* .... 6 May 7v
V.C General Lord Roberts *of
  Kandahar, GCB. GCSI.
  GCIE. R.* (Bengal) *Art.* 20 Dec. 88

LT. COLONELS.
Wm.LangtonCoke, (*t*), *JP.,
  DL. late Cornet* 4 *Hussars;
  Hon.Colonel* ....15 May 87
Joseph Hall Moore, *Hon.
  Colonel*.....................17 Mar. 88

MAJORS.
Henry Pearson, *p.s.* (*H*), (*t*)
  Hon. Lt. Colonel ....24 Mar. 88
Albert L. Salmond, *p.s.* (*t*),
  (S), *Hon. Major* 1 *Cadet
  Bn. West Surrey Regt.* ...10 Sept 92

CAPTAINS.
*Hon.*Alfred N.Curzon,*Hon.
  Major* ....11 Mar. 85
Vernon Henry Mellor, *p.s.* ... 5 Nov. 87
Edward Ranulph Leacroft 2 June 88
Gerard R. Oakes, *p.s.*.......22 Aug. 88
Arthur Webster Young,
  Hon. Lieut. 1 *Cadet Bn.
  West Surrey Regt.* 5 Sept.91
R.CollingwoodFenwick,*p.s.*22 Mar. 93
Herbert Waldy, *p.s.*..........22 Mar. 93
Geo. D.MarshallHughes,*p.s.*12 Aug. 93
Maximilian M. Litkie, *p.s.* 12 Sept.94

LIEUTENANTS.
Geo. Hy. Benton Fletcher,
  p.s. Hon. Captain 1 *Cadet
  Bn.West Surrey Regiment*22 Mar. 93
Laurence B. Asshetou
  Craven ....22 Mar. 93
Victor C. Patrick Martin,*p.s.*27 Jan. 94
Edward Charles Heath, *p.s.*27 Jan. 94
Henry Edw. Disbrowe Wise12 Sept.94
Cecil Arbuthnot White..... 12 Sept.94
Ralph Henry S. Wilmot ...12 Sept.94
Evan J. MurrayBurgoyne 12 Sept. 94

SECOND LIEUTENANTS.
Hugo Meynell................. 5 Sept. 94
Ernest Elborough Wood-
  cock .... 5 Feb. 95
Adjts.—F. C. Shaw, *Capt.*
  1 *Battalion*................. 18 Aug. 90
Qr. Master.—Wm. Lynch,
  Hon. Captain .... 1 May 78
Med. Off.—Surg. Lt.Colonel
  Alf. O. Francis .... 1 Dec. 91

White Facings.

4TH BATTALION.
(*Formerly the Nottingham, or Royal
  Sherwood Foresters.*)
Head Quarters, Newark.

HONORARY COLONEL.
Rt. Hon. Wm. J. A. C. J.
  Duke of Portland............ 8 June 89

LT. COLONEL.
John W. Keyworth,(*H*),*late
  Capt.* 48 *F., Hon. Colonel* 7 July 94

Militia Infantry.

MAJORS.
Geo. Redmond Prior, *Hon. Lt. Colonel* .... 24 June 90
Napier Langford Pearse,[1] *late 1 Battalion* ...... 11 July 94

CAPTAINS.
Arthur Steffe Crisp, *late Lt. 6 F. p.s.; Hon. Major* ... 7 Sept. 71
Geo. E. Mackarness, p.s. *Hon. Major* .... 26 Aug. 76
John A. Winstanley, *Hon. Major* .... 4 Feb. 80
George A. E. Wilkinson ... 3 May 84
John Humber .... 10 May 90
Gilbert Lloyd Elliott, *p.s. (I), late Lt.* 46 Foot & 13 *Hussars* .... 27 June 88
John R. Prescott, *ret. pay 1 Battalion* .... 27 June 94
George Seaton de Winton 6 Mar. 95

LIEUTENANTS.
Robert Chris. Thomas, *late Lt.* 3 *Brig. W. Div. R. Art.* 9 Jan. 89
Frederic Rupert Slade ...... 14 Feb. 91
Harold Evelyn Dolphin ... 3 Dec. 92
Charles Pigott Piers, (*H*), *Instructor of Musketry* ... 3 Dec. 92
Alfred Herbert Lyon......... 13 May 93
Godfrey James King......... 13 May 93
Robt. B. Fraser Robertson 13 May 93
Laurence Beaumont Chamberlain .... 20 Jan. 94
Gilbert Mortimore Hunt ... 20 Jan. 94
Lord Osborne de Vere Beauclerk .... 6 Mar. 95
David Henry Græme......... 6 Mar. 95
Greville H. Woodley Bernal 6 Mar. 95

SECOND LIEUTENANTS.
Arthur Persse Pollok ...... 3 July 93
Algernon J. Fred. Platt ... 13 Jan. 94
John Heugh Melville ...... 28 Mar. 94
Cecil Fane.................. 31 Mar. 94
Hon. Hy. W. W. Horsley-Beresford .... 23 Jan. 95

Adjt. & Capt.—R. Brittan, *ridge, Captain* 1 *Battalion* 1 Mar. 95
Qr. Master.—William Fox,[2] *Hon. Lieut* .... 6 July 87
Med. Off.—*Surg. Lt. Colonel* Thos. Fred. Greenwood... 1 Dec. 91

White Facings.

Loyal North Lancashire Regt.
3RD AND 4TH BATTALIONS.
(*Formerly the Duke of Lancaster's Own.*)
Head Quarters, Preston.
"*Mediterranean.*"

HONORARY COLONEL.
Thomas R. Crosse .... 10 Sept. 92

LT. COLONEL COMMANDANT.
Thomas Myles Sandys,[1] *MP. DL. late Capt.* 7 F. 5 Oct. 92

LT. COLONEL.
Charles Birch, (*T*), *Hon. Colonel*......... 5 Oct. 92

MAJORS.
Leith Bonhôte .... 23 July 94
James H. W. Pedder ...... 14 Nov. 94

CAPTAINS.
Arthur E. Da Costa, *p.s.(H)*, *Inst. of Musketry* ...... 27 Apr. 78
Thomas Cowper .... 11 Aug. 86
Reginald G. Chambres, *p.s., Hon. Major*............ 24 Mar. 80
William Harrison,[2] *Capt. ret. pay* 11 *Hussars, Hon. Major* .... 14 Aug. 89
Peter Ormrod, p.s.(*H*) ...... 8 July 91
Stephen Bibbins Allen ...... 26 July 93
Percy Wordsworth Harrison 5 June 93
Henry A. Pole Soppitt...... 14 Apr. 94

LIEUTENANTS.
Alfred Henry Turner, (*H*), *serving under the Royal Niger Company* .... 27 Aug. 90
Horbert Alex. C. Roberts...27 Aug. 90
Charles Hutchinson Orpen 24 Oct. 91
Charles Michael Quarry ... 6 Aug. 92
Cyril de Putron, *p.s.* ...... 10 Mar. 94
George Francis FitzRoy ...10 Mar. 94
Wm. Chamberlen Salmon 10 Mar. 94
Robert Esmé Berkeley ...... 5 May 94
Percy Strahan .... 5 May 94
Douglas Cyril Smith......... 29 Aug. 94
Harry Vernon Lockwood... 6 Mar. 95
Geoffrey Gregory .... 6 Mar. 95

SECOND LIEUTENANTS.
Edwin George Case .... 3 Feb. 94
Wm. Geo. Percival Miller 3 Apr. 94
Thomas Edwards-Moss...... 16 June 94
Alexander Gillespie Cowan 22 July 94
Percy G. Deslandes Winter 1 Aug. 94

Adjt. & Capt.—H. G. Leonard, *Capt.* 1 *Battalion* .... 28 Mar. 92
Qr. Masters.—J. A. Furlong, *Hon. Captain* .... 28 Mar. 77
Med. Off.—

White Facings.

The Northamptonshire Regt.
3RD AND 4TH BATTALIONS.
(*Formerly the Northampton and Rutland Militia.*)
Head Quarters, Northampton.
"*Mediterranean.*"

HONORARY COLONEL.
The Marq. of Exeter, *Aide de Camp to the Queen* ...... 26 Oct. 87

LT. COLONEL COMMANDANT.
Rt. Hon. Lord Burghley, *MP. p.s. late Lt. and Capt. Gr. Gds. Hon. Colonel*...... 3 Dec. 87

LT. COLONEL.
Sackville George Stopford-Sackville, *p.s., Hon. Colonel* 13 Apr. 89

MAJORS.
Edward Philip Monckton, *Hon. Lt. Colonel* .... 21 Apr. 86
Arthur John Fludyer, *Hon. Lt. Colonel* .... 23 May 91

CAPTAINS.
Joseph Hill, *Hon. Major* .. 3 Mar. 75
Frank A. White, *Hon. Major* 1 May 82
Henry W. K. Markham, *Hon. Major* .... 29 Dec. 85
William Rhodes .... 11 May 89
John Hume Smith............ 4 May 91
Henry M. Stockdale, *p.s.* 11 Apr. 92
Geo. H. C. Holden de Crespigny, (*H*), *late Lt.* 1 *Bn.* 12 Apr. 92
John A. Shiel Bouverie, Jun. 19 May 92
Christopher Alex. Markham, (*H*), (t) .... 6 May 93
Hon. John Powys, *p.s.* ...... 12 May 93
Sir Ar. R. de Capell Brooke, Bart............ 27 Mar. 95

LIEUTENANTS.
Charles Milnes Pencock ... 25 May 92
Charles Pigott Harvey ...... 6 May 93
Charles Robt. Ingham Hull, (*H*), *Instructor of Musketry* 6 May 93
Lord Sholto Geo. Douglas 12 May 93
James Douglas Waddell... 11 Nov. 93
Lisle Arthur Finch Dawson 3 Mar. 94
Chas. J. Eustace Moorsom 1 Aug. 94
Geo. Sherwin H. Pearson 1 Aug. 94
Buckley C. L. Mackworth Praed... .... 1 Aug. 94
Herbert H. de Bohun Morris 1 Aug. 94
Lionel Hugh Martineau ... 1 Aug. 94

SECOND LIEUTENANTS.
C. FitzPatrick Burroughes 22 Mar. 94
Mervyn Owen Wayne Powys 24 May 94
Hon. Wm. Thos. B. Cecil...23 June 94
Arthur Hugh Sartoris ...... 5 Sept. 94
Harry Grant Thorold ...... 26 Sept. 94
Charles Frederick Pilcher 28 Nov. 94

Adjt. & Capt.—F. J. Parker, *Captain* 1 *Battalion* ...... 1 Oct. 94
Qr. Master.—Robert Wallace,[1] *Hon. Capt.* .... 19 Sept. 80
Med. Off.—*Surg. Lt. Colonel* H. B. Spurgin .... 1 Dec. 91

White Facings.

Princess Charlotte of Wales' (Royal Berkshire Regiment).
3RD BATTALION.
(*Formerly the Royal Berks Militia.*)
Head Quarters, Reading.
"*Mediterranean.*"

HONORARY COLONEL.
M. A. Earl of Abingdon, *p.s.* 27 Oct. 80

LT. COLONEL.
Thomas John Bowles, *p.s.* ... 21 Apr. 94

MAJORS.
Tristram J. Wheble .... 2 Feb. 89

CAPTAINS.
Lord George Murray Pratt, *JP., late Lt. and Capt. Gren. Gds., Hon. Major* 24 Nov. 83
Arthur Wm. H. Hay, *p.s....*22 May 86
Francis Mildred Birch ...... 12 June 86
John Robin Gray, *late Lieut. King's R. Rifles...* ...... 17 Apr. 89
Walter Thornton, (*H*) ...... 4 May 90
Chas. E. M. Y. Nepean, *p.s.* 18 Feb. 91
Frederick George Barker...25 Mar. 91

LIEUTENANTS.
Wm. Jn. B. Van De Weyer 7 Feb. 91
Robert Hargreaves .... 7 Feb. 91
Wm. Arthur Fred. White.. 7 Feb. 91
Reginald Fredk. Cazenove 9 May 92
Hubert Victor Rhodes ...... 20 Feb. 95
Percy Cazenove .... 20 Feb. 95

SECOND LIEUTENANTS.
Harold Greenwood Henderson .... 3 Mar. 94
Harry Claude Fred. Hay, 1 *Cadet Bn. W. Surrey Regt.* 12 Mar. 94
Bates G. Van De Weyer ... 7 July 94
Albert Henry Royds .... 3 Oct. 94
Wm. Hugh Neville Bagot 1 Mar. 95

Adjt. & Capt.—C. M. Edwards, *Major* 1 *Battalion* .... 30 Oct. 90
Qr. Master.—Walter Hollyer,[1] *Hon. Captain*............... 18 June 81
Med. Off.—

Blue Facings.

The Queen's Own (Royal West Kent Regiment).
3RD BATTALION.
(*Formerly the West Kent Lt. Infantry.*)
Head Quarters, Maidstone.

HONORARY COLONEL.
Lt. General H.R.H. Arthur Wm. Patrick Albert, *Duke of Connaught, KG. KT. KP. GCSI. GCMG. GCIE. KCB.* .... 23 Aug. 84

LT. COLONEL COMMANDANT.
Everard Thomas Luck, *p.s. Hon. Colonel* .... 9 Jan. 92

LT. COLONEL.

MAJORS.
John Bonhote, *late Lt.* 84 F. *Hon. Lt. Colonel*............ 4 May 89
Edmund W. G. Bailey......... 6 Feb. 92

CAPTAINS.
Robert Waters Coombs, *Hon. Major*............ 27 Sept. 84
Charles Dundas Hohler, *p.s.* 11 Feb. 88
William Bradish,[1] *p.s., Hon. Major* .... 21 May 79
J. H. Kennedy,[2] *ret. pay* 2 *Battalion*............ 24 June 91
Edward Fleming .... 5 Oct. 89
Cecil Fred. Beeching......... 28 Apr. 94
Arthur Jas. P. Annesley (*H*), *serving with Gold Coast Constabulary* .... 6 Mar. 95

Militia Infantry. 599

LIEUTENANTS.
Jas. S. Drummond Gage, employed with the Egyptian Police ....28 May 92
George Wilson..............29 Apr. 93
Sidney Stanley Williams... 5 Dec. 94
Arthur Corbett Edwards ... 5 Dec. 94
Richard Whitehead .... 5 Dec. 94
Harry Kirwan Umfreville 5 Dec. 94
JustinianJ.Edwards-Heathcote .... 5 Dec. 94

SECOND LIEUTENANTS.
Fred. Ernest Swainson...... 1 June 93
Charles Lloyd Harford......20 Jan. 94
Edward Hoare Reeves ......17 Feb. 94
Herbert Chaplin Nisbet ...21 Apr. 94
Jas. Hy. Sydney Annesley12 May 94
William Beresford Molony 26 Sept.94
Gilbert S. Tritton Fenning 28 Nov. 94
Aylmer Cameron ....12 Dec. 94
Hy. Bourchier Wrey Gardiner ....30 Jan. 95
Charles Edward Martin ... 6 Mar. 95
Fred. W. Bagnall Willett...13 Mar. 95
Adjt. & Capt.—L. Brock-Hollinshead,*Major* 2 *Bn.*26 Apr. 93
Qr.Master.—Jas. Clifford,[4]
Hon. Captain .... 1 Apr. 83
Blue Facings.

The King's Own Yorkshire Light Infantry.
3RD BATTALION.
(*Formerly the 1st West York Militia.*)
Head Quarters, Pontefract.

HONORARY COLONEL.
c. Alex. Aitken, *late Capt.*
77 *F.* ....31 May 82

LT.COLONEL.
Theodore Henry Skinner, *p.s.* (*H*), [*t*], *late Lieut.* 8 *F., Hon. Colonel* ....15 Oct. 92

MAJORS.
Reginald Hayes-Sadler,*p.s. late Lt. Yorkshire Regt.; A. D. C. to Col. W. H. Richards, Com. S.E. Brig. Vol. Inf.* ....19 May 94

CAPTAINS.
Chas. Edw. Whalley, (*T*), *late Capt.retired pay* 107 *F. Hon. Major*....................26 July 82
Albert Gustavus Momber...20 Nov. 86
Albert Edward Bright, *p.s.* 21 Jan. 88
William Hotham,[1] *ret. pay Shropshire Lt. Infantry* ...19 Mar. 90
James Edw. Aikin, *ret. pay York & Lancaster Regt.*...30 Sept.91
George Earl Alt, *p.s.* ....21 May 92
Walter Spencer-Stanhope,[2] *ret. pay* 14 *Hussars*.........21 Sept. 92
Thomas Henry Lindberg, *p.s.* (*H*), *Inst. of Musketry*22 July 93
William HentonCarver,*p.s.* 9 June 94

LIEUTENANTS.
Claud Hy. M. Tabuteau,*p.s.* 9 June 94
Rupert Riley,*p.s.* .... 9 June 94

SECOND LIEUTENANTS.
Alex. Bannatyne Stewart...26 Aug. 93
Montg. Sidney Williams ...26 Aug. 93
Arthur Gorham ....24 Feb. 94
Mathew Richd. Hy. Wilson10 Mar. 94
Arthur H.WilliamsTempler17 Mar. 94
Frank Simeon Exham ...... 5 Apr. 94
George Frederick Hibbert 31 Oct. 94
Claude E. Myln Walker ...31 Oct. 94
Gerald Cecil M. Rouse ......27 Feb. 95
Reginald Kerr Granville...20 Mar. 95
Adjt. & Capt.—R. C. Money, *Captain* 2 *Battalion*.........19 Nov. 90
Qr.Master.—William Nice, *Hon. Captain* .... 8 July 86
Med. Off.—
Blue Facings.

The King's (Shropshire Light Infantry).
3RD BATTALION.
(*Formerly the Shropshire Militia.*)
Head Quarters, Shrewsbury.

HONORARY COLONEL.
Edward Corbett, *late Lt.* 72 *F.*............................ 6 Sept. 90

LT.COLONEL.
Sir Thomas Meyrick, *Bart. Hon. Colonel* .... 4 Oct. 84

MAJORS.
Fra. Alex. W. Whitmore, *Hon. Lt. Colonel* ....10 Jan. 83
Edw. MaltbyWakeman (*H*), *Hon. Lt.Colonel*............... 8 Nov. 84

CAPTAINS.
Harry Vane Russell 6 Sept.84
Walter Charlton Pryce,*p.s.* 26 Nov. 87
Ellis Sparling Cunliffe, *p.s.* 24 Nov. 88
F.R. HartlandAtcherley,*p.s.*15 June89
Geo. J. Scott,[1] *Captain ret. pay*18 *Hussars,Hon.Major*14 Aug. 89
William Norman Leslie......18 Feb. 93
Thomas Dickin, *p.s.* .... 3 Apr. 93

LIEUTENANTS.
John Chas. O. Aldworth ... 6 July 89
Edw. Pearkes Gundry, (*H*), *Instructor of Musketry* ... 8 Nov. 90
Fras. H. C. Weld-Forester.19 Sept.91
John Rowden Freme .... 6 Feb. 92
William Tayleur .... 4 Jan. 93
Chas. R. Borlase Wingfield 6 May 93
RowlandJ.Venables Lovett 6 May 93
John Derby Allcroft .... 7 May 94

SECOND LIEUTENANTS.
Edward Spencer Dickin ...2: Jan. 93
Thos. Brassey Maddocks ... 7 Oct. 93
Reginald Gordon Patchett 7 Mar. 94
Adjt. & Capt.—
Qr.Master.—GeorgePecker, *Hon. Lieut.*....................27 June 92
Med. Off.—*Surgeon Lt.Col.* H. Nelson Edwards ...... 1 Dec. 91
Blue Facings.

4TH BATTALION.
(*Formerly the Hereford Militia.*)
Head Quarters, Hereford.

HONORARY COLONEL.
W. B. B. H. *Lord* Bateman, *Lord Lieutenant*..............19 May 64

LT.COLONEL.
Hugh Powell Williams,*p.s.*17 Sept.92

MAJORS.
EdwardPodmoreClark(*H*), *late Lt.* 62 *F., p.s.; Hon. Lt.Colonel* ....21 Jan. 88
Henry B. K. Davies, *Hon. Lt.Colonel* ....15 Oct. 92

CAPTAINS.
E. S. Lucas, p.s.*Hon.Major*16 Apr. 79
Godfrey L.Clark, *Hon. Maj.* 8 Feb. 82
Robert Cockburn 6 Sept.84
Gilbert Charles Bourne ... 2 Oct. 86
Charles Orby Shipley (*H*), *Instructor of Musketry* ...17 May 90
John George O'Brien, *p.s.*13 Feb. 92
Richard H. T. Symonds-Tayler .... 6 Aug. 92
William Edwd. Norris, *p.s.*18 Mar. 93

LIEUTENANTS.
Herbert Hudson .... 6 Feb. 92
Thomas Henry Luke.........20 Aug. 92
Robert Lambert ....20 Aug. 92
Frank Sandiford Cooper ...17 Mar. 94
John Gordon Woodhouse...17 Mar. 94
Trevor C. G. James-Trevcr17 Mar. 94

SECOND LIEUTENANTS.
Henry Roland M. Bourne 24 Feb. 94
Reginald Henry Radford...24 Feb. 94
William Rumney Robins... 6 Mar. 94
Edward Hutchinson ....12 Mar. 94
Darcy Arthur Rasbotham 3 Oct. 94
Adjutant.— R. A. Smith, *Captain* 1 *Battalion*.........19 Sept. 93
Qr.Master.—Frank Charles Guest,[2] *Hon. Captain* ......19 Nov. 81
Med. Off.—
Blue Facings.

The Duke of Cambridge's Own (Middlesex Regiment).
3RD BATTALION.
(*Formerly the Royal Elthorne Light Infantry.*)
Head Quarters, Hounslow.

HONORARY COLONEL.

LIEUTENANT COLONEL.
Chas. Brome Bashford, *JP. late Capt.* 9 *Lancers, p.s. Hon.Colonel*..................10 July 78

MAJORS.
Vilett Rolleston, *p.s.* [*t*] ... 4 May 91
George Moore, *p.s.*............ 2 Dec. 93

CAPTAINS.
Fras.Andrew Lamb,*p.s.*(*H*)20 June85
Ernest MortimerGriffin(*H*)27 June 85
Charles James Fox, *p.s.*......14 Apr. 90
ThomasClyde Goldsworthy, *p.s.* (*H*) .... 5 May 90
George William Redway, *p.s.* (*t*) .... 9 July 91
Reginald Percy Jessel ...... 5 Mar. 92
George Anderson, *Instructor of Musketry*.............19 May 94
Andrew Bennet Black ......26 May 94

LIEUTENANTS.
Charles William Blake...... 6 May 93
Gerald Achilles Burgoyne 19 May 94
Leslie Fletcher ....19 May 94
Vernon Aubrey Scott Keighley .... 6 Mar. 95

SECOND LIEUTENANTS.
Wallace Duffield Wright ...24 Oct. 94
Robert Henry Parnall ......14 Nov. 94
Avenel de B. Wm. W. Bradford....................20 Feb. 95
Adjt. and Capt.—George B. Lempriere, *Capt.* 2 *Bn.* ...14 May 91
Qr. Master.— John Reed, *Hon. Lieut.* ....11 June 90
Med. Off.—
White Facings.

4TH BATTALION.
(*Formerly the Royal East Middlesex Militia.*)
Head Quarters, Hounslow.

HONORARY COLONEL.
Henry Kent,[1] *Lt. General retired list* ....14 June 90

LT.COLONEL.
George Coope Helme, *ret. pay Wilts Regt. Hon. Col.* 20 Feb. 89

MAJORS.
Joseph W. R. Adams, *JP., p.s.* (*H*) [*t*] *Hon. Lt.Col.* 20 Sept. 90
Gerard R. Rushbrooke, *p.s.*28 Apr. 94

Militia Infantry.

CAPTAINS.
John Edward Elin, *Hon.*
 Major .... 10 Jan. 85
Herbert W. H. Brenchley 19 Mar. 87
Stanley Mundey .... 26 May 88
Gerald Edgar Barker, *p.s.* 13 Apr. 89
Alex. Wentworth Kitson, p.s.
 Inspector of Civil Police,
 Gold Coast................... 20 Dec. 90
Robert Edward Neale ...... 10 Feb. 94
Frank Bennett Goldney ..... 10 Feb. 94
Percival Hope Graves, (*H*),
 (*t*), *p.s. Inst. of Musketry.* 6 Feb. 95

LIEUTENANTS.
Edward Morse .... 19 Mar. 90
Noel Edw. G. Willoughby 25 Feb. 91
Arthur Reginald Carey ...... 3 June 92
Robt. Peel D. S. Chichester 3 Mar. 94
Geo. W. Bulkeley Tattersall 3 Mar. 94
Wm. Ernest W. Elkington 20 Feb. 95

SECOND LIEUTENANTS.
Stephen Thomas Hardwick 30 Jan. 95
Greville John Prodgers ..... 30 Jan. 95
Adjt. & Capt.—C. R. Dyer,
 Captain 2 Battalion...... 25 Nov. 92
Qr. Master.—Samuel John
 Miller,[5] *Hon. Captain*... 1 Apr. 82
Med. Off.—

White Facings.

The King's Royal Rifle Corps.

5TH BATTALION.
(*Formerly the Huntingdon Rifles.*)
Head Quarters, Huntingdon.

HONORARY COLONEL.
Lieutenant Colonel.
Edward G. H. *Earl of Sand-*
 wich, Lord Lieut. of Hunts,
 Col. late Grenadier Guards,
 Hon. Colonel, Commanding
 South Midland Brigade
 Rifle Volunteers............... 18 Sept. 86

MAJOR.
Fred. Robert Beart, *p.s.* ... 10 Apr. 86

CAPTAINS.
John G. Green, (*H*), *Inst. of*
 Musketry .... 14 Apr. 86
Gerald Otho FitzGerald,
 Aide de Camp South Mid-
 land Brig. Inf. Vols. ...... 11 June 87
Herbert Charles Jones ...... 4 Mar. 91
Arthur Dunbar Pixley,[6] *ret.*
 pay King's Royal Rifles ... 26 Mar. 90

LIEUTENANTS.
Stanley Edwards .... 24 Oct. 94
Henry Francis Stirling ...... 24 Oct. 94
James Marshall .... 24 Oct. 94
Hervey Ronald Bruce .... 27 Feb. 95

SECOND LIEUTENANTS.
Charles Hugh Napier
 Seymour .... 24 Feb. 94
Grey William Duberly ...... 27 Feb. 95
Adjt. & Capt.—H. A. Kin-
 loch, *Capt. 3 Battalion* ... 2 Mar. 91
Med. Off.—

Scarlet Facings.

6TH BATTALION.
(*Formerly the Royal Flint Rifles.*)
[Disbanded 30 June 1889.]

7TH BATTALION.
(*Formerly the 2nd or Edmonton Royal*
Middlesex Rifles.)
Head Quarters, Barnet.

HONORARY COLONEL.
Hon. H. W. J. Byng, *late*
 Capt. & Lt. Col. Coldst. Gds.,
 Equerry to Her Majesty ... 15 June 78

LT. COLONEL.
George Robert Stewart
 Black,[1] (*H*), *late Capt. 60*
 Rifles, Hon. Colonel......... 4 Feb. 80

MAJORS.
Jas. L. Brooke Templer,[3]
 Hon. Lt. Colonel; Instructor
 in Ballooning, Aldershot... 4 Apr. 83

Edm. C. C. Hartopp, *late*
 Lt. Rifle Brigade; Hon.
 Lt. Colonel .... 16 Apr. 85
P. W. G. Copland-Crawford,
 serving in the Niger Coast
 Protectorate .... 5 Dec. 91
Francis R. W. Sampson ... 27 Jan. 94

CAPTAINS.
Robert Story,[7] *Capt. retired*
 pay King's Royal Rifles,
 Hon. Major.................. 15 Mar. 84
J. Nugent Blackwood-
 Price,[11] *Bt. Major ret. pay*
 King's R. Rifles............. 14 Feb. 85
Arthur S. Heathcote, (*H*)...27 Feb. 86
Charles Edw. Clowes (*H*),
 Capt. ret. pay King's R.
 Rifles, Hon. Major .... 23 May 88
Daniel Chas. Wm. Lysons,[8]
 Hon. Major .... 4 Oct. 90
Robt. Lister Bower,[9] *ret. pay*
 King's Royal Rifles, Assist.
 Inspector of Constabulary,
 Lagos .... 6 May 91
Fred. Savill Marsham, *Hon.*
 Major .... 10 Oct. 91
Wm. A. Hicks Beach, *ret.*
 pay King's Royal Rifles,
 Hon. Major .... 11 June 90
Charles H. Fenwick, *late*
 King's Royal Rifles ..... 12 Aug. 93
Fred. Arthur Irby,[10] *ret.*
 pay Rifle Brigade........... 13 Mar. 95

LIEUTENANTS.
Francis Wm. B. Sandwith,
 serving with Egyptian Police 26 Apr. 82
Francis Richard Gosling,
 (*H*), *Inst. of Musketry* ... 4 May 89
Hubert A. Courtenay
 Brooking .... 27 May 91
Felix Edm. Powell, *p.s.* (*H*),
 serving with the Egyptian
 Police .... 30 July 92
Alfred Edward FitzGerald 25 Mar. 93
George Charles Lambton 4 June 94
William Wilfred Rhodes ... 7 June 94
Chas. L. M. Willoughby Wallace 7 June 94
Bertram Gerald R. Oldfield 31 Oct. 94
John Gordon Stirling ...... 6 Feb. 95
Hon. Hugh Edwardes ...... 6 Feb. 95

SECOND LIEUTENANTS.
Gerard E. Byng Stephens ... 7 July 94
Harold Farnell Watson ... 31 Oct. 94
Chas. Alexander Cardwell 16 Jan. 95
Fras. Edw. Basil Napier ... 6 Feb. 95
Haughton Ealdred Okeover 13 Feb. 95
Adjt. & Capt.—C. A. T. Boult-
 bee, *Major K. R. Rifles* ... 20 Dec. 91
Qr. Master.—Evi John
 Crane,[14] *Hon. Captain* ... 15 Mar. 79
Med. Off.—

Scarlet Facings.

8TH BATTALION.
(*Formerly the Carlow Rifles.*)
Head Quarters, Carlow.

HONORARY COLONEL.
Sir Thomas Pierce Butler,[4]
 Bart. .... 20 July 89

LT. COLONEL.
J. J. H. R. Eustace .... 23 May 94

MAJOR.
Geo. Wellington L'Estrange 28 May 94

CAPTAINS.
Lord Walter Fitz Gerald,
 ret. pay 2 Battalion, Hon.
 Major .... 27 June 88
Joshua Kearney Millner,
 (*H*), *Instructor of Mus-*
 ketry........................... 18 Aug. 88
Chas. Edw. Henry Duckett-
 Steuart .... 20 July 89
Wilfred T. Richardson, *p.s.* 28 May 94

LIEUTENANTS.
John Hubert Grogan .... 11 Feb. 93
Mervyn Pratt .... 8 July 93
Charles Claude Wallace,
 late 14th Hussars............ 4 June 94

SECOND LIEUTENANTS.
Charles Howard Crosbie ... 16 Mar. 94
Adjt. & Capt.—Sir H. H. A.
 Walsh, *Bart. Capt. 2 Bn.* 1 Nov. 93
Med. Off.—*Surgeon Lt. Col.*
 Edward A. Rawson, *MD.* 1 Dec. 91

Scarlet Facings.

9TH BATTALION.
(*Formerly the North Cork Rifles.*)
Head Quarters, Mallow.

HONORARY COLONEL.
Richard Wm. Aldworth,[2]
 Colonel late 7 Foot .... 14 Jan. 88

LT. COLONEL.
William Cooke-Collis,[5] *late*
 Irish Rifles................... 12 Dec. 94

MAJORS.
William Stopford............... 10 Dec. 87

CAPTAINS.
Ludwig H. F. A. Bullen ...15 Sept. 88
Corliss Hawkes Bolster......27 Nov. 89
Richd. S. Brasier-Creagh
 p.s. .... 20 May 91
Albert William Clerke ...... 27 May 92
John H. D. Todd, *p.s.* ......10 July 93
Geo. G. de Courcy Harrison,
 (*H*), *Instructor of Musketry* 10 July 93
Francis George Davies ... 8 July 94

LIEUTENANTS.
Kenneth Wm. Millican, *p.s.* 28 May 92
Joseph Boyle Coghlan ...... 5 Nov. 92
William Speer Clerke ...... 17 June 93
Edw. W. Cotter Dillon ..... 20 Jan. 94
Edward Herbert Hobart ... 20 Jan. 94

SECOND LIEUTENANTS.
Thomas Roche .... 1 Mar. 93
John Ewan Martin .... 9 Mar. 94
Thos. Wm. Marshall Fuge 23 Sept. 94
Adjt. and Capt.—A. W. H.
 Bell, *Captain Connaught*
 Rangers .... 16 Aug. 94
Qr. Master.—Wm. Holmes,[16]
 Hon. Lieut.................... 14 Apr. 86
Med. Off.—*Surgeon Captain*
 James Creagh................. 18 June 73

Scarlet Facings.

The Duke of Edinburgh's (Wiltshire Regiment).

3RD BATTALION.
(*Formerly the Royal Wiltshire Militia.*)
Head Quarters, Devizes.
"*Mediterranean.*"

HONORARY COLONEL.
Major Gen. Paul Sanford,
 Lord Methuen, CB.CMG. 25 June 92

LT. COLONEL.
Edward C. A. Sanford, *p.s.* 4 Apr. 94

MAJORS.
Reginald Barclay .... 22 Aug. 94

CAPTAINS.
Ernest Wyndham Barnard,
 p.s. (*H*) .... 31 July 86
Cecil William P. Slade, *p.s.* 3 Mar. 88
Henry Wm. Harris, *p.s.* ...29 Nov. 90
Charles Henry Stilwell...... 5 Oct. 92
Walter T. Coleman, (*H*) ... 5 July 93
Abdy Locke Morant, *p.s.*
 (*t*) (*H*)............................ 19 Dec. 94

LIEUTENANTS.
Charles Joseph Harford, *serv-*
 ing with the British South
 African Company............ 8 Dec. 88
Reginald Benett Graves ... 10 May 93
John Elliot Carless............ 10 May 93

Militia Infantry. 601

The Manchester Regiment.

SECOND LIEUTENANTS.
Wm. B. Stuart Johnson......24 Dec. 92
John P. Hillier Winterscale 7 Jan. 93
Lionel Wallace Spiller......14 Jan. 93
Freeman Astley Jackson...25 Feb. 93
Henry Sanderson Laverton24 Mar. 93
Herbert Curling Laverton 23 Sept. 93
Ernest Radcliffe Cockburn11 Nov. 93
Hubert Peel Yates............ 6 Jan. 94
Myles Lonsdull Formby ...10 Feb. 94
Constantine Hotham Crichton ....28 Nov. 94
Adjt. & Capt.—H. W. Rowden, *Major* 2 *Battalion* ... 1 Sept. 90
Qr. Master.—Dav. Strachan,¹
Hon. Captain............... 7 Jan. 82
Med. Off.—

White Facings.

The Manchester Regiment.

3RD AND 4TH BATTALIONS.
(*Formerly 6th Royal Lancashire Militia.*)
Head Quarters, Ashton.
HONORARY COLONEL.
John H. Chambers, *DL.JP.*
late Capt. 46 *F.*............25 Apr. 88
LT. COLONEL COMMANDANT.
Aug. Graham P. Foley (*Lt. Colonel* 23 Sept. 93).........19 May 94
LIEUTENANT COLONEL.
Charles Dominic Leyden ...19 Sept. 94
MAJORS.
Wm. Ingersoll Merritt, *late Lt.* 30 *Foot* ....18 June 92
Wm. Gilbert Hyde Lees ... 3 Mar. 94
Herbert Alfred Johnson ...17 Oct. 94
John B. Irving,¹ p.s., (*H*),
ret. pay late Commt. & Transport Dept. Hon. Lt. Colonel 7 Nov. 94
CAPTAINS.
Stephen Lancaster Lucena 22 June 89
A. Hargraves Silverthorne,
(*H*), *Inst. of Musketry*......12 June 87
Robert Stewart Johnstone,
BA. LLB. p.s., District Commissioner, Lagos......... 9 July 87
John Brunt, *late Surg. RN.*
p.s.; Hon. Major............12 July 89
David C. Da Costa, *Capt.*
ret. pay Royal Scots; Hon. Major ....11 Sept. 89
Abel Henry Bayley...........27 Sept. 90
Sydney Calveley Goldsmith 22 Nov. 90
Thomas Langton Butler,
p.s. (*H*) ....18 June 92
William John Bosworth ... 2 Dec. 93
John Henry Dresser, p.s.[t]12 May 94
John Joseph O'Sullivan ...17 Oct. 94
Leslie Masters Silverthorne 2 Jan. 95
John Reginald Shaw......16 Jan. 95
LIEUTENANTS.
Vincent Cameron Gauntlett25 Apr. 91
W. J. Richardson Matthews 13 Feb. 92
Claude Champion-de-Crespigny .... 2 Apr. 92
Lestock F. R. Livingstone-Learmonth................. 4 May 92
Gerald Robinson ....14 May 92
John Barton Aiken...........23 July 92
Norman Zeal Emerson.....27 May 94
Cecil Arthur Vanderzee ...28 Oct. 93
Myles Aspinall Whittaker 17 Oct. 94
Ralph E. Haweis James ...17 Oct. 94
Arthur Clyde Perry, *Instructor of Musketry*.....17 Oct. 94
SECOND LIEUTENANTS.
Henry Francis Fraser ......14 July 92
Eustace E. M'Leod Beckles 7 June 93
Hy. Terence Frs. Dolan...10 Mar. 94
Alfred Granville Sharp ...15 Mar. 94
Fras. Montgomery Jennings 11 Apr. 94
Chas. Braithwaite Wallis 14 Apr. 94
George Burrows............14 Apr. 94
George Fraser MacCall ...23 July 94
Walter Allason ....23 July 94
Henry Trevellis Rawlings 14 Nov. 94
Eustace William Blois......19 Dec. 94
Adjts. & Capts.—W. R. N. Annesley, *DSO. Capt. W. Kent Regt.* ....23 Jan. 93
E. H. Burney, *Major, Berkshire Regiment* ....13 Nov. 93
Qr. Mr.—Abraham Hobbs,
Hon. Captain............19 Nov. 90
Med. Off.—

White Facings.

The Prince of Wales' North Staffordshire Regt.

3RD BATTALION.
(*Formerly the King's Own 2nd Stafford Light Infantry.*)
Head Quarters, Lichfield.
HONORARY COLONEL.
Sir Morton Edw. Buller, *Bt.* 11 Aug. 88
LT. COLONEL.
Sir Charles Forster, *Bart. Hon. Colonel* .... 2 Apr. 92
MAJORS.
John Henry Monckton, *p.s.*
(*H*), [t], *Hon. Lt. Colonel*20 June 88
George Crampton Hall......20 June 92
CAPTAINS.
Henry H. Ward, *Hon. Major*29 Mar. 82
George William H. Tudor,
p.s. [t], *Hon. Major*......... 7 Feb. 83
Robert H. Hargreaves, *Hon. Major* ....28 Jan. 88
George Henry Tunnicliffe 25 May 89
Fredk. Martin Madan, *p.s.*
(*H*), *Inst. of Musketry*......26 May 89
Chas. Holland James, *p.s.*(*H*) 9 Apr. 91
Alfred Richard Wood ....20 June 92
Guy L. Thorne Seckham,
p.s. (*H*) ....11 Feb. 93
LIEUTENANTS.
William L. Penrose Markwardlaw, *p.s.* (t) ....28 July 88
Charles Villiers Jameson... 9 Apr. 91
Reginald Francis Wynne...15 Mar. 93
Bertram Barré Waddell-Dodley .... 7 May 94
Montague Furber ....13 Feb. 95
SECOND LIEUTENANTS.
Geo. Edm. Stevenson Salt 14 Apr. 94
Walter Wm. MacGregor ...27 Apr. 94
Adjt. & Capt.—A. George,
Capt. 1 *Battalion* .... 1 May 93
Med. Off.—
Qr. Master.—Wm. Sandland,
Hon. Lieut. ....19 Oct. 94

White Facings.

4TH BATTALION.

(*Formerly the King's Own 3rd Stafford Rifles.*)
Head Quarters, Lichfield.
HONORARY COLONEL.
Hamar Alfred Bass, *MP. p.s.* 8 July 93
LT. COLONEL.
Chas. Bill,¹ *MP.* ....29 May 93
MAJORS.
Richard W. B. Mirehouse,³
Hon. Lt. Colonel ....12 Sept. 91
Francis R. Twemlow......29 May 93
CAPTAINS.
Cecil Wedgwood .... 9 May 87
Graham Lionel J. Wilson...15 Dec. 88
David G. O. Saunders-Davies 8 May 89
George Parker Bull .... 8 Apr. 93
Cecil C. Walter Troughton,
p.s. (t), (*H*) *Inspector Sierra Leone Police* ....30 May 93
Ralph Nevile Fane ....13 Jan. 94
Fras. Hamilton Wedgwood 2 July 94
Charles Boyer Webb ....14 Nov. 94
LIEUTENANTS.
Charles FitzHerbert Bill 14 Nov. 94
Walter Edward Blagg ......14 Nov. 94
Henry Edmendes ....14 Nov. 94
Harold Twyford............14 Nov. 94
Washington C. T. Hibbert 14 Nov. 94
Oliver Hawkshaw ....14 Nov. 94
George Augustus Riddell 14 Nov. 94
Walter Mackenzie Lovett 16 Jan. 95
SECOND LIEUTENANTS.
Charles Percival Parker...10 Apr. 94
Henry Claud Leicester......10 May 94
Alex. Edw. Wrottesley Salt 5 Dec. 94
Adjt. & Capt.—G. Chichester,
Captain 2 *Battalion*... ... 27 Feb. 94
Qr. Master.—James Couch,
Hon. Captain ....27 July 81
Med. Off.—

White Facings.

The York and Lancaster Regiment.

3RD BATTALION.
(*Formerly the 3rd West York Light Infantry.*)
Head Quarters, Pontefract.
HONORARY COLONEL.
Major General Frederick Hardy,¹ *retired list* ...... 4 Apr. 88
LT. COLONEL.
John Gerald Wilson, (t), *Hon. Colonel* ....20 Jan. 83
MAJORS.
John Edmund Groom ...... 4 June 92
Luis F. H. C. Morgan-Grenville .... 8 Apr. 93
CAPTAINS.
Grenfell Todd Naylor, *Hon. Major* ....21 Feb. 77
Charles Kean O'Hara, (*H*) 30 Jan. 84
Donald F. D. Maclean, [t],
late 4 Bn. Middlesex Regt. Hon. Major...................29 May 86
Fras. Davison Bland, p.s. (t)30 Oct. 86
Jas. Augustine de Castro, p.s.
late Lt. 6 *West York Mil.* 14 July 88
Chas. Ward Grant, p.s. (*H*),
serving with Gold Coast Constabulary .... 3 Apr. 91
Reginald B. Learoyd, (*H*), [t] 6 May 91
Ernest Fred. Lowthorpe, p.s. 16 Sept. 93
Herbert Morris Bower, p.s.
(*H*), (*T*) ....14 Apr. 94
LIEUTENANTS.
Robert D'Arcy C. Harley,
employed in British Guiana Constabulary .... 4 July 90
Wm. Godwine Robinson, p.s. 12 Nov. 92
Hugh Owen Swanston, p.s. 12 Nov. 92
Musgrave Robert Hall, p.s. 12 Nov. 92
Frederick Adrian Cathcart 12 Nov. 92
Wm. Scobie MacKenzie, p.s. 12 Nov. 92
James Ernest Forster, *p.s.*,
(*H*), *Inst. of Musketry* ...29 Apr. 93
John Francis Coston ....17 Mar. 94
Christian F. Hales Rumbold,
p.s. .... 5 May 94
Percy Frederick Hunt ...... 2 July 94
Philip Edmund Vaughan...20 Feb. 95
SECOND LIEUTENANTS.
Harold Philip Muir White 17 Mar. 94
Francis H. D. Vickerman...26 Sept. 94
Fred. Jas. Osbaldeston Montagu................. 9 Feb. 95
Robert Ronald Henderson 6 Feb. 95.
Adj. & Capt.—C. K. Colhoun,
Major 1 *Battalion* .... 9 Mar. 92
Qr. Master.—Robert Fitz-Patrick, *Hon. Captain* ... 1 Apr. 83
Med. Off.—

White Facings.

The Durham Light Infantry.

3RD BATTALION.
(*Formerly the 1st Durham Fusiliers.*)
Head Quarters, Barnard Castle.
HONORARY COLONEL.
Charles Freville Surtees,
late Capt. 3 *Hussars*......15 Mar. 73
LT. COLONEL.
Richard B. Wilson, [t], *Hon. Colonel*.................. 3 July 93
MAJORS.
James Allison, [t] *Hon. Lt. Colonel*..................18 June 90
Edw. S. V. Grinshawe, *p.s.* 3 July 93
CAPTAINS.
Henry Powys Greenwood,
(*H*) *p.s.* ....29 Oct. 87
James Brooke Fairbairn,
(t), *p.s.* ....27 June 88
Thomas George Sowerby... 2 Mar. 89
Harry John Sowerby ...... 8 Nov. 90
Herbert de Mussenden Leathes .... 8 Nov. 92
Philip Thurstane B. Basset,
p.s. .... 4 Nov. 93
Louis Edward Walker ...... 4 Nov. 93
William Hilton Briggs...... 4 Nov. 93

P P

Militia Infantry.

LIEUTENANTS.
Hy. Siward Baliol Sartees..30 Jan. 92
Owen M. Powell, p.s. (T),
  lateCapt.19Middlesex R.V. 2 Apr. 92
Fonton Weiss Graham ......21 July 94
George Douglas Lister ......21 July 94
William Gowans ......21 July 94
Edw. Chaytor Sowerby......21 July 94
Hon. Malcolm Bowes-Lyon21 July 94
  SECOND LIEUTENANTS.
Robert Whitbread ....23 Apr. 94
David Lloyd Brereton ......12 Sept. 94
Rodolph Feilden...............31 Oct. 94
Henry Frederic Low........ 9 Jan. 95
Edward Burnaby Thresher13 Feb. 95
Adjt. & Capt.—R. Eccles,
  Major Oxford Lt. Inf...... 2 May 92
Qr. Master.—Jas. A. Parkes,
  Hon. Lieut. ....31 Dec. 87
Med. Off. — Surgeon Lt.Col.
  James Munro, MD........ 1 Dec. 91

White Facings.

4TH BATTALION.
(Formerly the 2nd or North Durham Militia.)
Head Quarters, Newcastle.
  HONORARY COLONEL.
James J. Allison, CB........20 Aug. 92
  LT. COLONEL.
Edw. Leadbitter Smith, p.s.,
  Hon. Colonel ....15 Oct. 92
  MAJORS.
Alfred Reid, p.s. (H), Hon.
  Lt. Colonel ....10 Oct. 91
Mark H. Lambert, p.s.(H),[t] 12 Nov. 92
  CAPTAINS.
Thomas Lockhart, p.s. [t]
  Hon. Major..............17 Aug. 81
W. Mackay Stanford, p.s.,[t]20 Oct. 83
Ernest Frederick Gales, p.s.15 June 85
Nathan Horn Scott, p.s. ...23 June 86
Herbert M. Greenwell, p.s. 25 Apr. 88
Chas. Thurston. Fogg-Elliot 19 Nov. 92
Richard Henry W. Cardiff 19 Nov. 92
Charles Fred. Linisell,[1] late
  Scots Fusiliers, serving under the Colonial Office....... 7 Oct. 93
  LIEUTENANTS.
Douglas Henry Garden......10 Oct. 91
Chas. Edgar Shuttleworth 4 Nov. 93
John Cyril May .... 4 Nov. 93
William Ernest Rogerson...17 Oct. 94
Thomas Hodgson ....17 Oct. 94
Charles S. Dudlow Wildes17 Oct. 94
  SECOND LIEUTENANTS.
Edward Francis Green ...31 Oct. 94
William Joseph Roskell ...30 Jan. 95
Gaspard Fred. de Pledge,.. 6 Feb. 95
Adjt. & Capt.—C. N. Evelegh,
  Capt. Duke of Cornwall's
  Lt. Inf. ....19 Feb. 95
Qr. Master.—Joseph Magee
  Byrne, Hon. Lieut.........24 June 85
  White Facings.

The Highland Light Infantry.
3RD AND 4TH BATTALIONS.
(Formerly the 1st Royal Lanark Militia.)
Head Quarters, Hamilton.
  HONORARY COLONEL.
W. A. L. S. Duke of Hamilton and Brandon, KT. ...13 Mar. 78
  LT. COLONEL COMMANDANT.
John W. Thackeray, late
  Lt. 41 F. Hon. Colonel ... 4 Aug. 88
  LIEUTENANT COLONEL.
Wm. Fred. Story, Hon. Col. 24 Oct. 88
  MAJORS.
Fra. John Oathwaite, p.s.
  (t), Hon. Lt. Colonel .....30 Jan. 86
Thomas S. G. H. Robertson-Aikman, p.s. ....24 Oct. 88
Henry Lucas St. G. Stewart,
  late Lt. 74 Ft .... 2 July 90
Jas. Otway Graham Toler,
  late Captain 2nd Battalion;
  Hon. Lt. Colonel ....30 June 94
  CAPTAINS.
William Lindsay Stewart, 21 Nov. 85
G. E. Blake-Aughton, p.s.
  (H), Inst. of Musketry,
  Hon. Major .... 9 May 81
Edwin Awdry Everett ......16 June 88
Jocelyn Henry Cramer, p.s.
  (H), serving with Gold Coast
  Constabulary .... 4 May 89

Gilbert Alex. Pagan,[1] ret.
  pay Northumberland Fus.
  Hon. Major .... 30 Dec. 91
Frank John M'Ewan........16 Jan. 92
Chas. J. G. Mounsey Grant16 Jan. 92
Thomas Smijth O'Dell ......16 Jan. 92
John Hamilton E. Allen,
  late Lt. Royal Navy, Hon.
  Major ....30 May 92
Arch. O. Lyttelton Kindersley,
  serving with the Irregular
  Force in the Niger Coast
  Protectorate ....17 Sept. 92
Harry R. R. R. Cuninghame 24 Sept. 92
Chas. D. Hopwood, p.s. (H),
  Assistant Inspector Gold
  Coast Constabulary ...... 4 Feb. 93
Reginald H. Parkinson, late
  Lieut. South Stafford Regt.,
  Hon. Major ....13 Apr. 89
Thomas Ulric Thynne, late
  Lt. Royal Navy, Hon. Maj. 28 Oct. 93
Robert Greig, (1), late Maj.
  3 Brig. Scottish Division;
  Hon. Major ....15 Oct. 87
Duncan F. Robertson-Aikman, late Lt. 13 Hussars 29 July 94
Launcelot C. E. Wyndham14 Nov. 94
HughH. Robertson-Aikman,
  ret. pay 1 Dragoons ......27 Feb. 95
  LIEUTENANTS.
Aubrey C. Bertram Ingle 11 Mar. 91
Claude Roderick Morrison 13 Feb. 92
John Lovett H. Bennett ...11 June 92
Hon. Alex. G. A. Hore-Ruthven ....27 Apr. 93
Charles A. Murray Lyon-Campbell .... 5 July 93
Andrew Gillon .... 5 July 93
Archibald Wilson Jones, (H),
  Instructor of Musketry...... 5 July 93
  SECOND LIEUTENANTS.
William Basil Chas. Bridge 23 Sept. 93
Marcus S. Beresford Gubbins 11 Nov. 93
Alex. Richard Chancellor...18 Nov. 93
William Mearns .... 6 Jan. 94
Wm. Frederick Hamilton 27 Jan. 94
William Eric Segrave ...... 2 Apr. 94
James Finlay Anderson ...13 Apr. 94
Reginald H. Foster-Barham ....12 Dec. 94
Adjts. & Capts.—E. W. M.
M. Edwards, Capt. 1 Bn. 1 Jan. 92
A. F. Evans-Lombe, Capt.
  1 Bn. .... 1 Jan. 95
Qr. Master.—William Mackinnon,[5] Hon. Captain ...27 Feb. 84
Med. Off.—

Yellow Facings.

Seaforth Highlanders
(Ross-shire Buffs, The Duke of Albany's).
3RD BATTALION.
(Formerly the Highland Rifle Militia.)
Head Quarters, Dingwall.
  HONORARY COLONEL.
  LT. COLONEL.
Alex. C. Macleay, p.s. (t),
  Hon. Colonel .... 2 Mar. 82
  MAJORS.
Sir Hector Munro, Bart. p.s.
  Hon. Lt. Colonel ......25 Mar. 85
James H. Henderson, p.s.
  Hon. Major ....17 Dec. 92
  CAPTAINS.
Edw. Wm. Horne, late Lt.
  1 Bn. Highland Light Inf.
  Hon. Major ....11 Nov. 82
Henry Robert Baird, Hon.
  Major .... 5 July 84
Evan Sinclair Wemyss, p.s. 8 Feb. 90
Charles L. Doneton Monro,
  serving with the Bechuanaland Border Police ......20 Nov. 91
John Baillie Rose, p.s. ......21 Nov. 91
William Ingham Whitaker,
  p.s. ....22 Mar. 92
Hugh Davidson,[1] (H), late
  Capt. 2 Bn. Hon. Major...23 Mar. 92
Hercules Langford Brown,
  ....17 Mar. 94
Ranald J. M. Livingston-Macdonald, p.s. .... 4 Apr. 94

LIEUTENANTS.
James Menteith Middlemist,
  (H), serving with Gold
  Coast Constabulary ......11 Mar. 91
James Ernest Bayne ....21 Nov. 91
Hugh Middleton Ingle, p.s.
  Instructor of Musketry ...16 Jan. 92
Hy. Aug. Nugent Rose, p.s. 5 Nov. 92
John Charles Clarke, p.s. ... 6 May 93
Gilbert Robertson .... 4 Apr. 94
Walter Gabriel Home ...... 4 Apr. 94
  SECOND LIEUTENANTS.
Archibald Gordon Bruce ...19 Jan. 94
Alexander Horne............24 Oct. 94
Adam Robertson Stark ...16 Jan. 95
Adjt. & Capt.—H. S. Barlow,
  Major 2 Battalion.........10 May 93
Qr. Master.—Robert R. Lander,[3] Hon. Lieut............. 6 Oct. 86
Med. Off.—Surgeon Major J.
  Corbett .... 6 May 69

Yellow Facings.

The Gordon Highlanders.
3RD BATTALION.
(Formerly the Royal Aberdeenshire Highlanders.)
Head Quarters, Aberdeen.
  HONORARY COLONEL.
Field Marshal H.R.H. the
  Prince of Wales, KG. KT.
  KP. GCB. GCSI. GCMG.
  GCIE...............20 Nov. 72
  LT. COLONELS.
John Alexander Man,[1] (H),
  (S), Hon. Colonel, Commandant Local Forces,
  Trinidad and Tobago ...... 1 Feb. 89
Rt. Hon. A. H. T. Earl of
  Kintore, GCMG. Hon. Col.,
  Governor of South Australia 17 Oct. 91
Robert T. Caldwell, p.s. (T),
  Hon. Colonel ....17 Oct. 91
  MAJORS.
A. W. F. Lord Saltoun, late
  Major Gren. Guards ... 7 May 90
W. J. B. Stewart-Menzies, p.s.13 Apr. 92
  CAPTAINS.
Geo. Cosmo Abercromby,[3]
  (H), (t) ret. pay Manchester
  Regt., Hon. Major ....27 June 88
William Thomas Reid ......25 May 89
Cecil W. Kennard ....14 Mar. 91
Jas. Grant Malcolmson, p.s.
  (H) Instructor of Musketry 9 May 92
Alex. Hy. Leith, late Lt.
  Welsh Regt............... 3 Feb. 94
Charles Frederick Whitley-Deans-Dundas .... 5 May 94
Egbert Caldwell Cooper, p.s.
  (H), Assistant Inspector
  Gold Coast Constabulary... 7 Nov. 94
Jas. Ochoncar Forbes, p.s. 7 Nov. 94
  LIEUTENANTS.
Gambier Middleton .... 9 May 92
Arthur Abercromby Duff 6 Jan. 94
Hamilton Gatliff ....10 Oct. 94
James Johnston Fergusson10 Oct. 94
Robt. Michael Douglas Fox10 Oct. 94
Jn. Douglas Dalrymple-Hay10 Oct. 94
  SECOND LIEUTENANTS.
Alex. Edw. Forbes Morison17 Feb. 94
Ian R. I. Foster Forbes ...10 Oct. 94
Ian D. M. Lord Inverarie... 2 Jan. 95
Robt. Hamilton Kemp..... 2 Jan. 95
Adjt. & Capt.—C. H. Payne,
  Major 2 Battalion .... 1 May 90
Qr. Master.—Jas. Ross,[5] Hon.
  Captain .... 1 May 82
Med. Off.—Surg. Lt. Col. C.
  M. Macquibban, MD. ... 1 Dec. 91

Yellow Facings.

The Queen's Own Cameron Highlanders.
2ND BATTALION.
(Formerly the Highland Light Infantry Militia.)
Head Quarters, Inverness.
  LIEUTENANT COLONEL.
John Andrew Macdonald,
  Hon. Colonel .... 7 Sept. 87

Militia Infantry.

MAJORS.
Alfred D. Macintosh of Macintosh, *p.s., late Lt.* 71 *F.; Hon. Lt. Colonel*......17 Apr. 89
Colin L. M'Kenzie ....27 Aug. 92

CAPTAINS.
Robt.Arth.Paterson (*H*),[*t*]19 May 88
Charles Duncan Stewart ...13 Apr. 89
Joseph H. F. Radcliffe ......13 Apr. 89
Arth. Baird Douglas(*t*), *p.s.*
Hon. Major ....26 June 79
Wm. R. Dalziel Mackenzie, *p.s.* ....15 Aug. 91
Norman MacLeod,[1] *Hon. Major* ....23 Apr. 92
Kenneth J. Mackenzie,[2] *ret. pay Rifle Brigade*....... 4 May 92
ÆneasNormanMackintosh, *Aide de Camp to Colonel E. H. D. Macpherson, p.s.*29 Oct. 92
Hon. Arthur Hay,[3] *late Lt. Scots Guards* .... 8 June 94

LIEUTENANTS.
J. Y. M. *Lord Abinger* ...... 9 Aug. 90
Montagu J. Grant-Peterkin 15 Aug. 91
Archibald Wm. M'Donald 4 May 92
Wm. Eneas Mackintosh ...27 Aug. 92
Ronald Hugh Brodie........27 Aug. 92
Bernard S. Cuddon Fletcher 7 Apr. 94
Arthur D. Forbes-Gordon 22 Aug. 94
George Alastair Chas. Davy 22 Aug. 94
Jas. Sidgreaves Macdonell 22 Aug. 94

SECOND LIEUTENANTS.
David Price Haig .... 1 Mar. 93
Edw. Baskerville Mackenzie 1 Mar. 93
Cecil George de Pré ....10 Apr. 93
Douglas N. O. Capel Miers.24 Feb. 94
Wm. Robert Macpherson...19 Sept. 94
William Mosse Macdonald 20 Mar. 95
Adjt. & Capt.—T. A. Mackenzie, *Capt.* 1 *Battalion* 3 Nov. 90
Qr. Master.—John Emslie,[5] *Hon. Lieut.* ....13 Apr. 87
Med. Off.—*Surg. Lt. Colonel* Duncan M'Fadyen ...... 2 May 93

Blue Facings.

The Royal Irish Rifles,
3RD BATTALION.
(*Formerly the Royal North Down Rifles.*)
Head Quarters, Newtown Ards.

HONORARY COLONEL.
Marquis of Dufferin and Ava, *KP. GCB. GCSI. GCMG.* ......18 Jan. 65

LT.-COLONEL.
John M'Cance, *p.s. Hon. Colonel* .... 2 Dec. 93

MAJORS.
Daniel Louis Delacherois, (*H*), *late Lieut.* 4 *Hussars; Hon. Lt. Colonel*........... 5 Dec. 91
Robt. G. Sharman-Crawford, *late Capt.* 16 *Lancers* ......22 Aug. 94

CAPTAINS.
Francis Findlay, *p.s. Hon. Major* .... 1 Sept. 83
Edward Tatton Pakenham, *ret. pay King's R. Rifles, Hon. Major* ....19 Dec. 88
Stuart Alex. Menzies,[3] *late Capt. Seaforth Highlanders, Hon. Major* ....28 Sept. 89
Charles Dennis O'Callaghan 12 June 91
John Chas. Fitzmaurice Finn 43 Dec. 91
Robert Curzon Newton, *late Lieut.* 5 *Dragoon Gds.*......18 May 92
Edwin C. Oppenheim ....24 June 93
Wm. Arthur Chas. Mills, (*H*), *Inst. of Musketry* ... 3 Mar. 94

LIEUTENANT.
Daniel Dixon ....16 Sept. 93
James Frederick Humby ...16 Sept. 93
Geo. Alex. M. Kirkpatrick 16 Sept. 93

SECOND LIEUTENANTS.
James Rosborough........... 8 June 93
Lord Fred. T. Hamilton-Blackwood..................28 June 93
Blyth Ritchie .... 3 Feb. 94
Sydney O. Rowan-Hamilton 12 Dec. 94
Adjt. & Capt.—Edw. Allen, *Capt. Irish Rifles,*..........1 Feb. 94
Qr. Master.—Abraham Pecknold, *Hon. Lieut.* ....13 June 94
Med. Off.—

Dark Green Facings.

4TH BATTALION.
(*Formerly the Queen's Royal Rifles.*)
Head Quarters, Belfast.

HONORARY COLONEL.
Sir Fras. Edm. Macnaghten, *Bart.*[1] *late* 8 *Hussars* 1 Feb. 90

LT. COLONEL.
Edw. Vandeleur, *late Capt.* 2 *Dragoon Guards, p.s. Hon. Colonel* .... 5 Dec. 91

MAJORS.
Jas. Alexander Whitla, *late Lieut. Inniskilling Fus.* ...23 July 92
John Alex. Montgomery ...13 Mar. 95

CAPTAINS.
John H. Reginald Cox,[6](*H*), *ret. pay* 6 *Dragoons, Hon. Major* ....23 May 91
Ernest Carrington Arnold, *p.s.* .... 6 Feb. 92
Chas. Stephenson Murray 23 July 92
Wilfred Stanley Sharpe, late Lt. 6 *Dragoons, Inspector SierraLeoneFrontierPolice*17 June 93
Crawford Singleton Donnelly....................17 Mar. 94
Francis Jas. Montgomery 31 Oct. 94
Ashworth Peter M. Burke, *late Lt.* 1 *Battalion*.........28 Nov. 94
Robert Dixon, *Hon. Major, late Major* 2 *Vol. Bn. West Surrey Regiment* .... 5 Dec. 94

LIEUTENANTS.
Walter E. Carson M'Cammond 3 Sept.92
Jas. Madgewick Wilcocks 3 Sept.92
John Patrick.................. 3 Sept.92
Arthur G. Catton-Watson 10 June 93
James Ferguson..............31 Oct. 94
Charles Stewart Dixon......31 Oct. 94
Ed. Brownlow D. Chichester 31 Oct. 94
Kenneth Wm. Macnaghten 14 Nov. 94

SECOND LIEUTENANTS.
Charles Brownlow Strutt...12 Mar. 94
Audley S. Thos. John Leary 13 Feb. 95
Adjt. & Capt.—W. H. Dunlop, *Capt.* 1 *Battalion* ...... 2 Mar. 93
Qr. Mr.—John Foley, *Hon. Lieut.* ....17 Aug. 92
Med. Off.—

Dark Green Facings.

5TH BATTALION.
(*Formerly the Royal South Down Light Infantry.*)
Head Quarters, Downpatrick.

HONORARY COLONEL.
William Brownlow Forde, *late of* 67 *F., JP. DL.* 7 Sept.81

LIEUTENANT COLONEL.
Thos. Andrew M'Cammon, *Hon. Colonel* .... 8 Dec. 92

MAJORS.
Hon. Hy. Lyle Mulholland, *late Lt. R. Engineers* ...... 1 Nov. 90
Robert Hugh Wallace, (*H*) 24 Dec. 92

CAPTAINS.
Samuel S. F. Warren, *Hon. Major* .... 8 Aug. 83
William George Forde ......29 Nov. 90
Andrew Munro Ross (*H*), *late Lt. Black Watch, Instructor of Musketry* ..... 3 Jan. 91
Nicholas A. Delacherois-Crommelin...................21 Jan. 93
James Maidment Morrison 12 June 93
Randal Wm. Johnston, *late Capt. K.O. Scottish Bords.* 2 Sept.93
Arthur Norman Wilkinson 8 Aug. 94

LIEUTENANTS.
Thomas Hughes ....19 Oct. 89
Thomas V. Plaisted M'Cammon .... 4 Oct. 93
Waldegrave Percy Thompson 4 Oct. 93
Charles Henry Edye .... 4 Oct. 93
Gerald E. H. Barrett-Hamilton........................... 3 Feb. 94
Percy Hamilton Short ...... 8 Aug. 94

SECOND LIEUTENANTS.
Lennox G. Brydges Rodney 19 Sept.94
Douglas Moncrieff Govan 28 Nov. 94
Adjt. & Capt.—A. C. D. Spencer, *Capt.* 1 *Bn.*...... 1 Feb. 95

Qr. Mr.—Samuel M'Clonahan, *Hon. Lieut.* .... 7 Apr. 86
Med. Off.—*Surgeon Major* Edwin F. Nelson, *MD.*... 1 Aug. 70

Dark Green Facings.

6TH BATTALION.
(*Formerly the Louth Rifles.*)
Head Quarters, Dundalk.

HONORARY COLONEL.
Sir John S. Robinson, *Bart., CB. JP. late Lieut.* 60 *Rifles* ....26 Nov. 84

LT. COLONEL.
Matthew Robert Murphy, *Hon. Colonel* ....22 Oct. 84

MAJORS.
Harry Wm. Jamieson, *Hon. Lt. Colonel* ....26 June 86
Matthew John D'Arcy ......27 Aug. 87

CAPTAINS.
Alexander Henry............25 Mar. 85
Matthew C. E. Fortescue... 6 Mar. 86
Chas. Gerald Harris,[5] [*t*], (*H*), *ret. pay* 1 *Bn.. Inst. of Musketry, Hon. Major* 10 Oct. 88
John Cecil Thornhill ....13 April 89
John P. F. Macartney Filgate 14 July 89
Kelynge Greenway, jun...26 Sept. 91
Sidney Partis Borman......20 Aug. 92
Charles O'Brien Jameson...19 Sept.94

LIEUTENANTS.

SECOND LIEUTENANTS.
Percy Wallace, Jun. .... 9 Apr. 94
Wm. F. Colborne Garstin...15 Aug. 94
Adjt. & Capt.—A. T. Swaine, *Major* 1 *Battalion* ......16 May 92
Qr. Master.—Thos. Pike, *Hon. Lieut.* .... 7 Apr. 86

Dark Green Facings.

Princess Victoria's (Royal Irish Fusiliers).
3RD BATTALION.
(*Formerly the Armagh Light Infantry.*)
Head Quarters, Armagh.

HONORARY COLONEL.
Hon. Edw. Brownlow,[1] *late Lt. and Capt. Scots Guards* 7 Oct. 67

LT. COLONEL.
Robt. Cuming, *late Capt.* 99 *F. Hon. Colonel* ....13 June 92

MAJORS.
James Robert Jameson...... 2 Apr. 90
Henry Holden,[2] *p.s.* ....13 Aug. 92

CAPTAINS.
Arthur B. R. Kaye,[3] *Comdt. of Constabulary, British Honduras, Hon. Major* ... 29 Oct. 87
William C. FitzGerald (*H*) 29 Oct. 87
Francis Henry Murray ..... 3 Oct. 88
Percy Harland Atkin.........25 May 89
Matthew Boyd Bredon, p.s. *Hon. Major; serving in the Chinese Customs Service* ...19 May 91
Cecil Cromwell Collier ...... 4 Oct. 91
Wm. H. Alex. Theed ....13 Aug. 92
Clifford Cullen, *ret. pay Derbyshire Regt. Instructor of Musketry* .... 2 Nov. 92
Edw. Colburn Mayne, *p.s.*(*H*)10 May 93
Charles Edmund Pearson 17 June 93

LIEUTENANTS.
Robert Arthur Lidwill ...... 4 Oct. 93
James Edwards Harden ... 4 Oct. 93
John Lawrence Lawlor...... 4 Oct. 93
Charles Fred. Drielsma..... 4 Oct. 93
Reginald Osborne Fraser 4 Oct. 93
Chs. Home Douglas St. Clair 4 Oct. 93
William Dundas Dooner ...12 Sept.94

SECOND LIEUTENANTS.
John Charles Angell ....10 Feb. 94
Henry Charles Upton ......19 May 94
Christopher F. Maitland Lilly, *late Lt.* 3 *Hussars*...24 Oct. 94
Walter Hughes Ferrar......20 Feb. 95
Adjutant & Capt.—C. S. Kincaid, *Capt.* 2 *Bn.* ......22 Aug. 91
Qr. Master.—Nathaniel John Drewin, *Hon. Lieut.* ......17 Dec. 81
Med. Off.—

Blue Facings.

P P 2

Militia Infantry.

4TH BATTALION.
(Formerly the Cavan Militia.)
Head Quarters, Cavan.

HONORARY COLONEL.
Gerald Richard Dease,
*Chamberlain to the Lord
Lieut. of Ireland* ....19 Dec. 94

LT.COLONEL.
Sir Robert A. Hodson, *Bt. p.s.* 2 Dec. 93

MAJORS.
Edmund J. C. Dease ....28 Apr. 94

CAPTAINS.
William H. Malcolmson ...18 Aug. 86
Edgar J. Mayor, *p. s.* [*t*]
 Hon. Major...................31 July 86
John Douglas Hamilton,
 *late Lt. 14 Hussars, Assist.
 Insp. Lagos Constabulary* 25 Feb. 93
Herbert Hart, *Hon. Major*...12 Apr. 93
Charles Cecil Keenan ......25 May 93
Wm. W. Fras. Molony ....11 July 94
Wm. Joseph Hamilton ...... 2 Jun. 95

LIEUTENANTS.
Robert Sydney Mills.........17 May 93
Wilfrid Hubert Wild ....18 Apr. 94
Arthur T. C. Rundle ....18 Apr. 94
Allen R. Betham Shuttleworth ....16 Jan. 95
Alex. Ey. C. MacGregor ...16 Jan. 95
Eustace Malim Harris ......16 Jan. 95

SECOND LIEUTENANTS.
Harvey George de M. Prior 19 Sept. 94
Alex. L. Jos. Miller Kelly 13 Feb. 95
Adjt. & Capt.—C.U. Sandys,
 Captain 1 Battalion .... 1 Dec. 93
Qr. Master.—Jn. Watkins,[8]
 Hon. Captain ....30 Apr. 79
Med. Off.—

Blue Facings.

5TH BATTALION.
(Formerly the Monaghan Militia.)
Head Quarters, Monaghan.

HONORARY COLONEL.
Sir Thos. Oriel Forster, *Bart.
CB., late Captain 77 Foot* 26 Nov. 84

LT.COLONEL.
John Leslie,[6] *late Lt. Grenadier Guards*...................18 Apr. 91

MAJORS.
Wm. H. Broughton, *p.s.* [*t*]
 Hon. Lt. Colonel... ....21 May 94

CAPTAINS.
Cecil Hamilton Browne...... 3 Oct. 85
Charles William Hall, (*H*) 21 Jan. 88
Hon. Peter Westenra ...... 3 Oct. 91
J.C. Waterhouse Madden, *p.s.* 24 Oct. 91
C. A. Owen-Lewis ....13 Jan. 94

LIEUTENANTS.
Ricardo Adolfo Robinson... 4 Feb. 91
Fras. Berry Fetherstonhaugh ....24 Oct. 91
Jn. Jas. Davidge Cleminson,
 p.s. ....11 May 92
Victor Robt. Beatty West 11 May 92
Edward John Richardson 12 Sept. 94
Herbert Greenough Woolf,
 p.s. (*H*), *Inst. of Musketry* 30 Jan. 95

SECOND LIEUTENANTS.
Roger Walter Strickland...27 Feb. 92
William Henry Annesley...31 Jan. 94
William Haire-Forster ...... 6 Feb. 95
Adj. & Capt.—W.H.P. Plomer,
 Captain 2 Battalion ......24 Mar. 90
Qr. Master. — Matthew
 Toobey, *Hon. Lieut.* ....25 Oct. 93
Med. Off.—

Blue Facings.

The Connaught Rangers.
3RD BATTALION.
(Formerly the South Mayo Rifles and the North Mayo Militia.)
Head Quarters, Castlebar.

HONORARY COLONELS.
Geo. Marq. of Sligo, *DL, JP.* 5 July 41
Charles H. C. Knox, *late Capt. 8 Hussars*.............29 July 85

LT.COLONEL.
Maurice C. J. Blake, *p.s.*,
 Hon. Colonel ....31 Jan. 85

MAJORS.

CAPTAINS.
Henry Bourke Jordan ......17 Sept. 87
Maurice Owen O'Conor......28 June 90
David Ruttledge ....27 June 92
Victor Fred. Finlay Malley,
 (*H*), *Inst. of Musketry* ...25 Nov. 93

LIEUTENANTS.
Henry Howe Cuffe Knox...19 Mar. 92
Thos. B. G. Fairfax Eames 19 Mar. 92
Audley Charles Pratt........25 Nov. 93
Hon. John M. V. J. ffrench 9 June 94

SECOND LIEUTENANTS.
John H. N. Hamilton Burke 7 Oct. 93
Ernest Cecil Cochrane...... 3 Mar. 94
Francis Osborne Bowen ...20 Mar. 95
Adjts. & Capts.—A. W. D.
 Maclean, *Captain 2 Bn.*...17 Aug. 92
Paymast.—Stanhope Kenny 23 Feb. 55
Qr. Master.—Jas. M'Nally,
 Hon. Lieut. .... 6 June 94
Medical Officers.— Surgeon
 Major G. W. Hatchell ...11 Apr. 71
Surg. Lt. Col. Thos. Allman 23 Apr. 92

Green Facings.

4TH BATTALION.
(Formerly the Galway Militia.)
Head Quarters, Galway.

HONORARY COLONEL.
John Archer Daly ....11 July 91

LT.COLONEL.
Rich. Lynch Staunton ......19 Feb. 90

MAJORS.
George Patrick Chevers,
 Hon. Lt. Colonel..............16 June 90

CAPTAINS.
James Fras. Jameson, *late
 Lt. 7 Dragoon Guards,
 Hon. Major* ....27 Jan. 83
John Robert Lopdell, *p.s.* 14 May 87
E. Melvill Rennie Brewer,(*H*),
 p.s. ....4 June 90
Anderson L. Kelly, *late Capt.
 7 Hussars* .... 2 Apr. 92
John J. Chevers ....19 Sept. 94
Robert William Smyth......19 Sept. 94

LIEUTENANTS.
John C. Rennie Brewer,
 p.s. (*H*), *Inst. of Musketry* 11 June 92
William L. C. N. de K.
 Fitzgerald-Kenney ....11 June 92
Willoughby Chaplin Newton 22 Apr. 93
Percival Hedley Anderson 22 Apr. 93

SECOND LIEUTENANTS.
Fras. A. Emilio Dolmage... 4 Feb. 93
Percy J. Victor MacDermot 10 Feb. 94
Arthur Corrie Lewin .... 3 Mar. 94
Richard Garratt ....12 Sept. 94

Adjt.—R. N. A. Flanagan,
 Captain Irish Regt. .... 1 Jan. 95
Qr. Master.—Robert York,
 Hon. Lieut. ....29 Apr. 91
Med. Off.—

Green Facings.

5TH BATTALION.
(Formerly the Roscommon Militia.)
Head Quarters, Boyle.

HONORARY COLONEL.
Arthur, Lord De Freyne ...10 Aug. 89

LT.COLONEL.
Caleb Robertson,[1] *late Capt.
 88 Foot; Hon. Colonel* ...27 Apr. 89

MAJORS.
Hon. E. N. *Earl of* Kingston,
 Hon. Lt. Colonel..............13 Aug. 92
Thos. Y. L. Kirkwood, *Hon.
 Lt. Colonel* .... 2 Dec. 93

CAPTAINS.
John F. C. Beare..............22 Sept. 88
Wm. Lloyd (*H*), *Hon. Major* 14 Mar. 85
Michael J. Balfe, *Hon. Major* 1 Feb. 90
Hon. Richard P. French,
 Hon. Major .... 1 Feb. 90
Leslie Tulnell Peacocke .. 29 June 91
Basil Phibbs ....29 June 91
John Wynne Smith ....20 Aug. 92
Dayrell T. Hammond,[2] *ret.
 pay 1 Bn., Hon. Major* ...13 Jan. 94

LIEUTENANTS.
Edw. M. Woulfe Flanagan 2 Aug. 90
William Henry Parke ...... 2 Aug. 90
Francis Glancy .... 3 Oct. 91
Maurice Fitzm. Murray ...13 Aug. 92
Robt. Wm. Geo. Harrison 11 Mar. 93
Clement Joseph Murphy...26 May 94
Joseph O'Beirne ....26 May 94

SECOND LIEUTENANTS.
Frederick Whitfield Barretto 1 Feb. 94
John Hall-Dalwood .... 13 June 94
Adjt. & Capt.—M. G. Moore,
 Major 1 Battalion. .... 4 May 92
Qr. Mr.—Chas. Morrison,[8]
 Hon. Captain .... 8 Feb. 86
Med. Off.—

Green Facings.

Princess Louise's (Argyll and Sutherland Highlanders).
3RD BATTALION.
(Formerly Highland Borderers Lt. Inf.)
Head Quarters, Stirling.

HONORARY COLONEL.

LT.COLONEL.
The Duke of Montrose, *KT.
 late Lt. 5 Lancers, Hon.
 Colonel*...........................22 Oct. 81

MAJORS.
T. Robertson-Chaplin, *p.s.*[*t*],
 Hon. Lt. Colonel .... 8 Dec. 83

CAPTAINS.
Roderick W. Colquhoun, *p.s.
 Hon. Major* ....23 June 83
Sir William Orr-Ewing,
 Bart. p.s., Hon. Major ...19 Jan. 84
Alfred H. Middleton, (*H*),
 *late Capt. 2 Battalion, Hon.
 Major* ....22 Nov. 84
Graeme Alex. L. Whitelaw,
 p.s. .... 6 July 89
J.W. Scott-Plummer, *p.s.* (*t*) 3 May 90
Maxwell Emsley Rouse, *p.s.* 19 May 94

LIEUTENANTS.
Geo. Wm. Jas. C. *Earl of*
 Cardigan .... 9 July 92
Chris. Robt. Alex. Magnay 9 July 92
George Thomson Neilson,
 p.s. (*H*) .... 9 July 92
John Fyfe Jamieson ....18 Mar. 93
Jas. Dunsterville Graham 6 Jan. 94
James Barratt Gillatt ....12 Dec. 94

SECOND LIEUTENANTS.
Allan Bingham Pollok......10 Feb. 94
Geoffrey Goyer Gilligan ...19 Dec. 94

Militia Infantry.

Adjt.—A. Aytoun, *Capt.*1 Bn.19 Sept.92
Qr.Mr.—J. Denholm,³ *Hon.*
Captain ....20 June 87
Med. Off.—

Yellow Facings.

4TH BATTALION.
(*Formerly the Renfrew Militia—Prince of Wales' Royal Regt.*).
Head Quarters, Paisley.

HONORARY COLONEL.
Wm. Cuninghame, *late Capt.*
  11 *Hussars* ....22 Oct. 90

LT.COLONEL.
Archibald Campbell, Lord Blythswood,¹ *late Capt. & Lt. Col. Scots Gds. Hon. Col.*20 Feb. 78

MAJORS.
Arch. C. Drummond Dick, (*H*), *Hon. Lt. Colonel* ...... 1 Nov. 90
Montague D. Campbell, *p.s.* (*H*), *Hon. Lt. Colonel*...... 2 June 94

CAPTAINS.
John Chas. Cunninghame, *Hon. Major* 26 Sept.83
Hon. T. H. A. E. Cochrane, *MP. late Lt. Scots Guards* 26 Sept.83
Hugh Robert Wallace ......26 July 90
Jas. Thos. Scott, *late Capt.*
  1 *Bn. Dublin Fus. Hon. Maj.*29 Apr. 91
Alexander Archibald Speirs 3 Oct. 91
William Mure ....27 Aug. 92
Arthur R. Cole-Hamilton,² *late Scots Fusiliers, Inst. of Musketry, Hon. Major* ...24 Sept.92
Boyd Alex. Cuninghame ... 5 May 94
Louis Gairdner Pearson ...20 Mar. 95

LIEUTENANTS.
Henry H. Houldsworth ...12 Apr. 93
William Hall...............12 Apr. 93
Arthur Grenfell Wauchope 2 Dec. 93
Francis Douglas Farquhar 2 Dec. 93
Reginald J. Ponsonby Cox 2 Dec. 93
D. Churchill Marjoribanks 5 May 94
Walter Herbert Robinson 5 May 94
Barnett Albert Harvey ... 5 May 94

SECOND LIEUTENANTS.
Charles Neil Macdonald ...16 Sept.93
John U. Macdowall Ingilby 14 Oct. 93
James Arthur Moffat ...... 3 Feb. 94
Charles Caryl Clifton ......13 Feb. 95
Hon. Arthur Edw. B. O'Neill 13 Mar. 95
Adjt. & Capt.—A. Foster, *Captain* 1 *Battalion*.........10 Sept.94
Qr.Mr.—Alex. M'Rae, *Hon. Lieut.* .... 1 Apr. 87
Med. Off.—

Yellow Facings.

The Prince of Wales' Leinster Regt. (Royal Canadians).

3RD BATTALION.
(*Formerly the King's County Militia—Royal Rifles.*)
Head Quarters, Birr.

HONORARY COLONEL.
Robert Godolphin Cosby, *late Lt.* 6 *Drs.* .... 4 Nov. 93

LT.COLONEL.
John H. G. Smyth, (*H*).......18 Nov. 93

MAJOR.
W. F. J. P. *Earl of* Huntingdon................... 9 Dec. 93

CAPTAINS.
James W. H. FitzGerald, *late Lt. Berkshire Regt.*... 4 Nov. 91
Edward William Pritchard 22 Oct. 92
Edw. Patrick Smith, *p.s.* ...19 Nov. 92
Charles Thomas Biddulph 9 June 94

LIEUTENANTS.
Rowland H. Tyssen Smyth 9 Dec. 93
Randal Kingsmill Moore... 9 Dec. 93
William Gibson .... 9 Dec. 93

SECOND LIEUTENANTS.
Owen E. Moore Saunders 1 Mar. 93
Hy. Goddington Sheppard 25 May 93
Adjt. & Capt.—S. R. L. White, *Captain* 1 *Battalion* ... 5 Dec. 94
Qr.Master.—H. T. Garnett, *Hon. Lieut.* ....25 Apr. 85
Med. Off.—*Surg. Lt.Colonel* Chas. Baker Stoney, *MB.* 1 Dec. 91

Blue Facings.

4TH BATTALION.
(*Formerly the Queen's County Militia—Royal Rifles.*)
Head Quarters, Maryborough.

HONORARY COLONEL.
L. G. H. S. *Earl of* Portarlington, *p.s. late Lt. Scots Guards* ....24 Feb. 94

LT.COLONEL.
Frederick Kevan Izod ......28 Oct. 93

MAJORS.
Robert Maxwell Marsh ......25 Nov. 93

CAPTAINS.
Anthony Arthur Weldon, *p.s.*27 Aug.87
Theobald E. Woods Willington, *p.s.* ....10 Nov. 88
Richard R. W. Fitz Herbert 8 Jan. 90
Lancelot Croasdaile, *ret. pay Bedford Regt., Instructor of Musketry, Hon. Major* 1 Nov. 90
Dudley Colley Palmer ...... 5 Aug. 93
Thomas R. A. Stannus, (*H*) 2 June 94

LIEUTENANTS.
Francis Marsh ....13 Feb. 92
Geoffrey Hy. J. S. Smyth 19 Nov. 92
Derrick Alfred Carden......16 Sept.92
Chas. S. Musgrave Trench 7 July 94

SECOND LIEUTENANTS.
Hon. Chas. Hy. S. Monck 30 Jan. 95
Theobold William Butler-Kearney ....20 Feb. 95
Adjt.& Capt.—Geo. Hastings Brooke, *late Lt.* 48 *F.*, *Hon. Major* ....23 Oct. 75
Qr.Master.—Chas. Holden, *Hon. Lieut.* ....17 Dec. 81
Med. Off.—*Surg. Lt.Colonel* Dav. Jacob, *MD.* .... 1 Dec. 91

Blue Facings.

5TH BATTALION.
(*Formerly the Royal Meath Militia.*)
Head Quarters, Navan.

HONORARY COLONEL.
Hon. H. L. B. Rowley ......25 Oct. 90

LT.COLONEL.
Henry Stuart Johnston, *Hon. Colonel* .... 8 Nov. 90

MAJORS.
John P. Kearney, *Hon. Lt.Colonel* .... 7 Jan. 91

CAPTAINS.
Sinclair E. de Satgé-de Thoren, *p.s., Hon. Major*20 May 76
Chas. Pepper, *Hon. Major* 6 Aug. 79
Gustavus F. W. Lambart, *Hon. Major* .... 7 Aug. 79
Nugent Talbot Everard, *Hon. Major* ....15 Oct. 81
Wm. E. A. Barry, *p.s.* (*H*), [*t*], *Hon. Major, Inst. of Musketry* ....12 June 86
Richard Taylor Woods (*H*), *Hon. Major* ....26 May 94

LIEUTENANTS.
Edw. F. Jenico J. Farrell...17July 86
James Tottenham Butler 24 June 93
Richard William Everard 12 Sept.94
Edmund James Jameson...13 Mar. 95

SECOND LIEUTENANTS.
Robt. Hugh Morgan-Tighe 30 May 94
Jas. Geo. Richd. Lambart 4 June 94
Claude M. Bruce Hamilton 6 Mar. 95
Adjt.& Capt.—G. J. D. Browne, *Captain* 2 *Battalion* .... 2 Jan. 93
Qr.Mr.—Samuel Preston, *Hon. Lieut.* .... 2 Mar. 87
Med. Off.—

Blue Facings.

The Royal Munster Fusiliers.

3RD BATTALION.
(*Formerly the South Cork Light Infantry.*)
Head Quarters, Kinsale.

HONORARY COLONEL.
Hon. H. B. Bernard............ 5 July 76

LT.COLONEL.
Sir Aug. Riversdale Warren,¹ *Bart., late Major* 20 *F. Hon. Colonel* .... 6 July 65

MAJORS.
Fred. Wm. Bell, *Hon. Lt. Colonel*................ 9 Jan. 86
George Lucas, (*H*) ....12 Dec. 94

CAPTAINS.
Richard W. Cooper .... 5 Sept. 83
John Edward H. Herrick ...13 Sept.84
Morgan Wm. O'Donovan...13 Sept.84
Albert Louis Coppinger ... 7 Nov. 85
Thomas Romayne Sarsfield 4 Sept.86
Ludlow S. H. Payne, *late Lieut.* 61 *Foot* ....10 Mar. 88
Byam M. Loveday Roberts 28 Apr. 94

LIEUTENANTS.
Edward Osborne Sealy Allen 4 Sept 89
Wm. John H. M'Corquodaler 7 June 91
John M'Namara ....23 Jan. 92
Hy. Geo. Lindsay Davidson 6 Feb. 91
Chris. Copinger Mahony 21 Jan. 93
Thomas Arthur Clarke...... 7 Oct. 93
Wm. Delacour Beamish ...21 Apr. 94
Chudleigh Garvice............19 Sept. 94

SECOND LIEUTENANTS.
George Wensley C. Soden 8 May 94
Harold George Richardson 10 Oct. 94
Adjt. & Capt.—W. B. Butler-Creagh, *Maj. York Lt. Inf.*17 Aug. 91
Qr. Master. - Thos. Shattock, *Hon. Captain*............ 4 Dec. 89

Blue Facings.

4TH BATTALION.
(*Formerly the Kerry Militia.*)
Head Quarters, Tralee.

HONORARY COLONEL.
V. A., *Earl of* Kenmare, *KP.*26 Mar. 66

LT.COLONEL.
Wm. S. Hickie, *Hon. Col.* 13 Aug. 92

MAJORS.
Richard J. Rice, *Hon. Lt. Col.*25 June88
Wm. John Neligan .... 7 June 93

CAPTAINS.
Arthur Blennerhassett...... 1 June 86
James Marmaduke Sugrue, (*H*), *Inst. of Musketry* ...13 Sept. 9.
Harry North .... 8 Aug. 91
John Sandes................24 Sept.92
John MacGillycuddy 9 Sept.92
Henry Patrick Magill ...... 4 Apr. 94
Arthur H. C. Walker-Leigh 27 June 94
Montague Wm. Hawtrey, (*H*), *Inspector Sierra Leone Frontier Police* ....27 June 94

LIEUTENANTS.
Geo. A. Molineux Smallpeice ....26 Nov. 92
Thos. Hy. Wm. Lister ......28 Apr. 94
Henry Arthur Carroll ......28 Apr. 94
Nicholas Chas. L. Biale, *p.s.* 9 June 94
Cecil Rowland Leslie 27 Mar.95
Stewart B. Bythesea Dyer 27 Mar. 95
Robt. Edw. Michael Pakenham ....27 Mar. 95

SECOND LIEUTENANTS.
John Rendall ....19 June 93
William Marriott Sutton ...14 June 94
Adjt. & Capt.—B. Stewart, *Captain* 1 *Battalion*......... 1 Mar. 92
Qr. Master.—Tom Jessop, *Hon. Captain*............28 June 89

Blue Facings.

5TH BATTALION.
(*Formerly the Royal Limerick County Militia.*)
Head Quarters, Limerick.

HONORARY COLONELS.
W. H. J. C. *Earl of* Limerick, *KP. Aide de Camp to the Queen* ....19 May 94

LT.COLONEL.
Henry Jas. Brown, *ret. pay* 105 *Foot, Hon. Colonel* ...22 Nov. 90

MAJORS.
John Massy-Westropp, *ret. pay* 12 *Lancers* ....22 Nov. 90
Thomas Gloster, (*H*), *Hon. Lt. Colonel* ....18 Apr. 91

Militia Infantry.

CAPTAINS.
Wm. G. Gubbins, *Hon. Major* 16 May 74
Eyre Herbert Ievers ....26 July 50
Wm. H. E. de V. S. *Visct.*
 Glentworth, *late Lt. Rifle*
 Brigade ....25 Feb. 91
Wm. Fitzgerald Plummer,
 (H), Inst. of Musketry ... 9 June 91
Harry Thomson, *p.s. (H)*...30 May 92
James Wm. Stopford........26 Aug. 93
John R. Bramston Newman,
 p.s. ....3 Mar. 94
Gerald Rose Shine, *(H)* ...18 June 94
LIEUTENANTS.
Herbert Burton Morony ...15 June 91
Richbell Napier C. Curling 20 Aug. 92
Herbert J. Collett Leland...20 Aug. 92
Jos. Sutherland Matterson 26 Aug. 93
Edward Chute Atkinson ...26 Aug 93
Henry William d'Esterre...11 Feb. 93
Hugh Mortimer Travers ... 7 Nov. 94
SECOND LIEUTENANTS.
Herbert Prescott Hampson 23 Sept. 93
George Shields Eckford ...22 Apr. 94
Adjt. and Capt.—Jas. M.
 Chadwick, *Capt. Munster*
 Fusiliers ....11 Dec. 93
Paymaster.—Edw.C.D.Bell 25 Aug. 59
Qr. Master.—Michael C.
 Rowland, *Hon. Lieut.* ...... 6 Mar. 95
Med. Off.—
 Blue Facings.

The Royal Dublin Fusiliers.
3RD BATTALION.
(Formerly the *Kildare Rifles.*)
Head Quarters, Naas.
HONORARY COLONEL.
LT. COLONEL.
Fortescue J. Tynte, *p.s. Hon.*
 Colonel.............................16 Mar. 89
MAJORS.
William A. Gresson, *(H)* ...20 Mar. 94
CAPTAINS.
Hon. Ernest A. G. Pomeroy,
 late and Lt. 20 Hussars ... 4 May 92
George Haughton Gason ... 6 June 92
Hugh Arthur Henry, *(H)*,
 Instructor of Musketry ... 4 Mar. 93
Edw. Jos. Lorcan Keogh... 1 May 93
Frns. Wm. J. MacDonnell 30 Mar. 94
Henry Stewart Orpen, *(H)* 2 June 94
LIEUTENANTS.
Maurice Falkiner Dennis,
 p.s. ....25 Feb. 94
Theo. Stuart R. Verschoyle 5 May 94
Wm. C. Browne-Clayton... 5 May 94
Gordon Shakespear Hig-
 ginson ....5 May 94
Geo. Edw. Russell Patey... 5 May 94
SECOND LIEUTENANTS.
Butler Brooke ....23 Sept. 94
Harold Wilson Savage......26 Mar. 94
Edward Algernon Moles-
 worth ....30 Mar. 94
Ferdinand Ewing M'Clellan 28 Nov. 94
Adj. & Capt.—G. A. Shad-
 forth, *Major 2 Battalion* 9 Feb. 91
Qr. Mr.—Chas. Mathews,
 Hon. Lieut....................11 Nov. 91
M d. Off.—
 Blue Facings.

4TH BATTALION.
Formerly the *Royal Dublin City Mil.*—
 Queen's Own Royal Regiment.)
Head Quarters, Dublin.
HONORARY COLONEL.
Robert Eglinton Seton,
 late Lieut. 93 *F., p.s.* ...... 3 Dec. 88
LT. COLONEL.
Reginald Jas. Morrison, *ret.*
 pay Dublin Fus. Hon.
 Colonel ....24 Oct. 94
MAJORS.
Michael C. Hackett, *p.s.*......15 June 89
CAPTAINS.
Henry Wm. Phepoe, *Hon.*
 Major ....25 Apr. 77
Charles William Soden, *p.s.* 28 May 88
Percival Wormser-Harris 14 July 88

Walter Thaddeus M'Donnell 1 July 80
John Gibbs, *p.s., late Capt.*
 5 West York Militia ...... 5 Oct. 89
Edward C. D'H. Fairtlough,
 p.s. (H), Assistant Inspector
 Sierra Leone Frontier Police 10 Dec. 92
Abraham Jagoe (*H*).........12 June 93
LIEUTENANTS.
Valentine Alex. Blake, *(H)* 27 June 91
Cecil C. Butler Clarke ......18 Nov. 93
SECOND LIEUTENANTS.
Theodore Young Kellott... 2 May 93
Jas. Alexander Armstrong 29 May 93
Chas. Lambert Anderson...16 Dec. 93
Adjt. & Capt.—A. H. Bacon,
 Capt. Dublin Fusiliers ...16 Sept. 92
Qr. Master.—Charles Hills,
 Hon. Lieut. ....29 Oct. 81
Med. Off.—
 Blue Facings.

5TH BATTALION.
(*Formerly the Dublin County Light*
 Infantry.)
Head Quarters, Dublin.
HONORARY COLONEL.
Reginald, *Earl of Meath*, (t) 9 July 87
LT. COLONEL.
Edw. Vernon, *Hon. Colonel* 11 May 85
MAJORS.
Henry C. Gernon, (*H*),
 Hon. Lt. Colonel ....29 July 87
Guy L. Bence-Lambert,
 Hon. Lt. Colonel ....12 Nov. 87
CAPTAINS.
Henry Thomas Finlay, (*H*),
 late Ensign 6 *F. Hon. Maj.* 7 Apr. 83
Richard Arthur Hartley,
 Hon. Major ....30 Apr. 84
William Caldbeck Roper-
 Caldbeck, *p.s.* (*H*) ....23 Aug. 84
Peter La Touche, (*H*), *Inst.*
 of Musketry ....29 Oct. 87
George Aug. Luscombe, (*H*),
 Sub Inspector of Constabu-
 lary, British Honduras ...24 Apr. 88
Frederick Wm. Shaw, *late*
 Lt. 1 *Dragoons* ....10 Aug. 89
Wilfred B. Davidson-Houston,
 p.s., serving with Gold Coast
 Constabulary ....26 Nov. 92
Alex. Delapere Kirkpatrick,
 p.s. ....26 Nov. 92
LIEUTENANTS.
Sydney Douglas Stewart... 6 Dec. 90
William Henry Beamish ...16 Jan. 92
Seymour Anketell-Jones ...16 Jan. 92
Matthew J. Patrick Cor-
 bally ....26 Nov. 92
Hon. A. L. le N. Brabazon 16 Sept. 93
SECOND LIEUTENANTS.
Albemarle Cator Annesley 1 Mar. 93
Theodore W. Carte Moriarty 7 Mar. 93
Cecil T. Wrigley Grimshaw 9 Dec. 93
Edward W. Tunstall-Moore 20 Jan. 94
Spencer Anketell Jones ...19 Mar. 94
Adjt. & Capt.—Richd. S.
 Gage, *Capt. 1 Battalion*...20 Dec. 94
Qr. Master.—Walter Lowsey,
 Hon. Captain.................. 1 May 82
Med. Off.—
 Blue Facings.

The Rifle Brigade (The Prince Consort's Own).
5TH BATTALION.
(*Formerly the Queen's Own Royal*
 Tower Hamlets Light Infantry.)
Head Quarters, Victoria Park Square.
HONORARY COLONEL.
Geo. Shirley Maxwell (*H*),
 late Lieut. 20 *F.*...............27 July 89
LT. COLONEL.
John Wm. Lee, *Hon. Colonel* 27 July 89
MAJORS.
Oliver Thomas Duke,[1] *p.s.*
 [*t*], (*H*), *Hon. Lt. Colonel* 21 Sept. 89
Wm. Chas. Eldon Serjeant,[3]
 p.s.................................27 May 93

CAPTAINS.
Richard Rivarola Cole, *p.s.*
 (*H*), [*t*], *Instructor of*
 Musketry, Hon. Major ... 21 Feb. 80
George Croker Bayly, *p.s.*
 (*H*), *Aide de Camp to Gov.*
 of British Honduras, Hon.
 Major .... 5 June 82
Henry Daily Marshall, *p.s.*
 [*t*], (*H*) ....11 Aug. 86
E. H. Warren-Wright, *p.s.* 22 Mar. 90
Frank Boghurst Ditmas, *p.s.* 18 June 90
Percy Arthur Matthews, *p.s.*
 (*H*), *Assist. Inspector Gold*
 Coast Constabulary ....31 Mar. 91
Charles Mitford Burgess ...13 June 92
Jas. M'Laren Stuart Smith 6 Sept. 93
Lord Edw. Wm. J. Manners,
 ret. pay Rifle Brigade......16 May 94
John Barton Doré, *p.s.* ...... 6 Feb. 95
LIEUTENANTS.
Henry Francis Large .... 6 Aug. 92
Philip Martin Large .... 6 Aug. 92
Hugh T. Walford Wyllie ...11 Nov. 93
Robert Alexander ....11 Nov. 93
Vivian George Kennard ...11 Nov. 93
Gilbert Chas. D. Fergusson 30 Jan. 95
Rowland Harry M. Moody 30 Jan. 95
Wilbraham Taylor ....30 Jan. 95
SECOND LIEUTENANTS.
Alexander Graham Forbes 5 Sept. 94
Wyndham Fred. Tufnell ...16 Jan. 95
Lothian Graeme Scott ......20 Mar. 95
Adjt. & Capt.—H.F. M. Wil-
 son, *Capt.* 1 *Battalion* ... 1 Apr. 92
Qr. Master.—Wm. Wadham,
 Hon. Lieut......................19 Feb. 87
Med. Off.—Surgeon Major G.
 P. Bate, *M.D.*................... 4 Aug. 71
 Black Facings.

6TH BATTALION.
(*Formerly the Prince of Wales' Royal*
 Regiment of Longford Rifles.)
Head Quarters, Longford.
HONORARY COLONEL.
John Thos. Davys .... 3 Aug. 89
LT. COLONEL.
Charles E. Lefroy ....23 Dec. 93
MAJOR.
Henry Seton L. Stein ......18 June 94
CAPTAINS.
Charles Stuart Molony, *ret.*
 *pay York Regt., Inst. of Musk.*11 Feb. 88
William Alexander White... 2 July 92
LIEUTENANTS.
Frederick Geo. Mansford... 3 June 90
Jocelyn Fred. de F. Shaw. 2 Jan. 95
Jn. Kenelm Foster-Melliar 2 Jan. 95
Edwy Lewis Willcox......... 2 Jan. 95
SECOND LIEUTENANTS.
Wm. Preston Anslow Sole 14 Apr. 94
John Francis Duncan ...... 2 Jan. 95
Adj. & Capt.—H. L. Welman,
 Captain Irish Rifles........20 Nov. 93
 Black Facings.

7TH BATTALION.
(*Formerly the King's Own Royal Tower*
 Hamlets Light Infantry.)
Head Quarters, Dalston.
HONORARY COLONEL.
Alfred P. F. C. Somerset,
 CB. DL. JP. late Lt. 13 *F.* 18 June 92
LT. COLONEL.
Chas. Lawson de Salis,[2]
 (*H*), *Hon. Colonel* ....11 June 92
MAJORS.
Bernard Tindal Bosanquet,
 Hon. Lt. Colonel ....19 Dec. 77
Henry F. Bowles, *MP. p.s.* 5 Dec. 94

Militia Infantry.

CAPTAINS.
James J.C. Henry, p.s. Hon.
 Major .... 15 July 82
John Dunn .... 28 Apr. 88
Godfrey Herbert Bloomfield 5 Oct. 89
Arthur B. Williams, (T),
 p.s., Hon. Major .... 26 Mar. 90
William Hedley Drake, p.s. 14 Mar. 91
John Hautenville Cope, serving
 with the Selangor Police..11 June 92
Ralph L. Fenner, p.s. ......15 Apr. 93
Douglas George Lamb .....26 Aug. 93
Edwin Hunt .... 11 Nov. 93
Alexis Chas. Doxat, p.s. (H) 27 Feb. 94
Herbert Huntington, p.s.
 [t], Hon. Major .... 18 Nov. 82

LIEUTENANTS.
Cecil Stafford Northcote...11 Mar. 91
Duncan Wilfrid Panton, p.s.
 (H), Inst. of Musketry 19 Sept.91
Edw. Aug. Alfred de Salis 30 July 92
Gerald W. Paul Haslam ...28 Jan. 93
Robt. Stopford Woodward 11 Mar. 93
Edward Trevor Aspinall ...23 Sept. 93
Louis A. Fred. Weigall.... 7 Oct. 93
Boyd Alexander .... 18 Apr. 94
Servante Morland ....29 Aug. 94
John Dauncey .... 6 Feb. 95

SECOND LIEUTENANTS.
Duncan Keith Macpherson 10 Feb. 94
Frank W.S. Douglas Murray 10 Feb. 94
Hon. Henry Cavendish...... 5 Mar. 94
Neville Skottowe Parker... 9 June 94
Robt. Hy. Seymour Dash-
 wood .... 30 Jan. 95
Adjt. & Capt.—Hon. A. C. E.
Somerset, Captain 2 Bn.11 Aug. 90
Quarter Master.—Edmund
Teed,7 Hon. Lieut. ....18 Dec. 89
Med. Off.—

Black Facings.

8TH BATTALION.
(Formerly the Leitrim Rifles.)
[Disbanded 31 July 1889.]

9TH BATTALION.
(Formerly the Westmeath Rifles.)
Head Quarters, Mullingar.
HONORARY COLONEL.
John Jas. Nugent, DL, retired 4 Apr. 94
LT.-COLONEL.
John Richard Malone, late
 Lt. 12 Lancers, Hon. Col. 25 Aug. 86
MAJOR.
William G. Fitzgerald,
 (H), Hon. Lt.-Colonel ......19 Mar. 90

CAPTAINS.
Edw. W. Purdon, Hon. Major 5 Sept. 83
Gilbert Lavallan J. J. G.
Nugent, Hon. Major ......27 June 84
Wm. Barry Ritchie .... 18 Aug. 88
William Murray, (H), In-
 structor of Musketry ......29 Mar. 90
Percy Philip O'Reilly........10 May 93
Richard Pearce O'Reilly ... 6 July 93

LIEUTENANTS.
Chas. S. Dornford Robinson 5 June 91

SECOND LIEUTENANTS.
Andrew Samuel Kirkwood 20 Aug. 92
Robert Culley Barton ......22 Aug. 94
John Loftus Richards ...... 2 Jan. 95
Percy Redfern Creed........20 Feb. 95
Adjt. & Capt.—B. G. Lewis,
 Capt. E. Lancashire Regt. 18 Feb. 93
Qr. Master.—Charles Clark,
 Hon. Captain .... 4 Feb. 85
Med. Off.—

Black Facings.

Channel Islands Militia.

Royal Jersey.
Assistant Adj. General (with
 rank of Major in the Army).
Lt. Col. Chas. P. Le Cornu.
Government Secretary.
Lt. Col. A. W. Simpson.

ARTILLERY.
Lt. Col. S. Robin, p.
Adjutant.
F. W. G. Tothill, Captain
 R. Artillery, 24 Oct. 92.

1ST, or WEST REGIMENT.
(Light Infantry.)
"JERSEY."
Adjutant.
P. Palmes, Capt. N. Lan-
 cashire Regiment, 7 Oct. 92.

2ND, or EAST REGIMENT.
(Light Infantry.)
"JERSEY."
Lt. Col. Sir J. Godfray, Knt.
 Col. and Aide de Camp to
 the Queen.

Adjutant.
G. P. Stewart, Captain Inniskilling Fusiliers, 17 Dec. 94.

3RD, or SOUTH REGIMENT.
(Light Infantry.)
"JERSEY."
Lt. Col. J. Dumaresq, p.
Adjutant.
G. A. Norcott, Capt. North
 Lancashire Regt. 1 Oct. 91.

Royal Guernsey.
Dep. Assist. Adj. General (with
 rank of Major in the Army)
Lt. Col. J. E. Le Mottée,
 late Captain 64 F., Hon.
 Colonel.
Government Secretary.
Col. Wm. Bell, CB, late 64 F
 Aide de Camp to the Queen

Militia Aides de Camp to the
 Lt. Governor.
Capt. C. A. Carey.
Lieut. A. W. Carey.

ARTILLERY REGIMENT.
Lt. Col. P. Groves, p.s.
Adjutant.
H. B. Dodgson, Captain R.
 Artillery, 17 Oct. 92.

1ST, or EAST REGIMENT.
(Light Infantry.)
Lt. Col. A. H. Collings, p
 Hon. Colonel.
Adjutant (with rank of Cap-
 tain in the Army), C. R. M.
 O'Brien, Capt. E. Lanca-
 shire Regt. 9 Apr. 94+

2ND, or NORTH REGIMENT.
(Light Infantry.)
Lt. Col. J. Naftel, Hon. Colonel.

Adjutant (with rank of Cap-
 tain in the Army), O. A.
 A. Taylor, Captain West
 Riding Regiment, 2 Mar. 91.

3RD, or SOUTH REGIMENT.
(Light Infantry.)
Lt. Col. J. M. Tardif, p. Hon.
 Colonel.
Adjutant, C. H. T. Whitaker,
 Capt. York Lt. Infantry,
 21 Mar. 92.

Royal Alderney.
ARTILLERY.
Lt. Col. Com. W. Barton.
Adjutant (with rank of Cap-
 tain in the Army), Wm.
 Parker, District Officer
 R. Artillery, 2 Apr. 90.

Royal Sark.
Lt. Col. Com.
Adjutant.

Royal Malta Regiment of Militia.
"1800."

Hon. Colonel, Gen. Sir H. A. Smyth, KCMG, R. Art.
Lt. Colonel, H. Vella.

Adjutant (with rank of Captain in the Army), A. G. Chesney, Captain S. Stafford Regt. 1 Feb. 90.

Yeomanry Cavalry of Great Britain.

Ayrshire.
[11th Brigade.]
Head Quarters, Ayr.
HONORARY COLONEL.
Wm. Parker Adam............30 May 91
LT.-COLONEL.
Robt. Morrice Pollok, p.s.
 Hon. Colonel ....13 June 91
MAJOR.
John Geo. A. Baird, MP.
 late Lt. 16 Lancers .... 21 July 94
CAPTAINS.
Charles Edward Grant, p.s.,
 Aide de Camp to Sir D.
 Matheson, Com. Clyde
 Brig. Inf. Vols. ....19 Mar. 87
John C. C. Hamilton, p.s...18 June 88
David William Shaw, p.s.
 Assist. Brig. Adj. 11 Brig. 9 Mar. 89
Wm. K. Hamilton-Camp-
 bell, p.s .... 5 June 91
Francis S. Hamilton, p.s..25 Feb. 93
J. H. N. G. H. Visc. Dalrymple 29 July 93

LIEUTENANTS.
Allan George Pollok, p.s....12 Dec. 94
Oscar Evan Boulton..........12 Dec. 94
John Douglas Boswell, p.s. 12 Dec. 94
SECOND LIEUTENANTS.

Adj.—
Med. Officer.—Surg. Major.
Wm. J. Naismith, MD....2 July 92
Vet. Officers.—Vet. Lieut.
James Dickie ....19 Sept. 94
Vet. Lieut. Arthur Fletcher 15 Dec. 94
Blue—Scarlet Facings.

Berks.
(Hungerford.)
[1st Brigade.]
Head Quarters, Hungerford.
HONORARY COLONEL.

LT.-COLONEL.
Hon. Osbert Wm. Craven... 5 May 94
MAJORS.
Gerald Craven Ricardo, late
 Lt. 14 Hussars .... 5 May 94

CAPTAINS.
Edw. David Stern, p.s. (t) 6 Oct. 88
W. G. R. Earl of Craven, p.s. 17 Oct. 91
Wm. Henry Bishop, (p.s.) 10 Feb. 94

LIEUTENANTS.
Lionel George Thower ......27 June 94
Henry Caversham Simonds,
 (p.s.) ....27 June 94
C. Kingsley Milbourne, p.s.27 June 94
Arthur Roberts, (p.s.) ......27 June 94

SECOND LIEUTENANTS.
Hubert Gould Wm. Thorold 7 July 94
John B. Preston Kursinke 7 July 94
Harry V. Rudston Read ... 2 Jan. 95

Adj.—
Medical Officers.—Surgeon Lieutenant
 J. H. Walters, MD.......... 8 Apr. 93

Hon. Chap.—Rev. C. F.
 Trower, MA.................16 July 92
Scarlet—Blue Facings.

Buckinghamshire.

(*Royal Bucks Hussars.*)
[2nd Brigade.]
Head Quarters, Buckingham.

HONORARY COLONEL.

LT.COLONEL.
C. C. W. *Lord* Chesham,
late Captain 16 *Lancers,*
Hon. Colonel..................24 Apr. 89

MAJORS.
Henry Leslie Ellis,[1] *late*
Major 6 *Dragoons, Hon.*
Lt. Colonel .... 3 Dec. 87
James Poynter, *p.s. late Lt.*
14 *Hussars,Hon.Lt.Colonel* 8 June 89

CAPTAINS.
James F. H. Harter, *p.s.*
Hon. Major .... 9 June 80
Alfred Basil Loder, *p.s.*......29 Jan. 87
Harry Lawson W. Lawson, *p.s.* ....4 May 87
James Bogle Delap, *p.s.* [*t*] 14 July 88
William John Levi, *p.s.* ... 8 June 89
Reg. Bernhard Loder, *p.s.* 27 July 89
Richd. Saml. Budgett, *p.s.* 5 May 91
Hon. Edw. Sholto Douglas-Pennant, *late Lieut*, 1 *Life*
Guards........................ 6 Feb. 92
Walter de Winton, *late Lt.*
1 *Life Guards*..............12 June 93

LIEUTENANTS.
Wm. Walter Carlile, (*p.s.*)...25 Jan. 89
Sydney Loder, (*p.s.*) .... 9 Nov. 89
William Henry Allen, *p.s.* 1 Nov. 90
Cecil Alfred Grenfell, *p.s.* ...20 June 91
Henry Wickham,[3] *late Lt.*
Scots Guards.................16 Dec. 93

SECOND LIEUTENANTS.
Ernest Guy Fenwick.........16 Dec. 93
Adj.—
Hon. Chap.—Rev. Charles
W. S. Lowndes...............27 Feb. 78
Med. Officer.— Surg. Lt.Col.
Henry W. Kiallmark[4] ...27 Feb. 92
*Vet. Officer.—Vet.Capt.*Hon.
G. Lepper .... 1 Dec. 91
Green—Scarlet Facings.

Cheshire.

(*Earl of Chester's.*)
[9th Brigade.]
Head Quarters, Chester.

HONORARY COLONEL.
H. L. *Duke of* Westminster,
KG., Aide de Camp to the
Queen ....21 Feb. 91

LT.COLONEL COMMANDANT.

LT.COLONEL.
Piers E. Warburton, *p.Hon.*
Colonel........................18 Mar. 91

MAJORS.
C. A. *Earl of* Harrington,
Hon. Lt. Colonel...............23 May 91

CAPTAINS.
Jas. Tomkinson, *Hon.Maj.* 10 Jan. 77
Chris. Kay, *p. Hon. Major* 12 Jan. 84
Hugh A. Birley, *p. Hon.*
Major .... 7 Jan. 88
Hon. Alan de Tatton Egerton, *MP, p.s., Hon. Major* 7 Jan. 88
Lord Arthur Hugh Grosvenor, *p.s.*...................11 Aug. 88
W. B. Brocklehurst, *p.s.*
Hon. Major ....23 May 91
George Wyndham,[1] *MP,*
*late Lt.Coldstream Guards*10 Feb. 94
Oswald Mosley Leigh, *p.s.* 11 May 94

LIEUTENANTS.
Robt. Walter D. Phillips, *p.s.*16 Apr. 84
Wm. Roylance Court, *p.s.*...24 May 84
Edm. Wilson Swetenham,
(*p.s.*)...........................23 Nov. 89
Walter J. Henry Jones, *p.s.* 27 Aug. 92
Wm. T. Birchenough,(*p.s.*)27 Aug. 92
Edward Lee Townshend,
late Capt. 3 *Bn. Cheshire*
Regt. .... 5 May 94

SECOND LIEUTENANTS.
Charles Edw. Hope, (*p.s.*) 23 Aug. 90
Harry Barnston...............10 Oct. 94
Adj.
Med. Officer.—Surg.Capt. G.
Harrison ....27 May 85
Vet.Officer.—Vet. Lieut. R.
C. Edwards ....25 Mar. 93
Blue—Scarlet Facings.

Denbighshire.

(*Hussars.*)
[15th Brigade.]
Head Quarters, Wrexham.

HONORARY COLONEL.
Arth. Mesham, *p. late Capt.*
1 *Dragoons* ....20 Feb. 92

LT.COLONEL.
Henry Richd. L. Howard,[1]
late Major 16 *Lancers,*
Hon. Colonel ....18 May 92

MAJOR.
Sidney L. Parry ....18 June 92

CAPTAINS.
Oliver Ormrod, *p.s.* ....26 May 84
Harry Wm. Buddicom, *p.s.*18 June 92
George Blezard, *p.s.* ... 5 May 94

LIEUTENANTS.
Francis E. Cotton, (*p.s.*) ... 7 Mar. 77
Charles Edw. Wynne-Eyton,
(*p.s.*), *Assistant Brigade*
Adjutant 15th *Brigade* ... 5 July 93

SECOND LIEUTENANTS.
HenryEgertonPiercy,(*p.s.*) 3 Dec. 92
Adj.—
Med. Officer.—Surg. Lieut.
Richard Williams ....18 June 92
Blue—Scarlet Facings.

Derbyshire.

[6th Brigade.]
Head Quarters, Derby.

LT.COLONEL.
Paget P. Mosley, *late Capt.*
11 *Hussars, Hon. Colonel* 5 Aug. 78

MAJOR.
Walter Boden, *Hon. Lt.*
Colonel...................... 6 Feb. 86

CAPTAINS.
Reg. W. Chandos Pole, *late*
Lt. Gren.Gds. Hon. Major 9 June 77
Sir Peter Carlaw Walker,
Bart. p.s., Hon. Major ...26 July 90
Herbert Christian Holland,
p.s., late Lt. 15 *Hussars*...23 Mar. 92
Edward C. Shuttleworth
Holden, *p.s.* .... 8 July 93

LIEUTENANTS.
*Lord*H.CavendishBentinck,
(*p.s.*)...........................10 Apr 86
Victor C. W. Cavendish,
MP. (*p.s.*) .... 6 Feb. 95

SECOND LIEUTENANTS.
Fredk. Wm. Peacock,(*p.s.*)24 May 90
Alex. Weston Jarvis, *p.s.*... 2 Apr. 92
Lionel Guy Gisborne ....25 May. 93
Oswald Mosley.................20 Jan. 94
Adj.—
Med. Officer.—Surg. Capt.
Charles H. Hough ....28 Apr. 86
Hon. Chap. — Rev. Fred.
James Lyall, *MA.* 24 Sept.87
Blue—Scarlet Facings.

Royal 1st Devon.

(*Exeter.*)
[Devon Brigade.]
Head Quarters, Exeter.

HONORARY COLONEL.
H. R. *Lord* Courtenay ...... 8 Aug. 94

LT.COLONEL.
Charles A. W. Troyte, *p.s.*
(*t*), (S), *Hon. Colonel* ......21 July 94

MAJOR.
Sir John Shelley, *Bt. p.s.*
Hon. Lt.Colonel .... 3 Aug. 94

CAPTAINS.
Edward J. Sanders, *p.s.* ... 5 Oct. 81
Benjamin C. Cleave,*p.s. late*
*Lt.*4*Bn.Shropshire Lt.Inf.*
Hon. Major ....17 Nov. 83
HenryLewis,*p.s.Hon.Major*21 Apr. 85
John E. Heugh Balfour,*late*
Capt. 11 *Hussars* ....28 Jan. 93
Alf. Dyke Acland, *p.s.* (S)(*t*)19 Sept.94
Wm. Edw. T. Bolitho, *p.s.* 6 Mar. 95

LIEUTENANTS.
EdwardHerbertGifford,*p.s.* 7 Feb. 85
Rennell Coleridge (*p.s.*) ... 9 Aug. 90
Hon. Wm. Fred. Danvers
Smith, *MP. p.s.* .... 3 Dec. 92
Oliver A.V. *Lord* Ampthill,
p.s.............................11 Mar. 93

SECOND LIEUTENANTS.
John Williams .... 4 May 92
Merrik R. A. Wyatt-Edgell,
p.s............................. 9 July 92
John Geo E. Templer,[1]*late*
Capt. Highland Lt.Inf.... 7 July 94
Robert Lydston Newman17 Oct. 94
Charles Marwood-Tucker24 Oct. 94
Adj.—
Hon. Chap.—Rev. Edw. J.
G. Dupuis, *M.d.* ....15 Mar. 90
Med. Officer.—Surg. Captain
Frederick Morgan......... 4 May 92
Vet. Officer — Vet. Major J.
A. Collings .... 1 Dec. 91
Scarlet—Blue Facings.

Royal North Devon.

(*Hussars.*)
[Devon Brigade.]
Head Quarters, Barnstaple.

HONORARY COLONEL.
Sir Arthur Chichester, *Bt.*
*late Capt.*7 *Hussars*.........23 Nov. 89

LIEUTENANT COLONEL.
H. F. *Visct.* Ebrington, *Hon.*
Colonel ....11 Jan. 90

MAJOR.
*Hon.*Charles J.R. Hepburn-Stuart - Forbes - Trefusis,
p.s. ....25 June 90

CAPTAINS.
Wilson Noble Hoare, *p.s.*
late Royal Navy.............25 Apr. 85
Frederick Ward, p.s., *late*
Major East Surrey Regt.,
Hon. Lt. Colonel..............26 Nov. 87
H.Hy.J.W.Drummond,*p.s.,*
late Lieut. Rifle Brigade 14 Mar. 91
Arthur Scott Browne, *late*
Lieut. 16 *Lancers* .... 9 Jan. 92
John Skirrow Follett, *p.s.*...14 May 92
Wm. Edwin Pitts-Tucker,
p.s.............................14 May 92
Francis Alex. Barton,[1] *late*
Capt. 7 *Dragoon Guards*...26 Nov. 92
Vincent W. Calmady Hamlyn, *p.s.*.......................13 Jan. 94
Manuel De Las Casas, *p.s.* 16 June 94

LIEUTENANTS.
Wm. Roberts North-Row,
p.s. ....13 Jan. 94
John Bayly, *p.s.* ....10 May 94

SECOND LIEUTENANTS.
Arthur Francis Basset ......14 Jan. 93
John Byres-Leake, *p.s.* ...29 Apr. 93
Walter Bassett Basset ..... 4 Oct. 93
Robert Arthur Sanders ...18 Apr. 94
Adj.—
Med. Officer.— Surg. Lieut.
John R. Harper ....28 Mar. 94
*Vet.Officer.—Vet.Lieut.*Wm.
Penhale .... 8 Nov. 4
Hon. Chaplain.— Rev. Albany B. S. Wrey, *MA.* ... 5 May 94
Blue—Scarlet Facings.

Yeomanry Cavalry of Great Britain.

Dorset.
(*Queen's Own.*)
[Portsmouth Brigade.]
Head Quarters, Weymouth.
HONORARY COLONEL.

LIEUTENANT COLONEL.
John R.P. Goodden, *late Lt.*
4 *Dr.Gds.; Hon. Colonel*... 2 Apr. 90

MAJOR.
Wm. E. Brymer, *p. Hon.*
Lt.Colonel .... 8 Apr. 93

CAPTAINS.
Jno. K. Wingfield-Digby,
M.P., p.s. .... 9 Jan. 84
Elliott Lees, *p.s.* ....17 Apr. 89
Edm. M. Mansel-Pleydell,
Lt.Colonel late 12 *Lancers;*
Hon. Major ....24 Apr. 89
Hon. Berkeley Portman, *p.s.*25 Apr. 91
Montague S. Williams ..... 5 Mar. 92

LIEUTENANTS.
Wanley Ellis Sawbridge-
Erle-Drax, *p.s.* ....19 Mar. 90
Joseph Gundry, *p.s.* .....19 Mar. 90
Thomas Alfred Colfox, *p.s.*19 Mar. 90
Henry Rupert Fetherston-
haugh Frampton, (*p.s.*)... 2 Apr. 90

SECOND LIEUTENANTS.
Hon. Ivor Churchill Guest 3 Jan. 91
William Reginald Currie...25 Apr. 91
Hy.Cha. Thos. Hambro,*p.s.*10 June 91
Charles Louis Faber........ 9 Jan. 95
Adj.—
Med.Officers.—Surg. Lt. Col.
George W. Daniell .... 1 Dec. 91
Surg. Lieut. Wm. Rendall...28 July 88
Vet. Officer.— Vet. Lt. Oscar
Gordon Barrow .... 1 Nov. 90
Hon. Chaplain.—Rev. John
L. Gwatkin Hadow, *MA*. 3 May 90
Blue—Scarlet Facings.

Gloucestershire.
(*Royal Gloucestershire Hussars.*)
[3rd Brigade.]
Head Quarters, Gloucester.

HONORARY COLONEL.
F. W. F. Lord Fitzhardinge,
late Capt. R. Horse Gds.... 6 Aug. 87

LT.COLONEL.
H. A. W. F., *Marq. of Wor-
cester, late Capt. Royal
Horse Guards,Hon.Colonel*11 June 87

MAJOR.
Francis Henry, *p., late Lt.*9
Lancers; Hon.Lt.Colonel 30 July 87

CAPTAINS.
Sir Gerald W. H. Codring-
ton, *Bt., p.s., Hon. Major*15 May 75
Thomas Butt Miller, *p.s.* ... 5 Dec. 85
Lord H. E. Brudenell Somer-
set,[1] *p. Gentleman at Arms
and late Lt. R. Horse Gds.
Hon. Major* ....28 Apr. 86
Hedley Hunt Calvert,[2]*p.Assist.
Brigade Adjutant* 3 *Yeo-
manry Brigade* .... 9 June 88
Chas. Harvey Palairet, *p.
late Capt.*9*Lanc.Hon.Maj.*15 Sept.88
Robert P. Sandeman, *late
Capt.* 10 *Hussars* ....23 Apr. 92
H. de la P. Beresford Hey-
wood,*p.s.* ....17 Feb. 94
Arthur Evans (*p.s.*) .... 7 Apr. 94
J. E.Chapman Mathews,*p.s.*27 Feb. 95

LIEUTENANTS.
Thos. Holme Cardwell, *p.s.* 1 July 81
George John G. C. Cod-
rington (*p.s.*)..............27 July 81
Sir C. P. Van-Notten-Pole,
Bart., p.s. ....25 Oct. 90
D. Balcarres Lindsay, (*p.s.*)30 Jan. 92
H. A. M. *Earl* Cowley,(*p.s.*) 5 July 93
Darcy Edm. Taylor, (*p.s.*) 22 July 93
Vincent Wodehouse Yorke28 Apr. 04
Lionel Edward Barry .....27 Feb. 95

SECOND LIEUTENANTS.
Edw. Humphry de Freville24 Oct. 94
William Heyworth Playne 6 Feb. 95
Adj.—
Med. Officers.—Surg.Lt.Col.
William Wickham.........28 May 92
Surg. Lt. Col. Alfred Grace28 May 92
Vet. Officer.— Vet. Lieut. F.
B. Jones, *p.* ....17 Sept. 87
Blue—Scarlet Busby-Bag.

Hampshire.
(*Carabiniers.*)
[Portsmouth Brigade.]
Head Quarters, Southampton.

HONORARY COLONEL.
Rt. Hon. Thos. Geo. *Earl of
Northbrook, GCSI.* ......26 Jan. 89

LT.COLONEL.
Hon. Henry G. L. Crichton,
late Major 21 *Hussars,
Hon. Colonel* ....16 Jan. 84

MAJOR.
William Woods, *p.s.* ....23 Dec. 91

CAPTAINS.
Herman LeRoy-Lewis, p.s.27 Feb. 86
F. Vaughan Williams,*p.s.*[!]
Hon. Major ....26 Jan. 89
William Cory, *p.s.* .... 23 Dec. 91
Henry Albert Barclay, *p.s.* 5 Mar. 92
Thos. Geo. Best, *late Capt.
R. Art.*...................... 4 May 92
John Edw. B. Seely, *p.s.*...31 May 92

LIEUTENANTS.
Arthur Carleton Nicholson,
(*p.s.*).......................20 July 89
Harold Edw. Sherwin Holt,
p.s. ....20 July 89
Henry G. Philip Hoare(*p.s.*) 9 Apr. 92
Arthur A. W. B. Bright-
Smith,*late Capt.*3 *Hussars*15 Mar. 93

SECOND LIEUTENANTS.
Jas. Edw.*Visct.* FitzHarris,
(*p.s.*).......................20 Feb. 92
Granville C. G. Leveson
Gower ....23 May 92
Walter J.Ellery Cartwright22 July 93
Charles Hervey Hoare......13 Mar. 95
Adj.—
Med. Officer.— Surg. Capt.
G. F. A. England, *MB*, 7 Jan. 93
Vet. Officer.—
Hon. Chap.—Rev. Andrew
Wallace Milroy, *MA*....... ? Feb. 89
Blue.

Herts.
[7th Brigade.]
Head Quarters, St. Albans.

LIEUTENANT COLONEL.
E. H. *Earl of* Clarendon,
Hon. Colonel ....19 July 79

MAJOR.
G. Devereux deVere,*Earl of
Essex,p.s., late Lt.* Gren-
adier Guards ....25 Nov. 93

CAPTAINS.
Reginald A. Smith, *p.s.* ...11 Feb. 88
Abel Henry Smith, *MP.p.s.*16 Nov. 89
Edward Hy. Loyd, *p.s. DL*. 4 Mar. 91
Jno. Babington Gilliatt.*p.s.* 25 Nov. 91
John Medlicott Vereker,[1]
late Capt. 4 *Dragoon Gds.*25 July 94

LIEUTENANTS.
Sir George C. A. Arthur,[2]
Bart. p. late Lt. 2 *Life Gds.* 7 Aug. 86
G.R.Smith-Bosanquet(*p.s.*)25 Nov. 93

SECOND LIEUTENANTS.
Adj.—
Med. Officer.—Surg. Lieut.
Lovell Drage, *MB*..........14 Dec. 89
*Vet. Officer.— Vet.Lieut*W. C.
B. Revill .... 5 Nov. 92
Hon. Chap.—Rev. R. Lee-
James ....23 June 70
Scarlet—White Facings.

Royal East Kent.
(*The Duke of Connaught's Own.*)
(*Mounted Rifles.*)
[Kent Brigade.]
Head Quarters, Canterbury.

HONORARY COLONEL.
General H.R.H. Arthur
W. P. A. *Duke of Con-
naught, KG. KT. KP.
GCSI. GCMG. GCIE.
KCB.* ....27 Feb. 86

LT.COLONEL.
MAJOR.
Chas. Stewart Hardy, *late
Lt.* 37 *F., Hon. Lt.Colonel*19 Jan. 84

CAPTAINS.
G. R. C. *Lord Harris, GCIE.
p.s., Hon.Major; Governor
of Bombay* .... 8 Mar. 73
Edward Frewen, *p.s. Hon.
Major, Assist. Adj. Kent
Yeomanry Brigade* .... 8 July 81
George Edward, *Earl*
Sondes, *p.s.* ....25 June 84
John H. Monins, *p.s.* ..... 1 Feb. 90
Richard James Tylden, *p.s.*19 Feb. 90

LIEUTENANTS.
Ranald M. Laurie ....17 Apr. 89
*Hon.*Henry Aug. Milles,*p.s.* 4 July 91
Robt. Wm. Wynne Eyton 4 July 91
John Howard, *p.s.* ....16 May 92

SECOND LIEUTENANTS.
Adj.—
Hon. Chaplain.—Rev. L. E.
Goodwin, *MA* .... 3 Jan. 91
Med. Officer.—Surg. Lieut.
W. P. Thornton .... 4 May 92
Vet. Officer.— Vet. Lieut. J.
F. B. Moody................ 4 May 92
Rifle-Green—Scarlet Facings.

West Kent.
(*Queen's Own.*)
[Kent Brigade.]
Head Quarters, Maidstone.

HONORARY COLONEL.
William, *Marq. of* Aberga-
venny, *KG. late Cor. and
Sub Lt.* 2 *Life Gds.* ......17 Feb. 75

LT.COLONEL.
Sir Fitzroy D. Maclean,[1]
Bart., late Lt.Col. 13 *Hus.,
Hon. Colonel* ....13 May 80

MAJOR.
Charles Edw. Warde, *late* 4
Hussars,MP.Hon.Lt.Col. 8 Oct. 92

CAPTAINS.
JamesFrederick Edmendes,
Hon.Major ....16 Dec. 76
Edward Henry Hills, *p.s.*...19 Mar. 90
Phil. B.Beresford-Hope,*p.s.
Hon. Major* .... 6 May 91
Fiennes S. W. Cornwallis,
MP. p.s. ....27 June 91
Francis Bingham Mid-
may, *MP. p.s.* ....17 May 93

LIEUTENANTS.
Robert Stewart-Savile(*p.s.*)23 May 85
Hon. Thos. Allnutt Brassey,
p.s. ....19 Dec. 89
*Hon.*Egremont John Mills,
p.s. ....19 Dec. 91
Hy. L. Campbell Brassey 17 May 93

SECOND LIEUTENANTS.
Chas. Wm. Sofer Whitburn,
(*p.s.*).......................29 Aug. 91
Arthur Pearson Davison,*p.s.* 2 July 92
John Charles, *Marquis of*
Camden, *p.s.* 10 Sept.92
Lionel E. Sackville-West 9 Jan. 95
Adj.—
Med. Officer.—Surg. Capt.
Isaac Stephenson Jones 16 Apr. 84
Hon. Chap.—Rev. Harry
Harbord .... Dec. 76
Blue—Scarlet Facings.

Lanarkshire.

[11th Brigade.]
Head Quarters, Lanark.
Lt.Colonel Commandant.
Rt. Hon. C. A. Earl of Home, Aide de Camp to the Queen, and Colonel ....10 Apr. 66

MAJOR.

CAPTAINS.
Colonel Hon.W. S. D. Home, Lt.Col.&Col.h.p.Gr.Gds. 27 June 67
Sir Simon M.Lockhart, Bart. Lt.Colonel 1 Life Gds. (p.s.)......11 May 72
James Addie, *Hon. Major*... 2 Sept. 82
Henry E. Gordon, *p.s., Hon. Major* .... 2 Sept. 82
James C. Hope-Vere, *p.s.* .... 3 Sept. 87
Jas. Dennistoun Mitchell, jun., *p.s.* ....25 Feb. 9:

LIEUTENANTS.
Rt. Hon. John A. L. Earl of Hopetoun, GCMG. Lord in Waiting to the Queen... 1 July 81
C.W.A.N. Lord Lamington, *p.s.* .... 9 May 83
Alexander Whitelaw,*p.s.*...27 May 85
William Whitelaw,*MP.p.s.* 4 June 90
Robert Findlay, *p.s.*........27 June 94

SECOND LIEUTENANTS.
Harry D. Mann-Thomson, (*p.s.*).......................17 May 90
Adj.—

Med. Officer.—Surgeon Capt.
Russell Eliott Wood ......26 Apr. 82
Vet. Officer.—

Blue—Scarlet Facings.

Lanarkshire.

(*Queen's Own Royal Glasgow and Lower Ward of Lanarkshire.*)
[11th Brigade.]
Head Quarters, 124, South Portland Street, Glasgow.
HONORARY COLONEL.
W. A. L. S. *Duke of* Hamilton and Brandon, *KT.* ... 7 Oct. 82

LT.COLONEL.
James Neilson, *p.s., Hon. Colonel*......................31 Oct. 94

MAJOR.
Robert K. Stewart, *p.s.* ...21 Nov. 94

CAPTAINS.
Richard M'Farlane, *p.s. Hon. Major* .... 2 Oct. 86
John Alex. Neilson, *p.s.* ...12 Dec. 91
Andrew Coats, *p.s.*............ 2 June 94

LIEUTENANTS.
Andrew Arthur, *p.s.* ....12 Dec. 91
Alexander Neilson, *p.s.*........15 Apr. 93

SECOND LIEUTENANTS.
Charles William Forbes ...28 Nov. 91
John Lawrence Baird ......29 Apr. 93
Adj.—

Med. Officer.—

Vet. Officer.— Vet. Lieut.
William Boyle ....24 Apr. 77

Dark Blue—Scarlet Facings.

Duke of Lancaster's Own.

[14th Brigade.]
Head Quarters, Worsley.
HONORARY COLONEL.

LT.COLONEL.
Francis C. G. *Earl of* Ellesmere, *p.* .... 24 Jan. 91

MAJOR.
Clement M. Royds, *p. Hon. Lt.Colonel, Hon. Colonel 2 Vol. Bn. Lancashire Fusiliers* ....25 Feb. 91

CAPTAINS.
James E. Platt,*p.s.Hon.Maj.*22 Aug. 83
Wm. Chas. Jones ....17 July 86
Percy Hargreaves, *p.s.*......17 July 86
John Rutherford, *p.* .... 3 Sept. 87
Frederick Platt,*p.Hon.Maj.*27 June 88
George Kemp, *p.s.* ....18 July 91

LIEUTENANTS.
Albert Ernest Lees, *p.s.* ...21 Sept. 89
Robert Henry Tilney, *p.s.* 18 July 91
Henry Marmaduke Hardcastle, (*p.s.*) ....10 Oct. 94

SECOND LIEUTENANTS.
James Reginald Ormrod...22 Oct. 92
Walter Longley Bourke,*p.s.* 6 May 93
Arthur William Huntington 12 May 93
Hon. Fras. Wm. G. Egerton 7 Nov. 94
Adjutant :—
Med. Officer.—Surgeon Capt.
W. W. Saul, *MD.* ....23 Feb. 81
Hon. Chaplain.—Rev. Canon
John Allen, *BA.*............25 July 91

Scarlet—Blue Facings.

Lancashire Hussars.

[9th Brigade.]
Head Quarters, Ashton-in-Makerfield.
HONORARY COLONEL.
Rt. Hon. E. R. W. *Earl of* Lathom, *GCB.* ....25 Mar. 93

LT.COLONEL.
Wm. C. *Lord* Gerard, *late Lt. 2 Life Guards, Hon. Colonel*......................25 Feb. 93

MAJORS.
Edward R. G. Hopwood, *p. Hon. Lt.Colonel* ....22 Mar. 93

CAPTAINS.
Thomas W. Legh, *MP. JP. p.s. Hon. Major* ......28 June 90
Wm. Lee Pilkington, *p.s. Hon. Major* ....12 Mar. 92
Sir Humphrey Francis de Trafford, *Bt.,p.s.*................28 Apr. 93
James Henry Stock, *p.s.* ...29 Apr. 93
Thomas Algernon Earle,*p.s.*13 Jan. 94
Harold M'Corquodale, *p.s.* 28 Apr. 94

LIEUTENANTS.
Charles W. H. *Visct.* Molyneux, (*p.s.*).....................24 July 86
Arthur Lionel Peczenik (p.s.)18 Nov. 93

SECOND LIEUTENANTS.
Ernest Sinclair Pilkington, *p.s.*..........................11 Apr. 91
Rd. Atherton de A. Willis, (*p.s.*).........................29 July 93
Fred. B. J. Stapleton-Bretherton (*p.s.*)................26 Aug. 93
James Monro Walker.........18 May 94
Adjutant.—
Med. Officer.—Surgeon Capt.
Damer Harrisson ....21 Apr. 86
Vet. Officer.—Vet. Lieut.
William G. Dixon ....18 Mar. 91

Blue—Crimson Busby-Bag.

Leicestershire.

("*Prince Albert's Own.*")
[6th Brigade.]
Head Quarters, Leicester.
HONORARY COLONEL.
*Gen.*R.W.P.*Earl* Howe,[1] *CB. Col. 2 Life Guards* ....28 June 76

LT.COLONEL.
James W. Baillie,[2] *Hon. Col.* 5 July 82

MAJOR.
Frederick Gordon Blair, *late Capt. 16 Lancers* ......13 Mar. 95

CAPTAINS.
Sam Tudor Ashton, *late Capt. 14 Hussars, Hon. Major* ....11 Apr. 85
William John Martin, *p.s.*21 Apr. 86
Walter A. Peake, *p.s. Hon. Major* ....28 May 87
Geo. Stanley Williams, *late Capt. 8 Hussars*............27 June 90
G. R. P. *Visct.* Curzon, *MP.* 19 July 90

H. Geo. Clough-Taylor, *p.s. Assist. Adj. 6 Yeomanry Brigade* ....28 Nov. 91[1]
Eustace Reginald Maudslay, *late Capt. 16 Lancers* 19 Mar. 92
Everard March Phillipps De Lisle .... 2 July 92
Robt. Andrew Falkner,*p.s.*13 Mar. 95
Walter Gore Marshall, *p.s.*13 Mar. 95

LIEUTENANTS.
Gilbert, *Lord* Willoughby de Eresby, *MP., p.s.* ...... 6 June 85
Edw.deC.W.Oakeley,(*p.s.*) 20 June 85
Wm. G. S. Rolleston, *p.s.*... 6 Mar. 86
James Wm. Hornsby,(*p.s.*) 4 Apr. 91
Robert Bunten Muir, *p.s.* 30 Dec. 91
Thomas Elliot Harrison ...23 July 92

SECOND LIEUTENANTS.
Abbot Harold Robinson.*p.s.*20 Feb. 92
William Eustace Chaplin, (*p.s.*) ....18 June 92
Richard Hy. Ratcliff, (*p.s.*)18 June 92
Augustus Wm. Byron, (*p.s.*)25 June 92
Wilfrid Byron, *p.s.* ....18 Nov. 93
Adj.—E. C. P. Curzon, *Captain* 18 *Hussars* .... 1 Jan. 90
Med. Officer.—Surgeon Capt.
J. T. Jacques .... 7 Jan. 85
Vet. Officer. — Vet. Major
Edward Bailey .... 1 Dec. 91
Hon. Chap.—Rev. F. Thorpe 20 Sept.76

Blue—Scarlet Facings.

Lothian and Berwickshire.

[12th Brigade.]
Head Quarters, Dunbar.
HONORARY COLONEL.
G.*Earl of* Haddington,*Aide de Camp to the Queen, and Colonel* ....24 Oct. 94

MAJOR.
W.A.B. Hamilton,*CMG.*[t], *Hon. Lt.Colonel* ....18 July 83

CAPTAINS.
George, *Lord* Binning, *p.s., Capt. R. Horse Guards* ...13 Sept. 79
Wm. Jas. Gardiner Baird, *late Lt. 7 Hus.Hon.Major*18 July 83
Walter Wingate Gray, *p.s.*10 Aug. 89
Henry Callander, *p.s.* ......27 May 93

LIEUTENANTS.
Thos. Broadwood,(*p.s.*)*Assist. Brigade Adj.* 12*th Brigade* 1 July 81
Harold Beckwith Towse,*p.s.*17 Feb. 94

SECOND LIEUTENANTS.
Henry Kidd ....21 Apr. 94
Adjutant.—
Med. Officer.—Surgeon Capt.
Thos. Fras. S. Caverhill 2 May 83
*Vet.Officer.—Vet.Lieut.*Wm. O. Williams ....28 Jan. 88
Acting Qr. Mr.— William M'Nab.................. 6 May 93
Honorary Chaplain.— Rev.
Robert Buchanan ....30 Apr. 84

Scarlet—Blue Facings.

Middlesex.

(*Duke of Cambridge's Hussars.*)
[1st Brigade.]
Head Quarters, Knightsbridge.
HONORARY COLONEL.
H.R.H. G. W. F. C. *Duke of* Cambridge, *KG. KT. KP. GCB. GCSI. GCMG. GCIE*.................... 6 Jan. 94

LT.COLONEL.
Wm. Kenyon Mitford,[1] *late Capt. 8 Hussars* ....23 Apr. 92

MAJOR.
Fred. A. Heygate-Lambert, *p.s.* .... 8 Aug. 91

CAPTAINS.
Edw. Albert Sassoon, *p.s.*...25 May 89
Theodore V. Samuel Angier, *p.s.*.........................28 May 90
William Duncan, *p.s.*......... 4 June 92
Richd. Hamilton Rawson, *late Capt. 1 Life Guards* 4 Oct. 93
Hon. Victor R. Anderson-Pelham, *late Lt. 9 Lancers*19 Dec. 94

LIEUTENANTS.
Harold Wm. Edwards, *p.s.*13 Sept. 90
Alf. U.Miller Lambert,(*p.s.*)21 July 94
Chas. Richard Rivers, (*p.s.*)21 July 94

SECOND LIEUTENANTS.
Edward Stephen Revett... 7 July 94
Adjutant.—
Acting Qr.Mr.—Wm. Henry
Gastrell ....24 June 93
Med. Officer.—Surg. Lieut.
C. E. L. B. Hudson ......16 July 92
Hon. Chaplain.—Rev. P.J.T.
Blakeway, B.A. ....11 July 94
Vet. Officer.—

Green—Black Facings.

Montgomeryshire.
[15th Brigade.]
Head Quarters, Welshpool.
HONORARY COLONEL.

LT.COLONEL.
Sir H. L. W. Williams-
Wynn, *Bart. p.s.* .... 9 Feb. 89
MAJOR.
Arthur W. Williams-Wynn 21 May 92
CAPTAINS.
Nicholas Robinson, *p.s.*...... 8 July 82
Edward Pryce Jones, *p.s.*.... 1 Sept. 83
Robt. W. H. W. Williams-
Wynn, *p.s.* ....13 Aug. 87
Chas. Tertius Dugdale, *p.s.*13 July 89
LIEUTENANTS.
Josias A. Nussey Booker,
p.s. DL. ....28 July 88
Ernest Murray Lucas, *p.s.* 24 Apr. 85
Fred Rowland Williams-
Wynn (*p.s.*) ....21 May 90
John Culcairn Munro (*p.s.*) 4 July 91
Aymor Powlett Lane, (*p.s.*) 9 July 92
Hugh Edm. Ethelston Peel,
(*p.s.*)..............................22 July 93
SECOND LIEUTENANT.
Edw. G.Williams-Vaughan 9 May 94
Godfrey FitzHugh............16 June 94
Adj.—
Med. Officer.—Surgeon Capt.
John Gill 15 Aug.83
Vet. Officer. — Vet. Lieut.
John Chris. Rowlands ...28 Sept.89
Scarlet—Black Facings.

Northumberland.
(*Hussars.*)
[12th Brigade.]
Head Quarters, Newcastle-on-Tyne.
HONORARY COLONEL.
H. G. *Earl of* Ravensworth 7 Nov. 85
LT.COLONEL.
Sir Matt. W. Ridley, *Bart.,*
MP. Hon. Colonel .... 7 Nov. 85
MAJOR.
John B. Cookson, *Hon.*
Lt.Colonel 25 Sept.86
CAPTAINS.
John C. Straker, *p.s., Hon.*
Major ....10 June 74
Aug. E. Burdon, *late Cor.*
17 *Lancers ; Hon. Major*...23 Aug. 82
Chas. E. Hunter, *p.s., Hon.*
Major ....15 Mar. 84
Charles B. Lamb, *p.s. Hon.*
Major .... 6 Aug. 87
Herbert Straker, *p.s.*..........25 June 92
John Bertram Clayton, *p.s.*29 July 93
LIEUTENANTS.
Edw. Francis Riddell,(*p.s.*)21 Apr. 86
Wm. Armstrong Watson-
Armstrong (*p.s.*) .... 5 Nov. 92
Charles Oswin Hall (*p.s.*) .. 5 Nov. 92
George Savile Clayton, *p.s.* 8 Aug. 94
Frank Buddle Atkinson ... 8 Aug. 94
SECOND LIEUTENANTS.

Adj.—
Chap.—
Med. Officer.--Surg. Lieut.
Arthur Brumell ....21 May 92
Vet.Officer.—Vet. Capt. Geo.
Elphick .... 8 July 93
Blue—Scarlet Busby Bag.

Nottinghamshire.
(*Southern Nottinghamshire.*)
[17th Brigade.]
Head Quarters, Nottingham.
HONORARY COLONEL.
S. W. H. *Earl* Manvers ... 9 July 79
LT. COLONEL.
Henry *Lord* Belper, *Aide de Camp to the Queen, and Colonel* ....16 Aug. 79
MAJOR.
John L. Francklin, *Hon.*
Lt. Colonel ....11 Aug. 88
CAPTAINS.
Lancelot Rolleston, p.s. *Hon.*
Major ....23 June 75
Arch. Pratt-Barlow, *p.s.* ... 5 May 88
John Ralph Starkey, *p.s.*...29 May 89
Herbert Francis Smith,*p.s.*12 Mar. 92
Chas. Bingham Wright,*p.s.*28 Jan. 93
George Fellows, *p.s. Assist.*
Brig. Adj. 17 *Brigade ;*
Hon. Major .... 9 May 93
Francis Abel Smith, *p.s.* ... 4 Apr. 94
LIEUTENANTS.
Charles Wm. Trotter, *p.s.* 6 July 89
Frank Evelyn Seely, *p.s.*.... 6 July 89
George Murray Smith, *p.s.*15 Mar. 90
Charles Wm. Wright, *p.s.* 20 May 93
Richard Leslie Birkin, *p.s.*20 May 93
SECOND LIEUTENANTS.
C. A. A. V. de V. *Earl of*
Burford ....28 Mar. 94
Adj.—
*Acting Qr.Mr.—*J. H. Brad-
well .... 11 May 89
Med. Officer.—Surgeon Capt.
J. F. D. Willoughby ......12 May 94
Vet. Officer.—Vet. Lieut. E.
D. Johnson ....23 Jan. 92
Blue.

Nottinghamshire.
(*Sherwood Rangers.*)
[17th Brigade.]
Head Quarters, Retford.
HONORARY COLONEL.

LT. COLONEL.
G. E. M. *Visct.* Galway,
Hon. Colonel ....15 Mar. 82
MAJOR.
John Savile-Lumley, *p.s.* ... 5 Dec. 91
CAPTAINS.
Henry Denison, *p.s., late*
Lt.Col. R. Engineers ......20 Aug. 87
Thos. Randle Starkey (*p.s.*)24 Oct. 94
Joseph Fred. Laycock, *p.s.* 6 Mar. 95
LIEUTENANTS.
William Hollins, jun. (*p.s.*)29 Nov. 90
Richd. Castell Bacon (*p.s.*) 29 Nov. 90
Henry Bromley ....13 Jan. 91
Matthew Smith Dawson,*p.s.* 6 Mar. 95
SECOND LIEUTENANTS.
Horace Ogilvie Peacock ...19 Apr. 94
William FitzHerbert ...... 6 Mar. 95
Adj.—
Med. Officer.—Surg.Lieut. C.
Fleming .... 4 Apr. 94
Chap.—Rev. Richard Fitz
Herbert, *MA.* ....18 Apr. 85
Green.

Oxfordshire.
(*Queen's Own Oxfordshire Hussars.*)
[2nd Brigade.]
Head Quarters, Oxford.
HONORARY COLONEL.
Henry Barnett..................10 July 78
LT.COLONEL.
Art. *Visct.* Valentia, *late Lt.*
10 *Hussars* ....19 Dec. 94
MAJOR.
H. Crawley Norris, *late*
Capt. 8 *Hus.; Hon.Lt.Col.*23 Jan. 95
CAPTAINS.
Wm. D. Mackenzie, *p.s.*
Hon. Major ....29 May 78
James Francis Mason, *p.s.* 9 May 90

Sir Algernon Fras. Peyton,
Bt., late Capt. 11 *Hussars* 11 Mar. 91
Leonard Noble, *p.s., Hon.*
Major .... 4 May 92
R. T. Hermon-Hodge, *p.s.,*
Hon. Major .... 4 May 92
LIEUTENANTS.
Robert S. B. Davis............12 June 86
Alex. Nelson Hall, (*p.s.*) ...23 June 86
Cecil William Boyle, (*p.s.*) 2 Oct. 86
Hon. Wm. Fred. J. North,
p.s. ....25 Mar. 91
SECOND LIEUTENANTS.
Arthur Dugdale, *p.s.*......... 4 May 92
William Conolly ....16 July 92
Chas. R. J. *Duke of* Marl-
borough, (*p.s.*).............. 11 Feb. 93
Adj.—
Med. Officer.—Surg. Major
Horatio P. Symonds......21 July 94
Vet. Officer.—
Hon. Chap.—Very Rev. Fras.
Paget, *DD*....................23 June 94
Dark Blue—Crimson Facings.

Pembroke.
(*Castlemartin.*)
Head Quarters, Haverfordwest.
HONORARY COLONEL.
Sir Owen H. P. Scourfield,
Bart., Hon. Lt.Colonel ... 2 Aug. 90
LT.COLONEL.
Morgan J. Saurin, *p.s. late*
Capt. 6 *Dr. Gds., Hon.Col.*26 June 78
MAJOR.
Sir Charles E. G. Philipps,
Bart. p.s. Hon. Lt.Colonel 8 Aug. 91
CAPTAINS.
p.s.c. Thomas James Roch,
late Capt. R. Artillery,
Hon. Major ....24 Aug. 89
Arthur P.Saunders Davies,
p.s. ....25 Oct. 90
Ernest S. Saurin, *p.s. Hon.*
Major ....17 Oct. 91
Edw. Denman Cropper,¹*p.s.*15 June 93
LIEUTENANTS.
Antony W. J. Stokes, *p.s.*...17 Oct. 91
H. G. Saunders-Davies, *p.s.*17 Oct. 91
SECOND LIEUTENANTS.
Fred.Wm.A.H.Gillett,(*p.s.*) 5 Apr. 92
Jas. Fras. Hughes Buckley 6 Mar. 95
*Adj.—*G. B. Gench, *Captain*
4 *Dragoon Guards* ....15 Apr. 91
Med. Officer.—Surgeon Capt.
Geo. R. T. Phillips ....24 July 80
Blue—White Facings.

Shropshire.
[5th Brigade.]
Head Quarters, Shrewsbury.
HONORARY COLONEL.
F. C. *Earl of* Kilmorey, *KP.*
Hon. Colonel ....13 Apr. 89
MAJOR.
Edward H. Baldock, *p.s.*
late Lieut. Shropshire Mil.
Hon. Lt.Colonel ....22 Feb. 90
Hillyar D. Chapman ....30 Apr. 90
CAPTAINS.
Willoughby Baskerville My-
nors,² *late Lt.* 7 *Hussars* 11 Apr. 85
Hon. George R. C. Ormsby-
Gore, *p.s. late Lt.* Cold-
stream Guards, *Hon. Major* 4 Oct. 85
Charles Baldwyn Childe,³
late Capt. R. Horse Gds. 14 May 87
Thomas R. Cholmondeley 13 Apr. 89
Lloyd, *Lord* Kenyon, *p.s.* 9 May 90
G. B. H. D. *Lord* Rodney,⁴
late Capt. 1 *Life Guards*...10 May 90
Ralph Beaumont Benson,
p.s. 26 Sept.91
LIEUTENANTS.
Francis Hurt Sitwell, (*p.s.*) 11 Apr. 85
Alfred Wynne Corrie, *p.s.* 4 Sept. 89
Gordon Edw.Boileau Wood,
p.s. ....21 May 92
SECOND LIEUTENANTS.
John Brooke Cunliffe, *p.s.*16 July 90
Bryan Baldwin M. Leighton..25 Feb. 91
Walter Dugdale, *p.s.*..........12 Mar. 92
J. P. H.Heywood-Lonsdale 3 June 93
W.Walt. Graham Phillipps 14 Nov. 94

Adj.—E. A. Critchley, *Capt.*
4 Hussars .... 1 May 90
Med. Officer.—*Surgeon Capt.*
John D. Lloyd .... 1 May 80
Vet. Officer.—*Vet. Captain*
Henry Barnes ....24 Dec. 92
Blue—Scarlet Facings.

North Somerset.
[4th Brigade.]
Head Quarters, Bath.
HONORARY COLONEL.
Rt. Hon. R. E. St. L. *Earl of Cork and Orrery, KP.; Aide de Camp to the Queen, and Colonel, Master of the Horse* ....27 May 93
LT. COLONEL.
C. S. C. *Visct.* Dungarvan,
p.s., DL..................27 May 93
MAJOR.

CAPTAINS.
Charles Gathorne Hill, *p.* 30 July 87
Richd. J. BayntunHippisley,
p.s. .... 8 Nov. 90
Roger Marriott-Dodington,
p.s. .... 4 June 92
J. Lawrence Benthall, *p.s.*10 June 93
Douglas Hamilton M'Lean,
p.s. .... 4 Oct. 93
LIEUTENANTS.
John G. Blagrave ......18 Apr. 74
Robert Edm. Dickinson,*p.s.*25 July 83
Lord CharlesW.A.Montagu,
p.s. .... 7 Aug. 86
T. Raymond Symons, (*p.s.*) 6 May 91
SECOND LIEUTENANTS.
Henry G. *Visct.* Clifden,*p.s.*17 June 91
George Abraham Gibbs ...28 Jan. 93
Hon. Geoffrey Carr Glyn...23 Dec. 93
Sir Cecil Leopold Miles, *Bt.*24 Feb. 94
Adj.—
Med. Officer.—*Surg. Lt. Col.*
John J. Saville..............13 Apr. 92
Vet. Officer.—*Vet. Lt.* Frank
William Leigh .... 4 Nov. 93
Hon. Chap.—Rev. Wm. M.
Loir ....24 June 74
Blue—Scarlet Facings.

West Somerset.
[4th Brigade.]
Head Quarters, Taunton.
LT. COLONEL.
Hon. Arthur W. A. N. Hood,
CB., late Capt. 25 F. *Hon. Colonel*..................23 Mar. 72
MAJOR.

CAPTAINS.
Henry Thomas Daniel, *p.s.* 12 May 88
Jefferys PhilipT. Allen, *p.s.* 13 Apr. 89
Wm. Barrett, *late Lieut.* 5
Dragoon Guards .... 9 Apr. 92
LIEUTENANTS.
Lewis Harold G. Morgan,
(*p.s.*)..................12 July 84
Arthur Francis Levita,*p.s.* 5 Mar. 90
SECOND LIEUTENANT.
Alex. Gould Barrett, (*p.s.*) 17 Oct. 91
Adj.—
Med. Officer.—*Surg. Lt. Col.*
Samuel Farrant ....23 Sept. 93
Vet. Officer.—*Vet. Lieut.*
George Hill Elder .... 4 Apr. 83
Hon. Chaplain.—*Rev.* Charles
E. Chard, *BA*..............28 Mar. 94
Blue—Scarlet Facings.

Staffordshire.
(*Queen's Own Royal Regiment.*)
[8th Brigade.]
Head Quarters, Lichfield.
HONORARY COLONEL.
Henry, *Marquis of* Anglesey 5 Mar. 87

LT. COLONEL.
Cromartie, *Duke of* Sutherland, *p. Hon. Colonel* ...... 6 May 91
MAJOR.
Gerald F. Talbot, *Hon. Lt. Colonel*..................13 Apr. 87
CAPTAINS.
James Heath, *MP. p. Hon. Major* ....14 June 76
William *Lord* Bagot, *Hon. Major, Gentleman Usher to the Queen* ....21 Feb. 80
Sir Reginald Hardy, *Bt.*,
p.s., (l), Hon. Major ......13 Sept. 84
Albert O. Worthington,
Hon. Major .... 2 May 85
Fras. Edw. Fitzherbert,*p.s.*
Hon. Major .... 6 June 85
Arthur H. Heath, *p.s.* ......16 Oct. 86
Hon. Hy. Stuart Littleton,*p.s.*18 June 87
William Bromley-Davenport, *p.s.*..................30 Dec. 91
Henry Staveley Hill, *p.s.*....10 Sept. 92
LIEUTENANTS.
Ralph Sneyd, *p.s.* .... 6 Jan. 83
Hugh Spencer Charrington,
(*p.s.*)..................28 Mar. 85
Chas. Tertius Mander, *p.s.* 23 Aug. 90
Gerald Holbech Hardy, *p.s.*23 Aug. 90
Frank Addison Brace, *p.s.*23 Aug. 90
Philip Staveley Foster, *p.s.*30 July 92
William Moat, *p.s.* ....30 July 92
Thos. A. Wight-Boycott ...15 Mar. 93
SECOND LIEUTENANTS.
Adj.—
Med. Officer—*Surgeon Capt.*
E. W. Welchman............ 1 Aug. 94
Vet. Officer.—*Vet. Lieut.* F.
G. Warmington ....29 Apr. 93
Hon. Chaplain.—*Rev.* J. Gillart, *BA*.................. 2 May 85
Blue—Scarlet Facings.

The Loyal Suffolk Hussars.
(*The Duke of York's Own.*)
[7th Brigade.]
Head Quarters, Bury St. Edmunds.
HONORARY COLONEL.
H.R.H. G. F. E. A. *Duke of* York, *KG.* ....30 July 92
LT. COLONEL.
Alfred George Lucas,*p.s.*...18 Apr. 91
MAJOR.
Richard Beale Colvin, *p.s., Aide de Camp to Colonel N. Barnardiston, Comdg. the Brigade*..................17 May 92
CAPTAINS.
Arthur Wm. Fulcher, *p.s.*....24 May 90
Fletcher H. G. Cruickshank,
p.s., late Capt. R. Art. Hon. Major .... 4 May 92
Henry Basham Dickinson,
p.s...................17 May 92
Hugh Rose, *p.s.*..................20 May 93
Walter Raymond Greene,
p.s...................14 Oct. 93
Sir Geo. R. Leigh Hare,
Bart. late Lt. 2 *Life Gds.*10 Feb. 94
LIEUTENANT.
Percival A. O. Whitaker,
late Lt. 4 *Bn. Essex Regt.* 18 June 92
Hon. Douglas A. Tollemache, *p.s.* ....21 July 94
Hon. Joseph L. Hy. Petre21 July 94
Prince Frederick V. Duleep
Singh ....21 July 94
SECOND LIEUTENANTS.
Hon. Hy. Jacob Astley......10 Mar. 94
Roger Orme Kerrison ...... 7 July 94
Adj.—H. Alexander, *Capt.*
10 Hussars .... 1 Feb. 90
Med. Officer.—*Surg. Capt.*
Robt. Harry Lucas..........14 May 87
Hon. Chap.— *Rev.* L. D.
Kenyon-Stow ....14 May 92
Green—Scarlet Facings.

Warwickshire.
[8th Brigade.]
Head Quarters, Warwick.
HONORARY COLONEL.
LT. COLONEL.
H. *Lord* Willoughby de
Broke, *Hon. Colonel* ......12 Dec. 91

MAJORS.
Hugh de G. *Marq. of* Hertford, *late Lt. and Capt. Gr. Gds., Hon. Lt. Colonel* 16 Jan. 92
CAPTAINS.
William Charles Alston,
Hon. Major .... 9 Mar. 77
Fra. R. C. G. *Earl of* Warwick, *Hon. Major* ....26 Aug. 76
Arthur J. Armstrong, *late Capt.*16 *Lancers,Hon.Maj.* 8 Aug. 77
C. W. *Earl of* Aylesford,
late Major 3 *Bn. S. Stafford Regiment, Hon. Major*...16 Jan. 86
James B. Dugdale, *Hon. Major* ....21 Apr. 86
Rowland John Beech,[1] *late Lt.* 2 *LifeGuards, Hon.Maj.*29 May 86
Hon. Fra. Dudley Leigh, *p.s.* 24 Mar. 88
William Mackay Low, *p.s.*...26 Apr. 90
LIEUTENANTS.
Henry A. Adderley, (*p.s.*)... 2 May 77
Frank Dugdale, (*p.s.*) .... 1 July 80
Oswald Hon. P. Petre, *p.s.*17 Aug. 81
Basil Hanbury, (*p.s.*)..........16 Dec. 85
John Peter ArkFitzwright,(*p.s.*) 6 Feb. 86
Morton Peto Lucas, (*p.s.*)...22 Oct. 92
Rich. Butler Charteris, *p.s.* 22 Oct. 92
SECOND LIEUTENANTS.
Hon. A. H. Fulke Greville 21 June 90
Hon. Richard Greville Verney, (*p.s.*) .... 3 Oct. 91
Adj.—
Med. Officer.—*Surg. Lt. Col.*
Thos. Wm. Bullock ...... 1 Dec. 91
Vet. Officer.—*Vet. Lieut.*
Thomas Horton ....13 Feb. 92
Hon. Chap.—*Hon. and Rev.*
W. R. Verney ....18 Mar. 74
Dark Blue—White Facings.

Westmoreland and Cumberland.
[14th Brigade.]
Head Quarters, Penrith.
HONORARY COLONEL.
Sir H. Ralph Vane, *Bart.* 29 Aug. 91
LT. COLONEL.
Humphrey P. Senhouse, *p. Hon. Colonel*.................. 4 Oct. 93
MAJORS.
Hugh Cecil, *Earl of* Lonsdale ....28 Nov. 91
CAPTAINS.
Francis Markham, *p. late Capt. Rif.Brig.Hon. Major* 25 Oct. 84
Josceline FitzRoy Bagot,
MP. p.s., late Capt. Gren. Gds. Hon. Major .... 2 May 88
George G. Kirklinton, *p.s.*...16 Jan. 92
Joseph Harris, *p.s.*..............16 July 92
Arthur Paul Bridson, *p.s.*....24 June 93
Stanley Hughes le Fleming,
p.s. ....13 Mar. 95
LIEUTENANTS.
Robert Jefferson, *p.s.*..........20 Mar. 86
Hamlet Riley, *p.s.*..............12 Mar. 92
Jos. Hugh Jefferson, (*p.s.*) 13 Mar. 95
Charles Edw. Fisher, *Assist. Brig. Adjt.* 14 *Brigade* ...13 Mar. 95
SECOND LIEUTENANTS.

Adj.—
Med. Officer.—*Surg. Capt.*
J. E. Bowser, *MB*......12 Sept. 91
Vet. Officer.—
Hon. Chap.—*Rev.* George E.
Hasell ....29 Apr. 74
Scarlet—White Facings.

Royal Wiltshire.

Prince of Wales' Own Royal Regiment.)
[3rd Brigade.]
Head Quarters, Salisbury.
HONORARY COLONEL.
J. Alexander, *Marq. of* Bath 15 Nov. 90
LT. COLONEL.
George Sotheron Estcourt,
 Hon. Colonel ....15 Nov. 90
MAJOR.
Walter H. Long, *Hon. Lt.*
 Colonel ....13 Dec. 90
CAPTAINS.
Rt. Hon. Lord C. F. Brudenell-
 Bruce, p.s., *Hon. Major*...27 Apr. 82
Sir Algernon Neeld, *Bart.*
 Hon. Major ....2 Oct. 82
Sir H. Bruce Meux, Bt., p.s.
 Hon. Major......................29 Dec. 83
Fitzroy Pleydell Goddard,
 p.s. .... 8 Sept. 86
Joshua R. G. Gwatkin, p.s. 25 May 89
G. Prior Goldney, p.s., *Hon.*
 Major ....13 Dec. 90
Thos. Henry, *Visct.* Wey-
 mouth, p.s. .... 2 Sept. 93
Geo. Llewellen Palmer, p. 2 Sept. 93
Arch. Edward Miles,[1] *late*
 King's R. Rifles ....23 Jan. 95
LIEUTENANTS.
John Michael F. Fuller,
 Aide de Camp to the Gov-
 ernor General of India...19 Jan. 84
John Fred. Stancomb, (p.s.)16 Jan. 92
John M. Benett-Stanford,
 late Lieut. 1 *Dragoons* ...17 Dec. 92
SECOND LIEUTENANTS.
Henry Ludlow Lopes, (p.s.) 5 Dec. 88
Sir J. P. Dickson-Poynder,
 Bt. MP. p.s. late Lt. 3 *Bn.*
 Royal Scots.................. 8 Jan. 90
James Joicey, p.s. .... 6 May 91
Sir Thos. Fowler, Burt.(p.s.)20 Feb. 92
Roger Alvin Poore ....11 Feb. 93
George Eric Mackay ...... 4 Apr. 94
Adj.—H. J. Scobell, *Capt.*
 2 *Dragoons* .... 9 Oct. 89
Med. Officers.—Surg. Lt. G.
 T. K. Maurice .... 9 May 92
Surg. Lt. Ernest Kings-
 cote, *MB.* ....17 Mar. 94
Vet. Officer. — Vet. Lieut.
 Tom V. Pettifer ....13 Mar. 95
Blue—Scarlet Facings.

Worcestershire.

(The Queen's Own Worcestershire Hussars.)
[5th Brigade.]
Head Quarters, Worcester.
HONORARY COLONEL.
Aug. F. A. *Lord* Sandys ...4 July 85
LT. COLONEL.
Robert G. *Lord* Windsor...10 May 93
MAJORS.
W. H. *Earl of* Dudley, p.s.
 DL. ....23 Sept. 93
Sanford G. T. Scobell, p.
 Hon. Lt. Colonel ....25 July 94

CAPTAINS.
Sir H. F. Lambert, *Bt.* p.s. 6 June 85
Joseph Henry Smith, p.s..... 6 June 85
Henry Howard, p.s. ....2 Sept. 85
James Baldwin, p.s............16 July 90
John Howard Cartland, p.s. 6 Jan. 94
John Henry Crane, p.s. ... 6 Jan. 94
LIEUTENANTS.
Edward Alfred Broome......29 May 86
Ronald Moncreiffe, p.s.......19 Sept. 91
Henry R. Mansel Porter, *late*
 2nd Lt. 1 *Dragoons* ....26 Sept. 91
E. G. Bromley-Martin, p.s. 16 May 94
Walter Wm. Wiggin, p.s. 16 May 94
Henry Bennett Dain, (p.s.)16 May 94
SECOND LIEUTENANTS.
Hon. Robert A. Ward ......22 Sept. 88
Adj.—H. C. Page-Hender-
 son, *Major* 6 *Dragoons* ... 8 June 91
Chap.—Rev. David Melville 9 June 68
Med. Officer.—Surg. Capt.
 Arthur O. Holbeche ......19 Sept. 85
Vet. Officer.—
Blue—Scarlet Busby-Bag and Plume.

Yorkshire Hussars.

(Princess of Wales's Own.)
[13th Brigade.]
Head Quarters, York.
HONORARY COLONEL.
William Henry Harrison-
 Broadley....................... 5 Oct. 81
LT. COLONEL.
H. U. *Earl of* Harewood,
 late Lt. & Capt. Gr. Gds.,
 Hon. Colonel.................. 5 Nov. 8:
MAJOR.
Hon. William T. O. Powlett,
 Hon. Lt. Colonel .... 5 Nov. 81
CAPTAINS.
Beilby *Lord* Wenlock, *Hon.*
 *Major, Governor of Madras*18 Nov. 74
Ernest W. Beckett, *MP.* p.s.
 Hon. Major ....12 Jan. 84
Richard F. T. Gascoigne,
 Hon. Major, late Capt.
 R. Horse Guards .... 9 Aug. 84
Fras. Rich. H. S. Sutton, p.s. 12 June 86
Hon. Fras. Hbt. Dawnay, p.s. 5 May 88
Joseph J. D. Jefferson, p.s.
 Hon. Major ....10 Feb. 91
Chas. W. Ernest Duncombe
 (p.s.) .... 5 May 94
James J. Harrison, p.s. ... 5 May 94
Edwin Wilfrid Stanyforth,
 p.s. .... 5 May 94
Denis St. George Daly, late
 Capt. 18 *Hussars* ....19 May 94
LIEUTENANTS.
Darcy Bruce Wilson, p.s. ...14 Sept. 81
Hon. Tatton L. Fox-Wil-
 loughby (p.s.) .... 2 Sept. 85
Wm. Frns. H. *Visct.* Rain-
 cliffe, (p.s.)..................28 Nov. 85
Wentworth C. Blackett
 Beaumont, (p.s.) ....12 June 86
James Lionel Dugdale, (p.s.) 30 Oct. 86

SECOND LIEUTENANTS.
Wm. Gervase Beckett, p.s....14 Jan. 88
George Elliot, p.s. .... 8 Sept. 88
Rupert Evelyn Beckett, p s. 6 Feb. 92
Chas. Lionel Ward-Jackson,
 (p.s.) .... 5 Oct. 92
Stephen F. Wombwell (p.s.)26 Nov. 92
Robt. Wilfrid *Lord* Dora-
 more, p.s. .... 4 Jan. 93
Ernest C. Meysey-Thompson 22 Aug. 94
Chas. Hy. Wellesley Wilson 5 Sept. 94
Henry B. de la P. Beresford
 Peirse ....26 Sept. 94
Digby Leonard A. Cayley 26 Sept. 94
Adj.—
Med. Officer.—Surg. Lt. Col.
 Richard Hewetson ....27 Feb. 92
Vet. Officer.—Vet. Lieut.
 George Thomas Pickering 7 June 84
Blue.

Yorkshire Dragoons.

[13th Brigade.]
Head Quarters, Doncaster.
HONORARY COLONEL.
W. T. S. *Earl* Fitzwilliam,
 KG. ....25 Dec. 86
LT. COLONEL.
Aldred Fred. Geo. Beresford,
 Earl of Scarborough, *late*
 Lt. 7 *Hussars*..................24 Oct. 91
MAJOR.
Richd. H. Heywood-Jones,
 p.s. ....16 Jan. 95
CAPTAINS.
Wm. F. Lee, p.s., *Hon. Major* 13 Apr. 87
Mark Firth, p.s. ....23 June 88
Richd. Jas. Streatfeild, *late*
 Lieut. 5 *Dragoon Guards* 5 Sept. 88
Cecil Harold Simpson ...... 4 Mar. 93
Richard Key Micklethwait,
 p.s. ....20 Feb. 95
Thomas Wilson (p.s.)........ 20 Feb. 95
LIEUTENANTS.
Chas. Edw. Jeffcock, p.s.....11 Mar. 93
Charles Brook, p.s.............14 Oct. 93
Jno. Skipwith H. Fullerton,
 (p.s.) ....20 Feb. 95
F. S. Utterton Hatchard (p.s.)20 Feb. 95
Francis William Green......20 Feb. 95
William M'Kenzie Smith,
 p.s. ....20 Feb. 95
SECOND LIEUTENANTS.
Samuel Suckley ....23 July 92
Samuel Roberts ....28 Mar. 94
Henry J. Hope Barton ...16 Jan. 95
Adj.—
Acting Qr. Mr. — Hugh
 M'Carter Joel ....25 July 91
Med. Officer.—Surg. Lieut.
 Percy Barnard Mackay 18 Mar. 93
Hon. Chap.—Rev. Canon H.
 J. Tebbutt, *MA.* ....28 Sept. 89
Vet. Officer.—Vet. Lieut. R.
 C. Thompson...................25 Oct. 90
Dark Blue.

YEOMANRY BRIGADES.

1st BRIGADE, 7, Montpelier Terrace, London.—BERKS, MIDDLESEX.
Commanding Brigade, The Senior Commanding Officer. *Adjutant*, Captain F. F. Colvin, Lancers, 17 Sept. 94.

2nd BRIGADE, Buckingham.—BUCKINGHAMSHIRE, OXFORDSHIRE.
Commanding Brigade, The Senior Commanding Officer. *Adjutant*, Captain J. H. Aspinwall, 5 Dr. Gds. 1 June 93.

3rd BRIGADE, Gloucester.—ROYAL WILTSHIRE, GLOUCESTERSHIRE.
Commanding Brigade, The Senior Commanding Officer.
- *Adj.* Major W. H. Wyndham-Quin, 16 Lancers, 9 Oct. 94.
- *Assist. Adjutant*, Captain H. H. Calvert, Gloucestershire Hussars, 30 Nov. 94.

4th BRIGADE, Taunton.—NORTH SOMERSET, WEST SOMERSET.
Commanding Brigade, The Senior Commanding Officer. *Adjutant*. Captain W. E. R. Collis, 5 Lancers, 28 Oct. 94.

5th BRIGADE, Worcester.—WORCESTERSHIRE, SHROPSHIRE.
Commanding Brigade, The Senior Commanding Officer. *Adjutant*,

6th BRIGADE, Leicester.—DERBYSHIRE, LEICESTERSHIRE.
Commanding Brigade, The Senior Commanding Officer. *Adjutant*, Captain H. C. Dugdale, 16 Lancers, 1 Jan. 95.

7th BRIGADE, St. Albans.—SUFFOLK, HERTS.
Commanding Brigade, The Senior Commanding Officer. *Adjutant*, Major C. H. E. Coote, 11 Hussars, 1 Feb. 95.

8th BRIGADE, Lichfield.—STAFFORDSHIRE, WARWICKSHIRE.
Commanding Brigade, The Senior Commanding Officer. *Adjutant*, Captain L. Stamer, 16 Lancers, 1 Sept. 94.

9th BRIGADE, Chester.—CHESHIRE, LANCASHIRE HUSSARS.
Commanding Brigade, The Senior Commanding Officer. *Adjutant*, Major S. Frewen, 16 Lancers, 1 Apr. 93.

11th BRIGADE, Glasgow.—AYRSHIRE, LANARKSHIRE, LANARKSHIRE (QUEEN'S OWN ROYAL GLASGOW).
Commanding Brigade, The Senior Commanding Officer.
- *Adjutant*, Captain F. W. Duff, 9 Lancers, 8 Sept. 93.
- *Assist. Adj.* Captain D. W. Shaw, Ayrshire Yeomanry, 27 June 94.

12th BRIGADE, Newcastle-on-Tyne.—NORTHUMBERLAND, LOTHIANS AND BERWICKSHIRE.
Commanding Brigade, The Senior Commanding Officer.
- *Adj.* Captain R. H. Carr-Ellison, 1 Dragoons, 25 Sept. 94.
- *Assist. Adj.* Lieut. T. Broadwood, Lothians and Berwick Yeomanry, 2 Apr. 94.

13th BRIGADE, Cemetery Road, York.—YORKSHIRE HUSSARS, YORKSHIRE DRAGOONS.
Commanding Brigade, The Senior Commanding Officer. *Adjutant*, Captain L. J. Richardson, 14 Hussars, 1 June 93.

14th BRIGADE, Worsley.—WESTMORELAND AND CUMBERLAND, DUKE OF LANCASTER'S OWN.
Commanding Brigade, The Senior Commanding Officer.
- *Adjutant*, Capt. T. M. Jones Tailby, 11 Hussars, 1 Apr. 9.
- *Assist. Adj.* Second Lieut. C. E. Fisher, Westmoreland and Cumberland Yeomanry, 30 Jan. 95.

15th BRIGADE, Wrexham.—DENBIGHSHIRE, MONTGOMERYSHIRE.
Commanding Brigade, The Senior Commanding Officer.
- *Adjutant*, Capt. H. E. S. Pocklington, 15 Hussars, 23 Oct. 93.
- *Assist. Adj.* Lieut. C. E. Wynne-Eyton, Denbigh Hussars, 7 Feb. 94.

17th BRIGADE, Park Row, Nottingham.—SOUTH NOTTINGHAMSHIRE, SHERWOOD RANGERS.
Commanding Brigade, The Senior Commanding Officer.
- *Adjutant*, Captain C. B. Harvey, 10 Hussars, 24 July 94.
- *Assist. Adj.* Maj. G. Fellows, S. Notts Yeomanry, 9 May 93.

PORTSMOUTH BRIGADE, Netley.—HAMPSHIRE, DORSET.
Commanding Brigade, The Senior Commanding Officer. *Adjutant*, Captain K. R. Balfour, 1 Dragoons, 20 Nov. 93.

DEVON BRIGADE, Exeter.—ROYAL 1ST DEVON, ROYAL NORTH DEVON
Commanding Brigade, The Senior Commanding Officer. *Adjutant*, Captain H. C. Higgs, 21 Hussars, 1 June 93.

KENT BRIGADE, Cavalry Depot, Canterbury.—ROYAL EAST KENT, WEST KENT.
Commanding Brigade, The Senior Commanding Officer.
- *Adjutant*, Captain A. H. R. Ogilvy, 13 Hussars, 11 June 94.
- *Assist. Adj.* Major E. Frewen, East Kent Yeomanry, 20 Feb. 95.

War Services of the Officers of the Militia Artillery and Engineers.

[1] Sir E. S. Smyth.—For War Services, see West Surrey Regiment, p. 236.

[2] Colonel Pottinger served at the attack on the Burda Hills 19 December 1859.

[3] Major Heron-Maxwell served in Natal and the Transvaal during the latter part of the Zulu war of 1879 (mentioned in despatches, Medal with Clasp). Served in the Boer war of 1881 in Barrow's Mounted Infantry.

[4] Lt.Colonel W. Taylor served in the Egyptian war of 1882, and was present at the battle of Tel-el-Kebir (Medal with Clasp, 4th Class of the Medjidie, and Khedive's Star). Served with the Burmese Expedition in 1886-87 (mentioned in despatches, Medal with Clasp).

[5] Lord Coke served with the 1st Battalion Scots Guards in the Egyptian war of 1882, and was present at the battle of Tel-el-Kebir (Medal with Clasp, and Khedive's Star). Served in the expedition to the Soudan in 1885 with the 2nd Battalion of the Scots Guards, and was present in the engagements at Hasheen and Temai (Clasp).

[6] Colonel Tottenham served with the Scots Fusilier Guards in the Crimean campaign from 17th Jan. 1855 including the siege and fall of Sebastopol (Medal with one Clasp, 5th Class of the Medjidie, and Turkish Medal).

[7] Captain Hillas served in the Zulu war of 1879, and was present in the engagement at Ulundi (Medal with Clasp).

[8] Colonel Lawrence served with the 14th Regiment in the New Zealand war of 1860-61, and in that of 1863-64, including the action at Kohewa (Medal).

[9] Captain Larymore served with the expedition against the Jebus, Lagos, in 1892 (mentioned in despatches, Medal with Clasp).

[9†] Colonel Lowther served on the Gold Coast from December 1873 to the end of the Ashanti campaign (Medal).

[10] Sir Henry Havelock-Allan served as D.A.Q.M. General in the Persian Expedition from 15th Feb. 1857, including the bombardment and capture of Mohumrah (Medal). Served throughout the Indian campaigns of 1857-59 as Aide de Camp to General Havelock from 7th July, in the actions of Futtehpore, Aoung, Pandoo Nuddee, and Cawnpore, and as D. A. Adj. General to the force from 20th July 1857, in the actions of Oonao, Busseerutgunge (horse shot), Nawabgunge, Boorbeeake Chowkee, Bithoor, Mungarwar, and Alumbagh, and relief of Lucknow on 25th Sept.— langerously wounded by musket-ball through left elbow, and horse shot; defence of the Residency until relieved by Lord Clive on 17th Nov., on which day again severely wounded by a rifle-ball through left shoulder. Within a month joined the Joonpore Field Force under General Franks as D. A. Adj. General and was present at the actions of Nusrutpore, Chanda, Umeerpore, and Sultanpore. Present with the 4th Division before Lucknow from 4th March till its fall, including the storming of the Lesser Emaumbarra and the Kaiserbagh. Served as D. A. Adj. General from 29th March with Lugard's Column, and present at the relief of Azimghur; operations to 4th June (sabre cut on right

War Services of the Officers of the Militia Artillery and Engineers. 615

hand) against the Jugdespore rebels, including the attack on that stronghold and eight minor skirmishes. As D. A. General in the disturbed districts of Ghazeepore and Behar under Brigadier Douglas from 15th June to Nov. 1858, including the operations in the former district in July and August, and the campaign in Shahabad in Oct. and November. Commanded a detached body of 250. Mounted Riflemen and Cavalry in pursuit of the rebels after they evacuated Jugdespore on 18th Oct., intercepted and turned them from the Soane river, and three times engaged and defeated them, once at Nonadee on 20th Oct., inflicting considerable slaughter. Commanded a Detachment of Hodson's Horse with the Army in Oude under Lord Clyde, and present at the skirmish at Burgudeca, capture of Musjeedia, and final action on the Raptee on 31st Dec. 1858. Served till the conclusion of the campaign in command of the 1st Regt. Hodson's Horse. Was repeatedly mentioned in despatches, has received the Victoria Cross, the Brevets of Major and Lt.Colonel, a year's service for Lucknow, and Medal with two Clasps : was awarded the V℃ under the following circumstances : "'In the combat at Cawnpore Lieutenant Havelock was my Aide de Camp. The 64th Regiment had been much under artillery fire, from which it had severely suffered. The whole of the infantry were lying down in line, when, perceiving that the enemy had brought out the last reserved gun, a 24-pounder, and were rallying round it, I called up the regiment to rise and advance. Without any other word from me, Lieutenant Havelock placed himself on his horse, in front of the centre of the 64th, opposite the muzzle of the gun. Major Sterling, commanding the regiment, was in front, dismounted, but the Lieutenant continued to move steadily on in front of the regiment at a foot pace, on his horse. The gun discharged shot until the troops were within a short distance, when they fired grape. In went the corps, led by the Lieutenant, who still steered steadily on the gun's muzzle until it was mastered by a rush of the 64th.'—*Extract of a Telegram from the late Major General Sir Henry Havelock to the Commander in Chief in India, dated Cawnpore, 18th August 1857.*" Served in the New Zealand war of 1863 and to the end of 1864 (Medal), and present at Rangariri, Paterangi, and Orakau; commanded at the skirmish of Waiare, where the enemy's loss fell wholly on the Ngatimaniapoto tribe, the originators of the war.

[11] Colonel Younger served in the Afghan war in 1878-79 with the Royal Horse Artillery (Medal).
[12] Captain Stoughton served in the Boer war of 1881.
[13] Lt.Colonel Edwards served in the expedition to the Soudan in 1885 with the Commissariat and Transport Staff (Medal with Clasp, and Khedive's Star).
[14] Major Dalrymple served in the Boer war of 1881 with the Natal Field Force.
[15] Colonel Brooksbank served the Eastern campaign of 1854-55 with the 38th Regiment, and was present at the battle of Inkerman, siege and fall of Sebastopol, including the repulse of a sortie on the 21st December, attack and occupation of the Cemetery (Medal with two Clasps, 5th Class of the Medjidie, and Turkish Medal).
[16] Colonel Legard served in the Zulu war in 1879 as Acting Deputy Assistant Quarter Master General to the 1st Division (Medal with Clasp).
[17] Colonel Lewes served with the Buffs at the siege of Sebastopol in 1855, and commanded the covering party of the Buffs at the assault of the Redan on the 8th Sept. (Medal with Clasp, Brevet of Major, Knight of the Legion of Honor, 5th Class of the Medjidie, and Turkish Medal).
[18] Sir James Hills-Johnes served in suppression of the Indian mutiny in 1857-58, including the actions on the 30th and 31st May on the Hindun, battles of Budleekeserai and Nujjufghur, siege and capture of Delhi (severely wounded on 9th July 1857), siege and capture of Lucknow, Rohilcund campaign, taking of Bareilly, and action of Mohumdee (several times mentioned in despatches, also by the Governor General in Council, Victoria Cross, Medal with two Clasps, and Brevet of Major) : was awarded the V℃ "for very gallant conduct before Delhi, on the 9th July 1857, in defending the position assigned to him in case of alarm, and for noble behaviour on the part of Major Tombs in twice coming to his Subaltern's rescue, and on each occasion killing his man.—'Yesterday, the 9th July 1857, Lieutenant J. Hills was on piquet duty, with two guns, at the mound to the right of the camp. About 11 o'clock a.m. there was a rumour that the enemy's cavalry were coming down on his post. Lieutenant Hills proceeded to take up the position assigned in case of alarm, but, before he reached the spot, he saw the enemy close upon his guns before they had time to form up. To enable him to do this he boldly charged, single-handed, the head of the enemy's column, cut down the first man, struck the second, and was then ridden down, horse and all. On getting up and searching for his sword, three more men came at him (two mounted); the first man he wounded with his pistol; he caught the lance of the second in his left hand, and wounded him with his sword; the first man then came on again, and was cut down; the third man (on foot) then came up, and wrenched the sword from Lieutenant Hills, who fell in the struggle, and the enemy was about to cut him down when Major Tombs, who had gone up to visit his two guns, saw what was going on, rushed in and shot the man and saved Lieutenant Hills. By this time the enemy's cavalry had passed by, and Major Tombs and Lieutenant Hills went to look after the wounded men, when one of the enemy passed with Lieutenant Hills' pistol; he first cut at Lieutenant Hills who parried the blow, and he then turned on Major Tombs, who received the blow in the same manner. His second attack on the Lieutenant was more successful, as he was cut down with a bad sword-cut on the head, and would have been, no doubt, killed, had not Major Tombs rushed in and put his sword through the man.'—*Extract from Despatch of Lt.Colonel M. Mackenzie, Commanding 1st Brigade of Horse Artillery, dated Camp near Delhi, 10th July 1857, and published in the Supplement of the London Gazette of 15th January 1858.*" Commanded the 8-inch Mortars in the Abyssinian campaign from the 6th Feb. 1868, and was present at the capture of Magdala (mentioned in despatches, Brevet of Lt.Colonel, and Medal). Commanded the Peshawur Mountain Battery throughout the Looshai Expedition, Chittagong Column, 1871-72 (mentioned in despatches, CB., Medal with Clasp). Served in the Afghan war of 1878-80, and was present at the occupation of Candahar and Khelat-i-Ghilzie, in the engagement at Charasiab on the 6th October 1879 (mentioned in despatches), in the occupation of Cabul, and in the operations around Sherpore as Assistant Adjutant General of the Candahar Field Force (mentioned in despatches) ; was afterwards appointed Military Governor of the city of Cabul and Commander of a portion of the line of defences at Sherpore and of the 3rd Division of the Northern Afghanistan Field Force (received the thanks of both Houses of Parliament, KCB. and Medal with two Clasps).
[19] Colonel Lewis served with the 5th Dragoon Guards in the Crimean campaign in 1854-55, including the battles of Balaklava and Inkerman, battle of the Tchernaya, and siege of Sebastopol (Medal with three Clasps, Turkish War Medal, and 5th Class of the Medjidie).
[20] Lord Tredegar served in the Eastern campaign in 1854-55 with the 17th Lancers, and was present at the battle of Balaklava (Medal with Clasp).
[21] Lord Raglan served in the Afghan war in 1879-80, and took part in the march to Candahar with the force under Major General Phayre (mentioned in despatches, Medal).
[22] Major Lindsay served in the Boer war of 1881. Served in the Soudan campaign in 1885, and was present in the engagement at the Tofrek zereba (Medal with two Clasps, and Khedive's Star).
[23] Lt.Colonel Robbins served with the 91st Highlanders in the Zulu war of 1879, during the latter portion of the campaign as Acting Adjutant, and was present in the action of Gingindhlovu and relief of Ekowe (Medal with Clasp).

War Services of the Officers of the Militia Infantry.

Royal Scots.—[1] Lord Lothian served on the Staff of Sir J. Outram in the Persian war; was present at the taking of Mohumrah, and accompanied the troops in their advance upon Ahwaz (Medal with Clasp).
[2] Colonel Gordon served throughout the Eastern campaign of 1854-55, including the battles of Alma, Balaklava, and Inkerman, siege and fall of Sebastopol, and sortie of 26th Oct.; was Aide de Camp to General Simpson from 22nd Aug. to 12th Nov. 1855 (Medal with four Clasps, 5th Class of the Medjidie, and Turkish Medal).
[3] Lt.Colonel Scobie served throughout the second phase of the Ashanti war in 1874 with the 42nd Highlanders, and was present at the battles of Amoaful and Ordahsu and at the capture of Coomassie (Medal with Clasp).
[4] Major Grant served in the Egyptian war of 1882, and was present at the battle of Tel-el-Kebir (Medal with Clasp, and Khedive's Star).
[5] Major Dundas served with the 1st Battalion Scots Guards in the Egyptian war of 1882, and was present at the battle of Tel-el-Kebir (Medal with Clasp, and Khedive's Star).
[7] Lieut. Horniblow served with the Bechuanaland Expedition under Sir Charles Warren in 1884-85 with the 1st Battalion of the Royal Scots.
West Surrey Regiment.—[1] Lieut. Dyke served in the Burmese Expedition in 1885-87 with the 2nd Battalion Queen's Royal West Surrey Regiment under Brigadier General Lockhart (Medal with Clasp).

The Buffs.—¹ Captain Colley served with the Buffs throughout the operations in the Malay Peninsula in 1875-76, including the actions of the 4th 14th and 20th January (Medal with Clasp).

Lancaster Regiment.—¹ Major North served in the Soudan campaign in 1885 with the Commissariat and Transport Staff (Medal with Clasp, and Khedive's Star).

Warwickshire Regiment.—² Major Gretton.—See Civil Decorations for Gallantry, "Hart's Annual Army List," p. 786.

Royal Fusiliers.—¹ Colonel Dundas served with the 62nd Regiment in the Crimea from the 16th August 1855, including the siege and fall of Sebastopol, and attack of the Redan on the 8th September (Medal with Clasp, and Turkish Medal).

² Lt.Colonel Bircham served with the 3rd Battalion 60th Rifles in the Zulu war of 1879, and was present at the action of Gingindhlovu and relief of Ekowe (Medal with Clasp).

³ Colonel Wynter served with the 33rd Regiment throughout the Abyssinian campaign of 1867-68, and was present at the storming and capture of Magdala (Medal). Served in the Ashanti war, and was present at the capture of Adubiassie (Medal with Clasp). Served in the Afghan war in 1879-80, and was present in the engagement at Charasiab on the 6th October 1879 and in the operations round Cabul in December 1879, including the investment of Sherpore (mentioned in despatches); accompanied Sir Frederick Roberts in the march to Candahar, and was present at the battle of Candahar (mentioned in despatches, Brevet of Major, Medal with three Clasps, and Bronze Decoration).

⁴ Major La Terrière served with the 19th Hussars in the Egyptian war of 1882, and was present at the battle of Tel-el-Kebir (Medal with Clasp, and Khedive's Star). Served during the Nile expedition in 1884-85 with the Egyptian Army on the Bedouin Frontier and on the Lines of Communication; carried the despatches from the front to Korti on several occasions, and the Senior Staff Officer at Korti until its evacuation (Clasp).

⁵ Major Griesbach served in the Afghan war in 1880 as Orderly Officer to Brigadier General Nuttall, Commanding Cavalry Brigade, in the engagements on the Helmund and at Maiwand; took part in the defence of Candahar and was present at the battle of Canhahar (Medal with Clasp).

⁶ Major Pearce served with the 2nd Battalion Manchester Regiment throughout the Egyptian war of 1882 (Medal, and Khedive's Star).

Liverpool Regiment.—¹ Colonel Woodward served in the Soudan campaign in 1885 with the Commissariat and Transport Staff (Medal with Clasp, and Khedive's Star).

Norfolk Regiment.—¹ Major Thatcher served with the 1st Battalion Shropshire Light Infantry in the Egyptian war of 1882, and was present at the surrender of Kafr Dowar and Damietta (Medal, and Khedive's Star). Served in the expedition to the Soudan in 1885 with the 1st Battalion Shropshire Light Infantry (Clasp).

² Captain Halpin served with the Burmese Expedition in 1885-88 (Medal with two Clasps).

⁴ Captain Grehan served with the Burmese Expedition in 1888-89 with the 2nd Battalion Norfolk Regiment (Medal with Clasp).

Lincolnshire Regiment.—¹ Lord William Cecil served in the Soudan campaign in 1885 (Medal with Clasp, and Khedive's Star).

² Sir James de Hoghton served in the Ashanti war from the 17th December 1873, including the battle of Amoaful, attack and capture of Becquah, and advanced guard engagement at Jarbinbah (Medal with Clasp). [See also Civil Decorations for Gallantry, p. 786.]

Devonshire Regiment.—¹ Captain Dumbreck served in the Zulu war in 1879 on Commissariat duty (Medal with Clasp).

² Major Keene served with the 25th King's Own Borderers in the Afghan war in 1879-80 with the Khyber Line Force under Lieut.General Bright (Medal). Served with the 2nd Battalion King's Own Scottish Borderers with the Suakin Field Force in December 1888 during the investment of Suakin, and was present in the engagement at Gemaizah (Medal with Clasp).

⁵ Captain Carr served in the Afghan war in 1879-80 with the 2nd Battalion 11th Regiment in Southern Afghanistan (Medal).

Suffolk Regiment.—¹ Colonel Browning served with the 89th Regt. in the Crimea from 20th Aug. 1855, including the siege and fall of Sebastopol and attack of the 8th Sept. (Medal with Clasp, and Turkish Medal). Served during the Indian mutiny in 1875-58 as Staff Officer to a Field Force in Guzerat, including the attack on the Taringa Hills (mentioned in despatches); acted in the same capacity to another Field Force in Aug. 1858, and was present at the attack and capture of Mandeth—horse shot.

² Lt.Colonel Turner served in the Afghan war in 1878-79 as Orderly Officer to Brigadier General Thelwall and Brigadier General Forbes, and was present in the operations in the Koorum Valley, and at the capture of the Peiwar Kotal (mentioned in despatches); took part in the Zaimusht Expedition in command of a company of the 2nd Battalion of the 8th Foot, and was present at the assault of Zawa (Medal with Clasp).

³ Captain Francis.—See Civil Decorations for Gallantry, "Hart's Annual Army List," p. 786.

⁵ Lieut. James served in the New Zealand war in 1864-66 (Medal).

Somersetshire Light Infantry.—¹ Major Gore Langton served with the Koorum Field Force in the Afghan war in 1878-79, and was present with the expedition into the Khost Valley and in the engagement at Mattoon; accompanied Sir Frederick Roberts in the march to Candahar, and was present at the reconnaissance of 31st August and at the battle of Candahar (Medal with Clasp, and Bronze Decoration).

⁷ Captain West served throughout the Zulu war of 1879, and was present in the engagements at Zungin Nek, Kambula Hill, and Ulundi (Medal with Clasp).

⁸ Major Shephard served in the Zulu war in 1879 (Medal). Served with the Burmese Expedition in 1886-87 as Staff Officer to Brigadier General Anderson (mentioned in despatches, *DSO.*, and Medal with Clasp).

West Yorkshire Regiment—¹ Colonel Prideaux-Brune embarked for the Gold Coast with the 2nd Battalion Rifle Brigade, and served throughout the second phase of the Ashanti war in 1874, including the battle of Amonful, advanced guard skirmishes and ambuscade affairs between Adwabin and the river Ordah, battle of Ordahsu and capture of Coomassie (Medal with Clasp).

East Yorkshire Regiment.—¹ Colonel Grimston served with the 2nd Queen's Royals in the Kaffir war of 1851-52 (Medal); also with the expedition North of the Orange River in 1852-53.

² Lt.Colonel Buratall served with the 1st Battalion of the 60th Rifles on the Red River Expedition of 1870.

Bedfordshire Regiment.—¹ Captain Haggard served in the expedition to the Soudan in 1885 with the 1st Battalion Shropshire Light Infantry (Medal with Clasp, and Khedive's Star), and in the subsequent occupation of Suakin by British troops in 1885-86.

Leicestershire Regiment.—¹ Colonel Pearson served with the 95th Regt. in the Indian campaign in 1858, including the siege assault and capture of Kotah, battle of Kota ka Serai, general action resulting in the capture of Gwalior, siege and capture of Powrie, acted as Assistant Field Engineer, and mentioned in despatches (Medal with Clasp).

Irish Regiment.—¹ Captain Hon. E. B. L. H. Stopford served with the 1st Battalion Royal Irish Fusiliers in the Egyptian war of 1882, and was present at the battle of Tel-el-Kebir (Medal with Clasp, and Khedive's Star).

³ Major Cane served in the Egyptian war of 1882, and was present at the battle of Tel-el-Kebir (Medal with Clasp, and Khedive's Star).

⁴ Captain Trant served in the Boer war of 1881 with the Natal Field Force.

⁵ Captain Crabbe served as a volunteer with the 6th Inniskilling Dragoons in the Boer war of 1881. Served as a volunteer in the 19th Hussars in the Egyptian war of 1882, and was present at the battle of Tel-el-Kebir (Medal with Clasp, and Khedive's Star).

⁷ Captain Griffiths served in the Egyptian war of 1882 with the 1st Battalion Shropshire Light Infantry, and was present at the surrender of Kafr Dowar and Damietta (Medal, and Khedive's Star). Served in the expedition to the Soudan in 1885 with the 1st Battalion Shropshire Light Infantry (Clasp).

Yorkshire Regiment.—¹ Colonel Gunter served with the 4th Dragoon Guards in the Crimea in October 1854 including the siege of Sebastopol (Medal with Clasp, and Turkish Medal).

² Colonel Howard served in the Afghan war in 1878-79 with the Peshawur Valley Field Force and was present at the attack and capture of Ali Musjid (Medal with Clasp). Served with the Burmese Expedition in 1888-89 with the 4th Battalion Rifle Brigade (Medal with Clasp).

³ Captain de Teissier served in the expedition to the Soudan in 1885 with the 1st Battalion Shropshire Light

Infantry (Medal with Clasp, and Khedive's Star), and in the subsequent occupation of Suakin by British troops in 1885-36.

Lancashire Fusiliers.—[1] Major Hamilton served in the Nile Expedition in 1884-85 with the 1st Battalion of the South Staffordshire Regiment, and was present at the action of Kirbekan (Medal with two Clasps, and Khedive's Star).

Scots Fusiliers.—[1] Captain Toogood served in the Nile Expedition in 1884-85 with the 1st Battalion of the West Kent Regiment (Medal with Clasp, and Khedive's Star). Served with the Burmese Expedition in 1886-87 (mentioned in despatches, Medal with Clasp).

[2] Captain D'Aeth served in the Boer war of 1881 and took part in the defence of Pretoria.

[3] Lieut. Vaughan served with the Burmese Expedition in 1886-87 (mentioned in despatches, Medal with Clasp).

Cheshire Regiment.—[1] Sir Henry Loch served with the 3rd Bengal Cavalry in the Sutlej campaign in 1846 and was present at the battle of Sobraon (Medal). Was sent early in 1854 by the Foreign Office, under General Beatson, to the Danubian Provinces to organize the Turkish Irregular Cavalry, with rank of Lt. Colonel in the Turkish service; crossed to the Crimea, and was invalided shortly after the battle of Alma (Turkish Medal). Attached to Head Quarters of Commander in Chief in China in 1857 and present at the operations before and capture of Canton. Was on board the gunboat *Bustard* at the capture of the Peiho and upper forts in 1858. Was attacked to the head quarters of Sir Hope Grant in 1860 and present at the various operations previous to and at the capture of Sinho, Taugku, and the Taku forts (Medal with three Clasps). Accompanied the Earl of Elgin with the army on advance on Pekin, and was captured with Mr. Parkes and sent prisoner to Pekin; on release brought home the Convention of Pekin and ratified treaty of Tien-tsin, and made CB.

[2] Colonel Franco Hayhurst served in the Eastern campaign in 1854-55, including the battle of the Alma and siege of Sebastopol (Medal with two Clasps, and Turkish Medal).

South Wales Borderers.—[1] Colonel Thomas served with the 2nd Dragoon Guards the Oude campaign of 1858-59, including the assault and capture of Birwah, and Trans-Gogra affairs at Bungaon (Medal).

King's Own Scottish Borderers.—[1] Lieut. Howe served in the Afghan war of 1878-80 with the 25th King's Own Borderers with the Peshawur Valley Field Force under Lieut. General Maude, and afterwards with the Khyber Line Force under Lieut. General Bright (Medal).

Scottish Rifles.—[1] Lieut. Wishart served in the Zulu war in 1879, and was present in the engagements at Zungin Nek and Kambula and at the battle of Ulundi (Medal with Clasp).

Inniskilling Fusiliers.—[1] Colonel Buchanan served with the 88th Regt. in the Indian campaign of 1857-58, including the actions at Cawnpore under Major General Windham, battle of Cawnpore on 6th Dec., capture of Lucknow, operations in the Doab with the Column under Colonel G. V. Maxwell, to whom he was Orderly Officer, and siege and capture of Calpee in May 1858 (Medal with Clasp).

[3] Lord Caledon served with the Household Cavalry in the Egyptian war of 1882, and was present in the engagements of El Magfar and Mahsama, in the two actions at Kassasin, and at the battle of Tel-el-Kebir and the march to and capture of Cairo (Medal with Clasp, and Khedive's Star).

[4] Colonel Barton served in the Abyssinian war in 1867-68 with the 33rd Regiment, and was present at the capture of Magdala (Medal).

Worcestershire Regiment.—[1] Colonel Norbury served as Captain in the 6th Dragoon Guards in the Crimean campaign from 2nd July to 4th Sept. 1855, and was present at the battle of the Tchernaya and siege of Sebastopol (Medal with Clasp, and Turkish Medal).

[2] Major Holden served in the operations on the Soudan frontier in 1889, first as a volunteer with the British Brigade under Major General the Hon. R. H. de Montmorency, and subsequently in company with Colonel Wodehouse, Commanding Egyptian Infantry.

[3] Captain Montagu-Douglas-Scott served in the Soudan Frontier Field Force in 1885-86 with the Mounted Infantry under Brigadier General Butler, and was present in the engagement at Giniss (Medal, and Khedive's Star).

East Surrey Regiment.—[1] Colonel Haines served in the New Zealand war of 1863-66 (Medal).

Duke of Cornwall's Light Infantry.—[1] Captain Lloyd served with the 2nd Battalion of the Duke of Cornwall's Light Infantry throughout the Egyptian war of 1882, and was present at the reconnaissance in force from Alexandria on the 5th August, in the engagements at El Magfar and Tel-el-Mahuta, in the two actions at Kassasin, and at the battle of Tel-el-Kebir (Medal with Clasp, and Khedive's Star). Served in the Nile Expedition in 1884-85 with the 2nd Battalion of the Duke of Cornwall's Light Infantry, and took part in the operations of the Advance Column under Major General Earle (Clasp).

[2] Captain Hart served in the Egyptian war of 1882, and was present at the battle of Tel-el-Kebir (Medal with Clasp, and Khedive's Star); also served with the Nile Expedition in 1884-85 (Clasp).

West Riding Regiment.—[1] Captain Williams.—See Civil Decorations for Gallantry, "Hart's Annual Army List," p. 786.

[2] Captain FitzPatrick served in the Zulu war in 1879, and was present in the engagement at Gingindhlovu and at the relief of Ekowe (Medal with Clasp).

Border Regiment.—[1] Captain Jones served in the Nile Expedition in 1884-85 with the 1st Battalion of the Royal Sussex Regiment, and took part in the operations of the Desert Column under Sir Herbert Stewart, including the action at Abu Klea and the engagement at Metammeh (Medal with two Clasps, and Khedive's Star).

[3] Captain T. R. Morse served with the Burmese Expedition in 1885-87 (Medal with Clasp).

Sussex Regiment.—[1] Sir C. C. Goring served with the 33rd Regiment in the Abyssinian campaign of 1867-68 (Medal).

Dorsetshire Regiment.—[1] Lord Digby served in the expedition to the Soudan in 1885 with the 1st Battalion of the Coldstream Guards, and was present in the engagement at Hasheen, at that near Tofrek on the 24th March, and at the destruction of Temai (Medal with Clasp, and Khedive's Star).

[2] Colonel Hall served with the 14th Regiment in the Crimea in 1855, including the siege and fall of Sebastopol and assaults of the 18th June and 8th September (Medal with Clasp, and Turkish Medal).

[3] Captain Clinch served with the 39th Regiment throughout the Eastern campaign of 1854-56, and was present at the siege and fall of Sebastopol, and at the attacks of the 18th June and 8th September 1855 (Medal with Clasp, and Turkish Medal). Has received the Medal for Long Service and Good Conduct.

South Lancashire Regiment.—[1] Captain Tarbet served with the expedition against the Jebus, Lagos, in 1892 (mentioned in despatches, Medal with Clasp).

Black Watch.—[1] Lt. Colonel D. M. Smythe served in the Zulu war in 1879 with the Natal Native Contingent (Medal with Clasp).

[2] Lord Alexander Kennedy served with the 1st Battalion Black Watch in the Egyptian war of 1882, and was present at the battle of Tel-el-Kebir (Medal with Clasp, and Khedive's Star). Served in the Soudan Expedition in 1884 with the 1st Battalion Black Watch, and was present in the engagement at El Teb and Temai (two Clasps). Served in the Nile Expedition in 1884-85 with the 1st Battalion of the Black Watch, took part with the River Column under Major General Earle, and was present in the engagement at Kirbekan (mentioned in despatches, Brevet of Major, two Clasps).

[3] Major W. A. Scott served in the Egyptian war of 1882 with the Cameron Highlanders (Medal, and Khedive's Star); also served in the expedition to the Soudan in 1884 as Aide de Camp to Sir Gerald Graham and Press Censor to the Forces, and was present at the engagements at El Teb and Temai (mentioned in despatches, two Clasps).

Oxfordshire Light Infantry.—[1] Major Williams served during the operations against Sekukuni in 1879 including the storming of the stronghold (Medal with Clasp).

[4] Major Boyle served with the Commissariat in the Zulu war of 1879, and was Senior Commissariat Officer at Pinetown, Natal, from July to December 1879 (Medal).

Essex Regiment.—[1] Colonel Holroyd served with the 34th Regiment in the Crimea from the 10th August 1855 including the siege and fall of Sebastopol and assault of the Redan on the 8th September (Medal with Clasp, and Turkish Medal). Also in the Indian campaigns in 1857-59, including the actions at Cawnpore on the 26th, 27th, and 28th (wounded) Nov. 1857, capture of Meeangunge, siege and capture of Lucknow, relief of Azimghur (was Staff Officer to the Azimghur column in the winter of 1858-9), and defeat of the rebels at Bootwul (Medal with Clasp).

[6] Captain Colvin served in the Nile Expedition in 1884-85 with the 2nd Battalion of the Essex Regiment (Medal with Clasp, and Khedive's Star).

Derbyshire Regiment.—[1] Major Pearse served in the Egyptian war of 1882 with the 2nd Battalion of the Irish Regiment, and was present at the action at Kassasin on the 9th September and at the battle of Tel-el-Kebir (Medal with Clasp, and Khedive's Star).
[2] Lieut. Fox served in the Egyptian war of 1882 with the 2nd Battalion Derbyshire Regiment (Medal with Clasp, and Khedive's Star). Served with the Sikkim Expedition in 1888 with the 2nd Battalion Derbyshire Regiment (Medal with Clasp).

North Lancashire Regiment.—[1] Lt. Colonel Sandys served in Bengal through the Sepoy Mutiny in 1857-58.
[2] Major Harrison served in the Boer war in 1881 as a volunteer with the 14th Hussars. Served as a volunteer with the 4th Dragoon Guards in the Egyptian war of 1882, and was present in the engagement at Mahsama, the two actions at Kassasin, the battle at Tel-el-Kebir, and at the capture of Cairo (Medal with Clasp, and Khedive's Star). Served throughout the Nile Expedition in 1884-85 with the Light Camel Regiment, and took part in the operations of the Desert Column, including the engagement at Abu Klea Wells on the 16th and 17th February (Clasp).

Northamptonshire Regiment.—[1] Captain Wallace served in the Boer war of 1881, and was present in the engagement at Lang's Nek.

Berkshire Regiment.—[1] Captain Hollyer served with the 66th Regiment in the Afghan war in 1879-80, and took part in the defence of Candahar, and was present at the battle of Candahar (Medal with Clasp).

West Kent Regiment.—[1] Captain Bradish served in the Afghan war in 1880, and took part in the defence of Candahar (Medal).
[2] Captain Kennedy served in the Boer war of 1881 with the Natal Field Force. Served in the Nile Expedition in 1884-85 with the 1st Battalion of the West Kent Regiment (Medal with Clasp, and Khedive's Star).
[4] Captain Clifford served with the 21st Fusiliers in the Zulu war of 1879, and was present in the engagement at Ulundi (Medal with Clasp). Served in the Boer war in 1880-81, and took part in the defence of Pretoria.

Yorkshire Light Infantry.—[1] Captain Hotham served in the Hazara campaign in 1888 with the 2nd Battalion Royal Sussex Regiment (Medal with Clasp).
[2] Captain Spencer Stanhope served in the Soudan Expedition in 1884 with the 19th Hussars, and was present in the engagements at El Teb and Temai (Medal with Clasp, and Khedive's Star). Served in the Nile Expedition in 1884-85 with the 19th Hussars, and was present in the action at Kirbekan (two Clasps).

Shropshire Light Infantry.—[1] Major Scott served in the Egyptian war of 1882 with the 7th Dragoon Guards, and was present at the battle of Tel-el-Kebir (Medal with Clasp, and Khedive's Star).
[2] Captain Guest served in the Afghan war of 1878-80 (Medal).

Middlesex Regiment.—[1] Lt. General Kent served the Eastern campaign of 1854 and up to the 26th March 1855 with the 77th Regiment, including the battles of Alma and Inkerman, and siege of Sebastopol (Medal with three Clasps, 5th Class of the Medjidie, and Turkish Medal). Nominated to the 1st Class of the Medjidie for services rendered to the Sultan of Turkey.
[5] Captain S. J. Miller served in the Zulu war in 1879, and was present at the battle of Gingindhlovu and at the relief of Ekowe (Medal with Clasp).

King's Royal Rifle Corps.—[1] Colonel Black served with the 99th Regiment in the campaign of 1860 in North China, and was present at the surrender of Pekin (Medal with Clasp).
[2] Colonel Aldworth served the Eastern campaign of 1854 up to the 8th Nov. with the 7th Fusiliers, including the battles of Alma and Inkerman, siege of Sebastopol, and sortie of 6th Oct. (Medal with three Clasps, and Turkish Medal).
[3] Lt. Colonel Templer served in the Egyptian war of 1882 (Medal, and Khedive's Star). Served in the Soudan campaign in 1885 as Commandant of the Balloon Detachment, and was present in the engagement at Hasheen (mentioned in despatches, Clasp).
[4] Sir Thomas Butler served in the Eastern campaign in 1855 as Lieutenant 56th Regiment, and was present at the siege and capture of Sebastopol (Medal with Clasp, and Turkish Medal).
[5] Lt. Colonel W. Cooke-Collis served in the Afghan war in 1879-80, and took part in the march to Candahar with the force under Major General Phayre (mentioned in despatches, Medal). Served in the Soudan campaign in 1885 as Deputy Assistant Adjutant and Quarter Master General (mentioned in despatches, Medal with Clasp, and Khedive's Star).
[6] Captain Pixley served as Column Transport Officer in the Boer war of 1881, and was present in the engagements at Lang's Nek and the Ingogo River—severely wounded.
[7] Major Story served in the Afghan war in 1880 (Medal).
[8] Major Lysons served with the 2nd Battalion 60th Rifles in the Afghan war from October 1878 to October 1879, and took part in the advance on and occupation of Candahar and Khelat-i-Ghilzie (Medal). Served in the Boer war of 1881 with the Natal Field Force.
[9] Captain Bower served with the 3rd Battalion King's Royal Rifle Corps in the Egyptian war of 1882, and was present in the reconnaissance in force from Alexandria on 5th August, in the engagement at Tel-el-Mahuta, in the action at Kassasin (9th September), and at the battle of Tel-el-Kebir (Medal with Clasp, and Khedive's Star); also served in the Soudan Expedition under Sir Gerald Graham in 1884 with the 3rd Battalion King's Royal Rifle Corps in charge of the Regimental Transport, and was present in the engagements at El Teb and Temai (mentioned in despatches, two Clasps). Served in the Nile Expedition in 1884-85 with the Mounted Infantry, and commanded the picked shots who accompanied Lord Charles Beresford up the Nile to the relief of Sir Charles Wilson when wrecked near Khartoum (mentioned in despatches, Clasp).
[10] Captain Irby served with the Burmese Expedition in 1886-87 (Medal with Clasp).
[11] Major J. N. Blackwood-Price served with the 2nd Battalion 60th Rifles in the Afghan war from October 1878 to November 1880, took part in the advance on and occupation of Candahar and Khelat-i-Ghilzie, and was present in the engagements at Ahmed Kheyl and Urzoo near Ghuznee; accompanied Sir Frederick Roberts in the march to Candahar, and was present at the battle of Candahar (mentioned in despatches, Brevet of Major, Medal with two Clasps, and Bronze Decoration). Served in the Marri Expedition under Brigadier General MacGregor. Served in the Boer war in 1881 with the Natal Field Force.
[14] Captain Crane served with the Manipore Expedition in 1891 (Medal with Clasp).
[16] Lieut. Holmes served in the Afghan war in 1879-80, and was present in the engagements at Ahmed Kheyl and Urzoo near Ghuznee; accompanied Sir Frederick Roberts in the march to Candahar and was present at the battle of Candahar (Medal with two Clasps, and Bronze Decoration). Also served with the Marri Expedition in 1881 under Brigadier General MacGregor. Served in the Boer war of 1881 with the Natal Field Force.

Wiltshire Regiment.—[1] Captain Strachan served in the Zulu war in 1879, and was present in the engagement at Inyezane and at the investment of Ekowe (Medal with Clasp).

Manchester Regiment.—[1] Lt. Colonel Irving served with the 4th Regiment throughout the Abyssinian campaign in 1868, and was present at the action of Arogee and capture of Magdala.

North Staffordshire Regiment—[1] Lt. Colonel Bill served with the Burmese Expedition in 1886 attached to Brigadier General Stewart's Staff in the Ruby Mines Expedition (Medal with Clasp).

York and Lancaster Regiment.—[1] Major General F. Hardy served as Orderly Officer to Brigadier General Russell at the second relief of Lucknow, at the Alumbagh, and at the siege and capture of Lucknow; also present with the 84th Regiment at the relief of Azimghur and pursuit of Koer Sing (mentioned in despatches, Medal with two Clasps).
[3] Lt. Colonel Mirehouse.—See Civil Decorations for Gallantry, "Hart's Annual Army List," p. 786.

Durham Light Infantry.—[1] Captain Lindsell served with the 21st Fusiliers in the Zulu war of 1879 (Medal with Clasp). Also served in the Boer war of 1881, and took part in the defence of Potchefstroom. Served in the Burmese Expedition in 1885-86 with the Mounted Infantry (Medal with Clasp).

Highland Light Infantry.—[1] Major Pagan served with the 2nd Battalion Highland Light Infantry in the Egyptian war of 1882, and was present at the battle of Tel-el-Kebir (Medal with Clasp, and Khedive's Star).
[5] Captain Mackinnon served in the Egyptian war of 1882 (Medal, and Khedive's Star).

Seaforth Highlanders.—[1] Major Davidson served with the 78th Highlanders in the Afghan war in 1880 (Medal).
[3] Lieut. Lauder served throughout the Afghan war of 1878-80 with the 72nd Highlanders, and was present in the engagement at Charasiah on the 6th October 1879 and in the operations round Cabul in December 1879; accompanied

War Services of the Officers of the Militia Infantry. 619

Sir Frederick Roberts in the march to Candahar and was present at the battle of Candahar (mentioned in despatches, Medal with three Clasps, Bronze Decoration, and additional Medal with Clasp for distinguished conduct in the field. Served in the Egyptian war of 1882, and was present at the battle of Tel-el-Kebir (Medal with Clasp, and Khedive's Star).

Gordon Highlanders.—¹ Colonel Man served with the field force under Brigadier Murray, R. Artillery, employé on the 30-mile radius round Shanghai during the summer of 1863 (Medal). Also with the Anglo-Chinese Contingent in Colonel Gordon's Taeping campaigns of 1863-64, and was present during the operations before Soochow and at the siege and storming of Changchow (Chinese Medal, and 2nd Class of the order of the Precious Star). Was selected in 1873 to raise a corps of Military Police for the treaty district of Newchwang, Southern Manchuria, at that time infested by mounted banditti, and subsequently commanded the force embodied (received the thanks of the British and Italian Ministers and of the Imperial Commissioner, with the Brevet of Colonel in the Chinese army and the Cross of the Italian Crown 4th Class). Served with the Nile Expedition in 1884-85 as Boat Officer and Staff Officer and afterwards as Commandant at Dal (Medal with Clasp, and Khedive's Star). Received the thanks of the Egyptian Government and the 4th Class of the Osmanieh for his services as Aide de Camp to General Valentine Baker, Pasha, and Acting Deputy Inspector General of Gendarmerie in 1886-88.

³ Major Abercromby served with the 1st Battalion Scots Guards in the Egyptian war of 1882, and was present at the battle of Tel-el-Kebir (Medal with Clasp, and Khedive's Star).

⁵ Captain J. Ross served in the Afghan war of 1878-80, and was present in the engagement at Charasiab on the 6th October 1879 and the subsequent pursuit of the Afghans, and in the operations around Cabul in December 1879 including the investment of Sherpore; accompanied Sir Frederick Roberts in the march to Candahar, and was present at the battle of Candahar (Medal with three Clasps, and Bronze Decoration). Served in the Boer war of 1881.

Cameron Highlanders.—¹ Major Norman MacLeod served in the Egyptian war of 1882 (Medal, and Khedive's Star). Served in the Soudan Expedition in 1884 with the 1st Battalion Black Watch, and was present in the engagements at El Teb (slightly wounded) and Temai (mentioned in despatches, two Clasps).

² Captain Mackenzie served in the Burmese Expedition in 1888-89 with the 4th Battalion Rifle Brigade (Medal with Clasp).

³ Captain the Hon. Arthur Hay served with the 1st Battalion Scots Guards in the Egyptian war of 1882, and was present at the battle of Tel-el-Kebir (Medal with Clasp, and Khedive's Star).

⁵ Lieut. Emslie served throughout the Egyptian war of 1882 with the Cameron Highlanders, and was present at the battle of Tel-el-Kebir (Medal with Clasp, and Khedive's Star). Served throughout the Nile Expedition in 1884-85 with the Cameron Highlanders (Clasp); also served throughout the operations of the Soudan Frontier Field Force in 1885-86 with the Cameron Highlanders, including the investment of Kosheh, the reconnaissance on the 16th December, and the engagement at Giniss (mentioned in despatches, Medal for distinguished conduct in the field).

Irish Rifles.—¹ Sir Francis Edmund Macnaghten served the Eastern campaign of 1854-55 with the 8th Hussars, including the battles of Alma, Balaklava, and Inkerman, affairs of Bulganak and M'Kenzie's Farm, and siege of Sebastopol (Medal with four Clasps, and Turkish Medal). Served in Rajpootana and Central India in 1858-59, and was present at the capture of Kotah, reoccupation of Chundaree, battle of Kotah ke Serai, capture of Gwalior, actions of Koondrye (horse wounded) and Boordah (Medal with Clasp).

³ Major Menzies served with the 92nd Highlanders in the Afghan war in 1879-80, and was present in the engagement at Charasiab on the 6th October 1879 and subsequent pursuit of the enemy, in the operations around Cabul in December 1879 including the investment of Sherpore, and in the engagement at Charasiab on the 25th April 1880; accompanied Sir Frederick Roberts in the march to Candahar, and was present at the reconnaissance on the 31st August and in the battle of Candahar—severely wounded (Medal with three Clasps, and Bronze Decoration). Served with the 92nd Highlanders in the Boer war of 1881.

⁵ Major Harris served in the Boer war of 1881 with the Natal Field Force.

⁶ Major Cox served in the Bechuanaland Expedition in 1884-85 under Sir Charles Warren with the Inniskilling Dragoons.

Irish Fusiliers.—¹ Colonel Hon. Edward Brownlow served with the Scots Fusilier Guards in the Crimea from the 8th Sept. 1855 (Medal with Clasp for Sebastopol, and Turkish Medal).

² Major Holden served with the Bechuanaland Expedition under Sir Charles Warren in 1884-85.

³ Major Kaye served in the rebellion in the North West Territory of Canada in 1-85 with Boulton's Mounted Infantry, and was present in the engagements at Fish Creek and Batoche (Medal with Clasp).

⁶ Lt. Colonel Leslie served with the 2nd Battalion Grenadier Guards in the Egyptian war of 1882, and was present at the battle of Tel-el-Kebir (Medal with Clasp, and Khedive's Star).

⁸ Captain Watkins served with the 2nd Battalion of the Royal Irish Fusiliers in the Soudan Expedition in 1884, and was present in the engagements at El Teb and Temai (Honorary rank of Captain, Medal with Clasp, and Khedive's Star).

Connaught Rangers.—¹ Colonel Robertson served in the Crimea in 1855-56 subsequent to the fall of Sebastopol. Served in the Indian Mutiny campaign in 1857-58 and was present at the action of Bugnapore, at the siege of Lucknow, and with the 88th Connaught Rangers at the siege of Calpee (Medal with Clasp).

² Major Hammond served with the 88th Regiment throughout the Kafir war of 1877-78, and as Adjutant of the Regiment throughout the Zulu war of 1879 (Medal with Clasp).

³ Captain Morrison served with the 88th Regiment throughout the Kafir war of 1877-78, and the Zulu war of 1879 (Medal with Clasp).

Argyll and Sutherland Highlanders.—¹ Lord Blythswood served with the Scots Fusilier Guards in the Crimea from the 22nd May to the end of Aug. 1855; was present at the siege of Sebastopol, and wounded in the Trenches by a shell on the 22nd Aug. 1855 (Medal with Clasp, and Turkish Medal).

² Major Cole-Hamilton served with the 1st Battalion Shropshire Light Infantry in the Egyptian war of 1882, and was present at the surrender of Kafr Dowar and Damietta (Medal, and Khedive's Star). Served in the expedition to the Soudan in 1885 with the 1st Battalion Shropshire Light Infantry (Clasp). Served in the occupation of Suakin by British troops in 1885-86.

³ Captain Denholm served with the 91st Highlanders in the Zulu war of 1879 and was present in the action of Gingindhlovu and the relief of Ekowe (Medal with Clasp).

Munster Fusiliers.—¹ Sir Augustus Riversdale Warren served with the 20th Regiment in the Crimea from the 26th January 1855, including the siege and fall of Sebastopol, and capture of Kinbourn (Medal with Clasp, 5th Class of the Medjidie, and Turkish Medal). Served in the Indian campaign of 1857-58, including the actions of Chanda, Umeerpore, and Sultanpore, siege and capture of Lucknow (wounded), subsequent operations in Oude and affairs of Pohan and Meangunge, also at Churda, and Fort of Musjeedin (Medal with Clasp).

Dublin Fusiliers.—¹ Captain W. T. M'Donnell.—See Civil Decorations for Gallantry, "Hart's Annual Army List," p. 786.

Rifle Brigade.—¹ Lt. Colonel Duke served in the Afghan war of 1878-80 as Assistant Agent to the Governor General for Beloochistan, and was present in the engagement at Syud Boot (mentioned in despatches, Medal).

² Lt. Colonel de Salis served as a volunteer with the Cape Mounted Riflemen during the Kafir war of 1851-52 (Medal).

³ Major Serjeant served throughout the Bechuanaland Expedition in 1884-85 under Sir Charles Warren with the Mounted Rifles and the Pioneer Regiment.

⁷ Lieut. Teed embarked for the Gold Coast with the 2nd Battalion Rifle Brigade and served throughout the second phase of the Ashanti war in 1874, including the battle of Amoaful, battle of Ordahsu, and capture of Coomassie (Medal with Clasp).

Buckinghamshire.—¹ Lt. Colonel Ellis served in the Boer war of 1881 with the Inniskilling Dragoons.

³ Lieut. Wickham served with the 1st Battalion Scots Guards in the Egyptian war of 1882, and was present at the battle of Tel-el-Kebir (Medal with Clasp, and Khedive's Star).

⁴ Surgeon Lt. Colonel Kiallmark served in the Eastern campaign in 1855 as Staff Surgeon attached to the Ottoman Cavalry, and was present at the battles of Balaklava and the Tchernaya and at the siege of Sebastopol (Medal with Clasp, and Turkish Medal).

Q Q 2

Cheshire.—¹ Captain Wyndham served in the expedition to the Soudan in 1885 with the 1st Battalion of the Coldstream Guards, and was present in the engagement at Hashoen, at that near Tofrek on the 24th March, and at the destruction of Temai (Medal with Clasp, and Khedive's Star).

Denbigh.—¹ Colonel Howard served in the Zulu war in 1879 (Medal with Clasp).

Royal 1st Devon.—¹ Captain J. G. E. Templer served with the 2nd Battalion Highland Light Infantry in the Egyptian war of 1882, and was present at the battle of Tel-el-Kebir (Medal with Clasp, and Khedive's Star).

North Devon.—¹ Captain Barton served with the 7th Dragoon Guards in the Egyptian war of 1882, and was present in the engagement at Mahsama and in the two actions at Kassasin (Medal, and Khedive's Star).

Gloucestershire.—¹ Lord Henry Somerset.—For War Services, see the Honourable Corps of Gentlemen at Arms.

² Captain Calvert served with the 7th Dragoon Guards in the Egyptian war of 1882, and was present in the engagement at Mahsama, in the action at Kassasin on the 28th August, and at the battle of Tel-el-Kebir and the capture of Cairo (Medal with Clasp, and Khedive's Star).

Herts.—¹ Captain Vereker served in the Nile Expedition in 1884-85 with the Light Camel Corps (Medal with Clasp, and Khedive's Star).

² Sir George Arthur served in the Egyptian war of 1882 with the 19th Hussars, and acted as Orderly Officer to Brigadier General Wilkinson, and was present at the action at Kassasin on the 9th September and at the battle of Tel-el-Kebir (Medal with Clasp, and Khedive's Star). Served in the Nile Expedition in 1885 as Staff Captain (Clasp).

West Kent.—¹ Sir F. D. Maclean served in the Eastern campaign in 1854-55, and was present at the affair of Bulganak and at the battle of the Alma (Medal with two Clasps, and Turkish Medal).

Leicestershire.—¹ Lord Howe.—For War Services, see 2nd Life Guards.

² Colonel Baillie, when a Lieutenant in the Royal Horse Guards, served in the Eastern campaign in 1855 as Aide de Camp to Lord Rokeby, Commanding the Brigade of Guards, and was present at the siege of Sebastopol, until he was invalided in August (Medal with Clasp, and Turkish Medal).

Middlesex.—¹ Captain Mitford served with the 8th Hussars in the Afghan war in 1879-80 (Medal).

Pembroke.—¹ Captain Cropper served in the Zulu war in 1879, and was present in the engagement at Ulm i (mentioned in despatches, Medal with Clasp). Served in the Boer war of 1881.

Shropshire.—¹ Colonel Wingfield served in the Eastern campaign with the 71st Highland Light Infantry from December 1854 to November 1855, and was present at the siege of Sebastopol and at the capture of Kertch and Yenikale (Medal with Clasp, and Turkish Medal).

² Captain Mynors served with the 4th Dragoon Guards in the Egyptian war of 1882, and was present at the battle of Tel-el-Kebir and at the capture of Cairo (Medal with Clasp, and Khedive's Star).

³ Captain Childe served in the Egyptian war of 1882 and was present at the battle of Tel-el-Kebir (Medal with Clasp, and Khedive's Star).

⁴ Lord Rodney served with the 1st Life Guards in the Egyptian war of 1882, and was present in the engagements at El Magfar and Mahsama, in the two actions at Kassasin, at the battle of Tel-el-Kebir, and at the capture of Cairo (Medal with Clasp, and Khedive's Star). Served in the Nile Expedition in 1884-85 with the Heavy Camel Regiment, and was present in the engagements at Abu Klea, El Gubat and Metammeh, and at the attack on the convoy on the 14th February 1885 (two Clasps).

Warwickshire.—¹ Major Beech served in the Nile Expedition in 1884-85 with the 2nd Life Guards detachment of the Camel Corps, and was present at the action at Abu Klea—wounded (Medal with two Clasps, and Khedive's Star).

Wiltshire.—¹ Captain Miles served with the 3rd Battalion 60th Rifles in the Zulu war from April to September 1879 (Medal with Clasp). Also served in the Boer war in 1881. Served in the Nile Expedition in 1884-85 with the Mounted Infantry Camel Corps, and was present in the actions at Abu Klea and Gubat—wounded (Medal with two Clasps, and Khedive's Star).

West York.—¹ Lt.Colonel Greenwood served with the 10th Hussars in the Afghan war in 1878-79, and was present at the attack and capture of Ali Musjid (Medal with Clasp). Served in the Soudan Expedition in 1884 with the 10th Hussars, and was present in the engagements at El Teb and Temai (Medal with Clasp, and Khedive's Star). [See also Civil Decorations for Gallantry, "Hart's Annual Army List," p. 786.]

PROMOTIONS, APPOINTMENTS, &c., SINCE LAST PUBLICATION.

1st LIFE GUARDS.—2nd Lt. Schreiber, Lt. to complete Establishment...... 13 Feb. 95
Riding Mr. Hall, from 20 Hussars, Riding Mr. vice Hibbard, retired ... 20 Feb.
2nd LIFE GUARDS.—Major and Col. *Earl of* Dundonald, Lt.Col. vice Bt.Col. Hanning-Lee, placed on h.p. .... 12 Jan. 95
Capt. Anstruther-Thomson, Major, vice Col. *Earl of* Dundonald .... do.
Lt. *Earl of* Longford, Capt. vice Anstruther-Thomson .... do.
2nd Lt. Low, Lieut. vice *Earl of* Longford .... do.
2nd Lt. *Hon.* O. C. Molyneux, from R. Horse Gds. 2nd Lt. vice Low ... 6 Feb.
ROYAL HORSE GUARDS.—Capt. *Lord* Binning, Major, vice Atherley, retired .... 22 Dec. 94
Lt. Villiers, Capt. vice *Lord* Binning.. do.
2nd Lt. Charteris, Lt. vice Villiers... do.
Lt. *Hon.* O. C. Molyneux, from 3 Bn. Lancashire Fus. 2nd Lt. vice Charteris (2nd Life Gds. 6 Feb. 95).. 2 Jan. 95
Bt.Lt.Col. Brocklehurst, Lt.Col. vice Bt.Col. *Earl of* Erroll, placed on h.p. .... 18 Jan.
Capt. *Sir* J. C. Willoughby, *Bart.* Major, vice Bt.Lt.Col. Brocklehurst do.
Capt. Ferguson, Major, vice *Hon.* L. F. G. Byng, retired .... 6 Feb.
Lt. Ricardo, Capt. vice Ferguson.. do.
2nd Lt. *Sir* S. E. Scott, *Bart.* Lt. vice Ricardo .... do.
Lt. *Hon.* R. Ward, from 4 Bn. Worcester Regt. 2nd Lt. vice *Sir* S. E. Scott, *Bart.* .... do.
Lt. *Hon.* A. V. Meade, from 7 Bn. K. R. Rifles, do. vice *Hon.* O. C. Molyneux, 2 Life Gds. .... 13 Feb.
1st DRAGOON GUARDS.—Serg. Parker, from West Surrey Regt. 2nd Lt. in suc. to Lt. Eastwood, prom. .... 30 Jan. 95
Lt. Wynne, from 5 Bn. Munster Fus. do. in suc. to Lt. Berners, resigned 13 Feb.
Gent. Cadet Searight, from R. M. College, 2nd Lt. in suc. to Lt. Wildes placed on h p... 6 Mar.
2nd Lt. Tuthill, Lt. vice Wildes, do. .... 20 Feb.
2nd DRAGOON GUARDS.—Gen. Seymour, from 11 Hussars, Colonel, vice General *Sir* C. P. B. Walker, dead.. 20 Jan. 94
3rd DRAGOON GUARDS.—Squad Serg. Major Rough Rider Sykes, from Cavalry Depot Staff, Riding Mr. vice Marshall, retired .... 20 Feb. 95
Gent. Cadet Longfield, from R. M. College, 2nd Lt. in suc. to Lt. McCorquodale .... 6 Mar.
2nd Lt. Mitchell, Lt. vice McCorquodale, seconded........................... 23 Feb.
4th DRAGOON GUARDS.—Lt. Gen. Massy, Col. vice Gen. *Sir* E. C. Hodge, dead .... 11 Dec. 94
2nd Lt. Philips, from Coldstream Gds. 2nd Lt. in suc. to Lt. Brigstocke, resigned... 16 Jan. 95
5th DRAGOON GUARDS.—Lt. Eustace, Capt. vice Hoare, apptd. Adj. ...... 15 Jan. 95
2nd Lt. Hodgkinson, Lt. to complete Establishment .... 24 Jan.
7th DRAGOON GUARDS.—Major du Boulay, from h.p. Major, supernumerary 6 Mar. 95
1st DRAGOONS.—2nd Lts. Webb and M'Neile, Lts. to complete Establishment 9 Jan. 95
Capt. *Hon.* H. W. Mansfield, from 20 Hussars, Capt. vice Hardman, apptd. Adjt. .... 13 Feb.
2nd Lt. Pitt, Lt. to complete Establishment................................... 27 Feb.
2nd DRAGOONS.—Capt. Middleton, Major, vice Torrens, retired .... 9 Jan. 95
Gent. Cadet Bramby, from R. M. College, 2nd Lt. in suc. to Lt. Houldsworth, resigned .... 6 Mar.
3rd HUSSARS.—2nd Lt. Lethbridge, from 3 Bn. Northumberland Fus. 2nd Lt. in suc. to Lt. Lockhart, resigned .... 6 Feb. 95
4th HUSSARS.—Lt. Sunderland, from 6 Dr. Gds. Capt. vice Hillas, retired 6 Feb. 95
Gent. Cadet Churchill, from R. M. College, 2nd Lt. in suc. to Lt. Gaine, seconded .... 20 Feb.
Lt. Underwood, Capt. vice Follett, 9 Lancers .... 13 Feb.

5th LANCERS.—2nd Lt. Haworth, Lt. vice Wilson, prom. ...... 28 Oct. 94
Gent. Cadet M'Taggart, from R. M. College, 2nd Lt. in suc. to Lt. Wilson, do. ...... 20 Feb. 95
6th DRAGOONS.—2nd Lt. Paterson, Lt. vice Atkinson, seconded ...... 1 Jan. 95
Capt. O'Connor, from 2 Dr. Gds. Major, vice Pennefather, ret. pay ...... 6 Mar.
Gent. Cadet E. M. Bruce, from R. M. College, 2nd Lt. in suc. to Lt. Atkinson, seconded..... do.
8th HUSSARS.—Gent. Cadet A. G. C. Bruce, from R. M. College, 2nd Lt. in suc. to Lt. Bedingfeld, prom. ...... 6 Mar. 95
9th LANCERS. - Capt. Follett, from 4 Hussars, Major, vice Morland, retired 13 Feb. 95
Squad.Serg.Major Rough Rider Parker, Riding Master, vice Nicholson, do. 27 Feb.
11th HUSSARS.—Capt. Coote, Major, vice Borrowes, prom. Lt.Col. on h.p. 30 Jan. 95
Lt. Bailey, Capt in suc. to Major Coote, Adjt. of Yeomanry...... do.
Gent. Cadet Home, from R. M. College, 2nd Lt. in suc. to Lt. Tyndale-Biscoe, prom. ...... 20 Feb.
Gent. Cadet Yorke, from R. M. College, 2nd Lt. in suc. to Lt. Bailey... 6 Mar.
2nd Lt. Johnstone, Lt. vice Bailey ...... 30 Jan.
12th LANCERS.—Gent. Cadet Greenly, from R. M. College, 2nd Lt. vice Holder, resigned ...... 20 Feb. 95
16th LANCERS.—Capt. Oswald, Major, vice James, dead.. ...... 22 Dec. 94
Lt. *Hon*. L. A. Milles, Capt. vice Stamer, seconded...... 1 Sept.
Lt. Gough, do. vice Oswald ...... 22 Dec.
2nd Lts. Maling (vice *Hon*. L. A. Milles) and A. E. *Visct*. Fincastle (vice Maling, seconded), Lts ...... 1 Sept.
Gent. Cadet Campbell, from R. M. College, 2nd Lt. vice A. E. *Visct*. Fincastle ...... 13 Feb. 95
Gent. Cadet Hesketh, do. do. in suc. to Lt. Gough, prom...... 20 Feb.
2nd Lt. Macnaghten, Lt. to complete Establishment ...... 13 Mar.
17th LANCERS.—Lt. Warner, Capt. vice Herbert, prom...... 5 Dec. 94
2nd Lt. Tilney, Lt. vice Warner ...... do.
Lt. Portal, Capt. vice *Hon*. L. H. D. Fortescue, seconded ...... 1 Jan. 95
Gent. Cadets *Hon*. A. W. J. C. Skeffington (in suc. to Lt. Portal) and Montgomery (in suc. to Lt. Warner, prom.), from R. M. College, 2nd Lts...... 20 Feb.
2nd Lt. *Sir* Francis Burdett, *Bart*., Lt. vice Portal, prom...... 1 Jan.
18th HUSSARS.—Squad. Serg. Major Rough Rider Mummery, from Cavalry Depot Staff, Riding Mr., vice Jackson, placed on h.p...... 30 Jan. 95
20th HUSSARS.—Lt. Carew, Capt. vice *Hon*. H. W. Maustield, 1 Dragoons 13 Feb. 95
Gent. Cadet Lee, from R. M. College, 2nd Lt. in suc. to Lt. Carew, prom. 20 Feb.
Serg. Crawshaw, from 6 Dr. Gds. Riding Mr., vice Hall, 1 Life Gds.... 27 Feb.
21st HUSSARS.—Lt. Cordeaux, from 2 Dr. Gds. Capt. vice Pilkington, retired . ... 30 Jan. 95
ROYAL ARTILLERY.—Lt.Col. Scott, Ord. Consulting Officer for India, Lt.Col. ...... 4 Jan. 95
Major Curling, Lt.Col. vice Col. Sandes, retired ...... do.
Capt. Fountain (District Officer), Major, vice Marsh, do. ...... 3 Jan.
Capt. Ward, Major, vice Curling, prom. ...... 4 Jan.
Lts. Campbell and Freeth (upon the Seconded List), and Hall (vice Lyle, seconded), Capts. ...... 1 Jan.
Lt. Harrison, Capt. vice Ward, prom. ...... 4 Jan.
Lt. Peake, do. vice Harrison, seconded ...... 5 Jan.
Lt. White-Thomson, do. vice Brook-Smith, do...... 9 Jan.
Gent. Cadet Finch, from R. M. Academy, 2nd Lt. in suc. to Lt. Hall, prom...... 1 Jan.
Gent. Cadet Lloyd-Thomas, do. do. in suc. to Lt. Harrison, do. ...... 4 Jan.
Gent. Cadet Wheeler, do. do. in suc. to Lt. Peake, do. ...... 5 Jan.
Gent. Cadet Ravenhill, do. do. in suc. to Lt. White-Thomson, do. ...... 9 Jan.
Major Purdy, Lt.Col. vice Bt.Col. Perry, retired ...... 1 Feb.
Capt. M'Crea, Major, vice Purdy, prom...... do.
Lt. Forestier-Walker, Capt. vice M'Crea, do. ...... do.
2nd Lts. Gooding, Becke and Wyatt, Lts...... 1 Jan.
2nd Lts. Jeffcoat and Wheeler, do. ...... 27 Jan.
Gent. Cadet Grose, from R. M. Academy, 2nd Lt. in suc. to Lt. Forestier-Walker, prom. ...... 1 Feb.
Major Fowler, Lt.Col. vice Col. Lockyer, placed on h.p...... 20 Feb.
Capt. Massy, from Seconded List, Major, vice Fowler ...... do.
Lt. Lamb, do Capt. vice Parry, seconded...... do.

ROYAL ARTILLERY.—2nd Lts. Nicholl, Lloyd, Mackenzie, Freeth, Liveing,
Davson, Tyrrell, Maule, Owen, Spencer, Smithett and Wardropp, Lts. 12 Feb. 95
2nd Lts. M'Cheane and Robinson, do.. 15 Feb.
2nd Lts. Rowcroft, Bridges and Forman, do. .... 19 Feb.
2nd Lts. Sturrock and Johnstone, do.. 3 Mar.
Gent. Cadet Ingham, from R. M. College, 2nd Lt. in suc. to Lt. Scott,
seconded .... 1 Mar.
Serg. Major Clarke, Riding Master, vice Pawson, retired .... 6 Mar.
Gen. *Sir* R. Biddulph, Col. Com. vice Copland-Crawford, dead............ do.
Capt. Talbot, Major, vice Jones, retired pay .... 20 Mar.
The prom. to Lt. of 2nd Lt. Crawford is cancelled, he having been
transferred to Indian S. C. with anterior date.

ROYAL ENGINEERS.—Major Orpen, Lt.Col. vice Bt.Col. M'Cullagh, retired 1 Jan. 95
Capt. Randolph, Major, vice Orpen, prom.. do.
Lt. Travers, Capt. vice Randolph, do... do.
Major Savage, Lt.Col. vice Bt.Col. Rathborne, placed on h.p. .... 24 Jan.
Capt. Jackson, Major, vice Savage .... do.
Lt. Dunsterville, Capt. vice Jackson .... do.
Lt. Gen. *Sir* T. L. J. Gallwey, Col. Comdt. vice Gen. *Sir* J. S. Hawkins,
dead .... 11 Jan.
The apptmt. of 2nd Lt. Meyricke is antedated to.............................. 17 Nov. 94
The apptmt. of 2nd Lt. Heath is antedated to .... 1 Dec.
The apptmt. of 2nd Lt. Carden is antedated to.................................. 12 Dec.
The apptmt. of 2nd Lt. Stevens is antedated to .... 17 Dec.
Major Haslett, Lt.Col. vice Col. Galwey, placed on h.p. .... 1 Mar. 95
Capt. Littledale, Major, vice Haslett .... do.
Lt. Biggs, Capt. vice Littledale .... do.
2nd Lts. Grubb, Moir, Ley, Howard, Hall, Tylden-Pattenson, Sandys,
Jones, Garwood, Wood, Osborn, Pridham, Gillespie and Jelf, Lts. ... 12 Feb.

GRENADIER GUARDS.—Lt. Taylor, from h.p. Lt. Supernumerary............ 20 Feb. 95
Gent. Cadet Lethbridge, from R. M. College, 2nd Lt. in suc. to Lt.
Halford, prom.. do.

COLDSTREAM GUARDS.—Col. *Visct.* Falmouth, Col. to command the Regt.
and Regtl. Dist. vice Col. Sterling, placed on h.p............................... 5 Feb. 95
Col. Pole-Carew, Lt.Col. vice Col. *Visct.* Falmouth, apptd. to command
the Regt. .... do.
Capt. Surtees, Major, vice Col. Pole-Carew .... do.
Gent. Cadet Graham, from R. M. College, 2nd Lt. vice Philips, 4 Dr. Gds. 6 Mar.

SCOTS GUARDS.—Bt. Major Romilly, Major, vice Col. Montgomery, retired 12 Dec. 94
Gent. Cadet Elwes, from R. M. College, 2nd Lt. in suc. to Lt. Malcolm,
resigned .... 6 Mar. 95

GUARDS' DEPOT.—Major *Hon.* A. H. Henniker-Major, Coldstream Gds. to
Command the Depot, vice Major Crauford, Grenadier Gds. resigned... 1 Jan. 95

REGIMENTAL DISTRICT.—Col. M'Dougal, from Lt.Col. h.p. Col. to Command 28th Regtl. Dist. vice Col. Salis-Schwabe, period of service
expired .. .. 18 Jan. 95
Col. de Wend, do. do. to Command 15th Regtl. Dist. vice Col. Hallowes,
apptd. to command the Troops in Jamaica....................................... 19 Dec. 94
Col. Rogers, do. do. to command 100th Regtl. Dist. vice Crawford, retired 17 Feb. 95
Col. Dickson, do. do. to command 49th Regtl. Dist. vice Borrett, period
of service expired.. 10 Mar.

WEST SURREY REGIMENT.—Lt. Glasgow, Capt. vice King-King, apptd.
Adjt. .... 1 Dec. 94
2nd Lt. Mudge, Lt. on augmentation .... 16 Jan. 95
Gent. Cadet Longridge, from R. M. College, 2nd Lt. do.... .... 20 Feb.

EAST KENT REGIMENT.—Lt. Essell, Capt. vice Vyvyan, seconded .... 1 Jan. 95
2nd Lt. Perkins, Lt. vice Essell .... do.
2nd Lt. Monsell, from R. Fus. 2nd Lt. vice Perkins............................ 13 Mar.

LANCASTER REGIMENT.—2nd Lt. Lloyd, Lt. vice Tomkins, seconded ...... 14 Oct. 94
Serg. Major T. Batchelor, Qr. Mr. vice W. Batchelor, retired .... 20 Feb. 95
Capt. Bonomi, Major, vice Crofton, prom. Lt.Col. on h.p.................. 25 Jan.
Serg. Major Daly, Qr. Mr. vice Danby, retired................................... 27 Feb.
Gent. Cadet Lethbridge, from R. M. College, 2nd Lt. in suc. to Lt.
Boyce, prom. .... 6 Mar.
Hon. Queen's Cadet Davidson, do. do. in suc. to Lt. Tomkins, seconded do.
Lt. Stokes, Capt. vice Bonomi .... 25 Jan.

NORTHUMBERLAND FUSILIERS.—Capt. Hon. C. Lambton, Major, vice Dyke, prom. Lt.Col. on h.p......... 21 Jan. 95
Lt. Wilkinson, Capt. in suc. to Major Pennington, apptd. to the Staff... 27 Oct. 94
Lts. Leather (vice *Hon.* C. Lambton) and Booth (to complete Establishment), Capts............ 21 Jan. 95
2nd Lt. Somerville, Lt. vice Casson, prom............ 17 Oct. 94
2nd Lts. Craster (vice Wilkinson, prom.) and Percival (vice Stewart, seconded), Lts............ 27 Oct
2nd Lts. Heale (vice Leather) and Fishbourne (to complete Establishment), Lts. .... 21 Jan. 95
Lt. Turner, from h.p. Lt. Supernumerary............ 20 Feb.
Gent. Cadets Bevan (vice Wood, seconded), Buckley (in suc. to Lt. Leather, prom.), and Toppin (in suc. to Lt. Wilkinson, prom.), from R. M. College, 2nd Lts............ do.
Capt. Armstrong, Major, vice Kilgour, prom. Lt.Col. on h.p............ 27 Jan.
Capt. Sturges, do. vice Biddulph, do. ... . 30 Jan.
Lt. Dawkins, Capt. vice Armstrong............ 27 Jan.
Hon. Queen's Cadet Lennox, from R. M. College, 2nd Lt. in suc. to Lt. Stewart, seconded............ 6 Mar.
WARWICKSHIRE REGIMENT.—2nd Lt. Murray, Lt. vice Walton, seconded 25 Oct. 94
ROYAL FUSILIERS.—Serg. Major Bell, Qr. Mr. vice Clowes, retired......... 16 Jan. 95
Lt. Monsell, from 3 Bn. The Buffs, 2nd Lt. in suc. to Lt. Burne, seconded 6 Feb.
2nd Lt. Sanders, Lt. vice Burne, do............ 1 Jan.
Gent. Cadet Stone, from R. M. College, 2nd Lt. vice Cookson, cashiered 6 Mar.
LIVERPOOL REGIMENT.—Major Stone, Lt.Col.vice Hamilton, placed on h p. 4 Feb. 95
Capt. Evans, Major, vice Stone .... do.
2nd Lt. Harington, Lt. vice Steavenson, apptd. Adjt............ do.
Hon. Queen's Cadet Howard-Vyse, from R. M. College, 2nd Lt. in suc. to Lt. Steavenson, apptd. Adjt............ 6 Mar.
NORFOLK REGIMENT.—Lt. Peebles, Capt. vice Leathes. placed on h p. 5 Dec. 94
Gent. Cadet Wheatley, from R. M. College, 2nd Lt. vice Stewart, seconded .... 20 Feb. 95
The prom. to Lt. of 2nd Lt. Thomson is cancelled, he being transferred to Indian S.C. with anterior date.
LINCOLNSHIRE REGIMENT. 2nd Lt. Orr, Lt. vice Jenkins, resigned ...... 5 Dec. 94
Gent. Cadet Hodgson, from R. M. College, 2nd Lt. in suc. to Lt. Boothby, prom. .... 20 Feb. 95
Gent. Cadet Morant, do. do. in suc. to Lt. Gaitskell, prom............ 6 Mar.
DEVONSHIRE REGIMENT.—2nd Lt. Thomas, Lt. vice Lander, seconded ... 23 Nov. 94
SUFFOLK REGIMENT.—Major Dowse, Lt.Col. vice Bt. Col. Glasgow, placed on h.p............ 9 Dec. 94
Capt. Graham, Major, vice Dowse .... do.
The prom. to Capt. of Lt. Saunders is vice Shadwell, seconded, and is antedated to .... 3 Oct.
Lt. Thomson, Capt. vice Tombe, retired............ 14 Nov.
The proms. to Lt. of 2nd Lts. Wynter and Brackenbury are antedated to 3 Oct.
2nd Lt. Labertouche, Lt. vice Thomson .... 14 Nov.
Gent. Cadet Carey, from R. M. College, 2nd Lt. in suc. to Lt. Thomson 20 Feb. 95
Lt. Leader, Capt. vice Graham............ 9 Dec. 94
2nd Lt. Crooke, Lt. vice Leader .... do.
SOMERSET LT. INFANTRY.—2nd Lt. Troyte-Bullock, Lt. vice Keith-Falconer, apptd Adjt............ 30 Dec. 94
Gent. Cadet Dickinson, from R. M. College, 2nd Lt. in suc. to Lt. Keith-Falconer, do............ 20 Feb. 95
Gent. Cadet Yatman, do. do. in suc. to Lt. Elger, prom. .... 6 Mar.
WEST YORKSHIRE REGIMENT.—Lt. Berney, Capt. vice Alexander, seconded .... 3 Sept. 94
Lt. Lush, do. vice Bouford, dead .... 2 Dec.
The prom. to Lt. of 2nd Lt. Fulton is vice Berney, and is antedated to... 3 Sept.
2nd Lt. Ames, Lt. to complete Establishment .... do.
2nd Lt Paget, do. vice Carlyon, dead............ 29 Sept.
The prom. to Lt. of 2nd Lt. Paget is vice Luard, seconded, and is antedated to .... 26 Sept.
2nd Lt. Howard, Lt. vice Carlyon, dead............ 29 Sept.
2nd Lt. King, do. vice Lush, prom............ 2 Dec.
Gent. Cadets Worsley (vice Fulton, seconded) and Isaacke (in suc. to Lt. Berney, prom.), from R. M. College, 2nd Lts. .... do.

WEST YORKSHIRE REGIMENT.—Gent. Cadets Thompson (vice Costello, Indian S. C.) and Deverell and Mourilyan (on augmentation), do. do. ... 6 Mar. 95
Lt. Fisher, Capt. in suc. to Major Hobbs, Adjt. of Volunteers .... 20 Feb.
EAST YORKSHIRE REGIMENT.—2nd Lt. Cobb, Lt. vice Cureton, placed on h.p. .... 5 Dec. 94
The apptmt. to 2nd Lt. of Lt. Jamieson, from Local Military Forces, Cape of Good Hope, is cancelled.
Gent. Cadet Davis, from R. M. College, 2nd Lt. vice M'Bride, resigned 20 Feb. 95
BEDFORDSHIRE REGIMENT.—Gent. Cadet Strong, from R. M. College, 2nd Lt. vice McVittie, seconded .... 6 Mar. 95
LEICESTERSHIRE REGIMENT.—Major Gregg, Lt.Col. vice Bt.Col. Moir, placed on h.p. .... 3 Dec. 94
Capt. Peacock, Major, vice Gregg .... do.
IRISH REGIMENT.— Major Spyer, Lt.Col. vice Edge, dead .... 17 Dec. 94
Capt. Baskerville, Major, vice Spyer .... do.
Lts. Owens (from Bedford Regt. vice Baskerville) and Forbes (vice Flanagan, apptd. Adjt. 4 Bn. Connaught Rangers), Capts............ 30 Jan. 95
Gen. Fraser, from Dublin Fus. Col. vice Gen. Call, dead .... 8 Jan.
YORKSHIRE REGIMENT.—Lt. Maitland, from h.p. Lt............................ 30 Jan. 95
Gent. Cadet Chapman, from R. M. College, 2nd Lt. vice Corbett, seconded 20 Feb.
Lt. Bulfin, Capt. vice Hood, retired .... 30 Jan.
LANCASHIRE FUSILIERS.—2nd Lt. Lloyd, Lt. vice Dobbs, seconded ...... 11 Oct. 94
Serg. Major Gribble, Qr.Mr. vice Smyth, apptd. Qr.Mr. and Adjt. Hibernian Mil. School .... 13 Feb. 95
Gent. Cadet Awdry, from R. M. College, 2nd Lt. in suc. to Lt. Dobbs, seconded .... 20 Feb.
SCOTS FUSILIERS.—2nd Lt. Buchanan, Lt. vice W. D. Smith, prom. ...... 14 Nov. 94
WELSH FUSILIERS.—Lt. Delmé-Radcliffe, Capt. vice Webber, seconded... 1 Nov. 94
Serg.Major Ransome, Qr.Mr. vice Gray, retired .... 20 Feb. 95
Lt. Cobb, from 4 Bn. 2nd Lt. in suc. to Lt. Grey, placed on h.p......... 13 Mar.
SOUTH WALES BORDERERS.—Serg. Day, from Middlesex Regt. 2nd Lt. vice Puckle, seconded .... 20 Feb. 95
Gent. Cadet Airey, from R. M. College, do. vice Hunnard, do........... 6 Mar.
KING'S OWN SCOTTISH BORDERERS.—Major Dixon, Lt.Col. vice Dering, dead .... 3 Dec. 94
Capt. Gordon, Major, vice Dixon... do.
Lt. Davidson, Capt. vice Gordon.. do.
2nd Lt. Chamberlain, Lt. vice Davidson .... do.
Queen's Cadet Allan, from R. M. College, 2nd Lt. in suc. to Lt. Davidson, prom. .... 6 Mar.
The prom. to Lt. of 2nd Lt. Pennington is cancelled, he being transferred to Indian S. C with anterior date.
SCOTTISH RIFLES.—Lt. Wollstein, from Local Mil. Forces, New Zealand, 2nd Lt. in suc. to Lt. Churchill, prom. .... 9 Jan. 95
Major Rawlins, Lt.Col. vice Bt.Col. Mecham, placed on h.p............. 15 Dec. 94
Capt. Grant, Major, vice Rawlins .... do.
Lt. Head, Capt. vice Grant .... do.
2nd Lts. Turton (vice Head) and Walter (to complete Establishment), Lts. do.
Serg. Lawrence, from 6 Dragoons, 2nd Lt. in suc. to Lt. Bainbridge, seconded .... 20 Feb. 95
2nd Lt. Pears, Lt. vice Newnham, do. .... 14 Jan.
Gent. Cadets Clarke (in suc. to Lt. Head) and Stewart (in suc. to Lt. Newnham, seconded), from R. M. College, 2nd Lts. .... 6 Mar.
INNISKILLING FUSILIERS.—2nd Lt. Sime, Lt. vice Brooke, seconded ...... 1 Jan. 95
Gent. Cadet Arbuthnot, from R. M. College, 2nd Lt. in suc. to Lt. Brooke, seconded.. 6 Mar.
Lt. Leverson, from W. I. Regt. Lt. vice Peacocke, who exchanges......... 13 Mar.
GLOUCESTERSHIRE REGIMENT.—2nd Lt. Rising, Lt. vice Carmichael, seconded .... 2 Sept. 94
WORCESTERSHIRE REGIMENT.—Gent. Cadet Richards, from R. M. College, 2nd Lt. vice Fisher, seconded .... 20 Feb. 95
Major Clarke, Lt.Col. vice Spratt, placed on h.p................................ 2 Mar.
EAST LANCASHIRE REGIMENT.—Qr.Mr. Serg. Holbourn, Qr.Mr. vice Hornsby, dead .... 30 Jan. 95
Major Evans, Lt.Col. vice Goodwyn, placed on h.p. .... 18 Mar.

EAST SURREY REGIMENT.—2nd Lt. Porch, Lt. vice Pochin, prom. .... 28 Nov. 94
Lt. Williams, from Scots Fus. Capt. vice Wynyard, prom .... 6 Mar. 95
Gent. Cadet North, from R. M. College, 2nd Lt. in suc. to Lt. Packman,
  seconded .... do.
Capt. Benson, Major, vice Harris, placed on h.p. .... 8 Feb.
DUKE OF CORNWALL'S LIGHT INFANTRY.—Gent. Cadet de la Condamine,
  from R. M. College, 2nd Lt. vice Hamilton, dead .... 30 Jan. 95
Lt. Rawlinson, Capt. vice Evelegh, apptd. Adjt. of Militia .... 19 Feb.
2nd Lt. Petavel, Lt. vice Rawlinson... do.
WEST RIDING REGIMENT.—2nd Lt. Siordet, Lt. vice Kingston, resigned 30 Jan. 95
Gent. Cadets Tyndall (in suc. to Lt. Kingston, resigned) and Bennett
  (in suc. to Lt. Somerset, placed on h.p.), 2nd Lts. .... 6 Mar.
BORDER REGIMENT.—2nd Lt. Earle, Lt. vice Leishman, seconded .... 8 Dec. 94
Gent. Cadet du Boulay, from R. M. College, 2nd Lt. in suc. to Lt.
  Leishman, do. .... 6 Mar. 95
SUSSEX REGIMENT.—Lt. M'Farlane, Capt. vice Trevor, retired............ 23 Jan. 95
Major Cafe, Lt.Col. vice Dorling, placed on h.p. .... 2 Feb.
2nd Lt. Woodall, Lt. vice McFarlane, prom...................................... 23 Jan.
2nd Lt. Julius, from Munster Fus. 2nd Lt. vice Cooke, seconded .... 13 Feb.
Capt. Wheeler, Major, vice Cafe .... 2 Feb.
Lt. Jellicorse, Capt. vice Wheeler .... do.
2nd Lts. Cooke (vice Jellicorse) and Griffin (to complete Establish-
  ment), Lts. .... do.
Gent. Cadet Crawley-Boevey, from R. M. College, 2nd Lt. in suc. to Lt.
  McFarlane.. 6 Mar.
HAMPSHIRE REGIMENT.—Lt. Faith, from 3 Bn. 2nd Lt. vice Connell,
  seconded .... 23 Jan. 95
2nd Lt. Parker, Lt. vice Hicks, seconded .... 13 Oct. 94
Gent. Cadet Hennell, from R. M. College, 2nd Lt. in suc. to Lt.
  Hicks, do.. 20 Feb. 95
SOUTH STAFFORDSHIRE REGIMENT.—2nd Lt. Skinner, Lt. vice Home,
  seconded .... 9 Nov. 94
Major Horsbrugh, Lt.Col. vice Thomas, placed on h.p. .... 11 Feb. 95
Capt. Wylly, Major, vice Horsbrugh .... do.
2nd Lt. Wardell, from Oxford Lt. Inf. 2nd Lt. in suc. to Lt. Whishaw,
  apptd. Adjt. .... 13 Mar.
DORSETSHIRE REGIMENT.—Capt. Tyrwhitt-Walker, from Derby Regt.
  Major, vice Lushington, retired .... 13 Feb. 95
Lt. Boxer, Capt. vice Lamb, prom. .... 28 Aug. 94
2nd Lt. Cowie, Lt. vice Boxer .... do.
2nd Lt. Waymouth, do. vice Mansel, seconded................................ 29 Oct.
Gent. Cadet Hill, from R. M. College, 2nd Lt. in suc. to Lt. Mansel, do. 20 Feb. 95
Gent. Cadet Mercer, do. do. in suc. to Lt. Boxer, prom..................... 6 Mar.
SOUTH LANCASHIRE REGIMENT.—2nd Lt. Shuttleworth, Lt. vice Bundock,
  prom. .... 7 Nov. 94
2nd Lt. Skinner, do. on augmentation .... 19 Feb. 95
Gent. Cadet Gardiner, from R. M. College, 2nd Lt. vice Thacker, resigned 6 Mar.
Hon. Queen's Cadet Ewart, do. do. in suc. to Lt. Upperton, prom. ...... do.
WELSH REGIMENT.—Gent. Cadet Wyllie, from R. M. College, 2nd Lt. in
  suc. to Lt. Astley, apptd. Adjt. .... 20 Feb. 95
BLACK WATCH.—Capt. Maxwell, Major, vice Bushman, dead .... 3 Jan. 95
OXFORDSHIRE LIGHT INFANTRY.—Capt. Terry, Major, vice *Lord C. R.
  Pratt*, prom. Lt.Col. on h.p. .... 22 Dec. 94
Lt. Colville, Capt. vice Porter, prom... 9 Nov.
2nd Lt. Osborn, Lt. vice Colvile .... do.
2nd Lt. Marriott-Dodington, do. vice *Sir C. Cuyler, Bart.* apptd. Adjt. 16 Jan. 95
Gent. Cadets Chichester (in suc. to Lt. Colvile) and Wardell (in suc.
  to Lt. *Sir C. Cuyler, Bart.* apptd. Adjt.), from R. M. College, 2nd Lts. 6 Mar.
2nd Lt. Bennett, from West Riding Regt. 2nd Lt. vice Wardell,
  S. Stafford Regt. .... 13 Mar.
The prom. to Lt. of 2nd Lt. Stewart is cancelled, he being transferred
  to Indian S. C. with anterior date.
ESSEX REGIMENT.—2nd Lt. Vandeleur, Lt. vice Beaman, seconded......... 25 Oct. 94
Serg. Major Ames, from 65 Regtl. Dist. Qr.Mr. vice Cousins, retired ... 13 Feb. 95
Major Blest, Lt.Col. vice Prickett, placed on h.p. .... 8 Jan.
Gent. Cadet Bundock, from R. M. College, 2nd Lt. in suc. to Lt. Bea-
  man, seconded... 6 Mar.

Promotions, Appointments, &c. 640a

NORTH LANCASHIRE REGIMENT.—Lt. Powell, Capt. vice Brooker, seconded ... 3 Dec. 94
2nd Lt. Greene, Lt. vice Powell .... do.
Colour Serg. Cadell, from W. Riding Regt. 2nd Lt. in suc. to Lt. Powell, prom. .... 6 Feb. 95
NORTHAMPTON REGIMENT.—Lt. Bramwell, Capt. vice Metcalfe, seconded 30 May 94
2nd Lt. Faunce, Lt. vice Lloyd, prom. .... 1 Apr.
2nd Lt. M'Gill, do. vice Bramwell, do. .... 30 May
2nd Lt. Layard, do. vice Faunce, seconded .... 9 Oct.
Gent. Cadets Royston-Pigott (in suc. to Lt. Bramwell, prom.) and Wood-Martin (vice Faunce, seconded), from R. M. College, 2nd Lts. .... 20 Feb. 95
BERKSHIRE REGIMENT.—Capt. Burney, Major, vice Rathborne, retired... 29 Nov. 94
Serg. Major Cloke, Qr.Mr. vice Smith, do. .... 16 Jan. 95
2nd Lt. Lees, Lt. vice Maurice, apptd. Adjt. .... 29 Dec. 94
Gent. Cadets Hincks (in suc. to Lt. Climo, seconded) and Striedinger (in suc. to Lt. Maurice, apptd. Adjt.), from R. M. College, 2nd Lts. 20 Feb. 95
2nd Lt. Collins, Lt. vice Climo, seconded .... 8 Jan.
WEST KENT REGIMENT.—Lt. Hotham, Capt. vice Bt. Major Wintour, seconded .... 10 Sept. 94
2nd Lt. Davies, Lt. vice Hotham .... do.
Gent. Cadet Hope, from R. M. College, 2nd Lt. in suc. to Lt. Hotham 20 Feb. 95
YORKSHIRE LIGHT INFANTRY.—The prom. to Lt. of 2nd Lt. Cotton is cancelled, he being transferred to Indian S. C. with anterior date.
Serg. Hughes, from Shropshire Lt. Inf. 2nd Lt. in suc. to Lt. Muscroft, seconded .... 20 Mar. 95
SHROPSHIRE LIGHT INFANTRY.—2nd Lt. Smith, Lt. on augmentation ... 22 Dec. 94
Gent. Cadets Atchison (on augmentation), and Grover (in suc. to Lt. Mackenzie, seconded), from R. M. College, 2nd Lts. .... 20 Feb. 95
MIDDLESEX REGIMENT.—Capt. Longe, Major, vice Warden, retired......... 9 Jan. 95
2nd Lt. Preston, Lt. vice Ross, apptd. Adjt... 1 Dec. 94
Lt. Rowley, Capt. vice Harvest, seconded .... 21 Feb. 95
2nd Lt. Barnes, Lt. vice Rowley .... do.
KING'S ROYAL RIFLES.—Capt. Ryder, Major, vice Mends, prom. .... 9 Jan. 95
Lt. Hon. J. R. Brownlow, Capt. in suc. to Major Herbert, apptd. to the Staff .... 3 Jan.
Queen's India Cadet Johnstone, from R. M. College, 2nd Lt. in suc. to Lt. Hon. J. R. Brownlow, prom. .... 6 Feb.
2nd Lt. Thynne, Lt. vice *Hon.* J. R. Brownlow, do. .... 3 Jan.
Lt. Christian, Capt. vice Ryder, prom. .... 9 Jan.
2nd Lt. Green, Lt. vice Christian .... do.
Lt. Foljambe, from 4 Bn. Leinster Regt. 2nd Lt. in suc. to Lt. Christian 6 Mar.
Lt. Taylor, from 1 Vol. Bn. Hampshire Regt. 2nd Lt. in suc. to Lt. Cobbold, resigned .... 13 Mar.
WILTSHIRE REGIMENT.—Gent. Cadet Armstrong, from R. M. College, 2nd Lt. in suc. to Lt. Raikes, seconded... 20 Feb. 95
Lt. Barnes, Capt. vice Macmillen, do. .... 15 Jan.
2nd Lt. Shaw, Lt. vice Barnes.. do.
MANCHESTER REGIMENT.—2nd Lt. Walker, Lt. vice Maclure, seconded... 15 Apr. 94
Gent. Cadets Hirst (in suc. to Lt. Maclure, seconded), Tillard (in suc. to Lt. Ravenscroft, seconded), Godbold (vice Bromhead, seconded) and Stevenson (vice Jackson, resigned), from R. M. College, 2nd Lts. 20 Feb. 95
2nd Lt. Anderson, Lt. vice Ravenscroft, seconded .... 14 Dec. 94
NORTH STAFFORDSHIRE REGIMENT.—Capt. Higginson, Major, vice Sawyer, retired... 9 Jan. 95
Major Williams, Lt.Col. vice Bowles, placed on h.p. .... 6 Mar.
YORK AND LANCASTER REGIMENT.—Serg. Brown, from 4 Dr. Gds. 2nd Lt. in suc. to Lt. FitzGerald, seconded .... 23 Jan. 95
2nd Lt. Ashton, Lt. vice FitzGerald, seconded .... 27 Nov. 94
2nd Lt. Palmer, do. vice Stewart, resigned .... 29 Dec.
Gent. Cadet Hill, from R. M. College, 2nd Lt. in suc. to Lt. Stewart, resigned... 6 Mar. 95
Lt. Cobbold, Capt. vice Money, seconded .... 16 Jan.
2nd Lt. Armstrong, Lt. vice Cobbold .... do.
DURHAM LT. INFANTRY.—Lt. Luard, Capt. vice Murphy, retired .... 13 Feb. 95
2nd Lt. Martin, Lt. vice Luard, prom. .... do.
Gent. Cadet Davies, from R. M. College, 2nd Lt. in suc. to Lt. Luard... 6 Mar.

HIGHLAND LT. INFANTRY.—Lt. Fergusson, Capt. vice Mitchell-Innes,
  prom. .... 22 Nov. 94
2nd Lt. Grahame, Lt. vice Fergusson .... do.
Lt. Noyes, Capt. vice Evans-Lombe, apptd. Adjt. 4 Bn............ .... 1 Jan. 95.
2nd Lt. Armstrong, Lt. vice Noyes .... do.
Gent. Cadet Maxwell, from R. M. College, 2nd Lt. in suc. to Lt.
  Fergusson, prom. .... 20 Feb.
Gent. Cadets Ronald (on augmentation) and Rolland (in suc. to Lt.
  Noyes) from R. M. College, 2nd Lts. .... 6 Mar.
Hon. Queen's Cadets Home and Singleton, from R. M. College, 2nd Lts.
  on augmentation .... do.
GORDON HIGHLANDERS.—Major Mathias, Lt. Col. vice Gildea, placed
  on h.p. .... 14 Feb. 95
Gent. Cadets Allan (in suc. to Lt. Walker-Leigh, resigned) and
  Marshall (in suc. to Lt. Lindsay, resigned) from R. M.College, 2nd Lts. 6 Mar.
Capt. Wright, Major, vice Mathias .... 14 Feb.
IRISH RIFLES.—2nd Lt. Baker, Lt. to complete Establishment .... 18 Nov. 94
Gent. Cadet Low, from R. M. College, 2nd Lt. on augmentation......... 23 Jan. 95
Lt. Addison, Capt. vice Wilkinson, retired .... 20 Feb.
2nd Lt. King-Harman, Lt. vice Addison .... do.
IRISH FUSILIERS.—2nd Lt. Gray, Lt. vice Morgan, seconded .....:........... 1 Jan. 95
Gent. Cadet Knocker, from R. M. College, 2nd Lt. in suc. to Lt.
  Morgan, seconded .... 6 Mar.
CONNAUGHT RANGERS.—2nd Lt. Blunt, Lt. vice Church, seconded......... 1 Jan. 95
Gent. Cadet Wise, from R. M. College, 2nd Lt. in suc. to Lt. Church,
  seconded .... 6 Mar.
ARGYLL AND SUTHERLAND HIGHLANDERS.—Gent. Cadets Pattison (in suc.
  to Lt. Douglas, prom.), and Courtenay (in suc. to Lt. Grant, apptd.
  Adjt.), from R. M. College, 2nd Lts. .... 20 Feb. 95
Lt. M'Neill, Capt. vice Davidson, seconded .... 7 Nov. 94
Qr. Mr. Serg. Beattie, Qr.Mr. vice Forbes, retired .. .. 27 Feb. 95
LEINSTER REGIMENT.—Lt. Twist, Capt. vice White, apptd. Adjt. 3 Bn. 5 Dec. 94
2nd Lt. Legg, Lt. vice Sharp, seconded .... 4 Sept.
2nd Lt. Cochrane, do. vice Searle, do. .... 6 Oct.
2nd Lt. O'Shee, do. vice Reeve, prom. .... 10 Oct.
Capt. Northcott, Major, vice Murphy, prom. Lt.Col. on h.p................ 17 Oct.
Serg. Moffatt, from Yorkshire Regt. 2nd Lt. in suc. to Lt. Magee, prom. 30 Jan. 95
The prom. to Capt. of Lt. Twist is in suc. to Major Northcott, holding
  Staff apptmt. and is antedated to... 17 Oct. 94
Lt. Campbell, Capt. vice White, Adjt. 3 Bn. .... 5 Dec.
2nd Lt. Carlisle, Lt. vice Twist .... 17 Oct.
2nd Lt. Mather, do. vice Campbell .... 5 Dec.
Gent. Cadets Wakefield (in suc. to Lt. Owens, seconded), Fox (in suc.
  to Lt. Reeve, prom.), and Macdonald (on augmentation), from R. M.
  College, 2nd Lts.. 6 Mar. 95
The prom. to Lt. of 2nd Lt. Carlisle is vice Chanier, seconded, and is
  antedated to .... 11 Oct. 94
The prom. to Lt. of 2nd Lt. Mather is vice Twist, prom. and is ante-
  dated to... 17 Oct.
2nd Lt. Taylor, Lt. vice Campbell .... 5 Dec.
MUNSTER FUSILIERS.—2nd Lt. Cummin, Lt. vice Ottley, seconded......... 7 Nov. 94
Gent. Cadet Fagan, from R. M. College, 2nd Lt. vice Julius, Sussex Regt. 6 Mar. 95
Hon. Queen's Cadet Hutchinson, do. do. in suc. to Lt. Ottley, seconded do.
Qr.Mr. Serg. Rowland, Qr.Mr. vice Campbell, ret. pay .... do.
DUBLIN FUSILIERS.—Lt. Loveband, Capt. vice Gage, apptd. Adjt. 5 Bn. 20 Dec. 94.
Lt. Gen. Sir J. B. Spurgin, Col. vice Gen. Fraser, Irish Regt. .... 8 Jan. 95
RIFLE BRIGADE.—Bt. Lt.Col. Howard, Lt.Col. vice Col. Hon. N. G.
  Lyttelton, placed on h.p. .... 5 Dec. 94
Capt. Leslie, Major, vice Bt. Lt.Col. Howard .... do.
Lt. Irby, Capt. vice Leslie .... do.
Gent. Cadet Close, from R. M. College, 2nd Lt. in suc. to Lt. Irby, prom. 13 Feb. 95
Lt. Radclyffe, Capt. vice Rokeby, retired . ... 12 Dec. 94
2nd Lt. Thresher, Lt. vice Irby, prom. .... 5 Dec.
2nd Lt. Hon. C. F. H. Napier, do. vice Radclyffe .... 12 Dec.
2nd Lt. Thornton, from 4 Middlesex Vol. Rifles, 2nd Lt. in suc. to Lt.
  Radclyffe .... 6 Mar. 95.

RIFLE BRIGADE.—Gent. Cadet Burnett-Stuart, from R. M. College, do.
in suc. to Lt. Thesiger, apptd. Adjt. .... 6 Mar. 95
Lt. Green-Wilkinson, Capt. vice Lascelles, seconded .... 10 Feb.
WEST INDIA REGIMENT.—Lts. Hadow (vice Westmorland, seconded) and
Hill (vice Cotterill, dead), Capts. .... 22 Dec. 94
2nd Lt. Duffey, Lt. vice Hadow .... do.
Gent. Cadet Hutchinson, from R. M. College, 2nd Lt. in suc. to Lt.
Hill, prom. .... 13 Feb. 95
Gent. Cadet Craig-Brown, do. do. in suc. to Lt. Hadow, do............... 20 Feb.
2nd Lt. Martin, Lt. vice Hill, prom. .... 22 Dec. 94
Gent. Cadet Swabey, from R. M College, 2nd Lt. vice Prichard, resigned 6 Mar. 95
Lt. Peacocke, from Inniskilling Fus. Lt. vice Leverson, who exchanges 13 Mar.
UNATTACHED LIST.—Gent.Cadets Pakenham, Henderson,Pryce and Battye,
Queen's Cadet Kidd, Queen's India Cadet Pollock, Gent. Cadet Rivett-
Carnac, Queen's Cadets Simpson and Hoskyn, Gent. Cadet Villiers-
Stuart, Queen's India Cadet Channer, Gent. Cadet Palmer, Queen's
Cadet Godwin, Queen's India Cadets Strong, Keyes and Tyndall,
Queen's Cadet Buckley, Queen's India Cadet Ashburner, Gent Cadet.
Conway-Gordon, Queen's India Cadets Swinley and Goodfellow, Gent
Cadet Graham, Queen's India Cadet Bruce, Queen's Cadets Skeen and
Geddes, Queen's India Cadet Smith, Hon. Queen's India Cadet Lance,
Queen's India Cadet Birch and Hon. Queen's India Cadet Luckhardt,
from R. M. College, 2nd Lts. with a view to their apptmt. to Indian
Staff Corps .... 16 Jan. 95
ARMY SERVICE CORPS.—1st Class Staff Serg. Major Woods, Qr.Mr. vice
Cassell, retired .... 9 Jan. 95
Lt. Hardy, Capt. vice Morris, resigned .... do.
Lts. C. C. Macdonald, Mylrea and K. Macdonald (R. Marines), Burne
(R. Fus.), Christopher (Derby Regt.), Atkinson (6 Dragoons), Morgan
(Irish Fus.) and Brooke (Inniskilling Fus.), are transferred on prob. 1 Oct. 94
2nd Lts. Stewart (Norfolk Regt.), Fisher (Worcester Regt.), Hunnard
and Puckle (S. Wales Bordrs.) and M'Vittie (Bedford Regt.), do. ... do.
1st Class Staff Serg. Major Chase, Qr.Mr. vice De Lisle, retired .... 22 Jan. 95
1st Class Staff Serg. Major Wallace, Qr.Mr. vice Forde, retired .... 14 Feb.
Major French, Lt.Col. on the Supernumerary List .... 3 Feb.
Major Day, do. do. .... 13 Feb.
1st Class Staff Serg. Major Thornley, Qr.Mr. vice M'Caffery, ret. pay... 6 Mar.
1st Class Staff Serg. Major Gleeson, do. vice Nichols, do. .... 8 Mar.
ORDNANCE STORE DEPARTMENT.—Conductor Hunter, Ord. Store Corps,
Qr.Mr. vice Deeves, retired .... 4 Jan. 95
Capt. Butcher, from Cheshire Regt. Dep. Assist. Com. Gen. of Ord....... 27 Feb.
Conductor Swan, Qr.Mr. vice Pitt, ret pay .... 18 Mar.
ARMY PAY DEPARTMENT.—Lt. Maclure, Manchester Regt. Paym. .... 15 Jan. 94
Capt. Trevelyan, N. Stafford Regt. do. .... 30 Jan.
Paym. Irving, Staff Paym., vice Playfair, prom .... 16 Oct.
Paym. Newbury, do. vice Richmond, do. .... 16 Nov.
Paym. Chisholm-Batten, do. vice Wood, retired .... 8 Jan. 95
Paym. Webb, do. vice Ballard, do. .... 27 Feb.
Major Medhurst, from E. Lancs. Regt. Paym................................... 14 Mar 90
Major Benbow, 1 Dr. Gds. do. .... 8 May 94
Capt. Pereira, Bedford Regt. do. .... 9 May
ARMY MEDICAL STAFF.—Surg. Capt. Farmer-Bringhurst, Surg. Major ... 16 Jan. 95
Surg. Lt.Col. Irving, Brig. Surg. Lt Col. vice Clapp, retired............... 16 Dec. 94
Surg. Lts. Pilcher, Johnson, Beyts, Stalkartt, Dunn, Withers, Morphew,
Anderson, Tyacke, Holt, Mitchell, Fleming, Hennessy, Martin,
Buchanan, Lawson, Hughes, Kelly, Crawford, and Alexander, Surg.
Capts.. 30 Jan. 95
Surg. Capts. Macpherson, Simpson, Phipps, Baird, Hamilton, Semple,
Stuart, Deeble, Bond, Thomas, and Colman, Surg. Majors............... 3 Feb.
Surgs. on prob. Harrison, Howell, Lawson, Steel, Profeit, Kiddle,
Staddon, Whitehead, Murison, Tomlinson, Perry, and Heaton,
Surg. Lts. .... 29 Jan.
The prom. of Surg. Lt.Col. Swayne is antedated to .... 21 Aug. 94
Serg. Major Blackman, Med. Staff Corps, Qr.Mr. vice Tighe, retired ... 27 Feb. 95
Surg. Capt. Forrest, from h.p. Surg. Capt. vice Deacon, retired .... 17 Feb.
Brig. Surg. Lt.Col. Price, Surg. Col. vice Robinson, do...................... 27 Feb.
Surg. Lt.Col. Beamish, Brig. Surg. Lt.Col. vice Price...................... do.

HALF PAY.—Major Dyke, from Northumberland Fus. Lt.Col. .... 21 Jan. 95
Major Crofton, from Lancaster Regt. do .... 25 Jan.
Major Kilgour, from Northumberland Fus. do. .... 27 Jan.
Majors Biddulph (from Northumberland Fus.) and Borrowes (from 11
   Hussars), Lt.Cols. .... 30 Jan.
Major O'Sullivan, from R. Art. Lt.Col. .... 6 Mar.
ROYAL MARINE ARTILLERY.—2nd Lts. Nugent, Schreiber, Spurway, and
   Foulis, Lts. .... 1 July 93
Serg. Major Hill, Qr.Mr. vice Burton, retired .... 17 Mar. 95
ROYAL MARINES.—2nd Lts. Simmons, Nelson, Cartwright, Deed, Molloy,
   Coles, Willis, and Strong, Lts. .... 1 Jan. 95
Capt. Plumbe, Major, vice Hobart, to Half Pay List on apptmt. as Paym. 22 Jan.
Messrs. Hall, Heycock, Wilson, Mayhew, Simpson, Nixon, Walthall,
   Saunders, and Burge, 2nd Lts. .... 1 Feb.
Lt. Gibsone, Capt. vice Saunders, retired .... 5 Jan.
Capt. Maclurean, Major, vice Robinson, retired .... 25 Jan.
Lt. Bayliff, Capt. vice Maclurean, prom .... do.
Col. 2nd Com. Colwell, Col. Com. vice Scott, retired .... 23 Mar.
Col. Bird, Col. 2nd Com. Supernumerary, vice Colwell .... do.
Col. Sweny, do. vice Bird, Supernumerary .... do.

ALTERATIONS WHILE PRINTING.

ROYAL MARINE ARTILLERY.—Qr.Mr. and Hon. Capt. J. Muir, Hon. Major 17 Mar. 95.
ROYAL MARINES.—Lieut. J. C. Adams, being physically unfit for further
   service, is removed from Royal Marines .... 5 Feb. 95.

Retirements on Full or Retired Pay or on a Pension.

Colonels.
J. Rudge, h.p. Regimental District.
F. M. Drew, h.p. 7 Hussars.
G. B. B. Hobart, h.p. Royal Artillery.
W. B. R. Hall, ditto, ditto.
L. F. Perry, Royal Artillery.
H. G. MacGregor, Worcester Regiment.
R. A. Crawford, Regimental District.
E. Hughes, Army Service Corps.
C. W. I. Harrison, Royal Engineers.
A. J. Poole, h.p. Hampshire Regiment.
J. R. M'Cullagh, Royal Engineers.
H. W. D. Riley, h.p. Border Regiment.
H. T. T. Sandes, Royal Artillery.
A. Logan, ditto.
J. W. Scott, Royal Marines.
W. J. Galwey, h.p. Royal Engineers.

Lieutenant Colonels.
E. G. Pennefather, 6 Dragoons.
G. J. Parkyn, Army Service Corps.
C. J. Uniacke, ditto.
R. A. Livesay, h.p. Royal Engineers.
C. W. S. Lowndes, h.p. Highland Lt. Inf.
S. F. Foster, h.p. West India Regiment.
E. M. Alexander, h.p. Seaforth Highldrs.
V. G. L. Eyre, Indian Staff Corps.
A. C. Spencer, h.p. 1 Dragoon Guards.
M. W. Biddulph, h.p. Northumberland F.
K. Borrowes, h.p. 11 Hussars.
E. O. O'Sullivan, h.p. Royal Artillery.
W. H. M'Cheane, Royal Marines.

Majors.
W. T. Miller, h.p. Royal Marines.
H. C. Morland, 9 Lancers.
H. D. Robinson, Royal Marines.
T. W. L. Penno, West Yorkshire Regt.
W. H. Sawyer, North Staffordshire Regt.
Hon. L. F. G. Byng, Royal Horse Guards.
G. S. Jones, Royal Artillery.
A. J. Lushington, Dorsetshire Regiment.
C. W. Warden, Middlesex Regiment.
G. S. Marsh (District Officer); R. Art.
E. Fountain, ditto, ditto.
D. C. W. Harrison, Indian Staff Corps.

Captains.
H. H. Robertson-Aikman, 1 Dragoons.
B. C. Hood, Yorkshire Regiment.
E. T. C. Bower, Oxfordshire Light Inf.
W. S. Watson, Essex Regiment.
T. G. Hopkins, ditto.
W. D. H. Green, King's Royal Rifles.
W. J. Murphy, Durham Light Infantry.
F. A. Irby, Rifle Brigade.
E. E. Forbes, Indian Staff Corps.
J. E. Acland, h.p. Essex Regiment.

Quarter Masters.
J. Kelly, Royal Artillery.
W. Batchelor, Lancaster Regiment.
W. Gray, Welsh Fusiliers.
P. Hastings, Inniskilling Fusiliers.
J. Rorke, Welsh Regiment.
S. Forbes, Argyll and Sutherland Hldrs.
F. de Lisle, Army Service Corps.
J. M'Caffery, ditto.
R. Nichols, ditto.
G. Forde, ditto.
J. Pitt, Ordnance Store Department.
F. Tighe, Army Medical Staff.

Riding Masters.
H. Hibbard, 1 Life Guards.
E. H. Nicholson, 9 Lancers.
J. Pawson, Royal Artillery.

Staff Paymasters.
S. E. Wood.
J. R. Ballard.

Surgeon Colonel.
W. C. Robinson.

Surgeon Lt. Colonels.
B. W. Wellings.
J. Hoysted.

Veterinary Lt. Colonel.
G. A. A. Oliver.

Sub-Inspector of Schools.
T. Smith, Royal Marine Artillery.

Allowed to Withdraw.

Second Lieutenant.

W. F. Newberry, Royal Marines.

Retirements with Gratuity.

Majors.

J. A. W. O'N. Torrens, 2 Dragoons.
P. O'Brien, West India Regiment.

Captains.

W. H. Hillas, 4 Hussars.
P. W. Forbes, 6 Dragoons.

H. L. Pilkington, 21 Hussars.
C. P. Lloyd, East Kent Regiment.
F. de C. H. Helbert, Devonshire Regiment.
R. D. Wynyard, East Surrey Regiment.
G. A. Trevor, Sussex Regiment.
W. F. A. Wallace, Shropshire Light Inf.
L. T. V. Wilkinson, Irish Rifles.
C. W. H. Sanders, Royal Marines.

Resignations.

Major.

A. B. Cook, Reserve.

Captains.

Hon. L. F. K. Noel, 9 Lancers.
C. H. G. Wood, 15 Hussars.
A. W. Moon, West India Regiment.
J. Morris, Army Service Corps.
J. H. How, Reserve.
C. R. D. G. Cuninghame, ditto.

Lieutenants.

L. A. Kingston, West Riding Regiment.

R. P. Cobbold, King's Royal Rifles.
H. S. Ferguson, Reserve.

Second Lieutenants.

A. C. Holder, 12 Lancers.
S. W. Nicholson, Royal Artillery.
F. S. de M. Maude, Yorkshire Regiment.
R. B. Chapman, Inniskilling Fusiliers.
A. W. N. Thacker, S. Lancashire Regt.
F. G. K. Jackson, Manchester Regiment.
H. C. J. Biss, Highland Light Infantry.
B. C. Prichard, West India Regiment.

Cashiered.

Second Lieutenant.

S. Cookson, Royal Fusiliers.

Deaths.

Quarter Masters.

E. Vine, Scottish Rifles, Shahjehanpore, India, aged 48 .... 13 Feb. 95
H. Blissett, ret. pay, 77 Foot, Westbourne, Sussex .... 4 Dec. 94
J. Forbes, ret. pay, Black Watch .... 25 Jan. 95
J. Masterson, ret. pay, Southsea, aged 66 .... 22 Feb.
G. Mathews, ret. pay, 3 Hussars .... 5 Feb.
T. Muir, ret. pay, Culross, Fifeshire .... 1 Feb.
J. Walsh, ret. pay, Seaforth Highlanders, Bermuda .... 1 Nov. 94

Staff Paymasters.

W. Franklin, Shrewsbury .... 10 Mar. 95
J. Wray, ret. pay, Leyburn, Yorkshire .... 28 Dec. 94

Paymasters.

W. Sugden, Milan, aged 49 .... 25 Feb. 95
S. Daniel, ret. pay, Brigade Depot, Lee, Kent, aged 84 .... 15 Feb.
W. F. Nixon, ret. pay, 60 Foot, Bedford, aged 84 .... 8 Mar.

Commissaries General.

H. Tatum, half pay, Bedford, aged 76 .... 15 Mar. 95
J. S. Robertson, ditto, Bray, co. Wicklow .... 18 Feb.
J. L. Robertson, ret. pay, Butterglen, aged 56 .... 20 Feb.

Surgeon Major General.

J. Rudd, ret. pay, San Remo, Italy .... 24 Feb. 95

Brigade Surgeons.

J. Candy, ret. pay, Torquay .... 23 Jan. 95
J. Coates, ditto, Hythe, Kent, aged 68 .... 15 Mar.
T. J. Orton, ditto, London .... 9 Jan.

Surgeon Major.

C. M. M. Miller, ret. pay, Eastbourne, aged 69 .... 9 Feb. 95

Surgeon.

B. Stiles, ret. pay, Ollerton, Newark .... 11 Feb. 95

Assistant Surgeon.

C. J. Kirwan, ret. pay .... 19 Dec. 94

Inspectors of Army Schools.

R. Kirk, ret. pay, Portsmouth, aged 70 .... 26 Feb. 95
W. Thacker, ret. pay .... 10 Jan.

Chaplain.

J. F. Browne, ret. pay, 1st Class, Portchester .... 6 Nov. 94

www.ingramcontent.com/pod-product-compliance
Lightning Source LLC
Chambersburg PA
CBHW070312240426
43663CB00038BA/1485